FRENCH-ENGLISH
ENGLISH-FRENCH
THE IDEAL COMPANION FOR
ALL LEARNERS OF FRENCH

BBC

FRENCH

LEARNER'S **DICTIONARY**

D0993880

© Larousse-Bordas, 1997

ISBN 0-563-40087-0

Published by BBC Books, a division of BBC Worldwide Ltd,
Woodlands, 80 Wood Lane, London W12 0TT
First published 1997

Printed and bound in Great Britain by Mackays of Chatham
Cover printed by Belmont Press Ltd, Northampton

Introduction

The BBC *French Learner's Dictionary* is the result of a collaboration between the BBC and the Larousse Language Reference team. It is aimed at all learners of French and can be used either independently or alongside the BBC's best-selling *The French Experience* course.

Containing over 78,000 translations, the dictionary provides thorough coverage of everyday French and detailed coverage of GCSE word lists, along with business terms and computing vocabulary. There are also handy cultural notes throughout, giving a useful insight into the language as well as into French-speaking countries and their traditions.

Whether you are reading, writing, listening or speaking, the dictionary makes communication simpler as each word is clearly divided, where appropriate, into its different meanings and parts of speech, while there is essential guidance on French pronunciation.

Up-to-date and easy to use, this dictionary is the ideal companion for all learners, whether at school, at home or travelling abroad.

Abbreviations

Abréviations

abbreviation	*abbr/abr*	abréviation
adjective	*adj*	adjectif
administration, administrative	ADMIN	administration
adverb	*adv*	adverbe
aeronautics, aviation	AERON/AÉRON	aéronautique
agriculture, farming	AGR(IC)	agriculture
American English	Am	anglais américain
anatomy	ANAT	anatomie
archaeology	ARCHAEOL/ ARCHÉOL	archéologie
architecture	ARCHIT	architecture
slang	*arg*	argot
article	*art*	article
astrology	ASTROL	astrologie
astronomy	ASTRON	astronomie
automobile, cars	AUT(OM)	automobile
auxiliary	*aux*	auxiliaire
before noun – indicates that the translation is always used directly before the noun which it modifies	*avant n*	avant le nom – appliqué à la traduction d'un adjectif français, indique l'emploi d'un nom anglais avec valeur d'adjectif; souligne aussi les cas où la traduction d'un adjectif est nécessairement antéposée
Belgian French	Belg	belgicisme
biology	BIOL	biologie
botany	BOT	botanique
British English	Br	anglais britannique
Canadian English/French	Can	canadianisme
chemistry	CHEM/CHIM	chimie
cinema, film-making	CIN(EMA)	cinéma
commerce, business	COMM	commerce
compound	*comp*	nom anglais utilisé en apposition
comparative	*compar*	comparatif
computers, computer science	COMPUT	informatique
conjunction	*conj*	conjonction
construction, building trade	CONSTR	construction, bâtiment
continuous	*cont*	progressif
sewing	COUT	couture
culinary, cooking	CULIN	cuisine, art culinaire
definite	*def/déf*	défini
demonstrative	*dem*	démonstratif
ecology	ÉCOL	écologie
economics	ECON/ÉCON	économie
electricity	ELEC/ÉLECTR	électricité
electronics	ELECTRON/ ÉLECTRON	électronique
especially	*esp*	particulièrement

exclamation	*excl*	interjection
feminine	*f*	féminin
informal	*fam*	familier
figurative	*fig*	figuré
finance, financial	FIN	finances
formal	*fml*	soutenu
soccer	FTBL	football
inseparable	*fus*	non séparable

inseparable — *fus* — non séparable
— shows that a phrasal verb is 'fused', i.e. inseparable, e.g. **look after** where the object cannot come between the verb and the particle, e.g. I *looked* after him but not *I *looked* him after

— indique qu'un verbe anglais à particule ('phrasal verb') ne peut pas être séparé de sa particule, c'est-à-dire qu'un complément d'objet ne peut être inséré entre les deux, par exemple, I *looked* after him et non *I *looked* him after

generally, in most cases	*gen/gén*	généralement
geography, geographical	GEOGR/GÉOGR	géographie
geology, geological	GEOL/GÉOL	géologie
geometry	GEOM/GÉOM	géométrie
grammar	GRAM(M)	grammaire
Swiss French	*Helv*	helvétisme
history	HIST	histoire
humorous	*hum*	humoristique
industry	IND	industrie
indefinite	*indef/indéf*	indéfini
informal	*inf*	familier
infinitive	*infin*	infinitif
computers, computer science	INFORM	informatique
exclamation	*interj*	interjection
interrogative	*interr*	interrogatif
invariable	*inv*	invariable
ironic	*iro/iron*	ironique
juridical, legal	JUR	juridique
linguistics	LING	linguistique
literal	*lit/litt*	littéral
phrase(s)	*loc*	locution(s)
adjectival phrase	*loc adj*	locution adjectivale
adverbial phrase	*loc adv*	locution adverbiale
conjunctival phrase	*loc conj*	locution conjonctive
prepositional phrase	*loc prép*	locution prépositionnelle

prepositional phrase — *loc prép* — locution prépositionnelle
— adjectives, adverbs and prepositions consisting of more than one word, e.g. **d'affilée**, **par dépit**

— adjectifs, adverbes et prépositions composés de plusieurs mots, **d'affilée**, **par dépit**, par exemple

masculine	*m*	masculin
mathematics	MATH(S)	mathématiques
medicine	MED/MÉD	médecine
weather, meteorology	METEOR/ MÉTÉOR	météorologie
military	MIL	domaine militaire
music	MUS	musique

mythology	MYTH	mythologie
noun	*n*	nom
nautical, maritime	NAUT/NAVIG	navigation
numeral	*num*	numéral
oneself	*o.s.*	
pejorative	*pej/péj*	péjoratif
personal	*pers*	personnel
pharmacology, pharmaceutics	PHARM	pharmacologie
philosophy	PHILO	philosophie
photography	PHOT	photographie
phrase(s)	*phr*	locution(s)
physics	PHYS	physique
plural	*pl*	pluriel
politics	POL(IT)	politique
possessive	*poss*	possessif
past participle	*pp*	participe passé
present participle	*ppr*	participe présent
preposition	*prep/prép*	préposition
pronoun	*pron*	pronom
psychology, psychiatry	PSYCH(OL)	psychologie
past tense	*pt*	passé
	qqch	quelque chose
	qqn	quelqu'un
registered trademark	®	nom déposé
railways	RAIL	rail
relative	*rel*	relatif
religion	RELIG	religion
someone, somebody	*sb*	
school	SCH/SCOL	scolarité
Scottish English	*Scot*	anglais écossais
separable	*sep*	séparable

separable – shows that a phrasal verb is separable, e.g. **let in**, **help out** where the object can come between the verb and the particle, e.g. *I let her in, he helped me out*

séparable – indique qu'un verbe anglais à postposition ('phrasal verb') peut être séparé de sa particule, c'est-à-dire qu'un complément d'objet peut être inséré entre les deux, par exemple *I let her in, he helped me out*

singular	*sg*	singulier
slang	*sl*	argot
sociology	SOCIOL	sociologie
formal	*sout*	soutenu
stock exchange	ST EX	Bourse
something	*sthg*	
subject	*subj/suj*	sujet
superlative	*superl*	superlatif
technology, technical	TECH(NOL)	domaine technique et technologique
telecommunications	TELEC/TÉLÉCOM	télécommunications
very informal	*tfam*	très familier
television	TV/TÉLÉ	télévision

printing, typography	TYPO	typographie
uncountable noun	U	substantif non comptable
– i.e. an English noun which is never used in the plural or with 'a'; used when the French word is or can be a plural, e.g. **applause** *n* (U) applaudissements *mpl*, **battement** *nm* beat, beating (U)		– désigne en anglais les noms qui ne sont jamais utilisés au pluriel, lorsque le terme français est un pluriel, ou peut être mis au pluriel, par exemple **applause** *n* (U) applaudissements *mpl*, **battement** *nm* beat, beating (U)
university	UNIV	université
usually	*usu*	habituellement
link verb followed by a predicative adjective or noun	*v attr*	verbe suivi d'un attribut
verb	*vb/v*	verbe
veterinary science	VETER	médecine vétérinaire
intransitive verb	*vi*	verbe intransitif
impersonal verb	*v impers*	verbe impersonnel
very informal	*v inf*	très familier
pronominal verb	*vp*	verbe pronominal
transitive verb	*vt*	verbe transitif
vulgar	*vulg*	vulgaire
zoology	ZOOL	zoologie
cultural equivalent	≃	équivalence culturelle

English compounds

A compound is a word or expression which has a single meaning but is made up of more than one word, e.g. **point of view**, **kiss of life**, **virtual reality**, **West Indies** and **Confederation of British Industry**. It is a feature of this dictionary that English compounds appear in the A–Z list in strict alphabetical order. The compound **blood poisoning** will therefore come after **bloodhound** which itself follows **blood group**.

Mots composés anglais

On désigne par composés des entités lexicales ayant un sens autonome mais qui sont composées de plus d'un mot. Nous avons pris le parti de faire figurer les composés anglais dans l'ordre alphabétique général. Le composé **blood poisoning** est ainsi présenté après **bloodhound** qui suit **blood group**.

Trademarks

Words considered to be trademarks have been designated in this dictionary by the symbol ®. However, neither the presence nor the absence of such designation should be regarded as affecting the legal status of any trademark.

Noms de marque

Les noms de marque sont désignés dans ce dictionnaire par le symbole ®. Néanmoins, ni ce symbole ni son absence éventuelle ne peuvent être considérés comme susceptibles d'avoir une incidence quelconque sur le statut légal d'une marque.

Phonetic Transcription

English vowels

[ɪ]	pit, big, rid
[e]	pet, tend
[æ]	pat, bag, mad
[ʌ]	putt, cut
[ɒ]	pot, log
[ʊ]	put, full
[ə]	mother, suppose
[iː]	bean, weed
[ɑː]	barn, car, laugh
[ɔː]	born, lawn
[uː]	loop, loose
[ɜː]	burn, learn, bird

English diphthongs

[eɪ]	bay, late, great
[aɪ]	buy, light, aisle
[ɔɪ]	boy, foil
[əʊ]	no, road, blow
[aʊ]	now, shout, town
[ɪə]	peer, fierce, idea
[eə]	pair, bear, share
[ʊə]	poor, sure, tour

Transcription Phonétique

Voyelles françaises

[i]	fille, île
[e]	pays, année
[ɛ]	bec, aime
[a]	lac, papillon
[ɑ]	tas, âme
[o]	drôle, aube
[u]	outil, goût
[y]	usage, lune
[ø]	aveu, jeu
[œ]	peuple, bœuf
[ə]	le, je

Nasales françaises

[ɛ̃]	limbe, main
[ɑ̃]	champ, ennui
[ɔ̃]	ongle, mon
[œ̃]	parfum, brun

Semi-vowels / Semi-voyelles

you, spaniel	[j]	yeux, lieu
wet, why, twin	[w]	ouest, oui
	[ɥ]	lui, nuit

Consonants / Consonnes

pop, people	[p]	prendre, grippe
bottle, bib	[b]	bateau, rosbif
train, tip	[t]	théâtre, temps
dog, did	[d]	dalle, ronde
come, kitchen	[k]	coq, quatre
gag, great	[g]	garder, épilogue
chain, wretched	[tʃ]	
jig, fridge	[dʒ]	
fib, physical	[f]	physique, fort
vine, livid	[v]	voir, rive
think, fifth	[θ]	
this, with	[ð]	
seal, peace	[s]	cela, savant
zip, his	[z]	fraise, zéro
sheep, machine	[ʃ]	charrue, schéma
usual, measure	[ʒ]	rouge, jabot
loch	[x]	
how, perhaps	[h]	
metal, comb	[m]	mât, drame
night, dinner	[n]	nager, trône
sung, parking	[ŋ]	
	[ɲ]	agneau, peigner
little, help	[l]	halle, lit
right, carry	[r]	arracher, sabre

The symbol ['] has been used to represent the French 'h aspiré', e.g. **hachis** [ˈaʃi].

Le symbole ['] représente le 'h aspiré' français, e.g. **hachis** [ˈaʃi].

The symbol ['] indicates that the following syllable carries primary stress and the symbol [,] that the following syllable carries secondary stress.

Les symboles ['] et [,] indiquent respectivement un accent primaire et un accent secondaire sur la syllabe suivante.

The symbol [ʳ] in English phonetics indicates that the final 'r' is pronounced only when followed by a word beginning with a vowel. Note that it is nearly always pronounced in American English.

Le symbole [ʳ] indique que le 'r' final d'un mot anglais ne se prononce que lorsqu'il forme une liaison avec la voyelle du mot suivant; le 'r' final est presque toujours prononcé en anglais américain.

A phonetic transcription has been given where appropriate after every French headword (the main word which starts an entry). All one-word English headwords similarly have phonetics. For English compound headwords, whether hyphenated or of two or more words, phonetics are given for any element which does not appear elsewhere in the dictionary as a headword in its own right.

Une transcription phonétique – quand elle a été jugée nécessaire – suit chaque libellé (terme-vedette de l'entrée) français, ainsi que chaque libellé anglais écrit en un seul mot. Pour les mots composés anglais (avec ou sans trait d'union, et composés de deux éléments ou plus), la phonétique est présente pour ceux des éléments qui n'apparaissent pas dans le dictionnaire en tant que libellé à part entière.

French Verbs

Key: *prp* = present participle, *pp* = past participle, *pr ind* = present indicative, *imperf* = imperfect, *fut* = future, *cond* = conditional, *pr subj* = present subjunctive

acquérir: *pp* acquis, *pr ind* acquiers, acquérons, acquièrent, *imperf* acquérais, *fut* acquerrai, *pr subj* acquière

aller: *pp* allé, *pr ind* vais, vas, va, allons, allez, vont, *imperf* allais, *fut* irai, *cond* irais, *pr subj* aille

asseoir: *prp* asseyant, *pp* assis, *pr ind* assieds, asseyons, *imperf* asseyais, *fut* assiérai, *pr subj* asseye

atteindre: *prp* atteignant, *pp* atteint, *pr ind* atteins, atteignons, *imperf* atteignais, *pr subj* atteigne

avoir: *prp* ayant, *pp* eu, *pr ind* ai, as, a, avons, avez, ont, *imperf* avais, *fut* aurai, *cond* aurais, *pr subj* aie, aies, ait, ayons, ayez, aient

boire: *prp* buvant, *pp* bu, *pr ind* bois, buvons, boivent, *imperf* buvais, *pr subj* boive

conduire: *prp* conduisant, *pp* conduit, *pr ind* conduis, conduisons, *imperf* conduisais, *pr subj* conduise

connaître: *prp* connaissant, *pp* connu, *pr ind* connais, connaît, connaissons, *imperf* connaissais, *pr subj* connaisse

coudre: *prp* cousant, *pp* cousu, *pr ind* couds, cousons, *imperf* cousais, *pr subj* couse

courir: *pp* couru, *pr ind* cours, courons, *imperf* courais, *fut* courrai, *pr subj* coure

couvrir: *pp* couvert, *pr ind* couvre, couvrons, *imperf* couvrais, *pr subj* couvre

craindre: *prp* craignant, *pp* craint, *pr ind* crains, craignons, *imperf* craignais, *pr subj* craigne

croire: *prp* croyant, *pp* cru, *pr ind* crois, croyons, croient, *imperf* croyais, *pr subj* croie

cueillir: *pp* cueilli, *pr ind* cueille, cueillons, *imperf* cueillais, *fut* cueillerai, *pr subj* cueille

devoir: *pp* dû, due, *pr ind* dois, devons, doivent, *imperf* devais, *fut* devrai, *pr subj* doive

dire: *prp* disant, *pp* dit, *pr ind* dis, disons, dites, disent, *imperf* disais, *pr subj* dise

dormir: *pp* dormi, *pr ind* dors, dormons, *imperf* dormais, *pr subj* dorme

écrire: *prp* écrivant, *pp* écrit, *pr ind* écris, écrivons, *imperf* écrivais, *pr subj* écrive

essuyer: *pp* essuyé, *pr ind* essuie, essuyons, essuient, *imperf* essuyais, *fut* essuierai, *pr subj* essuie

être: *prp* étant, *pp* été, *pr ind* suis, es, est, sommes, êtes, sont, *imperf* étais, *fut* serai, *cond* serais, *pr subj* sois, sois, soit, soyons, soyez, soient

faire: *prp* faisant, *pp* fait, *pr ind* fais, fais, fait, faisons, faites, font, *imperf* faisais, *fut* ferai, *cond* ferais, *pr subj* fasse

falloir: *pp* fallu, *pr ind* faut, *imperf* fallait, *fut* faudra, *pr subj* faille

FINIR: *prp* finissant, *pp* fini, *pr ind* finis, finis, finit, finissons, finissez, finissent, *imperf* finissais, finissais, finissait, finissions, finissiez, finissaient, *fut* finirai, finiras, finira, finirons, finirez, finiront, *cond* finirais, finirais, finirait, finirions, finiriez, finiraient, *pr subj* finisse, finisses, finisse, finissions, finissiez, finissent

fuir: *prp* fuyant, *pp* fui, *pr ind* fuis, fuyons, fuient, *imperf* fuyais, *pr subj* fuie

haïr: *prp* haïssant, *pp* haï, *pr ind* hais, haïssons, *imperf* haïssais, *pr subj* haïsse

joindre: *comme* **atteindre**

lire: *prp* lisant, *pp* lu, *pr ind* lis, lisons, *imperf* lisais, *pr subj* lise

mentir: *pp* menti, *pr ind* mens, mentons, *imperf* mentais, *pr subj* mente

mettre: *prp* mettant, *pp* mis, *pr ind* mets, mettons, *imperf* mettais, *pr subj* mette

mourir: *pp* mort, *pr ind* meurs, mourons, meurent, *imperf* mourais, *fut* mourrai, *pr subj* meure

naître: *prp* naissant, *pp* né, *pr ind* nais, naît, naissons, *imperf* naissais, *pr subj* naisse

offrir: *pp* offert, *pr ind* offre, offrons, *imperf* offrais, *pr subj* offre

paraître: *comme* **connaître**

PARLER: *prp* parlant, *pp* parlé, *pr ind* parle, parles, parle, parlons, parlez, parlent, *imperf* parlais, parlais, parlait, parlions, parliez, parlaient, *fut* parlerai, parleras, parlera, parlerons, parlerez, parleront, *cond* parlerais, parlerais, parlerait, parlerions, parleriez, parleraient, *pr subj* parle, parles, parle, parlions, parliez, parlent

partir: *pp* parti, *pr ind* pars, partons, *imperf* partais, *pr subj* parte

plaire: *prp* plaisant, *pp* plu, *pr ind* plais, plaît, plaisons, *imperf* plaisais, *pr subj* plaise

pleuvoir: *pp* plu, *pr ind* pleut, *imperf* pleuvait, *fut* pleuvra, *pr subj* pleuve

pouvoir: *pp* pu, *pr ind* peux, peux, peut, pouvons, pouvez, peuvent, *imperf* pouvais, *fut* pourrai, *pr subj* puisse

prendre: *prp* prenant, *pp* pris, *pr ind* prends, prenons, prennent, *imperf* prenais, *pr subj* prenne

prévoir: *prp* prévoyant, *pp* prévu, *pr ind* prévois, prévoyons, prévoient, *imperf* prévoyais, *fut* prévoirai, *pr subj* prévoie

recevoir: *pp* reçu, *pr ind* reçois, recevons, reçoivent, *imperf* recevais, *fut* recevrai, *pr subj* reçoive

RENDRE: *prp* rendant, *pp* rendu, *pr ind* rends, rends, rend, rendons, rendez, rendent, *imperf* rendais, rendais, rendait, rendions, rendiez, rendaient, *fut* rendrai, rendras, rendra, rendrons, rendrez, rendront, *cond* rendrais, rendrais, rendrait, rendrions, rendriez, rendraient, *pr subj* rende, rendes, rende, rendions, rendiez, rendent

résoudre: *prp* résolvant, *pp* résolu, *pr ind* résous, résolvons, *imperf* résolvais, *pr subj* résolve

rire: *prp* riant, *pp* ri, *pr ind* ris, rions, *imperf* riais, *pr subj* rie

savoir: *prp* sachant, *pp* su, *pr ind* sais, savons, *imperf* savais, *fut* saurai, *pr subj* sache

servir: *pp* servi, *pr ind* sers, servons, *imperf* servais, *pr subj* serve

sortir: *comme* **partir**

suffire: *prp* suffisant, *pp* suffi, *pr ind* suffis, suffisons, *imperf* suffisais, *pr subj* suffise

suivre: *prp* suivant, *pp* suivi, *pr ind* suis, suivons, *imperf* suivais, *pr subj* suive

taire: *prp* taisant, *pp* tu, *pr ind* tais, taisons, *imperf* taisais, *pr subj* taise

tenir: *pp* tenu, *pr ind* tiens, tenons, tiennent, *imperf* tenais, *fut* tiendrai, *pr subj* tienne

vaincre: *prp* vainquant, *pp* vaincu, *pr ind* vaincs, vainc, vainquons, *imperf* vainquais, *pr subj* vainque

valoir: *pp* valu, *pr ind* vaux, valons, *imperf* valais, *fut* vaudrai, *pr subj* vaille

venir: *comme* **tenir**

vivre: *prp* vivant, *pp* vécu, *pr ind* vis, vivons, *imperf* vivais, *pr subj* vive

voir: *prp* voyant, *pp* vu, *pr ind* vois, voyons, voient, *imperf* voyais, *fut* verrai, *pr subj* voie

vouloir: *pp* voulu, *pr ind* veux, veux, veut, voulons, voulez, veulent, *imperf* voulais, *fut* voudrai, *pr subj* veuille

Numbers

Cardinal numbers are used for counting. The most important ones are:

0 zéro	16 seize	80 quatre-vingts
1 un (f une)	17 dix-sept	81 quatre-vingt-un (f une)
2 deux	18 dix-huit	82 quatre-vingt-deux
3 trois	19 dix-neuf	90 quatre-vingt-dix
4 quatre	20 vingt	91 quatre-vingt-onze
5 cinq	21 vingt et un (f une)	92 quatre-vingt-douze
6 six	22 vingt-deux	93 quatre-vingt-treize
7 sept	23 vingt-trois	100 cent
8 huit	30 trente	101 cent un (f une)
9 neuf	40 quarante	102 cent deux
10 dix	50 cinquante	110 cent dix
11 onze	60 soixante	120 cent vingt
12 douze	70 soixante-dix	121 cent vingt et un (f une)
13 treize	71 soixante et onze	200 deux cents
14 quatorze	72 soixante-douze	300 trois cents
15 quinze	73 soixante-treize	900 neuf cents

1 000	mille	2 000	deux mille
1 001	mille un (f une)	3 000	trois mille
1 002	mille deux	1 000 000	un million
1 100	mille cent, onze cents	2 000 000	deux millions
1 200	mille deux cents, douze cents	1 000 000 000	un milliard
1 900	mille neuf cents, dix-neuf cents		

NOTES:

– **mille** never adds an **-s** in the plural.

– **quatre-vingt** takes an **-s** when it comes at the end of a number: **quatre-vingts**, **deux cent quatre-vingts**. **Cent** also adds an **-s** if it refers to two hundred or more and comes at the end of a number: **cinq cents**, **trois mille sept cents**. However, when **cent** and **vingt** do not come at the end of the number, they do not take **-s** in the plural: **trois cent vingt-cinq**, **quatre-vingt-huit**.

– both **million** and **milliard** are always followed by **de** if they are used with another noun. Unlike their English equivalents, they also add an **-s** when they are preceded by a plural number: **deux millions de chômeurs**, **trois milliards de francs**.

Contrary to English, French uses a comma to mark the decimal part of a number: **6,5** (**six virgule cinq** = six point five); **8,34** (**huit virgule trente-quatre** = eight point three four). Numbers of four digits and above (**2 000**, **10 321**) are normally written with a space before the last three digits.

Ordinal numbers (first, second, third etc.) are used for putting things in order. They are formed by adding **-ième** to the end of the cardinal number, e.g. **deuxième**, **dixième**. If the cardinal number ends in **-e**, this is dropped, e.g. **onzième**, **seizième**. There are minor spelling changes with **cinq** and **neuf**: **cinquième**, **neuvième**. The French for first is **premier** (f **première**). Twenty-first, thirty-first etc. are translated as **vingt et unième**, **trente et unième** etc.

For more information on numbers, look at the entries for **six** and **sixième** on the French-English side of your dictionary, and at **six** and **sixth** on the English-French side.

Dates

The most usual ways of asking the date are: **quelle date sommes-nous?** or **quelle est la date aujourd'hui?** The reply will normally start with **c'est ...** or **nous sommes ...**

Remember that the cardinal numbers are used in dates in French: **le dix janvier**, **le vingt-cinq février**. For the first of the month, however, **premier** is used: **le premier septembre**.

To say the year in French: 1995 can be pronounced as either **mille neuf cent quatre-vingt-quinze** or **dix-neuf cent quatre-vingt-quinze**.

The days of the week are:

Monday	**lundi**
Tuesday	**mardi**
Wednesday	**mercredi**
Thursday	**jeudi**
Friday	**vendredi**
Saturday	**samedi**
Sunday	**dimanche**

The months of the year are:

January	**janvier**
February	**février**
March	**mars**
April	**avril**
May	**mai**
June	**juin**
July	**juillet**
August	**août**
September	**septembre**
October	**octobre**
November	**novembre**
December	**décembre**

Note that the days of the week and the months of the year start with a small letter in French.

For more information on days and months, look at the entries for **samedi** and **septembre** on the French-English side of your dictionary, and at **Saturday** and **September** on the English-French side.

The Time

The most usual way of asking the time is: **quelle heure est-il?** Here are some possible answers:

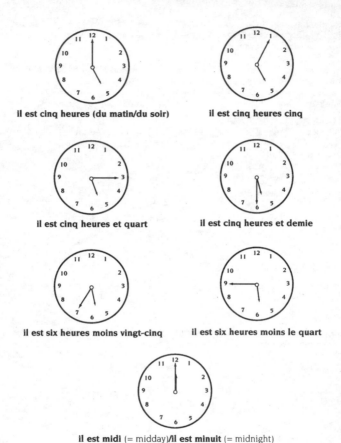

il est cinq heures (du matin/du soir)   **il est cinq heures cinq**

il est cinq heures et quart   **il est cinq heures et demie**

il est six heures moins vingt-cinq   **il est six heures moins le quart**

il est midi (= midday)/**il est minuit** (= midnight)

In French you may find times expressed using the 24-hour clock: a train departing at **quatorze heures vingt**, for example, would leave at 2.20 p.m.

a¹, A [a] *nm inv* a, A; **de A à Z** from beginning to end. ► **A 1.** (*abr de* **ampère**) A, amp. **2.** (*abr de* **autoroute**) M.
a² → **avoir**.

à [a] *prép* (*contraction de à + le =* **au**, *contraction de à + les =* **aux**) **1.** (*introduisant un complément d'objet indirect*) to; **parler à qqn** to speak to sb; **donner qqch à qqn** to give sth to sb, to give sb sth. **2.** (*introduisant un complément de lieu - situation*) at, in; (*- direction*) to; **être à la maison/au bureau** to be at home/at the office; **il habite à Paris/à la campagne** he lives in Paris/in the country; **aller à Paris/à la campagne/au Pérou** to go to Paris/to the country/to Peru; **un voyage à Londres/aux Seychelles** a journey to London/to the Seychelles. **3.** (*introduisant un complément de temps*): **à onze heures** at eleven o'clock; **au mois de février** in the month of February; **à plus tard!** see you later!; **de huit à dix heures** from eight to ten o'clock; **se situer à une heure/à 10 kilomètres de l'aéroport** to be situated an hour/10 kilometres (away) from the airport. **4.** (*introduisant un complément de manière, de moyen*): **à haute voix** out loud, aloud; **rire aux éclats** to roar with laughter; **acheter à crédit** to buy on credit; **à pied/cheval** on foot/horseback. **5.** (*indiquant une caractéristique*) with; **une fille aux cheveux longs** a girl with long hair; **l'homme à l'imperméable** the man with the raincoat. **6.** (*introduisant un chiffre*): **ils sont venus à dix** ten of them came; **un livre à 30 francs** a 30-franc book, a book costing 30 francs; **la vitesse est limitée à 50 km à l'heure** the speed limit is 50 km per ou an hour; **un groupe de 10 à 12 personnes** a group of 10 to 12 people, a group of between 10 and 12 people; **deux à deux** two by two. **7.** (*marque l'appartenance*): **c'est à moi/toi/lui/elle** it's mine/yours/his/hers; **ce vélo est à ma sœur** this bike is my sister's ou belongs to my sister; **une amie à moi** a friend of mine. **8.** (*introduit le but*): **coupe à champagne** champagne goblet; **le courrier à poster** the mail to be posted; **appartement à vendre/louer** flat for sale/to let.

AB (*abr de* **assez bien**) *fair grade* (*as assessment of schoolwork*).

abaisser [abese] *vt* **1.** (*rideau, voile*) to lower; (*levier, manette*) to push ou pull down. **2.** (*diminuer*) to reduce, to lower. ► **s'abaisser** *vp* **1.** (*descendre - rideau*) to fall, to come down; (*- terrain*) to fall away. **2.** (*s'humilier*) to demean o.s.; **s'~ à faire qqch** to lower o.s. to do sthg.

abandon [abādɔ̃] *nm* **1.** (*désertion, délaissement*) desertion; **à l'~** (*jardin, maison*) neglected, in a state of neglect. **2.** (*renonciation*) abandoning, giving up. **3.** (*nonchalance, confiance*) abandon.

abandonner [abādɔne] *vt* **1.** (*quitter - femme, enfants*) to abandon, to desert; (*- voiture, propriété*) to abandon. **2.** (*renoncer à*) to give up, to abandon. **3.** (*se retirer de - course, concours*) to withdraw from. **4.** (*céder*): **~ qqch à qqn** to leave sth to sb, to leave sb sthg.

abasourdi, -e [abazurdi] *adj* stunned.

abat-jour [abaʒur] *nm inv* lampshade.

abats [aba] *nmpl* (*d'animal*) offal (U); (*de volaille*) giblets.

abattement [abatmã] *nm* **1.** (*faiblesse physique*) weakness. **2.** (*désespoir*) dejection. **3.** (*déduction*) reduction; **~ fiscal** tax allowance.

abattis [abati] *nmpl* giblets.

abattoir [abatwar] *nm* abattoir, slaughterhouse.

abattre [abatr] *vt* 1. (*faire tomber - mur*) to knock down; (- *arbre*) to cut down, to fell; (- *avion*) to bring down. 2. (*tuer - gén*) to kill; (- *dans un abattoir*) to slaughter. 3. (*épuiser*) to wear out; (*démoraliser*) to demoralize.

abbaye [abei] *nf* abbey.

abbé [abe] *nm* 1. (*prêtre*) priest. 2. (*de couvent*) abbot.

abc *nm* basics (*pl*).

abcès [apsɛ] *nm* abscess.

abdiquer [abdike] ◆ *vt* (*renoncer à*) to renounce. ◆ *vi* (*roi*) to abdicate.

abdomen [abdomɛn] *nm* abdomen.

abdominaux [abdomino] *nmpl* 1. (*muscles*) abdominal ou stomach muscles. 2. (*exercices*): **faire des abdominaux** to do exercises for the stomach muscles.

abeille [abɛj] *nf* bee.

aberrant, -e [aberɑ̃, ɑ̃t] *adj* absurd.

abîme [abim] *nm* abyss, gulf.

abîmer [abime] *vt* (*détériorer - objet*) to damage; (- *partie du corps, vue*) to ruin. ▶ **s'abîmer** *vp* (*gén*) to be damaged; (*fruits*) to go bad.

abject, -e [abʒɛkt] *adj* despicable, contemptible.

aboiement [abwamɑ̃] *nm* bark, barking (U).

abolir [abolir] *vt* to abolish.

abominable [abominabl] *adj* appalling, awful.

abondance [abɔ̃dɑ̃s] *nf* 1. (*profusion*) abundance. 2. (*opulence*) affluence.

abondant, -e [abɔ̃dɑ̃, ɑ̃t] *adj* (*gén*) plentiful; (*végétation, chevelure*) luxuriant; (*pluie*) heavy.

abonder [abɔ̃de] *vi* to abound, to be abundant; **~ en qqch** to be rich in sthg; **~ dans le sens de qqn** to be entirely of sb's opinion.

abonné, -e [abɔne] *nm, f* 1. (*à un journal, à une chaîne de télé*) subscriber; (*à un théâtre*) season-ticket holder. 2. (*à un service public*) consumer.

abonnement [abɔnmɑ̃] *nm* 1. (*à un journal, à une chaîne de télé*) subscription; (*à un théâtre*) season ticket. 2. (*au téléphone*) rental; (*au gaz, à l'électricité*) standing charge.

abonner [abɔne] ▶ **s'abonner** *vp*: **s'~ à qqch** (*journal, chaîne de télé*) to take out a subscription to sthg; (*service public*) to get connected to sthg; (*théâtre*) to buy a season ticket for sthg.

abord [abɔr] *nm*: **être d'un ~ facile/difficile** to be very/not very approachable. ▶ **abords** *nmpl* (*gén*) surrounding area (*sg*); (*de ville*) outskirts. ▶ **d'abord** *loc adv* 1. (*en premier lieu*) first. 2. (*avant tout*): (**tout**) **d'~** first (of all), in the first place.

abordable [abɔrdabl] *adj* (*lieu*) accessible; (*personne*) approachable; (*de prix modéré*) affordable.

aborder [abɔrde] ◆ *vi* to land. ◆ *vt* 1. (*personne, lieu*) to approach. 2. (*question*) to tackle.

aborigène [abɔriʒɛn] *adj* aboriginal. ▶ **Aborigène** *nmf* (Australian) aborigine.

abouti, -e [abuti] *adj* (*projet, démarche*) successful.

aboutir [abutir] *vi* 1. (*chemin*): **~ à/dans** to end at/in. 2. (*négociation*) to be successful; **~ à qqch** to result in sthg.

aboutissement [abutismɑ̃] *nm* outcome.

aboyer [abwaje] *vi* to bark.

abrasif, -ive [abrazif, iv] *adj* abrasive.

abrégé, -e [abreʒe] *adj* abridged.

abréger [abreʒe] *vt* (*visite, réunion*) to cut short; (*discours*) to shorten; (*mot*) to abbreviate.

abreuvoir [abrœvwar] *nm* (*lieu*) watering place; (*installation*) drinking trough.

abréviation [abrevjasjɔ̃] *nf* abbreviation.

abri [abri] *nm* shelter; **à l'~ de** sheltered from; *fig* safe from; **~ de jardin** garden shed.

abricot [abriko] *nm & adj inv* apricot.

abricotier [abrikɔtje] *nm* apricot tree.

abriter [abrite] *vt* 1. (*protéger*): **~ qqn/qqch (de)** to shelter sb/sthg (from). 2. (*héberger*) to accommodate. ▶ **s'abriter** *vp*: **s'~ (de)** to shelter (from).

abroger [abrɔʒe] *vt* to repeal.

abrupt, -e [abrypt] *adj* 1. (*raide*) steep. 2. (*rude*) abrupt, brusque.

abruti, -e [abryti] *fam nm, f* moron.

abrutir [abrytir] *vt* 1. (*abêtir*): **~ qqn** to deaden sb's mind. 2. (*accabler*): **~ qqn de travail** to work sb silly.

abrutissant, -e [abrytisɑ̃, ɑ̃t] *adj* 1. (*bruit, travail*) stupefying. 2. (*jeu, feuilleton*) moronic.

absence [apsɑ̃s] *nf* 1. (*de personne*) absence. 2. (*carence*) lack.

absent, -e [apsɑ̃, ɑ̃t] ◆ *adj* 1. (*personne*): **~ (de)** (*gén*) away (from); (*pour maladie*) absent (from). 2. (*regard, air*)

vacant, absent. **3.** (*manquant*) lacking.
♦ *nm, f* absentee.

absenter [apsɑ̃te] ▶ **s'absenter** *vp*:
s'~ (de la pièce) to leave (the room).

absinthe [apsɛ̃t] *nf* (*plante*) worm-wood; (*boisson*) absinth.

absolu, -e [apsɔly] *adj* (*gén*) absolute;
(*décision, jugement*) uncompromising.

absolument [apsɔlymɑ̃] *adv* absolute-ly.

absorbant, -e [apsɔrbɑ̃, ɑ̃t] *adj*
1. (*matière*) absorbent. **2.** (*occupation*)
absorbing.

absorber [apsɔrbe] *vt* **1.** (*gén*) to
absorb. **2.** (*manger*) to take.

abstenir [apstənir] ▶ **s'abstenir** *vp*
1. (*ne rien faire*): **s'~ (de qqch/de faire
qqch)** to refrain (from sthg/from doing
sthg). **2.** (*ne pas voter*) to abstain.

abstention [apstɑ̃sjɔ̃] *nf* abstention.

abstinence [apstinɑ̃s] *nf* abstinence.

abstraction [apstraksjɔ̃] *nf* abstrac-tion; **faire ~ de** to disregard.

abstrait, -e [apstrɛ, ɛt] *adj* abstract.

absurde [apsyrd] *adj* absurd.

absurdité [apsyrdite] *nf* absurdity;
dire des ~s to talk nonsense (U).

abus [aby] *nm* abuse; **~ de confiance**
breach of trust; **~ de pouvoir** abuse of
power.

abuser [abyze] *vi* **1.** (*dépasser les bornes*)
to go too far. **2.** (*user*): **~ de** (*autorité, pou-voir*) to overstep the bounds of; (*temps*)
to take up too much of; **~ de ses forces**
to overexert o.s.

abusif, -ive [abyzif, iv] *adj* **1.** (*excessif*)
excessive. **2.** (*fautif*) improper.

acabit [akabi] *nm*: **du même ~** *péj* of the
same type.

acacia [akasja] *nm* acacia.

académicien, -enne [akademisjɛ̃,
ɛn] *nm, f* academician; (*de l'Académie
française*) member of the French
Academy.

académie [akademi] *nf* **1.** (SCOL &
UNIV) ≈ regional education authority
Br, ≈ school district Am. **2.** (*institut*)
academy; **l'Académie française** the
French Academy (*learned society of leading
men and women of letters*).

acajou [akaʒu] *nm & adj inv* mahogany.

acariâtre [akarjɑtr] *adj* bad-tempered, cantankerous.

acarien [akarjɛ̃] *nm* (*gén*) acarid; (*de
poussière*) dust mite.

accablant, -e [akablɑ̃, ɑ̃t] *adj* **1.** (*soleil,
chaleur*) oppressive. **2.** (*preuve, témoi-gnage*) overwhelming.

accabler [akable] *vt* **1.** (*surcharger*):
qqn de (*travail*) to overwhelm sb with; **~
qqn d'injures** to shower sb with abuse.
2. (*accuser*) to condemn.

accalmie [akalmi] *nf litt & fig* lull.

accéder [aksede] ▶ **accéder à** *vt*
1. (*pénétrer dans*) to reach, to get to.
2. (*parvenir à*) to attain. **3.** (*consentir à*)
comply with.

accélérateur [akseleratœr] *nm* accel-erator.

accélération [akselerasjɔ̃] *nf* (*de
voiture, machine*) acceleration; (*de projet*)
speeding up.

accélérer [akselere] ♦ *vt* to accelerate,
to speed up. ♦ *vi* (AUTOM) to accelerate.

accent [aksɑ̃] *nm* **1.** (*gén*) accent; **~
aigu/grave/circonflexe** acute/grave/cir-cumflex (accent). **2.** (*intonation*) tone;
mettre l'~ sur to stress, to emphasize.

accentuation [aksɑ̃tɥasjɔ̃] *nf* (*à l'écrit*)
accenting; (*en parlant*) stress.

accentuer [aksɑ̃tɥe] *vt* **1.** (*insister sur,
souligner*) to emphasize, to accentuate.
2. (*intensifier*) to intensify. **3.** (*à l'écrit*) to
put the accents on; (*en parlant*) to
stress. ▶ **s'accentuer** *vp* to become
more pronounced.

acceptable [aksɛptabl] *adj* satisfac-tory, acceptable.

acceptation [aksɛptasjɔ̃] *nf* accept-ance.

accepter [aksɛpte] *vt* to accept; **~ de
faire qqch** to agree to do sthg; **~ que** (+
subjonctif): **~ que qqn fasse qqch** to agree
to sb doing sthg; **je n'accepte pas qu'il
me parle ainsi** I won't have him talking
to me like that.

acception [aksɛpsjɔ̃] *nf* sense.

accès [aksɛ] *nm* **1.** (*entrée*) entry; **avoir/
donner ~ à** to have/to give access to; **'~
interdit'** 'no entry'. **2.** (*voie d'entrée*)
entrance. **3.** (*crise*) bout; **~ de colère** fit
of anger.

accessible [aksesibl] *adj* (*lieu, livre*)
accessible; (*personne*) approachable;
(*prix, équipement*) affordable.

accession [aksesjɔ̃] *nf*: **~ à** (*trône, prési-dence*) accession to; (*indépendance*)
attainment of.

accessoire [akseswar] ♦ *nm* **1.** (*gén*)
accessory. **2.** (*de théâtre, cinéma*) prop.
♦ *adj* secondary.

accident [aksidɑ̃] *nm* accident; **par ~**
by chance, by accident; **~ de la route/
de voiture** road/car accident.

accidenté, -e [aksidɑ̃te] ♦ *adj* **1.** (*ter-rain, surface*) uneven. **2.** (*voiture*) damaged. ◆ *nm, f* (*gén pl*): ~ **de la route** accident victim.

accidentel, -elle [aksidãtɛl] *adj* accidental.

acclamation [aklamasjɔ̃] *nf* (*gén pl*) cheers (*pl*), cheering (U).

acclamer [aklame] *vt* to cheer.

acclimatation [aklimatasjɔ̃] *nf* acclimatization.

acclimater [aklimate] *vt* to acclimatize; *fig* to introduce.

accolade [akɔlad] *nf* 1. (TYPO) brace. 2. (*embrassade*) embrace.

accommodant, -e [akɔmɔdã, ãt] *adj* obliging.

accommodement [akɔmɔdmã] *nm* compromise.

accommoder [akɔmɔde] *vt* (CULIN) to prepare.

accompagnateur, -trice [akɔ̃paɲatœr, tris] *nm, f* 1. (MUS) accompanist. 2. (*guide*) guide.

accompagnement [akɔ̃paɲmã] *nm* (MUS) accompaniment.

accompagner [akɔ̃paɲe] *vt* 1. (*personne*) to go with, to accompany. 2. (*agrémenter*): ~ **qqch de** to accompany sthg with. 3. (MUS) to accompany.

accompli, -e [akɔ̃pli] *adj* accomplished.

accomplir [akɔ̃plir] *vt* to carry out. ▶ **s'accomplir** *vp* to come about.

accomplissement [akɔ̃plismã] *nm* (*d'apprentissage*) completion; (*de travail*) fulfilment.

accord [akɔr] *nm* 1. (*gén & LING*) agreement. 2. (MUS) chord. 3. (*acceptation*) approval; **donner son ~ à qqch** to approve sthg. ▶ **d'accord** ◆ *loc adv* OK, all right. ◆ *loc adj*: **être d'~ (avec)** to agree (with); **tomber** OU **se mettre d'~** to come to an agreement, to agree.

accordéon [akɔrdeɔ̃] *nm* accordion.

accorder [akɔrde] *vt* 1. (*donner*): ~ **qqch à qqn** to grant sb sthg. 2. (*attribuer*): ~ **qqch à qqch** to accord sthg to sthg; ~ **de l'importance à** to attach importance to. 3. (*harmoniser*) to match. 4. (GRAM): ~ **qqch avec qqch** to make sthg agree with sthg. 5. (MUS) to tune. ▶ **s'accorder** *vp* 1. (*gén*): **s'~ (pour faire qqch)** to agree (to do sthg); **s'~ à faire qqch** to be unanimous in doing sthg. 2. (*être assorti*) to match. 3. (GRAM) to agree.

accoster [akɔste] ◆ *vt* 1. (NAVIG) to come alongside. 2. (*personne*) to accost. ◆ *vi* (NAVIG) to dock.

accotement [akɔtmã] *nm* (*de route*)

shoulder; ~ **non stabilisé** soft verge Br, soft shoulder Am.

accouchement [akuʃmã] *nm* childbirth; ~ **sans douleur** natural childbirth.

accoucher [akuʃe] *vi*: ~ **(de)** to give birth (to).

accouder [akude] ▶ **s'accouder** *vp* to lean on one's elbows; **s'~ à** to lean one's elbows on.

accoudoir [akudwar] *nm* armrest.

accouplement [akupləmã] *nm* mating, coupling.

accourir [akurir] *vi* to run up, to rush up.

accouru, -e [akury] *pp* → **accourir**.

accoutré, -e [akutre] *adj péj*: **être bizarrement ~** to be oddly got up.

accoutrement [akutrəmã] *nm péj* getup.

accoutumer [akutyme] *vt*: ~ **qqn à qqn/qqch** to get sb used to sb/sthg; ~ **qqn à faire qqch** to get sb used to doing sthg. ▶ **s'accoutumer** *vp*: **s'~ à qqn/qqch** to get used to sb/sthg; **s'~ à faire qqch** to get used to doing sthg.

accréditer [akredite] *vt* (*rumeur*) to substantiate; ~ **qqn auprès de** to accredit sb to.

accro [akro] *fam* ◆ *adj*: ~ **à** hooked on. ◆ *nmf*: **c'est une ~ de la planche** she's a windsurfing freak.

accroc [akro] *nm* 1. (*déchirure*) tear. 2. (*incident*) hitch.

accrochage [akrɔʃaʒ] *nm* 1. (*accident*) collision. 2. *fam* (*dispute*) row.

accroche [akrɔʃ] *nf* (COMM) catch line.

accrocher [akrɔʃe] *vt* 1. (*suspendre*): ~ **qqch (à)** to hang sthg up (on). 2. (*déchirer*): ~ **qqch (à)** to catch sthg (on). 3. (*attacher*): ~ **qqch (à)** to hitch sthg (to). ▶ **s'accrocher** *vp* 1. (*s'agripper*): **s'~ (à)** to hang on (to); **s'~ à qqn** *fig* to cling to sb. 2. *fam* (*se disputer*) to row, to have a row. 3. *fam* (*persévérer*) to stick at it.

accroissement [akrwasmã] *nm* increase, growth.

accroître [akrwatr] *vt* to increase. ▶ **s'accroître** *vp* to increase, to grow.

accroupir [akrupir] ▶ **s'accroupir** *vp* to squat.

accru, -e [akry] *pp* → **accroître**.

accueil [akœj] *nm* 1. (*lieu*) reception. 2. (*action*) welcome, reception.

accueillant, -e [akœjã, ãt] *adj* welcoming, friendly.

accueillir [akœjir] *vt* 1. (*gén*) to welcome. 2. (*loger*) to accommodate.

accumulateur [akymylatœr] *nm* accumulator, battery.

accumulation [akymylasjɔ̃] *nf* accumulation.

accumuler [akymyle] *vt* to accumulate; *fig* to store up. ▶ **s'accumuler** *vp* to pile up.

accusateur, -trice [akyzatœr, tris] ◆ *adj* accusing. ◆ *nm, f* accuser.

accusation [akyzasjɔ̃] *nf* 1. (*reproche*) accusation. 2. (JUR) charge; **mettre en ~** to indict; **l'~** the prosecution.

accusé, -e [akyze] *nm, f* accused, defendant. ▶ **accusé de réception** *nm* acknowledgement (of receipt).

accuser [akyze] *vt* 1. (*porter une accusation contre*): **~ qqn (de qqch)** to accuse sb (of sthg). 2. (JUR): **~ qqn de qqch** to charge sb with sthg.

acerbe [asɛrb] *adj* acerbic.

acéré, -e [asere] *adj* sharp.

achalandé, -e [aʃalɑ̃de] *adj* (*en marchandises*): **bien ~** well-stocked.

acharné, -e [aʃarne] *adj* (*combat*) fierce; (*travail*) unremitting.

acharnement [aʃarnəmɑ̃] *nm* relentlessness.

acharner [aʃarne] ▶ **s'acharner** *vp* 1. (*combattre*): **s'~ contre** ou **après** ou **sur qqn** (*ennemi, victime*) to hound sb; (*suj: malheur*) to dog sb. 2. (*s'obstiner*): **s'~ (à faire qqch)** to persist (in doing sthg).

achat [aʃa] *nm* purchase; **faire des ~s** to go shopping.

acheminer [aʃmine] *vt* to dispatch. ▶ **s'acheminer** *vp*: **s'~ vers** (*lieu, désastre*) to head for; (*solution, paix*) to move towards.

acheter [aʃte] *vt litt & fig* to buy; **~ qqch à** ou **pour qqn** to buy sthg for sb, to buy sb sthg.

acheteur, -euse [aʃtœr, øz] *nm, f* buyer, purchaser.

achevé, -e [aʃve] *adj sout*: **d'un ridicule ~** utterly ridiculous.

achèvement [aʃevmɑ̃] *nm* completion.

achever [aʃve] *vt* 1. (*terminer*) to complete, to finish (off). 2. (*tuer, accabler*) to finish off. ▶ **s'achever** *vp* to end, to come to an end.

achoppement [aʃɔpmɑ̃] → **pierre**.

acide [asid] ◆ *adj* 1. (*saveur*) sour. 2. (*propos*) sharp, acid. 3. (CHIM) acid. ◆ *nm* (CHIM) acid.

acidité [asidite] *nf* 1. (CHIM) acidity. 2. (*saveur*) sourness. 3. (*de propos*) sharpness.

acidulé, -e [asidyle] *adj* slightly acid. → **bonbon**.

acier [asje] *nm* steel; **~ inoxydable** stainless steel.

aciérie [asjeri] *nf* steelworks (*sg*).

acné [akne] *nf* acne.

acolyte [akɔlit] *nm péj* henchman.

acompte [akɔ̃t] *nm* deposit.

à-côté [akote] (*pl* **à-côtés**) *nm* 1. (*point accessoire*) side issue. 2. (*gain d'appoint*) extra.

à-coup [aku] (*pl* **à-coups**) *nm* jerk; **par ~s** in fits and starts.

acoustique [akustik] *nf* 1. (*science*) acoustics (U). 2. (*d'une salle*) acoustics (*pl*).

acquéreur [akerœr] *nm* buyer.

acquérir [akerir] *vt* (*gén*) to acquire.

acquiescement [akjɛsmɑ̃] *nm* approval.

acquiescer [akjese] *vi* to acquiesce; **~ à** to agree to.

acquis, -e [aki, iz] ◆ *pp* → **acquérir**. ◆ *adj* 1. (*caractère*) acquired. 2. (*droit, avantage*) established. ▶ **acquis** *nmpl* (*connaissances*) knowledge (U).

acquisition [akizisjɔ̃] *nf* acquisition.

acquit [aki] *nm* receipt; **pour ~** (COMM) received; **faire qqch par ~ de conscience** *fig* to do sthg to set one's mind at rest.

acquittement [akitmɑ̃] *nm* 1. (*d'obligation*) settlement. 2. (JUR) acquittal.

acquitter [akite] *vt* 1. (JUR) to acquit. 2. (*régler*) to pay. 3. (*libérer*): **~ qqn de** to release sb from.

âcre [akr] *adj* 1. (*saveur*) bitter. 2. (*fumée*) acrid.

acrobate [akrɔbat] *nmf* acrobat.

acrobatie [akrɔbasi] *nf* acrobatics (U).

acrylique [akrilik] *adj & nm* acrylic.

acte [akt] *nm* 1. (*action*) act, action; **faire ~ d'autorité** to exercise one's authority; **faire ~ de candidature** to submit an application. 2. (THÉÂTRE) act. 3. (JUR) deed; **~ d'accusation** charge; **~ de naissance/de mariage** birth/marriage certificate; **~ de vente** bill of sale. 4. (RELIG) certificate. 5. *loc*: **faire ~ de présence** to put in an appearance; **prendre ~ de** to note, to take note of. ▶ **actes** *nmpl* (*de colloque*) proceedings.

acteur, -trice [aktœr, tris] *nm, f* actor (*f* actress).

actif, -ive [aktif, iv] *adj* (*gén*) active; **la population active** the working population. ▶ **actif** *nm* 1. (FIN) assets (*pl*). 2. *loc*: **avoir qqch à son ~** to have sthg to one's credit.

action [aksjɔ̃] *nf* 1. (*gén*) action; **sous l'~ de** under the effect of. 2. (*acte*) action, act; **bonne/mauvaise ~** good/

bad deed. **3.** (JUR) action, lawsuit. **4.** (FIN) share.

actionnaire [aksjɔnɛr] *nmf* (FIN) shareholder.

actionner [aksjɔne] *vt* to work, to activate.

activement [aktivmã] *adv* actively.

activer [aktive] *vt* to speed up. ► **s'activer** *vp* to bustle about.

activiste [aktivist] *adj & nmf* activist.

activité [aktivite] *nf* (*gén*) activity; **en ~** (*volcan*) active.

actualiser [aktyalize] *vt* to bring up to date.

actualité [aktyalite] *nf* **1.** (*d'un sujet*) topicality. **2.** (*événements*): **l'~ sportive/ politique/littéraire** the current sports/ political/literary scene. ► **actualités** *nfpl*: **les ~s** the news (*sg*).

actuel, -elle [aktyɛl] *adj* (*contemporain, présent*) current, present; **à l'heure ~le** at the present time.

actuellement [aktyɛlmã] *adv* at present, currently.

acuité [akyite] *nf* acuteness.

acupuncture, acuponcture [akypɔ̃ktyr] *nf* acupuncture.

adage [adaʒ] *nm* adage, saying.

adaptateur, -trice [adaptatœr, tris] *nm, f* adapter. ► **adaptateur** *nm* (ÉLECTR) adapter.

adaptation [adaptasjɔ̃] *nf* adaptation.

adapter [adapte] *vt* **1.** (*gén*) to adapt. **2.** (*fixer*) to fit. ► **s'adapter** *vp*: **s'~ (à)** to adapt (to).

additif [aditif] *nm* **1.** (*supplément*) rider, additional clause. **2.** (*substance*) additive.

addition [adisjɔ̃] *nf* **1.** (*ajout, calcul*) addition. **2.** (*note*) bill Br, check Am.

additionner [adisjɔne] *vt* **1.** (*mélanger*): **~ une poudre d'eau** to add water to a powder. **2.** (*chiffres*) to add up.

adepte [adɛpt] *nmf* follower.

adéquat, -e [adekwa, at] *adj* suitable, appropriate.

adhérence [aderãs] *nf* (*de pneu*) grip.

adhérent, -e [aderã, ãt] *nm, f*: **~ (de)** member (of).

adhérer [adere] *vi* **1.** (*coller*) to stick, to adhere; **~ à** (*se fixer sur*) to stick ou adhere to; (*être d'accord avec*) *fig* to support, to adhere to. **2.** (*être membre*): **~ à** to become a member of, to join.

adhésif, -ive [adezif, iv] *adj* sticky, adhesive. ► **adhésif** *nm* adhesive.

adhésion [adezjɔ̃] *nf* **1.** (*à idée*): **~ (à)** support (for). **2.** (*à parti*): **~ (à)** membership (of).

adieu [adjø] ♦ *interj* goodbye!, farewell!; **dire ~ à qqch** *fig* to say goodbye to sthg. ♦ *nm* (*gén pl*) farewell; **faire ses ~x à qqn** to say one's farewells to sb.

adipeux, -euse [adipø, øz] *adj* (*tissu*) adipose; (*personne*) fat.

adjectif [adʒɛktif] *nm* (GRAM) adjective.

adjoint, -e [adʒwɛ̃, ɛ̃t] ♦ *adj* deputy (*avant n*), assistant (*avant n*). ♦ *nm, f* deputy, assistant; **~ au maire** deputy mayor.

adjonction [adʒɔ̃ksjɔ̃] *nf* addition.

adjudant [adʒydã] *nm* (*dans la marine*) warrant officer; (*dans l'armée*) company sergeant major.

adjuger [adʒyʒe] *vt*: **~ qqch (à qqn)** (*aux enchères*) to auction sthg (to sb); (*décerner*) to award sthg (to sb); **adjugé!** sold!

admettre [admɛtr] *vt* **1.** (*tolérer, accepter*) to allow, to accept. **2.** (*autoriser*) to allow. **3.** (*accueillir, reconnaître*) to admit.

administrateur, -trice [administratœr, tris] *nm, f* **1.** (*gérant*) administrator; **~ judiciaire** receiver. **2.** (*de conseil d'administration*) director.

administratif, -ive [administratif, iv] *adj* administrative.

administration [administrasjɔ̃] *nf* **1.** (*service public*): **l'Administration** ≃ the Civil Service. **2.** (*gestion*) administration.

administrer [administre] *vt* **1.** (*gérer*) to manage, to administer. **2.** (*médicament, sacrement*) to administer.

admirable [admirabl] *adj* **1.** (*personne, comportement*) admirable. **2.** (*paysage, spectacle*) wonderful.

admiratif, -ive [admiratif, iv] *adj* admiring.

admiration [admirasjɔ̃] *nf* admiration.

admirer [admire] *vt* to admire.

admis, -e [admi, iz] *pp* → **admettre**.

admissible [admisibl] *adj* **1.** (*attitude*) acceptable. **2.** (SCOL) eligible.

admission [admisjɔ̃] *nf* admission.

ADN (*abr de* **acide désoxyribonucléique**) *nm* DNA.

ado [ado] (*abr de* **adolescent**) *nmf fam* teenager.

adolescence [adɔlesãs] *nf* adolescence.

adolescent, -e [adɔlesã, ãt] *nm, f* adolescent, teenager.

affecter

adonner [adɔne] ▶ **s'adonner** vp: s'~ à (sport, activité) to devote o.s. to; (vice) to take to.

adopter [adɔpte] vt 1. (gén) to adopt. 2. (loi) to pass.

adoptif, -ive [adɔptif, iv] adj (famille) adoptive; (pays, enfant) adopted.

adoption [adɔpsjɔ̃] nf adoption; d'~ (pays, ville) adopted; (famille) adoptive.

adorable [adɔrabl] adj adorable, delightful.

adoration [adɔrasjɔ̃] nf 1. (amour) adoration. 2. (RELIG) worship.

adorer [adɔre] vt 1. (personne, chose) to adore. 2. (RELIG) to worship.

adosser [adose] vt: ~ qqch à qqch to place sthg against sthg. ▶ **s'adosser** vp: s'~ à ou contre qqch to lean against sthg.

adoucir [adusir] vt 1. (gén) to soften. 2. (chagrin, peine) to ease, to soothe. ▶ **s'adoucir** vp 1. (temps) to become ou get milder. 2. (personne) to mellow.

adoucissant, -e [adusisã, ãt] adj soothing. ▶ **adoucissant** nm softener.

adoucisseur [adusisœr] nm: ~ d'eau water softener.

adresse [adrɛs] nf 1. (gén & INFORM) address. 2. (habileté) skill.

adresser [adrese] vt 1. (faire parvenir): ~ qqch à qqn to address sthg to sb. 2. (envoyer): ~ qqn à qqn to refer sb to sb. ▶ **s'adresser** vp: s'~ à (parler à) to speak to; (être destiné à) to be aimed at, to be intended for.

Adriatique [adriatik] nf: l'~ the Adriatic.

adroit, -e [adrwa, at] adj skilful.

aduler [adyle] vt to adulate.

adulte [adylt] nmf & adj adult.

adultère [adyltɛr] ◆ nm (acte) adultery. ◆ adj adulterous.

advenir [advənir] v impers to happen; qu'advient-il de ...? what is happening to ...?; qu'est-il advenu de ...? what has happened to ou become of ...?

advenu [advəny] pp → **advenir**.

adverbe [advɛrb] nm adverb.

adversaire [advɛrsɛr] nmf adversary, opponent.

adverse [advɛrs] adj (opposé) opposing; → **parti**.

adversité [advɛrsite] nf adversity.

aération [aerasjɔ̃] nf (circulation d'air) ventilation; (action) airing.

aéré, -e [aere] adj 1. (pièce) well-ventilated; **mal ~** stuffy. 2. fig (présentation) well-spaced.

aérer [aere] vt 1. (pièce, chose) to air. 2. fig (présentation, mise en page) to lighten.

aérien, -enne [aerjɛ̃, ɛn] adj 1. (câble) overhead (avant n). 2. (transports, attaque) air (avant n); **compagnie aérienne** airline (company).

aérobic [aerɔbik] nm aerobics (U).

aérodrome [aerɔdrom] nm aerodrome.

aérodynamique [aerɔdinamik] adj streamlined, aerodynamic.

aérogare [aerɔgar] nf 1. (aéroport) airport. 2. (gare) air terminal.

aéroglisseur [aerɔglisœr] nm hovercraft.

aérogramme [aerɔgram] nm aerogramme.

aéronautique [aerɔnotik] nf aeronautics (U).

aéronaval, -e, -als [aerɔnaval] adj air and sea (avant n).

aérophagie [aerɔfaʒi] nf abdominal wind.

aéroport [aerɔpɔr] nm airport.

aéroporté, -e [aerɔpɔrte] adj airborne.

aérosol [aerɔsɔl] nm & adj inv aerosol.

aérospatial, -e, -aux [aerɔspasjal, o] adj aerospace (avant n). ▶ **aérospatiale** nf aerospace industry.

affable [afabl] adj 1. (personne) affable, agreeable. 2. (parole) kind.

affaiblir [afeblir] vt litt & fig to weaken. ▶ **s'affaiblir** vp litt & fig to weaken, to become weaker.

affaire [afɛr] nf 1. (question) matter. 2. (situation, polémique) affair. 3. (marché) deal; **faire une ~** to get a bargain ou a good deal. 4. (entreprise) business. 5. (procès) case. 6. loc: **avoir ~ à qqn** to deal with sb; **vous aurez ~ à moi!** you'll have me to deal with!; **faire l'~** to do nicely. ▶ **affaires** nfpl 1. (COMM) business (U). 2. (objets personnels) things, belongings. 3. (activités) affairs; **les Affaires étrangères** ≈ the Foreign Office (sg).

affairé, -e [afere] adj busy.

affairer [afere] ▶ **s'affairer** vp to bustle about.

affairisme [aferism] nm racketeering.

affaisser [afese] ▶ **s'affaisser** vp 1. (se creuser) to subside, to sink. 2. (tomber) to collapse.

affaler [afale] ▶ **s'affaler** vp to collapse.

affamé, -e [afame] adj starving.

affecter [afɛkte] vt 1. (consacrer): ~ qqch à to allocate sthg to. 2. (nommer):

~ **qqn à** to appoint sb to. **3.** (*feindre*) to feign. **4.** (*émouvoir*) to affect, to move.

affectif, -ive [afεktif, iv] *adj* emotional.

affection [afεksjɔ̃] *nf* **1.** (*sentiment*) affection; **avoir de l'~ pour** to be fond of. **2.** (*maladie*) complaint.

affectionner [afεksjɔne] *vt* to be fond of.

affectueusement [afεktɥøzmɑ̃] *adv* affectionately.

affectueux, -euse [afεktɥø, øz] *adj* affectionate.

affichage [afiʃaʒ] *nm* **1.** (*d'un poster, d'un avis*) putting up, displaying. **2.** (ÉLECTRON): ~ **à cristaux liquides** LCD, liquid crystal display; ~ **numérique** digital display.

affiche [afiʃ] *nf* (*gén*) poster; (*officielle*) notice.

afficher [afiʃe] *vt* **1.** (*liste, poster*) to put up; (*vente, réglementation*) to put up a notice about. **2.** (*laisser transparaître*) to display, to exhibit.

affilée [afile] ▶ **d'affilée** *loc adv*: **trois jours d'~** three days running.

affiler [afile] *vt* to sharpen.

affilier [afilje] ▶ **s'affilier** *vp*: **s'~ à** to join.

affiner [afine] *vt litt & fig* to refine.

affinité [afinite] *nf* affinity.

affirmatif, -ive [afirmatif, iv] *adj* **1.** (*réponse*) affirmative. **2.** (*personne*) positive. ▶ **affirmative** *nf*: **dans l'affirmative** if yes, if the answer is yes; **répondre par l'affirmative** to reply in the affirmative.

affirmation [afirmasjɔ̃] *nf* assertion.

affirmer [afirme] *vt* **1.** (*certifier*) to maintain, to claim. **2.** (*exprimer*) to assert.

affliction [afliksjɔ̃] *nf* affliction.

affligeant, -e [afliʒɑ̃, ɑ̃t] *adj* **1.** (*désolant*) saddening, distressing. **2.** (*lamentable*) appalling.

affliger [afliʒe] *vt sout* **1.** (*attrister*) to sadden, to distress. **2.** (*de défaut, de maladie*): **être affligé de** to be afflicted with.

affluence [aflyɑ̃s] *nf* crowd, crowds (*pl*).

affluent [aflyɑ̃] *nm* tributary.

affluer [aflye] *vi* **1.** (*choses*) to pour in, to flood in. **2.** (*personnes*) to flock. **3.** (*sang*): ~ **(à)** to rush (to).

afflux [afly] *nm* **1.** (*de liquide, dons, capitaux*) flow. **2.** (*de personnes*) flood.

affolement [afɔlmɑ̃] *nm* panic.

affoler [afɔle] *vt* (*inquiéter*) to terrify.

▶ **s'affoler** *vp* (*paniquer*) to panic.

affranchir [afrɑ̃ʃir] *vt* **1.** (*lettre - avec timbre*) to stamp; (- *à la machine*) to frank. **2.** (*esclave*) to set free, to liberate.

affreux, -euse [afrø, øz] *adj* **1.** (*repoussant*) horrible. **2.** (*effrayant*) terrifying. **3.** (*détestable*) awful, dreadful.

affriolant, -e [afrijɔlɑ̃, ɑ̃t] *adj* enticing.

affront [afrɔ̃] *nm* insult, affront.

affrontement [afrɔ̃tmɑ̃] *nm* confrontation.

affronter [afrɔ̃te] *vt* to confront.

▶ **s'affronter** *vp* to clash.

affubler [afyble] *vt péj*: **être affublé de** to be got up in.

affût [afy] *nm*: **être à l'~ (de)** to be lying in wait (for); *fig* to be on the lookout (for).

affûter [afyte] *vt* to sharpen.

Afghanistan [afganistɑ̃] *nm*: **l'~** Afghanistan.

afin [afɛ̃] ▶ **afin de** *loc prép* in order to.

▶ **afin que** *loc conj* (+ *subjonctif*) so that.

a fortiori [afɔrsjɔri] *adv* all the more.

africain, -e [afrikɛ̃, εn] *adj* African.

▶ **Africain, -e** *nm, f* African.

Afrique [afrik] *nf*: **l'~** Africa; **l'~ du Nord** North Africa; **l'~ du Sud** South Africa.

agacer [agase] *vt* to irritate.

âge [aʒ] *nm* age; **quel ~ as-tu?** how old are you?; **prendre de l'~** to age; **l'~ adulte** adulthood; **l'~ ingrat** the awkward ou difficult age; ~ **d'or** golden age; **le troisième ~** (*personnes*) the over-sixties.

âgé, -e [aʒe] *adj* old, elderly; **être ~ de 20 ans** to be 20 years old ou of age; **un enfant ~ de 3 ans** a 3-year-old child.

agence [aʒɑ̃s] *nf* agency; ~ **immobilière** estate agent's Br, real estate agent's Am; ~ **matrimoniale** marriage bureau; **Agence nationale pour l'emploi** = job centre; ~ **de publicité** advertising agency; ~ **de voyages** travel agent's, travel agency.

agencer [aʒɑ̃se] *vt* to arrange; *fig* to put together.

agenda [aʒɛ̃da] *nm* diary.

agenouiller [aʒnuje] ▶ **s'agenouiller** *vp* to kneel.

agent [aʒɑ̃] *nm* agent; ~ **de change** stockbroker; ~ **de police** police officer; ~ **secret** secret agent.

agglomération [aglɔmerasjɔ̃] *nf* (*ville*) conurbation.

aggloméré [aglɔmere] *nm* chipboard.

agglomérer [aglɔmere] vt to mix together.

agglutiner [aglytine] vt to stick together. ▶ **s'agglutiner** vp (foule) to gather, to congregate.

aggraver [agrave] vt to make worse. ▶ **s'aggraver** vp to get worse, to worsen.

agile [aʒil] adj agile, nimble.

agilité [aʒilite] nf litt & fig agility.

agios [aʒjo] nmpl (FIN) bank charges.

agir [aʒir] vi 1. (faire, être efficace) to act. 2. (se comporter) to behave. 3. (influer): ~ sur to have an effect on. ▶ **s'agir** v impers: il s'agit de ... it's a matter of ...; de quoi s'agit-il? what's it about?

agissements [aʒismā] nmpl péj schemes, intrigues.

agitateur, -trice [aʒitatœr, tris] nm, f (POLIT) agitator.

agitation [aʒitasjɔ̃] nf agitation; (politique, sociale) unrest.

agité, -e [aʒite] adj 1. (gén) restless; (enfant, classe) restless, fidgety; (journée, atmosphère) hectic; (mer) rough.

agiter [aʒite] vt 1. (remuer - flacon, objet) to shake; (- drapeau, bras) to wave. 2. (énerver) to perturb. ▶ **s'agiter** vp (personne) to move about, to fidget; (mer) to stir; (population) to get restless.

agneau [aɲo] nm 1. (animal, viande) lamb. 2. (cuir) lambskin.

agonie [agɔni] nf (de personne) mortal agony; fig death throes (pl).

agoniser [agɔnize] vi (personne) to be dying; fig to be on its last legs.

agrafe [agraf] nf 1. (de bureau) staple. 2. (MÉD) clip.

agrafer [agrafe] vt (attacher) to fasten.

agrafeuse [agraføz] nf stapler.

agrandir [agrɑ̃dir] vt 1. (élargir - gén & PHOT) to enlarge; (- rue, écart) to widen. 2. fig (développer) to expand. ▶ **s'agrandir** vp 1. (s'étendre) to grow. 2. fig (se développer) to expand.

agrandissement [agrɑ̃dismɑ̃] nm 1. (gén & PHOT) enlargement. 2. fig (développement) expansion.

agréable [agreabl] adj pleasant, nice.

agréé, -e [agree] adj (concessionnaire, appareil) authorized.

agréer [agree] vt sout (accepter): veuillez ~ mes salutations distinguées ou l'expression de mes sentiments distingués yours faithfully.

agrégation [agregasjɔ̃] nf competitive examination for secondary school and university teachers.

agrégé, -e [agreʒe] nm, f holder of the agrégation.

agrément [agremɑ̃] nm 1. (caractère agréable) attractiveness. 2. (approbation) consent, approval.

agrès [agrɛ] nmpl (SPORT) gym apparatus (U).

agresser [agrese] vt 1. (suj: personne) to attack. 2. fig (suj: bruit, pollution) to assault.

agresseur [agresœr] nm attacker.

agressif, -ive [agresif, iv] adj aggressive.

agression [agresjɔ̃] nf attack; (MIL & PSYCHOL) aggression.

agricole [agrikɔl] adj agricultural.

agriculteur, -trice [agrikyltœr, tris] nm, f farmer.

agriculture [agrikyltyr] nf agriculture, farming.

agripper [agripe] vt 1. (personne) to cling ou hang on to. 2. (objet) to grip, to clutch.

agronomie [agrɔnɔmi] nf agronomy.

agrume [agrym] nm citrus fruit.

aguets [agɛ] ▶ **aux aguets** loc adv: être/rester aux ~ to be ou keep on the lookout.

ahuri, -e [ayri] adj: être ~ (par qqch) to be taken aback (by sthg).

ahurissant, -e [ayrisɑ̃, ɑ̃t] adj astounding.

ai → avoir.

aide [ɛd] nf 1. (gén) help; appeler (qqn) à l'~ to call (to sb) for help; venir en ~ à qqn to come to sb's aid, to help sb; ~ ménagère home help. 2. (secours financier) aid; ~ sociale social security Br, welfare Am. ▶ **à l'aide de** loc prép with the help ou aid of.

aide-mémoire [ɛdmemwar] nm inv aide-mémoire; (pour examen) revision notes (pl).

aider [ede] vt to help; ~ qqn à faire qqch to help sb to do sthg. ▶ **s'aider** vp 1. (s'assister mutuellement) to help each other. 2. (avoir recours): s'~ de to use, to make use of.

aide-soignant, -e [ɛdswaɲɑ̃, ɑ̃t] nm, f nursing auxiliary Br, nurse's aide Am.

aie, aies etc → avoir.

aïe [aj] interj (exprime la douleur) ow!, ouch!

aïeul, -e [ajœl] nm, f sout grandparent, grandfather (f grandmother).

aïeux [ajø] nmpl ancestors.

aigle [ɛgl] nm eagle.

aigre [ɛgr] *adj* **1.** (*gén*) sour. **2.** (*propos*) harsh.

aigre-doux, -douce [ɛgrədu, dus] *adj* **1.** (CULIN) sweet-and-sour. **2.** (*propos*) bittersweet.

aigrelet, -ette [ɛgrələ, ɛt] *adj* **1.** (*vin*) vinegary. **2.** (*voix*) sharpish.

aigreur [ɛgrœr] *nf* **1.** (*d'un aliment*) sourness. **2.** (*d'un propos*) harshness. ▶ **aigreurs d'estomac** *nfpl* heartburn (U).

aigri, -e [egri] *adj* embittered.

aigu, -uë [egy] *adj* **1.** (*son*) high-pitched. **2.** (*objet, lame*) sharp; (*angle*) acute. **3.** (*douleur*) sharp, acute. **4.** (*intelligence, sens*) acute, keen. ▶ **aigu** *nm* high note.

aiguillage [eguijaʒ] *nm* (RAIL - *manœuvre*) shunting Br, switching Am; (- *dispositif*) points (*pl*) Br, switch Am.

aiguille [eguij] *nf* **1.** (*gén*) needle; ~ **à tricoter** knitting needle; ~ **de pin** pine needle. **2.** (*de pendule*) hand.

aiguiller [eguije] *vt* **1.** (RAIL) to shunt Br, to switch Am. **2.** (*personne, conversation*) to steer, to direct.

aiguilleur [eguijœr] *nm* **1.** (RAIL) pointsman Br, switchman Am. **2.** (AÉRON): ~ **du ciel** air traffic controller.

aiguiser [egize] *vt litt & fig* to sharpen.

ail [aj] (*pl* **ails** *ou* **aulx** [o]) *nm* garlic (U); ~ **des bois** Can wild leek.

aile [ɛl] *nf* (*gén*) wing.

aileron [ɛlrɔ̃] *nm* **1.** (*de requin*) fin. **2.** (*d'avion*) aileron.

ailier [elje] *nm* winger.

aille, ailles *etc* → **aller**.

ailleurs [ajœr] *adv* elsewhere, somewhere else; **nulle part/partout** ~ nowhere/everywhere else. ▶ **d'ailleurs** *loc adv* moreover, besides. ▶ **par ailleurs** *loc adv* moreover.

aimable [ɛmabl] *adj* kind, nice.

aimablement [ɛmabləmɑ̃] *adv* kindly.

aimant¹, -e [ɛmɑ̃, ɑ̃t] *adj* loving.

aimant² [ɛmɑ̃] *nm* magnet.

aimer [eme] *vt* **1.** (*gén*) to like; ~ **bien qqch/qqn** to like sthg/sb, to be fond of sthg/sb; ~ **bien faire qqch** to (really) like doing sthg; ~ **(à) faire qqch** to like to do sthg, to like doing sthg; **j'aime à croire que ...** I like to think that ...; **je n'aime pas que tu rentres seule le soir** I don't like you coming home alone at night; **j'aimerais (bien) que tu viennes avec moi** I'd like you to come with me; **j'aimerais bien une autre tasse de café** I wouldn't mind another cup of coffee; ~ **mieux qqch** to prefer sthg; ~ **mieux faire qqch** to prefer doing *ou* to do sthg. **2.** (*d'amour*) to love. ▶ **s'aimer** *vp* (*emploi réciproque*) to love each other; **s'~ bien** to like each other.

aine [ɛn] *nf* groin.

aîné, -e [ene] ◆ *adj* (*plus âgé*) elder, older; (*le plus âgé*) eldest, oldest. ◆ *nm, f* (*plus âgé*) older *ou* elder child, older *ou* eldest son/daughter; (*le plus âgé*) oldest *ou* eldest *ou* oldest *ou* eldest son/daughter; **elle est mon ~e de deux ans** she is two years older than me.

aînesse [ɛnɛs] → **droit**.

ainsi [ɛ̃si] *adv* **1.** (*manière*) in this way, like this. **2.** (*valeur conclusive*) thus; **et ~ de suite** and so on, and so forth; **pour ~ dire** so to speak. ▶ **ainsi que** *loc conj* (*et*) as well as.

air [ɛr] *nm* **1.** (*gén*) air; **en plein ~** (out) in the open air, outside; **en l'~** (*projet*) (up) in the air; *fig* (*paroles*) empty; ~ **conditionné** air-conditioning. **2.** (*apparence, mine*) air, look; **il a l'~ triste** he looks sad; **il a l'~ de bouder** it looks as if he's sulking; **il a l'~ de faire beau** it looks like being a nice day. **3.** (MUS) tune.

aire [ɛr] *nf* (*gén*) area; ~ **d'atterrissage** landing strip; ~ **de jeu** playground; ~ **de repos** lay-by; ~ **de stationnement** parking area.

aisance [ɛzɑ̃s] *nf* **1.** (*facilité*) ease. **2.** (*richesse*): **il vit dans l'~** he has an affluent lifestyle.

aise [ɛz] *nf sout* pleasure; **être à l'~** *ou* **à son ~** (*confortable*) to feel comfortable; (*financièrement*) to be comfortably off; **mettez-vous à l'~** make yourself comfortable; **mettre qqn mal à l'~** to make sb feel ill at ease *ou* uneasy. ▶ **aises** *nfpl*: **aimer ses ~s** to like one's (home) comforts; **prendre ses ~s** to make o.s. comfortable.

aisé, -e [eze] *adj* **1.** (*facile*) easy. **2.** (*riche*) well-off.

aisselle [ɛsɛl] *nf* armpit.

ajourner [aʒurne] *vt* **1.** (*reporter - décision etc*) to postpone; (- *réunion, procès*) to adjourn. **2.** (*candidat*) to refer.

ajout [aʒu] *nm* addition.

ajouter [aʒute] *vt* to add; ~ **foi à qqch** *sout* to give credence to sthg. ▶ **s'ajouter** *vp*: **s'~ à qqch** to be in addition to sthg.

ajuster [aʒyste] *vt* **1.** (*monter*): ~ **qqch (à)** to fit sthg (to). **2.** (*régler*) to adjust. **3.** (*vêtement*) to alter. **4.** (*tir, coup*) to aim.

▶ **s'ajuster** *vp* to be adaptable.

alarme [alarm] *nf* alarm; **donner l'~** to give ou raise the alarm.

alarmer [alarme] *vt* to alarm.

▶ **s'alarmer** *vp* to get ou become alarmed.

albanais, -e [albanɛ, ɛz] *adj* Albanian.

▶ **albanais** *nm* (*langue*) Albanian.

▶ **Albanais, -e** *nm, f* Albanian.

Albanie [albani] *nf*: **l'~** Albania.

albâtre [albatr] *nm* alabaster.

albatros [albatros] *nm* albatross.

albinos [albinos] *nmf & adj inv* albino.

album [albɔm] *nm* album; **~ (de) photo** photo album.

alcool [alkɔl] *nm* alcohol; **~ à brûler** methylated spirits (*pl*); **~ à 90 degrés** surgical spirit.

alcoolique [alkɔlik] *nmf & adj* alcoholic.

alcoolisé, -e [alkɔlize] *adj* alcoholic.

alcoolisme [alkɔlism] *nm* alcoholism.

Alc(o)otest® [alkɔtɛst] *nm* ≃ Breathalyser®.

alcôve [alkov] *nf* recess.

aléatoire [aleatwar] *adj* 1. (*avenir*) uncertain. 2. (*choix*) random.

alémanique [alemanik] *adj*: **la Suisse ~** German-speaking (part of) Switzerland.

alentour [alɑ̃tur] *adv* around, round about. ▶ **alentours** *nmpl* surroundings; **aux ~s de** (*spatial*) in the vicinity of; (*temporel*) around.

alerte [alɛrt] ♦ *adj* 1. (*personne, esprit*) agile, alert. 2. (*style, pas*) lively. ♦ *nf* alarm, alert; **donner l'~** to sound the alert; **~ à la bombe** bomb scare.

alerter [alɛrte] *vt* to warn, to alert.

algèbre [alʒɛbr] *nf* algebra.

Alger [alʒe] *n* Algiers.

Algérie [alʒeri] *nf*: **l'~** Algeria.

algérien, -enne [alʒerjɛ̃, ɛn] *adj* Algerian. ▶ **Algérien, -enne** *nm, f* Algerian.

algue [alg] *nf* seaweed (U).

alibi [alibi] *nm* alibi.

aliénation [aljenasjɔ̃] *nf* alienation; **~ mentale** insanity.

aliéné, -e [aljene] ♦ *adj* 1. (MÉD) insane. 2. (JUR) alienated. ♦ *nm, f* (MÉD) insane person.

aliéner [aljene] *vt* to alienate.

alignement [aliɲmɑ̃] *nm* alignment, lining up.

aligner [aliɲe] *vt* 1. (*disposer en ligne*) to line up, to align. 2. (*adapter*): **~ qqch sur** to align sthg with, to bring sthg into line with. ▶ **s'aligner** *vp* to line up;

s'~ sur (POLIT) to align o.s. with.

aliment [alimɑ̃] *nm* (*nourriture*) food (U).

alimentaire [alimɑ̃tɛr] *adj* 1. (*gén*) food (*avant n*); **c'est juste un travail ~** I'm doing this job just for the money. 2. (JUR) maintenance (*avant n*).

alimentation [alimɑ̃tasjɔ̃] *nf* 1. (*nourriture*) diet; **magasin d'~** food store. 2. (*approvisionnement*): **~ (en)** supply ou supplying (U) (of).

alimenter [alimɑ̃te] *vt* 1. (*nourrir*) to feed. 2. (*approvisionner*): **~ qqch en** to supply sthg with.

alinéa [alinea] *nm* 1. (*retrait de ligne*) indent. 2. (*dans document officiel*) paragraph.

aliter [alite] *vt*: **être alité** to be bedridden. ▶ **s'aliter** *vp* to take to one's bed.

alizé [alize] *nm* trade wind.

allaitement [alɛtmɑ̃] *nm* (*d'enfant*) breast-feeding; (*d'animal*) suckling.

allaiter [alete] *vt* (*enfant*) to breast-feed; (*animal*) to suckle.

allé, -e [ale] *pp* → **aller**.

alléchant, -e [aleʃɑ̃, ɑ̃t] *adj* mouth-watering, tempting.

allécher [aleʃe] *vt*: **il a été alléché par l'odeur/la perspective** the smell/prospect made his mouth water.

allée [ale] *nf* 1. (*dans un jardin*) path; (*dans une ville*) avenue. 2. (*trajet*): **~s et venues** comings and goings. 3. Can (GOLF) fairway.

allégé, -e [aleʒe] *adj* (*régime, produit*) low-fat.

alléger [aleʒe] *vt* 1. (*fardeau*) to lighten. 2. (*douleur*) to soothe.

allégorie [alegɔri] *nf* allegory.

allègre [alɛgr] *adj* 1. (*ton*) cheerful. 2. (*démarche*) jaunty.

allégresse [alegrɛs] *nf* elation.

alléguer [alege] *vt*: **~ une excuse** to put forward an excuse; **~ que** to plead (that).

Allemagne [almaɲ] *nf*: **l'~** Germany; **l'(ex-)~ de l'Est** (former) East Germany; **l'(ex-)~ de l'Ouest** (former) West Germany.

allemand, -e [almɑ̃, ɑ̃d] *adj* German. ▶ **allemand** *nm* (*langue*) German. ▶ **Allemand, -e** *nm, f* German; **un Allemand de l'Est/l'Ouest** an East/a West German.

aller [ale] ♦ *nm* 1. (*trajet*) outward journey. 2. (*billet*) single ticket *Br*, one-way ticket *Am*. ♦ *vi* 1. (*gén*) to go; **allez!** come on!; **vas-y!** go on!; **allons-y!, on y**

va! let's go!, off we go! **2.** (+ *infinitif*): ~ **faire qqch** to go and do sthg; ~ **chercher les enfants à l'école** to go and fetch the children from school; ~ **travailler/se promener** to go to work/for a walk. **3.** (*indiquant un état*): **comment vas-tu?** how are you?; **je vais bien** I'm very well, I'm fine; **comment ça va? – ça va** (*santé*) how are you? – fine ou all right; (*situation*) how are things? – fine ou all right; ~ **mieux** to be better. **4.** (*convenir*): **ce type de clou ne va pas pour ce travail** this kind of nail won't do ou isn't suitable for this job; ~ **avec** to go with; ~ **à qqn** to suit sb; (*suj: vêtement, taille*) to fit sb; **ces couleurs ne vont pas ensemble** these colours don't go well together. **5.** *loc:* **cela va de soi, cela va sans dire** that goes without saying; **il en va de ... comme ...** the same goes for ... as ...; **il en va de même pour lui** the same goes for him. ◆ *v aux* (+ *infinitif*) (*exprime le futur proche*) to be going to, will; **je vais arriver en retard** I'm going to arrive late, I'll arrive late; **nous allons bientôt avoir fini** we'll soon have finished. ▶ **s'en aller** *vp* **1.** (*partir*) to go, to be off; **allez-vous-en!** go away! **2.** (*disparaître*) to go away.

allergie [alɛrʒi] *nf* allergy.

allergique [alɛrʒik] *adj:* ~ **(à)** allergic (to).

aller-retour [alerətur] *nm* return (ticket).

alliage [aljaʒ] *nm* alloy.

alliance [aljɑ̃s] *nf* **1.** (*union - stratégique*) alliance; (*- par le mariage*) union, marriage; **cousin par** ~ cousin by marriage. **2.** (*bague*) wedding ring.

allié, -e [alje] ◆ *adj:* ~ **(à)** allied (to). ◆ *nm, f* ally. ▶ **Alliés** *nmpl:* **les Alliés** the Allies.

allier [alje] *vt* (*associer*) to combine. ▶ **s'allier** *vp* to become allies; **s'~ qqn** to win sb over as an ally; **s'~ à qqn** to ally with sb.

alligator [aligatɔr] *nm* alligator.

allô [alo] *interj* hello!

allocation [alɔkasjɔ̃] *nf* **1.** (*attribution*) allocation. **2.** (*aide financière*): ~ **chômage** unemployment benefit (U); ~ **logement** housing benefit (U); ~**s familiales** child benefit (U).

allocution [alɔkysjɔ̃] *nf* short speech.

allongé, -e [alɔ̃ʒe] *adj* **1.** (*position*): **être** ~ to be lying down ou stretched out. **2.** (*forme*) elongated.

allonger [alɔ̃ʒe] *vt* **1.** (*gén*) to lengthen, to make longer. **2.** (*jambe, bras*) to

stretch (out). **3.** (*personne*) to lay down. ▶ **s'allonger** *vp* **1.** (*gén*) to get longer. **2.** (*se coucher*) to lie down.

allumage [alymaʒ] *nm* **1.** (*de feu*) lighting. **2.** (*d'appareil électrique*) switching ou turning on. **3.** (*de moteur*) ignition.

allume-cigares [alymsigar] *nm inv* cigar lighter.

allume-gaz [alymgaz] *nm inv* gas lighter.

allumer [alyme] *vt* **1.** (*lampe, radio, télévision*) to turn ou switch on; **allume dans la cuisine** turn the kitchen light on. **2.** (*gaz*) to light; (*cigarette*) to light (up). **3.** *fam* (*personne*) to turn on.

allumette [alymɛt] *nf* match.

allumeuse [alymøz] *nf fam péj* tease.

allure [alyr] *nf* **1.** (*vitesse*) speed; **à toute** ~ at top ou full speed. **2.** (*prestance*) presence; **avoir de l'~** to have style. **3.** (*apparence générale*) appearance.

allusion [alyzjɔ̃] *nf* allusion; **faire** ~ **à** to refer ou allude to.

almanach [almana] *nm* almanac.

aloi [alwa] *nm:* **de bon** ~ (*mesure*) of real worth; **de mauvais** ~ (*gaîté*) not genuine; (*plaisanterie*) in bad taste.

alors [alɔr] *adv* **1.** (*jadis*) then, at that time. **2.** (*à ce moment-là*) then. **3.** (*exprimant la conséquence*) then, so; **et** ~, **qu'est-ce qui s'est passé?** so what happened?; **il va se mettre en colère – et** ~? he'll be angry – so what? **4.** (*emploi expressif*) well (then); ~, **qu'est-ce qu'on fait?** well, what are we doing?; **ça** ~! well fancy that! ▶ **alors que** *loc conj* **1.** (*exprimant le temps*) while, when. **2.** (*exprimant l'opposition*) even though; **elle est sortie** ~ **que c'était interdit** she went out even though it was forbidden; **ils aiment le café** ~ **que nous, nous buvons du thé** they like coffee whereas we drink tea.

alouette [alwɛt] *nf* lark.

alourdir [alurdir] *vt* **1.** (*gén*) to weigh down, to make heavy. **2.** *fig* (*impôts*) to increase.

aloyau [alwajo] *nm* sirloin.

Alpes [alp] *nfpl:* **les** ~ the Alps.

alphabet [alfabɛ] *nm* alphabet.

alphabétique [alfabetik] *adj* alphabetical.

alphabétiser [alfabetize] *vt:* ~ **qqn** to teach sb (how) to read and write; ~ **un pays** to eliminate illiteracy from a country.

alpin, -e [alpɛ̃, in] *adj* alpine.

alpinisme [alpinism] *nm* mountaineering.

Alsace [alzas] *nf*: l'~ Alsace.

altérer [altere] *vt* **1.** (*détériorer*) to spoil. **2.** (*santé*) to harm, to affect; (*vérité, récit*) to distort. ► **s'altérer** *vp* **1.** (*matière - métal*) to deteriorate; (- *aliment*) to go off, to spoil. **2.** (*santé*) to deteriorate.

alternance [alternãs] *nf* **1.** (*succession*) alternation; **en ~** alternately. **2.** (POLIT) change of government party.

alternatif, -ive [alternatif, iv] *adj* **1.** (*périodique*) alternating. **2.** (*parallèle*) alternative. ► **alternative** *nf* alternative.

alternativement [alternativmã] *adv* alternately.

alterner [alterne] *vi* (*se succéder*): ~ **(avec)** to alternate (with).

altier, -ère [altje, εr] *adj* haughty.

altitude [altityd] *nf* altitude, height; **en ~** at (high) altitude.

alto [alto] *nm* (MUS - *voix*) alto; (- *instrument*) viola.

aluminium [alyminjɔm] *nm* aluminium Br, aluminum Am.

alvéole [alveɔl] *nf* **1.** (*cavité*) cavity. **2.** (*de ruche, poumon*) alveolus.

amabilité [amabilite] *nf* kindness; **avoir l'~ de faire qqch** to be so kind as to do sthg.

amadouer [amadwe] *vt* (*adoucir*) to tame, to pacify; (*persuader*) to coax.

amaigrir [amegrir] *vt* to make thin ou thinner.

amaigrissant, -e [amegrisã, ãt] *adj* slimming (*avant n*) Br, reducing (*avant n*) Am.

amaigrissement [amegrismã] *nm* loss of weight.

amalgame [amalgam] *nm* **1.** (TECHNOL) amalgam. **2.** (*de styles*) mixture. **3.** (*d'idées, de notions*): **il ne faut pas faire l'~ entre ces deux questions** the two issues must not be confused.

amalgamer [amalgame] *vt* to combine.

amande [amãd] *nf* almond.

amandier [amãdje] *nm* almond tree.

amant [amã] *nm* lover.

amarre [amar] *nf* rope, cable.

amarrer [amare] *vt* **1.** (NAVIG) to moor. **2.** (*fixer*) to tie down.

amas [ama] *nm* pile.

amasser [amase] *vt* **1.** (*objets*) to pile up. **2.** (*argent*) to accumulate.

amateur [amatœr] *nm* **1.** (*connaisseur - d'art, de bon café*): ~ **de** lover of. **2.** (*non-professionnel*) amateur; **faire**

qqch en ~ to do sthg as a hobby. **3.** *péj* (*dilettante*) amateur.

amazone [amazon] *nf* horsewoman; **monter en ~** to ride sidesaddle.

Amazonie [amazoni] *nf*: l'~ the Amazon (Basin).

amazonien, -enne [amazonjẽ, εn] *adj* Amazonian; **la forêt ~ne** the Amazon rain forest.

ambassade [ãbasad] *nf* embassy.

ambassadeur, -drice [ãbasadœr, dris] *nm, f* ambassador.

ambiance [ãbjãs] *nf* atmosphere.

ambiant, -e [ãbjã, ãt] *adj*: **température ~e** room temperature.

ambidextre [ãbidεkstr] *adj* ambidextrous.

ambigu, -uë [ãbigy] *adj* ambiguous.

ambiguïté [ãbigɥite] *nf* ambiguity.

ambitieux, -euse [ãbisjø, øz] *adj* ambitious.

ambition [ãbisjɔ̃] *nf* **1.** *péj* (*arrivisme*) ambitiousness. **2.** (*désir*) ambition; **avoir l'~ de faire qqch** to have an ambition to do sthg.

ambivalent, -e [ãbivalã, ãt] *adj* ambivalent.

ambre [ãbr] *nm* **1.** (*couleur*) amber. **2.** (*matière*): ~ **(gris)** ambergris.

ambré, -e [ãbre] *adj* (*couleur*) amber.

ambulance [ãbylãs] *nf* ambulance.

ambulant, -e [ãbylã, ãt] *adj* travelling (*avant n*).

âme [am] *nf* **1.** (*gén*) soul; **avoir une ~ de comédien** to be a born actor; **~ sœur** soulmate. **2.** (*caractère*) spirit, soul.

amélioration [ameljɔrasjɔ̃] *nf* improvement.

améliorer [ameljɔre] *vt* to improve. ► **s'améliorer** *vp* to improve.

amen [amεn] *adv* amen.

aménagement [amenaʒmã] *nm* **1.** (*de lieu*) fitting out. **2.** (*de programme*) planning, organizing.

aménager [amenaʒe] *vt* **1.** (*pièce*) to fit out. **2.** (*programme*) to plan, to organize.

amende [amãd] *nf* fine.

amendement [amãdmã] *nm* (POLIT) amendment.

amender [amãde] *vt* **1.** (POLIT) to amend. **2.** (AGRIC) to enrich. ► **s'amender** *vp* to mend one's ways.

amener [amne] *vt* **1.** (*mener*) to bring. **2.** (*inciter*): ~ **qqn à faire qqch** (*suj: circonstances*) to lead sb to do sthg; (*suj: personne*) to get sb to do sthg. **3.** (*occasionner, préparer*) to bring about.

amenuiser [amənɥize] *vt* **1.** (*rendre plus*

petit): **ses cheveux amenuisent son visage** her hair makes her face look thinner. **2.** (*réduire*) to diminish, to reduce. ▶ **s'amenuiser** *vp* to dwindle, to diminish.

amer, -ère [amɛr] *adj* bitter.

américain, -e [amerikɛ̃, ɛn] *adj* American. ▶ **américain** *nm* (*langue*) American English. ▶ **Américain, -e** *nm, f* American.

américanisme [amerikanism] *nm* Americanism.

Amérique [amerik] *nf*: **l'~** America; **l'~ centrale** Central America; **l'~ du Nord** North America; **l'~ du Sud** South America; **l'~ latine** Latin America.

amertume [amɛrtym] *nf* bitterness.

améthyste [ametist] *nf* amethyst.

ameublement [amœbləmã] *nm* (*meubles*) furniture; (*action de meubler*) furnishing.

ami, -e [ami] ◆ *adj* friendly. ◆ *nm, f* **1.** (*camarade*) friend; **petit ~** boyfriend; **petite ~e** girlfriend. **2.** (*partisan*) supporter, friend.

amiable [amjabl] *adj* (*accord*) friendly, informal. ▶ **à l'amiable** *loc adv & loc adj* out of court.

amiante [amjãt] *nm* asbestos.

amibe [amib] *nf* amoeba.

amical, -e, -aux [amikal, o] *adj* friendly. ▶ **amicale** *nf* association, club (*for people with a shared interest*).

amicalement [amikalmã] *adv* **1.** (*de façon amicale*) amicably, in a friendly way. **2.** (*dans une lettre*) yours (ever), (with) best wishes.

amidon [amidɔ̃] *nm* starch.

amidonner [amidɔne] *vt* to starch.

amincissant, -e [amɛ̃sisɑ̃, ɑ̃t] *adj* slimming.

amiral, -aux [amiral, o] *nm* admiral.

amitié [amitje] *nf* **1.** (*affection*) affection; **prendre qqn en ~** to befriend sb. **2.** (*rapports amicaux*) friendship; **faire ses ~s à qqn** to give sb one's best wishes.

ammoniac, -aque [amɔnjak] *adj* (CHIM) ammoniac. ▶ **ammoniac** *nm* ammonia. ▶ **ammoniaque** *nf* ammonia (water).

amnésie [amnezi] *nf* amnesia.

amniocentèse [amnjosɛ̃tɛz] *nf* amniocentesis.

amnistie [amnisti] *nf* amnesty.

amnistier [amnistje] *vt* to amnesty.

amoindrir [amwɛ̃drir] *vt* to diminish.

amonceler [amɔ̃sle] *vt* to accumulate.

amont [amɔ̃] *nm* upstream (water); **en**

~ de (*rivière*) upriver ou upstream from; *fig* prior to.

amoral, -e, -aux [amɔral, o] *adj* (*qui ignore la morale*) amoral.

amorce [amɔrs] *nf* **1.** (*d'explosif*) priming; (*de cartouche, d'obus*) cap. **2.** (PÊCHE) bait. **3.** *fig* (*commencement*) beginnings (*pl*), germ.

amorcer [amɔrse] *vt* **1.** (*explosif*) to prime. **2.** (PÊCHE) to bait. **3.** *fig* (*commencer*) to begin, to initiate.

amorphe [amɔrf] *adj* (*personne*) lifeless.

amortir [amɔrtir] *vt* **1.** (*atténuer - choc*) to absorb; (- *bruit*) to deaden, to muffle. **2.** (*dette*) to pay off. **3.** (*achat*) to write off.

amour [amur] *nm* (*gén*) love; **faire l'~** to make love. ▶ **amours** *nfpl* (*vie sentimentale*) love-life.

amoureux, -euse [amurø, øz] ◆ *adj* **1.** (*personne*) in love; **être/tomber ~ (de)** to be/fall in love (with). **2.** (*regard, geste*) loving. ◆ *nm, f* **1.** (*prétendant*) suitor. **2.** (*passionné*): **~ de** lover of; **un ~ de la nature** a nature lover.

amour-propre [amurprɔpr] *nm* pride, self-respect.

ampère [ɑ̃pɛr] *nm* amp, ampere.

amphétamine [ɑ̃fetamin] *nf* amphetamine.

amphi [ɑ̃fi] *nm fam* lecture hall ou theatre; **cours en ~** lecture.

amphibie [ɑ̃fibi] *adj* amphibious.

amphithéâtre [ɑ̃fiteatr] *nm* **1.** (HIST) amphitheatre. **2.** (*d'université*) lecture hall ou theatre.

ample [ɑ̃pl] *adj* **1.** (*vêtement - gén*) loose-fitting; (- *jupe*) full. **2.** (*projet*) extensive; **pour de plus ~s informations** for further details. **3.** (*geste*) broad, sweeping.

amplement [ɑ̃pləmã] *adv* (*largement*) fully, amply.

ampleur [ɑ̃plœr] *nf* **1.** (*de vêtement*) fullness. **2.** (*d'événement, de dégâts*) extent.

ampli [ɑ̃pli] *nm* amp.

amplificateur, -trice [ɑ̃plifikatœr, tris] *adj* (ÉLECTR) amplifying; **un phénomène ~ de la croissance** *fig* a phenomenon which increases growth. ▶ **amplificateur** *nm* **1.** (*gén*) amplifier. **2.** (PHOT) enlarger.

amplifier [ɑ̃plifje] *vt* **1.** (*mouvement, son*) to amplify; (*image*) to magnify, to enlarge. **2.** (*scandale*) to increase; (*événe-*

ment, problème) to highlight.

amplitude [ɑ̃plityd] nf **1.** (de geste) full-ness. **2.** (d'onde) amplitude. **3.** (de tem-pérature) range.

ampoule [ɑ̃pul] nf **1.** (de lampe) bulb. **2.** (sur la peau) blister. **3.** (médicament) ampoule, phial.

amputation [ɑ̃pytasjɔ̃] nf (MÉD) amputation.

amputer [ɑ̃pyte] vt (MÉD) to amputate; fig (couper) to cut (back ou down).

amulette [amylɛt] nf amulet.

amusant, -e [amyzɑ̃, ɑ̃t] adj (drôle) funny; (distrayant) amusing; **c'est très ~** it's great fun.

amuse-gueule [amyzgœl] nm inv fam cocktail snack, (party) nibble.

amusement [amyzmɑ̃] nm amuse-ment (U).

amuser [amyze] vt to amuse, to enter-tain. ▶ **s'amuser** vp to have fun, to have a good time; **s'~ à faire qqch** to amuse o.s. (by) doing sthg.

amygdale [amidal] nf tonsil.

an [ɑ̃] nm year; **avoir sept ~s** to be seven (years old); **en l'~ 2000** in the year 2000; **le nouvel ~** the New Year.

anabolisant [anabolizɑ̃] nm anabolic steroid.

anachronique [anakrɔnik] adj anachronistic.

anagramme [anagram] nf anagram.

anal, -e, -aux [anal, o] adj anal.

analgésique [analʒezik] nm & adj analgesic.

anallergique [analɛrʒik] adj hypoal-lergenic.

analogie [analɔʒi] nf analogy.

analogique [analɔʒik] adj analogue.

analogue [analɔg] adj analogous, comparable.

analphabète [analfabɛt] nmf & adj illiterate.

analyse [analiz] nf **1.** (étude) analysis. **2.** (CHIM & MÉD) test, analysis. **3.** (psy-chanalyse) analysis (U).

analyser [analize] vt **1.** (étudier, psy-chanalyser) to analyse. **2.** (CHIM & MÉD) to test, to analyse.

analyste [analist] nmf analyst.

analyste-programmeur, -euse [analistprɔgramœr, øz] nm, f systems analyst.

analytique [analitik] adj analytical.

ananas [anana(s)] nm pineapple.

anarchie [anarʃi] nf **1.** (POLIT) anarchy. **2.** (désordre) chaos, anarchy.

anarchique [anarʃik] adj anarchic.

anarchiste [anarʃist] nmf & adj anar-chist.

anatomie [anatɔmi] nf anatomy.

anatomique [anatɔmik] adj anatomi-cal.

ancestral, -e, -aux [ɑ̃sɛstral, o] adj ancestral.

ancêtre [ɑ̃sɛtr] nmf (aïeul) ancestor; fig (forme première) forerunner, ancestor; fig (initiateur) father (f mother).

anchois [ɑ̃ʃwa] nm anchovy.

ancien, -enne [ɑ̃sjɛ̃, ɛn] adj **1.** (gén) old. **2.** (avant n) (précédent) former, old. **3.** (qui a de l'ancienneté) senior. **4.** (du passé) ancient.

anciennement [ɑ̃sjɛnmɑ̃] adv former-ly, previously.

ancienneté [ɑ̃sjɛnte] nf **1.** (d'une tradi-tion) oldness. **2.** (d'un employé) seniority.

ancre [ɑ̃kr] nf (NAVIG) anchor; **jeter l'~** to drop anchor; **lever l'~** to weigh anchor; fam (partir) to make tracks.

ancrer [ɑ̃kre] vt (bateau) to anchor; fig (idée, habitude) to root.

Andes [ɑ̃d] nfpl: **les ~** the Andes.

Andorre [ɑ̃dɔr] nf: **(la principauté d')~** (the principality of) Andorra.

andouille [ɑ̃duj] nf **1.** (charcuterie) type of sausage made of chitterlings (pig's intestines eaten cold). **2.** fam (imbécile) prat, twit.

âne [an] nm **1.** (ZOOL) ass, donkey. **2.** fam (imbécile) ass.

anéantir [aneɑ̃tir] vt **1.** (détruire) to annihilate; fig to ruin, to wreck. **2.** (démoraliser) to crush, to overwhelm.

anecdote [anɛkdɔt] nf anecdote.

anecdotique [anɛkdɔtik] adj anecdo-tal.

anémie [anemi] nf (MÉD) anaemia; fig enfeeblement.

anémié, -e [anemje] adj anaemic.

anémique [anemik] adj anaemic.

anémone [anemɔn] nf anemone.

ânerie [anri] nf fam (parole, acte): **dire/faire une ~** to say/do something stupid.

ânesse [anɛs] nf she-ass, she-donkey.

anesthésie [anɛstezi] nf anaesthesia; **~ locale/générale** local/general anaes-thetic.

anesthésier [anɛstezje] vt to anaes-thetize.

anesthésique [anɛstezik] nm & adj anaesthetic.

anesthésiste [anɛstezist] nmf anaes-thetist.

ange [ɑ̃ʒ] nm angel; **~ gardien** guardian angel; **être aux ~s** fig to be in one's seventh heaven.

angélique [ãʒelik] adj angelic.

angélus [ãʒelys] nm (sonnerie) angelus (bell).

angine [ãʒin] nf (pharyngite) pharyngitis; (amygdalite) tonsillitis.

anglais, -e [ãglɛ, ɛz] adj English.
▸ **anglais** nm (langue) English.
▸ **Anglais, -e** nm, f Englishman (f Englishwoman); **les Anglais** the English.
▸ **anglaises** nfpl ringlets.

angle [ãgl] nm 1. (coin) corner. 2. (MATHS) angle; ~ **droit/aigu/obtus** right/acute/obtuse angle.

Angleterre [ãglətɛr] nf: l'~ England.

anglican, -e [ãglikã, an] adj & nm, f Anglican.

anglophone [ãglɔfɔn] ◆ nmf English-speaker. ◆ adj English-speaking, anglophone.

anglo-saxon, -onne [ãglosaksɔ̃, ɔn] adj Anglo-Saxon. ▸ **anglo-saxon** nm (langue) Anglo-Saxon, Old English. ▸ **Anglo-Saxon, -onne** nm, f Anglo-Saxon.

angoisse [ãgwas] nf anguish.

angoisser [ãgwase] vt (effrayer) to cause anxiety to. ▸ **s'angoisser** vp 1. (être anxieux) to be overcome with anxiety. 2. fam (s'inquiéter) to fret.

anguille [ãgij] nf eel.

anguleux, -euse [ãgylø, øz] adj angular.

anicroche [anikrɔʃ] nf hitch.

animal, -e, -aux [animal, o] adj 1. (propre à l'animal) animal (avant n). 2. (instinctif) instinctive. ▸ **animal** nm (bête) animal; ~ **sauvage/domestique** wild/domestic animal.

animateur, -trice [animatœr, tris] nm, f 1. (RADIO & TÉLÉ) presenter. 2. (socioculturel, sportif) activities organizer.

animation [animasjɔ̃] nf 1. (de rue) activity, life; (de conversation, visage) animation. 2. (activités) activities (pl). 3. (CIN) animation.

animé, -e [anime] adj (rue) lively; (conversation, visage) animated; (objet) animate.

animer [anime] vt 1. (mettre de l'entrain dans) to animate, to liven up. 2. (présenter) to present. 3. (organiser des activités pour) to organize activities for. ▸ **s'animer** vp 1. (visage) to light up. 2. (rue) to come to life, to liven up.

animosité [animozite] nf animosity.

anis [ani(s)] nm (BOT) anise; (CULIN) aniseed.

ankylosé, -e [ãkiloze] adj (paralysé) stiff; (engourdi) numb.

annales [anal] nfpl 1. (d'examen) past papers. 2. (chronique annuelle) chronicle (sg), annals.

anneau, -x [ano] nm 1. (gén) ring. 2. (maillon) link.

année [ane] nf year; **souhaiter la bonne ~ à qqn** to wish sb a Happy New Year; ~ **bissextile** leap year; ~-**lumière** light year; ~ **scolaire** school year.

annexe [anɛks] ◆ nf 1. (de dossier) appendix, annexe. 2. (de bâtiment) annexe. ◆ adj related, associated.

annexer [anɛkse] vt 1. (incorporer): ~ **qqch (à qqch)** to append ou annex sthg (to sthg). 2. (pays) to annex.

annexion [anɛksjɔ̃] nf annexation.

annihiler [aniile] vt (réduire à néant) to destroy, to wreck.

anniversaire [anivɛrsɛr] ◆ nm (de mariage, mort, événement) anniversary; (de naissance) birthday; **bon** ou **joyeux ~!** happy birthday! ◆ adj anniversary (avant n).

annonce [anɔ̃s] nf 1. (déclaration) announcement; fig sign, indication. 2. (texte) advertisement; **petite ~** classified advertisement, small ad.

annoncer [anɔ̃se] vt 1. (faire savoir) to announce. 2. (prédire) to predict.

annonciateur, -trice [anɔ̃sjatœr, tris] adj: ~ **de qqch** heralding sthg.

annoter [anɔte] vt to annotate.

annuaire [anɥɛr] nm annual, year-book; ~ **téléphonique** telephone directory, phone book.

annuel, -elle [anɥɛl] adj 1. (tous les ans) annual, yearly. 2. (d'une année) annual.

annuité [anɥite] nf 1. (paiement) annual payment ou instalment. 2. (année de service) year (of service).

annulaire [anɥlɛr] nm ring finger.

annulation [anylasjɔ̃] nf 1. (de rendez-vous, réservation) cancellation. 2. (de mariage) annulment.

annuler [anyle] vt 1. (rendez-vous, réservation) to cancel. 2. (mariage) to annul. ▸ **s'annuler** vp to cancel each other out.

anoblir [anɔblir] vt to ennoble.

anodin, -e [anɔdɛ̃, in] adj 1. (blessure) minor. 2. (propos) harmless. 3. (détail, personne) insignificant.

anomalie [anɔmali] nf anomaly.

ânon [anɔ̃] nm young donkey ou ass.

ânonner [anɔne] vt & vi to recite in a drone.

anonymat [anɔnima] *nm* anonymity.
anonyme [anɔnim] *adj* anonymous.
anorak [anɔrak] *nm* anorak.
anorexie [anɔrɛksi] *nf* anorexia.
anormal, -e, -aux [anɔrmal, o] ♦ *adj*
1. (*inhabituel*) abnormal, not normal.
2. (*intolérable, injuste*) wrong, not right.
3. (*arriéré*) (mentally) subnormal.
♦ *nm, f* mental defective.
ANPE (*abr de* **Agence nationale pour
l'emploi**) *nf* French national employment
agency, = job centre Br.
anse [ɑ̃s] *nf* 1. (*d'ustensile*) handle.
2. (GÉOGR) cove.
antagoniste [ɑ̃tagɔnist] *adj* antago-
nistic.
antan [ɑ̃tɑ̃] ▶ **d'antan** *loc adj littéraire*
of old, of yesteryear.
antarctique [ɑ̃tarktik] *adj* Antarctic; **le
cercle polaire ~** the Antarctic Circle.
▶ **Antarctique** *nm* 1. (*continent*): **l'~**
Antarctica. 2. (*océan*): **l'~** the Antarctic
(Ocean).
antécédent [ɑ̃tesedɑ̃] *nm* (*gén pl*)
(*passé*) history (*sg*).
antenne [ɑ̃tɛn] *nf* 1. (*d'insecte*) antenna, feeler. 2. (*de télévision, de radio*) aerial
Br, antenna. 3. (*succursale*) branch,
office.
antérieur, -e [ɑ̃terjœr] *adj* 1. (*dans le
temps*) earlier, previous; **~ à** previous ou
prior to. 2. (*dans l'espace*) front (*avant n*).
antérieurement [ɑ̃terjœrmɑ̃] *adv* earlier, previously; **~ à** prior to.
anthologie [ɑ̃tɔlɔʒi] *nf* anthology.
anthracite [ɑ̃trasit] ♦ *nm* anthracite.
♦ *adj inv* charcoal (grey).
anthropologie [ɑ̃trɔpɔlɔʒi] *nf* anthro-
pology.
anthropophage [ɑ̃trɔpɔfaʒ] *nmf* cannibal.
antialcoolique [ɑ̃tialkɔlik] *adj*: **ligue ~**
temperance league.
antibiotique [ɑ̃tibjɔtik] *nm & adj*
antibiotic.
antibrouillard [ɑ̃tibrujar] *nm & adj
inv*: (**phare** ou **feu**) **~** fog lamp Br, fog-
light Am.
antichambre [ɑ̃tiʃɑ̃br] *nf* antecham-
ber; **faire ~** *fig* to wait patiently (*to see
somebody*).
anticipation [ɑ̃tisipasjɔ̃] *nf* (LITTÉRA-
TURE): **roman d'~** science fiction novel.
anticipé, -e [ɑ̃tisipe] *adj* early.
anticiper [ɑ̃tisipe] ♦ *vt* to anticipate.
♦ *vi*: **~ (sur qqch)** to anticipate (sthg).
anticonformiste [ɑ̃tikɔ̃fɔrmist] *adj &
nmf* non-conformist.

anticorps [ɑ̃tikɔr] *nm* antibody.
anticyclone [ɑ̃tisiklɔn] *nm* anticyclone.
antidater [ɑ̃tidate] *vt* to backdate.
antidémarrage [ɑ̃tidemaraʒ] *adj inv*:
système ~ immobilizer.
antidépresseur [ɑ̃tidepresœr] *nm &
adj m* antidepressant.
antidopage [ɑ̃tidɔpaʒ] *adj inv*: **contrôle
~** drug test.
antidote [ɑ̃tidɔt] *nm* antidote.
antigel [ɑ̃tiʒɛl] *nm inv & adj inv*
antifreeze.
antillais, -e [ɑ̃tijɛ, ɛz] *adj* West Indian.
▶ **Antillais, -e** *nm, f* West Indian.
Antilles [ɑ̃tij] *nfpl*: **les ~** the West
Indies.
antilope [ɑ̃tilɔp] *nf* antelope.
antimilitariste [ɑ̃timilitarist] *nmf & adj*
antimilitarist.
antimite [ɑ̃timit] *adj inv*: **boule ~** mothball.
antipathie [ɑ̃tipati] *nf* antipathy, hostility.
antipathique [ɑ̃tipatik] *adj* unpleasant; **elle m'est ~** I dislike her, I don't like
her.
antipelliculaire [ɑ̃tipelikylɛr] *adj*:
shampooing ~ anti-dandruff shampoo.
antiquaire [ɑ̃tikɛr] *nmf* antique dealer.
antique [ɑ̃tik] *adj* 1. (*de l'antiquité - civilisation*) ancient; (*- vase, objet*) antique.
2. (*vieux*) antiquated, ancient.
antiquité [ɑ̃tikite] *nf* 1. (*époque*):
l'Antiquité antiquity. 2. (*objet*) antique.
antirabique [ɑ̃tirabik] *adj*: **vaccin ~**
rabies vaccine.
antiraciste [ɑ̃tirasist] *adj & nmf*
antiracist.
antirides [ɑ̃tirid] *adj inv* anti-wrinkle.
antirouille [ɑ̃tiruj] *adj inv* (*traitement*)
rust (*avant n*); (*revêtement, peinture*) rust-
proof.
antisèche [ɑ̃tisɛʃ] *nm* ou *nf arg scol* crib
Br, cheat sheet Am.
antisémite [ɑ̃tisemit] ♦ *nmf* anti-
Semite. ♦ *adj* anti-Semitic.
antiseptique [ɑ̃tisɛptik] *nm & adj* antiseptic.
antisismique [ɑ̃tisismik] *adj*
earthquake-proof.
antithèse [ɑ̃titɛz] *nf* antithesis.
antiviral, -aux [ɑ̃tiviral, o] *nm*
antivirus.
antivol [ɑ̃tivɔl] *nm inv* anti-theft
device.
antre [ɑ̃tr] *nm* den, lair.

anus [anys] nm anus.

anxiété [ãksjete] nf anxiety.

anxieux, -euse [ãksjø, øz] ◆ adj anxious, worried; **être ~ de qqch** to be worried ou anxious about sthg; **être ~ de faire qqch** to be anxious to do sthg. ◆ nm, f worrier.

aorte [ɔʀt] nf aorta.

août [u(t)] nm August; *voir aussi* **septembre**.

apaisement [apεzmã] nm 1. (*moral*) comfort. 2. (*de douleur*) alleviation. 3. (*de tension, de crise*) calming.

apaiser [apeze] vt 1. (*personne*) to calm down, to pacify. 2. (*conscience*) to salve; (*douleur*) to soothe; (*soif*) to slake, to quench; (*faim*) to assuage. ▶ **s'apaiser** vp 1. (*personne*) to calm down. 2. (*besoin*) to be assuaged; (*tempête*) to subside, to abate; (*douleur*) to die down; (*scrupules*) to be allayed.

apanage [apanaʒ] nm sout privilege; **être l'~ de qqn/qqch** to be the prerogative of sb/sthg.

aparté [aparte] nm 1. (THÉÂTRE) aside. 2. (*conversation*) private conversation; **prendre qqn en ~** to take sb aside.

apartheid [aparted] nm apartheid.

apathie [apati] nf apathy.

apathique [apatik] adj apathetic.

apatride [apatrid] nmf stateless person.

apercevoir [apεrsəvwar] vt (*voir*) to see, to catch sight of. ▶ **s'apercevoir** vp: **s'~ de qqch** to notice sthg; **s'~ que** to notice (that).

aperçu, -e [apεrsy] pp → **apercevoir**. ▶ **aperçu** nm general idea.

apéritif, -ive [aperitif, iv] adj which whets the appetite. ▶ **apéritif** nm aperitif.

apesanteur [apəzãtœr] nf weightlessness.

à-peu-près [apøprε] nm inv approximation.

aphone [afɔn] adj voiceless.

aphrodisiaque [afrɔdizjak] nm & adj aphrodisiac.

aphte [aft] nm mouth ulcer.

apiculteur, -trice [apikyltœr, tris] nm, f beekeeper.

apitoyer [apitwaje] vt to move to pity. ▶ **s'apitoyer** vp to feel pity; **s'~ sur** to feel sorry for.

ap. J.-C. (*abr de* après Jésus-Christ) AD.

aplanir [aplanir] vt 1. (*aplatir*) to level. 2. *fig* (*difficulté, obstacle*) to smooth away, to iron out.

aplatir [aplatir] vt (*gén*) to flatten; (*couture*) to press flat; (*cheveux*) to smooth down.

aplomb [aplɔ̃] nm 1. (*stabilité*) balance. 2. (*audace*) nerve, cheek. ▶ **d'aplomb** loc adv steady.

apocalypse [apɔkalips] nf apocalypse.

apogée [apɔʒe] nm (ASTRON) apogee; *fig* peak.

apolitique [apɔlitik] adj apolitical, unpolitical.

apologie [apɔlɔʒi] nf justification, apology.

apoplexie [apɔplεksi] nf apoplexy.

apostrophe [apɔstrɔf] nf (*signe graphique*) apostrophe.

apostropher [apɔstrɔfe] vt: **~ qqn** to speak rudely to sb.

apothéose [apɔteoz] nf 1. (*consécration*) great honour. 2. (*point culminant - d'un spectacle*) grand finale; (- *d'une carrière*) crowning glory.

apôtre [apotr] nm apostle, disciple.

apparaître [aparεtr] ◆ vi 1. (*gén*) to appear. 2. (*se dévoiler*) to come to light. ◆ v impers: **il apparaît que** it seems ou appears that.

apparat [apara] nm pomp; **d'~** (*dîner, habit*) ceremonial.

appareil [aparεj] nm 1. (*gén*) device; (*électrique*) appliance. 2. (*téléphone*) phone, telephone; **qui est à l'~?** who's speaking? 3. (*avion*) aircraft. ▶ **appareil digestif** nm digestive system. ▶ **appareil photo** nm camera.

appareillage [aparεjaʒ] nm 1. (*équipement*) equipment. 2. (NAVIG) getting under way.

appareiller [aparεje] ◆ vt (*assortir*) to match up. ◆ vi (NAVIG) to get under way.

apparemment [aparamã] adv apparently.

apparence [aparãs] nf appearance. ▶ **en apparence** loc adv seemingly, apparently.

apparent, -e [aparã, ãt] adj 1. (*superficiel, illusoire*) apparent. 2. (*visible*) visible.

apparenté, -e [aparãte] adj: **~ à** (*personne*) related to; *fig* (*ressemblant*) similar to.

appariteur [aparitœr] nm porter (*in university*).

apparition [aparisjɔ̃] nf 1. (*gén*) appearance. 2. (*vision -* RELIG) vision; (- *de fantôme*) apparition.

appart [apart] (*abr de* **appartement**) nm fam flat Br, apartment Am.

appartement [apartəmã] *nm* flat Br, apartment Am.

appartenir [apartənir] *vi* **1.** (*être la propriété de*): ~ à qqn to belong to sb. **2.** (*faire partie de*): ~ à qqch to belong to sthg, to be a member of sthg; **il ne m'appartient pas de faire ...** *fig & sout* it's not up to me to do ...

appartenu [apartəny] *pp inv* → **appartenir**.

apparu, -e [apary] *pp* → **apparaître**.

appâter [apate] *vt litt & fig* to lure.

appauvrir [apovrir] *vt* to impoverish. ▸ **s'appauvrir** *vp* to grow poorer, to become impoverished.

appel [apɛl] *nm* **1.** (*gén*) call; **faire ~ à qqn** to appeal for sb; **faire ~ à qqch** (*nécessiter*) to call for sthg; (*avoir recours à*) to call on sthg; ~ (**téléphonique**) (phone) call. **2.** (JUR) appeal; **faire ~** (JUR) to appeal; **sans ~** final. **3.** (*pour vérifier - gén*) roll-call; (- SCOL) registration. **4.** (COMM): ~ **d'offre** invitation to tender. **5.** (*signe*): **faire un ~ de phares** to flash one's headlights.

appelé [aple] *nm* conscript.

appeler [aple] *vt* **1.** (*gén*) to call. **2.** (*téléphoner*) to ring, to call. **3.** (*exiger*) to call for. ▸ **s'appeler** *vp* **1.** (*se nommer*) to be called; **comment cela s'appelle?** what is it called?; **il s'appelle Patrick** his name is Patrick, he's called Patrick. **2.** (*se téléphoner*): **on s'appelle demain?** shall we talk tomorrow?

appendice [apɛ̃dis] *nm* appendix.

appendicite [apɛ̃disit] *nf* appendicitis.

appentis [apɑ̃ti] *nm* lean-to.

appesantir [apəzɑ̃tir] *vt* (*démarche*) to slow down. ▸ **s'appesantir** *vp* **1.** (*s'alourdir*) to become heavy. **2.** (*insister*): **s'~ sur qqch** to dwell on sthg.

appétissant, -e [apetisɑ̃, ɑ̃t] *adj* (*nourriture*) appetizing.

appétit [apeti] *nm* appetite; **bon ~!** enjoy your meal!

applaudir [aplodir] ♦ *vt* to applaud. ♦ *vi* to clap, to applaud; ~ **à qqch** *fig* to applaud sthg; ~ **à tout rompre** *fig* to bring the house down.

applaudissements [aplodismã] *nmpl* applause (U), clapping (U).

applicable [aplikabl] *adj* applicable.

application [aplikasjɔ̃] *nf* (*gén* & INFORM) application.

applique [aplik] *nf* wall lamp.

appliquer [aplike] *vt* (*gén*) to apply;

(*loi*) to enforce. ▸ **s'appliquer** *vp* **1.** (*s'étaler, se poser*): **cette peinture s'applique facilement** this paint goes on easily. **2.** (*se concentrer*): **s'~ (à faire qqch)** to apply o.s. (to doing sthg).

appoint [apwɛ̃] *nm* **1.** (*monnaie*) change; **faire l'~** to give the right money. **2.** (*aide*) help, support; **d'~** (*salaire, chauffage*) extra; **lit d'~** spare bed.

appointements [apwɛ̃tmã] *nmpl* salary (*sg*).

apport [apɔr] *nm* **1.** (*gén* & FIN) contribution. **2.** (*de chaleur*) input.

apporter [apɔrte] *vt* **1.** (*gén*) to bring; **ça m'a beaucoup apporté** *fig* I got a lot from it. **2.** (*raison, preuve*) to provide, to give. **3.** (*mettre - soin*) to exercise; (- *attention*) to give.

apposer [apoze] *vt* **1.** (*affiche*) to put up. **2.** (*signature*) to append.

apposition [apozisjɔ̃] *nf* (GRAM) apposition.

appréciable [apresjabl] *adj* **1.** (*notable*) appreciable. **2.** (*précieux*): **un grand jardin, c'est ~!** I/we really appreciate having a big garden.

appréciation [apresjasjɔ̃] *nf* **1.** (*de valeur*) valuation; (*de distance, poids*) estimation. **2.** (*jugement*) judgment. **3.** (SCOL) assessment.

apprécier [apresje] *vt* **1.** (*gén*) to appreciate. **2.** (*évaluer*) to estimate, to assess.

appréhender [apreɑ̃de] *vt* **1.** (*arrêter*) to arrest. **2.** (*craindre*): ~ **qqch/de faire qqch** to dread sthg/doing sthg.

appréhension [apreɑ̃sjɔ̃] *nf* apprehension.

apprendre [aprɑ̃dr] *vt* **1.** (*étudier*) to learn; ~ **à faire qqch** to learn (how) to do sthg. **2.** (*enseigner*) to teach; ~ **qqch à qqn** to teach sb sthg; ~ **à qqn à faire qqch** to teach sb (how) to do sthg. **3.** (*nouvelle*) to hear of, to learn of; ~ **que** to hear that, to learn that; ~ **qqch à qqn** to tell sb of sthg.

apprenti, -e [aprɑ̃ti] *nm, f* (*élève*) apprentice; *fig* beginner.

apprentissage [aprɑ̃tisaʒ] *nm* **1.** (*de métier*) apprenticeship. **2.** (*formation*) learning.

apprêter [aprete] *vt* to prepare. ▸ **s'apprêter** *vp* **1.** (*être sur le point*): **s'~ à faire qqch** to get ready to do sthg. **2.** (*s'habiller*): **s'~ pour qqch** to dress up for sthg.

appris, -e [apri, iz] *pp* → **apprendre**.

apprivoiser [aprivwaze] *vt* to tame.

approbateur, -trice [aprɔbatœr, tris] *adj* approving.

approbation [aprɔbasjɔ̃] *nf* approval.

approchant, -e [aprɔʃɑ̃, ɑ̃t] *adj* similar.

approche [aprɔʃ] *nf* (*arrivée*) approach; **à l'~ des fêtes** as the Christmas holidays draw near; **il a pressé le pas à l'~ de la maison** he quickened his step as he drew near the house.

approcher [aprɔʃe] ◆ *vt* 1. (*mettre plus près*) to move near, to bring near; **~ qqch de qqn/qqch** to move sthg near (to) sb/sthg. 2. (*aborder*) to go up to, to approach. ◆ *vi* to approach, to go/come near; **approchez!** come nearer!; **n'approchez pas!** keep ou stay away!; **~ de** (*moment, fin*) to approach. ▶ **s'approcher** *vp* to come/go near, to approach; **s'~ de qqn/qqch** to approach sb/sthg.

approfondir [aprɔfɔ̃dir] *vt* 1. (*creuser*) to make deeper. 2. (*développer*) to go further into.

approprié, -e [aprɔprije] *adj* : **~ (à)** appropriate (to).

approprier [aprɔprije] *vt* 1. (*adapter*) to adapt. 2. *Belg* to clean. ▶ **s'approprier** *vp* (*s'adjuger*) to appropriate.

approuver [apruve] *vt* (*gén*) to approve of.

approvisionnement [aprɔvizjɔnmɑ̃] *nm* supplies (*pl*), stocks (*pl*).

approvisionner [aprɔvizjɔne] *vt* 1. (*compte en banque*) to pay money into. 2. (*magasin, pays*) to supply.

approximatif, -ive [aprɔksimatif, iv] *adj* approximate, rough.

approximation [aprɔksimasjɔ̃] *nf* approximation.

approximativement [aprɔksimativmɑ̃] *adv* approximately, roughly.

appt *abr de* **appartement**.

appui [apɥi] *nm* (*soutien*) support.

appui-tête [apɥitɛt] (*pl* **appuis-tête**) *nm* headrest.

appuyer [apɥije] ◆ *vt* 1. (*poser*) : **~ qqch sur/contre qqch** to lean sthg on/against sthg, to rest sthg on/against sthg. 2. (*presser*) : **~ qqch sur/contre** to press sthg on/against. 3. *fig* (*soutenir*) to support. ◆ *vi* 1. (*reposer*) : **~ sur** to lean ou rest on. 2. (*presser*) to push; **~ sur** (*bouton*) to press. 3. *fig* (*insister*) : **~ sur** to stress. 4. (*se diriger*) : **~ sur la** ou **à droite** to bear right. ▶ **s'appuyer** *vp* 1. (*se tenir*) : **s'~ contre/sur** to lean against/on,

to rest against/on. 2. (*se baser*) : **s'~ sur** to rely on.

âpre [apr] *adj* 1. (*goût, discussion, combat*) bitter. 2. (*ton, épreuve, critique*) harsh. 3. (*concurrence*) fierce.

après [aprɛ] ◆ *prép* 1. (*gén*) after; **~ avoir mangé, ils ...** after having eaten ou after they had eaten, they ...; **~ cela** after that; **~ quoi** after which. 2. (*indiquant l'attirance, l'attachement, l'hostilité*) : **soupirer ~ qqn** to yearn for sb; **aboyer ~ qqn** to bark at sb. ◆ *adv* 1. (*temps*) afterwards; **un mois ~** one month later; **le mois d'~** the following ou next month. 2. (*lieu, dans un ordre, dans un rang*) : **la rue d'~** the next street; **c'est ma sœur qui vient ~** my sister's next. ▶ **après coup** *loc adv* afterwards, after the event. ▶ **après que** *loc conj* (+ *indicatif*) after; **je le verrai ~ qu'il aura fini** I'll see him after ou when he's finished; **~ qu'ils eurent dîné, ...** after dinner ou after they had dined, ... ▶ **après tout** *loc adv* after all. ▶ **d'après** *loc prép* according to; **d'~ moi** in my opinion; **d'~ lui** according to him. ▶ **et après** *loc adv* (*employée interrogative ment*) 1. (*questionnement sur la suite*) and then what? 2. (*exprime l'indifférence*) so what?

après-demain [aprɛdmɛ̃] *adv* the day after tomorrow.

après-guerre [aprɛgɛr] *nm* post-war years (*pl*); **d'~** post-war.

après-midi [aprɛmidi] *nm inv* ou *nf inv* afternoon.

après-rasage [aprɛrazaʒ] *nm & adj inv* aftershave.

après-ski [aprɛski] *nm* (*chaussure*) snow-boot.

après-soleil [aprɛsɔlɛj] *adj inv* after-sun (*avant n*).

après-vente [aprɛvɑ̃t] → **service**.

à-propos [apropo] *nm inv* (*de remarque*) aptness; **faire preuve d'~** to show presence of mind.

apte [apt] *adj* : **~ à qqch/à faire qqch** capable of sthg/of doing sthg; **~ (au service)** (MIL) fit (for service).

aptitude [aptityd] *nf* aptitude.

aquarelle [akwarɛl] *nf* watercolour.

aquarium [akwarjɔm] *nm* aquarium.

aquatique [akwatik] *adj* (*plante, animal*) aquatic; (*milieu, paysage*) watery, marshy.

aqueduc [akdyk] *nm* aqueduct.

aqueux, -euse [akø, øz] *adj* watery.

aquilin [akilɛ̃] → **nez**.

arabe [arab] ◆ *adj* (*peuple*) Arab; (*désert*)

Arabian. ♦ *nm* (*langue*) Arabic.
▶ **Arabe** *nmf* Arab.

arabesque [arabɛsk] *nf* **1.** (*ornement*) arabesque. **2.** (*ligne sinueuse*) flourish.

Arabie [arabi] *nf*: **l'~** Arabia; **l'~ Saoudite** Saudi Arabia.

arabophone [arabɔfɔn] ♦ *adj* Arabic-speaking. ♦ *nmf* Arabic speaker.

arachide [araʃid] *nf* **1.** (*plante*) groundnut. **2.** (*graine*) peanut, groundnut.

araignée [areɲe] *nf* spider.
▶ **araignée de mer** *nf* spider crab.

arbalète [arbalɛt] *nf* crossbow.

arbitrage [arbitraʒ] *nm* **1.** (SPORT - *gén*) refereeing; (- *au tennis, cricket*) umpiring. **2.** (JUR) arbitration.

arbitraire [arbitrɛr] *adj* arbitrary.

arbitre [arbitr] *nm* **1.** (SPORT - *gén*) referee; (- *au tennis, cricket*) umpire. **2.** (*conciliateur*) arbitrator.

arbitrer [arbitre] *vt* **1.** (SPORT - *gén*) to referee; (- *au tennis, cricket*) to umpire. **2.** (*conflit*) to arbitrate.

arbre [arbr] *nm* **1.** (BOT & *fig*) tree; **~ généalogique** family tree. **2.** (*axe*) shaft.

arbrisseau, -x [arbriso] *nm* shrub.

arbuste [arbyst] *nm* shrub.

arc [ark] *nm* **1.** (*arme*) bow. **2.** (*courbe*) arc; **~ de cercle** arc of a circle. **3.** (ARCHIT) arch.

arcade [arkad] *nf* **1.** (ARCHIT) arch; **~s** arcade (*sg*). **2.** (ANAT): **~ sourcilière** arch of the eyebrows.

arc-bouter [arkbute] ▶ **s'arc-bouter** *vp* to brace o.s.

arceau, -x [arso] *nm* **1.** (ARCHIT) arch. **2.** (*objet métallique*) hoop.

arc-en-ciel [arkɑ̃sjɛl] (*pl* **arcs-en-ciel**) *nm* rainbow.

archaïque [arkaik] *adj* archaic.

arche [arʃ] *nf* (ARCHIT) arch.

archéologie [arkeɔlɔʒi] *nf* archaeology.

archéologique [arkeɔlɔʒik] *adj* archaeological.

archéologue [arkeɔlɔg] *nmf* archaeologist.

archet [arʃɛ] *nm* (MUS) bow.

archevêque [arʃəvɛk] *nm* archbishop.

archipel [arʃipɛl] *nm* archipelago.

architecte [arʃitɛkt] *nmf* architect.

architecture [arʃitɛktyr] *nf* architecture; *fig* structure.

archiver [arʃive] *vt* to file ou to store (away).

archives [arʃiv] *nfpl* (*de bureau*) records; (*de musée*) archives.

archiviste [arʃivist] *nmf* archivist.

arctique [arktik] *adj* Arctic; **le cercle polaire ~** the Arctic Circle. ▶ **Arctique** *nm*: **l'~** the Arctic.

ardemment [ardamɑ̃] *adv* fervently, passionately.

ardent, -e [ardɑ̃, ɑ̃t] *adj* **1.** (*soleil*) blazing. **2.** (*soif, fièvre*) raging; (*passion*) burning.

ardeur [ardœr] *nf* **1.** (*vigueur*) fervour, enthusiasm. **2.** (*chaleur*) blazing heat.

ardoise [ardwaz] *nf* slate.

ardu, -e [ardy] *adj* (*travail*) arduous; (*problème*) difficult.

are [ar] *nm* 100 *square metres*.

arène [arɛn] *nf* arena. ▶ **arènes** *nfpl* (*romaines*) amphitheatre (*sg*); (*pour corridas*) bullring (*sg*).

arête [arɛt] *nf* **1.** (*de poisson*) bone. **2.** (*du nez*) bridge.

argent [arʒɑ̃] *nm* **1.** (*métal, couleur*) silver. **2.** (*monnaie*) money; **~ liquide** (ready) cash; **~ de poche** pocket money.

argenté, -e [arʒɑ̃te] *adj* silvery, silver.

argenterie [arʒɑ̃tri] *nf* silverware.

Argentine [arʒɑ̃tin] *nf*: **l'~** Argentina.

argile [arʒil] *nf* clay.

argileux, -euse [arʒilø, øz] *adj* clayey.

argot [argo] *nm* slang.

argotique [argɔtik] *adj* slang (*avant n*), slangy.

argument [argymɑ̃] *nm* argument.

argumentation [argymɑ̃tasjɔ̃] *nf* argumentation.

argus [argys] *nm*: **coté à l'~** rated in the *guide to secondhand car prices*.

aride [arid] *adj* litt & *fig* arid; (*travail*) thankless.

aristocrate [aristɔkrat] *nmf* aristocrat.

aristocratie [aristɔkrasi] *nf* aristocracy.

arithmétique [aritmetik] *nf* arithmetic.

armateur [armatœr] *nm* ship owner.

armature [armatyr] *nf* **1.** (CONSTR & *fig*) framework. **2.** (*de parapluie*) frame; (*de soutien-gorge*) underwiring.

arme [arm] *nf* litt & *fig* weapon; **~ blanche** blade; **~ à feu** firearm. ▶ **armes** *nfpl* **1.** (*armée*): **les ~s** the army. **2.** (*blason*) coat of arms (*sg*). **3.** *loc*: **partir avec ~s et bagages** to leave taking everything.

armée [arme] *nf* army; **l'~ de l'air** the air force; **l'~ de terre** the army. ▶ **Armée du salut** *nf*: **l'Armée du salut** the Salvation Army.

armement [arməmɑ̃] nm (MIL - de personne) arming; (- de pays) armament; (- ensemble d'armes) arms (pl); **la course aux ~s** the arms race.

armer [arme] vt 1. (pourvoir en armes) to arm; **être armé pour qqch/pour faire qqch** fig (préparé) to be equipped for sthg/to do sthg. 2. (fusil) to cock. 3. (appareil photo) to wind on. 4. (navire) to fit out.

armistice [armistis] nm armistice.

armoire [armwar] nf (gén) cupboard Br, closet Am; (garde-robe) wardrobe; **c'est une ~ à glace!** fam fig he's built like a tank!; **~ à pharmacie** medicine cabinet.

armoiries [armwari] nfpl coat of arms (sg).

armure [armyr] nf armour.

armurier [armyrje] nm (d'armes à feu) gunsmith; (d'armes blanches) armourer.

arnaque [arnak] nf fam rip-off.

arnaquer [arnake] vt fam to do Br, to swindle; **se faire ~** to be had.

aromate [arɔmat] nm (épice) spice; (fine herbe) herb.

aromatiser [arɔmatize] vt to flavour.

arôme [arom] nm 1. (gén) aroma; (de fleur, parfum) fragrance. 2. (goût) flavour.

arpège [arpɛʒ] nm arpeggio.

arpenter [arpɑ̃te] vt (marcher) to pace up and down.

arqué, -e [arke] adj 1. (objet) curved. 2. (jambe) bow (avant n), bandy; (nez) hooked; (sourcil) arched.

arr. abr de **arrondissement**.

arrache-pied [araʃpje] ▶ **d'arrache-pied** loc adv: **travailler d'~** to work away furiously.

arracher [araʃe] vt 1. (extraire - plante) to pull up ou out; (- dent) to extract. 2. (déchirer - page) to tear off ou out; (- chemise, bras) to tear off. 3. (prendre): **~ qqch à qqn** to snatch sthg from sb; (susciter) to wring sthg from sb. 4. (soustraire): **~ qqn à** (milieu, lieu) to drag sb away from; (lit, sommeil) to drag sb from; (habitude, torpeur) to force sb out of.

arrangeant, -e [arɑ̃ʒɑ̃, ɑ̃t] adj obliging.

arrangement [arɑ̃ʒmɑ̃] nm 1. (gén) arrangement. 2. (accord) agreement, arrangement.

arranger [arɑ̃ʒe] vt 1. (gén) to arrange. 2. (convenir à) to suit. 3. (régler) to settle. 4. (améliorer) to sort out. 5. (réparer) to fix. ▶ **s'arranger** vp to come to an agreement; **s'~ pour faire qqch** to man-

age to do sthg; **arrangez-vous pour être là à cinq heures** make sure you're there at five o'clock; **cela va s'~** things will work out.

arrdt. abr de **arrondissement**.

arrestation [arɛstasjɔ̃] nf arrest; **être en état d'~** to be under arrest.

arrêt [arɛ] nm 1. (d'un mouvement) stopping; **à l'~** (véhicule) stationary; (machine) (switched) off; **tomber en ~ devant qqch** to stop dead in front of sthg. 2. (interruption) interruption; **sans ~** (sans interruption) non-stop; (sans relâche) constantly, continually; **être en ~ maladie** to be on sick leave; **~ maladie** ou **de travail** doctor's certificate; **~ du travail** stoppage. 3. (station): **~ (d'autobus)** (bus) stop. 4. (JUR) decision, judgment.

arrêté [arete] nm (ADMIN) order, decree.

arrêter [arete] ◆ vt 1. (gén) to stop. 2. (cesser): **~ de faire qqch** to stop doing sthg; **~ de fumer** to stop smoking. 3. (voleur) to arrest. ◆ vi to stop. ▶ **s'arrêter** vp to stop; **s'~ à qqch**: **il ne s'arrête pas à ces détails** he's not going to dwell on these details; **s'~ de faire** to stop doing.

arrhes [ar] nfpl deposit (sg).

arrière [arjɛr] ◆ adj inv back, rear; **roue ~** rear ou back wheel; **marche ~** reverse gear. ◆ nm 1. (partie postérieure) back; **à l'~** at the back Br, in back Am. 2. (SPORT) back. ▶ **en arrière** loc adv 1. (dans la direction opposée) back, backwards; **faire un pas en ~** to take a step back ou backwards. 2. (derrière, à la traîne) behind; **rester en ~** to lag behind.

arriéré, -e [arjere] adj (mentalité, pays) backward. ▶ **arriéré** nm arrears (pl).

arrière-boutique [arjɛrbutik] (pl **arrière-boutiques**) nf back shop.

arrière-garde [arjɛrgard] (pl **arrière-gardes**) nf rearguard.

arrière-goût [arjɛrgu] (pl **arrière-goûts**) nm aftertaste.

arrière-grand-mère [arjɛrgrɑ̃mɛr] (pl **arrière-grands-mères**) nf great-grandmother.

arrière-grand-père [arjɛrgrɑ̃pɛr] (pl **arrière-grands-pères**) nm great-grandfather.

arrière-pays [arjɛrpei] nm inv hinterland.

arrière-pensée [arjɛrpɑ̃se] (pl **arrière-pensées**) nf (raison intéressée) ulterior motive.

arrière-plan [arjɛrplɑ̃] (pl **arrière-**

plans) nm background.

arrière-saison [arjɛrsɛzɔ̃] (pl **arrière-saisons**) nf late autumn.

arrière-train [arjɛrtrɛ̃] (pl **arrière-trains**) nm hindquarters (pl).

arrimer [arime] vt 1. (attacher) to secure. 2. (NAVIG) to stow.

arrivage [arivaʒ] nm (de marchandises) consignment, delivery.

arrivée [arive] nf 1. (venue) arrival. 2. (TECHNOL) inlet.

arriver [arive] ◆ vi 1. (venir) to arrive; **j'arrive!** (I'm) coming!; ~ **à Paris** to arrive in ou reach Paris; **l'eau m'arrivait aux genoux** the water came up to my knees. 2. (parvenir): ~ **à faire qqch** to manage to do sthg, to succeed in doing sthg; **il n'arrive pas à faire ses devoirs** he can't do his homework. ◆ v impers to happen; **il arrive que** (+ subjonctif): **il arrive qu'il soit en retard** he is sometimes late; **il arrive à tout le monde de se tromper** anyone can make a mistake; **il lui arrive d'oublier quel jour on est** he sometimes forgets what day it is; **quoi qu'il arrive** whatever happens.

arrivisme [arivism] nm péj ambition.

arrogance [arɔgɑ̃s] nf arrogance.

arrogant, -e [arɔgɑ̃, ɑ̃t] adj arrogant.

arroger [arɔʒe] ▶ **s'arroger** vp: **s'~ le droit de faire qqch** to take it upon o.s. to do sthg.

arrondi [arɔ̃di] nm (de jupe) hemline.

arrondir [arɔ̃dir] vt 1. (forme) to make round. 2. (chiffre - en haut) to round up; (- en bas) to round down.

arrondissement [arɔ̃dismɑ̃] nm (ADMIN) arrondissement (administrative division of a département or city).

arroser [aroze] vt 1. (jardin) to water, to spray. 2. fam (célébrer) to celebrate.

arrosoir [arozwar] nm watering can.

arsenal, -aux [arsənal, o] nm 1. (de navires) naval dockyard. 2. (d'armes) arsenal.

arsenic [arsənik] nm arsenic.

art [ar] nm art; **le septième ~** cinema; **~s et métiers** state-funded institution offering vocational courses by correspondence or evening classes.

art. abr de **article**.

artère [arter] nf 1. (ANAT) artery. 2. (rue) arterial road.

artériel, -elle [arterjɛl] adj arterial.

artériosclérose [arterjoskleroz] nf arteriosclerosis.

arthrite [artrit] nf arthritis.

arthrose [artroz] nf osteoarthritis.

artichaut [artiʃo] nm artichoke.

article [artikl] nm 1. (gén) article; ~ **de fond** feature. 2. loc: **à l'~ de la mort** at death's door.

articulation [artikylasjɔ̃] nf 1. (ANAT & TECHNOL) joint. 2. (prononciation) articulation.

articuler [artikyle] vt 1. (prononcer) to articulate. 2. (ANAT & TECHNOL) to articulate, to joint.

artifice [artifis] nm 1. (moyen astucieux) clever device ou trick. 2. (tromperie) trick.

artificiel, -elle [artifisjɛl] adj artificial.

artillerie [artijri] nf (MIL) artillery.

artisan, -e [artizɑ̃, an] nm, f craftsman (f craftswoman).

artisanal, -e, -aux [artizanal, o] adj craft (avant n).

artisanat [artizana] nm (métier) craft; (classe) craftsmen.

artiste [artist] nmf 1. (créateur) artist; ~ **peintre** painter. 2. (interprète) performer.

artistique [artistik] adj artistic.

as¹ [a] → **avoir**.

as² [as] nm 1. (carte) ace. 2. (champion) star, ace.

ascendant, -e [asɑ̃dɑ̃, ɑ̃t] adj rising. ▶ **ascendant** nm 1. (influence) influence, power. 2. (ASTROL) ascendant.

ascenseur [asɑ̃sœr] nm lift Br, elevator Am.

ascension [asɑ̃sjɔ̃] nf 1. (de montagne) ascent. 2. (progression) rise. ▶ **Ascension** nf: **l'Ascension** Ascension (Day).

ascète [asɛt] nmf ascetic.

asiatique [azjatik] adj 1. (de l'Asie en général) Asian. 2. (d'Extrême-Orient) oriental. ▶ **Asiatique** nmf Asian.

Asie [azi] nf: **l'~** Asia; **l'~ du Sud-Est** Southeast Asia.

asile [azil] nm 1. (refuge) refuge. 2. (POLIT): **demander/accorder l'~ politique** to seek/to grant political asylum. 3. vieilli (psychiatrique) asylum.

asocial, -e, -aux [asɔsjal, o] ◆ adj antisocial. ◆ nm, f social misfit.

aspect [aspɛ] nm 1. (apparence) appearance; **d'~ agréable** nice-looking. 2. (angle & LING) aspect.

asperge [aspɛrʒ] nf (légume) asparagus.

asperger [aspɛrʒe] vt: ~ **qqch de qqch** to spray sthg with sthg; ~ **qqn de qqch** (arroser) to spray sb with sthg; (éclabousser) to splash sb with sthg.

aspérité [asperite] nf (du sol) bump.

asphalte [asfalt] nm asphalt.

asphyxier [asfiksje] *vt* 1. (MÉD) to asphyxiate, to suffocate. 2. *fig* (*économie*) to paralyse.

aspic [aspik] *nm* (*vipère*) asp.

aspirant, -e [aspirã, ãt] *adj*: **hotte ~e** cooker hood Br, cooker range Am; **pompe ~e** suction pump. ► **aspirant** *nm* (*armée*) = officer cadet; (*marine*) = midshipman.

aspirateur [aspiratœr] *nm* Hoover® Br, vacuum cleaner; **passer l'~** to do the vacuuming ou hoovering.

aspiration [aspirasjɔ̃] *nf* 1. (*souffle*) inhalation. 2. (TECHNOL) suction. ► **aspirations** *nfpl* aspirations.

aspirer [aspire] *vt* 1. (*air*) to inhale; (*liquide*) to suck up. 2. (TECHNOL) to suck up, to draw up. 3. (*désirer*): **~ à qqch/à faire qqch** to aspire to sthg/to do sthg.

aspirine [aspirin] *nf* aspirin.

assagir [asaʒir] *vt* to quieten down.

assaillant, -e [asajã, ãt] *nm, f* assailant, attacker.

assaillir [asajir] *vt* to attack, to assault; **~ qqn de qqch** *fig* to assail ou bombard sb with sthg.

assainir [asenir] *vt* 1. (*logement*) to clean up. 2. (*eau*) to purify. 3. (ÉCON) to rectify, to stabilize.

assaisonnement [asɛzɔnmã] *nm* (*sauce*) dressing; (*condiments*) seasoning.

assaisonner [asɛzɔne] *vt* (*salade*) to dress; (*viande, plat*) to season.

assassin, -e [asasɛ̃, in] *adj* provocative. ► **assassin** *nm* (*gén*) murderer, (POLIT) assassin.

assassinat [asasina] *nm* (*gén*) murder, (POLIT) assassination.

assassiner [asasine] *vt* (*tuer - gén*) to murder; (- POLIT) to assassinate.

assaut [aso] *nm* (*attaque*) assault, attack; **prendre d'~** (*lieu*) to storm; (*personne*) to attack.

assécher [aseʃe] *vt* to drain.

ASSEDIC, Assedic [asedik] (*abr de Associations pour l'emploi dans l'industrie et le commerce*) *nfpl* French unemployment insurance scheme; **toucher les ~** to get unemployment benefit Br ou welfare Am.

assemblage [asãblaʒ] *nm* (*gén*) assembly.

assemblée [asãble] *nf* 1. (*réunion*) meeting. 2. (*public*) gathering. 3. (ADMIN & POLIT) assembly; **l'Assemblée nationale** *lower house of the French parliament*.

assembler [asãble] *vt* 1. (*monter*) to put together. 2. (*réunir - objets*) to gather (together). 3. (*personnes - gén*) to bring

together, to assemble. ► **s'assembler** *vp* to gather.

assener [asəne], **asséner** [asene] *vt*: **~ un coup à qqn** (*frapper*) to strike sb, to deal sb a blow.

assentiment [asãtimã] *nm* assent.

asseoir [aswar] ◆ *vt* 1. (*sur un siège*) to put. 2. (*fondations*) to lay. 3. *fig* (*réputation*) to establish. ◆ *vi*: **faire ~ qqn** to seat sb, to ask sb to take a seat. ► **s'asseoir** *vp* to sit (down).

assermenté, -e [asɛrmãte] *adj* (*fonctionnaire, expert*) sworn.

assertion [asɛrsjɔ̃] *nf* assertion.

asseseur [asesœr] *nm* assessor.

assez [ase] *adv* 1. (*suffisamment*) enough; **~ grand pour qqch/pour faire qqch** big enough for sthg/to do sthg; **~ de** enough; **~ de lait/chaises** enough milk/chairs; **en avoir ~ de qqn/qqch** to have had enough of sb/sthg, to be fed up with sb/sthg. 2. (*plutôt*) quite, rather.

assidu, -e [asidy] *adj* 1. (*élève*) diligent. 2. (*travail*) painstaking. 3. (*empressé*): **~ (auprès de qqn)** attentive (to sb).

assiduité [asidyite] *nf* 1. (*zèle*) diligence. 2. (*fréquence*): **avec ~** regularly. ► **assiduités** *nfpl* *péj & sout* attentions.

assiéger [asjeʒe] *vt* to besiege.

assiette [asjɛt] *nf* 1. (*vaisselle*) plate; **~ creuse** ou **à soupe** soup plate; **~ à dessert** dessert plate; **~ plate** dinner plate. 2. (*d'impôt*) base. 3. (CULIN): **~ anglaise** assorted cold meats (*pl*) Br, cold cuts (*pl*) Am.

assigner [asiɲe] *vt* (JUR): **~ qqn en justice** to issue a writ against sb.

assimiler [asimile] *vt* 1. (*aliment, connaissances*) to assimilate. 2. (*confondre*): **~ qqch (à qqch)** to liken sthg (to sthg); **~ qqn à qqn** to compare sb to ou with sb.

assis, -e [asi, iz] ◆ *pp* → **asseoir**. ◆ *adj* sitting, seated; **place ~e** seat. ► **assise** *nf* (*base*) seat, seating. ► **assises** *nfpl* 1. (JUR): (**cour d'**)**~es** Crown Court Br, Circuit court Am. 2. (*congrès*) conference (*sg*).

assistance [asistãs] *nf* 1. (*aide*) assistance; **l'Assistance publique** *French authority which manages the social services and state-owned hospitals*. 2. (*auditoire*) audience.

assistant, -e [asistã, ãt] *nm, f* 1. (*auxiliaire*) assistant; **~e sociale** social worker. 2. (UNIV) assistant lecturer.

assister [asiste] ◆ *vi*: **~ à qqch** to be at

sthg, to attend sthg. ◆ *vt* to assist.
association [asɔsjasjɔ̃] *nf* **1.** (*gén*)
association. **2.** (*union*) society, association; ~ **sportive** sports club. **3.** (COMM)
partnership.
associé, -e [asɔsje] ◆ *adj* associated.
◆ *nm, f* **1.** (*collaborateur*) associate.
2. (*actionnaire*) partner.
associer [asɔsje] *vt* **1.** (*personnes*) to
bring together. **2.** (*idées*) to associate.
3. (*faire participer*): ~ **qqn à qqch** (*inclure*)
to bring sb in on sthg; (*prendre pour
partenaire*) to make sb a partner in sthg.
▶ **s'associer** *vp* **1.** (*prendre part*): s'~ à
qqch (*participer*) to join ou participate in
sthg; (*partager*) to share sthg. **2.** (*collaborer*): s'~ à ou avec **qqn** to join forces
with sb.
assoiffé, -e [aswafe] *adj* thirsty; ~ **de
pouvoir** *fig* power-hungry.
assombrir [asɔ̃brir] *vt* **1.** (*plonger dans
l'obscurité*) to darken. **2.** *fig* (*attrister*) to
cast a shadow over. ▶ **s'assombrir** *vp*
1. (*devenir sombre*) to grow dark. **2.** *fig*
(*s'attrister*) to darken.
assommer [asɔme] *vt* **1.** (*frapper*) to
knock out. **2.** (*ennuyer*) to bore stiff.
Assomption [asɔ̃psjɔ̃] *nf*: l'~ the
Assumption.
assorti, -e [asɔrti] *adj* (*accordé*): bien ~
well-matched; mal ~ ill-matched; une
cravate ~e au costume a tie which
matches the suit.
assortiment [asɔrtimɑ̃] *nm* assortment, selection.
assortir [asɔrtir] *vt* (*objets*): ~ **qqch à
qqch** to match sthg to ou with sthg.
assoupi, -e [asupi] *adj* (*endormi*) doz-
ing.
assoupir [asupir] *vt sout* (*enfant*) to
send to sleep. ▶ **s'assoupir** *vp* (*s'endormir*) to doze off.
assouplir [asuplir] *vt* **1.** (*corps*) to make
supple. **2.** (*matière*) to soften. **3.** (*règlement*) to relax.
assourdir [asurdir] *vt* **1.** (*rendre sourd*)
to deafen. **2.** (*amortir*) to deaden, to
muffle.
assouvir [asuvir] *vt* to satisfy.
assujettir [asyʒetir] *vt* **1.** (*peuple*) to
subjugate. **2.** (*soumettre*): ~ **qqn à qqch**
to subject sb to sthg.
assumer [asyme] *vt* **1.** (*fonction -
exercer*) to carry out. **2.** (*risque, responsabilité*) to accept. **3.** (*condition*) to come to
terms with. **4.** (*frais*) to meet.
assurance [asyrɑ̃s] *nf* **1.** (*gén*) assurance. **2.** (*contrat*) insurance; ~ **maladie**

health insurance; ~ **tous risques** (AUTOM)
comprehensive insurance; ~~**vie** life
assurance.
assuré, -e [asyre] *nm, f* policy holder;
~ **social** National Insurance Br ou Social
Security Am contributor.
assurément [asyremɑ̃] *adv sout* certainly.
assurer [asyre] *vt* **1.** (*promettre*): ~ **à
qqn que** to assure sb (that); ~ **qqn de
qqch** to assure sb of sthg. **2.** (*permanence, liaison*) to provide. **3.** (*voiture*) to
insure. ▶ **s'assurer** *vp* **1.** (*vérifier*): s'~
que to make sure (that); s'~ **de qqch** to
ensure sthg, to make sure of sthg.
2. (COMM): s'~ (**contre qqch**) to insure
o.s. (against sthg). **3.** (*obtenir*): s'~ **qqch**
to secure sthg.
astérisque [asterisk] *nm* asterisk.
asthme [asm] *nm* (MÉD) asthma.
asticot [astiko] *nm* maggot.
astiquer [astike] *vt* to polish.
astre [astr] *nm* star.
astreignant, -e [astreɲɑ̃, ɑ̃t] *adj*
demanding.
astreindre [astrɛ̃dr] *vt*: ~ **qqn à qqch**
to subject sb to sthg; ~ **qqn à faire qqch**
to compel sb to do sthg.
astreint, -e [astrɛ̃, ɛ̃t] *pp* → **astreindre**.
astringent, -e [astrɛ̃ʒɑ̃, ɑ̃t] *adj* astringent.
astrologie [astrɔlɔʒi] *nf* astrology.
astrologue [astrɔlɔg] *nm* astrologer.
astronaute [astrɔnot] *nmf* astronaut.
astronomie [astrɔnɔmi] *nf* astronomy.
astronomique [astrɔnɔmik] *adj* astronomical.
astuce [astys] *nf* **1.** (*ruse*) (clever) trick.
2. (*ingéniosité*) shrewdness (U).
astucieux, -euse [astysjø, øz] *adj*
1. (*idée*) clever. **2.** (*personne*) shrewd.
asymétrique [asimetrik] *adj* asym-
metric, asymmetrical.
atelier [atəlje] *nm* **1.** (*d'artisan*) workshop. **2.** (*de peintre*) studio.
athée [ate] ◆ *nmf* atheist. ◆ *adj* atheis-
tic.
Athènes [atɛn] *n* Athens.
athlète [atlɛt] *nmf* athlete.
athlétisme [atletism] *nm* athletics (U).
atlantique [atlɑ̃tik] *adj* Atlantic.
▶ **Atlantique** *nm*: l'**Atlantique** the
Atlantic (Ocean).
atlas [atlas] *nm* atlas.
atmosphère [atmɔsfer] *nf* atmosphere.
atome [atom] *nm* atom.

atomique [atɔmik] *adj* **1.** (*gén*) nuclear. **2.** (CHIM & PHYS) atomic.

atomiseur [atɔmizœr] *nm* spray.

atone [atɔn] *adj* (*inexpressif*) lifeless.

atout [atu] *nm* **1.** (*carte*) trump; ~ cœur/pique/trèfle/carreau hearts/spades/clubs/diamonds are trumps. **2.** *fig* (*ressource*) asset, advantage.

âtre [atr] *nm littéraire* hearth.

atroce [atrɔs] *adj* **1.** (*crime*) atrocious, dreadful. **2.** (*souffrance*) horrific, atrocious.

atrocité [atrɔsite] *nf* **1.** (*horreur*) atrocity. **2.** (*calomnie*) insult.

atrophier [atrɔfje] ▶ **s'atrophier** *vp* to atrophy.

attabler [atable] ▶ **s'attabler** *vp* to sit down (at the table).

attachant, -e [ataʃɑ̃, ɑ̃t] *adj* lovable.

attache [ataʃ] *nf* (*lien*) fastening. ▶ **attaches** *nfpl* links, connections.

attaché, -e [ataʃe] *nm, f* attaché; ~ de presse (*diplomatique*) press attaché; (*d'organisme, d'entreprise*) press officer.

attaché-case [ataʃekɛz] (*pl* **attachés-cases**) *nm* attaché case.

attachement [ataʃmɑ̃] *nm* attachment.

attacher [ataʃe] ◆ *vt* **1.** (*lier*): ~ qqch (à) to fasten ou tie sthg (to). **2.** (*paquet*) to tie up. **3.** (*lacet*) to do up; (*ceinture de sécurité*) to fasten. ◆ *vi* (CULIN): ~ (à) to stick (to). ▶ **s'attacher** *vp* **1.** (*émotionnellement*): s'~ à qqn/qqch to become attached to sb/sthg. **2.** (*se fermer*) to fasten; s'~ avec ou par qqch to do up ou fasten with sthg. **3.** (*s'appliquer*): s'~ à qqch/à faire qqch to devote o.s. to sthg/to doing sthg, to apply o.s. to sthg/to doing sthg.

attaquant, -e [atakɑ̃, ɑ̃t] *nm, f* attacker.

attaque [atak] *nf* (*gén* & MÉD) attack; *fig*: ~ contre qqn/qqch attack on sb/sthg.

attaquer [atake] *vt* **1.** (*gén*) to attack. **2.** (JUR - *personne*) to take to court; (- *jugement*) to contest. **3.** *fam* (*plat*) to tuck into. ▶ **s'attaquer** *vp* **1.** (*combattre*): s'~ à qqn to attack sb. **2.** *fig*: s'~ à qqch (*tâche*) to tackle sthg.

attardé, -e [atarde] *adj* **1.** (*idées*) outdated. **2.** (*passants*) late. **3.** (*enfant*) backward.

attarder [atarde] ▶ **s'attarder** *vp*: s'~ sur qqch to dwell on sthg; s'~ à faire qqch to stay on to do sthg, to stay behind to do sthg.

atteindre [atɛdr] *vt* **1.** (*gén*) to reach.

2. (*toucher*) to hit. **3.** (*affecter*) to affect.

atteint, -e [atɛ̃, ɛ̃t] ◆ *pp* → **atteindre**. ◆ *adj* (*malade*): être ~ de to be suffering from. ▶ **atteinte** *nf* **1.** (*préjudice*): porter ~e à to undermine; hors d'~e (*hors de portée*) out of reach; (*inattaquable*) beyond reach. **2.** (*effet*) effect.

attelage [atlaʒ] *nm* (*chevaux*) team.

atteler [atle] *vt* (*animaux, véhicules*) to hitch up; (*wagons*) to couple.

attelle [atɛl] *nf* splint.

attenant, -e [atnɑ̃, ɑ̃t] *adj*: ~ (à qqch) adjoining (sthg).

attendre [atɑ̃dr] ◆ *vt* **1.** (*gén*) to wait for; le déjeuner nous attend lunch is ready; ~ que (+ *subjonctif*): ~ que la pluie s'arrête to wait for the rain to stop; faire ~ qqn (*personne*) to keep sb waiting. **2.** (*espérer*): ~ qqch (de qqn/qqch) to expect sthg (from sb/sthg). **3.** (*suj: surprise, épreuve*) to be in store for. ◆ *vi* to wait; attends! hang on! ▶ **s'attendre** *vp*: s'~ à to expect. ▶ **en attendant** *loc adv* **1.** (*pendant ce temps*) meanwhile, in the meantime. **2.** (*quand même*) all the same.

attendrir [atɑ̃drir] *vt* **1.** (*viande*) to tenderize. **2.** (*personne*) to move. ▶ **s'attendrir** *vp*: s'~ (sur qqn/qqch) to be moved (by sb/sthg).

attendrissant, -e [atɑ̃drisɑ̃, ɑ̃t] *adj* moving, touching.

attendu, -e [atɑ̃dy] *pp* → **attendre**. ▶ **attendu que** *loc conj* since, considering that.

attentat [atɑ̃ta] *nm* attack; ~ à la bombe bomb attack, bombing.

attente [atɑ̃t] *nf* **1.** (*station*) wait; en ~ in abeyance. **2.** (*espoir*) expectation; répondre aux ~s de qqn to live up to sb's expectations.

attenter [atɑ̃te] *vi*: ~ à (*liberté, droit*) to violate; ~ à ses jours to attempt suicide; ~ à la vie de qqn to make an attempt on sb's life.

attentif, -ive [atɑ̃tif, iv] *adj* (*auditoire*): ~ (à qqch) attentive (to sthg).

attention [atɑ̃sjɔ̃] ◆ *nf* attention; à l'~ de for the attention of; faire ~ à (*prudence*) to be careful of; (*concentration*) to pay attention to. ◆ *interj* watch out!, be careful!

attentionné, -e [atɑ̃sjɔne] *adj* thoughtful.

attentivement [atɑ̃tivmɑ̃] *adv* attentively, carefully.

atténuer [atenɥe] *vt* (*douleur*) to ease; (*propos, ton*) to tone down; (*lumière*) to dim, to subdue; (*bruit*) to quieten.

▶ **s'atténuer** *vp* (*lumière*) to dim, to fade; (*bruit*) to fade; (*douleur*) to ease.

atterrer [atere] *vt* to stagger.

atterrir [aterir] *vi* to land; ~ **dans qqch** *fig* to land up in sthg.

atterrissage [aterisaʒ] *nm* landing.

attestation [atɛstasjɔ̃] *nf* (*certificat*) certificate.

attester [atɛste] *vt* 1. (*confirmer*) to vouch for. 2. (*certifier*) to attest.

attirail [atiraj] *nm fam* (*équipement*) gear.

attirance [atirɑ̃s] *nf* attraction.

attirant, -e [atirɑ̃, ɑ̃t] *adj* attractive.

attirer [atire] *vt* 1. (*gén*) to attract. 2. (*amener vers soi*): ~ **qqn à/vers soi** to draw sb to/towards one. 3. (*provoquer*): ~ **des ennuis à qqn** to cause trouble for sb. ▶ **s'attirer** *vp*: **s'~ qqch** to bring sthg on o.s.

attiser [atize] *vt* 1. (*feu*) to poke. 2. *fig* (*haine*) to stir up.

attitré, -e [atitre] *adj* 1. (*habituel*) usual. 2. (*titulaire - fournisseur*) by appointment; (- *représentant*) accredited.

attitude [atityd] *nf* 1. (*comportement, approche*) attitude. 2. (*posture*) posture.

attouchement [atuʃmɑ̃] *nm* caress.

attractif, -ive [atraktif, iv] *adj* 1. (*force*) magnetic. 2. (*prix*) attractive.

attraction [atraksjɔ̃] *nf* 1. (*gén*) attraction. 2. (*force*): ~ **magnétique** magnetic force. ▶ **attractions** *nfpl* 1. (*jeux*) amusements. 2. (*spectacle*) attractions.

attrait [atrɛ] *nm* 1. (*séduction*) appeal. 2. (*intérêt*) attraction.

attrape-nigaud [atrapnigo] (*pl* **attrape-nigauds**) *nm* con.

attraper [atrape] *vt* 1. (*gén*) to catch. 2. *fam* (*gronder*) to tell off. 3. *fam* (*tromper*) to take in.

attrayant, -e [atrɛjɑ̃, ɑ̃t] *adj* attractive.

attribuer [atribɥe] *vt* 1. (*tâche, part*): ~ **qqch à qqn** to assign ou allocate sthg to sb, to assign ou allocate sb sthg; (*privilège*) to grant sthg to sb, to grant sb sthg; (*récompense*) to award sthg to sb, to award sb sthg. 2. (*faute*): ~ **qqch à qqn** to attribute sthg to sb, to put sthg down to sb. ▶ **s'attribuer** *vp* 1. (*s'approprier*) to appropriate (for o.s.). 2. (*revendiquer*) to claim (for o.s.).

attribut [atriby] *nm* 1. (*gén*) attribute. 2. (GRAM) complement.

attribution [atribysjɔ̃] *nf* 1. (*de prix*) awarding, award. 2. (*de part, tâche*) allocation, assignment. 3. (*d'avantage*) bestowing. ▶ **attributions** *nfpl* (*fonctions*) duties.

attrister [atriste] *vt* to sadden. ▶ **s'attrister** *vp* to be saddened.

attroupement [atrupmɑ̃] *nm* crowd.

attrouper [atrupe] ▶ **s'attrouper** *vp* to form a crowd, to gather.

au [o] → **à**.

aubade [obad] *nf* dawn serenade.

aubaine [obɛn] *nf* piece of good fortune.

aube [ob] *nf* (*aurore*) dawn, daybreak; **à l'~** at dawn.

aubépine [obepin] *nf* hawthorn.

auberge [obɛrʒ] *nf* (*hôtel*) inn; ~ **de jeunesse** youth hostel.

aubergine [obɛrʒin] *nf* 1. (BOT) aubergine Br, eggplant Am. 2. *péj* (*contractuelle*) traffic warden Br, meter maid Am.

aubergiste [obɛrʒist] *nmf* innkeeper.

auburn [obœrn] *adj inv* auburn.

aucun, -e [okœ̃, yn] ◆ *adj* 1. (*sens négatif*): **ne ... ~** no; **il n'y a ~e voiture dans la rue** there aren't any cars in the street, there are no cars in the street; **sans faire ~ bruit** without making a sound. 2. (*sens positif*) any; **il lit plus qu'~ autre enfant** he reads more than any other child. ◆ *pron* 1. (*sens négatif*) none; ~ **des enfants** none of the children; ~ **d'entre nous** none of us; ~ (**des deux**) neither (of them). 2. (*sens positif*): **plus qu'~ de nous** more than any of us.

aucunement [okynmɑ̃] *adv* not at all, in no way.

audace [odas] *nf* 1. (*hardiesse*) daring, boldness. 2. (*insolence*) audacity. 3. (*innovation*) daring innovation.

audacieux, -euse [odasjø, øz] *adj* 1. (*projet*) daring, bold. 2. (*personne, geste*) bold.

au-dedans [odədɑ̃] *loc adv* inside. ▶ **au-dedans de** *loc prép* inside.

au-dehors [odəɔr] *loc adv* outside. ▶ **au-dehors de** *loc prép* outside.

au-delà [odəla] ◆ *loc adv* 1. (*plus loin*) beyond. 2. (*davantage, plus*) more. ◆ *nm*: **l'~** the hereafter, the afterlife. ▶ **au-delà de** *loc prép* beyond.

au-dessous [odəsu] *loc adv* below, underneath. ▶ **au-dessous de** *loc prép* below, under.

au-dessus [odəsy] *loc adv* above. ▶ **au-dessus de** *loc prép* above, over.

au-devant [odəvɑ̃] *loc adv* ahead. ▶ **au-devant de** *loc prép*: **aller ~ de** to go to meet; **aller ~ du danger** to court danger.

audible [odibl] *adj* audible.

audience [odjɑ̃s] *nf* **1.** (*public, entretien*) audience. **2.** (JUR) hearing.

Audimat® [odimat] *nm* audience rating.

audionumérique [odjɔnymerik] *adj* digital audio.

audiovisuel, -elle [odjɔvizɥɛl] *adj* audio-visual. ▶ **audiovisuel** *nm* TV and radio.

audit [odit] *nm* audit.

auditeur, -trice [oditœr, tris] *nm, f* listener. ▶ **auditeur** *nm* **1.** (UNIV): ~ **libre** *person allowed to attend lectures without being registered*, auditor *Am.* **2.** (FIN) auditor.

audition [odisjɔ̃] *nf* **1.** (*fait d'entendre*) hearing. **2.** (JUR) examination. **3.** (THÉÂTRE) audition. **4.** (MUS) recital.

auditionner [odisjɔne] *vt & vi* to audition.

auditoire [oditwar] *nm* (*public*) audience.

auditorium [oditɔrjɔm] *nm* (*de concert*) auditorium; (*d'enregistrement*) studio.

auge [oʒ] *nf* (*pour animaux*) trough.

augmentation [ogmɑ̃tasjɔ̃] *nf*: ~ **(de)** increase (in); ~ **(de salaire)** rise (in salary).

augmenter [ogmɑ̃te] ◆ *vt* to increase; (*prix, salaire*) to raise; (*personne*) to give a rise Br ou raise Am to. ◆ *vi* to increase, to rise; **la douleur augmente** the pain is getting worse.

augure [ogyr] *nm* (*présage*) omen; **être de bon/mauvais** ~ to be a good/bad sign.

aujourd'hui [oʒurdɥi] *adv* today.

aulx → **ail**.

aumône [omon] *nf*: **faire l'**~ **à qqn** to give alms to sb.

auparavant [oparavɑ̃] *adv* **1.** (*tout d'abord*) first (of all). **2.** (*avant*) before, previously.

auprès [oprɛ] ▶ **auprès de** *loc prép* **1.** (*à côté de*) beside, next to. **2.** (*comparé à*) compared with. **3.** (*en s'adressant à*) to.

auquel [okɛl] → **lequel**.

aurai, auras *etc* → **avoir**.

auréole [oreɔl] *nf* **1.** (ASTRON & RELIG) halo. **2.** (*trace*) ring.

auriculaire [orikylɛr] *nm* little finger.

aurore [orɔr] *nf* dawn.

ausculter [oskylte] *vt* (MÉD) to sound.

auspice [ospis] *nm* (*gén pl*) sign, auspice; **sous les** ~**s de qqn** under the auspices of sb.

aussi [osi] *adv* **1.** (*pareillement, en plus*) also, too; **moi** ~ me too; **j'y vais** ~ I'm

going too ou as well. **2.** (*dans une comparaison*): ~ ... **que** as ... as; **il n'est pas** ~ **intelligent que son frère** he's not as clever as his brother; **je n'ai jamais rien vu d'**~ **beau** I've never seen anything so beautiful; ~ **incroyable que cela paraisse** incredible though ou as it may seem. ▶ **(tout) aussi bien** *loc adv* just as easily, just as well; **j'aurais pu (tout)** ~ **bien refuser** I could just as easily have said no. ▶ **aussi bien ... que** *loc conj* as well ... as; **tu le sais** ~ **bien que moi** you know as well as I do.

aussitôt [osito] *adv* immediately. ▶ **aussitôt que** *loc conj* as soon as.

austère [ostɛr] *adj* **1.** (*personne, vie*) austere. **2.** (*vêtement*) severe; (*paysage*) harsh.

austérité [osterite] *nf* **1.** (*de personne, vie*) austerity. **2.** (*de vêtement*) severeness; (*de paysage*) harshness.

austral, -e [ostral] (*pl* **australs** ou **austraux** [ostro]) *adj* southern.

Australie [ostrali] *nf*: **l'**~ Australia.

australien, -enne [ostraljɛ̃, ɛn] *adj* Australian. ▶ **Australien, -enne** *nm, f* Australian.

autant [otɑ̃] *adv* **1.** (*comparatif*): ~ **que** as much as; **ce livre coûte** ~ **que l'autre** this book costs as much as the other one; ~ **de (... que)** (*quantité*) as much (... as); (*nombre*) as many (... as); **il a dépensé** ~ **d'argent que moi** he spent as much money as I did; **il y a** ~ **de femmes que d'hommes** there are as many women as men. **2.** (*à un tel point, en si grande quantité*) so much; (*en si grand nombre*) so many; ~ **de patience** so much patience; ~ **de gens** so many people; **il ne peut pas en dire** ~ he can't say the same; **en faire** ~ to do likewise. **3.** (*il vaut mieux*): ~ **dire la vérité** we/you *etc* may as well tell the truth. ▶ **autant que** *loc conj*: **(pour)** ~ **que je sache** as far as I know. ▶ **d'autant** *loc adv* accordingly, in proportion. ▶ **d'autant mieux** *loc adv* all the better; **d'**~ **mieux que** all the better since. ▶ **d'autant que** *loc conj*: **d'**~ **(plus) que** all the more so since; **d'**~ **moins que** all the less so since. ▶ **pour autant** *loc adv* for all that.

autel [otɛl] *nm* altar.

auteur [otœr] *nm* **1.** (*d'œuvre*) author. **2.** (*responsable*) perpetrator.

authentique [otɑ̃tik] *adj* authentic, genuine.

autiste [otist] *adj* autistic.

auto [oto] *nf* car.

autobiographie [otɔbjɔgrafi] *nf* autobiography.

autobronzant, -e [otɔbrɔ̃zɑ̃, ɑ̃t] *adj* self-tanning.

autobus [otɔbys] *nm* bus.

autocar [otɔkar] *nm* coach.

autochtone [otɔktɔn] *nmf & adj* native.

autocollant, -e [otɔkɔlɑ̃, ɑ̃t] *adj* self-adhesive, sticky. ► **autocollant** *nm* sticker.

autocouchettes [otɔkuʃɛt] *adj inv*: **train ~** ≃ Motorail® train.

autocritique [otɔkritik] *nf* self-criticism.

autocuiseur [otɔkɥizœr] *nm* pressure cooker.

autodéfense [otɔdefɑ̃s] *nf* self-defence.

autodétruire [otɔdetrɥir] ► **s'autodétruire** *vp* 1. (*machine*) to self-destruct. 2. (*personne*) to destroy o.s.

autodidacte [otɔdidakt] *nmf* self-taught person.

auto-école [otɔekɔl] (*pl* **auto-écoles**) *nf* driving school.

autofinancement [otɔfinɑ̃smɑ̃] *nm* self-financing.

autofocus [otɔfɔkys] *nm & adj inv* autofocus.

autographe [otɔgraf] *nm* autograph.

automate [otɔmat] *nm* (*robot*) automaton.

automatique [otɔmatik] ◆ *nm* 1. (*pistolet*) automatic. 2. (TÉLÉCOM) ≃ direct dialling. ◆ *adj* automatic.

automatisation [otɔmatizasjɔ̃] *nf* automation.

automatisme [otɔmatism] *nm* 1. (*de machine*) automatic operation. 2. (*réflexe*) automatic reaction, automatism.

automédication [otɔmedikasjɔ̃] *nf* self-medication.

automne [otɔn] *nm* autumn, fall *Am*; **en ~** in the autumn, in the fall *Am*.

automobile [otɔmɔbil] ◆ *nf* car, automobile *Am*. ◆ *adj* (*industrie, accessoires*) car (*avant n*), automobile (*avant n*) *Am*; (*véhicule*) motor (*avant n*).

automobiliste [otɔmɔbilist] *nmf* motorist.

autonettoyant, -e [otɔnɛtwajɑ̃, ɑ̃t] *adj* self-cleaning.

autonome [otɔnɔm] *adj* 1. (*gén*) autonomous, independent. 2. (*appareil*) self-contained.

autonomie [otɔnɔmi] *nf* 1. (*indépendance*) autonomy, independence.

2. (AUTOM & AVIAT) range. 3. (POLIT) autonomy, self-government.

autonomiste [otɔnɔmist] *nmf & adj* separatist.

autoportrait [otɔpɔrtrɛ] *nm* self-portrait.

autopsie [otɔpsi] *nf* post-mortem, autopsy.

autoradio [otɔradjo] *nm* car radio.

autorail [otɔraj] *nm* railcar.

autorisation [otɔrizasjɔ̃] *nf* 1. (*permission*) permission, authorization; **avoir l'~ de faire qqch** to be allowed to do sthg. 2. (*attestation*) pass, permit.

autorisé, -e [otɔrize] *adj* (*personne*) in authority; **milieux ~s** official circles.

autoriser [otɔrize] *vt* to authorize, to permit; **~ qqn à faire qqch** (*permission*) to give sb permission to do sthg; (*possibilité*) to permit ou allow sb to do sthg.

autoritaire [otɔritɛr] *adj* authoritarian.

autorité [otɔrite] *nf* authority; **faire ~** (*ouvrage*) to be authoritative; (*personne*) to be an authority.

autoroute [otɔrut] *nf* motorway *Br*, highway *Am*, freeway *Am*; **~ à péage** toll motorway *Br*, turnpike *Am*.

auto-stop [otɔstɔp] *nm* hitchhiking; **faire de l'~** to hitchhike, to hitch.

auto-stoppeur, -euse [otɔstɔpœr, øz] (*mpl* **auto-stoppeurs**, *fpl* **auto-stoppeuses**) *nm, f* hitchhiker, hitcher.

autour [otur] *adv* round, around. ► **autour de** *loc prép* 1. (*sens spatial*) round, around. 2. (*sens temporel*) about, around.

autre [otr] ◆ *adj indéf* 1. (*distinct, différent*) other, different; **je préfère une ~ marque de café** I prefer another ou a different brand of coffee; **l'un et l'~ projets** both projects; **~ chose** something else. 2. (*supplémentaire*) other; **tu veux une ~ tasse de café?** would you like another cup of coffee? 3. (*qui reste*) other, remaining; **les ~s passagers ont été rapatriés en autobus** the other ou remaining passengers were bussed home. ◆ *pron indéf*: **l'~** the other (one); **un ~** another (one); **les ~s** (*personnes*) the others; (*objets*) the others, the other ones; **l'un à côté de l'~** side by side; **d'une semaine à l'~** from one week to the next; **aucun ~, nul ~, personne d'~** no one else, nobody else; **quelqu'un d'~** somebody else, someone else; **rien d'~** nothing else; **l'un et l'~ sont venus** they both came, both of them came;

l'un ou l'~ ira one or other (of them) will go; **ni l'un ni l'~ n'est venu** neither (of them) came.

autrefois [otrəfwa] *adv* in the past, formerly.

autrement [otrəmã] *adv* **1.** (*différemment*) otherwise, differently; **je n'ai pas pu faire ~ que d'y aller** I had no choice but to go; **~ dit** in other words. **2.** (*sinon*) otherwise.

Autriche [otriʃ] *nf*: **l'~** Austria.

autrichien, -enne [otriʃjɛ̃, ɛn] *adj* Austrian. ▶ **Autrichien, -enne** *nm, f* Austrian.

autruche [otryʃ] *nf* ostrich.

autrui [otryi] *pron* others, other people.

auvent [ovã] *nm* canopy.

aux [o] → **à**.

auxiliaire [oksiljɛr] ◆ *nmf* (*assistant*) assistant. ◆ *nm* (GRAM) auxiliary (verb). ◆ *adj* **1.** (*secondaire*) auxiliary. **2.** (ADMIN) assistant (*avant n*).

auxquels, auxquelles [okɛl] → **lequel**.

av. *abr de* **avenue**.

avachi, -e [avaʃi] *adj* **1.** (*gén*) misshapen. **2.** (*personne*) listless; **il était ~ dans un fauteuil** he was slumped in an armchair.

aval, -als [aval] *nm* backing (U), endorsement. ▶ **en aval** *loc adv litt & fig* downstream.

avalanche [avalãʃ] *nf litt & fig* avalanche.

avaler [avale] *vt* **1.** (*gén*) to swallow. **2.** *fig* (*supporter*) to take; **dur à ~** difficult to swallow.

avance [avãs] *nf* **1.** (*progression, somme d'argent*) advance. **2.** (*distance, temps*) lead; **le train a dix minutes d'~** the train is ten minutes early; **prendre de l'~ (dans qqch)** to get ahead (in sthg). ▶ **avances** *nfpl*: **faire des ~s à qqn** to make advances towards sb. ▶ **à l'avance** *loc adv* in advance. ▶ **d'avance** *loc adv* in advance. ▶ **en avance** *loc adv*: **être en ~** to be early; **être en ~ sur qqch** to be ahead of sthg. ▶ **par avance** *loc adv* in advance.

avancement [avãsmã] *nm* **1.** (*développement*) progress. **2.** (*promotion*) promotion.

avancer [avãse] ◆ *vt* **1.** (*objet, tête*) to move forward; (*date, départ*) to bring forward; (*main*) to hold out. **2.** (*projet, travail*) to advance. **3.** (*montre, horloge*) to put forward. **4.** (*argent*): **~ qqch à qqn** to

advance sb sthg. ◆ *vi* **1.** (*approcher*) to move forward. **2.** (*progresser*) to advance; **~ dans qqch** to make progress in sthg. **3.** (*faire saillie*): **~ (dans/sur)** to jut out (into/over), to project (into/over). **4.** (*montre, horloge*): **ma montre avance de dix minutes** my watch is ten minutes fast. **5.** (*servir*): **ça n'avance à rien** that won't get us/you anywhere. ▶ **s'avancer** *vp* **1.** (*s'approcher*) to move forward; **s'~ vers qqn/qqch** to move towards sb/sthg. **2.** (*s'engager*) to commit o.s.

avant [avã] ◆ *prép* before. ◆ *adv* before; **quelques jours ~** a few days earlier ou before; **tu connais le cinéma? ma maison se situe un peu ~** do you know the cinema? my house is just this side of it. ◆ *adj inv* front; **les roues ~** the front wheels. ◆ *nm*. **1.** (*partie antérieure*) front. **2.** (SPORT) forward. ▶ **avant de** *loc prép*: **~ de faire qqch** before doing sthg; **~ de partir** before leaving. ▶ **avant que** *loc conj* (+ *subjonctif*): **je dois te parler ~ que tu partes** I must speak to you before you leave. ▶ **avant tout** *loc adv* above all; **sa carrière passe ~ tout** his career comes first. ▶ **en avant** *loc adv* forward, forwards.

avantage [avãtaʒ] *nm* (*gén* & TENNIS) advantage; **se montrer à son ~** to look one's best.

avantager [avãtaʒe] *vt* **1.** (*favoriser*) to favour. **2.** (*mettre en valeur*) to flatter.

avantageux, -euse [avãtaʒø, øz] *adj* **1.** (*profitable*) profitable, lucrative. **2.** (*flatteur*) flattering. **3.** (*économique*) reasonable.

avant-bras [avãbra] *nm inv* forearm.

avant-centre [avãsãtr] (*pl* **avants-centres**) *nm* centre forward.

avant-coureur [avãkurœr] → **signe**.

avant-dernier, -ère [avãdɛrnje, ɛr] (*mpl* **avant-derniers**, *fpl* **avant-dernières**) *adj* second to last, penultimate.

avant-garde [avãgard] (*pl* **avant-gardes**) *nf* **1.** (MIL) vanguard. **2.** (*idées*) avant-garde.

avant-goût [avãgu] (*pl* **avant-goûts**) *nm* foretaste.

avant-hier [avãtjɛr] *adv* the day before yesterday.

avant-première [avãprəmjɛr] (*pl* **avant-premières**) *nf* preview.

avant-projet [avãprɔʒɛ] (*pl* **avant-projets**) *nm* draft.

avant-propos [avãprɔpo] *nm inv* foreword.

avant-veille [avãvɛj] (*pl* **avant-veilles**) *nf*: **l'~** two days earlier.

avare [avar] ◆ *nmf* miser. ◆ *adj* miserly; **être ~ de qqch** *fig* to be sparing with sthg.

avarice [avaris] *nf* avarice.

avarie [avari] *nf* damage (U).

avarié, -e [avarje] *adj* rotting, bad.

avatar [avatar] *nm* (*transformation*) metamorphosis. ▶ **avatars** *nmpl* (*mésaventures*) misfortunes.

avec [avɛk] ◆ *prép* **1.** (*gén*) with; **~ respect** with respect, respectfully; **c'est fait ~ du cuir** it's made from leather; **et ~ ça?** *fam*, **et ~ ceci?** (*dans un magasin*) anything else? **2.** (*vis-à-vis de*) to, towards. ◆ *adv fam* with it/him *etc*; **tiens mon sac, je ne peux pas courir ~!** hold my bag, I can't run with it!

Ave (Maria) [ave(marja)] *nm inv* Hail Mary.

avenant, -e [avnã, ãt] *adj* pleasant. ▶ **avenant** *nm* (JUR) additional clause. ▶ **à l'avenant** *loc adv* in the same vein.

avènement [avɛnmã] *nm* **1.** (*d'un roi*) accession. **2.** *fig* (*d'un*) advent.

avenir [avnir] *nm* future; **avoir de l'~** to have a future; **d'~** (*profession, concept*) with a future, with prospects. ▶ **à l'avenir** *loc adv* in future.

Avent [avã] *nm*: **l'~** Advent.

aventure [avãtyr] *nf* **1.** (*gén*) adventure. **2.** (*liaison amoureuse*) affair.

aventurer [avãtyre] *vt* (*risquer*) to risk. ▶ **s'aventurer** *vp* to venture (out); **s'~ à faire qqch** *fig* to venture to do sthg.

aventureux, -euse [avãtyrø, øz] *adj* **1.** (*personne, vie*) adventurous. **2.** (*projet*) risky.

aventurier, -ère [avãtyrje, ɛr] *nm, f* adventurer.

avenu [avny] *adj m*: **nul et non ~** (JUR) null and void.

avenue [avny] *nf* avenue.

avérer [avere] ▶ **s'avérer** *vp*: **il s'est avéré (être) à la hauteur** he proved (to be) up to it.

averse [avɛrs] *nf* downpour; **~ de neige** snowflurry.

averti, -e [avɛrti] *adj* **1.** (*expérimenté*) experienced. **2.** (*initié*): **~ (de)** informed ou well-informed (about).

avertir [avɛrtir] *vt* **1.** (*mettre en garde*) to warn. **2.** (*prévenir*) to inform; **avertissez-moi dès que possible** let me know as soon as possible.

avertissement [avɛrtismã] *nm*

1. (*gén*) warning. **2.** (*avis*) notice, notification.

avertisseur, -euse [avɛrtisœr, øz] *nm* **1.** (Klaxon®) horn. **2.** (*d'incendie*) alarm.

aveu, -x [avø] *nm* confession.

aveugle [avœgl] ◆ *nmf* blind person; **les ~s** the blind. ◆ *adj litt & fig* blind.

aveuglement [avœgləmã] *nm* blindness.

aveuglément [avœglemã] *adv* blindly.

aveugler [avœgle] *vt litt & fig* (*priver de la vue*) to blind.

aveuglette [avœglɛt] *loc adv*: **à l'aveuglette** *loc adv*: **marcher à l'~** to grope one's way; **avancer à l'~** *fig* to be in the dark.

aviateur, -trice [avjatœr, tris] *nm, f* aviator.

aviation [avjasjɔ̃] *nf* **1.** (*transport aérien*) aviation. **2.** (MIL) airforce.

avide [avid] *adj* **1.** (*vorace, cupide*) greedy. **2.** (*désireux*): **~ (de qqch/de faire qqch)** eager (for sthg/to do sthg).

avidité [avidite] *nf* **1.** (*voracité, cupidité*) greed. **2.** (*passion*) eagerness.

avilir [avilir] *vt* (*personne*) to degrade. ▶ **s'avilir** *vp* **1.** (*personne*) to demean o.s. **2.** (*monnaie, marchandise*) to depreciate.

aviné, -e [avine] *adj* **1.** (*personne*) inebriated. **2.** (*haleine*) smelling of alcohol.

avion [avjɔ̃] *nm* plane, aeroplane, airplane *Am*; **en ~** by plane, by air; **par ~** (*courrier*) airmail; **~ à réaction** jet (plane).

aviron [avirɔ̃] *nm* **1.** (*rame*) oar. **2.** (SPORT): **l'~** rowing.

avis [avi] *nm* **1.** (*opinion*) opinion; **changer d'~** to change one's mind; **être d'~ que** to think that, to be of the opinion that; **à mon ~** in my opinion. **2.** (*conseil*) advice (U). **3.** (*notification*) notification, notice; **sauf ~ contraire** unless otherwise informed.

avisé, -e [avize] *adj* (*sensé*) sensible; **être bien/mal ~ de faire qqch** to be well-advised/ill-advised to do sthg.

aviser [avize] ◆ *vt* (*informer*): **~ qqn de qqch** to inform sb of sthg. ◆ *vi* to reassess the situation. ▶ **s'aviser** *vp* **1.** *sout* (*s'apercevoir*): **s'~ de qqch** to notice sthg. **2.** (*oser*): **s'~ de faire qqch** to take it into one's head to do sthg; **ne t'avise pas de répondre!** don't you dare answer me back!

av. J.-C. (*abr de* **avant Jésus-Christ**) BC.

avocat, -e [avɔka, at] *nm, f* (JUR) barrister Br, attorney-at-law Am; **~ de la défense** counsel for the defence Br, defense counsel Am; **~ général** ≃ counsel for the prosecution Br, prosecuting attorney Am. ▶ **avocat** *nm* (*fruit*) avocado.

avoine [avwan] *nf* oats (*pl*).

avoir [avwar] ♦ *nm* **1.** (*biens*) assets (*pl*). **2.** (*document*) credit note. ♦ *v aux* to have; **j'ai fini** I have finished; **il a attendu pendant deux heures** he waited for two hours. ♦ *vt* **1.** (*posséder*) to have (got); **il a deux enfants/les cheveux bruns** he has (got) two children/brown hair; **la maison a un grand jardin** the house has (got) a large garden. **2.** (*être âgé de*): **il a 20 ans** he is 20 (years old); **il a deux ans de plus que son frère** he is two years older than his brother. **3.** (*obtenir*) to get. **4.** (*éprouver*) to have; **~ du chagrin** to feel sorrowful; **~ de la sympathie pour qqn** to have a liking for sb; *voir aussi* **faim, peur, soif** *etc*. **5.** *loc*: **se faire ~** *fam* to be had ou conned; **en ~ assez (de qqch/de faire qqch)** to have had enough (of sthg/of doing sthg); **j'en ai pour cinq minutes** it'll take me five minutes; **en ~ après qqn** to have (got) it in for sb. ▶ **avoir à** *vi + prép* (*devoir*): **~ à faire qqch** to have to do sthg; **tu n'avais pas à lui parler sur ce ton** you had no need to speak to him like that, you shouldn't have spoken to him like that; **tu n'avais qu'à me demander** you only had to ask me; **tu n'as qu'à y aller toi-même** just go (there) yourself, why don't you just go (there) yourself? ▶ **il y a** *v impers* **1.** (*présentatif*) there is/are; **il y a un problème** there's a problem; **il y a des problèmes** there are (some) problems; **qu'est-ce qu'il y a?** what's the matter?, what is it?; **il n'y a qu'à en finir** we'll/you'll *etc* just have to have done (with it). **2.** (*temporel*): **il y a trois ans** three years ago; **il y a longtemps de cela** that was a long time ago; **il y a longtemps qu'il est parti** he left a long time ago; **il va y ~ quatorze ans** it will be fourteen years.

avoisinant, -e [avwazinɑ̃, ɑ̃t] *adj* **1.** (*lieu, maison*) neighbouring. **2.** (*sens, couleur*) similar.

avortement [avɔrtəmɑ̃] *nm* (MÉD) abortion.

avorter [avɔrte] *vi* **1.** (MÉD): **(se faire) ~** to have an abortion. **2.** (*échouer*) to fail.

avorton [avɔrtɔ̃] *nm péj* (*nabot*) runt.

avouer [avwe] *vt* **1.** (*confesser*) to confess (to). **2.** (*reconnaître*) to admit.

avril [avril] *nm* April; **le premier ~** April Fools' Day; *voir aussi* **septembre**.

LE PREMIER AVRIL

In France it is traditional on April Fools' Day for children to stick cut-out paper fishes on the backs of their friends, or even passers-by in the street, without them knowing.

axe [aks] *nm* **1.** (GÉOM & PHYS) axis. **2.** (*de roue*) axle. **3.** (*prolongement*): **dans l'~ de** directly in line with.

axer [akse] *vt*: **~ qqch sur/autour de qqch** to centre sthg on/around sthg.

ayant [εjɑ̃] *ppr* → **avoir**.

azalée [azale] *nf* azalea.

azimut [azimyt] ▶ **tous azimuts** *loc adj* (*défense, offensive*) all-out.

azote [azɔt] *nm* nitrogen.

azur [azyr] *nm littéraire* **1.** (*couleur*) azure. **2.** (*ciel*) skies (*pl*).

B

b, B [be] *nm inv* b, B. ▶ **B** (*abr de* **bien**) *good grade (as assessment on schoolwork)*, ≃ B.

BA (*abr de* **bonne action**) *nf fam* good deed.

baba [baba] *nm*: **~ au rhum** rum baba.

babiller [babije] *vi* to babble.

babines [babin] *nfpl* chops.

bâbord [babɔr] *nm* port; **à ~** to port, on the port side.

babouin [babwɛ̃] *nm* baboon.

baby-sitter [bebisitœr] (*pl* **baby-sitters**) *nmf* baby-sitter.

baby-sitting [bebisitiŋ] *nm*: **faire du ~** to baby-sit.

bac [bak] *nm* **1.** = **baccalauréat**. **2.** (*bateau*) ferry. **3.** (*de réfrigérateur*): **~ à glace** ice tray; **~ à légumes** vegetable drawer.

baccalauréat [bakalɔrea] *nm school-leaving examinations leading to university entrance qualification.*

BACCALAURÉAT

In France the 'baccalauréat' is the exam taken by students in their final year at 'lycée' who want to go on to further education. It covers a wide range of subjects but students may select one major subject area relevant to their chosen career, e.g. arts, science, engineering or fine art.

bâche [baʃ] *nf* (*toile*) tarpaulin.

bachelier, -ère [baʃəlje, ɛr] *nm, f* holder of the baccalauréat.

bacille [basil] *nm* bacillus.

bâcler [bakle] *vt* to botch.

bacon [bekɔn] *nm* bacon.

bactérie [bakteri] *nf* bacterium.

badaud, -e [bado, od] *nm, f* gawper.

badge [badʒ] *nm* badge.

badigeonner [badiʒɔne] *vt* (*mur*) to whitewash.

badiner [badine] *vi sout* to joke; **ne pas ~ avec qqch** not to treat sthg lightly.

badminton [badmintɔn] *nm* badminton.

baffe [baf] *nf fam* slap.

baffle [bafl] *nm* speaker.

bafouiller [bafuje] *vi & vt* to mumble.

bâfrer [bafre] *fam vi* to guzzle.

bagage [bagaʒ] *nm* 1. (*gén pl*) (*valises, sacs*) luggage (U), baggage (U); **faire ses ~s** to pack; **~s à main** hand luggage. 2. (*connaissances*) (fund of) knowledge; **intellectuel/culturel** intellectual/cultural baggage.

bagagiste [bagaʒist] *nmf* (*chargement des avions*) baggage handler; (*à l'hôtel etc*) porter; (*fabricant*) travel goods manufacturer.

bagarre [bagar] *nf* brawl, fight.

bagarrer [bagare] *vi* to fight. ► **se bagarrer** *vp* to fight.

bagatelle [bagatɛl] *nf* 1. (*objet*) trinket. 2. (*somme d'argent*): **acheter qqch pour une ~** to buy sthg for next to nothing; **la ~ de X francs** *iron* a mere X francs. 3. (*chose futile*) trifle.

bagnard [baɲar] *nm* convict.

bagne [baɲ] *nm* (*prison*) labour camp.

bagnole [baɲɔl] *nf fam* car.

bague [bag] *nf* 1. (*bijou, anneau*) ring; **~ de fiançailles** engagement ring. 2. (TECH): **~ de serrage** clip.

baguer [bage] *vt* (*oiseau, arbre*) to ring.

baguette [bagɛt] *nf* 1. (*pain*) French stick. 2. (*petit bâton*) stick; **~ magique** magic wand; **~ de tambour** drumstick; **mener qqn à la ~** to rule sb with a rod of iron. 3. (*pour manger*) chopstick. 4. (*de chef d'orchestre*) baton.

bahut [bay] *nm* 1. (*buffet*) sideboard. 2. *arg scol* (*lycée*) secondary school.

baie [bɛ] *nf* 1. (*fruit*) berry. 2. (GÉOGR) bay. 3. (*fenêtre*): **~ vitrée** picture window.

baignade [bɛɲad] *nf* (*action*) bathing (U) Br, swimming (U); **'~ interdite'** 'no bathing/swimming'.

baigner [bɛɲe] ◆ *vt* 1. (*donner un bain à*) to bath. 2. (*tremper, remplir*) to bathe; **baigné de soleil** bathed in sunlight. ◆ *vi*: **~ dans son sang** to lie in a pool of blood; **les tomates baignaient dans l'huile** the tomatoes were swimming in oil. ► **se baigner** *vp* 1. (*dans la mer*) to go swimming, to swim. 2. (*dans une baignoire*) to have a bath.

baigneur, -euse [bɛɲœr, øz] *nm, f* bather Br, swimmer. ► **baigneur** *nm* (*poupée*) baby doll.

baignoire [bɛɲwar] *nf* bath.

bail [baj] (*pl* **baux** [bo]) *nm* (JUR) lease.

bâillement [bajmɑ̃] *nm* yawning (U), yawn.

bâiller [baje] *vi* 1. (*personne*) to yawn. 2. (*vêtement*) to gape.

bailleur, -eresse [bajœr, bajrɛs] *nm, f* lessor; **~ de fonds** backer.

bâillon [bajɔ̃] *nm* gag.

bâillonner [bajɔne] *vt* to gag.

bain [bɛ̃] *nm* 1. (*gén*) bath; **prendre un ~** to have ou take a bath; **~ moussant** foaming bath oil; **~ à remous** Jacuzzi®; **~s-douches** public baths. 2. (*dans mer, piscine*) swim; **~ de mer** sea bathing Br ou swimming. 3. *loc*: **prendre un ~ de soleil** to sunbathe.

bain-marie [bɛ̃mari] (*pl* **bains-marie**) *nm*: **au ~** in a bain-marie.

baïonnette [bajɔnɛt] *nf* 1. (*arme*) bayonet. 2. (ÉLECTR) bayonet fitting.

baiser [beze] *nm* kiss.

baisse [bɛs] *nf* (*gén*): **~ (de)** drop (in), fall (in); **en ~** falling; **la tendance est à la ~** there is a downward trend.

baisser [bese] ◆ *vt* (*gén*) to lower; (*radio*) to turn down. ◆ *vi* 1. (*descendre*) to go down; **le jour baisse** it's getting dark. 2. (*santé, vue*) to fail. 3. (*prix*) to fall. ► **se baisser** *vp* to bend down.

bajoues [baʒu] *nfpl* jowls.

bal [bal] *nm* ball; **~ masqué/costumé** masked/fancy-dress ball; **~ populaire** ou **musette** popular old-fashioned dance accompanied by accordion.

balade [balad] *nf fam* stroll.

balader [balade] *vt* 1. *fam* (*traîner avec soi*) to trail around. 2. (*emmener en promenade*) to take for a walk. ► **se balader** *vp fam* (*se promener - à pied*) to go for a walk; (- *en voiture*) to go for a drive.

baladeur, -euse [baladœr, øz] adj wandering. ▶ **baladeur** nm personal stereo.

balafre [balafr] nf 1. (blessure) gash. 2. (cicatrice) scar.

balafré, -e [balafre] adj scarred.

balai [balɛ] nm 1. (de nettoyage) broom, brush. 2. fam (an): **il a 50 ~s** he's 50 years old.

balai-brosse [balɛbrɔs] nm (long-handled) scrubbing brush.

balance [balɑ̃s] nf 1. (instrument) scales (pl). 2. (COMM & POLIT) balance. ▶ **Balance** nf (ASTROL) Libra.

balancer [balɑ̃se] vt 1. (bouger) to swing. 2. fam (lancer) to chuck. 3. fam (jeter) to chuck out. ▶ **se balancer** vp 1. (sur une chaise) to rock backwards and forwards. 2. (sur une balançoire) to swing. 3. fam: **se ~ de qqch** not to give a damn about sthg.

balancier [balɑ̃sje] nm 1. (de pendule) pendulum. 2. (de funambule) pole.

balançoire [balɑ̃swar] nf (suspendue) swing; (bascule) see-saw.

balayage [balɛjaʒ] nm (gén) sweeping; (TECHNOL) scanning.

balayer [balɛje] vt 1. (nettoyer) to sweep. 2. (chasser) to sweep away. 3. (suj: radar) to scan; (suj: projecteurs) to sweep (across).

balayette [balɛjɛt] nf small brush.

balayeur, -euse [balɛjœr, øz] nm, f roadsweeper Br, streetsweeper Am. ▶ **balayeuse** nf (machine) roadsweeper.

balbutier [balbysje] ◆ vi (bafouiller) to stammer. ◆ vt (bafouiller) to stammer (out).

balcon [balkɔ̃] nm 1. (de maison - terrasse) balcony; (- balustrade) parapet. 2. (de théâtre, de cinéma) circle.

balconnet [balkɔnɛ] nm: **soutien-gorge à ~** half-cup bra.

baldaquin [baldakɛ̃] → **lit**.

Bâle [bal] n Basel.

baleine [balɛn] nf 1. (mammifère) whale. 2. (de corset) whalebone. 3. (de parapluie) rib.

balise [baliz] nf 1. (NAVIG) marker (buoy). 2. (AÉRON) runway light. 3. (AUTOM) road sign. 4. (INFORM) tag.

baliser [balize] vt to mark out.

balivernes [balivɛrn] nfpl nonsense (U).

Balkans [balkɑ̃] nmpl: **les ~** the Balkans.

ballade [balad] nf ballad.

ballant, -e [balɑ̃, ɑ̃t] adj: **les bras ~s** arms dangling.

ballast [balast] nm 1. (chemin de fer) ballast. 2. (NAVIG) ballast tank.

balle [bal] nf 1. (d'arme à feu) bullet; **~ perdue** stray bullet. 2. (de jeu) ball. 3. (de marchandises) bale. 4. fam (argent) franc.

ballerine [balrin] nf 1. (danseuse) ballerina. 2. (chaussure) ballet shoe.

ballet [balɛ] nm (gén) ballet; fig (activité intense) to-ing and fro-ing.

ballon [balɔ̃] nm 1. (JEU & SPORT) ball; **~ de football** football. 2. (montgolfière, de fête) balloon.

ballonné, -e [balɔne] adj: **avoir le ventre ~, être ~** to be bloated.

ballot [balo] nm 1. (de marchandises) bundle. 2. vieilli (imbécile) twit.

ballottage [balɔtaʒ] nm (POLIT) second ballot; **en ~** standing for a second ballot.

ballotter [balɔte] ◆ vt to toss about. ◆ vi (chose) to roll around.

ballottine [balɔtin] nf: **~ de foie gras** type of galantine made with foie gras.

ball-trap [baltrap] nm clay pigeon shooting.

balluchon = **baluchon**.

balnéaire [balneɛr] adj: **station ~** seaside resort.

balourd, -e [balur, urd] adj clumsy.

balte [balt] adj Baltic. ▶ **Balte** nmf native of the Baltic states.

Baltique [baltik] nf: **la ~** the Baltic (Sea).

baluchon, balluchon [balyʃɔ̃] nm bundle; **faire son ~** fam to pack one's bags (and leave).

balustrade [balystrad] nf 1. (de terrasse) balustrade. 2. (rambarde) guardrail.

bambin [bɑ̃bɛ̃] nm kiddie.

bambou [bɑ̃bu] nm (plante) bamboo.

ban [bɑ̃] nm 1. (de mariage): **publier** ou **afficher les ~s** to publish ou display the banns. 2. loc: **être/mettre qqn au ~ de la société** to be outlawed/to outlaw sb (from society); **le ~ et l'arrière-~** the whole lot of them.

banal, -e, -als [banal] adj commonplace, banal.

banaliser [banalize] vt: **voiture banalisée** unmarked police car.

banalité [banalite] nf 1. (caractère banal) banality. 2. (cliché) commonplace.

banane [banan] nf 1. (fruit) banana. 2. (sac) bum-bag. 3. (coiffure) quiff.

bananier, -ère [bananje, ɛr] adj

banana (*avant n*). ▶ **bananier** *nm*
1. (*arbre*) banana tree. 2. (*cargo*) banana
boat.

banc [bɑ̃] *nm* (*siège*) bench; **le ~ des
accusés** (JUR) the dock; **~ d'essai** test-
bed; **être au ~ d'essai** *fig* to be at the
test stage; **~ de sable** sandbank.

bancaire [bɑ̃kɛʀ] *adj* bank (*avant n*),
banking (*avant n*).

bancal, -e, -als [bɑ̃kal] *adj* 1. (*meuble*)
wobbly. 2. (*théorie, idée*) unsound.

bandage [bɑ̃daʒ] *nm* (*de blessé*)
bandage.

bande [bɑ̃d] *nf* 1. (*de tissu, de papier*)
strip; **~ dessinée** comic strip. 2. (*bandage*) bandage; **~ Velpeau®** crepe bandage. 3. (*de billard*) cushion; **par la ~** *fig* by
a roundabout route. 4. (*groupe*) band;
en ~ in a group. 5. (*pellicule de film*) film.
6. (*d'enregistrement*) tape; **~ magnétique**
(magnetic) tape; **~ originale** (CIN) original soundtrack; **~ vidéo** video (tape).
7. (*voie*): **~ d'arrêt d'urgence** hard shoulder. 8. (RADIO): **~ de fréquence** wave-
band. 9. (NAVIG): **donner de la ~** to list.

bande-annonce [bɑ̃dɑnɔ̃s] *nf* trailer.

bandeau [bɑ̃do] *nm* 1. (*sur les yeux*)
blindfold. 2. (*dans les cheveux*) headband.

bandelette [bɑ̃dlɛt] *nf* strip (of cloth).

bander [bɑ̃de] ◆ *vt* 1. (MÉD) to bandage; **~ les yeux de qqn** to blindfold sb.
2. (*arc*) to draw back. 3. (*muscle*) to flex.
◆ *vi vulg* to have a hard-on.

banderole [bɑ̃dʀɔl] *nf* streamer.

bande-son [bɑ̃dsɔ̃] (*pl* **bandes-son**) *nf*
soundtrack.

bandit [bɑ̃di] *nm* (*voleur*) bandit.

banditisme [bɑ̃ditism] *nm* serious
crime.

bandoulière [bɑ̃duljɛʀ] *nf* bandolier;
en ~ across the shoulder.

banlieue [bɑ̃ljø] *nf* suburbs (*pl*).

banlieusard, -e [bɑ̃ljøzaʀ, aʀd] *nm, f*
person living in the suburbs.

bannière [banjɛʀ] *nf* (*étendard*) banner.

bannir [baniʀ] *vt*: **~ qqn/qqch (de)** to
banish sb/sthg (from).

banque [bɑ̃k] *nf* 1. (*activité*) banking.
2. (*établissement, au jeu*) bank. 3.
(INFORM): **~ de données** data bank.
4. (MÉD): **~ d'organes/du sang/du
sperme** organ/blood/sperm bank.

banqueroute [bɑ̃kʀut] *nf* bankruptcy;
faire ~ to go bankrupt.

banquet [bɑ̃kɛ] *nm* (celebration) dinner; (*de gala*) banquet.

banquette [bɑ̃kɛt] *nf* seat.

banquier, -ère [bɑ̃kje, ɛʀ] *nm, f*
banker.

banquise [bɑ̃kiz] *nf* ice field.

baptême [batɛm] *nm* 1. (RELIG) baptism, christening. 2. (*première fois*): **~ de
l'air** maiden flight.

baptiser [batize] *vt* to baptize, to
christen.

baquet [bakɛ] *nm* (*cuve*) tub.

bar [baʀ] *nm* 1. (*café, unité de pression*)
bar. 2. (*poisson*) bass.

baraque [baʀak] *nf* 1. (*cabane*) hut. 2.
fam (*maison*) house. 3. (*de forain*) stall,
stand.

baraqué, -e [baʀake] *adj fam* well-
built.

baraquement [baʀakmɑ̃] *nm* camp (*of
huts for refugees, workers etc*).

baratin [baʀatɛ̃] *nm fam* smooth talk;
faire du ~ à qqn to sweet-talk sb.

baratiner [baʀatine] *fam* ◆ *vt* (*femme*)
to chat up; (*client*) to give one's sales
pitch to. ◆ *vi* to be a smooth talker.

barbare [baʀbaʀ] ◆ *nm* barbarian.
◆ *adj* 1. *péj* (*non civilisé*) barbarous.
2. (*cruel*) barbaric.

barbe [baʀb] *nf* beard; **se laisser pousser la ~** to grow a beard; **~ à papa** candy
floss Br, cotton candy Am; **quelle** OU **la
~!** *fam* what a drag!

barbelé, -e [baʀbəle] *adj* barbed.
▶ **barbelé** *nm* barbed wire (U).

barbiche [baʀbiʃ] *nf* goatee (beard).

barbiturique [baʀbityʀik] *nm* barbiturate.

barboter [baʀbɔte] *vi* to paddle.

barboteuse [baʀbɔtøz] *nf* romper-
suit.

barbouillé, -e [baʀbuje] *adj*: **être ~,
avoir l'estomac ~** to feel sick.

barbouiller [baʀbuje] *vt* (*salir*): **~ qqch
(de)** to smear sthg (with).

barbu, -e [baʀby] *adj* bearded.
▶ **barbu** *nm* bearded man.

bardé, -e [baʀde] *adj*: **il est ~ de
diplômes** he's got heaps of diplomas.

barder [baʀde] ◆ *vt* (CULIN) to bard.
◆ *vi fam*: **ça va ~** there'll be trouble.

barème [baʀɛm] *nm* (*de référence*) table;
(*de salaires*) scale.

baril [baʀil] *nm* barrel.

bariolé, -e [baʀjɔle] *adj* multicoloured.

barjo(t) [baʀʒo] *adj inv fam* nuts.

barmaid [baʀmɛd] *nf* barmaid.

barman [baʀman] (*pl* **barmans** OU **bar-
men** [baʀmɛn]) *nm* barman.

baromètre [baʀɔmɛtʀ] *nm* barometer.

baron, -onne [barɔ̃, ɔn] *nm, f* baron (*f* baroness).

baroque [barɔk] *adj* 1. (*style*) baroque. 2. (*bizarre*) weird.

barque [bark] *nf* small boat.

barquette [barkɛt] *nf* 1. (*tartelette*) pastry boat. 2. (*récipient - de fruits*) punnet; (*- de crème glacée*) tub.

barrage [baraʒ] *nm* 1. (*de rue*) roadblock. 2. (CONSTR) dam.

barre [bar] *nf* 1. (*gén & JUR*) bar; ~ **fixe** (GYM) high bar; ~ **des témoins** (JUR) witness box Br ou stand Am. 2. (NAVIG) helm. 3. (*trait*) stroke. 4. (INFORM): ~ **d'espacement** space bar.

barreau [baro] *nm* bar; **le** ~ (JUR) the Bar.

barrer [bare] *vt* 1. (*rue, route*) to block. 2. (*mot, phrase*) to cross out. 3. (*bateau*) to steer. ► **se barrer** *vp fam* to clear off.

barrette [barɛt] *nf* (*pince à cheveux*) (hair) slide Br, barrette Am.

barreur, -euse [barœr, øz] *nm, f* (NAVIG) helmsman; (*à l'aviron*) cox.

barricade [barikad] *nf* barricade.

barrière [barjɛr] *nf litt & fig* barrier.

barrique [barik] *nf* barrel.

baryton [baritɔ̃] *nm* baritone.

bas, basse [ba, baz *devant nm commençant par voyelle ou h muet*, bas] *adj* 1. (*gén*) low. 2. *péj* (*vil*) base, low. 3. (MUS) bass. ► **bas** ◆ *nm* 1. (*partie inférieure*) bottom, lower part; **avoir/connaître des hauts et des** ~ to have/go through ups and downs. 2. (*vêtement*) stocking; ~ **de laine** woollen stocking; *fig* nest egg. ◆ *adv* low; **à** ~ ~ ...! down with ...!; **parler** ~ to speak in a low voice, to speak softly; **mettre** ~ (*animal*) to give birth. ► **en bas** *loc adv* at the bottom; (*dans une maison*) downstairs. ► **en bas de** *prép* at the bottom of; **attendre qqn en** ~ **de chez lui** to wait for sb downstairs. ► **bas de gamme** ◆ *adj* downmarket. ◆ *nm* bottom of the range.

basalte [bazalt] *nm* basalt.

basané, -e [bazane] *adj* tanned.

bas-côté [bakote] *nm* (*de route*) verge.

bascule [baskyl] *nf* (*balançoire*) seesaw.

basculer [baskyle] ◆ *vi* to fall over, to overbalance; (*benne*) to tip up; ~ **dans qqch** *fig* to tip over into sthg. ◆ *vt* to tip up, to tilt.

base [baz] *nf* 1. (*partie inférieure*) base. 2. (*principe fondamental*) basis; **à** ~ **de** based on; **de** ~ basic; **une boisson à** ~ **d'orange** an orange-based drink; **sur la** ~ **de** on the basis of. 3. (INFORM): ~ **de données** database.

baser [baze] *vt* to base. ► **se baser** *vp*: **sur quoi vous basez-vous pour affirmer cela?** what are you basing this statement on?

bas-fond [bafɔ̃] *nm* (*de l'océan*) shallow. ► **bas-fonds** *nmpl fig* 1. (*de la société*) dregs. 2. (*quartiers pauvres*) slums.

basilic [bazilik] *nm* (*plante*) basil.

basilique [bazilik] *nf* basilica.

basique [bazik] *adj* basic.

basket [baskɛt] ◆ *nm* = **basket-ball**. ◆ *nf* (*chaussure*) trainer Br, sneaker Am; **lâche-moi les ~s!** *fam fig* get off my back!

basket-ball [baskɛtbol] *nm* basketball.

basque [bask] ◆ *adj* Basque; **le Pays** ~ the Basque country. ◆ *nm* (*langue*) Basque. ◆ *nf* (*vêtement*) tail (*of coat*); **être toujours pendu aux ~s de qqn** *fam fig* to be always tagging along after sb. ► **Basque** *nmf* Basque.

bas-relief [barəljɛf] *nm* bas-relief.

basse [bas] ◆ *adj* → **bas**. ◆ *nf* (MUS) bass.

basse-cour [baskur] *nf* 1. (*volaille*) poultry. 2. (*partie de ferme*) farmyard.

bassement [basmɑ̃] *adv* despicably.

basset [basɛ] *nm* basset hound.

bassin [basɛ̃] *nm* 1. (*cuvette*) bowl. 2. (*pièce d'eau*) (ornamental) pond. 3. (*de piscine*): **petit/grand** ~ children's/main pool. 4. (ANAT) pelvis. 5. (GÉOL) basin; **houiller** coalfield; **le Bassin parisien** the Paris basin.

bassine [basin] *nf* bowl, basin.

bassiste [basist] *nmf* bass player.

basson [basɔ̃] *nm* (*instrument*) bassoon; (*personne*) bassoonist.

bastide [bastid] *nf* traditional farmhouse or country house in southern France; walled town (*in south-west France*).

bastingage [bastɛ̃gaʒ] *nm* (ship's) rail.

bastion [bastjɔ̃] *nm litt & fig* bastion.

baston [bastɔ̃] *nf tfam* punch-up.

bas-ventre [bavɑ̃tr] *nm* stomach.

bataille [bataj] *nf* 1. (MIL) battle. 2. (*bagarre*) fight. 3. (*jeu de cartes*) ≃ beggar-my-neighbour. 4. *loc*: **en** ~ (*cheveux*) dishevelled.

bataillon [batajɔ̃] *nm* (MIL) battalion; *fig* horde.

bâtard, -e [batar, ard] ◆ *adj* 1. (*enfant*) illegitimate. 2. *péj* (*style, solution*) hybrid. ◆ *nm, f* illegitimate child. ► **bâtard** *nm* 1. (*pain*) = Vienna loaf. 2. (*chien*) mongrel.

batavia [batavja] nf Webb lettuce.

bateau [bato] nm **1.** (*embarcation - gén*) boat; (*- plus grand*) ship; ~ **à voile/moteur** sailing/motor boat; ~ **de pêche** fishing boat; **mener qqn en** ~ *fig* to take sb for a ride. **2.** (*de trottoir*) driveway entrance (*low kerb*). **3.** (*en apposition inv*) (*sujet, thème*) well-worn; **c'est ~!** it's the same old stuff!

bateau-mouche [batomuʃ] (*pl* **bateaux-mouches**) nm river boat (*on the Seine*).

bâti, -e [bati] *adj* **1.** (*terrain*) developed. **2.** (*personne*): **bien** ~ well-built. ▶ **bâti** nm **1.** (COUTURE) tacking. **2.** (CONSTR) frame, framework.

batifoler [batifɔle] *vi* to frolic.

bâtiment [batimɑ̃] nm **1.** (*édifice*) building. **2.** (IND): **le** ~ the building trade. **3.** (NAVIG) ship, vessel.

bâtir [batir] *vt* **1.** (CONSTR) to build. **2.** *fig* (*réputation, fortune*) to build (up); (*théorie, phrase*) to construct. **3.** (COUTURE) to tack.

bâtisse [batis] nf souvent péj house.

bâton [batɔ̃] nm **1.** (*gén*) stick; ~ **de ski** ski pole. **2.** *fam fig* 10,000 francs. **3.** *loc:* **mettre des ~s dans les roues à qqn** to put a spoke in sb's wheel; **parler à ~s rompus** to talk of this and that.

bâtonnet [batɔnɛ] nm rod.

batracien [batrasjɛ̃] nm amphibian.

battage [bataʒ] nm: ~ (**publicitaire** ou **médiatique**) (media) hype.

battant, -e [batɑ̃, ɑ̃t] ◆ *adj:* **sous une pluie ~e** in the pouring ou driving rain; **le cœur** ~ with beating heart. ◆ nm, f fighter. ▶ **battant** nm **1.** (*de porte*) door (*of double doors*); (*de fenêtre*) half (*of double window*). **2.** (*de cloche*) clapper.

battement [batmɑ̃] nm **1.** (*mouvement - d'ailes*) flap, beating (U); (*- de cœur, pouls*) beat, beating (U); (*- de cils, paupières*) flutter, fluttering (U). **2.** (*intervalle de temps*) break; **une heure de** ~ an hour free.

batterie [batri] nf **1.** (ÉLECTR & MIL) battery; **recharger ses ~s** *fig* to recharge one's batteries. **2.** (*attirail*): ~ **de cuisine** kitchen utensils (*pl*). **3.** (MUS) drums (*pl*). **4.** (*série*): **une** ~ **de** a string of.

batteur [batœr] nm **1.** (MUS) drummer. **2.** (CULIN) beater, whisk. **3.** (SPORT - *de cricket*) batsman; (*- de base-ball*) batter.

battre [batr] ◆ *vt* **1.** (*gén*) to beat; ~ **en neige** (*blancs d'œufs*) to beat until stiff. **2.** (*cartes*) to shuffle. ◆ *vi* (*gén*) to beat; ~ **des cils** to blink; ~ **des mains** to clap (one's hands). ▶ **se battre** *vp* to fight;

se ~ **contre qqn** to fight sb.

battu, -e [baty] ◆ *pp* → **battre**. ◆ *adj* **1.** (*tassé*) hard-packed; **jouer sur terre ~e** (TENNIS) to play on clay. **2.** (*fatigué*): **avoir les yeux ~s** to have shadows under one's eyes. ▶ **battue** nf **1.** (*chasse*) beat. **2.** (*chasse à l'homme*) manhunt.

baume [bom] nm *litt & fig* balm; **mettre du** ~ **au cœur de qqn** to comfort sb.

baux → **bail**.

bavard, -e [bavar, ard] ◆ *adj* talkative. ◆ nm, f chatterbox; *péj* gossip.

bavardage [bavardaʒ] nm **1.** (*papotage*) chattering. **2.** (*gén pl*) (*racontar*) gossip (U).

bavarder [bavarde] *vi* to chatter; *péj* to gossip.

bave [bav] nf **1.** (*salive*) dribble. **2.** (*d'animal*) slaver. **3.** (*de limace*) slime.

baver [bave] *vi* **1.** (*personne*) to dribble. **2.** (*animal*) to slaver. **3.** (*limace*) to leave a trail. **4.** (*stylo*) to leak. **5.** *loc:* **en** ~ *fam* to have a hard ou rough time of it.

bavette [bavɛt] nf **1.** (*bavoir, de tablier*) bib. **2.** (*viande*) flank. **3.** *loc:* **tailler une** ~ (**avec qqn**) *fam* to have a chinwag (with sb).

baveux, -euse [bavø, øz] *adj* **1.** (*bébé*) dribbling. **2.** (*omelette*) runny.

bavoir [bavwar] nm bib.

bavure [bavyr] nf **1.** (*tache*) smudge. **2.** (*erreur*) blunder.

bayer [baje] *vi:* ~ **aux corneilles** to stand gazing into space.

bazar [bazar] nm **1.** (*boutique*) general store. **2.** *fam* (*désordre*) jumble, clutter.

bazarder [bazarde] *vt fam* to chuck out, to get rid of.

BCBG (*abr de* **bon chic bon genre**) *nmf & adj* term used to describe an upper-class lifestyle reflected especially in expensive but conservative clothes.

bcp *abr de* **beaucoup**.

bd *abr de* **boulevard**.

BD, bédé [bede] (*abr de* **bande dessinée**) nf: **une** ~ a comic strip.

béant, -e [beɑ̃, ɑ̃t] *adj* (*plaie, gouffre*) gaping; (*yeux*) wide open.

béat, -e [bea, at] *adj* (*heureux*) blissful.

beau, belle, beaux [bo, bɛl] *adj* (**bel** *devant voyelle ou h muet*) **1.** (*joli - femme*) beautiful, good-looking; (*- homme*) handsome, good-looking; (*- chose*) beautiful. **2.** (*temps*) fine, good. **3.** (*toujours avant le nom*) (*important*) fine, excellent; **une belle somme** a tidy sum (of money). **4.** *iron* (*mauvais*): **une belle**

grippe a nasty dose of the flu; **un ~ travail** a fine piece of work. **5.** (*sens intensif*): **un ~ jour** one fine day. **6.** *loc*: **elle a ~ jeu de dire ça** it's easy ou all very well for her to say that. ▶ **beau** ♦ *adv*: **il fait ~ the** weather is good ou fine; **j'ai ~ essayer ...** however hard I try ..., try as I may ...; **j'ai ~ dire ...** whatever I say ... ♦ *nm*: **être au ~ fixe** to be set fair; **avoir le moral au ~ fixe** *fig* to have a sunny disposition; **faire le ~** (*chien*) to sit up and beg. ▶ **belle** *nf* **1.** (*femme*) lady friend. **2.** (*dans un jeu*) decider. ▶ **de plus belle** *loc adv* more than ever.

beaucoup [boku] ♦ *adv* **1.** (*un grand nombre*): **~ de** a lot of, many; **il y en a ~ there** are many ou a lot (of them). **2.** (*une grande quantité*): **~ de** a lot of; **~ d'énergie** a lot of energy; **il n'a pas ~ de temps** he hasn't a lot of ou much time; **il n'en a pas ~** he doesn't have much ou a lot (of it). **3.** (*modifiant un verbe*) a lot; **il boit ~** he drinks a lot; **c'est ~ dire** that's saying a lot. **4.** (*modifiant un adjectif comparatif*) much, a lot; **c'est ~ mieux** it's much ou a lot better. ♦ *pron inv* many; **nous sommes ~ à penser que ...** many of us think that ... ▶ **de beaucoup** *loc adv* by far.

beauf [bɔf] *nm* **1.** *péj* stereotype of average French man with narrow views. **2.** *fam* (*beau-frère*) brother-in-law.

beau-fils [bofis] *nm* **1.** (*gendre*) son-in-law. **2.** (*de remariage*) stepson.

beau-frère [bofrɛr] *nm* brother-in-law.

beau-père [bopɛr] *nm* **1.** (*père du conjoint*) father-in-law. **2.** (*de remariage*) stepfather.

beauté [bote] *nf* beauty; **de toute ~** absolutely beautiful; **en ~** (*magnifiquement*) in great style.

beaux-arts [bozar] *nmpl* fine art (*sg*). ▶ **Beaux-Arts** *nmpl*: **les Beaux-Arts** French national art school.

beaux-parents [boparã] *nmpl* **1.** (*de l'homme*) husband's parents, in-laws. **2.** (*de la femme*) wife's parents, in-laws.

bébé [bebe] *nm* baby.

bébé-éprouvette [bebeepruvɛt] (*pl bébés-éprouvette*) *nm* test-tube baby.

bébête [bebɛt] *adj* silly.

bec [bɛk] *nm* **1.** (*d'oiseau*) beak. **2.** (*d'instrument de musique*) mouthpiece. **3.** (*de casserole etc*) lip; **~ de gaz** (*réverbère*) gaslamp (*in street*); **~ verseur** spout. **4.** *fam* (*bouche*) mouth; **ouvrir le ~** to open one's mouth; **clouer le ~ à qqn** to shut sb up.

bécane [bekan] *nf fam* **1.** (*moto, vélo*) bike. **2.** (*ordinateur etc*) machine.

bécasse [bekas] *nf* **1.** (*oiseau*) woodcock. **2.** *fam* (*femme sotte*) silly goose.

bec-de-lièvre [bɛkdəljɛvr] (*pl becs-de-lièvre*) *nm* harelip.

bêche [bɛʃ] *nf* spade.

bêcher [beʃe] *vt* to dig.

bécoter [bekɔte] *vt fam* to snog *Br* ou smooch with. ▶ **se bécoter** *vp* to snog *Br*, to smooch.

becquée [beke] *nf*: **donner la ~ à** to feed.

becqueter, béqueter [bɛkte] *vt* to peck at.

bedaine [bədɛn] *nf* potbelly.

bédé = **BD**.

bedonnant, -e [bədɔnã, ãt] *adj* pot-bellied.

bée [be] *adj*: **bouche ~** open-mouthed.

bégayer [begeje] ♦ *vi* to have a stutter ou stammer. ♦ *vt* to stammer (out).

bégonia [begɔnja] *nm* begonia.

bègue [bɛg] ♦ *adj*: **être ~** to have a stutter ou stammer. ♦ *nmf* stutterer, stammerer.

béguin [begɛ̃] *nm fam*: **avoir le ~ pour qqn** to have a crush on sb.

beige [bɛʒ] *adj & nm* beige.

beignet [bɛɲɛ] *nm* fritter.

bel [bɛl] → **beau**.

bêler [bele] *vi* to bleat.

belette [bəlɛt] *nf* weasel.

belge [bɛlʒ] *adj* Belgian. ▶ **Belge** *nmf* Belgian.

Belgique [bɛlʒik] *nf*: **la ~** Belgium.

bélier [belje] *nm* **1.** (*animal*) ram. **2.** (*poutre*) battering ram. ▶ **Bélier** *nm* (ASTROL) Aries.

belladone [beladɔn] *nf* deadly nightshade.

belle [bɛl] *adj & nf* → **beau**.

belle-famille [bɛlfamij] *nf* **1.** (*de l'homme*) husband's family, in-laws (*pl*). **2.** (*de la femme*) wife's family, in-laws (*pl*).

belle-fille [bɛlfij] *nf* **1.** (*épouse du fils*) daughter-in-law. **2.** (*de remariage*) step-daughter.

belle-mère [bɛlmɛr] *nf* **1.** (*mère du conjoint*) mother-in-law. **2.** (*de remariage*) stepmother.

belle-sœur [bɛlsœr] *nf* sister-in-law.

belligérant, -e [beliʒerã, ãt] *adj & nm, f* belligerent.

belliqueux, -euse [belikø, øz] *adj* (*peuple*) warlike; (*humeur, tempérament*) aggressive.

belvédère [bɛlvedɛr] nm 1. (construction) belvedere. 2. (terrasse) viewpoint.

bémol [bemɔl] adj & nm (MUS) flat.

ben [bɛ̃] adv fam: ~ quoi? so what?; ~ non well, no.

bénédiction [benediksjɔ̃] nf blessing.

bénéfice [benefis] nm 1. (avantage) advantage, benefit; au ~ de in aid of. 2. (profit) profit.

bénéficiaire [benefisjɛr] ◆ nmf (gén) beneficiary; (de chèque) payee. ◆ adj (marge) profit (avant n); (résultat, société) profit-making.

bénéficier [benefisje] vi: ~ de (profiter de) to benefit from; (jouir de) to have, to enjoy; (obtenir) to have, to get.

bénéfique [benefik] adj beneficial.

Bénélux [benelyks] nm: le ~ Benelux.

benêt [bənɛ] nm clod.

bénévole [benevɔl] ◆ adj voluntary. ◆ nmf volunteer, voluntary worker.

bénin, -igne [benɛ̃, iɲ] adj (maladie, accident) minor; (tumeur) benign.

bénir [benir] vt 1. (gén) to bless. 2. (se réjouir de) to thank God for.

bénitier [benitje] nm holy water font.

benjamin, -e [bɛ̃ʒamɛ̃, in] nm, f (de famille) youngest child; (de groupe) youngest member.

benne [bɛn] nf 1. (de camion) tipper. 2. (de téléphérique) car. 3. (pour déchets) skip.

benzine [bɛ̃zin] nf benzine.

béotien, -enne [beɔsjɛ̃, ɛn] nm, f philistine.

BEP, Bep (abr de brevet d'études professionnelles) nm school-leaver's diploma (taken at age 18).

BEPC, Bepc (abr de brevet d'études du premier cycle) nm former school certificate (taken at age 16).

béquille [bekij] nf 1. (pour marcher) crutch. 2. (d'un deux-roues) stand.

berbère [bɛrbɛr] adj & nm Berber. ▸ **Berbère** nmf Berber.

berceau, -x [bɛrso] nm cradle.

bercer [bɛrse] vt (bébé, bateau) to rock.

berceuse [bɛrsøz] nf 1. (chanson) lullaby. 2. Can (fauteuil) rocking chair.

béret [berɛ] nm beret.

berge [bɛrʒ] nf 1. (bord) bank. 2. fam (an): il a plus de 50 ~s he's over 50.

berger, -ère [bɛrʒe, ɛr] nm, f shepherd (f shepherdess). ▸ **berger allemand** nm alsatian Br, German shepherd.

bergerie [bɛrʒəri] nf sheepfold.

berk [bɛrk] interj fam yuck!

Berlin [bɛrlɛ̃] n Berlin.

berline [bɛrlin] nf saloon (car) Br, sedan Am.

berlingot [bɛrlɛ̃go] nm 1. (de lait) carton. 2. (bonbon) boiled sweet.

berlue [bɛrly] nf: j'ai la ~! I must be seeing things!

bermuda [bɛrmyda] nm bermuda shorts (pl).

berne [bɛrn] nf: en ~ ≃ at half-mast.

berner [bɛrne] vt to fool.

besogne [bəzɔɲ] nf job, work (U).

besoin [bəzwɛ̃] nm need; avoir ~ de qqch/de faire qqch to need sthg/to do sthg; au ~ if necessary, if need ou needs be. ▸ **besoins** nmpl 1. (exigences) needs. 2. loc: faire ses ~s to relieve o.s.

bestial, -e, -aux [bɛstjal, o] adj bestial, brutish.

bestiole [bɛstjɔl] nf (little) creature.

bétail [betaj] nm cattle (pl).

bête [bɛt] ◆ nf (animal) animal; (insecte) insect; ~ de somme beast of burden. ◆ adj (stupide) stupid.

bêtise [betiz] nf 1. (stupidité) stupidity. 2. (action, remarque) stupid thing; faire/dire une ~ to do/say something stupid.

béton [betɔ̃] nm (matériau) concrete; ~ armé reinforced concrete.

bétonnière [betɔnjɛr] nf cement mixer.

betterave [bɛtrav] nf beetroot Br, beet Am; ~ sucrière ou à sucre sugar beet.

beugler [bøgle] vi (bovin) to moo.

beurk [bœrk] fam = berk.

beurre [bœr] nm (aliment) butter.

beurrer [bœre] vt to butter.

beurrier [bœrje] nm butter dish.

beuverie [bœvri] nf drinking session.

bévue [bevy] nf blunder.

biais [bjɛ] nm 1. (ligne oblique) slant; en ou de ~ (de travers) at an angle; fig indirectly. 2. (COUTURE) bias. 3. (moyen détourné) expedient; par le ~ de by means of.

biaiser [bjeze] vi fig to dodge the issue.

bibelot [biblo] nm trinket, curio.

biberon [bibrɔ̃] nm baby's bottle.

bible [bibl] nf bible.

bibliographie [bibljɔgrafi] nf bibliography.

bibliophile [bibljɔfil] nmf book lover.

bibliothécaire [bibljɔtekɛr] nmf librarian.

bibliothèque [bibljɔtɛk] nf 1. (meuble) bookcase. 2. (édifice, collection) library.

biblique [biblik] *adj* biblical.

bicarbonate [bikarbɔnat] *nm*: ~ (de soude) bicarbonate of soda.

biceps [bisɛps] *nm* biceps.

biche [biʃ] *nf* (ZOOL) hind, doe.

bicolore [bikɔlɔr] *adj* two-coloured.

bicoque [bikɔk] *nf péj* house.

bicorne [bikɔrn] *nm* cocked hat.

bicyclette [bisiklɛt] *nf* bicycle; **rouler à ~** to cycle.

bide [bid] *nm fam* **1.** (*ventre*) belly. **2.** (*échec*) flop.

bidet [bidɛ] *nm* **1.** (*sanitaire*) bidet. **2.** *hum* (*cheval*) nag.

bidon [bidɔ̃] *nm* **1.** (*récipient*) can. **2.** *fam* (*ventre*) belly. **3.** (*en apposition inv*) *fam* (*faux*) phoney.

bidonville [bidɔ̃vil] *nm* shantytown.

bielle [bjɛl] *nf* connecting rod.

bien [bjɛ̃] (*compar & superl* **mieux**) ◆ *adj inv* **1.** (*satisfaisant*) good; **il est ~ comme prof** he's a good teacher. **2.** (*en bonne santé*) well; **je ne me sens pas ~** I don't feel well. **3.** (*joli*) good-looking; **tu ne trouves pas qu'elle est ~ comme ça?** don't you think she looks good ou nice like that? **4.** (*à l'aise*) comfortable. **5.** (*convenable*) respectable. ◆ *nm* **1.** (*sens moral*): **le ~ et le mal** good and evil. **2.** (*intérêt*) good; **je te dis ça pour ton ~** I'm telling you this for your own good. **3.** (*richesse, propriété*) property, possession; **~s de consommation** consumer goods. **4.** *loc*: **faire du ~ à qqn** to do sb good; **dire du ~ de qqn/qqch** to speak well of sb/sthg; **mener à ~** to bring to fruition, to complete. ◆ *adv* **1.** (*de manière satisfaisante*) well; **on mange ~ ici** the food's good here; **il ne s'est pas ~ conduit** he didn't behave well; **tu as ~ fait** you did the right thing; **tu ferais ~ d'y aller** you would be wise to go; **c'est ~ fait!** it serves him/her *etc* right! **2.** (*sens intensif*) quite, really; **~ souvent** quite often; **j'espère ~ que ...** I DO hope that ...; **on a ~ ri** we had a good laugh; **il y a ~ trois heures que j'attends** I've been waiting for at least three hours; **c'est ~ aimable à vous** it's very kind ou good of you. **3.** (*renforçant un comparatif*): **il est parti ~ plus tard** he left much later; **on était ~ moins riches** we were a lot worse off ou poorer. **4.** (*servant à conclure ou à introduire*): **~, je t'écoute** well, I'm listening. **5.** (*en effet*): **c'est ~ lui** it really IS him; **c'est ~ ce que je disais** that's just what I said. ◆ *interj*: **eh ~!** oh well!; **eh ~, qu'en penses-tu?** well, what do you think?

▶ **biens** *nmpl* property (U). ▶ **bien de, bien des** *loc adj*: **~ des gens sont venus** quite a lot of people came; **~ des fois** many times; **il a ~ de la chance** he's very ou really lucky. ▶ **bien entendu** *loc adv* of course. ▶ **bien que** *loc conj* (+ *subjonctif*) although, though. ▶ **bien sûr** *loc adv* of course, certainly.

bien-aimé, -e [bjɛ̃neme] (*mpl* **bien-aimés**, *fpl* **bien-aimées**) *adj & nm, f* beloved.

bien-être [bjɛ̃nɛtr] *nm inv* (*physique*) wellbeing.

bienfaisance [bjɛ̃fəzɑ̃s] *nf* charity.

bienfaisant, -e [bjɛ̃fəzɑ̃, ɑ̃t] *adj* beneficial.

bienfait [bjɛ̃fɛ] *nm* **1.** (*effet bénéfique*) benefit. **2.** (*faveur*) kindness.

bienfaiteur, -trice [bjɛ̃fɛtœr, tris] *nm, f* benefactor.

bien-fondé [bjɛ̃fɔ̃de] (*pl* **bien-fondés**) *nm* validity.

bienheureux, -euse [bjɛ̃nørø, øz] *adj* **1.** (RELIG) blessed. **2.** (*heureux*) happy.

bientôt [bjɛ̃to] *adv* soon; **à ~!** see you soon!

bienveillance [bjɛ̃vejɑ̃s] *nf* kindness.

bienveillant, -e [bjɛ̃vejɑ̃, ɑ̃t] *adj* kindly.

bienvenu, -e [bjɛ̃vny] ◆ *adj* (*qui arrive à propos*) welcome. ◆ *nm, f*: **être le ~/la ~e** to be welcome; **soyez le ~!** welcome! ▶ **bienvenue** *nf* welcome; **souhaiter la ~e à qqn** to welcome sb.

bière [bjɛr] *nf* **1.** (*boisson*) beer; **~ blonde** lager; **~ brune** brown ale; **~ pression** draught beer. **2.** (*cercueil*) coffin.

bifteck [biftɛk] *nm* steak.

bifurcation [bifyrkasjɔ̃] *nf* (*embranchement*) fork; *fig* new direction.

bifurquer [bifyrke] *vi* **1.** (*route, voie ferrée*) to fork. **2.** (*voiture*) to turn off. **3.** *fig* (*personne*) to branch off.

bigamie [bigami] *nf* bigamy.

bigoudi [bigudi] *nm* curler.

bijou, -x [biʒu] *nm* **1.** (*joyau*) jewel. **2.** *fig* (*chef d'œuvre*) gem.

bijouterie [biʒutri] *nf* (*magasin*) jeweller's (shop).

bijoutier, -ère [biʒutje, ɛr] *nm, f* jeweller.

Bikini® [bikini] *nm* bikini.

bilan [bilɑ̃] *nm* **1.** (FIN) balance sheet; **déposer son ~** to declare bankruptcy. **2.** (*état d'une situation*) state of affairs; **faire le ~ (de)** to take stock (of); **~ de santé** checkup.

bilatéral, -e, -aux [bilateral, o] adj
1. (*stationnement*) on both sides (of the
road). 2. (*contrat, accord*) bilateral.

bile [bil] nf bile; **se faire de la ~** fam to
worry.

biliaire [biljɛr] adj biliary; **calcul ~** gallstone; **vésicule ~** gall bladder.

bilingue [bilɛ̃g] adj bilingual.

billard [bijar] nm 1. (*jeu*) billiards (U).
2. (*table de jeu*) billiard table.

bille [bij] nf 1. (*d'enfant*) marble. 2. (*de
bois*) block of wood.

billet [bijɛ] nm 1. (*lettre*) note.
2. (*argent*): **~ (de banque)** (bank) note;
un ~ de 100 francs a 100-franc note.
3. (*ticket*) ticket; **~ de train/d'avion** train/
plane ticket; **~ de loterie** lottery ticket.

billetterie [bijɛtri] nf 1. (*à l'aéroport*)
ticket desk; (*à la gare*) booking office ou
hall. 2. (BANQUE) cash dispenser.

billion [biljɔ̃] nm billion Br, trillion Am.

bimensuel, -elle [bimɑ̃sɥɛl] adj fortnightly Br, twice monthly. ▶ **bimensuel** nm fortnightly review Br, semi-
monthly Am.

bimoteur [bimɔtœr] nm twin-engined
plane.

binaire [binɛr] adj binary.

biner [bine] vt to hoe.

binocle [binɔkl] nm pince-nez. ▶ **bi-
nocles** nmpl fam vieilli specs.

bio [bjo] adj inv natural; **aliments ~**
wholefood, health food.

biochimie [bjoʃimi] nf biochemistry.

biodégradable [bjodegradabl] adj
biodegradable.

biographie [bjografi] nf biography.

biologie [bjolɔʒi] nf biology.

biologique [bjolɔʒik] adj 1. (SCIENCE)
biological. 2. (*naturel*) organic.

biopsie [bjopsi] nf biopsy.

biorythme [bjoritm] nm biorhythm.

bip [bip] nm beep; **'parlez après le ~
(sonore)'** 'please speak after the beep
ou tone'.

biréacteur [bireaktœr] nm twin-
engined jet.

bis¹, -e [bi, biz] adj greyish-brown;
pain ~ brown bread.

bis² [bis] adv 1. (*dans adresse*): **5 ~** 5a.
2. (*à la fin d'un spectacle*) encore.

bisannuel, -elle [bizanɥɛl] adj bien-
nial.

biscornu, -e [biskɔrny] adj 1. (*difforme*)
irregularly shaped. 2. (*bizarre*) weird.

biscotte [biskɔt] nf toasted bread sold in
packets and often eaten for breakfast.

biscuit [biskɥi] nm 1. (*sec*) biscuit Br,

cookie Am; (*salé*) cracker. 2. (*gâteau*)
sponge.

bise [biz] nf 1. (*vent*) north wind. 2.
fam (*baiser*) kiss; **grosses ~s** love and
kisses.

biseau, -x [bizo] nm bevel; **en ~** bev-
elled.

bison [bizɔ̃] nm bison; **Bison Futé** French
road traffic information organization.

BISON FUTÉ

This organization was created in 1975
to provide information on traffic flow
and road conditions at busy times of
the year. It also suggests 'itinéraires
bis', less busy roads often through
attractive countryside, which are indi-
cated by green signposts.

bisou [bizu] nm fam kiss.

bissextile [bisɛkstil] → **année**.

bistouri [bisturi] nm lancet.

bistro(t) [bistro] nm fam cafe, bar.

bit [bit] nm (INFORM) bit.

bivouac [bivwak] nm bivouac.

bivouaquer [bivwake] vi to bivouac.

bizarre [bizar] adj strange, odd.

bizutage [bizytaʒ] nm practical jokes
played on new arrivals in a school or college.

black-out [blakawt] nm blackout.

blafard, -e [blafar, ard] adj pale.

blague [blag] nf (*plaisanterie*) joke.

blaguer [blage] fam vi to joke.

blagueur, -euse [blagœr, øz] fam
♦ adj jokey. ♦ nm, f joker.

blaireau, -x [blɛro] nm 1. (*animal*)
badger. 2. (*de rasage*) shaving brush.

blâme [blam] nm 1. (*désapprobation*)
disapproval. 2. (*sanction*) reprimand.

blâmer [blame] vt 1. (*désapprouver*) to
blame. 2. (*sanctionner*) to reprimand.

blanc, blanche [blɑ̃, blɑ̃ʃ] adj 1. (*gén*)
white. 2. (*non écrit*) blank. 3. (*pâle*) pale.
▶ **blanc** nm 1. (*couleur*) white. 2. (*personne*) white (man). 3. (*linge de maison*): **le
~** the (household) linen. 4. (*sur page*)
blank (space); **en ~** (*chèque*) blank. 5. (*de
volaille*) white meat. 6. (*vin*) white
(wine). 7. loc: **chauffé à ~** white-hot.
▶ **blanche** nf 1. (*personne*) white
(woman). 2. (MUS) minim. ▶ **blanc
d'œuf** nm egg white.

blancheur [blɑ̃ʃœr] nf whiteness.

blanchir [blɑ̃ʃir] ♦ vt 1. (*mur*) to whitewash. 2. (*linge, argent*) to launder.
3. (*légumes*) to blanch. 4. (*sucre*) to
refine; (*papier, tissu*) to bleach. ♦ vi: **~
(de)** to go white (with).

blanchissage [blɑ̃ʃisaʒ] nm (de linge) laundering.

blanchisserie [blɑ̃ʃisri] nf laundry.

blanquette [blɑ̃kɛt] nf (CULIN) stew of veal, lamb or chicken served in a white sauce; ~ de veau veal blanquette.

blasé, -e [blaze] adj blasé.

blason [blazɔ̃] nm coat of arms.

blasphème [blasfɛm] nm blasphemy.

blasphémer [blasfeme] vt & vi to blaspheme.

blatte [blat] nf cockroach.

blazer [blazɛr] nm blazer.

blé [ble] nm 1. (céréale) wheat, corn. 2. fam (argent) dough.

blême [blɛm] adj: ~ (de) pale (with).

blennorragie [blenɔraʒi] nf gonorrhoea.

blessant, -e [blɛsɑ̃, ɑ̃t] adj hurtful.

blessé, -e [blese] nm, f wounded ou injured person.

blesser [blese] vt 1. (physiquement - accidentellement) to injure, to hurt; (- par arme) to wound. 2. (moralement) to hurt. ▶ **se blesser** vp to injure ou hurt o.s.

blessure [blesyr] nf litt & fig wound.

blet, blette [blɛ, blɛt] adj overripe.

bleu, -e [blø] adj 1. (couleur) blue. 2. (viande) very rare. ▶ **bleu** nm 1. (couleur) blue. 2. (meurtrissure) bruise. 3. fam (novice - à l'armée) raw recruit; (- à l'université) freshman, fresher Br. 4. (fromage) blue cheese. 5. (vêtement): ~ de travail overalls (pl).

bleuet [bløɛ] nm cornflower; Can (fruit) blueberry.

bleuir [bløir] vt & vi to turn blue.

bleuté, -e [bløte] adj bluish.

blindé, -e [blɛ̃de] adj (véhicule) armoured; (porte, coffre) armour-plated. ▶ **blindé** nm armoured car.

blinder [blɛ̃de] vt (véhicule) to armour; (porte, coffre) to armour-plate.

blizzard [blizar] nm blizzard.

bloc [blɔk] nm 1. (gén) block; en ~ wholesale. 2. (assemblage) unit; ~ d'alimentation (INFORM) power pack; ~ opératoire operating theatre.

blocage [blɔkaʒ] nm 1. (ÉCON) freeze, freezing (U). 2. (de roue) locking. 3. (PSYCHOL) (mental) block.

blockhaus [blɔkos] nm blockhouse.

bloc-notes [blɔknɔt] nm notepad.

blocus [blɔkys] nm blockade.

blond, -e [blɔ̃, blɔ̃d] ♦ adj fair, blond. ♦ nm, f fair-haired ou blond man (f fair-haired ou blonde woman). ▶ **blond** nm: ~ cendré/vénitien/platine ash/straw-berry/platinum blond. ▶ **blonde** nf 1. (cigarette) Virginia cigarette. 2. (bière) lager.

blondeur [blɔ̃dœr] nf blondness, fairness.

bloquer [blɔke] vt 1. (porte, freins) to jam; (roues) to lock. 2. (route, chemin) to block; (personne): être bloqué to be stuck. 3. (prix, salaires, crédit) to freeze. 4. (PSYCHOL): être bloqué to have a (mental) block. ▶ **se bloquer** vp (se coincer) to jam.

blottir [blɔtir] ▶ **se blottir** vp: se ~ (contre) to snuggle up (to).

blouse [bluz] nf (de travail, d'écolier) smock.

blouson [bluzɔ̃] nm bomber jacket, blouson.

blue-jean [bludʒin] (pl blue-jeans [bludʒins]) nm jeans (pl).

blues [bluz] nm inv blues.

bluffer [blœfe] fam vi & vt to bluff.

blush [blœʃ] nm blusher.

boa [bɔa] nm boa.

bobard [bɔbar] nm fam fib.

bobine [bɔbin] nf 1. (cylindre) reel, spool. 2. (ÉLECTR) coil.

bobsleigh [bɔbslɛg] nm bobsleigh.

bocage [bɔkaʒ] nm (GÉOGR) bocage.

bocal, -aux [bɔkal, o] nm jar.

body-building [bɔdibildiŋ] nm: le ~ body building (U).

bœuf [bœf, pl bø] nm 1. (animal) ox. 2. (viande) beef; ~ bourguignon beef stew in a red-wine sauce.

bof [bɔf] interj fam (exprime le mépris) so what?; (exprime la lassitude) I don't really care.

bohème [bɔɛm] adj bohemian.

bohémien, -enne [bɔemjɛ̃, ɛn] nm, f 1. (tsigane) gipsy. 2. (non-conformiste) bohemian.

boire [bwar] ♦ vt 1. (s'abreuver) to drink. 2. (absorber) to soak up, to absorb. ♦ vi to drink.

bois [bwa] ♦ nm wood; en ~ wooden. ♦ nmpl 1. (MUS) woodwind (U). 2. (cornes) antlers.

boisé, -e [bwaze] adj wooded.

boiserie [bwazri] nf panelling (U).

boisson [bwasɔ̃] nf (breuvage) drink.

boîte [bwat] nf 1. (récipient) box; en ~ tinned Br, canned; ~ de conserve tin Br, can; ~ à gants glove compartment; ~ aux lettres (pour la réception) letterbox; (pour l'envoi) postbox Br, mailbox Am; ~ à musique musical box Br, music box Am; ~ postale post office box; ~ de

vitesses gearbox. **2.** *fam (entreprise)* company, firm; *(lycée)* school. **3.** *fam (discothèque):* ~ **(de nuit)** nightclub, club.
boiter [bwate] *vi (personne)* to limp.
boiteux, -euse [bwatø, øz] *adj* **1.** *(personne)* lame. **2.** *(meuble)* wobbly. **3.** *fig (raisonnement)* shaky.
boîtier [bwatje] *nm* **1.** *(boîte)* case. **2.** (TECHNOL) casing.
bol [bɔl] *nm* **1.** *(récipient)* bowl. **2.** *(contenu)* bowl, bowlful. **3.** *loc:* **prendre un ~ d'air** to get some fresh air.
bolet [bɔlɛ] *nm* boletus.
bolide [bɔlid] *nm (véhicule)* racing car.
Bolivie [bɔlivi] *nf:* **la ~** Bolivia.
bombance [bɔ̃bɑ̃s] *nf:* **faire ~** *fam* to have a feast.
bombardement [bɔ̃baʀdəmɑ̃] *nm* bombardment, bombing (U).
bombarder [bɔ̃baʀde] *vt* **1.** (MIL) to bomb. **2.** *(assaillir):* ~ **qqn/qqch de** to bombard sb/sthg with.
bombardier [bɔ̃baʀdje] *nm* **1.** *(avion)* bomber. **2.** *(aviateur)* bombardier.
bombe [bɔ̃b] *nf* **1.** *(projectile)* bomb; *fig* bombshell; ~ **atomique** atomic bomb; ~ **à retardement** time bomb. **2.** *(casquette)* riding hat. **3.** *(atomiseur)* spray, aerosol.
bombé, -e [bɔ̃be] *adj* bulging, rounded.
bon, bonne [bɔ̃, bɔn] *(compar & superl* **meilleur)** *adj* **1.** *(gén)* good. **2.** *(généreux)* good, kind. **3.** *(utilisable - billet, carte)* valid. **4.** *(correct)* right. **5.** *(dans l'expression d'un souhait):* **bonne année!** Happy New Year!; **bonne chance!** good luck!; **bonne idée!** good idea!; **bonne journée!** have a nice day!; **bonnes vacances!** have a nice holiday! **6.** *loc:* **être ~ pour qqch/pour faire qqch** *fam* to be fit for sthg/for doing sthg; **tu es ~ pour une contravention** you'll end up with a parking ticket; **~ à (+** *infinitif)* fit to; **c'est ~ à savoir** that's worth knowing. ▶ **bon** ◆ *adv:* **il fait ~** the weather's fine, it's fine; **sentir ~** to smell good; **tenir ~** to stand firm. ◆ *interj* **1.** *(marque de satisfaction)* good! **2.** *(marque de surprise):* **ah ~!** really? ◆ *nm* **1.** *(constatant un droit)* voucher; ~ **de commande** order form; ~ **du Trésor** (FIN) Treasury bill *ou* bond. **2.** *(gén pl) (personne):* **les ~s et les méchants** good people and wicked people. ▶ **pour de bon** *loc adv* seriously, really.
bonbon [bɔ̃bɔ̃] *nm* **1.** *(friandise)* sweet Br, piece of candy Am. **2.** Belg *(gâteau)* biscuit.

bonbonne [bɔ̃bɔn] *nf* demijohn.
bonbonnière [bɔ̃bɔnjɛʀ] *nf (boîte)* sweet-box Br, candy box Am.
bond [bɔ̃] *nm (d'animal, de personne)* leap, bound; *(de balle)* bounce; **faire un ~** to leap (forward).
bonde [bɔ̃d] *nf* **1.** *(d'évier)* plug. **2.** *(trou)* bunghole. **3.** *(bouchon)* bung.
bondé, -e [bɔ̃de] *adj* packed.
bondir [bɔ̃diʀ] *vi* **1.** *(sauter)* to leap, to bound; ~ **sur qqn/qqch** to pounce on sb/sthg. **2.** *(s'élancer)* to leap forward.
bonheur [bɔnœʀ] *nm* **1.** *(félicité)* happiness. **2.** *(chance)* (good) luck, good fortune; **par ~** happily, fortunately; **porter ~** to be lucky, to bring good luck.
bonhomme [bɔnɔm] *(pl* **bonshommes** [bɔ̃zɔm]) *nm* **1.** *fam péj (homme)* fellow. **2.** *(représentation)* man; ~ **de neige** snowman.
bonification [bɔnifikasjɔ̃] *nf* **1.** *(de terre, de vin)* improvement. **2.** (SPORT) bonus points *(pl)*.
bonjour [bɔ̃ʒuʀ] *nm* hello; *(avant midi)* good morning; *(après midi)* good afternoon.
bonne [bɔn] ◆ *nf* maid. ◆ *adj* → **bon**.
bonnet [bɔnɛ] *nm* **1.** *(coiffure)* (woolly) hat; ~ **de bain** swimming cap. **2.** *(de soutien-gorge)* cup.
bonneterie [bɔnɛtʀi] *nf (commerce)* hosiery (business *ou* trade).
bonsoir [bɔ̃swaʀ] *nm (en arrivant)* hello, good evening; *(en partant)* goodbye, good evening; *(en se couchant)* good night.
bonté [bɔ̃te] *nf* **1.** *(qualité)* goodness, kindness; **avoir la ~ de faire qqch** *sout* to be so good *ou* kind as to do sthg. **2.** *(gén pl) (acte)* act of kindness.
bonus [bɔnys] *nm (prime d'assurance)* no-claims bonus.
bord [bɔʀ] *nm* **1.** *(de table, de vêtement)* edge; *(de verre, de chapeau)* rim; **à ras ~s** to the brim. **2.** *(de rivière)* bank; *(de lac)* edge, shore; **au ~ de la mer** at the seaside. **3.** *(de bois, jardin)* edge; *(de route)* edge, side. **4.** *(d'un moyen de transport):* **passer par-dessus ~** to fall overboard. ▶ **à bord de** *loc prép:* **~ de qqch** on board sthg. ▶ **au bord de** *loc prép* on the edge of; *fig* on the verge of.
bordeaux [bɔʀdo] ◆ *nm* **1.** *(vin)* Bordeaux. **2.** *(couleur)* claret. ◆ *adj inv* claret.
bordel [bɔʀdɛl] *nm vulg* **1.** *(maison close)* brothel. **2.** *(désordre)* shambles *(sg)*.
border [bɔʀde] *vt* **1.** *(vêtement):* ~ **qqch**

de to edge sthg with. **2.** (*être en bordure de*) to line. **3.** (*couverture, personne*) to tuck in.

bordereau, -x [bɔrdəro] *nm* **1.** (*liste*) schedule. **2.** (*facture*) invoice. **3.** (*relevé*) slip.

bordure [bɔrdyr] *nf* **1.** (*bord*) edge; **en ~ de** on the edge of. **2.** (*de fleurs*) border.

borgne [bɔrɲ] *adj* (*personne*) one-eyed.

borne [bɔrn] *nf* **1.** (*marque*) boundary marker. **2.** *fam* (*kilomètre*) kilometre. **3.** (*limite*) limit, bounds (*pl*); **dépasser les ~s** to go too far; **sans ~s** boundless. **4.** (ÉLECTR) terminal.

borné, -e [bɔrne] *adj* (*personne*) narrow-minded; (*esprit*) narrow.

borner [bɔrne] *vt* (*terrain*) to limit; (*projet, ambition*) to limit, to restrict. ▶ **se borner** *vp*: **se ~ à qqch/à faire qqch** (*suj: personne*) to confine o.s. to sthg/to doing sthg.

bosniaque [bɔsnjak] *adj* Bosnian. ▶ **Bosniaque** *nmf* Bosnian.

Bosnie [bɔsni] *nf*: **la ~** Bosnia.

bosquet [bɔskɛ] *nm* copse.

bosse [bɔs] *nf* **1.** (*sur tête, sur route*) bump. **2.** (*de bossu, chameau*) hump.

bosser [bɔse] *vi fam* to work hard.

bossu, -e [bɔsy] ◆ *adj* hunchbacked. ◆ *nm, f* hunchback.

bot [bo] → **pied**.

botanique [bɔtanik] ◆ *adj* botanical. ◆ *nf*: **la ~** botany.

botte [bɔt] *nf* **1.** (*chaussure*) boot. **2.** (*de légumes*) bunch. **3.** (*en escrime*) thrust, lunge.

botter [bɔte] *vt* **1.** (*chausser*): **être botté de cuir** to be wearing leather boots. **2.** *fam* (*donner un coup de pied à*) to boot. **3.** *fam vieilli* (*plaire à*): **ça me botte** I dig it.

bottier [bɔtje] *nm* (*de bottes*) bootmaker; (*de chaussures*) shoemaker.

Bottin® [bɔtɛ̃] *nm* phone book.

bottine [bɔtin] *nf* (ankle) boot.

bouc [buk] *nm* **1.** (*animal*) (billy) goat; **~ émissaire** *fig* scapegoat. **2.** (*barbe*) goatee.

boucan [bukɑ̃] *nm fam* row, racket.

bouche [buʃ] *nf* (*gén*) mouth; **~ d'incendie** fire hydrant; **~ de métro** metro entrance ou exit.

bouché, -e [buʃe] *adj* **1.** (*en bouteille*) bottled. **2.** *fam* (*personne*) thick Br, dumb.

bouche-à-bouche [buʃabuʃ] *nm inv*: **faire du ~ à qqn** to give sb mouth-to-mouth resuscitation.

bouchée [buʃe] *nf* mouthful.

boucher[1] [buʃe] *vt* **1.** (*fermer - bouteille*) to cork; (*- trou*) to fill (**in** ou **up**). **2.** (*passage, vue*) to block.

boucher[2]**, -ère** [buʃe, ɛr] *nm, f* butcher.

boucherie [buʃri] *nf* **1.** (*magasin*) butcher's (shop). **2.** *fig* (*carnage*) slaughter.

bouche-trou [buʃtru] (*pl* **bouche-trous**) *nm* **1.** (*personne*): **servir de ~** to make up (the) numbers. **2.** (*objet*) stopgap.

bouchon [buʃɔ̃] *nm* **1.** (*pour obturer - gén*) top; (*- de réservoir*) cap; (*- de bouteille*) cork. **2.** (*de canne à pêche*) float. **3.** (*embouteillage*) traffic jam.

boucle [bukl] *nf* **1.** (*de ceinture, soulier*) buckle. **2.** (*bijou*): **~ d'oreille** earring. **3.** (*de cheveux*) curl. **4.** (*de fleuve, d'avion &* INFORM) loop.

bouclé, -e [bukle] *adj* (*cheveux*) curly; (*personne*) curly-haired.

boucler [bukle] *vt* **1.** (*attacher*) to buckle; (*ceinture de sécurité*) to fasten. **2.** (*fermer*) to shut. **3.** *fam* (*enfermer - voleur*) to lock up; (*- malade*) to shut away. **4.** (*encercler*) to seal off. **5.** (*terminer*) to finish.

bouclier [buklije] *nm litt & fig* shield.

bouddhiste [budist] *nmf & adj* Buddhist.

bouder [bude] ◆ *vi* to sulk. ◆ *vt* (*chose*) to dislike; (*personne*) to shun; **elle me boude depuis que je lui ai fait faux-bond** she has cold-shouldered me ever since I let her down.

boudeur, -euse [budœr, øz] *adj* sulky.

boudin [budɛ̃] *nm* (CULIN) blood pudding.

boue [bu] *nf* mud.

bouée [bwe] *nf* **1.** (*balise*) buoy. **2.** (*pour flotter*) rubber ring; **~ de sauvetage** lifebelt.

boueux, -euse [buø, øz] *adj* muddy.

bouffe [buf] *nf fam* grub.

bouffée [bufe] *nf* **1.** (*de fumée*) puff; (*de parfum*) whiff; (*d'air*) breath. **2.** (*accès*) surge; **~s délirantes** mad fits.

bouffer [bufe] *vt fam* (*manger*) to eat.

bouffi, -e [bufi] *adj*: **~ (de)** swollen (with).

bouffon, -onne [bufɔ̃, ɔn] *adj* farcical. ▶ **bouffon** *nm* **1.** (HIST) jester. **2.** (*pitre*) clown.

bouge [buʒ] *nm péj* **1.** (*taudis*) hovel. **2.** (*café*) dive.

bougeoir [buʒwar] *nm* candlestick.

bougeotte [buʒɔt] *nf*: **avoir la ~** to have itchy feet.

bouger [buʒe] ◆ vt (déplacer) to move. ◆ vi **1.** (remuer) to move. **2.** (changer) to change. **3.** (s'agiter): **ça bouge partout dans le monde** there is unrest all over the world.

bougie [buʒi] nf **1.** (chandelle) candle. **2.** (de moteur) spark plug, sparking plug.

bougon, -onne [bugɔ̃, ɔn] adj grumpy.

bougonner [bugɔne] vt & vi to grumble.

bouillant, -e [bujã, ãt] adj **1.** (qui bout) boiling. **2.** (très chaud) boiling hot.

bouillie [buji] nf baby's cereal; **réduire en ~** (légumes) to puree; (personne) to reduce to a pulp.

bouillir [bujir] vi (aliments) to boil; **faire ~** to boil.

bouilloire [bujwar] nf kettle.

bouillon [bujɔ̃] nm **1.** (soupe) stock. **2.** (bouillonnement) bubble; **faire bouillir à gros ~s** to bring to a rolling boil.

bouillonner [bujɔne] vi **1.** (liquide) to bubble. **2.** (torrent) to foam. **3.** fig (personne) to seethe.

bouillotte [bujɔt] nf hot-water bottle.

boul. abr de **boulevard**.

boulanger, -ère [bulãʒe, ɛr] nm, f baker.

boulangerie [bulãʒri] nf **1.** (magasin) baker's (shop). **2.** (commerce) bakery trade.

boulangerie-pâtisserie [bulãʒripatisri] (pl **boulangeries-pâtisseries**) nf = baker's (shop).

boule [bul] nf (gén) ball; (de loto) counter; (de pétanque) bowl; **~ de neige** snowball. ► **boules** nfpl (JEUX) game played on bare ground with steel bowls.

bouleau, -x [bulo] nm silver birch.

bouledogue [buldɔg] nm bulldog.

boulet [bulɛ] nm **1.** (munition): **~ de canon** cannonball. **2.** (de forçat) ball and chain. **3.** fig (fardeau) millstone (round one's neck).

boulette [bulɛt] nf **1.** (petite boule) pellet. **2.** (de viande) meatball.

boulevard [bulvar] nm **1.** (rue) boulevard. **2.** (THÉÂTRE) light comedy (U).

bouleversant, -e [bulvɛrsã, ãt] adj distressing.

bouleversement [bulvɛrsəmã] nm disruption.

bouleverser [bulvɛrse] vt **1.** (objets) to turn upside down. **2.** (modifier) to disrupt. **3.** (émouvoir) to distress.

boulier [bulje] nm abacus.

boulimie [bulimi] nf bulimia.

boulon [bulɔ̃] nm bolt.

boulonner [bulɔne] ◆ vt to bolt. ◆ vi fam to slog (away).

boulot [bulo] nm fam **1.** (travail) work. **2.** (emploi) job.

boum [bum] nf fam vieilli party.

bouquet [bukɛ] nm **1.** (de fleurs - gén) bunch (of flowers). **2.** (de vin) bouquet. **3.** (de feu d'artifice) crowning piece.

bouquin [bukɛ̃] nm fam book.

bouquiner [bukine] vi & vt fam to read.

bouquiniste [bukinist] nmf second-hand bookseller.

bourbier [burbje] nm (lieu) quagmire, mire; fig mess.

bourde [burd] nf fam (erreur) blunder.

bourdon [burdɔ̃] nm (insecte) bumble-bee.

bourdonnement [burdɔnmã] nm (d'insecte, de voix, de moteur) buzz (U).

bourdonner [burdɔne] vi **1.** (insecte, machine, voix) to buzz. **2.** (oreille) to ring.

bourgeois, -e [burʒwa, az] ◆ adj **1.** (valeur) middle-class. **2.** (cuisine) plain. **3.** péj (personne) bourgeois. ◆ nm, f bourgeois.

bourgeoisie [burʒwazi] nf = middle classes (pl).

bourgeon [burʒɔ̃] nm bud.

bourgeonner [burʒɔne] vi to bud.

Bourgogne [burgɔɲ] nf: **la ~** Burgundy.

bourlinguer [burlɛ̃ge] vi fam (voyager) to bum around the world.

bourrade [burad] nf thump.

bourrage [buraʒ] nm (de coussin) stuffing. ► **bourrage de crâne** nm **1.** (bachotage) swotting. **2.** (propagande) brainwashing.

bourrasque [burask] nf gust of wind.

bourratif, -ive [buratif, iv] adj stodgy.

bourreau, -x [buro] nm (HIST) executioner.

bourrelet [burlɛ] nm (de graisse) roll of fat.

bourrer [bure] vt **1.** (remplir - coussin) to stuff; (- sac, armoire): **~ qqch (de)** to cram sthg full (with). **2.** fam (gaver): **~ qqn (de)** to stuff sb (with).

bourrique [burik] nf **1.** (ânesse) she-ass. **2.** fam (personne) pigheaded person.

bourru, -e [bury] adj (peu aimable) surly.

bourse [burs] nf **1.** (porte-monnaie) purse. **2.** (d'études) grant. ► **Bourse** nf **1.** (lieu) = Stock Exchange Br, = Wall Street Am. **2.** (opérations): **Bourse des**

valeurs stock market, stock exchange; **Bourse de commerce** commodity market.

boursier, -ère [bursje, ɛr] adj 1. (élève) on a grant. 2. (FIN) stock-market (avant n).

boursouflé, -e [bursufle] adj (enflé) swollen.

bousculade [buskylad] nf 1. (cohue) crush. 2. (agitation) rush.

bousculer [buskyle] vt 1. (faire tomber) to knock over. 2. (presser) to rush. 3. (modifier) to overturn.

bouse [buz] nf: ~ de vache cow dung.

bousiller [buzije] vt fam (abîmer) to ruin, to knacker Br.

boussole [busɔl] nf compass.

bout [bu] nm 1. (extrémité, fin) end; **au ~ de** (temps) after; (espace) at the end of; **d'un ~ à l'autre** (de ville etc) from one end to the other; (de livre) from beginning to end. 2. (morceau) bit. 3. loc: **être à ~ de** to be exhausted; **à ~ portant** at point-blank range; **pousser qqn à ~** to drive sb to distraction; **venir à ~ de** (personne) to get the better of; (difficulté) to overcome.

boutade [butad] nf (plaisanterie) jest.

boute-en-train [butɑ̃trɛ̃] nm inv live wire; **il était le ~ de la soirée** he was the life and soul of the party.

bouteille [butɛj] nf bottle.

boutique [butik] nf (gén) shop; (de mode) boutique.

bouton [butɔ̃] nm 1. (COUTURE) button; **~ de manchette** cuff link. 2. (sur la peau) spot. 3. (de porte) knob. 4. (commutateur) switch. 5. (bourgeon) bud.

bouton-d'or [butɔ̃dɔr] (pl **boutons-d'or**) nm buttercup.

boutonner [butɔne] vt to button (up).

boutonneux, -euse [butɔnø, øz] adj spotty.

boutonnière [butɔnjɛr] nf (de vêtement) buttonhole.

bouton-pression [butɔ̃presjɔ̃] (pl **boutons-pression**) nm press-stud Br, snap fastener Am.

bouture [butyr] nf cutting.

bovin, -e [bɔvɛ̃, in] adj bovine. ▶ **bovins** nmpl cattle (pl).

bowling [buliŋ] nm 1. (jeu) bowling. 2. (lieu) bowling alley.

box [bɔks] (pl **boxes**) nm 1. (d'écurie) loose box. 2. (compartiment) cubicle; **le ~ des accusés** the dock. 3. (parking) lock-up garage.

boxe [bɔks] nf boxing.

boxer¹ [bɔkse] ◆ vi to box. ◆ vt fam to thump.

boxer² [bɔksɛr] nm (chien) boxer.

boxeur [bɔksœr] nm (SPORT) boxer.

boyau [bwajo] nm 1. (chambre à air) inner tube. 2. (corde) catgut. 3. (galerie) narrow gallery. ▶ **boyaux** nmpl (intestins) guts.

boycotter [bɔjkɔte] vt to boycott.

BP (abr de **boîte postale**) nf PO Box.

bracelet [braslɛ] nm 1. (bijou) bracelet. 2. (de montre) strap.

bracelet-montre [braslɛmɔ̃tr] nm wristwatch.

braconner [brakɔne] vi to go poaching, to poach.

braconnier [brakɔnje] nm poacher.

brader [brade] vt (solder) to sell off; (vendre à bas prix) to sell for next to nothing.

braderie [bradri] nf clearance sale.

braguette [bragɛt] nf flies (pl).

braille [braj] nm Braille.

brailler [braje] vi to bawl.

braire [brɛr] vi (âne) to bray.

braise [brɛz] nf embers (pl).

bramer [brame] vi (cerf) to bell.

brancard [brɑ̃kar] nm 1. (civière) stretcher. 2. (de charrette) shaft.

brancardier, -ère [brɑ̃kardje, ɛr] nm, f stretcher-bearer.

branchage [brɑ̃ʃaʒ] nm branches (pl).

branche [brɑ̃ʃ] nf 1. (gén) branch. 2. (de lunettes) arm.

branché, -e [brɑ̃ʃe] adj 1. (ÉLECTR) plugged in, connected. 2. fam (à la mode) trendy.

branchement [brɑ̃ʃmɑ̃] nm (raccordement) connection, plugging in.

brancher [brɑ̃ʃe] vt 1. (raccorder & INFORM) to connect; **~ qqch sur** (ÉLECTR) to plug sthg into. 2. fam (orienter) to steer; **~ qqn sur qqch** to start sb off on sthg. 3. fam (plaire) to appeal to.

branchies [brɑ̃ʃi] nfpl (de poisson) gills.

brandir [brɑ̃dir] vt to wave.

branlant, -e [brɑ̃lɑ̃, ɑ̃t] adj (escalier, mur) shaky; (meuble, dent) wobbly.

branle-bas [brɑ̃lba] nm inv pandemonium (U).

braquage [brakaʒ] nm 1. (AUTOM) lock. 2. (attaque) holdup.

braquer [brake] ◆ vt 1. (diriger): **~ qqch sur** (arme) to aim sthg at; (regard) to fix sthg on. 2. fam (attaquer) to hold up. ◆ vi to turn (the wheel). ▶ **se braquer** vp (personne) to take a stand.

bras [bra] nm 1. (gén) arm; **~ droit** right-hand man ou woman; **~ de fer** (jeu) arm wrestling; fig trial of strength; **avoir le ~ long** (avoir de l'influence) to have pull.

2. (*de cours d'eau*) branch; ~ **de mer** arm of the sea.

brasier [brazje] *nm* (*incendie*) blaze, inferno.

bras-le-corps [bralkɔr] ▶ **à bras-le-corps** *loc adv* bodily.

brassage [brasaʒ] *nm* **1.** (*de bière*) brewing. **2.** *fig* (*mélange*) mixing.

brassard [brasar] *nm* armband.

brasse [bras] *nf* (*nage*) breaststroke; ~ **papillon** butterfly (stroke).

brassée [brase] *nf* armful.

brasser [brase] *vt* **1.** (*bière*) to brew. **2.** (*mélanger*) to mix. **3.** *fig* (*manier*) to handle.

brasserie [brasri] *nf* **1.** (*usine*) brewery. **2.** (*café-restaurant*) brasserie.

brassière [brasjɛr] *nf* **1.** (*de bébé*) (baby's) vest Br ou undershirt Am. **2.** Can (*soutien-gorge*) bra.

bravade [bravad] *nf:* **par ~** out of bravado.

brave [brav] ◆ *adj* **1.** (*après n*) (*courageux*) brave. **2.** (*avant n*) (*honnête*) decent. **3.** (*naïf et gentil*) nice. ◆ *nmf:* **mon ~** my good man.

braver [brave] *vt* **1.** (*parents, règlement*) to defy. **2.** (*mépriser*) to brave.

bravo [bravo] *interj* bravo! ▶ **bravos** *nmpl* cheers.

bravoure [bravur] *nf* bravery.

break [brɛk] *nm* **1.** (*voiture*) estate (car) Br, station wagon Am. **2.** (*pause*) break.

brebis [brəbi] *nf* ewe; ~ **galeuse** black sheep.

brèche [brɛʃ] *nf* **1.** (*de mur*) gap. **2.** (MIL) breach.

bredouiller [brəduje] *vi* to stammer.

bref, brève [brɛf, brɛv] *adj* **1.** (*gén*) short, brief; **soyez ~!** make it brief! **2.** (LING) short. ▶ **bref** *adv* in short, in a word. ▶ **brève** *nf* (PRESSE) brief news item.

brelan [brəlɑ̃] *nm:* **un ~** three of a kind; **un ~ de valets** three jacks.

Brésil [brezil] *nm:* **le ~** Brazil.

Bretagne [brətaɲ] *nf:* **la ~** Brittany.

bretelle [brətɛl] *nf* **1.** (*d'autoroute*) access road, slip road Br. **2.** (*de pantalon*): ~**s** braces Br, suspenders Am. **3.** (*de bustier*) strap.

breton, -onne [brətɔ̃, ɔn] *adj* Breton. ▶ **breton** *nm* (*langue*) Breton.

breuvage [brœvaʒ] *nm* (*boisson*) beverage.

brève → **bref**.

brevet [brəvɛ] *nm* **1.** (*certificat*) certificate; ~ **de secouriste** first-aid certificate.

2. (*diplôme*) diploma. **3.** (*d'invention*) patent.

breveter [brəvte] *vt* to patent.

bréviaire [brevjɛr] *nm* breviary.

bribe [brib] *nf* (*fragment*) scrap, bit; *fig* snippet; ~**s de conversation** snatches of conversation.

bric [brik] ▶ **de bric et de broc** *loc adv* any old how.

bric-à-brac [brikabrak] *nm inv* bric-a-brac.

bricolage [brikɔlaʒ] *nm* **1.** (*travaux*) do-it-yourself, DIY. **2.** (*réparation provisoire*) patching up.

bricole [brikɔl] *nf* **1.** (*babiole*) trinket. **2.** (*chose insignifiante*) trivial matter.

bricoler [brikɔle] ◆ *vi* to do odd jobs (around the house). ◆ *vt* **1.** (*réparer*) to fix, to mend. **2.** (*fabriquer*) to make, to knock up Br.

bricoleur, -euse [brikɔlœr, øz] *nm, f* home handyman (*f* handywoman).

bride [brid] *nf* **1.** (*de cheval*) bridle. **2.** (*de chapeau*) string. **3.** (COUTURE) bride, bar. **4.** (TECHNOL) flange.

bridé [bride] → **œil**.

brider [bride] *vt* (*cheval*) to bridle; *fig* to rein (in).

bridge [bridʒ] *nm* bridge.

brie [bri] *nm* Brie.

briefer [brife] *vt* to brief.

briefing [brifiŋ] *nm* briefing.

brièvement [brijɛvmɑ̃] *adv* briefly.

brièveté [brijɛvte] *nf* brevity, briefness.

brigade [brigad] *nf* **1.** (*d'ouvriers, de soldats*) brigade. **2.** (*détachement*) squad; ~ **volante** flying squad.

brigand [brigɑ̃] *nm* (*bandit*) bandit.

brillamment [brijamɑ̃] *adv* (*gén*) brilliantly; (*réussir un examen*) with flying colours.

brillant, -e [brijɑ̃, ɑ̃t] *adj* **1.** (*qui brille - gén*) sparkling; (- *cheveux*) glossy; (- *yeux*) bright. **2.** (*remarquable*) brilliant. ▶ **brillant** *nm* (*diamant*) brilliant.

briller [brije] *vi* to shine.

brimer [brime] *vt* to victimize, to bully.

brin [brɛ̃] *nm* **1.** (*tige*) twig; ~ **d'herbe** blade of grass. **2.** (*fil*) strand. **3.** (*petite quantité*): **un ~ (de)** a bit (of); **faire un ~ de toilette** to have a quick wash.

brindille [brɛ̃dij] *nf* twig.

bringuebaler, brinquebaler [brɛ̃gbale] *vi* (*voiture*) to jolt along.

brio [brijo] *nm* (*talent*): **avec ~** brilliantly.

brioche [brijɔʃ] *nf* **1.** (*pâtisserie*)

brioche. 2. *fam (ventre)* paunch.

brioché, -e [brijɔʃe] *adj (pain)* brioche-style.

brique [brik] *nf* 1. *(pierre)* brick. 2. *(emballage)* carton. 3. *fam (argent)* 10,000 *francs*.

briquer [brike] *vt* to scrub.

briquet [brikɛ] *nm (cigarette)* lighter.

brisant [brizɑ̃] *nm (écueil)* reef. ▶ **brisants** *nmpl (récif)* breakers.

brise [briz] *nf* breeze.

brise-glace(s) [brizglas] *nm inv (navire)* icebreaker.

brise-lames [brizlam] *nm inv* breakwater.

briser [brize] *vt* 1. *(gén)* to break. 2. *fig (carrière)* to ruin; *(conversation)* to break off; *(espérances)* to shatter. ▶ **se briser** *vp* 1. *(gén)* to break. 2. *fig (espoir)* to be dashed; *(efforts)* to be thwarted.

briseur, -euse [brizœr, øz] *nm, f:* ~ **de grève** strike-breaker.

britannique [britanik] *adj* British. ▶ **Britannique** *nmf* British person, Briton; **les Britanniques** the British.

broc [bro] *nm* jug.

brocante [brɔkɑ̃t] *nf* 1. *(commerce)* secondhand trade. 2. *(objets)* secondhand goods *(pl)*.

brocanteur, -euse [brɔkɑ̃tœr, øz] *nm, f* dealer in secondhand goods.

broche [brɔʃ] *nf* 1. *(bijou)* brooch. 2. (CULIN) spit; **cuire à la** ~ to spit-roast. 3. (ÉLECTR & MÉD) pin.

broché, -e [brɔʃe] *adj* 1. *(tissu)* brocade *(avant n)*, brocaded. 2. (TYPO): **livre** ~ paperback (book).

brochet [brɔʃɛ] *nm* pike.

brochette [brɔʃɛt] *nf* 1. *(ustensile)* skewer. 2. *(plat)* kebab. 3. *fam fig (groupe)* string, row.

brochure [brɔʃyr] *nf (imprimé)* brochure, booklet.

broder [brɔde] *vt & vi* to embroider.

broderie [brɔdri] *nf* 1. *(art)* embroidery. 2. *(ouvrage)* (piece of) embroidery.

bromure [brɔmyr] *nm* bromide.

bronche [brɔ̃ʃ] *nf* bronchus; **j'ai des problèmes de** ~**s** I've got chest problems.

broncher [brɔ̃ʃe] *vi:* **sans** ~ without complaining, uncomplainingly.

bronchite [brɔ̃ʃit] *nf* bronchitis (U).

bronzage [brɔ̃zaʒ] *nm (de peau)* tan, suntan.

bronze [brɔ̃z] *nm* bronze.

bronzé, -e [brɔ̃ze] *adj* tanned, sun-tanned.

bronzer [brɔ̃ze] *vi (peau)* to tan; *(personne)* to get a tan.

brosse [brɔs] *nf* brush; ~ **à cheveux** hairbrush; ~ **à dents** toothbrush; **avoir les cheveux en** ~ to have a crew cut.

brosser [brɔse] *vt* 1. *(habits, cheveux)* to brush. 2. *(paysage, portrait)* to paint. ▶ **se brosser** *vp:* **se** ~ **les cheveux/les dents** to brush one's hair/teeth.

brouette [bruɛt] *nf* wheelbarrow.

brouhaha [bruaa] *nm* hubbub.

brouillard [brujar] *nm (léger)* mist; *(dense)* fog; ~ **givrant** freezing fog.

brouille [bruj] *nf* quarrel.

brouillé, -e [bruje] *adj* 1. *(fâché):* **être** ~ **avec qqn** to be on bad terms with sb; **être** ~ **avec qqch** *fig* to be hopeless ou useless at sthg. 2. *(teint)* muddy. 3. → **œuf**.

brouiller [bruje] *vt* 1. *(désunir)* to set at odds, to put on bad terms. 2. *(vue)* to blur. 3. (RADIO) to cause interference to; *(- délibérément)* to jam. 4. *(rendre confus)* to muddle (up). ▶ **se brouiller** *vp* 1. *(se fâcher)* to fall out; **se** ~ **avec qqn (pour qqch)** to fall out with sb (over sthg). 2. *(se troubler)* to become blurred. 3. (MÉTÉOR) to cloud over.

brouillon, -onne [brujɔ̃, ɔn] *adj* careless, untidy. ▶ **brouillon** *nm* rough copy, draft.

broussaille [brusaj] *nf:* **les** ~**s** the undergrowth; **en** ~ *fig (cheveux)* untidy; *(sourcils)* bushy.

brousse [brus] *nf* (GÉOGR) scrubland, bush.

brouter [brute] ♦ *vt* to graze on. ♦ *vi* 1. *(animal)* to graze. 2. (TECHNOL) to judder.

broutille [brutij] *nf* trifle.

broyer [brwaje] *vt* to grind, to crush.

bru [bry] *nf sout* daughter-in-law.

brugnon [bryɲɔ̃] *nm* nectarine.

bruine [brɥin] *nf* drizzle.

bruissement [brɥismɑ̃] *nm (de feuilles, d'étoffe)* rustle, rustling (U); *(d'eau)* murmur, murmuring (U).

bruit [brɥi] *nm* 1. *(son)* noise, sound; ~ **de fond** background noise. 2. *(vacarme &* TECHNOL*)* noise; **faire du** ~ to make a noise; **sans** ~ silently, noiselessly. 3. *(rumeur)* rumour. 4. *(retentissement)* fuss; **faire du** ~ to cause a stir.

bruitage [brɥitaʒ] *nm* sound-effects *(pl)*.

brûlant, -e [brylɑ̃, ɑ̃t] *adj* 1. *(gén)*

bureau

burning (hot); (liquide) boiling (hot); (plat) piping hot. **2.** fig (amour, question) burning.

brûle-pourpoint [brylpurpwɛ̃] ► **à brûle-pourpoint** loc adv point-blank, straight out.

brûler [bryle] ◆ vt **1.** (gén) to burn; (suj: eau bouillante) to scald; **la fumée me brûle les yeux** the smoke is making my eyes sting. **2.** (feu rouge) to drive through; (étape) to miss out, to skip. ◆ vi **1.** (gén) to burn; (maison, forêt) to be on fire. **2.** (être brûlant) to be burning (hot); ~ de fig to be consumed with; ~ **de faire qqch** to be longing ou dying to do sthg; ~ **de fièvre** to be running a high temperature. ► **se brûler** vp to burn o.s.

brûlure [brylyr] nf **1.** (lésion) burn; ~ **au premier/troisième degré** first-degree/third-degree burn. **2.** (sensation) burning (sensation); **avoir des ~s d'estomac** to have heartburn.

brume [brym] nf mist.

brumeux, -euse [brymø, øz] adj misty; fig hazy.

brun, -e [brœ̃, bryn] ◆ adj brown; (cheveux) dark. ◆ nm, f dark-haired man (f woman). ► **brun** nm (couleur) brown. ► **brune** nf **1.** (cigarette) cigarette made of dark tobacco. **2.** (bière) brown ale.

brunir [brynir] vi (personne) to get a tan; (peau) to tan.

Brushing® [brœʃiŋ] nm: **faire un ~ à qqn** to give sb a blow-dry, to blow-dry sb's hair.

brusque [brysk] adj abrupt.

brusquement [bryskəmɑ̃] adv abruptly.

brusquer [bryske] vt to rush; (élève) to push.

brusquerie [bryskəri] nf abruptness.

brut, -e [bryt] adj **1.** (pierre précieuse, bois) rough; (sucre) unrefined; (métal, soie) raw; (champagne) extra dry; **(pétrole)** ~ crude (oil). **2.** fig (fait, idées) crude, raw. **3.** (ÉCON) gross. ► **brute** nf brute.

brutal, -e, -aux [brytal, o] adj **1.** (violent) violent, brutal. **2.** (soudain) sudden. **3.** (manière) blunt.

brutaliser [brytalize] vt to mistreat.

brutalité [brytalite] nf **1.** (violence) violence, brutality. **2.** (caractère soudain) suddenness.

Bruxelles [bry(k)sɛl] n Brussels.

bruyamment [bruijamɑ̃] adv noisily.

bruyant, -e [bruijɑ̃, ɑ̃t] adj noisy.

bruyère [bruijɛr] nf (plante) heather.

BT nm (abr de **brevet de technicien**) voca-

tional training certificate (taken at age 18).

BTP (abr de **bâtiments et travaux publics**) nmpl building and public works sector.

BTS (abr de **brevet de technicien supérieur**) nm advanced vocational training certificate (taken at the end of a 2-year higher education course).

bu, -e [by] pp → **boire**.

buanderie [byɑ̃dri] nf laundry.

buccal, -e, -aux [bykal, o] adj buccal.

bûche [byʃ] nf (bois) log; ~ **de Noël** Yule log; **prendre** ou **ramasser une** ~ fam to fall flat on one's face.

bûcher¹ [byʃe] nm **1.** (supplice): **le** ~ the stake. **2.** (funéraire) pyre.

bûcher² [byʃe] ◆ vi to swot. ◆ vt to swot up.

bûcheron, -onne [byʃrɔ̃, ɔn] nm, f forestry worker.

bûcheur, -euse [byʃœr, øz] ◆ adj hard-working. ◆ nm, f fam swot.

bucolique [bykɔlik] adj pastoral.

budget [bydʒɛ] nm budget.

budgétaire [bydʒetɛr] adj budgetary; **année** ~ financial year.

buée [bɥe] nf (sur vitre) condensation.

buffet [byfɛ] nm **1.** (meuble) sideboard. **2.** (repas) buffet. **3.** (café-restaurant): ~ **de gare** station buffet.

buffle [byfl] nm (animal) buffalo.

buis [bɥi] nm box(wood).

buisson [bɥisɔ̃] nm bush.

buissonnière [bɥisɔnjɛr] → **école**.

bulbe [bylb] nm bulb.

bulgare [bylgar] adj Bulgarian. ► **bulgare** nm (langue) Bulgarian. ► **Bulgare** nmf Bulgarian.

Bulgarie [bylgari] nf: **la** ~ Bulgaria.

bulldozer [byldozɛr] nm bulldozer.

bulle [byl] nf **1.** (gén) bubble; ~ **de savon** soap bubble. **2.** (de bande dessinée) speech balloon.

bulletin [byltɛ̃] nm **1.** (communiqué) bulletin; ~ **(de la) météo** weather forecast; ~ **de santé** medical bulletin. **2.** (imprimé) form; ~ **de vote** ballot paper. **3.** (SCOL) report. **4.** (certificat) certificate; ~ **de salaire** ou **de paye** pay slip.

bulletin-réponse [byltɛ̃repɔ̃s] (pl **bulletins-réponse**) nm reply form.

buraliste [byralist] nmf (d'un bureau de tabac) tobacconist.

bureau [byro] nm **1.** (gén) office; ~ **d'aide sociale** social security office; ~ **de change** bureau de change; ~ **d'études** design office; ~ **de poste** post office; ~ **de tabac** tobacconist's; ~ **de vote** polling station. **2.** (meuble) desk.

bureaucrate [byrokrat] *nmf* bureaucrat.

bureaucratie [byrokrasi] *nf* bureaucracy.

bureautique [byrotik] *nf* office automation.

burette [byrɛt] *nf* (*de mécanicien*) oilcan.

burin [byrɛ̃] *nm* (*outil*) chisel.

buriné, -e [byrine] *adj* engraved; (*visage, traits*) lined.

burlesque [byrlɛsk] *adj* 1. (*comique*) funny. 2. (*ridicule*) ludicrous, absurd. 3. (THÉÂTRE) burlesque.

bus [bys] *nm* bus.

busqué [byske] → **nez**.

buste [byst] *nm* (*torse*) chest; (*poitrine de femme, sculpture*) bust.

bustier [bystje] *nm* (*corsage*) strapless top; (*soutien-gorge*) longline bra.

but [byt] *nm* 1. (*point visé*) target. 2. (*objectif*) goal, aim, purpose; **errer sans ~** to wander aimlessly; **il touche au ~** he's nearly there; **à ~ non lucratif** (JUR) non-profit-making Br, non-profit Am; **aller droit au ~** to go straight to the point; **dans le ~ de faire qqch** with the aim ou intention of doing sthg. 3. (SPORT) goal; **marquer un ~** to score a goal. 4. *loc*: **de ~ en blanc** point-blank, straight out.

butane [bytan] *nm*: (**gaz**) **~** butane; (*domestique*) Calor gas® Br, butane.

buté, -e [byte] *adj* stubborn.

buter [byte] ◆ *vi* (*se heurter*): **~ sur/contre qqch** to stumble on/over sthg, to trip on/over sthg. ◆ *vt* *tfam* (*tuer*) to do in, to bump off. ▶ **se buter** *vp* to dig one's heels in; **se ~ contre** *fig* to refuse to listen to.

butin [bytɛ̃] *nm* (*de guerre*) booty; (*de vol*) loot; (*de recherche*) finds (*pl*).

butiner [bytine] *vi* to collect nectar.

butte [byt] *nf* (*colline*) mound, rise; **être en ~ à** *fig* to be exposed to.

buvard [byvar] *nm* (*papier*) blotting-paper; (*sous-main*) blotter.

buvette [byvɛt] *nf* (*café*) refreshment room, buffet.

buveur, -euse [byvœr, øz] *nm, f* drinker.

c¹, C [se] *nm inv* c, C. ▶ **C** (*abr de* **celsius, centigrade**) C.

c² *abr de* **centime**.

c' → **ce**.

CA *nm abr de* **chiffre d'affaires**.

ça [sa] *pron dém* 1. (*pour désigner*) that; (*- plus près*) this. 2. (*sujet indéterminé*) it, that; **comment ~ va?** how are you?, how are things?; **~ ira comme ~** that will be fine; **~ y est** that's it; **c'est ~** that's right. 3. (*renforcement expressif*): **où ~?** where?; **qui ~?** who?

çà [sa] *adv*: **~ et là** here and there.

caban [kabɑ̃] *nm* reefer (jacket).

cabane [kaban] *nf* (*abri*) cabin, hut; (*remise*) shed; **~ à lapins** hutch.

cabanon [kabanɔ̃] *nm* 1. (*à la campagne*) cottage. 2. (*sur la plage*) chalet. 3. (*cellule*) padded cell. 4. (*de rangement*) shed.

cabaret [kabarɛ] *nm* cabaret.

cabas [kaba] *nm* shopping-bag.

cabillaud [kabijo] *nm* (fresh) cod.

cabine [kabin] *nf* 1. (*de navire, d'avion, de véhicule*) cabin. 2. (*compartiment, petit local*) cubicle; **~ d'essayage** fitting room; **~ téléphonique** phone box.

cabinet [kabinɛ] *nm* 1. (*pièce*): **~ de toilette** = bathroom. 2. (*local professionnel*) office; **~ dentaire/médical** dentist's/doctor's surgery Br, dentist's/doctor's office Am. 3. (*de ministre*) advisers (*pl*). ▶ **cabinets** *nmpl* toilet (*sg*).

câble [kabl] *nm* cable; **télévision par ~** cable television.

câblé, -e [kable] *adj* (TÉLÉ) equipped with cable TV.

cabosser [kabɔse] *vt* to dent.

cabotage [kabɔtaʒ] *nm* coastal navigation.

caboteur [kabɔtœr] *nm* (*navire*) coaster.

cabrer [kabre] ▶ **se cabrer** *vp* 1. (*cheval*) to rear (up); (*avion*) to climb steeply. 2. *fig* (*personne*) to take offence.

cabri [kabri] *nm* kid.

cabriole [kabrijɔl] *nf* (*bond*) caper; (*pirouette*) somersault.

cabriolet [kabrijɔlɛ] *nm* convertible.

CAC, Cac [kak] (*abr de* **Compagnie des**

agents de change *nf*: **l'indice ~-40** *the French stock exchange shares index.*

caca [kaka] *nm fam* pooh; **faire ~** to do a pooh; **~ d'oie** greeny-yellow.

cacahouète, cacahuète [kakawɛt] *nf* peanut.

cacao [kakao] *nm* **1.** (*poudre*) cocoa (powder). **2.** (*boisson*) cocoa.

cachalot [kaʃalo] *nm* sperm whale.

cache [kaʃ] ◆ *nf* (*cachette*) hiding place. ◆ *nm* (*masque*) card (*for masking text etc*).

cache-cache [kaʃkaʃ] *nm inv*: **jouer à ~** to play hide and seek.

cachemire [kaʃmir] *nm* **1.** (*laine*) cashmere. **2.** (*dessin*) paisley.

cache-nez [kaʃne] *nm inv* scarf.

cache-pot [kaʃpo] *nm inv* flowerpot-holder.

cacher [kaʃe] *vt* **1.** (*gén*) to hide; **je ne vous cache pas que ...** to be honest, ... **2.** (*vue*) to mask. ► **se cacher** *vp*: **se ~ (de qqn)** to hide (from sb).

cachet [kaʃɛ] *nm* **1.** (*comprimé*) tablet, pill. **2.** (*marque*) postmark. **3.** (*style*) style, character; **avoir du ~** to have character. **4.** (*rétribution*) fee.

cacheter [kaʃte] *vt* to seal.

cachette [kaʃɛt] *nf* hiding place; **en ~** secretly.

cachot [kaʃo] *nm* (*cellule*) cell.

cachotterie [kaʃɔtri] *nf* little secret; **faire des ~s (à qqn)** to hide things (from sb).

cachottier, -ère [kaʃɔtje, ɛr] *nm, f* secretive person.

cactus [kaktys] *nm* cactus.

c.-à-d. (*abr de c'est-à-dire*) i.e.

cadastre [kadastr] *nm* (*registre*) ≃ land register; (*service*) ≃ land registry, ≃ land office *Am*.

cadavérique [kadaverik] *adj* deathly.

cadavre [kadavr] *nm* corpse, (dead) body.

Caddie® [kadi] *nm* (*chariot*) trolley.

cadeau, -x [kado] ◆ *nm* present, gift; **faire ~ de qqch à qqn** to give sthg to sb (as a present). ◆ *adj inv*: **idée ~** gift idea.

cadenas [kadna] *nm* padlock.

cadenasser [kadnase] *vt* to padlock.

cadence [kadɑ̃s] *nf* **1.** (*rythme musical*) rhythm; **en ~** in time. **2.** (*de travail*) rate.

cadencé, -e [kadɑ̃se] *adj* rhythmical.

cadet, -ette [kadɛ, ɛt] *nm, f* **1.** (*de deux enfants*) youngest; (*de plusieurs enfants*) youngest; **il est mon ~ de deux ans** he's two years younger than me. **2.** (SPORT) junior.

cadran [kadrɑ̃] *nm* dial; **~ solaire** sun-dial.

cadre [kadr] *nm* **1.** (*de tableau, de porte*) frame. **2.** (*contexte*) context. **3.** (*décor, milieu*) surroundings (*pl*). **4.** (*responsable*): **~ moyen/supérieur** middle/senior manager. **5.** (*sur formulaire*) box.

cadrer [kadre] ◆ *vi* to agree, to tally. ◆ *vt* (CIN, PHOT & TÉLÉ) to frame.

caduc, caduque [kadyk] *adj* **1.** (*feuille*) deciduous. **2.** (*qui n'est plus valide*) obsolete.

cafard [kafar] *nm* **1.** (*insecte*) cockroach. **2.** *fig* (*mélancolie*): **avoir le ~** to feel low ou down.

café [kafe] *nm* **1.** (*plante, boisson*) coffee; **~ crème** *coffee with frothy milk*; **~ en grains** *coffee beans*; **~ au lait** *white coffee (with hot milk)*; **~ moulu** *ground coffee*; **~ noir** *black coffee*; **~ en poudre** ou **soluble** *instant coffee*. **2.** (*lieu*) bar, cafe.

CAFÉ

French cafés serve a wide range of drinks and sometimes sandwiches or light meals. They often have pavement seating areas or large plate-glass windows looking directly onto the street. Paris cafés have also traditionally played an important role in French political, cultural and literary life.
Coffee served in French cafés comes in various forms such as 'café crème' (served with frothy hot milk), 'grand crème' (a large 'café crème'), 'café noisette' (with just a tiny amount of milk) and 'express' or 'expresso' (strong black coffee served in small cups). The expression 'café au lait' is used at home to mean the same as a 'grand crème'.

---

caféine [kafein] *nf* caffeine.

cafétéria [kafeterja] *nf* cafeteria.

café-théâtre [kafeteatr] *nm* ≃ cabaret.

cafetière [kaftjer] *nf* **1.** (*récipient*) coffee-pot. **2.** (*électrique*) coffee-maker; (*italienne*) percolator.

cafouiller [kafuje] *vi fam* **1.** (*s'embrouiller*) to get into a mess. **2.** (*moteur*) to misfire; (TÉLÉ) to be on the blink.

cage [kaʒ] *nf* **1.** (*pour animaux*) cage. **2.** (*dans une maison*): **~ d'escalier** stairwell. **3.** (ANAT): **~ thoracique** rib cage.

cageot [kaʒo] *nm* (*caisse*) crate.

cagibi [kaʒibi] *nm* boxroom *Br*, storage room *Am*.

cagneux, -euse [kaɲø, øz] *adj*: **avoir les genoux ~** to be knock-kneed.

cagnotte [kaɲɔt] nf 1. (caisse commune) kitty. 2. (économies) savings (pl).

cagoule [kagul] nf 1. (passe-montagne) balaclava. 2. (de voleur, de pénitent) hood.

cahier [kaje] nm 1. (de notes) exercise book, notebook; ~ de brouillon rough book; ~ de rapport logbook; ~ de textes homework book. 2. (COMM): ~ des charges specification.

cahin-caha [kaɛ̃kaa] adv: aller ~ to be jogging along.

cahot [kao] nm bump, jolt.

cahoter [kaɔte] vi to jolt around.

cahute [kayt] nf shack.

caille [kaj] nf quail.

caillé, -e [kaje] adj (lait) curdled; (sang) clotted.

caillot [kajo] nm clot.

caillou, -x [kaju] nm 1. (pierre) stone, pebble. 2. fam (crâne) head.

caillouteux, -euse [kajutø, øz] adj stony.

caïman [kaimã] nm cayman.

Caire [kɛr] n: Le ~ Cairo.

caisse [kɛs] nf 1. (boîte) crate, box; ~ à outils toolbox. 2. (TECHNOL) case. 3. (guichet) cash desk, till; (de supermarché) checkout, till; ~ enregistreuse cash register. 4. (recette) takings (pl). 5. (organisme): ~ d'allocation ≃ social security office; ~ d'épargne (fonds) savings fund; (établissement) savings bank; ~ de retraite pension fund.

caissier, -ère [kesje, ɛr] nm, f cashier.

caisson [kɛsɔ̃] nm 1. (MIL & TECHNOL) caisson. 2. (ARCHIT) coffer.

cajoler [kaʒɔle] vt to make a fuss of, to cuddle.

cajou [kaʒu] → noix.

cake [kɛk] nm fruit-cake.

cal¹ [kal] nm callus.

cal² (abr de calorie) cal.

calamar [kalamar], **calmar** [kalmar] nm squid.

calamité [kalamite] nf disaster.

calandre [kalɑ̃dr] nf 1. (de voiture) radiator grille. 2. (machine) calender.

calanque [kalɑ̃k] nf rocky inlet.

calcaire [kalkɛr] ◆ adj (eau) hard; (sol) chalky; (roche) limestone (avant n). ◆ nm limestone.

calciner [kalsine] vt to burn to a cinder.

calcium [kalsjɔm] nm calcium.

calcul [kalkyl] nm 1. (opération): le ~ arithmetic; ~ mental mental arithmetic. 2. (compte) calculation. 3. fig (plan) plan. 4. (MÉD): ~ (rénal) kidney stone.

calculateur, -trice [kalkylatœr, tris] adj péj calculating. ► **calculateur** nm computer. ► **calculatrice** nf calculator.

calculer [kalkyle] ◆ vt 1. (déterminer) to calculate, to work out. 2. (prévoir) to plan; mal/bien ~ qqch to judge sthg badly/well. ◆ vi péj (dépenser avec parcimonie) to count the pennies.

calculette [kalkylɛt] nf pocket calculator.

cale [kal] nf 1. (de navire) hold; ~ sèche dry dock. 2. (pour immobiliser) wedge.

calé, -e [kale] adj fam (personne) clever, brainy; être ~ en to be good at.

calèche [kalɛʃ] nf (horse-drawn) carriage.

caleçon [kalsɔ̃] nm 1. (sous-vêtement masculin) boxer shorts (pl), pair of boxer shorts. 2. (vêtement féminin) leggings (pl), pair of leggings.

calembour [kalãbur] nm pun, play on words.

calendrier [kalãdrije] nm 1. (système, agenda, d'un festival) calendar. 2. (emploi du temps) timetable. 3. (d'un voyage) schedule.

calepin [kalpɛ̃] nm notebook.

caler [kale] ◆ vt 1. (avec cale) to wedge. 2. (stabiliser, appuyer) to prop up. 3. fam (remplir): ça cale (l'estomac) it's filling. ◆ vi 1. (moteur, véhicule) to stall. 2. fam (personne) to give up.

calfeutrer [kalføtre] vt to draughtproof. ► **se calfeutrer** vp to shut o.s. up ou away.

calibre [kalibr] nm 1. (de tuyau) diameter, bore; (de fusil) calibre; (de fruit, d'œuf) size. 2. fam fig (envergure) calibre.

calibrer [kalibre] vt 1. (machine, fusil) to calibrate. 2. (fruit, œuf) to grade.

Californie [kalifɔrni] nf: la ~ California.

califourchon [kalifurʃɔ̃] ► à califourchon loc adv astride; être (assis) à ~ sur qqch to sit astride sthg.

câlin, -e [kalɛ̃, in] adj affectionate. ► **câlin** nm cuddle.

câliner [kaline] vt to cuddle.

calleux, -euse [kalø, øz] adj calloused.

calligraphie [kaligrafi] nf calligraphy.

calmant, -e [kalmã, ãt] adj soothing. ► **calmant** nm (pour la douleur) painkiller; (pour l'anxiété) tranquillizer, sedative.

calmar → calamar.

calme [kalm] ◆ adj quiet, calm. ◆ nm 1. (gén) calm, calmness. 2. (absence de bruit) peace (and quiet); être au ~ to have ou to enjoy peace and quiet.

calmer [kalme] vt 1. (apaiser) to calm (down). 2. (réduire - douleur) to soothe; (- inquiétude) to allay. ► **se calmer** vp 1. (s'apaiser - personne, discussion) to calm down; (- tempête) to abate; (- mer) to become calm. 2. (diminuer - douleur) to ease; (- fièvre, inquiétude, désir) to subside.

calomnie [kalɔmni] nf (écrits) libel; (paroles) slander.

calorie [kalɔri] nf calorie.

calorique [kalɔrik] adj calorific.

calot [kalo] nm (bille) (large) marble.

calotte [kalɔt] nf 1. (bonnet) skullcap. 2. (GÉOGR): ~ **glaciaire** ice cap.

calque [kalk] nm 1. (dessin) tracing. 2. (papier): (papier) ~ tracing paper. 3. fig (imitation) (exact) copy.

calquer [kalke] vt 1. (carte) to trace. 2. (imiter) to copy exactly; ~ **qqch sur qqch** to model sthg on sthg.

calvaire [kalver] nm 1. (croix) wayside cross. 2. fig (épreuve) ordeal.

calvitie [kalvisi] nf baldness.

camaïeu [kamajø] nm monochrome.

camarade [kamarad] nmf 1. (compagnon, ami) friend; ~ **de classe** classmate; ~ **d'école** schoolfriend. 2. (POLIT) comrade.

camaraderie [kamaradri] nf 1. (familiarité, entente) friendship. 2. (solidarité) comradeship, camaraderie.

Cambodge [kɑ̃bɔdʒ] nm: **le** ~ Cambodia.

cambouis [kɑ̃bwi] nm dirty grease.

cambré, -e [kɑ̃bre] adj arched.

cambriolage [kɑ̃brijɔlaʒ] nm burglary.

cambrioler [kɑ̃brijɔle] vt to burgle Br, to burglarize Am.

cambrioleur, -euse [kɑ̃brijɔlœr, øz] nm, f burglar.

camée [kame] nm cameo.

caméléon [kamele5] nm litt & fig chameleon.

camélia [kamelja] nm camellia.

camelote [kamlɔt] nf (marchandise de mauvaise qualité) rubbish.

camembert [kamɑ̃ber] nm Camembert.

caméra [kamera] nf 1. (CIN & TÉLÉ) camera. 2. (d'amateur) cinecamera.

cameraman [kameraman] (pl **cameramen** [kameramɛn] ou **cameramans**) nm cameraman.

Cameroun [kamrun] nm: **le** ~ Cameroon.

Caméscope® [kameskɔp] nm camcorder.

camion [kamj5] nm lorry Br, truck Am; ~ **de déménagement** removal van Br, moving van Am.

camion-citerne [kamj5sitern] nm tanker Br, tanker truck Am.

camionnage [kamjɔnaʒ] nm road haulage Br, trucking Am.

camionnette [kamjɔnet] nf van.

camionneur [kamjɔnœr] nm 1. (conducteur) lorry-driver Br, truck-driver Am. 2. (entrepreneur) road haulier Br, trucker Am.

camisole [kamizɔl] ► **camisole de force** nf straitjacket.

camouflage [kamuflaʒ] nm (déguisement) camouflage; fig (dissimulation) concealment.

camoufler [kamufle] vt (déguiser) to camouflage; fig (dissimuler) to conceal, to cover up.

camp [kɑ̃] nm 1. (gén) camp; ~ **de concentration** concentration camp. 2. (SPORT) half (of the field). 3. (parti) side.

campagnard, -e [kɑ̃paɲar, ard] adj 1. (de la campagne) country (avant n). 2. (rustique) rustic.

campagne [kɑ̃paɲ] nf 1. (régions rurales) country; **à la** ~ in the country. 2. (MIL, POLIT & PUBLICITÉ) campaign; **faire** ~ **pour/contre** to campaign for/against; ~ **électorale** election campaign; ~ **de presse** press campaign; ~ **publicitaire** advertising campaign.

campement [kɑ̃pmɑ̃] nm camp, encampment.

camper [kɑ̃pe] ◆ vi to camp. ◆ vt 1. (poser solidement) to place firmly. 2. fig (esquisser) to portray.

campeur, -euse [kɑ̃pœr, øz] nm, f camper.

camphre [kɑ̃fr] nm camphor.

camping [kɑ̃piŋ] nm 1. (activité) camping; **faire du** ~ to go camping. 2. (terrain) campsite.

Canada [kanada] nm: **le** ~ Canada.

canadien, -enne [kanadjɛ̃, ɛn] adj Canadian. ► **canadienne** nf (veste) sheepskin jacket. ► **Canadien, -enne** nm, f Canadian.

canaille [kanaj] ◆ adj 1. (coquin) roguish. 2. (vulgaire) crude. ◆ nf 1. (scélérat) scoundrel. 2. hum (coquin) little devil.

canal, -aux [kanal, o] nm 1. (gén) channel; **par le** ~ **de qqn** fig (par l'entremise de) through sb. 2. (voie d'eau) canal. 3. (ANAT) canal, duct. ► **Canal** nm: **Canal+** French TV pay channel.

canalisation [kanalizasjɔ̃] nf (conduit) pipe.

canaliser [kanalize] vt 1. (cours d'eau) to canalize. 2. fig (orienter) to channel.

canapé [kanape] nm (siège) sofa.

canapé-lit [kanapeli] nm sofa bed.

canaque, kanak [kanak] adj Kanak. ▶ **Canaque** nmf Kanak.

canard [kanar] nm 1. (oiseau) duck. 2. (fausse note) wrong note. 3. fam (journal) rag.

canari [kanari] nm canary.

cancan [kɑ̃kɑ̃] nm 1. (ragot) piece of gossip. 2. (danse) cancan.

cancer [kɑ̃sɛr] nm (MÉD) cancer. ▶ **Cancer** nm (ASTROL) Cancer.

cancéreux, -euse [kɑ̃serø, øz] ◆ adj 1. (personne) suffering from cancer. 2. (tumeur) cancerous. ◆ nm, f (personne) cancer sufferer.

cancérigène [kɑ̃seriʒɛn] adj carcinogenic.

cancre [kɑ̃kr] nm fam dunce.

cancrelat [kɑ̃krəla] nm cockroach.

candélabre [kɑ̃delabr] nm candelabra.

candeur [kɑ̃dœr] nf ingenuousness.

candi [kɑ̃di] adj: sucre ~ (sugar) candy.

candidat, -e [kɑ̃dida, at] nm, f: ~ (à) candidate (for).

candidature [kɑ̃didatyr] nf 1. (à un poste) application; **poser sa ~ pour qqch** to apply for sthg. 2. (à une élection) candidature.

candide [kɑ̃did] adj ingenuous.

cane [kan] nf (female) duck.

caneton [kantɔ̃] nm (male) duckling.

canette [kanɛt] nf 1. (de fil) spool. 2. (petite cane) (female) duckling. 3. (de boisson - bouteille) bottle; (- boîte) can.

canevas [kanva] nm (COUTURE) canvas.

caniche [kaniʃ] nm poodle.

canicule [kanikyl] nf heatwave.

canif [kanif] nm penknife.

canin, -e [kanɛ̃, in] adj canine; **exposition ~e** dog show. ▶ **canine** nf canine (tooth).

caniveau, -x [kanivo] nm gutter.

canne [kan] nf 1. (bâton) walking stick; ~ **à pêche** fishing rod. 2. fam (jambe) pin. ▶ **canne à sucre** nf sugar cane.

cannelle [kanɛl] nf (aromate) cinnamon.

cannelure [kanlyr] nf (de colonne) flute.

cannibale [kanibal] nmf & adj cannibal.

canoë [kanɔe] nm canoe; **faire du ~** to go canoeing.

canoë-kayak [kanɔekajak] nm kayak.

canon [kanɔ̃] nm 1. (arme) gun; (HIST) cannon. 2. (tube d'arme) barrel. 3. (MUS): **chanter en ~** to sing in canon. 4. (norme & RELIG) canon. 5. (SPORT): ~ **à neige** snow-making machine.

canot [kano] nm dinghy; ~ **pneumatique** inflatable dinghy; ~ **de sauvetage** lifeboat.

canotage [kanɔtaʒ] nm boating; **faire du ~** to go boating.

cantatrice [kɑ̃tatris] nf prima donna.

cantine [kɑ̃tin] nf 1. (réfectoire) canteen. 2. (malle) trunk.

cantique [kɑ̃tik] nm hymn.

canton [kɑ̃tɔ̃] nm 1. (en France) = district. 2. (en Suisse) canton.

CANTON

Switzerland is a confederation of 23 districts known as 'cantons', three of which are themselves divided into 'demi-cantons'. Although they are to a large extent self-governing, the federal government reserves control over certain areas such as foreign policy, the treasury, customs and the postal service.

cantonade [kɑ̃tɔnad] ▶ **à la cantonade** loc adv: **parler à la ~** to speak to everyone (in general).

cantonais, -e [kɑ̃tɔnɛ, ɛz] adj Cantonese; **riz ~** egg fried rice. ▶ **cantonais** nm (langue) Cantonese.

cantonner [kɑ̃tɔne] vt 1. (MIL) to quarter, to billet Br. 2. (maintenir) to confine; ~ **qqn à** ou **dans** to confine sb to.

cantonnier [kɑ̃tɔnje] nm roadman.

canular [kanylar] nm fam hoax.

caoutchouc [kautʃu] nm 1. (substance) rubber. 2. (plante) rubber plant.

caoutchouteux, -euse [kautʃutø, øz] adj rubbery.

cap [kap] nm 1. (GÉOGR) cape; **le ~ de Bonne-Espérance** the Cape of Good Hope; **le ~ Horn** Cape Horn; **passer le ~ de qqch** fig to get through sthg; **passer le ~ de la quarantaine** fig to turn forty. 2. (direction) course; **changer de ~** to change course; **mettre le ~ sur** to head for. ▶ **Cap** nm: **Le Cap** Cape Town.

CAP (abr de **certificat d'aptitude professionnelle**) nm vocational training certificate (taken at secondary school).

capable [kapabl] adj 1. (apte): ~ **(de qqch/de faire qqch)** capable (of sthg/of doing sthg). **2.** (*à même*): ~ **de faire qqch** likely to do sthg.

capacité [kapasite] *nf* **1.** (*de récipient*) capacity. **2.** (*de personne*) ability. **3.** (UNIV): ~ **en droit** (*diplôme*) qualifying certificate in law gained by examination after 2 years' study.

cape [kap] *nf* (*vêtement*) cloak; **rire sous** ~ *fig* to laugh up one's sleeve.

CAPES, Capes [kapɛs] (*abr de* **certificat d'aptitude au professorat de l'enseignement du second degré**) *nm* secondary school teaching certificate.

capharnaüm [kafarnaɔm] *nm* mess.

capillaire [kapilɛr] ◆ *adj* **1.** (*lotion*) hair (*avant n*). **2.** (ANAT & BOT) capillary. ◆ *nm* **1.** (BOT) maidenhair fern. **2.** (ANAT) capillary.

capitaine [kapitɛn] *nm* captain.

capitainerie [kapitɛnri] *nf* harbour master's office.

capital, -e, -aux [kapital, o] *adj* **1.** (*décision, événement*) major. **2.** (JUR) capital. ▶ **capital** *nm* (FIN) capital; ~ **santé** *fig* reserves (*pl*) of health; ~ **social** authorized ou share capital. ▶ **capitale** *nf* (*ville, lettre*) capital. ▶ **capitaux** *nmpl* capital (U).

capitaliser [kapitalize] ◆ *vt* (FIN) to capitalize; *fig* to accumulate. ◆ *vi* to save.

capitalisme [kapitalism] *nm* capitalism.

capitaliste [kapitalist] *nmf & adj* capitalist.

capiteux, -euse [kapitø, øz] *adj* (*vin*) intoxicating; (*parfum*) heady.

capitonné, -e [kapitɔne] *adj* padded.

capituler [kapityle] *vi* to surrender; ~ **devant qqn/qqch** to surrender to sb/sthg.

caporal, -aux [kapɔral, o] *nm* **1.** (MIL) lance-corporal. **2.** (*tabac*) caporal.

capot [kapo] *nm* **1.** (*de voiture*) bonnet Br, hood Am. **2.** (*de machine*) (protective) cover.

capote [kapɔt] *nf* **1.** (*de voiture*) hood Br, top Am. **2.** *fam* (*préservatif*): ~ **(anglaise)** condom.

câpre [kapr] *nf* caper.

caprice [kapris] *nm* whim.

capricieux, -euse [kaprisjø, øz] ◆ *adj* (*changeant*) capricious; (*coléreux*) temperamental. ◆ *nm, f* temperamental person.

capricorne [kaprikɔrn] *nm* (ZOOL) capricorn beetle. ▶ **Capricorne** *nm* (ASTROL) Capricorn.

capsule [kapsyl] *nf* **1.** (*de bouteille*) cap. **2.** (ASTRON, BOT & MÉD) capsule.

capter [kapte] *vt* **1.** (*recevoir sur émetteur*) to pick up. **2.** (*source, rivière*) to harness. **3.** *fig* (*attention, confiance*) to gain, to win.

captif, -ive [kaptif, iv] ◆ *adj* captive. ◆ *nm, f* prisoner.

captivant, -e [kaptivɑ̃, ɑ̃t] *adj* (*livre, film*) enthralling; (*personne*) captivating.

captiver [kaptive] *vt* to captivate.

captivité [kaptivite] *nf* captivity.

capture [kaptyr] *nf* **1.** (*action*) capture. **2.** (*prise*) catch.

capturer [kaptyre] *vt* to catch, to capture.

capuche [kapyʃ] *nf* (detachable) hood.

capuchon [kapyʃɔ̃] *nm* **1.** (*bonnet - d'imperméable*) hood. **2.** (*bouchon*) cap, top.

capucine [kapysin] *nf* (*fleur*) nasturtium.

Cap-Vert [kapvɛr] *nm*: **le** ~ Cape Verde.

caquet [kakɛ] *nm* *péj* (*bavardage*): **rabattre le** ~ **à** ou **de qqn** to shut sb up.

caqueter [kakte] *vi* **1.** (*poule*) to cackle. **2.** *péj* (*personne*) to chatter.

car¹ [kar] *nm* coach Br, bus Am.

car² [kar] *conj* for, because.

carabine [karabin] *nf* rifle.

caractère [karaktɛr] *nm* (*gén*) character; **avoir du** ~ to have character; **avoir mauvais** ~ to be bad-tempered; **en petits/gros** ~**s** in small/large print; ~**s d'imprimerie** block capitals.

caractériel, -elle [karakterjɛl] *adj* (*troubles*) emotional; (*personne*) emotionally disturbed.

caractérisé, -e [karakterize] *adj* (*net*) clear.

caractériser [karakterize] *vt* to be characteristic of. ▶ **se caractériser** *vp*: **se** ~ **par qqch** to be characterized by sthg.

caractéristique [karakteristik] ◆ *nf* characteristic, feature. ◆ *adj*: ~ **(de)** characteristic (of).

carafe [karaf] *nf* (*pour vin, eau*) carafe; (*pour alcool*) decanter.

Caraïbes [karaib] *nfpl*: **les** ~ the Caribbean.

carambolage [karɑ̃bɔlaʒ] *nm* pile-up.

caramel [karamel] *nm* **1.** (CULIN) caramel. **2.** (*bonbon - dur*) toffee, caramel; (- *mou*) fudge.

carapace [karapas] *nf* shell; *fig* protection, shield.

carapater [karapate] ▶ **se carapater** *vp fam* to scarper, to hop it.
carat [kara] *nm* carat; **or à 9 ~s** 9-carat gold.
caravane [karavan] *nf* (*de camping, de désert*) caravan.
caravaning [karavaniŋ] *nm* caravanning.
carbone [karbɔn] *nm* carbon; **(papier)** ~ carbon paper.
carbonique [karbɔnik] *adj*: **gaz** ~ carbon dioxide; **neige** ~ dry ice.
carboniser [karbɔnize] *vt* to burn to a cinder.
carburant [karbyrɑ̃] *nm* fuel.
carburateur [karbyratœr] *nm* carburettor.
carcan [karkɑ̃] *nm* (HIST) iron collar; *fig* yoke.
carcasse [karkas] *nf* **1.** (*d'animal*) carcass. **2.** (*de bâtiment, navire*) framework. **3.** (*de véhicule*) shell.
cardiaque [kardjak] *adj* cardiac; **être** ~ to have a heart condition; **crise** ~ heart attack.
cardigan [kardigɑ̃] *nm* cardigan.
cardinal, -e, -aux [kardinal, o] *adj* cardinal. ▶ **cardinal** *nm* **1.** (RELIG) cardinal. **2.** (*nombre*) cardinal number.
cardiologue [kardjɔlɔg] *nmf* heart specialist, cardiologist.
cardio-vasculaire [kardjovaskyler] (*pl* **cardio-vasculaires**) *adj* cardiovascular.
Carême [karɛm] *nm*: **le** ~ Lent.
carence [karɑ̃s] *nf* (*manque*): ~ **(en)** deficiency (in).
carène [karɛn] *nf* (NAVIG) hull.
caressant, -e [karesɑ̃, ɑ̃t] *adj* affectionate.
caresse [kares] *nf* caress.
caresser [karese] *vt* **1.** (*personne*) to caress; (*animal, objet*) to stroke. **2.** *fig* (*espoir*) to cherish.
cargaison [kargezɔ̃] *nf* (TRANSPORT) cargo.
cargo [kargo] *nm* **1.** (*navire*) freighter. **2.** (*avion*) cargo plane.
caricature [karikatyr] *nf* **1.** (*gén*) caricature. **2.** *péj* (*personne*) sight.
carie [kari] *nf* (MÉD) caries.
carillon [karijɔ̃] *nm* **1.** (*cloches*) bells (*pl*). **2.** (*d'horloge, de porte*) chime.
carlingue [karlɛ̃g] *nf* **1.** (*d'avion*) cabin. **2.** (*de navire*) keelson.
carmin [karmɛ̃] *adj inv* crimson.
carnage [karnaʒ] *nm* slaughter, carnage.

carnassier [karnasje] *nm* carnivore.
carnaval [karnaval] *nm* carnival.

CARNAVAL

During February in some French towns there are large processions of carnival floats and people in fancy dress. The most famous carnival is held in Nice and is known for its colourful floats decked with flowers. In Belgium the most famous carnival is held in the town of Binche where people dress up as giant characters called 'gilles'.

---

carnet [karnɛ] *nm* **1.** (*petit cahier*) notebook; ~ **d'adresses** address book; ~ **de notes** (SCOL) report card. **2.** (*bloc de feuilles*) book; ~ **de chèques** cheque book; ~ **de tickets** book of tickets.
carnivore [karnivɔr] ◆ *adj* carnivorous. ◆ *nm* carnivore.
carotte [karɔt] *nf* carrot.
carpe [karp] *nf* carp.
carpette [karpɛt] *nf* **1.** (*petit tapis*) rug. **2.** *fam péj* (*personne*) doormat.
carquois [karkwa] *nm* quiver.
carré, -e [kare] *adj* (*gén*) square; **20 mètres ~s** 20 square metres. ▶ **carré** *nm* **1.** (*quadrilatère*) square; **élever un nombre au ~** (MATHS) to square a number; ~ **blanc** (TV) *white square in the corner of the screen indicating that a television programme is not recommended for children.* **2.** (CARTES) **un ~ d'as** four aces. **3.** (*petit terrain*) patch, plot.
carreau, -x [karo] *nm* **1.** (*carrelage*) tile. **2.** (*vitre*) window pane. **3.** (*motif carré*) check; **à ~x** checked; (*papier*) squared. **4.** (CARTES) diamond.
carrefour [karfur] *nm* (*de routes, de la vie*) crossroads (*sg*).
carrelage [karlaʒ] *nm* (*surface*) tiles (*pl*).
carrément [karemɑ̃] *adv* **1.** (*franchement*) bluntly. **2.** (*complètement*) completely, quite. **3.** (*sans hésiter*) straight.
carrière [karjer] *nf* **1.** (*profession*) career; **faire ~ dans qqch** to make a career (for o.s.) in sthg. **2.** (*gisement*) quarry.
carriériste [karjerist] *nmf péj* careerist.
carriole [karjɔl] *nf* **1.** (*petite charrette*) cart. **2.** Can (*traîneau*) sleigh.
carrossable [karɔsabl] *adj* suitable for vehicles.
carrosse [karɔs] *nm* (horse-drawn) coach.
carrosserie [karɔsri] *nf* (*de voiture*)

cassette

bodywork, body.

carrossier [karɔsje] *nm* coachbuilder.

carrure [karyr] *nf* (*de personne*) build; *fig* stature.

cartable [kartabl] *nm* schoolbag.

carte [kart] *nf* 1. (*gén*) card; ~ **d'abonnement** season ticket; ~ **bancaire** cash card Br; ~ **de crédit** credit card; ~ **d'étudiant** student card; ~ **à gratter** scratch card; ~ **grise** ≃ logbook Br, ≃ car registration papers Am; ~ **(nationale) d'identité** identity card; **Carte Orange** season ticket (*for use on public transport in Paris*); ~ **postale** postcard; ~ **à puce** smart card; ~ **de séjour** residence permit; **Carte Vermeil** *card entitling senior citizens to reduced rates in cinemas, on public transport etc*; ~ **de visite** visiting card Br, calling card Am; **donner ~ blanche à qqn** *fig* to give sb a free hand. 2. (*de jeu*): ~ **(à jouer)** (playing) card. 3. (GÉOGR) map; ~ **d'état-major** ≃ Ordnance Survey map Br, ≃ Geological Survey map Am; ~ **routière** road map. 4. (*au restaurant*) menu; **à la ~** (*menu*) à la carte; (*horaires*) flexible; ~ **des vins** wine list.

CARTE (NATIONALE) D'IDENTITÉ

Official documents giving personal details (name, address, age, height etc) and a photograph of the holder, identity cards must be carried by all French citizens and presented to the police on request (at checks in the street or on public transport, for example). They can also be used instead of a passport for travel within the European Union and may be asked for as proof of identity when paying by cheque.

---

cartilage [kartilaʒ] *nm* cartilage.

cartomancien, -enne [kartɔmɑ̃sjɛ̃, ɛn] *nm, f* fortune-teller (*using cards*).

carton [kartɔ̃] *nm* 1. (*matière*) cardboard. 2. (*emballage*) cardboard box; ~ **à dessin** portfolio.

cartonné, -e [kartɔne] *adj* (*livre*) hardback.

carton-pâte [kartɔ̃pat] *nm* pasteboard.

cartouche [kartuʃ] *nf* 1. (*gén* & INFORM) cartridge. 2. (*de cigarettes*) carton.

cas [ka] *nm* case; **au ~ où** in case; **en aucun ~** under no circumstances; **en tout ~** in any case, anyway; **en ~ de** in case of; **en ~ de besoin** if need be; **le ~ échéant** if the need arises, if need be; ~ **de conscience** matter of conscience; ~

social person with social problems.

casanier, -ère [kazanje, ɛr] *adj* & *nm, f* stay-at-home.

casaque [kazak] *nf* 1. (*veste*) overblouse. 2. (HIPPISME) blouse.

cascade [kaskad] *nf* 1. (*chute d'eau*) waterfall; *fig* stream, torrent. 2. (CIN) stunt.

cascadeur, -euse [kaskadœr, øz] *nm, f* (CIN) stuntman (*f* stuntwoman).

cascher = **kas(c)her**.

case [kaz] *nf* 1. (*habitation*) hut. 2. (*de boîte, tiroir*) compartment; (*d'échiquier*) square; (*sur un formulaire*) box.

caser [kaze] *vt* 1. *fam* (*trouver un emploi pour*) to get a job for. 2. *fam* (*marier*) to marry off. 3. (*placer*) to put. ▶ **se caser** *vp fam* 1. (*trouver un emploi*) to get (o.s.) a job. 2. (*se marier*) to get hitched.

caserne [kazɛrn] *nf* barracks.

cash [kaʃ] *nm* cash; **payer ~** to pay (in) cash.

casier [kazje] *nm* 1. (*compartiment*) compartment; (*pour le courrier*) pigeonhole. 2. (*meuble - à bouteilles*) rack; (- *à courrier*) set of pigeonholes. 3. (PÊCHE) lobster pot. ▶ **casier judiciaire** *nm* police record.

casino [kazino] *nm* casino.

casque [kask] *nm* 1. (*de protection*) helmet. 2. (*à écouteurs*) headphones (*pl*). ▶ **Casques bleus** *nmpl*: **les Casques bleus** the UN peace-keeping force.

casquette [kaskɛt] *nf* cap.

cassant, -e [kasɑ̃, ɑ̃t] *adj* 1. (*fragile - verre*) fragile; (- *cheveux*) brittle. 2. (*dur*) brusque.

cassation [kasasjɔ̃] → **cour**.

casse [kas] ◆ *nf* 1. *fam* (*violence*) aggro. 2. (*de voitures*) scrapyard. ◆ *nm fam* (*cambriolage*) break-in.

casse-cou [kasku] *nmf inv* (*personne*) daredevil.

casse-croûte [kaskrut] *nm inv* snack.

casse-noisettes [kasnwazɛt], **casse-noix** [kasnwa] *nm inv* nutcrackers (*pl*).

casse-pieds [kaspje] ◆ *adj inv fam* annoying. ◆ *nmf inv* pain (in the neck).

casser [kase] ◆ *vt* 1. (*briser*) to break. 2. (JUR) to quash. 3. (COMM) to slash prices. ◆ *vi* to break. ▶ **se casser** *vp* 1. (*se briser*) to break. 2. (*membre*): **se ~ un bras** to break one's arm.

casserole [kasrɔl] *nf* (*ustensile*) saucepan.

casse-tête [kastɛt] *nm inv* 1. *fig* (*problème*) headache. 2. (*jeu*) puzzle.

cassette [kasɛt] *nf* 1. (*coffret*) casket.

2. (de musique, vidéo) cassette.

cassis [kasis] nm 1. (fruit) blackcurrant; (arbuste) blackcurrant bush; (liqueur) blackcurrant liqueur. 2. (sur la route) dip.

cassure [kasyr] nf break.

caste [kast] nf caste.

casting [kastiŋ] nm (acteurs) cast; (sélection) casting; **aller à un ~** to go to an audition.

castor [kastɔr] nm beaver.

castrer [kastre] vt to castrate; (chat) to neuter; (chatte) to spay.

cataclysme [kataklism] nm cataclysm.

catacombes [katakɔ̃b] nfpl catacombs.

catadioptre [katadjɔptr], **Cataphote®** [katafɔt] nm 1. (sur la route) cat's eye. 2. (de véhicule) reflector.

catalan, -e [katalɑ̃, an] adj Catalan, Catalonian. ▶ **catalan** nm (langue) Catalan.

catalogue [katalɔg] nm catalogue.

cataloguer [katalɔge] vt 1. (classer) to catalogue. 2. péj (juger) to label.

catalyseur [katalizœr] nm (CHIM & fig) catalyst.

catalytique [katalitik] → **pot**.

catamaran [katamarɑ̃] nm (voilier) catamaran.

Cataphote® = **catadioptre**.

cataplasme [kataplasm] nm poultice.

catapulter [katapylte] vt to catapult.

cataracte [katarakt] nf cataract.

catarrhe [katar] nm catarrh.

catastrophe [katastrɔf] nf disaster, catastrophe.

catastrophé, -e [katastrɔfe] adj shocked, upset.

catastrophique [katastrɔfik] adj disastrous, catastrophic.

catch [katʃ] nm wrestling.

catéchisme [kateʃism] nm catechism.

catégorie [kategɔri] nf (gén) category; (de personnel) grade; (de viande, fruits) quality; **~ socio-professionnelle** (ÉCON) socio-economic group.

catégorique [kategɔrik] adj categorical.

cathédrale [katedral] nf cathedral.

cathodique [katɔdik] → **tube**.

catholicisme [katɔlisism] nm Catholicism.

catholique [katɔlik] adj Catholic.

catimini [katimini] ▶ **en catimini** loc adv secretly.

cauchemar [koʃmar] nm litt & fig nightmare.

cauchemardesque [koʃmardɛsk] adj nightmarish.

cause [koz] nf 1. (gén) cause; **à ~ de** because of; **pour ~ de** on account of, because of. 2. (JUR) case. 3. loc: **être en ~** (intérêts) to be at stake; (honnêteté) to be in doubt ou in question; **remettre en ~** to challenge, to question.

causer [koze] ◆ vt: **~ qqch à qqn** to cause sb sthg. ◆ vi (bavarder): **~ (de)** to chat (about).

causerie [kozri] nf talk.

caustique [kostik] adj & nm caustic.

cautériser [koterize] vt to cauterize.

caution [kosjɔ̃] nf 1. (somme d'argent) guarantee. 2. (personne) guarantor; **se porter ~ pour qqn** to act as guarantor for sb.

cautionner [kosjɔne] vt 1. (se porter garant de) to guarantee. 2. fig (appuyer) to support, to back.

cavalcade [kavalkad] nf 1. (de cavaliers) cavalcade. 2. (d'enfants) stampede.

cavalerie [kavalri] nf (MIL) cavalry.

cavalier, -ère [kavalje, ɛr] nm, f 1. (à cheval) rider. 2. (partenaire) partner. ▶ **cavalier** nm (aux échecs) knight.

cavalièrement [kavaljɛrmɑ̃] adv in an offhand manner.

cave [kav] ◆ nf 1. (sous-sol) cellar. 2. (de vins) (wine) cellar. ◆ adj (joues) hollow; (yeux) sunken.

caveau, -x [kavo] nm 1. (petite cave) small cellar. 2. (sépulture) vault.

caverne [kavɛrn] nf cave.

caviar [kavjar] nm caviar.

cavité [kavite] nf cavity.

CB (abr de citizen's band, canaux banalisés) nf CB.

cc abr de **charges comprises**.

CCP (abr de **compte chèque postal, compte courant postal**) nm post office account; ≃ Giro Br.

CD nm (abr de **compact disc**) CD.

CDD nm abr de **contrat à durée déterminée**.

CDI nm 1. (abr de **centre de documentation et d'information**) school library. 2. abr de **contrat à durée indéterminée**.

ce [sə] ◆ adj dém (cet [sɛt] devant voyelle ou h muet, f cette [sɛt], pl ces [se]) (proche) this, these (pl); (éloigné) that, those (pl); **~ mois, ~ mois-ci** this month; **cette année, cette année-là** that year. ◆ pron dém (c' devant voyelle): **c'est** it is, it's; **~ sont** they are, they're; **c'est mon bureau** this is my office, it's my office; **~ sont mes enfants** these are my children, they're my children; **c'est à Paris** it's in Paris; **qui est~?** who is it?; **~ qui, ~ que** what; **ils ont eu ~ qui leur revenait** they got what they deserved; ..., **~ qui est étonnant** ..., which is surprising; **vous savez bien ~ à quoi je pense** you know exactly what I'm thinking about; **faites donc ~ pour quoi on vous paie** do what you're paid to do.

CE ◆ *nm* 1. *abr de* **comité d'entreprise**. 2. (*abr de* **cours élémentaire**): **~1** second year of primary school; **~2** third year of primary school. ◆ *nf* (*abr de* **Communauté européenne**) EC.

ceci [səsi] *pron dém* this; **à ~ près que** with the exception that, except that.

cécité [sesite] *nf* blindness.

céder [sede] ◆ *vt* 1. (*donner*) to give up; **'cédez le passage'** 'give way' Br, 'yield' Am. 2. (*revendre*) to sell. ◆ *vi* 1. (*personne*): **~ (à)** to give in (to), to yield (to). 2. (*chaise, plancher*) to give way.

CEDEX, Cedex [sedɛks] (*abr de* **courrier d'entreprise à distribution exceptionnelle**) *nm* accelerated postal service for bulk users.

cédille [sedij] *nf* cedilla.

cèdre [sɛdr] *nm* cedar.

CEE (*abr de* **Communauté économique européenne**) *nf* EEC.

CEI (*abr de* **Communauté d'États Indépendants**) *nf* CIS.

ceinture [sɛ̃tyr] *nf* 1. (*gén*) belt; **~ de sécurité** safety ou seat belt. 2. (ANAT) waist.

ceinturon [sɛ̃tyrɔ̃] *nm* belt.

cela [səla] *pron dém* that; **~ ne vous regarde pas** it's ou that's none of your business; **il y a des années de ~** that was many years ago; **c'est ~** that's right; **~ dit ...** having said that ...; **malgré ~** in spite of that, nevertheless.

célèbre [selɛbr] *adj* famous.

célébrer [selebre] *vt* 1. (*gén*) to celebrate. 2. (*faire la louange de*) to praise.

célébrité [selebrite] *nf* 1. (*renommée*) fame. 2. (*personne*) celebrity.

céleri [sɛlri] *nm* celery.

céleste [selɛst] *adj* heavenly.

célibat [seliba] *nm* celibacy.

célibataire [selibatɛr] ◆ *adj* single, unmarried. ◆ *nmf* single person, single man (*f* woman).

celle → **celui**.

celle-ci → **celui-ci**.

celle-là → **celui-là**.

celles → **celui**.

celles-ci → **celui-ci**.

celles-là → **celui-là**.

cellier [selje] *nm* storeroom.

Cellophane® [selɔfan] *nf* Cellophane®.

cellulaire [selylɛr] *adj* 1. (BIOL & TÉLÉCOM) cellular. 2. (*destiné aux prisonniers*): **régime ~** solitary confinement; **voiture ~** prison van.

cellule [selyl] *nf* 1. (*gén* & INFORM) cell. 2. (*groupe*) unit.

cellulite [selylit] *nf* cellulite.

celte [sɛlt] *adj* Celtic. ▶ **Celte** *nmf* Celt.

celui [səlɥi] (*f* **celle** [sɛl], *mpl* **ceux** [sø], *fpl* **celles** [sɛl]) *pron dém* 1. (*suivi d'un complément prépositionnel*) the one; **celle de devant** the one in front; **ceux d'entre vous qui ...** those of you who ... 2. (*suivi d'un pronom relatif*): **~ qui** (*objet*) the one which ou that; (*personne*) the one who; **c'est celle qui te va le mieux** that's the one which ou that suits you best; **~ que vous voyez** the one (which ou that) you can see, the one whom you can see; **ceux que je connais** those I know.

celui-ci [səlɥisi] (*f* **celle-ci** [sɛlsi], *mpl* **ceux-ci** [søsi], *fpl* **celles-ci** [sɛlsi]) *pron dém* this one, these ones (*pl*).

celui-là [səlɥila] (*f* **celle-là** [sɛlla], *mpl* **ceux-là** [søla], *fpl* **celles-là** [sɛlla]) *pron dém* that one, those ones (*pl*); **~ ... celui-ci** the former ... the latter.

cendre [sɑ̃dr] *nf* ash.

cendré, -e [sɑ̃dre] *adj* (*chevelure*): **blond ~** ash blond.

cendrier [sɑ̃drije] *nm* 1. (*de fumeur*) ashtray. 2. (*de poêle*) ashpan.

cène [sɛn] *nf* (Holy) Communion. ▶ **Cène** *nf*: **la Cène** the Last Supper.

censé, -e [sɑ̃se] *adj*: **être ~ faire qqch** to be supposed to do sthg.

censeur [sɑ̃sœr] *nm* 1. (SCOL) ≃ deputy head Br, ≃ vice-principal Am. 2. (CIN & PRESSE) censor.

censure [sɑ̃syr] *nf* 1. (CIN & presse - contrôle) censorship; (- *censeurs*) censors (*pl*). 2. (POLIT) censure. 3. (PSYCHOL) censor.

censurer [sɑ̃syre] *vt* 1. (CIN, PRESSE & PSYCHOL) to censor. 2. (*juger*) to censure.

cent [sɑ̃] ◆ *adj num* one hundred, a hundred. ◆ *nm* 1. (*nombre*) a hundred; *voir aussi* **six**. 2. (*mesure de proportion*): **pour ~** per cent.

centaine [sɑ̃tɛn] *nf* 1. (*cent unités*) hundred. 2. (*un grand nombre*): **une ~ de** about a hundred; **des ~s (de)** hundreds (of); **plusieurs ~s de** several hundred;

par ~s in hundreds.

centenaire [sɑ̃tner] ◆ adj hundred-year-old (avant n); être ~ to be a hundred years old. ◆ nmf centenarian. ◆ nm (anniversaire) centenary.

centiare [sɑ̃tjar] nm square metre.

centième [sɑ̃tjɛm] adj num, nm & nmf hundredth; voir aussi **sixième**.

centigrade [sɑ̃tigrad] → **degré**.

centilitre [sɑ̃tilitr] nm centilitre.

centime [sɑ̃tim] nm centime.

centimètre [sɑ̃timetr] nm 1. (mesure) centimetre. 2. (ruban, règle) tape measure.

central, -e, -aux [sɑ̃tral, o] adj central. ▶ **central** nm (de réseau): ~ **téléphonique** telephone exchange. ▶ **centrale** nf 1. (usine) power plant ou station; ~e **hydroélectrique** hydroelectric power station; ~e **nucléaire** nuclear power plant ou station. 2. (COMM): ~e **d'achat** buying group.

centraliser [sɑ̃tralize] vt to centralize.

centre [sɑ̃tr] nm (gén) centre; ~ **aéré** outdoor centre; ~ **commercial** shopping centre; ~ **culturel** arts centre; ~ **de gravité** centre of gravity.

centrer [sɑ̃tre] vt to centre.

centre-ville [sɑ̃trəvil] nm city centre, town centre.

centrifuge [sɑ̃trify ʒ] → **force**.

centrifugeuse [sɑ̃trify ʒøz] nf 1. (TECHNOL) centrifuge. 2. (CULIN) juice extractor.

centuple [sɑ̃typl] nm: être le ~ **de qqch** to be a hundred times sthg; au ~ a hundredfold.

cep [sɛp] nm stock.

cèpe [sɛp] nm cep.

cependant [səpɑ̃dɑ̃] conj however, yet.

céramique [seramik] nf (matière, objet) ceramic.

cerceau, -x [serso] nm hoop.

cercle [serkl] nm circle; ~ **vicieux** vicious circle.

cercueil [serkœj] nm coffin.

céréale [sereal] nf cereal.

cérémonial, -als [seremɔnjal] nm ceremonial.

cérémonie [seremɔni] nf ceremony.

cérémonieux, -euse [seremɔnjø, øz] adj ceremonious.

cerf [ser] nm stag.

cerf-volant [servɔlɑ̃] nm (jouet) kite.

cerise [səriz] nf & adj inv cherry.

cerisier [sərizje] nm (arbre) cherry (tree); (bois) cherry (wood).

cerne [sern] nm ring.

cerné [serne] → **œil**.

cerner [serne] vt 1. (encercler) to surround. 2. fig (sujet) to define.

certain, -e [sertɛ̃, ɛn] ◆ adj certain; être ~ **de qqch** to be certain ou sure of sthg; je suis pourtant ~ d'avoir mis mes clés là but I'm certain ou sure I left my keys there. ◆ adj indéf (avant n) certain; il a un ~ **talent** he has some talent ou a certain talent; un ~ **temps** for a while; c'est un monsieur d'un ~ âge he's getting on a bit; un ~ M. Lebrun a Mr Lebrun. ▶ **certains** (fpl certaines) pron indéf pl some.

certainement [sertɛnmɑ̃] adv certainly.

certes [sert] adv of course.

certificat [sertifika] nm (attestation, diplôme) certificate; ~ **médical** medical certificate.

certifié, -e [sertifje] adj: professeur ~ qualified teacher.

certifier [sertifje] vt 1. (assurer): ~ **qqch à qqn** to assure sb of sthg. 2. (authentifier) to certify.

certitude [sertityd] nf certainty.

cerveau [servo] nm brain.

cervelle [servel] nf 1. (ANAT) brain. 2. (facultés mentales, aliment) brains (pl).

cervical, -e, -aux [servikal, o] adj cervical.

ces → **ce**.

CES (abr de **collège d'enseignement secondaire**) nm former secondary school.

césarienne [sezarjɛn] nf caesarean (section).

cesse [ses] nf: n'avoir de ~ que (+ subjonctif) sout not to rest until. ▶ **sans cesse** loc adv continually, constantly.

cesser [sese] ◆ vi to stop, to cease. ◆ vt to stop; ~ **de faire qqch** to stop doing sthg.

cessez-le-feu [seselfø] nm inv ceasefire.

cession [sesjɔ̃] nf transfer.

c'est-à-dire [setadir] conj 1. (en d'autres termes): ~ **(que)** that is (to say). 2. (introduit une restriction, précision, réponse): ~ **que** well ..., actually ...

cet → **ce**.

cétacé [setase] nm cetacean.

cette → **ce**.

ceux → **celui**.

ceux-ci → **celui-ci**.

ceux-là → **celui-là**.

cf. (abr de confer) cf.

CFA nf (abr de **Communauté financière**

africaine): **franc ~** currency used in former French African colonies.

CFC (abr de **chlorofluorocarbone**) nm CFC.

chacal [ʃakal] nm jackal.

chacun, -e [ʃakœ̃, yn] pron indéf each (one); (tout le monde) everyone, everybody; **~ de nous/de vous/d'eux** each of us/you/them; **~ pour soi** every man for himself; **tout un; ~** every one of us/them.

chagrin, -e [ʃagrɛ̃, in] adj (personne) grieving; (caractère, humeur) morose. ▶ **chagrin** nm grief; **avoir du ~** to grieve.

chagriner [ʃagrine] vt 1. (peiner) to grieve, to distress. 2. (contrarier) to upset.

chahut [ʃay] nm uproar.

chahuter [ʃayte] ♦ vi to cause an uproar. ♦ vt 1. (importuner - professeur) to rag, to tease; (- orateur) to heckle. 2. (bousculer) to jostle.

chaîne [ʃɛn] nf 1. (gén) chain; **~ de montagnes** mountain range. 2. (IND): **~ de fabrication/de montage** production/assembly line; **travail à la ~** production-line work; **produire qqch à la ~** to mass-produce sthg. 3. (TÉLÉ) channel. 4. (appareil) stereo (system); **~ hi-fi** hi-fi system. ▶ **chaînes** nfpl fig chains, bonds.

chaînon [ʃɛnɔ̃] nm litt & fig link.

chair [ʃɛr] nf flesh; **~ à saucisse** sausage meat; **avoir la ~ de poule** fig to have goosepimples Br, to have goosebumps Am.

chaire [ʃɛr] nf 1. (estrade - de prédicateur) pulpit; (- de professeur) rostrum. 2. (UNIV) chair.

chaise [ʃɛz] nf chair; **~ longue** deckchair.

châle [ʃal] nm shawl.

chalet [ʃalɛ] nm 1. (de montagne) chalet. 2. Can (maison de campagne) (holiday) cottage.

chaleur [ʃalœr] nf heat; (agréable) warmth.

chaleureux, -euse [ʃalœrø, øz] adj warm.

challenge [ʃalɑ̃ʒ] nm 1. (SPORT) tournament. 2. fig (défi) challenge.

chaloupe [ʃalup] nf rowing boat Br, rowboat Am.

chalumeau [ʃalymo] nm (TECHNOL) blowlamp Br, blowtorch Am.

chalutier [ʃalytje] nm (bateau) trawler.

chamailler [ʃamaje] ▶ **se chamailler** vp fam to squabble.

chambranle [ʃɑ̃brɑ̃l] nm (de porte, fenêtre) frame; (de cheminée) mantelpiece.

chambre [ʃɑ̃br] nf 1. (où l'on dort): **~ (à coucher)** bedroom; **~ à un lit, ~ pour une personne** single room; **~ pour deux personnes** double room; **~ à deux lits** twin-bedded room; **~ d'amis** spare room; **~ d'hôte** bed and breakfast. 2. (local) room; **~ forte** strongroom; **~ froide** cold store; **~ noire** darkroom. 3. (JUR) division; **~ d'accusation** court of criminal appeal. 4. (POLIT) chamber, house; **Chambre des députés** = House of Commons Br, ≃ House of Representatives Am. 5. (TECHNOL) chamber; **~ à air** (de pneu) inner tube.

chambrer [ʃɑ̃bre] vt 1. (vin) to bring to room temperature. 2. fam (se moquer): **~ qqn** to pull sb's leg, to wind sb up Br.

chameau, -x [ʃamo] nm (mammifère) camel.

chamois [ʃamwa] nm chamois; (peau) chamois (leather).

champ [ʃɑ̃] nm 1. (gén & INFORM) field; **~ de bataille** battlefield; **~ de courses** racecourse. 2. (étendue) area.

champagne [ʃɑ̃paɲ] nm champagne.

CHAMPAGNE

The famous sparkling wine can properly speaking only be called champagne if it is made from grapes grown in the Champagne region in northeast France. It can be combined with blackcurrant liqueur to make the cocktail 'kir royal'.

champêtre [ʃɑ̃pɛtr] adj rural.

champignon [ʃɑ̃piɲɔ̃] nm 1. (BOT & MÉD) fungus. 2. (comestible) mushroom; **~ vénéneux** toadstool.

champion, -onne [ʃɑ̃pjɔ̃, ɔn] ♦ nm, f champion. ♦ adj fam brilliant.

championnat [ʃɑ̃pjɔna] nm championship.

chance [ʃɑ̃s] nf 1. (bonheur) luck (U); **avoir de la ~** to be lucky; **ne pas avoir de ~** to be unlucky; **porter ~** to bring good luck. 2. (probabilité, possibilité) chance, opportunity; **avoir des ~s de faire qqch** to have a chance of doing sthg.

chanceler [ʃɑ̃sle] vi (personne, gouvernement) to totter; (meuble) to wobble.

chancelier [ʃɑ̃səlje] nm 1. (premier ministre) chancellor. 2. (de consulat, d'ambassade) secretary.

chanceux, -euse [ʃɑ̃sø, øz] adj lucky.

chandail [ʃɑ̃daj] *nm* (thick) sweater.
Chandeleur [ʃɑ̃dlœr] *nf* Candlemas.

CHANDELEUR
The French celebrate Candlemas, 2 February, by making pancakes which they toss in a frying pan held in one hand whilst holding a coin in the other hand. Tradition has it that you will have good luck in the coming year if you successfully catch the pancake.

---

chandelier [ʃɑ̃dəlje] *nm* (*pour une bougie*) candlestick; (*à plusieurs branches*) candelabra.
chandelle [ʃɑ̃dɛl] *nf* (*bougie*) candle.
change [ʃɑ̃ʒ] *nm* 1. (*troc* & FIN) exchange. 2. (*couche de bébé*) disposable nappy Br, diaper Am.
changeant, -e [ʃɑ̃ʒɑ̃, ɑ̃t] *adj* 1. (*temps, humeur*) changeable. 2. (*reflet*) shimmering.
changement [ʃɑ̃ʒmɑ̃] *nm* change.
changer [ʃɑ̃ʒe] ◆ *vt* 1. (*gén*) to change; ~ **qqch contre** to change ou exchange sthg for; ~ **qqn en** to change sb into; ~ **des francs en livres** to change francs into pounds, to exchange francs for pounds. 2. (*modifier*) to change, to alter; **ça me/te change** that will be a (nice) change for me/you. ◆ *vi* (*gén*) to change; ~ **de train (à)** to change trains (at); ~ **d'avis** to change one's mind; **ça changera!** that'll make a change!; ~ **de direction** to change direction; ~ **de place (avec qqn)** to change places (with sb); **pour** ~ for a change.
chanson [ʃɑ̃sɔ̃] *nf* song; **c'est toujours la même** ~ *fig* it's the same old story.
chansonnier, -ère [ʃɑ̃sɔnje, ɛr] *nm, f* cabaret singer-songwriter.
chant [ʃɑ̃] *nm* 1. (*chanson*) song, singing (U); (*sacré*) hymn. 2. (*art*) singing.
chantage [ʃɑ̃taʒ] *nm litt* & *fig* blackmail; **faire du** ~ to use ou resort to blackmail; **faire du** ~ **à qqn** to blackmail sb.
chanter [ʃɑ̃te] ◆ *vt* 1. (*chanson*) to sing. 2. *littéraire* (*célébrer*) to sing ou tell of; ~ **les louanges de qqn** to sing sb's praises. ◆ *vi* 1. (*gén*) to sing. 2. *loc*: **faire** ~ **qqn** to blackmail sb; **si ça vous chante!** *fam* if you feel like ou fancy it!
chanteur, -euse [ʃɑ̃tœr, øz] *nm, f* singer.
chantier [ʃɑ̃tje] *nm* 1. (CONSTR) (building) site; (*sur la route*) roadworks (*pl*); ~

naval shipyard, dockyard. 2. *fig* (*désordre*) shambles (*sg*), mess.
Chantilly [ʃɑ̃tiji] *nf*: (**crème**) ~ stiffly whipped cream sweetened and flavoured.
chantonner [ʃɑ̃tɔne] *vt* & *vi* to hum.
chanvre [ʃɑ̃vr] *nm* hemp.
chaos [kao] *nm* chaos.
chap. (*abr de chapitre*) ch.
chaparder [ʃaparde] *vt* to steal.
chapeau, -x [ʃapo] *nm* 1. (*coiffure*) hat. 2. (PRESSE) introductory paragraph.
chapeauter [ʃapote] *vt* (*service*) to head; (*personnes*) to supervise.
chapelet [ʃaplɛ] *nm* 1. (RELIG) rosary. 2. *fig* (*d'injures*) string, torrent.
chapelle [ʃapɛl] *nf* (*petite église*) chapel; (*partie d'église*) choir.
chapelure [ʃaplyr] *nf* (dried) breadcrumbs (*pl*).
chaperon [ʃaprɔ̃] *nm* chaperone.
chapiteau [ʃapito] *nm* (*de cirque*) big top.
chapitre [ʃapitr] *nm* (*de livre* & RELIG) chapter.
chaque [ʃak] *adj indéf* each, every; ~ **personne** each person, everyone; **j'ai payé ces livres 100 francs** ~ I paid 100 francs each for these books.
char [ʃar] *nm* 1. (MIL): ~ (**d'assaut**) tank. 2. (*de carnaval*) float. 3. Can (*voiture*) car.
charabia [ʃarabja] *nm* gibberish.
charade [ʃarad] *nf* charade.
charbon [ʃarbɔ̃] *nm* (*combustible*) coal; ~ **de bois** charcoal.
charcuter [ʃarkyte] *vt fam péj* to butcher.
charcuterie [ʃarkytri] *nf* 1. (*magasin*) pork butcher's. 2. (*produits*) pork meat products.
charcutier, -ère [ʃarkytje, ɛr] *nm, f* (*commerçant*) pork butcher.
chardon [ʃardɔ̃] *nm* (*plante*) thistle.
charge [ʃarʒ] *nf* 1. (*fardeau*) load. 2. (*fonction*) office. 3. (*responsabilité*) responsibility; **être à la** ~ **de** (*personne*) to be dependent on; **les travaux sont à la** ~ **du propriétaire** the owner is liable for the cost of the work; **prendre qqch en** ~ (*payer*) to pay (for) sthg; (*s'occuper de*) to take charge of sthg; **prendre qqn en** ~ to take charge of sb. 4. (ÉLECTR, JUR & MIL) charge. ▶ **charges** *nfpl* 1. (*d'appartement*) service charge. 2. (ÉCON) expenses, costs; **~s sociales** ≃ employer's contributions.
chargé, -e [ʃarʒe] ◆ *adj* 1. (*véhicule, personne*): ~ (**de**) loaded (with). 2. (*responsable*): ~ (**de**) responsible (for).

3. (*occupé*) full, busy. ◆ *nm, f:* ~ **d'affaires** chargé d'affaires; ~ **de mission** head of mission.

chargement [ʃaʀʒəmã] *nm* **1.** (*action*) loading. **2.** (*marchandises*) load.

charger [ʃaʀʒe] *vt* **1.** (*gén & INFORM*) to load. **2.** (ÉLECTR, JUR & MIL) to charge. **3.** (*donner une mission à*): ~ **qqn de faire qqch** to put sb in charge of doing sthg. ▶ **se charger** *vp:* **se** ~ **de qqn/qqch** to take care of sb/sthg, to take charge of sb/sthg; **se** ~ **de faire qqch** to undertake to do sthg.

chargeur [ʃaʀʒœʀ] *nm* **1.** (ÉLECTR) charger. **2.** (*d'arme*) magazine.

chariot [ʃaʀjo] *nm* **1.** (*charrette*) handcart. **2.** (*à bagages, dans un hôpital*) trolley *Br*, wagon *Am*. **3.** (*de machine à écrire*) carriage.

charisme [kaʀism] *nm* charisma.

charitable [ʃaʀitabl] *adj* charitable; (*conseil*) friendly.

charité [ʃaʀite] *nf* **1.** (*aumône & RELIG*) charity. **2.** (*bonté*) kindness.

charlatan [ʃaʀlatã] *nm péj* charlatan.

charlotte [ʃaʀlɔt] *nf* (*cuite*) charlotte; (*froide*) cold dessert of chocolate or fruit mousse encased in sponge fingers.

charmant, -e [ʃaʀmã, ãt] *adj* charming.

charme [ʃaʀm] *nm* **1.** (*séduction*) charm. **2.** (*enchantement*) spell. **3.** (*arbre*) ironwood, hornbeam.

charmer [ʃaʀme] *vt* to charm; **être charmé de faire qqch** to be delighted to do sthg.

charmeur, -euse [ʃaʀmœʀ, øz] ◆ *adj* charming. ◆ *nm, f* charmer; ~ **de serpents** snake charmer.

charnel, -elle [ʃaʀnɛl] *adj* carnal.

charnier [ʃaʀnje] *nm* mass grave.

charnière [ʃaʀnjɛʀ] ◆ *nf* hinge; *fig* turning point. ◆ *adj* (*période*) transitional.

charnu, -e [ʃaʀny] *adj* fleshy.

charogne [ʃaʀɔɲ] *nf* (*d'animal*) carrion (U).

charpente [ʃaʀpãt] *nf* **1.** (*de bâtiment, de roman*) framework. **2.** (*ossature*) frame.

charpentier [ʃaʀpãtje] *nm* carpenter.

charretier, -ère [ʃaʀtje, ɛʀ] *nm, f* carter.

charrette [ʃaʀɛt] *nf* cart.

charrier [ʃaʀje] ◆ *vt* **1.** to carry. **2.** *fam* (*se moquer de*): ~ **qqn** to take sb for a ride. ◆ *vi fam* (*exagérer*) to go too far.

charrue [ʃaʀy] *nf* plough, plow *Am*.

charte [ʃaʀt] *nf* charter.

charter [ʃaʀtɛʀ] *nm* chartered plane.

chartreuse [ʃaʀtʀøz] *nf* **1.** (RELIG) Carthusian monastery. **2.** (*liqueur*) Chartreuse.

chas [ʃa] *nm* eye (*of needle*).

chasse [ʃas] *nf* **1.** (*action*) hunting; ~ **à courre** hunting (*on horseback with hounds*). **2.** (*période*): **la** ~ **est ouverte/fermée** it's the open/close season. **3.** (*domaine*): ~ **gardée** private hunting ou shooting preserve; *fig* preserve. **4.** (*poursuite*) chase; **faire la** ~ **à qqn/qqch** *fig* to hunt (for) sb/sthg, to hunt sb/sthg down; **prendre qqn/qqch en** ~ to give chase to sb/sthg. **5.** (*des cabinets*): ~ **(d'eau)** flush; **tirer la** ~ to flush the toilet.

chassé-croisé [ʃasekʀwaze] *nm* toing and froing.

chasse-neige [ʃasnɛʒ] *nm inv* snowplough.

chasser [ʃase] *vt* **1.** (*animal*) to hunt. **2.** (*faire partir - personne*) to drive ou chase away; (*- odeur, souci*) to dispel.

chasseur, -euse [ʃasœʀ, øz] *nm, f* hunter. ▶ **chasseur** *nm* **1.** (*d'hôtel*) page, messenger. **2.** (MIL): ~ **alpin** soldier specially trained for operations in mountainous terrain. **3.** (*avion*) fighter.

châssis [ʃasi] *nm* **1.** (*de fenêtre, de porte, de machine*) frame. **2.** (*de véhicule*) chassis.

chaste [ʃast] *adj* chaste.

chasteté [ʃastəte] *nf* chastity.

chasuble [ʃazybl] *nf* chasuble.

chat, chatte [ʃa, ʃat] *nm, f* cat.

châtaigne [ʃatɛɲ] *nf* **1.** (*fruit*) chestnut. **2.** *fam* (*coup*) clout.

châtaignier [ʃatɛɲe] *nm* (*arbre*) chestnut (tree); (*bois*) chestnut.

châtain [ʃatɛ̃] *adj & nm* chestnut, chestnut-brown.

château, -x [ʃato] *nm* **1.** (*forteresse*): ~ **(fort)** castle. **2.** (*résidence - seigneuriale*) mansion; (*- de monarque, d'évêque*) palace; ~ **de sable** sandcastle. **3.** (*réservoir*): ~ **d'eau** water tower.

CHÂTEAUX DE LA LOIRE

The Renaissance 'châteaux' found in the Loire valley in the west of France are royal or stately residences built in the 15th and 16th centuries. The best-known 'châteaux' include the one at Chambord, which was built for François I; Chenonceaux, where the 'château' stands on arches over the river Cher; and Azay-le-Rideau, where the 'château' stands on a tiny island in the river Indre.

châtiment [ʃatimã] nm punishment.

chaton [ʃatɔ̃] nm 1. (petit chat) kitten. 2. (BOT) catkin.

chatouiller [ʃatuje] vt 1. (faire des chatouilles à) to tickle. 2. fig (titiller) to titillate.

chatoyant, -e [ʃatwajã, ãt] adj (reflet, étoffe) shimmering; (bijou) sparkling.

châtrer [ʃatre] vt to castrate; (chat) to neuter; (chatte) to spay.

chatte → chat.

chaud, -e [ʃo, ʃod] adj 1. (gén) warm; (de température très élevée, sensuel) hot. 2. fig (enthousiaste): être ~ pour qqch/pour faire qqch to be keen on sthg/on doing sthg. ► **chaud** ◆ adv: avoir ~ to be warm ou hot; il fait ~ it's warm ou hot; manger ~ to have something hot (to eat). ◆ nm heat; rester au ~ to stay in the warm.

chaudement [ʃodmã] adv warmly.

chaudière [ʃodjɛr] nf boiler.

chaudron [ʃodrɔ̃] nm cauldron.

chauffage [ʃofaʒ] nm (appareil) heating (system); ~ central central heating; ~ central au mazout oil-fired central heating; ~ au gaz gas heating.

chauffant, -e [ʃofã, ãt] adj heating; plaque ~e hotplate.

chauffard [ʃofar] nm péj reckless driver.

chauffe-eau [ʃofo] nm inv waterheater.

chauffer [ʃofe] ◆ vt (rendre chaud) to heat (up). ◆ vi 1. (devenir chaud) to heat up. 2. (moteur) to overheat. 3. fam (barder): ça va ~ there's going to be trouble.

chauffeur [ʃofœr] nm (AUTOM) driver.

chaume [ʃom] nm (paille) thatch.

chaumière [ʃomjɛr] nf cottage.

chaussée [ʃose] nf road, roadway; '~ déformée' 'uneven road surface'.

chausse-pied [ʃospje] (pl chaussepieds) nm shoehorn.

chausser [ʃose] ◆ vt (chaussures, lunettes, skis) to put on. ◆ vi: ~ du 39 to take size 39 (shoes). ► **se chausser** vp to put one's shoes on.

chaussette [ʃosɛt] nf sock.

chausson [ʃosɔ̃] nm 1. (pantoufle) slipper. 2. (de danse) ballet shoe. 3. (de bébé) bootee. 4. (CULIN) turnover; ~ aux pommes apple turnover.

chaussure [ʃosyr] nf 1. (soulier) shoe; ~ basse low-heeled shoe, flat shoe; ~ de marche (de randonnée) hiking ou walking boot; (confortable) walking shoe; ~ de

ski ski boot. 2. (industrie) footwear industry.

chauve [ʃov] adj (sans cheveux) bald.

chauve-souris [ʃovsuri] nf bat.

chauvin, -e [ʃovɛ̃, in] adj chauvinistic.

chaux [ʃo] nf lime; blanchi à la ~ whitewashed.

chavirer [ʃavire] vi 1. (bateau) to capsize. 2. fig (tourner) to spin.

chef [ʃɛf] nm 1. (d'un groupe) head, leader; (au travail) boss; en ~ in chief; ~ d'entreprise company head; ~ d'État head of state; ~ de famille head of the family; ~ de file (POLIT) (party) leader; ~ de gare stationmaster; ~ d'orchestre conductor; ~ de rayon departmental manager ou supervisor; ~ de service (ADMIN) departmental manager. 2. (cuisinier) chef. ► **chef d'accusation** nm charge, count.

chef-d'œuvre [ʃɛdœvr] (pl chefsd'œuvre) nm masterpiece.

chef-lieu [ʃɛfljø] nm ≃ county town.

cheik [ʃɛk] nm sheikh.

chemin [ʃəmɛ̃] nm 1. (voie) path; ~ de fer railway; ~ vicinal byroad, minor road. 2. (parcours) way; fig road; en ~ on the way.

cheminée [ʃəmine] nf 1. (foyer) fireplace. 2. (conduit d'usine) chimney. 3. (encadrement) mantelpiece. 4. (de paquebot, locomotive) funnel.

cheminement [ʃəminmã] nm (progression) advance; fig (d'idée) development.

cheminer [ʃəmine] vi (avancer) to make one's way; fig (idée) to develop.

cheminot [ʃəmino] nm railwayman Br, railroad man Am.

chemise [ʃəmiz] nf 1. (d'homme) shirt; ~ de nuit (de femme) nightdress. 2. (dossier) folder.

chemisette [ʃəmizɛt] nf (d'homme) short-sleeved shirt; (de femme) shortsleeved blouse.

chemisier [ʃəmizje] nm (vêtement) blouse.

chenal, -aux [ʃənal, o] nm (canal) channel.

chêne [ʃɛn] nm (arbre) oak (tree); (bois) oak.

chenet [ʃənɛ] nm firedog.

chenil [ʃənil] nm (pour chiens) kennel.

chenille [ʃənij] nf 1. (insecte) caterpillar. 2. (courroie) caterpillar track.

chenillette [ʃənijɛt] nf (au ski) snowmobile.

chèque [ʃɛk] nm cheque; faire/toucher un ~ to write/cash a cheque; ~ (ban-

caire) (bank) cheque; **~ barré** crossed cheque; **~ postal** post office cheque; **~ sans provision** bad cheque; **~ de voyage** traveller's cheque.

chèque-cadeau [ʃɛkkado] *nm* gift token.

chèque-repas [ʃɛkrəpa] (*pl* **chèques-repas**), **chèque-restaurant** [ʃɛkrɛstɔrã] (*pl* **chèques-restaurant**) *nm* luncheon voucher.

chéquier [ʃekje] *nm* chequebook.

cher, chère [ʃɛr] ♦ *adj* **1.** (*aimé*): **~ (à qqn)** dear (to sb); **Cher Monsieur** (*au début d'une lettre*) Dear Sir; **Chère Madame** (*au début d'une lettre*) Dear Madam. **2.** (*produit, vie, commerçant*) expensive. ♦ *nm, f hum:* **mon ~** dear. ▶ **cher** *adv:* **valoir ~, coûter ~** to be expensive, to cost a lot; **payer ~** to pay a lot; **je l'ai payé ~** *litt & fig* it cost me a lot.

chercher [ʃɛrʃe] ♦ *vt* **1.** (*gén*) to look for. **2.** (*prendre*) **aller/venir ~ qqn** (*à un rendez-vous*) to (go/come and) meet sb; (*en voiture*) to (go/come and) pick sb up; **aller/venir ~ qqch** to (go/come and) get sthg. ♦ *vi:* **~ à faire qqch** to try to do sthg.

chercheur, -euse [ʃɛrʃœr, øz] *nm, f* (*scientifique*) researcher.

chéri, -e [ʃeri] ♦ *adj* dear. ♦ *nm, f* darling.

chérir [ʃerir] *vt* (*personne*) to love dearly; (*chose, idée*) to cherish.

chétif, -ive [ʃetif, iv] *adj* (*malingre*) sickly, weak.

cheval, -aux [ʃəval, o] *nm* **1.** (*animal*) horse; **~** on horseback; **être à ~ sur qqch** (*être assis*) to be sitting astride sthg; *fig* (*siècles*) to straddle sthg; *fig* (*tenir à*) to be a stickler for sthg; **~ d'arçons** horse (*in gymnastics*). **2.** (*équitation*) riding, horse-riding; **faire du ~** to ride. **3.** (AUTOM): **~, ~-vapeur** horsepower.

chevalerie [ʃəvalri] *nf* **1.** (*qualité*) chivalry. **2.** (HIST) knighthood.

chevalet [ʃəvalɛ] *nm* (*de peintre*) easel.

chevalier [ʃəvalje] *nm* knight.

chevalière [ʃəvaljɛr] *nf* (*bague*) signet ring.

chevauchée [ʃəvoʃe] *nf* (*course*) ride, horse-ride.

chevaucher [ʃəvoʃe] *vt* (*être assis*) to sit on horseback. ▶ **se chevaucher** *vp* to overlap.

chevelu, -e [ʃəvly] *adj* hairy.

chevelure [ʃəvlyr] *nf* (*cheveux*) hair.

chevet [ʃəvɛ] *nm* head (*of bed*); **être au**

~ de qqn to be at sb's bedside.

cheveu, -x [ʃəvø] *nm* (*chevelure*) hair; **se faire couper les ~x** to have one's hair cut.

cheville [ʃəvij] *nf* **1.** (ANAT) ankle. **2.** (*pour fixer une vis*) Rawlplug®.

chèvre [ʃɛvr] ♦ *nf* (*animal*) goat. ♦ *nm* (*fromage*) goat's cheese.

chevreau, -x [ʃəvro] *nm* kid.

chèvrefeuille [ʃɛvrəfœj] *nm* honeysuckle.

chevreuil [ʃəvrœj] *nm* **1.** (*animal*) roe deer. **2.** (CULIN) venison.

chevronné, -e [ʃəvrɔne] *adj* (*expérimenté*) experienced.

chevrotant, -e [ʃəvrɔtã, ãt] *adj* tremulous.

chevrotine [ʃəvrɔtin] *nf* buckshot.

chewing-gum [ʃwiŋgɔm] (*pl* **chewing-gums**) *nm* chewing gum (U).

chez [ʃe] *prép* **1.** (*dans la maison de*): **il est ~ lui** he's at home; **il rentre ~ lui** he's going home; **être ~ le coiffeur/médecin** to be at the hairdresser's/doctor's; **aller ~ le coiffeur/médecin** to go to the hairdresser's/doctor's; **il va venir ~ nous** he is going to come to our place *ou* house; **il habite ~ nous** he lives with us. **2.** (*en ce qui concerne*): **~ les jeunes** among young people; **~ les Anglais** in England. **3.** (*dans les œuvres de*): **~ Proust** in (the works of) Proust. **4.** (*dans le caractère de*): **ce que j'apprécie ~ lui, c'est sa gentillesse** what I like about him is his kindness.

chez-soi [ʃeswa] *nm inv* home, place of one's own.

chic [ʃik] ♦ *adj* (*inv en genre*) **1.** (*élégant*) smart, chic. **2.** *vieilli* (*serviable*) nice. ♦ *nm* style. ♦ *interj:* **~ (alors)!** great!

chiche [ʃiʃ] *adj* **1.** (*avare*) mean. **2.** (*peu abondant*) meagre, scanty.

chicorée [ʃikɔre] *nf* (*salade*) endive; (*à café*) chicory.

chien [ʃjɛ̃] *nm* **1.** (*animal*) dog; **~ de chasse** (*d'arrêt*) gundog; **~ de garde** guard dog. **2.** (*d'arme*) hammer. **3.** *loc:* **avoir un mal de ~ à faire qqch** to have a lot of trouble doing sthg; **en ~ de fusil** curled up.

chiendent [ʃjɛ̃dã] *nm* couch grass.

chien-loup [ʃjɛ̃lu] *nm* Alsatian (dog).

chienne [ʃjɛn] *nf* (*female*) dog, bitch.

chiffe [ʃif] *nf:* **c'est une ~ molle** he's spineless, he's a weed.

chiffon [ʃifɔ̃] *nm* (*linge*) rag.

chiffonné, -e [ʃifɔne] *adj* (*visage, mine*) worn.

chiffre [ʃifr] *nm* **1.** (*caractère*) figure,

number; ~ **arabe/romain** Arabic/Roman numeral. 2. (*montant*) sum; ~ **d'affaires** (COMM) turnover Br, net revenue Am; ~ **rond** round number; ~ **de ventes** sales figures (*pl*).

chiffrer [ʃifre] ♦ *vt* 1. (*évaluer*) to calculate, to assess. 2. (*coder*) to encode. ♦ *vi* *fam* to mount up. ▶ **se chiffrer** *vp*: **se ~ à** to add up to.

chignole [ʃiɲɔl] *nf* drill.

chignon [ʃiɲɔ̃] *nm* bun (*in hair*); **se crêper le ~** *fig* to scratch each other's eyes out.

Chili [ʃili] *nm*: **le ~** Chile.

chimère [ʃimɛr] *nf* 1. (MYTH) chimera. 2. (*illusion*) illusion, dream.

chimie [ʃimi] *nf* chemistry.

chimiothérapie [ʃimjɔterapi] *nf* chemotherapy.

chimique [ʃimik] *adj* chemical.

chimiste [ʃimist] *nmf* chemist.

chimpanzé [ʃɛ̃pɑ̃ze] *nm* chimpanzee.

Chine [ʃin] *nf*: **la ~** China.

chiné, -e [ʃine] *adj* mottled.

chiner [ʃine] *vi* to look for bargains.

chinois, -e [ʃinwa, az] *adj* Chinese. ▶ **chinois** *nm* 1. (*langue*) Chinese. 2. (*passoire*) conical sieve. ▶ **Chinois, -e** *nm, f* Chinese person; **les Chinois** the Chinese.

chiot [ʃjo] *nm* puppy.

chipie [ʃipi] *nf* vixen *péj*.

chips [ʃips] *nfpl*: (**pommes**) ~ (potato) crisps Br, (potato) chips Am.

chiquenaude [ʃiknod] *nf* flick.

chiquer [ʃike] ♦ *vt* to chew. ♦ *vi* to chew tobacco.

chirurgical, -e, -aux [ʃiryrʒikal, o] *adj* surgical.

chirurgie [ʃiryrʒi] *nf* surgery.

chirurgien [ʃiryrʒjɛ̃] *nm* surgeon.

chiure [ʃjyr] *nf*: ~ (**de mouche**) flyspecks (*pl*).

chlore [klɔr] *nm* chlorine.

chloroforme [klɔrɔfɔrm] *nm* chloroform.

chlorophylle [klɔrɔfil] *nf* chlorophyll.

choc [ʃɔk] *nm* 1. (*heurt, coup*) impact. 2. (*conflit*) clash. 3. (*émotion*) shock. 4. (*en apposition*): **images-~s** shock pictures; **prix-~** amazing bargain.

chocolat [ʃɔkɔla] ♦ *nm* chocolate; ~ **au lait/noir** milk/plain chocolate; ~ **à cuire/à croquer** cooking/eating chocolate. ♦ *adj inv* chocolate (brown).

chœur [kœr] *nm* 1. (*chorale*) choir; (*d'opéra & fig*) chorus; **en ~** *fig* all together. 2. (*d'église*) choir, chancel.

choisi, -e [ʃwazi] *adj* selected; (*termes, langage*) carefully chosen.

choisir [ʃwazir] ♦ *vt*: ~ (**de faire qqch**) to choose (to do sthg). ♦ *vi* to choose.

choix [ʃwa] *nm* 1. (*gén*) choice; **le livre de ton** ~ any book you like; **au** ~ as you prefer; **avoir le** ~ to have the choice. 2. (*qualité*): **de premier** ~ grade OU class one; **articles de second** ~ seconds.

choléra [kɔlera] *nm* cholera.

cholestérol [kɔlɛsterɔl] *nm* cholesterol.

chômage [ʃomaʒ] *nm* unemployment; **en ~, au** ~ unemployed; **être mis au** ~ **technique** to be laid off.

chômeur, -euse [ʃomœr, øz] *nm, f*: **les ~s** the unemployed.

chope [ʃɔp] *nf* tankard.

choper [ʃɔpe] *vt fam* 1. (*voler, arrêter*) to nick Br, to pinch. 2. (*attraper*) to catch.

choquant, -e [ʃɔkɑ̃, ɑ̃t] *adj* shocking.

choquer [ʃɔke] *vt* 1. (*scandaliser*) to shock. 2. (*traumatiser*) to shake (up).

choral, -e, -als OU **-aux** [kɔral, o] *adj* choral. ▶ **chorale** *nf* (*groupe*) choir.

chorégraphie [kɔregrafi] *nf* choreography.

choriste [kɔrist] *nmf* chorister.

chose [ʃoz] *nf* thing; **c'est (bien) peu de** ~ it's nothing really; **c'est la même** ~ it's the same thing; **c'est la moindre des ~s** it's the least I/we can do; **de deux ~s l'une** (it's got to be) one thing or the other; **parler de ~s et d'autres** to talk of this and that.

chou, -x [ʃu] ♦ *nm* 1. (*légume*) cabbage. 2. (*pâtisserie*) choux bun. ♦ *adj inv* sweet, cute.

chouchou, -oute [ʃuʃu, ut] *nm, f* favourite; (*élève*) teacher's pet.

choucroute [ʃukrut] *nf* sauerkraut.

chouette [ʃwɛt] ♦ *nf* (*oiseau*) owl. ♦ *adj fam vieilli* smashing Br, great. ♦ *interj*: ~ (**alors**)! great!

chou-fleur [ʃuflœr] *nm* cauliflower.

chrétien, -enne [kretjɛ̃, ɛn] *adj & nm, f* Christian.

chrétienté [kretjɛ̃te] *nf* Christendom.

Christ [krist] *nm* Christ.

christianisme [kristjanism] *nm* Christianity.

chrome [krom] *nm* (CHIM) chromium.

chromé, -e [krome] *adj* chrome-plated; **acier** ~ chrome steel.

chromosome [krɔmɔzom] *nm* chromosome.

chronique [krɔnik] ♦ *nf* 1. (*annales*) chronicle. 2. (PRESSE): ~ **sportive** sports section. ♦ *adj* chronic.

chronologie [krɔnɔlɔʒi] *nf* chronology.

chronologique [krɔnɔlɔʒik] *adj* chronological.

chronomètre [krɔnɔmɛtr] *nm* (SPORT) stopwatch.

chronométrer [krɔnɔmetre] *vt* to time.

chrysalide [krizalid] *nf* chrysalis.

chrysanthème [krizɑ̃tɛm] *nm* chrysanthemum.

chuchotement [ʃyʃɔtmɑ̃] *nm* whisper.

chuchoter [ʃyʃɔte] *vt & vi* to whisper.

chut [ʃyt] *interj* sh!, hush!

chute [ʃyt] *nf* 1. (*gén*) fall; ~ **d'eau** waterfall. 2. (*de tissu*) scrap.

chuter [ʃyte] *vi* 1. (*baisser*) to fall dramatically. 2. (*tomber*) to fall.

ci [si] *adv* (*après n*): **ce livre-~** this book; **ces jours-~** these days.

ci-après [siapre] *adv* below.

cible [sibl] *nf litt & fig* target.

cicatrice [sikatris] *nf* scar.

cicatriser [sikatrize] *vt litt & fig* to heal.

ci-contre [sikɔ̃tr] *adv* opposite.

ci-dessous [sidəsu] *adv* below.

ci-dessus [sidəsy] *adv* above.

cidre [sidr] *nm* cider.

Cie (*abr de* **compagnie**) Co.

ciel [sjɛl] (*pl sens 1* **ciels**, *pl sens 2* **cieux** [sjø]) *nm* 1. (*firmament*) sky; **à ~ ouvert** open-air. 2. (*paradis, providence*) heaven. ▶ **cieux** *nmpl* heaven (*sg*).

cierge [sjɛrʒ] *nm* (RELIG) (votive) candle.

cigale [sigal] *nf* cicada.

cigare [sigar] *nm* cigar.

cigarette [sigaret] *nf* cigarette.

ci-gît [siʒi] *adv* here lies.

cigogne [sigɔɲ] *nf* stork.

ci-inclus, -e [siɛ̃kly, yz] *adj* enclosed. ▶ **ci-inclus** *adv* enclosed.

ci-joint, -e [siʒwɛ̃, ɛ̃t] *adj* enclosed. ▶ **ci-joint** *adv*: **veuillez trouver ~ ...** please find enclosed ...

cil [sil] *nm* (ANAT) eyelash, lash.

ciller [sije] *vi* to blink (one's eyes).

cime [sim] *nf* (*d'arbre, de montagne*) top; *fig* height.

ciment [simɑ̃] *nm* cement.

cimenter [simɑ̃te] *vt* to cement.

cimetière [simtjɛr] *nm* cemetery.

ciné [sine] *nm fam* cinema.

cinéaste [sineast] *nmf* film-maker.

ciné-club [sineklœb] (*pl* **ciné-clubs**) *nm* film club.

cinéma [sinema] *nm* 1. (*salle, industrie*) cinema. 2. (*art*) cinema, film; **un acteur de ~** a film star.

cinémathèque [sinematek] *nf* film archive.

cinématographique [sinematɔgrafik] *adj* cinematographic.

cinéphile [sinefil] *nmf* film buff.

cinglé, -e [sɛ̃gle] *fam adj* nuts, nutty.

cingler [sɛ̃gle] *vt* to lash.

cinq [sɛ̃k] ♦ *adj num* five. ♦ *nm* five; *voir aussi* **six**.

cinquantaine [sɛ̃kɑ̃tɛn] *nf* 1. (*nombre*): **une ~ de** about fifty. 2. (*âge*): **avoir la ~** to be in one's fifties.

cinquante [sɛ̃kɑ̃t] *adj num & nm* fifty; *voir aussi* **six**.

cinquantième [sɛ̃kɑ̃tjem] *adj num, nm & nmf* fiftieth; *voir aussi* **sixième**.

cinquième [sɛ̃kjem] ♦ *adj num, nm & nmf* fifth. ♦ *nf* (SCOL) ≃ second year *ou* form Br, ≃ seventh grade Am; *voir aussi* **sixième**.

cintre [sɛ̃tr] *nm* (*pour vêtements*) coat hanger.

cintré, -e [sɛ̃tre] *adj* (COUTURE) waisted.

cirage [siraʒ] *nm* (*produit*) shoe polish.

circoncision [sirkɔ̃sizjɔ̃] *nf* circumcision.

circonférence [sirkɔ̃ferɑ̃s] *nf* 1. (GÉOM) circumference. 2. (*pourtour*) boundary.

circonflexe [sirkɔ̃flɛks] → **accent**.

circonscription [sirkɔ̃skripsjɔ̃] *nf* district.

circonscrire [sirkɔ̃skrir] *vt* 1. (*incendie, épidémie*) to contain. 2. *fig* (*sujet*) to define.

circonspect, -e [sirkɔ̃spe, ɛkt] *adj* cautious.

circonstance [sirkɔ̃stɑ̃s] *nf* 1. (*occasion*) occasion. 2. (*gén pl*) (*contexte, conjoncture*) circumstance; **~s atténuantes** (JUR) mitigating circumstances.

circonstancié, -e [sirkɔ̃stɑ̃sje] *adj* detailed.

circonstanciel, -elle [sirkɔ̃stɑ̃sjɛl] *adj* (GRAM) adverbial.

circuit [sirkɥi] *nm* 1. (*chemin*) route. 2. (*parcours touristique*) tour. 3. (SPORT & TECHNOL) circuit; **en ~ fermé** (*en boucle*) closed-circuit (*avant n*).

circulaire [sirkyler] ♦ *nf* circular. ♦ *adj* circular; **voyage ~** round trip.

circulation [sirkylasjɔ̃] *nf* 1. (*mouvement*) circulation; **mettre en ~** to circulate; **~ (du sang)** circulation. 2. (*trafic*) traffic.

circuler [sirkyle] *vi* **1.** (*sang, air, argent*) to circulate; **faire ~ qqch** to circulate sthg. **2.** (*voitures*) to move (along); (*conducteurs*) to drive; **on circule mal en ville** the traffic is bad in town. **3.** (*train, bus*) to run. **4.** *fig* (*rumeur, nouvelle*) to spread.

cire [sir] *nf* **1.** (*matière*) wax. **2.** (*encaustique*) polish.

ciré, -e [sire] *adj* **1.** (*parquet*) polished. **2.** → **toile.** ◆ **ciré** *nm* oilskin.

cirer [sire] *vt* to polish.

cirque [sirk] *nm* **1.** (*gén*) circus. **2.** (GÉOL) cirque. **3.** *fam fig* (*désordre, chahut*) chaos (U).

cirrhose [siroz] *nf* cirrhosis (U).

cisaille [sizaj] *nf* shears (*pl*).

cisailler [sizaje] *vt* (*métal*) to cut; (*branches*) to prune.

ciseau, -x [sizo] *nm* chisel. ▶ **ciseaux** *nmpl* scissors.

ciseler [sizle] *vt* **1.** (*pierre, métal*) to chisel. **2.** (*bijou*) to engrave.

citadelle [sitadɛl] *nf litt & fig* citadel.

citadin, -e [sitadɛ̃, in] ◆ *adj* city (*avant n*), urban. ◆ *nm, f* city dweller.

citation [sitasjɔ̃] *nf* **1.** (JUR) summons (*sg*). **2.** (*extrait*) quote, quotation.

cité [site] *nf* **1.** (*ville*) city. **2.** (*lotissement*) housing estate; **~ universitaire** halls (*pl*) of residence.

citer [site] *vt* **1.** (*exemple, propos, auteur*) to quote. **2.** (JUR) (*convoquer*) to summon. **3.** (MIL): **être cité à l'ordre du jour** to be mentioned in dispatches.

citerne [sitɛrn] *nf* **1.** (*d'eau*) water tank. **2.** (*cuve*) tank.

cité U [sitey] *nf fam abr de* **cité universitaire.**

citoyen, -enne [sitwajɛ̃, ɛn] *nm, f* citizen.

citoyenneté [sitwajɛnte] *nf* citizenship.

citron [sitrɔ̃] *nm* lemon; **~ pressé** fresh lemon juice; **~ vert** lime.

citronnade [sitrɔnad] *nf* (still) lemonade.

citronnier [sitrɔnje] *nm* lemon tree.

citrouille [sitruj] *nf* pumpkin.

civet [sivɛ] *nm* stew; **~ de lièvre** jugged hare.

civière [sivjɛr] *nf* stretcher.

civil, -e [sivil] ◆ *adj* **1.** (*gén*) civil. **2.** (*non militaire*) civilian. ◆ *nm, f* civilian; **dans le ~** in civilian life; **policier en ~** plain-clothes policeman (*f* policewoman); **soldat en ~** soldier in civilian clothes.

civilement [sivilmɑ̃] *adv*: **se marier ~** to get married at a registry office.

civilisation [sivilizasjɔ̃] *nf* civilization.

civilisé, -e [sivilize] *adj* civilized.

civiliser [sivilize] *vt* to civilize.

civique [sivik] *adj* civic; **instruction ~** civics (U).

civisme [sivism] *nm* sense of civic responsibility.

cl (*abr de* **centilitre**) cl.

clafoutis [klafuti] *nm flan made with cherries or other fruit.*

clair, -e [klɛr] *adj* **1.** (*gén*) clear; **c'est ~ et net** there's no two ways about it. **2.** (*lumineux*) bright. **3.** (*pâle - couleur, teint*) light; (*- tissu, cheveux*) light-coloured. ▶ **clair** ◆ *adv*: **voir ~ (dans qqch)** *fig* to have a clear understanding (of sthg). ◆ *nm*: **mettre** OU **tirer qqch au ~** to shed light upon sthg. ▶ **clair de lune** (*pl* **clairs de lune**) *nm* moonlight (U). ▶ **en clair** *loc adv* (TÉLÉ) unscrambled (*esp of a private TV channel*).

clairement [klɛrmɑ̃] *adv* clearly.

claire-voie [klɛrvwa] ▶ **à claire-voie** *loc adv* openwork (*avant n*).

clairière [klɛrjɛr] *nf* clearing.

clairon [klɛrɔ̃] *nm* bugle.

claironner [klɛrɔne] *vt fig* (*crier*): **~ qqch** to shout sthg from the rooftops.

clairsemé, -e [klɛrsəme] *adj* (*cheveux*) thin; (*arbres*) scattered; (*population*) sparse.

clairvoyant, -e [klɛrvwajɑ̃, ɑ̃t] *adj* perceptive.

clamer [klame] *vt* to proclaim.

clameur [klamœr] *nf* clamour.

clan [klɑ̃] *nm* clan.

clandestin, -e [klɑ̃dɛstɛ̃, in] ◆ *adj* (*journal, commerce*) clandestine; (*activité*) covert. ◆ *nm, f* (*étranger*) illegal immigrant OU alien; (*voyageur*) stowaway.

clapier [klapje] *nm* (*à lapins*) hutch.

clapoter [klapɔte] *vi* (*vagues*) to lap.

claquage [klakaʒ] *nm* (MÉD) strain; **se faire un ~** to pull OU to strain a muscle.

claque [klak] *nf* **1.** (*gifle*) slap. **2.** (THÉÂTRE) claque.

claquer [klake] ◆ *vt* **1.** (*fermer*) to slam. **2. faire ~** (*langue*) to click; (*doigts*) to snap; (*fouet*) to crack. **3.** *fam* (*gifler*) to slap. **4.** *fam* (*dépenser*) to blow. ◆ *vi* (*porte, volet*) to bang.

claquettes [klakɛt] *nfpl* (*danse*) tap dancing (U).

clarifier [klarifje] *vt litt & fig* to clarify.

clarinette [klarinɛt] *nf* (*instrument*) clarinet.

clarté [klarte] nf 1. (lumière) brightness. 2. (netteté) clarity.

classe [klas] nf 1. (gén) class; **voyager en première/seconde ~** to travel first/second class; **~ touriste** economy class. 2. (SCOL): **aller en ~** to go to school; **~ de mer** seaside trip (with school); **~ de neige** skiing trip (with school); **~ verte** field trip (with school). 3. (MIL) rank. 4. loc: **faire ses ~s** (MIL) to do one's training.

CLASSE VERTE/DE MER/DE NEIGE

In France schools organize trips for one or two weeks to the countryside, to the seaside, or to go skiing. As well as offering sporting activities, they are intended to encourage children to explore their environment and mix with the local people.

classé, -e [klase] adj (monument) listed.

classement [klasmã] nm 1. (rangement) filing. 2. (classification) classification. 3. (rang - SCOL) position; (- SPORT) placing. 4. (liste - SCOL) class list; (- SPORT) final placings (pl).

classer [klase] vt 1. (ranger) to file. 2. (plantes, animaux) to classify. 3. (cataloguer): **~ qqn (parmi)** to label sb (as). 4. (attribuer un rang à) to rank. ► **se classer** vp to be classed, to rank; **se ~ troisième** to come third.

classeur [klasœr] nm 1. (meuble) filing cabinet. 2. (d'écolier) ring binder.

classification [klasifikasjõ] nf classification.

classique [klasik] ◆ nm 1. (auteur) classical author. 2. (œuvre) classic. ◆ adj 1. (ART & MUS) classical. 2. (sobre) classic. 3. (habituel) classic; **ça c'est l'histoire ~!** it's the usual story!

clause [kloz] nf clause.

claustrophobie [klostrofobi] nf claustrophobia.

clavecin [klavsẽ] nm harpsichord.

clavicule [klavikyl] nf collarbone.

clavier [klavje] nm keyboard.

clé, clef [kle] ◆ nf 1. (gén) key; **la ~ du mystère** the key to the mystery; **mettre qqn/qqch sous ~** to lock sb/sthg up; **~ de contact** (AUTOM) ignition key. 2. (outil): **~ anglaise ou à molette** adjustable spanner Br ou wrench Am, monkey wrench. 3. (MUS) (signe) clef; **~ de sol/fa** treble/bass clef. ◆ adj: **industrie/rôle ~** key industry/role. ► **clé de voûte** nf litt & fig keystone.

clément, -e [klemã, ãt] adj 1. (indul-gent) lenient. 2. fig (température) mild.

clémentine [klemãtin] nf clementine.

cleptomane = **kleptomane**.

clerc [kler] nm (assistant) clerk.

clergé [klerʒe] nm clergy.

cliché [kliʃe] nm 1. (PHOT) negative. 2. (banalité) cliché.

client, -e [klijã, ãt] nm, f 1. (de notaire, d'agence) client; (de médecin) patient. 2. (acheteur) customer. 3. (habitué) regular (customer).

clientèle [klijãtel] nf 1. (ensemble des clients) customers (pl); (de profession libérale) clientele. 2. (fait d'être client): **accorder sa ~ à** to give one's custom to.

cligner [kliɲe] vi: **~ de l'œil** to wink; **~ des yeux** to blink.

clignotant, -e [kliɲɔtã, ãt] adj (lumière) flickering. ► **clignotant** nm (AUTOM) indicator.

clignoter [kliɲɔte] vi 1. (yeux) to blink. 2. (lumière) to flicker.

climat [klima] nm litt & fig climate.

climatique [klimatik] adj climatic.

climatisation [klimatizasjõ] nf air-conditioning.

climatisé, -e [klimatize] adj air-conditioned.

clin [klẽ] ► **clin d'œil** nm: **faire un ~ d'œil (à)** to wink (at); **en un ~ d'œil** in a flash.

clinique [klinik] ◆ nf clinic. ◆ adj clinical.

clip [klip] nm 1. (vidéo) pop video. 2. (boucle d'oreilles) clip-on earring.

cliquer [klike] vi (INFORM) to click.

cliqueter [klikte] vi 1. (pièces, clés, chaînes) to jingle, to jangle. 2. (verres) to clink.

clivage [klivaʒ] nm fig (division) division.

clochard, -e [kloʃar, ard] nm, f tramp.

cloche [kloʃ] ◆ nf 1. (d'église) bell. 2. fam (idiot) idiot, clot Br. ◆ adj fam: **ce qu'elle peut être ~, celle-là!** she can be a right idiot!

cloche-pied [kloʃpje] ► **à cloche-pied** loc adv hopping; **sauter à ~** to hop.

clocher [kloʃe] nm (d'église) church tower.

clochette [kloʃet] nf 1. (petite cloche) (little) bell. 2. (de fleur) bell.

clodo [klodo] nmf fam tramp.

cloison [klwazõ] nf (mur) partition.

cloisonner [klwazone] vt (pièce, maison) to partition (off); fig to compartmentalize.

cloître [klwatr] nm cloister.

clopiner [klɔpine] *vi* to hobble along.

cloporte [klɔpɔrt] *nm* woodlouse.

cloque [klɔk] *nf* blister.

clore [klɔr] *vt* to close; (*négociations*) to conclude.

clos, -e [klo, kloz] ◆ *pp* → **clore**. ◆ *adj* closed.

clôture [klotyr] *nf* **1.** (*haie*) hedge; (*de fil de fer*) fence. **2.** (*fermeture*) closing, closure. **3.** (*fin*) end, conclusion.

clôturer [klotyre] *vt* **1.** (*terrain*) to enclose. **2.** (*négociation*) to close, to conclude.

clou [klu] *nm* **1.** (*pointe*) nail; ~ **de girofle** (CULIN) clove. **2.** (*attraction*) highlight.

clouer [klue] *vt* (*fixer - couvercle, planche*) to nail (down); (- *tableau, caisse*) to nail (up); *fig* (*immobiliser*): **rester cloué sur place** to be rooted to the spot.

clouté, -e [klute] *adj* (*vêtement*) studded.

clown [klun] *nm* clown; **faire le ~** to clown around, to act the fool.

club [klœb] *nm* club.

cm (*abr de* **centimètre**) cm.

CM *nm* (*abr de* **cours moyen**): **~1** *fourth year of primary school;* **~2** *fifth year of primary school.*

CNAM [knam] (*abr de* **Conservatoire national des arts et métiers**) *nm science and technology school in Paris.*

CNRS (*abr de* **Centre national de la recherche scientifique**) *nm national scientific research organization.*

coaguler [kɔagyle] *vi* **1.** (*sang*) to clot. **2.** (*lait*) to curdle.

coalition [kɔalisjɔ̃] *nf* coalition.

coasser [kɔase] *vi* (*grenouille*) to croak.

cobaye [kɔbaj] *nm litt & fig* guinea pig.

cobra [kɔbra] *nm* cobra.

Coca® [kɔka] *nm* (*boisson*) Coke®.

cocaïne [kɔkain] *nf* cocaine.

cocaïnomane [kokainɔman] *nmf* cocaine addict.

cocarde [kɔkard] *nf* **1.** (*insigne*) roundel. **2.** (*distinction*) rosette.

cocardier, -ère [kɔkardje, ɛr] *adj* (*chauvin*) jingoistic.

cocasse [kɔkas] *adj* funny.

coccinelle [kɔksinɛl] *nf* **1.** (*insecte*) ladybird *Br*, ladybug *Am*. **2.** (*voiture*) Beetle.

coccyx [kɔksis] *nm* coccyx.

cocher¹ [kɔʃe] *nm* coachman.

cocher² [kɔʃe] *vt* to tick (off) *Br*, to check (off) *Am*.

cochon, -onne [kɔʃɔ̃, ɔn] ◆ *adj* dirty, smutty. ◆ *nm, f fam péj* pig; **un tour de ~**

a dirty trick. ▶ **cochon** *nm* pig.

cochonnerie [kɔʃɔnri] *nf fam* **1.** (*nourriture*) muck (U). **2.** (*chose*) rubbish (U). **3.** (*saleté*) mess (U). **4.** (*obscénité*) dirty joke, smut (U).

cochonnet [kɔʃɔnɛ] *nm* (JEU) jack.

cocktail [kɔktɛl] *nm* **1.** (*réception*) cocktail party. **2.** (*boisson*) cocktail. **3.** *fig* (*mélange*) mixture.

coco [kɔko] *nm* **1.** → **noix**. **2.** *péj* (*communiste*) commie.

cocon [kɔkɔ̃] *nm* (ZOOL & *fig*) cocoon.

cocorico [kɔkɔriko] *nm* (*du coq*) cock-a-doodle-doo.

cocotier [kɔkɔtje] *nm* coconut tree.

cocotte [kɔkɔt] *nf* **1.** (*marmite*) casserole (dish). **2.** (*poule*) hen. **3.** *péj* (*courtisane*) tart.

Cocotte-Minute® [kɔkɔtminyt] *nf* pressure cooker.

cocu, -e [kɔky] *nm, f & adj fam* cuckold.

code [kɔd] *nm* **1.** (*gén*) code; ~ **barres** bar code; ~ **pénal** penal code; ~ **postal** postcode *Br*, zip code *Am*; ~ **de la route** highway code; ~ **secret** (*pour carte de crédit*) PIN number. **2.** (*phares*) dipped headlights (*pl*).

coder [kɔde] *vt* to code.

coefficient [kɔefisjɑ̃] *nm* coefficient.

coéquipier, -ère [kɔekipje, ɛr] *nm, f* teammate.

cœur [kœr] *nm* heart; **au ~ de l'hiver** in the depths of winter; **au ~ de l'été** at the height of summer; **de bon ~** willingly; **de tout son ~** with all one's heart; **apprendre par ~** to learn by heart; **avoir bon ~** to be kind-hearted; **avoir un coup de ~ pour qqch** to fall in love with sthg; **avoir mal au ~** to feel sick; **s'en donner à ~ joie** (*prendre beaucoup de plaisir*) to have a whale of a time; **soulever le ~ à qqn** to make sb feel sick; **ça me tient à ~** it's close to my heart.

coexister [kɔɛgziste] *vi* to coexist.

coffre [kɔfr] *nm* **1.** (*meuble*) chest. **2.** (*de voiture*) boot *Br*, trunk *Am*. **3.** (*coffre-fort*) safe.

coffre-fort [kɔfrəfɔr] *nm* safe.

coffret [kɔfrɛ] *nm* **1.** (*petit coffre*) casket; ~ **à bijoux** jewellery box. **2.** (*de disques*) boxed set.

cogner [kɔɲe] *vi* **1.** (*heurter*) to bang. **2.** *fam* (*donner des coups*) to hit. **3.** (*soleil*) to beat down. ▶ **se cogner** *vp* (*se heurter*) to bump o.s.; **se ~ à** OU **contre qqch** to bump into sthg; **se ~ la tête/le genou** to hit one's head/knee.

cohabiter [kɔabite] *vi* **1.** (*habiter ensem-*

collier

ble) to live together. **2.** (POLIT) to cohabit.

cohérence [kɔerɑ̃s] *nf* consistency, coherence.

cohérent, -e [kɔerɑ̃, ɑ̃t] *adj* **1.** (*logique*) consistent, coherent. **2.** (*unifié*) coherent.

cohésion [kɔezjɔ̃] *nf* cohesion.

cohorte [kɔɔrt] *nf* (*groupe*) troop.

cohue [kɔy] *nf* **1.** (*foule*) crowd. **2.** (*bousculade*) crush.

coi, coite [kwa, kwat] *adj*: **rester ~ sout** to remain silent.

coiffe [kwaf] *nf* headdress.

coiffé, -e [kwafe] *adj*: **être bien/mal ~** to have tidy/untidy hair; **être ~ d'une casquette** to be wearing a cap.

coiffer [kwafe] *vt* **1.** (*mettre sur la tête*): **~ qqn de qqch** to put sthg on sb's head. **2.** (*les cheveux*): **~ qqn** to do sb's hair. ▶ **se coiffer** *vp* **1.** (*les cheveux*) to do one's hair. **2.** (*mettre sur sa tête*): **se ~ de** to wear, to put on.

coiffeur, -euse [kwafœr, øz] *nm, f* hairdresser. ▶ **coiffeuse** *nf* (*meuble*) dressing table.

coiffure [kwafyr] *nf* **1.** (*chapeau*) hat. **2.** (*cheveux*) hairstyle.

coin [kwɛ̃] *nm* **1.** (*angle*) corner; **au ~ du feu** by the fireside; **au ~ de la rue** on the street corner. **2.** (*parcelle, endroit*) place, spot; **dans le ~** in the area; **un ~ de ciel bleu** a patch of blue sky; **~ cuisine** kitchen area; **le petit ~** *fam* the little boys'/girls' room. **3.** (*outil*) wedge.

coincer [kwɛ̃se] *vt* **1.** (*bloquer*) to jam. **2.** *fam* (*prendre*) to nab; *fig* to catch out. **3.** (*acculer*) to corner, to trap.

coïncidence [kɔɛ̃sidɑ̃s] *nf* coincidence.

coïncider [kɔɛ̃side] *vi* to coincide.

coing [kwɛ̃] *nm* (*fruit*) quince.

coït [kɔit] *nm* coitus.

col [kɔl] *nm* **1.** (*de vêtement*) collar; **~ roulé** polo neck Br, turtleneck Am. **2.** (*partie étroite*) neck. **3.** (ANAT): **~ du fémur** neck of the thighbone ou femur; **~ de l'utérus** cervix, neck of the womb. **4.** (GÉOGR) pass.

coléoptère [kɔleɔptɛr] *nm* beetle.

colère [kɔlɛr] *nf* **1.** (*irritation*) anger; **être/se mettre en ~** to be/get angry. **2.** (*accès d'humeur*) fit of anger ou rage; **piquer une ~** to fly into a rage.

coléreux, -euse [kɔlerø, øz], **colérique** [kɔlerik] *adj* (*tempérament*) fiery; (*personne*) quick-tempered.

colimaçon [kɔlimasɔ̃] ▶ **en coli-**

maçon *loc adv* spiral.

colique [kɔlik] *nf* **1.** (*gén pl*) (*douleur*) colic (U). **2.** (*diarrhée*) diarrhoea.

colis [kɔli] *nm* parcel.

collaborateur, -trice [kɔlabɔratœr, tris] *nm, f* **1.** (*employé*) colleague. **2.** (HIST) collaborator.

collaboration [kɔlabɔrasjɔ̃] *nf* collaboration.

collaborer [kɔlabɔre] *vi* **1.** (*coopérer, sous l'Occupation*) to collaborate. **2.** (*participer*): **~ à** to contribute to.

collant, -e [kɔlɑ̃, ɑ̃t] *adj* **1.** (*substance*) sticky. **2.** *fam* (*personne*) clinging, clingy. ▶ **collant** *nm* tights (*pl*) Br, panty hose (*pl*) Am.

colle [kɔl] *nf* **1.** (*substance*) glue. **2.** (*question*) poser. **3.** (SCOL - *interrogation*) test; (- *retenue*) detention.

collecte [kɔlɛkt] *nf* collection.

collectif, -ive [kɔlɛktif, iv] *adj* **1.** (*responsabilité, travail*) collective. **2.** (*billet, voyage*) group (*avant n*). ▶ **collectif** *nm* **1.** (*équipe*) team. **2.** (LING) collective noun. **3.** (FIN): **~ budgétaire** collection of budgetary measures.

collection [kɔlɛksjɔ̃] *nf* **1.** (*d'objets, livres, de vêtements*) collection; **faire la ~ de** to collect. **2.** (COMM) line.

collectionner [kɔlɛksjɔne] *vt litt & fig* to collect.

collectionneur, -euse [kɔlɛksjɔnœr, øz] *nm, f* collector.

collectivité [kɔlɛktivite] *nf* community; **les ~s locales** (ADMIN) the local communities.

collège [kɔlɛʒ] *nm* **1.** (SCOL) ≃ secondary school. **2.** (*de personnes*) college.

collégien, -enne [kɔleʒjɛ̃, ɛn] *nm, f* schoolboy (*f* schoolgirl).

collègue [kɔlɛg] *nmf* colleague.

coller [kɔle] ◆ *vt* **1.** (*fixer - affiche*) to stick (up); (- *timbre*) to stick. **2.** (*appuyer*) to press. **3.** *fam* (*mettre*) to stick, to dump. **4.** (SCOL) to give (a) detention to, to keep behind. ◆ *vi* **1.** (*adhérer*) to stick. **2.** (*être adapté*): **~ à qqch** (*vêtement*) to cling to sthg; *fig* to fit in with sthg, to adhere to sthg. ▶ **se coller** *vp* (*se plaquer*): **se ~ contre qqn/qqch** to press o.s. against sb/sthg.

collerette [kɔlrɛt] *nf* (*de vêtement*) ruff.

collet [kɔlɛ] *nm* **1.** (*de vêtement*) collar; **être ~ monté** (*affecté, guindé*) to be straitlaced. **2.** (*piège*) snare.

collier [kɔlje] *nm* **1.** (*bijou*) necklace. **2.** (*d'animal*) collar. **3.** (*barbe*) fringe of beard along the jawline.

colline [kɔlin] *nf* hill.

collision [kɔlizjɔ̃] *nf* (*choc*) collision, crash; **entrer en ~ avec** to collide with.

colloque [kɔlɔk] *nm* colloquium.

colmater [kɔlmate] *vt* 1. (*fuite*) to plug, to seal off. 2. (*brèche*) to fill, to seal.

colombe [kɔlɔ̃b] *nf* dove.

Colombie [kɔlɔ̃bi] *nf*: **la ~** Colombia.

colon [kɔlɔ̃] *nm* settler.

côlon [kolɔ̃] *nm* colon.

colonel [kɔlɔnɛl] *nm* colonel.

colonial, -e, -aux [kɔlɔnjal, o] *adj* colonial.

colonialisme [kɔlɔnjalism] *nm* colonialism.

colonie [kɔlɔni] *nf* 1. (*territoire*) colony. 2. (*d'expatriés*) community; **~ de vacances** holiday *Br* ou vacation *Am* camp (*for children*).

colonisation [kɔlɔnizasjɔ̃] *nf* colonization.

coloniser [kɔlɔnize] *vt litt & fig* to colonize.

colonne [kɔlɔn] *nf* column. ► **colonne vertébrale** *nf* spine, spinal column.

colorant, -e [kɔlɔrɑ̃, ɑ̃t] *adj* colouring. ► **colorant** *nm* colouring.

coloré, -e [kɔlɔre] *adj* 1. (*de couleur*) coloured. 2. (*imagé*) colourful.

colorer [kɔlɔre] *vt* (*teindre*) to colour.

colorier [kɔlɔrje] *vt* to colour in.

coloris [kɔlɔri] *nm* shade.

colorisation [kɔlɔrizasjɔ̃] *nf* (CIN) colourization.

coloriser [kɔlɔrize] *vt* (CIN) to colourize.

colossal, -e, -aux [kɔlɔsal, o] *adj* colossal, huge.

colporter [kɔlpɔrte] *vt* (*marchandise*) to hawk; (*information*) to spread.

coma [kɔma] *nm* coma; **être dans le ~** to be in a coma.

comateux, -euse [kɔmatø, øz] *adj* comatose.

combat [kɔ̃ba] *nm* 1. (*bataille*) battle, fight. 2. *fig* (*lutte*) struggle. 3. (SPORT) fight.

combatif, -ive [kɔ̃batif, iv] *adj* (*humeur*) fighting (*avant n*); (*troupes*) willing to fight.

combattant, -e [kɔ̃batɑ̃, ɑ̃t] *nm, f* (*en guerre*) combatant; (*dans bagarre*) fighter; **ancien ~** veteran.

combattre [kɔ̃batr] ♦ *vt litt & fig* to fight (against). ♦ *vi* to fight.

combattu, -e [kɔ̃baty] *pp* → **combattre**.

combien [kɔ̃bjɛ̃] ♦ *conj* how much; **~ de** (*nombre*) how many; (*quantité*) how much;

~ de temps? how long?; **ça fait ~?** (*prix*) how much is that?; (*longueur, hauteur etc*) how long/high *etc* is it? ♦ *adv* how (much). ♦ *nm inv*: **le ~ sommes-nous?** what date is it?; **tous les ~?** how often?

combinaison [kɔ̃binɛzɔ̃] *nf* 1. (*d'éléments*) combination. 2. (*de femme*) slip. 3. (*vêtement - de mécanicien*) boiler suit *Br*, overalls (*pl*) *Br*, overall *Am*; (*- de ski*) ski suit. 4. (*de coffre*) combination.

combine [kɔ̃bin] *nf fam* trick.

combiné [kɔ̃bine] *nm* receiver.

combiner [kɔ̃bine] *vt* 1. (*arranger*) to combine. 2. (*organiser*) to devise. ► **se combiner** *vp* to turn out.

comble [kɔ̃bl] ♦ *nm* height; **c'est un** ou **le ~!** that beats everything! ♦ *adj* packed. ► **combles** *nmpl* attic (*sg*), loft (*sg*).

combler [kɔ̃ble] *vt* 1. (*gâter*): **~ qqn de** to shower sb with. 2. (*boucher*) to fill in. 3. (*déficit*) to make good; (*lacune*) to fill.

combustible [kɔ̃bystibl] ♦ *nm* fuel. ♦ *adj* combustible.

combustion [kɔ̃bystjɔ̃] *nf* combustion.

comédie [kɔmedi] *nf* 1. (CIN & THÉÂTRE) comedy; **~ musicale** musical. 2. (*complication*) palaver.

comédien, -enne [kɔmedjɛ̃, ɛn] *nm, f* (*acteur*) actor (*f* actress); *fig & péj* sham.

comestible [kɔmɛstibl] *adj* edible.

comète [kɔmɛt] *nf* comet.

comique [kɔmik] ♦ *nm* (THÉÂTRE) comic actor. ♦ *adj* 1. (*style*) comic. 2. (*drôle*) comical, funny.

comité [kɔmite] *nm* committee; **~ d'entreprise** works council (*also organizing leisure activities*).

commandant [kɔmɑ̃dɑ̃] *nm* commander.

commande [kɔmɑ̃d] *nf* 1. (*de marchandises*) order; **passer une ~** to place an order; **sur ~** to order; **disponible sur ~** available on request. 2. (TECHNOL) control. 3. (INFORM) command; **~ numérique** digital control.

commander [kɔmɑ̃de] ♦ *vt* 1. (MIL) to command. 2. (*contrôler*) to operate, to control. 3. (COMM) to order. ♦ *vi* to be in charge; **~ à qqn de faire qqch** to order sb to do sthg.

commanditer [kɔmɑ̃dite] *vt* 1. (*entreprise*) to finance. 2. (*meurtre*) to put up the money for.

commando [kɔmɑ̃do] *nm* commando (unit).

comme [kɔm] ♦ *conj* 1. (*introduisant une*

comparaison) like; **il sera médecin ~ son père** he'll become a doctor (just like his father. **2.** (*exprimant la manière*) as; **fais ~ il te plaira** do as you wish; **~ prévu/convenu** as planned/agreed; **~ bon vous semble** as you think best; **~ ci ~ ça** *fam* so-so. **3.** (*tel que*) like, such as; **les arbres ~ le marronnier** trees such as ou like the chestnut. **4.** (*en tant que*) as. **5.** (*ainsi que*): **les filles ~ les garçons iront jouer au foot** both girls and boys will play football; **l'un ~ l'autre sont très gentils** the one is as kind as the other, they are equally kind. **6.** (*introduisant une cause*) as, since; **~ il pleuvait nous sommes rentrés** as it was raining we went back. ◆ *adv* (*marquant l'intensité*) how; **~ tu as grandi!** how you've grown!; **~ c'est difficile!** it's so difficult!; **regarde ~ il nage bien!** (just) look what a good swimmer he is!, (just) look how well he swims!

commémoration [kɔmemɔrasjɔ̃] *nf* commemoration.

commémorer [kɔmemɔre] *vt* to commemorate.

commencement [kɔmãsmã] *nm* beginning, start.

commencer [kɔmãse] ◆ *vt* (*entreprendre*) to begin, to start; (*être au début de*) to begin. ◆ *vi* to start, to begin; **~ à faire qqch** to begin ou start to do sthg, to begin ou start doing sthg; **~ par faire qqch** to begin ou start by doing sthg.

comment [kɔmã] ◆ *adv* how; **~?** what?; **~ ça va?** how are you?; **~ cela?** how come? ◆ *nm inv* → **pourquoi**.

commentaire [kɔmãtɛr] *nm* **1.** (*explication*) commentary. **2.** (*observation*) comment.

commentateur, -trice [kɔmãtatœr, tris] *nm, f* (RADIO & TÉLÉ) commentator.

commenter [kɔmãte] *vt* to comment on.

commérage [kɔmeraʒ] *nm péj* gossip (U).

commerçant, -e [kɔmɛrsã, ãt] ◆ *adj* (*rue*) shopping (*avant n*); (*quartier*) commercial; (*personne*) business-minded. ◆ *nm, f* shopkeeper.

commerce [kɔmɛrs] *nm* **1.** (*achat et vente*) commerce, trade; **~ de gros/détail** wholesale/retail trade; **~ extérieur** foreign trade. **2.** (*magasin*) business; **le petit ~** small shopkeepers (*pl*).

commercial, -e, -aux [kɔmɛrsjal, o] ◆ *adj* (*entreprise, valeur*) commercial; (*politique*) trade (*avant n*). ◆ *nm, f* mar-

keting man (*f* woman).

commercialiser [kɔmɛrsjalize] *vt* to market.

commère [kɔmɛr] *nf péj* gossip.

commettre [kɔmɛtr] *vt* to commit.

commis, -e [kɔmi, iz] *pp* → **commettre**. ▶ **commis** *nm* assistant; **~ voyageur** commercial traveller.

commisération [kɔmizerasjɔ̃] *nf sout* commiseration.

commissaire [kɔmisɛr] *nm* commissioner; **~ de police** (police) superintendent *Br*, (police) captain *Am*.

commissaire-priseur [kɔmiser-prizœr] *nm* auctioneer.

commissariat [kɔmisarja] *nm*: **~ de police** police station.

commission [kɔmisjɔ̃] *nf* **1.** (*délégation*) commission, committee. **2.** (*message*) message. **3.** (*rémunération*) commission. ▶ **commissions** *nfpl* shopping (U); **faire les ~s** to do the shopping.

commissure [kɔmisyr] *nf*: **la ~ des lèvres** the corner of the mouth.

commode [kɔmɔd] ◆ *nf* chest of drawers. ◆ *adj* **1.** (*pratique - système*) convenient; (- *outil*) handy. **2.** (*aimable*): **pas ~** awkward.

commodité [kɔmɔdite] *nf* convenience.

commotion [kɔmɔsjɔ̃] *nf* (MÉD) shock; **~ cérébrale** concussion.

commuer [kɔmɥe] *vt*: **~ qqch en** to commute sthg to.

commun, -e [kɔmœ̃, yn] *adj* **1.** (*gén*) common; (- *décision, effort*) joint; (- *salle*) shared; **avoir qqch en ~** to have sthg in common. **2.** (*courant*) usual, common. ▶ **commune** *nf* town.

communal, -e, -aux [kɔmynal, o] *adj* (*école*) local; (*bâtiments*) council (*avant n*).

communauté [kɔmynote] *nf* **1.** (*groupe*) community. **2.** (*de sentiments, d'idées*) identity. **3.** (POL): **la Communauté européenne** the European Community.

commune → **commun**.

communément [kɔmynemã] *adv* commonly.

communiant, -e [kɔmynjã, ãt] *nm, f* communicant; **premier ~** child taking first communion.

communication [kɔmynikasjɔ̃] *nf* **1.** (*gén*) communication. **2.** (TÉLÉCOM): **~ (téléphonique)** (phone) call; **être en ~ avec qqn** to be talking to sb; **obtenir la ~** to get through; **~ interurbaine** long-distance (phone) call.

communier [kɔmynje] *vi* (RELIG) to

take communion.

communion [kɔmynjɔ̃] *nf* (RELIG) communion.

communiqué [kɔmynike] *nm* communiqué; ~ **de presse** press release.

communiquer [kɔmynike] *vt*: ~ **qqch à** (*information, sentiment*) to pass on ou communicate sthg to; (*chaleur*) to transmit sthg to.

communisme [kɔmynism] *nm* communism.

communiste [kɔmynist] *nmf & adj* communist.

commutateur [kɔmytatœr] *nm* switch.

compact, -e [kɔ̃pakt] *adj* 1. (*épais, dense*) dense. 2. (*petit*) compact. ▶ **compact** *nm* (*disque laser*) compact disc, CD.

compagne → **compagnon**.

compagnie [kɔ̃paɲi] *nf* 1. (*gén & COMM*) company; **tenir ~ à qqn** to keep sb company; **en ~ de** in the company of. 2. (*assemblée*) gathering.

compagnon [kɔ̃paɲɔ̃], **compagne** [kɔ̃paɲ] *nm, f* companion. ▶ **compagnon** *nm* (HIST) journeyman.

comparable [kɔ̃parabl] *adj* comparable.

comparaison [kɔ̃parɛzɔ̃] *nf* (*parallèle*) comparison; **en ~ de, par ~ avec** compared with, in ou by comparison with.

comparaître [kɔ̃parɛtr] *vi* (JUR): ~ (**devant**) to appear (before).

comparatif, -ive [kɔ̃paratif, iv] *adj* comparative.

comparé, -e [kɔ̃pare] *adj* comparative; (*mérites*) relative.

comparer [kɔ̃pare] *vt* 1. (*confronter*): ~ (**avec**) to compare (with). 2. (*assimiler*): ~ **qqch à** to compare ou liken sthg to.

comparse [kɔ̃pars] *nmf péj* stooge.

compartiment [kɔ̃partimɑ̃] *nm* compartment.

comparu, -e [kɔ̃pary] *pp* → **comparaître**.

comparution [kɔ̃parysjɔ̃] *nf* (JUR) appearance.

compas [kɔ̃pa] *nm* 1. (*de dessin*) pair of compasses, compasses (*pl*). 2. (NAVIG) compass.

compassion [kɔ̃pasjɔ̃] *nf sout* compassion.

compatible [kɔ̃patibl] *adj*: ~ (**avec**) compatible (with).

compatir [kɔ̃patir] *vi*: ~ (**à**) to sympathize (with).

compatriote [kɔ̃patrijɔt] *nmf* compatriot, fellow countryman (*f* countrywoman).

compensation [kɔ̃pɑ̃sasjɔ̃] *nf* (*dédommagement*) compensation.

compensé, -e [kɔ̃pɑ̃se] *adj* built-up.

compenser [kɔ̃pɑ̃se] *vt* to compensate ou make up for.

compétence [kɔ̃petɑ̃s] *nf* 1. (*qualification*) skill, ability. 2. (JUR) competence; **cela n'entre pas dans mes ~s** that's outside my scope.

compétent, -e [kɔ̃petɑ̃, ɑ̃t] *adj* 1. (*capable*) capable, competent. 2. (ADMIN & JUR) competent; **les autorités ~es** the relevant authorities.

compétitif, -ive [kɔ̃petitif, iv] *adj* competitive.

compétition [kɔ̃petisjɔ̃] *nf* competition; **faire de la ~** to go in for competitive sport.

complainte [kɔ̃plɛ̃t] *nf* lament.

complaisant, -e [kɔ̃plɛzɑ̃, ɑ̃t] *adj* 1. (*aimable*) obliging, kind. 2. (*indulgent*) indulgent.

complément [kɔ̃plemɑ̃] *nm* 1. (*gén & GRAM*) complement. 2. (*reste*) remainder.

complémentaire [kɔ̃plemɑ̃tɛr] *adj* 1. (*supplémentaire*) supplementary. 2. (*caractères, couleurs*) complementary.

complet, -ète [kɔ̃plɛ, ɛt] *adj* 1. (*gén*) complete. 2. (*plein*) full. ▶ **complet(-veston)** *nm* suit.

complètement [kɔ̃plɛtmɑ̃] *adv* 1. (*vraiment*) absolutely, totally. 2. (*entièrement*) completely.

compléter [kɔ̃plete] *vt* (*gén*) to complete, to complement; (*somme d'argent*) to make up.

complexe [kɔ̃plɛks] ◆ *nm* 1. (PSYCHOL) complex; ~ **d'infériorité/de supériorité** inferiority/superiority complex. 2. (*ensemble*) complex. ◆ *adj* complex, complicated.

complexé, -e [kɔ̃plɛkse] *adj* hung up, mixed up.

complexifier [kɔ̃plɛksifje] *vt* to make (more) complex.

complexité [kɔ̃plɛksite] *nf* complexity.

complication [kɔ̃plikasjɔ̃] *nf* intricacy, complexity. ▶ **complications** *nfpl* complications.

complice [kɔ̃plis] ◆ *nmf* accomplice. ◆ *adj* (*sourire, regard, air*) knowing.

complicité [kɔ̃plisite] *nf* complicity.

compliment [kɔ̃plimɑ̃] *nm* compliment.

complimenter [kɔ̃plimɑ̃te] vt to compliment.

compliqué, -e [kɔ̃plike] adj (problème) complex, complicated; (personne) complicated.

compliquer [kɔ̃plike] vt to complicate.

complot [kɔ̃plo] nm plot.

comploter [kɔ̃plɔte] vt & vi litt & fig to plot.

comportement [kɔ̃pɔrtəmɑ̃] nm behaviour.

comportemental, -e, -aux [kɔ̃pɔrtəmɑ̃tal, o] adj behavioural.

comporter [kɔ̃pɔrte] vt 1. (contenir) to include, to contain. 2. (être composé de) to consist of, to be made up of. ▶ **se comporter** vp to behave.

composant, -e [kɔ̃pozɑ̃, ɑ̃t] adj constituent, component. ▶ **composant** nm component. ▶ **composante** nf component.

composé, -e [kɔ̃poze] adj compound. ▶ **composé** nm 1. (mélange) combination. 2. (CHIM & LING) compound.

composer [kɔ̃poze] ◆ vt 1. (constituer) to make up, to form. 2. (créer - musique) to compose, to write. 3. (numéro de téléphone) to dial; (code) to key in. ◆ vi to compromise. ▶ **se composer** vp (être constitué): **se ~ de** to be composed of, to be made up of.

composite [kɔ̃pozit] adj 1. (disparate - mobilier) assorted, of various types; (- foule) heterogeneous. 2. (matériau) composite.

compositeur, -trice [kɔ̃pozitœr, tris] nm, f 1. (MUS) composer. 2. (TYPO) typesetter.

composition [kɔ̃pozisjɔ̃] nf 1. (gén) composition; (de roman) writing, composition. 2. (SCOL) test. 3. (caractère): **être de bonne ~** to be good-natured.

composter [kɔ̃pɔste] vt (ticket, billet) to date-stamp.

compote [kɔ̃pɔt] nf compote; **~ de pommes** stewed apple.

compréhensible [kɔ̃preɑ̃sibl] adj (texte, parole) comprehensible; fig (réaction) understandable.

compréhensif, -ive [kɔ̃preɑ̃sif, iv] adj understanding.

compréhension [kɔ̃preɑ̃sjɔ̃] nf 1. (de texte) comprehension, understanding. 2. (indulgence) understanding.

comprendre [kɔ̃prɑ̃dr] vt 1. (gén) to understand; **je comprends!** I see!; **se faire ~** to make o.s. understood; **mal ~** to misunderstand. 2. (comporter) to

comprise, to consist of. 3. (inclure) to include.

compresse [kɔ̃prɛs] nf compress.

compresseur [kɔ̃presœr] → **rouleau**.

compression [kɔ̃presjɔ̃] nf (de gaz) compression; fig cutback, reduction.

comprimé, -e [kɔ̃prime] adj compressed. ▶ **comprimé** nm tablet; **~ effervescent** effervescent tablet.

comprimer [kɔ̃prime] vt 1. (gaz, vapeur) to compress. 2. (personnes): **être comprimés dans** to be packed into.

compris, -e [kɔ̃pri, iz] ◆ pp → **comprendre**. ◆ adj 1. (situé) lying, contained. 2. (inclus): **charges (non) ~es** (not) including bills, bills (not) included; **tout ~** all inclusive, all in; **y ~** including.

compromettre [kɔ̃prɔmetr] vt to compromise.

compromis, -e [kɔ̃prɔmi, iz] pp → **compromettre**. ▶ **compromis** nm compromise.

compromission [kɔ̃prɔmisjɔ̃] nf péj base action.

comptabilité [kɔ̃tabilite] nf (comptes) accounts (pl); (service): **la ~** accounts, the accounts department.

comptable [kɔ̃tabl] nmf accountant.

comptant [kɔ̃tɑ̃] adv: **payer** ou **régler ~** to pay cash. ▶ **au comptant** loc adv: **payer au ~** to pay cash.

compte [kɔ̃t] nm 1. (action) count, counting (U); (total) number; **faire le ~ (de)** to add up; **~ à rebours** countdown. 2. (BANQUE, COMM & COMPTABILITÉ) account; **ouvrir un ~** to open an account; **~ bancaire** ou **en banque** bank account; **~ courant** current account, checking account Am; **~ créditeur** account in credit; **~ débiteur** overdrawn account; **~ de dépôt** deposit account; **~ d'épargne** savings account; **~ d'exploitation** operating account; **~ postal** post office account. 3. loc: **avoir son ~** to have had enough; **être/se mettre à son ~** to be/become self-employed; **prendre qqch en ~, tenir ~ de qqch** to take sthg into account; **se rendre ~ de qqch** to realize sthg; **s'en tirer à bon ~** to get off lightly; **tout ~ fait** all things considered. ▶ **comptes** nmpl accounts; **faire ses ~s** to do one's accounts.

compte-chèques, compte chèques [kɔ̃tʃɛk] nm current account, checking account Am.

compte-gouttes [kɔ̃tgut] nm inv dropper.

compter [kɔ̃te] ◆ vt 1. (dénombrer) to count. 2. (avoir l'intention de): ~ **faire qqch** to intend to do sthg, to plan to do sthg. 3. (avoir): to have; **la capitale compte deux millions d'habitants** the capital has two million inhabitants. ◆ vi 1. (calculer) to count. 2. (être important) to count, to matter; ~ **pour** to count for. 3. ~ **sur** (se fier à) to rely ou count on. ▶ **sans compter que** loc conj besides which.

compte rendu, compte-rendu [kɔ̃trãdy] nm report, account.

compteur [kɔ̃tœr] nm meter.

comptine [kɔ̃tin] nf nursery rhyme.

comptoir [kɔ̃twar] nm 1. (de bar) bar; (de magasin) counter. 2. (HIST) trading post. 3. Helv (foire) trade fair.

compulser [kɔ̃pylse] vt to consult.

comte [kɔ̃t] nm count.

comté [kɔ̃te] nm type of cheese similar to Gruyère.

comtesse [kɔ̃tɛs] nf countess.

con, conne [kɔ̃, kɔn] tfam ◆ adj bloody Br ou damned stupid. ◆ nm, f stupid bastard (f bitch).

concave [kɔ̃kav] adj concave.

concéder [kɔ̃sede] vt: ~ **qqch à** (droit, terrain) to grant sthg to; (point, victoire) to concede sthg to; ~ **que** to admit (that), to concede (that).

concentration [kɔ̃sɑ̃trasjɔ̃] nf concentration.

concentré, -e [kɔ̃sɑ̃tre] adj 1. (gén) concentrated. 2. (personne): **elle était très ~e** she was concentrating hard. 3. → **lait.** ▶ **concentré** nm concentrate; ~ **de tomates** tomato puree.

concentrer [kɔ̃sɑ̃tre] vt to concentrate. ▶ **se concentrer** vp 1. (se rassembler) to be concentrated. 2. (personne) to concentrate.

concentrique [kɔ̃sɑ̃trik] adj concentric.

concept [kɔ̃sept] nm concept.

conception [kɔ̃sɛpsjɔ̃] nf 1. (gén) conception. 2. (d'un produit, d'une campagne) design, designing (U).

concernant [kɔ̃sɛrnɑ̃] prép regarding, concerning.

concerner [kɔ̃sɛrne] vt to concern; **être/se sentir concerné par qqch** to be/feel concerned by sthg; **en ce qui me concerne** as far as I'm concerned.

concert [kɔ̃sɛr] nm (MUS) concert.

concertation [kɔ̃sɛrtasjɔ̃] nf consultation.

concerter [kɔ̃sɛrte] vt (organiser) to devise (jointly). ▶ **se concerter** vp to

consult (each other).

concerto [kɔ̃sɛrto] nm concerto.

concession [kɔ̃sesjɔ̃] nf 1. (compromis & GRAM) concession. 2. (autorisation) rights (pl), concession.

concessionnaire [kɔ̃sesjɔnɛr] nmf 1. (automobile) (car) dealer. 2. (qui possède une franchise) franchise holder.

concevable [kɔ̃səvabl] adj conceivable.

concevoir [kɔ̃səvwar] vt 1. (enfant, projet) to conceive. 2. (comprendre) to conceive of; **je ne peux pas ~ comment/pourquoi** I cannot conceive how/why.

concierge [kɔ̃sjɛrʒ] nmf caretaker, concierge.

conciliation [kɔ̃siljasjɔ̃] nf 1. (règlement d'un conflit) reconciliation, reconciling. 2. (accord & JUR) conciliation.

concilier [kɔ̃silje] vt (mettre d'accord, allier) to reconcile; ~ **qqch et** ou **avec qqch** to reconcile sthg with sthg.

concis, -e [kɔ̃si, iz] adj (style, discours) concise; (personne) terse.

concision [kɔ̃sizjɔ̃] nf conciseness, concision.

concitoyen, -enne [kɔ̃sitwajɛ̃, ɛn] nm, f fellow citizen.

conclu, -e [kɔ̃kly] pp → **conclure.**

concluant, -e [kɔ̃klyɑ̃, ɑ̃t] adj (convaincant) conclusive.

conclure [kɔ̃klyr] ◆ vt to conclude; **en ~ que** to deduce (that). ◆ vi: ~ **à qqch**: **les experts ont conclu à la folie** the experts concluded he/she was mad.

conclusion [kɔ̃klyzjɔ̃] nf 1. (gén) conclusion. 2. (partie finale) close.

concombre [kɔ̃kɔ̃br] nm cucumber.

concordance [kɔ̃kɔrdɑ̃s] nf (conformité) agreement; ~ **des temps** (GRAM) sequence of tenses.

concorder [kɔ̃kɔrde] vi 1. (coïncider) to agree, to coincide. 2. (être en accord): ~ **(avec)** to be in accordance (with).

concourir [kɔ̃kurir] vi 1. (contribuer): ~ **à** to work towards. 2. (participer à un concours) to compete.

concours [kɔ̃kur] nm 1. (examen) competitive examination. 2. (compétition) competition, contest. 3. (coïncidence): ~ **de circonstances** combination of circumstances.

concret, -ète [kɔ̃krɛ, ɛt] adj concrete.

concrétiser [kɔ̃kretize] vt (projet) to give shape to; (rêve, espoir) to give solid form to. ▶ **se concrétiser** vp (projet) to take shape; (rêve, espoir) to materialize.

conçu, -e [kɔ̃sy] pp → **concevoir.**

concubin, -e [kɔ̃kybɛ̃, in] nm, f partner (not married).

concubinage [kɔ̃kybinaʒ] nm living together, cohabitation.

concupiscent, -e [kɔ̃kypisɑ̃, ɑ̃t] adj concupiscent.

concurremment [kɔ̃kyramɑ̃] adv jointly.

concurrence [kɔ̃kyrɑ̃s] nf 1. (rivalité) rivalry. 2. (ÉCON) competition.

concurrent, -e [kɔ̃kyrɑ̃, ɑ̃t] ◆ adj rival, competing. ◆ nm, f competitor.

concurrentiel, -elle [kɔ̃kyrɑ̃sjɛl] adj competitive.

condamnation [kɔ̃danasjɔ̃] nf 1. (JUR) sentence. 2. (dénonciation) condemnation.

condamné, -e [kɔ̃dane] nm, f convict, prisoner.

condamner [kɔ̃dane] vt 1. (JUR): ~ qqn (à) to sentence sb (to); ~ qqn à une amende to fine sb. 2. fig (obliger): ~ qqn à qqch to condemn sb to sthg. 3. (malade): être condamné to be terminally ill. 4. (interdire) to forbid. 5. (blâmer) to condemn. 6. (fermer) to fill in, to block up.

condensation [kɔ̃dɑ̃sasjɔ̃] nf condensation.

condensé [kɔ̃dɑ̃se] ◆ nm summary. ◆ adj → lait.

condenser [kɔ̃dɑ̃se] vt to condense.

condescendant, -e [kɔ̃desɑ̃dɑ̃, ɑ̃t] adj condescending.

condiment [kɔ̃dimɑ̃] nm condiment.

condisciple [kɔ̃disipl] nm fellow student.

condition [kɔ̃disjɔ̃] nf 1. (gén) condition; se mettre en ~ (physiquement) to get into shape. 2. (place sociale) station; la ~ des ouvriers the workers' lot. ▶ **conditions** nfpl 1. (circonstances) conditions; ~s de vie living conditions. 2. (de paiement) terms. ▶ **à condition de** loc prép providing ou provided (that). ▶ **à condition que** loc conj (+ subjonctif) providing ou provided (that). ▶ **sans conditions** ◆ loc adj unconditional. ◆ loc adv unconditionally.

conditionné, -e [kɔ̃disjɔne] adj 1. (emballé): ~ sous vide vacuum-packed. 2. → air.

conditionnel, -elle [kɔ̃disjɔnɛl] adj conditional. ▶ **conditionnel** nm (GRAM) conditional.

conditionnement [kɔ̃disjɔnmɑ̃] nm 1. (action d'emballer) packaging, packing. 2. (emballage) package. 3. (PSYCHOL & TECHNOL) conditioning.

conditionner [kɔ̃disjɔne] vt 1. (déterminer) to govern. 2. (PSYCHOL & TECHNOL) to condition. 3. (emballer) to pack.

condoléances [kɔ̃dɔleɑ̃s] nfpl condolences.

conducteur, -trice [kɔ̃dyktœr, tris] ◆ adj conductive. ◆ nm, f (de véhicule) driver. ▶ **conducteur** nm (ÉLECTR) conductor.

conduire [kɔ̃dɥir] ◆ vt 1. (voiture, personne) to drive. 2. (transmettre) to conduct. 3. (diriger) to manage. 4. fig (à la ruine, au désespoir): ~ qqn à qqch to drive sb to sthg. ◆ vi 1. (AUTOM) to drive. 2. (mener): ~ à to lead to. ▶ **se conduire** vp to behave.

conduit, -e [kɔ̃dɥi, it] pp → conduire. ▶ **conduit** nm 1. (tuyau) conduit, pipe. 2. (ANAT) duct, canal. ▶ **conduite** nf 1. (pilotage d'un véhicule) driving; ~e à droite/gauche right-hand/left-hand drive. 2. (comportement) behaviour (U). 3. (canalisation): ~e de gaz/d'eau gas/water main, gas/water pipe.

cône [kon] nm (GÉOM) cone.

confection [kɔ̃fɛksjɔ̃] nf 1. (réalisation) making. 2. (industrie) clothing industry.

confectionner [kɔ̃fɛksjɔne] vt to make.

confédération [kɔ̃federasjɔ̃] nf 1. (d'États) confederacy. 2. (d'associations) confederation.

conférence [kɔ̃ferɑ̃s] nf 1. (exposé) lecture. 2. (réunion) conference; ~ de presse press conference.

conférencier, -ère [kɔ̃ferɑ̃sje, ɛr] nm, f lecturer.

conférer [kɔ̃fere] vt (accorder): ~ qqch à qqn to confer sthg on sb.

confesser [kɔ̃fese] vt (avouer) to confess. ▶ **se confesser** vp to go to confession.

confession [kɔ̃fesjɔ̃] nf confession.

confessionnal, -aux [kɔ̃fesjɔnal, o] nm confessional.

confetti [kɔ̃feti] nm confetti (U).

confiance [kɔ̃fjɑ̃s] nf confidence; avoir ~ en to have confidence ou faith in; avoir ~ en soi to be self-confident; en toute ~ with complete confidence; de ~ trustworthy; faire ~ à qqn/qqch to trust sb/sthg.

confiant, -e [kɔ̃fjɑ̃, ɑ̃t] adj (sans méfiance) trusting.

confidence [kɔ̃fidɑ̃s] nf confidence.

confident, -e [kɔ̃fidɑ̃, ɑ̃t] nm, f confidant (f confidante).

confidentiel, -elle [kɔ̃fidɑ̃sjɛl] adj confidential.

confier [kɔ̃fje] vt 1. (donner): ~ qqn/qqch à qqn to entrust sb/sthg to sb. 2. (dire): ~ qqch à qqn to confide sthg to sb. ▶ **se confier** vp: se ~ à qqn to confide in sb.

confiné, -e [kɔ̃fine] adj 1. (air) stale; (atmosphère) enclosed. 2. (enfermé) shut away.

confins [kɔ̃fɛ̃] nmpl: **aux ~ de** on the borders of.

confirmation [kɔ̃firmasjɔ̃] nf confirmation.

confirmer [kɔ̃firme] vt (certifier) to confirm. ▶ **se confirmer** vp to be confirmed.

confiscation [kɔ̃fiskasjɔ̃] nf confiscation.

confiserie [kɔ̃fizri] nf 1. (magasin) sweet shop Br, candy store Am, confectioner's. 2. (sucreries) sweets (pl) Br, candy (U) Am, confectionery (U).

confiseur, -euse [kɔ̃fizœr, øz] nm, f confectioner.

confisquer [kɔ̃fiske] vt to confiscate.

confit [kɔ̃fi] nm: ~ **de canard/d'oie** potted duck/goose.

confiture [kɔ̃fityr] nf jam.

conflit [kɔ̃fli] nm 1. (situation tendue) clash, conflict. 2. (entre États) conflict.

confondre [kɔ̃fɔ̃dr] vt 1. (ne pas distinguer) to confuse, to mix up. 2. (accusé) to confound. 3. (stupéfier) to astound.

confondu, -e [kɔ̃fɔ̃dy] pp → **confondre**.

conformation [kɔ̃fɔrmasjɔ̃] nf structure.

conforme [kɔ̃fɔrm] adj: ~ **à** in accordance with.

conformément [kɔ̃fɔrmemɑ̃] ▶ **conformément à** loc prép in accordance with.

conformer [kɔ̃fɔrme] vt: ~ **qqch à** to shape sthg according to. ▶ **se conformer** vp: se ~ **à** (s'adapter) to conform to; (obéir) to comply with.

conformiste [kɔ̃fɔrmist] ◆ nmf conformist. ◆ adj (traditionaliste) conformist.

conformité [kɔ̃fɔrmite] nf (accord): **être en ~ avec** to be in accordance with.

confort [kɔ̃fɔr] nm comfort; **tout ~** with all mod cons Br, with all modern conveniences Am.

confortable [kɔ̃fɔrtabl] adj comfortable.

confortablement [kɔ̃fɔrtabləmɑ̃] adv comfortably.

confrère, consœur [kɔ̃frɛr, kɔ̃sœr] nm, f colleague.

confrontation [kɔ̃frɔ̃tasjɔ̃] nf (face à face) confrontation.

confronter [kɔ̃frɔ̃te] vt (mettre face à face) to confront; fig: **être confronté à** to be confronted ou faced with.

confus, -e [kɔ̃fy, yz] adj 1. (indistinct, embrouillé) confused. 2. (gêné) embarrassed.

confusion [kɔ̃fyzjɔ̃] nf 1. (gén) confusion. 2. (embarras) confusion, embarrassment.

congé [kɔ̃ʒe] nm 1. (arrêt de travail) leave (U); ~ **(de) maladie** sick leave; ~ **de maternité** maternity leave. 2. (vacances) holiday Br, vacation Am; **en ~** on holiday; **~s payés** paid holiday (U) ou holidays ou leave (U) Br, paid vacation Am; **une journée/semaine de ~** a day/week off. 3. (renvoi) notice; **donner son ~ à qqn** to give sb his/her notice; **prendre ~ (de qqn)** sout to take one's leave (of sb).

congédier [kɔ̃ʒedje] vt to dismiss.

congélateur [kɔ̃ʒelatœr] nm freezer.

congeler [kɔ̃ʒle] vt to freeze.

congénital, -e, -aux [kɔ̃ʒenital, o] adj congenital.

congère [kɔ̃ʒɛr] nf snowdrift.

congestion [kɔ̃ʒɛstjɔ̃] nf congestion; ~ **pulmonaire** pulmonary congestion.

Congo [kɔ̃go] nm: **le ~** the Congo.

congratuler [kɔ̃gratyle] vt to congratulate.

congrégation [kɔ̃gregasjɔ̃] nf congregation.

congrès [kɔ̃grɛ] nm (colloque) assembly.

conifère [kɔnifɛr] nm conifer.

conjecture [kɔ̃ʒɛktyr] nf conjecture.

conjecturer [kɔ̃ʒɛktyre] vt & vi to conjecture.

conjoint, -e [kɔ̃ʒwɛ̃, ɛ̃t] ◆ adj joint. ◆ nm, f spouse.

conjonction [kɔ̃ʒɔ̃ksjɔ̃] nf conjunction.

conjonctivite [kɔ̃ʒɔ̃ktivit] nf conjunctivitis (U).

conjoncture [kɔ̃ʒɔ̃ktyr] nf (ÉCON) situation, circumstances (pl).

conjugaison [kɔ̃ʒygɛzɔ̃] nf 1. (union) uniting. 2. (GRAM) conjugation.

conjugal, -e, -aux [kɔ̃ʒygal, o] adj conjugal.

conjuguer [kɔ̃ʒyge] vt 1. (unir) to combine. 2. (GRAM) to conjugate.

conjuration [kɔ̃ʒyrasjɔ̃] nf 1. (conspira-

tion) conspiracy. **2.** (*exorcisme*) exorcism.
connaissance [kɔnɛsɑ̃s] *nf* **1.** (*savoir*)
knowledge (U); **à ma ~ to** (the best of)
my knowledge; **en ~ de cause** with full
knowledge of the facts; **prendre ~ de
qqch** to study sthg, to examine sthg.
2. (*personne*) acquaintance; **faire ~ (avec
qqn)** to become acquainted (with sb);
faire la ~ de to meet. **3.** (*conscience*): **per-
dre/reprendre ~** to lose/regain consciousness.
connaisseur, -euse [kɔnɛsœr, øz]
◆ *adj* expert (*avant n*). ◆ *nm, f* connoisseur.
connaître [kɔnɛtr] *vt* **1.** (*gén*) to know;
~ qqn de nom/de vue to know sb by
name/sight. **2.** (*éprouver*) to experience.
▶ **se connaître** *vp* **1.** s'y **~ en** (*être
expert*) to know about; **il s'y connaît** he
knows what he's talking about/doing.
2. (*soi-même*) to know o.s. **3.** (*se rencontrer*) to meet (each other); **ils se connaissent** they've met (each other).
connecter [kɔnɛkte] *vt* to connect.
connexion [kɔnɛksjɔ̃] *nf* connection.
connu, -e [kɔny] ◆ *pp* → **connaître**.
◆ *adj* (*célèbre*) well-known, famous.
conquérant, -e [kɔ̃kerɑ̃, ɑ̃t] ◆ *adj*
conquering. ◆ *nm, f* conqueror.
conquérir [kɔ̃kerir] *vt* to conquer.
conquête [kɔ̃kɛt] *nf* conquest.
conquis, -e [kɔ̃ki, iz] *pp* → **conquérir**.
consacrer [kɔ̃sakre] *vt* **1.** (RELIG) to consecrate. **2.** (*employer*): **~ qqch à** to devote
sthg to. ▶ **se consacrer** *vp*: **se ~ à** to
dedicate o.s. to, to devote o.s. to.
conscience [kɔ̃sjɑ̃s] *nf* **1.** (*connaissance
& PSYCHOL*) consciousness; **avoir ~ de
qqch** to be aware of sthg. **2.** (*morale*)
conscience; **bonne/mauvaise ~** clear/
guilty conscience; **~ professionnelle** professional integrity, conscientiousness.
consciencieux, -euse [kɔ̃sjɑ̃sjø, øz]
adj conscientious.
conscient, -e [kɔ̃sjɑ̃, ɑ̃t] *adj* conscious; **être ~ de qqch** (*connaître*) to be
conscious of sthg.
conscription [kɔ̃skripsjɔ̃] *nf* conscription, draft *Am*.
conscrit [kɔ̃skri] *nm* conscript, recruit,
draftee *Am*.
consécration [kɔ̃sekrasjɔ̃] *nf* **1.** (*reconnaissance*) recognition; (*de droit, coutume*)
establishment. **2.** (RELIG) consecration.
consécutif, -ive [kɔ̃sekytif, iv] *adj*
1. (*successif & GRAM*) consecutive.
2. (*résultant*): **~ à** resulting from.
conseil [kɔ̃sɛj] *nm* **1.** (*avis*) piece of

advice, advice (U); **donner un ~ ou des
~s (à qqn)** to give (sb) advice. **2.** (*personne*): **~ (en)** consultant (in). **3.** (*assemblée*) council; **~ d'administration** board of
directors; **~ de classe** staff meeting; **~
de discipline** disciplinary committee.
conseiller[1] [kɔ̃seje] ◆ *vt* **1.** (*recommander*) to advise; **~ qqch à qqn** to recommend sthg to sb. **2.** (*guider*) to advise,
to counsel. ◆ *vi* (*donner un conseil*): **~ à
qqn de faire qqch** to advise sb to do
sthg.
conseiller[2]**, -ère** [kɔ̃seje, ɛr] *nm, f*
1. (*guide*) counsellor. **2.** (*d'un conseil*)
councillor; **~ municipal** town councillor
Br, city councilman (*f* -woman) *Am*.
consensuel, -elle [kɔ̃sɑ̃sɥel] *adj*: **politique ~le** consensus politics.
consentement [kɔ̃sɑ̃tmɑ̃] *nm* consent.
consentir [kɔ̃sɑ̃tir] *vi*: **~ à qqch** to consent to sthg.
conséquence [kɔ̃sekɑ̃s] *nf* consequence, result; **ne pas tirer à ~** to be of
no consequence.
conséquent, -e [kɔ̃sekɑ̃, ɑ̃t] *adj* **1.**
(*cohérent*) consistent. **2.** (*important*) sizeable, considerable. ▶ **par consé-
quent** *loc adv* therefore, consequently.
conservateur, -trice [kɔ̃sɛrvatœr,
tris] ◆ *adj* conservative. ◆ *nm, f* **1.**
(POLIT) conservative. **2.** (*administrateur*)
curator. ▶ **conservateur** *nm* preservative.
conservation [kɔ̃sɛrvasjɔ̃] *nf* **1.** (*état,
entretien*) preservation. **2.** (*d'aliment*)
preserving.
conservatoire [kɔ̃sɛrvatwar] *nm*
academy; **~ de musique** music college.
conserve [kɔ̃sɛrv] *nf* tinned *Br* ou
canned food; **en ~** (*en boîte*) tinned,
canned; (*en bocal*) preserved, bottled.
conserver [kɔ̃sɛrve] *vt* **1.** (*garder,
entretenir*) to keep. **2.** (*entreposer - en boîte*)
to can; (*- en bocal*) to bottle.
considérable [kɔ̃siderabl] *adj* considerable.
considération [kɔ̃siderasjɔ̃] *nf* **1.**
(*réflexion, motivation*) consideration; **prendre qqch en ~** to take sthg into consideration. **2.** (*estime*) respect.
considérer [kɔ̃sidere] *vt* to consider;
tout bien considéré all things considered.
consigne [kɔ̃siɲ] *nf* **1.** (*gén pl*) (*instruction*) instructions (*pl*). **2.** (*entrepôt de
bagages*) left-luggage office *Br*, check-
room *Am*, baggage room *Am*; **~ automa-**

tique left-luggage lockers (pl) Br.
3. (somme d'argent) deposit.

consigné, -e [kɔ̃siɲe] adj returnable.

consistance [kɔ̃sistɑ̃s] nf (solidité) consistency; fig substance.

consistant, -e [kɔ̃sistɑ̃, ɑ̃t] adj
1. (épais) thick. 2. (nourrissant) substantial. 3. (fondé) sound.

consister [kɔ̃siste] vi: ~ en to consist of; ~ à faire qqch to consist in doing sthg.

consœur → **confrère**.

consolation [kɔ̃sɔlasjɔ̃] nf consolation.

console [kɔ̃sɔl] nf 1. (table) console (table). 2. (INFORM): ~ de jeux video game console; ~ de visualisation VDU, visual display unit.

consoler [kɔ̃sɔle] vt (réconforter): ~ qqn (de qqch) to comfort sb (in sthg).

consolider [kɔ̃sɔlide] vt litt & fig to strengthen.

consommateur, -trice [kɔ̃sɔmatœr, tris] nm, f (acheteur) consumer; (d'un bar) customer.

consommation [kɔ̃sɔmasjɔ̃] nf
1. (utilisation) consumption; faire une grande ou grosse ~ de to use (up) a lot of. 2. (boisson) drink.

consommé, -e [kɔ̃sɔme] adj sout consummate. ▶ **consommé** nm consommé.

consommer [kɔ̃sɔme] ◆ vt 1. (utiliser) to use (up). 2. (manger) to eat. 3. (énergie) to consume, to use. ◆ vi 1. (boire) to drink. 2. (voiture): cette voiture consomme beaucoup this car uses a lot of fuel.

consonance [kɔ̃sɔnɑ̃s] nf consonance.

consonne [kɔ̃sɔn] nf consonant.

conspirateur, -trice [kɔ̃spiratœr, tris] nm, f conspirator.

conspirer [kɔ̃spire] ◆ vt (comploter) to plot. ◆ vi to conspire.

constamment [kɔ̃stamɑ̃] adv constantly.

constant, -e [kɔ̃stɑ̃, ɑ̃t] adj constant.

constat [kɔ̃sta] nm 1. (procès-verbal) report. 2. (constatation) established fact.

constatation [kɔ̃statasjɔ̃] nf 1. (révélation) observation. 2. (fait retenu) finding.

constater [kɔ̃state] vt 1. (se rendre compte de) to see, to notice. 2. (consigner - fait, infraction) to record; (- décès, authenticité) to certify.

constellation [kɔ̃stelasjɔ̃] nf (ASTRON) constellation.

consternation [kɔ̃stɛrnasjɔ̃] nf dismay.

consterner [kɔ̃stɛrne] vt to dismay.

constipation [kɔ̃stipasjɔ̃] nf constipation.

constipé, -e [kɔ̃stipe] adj 1. (MÉD) constipated. 2. fam fig (manière, air) ill at ease.

constituer [kɔ̃stitɥe] vt 1. (élaborer) to set up. 2. (composer) to make up. 3. (représenter) to constitute.

constitution [kɔ̃stitɥsjɔ̃] nf 1. (création) setting up. 2. (de pays, de corps) constitution.

constructeur [kɔ̃stryktœr] nm 1. (fabricant) manufacturer; (de navire) shipbuilder. 2. (bâtisseur) builder.

construction [kɔ̃stryksjɔ̃] nf 1. (IND) building, construction; ~ navale shipbuilding. 2. (édifice) structure, building. 3. (GRAM & fig) construction.

construire [kɔ̃strɥir] vt 1. (bâtir, fabriquer) to build. 2. (théorie, phrase) to construct.

construit, -e [kɔ̃strɥi, it] pp → **construire**.

consulat [kɔ̃syla] nm (résidence) consulate.

consultation [kɔ̃syltasjɔ̃] nf (MÉD & POLIT) consultation.

consulter [kɔ̃sylte] ◆ vt 1. (compulser) to consult. 2. (interroger, demander conseil à) to consult, to ask. 3. (spécialiste) to consult, to see. ◆ vi (médecin) to take ou hold surgery; (avocat) to be available for consultation. ▶ **se consulter** vp to confer.

contact [kɔ̃takt] nm 1. (gén) contact; le ~ du marbre est froid marble is cold to the touch; prendre ~ avec to make contact with; rester en ~ (avec) to stay in touch (with); au ~ de on contact with; avoir le sens du ~ to be good with people. 2. (AUTOM) ignition; mettre/couper le ~ to switch on/off the ignition.

contacter [kɔ̃takte] vt to contact.

contagieux, -euse [kɔ̃taʒjø, øz] adj (MÉD) contagious; fig infectious.

contagion [kɔ̃taʒjɔ̃] nf (MÉD) contagion; fig infectiousness.

contaminer [kɔ̃tamine] vt (infecter) to contaminate; fig to contaminate, to infect.

conte [kɔ̃t] nm story; ~ de fées fairy tale.

contemplation [kɔ̃tɑ̃plasjɔ̃] nf contemplation.

contempler [kɔ̃tɑ̃ple] vt to contemplate.

contemporain, -e [kɔ̃tɑ̃pɔrɛ̃, ɛn]

nm, f contemporary.

contenance [kɔ̃tnɑ̃s] *nf* **1.** (*capacité volumique*) capacity. **2.** (*attitude*): **se donner une ~** to give an impression of composure; **perdre ~** to lose one's composure.

contenir [kɔ̃tnir] *vt* to contain, to hold, to take. ▶ **se contenir** *vp* to contain o.s., to control o.s.

content, -e [kɔ̃tɑ̃, ɑ̃t] *adj* (*satisfait*): **~ (de qqn/qqch)** happy (with sb/sthg), content (with sb/sthg); **~ de faire qqch** happy to do sthg.

contentement [kɔ̃tɑ̃tmɑ̃] *nm* satisfaction.

contenter [kɔ̃tɑ̃te] *vt* to satisfy. ▶ **se contenter** *vp*: **se ~ de qqch/de faire qqch** to content o.s. with sthg/with doing sthg.

contentieux [kɔ̃tɑ̃sjø] *nm* (*litige*) dispute; (*service*) legal department.

contenu, -e [kɔ̃tny] *pp* → **contenir**. ▶ **contenu** *nm* **1.** (*de récipient*) contents (*pl*). **2.** (*de texte, discours*) content.

conter [kɔ̃te] *vt* to tell.

contestable [kɔ̃tɛstabl] *adj* questionable.

contestation [kɔ̃tɛstasjɔ̃] *nf* **1.** (*protestation*) protest, dispute. **2.** (POLIT): **la ~** anti-establishment activity.

conteste [kɔ̃tɛst] ▶ **sans conteste** *loc adv* unquestionably.

contester [kɔ̃tɛste] ♦ *vt* to dispute, to contest. ♦ *vi* to protest.

conteur, -euse [kɔ̃tœr, øz] *nm, f* storyteller.

contexte [kɔ̃tɛkst] *nm* context.

contigu, -uë [kɔ̃tigy] *adj*: **~ (à)** adjacent (to).

continent [kɔ̃tinɑ̃] *nm* continent.

continental, -e, -aux [kɔ̃tinɑ̃tal, o] *adj* continental.

contingence [kɔ̃tɛ̃ʒɑ̃s] *nf* (*gén pl*) contingency.

contingent [kɔ̃tɛ̃ʒɑ̃] *nm* **1.** (MIL) national service conscripts (*pl*), draft Am. **2.** (COMM) quota.

continu, -e [kɔ̃tiny] *adj* continuous.

continuation [kɔ̃tinɥasjɔ̃] *nf* continuation.

continuel, -elle [kɔ̃tinɥɛl] *adj* **1.** (*continu*) continuous. **2.** (*répété*) continual.

continuellement [kɔ̃tinɥɛlmɑ̃] *adv* continually.

continuer [kɔ̃tinɥe] ♦ *vt* (*poursuivre*) to carry on with, to continue (with). ♦ *vi* to continue, to go on; **~ à ou de faire qqch**

to continue to do ou doing sthg.

continuité [kɔ̃tinɥite] *nf* continuity.

contorsionner [kɔ̃tɔrsjɔne] ▶ **se contorsionner** *vp* to contort (o.s.), to writhe.

contour [kɔ̃tur] *nm* **1.** (*limite*) outline. **2.** (*gén pl*) (*courbe*) bend.

contourner [kɔ̃turne] *vt litt & fig* to bypass, to get round.

contraceptif, -ive [kɔ̃trasɛptif, iv] *adj* contraceptive. ▶ **contraceptif** *nm* contraceptive.

contraception [kɔ̃trasɛpsjɔ̃] *nf* contraception.

contracter [kɔ̃trakte] *vt* **1.** (*muscle*) to contract, to tense; (*visage*) to contort. **2.** (*maladie*) to contract, to catch. **3.** (*engagement*) to contract; (*assurance*) to take out.

contraction [kɔ̃traksjɔ̃] *nf* contraction; (*état de muscle*) tenseness.

contractuel, -elle [kɔ̃traktɥɛl] *nm, f* traffic warden Br.

contradiction [kɔ̃tradiksjɔ̃] *nf* contradiction.

contradictoire [kɔ̃tradiktwar] *adj* contradictory; **débat ~** open debate.

contraignant, -e [kɔ̃trɛɲɑ̃, ɑ̃t] *adj* restricting.

contraindre [kɔ̃trɛ̃dr] *vt*: **~ qqn à faire qqch** to compel ou force sb to do sthg; **être contraint de faire qqch** to be compelled ou forced to do sthg.

contraint, -e [kɔ̃trɛ̃, ɛ̃t] ♦ *pp* → **contraindre**. ♦ *adj* forced. ▶ **contrainte** *nf* constraint.

contraire [kɔ̃trɛr] ♦ *nm*: **le ~** the opposite; **je n'ai jamais dit le ~** I have never denied it. ♦ *adj* opposite; **~ à** (*non conforme à*) contrary to. ▶ **au contraire** *loc adv* on the contrary. ▶ **au contraire de** *loc prép* unlike.

contrairement [kɔ̃trɛrmɑ̃] ▶ **contrairement à** *loc prép* contrary to.

contrarier [kɔ̃trarje] *vt* **1.** (*contrecarrer*) to thwart, to frustrate. **2.** (*irriter*) to annoy.

contrariété [kɔ̃trarjete] *nf* annoyance.

contraste [kɔ̃trast] *nm* contrast.

contraster [kɔ̃traste] *vt & vi* to contrast.

contrat [kɔ̃tra] *nm* contract, agreement; **~ à durée déterminée/indéterminée** fixed-term/permanent contract.

contravention [kɔ̃travɑ̃sjɔ̃] *nf* (*amende*) fine; **~ pour stationnement interdit** parking ticket; **dresser une ~ à qqn** to fine sb.

contre [kɔ̃tr] ◆ *prép* **1.** (*juxtaposition, opposition*) against. **2.** (*proportion, comparaison*): **élu à 15 voix ~ 9** elected by 15 votes to 9. **3.** (*échange*) (in exchange) for. ◆ *adv* (*juxtaposition*): **prends la rampe et appuie-toi ~** take hold of the rail and lean against it. ▶ **par contre** *loc adv* on the other hand.

contre-attaque [kɔ̃tratak] (*pl* **contre-attaques**) *nf* counterattack.

contrebalancer [kɔ̃trəbalɑ̃se] *vt* to counterbalance, to offset.

contrebande [kɔ̃trəbɑ̃d] *nf* (*activité*) smuggling; (*marchandises*) contraband.

contrebandier, -ère [kɔ̃trəbɑ̃dje, ɛr] *nm, f* smuggler.

contrebas [kɔ̃trəba] ▶ **en contrebas** *loc adv* (down) below.

contrebasse [kɔ̃trəbas] *nf* (*instrument*) (double) bass.

contrecarrer [kɔ̃trəkare] *vt* to thwart, to frustrate.

contrecœur [kɔ̃trəkœr] ▶ **à contre-cœur** *loc adv* grudgingly.

contrecoup [kɔ̃trəku] *nm* consequence.

contre-courant [kɔ̃trəkurɑ̃] ▶ **à contre-courant** *loc adv* against the current.

contredire [kɔ̃trədir] *vt* to contradict. ▶ **se contredire** *vp* **1.** (*emploi réciproque*) to contradict (each other). **2.** (*emploi réfléchi*) to contradict o.s.

contredit, -e [kɔ̃trədi, it] *pp* → **contredire**.

contrée [kɔ̃tre] *nf* (*pays*) land; (*région*) region.

contre-espionnage [kɔ̃trɛspjɔnaʒ] *nm* counterespionage.

contre-expertise [kɔ̃trɛkspertiz] (*pl* **contre-expertises**) *nf* second (expert) opinion.

contrefaçon [kɔ̃trəfasɔ̃] *nf* (*activité*) counterfeiting; (*produit*) forgery.

contrefaire [kɔ̃trəfɛr] *vt* **1.** (*signature, monnaie*) to counterfeit, to forge. **2.** (*voix*) to disguise.

contrefort [kɔ̃trəfɔr] *nm* **1.** (*pilier*) buttress. **2.** (*de chaussure*) back. ▶ **contreforts** *nmpl* foothills.

contre-indication [kɔ̃trɛ̃dikasjɔ̃] (*pl* **contre-indications**) *nf* contraindication.

contre-jour [kɔ̃trəʒur] ▶ **à contre-jour** *loc adv* against the light.

contremaître, -esse [kɔ̃trəmetr, ɛs] *nm, f* foreman (*f* forewoman).

contremarque [kɔ̃trəmark] *nf* (*pour* *sortir d'un spectacle*) pass-out ticket.

contre-offensive [kɔ̃trɔfɑ̃siv] (*pl* **contre-offensives**) *nf* counteroffensive.

contre-ordre = **contrordre**.

contrepartie [kɔ̃trəparti] *nf* **1.** (*compensation*) compensation. **2.** (*contraire*) opposing view. ▶ **en contrepartie** *loc adv* in return.

contre-performance [kɔ̃trəperfɔrmɑ̃s] (*pl* **contre-performances**) *nf* disappointing performance.

contrepèterie [kɔ̃trəpetri] *nf* spoonerism.

contre-pied [kɔ̃trəpje] *nm*: **prendre le ~ de** to do the opposite of.

contreplaqué, contre-plaqué [kɔ̃trəplake] *nm* plywood.

contrepoids [kɔ̃trəpwa] *nm litt & fig* counterbalance, counterweight.

contre-pouvoir [kɔ̃trəpuvwar] (*pl* **contre-pouvoirs**) *nm* counterbalance.

contrer [kɔ̃tre] *vt* **1.** (*s'opposer à*) to counter. **2.** (CARTES) to double.

contresens [kɔ̃trəsɑ̃s] *nm* **1.** (*erreur - de traduction*) mistranslation; (- *d'interprétation*) misinterpretation. **2.** (*absurdité*) nonsense (U). ▶ **à contresens** *loc adv litt & fig* the wrong way.

contresigner [kɔ̃trəsiɲe] *vt* to countersign.

contretemps [kɔ̃trətɑ̃] *nm* hitch, mishap. ▶ **à contretemps** *loc adv* (MUS) out of time; *fig* at the wrong moment.

contrevenir [kɔ̃trəvnir] *vi*: **~ à** to contravene, to infringe.

contribuable [kɔ̃tribɥabl] *nmf* taxpayer.

contribuer [kɔ̃tribɥe] *vi*: **~ à** to contribute to ou towards.

contribution [kɔ̃tribysjɔ̃] *nf*: **~ (à)** contribution (to); **mettre qqn à ~** to call on sb's services. ▶ **contributions** *nfpl* taxes; **~s directes/indirectes** direct/indirect taxation.

contrit, -e [kɔ̃tri, it] *adj* contrite.

contrôle [kɔ̃trol] *nm* **1.** (*vérification - de déclaration*) check, checking (U); (- *de documents, billets*) inspection; **~ d'identité** identity check. **2.** (*maîtrise, commande*) control; **perdre le ~ de qqch** to lose control of sthg; **~ des naissances** birth control; **~ des prix** price control. **3.** (SCOL) test.

contrôler [kɔ̃trole] *vt* **1.** (*vérifier - documents, billets*) to inspect; (- *déclaration*) to check; (- *connaissances*) to test. **2.** (*maîtriser, diriger*) to control. **3.** (TECHNOL) to monitor, to control.

contrôleur, -euse [kɔ̃trolœr, øz] *nm, f*
(*de train*) ticket inspector; (*d'autobus*)
(bus) conductor (*f* conductress); **~**
aérien air traffic controller.

contrordre, **contre-ordre** (*pl*
contre-ordres) [kɔ̃trɔrdr] *nm* countermand; **sauf ~** unless otherwise instructed.

controverse [kɔ̃trɔvɛrs] *nf* controversy.

controversé, -e [kɔ̃trɔvɛrse] *adj* (*personne, décision*) controversial.

contumace [kɔ̃tymas] *nf* (JUR):
condamné par ~ sentenced in absentia.

contusion [kɔ̃tyzjɔ̃] *nf* bruise, contusion.

convaincant, -e [kɔ̃vɛ̃kɑ̃, ɑ̃t] *adj* convincing.

convaincre [kɔ̃vɛ̃kr] *vt* 1. (*persuader*): **~**
qqn (de qqch) to convince sb (of sthg); **~**
qqn (de faire qqch) to persuade sb (to
do sthg). 2. (JUR): **~ qqn de** to find sb
guilty of, to convict sb of.

convaincu, -e [kɔ̃vɛ̃ky] ◆ *pp* →
convaincre. ◆ *adj* (*partisan*) committed;
d'un ton ~, d'un air ~ with conviction.

convainquant [kɔ̃vɛ̃kɑ̃] *ppr* →
convaincre.

convalescence [kɔ̃valesɑ̃s] *nf* convalescence; **être en ~** to be convalescing
ou recovering.

convalescent, -e [kɔ̃valesɑ̃, ɑ̃t] *adj &
nm, f* convalescent.

convenable [kɔ̃vnabl] *adj* 1. (*manières,
comportement*) polite; (*tenue, personne*)
decent, respectable. 2. (*acceptable*) adequate, acceptable.

convenance [kɔ̃vnɑ̃s] *nf*: **à ma/votre ~**
to my/your convenience. ▶ **convenances** *nfpl* proprieties.

convenir [kɔ̃vnir] *vi* 1. (*décider*): **~ de
qqch/de faire qqch** to agree on sthg/to
do sthg. 2. (*plaire*): **~ à qqn** to suit sb, to
be convenient for sb. 3. (*être approprié*):
~ à ou **pour** to be suitable for. 4. *sout*
(*admettre*): **~ de qqch** to admit to sthg; **~**
que to admit (that).

convention [kɔ̃vɑ̃sjɔ̃] *nf* 1. (*règle,
assemblée*) convention. 2. (*accord*) agreement; **~ collective** collective agreement.

conventionné, -e [kɔ̃vɑ̃sjɔne] *adj* ≃
National Health (*avant n*) Br.

conventionnel, -elle [kɔ̃vɑ̃sjɔnɛl] *adj*
conventional.

convenu, -e [kɔ̃vny] ◆ *pp* → **convenir.**
◆ *adj* (*décidé*): **comme ~** as agreed.

convergent, -e [kɔ̃vɛrʒɑ̃, ɑ̃t] *adj* convergent.

converger [kɔ̃vɛrʒe] *vi*: **~ (vers)** to converge (on).

conversation [kɔ̃vɛrsasjɔ̃] *nf* conversation.

converser [kɔ̃vɛrse] *vi sout*: **~ (avec)** to
converse (with).

conversion [kɔ̃vɛrsjɔ̃] *nf* (*gén*): **~ (à/
en)** conversion (to/into).

convertible [kɔ̃vɛrtibl] *nm* (*canapé-lit*)
sofa-bed.

convertir [kɔ̃vɛrtir] *vt*: **~ qqn (à)** to
convert sb (to); **~ qqch (en)** to convert
sthg (into). ▶ **se convertir** *vp*: **se ~ (à)**
to be converted (to).

convexe [kɔ̃vɛks] *adj* convex.

conviction [kɔ̃viksjɔ̃] *nf* conviction.

convier [kɔ̃vje] *vt*: **~ qqn à** to invite sb
to.

convive [kɔ̃viv] *nmf* guest (*at a meal*).

convivial, -e, -aux [kɔ̃vivjal, o] *adj*
1. (*réunion*) convivial. 2. (INFORM) user-
friendly.

convocation [kɔ̃vɔkasjɔ̃] *nf* (*avis écrit*)
summons (*sg*), notification to attend.

convoi [kɔ̃vwa] *nm* 1. (*de véhicules*) convoy. 2. (*train*) train.

convoiter [kɔ̃vwate] *vt* to covet.

convoitise [kɔ̃vwatiz] *nf* covetous-
ness.

convoquer [kɔ̃vɔke] *vt* 1. (*assemblée*) to
convene. 2. (*pour un entretien*) to invite.
3. (*subalterne, témoin*) to summon. 4. (*à
un examen*): **~** to ask sb to attend.

convoyer [kɔ̃vwaje] *vt* to escort.

convoyeur, -euse [kɔ̃vwajœr, øz]
nm, f escort; **~ de fonds** security guard.

convulsion [kɔ̃vylsjɔ̃] *nf* convulsion.

coopération [kɔɔperasjɔ̃] *nf* 1. (*collaboration*) cooperation. 2. (*aide*): **la ~ ≃**
overseas development.

coopérer [kɔɔpere] *vi*: **~ (à)** to cooperate (in).

coordination [kɔɔrdinasjɔ̃] *nf* coordination.

coordonnée [kɔɔrdɔne] *nf* (MATHS)
coordinate. ▶ **coordonnées** *nfpl*
1. (GÉOGR) coordinates. 2. (*adresse*)
address and phone number, details.

coordonner [kɔɔrdɔne] *vt* to coordinate.

copain, -ine [kɔpɛ̃, in] ◆ *adj* matey;
être très ~s to be great pals. ◆ *nm, f*
(*ami*) friend, mate; (*petit ami*) boyfriend
(*f* girlfriend).

copeau, -x [kɔpo] *nm* (*de bois*) (wood)
shaving.

Copenhague [kɔpɛnag] *n* Copenhagen.

copie [kɔpi] nf 1. (double, reproduction) copy. 2. (SCOL - de devoir) fair copy; (- d'examen) paper, script.

copier [kɔpje] ◆ vt to copy. ◆ vi: ~ sur qqn to copy from sb.

copieux, -euse [kɔpjø, øz] adj copious.

copilote [kɔpilɔt] nmf copilot.

copine → copain.

coproduction [kɔprɔdyksjɔ̃] nf coproduction.

copropriété [kɔprɔprijete] nf co-ownership, joint ownership.

coq [kɔk] nm cock, cockerel; ~ au vin chicken cooked with red wine, bacon, mushrooms and shallots; **sauter** OU **passer du** ~ à l'âne to jump from one subject to another.

coque [kɔk] nf 1. (de noix) shell. 2. (de navire) hull.

coquelicot [kɔkliko] nm poppy.

coqueluche [kɔklyʃ] nf whooping cough.

coquet, -ette [kɔkɛ, ɛt] adj 1. (vêtements) smart, stylish; (ville, jeune fille) pretty. 2. (avant n) hum (important): **la ~te somme de 100 livres** the tidy sum of £100. ▶ **coquette** nf flirt.

coquetier [kɔktje] nm eggcup.

coquetterie [kɔketri] nf (désir de plaire) coquettishness.

coquillage [kɔkijaʒ] nm 1. (mollusque) shellfish. 2. (coquille) shell.

coquille [kɔkij] nf 1. (de mollusque, noix, œuf) shell; ~ **de noix** (embarcation) cockleshell. 2. (TYPO) misprint.

coquillettes [kɔkijɛt] nfpl pasta shells.

coquin, -e [kɔkɛ̃, in] ◆ adj (sous-vêtement) sexy, naughty; (regard, histoire) saucy. ◆ nm, f rascal.

cor [kɔr] nm 1. (instrument) horn. 2. (au pied) corn. ▶ **à cor et à cri** loc adv: **réclamer qqch à ~ et à cri** to clamour for sthg.

corail, -aux [kɔraj, o] nm 1. (gén) coral. 2. (RAIL): **train ~** ≃ express train.

Coran [kɔrɑ̃] nm: **le ~** the Koran.

corbeau, -x [kɔrbo] nm 1. (oiseau) crow. 2. (délateur) writer of poison-pen letters.

corbeille [kɔrbɛj] nf 1. (panier) basket; ~ **à papier** waste paper basket. 2. (THÉÂTRE) (dress) circle. 3. (de Bourse) stockbrokers' enclosure (at Paris Stock Exchange).

corbillard [kɔrbijar] nm hearse.

cordage [kɔrdaʒ] nm 1. (de bateau) rig-

ging (U). 2. (de raquette) strings (pl).

corde [kɔrd] nf 1. (filin) rope; ~ **à linge** washing OU clothes line; ~ **à sauter** skipping rope. 2. (d'instrument, arc) string. 3. (ANAT): ~**s vocales** vocal cords. 4. (HIPPISME) rails (pl); (ATHLÉTISME) inside (lane).

cordée [kɔrde] nf (ALPINISME) roped party (of mountaineers).

cordial, -e, -aux [kɔrdjal, o] adj warm, cordial.

cordon [kɔrdɔ̃] nm string, cord; ~ **ombilical** umbilical cord; ~ **de police** police cordon.

cordon-bleu [kɔrdɔ̃blø] nm cordon bleu cook.

cordonnerie [kɔrdɔnri] nf (magasin) shoe repairer's, cobbler's.

cordonnier, -ère [kɔrdɔnje, ɛr] nm, f shoe repairer, cobbler.

Corée [kɔre] nf Korea.

coriace [kɔrjas] adj litt & fig tough.

cormoran [kɔrmɔrɑ̃] nm cormorant.

corne [kɔrn] nf 1. (gén) horn; (de cerf) antler. 2. (callosité) hard skin (U), callus.

cornée [kɔrne] nf cornea.

corneille [kɔrnɛj] nf crow.

cornemuse [kɔrnəmyz] nf bagpipes (pl).

corner¹ [kɔrne] vt (page) to turn down the corner of.

corner² [kɔrner] nm (FOOTBALL) corner (kick).

cornet [kɔrnɛ] nm 1. (d'aliment) cornet, cone. 2. (de jeu) (dice) shaker.

corniaud, corniot [kɔrnjo] nm 1. (chien) mongrel. 2. fam (imbécile) twit.

corniche [kɔrniʃ] nf 1. (route) cliff road. 2. (moulure) cornice.

cornichon [kɔrniʃɔ̃] nm 1. (condiment) gherkin. 2. fam (imbécile) twit.

corniot = corniaud.

Cornouailles [kɔrnwaj] nf: **la ~** Cornwall.

corollaire [kɔrɔlɛr] nm corollary.

corolle [kɔrɔl] nf corolla.

coron [kɔrɔ̃] nm (village) mining village.

corporation [kɔrpɔrasjɔ̃] nf corporate body.

corporel, -elle [kɔrpɔrel] adj (physique - besoin) bodily; (- châtiment) corporal.

corps [kɔr] nm 1. (gén) body. 2. (groupe): ~ **d'armée** (army) corps; ~ **enseignant** (profession) teaching profession; (d'école) teaching staff.

corpulent, -e [kɔrpylɑ̃, ɑ̃t] adj corpulent, stout.

côtelé

correct, -e [kɔrɛkt] adj 1. (exact) correct, right. 2. (honnête) correct, proper. 3. (acceptable) decent; (travail) fair.

correcteur, -trice [kɔrɛktœr, tris] ◆ adj corrective. ◆ nm, f 1. (d'examen) examiner, marker Br, grader Am. 2. (TYPO) proofreader.

correction [kɔrɛksjɔ̃] nf 1. (d'erreur) correction. 2. (punition) punishment. 3. (TYPO) proofreading. 4. (notation) marking. 5. (bienséance) propriety.

corrélation [kɔrelasjɔ̃] nf correlation.

correspondance [kɔrɛspɔ̃dãs] nf 1. (gén) correspondence; **cours par ~** correspondence course. 2. (TRANSPORT) connection; **assurer la ~ avec** to connect with.

correspondant, -e [kɔrɛspɔ̃dã, ãt] ◆ adj corresponding. ◆ nm, f 1. (par lettres) penfriend, correspondent. 2. (par téléphone): **je vous passe votre ~** I'll put you through. 3. (PRESSE) correspondent.

correspondre [kɔrɛspɔ̃dr] vi 1. (être conforme): **~ à** to correspond to. 2. (par lettres): **~ avec** to correspond with.

corridor [kɔridɔr] nm corridor.

corrigé [kɔriʒe] nm correct version.

corriger [kɔriʒe] vt 1. (TYPO) to correct, to proofread. 2. (noter) to mark. 3. (modifier) to correct. 4. (punir) to give a good hiding to. ▶ **se corriger** vp (d'un défaut): **se ~ de** to cure o.s. of.

corroborer [kɔrɔbɔre] vt to corroborate.

corroder [kɔrɔde] vt (ronger) to corrode; fig to erode.

corrompre [kɔrɔ̃pr] vt 1. (soudoyer) to bribe. 2. (dépraver) to corrupt.

corrosion [kɔrozjɔ̃] nf corrosion.

corruption [kɔrypsjɔ̃] nf 1. (subornation) bribery. 2. (dépravation) corruption.

corsage [kɔrsaʒ] nm 1. (chemisier) blouse. 2. (de robe) bodice.

corsaire [kɔrsɛr] nm 1. (navire, marin) corsair, privateer. 2. (pantalon) pedal-pushers (pl).

corse [kɔrs] ◆ adj Corsican. ◆ nm (langue) Corsican. ▶ **Corse** ◆ nmf Corsican. ◆ nf: **la Corse** Corsica.

corsé, -e [kɔrse] adj (café) strong; (vin) full-bodied; (plat, histoire) spicy.

corset [kɔrsɛ] nm corset.

cortège [kɔrtɛʒ] nm procession.

corvée [kɔrve] nf 1. (MIL) fatigue (duty). 2. (activité pénible) chore.

cosmétique [kɔsmetik] nm & adj cosmetic.

cosmique [kɔsmik] adj cosmic.

cosmonaute [kɔsmɔnot] nmf cosmonaut.

cosmopolite [kɔsmɔpɔlit] adj cosmopolitan.

cosmos [kɔsmos] nm 1. (univers) cosmos. 2. (espace) outer space.

cossu, -e [kɔsy] adj (maison) opulent.

Costa Rica [kɔstarika] nm: **le ~** Costa Rica.

costaud (f costaud ou -e) [kɔsto, od] adj sturdily built.

costume [kɔstym] nm 1. (folklorique, de théâtre) costume. 2. (vêtement d'homme) suit; **en ~-cravate** wearing a suit and a tie.

costumé, -e [kɔstyme] adj fancy-dress (avant n).

costumier, -ère [kɔstymje, ɛr] nm, f (THÉÂTRE) wardrobe master (f mistress).

cotation [kɔtasjɔ̃] nf (FIN) quotation.

cote [kɔt] nf 1. (marque de classement) classification mark; (marque numérale) serial number. 2. (FIN) quotation. 3. (popularité) rating. 4. (niveau) level; **~ d'alerte** (de cours d'eau) danger level; fig crisis point.

côte [kot] nf 1. (ANAT, BOT & de bœuf) rib; (de porc, mouton, agneau) chop; **~ à ~** side by side. 2. (pente) hill. 3. (littoral) coast; **la Côte d'Azur** the French Riviera.

côté [kote] nm 1. (gén) side; **être couché sur le ~** to be lying on one's side; **être aux ~s de qqn** fig to be by sb's side; **d'un ~ ..., de l'autre ~ ...** on the one hand ..., on the other hand ...; **de mon ~** for my part; **et ~ finances, ça va?** fam how are things moneywise? 2. (endroit, direction) direction, way; **de quel ~ est-il parti?** which way did he go?; **de l'autre ~ de** on the other side of; **de tous ~s** from all directions; **du ~ de** (près de) near; (direction) towards; (provenance) from. ▶ **à côté** loc adv 1. (lieu - gén) nearby; (- dans la maison adjacente) next door. 2. (cible): **tirer à ~** to shoot wide (of the target). ▶ **à côté de** loc prép 1. (proximité) beside, next to. 2. (en comparaison avec) beside, compared to. 3. (en dehors de): **être à ~ du sujet** to be off the point. ▶ **de côté** loc adv 1. (se placer, marcher) sideways. 2. (en réserve) aside.

coteau [kɔto] nm 1. (colline) hill. 2. (versant) slope.

Côte-d'Ivoire [kotdivwar] nf: **la ~** the Ivory Coast.

côtelé, -e [kotle] adj ribbed; **velours ~** corduroy.

côtelette [kotlɛt] nf (de porc, mouton, d'agneau) chop; (de veau) cutlet.

coter [kɔte] vt 1. (marquer, noter) to mark. 2. (FIN) to quote.

côtier, -ère [kotje, ɛr] adj coastal.

cotisation [kɔtizasjɔ̃] nf (à club, parti) subscription; (à la Sécurité sociale) contribution.

cotiser [kɔtize] vi (à un club, un parti) to subscribe; (à la Sécurité sociale) to contribute. ► **se cotiser** vp to club together.

coton [kɔtɔ̃] nm cotton; ~ **(hydrophile)** cotton wool.

Coton-Tige® [kɔtɔ̃tiʒ] nm cotton bud.

côtoyer [kotwaje] vt fig (fréquenter) to mix with.

cotre [kɔtr] nm cutter.

cou [ku] nm (de personne, bouteille) neck.

couchant [kuʃɑ̃] ◆ adj → **soleil.** ◆ nm west.

couche [kuʃ] nf 1. (de peinture, de vernis) coat, layer; (de poussière) film, layer. 2. (épaisseur) layer; ~ **d'ozone** ozone layer. 3. (de bébé) nappy Br, diaper Am. 4. (classe sociale) stratum. ► **fausse couche** nf miscarriage.

couché, -e [kuʃe] adj: **être ~** (étendu) to be lying down; (au lit) to be in bed.

couche-culotte [kuʃkylɔt] nf disposable nappy Br ou diaper Am.

coucher¹ [kuʃe] ◆ vt 1. (enfant) to put to bed. 2. (objet, blessé) to lay down. ◆ vi 1. (passer la nuit) to spend the night. 2. fam (avoir des rapports sexuels): ~ **avec** to sleep with. ► **se coucher** vp 1. (s'allonger) to lie down. 2. (se mettre au lit) to go to bed. 3. (astre) to set.

coucher² [kuʃe] nm (d'astre) setting; **au ~ du soleil** at sunset.

couchette [kuʃɛt] nf 1. (de train) couchette. 2. (de navire) berth.

coucou [kuku] ◆ nm 1. (oiseau) cuckoo. 2. (pendule) cuckoo clock. 3. péj (avion) crate. ◆ interj peekaboo!

coude [kud] nm 1. (de personne, de vêtement) elbow. 2. (courbe) bend.

cou-de-pied [kudpje] (pl **cous-de-pied**) nm instep.

coudre [kudr] vt (bouton) to sew on.

couette [kwɛt] nf 1. (édredon) duvet. 2. (coiffure) bunches (pl).

couffin [kufɛ̃] nm (berceau) Moses basket.

couille [kuj] nf (gén pl) vulg ball.

couiner [kwine] vi 1. (animal) to squeal. 2. (pleurnicher) to whine.

coulée [kule] nf 1. (de matière liquide): ~ **de lave** lava flow; ~ **de boue** mudslide.

2. (de métal) casting.

couler [kule] ◆ vi 1. (liquide) to flow; **faire ~ un bain** to run a bath. 2. (beurre, fromage, nez) to run. 3. (navire, entreprise) to sink. ◆ vt 1. (navire) to sink. 2. (métal, bronze) to cast.

couleur [kulœr] ◆ nf 1. (teinte, caractère) colour. 2. (linge) coloureds (pl). 3. (CARTES) suit. ◆ adj inv (télévision, pellicule) colour (avant n).

couleuvre [kulœvr] nf grass snake.

coulis [kuli] nm liquid puree of fruit, vegetables or shellfish.

coulisse [kulis] nf (glissière): **fenêtre/porte à ~** sliding window/door. ► **coulisses** nfpl (THÉÂTRE) wings.

coulisser [kulise] vi to slide.

couloir [kulwar] nm 1. (corridor) corridor. 2. (GÉOGR) gully. 3. (SPORT & TRANSPORT) lane.

coup [ku] nm 1. (choc - physique, moral) blow; ~ **de couteau** stab (with a knife); **un ~ dur** fig a heavy blow; **donner un ~ de fouet à qqn** fig to give sb a shot in the arm; ~ **de grâce** litt & fig coup de grâce, death-blow; ~ **de pied** kick; ~ **de poing** punch. 2. (action nuisible) trick. 3. (SPORT - au tennis) stroke; (- en boxe) blow, punch; (- au football) kick; ~ **franc** free kick. 4. (d'éponge, de chiffon) wipe; **un ~ de crayon** a pencil stroke. 5. (bruit) noise; ~ **de feu** shot, gunshot; ~ **de tonnerre** thunderclap. 6. (action spectaculaire): ~ **d'État** coup (d'état); ~ **de théâtre** fig dramatic turn of events. 7. fam (fois) time. 8. loc: **boire un ~** to have a drink; **donner un ~ de main à qqn** to give sb a helping hand; **jeter un ~ d'œil à** to glance at; **tenir le ~** to hold out; **valoir le ~** to be well worth it. ► **coup de fil** nm phone call. ► **coup de foudre** nm love at first sight. ► **coup du lapin** nm (AUTOM) whiplash (U). ► **coup de soleil** nm sunburn (U). ► **coup de téléphone** nm telephone ou phone call; **donner** ou **passer un ~ de téléphone à qqn** to telephone ou phone sb. ► **coup de vent** nm gust of wind; **partir en ~ de vent** to rush off. ► **du coup** loc adv as a result. ► **coup sur coup** loc adv one after the other. ► **du premier coup** loc adv first time, at the first attempt. ► **tout à coup** loc adv suddenly. ► **à coup sûr** loc adv definitely. ► **sous le coup de** loc prép (sous l'effet de) in the grip of.

coupable [kupabl] ◆ adj 1. (personne, pensée) guilty. 2. (action, dessein) culpable, reprehensible; (*négligence, oubli*) sinful. ◆ *nmf* guilty person ou party.

coupant, -e [kupã, ãt] *adj* **1.** (*tranchant*) cutting. **2.** *fig* (*sec*) sharp.

coupe [kup] *nf* **1.** (*verre*) glass. **2.** (*à fruits*) dish. **3.** (SPORT) cup. **4.** (*de vêtement, aux cartes*) cut. **5.** (*plan, surface*) (*cross*) section. **6.** (*réduction*) cut, cutback.

coupé, -e [kupe] *adj* : **bien/mal ~** well/badly cut.

coupe-ongles [kupõgl] *nm inv* nail clippers.

coupe-papier [kuppapje] (*pl inv* ou **coupe-papiers**) *nm* paper knife.

couper [kupe] ◆ *vt* **1.** (*matériau, cheveux, blé*) to cut. **2.** (*interrompre, trancher*) to cut off. **3.** (*traverser*) to cut across. **4.** (*pain, au tennis*) to slice; (*rôti*) to carve. **5.** (*mélanger*) to dilute. **6.** (CARTES - *avec atout*) to trump; (- *paquet*) to cut. **7.** (*envie, appétit*) to take away. ◆ *vi* (*gén*) to cut. ▶ **se couper** *vp* **1.** (*se blesser*) to cut o.s. **2.** (*se croiser*) to cross. **3.** (*s'isoler*) : **se ~ de** to cut o.s. off from.

couperet [kuprɛ] *nm* **1.** (*de boucher*) cleaver. **2.** (*de guillotine*) blade.

couperosé, -e [kuproze] *adj* blotchy.

couple [kupl] *nm* (*de personnes*) couple; (*d'animaux*) pair.

coupler [kuple] *vt* (*objets*) to couple.

couplet [kuplɛ] *nm* verse.

coupole [kupɔl] *nf* (ARCHIT) dome, cupola.

coupon [kupõ] *nm* **1.** (*d'étoffe*) remnant. **2.** (*billet*) ticket.

coupon-réponse [kupõrepõs] (*pl* **coupons-réponse**) *nm* reply coupon.

coupure [kupyr] *nf* **1.** (*gén*) cut; (*billet de banque*) : **petite ~** small denomination note; **~ de courant** (ÉLECT) power cut; (INFORM) blackout. **2.** *fig* (*rupture*) break.

cour [kur] *nf* **1.** (*espace*) courtyard. **2.** (*du roi, tribunal*) court; *fig & hum* following; **Cour de cassation** Court of Appeal; **~ martiale** court-martial. **3.** *loc* : **faire la ~ à qqn** to court sb.

courage [kuraʒ] *nm* courage; **bon ~!** good luck!; **je n'ai pas le ~ de faire mes devoirs** I can't bring myself to do my homework.

courageux, -euse [kuraʒø, øz] *adj* **1.** (*brave*) brave. **2.** (*audacieux*) bold.

couramment [kuramã] *adv* **1.** (*parler une langue*) fluently. **2.** (*communément*) commonly.

courant, -e [kurã, ãt] *adj* **1.** (*habituel*) everyday (*avant n*); (*commun*) common; **'anglais ~'** 'fluent English'. **2.** (*en cours*)

present. ▶ **courant** *nm* **1.** (*marin, atmosphérique, électrique*) current; **~ d'air** draught. **2.** (*d'idées*) current. **3.** (*laps de temps*) : **dans le ~ du mois/de l'année** in the course of the month/the year. **4.** (*mouvement*) flow, movement. ▶ **au courant** *loc adv* : **être au ~** to know (about it); **mettre qqn au ~ (de)** to tell sb (about); **tenir qqn au ~ (de)** to keep sb informed (about); **se mettre/se tenir au ~ (de)** to get/keep up to date (with).

courbature [kurbatyr] *nf* ache.

courbaturé, -e [kurbatyre] *adj* aching.

courbe [kurb] ◆ *nf* curve; **~ de niveau** (*sur une carte*) contour (line). ◆ *adj* curved.

courber [kurbe] ◆ *vt* **1.** (*tige*) to bend. **2.** (*tête*) to bow. ◆ *vi* to bow. ▶ **se courber** *vp* **1.** (*chose*) to bend. **2.** (*personne*) to bow, to bend down.

courbette [kurbɛt] *nf* (*révérence*) bow; **faire des ~s** *fig* to bow and scrape.

coureur, -euse [kurœr, øz] *nm, f* (SPORT) runner; **~ cycliste** racing cyclist.

courge [kurʒ] *nf* **1.** (*légume*) marrow Br, squash Am. **2.** *fam* (*imbécile*) dimwit.

courgette [kurʒɛt] *nf* courgette Br, zucchini Am.

courir [kurir] ◆ *vi* **1.** (*aller rapidement*) to run. **2.** (SPORT) to race. **3.** (*se précipiter, rivière*) to rush. **4.** (*se propager*) : **le bruit court que ...** rumour has it that ...; **faire ~ un bruit** to spread a rumour. ◆ *vt* **1.** (SPORT) to run in. **2.** (*parcourir*) to roam (through). **3.** (*fréquenter - bals, musées*) to do the rounds of.

couronne [kurɔn] *nf* **1.** (*ornement, autorité*) crown. **2.** (*de fleurs*) wreath. **3.** (*monnaie - de Suède, d'Islande*) krona; (- *du Danemark, de Norvège*) krone; (- *de Tchécoslovaquie*) crown.

couronnement [kurɔnmã] *nm* **1.** (*de monarque*) coronation. **2.** *fig* (*apogée*) crowning achievement.

couronner [kurɔne] *vt* **1.** (*monarque*) to crown. **2.** (*récompenser*) to give a prize to.

courre [kur] → **chasse**.

courrier [kurje] *nm* mail, letters (*pl*); **~ du cœur** agony column.

courroie [kurwa] *nf* (TECHNOL) belt; (*attache*) strap; **~ de transmission** driving belt; **~ de ventilateur** fanbelt.

courroucer [kuruse] *vt littéraire* to anger.

cours [kur] *nm* **1.** (*écoulement*) flow; **~ d'eau** waterway; **donner** ou **laisser libre ~ à** *fig* to give free rein to. **2.** (*déroulement*) course; **au ~ de** during, in the course of; **en ~** (*année, dossier*) current; (*affaires*) in hand; **en ~ de route** on the way. **3.** (FIN) price; **avoir ~** (*monnaie*) to be legal tender. **4.** (*leçon*) class, lesson; **donner des ~** (**à qqn**) to teach (sb). **5.** (*classe*): **~ élémentaire** *years two and three of primary school*; **~ moyen** *last two years of primary school*; **~ préparatoire** = *first-year infants* Br, = *nursery school* Am.

course [kurs] *nf* **1.** (*action*) running (U); **au pas de ~** at a run. **2.** (*compétition*) race. **3.** (*en taxi*) journey. **4.** (*mouvement*) flight, course. **5.** (*commission*) errand; **faire des ~s** to go shopping.

coursier, -ère [kursje, ɛr] *nm, f* messenger.

court, -e [kur, kurt] *adj* short. ▶ **court** ◆ *adv*: **être à ~ d'argent/d'idées/d'arguments** to be short of money/ideas/arguments; **prendre qqn de ~** to catch sb unawares; **tourner ~** to stop suddenly. ◆ *nm*: **~ de tennis** tennis court.

court-bouillon [kurbujɔ̃] *nm* court-bouillon.

court-circuit [kursirkɥi] *nm* short circuit.

courtier, -ère [kurtje, ɛr] *nm, f* broker.

courtisan, -e [kurtizɑ̃, an] *nm, f* **1.** (HIST) courtier. **2.** (*flatteur*) sycophant. ▶ **courtisane** *nf* courtesan.

courtiser [kurtize] *vt* **1.** (*femme*) to woo, to court. **2.** *péj* (*flatter*) to flatter.

court-métrage [kurmetraʒ] *nm* short (film).

courtois, -e [kurtwa, az] *adj* courteous.

courtoisie [kurtwazi] *nf* courtesy.

couru, -e [kury] ◆ *pp* → **courir**. ◆ *adj* popular.

couscous [kuskus] *nm* couscous (*traditional North African dish of semolina served with a spicy stew of meat and vegetables*).

cousin, -e [kuzɛ̃, in] *nm, f* cousin; **~ germain** first cousin.

coussin [kusɛ̃] *nm* (*de siège*) cushion.

cousu, -e [kuzy] *pp* → **coudre**.

coût [ku] *nm* cost.

coûtant [kutɑ̃] → **prix**.

couteau, -x [kuto] *nm* **1.** (*gén*) knife; **à cran d'arrêt** flick knife. **2.** (*coquillage*) razor shell Br, razor clam Am.

coûter [kute] ◆ *vi* **1.** (*valoir*) to cost; **ça coûte combien?** how much is it?; **~ cher à qqn** to cost sb a lot; *fig* to cost sb dear ou dearly. **2.** *fig* (*être pénible*) to be difficult. ◆ *vt fig* to cost. ▶ **coûte que coûte** *loc adv* at all costs.

coûteux, -euse [kutø, øz] *adj* costly, expensive.

coutume [kutym] *nf* (*gén & JUR*) custom.

couture [kutyr] *nf* **1.** (*action*) sewing. **2.** (*points*) seam. **3.** (*activité*) dress-making; **haute ~** designer fashion.

couturier, -ère [kutyrje, ɛr] *nm, f* couturier.

couvée [kuve] *nf* (*d'œufs*) clutch; (*de poussins*) brood.

couvent [kuvɑ̃] *nm* (*de sœurs*) convent; (*de moines*) monastery.

couver [kuve] ◆ *vt* **1.** (*œufs*) to sit on. **2.** (*dorloter*) to mollycoddle. **3.** (*maladie*) to be sickening for. ◆ *vi* (*poule*) to brood; *fig* (*complot*) to hatch.

couvercle [kuvɛrkl] *nm* (*de casserole, boîte*) lid, cover.

couvert, -e [kuvɛr, ɛrt] ◆ *pp* → **couvrir**. ◆ *adj* **1.** (*submergé*) covered; **~ de** covered with. **2.** (*habillé*) dressed; **être bien ~** to be well wrapped up. **3.** (*nuageux*) overcast. ▶ **couvert** *nm* **1.** (*abri*): **se mettre à ~** to take shelter. **2.** (*place à table*) place (setting); **mettre ou dresser le ~** to set ou lay the table. ▶ **couverts** *nmpl* cutlery (U).

couverture [kuvɛrtyr] *nf* **1.** (*gén*) cover. **2.** (*de lit*) blanket; **~ chauffante** electric blanket. **3.** (*toit*) roofing (U).

couveuse [kuvøz] *nf* **1.** (*poule*) sitting hen. **2.** (*machine*) incubator.

couvre-chef [kuvrəʃɛf] (*pl* **couvre-chefs**) *nm hum* hat.

couvre-feu [kuvrəfø] (*pl* **couvre-feux**) *nm* curfew.

couvreur [kuvrœr] *nm* roofer.

couvrir [kuvrir] *vt* **1.** (*gén*) to cover; **~ qqn/qqch de** *litt & fig* to cover sb/sthg with. **2.** (*protéger*) to shield. ▶ **se couvrir** *vp* **1.** (*se vêtir*) to wrap up. **2.** (*se recouvrir*): **se ~ de feuilles/de fleurs** to come into leaf/blossom. **3.** (*ciel*) to cloud over. **4.** (*se protéger*) to cover o.s.

covoiturage [kɔvwatyraʒ] *nm* car sharing; **pratiquer le ~** to belong to a car pool.

CP *nm abr de* **cours préparatoire**.

crabe [krab] *nm* crab.

crachat [kraʃa] *nm* spit (U).

cracher [kraʃe] ◆ *vi* **1.** (*personne*) to spit. **2.** *fam* (*dédaigner*): **ne pas ~ sur qqch** not to turn one's nose up at sthg. ◆ *vt* (*sang*) to spit (up); (*lave, injures*) to spit (out).

crachin [kraʃɛ̃] *nm* drizzle.

crachoir [kraʃwar] *nm* spittoon.

craie [krɛ] *nf* chalk.

craindre [krɛ̃dr] *vt* **1.** (*redouter*) to fear, to be afraid of; ~ **de faire qqch** to be afraid of doing sthg; **je crains d'avoir oublié mes papiers** I'm afraid I've forgotten my papers; ~ **que** (+ *subjonctif*) to be afraid (that); **je crains qu'il oublie** ou **n'oublie** I'm afraid he may forget. **2.** (*être sensible à*) to be susceptible to.

craint, -e [krɛ̃, ɛ̃t] *pp* → **craindre**.

crainte [krɛ̃t] *nf* fear; **de** ~ **de faire qqch** for fear of doing sthg; **de** ~ **que** (+ *subjonctif*) for fear that; **il a fui de** ~ **qu'on ne le voie** he fled for fear that he might be seen ou for fear of being seen.

craintif, -ive [krɛ̃tif, iv] *adj* timid.

cramoisi, -e [kramwazi] *adj* crimson.

crampe [krɑ̃p] *nf* cramp.

crampon [krɑ̃pɔ̃] *nm* (*crochet - gén*) clamp; (- *pour alpinisme*) crampon.

cramponner [krɑ̃pɔne] ► **se cramponner** *vp* (*s'agripper*) to hang on; **se** ~ **à qqn/qqch** *litt & fig* to cling to sb/sthg.

cran [krɑ̃] *nm* **1.** (*entaille, degré*) notch, cut. **2.** (U) (*audace*) guts (*pl*).

crâne [kran] *nm* skull.

crâner [krane] *vi fam* to show off.

crânien, -enne [kranjɛ̃, ɛn] *adj*: **boîte** ~**ne** skull; **traumatisme** ~ head injury.

crapaud [krapo] *nm* toad.

crapule [krapyl] *nf* scum (U).

craquelure [kraklyr] *nf* crack.

craquement [krakmɑ̃] *nm* crack, cracking (U).

craquer [krake] ◆ *vi* **1.** (*produire un bruit*) to crack; (*plancher, chaussure*) to creak. **2.** (*se déchirer*) to split. **3.** (*s'effondrer - personne*) to crack up. **4.** (*être séduit par*): ~ **pour** to fall for. ◆ *vt* (*allumette*) to strike.

crasse [kras] *nf* **1.** (*saleté*) dirt, filth. **2.** *fam* (*mauvais tour*) dirty trick.

crasseux, -euse [krasø, øz] *adj* filthy.

cratère [kratɛr] *nm* crater.

cravache [kravaʃ] *nf* riding crop.

cravate [kravat] *nf* tie.

crawl [krol] *nm* crawl.

crayon [krɛjɔ̃] *nm* **1.** (*gén*) pencil; ~ **à bille** ballpoint (pen); ~ **de couleur** crayon. **2.** (TECHNOL) pen; ~ **optique** light pen.

créancier, -ère [kreɑ̃sje, ɛr] *nm, f* creditor.

créateur, -trice [kreatœr, tris] ◆ *adj* creative. ◆ *nm, f* creator. ► **Créateur** *nm*: **le Créateur** the Creator.

créatif, -ive [kreatif, iv] *adj* creative.

création [kreasjɔ̃] *nf* creation.

créativité [kreativite] *nf* creativity.

créature [kreatyr] *nf* creature.

crécelle [kresɛl] *nf* rattle.

crèche [krɛʃ] *nf* **1.** (*de Noël*) crib. **2.** (*garderie*) crèche.

crédible [kredibl] *adj* credible.

crédit [kredi] *nm* **1.** (*gén*) credit; **faire** ~ **à qqn** to give sb credit; **acheter/vendre qqch à** ~ to buy/sell sthg on credit; ~ **municipal** pawnshop. **2.** *fig & sout* influence.

crédit-bail [kredibaj] (*pl* **crédits-bails**) *nm* leasing.

créditeur, -trice [kreditœr, tris] ◆ *adj* in credit. ◆ *nm, f* creditor.

crédule [kredyl] *adj* credulous.

crédulité [kredylite] *nf* credulity.

créer [kree] *vt* **1.** (RELIG & *inventer*) to create. **2.** (*fonder*) to found, to start up.

crémaillère [kremajɛr] *nf* **1.** (*de cheminée*) trammel; **pendre la** ~ *fig* to have a housewarming (party). **2.** (TECHNOL) rack.

crémation [kremasjɔ̃] *nf* cremation.

crématoire [krematwar] → **four**.

crème [krɛm] ◆ *nf* (*gén*) cream; ~ **fouettée/fraîche/glacée** whipped/fresh/ice cream; ~ **anglaise** custard; ~ **hydratante** moisturizer. ◆ *adj inv* cream.

crémerie [krɛmri] *nf* dairy.

crémier, -ère [kremje, ɛr] *nm, f* dairyman (*f* dairywoman).

créneau, -x [kreno] *nm* **1.** (*de fortification*) crenel. **2.** (*pour se garer*): **faire un** ~ to reverse into a parking space. **3.** (*de marché*) niche. **4.** (*horaire*) window, gap.

créole [kreɔl] *adj & nm* creole.

crêpe [krɛp] ◆ *nf* (CULIN) pancake. ◆ *nm* (*tissu*) crepe.

crêperie [krɛpri] *nf* pancake restaurant.

crépi [krepi] *nm* roughcast.

crépir [krepir] *vt* to roughcast.

crépiter [krepite] *vi* (*feu, flammes*) to crackle; (*pluie*) to patter.

crépon [krepɔ̃] ◆ *adj* → **papier**. ◆ *nm* seersucker.

crépu, -e [krepy] *adj* frizzy.

crépuscule [krepyskyl] *nm* (*du jour*) dusk, twilight; *fig* twilight.

crescendo [kreʃɛndo, kreʃɛ̃do] ◆ *adv* crescendo; **aller** ~ *fig* (*bruit*) to get ou grow louder and louder. ◆ *nm inv* (MUS & *fig*) crescendo.

cresson [kresɔ̃] *nm* watercress.

Crète [krɛt] *nf*: **la** ~ Crete.

crête [krɛt] *nf* **1.** (*de coq*) comb. **2.** (*de montagne, vague, oiseau*) crest.

crétin, -e [kretɛ̃, in] *fam* ♦ *adj* cretinous, idiotic. ♦ *nm, f* cretin, idiot.

creuser [krøze] *vt* **1.** (*trou*) to dig. **2.** (*objet*) to hollow out. **3.** *fig* (*approfondir*) to go into deeply.

creux, creuse [krø, krøz] *adj* **1.** (*vide, concave*) hollow. **2.** (*période - d'activité réduite*) slack; (- *à tarif réduit*) off-peak. **3.** (*paroles*) empty. ▶ **creux** *nm* **1.** (*concavité*) hollow. **2.** (*période*) lull.

crevaison [krəvɛzõ] *nf* puncture.

crevant, -e [krəvã, ãt] *adj fam* (*fatigant*) exhausting, knackering Br.

crevasse [krəvas] *nf* (*de mur*) crevice, crack; (*de glacier*) crevasse; (*sur la main*) crack.

crevé, -e [krəve] *adj* **1.** (*pneu*) burst, punctured. **2.** *fam* (*fatigué*) dead, shattered Br.

crève-cœur [krɛvkœr] *nm inv* heartbreak.

crever [krəve] ♦ *vi* **1.** (*éclater*) to burst. **2.** *tfam* (*mourir*) to die; ~ **de** *fig* (*jalousie, orgueil*) to be bursting with. ♦ *vt* **1.** (*percer*) to burst. **2.** *fam* (*épuiser*) to wear out.

crevette [krəvɛt] *nf*: ~ (**grise**) shrimp; ~ (**rose**) prawn.

cri [kri] *nm* **1.** (*de personne*) cry, shout; (*perçant*) scream; (*d'animal*) cry; **pousser un** ~ to cry (out), to shout; **pousser un** ~ **de douleur** to cry out in pain. **2.** (*appel*) cry; **le dernier** ~ *fig* the latest thing.

criant, -e [krijã, ãt] *adj* (*injustice*) blatant.

criard, -e [krijar, ard] *adj* **1.** (*voix*) strident, piercing. **2.** (*couleur*) loud.

crible [kribl] *nm* (*instrument*) sieve; **passer qqch au** ~ *fig* to examine sthg closely.

criblé, -e [krible] *adj* riddled; **être** ~ **de dettes** to be up to one's eyes in debt.

cric [krik] *nm* jack.

cricket [krikɛt] *nm* cricket.

crier [krije] ♦ *vi* **1.** (*pousser un cri*) to shout (out), to yell. **2.** (*parler fort*) to shout. **3.** (*protester*): ~ **contre** ou **après** **qqn** to nag sb, to go on at sb. ♦ *vt* to shout (out).

crime [krim] *nm* **1.** (*délit*) crime. **2.** (*meurtre*) murder.

criminalité [kriminalite] *nf* crime.

criminel, -elle [kriminɛl] ♦ *adj* criminal. ♦ *nm, f* criminal; ~ **de guerre** war criminal.

crin [krɛ̃] *nm* (*d'animal*) hair.

crinière [krinjɛr] *nf* mane.

crique [krik] *nf* creek.

criquet [krikɛ] *nm* locust; (*sauterelle*) grasshopper.

crise [kriz] *nf* **1.** (MÉD) attack; ~ **cardiaque** heart attack; ~ **de foie** bilious attack. **2.** (*accès*) fit; ~ **de nerfs** attack of nerves. **3.** (*phase critique*) crisis.

crispation [krispasjõ] *nf* **1.** (*contraction*) contraction. **2.** (*agacement*) irritation.

crispé, -e [krispe] *adj* tense, on edge.

crisper [krispe] *vt* **1.** (*contracter - visage*) to tense; (- *poing*) to clench. **2.** (*agacer*) to irritate. ▶ **se crisper** *vp* **1.** (*se contracter*) to tense (up). **2.** (*s'irriter*) to get irritated.

crisser [krise] *vi* (*pneu*) to screech; (*étoffe*) to rustle.

cristal, -aux [kristal, o] *nm* crystal; ~ **de roche** quartz.

cristallin, -e [kristalɛ̃, in] *adj* **1.** (*limpide*) crystal clear, crystalline. **2.** (*roche*) crystalline. ▶ **cristallin** *nm* crystalline lens.

critère [kritɛr] *nm* criterion.

critique [kritik] ♦ *adj* critical. ♦ *nmf* critic. ♦ *nf* criticism.

critiquer [kritike] *vt* to criticize.

croasser [krɔase] *vi* to croak, to caw.

croate [krɔat] *adj* Croat, Croatian. ▶ **Croate** *nmf* Croat, Croatian.

Croatie [krɔasi] *nf*: **la** ~ Croatia.

croc [kro] *nm* (*de chien*) fang.

croche [krɔʃ] *nf* quaver Br, eighth (note) Am.

croche-pied [krɔʃpje] (*pl* **croche-pieds**) *nm*: **faire un** ~ **à qqn** to trip sb up.

crochet [krɔʃɛ] *nm* **1.** (*de métal*) hook; **vivre aux** ~**s de qqn** to live off sb. **2.** (TRICOT) crochet hook. **3.** (TYPO) square bracket. **4.** (BOXE): ~ **du gauche/du droit** left/right hook.

crochu, -e [krɔʃy] *adj* (*doigts*) claw-like; (*nez*) hooked.

crocodile [krɔkɔdil] *nm* crocodile.

croire [krwar] ♦ *vt* **1.** (*chose, personne*) to believe. **2.** (*penser*) to think; **tu crois?** do you think so?; **il le croyait parti** he thought you'd left; ~ **que** to think (that). ♦ *vi*: ~ **à** to believe in; ~ **en** to believe in, to have faith in.

croisade [krwazad] *nf* (HIST & *fig*) crusade.

croisé, -e [krwaze] *adj* (*veste*) double-breasted. ▶ **croisé** *nm* (HIST) crusader.

croisement [krwazmã] *nm* **1.** (*intersection*) junction, intersection. **2.** (BIOL) crossbreeding.

croiser [krwaze] ♦ *vt* **1.** (*jambes*) to cross; (*bras*) to fold. **2.** (*passer à côté de*) to pass. **3.** (*chemin*) to cross, to cut across. **4.** (*métisser*) to interbreed. ◆ *vi* (NAVIG) to cruise. ▶ **se croiser** *vp* (*chemins*) to cross, to intersect; (*personnes*) to come across each other; (*lettres*) to cross; (*regards*) to meet.

croisière [krwazjɛr] *nf* cruise.

croisillon [krwazijɔ̃] *nm*: **à ~s** lattice (*avant n*).

croissance [krwasɑ̃s] *nf* growth, development; **~ économique** economic growth ou development.

croissant, -e [krwasɑ̃, ɑ̃t] *adj* increasing, growing. ▶ **croissant** *nm* **1.** (*de lune*) crescent. **2.** (CULIN) croissant.

croître [krwatr] *vi* **1.** (*grandir*) to grow. **2.** (*augmenter*) to increase.

croix [krwa] *nf* cross; **en ~** in the shape of a cross; **~ gammée** swastika.

Croix-Rouge [krwaruʒ] *nf*: **la ~** the Red Cross.

croquant, -e [krɔkɑ̃, ɑ̃t] *adj* crisp, crunchy.

croque-mitaine [krɔkmitɛn] (*pl* **croque-mitaines**) *nm* bogeyman.

croque-monsieur [krɔkməsjø] *nm inv* toasted cheese and ham sandwich.

croque-mort [krɔkmɔr] (*pl* **croque-morts**) *nm fam* undertaker.

croquer [krɔke] ◆ *vt* **1.** (*manger*) to crunch. **2.** (*dessiner*) to sketch. ◆ *vi* to be crunchy.

croquette [krɔkɛt] *nf* croquette.

croquis [krɔki] *nm* sketch.

cross [krɔs] *nm* (*exercice*) cross-country (running); (*course*) cross-country race.

crotte [krɔt] *nf* (*de lapin etc*) droppings (*pl*); (*de chien*) dirt.

crottin [krɔtɛ̃] *nm* (*de cheval*) (horse) manure.

crouler [krule] *vi* to crumble; **~ sous** *litt & fig* to collapse under.

croupe [krup] *nf* rump; **monter en ~** to ride pillion.

croupier [krupje] *nm* croupier.

croupir [krupir] *vi litt & fig* to stagnate.

CROUS [krus] (*abr de* **Centre régional des œuvres universitaires et scolaires**) *nm* student representative body dealing with accommodation, catering etc.

croustillant, -e [krustijɑ̃, ɑ̃t] *adj* (*croquant - pain*) crusty; (*- biscuit*) crunchy.

croûte [krut] *nf* **1.** (*du pain, terrestre*) crust. **2.** (*de fromage*) rind. **3.** (*de plaie*) scab. **4.** *fam péj* (*tableau*) daub.

croûton [krutɔ̃] *nm* **1.** (*bout du pain*) crust. **2.** (*pain frit*) crouton. **3.** *fam péj* (*personne*) fuddy-duddy.

croyance [krwajɑ̃s] *nf* belief.

croyant, -e [krwajɑ̃, ɑ̃t] ◆ *adj*: **être ~** to be a believer. ◆ *nm, f* believer.

CRS (*abr de* **Compagnie républicaine de sécurité**) *nm* member of the French riot police.

cru, -e [kry] ◆ *pp* → **croire**. ◆ *adj* **1.** (*non cuit*) raw. **2.** (*violent*) harsh. **3.** (*direct*) blunt. **4.** (*grivois*) crude. ▶ **cru** *nm* (*vin*) vintage, wine; (*vignoble*) vineyard; **du ~** *fig* local.

crû [kry] *pp* → **croître**.

cruauté [kryote] *nf* cruelty.

cruche [kryʃ] *nf* **1.** (*objet*) jug. **2.** *fam péj* (*personne niaise*) twit.

crucial, -e, -aux [krysjal, o] *adj* crucial.

crucifix [krysifi] *nm* crucifix.

crudité [krydite] *nf* crudeness. ▶ **crudités** *nfpl* crudités.

crue [kry] *nf* rise in the water level.

cruel, -elle [kryɛl] *adj* cruel.

crustacé [krystase] *nm* shellfish, crustacean; **~s** shellfish (U).

Cuba [kyba] *n* Cuba.

cubain, -e [kybɛ̃, ɛn] *adj* Cuban. ▶ **Cubain, -e** *nm, f* Cuban.

cube [kyb] *nm* cube; **4 au ~ = 64** 4 cubed is 64; **mètre ~** cubic metre.

cueillette [kœjɛt] *nf* picking, harvesting.

cueilli, -e [kœji] *pp* → **cueillir**.

cueillir [kœjir] *vt* (*fruits, fleurs*) to pick.

cuillère, cuiller [kɥijɛr] *nf* spoon; **~ à café** coffee spoon; **~ à dessert** dessertspoon; **~ à soupe** soup spoon; (CULIN) tablespoon; **petite ~** teaspoon.

cuillerée [kɥijere] *nf* spoonful; **~ à café** (CULIN) teaspoonful; **~ à soupe** (CULIN) tablespoonful.

cuir [kɥir] *nm* leather; (*non tanné*) hide; **~ chevelu** (ANAT) scalp.

cuirasse [kɥiras] *nf* (*de chevalier*) breastplate; *fig* armour.

cuirassé [kɥirase] *nm* battleship.

cuire [kɥir] ◆ *vt* (*viande, œuf*) to cook; (*tarte, gâteau*) to bake. ◆ *vi* **1.** (*viande, œuf*) to cook; (*tarte, gâteau*) to bake; **faire ~ qqch** to cook/bake sthg. **2.** *fig* (*personne*) to roast, to be boiling.

cuisine [kɥizin] *nf* **1.** (*pièce*) kitchen. **2.** (*art*) cooking, cookery; **faire la ~** to do the cooking, to cook.

cuisiné, -e [kɥizine] *adj*: **plat ~** ready-cooked meal.

cuisiner [kɥizine] ◆ *vt* **1.** (*aliment*) to cook. **2.** *fam* (*personne*) to grill. ◆ *vi* to cook; **bien/mal ~** to be a good/bad cook.

cuisinette [kчizinɛt] *nf* kitchenette.
cuisinier, -ère [kчizinje, ɛr] *nm, f*
cook. ▶ **cuisinière** *nf* cooker; **cuisinière**
électrique/à gaz electric/gas cooker.
cuisse [kчis] *nf* 1. (ANAT) thigh.
2. (CULIN) leg.
cuisson [kчisɔ̃] *nf* cooking.
cuit, -e [kчi, kчit] ◆ *pp* → **cuire**. ◆ *adj*:
bien ~ (*steak*) well-done.
cuivre [kчivr] *nm* (*métal*): **~ (rouge)** copper; **~ jaune** brass. ▶ **cuivres** *nmpl*: **les**
~s (MUS) the brass.
cuivré, -e [kчivre] *adj* (*couleur, reflet*)
coppery; (*teint*) bronzed.
cul [ky] *nm* 1. *tfam* (*postérieur*) bum.
2. (*de bouteille*) bottom.
culbute [kylbyt] *nf* 1. (*saut*) somersault. 2. (*chute*) tumble, fall.
cul-de-sac [kydsak] (*pl* **culs-de-sac**) *nm*
dead end.
culinaire [kylinɛr] *adj* culinary.
culminant [kylminã] → **point**.
culot [kylo] *nm* 1. *fam* (*toupet*) cheek,
nerve; **avoir du ~** to have a lot of nerve.
2. (*de cartouche, ampoule*) cap.
culotte [kylɔt] *nf* (*sous-vêtement féminin*)
knickers (*pl*), panties (*pl*), pair of knickers ou panties.
culotté, -e [kylɔte] *adj* (*effronté*): **elle est**
~e she's got a nerve.
culpabilité [kylpabilite] *nf* guilt.
culte [kylt] *nm* 1. (*vénération, amour*)
worship. 2. (*religion*) religion.
cultivateur, -trice [kyltivatœr, tris]
nm, f farmer.
cultivé, -e [kyltive] *adj* (*personne*) educated, cultured.
cultiver [kyltive] *vt* 1. (*terre, goût, rela-*
tion) to cultivate. 2. (*plante*) to grow.
culture [kyltyr] *nf* 1. (AGRIC) cultivation, farming; **les ~s** cultivated land.
2. (*savoir*) culture, knowledge; **~**
physique physical training. 3. (*civilisa-*
tion) culture.
culturel, -elle [kyltyrɛl] *adj* cultural.
culturisme [kyltyrism] *nm* bodybuild-
ing.
cumin [kymɛ̃] *nm* cumin.
cumuler [kymyle] *vt* (*fonctions, titres*) to
hold simultaneously; (*salaires*) to draw
simultaneously.
cupide [kypid] *adj* greedy.
cure [kyr] *nf* (*course of*) treatment;
faire une ~ de fruits to go on a fruit-
based diet; **~ de désintoxication**
(*d'alcool*) drying-out treatment; (*de*
drogue) detoxification treatment; **~ de**
sommeil sleep therapy; **faire une ~ ther-**

male to take the waters.
curé [kyre] *nm* parish priest.
cure-dents [kyrdã] *nm inv* toothpick.
curer [kyre] *vt* to clean out.
curieux, -euse [kyrjø, øz] ◆ *adj*
1. (*intéressé*) curious; **~ de qqch/de faire**
qqch curious about sthg/to do sthg.
2. (*indiscret*) inquisitive. 3. (*étrange*)
strange, curious. ◆ *nm, f* busybody.
curiosité [kyrjozite] *nf* curiosity.
curriculum vitae [kyrikylɔmvite] *nm*
inv curriculum vitae.
curry [kyri], **carry** [kari], **cari** [kari]
nm 1. (*épice*) curry powder. 2. (*plat*)
curry.
curseur [kyrsœr] *nm* cursor.
cutané, -e [kytane] *adj* cutaneous,
skin (*avant n*).
cutiréaction, cuti-réaction (*pl*
cuti-réactions) [kytireaksjɔ̃] *nf* skin test.
cuve [kyv] *nf* 1. (*citerne*) tank. 2. (*à vin*)
vat.
cuvée [kyve] *nf* (*récolte*) vintage.
cuvette [kyvɛt] *nf* 1. (*récipient*) basin,
bowl. 2. (*de lavabo*) basin; (*de W.-C.*)
bowl. 3. (GÉOGR) basin.
CV *nm* 1. (*abr de* **curriculum vitae**) CV.
2. (*abr de* **cheval-vapeur**) hp; (*puissance*
fiscale) *classification for scaling of car tax*.
cyanure [sjanyr] *nm* cyanide.
cybercafé [siberkafe] *nm* cybercafe.
cyberespace [siberɛspas] *nm* cyberspace.
cyclable [siklabl] → **piste**.
cycle [sikl] *nm* cycle; **premier ~** (UNIV) =
first and second year; (SCOL) middle
school *Br*, junior high school *Am*; **se-**
cond ~ (UNIV) = final year *Br*, = senior
year *Am*; (SCOL) upper school *Br*, high
school *Am*; **troisième ~** (UNIV) = postgraduate year ou years.
cyclique [siklik] *adj* cyclic, cyclical.
cyclisme [siklism] *nm* cycling.
cycliste [siklist] *nmf* cyclist.
cyclone [siklon] *nm* cyclone.
cygne [siɲ] *nm* swan.
cylindre [silɛ̃dr] *nm* 1. (AUTOM & GÉOM)
cylinder. 2. (*rouleau*) roller.
cymbale [sɛ̃bal] *nf* cymbal.
cynique [sinik] *adj* cynical.
cynisme [sinism] *nm* cynicism.
cyprès [sipre] *nm* cypress.
cyrillique [sirilik] *adj* Cyrillic.

D

d, D [de] *nm inv* d, D.

d' → **de**.

d'abord [dabɔr] → **abord**.

d'accord [dakɔr] *loc adv*: ~**!** all right!, OK!; **être ~ avec** to agree with.

dactylo [daktilo] *nf* (*personne*) typist; (*procédé*) typing.

dactylographier [daktilɔgrafje] *vt* to type.

dada [dada] *nm* **1.** *fam* (*occupation*) hobby. **2.** *fam* (*idée*) hobbyhorse.

dahlia [dalja] *nm* dahlia.

daigner [deɲe] *vi* to deign.

daim [dɛ̃] *nm* **1.** (*animal*) fallow deer. **2.** (*peau*) suede.

dallage [dalaʒ] *nm* (*action*) paving; (*dalles*) pavement.

dalle [dal] *nf* (*de pierre*) slab; (*de lino*) tile.

dalmatien, -enne [dalmasjɛ̃, ɛn] *nm, f* dalmatian.

daltonien, -enne [daltɔnjɛ̃, ɛn] *adj* colour-blind.

dame [dam] *nf* **1.** (*femme*) lady. **2.** (CARTES & ÉCHECS) queen. ▶ **dames** *nfpl* draughts Br, checkers Am.

damier [damje] *nm* **1.** (*de jeu*) draughtboard Br, checkerboard Am. **2.** (*motif*): **à ~** checked.

damné, -e [dane] *adj fam* damned.

damner [dane] *vt* to damn.

dancing [dɑ̃siŋ] *nm* dance hall.

dandiner [dɑ̃dine] ▶ **se dandiner** *vp* to waddle.

Danemark [danmark] *nm*: **le ~** Denmark.

danger [dɑ̃ʒe] *nm* danger; **en ~** in danger; **courir un ~** to run a risk.

dangereux, -euse [dɑ̃ʒrø, øz] *adj* dangerous.

danois, -e [danwa, az] *adj* Danish. ▶ **danois** *nm* **1.** (*langue*) Danish. **2.** (*chien*) Great Dane. ▶ **Danois, -e** *nm, f* Dane.

dans [dɑ̃] *prép* **1.** (*dans le temps*) in; **je reviens ~ un mois** I'll be back in a month ou in a month's time. **2.** (*dans l'espace*) in; **~ une boîte** in ou inside a box. **3.** (*avec mouvement*) into; **entrer ~ une chambre** to come into a room, to enter a room.

4. (*indiquant état, manière*) in; **vivre ~ la misère** to live in poverty; **il est ~ le commerce** he's in business. **5.** (*environ*): **~ les ...** about ...; **ça coûte ~ les 200 francs** it costs about 200 francs.

dansant, -e [dɑ̃sɑ̃, ɑ̃t] *adj litt & fig* dancing; **soirée ~e** dance; **thé ~** tea dance.

danse [dɑ̃s] *nf* **1.** (*art*) dancing. **2.** (*musique*) dance.

danser [dɑ̃se] ◆ *vi* **1.** (*personne*) to dance. **2.** (*bateau*) to bob; (*flammes*) to flicker. ◆ *vt* to dance.

danseur, -euse [dɑ̃sœr, øz] *nm, f* dancer.

dard [dar] *nm* (*d'animal*) sting.

date [dat] *nf* **1.** (*jour+mois+année*) date; **de longue ~** long-standing; **~ de naissance** date of birth. **2.** (*moment*) event.

dater [date] ◆ *vt* to date. ◆ *vi* **1.** (*marquer*) to be ou mark a milestone. **2.** *fam* (*être démodé*) to be dated. ▶ **à dater de** *loc prép* as of ou from.

datte [dat] *nf* date.

dattier [datje] *nm* date palm.

daube [dob] *nf*: (**bœuf en**) **~** beef stew cooked with wine.

dauphin [dofɛ̃] *nm* **1.** (*mammifère*) dolphin. **2.** (HIST) heir apparent.

daurade [dɔrad] *nf* sea bream.

davantage [davɑ̃taʒ] *adv* **1.** (*plus*) more; **~ de** more. **2.** (*plus longtemps*) (any) longer.

de [də] (*contraction de de + le* = **du** [dy], *de + les* = **des** [de]) ◆ *prép* **1.** (*provenance*) from; **revenir ~ Paris** to come back ou return from Paris; **il est sorti ~ la maison** he left the house, he went out of the house. **2.** (*avec à*): **~ ... à** from ... to; **~ dix heures à midi** from ten o'clock to ou till midday; **il y avait ~ quinze à vingt mille spectateurs** there were between fifteen and twenty thousand spectators. **3.** (*appartenance*) of; **la porte du salon** the door of the sitting room, the sitting-room door; **le frère ~ Pierre** Pierre's brother. **4.** (*indique la détermination, la qualité*): **un verre d'eau** a glass of water; **un peignoir ~ soie** a silk dressing gown; **un appartement ~ 60m²** a flat 60 metres square; **un bébé ~ trois jours** a three-day-old baby; **une ville ~ 500 000 habitants** a town with ou of 500,000 inhabitants; **le train ~ 9 h 30** the 9.30 train. ◆ *article partitif* **1.** (*dans une phrase affirmative*) some; **je voudrais du vin/du lait** I'd like (some) wine/(some) milk; **boire ~ l'eau** to drink (some) water;

acheter des légumes to buy some vegetables. **2.** (*dans une interrogation ou une négation*) any; **ils n'ont pas d'enfants** they don't have any children, they have no children; **avez-vous du pain?** do you have any bread?, have you got any bread?; **voulez-vous du thé?** would you like some tea?

dé [de] *nm* **1.** (*à jouer*) dice, die. **2.** (COUTURE): ~ **(à coudre)** thimble.

DEA (*abr de* **diplôme d'études approfondies**) *nm* postgraduate diploma.

dealer[1] [dile] *vt* to deal.

dealer[2] [dilœr] *nm fam* dealer.

déambuler [deɑ̃byle] *vi* to stroll (around).

débâcle [debakl] *nf* (*débandade*) rout; *fig* collapse.

déballer [debale] *vt* to unpack; *fam fig* to pour out.

débandade [debɑ̃dad] *nf* dispersal.

débarbouiller [debarbuje] *vt*: ~ **qqn** to wash sb's face. ► **se débarbouiller** *vp* to wash one's face.

débarcadère [debarkadɛr] *nm* landing stage.

débardeur [debardœr] *nm* **1.** (*ouvrier*) docker. **2.** (*vêtement*) slipover.

débarquement [debarkəmɑ̃] *nm* (*de marchandises*) unloading.

débarquer [debarke] ♦ *vt* (*marchandises*) to unload; (*passagers & MIL*) to land. ♦ *vi* **1.** (*d'un bateau*) to disembark. **2.** (MIL) to land. **3.** *fam* (*arriver à l'improviste*) to turn up; *fig* to know nothing.

débarras [debara] *nm* junk room; **bon ~!** *fig* good riddance!

débarrasser [debarase] *vt* **1.** (*pièce*) to clear up; (*table*) to clear. **2.** (*ôter*): ~ **qqn de qqch** to take sthg from sb. ► **se débarrasser** *vp*: **se ~ de** to get rid of.

débat [deba] *nm* debate.

débattre [debatr] *vt* to debate, to discuss. ► **se débattre** *vp* to struggle.

débattu, -e [debaty] *pp* → **débattre**.

débauche [deboʃ] *nf* debauchery.

débaucher [deboʃe] *vt* **1.** (*corrompre*) to debauch, to corrupt. **2.** (*licencier*) to make redundant.

débile [debil] ♦ *nmf* **1.** (*attardé*) retarded person; ~ **mental** mentally retarded person. **2.** *fam* (*idiot*) moron. ♦ *adj fam* stupid.

débit [debi] *nm* **1.** (*de marchandises*) (retail) sale. **2.** (*magasin*): ~ **de boissons** bar; ~ **de tabac** tobacconist's Br, tobacco shop Am. **3.** (*coupe*) sawing up, cutting up. **4.** (*de liquide*) (rate of) flow.

5. (*élocution*) delivery. **6.** (FIN) debit; **avoir un ~ de 500 francs** to be 500 francs overdrawn.

débitant, -e [debitɑ̃, ɑ̃t] *nm, f* **1.** (*de boissons*) publican Br, bar owner Am. **2.** (*de tabac*) tobacconist Br, tobacco dealer Am.

débiter [debite] *vt* **1.** (*marchandises*) to sell. **2.** (*arbre*) to saw up; (*viande*) to cut up. **3.** (*suj: robinet*) to have a flow of. **4.** *fam fig* (*prononcer*) to spout. **5.** (FIN) to debit.

débiteur, -trice [debitœr, tris] ♦ *adj* **1.** (*personne*) debtor (*avant n*). **2.** (FIN) debit (*avant n*), in the red. ♦ *nm, f* debtor.

déblayer [debleje] *vt* (*dégager*) to clear; ~ **le terrain** *fig* to clear the ground.

débloquer [debloke] ♦ *vt* **1.** (*machine*) to get going again. **2.** (*crédit*) to release. **3.** (*compte, salaires, prix*) to unfreeze. ♦ *vi fam* to talk rubbish.

déboires [debwar] *nmpl* **1.** (*déceptions*) disappointments. **2.** (*échecs*) setbacks. **3.** (*ennuis*) trouble (U), problems.

déboiser [debwaze] *vt* (*région*) to deforest; (*terrain*) to clear (of trees).

déboîter [debwate] ♦ *vt* **1.** (*objet*) to dislodge. **2.** (*membre*) to dislocate. ♦ *vi* (AUTOM) to pull out. ► **se déboîter** *vp* **1.** (*se démonter*) to come apart; (*porte*) to come off its hinges. **2.** (*membre*) to dislocate.

débonnaire [debɔnɛr] *adj* good-natured, easy-going.

déborder [debɔrde] *vi* (*fleuve, liquide*) to overflow; *fig* to flood; ~ **de** (*vie, joie*) to be bubbling with.

débouché [debuʃe] *nm* **1.** (*issue*) end. **2.** (*gén pl*) (COMM) outlet. **3.** (*de carrière*) prospect, opening.

déboucher [debuʃe] ♦ *vt* **1.** (*bouteille*) to open. **2.** (*conduite, nez*) to unblock. ♦ *vi*: ~ **sur** (*arriver*) to open out into; *fig* to lead to, to achieve.

débourser [deburse] *vt* to pay out.

debout [dəbu] *adv* **1.** (*gén*): **être ~** (*sur ses pieds*) to be standing (up); (*réveillé*) to be up; (*objet*) to be standing up ou upright; **mettre qqch ~** to stand sthg up; **se mettre ~** to stand up; **~!** get up!, on your feet! **2.** *loc*: **tenir ~** (*bâtiment*) to remain standing; (*argument*) to stand up.

déboutonner [debutɔne] *vt* to unbutton, to undo.

débraillé, -e [debraje] *adj* dishevelled.

débrayage [debrejaʒ] *nm* (*arrêt de travail*) stoppage.

débrayer [debreje] vi (AUTOM) to disengage the clutch, to declutch.

débris [debri] ◆ nm piece, fragment. ◆ nmpl (restes) leftovers.

débrouillard, -e [debrujar, ard] fam adj resourceful.

débrouiller [debruje] vt 1. (démêler) to untangle. 2. fig (résoudre) to unravel, to solve. ▶ **se débrouiller** vp: se ~ **(pour faire qqch)** to manage (to do sthg); se ~ **en anglais/math** to get by in English/maths; **débrouille-toi!** you'll have to sort it out (by) yourself!

débroussailler [debrusaje] vt (terrain) to clear; fig to do the groundwork for.

début [deby] nm beginning, start; au ~ at the start ou beginning; au ~ de at the beginning of; dès le ~ (right) from the start.

débutant, -e [debytã, ãt] nm, f beginner.

débuter [debyte] vi 1. (commencer): ~ **(par)** to begin (with), to start (with). 2. (faire ses débuts) to start out.

deçà [dəsa] ▶ **en deçà de** loc prép 1. (de ce côté-ci de) on this side of. 2. (en dessous de) short of.

décacheter [dekaʃte] vt to open.

décadence [dekadãs] nf 1. (déclin) decline. 2. (débauche) decadence.

décadent, -e [dekadã, ãt] adj decadent.

décaféiné, -e [dekafeine] adj decaffeinated. ▶ **décaféiné** nm decaffeinated coffee.

décalage [dekalaʒ] nm gap; fig gulf, discrepancy; ~ **horaire** (entre zones) time difference; (après un vol) jet lag.

décaler [dekale] vt 1. (dans le temps - avancer) to bring forward; (- retarder) to put back. 2. (dans l'espace) to move, to shift.

décalquer [dekalke] vt to trace.

décamper [dekãpe] vi fam to clear off.

décapant, -e [dekapã, ãt] adj 1. (nettoyant) stripping. 2. fig (incisif) cutting, caustic. ▶ **décapant** nm (paint) stripper.

décaper [dekape] vt to strip, to sand.

décapiter [dekapite] vt (personne) to behead; (- accidentellement) to decapitate; (arbre) to cut the top off; fig to remove the leader ou leaders of.

décapotable [dekapɔtabl] nf & adj convertible.

décapsuler [dekapsyle] vt to take the top off, to open.

décapsuleur [dekapsylœr] nm bottle opener.

décédé, -e [desede] adj deceased.

décéder [desede] vi to die.

déceler [desle] vt (repérer) to detect.

décembre [desãbr] nm December; voir aussi **septembre**.

décemment [desamã] adv 1. (convenablement) properly. 2. (raisonnablement) reasonably.

décence [desãs] nf decency.

décennie [deseni] nf decade.

décent, -e [desã, ãt] adj decent.

décentralisation [desãtralizasjõ] nf decentralization.

décentrer [desãtre] vt to move off-centre ou away from the centre.

déception [desɛpsjõ] nf disappointment.

décerner [desɛrne] vt: ~ **qqch à** to award sthg to.

décès [desɛ] nm death.

décevant, -e [desəvã, ãt] adj disappointing.

décevoir [desəvwar] vt to disappoint.

déchaîné, -e [deʃene] adj 1. (vent, mer) stormy, wild. 2. (personne) wild.

déchaîner [deʃene] vt (passion) to unleash; (rires) to cause an outburst of. ▶ **se déchaîner** vp 1. (éléments naturels) to erupt. 2. (personne) to fly into a rage.

déchanter [deʃãte] vi to become disillusioned.

décharge [deʃarʒ] nf 1. (JUR) discharge. 2. (ÉLECTR) discharge; ~ **électrique** electric shock. 3. (dépotoir) rubbish tip ou dump Br, garbage dump Am.

déchargement [deʃarʒəmã] nm unloading.

décharger [deʃarʒe] vt 1. (véhicule, marchandises) to unload. 2. (arme - tirer) to fire, to discharge; (- enlever la charge) to unload. 3. (soulager - cœur) to unburden; (- conscience) to salve; (- colère) to vent. 4. (libérer): ~ **qqn de** to release sb from.

décharné, -e [deʃarne] adj (maigre) emaciated.

déchausser [deʃose] vt: ~ **qqn** to take sb's shoes off. ▶ **se déchausser** vp 1. (personne) to take one's shoes off. 2. (dent) to come loose.

déchéance [deʃeãs] nf (déclin) degeneration, decline.

déchet [deʃɛ] nm (de matériau) scrap. ▶ **déchets** nmpl refuse (U), waste (U).

déchiffrer [deʃifre] vt 1. (inscription, hiéroglyphes) to decipher; (énigme) to unravel. 2. (MUS) to sight-read.

déchiqueter [deʃikte] vt to tear to shreds.

déchirant, -e [deʃirɑ̃, ɑ̃t] adj heartrending.

déchirement [deʃirmɑ̃] nm (souffrance morale) heartbreak, distress.

déchirer [deʃire] vt (papier, tissu) to tear up, to rip up. ▶ **se déchirer** vp 1. (personnes) to tear each other apart. 2. (matériau, muscle) to tear.

déchirure [deʃiryr] nf tear; fig wrench; ~ **musculaire** (MÉD) torn muscle.

déchu, -e [deʃy] adj 1. (homme, ange) fallen; (souverain) deposed. 2. (JUR): être ~ **de** to be deprived of.

décibel [desibɛl] nm decibel.

décidé, -e [deside] adj 1. (résolu) determined. 2. (arrêté) settled.

décidément [desidemɑ̃] adv really.

décider [deside] vt 1. (prendre une décision): ~ **(de faire qqch)** to decide (to do sthg). 2. (convaincre): ~ **qqn à faire qqch** to persuade sb to do sthg. ▶ **se décider** vp 1. (personne): **se** ~ **(à faire qqch)** to make up one's mind (to do sthg). 2. (choisir): **se** ~ **pour** to decide on, to settle on.

décilitre [desilitr] nm decilitre.

décimal, -e, -aux [desimal, o] adj decimal. ▶ **décimale** nf decimal.

décimer [desime] vt to decimate.

décimètre [desimetr] nm 1. (dixième de mètre) decimetre. 2. (règle) ruler; **double** ~ = foot rule.

décisif, -ive [desizif, iv] adj decisive.

décision [desizjɔ̃] nf decision.

décisionnaire [desizjɔnɛr] nmf decision-maker.

déclamer [deklame] vt to declaim.

déclaration [deklarasjɔ̃] nf 1. (orale) declaration, announcement. 2. (écrite) report, declaration; (d'assurance) claim; ~ **de naissance/de décès** registration of birth/death; ~ **d'impôts** tax return; ~ **de revenus** statement of income.

déclarer [deklare] vt 1. (annoncer) to declare. 2. (signaler) to report; **rien à** ~ nothing to declare; ~ **une naissance** to register a birth. ▶ **se déclarer** vp 1. (se prononcer): **se** ~ **pour/contre qqch** to come out in favour of/against sthg. 2. (se manifester) to break out.

déclenchement [deklɑ̃ʃmɑ̃] nm (de mécanisme) activating, setting off; fig launching.

déclencher [deklɑ̃ʃe] vt (mécanisme) to activate, to set off; fig to launch. ▶ **se déclencher** vp (mécanisme) to go off, to

be activated; fig to be triggered off.

déclic [deklik] nm 1. (mécanisme) trigger. 2. (bruit) click.

déclin [deklɛ̃] nm 1. (de civilisation, population, santé) decline. 2. (fin) close.

déclinaison [deklinɛzɔ̃] nf (GRAM) declension.

décliner [dekline] ◆ vi (santé, population, popularité) to decline. ◆ vt 1. (offre, honneur) to decline. 2. (GRAM) to decline; fig (gamme de produits) to develop.

décoder [dekɔde] vt to decode.

décoiffer [dekwafe] vt (cheveux) to mess up.

décoincer [dekwɛ̃se] vt 1. (chose) to loosen; (mécanisme) to unjam. 2. fam (personne) to loosen up.

décollage [dekɔlaʒ] nm takeoff.

décoller [dekɔle] ◆ vt (étiquette, timbre) to unstick; (papier peint) to strip (off). ◆ vi litt & fig to take off.

décolleté, -e [dekɔlte] adj (vêtement) low-cut. ▶ **décolleté** nm 1. (de personne) neck and shoulders (pl). 2. (de vêtement) neckline, neck.

décolonisation [dekɔlɔnizasjɔ̃] nf decolonization.

décolorer [dekɔlɔre] vt (par décolorant) to bleach, to lighten; (par usure) to fade.

décombres [dekɔ̃br] nmpl debris (U).

décommander [dekɔmɑ̃de] vt to cancel.

décomposé, -e [dekɔ̃poze] adj 1. (pourri) decomposed. 2. (visage) haggard; (personne) in shock.

décomposer [dekɔ̃poze] vt (gén): ~ **(en)** to break down (into). ▶ **se décomposer** vp 1. (se putréfier) to rot, to decompose. 2. (se diviser): **se** ~ **en** to be broken down into.

décomposition [dekɔ̃pozisjɔ̃] nf 1. (putréfaction) decomposition. 2. fig (analyse) breaking down, analysis.

décompresser [dekɔ̃prese] ◆ vt (TECHNOL) to decompress. ◆ vi to unwind.

décompression [dekɔ̃presjɔ̃] nf decompression.

décompte [dekɔ̃t] nm (calcul) breakdown (of an amount).

déconcentrer [dekɔ̃sɑ̃tre] vt (distraire) to distract. ▶ **se déconcentrer** vp to be distracted.

déconcerter [dekɔ̃sɛrte] vt to disconcert.

déconfiture [dekɔ̃fityr] nf collapse, ruin.

décongeler [dekɔ̃ʒle] vt to defrost.

décongestionner [dekɔ̃ʒɛstjɔne] *vt* to relieve congestion in.

déconnecter [dekɔnɛkte] *vt* to disconnect.

déconseillé, -e [dekɔ̃seje] *adj*: **c'est fortement ~** it's extremely inadvisable.

déconseiller [dekɔ̃seje] *vt*: **~ qqch à qqn** to advise sb against sthg; **~ à qqn de faire qqch** to advise sb against doing sthg.

déconsidérer [dekɔ̃sidere] *vt* to discredit.

décontaminer [dekɔ̃tamine] *vt* to decontaminate.

décontenancer [dekɔ̃tnɑ̃se] *vt* to put out.

décontracté, -e [dekɔ̃trakte] *adj* 1. (*muscle*) relaxed. 2. (*détendu*) casual, laid-back.

décontracter [dekɔ̃trakte] *vt* to relax. ► **se décontracter** *vp* to relax.

décor [dekɔr] *nm* 1. (*cadre*) scenery. 2. (THÉÂTRE) scenery (U); (CIN) sets (*pl*), décor.

décorateur, -trice [dekɔratœr, tris] *nm, f* (CIN & THÉÂTRE) designer; **~ d'intérieur** interior decorator.

décoratif, -ive [dekɔratif, iv] *adj* decorative.

décoration [dekɔrasjɔ̃] *nf* decoration.

décorer [dekɔre] *vt* to decorate.

décortiquer [dekɔrtike] *vt* (*noix*) to shell; (*graine*) to husk; *fig* to analyse in minute detail.

découcher [dekuʃe] *vi* to stay out all night.

découdre [dekudr] *vt* (COUTURE) to unpick.

découler [dekule] *vi*: **~ de** to follow from.

découpage [dekupaʒ] *nm* 1. (*action*) cutting out; (*résultat*) paper cutout. 2. (ADMIN): **~ (électoral)** division into constituencies.

découper [dekupe] *vt* 1. (*couper*) to cut up. 2. *fig* (*diviser*) to cut out.

découpure [dekupyr] *nf* (*bord*) indentations (*pl*), jagged outline.

découragement [dekuraʒmɑ̃] *nm* discouragement.

décourager [dekuraʒe] *vt* to discourage; **~ qqn de qqch** to put sb off sthg; **~ qqn de faire qqch** to discourage sb from doing sthg. ► **se décourager** *vp* to lose heart.

décousu, -e [dekuzy] ◆ *pp* → **découdre**. ◆ *adj fig* (*conversation*) disjointed.

découvert, -e [dekuvɛr, ɛrt] ◆ *pp* → **découvrir**. ◆ *adj* (*tête*) bare; (*terrain*) exposed. ► **découvert** *nm* (BANQUE) overdraft; **être à ~ (de 6 000 francs)** to be (6,000 francs) overdrawn. ► **découverte** *nf* discovery; **aller à la ~e de** to explore.

découvrir [dekuvrir] *vt* 1. (*trouver, surprendre*) to discover. 2. (*ôter ce qui couvre, mettre à jour*) to uncover.

décrasser [dekrase] *vt* to scrub.

décret [dekre] *nm* decree.

décréter [dekrete] *vt* (*décider*): **~ que** to decide that.

décrire [dekrir] *vt* to describe.

décrit, -e [dekri, it] *pp* → **décrire**.

décrocher [dekrɔʃe] ◆ *vt* 1. (*enlever*) to take down. 2. (*téléphone*) to pick up. 3. *fam* (*obtenir*) to land. ◆ *vi fam* (*abandonner*) to drop out.

décroissant, -e [dekrwasɑ̃, ɑ̃t] *adj* (*courbe*) decreasing; (*influence*) diminishing.

décroître [dekrwatr] *vi* to decrease, to diminish; (*jours*) to get shorter.

décrypter [dekripte] *vt* to decipher.

déçu, -e [desy] ◆ *pp* → **décevoir**. ◆ *adj* disappointed.

déculotter [dekylɔte] *vt*: **~ qqn** to take sb's trousers off.

dédaigner [dedɛɲe] *vt* 1. (*mépriser - personne*) to despise; (- *conseils, injures*) to scorn. 2. (*refuser*): **~ de faire qqch** *sout* to disdain to do sthg; **ne pas ~ qqch/de faire qqch** not to be above sthg/above doing sthg.

dédaigneux, -euse [dedɛɲø, øz] *adj* disdainful.

dédain [dedɛ̃] *nm* disdain, contempt.

dédale [dedal] *nm litt & fig* maze.

dedans [dədɑ̃] *adv & nm* inside. ► **de dedans** *loc adv* from inside, from within. ► **en dedans** *loc adv* inside, within. ► **en dedans de** *loc prép* inside, within; *voir aussi* **là-dedans**.

dédicace [dedikas] *nf* dedication.

dédicacer [dedikase] *vt*: **~ qqch (à qqn)** to sign ou autograph sthg (for sb).

dédier [dedje] *vt*: **~ qqch (à qqn/à qqch)** to dedicate sthg (to sb/to sthg).

dédire [dedir] ► **se dédire** *vp sout* to go back on one's word.

dédommagement [dedɔmaʒmɑ̃] *nm* compensation.

dédommager [dedɔmaʒe] *vt* 1. (*indemniser*) to compensate. 2. *fig* (*remercier*) to repay.

dédouaner [dedwane] *vt* (*marchandi-*

ses) to clear through customs.

dédoubler [deduble] *vt* to halve, to split; (*fil*) to separate.

déduction [dedyksjɔ̃] *nf* deduction.

déduire [dedɥir] *vt*: ~ qqch (de) (*ôter*) to deduct sthg (from); (*conclure*) to deduce sthg (from).

déduit, -e [dedɥi, it] *pp* → **déduire**.

déesse [deɛs] *nf* goddess.

défaillance [defajɑ̃s] *nf* **1.** (*incapacité - de machine*) failure; (*- de personne, organisation*) weakness. **2.** (*malaise*) blackout, fainting fit.

défaillant, -e [defajɑ̃, ɑ̃t] *adj* (*faible*) failing.

défaillir [defajir] *vi* (*s'évanouir*) to faint.

défaire [defɛr] *vt* (*détacher*) to undo; (*valise*) to unpack; (*lit*) to strip. ▶ **se défaire** *vp* **1.** (*ne pas tenir*) to come undone. **2.** *sout* (*se séparer*): **se ~ de** to get rid of.

défait, -e [defɛ, ɛt] ♦ *pp* → **défaire**. ♦ *adj fig* (*épuisé*) haggard. ▶ **défaite** *nf* defeat.

défaitiste [defetist] *nmf* & *adj* defeatist.

défaut [defo] *nm* **1.** (*imperfection*) flaw; (*- de personne*) fault, shortcoming; **~ de fabrication** manufacturing fault. **2.** (*manque*) lack; **à ~ de** for lack ou want of; **l'eau fait (cruellement) ~** there is a serious water shortage.

défaveur [defavœr] *nf* disfavour; **être/ tomber en ~** to be/fall out of favour.

défavorable [defavɔrabl] *adj* unfavourable.

défavorisé, -e [defavɔrize] *adj* disadvantaged, underprivileged.

défavoriser [defavɔrize] *vt* to handicap, to penalize.

défection [defɛksjɔ̃] *nf* **1.** (*absence*) absence. **2.** (*abandon*) defection.

défectueux, -euse [defɛktɥø, øz] *adj* faulty, defective.

défendeur, -eresse [defɑ̃dœr, rɛs] *nm, f* defendant.

défendre [defɑ̃dr] *vt* **1.** (*personne, opinion, client*) to defend. **2.** (*interdire*) to forbid; **~ qqch à qqn** to forbid sb sthg; **~ à qqn de faire qqch** to forbid sb to do sthg; **~ que qqn fasse qqch** to forbid sb to do sthg. ▶ **se défendre** *vp* **1.** (*se battre, se justifier*) to defend o.s. **2.** (*nier*): **se ~ de faire qqch** to deny doing sthg. **3.** (*thèse*) to stand up.

défendu, -e [defɑ̃dy] ♦ *pp* → **défendre**. ♦ *adj*: **'il est ~ de jouer au ballon'** 'no ball games'.

défense [defɑ̃s] *nf* **1.** (*d'éléphant*) tusk. **2.** (*interdiction*) prohibition, ban; **'~ de fumer/de stationner/d'entrer'** 'no smoking/parking/entry'; **'~ d'afficher'** 'stick no bills'. **3.** (*protection*) defence; **prendre la ~ de** to stand up for; **légitime ~** (JUR) self-defence.

LA DÉFENSE

This business district to the west of Paris was started during the 1960s and 70s. It consists mainly of ultramodern glass skyscrapers and its most recognizable landmark is the 'Grande Arche', a huge office building shaped like a square archway.

---

défenseur [defɑ̃sœr] *nm* (*partisan*) champion.

défensif, -ive [defɑ̃sif, iv] *adj* defensive. ▶ **défensive** *nf*: **être sur la défensive** to be on the defensive.

déférence [deferɑ̃s] *nf* deference.

déferlement [defɛrləmɑ̃] *nm* (*de vagues*) breaking; *fig* surge, upsurge.

déferler [defɛrle] *vi* (*vagues*) to break; *fig* to surge.

défi [defi] *nm* challenge.

défiance [defjɑ̃s] *nf* distrust, mistrust.

déficience [defisjɑ̃s] *nf* deficiency.

déficit [defisit] *nm* (FIN) deficit; **être en ~** to be in deficit.

déficitaire [defisiter] *adj* in deficit.

défier [defje] *vt* (*braver*): **~ qqn de faire qqch** to defy sb to do sthg.

défigurer [defigyre] *vt* **1.** (*blesser*) to disfigure. **2.** (*enlaidir*) to deface.

défilé [defile] *nm* **1.** (*parade*) parade. **2.** (*couloir*) defile, narrow pass.

défiler [defile] *vi* **1.** (*dans une parade*) to march past. **2.** (*se succéder*) to pass. ▶ **se défiler** *vp fam* to back out.

défini, -e [defini] *adj* **1.** (*précis*) clear, precise. **2.** (GRAM) definite.

définir [definir] *vt* to define.

définitif, -ive [definitif, iv] *adj* definitive, final. ▶ **en définitive** *loc adv* in the end.

définition [definisjɔ̃] *nf* definition.

définitivement [definitivmɑ̃] *adv* for good, permanently.

défiscaliser [defiskalize] *vt* to exempt from taxation.

déflationniste [deflasjɔnist] *adj* deflationary, deflationist.

défoncer [defɔ̃se] *vt* (*caisse, porte*) to smash in; (*route*) to break up; (*mur*) to smash down; (*chaise*) to break.

déformation [deformasjɔ̃] nf 1. (d'objet, de théorie) distortion. 2. (MÉD) deformity; ~ **professionnelle** mental conditioning caused by one's job.

déformer [deforme] vt to distort. ► se **déformer** vp (changer de forme) to be distorted, to be deformed; (se courber) to bend.

défouler [defule] vt fam to unwind. ► se **défouler** vp fam to let off steam, to unwind.

défricher [defriʃe] vt (terrain) to clear; fig (question) to do the groundwork for.

défunt, -e [defœ̃, œ̃t] ◆ adj (décédé) late. ◆ nm, f deceased.

dégagé, -e [degaʒe] adj 1. (ciel, vue) clear; (partie du corps) bare. 2. (désinvolte) casual, airy. 3. (libre): ~ **de** free from.

dégager [degaʒe] ◆ vt 1. (odeur) to produce, to give off. 2. (délivrer - blessé) to free, to extricate. 3. (bénéfice) to show. 4. (pièce) to clear. 5. (libérer): ~ **qqn de** to release sb from. ◆ vi fam (partir) to clear off. ► se **dégager** vp 1. (se délivrer): se ~ **de qqch** to free o.s. from sthg; fig to get out of sthg. 2. (émaner) to be given off. 3. (émerger) to emerge.

dégarnir [degarnir] vt to strip, to clear. ► se **dégarnir** vp (vitrine) to be cleared; (arbre) to lose its leaves; **sa tête se dégarnit, il se dégarnit** he's going bald.

dégât [dega] nm litt & fig damage (U); **faire des ~s** to cause damage.

dégel [deʒɛl] nm (fonte des glaces) thaw.

dégeler [deʒle] ◆ vt (produit surgelé) to thaw. ◆ vi to thaw.

dégénéré, -e [deʒenere] adj & nm, f degenerate.

dégénérer [deʒenere] vi to degenerate; ~ **en** to degenerate into.

dégivrer [deʒivre] vt (pare-brise) to de-ice; (réfrigérateur) to defrost.

dégonfler [degɔ̃fle] ◆ vt to deflate, to let down. ◆ vi to go down. ► se **dégonfler** vp 1. (objet) to go down. 2. fam (personne) to chicken out.

dégorger [degɔrʒe] vi: **faire ~** (légumes) to drain of water (by sprinkling with salt).

dégouliner [deguline] vi to trickle.

dégourdi, -e [degurdi] adj clever.

dégourdir [degurdir] vt 1. (membres - ankylosés) to restore the circulation to. 2. fig (déniaiser): ~ **qqn** to teach sb a thing or two. ► se **dégourdir** vp 1. (membres): se ~ **les jambes** to stretch one's legs. 2. fig (acquérir de l'aisance) to learn a thing or two.

dégoût [degu] nm disgust, distaste.

dégoûtant, -e [degutɑ̃, ɑ̃t] adj 1. (sale) filthy, disgusting. 2. (révoltant, grossier) disgusting.

dégoûter [degute] vt to disgust.

dégoutter [degute] vi: ~ **(de qqch)** to drip (with sthg).

dégradé, -e [degrade] adj (couleur) shading off. ► **dégradé** nm gradation; **un ~ de bleu** a blue shading. ► **en dégradé** loc adv (cheveux) layered.

dégrader [degrade] vt 1. (officier) to degrade. 2. (abîmer) to damage. 3. fig (avilir) to degrade, to debase. ► se **dégrader** vp 1. (bâtiment, santé) to deteriorate. 2. fig (personne) to degrade o.s.

dégrafer [degrafe] vt to undo, to unfasten.

dégraissage [degresaʒ] nm 1. (de vêtement) dry-cleaning. 2. (de personnel) trimming, cutting back.

degré [degre] nm (gén) degree; ~**s centigrades** ou **Celsius** degrees centigrade ou Celsius; **prendre qqn/qqch au premier ~** to take sb/sthg at face value.

dégressif, -ive [degresif, iv] adj: **tarif ~** decreasing price scale.

dégringoler [degrɛ̃gɔle] fam vi (tomber) to tumble; fig to crash.

dégueniller, -e [degənije] adj ragged.

déguerpir [degɛrpir] vi to clear off.

dégueulasse [degœlas] ◆ fam ◆ adj 1. (très sale, grossier) filthy. 2. (révoltant) dirty, rotten. ◆ nmf scum (U).

dégueuler [degœle] vi fam to throw up.

déguisement [degizmɑ̃] nm disguise; (pour bal masqué) fancy dress.

déguiser [degize] vt to disguise. ► se **déguiser** vp: se ~ **en** (pour tromper) to disguise o.s. as; (pour s'amuser) to dress up as.

dégustation [degystasjɔ̃] nf tasting, sampling; ~ **de vin** wine tasting.

déguster [degyste] ◆ vt (savourer) to taste, to sample. ◆ vi fam (subir): **il va ~!** he'll be for it!

déhancher [deɑ̃ʃe] ► se **déhancher** vp (en marchant) to swing one's hips; (en restant immobile) to put all one's weight on one leg.

dehors [dəɔr] ◆ adv outside; **aller ~** to go outside; **dormir ~** to sleep out of doors, to sleep out; **jeter** ou **mettre qqn ~** to throw sb out. ◆ nm outside. ◆ nmpl: **les ~** (les apparences) appearances. ► **en dehors** loc adv outside, outwards. ► **en dehors de** loc prép (*excepté*) apart from.

déjà [deʒa] *adv* **1.** (*dès cet instant*) already. **2.** (*précédemment*) already, before. **3.** (*au fait*): **quel est ton nom ~?** what did you say your name was? **4.** (*renforce une affirmation*): **ce n'est ~ pas si mal** that's not bad at all.

déjeuner [deʒœne] ◆ *vi* **1.** (*le matin*) to have breakfast. **2.** (*à midi*) to have lunch. ◆ *nm* **1.** (*repas de midi*) lunch. **2.** Can (*dîner*) dinner.

déjouer [deʒwe] *vt* to frustrate; **~ la surveillance de qqn** to elude sb's surveillance.

delà [dəla] → **au-delà**.

délabré, -e [delabre] *adj* ruined.

délacer [delase] *vt* to unlace, to undo.

délai [delɛ] *nm* **1.** (*temps accordé*) period; **sans ~** immediately, without delay; **~ de livraison** delivery time, lead time. **2.** (*sursis*) extension (of deadline).

délaisser [delese] *vt* **1.** (*abandonner*) to leave. **2.** (*négliger*) to neglect.

délassement [delasmɑ̃] *nm* relaxation.

délasser [delase] *vt* to refresh. ▶ **se délasser** *vp* to relax.

délation [delasjɔ̃] *nf* informing.

délavé, -e [delave] *adj* faded.

délayer [deleje] *vt* (*diluer*): **~ qqch dans qqch** to mix sthg with sthg.

délecter [delɛkte] ▶ **se délecter** *vp*: se **~ de qqch/à faire qqch** to delight in sthg/in doing sthg.

délégation [delegasjɔ̃] *nf* delegation.

délégué, -e [delege] ◆ *adj* (*personne*) delegated. ◆ *nm, f* (*représentant*): **~ (à)** delegate (to).

déléguer [delege] *vt*: **~ qqn (à qqch)** to delegate sb (to sthg).

délester [delɛste] *vt* **1.** (*circulation routière*) to set up a diversion on, to divert. **2.** *fig & hum* (*voler*): **~ qqn de qqch** to relieve sb of sthg.

délibération [deliberasjɔ̃] *nf* deliberation.

délibéré, -e [delibere] *adj* **1.** (*intentionnel*) deliberate. **2.** (*résolu*) determined.

délibérer [delibere] *vi*: **~ (de ou sur)** to deliberate (on ou over).

délicat, -e [delika, at] *adj* **1.** (*gén*) delicate. **2.** (*exigeant*) fussy, difficult.

délicatement [delikatmɑ̃] *adv* delicately.

délicatesse [delikatɛs] *nf* **1.** (*gén*) delicacy. **2.** (*tact*) delicacy, tact.

délice [delis] *nm* delight.

délicieux, -euse [delisjø, øz] *adj*

1. (*savoureux*) delicious. **2.** (*agréable*) delightful.

délié, -e [delje] *adj* (*doigts*) nimble.

délier [delje] *vt* to untie.

délimiter [delimite] *vt* (*frontière*) to fix; *fig* (*question, domaine*) to define, to demarcate.

délinquance [delɛ̃kɑ̃s] *nf* delinquency.

délinquant, -e [delɛ̃kɑ̃, ɑ̃t] *nm, f* delinquent.

délirant, -e [delirɑ̃, ɑ̃t] *adj* **1.** (MÉD) delirious. **2.** (*extravagant*) frenzied. **3.** *fam* (*extraordinaire*) crazy.

délire [delir] *nm* (MÉD) delirium; **en ~** *fig* frenzied.

délirer [delire] *vi* (MÉD) to be ou become delirious; *fam fig* to rave.

délit [deli] *nm* crime, offence; **en flagrant ~** red-handed, in the act.

délivrance [delivrɑ̃s] *nf* **1.** (*libération*) freeing, release. **2.** (*soulagement*) relief. **3.** (*accouchement*) delivery.

délivrer [delivre] *vt* **1.** (*prisonnier*) to free, to release. **2.** (*pays*) to deliver, to free; **~ de** to free from; *fig* to relieve from. **3.** (*remettre*): **~ qqch (à qqn)** to issue sthg (to sb). **4.** (*marchandise*) to deliver.

déloger [delɔʒe] *vt*: **~ (de)** to dislodge (from).

déloyal, -e, -aux [delwajal, o] *adj* **1.** (*infidèle*) disloyal. **2.** (*malhonnête*) unfair.

delta [dɛlta] *nm* delta.

deltaplane, delta-plane (*pl* **delta-planes**) [dɛltaplan] *nm* hang glider.

déluge [delyʒ] *nm* (RELIG): **le Déluge** the Flood. **2.** (*pluie*) downpour, deluge; **un ~ de** *fig* a flood of.

déluré, -e [delyre] *adj* (*malin*) quick-witted; *péj* (*dévergondé*) saucy.

démagogie [demagɔʒi] *nf* pandering to public opinion, demagogy.

demain [dəmɛ̃] ◆ *adv* **1.** (*le jour suivant*) tomorrow; **~ matin** tomorrow morning. **2.** *fig* (*plus tard*) in the future. ◆ *nm* tomorrow; **à ~!** see you tomorrow!

demande [dəmɑ̃d] *nf* **1.** (*souhait*) request. **2.** (*démarche*) proposal; **~ en mariage** proposal of marriage. **3.** (*candidature*) application; **~ d'emploi** job application; **'~s d'emploi'** 'situations wanted'. **4.** (ÉCON) demand.

demandé, -e [dəmɑ̃de] *adj* in demand.

demander [dəmɑ̃de] ◆ *vt* **1.** (*réclamer, s'enquérir*) to ask for; **~ qqch à qqn** to ask

demi-frère

sb for sthg. **2.** (*appeler*) to call; **on vous demande à la réception/au téléphone** you're wanted at reception/on the telephone. **3.** (*désirer*) to ask, to want; **je ne demande pas mieux** I'd be only too pleased (to), I'd love to. **4.** (*exiger*): **tu m'en demandes trop** you're asking too much of me. **5.** (*nécessiter*) to require. ◆ *vi* **1.** (*réclamer*): **~ à qqn de faire qqch** to ask sb to do sthg; **ne ~ qu'à ...** to be ready to ... **2.** (*nécessiter*): **ce projet demande à être étudié** this project requires investigation ou needs investigating. ▶ **se demander** *vp*: **se ~ (si)** to wonder (if ou whether).

demandeur, -euse [dəmɑ̃dœr, øz] *nm, f* (*solliciteur*): **~ d'asile** asylum-seeker; **~ d'emploi** job-seeker.

démangeaison [demɑ̃ʒɛzɔ̃] *nf* (*irritation*) itch, itching (U); *fam* big urge.

démanger [demɑ̃ʒe] *vi* (*gratter*) to itch; **ça me démange de ...** *fig* I'm itching ou dying to ...

démanteler [demɑ̃tle] *vt* (*construction*) to demolish; *fig* to break up.

démaquillant, -e [demakijɑ̃, ɑ̃t] *adj* make-up-removing (*avant n*). ▶ **démaquillant** *nm* make-up remover.

démaquiller [demakije] *vt* to remove make-up from. ▶ **se démaquiller** *vp* to remove one's make-up.

démarche [demarʃ] *nf* **1.** (*manière de marcher*) gait, walk. **2.** (*raisonnement*) approach, method. **3.** (*requête*) step; **faire les ~s pour faire qqch** to take the necessary steps to do sthg.

démarcheur, -euse [demarʃœr, øz] *nm, f* (*représentant*) door-to-door salesman (*f* saleswoman).

démarquer [demarke] *vt* **1.** (*solder*) to mark down. **2.** (SPORT) not to mark. ▶ **se démarquer** *vp fig* (*se distinguer*): **se ~ (de)** to distinguish o.s. (from).

démarrage [demaraʒ] *nm* starting, start; **~ en côte** hill start.

démarrer [demare] ◆ *vi* **1.** (*véhicule*) to start (up); (*conducteur*) to drive off. **2.** *fig* (*affaire, projet*) to get off the ground. ◆ *vt* **1.** (*véhicule*) to start (up). **2.** *fam fig* (*commencer*): **~ qqch** to get sthg going.

démarreur [demarœr] *nm* starter.

démasquer [demaske] *vt* **1.** (*personne*) to unmask. **2.** *fig* (*complot, plan*) to unveil.

démêlant, -e [demɛlɑ̃, ɑ̃t] *adj* conditioning (*avant n*). ▶ **démêlant** *nm* conditioner.

démêlé [demele] *nm* quarrel; **avoir des**

~s avec la justice to get into trouble with the law.

démêler [demele] *vt* (*cheveux, fil*) to untangle; *fig* to unravel. ▶ **se démêler** *vp*: **se ~ de** *fig* to extricate o.s. from.

déménagement [demenaʒmɑ̃] *nm* removal.

déménager [demenaʒe] ◆ *vt* to move. ◆ *vi* to move (house).

déménageur [demenaʒœr] *nm* removal man Br, mover Am.

démence [demɑ̃s] *nf* (MÉD) dementia; (*bêtise*) madness.

démener [demne] ▶ **se démener** *vp litt & fig* to struggle.

dément, -e [demɑ̃, ɑ̃t] ◆ *adj* (MÉD) demented; *fam* (*extraordinaire, extravagant*) crazy. ◆ *nm, f* demented person.

démenti [demɑ̃ti] *nm* denial.

démentiel, -elle [demɑ̃sjɛl] *adj* (MÉD) demented; *fam* (*incroyable*) crazy.

démentir [demɑ̃tir] *vt* **1.** (*réfuter*) to deny. **2.** (*contredire*) to contradict.

démesure [deməzyr] *nf* excess, immoderation.

démettre [demɛtr] *vt* **1.** (MÉD) to put out (of joint). **2.** (*congédier*): **~ qqn de** to dismiss sb from. ▶ **se démettre** *vp* **1.** (MÉD): **se ~ l'épaule** to put one's shoulder out (of joint). **2.** (*démissionner*): **se ~ de ses fonctions** to resign.

demeurant [dəmœrɑ̃] ▶ **au demeurant** *loc adv* all things considered.

demeure [dəmœr] *nf sout* (*domicile, habitation*) residence. ▶ **à demeure** *loc adv* permanently.

demeuré, -e [dəmœre] ◆ *adj* simple, half-witted. ◆ *nm, f* half-wit.

demeurer [dəmœre] *vi* **1.** (*aux: avoir*) (*habiter*) to live. **2.** (*aux: être*) (*rester*) to remain.

demi, -e [dəmi] *adj* half; **un kilo et ~** one and a half kilos; **il est une heure et ~e** it's half past one; **à ~** half; **dormir à ~** to be nearly asleep; **ouvrir à ~** to half-open; **faire les choses à ~** to do things by halves. ▶ **demi** *nm* **1.** (*bière*) beer, ≈ half-pint Br. **2.** (FOOTBALL) midfielder. ▶ **demie** *nf*: **à la ~e** on the half-hour.

demi-cercle [dəmisɛrkl] (*pl* **demi-cercles**) *nm* semicircle.

demi-douzaine [dəmiduzɛn] (*pl* **demi-douzaines**) *nf* half-dozen; **une ~ (de)** half a dozen.

demi-finale [dəmifinal] (*pl* **demi-finales**) *nf* semifinal.

demi-frère [dəmifrɛr] (*pl* **demi-frères**) *nm* half-brother.

demi-gros [dəmigro] nm: (commerce de) ~ cash and carry.

demi-heure [dəmijœr] (pl **demi-heures**) nf half an hour, half-hour.

demi-journée [dəmiʒurne] (pl **demi-journées**) nf half a day, half-day.

demi-litre [dəmilitr] (pl **demi-litres**) nm half a litre, half-litre.

demi-mesure [dəmiməzyr] (pl **demi-mesures**) nf 1. (quantité) half a measure. 2. (compromis) half-measure.

demi-mot [dəmimo] ▶ **à demi-mot** loc adv: **comprendre à ~** to understand without things having to be spelled out.

déminer [demine] vt to clear of mines.

demi-pension [dəmipãsjɔ̃] (pl **demi-pensions**) nf 1. (d'hôtel) half-board. 2. (d'école): **être en ~** to take school dinners (pl).

démis, -e [demi, iz] pp → **démettre**.

demi-sœur [dəmisœr] (pl **demi-sœurs**) nf half-sister.

démission [demisjɔ̃] nf resignation.

démissionner [demisjɔne] vi (d'un emploi) to resign; fig to give up.

demi-tarif [dəmitarif] (pl **demi-tarifs**) ◆ adj half-price. ◆ nm 1. (tarification) half-fare. 2. (billet) half-price ticket.

demi-tour [dəmitur] (pl **demi-tours**) nm (gén) half-turn; (MIL) about-turn; **faire ~** to turn back.

démocrate [demɔkrat] nmf democrat.

démocratie [demɔkrasi] nf democracy.

démocratique [demɔkratik] adj democratic.

démocratiser [demɔkratize] vt to democratize.

démodé, -e [demɔde] adj old-fashioned.

démographique [demɔgrafik] adj demographic.

demoiselle [dəmwazɛl] nf (jeune fille) maid; **~ d'honneur** bridesmaid.

démolir [demɔlir] vt (gén) to demolish.

démolition [demɔlisjɔ̃] nf demolition.

démon [demɔ̃] nm (diable, personne) devil, demon; **le ~** (RELIG) the Devil.

démoniaque [demɔnjak] adj (diabolique) diabolical.

démonstratif, -ive [demɔ̃stratif, iv] adj (personne & GRAM) demonstrative. ▶ **démonstratif** nm (GRAM) demonstrative.

démonstration [demɔ̃strasjɔ̃] nf (gén) demonstration.

démontable [demɔ̃tabl] adj which can be taken to pieces.

démonter [demɔ̃te] vt 1. (appareil) to dismantle, to take apart. 2. (troubler): ~ qqn to put sb out. ▶ **se démonter** vp fam to be put out.

démontrer [demɔ̃tre] vt 1. (prouver) to prove, to demonstrate. 2. (témoigner de) to show, to demonstrate.

démoralisant, -e [demɔralizã, ãt] adj demoralizing.

démoraliser [demɔralize] vt to demoralize. ▶ **se démoraliser** vp to lose heart.

démordre [demɔrdr] vt: **ne pas ~ de** to stick to.

démotiver [demɔtive] vt to demotivate.

démouler [demule] vt to turn out of a mould, to remove from a mould.

démunir [demynir] vt to deprive. ▶ **se démunir** vp: **se ~ de** to part with.

dénaturer [denatyre] vt 1. (goût) to impair, to mar. 2. (TECHNOL) to denature. 3. (déformer) to distort.

dénégation [denegasjɔ̃] nf denial.

dénicher [deniʃe] vt fig 1. (personne) to flush out. 2. fam (objet) to unearth.

dénigrer [denigre] vt to denigrate, to run down.

dénivelé [denivle] nm difference in level ou height.

dénivellation [denivɛlasjɔ̃] nf 1. (différence de niveau) difference in height ou level. 2. (pente) slope.

dénombrer [denɔ̃bre] vt (compter) to count; (énumérer) to enumerate.

dénominateur [denɔminatœr] nm denominator.

dénomination [denɔminasjɔ̃] nf name.

dénommé, -e [denɔme] adj: **un ~ Robert** someone by the name of Robert.

dénoncer [denɔ̃se] vt 1. (gén) to denounce; **~ qqn à qqn** to denounce sb to sb, to inform on sb. 2. fig (trahir) to betray.

dénonciation [denɔ̃sjasjɔ̃] nf denunciation.

dénoter [denɔte] vt to show, to indicate.

dénouement [denumã] nm 1. (issue) outcome. 2. (d'un film, d'un livre) denouement.

dénouer [denwe] vt (nœud) to untie, undo; fig to unravel.

dénoyauter [denwajote] vt (fruit) to stone.

denrée [dɑ̃re] *nf* (*produit*) produce (U); **~s alimentaires** foodstuffs.

dense [dɑ̃s] *adj* **1.** (*gén*) dense. **2.** (*style*) condensed.

densité [dɑ̃site] *nf* density.

dent [dɑ̃] *nf* **1.** (*de personne, d'objet*) tooth; **faire ses ~s** to cut one's teeth, to teethe; **~ de lait/de sagesse** milk/wisdom tooth. **2.** (GÉOGR) peak.

dentaire [dɑ̃tɛr] *adj* dental.

dentelé, -e [dɑ̃tle] *adj* serrated, jagged.

dentelle [dɑ̃tɛl] *nf* lace (U).

dentier [dɑ̃tje] *nm* (*dents*) dentures (*pl*).

dentifrice [dɑ̃tifris] *nm* toothpaste.

dentiste [dɑ̃tist] *nmf* dentist.

dentition [dɑ̃tisjɔ̃] *nf* teeth (*pl*), dentition.

dénuder [denyde] *vt* to leave bare; (*fil électrique*) to strip.

dénué, -e [denɥe] *adj sout*: **~ de** devoid of.

dénuement [denymɑ̃] *nm* destitution (U).

déodorant, -e [deɔdɔrɑ̃, ɑ̃t] *adj* deodorant. ▶ **déodorant** *nm* deodorant.

déontologie [deɔ̃tɔlɔʒi] *nf* professional ethics (*pl*).

dépannage [depanaʒ] *nm* repair; **service de ~** (AUT) breakdown service.

dépanner [depane] *vt* **1.** (*réparer*) to repair, to fix. **2.** *fam* (*aider*) to bail out.

dépanneur, -euse [depanœr, øz] *nm, f* repairman (*f* repairwoman). ▶ **dépanneuse** *nf* (*véhicule*) (break-down) recovery vehicle.

dépareillé, -e [depareje] *adj* (*ensemble*) non-matching; (*paire*) odd.

départ [depar] *nm* **1.** (*de personne*) departure, leaving; (*de véhicule*) departure; **les grands ~s** the holiday exodus (*sg*). **2.** (SPORT & *fig*) start. ▶ **au départ** *loc adv* to start with.

départager [departaʒe] *vt* **1.** (*concurrents, opinions*) to decide between. **2.** (*séparer*) to separate.

département [departəmɑ̃] *nm* **1.** (*territoire*) territorial and administrative division of France. **2.** (*service*) department.

départemental, -e, -aux [departəmɑ̃tal, o] *adj* of a French 'département'. ▶ **départementale** *nf* secondary road, ≃ B road Br.

dépassé, -e [depase] *adj* **1.** (*périmé*) old-fashioned. **2.** *fam* (*déconcerté*): **~ par** overwhelmed by.

dépassement [depasmɑ̃] *nm* (*en voiture*) overtaking.

dépasser [depase] ◆ *vt* **1.** (*doubler*) to overtake. **2.** (*être plus grand que*) to be taller than. **3.** (*excéder*) to exceed, to be more than. **4.** (*durer plus longtemps que*): **~ une heure** to go on for more than an hour. **5.** (*aller au-delà de*) to exceed. **6.** (*franchir*) to pass. ◆ *vi*: **~ (de)** to stick out (from).

dépayser [depeize] *vt* **1.** (*désorienter*) to disorientate Br, to disorient Am. **2.** (*changer agréablement*) to make a change of scene for.

dépecer [depəse] *vt* **1.** (*découper*) to chop up. **2.** (*déchiqueter*) to tear apart.

dépêche [depɛʃ] *nf* dispatch.

dépêcher [depeʃe] *vt sout* (*envoyer*) to dispatch. ▶ **se dépêcher** *vp* to hurry up; **se ~ de faire qqch** to hurry to do sthg.

dépeindre [depɛ̃dr] *vt* to depict, to describe.

dépeint, -e [depɛ̃, ɛ̃t] *pp* → **dépeindre**.

dépendance [depɑ̃dɑ̃s] *nf* **1.** (*de personne*) dependence. **2.** (*à la drogue*) dependency. **3.** (*de bâtiment*) outbuilding.

dépendre [depɑ̃dr] *vt* **1.** (*être soumis*): **~ de** to depend on; **ça dépend** it depends. **2.** (*appartenir*): **~ de** to belong to.

dépens [depɑ̃] *nmpl* (JUR) costs; **aux ~ de qqn** at sb's expense; **je l'ai appris à mes ~** I learned this to my cost.

dépense [depɑ̃s] *nf* **1.** (*frais*) expense. **2.** (FIN & *fig*) expenditure (U); **les ~s publiques** public spending (U).

dépenser [depɑ̃se] *vt* **1.** (*argent*) to spend. **2.** *fig* (*énergie*) to expend. ▶ **se dépenser** *vp litt & fig* to exert o.s.

dépensier, -ère [depɑ̃sje, ɛr] *adj* extravagant.

déperdition [deperdisjɔ̃] *nf* loss.

dépérir [deperir] *vi* **1.** (*personne*) to waste away. **2.** (*santé, affaire*) to decline. **3.** (*plante*) to wither.

dépeupler [depœple] *vt* **1.** (*pays*) to depopulate. **2.** (*étang, rivière, forêt*) to drive the wildlife from.

déphasé, -e [defaze] *adj* (ÉLECTR) out of phase; *fam fig* out of touch.

dépilatoire [depilatwar] *adj*: **crème/lotion ~** depilatory cream/lotion.

dépistage [depistaʒ] *nm* (*de maladie*) screening; **~ du SIDA** AIDS testing.

dépister [depiste] *vt* **1.** (*gibier, voleur*) to track down. **2.** (*maladie*) to screen for.

dépit [depi] *nm* pique, spite. ▶ **en**

dépit de loc prép in spite of.
déplacé, -e [deplase] adj **1.** (propos, attitude, présence) out of place. **2.** (personne) displaced.
déplacement [deplasmã] nm **1.** (d'objet) moving. **2.** (voyage) travelling (U).
déplacer [deplase] vt **1.** (objet) to move, to shift; fig (problème) to shift the emphasis of. **2.** (muter) to transfer. ▶ **se déplacer** vp **1.** (se mouvoir - animal) to move (around); (- personne) to walk. **2.** (voyager) to travel. **3.** (MÉD): **se ~ une vertèbre** to slip a disc.
déplaire [depler] vt **1.** (ne pas plaire): **cela me déplaît** I don't like it. **2.** (irriter) to displease.
déplaisant, -e [deplezã, ãt] adj sout unpleasant.
dépliant [deplijã] nm leaflet; **~ touristique** tourist brochure.
déplier [deplije] vt to unfold.
déploiement [deplwamã] nm **1.** (MIL) deployment. **2.** (d'ailes) spreading. **3.** fig (d'efforts) display.
déplorer [deplore] vt (regretter) to deplore.
déployer [deplwaje] vt **1.** (déplier - gén) to unfold; (- plan, journal) to open; (ailes) to spread. **2.** (MIL) to deploy. **3.** (mettre en œuvre) to expend.
déplu [deply] pp → **déplaire**.
déportation [deportasjõ] nf **1.** (exil) deportation. **2.** (internement) transportation to a concentration camp.
déporté, -e [deporte] nm, f **1.** (exilé) deportee. **2.** (interné) prisoner (in a concentration camp).
déporter [deporte] vt **1.** (dévier) to carry off course. **2.** (exiler) to deport. **3.** (interner) to send to a concentration camp.
déposé, -e [depoze] adj: **marque ~e** registered trademark; **modèle ~** patented design.
déposer [depoze] ◆ vt **1.** (poser) to put down. **2.** (personne, paquet) to drop. **3.** (argent, sédiment) to deposit. **4.** (JUR) to file; **~ son bilan** (FIN) to go into liquidation. **5.** (monarque) to depose. ◆ vi (JUR) to testify, to give evidence. ▶ **se déposer** vp to settle.
dépositaire [depoziter] nmf **1.** (COMM) agent. **2.** (d'objet) bailee; **~ de** fig person entrusted with.
déposition [depozisjõ] nf deposition.
déposséder [deposede] vt: **~ qqn de** to dispossess sb of.
dépôt [depo] nm **1.** (d'objet, d'argent, de

sédiment) deposit, depositing (U); **verser un ~ (de garantie)** to put down a deposit; **~ d'ordures** (rubbish) dump Br, garbage dump Am. **2.** (ADMIN) registration; **~ légal** copyright registration. **3.** (garage) depot. **4.** (entrepôt) store, warehouse. **5.** (prison) = police cells (pl).
dépotoir [depotwar] nm (décharge) (rubbish) dump Br, garbage dump Am; fam fig dump, tip.
dépouille [depuj] nf **1.** (peau) hide, skin. **2.** (humaine) remains (pl).
dépouillement [depujmã] nm (sobriété) austerity, sobriety.
dépouiller [depuje] vt **1.** (priver): **~ qqn (de)** to strip sb (of). **2.** (examiner) to peruse; **~ un scrutin** to count the votes.
dépourvu, -e [depurvy] adj: **~ de** without, lacking in. ▶ **au dépourvu** loc adv: **prendre qqn au ~** to catch sb unawares.
dépoussiérer [depusjere] vt to dust (off).
dépravé, -e [deprave] ◆ adj depraved. ◆ nm, f degenerate.
dépréciation [depresjasjõ] nf depreciation.
déprécier [depresje] vt **1.** (marchandise) to reduce the value of. **2.** (œuvre) to disparage. ▶ **se déprécier** vp **1.** (marchandise) to depreciate. **2.** (personne) to put o.s. down.
dépressif, -ive [depresif, iv] adj depressive.
dépression [depresjõ] nf depression; **~ nerveuse** nervous breakdown.
déprimant, -e [deprimã, ãt] adj depressing.
déprime [deprim] nf fam: **faire une ~** to be (feeling) down.
déprimé, -e [deprime] adj depressed.
déprimer [deprime] ◆ vt to depress. ◆ vi fam to be (feeling) down.
déprogrammer [deprograme] vt to remove from the schedule; (TÉLÉ) to take off the air.
dépuceler [depysle] vt fam: **~ qqn** to take sb's virginity.
depuis [dəpɥi] ◆ prép **1.** (à partir d'une date ou d'un moment précis) since; **je ne l'ai pas vu ~ son mariage** I haven't seen him since he got married; **il est parti ~ hier** he's been away since yesterday; **~ le début jusqu'à la fin** from beginning to end. **2.** (exprimant une durée) for; **il est malade ~ une semaine** he has been ill for a week; **~ 10 ans/longtemps** for 10 years/a long time; **~ toujours** always.

3. (*dans l'espace*) from; ~ **la route, on pouvait voir la mer** you could see the sea from the road. ◆ *adv* since (then); ~, **nous ne l'avons pas revu** we haven't seen him since (then). ▶ **depuis que** *loc conj* since; **je ne l'ai pas revu ~ qu'il s'est marié** I haven't seen him since he got married.

député [depyte] *nm* (*au parlement*) member of parliament Br, representative Am.

déraciner [derasine] *vt litt & fig* to uproot.

déraillement [derajmɑ̃] *nm* derailment.

dérailler [deraje] *vi* **1.** (*train*) to leave the rails, to be derailed. **2.** *fam fig* (*mécanisme*) to go on the blink. **3.** *fam fig* (*personne*) to go to pieces.

dérailleur [derajœr] *nm* (*de bicyclette*) derailleur.

déraisonnable [derezɔnabl] *adj* unreasonable.

dérangement [derɑ̃ʒmɑ̃] *nm* trouble; **en ~** out of order.

déranger [derɑ̃ʒe] ◆ *vt* **1.** (*personne*) to disturb, to bother; **ça vous dérange si je fume?** do you mind if I smoke? **2.** (*plan*) to disrupt. **3.** (*maison, pièce*) to disarrange, to make untidy. ◆ *vi* to be disturbing. ▶ **se déranger** *vp* **1.** (*se déplacer*) to move. **2.** (*se gêner*) to put o.s. out.

dérapage [derapaʒ] *nm* (*glissement*) skid; *fig* excess.

déraper [derape] *vi* (*glisser*) to skid; *fig* to get out of hand.

déréglementer [dereglǝmɑ̃te] *vt* to deregulate.

dérégler [deregle] *vt* (*mécanisme*) to put out of order; *fig* to upset. ▶ **se dérégler** *vp* (*mécanisme*) to go wrong; *fig* to be upset ou unsettled.

dérider [deride] *vt fig*: ~ **qqn** to cheer sb up.

dérision [derizjɔ̃] *nf* derision; **tourner qqch en ~** to hold sthg up to ridicule.

dérisoire [derizwar] *adj* derisory.

dérivatif, -ive [derivatif, iv] *adj* derivative. ▶ **dérivatif** *nm* distraction.

dérive [deriv] *nf* (*mouvement*) drift, drifting (U); **aller** ou **partir à la ~** *fig* to fall apart.

dérivé [derive] *nm* derivative.

dériver [derive] ◆ *vt* (*détourner*) to divert. ◆ *vi* **1.** (*aller à la dérive*) to drift. **2.** *fig* (*découler*): ~ **de** to derive from.

dériveur [derivœr] *nm* sailing dinghy (*with centreboard*).

dermatologie [dermatɔlɔʒi] *nf* dermatology.

dermatologue [dermatɔlɔg] *nmf* dermatologist.

dernier, -ère [dɛrnje, ɛr] ◆ *adj* **1.** (*gén*) last; **l'année dernière** last year. **2.** (*ultime*) last, final. **3.** (*plus récent*) latest. ◆ *nm, f* last; **ce ~** the latter. ▶ **en dernier** *loc adv* last.

dernièrement [dɛrnjɛrmɑ̃] *adv* recently, lately.

dernier-né, dernière-née [dɛrnje-ne, dɛrnjɛrne] *nm, f* (*bébé*) youngest (child).

dérobade [derɔbad] *nf* evasion, shirking (U).

dérobé, -e [derɔbe] *adj* **1.** (*volé*) stolen. **2.** (*caché*) hidden. ▶ **à la dérobée** *loc adv* surreptitiously.

dérober [derɔbe] *vt sout* to steal. ▶ **se dérober** *vp* **1.** (*se soustraire*): **se ~ à qqch** to shirk sthg. **2.** (*s'effondrer*) to give way.

dérogation [derɔgasjɔ̃] *nf* (*action*) dispensation; (*résultat*) exception.

déroulement [derulmɑ̃] *nm* **1.** (*de bobine*) unwinding. **2.** *fig* (*d'événement*) development.

dérouler [derule] *vt* (*fil*) to unwind; (*papier, tissu*) to unroll. ▶ **se dérouler** *vp* to take place.

déroute [derut] *nf* (MIL) rout; *fig* collapse.

dérouter [derute] *vt* **1.** (*déconcerter*) to disconcert, to put out. **2.** (*dévier*) to divert.

derrière [dɛrjɛr] ◆ *prép & adv* behind. ◆ *nm* **1.** (*partie arrière*) back; **la porte de ~** the back door. **2.** (*partie du corps*) bottom, behind.

des [de] ◆ *art indéf* → **un**. ◆ *prép* → **de**.

dès [dɛ] *prép* from; ~ **son arrivée** the minute he arrives/arrived, as soon as he arrives/arrived; ~ **l'enfance** since childhood; ~ **1900** as far back as 1900, as early as 1900; ~ **maintenant** from now on. ▶ **dès que** *loc conj* as soon as.

désabusé, -e [dezabyze] *adj* disillusioned.

désaccord [dezakɔr] *nm* disagreement.

désaccordé, -e [dezakɔrde] *adj* out of tune.

désaffecté, -e [dezafɛkte] *adj* disused.

désagréable [dezagreabl] *adj* unpleasant.

désagréger [dezagreʒe] *vt* to break up. ▶ **se désagréger** *vp* to break up.

désagrément [dezagremã] *nm* annoyance.

désaltérant, -e [dezalterã, ãt] *adj* thirst-quenching.

désaltérer [dezaltere] ▶ **se désaltérer** *vp* to quench one's thirst.

désamorcer [dezamɔrse] *vt* (*arme*) to remove the primer from; (*bombe*) to defuse; *fig* (*complot*) to nip in the bud.

désappointer [dezapwɛte] *vt* to disappoint.

désapprobation [dezaprɔbasjɔ̃] *nf* disapproval.

désapprouver [dezapruve] ♦ *vt* to disapprove of. ♦ *vi* to be disapproving.

désarmement [dezarməmã] *nm* disarmament.

désarmer [dezarme] *vt* to disarm; (*fusil*) to unload.

désarroi [dezarwa] *nm* confusion.

désastre [dezastr] *nm* disaster.

désastreux, -euse [dezastrø, øz] *adj* disastrous.

désavantage [dezavãtaʒ] *nm* disadvantage.

désavantager [dezavãtaʒe] *vt* to disadvantage.

désavantageux, -euse [dezavãtaʒø, øz] *adj* unfavourable.

désavouer [dezavwe] *vt* to disown.

désaxé, -e [dezakse] ♦ *adj* (*mentalement*) disordered, unhinged. ♦ *nm, f* unhinged person.

descendance [desãdãs] *nf* (*progéniture*) descendants (*pl*).

descendant, -e [desãdã, ãt] *nm, f* (*héritier*) descendant.

descendre [desãdr] ♦ *vt* (*aux: avoir*) **1.** (*escalier, pente*) to go/come down; ~ **la rue en courant** to run down the street. **2.** (*rideau, tableau*) to lower. **3.** (*apporter*) to bring/take down. **4.** *fam* (*personne, avion*) to shoot down. ♦ *vi* (*aux: être*) **1.** (*gén*) to go/come down; (*température, niveau*) to fall. **2.** (*passager*) to get off; ~ **d'un bus** to get off a bus; ~ **d'une voiture** to get out of a car. **3.** (*être issu*): ~ **de** to be descended from. **4.** (*marée*) to go out.

descendu, -e [desãdy] *pp* → **descendre.**

descente [desãt] *nf* **1.** (*action*) descent. **2.** (*pente*) downhill slope ou stretch. **3.** (*irruption*) raid. **4.** (*tapis*): ~ **de lit** bedside rug.

descriptif, -ive [dɛskriptif, iv] *adj* descriptive. ▶ **descriptif** *nm* (*de lieu*) particulars (*pl*); (*d'appareil*) specification.

description [dɛskripsjɔ̃] *nf* description.

désemparé, -e [dezãpare] *adj* (*personne*) helpless; (*avion, navire*) disabled.

désendettement [dezãdɛtmã] *nm* degearing, debt reduction.

désenfler [dezãfle] *vi* to go down, to become less swollen.

désensibiliser [desãsibilize] *vt* to desensitize.

déséquilibre [dezekilibr] *nm* imbalance.

déséquilibré, -e [dezekilibre] *nm, f* unbalanced person.

déséquilibrer [dezekilibre] *vt* **1.** (*physiquement*): ~ **qqn** to throw sb off balance. **2.** (*perturber*) to unbalance.

désert, -e [dezɛr, ɛrt] *adj* (*désertique - île*) desert (*avant n*); (*peu fréquenté*) deserted. ▶ **désert** *nm* desert.

déserter [dezɛrte] *vt & vi* to desert.

déserteur [dezɛrtœr] *nm* (MIL) deserter; *fig & péj* traitor.

désertion [dezɛrsjɔ̃] *nf* desertion.

désertique [dezɛrtik] *adj* desert (*avant n*).

désespéré, -e [dezɛspere] *adj* **1.** (*regard*) desperate. **2.** (*situation*) hopeless.

désespérément [dezɛsperemã] *adv* **1.** (*sans espoir*) hopelessly. **2.** (*avec acharnement*) desperately.

désespérer [dezɛspere] ♦ *vt* **1.** (*décourager*): ~ **qqn** to drive sb to despair. **2.** (*perdre espoir*): ~ **que qqch arrive** to give up hope of sthg happening. ♦ *vi*: ~ (**de**) to despair (of). ▶ **se désespérer** *vp* to despair.

désespoir [dezɛspwar] *nm* despair; **en** ~ **de cause** as a last resort.

déshabillé [dezabije] *nm* negligee.

déshabiller [dezabije] *vt* to undress. ▶ **se déshabiller** *vp* to undress, to get undressed.

désherbant, -e [dezɛrbã, ãt] *adj* weed-killing. ▶ **désherbant** *nm* weed-killer.

déshérité, -e [dezerite] ♦ *adj* **1.** (*privé d'héritage*) disinherited. **2.** (*pauvre*) deprived. ♦ *nm, f* (*pauvre*) deprived person.

déshériter [dezerite] *vt* to disinherit.

déshonneur [dezɔnœr] *nm* disgrace.

déshonorer [dezɔnɔre] *vt* to disgrace, to bring disgrace on.

déshydrater [dezidrate] *vt* to dehydrate. ▶ **se déshydrater** *vp* to become dehydrated.

désigner [deziɲe] *vt* 1. (*choisir*) to appoint. 2. (*signaler*) to point out. 3. (*nommer*) to designate.

désillusion [dezilyzjɔ̃] *nf* disillusion.

désincarné, -e [dezɛ̃karne] *adj* 1. (RELIG) disembodied. 2. (*éthéré*) unearthly.

désinfectant, -e [dezɛ̃fɛktɑ̃, ɑ̃t] *adj* disinfectant. ► **désinfectant** *nm* disinfectant.

désinfecter [dezɛ̃fɛkte] *vt* to disinfect.

désinflation [dezɛ̃flasjɔ̃] *nf* disinflation.

désintégrer [dezɛ̃tegre] *vt* to break up. ► **se désintégrer** *vp* to disintegrate, to break up.

désintéressé, -e [dezɛ̃terese] *adj* disinterested.

désintéresser [dezɛ̃terese] ► **se désintéresser** *vp*: se ~ de to lose interest in.

désintoxication [dezɛ̃tɔksikasjɔ̃] *nf* detoxification.

désinvolte [dezɛ̃vɔlt] *adj* 1. (*à l'aise*) casual. 2. *péj* (*sans-gêne*) offhand.

désinvolture [dezɛ̃vɔltyr] *nf* 1. (*légèreté*) casualness. 2. *péj* (*sans-gêne*) offhandedness.

désir [dezir] *nm* 1. (*souhait*) desire, wish. 2. (*charnel*) desire.

désirable [dezirabl] *adj* desirable.

désirer [dezire] *vt* 1. *sout* (*chose*): ~ faire qqch to wish to do sthg; **vous désirez?** (*dans un magasin*) can I help you?; (*dans un café*) what can I get you? 2. (*sexuellement*) to desire.

désistement [dezistəmɑ̃] *nm*: ~ (**de**) withdrawal (from).

désister [deziste] ► **se désister** *vp* (*se retirer*) to withdraw, to stand down.

désobéir [dezɔbeir] *vi*: ~ (**à qqn**) to disobey (sb).

désobéissant, -e [dezɔbeisɑ̃, ɑ̃t] *adj* disobedient.

désobligeant, -e [dezɔbliʒɑ̃, ɑ̃t] *adj sout* offensive.

désodorisant, -e [dezɔdɔrizɑ̃, ɑ̃t] *adj* deodorant. ► **désodorisant** *nm* air freshener.

désœuvré, -e [dezœvre] *adj* idle.

désolation [dezɔlasjɔ̃] *nf* 1. (*destruction*) desolation. 2. *sout* (*affliction*) distress.

désolé, -e [dezɔle] *adj* 1. (*ravagé*) desolate. 2. (*contrarié*) very sorry.

désoler [dezɔle] *vt* 1. (*affliger*) to sadden. 2. (*contrarier*) to upset, to make

sorry. ► **se désoler** *vp* (*être contrarié*) to be upset.

désolidariser [desɔlidarize] *vt* 1. (*choses*): ~ qqch (**de**) to disengage ou disconnect sthg (from). 2. (*personnes*) to estrange. ► **se désolidariser** *vp*: se ~ de to dissociate o.s. from.

désopilant, -e [dezɔpilɑ̃, ɑ̃t] *adj* hilarious.

désordonné, -e [dezɔrdɔne] *adj* (*maison, personne*) untidy; *fig* (*vie*) disorganized.

désordre [dezɔrdr] *nm* 1. (*fouillis*) untidiness; **en ~** untidy. 2. (*agitation*) disturbances (*pl*), disorder (U).

désorganiser [dezɔrganize] *vt* to disrupt.

désorienté, -e [dezɔrjɑ̃te] *adj* disoriented, disorientated.

désormais [dezɔrmɛ] *adv* from now on, in future.

désosser [dezɔse] *vt* to bone.

despote [dɛspɔt] *nm* (*chef d'État*) despot; *fig & péj* tyrant.

despotisme [dɛspɔtism] *nm* (*gouvernement*) despotism; *fig & péj* tyranny.

desquels, desquelles [dekɛl] → **lequel**.

DESS (*abr de* **diplôme d'études supérieures spécialisées**) *nm* postgraduate diploma.

dessécher [deseʃe] *vt* (*peau*) to dry (out); *fig* (*cœur*) to harden. ► **se dessécher** *vp* (*peau, terre*) to dry out; (*plante*) to wither; *fig* to harden.

desserrer [desere] *vt* to loosen; (*poing, dents*) to unclench; (*frein*) to release.

dessert [desɛr] *nm* dessert.

desserte [desɛrt] *nf* 1. (TRANSPORT) (transport) service. 2. (*meuble*) sideboard.

desservir [deservir] *vt* 1. (TRANSPORT) to serve. 2. (*table*) to clear. 3. (*désavantager*) to do a disservice to.

dessin [desɛ̃] *nm* 1. (*graphique*) drawing; ~ animé cartoon (*film*); ~ humoristique cartoon (*drawing*). 2. *fig* (*contour*) outline.

dessinateur, -trice [desinatœr, tris] *nm, f* artist, draughtsman (*f* draughtswoman).

dessiner [desine] ◆ *vt* (*représenter*) to draw; *fig* to outline. ◆ *vi* to draw.

dessous [dəsu] ◆ *adv* underneath. ◆ *nm* (*partie inférieure - gén*) underside; (*- d'un tissu*) wrong side. ◆ *nmpl* (*sous-vêtements féminins*) underwear (U). ► **en dessous** *loc adv* underneath; (*plus* *bas*) below; **ils habitent l'appartement d'en ~** they live in the flat below ou downstairs.

dessous-de-plat [dəsudpla] *nm inv* tablemat.

dessus [dəsy] ◆ *adv* on top; **faites attention à ne pas marcher ~** be careful not to walk on it. ◆ *nm* 1. (*partie supérieure*) top. 2. (*étage supérieur*) upstairs; **les voisins du ~** the upstairs neighbours. 3. *loc*: **avoir le ~** to have the upper hand; **reprendre le ~** to get over it. ▶ **en dessus** *loc adv* on top.

dessus-de-lit [dəsydli] *nm inv* bedspread.

déstabiliser [destabilize] *vt* to destabilize.

destin [dɛstɛ̃] *nm* fate.

destinataire [dɛstinatɛr] *nmf* addressee.

destination [dɛstinasjɔ̃] *nf* 1. (*direction*) destination; **un avion à ~ de Paris** a plane to ou for Paris. 2. (*rôle*) purpose.

destinée [dɛstine] *nf* destiny.

destiner [dɛstine] *vt* 1. (*consacrer*): **~ qqch à** to intend sthg for, to mean sthg for. 2. (*vouer*): **~ qqn à qqch/à faire qqch** (*à un métier*) to destine sb for sthg/to do sthg.

destituer [dɛstitɥe] *vt* to dismiss.

destructeur, -trice [dɛstryktœr, tris] ◆ *adj* destructive. ◆ *nm, f* destroyer.

destruction [dɛstryksjɔ̃] *nf* destruction.

désuet, -ète [dezɥɛ, ɛt] *adj* (*expression, coutume*) obsolete; (*style, tableau*) outmoded.

désuni, -e [dezyni] *adj* divided.

détachable [detaʃabl] *adj* detachable, removable.

détachant, -e [detaʃɑ̃, ɑ̃t] *adj* stain-removing. ▶ **détachant** *nm* stain remover.

détaché, -e [detaʃe] *adj* detached.

détachement [detaʃmɑ̃] *nm* 1. (*d'esprit*) detachment. 2. (*de fonctionnaire*) secondment. 3. (MIL) detachment.

détacher [detaʃe] *vt* 1. (*enlever*): **~ qqch (de)** (*objet*) to detach sthg (from); *fig* to free sthg (from). 2. (*nettoyer*) to remove stains from, to clean. 3. (*délier*) to undo; (*cheveux*) to untie. 4. (ADMIN): **~ qqn auprès de** to second sb to. ▶ **se détacher** *vp* 1. (*tomber*): **se ~ (de)** to come off; *fig* to free o.s. (from). 2. (*se défaire*) to come undone. 3. (*ressortir*): **se ~ sur** to stand out on. 4. (*se désintéresser*): **se ~ de qqn** to drift apart from sb.

détail [detaj] *nm* 1. (*précision*) detail. 2. (COMM): **le ~** retail. ▶ **au détail** *loc adj* & *loc adv* retail. ▶ **en détail** *loc adv* in detail.

détaillant, -e [detajɑ̃, ɑ̃t] *nm, f* retailer.

détaillé, -e [detaje] *adj* detailed.

détailler [detaje] *vt* 1. (*expliquer*) to give details of. 2. (*vendre*) to retail.

détaler [detale] *vi* 1. (*personne*) to clear out. 2. (*animal*) to bolt.

détartrant, -e [detartrɑ̃, ɑ̃t] *adj* descaling. ▶ **détartrant** *nm* descaling agent.

détaxe [detaks] *nf*: **~ (sur)** (*suppression*) removal of tax (from); (*réduction*) reduction in tax (on).

détecter [detɛkte] *vt* to detect.

détecteur, -trice [detɛktœr, tris] *adj* detecting, detector (*avant n*). ▶ **détecteur** *nm* detector.

détection [detɛksjɔ̃] *nf* detection.

détective [detɛktiv] *nm* detective; **~ privé** private detective.

déteindre [detɛ̃dr] *vi* to fade.

déteint, -e [detɛ̃, ɛ̃t] *pp* → **déteindre**.

dételer [detle] *vt* (*cheval*) to unharness.

détendre [detɑ̃dr] *vt* 1. (*corde*) to loosen, to slacken; *fig* to ease. 2. (*personne*) to relax. ▶ **se détendre** *vp* 1. (*se relâcher*) to slacken; *fig* (*situation*) to ease; (*atmosphère*) to become more relaxed. 2. (*se reposer*) to relax.

détendu, -e [detɑ̃dy] ◆ *pp* → **détendre**. ◆ *adj* 1. (*corde*) loose, slack. 2. (*personne*) relaxed.

détenir [detnir] *vt* 1. (*objet*) to have, to hold. 2. (*personne*) to detain, to hold.

détente [detɑ̃t] *nf* 1. (*de ressort*) release. 2. (*d'une arme*) trigger. 3. (*repos*) relaxation. 4. (POLIT) détente.

détenteur, -trice [detɑ̃tœr, tris] *nm, f* (*d'objet, de secret*) possessor; (*de prix, record*) holder.

détention [detɑ̃sjɔ̃] *nf* 1. (*possession*) possession. 2. (*emprisonnement*) detention.

détenu, -e [detny] ◆ *pp* → **détenir**. ◆ *adj* detained. ◆ *nm, f* prisoner.

détergent, -e [detɛrʒɑ̃, ɑ̃t] *adj* detergent (*avant n*). ▶ **détergent** *nm* detergent.

détérioration [deterjɔrasjɔ̃] *nf* (*de bâtiment*) deterioration; (*de situation*) worsening.

détériorer [deterjɔre] *vt* 1. (*abîmer*) to damage. 2. (*altérer*) to ruin. ▶ **se détériorer** *vp* 1. (*bâtiment*) to deteriorate; (*situation*) to worsen. **2.** (*s'altérer*) to be spoiled.

déterminant, -e [detɛrminɑ̃, ɑ̃t] *adj* decisive, determining. ▸ **déterminant** *nm* (LING) determiner.

détermination [detɛrminasjɔ̃] *nf* (*résolution*) decision.

déterminé, -e [detɛrmine] *adj* **1.** (*quantité*) given (*avant n*). **2.** (*expression*) determined.

déterminer [detɛrmine] *vt* **1.** (*préciser*) to determine, to specify. **2.** (*provoquer*) to bring about.

déterrer [detere] *vt* to dig up.

détestable [detɛstabl] *adj* dreadful.

détester [detɛste] *vt* to detest.

détonateur [detɔnatœr] *nm* (TECHNOL) detonator; *fig* trigger.

détoner [detɔne] *vi* to detonate.

détonner [detɔne] *vi* (MUS) to be out of tune; (*couleur*) to clash; (*personne*) to be out of place.

détour [detur] *nm* **1.** (*crochet*) detour. **2.** (*méandre*) bend; **sans ~** *fig* directly.

détourné, -e [deturne] *adj* (*dévié*) indirect; *fig* roundabout (*avant n*).

détournement [deturnəmɑ̃] *nm* diversion; **~ d'avion** hijacking; **~ de fonds** embezzlement; **~ de mineur** corruption of a minor.

détourner [deturne] *vt* **1.** (*dévier - gén*) to divert; (*- avion*) to hijack. **2.** (*écarter*): **~ qqn de** to distract sb from, to divert sb from. **3.** (*tourner ailleurs*) to turn away. **4.** (*argent*) to embezzle. ▸ **se détourner** *vp* to turn away; **se ~ de** *fig* to move away from.

détraquer [detrake] *vt fam* (*dérégler*) to break; *fig* to upset. ▸ **se détraquer** *vp fam* (*se dérégler*) to go wrong; *fig* to become unsettled.

détresse [detrɛs] *nf* distress.

détriment [detrimɑ̃] ▸ **au détriment de** *loc prép* to the detriment of.

détritus [detrity(s)] *nm* detritus.

détroit [detrwa] *nm* strait.

détromper [detrɔ̃pe] *vt* to disabuse.

détrôner [detrone] *vt* (*souverain*) to dethrone; *fig* to oust.

détruire [detrɥir] *vt* **1.** (*démolir, éliminer*) to destroy. **2.** *fig* (*anéantir*) to ruin.

détruit, -e [detrɥi, it] *pp* → **détruire**.

dette [dɛt] *nf* debt.

DEUG, Deug [dœg] (*abr de* **diplôme d'études universitaires générales**) *nm* university diploma taken after two years of arts courses.

deuil [dœj] *nm* (*douleur, mort*) bereavement; (*vêtements, période*) mourning (U); **porter le ~** to be in ou wear mourning.

DEUST, Deust [dœst] (*abr de* **diplôme d'études universitaires scientifiques et techniques**) *nm* university diploma taken after two years of science courses; *voir aussi* **DEUG**.

deux [dø] ◆ *adj num* two; **ses ~ fils** both his sons, his two sons; **tous les ~ jours** every other day, every two days, every second day. ◆ *nm* two; **les ~** both; **par ~** in pairs; *voir aussi* **six**.

deuxième [døzjɛm] *adj num, nm & nmf* second; *voir aussi* **sixième**.

deux-pièces [døpjɛs] *nm inv* **1.** (*appartement*) two-room flat Br ou apartment Am. **2.** (*bikini*) two-piece (swimming costume).

deux-points [døpwɛ̃] *nm inv* colon.

deux-roues [døru] *nm inv* two-wheeled vehicle.

dévaler [devale] *vt* to run down.

dévaliser [devalize] *vt* (*cambrioler - maison*) to ransack; (*- personne*) to rob; *fig* to strip bare.

dévaloriser [devalɔrize] *vt* **1.** (*monnaie*) to devalue. **2.** (*personne*) to run ou put down. ▸ **se dévaloriser** *vp* **1.** (*monnaie*) to fall in value. **2.** (*personne*) *fig* to run ou put o.s. down.

dévaluation [devalɥasjɔ̃] *nf* devaluation.

dévaluer [devalɥe] *vt* to devalue. ▸ **se dévaluer** *vp* to devalue.

devancer [dəvɑ̃se] *vt* **1.** (*précéder*) to arrive before. **2.** (*anticiper*) to anticipate.

devant [dəvɑ̃] ◆ *prép* **1.** (*en face de*) in front of. **2.** (*en avant de*) ahead of, in front of; **aller droit ~ soi** to go straight ahead ou on. **3.** (*en présence de, face à*) in the face of. ◆ *adv* **1.** (*en face*) in front. **2.** (*en avant*) in front, ahead. ◆ *nm* front; **prendre les ~s** to make the first move, to take the initiative. ▸ **de devant** *loc adj* (*pattes, roues*) front (*avant n*).

devanture [dəvɑ̃tyr] *nf* shop window.

dévaster [devaste] *vt* to devastate.

développement [devlɔpmɑ̃] *nm* **1.** (*gén*) development. **2.** (PHOT) developing.

développer [devlɔpe] *vt* to develop; (*industrie, commerce*) to expand. ▸ **se développer** *vp* **1.** (*s'épanouir*) to spread. **2.** (ÉCON) to grow, to expand.

devenir [dəvnir] *vi* to become; **que devenez-vous?** *fig* how are you doing?

devenu, -e [dəvny] *pp* → **devenir**.

dévergondé, -e [devɛrgɔ̃de] ♦ *adj* shameless, wild. ♦ *nm, f* shameless person.

déverser [devɛrse] *vt* **1.** (*liquide*) to pour out. **2.** (*ordures*) to tip (out). **3.** *fig* (*injures*) to pour out.

déviation [devjasjɔ̃] *nf* **1.** (*gén*) deviation. **2.** (*d'itinéraire*) diversion.

dévier [devje] ♦ *vi*: **~ de** to deviate from. ♦ *vt* to divert.

devin, devineresse [dəvɛ̃, dəvinrɛs] *nm, f*: **je ne suis pas ~!** I'm not psychic!

deviner [dəvine] *vt* to guess.

devinette [dəvinɛt] *nf* riddle.

devis [dəvi] *nm* estimate; **faire un ~** to (give an) estimate.

dévisager [devizaʒe] *vt* to stare at.

devise [dəviz] *nf* **1.** (*formule*) motto. **2.** (*monnaie*) currency. ▶ **devises** *nfpl* (*argent*) currency (U).

dévisser [devise] *vt* to unscrew.

dévoiler [devwale] *vt* to unveil; *fig* to reveal.

devoir [dəvwar] ♦ *nm* **1.** (*obligation*) duty. **2.** (SCOL) homework (U); **faire ses ~s** to do one's homework. ♦ *vt* **1.** (*argent, respect*): **~ qqch (à qqn)** to owe (sb) sthg. **2.** (*marque l'obligation*): **~ faire qqch** to have to do sthg; **je dois partir à l'heure ce soir** I have to ou must leave on time tonight; **tu devrais faire attention** you should be ou ought to be careful; **il n'aurait pas dû mentir** he shouldn't have lied, he ought not to have lied. **3.** (*marque la probabilité*): **il doit faire chaud là-bas** it must be hot over there. **4.** (*marque le futur, l'intention*): **~ faire qqch** to be going to do sthg, to be going to do sthg; **elle doit arriver à 6 heures** she's due to arrive at 6 o'clock; **je dois voir mes parents ce week-end** I'm seeing ou going to see my parents this weekend. **5.** (*être destiné à*): **il devait mourir trois ans plus tard** he was to die three years later; **cela devait arriver** it had to happen, it was bound to happen. ▶ **se devoir** *vp*: **se ~ de faire qqch** to be duty-bound to do sthg; **comme il se doit** as is proper.

dévolu, -e [devɔly] *adj sout*: **~ à** allotted to. ▶ **dévolu** *nm*: **jeter son ~ sur** to set one's sights on.

dévorant, -e [devɔrɑ̃, ɑ̃t] *adj* **1.** (*faim*) gnawing; (*soif*) burning. **2.** (*passion*) consuming.

dévorer [devɔre] *vt* to devour.

dévotion [devɔsjɔ̃] *nf* devotion; **avec ~** (*prier*) devoutly; (*soigner, aimer*) devotedly.

dévoué, -e [devwe] *adj* devoted.

dévouement [devumɑ̃] *nm* devotion.

dévouer [devwe] ▶ **se dévouer** *vp* **1.** (*se consacrer*): **se ~ à** to devote o.s. to. **2.** *fig* (*se sacrifier*): **se ~ pour qqch/pour faire qqch** to sacrifice o.s. for sthg/to do sthg.

dévoyé, -e [devwaje] *adj & nm, f* delinquent.

devrai, devras *etc* → **devoir**.

dextérité [dɛksterite] *nf* dexterity, skill.

diabète [djabɛt] *nm* diabetes (U).

diabétique [djabetik] *nmf & adj* diabetic.

diable [djabl] *nm* devil.

diabolique [djabɔlik] *adj* diabolical.

diabolo [djabɔlo] *nm* (*boisson*) fruit cordial and lemonade; **~ menthe** mint (cordial) and lemonade.

diadème [djadɛm] *nm* diadem.

diagnostic [djagnɔstik] *nm* (MÉD & *fig*) diagnosis.

diagnostiquer [djagnɔstike] *vt* (MÉD & *fig*) to diagnose.

diagonale [djagɔnal] *nf* diagonal.

dialecte [djalɛkt] *nm* dialect.

dialogue [djalɔg] *nm* discussion.

dialoguer [djalɔge] *vi* **1.** (*converser*) to converse. **2.** (INFORM) to interact.

diamant [djamɑ̃] *nm* (*pierre*) diamond.

diamètre [djamɛtr] *nm* diameter.

diapason [djapazɔ̃] *nm* (*instrument*) tuning fork.

diapositive [djapozitiv] *nf* slide.

diarrhée [djare] *nf* diarrhoea.

dictateur [diktatœr] *nm* dictator.

dictature [diktatyr] *nf* dictatorship.

dictée [dikte] *nf* dictation.

dicter [dikte] *vt* to dictate.

diction [diksjɔ̃] *nf* diction.

dictionnaire [diksjɔnɛr] *nm* dictionary.

dicton [diktɔ̃] *nm* saying, dictum.

dièse [djɛz] ♦ *adj* sharp; **do/fa ~** C/F sharp. ♦ *nm* sharp.

diesel [djezɛl] *adj inv* diesel.

diète [djɛt] *nf* diet.

diététicien, -enne [djetetisjɛ̃, ɛn] *nm, f* dietician.

diététique [djetetik] ♦ *nf* dietetics (U). ♦ *adj* (*considération, raison*) dietary; (*produit, magasin*) health (*avant n*).

dieu, -x [djø] *nm* God; **mon Dieu!** my God! ▶ **Dieu** *nm* God; **mon Dieu!** my God!

diffamation [difamasjɔ̃] *nf* (*écrite*) libel; (*orale*) slander.

différé, -e [difere] *adj* recorded.

▶ **différé** *nm*: en ~ (TÉLÉ) recorded; (INFORM) off-line.

différence [diferɑ̃s] *nf* difference.

différencier [diferɑ̃sje] *vt*: ~ qqch de qqch to differentiate sthg from sthg. ▶ **se différencier** *vp*: se ~ de to be different from.

différend [diferɑ̃] *nm* (*désaccord*) difference of opinion.

différent, -e [diferɑ̃, ɑ̃t] *adj*: ~ (de) different (from).

différer [difere] ◆ *vt* (*retarder*) to postpone. ◆ *vi*: ~ de to differ from, to be different from.

difficile [difisil] *adj* difficult.

difficilement [difisilmɑ̃] *adv* with difficulty.

difficulté [difikylte] *nf* 1. (*complexité, peine*) difficulty. 2. (*obstacle*) problem.

difforme [difɔrm] *adj* deformed.

diffuser [difyze] *vt* 1. (*lumière*) to diffuse. 2. (*émission*) to broadcast. 3. (*livres*) to distribute.

diffuseur [difyzœr] *nm* 1. (*appareil*) diffuser. 2. (*de livres*) distributor.

diffusion [difyzjɔ̃] *nf* 1. (*d'émission, d'onde*) broadcast. 2. (*de livres*) distribution. 3. (*propagation*) spread.

digérer [diʒere] ◆ *vi* to digest. ◆ *vt* 1. (*repas, connaissance*) to digest. 2. *fam fig* (*désagrément*) to put up with.

digestif, -ive [diʒɛstif, iv] *adj* digestive. ▶ **digestif** *nm* liqueur.

digestion [diʒɛstjɔ̃] *nf* digestion.

digital, -e, -aux [diʒital, o] *adj* 1. (TECHNOL) digital. 2. → **empreinte**.

digne [diɲ] *adj* 1. (*honorable*) dignified. 2. (*méritant*): ~ de worthy of.

dignité [diɲite] *nf* dignity.

digression [digresjɔ̃] *nf* digression.

digue [dig] *nf* dike.

dilapider [dilapide] *vt* to squander.

dilater [dilate] *vt* to dilate.

dilemme [dilɛm] *nm* dilemma.

diligence [diliʒɑ̃s] *nf* (HIST & *sout*) diligence.

diluant [dilɥɑ̃] *nm* thinner.

diluer [dilɥe] *vt* to dilute.

diluvien, -enne [dilyvjɛ̃, ɛn] *adj* torrential.

dimanche [dimɑ̃ʃ] *nm* Sunday; *voir aussi* **samedi**.

dimension [dimɑ̃sjɔ̃] *nf* 1. (*mesure*) dimension. 2. (*taille*) dimensions (*pl*), size. 3. *fig* (*importance*) magnitude.

diminuer [diminɥe] ◆ *vt* (*réduire*) to diminish, to reduce. ◆ *vi* (*intensité*) to diminish, to decrease.

▶ **diminutif, -ive** [diminytif, iv] *adj* diminutive. ▶ **diminutif** *nm* diminutive.

diminution [diminysjɔ̃] *nf* diminution.

dinde [dɛ̃d] *nf* 1. (*animal*) turkey. 2. *péj* (*femme*) stupid woman.

dindon [dɛ̃dɔ̃] *nm* turkey; être le ~ de la farce *fig* to be made a fool of.

dîner [dine] ◆ *vi* to dine. ◆ *nm* dinner.

dingue [dɛ̃g] *fam* ◆ *adj* 1. (*personne*) crazy. 2. (*histoire*) incredible. ◆ *nmf* loony.

dinosaure [dinozɔr] *nm* dinosaur.

diplomate [diplɔmat] ◆ *nmf* (*ambassadeur*) diplomat. ◆ *adj* diplomatic.

diplomatie [diplɔmasi] *nf* diplomacy.

diplomatique [diplɔmatik] *adj* diplomatic.

diplôme [diplom] *nm* diploma.

diplômé, -e [diplome] ◆ *adj*: être ~ de/ en to be a graduate of/in. ◆ *nm, f* graduate.

dire [dir] *vt*: ~ qqch (à qqn) (*parole*) to say sthg (to sb); (*vérité, mensonge, secret*) to tell (sb) sthg; ~ à qqn de faire qqch to tell sb to do sthg; il m'a dit que ... he told me (that) ...; la ville proprement dite the actual town; ~ du bien/du mal (de) to speak well/ill (of); que dirais-tu de ...? what would you say to ...?; qu'en dis-tu? what do you think (of it)?; on dirait que ... it looks as if ...; on dirait de la soie it looks like silk, you'd think it was silk; et ~ que je n'étais pas là! and to think I wasn't there!; ça ne me dit rien (*pas envie*) I don't fancy that; (*jamais entendu*) I've never heard of it. ▶ **se dire** *vp* 1. (*penser*) to think (to o.s.). 2. (*s'employer*): ça ne se dit pas (*par décence*) you mustn't say that; (*par usage*) people don't say that, nobody says that. 3. (*se traduire*): 'chat' se dit 'gato' en espagnol the Spanish for 'cat' is 'gato'. ▶ **cela dit** *loc adv* having said that. ▶ **dis donc** *loc adv fam* so; (*au fait*) by the way; (*à qqn qui exagère*) look here! ▶ **pour ainsi dire** *loc adv* so to speak. ▶ **à vrai dire** *loc adv* to tell the truth.

direct, -e [dirɛkt] *adj*. ▶ **direct** *nm* 1. (BOXE) jab. 2. (*train*) direct train. 3. (RADIO & TÉLÉ): le ~ live transmission (U); en ~ live.

directement [dirɛktəmɑ̃] *adv* directly.

directeur, -trice [dirɛktœr, tris] ◆ *adj* 1. (*dirigeant*) leading; comité ~ steering committee. 2. (*central*) guiding. ◆ *nm, f* director, manager; ~ général general manager, managing director *Br*, chief executive officer Am.

direction [dirɛksjɔ̃] nf 1. (gestion, ensemble des cadres) management; **sous la ~ de** under the management of. 2. (orientation) direction; **en** ou **dans la ~ de** in the direction of. 3. (AUTOM) steering.

directive [dirɛktiv] nf directive.

directrice → directeur.

dirigeable [diriʒabl] nm : (ballon) ~ airship.

dirigeant, -e [diriʒɑ̃, ɑ̃t] ◆ adj ruling. ◆ nm, f (de pays) leader; (d'entreprise) manager.

diriger [diriʒe] vt 1. (mener - entreprise) to run, to manage; (- orchestre) to conduct; (- film, acteurs) to direct; (- recherches, projet) to supervise. 2. (conduire) to steer. 3. (orienter) : ~ qqch sur/vers to aim sthg at/towards. **▶ se diriger** vp : **se ~ vers** to go ou head towards.

discernement [disɛrnəmɑ̃] nm (jugement) discernment.

discerner [disɛrne] vt 1. (distinguer) : ~ qqch de to distinguish sthg from. 2. (deviner) to discern.

disciple [disipl] nmf disciple.

disciplinaire [disipliner] adj disciplinary.

discipline [disiplin] nf discipline.

discipliner [discipline] vt (personne) to discipline; (cheveux) to control.

disco [disko] nm disco (music).

discontinu, -e [diskɔ̃tiny] adj (ligne) broken; (bruit, effort) intermittent.

discordant, -e [diskɔrdɑ̃, ɑ̃t] adj discordant.

discorde [diskɔrd] nf discord.

discothèque [diskɔtɛk] nf 1. (boîte de nuit) discothèque. 2. (de prêt) record library.

discourir [diskurir] vi to talk at length.

discours [diskur] nm (allocution) speech.

discréditer [diskredite] vt to discredit.

discret, -ète [diskrɛ, ɛt] adj (gén) discreet; (réservé) reserved.

discrètement [diskrɛtmɑ̃] adv discreetly.

discrétion [diskresjɔ̃] nf (réserve, tact, silence) discretion.

discrimination [diskriminasjɔ̃] nf discrimination; **sans ~** indiscriminately.

discriminatoire [diskriminatwar] adj discriminatory.

disculper [diskylpe] vt to exonerate. **▶ se disculper** vp to exonerate o.s.

discussion [diskysjɔ̃] nf 1. (conversation, examen) discussion. 2. (contestation, altercation) argument.

discutable [diskytabl] adj (contestable) questionable.

discuter [diskyte] ◆ vt 1. (débattre) : ~ (de) qqch to discuss sthg. 2. (contester) to dispute. ◆ vi 1. (parlementer) to discuss. 2. (converser) to talk. 3. (contester) to argue.

diseur, -euse [dizœr, øz] nm, f : ~ **de bonne aventure** fortune-teller.

disgracieux, -euse [disgrasjø, øz] adj 1. (sans grâce) awkward, graceless. 2. (laid) plain.

disjoncteur [disʒɔ̃ktœr] nm trip switch, circuit breaker.

disloquer [dislɔke] vt 1. (MÉD) to dislocate. 2. (machine, empire) to dismantle. **▶ se disloquer** vp (machine) to fall apart ou to pieces; fig (empire) to break up.

disparaître [disparɛtr] vi 1. (gén) to disappear, to vanish; **faire ~** (personne) to get rid of; (obstacle) to remove. 2. (mourir) to die.

disparité [disparite] nf (différence - d'éléments) disparity; (- de couleurs) mismatch.

disparition [disparisjɔ̃] nf 1. (gén) disappearance; (d'espèce) extinction; **en voie de ~** endangered. 2. (mort) passing.

disparu, -e [dispary] ◆ pp → **disparaître.** ◆ nm, f dead person, deceased.

dispensaire [dispɑ̃ser] nm community clinic Br, free clinic Am.

dispense [dispɑ̃s] nf (exemption) exemption.

dispenser [dispɑ̃se] vt 1. (distribuer) to dispense. 2. (exempter) : ~ qqn de qqch (corvée) to excuse sb sthg, to let sb off sthg; **je te dispense de tes réflexions!** fig spare us the comments!, keep your comments to yourself!

disperser [dispɛrse] vt to scatter (about ou around); (collection, brume, foule) to break up; fig (efforts, forces) to dissipate, to waste. **▶ se disperser** vp 1. (feuilles, cendres) to scatter; (brume, foule) to break up, to clear. 2. (personne) to take on too much at once, to spread o.s. too thin.

dispersion [dispɛrsjɔ̃] nf scattering; (de collection, brume, foule) breaking up; fig (d'efforts, de forces) waste, squandering.

disponibilité [disponibilite] nf 1. (de choses) availability. 2. (de fonctionnaire) leave of absence. 3. (d'esprit) alertness, receptiveness.

disponible [dispɔnibl] *adj* (*place, personne*) available, free.

disposé, -e [dispoze] *adj*: **être ~ à faire qqch** to be prepared ou willing to do sthg; **être bien ~ envers qqn** to be well-disposed towards ou to sb.

disposer [dispoze] ◆ *vt* (*arranger*) to arrange. ◆ *vi*: **~ de** (*moyens, argent*) to have available (to one), to have at one's disposal; (*chose*) to have the use of; (*temps*) to have free ou available.

dispositif [dispozitif] *nm* (*mécanisme*) device, mechanism.

disposition [dispozisjɔ̃] *nf* 1. (*arrangement*) arrangement. 2. (*disponibilité*): **à la ~ de** at the disposal of, available to. ▶ **dispositions** *nfpl* 1. (*mesures*) arrangements, measures. 2. (*dons*): **avoir des ~s pour** to have a gift for.

disproportionné, -e [disprɔpɔrsjɔne] *adj* out of proportion.

dispute [dispyt] *nf* argument, quarrel.

disputer [dispyte] *vt* 1. (SPORT - *course*) to run; (- *match*) to play. 2. (*lutter pour*) to fight for. ▶ **se disputer** *vp* 1. (*se quereller*) to quarrel, to fight. 2. (*lutter pour*) to fight over ou for.

disquaire [diskɛr] *nm* record dealer.

disqualifier [diskalifje] *vt* to disqualify.

disque [disk] *nm* 1. (MUS) record; (*vidéo*) video disc; **~ compact** ou **laser** compact disc. 2. (ANAT) disc. 3. (INFORM) disk; **~ dur** hard disk. 4. (SPORT) discus.

disquette [diskɛt] *nf* diskette, floppy disk; **~ système** system diskette.

dissection [disɛksjɔ̃] *nf* dissection.

dissemblable [disãblabl] *adj* dissimilar.

disséminer [disemine] *vt* (*graines, maisons*) to scatter, to spread (out); *fig* (*idées*) to disseminate, to spread.

disséquer [diseke] *vt* *litt* & *fig* to dissect.

dissertation [disɛrtasjɔ̃] *nf* essay.

dissident, -e [disidã, ãt] *adj* & *nm, f* dissident.

dissimulation [disimylasjɔ̃] *nf* 1. (*hypocrisie*) duplicity. 2. (*de la vérité*) concealment.

dissimuler [disimyle] *vt* to conceal. ▶ **se dissimuler** *vp* 1. (*se cacher*) to conceal o.s., to hide. 2. (*refuser de voir*): **se ~ qqch** to close one's eyes to sthg.

dissipation [disipasjɔ̃] *nf* (*indiscipline*) indiscipline, misbehaviour.

dissiper [disipe] *vt* 1. (*chasser*) to break up, to clear; *fig* to dispel. 2. (*distraire*) to

lead astray. ▶ **se dissiper** *vp* 1. (*brouillard, fumée*) to clear. 2. (*élève*) to misbehave. 3. *fig* (*malaise, fatigue*) to go away; (*doute*) to be dispelled.

dissocier [disɔsje] *vt* (*séparer*) to separate, to distinguish.

dissolution [disɔlysjɔ̃] *nf* 1. (JUR) dissolution. 2. (*mélange*) dissolving. 3. *sout* (*débauche*) dissipation.

dissolvant, -e [disɔlvã, ãt] *adj* solvent. ▶ **dissolvant** *nm* (*solvant*) solvent; (*pour vernis à ongles*) nail varnish remover.

dissoudre [disudr] *vt*: **(faire) ~** to dissolve. ▶ **se dissoudre** *vp* (*substance*) to dissolve.

dissous, -oute [disu, ut] *pp* → **dissoudre**.

dissuader [disɥade] *vt* to dissuade.

dissuasion [disɥazjɔ̃] *nf* dissuasion; **force de ~** deterrent (effect).

distance [distãs] *nf* 1. (*éloignement*) distance; **à ~** at a distance; (*télécommander*) by remote control; **à une ~ de 300 mètres** 300 metres away. 2. (*intervalle*) interval. 3. (*écart*) gap.

distancer [distãse] *vt* to outstrip.

distant, -e [distã, ãt] *adj* 1. (*éloigné*): **une ville ~e de 10 km** a town 10 km away; **des villes ~es de 10 km** towns 10 km apart. 2. (*froid*) distant.

distendre [distãdr] *vt* (*ressort, corde*) to stretch; (*abdomen*) to distend. ▶ **se distendre** *vp* to distend.

distendu, -e [distãdy] *pp* → **distendre**.

distiller [distile] *vt* (*alcool*) to distil; (*pétrole*) to refine; (*miel*) to secrete; *fig* & *littéraire* to exude.

distinct, -e [distɛ̃, ɛ̃kt] *adj* distinct.

distinctement [distɛ̃ktəmã] *adv* distinctly, clearly.

distinctif, -ive [distɛ̃ktif, iv] *adj* distinctive.

distinction [distɛ̃ksjɔ̃] *nf* distinction.

distingué, -e [distɛ̃ge] *adj* distinguished.

distinguer [distɛ̃ge] *vt* 1. (*différencier*) to tell apart, to distinguish. 2. (*percevoir*) to make out, to distinguish. 3. (*rendre différent*): **~ de** to distinguish from, to set apart from. ▶ **se distinguer** *vp* 1. (*se différencier*): **se ~ (de)** to stand out (from). 2. (*s'illustrer*) to distinguish o.s.

distraction [distraksjɔ̃] *nf* 1. (*inattention*) inattention, absent-mindedness. 2. (*passe-temps*) leisure activity.

distraire [distrɛr] *vt* 1. (*déranger*) to

distract. **2.** (*divertir*) to amuse, to entertain. ► **se distraire** *vp* to amuse o.s.

distrait, -e [distrɛ, ɛt] ◆ *pp* → **distraire**. ◆ *adj* absent-minded.

distribuer [distribɥe] *vt* to distribute;
(*courrier*) to deliver; (*ordres*) to give out;
(*cartes*) to deal; (*coups, sourires*) to dispense.

distributeur, -trice [distribytœr, tris]
nm, f distributor. ► **distributeur** *nm*
1. (AUTOM & COMM) distributor. **2.**
(*machine*): ~ **(automatique) de billets**
(BANQUE) cash machine, cash dispenser; (TRANSPORT) ticket machine; ~
de boissons drinks machine.

distribution [distribysjɔ̃] *nf* **1.** (*répartition, diffusion, disposition*) distribution; ~
des prix (SCOL) prize-giving. **2.** (CIN &
THÉÂTRE) cast.

dit, dite [di, dit] ◆ *pp* → **dire**. ◆ *adj*
1. (*appelé*) known as. **2.** (JUR) said,
above. **3.** (*fixé*): **à l'heure ~e** at the
appointed time.

divagation [divagasjɔ̃] *nf* wandering.

divaguer [divage] *vi* to ramble.

divan [divɑ̃] *nm* divan (*seat*).

divergence [divɛrʒɑ̃s] *nf* divergence,
difference; (*d'opinions*) difference.

diverger [divɛrʒe] *vi* to diverge; (*opinions*) to differ.

divers, -e [divɛr, ɛrs] *adj* **1.** (*différent*)
different, various. **2.** (*disparate*) diverse.
3. (*avant n*) (*plusieurs*) various, several.

diversifier [divɛrsifje] *vt* to vary, to
diversify. ► **se diversifier** *vp* to diversify.

diversion [divɛrsjɔ̃] *nf* diversion.

diversité [divɛrsite] *nf* diversity.

divertir [divɛrtir] *vt* (*distraire*) to entertain, to amuse. ► **se divertir** *vp* to
amuse o.s., to entertain o.s.

divertissement [divɛrtismɑ̃] *nm*
(*passe-temps*) form of relaxation.

divin, -e [divɛ̃, in] *adj* divine.

divinité [divinite] *nf* divinity.

diviser [divize] *vt* **1.** (*gén*) to divide, to
split up. **2.** (MATHS) to divide; ~ **8 par 4**
to divide 8 by 4.

division [divizjɔ̃] *nf* division.

divorce [divɔrs] *nm* **1.** (JUR) divorce. **2.**
fig (*divergence*) gulf, separation.

divorcé, -e [divɔrse] ◆ *adj* divorced.
◆ *nm, f* divorcee, divorced person.

divorcer [divɔrse] *vi* to divorce.

divulguer [divylge] *vt* to divulge.

dix [dis] *adj num & nm* ten; *voir aussi* **six**.

dix-huit [dizɥit] *adj num & nm* eighteen; *voir aussi* **six**.

dix-huitième [dizɥitjɛm] *adj num, nm
& nmf* eighteenth; *voir aussi* **sixième**.

dixième [dizjɛm] *adj num, nm & nmf*
tenth; *voir aussi* **sixième**.

dix-neuf [diznœf] *adj num & nm* nineteen; *voir aussi* **six**.

dix-neuvième [diznœvjɛm] *adj num,
nm & nmf* nineteenth; *voir aussi* **sixième**.

dix-sept [disɛt] *adj num & nm* seventeen; *voir aussi* **six**.

dix-septième [disɛtjɛm] *adj num, nm
& nmf* seventeenth; *voir aussi* **sixième**.

dizaine [dizɛn] *nf* **1.** (MATHS) ten.
2. (*environ dix*): **une ~** about ten; **par
~s** (*en grand nombre*) in their dozens.

DM (*abr de deutsche Mark*) DM.

do [do] *nm inv* (MUS) C; (*chanté*) doh.

doc [dɔk] (*abr de documentation*) *nf* literature, brochures (*pl*).

doc. (*abr de document*) doc.

docile [dɔsil] *adj* (*obéissant*) docile.

dock [dɔk] *nm* **1.** (*bassin*) dock. **2.**
(*hangar*) warehouse.

docker [dɔkɛr] *nm* docker.

docteur [dɔktœr] *nm* **1.** (*médecin*) doctor. **2.** (UNIV): ~ **ès lettres/sciences** ≃
PhD.

doctorat [dɔktɔra] *nm* (*grade*) doctorate.

doctrine [dɔktrin] *nf* doctrine.

document [dɔkymɑ̃] *nm* document.

documentaire [dɔkymɑ̃tɛr] *nm & adj*
documentary.

documentaliste [dɔkymɑ̃talist] *nmf*
(*d'archives*) archivist; (PRESSE & TÉLÉ)
researcher.

documentation [dɔkymɑ̃tasjɔ̃] *nf*
1. (*travail*) research. **2.** (*documents*)
paperwork, papers (*pl*). **3.** (*brochures*)
documentation.

documenter [dɔkymɑ̃te] *vt* to document. ► **se documenter** *vp* to do
some research.

dodo [dodo] *nm fam* beddy-byes; **faire
~** to sleep.

dodu, -e [dody] *adj fam* (*enfant, joue,
bras*) chubby; (*animal*) plump.

dogme [dɔgm] *nm* dogma.

dogue [dɔg] *nm* mastiff.

doigt [dwa] *nm* finger; **un ~ de** (just) a
drop OU finger of; **montrer qqch du ~** to
point at sthg; ~ **de pied** toe.

dois → **devoir**.

doive → **devoir**.

dollar [dɔlar] *nm* dollar.

domaine [dɔmɛn] *nm* **1.** (*propriété*)
estate. **2.** (*secteur, champ d'activité*) field,
domain.

dôme [dom] *nm* **1.** (ARCHIT) dome. **2.** (GÉOGR) rounded peak.

domestique [dɔmɛstik] ◆ *nmf* (domestic) servant. ◆ *adj* family (*avant n*); (*travaux*) household (*avant n*).

domestiquer [dɔmɛstike] *vt* **1.** (*animal*) to domesticate. **2.** (*éléments naturels*) to harness.

domicile [dɔmisil] *nm* (*gén*) (place of) residence; **travailler à ~** to work from ou at home; **ils livrent à ~** they do deliveries.

domicilié, -e [dɔmisilje] *adj*: **~ à** resident in ou at.

dominant, -e [dɔminɑ̃, ɑ̃t] *adj* (*qui prévaut*) dominant.

domination [dɔminasjɔ̃] *nf* **1.** (*autorité*) domination, dominion. **2.** (*influence*) influence.

dominer [dɔmine] ◆ *vt* **1.** (*surplomber, avoir de l'autorité sur*) to dominate. **2.** (*surpasser*) to outclass. **3.** (*maîtriser*) to control, to master. **4.** *fig* (*connaître*) to master. ◆ *vi* **1.** (*régner*) to dominate, to be dominant. **2.** (*prédominer*) to predominate. **3.** (*triompher*) to be on top, to hold sway. ▶ **se dominer** *vp* to control o.s.

dominical, -e, -aux [dɔminikal, o] *adj* Sunday (*avant n*).

Dominique [dɔminik] *nf*: **la ~** Dominica.

domino [dɔmino] *nm* domino.

dommage [dɔmaʒ] *nm* **1.** (*préjudice*) harm (U); **~s et intérêts, ~s-intérêts** damages; **quel ~!** what a shame!; **c'est ~ que** (+ subjonctif) it's a pity ou shame (that). **2.** (*dégâts*) damage (U).

dompter [dɔ̃te] *vt* **1.** (*animal, fauve*) to tame. **2.** *fig* (*maîtriser*) to overcome, to control.

dompteur, -euse [dɔ̃tœr, øz] *nm, f* (*de fauves*) tamer.

DOM-TOM [dɔmtɔm] (*abr de* **départements d'outre-mer/territoires d'outre-mer**) *nmpl* French overseas départements and territories.

DOM-TOM

The 'DOM' (French overseas 'départements' with the same status as mainland 'départements') include the islands of Martinique, Guadeloupe, Réunion, and St Pierre and Miquelon. The 'TOM' (French overseas territories having more independence than the 'DOM') include the islands of New Caledonia, Wallis and Futuna, French Polynesia and Mayotte. Their inhabitants are all French citizens.

---

don [dɔ̃] *nm* **1.** (*cadeau*) gift. **2.** (*aptitude*) knack.

donateur, -trice [dɔnatœr, tris] *nm, f* donor.

donation [dɔnasjɔ̃] *nf* settlement.

donc [dɔ̃k] *conj* so; **je disais ~ ...** so as I was saying ...; **allons ~!** come on!; **tais-toi ~!** will you be quiet!; **tiens ~!** well, well, well!

donjon [dɔ̃ʒɔ̃] *nm* keep.

donné, -e [dɔne] *adj* given; **étant ~ que** given that, considering (that). ▶ **donnée** *nf* **1.** (INFORM & MATHS) datum, piece of data; **~es numériques** numerical data. **2.** (*élément*) fact, particular.

donner [dɔne] ◆ *vt* **1.** (*gén*) to give; (*se débarrasser de*) to give away; **~ qqch à qqn** to give sb sthg, to give sthg to sb; **~ qqch à faire à qqn** to give sb sthg to do, to give sthg to sb to do; **~ sa voiture à réparer** to leave one's car to be repaired; **quel âge lui donnes-tu?** how old do you think he/she is? **2.** (*occasionner*) to give, to cause. ◆ *vi* **1.** (*s'ouvrir*): **~ sur** to look out onto. **2.** (*produire*) to produce, to yield.

donneur, -euse [dɔnœr, øz] *nm, f* **1.** (MÉD) donor. **2.** (CARTES) dealer.

dont [dɔ̃] *pron rel* **1.** (*complément de verbe ou d'adjectif*): **la personne ~ tu parles** the person you're speaking about, the person about whom you are speaking; **l'accident ~ il est responsable** the accident for which he is responsible. **2.** (*complément de nom ou de pronom - relatif à l'objet*) of which, whose; (- *relatif à personne*) whose; **la boîte ~ le couvercle est jaune** the box whose lid is yellow, the box with the yellow lid; **c'est quelqu'un ~ j'apprécie l'honnêteté** he's someone whose honesty I appreciate; **celui ~ les parents sont divorcés** the one whose parents are divorced. **3.** (*indiquant la partie d'un tout*): **plusieurs personnes ont téléphoné, ~ ton frère** several people phoned, one of which was your brother ou and among them was your brother.

dopage [dɔpaʒ] *nm* doping.

doper [dɔpe] *vt* to dope. ▶ **se doper** *vp* to take stimulants.

dorade [dɔrad] = **daurade**.

doré, -e [dɔre] *adj* **1.** (*couvert de dorure*) gilded, gilt. **2.** (*couleur*) golden.

dorénavant [dɔrenavɑ̃] *adv* from now on, in future.

dorer [dɔʀe] vt 1. (couvrir d'or) to gild.
2. (peau) to tan. 3. (CULIN) to glaze.

dorloter [dɔʀlɔte] vt to pamper, to cosset.

dormir [dɔʀmiʀ] vi 1. (sommeiller) to sleep. 2. (rester inactif - personne) to slack, to stand around (doing nothing); (- capitaux) to lie idle.

dortoir [dɔʀtwaʀ] nm dormitory.

dos [do] nm back; de ~ from behind; 'voir au ~' 'see over'; ~ crawlé backstroke.

DOS, Dos [dɔs] (abr de **Disk Operating System**) nm DOS.

dosage [dozaʒ] nm (de médicament) dose; (d'ingrédient) amount.

dos-d'âne [dodan] nm bump.

dose [doz] nf 1. (quantité de médicament) dose. 2. (quantité) share; **forcer la** ~ fam fig to overdo it; **une (bonne)** ~ **de bêtise** fam fig a lot of silliness.

doser [doze] vt (médicament, ingrédient) to measure out; fig to weigh up.

dossard [dosaʀ] nm number (on competitor's back).

dossier [dosje] nm 1. (de fauteuil) back. 2. (documents) file, dossier. 3. (classeur) file, folder. 4. fig (question) question.

dot [dɔt] nf dowry.

doter [dɔte] vt (pourvoir): ~ **de** (talent) to endow with; (machine) to equip with.

douane [dwan] nf 1. (service, lieu) customs (pl); **passer la** ~ to go through customs. 2. (taxe) (import) duty.

douanier, -ère [dwanje, ɛʀ] ◆ adj customs (avant n). ◆ nm, f customs officer.

doublage [dublaʒ] nm 1. (renforcement) lining. 2. (de film) dubbing. 3. (d'acteur) understudying.

double [dublə] ◆ adj double. ◆ adv double. ◆ nm 1. (quantité): **le** ~ double. 2. (copie) copy; **en** ~ in duplicate. 3. (TENNIS) doubles (pl).

doublé [duble] nm (réussite double) double.

doublement [dubləmɑ̃] adv doubly.

doubler [duble] ◆ vt 1. (multiplier) to double. 2. (plier) to (fold) double. 3. (renforcer): ~ **(de)** to line (with). 4. (dépasser) to overtake. 5. (film, acteur) to dub. 6. (augmenter) to double. ◆ vi 1. (véhicule) to overtake. 2. (augmenter) to double.

doublure [dublyʀ] nf 1. (renforcement) lining. 2. (CIN) stand-in.

douce → **doux.**

doucement [dusmɑ̃] adv 1. (descendre) carefully; (frapper) gently. 2. (traiter) gently; (parler) softly.

douceur [dusœʀ] nf 1. (de saveur, parfum) sweetness. 2. (d'éclairage, de peau, de musique) softness. 3. (de climat) mildness. 4. (de caractère) gentleness. ▶ **douceurs** nfpl (friandises) sweets.

douche [duʃ] nf 1. (appareil, action) shower. 2. fam fig (déception) letdown.

doucher [duʃe] vt 1. (donner une douche à): ~ **qqn** to give sb a shower. 2. fam fig (décevoir) to let down. ▶ **se doucher** vp to take ou have a shower, to shower.

doué, -e [dwe] adj talented; **être** ~ **pour** to have a gift for.

douillet, -ette [dujɛ, ɛt] ◆ adj 1. (confortable) snug, cosy. 2. (sensible) soft. ◆ nm, f wimp.

douleur [dulœʀ] nf litt & fig pain.

douloureux, -euse [duluʀø, øz] adj 1. (physiquement) painful. 2. (moralement) distressing. 3. (regard, air) sorrowful.

doute [dut] nm doubt. ▶ **sans doute** loc adv no doubt; **sans aucun** ~ without (a) doubt.

douter [dute] ◆ vt (ne pas croire): ~ **que** (+ subjonctif) to doubt (that). ◆ vi (ne pas avoir confiance): ~ **de qqn/de qqch** to doubt sb/sthg, to have doubts about sb/sthg; **j'en doute** I doubt it. ▶ **se douter** vp: **se** ~ **de qqch** to suspect sthg; **je m'en doutais** I thought so.

douteux, -euse [dutø, øz] adj 1. (incertain) doubtful. 2. (contestable) questionable. 3. péj (mœurs) dubious; (vêtements, personne) dubious-looking.

Douvres [duvʀ] n Dover.

doux, douce [du, dus] adj 1. (éclairage, peau, musique) soft. 2. (saveur, parfum) sweet. 3. (climat, condiment) mild. 4. (pente, regard, caractère) gentle.

douzaine [duzɛn] nf 1. (douze) dozen. 2. (environ douze): **une** ~ **de** about twelve.

douze [duz] adj num & nm twelve; voir aussi **six.**

douzième [duzjɛm] adj num, nm & nmf twelfth; voir aussi **sixième.**

doyen, -enne [dwajɛ̃, ɛn] nm, f (le plus ancien) most senior member.

Dr (abr de **Docteur**) Dr.

draconien, -enne [dʀakɔnjɛ̃, ɛn] adj draconian.

dragée [dʀaʒe] nf 1. (confiserie) sugared almond. 2. (comprimé) pill.

dragon [dʀagɔ̃] nm 1. (monstre, personne autoritaire) dragon. 2. (soldat) dragoon.

draguer [dʀage] vt 1. (nettoyer) to dredge. 2. fam (personne) to chat up, to get off with.

dragueur, -euse [dragœr, øz] nm, f fam (homme) womanizer; **quelle dragueuse!** she's always chasing after men!

drainage [drɛnaʒ] nm draining.

drainer [drene] vt 1. (terrain, plaie) to drain. 2. fig (attirer) to drain off.

dramatique [dramatik] ◆ nf play. ◆ adj 1. (THÉÂTRE) dramatic. 2. (grave) tragic.

dramatiser [dramatize] vt (exagérer) to dramatize.

drame [dram] nm 1. (catastrophe) tragedy; **faire un ~ de qqch** fig to make a drama of sthg. 2. (LITTÉRATURE) drama.

drap [dra] nm 1. (de lit) sheet. 2. (tissu) woollen cloth.

drapeau, -x [drapo] nm flag; **être sous les ~x** fig to be doing military service.

draper [drape] vt to drape.

draperie [drapri] nf (tenture) drapery.

dresser [drese] vt 1. (lever) to raise. 2. (faire tenir) to put up. 3. sout (construire) to erect. 4. (acte, liste, carte) to draw up; (procès-verbal) to make out. 5. (dompter) to train. 6. fig (opposer): **~ qqn contre qqn** to set sb against sb. ▶ **se dresser** vp 1. (se lever) to stand up. 2. (s'élever) to rise (up); fig to stand; **se ~ contre qqch** to rise up against sthg.

dresseur, -euse [dresœr, øz] nm, f trainer.

dribbler [drible] (SPORT) ◆ vi to dribble. ◆ vt: **~ qqn** to dribble past sb.

drogue [drɔg] nf (stupéfiant & fig) drug; **la ~** drugs (pl).

drogué, -e [drɔge] ◆ adj drugged. ◆ nm, f drug addict.

droguer [drɔge] vt (victime) to drug. ▶ **se droguer** vp (de stupéfiants) to take drugs.

droguerie [drɔgri] nf hardware shop.

droguiste [drɔgist] nmf: **chez le ~** at the hardware shop.

droit, -e [drwa, drwat] adj 1. (du côté droit) right. 2. (rectiligne, vertical, honnête) straight. ▶ **droit** ◆ adv straight; **tout ~** straight ahead. ◆ nm 1. (JUR) law. 2. (prérogative) right; **avoir ~ à** to be entitled to; **avoir le ~ de faire qqch** to be allowed to do sthg; **être en ~ de faire qqch** to have a right to do sthg; **~ d'aînesse** birthright; **~ de vote** right to vote; **~s de l'homme** human rights. ▶ **droite** nf 1. (gén) right, right-hand side; **à ~e** on the right; **à ~e de** to the right of. 2. (POLIT): **la ~e** the right (wing); **de ~e** right-wing.

droitier, -ère [drwatje, ɛr] ◆ adj right-handed. ◆ nm, f right-handed person, right-hander.

drôle [drol] adj 1. (amusant) funny. 2. **~ de** (bizarre) funny; fam (remarquable) amazing.

dromadaire [drɔmadɛr] nm dromedary.

dru, -e [dry] adj thick.

ds abr de **dans**.

du → **de**.

dû, due [dy] ◆ pp → **devoir**. ◆ adj due, owing. ▶ **dû** nm due.

Dublin [dyblɛ̃] n Dublin.

duc [dyk] nm duke.

duchesse [dyʃɛs] nf duchess.

duel [dɥɛl] nm duel.

dûment [dymã] adv duly.

dune [dyn] nf dune.

duo [dɥo] nm 1. (MUS) duet. 2. (couple) duo.

dupe [dyp] ◆ nf dupe. ◆ adj gullible.

duper [dype] vt sout to dupe, to take sb in.

duplex [dypleks] nm 1. (appartement) split-level flat, maisonette Br, duplex Am. 2. (RADIO & TÉLÉ) link-up.

duplicata [dyplikata] nm inv duplicate.

dupliquer [dyplike] vt (document) to duplicate.

duquel [dykel] → **lequel**.

dur, -e [dyr] ◆ adj 1. (matière, personne, travail) hard. 2. (carton) stiff. 3. (viande) tough. 3. (climat, punition, loi) harsh. ◆ nm, f fam: **~ (à cuire)** tough nut. ▶ **dur** adv hard.

durable [dyrabl] adj lasting.

durant [dyrã] prép 1. (pendant) for. 2. (au cours de) during.

durcir [dyrsir] ◆ vt litt & fig to harden. ◆ vi to harden, to become hard.

durée [dyre] nf (longueur) length; (période) period.

durement [dyrmã] adv 1. (violemment) hard, vigorously. 2. (péniblement) severely. 3. (méchamment) harshly.

durer [dyre] vi to last.

dureté [dyrte] nf 1. (de matériau, de l'eau) hardness. 2. (d'époque, de climat, de personne) harshness. 3. (de punition) severity.

dus, dut etc → **devoir**.

DUT (abr de **diplôme universitaire de technologie**) nm university diploma in technology.

duvet [dyvɛ] nm 1. (plumes, poils fins) down. 2. (sac de couchage) sleeping bag.

dynamique [dinamik] adj dynamic.

dynamisme [dinamism] *nm* dynamism.

dynamite [dinamit] *nf* dynamite.

dynastie [dinasti] *nf* dynasty.

dyslexique [dislɛksik] *adj* dyslexic.

e, E [ə] *nm inv* e, E. ▶ **E** (*abr de* **est**) E.

eau, -x [o] *nf* water; **~ douce/salée/de mer** fresh/salt/sea water; **~ gazeuse/ plate** fizzy/still water; **~ courante** running water; **~ minérale** mineral water; **~ oxygénée** hydrogen peroxide; **~ de toilette** toilet water; **tomber à l'~** *fig* to fall through.

eau-de-vie [odvi] (*pl* **eaux-de-vie**) *nf* brandy.

ébahi, -e [ebai] *adj* staggered, astounded.

ébattre [ebatr] ▶ **s'ébattre** *vp littéraire* to frolic.

ébauche [eboʃ] *nf* (*esquisse*) sketch; *fig* outline; **l'~ d'un sourire** the ghost of a smile.

ébaucher [eboʃe] *vt* 1. (*esquisser*) to rough out. 2. *fig* (*commencer*): **~ un geste** to start to make a gesture.

ébène [ebɛn] *nf* ebony.

ébéniste [ebenist] *nm* cabinet-maker.

éberlué, -e [ebɛrlɥe] *adj* flabbergasted.

éblouir [ebluir] *vt* to dazzle.

éblouissement [ebluismɑ̃] *nm* 1. (*aveuglement*) glare, dazzle. 2. (*vertige*) dizziness. 3. (*émerveillement*) amazement.

éborgner [ebɔrɲe] *vt*: **~ qqn** to put sb's eye out.

éboueur [ebwœr] *nm* dustman Br, garbage collector Am.

ébouillanter [ebujɑ̃te] *vt* to scald.

éboulement [ebulmɑ̃] *nm* caving in, fall.

éboulis [ebuli] *nm* mass of fallen rocks.

ébouriffer [eburife] *vt* (*cheveux*) to ruffle.

ébranler [ebrɑ̃le] *vt* 1. (*bâtiment, opinion*) to shake. 2. (*gouvernement, nerfs*) to weaken. ▶ **s'ébranler** *vp* (*train*) to move off.

ébrécher [ebreʃe] *vt* (*assiette, verre*) to chip; *fam fig* to break into.

ébriété [ebrijete] *nf* drunkenness.

ébrouer [ebrue] ▶ **s'ébrouer** *vp* (*animal*) to shake o.s.

ébruiter [ebrɥite] *vt* to spread.

ébullition [ebylisjɔ̃] *nf* 1. (*de liquide*) boiling point. 2. (*effervescence*): **en ~** *fig* in a state of agitation.

écaille [ekaj] *nf* 1. (*de poisson, reptile*) scale; (*de tortue*) shell. 2. (*de plâtre, peinture, vernis*) flake. 3. (*matière*) tortoise-shell; **en ~** (*lunettes*) horn-rimmed.

écailler [ekaje] *vt* 1. (*poisson*) to scale. 2. (*huîtres*) to open. ▶ **s'écailler** *vp* to flake ou peel off.

écarlate [ekarlat] *adj & nf* scarlet.

écarquiller [ekarkije] *vt*: **~ les yeux** to stare wide-eyed.

écart [ekar] *nm* 1. (*espace*) space. 2. (*temps*) gap. 3. (*différence*) difference. 4. (*déviation*): **faire un ~** (*personne*) to step aside; (*cheval*) to shy; **être à l'~** to be in the background.

écarteler [ekartəle] *vt fig* to tear apart.

écartement [ekartəmɑ̃] *nm*: **~ entre** space between.

écarter [ekarte] *vt* 1. (*bras, jambes*) to open, to spread; **~ qqch de** to move sthg away from. 2. (*obstacle, danger*) to brush aside. 3. (*foule, rideaux*) to push aside; (*solution*) to dismiss; **~ qqn de** to exclude sb from. ▶ **s'écarter** *vp* 1. (*se séparer*) to part. 2. (*se détourner*): **s'~ de** to deviate from.

ecchymose [ekimoz] *nf* bruise.

ecclésiastique [eklezjastik] ♦ *nm* clergyman. ♦ *adj* ecclesiastical.

écervelé, -e [esɛrvəle] ♦ *adj* scatty, scatterbrained. ♦ *nm, f* scatterbrain.

échafaud [eʃafo] *nm* scaffold.

échafaudage [eʃafodaʒ] *nm* 1. (CONSTR) scaffolding. 2. (*amas*) pile.

échalote [eʃalɔt] *nf* shallot.

échancrure [eʃɑ̃kryr] *nf* 1. (*de robe*) low neckline. 2. (*de côte*) indentation.

échange [eʃɑ̃ʒ] *nm* (*de choses*) exchange; **en ~ (de)** in exchange (for).

échangeable [eʃɑ̃ʒabl] *adj* exchangeable.

échanger [eʃɑ̃ʒe] *vt* 1. (*troquer*) to swap, to exchange. 2. (*marchandise*): **~ qqch (contre)** to change sthg (for). 3. (*communiquer*) to exchange.

échantillon [eʃɑ̃tijɔ̃] *nm* (*de produit, de population*) sample; *fig* example.

échappatoire [eʃapatwar] *nf* way out.

échappement [eʃapmã] *nm* (AUTOM) exhaust; → **pot**.

échapper [eʃape] *vi* **1.** **~ à** (*personne, situation*) to escape from; (*danger, mort*) to escape; (*suj: détail, parole, sens*) to escape. **2.** (*glisser*): **laisser ~** to let slip. ▶ **s'échapper** *vp*: **s'~ (de)** to escape (from).

écharde [eʃard] *nf* splinter.

écharpe [eʃarp] *nf* scarf; **en ~** in a sling.

écharper [eʃarpe] *vt* to rip to pieces ou shreds.

échasse [eʃas] *nf* (*de berger, oiseau*) stilt.

échassier [eʃasje] *nm* wader.

échauffement [eʃofmã] *nm* (SPORT) warm-up.

échauffer [eʃofe] *vt* **1.** (*chauffer*) to overheat. **2.** (*exciter*) to excite. **3.** (*énerver*) to irritate. ▶ **s'échauffer** *vp* **1.** (SPORT) to warm up. **2.** *fig* (*s'animer*) to become heated.

échéance [eʃeãs] *nf* **1.** (*délai*) expiry; **à longue ~** in the long term. **2.** (*date*) payment date; **arriver à ~** to fall due.

échéant [eʃeã] *adj*: **le cas ~** if necessary, if need be.

échec [eʃɛk] *nm* **1.** (*insuccès*) failure. **2.** (JEU): **~ et mat** checkmate. ▶ **échecs** *nmpl* chess (U).

échelle [eʃɛl] *nf* **1.** (*objet*) ladder. **2.** (*ordre de grandeur*) scale.

échelon [eʃlɔ̃] *nm* **1.** (*barreau*) rung. **2.** *fig* (*niveau*) level.

échelonner [eʃlɔne] *vt* (*espacer*) to spread out.

échevelé, -e [eʃəvle] *adj* **1.** (*ébouriffé*) dishevelled. **2.** (*frénétique*) wild.

échine [eʃin] *nf* (ANAT) spine.

échiquier [eʃikje] *nm* (JEU) chessboard.

écho [eko] *nm* echo.

échographie [ekɔgrafi] *nf* (*examen*) ultrasound (scan).

échoir [eʃwar] *vi* **1.** (*être dévolu*): **~ à** to fall to. **2.** (*expirer*) to fall due.

échoppe [eʃɔp] *nf* stall.

échouer [eʃwe] *vi* (*ne pas réussir*) to fail; **~ à un examen** to fail an exam. ▶ **s'échouer** *vp* (*navire*) to run aground.

échu, -e [eʃy] *pp* → **échoir**.

éclabousser [eklabuse] *vt* **1.** (*suj: liquide*) to spatter. **2.** *fig* (*compromettre*) to compromise.

éclair [eklɛr] ◆ *nm* **1.** (*de lumière*) flash of lightning. **2.** *fig* (*instant*): **~ de** flash of. **3.** (*gâteau*): **~ au chocolat/café** chocolate/coffee éclair. ◆ *adj inv*: **visite ~** flying visit; **guerre ~** blitzkrieg.

éclairage [eklɛraʒ] *nm* **1.** (*lumière*) lighting. **2.** *fig* (*point de vue*) light.

éclaircie [eklɛrsi] *nf* bright interval, sunny spell.

éclaircir [eklɛrsir] *vt* **1.** (*rendre plus clair*) to lighten. **2.** (*rendre moins épais*) to thin. **3.** *fig* (*clarifier*) to clarify. ▶ **s'éclaircir** *vp* **1.** (*devenir plus clair*) to clear. **2.** (*devenir moins épais*) to thin. **3.** (*se clarifier*) to become clearer.

éclaircissement [eklɛrsismã] *nm* (*explication*) explanation.

éclairer [eklere] *vt* **1.** (*de lumière*) to light up. **2.** (*expliquer*) to clarify. ▶ **s'éclairer** *vp* **1.** (*personne*) to light one's way. **2.** (*regard, visage*) to light up. **3.** (*rue, ville*) to light up.

éclaireur [eklɛrœr] *nm* scout.

éclat [ekla] *nm* **1.** (*de verre, d'os*) splinter; (*de pierre*) chip. **2.** (*de lumière*) brilliance. **3.** (*de couleur*) vividness. **4.** (*beauté*) radiance. **5.** (*faste*) splendour. **6.** (*bruit*) burst; **~ de rire** burst of laughter; **~s de voix** shouts; **faire un ~** to cause a scandal. **7.** *loc*: **rire aux ~s** to roar ou shriek with laughter.

éclater [eklate] *vi* **1.** (*exploser - pneu*) to burst; (*- verre*) to shatter; (*- obus*) to explode; **faire ~** (*ballon*) to burst; (*bombe*) to explode; (*pétard*) to let off. **2.** (*incendie, rires*) to break out. **3.** (*joie*) to shine; **laisser ~** to give vent to. **4.** *fig* (*nouvelles, scandale*) to break. ▶ **s'éclater** *vp fam* to have a great time.

éclectique [eklɛktik] *adj* eclectic.

éclipse [eklips] *nf* (ASTRON) eclipse; **~ de lune/soleil** eclipse of the moon/sun.

éclipser [eklipse] *vt* to eclipse. ▶ **s'éclipser** *vp* **1.** (ASTRON) to go into eclipse. **2.** *fam* (*s'esquiver*) to slip away.

éclopé, -e [eklɔpe] ◆ *adj* lame. ◆ *nm, f* lame person.

éclore [eklɔr] *vi* (*s'ouvrir - fleur*) to open out, to blossom; (*- œuf*) to hatch.

éclos, -e [eklo, oz] *pp* → **éclore**.

écluse [eklyz] *nf* lock.

écœurant, -e [ekœrã, ãt] *adj* **1.** (*gén*) disgusting. **2.** (*démoralisant*) sickening.

écœurer [ekœre] *vt* **1.** (*dégoûter*) to sicken, to disgust. **2.** *fig* (*indigner*) to sicken. **3.** (*décourager*) to discourage.

école [ekɔl] *nf* **1.** (*gén*) school; **~ maternelle** nursery school; **~ normale** = teacher training college Br, = teachers college Am; **École normale supérieure** *grande école for secondary and university teachers*; **~ primaire/secondaire** primary/

secondary school *Br*, grade/high school *Am*; **grande ~** *specialist training establishment, entered by competitive exam and highly prestigious*; **faire l'~ buissonnière** to play truant *Br ou* hooky *Am*; **faire ~** to be accepted. **2.** (*éducation*) schooling; **l'~ privée** private education.

écolier, -ère [ekɔlje, ɛr] *nm, f* (*élève*) pupil.

écolo [ekɔlo] *nmf fam* ecologist; **les ~s** the Greens.

écologie [ekɔlɔʒi] *nf* ecology.

écologiste [ekɔlɔʒist] *nmf* ecologist.

écomusée [ekɔmyze] *nm* museum of the environment.

éconduire [ekɔ̃dɥir] *vt* (*repousser - demande*) to dismiss; (*- visiteur, soupirant*) to show to the door.

économe [ekɔnɔm] ◆ *nmf* bursar. ◆ *adj* careful, thrifty.

économie [ekɔnɔmi] *nf* **1.** (*science*) economics (*U*). **2.** (POLIT) economy; **~ de marché** market economy. **3.** (*parcimonie*) economy, thrift. **4.** (*gén pl*) (*pécule*) savings (*pl*); **faire des ~s** to save up.

économique [ekɔnɔmik] *adj* **1.** (ÉCON) economic. **2.** (*avantageux*) economical.

économiser [ekɔnɔmize] *vt* to save.

économiste [ekɔnɔmist] *nmf* economist.

écoper [ekɔpe] *vt* **1.** (NAVIG) to bale out. **2.** *fam* (*sanction*): **~ (de) qqch** to get sthg.

écoproduit [ekɔprɔdɥi] *nm* green product.

écorce [ekɔrs] *nf* **1.** (*d'arbre*) bark. **2.** (*d'agrume*) peel. **3.** (GÉOL) crust.

écorcher [ekɔrʃe] *vt* **1.** (*lapin*) to skin. **2.** (*bras, jambe*) to scratch. **3.** *fig* (*langue, nom*) to mispronounce.

écorchure [ekɔrʃyr] *nf* graze, scratch.

écossais, -e [ekɔsɛ, ɛz] *adj* **1.** (*de l'É-cosse*) Scottish; (*whisky*) Scotch. **2.** (*tissu*) tartan. ▶ **écossais** *nm* (*langue*) Scots. ▶ **Écossais, -e** *nm, f* Scot, Scotsman (*f* Scotswoman).

Écosse [ekɔs] *nf*: **l'~** Scotland.

écosser [ekɔse] *vt* to shell.

écosystème [ekɔsistɛm] *nm* ecosystem.

écouler [ekule] *vt* to sell. ▶ **s'écouler** *vp* **1.** (*eau*) to flow. **2.** (*personnes*) to flow out. **3.** (*temps*) to pass.

écourter [ekurte] *vt* to shorten.

écoute [ekut] *nf* **1.** (*action d'écouter*): **être à l'~ de** to be listening to. **2.** (RADIO) listening; **heures de grande ~** (RADIO) peak listening time; (TÉLÉ) peak viewing

time, prime time.

écouter [ekute] *vt* to listen to.

écouteur [ekutœr] *nm* (*de téléphone*) earpiece. ▶ **écouteurs** *nmpl* (*de radio*) headphones.

écoutille [ekutij] *nf* hatchway.

écran [ekrã] *nm* **1.** (*de protection*) shield. **2.** (CIN & INFORM) screen; **le petit ~** television.

écrasant, -e [ekrazã, ãt] *adj fig* (*accablant*) overwhelming.

écraser [ekraze] *vt* **1.** (*comprimer - cigarette*) to stub out; (*- pied*) to tread on; (*- insecte, raisin*) to crush. **2.** (*accabler*): **~ qqn (de)** to burden sb (with). **3.** (*vaincre*) to crush. **4.** (*renverser*) to run over. ▶ **s'écraser** *vp* (*avion, automobile*): **s'~ (contre)** to crash (into).

écrémer [ekreme] *vt* (*lait*) to skim.

écrevisse [ekrəvis] *nf* crayfish.

écrier [ekrije] ▶ **s'écrier** *vp* to cry out.

écrin [ekrɛ̃] *nm* case.

écrire [ekrir] *vt* **1.** (*phrase, livre*) to write. **2.** (*orthographier*) to spell. ▶ **s'écrire** *vp* (*s'épeler*) to be spelled.

écrit, -e [ekri, it] ◆ *pp* → **écrire**. ◆ *adj* written. ▶ **écrit** *nm* **1.** (*ouvrage*) writing. **2.** (*examen*) written exam. **3.** (*document*) piece of writing. ▶ **par écrit** *loc adv* in writing.

écriteau, -x [ekrito] *nm* notice.

écriture [ekrityr] *nf* **1.** (*gén*) writing. **2.** (*gén pl*) (COMM) (*comptes*) books (*pl*).

écrivain [ekrivɛ̃] *nm* writer, author.

écrou [ekru] *nm* (TECHNOL) nut.

écrouer [ekrue] *vt* to imprison.

écrouler [ekrule] ▶ **s'écrouler** *vp litt & fig* to collapse.

écru, -e [ekry] *adj* (*naturel*) unbleached.

ECU [eky] (*abr de* **European Currency Unit**) *nm* ECU.

écu [eky] *nm* **1.** (*bouclier, armoiries*) shield. **2.** (*monnaie ancienne*) crown. **3.** = **ECU**.

écueil [ekœj] *nm* **1.** (*rocher*) reef. **2.** *fig* (*obstacle*) stumbling block.

écuelle [ekɥɛl] *nf* (*objet*) bowl.

éculé, -e [ekyle] *adj* **1.** (*chaussure*) down-at-heel. **2.** *fig* (*plaisanterie*) hackneyed.

écume [ekym] *nf* (*mousse, bave*) foam.

écumoire [ekymwar] *nf* skimmer.

écureuil [ekyrœj] *nm* squirrel.

écurie [ekyri] *nf* **1.** (*pour chevaux & SPORT*) stable. **2.** *fig* (*local sale*) pigsty.

écusson [ekysɔ̃] *nm* **1.** (*d'armoiries*) coat-of-arms. **2.** (MIL) badge.

écuyer, -ère [ekɥije, ɛr] *nm, f* (*de*

cirque) rider. ▶ **écuyer** *nm* (*de chevalier*) squire.

eczéma [ɛgzema] *nm* eczema.

édenté, -e [edɑ̃te] *adj* toothless.

EDF, Edf (*abr de* Électricité de France) *nf* French national electricity company.

édifice [edifis] *nm* 1. (*construction*) building. 2. *fig* (*institution*): **l'~ social** the fabric of society.

édifier [edifje] *vt* 1. (*ville, église*) to build. 2. *fig* (*théorie*) to construct. 3. (*personne*) to edify; *iron* to enlighten.

Édimbourg [edɛ̃bur] *n* Edinburgh.

éditer [edite] *vt* to publish.

éditeur, -trice [editœr, tris] *nm, f* publisher.

édition [edisjɔ̃] *nf* 1. (*profession*) publishing. 2. (*de journal, livre*) edition.

éditorial, -aux [editɔrjal, o] *nm* leader, editorial.

édredon [edrədɔ̃] *nm* eiderdown.

éducateur, -trice [edykatœr, tris] *nm, f* teacher; **~ spécialisé** *teacher of children with special educational needs.*

éducatif, -ive [edykatif, iv] *adj* educational.

éducation [edykasjɔ̃] *nf* 1. (*apprentissage*) education; **l'Éducation nationale** ≈ the Department for Education Br, ≈ the Department of Education Am. 2. (*parentale*) upbringing. 3. (*savoir-vivre*) breeding.

édulcorant [edylkɔrɑ̃] *nm*: **~ (de synthèse)** (*artificiel*) sweetener.

édulcorer [edylkɔre] *vt* 1. *sout* (*tisane*) to sweeten. 2. *fig* (*propos*) to tone down.

éduquer [edyke] *vt* (*enfant*) to bring up; (*élève*) to educate.

effacé, -e [efase] *adj* 1. (*teinte*) faded. 2. (*modeste - rôle*) unobtrusive; (- *personne*) self-effacing.

effacer [efase] *vt* 1. (*mot*) to erase, to rub out; (INFORM) to delete. 2. (*souvenir*) to erase. 3. (*réussite*) to eclipse. ▶ **s'effacer** *vp* 1. (*s'estomper*) to fade (away). 2. *sout* (*s'écarter*) to move aside. 3. *fig* (*s'incliner*) to give way.

effarant, -e [efarɑ̃, ɑ̃t] *adj* frightening.

effarement [efarmɑ̃] *nm* alarm.

effarer [efare] *vt* to frighten, to scare.

effaroucher [efaruʃe] *vt* 1. (*effrayer*) to scare off. 2. (*intimider*) to overawe.

effectif, -ive [efɛktif, iv] *adj* 1. (*remède*) effective. 2. (*aide*) positive. ▶ **effectif** *nm* 1. (MIL) strength. 2. (*de groupe*) total number.

effectivement [efɛktivmɑ̃] *adv* 1. (*réellement*) effectively. 2. (*confirmation*) in fact.

effectuer [efɛktɥe] *vt* (*réaliser - manœuvre*) to carry out; (- *trajet, paiement*) to make. ▶ **s'effectuer** *vp* to be carried out; **le trajet s'effectue en deux heures** the journey takes two hours.

efféminé, -e [efemine] *adj* effeminate.

effervescent, -e [efɛrvesɑ̃, ɑ̃t] *adj* (*boisson*) effervescent; *fig* (*pays*) in turmoil.

effet [efɛ] *nm* 1. (*gén*) effect; **sous l'~ de** under the effects of; **~ de serre** greenhouse effect. 2. (*impression recherchée*) impression. 3. (COMM) (*titre*) bill. ▶ **en effet** *loc adv* in fact, indeed.

effeuiller [efœje] *vt* (*arbre*) to remove the leaves from; (*fleur*) to remove the petals from.

efficace [efikas] *adj* 1. (*remède, mesure*) effective. 2. (*personne, machine*) efficient.

effigie [efiʒi] *nf* effigy.

effilé, -e [efile] *adj* (*doigt*) slender; (*lame*) sharp; (*voiture*) streamlined; **amandes ~es** flaked almonds.

effiler [efile] *vt* 1. (*tissu*) to fray. 2. (*lame*) to sharpen. 3. (*cheveux*) to thin.

effilocher [efilɔʃe] *vt* to fray. ▶ **s'effilocher** *vp* to fray.

efflanqué, -e [eflɑ̃ke] *adj* emaciated.

effleurer [eflœre] *vt* 1. (*visage, bras*) to brush (against). 2. *fig* (*problème, thème*) to touch on. 3. *fig* (*suj: pensée, idée*): **~ qqn** to cross sb's mind.

effluve [eflyv] *nm* exhalation.

effondrement [efɔ̃drəmɑ̃] *nm* collapse.

effondrer [efɔ̃dre] ▶ **s'effondrer** *vp litt & fig* to collapse.

efforcer [efɔrse] ▶ **s'efforcer** *vp*: **s'~ de faire qqch** to make an effort to do sthg.

effort [efɔr] *nm* (*de personne*) effort.

effraction [efraksjɔ̃] *nf* breaking in; **entrer par ~ dans** to break into.

effrayer [efreje] *vt* to frighten, to scare.

effréné, -e [efrene] *adj* (*course*) frantic.

effriter [efrite] *vt* to cause to crumble. ▶ **s'effriter** *vp* (*mur*) to crumble.

effroi [efrwa] *nm* fear, dread.

effronté, -e [efrɔ̃te] ◆ *adj* insolent. ◆ *nm, f* insolent person.

effronterie [efrɔ̃tri] *nf* insolence.

effroyable [efrwajabl] *adj* 1. (*catastrophe, misère*) appalling. 2. (*laideur*) hideous.

effusion [efyzjɔ̃] *nf* 1. (*de liquide*) effusion. 2. (*de sentiments*) effusiveness.

égal, -e, -aux [egal, o] ◆ *adj* 1. (*équivalent*) equal. 2. (*régulier*) even. ◆ *nm, f* equal.

également [egalmã] *adv* 1. (*avec égalité*) equally. 2. (*aussi*) as well, too.

égaler [egale] *vt* 1. (MATHS) to equal. 2. (*beauté*) to match, to compare with.

égaliser [egalize] ◆ *vt* (*haie, cheveux*) to trim. ◆ *vi* (SPORT) to equalize Br, to tie Am.

égalitaire [egalitɛr] *adj* egalitarian.

égalité [egalite] *nf* 1. (*gén*) equality. 2. (*d'humeur*) evenness. 3. (SPORT): **être à ~** to be level.

égard [egar] *nm* consideration; **à cet ~** in this respect. ▶ **à l'égard de** *loc prép* with regard to, towards.

égarement [egarmã] *nm* 1. (*de jeunesse*) wildness. 2. (*de raisonnement*) aberration.

égarer [egare] *vt* 1. (*objet*) to mislay, to lose. 2. (*personne*) to mislead. 3. *fig & sout* (*suj: passion*) to lead astray. ▶ **s'égarer** *vp* 1. (*lettre*) to get lost, to go astray; (*personne*) to get lost, to lose one's way. 2. *fig & sout* (*personne*) to stray from the point.

égayer [egeje] *vt* 1. (*personne*) to cheer up. 2. (*pièce*) to brighten up.

égide [eʒid] *nf* protection; **sous l'~ de** *littéraire* under the aegis of.

église [egliz] *nf* church. ▶ **Église** *nf*: **l'Église** the Church.

égocentrique [egosãtrik] *adj* self-centred, egocentric.

égoïsme [egoism] *nm* selfishness, egoism.

égoïste [egoist] ◆ *nmf* selfish person. ◆ *adj* selfish, egoistic.

égorger [egorʒe] *vt* (*animal, personne*) to cut the throat of.

égosiller [egozije] ▶ **s'égosiller** *vp fam* 1. (*crier*) to bawl, to shout. 2. (*chanter*) to sing one's head off.

égout [egu] *nm* sewer.

égoutter [egute] *vt* 1. (*vaisselle*) to leave to drain. 2. (*légumes, fromage*) to drain. ▶ **s'égoutter** *vp* to drip, to drain.

égouttoir [egutwar] *nm* 1. (*à légumes*) colander, strainer. 2. (*à vaisselle*) rack (*for washing-up*).

égratigner [egratiɲe] *vt* to scratch; *fig* to have a go ou dig at. ▶ **s'égratigner** *vp*: **s'~ la main** to scratch one's hand.

égratignure [egratiɲyr] *nf* scratch, graze; *fig* dig.

égrener [egrəne] *vt* 1. (*détacher les grains de - épi, cosse*) to shell; (- *grappe*) to pick grapes from. 2. (*chapelet*) to tell. 3. *fig* (*marquer*) to mark.

égrillard, -e [egrijar, ard] *adj* ribald, bawdy.

Égypte [eʒipt] *nf*: **l'~** Egypt.

égyptien, -enne [eʒipsjɛ̃, ɛn] *adj* Egyptian. ▶ **égyptien** *nm* (*langue*) Egyptian. ▶ **Égyptien, -enne** *nm, f* Egyptian.

égyptologie [eʒiptɔlɔʒi] *nf* Egyptology.

eh [e] *interj* hey!; **~ bien** well.

éhonté, -e [eɔ̃te] *adj* shameless.

Eiffel [efɛl] *n*: **la tour ~** the Eiffel Tower.

éjaculation [eʒakylasjɔ̃] *nf* ejaculation.

éjectable [eʒɛktabl] *adj*: **siège ~** ejector seat.

éjecter [eʒɛkte] *vt* 1. (*douille*) to eject. 2. *fam* (*personne*) to kick out.

élaboration [elabɔrasjɔ̃] *nf* (*de plan, système*) working out, development.

élaboré, -e [elabɔre] *adj* elaborate.

élaborer [elabɔre] *vt* (*plan, système*) to work out, to develop.

élaguer [elage] *vt litt & fig* to prune.

élan [elã] *nm* 1. (ZOOL) elk. 2. (SPORT) run-up; *Can* (GOLF) swing; **prendre son ~** to take a run-up, to gather speed. 3. *fig* (*de joie*) outburst.

élancé, -e [elãse] *adj* slender.

élancer [elãse] *vi* (MÉD) to give shooting pains. ▶ **s'élancer** *vp* 1. (*se précipiter*) to rush, to dash. 2. (SPORT) to take a run-up. 3. *fig* (*s'envoler*) to soar.

élargir [elarʒir] *vt* to widen; (*vêtement*) to let out; *fig* to expand. ▶ **s'élargir** *vp* (*s'agrandir*) to widen; (*vêtement*) to stretch; *fig* to expand.

élasticité [elastisite] *nf* (PHYS) elasticity.

élastique [elastik] ◆ *nm* 1. (*pour attacher*) elastic band. 2. (*matière*) elastic. ◆ *adj* 1. (PHYS) elastic. 2. (*corps*) flexible. 3. *fig* (*conscience*) accommodating.

électeur, -trice [elɛktœr, tris] *nm, f* voter, elector.

élection [elɛksjɔ̃] *nf* (*vote*) election; **~ présidentielle** presidential election; **~s municipales** local elections.

électoral, -e, -aux [elɛktɔral, o] *adj* electoral; (*campagne, réunion*) election (*avant n*).

électricien, -enne [elɛktrisjɛ̃, ɛn] *nm, f* electrician.

électricité [elɛktrisite] *nf* electricity.

électrifier [elɛktrifje] *vt* to electrify.

électrique [elɛktrik] *adj litt & fig* electric.

électrocardiogramme [elɛktrɔkardjɔgram] *nm* electrocardiogram.

électrochoc [elɛktrɔʃɔk] *nm* electroshock therapy.

électrocuter [elɛktrɔkyte] *vt* to electrocute.

électrode [elɛktrɔd] *nf* electrode.

électroencéphalogramme [elɛktrɔɑ̃sefalɔgram] *nm* electroencephalogram.

électrogène [elɛktrɔʒɛn] *adj* : **groupe ~** generating unit.

électrolyse [elɛktrɔliz] *nf* electrolysis.

électromagnétique [elɛktrɔmaɲetik] *adj* electromagnetic.

électroménager [elɛktrɔmenaʒe] *nm* household electrical appliances (*pl*).

électron [elɛktrɔ̃] *nm* electron.

électronicien, -enne [elɛktrɔnisjɛ̃, ɛn] *nm, f* electronics specialist.

électronique [elɛktrɔnik] ◆ *nf* (SCIENCE) electronics (U). ◆ *adj* electronic; (*microscope*) electron (*avant n*).

électrophone [elɛktrɔfɔn] *nm* record player.

élégance [elegɑ̃s] *nf* (*de personne, style*) elegance.

élégant, -e [elegɑ̃, ɑ̃t] *adj* **1.** (*personne, style*) elegant. **2.** (*délicat - solution, procédé*) elegant; (*- conduite*) generous.

élément [elemɑ̃] *nm* **1.** (*gén*) element; **être dans son ~** to be in one's element. **2.** (*de machine*) component.

élémentaire [elemɑ̃tɛr] *adj* **1.** (*gén*) elementary. **2.** (*installation, besoin*) basic.

éléphant [elefɑ̃] *nm* elephant.

élevage [ɛlvaʒ] *nm* breeding, rearing; (*installation*) farm.

élévateur, -trice [elevatœr, tris] *adj* elevator (*avant n*).

élevé, -e [ɛlve] *adj* **1.** (*haut*) high. **2.** *fig* (*sentiment, âme*) noble. **3.** (*enfant*): **bien/mal ~** well/badly brought up.

élève [elɛv] *nmf* (*écolier, disciple*) pupil.

élever [ɛlve] *vt* **1.** (*gén*) to raise. **2.** (*statue*) to put up, to erect. **3.** (*à un rang supérieur*) to elevate. **4.** (*esprit*) to improve. **5.** (*enfant*) to bring up. **6.** (*poulets*) to rear, to breed. ▶ **s'élever** *vp* **1.** (*gén*) to rise. **2.** (*montant*): **s'~ à** to add up to. **3.** (*protester*): **s'~ contre qqn/qqch** to protest against sb/sthg.

éleveur, -euse [ɛlvœr, øz] *nm, f* breeder.

elfe [ɛlf] *nm* elf.

éligible [eliʒibl] *adj* eligible.

élimé, -e [elime] *adj* threadbare.

élimination [eliminasjɔ̃] *nf* elimination.

éliminatoire [eliminatwar] ◆ *nf* (*gén pl*) (SPORT) qualifying heat *ou* round. ◆ *adj* qualifying (*avant n*).

éliminer [elimine] *vt* to eliminate.

élire [elir] *vt* to elect.

élite [elit] *nf* elite; **d'~** choice, select.

élitiste [elitist] *nmf & adj* elitist.

elle [ɛl] *pron pers* **1.** (*sujet - personne*) she; (*- animal*) it, she; (*- chose*) it. **2.** (*complément - personne*) her; (*- animal*) it, her; (*- chose*) it. ▶ **elles** *pron pers pl* **1.** (*sujet*) they. **2.** (*complément*) them. ▶ **elle-même** *pron pers* (*personne*) herself; (*animal*) itself, herself; (*chose*) itself. ▶ **elles-mêmes** *pron pers pl* themselves.

ellipse [elips] *nf* **1.** (GÉOM) ellipse. **2.** (LING) ellipsis.

élocution [elɔkysjɔ̃] *nf* delivery; **défaut d'~** speech defect.

éloge [elɔʒ] *nm* (*louange*) praise; **faire l'~ de qqn/qqch** (*louer*) to speak highly of sb/sthg; **couvrir qqn d'~s** to shower sb with praise.

élogieux, -euse [elɔʒjø, øz] *adj* laudatory.

éloignement [elwaɲmɑ̃] *nm* **1.** (*mise à l'écart*) removal. **2.** (*séparation*) absence. **3.** (*dans l'espace, le temps*) distance.

éloigner [elwaɲe] *vt* **1.** (*écarter*) to move away; **~ qqch de** to move sthg away from. **2.** (*détourner*) to turn away. **3.** (*chasser*) to dismiss. ▶ **s'éloigner** *vp* **1.** (*partir*) to move *ou* go away. **2.** *fig* (*du sujet*) to stray from the point. **3.** (*se détacher*) to distance o.s.

éloquence [elɔkɑ̃s] *nf* (*d'orateur, d'expression*) eloquence.

éloquent, -e [elɔkɑ̃, ɑ̃t] *adj* **1.** (*avocat, silence*) eloquent. **2.** (*données*) significant.

élu, -e [ely] ◆ *pp* → **élire**. ◆ *adj* (POLIT) elected. ◆ *nm, f* **1.** (POLIT) elected representative. **2.** (RELIG) chosen one; **l'~ de son cœur** *hum ou sout* one's heart's desire.

élucider [elyside] *vt* to clear up.

éluder [elyde] *vt* to evade.

Élysée [elize] *nm* : **l'~** *the official residence of the French President and, by extension, the President himself.*

émacié, -e [emasje] *adj littéraire* emaciated.

émail, -aux [emaj, emo] *nm* enamel;

en ~ enamel, enamelled.

émanciper [emãsipe] vt to emancipate. ▶ **s'émanciper** vp 1. (se libérer) to become free ou liberated. 2. fam (se dévergonder) to become emancipated.

émaner [emane] vi : ~ **de** to emanate from.

émarger [emarʒe] vt (signer) to sign.

émasculer [emaskyle] vt to emasculate.

emballage [ãbalaʒ] nm packaging.

emballer [ãbale] vt 1. (objet) to pack (up), to wrap (up). 2. fam (plaire) to thrill. ▶ **s'emballer** vp 1. (moteur) to race. 2. (cheval) to bolt. 3. fam (personne - s'enthousiasmer) to get carried away; (- s'emporter) to lose one's temper.

embarcadère [ãbarkadɛr] nm landing stage.

embarcation [ãbarkasjɔ̃] nf small boat.

embardée [ãbarde] nf swerve; **faire une ~** to swerve.

embargo [ãbargo] nm embargo.

embarquement [ãbarkəmã] nm 1. (de marchandises) loading. 2. (de passagers) boarding.

embarquer [ãbarke] ♦ vt 1. (marchandises) to load. 2. (passagers) to take on board. 3. fam (arrêter) to pick up. 4. fam fig (engager) : ~ **qqn dans** to involve sb in. 5. fam (emmener) to cart off. ♦ vi : ~ **(pour)** to sail (for). ▶ **s'embarquer** vp 1. (sur un bateau) to (set) sail. 2. fam fig (s'engager) : **s'~ dans** to get involved in.

embarras [ãbara] nm 1. (incertitude) (state of) uncertainty; **avoir l'~ du choix** to be spoilt for choice. 2. (situation difficile) predicament; **être dans l'~** to be in a predicament; **mettre qqn dans l'~** to place sb in an awkward position; **tirer qqn d'~** to get sb out of a tight spot. 3. (gêne) embarrassment. 4. (souci) difficulty, worry.

embarrassé, -e [ãbarase] adj 1. (encombré - pièce, bureau) cluttered; **avoir les mains ~es** to have one's hands full. 2. (gêné) embarrassed. 3. (confus) confused.

embarrasser [ãbarase] vt 1. (encombrer - pièce) to clutter up; (- personne) to hamper. 2. (gêner) to put in an awkward position. ▶ **s'embarrasser** vp (se charger) : **s'~ de qqch** to burden o.s. with sthg; fig to bother about sthg.

embauche [ãboʃ] nf, **embauchage** [ãboʃaʒ] nm hiring, employment.

embaucher [ãboʃe] vt 1. (employer) to

employ, to take on. 2. fam (occuper) : **je t'embauche!** I need your help!

embaumer [ãbome] ♦ vt 1. (cadavre) to embalm. 2. (parfumer) to scent. ♦ vi to be fragrant.

embellir [ãbelir] ♦ vt 1. (agrémenter) to brighten up. 2. fig (enjoliver) to embellish. ♦ vi (devenir plus beau) to become more attractive; fig & hum to grow, to increase.

embêtant, -e [ãbɛtã, ãt] adj fam annoying.

embêtement [ãbɛtmã] nm fam trouble.

embêter [ãbɛte] vt fam (contrarier, importuner) to annoy. ▶ **s'embêter** vp fam (s'ennuyer) to be bored.

emblée [ãble] ▶ **d'emblée** loc adv right away.

emblème [ãblɛm] nm emblem.

emboîter [ãbwate] vt : ~ **qqch dans qqch** to fit sthg into sthg. ▶ **s'emboîter** vp to fit together.

embonpoint [ãbɔ̃pwɛ̃] nm stoutness.

embouché, -e [ãbuʃe] adj fam : **mal ~** foul-mouthed.

embouchure [ãbuʃyr] nf (de fleuve) mouth.

embourber [ãburbe] ▶ **s'embourber** vp (s'enliser) to get stuck in the mud; fig to get bogged down.

embourgeoiser [ãburʒwaze] vt (personne) to instil middle-class values in; (quartier) to gentrify. ▶ **s'embourgeoiser** vp (personne) to adopt middle-class values; (quartier) to become gentrified.

embout [ãbu] nm (protection) tip; (extrémité d'un tube) nozzle.

embouteillage [ãbutejaʒ] nm (circulation) traffic jam.

emboutir [ãbutir] vt 1. fam (voiture) to crash into. 2. (TECHNOL) to stamp.

embranchement [ãbrãʃmã] nm (carrefour) junction.

embraser [ãbraze] vt (incendier, éclairer) to set ablaze; fig (d'amour) to (set on) fire, to inflame. ▶ **s'embraser** vp (prendre feu, s'éclairer) to be ablaze.

embrassade [ãbrasad] nf embrace.

embrasser [ãbrase] vt 1. (donner un baiser à) to kiss. 2. (étreindre) to embrace. 3. fig (du regard) to take in. ▶ **s'embrasser** vp to kiss (each other).

embrasure [ãbrazyr] nf : **dans l'~ de la fenêtre** in the window.

embrayage [ãbrɛjaʒ] nm (mécanisme) clutch.

embrayer [ābreje] vi (AUTOM) to engage the clutch.

embrocher [ābrɔʃe] vt to skewer.

embrouillamini [ābrujamini] nm fam muddle.

embrouiller [ābruje] vt 1. (mélanger) to mix (up), to muddle (up). 2. fig (compliquer) to confuse.

embruns [ābrœ̃] nmpl spray (U).

embryon [ābrijɔ̃] nm litt & fig embryo.

embûche [ābyʃ] nf pitfall.

embuer [ābɥe] vt 1. (de vapeur) to steam up. 2. (de larmes) to mist (over).

embuscade [ābyskad] nf ambush.

éméché, -e [emeʃe] adj fam merry, tipsy.

émeraude [emrod] nf emerald.

émerger [emɛrʒe] vi 1. (gén) to emerge. 2. (NAVIG & fig) to surface.

émeri [emri] nm: papier OU toile ~ emery paper.

émérite [emerit] adj distinguished, eminent.

émerveiller [emɛrveje] vt to fill with wonder.

émetteur, -trice [emetœr, tris] adj transmitting; poste ~ transmitter. ▶ **émetteur** nm (appareil) transmitter.

émettre [emɛtr] vt 1. (produire) to emit. 2. (diffuser) to transmit, to broadcast. 3. (mettre en circulation) to issue. 4. (exprimer) to express.

émeute [emøt] nf riot.

émietter [emjete] vt 1. (du pain) to crumble. 2. (morceler) to divide up.

émigrant, -e [emigrā, āt] adj & nm, f emigrant.

émigré, -e [emigre] ◆ adj migrant. ◆ nm, f emigrant.

émigrer [emigre] vi 1. (personnes) to emigrate. 2. (animaux) to migrate.

émincé, -e [emēse] adj sliced thinly. ▶ **émincé** nm thin slices of meat served in a sauce.

éminemment [eminamā] adv eminently.

éminence [eminās] nf hill.

éminent, -e [eminā, āt] adj eminent, distinguished.

émir [emir] nm emir.

émirat [emira] nm emirate. ▶ **Émirat** nm: les Émirats arabes unis the United Arab Emirates.

émis, -e [emi, iz] pp → émettre.

émissaire [emiser] ◆ nm (envoyé) emissary, envoy. ◆ adj → bouc.

émission [emisjɔ̃] nf 1. (de gaz, de son etc) emission. 2. (RADIO & TÉLÉ - transmis-sion) transmission, broadcasting; (- programme) programme Br, program Am. 3. (mise en circulation) issue.

emmagasiner [āmagazine] vt 1. (stocker) to store. 2. fig (accumuler) to store up.

emmailloter [āmajɔte] vt to wrap up.

emmanchure [āmāʃyr] nf armhole.

emmêler [āmele] vt 1. (fils) to tangle up. 2. fig (idées) to muddle up, to confuse. ▶ **s'emmêler** vp 1. (fils) to get into a tangle. 2. fig (personne) to get mixed up.

emménagement [āmenaʒmā] nm moving in.

emménager [āmenaʒe] vi to move in.

emmener [āmne] vt to take.

emmerder [āmerde] vt tfam to piss off. ▶ **s'emmerder** vp tfam (s'embêter) to be bored stiff.

emmitoufler [āmitufle] vt to wrap up. ▶ **s'emmitoufler** vp to wrap o.s. up.

émoi [emwa] nm (émotion) emotion.

émotif, -ive [emotif, iv] adj emotional.

émotion [emosjɔ̃] nf 1. (sentiment) emotion. 2. (peur) fright, shock.

émotionnel, -elle [emosjonel] adj emotional.

émousser [emuse] vt litt & fig to blunt.

émouvant, -e [emuvā, āt] adj moving.

émouvoir [emuvwar] vt 1. (troubler) to disturb, to upset. 2. (susciter la sympathie de) to move, to touch. ▶ **s'émouvoir** vp to show emotion, to be upset.

empailler [āpaje] vt 1. (animal) to stuff. 2. (chaise) to upholster (with straw).

empaler [āpale] vt to impale.

empaqueter [āpakte] vt to pack (up), to wrap (up).

empâter [āpate] vt 1. (visage, traits) to fatten out. 2. (bouche, langue) to coat, to fur up. ▶ **s'empâter** vp to put on weight.

empêchement [āpeʃmā] nm obstacle; j'ai un ~ something has come up.

empêcher [āpeʃe] vt to prevent; ~ qqn/qqch de faire qqch to prevent sb/ sthg from doing sthg; ~ que qqn (ne) fasse qqch to prevent sb from doing sthg; (il) n'empêche que nevertheless, all the same.

empereur [āprœr] nm emperor.

empesé, -e [āpəze] adj 1. (linge) starched. 2. fig (style) stiff.

empester [āpeste] vi to stink.

empêtrer [ɑ̃petre] *vt*: **être empêtré dans** to be tangled up in. ▶ **s'empêtrer** *vp*: **s'~ (dans)** to get tangled up (in).

emphase [ɑ̃faz] *nf péj* pomposity.

empiéter [ɑ̃pjete] *vi*: **~ sur** to encroach on.

empiffrer [ɑ̃pifre] ▶ **s'empiffrer** *vp fam* to stuff o.s.

empiler [ɑ̃pile] *vt (entasser)* to pile up, to stack up.

empire [ɑ̃pir] *nm* **1.** (HIST & *fig*) empire. **2.** *sout (contrôle)* influence.

empirer [ɑ̃pire] *vi & vt* to worsen.

empirique [ɑ̃pirik] *adj* empirical.

emplacement [ɑ̃plasmɑ̃] *nm (gén)* site, location; *(dans un camping)* place.

emplette [ɑ̃plɛt] *nf (gén pl)* purchase.

emplir [ɑ̃plir] *vt sout*: **~ (de)** to fill (with). ▶ **s'emplir** *vp*: **s'~ (de)** to fill (with).

emploi [ɑ̃plwa] *nm* **1.** *(utilisation)* use; **~ du temps** timetable; **mode d'~** instructions *(pl)* (for use). **2.** *(travail)* job.

employé, -e [ɑ̃plwaje] *nm, f* employee; **~ de bureau** office employee *ou* worker.

employer [ɑ̃plwaje] *vt* **1.** *(utiliser)* to use. **2.** *(salarier)* to employ.

employeur, -euse [ɑ̃plwajœr, øz] *nm, f* employer.

empocher [ɑ̃pɔʃe] *vt fam* to pocket.

empoignade [ɑ̃pwaɲad] *nf* row.

empoigner [ɑ̃pwaɲe] *vt (saisir)* to grasp. ▶ **s'empoigner** *vp fig* to come to blows.

empoisonnement [ɑ̃pwazɔnmɑ̃] *nm (intoxication)* poisoning.

empoisonner [ɑ̃pwazɔne] *vt* **1.** *(gén)* to poison. **2.** *fam (ennuyer)* to annoy, to bug.

emporté, -e [ɑ̃pɔrte] *adj* short-tempered.

emportement [ɑ̃pɔrtəmɑ̃] *nm* anger.

emporter [ɑ̃pɔrte] *vt* **1.** *(emmener)* to take (away); **à ~** *(plats)* to take away, to go *Am*. **2.** *(entraîner)* to carry along. **3.** *(arracher)* to tear off, to blow off. **4.** *(faire mourir)* to carry off. **5.** *(surpasser)*: **l'~ sur** to get the better of. ▶ **s'emporter** *vp* to get angry, to lose one's temper.

empoté, -e [ɑ̃pɔte] *fam* ◆ *adj* clumsy. ◆ *nm, f* clumsy person.

empreinte [ɑ̃prɛt] *nf (trace)* print; *fig* mark, trace; **~s digitales** fingerprints.

empressement [ɑ̃prɛsmɑ̃] *nm* **1.** *(zèle)* attentiveness. **2.** *(enthousiasme)* eagerness.

empresser [ɑ̃prese] ▶ **s'empresser** *vp*: **s'~ de faire qqch** to hurry to do sthg;

s'~ auprès de qqn to be attentive to sb.

emprise [ɑ̃priz] *nf (ascendant)* influence.

emprisonnement [ɑ̃prizɔnmɑ̃] *nm* imprisonment.

emprisonner [ɑ̃prizɔne] *vt (voleur)* to imprison.

emprunt [ɑ̃prœ̃] *nm* **1.** (FIN) loan. **2.** (LING & *fig*) borrowing.

emprunté, -e [ɑ̃prœ̃te] *adj* awkward, self-conscious.

emprunter [ɑ̃prœ̃te] *vt* **1.** *(gén)* to borrow; **~ qqch à** to borrow sthg from. **2.** *(route)* to take.

ému, -e [emy] ◆ *pp* → **émouvoir.** ◆ *adj (personne)* moved, touched; *(regard, sourire)* emotional.

émulation [emylasjɔ̃] *nf* **1.** *(concurrence)* rivalry. **2.** *(imitation)* emulation.

émule [emyl] *nmf* **1.** *(imitateur)* emulator. **2.** *(concurrent)* rival.

émulsion [emylsjɔ̃] *nf* emulsion.

en [ɑ̃] ◆ *prép* **1.** *(temps)* in; **~ 1994** in 1994; **~ hiver/septembre** in winter/September. **2.** *(lieu)* in; *(direction)* to; **habiter ~ Sicile/ville** to live in Sicily/town; **aller ~ Sicile/ville** to go to Sicily/town. **3.** *(matière)* made of; **c'est ~ métal** it's (made of) metal; **une théière ~ argent** a silver teapot. **4.** *(état, forme, manière)*: **les arbres sont ~ fleurs** the trees are in blossom; **du sucre ~ morceaux** sugar cubes; **je l'ai eu ~ cadeau** I was given it as a present; **dire qqch ~ anglais** to say sthg in English; **~ vacances** on holiday. **5.** *(moyen)* by; **~ avion/bateau/train** by plane/boat/train. **6.** *(mesure)* in; **vous l'avez ~ 38?** do you have it in a 38?; **compter ~ dollars** to calculate in dollars. **7.** *(devant un participe présent)*: **arrivant à Paris** on arriving in Paris, as he/she *etc* arrived in Paris; **~ faisant un effort** by making an effort; **~ mangeant** while eating; **elle répondit ~ souriant** she replied with a smile. ◆ *pron adv* **1.** *(complément de verbe, de nom, d'adjectif)*: **il s'~ est souvenu** he remembered it; **nous ~ avons déjà parlé** we've already spoken about it; **je m'~ porte garant** I'll vouch for it. **2.** *(avec un indéfini, exprimant une quantité)*: **j'ai du chocolat, tu ~ veux?** I've got some chocolate, do you want some?; **tu ~ as?** have you got any?, do you have any?; **il y ~ a plusieurs** there are several (of them). **3.** *(provenance)* from there.

ENA, Ena [ena] *(abr de École nationale d'administration)* *nf prestigious grande école* *training future government officials.*

encadrement [ɑ̃kadrəmɑ̃] *nm* **1.** (*de tableau, porte*) frame. **2.** (*dans une entreprise*) managerial staff; (*à l'armée*) officers (*pl*); (*à l'école*) staff. **3.** (*du crédit*) restriction.

encadrer [ɑ̃kadre] *vt* **1.** (*photo, visage*) to frame. **2.** (*employés*) to supervise; (*soldats*) to be in command of; (*élèves*) to teach.

encaissé, -e [ɑ̃kese] *adj* (*vallée*) deep and narrow; (*rivière*) steep-banked.

encaisser [ɑ̃kese] *vt* **1.** (*argent, coups, insultes*) to take. **2.** (*chèque*) to cash.

encart [ɑ̃kar] *nm* insert.

encastrer [ɑ̃kastre] *vt* to fit. ▸ **s'encastrer** *vp* to fit (exactly).

encaustique [ɑ̃kostik] *nf* (*cire*) polish.

enceinte [ɑ̃sɛ̃t] ◆ *adj f* pregnant; **~ de 4 mois** 4 months pregnant. ◆ *nf* **1.** (*muraille*) wall. **2.** (*espace*) **dans l'~ de** within (the confines of). **3.** (*baffle*) **~ (acoustique)** speaker.

encens [ɑ̃sɑ̃] *nm* incense.

encenser [ɑ̃sɑ̃se] *vt* **1.** (*brûler de l'encens dans*) to burn incense in. **2.** *fig* (*louer*) to flatter.

encensoir [ɑ̃sɑ̃swar] *nm* censer.

encercler [ɑ̃sɛrkle] *vt* **1.** (*cerner, environner*) to surround. **2.** (*entourer*) to circle.

enchaînement [ɑ̃ʃɛnmɑ̃] *nm* **1.** (*succession*) series. **2.** (*liaison*) link.

enchaîner [ɑ̃ʃene] ◆ *vt* **1.** (*attacher*) to chain up. **2.** *fig* (*asservir*) to enslave. **3.** (*coordonner*) to link. ◆ *vi*: **~ (sur)** to move on (to). ▸ **s'enchaîner** *vp* (*se suivre*) to follow on from each other.

enchanté, -e [ɑ̃ʃɑ̃te] *adj* **1.** (*ravi*) delighted; **~ de faire votre connaissance** pleased to meet you. **2.** (*ensorcelé*) enchanted.

enchantement [ɑ̃ʃɑ̃tmɑ̃] *nm* **1.** (*sortilège*) magic spell; **comme par ~** as if by magic. **2.** *sout* (*ravissement*) delight. **3.** (*merveille*) wonder.

enchanter [ɑ̃ʃɑ̃te] *vt* **1.** (*ensorceler, charmer*) to enchant. **2.** (*ravir*) to delight.

enchâsser [ɑ̃ʃase] *vt* **1.** (*encastrer*) to fit. **2.** (*sertir*) to set.

enchère [ɑ̃ʃɛr] *nf* bid; **vendre qqch aux ~s** to sell sthg at ou by auction.

enchevêtrer [ɑ̃ʃəvɛtre] *vt* (*emmêler*) to tangle up; *fig* to muddle, to confuse.

enclave [ɑ̃klav] *nf* enclave.

enclencher [ɑ̃klɑ̃ʃe] *vt* (*mécanisme*) to engage. ▸ **s'enclencher** *vp* **1.** (TECHNOL) to engage. **2.** *fig* (*commencer*) to begin.

enclin, -e [ɑ̃klɛ̃, in] *adj*: **~ à qqch/à faire qqch** inclined to sthg/to do sthg.

enclore [ɑ̃klɔr] *vt* to fence in, to enclose.

enclos, -e [ɑ̃klo, oz] *pp* → **enclore**. ▸ **enclos** *nm* enclosure.

enclume [ɑ̃klym] *nf* anvil.

encoche [ɑ̃kɔʃ] *nf* notch.

encoignure [ɑ̃kwaɲyr, ɑ̃kɔɲyr] *nf* (*coin*) corner.

encolure [ɑ̃kɔlyr] *nf* neck.

encombrant, -e [ɑ̃kɔ̃brɑ̃, ɑ̃t] *adj* cumbersome; *fig* (*personne*) undesirable.

encombre [ɑ̃kɔ̃br] ▸ **sans encombre** *loc adv* without a hitch.

encombré, -e [ɑ̃kɔ̃bre] *adj* (*lieu*) busy, congested; *fig* saturated.

encombrement [ɑ̃kɔ̃brəmɑ̃] *nm* **1.** (*d'une pièce*) clutter. **2.** (*d'un objet*) overall dimensions (*pl*). **3.** (*embouteillage*) traffic jam. **4.** (INFORM) footprint.

encombrer [ɑ̃kɔ̃bre] *vt* to clutter (up).

encontre [ɑ̃kɔ̃tr] ▸ **à l'encontre de** *loc prép*: **aller à l'~ de** to go against, to oppose.

encore [ɑ̃kɔr] *adv* **1.** (*toujours*) still; **~ un mois** one more month; **pas ~** not yet; **elle ne travaille pas ~** she's not working yet. **2.** (*de nouveau*) again; **il m'a ~ menti** he's lied to me again; **quoi ~?** what now?; **l'ascenseur est en panne – ~!** the lift's out of order – not again!; **~ de la glace?** some more ice cream?; **~ une fois** once more, once again. **3.** (*marque le renforcement*) even; **~ mieux/pire** even better/worse. ▸ **et encore** *loc adv*: **j'ai eu le temps de prendre un sandwich, et ~!** I had time for a sandwich, but only just! ▸ **si encore** *loc adv* if only. ▸ **encore que** *loc conj* (+ *subjonctif*) although.

encouragement [ɑ̃kuraʒmɑ̃] *nm* (*parole*) (word of) encouragement.

encourager [ɑ̃kuraʒe] *vt* to encourage; **~ qqn à faire qqch** to encourage sb to do sthg.

encourir [ɑ̃kurir] *vt sout* to incur.

encouru, -e [ɑ̃kury] *pp* → **encourir**.

encrasser [ɑ̃krase] *vt* **1.** (TECHNOL) to clog up. **2.** *fam* (*salir*) to make dirty ou filthy. ▸ **s'encrasser** *vp* **1.** (TECHNOL) to clog up. **2.** *fam* (*se salir*) to get dirty ou filthy.

encre [ɑ̃kr] *nf* ink.

encrer [ɑ̃kre] *vt* to ink.

encrier [ɑ̃krije] *nm* inkwell.

encroûter [ɑ̃krute] ▸ **s'encroûter** *vp fam* to get into a rut; **s'~ dans ses habi-**

tudes to become set in one's ways.
encyclopédie [ɑ̃siklɔpedi] nf encyclopedia.

encyclopédique [ɑ̃siklɔpedik] adj encyclopedic.

endémique [ɑ̃demik] adj endemic.

endetter [ɑ̃dete] ▶ **s'endetter** vp to get into debt.

endeuiller [ɑ̃dœje] vt to plunge into mourning.

endiablé, -e [ɑ̃djable] adj (frénétique) frantic, frenzied.

endiguer [ɑ̃dige] vt 1. (fleuve) to dam. 2. fig (réprimer) to stem.

endimanché, -e [ɑ̃dimɑ̃ʃe] adj in one's Sunday best.

endive [ɑ̃div] nf chicory (U).

endoctriner [ɑ̃dɔktrine] vt to indoctrinate.

endommager [ɑ̃dɔmaʒe] vt to damage.

endormi, -e [ɑ̃dɔrmi] adj 1. (personne) sleeping, asleep. 2. fig (village) sleepy; (jambe) numb; (passion) dormant; fam (apathique) sluggish.

endormir [ɑ̃dɔrmir] vt 1. (assoupir, ennuyer) to send to sleep. 2. (anesthésier - patient) to anaesthetize; (- douleur) to ease. 3. fig (tromper) to allay. ▶ **s'endormir** vp (s'assoupir) to fall asleep.

endosser [ɑ̃dose] vt 1. (vêtement) to put on. 2. (FIN & JUR) to endorse; ~ un chèque to endorse a cheque. 3. fig (responsabilité) to take on.

endroit [ɑ̃drwa] nm 1. (lieu, point) place; à quel ~? where? 2. (passage) part. 3. (côté) right side; à l'~ the right way round.

enduire [ɑ̃dɥir] vt: ~ qqch (de) to coat sthg (with).

enduit, -e [ɑ̃dɥi, it] pp → **enduire**. ▶ **enduit** nm coating.

endurance [ɑ̃dyrɑ̃s] nf endurance.

endurcir [ɑ̃dyrsir] vt to harden. ▶ **s'endurcir** vp: s'~ à to become hardened to.

endurer [ɑ̃dyre] vt to endure.

énergétique [enɛrʒetik] adj 1. (ressource) energy (avant n). 2. (aliment) energy-giving.

énergie [enɛrʒi] nf energy.

énergique [enɛrʒik] adj (gén) energetic; (remède) powerful; (mesure) drastic.

énergumène [enɛrgymɛn] nmf rowdy character.

énerver [enɛrve] vt to irritate, to annoy. ▶ **s'énerver** vp to get annoyed.

enfance [ɑ̃fɑ̃s] nf 1. (âge) childhood. 2. (enfants) children (pl).

enfant [ɑ̃fɑ̃] nmf (gén) child; attendre un ~ to be expecting a baby. ▶ **bon enfant** loc adj good-natured.

enfanter [ɑ̃fɑ̃te] vt littéraire to give birth to.

enfantillage [ɑ̃fɑ̃tijaʒ] nm childishness (U).

enfantin, -e [ɑ̃fɑ̃tɛ̃, in] adj 1. (propre à l'enfance) childlike; péj childish; (jeu, chanson) children's (avant n). 2. (facile) childishly simple.

enfer [ɑ̃fɛr] nm (RELIG & fig) hell. ▶ **Enfers** nmpl: les Enfers the Underworld (sg).

enfermer [ɑ̃fɛrme] vt (séquestrer, ranger) to shut away. ▶ **s'enfermer** vp to shut o.s. away ou up; s'~ dans fig to retreat into.

enfilade [ɑ̃filad] nf row.

enfiler [ɑ̃file] vt 1. (aiguille, sur un fil) to thread. 2. (vêtements) to slip on.

enfin [ɑ̃fɛ̃] adv 1. (en dernier lieu) finally, at last; (dans une liste) lastly. 2. (avant une récapitulation) in a word, in short. 3. (introduit une rectification) that is, well. 4. (introduit une concession) anyway.

enflammer [ɑ̃flame] vt 1. (bois) to set fire to. 2. fig (exalter) to inflame. ▶ **s'enflammer** vp 1. (bois) to catch fire. 2. fig (s'exalter) to flare up.

enflé, -e [ɑ̃fle] adj (style) turgid.

enfler [ɑ̃fle] vi to swell (up).

enfoncer [ɑ̃fɔ̃se] vt 1. (faire pénétrer) to drive in; ~ qqch dans qqch to drive sthg into sthg. 2. (enfouir): ~ ses mains dans ses poches to thrust one's hands into one's pockets. 3. (défoncer) to break down. ▶ **s'enfoncer** vp 1. s'~ dans (eau, boue) to sink into; (bois, ville) to disappear into. 2. (céder) to give way.

enfouir [ɑ̃fwir] vt 1. (cacher) to hide. 2. (ensevelir) to bury.

enfourcher [ɑ̃furʃe] vt to get on, to mount.

enfourner [ɑ̃furne] vt 1. (pain) to put in the oven. 2. fam (avaler) to gobble up.

enfreindre [ɑ̃frɛ̃dr] vt to infringe.

enfreint, -e [ɑ̃frɛ̃, ɛ̃t] pp → **enfreindre**.

enfuir [ɑ̃fɥir] ▶ **s'enfuir** vp (fuir) to run away.

enfumer [ɑ̃fyme] vt to fill with smoke.

engagé, -e [ɑ̃gaʒe] adj committed.

engageant, -e [ɑ̃gaʒɑ̃, ɑ̃t] adj engaging.

engagement [ɑ̃gaʒmɑ̃] nm 1. (pro-

messe) commitment. **2.** (JUR) contract. **3.** (MIL - *de soldats*) enlistment; (- *combat*) engagement. **4.** (FOOTBALL & RUGBY) kick-off.

engager [ɑ̃gaʒe] *vt* **1.** (*lier*) to commit. **2.** (*embaucher*) to take on, to engage. **3.** (*faire entrer*): ~ **qqch dans** to insert sthg into; ~ **une vitesse** to put the car into gear. **4.** (*commencer*) to start. **5.** (*impliquer*) to involve. **6.** (*encourager*): ~ **qqn à faire qqch** to urge sb to do sthg. ▶ **s'engager** *vp* **1.** (*promettre*): **s'~ à qqch/à faire qqch** to commit o.s. to sthg/to doing sthg. **2.** (MIL): **s'~ (dans)** to enlist (in). **3.** (*pénétrer*): **s'~ dans** to enter.

engelure [ɑ̃ʒlyr] *nf* chilblain.

engendrer [ɑ̃ʒɑ̃dre] *vt* **1.** littéraire to father. **2.** *fig* (*produire*) to cause, to give rise to; (*sentiment*) to engender.

engin [ɑ̃ʒɛ̃] *nm* **1.** (*machine*) machine. **2.** (MIL) missile. **3.** *fam péj* (*objet*) thing.

englober [ɑ̃glɔbe] *vt* to include.

engloutir [ɑ̃glutir] *vt* **1.** (*dévorer*) to gobble up. **2.** (*faire disparaître*) to engulf. **3.** *fig* (*dilapider*) to squander.

engorger [ɑ̃gɔrʒe] *vt* **1.** (*obstruer*) to block, to obstruct. **2.** (MÉD) to engorge. ▶ **s'engorger** *vp* to become blocked.

engouement [ɑ̃gumɑ̃] *nm* (*enthousiasme*) infatuation.

engouffrer [ɑ̃gufre] *vt fam* (*dévorer*) to wolf down. ▶ **s'engouffrer** *vp*: **s'~ dans** to rush into.

engourdi, -e [ɑ̃gurdi] *adj* numb; *fig* dull.

engourdir [ɑ̃gurdir] *vt* to numb; *fig* to dull. ▶ **s'engourdir** *vp* to go numb.

engrais [ɑ̃grɛ] *nm* fertilizer.

engraisser [ɑ̃grese] ◆ *vt* **1.** (*animal*) to fatten. **2.** (*terre*) to fertilize. ◆ *vi* to put on weight.

engrenage [ɑ̃grənaʒ] *nm* **1.** (TECHNOL) gears (*pl*). **2.** *fig* (*circonstances*): **être pris dans l'~** to be caught up in the system.

engueulade [ɑ̃gœlad] *nf fam* bawling out.

engueuler [ɑ̃gœle] *vt fam*: ~ **qqn** to bawl sb out. ▶ **s'engueuler** *vp fam* to have a row, to have a slanging match Br.

enhardir [ɑ̃ardir] *vt* to make bold. ▶ **s'enhardir** *vp* to pluck up one's courage.

énième [enjɛm] *adj fam*: **la ~ fois** the nth time.

énigmatique [enigmatik] *adj* enigmatic.

énigme [enigm] *nf* **1.** (*mystère*) enigma. **2.** (*jeu*) riddle.

enivrant, -e [ɑ̃nivrɑ̃, ɑ̃t] *adj litt & fig* intoxicating.

enivrer [ɑ̃nivre] *vt litt* to get drunk; *fig* to intoxicate. ▶ **s'enivrer** *vp*: **s'~ (de)** to get drunk (on); *fig* to become intoxicated (with).

enjambée [ɑ̃ʒɑ̃be] *nf* stride.

enjamber [ɑ̃ʒɑ̃be] *vt* **1.** (*obstacle*) to step over. **2.** (*cours d'eau*) to straddle.

enjeu [ɑ̃ʒø] *nm* (*mise*) stake; **quel est l'~ ici?** *fig* what's at stake here?

enjoindre [ɑ̃ʒwɛ̃dr] *vt littéraire*: ~ **à qqn de faire qqch** to enjoin sb to do sthg.

enjoint [ɑ̃ʒwɛ̃] *pp inv* → **enjoindre**.

enjôler [ɑ̃ʒole] *vt* to coax.

enjoliver [ɑ̃ʒolive] *vt* to embellish.

enjoliveur [ɑ̃ʒolivœr] *nm* (*de roue*) hubcap; (*de calandre*) badge.

enjoué, -e [ɑ̃ʒwe] *adj* cheerful.

enlacer [ɑ̃lase] *vt* (*prendre dans ses bras*) to embrace, to hug. ▶ **s'enlacer** *vp* (*s'embrasser*) to embrace, to hug.

enlaidir [ɑ̃ledir] ◆ *vt* to make ugly. ◆ *vi* to become ugly.

enlèvement [ɑ̃levmɑ̃] *nm* **1.** (*action d'enlever*) removal. **2.** (*rapt*) abduction.

enlever [ɑ̃lve] *vt* **1.** (*gén*) to remove; (*vêtement*) to take off. **2.** (*prendre*): ~ **qqch à qqn** to take sthg away from sb. **3.** (*kidnapper*) to abduct.

enliser [ɑ̃lize] ▶ **s'enliser** *vp* **1.** (*s'embourber*) to sink, to get stuck. **2.** *fig* (*piétiner*): **s'~ dans qqch** to get bogged down in sthg.

enluminure [ɑ̃lyminyr] *nf* illumination.

enneigé, -e [ɑ̃neʒe] *adj* snow-covered.

enneigement [ɑ̃neʒmɑ̃] *nm* snow cover.

ennemi, -e [ɛnmi] ◆ *adj* enemy (*avant n*). ◆ *nm, f* enemy.

ennui [ɑ̃nɥi] *nm* **1.** (*lassitude*) boredom. **2.** (*contrariété*) annoyance; **l'~, c'est que ...** the annoying thing is that ... **3.** (*problème*) trouble (U); **avoir des ~s** to have problems.

ennuyer [ɑ̃nɥije] *vt* **1.** (*agacer, contrarier*) to annoy; **cela t'ennuierait de venir me chercher?** would you mind picking me up? **2.** (*lasser*) to bore. **3.** (*inquiéter*) to bother. ▶ **s'ennuyer** *vp* **1.** (*se morfondre*) to be bored. **2.** (*déplorer l'absence*): **s'~ de qqn/qqch** to miss sb/sthg.

ennuyeux, -euse [ɑ̃nɥijø, øz] *adj* **1.** (*lassant*) boring. **2.** (*contrariant*) annoying.

énoncé [enɔ̃se] *nm* (*libellé*) wording.
énoncer [enɔ̃se] *vt* **1.** (*libeller*) to word. **2.** (*exposer*) to expound; (*théorème*) to set forth.

énorme [enɔrm] *adj* **1.** *litt & fig* (*immense*) enormous. **2.** *fam fig* (*incroyable*) far-fetched.

énormément [enɔrmemɑ̃] *adv* enormously; ~ **de** a great deal of.

enquête [ɑ̃kɛt] *nf* **1.** (*de police, recherches*) investigation. **2.** (*sondage*) survey.

enquêter [ɑ̃kete] *vi* **1.** (*police, chercheur*) to investigate. **2.** (*sonder*) to conduct a survey.

enragé, -e [ɑ̃raʒe] *adj* **1.** (*chien*) rabid, with rabies. **2.** *fig* (*invétéré*) keen.

enrager [ɑ̃raʒe] *vi* to be furious; **faire ~ qqn** to infuriate sb.

enrayer [ɑ̃reje] *vt* **1.** (*épidémie*) to check, to stop. **2.** (*mécanisme*) to jam. ▶ **s'enrayer** *vp* (*mécanisme*) to jam.

enregistrement [ɑ̃rəʒistrəmɑ̃] *nm* **1.** (*de son, d'images, d'informations*) recording. **2.** (*inscription*) registration. **3.** (*à l'aéroport*) check-in; ~ **des bagages** baggage registration.

enregistrer [ɑ̃rəʒistre] *vt* **1.** (*son, images, informations*) to record. **2.** (INFORM) to store. **3.** (*inscrire*) to register. **4.** (*à l'aéroport*) to check in. **5.** *fam* (*mémoriser*) to make a mental note of.

enrhumé, -e [ɑ̃ryme] *adj*: **je suis ~** I have a cold.

enrhumer [ɑ̃ryme] ▶ **s'enrhumer** *vp* to catch (a) cold.

enrichir [ɑ̃riʃir] *vt* **1.** (*financièrement*) to make rich. **2.** (*terre & fig*) to enrich. ▶ **s'enrichir** *vp* **1.** (*financièrement*) to grow rich. **2.** (*sol & fig*) to become enriched.

enrobé, -e [ɑ̃rɔbe] *adj* **1.** (*recouvert*): ~ **de** coated with. **2.** *fam* (*grassouillet*) plump.

enrober [ɑ̃rɔbe] *vt* (*recouvrir*): ~ **qqch de** to coat sthg with. ▶ **s'enrober** *vp* to put on weight.

enrôler [ɑ̃role] *vt* to enrol; (MIL) to enlist. ▶ **s'enrôler** *vp* to enrol; (MIL) to enlist.

enroué, -e [ɑ̃rwe] *adj* hoarse.

enrouler [ɑ̃rule] *vt* to roll up; ~ **qqch autour de qqch** to wind sthg round sthg. ▶ **s'enrouler** *vp* **1.** (*entourer*): **s'~ sur** OU **autour de qqch** to wind around sthg. **2.** (*se pelotonner*): **s'~ dans qqch** to wrap o.s. up in sthg.

ensabler [ɑ̃sable] *vt* to silt up. ▶ **s'ensabler** *vp* to silt up.

enseignant, -e [ɑ̃seɲɑ̃, ɑ̃t] ◆ *adj* teaching (*avant n*). ◆ *nm, f* teacher.

enseigne [ɑ̃seɲ] *nf* **1.** (*de commerce*) sign. **2.** (*drapeau, soldat*) ensign.

enseignement [ɑ̃seɲmɑ̃] *nm* (*gén*) teaching; ~ **primaire/secondaire** primary/secondary education.

enseigner [ɑ̃seɲe] *vt litt & fig* to teach; ~ **qqch à qqn** to teach sb sthg, to teach sthg to sb.

ensemble [ɑ̃sɑ̃bl] ◆ *adv* together; **aller ~** to go together. ◆ *nm* **1.** (*totalité*) whole; **idée d'~** general idea; **dans l'~** on the whole. **2.** (*harmonie*) unity. **3.** (*vêtement*) outfit, suit. **4.** (*série*) collection. **5.** (MATHS) set. **6.** (MUS) ensemble.

ensemencer [ɑ̃səmɑ̃se] *vt* **1.** (*terre*) to sow. **2.** (*rivière*) to stock.

enserrer [ɑ̃sere] *vt* (*entourer*) to encircle; *fig* to imprison.

ensevelir [ɑ̃səvlir] *vt litt & fig* to bury.

ensoleillé, -e [ɑ̃sɔleje] *adj* sunny.

ensoleillement [ɑ̃sɔlejmɑ̃] *nm* sunshine.

ensommeillé, -e [ɑ̃sɔmeje] *adj* sleepy.

ensorceler [ɑ̃sɔrsəle] *vt* to bewitch.

ensuite [ɑ̃sɥit] *adv* **1.** (*après, plus tard*) after, afterwards, later. **2.** (*puis*) then, next, after that; **et ~?** what then?, what next?

ensuivre [ɑ̃sɥivr] ▶ **s'ensuivre** *vp* to follow; **il s'ensuit que** it follows that.

entaille [ɑ̃taj] *nf* cut.

entailler [ɑ̃taje] *vt* to cut.

entamer [ɑ̃tame] *vt* **1.** (*commencer*) to start (on); (- *bouteille*) to start, to open. **2.** (*capital*) to dip into. **3.** (*cuir, réputation*) to damage. **4.** (*courage*) to shake.

entartrer [ɑ̃tartre] *vt* to fur up. ▶ **s'entartrer** *vp* to fur up.

entasser [ɑ̃tase] *vt* **1.** (*accumuler, multiplier*) to pile up. **2.** (*serrer*) to squeeze. ▶ **s'entasser** *vp* **1.** (*objets*) to pile up. **2.** (*personnes*): **s'~ dans** to squeeze into.

entendement [ɑ̃tɑ̃dmɑ̃] *nm* understanding.

entendre [ɑ̃tɑ̃dr] *vt* **1.** (*percevoir, écouter*) to hear; ~ **parler de qqch** to hear of OU about sthg. **2.** *sout* (*comprendre*) to understand; **laisser ~ que** to imply that. **3.** *sout* (*vouloir*): ~ **faire qqch** to intend to do sthg. **4.** (*vouloir dire*) to mean. ▶ **s'entendre** *vp* **1.** (*sympathiser*): **s'~ avec qqn** to get on with sb. **2.** (*s'accorder*) to agree.

entendu, -e [ɑ̃tɑ̃dy] ◆ *pp* → **entendre**. ◆ *adj* **1.** (*compris*) agreed, understood.

2. (*complice*) knowing.

entente [ātāt] *nf* **1.** (*harmonie*) understanding. **2.** (*accord*) agreement.

entériner [āterine] *vt* to ratify.

enterrement [āterrmā] *nm* burial.

enterrer [ātere] *vt litt & fig* to bury; ~ **sa vie de garçon** to have a stag party.

en-tête [ātɛt] (*pl* **en-têtes**) *nm* heading.

entêté, -e [ātete] *adj* stubborn.

entêter [ātete] ▶ **s'entêter** *vp* to persist; **s'~ à faire qqch** to persist in doing sthg.

enthousiasme [ātuzjasm] *nm* enthusiasm.

enthousiasmer [ātuzjasme] *vt* to fill with enthusiasm. ▶ **s'enthousiasmer** *vp*: **s'~ pour** to be enthusiastic about.

enticher [ātiʃe] ▶ **s'enticher** *vp*: **s'~ de qqn/qqch** to become obsessed with sb/sthg.

entier, -ère [ātje, ɛr] *adj* whole, entire. ▶ **en entier** *loc adv* in its/their entirety.

entièrement [ātjɛrmā] *adv* **1.** (*complètement*) fully. **2.** (*pleinement*) wholly, entirely.

entité [ātite] *nf* entity.

entonner [ātɔne] *vt* (*chant*) to strike up.

entonnoir [ātɔnwar] *nm* **1.** (*instrument*) funnel. **2.** (*cavité*) crater.

entorse [ātɔrs] *nf* (MÉD) sprain; **se faire une ~ à la cheville/au poignet** to sprain one's ankle/wrist.

entortiller [ātɔrtije] *vt* **1.** (*entrelacer*) to twist. **2.** (*envelopper*): ~ **qqch autour de qqch** to wrap sthg round sthg. **3.** *fam fig* (*personne*) to sweet-talk.

entourage [āturaʒ] *nm* (*gén*) circle; (*d'un roi, d'un président*) entourage.

entourer [āture] *vt* **1.** (*enclore, encercler*): ~ **(de)** to surround (with). **2.** *fig* (*soutenir*) to rally round.

entourloupette [āturlupɛt] *nf fam* dirty trick.

entracte [ātrakt] *nm* interval; *fig* interlude.

entraide [ātrɛd] *nf* mutual assistance.

entrailles [ātraj] *nfpl* **1.** (*intestins*) entrails. **2.** *sout* (*profondeurs*) depths.

entrain [ātrɛ̃] *nm* drive.

entraînement [ātrɛnmā] *nm* (*préparation*) practice; (SPORT) training.

entraîner [ātrene] *vt* **1.** (TECHNOL) to drive. **2.** (*tirer*) to pull. **3.** (*susciter*) to lead to. **4.** (SPORT) to coach. **5.** (*emmener*) to take along. **6.** (*séduire*) to influence; ~ **qqn à faire qqch** to talk sb into

sthg. ▶ **s'entraîner** *vp* to practise; (SPORT) to train; **s'~ à faire qqch** to practise doing sthg.

entraîneur, -euse [ātrɛnœr, øz] *nm, f* trainer, coach.

entrave [ātrav] *nf* hobble; *fig* obstruction.

entraver [ātrave] *vt* to hobble; *fig* to hinder.

entre [ātr] *prép* **1.** (*gén*) between; ~ **nous** between you and me, between ourselves. **2.** (*parmi*) among; **l'un d'~ nous ira** one of us will go; **généralement ils restent ~ eux** they tend to keep themselves to themselves; **ils se battent ~ eux** they're fighting among ou amongst themselves.

entrebâiller [ātrəbaje] *vt* to open slightly.

entrechoquer [ātrəʃɔke] *vt* to bang together. ▶ **s'entrechoquer** *vp* to bang into each other.

entrecôte [ātrəkot] *nf* entrecôte.

entrecouper [ātrəkupe] *vt* to intersperse.

entrecroiser [ātrəkrwaze] *vt* to interlace. ▶ **s'entrecroiser** *vp* to intersect.

entrée [ātre] *nf* **1.** (*arrivée, accès*) entry, entrance; '~ **interdite**' 'no admittance'; '~ **libre**' (*dans musée*) 'admission free'; (*dans boutique*) 'browsers welcome'. **2.** (*porte*) entrance. **3.** (*vestibule*) (entrance) hall. **4.** (*billet*) ticket. **5.** (*plat*) starter, first course.

entrefaites [ātrəfɛt] *nfpl*: **sur ces ~** just at that moment.

entrefilet [ātrəfilɛ] *nm* paragraph.

entrejambe, entre-jambes [ātrəʒāb] *nm* crotch.

entrelacer [ātrəlase] *vt* to intertwine.

entrelarder [ātrəlarde] *vt* **1.** (CULIN) to lard. **2.** *fam fig* (*discours*): ~ **de** to lace with.

entremêler [ātrəmele] *vt* to mix; ~ **de** to mix with.

entremets [ātrəmɛ] *nm* dessert.

entremettre [ātrəmɛtr] ▶ **s'entremettre** *vp*: **s'~ (dans)** to mediate (in).

entremise [ātrəmiz] *nf* intervention; **par l'~ de** through.

entrepont [ātrəpɔ̃] *nm* steerage.

entreposer [ātrəpoze] *vt* to store.

entrepôt [ātrəpo] *nm* warehouse.

entreprendre [ātrəprādr] *vt* to undertake; (*commencer*) to start; ~ **de faire qqch** to undertake to do sthg.

entrepreneur, -euse [ātrəprənœr,

øz] *nm, f* (*de services & CONSTR*) contractor.
entrepris, -e [ātrəpri, iz] *pp* → **entreprendre**.
entreprise [ātrəpriz] *nf* **1.** (*travail, initiative*) enterprise. **2.** (*société*) company.
entrer [ātre] ◆ *vi* (*aux: être*) **1.** (*pénétrer*) to enter, to go/come in; ~ **dans** (*gén*) to enter; (*pièce*) to go/come into; (*bain, voiture*) to get into; *fig* (*sujet*) to go into; ~ **par** to go in *ou* enter by; **faire** ~ **qqn** to show sb in; **faire** ~ **qqch** to bring sthg in. **2.** (*faire partie*): ~ **dans** to go into, to be part of. **3.** (*être admis, devenir membre*): ~ **à** (*club, parti*) to join; ~ **dans** (*les affaires, l'enseignement*) to go into; (*la police, l'armée*) to join; ~ **à l'université** to enter university; ~ **à l'hôpital** to go into hospital. ◆ *vt* (*aux: avoir*) **1.** (*gén*) to bring in. **2.** (*INFORM*) to enter, to input.
entresol [ātrəsɔl] *nm* mezzanine.
entre-temps [ātrətā] *adv* meanwhile.
entretenir [ātrətnir] *vt* **1.** (*faire durer*) to keep alive. **2.** (*cultiver*) to maintain. **3.** (*soigner*) to look after. **4.** (*personne, famille*) to support. **5.** (*parler à*): ~ **qqn de qqch** to speak to sb about sthg. ▶ **s'entretenir** *vp* (*se parler*): **s'~ (de)** to talk (about).
entretien [ātrətjē] *nm* **1.** (*de voiture, jardin*) maintenance, upkeep. **2.** (*conversation*) discussion; (*colloque*) debate.
entre-tuer [ātrətɥe] ▶ **s'entre-tuer** *vp* to kill each other.
entrevoir [ātrəvwar] *vt* **1.** (*distinguer*) to make out. **2.** (*voir rapidement*) to see briefly. **3.** *fig* (*deviner*) to glimpse.
entrevu, -e [ātrəvy] *pp* → **entrevoir**.
entrevue [ātrəvy] *nf* meeting.
entrouvert, -e [ātruver, ɛrt] ◆ *pp* → **entrouvrir**. ◆ *adj* half-open.
entrouvrir [ātruvrir] *vt* to open partly. ▶ **s'entrouvrir** *vp* to open partly.
énumération [enymerasjɔ̃] *nf* enumeration.
énumérer [enymere] *vt* to enumerate.
env. (*abr de* environ) approx.
envahir [āvair] *vt* **1.** (*gén & MIL*) to invade. **2.** *fig* (*suj: sommeil, doute*) to overcome. **3.** *fig* (*déranger*) to intrude on.
envahissant, -e [āvaisā, āt] *adj* **1.** (*herbes*) invasive. **2.** (*personne*) intrusive.
envahisseur [āvaisœr] *nm* invader.
enveloppe [āvlɔp] *nf* **1.** (*de lettre*) envelope. **2.** (*d'emballage*) covering. **3.** (*membrane*) membrane; (*de graine*) husk.
envelopper [āvlɔpe] *vt* **1.** (*emballer*) to

wrap (up). **2.** (*suj: brouillard*) to envelop. **3.** (*déguiser*) to mask. ▶ **s'envelopper** *vp*: **s'~ dans** to wrap o.s. up in.
envenimer [āvnime] *vt* **1.** (*blessure*) to infect. **2.** *fig* (*querelle*) to poison. ▶ **s'envenimer** *vp* **1.** (*s'infecter*) to become infected. **2.** *fig* (*se détériorer*) to become poisoned.
envergure [āvɛrgyr] *nf* **1.** (*largeur*) span; (*d'oiseau, d'avion*) wingspan. **2.** *fig* (*qualité*) calibre. **3.** *fig* (*importance*) scope; **prendre de l'~** to expand.
envers¹ [āvɛr] *prép* towards.
envers² [āver] *nm* **1.** (*de tissu*) wrong side; (*de feuillet etc*) back; (*de médaille*) reverse. **2.** (*face cachée*) other side. ▶ **à l'envers** *loc adv* (*vêtement*) inside out; (*portrait, feuille*) upside down; *fig* the wrong way.
envi [āvi] ▶ **à l'envi** *loc adv littéraire* trying to outdo each other.
envie [āvi] *nf* **1.** (*désir*) desire; **avoir ~ de qqch/de faire qqch** to feel like sthg/like doing sthg, to want sthg/to do sthg. **2.** (*convoitise*) envy; **ce tailleur me fait ~** I covet that suit.
envier [āvje] *vt* to envy.
envieux, -euse [āvjø, øz] ◆ *adj* envious. ◆ *nm, f* envious person; **faire des ~** to make other people envious.
environ [āvirɔ̃] *adv* (*à peu près*) about.
environnement [āvirɔnmā] *nm* environment.
environs [āvirɔ̃] *nmpl* (surrounding) area (*sg*); **aux ~ de** (*lieu*) near; (*époque*) round about, around.
envisager [āvizaʒe] *vt* to consider; ~ **de faire qqch** to be considering doing sthg.
envoi [āvwa] *nm* **1.** (*action*) sending, dispatch. **2.** (*colis*) parcel.
envol [āvɔl] *nm* takeoff.
envolée [āvɔle] *nf* **1.** (*d'oiseaux & fig*) flight. **2.** (*augmentation*): **l'~ du dollar** the rapid rise in the value of the dollar.
envoler [āvɔle] ▶ **s'envoler** *vp* **1.** (*oiseau*) to fly away. **2.** (*avion*) to take off. **3.** (*disparaître*) to disappear into thin air.
envoûter [āvute] *vt* to bewitch.
envoyé, -e [āvwaje] ◆ *adj*: **bien ~** well-aimed. ◆ *nm, f* envoy.
envoyer [āvwaje] *vt* to send; ~ **qqch à qqn** (*expédier*) to send sb sthg, to send sthg to sb; (*jeter*) to throw sb sthg, to throw sthg to sb; ~ **qqn faire qqch** to send sb to do sthg; ~ **chercher qqn/qqch** to send for sb/sthg.

épagneul [epaɲœl] nm spaniel.

épais, -aisse [epɛ, ɛs] adj 1. (large, dense) thick. 2. (grossier) crude.

épaisseur [epɛsœr] nf 1. (largeur, densité) thickness. fig (consistance) depth.

épaissir [epesir] vt & vi to thicken. ► **s'épaissir** vp 1. (liquide) to thicken. 2. fig (mystère) to deepen.

épanchement [epɑ̃ʃmɑ̃] nm 1. (effusion) outpouring. 2. (MÉD) effusion.

épancher [epɑ̃ʃe] vt to pour out. ► **s'épancher** vp (se confier) to pour one's heart out.

épanoui, -e [epanwi] adj 1. (fleur) in full bloom. 2. (expression) radiant. 3. (corps) fully formed; **aux formes ~es** well-rounded.

épanouir [epanwir] vt (personne) to make happy. ► **s'épanouir** vp 1. (fleur) to open. 2. (visage) to light up. 3. (corps) to fill out. 4. (personnalité) to blossom.

épanouissement [epanwismɑ̃] nm 1. (de fleur) blooming, opening. 2. (de visage) brightening. 3. (de corps) filling out. 4. (de personnalité) flowering.

épargnant, -e [eparɲɑ̃, ɑ̃t] nm, f saver.

épargne [eparɲ] nf 1. (action, vertu) saving. 2. (somme) savings (pl); **~ logement** savings account (to buy property).

épargner [eparɲe] vt 1. (gén) to spare; **~ qqch à qqn** to spare sb sthg. 2. (économiser) to save.

éparpiller [eparpije] vt 1. (choses, personnes) to scatter. 2. fig (forces) to dissipate. ► **s'éparpiller** vp 1. (se disperser) to scatter. 2. fig (perdre son temps) to lack focus.

épars, -e [epar, ars] adj sout (objets) scattered; (végétation, cheveux) sparse.

épatant, -e [epatɑ̃, ɑ̃t] adj fam great.

épaté, -e [epate] adj 1. (nez) flat. 2. fam (étonné) amazed.

épaule [epol] nf shoulder.

épauler [epole] vt to support, to back up.

épaulette [epolet] nf 1. (MIL) epaulet. 2. (rembourrage) shoulder pad.

épave [epav] nf wreck.

épée [epe] nf sword.

épeler [eple] vt to spell.

épépiner [epepine] vt to seed.

éperdu, -e [eperdy] adj (sentiment) passionate; **~ de** (personne) overcome with.

éperon [eprɔ̃] nm (de cavalier, de montagne) spur; (de navire) ram.

éperonner [eprɔne] vt to spur on.

épervier [epervje] nm sparrowhawk.

éphémère [efemɛr] ◆ adj (bref) ephemeral, fleeting. ◆ nm (ZOOL) mayfly.

éphéméride [efemerid] nf tear-off calendar.

épi [epi] nm 1. (de céréale) ear. 2. (cheveux) tuft.

épice [epis] nf spice.

épicé, -e [epise] adj spicy.

épicéa [episea] nm spruce.

épicer [epise] vt (plat) to spice.

épicerie [episri] nf 1. (magasin) grocer's (shop). 2. (denrées) groceries (pl).

épicier, -ère [episje, ɛr] nm, f grocer.

épidémie [epidemi] nf epidemic.

épiderme [epiderm] nm epidermis.

épier [epje] vt 1. (espionner) to spy on. 2. (observer) to look for.

épilation [epilasjɔ̃] nf hair removal.

épilepsie [epilɛpsi] nf epilepsy.

épiler [epile] vt (jambes) to remove hair from; (sourcils) to pluck. ► **s'épiler** vp: **s'~ les jambes** to remove the hair from one's legs; **s'~ les sourcils** to pluck one's eyebrows.

épilogue [epilɔg] nm 1. (de roman) epilogue. 2. (d'affaire) outcome.

épinards [epinar] nmpl spinach (U).

épine [epin] nf (piquant - de rosier) thorn; (- de hérisson) spine.

épineux, -euse [epinø, øz] adj thorny.

épingle [epɛ̃gl] nf (instrument) pin.

épingler [epɛ̃gle] vt 1. (fixer) to pin (up). 2. fam fig (arrêter) to nab, to nick Br.

épinière [epinjɛr] → **moelle**.

Épiphanie [epifani] nf Epiphany.

épique [epik] adj epic.

épiscopal, -e, -aux [episkɔpal, o] adj episcopal.

épisode [epizɔd] nm episode.

épisodique [epizɔdik] adj 1. (occasionnel) occasional. 2. (secondaire) minor.

épistolaire [epistɔlɛr] adj 1. (échange) of letters; **être en relations ~s avec qqn** to be in (regular) correspondence with sb. 2. (roman) epistolary.

épitaphe [epitaf] nf epitaph.

épithète [epitɛt] ◆ nf 1. (GRAM) attribute. 2. (qualificatif) term. ◆ adj attributive.

épître [epitr] nf epistle.

éploré, -e [eplɔre] adj (personne) in tears; (visage, air) tearful.

épluche-légumes [eplyʃlegym] nm inv potato peeler.

éplucher [eplyʃe] vt 1. (légumes) to

peel. **2.** (*textes*) to dissect; (*comptes*) to scrutinize.

épluchure [eplyʃyr] *nf* peelings (*pl*).

éponge [epɔ̃ʒ] *nf* sponge.

éponger [epɔ̃ʒe] *vt* **1.** (*liquide, déficit*) to mop up. **2.** (*visage*) to mop, to wipe.

épopée [epɔpe] *nf* epic.

époque [epɔk] *nf* **1.** (*de l'année*) time; à l'~ at the time. **2.** (*de l'histoire*) period.

épouiller [epuje] *vt* to delouse.

époumoner [epumɔne] ▶ **s'époumoner** *vp* to shout o.s. hoarse.

épouse → **époux**.

épouser [epuze] *vt* **1.** (*personne*) to marry. **2.** (*forme*) to hug. **3.** *fig* (*idée, principe*) to espouse.

épousseter [epuste] *vt* to dust.

époustouflant, -e [epustuflɑ̃, ɑ̃t] *adj fam* amazing.

épouvantable [epuvɑ̃tabl] *adj* dreadful.

épouvantail [epuvɑ̃taj] *nm* (*à moineaux*) scarecrow; *fig* bogeyman.

épouvanter [epuvɑ̃te] *vt* to terrify.

époux, épouse [epu, epuz] *nm, f* spouse.

éprendre [eprɑ̃dr] ▶ **s'éprendre** *vp sout*: **s'~ de** to fall in love with.

épreuve [eprœv] *nf* **1.** (*essai, examen*) test; à l'~ **du feu** fireproof; à l'~ **des balles** bullet-proof; ~ **de force** *fig* trial of strength. **2.** (*malheur*) ordeal. **3.** (SPORT) event. **4.** (TYPO) proof. **5.** (PHOT) print.

épris, -e [epri, iz] ♦ *pp* → **éprendre**. ♦ *adj sout*: ~ **de** in love with.

éprouver [epruve] *vt* **1.** (*tester*) to test. **2.** (*ressentir*) to feel. **3.** (*faire souffrir*) to distress; **être éprouvé par** to be afflicted by. **4.** (*difficultés, problèmes*) to experience.

éprouvette [epruvɛt] *nf* **1.** (*tube à essai*) test tube. **2.** (*échantillon*) sample.

EPS (*abr de* **éducation physique et sportive**) *nf* PE.

épuisé, -e [epɥize] *adj* **1.** (*personne, corps*) exhausted. **2.** (*marchandise*) sold out, out of stock; (*livre*) out of print.

épuisement [epɥizmɑ̃] *nm* exhaustion.

épuiser [epɥize] *vt* to exhaust.

épuisette [epɥizɛt] *nf* landing net.

épurer [epyre] *vt* **1.** (*eau, huile*) to purify. **2.** (POLIT) to purge.

équarrir [ekarir] *vt* **1.** (*animal*) to cut up. **2.** (*poutre*) to square.

équateur [ekwatœr] *nm* equator.

Équateur [ekwatœr] *nm*: l'~ Ecuador.

équation [ekwasjɔ̃] *nf* equation.

équatorial, -e, -aux [ekwatɔrjal, o] *adj* equatorial.

équerre [ekɛr] *nf* (*instrument*) set square; (*en T*) T-square.

équestre [ekɛstr] *adj* equestrian.

équilatéral, -e, -aux [ekɥilateral, o] *adj* equilateral.

équilibre [ekilibr] *nm* **1.** (*gén*) balance. **2.** (*psychique*) stability.

équilibré, -e [ekilibre] *adj* **1.** (*personne*) well-balanced. **2.** (*vie*) stable. **3.** (ARCHIT): **aux proportions ~es** well-proportioned.

équilibrer [ekilibre] *vt* to balance. ▶ **s'équilibrer** *vp* to balance each other out.

équilibriste [ekilibrist] *nmf* tightrope walker.

équipage [ekipaʒ] *nm* crew.

équipe [ekip] *nf* team.

équipé, -e [ekipe] *adj*: **cuisine ~e** fitted kitchen.

équipement [ekipmɑ̃] *nm* **1.** (*matériel*) equipment. **2.** (*aménagement*) facilities (*pl*); ~s **sportifs/scolaires** sports/educational facilities.

équiper [ekipe] *vt* **1.** (*navire, armée*) to equip. **2.** (*personne, local*) to equip, to fit out; ~ **qqn/qqch de** to equip sb/sthg with, to fit sb/sthg out with. ▶ **s'équiper** *vp*: **s'~ (de)** to equip o.s. (with).

équipier, -ère [ekipje, ɛr] *nm, f* team member.

équitable [ekitabl] *adj* fair.

équitation [ekitasjɔ̃] *nf* riding, horse-riding.

équité [ekite] *nf* fairness.

équivalent, -e [ekivalɑ̃, ɑ̃t] *adj* equivalent. ▶ **équivalent** *nm* equivalent.

équivaloir [ekivalwar] *vi*: ~ **à** to be equivalent to.

équivoque [ekivɔk] ♦ *adj* **1.** (*ambigu*) ambiguous. **2.** (*mystérieux*) dubious. ♦ *nf* ambiguity; **sans** ~ unequivocal (*adj*), unequivocally (*adv*).

érable [erabl] *nm* maple.

éradiquer [eradike] *vt* to eradicate.

érafler [erafle] *vt* **1.** (*peau*) to scratch. **2.** (*mur, voiture*) to scrape.

éraflure [eraflyr] *nf* **1.** (*de peau*) scratch. **2.** (*de mur, voiture*) scrape.

éraillé, -e [eraje] *adj* (*voix*) hoarse.

ère [ɛr] *nf* era.

érection [erɛksjɔ̃] *nf* erection.

éreintant, -e [erɛ̃tɑ̃, ɑ̃t] *adj* exhausting.

éreinter [erɛ̃te] *vt* **1.** (*fatiguer*) to

exhaust. **2.** (*critiquer*) to pull to pieces.
ergonomique [ɛrgɔnɔmik]   *adj*
ergonomic.
ériger [eriʒe] *vt* **1.** (*monument*) to erect.
2. (*tribunal*) to set up. **3.** *fig* (*transformer*):
~ qqn en to set sb up as.
ermite [ɛrmit] *nm* hermit.
éroder [erɔde] *vt* to erode.
érogène [erɔʒɛn] *adj* erogenous.
érosion [erozjɔ̃] *nf* erosion.
érotique [erɔtik] *adj* erotic.
érotisme [erɔtism] *nm* eroticism.
errance [ɛrɑ̃s] *nf* wandering.
erratum [eratɔm] (*pl* **errata** [erata]) *nm*
erratum.
errer [ere] *vi* to wander.
erreur [ɛrœr] *nf* mistake; **par ~** by mistake.
erroné, -e [ɛrɔne] *adj* sout wrong.
ersatz [ɛrzats] *nm inv* ersatz.
éructer [erykte] *vi* to belch.
érudit, -e [erydi, it] ◆ *adj* erudite,
learned. ◆ *nm, f* learned person.
éruption [erypsjɔ̃] *nf* **1.** (MÉD) rash.
2. (*de volcan*) eruption.
es → **être**.
ès [ɛs] *prép* of (*in certain titles*); **docteur ~
lettres** ≃ PhD, doctor of philosophy.
escabeau, -x [ɛskabo] *nm* **1.** (*échelle*)
stepladder. **2.** *vieilli* (*tabouret*) stool.
escadre [ɛskadr] *nf* **1.** (*navires*) fleet.
2. (*avions*) wing.
escadrille [ɛskadrij]   *nf* **1.** (*navires*)
flotilla. **2.** (*avions*) flight.
escadron [ɛskadrɔ̃] *nm* squadron.
escalade [ɛskalad] *nf* **1.** (*de montagne,
grille*) climbing; **mur d'~** climbing wall.
2. (*des prix, de violence*) escalation.
escalader [ɛskalade] *vt* to climb.
escale [ɛskal] *nf* **1.** (*lieu - pour navire*)
port of call; (*- pour avion*) stopover.
2. (*arrêt - de navire*) call; (*- d'avion*)
stopover, stop; **faire ~ à** (*navire*) to put
in at, to call at; (*avion*) to stop over at.
escalier [ɛskalje]   *nm* stairs (*pl*);
descendre/monter l'~ to go downstairs/
upstairs; **~ roulant** ou **mécanique** escalator.
escalope [ɛskalɔp] *nf* escalope.
escamotable [ɛskamɔtabl] *adj* **1.** (*train
d'atterrissage*) retractable; (*antenne*) telescopic. **2.** (*table*) folding.
escamoter [ɛskamɔte] *vt* **1.** (*faire disparaître*) to make disappear. **2.** (*voler*) to
lift. **3.** (*rentrer*) to retract. **4.** (*phrase, mot*)
to swallow. **5.** (*éluder - question*) to
evade; (*- objection*) to get round.
escapade [ɛskapad] *nf* **1.** (*voyage*) out-

ing. **2.** (*fugue*) escapade.
escargot [ɛskargo] *nm* snail.
escarmouche [ɛskarmuʃ] *nf* skirmish.
escarpé, -e [ɛskarpe] *adj* steep.
escarpement [ɛskarpəmɑ̃] *nm* **1.** (*de
pente*) steep slope. **2.** (GÉOGR) escarp-
ment.
escarpin [ɛskarpɛ̃] *nm* court shoe Br,
pump Am.
escarre [ɛskar] *nf* bedsore, pressure
sore.
escient [esjɑ̃] *nm*: **à bon ~** advisedly; **à
mauvais ~** ill-advisedly.
esclaffer [ɛsklafe] ► **s'esclaffer** *vp* to
burst out laughing.
esclandre [ɛsklɑ̃dr] *nm sout* scene.
esclavage [ɛsklavaʒ] *nm* slavery.
esclave [ɛsklav] ◆ *nmf* slave. ◆ *adj*:
être ~ de to be a slave to.
escompte [ɛskɔ̃t] *nm* discount.
escompter [ɛskɔ̃te] *vt* **1.** (*prévoir*) to
count on. **2.** (FIN) to discount.
escorte [ɛskɔrt] *nf* escort.
escorter [ɛskɔrte] *vt* to escort.
escouade [ɛskwad] *nf* squad.
escrime [ɛskrim] *nf* fencing.
escrimer [ɛskrime] ► **s'escrimer** *vp*:
s'~ à faire qqch to work (away) at doing
sthg.
escroc [ɛskro] *nm* swindler.
escroquer [ɛskrɔke] *vt* to swindle; **~
qqch à qqn** to swindle sb out of sthg.
escroquerie [ɛskrɔkri] *nf* swindle,
swindling (U).
eskimo, Eskimo → **esquimau**.
espace [ɛspas] *nm* space; **~ vert** green
space, green area.
espacer [ɛspase] *vt* **1.** (*dans l'espace*) to
space out. **2.** (*dans le temps - visites*) to
space out; (*- paiements*) to spread out.
espadon [ɛspadɔ̃] *nm* (*poisson*) swordfish.
espadrille [ɛspadrij] *nf* espadrille.
Espagne [ɛspaɲ] *nf*: **l'~** Spain.
espagnol, -e [ɛspaɲɔl] *adj* Spanish.
► **espagnol** *nm* (*langue*) Spanish.
► **Espagnol, -e** *nm, f* Spaniard; **les
Espagnols** the Spanish.
espèce [ɛspɛs] *nf* **1.** (BIOL, BOT & ZOOL)
species. **2.** (*sorte*) kind, sort; **~ d'idiot!**
you stupid fool! ► **espèces** *nfpl* cash;
payer en ~s to pay (in) cash.
espérance [ɛsperɑ̃s] *nf* hope; **~ de vie**
life expectancy.
espérer [ɛspere] ◆ *vt* to hope for; **~
que** to hope (that); **~ faire qqch** to hope
to do sthg. ◆ *vi* to hope; **~ en qqn/qqch**
to trust in sb/sthg.

espiègle [ɛspjɛgl] *adj* mischievous.

espion, -onne [ɛspjɔ̃, ɔn] *nm, f* spy.

espionnage [ɛspjɔnaʒ] *nm* spying; ~ **industriel** industrial espionage.

espionner [ɛspjɔne] *vt* to spy on.

esplanade [ɛsplanad] *nf* esplanade.

espoir [ɛspwar] *nm* hope.

esprit [ɛspri] *nm* **1.** (*entendement, personne, pensée*) mind; **reprendre ses ~s** to recover. **2.** (*attitude*) spirit; ~ **de compétition** competitive spirit; ~ **critique** critical acumen. **3.** (*humour*) wit. **4.** (*fantôme*) spirit, ghost.

esquimau, -aude, -aux, eskimo [ɛskimo, od] *adj* Eskimo. ▶ **Esquimau, -aude** *nm, f*, **Eskimo** *nmf* Eskimo (*beware: the term 'Esquimau', like its English equivalent, is often considered offensive in North America. The term 'Inuit' is preferred*).

esquinter [ɛskɛ̃te] *vt fam* **1.** (*abîmer*) to ruin. **2.** (*critiquer*) to slate Br, to pan. ▶ **s'esquinter** *vp:* **s'~ à faire qqch** to kill o.s. doing sthg.

esquiver [ɛskive] *vt* to dodge. ▶ **s'esquiver** *vp* to slip away.

essai [ɛsɛ] *nm* **1.** (*vérification*) test, testing (U); **à l'~** on trial. **2.** (*tentative*) attempt. **3.** (RUGBY) try.

essaim [ɛsɛ̃] *nm litt & fig* swarm.

essayage [ɛsejaʒ] *nm* fitting.

essayer [ɛseje] *vt* to try; ~ **de faire qqch** to try to do sthg.

essence [ɛsɑ̃s] *nf* **1.** (*fondement, de plante*) essence; **par ~** *sout* in essence. **2.** (*carburant*) petrol Br, gas Am. **3.** (*d'arbre*) species.

essentiel, -elle [ɛsɑ̃sjɛl] *adj* **1.** (*indispensable*) essential. **2.** (*fondamental*) basic. ▶ **essentiel** *nm* **1.** (*point*): **l'~** (*le principal*) the essential ou main thing; (*objets*) the essentials (*pl*). **2.** (*quantité*): **l'~ de** the main ou greater part of.

essentiellement [ɛsɑ̃sjɛlmɑ̃] *adv* **1.** (*avant tout*) above all. **2.** (*par essence*) essentially.

esseulé, -e [ɛsœle] *adj littéraire* forsaken.

essieu [ɛsjø] *nm* axle.

essor [ɛsɔr] *nm* flight, expansion, boom; **prendre son ~** to take flight; *fig* to take off.

essorer [ɛsɔre] *vt* (*à la main, à rouleaux*) to wring out; (*à la machine*) to spin-dry; (*salade*) to spin, to dry.

essoreuse [ɛsɔrøz] *nf* (*à rouleaux*) mangle; (*électrique*) spin-dryer; (*à salade*) salad spinner.

essouffler [ɛsufle] *vt* to make breath-

less. ▶ **s'essouffler** *vp* to be breathless ou out of breath; *fig* to run out of steam.

essuie-glace [ɛsɥiglas] (*pl* **essuie-glaces**) *nm* windscreen wiper Br, windshield wiper Am.

essuie-mains [ɛsɥimɛ̃] *nm inv* hand towel.

essuie-tout [ɛsɥitu] *nm inv* kitchen roll.

essuyer [ɛsɥije] *vt* **1.** (*sécher*) to dry. **2.** (*nettoyer*) to wipe. **3.** *fig* (*subir*) to suffer. ▶ **s'essuyer** *vp* to dry o.s.

est¹ [ɛst] ◆ *nm* east; **un vent d'~** an easterly wind; **à l'~** in the east; **à l'~ (de)** to the east (of). ◆ *adj inv* (*gén*) east; (*province, région*) eastern.

est² [ɛ] → **être**.

estafette [ɛstafɛt] *nf* dispatch-rider; (MIL) liaison officer.

estafilade [ɛstafilad] *nf* slash, gash.

est-allemand, -e [ɛstalmɑ̃, ɑ̃d] *adj* East German.

estampe [ɛstɑ̃p] *nf* print.

estampille [ɛstɑ̃pij] *nf* stamp.

est-ce que [ɛskə] *adv interr:* **est-ce qu'il fait beau?** is the weather good?; ~ **vous aimez l'accordéon?** do you like the accordion?; **où ~ tu es?** where are you?

esthète [ɛstɛt] *nmf* aesthete.

esthétique [ɛstetik] *adj* **1.** (*relatif à la beauté*) aesthetic. **2.** (*harmonieux*) attractive.

estimation [ɛstimasjɔ̃] *nf* estimate, estimation.

estime [ɛstim] *nf* respect, esteem.

estimer [ɛstime] *vt* **1.** (*expertiser*) to value. **2.** (*évaluer*) to estimate; **j'estime la durée du voyage à 2 heures** I reckon the journey time is 2 hours. **3.** (*respecter*) to respect. **4.** (*penser*): ~ **que** to feel (that).

estival, -e, -aux [ɛstival, o] *adj* summer (*avant n*).

estivant, -e [ɛstivɑ̃, ɑ̃t] *nm, f* (summer) holiday-maker Br ou vacationer Am.

estomac [ɛstɔma] *nm* (ANAT) stomach.

estomper [ɛstɔ̃pe] *vt* to blur; *fig* (*douleur*) to lessen. ▶ **s'estomper** *vp* to become blurred; *fig* (*douleur*) to lessen.

Estonie [ɛstɔni] *nf:* **l'~** Estonia.

estrade [ɛstrad] *nf* dais.

estragon [ɛstragɔ̃] *nm* tarragon.

estropié, -e [ɛstrɔpje] ◆ *adj* crippled. ◆ *nm, f* cripple.

estuaire [ɛstɥɛr] *nm* estuary.

esturgeon [ɛstyrʒɔ̃] *nm* sturgeon.

et [e] *conj* **1.** (*gén*) and; **~ moi?** what about me? **2.** (*dans les fractions et les nombres composés*): **vingt ~ un** twenty-one; **il y a deux ans ~ demi** two and a half years ago; **à deux heures ~ demie** at half past two.

ét. (*abr de* **étage**) fl.

ETA (*abr de* **Euskadi ta Askatasuna**) *nf* ETA.

étable [etabl] *nf* cowshed.

établi [etabli] *nm* workbench.

établir [etablir] *vt* **1.** (*gén*) to establish; (*record*) to set. **2.** (*dresser*) to draw up. ▶ **s'établir** *vp* **1.** (*s'installer*) to settle. **2.** (*s'instaurer*) to become established.

établissement [etablismã] *nm* establishment; **~ hospitalier** hospital; **~ scolaire** educational establishment.

étage [etaʒ] *nm* **1.** (*de bâtiment*) storey, floor; **un immeuble à quatre ~s** a four-storey block of flats; **au premier ~** on the first floor Br, on the second floor Am; **~** upstairs. **2.** (*de fusée*) stage.

étagère [etaʒɛr] *nf* **1.** (*rayon*) shelf. **2.** (*meuble*) shelves (*pl*), set of shelves.

étain [etɛ̃] *nm* (*métal*) tin; (*alliage*) pewter.

étais, était *etc* → **être**.

étal [etal] (*pl* **-s** *ou* **étaux** [eto]) *nm* **1.** (*éventaire*) stall. **2.** (*de boucher*) butcher's block.

étalage [etalaʒ] *nm* **1.** (*action, ensemble d'objets*) display; **faire ~ de** *fig* to flaunt. **2.** (*devanture*) window display.

étalagiste [etalaʒist] *nmf* **1.** (*décorateur*) window-dresser. **2.** (*vendeur*) stall-holder.

étaler [etale] *vt* **1.** (*exposer*) to display. **2.** (*étendre*) to spread out. **3.** (*dans le temps*) to stagger. **4.** (*mettre une couche de*) to spread. **5.** (*exhiber*) to parade. ▶ **s'étaler** *vp* **1.** (*s'étendre*) to spread. **2.** (*dans le temps*): **s'~ (sur)** to be spread (over). **3.** *fam* (*tomber*) to come a cropper Br, to fall flat on one's face.

étalon [etalɔ̃] *nm* **1.** (*cheval*) stallion. **2.** (*mesure*) standard.

étamine [etamin] *nf* (*de fleur*) stamen.

étanche [etɑ̃ʃ] *adj* watertight; (*montre*) waterproof.

étancher [etɑ̃ʃe] *vt* **1.** (*sang, larmes*) to stem (the flow of). **2.** (*assouvir*) to quench.

étang [etɑ̃] *nm* pond.

étant → **être**.

étape [etap] *nf* **1.** (*gén*) stage. **2.** (*halte*) stop; **faire ~ à** to break one's journey at.

état [eta] *nm* **1.** (*manière d'être*) state;

être en ~/hors d'~ de faire qqch to be in a/in no fit state to do sthg; **en bon/mauvais ~** in good/poor condition; **en ~ de marche** in working order; **~ d'âme** mood; **~ d'esprit** state of mind; **~ de santé** (state of) health; **être dans tous ses ~s** *fig* to be in a state. **2.** (*métier, statut*) status; **~ civil** (ADMIN) = marital status. **3.** (*inventaire - gén*) inventory; (*- de dépenses*) statement; **~ des lieux** *inventory and inspection of rented property.* ▶ **État** *nm* (*nation*) state; **l'État** the State.

état-major [etamaʒɔr] *nm* **1.** (ADMIN & MIL) staff; (*de parti*) leadership. **2.** (*lieu*) headquarters (*pl*).

États-Unis [etazyni] *nmpl*: **les ~ (d'Amérique)** the United States (of America).

étau [eto] *nm* vice.

étayer [eteje] *vt* to prop up; *fig* to back up.

etc. (*abr de* **et cætera**) etc.

été [ete] ◆ *pp inv* → **être**. ◆ *nm* summer; **en ~** in (the) summer.

éteindre [etɛ̃dr] *vt* (*incendie, bougie, cigarette*) to put out; (*radio, chauffage, lampe*) to turn off, to switch off. ▶ **s'éteindre** *vp* **1.** (*feu, lampe*) to go out. **2.** (*bruit, souvenir*) to fade (away). **3.** *fig & littéraire* (*personne*) to pass away. **4.** (*race*) to die out.

étendard [etɑ̃dar] *nm* standard.

étendre [etɑ̃dr] *vt* **1.** (*déployer*) to stretch; (*journal, linge*) to spread (out). **2.** (*coucher*) to lay. **3.** (*appliquer*) to spread. **4.** (*accroître*) to extend. **5.** (*diluer*) to dilute; (*sauce*) to thin. ▶ **s'étendre** *vp* **1.** (*se coucher*) to lie down. **2.** (*s'étaler au loin*): **s'~ (de/jusqu'à)** to stretch (from/as far as). **3.** (*croître*) to spread. **4.** (*s'attarder*): **s'~ sur** to elaborate on.

étendu, -e [etɑ̃dy] ◆ *pp* → **étendre**. ◆ *adj* **1.** (*bras, main*) outstretched. **2.** (*plaine, connaissances*) extensive. ▶ **étendue** *nf* **1.** (*surface*) area, expanse. **2.** (*durée*) length. **3.** (*importance*) extent. **4.** (MUS) range.

éternel, -elle [etɛrnɛl] *adj* eternal; **ce ne sera pas ~** this won't last for ever.

éterniser [etɛrnize] *vt* (*prolonger*) to drag out. ▶ **s'éterniser** *vp* **1.** (*se prolonger*) to drag out. **2.** *fam* (*rester*) to stay for ever.

éternité [etɛrnite] *nf* eternity.

éternuer [etɛrnɥe] *vi* to sneeze.

êtes → **être**.

étêter [etete] *vt* to cut the head off.

éther [etɛr] *nm* ether.

Éthiopie [etjɔpi] *nf*: **l'~** Ethiopia.

éthique [etik] ◆ *nf* ethics (U or *pl*). ◆ *adj* ethical.

ethnie [ɛtni] *nf* ethnic group.

ethnique [ɛtnik] *adj* ethnic.

ethnologie [ɛtnɔlɔʒi] *nf* ethnology.

éthylisme [etilism] *nm* alcoholism.

étiez, étions *etc* → **être**.

étincelant, -e [etɛ̃slɑ̃, ɑ̃t] *adj* sparkling.

étinceler [etɛ̃sle] *vi* to sparkle.

étincelle [etɛ̃sɛl] *nf* spark.

étioler [etjɔle] ▶ **s'étioler** *vp* (*plante*) to wilt; (*personne*) to weaken; (*mémoire*) to go.

étiqueter [etikte] *vt litt & fig* to label.

étiquette [etiket] *nf* 1. (*marque & fig*) label. 2. (*protocole*) etiquette.

étirer [etire] *vt* to stretch. ▶ **s'étirer** *vp* to stretch.

étoffe [etɔf] *nf* fabric, material.

étoile [etwal] *nf* star; **~ filante** shooting star; **à la belle ~** *fig* under the stars. ▶ **étoile de mer** *nf* starfish.

étoilé, -e [etwale] *adj* 1. (*ciel, nuit*) starry; **la bannière ~e** the Star-Spangled Banner. 2. (*vitre, pare-brise*) shattered.

étole [etɔl] *nf* stole.

étonnant, -e [etɔnɑ̃, ɑ̃t] *adj* astonishing.

étonnement [etɔnmɑ̃] *nm* astonishment, surprise.

étonner [etɔne] *vt* to surprise, to astonish. ▶ **s'étonner** *vp*: **s'~ (de)** to be surprised (by); **s'~ que** (+ *subjonctif*) to be surprised (that).

étouffant, -e [etufɑ̃, ɑ̃t] *adj* stifling.

étouffée [etufe] ▶ **à l'étouffée** *loc adv* steamed; (*viande*) braised.

étouffer [etufe] ◆ *vt* 1. (*gén*) to stifle. 2. (*asphyxier*) to suffocate. 3. (*feu*) to smother. 4. (*scandale, révolte*) to suppress. ◆ *vi* to suffocate. ▶ **s'étouffer** *vp* (*s'étrangler*) to choke.

étourderie [eturdəri] *nf* 1. (*distraction*) thoughtlessness. 2. (*bévue*) careless mistake; (*acte irréfléchi*) thoughtless act.

étourdi, -e [eturdi] ◆ *adj* scatterbrained. ◆ *nm, f* scatterbrain.

étourdir [eturdir] *vt* (*assommer*) to daze.

étourdissement [eturdismɑ̃] *nm* dizzy spell.

étourneau, -x [eturno] *nm* starling.

étrange [etrɑ̃ʒ] *adj* strange.

étranger, -ère [etrɑ̃ʒe, ɛr] ◆ *adj* 1. (*gén*) foreign. 2. (*différent, isolé*) unknown, unfamiliar; **être ~ à qqn** to be unknown to sb; **être ~ à qqch** to have no connection with sthg; **se sentir ~** to feel like an outsider. ◆ *nm, f* 1. (*de nationalité différente*) foreigner. 2. (*inconnu*) stranger. 3. (*exclu*) outsider. ▶ **étranger** *nm*: **à l'~** abroad.

étrangeté [etrɑ̃ʒte] *nf* strangeness.

étranglement [etrɑ̃gləmɑ̃] *nm* 1. (*strangulation*) strangulation. 2. (*rétrécissement*) constriction.

étrangler [etrɑ̃gle] *vt* 1. (*gén*) to choke. 2. (*étrangler*) to strangle. 3. (*réprimer*) to stifle. 4. (*serrer*) to constrict. ▶ **s'étrangler** *vp* (*s'étouffer*) to choke.

étrave [etrav] *nf* stem.

être [ɛtr] ◆ *nm* being; **les ~s vivants/humains** living/human beings. ◆ *v aux* 1. (*pour les temps composés*) to have/to be; **il est parti hier** he left yesterday; **il est déjà arrivé** he has already arrived; **il est né en 1952** he was born in 1952. 2. (*pour le passif*) to be; **la maison a été vendue** the house has been ou was sold. ◆ *v attr* 1. (*état*) to be; **la maison est blanche** the house is white; **il est médecin** he's a doctor; **sois sage!** be good! 2. (*possession*): **~ à qqn** to be sb's, to belong to sb; **c'est à vous, cette voiture?** is this your car?, is this car yours? ◆ *v impers* 1. (*exprimant le temps*): **quelle heure est-il?** what time is it?, what's the time?; **il est dix heures dix** it's ten past ten *Br*, it's ten after ten *Am*. 2. (*suivi d'un adjectif*): **il est ...** it is ...; **il est inutile de** it's useless to; **il serait bon de/que** it would be good to/if, it would be a good idea to/if. ◆ *vi* 1. (*exister*) to be; **n'~ plus** *sout* (*être décédé*) to be no more. 2. (*indique une situation, un état*) to be; **il est à Paris** he's in Paris; **nous sommes au printemps/en été** it's spring/summer. 3. (*indiquant une origine*): **il est de Paris** he's from Paris. ▶ **être à** *v + prép* 1. (*indiquant une obligation*): **c'est à vérifier** it needs to be checked; **c'est à voir** that remains to be seen. 2. (*indiquant une continuité*): **il est toujours à ne rien faire** he never does a thing.

étreindre [etrɛ̃dr] *vt* 1. (*embrasser*) to hug, to embrace. 2. *fig* (*tenailler*) to grip, to clutch. ▶ **s'étreindre** *vp* to embrace each other.

étreinte [etrɛ̃t] *nf* 1. (*enlacement*) embrace. 2. (*pression*) stranglehold.

étrenner [etrene] *vt* to use for the first time.

étrennes [etʀɛn] *nfpl* Christmas box (*sg*).

étrier [etʀije] *nm* stirrup.

étriller [etʀije] *vt* 1. (*cheval*) to curry. 2. (*personne*) to wipe the floor with; (*film*) to tear to pieces.

étriper [etʀipe] *vt* 1. (*animal*) to disembowel. 2. *fam fig* (*tuer*) to murder. ▶ **s'étriper** *vp fam* to tear each other to pieces.

étriqué, -e [etʀike] *adj* 1. (*vêtement*) tight; (*appartement*) cramped. 2. (*mesquin*) narrow.

étroit, -e [etʀwa, at] *adj* 1. (*gén*) narrow. 2. (*intime*) close. 3. (*serré*) tight. ▶ **à l'étroit** *loc adj*: **être à l'~** to be cramped.

étroitesse [etʀwatɛs] *nf* narrowness.

étude [etyd] *nf* 1. (*gén*) study; **à l'~** under consideration; **~ de marché** market research (U). 2. (*de notaire - local*) office; (*- charge*) practice. 3. (*MUS*) étude. ▶ **études** *nfpl* studies; **faire des ~s** to study.

étudiant, -e [etydjɑ̃, ɑ̃t] *nm, f* student.

étudié, -e [etydje] *adj* studied.

étudier [etydje] *vt* to study.

étui [etɥi] *nm* case; **~ à cigarettes/ lunettes** cigarette/glasses case.

étuve [etyv] *nf* 1. (*local*) steam room; *fig* oven. 2. (*appareil*) sterilizer.

étuvée [etyve] ▶ **à l'étuvée** *loc adv* braised.

étymologie [etimɔlɔʒi] *nf* etymology.

eu, -e [y] *pp* → **avoir**.

E-U, E-U A (*abr de* États-Unis (d'Amérique)) *nmpl* US, USA.

eucalyptus [økaliptys] *nm* eucalyptus.

euh [ø] *interj* er.

eunuque [ønyk] *nm* eunuch.

euphémisme [øfemism] *nm* euphemism.

euphorie [øfɔʀi] *nf* euphoria.

euphorisant, -e [øfɔʀizɑ̃, ɑ̃t] *adj* exhilarating. ▶ **euphorisant** *nm* antidepressant.

eurent → **avoir**.

eurodéputé [øʀɔdepyte] *nm* Euro MP.

Europe [øʀɔp] *nf*: **l'~** Europe.

européen, -enne [øʀɔpeɛ̃, ɛn] *adj* European. ▶ **Européen, -enne** *nm, f* European.

eus, eut *etc* → **avoir**.

eût → **avoir**.

euthanasie [øtanazi] *nf* euthanasia.

eux [ø] *pron pers* 1. (*sujet*) they; **ce sont ~ qui me l'ont dit** they're the ones who

told me. 2. (*complément*) them. ▶ **eux-mêmes** *pron pers* themselves.

évacuer [evakɥe] *vt* 1. (*gén*) to evacuate. 2. (*liquide*) to drain.

évadé, -e [evade] *nm, f* escaped prisoner.

évader [evade] ▶ **s'évader** *vp*: **s'~ (de)** to escape (from).

évaluation [evalɥasjɔ̃] *nf* (*action*) valuation; (*résultat*) estimate.

évaluer [evalɥe] *vt* (*distance*) to estimate; (*tableau*) to value; (*risque*) to assess.

évangélique [evɑ̃ʒelik] *adj* evangelical.

évangéliser [evɑ̃ʒelize] *vt* to evangelize.

évangile [evɑ̃ʒil] *nm* gospel.

évanouir [evanwiʀ] ▶ **s'évanouir** *vp* 1. (*défaillir*) to faint. 2. (*disparaître*) to fade.

évanouissement [evanwismɑ̃] *nm* (*syncope*) fainting fit.

évaporer [evapɔʀe] ▶ **s'évaporer** *vp* to evaporate.

évasé, -e [evaze] *adj* flared.

évasif, -ive [evazif, iv] *adj* evasive.

évasion [evazjɔ̃] *nf* escape.

évêché [eveʃe] *nm* (*territoire*) diocese; (*résidence*) bishop's palace.

éveil [evɛj] *nm* awakening; **en ~** on the alert.

éveillé, -e [eveje] *adj* 1. (*qui ne dort pas*) wide awake. 2. (*vif, alerte*) alert.

éveiller [eveje] *vt* to arouse; (*intelligence, dormeur*) to awaken. ▶ **s'éveiller** *vp* 1. (*dormeur*) to wake, to awaken. 2. (*curiosité*) to be aroused. 3. (*esprit, intelligence*) to be awakened. 4. (*s'ouvrir*): **s'~ à qqch** to discover sthg.

événement [evɛnmɑ̃] *nm* event.

événementiel, -elle [evɛnmɑ̃sjɛl] *adj* (*histoire*) factual.

éventail [evɑ̃taj] *nm* 1. (*objet*) fan; **en ~** fan-shaped. 2. (*choix*) range.

éventaire [evɑ̃tɛʀ] *nm* 1. (*étalage*) stall, stand. 2. (*corbeille*) tray.

éventer [evɑ̃te] *vt* 1. (*rafraîchir*) to fan. 2. (*divulguer*) to give away. ▶ **s'éventer** *vp* 1. (*se rafraîchir*) to fan o.s. 2. (*parfum, vin*) to go stale.

éventrer [evɑ̃tʀe] *vt* 1. (*étriper*) to disembowel. 2. (*fendre*) to rip open.

éventualité [evɑ̃tɥalite] *nf* 1. (*possibilité*) possibility. 2. (*circonstance*) eventuality; **dans l'~ de** in the event of.

éventuel, -elle [evɑ̃tɥɛl] *adj* possible.

éventuellement [evɑ̃tɥɛlmɑ̃] *adv* possibly.

évêque [evɛk] nm bishop.

évertuer [evɛrtɥe] ► **s'évertuer** vp: **s'~ à faire qqch** to strive to do sthg.

évidemment [evidamã] adv obviously.

évidence [evidãs] nf (caractère) evidence; (fait) obvious fact; **mettre en ~** to emphasize, to highlight.

évident, -e [evidã, ãt] adj obvious.

évider [evide] vt to hollow out.

évier [evje] nm sink.

évincer [evɛ̃se] vt: **~ qqn (de)** to oust sb (from).

éviter [evite] vt 1. (esquiver) to avoid. 2. (s'abstenir): **~ de faire qqch** to avoid doing sthg. 3. (épargner): **~ qqch à qqn** to save sb sthg.

évocateur, -trice [evɔkatœr, tris] adj (geste, regard) meaningful.

évocation [evɔkasjɔ̃] nf evocation.

évolué, -e [evɔlɥe] adj 1. (développé) developed. 2. (libéral, progressiste) broad-minded.

évoluer [evɔlɥe] vi 1. (changer) to evolve; (personne) to change. 2. (se mouvoir) to move about.

évolution [evɔlysjɔ̃] nf 1. (transformation) development. 2. (BIOL) evolution. 3. (MÉD) progress.

évoquer [evɔke] vt 1. (souvenir) to evoke. 2. (problème) to refer to.

exacerber [ɛgzasɛrbe] vt to heighten.

exact, -e [ɛgzakt] adj 1. (calcul) correct. 2. (récit, copie) exact. 3. (ponctuel) punctual.

exactement [ɛgzaktəmã] adv exactly.

exaction [ɛgzaksjɔ̃] nf extortion.

exactitude [ɛgzaktityd] nf 1. (de calcul, montre) accuracy. 2. (ponctualité) punctuality.

ex æquo [ɛgzeko] ◆ adj inv & nmf inv equal. ◆ adv equal; **troisième ~** third equal.

exagération [ɛgzaʒerasjɔ̃] nf exaggeration.

exagéré, -e [ɛgzaʒere] adj exaggerated.

exagérer [ɛgzaʒere] vt & vi to exaggerate.

exalté, -e [ɛgzalte] ◆ adj (sentiment) elated; (tempérament) over-excited; (imagination) vivid. ◆ nm, f fanatic.

exalter [ɛgzalte] vt to excite. ► **s'exalter** vp to get carried away.

examen [ɛgzamɛ̃] nm examination; (SCOL) exam, examination; **~ médical** medical (examination).

examinateur, -trice [ɛgzaminatœr, tris] nm, f examiner.

examiner [ɛgzamine] vt to examine.

exaspération [ɛgzasperasjɔ̃] nf exasperation.

exaspérer [ɛgzaspere] vt to exasperate.

exaucer [ɛgzose] vt to grant; **~ qqn** to answer sb's prayers.

excédent [ɛksedã] nm surplus; **en ~** surplus (avant n).

excéder [ɛksede] vt 1. (gén) to exceed. 2. (exaspérer) to exasperate.

excellence [ɛkselãs] nf excellence.

excellent, -e [ɛkselã, ãt] adj excellent.

exceller [ɛksele] vi: **~ en ou dans qqch** to excel in ou at sthg; **~ à faire qqch** to excel at doing sthg.

excentré, -e [ɛksãtre] adj: **c'est très ~** it's quite a long way out.

excentrique [ɛksãtrik] ◆ nmf eccentric. ◆ adj 1. (gén) eccentric. 2. (quartier) outlying.

excepté, -e [ɛksɛpte] adj: **tous sont venus, lui ~** everyone came except (for) him. ► **excepté** prép apart from, except.

exception [ɛksɛpsjɔ̃] nf exception; **à l'~ de** except for.

exceptionnel, -elle [ɛksɛpsjɔnɛl] adj exceptional.

excès [ɛksɛ] ◆ nm excess; **~ de zèle** overzealousness. ◆ nmpl excesses.

excessif, -ive [ɛksesif, iv] adj 1. (démesuré) excessive. 2. (extrême) extreme.

excitant, -e [ɛksitã, ãt] adj (stimulant, passionnant) exciting. ► **excitant** nm stimulant.

excitation [ɛksitasjɔ̃] nf 1. (énervement) excitement. 2. (stimulation) encouragement. 3. (MÉD) stimulation.

excité, -e [ɛksite] ◆ adj (énervé) excited. ◆ nm, f hothead.

exciter [ɛksite] vt 1. (gén) to excite. 2. (inciter): **~ qqn (à qqch/à faire qqch)** to incite sb (to sthg/to do sthg). 3. (MÉD) to stimulate.

exclamation [ɛksklamasjɔ̃] nf exclamation.

exclamer [ɛksklame] ► **s'exclamer** vp: **s'~ (devant)** to exclaim (at ou over).

exclu, -e [ɛkskly] ◆ pp → **exclure**. ◆ adj excluded. ◆ nm, f outsider.

exclure [ɛksklyr] vt to exclude; (expulser) to expel.

exclusif, -ive [ɛksklyzif, iv] adj exclusive.

exclusion [ɛksklyzjɔ̃] nf expulsion; à l'~ **de** to the exclusion of.

exclusivement [ɛksklyzivmã] adv (uniquement) exclusively.

exclusivité [ɛksklyzivite] nf 1. (COMM) exclusive rights (pl). 2. (CIN) sole screening rights (pl); **en** ~ exclusively. 3. (de sentiment) exclusiveness.

excommunier [ɛkskɔmynje] vt to excommunicate.

excrément [ɛkskremã] nm (gén pl) excrement (U).

excroissance [ɛkskrwasãs] nf excrescence.

excursion [ɛkskyrsjɔ̃] nf excursion.

excursionniste [ɛkskyrsjɔnist] nmf day-tripper Br, vacationer Am.

excuse [ɛkskyz] nf excuse.

excuser [ɛkskyze] vt to excuse; **excusez-moi** (pour réparer) I'm sorry; (pour demander) excuse me. ► **s'excuser** vp (demander pardon) to apologize; **s'~ de qqch/de faire qqch** to apologize for sth/for doing sth.

exécrable [ɛgzekrabl] adj atrocious.

exécutant, -e [ɛgzekytã, ãt] nm, f 1. (personne) underling. 2. (MUS) performer.

exécuter [ɛgzekyte] vt 1. (réaliser) to carry out; (tableau) to paint. 2. (MUS) to play, to perform. 3. (mettre à mort) to execute. ► **s'exécuter** vp to comply.

exécutif, -ive [ɛgzekytif, iv] adj executive. ► **exécutif** nm: **l'~** the executive.

exécution [ɛgzekysjɔ̃] nf 1. (réalisation) carrying out; (de tableau) painting. 2. (MUS) performance. 3. (mise à mort) execution.

exemplaire [ɛgzãplɛr] ◆ nm copy. ◆ adj exemplary.

exemple [ɛgzãpl] nm example; **par** ~ for example, for instance.

exempté, -e [ɛgzãte] adj: ~ **(de)** exempt (from).

exercer [ɛgzɛrse] vt 1. (entraîner, mettre en usage) to exercise; (autorité, influence) to exert. 2. (métier) to carry on; (médecine) to practise. ► **s'exercer** vp 1. (s'entraîner) to practise; **s'~ à qqch/à faire qqch** to practise sth/doing sth. 2. (se manifester): **s'~ (sur** ou **contre)** to be exerted (on).

exercice [ɛgzɛrsis] nm 1. (gén) exercise. 2. (entraînement) practice. 3. (de métier, fonction) carrying out; **en** ~ in office.

exhaler [ɛgzale] vt littéraire 1. (odeur) to give off. 2. (plainte, soupir) to utter.

► **s'exhaler** vp 1. (odeur) to rise. 2. (plainte, soupir): **s'~ de** to rise from.

exhaustif, -ive [ɛgzostif, iv] adj exhaustive.

exhiber [ɛgzibe] vt (présenter) to show; (faire étalage de) to show off. ► **s'exhiber** vp to make an exhibition of o.s.

exhibitionniste [ɛgzibisjɔnist] nmf exhibitionist.

exhorter [ɛgzɔrte] vt: ~ **qqn à qqch/à faire qqch** to urge sb to sth/to do sth.

exhumer [ɛgzyme] vt to exhume; fig to unearth, to dig up.

exigeant, -e [ɛgziʒã, ãt] adj demanding.

exigence [ɛgziʒãs] nf (demande) demand.

exiger [ɛgziʒe] vt 1. (demander) to demand; ~ **que** (+ subjonctif) to demand that; ~ **qqch de qqn** to demand sth from sb. 2. (nécessiter) to require.

exigible [ɛgziʒibl] adj payable.

exigu, -ë [ɛgzigy] adj cramped.

exil [ɛgzil] nm exile; **en** ~ exiled.

exilé, -e [ɛgzile] nm, f exile.

exiler [ɛgzile] vt to exile. ► **s'exiler** vp 1. (POLIT) to go into exile. 2. fig (partir) to go into seclusion.

existence [ɛgzistãs] nf existence.

exister [ɛgziste] ◆ vi to exist. ◆ v impers: **il existe** (il y a) there is/are.

exode [ɛgzɔd] nm exodus.

exonération [ɛgzɔnerasjɔ̃] nf exemption; ~ **d'impôts** tax exemption.

exorbitant, -e [ɛgzɔrbitã, ãt] adj exorbitant.

exorbité, -e [ɛgzɔrbite] → **œil**.

exorciser [ɛgzɔrsize] vt to exorcize.

exotique [ɛgzɔtik] adj exotic.

exotisme [ɛgzɔtism] nm exoticism.

expansif, -ive [ɛkspãsif, iv] adj expansive.

expansion [ɛkspãsjɔ̃] nf expansion.

expansionniste [ɛkspãsjɔnist] nmf & adj expansionist.

expatrié, -e [ɛkspatrije] adj & nm, f expatriate.

expatrier [ɛkspatrije] vt to expatriate. ► **s'expatrier** vp to leave one's country.

expédier [ɛkspedje] vt 1. (lettre, marchandise) to send, to dispatch. 2. (personne) to get rid of; (question) to dispose of. 3. (travail) to dash off.

expéditeur, -trice [ɛkspeditœr, tris] nm, f sender.

expéditif, -ive [ɛkspeditif, iv] adj quick, expeditious.

expédition [εkspedisjɔ̃] nf 1. (envoi) sending. 2. (voyage, campagne militaire) expedition.

expérience [εksperjɑ̃s] nf 1. (pratique) experience; **avoir de l'~** to have experience, to be experienced. 2. (essai) experiment.

expérimental, -e, -aux [εksperimɑ̃tal, o] adj experimental.

expérimenté, -e [εksperimɑ̃te] adj experienced.

expert, -e [εkspεr, εrt] adj expert. ▶ **expert** nm expert.

expert-comptable [εkspεrkɔ̃tabl] nm chartered accountant Br, certified public accountant Am.

expertise [εkspεrtiz] nf 1. (examen) expert appraisal; (estimation) (expert) valuation. 2. (compétence) expertise.

expertiser [εkspεrtize] vt to value; (dégâts) to assess.

expier [εkspje] vt to pay for.

expiration [εkspirasjɔ̃] nf 1. (d'air) exhalation. 2. (de contrat) expiry.

expirer [εkspire] ◆ vt to breathe out. ◆ vi (contrat) to expire.

explicatif, -ive [εksplikatif, iv] adj explanatory.

explication [εksplikasjɔ̃] nf explanation; **~ de texte** (literary) criticism.

explicite [εksplisit] adj explicit.

expliciter [εksplisite] vt to make explicit.

expliquer [εksplike] vt 1. (gén) to explain. 2. (texte) to criticize. ▶ **s'expliquer** vp 1. (se justifier) to explain o.s. 2. (comprendre) to understand. 3. (discuter) to have it out. 4. (devenir compréhensible) to be explained.

exploit [εksplwa] nm exploit, feat; iron (maladresse) achievement.

exploitant, -e [εksplwatɑ̃, ɑ̃t] nm, f farmer.

exploitation [εksplwatasjɔ̃] nf 1. (mise en valeur) running; (de mine) working. 2. (entreprise) operation, concern; **~ agricole** farm. 3. (d'une personne) exploitation.

exploiter [εksplwate] vt 1. (gén) to exploit. 2. (entreprise) to operate, to run.

explorateur, -trice [εksplɔratœr, tris] nm, f explorer.

explorer [εksplɔre] vt to explore.

exploser [εksploze] vi to explode.

explosif, -ive [εksplozif, iv] adj explosive. ▶ **explosif** nm explosive.

explosion [εksplozjɔ̃] nf explosion; (de colère, joie) outburst.

exportateur, -trice [εkspɔrtatœr, tris] ◆ adj exporting. ◆ nm, f exporter.

exportation [εkspɔrtasjɔ̃] nf export.

exporter [εkspɔrte] vt to export.

exposé, -e [εkspoze] adj 1. (orienté): **bien ~** facing the sun. 2. (vulnérable) exposed. ▶ **exposé** nm account; (SCOL) talk.

exposer [εkspoze] vt 1. (orienter, mettre en danger) to expose. 2. (présenter) to display; (- tableaux) to show, to exhibit. 3. (expliquer) to explain, to set out. ▶ **s'exposer** vp: **s'~ à qqch** to expose o.s. to sthg.

exposition [εkspozisjɔ̃] nf 1. (présentation) exhibition. 2. (orientation) aspect.

exprès¹, -esse [εksprεs] adj (formel) formal, express. ▶ **exprès** adj inv (urgent) express.

exprès² [εksprε] adv on purpose; **faire ~ de faire qqch** to do sthg deliberately ou on purpose.

express [εksprεs] ◆ nm inv 1. (train) express. 2. (café) espresso. ◆ adj inv express.

expressément [εkspresemɑ̃] adv expressly.

expressif, -ive [εkspresif, iv] adj expressive.

expression [εkspresjɔ̃] nf expression.

exprimer [εksprime] vt (pensées, sentiments) to express. ▶ **s'exprimer** vp to express o.s.

expropriation [εksprɔprijasjɔ̃] nf expropriation.

exproprier [εksprɔprije] vt to expropriate.

expulser [εkspylse] vt: **~ (de)** to expel (from); (locataire) to evict (from).

expulsion [εkspylsjɔ̃] nf expulsion; (de locataire) eviction.

exquis, -e [εkski, iz] adj 1. (délicieux) exquisite. 2. (distingué, agréable) delightful.

extase [εkstaz] nf ecstasy.

extasier [εkstazje] ▶ **s'extasier** vp: **s'~ devant** to go into ecstasies over.

extensible [εkstɑ̃sibl] adj stretchable.

extension [εkstɑ̃sjɔ̃] nf 1. (étirement) stretching. 2. (élargissement) extension; **par ~** by extension.

exténuer [εkstenɥe] vt to exhaust.

extérieur, -e [εksterjœr] adj 1. (au dehors) outside; (étranger) external; (apparent) outward. 2. (ÉCON & POLIT) foreign. ▶ **extérieur** nm (dehors) outside; (de maison) exterior; **à l'~ de qqch** outside sthg.

extérieurement [ɛksterjœrmɑ̃] adv
1. (à l'extérieur) on the outside, externally. **2.** (en apparence) outwardly.

extérioriser [ɛksterjɔrize] vt to show.

exterminer [ɛkstɛrmine] vt to exterminate.

externat [ɛkstɛrna] nm **1.** (SCOL) day school. **2.** (MÉD) non-resident medical studentship.

externe [ɛkstɛrn] ◆ nmf **1.** (SCOL) day pupil. **2.** (MÉD) non-resident medical student, ≃ extern Am. ◆ adj outer, external.

extincteur [ɛkstɛ̃ktœr] nm (fire) extinguisher.

extinction [ɛkstɛ̃ksjɔ̃] nf **1.** (action d'éteindre) putting out, extinguishing. **2.** fig (disparition) extinction; ~ **de voix** loss of one's voice.

extirper [ɛkstirpe] vt: ~ **(de)** (épine, réponse, secret) to drag (out of); (erreur, préjugé) to root out (of).

extorquer [ɛkstɔrke] vt: ~ **qqch à qqn** to extort sthg from sb.

extra [ɛkstra] ◆ nm inv **1.** (employé) extra help (U). **2.** (chose inhabituelle) (special) treat. ◆ adj inv **1.** (de qualité) top-quality. **2.** fam (génial) great, fantastic.

extraction [ɛkstraksjɔ̃] nf extraction.

extrader [ɛkstrade] vt to extradite.

extraire [ɛkstrɛr] vt: ~ **(de)** to extract (from).

extrait, -e [ɛkstrɛ, ɛt] pp → **extraire**. ▶ **extrait** nm extract; ~ **de naissance** birth certificate.

extraordinaire [ɛkstraɔrdinɛr] adj extraordinary.

extrapoler [ɛkstrapɔle] vt & vi to extrapolate.

extraterrestre [ɛkstratɛrɛstr] nmf & adj extraterrestrial.

extravagance [ɛkstravagɑ̃s] nf extravagance.

extravagant, -e [ɛkstravagɑ̃, ɑ̃t] adj extravagant; (idée, propos) wild.

extraverti, -e [ɛkstravɛrti] nm, f & adj extrovert.

extrême [ɛkstrɛm] ◆ nm extreme; **d'un ~ à l'autre** from one extreme to the other. ◆ adj extreme; (limite) furthest.

extrêmement [ɛkstrɛmmɑ̃] adv extremely.

extrême-onction [ɛkstrɛmɔ̃ksjɔ̃] nf last rites (pl), extreme unction.

Extrême-Orient [ɛkstrɛmɔrjɑ̃] nm: **l'~** the Far East.

extrémiste [ɛkstremist] nmf & adj extremist.

extrémité [ɛkstremite] nf **1.** (bout) end. **2.** (situation critique) straights (pl).

exubérant, -e [ɛgzyberɑ̃, ɑ̃t] adj **1.** (personne) exuberant. **2.** (végétation) luxuriant.

exulter [ɛgzylte] vi to exult.

F

f, F [ɛf] nm inv f, F; **F3** three-room flat Br ou apartment Am. ▶ **F 1.** (abr de **Fahrenheit**) F. **2.** (abr de franc) F, Fr.

fa [fa] nm inv F; (chanté) fa.

fable [fabl] nf fable.

fabricant, -e [fabrikɑ̃, ɑ̃t] nm, f manufacturer.

fabrication [fabrikasjɔ̃] nf manufacture, manufacturing.

fabrique [fabrik] nf (usine) factory.

fabriquer [fabrike] vt **1.** (confectionner) to manufacture, to make. **2.** fam (faire): **qu'est-ce que tu fabriques?** what are you up to? **3.** (inventer) to fabricate.

fabulation [fabylasjɔ̃] nf fabrication.

fabuleux, -euse [fabylø, øz] adj fabulous.

fac [fak] nf fam college, uni Br.

façade [fasad] nf litt & fig facade.

face [fas] nf **1.** (visage) face. **2.** (côté) side; **faire ~ à qqch** (maison) to face sthg, to be opposite sthg; fig (affronter) to face up to sthg; **de ~** from the front; **en ~ de qqn/qqch** opposite sb/sthg. **3.** (aspect) aspect.

face-à-face [fasafas] nm inv debate.

facétie [fasesi] nf practical joke.

facette [fasɛt] nf litt & fig facet.

fâché, -e [faʃe] adj **1.** (en colère) angry; (contrarié) annoyed. **2.** (brouillé) on bad terms.

fâcher [faʃe] vt (mettre en colère) to anger, to make angry; (contrarier) to annoy, to make annoyed. ▶ **se fâcher** vp **1.** (se mettre en colère): **se ~ (contre qqn)** to get angry (with sb). **2.** (se brouiller): **se ~ (avec qqn)** to fall out (with sb).

fâcheux, -euse [faʃø, øz] adj unfortunate.

facile [fasil] adj **1.** (aisé) easy; ~ **à faire/prononcer** easy to do/pronounce.

2. (*peu subtil*) facile. 3. (*conciliant*) easy-going.

facilement [fasilmɑ̃] *adv* easily.

facilité [fasilite] *nf* 1. (*de tâche, problème*) easiness. 2. (*capacité*) ease. 3. (*dispositions*) aptitude. 4. (COMM): **~s de paiement** easy (payment) terms.

faciliter [fasilite] *vt* to make easier.

façon [fasɔ̃] *nf* 1. (*manière*) way. 2. (*travail*) work; (COUTURE) making-up. 3. (*imitation*): **~** imitation leather. ▶ **de façon à** *loc prép* so as to. ▶ **de façon que** *loc conj* (+ *subjonctif*) so that. ▶ **de toute façon** *loc adv* anyway, in any case.

fac-similé [faksimile] (*pl* **fac-similés**) *nm* facsimile.

facteur, -trice [faktœr, tris] *nm, f* (*des postes*) postman (*f* postwoman) Br, mailman (*f* mailwoman) Am. ▶ **facteur** *nm* (*élément & MATHS*) factor.

factice [faktis] *adj* artificial.

faction [faksjɔ̃] *nf* 1. (*groupe*) faction. 2. (MIL): **être en** ou **de ~** to be on guard (duty) ou on sentry duty.

facture [faktyr] *nf* 1. (COMM) invoice; (*de gaz, d'électricité*) bill. 2. (ART) technique.

facturer [faktyre] *vt* (COMM) to invoice.

facultatif, -ive [fakyltatif, iv] *adj* optional.

faculté [fakylte] *nf* 1. (*don & UNIV*) faculty; **~ de lettres/de droit/de médecine** Faculty of Arts/Law/Medicine. 2. (*possibilité*) freedom. 3. (*pouvoir*) power. ▶ **facultés** *nfpl* (*mental*) faculties.

fadaises [fadɛz] *nfpl* drivel (U).

fade [fad] *adj* 1. (*sans saveur*) bland. 2. (*sans intérêt*) insipid.

fagot [fago] *nm* bundle of sticks.

faible [fɛbl] ◆ *adj* 1. (*gén*) weak; **être ~ en maths** to be not very good at maths. 2. (*petit - montant, proportion*) small; (- *revenu*) low. 3. (*lueur, bruit*) faint. ◆ *nmf* weak person; **~ d'esprit** feeble-minded person. ◆ *nm* weakness.

faiblement [fɛbləmɑ̃] *adv* 1. (*mollement*) weakly, feebly. 2. (*imperceptiblement*) faintly. 3. (*peu*) slightly.

faiblesse [fɛblɛs] *nf* 1. (*gén*) weakness. 2. (*petitesse*) smallness.

faiblir [feblir] *vi* 1. (*personne, monnaie*) to weaken. 2. (*forces*) to diminish, to fail. 3. (*tempête, vent*) to die down.

faïence [fajɑ̃s] *nf* earthenware.

faignant, -e = **fainéant**.

faille [faj] ◆ → **falloir**. ◆ *nf* 1. (GÉOL) fault. 2. (*défaut*) flaw.

faillible [fajibl] *adj* fallible.

faillir [fajir] *vi* 1. (*manquer*): **~ à** (*promesse*) not to keep; (*devoir*) not to do. 2. (*être sur le point de*): **~ faire qqch** to nearly ou almost do sthg.

faillite [fajit] *nf* (FIN) bankruptcy; **faire ~** to go bankrupt; **en ~** bankrupt.

faim [fɛ̃] *nf* hunger; **avoir ~** to be hungry.

fainéant, -e [feneɑ̃, ɑ̃t], **feignant, -e, faignant, -e** [fɛɲɑ̃, ɑ̃t] ◆ *adj* lazy, idle. ◆ *nm, f* lazybones.

faire [fɛr] ◆ *vt* 1. (*fabriquer, préparer*) to make; **~ une tarte/du café/un film** to make a tart/coffee/a film; **~ qqch de qqch** (*transformer*) to make sthg into sthg; **~ qqch de qqn** *fig* to make sthg of sb; **il veut en ~ un avocat** he wants him to be a lawyer, he wants to make a lawyer of him. 2. (*s'occuper à, entreprendre*) to do; **qu'est-ce qu'il fait dans la vie?** what does he do (for a living)?; **que fais-tu dimanche?** what are you doing on Sunday? 3. (*étudier*) to do; **~ de l'anglais/des maths/du droit** to do English/maths/law. 4. (*sport, musique*) to play; **~ du football/de la clarinette** to play football/the clarinet. 5. (*effectuer*) to do; **~ le ménage** to do the housework; **~ la cuisine** to cook, to do the cooking; **~ la lessive** to do the washing. 6. (*occasionner*): **~ de la peine à qqn** to hurt sb; **~ du mal à** to harm; **~ du bruit** to make a noise; **ça ne fait rien** it doesn't matter. 7. (*imiter*): **~ le sourd/l'innocent** to act deaf/the innocent. 8. (*calcul, mesure*): **un et un font deux** one and one are ou make two; **ça fait combien (de kilomètres) jusqu'à la mer?** how far is it to the sea?; **la table fait 2 mètres de long** the table is 2 metres long; **~ du 38** to take a size 38. 9. (*coûter*) to be, to cost; **ça vous fait 50 francs en tout** that'll be 50 francs altogether. 10. (*dire*): **'tiens', fit-elle** 'really', she said. 11. **ne ~ que** (*faire sans cesse*) to do nothing but; **elle ne fait que bavarder** she does nothing but gossip, she's always gossiping; **je ne fais que passer** I've just popped in. ◆ *vi* (*agir*) to do, to act; **fais vite!** hurry up!; **que ~?** what is to be done?; **tu ferais bien d'aller voir ce qui se passe** you ought to ou you'd better go and see what's happening; **~ comme chez soi** to make o.s. at home. ◆ *v attr* (*avoir l'air*) to look; **~ démodé/joli** to look old-fashioned/pretty; **ça fait jeune** it makes you look young. ◆ *v substitut* to do; **je lui**

ai dit de prendre une échelle mais il ne l'a pas fait I told him to use a ladder but he didn't; **faites!** please do! ◆ *v impers* **1.** (*climat, temps*): **il fait beau/froid** it's fine/cold; **il fait 20 degrés** it's 20 degrees; **il fait jour/nuit** it's light/dark. **2.** (*exprime la durée, la distance*): **ça fait six mois que je ne l'ai pas vu** it's six months since I last saw him; **ça fait six mois que je fais du portugais** I've been going to Portuguese classes for six months; **ça fait 30 kilomètres qu'on roule sans phares** we've been driving without lights for 30 kilometres. ◆ *v auxiliaire* **1.** (*à l'actif*) to make; **~ démarrer une voiture** to start a car; **~ tomber qqch** to make sthg fall; **l'aspirine fait tomber la fièvre** aspirin brings down the temperature; **~ travailler qqn** to make sb work; **~ traverser la rue à un aveugle** to help a blind man cross the road. **2.** (*au passif*): **~ faire qqch (par qqn)** to have sthg done (by sb); **~ réparer sa voiture/nettoyer ses vitres** to have one's car repaired/one's windows cleaned. ▶ **se faire** *vp* **1.** (*avoir lieu*) to take place. **2.** (*être convenable*): **ça ne se fait pas (de faire qqch)** it's not done (to do sthg). **3.** (*devenir*): **se ~** (+ *adjectif*) to get, to become; **il se fait tard** it's getting late; **se ~ beau** to make o.s. beautiful. **4.** (*causer*) (+ *nom*): **se ~ mal** to hurt o.s.; **se ~ des amis** to make friends; **se ~ une idée sur qqch** to get some idea about sthg. **5.** (+ *infinitif*): **se ~ écraser** to get run over; **se ~ opérer** to have an operation; **se ~ aider (par qqn)** to get help (from sb); **se ~ faire un costume** to have a suit made (for o.s.). **6.** *loc*: **comment se fait-il que ...?** how is it that ...?, how come ...?; **s'en ~** to worry; **ne vous en faites pas!** don't worry! ▶ **se faire à** *vp + prép* to get used to.

faire-part [fɛrpar] *nm inv* announcement.

fais, fait *etc* → **faire**.

faisable [fəzabl] *adj* feasible.

faisan, -e [fəzɑ̃, an] *nm, f* pheasant.

faisandé, -e [fəzɑ̃de] *adj* (CULIN) high.

faisceau, -x [fɛso] *nm* (*rayon*) beam.

faisons → **faire**.

fait, faite [fɛ, fɛt] ◆ *pp* → **faire**. ◆ *adj* **1.** (*fabriqué*) made; **il n'est pas ~ pour mener cette vie** he's not cut out for that kind of life. **2.** (*physique*): **bien ~** well-built. **3.** (*fromage*) ripe. **4.** *loc*: **c'est bien ~ pour lui** (it) serves him right; **c'en est ~ de nous** we're done for. ▶ **fait** *nm* **1.** (*acte*) act; **mettre qqn devant le ~**

accompli to present sb with a fait accompli; **prendre qqn sur le ~** to catch sb in the act; **~s et gestes** doings, actions. **2.** (*événement*) event; **~s divers** news in brief. **3.** (*réalité*) fact. ▶ **au fait** *loc adv* by the way. ▶ **en fait** *loc adv* in (actual) fact. ▶ **en fait de** *loc prép* by way of. ▶ **du fait de** *loc prép* because of.

faîte [fɛt] *nm* **1.** (*de toit*) ridge. **2.** (*d'arbre*) top. **3.** *fig* (*sommet*) pinnacle.

faites → **faire**.

fait-tout (*pl inv*), **faitout** (*pl faitouts*) [fɛtu] *nm* stewpan.

fakir [fakir] *nm* fakir.

falaise [falɛz] *nf* cliff.

fallacieux, -euse [falasjø, øz] *adj* **1.** (*promesse*) false. **2.** (*argument*) fallacious.

falloir [falwar] *v impers*: **il me faut du temps** I need (some) time; **il faut que tu partes** you must go ou leave, you'll have to go ou leave; **il faut toujours qu'elle intervienne!** she always has to interfere!; **il faut faire attention** we/you *etc* must be careful, we'll/you'll *etc* have to be careful; **s'il le faut** if necessary. ▶ **s'en falloir** *v impers*: **il s'en faut de peu qu'il puisse acheter cette maison** he can almost afford to buy the house; **il s'en faut de 20 cm pour que l'armoire tienne dans le coin** the cupboard is 20 cm too big to fit into the corner; **il s'en faut de beaucoup pour qu'il ait l'examen** it'll take a lot for him to pass the exam; **peu s'en est fallu qu'il démissionne** he very nearly resigned, he came close to resigning.

fallu [faly] *pp inv* → **falloir**.

falot, -e [falo, ɔt] *adj* dull.

falsifier [falsifje] *vt* (*document, signature, faits*) to falsify.

famé, -e [fame] *adj*: **mal ~** with a (bad) reputation.

famélique [famelik] *adj* half-starved.

fameux, -euse [famø, øz] *adj* **1.** (*célèbre*) famous. **2.** *fam* (*remarquable*) great.

familial, -e, -aux [familjal, o] *adj* family (*avant n*).

familiariser [familjarize] *vt*: **~ qqn avec** to familiarize sb with.

familiarité [familjarite] *nf* familiarity. ▶ **familiarités** *nfpl* liberties.

familier, -ère [familje, ɛr] *adj* familiar. ▶ **familier** *nm* regular (customer).

famille [famij] *nf* family; (*ensemble des parents*) relatives, relations.

famine [famin] nf famine.

fan [fan] nmf fam fan.

fanal, -aux [fanal, o] nm 1. (de phare) beacon. 2. (lanterne) lantern.

fanatique [fanatik] ♦ nmf fanatic. ♦ adj fanatical.

fanatisme [fanatism] nm fanaticism.

faner [fane] ♦ vt (altérer) to fade. ♦ vi 1. (fleur) to wither. 2. (beauté, couleur) to fade. ▶ **se faner** vp 1. (fleur) to wither. 2. (beauté, couleur) to fade.

fanfare [fɑ̃far] nf 1. (orchestre) brass band. 2. (musique) fanfare.

fanfaron, -onne [fɑ̃farɔ̃, ɔn] ♦ adj boastful. ♦ nm, f braggart.

fange [fɑ̃ʒ] nf littéraire mire.

fanion [fanjɔ̃] nm pennant.

fantaisie [fɑ̃tezi] ♦ nf 1. (caprice) whim. 2. (U) (goût) fancy. 3. (imagination) imagination. ♦ adj inv: chapeau ~ fancy hat; bijoux ~ fake jewellery.

fantaisiste [fɑ̃tezist] ♦ nmf entertainer. ♦ adj (bizarre) fanciful; (farfelu) unconventional.

fantasme [fɑ̃tasm] nm fantasy.

fantasque [fɑ̃task] adj 1. (personne) whimsical. 2. (humeur) capricious.

fantassin [fɑ̃tasɛ̃] nm infantryman.

fantastique [fɑ̃tastik] ♦ adj fantastic. ♦ nm: le ~ the fantastic.

fantoche [fɑ̃tɔʃ] ♦ adj puppet (avant n). ♦ nm puppet.

fantôme [fɑ̃tom] ♦ nm ghost. ♦ adj (inexistant) phantom.

faon [fɑ̃] nm fawn.

far [far] nm: ~ **breton** Breton custard tart with prunes.

farandole [farɑ̃dɔl] nf farandole.

farce [fars] nf 1. (CULIN) stuffing. 2. (blague) (practical) joke; ~s et attrapes jokes and novelties.

farceur, -euse [farsœr, øz] nm, f (practical) joker.

farcir [farsir] vt 1. (CULIN) to stuff. 2. (remplir): ~ qqch de to stuff ou cram sthg with.

fard [far] nm make-up.

fardeau, -x [fardo] nm (poids) load; fig burden.

farder [farde] vt (maquiller) to make up. ▶ **se farder** vp to make o.s. up, to put on one's make-up.

farfelu, -e [farfəly] fam ♦ adj weird. ♦ nm, f weirdo.

farfouiller [farfuje] vi fam to rummage.

farine [farin] nf flour.

farniente [farnjɛnte] nm idleness.

farouche [faruʃ] adj 1. (animal) wild, not tame; (personne) shy, withdrawn. 2. (sentiment) fierce.

fart [far(t)] nm (ski) wax.

fascicule [fasikyl] nm part, instalment.

fascination [fasinasjɔ̃] nf fascination.

fasciner [fasine] vt to fascinate.

fascisme [faʃism] nm fascism.

fasse, fassions etc → **faire**.

faste [fast] ♦ nm splendour. ♦ adj (favorable) lucky.

fastidieux, -euse [fastidjø, øz] adj boring.

fastueux, -euse [fastɥø, øz] adj luxurious.

fatal, -e [fatal] adj 1. (mortel, funeste) fatal. 2. (inévitable) inevitable.

fataliste [fatalist] adj fatalistic.

fatalité [fatalite] nf 1. (destin) fate. 2. (inéluctabilité) inevitability.

fatigant, -e [fatigɑ̃, ɑ̃t] adj 1. (épuisant) tiring. 2. (ennuyeux) tiresome.

fatiguant, -e [fatigɑ̃] ppr → **fatiguer**.

fatigue [fatig] nf tiredness.

fatigué, -e [fatige] adj tired; (cœur, yeux) strained.

fatiguer [fatige] ♦ vt 1. (épuiser, affecter) to tire; (- cœur, yeux) to strain. 2. (ennuyer) to wear out. ♦ vi 1. (personne) to grow tired. 2. (moteur) to strain. ▶ **se fatiguer** vp to get tired; se ~ de qqch to get tired of sthg; se ~ à faire qqch to wear o.s. out doing sthg.

fatras [fatra] nm jumble.

faubourg [fobur] nm suburb.

fauché, -e [foʃe] adj fam broke, hard-up.

faucher [foʃe] vt 1. (couper - herbe, blé) to cut. 2. fam (voler): ~ qqch à qqn to pinch sthg from sb. 3. (piéton) to run over. 4. fig (suj: mort, maladie) to cut down.

faucille [fosij] nf sickle.

faucon [fokɔ̃] nm hawk.

faudra → **falloir**.

faufiler [fofile] vt to tack, to baste. ▶ **se faufiler** vp: se ~ dans to slip into; se ~ entre to thread one's way between.

faune [fon] ♦ nf 1. (animaux) fauna. 2. péj (personnes): la ~ qui fréquente ce bar the sort of people who hang round that bar. ♦ nm (MYTH) faun.

faussaire [fosɛr] nmf forger.

faussement [fosmɑ̃] adv 1. (à tort) wrongly. 2. (prétendument) falsely.

fausser [fose] vt 1. (déformer) to bend. 2. (rendre faux) to distort.

fausseté [foste] nf 1. (hypocrisie)

duplicity. **2.** (*de jugement, d'idée*) falsity.

faut → **falloir**.

faute [fot] *nf* **1.** (*erreur*) mistake, error; ~ **de frappe** (*à la machine à écrire*) typing error; (*à l'ordinateur*) keying error; ~ **d'orthographe** spelling mistake. **2.** (*méfait, infraction*) offence; **prendre qqn en ~** to catch sb out; ~ **professionnelle** professional misdemeanour. **3.** (TENNIS) fault; (FOOTBALL) foul. **4.** (*responsabilité*) fault; **de ma/ta** *etc* ~ my/your *etc* fault; **par la ~ de qqn** because of sb. ► **faute de** *loc prép* for want ou lack of; ~ **de mieux** for want ou lack of anything better. ► **sans faute** *loc adv* without fail.

fauteuil [fotœj] *nm* **1.** (*siège*) armchair; ~ **roulant** wheelchair. **2.** (*de théâtre*) seat. **3.** (*de président*) chair; (*d'académicien*) seat.

fautif, -ive [fotif, iv] ◆ *adj* **1.** (*coupable*) guilty. **2.** (*défectueux*) faulty. ◆ *nm, f* guilty party.

fauve [fov] ◆ *nm* **1.** (*animal*) big cat. **2.** (*couleur*) fawn. **3.** (ART) Fauve. ◆ *adj* **1.** (*animal*) wild. **2.** (*cuir, cheveux*) tawny. **3.** (ART) Fauvist.

fauvette [fovɛt] *nf* warbler.

faux, fausse [fo, fos] *adj* **1.** (*incorrect*) wrong. **2.** (*postiche, mensonger, hypocrite*) false; ~ **témoignage** (JUR) perjury. **3.** (*monnaie, papiers*) forged, fake. **4.** (*injustifié*) : **fausse alerte** false alarm; **c'est un ~ problème** that's not an issue (here). ► **faux** ◆ *nm* (*document, tableau*) forgery, fake. ◆ *nf* scythe. ◆ *adv* : **chanter/jouer ~** (MUS) to sing/play out of tune; **sonner ~** *fig* not to ring true.

faux-filet, faux filet [fofilɛ] *nm* sirloin.

faux-fuyant [fofɥijã] *nm* excuse.

faux-monnayeur [fomɔnɛjœr] *nm* counterfeiter.

faux-sens [fosãs] *nm inv* mistranslation.

faveur [favœr] *nf* favour. ► **à la faveur de** *loc prép* thanks to. ► **en faveur de** *loc prép* in favour of.

favorable [favɔrabl] *adj* : ~ (**à**) favourable (to).

favori, -ite [favɔri, it] *adj & nm, f* favourite.

favoriser [favɔrize] *vt* **1.** (*avantager*) to favour. **2.** (*contribuer à*) to promote.

fax [faks] *nm* fax.

faxer [fakse] *vt* to fax.

fayot [fajo] *nm* **1.** (*haricot*) bean. **2.** *fam* (*personne*) creep, crawler.

fébrile [febril] *adj* feverish.

fécond, -e [fekɔ̃, ɔ̃d] *adj* **1.** (*femelle, terre, esprit*) fertile. **2.** (*écrivain*) prolific.

fécondation [fekɔ̃dasjɔ̃] *nf* fertilization; ~ **in vitro** in vitro fertilization.

féconder [fekɔ̃de] *vt* **1.** (*ovule*) to fertilize. **2.** (*femme, femelle*) to impregnate.

fécondité [fekɔ̃dite] *nf* **1.** (*gén*) fertility. **2.** (*d'écrivain*) productiveness.

fécule [fekyl] *nf* starch.

féculent, -e [fekylã, ãt] *adj* starchy. ► **féculent** *nm* starchy food.

fédéral, -e, -aux [federal, o] *adj* federal.

fédération [federasjɔ̃] *nf* federation.

fée [fe] *nf* fairy.

féerique [fe(e)rik] *adj* (*enchanteur*) enchanting.

feignant, -e = **fainéant**.

feindre [fɛ̃dr] ◆ *vt* to feign; ~ **de faire qqch** to pretend to do sthg. ◆ *vi* to pretend.

feint, -e [fɛ̃, fɛ̃t] *pp* → **feindre**.

feinte [fɛ̃t] *nf* **1.** (*ruse*) ruse. **2.** (FOOTBALL) dummy; (BOXE) feint.

fêlé, -e [fele] *adj* **1.** (*assiette*) cracked. **2.** *fam* (*personne*) cracked, loony.

fêler [fele] *vt* to crack.

félicitations [felisitasjɔ̃] *nfpl* congratulations.

féliciter [felisite] *vt* to congratulate. ► **se féliciter** *vp* : **se ~ de** to congratulate o.s. on.

félin, -e [felɛ̃, in] *adj* feline. ► **félin** *nm* big cat.

félon, -onne [felɔ̃, ɔn] *littéraire* ◆ *adj* traitorous. ◆ *nm, f* traitor.

fêlure [felyr] *nf* crack.

femelle [fəmɛl] *nf & adj* female.

féminin, -e [feminɛ̃, in] *adj* **1.** (*gén*) feminine. **2.** (*revue, équipe*) women's (*avant n*). ► **féminin** *nm* (GRAM) feminine.

féminisme [feminism] *nm* feminism.

féminité [feminite] *nf* femininity.

femme [fam] *nf* **1.** (*personne de sexe féminin*) woman; ~ **de chambre** chambermaid; ~ **de ménage** cleaning woman. **2.** (*épouse*) wife.

fémur [femyr] *nm* femur.

fendre [fãdr] *vt* **1.** (*bois*) to split. **2.** (*foule, flots*) to cut through. ► **se fendre** *vp* (*se crevasser*) to crack.

fendu, -e [fãdy] *pp* → **fendre**.

fenêtre [fənɛtr] *nf* (*gén & INFORM*) window.

fenouil [fənuj] *nm* fennel.

fente [fãt] *nf* **1.** (*fissure*) crack. **2.** (*inters-*

tice, de vêtement) slit.

féodal, -e, -aux [feɔdal, o] *adj* feudal.

féodalité [feɔdalite] *nf* feudalism.

fer [fɛr] *nm* iron; ~ **à cheval** horseshoe;
~ **forgé** wrought iron; ~ **à repasser** iron;
~ **à souder** soldering iron.

ferai, feras *etc* → **faire**.

fer-blanc [fɛrblɑ̃] *nm* tinplate, tin.

ferblanterie [fɛrblɑ̃tri] *nf* **1.** (*commerce*)
tin industry. **2.** (*ustensiles*) tinware.

férié, -e [ferje] → **jour**.

férir [ferir] *vt*: **sans coup** ~ without
meeting any resistance ou obstacle.

ferme¹ [fɛrm] *nf* farm; ~ **auberge** *farm
providing holiday accommodation*.

ferme² [fɛrm] ◆ *adj* firm; **être** ~ **sur ses
jambes** to be steady on one's feet.
◆ *adv* **1.** (*beaucoup*) a lot. **2.** (*définitivement*): **acheter/vendre** ~ to make a firm
purchase/sale.

fermement [fɛrməmɑ̃] *adv* firmly.

ferment [fɛrmɑ̃] *nm* **1.** (*levure*) ferment. **2.** *fig* (*germe*) seeds, seeds (*pl*).

fermentation [fɛrmɑ̃tasjɔ̃] *nf* (CHIM)
fermentation; *fig* ferment.

fermer [fɛrme] ◆ *vt* **1.** (*porte, tiroir, yeux*)
to close, to shut; (*rideaux*) to close, to
draw; (*store*) to pull down; (*enveloppe*) to
seal. **2.** (*bloquer*) to close; ~ **son esprit à
qqch** to close one's mind to sthg.
3. (*gaz, lumière*) to turn off. **4.** (*vêtement*)
to do up. **5.** (*entreprise*) to close down.
6. (*interdire*): ~ **qqch à qqn** to close sthg
to sb. ◆ *vi* **1.** (*gén*) to shut, to close.
2. (*vêtement*) to do up. **3.** (*entreprise*) to
close down. ▶ **se fermer** *vp* **1.** (*porte*)
to close, to shut. **2.** (*plaie*) to close up.
3. (*vêtement*) to do up.

fermeté [fɛrməte] *nf* firmness.

fermeture [fɛrmətyr] *nf* **1.** (*de porte*)
closing. **2.** (*de vêtement, sac*) fastening; ~
Éclair® zip Br, zipper Am. **3.** (*d'établissement - temporaire*) closing; (*- définitive*)
closure; ~ **hebdomadaire/annuelle**
weekly/annual closing.

fermier, -ère [fɛrmje, ɛr] *nm, f* farmer.

fermoir [fɛrmwar] *nm* clasp.

féroce [ferɔs] *adj* (*animal, appétit*) ferocious; (*personne, désir*) fierce.

ferraille [fɛraj] *nf* **1.** (*vieux fer*) scrap
iron (U); **bon à mettre à la** ~ fit for the
scrap heap. **2.** *fam* (*monnaie*) loose
change.

ferronnerie [fɛrɔnri] *nf* **1.** (*objet, métier*)
ironwork (U). **2.** (*atelier*) ironworks (*sg*).

ferroviaire [fɛrɔvjɛr] *adj* rail (*avant
n*).

ferry-boat [fɛribot] (*pl* **ferry-boats**) *nm*
ferry.

fertile [fɛrtil] *adj litt & fig* fertile; ~ **en** *fig*
filled with, full of.

fertiliser [fɛrtilize] *vt* to fertilize.

fertilité [fɛrtilite] *nf* fertility.

féru, -e [fery] *adj sout* (*passionné*): **être** ~
de qqch to have a passion for sthg.

fervent, -e [fɛrvɑ̃, ɑ̃t] *adj* (*chrétien*) fervent; (*amoureux, démocrate*) ardent.

ferveur [fɛrvœr] *nf* (*dévotion*) fervour.

fesse [fɛs] *nf* buttock.

fessée [fese] *nf* spanking, smack (on
the bottom).

festin [fɛstɛ̃] *nm* banquet, feast.

festival, -als [fɛstival] *nm* festival.

FESTIVAL D'AVIGNON

Founded in 1947 by Jean Vilar, a leading
French theatre director, this festival
takes place each year in and around the
town of Avignon in southeast France.
As well as important new plays and
dance pieces performed here for the
first time before touring France, more
informal street performances take place
throughout the town.

FESTIVAL DE CANNES

During this international film festival
held each year in May in this fashionable seaside resort in the south of
France, prizes are awarded for acting,
directing etc. The most sought-after
prize is the Palme d'Or, given to the
best film in the festival.

festivités [fɛstivite] *nfpl* festivities.

feston [fɛstɔ̃] *nm* (COUTURE) scallop.

festoyer [fɛstwaje] *vi* to feast.

fêtard, -e [fɛtar, ard] *nm, f* fun-loving
person.

fête [fɛt] *nf* **1.** (*congé*) holiday; **les** ~**s** (**de
fin d'année**) the Christmas holidays; ~
nationale national holiday. **2.** (*réunion,
réception*) celebration. **3.** (*kermesse*) fair; ~
foraine funfair; **la** ~ **de la Musique** *annual
music festival which takes place in the streets*.
4. (*jour de célébration - de personne*) saint's
day; (*- de saint*) feast (day); **bonne** ~!
Happy Saint's Day! **5.** (*soirée*) party. **6.**
loc: **faire** ~ **à qqn** to make a fuss of sb;
faire la ~ to have a good time.

BONNE FÊTE!

In France each day is associated with a
certain saint. It is traditional to wish
'bonne fête' (Happy Saint's Day) to peo-

ple whose Christian name is the same as the saint for that day.

FÊTE DE LA MUSIQUE
This public event was started at the beginning of the 1980s to promote music in France. It takes place every year on 21 June when both professional and amateur musicians play for free in the streets in the evening.

fêter [fete] *vt* (*événement*) to celebrate; (*personne*) to have a party for.

fétiche [fetiʃ] *nm* **1.** (*objet de culte*) fetish. **2.** (*mascotte*) mascot.

fétichisme [fetiʃism] *nm* (*culte, perversion*) fetishism.

fétide [fetid] *adj* fetid.

fétu [fety] *nm*: ~ (**de paille**) wisp (of straw).

feu¹, -x [fø] *nm* **1.** (*flamme, incendie*) fire; **au ~!** fire!; **en ~** *litt* & *fig* on fire; **avez-vous du ~?** have you got a light?; **faire ~** (MIL) to fire; **mettre le ~ à qqch** to set fire to sthg, to set sthg on fire; **prendre ~** to catch fire; **~ de camp** camp fire; **~ de cheminée** chimney fire; **~ follet** will-o'-the-wisp. **2.** (*signal*) light; **~ rouge/vert** red/green light; **~x de croisement** dipped headlights; **~x de position** sidelights; **~x de route** headlights on full beam. **3.** (CULIN) ring *Br*, burner *Am*; **à ~ doux/vif** on a low/high flame; **à petit ~** gently. **4.** (CIN & THÉÂTRE) light (U). ▶ **feu d'artifice** *nm* firework.

feu², -e [fø] *adj*: **~ M. X** the late Mr X; **~ mon mari** my late husband.

feuillage [fœjaʒ] *nm* foliage.

feuille [fœj] *nf* **1.** (*d'arbre*) leaf; **~ morte** dead leaf; **~ de vigne** (BOT) vine leaf. **2.** (*page*) sheet; **~ de papier** sheet of paper. **3.** (*document*) form; **~ de soins** claim form for reimbursement of medical expenses.

feuillet [fœjɛ] *nm* page.

feuilleté, -e [fœjte] *adj* **1.** (CULIN): **pâte ~e** puff pastry. **2.** (GÉOL) foliated.

feuilleter [fœjte] *vt* to flick through.

feuilleton [fœjtɔ̃] *nm* serial.

feutre [føtr] *nm* **1.** (*étoffe*) felt. **2.** (*chapeau*) felt hat. **3.** (*crayon*) felt-tip pen.

feutré, -e [føtre] *adj* **1.** (*garni de feutre*) trimmed with felt; (*qui a l'aspect du feutre*) felted. **2.** (*bruit, cri*) muffled.

feutrine [føtrin] *nf* lightweight felt.

fève [fɛv] *nf* broad bean.

février [fevrije] *nm* February; *voir aussi* **septembre**.

fg *abr de* **faubourg**.

fi [fi] *interj*: **faire ~ de** to scorn.

fiable [fjabl] *adj* reliable.

fiacre [fjakr] *nm* hackney carriage.

fiançailles [fjɑ̃saj] *nfpl* engagement (*sg*).

fiancé, -e [fjɑ̃se] *nm, f* fiancé (*f* fiancée).

fiancer [fjɑ̃se] ▶ **se fiancer** *vp*: **se ~ (avec)** to get engaged (to).

fibre [fibr] *nf* (ANAT, BIOL & TECHNOL) fibre; **~ de verre** fibreglass, glass fibre.

ficelé, -e [fisle] *adj fam* dressed.

ficeler [fisle] *vt* (*lier*) to tie up.

ficelle [fisɛl] *nf* **1.** (*fil*) string. **2.** (*pain*) thin French stick. **3.** (*gén pl*) (*truc*) trick.

fiche [fiʃ] *nf* **1.** (*document*) card; **~ de paie** pay slip. **2.** (ÉLECTR & TECHNOL) pin.

ficher [fiʃe] (*pp vt sens 1 & 2* **fiché**, *pp vt sens 3 & 4* **fichu**) *vt* **1.** (*enfoncer*): **~ qqch dans** to stick sthg into. **2.** (*inscrire*) to put on file. **3.** *fam* (*faire*): **qu'est-ce qu'il fiche?** what's he doing? **4.** *fam* (*mettre*) to put; **~ qqch par terre** *fig* to mess ou muck sthg up. ▶ **se ficher** *vp* **1.** (*s'enfoncer - suj: clou, pique*): **se ~ dans** to go into. **2.** *fam* (*se moquer*): **se ~ de** to make fun of. **3.** *fam* (*ne pas tenir compte*): **se ~ de** not to give a damn about.

fichier [fiʃje] *nm* file.

fichu, -e [fiʃy] *adj* **1.** *fam* (*cassé, fini*) done for. **2.** (*avant n*) (*désagréable*) nasty. **3.** *loc*: **être mal ~** *fam* (*personne*) to feel rotten; (*objet*) to be badly made; **il n'est même pas ~ de faire son lit** *fam* he can't even make his own bed. ▶ **fichu** *nm* scarf.

fictif, -ive [fiktif, iv] *adj* **1.** (*imaginaire*) imaginary. **2.** (*faux*) false.

fiction [fiksjɔ̃] *nf* **1.** (LITTÉRATURE) fiction. **2.** (*monde imaginaire*) dream world.

fidèle [fidɛl] ◆ *nmf* **1.** (RELIG) believer. **2.** (*adepte*) fan. ◆ *adj* **1.** (*loyal, exact, semblable*): **~ (à)** faithful (to); **~ à la réalité** accurate. **2.** (*habitué*) regular.

fidélité [fidelite] *nf* faithfulness.

fief [fjɛf] *nm* fief; *fig* stronghold.

fiel [fjɛl] *nm litt* & *fig* gall.

fier¹, fière [fjɛr] *adj* **1.** (*gén*) proud; **~ de qqn/qqch** proud of sb/sthg; **~ de faire qqch** proud to be doing sthg. **2.** (*noble*) noble.

fier² [fje] ▶ **se fier** *vp*: **se ~ à** to trust, to rely on.

fierté [fjɛrte] *nf* **1.** (*satisfaction, dignité*) pride. **2.** (*arrogance*) arrogance.

fièvre [fjɛvr] *nf* **1.** (MÉD) fever; **avoir 40 de ~** to have a temperature of 105 (degrees). 2. *fig* (*excitation*) excitement.

fiévreux, -euse [fjevrø, øz] *adj litt &*
fig feverish.

fig. *abr de* **figure.**

figer [fiʒe] *vt* to paralyse. ▶ **se figer**
vp 1. (*s'immobiliser*) to freeze. 2. (*se solidi-*
fier) to congeal.

fignoler [fiɲɔle] *vt* to put the finishing
touches to.

figue [fig] *nf* fig.

figuier [figje] *nm* fig-tree.

figurant, -e [figyrã, ãt] *nm, f* extra.

figuratif, -ive [figyratif, iv] *adj* figurative.

figure [figyr] *nf* 1. (*gén*) figure; **faire ~**
de to look like. 2. (*visage*) face.

figuré, -e [figyre] *adj* (*sens*) figurative.
▶ **figuré** *nm*: **au ~** in the figurative
sense.

figurer [figyre] ◆ *vt* to represent. ◆ *vi*:
~ dans/parmi to figure in/among.

figurine [figyrin] *nf* figurine.

fil [fil] *nm* 1. (*brin*) thread; **~ à plomb**
plumb line; **perdre le ~ (de qqch)** *fig* to
lose the thread (of sthg). 2. (*câble*) wire;
~ de fer wire. 3. (*cours*) course; **au ~ de**
in the course of. 4. (*tissu*) linen. 5. (*tran-*
chant) edge.

filament [filamã] *nm* 1. (ANAT & ÉLECTR)
filament. 2. (*végétal*) fibre. 3. (*de colle,*
bave) thread.

filandreux, -euse [filãdrø, øz] *adj*
(*viande*) stringy.

filasse [filas] ◆ *nf* tow. ◆ *adj inv* flaxen.

filature [filatyr] *nf* 1. (*usine*) mill; (*fabri-*
cation) spinning. 2. (*poursuite*) tailing.

file [fil] *nf* line; **à la ~** in a line; **se garer**
en double ~ to double-park; **~ d'attente**
queue Br, line Am.

filer [file] ◆ *vt* 1. (*soie, coton*) to spin.
2. (*personne*) to tail. 3. *fam* (*donner*):
~ qqch à qqn to slip sthg to sb, to slip sb
sthg. ◆ *vi* 1. (*bas*) to ladder Br, to run
Am. 2. (*aller vite - temps, véhicule*) to fly
(by). 3. *fam* (*partir*) to dash off. 4. *loc*: **~**
doux to behave nicely.

filet [file] *nm* 1. (*à mailles*) net; **~ de**
pêche fishing net; **~ à provisions** string
bag. 2. (CULIN) fillet. 3. (*de liquide*) drop,
dash; (*de lumière*) shaft.

filial, -e, -aux [filjal, o] *adj* filial.
▶ **filiale** *nf* (ÉCON) subsidiary.

filiation [filjasjɔ̃] *nf* (*lien de parenté*)
line.

filière [filjɛr] *nf* 1. (*voie*): **~ scientifique**
(SCOL) science subjects (*pl*); **suivre la ~**
(*professionnelle*) to work one's way up;
suivre la ~ hiérarchique to go through

the right channels. 2. (*réseau*) network.

filiforme [filifɔrm] *adj* skinny.

filigrane [filigran] *nm* (*dessin*) watermark; **en ~** *fig* between the lines.

filin [filɛ̃] *nm* rope.

fille [fij] *nf* 1. (*enfant*) daughter.
2. (*femme*) girl; **jeune ~** girl; **~ mère** *péj*
single mother; **vieille ~** *péj* spinster.

fillette [fijɛt] *nf* little girl.

filleul, -e [fijœl] *nm, f* godchild.

film [film] *nm* 1. (*gén*) film; **~ catastro-**
phe disaster movie; **~ d'épouvante** horror film; **~ policier** detective film. 2. *fig*
(*déroulement*) course.

filmer [filme] *vt* to film.

filmographie [filmɔgrafi] *nf* filmogra-
phy, films (*pl*).

filon [filɔ̃] *nm* 1. (*de mine*) vein. 2. *fam*
fig (*possibilité*) cushy number.

fils [fis] *nm* son; **~ de famille** boy from a
privileged background.

filtrant, -e [filtrã, ãt] *adj* (*verre*) tinted.

filtre [filtr] *nm* filter; **~ à café** coffee filter.

filtrer [filtre] ◆ *vt* to filter; *fig* to screen.
◆ *vi* to filter; *fig* to filter through.

fin, fine [fɛ̃, fin] ◆ *adj* 1. (*gén*) fine. 2.
(*partie du corps*) slender; (*couche, papier*)
thin. 3. (*subtil*) shrewd. 4. (*ouïe, vue*)
keen. ◆ *adv* finely; **~ prêt** quite ready.
▶ **fin** *nf* end; **~ mars** at the end of
March; **mettre ~ à** to put a stop ou an
end to; **prendre ~** to come to an end;
tirer ou toucher à sa ~ to draw to a close;
arriver ou parvenir à ses ~s to achieve
one's ends ou aims. ▶ **fin de série** *nf*
oddment. ▶ **à la fin** *loc adv*: **tu vas m'é-**
couter, à la ~? will you listen to me?
▶ **à la fin de** *loc prép* at the end of.
▶ **sans fin** *loc adj* endless.

final, -e [final] (*pl* **finals** ou **finaux**
[fino]) *adj* final. ▶ **finale** *nf* (SPORT) final.

finalement [finalmã] *adv* finally.

finaliste [finalist] *nmf & adj* finalist.

finalité [finalite] *nf sout* (*fonction*) purpose.

finance [finãs] *nf* finance. ▶ **finances**
nfpl finances.

financer [finãse] *vt* to finance, to fund.

financier, -ère [finãsje, ɛr] *adj* financial. ▶ **financier** *nm* financier.

finaud, -e [fino, od] *adj* wily, crafty.

finement [finmã] *adv* 1. (*de façon fine*)
finely. 2. (*subtilement*) subtly.

finesse [finɛs] *nf* 1. (*gén*) fineness.
2. (*minceur*) slenderness. 3. (*perspicacité*)
shrewdness. 4. (*subtilité*) subtlety.

fini, -e [fini] *adj* 1. *péj* (*fieffé*): **un crétin ~**

a complete idiot. **2.** *fam* (*usé, diminué*) finished. **3.** (*limité*) finite. ▶ **fini** *nm* (*d'objet*) finish.

finir [finiʀ] ◆ *vt* **1.** (*gén*) to finish, to end; **c'est fini pour aujourd'hui** that's it for today. **2.** (*vider*) to empty. ◆ *vi* **1.** (*gén*) to finish, to end; **~ par faire qqch** to do sthg eventually; **tu vas ~ par tomber!** you're going to fall!; **mal ~** to end badly. **2.** (*arrêter*): **~ de faire qqch** to stop doing sthg; **en ~ (avec)** to finish (with).

finition [finisjɔ̃] *nf* (*d'objet*) finish.

finlandais, -e [fɛ̃lɑ̃dɛ, ɛz] *adj* Finnish. ▶ **Finlandais, -e** *nm, f* Finn.

Finlande [fɛ̃lɑ̃d] *nf*: **la ~** Finland.

finnois, -e [finwa, az] *adj* Finnish. ▶ **finnois** *nm* (*langue*) Finnish. ▶ **Finnois, -e** *nm, f* Finn.

fiole [fjɔl] *nf* flask.

fioriture [fjɔʀityʀ] *nf* flourish.

fioul = **fuel**.

firmament [fiʀmamɑ̃] *nm* firmament.

firme [fiʀm] *nf* firm.

fis, fit etc → **faire**.

fisc [fisk] *nm* ≃ Inland Revenue *Br*, ≃ Internal Revenue *Am*.

fiscal, -e, -aux [fiskal, o] *adj* tax (*avant n*), fiscal.

fiscalité [fiskalite] *nf* tax system.

fissure [fisyʀ] *nf litt & fig* crack.

fissurer [fisyʀe] *vt* (*fendre*) to crack; *fig* to split. ▶ **se fissurer** *vp* to crack.

fiston [fistɔ̃] *nm fam* son.

FIV [fiv] (*abr de* **fécondation in vitro**) *nf* IVF.

fixation [fiksasjɔ̃] *nf* **1.** (*action de fixer*) fixing. **2.** (*attache*) fastening, fastener; (*de ski*) binding. **3.** (PSYCHOL) fixation.

fixe [fiks] *adj* fixed; (*encre*) permanent. ▶ **fixe** *nm* fixed salary.

fixement [fiksəmɑ̃] *adv* fixedly.

fixer [fikse] *vt* **1.** (*gén*) to fix; (*règle*) to set; **~ son choix sur** to decide on. **2.** (*monter*) to hang. **3.** (*regarder*) to stare at. **4.** (*renseigner*): **~ qqn sur qqch** to put sb in the picture about sthg; **être fixé sur qqch** to know all about sthg. ▶ **se fixer** *vp* to settle; **se ~ sur** (*suj: choix, personne*) to settle on; (*suj: regard*) to rest on.

fjord [fjɔʀd] *nm* fjord.

flacon [flakɔ̃] *nm* small bottle.

flageller [flaʒele] *vt* (*fouetter*) to flagellate.

flageoler [flaʒɔle] *vi* to tremble.

flageolet [flaʒɔlɛ] *nm* **1.** (*haricot*) flageolet bean. **2.** (MUS) flageolet.

flagrant, -e [flagʀɑ̃, ɑ̃t] *adj* flagrant; → **délit**.

flair [flɛʀ] *nm* sense of smell.

flairer [flɛʀe] *vt* to sniff, to smell; *fig* to scent.

flamand, -e [flamɑ̃, ɑ̃d] *adj* Flemish. ▶ **flamand** *nm* (*langue*) Flemish. ▶ **Flamand, -e** *nm, f* Flemish person, Fleming.

flamant [flamɑ̃] *nm* flamingo; **~ rose** pink flamingo.

flambeau, -x [flɑ̃bo] *nm* torch; *fig* flame.

flamber [flɑ̃be] ◆ *vi* **1.** (*brûler*) to blaze. **2.** *fam* (JEU) to play for high stakes. ◆ *vt* **1.** (*crêpe*) to flambé. **2.** (*volaille*) to singe.

flamboyant, -e [flɑ̃bwajɑ̃, ɑ̃t] *adj* **1.** (*ciel, regard*) blazing; (*couleur*) flaming. **2.** (ARCHIT) flamboyant.

flamboyer [flɑ̃bwaje] *vi* to blaze.

flamme [flam] *nf* flame; *fig* fervour, fire.

flan [flɑ̃] *nm* baked custard.

flanc [flɑ̃] *nm* (*de personne, navire, montagne*) side; (*d'animal, d'armée*) flank.

flancher [flɑ̃ʃe] *vi fam* to give up.

flanelle [flanɛl] *nf* flannel.

flâner [flane] *vi* (*se promener*) to stroll.

flanquer [flɑ̃ke] *vt* **1.** *fam* (*jeter*): **~ qqch par terre** to fling sthg to the ground; **~ qqn dehors** to chuck *ou* fling sb out. **2.** *fam* (*donner*): **une gifle à qqn** to clout sb round the ear; **~ la frousse à qqn** to put the wind up sb. **3.** (*accompagner*): **être flanqué de** to be flanked by.

flapi, -e [flapi] *adj fam* dead beat.

flaque [flak] *nf* pool.

flash [flaʃ] *nm* **1.** (PHOT) flash. **2.** (RADIO & TÉLÉ): **~ (d'information)** newsflash; **~ de publicité** commercial.

flash-back [flaʃbak] (*pl inv ou* **flash-backs**) *nm* (CIN) flashback.

flasher [flaʃe] *vi fam*: **~ sur qqn/qqch** to be turned on by sb/sthg.

flasque [flask] ◆ *nf* flask. ◆ *adj* flabby, limp.

flatter [flate] *vt* **1.** (*louer*) to flatter. **2.** (*caresser*) to stroke. ▶ **se flatter** *vp* to flatter o.s.; **je me flatte de le convaincre** I flatter myself that I can convince him.

flatterie [flatʀi] *nf* flattery.

flatteur, -euse [flatœʀ, øz] ◆ *adj* flattering. ◆ *nm, f* flatterer.

FLE, fle [flə] (*abr de* **français langue étrangère**) *nm* French as a foreign language.

fléau, -x [fleo] *nm* **1.** *litt & fig* (*calamité*) scourge. **2.** (*instrument*) flail.

flèche [flɛʃ] *nf* **1.** (*gén*) arrow. **2.**

(*d'église*) spire. **3.** *fig* (*critique*) shaft.
fléchette [fleʃɛt] *nf* dart. ► **fléchettes** *nfpl* darts (*sg*).
fléchir [fleʃir] ♦ *vt* to bend, to flex; *fig* to sway. ♦ *vi* to bend; *fig* to weaken.
fléchissement [fleʃismɑ̃] *nm* flexing, bending; *fig* weakening.
flegmatique [flɛgmatik] *adj* phlegmatic.
flegme [flɛgm] *nm* composure.
flemmard, -e [flɛmar, ard] *fam* ♦ *adj* lazy. ♦ *nm, f* lazybones (*sg*).
flemme [flɛm] *nf fam* laziness; **j'ai la ~ (de sortir)** I can't be bothered (to go out).
flétrir [fletrir] *vt* (*fleur, visage*) to wither. ► **se flétrir** *vp* to wither.
fleur [flœr] *nf* (BOT & *fig*) flower; **en ~, en ~s** (*arbre*) in flower, in blossom; **à ~s** (*motif*) flowered.
fleuret [flœrɛ] *nm* foil.
fleuri, -e [flœri] *adj* **1.** (*jardin, pré*) in flower; (*vase*) of flowers; (*tissu*) flowered; (*table, appartement*) decorated with flowers. **2.** *fig* (*style*) flowery.
fleurir [flœrir] ♦ *vi* to blossom; *fig* to flourish. ♦ *vt* (*maison*) to decorate with flowers; (*tombe*) to lay flowers on.
fleuriste [flœrist] *nmf* florist.
fleuron [flœrɔ̃] *nm fig* jewel.
fleuve [flœv] *nm* **1.** (*cours d'eau*) river. **2.** (*en apposition*) (*interminable*) lengthy, interminable.
flexible [flɛksibl] *adj* flexible.
flexion [flɛksjɔ̃] *nf* **1.** (*de genou, de poutre*) bending. **2.** (LING) inflexion.
flibustier [flibystje] *nm* buccaneer.
flic [flik] *nm fam* cop.
flinguer [flɛ̃ge] *vt fam* to gun down. ► **se flinguer** *vp fam* to blow one's brains out.
flipper [flipœr] *nm* pin-ball machine.
flirter [flœrte] *vi*: **~ (avec qqn)** to flirt (with sb); **~ avec qqch** *fig* to flirt with sthg.
flocon [flɔkɔ̃] *nm* flake; **~ de neige** snowflake.
flonflon [flɔ̃flɔ̃] *nm* (*gén pl*) blare.
flop [flɔp] *nm* (*échec*) flop, failure.
floraison [flɔrɛzɔ̃] *nf litt* & *fig* flowering, blossoming.
floral, -e, -aux [flɔral, o] *adj* floral.
flore [flɔr] *nf* flora.
Floride [flɔrid] *nf*: **la ~** Florida.
florissant, -e [flɔrisɑ̃, ɑ̃t] *adj* (*santé*) blooming; (*économie*) flourishing.
flot [flo] *nm* flood, stream; **être à ~** (*navire*) to be afloat; *fig* to be back to

normal. ► **flots** *nmpl littéraire* waves.
flottaison [flɔtɛzɔ̃] *nf* floating.
flottant, -e [flɔtɑ̃, ɑ̃t] *adj* **1.** (*gén*) floating; (*esprit*) irresolute. **2.** (*robe*) loose-fitting.
flotte [flɔt] *nf* **1.** (AÉRON & NAVIG) fleet. **2.** *fam* (*eau*) water. **3.** *fam* (*pluie*) rain.
flottement [flɔtmɑ̃] *nm* **1.** (*indécision*) hesitation, wavering. **2.** (*de monnaie*) floating.
flotter [flɔte] ♦ *vi* **1.** (*sur l'eau*) to float. **2.** (*drapeau*) to flap; (*brume, odeur*) to drift. **3.** (*dans un vêtement*): **tu flottes dedans** it's baggy on you. ♦ *v impers fam*: **il flotte** it's raining.
flotteur [flɔtœr] *nm* (*de ligne de pêche, d'hydravion*) float; (*de chasse d'eau*) ballcock.
flou, -e [flu] *adj* **1.** (*couleur, coiffure*) soft. **2.** (*photo*) blurred, fuzzy. **3.** (*pensée*) vague, woolly. ► **flou** *nm* (*de photo*) fuzziness; (*de décision*) vagueness.
flouer [flue] *vt fam* to do, to swindle.
fluctuer [flyktɥe] *vi* to fluctuate.
fluet, -ette [flyɛ, ɛt] *adj* (*personne*) thin, slender; (*voix*) thin.
fluide [flɥid] ♦ *nm* **1.** (*matière*) fluid. **2.** *fig* (*pouvoir*) (occult) power. ♦ *adj* (*matière*) fluid; (*circulation*) flowing freely.
fluidifier [flɥidifje] *vt* (*trafic*) to improve the flow of.
fluidité [flɥidite] *nf* (*gén*) fluidity; (*de circulation*) easy flow.
fluor [flyɔr] *nm* fluorine.
fluorescent, -e [flyɔrɛsɑ̃, ɑ̃t] *adj* fluorescent.
flûte [flyt] ♦ *nf* **1.** (MUS) flute. **2.** (*verre*) flute (glass). ♦ *interj fam* bother!
flûtiste [flytist] *nmf* flautist.
fluvial, -e, -aux [flyvjal, o] *adj* (*eaux, pêche*) river (*avant n*); (*alluvions*) fluvial.
flux [fly] *nm* **1.** (*écoulement*) flow. **2.** (*marée*) flood tide. **3.** (PHYS) flux.
fluxion [flyksjɔ̃] *nf* inflammation.
FM (*abr de* **frequency modulation**) *nf* FM.
FMI (*abr de* **Fonds monétaire international**) *nm* IMF.
FN (*abr de* **Front national**) *nm* extreme right-wing French political party.
foc [fɔk] *nm* jib.
focal, -e, -aux [fɔkal, o] *adj* focal.
fœtal, -e, -aux [fetal, o] *adj* foetal.
fœtus [fetys] *nm* foetus.
foi [fwa] *nf* **1.** (RELIG) faith. **2.** (*confiance*) trust; **avoir ~ en qqn/qqch** to trust sb/sthg, to have faith in sb/sthg. **3.** *loc*: **être de bonne/mauvaise ~** to be in good/bad faith.

foie [fwa] *nm* (ANAT & CULIN) liver.

foin [fwɛ̃] *nm* hay.

foire [fwar] *nf* 1. (*fête*) funfair. 2. (*exposition, salon*) trade fair.

fois [fwa] *nf* time; **une ~** once; **deux ~** twice; **trois/quatre ~** three/four times; **deux ~ plus long** twice as long; **neuf ~ sur dix** nine times out of ten; **deux ~ trois** two times three; **cette ~** this time; **il était une ~ ...** once upon a time there was ...; **une (bonne) ~ pour toutes** once and for all. ▶ **à la fois** *loc adv* at the same time, at once. ▶ **des fois** *loc adv* (*parfois*) sometimes. ▶ **une fois que** *loc conj* once.

foison [fwazɔ̃] ▶ **à foison** *loc adv* in abundance.

foisonner [fwazɔne] *vi* to abound.

folâtre [fɔlatr] *adj* playful.

folâtrer [fɔlatre] *vi* to romp (about).

folie [fɔli] *nf litt & fig* madness.

folklore [fɔlklɔr] *nm* (*de pays*) folklore.

folklorique [fɔlklɔrik] *adj* 1. (*danse*) folk. 2. *fig* (*situation, personne*) bizarre, quaint.

folle → **fou**.

follement [fɔlmɑ̃] *adv* madly, wildly.

follet [fɔlɛ] → **feu**.

fomenter [fɔmɑ̃te] *vt* to foment.

foncé, -e [fɔ̃se] *adj* dark.

foncer [fɔ̃se] *vi* 1. (*teinte*) to darken. 2. (*se ruer*): **~ sur** to rush at. 3. *fam* (*se dépêcher*) to get a move on.

foncier, -ère [fɔ̃sje, ɛr] *adj* 1. (*impôt*) land (*avant n*); **propriétaire ~** landowner. 2. (*fondamental*) basic, fundamental.

foncièrement [fɔ̃sjɛrmɑ̃] *adv* basically.

fonction [fɔ̃ksjɔ̃] *nf* 1. (*gén*) function; **faire ~ de** to act as. 2. (*profession*) post; **entrer en ~** to take up one's post ou duties. ▶ **en fonction de** *loc prép* according to.

fonctionnaire [fɔ̃ksjɔnɛr] *nmf* (*de l'État*) state employee; (*dans l'administration*) civil servant; **haut ~** senior civil servant.

fonctionnel, -elle [fɔ̃ksjɔnɛl] *adj* functional.

fonctionnement [fɔ̃ksjɔnmɑ̃] *nm* working, functioning.

fonctionner [fɔ̃ksjɔne] *vi* to work, to function.

fond [fɔ̃] *nm* 1. (*de récipient, puits, mer*) bottom; (*de pièce*) back; **sans ~** bottomless. 2. (*substance*) heart, root; **le ~ de ma pensée** what I really think; **le ~ et la forme** content and form. 3. (*arrière-plan*)

background. ▶ **fond de teint** *nm* foundation. ▶ **à fond** *loc adv* 1. (*entièrement*) thoroughly; **se donner à ~** to give one's all. 2. (*très vite*) at top speed. ▶ **au fond, dans le fond** *loc adv* basically. ▶ **au fond de** *loc prép*: **au ~ de moi-même/lui-même** *etc* at heart, deep down.

fondamental, -e, -aux [fɔ̃damɑ̃tal, o] *adj* fundamental.

fondant, -e [fɔ̃dɑ̃, ɑ̃t] *adj* (*neige, glace*) melting; (*aliment*) which melts in the mouth.

fondateur, -trice [fɔ̃datœr, tris] *nm, f* founder.

fondation [fɔ̃dasjɔ̃] *nf* foundation. ▶ **fondations** *nfpl* (CONSTR) foundations.

fondé, -e [fɔ̃de] *adj* (*craintes, reproches*) justified, well-founded; **non ~** unfounded. ▶ **fondé de pouvoir** *nm* authorized representative.

fondement [fɔ̃dmɑ̃] *nm* (*base, motif*) foundation; **sans ~** groundless, without foundation.

fonder [fɔ̃de] *vt* 1. (*créer*) to found. 2. (*baser*): **~ qqch sur** to base sthg on; **~ de grands espoirs sur qqn** to pin one's hopes on sb. ▶ **se fonder** *vp*: **se ~ sur** (*suj: personne*) to base o.s. on; (*suj: argument*) to be based on.

fonderie [fɔ̃dri] *nf* (*usine*) foundry.

fondre [fɔ̃dr] ◆ *vt* 1. (*beurre, neige*) to melt; (*sucre, sel*) to dissolve; (*métal*) to melt down. 2. (*mouler*) to cast. 3. (*mêler*) to blend. ◆ *vi* 1. (*beurre, neige*) to melt; (*sucre, sel*) to dissolve; *fig* to melt away. 2. (*maigrir*) to lose weight. 3. (*se ruer*): **~ sur** to swoop down on.

fonds [fɔ̃] ◆ *nm* 1. (*ressources*) fund; **le Fonds monétaire international** the International Monetary Fund. 2. (*bien immobilier*): **~ (de commerce)** business. ◆ *nmpl* funds.

fondu, -e [fɔ̃dy] *pp* → **fondre**. ▶ **fondue** *nf* fondue.

font → **faire**.

fontaine [fɔ̃tɛn] *nf* (*naturelle*) spring; (*publique*) fountain.

fonte [fɔ̃t] *nf* 1. (*de glace, beurre*) melting; (*de métal*) melting down. 2. (*alliage*) cast iron.

foot [fut] = **football**.

football [futbol] *nm* football *Br*, soccer.

footballeur, -euse [futbolœr, øz] *nm, f* footballer *Br*, soccer player.

footing [futiŋ] *nm* jogging.

for [fɔr] *nm*: **dans son ~ intérieur** in his/her heart of hearts.

forage [fɔraʒ] *nm* drilling.

forain, -e [fɔrɛ̃, ɛn] → **fête**. ▶ **forain** *nm* stallholder.

forçat [fɔrsa] *nm* convict.

force [fɔrs] *nf* **1.** (*vigueur*) strength; **c'est ce qui fait sa ~** that's where his strength lies. **2.** (*violence, puissance,* MIL & PHYS) force; **faire faire qqch à qqn de ~** to force sb to do sthg; **avoir ~ de loi** to have force of law; **obtenir qqch par la ~** to obtain sthg by force; **~ centrifuge** (PHYS) centrifugal force. ▶ **forces** *nfpl* (*physique*) strength (*sg*); **de toutes ses ~s** with all his/her strength. ▶ **à force de** *loc prép* by dint of, as the result of.

forcément [fɔrsemɑ̃] *adv* inevitably.

forcené, -e [fɔrsəne] *nm, f* maniac.

forceps [fɔrsɛps] *nm* forceps (*pl*).

forcer [fɔrse] ◆ *vt* **1.** (*gén*) to force; **~ qqn à qqch/à faire qqch** to force sb into sthg/to do sthg. **2.** (*admiration, respect*) to compel, to command. **3.** (*talent, voix*) to strain. ◆ *vi*: **ça ne sert à rien de ~, ça ne passe pas** there's no point in forcing it, it won't go through; **~ sur qqch** to overdo sthg. ▶ **se forcer** *vp* (*s'obliger*): **se ~ à faire qqch** to force o.s. to do sthg.

forcir [fɔrsir] *vi* to put on weight.

forer [fɔre] *vt* to drill.

forestier, -ère [fɔrɛstje, ɛr] *adj* forest (*avant n*).

forêt [fɔrɛ] *nf* forest.

forfait [fɔrfɛ] *nm* **1.** (*prix fixe*) fixed price. **2.** (SPORT): **déclarer ~** (*abandonner*) to withdraw; *fig* to give up. **3.** *littéraire* (*crime*) heinous crime.

forfaitaire [fɔrfɛtɛr] *adj* inclusive.

forge [fɔrʒ] *nf* forge.

forger [fɔrʒe] *vt* **1.** (*métal*) to forge. **2.** *fig* (*caractère*) to form.

forgeron [fɔrʒərɔ̃] *nm* blacksmith.

formaliser [fɔrmalize] *vt* to formalize. ▶ **se formaliser** *vp*: **se ~ (de)** to take offence (at).

formalisme [fɔrmalism] *nm* formality.

formaliste [fɔrmalist] ◆ *nmf* formalist. ◆ *adj* (*milieu*) conventional; (*personne*): **être ~** to be a stickler for the rules.

formalité [fɔrmalite] *nf* formality.

format [fɔrma] *nm* (*dimension*) size.

formatage [fɔrmataʒ] *nm* (INFORM) formatting.

formater [fɔrmate] *vt* (INFORM) to format.

formateur, -trice [fɔrmatœr, tris] ◆ *adj* formative. ◆ *nm, f* trainer.

formation [fɔrmasjɔ̃] *nf* **1.** (*gén*) formation. **2.** (*apprentissage*) training.

forme [fɔrm] *nf* **1.** (*aspect*) shape, form; **en ~ de** in the shape of. **2.** (*état*) form; **être en (pleine) ~** to be in (great) shape, to be on (top) form. ▶ **formes** *nfpl* figure (*sg*).

formel, -elle [fɔrmɛl] *adj* **1.** (*définitif, ferme*) positive, definite. **2.** (*poli*) formal.

former [fɔrme] *vt* **1.** (*gén*) to form. **2.** (*personnel, élèves*) to train. **3.** (*goût, sensibilité*) to develop. ▶ **se former** *vp* **1.** (*se constituer*) to form. **2.** (*s'instruire*) to train o.s.

Formica® [fɔrmika] *nm inv* Formica®.

formidable [fɔrmidabl] *adj* **1.** (*épatant*) great, tremendous. **2.** (*incroyable*) incredible.

formol [fɔrmɔl] *nm* formalin.

formulaire [fɔrmyler] *nm* form; **remplir un ~** to fill in a form.

formule [fɔrmyl] *nf* **1.** (*expression*) expression; **~ de politesse** (*orale*) polite phrase; (*épistolaire*) letter ending. **2.** (CHIM & MATHS) formula. **3.** (*méthode*) way, method.

formuler [fɔrmyle] *vt* to formulate, to express.

fort, -e [fɔr, fɔrt] ◆ *adj* **1.** (*gén*) strong; **et le plus ~, c'est que ...** and the most amazing thing about it is ...; **c'est plus ~ que moi** I can't help it. **2.** (*corpulent*) heavy, big. **3.** (*doué*) gifted; **être ~ en qqch** to be good at sthg. **4.** (*puissant - voix*) loud; (- *vent, lumière, accent*) strong. **5.** (*considérable*) large; **il y a de ~es chances qu'il gagne** there's a good chance he'll win. ◆ *adv* **1.** (*frapper, battre*) hard; (*sonner, parler*) loud, loudly. **2.** *sout* (*très*) very. ◆ *nm* **1.** (*château*) fort. **2.** (*spécialité*): **ce n'est pas mon ~** it's not my forte ou strong point.

forteresse [fɔrtərɛs] *nf* fortress.

fortifiant, -e [fɔrtifjɑ̃, ɑ̃t] *adj* fortifying. ▶ **fortifiant** *nm* tonic.

fortification [fɔrtifikasjɔ̃] *nf* fortification.

fortifier [fɔrtifje] *vt* (*personne, ville*) to fortify.

fortuit, -e [fɔrtɥi, it] *adj* chance (*avant n*), fortuitous.

fortune [fɔrtyn] *nf* **1.** (*richesse*) fortune. **2.** (*hasard*) luck, fortune.

fortuné, -e [fɔrtyne] *adj* **1.** (*riche*) wealthy. **2.** (*chanceux*) fortunate, lucky.

forum [fɔrɔm] *nm* forum.

fosse [fos] *nf* **1.** (*trou*) pit. **2.** (*tombe*) grave.

fossé [fose] nm ditch; fig gap.

fossette [foset] nf dimple.

fossile [fosil] nm 1. (de plante, d'animal) fossil. 2. fig & péj (personne) fossil, fogy.

fossoyeur, -euse [foswajœr, øz] nm, f gravedigger.

fou, folle [fu, fɔl] ◆ adj (**fol** devant voyelle ou h muet) mad, insane; (prodigieux) tremendous. ◆ nm, f madman (f madwoman).

foudre [fudr] nf lightning.

foudroyant, -e [fudrwajã, ãt] adj 1. (progrès, vitesse) lightning (avant n); (succès) stunning. 2. (nouvelle) devastating; (regard) withering.

foudroyer [fudrwaje] vt 1. (suj: foudre) to strike; **l'arbre a été foudroyé** the tree was struck by lightning. 2. fig (abattre) to strike down, to kill; ~ qqn du regard to glare at sb.

fouet [fwɛ] nm 1. (en cuir) whip. 2. (CULIN) whisk.

fouetter [fwete] vt 1. (gén) to whip; (suj: pluie) to lash (against). 2. (stimuler) to stimulate.

fougère [fuʒɛr] nf fern.

fougue [fug] nf ardour.

fougueux, -euse [fugø, øz] adj ardent, spirited.

fouille [fuj] nf 1. (de personne, maison) search. 2. (du sol) dig, excavation.

fouiller [fuje] ◆ vt 1. (gén) to search. 2. fig (approfondir) to examine closely. ◆ vi: ~ dans to go through.

fouillis [fuji] nm jumble, muddle.

fouine [fwin] nf stone-marten.

fouiner [fwine] vi to ferret about.

foulard [fular] nm scarf.

foule [ful] nf (de gens) crowd.

foulée [fule] nf (de coureur) stride.

fouler [fule] vt (raisin) to press; (sol) to walk on. ▶ **se fouler** vp (MÉD): **se ~ le poignet/la cheville** to sprain one's wrist/ankle.

foulure [fulyr] nf sprain.

four [fur] nm 1. (de cuisson) oven; ~ **électrique/à micro-ondes** electric/microwave oven; ~ **crématoire** (HIST) oven. 2. (THÉÂTRE) flop.

fourbe [furb] adj treacherous, deceitful.

fourbu, -e [furby] adj tired out, exhausted.

fourche [furʃ] nf 1. (outil) pitchfork. 2. (de vélo, route) fork. 3. Belg (SCOL) free period.

fourchette [furʃɛt] nf 1. (couvert) fork. 2. (écart) range, bracket.

fourgon [furgɔ̃] nm 1. (camionnette) van; ~ **cellulaire** police van Br, patrol wagon Am. 2. (ferroviaire): ~ **à bestiaux** cattle truck; ~ **postal** mail van.

fourgonnette [furgɔnɛt] nf small van.

fourmi [furmi] nf (insecte) ant; fig hard worker.

fourmilière [furmiljɛr] nf anthill.

fourmiller [furmije] vi (pulluler) to swarm; ~ de fig to be swarming with.

fournaise [furnɛz] nf furnace.

fourneau, -x [furno] nm 1. (cuisinière, poêle) stove. 2. (de fonderie) furnace.

fournée [furne] nf batch.

fourni, -e [furni] adj (barbe, cheveux) thick.

fournil [furnil] nm bakery.

fournir [furnir] vt 1. (procurer): ~ qqch à qqn to supply ou provide sb with sthg. 2. (produire): ~ **un effort** to make an effort. 3. (approvisionner): ~ qqn (en) to supply sb (with).

fournisseur, -euse [furnisœr, øz] nm, f supplier.

fourniture [furnityr] nf supply, supplying (U). ▶ **fournitures** nfpl: ~s de bureau office supplies; ~s scolaires school supplies.

fourrage [furaʒ] nm fodder.

fourré [fure] nm thicket.

fourreau, -x [furo] nm 1. (d'épée) sheath; (de parapluie) cover. 2. (robe) sheath dress.

fourrer [fure] vt 1. (CULIN) to stuff, to fill. 2. fam (mettre): ~ qqch (dans) to stuff sthg (into). ▶ **se fourrer** vp: se ~ une idée dans la tête to get an idea into one's head; je ne savais plus où me ~ I didn't know where to put myself.

fourre-tout [furtu] nm inv 1. (pièce) lumber room Br, junk room Am. 2. (sac) holdall.

fourreur [furœr] nm furrier.

fourrière [furjɛr] nf pound.

fourrure [furyr] nf fur.

fourvoyer [furvwaje] ▶ **se fourvoyer** vp sout (s'égarer) to lose one's way; (se tromper) to go off on the wrong track.

foutre [futr] vt tfam 1. (mettre) to shove, to stick; ~ qqn dehors ou à la porte to chuck sb out. 2. (donner): ~ la trouille à qqn to put the wind up sb; il lui a foutu une baffe he thumped him one. 3. (faire) to do; ne rien ~ de la journée to do damn all all day; j'en ai rien à ~ I don't give a toss. ▶ **se foutre** vp tfam 1. (se mettre): se ~ dans (situation) to get o.s. into. 2. (se moquer): se ~ de (la gueule

de) qqn to laugh at sb, to take the mickey out of sb Br. **3.** (*ne pas s'intéresser*): **je m'en fous** I don't give a damn about it.

foyer [fwaje] *nm* **1.** (*maison*) home; **être mère au ~** to be a housewife and mother. **2.** (*résidence*) home, hostel. **3.** (*point central*) centre. **4.** (*de lunettes*) focus; **verres à double ~** bifocals.

fracas [fraka] *nm* roar.

fracasser [frakase] *vt* to smash, to shatter.

fraction [fraksjɔ̃] *nf* fraction.

fractionner [fraksjɔne] *vt* to divide (up), to split up.

fracture [fraktyr] *nf* (MÉD) fracture.

fracturer [fraktyre] *vt* **1.** (MÉD) to fracture. **2.** (*coffre, serrure*) to break open.

fragile [fraʒil] *adj* (*gén*) fragile; (*peau, santé*) delicate.

fragiliser [fraʒilize] *vt* to weaken.

fragilité [fraʒilite] *nf* fragility.

fragment [fragmɑ̃] *nm* **1.** (*morceau*) fragment. **2.** (*extrait - d'œuvre*) extract; (*- de conversation*) snatch.

fragmenter [fragmɑ̃te] *vt* to fragment, to break up.

fraîche → **frais**.

fraîcheur [frɛʃœr] *nf* **1.** (*d'air, d'accueil*) coolness. **2.** (*de teint, d'aliment*) freshness.

frais, fraîche [frɛ, frɛʃ] *adj* **1.** (*air, accueil*) cool; **une boisson fraîche** a cold drink. **2.** (*récent - trace*) fresh; (*- encre*) wet. **3.** (*teint*) fresh, clear. ▶ **frais** ◆ *nm*: **mettre qqch au ~** to put sthg in a cool place. ◆ *nmpl* (*dépenses*) expenses, costs; **aux ~ de la maison** at the company's expense; **faire des ~** to spend a lot of money; **rentrer dans ses ~** to cover one's expenses; **~ fixes** fixed costs. ◆ *adv*: **il fait ~** it's cool.

fraise [frɛz] *nf* **1.** (*fruit*) strawberry. **2.** (*de dentiste*) drill; (*de menuisier*) bit.

fraiseuse [frɛzøz] *nf* milling machine.

fraisier [frɛzje] *nm* **1.** (*plante*) strawberry plant. **2.** (*gâteau*) strawberry sponge.

framboise [frɑ̃bwaz] *nf* **1.** (*fruit*) raspberry. **2.** (*liqueur*) raspberry liqueur.

franc, franche [frɑ̃, frɑ̃ʃ] *adj* **1.** (*sincère*) frank. **2.** (*net*) clear, definite. ▶ **franc** *nm* franc.

français, -e [frɑ̃sɛ, ɛz] *adj* French. ▶ **français** *nm* (*langue*) French. ▶ **Français, -e** *nm, f* Frenchman (*f* Frenchwoman); **les Français** the French.

France [frɑ̃s] *nf*: **la ~** France; **~ 2, ~ 3** (TÉLÉ) *French state-owned television channels.*

franche → **franc**.

franchement [frɑ̃ʃmɑ̃] *adv* **1.** (*sincèrement*) frankly. **2.** (*nettement*) clearly. **3.** (*tout à fait*) completely, downright.

franchir [frɑ̃ʃir] *vt* **1.** (*obstacle*) to get over. **2.** (*porte*) to go through; (*seuil*) to cross. **3.** (*distance*) to cover.

franchise [frɑ̃ʃiz] *nf* **1.** (*sincérité*) frankness. **2.** (COMM) franchise. **3.** (*d'assurance*) excess. **4.** (*détaxe*) exemption.

franciscain, -e [frɑ̃siskɛ̃, ɛn] *adj & nm, f* Franciscan.

franciser [frɑ̃size] *vt* to frenchify.

franc-jeu [frɑ̃ʒø] *nm*: **jouer ~** to play fair.

franc-maçon, -onne [frɑ̃masɔ̃, ɔn] (*mpl* francs-maçons, *fpl* franc-maçonnes) *adj* masonic. ▶ **franc-maçon** *nm* freemason.

franc-maçonnerie [frɑ̃masɔnri] *nf* freemasonry (U).

franco [frɑ̃ko] *adv* (COMM): **~ de port** carriage paid.

francophone [frɑ̃kɔfɔn] ◆ *adj* French-speaking. ◆ *nmf* French speaker.

francophonie [frɑ̃kɔfɔni] *nf*: **la ~** French-speaking nations (*pl*).

franc-parler [frɑ̃parle] *nm*: **avoir son ~** to speak one's mind.

franc-tireur [frɑ̃tirœr] *nm* (MIL) irregular.

frange [frɑ̃ʒ] *nf* fringe.

frangipane [frɑ̃ʒipan] *nf* almond paste.

franglais [frɑ̃glɛ] *nm* Franglais.

franquette [frɑ̃kɛt] ▶ **à la bonne franquette** *loc adv* informally, without any ceremony.

frappant, -e [frapɑ̃, ɑ̃t] *adj* striking.

frapper [frape] ◆ *vt* **1.** (*gén*) to strike. **2.** (*boisson*) to chill. ◆ *vi* to knock.

frasques [frask] *nfpl* pranks, escapades.

fraternel, -elle [fratɛrnɛl] *adj* fraternal, brotherly.

fraterniser [fratɛrnize] *vi* to fraternize.

fraternité [fratɛrnite] *nf* brotherhood.

fratricide [fratrisid] *nmf* fratricide.

fraude [frod] *nf* fraud.

frauder [frode] *vt & vi* to cheat.

frauduleux, -euse [frodylø, øz] *adj* fraudulent.

frayer [freje] ▶ **se frayer** *vp*: **se ~ un chemin (à travers une foule)** to force one's way through (a crowd).

frayeur [frejœr] *nf* fright, fear.

fredaines [frədɛn] *nfpl* pranks.

fredonner [frədɔne] *vt & vi* to hum.

freezer [frizœr] *nm* freezer compartment.

frégate [fregat] *nf* (*bateau*) frigate.

frein [frɛ̃] *nm* **1.** (AUTOM) brake; **~ à main** handbrake. **2.** *fig* (*obstacle*) brake, check.

freinage [frɛnaʒ] *nm* braking.

freiner [frene] ♦ *vt* **1.** (*mouvement, véhicule*) to slow down; (*inflation, dépenses*) to curb. **2.** (*personne*) to restrain. ♦ *vi* to brake.

frelaté, -e [frəlate] *adj* (*vin*) adulterated; *fig* corrupt.

frêle [frɛl] *adj* (*enfant, voix*) frail.

frelon [frəlɔ̃] *nm* hornet.

frémir [fremir] *vi* **1.** (*corps, personne*) to tremble. **2.** (*eau*) to simmer.

frémissement [fremismɑ̃] *nm* **1.** (*de corps, personne*) shiver, trembling (U). **2.** (*d'eau*) simmering.

frêne [frɛn] *nm* ash.

frénésie [frenezi] *nf* frenzy.

frénétique [frenetik] *adj* frenzied.

fréquemment [frekamɑ̃] *adv* frequently.

fréquence [frekɑ̃s] *nf* frequency.

fréquent, -e [frekɑ̃, ɑ̃t] *adj* frequent.

fréquentation [frekɑ̃tasjɔ̃] *nf* **1.** (*d'endroit*) frequenting. **2.** (*de personne*) association. ▶ **fréquentations** *nfpl* company (U).

fréquenté, -e [frekɑ̃te] *adj*: **très ~** busy; **c'est très bien/mal ~** the right/wrong sort of people go there.

fréquenter [frekɑ̃te] *vt* **1.** (*endroit*) to frequent. **2.** (*personne*) to associate with; (*petit ami*) to go out with, to see. ▶ **se fréquenter** *vp* to meet each other.

frère [frɛr] ♦ *nm* brother. ♦ *adj* (*parti, pays*) sister (*avant n*).

fresque [frɛsk] *nf* fresco.

fret [frɛ] *nm* freight.

frétiller [fretije] *vi* (*poisson, personne*) to wriggle.

fretin [frətɛ̃] *nm*: **le menu ~** the small fry.

friable [frijabl] *adj* crumbly.

friand, -e [frijɑ̃, ɑ̃d] *adj*: **être ~ de** to be partial to.

friandise [frijɑ̃diz] *nf* delicacy.

fric [frik] *nm fam* cash.

friche [friʃ] *nf* fallow land; **en ~** fallow.

friction [friksjɔ̃] *nf* **1.** (*massage*) massage. **2.** *fig* (*désaccord*) friction.

frictionner [friksjɔne] *vt* to rub.

Frigidaire® [friʒidɛr] *nm* fridge, refrigerator.

frigide [friʒid] *adj* frigid.

frigo [frigo] *nm fam* fridge.

frigorifié, -e [frigɔrifje] *adj fam* frozen.

frileux, -euse [frilø, øz] *adj* (*craignant le froid*) sensitive to the cold.

frimas [frima] *nm littéraire* foggy winter weather.

frimer [frime] *vi fam* (*bluffer*) to pretend; (*se mettre en valeur*) to show off.

frimousse [frimus] *nf fam* dear little face.

fringale [frɛ̃gal] *nf fam*: **avoir la ~** to be starving.

fringant, -e [frɛ̃gɑ̃, ɑ̃t] *adj* high-spirited.

fripe [frip] *nf*: **les ~s** secondhand clothes.

fripon, -onne [fripɔ̃, ɔn] ♦ *nm, f fam vieilli* rogue, rascal. ♦ *adj* mischievous, cheeky.

fripouille [fripuj] *nf fam* scoundrel; **petite ~** little devil.

frire [frir] ♦ *vt* to fry. ♦ *vi* to fry.

frise [friz] *nf* (ARCHIT) frieze.

frisé, -e [frize] *adj* (*cheveux*) curly; (*personne*) curly-haired.

friser [frize] ♦ *vt* **1.** (*cheveux*) to curl. **2.** *fig* (*ressembler à*) to border on. ♦ *vi* to curl.

frisquet [friskɛ] *adj m*: **il fait ~** it's chilly.

frisson [frisɔ̃] *nm* (*gén*) shiver; (*de dégoût*) shudder.

frissonner [frisɔne] *vi* (*trembler*) to shiver; (*de dégoût*) to shudder.

frit, -e [fri, frit] *pp* → **frire**.

frite [frit] *nf* chip *Br*, (French) fry *Am*.

friteuse [fritøz] *nf* deep fat fryer.

friture [frityr] *nf* **1.** (*poisson*) fried fish. **2.** *fam* (RADIO) crackle.

frivole [frivɔl] *adj* frivolous.

frivolité [frivɔlite] *nf* frivolity.

froid, froide [frwa, frwad] *adj litt & fig* cold; **rester ~** to be unmoved. ▶ **froid** ♦ *nm* **1.** (*température*) cold; **prendre ~** to catch (a) cold. **2.** (*tension*) coolness. ♦ *adv*: **il fait ~** it's cold; **avoir ~** to be cold.

froidement [frwadmɑ̃] *adv* **1.** (*accueillir*) coldly. **2.** (*écouter, parler*) coolly. **3.** (*tuer*) cold-bloodedly.

froideur [frwadœr] *nf* **1.** (*indifférence*) coldness. **2.** (*impassibilité*) coolness.

froisser [frwase] *vt* **1.** (*tissu, papier*) to crumple, to crease. **2.** *fig* (*offenser*) to offend. ▶ **se froisser** *vp* **1.** (*tissu*) to crumple, to crease. **2.** (MÉD): **se ~ un muscle** to strain a muscle. **3.** (*se vexer*) to take offence.

frôler [frole] vt to brush against; fig to have a brush with, to come close to.

fromage [fromaʒ] nm cheese; ~ de brebis/de chèvre sheep's milk/goat's cheese.

FROMAGE

There are about 350 types of French cheese, which can be divided into soft cheeses (such as Camembert, Brie and Pont-l'Évêque), hard cheeses (such as Tomme and Comté) and blue cheeses (such as Bleu d'Auvergne), all made from cow's milk. There are also many cheeses made from goat's milk and sheep's milk. In France cheese is eaten with bread before dessert.

fromager, -ère [fromaʒe, ɛr] nm, f (fabricant) cheesemaker.

fromagerie [fromaʒri] nf cheese shop.

froment [fromã] nm wheat.

froncer [frõse] vt 1. (COUTURE) to gather. 2. (plisser): ~ les sourcils to frown.

frondaison [frõdɛzõ] nf 1. (phénomène) foliation. 2. (feuillage) foliage.

fronde [frõd] nf 1. (arme) sling; (jouet) catapult Br, slingshot Am. 2. (révolte) rebellion.

front [frõ] nm 1. (ANAT) forehead. 2. fig (audace) cheek. 3. (avant) front; (de bâtiment) front, façade; ~ de mer (sea) front. 4. (MÉTÉOR, MIL & POLIT) front.

frontal, -e, -aux [frõtal, o] adj 1. (ANAT) frontal. 2. (collision, attaque) head-on.

frontalier, -ère [frõtalje, ɛr] ♦ adj frontier (avant n); travailleur ~ person who lives on one side of the border and works on the other. ♦ nm, f inhabitant of border area.

frontière [frõtjɛr] ♦ adj border (avant n). ♦ nf frontier, border; fig frontier.

fronton [frõtõ] nm (ARCHIT) pediment.

frottement [frotmã] nm 1. (action) rubbing. 2. (contact, difficulté) friction.

frotter [frote] ♦ vt to rub; (parquet) to scrub. ♦ vi to rub, to scrape.

frottis [froti] nm smear.

fructifier [fryktifje] vi 1. (investissement) to give ou yield a profit. 2. (terre) to be productive. 3. (arbre, idée) to bear fruit.

fructueux, -euse [fryktɥø, øz] adj fruitful, profitable.

frugal, -e, -aux [frygal, o] adj frugal.

fruit [frɥi] nm litt & fig fruit (U); ~s de mer seafood (U).

fruité, -e [frɥite] adj fruity.

fruitier, -ère [frɥitje, ɛr] ♦ adj (arbre) fruit (avant n). ♦ nm, f fruiterer.

fruste [fryst] adj uncouth.

frustration [frystrasjõ] nf frustration.

frustrer [frystre] vt 1. (priver): ~ qqn de to deprive sb of. 2. (décevoir) to frustrate.

fuchsia [fyʃja] nm fuchsia.

fuel, fioul [fjul] nm 1. (de chauffage) fuel. 2. (carburant) fuel oil.

fugace [fygas] adj fleeting.

fugitif, -ive [fyʒitif, iv] ♦ adj fleeting. ♦ nm, f fugitive.

fugue [fyg] nf 1. (de personne) flight; faire une ~ to run away. 2. (MUS) fugue.

fui [fɥi] pp inv → fuir.

fuir [fɥir] ♦ vi 1. (détaler) to flee. 2. (tuyau) to leak. 3. fig (s'écouler) to fly by. ♦ vt (éviter) to avoid, to shun.

fuite [fɥit] nf 1. (de personne) escape, flight. 2. (écoulement, d'information) leak.

fulgurant, -e [fylgyrã, ãt] adj 1. (découverte) dazzling. 2. (vitesse) lightning (avant n). 3. (douleur) searing.

fulminer [fylmine] vi (personne): ~ (contre) to fulminate (against).

fumé, -e [fyme] adj 1. (CULIN) smoked. 2. (verres) tinted.

fumée [fyme] nf (de combustion) smoke.

fumer [fyme] ♦ vi 1. (personne, cheminée) to smoke. 2. (bouilloire, plat) to steam. ♦ vt 1. (cigarette, aliment) to smoke. 2. (AGRIC) to spread manure on.

fumeur, -euse [fymœr, øz] nm, f smoker.

fumier [fymje] nm (AGRIC) dung, manure.

fumiste [fymist] nmf péj skiver Br, shirker.

fumisterie [fymistəri] nf fam skiving Br, shirking.

fumoir [fymwar] nm 1. (pour aliments) smokehouse. 2. (pièce) smoking room.

funambule [fynãbyl] nmf tightrope walker.

funèbre [fynɛbr] adj 1. (de funérailles) funeral (avant n). 2. (lugubre) funereal; (sentiments) dismal.

funérailles [fyneraj] nfpl funeral (sg).

funéraire [fynerɛr] adj funeral (avant n).

funeste [fynɛst] adj 1. (accident) fatal. 2. (initiative, erreur) disastrous. 3. (présage) of doom.

funiculaire [fynikylɛr] nm funicular railway.

fur [fyr] ► au fur et à mesure loc adv as I/you etc go along; au ~ et à mesure des besoins as (and when) needed.

▶ **au fur et à mesure que** *loc conj* as (and when).

furet [fyrɛ] *nm* (*animal*) ferret.

fureter [fyrte] *vi* (*fouiller*) to ferret around.

fureur [fyrœr] *nf* (*colère*) fury.

furibond, -e [fyribɔ̃, ɔ̃d] *adj* furious.

furie [fyri] *nf* **1.** (*colère, agitation*) fury; **en ~** (*personne*) infuriated; (*éléments*) raging. **2.** *fig* (*femme*) shrew.

furieux, -euse [fyrjø, øz] *adj* **1.** (*personne*) furious. **2.** (*énorme*) tremendous.

furoncle [fyrɔ̃kl] *nm* boil.

furtif, -ive [fyrtif, iv] *adj* furtive.

fus, fut *etc* → **être**.

fusain [fyzɛ̃] *nm* **1.** (*crayon*) charcoal. **2.** (*dessin*) charcoal drawing.

fuseau, -x [fyzo] *nm* **1.** (*outil*) spindle. **2.** (*pantalon*) ski-pants (*pl*). ▶ **fuseau horaire** time zone.

fusée [fyze] *nf* (*pièce d'artifice & AÉRON*) rocket.

fuselage [fyzlaʒ] *nm* fuselage.

fuselé, -e [fyzle] *adj* (*doigts*) tapering; (*jambes*) slender.

fuser [fyze] *vi* (*cri, rire*) to burst forth ou out.

fusible [fyzibl] *nm* fuse.

fusil [fyzi] *nm* (*arme*) gun.

fusillade [fyzijad] *nf* (*combat*) gunfire (U), fusillade.

fusiller [fyzije] *vt* (*exécuter*) to shoot.

fusion [fyzjɔ̃] *nf* **1.** (*gén*) fusion. **2.** (*fonte*) smelting. **3.** (*ÉCON & POLIT*) merger.

fusionner [fyzjɔne] *vt & vi* to merge.

fustiger [fystiʒe] *vt* to castigate.

fut → **être**.

fût [fy] *nm* **1.** (*d'arbre*) trunk. **2.** (*tonneau*) barrel, cask. **3.** (*d'arme*) stock. **4.** (*de colonne*) shaft.

futaie [fyte] *nf* wood.

futile [fytil] *adj* **1.** (*insignifiant*) futile. **2.** (*frivole*) frivolous.

futur, -e [fytyr] ◆ *adj* future (*avant n*). ◆ *nm, f* (*fiancé*) intended. ▶ **futur** *nm* future.

futuriste [fytyrist] *adj* futuristic.

fuyant, -e [fɥijɑ̃, ɑ̃t] *adj* **1.** (*perspective, front*) receding (*avant n*). **2.** (*regard*) evasive.

fuyard, -e [fɥijar, ard] *nm, f* runaway.

G

g, G [ʒe] *nm inv* g, G.

gabardine [gabardin] *nf* gabardine.

gabarit [gabari] *nm* (*dimension*) size.

Gabon [gabɔ̃] *nm*: **le ~** Gabon.

gâcher [gaʃe] *vt* **1.** (*gaspiller*) to waste. **2.** (*gâter*) to spoil. **3.** (*CONSTR*) to mix.

gâchette [gaʃɛt] *nf* trigger.

gâchis [gaʃi] *nm* (*gaspillage*) waste (U).

gadget [gadʒɛt] *nm* gadget.

gadoue [gadu] *nf fam* (*boue*) mud.

gaélique [gaelik] ◆ *adj* Gaelic. ◆ *nm* Gaelic.

gaffe [gaf] *nf* **1.** *fam* (*maladresse*) clanger. **2.** (*outil*) boat hook.

gaffer [gafe] *vi fam* to put one's foot in it.

gag [gag] *nm* gag.

gage [gaʒ] *nm* **1.** (*dépôt*) pledge; **mettre qqch en ~** to pawn sthg. **2.** (*assurance, preuve*) proof. **3.** (*dans jeu*) forfeit.

gager [gaʒe] *vt*: **~ que** to bet (that).

gageure [gaʒyr] *nf* challenge.

gagnant, -e [gaɲɑ̃, ɑ̃t] ◆ *adj* winning (*avant n*). ◆ *nm, f* winner.

gagne-pain [gaɲpɛ̃] *nm inv* livelihood.

gagner [gaɲe] ◆ *vt* **1.** (*salaire, argent, repos*) to earn. **2.** (*course, prix, affection*) to win. **3.** (*obtenir, économiser*) to gain; **~ du temps/de la place** to gain time/space. **4.** (*atteindre*) to reach; (- *suj: feu, engourdissement*) to spread to; (- *suj: sommeil, froid*) to overcome. ◆ *vi* **1.** (*être vainqueur*) to win. **2.** (*bénéficier*) to gain; **~ à faire qqch** to be better off doing sthg; **qu'est-ce que j'y gagne?** what do I get out of it? **3.** (*s'améliorer*): **~ en** to increase in.

gai, -e [gɛ] *adj* **1.** (*joyeux*) cheerful, happy. **2.** (*vif, plaisant*) bright.

gaieté [gete] *nf* **1.** (*joie*) cheerfulness. **2.** (*vivacité*) brightness.

gaillard, -e [gajar, ard] *nm, f* strapping individual.

gain [gɛ̃] *nm* **1.** (*profit*) gain, profit. **2.** (*succès*) winning. **3.** (*économie*) saving. ▶ **gains** *nmpl* earnings.

gaine [gɛn] *nf* **1.** (*étui, enveloppe*) sheath. **2.** (*sous-vêtement*) girdle, corset.

gainer [gene] *vt* to sheathe.

gala [gala] *nm* gala, reception.

galant, -e [galɑ̃, ɑ̃t] adj 1. (courtois) gallant. 2. (amoureux) flirtatious. ▶ **galant** nm admirer.

galanterie [galɑ̃tri] nf 1. (courtoisie) gallantry, politeness. 2. (flatterie) compliment.

galaxie [galaksi] nf galaxy.

galbe [galb] nm curve.

gale [gal] nf (MÉD) scabies (U).

galère [galɛr] nf (NAVIG) galley; **quelle ~!** fig what a hassle!, what a drag!

galérer [galere] vi fam to have a hard time.

galerie [galri] nf 1. (gén) gallery; **~ marchande** ou **commerciale** shopping arcade. 2. (THÉÂTRE) circle. 3. (porte-bagages) roof rack.

galet [galɛ] nm 1. (caillou) pebble. 2. (TECHNOL) wheel, roller.

galette [galɛt] nf (CULIN) pancake (made from buckwheat flour); **~ des Rois** cake traditionally eaten on Twelfth Night.

GALETTE DES ROIS

This large round pastry, often filled with almond paste, is traditionally eaten on Twelfth Night, 6 January. It contains a small porcelain figurine (the 'fève'). The cake is shared out and the person who finds the 'fève' becomes the king or queen and is given a cardboard crown to wear.

galipette [galipɛt] nf fam somersault.

Galles [gal] → **pays**.

gallicisme [galisism] nm (expression) French idiom; (dans une langue étrangère) gallicism.

gallois, -e [galwa, az] adj Welsh. ▶ **gallois** nm (langue) Welsh. ▶ **Gallois, -e** nm, f Welshman (f Welshwoman); **les Gallois** the Welsh.

galon [galɔ̃] nm 1. (COUTURE) braid (U). 2. (MIL) stripe.

galop [galo] nm (allure) gallop; **au ~** (cheval) at a gallop; fig at the double.

galoper [galope] vi 1. (cheval) to gallop. 2. (personne) to run about. 3. (imagination) to run riot.

galopin [galopɛ̃] nm fam brat.

galvaniser [galvanize] vt litt & fig to galvanize.

galvauder [galvode] vt (ternir) to tarnish.

gambader [gɑ̃bade] vi (sautiller) to leap about; (agneau) to gambol.

gamelle [gamɛl] nf (plat) mess tin Br, kit Am.

gamin, -e [gamɛ̃, in] ◆ adj (puéril) childish. ◆ nm, f fam (enfant) kid.

gamme [gam] nf 1. (série) range; **~ de produits** product range. 2. (MUS) scale.

ganglion [gɑ̃gliɔ̃] nm ganglion.

gangrène [gɑ̃grɛn] nf gangrene; fig corruption, canker.

gangue [gɑ̃g] nf 1. (de minerai) gangue. 2. fig (carcan) straitjacket.

gant [gɑ̃] nm glove; **~ de toilette** face cloth, flannel Br.

garage [garaʒ] nm garage.

garagiste [garaʒist] nmf (propriétaire) garage owner; (réparateur) garage mechanic.

garant, -e [garɑ̃, ɑ̃t] nm, f (responsable) guarantor; **se porter ~ de** to vouch for. ▶ **garant** nm (garantie) guarantee.

garantie [garɑ̃ti] nf (gén) guarantee.

garantir [garɑ̃tir] vt 1. (assurer & COMM) to guarantee; **~ à qqn que** to assure ou guarantee sb that. 2. (protéger): **~ qqch (de)** to protect sthg (from).

garçon [garsɔ̃] nm 1. (enfant) boy. 2. (célibataire): **vieux ~** confirmed bachelor. 3. (serveur): **~ (de café)** waiter.

garçonnet [garsɔnɛ] nm little boy.

garçonnière [garsɔnjɛr] nf bachelor flat Br ou apartment Am.

garde [gard] ◆ nf 1. (surveillance) protection. 2. (veille): **pharmacie de ~** duty chemist. 3. (MIL) guard; **monter la ~** to go on guard. 4. loc: **être/se tenir sur ses ~s** to be/stay on one's guard; **mettre qqn en ~ contre qqch** to put sb on their guard about sthg; **mise en ~** warning. ◆ nmf keeper; **~ du corps** bodyguard; **~ d'enfants** childminder.

garde-à-vous [gardavu] nm inv attention; **se mettre au ~** to stand to attention.

garde-boue [gardəbu] nm inv mudguard Br, fender Am.

garde-chasse [gardəʃas] (pl **gardes-chasse** ou **gardes-chasses**) nm gamekeeper.

garde-fou [gardəfu] (pl **garde-fous**) nm railing, parapet.

garde-malade [gardəmalad] (pl **gardes-malades**) nmf nurse.

garde-manger [gardəmɑ̃ʒe] nm inv (pièce) pantry, larder; (armoire) meat safe Br, cooler Am.

garde-pêche [gardəpɛʃ] (pl **gardes-pêche**) nm (personne) water bailiff Br, fishwarden Am.

garder [garde] vt 1. (gén) to keep; (vêtement) to keep on. 2. (surveiller) to mind, to look after; (*défendre*) to guard. **3.** (*protéger*) **~ qqn de qqch** to save sb from sthg. ▶ **se garder** *vp* **1.** (*se conserver*) to keep. **2.** (*se méfier*): **se ~ de qqn/ qqch** to beware of sb/sthg. **3.** (*s'abstenir*): **se ~ de faire qqch** to take care not to do sthg.

garderie [gardəri] *nf* crèche Br, day nursery Br, day-care center Am.

garde-robe [gardərɔb] (*pl* **garde-robes**) *nf* wardrobe.

gardien, -enne [gardjɛ̃, ɛn] *nm, f* **1.** (*surveillant*) guard, keeper; **~ de but** goalkeeper; **~ de nuit** night watchman. **2.** *fig* (*défenseur*) protector, guardian. **3.** (*agent*): **~ de la paix** policeman.

gare¹ [gar] *nf* station; **~ routière** (*de marchandises*) road haulage depot; (*pour passagers*) bus station.

gare² [gar] *interj* (*attention*) watch out!; **~ aux voleurs** beware of pickpockets.

garer [gare] *vt* **1.** (*ranger*) to park. **2.** (*mettre à l'abri*) to put in a safe place. ▶ **se garer** *vp* **1.** (*stationner*) to park. **2.** (*se ranger*) to pull over.

gargariser [gargarize] ▶ **se gargariser** *vp* **1.** (*se rincer*) to gargle. **2.** *péj* (*se délecter*): **se ~ de** to delight ou revel in.

gargouiller [garguje] *vi* **1.** (*eau*) to gurgle. **2.** (*intestins*) to rumble.

garnement [garnəmɑ̃] *nm* rascal, pest.

garni [garni] *nm* *vieilli* furnished accommodation (U).

garnir [garnir] *vt* **1.** (*équiper*) to fit out, to furnish. **2.** (*remplir*) to fill. **3.** (*orner*): **~ qqch de** to decorate sthg with; (COUTURE) to trim sthg with.

garnison [garnizɔ̃] *nf* garrison.

garniture [garnityr] *nf* **1.** (*ornement*) trimming; (*de lit*) bed linen. **2.** (CULIN - *pour accompagner*) garnish Br, fixings (*pl*) Am; (- *pour remplir*) filling.

garrigue [garig] *nf* scrub.

garrot [garo] *nm* **1.** (*de cheval*) withers (*pl*). **2.** (MÉD) tourniquet.

gars [ga] *nm* *fam* **1.** (*garçon, homme*) lad. **2.** (*type*) guy, bloke Br.

gas-oil [gazɔjl, gazwal], **gazole** [gazɔl] *nm* diesel oil.

gaspillage [gaspijaʒ] *nm* waste.

gaspiller [gaspije] *vt* to waste.

gastrique [gastrik] *adj* gastric.

gastro-entérite [gastrɔɑ̃terit] (*pl* **gastro-entérites**) *nf* gastroenteritis (U).

gastronome [gastrɔnɔm] *nmf* gourmet.

gastronomie [gastrɔnɔmi] *nf* gastronomy.

gastronomique [gastrɔnɔmik] *adj* gastronomic; **guide ~** restaurant guide.

gâteau, -x [gato] *nm* cake; **~ sec** biscuit Br, cookie Am.

gâter [gate] *vt* **1.** (*gén*) to spoil; (*vacances, affaires*) to ruin, to spoil. **2.** *iron* (*combler*) to be too good to; **on est gâté!** just marvellous! ▶ **se gâter** *vp* **1.** (*temps*) to change for the worse. **2.** (*situation*) to take a turn for the worse.

gâteux, -euse [gatø, øz] *adj* senile.

gauche [goʃ] ◆ *nf* **1.** (*côté*) left, left-hand side; **à ~ (de)** on the left (of). **2.** (POLIT): **la ~** the left (wing); **de ~** left-wing. ◆ *adj* **1.** (*côté*) left. **2.** (*personne*) clumsy.

gaucher, -ère [goʃe, ɛr] ◆ *adj* left-handed. ◆ *nm, f* left-handed person.

gauchiste [goʃist] *nmf* leftist.

gaufre [gofr] *nf* waffle.

gaufrer [gofre] *vt* to emboss.

gaufrette [gofrɛt] *nf* wafer.

gaule [gol] *nf* **1.** (*perche*) pole. **2.** (*canne à pêche*) fishing rod.

gauler [gole] *vt* to bring ou shake down.

gaulliste [golist] *nmf & adj* Gaullist.

gaulois, -e [golwa, az] *adj* (*de Gaule*) Gallic. ▶ **Gaulois, -e** *nm, f* Gaul.

gaver [gave] *vt* **1.** (*animal*) to force-feed. **2.** (*personne*): **~ qqn de** to feed sb full of.

gay [gɛ] *adj inv & nm* gay.

gaz [gaz] *nm inv* gas.

gaze [gaz] *nf* gauze.

gazelle [gazɛl] *nf* gazelle.

gazer [gaze] *vt* to gas.

gazette [gazɛt] *nf* newspaper, gazette.

gazeux, -euse [gazø, øz] *adj* **1.** (CHIM) gaseous. **2.** (*boisson*) fizzy.

gazoduc [gazɔdyk] *nm* gas pipeline.

gazole = **gas-oil**.

gazon [gazɔ̃] *nm* (*herbe*) grass; (*terrain*) lawn.

gazouiller [gazuje] *vi* **1.** (*oiseau*) to chirp, to twitter. **2.** (*bébé*) to gurgle.

GB, G-B (*abr de* **Grande-Bretagne**) *nf* GB.

gd *abr de* **grand**.

GDF, Gdf (*abr de* **Gaz de France**) *French national gas company.*

geai [ʒɛ] *nm* jay.

géant, -e [ʒeɑ̃, ɑ̃t] ◆ *adj* gigantic, giant. ◆ *nm, f* giant.

geindre [ʒɛ̃dr] *vi* **1.** (*gémir*) to moan. **2.** *fam* (*pleurnicher*) to whine.

gel [ʒɛl] *nm* **1.** (MÉTÉOR) frost. **2.** (*d'eau*) freezing. **3.** (*cosmétique*) gel.

gélatine [ʒelatin] *nf* gelatine.

gelée [ʒəle] *nf* **1.** (MÉTÉOR) frost. **2.** (CULIN) jelly.

geler [ʒəle] *vt & vi* **1.** (*gén*) to freeze. **2.** (*projet*) to halt.

gélule [ʒelyl] *nf* capsule.

Gémeaux [ʒemo] *nmpl* (ASTROL) Gemini.

gémir [ʒemir] *vi* **1.** (*gén*) to moan. **2.** (*par déception*) to groan.

gémissement [ʒemismɑ̃] *nm* **1.** (*gén*) moan; (*du vent*) moaning (U). **2.** (*de déception*) groan.

gemme [ʒɛm] *nf* gem, precious stone.

gênant, -e [ʒenɑ̃, ɑ̃t] *adj* **1.** (*encombrant*) in the way. **2.** (*embarrassant*) awkward, embarrassing. **3.** (*énervant*): **être ~** to be a nuisance.

gencive [ʒɑ̃siv] *nf* gum.

gendarme [ʒɑ̃darm] *nm* policeman.

gendarmerie [ʒɑ̃darməri] *nf* **1.** (*corps*) police force. **2.** (*lieu*) police station.

gendre [ʒɑ̃dr] *nm* son-in-law.

gène [ʒɛn] *nm* gene.

gêne [ʒɛn] *nf* **1.** (*physique*) difficulty. **2.** (*psychologique*) embarrassment. **3.** (*financière*) difficulty.

généalogie [ʒenealɔʒi] *nf* genealogy.

généalogique [ʒenealɔʒik] *adj* genealogical; **arbre ~** family tree.

gêner [ʒene] *vt* **1.** (*physiquement - gén*) to be too tight for; (*- suj: chaussures*) to pinch. **2.** (*moralement*) to embarrass. **3.** (*incommoder*) to bother. **4.** (*encombrer*) to hamper.

général, -e, -aux [ʒeneral, o] *adj* general; **en ~** generally, in general; **répétition ~e** dress rehearsal. ▶ **général** *nm* (MIL) general. ▶ **générale** *nf* (THÉÂTRE) dress rehearsal.

généralement [ʒeneralmɑ̃] *adv* generally.

généralisation [ʒeneralizasjɔ̃] *nf* generalization.

généraliser [ʒeneralize] *vt & vi* to generalize. ▶ **se généraliser** *vp* to become general ou widespread.

généraliste [ʒeneralist] ♦ *nmf* GP Br, family doctor. ♦ *adj* general.

généralité [ʒeneralite] *nf* **1.** (*idée*) generality. **2.** (*universalité*) general nature. ▶ **généralités** *nfpl* generalities.

générateur, -trice [ʒeneratœr, tris] *adj* generating. ▶ **générateur** *nm* (TECHNOL) generator.

génération [ʒenerasjɔ̃] *nf* generation.

générer [ʒenere] *vt* to generate.

généreux, -euse [ʒenerø, øz] *adj* generous; (*terre*) fertile.

générique [ʒenerik] ♦ *adj* generic. ♦ *nm* credits (*pl*).

générosité [ʒenerozite] *nf* generosity.

genèse [ʒənɛz] *nf* (*création*) genesis. ▶ **Genèse** *nf* (BIBLE) Genesis.

genêt [ʒənɛ] *nm* broom.

génétique [ʒenetik] ♦ *adj* genetic. ♦ *nf* genetics (U).

Genève [ʒənɛv] *n* Geneva.

génial, -e, -aux [ʒenjal, o] *adj* **1.** (*personne*) of genius. **2.** (*idée, invention*) inspired. **3.** *fam* (*formidable*): **c'est ~!** that's great!, that's terrific!

génie [ʒeni] *nm* **1.** (*personne, aptitude*) genius. **2.** (MYTH) spirit, genie. **3.** (TECHNOL) engineering; **le ~** (MIL) ≃ the Royal Engineers Br, ≃ the (Army) Corps of Engineers Am.

genièvre [ʒənjɛvr] *nm* juniper.

génisse [ʒenis] *nf* heifer.

génital, -e, -aux [ʒenital, o] *adj* genital.

génitif [ʒenitif] *nm* genitive (case).

génocide [ʒenɔsid] *nm* genocide.

genou, -x [ʒənu] *nm* knee; **à ~x** on one's knees, kneeling.

genouillère [ʒənujer] *nf* **1.** (*bandage*) knee bandage. **2.** (SPORT) kneepad.

genre [ʒɑ̃r] *nm* **1.** (*type*) type, kind. **2.** (LITTÉRATURE) genre. **3.** (*style de personne*) style. **4.** (GRAM) gender.

gens [ʒɑ̃] *nmpl* people.

gentiane [ʒɑ̃sjan] *nf* gentian.

gentil, -ille [ʒɑ̃ti, ij] *adj* **1.** (*agréable*) nice. **2.** (*aimable*) kind, nice.

gentillesse [ʒɑ̃tijɛs] *nf* kindness.

gentiment [ʒɑ̃timɑ̃] *adv* **1.** (*sagement*) nicely. **2.** (*aimablement*) kindly, nicely. **3.** *Helv* (*tranquillement*) calmly, quietly.

génuflexion [ʒenyflɛksjɔ̃] *nf* genuflexion.

géographie [ʒeɔgrafi] *nf* geography.

geôlier, -ère [ʒolje, ɛr] *nm, f* gaoler.

géologie [ʒeɔlɔʒi] *nf* geology.

géologique [ʒeɔlɔʒik] *adj* geological.

géologue [ʒeɔlɔg] *nmf* geologist.

géomètre [ʒeɔmɛtr] *nmf* **1.** (*spécialiste*) geometer, geometrician. **2.** (*technicien*) surveyor.

géométrie [ʒeɔmetri] *nf* geometry.

gérance [ʒerɑ̃s] *nf* management.

géranium [ʒeranjɔm] *nm* geranium.

gérant, -e [ʒerɑ̃, ɑ̃t] *nm, f* manager.

gerbe [ʒɛrb] *nf* **1.** (*de blé*) sheaf; (*de fleurs*) spray. **2.** (*d'étincelles, d'eau*) shower.

gercé, -e [ʒɛrse] *adj* chapped.

gérer [ʒere] *vt* to manage.

gériatrie [ʒerjatri] *nf* geriatrics (U).

germain, -e [ʒɛrmɛ̃, ɛn] → **cousin**.

germanique [ʒɛrmanik] *adj* Germanic.

germe [ʒɛrm] *nm* **1.** (BOT & MÉD) germ; (*de pomme de terre*) eye. **2.** *fig* (*origine*) seed, cause.

germer [ʒɛrme] *vi* to germinate.

gésier [ʒezje] *nm* gizzard.

gésir [ʒezir] *vi littéraire* to lie.

gestation [ʒɛstasjɔ̃] *nf* gestation.

geste [ʒɛst] *nm* **1.** (*mouvement*) gesture. **2.** (*acte*) act, deed.

gesticuler [ʒɛstikyle] *vi* to gesticulate.

gestion [ʒɛstjɔ̃] *nf* management; (JUR) administration; **~ de fichiers** (INFORM) file management.

Ghana [gana] *nm:* **le ~** Ghana.

ghetto [geto] *nm litt & fig* ghetto.

gibet [ʒibɛ] *nm* gallows (*sg*), gibbet.

gibier [ʒibje] *nm* game; *fig* (*personne*) prey.

giboulée [ʒibule] *nf* sudden shower.

gicler [ʒikle] *vi* to squirt, to spurt.

gifle [ʒifl] *nf* slap.

gifler [ʒifle] *vt* to slap; *fig* (*suj: vent, pluie*) to whip, to lash.

gigantesque [ʒigɑ̃tɛsk] *adj* gigantic.

gigolo [ʒigolo] *nm* gigolo.

gigot [ʒigo] *nm* (CULIN) leg.

gigoter [ʒigote] *vi* to squirm, to wriggle.

gilet [ʒile] *nm* **1.** (*cardigan*) cardigan. **2.** (*sans manches*) waistcoat Br, vest Am.

gin [dʒin] *nm* gin.

gingembre [ʒɛ̃ʒɑ̃br] *nm* ginger.

girafe [ʒiraf] *nf* giraffe.

giratoire [ʒiratwar] *adj* gyrating; **sens ~** roundabout Br, traffic circle Am.

girofle [ʒirɔfl] → **clou**.

girouette [ʒirwɛt] *nf* weathercock.

gisement [ʒizmɑ̃] *nm* deposit.

gît → **gésir**.

gitan, -e [ʒitɑ̃, an] *adj* Gipsy (*avant n*). ► **Gitan, -e** *nm, f* Gipsy.

gîte [ʒit] *nm* **1.** (*logement*): **~ rural** gîte, *self-catering accommodation in the country.* **2.** (*du bœuf*) shin Br, shank Am.

GÎTE (RURAL)

Often quite large converted farmhouses or outbuildings, 'gîtes' can be rented out as self-catering accommodation by holidaymakers. They are classified according to the level of comfort and amenities provided.

---

givre [ʒivr] *nm* frost.

glabre [glabr] *adj* hairless.

glace [glas] *nf* **1.** (*eau congelée*) ice. **2.** (*crème glacée*) ice cream. **3.** (*vitre*) pane; (*- de voiture*) window. **4.** (*miroir*) mirror.

glacé, -e [glase] *adj* **1.** (*gelé*) frozen. **2.** (*très froid*) freezing. **3.** *fig* (*hostile*) cold. **4.** (*dessert*) iced; (*viande*) glazed; (*fruit*) glacé.

glacer [glase] *vt* **1.** (*geler, paralyser*) to chill. **2.** (*étoffe, papier*) to glaze. **3.** (*gâteau*) to ice Br, to frost Am.

glacial, -e, -aux [glasjal, o] *adj litt & fig* icy.

glacier [glasje] *nm* **1.** (GÉOGR) glacier. **2.** (*marchand*) ice cream seller *ou* man.

glaçon [glasɔ̃] *nm* **1.** (*dans boisson*) ice cube. **2.** (*sur toit*) icicle. **3.** *fam fig* (*personne*) iceberg.

glaïeul [glajœl] *nm* gladiolus.

glaire [glɛr] *nf* (MÉD) phlegm.

glaise [glɛz] *nf* clay.

glaive [glɛv] *nm* sword.

gland [glɑ̃] *nm* **1.** (*de chêne*) acorn. **2.** (*ornement*) tassel. **3.** (ANAT) glans.

glande [glɑ̃d] *nf* gland.

glaner [glane] *vt* to glean.

glapir [glapir] *vi* to yelp, to yap.

glas [gla] *nm* knell.

glauque [glok] *adj* **1.** (*couleur*) blueygreen. **2.** *fam* (*lugubre*) gloomy. **3.** *fam* (*sordide*) sordid.

glissade [glisad] *nf* slip.

glissant, -e [glisɑ̃, ɑ̃t] *adj* slippery.

glissement [glismɑ̃] *nm* **1.** (*action de glisser*) gliding, sliding. **2.** *fig* (*électoral*) swing, shift.

glisser [glise] ◆ *vi* **1.** (*se déplacer*): **~ (sur)** to glide (over), to slide (over). **2.** (*déraper*): **~ (sur)** to slip (on). **3.** *fig* (*passer rapidement*): **~ sur** to skate over. **4.** (*surface*) to be slippery. **5.** (*progresser*) to slip; **~ dans/vers** to slip into/ towards, to slide into/towards. ◆ *vt* to slip; **~ un regard à qqn** *fig* to give sb a sidelong glance. ► **se glisser** *vp* to slip; **se ~ dans** (*lit*) to slip *ou* slide into; *fig* to slip *ou* creep into.

glissière [glisjɛr] *nf* runner.

global, -e, -aux [global, o] *adj* global.

globalement [globalmɑ̃] *adv* on the whole.

globe [glob] *nm* **1.** (*sphère, terre*) globe. **2.** (*de verre*) glass cover.

globule [glɔbyl] *nm* corpuscle, blood cell; ~ **blanc/rouge** white/red corpuscle.

globuleux [glɔbylø] → **œil**.

gloire [glwar] *nf* 1. (*renommée*) glory; (*de vedette*) fame, stardom. 2. (*mérite*) credit.

glorieux, -euse [glɔrjø, øz] *adj* (*mort, combat*) glorious; (*héros, soldat*) renowned.

glossaire [glɔsɛr] *nm* glossary.

glousser [gluse] *vi* 1. (*poule*) to cluck. 2. *fam* (*personne*) to chortle, to chuckle.

glouton, -onne [glutɔ̃, ɔn] ◆ *adj* greedy. ◆ *nm, f* glutton.

glu [gly] *nf* (*colle*) glue.

gluant, -e [glyɑ̃, ɑ̃t] *adj* sticky.

glucide [glysid] *nm* glucide.

glycémie [glisemi] *nf* glycaemia.

glycine [glisin] *nf* wisteria.

go [go] ► **tout de go** *loc adv* straight.

GO (*abr de* **grandes ondes**) *nfpl* LW.

goal [gol] *nm* goalkeeper.

gobelet [gɔblɛ] *nm* beaker, tumbler.

gober [gɔbe] *vt* 1. (*avaler*) to gulp down. 2. *fam* (*croire*) to swallow.

godet [gɔdɛ] *nm* 1. (*récipient*) jar, pot. 2. (COUTURE) flare.

godiller [gɔdije] *vi* 1. (*rameur*) to scull. 2. (*skieur*) to wedeln.

goéland [gɔelɑ̃] *nm* gull, seagull.

goélette [gɔelɛt] *nf* schooner.

goguenard, -e [gɔgnar, ard] *adj* mocking.

goinfre [gwɛ̃fr] *nmf fam* pig.

goitre [gwatr] *nm* goitre.

golf [gɔlf] *nm* (*sport*) golf; (*terrain*) golf course.

golfe [gɔlf] *nm* gulf, bay; **le ~ de Gascogne** the Bay of Biscay; **le ~ Persique** the (Persian) Gulf.

gomme [gɔm] *nf* 1. (*substance, bonbon*) gum. 2. (*pour effacer*) rubber *Br*, eraser.

gommer [gɔme] *vt* to rub out, to erase; *fig* to erase.

gond [gɔ̃] *nm* hinge.

gondole [gɔ̃dɔl] *nf* gondola.

gondoler [gɔ̃dɔle] *vi* (*bois*) to warp; (*carton*) to curl.

gonfler [gɔ̃fle] ◆ *vt* 1. (*ballon, pneu*) to blow up, to inflate; (*rivière, poitrine, yeux*) to swell; (*joues*) to blow out. 2. *fig* (*grossir*) to exaggerate. ◆ *vi* to swell.

gonflette [gɔ̃flɛt] *nf fam:* **faire de la ~** to pump iron.

gong [gɔ̃g] *nm* gong.

gorge [gɔrʒ] *nf* 1. (*gosier, cou*) throat. 2. (*gén pl*) (*vallée*) gorge.

gorgée [gɔrʒe] *nf* mouthful.

gorger [gɔrʒe] *vt:* ~ **qqn de qqch** (*gaver*) to stuff sb with sthg; (*combler*) to heap sthg on sb; ~ **qqch de** to fill sthg with.

gorille [gɔrij] *nm* (*animal*) gorilla.

gosier [gozje] *nm* throat, gullet.

gosse [gɔs] *nmf fam* kid.

gothique [gɔtik] *adj* 1. (ARCHIT) Gothic. 2. (TYPO): **écriture** ~ Gothic script.

gouache [gwaʃ] *nf* gouache.

goudron [gudrɔ̃] *nm* tar.

goudronner [gudrɔne] *vt* to tar.

gouffre [gufr] *nm* abyss.

goujat [guʒa] *nm* boor.

goulet [gulɛ] *nm* narrows (*pl*).

goulot [gulo] *nm* neck.

goulu, -e [guly] *adj* greedy, gluttonous. ◆ *nm, f* glutton.

goupillon [gupijɔ̃] *nm* 1. (RELIG) (*holy water*) sprinkler. 2. (*à bouteille*) bottle brush.

gourd, -e [gur, gurd] *adj* numb.

gourde [gurd] ◆ *nf* 1. (*récipient*) flask, waterbottle. 2. *fam* (*personne*) clot *Br*. ◆ *adj fam* thick.

gourdin [gurdɛ̃] *nm* club.

gourmand, -e [gurmɑ̃, ɑ̃d] ◆ *adj* greedy. ◆ *nm, f* glutton.

gourmandise [gurmɑ̃diz] *nf* 1. (*caractère*) greed, greediness. 2. (*sucrerie*) sweet thing.

gourmette [gurmɛt] *nf* chain bracelet.

gousse [gus] *nf* pod; ~ **d'ail** clove of garlic.

goût [gu] *nm* taste; **de mauvais ~** tasteless, in bad taste; **chacun ses ~s, à chacun son ~** everyone to his own taste.

goûter [gute] ◆ *vt* 1. (*déguster*) to taste. 2. (*savourer*) to enjoy. ◆ *vi* to have an afternoon snack; ~ **à** to taste. ◆ *nm* afternoon snack for children, typically consisting of bread, butter, chocolate and a drink.

goutte [gut] *nf* 1. (*de pluie, d'eau*) drop. 2. (MÉD) (*maladie*) gout. ► **gouttes** *nfpl* (MÉD) drops.

goutte-à-goutte [gutagut] *nm inv* (intravenous) drip *Br*, IV *Am*.

gouttelette [gutlɛt] *nf* droplet.

gouttière [gutjɛr] *nf* 1. (CONSTR - *horizontale*) gutter; (- *verticale*) drainpipe. 2. (MÉD) splint.

gouvernail [guvɛrnaj] *nm* rudder.

gouvernante [guvɛrnɑ̃t] *nf* 1. (*d'enfants*) governess. 2. (*de maison*) housekeeper.

gouvernement [guvɛrnəmɑ̃] *nm* government.

gouverner [guvɛrne] *vt* to govern.

gouverneur [guvɛrnœr] *nm* governor.

grâce [gras] *nf* 1. (*charme*) grace; **de**

bonne ~ with good grace, willingly; **de mauvaise ~** with bad grace, reluctantly. **2.** (*faveur*) favour. **3.** (*miséricorde*) mercy. ▶ **grâce à** *loc prép* thanks to.

gracier [grasje] *vt* to pardon.

gracieusement [grasjøzmã] *adv* **1.** (*avec grâce*) graciously. **2.** (*gratuitement*) free (of charge).

gracieux, -euse [grasjø, øz] *adj* **1.** (*charmant*) graceful. **2.** (*gratuit*) free.

gradation [gradasjɔ̃] *nf* gradation.

grade [grad] *nm* (*échelon*) rank; (*universitaire*) qualification.

gradé, -e [grade] ◆ *adj* non-commissioned. ◆ *nm, f* non-commissioned officer, NCO.

gradin [gradɛ̃] *nm* (*de stade, de théâtre*) tier; (*de terrain*) terrace.

graduation [gradɥasjɔ̃] *nf* graduation.

graduel, -elle [gradɥɛl] *adj* gradual; (*difficultés*) increasing.

graduer [gradɥe] *vt* **1.** (*récipient, règle*) to graduate. **2.** *fig* (*effort, travail*) to increase gradually.

graffiti [grafiti] *nm inv* graffiti (U).

grain [grɛ̃] *nm* **1.** (*gén*) grain; (*de moutarde*) seed; (*de café*) bean; (*de raisin*) grape. **2.** (*point*): **~ de beauté** beauty spot. **3.** (*averse*) squall.

graine [grɛn] *nf* (BOT) seed.

graisse [grɛs] *nf* **1.** (ANAT & CULIN) fat. **2.** (*pour lubrifier*) grease.

graisser [grɛse] *vt* **1.** (*machine*) to grease, to lubricate. **2.** (*vêtements*) to get grease on.

grammaire [gramɛr] *nf* grammar.

grammatical, -e, -aux [gramatikal, o] *adj* grammatical.

gramme [gram] *nm* gram, gramme.

grand, -e [grã, grãd] ◆ *adj* **1.** (*en hauteur*) tall; (*en dimensions*) big, large; (*en quantité, nombre*) large, great; **un ~ nombre de** a large ou great number of; **en ~** (*dimension*) full-size. **2.** (*âgé*) grown-up; **les ~es personnes** grown-ups; **~ frère** big ou older brother. **3.** (*important, remarquable*) great; **un ~ homme** a great man. **4.** (*intense*): **un ~ blessé/brûlé** a person with serious wounds/burns; **un ~ buveur/fumeur** a heavy drinker/smoker. ◆ *nm, f* (*gén pl*) **1.** (*personnage*) great man (*f* woman); **c'est l'un des ~s de l'électroménager** he's one of the big names in electrical appliances. **2.** (*enfant*) older ou bigger boy (*f* girl).

grand-angle [grãtãgl] *nm* wide-angle lens.

grand-chose [grãʃoz] ▶ **pas grand-chose** *pron indéf* not much.

Grande-Bretagne [grãdbrətaɲ] *nf*: **la ~** Great Britain.

grandeur [grãdœr] *nf* **1.** (*taille*) size. **2.** (*apogée & fig*) greatness; **~ d'âme** *fig* magnanimity.

grandir [grãdir] ◆ *vt*: **~ qqn** (*suj: chaussures*) to make sb look taller; *fig* to increase sb's standing. ◆ *vi* (*personne, plante*) to grow; (*obscurité, bruit*) to increase, to grow.

grandissant, -e [grãdisã, ãt] *adj* growing.

grand-mère [grãmɛr] *nf* grandmother; *fam fig* old biddy.

grand-père [grãpɛr] *nm* grandfather; *fam fig* old geezer.

grands-parents [grãparã] *nmpl* grandparents.

grange [grãʒ] *nf* barn.

granit(e) [granit] *nm* granite.

granulé, -e [granyle] *adj* (*surface*) granular. ▶ **granulé** *nm* tablet.

granuleux, -euse [granylø, øz] *adj* granular.

graphique [grafik] ◆ *nm* diagram; (*graphe*) graph. ◆ *adj* graphic.

graphisme [grafism] *nm* **1.** (*écriture*) handwriting. **2.** (ART) style of drawing. **3.** (*design*) design; (*image*) graphics (U).

graphiste [grafist] *nmf* graphic designer.

graphologie [grafɔlɔʒi] *nf* graphology.

grappe [grap] *nf* **1.** (*de fruits*) bunch; (*de fleurs*) stem. **2.** *fig* (*de gens*) knot.

grappiller [grapije] *vt litt & fig* to gather, to pick up.

grappin [grapɛ̃] *nm* (*ancre*) grapnel.

gras, grasse [gra, gras] *adj* **1.** (*personne, animal*) fat. **2.** (*plat, aliment*) fatty; **matières grasses** fats. **3.** (*cheveux, mains*) greasy. **4.** (*sol*) clayey; (*crayon*) soft. **5.** *fig* (*rire*) throaty; (*toux*) phlegmy. ▶ **gras** ◆ *nm* **1.** (*du jambon*) fat. **2.** (TYPO) bold (type). ◆ *adv*: **manger ~** to eat fatty foods.

grassement [grasmã] *adv* **1.** (*rire*) coarsely. **2.** (*payer*) a lot.

gratifier [gratifje] *vt* **1.** (*accorder*): **~ qqn de qqch** to present sb with sthg, to present sthg to sb; *fig* to reward sb with sthg. **2.** (*stimuler*) to gratify.

gratin [gratɛ̃] *nm* **1.** (CULIN) dish sprinkled with breadcrumbs or cheese and browned; **~ dauphinois** sliced potatoes baked with cream and browned on top. **2.** *fam fig* (*haute société*) upper crust.

gratiné, -e [gratine] *adj* 1. (CULIN) *sprinkled with breadcrumbs or cheese and browned.* 2. *fam fig* (ardu) stiff.

gratis [gratis] *adv* free.

gratitude [gratityd] *nf*: ~ **(envers)** gratitude (to ou towards).

gratte-ciel [gratsjɛl] *nm inv* skyscraper.

grattement [gratmã] *nm* scratching.

gratter [grate] ◆ *vt* (gén) to scratch; (pour enlever) to scrape off. ◆ *vi* 1. (démanger) to itch, to be itchy. 2. *fam* (écrire) to scribble. 3. (frapper): ~ **à la porte** to tap at the door. 4. *fam* (travailler) to slave, to slog. ▶ **se gratter** *vp* to scratch.

gratuit, -e [gratɥi, it] *adj* 1. (entrée) free. 2. (violence) gratuitous.

gratuitement [gratɥitmã] *adv* 1. (sans payer) free, for nothing. 2. (sans raison) gratuitously.

gravats [grava] *nmpl* rubble (U).

grave [grav] ◆ *adj* 1. (attitude, faute, maladie) serious, grave; **ce n'est pas ~** (ce n'est rien) don't worry about it. 2. (voix) deep. 3. (LING): **accent ~** grave accent. ◆ *nm* (gén pl) (MUS) low register.

gravement [gravmã] *adv* gravely, seriously.

graver [grave] *vt* 1. (gén) to engrave. 2. (bois) to carve. 3. (disque) to cut.

gravier [gravje] *nm* gravel (U).

gravillon [gravijɔ̃] *nm* fine gravel (U).

gravir [gravir] *vt* to climb.

gravité [gravite] *nf* 1. (importance) seriousness, gravity. 2. (PHYS) gravity.

graviter [gravite] *vi* 1. (astre) to revolve. 2. *fig* (évoluer) to gravitate.

gravure [gravyr] *nf* 1. (technique): ~ **(sur)** engraving (on). 2. (reproduction) print; (dans livre) plate.

gré [gre] *nm* 1. (goût): **à mon/son ~** for my/his taste, for my/his liking. 2. (volonté): **bon ~ mal ~** willy nilly; **de ~ ou de force** *fig* whether you/they *etc* like it or not; **de mon/son plein ~** of my/his own free will.

grec, grecque [grɛk] *adj* Greek. ▶ **grec** *nm* (langue) Greek. ▶ **Grec, Grecque** *nm, f* Greek.

Grèce [grɛs] *nf*: **la ~** Greece.

gréement [gremã] *nm* rigging.

greffe [grɛf] *nf* 1. (MÉD) transplant; (de peau) graft. 2. (BOT) graft.

greffer [grɛfe] *vt* 1. (MÉD) to transplant; (peau) to graft; ~ **un rein/un cœur à qqn** to give sb a kidney/heart transplant. 2. (BOT) to graft. ▶ **se greffer** *vp*:

se ~ sur qqch to be added to sthg.

greffier [grɛfje] *nm* clerk of the court.

grégaire [greger] *adj* gregarious.

grêle [grɛl] ◆ *nf* hail. ◆ *adj* 1. (jambes) spindly. 2. (son) shrill.

grêler [grele] *v impers* to hail; **il grêle** it's hailing.

grêlon [grelɔ̃] *nm* hailstone.

grelot [grəlo] *nm* bell.

grelotter [grəlɔte] *vi*: ~ **(de)** to shiver (with).

grenade [grənad] *nf* 1. (fruit) pomegranate. 2. (MIL) grenade.

grenat [grəna] *adj inv* dark red.

grenier [grənje] *nm* 1. (de maison) attic. 2. (à foin) loft.

grenouille [grənuj] *nf* frog.

grès [grɛ] *nm* 1. (roche) sandstone. 2. (poterie) stoneware.

grésiller [grezije] *vi* 1. (friture) to sizzle; (feu) to crackle. 2. (radio) to crackle.

grève [grɛv] *nf* 1. (arrêt du travail) strike; **être en ~** to be on strike; **faire ~** to strike, to go on strike. 2. (rivage) shore.

grever [grəve] *vt* to burden; (budget) to put a strain on.

gréviste [grevist] *nmf* striker.

gribouiller [gribuje] *vt & vi* 1. (écrire) to scrawl. 2. (dessiner) to doodle.

grief [grijɛf] *nm* grievance; **faire ~ de qqch à qqn** to hold sthg against sb.

grièvement [grijɛvmã] *adv* seriously.

griffe [grif] *nf* 1. (d'animal) claw. 2. *Belg* (éraflure) scratch.

griffer [grife] *vt* (suj: chat etc) to claw.

grignoter [griɲɔte] ◆ *vt* 1. (manger) to nibble. 2. *fam fig* (réduire - capital) to eat away (at). ◆ *vi* 1. (manger) to nibble. 2. *fam fig* (prendre): ~ **sur** to nibble away at.

gril [gril] *nm* grill.

grillade [grijad] *nf* (CULIN) grilled meat.

grillage [grijaʒ] *nm* 1. (de porte, de fenêtre) wire netting. 2. (clôture) wire fence.

grille [grij] *nf* 1. (portail) gate. 2. (d'orifice, de guichet) grille; (de fenêtre) bars (pl). 3. (de mots croisés, de loto) grid. 4. (tableau) table.

grille-pain [grijpɛ̃] *nm inv* toaster.

griller [grije] ◆ *vt* 1. (viande) to grill Br, to broil Am; (pain) to toast; (café, marrons) to roast. 2. *fig* (au soleil - personne) to burn; (- végétation) to shrivel. 3. *fam fig* (dépasser - concurrents) to outstrip; ~ **un feu rouge** to jump the lights. 4. *fig* (compromettre) to ruin. ◆ *vi* 1. (viande) to grill Br, to broil Am. 2. (ampoule) to blow.

grillon [grijɔ̃] nm (insecte) cricket.

grimace [grimas] nf grimace.

grimer [grime] vt (CIN & THÉÂTRE) to make up.

grimper [grɛ̃pe] ♦ vt to climb. ♦ vi to climb; ~ à un arbre/une échelle to climb a tree/a ladder.

grincement [grɛ̃smɑ̃] nm (de charnière) squeaking; (de porte, plancher) creaking.

grincer [grɛ̃se] vi (charnière) to squeak; (porte, plancher) to creak.

grincheux, -euse [grɛ̃ʃø, øz] ♦ adj grumpy. ♦ nm, f moaner, grumbler.

grippal, -e, -aux [gripal, o] adj: état ~ flu.

grippe [grip] nf (MÉD) flu (U).

grippé, -e [gripe] adj (malade): être ~ to have flu.

gripper [gripe] vi 1. (mécanisme) to jam. 2. fig (processus) to stall.

gris, -e [gri, griz] adj 1. (couleur) grey. 2. fig (morne) dismal. 3. (saoul) tipsy. 4. (temps) grey, cloudy. ▶ **gris** nm (couleur) grey.

grisaille [grizaj] nf 1. (de ciel) greyness. 2. fig (de vie) dullness.

grisant, -e [grizɑ̃, ɑ̃t] adj intoxicating.

griser [grize] vt to intoxicate.

grisonnant, -e [grizɔnɑ̃, ɑ̃t] adj greying.

grisonner [grizɔne] vi to turn grey.

grisou [grizu] nm firedamp.

grive [griv] nf thrush.

grivois, -e [grivwa, az] adj ribald.

Groenland [grɔɛnlɑ̃d] nm: le ~ Greenland.

grog [grɔg] nm (hot) toddy.

grognement [grɔɲmɑ̃] nm 1. (son) grunt; (d'ours, de chien) growl. 2. (protestation) grumble.

grogner [grɔɲe] vi 1. (émettre un son) to grunt; (ours, chien) to growl. 2. (protester) to grumble.

groin [grwɛ̃] nm snout.

grommeler [grɔmle] vt & vi to mutter.

grondement [grɔ̃dmɑ̃] nm (d'animal) growl; (de tonnerre, de train) rumble; (de torrent) roar.

gronder [grɔ̃de] ♦ vi (animal) to growl; (tonnerre) to rumble. ♦ vt to scold.

gros, grosse [gro, gros] adj (gén avant n) 1. (gén) large, big; péj big. 2. (avant ou après n) (corpulent) fat. 3. (grossier) coarse. 4. (fort, sonore) loud. 5. (important, grave - ennuis) serious; (- dépense) major. ▶ **gros** ♦ adv (beaucoup) a lot. ♦ nm (partie): le (plus) ~ (de qqch) the main part (of sthg). ▶ **en gros** loc adv & loc adj

1. (COMM) wholesale. 2. (en grands caractères) in large letters. 3. (grosso modo) roughly.

groseille [grozɛj] nf currant.

grosse [gros] → **gros**.

grossesse [grosɛs] nf pregnancy.

grosseur [grosœr] nf 1. (dimension, taille) size. 2. (MÉD) lump.

grossier, -ère [grosje, ɛr] adj 1. (matière) coarse. 2. (sommaire) rough. 3. (insolent) rude. 4. (vulgaire) crude. 5. (erreur) crass.

grossièrement [grosjɛrmɑ̃] adv 1. (sommairement) roughly. 2. (vulgairement) crudely.

grossir [grosir] ♦ vi 1. (prendre du poids) to put on weight. 2. (augmenter) to grow. 3. (s'intensifier) to increase. ♦ vt 1. (suj: microscope, verre) to magnify. 2. (suj: vêtement): ~ qqn to make sb look fatter. 3. (exagérer) to exaggerate.

grossiste [grosist] nmf wholesaler.

grosso modo [grosomɔdo] adv roughly.

grotte [grɔt] nf cave.

grouiller [gruje] vi: ~ (de) to swarm (with).

groupe [grup] nm group. ▶ **groupe sanguin** nm blood group.

groupement [grupmɑ̃] nm 1. (action) grouping. 2. (groupe) group.

grouper [grupe] vt to group. ▶ **se grouper** vp to come together.

grue [gry] nf (TECHNOL & ZOOL) crane.

grumeau, -x [grymo] nm lump.

gruyère [gryjɛr] nm Gruyère (cheese).

Guadeloupe [gwadlup] nf: la ~ Guadeloupe.

Guatemala [gwatemala] nm: le ~ Guatemala.

gué [ge] nm ford; traverser à ~ to ford.

guenilles [gənij] nfpl rags.

guenon [gənɔ̃] nf female monkey.

guépard [gepar] nm cheetah.

guêpe [gɛp] nf wasp.

guêpier [gepje] nm wasp's nest; fig hornet's nest.

guère [gɛr] adv (peu) hardly; ne (+ verbe) ~ (peu) hardly; il ne l'aime ~ he doesn't like him/her very much; il n'y a ~ plus de six ans qu'il est parti it's barely six years since he left.

guéridon [geridɔ̃] nm pedestal table.

guérilla [gerija] nf guerrilla warfare.

guérir [gerir] ♦ vt to cure. ♦ vi to recover, to get better.

guérison [gerizɔ̃] nf 1. (de malade) recovery. 2. (de maladie) cure.

guerre [gɛr] nf 1. (MIL & fig) war; faire la

~ **à un pays** to make ou wage war on a country; **Première/Seconde Guerre mondiale** First/Second World War. **2.** (*technique*) warfare (U).

guerrier, -ère [gɛrje, ɛr] *adj* **1.** (*de guerre*) war (*avant n*). **2.** (*peuple*) warlike. ▶ **guerrier** *nm* warrior.

guet-apens [gɛtapɑ̃] *nm* ambush; *fig* trap.

guêtre [gɛtr] *nf* gaiter.

guetter [gete] *vt* **1.** (*épier*) to lie in wait for. **2.** (*attendre*) to be on the look-out for, to watch for. **3.** (*menacer*) to threaten.

gueule [gœl] *nf* **1.** (*d'animal, ouverture*) mouth. **2.** *tfam* (*bouche de l'homme*) gob Br, yap Am. **3.** *fam* (*visage*) face.

gueuleton [gœltɔ̃] *nm fam* blowout.

gui [gi] *nm* mistletoe.

guichet [giʃɛ] *nm* counter; (*de gare, de théâtre*) ticket office.

guide [gid] *nm* **1.** (*gén*) guide. **2.** (*livre*) guidebook.

guider [gide] *vt* to guide.

guidon [gidɔ̃] *nm* handlebars (*pl*).

guignol [giɲɔl] *nm* **1.** (*marionnette*) glove puppet. **2.** (*théâtre*) ≃ Punch and Judy show.

guillemet [gijmɛ] *nm* inverted comma, quotation mark.

guilleret, -ette [gijrɛ, ɛt] *adj* perky.

guillotine [gijɔtin] *nf* **1.** (*instrument*) guillotine. **2.** (*de fenêtre*) sash.

guindé, -e [gɛ̃de] *adj* stiff.

Guinée [gine] *nf*: **la ~** Guinea.

guirlande [girlɑ̃d] *nf* **1.** (*de fleurs*) garland. **2.** (*de papier*) chain; (*de Noël*) tinsel (U).

guise [giz] *nf*: **à ma ~** as I please ou like; **en ~ de** by way of.

guitare [gitar] *nf* guitar.

guitariste [gitarist] *nmf* guitarist.

guttural, -e, -aux [gytyral, o] *adj* guttural.

Guyane [gɥijan] *nf*: **la ~ française** French Guiana.

gymnastique [ʒimnastik] *nf* (SPORT & *fig*) gymnastics (U); **faire de la ~** to do keep-fit exercises.

gynécologie [ʒinekɔlɔʒi] *nf* gynaecology.

gynécologue [ʒinekɔlɔg] *nmf* gynaecologist.

H

h¹, H [aʃ] *nm inv* h, H.

h² (*abr de* **heure**) hr.

ha (*abr de* **hectare**) ha.

hab. *abr de* **habitant**.

habile [abil] *adj* skilful; (*démarche*) clever.

habileté [abilte] *nf* skill.

habillement [abijmɑ̃] *nm* (*couture*) clothing trade Br, garment industry Am.

habiller [abije] *vt* **1.** (*vêtir*): ~ **qqn** (**de**) to dress sb (in). **2.** (*recouvrir*) to cover. ▶ **s'habiller** *vp* **1.** (*se vêtir*) to dress, to get dressed. **2.** (*se vêtir élégamment*) to dress up.

habit [abi] *nm* **1.** (*costume*) suit. **2.** (RELIG) habit. ▶ **habits** *nmpl* (*vêtements*) clothes.

habitacle [abitakl] *nm* (*d'avion*) cockpit; (*de voiture*) passenger compartment.

habitant, -e [abitɑ̃, ɑ̃t] *nm, f* **1.** (*de pays*) inhabitant. **2.** (*d'immeuble*) occupant. **3.** Can (*paysan*) farmer.

habitation [abitasjɔ̃] *nf* **1.** (*fait d'habiter*) housing. **2.** (*résidence*) house, home.

habiter [abite] ◆ *vt* (*résider*) to live in. ◆ *vi* to live; ~ **à** to live in.

habitude [abityd] *nf* (*façon de faire*) habit; **avoir l'~ de faire qqch** to be in the habit of doing sthg; **d'~** usually.

habituel, -elle [abitɥɛl] *adj* (*coutumier*) usual, customary.

habituellement [abitɥɛlmɑ̃] *adv* usually, normally.

habituer [abitɥe] *vt*: ~ **qqn à qqch/à faire qqch** to get sb used to sthg/to doing sthg. ▶ **s'habituer** *vp*: **s'~ à qqch/à faire qqch** to get used to sthg/to doing sthg.

hache ['aʃ] *nf* axe.

hacher ['aʃe] *vt* **1.** (*couper - gén*) to chop finely; (- *viande*) to mince Br, to grind Am. **2.** (*entrecouper*) to interrupt.

hachisch = **haschisch**.

hachoir ['aʃwar] *nm* **1.** (*couteau*) chopper. **2.** (*appareil*) mincer Br, grinder Am. **3.** (*planche*) chopping-board.

hachure ['aʃyr] *nf* hatching.

hagard, -e ['agar, ard] *adj* haggard.

haie ['ε] nf 1. (d'arbustes) hedge. 2. (de personnes) row; (de soldats, d'agents de police) line. 3. (SPORT) hurdle.

haillons ['ajɔ̃] nmpl rags.

haine ['εn] nf hatred.

haïr ['air] vt to hate.

Haïti [aiti] n Haiti.

hâle ['al] nm tan.

hâlé, -e ['ale] adj tanned.

haleine [alεn] nf breath.

haleter ['alte] vi to pant.

hall ['ol] nm 1. (vestibule, entrée) foyer, lobby. 2. (salle publique) concourse.

halle ['al] nf covered market.

hallucination [alysinasjɔ̃] nf hallucination.

halo ['alo] nm (cercle lumineux) halo.

halogène [alɔʒεn] nm & adj halogen.

halte ['alt] ◆ nf stop. ◆ interj stop!

haltère [altεr] nm dumbbell.

haltérophilie [alterɔfili] nf weightlifting.

hamac ['amak] nm hammock.

hamburger ['aburgœr] nm hamburger.

hameau, -x ['amo] nm hamlet.

hameçon [amsɔ̃] nm fish-hook.

hammam ['amam] nm Turkish bath.

hamster ['amstεr] nm hamster.

hanche ['ãʃ] nf hip.

handball ['ãdbal] nm handball.

handicap ['ãdikap] nm handicap.

handicapé, -e ['ãdikape] ◆ adj handicapped. ◆ nm, f handicapped person.

handicaper ['ãdikape] vt to handicap.

hangar ['ãgar] nm shed; (AÉRON) hangar.

hanneton ['antɔ̃] nm cockchafer.

hanter ['ãte] vt to haunt.

hantise ['ãtiz] nf obsession.

happer ['ape] vt (attraper) to snap up.

haranguer ['arãge] vt to harangue.

haras ['ara] nm stud (farm).

harassant, -e ['arasã, ãt] adj exhausting.

harceler ['arsəle] vt 1. (relancer) to harass. 2. (MIL) to harry. 3. (importuner): ~ qqn (de) to pester sb (with).

hardes ['ard] nfpl old clothes.

hardi, -e ['ardi] adj bold, daring.

hareng ['arã] nm herring.

hargne ['arɲ] nf spite (U), bad temper.

haricot ['ariko] nm bean; ~s verts/blancs/rouges green/haricot/kidney beans.

harmonica [armɔnika] nm harmonica, mouth organ.

harmonie [armɔni] nf 1. (gén) harmony. 2. (de visage) symmetry.

harmonieux, -euse [armɔnjø, øz] adj 1. (gén) harmonious. 2. (voix) melodious. 3. (traits, silhouette) regular.

harmoniser [armɔnize] vt (MUS & fig) to harmonize; (salaires) to bring into line.

harnacher ['arnaʃe] vt (cheval) to harness.

harnais ['arnε] nm 1. (de cheval, de parachutiste) harness. 2. (TECHNOL) train.

harpe ['arp] nf harp.

harpon ['arpɔ̃] nm harpoon.

harponner ['arpɔne] vt 1. (poisson) to harpoon. 2. fam (personne) to waylay.

hasard ['azar] nm chance; au ~ at random; par ~ by accident, by chance.

hasarder ['azarde] vt 1. (tenter) to venture. 2. (risquer) to hazard. ► **se hasarder** vp: se ~ à faire qqch to risk doing sthg.

haschisch, haschich, hachisch ['aʃiʃ] nm hashish.

hâte ['at] nf haste.

hâter ['ate] vt 1. (activer) to hasten. 2. (avancer) to bring forward. ► **hâter** vp to hurry; se ~ de faire qqch to hurry to do sthg.

hausse ['os] nf (augmentation) rise, increase; en ~ rising, increasing.

hausser ['ose] vt to raise.

haut, -e [o, ot] adj 1. (gén) high; ~ de 20 m 20 m high. 2. (classe sociale, pays, région) upper. 3. (responsable) senior. ► **haut** ◆ adv 1. (gén) high; (placé) highly. 2. (fort) loudly. ◆ nm 1. (hauteur) height; faire 2 m de ~ to be 2 m high ou in height. 2. (sommet, vêtement) top. 3. loc: avoir ou connaître des ~s et des bas to have one's ups and downs. ► de haut loc adv (avec dédain) haughtily; le prendre de ~ to react haughtily. ► de haut en bas loc adv from top to bottom. ► du haut de loc prép from the top of. ► en haut de loc prép at the top of.

hautain, -e ['otε̃, εn] adj haughty.

hautbois ['obwa] nm oboe.

haut de gamme [odgam] adj upmarket.

haute-fidélité [otfidelite] nf high fidelity, hi-fi.

hauteur ['otœr] nf height; à ~ d'épaule at shoulder level ou height.

haut-fourneau ['ofurno] nm blast furnace.

haut-parleur ['oparlœr] (pl **haut-parleurs**) nm loudspeaker.

havre ['avr] *nm* (*refuge*) haven.

Haye ['ɛ] *n*: **la ~** the Hague.

hayon ['ajɔ̃] *nm* hatchback.

hebdomadaire [ɛbdɔmadɛr] *nm & adj* weekly.

hébergement [eberʒəmɑ̃] *nm* accommodation.

héberger [eberʒe] *vt* **1.** (*loger*) to put up. **2.** (*suj: hôtel*) to take in.

hébété, -e [ebete] *adj* dazed.

hébraïque [ebraik] *adj* Hebrew.

hébreu, -x [ebrø] *adj* Hebrew.
▶ **hébreu** *nm* (*langue*) Hebrew.
▶ **Hébreu, -x** *nm* Hebrew.

hécatombe [ekatɔ̃b] *nf litt & fig* slaughter.

hectare [ɛktar] *nm* hectare.

hectolitre [ɛktɔlitr] *nm* hectolitre.

hégémonie [eʒemɔni] *nf* hegemony.

hein ['ɛ̃] *interj fam* eh?, what?; **tu m'en veux, ~?** you're cross with me, aren't you?

hélas [elas] *interj* unfortunately, alas.

héler [ele] *vt sout* to hail.

hélice [elis] *nf* **1.** (*d'avion, de bateau*) propeller. **2.** (MATHS) helix.

hélicoptère [elikɔptɛr] *nm* helicopter.

héliport [elipɔr] *nm* heliport.

hélium [eljɔm] *nm* helium.

Helsinki ['ɛlsiŋki] *n* Helsinki.

helvétique [ɛlvetik] *adj* Swiss.

hématome [ematom] *nm* (MÉD) haematoma.

hémicycle [emisikl] *nm* (POLIT): **l'~** the Assemblée Nationale.

hémisphère [emisfɛr] *nm* hemisphere.

hémophile [emɔfil] ◆ *nmf* haemophiliac. ◆ *adj* haemophilic.

hémorragie [emɔraʒi] *nf* **1.** (MÉD) haemorrhage. **2.** *fig* (*perte, fuite*) loss.

hémorroïdes [emɔrɔid] *nfpl* haemorrhoids, piles.

hennir ['enir] *vi* to neigh, to whinny.

hépatite [epatit] *nf* (MÉD) hepatitis.

herbe [ɛrb] *nf* **1.** (BOT) grass. **2.** (CULIN & MÉD) herb. **3.** *fam* (*marijuana*) grass.

herbicide [ɛrbisid] *nm* weedkiller, herbicide.

herboriste [ɛrbɔrist] *nmf* herbalist.

héréditaire [erediter] *adj* hereditary.

hérédité [eredite] *nf* (*génétique*) heredity.

hérésie [erezi] *nf* heresy.

hérisson ['erisɔ̃] *nm* (ZOOL) hedgehog.

héritage [eritaʒ] *nm* **1.** (*de biens*) inheritance. **2.** (*culturel*) heritage.

hériter [erite] ◆ *vi* to inherit; **~ de qqch** to inherit sthg. ◆ *vt*: **~ qqch de qqn** *litt &* *fig* to inherit sthg from sb.

héritier, -ère [eritje, ɛr] *nm, f* heir (*f* heiress).

hermétique [ɛrmetik] *adj* **1.** (*étanche*) hermetic. **2.** (*incompréhensible*) inaccessible, impossible to understand. **3.** (*impénétrable*) impenetrable.

hermine [ɛrmin] *nf* **1.** (*animal*) stoat. **2.** (*fourrure*) ermine.

hernie ['ɛrni] *nf* hernia.

héroïne [erɔin] *nf* **1.** (*personne*) heroine. **2.** (*drogue*) heroin.

héroïque [erɔik] *adj* heroic.

héroïsme [erɔism] *nm* heroism.

héron ['erɔ̃] *nm* heron.

héros ['ero] *nm* hero.

hertz ['ɛrts] *nm inv* hertz.

hésitant, -e [ezitɑ̃, ɑ̃t] *adj* hesitant.

hésitation [ezitasjɔ̃] *nf* hesitation.

hésiter [ezite] *vi* to hesitate; **~ entre/sur** to hesitate between/over; **~ à faire qqch** to hesitate to do sthg.

hétéroclite [eterɔklit] *adj* motley.

hétérogène [eterɔʒɛn] *adj* heterogeneous.

hétérosexuel, -elle [eterɔsɛksɥɛl] *adj & nm, f* heterosexual.

hêtre ['ɛtr] *nm* beech.

heure [œr] *nf* **1.** (*unité de temps*) hour; **250 km à l'~** 250 km per ou an hour; **faire des ~s supplémentaires** to work overtime. **2.** (*moment du jour*) time; **il est deux ~s** it's two o'clock; **quelle ~ est-il?** what time is it?; **être à l'~** to be on time; **à quelle ~?** when?, (at) what time?; **~ de pointe** rush hour; **~s de bureau** office hours; **à ~ fixe** at set times. **3.** (SCOL) class, period. **4.** *loc*: **c'est l'~ (de faire qqch)** it's time (to do sthg); **de bonne ~** early.

heureusement [œrøzmɑ̃] *adv* (*par chance*) luckily, fortunately.

heureux, -euse [œrø, øz] *adj* **1.** (*gén*) happy; (*favorable*) fortunate; **être ~ de faire qqch** to be happy to do sthg. **2.** (*réussi*) successful, happy.

heurt ['œr] *nm* **1.** (*choc*) collision, impact. **2.** (*désaccord*) clash.

heurter ['œrte] *vt* **1.** (*rentrer dans - gén*) to hit; (*- suj: personne*) to bump into. **2.** (*offenser - personne, sensibilité*) to offend. **3.** (*bon sens, convenances*) to go against. ▶ **se heurter** *vp* **1.** (*gén*): **se ~ (contre)** to collide (with). **2.** (*rencontrer*): **se ~ à qqch** to come up against sthg.

hexagonal, -e, -aux [ɛgzagɔnal, o] *adj* **1.** (GÉOM) hexagonal. **2.** (*français*) French.

hexagone [ɛgzagɔn] *nm* (GÉOM) hexagon. ▶ **Hexagone** *nm*: **l'Hexagone** (metropolitan) France.

hiatus [jatys] *nm inv* hiatus.

hiberner [ibɛʀne] *vi* to hibernate.

hibou, -x ['ibu] *nm* owl.

hideux, -euse ['idø, øz] *adj* hideous.

hier [ijɛʀ] *adv* yesterday.

hiérarchie ['jeʀaʀʃi] *nf* hierarchy.

hiéroglyphe [jeʀɔglif] *nm* hieroglyph, hieroglyphic.

hilare [ilaʀ] *adj* beaming.

hilarité [ilaʀite] *nf* hilarity.

Himalaya [imalaja] *nm*: **l'~** the Himalayas (*pl*).

hindou, -e [ɛ̃du] *adj* Hindu. ▶ **Hindou, -e** *nm, f* Hindu.

hippie, hippy ['ipi] (*pl* **hippies**) *nmf & adj* hippy.

hippique [ipik] *adj* horse (*avant n*).

hippodrome [ipɔdʀom] *nm* racecourse.

hippopotame [ipɔpɔtam] *nm* hippopotamus.

hirondelle [iʀɔ̃dɛl] *nf* swallow.

hirsute [iʀsyt] *adj* (*chevelure, barbe*) shaggy.

hispanique [ispanik] *adj* (*gén*) Hispanic.

hisser ['ise] *vt* 1. (*voile, drapeau*) to hoist. 2. (*charge*) to heave, to haul. ▶ **se hisser** *vp* 1. (*grimper*): **se ~ (sur)** to heave ou haul o.s. up (onto). 2. *fig* (*s'élever*): **se ~ à** to pull o.s. up to.

histoire [istwaʀ] *nf* 1. (*science*) history; **~ naturelle** natural history. 2. (*récit, mensonge*) story. 3. (*aventure*) funny ou strange thing. 4. (*gén pl*) (*ennui*) trouble (U).

historique [istɔʀik] *adj* 1. (*roman, recherches*) historical. 2. (*monument, événement*) historic.

hit-parade ['itpaʀad] (*pl* **hit-parades**) *nm*: **le ~** the charts (*pl*).

hiver [ivɛʀ] *nm* winter; **en ~** in (the) winter.

HLM (*abr de* **habitation à loyer modéré**) *nm ou nf* low-rent, state-owned housing, ≃ council house/flat Br, ≃ public housing unit Am.

hobby ['ɔbi] (*pl* **hobbies**) *nm* hobby.

hocher ['ɔʃe] *vt*: **~ la tête** (*affirmativement*) to nod (one's head); (*négativement*) to shake one's head.

hochet ['ɔʃɛ] *nm* rattle.

hockey ['ɔkɛ] *nm* hockey; **~ sur glace** ice hockey Br, hockey Am.

holding ['ɔldiŋ] *nm ou nf* holding company.

hold-up ['ɔldœp] *nm inv* hold-up.

hollandais, -e ['ɔlɑ̃dɛ, ɛz] *adj* Dutch. ▶ **hollandais** *nm* (*langue*) Dutch. ▶ **Hollandais, -e** *nm, f* Dutchman (*f* Dutchwoman).

Hollande ['ɔlɑ̃d] *nf*: **la ~** Holland.

holocauste ['ɔlɔkost] *nm* holocaust.

homard ['ɔmaʀ] *nm* lobster.

homéopathie [ɔmeɔpati] *nf* homeopathy.

homéopathique [ɔmeɔpatik] *adj* homeopathic.

homicide [ɔmisid] *nm* (*meurtre*) murder.

hommage [ɔmaʒ] *nm* (*témoignage d'estime*) tribute; **rendre ~ à qqn/qqch** to pay tribute to sb/sthg.

homme [ɔm] *nm* man; **~ d'affaires** businessman; **~ d'État** statesman; **~ politique** politician.

homme-grenouille [ɔmgʀənuj] *nm* frogman.

homogène [ɔmɔʒɛn] *adj* homogeneous.

homologue [ɔmɔlɔg] *nm* counterpart, opposite number.

homologuer [ɔmɔlɔge] *vt* (*ratifier*) to give official approval to; (SPORT) to recognize, to ratify.

homonyme [ɔmɔnim] *nm* 1. (LING) homonym. 2. (*personne, ville*) namesake.

homosexualité [ɔmɔsɛksɥalite] *nf* homosexuality.

homosexuel, -elle [ɔmɔsɛksɥel] *adj & nm, f* homosexual.

Honduras ['ɔ̃dyʀas] *nm*: **le ~** Honduras.

Hongrie ['ɔ̃gʀi] *nf*: **la ~** Hungary.

hongrois, -e ['ɔ̃gʀwa, az] *adj* Hungarian. ▶ **hongrois** *nm* (*langue*) Hungarian. ▶ **Hongrois, -e** *nm, f* Hungarian.

honnête [ɔnɛt] *adj* 1. (*intègre*) honest. 2. (*correct*) honourable. 3. (*convenable - travail, résultat*) reasonable.

honnêtement [ɔnɛtmɑ̃] *adv* 1. (*de façon intègre, franchement*) honestly. 2. (*correctement*) honourably.

honnêteté [ɔnɛtte] *nf* honesty.

honneur [ɔnœʀ] *nm* honour; **faire ~ à qqn/à qqch** to be a credit to sb/to sthg; **faire ~ à un repas** *fig* to do justice to a meal.

honorable [ɔnɔʀabl] *adj* 1. (*digne*) honourable. 2. (*convenable*) respectable.

honoraire [ɔnɔʀɛʀ] *adj* honorary. ▶ **honoraires** *nmpl* fee (*sg*), fees.

honorer [ɔnɔre] vt 1. (faire honneur à) to be a credit to. 2. (payer) to honour.

honte ['ɔ̃t] nf (sentiment) shame; **avoir ~ de qqn/qqch** to be ashamed of sb/sthg; **avoir ~ de faire qqch** to be ashamed of doing sthg.

honteux, -euse ['ɔ̃tø, øz] adj shameful; (personne) ashamed.

hôpital, -aux [ɔpital, o] nm hospital.

hoquet ['ɔke] nm hiccup.

horaire [ɔrer] ♦ nm 1. (de départ, d'arrivée) timetable. 2. (de travail) hours (pl) (of work). ♦ adj hourly.

horizon [ɔrizɔ̃] nm 1. (ligne, perspective) horizon. 2. (panorama) view.

horizontal, -e, -aux [ɔrizɔ̃tal, o] adj horizontal. ▶ **horizontale** nf (MATHS) horizontal.

horloge [ɔrlɔʒ] nf clock.

horlogerie [ɔrlɔʒri] nf clock (and watch)-making.

hormis ['ɔrmi] prép save.

hormone [ɔrmɔn] nf hormone.

horodateur [ɔrɔdatœr] nm (à l'usine) clock; (au parking) ticket machine.

horoscope [ɔrɔskɔp] nm horoscope.

horreur [ɔrœr] nf horror; **avoir ~ de qqn/qqch** to hate sb/sthg; **avoir ~ de faire qqch** to hate doing sthg; **quelle ~!** how dreadful!, how awful!

horrible [ɔribl] adj 1. (affreux) horrible. 2. fig (terrible) terrible, dreadful.

horrifier [ɔrifje] vt to horrify.

horripiler [ɔripile] vt to exasperate.

hors ['ɔr] prép → pair, service. ▶ **hors de** loc prép outside.

hors-bord [ɔrbɔr] nm inv speedboat.

hors-d'œuvre ['ɔrdœvr] nm inv hors d'oeuvre, starter.

hors-jeu ['ɔrʒø] nm inv & adj inv offside.

hors-la-loi ['ɔrlalwa] nm inv outlaw.

hors-piste ['ɔrpist] nm inv off-piste skiing.

hortensia [ɔrtɑ̃sja] nm hydrangea.

horticulture [ɔrtikyltyr] nf horticulture.

hospice [ɔspis] nm home.

hospitalier, -ère [ɔspitalje, ɛr] adj 1. (accueillant) hospitable. 2. (relatif aux hôpitaux) hospital (avant n).

hospitaliser [ɔspitalize] vt to hospitalize.

hospitalité [ɔspitalite] nf hospitality.

hostie [ɔsti] nf host.

hostile [ɔstil] adj: **~ (à)** hostile (to).

hostilité [ɔstilite] nf hostility. ▶ **hostilités** nfpl hostilities.

hôte, hôtesse [ot, otɛs] nm, f host (f hostess); **hôtesse d'accueil** receptionist; **hôtesse de l'air** air hostess. ▶ **hôte** nm (invité) guest.

hôtel [otɛl] nm 1. (d'hébergement) hotel. 2. (établissement public) public building; **~ de ville** town hall. 3. (demeure): **~ (particulier)** (private) mansion.

hôtelier, -ère [otəlje, ɛr] nm, f hotelier.

hôtellerie [otɛlri] nf (métier) hotel business.

hotte ['ɔt] nf 1. (panier) basket. 2. (d'aération) hood.

houblon ['ublɔ̃] nm 1. (BOT) hop. 2. (de la bière) hops (pl).

houille ['uj] nf coal.

houiller, -ère ['uje, ɛr] adj coal (avant n). ▶ **houillère** nf coalmine.

houle ['ul] nf swell.

houlette ['ulɛt] nf sout: **sous la ~ de qqn** under the guidance of sb.

houppe ['up] nf 1. (à poudre) powder puff. 2. (de cheveux) tuft.

hourra, hurrah ['ura] interj hurrah!

houspiller ['uspije] vt to tell off.

housse ['us] nf cover.

houx ['u] nm holly.

HS (abr de hors service) adj out of order.

hublot ['yblo] nm (de bateau) porthole.

huer ['ɥe] vt (siffler) to boo.

huile [ɥil] nf 1. (gén) oil; **~ d'arachide/ d'olive** groundnut/olive oil. 2. (peinture) oil painting. 3. fam (personnalité) bigwig.

huis [ɥi] nm littéraire door; **à ~ clos** (JUR) in camera.

huissier [ɥisje] nm 1. (appariteur) usher. 2. (JUR) bailiff.

huit ['ɥit] ♦ adj num eight. ♦ nm eight; **lundi en ~** a week on Br ou from Am Monday, Monday week Br; voir aussi **six**.

huitième ['ɥitjɛm] ♦ adj num & nmf eighth. ♦ nm eighth; **le ~ de finale** round before the quarterfinal. ♦ nf (SCOL) = second year ou form (at junior school) Br, = fourth grade Am; voir aussi **sixième**.

huître [ɥitr] nf oyster.

humain, -e [ymɛ̃, ɛn] adj 1. (gén) human. 2. (sensible) humane. ▶ **humain** nm (être humain) human (being).

humanitaire [ymaniter] adj humanitarian.

humanité [ymanite] nf humanity. ▶ **humanités** nfpl Belg humanities.

humble [œ̃bl] adj humble.

humecter [ymɛkte] vt to moisten.

humer ['yme] vt to smell.

humérus [ymerys] nm humerus.

humeur [ymœr] nf 1. (disposition) mood; être de bonne/mauvaise ~ to be in a good/bad mood. 2. (caractère) nature. 3. sout (irritation) temper.

humide [ymid] adj (air, climat) humid; (terre, herbe, mur) wet, damp; (saison) rainy; (front, yeux) moist.

humidité [ymidite] nf (de climat, d'air) humidity; (de terre, mur) dampness.

humiliation [ymiljasjɔ̃] nf humiliation.

humilier [ymilje] vt to humiliate.
▶ **s'humilier** vp: s'~ devant qqn to grovel to sb.

humilité [ymilite] nf humility.

humoristique [ymɔristik] adj humorous.

humour [ymur] nm humour.

humus [ymys] nm humus.

huppé, -e ['ype] adj 1. fam (société) upper-crust. 2. (oiseau) crested.

hurlement ['yrləmã] nm howl.

hurler ['yrle] vi (gén) to howl.

hurrah = **hourra**.

hutte ['yt] nf hut.

hybride [ibrid] nm & adj hybrid.

hydratant, -e [idratã, ãt] adj moisturizing.

hydrater [idrate] vt 1. (CHIM) to hydrate. 2. (peau) to moisturize.

hydraulique [idrolik] adj hydraulic.

hydravion [idravjɔ̃] nm seaplane, hydroplane.

hydrocarbure [idrokarbyr] nm hydrocarbon.

hydrocution [idrɔkysjɔ̃] nf immersion syncope.

hydroélectrique [idroelɛktrik] adj hydroelectric.

hydrogène [idrɔʒɛn] nm hydrogen.

hydroglisseur [idroglisœr] nm jetfoil, hydroplane.

hydrophile [idrɔfil] adj → **coton**.

hyène [jɛn] nf hyena.

hygiène [iʒjɛn] nf hygiene; ~ de vie healthy lifestyle.

hygiénique [iʒjenik] adj 1. (sanitaire) hygienic. 2. (bon pour la santé) healthy.

hymne [imn] nm hymn; ~ national national anthem.

hypermarché [ipɛrmarʃe] nm hypermarket.

hypermétrope [ipɛrmetrɔp] ◆ nmf longsighted person. ◆ adj longsighted.

hypertension [ipɛrtãsjɔ̃] nf high blood pressure, hypertension.

hypertrophié [ipɛrtrɔfje] adj hypertrophic; fig exaggerated.

hypnotiser [ipnɔtize] vt to hypnotize; fig to mesmerize.

hypoallergénique [ipɔalɛrʒenik] adj hypoallergenic.

hypocondriaque [ipɔkɔ̃drijak] nmf & adj hypochondriac.

hypocrisie [ipɔkrizi] nf hypocrisy.

hypocrite [ipɔkrit] ◆ nmf hypocrite.
◆ adj hypocritical.

hypoglycémie [ipɔglisemi] nf hypoglycaemia.

hypotension [ipɔtãsjɔ̃] nf low blood pressure.

hypothèque [ipɔtek] nf mortgage.

hypothèse [ipɔtez] nf hypothesis.

hystérie [isteri] nf hysteria.

hystérique [isterik] adj hysterical.

I

i, I [i] nm inv i, I; mettre les points sur les i to dot the i's and cross the t's.

ibérique [iberik] adj: la péninsule ~ the Iberian Peninsula.

iceberg [ajsbɛrg] nm iceberg.

ici [isi] adv 1. (lieu) here; par ~ (direction) this way; (alentour) around here. 2. (temps) now; d'~ là by then; d'~ une semaine in a week's time, a week from now. 3. (au téléphone): ~ Jacques Jacques speaking ou here.

icône [ikon] nf (INFORM & RELIG) icon.

idéal, -e [ideal] (pl idéals ou idéaux [ideo]) adj ideal. ▶ **idéal** nm ideal.

idéaliste [idealist] ◆ nmf idealist. ◆ adj idealistic.

idée [ide] nf idea; à l'~ de/que at the idea of/that; se faire des ~s to imagine things; cela ne m'est jamais venu à l'~ it never occurred to me.

identification [idãtifikasjɔ̃] nf: ~ (à) identification (with).

identifier [idãtifje] vt to identify.
▶ **s'identifier** vp: s'~ à qqn/qqch to identify with sb/sthg.

identique [idãtik] adj: ~ (à) identical (to).

identité [idãtite] nf identity.

idéologie [ideɔlɔʒi] nf ideology.

idiomatique [idjɔmatik] adj idiomatic.

idiot, -e [idjo, ɔt] ◆ adj idiotic; (MÉD) idiot (avant n). ◆ nm, f idiot.

idiotie [idjɔsi] nf 1. (stupidité) idiocy. 2. (action, parole) idiotic thing.

idolâtrer [idɔlatre] vt to idolize.

idole [idɔl] nf idol.

idylle [idil] nf (amour) romance.

idyllique [idilik] adj (idéal) idyllic.

if [if] nm yew.

igloo, iglou [iglu] nm igloo.

igname [iɲam] nf yam.

ignare [iɲar] ◆ nmf ignoramus. ◆ adj ignorant.

ignoble [iɲɔbl] adj 1. (abject) base. 2. (hideux) vile.

ignominie [iɲɔmini] nf 1. (état) disgrace. 2. (action) disgraceful act.

ignorance [iɲɔrɑ̃s] nf ignorance.

ignorant, -e [iɲɔrɑ̃, ɑ̃t] ◆ adj ignorant. ◆ nm, f ignoramus.

ignorer [iɲɔre] vt 1. (ne pas savoir) not to know, to be unaware of. 2. (ne pas tenir compte de) to ignore. 3. (ne pas connaître) to have no experience of.

il [il] pron pers 1. (sujet - personne) he; (- animal) it, he; (- chose) it. 2. (sujet d'un verbe impersonnel) it; ~ **pleut** it's raining.
▶ **ils** pron pers pl they.

île [il] nf island; **les ~s Anglo-Normandes** the Channel Islands; **les ~s Baléares** the Balearic Islands; **les ~s Britanniques** the British Isles; **les ~s Canaries** the Canary Islands; **les ~s Malouines** the Falkland Islands; **l'~ Maurice** Mauritius.

illégal, -e, -aux [ilegal, o] adj illegal.

illégalité [ilegalite] nf (fait d'être illégal) illegality.

illégitime [ileʒitim] adj 1. (enfant) illegitimate; (union) unlawful. 2. (non justifié) unwarranted.

illettré, -e [iletre] adj & nm, f illiterate.

illicite [ilisit] adj illicit.

illimité, -e [ilimite] adj 1. (sans limites) unlimited. 2. (indéterminé) indefinite.

illisible [ilizibl] adj 1. (indéchiffrable) illegible. 2. (incompréhensible & INFORM) unreadable.

illogique [ilɔʒik] adj illogical.

illumination [ilyminasjɔ̃] nf 1. (éclairage) lighting. 2. (idée soudaine) inspiration.

illuminer [ilymine] vt to light up; (bâtiment, rue) to illuminate. ▶ **s'illuminer** vp: **s'~ de joie** to light up with joy.

illusion [ilyzjɔ̃] nf illusion.

illusoire [ilyzwar] adj illusory.

illustration [ilystrasjɔ̃] nf illustration.

illustre [ilystr] adj illustrious.

illustré, -e [ilystre] adj illustrated.
▶ **illustré** nm illustrated magazine.

illustrer [ilystre] vt 1. (gén) to illustrate. 2. (rendre célèbre) to make famous.
▶ **s'illustrer** vp to distinguish o.s.

îlot [ilo] nm 1. (île) small island, islet. 2. fig (de résistance) pocket.

ils → **il**.

image [imaʒ] nf 1. (vision mentale, comparaison, ressemblance) image; ~ **de marque** (d'une personne) image; (d'une entreprise) corporate image; (d'un produit) brand image. 2. (dessin) picture.

imaginaire [imaʒinɛr] adj imaginary.

imagination [imaʒinasjɔ̃] nf imagination; **avoir de l'~** to be imaginative.

imaginer [imaʒine] vt 1. (supposer, croire) to imagine. 2. (trouver) to think of.
▶ **s'imaginer** vp 1. (se voir) to see o.s. 2. (croire) to imagine.

imam [imam] nm imam.

imbattable [ɛ̃batabl] adj unbeatable.

imbécile [ɛ̃besil] nmf imbecile.

imberbe [ɛ̃bɛrb] adj beardless.

imbiber [ɛ̃bibe] vt: ~ **qqch de qqch** to soak sthg with ou in sthg.

imbriqué, -e [ɛ̃brike] adj overlapping.

imbroglio [ɛ̃brɔljo] nm imbroglio.

imbu, -e [ɛ̃by] adj: **être ~ de** to be full of.

imbuvable [ɛ̃byvabl] adj 1. (eau) undrinkable. 2. fam (personne) unbearable.

imitateur, -trice [imitatœr, tris] nm, f 1. (comique) impersonator. 2. péj (copieur) imitator.

imitation [imitasjɔ̃] nf imitation.

imiter [imite] vt 1. (s'inspirer de, contrefaire) to imitate. 2. (reproduire l'aspect de) to look (just) like.

immaculé, -e [imakyle] adj immaculate.

immangeable [ɛ̃mɑ̃ʒabl] adj inedible.

immanquable [ɛ̃mɑ̃kabl] adj impossible to miss; (sort, échec) inevitable.

immatriculation [imatrikylasjɔ̃] nf registration.

immédiat, -e [imedja, at] adj immediate.

immédiatement [imedjatmɑ̃] adv immediately.

immense [imɑ̃s] adj immense.

immerger [imɛrʒe] vt to submerge. ▶ **s'immerger** vp to submerge o.s.

immérité, -e [imerite] adj undeserved.

immeuble [imœbl] nm building.

immigration [imigrasjɔ̃] nf immigration.

immigré, -e [imigre] adj & nm, f immigrant.

immigrer [imigre] vi to immigrate.

imminent, -e [iminã, ãt] adj imminent.

immiscer [imise] ▸ **s'immiscer** vp : s'~ **dans** to interfere in ou with.

immobile [imɔbil] adj 1. (personne, visage) motionless. 2. (mécanisme) fixed, stationary. 3. fig (figé) immovable.

immobilier, -ère [imɔbilje, ɛr] adj : biens ~s property (U) Br, real estate (U) Am.

immobiliser [imɔbilize] vt to immobilize. ▸ **s'immobiliser** vp to stop.

immobilité [imɔbilite] nf immobility; (de paysage, de lac) stillness.

immodéré, -e [imɔdere] adj inordinate.

immonde [imɔ̃d] adj 1. (sale) foul. 2. (abject) vile.

immondices [imɔ̃dis] nfpl waste (U), refuse (U).

immoral, -e, -aux [imɔral, o] adj immoral.

immortaliser [imɔrtalize] vt to immortalize.

immortel, -elle [imɔrtɛl] adj immortal. ▸ **immortel** nm fam member of the Académie française.

immuable [imɥabl] adj 1. (éternel - loi) immutable. 2. (constant) unchanging.

immuniser [imynize] vt 1. (vacciner) to immunize. 2. fig (garantir) : ~ qqn contre qqch to make sb immune to sthg.

immunité [imynite] nf immunity.

impact [ɛ̃pakt] nm impact; avoir de l'~ sur to have an impact on.

impair, -e [ɛ̃pɛr] adj odd. ▸ **impair** nm (faux-pas) gaffe.

imparable [ɛ̃parabl] adj 1. (coup) unstoppable. 2. (argument) unanswerable.

impardonnable [ɛ̃pardɔnabl] adj unforgivable.

imparfait, -e [ɛ̃parfɛ, ɛt] adj 1. (défectueux) imperfect. 2. (inachevé) incomplete. ▸ **imparfait** nm (GRAM) imperfect (tense).

impartial, -e, -aux [ɛ̃parsjal, o] adj impartial.

impartir [ɛ̃partir] vt : ~ qqch à qqn littéraire (délai, droit) to grant sthg to sb; (tâche) to assign sthg to sb.

impasse [ɛ̃pas] nf 1. (rue) dead end. 2. fig (difficulté) impasse, deadlock.

impassible [ɛ̃pasibl] adj impassive.

impatience [ɛ̃pasjɑ̃s] nf impatience.

impatient, -e [ɛ̃pasjɑ̃, ɑ̃t] adj impatient.

impatienter [ɛ̃pasjɑ̃te] vt to annoy. ▸ **s'impatienter** vp : s'~ **(de/contre)** to get impatient (at/with).

impayé, -e [ɛ̃peje] adj unpaid, outstanding. ▸ **impayé** nm outstanding payment.

impeccable [ɛ̃pekabl] adj 1. (parfait) impeccable, faultless. 2. (propre) spotless, immaculate.

impénétrable [ɛ̃penetrabl] adj impenetrable.

impénitent, -e [ɛ̃penitɑ̃, ɑ̃t] adj unrepentant.

impensable [ɛ̃pɑ̃sabl] adj unthinkable.

impératif, -ive [ɛ̃peratif, iv] adj 1. (ton, air) imperious. 2. (besoin) imperative, essential. ▸ **impératif** nm (GRAM) imperative.

impératrice [ɛ̃peratris] nf empress.

imperceptible [ɛ̃persɛptibl] adj imperceptible.

imperfection [ɛ̃pɛrfɛksjɔ̃] nf imperfection.

impérialisme [ɛ̃perjalism] nm (POLIT) imperialism; fig dominance.

impérieux, -euse [ɛ̃perjø, øz] adj 1. (ton, air) imperious. 2. (nécessité) urgent.

impérissable [ɛ̃perisabl] adj undying.

imperméabiliser [ɛ̃pɛrmeabilize] vt to waterproof.

imperméable [ɛ̃pɛrmeabl] ◆ adj waterproof; ~ à (étanche) impermeable to; fig impervious ou immune to. ◆ nm raincoat.

impersonnel, -elle [ɛ̃pɛrsɔnɛl] adj impersonal.

impertinence [ɛ̃pɛrtinɑ̃s] nf impertinence (U).

impertinent, -e [ɛ̃pɛrtinɑ̃, ɑ̃t] ◆ adj impertinent. ◆ nm, f impertinent person.

imperturbable [ɛ̃pɛrtyrbabl] adj imperturbable.

impétueux, -euse [ɛ̃petɥø, øz] adj (personne, caractère) impetuous.

impie [ɛ̃pi] adj littéraire & vieilli impious.

impitoyable [ɛ̃pitwajabl] adj merciless, pitiless.

implacable [ɛ̃plakabl] adj implacable.

implanter [ɛ̃plɑ̃te] vt 1. (entreprise, système) to establish. 2. fig (préjugé) to implant. ▸ **s'implanter** vp (entreprise) to set up; (coutume) to become established.

implication 176

implication [ɛ̃plikasjɔ̃] *nf* **1.** (*participation*): ~ **(dans)** involvement (in). **2.** (*gén pl*) (*conséquence*) implication.

implicite [ɛ̃plisit] *adj* implicit.

impliquer [ɛ̃plike] *vt* **1.** (*compromettre*): ~ **qqn dans** to implicate sb in. **2.** (*requérir, entraîner*) to imply. ▶ **s'impliquer** *vp*: **s'~ dans** *fam* to become involved in.

implorer [ɛ̃plɔre] *vt* to beseech.

implosion [ɛ̃plozjɔ̃] *nf* implosion.

impoli, -e [ɛ̃pɔli] *adj* rude, impolite.

impopulaire [ɛ̃pɔpylɛr] *adj* unpopular.

importance [ɛ̃pɔrtɑ̃s] *nf* **1.** (*gén*) importance; (*de problème, montant*) magnitude. **2.** (*de dommages*) extent. **3.** (*de ville*) size.

important, -e [ɛ̃pɔrtɑ̃, ɑ̃t] *adj* **1.** (*gén*) important. **2.** (*considérable*) considerable, sizeable; (*- dommages*) extensive.

importation [ɛ̃pɔrtasjɔ̃] *nf* (COMM & *fig*) import.

importer [ɛ̃pɔrte] ◆ *vt* to import. ◆ *v impers*: ~ **(à)** to matter (to); **il importe de/que** it is important to/that; **qu'importe! peu importe!** it doesn't matter!; **n'importe qui** anyone (at all); **n'importe quoi** anything (at all); **n'importe où** anywhere (at all); **n'importe quand** at any time (at all).

import-export [ɛ̃pɔrɛkspɔr] *nm* import-export.

importuner [ɛ̃pɔrtyne] *vt* to irk.

imposable [ɛ̃pozabl] *adj* taxable.

imposant, -e [ɛ̃pozɑ̃, ɑ̃t] *adj* imposing.

imposé, -e [ɛ̃poze] *adj* **1.** (*contribuable*) taxed. **2.** (SPORT) (*figure*) compulsory.

imposer [ɛ̃poze] *vt* **1.** (*gén*): ~ **qqch/qqn à qqn** to impose sthg/sb on sb. **2.** (*impressionner*): **en ~ à qqn** to impress sb. **3.** (*taxer*) to tax. ▶ **s'imposer** *vp* **1.** (*être nécessaire*) to be essential ou imperative. **2.** (*forcer le respect*) to stand out. **3.** (*avoir pour règle*): **s'~ de faire qqch** to make it a rule to do sthg.

impossibilité [ɛ̃pɔsibilite] *nf* impossibility; **être dans l'~ de faire qqch** to find it impossible to ou to be unable to do sthg.

impossible [ɛ̃pɔsibl] ◆ *adj* impossible. ◆ *nm*: **tenter l'~** to attempt the impossible.

imposteur [ɛ̃pɔstœr] *nm* impostor.

impôt [ɛ̃po] *nm* tax; **~s locaux** council tax Br, local tax Am; **~ sur le revenu** income tax.

impotent, -e [ɛ̃pɔtɑ̃, ɑ̃t] *adj* disabled.

impraticable [ɛ̃pratikabl] *adj* **1.** (*inapplicable*) impracticable. **2.** (*inaccessible*) impassable.

imprécis, -e [ɛ̃presi, iz] *adj* imprecise.

imprégner [ɛ̃preɲe] *vt* (*imbiber*): ~ **qqch de qqch** to soak sthg in sthg; ~ **qqn de qqch** *fig* to fill sb with sthg. ▶ **s'imprégner** *vp*: **s'~ de qqch** (*s'imbiber*) to soak sthg up; *fig* to soak sthg up, to steep o.s. in sthg.

imprenable [ɛ̃prǝnabl] *adj* **1.** (*forteresse*) impregnable. **2.** (*vue*) unimpeded.

imprésario, impresario [ɛ̃presarjo] *nm* impresario.

impression [ɛ̃presjɔ̃] *nf* **1.** (*gén*) impression; **avoir l'~ que** to have the impression ou feeling that. **2.** (*de livre, tissu*) printing. **3.** (PHOT) print.

impressionner [ɛ̃presjɔne] *vt* **1.** (*frapper*) to impress. **2.** (*choquer*) to shock, to upset. **3.** (*intimider*) to frighten. **4.** (PHOT) to expose.

impressionniste [ɛ̃presjɔnist] *nmf* & *adj* impressionist.

imprévisible [ɛ̃previzibl] *adj* unforeseeable.

imprévu, -e [ɛ̃prevy] *adj* unforeseen. ▶ **imprévu** *nm* unforeseen situation.

imprimante [ɛ̃primɑ̃t] *nf* printer.

imprimé, -e [ɛ̃prime] *adj* printed. ▶ **imprimé** *nm* **1.** (POSTES) printed matter (U). **2.** (*formulaire*) printed form. **3.** (*tissu*) print.

imprimer [ɛ̃prime] *vt* **1.** (*texte, tissu*) to print. **2.** (*mouvement*) to impart. **3.** (*marque, empreinte*) to leave.

imprimerie [ɛ̃primri] *nf* **1.** (*technique*) printing. **2.** (*usine*) printing works (*sg*).

improbable [ɛ̃prɔbabl] *adj* improbable.

improductif, -ive [ɛ̃prɔdyktif, iv] *adj* unproductive.

impromptu, -e [ɛ̃prɔ̃pty] *adj* impromptu.

impropre [ɛ̃prɔpr] *adj* **1.** (GRAM) incorrect. **2.** (*inadapté*): ~ **à** unfit for.

improviser [ɛ̃prɔvize] *vt* to improvise. ▶ **s'improviser** *vp* **1.** (*s'organiser*) to be improvised. **2.** (*devenir*): **s'~ metteur en scène** to act as director.

improviste [ɛ̃prɔvist] ▶ **à l'improviste** *loc adv* unexpectedly, without warning.

imprudence [ɛ̃prydɑ̃s] *nf* **1.** (*de personne, d'acte*) rashness. **2.** (*acte*) rash act.

imprudent, -e [ɛ̃prydɑ̃, ɑ̃t] ◆ *adj* rash. ◆ *nm, f* rash person.

impubère [ɛ̃pybɛr] *adj* (*avant la puberté*) pre-pubescent.

impudent, -e [ɛ̃pydɑ̃, ɑ̃t] ♦ *adj* impudent. ♦ *nm, f* impudent person.

impudique [ɛ̃pydik] *adj* shameless.

impuissant, -e [ɛ̃pɥisɑ̃, ɑ̃t] *adj* 1. (*incapable*): ~ (**à faire qqch**) powerless (to do sthg). 2. (*homme, fureur*) impotent. ▶ **impuissant** *nm* impotent man.

impulsif, -ive [ɛ̃pylsif, iv] ♦ *adj* impulsive. ♦ *nm, f* impulsive person.

impulsion [ɛ̃pylsjɔ̃] *nf* 1. (*poussée, essor*) impetus. 2. (*instinct*) impulse, instinct. 3. *fig*: **sous l'~ de qqn** (*influence*) at the prompting ou instigation of sb; **sous l'~ de qqch** (*effet*) impelled by sthg.

impunément [ɛ̃pynemɑ̃] *adv* with impunity.

impunité [ɛ̃pynite] *nf* impunity; **en toute ~** with impunity.

impur, -e [ɛ̃pyr] *adj* impure.

impureté [ɛ̃pyrte] *nf* impurity.

imputer [ɛ̃pyte] *vt*: ~ **qqch à qqn/à qqch** to attribute sthg to sb/to sthg; ~ **qqch à qqch** (FIN) to charge sthg to sthg.

imputrescible [ɛ̃pytresibl] *adj* (*bois*) rotproof; (*déchets*) non-degradable.

inabordable [inabɔrdabl] *adj* 1. (*prix*) prohibitive. 2. (GÉOGR) inaccessible (*by boat*). 3. (*personne*) unapproachable.

inacceptable [inaksɛptabl] *adj* unacceptable.

inaccessible [inaksesibl] *adj* (*destination, domaine, personne*) inaccessible; (*objectif, poste*) unattainable; ~ **à** (*sentiment*) impervious to.

inaccoutumé, -e [inakutyme] *adj* unaccustomed.

inachevé, -e [inaʃve] *adj* unfinished, uncompleted.

inactif, -ive [inaktif, iv] *adj* 1. (*sans occupation, non utilisé*) idle. 2. (*sans effet*) ineffective. 3. (*sans emploi*) non-working.

inaction [inaksjɔ̃] *nf* inaction.

inadapté, -e [inadapte] *adj* 1. (*non adapté*): ~ (**à**) unsuitable (for), unsuited (to). 2. (*asocial*) maladjusted.

inadmissible [inadmisibl] *adj* (*conduite*) unacceptable.

inadvertance [inadvɛrtɑ̃s] *nf littéraire* oversight; **par ~** inadvertently.

inaliénable [inaljenabl] *adj* inalienable.

inaltérable [inalterabl] *adj* 1. (*matériau*) stable. 2. (*sentiment*) unfailing.

inamovible [inamɔvibl] *adj* fixed.

inanimé, -e [inanime] *adj* 1. (*sans vie*) inanimate. 2. (*inerte, évanoui*) senseless.

inanition [inanisjɔ̃] *nf*: **tomber/mourir d'~** to faint with/die of hunger.

inaperçu, -e [inapɛrsy] *adj* unnoticed.

inappréciable [inapresjabl] *adj* (*précieux*) invaluable.

inapprochable [inaproʃabl] *adj*: **il est vraiment ~ en ce moment** you can't say anything to him at the moment.

inapte [inapt] *adj* 1. (*incapable*): ~ **à qqch/à faire qqch** incapable of sthg/of doing sthg. 2. (MIL) unfit.

inattaquable [inatakabl] *adj* 1. (*imprenable*) impregnable. 2. (*irréprochable*) irreproachable, beyond reproach. 3. (*irréfutable*) irrefutable.

inattendu, -e [inatɑ̃dy] *adj* unexpected.

inattention [inatɑ̃sjɔ̃] *nf* inattention; **faute d'~** careless mistake.

inaudible [inodibl] *adj* (*impossible à entendre*) inaudible.

inauguration [inogyrasjɔ̃] *nf* (*cérémonie*) inauguration, opening (ceremony).

inaugurer [inogyre] *vt* 1. (*monument*) to unveil; (*installation, route*) to open; (*procédé, édifice*) to inaugurate. 2. (*époque*) to usher in.

inavouable [inavwabl] *adj* unmentionable.

incalculable [ɛ̃kalkylabl] *adj* incalculable.

incandescence [ɛ̃kɑ̃desɑ̃s] *nf* incandescence.

incantation [ɛ̃kɑ̃tasjɔ̃] *nf* incantation.

incapable [ɛ̃kapabl] ♦ *nmf* (*raté*) incompetent. ♦ *adj*: ~ **de faire qqch** (*inapte à*) incapable of doing sthg; (*dans l'impossibilité de*) unable to do sthg.

incapacité [ɛ̃kapasite] *nf* 1. (*impossibilité*): ~ **à** ou **de faire qqch** inability to do sthg. 2. (*invalidité*) disability.

incarcération [ɛ̃karserasjɔ̃] *nf* incarceration.

incarner [ɛ̃karne] *vt* 1. (*personnifier*) to be the incarnation of. 2. (CIN & THÉÂTRE) to play.

incartade [ɛ̃kartad] *nf* misdemeanour.

incassable [ɛ̃kasabl] *adj* unbreakable.

incendie [ɛ̃sɑ̃di] *nm* fire; *fig* flames (*pl*).

incendier [ɛ̃sɑ̃dje] *vt* (*mettre le feu à*) to set alight, to set fire to.

incertain, -e [ɛ̃sɛrtɛ̃, ɛn] *adj* 1. (*gén*) uncertain; (*temps*) unsettled. 2. (*vague - lumière*) dim; (- *contour*) blurred.

incertitude [ɛ̃sɛrtityd] *nf* uncertainty.

incessamment [ɛ̃sesamɑ̃] *adv* at any

moment, any moment now.

incessant, -e [ɛ̃sesã, ãt] adj incessant.

inceste [ɛ̃sɛst] nm incest.

inchangé, -e [ɛ̃ʃɑ̃ʒe] adj unchanged.

incidence [ɛ̃sidɑ̃s] nf (conséquence) effect, impact (U).

incident, -e [ɛ̃sidɑ̃, ãt] adj (accessoire) incidental. ▶ **incident** nm (gén) incident; (ennui) hitch.

incinérer [ɛ̃sinere] vt 1. (corps) to cremate. 2. (ordures) to incinerate.

inciser [ɛ̃size] vt to incise, to make an incision in.

incisif, -ive [ɛ̃sizif, iv] adj incisive. ▶ **incisive** nf incisor.

inciter [ɛ̃site] vt 1. (provoquer): ~ qqn à qqch/à faire qqch to incite sb to sthg/to do sthg. 2. (encourager): ~ qqn à faire qqch to encourage sb to do sthg.

inclassable [ɛ̃klasabl] adj unclassifiable.

inclinable [ɛ̃klinabl] adj reclinable, reclining.

inclinaison [ɛ̃klinɛzɔ̃] nf 1. (pente) incline. 2. (de tête, chapeau) angle, tilt.

incliner [ɛ̃kline] vt (pencher) to tilt, to lean. ▶ **s'incliner** vp 1. (se pencher) to tilt, to lean. 2. (céder): s'~ (devant) to give in (to), to yield (to).

inclure [ɛ̃klyr] vt (mettre dedans): ~ qqch dans qqch to include sthg in sthg; (joindre) to enclose sthg with sthg.

inclus, -e [ɛ̃kly, yz] ♦ pp → **inclure**. ♦ adj (compris - taxe, frais) included; (joint - lettre) enclosed; (y compris): jusqu'à la page 10 ~e up to and including page 10.

incognito [ɛ̃kɔɲito] adv incognito.

incohérent, -e [ɛ̃kɔerã, ãt] adj (paroles) incoherent; (actes) inconsistent.

incollable [ɛ̃kɔlabl] adj 1. (riz) nonstick. 2. fam (imbattable) unbeatable.

incolore [ɛ̃kɔlɔr] adj colourless.

incomber [ɛ̃kɔ̃be] vi: ~ à qqn to be sb's responsibility; **il incombe à qqn de faire qqch** (emploi impersonnel) it falls to sb ou it is incumbent on sb to do sthg.

incommensurable [ɛ̃kɔmɑ̃syrabl] adj (immense) immeasurable.

incommoder [ɛ̃kɔmɔde] vt sout to trouble.

incomparable [ɛ̃kɔ̃parabl] adj 1. (différent) not comparable. 2. (sans pareil) incomparable.

incompatible [ɛ̃kɔ̃patibl] adj incompatible.

incompétent, -e [ɛ̃kɔ̃petã, ãt] adj (incapable) incompetent.

incomplet, -ète [ɛ̃kɔ̃plɛ, ɛt] adj incomplete.

incompréhensible [ɛ̃kɔ̃preãsibl] adj incomprehensible.

incompris, -e [ɛ̃kɔ̃pri, iz] ♦ adj misunderstood, not appreciated. ♦ nm, f misunderstood person.

inconcevable [ɛ̃kɔ̃svabl] adj unimaginable.

inconciliable [ɛ̃kɔ̃siljabl] adj irreconcilable.

inconditionnel, -elle [ɛ̃kɔ̃disjɔnɛl] ♦ adj 1. (total) unconditional. 2. (fervent) ardent. ♦ nm, f ardent supporter ou admirer.

inconfortable [ɛ̃kɔ̃fɔrtabl] adj uncomfortable.

incongru, -e [ɛ̃kɔ̃gry] adj 1. (malséant) unseemly, inappropriate. 2. (bizarre) incongruous.

inconnu, -e [ɛ̃kɔny] ♦ adj unknown. ♦ nm, f stranger. ▶ **inconnue** nf 1. (MATHS) unknown. 2. (variable) unknown (factor).

inconsciemment [ɛ̃kɔ̃sjamã] adv 1. (sans en avoir conscience) unconsciously, unwittingly. 2. (à la légère) thoughtlessly.

inconscient, -e [ɛ̃kɔ̃sjã, ãt] adj 1. (évanoui, machinal) unconscious. 2. (irresponsable) thoughtless. ▶ **inconscient** nm: l'~ the unconscious.

inconsidéré, -e [ɛ̃kɔ̃sidere] adj ill-considered, thoughtless.

inconsistant, -e [ɛ̃kɔ̃sistã, ãt] adj 1. (aliment) thin, watery. 2. (caractère) frivolous.

inconsolable [ɛ̃kɔ̃sɔlabl] adj inconsolable.

incontestable [ɛ̃kɔ̃tɛstabl] adj unquestionable, indisputable.

incontinent, -e [ɛ̃kɔ̃tinã, ãt] adj (MÉD) incontinent.

incontournable [ɛ̃kɔ̃turnabl] adj unavoidable.

inconvenant, -e [ɛ̃kɔ̃vnã, ãt] adj improper, unseemly.

inconvénient [ɛ̃kɔ̃venjã] nm 1. (obstacle) problem. 2. (désavantage) disadvantage, drawback. 3. (risque) risk.

incorporé, -e [ɛ̃kɔrpɔre] adj (intégré) built-in.

incorporer [ɛ̃kɔrpɔre] vt 1. (gén) to incorporate; ~ qqch dans to incorporate sthg into; ~ qqch à (CULIN) to mix ou blend sthg into. 2. (MIL) to enlist.

incorrect, -e [ɛ̃kɔrɛkt] adj 1. (faux) incorrect. 2. (inconvenant) inappropriate; (*impoli*) rude. **3.** (*déloyal*) unfair; **être ~ avec qqn** to treat sb unfairly.

incorrection [ɛ̃kɔrɛksjɔ̃] *nf* **1.** (*impolitesse*) impropriety. **2.** (*de langage*) grammatical mistake. **3.** (*malhonnêteté*) dishonesty.

incorrigible [ɛ̃kɔriʒibl] *adj* incorrigible.

incorruptible [ɛ̃kɔryptibl] *adj* incorruptible.

incrédule [ɛ̃kredyl] *adj* **1.** (*sceptique*) incredulous, sceptical. **2.** (RELIG) unbelieving.

increvable [ɛ̃krəvabl] *adj* **1.** (*ballon, pneu*) puncture-proof. **2.** *fam fig* (*personne*) tireless; (*machine*) that will withstand rough treatment.

incriminer [ɛ̃krimine] *vt* **1.** (*personne*) to incriminate. **2.** (*conduite*) to condemn.

incroyable [ɛ̃krwajabl] *adj* incredible, unbelievable.

incroyant, -e [ɛ̃krwajɑ̃, ɑ̃t] *nm, f* unbeliever.

incruster [ɛ̃kryste] *vt* **1.** (*insérer*): **~ qqch dans qqch** to inlay sthg in sthg. **2.** (*décorer*): **~ qqch de qqch** to inlay sthg with sthg. **3.** (*couvrir d'un dépôt*) to fur up. ► **s'incruster** *vp* (*s'insérer*): **s'~ dans qqch** to become embedded in sthg.

incubation [ɛ̃kybasjɔ̃] *nf* (*d'œuf, de maladie*) incubation; *fig* hatching.

inculpation [ɛ̃kylpasjɔ̃] *nf* charge.

inculper [ɛ̃kylpe] *vt* to charge; **~ qqn de** to charge sb with.

inculquer [ɛ̃kylke] *vt*: **~ qqch à qqn** to instil sthg in sb.

inculte [ɛ̃kylt] *adj* **1.** (*terre*) uncultivated. **2.** *péj* (*personne*) uneducated.

incurable [ɛ̃kyrabl] *adj* incurable.

incursion [ɛ̃kyrsjɔ̃] *nf* incursion, foray.

Inde [ɛ̃d] *nf*: **l'~** India.

indécent, -e [ɛ̃desɑ̃, ɑ̃t] *adj* **1.** (*impudique*) indecent. **2.** (*immoral*) scandalous.

indéchiffrable [ɛ̃deʃifrabl] *adj* **1.** (*texte, écriture*) indecipherable. **2.** *fig* (*regard*) inscrutable, impenetrable.

indécis, -e [ɛ̃desi, iz] ♦ *adj* **1.** (*personne - sur le moment*) undecided; (*- de nature*) indecisive. **2.** (*sourire*) vague. ♦ *nm, f* indecisive person.

indécision [ɛ̃desizjɔ̃] *nf* indecision; (*perpétuelle*) indecisiveness.

indécrottable [ɛ̃dekrɔtabl] *adj* *fam* **1.** (*borné*) incredibly dumb. **2.** (*incorrigible*) hopeless.

indéfendable [ɛ̃defɑ̃dabl] *adj* indefensible.

indéfini, -e [ɛ̃defini] *adj* (*quantité,*

pronom) indefinite.

indéfinissable [ɛ̃definisabl] *adj* indefinable.

indéformable [ɛ̃deformabl] *adj* that retains its shape.

indélébile [ɛ̃delebil] *adj* indelible.

indélicat, -e [ɛ̃delika, at] *adj* **1.** (*mufle*) indelicate. **2.** (*malhonnête*) dishonest.

indemne [ɛ̃dɛmn] *adj* unscathed, unharmed.

indemniser [ɛ̃dɛmnize] *vt*: **~ qqn de qqch** (*perte, préjudice*) to compensate sb for sthg; (*frais*) to reimburse sb for sthg.

indemnité [ɛ̃dɛmnite] *nf* **1.** (*de perte, préjudice*) compensation. **2.** (*de frais*) allowance.

indémodable [ɛ̃demɔdabl] *adj*: **ce style est ~** this style doesn't date.

indéniable [ɛ̃denjabl] *adj* undeniable.

indépendance [ɛ̃depɑ̃dɑ̃s] *nf* independence.

indépendant, -e [ɛ̃depɑ̃dɑ̃, ɑ̃t] *adj* **1.** (*gén*) independent; (*entrée*) separate; **~ de ma volonté** beyond my control. **2.** (*travailleur*) self-employed.

indéracinable [ɛ̃derasinabl] *adj* (*arbre*) impossible to uproot; *fig* ineradicable.

indescriptible [ɛ̃dɛskriptibl] *adj* indescribable.

indestructible [ɛ̃dɛstryktibl] *adj* indestructible.

indéterminé, -e [ɛ̃detɛrmine] *adj* **1.** (*indéfini*) indeterminate, indefinite. **2.** (*vague*) vague. **3.** (*personne*) undecided.

index [ɛ̃dɛks] *nm* **1.** (*doigt*) index finger. **2.** (*aiguille*) pointer, needle. **3.** (*registre*) index.

indexer [ɛ̃dɛkse] *vt* **1.** (ÉCON): **~ qqch sur qqch** to index sthg to sthg. **2.** (*livre*) to index.

indicateur, -trice [ɛ̃dikatœr, tris] *adj*: **poteau ~** signpost; **panneau ~** road sign. ► **indicateur** *nm* **1.** (*guide*) directory, guide; **~ des chemins de fer** railway timetable. **2.** (TECHNOL) gauge. **3.** (ÉCON) indicator. **4.** (*de police*) informer.

indicatif, -ive [ɛ̃dikatif, iv] *adj* indicative. ► **indicatif** *nm* **1.** (RADIO & TÉLÉ) signature tune. **2.** (*code*): **~ (téléphonique)** dialling code Br, dial code Am. **3.** (GRAM): **l'~** the indicative.

indication [ɛ̃dikasjɔ̃] *nf* **1.** (*mention*) indication. **2.** (*renseignement*) information (U). **3.** (*directive*) instruction; (THÉÂTRE) direction; **sauf ~ contraire** unless otherwise instructed.

indice [ɛ̃dis] *nm* **1.** (*signe*) sign. **2.** (*dans une enquête*) clue. **3.** (*taux*) rating; **~ du**

coût de la vie (ÉCON) cost-of-living index. **4.** (MATHS) index.

indicible [ɛ̃disibl] adj inexpressible.

indien, -enne [ɛ̃djɛ̃, ɛn] adj **1.** (d'Inde) Indian. **2.** (d'Amérique) American Indian, Native American. ▶ **Indien, -enne** nm, f **1.** (d'Inde) Indian. **2.** (d'Amérique) American Indian, Native American.

indifféremment [ɛ̃diferamɑ̃] adv indifferently.

indifférent, -e [ɛ̃diferɑ̃, ɑ̃t] ♦ adj (gén): ~ à indifferent to. ♦ nm, f uncon-cerned person.

indigence [ɛ̃diʒɑ̃s] nf poverty.

indigène [ɛ̃diʒɛn] ♦ nmf native. ♦ adj (peuple) native; (faune, flore) indigenous.

indigent, -e [ɛ̃diʒɑ̃, ɑ̃t] ♦ adj (pauvre) destitute, poverty-stricken; fig (intellec-tuellement) impoverished. ♦ nm, f poor person; les ~s the poor, the destitute.

indigeste [ɛ̃diʒɛst] adj indigestible.

indigestion [ɛ̃diʒɛstjɔ̃] nf **1.** (alimen-taire) indigestion. **2.** fig (saturation) sur-feit.

indignation [ɛ̃diɲasjɔ̃] nf indignation.

indigné, -e [ɛ̃diɲe] adj indignant.

indigner [ɛ̃diɲe] vt to make indignant. ▶ **s'indigner** vp: s'~ de ou contre qqch to get indignant about sthg.

indigo [ɛ̃digo] ♦ nm indigo. ♦ adj inv indigo (blue).

indiquer [ɛ̃dike] vt **1.** (désigner) to in-dicate, to point out. **2.** (afficher, mon-trer - suj: carte, pendule, aiguille) to show, to indicate. **3.** (recommander): ~ qqn/ qqch à qqn to tell sb of sb/sthg, to suggest sb/sthg to sb. **4.** (dire, renseigner sur) to tell; **pourriez-vous m'~ l'heure?** could you tell me the time? **5.** (fixer - heure, date, lieu) to name, to indicate.

indirect, -e [ɛ̃dirɛkt] adj (gén) indirect; (itinéraire) roundabout.

indiscipliné, -e [ɛ̃disipline] adj **1.** (éco-lier, esprit) undisciplined, unruly. **2.** fig (mèches de cheveux) unmanageable.

indiscret, -ète [ɛ̃diskrɛ, ɛt] ♦ adj indiscreet; (curieux) inquisitive. ♦ nm, f indiscreet person.

indiscrétion [ɛ̃diskresjɔ̃] nf indiscre-tion; (curiosité) curiosity.

indiscutable [ɛ̃diskytabl] adj unques-tionable, indisputable.

indispensable [ɛ̃dispɑ̃sabl] adj indis-pensable, essential; ~ à indispensable to, essential to; **il est ~ de faire qqch** it is essential ou vital to do sthg.

indisponible [ɛ̃dispɔnibl] adj unavail-able.

indisposer [ɛ̃dispoze] vt sout (rendre malade) to indispose.

indistinct, -e [ɛ̃distɛ̃(kt), ɛ̃kt] adj in-distinct; (souvenir) hazy.

individu [ɛ̃dividy] nm individual.

individuel, -elle [ɛ̃dividɥɛl] adj indi-vidual.

indivisible [ɛ̃divizibl] adj indivisible.

Indochine [ɛ̃dɔʃin] nf: l'~ Indo-china.

indolent, -e [ɛ̃dɔlɑ̃, ɑ̃t] adj **1.** (per-sonne) indolent, lethargic. **2.** (geste, regard) languid.

indolore [ɛ̃dɔlɔr] adj painless.

indomptable [ɛ̃dɔ̃tabl] adj **1.** (animal) untamable. **2.** (personne) indomitable.

Indonésie [ɛ̃dɔnezi] nf: l'~ Indonesia.

indu, -e [ɛ̃dy] adj (heure) ungodly, unearthly.

indubitable [ɛ̃dybitabl] adj indu-bitable, undoubted; **il est ~ que** it is indisputable ou beyond doubt that.

induire [ɛ̃dɥir] vt to induce; ~ qqn à faire qqch to induce sb to do sthg; ~ qqn en erreur to mislead sb; en ~ que to infer ou gather that.

induit, -e [ɛ̃dɥi, it] pp → **induire.**

indulgence [ɛ̃dylʒɑ̃s] nf (de juge) leniency; (de parent) indulgence.

indulgent, -e [ɛ̃dylʒɑ̃, ɑ̃t] adj (juge) lenient; (parent) indulgent.

indûment [ɛ̃dymɑ̃] adv unduly.

industrialiser [ɛ̃dystrijalize] vt to industrialize. ▶ **s'industrialiser** vp to become industrialized.

industrie [ɛ̃dystri] nf industry.

industriel, -elle [ɛ̃dystrijɛl] adj indus-trial. ▶ **industriel** nm industrialist.

inébranlable [inebrɑ̃labl] adj **1.** (roc) solid, immovable. **2.** fig (conviction) unshakeable.

inédit, -e [inedi, it] adj **1.** (texte) unpublished. **2.** (trouvaille) novel, origi-nal.

ineffable [inefabl] adj ineffable.

ineffaçable [inefasabl] adj indelible.

inefficace [inefikas] adj **1.** (personne, machine) inefficient. **2.** (solution, remède, mesure) ineffective.

inefficacité [inefikasite] nf **1.** (de per-sonne, machine) inefficiency. **2.** (de solu-tion, remède, mesure) ineffectiveness.

inégal, -e, -aux [inegal, o] adj **1.** (dif-férent, disproportionné) unequal. **2.** (ir-régulier) uneven. **3.** (changeant) change-able; (artiste, travail) erratic.

inégalé, -e [inegale] adj unequalled.

inégalité [inegalite] nf **1.** (injustice, dis-

proportion) inequality. **2.** (*différence*) difference, disparity. **3.** (*irrégularité*) unevenness. **4.** (*d'humeur*) changeability.

inélégant, -e [inelegɑ̃, ɑ̃t] *adj* **1.** (*dans l'habillement*) inelegant. **2.** *fig* (*indélicat*) discourteous.

inéligible [ineliʒibl] *adj* ineligible.

inéluctable [inelyktabl] *adj* inescapable.

inénarrable [inenarabl] *adj* very funny.

inepte [inɛpt] *adj* inept.

ineptie [inɛpsi] *nf* **1.** (*bêtise*) ineptitude. **2.** (*chose idiote*) nonsense (U).

inépuisable [inepɥizabl] *adj* inexhaustible.

inerte [inɛrt] *adj* **1.** (*corps, membre*) lifeless. **2.** (*personne*) passive, inert. **3.** (PHYS) inert.

inertie [inɛrsi] *nf* **1.** (*manque de réaction*) apathy, inertia. **2.** (PHYS) inertia.

inespéré, -e [inɛspere] *adj* unexpected, unhoped-for.

inesthétique [inɛstetik] *adj* unaesthetic.

inestimable [inɛstimabl] *adj*: **d'une valeur ~** priceless; *fig* invaluable.

inévitable [inevitabl] *adj* (*obstacle*) unavoidable; (*conséquence*) inevitable.

inexact, -e [inɛgza(kt), akt] *adj* **1.** (*faux, incomplet*) inaccurate, inexact. **2.** (*en retard*) unpunctual.

inexactitude [inɛgzaktityd] *nf* (*erreur, imprécision*) inaccuracy.

inexcusable [inɛkskyzabl] *adj* unforgivable, inexcusable.

inexistant, -e [inɛgzistɑ̃, ɑ̃t] *adj* nonexistent.

inexorable [inɛgzɔrabl] *adj* inexorable.

inexpérience [inɛksperjɑ̃s] *nf* lack of experience, inexperience.

inexplicable [inɛksplikabl] *adj* inexplicable, unexplainable.

inexpliqué, -e [inɛksplike] *adj* unexplained.

inexpressif, -ive [inɛkspresif, iv] *adj* inexpressive.

inexprimable [inɛksprimabl] *adj* inexpressible.

inextensible [inɛkstɑ̃sibl] *adj* **1.** (*matériau*) unstretchable. **2.** (*étoffe*) non-stretch.

in extremis [inɛkstremis] *adv* at the last minute.

inextricable [inɛkstrikabl] *adj* **1.** (*fouillis*) inextricable. **2.** *fig* (*affaire, mystère*) that cannot be unravelled.

infaillible [ɛ̃fajibl] *adj* (*personne, mé-*

thode) infallible; (*instinct*) unerring.

infâme [ɛ̃fam] *adj* **1.** (*ignoble*) despicable. **2.** *hum ou littéraire* (*dégoûtant*) vile.

infanterie [ɛ̃fɑ̃tri] *nf* infantry.

infanticide [ɛ̃fɑ̃tisid] ◆ *nmf* infanticide, child-killer. ◆ *adj* infanticidal.

infantile [ɛ̃fɑ̃til] *adj* **1.** (*maladie*) childhood (*avant n*). **2.** (*médecine*) for children. **3.** (*comportement*) infantile.

infarctus [ɛ̃farktys] *nm* infarction, infarct; **~ du myocarde** coronary thrombosis, myocardial infarction.

infatigable [ɛ̃fatigabl] *adj* **1.** (*personne*) tireless. **2.** (*attitude*) untiring.

infect, -e [ɛ̃fɛkt] *adj* (*dégoûtant*) vile.

infecter [ɛ̃fɛkte] *vt* **1.** (*eau*) to contaminate. **2.** (*plaie*) to infect. **3.** (*empoisonner*) to poison. ▸ **s'infecter** *vp* to become infected, to turn septic.

infectieux, -euse [ɛ̃fɛksjø, øz] *adj* infectious.

infection [ɛ̃fɛksjɔ̃] *nf* **1.** (MÉD) infection. **2.** *fig & péj* (*puanteur*) stench.

inférer [ɛ̃fere] *vt littéraire*: **~ qqch de qqch** to infer sthg from sthg.

inférieur, -e [ɛ̃ferjœr] ◆ *adj* **1.** (*qui est en bas*) lower. **2.** (*dans une hiérarchie*) inferior; **~ à** (*qualité*) inferior to; (*quantité*) less than. ◆ *nm, f* inferior.

infériorité [ɛ̃ferjɔrite] *nf* inferiority.

infernal, -e, -aux [ɛ̃fɛrnal, o] *adj* **1.** (*personne*) fiendish. **2.** *fig* (*bruit, chaleur, rythme*) infernal; (*vision*) diabolical.

infester [ɛ̃fɛste] *vt* to infest; **être infesté de** (*rats, moustiques*) to be infested with.

infidèle [ɛ̃fidɛl] *adj* **1.** (*mari, femme, ami*): **~ (à)** unfaithful (to). **2.** (*traducteur, historien*) inaccurate.

infidélité [ɛ̃fidelite] *nf* (*trahison*) infidelity.

infiltration [ɛ̃filtrasjɔ̃] *nf* infiltration.

infiltrer [ɛ̃filtre] *vt* to infiltrate. ▸ **s'infiltrer** *vp* **1.** (*pluie, lumière*): **s'~ par/dans** to filter through/into. **2.** (*hommes, idées*) to infiltrate.

infime [ɛ̃fim] *adj* minute, infinitesimal.

infini, -e [ɛ̃fini] *adj* **1.** (*sans bornes*) infinite, boundless. **2.** (MATHS, PHILO & RELIG) infinite. **3.** *fig* (*interminable*) endless, interminable. ▸ **infini** *nm* infinity. ▸ **à l'infini** *loc adv* **1.** (MATHS) to infinity. **2.** (*discourir*) ad infinitum, endlessly.

infiniment [ɛ̃finimɑ̃] *adv* extremely, immensely.

infinité [ɛ̃finite] *nf* infinity, infinite number.

infinitif, -ive [ɛ̃finitif, iv] *adj* infinitive. ▸ **infinitif** *nm* infinitive.

infirme [ɛ̃firm] ♦ adj (handicapé) disabled; (avec l'âge) infirm. ♦ nmf disabled person.

infirmer [ɛ̃firme] vt 1. (démentir) to invalidate. 2. (JUR) to annul.

infirmerie [ɛ̃firməri] nf infirmary.

infirmier, -ère [ɛ̃firmje, ɛr] nm, f nurse.

infirmité [ɛ̃firmite] nf (handicap) disability; (de vieillesse) infirmity.

inflammable [ɛ̃flamabl] adj inflammable, flammable.

inflammation [ɛ̃flamasjɔ̃] nf inflammation.

inflation [ɛ̃flasjɔ̃] nf (ÉCON) inflation; fig increase.

inflationniste [ɛ̃flasjɔnist] adj & nmf inflationist.

infléchir [ɛ̃fleʃir] vt fig (politique) to modify.

inflexible [ɛ̃flɛksibl] adj inflexible.

inflexion [ɛ̃flɛksjɔ̃] nf 1. (de tête) nod. 2. (de voix) inflection.

infliger [ɛ̃fliʒe] vt: ~ qqch à qqn to inflict sthg on sb; (amende) to impose sthg on sb.

influençable [ɛ̃flyɑ̃sabl] adj easily influenced.

influence [ɛ̃flyɑ̃s] nf influence; (de médicament) effect.

influencer [ɛ̃flyɑ̃se] vt to influence.

influent, -e [ɛ̃flyɑ̃, ɑ̃t] adj influential.

influer [ɛ̃flye] vi: ~ sur qqch to influence sthg, to have an effect on sthg.

Infographie® [ɛ̃fɔgrafi] nf computer graphics (U).

informaticien, -enne [ɛ̃fɔrmatisjɛ̃, ɛn] nm, f computer scientist.

information [ɛ̃fɔrmasjɔ̃] nf 1. (renseignement) piece of information. 2. (renseignements & INFORM) information (U). 3. (nouvelle) piece of news. ▶ **informations** nfpl (MÉDIA) news (sg).

informatique [ɛ̃fɔrmatik] ♦ nf 1. (technique) computers. 2. (science) computer science. ♦ adj data-processing (avant n), computer (avant n).

informatiser [ɛ̃fɔrmatize] vt to computerize.

informe [ɛ̃fɔrm] adj (masse, vêtement, silhouette) shapeless.

informel, -elle [ɛ̃fɔrmɛl] adj informal.

informer [ɛ̃fɔrme] vt to inform; ~ qqn sur ou de qqch to inform sb about sthg. ▶ **s'informer** vp to inform o.s.; s'~ de qqch to ask about sthg; s'~ sur qqch to find out about sthg.

infortune [ɛ̃fɔrtyn] nf misfortune.

infos [ɛ̃fo] (abr de **informations**) nfpl fam: les ~ the news (sg).

infraction [ɛ̃fraksjɔ̃] nf offence; être en ~ to be in breach of the law.

infranchissable [ɛ̃frɑ̃ʃisabl] adj insurmountable.

infrarouge [ɛ̃fraruʒ] nm & adj infrared.

infrastructure [ɛ̃frastryktyr] nf infrastructure.

infroissable [ɛ̃frwasabl] adj creaseresistant.

infructueux, -euse [ɛ̃fryktɥø, øz] adj fruitless.

infuser [ɛ̃fyze] vi (tisane) to infuse; (thé) to brew.

infusion [ɛ̃fyzjɔ̃] nf infusion.

ingénier [ɛ̃ʒenje] ▶ **s'ingénier** vp: s'~ à faire qqch to try hard to do sthg.

ingénieur [ɛ̃ʒenjœr] nm engineer.

ingénieux, -euse [ɛ̃ʒenjø, øz] adj ingenious.

ingéniosité [ɛ̃ʒenjozite] nf ingenuity.

ingénu, -e [ɛ̃ʒeny] adj littéraire (candide) artless; hum & péj (trop candide) naïve.

ingérable [ɛ̃ʒerabl] adj unmanageable.

ingérer [ɛ̃ʒere] vt to ingest. ▶ **s'ingérer** vp: s'~ dans to interfere in.

ingrat, -e [ɛ̃gra, at] ♦ adj 1. (personne) ungrateful. 2. (métier) thankless, unrewarding. 3. (sol) barren. 4. (physique) unattractive. ♦ nm, f ungrateful wretch.

ingratitude [ɛ̃gratityd] nf ingratitude.

ingrédient [ɛ̃gredjɑ̃] nm ingredient.

inguérissable [ɛ̃gerisabl] adj incurable.

ingurgiter [ɛ̃gyrʒite] vt 1. (avaler) to swallow. 2. fig (connaissances) to absorb.

inhabitable [inabitabl] adj uninhabitable.

inhabité, -e [inabite] adj uninhabited.

inhabituel, -elle [inabitɥɛl] adj unusual.

inhalateur, -trice [inalatœr, tris] adj: appareil ~ inhaler. ▶ **inhalateur** nm inhaler.

inhalation [inalasjɔ̃] nf inhalation.

inhérent, -e [inerɑ̃, ɑ̃t] adj: ~ à inherent in.

inhibition [inibisjɔ̃] nf inhibition.

inhospitalier, -ère [inɔspitalje, ɛr] adj inhospitable.

inhumain, -e [inymɛ̃, ɛn] adj inhuman.

inhumation [inymasjɔ̃] nf burial.

inhumer [inyme] vt to bury.

inimaginable [inimaʒinabl] adj incredible, unimaginable.

inimitable [inimitabl] *adj* inimitable.

ininflammable [inɛ̃flamabl] *adj* non-flammable.

inintelligible [inɛ̃teliʒibl] *adj* unintelligible.

inintéressant, -e [inɛ̃teresɑ̃, ɑ̃t] *adj* uninteresting.

ininterrompu, -e [inɛ̃terɔ̃py] *adj* (*file, vacarme*) uninterrupted; (*ligne, suite*) unbroken; (*travail, effort*) continuous.

inique [inik] *adj* iniquitous.

initial, -e, -aux [inisjal, o] *adj* (*lettre*) initial. ▶ **initiale** *nf* initial.

initiateur, -trice [inisjatœr, tris] *nm, f* **1.** (*maître*) initiator. **2.** (*précurseur*) innovator.

initiation [inisjasjɔ̃] *nf*: **~ (à)** (*discipline*) introduction (to); (*rituel*) initiation (into).

initiative [inisjativ] *nf* initiative; **prendre l'~ de qqch/de faire qqch** to take the initiative for sthg/in doing sthg.

initié, -e [inisje] ♦ *adj* initiated. ♦ *nm, f* initiate.

initier [inisje] *vt*: **~ qqn à** to initiate sb into. ▶ **s'initier** *vp*: **s'~ à** to familiarize o.s. with.

injecté, -e [ɛ̃ʒɛkte] *adj*: **yeux ~s de sang** bloodshot eyes.

injecter [ɛ̃ʒɛkte] *vt* to inject.

injection [ɛ̃ʒɛksjɔ̃] *nf* injection.

injoignable [ɛ̃jwaɲabl] *adj*: **j'ai essayé de lui téléphoner mais il est ~** I tried to phone him but I couldn't get through to him ou reach him ou get hold of him.

injonction [ɛ̃ʒɔ̃ksjɔ̃] *nf* injunction.

injure [ɛ̃ʒyr] *nf* insult.

injurier [ɛ̃ʒyrje] *vt* to insult.

injurieux, -euse [ɛ̃ʒyrjø, øz] *adj* abusive, insulting.

injuste [ɛ̃ʒyst] *adj* unjust, unfair.

injustice [ɛ̃ʒystis] *nf* injustice.

inlassable [ɛ̃lasabl] *adj* tireless.

inlassablement [ɛ̃lasabləmɑ̃] *adv* tirelessly.

inné, -e [ine] *adj* innate.

innocence [inɔsɑ̃s] *nf* innocence.

innocent, -e [inɔsɑ̃, ɑ̃t] ♦ *adj* innocent. ♦ *nm, f* **1.** (JUR) innocent person. **2.** (*inoffensif, candide*) innocent. **3.** *vieilli* (*idiot*) simpleton.

innocenter [inɔsɑ̃te] *vt* **1.** (JUR) to clear. **2.** *fig* (*excuser*) to justify.

innocuité [inɔkɥite] *nf* harmlessness.

innombrable [inɔ̃brabl] *adj* innumerable; (*foule*) vast.

innover [inɔve] *vi* to innovate.

inobservation [inɔpsɛrvasjɔ̃] *nf* inobservance.

inoccupé, -e [inɔkype] *adj* (*lieu*) empty, unoccupied.

inoculer [inɔkyle] *vt* (MÉD): **~ qqch à qqn** (*volontairement*) to inoculate sb with sthg.

inodore [inɔdɔr] *adj* odourless.

inoffensif, -ive [inɔfɑ̃sif, iv] *adj* harmless.

inondation [inɔ̃dasjɔ̃] *nf* **1.** (*action*) flooding. **2.** (*résultat*) flood.

inonder [inɔ̃de] *vt* to flood; **~ de** *fig* to flood with.

inopérable [inɔperabl] *adj* inoperable.

inopérant, -e [inɔperɑ̃, ɑ̃t] *adj* ineffective.

inopiné, -e [inɔpine] *adj* unexpected.

inopportun, -e [inɔpɔrtœ̃, yn] *adj* inopportune.

inoubliable [inublijabl] *adj* unforgettable.

inouï, -e [inwi] *adj* incredible, extraordinary.

Inox® [inɔks] *nm inv* & *adj inv* stainless steel.

inoxydable [inɔksidabl] *adj* stainless; (*casserole*) stainless steel (*avant n*).

inqualifiable [ɛ̃kalifjabl] *adj* unspeakable.

inquiet, -ète [ɛ̃kjɛ, ɛt] *adj* **1.** (*gén*) anxious. **2.** (*tourmenté*) feverish.

inquiéter [ɛ̃kjete] *vt* **1.** (*donner du souci à*) to worry. **2.** (*déranger*) to disturb. ▶ **s'inquiéter** *vp* **1.** (*s'alarmer*) to be worried. **2.** (*se préoccuper*): **s'~ de** (*s'enquérir de*) to enquire about; (*se soucier de*) to worry about.

inquiétude [ɛ̃kjetyd] *nf* anxiety, worry.

inquisiteur, -trice [ɛ̃kizitœr, tris] *adj* prying.

insaisissable [ɛ̃sezisabl] *adj* **1.** (*personne*) elusive. **2.** *fig* (*nuance*) imperceptible.

insalubre [ɛ̃salybr] *adj* unhealthy.

insatiable [ɛ̃sasjabl] *adj* insatiable.

insatisfait, -e [ɛ̃satisfɛ, ɛt] ♦ *adj* (*personne*) dissatisfied. ♦ *nm, f* malcontent.

inscription [ɛ̃skripsjɔ̃] *nf* **1.** (*action, écrit*) inscription. **2.** (*enregistrement*) enrolment, registration.

inscrire [ɛ̃skrir] *vt* **1.** (*écrire*) to write down; (- *sur la pierre, le métal*) to inscribe. **2.** (*personne*): **~ qqn à qqch** to enrol ou register sb for sthg; **~ qqn sur qqch** to put sb's name down on sthg. **3.** (SPORT) (*but*) to score. ▶ **s'inscrire** *vp* (*personne*): **s'~ à qqch** to enrol ou register for sthg; **s'~ sur qqch** to put one's name down on sthg.

inscrit, -e [ɛskri, it] ◆ *pp* → **inscrire**. ◆ *adj* (*sur liste*) registered; **être ~ sur une liste** to have one's name on a list. ◆ *nm, f* registered person.

insecte [ɛsɛkt] *nm* insect.

insecticide [ɛsɛktisid] *nm & adj* insecticide.

insécurité [ɛsekyrite] *nf* insecurity.

insémination [ɛseminasjɔ̃] *nf* insemination; **~ artificielle** artificial insemination.

insensé, -e [ɛsɑ̃se] *adj* 1. (*déraisonnable*) insane. 2. (*incroyable, excentrique*) extraordinary.

insensibiliser [ɛsɑ̃sibilize] *vt* to anaesthetize.

insensible [ɛsɑ̃sibl] *adj* 1. (*gén*): **~ (à)** insensitive (to). 2. (*imperceptible*) imperceptible.

insensiblement [ɛsɑ̃siblǝmɑ̃] *adv* imperceptibly.

inséparable [ɛseparabl] *adj*: **~ (de)** inseparable (from).

insérer [ɛsere] *vt* to insert; **~ une annonce dans un journal** to put an advertisement in a newspaper. ▶ **s'insérer** *vp* (*s'intégrer*): **s'~ dans** to fit into.

insidieux, -euse [ɛsidjø, øz] *adj* insidious.

insigne [ɛsiɲ] ◆ *nm* badge. ◆ *adj* 1. littéraire (*honneur*) distinguished. 2. *hum* (*maladresse*) remarkable.

insignifiant, -e [ɛsiɲifjɑ̃, ɑ̃t] *adj* insignificant.

insinuation [ɛsinɥasjɔ̃] *nf* insinuation, innuendo.

insinuer [ɛsinɥe] *vt* to insinuate, to imply. ▶ **s'insinuer** *vp*: **s'~ dans** (*eau, humidité, odeur*) to seep into; *fig* (*personne*) to insinuate o.s. into.

insipide [ɛsipid] *adj* (*aliment*) insipid, tasteless; *fig* insipid.

insistance [ɛsistɑ̃s] *nf* insistence.

insister [ɛsiste] *vi* to insist; **~ sur** to insist on; **~ pour faire qqch** to insist on doing sthg.

insolation [ɛsɔlasjɔ̃] *nf* (*malaise*) sunstroke (U).

insolence [ɛsɔlɑ̃s] *nf* insolence (U).

insolent, -e [ɛsɔlɑ̃, ɑ̃t] ◆ *adj* (*personne, acte*) insolent. ◆ *nm, f* insolent person.

insolite [ɛsɔlit] *adj* unusual.

insoluble [ɛsɔlybl] *adj* insoluble.

insolvable [ɛsɔlvabl] *adj* insolvent.

insomnie [ɛsɔmni] *nf* insomnia (U).

insondable [ɛsɔ̃dabl] *adj* (*gouffre, mys-*

tère) unfathomable; (*bêtise*) abysmal.

insonoriser [ɛsɔnɔrize] *vt* to soundproof.

insouciance [ɛsusjɑ̃s] *nf* (*légèreté*) carefree attitude.

insouciant, -e [ɛsusjɑ̃, ɑ̃t] *adj* (*sans-souci*) carefree.

insoumis, -e [ɛsumi, iz] *adj* 1. (*caractère*) rebellious. 2. (*peuple*) unsubjugated. 3. (*soldat*) deserting.

insoumission [ɛsumisjɔ̃] *nf* 1. (*caractère rebelle*) rebelliousness. 2. (MIL) desertion.

insoupçonné, -e [ɛsupsɔne] *adj* unsuspected.

insoutenable [ɛsutnabl] *adj* 1. (*rythme*) unsustainable. 2. (*scène, violence*) unbearable. 3. (*théorie*) untenable.

inspecter [ɛspɛkte] *vt* to inspect.

inspecteur, -trice [ɛspɛktœr, tris] *nm, f* inspector.

inspection [ɛspɛksjɔ̃] *nf* 1. (*contrôle*) inspection. 2. (*fonction*) inspectorate.

inspiration [ɛspirasjɔ̃] *nf* 1. (*gén*) inspiration; (*idée*) bright idea, brainwave; **avoir de l'~** to be inspired. 2. (*d'air*) breathing in.

inspiré, -e [ɛspire] *adj* inspired.

inspirer [ɛspire] *vt* 1. (*gén*) to inspire; **~ qqch à qqn** to inspire sb with sthg. 2. (*air*) to breathe in, to inhale. ▶ **s'inspirer** *vp* (*prendre modèle sur*): **s'~ de qqn/qqch** to be inspired by sb/sthg.

instable [ɛstabl] *adj* 1. (*gén*) unstable. 2. (*vie, temps*) unsettled.

installation [ɛstalasjɔ̃] *nf* 1. (*de gaz, eau, électricité*) installation. 2. (*de personne - comme médecin, artisan*) setting up; (*- dans appartement*) settling in. 3. (*gén pl*) (*équipement*) installations (*pl*), fittings (*pl*); (*industrielle*) plant (U); (*de loisirs*) facilities (*pl*); **~ électrique** wiring.

installer [ɛstale] *vt* 1. (*gaz, eau, électricité*) to install, to put in. 2. (*appartement*) to fit out. 3. (*rideaux, étagères*) to put up; (*meubles*) to put in. 4. (*personne*): **~ qqn** to get sb settled, to install sb. ▶ **s'installer** *vp* 1. (*comme médecin, artisan etc*) to set (o.s.) up. 2. (*emménager*) to settle in; **s'~ chez qqn** to move in with sb. 3. (*dans fauteuil*) to settle down. 4. *fig* (*maladie, routine*) to set in.

instamment [ɛstamɑ̃] *adv* insistently.

instance [ɛstɑ̃s] *nf* 1. (*autorité*) authority. 2. (JUR) proceedings (*pl*). 3. (*insistance*) entreaties (*pl*). ▶ **en instance** *loc adj* pending. ▶ **en instance de** *loc adv* on the point of.

instant [ɛ̃stɑ̃] *nm* instant; **à l'~** (*il y a peu de temps*) a moment ago; (*immédiatement*) this minute; **à tout ~** (*en permanence*) at all times; (*d'un moment à l'autre*) at any moment; **pour l'~** for the moment.

instantané, -e [ɛ̃stɑ̃tane] *adj* **1.** (*immédiat*) instantaneous. **2.** (*soluble*) instant. ▶ **instantané** *nm* snapshot.

instar [ɛ̃star] ▶ **à l'instar de** *loc prép* following the example of.

instaurer [ɛ̃stɔre] *vt* (*instituer*) to establish; *fig* (*peur, confiance*) to instil.

instigateur, -trice [ɛ̃stigatœr, tris] *nm, f* instigator.

instigation [ɛ̃stigasjɔ̃] *nf* instigation. ▶ **à l'instigation de, sur l'instigation de** *loc prép* at the instigation of.

instinct [ɛ̃stɛ̃] *nm* instinct.

instinctif, -ive [ɛ̃stɛ̃ktif, iv] ♦ *adj* instinctive. ♦ *nm, f* instinctive person.

instituer [ɛ̃stitɥe] *vt* **1.** (*pratique*) to institute. **2.** (JUR) (*personne*) to appoint.

institut [ɛ̃stity] *nm* **1.** (*gén*) institute. **2.** (*de soins*): **~ de beauté** beauty salon.

instituteur, -trice [ɛ̃stitytœr, tris] *nm, f* primary Br ou grade Am school teacher.

institution [ɛ̃stitysjɔ̃] *nf* **1.** (*gén*) institution. **2.** (*école privée*) private school. ▶ **institutions** *nfpl* (POLIT) institutions.

instructif, -ive [ɛ̃stryktif, iv] *adj* instructive, educational.

instruction [ɛ̃stryksjɔ̃] *nf* **1.** (*enseignement, savoir*) education. **2.** (*formation*) training. **3.** (*directive*) order. **4.** (JUR) (*pre-trial*) investigation. ▶ **instructions** *nfpl* instructions.

instruit, -e [ɛ̃strɥi, it] *adj* educated.

instrument [ɛ̃strymɑ̃] *nm* instrument; **~ de musique** musical instrument.

insu [ɛ̃sy] ▶ **à l'insu de** *loc prép*: **à l'~ de qqn** without sb knowing; **ils ont tout organisé à mon ~** they organized it all without my knowing.

insubmersible [ɛ̃sybmɛrsibl] *adj* unsinkable.

insubordination [ɛ̃sybɔrdinasjɔ̃] *nf* insubordination.

insuccès [ɛ̃syksɛ] *nm* failure.

insuffisance [ɛ̃syfizɑ̃s] *nf* **1.** (*manque*) insufficiency. **2.** (MÉD) deficiency. ▶ **insuffisances** *nfpl* (*faiblesses*) shortcomings.

insuffisant, -e [ɛ̃syfizɑ̃, ɑ̃t] *adj* **1.** (*en quantité*) insufficient. **2.** (*en qualité*) inadequate, unsatisfactory.

insuffler [ɛ̃syfle] *vt* **1.** (*air*) to blow. **2.**

fig (*sentiment*): **~ qqch à qqn** to inspire sb with sthg.

insulaire [ɛ̃sylɛr] ♦ *nmf* islander. ♦ *adj* (GÉOGR) island (*avant n*).

insuline [ɛ̃sylin] *nf* insulin.

insulte [ɛ̃sylt] *nf* insult.

insulter [ɛ̃sylte] *vt* to insult.

insupportable [ɛ̃sypɔrtabl] *adj* unbearable.

insurgé, -e [ɛ̃syrʒe] *adj & nm, f* insurgent, rebel.

insurger [ɛ̃syrʒe] ▶ **s'insurger** *vp* to rebel, to revolt.

insurmontable [ɛ̃syrmɔ̃tabl] *adj* (*difficulté*) insurmountable; (*dégoût*) uncontrollable.

insurrection [ɛ̃syrɛksjɔ̃] *nf* insurrection.

intact, -e [ɛ̃takt] *adj* intact.

intangible [ɛ̃tɑ̃ʒibl] *adj* **1.** *littéraire* (*impalpable*) intangible. **2.** (*sacré*) inviolable.

intarissable [ɛ̃tarisabl] *adj* inexhaustible; **il est ~** he could go on talking for ever.

intégral, -e, -aux [ɛ̃tegral, o] *adj* **1.** (*paiement*) in full; (*texte*) unabridged, complete. **2.** (MATHS): **calcul ~** integral calculus.

intégralement [ɛ̃tegralmɑ̃] *adv* fully, in full.

intégrant, -e [ɛ̃tegrɑ̃, ɑ̃t] → **parti**.

intègre [ɛ̃tɛgr] *adj* honest, of integrity.

intégré, -e [ɛ̃tegre] *adj* (*élément*) built-in.

intégrer [ɛ̃tegre] *vt* (*assimiler*): **~ (à ou dans)** to integrate (into). ▶ **s'intégrer** *vp* **1.** (*s'incorporer*): **s'~ dans** ou **à** to fit into. **2.** (*s'adapter*) to integrate.

intégrisme [ɛ̃tegrism] *nm* fundamentalism.

intégrité [ɛ̃tegrite] *nf* **1.** (*totalité*) entirety. **2.** (*honnêteté*) integrity.

intellectuel, -elle [ɛ̃telɛktɥel] *adj & nm, f* intellectual.

intelligence [ɛ̃teliʒɑ̃s] *nf* (*facultés mentales*) intelligence; **~ artificielle** artificial intelligence.

intelligent, -e [ɛ̃teliʒɑ̃, ɑ̃t] *adj* intelligent.

intelligible [ɛ̃teliʒibl] *adj* **1.** (*voix*) clear. **2.** (*concept, texte*) intelligible.

intello [ɛ̃telo] *adj inv & nmf péj* highbrow.

intempéries [ɛ̃tɑ̃peri] *nfpl* bad weather (U).

intempestif, -ive [ɛ̃tɑ̃pɛstif, iv] *adj* untimely.

intenable [ɛ̃tənabl] *adj* 1. (*chaleur, personne*) unbearable. 2. (*position*) untenable, indefensible.

intendance [ɛ̃tɑ̃dɑ̃s] *nf* 1. (MIL) commissariat; (SCOL & UNIV) bursar's office. 2. *fig* (*questions matérielles*) housekeeping.

intendant, -e [ɛ̃tɑ̃dɑ̃, ɑ̃t] *nm, f* 1. (SCOL & UNIV) bursar. 2. (*de manoir*) steward.

intense [ɛ̃tɑ̃s] *adj* (*gén*) intense.

intensif, -ive [ɛ̃tɑ̃sif, iv] *adj* intensive.

intensifier [ɛ̃tɑ̃sifje] *vt* to intensify. ▶ **s'intensifier** *vp* to intensify.

intensité [ɛ̃tɑ̃site] *nf* intensity.

intenter [ɛ̃tɑ̃te] *vt* (JUR): ~ qqch contre ou à qqn to bring sthg against sb.

intention [ɛ̃tɑ̃sjɔ̃] *nf* intention; avoir l'~ de faire qqch to intend to do sthg. ▶ **à l'intention de** *loc prép* for.

intentionné, -e [ɛ̃tɑ̃sjɔne] *adj*: bien ~ well-meaning; mal ~ ill-disposed.

intentionnel, -elle [ɛ̃tɑ̃sjɔnɛl] *adj* intentional.

interactif, -ive [ɛ̃teraktif, iv] *adj* interactive.

intercalaire [ɛ̃tɛrkalɛr] ♦ *nm* insert. ♦ *adj*: feuillet ~ insert.

intercaler [ɛ̃tɛrkale] *vt*: ~ qqch dans qqch (*feuillet, citation*) to insert sthg in sthg; (*dans le temps*) to fit sthg into thg.

intercéder [ɛ̃tɛrsede] *vi*: ~ pour ou en faveur de qqn auprès de qqn to intercede with sb on behalf of sb.

intercepter [ɛ̃tɛrsɛpte] *vt* 1. (*lettre, ballon*) to intercept. 2. (*chaleur*) to block.

interchangeable [ɛ̃tɛrʃɑ̃ʒabl] *adj* interchangeable.

interclasse [ɛ̃tɛrklas] *nm* break.

interdiction [ɛ̃tɛrdiksjɔ̃] *nf* 1. (*défense*): '~ de stationner' 'strictly no parking'. 2. (*prohibition, suspension*): ~ (de) ban (on), banning (of); ~ de séjour order banning released prisoner from living in certain areas.

interdire [ɛ̃tɛrdir] *vt* 1. (*prohiber*): ~ qqch à qqn to forbid sb sthg; ~ à qqn de faire qqch to forbid sb to do sthg. 2. (*empêcher*) to prevent; ~ à qqn de faire qqch to prevent sb from doing sthg. 3. (*bloquer*) to block.

interdit, -e [ɛ̃tɛrdi, it] ♦ *pp* → **interdire**. ♦ *adj* 1. (*défendu*) forbidden; 'film ~ aux moins de 18 ans' ≃ (18); il est ~ de fumer you're not allowed to smoke. 2. (*ébahi*): rester ~ to be stunned. 3. (*privé*): être ~ de chéquier to have had one's chequebook facilities withdrawn; ~ de séjour banned from entering the country.

intéressant, -e [ɛ̃teresɑ̃, ɑ̃t] *adj* 1. (*captivant*) interesting. 2. (*avantageux*) advantageous, good.

intéressé, -e [ɛ̃terese] *adj* (*concerné*) concerned, involved; *péj* (*motivé*) self-interested.

intéresser [ɛ̃terese] *vt* 1. (*captiver*) to interest; ~ qqn à qqch to interest sb in sthg. 2. (COMM) (*faire participer*): ~ les employés (aux bénéfices) to give one's employees a share in the profits; ~ qqn dans son commerce to give sb a financial interest in one's business. 3. (*concerner*) to concern. ▶ **s'intéresser** *vp*: s'~ à qqn/qqch to take an interest in sb/sthg, to be interested in sb/sthg.

intérêt [ɛ̃tere] *nm* 1. (*gén*) interest; ~ pour interest in; avoir ~ à faire qqch to be well advised to do sthg. 2. (*importance*) significance. ▶ **intérêts** *nmpl* 1. (FIN) interest (*sg*). 2. (COMM): avoir des ~s dans to have a stake in.

interface [ɛ̃tɛrfas] *nf* (INFORM) interface; ~ graphique graphic interface.

interférer [ɛ̃tɛrfere] *vi* 1. (PHYS) to interfere. 2. *fig* (*s'immiscer*): ~ dans qqch to interfere in sthg.

intérieur, -e [ɛ̃terjœr] *adj* 1. (*gén*) inner. 2. (*de pays*) domestic. ▶ **intérieur** *nm* 1. (*gén*) inside; de l'~ from the inside; à l'~ (de qqch) inside (sthg). 2. (*de pays*) interior.

intérim [ɛ̃terim] *nm* 1. (*période*) interim period; par ~ acting. 2. (*travail temporaire*) temporary ou casual work; (*dans bureau*) temping.

intérimaire [ɛ̃terimɛr] ♦ *adj* 1. (*ministre, directeur*) acting (*avant n*). 2. (*employé, fonctions*) temporary. ♦ *nmf* (*employé*) temp.

intérioriser [ɛ̃terjɔrize] *vt* to internalize.

interjection [ɛ̃terʒeksjɔ̃] *nf* (LING) interjection.

interligne [ɛ̃terliɲ] *nm* (line) spacing.

interlocuteur, -trice [ɛ̃terlɔkytœr, tris] *nm, f* 1. (*dans conversation*) speaker; mon ~ the person to whom I am/was speaking. 2. (*dans négociation*) negotiator.

interloquer [ɛ̃terlɔke] *vt* to disconcert.

interlude [ɛ̃terlyd] *nm* interlude.

intermède [ɛ̃termɛd] *nm* interlude.

intermédiaire [ɛ̃termedjer] ♦ *nm* intermediary, go-between; par l'~ de qqn/qqch through sb/sthg. ♦ *adj* intermediate.

interminable [ɛ̃tɛrminabl] *adj* never-ending, interminable.

intermittence [ɛ̃tɛrmitãs] *nf* (*discontinuité*): **par ~** intermittently, off and on.

intermittent, -e [ɛ̃tɛrmitã, ãt] *adj* intermittent.

internat [ɛ̃tɛrna] *nm* (SCOL - *établissement*) boarding school; (*- système*) boarding.

international, -e, -aux [ɛ̃tɛrnasjɔnal, o] *adj* international.

internaute [ɛ̃tɛrnɔt] *nmf* (INFORM) Internet user.

interne [ɛ̃tɛrn] ◆ *nmf* **1.** (*élève*) boarder. **2.** (MÉD & UNIV) houseman Br, intern Am. ◆ *adj* **1.** (ANAT) internal; (*oreille*) inner. **2.** (*du pays*) domestic; (*d'une société*) internal; **magazine (de communication)** OU **journal ~** in-house magazine.

internement [ɛ̃tɛrnəmã] *nm* **1.** (MÉD) committal (*to psychiatric hospital*). **2.** (POLIT) internment.

interner [ɛ̃tɛrne] *vt* **1.** (MÉD) to commit (*to psychiatric hospital*). **2.** (POLIT) to intern.

Internet [ɛ̃tɛrnɛt] *nm*: **l'~** the Internet.

interpeller [ɛ̃tɛrpəle] *vt* **1.** (*apostropher*) to call OU shout out to. **2.** (*interroger*) to take in for questioning.

Interphone® [ɛ̃tɛrfɔn] *nm* intercom; (*d'un immeuble*) entry phone.

interposer [ɛ̃tɛrpoze] *vt* to interpose. ► **s'interposer** *vp*: **s'~ entre qqn et qqn** to intervene OU come between sb and sb.

interprète [ɛ̃tɛrprɛt] *nmf* **1.** (*gén*) interpreter. **2.** (CIN, MUS & THÉÂTRE) performer.

interpréter [ɛ̃tɛrprete] *vt* to interpret.

interrogateur, -trice [ɛ̃tɛrɔgatœr, tris] *adj* inquiring (*avant n*).

interrogatif, -ive [ɛ̃tɛrɔgatif, iv] *adj* (GRAM) interrogative.

interrogation [ɛ̃tɛrɔgasjɔ̃] *nf* **1.** (*de prisonnier*) interrogation; (*de témoin*) questioning. **2.** (*question*) question. **3.** (SCOL) test.

interrogatoire [ɛ̃tɛrɔgatwar] *nm* **1.** (*de police, juge*) questioning. **2.** (*procès-verbal*) statement.

interrogeable [ɛ̃tɛrɔʒabl] *adj*: **répondeur ~ à distance** answerphone with remote playback facility.

interroger [ɛ̃tɛrɔʒe] *vt* **1.** (*questionner*) to question; (*accusé, base de données*) to interrogate; **~ qqn (sur qqch)** to question sb (about sthg). **2.** (*faits, conscience*) to examine. ► **s'interroger** *vp*: **s'~ sur**

to wonder about.

interrompre [ɛ̃tɛrɔ̃pr] *vt* to interrupt. ► **s'interrompre** *vp* to stop.

interrompu, -e [ɛ̃tɛrɔ̃py] *pp* → **interrompre**.

interrupteur [ɛ̃tɛryptœr] *nm* switch.

interruption [ɛ̃tɛrypsjɔ̃] *nf* **1.** (*arrêt*) break. **2.** (*action*) interruption.

intersection [ɛ̃tɛrsɛksjɔ̃] *nf* intersection.

interstice [ɛ̃tɛrstis] *nm* chink, crack.

interurbain [ɛ̃tɛryrbɛ̃, ɛn] *adj* long-distance. ► **interurbain** *nm*: **l'~** the long-distance telephone service.

intervalle [ɛ̃tɛrval] *nm* **1.** (*spatial*) space, gap. **2.** (*temporel*) interval, period (of time); **à 6 jours d'~** after 6 days. **3.** (MUS) interval.

intervenant, -e [ɛ̃tɛrvənã, ãt] *nm, f* (*orateur*) speaker.

intervenir [ɛ̃tɛrvənir] *vi* **1.** (*personne*) to intervene; **~ auprès de qqn** to intervene with sb; **~ dans qqch** to intervene in sthg; **faire ~ qqn** to bring OU call in sb. **2.** (*événement*) to take place.

intervention [ɛ̃tɛrvãsjɔ̃] *nf* **1.** (*gén*) intervention. **2.** (MÉD) operation; **subir une ~ chirurgicale** to have an operation, to have surgery. **3.** (*discours*) speech.

intervenu, -e [ɛ̃tɛrvəny] *pp* → **intervenir**.

intervertir [ɛ̃tɛrvɛrtir] *vt* to reverse, to invert.

interview [ɛ̃tɛrvju] *nf* interview.

interviewer [ɛ̃tɛrvjuve] *vt* to interview.

intestin [ɛ̃tɛstɛ̃] *nm* intestine.

intestinal, -e, -aux [ɛ̃tɛstinal, o] *adj* intestinal.

intime [ɛ̃tim] ◆ *nmf* close friend. ◆ *adj* (*gén*) intimate; (*vie, journal*) private.

intimider [ɛ̃timide] *vt* to intimidate.

intimité [ɛ̃timite] *nf* **1.** (*secret*) depths (*pl*). **2.** (*familiarité, confort*) intimacy. **3.** (*vie privée*) privacy.

intitulé [ɛ̃tityle] *nm* (*titre*) title; (*de paragraphe*) heading.

intituler [ɛ̃tityle] *vt* to call, to entitle. ► **s'intituler** *vp* (*ouvrage*) to be called OU entitled.

intolérable [ɛ̃tɔlerabl] *adj* intolerable.

intolérance [ɛ̃tɔlerãs] *nf* (*religieuse, politique*) intolerance.

intolérant, -e [ɛ̃tɔlerã, ãt] *adj* intolerant.

intonation [ɛ̃tɔnasjɔ̃] *nf* intonation.

intouchable [ɛ̃tuʃabl] *nmf & adj* untouchable.

intoxication [ɛ̃tɔksikasjɔ̃] *nf* (*empoisonnement*) poisoning.

intoxiquer [ɛ̃tɔksike] *vt*: ~ qqn par (*empoisonner*) to poison sb with.

intraduisible [ɛ̃tradɥizibl] *adj* (*texte*) untranslatable.

intraitable [ɛ̃trɛtabl] *adj*: ~ (sur) inflexible (about).

intransigeant, -e [ɛ̃trɑ̃ziʒɑ̃, ɑ̃t] *adj* intransigent.

intransitif, -ive [ɛ̃trɑ̃zitif, iv] *adj* intransitive.

intransportable [ɛ̃trɑ̃spɔrtabl] *adj*: **il est ~** he/it cannot be moved.

intraveineux, -euse [ɛ̃travenø, øz] *adj* intravenous.

intrépide [ɛ̃trepid] *adj* bold, intrepid.

intrigue [ɛ̃trig] *nf* 1. (*manœuvre*) intrigue. 2. (CIN, LITTÉRATURE & THÉÂTRE) plot.

intriguer [ɛ̃trige] ◆ *vt* to intrigue. ◆ *vi* to scheme, to intrigue.

introduction [ɛ̃trɔdyksjɔ̃] *nf* 1. (*gén*): ~ (à) introduction (to). 2. (*insertion*) insertion.

introduire [ɛ̃trɔdɥir] *vt* 1. (*gén*) to introduce. 2. (*faire entrer*) to show in. 3. (*insérer*) to insert. ▶ **s'introduire** *vp* 1. (*pénétrer*) to enter; **s'~ dans une maison** (*cambrioleur*) to get into ou enter a house. 2. (*s'implanter*) to be introduced.

introduit, -e [ɛ̃trɔdɥi, it] *pp* → **introduire**.

introspection [ɛ̃trɔspeksjɔ̃] *nf* introspection.

introuvable [ɛ̃truvabl] *adj* nowhere to be found.

introverti, -e [ɛ̃trɔverti] ◆ *adj* introverted. ◆ *nm, f* introvert.

intrus, -e [ɛ̃try, yz] *nm, f* intruder.

intrusion [ɛ̃tryzjɔ̃] *nf* 1. (*gén & GÉOL*) intrusion. 2. (*ingérence*) interference.

intuitif, -ive [ɛ̃tɥitif, iv] *adj* intuitive.

intuition [ɛ̃tɥisjɔ̃] *nf* intuition.

inusable [inyzabl] *adj* hardwearing.

inusité, -e [inyzite] *adj* unusual, uncommon.

inutile [inytil] *adj* (*objet, personne*) useless; (*effort, démarche*) pointless.

inutilisable [inytilizabl] *adj* unusable.

inutilité [inytilite] *nf* (*de personne, d'objet*) uselessness; (*de démarche, d'effort*) pointlessness.

invaincu, -e [ɛ̃vɛ̃ky] *adj* (SPORT) unbeaten.

invalide [ɛ̃valid] ◆ *nmf* disabled person; ~ **du travail** industrially disabled person. ◆ *adj* disabled.

invalidité [ɛ̃validite] *nf* 1. (JUR) invalidity. 2. (MÉD) disability.

invariable [ɛ̃varjabl] *adj* 1. (*immuable*) unchanging. 2. (GRAM) invariable.

invasion [ɛ̃vazjɔ̃] *nf* invasion.

invendable [ɛ̃vɑ̃dabl] *adj* unsaleable, unsellable.

invendu, -e [ɛ̃vɑ̃dy] *adj* unsold. ▶ **invendu** *nm* (*gén pl*) remainder.

inventaire [ɛ̃vɑ̃tɛr] *nm* 1. (*gén*) inventory. 2. (COMM - *activité*) stocktaking Br, inventory Am; (- *liste*) list.

inventer [ɛ̃vɑ̃te] *vt* to invent.

inventeur [ɛ̃vɑ̃tœr] *nm* (*de machine*) inventor.

invention [ɛ̃vɑ̃sjɔ̃] *nf* 1. (*découverte, mensonge*) invention. 2. (*imagination*) inventiveness.

inventorier [ɛ̃vɑ̃tɔrje] *vt* to make an inventory of.

inverse [ɛ̃vers] ◆ *nm* opposite, reverse. ◆ *adj* 1. (*sens*) opposite; (*ordre*) reverse; **en sens ~ (de)** in the opposite direction (to). 2. (*rapport*) inverse.

inversement [ɛ̃versəmɑ̃] *adv* 1. (MATHS) inversely. 2. (*au contraire*) on the other hand. 3. (*vice versa*) vice versa.

inverser [ɛ̃verse] *vt* to reverse.

invertébré, -e [ɛ̃vertebre] *adj* invertebrate. ▶ **invertébré** *nm* invertebrate.

investigation [ɛ̃vestigasjɔ̃] *nf* investigation.

investir [ɛ̃vestir] *vt* to invest.

investissement [ɛ̃vestismɑ̃] *nm* investment.

investisseur, -euse [ɛ̃vestisœr, øz] *nm, f* investor.

investiture [ɛ̃vestityr] *nf* investiture.

invétéré, -e [ɛ̃vetere] *adj* péj inveterate.

invincible [ɛ̃vɛ̃sibl] *adj* invincible.

inviolable [ɛ̃vjɔlabl] *adj* 1. (JUR) inviolable. 2. (*coffre*) impregnable.

invisible [ɛ̃vizibl] *adj* invisible.

invitation [ɛ̃vitasjɔ̃] *nf*: ~ (à) invitation (to); **sur ~** by invitation.

invité, -e [ɛ̃vite] ◆ *adj* (*hôte*) invited; (*professeur, conférencier*) guest (*avant n*). ◆ *nm, f* guest.

inviter [ɛ̃vite] *vt* to invite; ~ **qqn à faire qqch** to invite sb to do sthg; *fig* (*suj: chose*) to be an invitation to sb to do sthg; **je vous invite!** it's my treat!

in vitro [invitro] → **fécondation**.

invivable [ɛ̃vivabl] *adj* unbearable.

involontaire [ɛ̃vɔlɔ̃tɛr] *adj* (*acte*) involuntary.

invoquer [ɛ̃vɔke] vt **1.** (alléguer) to put forward. **2.** (citer, appeler à l'aide) to invoke; (paix) to call for.

invraisemblable [ɛ̃vrɛsɑ̃blabl] adj **1.** (incroyable) unlikely, improbable. **2.** (extravagant) incredible.

invulnérable [ɛ̃vylnerabl] adj invulnerable.

iode [jɔd] nm iodine.

ion [jɔ̃] nm ion.

IRA [ira] (abr de Irish Republican Army) nf IRA.

irai, iras etc → **aller**.

Irak, Iraq [irak] nm: **l'~** Iraq.

irakien, -enne, iraquien, -enne [irakjɛ̃, ɛn] adj Iraqi. ▶ **Irakien, -enne, Iraquien, -enne** nm, f Iraqi.

Iran [irɑ̃] nm: **l'~** Iran.

iranien, -enne [iranjɛ̃, ɛn] adj Iranian. ▶ **iranien** nm (langue) Iranian. ▶ **Iranien, -enne** nm, f Iranian.

Iraq = **Irak**.

iraquien = **irakien**.

irascible [irasibl] adj irascible.

iris [iris] nm (ANAT & BOT) iris.

irisé, -e [irize] adj iridescent.

irlandais, -e [irlɑ̃dɛ, ɛz] adj Irish. ▶ **irlandais** nm (langue) Irish. ▶ **Irlandais, -e** nm, f Irishman (f Irishwoman).

Irlande [irlɑ̃d] nf: **l'~** Ireland; **l'~ du Nord/Sud** Northern/Southern Ireland.

ironie [irɔni] nf irony.

ironique [irɔnik] adj ironic.

ironiser [irɔnize] vi to speak ironically.

irradier [iradje] ◆ vi to radiate. ◆ vt to irradiate.

irraisonné, -e [irɛzɔne] adj irrational.

irrationnel, -elle [irasjɔnɛl] adj irrational.

irréalisable [irealizabl] adj unrealizable.

irrécupérable [irekyperabl] adj **1.** (irrécouvrable) irretrievable. **2.** (irréparable) beyond repair. **3.** fam (personne) beyond hope.

irrécusable [irekyzabl] adj unimpeachable.

irréductible [iredyktibl] ◆ nmf diehard. ◆ adj **1.** (CHIM, MATHS & MÉD) irreducible. **2.** fig (volonté) indomitable; (personne) implacable; (communiste) diehard (avant n).

irréel, -elle [ireɛl] adj unreal.

irréfléchi, -e [irefleʃi] adj unthinking.

irréfutable [irefytabl] adj irrefutable.

irrégularité [iregylarite] nf **1.** (gén) irregularity. **2.** (de terrain, performance) unevenness.

irrégulier, -ère [iregylje, ɛr] adj **1.** (gén) irregular. **2.** (terrain, surface) uneven, irregular. **3.** (employé, athlète) erratic.

irrémédiable [iremedjabl] adj (irréparable) irreparable.

irremplaçable [irɑ̃plasabl] adj irreplaceable.

irréparable [ireparabl] adj **1.** (objet) beyond repair. **2.** fig (perte, erreur) irreparable.

irrépressible [irepresibl] adj irrepressible.

irréprochable [ireprɔʃabl] adj irreproachable.

irrésistible [irezistibl] adj **1.** (tentation, femme) irresistible. **2.** (amusant) entertaining.

irrésolu, -e [irezɔly] adj **1.** (indécis) irresolute. **2.** (sans solution) unresolved.

irrespirable [irespirabl] adj **1.** (air) unbreathable. **2.** fig (oppressant) oppressive.

irresponsable [irespɔ̃sabl] ◆ nmf irresponsible person. ◆ adj irresponsible.

irréversible [ireversibl] adj irreversible.

irrévocable [irevɔkabl] adj irrevocable.

irrigation [irigasjɔ̃] nf irrigation.

irriguer [irige] vt to irrigate.

irritable [iritabl] adj irritable.

irritation [iritasjɔ̃] nf irritation.

irriter [irite] vt **1.** (exaspérer) to irritate, to annoy. **2.** (MÉD) to irritate. ▶ **s'irriter** vp to get irritated; **s'~ contre qqn/de qqch** to get irritated with sb/at sthg.

irruption [irypsjɔ̃] nf **1.** (invasion) invasion. **2.** (entrée brusque) irruption.

islam [islam] nm Islam.

islamique [islamik] adj Islamic.

islandais, -e [islɑ̃dɛ, ɛz] adj Icelandic. ▶ **islandais** nm (langue) Icelandic. ▶ **Islandais, -e** nm, f Icelander.

Islande [islɑ̃d] nf: **l'~** Iceland.

isocèle [izɔsɛl] adj isoceles.

isolant, -e [izɔlɑ̃, ɑ̃t] adj insulating. ▶ **isolant** nm insulator, insulating material.

isolation [izɔlasjɔ̃] nf insulation.

isolé, -e [izɔle] adj isolated.

isoler [izɔle] vt **1.** (séparer) to isolate. **2.** (CONSTR & ÉLECTR) to insulate; **~ qqch du froid** to insulate sthg (against the cold); **~ qqch du bruit** to soundproof sthg. ▶ **s'isoler** vp: **s'~ (de)** to isolate o.s. (from).

isoloir [izɔlwar] nm polling booth.
isotherme [izɔtɛrm] adj isothermal.
Israël [israɛl] n Israel.
israélien, -enne [israeljɛ̃, ɛn] adj Israeli. ▶ **Israélien, -enne** nm, f Israeli.
israélite [israelit] adj Jewish. ▶ **Israélite** nmf Jew.
issu, -e [isy] adj: être ~ de (résulter de) to emerge ou stem from; (personne) to come from. ▶ **issue** nf 1. (sortie) exit; ~e de secours emergency exit. 2. fig (solution) way out, solution. 3. (terme) outcome.
isthme [ism] nm isthmus.
Italie [itali] nf: l'~ Italy.
italien, -enne [italjɛ̃, ɛn] adj Italian. ▶ **italien** nm (langue) Italian. ▶ **Italien, -enne** nm, f Italian.
italique [italik] nm (TYPO) italics (pl); en ~ in italics.
itinéraire [itinerɛr] nm itinerary, route.
itinérant, -e [itinerɑ̃, ɑ̃t] adj (spectacle, troupe) itinerant.
IUT (abr de institut universitaire de technologie) nm ≃ technical college.
IVG (abr de interruption volontaire de grossesse) nf abortion.
ivoire [ivwar] nm ivory.
ivoirien, -enne [ivwarjɛ̃, ɛn] adj of/from the Ivory Coast.
ivre [ivr] adj drunk.
ivresse [ivrɛs] nf drunkenness; (extase) rapture.
ivrogne [ivrɔɲ] nmf drunkard.

J

j, J [ʒi] nm inv j, J.
j' → je.
jabot [ʒabo] nm 1. (d'oiseau) crop. 2. (de chemise) frill.
jacasser [ʒakase] vi péj to chatter, to jabber.
jacinthe [ʒasɛ̃t] nf hyacinth.
Jacuzzi® [ʒakuzi] nm Jacuzzi®.
jade [ʒad] nm jade.
jadis [ʒadis] adv formerly, in former times.
jaguar [ʒagwar] nm jaguar.

jaillir [ʒajir] vi 1. (liquide) to gush; (flammes) to leap. 2. (cri) to ring out. 3. (personne) to spring out.
jais [ʒɛ] nm jet.
jalon [ʒalɔ̃] nm marker pole.
jalonner [ʒalɔne] vt to mark (out).
jalousie [ʒaluzi] nf 1. (envie) jealousy. 2. (store) blind.
jaloux, -ouse [ʒalu, uz] adj: ~ (de) jealous (of).
Jamaïque [ʒamaik] nf: la ~ Jamaica.
jamais [ʒamɛ] adv 1. (sens négatif) never; ne ... ~, ~ ne never; je ne reviendrai ~, ~ je ne reviendrai I'll never come back; je ne viendrai ~ plus, plus ~ je ne viendrai I'll never come here again. 2. (sens positif) plus que ~ more than ever; il est plus triste que ~ he's sadder than ever; si ~ tu le vois if you should happen to see him, should you happen to see him. ▶ **à jamais** loc adv for ever.
jambe [ʒɑ̃b] nf leg.
jambières [ʒɑ̃bjɛr] nfpl (de football) shin pads; (de cricket) pads.
jambon [ʒɑ̃bɔ̃] nm ham; ~ blanc boiled ou cooked ham; un ~ beurre fam a ham sandwich.
jante [ʒɑ̃t] nf (wheel) rim.
janvier [ʒɑ̃vje] nm January; voir aussi **septembre**.
Japon [ʒapɔ̃] nm: le ~ Japan.
japonais, -e [ʒapɔnɛ, ɛz] adj Japanese. ▶ **japonais** nm (langue) Japanese. ▶ **Japonais, -e** nm, f Japanese (person); les Japonais the Japanese.
japper [ʒape] vi to yap.
jaquette [ʒakɛt] nf 1. (vêtement) jacket. 2. (de livre) (dust) jacket.
jardin [ʒardɛ̃] nm garden; ~ public park.
jardinage [ʒardinaʒ] nm gardening.
jardinet [ʒardinɛ] nm small garden.
jardinier, -ère [ʒardinje, ɛr] nm, f gardener. ▶ **jardinière** nf (bac à fleurs) window box.
jargon [ʒargɔ̃] nm 1. (langage spécialisé) jargon. 2. fam (charabia) gibberish.
jarret [ʒarɛ] nm 1. (ANAT) back of the knee. 2. (CULIN) knuckle of veal.
jarretelle [ʒartɛl] nf suspender Br, garter Am.
jarretière [ʒartjɛr] nf garter.
jars [ʒar] nm gander.
jaser [ʒaze] vi (bavarder) to gossip.
jasmin [ʒasmɛ̃] nm jasmine.
jatte [ʒat] nf bowl.

jauge [ʒoʒ] nf (instrument) gauge.
jauger [ʒoʒe] vt to gauge.
jaunâtre [ʒonatr] adj yellowish.
jaune [ʒon] ◆ nm (couleur) yellow. ◆ adj
yellow. ▶ **jaune d'œuf** nm (egg) yolk.
jaunir [ʒonir] vt & vi to turn yellow.
jaunisse [ʒonis] nf (MÉD) jaundice.
java [ʒava] nf type of popular dance.
Javel [ʒavɛl] nf: **eau de ~** bleach.
javelot [ʒavlo] nm javelin.
jazz [dʒaz] nm jazz.
J.-C. (abr de Jésus-Christ) J.C.
je [ʒə], **j'** (devant voyelle et h muet) pron pers
I.
jean [dʒin], **jeans** [dʒins] nm jeans
(pl), pair of jeans.
Jeep® [dʒip] nf Jeep®.
jérémiades [ʒeremjad] nfpl moaning
(U), whining (U).
jerrycan, jerricane [ʒerikan] nm
jerry can.
jersey [ʒɛrzɛ] nm jersey.
jésuite [ʒezɥit] nm Jesuit.
Jésus-Christ [ʒezykri] nm Jesus
Christ.
jet¹ [ʒɛ] nm **1.** (action de jeter) throw.
2. (de liquide) jet.
jet² [dʒɛt] nm (avion) jet.
jetable [ʒətabl] adj disposable.
jeté, -e [ʒəte] pp → **jeter**.
jetée [ʒəte] nf jetty.
jeter [ʒəte] vt to throw; (se débarrasser de)
to throw away; **~ qqch à qqn** (lancer) to
throw sthg to sb, to throw sb sthg; (pour
faire mal) to throw sthg at sb. ▶ **se jeter**
vp: **se ~ sur** to pounce on; **se ~ dans** (suj:
rivière) to flow into.
jeton [ʒətɔ̃] nm (de jeu) counter; (de téléphone) token.
jeu, -x [ʒø] nm **1.** (divertissement) play
(U), playing (U); **~ de mots** play on
words, pun. **2.** (régi par des règles) game;
mettre un joueur hors ~ to put a player
offside; **~ de société** parlour game.
3. (d'argent): **le ~** gambling. **4.** (d'échecs,
de clés) set; **~ de cartes** pack of cards.
5. (manière de jouer - MUS) playing;
(- THÉÂTRE) acting; (- SPORT) game.
6. (TECHNOL) play. **7.** loc: **cacher son ~** to
play one's cards close to one's chest.
▶ **Jeux Olympiques** nmpl: **les Jeux
Olympiques** the Olympic Games.
jeudi [ʒødi] nm Thursday; voir aussi
samedi.
jeun [ʒœ̃] ▶ **à jeun** loc adv on an empty
stomach.
jeune [ʒœn] ◆ adj young; (style,
apparence) youthful; **~ homme/femme**

young man/woman. ◆ nm young person; **les ~s** young people.
jeûne [ʒøn] nm fast.
jeunesse [ʒœnɛs] nf **1.** (âge) youth; (de
style, apparence) youthfulness. **2.** (jeunes
gens) young people (pl).
jingle [dʒingəl] nm jingle.
JO nmpl (abr de Jeux Olympiques)
Olympic Games.
joaillier, -ère [ʒɔaje, ɛr] nm, f jeweller.
job [dʒɔb] nm fam job.
jockey [ʒɔkɛ] nm jockey.
jogging [dʒɔgin] nm **1.** (activité) jogging. **2.** (vêtement) tracksuit, jogging
suit.
joie [ʒwa] nf joy.
joindre [ʒwɛ̃dr] vt **1.** (rapprocher) to
join; (mains) to put together. **2.** (ajouter):
~ qqch (à) to attach sthg (to); (adjoindre)
to enclose sthg (with). **3.** (par téléphone)
to contact, to reach. ▶ **se joindre** vp:
se ~ à qqn to join sb; **se ~ à qqch** to join
in sthg.
joint, -e [ʒwɛ̃, ɛ̃t] pp → **joindre**.
▶ **joint** nm **1.** (d'étanchéité) seal. **2.** fam
(drogue) joint.
joker [ʒɔkɛr] nm joker.
joli, -e [ʒɔli] adj **1.** (femme, chose) pretty,
attractive. **2.** (somme, situation) nice.
joliment [ʒɔlimã] adv **1.** (bien) prettily,
attractively; iron nicely. **2.** fam (beaucoup)
really.
jonc [ʒɔ̃] nm rush, bulrush.
joncher [ʒɔ̃ʃe] vt to strew; **être jonché
de** to be strewn with.
jonction [ʒɔ̃ksjɔ̃] nf (de routes) junction.
jongler [ʒɔ̃gle] vi to juggle.
jongleur, -euse [ʒɔ̃glœr, øz] nm, f juggler.
jonquille [ʒɔ̃kij] nf daffodil.
Jordanie [ʒɔrdani] nf: **la ~** Jordan.
joue [ʒu] nf cheek; **tenir** OU **mettre qqn
en ~** fig to take aim at sb.
jouer [ʒwe] ◆ vi **1.** (gén) to play; **~ avec
qqn/qqch** to play with sb/sthg; **~ à qqch**
(jeu, sport) to play sthg; **~ de** (MUS) to
play; **à toi de ~!** (it's) your turn!; fig your
move! **2.** (CIN & THÉÂTRE) to act. **3.** (parier) to gamble. ◆ vt **1.** (carte, partie) to
play. **2.** (somme d'argent) to bet, to
wager; fig to gamble with. **3.**
(THÉÂTRE - personnage, rôle) to play; (- pièce)
to put on, to perform. **4.** (avoir à l'affiche)
to show. **5.** (MUS) to perform, to play.
jouet [ʒwɛ] nm toy.
joueur, -euse [ʒwœr, øz] nm, f
1. (SPORT) player; **~ de football** foot-

baller, football player. **2.** (*au casino*) gambler.

joufflu, -e [ʒufly] *adj* (*personne*) chubby-cheeked.

joug [ʒu] *nm* yoke.

jouir [ʒwir] *vi* **1.** (*profiter*): ~ **de** to enjoy. **2.** (*sexuellement*) to have an orgasm.

jouissance [ʒwisɑ̃s] *nf* **1.** (JUR) (*d'un bien*) use. **2.** (*sexuelle*) orgasm.

joujou, -x [ʒuʒu] *nm* toy.

jour [ʒur] *nm* **1.** (*unité de temps*) day; **huit ~s** a week; **quinze ~s** a fortnight Br, two weeks; **de ~ en ~** day by day; **au ~ le ~** from day to day; **~ et nuit** night and day; **le ~ de l'an** New Year's Day; **~ chômé** public holiday; **~ de congé** day off; **~ férié** public holiday; **~ ouvrable** working day. **2.** (*lumière*) daylight; **de ~** in the daytime, by day. **3.** *loc*: **mettre qqch à ~** to update sthg, to bring sthg up to date; **de nos ~s** these days, nowadays.

journal, -aux [ʒurnal, o] *nm* **1.** (*publication*) newspaper, paper; **~ d'information** serious ou quality newspaper. **2.** (TÉLÉ): **~ télévisé** television news. **3.** (*écrit*): **~ (intime)** diary, journal.

journalier, -ère [ʒurnalje, ɛr] *adj* daily.

journalisme [ʒurnalism] *nm* journalism.

journaliste [ʒurnalist] *nmf* journalist, reporter.

journée [ʒurne] *nf* day.

joute [ʒut] *nf* joust; *fig* duel.

jovial, -e, -aux [ʒɔvjal, o] *adj* jovial, jolly.

joyau, -x [ʒwajo] *nm* jewel.

joyeux, -euse [ʒwajø, øz] *adj* joyful, happy; **~ Noël!** Merry Christmas!

jubilé [ʒybile] *nm* jubilee.

jubiler [ʒybile] *vi fam* to be jubilant.

jucher [ʒyʃe] *vt*: **~ qqn sur qqch** to perch sb on sthg.

judaïque [ʒydaik] *adj* (*loi*) Judaic; (*tradition, religion*) Jewish.

judaïsme [ʒydaism] *nm* Judaism.

judas [ʒyda] *nm* (*ouverture*) peephole.

judéo-chrétien, -enne [ʒydeɔkretjɛ̃, ɛn] (*mpl* **judéo-chrétiens**, *fpl* **judéo-chrétiennes**) *adj* Judaeo-Christian.

judiciaire [ʒydisjɛr] *adj* judicial.

judicieux, -euse [ʒydisjø, øz] *adj* judicious.

judo [ʒydo] *nm* judo.

juge [ʒyʒ] *nm* judge; **~ d'instruction** examining magistrate.

jugé [ʒyʒe] ▶ **au jugé** *loc adv* by

guesswork; **tirer au ~** to fire blind.

jugement [ʒyʒmɑ̃] *nm* judgment; **prononcer un ~** to pass sentence.

jugeote [ʒyʒɔt] *nf fam* common sense.

juger [ʒyʒe] ◆ *vt* to judge; (*accusé*) to try; **~ que** to judge (that), to consider (that); **~ qqn/qqch inutile** to consider sb/sthg useless. ◆ *vi* to judge; **~ de qqch** to judge sthg; **si j'en juge d'après mon expérience** judging from my experience; **jugez de ma surprise!** imagine my surprise!

juif, -ive [ʒɥif, iv] *adj* Jewish. ▶ **Juif, -ive** *nm, f* Jew.

juillet [ʒɥijɛ] *nm* July; **le 14-Juillet** *national holiday to mark the anniversary of the storming of the Bastille*; *voir aussi* **septembre**.

LE 14-JUILLET

The fourteenth of July is a national holiday in France, in commemoration of the storming of the Bastille on the same day in 1789. Celebrations take place throughout France and often last several days, with outdoor public dances, firework displays etc. A grand military parade is held in Paris on the morning of the fourteenth, in the presence of the President of France.

juin [ʒɥɛ̃] *nm* June; *voir aussi* **septembre**.

juke-box [dʒukbɔks] *nm inv* jukebox.

jumeau, -elle, -x [ʒymo, ɛl, o] ◆ *adj* twin (*avant n*). ◆ *nm, f* twin. ▶ **jumelles** *nfpl* (OPTIQUE) binoculars.

jumelé, -e [ʒymle] *adj* (*villes*) twinned; (*maisons*) semidetached.

jumeler [ʒymle] *vt* to twin.

jumelle → **jumeau**.

jument [ʒymɑ̃] *nf* mare.

jungle [ʒœ̃gl] *nf* jungle.

junior [ʒynjɔr] *adj & nmf* (SPORT) junior.

junte [ʒœ̃t] *nf* junta.

jupe [ʒyp] *nf* skirt.

jupe-culotte [ʒypkylɔt] *nf* culottes (*pl*).

jupon [ʒypɔ̃] *nm* petticoat, slip.

juré [ʒyre] *nm* (JUR) juror.

jurer [ʒyre] ◆ *vt*: **~ qqch à qqn** to swear ou pledge sthg to sb; **~ (à qqn) que ...** to swear (to sb) that ...; **~ de faire qqch** to swear ou vow to do sthg. ◆ *vi* **1.** (*blasphémer*) to swear, to curse. **2.** (*ne pas aller ensemble*): **~ (avec)** to clash (with). ▶ **se jurer** *vp*: **se ~ de faire qqch** to swear ou vow to do sthg.

juridiction [ʒyridiksjɔ̃] nf jurisdiction.

juridique [ʒyridik] adj legal.

jurisprudence [ʒyrisprydɑ̃s] nf jurisprudence.

juriste [ʒyrist] nmf lawyer.

juron [ʒyrɔ̃] nm swearword, oath.

jury [ʒyri] nm 1. (JUR) jury. 2. (SCOL - d'examen) examining board; (- de concours) admissions board.

jus [ʒy] nm 1. (de fruits, légumes) juice. 2. (de viande) gravy.

jusque, jusqu' [ʒysk(ə)] ▶ **jusqu'à** loc prép 1. (sens temporel) until, till; **jusqu'à nouvel ordre** until further notice; **jusqu'à présent** up until now, so far. 2. (sens spatial) as far as; **jusqu'au bout** to the end. 3. (même) even. ▶ **jusqu'à ce que** loc conj until, till. ▶ **jusqu'en** loc prép up until. ▶ **jusqu'ici** loc adv (lieu) up to here; (temps) up until now, so far. ▶ **jusque-là** loc adv (lieu) up to there; (temps) up until then.

justaucorps [ʒystokɔr] nm (maillot) leotard.

juste [ʒyst] ◆ adj 1. (équitable) fair. 2. (exact) right, correct. 3. (trop petit) tight. ◆ adv 1. (bien) correctly, right. 2. (exactement, seulement) just.

justement [ʒystəmɑ̃] adv 1. (avec raison) rightly. 2. (précisément) exactly, precisely.

justesse [ʒystɛs] nf (de remarque) aptness; (de raisonnement) soundness. ▶ **de justesse** loc adv only just.

justice [ʒystis] nf 1. (JUR) justice; **passer en ~** to stand trial. 2. (équité) fairness.

justicier, -ère [ʒystisje, ɛr] nm, f righter of wrongs.

justifiable [ʒystifjabl] adj justifiable.

justificatif, -ive [ʒystifikatif, iv] adj supporting. ▶ **justificatif** nm written proof (U).

justification [ʒystifikasjɔ̃] nf justification.

justifier [ʒystifje] vt (gén) to justify. ▶ **se justifier** vp to justify o.s.

jute [ʒyt] nm jute.

juteux, -euse [ʒytø, øz] adj juicy.

juvénile [ʒyvenil] adj youthful.

juxtaposer [ʒykstapoze] vt to juxtapose.

K

k, K [ka] nm inv k, K.

K7 [kaset] (abr de cassette) nf cassette.

kaki [kaki] ◆ nm 1. (couleur) khaki. 2. (fruit) persimmon. ◆ adj inv khaki.

kaléidoscope [kaleidɔskɔp] nm kaleidoscope.

kamikaze [kamikaz] nm kamikaze pilot.

kanak = **canaque**.

kangourou [kɑ̃guru] nm kangaroo.

karaoké [karaɔke] nm karaoke.

karaté [karate] nm karate.

karting [kartiŋ] nm go-karting.

kas(c)her, cascher [kaʃɛr] adj inv kosher.

kayak [kajak] nm (bateau) kayak; **faire du ~** to go canoeing.

Kenya [kenja] nm : **le ~** Kenya.

képi [kepi] nm kepi.

kermesse [kɛrmɛs] nf 1. (foire) fair. 2. (fête de bienfaisance) fête.

KERMESSE

These outdoor events, organized to raise money and with stalls selling homemade produce, are similar to British fêtes. In the north of France a 'kermesse' is specifically a church fête held on the feast of the patron saint of the village or town (see box at **fête**).

kérosène [kerɔzɛn] nm kerosene.

ketchup [kɛtʃœp] nm ketchup.

kg (abr de kilogramme) kg.

kibboutz [kibuts] nm inv kibbutz.

kidnapper [kidnape] vt to kidnap.

kidnappeur, -euse [kidnapœr, øz] nm, f kidnapper.

kilo [kilo] nm kilo.

kilogramme [kilɔgram] nm kilogram.

kilométrage [kilɔmetraʒ] nm 1. (de voiture) ≃ mileage. 2. (distance) distance.

kilomètre [kilɔmɛtr] nm kilometre.

kilo-octet [kilɔɔktɛ] nm (INFORM) kilobyte.

kilowatt [kilɔwat] nm kilowatt.

kilt [kilt] nm kilt.

kimono [kimɔno] nm kimono.

kinésithérapeute [kineziterapøt] nmf

physiotherapist.

kiosque [kjɔsk] *nm* **1.** (*de vente*) kiosk. **2.** (*pavillon*) pavilion.

kir [kir] *nm* apéritif made with white wine and blackcurrant liqueur.

kirsch [kirʃ] *nm* cherry brandy.

kitchenette [kitʃənɛt] *nf* kitchenette.

kitsch [kitʃ] *adj inv* kitsch.

kiwi [kiwi] *nm* **1.** (*oiseau*) kiwi. **2.** (*fruit*) kiwi, kiwi fruit (U).

Klaxon® [klaksɔ̃] *nm* horn.

klaxonner [klaksɔne] *vi* to hoot.

kleptomane, cleptomane [klɛptɔman] *nmf* kleptomaniac.

km (*abr de* **kilomètre**) km.

km/h (*abr de* **kilomètre par heure**) kph.

Ko (*abr de* **kilo-octet**) K.

K.-O. [kao] *nm*: **mettre qqn ~** to knock sb out.

Koweït [kɔwɛt] *nm*: **le ~** Kuwait.

krach [krak] *nm* crash; **~ boursier** stock market crash.

kugelhof [kugɛlɔf] *nm* light dome-shaped cake with currants and almonds, a speciality of Alsace.

kung-fu [kuŋfu] *nm* kung fu.

kurde [kyrd] ◆ *adj* Kurdish. ◆ *nm* (*langue*) Kurdish. ▶ **Kurde** *nmf* Kurd.

kyrielle [kirjɛl] *nf fam* stream; (*d'enfants*) horde.

kyste [kist] *nm* cyst.

L

l, L [ɛl] ◆ *nm inv* l, L. ◆ (*abr de* **litre**) l.

l' → **le**.

la¹ [la] *art déf & pron déf* → **le**.

la² [la] *nm inv* (MUS) A; (*chanté*) la.

là [la] *adv* **1.** (*lieu*) there; **passe par ~** go that way; **c'est ~ que je travaille** that's where I work; **je suis ~** I'm here. **2.** (*temps*) then; **à quelques jours de ~** a few days later, a few days after that. **3.** (*avec une proposition relative*): **~ où** (*lieu*) where; (*temps*) when.

là-bas [laba] *adv* (over) there.

label [label] *nm* **1.** (*étiquette*): **~ de qualité** label guaranteeing quality. **2.** (*commerce*) label, brand name.

labeur [labœr] *nm sout* labour.

labo [labo] (*abr de* **laboratoire**) *nm fam* lab.

laborantin, -e [labɔrɑ̃tɛ̃, in] *nm, f* laboratory assistant.

laboratoire [labɔratwar] *nm* laboratory.

laborieux, -euse [labɔrjø, øz] *adj* (*difficile*) laborious.

labourer [labure] *vt* **1.** (AGRIC) to plough. **2.** *fig* (*creuser*) to make a gash in.

laboureur [laburœr] *nm* ploughman.

labyrinthe [labirɛ̃t] *nm* labyrinth.

lac [lak] *nm* lake; **les Grands Lacs** the Great Lakes; **le ~ Léman** Lake Geneva.

lacer [lase] *vt* to tie.

lacérer [lasere] *vt* **1.** (*déchirer*) to shred. **2.** (*blesser, griffer*) to slash.

lacet [lasɛ] *nm* **1.** (*cordon*) lace. **2.** (*de route*) bend. **3.** (*piège*) snare.

lâche [laʃ] ◆ *nmf* coward. ◆ *adj* **1.** (*nœud*) loose. **2.** (*personne, comportement*) cowardly.

lâcher [laʃe] ◆ *vt* **1.** (*libérer - bras, objet*) to let go of; (*- animal*) to let go, to release; *fig* (*- mot*) to let slip. **2.** (*desserrer*) to loosen. **3.** (*laisser tomber*): **~ qqch** to drop sthg. ◆ *vi* to give way.

lâcheté [laʃte] *nf* **1.** (*couardise*) cowardice. **2.** (*acte*) cowardly act.

lacis [lasi] *nm* (*labyrinthe*) maze.

laconique [lakɔnik] *adj* laconic.

lacrymogène [lakrimɔʒɛn] *adj* tear (*avant n*).

lacune [lakyn] *nf* (*manque*) gap.

lacustre [lakystr] *adj* (*faune, plante*) lake (*avant n*); (*cité, village*) on stilts.

lad [lad] *nm* stable lad.

là-dedans [ladədɑ̃] *adv* inside, in there; **il y a quelque chose qui m'intrigue ~** there's something in that which intrigues me.

là-dessous [ladsu] *adv* underneath, under there; *fig* behind that.

là-dessus [ladsy] *adv* on that; **~, il partit** at that point ou with that, he left; **je suis d'accord ~** I agree about that.

ladite → **ledit**.

lagon [lagɔ̃] *nm*, **lagune** [lagyn] *nf* lagoon.

là-haut [lao] *adv* up there.

laïc (*f* **laïque**), **laïque** [laik] *adj* lay (*avant n*); (*juridiction*) civil (*avant n*); (*école*) state (*avant n*).

laid, -e [lɛ, lɛd] *adj* **1.** (*esthétiquement*) ugly. **2.** (*moralement*) wicked.

laideron [lɛdrɔ̃] *nm* ugly woman.

laideur [lɛdœr] *nf* **1.** (*physique*) ugliness. **2.** (*morale*) wickedness.

lainage [lɛnaʒ] *nm* (*étoffe*) woollen

material; (*vêtement*) woolly ou woollen garment.

laine [lɛn] *nf* wool.

laineux, -euse [lɛnø, øz] *adj* woolly.

laïque = **laïc**.

laisse [lɛs] *nf* (*corde*) lead, leash; **tenir en ~** (*chien*) to keep on a lead ou leash.

laisser [lɛse] ◆ *v aux* (+ *infinitif*): **~ qqn faire qqch** to let sb do sthg; **laisse-le faire** leave him alone, don't interfere; **~ tomber qqch** *litt & fig* to drop sthg; **laisse tomber!** *fam* drop it! ◆ *vt* 1. (*gén*) to leave; **~ qqn/qqch à qqn** (*confier*) to leave sb/sthg with sb. 2. (*céder*): **~ qqch à qqn** to let sb have sthg. ▶ **se laisser** *vp*: **se ~ faire** to let o.s. be persuaded; **se ~ aller** to relax; (*dans son apparence*) to let o.s. go; **se ~ aller à qqch** to indulge in sthg.

laisser-aller [lɛseale] *nm inv* carelessness.

laissez-passer [lɛsepase] *nm inv* pass.

lait [lɛ] *nm* 1. (*gén*) milk; **~ entier/écrémé** whole/skimmed milk; **~ concentré** ou **condensé** (*sucré*) condensed milk; (*non sucré*) evaporated milk. 2. (*cosmétique*): **~ démaquillant** cleansing milk ou lotion.

laitage [lɛtaʒ] *nm* dairy product.

laiterie [lɛtri] *nf* dairy.

laitier, -ère [lɛtje, ɛr] ◆ *adj* dairy (*avant n*). ◆ *nm, f* milkman (*f* milkwoman).

laiton [lɛtɔ̃] *nm* brass.

laitue [lɛty] *nf* lettuce.

laïus [lajys] *nm* long speech.

lambeau, -x [lɑ̃bo] *nm* (*morceau*) shred.

lambris [lɑ̃bri] *nm* panelling.

lame [lam] *nf* 1. (*fer*) blade; **~ de rasoir** razor blade. 2. (*lamelle*) strip. 3. (*vague*) wave.

lamé, -e [lame] *adj* lamé. ▶ **lamé** *nm* lamé.

lamelle [lamɛl] *nf* 1. (*de champignon*) gill. 2. (*tranche*) thin slice. 3. (*de verre*) slide.

lamentable [lamɑ̃tabl] *adj* 1. (*résultats, sort*) appalling. 2. (*ton*) plaintive.

lamentation [lamɑ̃tasjɔ̃] *nf* 1. (*plainte*) lamentation. 2. (*gén pl*) (*jérémiade*) moaning (U).

lamenter [lamɑ̃te] ▶ **se lamenter** *vp* to complain.

laminer [lamine] *vt* (IND) to laminate; *fig* (*personne, revenus*) to eat away at.

lampadaire [lɑ̃padɛr] *nm* (*dans mai-* son) standard lamp Br, floor lamp Am; (*de rue*) street lamp ou light.

lampe [lɑ̃p] *nf* lamp, light; **~ de chevet** bedside lamp; **~ halogène** halogen light; **~ de poche** torch Br, flashlight Am.

lampion [lɑ̃pjɔ̃] *nm* Chinese lantern.

lance [lɑ̃s] *nf* 1. (*arme*) spear. 2. (*de tuyau*) nozzle; **~ d'incendie** fire hose.

lance-flammes [lɑ̃sflam] *nm inv* flame-thrower.

lancement [lɑ̃smɑ̃] *nm* (*d'entreprise, produit, navire*) launching.

lance-pierres [lɑ̃spjɛr] *nm inv* catapult.

lancer [lɑ̃se] ◆ *vt* 1. (*pierre, javelot*) to throw; **~ qqch sur qqn** to throw sthg at sb. 2. (*fusée, produit, style*) to launch. 3. (*émettre*) to give off; (*cri*) to let out; (*injures*) to hurl; (*ultimatum*) to issue. 4. (*moteur*) to start up. 5. (INFORM - *programme*) to start; (- *système*) to boot (up). 6. *fig* (*sur un sujet*): **~ qqn sur qqch** to get sb started on sthg. ◆ *nm* 1. (PÊCHE) casting. 2. (SPORT) throwing; **~ du poids** shotput. ▶ **se lancer** *vp* 1. (*débuter*) to make a name for o.s. 2. (*s'engager*): **se ~ dans** (*dépenses, explication*) to embark on.

lancinant, -e [lɑ̃sinɑ̃, ɑ̃t] *adj* 1. (*douleur*) shooting. 2. *fig* (*obsédant*) haunting. 3. (*monotone*) insistent.

landau [lɑ̃do] *nm* (*d'enfant*) pram.

lande [lɑ̃d] *nf* moor.

langage [lɑ̃gaʒ] *nm* language.

lange [lɑ̃ʒ] *nm* nappy Br, diaper Am.

langer [lɑ̃ʒe] *vt* to change.

langoureux, -euse [lɑ̃gurø, øz] *adj* languorous.

langouste [lɑ̃gust] *nf* crayfish.

langoustine [lɑ̃gustin] *nf* langoustine.

langue [lɑ̃g] *nf* 1. (ANAT & *fig*) tongue. 2. (LING) language; **~ maternelle** mother tongue; **~ morte/vivante** dead/modern language.

languette [lɑ̃gɛt] *nf* tongue.

langueur [lɑ̃gœr] *nf* 1. (*dépérissement, mélancolie*) languor. 2. (*apathie*) apathy.

languir [lɑ̃gir] *vi* 1. (*dépérir*): **~ (de)** to languish (with). 2. *sout* (*attendre*) to wait; **faire ~ qqn** to keep sb waiting.

lanière [lanjɛr] *nf* strip.

lanterne [lɑ̃tɛrn] *nf* 1. (*éclairage*) lantern. 2. (*phare*) light.

Laos [laɔs] *nm*: **le ~** Laos.

laper [lape] *vt & vi* to lap.

lapider [lapide] *vt* (*tuer*) to stone.

lapin, -e [lapɛ̃, in] *nm, f* (CULIN & ZOOL) rabbit. ▶ **lapin** *nm* (*fourrure*) rabbit fur.

Laponie [laponi] *nf*: **la ~** Lapland.

laps [laps] *nm*: **(dans) un ~ de temps** (in) a while.

lapsus [lapsys] *nm* slip (of the tongue/pen).

laquais [lakɛ] *nm* lackey.

laque [lak] *nf* 1. (*vernis, peinture*) lacquer. 2. (*pour cheveux*) hair spray, lacquer.

laqué, -e [lake] *adj* lacquered.

laquelle → **lequel**.

larbin [larbɛ̃] *nm* 1. (*domestique*) servant. 2. (*personne servile*) yes-man.

larcin [larsɛ̃] *nm* 1. (*vol*) larceny, theft. 2. (*butin*) spoils (*pl*).

lard [lar] *nm* 1. (*graisse de porc*) lard. 2. (*viande*) bacon.

lardon [lardɔ̃] *nm* 1. (CULIN) cube or strip of bacon. 2. *fam* (*enfant*) kid.

large [larʒ] ♦ *adj* 1. (*étendu, grand*) wide; **~ de 5 mètres** 5 metres wide. 2. (*important, considérable*) large, big. 3. (*esprit, sourire*) broad. 4. (*généreux - personne*) generous. ♦ *nm* 1. (*largeur*): **5 mètres de ~** 5 metres wide. 2. (*mer*): **le ~** the open sea; **au ~ de la côte française** off the French coast.

largement [larʒəmɑ̃] *adv* 1. (*diffuser, répandre*) widely. 2. (*donner, payer*) generously; (*dépasser*) considerably; (*récompenser*) amply; **avoir ~ le temps** to have plenty of time. 3. (*au moins*) easily.

largeur [larʒœr] *nf* 1. (*d'avenue, de cercle*) width. 2. *fig* (*d'idées, d'esprit*) breadth.

larguer [large] *vt* 1. (*voile*) to unfurl. 2. (*bombe, parachutiste*) to drop. 3. *fam fig* (*abandonner*) to chuck.

larme [larm] *nf* (*pleur*) tear; **être en ~s** to be in tears.

larmoyant, -e [larmwajɑ̃, ɑ̃t] *adj* 1. (*yeux, personne*) tearful. 2. *péj* (*histoire*) tearjerking.

larron [larɔ̃] *nm vieilli* (*voleur*) thief.

larve [larv] *nf* 1. (ZOOL) larva. 2. *péj* (*personne*) wimp.

laryngite [larɛ̃ʒit] *nf* laryngitis (U).

larynx [larɛ̃ks] *nm* larynx.

las, lasse [la, las] *adj littéraire* (*fatigué*) weary.

lascif, -ive [lasif, iv] *adj* lascivious.

laser [lazɛr] ♦ *nm* laser. ♦ *adj inv* laser (*avant n*).

lasser [lase] *vt sout* (*personne*) to weary; (*patience*) to try. ► **se lasser** *vp* to weary.

lassitude [lasityd] *nf* lassitude.

lasso [laso] *nm* lasso.

latent, -e [latɑ̃, ɑ̃t] *adj* latent.

latéral, -e, -aux [lateral, o] *adj* lateral.

latex [latɛks] *nm inv* latex.

latin, -e [latɛ̃, in] *adj* Latin. ► **latin** *nm* (*langue*) Latin.

latiniste [latinist] *nmf* (*spécialiste*) Latinist; (*étudiant*) Latin student.

latino-américain, -e [latinoamerikɛ̃, ɛn] (*mpl* **latino-américains**, *fpl* **latino-américaines**) *adj* Latin-American, Hispanic.

latitude [latityd] *nf litt & fig* latitude.

latrines [latrin] *nfpl* latrines.

latte [lat] *nf* lath, slat.

lauréat, -e [lɔrea, at] *nm, f* prize-winner, winner.

laurier [lɔrje] *nm* (BOT) laurel.

lavable [lavabl] *adj* washable.

lavabo [lavabo] *nm* 1. (*cuvette*) basin. 2. (*gén pl*) (*local*) toilet.

lavage [lavaʒ] *nm* washing.

lavande [lavɑ̃d] *nf* (BOT) lavender.

lave [lav] *nf* lava.

lave-glace [lavglas] (*pl* **lave-glaces**) *nm* windscreen washer Br, windshield washer Am.

lave-linge [lavlɛ̃ʒ] *nm inv* washing machine.

laver [lave] *vt* 1. (*nettoyer*) to wash. 2. *fig* (*disculper*): **~ qqn de qqch** to clear sb of sthg. ► **se laver** *vp* (*se nettoyer*) to wash o.s., to have a wash; **se ~ les mains/les cheveux** to wash one's hands/hair.

laverie [lavri] *nf* (*commerce*) laundry; **~ automatique** launderette.

lavette [lavɛt] *nf* 1. (*brosse*) washing-up brush; (*en tissu*) dishcloth. 2. *fam* (*homme*) drip.

laveur, -euse [lavœr, øz] *nm, f* washer; **~ de carreaux** window cleaner (*person*).

lave-vaisselle [lavvesɛl] *nm inv* dishwasher.

lavoir [lavwar] *nm* (*lieu*) laundry.

laxatif, -ive [laksatif, iv] *adj* laxative. ► **laxatif** *nm* laxative.

laxisme [laksism] *nm* laxity.

laxiste [laksist] *adj* lax.

layette [lɛjɛt] *nf* layette.

le [lə], **l'** (*devant voyelle ou h muet*) (*f* **la** [la], *pl* **les** [le]) ♦ *art déf* 1. (*gén*) the; **~ lac** the lake; **la fenêtre** the window; **l'homme** the man; **les enfants** the children. 2. (*devant les noms abstraits*): **l'amour** love; **la liberté** freedom. 3. (*temps*): **~ 15 janvier 1993** 15th January 1993; **je suis arrivé ~ 15 janvier 1993** I arrived on the 15th of January 1993; **~ lundi** (*habituellement*) on

Mondays; (*jour précis*) on (the) Monday.
4. (*possession*): **se laver les mains** to wash
one's hands; **avoir les cheveux blonds** to
have fair hair. 5. (*distributif*) per, a; **10
francs ~ mètre** 10 francs per ou a metre.
♦ *pron pers* 1. (*personne*) him (*f* her), *pl*
them; (*chose*) it, *pl* them; (*animal*) it, him
(*f* her), *pl* them **je ~/la/les connais bien** I
know him/her/them well; **tu dois avoir la
clé, donne-la moi** you must have the
key, give it to me. 2. (*représente une
proposition*): **je ~ sais bien** I know, I'm well
aware (of it).

LEA (*abr de* **langues étrangères
appliquées**) *nfpl* applied modern languages.
leader [lidœr] *nm* (*de parti, course*)
leader.
leadership [lidœrʃip] *nm* leadership.
lécher [leʃe] *vt* 1. (*passer la langue sur,
effleurer*) to lick; (*suj: vague*) to wash
against. 2. *fam* (*fignoler*) to polish (up).
lèche-vitrines [lɛʃvitrin] *nm inv*
window-shopping; **faire du ~** to go
window-shopping.
leçon [ləsɔ̃] *nf* 1. (*gén*) lesson; **~s de
conduite** driving lessons; **~s particulières**
private lessons ou classes. 2. (*conseil*)
advice (U); **faire la ~ à qqn** to lecture
sb.
lecteur, -trice [lɛktœr, tris] *nm, f* 1. (*de
livres*) reader. 2. (UNIV) foreign language
assistant. ► **lecteur** *nm* 1. (*gén*) head; **~
de cassettes/CD** cassette/CDplayer.
2. (INFORM) reader.
lecture [lɛktyr] *nf* reading.
ledit, ladite [lədi, ladit] (*mpl* **lesdits**
[ledi], *fpl* **lesdites** [ledit]) *adj* the said, the
aforementioned.
légal, -e, -aux [legal, o] *adj* legal.
légalement [legalmɑ̃] *adv* legally.
légaliser [legalize] *vt* (*rendre légal*) to
legalize.
légalité [legalite] *nf* 1. (*de contrat, d'acte*)
legality, lawfulness. 2. (*loi*) law.
légataire [legatɛr] *nmf* legatee.
légendaire [leʒɑ̃dɛr] *adj* legendary.
légende [leʒɑ̃d] *nf* 1. (*fable*) legend.
2. (*de carte, de schéma*) key.
léger, -ère [leʒe, ɛr] *adj* 1. (*objet, étoffe,
repas*) light. 2. (*bruit, différence, odeur*)
slight. 3. (*alcool, tabac*) low-strength.
4. (*femme*) flighty. 5. (*insouciant - ton*)
light-hearted; (*- conduite*) thoughtless.
► **à la légère** *loc adv* lightly, thoughtlessly.
légèrement [leʒɛrmɑ̃] *adv* 1. (*s'habiller,
poser*) lightly. 2. (*agir*) thoughtlessly.
3. (*blesser, remuer*) slightly.

légèreté [leʒɛrte] *nf* 1. (*d'objet, de repas,
de punition*) lightness. 2. (*de style*) grace-
fulness. 3. (*de conduite*) thoughtlessness. 4. (*de personne*) flightiness.
légiférer [leʒifere] *vi* to legislate.
légion [leʒjɔ̃] *nf* (MIL) legion.
légionnaire [leʒjɔnɛr] *nm* legionary.
législatif, -ive [leʒislatif, iv] *adj* legislative. ► **législatives** *nfpl*: **les législatives** the legislative elections, = the
general election (*sg*) Br.
législation [leʒislasjɔ̃] *nf* legislation.
légiste [leʒist] *adj* 1. (*juriste*) jurist. 2. →
médecin.
légitime [leʒitim] *adj* legitimate.
légitimer [leʒitime] *vt* 1. (*reconnaître*) to
recognize; (*enfant*) to legitimize. 2. (*justifier*) to justify.
legs [leg] *nm* legacy.
léguer [lege] *vt*: **~ qqch à qqn** (JUR) to
bequeath sthg to sb; *fig* to pass sthg on
to sb.
légume [legym] *nm* vegetable.
leitmotiv [lajtmɔtif, lɛtmɔtiv] *nm* leit-
motif.
Léman [lemɑ̃] → **lac**.
lendemain [lɑ̃dmɛ̃] *nm* (*jour*) day
after; **le ~ matin** the next morning; **au ~
de** after, in the days following.
lénifiant, -e [lenifjɑ̃, ɑ̃t] *adj litt & fig*
soothing.
lent, -e [lɑ̃, lɑ̃t] *adj* slow.
lente [lɑ̃t] *nf* nit.
lentement [lɑ̃tmɑ̃] *adv* slowly.
lenteur [lɑ̃tœr] *nf* slowness (U).
lentille [lɑ̃tij] *nf* 1. (BOT & CULIN) lentil.
2. (*d'optique*) lens; **~s de contact** contact
lenses.
léopard [leɔpar] *nm* leopard.
LEP, Lep (*abr de* **lycée d'enseignement
professionnel**) *nm* former secondary school
for vocational training.
lèpre [lɛpr] *nf* (MÉD) leprosy.
lequel [ləkɛl] (*f* **laquelle** [lakɛl], *mpl*
lesquels [lekɛl], *fpl* **lesquelles** [lekɛl])
(*contraction de à + lequel* = **auquel**, *de +
lequel* = **duquel**, *à + lesquels/lesquelles* =
auxquels/auxquelles, *de + lesquels/
lesquelles* = **desquels/desquelles**) ♦ *pron rel*
1. (*complément - personne*) whom; (*- chose*)
which. 2. (*sujet - personne*) who; (*- chose*)
which. ♦ *pron interr*: **~?** which (one)?
les → **le**.
lesbienne [lɛsbjɛn] *nf* lesbian.
lesdits, lesdites → **ledit**.
léser [leze] *vt* (*frustrer*) to wrong.
lésiner [lezine] *vi* to skimp; **ne pas ~ sur**
not to skimp on.

lésion [lezjɔ̃] *nf* lesion.

lesquels, lesquelles → lequel.

lessive [lɛsiv] *nf* **1.** (*linge*) washing, laundry; **faire la ~** to do the washing ou laundry. **2.** (*produit*) washing powder.

lest [lɛst] *nm* ballast.

leste [lɛst] *adj* **1.** (*agile*) nimble, agile. **2.** (*licencieux*) crude.

lester [lɛste] *vt* (*garnir de lest*) to ballast.

léthargie [letarʒi] *nf litt & fig* lethargy.

Lettonie [lɛtɔni] *nf*: **la ~** Latvia.

lettre [lɛtr] *nf* **1.** (*gén*) letter; **en toutes ~s** in words, in full. **2.** (*sens des mots*): **à la ~** to the letter. ▶ **lettres** *nfpl* **1.** (*culture littéraire*) letters. **2.** (UNIV) arts; **~s classiques** classics; **~s modernes** French language and literature.

leucémie [løsemi] *nf* leukemia.

leucocyte [løkɔsit] *nm* leucocyte.

leur [lœr] *pron pers inv* (to) them; **je voudrais ~ parler** I'd like to speak to them; **je ~ ai donné la lettre** I gave them the letter, I gave the letter to them. ▶ **leur** (*pl* **leurs**) *adj poss* their; **c'est ~ tour** it's their turn; **~s enfants** their children. ▶ **le leur** (*f* **la leur**, *pl* **les leurs**) *pron poss* theirs; **il faudra qu'ils y mettent du ~** they've got to pull their weight.

leurrer [lœre] *vt* to deceive. ▶ **se leurrer** *vp* to deceive o.s.

levain [ləvɛ̃] *nm* (CULIN): **pain au ~/sans ~** leavened/unleavened bread.

levant [ləvɑ̃] ◆ *nm* east. ◆ *adj* → **soleil.**

lever [ləve] ◆ *vt* **1.** (*objet, blocus, interdiction*) to lift. **2.** (*main, tête, armée*) to raise. **3.** (*scellés, difficulté*) to remove. **4.** (*séance*) to close, to end. **5.** (*impôts, courrier*) to collect. **6.** (*enfant, malade*): **~ qqn** to get sb up. ◆ *vi* **1.** (*plante*) to come up. **2.** (*pâte*) to rise. ◆ *nm* **1.** (*d'astre*) rising, rise; **~ du jour** daybreak; **~ du soleil** sunrise. **2.** (*de personne*): **il est toujours de mauvaise humeur au ~** he's always in a bad mood when he gets up. ▶ **se lever** *vp* **1.** (*personne*) to get up, to rise; (*vent*) to get up. **2.** (*soleil, lune*) to rise; (*jour*) to break. **3.** (*temps*) to clear.

lève-tard [lɛvtar] *nmf inv* late riser.

lève-tôt [lɛvto] *nmf inv* early riser.

levier [ləvje] *nm litt & fig* lever; **~ de vitesses** gear lever Br, gear shift Am.

lévitation [levitasjɔ̃] *nf* levitation.

lèvre [lɛvr] *nf* (ANAT) lip; (*de vulve*) labium.

lévrier, levrette [levrije, ləvrɛt] *nm, f* greyhound.

levure [ləvyr] *nf* yeast; **~ chimique** baking powder.

lexicographie [lɛksikɔgrafi] *nf* lexicography.

lexique [lɛksik] *nm* **1.** (*dictionnaire*) glossary. **2.** (*vocabulaire*) vocabulary.

lézard [lezar] *nm* (*animal*) lizard.

lézarder [lezarde] ◆ *vt* to crack. ◆ *vi fam* (*paresser*) to bask. ▶ **se lézarder** *vp* to crack.

liaison [ljezɔ̃] *nf* **1.** (*jonction, enchaînement*) connection. **2.** (CULIN & LING) liaison. **3.** (*contact, relation*) contact; **avoir une ~** to have an affair. **4.** (TRANSPORT) link.

liane [ljan] *nf* creeper.

liant, -e [ljɑ̃, ɑ̃t] *adj* sociable. ▶ **liant** *nm* (*substance*) binder.

liasse [ljas] *nf* bundle; (*de billets de banque*) wad.

Liban [libɑ̃] *nm*: **le ~** Lebanon.

libanais, -e [libanɛ, ɛz] *adj* Lebanese. ▶ **Libanais, -e** *nm, f* Lebanese (person); **les Libanais** the Lebanese.

libeller [libele] *vt* **1.** (*chèque*) to make out. **2.** (*lettre*) to word.

libellule [libelyl] *nf* dragonfly.

libéral, -e, -aux [liberal, o] ◆ *adj* (*attitude, idée, parti*) liberal. ◆ *nm, f* (POLIT) liberal.

libéraliser [liberalize] *vt* to liberalize.

libéralisme [liberalism] *nm* liberalism.

libération [liberasjɔ̃] *nf* **1.** (*de prisonnier*) release, freeing. **2.** (*de pays, de la femme*) liberation. **3.** (*d'énergie*) release.

libérer [libere] *vt* **1.** (*prisonnier, fonds*) to release, to free. **2.** (*pays, la femme*) to liberate; **~ qqn de qqch** to free sb from sthg. **3.** (*passage*) to clear. **4.** (*énergie*) to release. **5.** (*instincts, passions*) to give free rein to. ▶ **se libérer** *vp* **1.** (*se rendre disponible*) to get away. **2.** (*se dégager*): **se ~ de** (*lien*) to free o.s. from; (*engagement*) to get out of.

liberté [libɛrte] *nf* **1.** (*gén*) freedom; **en ~** free; **parler en toute ~** to speak freely; **~ d'expression** freedom of expression; **~ d'opinion** freedom of thought. **2.** (JUR) release. **3.** (*loisir*) free time.

libertin, -e [libɛrtɛ̃, in] *nm, f* libertine.

libidineux, -euse [libidinø, øz] *adj* lecherous.

libido [libido] *nf* libido.

libraire [librɛr] *nmf* bookseller.

librairie [librɛri] *nf* (*magasin*) bookshop.

libre [libr] *adj* **1.** (*gén*) free; **~ de qqch** free from sthg; **être ~ de faire qqch** to be free to do sthg. **2.** (*école, secteur*) private. **3.** (*passage*) clear.

libre-échange [librəʃɑ̃ʒ] *nm* free trade (U).

librement [librəmɑ̃] *adv* freely.

libre-service [librəsɛrvis] *nm* (*magasin*) self-service store ou shop; (*restaurant*) self-service restaurant.

Libye [libi] *nf*: **la ~** Libya.

libyen, -enne [libjɛ̃, ɛn] *adj* Libyan. ► **Libyen, -enne** *nm, f* Libyan.

licence [lisɑ̃s] *nf* **1.** (*permis*) permit; (COMM) licence. **2.** (UNIV) (first) degree; **~ ès lettres/en droit** ≃ Bachelor of Arts/Law degree. **3.** *littéraire* (*liberté*) licence.

licencié, -e [lisɑ̃sje] ◆ *adj* (UNIV) graduate (*avant n*). ◆ *nm, f* **1.** (UNIV) graduate. **2.** (*titulaire d'un permis*) permit-holder; (COMM) licence-holder.

licenciement [lisɑ̃simɑ̃] *nm* dismissal; (*économique*) layoff, redundancy Br.

licencier [lisɑ̃sje] *vt* to dismiss; (*pour cause économique*) to lay off, to make redundant Br.

lichen [likɛn] *nm* lichen.

licite [lisit] *adj* lawful, legal.

licorne [likɔrn] *nf* unicorn.

lie [li] *nf* (*dépôt*) dregs (*pl*), sediment.

lie-de-vin [lidəvɛ̃] *adj inv* burgundy, wine-coloured.

lié, -e [lje] *adj* **1.** (*mains*) bound. **2.** (*amis*): **être très ~ avec** to be great friends with.

Liechtenstein [liʃtɛnʃtajn] *nm*: **le ~** Liechtenstein.

liège [ljɛʒ] *nm* cork.

lien [ljɛ̃] *nm* **1.** (*sangle*) bond. **2.** (*relation, affinité*) bond, tie; **avoir des ~s de parenté avec** to be related to. **3.** *fig* (*enchaînement*) connection, link.

lier [lje] *vt* **1.** (*attacher*) to tie (up); **~ qqn/qqch à** to tie sb/sthg to. **2.** (*suj: contrat, promesse*) to bind; **~ qqn/qqch par** to bind sb/sthg by. **3.** (*relier par la logique*) to link, to connect; **~ qqch à** to link sthg to, to connect sthg with. **4.** (*commencer*): **~ connaissance/conversation avec** to strike up an acquaintance/a conversation with. **5.** (*suj: sentiment, intérêt*) to unite. **6.** (CULIN) to thicken. ► **se lier** *vp* (*s'attacher*): **se ~ (d'amitié) avec qqn** to make friends with sb.

lierre [ljɛr] *nm* ivy.

liesse [ljɛs] *nf* jubilation.

lieu, -x [ljø] *nm* **1.** (*endroit*) place; **en ~ sûr** in a safe place; **~ de naissance** birthplace. **2.** *loc*: **avoir ~** to take place. ► **lieux** *nmpl* **1.** (*scène*) scene (*sg*), spot (*sg*); **sur les ~x (d'un crime/d'un accident)** at the scene (of a crime/an accident).

2. (*domicile*) premises. ► **lieu commun** *nm* commonplace. ► **au lieu de** *loc prép*: **au ~ de qqch/de faire qqch** instead of sthg/of doing sthg. ► **en dernier lieu** *loc adv* lastly. ► **en premier lieu** *loc adv* in the first place.

lieu-dit [ljødi] (*pl* lieux-dits) *nm* locality, place.

lieue [ljø] *nf* league.

lieutenant [ljøtnɑ̃] *nm* lieutenant.

lièvre [ljɛvr] *nm* hare.

lifter [lifte] *vt* (TENNIS) to spin, to put a spin on.

lifting [liftiŋ] *nm* face-lift.

ligament [ligamɑ̃] *nm* ligament.

ligaturer [ligatyre] *vt* (MÉD) to ligature, to ligate.

ligne [liɲ] *nf* **1.** (*gén*) line; **à la ~** new line ou paragraph; **en ~** (*personnes*) in a line; (INFORM) on line; **restez en ~!** (TÉLÉCOM) hold the line!; **~ de départ/d'arrivée** starting/finishing line; **~ aérienne** airline; **~ de commande** (INFORM) command line; **~ de conduite** line of conduct; **~ directrice** guideline; **~s de la main** lines of the hand; **les grandes ~s** (TRANSPORT) the main lines. **2.** (*forme - de voiture, meuble*) lines (*pl*). **3.** (*silhouette*): **garder la ~** to keep one's figure; **surveiller sa ~** to watch one's waistline. **4.** (*de pêche*) fishing line; **pêcher à la ~** to go angling. **5.** *loc*: **dans les grandes ~s** in outline; **entrer en ~ de compte** to be taken into account.

lignée [liɲe] *nf* (*famille*) descendants (*pl*); **dans la ~ de** *fig* (*d'écrivains, d'artistes*) in the tradition of.

ligoter [ligɔte] *vt* (*attacher*) to tie up; **~ qqn à qqch** to tie sb to sthg.

ligue [lig] *nf* league.

liguer [lige] ► **se liguer** *vp* to form a league; **se ~ contre** to conspire against.

lilas [lila] *nm & adj inv* lilac.

limace [limas] *nf* (ZOOL) slug.

limaille [limaj] *nf* filings (*pl*).

limande [limɑ̃d] *nf* dab.

lime [lim] *nf* **1.** (*outil*) file; **~ à ongles** nail file. **2.** (BOT) lime.

limer [lime] *vt* (*ongles*) to file; (*aspérités*) to file down; (*barreau*) to file through.

limier [limje] *nm* **1.** (*chien*) bloodhound. **2.** (*détective*) sleuth.

limitation [limitasjɔ̃] *nf* limitation; (*de naissances*) control; **~ de vitesse** speed limit.

limite [limit] ◆ *nf* **1.** (*gén*) limit; **à la ~** (*au pire*) at worst; **à la ~, j'accepterais de le voir** if pushed, I'd agree to see him.

2. (*terme, échéance*) deadline; **~ d'âge** age limit. ◆ *adj* (*extrême*) maximum (*avant n*); **cas ~** borderline case; **date ~** deadline; **date ~ de vente/consommation** sell-by/use-by date.

limiter [limite] *vt* **1.** (*borner*) to border, to bound. **2.** (*restreindre*) to limit. ▶ **se limiter** *vp* **1.** (*se restreindre*): **se ~ à qqch/à faire qqch** to limit o.s. to sthg/to doing sthg. **2.** (*se borner*): **se ~ à** to be limited to.

limitrophe [limitrɔf] *adj* **1.** (*frontalier*) border (*avant n*); **être ~ de** to border on. **2.** (*voisin*) adjacent.

limoger [limɔʒe] *vt* to dismiss.

limon [limɔ̃] *nm* (GÉOL) alluvium, silt.

limonade [limɔnad] *nf* lemonade.

limpide [lɛ̃pid] *adj* **1.** (*eau*) limpid. **2.** (*ciel, regard*) clear. **3.** (*explication, style*) clear, lucid.

lin [lɛ̃] *nm* **1.** (BOT) flax. **2.** (*tissu*) linen.

linceul [lɛ̃sœl] *nm* shroud.

linéaire [lineɛr] *adj* (*mesure, perspective*) linear.

linge [lɛ̃ʒ] *nm* **1.** (*lessive*) washing, laundry. **2.** (*de lit, de table*) linen. **3.** (*sous-vêtements*) underwear. **4.** (*morceau de tissu*) cloth.

lingerie [lɛ̃ʒri] *nf* **1.** (*local*) linen room. **2.** (*sous-vêtements*) lingerie.

lingot [lɛ̃go] *nm* ingot.

linguiste [lɛ̃gɥist] *nmf* linguist.

linguistique [lɛ̃gɥistik] ◆ *nf* linguistics (*U*). ◆ *adj* linguistic.

linoléum [linɔleɔm] *nm* lino, linoleum.

lion, lionne [ljɔ̃, ljɔn] *nm, f* lion (*f* lioness). ▶ **Lion** *nm* (ASTROL) Leo.

lionceau, -x [ljɔ̃so] *nm* lion cub.

lipide [lipid] *nm* lipid.

liquéfier [likefje] *vt* to liquefy. ▶ **se liquéfier** *vp* **1.** (*matière*) to liquefy. **2.** *fig* (*personne*) to turn to jelly.

liqueur [likœr] *nf* liqueur.

liquidation [likidasjɔ̃] *nf* **1.** (*de compte & BOURSE*) settlement. **2.** (*de société, stock*) liquidation.

liquide [likid] ◆ *nm* **1.** (*substance*) liquid. **2.** (*argent*) cash; **en ~** in cash. ◆ *adj* (*corps & LING*) liquid.

liquider [likide] *vt* **1.** (*compte & BOURSE*) to settle. **2.** (*société, stock*) to liquidate. **3.** *arg crime* (*témoin*) to liquidate, to eliminate; *fig* (*problème*) to eliminate, to get rid of.

liquidité [likidite] *nf* liquidity. ▶ **liquidités** *nfpl* liquid assets.

liquoreux, -euse [likɔrø, øz] *adj* syrupy.

lire¹ [lir] *vt* to read; **lu et approuvé** read and approved.

lire² [lir] *nf* lira.

lis, lys [lis] *nm* lily.

Lisbonne [lizbɔn] *n* Lisbon.

liseré [lizre], **liséré** [lizere] *nm* **1.** (*ruban*) binding. **2.** (*bande*) border, edging.

liseron [lizrɔ̃] *nm* bindweed.

liseuse [lizøz] *nf* **1.** (*vêtement*) bed-jacket. **2.** (*lampe*) reading light.

lisible [lizibl] *adj* (*écriture*) legible.

lisière [lizjɛr] *nf* (*limite*) edge.

lisse [lis] *adj* (*surface, peau*) smooth.

lisser [lise] *vt* **1.** (*papier, vêtements*) to smooth (out). **2.** (*moustache, cheveux*) to smooth (down). **3.** (*plumes*) to preen.

liste [list] *nf* list; **~ d'attente** waiting list; **~ électorale** electoral roll; **~ de mariage** wedding present list; **être sur la ~ rouge** to be ex-directory.

lister [liste] *vt* to list.

listing [listiŋ] *nm* listing.

lit [li] *nm* (*gén*) bed; **faire son ~** to make one's bed; **garder le ~** to stay in bed; **se mettre au ~** to go to bed; **~ à baldaquin** four-poster bed; **~ de camp** camp bed.

litanie [litani] *nf* litany.

literie [litri] *nf* bedding.

lithographie [litɔgrafi] *nf* **1.** (*procédé*) lithography. **2.** (*image*) lithograph.

litière [litjɛr] *nf* litter.

litige [litiʒ] *nm* **1.** (JUR) lawsuit. **2.** (*désaccord*) dispute.

litigieux, -euse [litiʒjø, øz] *adj* **1.** (JUR) litigious. **2.** (*douteux*) disputed.

litre [litr] *nm* **1.** (*mesure, quantité*) litre. **2.** (*récipient*) litre bottle.

littéraire [literer] *adj* literary.

littéral, -e, -aux [literal, o] *adj* **1.** (*gén*) literal. **2.** (*écrit*) written.

littérature [literatyr] *nf* (*gén*) literature.

littoral, -e, -aux [litɔral, o] *adj* coastal. ▶ **littoral** *nm* coast, coastline.

Lituanie [litɥani] *nf*: **la ~** Lithuania.

liturgie [lityrʒi] *nf* liturgy.

livide [livid] *adj* (*blême*) pallid.

livraison [livrezɔ̃] *nf* (*de marchandise*) delivery; **~ à domicile** home delivery.

livre [livr] ◆ *nm* (*gén*) book; **~ de cuisine** cookery book; **~ d'or** visitors' book; **~ de poche** paperback. ◆ *nf* pound; **~ sterling** pound sterling.

livrée [livre] *nf* (*uniforme*) livery.

livrer [livre] *vt* **1.** (COMM) to deliver; **~ qqch à qqn** (*achat*) to deliver sthg to sb; *fig* (*secret*) to reveal *ou* give away sthg to sb. 2. (*coupable, complice*): ~ **qqn à qqn** to hand sb over to sb. 3. (*abandonner*): ~ **qqch à qqch** to give sth over to sthg; ~ **qqn à lui-même** to leave sb to his own devices. ▸ **se livrer** *vp* 1. (*se rendre*): **se ~ à** (*police, ennemi*) to give o.s. up to. 2. (*se confier*): **se ~ à** (*ami*) to open up to, to confide in. 3. (*se consacrer*): **se ~ à** (*occupation*) to devote o.s. to; (*excès*) to indulge in.

livret [livrɛ] *nm* 1. (*carnet*) booklet; ~ **de caisse d'épargne** passbook, bankbook; ~ **de famille** *official family record book, given by registrar to newlyweds*; ~ **scolaire** = school report. 2. (*catalogue*) catalogue. 3. (MUS) book, libretto.

livreur, -euse [livrœr, øz] *nm, f* delivery man (*f* woman).

lobby [lɔbi] (*pl* **lobbies**) *nm* lobby.

lobe [lɔb] *nm* (ANAT & BOT) lobe.

lober [lɔbe] *vt* to lob.

local, -e, -aux [lɔkal, o] *adj* local; (*douleur*) localized. ▸ **local** *nm* room, premises (*pl*). ▸ **locaux** *nmpl* premises, offices.

localiser [lɔkalize] *vt* 1. (*avion, bruit*) to locate. 2. (*épidémie, conflit*) to localize.

localité [lɔkalite] *nf* (small) town.

locataire [lɔkatɛr] *nmf* tenant.

location [lɔkasjɔ̃] *nf* 1. (*de propriété - par propriétaire*) letting Br, renting Am; (- *par locataire*) renting; (*de machine*) leasing; ~ **de voitures/vélos** car/bicycle hire Br, car/bicycle rent Am. 2. (*bail*) lease. 3. (*maison, appartement*) rented property. 4. (*réservation*) booking.

location-vente [lɔkasjɔ̃vɑ̃t] *nf* = hire purchase Br, = installment plan Am.

locomotion [lɔkɔmɔsjɔ̃] *nf* locomotion.

locomotive [lɔkɔmɔtiv] *nf* 1. (*machine*) locomotive. 2. *fig* (*leader*) moving force.

locution [lɔkysjɔ̃] *nf* expression, phrase.

loft [lɔft] *nm* (converted) loft.

logarithme [lɔgaritm] *nm* logarithm.

loge [lɔʒ] *nf* 1. (*de concierge, de francs-maçons*) lodge. 2. (*d'acteur*) dressing room.

logement [lɔʒmɑ̃] *nm* 1. (*hébergement*) accommodation. 2. (*appartement*) flat Br, apartment Am; ~ **de fonction** company flat Br ou apartment Am.

loger [lɔʒe] ▸ *vi* (*habiter*) to live. ▸ *vt* 1. (*amis, invités*) to put up. 2. (*suj: hôtel, maison*) to accommodate, to take. ▸ **se loger** *vp* 1. (*trouver un logement*) to find accommodation. 2. (*se placer - ballon,*

balle): **se ~ dans** to lodge in, to stick in.

logeur, -euse [lɔʒœr, øz] *nm, f* landlord (*f* landlady).

logiciel [lɔʒisjɛl] *nm* software (U); ~ **intégré** integrated software.

logique [lɔʒik] ◆ *nf* logic. ◆ *adj* logical.

logiquement [lɔʒikmɑ̃] *adv* logically.

logis [lɔʒi] *nm* abode.

logistique [lɔʒistik] *nf* logistics (*pl*).

logo [logo] *nm* logo.

loi [lwa] *nf* (*gén*) law.

loin [lwɛ̃] *adv* 1. (*dans l'espace*) far; **plus ~** further. 2. (*dans le temps - passé*) a long time ago; (- *futur*) a long way off. ▸ **au loin** *loc adv* in the distance, far off. ▸ **de loin** *loc adv* (*depuis une grande distance*) from a distance; **de plus ~** from further away. ▸ **loin de** *loc prép* 1. (*gén*) far from; ~ **de là!** *fig* far from it! 2. (*dans le temps*): **il n'est pas ~ de 9 h** it's nearly 9 o'clock, it's not far off 9 o'clock.

lointain, -e [lwɛ̃tɛ̃, ɛn] *adj* (*pays, avenir, parent*) distant.

loir [lwar] *nm* dormouse.

loisir [lwazir] *nm* 1. (*temps libre*) leisure. 2. (*gén pl*) (*distractions*) leisure activities (*pl*).

londonien, -enne [lɔ̃dɔnjɛ̃, ɛn] *adj* London (*avant n*). ▸ **Londonien, -enne** *nm, f* Londoner.

Londres [lɔ̃dr] *n* London.

long, longue [lɔ̃, lɔ̃g] *adj* 1. (*gén*) long. 2. (*lent*) slow; **être ~ à faire qqch** to take a long time doing sthg. ▸ **long** ◆ *nm* (*longueur*): **4 mètres de ~** 4 metres long ou in length; **de ~ en large** up and down, to and fro; **en ~ et en large** in great detail; (*tout*) **le ~ de** (*espace*) all along; **tout au ~ de** (*année, carrière*) throughout. ◆ *adv* (*beaucoup*): **en savoir ~ sur qqch** to know a lot about sthg. ▸ **à la longue** *loc adv* in the end.

long-courrier [lɔ̃kurje] *adj* (*navire*) ocean-going; (*vol*) long-haul.

longe [lɔ̃ʒ] *nf* (*courroie*) halter.

longer [lɔ̃ʒe] *vt* 1. (*border*) to go along ou alongside. 2. (*marcher le long de*) to walk along; (*raser*) to stay close to, to hug.

longévité [lɔ̃ʒevite] *nf* longevity.

longiligne [lɔ̃ʒiliɲ] *adj* long-limbed.

longitude [lɔ̃ʒityd] *nf* longitude.

longtemps [lɔ̃tɑ̃] *adv* (for) a long time; **depuis ~** (for) a long time; **il y a ~ que ...** it's been a long time since ...; **il y a ~ qu'il est là** he's been here a long time; **mettre ~ à faire qqch** to take a long time to do sthg.

longue → **long**.

longuement [lɔ̃gmɑ̃] *adv* 1. (*longtemps*)

for a long time. **2.** (*en détail*) at length.
longueur [lɔ̃gœr] *nf* length; **faire 5
mètres de ~** to be 5 metres long; **disposer qqch en ~** to put sthg lengthways; **à
~ de journée/temps** the entire day/time;
~ d'onde wavelength. ▶ **longueurs** *nfpl*
(*de film, de livre*) boring parts.
longue-vue [lɔ̃gvy] *nf* telescope.
look [luk] *nm* look; **avoir un ~** to have a
style.
looping [lupiŋ] *nm* loop the loop.
lopin [lɔpɛ̃] *nm*: **~ (de terre)** patch ou
plot of land.
loquace [lɔkas] *adj* loquacious.
loque [lɔk] *nf* **1.** (*lambeau*) rag. **2.** *fig*
(*personne*) wreck.
loquet [lɔkɛ] *nm* latch.
lorgner [lɔrɲe] *vt fam* **1.** (*observer*) to
eye. **2.** (*guigner*) to have one's eye on.
lors [lɔr] *adv*: **depuis ~** since that time;
~ de at the time of.
lorsque [lɔrsk(ə)] *conj* when.
losange [lɔzɑ̃ʒ] *nm* lozenge.
lot [lo] *nm* **1.** (*part*) share; (*de terre*) plot.
2. (*stock*) batch. **3.** (*prix*) prize. **4.** *fig* (*destin*) fate, lot.
loterie [lɔtri] *nf* lottery.
loti, -e [lɔti] *adj*: **être bien/mal ~** to be
well/badly off.
lotion [lɔsjɔ̃] *nf* lotion.
lotir [lɔtir] *vt* to divide up.
lotissement [lɔtismɑ̃] *nm* (*terrain*) plot.
loto [lɔto] *nm* **1.** (*jeu de société*) lotto.
2. (*loterie*) popular national lottery; **le ~
sportif** ≈ the football pools Br, ≈ the
soccer sweepstakes Am.

LOTO

The French national lottery, 'loto', has
been running since 1976 on a similar
basis to the lotteries in Britain and the
US with a twice-weekly televised prize
draw. French people can also bet on the
results of football matches in the 'loto
sportif'.

lotte [lɔt] *nf* monkfish.
lotus [lɔtys] *nm* lotus.
louable [lwabl] *adj* **1.** (*méritoire*) praiseworthy, laudable. **2.** (*location*): **facilement/difficilement ~** easy/difficult to let
Br, easy/difficult to rent Am.
louange [lwɑ̃ʒ] *nf* praise.
louche¹ [luʃ] *nf* ladle.
louche² [luʃ] *adj fam* (*personne, histoire*)
suspicious.
loucher [luʃe] *vi* **1.** (*être atteint de strabisme*) to squint. **2.** *fam fig* (*lorgner*): **~ sur**

to have one's eye on.
louer [lwe] *vt* **1.** (*glorifier*) to praise.
2. (*donner en location*) to rent (out); **à ~**
for rent. **3.** (*prendre en location*) to rent.
4. (*réserver*) to book. ▶ **se louer** *vp sout*
(*se féliciter*): **se ~ de qqch/de faire qqch** to
be very pleased about sthg/about
doing sthg.
loueur, -euse [lwœr, øz] *nm, f*: **c'est un
~ de voitures** he rents out cars.
loufoque [lufɔk] *fam adj* nuts, crazy.
loup [lu] *nm* **1.** (*carnassier*) wolf. **2.** (*poisson*) bass. **3.** (*masque*) mask.
loupe [lup] *nf* (*optique*) magnifying
glass.
louper [lupe] *vt fam* (*travail*) to make a
mess of; (*train*) to miss.
loup-garou [lugaru] (*pl* **loups-garous**)
nm werewolf.
lourd, -e [lur, lurd] *adj* **1.** (*gén*) heavy; **~
de** *fig* full of. **2.** (*tâche*) difficult; (*faute*)
serious. **3.** (*maladroit*) clumsy, heavyhanded. **4.** (MÉTÉOR) close. ▶ **lourd** *adv*:
peser ~ to be heavy, to weigh a lot; **il
n'en fait pas ~** *fam* he doesn't do much.
loutre [lutr] *nf* otter.
louve [luv] *nf* she-wolf.
louveteau, -x [luvto] *nm* **1.** (ZOOL)
wolf cub. **2.** (*scout*) cub.
louvoyer [luvwaje] *vi* **1.** (NAVIG) to
tack. **2.** *fig* (*tergiverser*) to beat about the
bush.
Louvre [luvr] *n*: **le ~** the Louvre
(museum).

LE LOUVRE

One of the largest museums in the
world, the Louvre contains a huge collection of antiques, sculptures and
paintings. Following the addition of
rooms which formerly housed the
French Treasury department and renovation of the exterior, the museum is
now referred to as the 'Grand Louvre'.
There is a new entrance via a glass
pyramid built in the front courtyard,
and an underground shopping centre
and car park have been built.

lover [lɔve] ▶ **se lover** *vp* (*serpent*) to
coil up.
loyal, -e, -aux [lwajal, o] *adj*
1. (*fidèle*) loyal. **2.** (*honnête*) fair.
loyauté [lwajote] *nf* **1.** (*fidélité*) loyalty.
2. (*honnêteté*) fairness.
loyer [lwaje] *nm* rent.
LP (*abr de* **lycée professionnel**) *nm* secondary school for vocational training.

lu, -e [ly] *pp* → **lire¹**.

lubie [lybi] *nf fam* whim.

lubrifier [lybrifje] *vt* to lubricate.

lubrique [lybrik] *adj* lewd.

lucarne [lykarn] *nf* **1.** (*fenêtre*) skylight. **2.** (FOOTBALL) top corner of the net.

lucide [lysid] *adj* lucid.

lucidité [lysidite] *nf* lucidity.

lucratif, -ive [lykratif, iv] *adj* lucrative.

ludique [lydik] *adj* play (*avant n*).

ludoéducatif [lydɔedykatif] *nm* edutainment.

ludothèque [lydɔtek] *nf* toy library.

lueur [lɥœr] *nf* **1.** (*de bougie, d'étoile*) light; **à la ~ de** by the light of. **2.** *fig* (*de colère*) gleam; (*de raison*) spark; **~ d'espoir** glimmer of hope.

luge [lyʒ] *nf* toboggan.

lugubre [lygybr] *adj* lugubrious.

lui¹ [lɥi] *pp inv* → **luire**.

lui² [lɥi] *pron pers* **1.** (*complément d'objet indirect - homme*) (to) him; (- *femme*) (to) her; (- *animal, chose*) (to) it; **je ~ ai parlé** I've spoken to him/to her; **il ~ a serré la main** he shook his/her hand. **2.** (*sujet, en renforcement de 'il'*) he. **3.** (*objet, après préposition, comparatif - personne*) him; (- *animal, chose*) it; **sans ~** without him; **je vais chez ~** I'm going to his place; **elle est plus jeune que ~** she's younger than him ou than he is. **4.** (*remplaçant 'soi' en fonction de pronom réfléchi - personne*) himself; (- *animal, chose*) itself; **il est content de ~** he's pleased with himself. ▶ **lui-même** *pron pers* (*personne*) himself; (*animal, chose*) itself.

luire [lɥir] *vi* (*soleil, métal*) to shine; *fig* (*espoir*) to glow, to glimmer.

luisant, -e [lɥizã, ãt] *adj* gleaming.

lumière [lymjer] *nf* (*éclairage & fig*) light.

lumineux, -euse [lyminø, øz] *adj* **1.** (*couleur, cadran*) luminous. **2.** *fig* (*visage*) radiant; (*idée*) brilliant. **3.** (*explication*) clear.

luminosité [lyminozite] *nf* **1.** (*du regard, ciel*) radiance. **2.** (SCIENCE) luminosity.

lump [lœp] *nm*: **œufs de ~** lumpfish roe.

lunaire [lyner] *adj* **1.** (ASTRON) lunar. **2.** *fig* (*visage*) moon (*avant n*); (*paysage*) lunar.

lunatique [lynatik] *adj* temperamental.

lunch [lœʃ] *nm* buffet lunch.

lundi [lœdi] *nm* Monday; *voir aussi* **samedi**.

lune [lyn] *nf* (ASTRON) moon; **pleine ~** full moon; **~ de miel** *fig* honeymoon.

lunette [lynet] *nf* (ASTRON) telescope.

▶ **lunettes** *nfpl* glasses; **~s de soleil** sunglasses.

lurette [lyret] *nf*: **il y a belle ~ que ...** *fam* it's been ages since ...

luron, -onne [lyrõ, ɔn] *nm, f fam*: **un joyeux ~** a bit of a lad.

lustre [lystr] *nm* **1.** (*luminaire*) chandelier. **2.** (*éclat*) sheen, shine; *fig* reputation.

lustrer [lystre] *vt* **1.** (*faire briller*) to make shine. **2.** (*user*) to wear.

luth [lyt] *nm* lute.

lutin, -e [lytɛ̃, in] *adj* mischievous. ▶ **lutin** *nm* imp.

lutte [lyt] *nf* **1.** (*combat*) fight, struggle; **la ~ des classes** the class struggle. **2.** (SPORT) wrestling.

lutter [lyte] *vi* to fight, to struggle; **~ contre** to fight (against).

lutteur, -euse [lytœr, øz] *nm, f* (SPORT) wrestler; *fig* fighter.

luxation [lyksasjõ] *nf* dislocation.

luxe [lyks] *nm* luxury; **de ~** luxury.

Luxembourg [lyksãbur] *nm* (*pays*): **le ~** Luxembourg.

luxueux, -euse [lyksɥø, øz] *adj* luxurious.

luxure [lyksyr] *nf* lust.

luzerne [lyzern] *nf* lucerne, alfalfa.

lycée [lise] *nm* ≃ secondary school Br, ≃ high school Am; **~ technique/professionnel** ≃ technical/training college.

lycéen, -enne [liseɛ̃, ɛn] *nm, f* secondary school pupil Br, high school pupil Am.

lymphatique [lɛ̃fatik] *adj* **1.** (MÉD) lymphatic. **2.** *fig* (*apathique*) sluggish.

lyncher [lɛ̃ʃe] *vt* to lynch.

lynx [lɛ̃ks] *nm* lynx.

Lyon [ljõ] *n* Lyons.

lyre [lir] *nf* lyre.

lyrique [lirik] *adj* (*poésie*) *fig* lyrical; (*drame, chanteur, poète*) lyric.

lys = **lis**.

m, M [ɛm] ◆ *nm inv* m, M. ◆ (*abr de mètre*) m. ▶ **M 1.** (*abr de Monsieur*) Mr. **2.** (*abr de million*) M.

m' → **me**.

ma → **mon**.

macabre [makabr] *adj* macabre.

macadam [makadam] *nm* (*revêtement*) macadam; (*route*) road.

macaron [makarɔ̃] *nm* **1.** (*pâtisserie*) macaroon. **2.** (*autocollant*) sticker.

macaronis [makarɔni] *nmpl* (CULIN) macaroni (U).

macédoine [masedwan] *nf* (CULIN): ~ de fruits fruit salad.

macérer [masere] ♦ *vt* to steep. ♦ *vi* **1.** (*mariner*) to steep; faire ~ to steep. **2.** *fig & péj* (*personne*) to wallow.

mâche [maʃ] *nf* lamb's lettuce.

mâcher [maʃe] *vt* (*mastiquer*) to chew.

machiavélique [makjavelik] *adj* Machiavellian.

machin [maʃɛ̃] *nm fam* (*chose*) thing, thingumajig.

Machin, -e [maʃɛ̃, in] *nm, f fam* what's his name (*f* what's her name).

machinal, -e, -aux [maʃinal, o] *adj* mechanical.

machination [maʃinasjɔ̃] *nf* machination.

machine [maʃin] *nf* **1.** (TECHNOL) machine; ~ à coudre sewing machine; ~ à écrire typewriter; ~ à laver washing machine. **2.** (*organisation*) machinery (U). **3.** (NAVIG) engine.

machine-outil [maʃinuti] *nf* machine tool.

machiniste [maʃinist] *nm* **1.** (CIN & THÉÂTRE) scene shifter. **2.** (TRANSPORT) driver.

macho [matʃo] *péj nm* macho man.

mâchoire [maʃwar] *nf* jaw.

mâchonner [maʃɔne] *vt* (*mâcher, mordiller*) to chew.

maçon [masɔ̃] *nm* mason.

maçonnerie [masɔnri] *nf* (*travaux*) building; (*construction*) masonry; (*franc-maçonnerie*) freemasonry.

macramé [makrame] *nm* macramé.

maculer [makyle] *vt* to stain.

madame [madam] (*pl* mesdames [medam]) *nf* (*titre*): ~ X Mrs X; bonjour ~! good morning!; (*dans hôtel, restaurant*) good morning, madam!; bonjour mesdames! good morning (ladies)!; Madame le Ministre n'est pas là the Minister is out.

mademoiselle [madmwazɛl] (*pl* mesdemoiselles [medmwazɛl]) *nf* (*titre*): ~ X Miss X; bonjour ~! good morning, miss!; (*à l'école, dans hôtel*) good morning, miss!; bonjour mesdemoiselles! good morning (ladies)!

madone [madɔn] *nf* (ART & RELIG) Madonna.

Madrid [madrid] *n* Madrid.

madrier [madrije] *nm* beam.

maf(f)ia [mafja] *nf* Mafia.

magasin [magazɛ̃] *nm* **1.** (*boutique*) shop *Br*, store *Am*; grand ~ department store; faire les ~s *fig* to go round the shops *Br* ou stores *Am*. **2.** (*d'arme, d'appareil photo*) magazine.

magazine [magazin] *nm* magazine.

mage [maʒ] *nm*: les Rois ~s the Three Wise Men.

Maghreb [magrɛb] *nm*: le ~ the Maghreb.

maghrébin, -e [magrebɛ̃, in] *adj* North African. ▶ **Maghrébin, -e** *nm, f* North African.

magicien, -enne [maʒisjɛ̃, ɛn] *nm, f* magician.

magie [maʒi] *nf* magic.

magique [maʒik] *adj* **1.** (*occulte*) magic. **2.** (*merveilleux*) magical.

magistère [maʒistɛr] *nm* postgraduate vocational qualification.

magistral, -e, -aux [maʒistral, o] *adj* **1.** (*œuvre, habileté*) masterly. **2.** (*dispute, fessée*) enormous. **3.** (*attitude, ton*) authoritative.

magistrat [maʒistra] *nm* magistrate.

magistrature [maʒistratyr] *nf* magistracy, magistrature.

magma [magma] *nm* **1.** (GÉOL) magma. **2.** *fig* (*mélange*) muddle.

magnanime [maɲanim] *adj* magnanimous.

magnat [maɲa] *nm* magnate, tycoon.

magnésium [maɲezjɔm] *nm* magnesium.

magnétique [maɲetik] *adj* magnetic.

magnétisme [maɲetism] *nm* (PHYS & *fascination*) magnetism.

magnéto(phone) [maɲetɔ(fɔn)] *nm* tape recorder.

magnétoscope [maɲetɔskɔp] *nm* videorecorder.

magnificence [maɲifisɑ̃s] *nf* magnificence.

magnifique [maɲifik] *adj* magnificent.

magnum [magnɔm] *nm* magnum.

magot [mago] *nm fam* tidy sum, packet.

mai [mɛ] *nm* May; le premier ~ May Day; *voir aussi* septembre.

PREMIER MAI

The first day of May is a national holiday in France celebrating Labour Day, and traditionally there are large processions led by trade unions in the larger cities. Also on this day, bunches of lilies of the valley are sold in the streets and given as presents. The flowers are supposed to bring good luck.

---

maigre [mɛgr] *adj* **1.** (*très mince*) thin. **2.** (*aliment*) low-fat; (*viande*) lean. **3.** (*peu important*) meagre; (*végétation*) sparse.

maigreur [mɛgrœr] *nf* thinness.

maigrir [megrir] *vi* to lose weight.

mailing [meliŋ] *nm* mailing, mailshot.

maille [maj] *nf* **1.** (*de tricot*) stitch. **2.** (*de filet*) mesh.

maillet [majɛ] *nm* mallet.

maillon [majɔ̃] *nm* link.

maillot [majo] *nm* (*de sport*) shirt, jersey; **~ de bain** swimsuit; **~ de corps** vest Br, undershirt Am.

main [mɛ̃] *nf* hand; **à la ~** by hand; **attaque à ~ armée** armed attack; **donner la ~ à qqn** to take sb's hand; **en ~ propre** in person; **avoir sous la ~** to have to hand; **haut les ~s!** hands up!

main-d'œuvre [mɛ̃dœvr] *nf* labour, workforce.

mainmise [mɛ̃miz] *nf* seizure.

maint, -e [mɛ̃, mɛ̃t] *adj littéraire* many a; **~s** many; **~es fois** time and time again.

maintenance [mɛ̃tnɑ̃s] *nf* maintenance.

maintenant [mɛ̃tnɑ̃] *adv* now. ► **maintenant que** *loc prép* now that.

maintenir [mɛ̃tnir] *vt* **1.** (*soutenir*) to support; **~ qqn à distance** to keep sb away. **2.** (*garder, conserver*) to maintain. **3.** (*affirmer*): **~ que** to maintain (that). ► **se maintenir** *vp* **1.** (*durer*) to last. **2.** (*rester*) to remain.

maintenu, -e [mɛ̃tny] *pp* → **maintenir**.

maintien [mɛ̃tjɛ̃] *nm* **1.** (*conservation*) maintenance; (*de tradition*) upholding. **2.** (*tenue*) posture.

maire [mɛr] *nm* mayor.

mairie [meri] *nf* **1.** (*bâtiment*) town hall Br, city hall Am. **2.** (*administration*) town council Br, city hall Am.

mais [mɛ] ◆ *conj* but; **~ non!** of course not!; **~ alors, tu l'as vu ou non?** so did you see him or not?; **il a pleuré, ~ pleuré** he cried, and how!; **non ~ ça ne va pas!** that's just not on! ◆ *adv* but; **vous êtes prêts? - ~ bien sûr!** are you ready? – but of course! ◆ *nm*: **il y a un ~** there's a hitch ou a snag; **il n'y a pas**

de **~** (there are) no buts.

maïs [mais] *nm* maize Br, corn Am.

maison [mɛzɔ̃] *nf* **1.** (*habitation, lignée & ASTROL*) house; **~ de campagne** house in the country; **~ individuelle** detached house. **2.** (*foyer*) home; (*famille*) family; **à la ~** (*au domicile*) at home. **3.** (COMM) company. **4.** (*institut*): **~ d'arrêt** prison; **~ de la culture** arts centre; **~ de retraite** old people's home. **5.** (*en apposition*) (*artisanal*) homemade; (*dans restaurant - vin*) house (*avant n*).

Maison-Blanche [mɛzɔ̃blɑ̃ʃ] *nf*: **la ~** the White House.

maisonnée [mɛzɔne] *nf* household.

maisonnette [mɛzɔnɛt] *nf* small house.

maître, -esse [mɛtr, mɛtrɛs] *nm, f* **1.** (*professeur*) teacher; **~ chanteur** blackmailer; **~ de conférences** (UNIV) ≃ senior lecturer; **~ d'école** schoolteacher; **~ nageur** swimming instructor. **2.** (*modèle, artiste & fig*) master. **3.** (*dirigeant*) ruler; (*d'animal*) master (*f* mistress); **~ d'hôtel** head waiter; **être ~ de soi** to be in control of oneself, to have self-control. **4.** (*en apposition*) (*principal*) main, principal. ► **Maître** *nm* form of address for lawyers. ► **maîtresse** *nf* (*amie*) mistress.

maître-assistant, -e [mɛtrasistɑ̃, ɑ̃t] *nm, f* ≃ lecturer Br, ≃ assistant professor Am.

maîtresse → **maître**.

maîtrise [metriz] *nf* **1.** (*sang-froid, domination*) control. **2.** (*connaissance*) mastery, command; (*habileté*) skill. **3.** (UNIV) ≃ master's degree.

maîtriser [metrize] *vt* **1.** (*animal, forcené*) to subdue. **2.** (*émotion, réaction*) to control, to master. **3.** (*incendie*) to bring under control. ► **se maîtriser** *vp* to control o.s.

majesté [maʒɛste] *nf* majesty. ► **Majesté** *nf*: **Sa Majesté** His/Her Majesty.

majestueux, -euse [maʒɛstɥø, øz] *adj* majestic.

majeur, -e [maʒœr] *adj* **1.** (*gén*) major. **2.** (*personne*) of age. ► **majeur** *nm* middle finger.

major [maʒɔr] *nm* (MIL) ≃ adjutant.

majordome [maʒɔrdɔm] *nm* majordomo.

majorer [maʒɔre] *vt* to increase.

majorette [maʒɔrɛt] *nf* majorette.

majoritaire [maʒɔritɛr] *adj* majority (*avant n*); **être ~** to be in the majority.

majorité [maʒɔrite] *nf* majority; **en**

(grande) ~ in the majority; ~ **absolue/ relative** (POLIT) absolute/relative majority.

majuscule [maʒyskyl] ♦ *nf* capital (letter). ♦ *adj* capital (*avant n*).

mal, maux [mal, mo] *nm* 1. (*ce qui est contraire à la morale*) evil. 2. (*souffrance physique*) pain; **avoir ~ au bras** to have a sore arm; **avoir ~ au cœur** to feel sick; **avoir ~ au dos** to have backache; **avoir ~ à la gorge** to have a sore throat; **avoir le ~ de mer** to be seasick; **avoir ~ aux dents/à la tête** to have toothache/a headache; **avoir ~ au ventre** to have (a) stomachache; **faire ~ à qqn** to hurt sb; **ça fait ~** it hurts; **se faire ~** to hurt o.s. 3. (*difficulté*) difficulty. 4. (*douleur morale*) pain, suffering (U); **être en ~ de qqch** to long for sthg; **faire du ~ (à qqn)** to hurt (sb). ▶ **mal** *adv* 1. (*malade*) ill; **aller ~** not to be well; **se sentir ~** to feel ill; **être au plus ~** to be extremely ill. 2. (*respirer*) with difficulty. 3. (*informé, se conduire*) badly; **~ prendre qqch** to take sthg badly; **~ tourner** to go wrong. 4. *loc*: **pas ~** not bad (*adj*), not badly (*adv*); **pas ~ de** quite a lot of.

malade [malad] ♦ *nmf* invalid, sick person; **~ mental** mentally ill person. ♦ *adj* 1. (*souffrant - personne*) ill, sick; (*- organe*) bad; **tomber ~** to fall ill ou sick. 2. *fam* (*fou*) crazy.

maladie [maladi] *nf* 1. (MÉD) illness; **~ de Creutzfeldt-Jakob** Creutzfeldt-Jakob disease. 2. (*passion, manie*) mania.

maladresse [maladrɛs] *nf* 1. (*inhabileté*) clumsiness. 2. (*bévue*) blunder.

maladroit, -e [maladrwa, at] *adj* clumsy.

malaise [malɛz] *nm* 1. (*indisposition*) discomfort. 2. (*trouble*) unease (U).

malaisé, -e [maleze] *adj* difficult.

Malaisie [malɛzi] *nf*: **la ~** Malaya.

malappris, -e [malapri, iz] *nm, f* lout.

malaria [malarja] *nf* malaria.

malaxer [malakse] *vt* to knead.

malchance [malʃɑ̃s] *nf* bad luck (U).

malchanceux, -euse [malʃɑ̃sø, øz] ♦ *adj* unlucky. ♦ *nm, f* unlucky person.

malcommode [malkɔmɔd] *adj* inconvenient; (*meuble*) impractical.

mâle [mal] ♦ *adj* 1. (*enfant, animal, hormone*) male. 2. (*voix, assurance*) manly. 3. (ÉLECTR) male. ♦ *nm* male.

malédiction [malediksjɔ̃] *nf* curse.

maléfique [malefik] *adj sout* evil.

malencontreux, -euse [malɑ̃kɔ̃trø, øz] *adj* (*hasard, rencontre*) unfortunate.

malentendant, -e [malɑ̃tɑ̃dɑ̃, ɑ̃t] *nm, f* person who is hard of hearing.

malentendu [malɑ̃tɑ̃dy] *nm* misunderstanding.

malfaçon [malfasɔ̃] *nf* defect.

malfaiteur [malfetœr] *nm* criminal.

malfamé, -e, mal famé, -e [malfame] *adj* disreputable.

malformation [malfɔrmasjɔ̃] *nf* malformation.

malfrat [malfra] *nm fam* crook.

malgré [malgre] *prép* in spite of; **~ tout** (*quoi qu'il arrive*) in spite of everything; (*pourtant*) even so, yet. ▶ **malgré que** *loc conj* (+ *subjonctif*) *fam* although, in spite of the fact that.

malhabile [malabil] *adj* clumsy.

malheur [malœr] *nm* misfortune; **par ~** unfortunately; **porter ~ à qqn** to bring sb bad luck.

malheureusement [malœrøzmɑ̃] *adv* unfortunately.

malheureux, -euse [malœrø, øz] ♦ *adj* 1. (*triste*) unhappy. 2. (*désastreux, regrettable*) unfortunate. 3. (*malchanceux*) unlucky. 4. (*avant n*) (*sans valeur*) pathetic, miserable. ♦ *nm, f* (*infortuné*) poor soul.

malhonnête [malɔnɛt] ♦ *nmf* dishonest person. ♦ *adj* 1. (*personne, affaire*) dishonest. 2. *hum* (*proposition, propos*) indecent.

malhonnêteté [malɔnɛtte] *nf* (*de personne*) dishonesty.

Mali [mali] *nm*: **le ~** Mali.

malice [malis] *nf* mischief.

malicieux, -euse [malisjø, øz] *adj* mischievous.

malin, -igne [malɛ̃, iɲ] ♦ *adj* 1. (*rusé*) crafty, cunning; (*regard, sourire*) knowing. 2. (*méchant*) malicious, spiteful. 3. (MÉD) malignant. ♦ *nm, f* cunning ou crafty person.

malingre [malɛ̃gr] *adj* sickly.

malle [mal] *nf* (*coffre*) trunk; (*de voiture*) boot Br, trunk Am.

malléable [maleabl] *adj* malleable.

mallette [malɛt] *nf* briefcase.

mal-logé, -e [malɔʒe] (*mpl* **mal-logés**, *fpl* **mal-logées**) *nm, f* person living in poor accommodation.

malmener [malməne] *vt* (*brutaliser*) to handle roughly, to ill-treat.

malnutrition [malnytrisjɔ̃] *nf* malnutrition.

malodorant, -e [malɔdɔrɑ̃, ɑ̃t] *adj* smelly.

malotru, -e [malɔtry] *nm, f* lout.

manœuvre

malpoli, -e [malpɔli] *nm, f* rude person.

malpropre [malprɔpr] *adj* (*sale*) dirty.

malsain, -e [malsɛ̃, ɛn] *adj* unhealthy.

malt [malt] *nm* **1.** (*céréale*) malt. **2.** (*whisky*) malt (whisky).

Malte [malt] *n* Malta.

maltraiter [maltrete] *vt* to ill-treat; (*en paroles*) to attack, to run down.

malus [malys] *nm increase in car insurance charges, due to loss of no-claims bonus.*

malveillant, -e [malvɛjã, ãt] *adj* spiteful.

malversation [malvɛrsasjɔ̃] *nf* embezzlement.

malvoyant, -e [malvwajã, ãt] *nm, f* person who is partially sighted.

maman [mamã] *nf* mummy.

mamelle [mamɛl] *nf* teat; (*de vache*) udder.

mamelon [mamlɔ̃] *nm* (*du sein*) nipple.

mamie, mamy [mami] *nf* granny, grandma.

mammifère [mamifɛr] *nm* mammal.

mammouth [mamut] *nm* mammoth.

mamy = **mamie**.

management [manadʒmɛnt] *nm* management.

manager [manadʒɛr] *nm* manager.

manche [mãʃ] ◆ *nf* **1.** (*de vêtement*) sleeve; **~s courtes/longues** short/long sleeves. **2.** (*de jeu*) round, game; (TENNIS) set. ◆ *nm* **1.** (*d'outil*) handle; **~ à balai** broomstick; (*d'avion*) joystick. **2.** (MUS) neck.

Manche [mãʃ] *nf* (*mer*): **la ~** the English Channel.

manchette [mãʃɛt] *nf* **1.** (*de chemise*) cuff. **2.** (*de journal*) headline. **3.** (*coup*) forearm blow.

manchon [mãʃɔ̃] *nm* **1.** (*en fourrure*) muff. **2.** (TECHNOL) casing, sleeve.

manchot, -ote [mãʃo, ɔt] ◆ *adj* one-armed. ◆ *nm, f* one-armed person. ▶ **manchot** *nm* penguin.

mandarine [mãdarin] *nf* mandarin (orange).

mandat [mãda] *nm* **1.** (*pouvoir, fonction*) mandate. **2.** (JUR) warrant; **~ de perquisition** search warrant. **3.** (*titre postal*) money order; **~ postal** postal order Br, money order Am.

mandataire [mãdatɛr] *nmf* proxy, representative.

mandibule [mãdibyl] *nf* mandible.

mandoline [mãdɔlin] *nf* mandolin.

manège [manɛʒ] *nm* **1.** (*attraction*) roundabout Br, carousel Am. **2.** (*de chevaux - lieu*) riding school. **3.** (*manœuvre*) scheme, game.

manette [manɛt] *nf* lever.

mangeable [mãʒabl] *adj* edible.

mangeoire [mãʒwar] *nf* manger.

manger [mãʒe] ◆ *vt* **1.** (*nourriture*) to eat. **2.** (*fortune*) to get through, to squander. ◆ *vi* to eat.

mangue [mãg] *nf* mango.

maniable [manjabl] *adj* (*instrument*) manageable.

maniaque [manjak] ◆ *nmf* **1.** (*méticuleux*) fusspot. **2.** (*fou*) maniac. ◆ *adj* **1.** (*méticuleux*) fussy. **2.** (*fou*) maniacal.

manie [mani] *nf* **1.** (*habitude*) funny habit; **avoir la ~ de qqch/de faire qqch** to have a mania for sthg/for doing sthg. **2.** (*obsession*) mania.

maniement [manimã] *nm* handling.

manier [manje] *vt* (*manipuler, utiliser*) to handle; *fig* (*ironie, mots*) to handle skilfully.

manière [manjɛr] *nf* (*méthode*) manner, way; **de toute ~** at any rate; **d'une ~ générale** generally speaking. ▶ **manières** *nfpl* manners. ▶ **de manière à** *loc conj* (in order) to; **de ~ à ce que** (+ *subjonctif*) so that. ▶ **de manière que** *loc conj* (+ *subjonctif*) in such a way that.

maniéré, -e [manjere] *adj* affected.

manif [manif] *nf fam* demo.

manifestant, -e [manifɛstã, ãt] *nm, f* demonstrator.

manifestation [manifɛstasjɔ̃] *nf* **1.** (*témoignage*) expression. **2.** (*mouvement collectif*) demonstration. **3.** (*apparition - de maladie*) appearance.

manifester [manifɛste] ◆ *vt* to show, to express. ◆ *vi* to demonstrate. ▶ **se manifester** *vp* **1.** (*apparaître*) to show ou manifest itself. **2.** (*se montrer*) to turn up, to appear.

manigancer [manigãse] *vt fam* to plot.

manioc [manjɔk] *nm* manioc.

manipuler [manipyle] *vt* **1.** (*colis, appareil*) to handle. **2.** (*statistiques, résultats*) to falsify, to rig. **3.** *péj* (*personne*) to manipulate.

manivelle [manivɛl] *nf* crank.

manne [man] *nf* (RELIG) manna; *fig & littéraire* godsend.

mannequin [mankɛ̃] *nm* **1.** (*forme humaine*) model, dummy. **2.** (*personne*) model, mannequin.

manœuvre [manœvr] ◆ *nf* **1.** (*d'appareil, de véhicule*) driving, handling. **2.** (MIL) manoeuvre, exercise. **3.** (*machi-*

nation) ploy, scheme. ◆ *nm* labourer.

manœuvrer [manœvre] ◆ *vi* to manoeuvre. ◆ *vt* 1. (*faire fonctionner*) to operate, to work; (*voiture*) to manoeuvre. 2. (*influencer*) to manipulate.

manoir [manwar] *nm* manor, country house.

manquant, -e [mākā, āt] *adj* missing.

manque [māk] *nm* 1. (*pénurie*) lack, shortage; **par ~ de** for want of. 2. (*de toxicomane*) withdrawal symptoms (*pl*). 3. (*lacune*) gap.

manqué, -e [māke] *adj* (*raté*) failed; (*rendez-vous*) missed.

manquer [māke] ◆ *vi* 1. (*faire défaut*) to be lacking, to be missing; **l'argent/le temps me manque** I don't have enough money/time; **tu me manques** I miss you. 2. (*être absent*): **~ (à)** to be absent (from), to be missing (from). 3. (*échouer*) to fail. 4. (*ne pas avoir assez*): **~ de qqch** to lack sthg, to be short of sthg. 5. (*faillir*): **il a manqué de se noyer** he nearly ou almost drowned; **ne manquez pas de lui dire** don't forget to tell him; **je n'y manquerai pas** I certainly will, I'll definitely do it. 6. (*ne pas respecter*): **~ à** (*devoir*) to fail in; **~ à sa parole** to break one's word. ◆ *vt* 1. (*gén*) to miss; **à ne pas ~** not to be missed. 2. (*échouer à*) to bungle, to botch. ◆ *v impers*: **il manque quelqu'un** somebody is missing; **il me manque 20 francs** I'm 20 francs short.

mansarde [māsard] *nf* attic.

mansardé, -e [māsarde] *adj* attic (*avant n*).

mansuétude [māsyetyd] *nf* *littéraire* indulgence.

mante [māt] *nf* (HIST) mantle. ▶ **mante religieuse** *nf* praying mantis.

manteau, -x [māto] *nm* (*vêtement*) coat.

manucure [manykyr] *nmf* manicurist.

manuel, -elle [manɥɛl] *adj* manual. ▶ **manuel** *nm* manual.

manufacture [manyfaktyr] *nf* (*fabrique*) factory.

manuscrit, -e [manyskri, it] *adj* handwritten. ▶ **manuscrit** *nm* manuscript.

manutention [manytāsjɔ̃] *nf* handling.

manutentionnaire [manytāsjɔnɛr] *nmf* packer.

mappemonde [mapmɔ̃d] *nf* 1. (*carte*) map of the world. 2. (*sphère*) globe.

maquereau, -elle, -x [makro, ɛl, o] *nm, f fam* pimp (*f* madam). ▶ **maque-**

reau *nm* mackerel.

maquette [makɛt] *nf* 1. (*ébauche*) paste-up. 2. (*modèle réduit*) model.

maquillage [makijaʒ] *nm* (*action, produits*) make-up.

maquiller [makije] *vt* 1. (*farder*) to make up. 2. (*fausser*) to disguise; (*- passeport*) to falsify; (*- chiffres*) to doctor. ▶ **se maquiller** *vp* to make up, to put on one's make-up.

maquis [maki] *nm* 1. (*végétation*) scrub, brush. 2. (HIST) Maquis.

marabout [marabu] *nm* 1. (ZOOL) marabou. 2. (*guérisseur*) marabout.

maraîcher, -ère [mareʃe, ɛr] ◆ *adj* market garden (*avant n*) Br, truck farming (*avant n*) Am. ◆ *nm, f* market gardener Br, truck farmer Am.

marais [marɛ] *nm* (*marécage*) marsh, swamp; **~ salant** saltpan.

LE MARAIS

This district in the fourth 'arrondissement' of Paris stretches between the Bastille and the Hôtel de Ville. It is famous for its many fashionable town houses built on and around the Place des Vosges, and is historically associated with the Jewish community.

marasme [marasm] *nm* (*récession*) stagnation.

marathon [maratɔ̃] *nm* marathon.

marâtre [maratr] *nf* vieilli 1. (*mauvaise mère*) bad mother. 2. (*belle-mère*) stepmother.

maraude [marod] *nf*, **maraudage** [marodaʒ] *nm* pilfering.

marbre [marbr] *nm* (*roche, objet*) marble.

marc [mar] *nm* 1. (*eau-de-vie*) spirit distilled from grape residue. 2. (*de fruits*) residue; (*de thé*) leaves; **~ de café** grounds (*pl*).

marcassin [markasɛ̃] *nm* young wild boar.

marchand, -e [marʃā, ād] ◆ *adj* (*valeur*) market (*avant n*); (*prix*) trade (*avant n*). ◆ *nm, f* (*commerçant*) merchant; (*détaillant*) shopkeeper Br, storekeeper Am; **~ de journaux** newsagent; **~ de légumes** greengrocer.

marchander [marʃāde] ◆ *vt* 1. (*prix*) to haggle over. 2. (*appui*) to begrudge. ◆ *vi* to bargain, to haggle.

marchandise [marʃādiz] *nf* merchandise (U), goods (*pl*).

marche [marʃ] *nf* 1. (*d'escalier*) step.

maroquinerie

2. (*de personne*) walking; (*promenade*) walk; **~ à pied** walking; **~ à suivre** *fig* correct procedure. **3.** (MUS) march. **4.** (*déplacement - du temps, d'astre*) course; **en ~ arrière** in reverse; **faire ~ arrière** to reverse; *fig* to backpedal, to backtrack. **5.** (*fonctionnement*) running, working; **en ~ running; se mettre en ~** to start (up).

marché [marʃe] *nm* **1.** (*gén*) market; **faire son ~** to go shopping, to do one's shopping; **le ~ du travail** the labour market; **~ noir** black market; **~ aux puces** flea market. **2.** (*contrat*) bargain, deal; **(à) bon ~** cheap. ▶ **Marché commun** *nm*: **le Marché commun** the Common Market.

MARCHÉ

Almost every French town, however small, has its own open-air or covered market which takes place once or twice a week. It usually consists of stalls selling fresh produce, flowers, clothes or household goods; but there are also specialized markets selling, for example, just flowers, cheese or livestock.

marchepied [marʃəpje] *nm* (*de train*) step; (*escabeau*) steps (*pl*) Br, stepladder; *fig* stepping-stone.

marcher [marʃe] *vi* **1.** (*aller à pied*) to walk. **2.** (*poser le pied*) to step. **3.** (*fonctionner, tourner*) to work; **son affaire marche bien** his business is doing well. **4.** *fam* (*accepter*) to agree. **5.** *loc*: **faire ~ qqn** *fam* to take sb for a ride.

mardi [mardi] *nm* Tuesday; **~ gras** Shrove Tuesday; *voir aussi* **samedi**.

mare [mar] *nf* pool.

marécage [mareka3] *nm* marsh, bog.

marécageux, -euse [mareka3ø, øz] *adj* (*terrain*) marshy, boggy.

maréchal, -aux [mareʃal, o] *nm* marshal.

marée [mare] *nf* **1.** (*de la mer*) tide; **(à) haute/basse ~** (at) high/low tide. **2.** *fig* (*de personnes*) wave, surge. ▶ **marée noire** *nf* oil slick.

marelle [marɛl] *nf* hopscotch.

margarine [margarin] *nf* margarine.

marge [mar3] *nf* **1.** (*espace*) margin; **vivre en ~ de la société** *fig* to live on the fringes of society. **2.** (*latitude*) leeway; **~ d'erreur** margin of error. **3.** (COMM) margin; **~ commerciale** gross margin.

margelle [mar3ɛl] *nf* coping.

marginal, -e, -aux [mar3inal, o] ◆ *adj* **1.** (*gén*) marginal. **2.** (*groupe*)

dropout (*avant n*). ◆ *nm, f* dropout.

marguerite [margərit] *nf* **1.** (BOT) daisy. **2.** (*d'imprimante*) daisy wheel.

mari [mari] *nm* husband.

mariage [marja3] *nm* **1.** (*union, institution*) marriage. **2.** (*cérémonie*) wedding; **~ civil/religieux** civil/church wedding. **3.** *fig* (*de choses*) blend.

Marianne [marjan] *n personification of the French Republic*.

marié, -e [marje] ◆ *adj* married. ◆ *nm, f* groom, bridegroom (*f* bride).

marier [marje] *vt* **1.** (*personne*) to marry. **2.** *fig* (*couleurs*) to blend. ▶ **se marier** *vp* **1.** (*personnes*) to get married; **se ~ avec qqn** to marry sb. **2.** *fig* (*couleurs*) to blend.

marihuana [marirwana], **marijuana** [mariʒɥana] *nf* marijuana.

marin, -e [marɛ̃, in] *adj* **1.** (*de la mer*) sea (*avant n*); (*faune, biologie*) marine. **2.** (NAVIG) (*carte, mille*) nautical. ▶ **marin** *nm* **1.** (*navigateur*) seafarer. **2.** (*matelot*) sailor; **~ pêcheur** deep-sea fisherman. ▶ **marine** ◆ *nf* **1.** (*navigation*) seamanship, navigation. **2.** (*navires*) navy; **~e marchande** merchant navy; **~e nationale** navy. ◆ *nm* **1.** (MIL) marine. **2.** (*couleur*) navy (blue). ◆ *adj inv* navy.

mariner [marine] ◆ *vt* to marinate. ◆ *vi* **1.** (*aliment*) to marinate; **faire ~ qqch** to marinate sthg. **2.** *fam fig* (*attendre*) to hang around; **faire ~ qqn** to let sb stew.

marinier [marinje] *nm* bargee Br, bargeman Am.

marionnette [marjɔnɛt] *nf* puppet.

marital, -e, -aux [marital, o] *adj*: **autorisation ~e** husband's permission.

maritime [maritim] *adj* (*navigation*) maritime; (*ville*) coastal.

mark [mark] *nm* (*monnaie*) mark.

marketing [marketiŋ] *nm* marketing; **~ téléphonique** telemarketing.

marmaille [marmaj] *nf fam* brood (of kids).

marmelade [marmaləd] *nf* stewed fruit.

marmite [marmit] *nf* (*casserole*) pot.

marmonner [marmɔne] *vt & vi* to mutter, to mumble.

marmot [marmo] *nm fam* kid.

marmotte [marmɔt] *nf* marmot.

Maroc [marɔk] *nm*: **le ~** Morocco.

marocain, -e [marɔkɛ̃, ɛn] *adj* Moroccan. ▶ **Marocain, -e** *nm, f* Moroccan.

maroquinerie [marɔkinri] *nf* (*magasin*) leather-goods shop Br ou store Am.

marotte [marɔt] nf (dada) craze.

marquant, -e [markɑ̃, ɑ̃t] adj outstanding.

marque [mark] nf 1. (signe, trace) mark; fig stamp, mark. 2. (label, fabricant) make, brand; de ~ designer (avant n); fig important; ~ déposée registered trademark. 3. (SPORT) score; à vos ~s, prêts, partez! on your marks, get set, go! 4. (témoignage) sign, token.

marqué, -e [marke] adj 1. (net) marked, pronounced. 2. (personne, visage) marked.

marquer [marke] ◆ vt 1. (gén) to mark. 2. fam (écrire) to write down, to note down. 3. (indiquer, manifester) to show. 4. (SPORT - but, point) to score; (- joueur) to mark. ◆ vi 1. (événement, expérience) to leave its mark. 2. (SPORT) to score.

marqueur [markœr] nm (crayon) marker (pen).

marquis, -e [marki, iz] nm, f marquis (f marchioness).

marraine [marɛn] nf 1. (de filleul) godmother. 2. (de navire) christener.

marrant, -e [marɑ̃, ɑ̃t] adj fam funny.

marre [mar] adv : en avoir ~ (de) fam to be fed up (with).

marrer [mare] ▶ **se marrer** vp fam to split one's sides.

marron, -onne [marɔ̃, ɔn] adj péj (médecin) quack (avant n); (avocat) crooked. ▶ **marron** ◆ nm 1. (fruit) chestnut. 2. (couleur) brown. ◆ adj inv brown.

marronnier [marɔnje] nm chestnut tree.

mars [mars] nm March; voir aussi **septembre**.

Marseille [marsɛj] n Marseilles.

marsouin [marswɛ̃] nm porpoise.

marteau, -x [marto] ◆ nm 1. (gén) hammer; ~ piqueur, ~ pneumatique pneumatic drill. 2. (heurtoir) knocker. ◆ adj fam barmy.

marteler [martəle] vt 1. (pieu) to hammer; (table, porte) to hammer on, to pound. 2. (phrase) to rap out.

martial, -e, -aux [marsjal, o] adj martial.

martien, -enne [marsjɛ̃, ɛn] adj & nm, f Martian.

martinet [martinɛ] nm 1. (ZOOL) swift. 2. (fouet) whip.

martingale [martɛ̃gal] nf 1. (de vêtement) half-belt. 2. (JEU) winning system.

Martini® [martini] nm Martini®.

Martinique [martinik] nf : la ~ Martinique.

martyr, -e [martir] ◆ adj martyred. ◆ nm, f martyr. ▶ **martyre** nm martyrdom.

martyriser [martirize] vt to torment.

marxisme [marksism] nm Marxism.

mascarade [maskarad] nf (mise en scène) masquerade.

mascotte [maskɔt] nf mascot.

masculin, -e [maskylɛ̃, in] adj (apparence & GRAM) masculine; (métier, population, sexe) male. ▶ **masculin** nm (GRAM) masculine.

maso [mazo] fam ◆ nm masochist. ◆ adj masochistic.

masochisme [mazɔʃism] nm masochism.

masque [mask] nm 1. (gén) mask; ~ à gaz gas mask. 2. fig (façade) front, façade.

masquer [maske] vt 1. (vérité, crime, problème) to conceal. 2. (maison, visage) to conceal, to hide.

massacre [masakr] nm litt & fig massacre.

massacrer [masakre] vt to massacre; (voiture) to smash up.

massage [masaʒ] nm massage.

masse [mas] nf 1. (de pierre) block; (d'eau) volume. 2. (grande quantité) : une ~ de masses (pl) ou loads (pl) of. 3. (PHYS) mass. 4. (ÉLECTR) earth Br, ground Am. 5. (maillet) sledgehammer. ▶ **en masse** loc adv (venir) en masse, all together; fam (acheter) in bulk.

masser [mase] vt 1. (assembler) to assemble. 2. (frotter) to massage. ▶ **se masser** vp 1. (s'assembler) to assemble, to gather. 2. (se frotter) : se ~ le bras to massage one's arm.

masseur, -euse [masœr, øz] nm, f (personne) masseur (f masseuse).

massicot [masiko] nm guillotine.

massif, -ive [masif, iv] adj 1. (monument, personne, dose) massive. 2. (or, chêne) solid. ▶ **massif** nm 1. (de plantes) clump. 2. (de montagnes) massif.

massue [masy] nf club.

mastic [mastik] nm mastic, putty.

mastiquer [mastike] vt (mâcher) to chew.

masturber [mastyrbe] ▶ **se masturber** vp to masturbate.

masure [mazyr] nf hovel.

mat, -e [mat] adj 1. (peinture, surface) matt. 2. (peau, personne) dusky. 3. (bruit, son) dull. 4. (aux échecs) checkmated. ▶ **mat** nm checkmate.

mât [ma] *nm* 1. (NAVIG) mast. 2. (*poteau*) pole, post.

match [matʃ] (*pl* matches OU matchs) *nm* match; (faire) ~ nul (to) draw; ~ aller/retour first/second leg.

matelas [matla] *nm inv* (*de lit*) mattress; ~ pneumatique airbed.

matelot [matlo] *nm* sailor.

mater [mate] *vt* 1. (*soumettre, neutraliser*) to subdue. 2. *fam* (*regarder*) to eye up.

matérialiser [materjalize] ► se **matérialiser** *vp* (*aspirations*) to be realized.

matérialiste [materjalist] ◆ *nmf* materialist. ◆ *adj* materialistic.

matériau, -x [materjo] *nm* material. ► **matériaux** *nmpl* (CONSTR) material (U), materials.

matériel, -elle [materjɛl] *adj* 1. (*être, substance*) material, physical; (*confort, avantage, aide*) material. 2. (*considération*) practical. ► **matériel** *nm* 1. (*gén*) equipment (U). 2. (INFORM) hardware (U).

maternel, -elle [matɛrnɛl] *adj* (*grands-parents, instinct*) maternal; (*amour*) motherly; (*langue*) mother (*avant n*). ► **maternelle** *nf* nursery school.

maternité [maternite] *nf* 1. (*qualité*) maternity, motherhood. 2. (*hôpital*) maternity hospital.

mathématicien, -enne [matematisjɛ̃, ɛn] *nm, f* mathematician.

mathématique [matematik] *adj* mathematical. ► **mathématiques** *nfpl* mathematics (U).

maths [mat] *nfpl fam* maths Br, math Am.

matière [matjɛr] *nf* 1. (*substance*) matter; ~s grasses fats; ~ grise grey matter. 2. (*matériau*) material; ~s premières raw materials. 3. (*discipline, sujet*) subject; en ~ de sport/littérature as far as sport/literature is concerned.

matin [matɛ̃] *nm* morning; le ~ in the morning; ce ~ this morning; à trois heures du ~ at 3 o'clock in the morning; du ~ au soir *fig* from dawn to dusk.

matinal, -e, -aux [matinal, o] *adj* 1. (*gymnastique, émission*) morning (*avant n*). 2. (*personne*): être ~ to be an early riser.

matinée [matine] *nf* 1. (*matin*) morning; faire la grasse ~ to have a lie in. 2. (*spectacle*) matinée, afternoon performance.

matou [matu] *nm* tom, tomcat.

matraque [matrak] *nf* truncheon.

matraquer [matrake] *vt* 1. (*frapper*) to beat, to club. 2. *fig* (*intoxiquer*) to bombard.

matriarcat [matrijarka] *nm* matriarchy.

matrice [matris] *nf* 1. (*moule*) mould. 2. (MATHS) matrix. 3. (ANAT) womb.

matricule [matrikyl] *nm*: (numéro) ~ number.

matrimonial, -e, -aux [matrimɔnjal, o] *adj* matrimonial.

matrone [matrɔn] *nf péj* old bag.

mature [matyr] *adj* mature.

mâture [matyr] *nf* masts (*pl*).

maturité [matyrite] *nf* maturity; (*de fruit*) ripeness.

maudire [modir] *vt* to curse.

maudit, -e [modi, it] ◆ *pp* → **maudire**. ◆ *adj* 1. (*réprouvé*) accursed. 2. (*avant n*) (*exécrable*) damned.

maugréer [mogree] ◆ *vt* to mutter. ◆ *vi* ~ (contre) to grumble (about).

Maurice [moris] → **île**.

mausolée [mozɔle] *nm* mausoleum.

maussade [mosad] *adj* 1. (*personne, air*) sullen. 2. (*temps*) gloomy.

mauvais, -e [movɛ, ɛz] *adj* 1. (*gén*) bad. 2. (*moment, numéro, réponse*) wrong. 3. (*mer*) rough. 4. (*personne, regard*) nasty. ► **mauvais** *adv*: il fait ~ the weather is bad; sentir ~ to smell bad.

mauve [mov] *nm & adj* mauve.

mauviette [movjɛt] *nf fam* 1. (*physiquement*) weakling. 2. (*moralement*) coward, wimp.

maux → **mal**.

max [maks] (*abr de* **maximum**) *nm fam*: un ~ de fric loads of money.

max. (*abr de* **maximum**) max.

maxillaire [maksilɛr] *nm* jawbone.

maximal, -e, -aux [maksimal, o] *adj* maximum; (*degré*) highest.

maxime [maksim] *nf* maxim.

maximum [maksimɔm] (*pl* maxima [maksima]) ◆ *nm* maximum; le ~ de personnes the greatest (possible) number of people; au ~ at the most. ◆ *adj* maximum.

maya [maja] *adj* Mayan. ► **Maya** *nmf*: les Mayas the Maya.

mayonnaise [majɔnɛz] *nf* mayonnaise.

mazout [mazut] *nm* fuel oil.

me [mə], **m'** (*devant voyelle ou* h *muet*) *pron pers* 1. (*complément d'objet direct*) me. 2. (*complément d'objet indirect*) (to) me. 3. (*réfléchi*) myself. 4. (*avec un présentatif*): ~ voici here I am.

méandre [meãdr] *nm* (*de rivière*) meander, bend. ▶ **méandres** *nmpl* (*détours sinueux*) meanderings (*pl*).

mec [mɛk] *nm fam* guy, bloke.

mécanicien, -enne [mekanisjɛ̃, ɛn] *nm, f* 1. (*de garage*) mechanic. 2. (*conducteur de train*) train driver Br, engineer Am.

mécanique [mekanik] ◆ *nf* 1. (TECHNOL) mechanical engineering. 2. (MATHS & PHYS) mechanics (U). 3. (*mécanisme*) mechanism. ◆ *adj* mechanical.

mécanisme [mekanism] *nm* mechanism.

mécène [mesɛn] *nm* patron.

méchamment [meʃamã] *adv* (*cruellement*) nastily.

méchanceté [meʃãste] *nf* 1. (*attitude*) nastiness. 2. *fam* (*rosserie*) nasty thing.

méchant, -e [meʃã, ãt] ◆ *adj* 1. (*malveillant, cruel*) nasty, wicked; (*animal*) vicious. 2. (*désobéissant*) naughty. ◆ *nm, f* (*en langage enfantin*) baddy.

mèche [mɛʃ] *nf* 1. (*de bougie*) wick. 2. (*de cheveux*) lock. 3. (*de bombe*) fuse.

méchoui [meʃwi] *nm* whole roast sheep.

méconnaissable [mekɔnɛsabl] *adj* unrecognizable.

méconnu, -e [mekɔny] *adj* unrecognized.

mécontent, -e [mekɔ̃tã, ãt] ◆ *adj* unhappy. ◆ *nm, f* malcontent.

mécontenter [mekɔ̃tãte] *vt* to displease.

Mecque [mɛk] *n*: **La ~** Mecca.

mécréant, -e [mekreã, ãt] *nm, f* nonbeliever.

médaille [medaj] *nf* 1. (*pièce, décoration*) medal. 2. (*bijou*) medallion. 3. (*de chien*) identification disc, tag.

médaillon [medajɔ̃] *nm* 1. (*bijou*) locket. 2. (ART & CULIN) medallion.

médecin [medsɛ̃] *nm* doctor; **~ conventionné** ≃ National Health doctor Br; **~ de famille** family doctor, GP Br; **~ de garde** doctor on duty, duty doctor; **~ généraliste** general practitioner, GP; **~ légiste** forensic scientist Br, medical examiner Am; **votre ~ traitant** your (usual) doctor.

médecine [medsin] *nf* medicine.

média [medja] *nm*: **les ~s** the (mass) media.

médian, -e [medjã, an] *adj* median. ▶ **médiane** *nf* median.

médiateur, -trice [medjatœr, tris] ◆ *adj* mediating (*avant n*). ◆ *nm, f* mediator; (*dans conflit de travail*) arbitrator.

▶ **médiateur** *nm* (ADMIN) ombudsman.
▶ **médiatrice** *nf* median.

médiathèque [medjatɛk] *nf* media library.

médiatique [medjatik] *adj* media (*avant n*).

médiatiser [medjatize] *vt péj* to turn into a media event.

médical, -e, -aux [medikal, o] *adj* medical.

médicament [medikamã] *nm* medicine, drug.

médicinal, -e, -aux [medisinal, o] *adj* medicinal.

médico-légal, -e, -aux [medikɔlegal, o] *adj* forensic.

médiéval, -e, -aux [medjeval, o] *adj* medieval.

médiocre [medjɔkr] *adj* mediocre.

médiocrité [medjɔkrite] *nf* mediocrity.

médire [medir] *vi* to gossip; **~ de qqn** to speak ill of sb.

médisant, -e [medizã, ãt] *adj* slanderous.

méditation [meditasjɔ̃] *nf* meditation.

méditer [medite] ◆ *vt* (*projeter*) to plan; **~ de faire qqch** to plan to do sthg. ◆ *vi*: **~ (sur)** to meditate (on).

Méditerranée [mediterane] *nf*: **la ~** the Mediterranean (Sea).

méditerranéen, -enne [mediteraneɛ̃, ɛn] *adj* Mediterranean. ▶ **Méditerranéen, -enne** *nm, f* person from the Mediterranean.

médium [medjɔm] *nm* (*personne*) medium.

médius [medjys] *nm* middle finger.

méduse [medyz] *nf* jellyfish.

méduser [medyze] *vt* to dumbfound.

meeting [mitiŋ] *nm* meeting.

méfait [mefɛ] *nm* misdemeanour, misdeed. ▶ **méfaits** *nmpl* (*du temps*) ravages.

méfiance [mefjãs] *nf* suspicion, distrust.

méfiant, -e [mefjã, ãt] *adj* suspicious, distrustful.

méfier [mefje] ▶ **se méfier** *vp* to be wary ou careful; **se ~ de qqn/qqch** to distrust sb/sthg.

mégalo [megalo] *nmf & adj fam* megalomaniac.

mégalomane [megalɔman] *nmf & adj* megalomaniac.

mégalomanie [megalɔmani] *nf* megalomania.

méga-octet [megaɔktɛ] *nm* megabyte.

ménagerie

mégapole [megapɔl] *nf* megalopolis, megacity.

mégarde [megard] ▶ **par mégarde** *loc adv* by mistake.

mégère [meʒɛr] *nf péj* shrew.

mégot [mego] *nm fam* fag-end Br, butt Am.

meilleur, -e [mɛjœr] ◆ *adj (compar)* better; *(superl)* best. ◆ *nm, f* best. ▶ **meilleur** ◆ *nm*: **le ~** the best. ◆ *adv* better.

mélancolie [melɑ̃kɔli] *nf* melancholy.

mélancolique [melɑ̃kɔlik] *adj* melancholy.

mélange [melɑ̃ʒ] *nm* **1.** *(action)* mixing. **2.** *(mixture)* mixture.

mélanger [melɑ̃ʒe] *vt* **1.** *(mettre ensemble)* to mix. **2.** *(déranger)* to mix up, to muddle up. ▶ **se mélanger** *vp* **1.** *(se mêler)* to mix. **2.** *(se brouiller)* to get mixed up.

mêlée [mele] *nf* **1.** *(combat)* fray. **2.** (RUGBY) scrum.

mêler [mele] *vt* **1.** *(mélanger)* to mix. **2.** *(déranger)* to muddle up, to mix up. **3.** *(impliquer)*: **~ qqn à qqch** to involve sb in sthg. ▶ **se mêler** *vp* **1.** *(se joindre)*: **se ~ à** *(groupe)* to join. **2.** *(s'ingérer)*: **se ~ de qqch** to get mixed up in sthg; **mêlez-vous de ce qui vous regarde!** mind your own business!

mélèze [melɛz] *nm* larch.

mélo [melo] *nm fam* melodrama.

mélodie [melɔdi] *nf* melody.

mélodieux, -euse [melɔdjø, øz] *adj* melodious, tuneful.

mélodrame [melɔdram] *nm* melodrama.

mélomane [melɔman] ◆ *nmf* music lover. ◆ *adj* music-loving.

melon [məlɔ̃] *nm* **1.** *(fruit)* melon. **2.** *(chapeau)* bowler (hat).

membrane [mɑ̃bran] *nf* membrane.

membre [mɑ̃br] ◆ *nm* **1.** *(du corps)* limb. **2.** *(personne, pays, partie)* member. ◆ *adj* member *(avant n)*.

mémé = **mémère**.

même [mɛm] ◆ *adj indéf* **1.** *(indique une identité ou une ressemblance)* same; **il a le ~ âge que moi** he's the same age as me. **2.** *(sert à souligner)*: **ce sont ses paroles ~s** those are his very words; **elle est la bonté ~** she's kindness itself. ◆ *pron indéf*: **le/la ~** the same one; **ce sont toujours les ~s qui gagnent** it's always the same people who win. ◆ *adv* even; **il n'est ~ pas diplômé** he isn't even qualified. ▶ **de même** *loc adv* similarly, like-wise; **il en va de ~ pour lui** the same goes for him. ▶ **de même que** *loc conj* just as. ▶ **tout de même** *loc adv* all the same. ▶ **à même** *loc prép*: **s'asseoir à ~ le sol** to sit on the bare ground. ▶ **à même de** *loc prép*: **être à ~ de faire qqch** to be able to do sthg, to be in a position to do sthg. ▶ **même si** *loc conj* even if.

mémento [memɛ̃to] *nm* **1.** *(agenda)* pocket diary. **2.** *(ouvrage)* notes *(title of school textbook)*.

mémère [memɛr], **mémé** [meme] *nf fam* **1.** *(grand-mère)* granny. **2.** *péj (vieille femme)* old biddy.

mémoire [memwar] ◆ *nf (gén &* INFORM*)* memory; **de ~** from memory; **avoir bonne/mauvaise ~** to have a good/bad memory; **mettre en ~** (INFORM) to store; **~ tampon** (INFORM) buffer; **~ vive** (INFORM) random access memory; **à la ~ de** in memory of. ◆ *nm* (UNIV) dissertation, paper. ▶ **mémoires** *nmpl* memoirs.

mémorable [memɔrabl] *adj* memorable.

mémorial, -aux [memɔrjal, o] *nm* *(monument)* memorial.

mémorisable [memɔrizabl] *adj* (INFORM) storable.

menaçant, -e [mənasɑ̃, ɑ̃t] *adj* threatening.

menace [mənas] *nf*: **~ (pour)** threat (to).

menacer [mənase] ◆ *vt* to threaten; **~ de faire qqch** to threaten to do sthg; **~ qqn de qqch** to threaten sb with sthg. ◆ *vi*: **la pluie menace** it looks like rain.

ménage [menaʒ] *nm* **1.** *(nettoyage)* housework (U); **faire le ~** to do the housework. **2.** *(couple)* couple. **3.** (ÉCON) household.

ménagement [menaʒmɑ̃] *nm* *(égards)* consideration; **sans ~** brutally.

ménager¹, -ère [menaʒe, ɛr] *adj* household *(avant n)*, domestic; **tâches ménagères** household tasks. ▶ **ménagère** *nf* **1.** *(femme)* housewife. **2.** *(de couverts)* canteen.

ménager² [menaʒe] *vt* **1.** *(bien traiter)* to treat gently. **2.** *(économiser - sucre, réserves)* to use sparingly; *(- argent, temps)* to use carefully; **~ ses forces** to conserve one's strength; **~ sa santé** to take care of one's health. **3** *(pratiquer - espace)* to make. ▶ **se ménager** *vp* to take care of o.s., to look after o.s.

ménagerie [menaʒri] *nf* menagerie.

mendiant, -e [mãdjã, ãt] *nm, f* beggar.

mendier [mãdje] ◆ *vt* (*argent*) to beg for. ◆ *vi* to beg.

mener [məne] ◆ *vt* 1. (*emmener*) to take. 2. (*diriger - débat, enquête*) to conduct; (- *affaires*) to manage, to run; ~ qqch à bonne fin ou à bien to see sthg through, to bring sthg to a successful conclusion. 3. (*être en tête de*) to lead. ◆ *vi* to lead.

meneur, -euse [mənœr, øz] *nm, f* (*chef*) ringleader; ~ d'hommes born leader.

menhir [menir] *nm* standing stone.

méningite [menēʒit] *nf* meningitis (U).

ménisque [menisk] *nm* meniscus.

ménopause [menɔpoz] *nf* menopause.

menotte [mənɔt] *nf* (*main*) little hand. ▶ **menottes** *nfpl* handcuffs; passer les ~s à qqn to handcuff sb.

mensonge [mãsɔ̃ʒ] *nm* (*propos*) lie.

mensonger, -ère [mãsɔ̃ʒe, ɛr] *adj* false.

menstruel, -elle [mãstryɛl] *adj* menstrual.

mensualiser [mãsɥalize] *vt* to pay monthly.

mensualité [mãsɥalite] *nf* 1. (*traite*) monthly instalment. 2. (*salaire*) (monthly) salary.

mensuel, -elle [mãsɥɛl] *adj* monthly. ▶ **mensuel** *nm* monthly (magazine).

mensuration [mãsyrasjɔ̃] *nf* measuring. ▶ **mensurations** *nfpl* measurements.

mental, -e, -aux [mãtal, o] *adj* mental.

mentalité [mãtalite] *nf* mentality.

menteur, -euse [mãtœr, øz] *nm, f* liar.

menthe [mãt] *nf* mint.

menti [mãti] *pp inv* → **mentir**.

mention [mãsjɔ̃] *nf* 1. (*citation*) mention. 2. (*note*) note; 'rayer la ~ inutile' 'delete as appropriate'. 3. (UNIV): avec ~ with distinction.

mentionner [mãsjɔne] *vt* to mention.

mentir [mãtir] *vi*: ~ (à) to lie (to).

menton [mãtɔ̃] *nm* chin.

menu, -e [məny] *adj* (*très petit*) tiny; (*mince*) thin. ▶ **menu** *nm* (*gén* & INFORM) menu; (*repas à prix fixe*) set menu; ~ gastronomique/touristique gourmet/tourist menu.

menuiserie [mənɥizri] *nf* 1. (*métier*) joinery, carpentry. 2. (*atelier*) joinery (workshop).

menuisier [mənɥizje] *nm* joiner, carpenter.

méprendre [meprãdr] ▶ **se méprendre** *vp littéraire*: se ~ sur to be mistaken about.

mépris, -e [mepri, iz] *pp* → **méprendre**. ▶ **mépris** *nm* 1. (*dédain*): ~ (pour) contempt (for), scorn (for). 2. (*indifférence*): ~ de disregard for. ▶ **au mépris de** *loc prép* regardless of.

méprisable [meprizabl] *adj* contemptible, despicable.

méprisant, -e [meprizã, ãt] *adj* contemptuous, scornful.

mépriser [meprize] *vt* to despise; (*danger, offre*) to scorn.

mer [mɛr] *nf* sea; en ~ at sea; prendre la ~ to put to sea; haute ou pleine ~ open sea; la ~ d'Irlande the Irish Sea; la ~ Morte the Dead Sea; la ~ Noire the Black Sea; la ~ du Nord the North Sea.

mercantile [mɛrkãtil] *adj péj* mercenary.

mercenaire [mɛrsənɛr] *nm & adj* mercenary.

mercerie [mɛrsəri] *nf* 1. (*articles*) haberdashery Br, notions (pl) Am. 2. (*boutique*) haberdasher's shop Br, notions store Am.

merci [mɛrsi] ◆ *interj* thank you!, thanks!; ~ beaucoup! thank you very much! ◆ *nm*: ~ (de ou pour) thank you (for); dire ~ à qqn to thank sb, to say thank you to sb. ◆ *nf* mercy; être à la ~ de to be at the mercy of.

mercier, -ère [mɛrsje, ɛr] *nm, f* haberdasher Br, notions dealer Am.

mercredi [mɛrkrədi] *nm* Wednesday; *voir aussi* **samedi**.

mercure [mɛrkyr] *nm* mercury.

merde [mɛrd] *tfam nf* shit.

mère [mɛr] *nf* mother; ~ de famille mother.

merguez [mɛrgɛz] *nf inv* North African spiced sausage.

méridien, -enne [meridjē, ɛn] *adj* (*ligne*) meridian. ▶ **méridien** *nm* meridian.

méridional, -e, -aux [meridjɔnal, o] *adj* southern; (*du sud de la France*) Southern (French).

meringue [mərēg] *nf* meringue.

merisier [mərizje] *nm* 1. (*arbre*) wild cherry (tree). 2. (*bois*) cherry.

mérite [merit] *nm* merit.

mériter [merite] *vt* 1. (*être digne de, encourir*) to deserve. 2. (*valoir*) to be worth, to merit.

merlan [mɛrlɑ̃] nm whiting.

merle [mɛrl] nm blackbird.

merveille [mɛrvɛj] nf marvel, wonder; **à ~** marvellously, wonderfully.

merveilleux, -euse [mɛrvɛjø, øz] adj 1. (remarquable, prodigieux) marvellous, wonderful. 2. (magique) magic, magical. ► **merveilleux** nm: **le ~** the supernatural.

mes → **mon.**

mésange [mezɑ̃ʒ] nf (ZOOL) tit.

mésaventure [mezavɑ̃tyr] nf misfortune.

mesdames → **madame.**

mesdemoiselles → **mademoiselle.**

mésentente [mezɑ̃tɑ̃t] nf disagreement.

mesquin, -e [mɛskɛ̃, in] adj mean, petty.

mesquinerie [mɛskinri] nf (étroitesse d'esprit) meanness, pettiness.

mess [mɛs] nm mess.

message [mesaʒ] nm message; **laisser un ~ à qqn** to leave a message for sb.

messager, -ère [mesaʒe, ɛr] nm, f messenger.

messagerie [mesaʒri] nf 1. (gén pl) (transport de marchandises) freight (U). 2. (INFORM): **~ électronique** electronic mail.

messe [mɛs] nf mass; **aller à la ~** to go to mass.

messie [mesi] nm Messiah; fig saviour.

messieurs → **monsieur.**

mesure [məzyr] nf 1. (disposition, acte) measure, step; **prendre des ~s** to take measures ou steps. 2. (évaluation, dimension) measurement; **prendre les ~s de qqn/qqch** to measure sb/sthg. 3. (étalon, récipient) measure. 4. (MUS) time, tempo. 5. (modération) moderation. 6. loc: **dans la ~ du possible** as far as possible; **être en ~ de** to be in a position to. ► **à la mesure de** loc prép worthy of. ► **à mesure que** loc conj as. ► **outre mesure** loc adv excessively. ► **sur mesure** loc adj custom-made; (costume) made-to-measure.

mesurer [məzyre] vt 1. (gén) to measure; **elle mesure 1,50 m** she's 5 feet tall; **la table mesure 1,50 m** the table is 5 feet long. 2. (risques, portée, ampleur) to weigh up; **~ ses paroles** to weigh one's words. ► **se mesurer** vp: **se ~ avec** ou **à qqn** to pit o.s. against sb.

métabolisme [metabɔlism] nm metabolism.

métal, -aux [metal, o] nm metal.

métallique [metalik] adj 1. (en métal) metal (avant n). 2. (éclat, son) metallic.

métallurgie [metalyrʒi] nf (industrie) metallurgical industry.

métamorphose [metamɔrfoz] nf metamorphosis.

métaphore [metafɔr] nf metaphor.

métaphysique [metafizik] ◆ nf metaphysics (U). ◆ adj metaphysical.

métayer, -ère [meteje, metɛjɛr] nm, f tenant farmer.

météo [meteo] nf 1. (bulletin) weather forecast. 2. (service) ≃ Met Office Br, ≃ National Weather Service Am.

météore [meteɔr] nm meteor.

météorite [meteɔrit] nm ou nf meteorite.

météorologie [meteɔrɔlɔʒi] nf (SCIENCE) meteorology.

météorologique [meteɔrɔlɔʒik] adj meteorological, weather (avant n).

méthane [metan] nm methane.

méthode [metɔd] nf 1. (gén) method. 2. (ouvrage - gén) manual; (- de lecture, de langue) primer.

méthodologie [metɔdɔlɔʒi] nf methodology.

méticuleux, -euse [metikylø, øz] adj meticulous.

métier [metje] nm (profession - manuelle) occupation, trade; (- intellectuelle) occupation, profession; **avoir du ~** to have experience.

métis, -isse [metis] nm, f half-caste, half-breed. ► **métis** nm (tissu) cottonlinen mix.

métrage [metraʒ] nm 1. (mesure) measurement, measuring. 2. (COUTURE - coupon) length. 3. (CIN) footage; **long ~** feature film; **court ~** short (film).

mètre [mɛtr] nm 1. (LITTÉRATURE & MATHS) metre; **~ carré/cube** square/cubic metre. 2. (instrument) rule.

métro [metro] nm underground Br, subway Am.

MÉTRO

The Paris 'métro' was built in 1900 and consists of fifteen lines serving the whole of the city with trains running between 5.30 am and 1.00 am. The entrances to 'métro' stations are known as 'bouches de métro' and some of the older ones feature ornate art nouveau wrought-iron railings and the sign 'Métropolitain'.

métronome [metronom] *nm* metronome.

métropole [metropol] *nf* 1. (*ville*) metropolis. 2. (*pays*) home country.

métropolitain, -e [metropolitɛ̃, ɛn] *adj* metropolitan; **la France ~e** metropolitan ou mainland France.

mets [mɛ] *nm* (CULIN) dish.

metteur [metœr] *nm*: **~ en scène** (THÉÂTRE) producer; (CIN) director.

mettre [mɛtr] *vt* 1. (*placer*) to put; **~ de l'eau à bouillir** to put some water on to boil. 2. (*revêtir*) to put on; **mets ta robe noire** put your black dress on; **je ne mets plus ma robe noire** I don't wear my black dress any more. 3. (*consacrer - temps*) to take; (*- argent*) to spend; **~ longtemps à faire qqch** to take a long time to do sthg. 4. (*allumer - radio, chauffage*) to put on, to switch on. 5. (*installer*) to put in; **faire ~ l'électricité** to have electricity put in; **faire ~ de la moquette** to have a carpet put down ou fitted. 6. (*inscrire*) to put (down). ▶ **se mettre** *vp* 1. (*se placer*): **où est-ce que ça se met?** where does this go?; **se ~ au lit** to get into bed; **se ~ à côté de qqn** to sit/ stand near to sb. 2. (*devenir*): **se ~ en colère** to get angry. 3. (*commencer*): **se ~ à qqch/à faire qqch** to start sthg/doing sthg. 4. (*revêtir*) to put on; **je n'ai rien à me ~** I haven't got a thing to wear.

meuble [mœbl] ◆ *nm* piece of furniture; **~s** furniture (U). ◆ *adj* 1. (*terre, sol*) easily worked. 2. (JUR) movable.

meublé, -e [mœble] *adj* furnished. ▶ **meublé** *nm* furnished room/flat Br, furnished apartment Am.

meubler [mœble] *vt* 1. (*pièce, maison*) to furnish. 2. *fig* (*occuper*): **~ qqch (de)** to fill sthg (with). ▶ **se meubler** *vp* to furnish one's home.

meugler [møgle] *vi* to moo.

meule [møl] *nf* 1. (*à moudre*) millstone. 2. (*à aiguiser*) grindstone. 3. (*de fromage*) round. 4. (AGRIC) stack; **~ de foin** haystack.

meunier, -ère [mønje, ɛr] *nm, f* miller (*f* miller's wife).

meurtre [mœrtr] *nm* murder.

meurtrier, -ère [mœrtrije, ɛr] ◆ *adj* (*épidémie, arme*) deadly; (*fureur*) murderous; (*combat*) bloody. ◆ *nm, f* murderer.

meurtrir [mœrtrir] *vt* 1. (*contusionner*) to bruise. 2. *fig* (*blesser*) to wound.

meurtrissure [mœrtrisyr] *nf* (*marque*) bruise.

meute [møt] *nf* pack.

mexicain, -e [mɛksikɛ̃, ɛn] *adj* Mexican. ▶ **Mexicain, -e** *nm, f* Mexican.

Mexique [mɛksik] *nm*: **le ~** Mexico.

mezzanine [mɛdzanin] *nf* mezzanine.

mezzo-soprano [mɛdzosoprano] (*pl* **mezzo-sopranos**) *nm* mezzo-soprano.

mi [mi] *nm inv* E; (*chanté*) mi.

mi- [mi] ◆ *adj inv* half; **à la ~juin** in mid-June. ◆ *adv* half-.

miasme [mjasm] *nm* (*gén pl*) putrid ou foul smell.

miaulement [mjolmã] *nm* miaowing.

miauler [mjole] *vi* to miaow.

mi-bas [miba] *nm inv* knee-sock.

mi-carême [mikarɛm] *nf* feast day on third Thursday in Lent.

mi-chemin [miʃmɛ̃] ▶ **à mi-chemin** *loc adv* halfway (there).

mi-clos, -e [miklo, oz] *adj* half-closed.

micro [mikro] ◆ *nm* 1. (*microphone*) mike. 2. (*micro-ordinateur*) micro. ◆ *nf* microcomputing.

microbe [mikrob] *nm* 1. (MÉD) microbe, germ. 2. *péj* (*avorton*) (little) runt.

microclimat [mikroklima] *nm* microclimate.

microcosme [mikrokɔsm] *nm* microcosm.

microfiche [mikrofiʃ] *nf* microfiche.

microfilm [mikrofilm] *nm* microfilm.

micro-ondes [mikroɔ̃d] *nfpl* microwaves; **four à ~** microwave (oven).

micro-ordinateur [mikroɔrdinatœr] (*pl* **micro-ordinateurs**) *nm* micro, microcomputer.

microphone [mikrofɔn] *nm* microphone.

microprocesseur [mikroprosesœr] *nm* microprocessor.

microscope [mikroskɔp] *nm* microscope.

midi [midi] *nm* 1. (*période du déjeuner*) lunchtime. 2. (*heure*) midday, noon. 3. (*sud*) south. ▶ **Midi** *nm*: **le Midi** the South of France.

mie [mi] *nf* (*de pain*) soft part, inside.

miel [mjɛl] *nm* honey.

mielleux, -euse [mjɛlø, øz] *adj* (*personne*) unctuous; (*paroles, air*) honeyed.

mien [mjɛ̃] ▶ **le mien** (*f* **la mienne** [lamjɛn], *mpl* **les miens** [lemjɛ̃], *fpl* **les miennes** [lemjɛn]) *pron poss* mine.

miette [mjɛt] *nf* 1. (*de pain*) crumb, breadcrumb. 2. (*gén pl*) (*débris*) shreds (*pl*).

mieux [mjø] ◆ *adv* 1. (*comparatif*): **~ (que)** better (than); **il pourrait ~ faire** he could do better; **il va ~** he's better; **faire ~ de faire qqch** to do better to do sthg; **vous feriez ~ de vous taire** you would do better to keep quiet, you would be well-advised to keep quiet. **2.** (*superlatif*) best; **il est le ~ payé du service** he's the best ou highest paid member of the department; **le ~ qu'il peut** as best he can. ◆ *adj* better. ◆ *nm* **1.** (*sans déterminant*): **j'espérais ~** I was hoping for something better. **2.** (*avec déterminant*) best; **il y a un ou du ~** there's been an improvement; **faire de son ~** to do one's best. ▶ **au mieux** *loc adv* at best. ▶ **pour le mieux** *loc adv* for the best. ▶ **de mieux en mieux** *loc adv* better and better.

mièvre [mjɛvr] *adj* insipid.

mignon, -onne [miɲõ, ɔn] ◆ *adj* **1.** (*charmant*) sweet, cute. **2.** (*gentil*) nice. ◆ *nm, f* darling, sweetheart.

migraine [migrɛn] *nf* headache; (MÉD) migraine.

migrant, -e [migrã, ãt] *nm, f* migrant.

migrateur, -trice [migratœr, tris] *adj* migratory.

migration [migrasjõ] *nf* migration.

mijoter [miʒɔte] ◆ *vt fam* (*tramer*) to cook up. ◆ *vi* (CULIN) to simmer.

mi-journée [miʒurne] *nf*: **les informations de la ~** the lunchtime news.

mil [mij] *nm* millet.

milan [milã] *nm* kite (*bird*).

milice [milis] *nf* militia.

milicien, -enne [milisjɛ̃, ɛn] *nm, f* militiaman (*f* militiawoman).

milieu, -x [miljø] *nm* **1.** (*centre*) middle; **au ~ de** (*au centre de*) in the middle of; (*parmi*) among, surrounded by. **2.** (*stade intermédiaire*) middle course. **3.** (BIOL & SOCIOL) environment; ~ **familial** family background. **4.** (*pègre*): **le ~** the underworld. **5.** (FOOTBALL): ~ **de terrain** midfielder, midfield player.

militaire [militɛr] ◆ *nm* soldier; ~ **de carrière** professional soldier. ◆ *adj* military.

militant, -e [militã, ãt] *adj & nm, f* militant.

militer [milite] *vi* to be active; ~ **pour/contre** to militate in favour of/against.

mille [mil] ◆ *nm inv* **1.** (*unité*) a ou one thousand. **2.** (*de cible*): **dans le ~** on target. **3.** (NAVIG): ~ **marin** nautical mile. **4.** (*distance*) mile. ◆ *adj inv* thousand; **c'est ~ fois trop** it's far too much; **je lui ai dit ~ fois** I've told him/her a thousand times; *voir aussi* **six**.

mille-feuille [milfœj] (*pl* **mille-feuilles**) *nm* = vanilla slice Br, = napoleon Am.

millénaire [milenɛr] ◆ *nm* millennium, thousand years (*pl*). ◆ *adj* thousand-year-old (*avant n*).

mille-pattes [milpat] *nm inv* centipede, millipede.

millésime [milezim] *nm* **1.** (*de pièce*) date. **2.** (*de vin*) vintage, year.

millésimé, -e [milezime] *adj* (*vin*) vintage (*avant n*).

millet [mijɛ] *nm* millet.

milliard [miljar] *nm* thousand million Br, billion Am; **par ~s** *fig* in (their) millions.

milliardaire [miljardɛr] *nmf* multimillionaire Br, billionaire Am.

millier [milje] *nm* thousand; **un ~ de francs/personnes** about a thousand francs/people; **par ~s** in (their) thousands.

milligramme [miligram] *nm* milligram, milligramme.

millilitre [mililitr] *nm* millilitre.

millimètre [milimɛtr] *nm* millimetre.

million [miljõ] *nm* million; **un ~ de francs** a million francs.

millionnaire [miljɔnɛr] *nmf* millionaire.

mime [mim] *nm* mime.

mimer [mime] *vt* **1.** (*exprimer sans parler*) to mime. **2.** (*imiter*) to mimic.

mimétisme [mimetism] *nm* mimicry.

mimique [mimik] *nf* **1.** (*grimace*) face. **2.** (*geste*) sign language (U).

mimosa [mimoza] *nm* mimosa.

min. (*abr de* minimum) min.

minable [minabl] *adj fam* **1.** (*misérable*) seedy, shabby. **2.** (*médiocre*) pathetic.

minaret [minarɛ] *nm* minaret.

minauder [minode] *vi* to simper.

mince [mɛ̃s] *adj* **1.** (*maigre - gén*) thin; (- *personne, taille*) slender, slim. **2.** *fig* (*faible*) small, meagre.

minceur [mɛ̃sœr] *nf* **1.** (*gén*) thinness; (*de personne*) slenderness, slimness. **2.** *fig* (*insuffisance*) meagreness.

mincir [mɛ̃sir] *vi* to get thinner ou slimmer.

mine [min] *nf* **1.** (*expression*) look; **avoir bonne/mauvaise ~** to look well/ill. **2.** (*apparence*) appearance. **3.** (*gisement &* *fig*) mine; (*exploitation*) mining; ~ **de charbon** coalmine. **4.** (*explosif*) mine. **5.** (*de crayon*) lead.

miner [mine] *vt* **1.** (MIL) to mine. **2.** (*ronger*) to undermine, to wear away; *fig* to wear down.

minerai [minrɛ] nm ore.
minéral, -e, -aux [mineral, o] adj
1. (CHIM) inorganic. 2. (eau, source) mineral (avant n). ▶ **minéral** nm mineral.
minéralogie [mineralɔʒi] nf mineralogy.
minéralogique [mineralɔʒik] adj
1. (AUTOM): **plaque ~** numberplate Br, license plate Am. 2. (GÉOL) mineralogical.
minet, -ette [minɛ, ɛt] nm, f fam
1. (chat) pussycat, pussy. 2. (personne) trendy.
mineur, -e [minœr] ◆ adj minor.
◆ nm, f (JUR) minor. ▶ **mineur** nm (ouvrier) miner; **~ de fond** face worker.
miniature [minjatyr] ◆ nf miniature.
◆ adj miniature.
miniaturiser [minjatyrize] vt to miniaturize.
minibus [minibys] nm minibus.
minichaîne [miniʃɛn] nf portable hi-fi.
minier, -ère [minje, ɛr] adj mining (avant n).
minijupe [miniʒyp] nf miniskirt.
minimal, -e, -aux [minimal, o] adj minimum.
minimalisme [minimalism] nm minimalism.
minime [minim] ◆ nmf (SPORT) = junior. ◆ adj minimal.
minimiser [minimize] vt to minimize.
minimum [minimɔm] (pl minimums ou **minima** [minima]) ◆ nm (gén & MATHS) minimum; **au ~** at least; **le strict ~** the bare minimum. ◆ adj minimum.
ministère [ministɛr] nm 1. (département) ministry Br, department. 2. (cabinet) government. 3. (RELIG) ministry.
ministériel, -elle [ministerjɛl] adj (du ministère) departmental, ministerial Br.
ministre [ministr] nm secretary, minister Br; **~ d'État** secretary of state, cabinet minister Br; **premier ~** prime minister.
Minitel® [minitɛl] nm teletext system run by the French national telephone company, providing an information and communication network.

MINITEL®

A French national information network, Minitel® is also the name of the computer hardware used to access this network. The services available are both informative (information on weather and road conditions, an electronic telephone directory etc) and interactive (allowing users to correspond by e-mail or, for example, to buy train or concert tickets). To access these services, the user dials a four-figure code (3614, 3615 etc) and then keys in the relevant codeword for the service they require.

minois [minwa] nm sweet (little) face.
minoritaire [minɔritɛr] adj minority (avant n); **être ~** to be in the minority.
minorité [minɔrite] nf minority; **en ~** in the minority.
minuit [minɥi] nm midnight.
minuscule [minyskyl] ◆ nf (lettre) small letter. ◆ adj 1. (lettre) small. 2. (très petit) tiny, minuscule.
minute [minyt] ◆ nf minute; **dans une ~** in a minute; **d'une ~ à l'autre** in next to no time. ◆ interj fam hang on (a minute)!
minuter [minyte] vt (chronométrer) to time (precisely).
minuterie [minytri] nf (d'éclairage) time switch, timer.
minuteur [minytœr] nm timer.
minutie [minysi] nf (soin) meticulousness; (précision) attention to detail; **avec ~** (avec soin) meticulously; (dans le détail) in minute detail.
minutieux, -euse [minysjø, øz] adj (méticuleux) meticulous; (détaillé) minutely detailed; **un travail ~** a job requiring great attention to detail.
mioche [mjɔʃ] nmf fam kiddy.
mirabelle [mirabɛl] nf 1. (fruit) mirabelle (plum). 2. (alcool) plum brandy.
miracle [mirakl] nm miracle; **par ~** by some ou a miracle, miraculously.
miraculeux, -euse [mirakylø, øz] adj miraculous.
mirador [miradɔr] nm (MIL) watchtower.
mirage [miraʒ] nm mirage.
mire [mir] nf 1. (TÉLÉ) test card. 2. (visée): **ligne de ~** line of sight.
mirifique [mirifik] adj fabulous.
mirobolant, -e [mirɔbɔlã, ãt] adj fabulous, fantastic.
miroir [mirwar] nm mirror.
miroiter [mirwate] vi to sparkle, to gleam; **faire ~ qqch à qqn** to hold out the prospect of sthg to sb.
mis, mise [mi, miz] pp → **mettre**.
misanthrope [mizãtrɔp] ◆ nmf misanthropist, misanthrope. ◆ adj misanthropic.
mise [miz] nf 1. (action) putting; **~ à jour** updating; **~ en page** making up, com-

posing; **~ au point** (PHOT) focusing; (TECHNOL.) adjustment; *fig* clarification; **~ en scène** production. **2.** (*d'argent*) stake. **3.** (*tenue*) appearance.

miser [mize] ◆ *vt* to bet. ◆ *vi*: **~ sur** to bet on; *fig* to count on.

misérable [mizerabl] *adj* **1.** (*pauvre*) poor, wretched. **2.** (*sans valeur*) paltry, miserable.

misère [mizɛr] *nf* **1.** (*indigence*) poverty. **2.** (*infortune*) misery. **3.** *fig* (*bagatelle*) trifle.

miséricorde [mizerikɔrd] *nf* (*clémence*) mercy.

misogyne [mizɔʒin] *adj* misogynous.

misogynie [mizɔʒini] *nf* misogyny.

missel [misɛl] *nm* missal.

missile [misil] *nm* missile.

mission [misjɔ̃] *nf* mission; **en ~** on a mission.

missionnaire [misjɔnɛr] *nmf* missionary.

missive [misiv] *nf* letter.

mistral [mistral] *nm* strong cold wind that blows down the Rhône Valley and through southern France.

mitaine [mitɛn] *nf* fingerless glove.

mite [mit] *nf* (*clothes*) moth.

mité, -e [mite] *adj* moth-eaten.

mi-temps [mitɑ̃] ◆ *nf inv* (SPORT - *période*) half; (- *pause*) half-time. ◆ *nm* part-time work. ▶ **à mi-temps** *loc adj & loc adv* part-time.

miteux, -euse [mitø, øz] *fam adj* seedy, dingy.

mitigé, -e [mitiʒe] *adj* **1.** (*tempéré*) lukewarm. **2.** *fam* (*mélangé*) mixed.

mitonner [mitɔne] ◆ *vt* **1.** (*faire cuire*) to simmer. **2.** (*préparer avec soin*) to prepare lovingly. ◆ *vi* (CULIN) to simmer.

mitoyen, -enne [mitwajɛ̃, ɛn] *adj* (*commun*) common; (*attenant*) adjoining; **mur ~** party wall.

mitrailler [mitraje] *vt* **1.** (MIL) to machinegun. **2.** *fam* (*photographier*) to click away at. **3.** *fig* (*assaillir*): **~ qqn (de)** to bombard sb (with).

mitraillette [mitrajɛt] *nf* submachine gun.

mitrailleuse [mitrajøz] *nf* machinegun.

mitre [mitr] *nf* (*d'évêque*) mitre.

mi-voix [mivwa] ▶ **à mi-voix** *loc adv* in a low voice.

mixage [miksaʒ] *nm* (CIN & RADIO) (sound) mixing.

mixer¹, mixeur [miksœr] *nm* (food) mixer.

mixer² [mikse] *vt* to mix.

mixte [mikst] *adj* mixed.

mixture [mikstyr] *nf* **1.** (CHIM & CULIN) mixture. **2.** *péj* (*mélange*) concoction.

MJC (*abr de* **maison des jeunes et de la culture**) *nf* youth and cultural centre.

ml (*abr de* **millilitre**) ml.

Mlle (*abr de* **Mademoiselle**) Miss.

mm (*abr de* **millimètre**) mm.

MM (*abr de* **Messieurs**) Messrs.

Mme (*abr de* **Madame**) Mrs.

mnémotechnique [mnemɔtɛknik] *adj* mnemonic.

Mo (*abr de* **méga-octet**) MB.

mobile [mɔbil] ◆ *nm* **1.** (*objet*) mobile. **2.** (*motivation*) motive. ◆ *adj* **1.** (*gén*) movable, mobile; (*partie, pièce*) moving. **2.** (*population, main-d'œuvre*) mobile.

mobilier, -ère [mɔbilje, ɛr] *adj* (JUR) movable. ▶ **mobilier** *nm* furniture.

mobilisation [mɔbilizasjɔ̃] *nf* mobilization.

mobiliser [mɔbilize] *vt* **1.** (*gén*) to mobilize. **2.** (*moralement*) to rally. ▶ **se mobiliser** *vp* to mobilize, to rally.

mobilité [mɔbilite] *nf* mobility.

Mobylette® [mɔbilɛt] *nf* moped.

mocassin [mɔkasɛ̃] *nm* moccasin.

moche [mɔʃ] *adj fam* **1.** (*laid*) ugly. **2.** (*triste, méprisable*) lousy, rotten.

modalité [mɔdalite] *nf* (*convention*) form; **~s de paiement** methods of payment.

mode [mɔd] ◆ *nf* **1.** (*gén*) fashion; **à la ~** in fashion, fashionable. **2.** (*coutume*) custom, style; **à la ~ de** in the style of. ◆ *nm* **1.** (*manière*) mode, form; **~ de vie** way of life. **2.** (*méthode*) method; **~ d'emploi** instructions (for use). **3.** (GRAM) mood. **4.** (MUS) mode.

modèle [mɔdɛl] *nm* **1.** (*gén*) model; **sur le ~ de** on the model of; **~ déposé** patented design. **2.** (*en apposition*) (*exemplaire*) model (*avant n*).

modeler [mɔdle] *vt* to shape; **~ qqch sur qqch** *fig* to model sthg on sthg.

modélisme [mɔdelism] *nm* modelling (*of scale models*).

modération [mɔderasjɔ̃] *nf* moderation.

modéré, -e [mɔdere] *adj & nm, f* moderate.

modérer [mɔdere] *vt* to moderate. ▶ **se modérer** *vp* to restrain o.s., to control o.s.

moderne [mɔdɛrn] *adj* modern; (*mathématiques*) new.

moderniser [mɔdɛrnize] *vt* to modernize. ▶ **se moderniser** *vp* to become (more) modern.

modeste [mɔdɛst] *adj* modest; (*origine*) humble.

modestie [mɔdɛsti] *nf* modesty; **fausse ~** false modesty.

modification [mɔdifikasjɔ̃] *nf* alteration, modification.

modifier [mɔdifje] *vt* to alter, to modify. ▶ **se modifier** *vp* to alter.

modique [mɔdik] *adj* modest.

modiste [mɔdist] *nf* milliner.

modulation [mɔdylasjɔ̃] *nf* modulation.

module [mɔdyl] *nm* module.

moduler [mɔdyle] *vt* **1.** (*air*) to warble. **2.** (*structure*) to adjust.

moelle [mwal] *nf* (ANAT) marrow. ▶ **moelle épinière** *nf* spinal cord.

moelleux, -euse [mwalø, øz] *adj* **1.** (*canapé, tapis*) soft. **2.** (*fromage, vin*) mellow.

moellon [mwalɔ̃] *nm* rubble stone.

mœurs [mœr(s)] *nfpl* **1.** (*morale*) morals. **2.** (*coutumes*) customs, habits. **3.** (ZOOL) behaviour (U).

mohair [mɔɛr] *nm* mohair.

moi [mwa] ◆ *pron pers* **1.** (*objet, après préposition, comparatif*) me; **aide-~** help me; **il me l'a dit, à ~** he told ME; **plus âgé que ~** older than me ou than I (am). **2.** (*sujet*) I; **~ non plus, je n'en sais rien** I don't know anything about it either; **qui est là? - (c'est)** who's there? – it's me; **je l'ai vu hier - ~ aussi** I saw him yesterday – me too; **c'est ~ qui lui ai dit de venir** I was the one who told him to come. ▶ **moi-même** *pron pers* myself.

moignon [mwaɲɔ̃] *nm* stump.

moindre [mwɛ̃dr] ◆ *adj superl*: **le/la ~** the least; (*avec négation*) the least ou slightest; **les ~s détails** the smallest details; **sans la ~ difficulté** without the slightest problem; **c'est la ~ des choses** it's the least I/you *etc* could do. ◆ *adj compar* less; (*prix*) lower; **à un ~ degré** to a lesser extent.

moine [mwan] *nm* monk.

moineau, -x [mwano] *nm* sparrow.

moins [mwɛ̃] ◆ *adv* **1.** (*quantité*) less; **~ de** less (than); **~ de lait** less milk; **~ de gens** fewer people; **~ de dix** less than ten; **il est un peu ~ de 10 heures** it's nearly 10 o'clock. **2.** (*comparatif*): **~ (que)** less (than); **il est ~ vieux que ton frère** he's not as old as your brother, he's younger than your brother; **bien ~ grand que** much smaller than; **~ il**

mange, **~ il travaille** the less he eats, the less he works; **ce n'en est pas ~ difficile** it is still difficult. **3.** (*superlatif*): **le ~** (the) least; **le ~ riche des hommes** the poorest man; **c'est lui qui travaille le ~** he works (the) least; **le ~ possible** as little as possible. ◆ *prép* **1.** (*gén*) minus; **dix ~ huit font deux** ten minus eight is two, ten take away eight is two; **il fait ~ vingt** it's twenty below, it's minus twenty. **2.** (*servant à indiquer l'heure*): **il est 3 heures ~ le quart** it's quarter to 3; **il est ~ dix** it's ten to. ◆ *nm* **1.** (*signe*) minus (sign). **2.** *loc*: **le ~ qu'on puisse dire, c'est que ...** it's an understatement to say ... ▶ **à moins de** *loc prép*: **à ~ de battre le record** unless I/you *etc* beat the record. ▶ **à moins que** *loc conj* (+ *subjonctif*) unless. ▶ **au moins** *loc adv* at least. ▶ **de moins en moins** *loc adv* less and less. ▶ **du moins** *loc adv* at least. ▶ **en moins** *loc adv*: **il a une dent en ~** he's missing ou minus a tooth; **c'était le paradis, les anges en ~** it was heaven, minus the angels. ▶ **pour le moins** *loc adv* at (the very) least. ▶ **tout au moins** *loc adv* at (the very) least.

moiré, -e [mware] *adj* **1.** (*tissu*) watered. **2.** *littéraire* (*reflet*) shimmering.

mois [mwa] *nm* (*laps de temps*) month.

moisi, -e [mwazi] *adj* mouldy. ▶ **moisi** *nm* mould.

moisir [mwazir] *vi* **1.** (*pourrir*) to go mouldy. **2.** *fig* (*personne*) to rot.

moisissure [mwazisyr] *nf* mould.

moisson [mwasɔ̃] *nf* **1.** (*récolte*) harvest; **faire la ~** ou **les ~s** to harvest, to bring in the harvest. **2.** *fig* (*d'idées, de projets*) wealth.

moissonner [mwasɔne] *vt* to harvest, to gather (in); *fig* to collect, to gather.

moissonneuse-batteuse [mwasɔnøzbatøz] *nf* combine (harvester).

moite [mwat] *adj* (*peau, mains*) moist, sweaty; (*atmosphère*) muggy.

moiteur [mwatœr] *nf* (*de peau, mains*) moistness; (*d'atmosphère*) mugginess.

moitié [mwatje] *nf* (*gén*) half; **à ~ vide** half-empty; **faire qqch à ~** to half-do sthg; **la ~ du temps** half the time; **à la ~ de qqch** halfway through sthg.

moka [mɔka] *nm* **1.** (*café*) mocha (coffee). **2.** (*gâteau*) coffee cake.

mol → **mou**.

molaire [mɔlɛr] *nf* molar.

molécule [mɔlekyl] *nf* molecule.

molester [mɔlɛste] *vt* to manhandle.

molle → **mou**.

mollement [mɔlmã] *adv* 1. (*faiblement*) weakly, feebly. 2. *littéraire* (*paresseusement*) sluggishly, lethargically.

mollesse [mɔlɛs] *nf* 1. (*de chose*) softness. 2. (*de personne*) lethargy.

mollet [mɔlɛ] ◆ *nm* calf. ◆ *adj* → **œuf**.

mollir [mɔlir] *vi* 1. (*physiquement, moralement*) to give way. 2. (*vent*) to drop, to die down.

mollusque [mɔlysk] *nm* (ZOOL) mollusc.

molosse [mɔlɔs] *nm* 1. (*chien*) large ferocious dog. 2. *fig & péj* (*personne*) hulking great brute ou fellow.

môme [mom] *fam nmf* (*enfant*) kid, youngster.

moment [mɔmã] *nm* 1. (*gén*) moment; **au ~ de l'accident** at the time of the accident, when the accident happened; **au ~ de partir** just as we/you *etc* were leaving; **au ~ où** just as; **dans un ~** in a moment; **d'un ~ à l'autre, à tout ~** (at) any moment, any moment now; **à un ~ donné** at a given moment; **par ~s** at times, now and then; **en ce ~** at the moment; **pour le ~** for the moment. 2. (*durée*) (short) time; **passer un mauvais ~** to have a bad time. 3. (*occasion*) time; **ce n'est pas le ~ (de faire qqch)** this is not the time (to do sthg). ▶ **du moment que** *loc prép* since, as.

momentané, -e [mɔmãtane] *adj* temporary.

momie [mɔmi] *nf* mummy.

mon [mɔ̃] (*f* **ma** [ma], *pl* **mes** [me]) *adj poss* my.

monacal, -e, -aux [mɔnakal, o] *adj* monastic.

Monaco [mɔnako] *n*: **(la principauté de) ~** (the principality of) Monaco.

monarchie [mɔnarʃi] *nf* monarchy; **~ absolue/constitutionnelle** absolute/constitutional monarchy.

monarque [mɔnark] *nm* monarch.

monastère [mɔnastɛr] *nm* monastery.

monceau, -x [mɔ̃so] *nm* (*tas*) heap.

mondain, -e [mɔ̃dɛ̃, ɛn] *adj* 1. (*chronique, journaliste*) society (*avant n*). 2. *péj* (*futile*) frivolous, superficial.

mondanités [mɔ̃danite] *nfpl* 1. (*événements*) society life (U). 2. (*paroles*) small talk (U); (*comportements*) formalities.

monde [mɔ̃d] *nm* 1. (*gén*) world; **le/la plus ..., au ~, le/la plus ... du ~** the most ... in the world; **pour rien au ~** not for the world, not for all the tea in China; **mettre un enfant au ~** to bring a child into the world. 2. (*gens*) people (*pl*);

beaucoup/peu de ~ a lot of/not many people; **tout le ~** everyone, everybody. 3. *loc*: **c'est une ~!** that's really the limit!; **se faire un ~ de qqch** to make too much of sthg; **noir de ~** packed with people.

mondial, -e, -aux [mɔ̃djal, o] *adj* world (*avant n*).

mondialement [mɔ̃djalmã] *adv* throughout ou all over the world.

mondialisation [mɔ̃djalizasjɔ̃] *nf* globalization.

monétaire [mɔnetɛr] *adj* monetary.

Mongolie [mɔ̃gɔli] *nf*: **la ~** Mongolia.

mongolien, -enne [mɔ̃gɔljɛ̃, ɛn] *vieilli nm, f* Mongol.

moniteur, -trice [mɔnitœr, tris] *nm, f* 1. (*enseignant*) instructor, coach; **~ d'auto-école** driving instructor. 2. (*de colonie de vacances*) supervisor, leader. ▶ **moniteur** *nm* (*appareil &* INFORM) monitor.

monnaie [mɔnɛ] *nf* 1. (*moyen de paiement*) money. 2. (*de pays*) currency. 3. (*pièces*) change; **avoir de la ~** to have change; **avoir la ~** to have the change; **faire (de) la ~** to get (some) change.

monnayer [mɔnɛje] *vt* 1. (*biens*) to convert into cash. 2. *fig* (*silence*) to buy.

monochrome [mɔnɔkrom] *adj* monochrome, monochromatic.

monocle [mɔnɔkl] *nm* monocle.

monocoque [mɔnɔkɔk] *nm & adj* (*bateau*) monohull.

monocorde [mɔnɔkɔrd] *adj* (*monotone*) monotonous.

monogramme [mɔnɔgram] *nm* monogram.

monolingue [mɔnɔlɛ̃g] *adj* monolingual.

monologue [mɔnɔlɔg] *nm* 1. (THÉÂTRE) soliloquy. 2. (*discours individuel*) monologue.

monologuer [mɔnɔlɔge] *vi* 1. (THÉÂTRE) to soliloquize. 2. *fig & péj* (*parler*) to talk away.

monoparental, -e, -aux [mɔnɔparãtal, o] *adj* single-parent (*avant n*).

monoplace [mɔnɔplas] *adj* single-seater (*avant n*).

monoplan [mɔnɔplã] *nm* monoplane.

monopole [mɔnɔpɔl] *nm* monopoly; **avoir le ~ de qqch** *litt & fig* to have a monopoly of ou on sthg; **~ d'État** state monopoly.

monopoliser [mɔnɔpɔlize] *vt* to monopolize.

monoski [mɔnɔski] *nm* 1. (*objet*) monoski. 2. (SPORT) monoskiing.

monosyllabe [mɔnɔsilab] ◆ *nm* monosyllable. ◆ *adj* monosyllabic.

monotone [mɔnɔtɔn] *adj* monotonous.

monotonie [mɔnɔtɔni] *nf* monotony.

monseigneur [mɔ̃sɛɲœr] (*pl* **messeigneurs** [mesɛɲœr]) *nm* (*titre - d'évêque, de duc*) His Grace; (*- de cardinal*) His Eminence; (*- de prince*) His (Royal) Highness.

monsieur [məsjø] (*pl* **messieurs** [mesjø]) *nm* **1.** (*titre*): ~ **X** Mr X; **bonjour ~** good morning; (*dans hôtel, restaurant*) good morning, sir; **bonjour messieurs** good morning (gentlemen); **messieurs dames** ladies and gentlemen; **Monsieur le Ministre n'est pas là** the Minister is out. **2.** (*homme quelconque*) gentleman.

monstre [mɔ̃str] *nm* **1.** (*gén*) monster. **2.** (*en apposition*) *fam* (*énorme*) colossal.

monstrueux, -euse [mɔ̃stryø, øz] *adj* **1.** (*gén*) monstrous. **2.** *fig* (*erreur*) terrible.

monstruosité [mɔ̃stryozite] *nf* monstrosity.

mont [mɔ̃] *nm* (GÉOGR) Mount; **le ~ Blanc** Mont Blanc; **le ~ Cervin** the Matterhorn; **le Mont-Saint-Michel** Mont-Saint-Michel.

MONT-SAINT-MICHEL

A rocky island standing off the northwest coast of France, Mont-Saint-Michel is joined to the mainland by a causeway. It is a popular tourist attraction famous for its Gothic Benedictine abbey which dominates the island, and has been designated by UNESCO as one of the most important heritage sites in the world. It has also entered into French folklore as the home of the 'omelette de la mère Poulard' ('Mother Poulard's omelette') named after a 19th-century cook who lived on the island.

montage [mɔ̃taʒ] *nm* **1.** (*assemblage*) assembly; (*de bijou*) setting. **2.** (PHOT) photomontage. **3.** (CIN) editing.

montagnard, -e [mɔ̃taɲar, ard] ◆ *adj* mountain (*avant n*). ◆ *nm, f* mountain dweller.

montagne [mɔ̃taɲ] *nf* **1.** (*gén*) mountain; **les ~s Rocheuses** the Rocky Mountains. **2.** (*région*): **la ~** the mountains (*pl*); **à la ~** in the mountains; **en haute ~** at high altitudes. ▶ **montagnes russes** *nfpl* big dipper (*sg*), roller coaster (*sg*).

montagneux, -euse [mɔ̃taɲø, øz] *adj* mountainous.

montant, -e [mɔ̃tã, ãt] *adj* (*mouvement*) rising. ▶ **montant** *nm* **1.** (*pièce verticale*) upright. **2.** (*somme*) total (amount).

mont-de-piété [mɔ̃dpjete] (*pl* **monts-de-piété**) *nm* pawnshop.

monte-charge [mɔ̃tʃarʒ] *nm inv* goods lift Br, service elevator Am.

montée [mɔ̃te] *nf* **1.** (*de montagne*) climb, ascent. **2.** (*de prix*) rise. **3.** (*relief*) slope, gradient.

monte-plats [mɔ̃tpla] *nm inv* dumbwaiter.

monter [mɔ̃te] ◆ *vi* (*aux: être*) **1.** (*personne*) to come/go up; (*température, niveau*) to rise; (*route, avion*) to climb; ~ **sur qqch** to climb onto sthg. **2.** (*passager*) to get on; ~ **dans un bus** to get on a bus; ~ **dans une voiture** to get into a car. **3.** (*cavalier*) to ride; ~ **à cheval** to ride. **4.** (*marée*) to go/come in. ◆ *vt* (*aux: avoir*) **1.** (*escalier, côte*) to climb, to come/go up; ~ **la rue en courant** to run up the street. **2.** (*chauffage, son*) to turn up. **3.** (*valise*) to take/bring up. **4.** (*meuble*) to assemble; (COUTURE) to assemble, to put ou sew together; (*tente*) to put up. **5.** (*cheval*) to mount. **6.** (THÉÂTRE) to put on. **7.** (*société, club*) to set up. **8.** (CULIN) to beat, to whisk (up). ▶ **se monter** *vp* (*atteindre*): **se ~ à** to amount to, to add up to.

monteur, -euse [mɔ̃tœr, øz] *nm, f* **1.** (TECHNOL) fitter. **2.** (CIN) editor.

monticule [mɔ̃tikyl] *nm* mound.

montre [mɔ̃tr] *nf* watch; ~ **à quartz** quartz watch; ~ **en main** to the minute, exactly; **contre la ~** (*sport*) time-trialling; (*épreuve*) time trial; **une course contre la ~** *fig* a race against time.

montre-bracelet [mɔ̃trəbraslɛ] *nf* wristwatch.

montrer [mɔ̃tre] *vt* **1.** (*gén*) to show; ~ **qqch à qqn** to show sb sthg, to show sthg to sb. **2.** (*désigner*) to show, to point out; ~ **qqch du doigt** to point at ou to sthg. ▶ **se montrer** *vp* **1.** (*se faire voir*) to appear. **2.** *fig* (*se présenter*) to show o.s. **3.** *fig* (*se révéler*) to prove (to be).

monture [mɔ̃tyr] *nf* **1.** (*animal*) mount. **2.** (*de lunettes*) frame.

monument [mɔnymã] *nm* (*gén*): ~ **(à)** monument (to); ~ **aux morts** war memorial.

monumental, -e, -aux [mɔnymãtal, o] *adj* monumental.

moquer [mɔke] ▶ **se moquer** *vp*: **se ~**

de (*plaisanter sur*) to make fun of, to laugh at; (*ne pas se soucier de*) not to give a damn about.

moquerie [mɔkri] *nf* mockery (U), jibe.

moquette [mɔkɛt] *nf* (fitted) carpet.

moqueur, -euse [mɔkœr, øz] *adj* mocking.

moral, -e, -aux [mɔral, o] *adj* moral. ▶ **moral** *nm* 1. (*mental*): **au ~ comme au physique** mentally as well as physically. 2. (*état d'esprit*) morale, spirits (*pl*); **avoir/ne pas avoir le ~** to be in good/bad spirits; **remonter le ~ à qqn** to cheer sb up. ▶ **morale** *nf* 1. (*science*) moral philosophy, morals (*pl*). 2. (*règle*) morality. 3. (*mœurs*) morals (*pl*). 4. (*leçon*) moral; **faire la ~e à qqn** to preach at ou lecture sb.

moralisateur, -trice [mɔralizatœr, tris] ♦ *adj* moralizing. ♦ *nm, f* moralizer.

moraliste [mɔralist] *nmf* moralist.

moralité [mɔralite] *nf* 1. (*gén*) morality. 2. (*enseignement*) morals.

moratoire [mɔratwar] *nm* moratorium.

morbide [mɔrbid] *adj* morbid.

morceau, -x [mɔrso] *nm* 1. (*gén*) piece. 2. (*de poème, de film*) passage.

morceler [mɔrsəle] *vt* to break up, to split up.

mordant, -e [mɔrdɑ̃, ɑ̃t] *adj* biting. ▶ **mordant** *nm* (*vivacité*) keenness, bite.

mordiller [mɔrdije] *vt* to nibble.

mordoré, -e [mɔrdɔre] *adj* bronze.

mordre [mɔrdr] ♦ *vt* (*blesser*) to bite. ♦ *vi* 1. (*saisir avec les dents*): **~ à** to bite. 2. (*croquer*): **~ dans qqch** to bite into sthg. 3. (SPORT): **~ sur la ligne** to step over the line.

mordu, -e [mɔrdy] ♦ *pp* → **mordre**. ♦ *adj* (*amoureux*) hooked. ♦ *nm, f*: **~ de foot/ski** *etc* football/ski *etc* addict.

morfondre [mɔrfɔ̃dr] ▶ **se morfondre** *vp* to mope.

morgue [mɔrg] *nf* 1. (*attitude*) pride. 2. (*lieu*) morgue.

moribond, -e [mɔribɔ̃, ɔ̃d] ♦ *adj* dying. ♦ *nm, f* dying person.

morille [mɔrij] *nf* morel.

morne [mɔrn] *adj* (*personne, visage*) gloomy; (*paysage, temps, ville*) dismal, dreary.

morose [mɔroz] *adj* gloomy.

morphine [mɔrfin] *nf* morphine.

morphologie [mɔrfɔlɔʒi] *nf* morphology.

mors [mɔr] *nm* bit.

morse [mɔrs] *nm* 1. (ZOOL) walrus. 2. (*code*) Morse (code).

morfondre

morsure [mɔrsyr] *nf* bite.

mort, -e [mɔr, mɔrt] ♦ *pp* → **mourir**. ♦ *adj* dead; **~ de fatigue** *fig* dead tired; **~ de peur** *fig* frightened to death. ♦ *nm, f* 1. (*cadavre*) corpse, dead body. 2. (*défunt*) dead person. ▶ **mort** ♦ *nm* 1. (*victime*) fatality. 2. (CARTES) dummy. ♦ *nf litt & fig* death; **de ~** (*silence*) deathly; **condamner qqn à ~** to sentence sb to death; **se donner la ~** to take one's own life, to commit suicide.

mortadelle [mɔrtadɛl] *nf* mortadella.

mortalité [mɔrtalite] *nf* mortality, death rate.

mort-aux-rats [mɔrora] *nf inv* rat poison.

Morte → **mer**.

mortel, -elle [mɔrtɛl] ♦ *adj* 1. (*humain*) mortal. 2. (*accident, maladie*) fatal. 3. *fig* (*ennuyeux*) deadly (dull). ♦ *nm, f* mortal.

morte-saison [mɔrtsɛzɔ̃] *nf* slack season, off-season.

mortier [mɔrtje] *nm* mortar.

mortification [mɔrtifikasjɔ̃] *nf* mortification.

mort-né, -e [mɔrne] (*mpl* **mort-nés**, *fpl* **mort-nées**) *adj* (*enfant*) still-born.

mortuaire [mɔrtɥer] *adj* funeral (*avant n*).

morue [mɔry] *nf* (ZOOL) cod.

mosaïque [mɔzaik] *nf litt & fig* mosaic.

Moscou [mɔsku] *n* Moscow.

mosquée [mɔske] *nf* mosque.

mot [mo] *nm* 1. (*gén*) word; **gros ~** swearword; **~ de passe** password; **~s croisés** crossword (puzzle) (*sg*); **petit ~** note. 2. (*message*) note, message.

motard [mɔtar] *nm* 1. (*motocycliste*) motorcyclist. 2. (*policier*) motorcycle policeman.

motel [mɔtɛl] *nm* motel.

moteur, -trice [mɔtœr, tris] *adj* (*force, énergie*) driving (*avant n*); **à quatre roues motrices** (AUTOM) with four-wheel drive. ▶ **moteur** *nm* (TECHNOL) motor, engine; *fig* driving force.

motif [mɔtif] *nm* 1. (*raison*) motive, grounds (*pl*). 2. (*dessin, impression*) motif.

motion [mɔsjɔ̃] *nf* (POLIT) motion; **~ de censure** motion of censure.

motiver [mɔtive] *vt* 1. (*stimuler*) to motivate. 2. (*justifier*) to justify.

moto [mɔto] *nf* motorbike.

motocross [mɔtokrɔs] *nm* motocross.

motoculteur [mɔtokyltœr] *nm* ≃ Rotavator®.

motocyclette [mɔtɔsiklɛt] *nf* motorcycle, motorbike.

motocycliste [mɔtɔsiklist] *nmf* motorcyclist.

motoneige [mɔtɔnɛʒ] *nf* snowmobile.

motorisé, -e [mɔtɔrize] *adj* motorized; **être ~** *fam* to have a car.

motrice → **moteur**.

motricité [mɔtrisite] *nf* motor functions (*pl*).

motte [mɔt] *nf*: **~ (de terre)** clod, lump of earth; **~ de beurre** slab of butter.

mou, molle [mu, mɔl] *adj* (**mol** *devant voyelle ou h muet*) **1.** (*gén*) soft. **2.** (*faible*) weak. **3.** (*résistance, protestation*) half-hearted. **4.** *fam* (*de caractère*) wet, wimpy. ▶ **mou** *nm* **1.** (*de corde*): **avoir du ~** to be slack. **2.** (*abats*) lungs (*pl*), lights (*pl*).

mouchard, -e [muʃar, ard] *nm, f fam* (*personne*) sneak. ▶ **mouchard** *nm fam* (*dans camion, train*) spy in the cab.

mouche [muʃ] *nf* **1.** (ZOOL) fly. **2.** (*accessoire féminin*) beauty spot.

moucher [muʃe] *vt* **1.** (*nez*) to wipe; **~ un enfant** to wipe a child's nose. **2.** (*chandelle*) to snuff out. **3.** *fam fig* (*personne*): **~ qqn** to put sb in his/her place. ▶ **se moucher** *vp* to blow ou wipe one's nose.

moucheron [muʃrɔ̃] *nm* (*insecte*) gnat.

moucheté, -e [muʃte] *adj* **1.** (*laine*) flecked. **2.** (*animal*) spotted, speckled.

mouchoir [muʃwar] *nm* handkerchief.

moudre [mudr] *vt* to grind.

moue [mu] *nf* pout; **faire la ~** to pull a face.

mouette [mwɛt] *nf* seagull.

moufle [mufl] *nf* mitten.

mouflon [muflɔ̃] *nm* wild sheep.

mouillage [mujaʒ] *nm* (NAVIG - *emplacement*) anchorage, moorings (*pl*).

mouillé, -e [muje] *adj* wet.

mouiller [muje] *vt* **1.** (*personne, objet*) to wet; **se faire ~** to get wet ou soaked. **2.** (NAVIG): **~ l'ancre** to drop anchor. **3.** *fam fig* (*compromettre*) to involve. ▶ **se mouiller** *vp* **1.** (*se tremper*) to get wet. **2.** *fam fig* (*prendre des risques*) to stick one's neck out.

moulage [mulaʒ] *nm* **1.** (*action*) moulding, casting. **2.** (*objet*) cast.

moule [mul] ◆ *nm* mould; **~ à gâteau** cake tin; **~ à tarte** flan dish. ◆ *nf* (ZOOL) mussel.

mouler [mule] *vt* **1.** (*objet*) to mould. **2.** (*forme*) to make a cast of.

moulin [mulɛ̃] *nm* mill; **~ à café** coffee mill; **~ à paroles** *fig* chatterbox.

moulinet [mulinɛ] *nm* **1.** (PÊCHE) reel. **2.** (*mouvement*): **faire des ~s** to whirl one's arms around.

Moulinette® [mulinɛt] *nf* food mill.

moulu, -e [muly] *adj* (*en poudre*) ground.

moulure [mulyr] *nf* moulding.

mourant, -e [murɑ̃, ɑ̃t] ◆ *adj* **1.** (*moribond*) dying. **2.** *fig* (*voix*) faint. ◆ *nm, f* dying person.

mourir [murir] *vi* **1.** (*personne*) to die; **s'ennuyer à ~** to be bored to death. **2.** (*feu*) to die down.

mousquetaire [muskətɛr] *nm* musketeer.

moussant, -e [musɑ̃, ɑ̃t] *adj* foaming.

mousse [mus] ◆ *nf* **1.** (BOT) moss. **2.** (*substance*) foam; **~ à raser** shaving foam. **3.** (CULIN) mousse. **4.** (*matière plastique*) foam rubber. ◆ *nm* (NAVIG) cabin boy.

mousseline [muslin] *nf* muslin.

mousser [muse] *vi* to foam, to lather.

mousseux, -euse [musø, øz] *adj* **1.** (*shampooing*) foaming, frothy. **2.** (*vin, cidre*) sparkling. ▶ **mousseux** *nm* sparkling wine.

mousson [musɔ̃] *nf* monsoon.

moussu, -e [musy] *adj* mossy, moss-covered.

moustache [mustaʃ] *nf* moustache. ▶ **moustaches** *nfpl* (*d'animal*) whiskers.

moustachu, -e [mustaʃy] *adj* with a moustache.

moustiquaire [mustikɛr] *nf* mosquito net.

moustique [mustik] *nm* mosquito.

moutarde [mutard] *nf* mustard.

mouton [mutɔ̃] *nm* **1.** (ZOOL & *fig*) sheep. **2.** (*viande*) mutton. **3.** *fam* (*poussière*) piece of fluff, fluff (U).

mouture [mutyr] *nf* **1.** (*de céréales, de café*) grinding. **2.** (*de thème, d'œuvre*) rehash.

mouvance [muvɑ̃s] *nf* (*domaine*) sphere of influence.

mouvant, -e [muvɑ̃, ɑ̃t] *adj* **1.** (*terrain*) unstable. **2.** (*situation*) uncertain.

mouvement [muvmɑ̃] *nm* **1.** (*gén*) movement; **en ~** on the move. **2.** (*de colère, d'indignation*) burst, fit.

mouvementé, -e [muvmɑ̃te] *adj* **1.** (*terrain*) rough. **2.** (*réunion, soirée*) eventful.

mouvoir [muvwar] *vt* to move. ▶ **se mouvoir** *vp* to move.

moyen, -enne [mwajɛ̃, ɛn] *adj*

1. (*intermédiaire*) medium. **2.** (*médiocre, courant*) average. ▶ **moyen** *nm* means (*sg*), way; **~ de communication** means of communication; **~ de locomotion** OU **transport** means of transport. ▶ **moyenne** *nf* average; **en moyenne** on average; **la moyenne d'âge** the average age. ▶ **moyens** *nmpl* **1.** (*ressources*) means; **avoir les ~s** to be comfortably off. **2.** (*capacités*) powers, ability; **faire qqch par ses propres ~s** to do sthg on one's own. ▶ **au moyen de** *loc prép* by means of.

Moyen Âge [mwajɛnaʒ] *nm*: **le ~** the Middle Ages (*pl*).

moyennement [mwajɛnmɑ̃] *adv* moderately, fairly.

Moyen-Orient [mwajɛnɔrjɑ̃] *nm*: **le ~** the Middle East.

mozzarelle [mɔdzarɛl] *nf* mozzarella.

MST *nf* **1.** (*abr de* **maladie sexuellement transmissible**) STD. **2.** (*abr de* **maîtrise de sciences et techniques**) *masters degree in science and technology*.

mû, mue [my] *pp* → **mouvoir**.

mue [my] *nf* **1.** (*de pelage*) moulting. **2.** (*de serpent*) skin, slough. **3.** (*de voix*) breaking.

muer [mɥe] *vi* **1.** (*mammifère*) to moult. **2.** (*serpent*) to slough its skin. **3.** (*voix*) to break; (*jeune homme*): **il mue** his voice is breaking.

muet, muette [mɥe, ɛt] ◆ *adj* **1.** (MÉD) dumb. **2.** (*silencieux*) silent; **~ d'admiration/d'étonnement** speechless with admiration/surprise. **3.** (LING) silent, mute. ◆ *nm, f* mute, dumb person. ▶ **muet** *nm*: **le ~** (CIN) silent films (*pl*).

muezzin [mɥedzin] *nm* muezzin.

mufle [myfl] *nm* **1.** (*d'animal*) muzzle, snout. **2.** *fig* (*goujat*) lout.

muflerie [myfləri] *nf* loutishness.

mugir [myʒir] *vi* **1.** (*vache*) to moo. **2.** (*vent, sirène*) to howl.

muguet [mygɛ] *nm* **1.** (*fleur*) lily of the valley. **2.** (MÉD) thrush.

mule [myl] *nf* mule.

mulet [mylɛ] *nm* **1.** (*âne*) mule. **2.** (*poisson*) mullet.

mulot [mylo] *nm* field mouse.

multicolore [myltikɔlɔr] *adj* multicoloured.

multifonction [myltifɔ̃ksjɔ̃] *adj inv* multifunction.

multilatéral, -e, -aux [myltilateral, o] *adj* multilateral.

multimédia [myltimedja] *nm & adj inv* multimedia.

multinational, -e, -aux [myltinasjɔnal, o] *adj* multinational. ▶ **multinationale** *nf* multinational (company).

multiple [myltipl] ◆ *nm* multiple. ◆ *adj* **1.** (*nombreux*) multiple, numerous. **2.** (*divers*) many, various.

multiplication [myltiplikasjɔ̃] *nf* multiplication.

multiplier [myltiplije] *vt* **1.** (*accroître*) to increase. **2.** (MATHS) to multiply; **X multiplié par Y égale Z** X multiplied by OU times Y equals Z. ▶ **se multiplier** *vp* to multiply.

multiracial, -e, -aux [myltirasjal, o] *adj* multiracial.

multirisque [myltirisk] *adj* comprehensive.

multitude [myltityd] *nf*: **~ (de)** multitude (of).

municipal, -e, -aux [mynisipal, o] *adj* municipal. ▶ **municipales** *nfpl*: **les ~es** the local government elections.

municipalité [mynisipalite] *nf* **1.** (*commune*) municipality. **2.** (*conseil*) town council.

munir [mynir] *vt*: **~ qqn/qqch de** to equip sb/sthg with. ▶ **se munir** *vp*: **se ~ de** to equip o.s. with.

munitions [mynisjɔ̃] *nfpl* ammunition (U), munitions.

muqueuse [mykøz] *nf* mucous membrane.

mur [myr] *nm* **1.** (*gén*) wall. **2.** *fig* (*obstacle*) barrier, brick wall; **~ du son** (AÉRON) sound barrier.

mûr, mûre [myr] *adj* ripe; (*personne*) mature. ▶ **mûre** *nf* **1.** (*de mûrier*) mulberry. **2.** (*de ronce*) blackberry, bramble.

muraille [myraj] *nf* wall.

murène [myrɛn] *nf* moray eel.

murer [myre] *vt* **1.** (*boucher*) to wall up, to block up. **2.** (*enfermer*) to wall in. ▶ **se murer** *vp* to shut o.s. up OU away; **se ~ dans** *fig* to retreat into.

muret [myrɛ] *nm* low wall.

mûrier [myrje] *nm* **1.** (*arbre*) mulberry tree. **2.** (*ronce*) blackberry bush, bramble bush.

mûrir [myrir] *vi* **1.** (*fruits, légumes*) to ripen. **2.** *fig* (*idée, projet*) to develop. **3.** (*personne*) to mature.

murmure [myrmyr] *nm* murmur.

murmurer [myrmyre] *vt & vi* to murmur.

musaraigne [myzarɛɲ] *nf* shrew.

musarder [myzarde] *vi fam* to dawdle.

muscade [myskad] *nf* nutmeg.

muscat [myska] *nm* **1.** (*raisin*) muscat grape. **2.** (*vin*) sweet wine.

muscle [myskl] nm muscle.

musclé, -e [myskle] adj 1. (personne) muscular. 2. fig (mesure, décision) forceful.

muscler [myskle] vt: ~ **son corps** to build up one's muscles. ▶ **se muscler** vp to build up one's muscles.

musculation [myskylasjɔ̃] nf: **faire de la ~** to do muscle-building exercises.

muse [myz] nf muse.

museau [myzo] nm 1. (d'animal) muzzle, snout. 2. fam (de personne) face.

musée [myze] nm museum; (d'art) art gallery.

museler [myzle] vt litt & fig to muzzle.

muselière [myzəljɛr] nf muzzle.

musette [myzɛt] nf haversack; (d'écolier) satchel.

musical, -e, -aux [myzikal, o] adj 1. (son) musical. 2. (émission, critique) music (avant n).

music-hall [myzikol] (pl **music-halls**) nm music-hall.

musicien, -enne [myzisjɛ̃, ɛn] ◆ adj musical. ◆ nm, f musician.

musique [myzik] nf music; ~ **de chambre** chamber music; ~ **de film** film Br ou movie Am score.

musulman, -e [myzylmɑ̃, an] adj & nm, f Muslim.

mutant, -e [mytɑ̃, ɑ̃t] adj & nm, f mutant.

mutation [mytasjɔ̃] nf 1. (BIOL) mutation. 2. fig (changement) transformation. 3. (de fonctionnaire) transfer.

muter [myte] vt to transfer.

mutilation [mytilasjɔ̃] nf mutilation.

mutilé, -e [mytile] nm, f disabled person.

mutiler [mytile] vt to mutilate.

mutinerie [mytinri] nf rebellion; (MIL & NAVIG) mutiny.

mutisme [mytism] nm silence.

mutualité [mytqalite] nf (assurance) mutual insurance.

mutuel, -elle [mytqɛl] adj mutual. ▶ **mutuelle** nf mutual insurance company.

mycose [mikoz] nf mycosis, fungal infection.

myocarde [mjɔkard] nm myocardium.

myopathie [mjɔpati] nf myopathy.

myope [mjɔp] ◆ nmf shortsighted person. ◆ adj shortsighted, myopic.

myopie [mjɔpi] nf shortsightedness, myopia.

myosotis [mjozɔtis] nm forget-me-not.

myrtille [mirtij] nf bilberry Br, blueberry Am.

mystère [mistɛr] nm (gén) mystery.

mystérieux, -euse [misterjø, øz] adj mysterious.

mysticisme [mistisism] nm mysticism.

mystification [mistifikasjɔ̃] nf (tromperie) hoax, practical joke.

mystifier [mistifje] vt (duper) to take in.

mystique [mistik] ◆ nmf mystic. ◆ adj mystic, mystical.

mythe [mit] nm myth.

mythique [mitik] adj mythical.

mythologie [mitɔlɔʒi] nf mythology.

mythomane [mitɔman] nmf pathological liar.

N

n, N [ɛn] nm inv (lettre) n, N. ▶ **N** (abr de **nord**) N.

n' → **ne**.

nacelle [nasɛl] nf (de montgolfière) basket.

nacre [nakr] nf mother-of-pearl.

nage [naʒ] nf 1. (natation) swimming; **traverser à la ~** to swim across. 2. loc: **en ~** bathed in sweat.

nageoire [naʒwar] nf fin.

nager [naʒe] vi 1. (se baigner) to swim. 2. (flotter) to float. 3. fig (dans vêtement): ~ **dans** to be lost in; ~ **dans la joie** to be incredibly happy.

nageur, -euse [naʒœr, øz] nm, f swimmer.

naguère [nagɛr] adv littéraire a short time ago.

naïf, naïve [naif, iv] adj 1. (ingénu, art) naive. 2. péj (crédule) gullible.

nain, -e [nɛ̃, nɛn] ◆ adj dwarf (avant n). ◆ nm, f dwarf.

naissance [nɛsɑ̃s] nf 1. (de personne) birth; **donner ~ à** to give birth to; **le contrôle des ~s** birth control. 2. (endroit) source; (du cou) nape. 3. fig (de science, nation) birth; **donner ~ à** to give rise to.

naissant, -e [nɛsɑ̃, ɑ̃t] adj 1. (brise) rising; (jour) dawning. 2. (barbe) incipient.

naître [nɛtr] vi 1. (enfant) to be born; **elle est née en 1965** she was born in 1965. 2. (espoir) to spring up; ~ **de** to arise from; **faire ~ qqch** to give rise to sthg.

naïveté [naivte] nf 1. (candeur) innocence. 2. *péj* (*crédulité*) gullibility.

nana [nana] *nf fam* (*jeune fille*) girl.

nanti, -e [nɑ̃ti] *nm, f* wealthy person.

nantir [nɑ̃tir] *vt littéraire*: ~ qqn de to provide sb with.

nappe [nap] *nf* 1. (*de table*) tablecloth, cloth. 2. *fig* (*étendue - gén*) sheet; (- *de brouillard*) blanket. 3. (*couche*) layer.

napper [nape] *vt* (CULIN) to coat.

napperon [naprɔ̃] *nm* tablemat.

narcisse [narsis] *nm* (BOT) narcissus.

narcissisme [narsisism] *nm* narcissism.

narcotique [narkɔtik] *nm & adj* narcotic.

narguer [narge] *vt* (*danger*) to flout; (*personne*) to scorn, to scoff at.

narine [narin] *nf* nostril.

narquois, -e [narkwa, az] *adj* sardonic.

narrateur, -trice [naratœr, tris] *nm, f* narrator.

narrer [nare] *vt littéraire* to narrate.

nasal, -e, -aux [nazal, o] *adj* nasal.

naseau, -x [nazo] *nm* nostril.

nasillard, -e [nazijar, ard] *adj* nasal.

nasse [nas] *nf* keep net.

natal, -e, -als [natal] *adj* (*d'origine*) native.

natalité [natalite] *nf* birth rate.

natation [natasjɔ̃] *nf* swimming; faire de la ~ to swim.

natif, -ive [natif, iv] ◆ *adj* (*originaire*): ~ de native of. ◆ *nm, f* native.

nation [nasjɔ̃] *nf* nation. ▶ **Nations unies** *nfpl*: les Nations unies the United Nations.

national, -e, -aux [nasjɔnal, o] *adj* national. ▶ **nationale** *nf*: (route) ~e ≃ A road Br, ≃ state highway Am.

nationaliser [nasjɔnalize] *vt* to nationalize.

nationalisme [nasjɔnalism] *nm* nationalism.

nationalité [nasjɔnalite] *nf* nationality; de ~ française of French nationality.

nativité [nativite] *nf* nativity.

natte [nat] *nf* 1. (*tresse*) plait. 2. (*tapis*) mat.

naturaliser [natyralize] *vt* 1. (*personne, plante*) to naturalize. 2. (*empailler*) to stuff.

naturaliste [natyralist] ◆ *nmf* 1. (LITTÉRATURE & ZOOL) naturalist. 2. (*empailleur*) taxidermist. ◆ *adj* naturalistic.

nature [natyr] ◆ *nf* nature. ◆ *adj inv* 1. (*simple*) plain. 2. *fam* (*spontané*) natural.

naturel, -elle [natyrɛl] *adj* natural. ▶ **naturel** *nm* 1. (*tempérament*) nature;

être d'un ~ **affable/sensible** *etc* to be affable/sensitive *etc* by nature. 2. (*aisance, spontanéité*) naturalness.

naturellement [natyrɛlmɑ̃] *adv* 1. (*gén*) naturally. 2. (*logiquement*) rationally.

naturiste [natyrist] *nmf* naturist.

naufrage [nofraʒ] *nm* 1. (*navire*) shipwreck; faire ~ to be wrecked. 2. *fig* (*effondrement*) collapse.

naufragé, -e [nofraʒe] ◆ *adj* shipwrecked. ◆ *nm, f* shipwrecked person.

nauséabond, -e [nozeabɔ̃, ɔ̃d] *adj* nauseating.

nausée [noze] *nf* 1. (MÉD) nausea; avoir la ~ to feel nauseous ou sick. 2. (*dégoût*) disgust.

nautique [notik] *adj* nautical; (*ski, sport*) water (*avant n*).

naval, -e, -als [naval] *adj* naval.

navarin [navarɛ̃] *nm* mutton and vegetable stew.

navet [navɛ] *nm* 1. (BOT) turnip. 2. *fam péj* (*œuvre*) load of rubbish.

navette [navɛt] *nf* shuttle; ~ spatiale (AÉRON) space shuttle; faire la ~ to shuttle.

navigable [navigabl] *adj* navigable.

navigateur, -trice [navigatœr, tris] *nm, f* navigator.

navigation [navigasjɔ̃] *nf* navigation; (COMM) shipping.

naviguer [navige] *vi* 1. (*voguer*) to sail. 2. (*piloter*) to navigate.

navire [navir] *nm* ship.

navrant, -e [navrɑ̃, ɑ̃t] *adj* 1. (*triste*) upsetting, distressing. 2. (*regrettable, mauvais*) unfortunate.

navrer [navre] *vt* to upset; être navré de qqch/de faire qqch to be sorry about sthg/to do sthg.

nazi, -e [nazi] *nm, f* Nazi.

nazisme [nazism] *nm* Nazism.

NB (*abr de* **Nota Bene**) NB.

NDLR (*abr de* **note de la rédaction**) editor's note.

NDT (*abr de* **note du traducteur**) translator's note.

ne [nə], **n'** (*devant voyelle ou h muet*) *adv* 1. (*négation*) → **pas²**, **plus**, **rien** *etc*. 2. (*négation implicite*): il se porte mieux que je ~ (le) croyais he's in better health than I thought (he would be). 3. (*avec verbes ou expressions marquant le doute, la crainte etc*): je crains qu'il n'oublie I'm afraid he'll forget.

né, -e [ne] *adj* born; ~ en 1965 born in 1965; ~ le 17 juin born on the 17th June; Mme X, ~ e Y Mrs X née Y.

néanmoins [neãmwẽ] adv neverthe-less.

néant [neã] nm 1. (absence de valeur) worth-lessness. 2. (absence d'existence) nothing-ness; **réduire à ~** to reduce to nothing.

nébuleux, -euse [nebylø, øz] adj 1. (ciel) cloudy. 2. (idée, projet) nebulous. ► **nébuleuse** nf (ASTRON) nebula.

nécessaire [neseser] ◆ adj necessary; **~ à** necessary for; **il est ~ de faire qqch** it is necessary to do sthg; **il est ~ que** (+ subjonctif): **il est ~ qu'elle vienne** she must come. ◆ nm 1. (biens) necessities (pl); **le strict ~** the bare essentials (pl). 2. (mesures): **faire le ~** to do the neces-sary. 3. (trousse) bag.

nécessité [nesesite] nf (obligation, situa-tion) necessity; **être dans la ~ de faire qqch** to have no choice ou alternative but to do sthg.

nécessiter [nesesite] vt to necessitate.

nécrologique [nekrɔlɔʒik] adj obitu-ary (avant n).

nectar [nektar] nm nectar.

nectarine [nektarin] nf nectarine.

néerlandais, -e [neerlãde, ɛz] adj Dutch. ► **néerlandais** nm (langue) Dutch. ► **Néerlandais, -e** nm, f Dutchman (f Dutchwoman); **les Néerlandais** the Dutch.

nef [nɛf] nf 1. (d'église) nave. 2. littéraire (bateau) vessel.

néfaste [nefast] adj 1. (jour, événement) fateful. 2. (influence) harmful.

négatif, -ive [negatif, iv] adj negative. ► **négatif** nm (PHOT) negative. ► **négative** nf: **répondre par la négative** to reply in the negative.

négation [negasjɔ̃] nf 1. (rejet) denial. 2. (GRAM) negative.

négligé, -e [negliʒe] adj 1. (travail, tenue) untidy. 2. (ami, jardin) neglected.

négligeable [negliʒabl] adj negligible.

négligemment [negliʒamɑ̃] adv 1. (sans soin) carelessly. 2. (avec indif-férence) casually.

négligence [negliʒɑ̃s] nf 1. (laisser-aller) carelessness. 2. (omission) negligence; **par ~** out of negligence.

négligent, -e [negliʒɑ̃, ɑ̃t] adj 1. (sans soin) careless. 2. (indifférent) casual.

négliger [negliʒe] vt 1. (ami, jardin) to neglect; **~ de faire qqch** to fail to do sthg. 2. (avertissement) to ignore. ► **se négliger** vp to neglect o.s.

négoce [negɔs] nm business.

négociable [negɔsjabl] adj nego-tiable.

négociant, -e [negɔsjã, ãt] nm, f deal-er.

négociateur, -trice [negɔsjatœr, tris] nm, f negotiator.

négociation [negɔsjasjɔ̃] nf negotia-tion; **~s de paix** peace negotiations.

négocier [negɔsje] vt to negotiate.

nègre, négresse [nɛgr, negrɛs] nm, f negro (f negress) (beware: the terms 'nègre' and 'négresse' are considered racist). ► **nègre** ◆ nm fam ghost writer. ◆ adj negro (avant n) (beware: the term 'nègre' is considered racist).

neige [nɛʒ] nf (flocons) snow.

neiger [neʒe] v impers: **il neige** it is snowing.

neigeux, -euse [nɛʒø, øz] adj snowy.

nénuphar [nenyfar] nm water-lily.

néologisme [neɔlɔʒism] nm neolo-gism.

néon [neɔ̃] nm 1. (gaz) neon. 2. (enseigne) neon light.

néophyte [neɔfit] nmf novice.

néo-zélandais, -e [neɔzelãde, ɛz] (mpl inv, fpl **néo-zélandaises**) adj New Zealand (avant n). ► **Néo-Zélandais, -e** nm, f New Zealander.

Népal [nepal] nm: **le ~** Nepal.

nerf [nɛr] nm 1. (ANAT) nerve. 2. fig (vigueur) spirit.

nerveux, -euse [nɛrvø, øz] adj 1. (gén) nervous. 2. (viande) stringy. 3. (style) vigorous; (voiture) nippy.

nervosité [nɛrvozite] nf nervousness.

nervure [nɛrvyr] nf (de feuille, d'aile) vein.

n'est-ce pas [nɛspa] adv: **vous me croyez, ~?** you believe me, don't you?; **c'est délicieux, ~?** it's delicious, isn't it?; **~ que vous vous êtes bien amusés?** you enjoyed yourselves, didn't you?

net, nette [nɛt] adj 1. (écriture, image, idée) clear. 2. (propre, rangé) clean, neat. 3. (COMM & FIN) net; **~ d'impôt** tax-free Br, tax-exempt Am. 4. (visible, manifeste) definite, distinct. ► **net** adv (sur le coup) on the spot; **s'arrêter ~** to stop dead; **se casser ~** to break clean off.

Net [nɛt] nm fam: **le ~** the Net; **surfer sur le ~** to surf the Net.

nettement [nɛtmɑ̃] adv 1. (clairement) clearly. 2. (incontestablement) definitely; **~ plus/moins** much more/less.

netteté [nɛtte] nf clearness.

nettoyage [netwajaʒ] nm (de vêtement) cleaning; **~ à sec** dry cleaning.

nettoyer [netwaje] vt 1. (gén) to clean. 2. (grenier) to clear out.

neuf¹, **neuve** [nœf, nœv] *adj* new. ► **neuf** *nm*: **vêtu de ~** wearing new clothes; **quoi de ~?** what's new?; **rien de ~** nothing new.

neuf² [nœf] *adj num & nm* nine; *voir aussi* **six**.

neurasthénique [nørastenik] *nmf & adj* depressive.

neurologie [nørɔlɔʒi] *nf* neurology.

neutraliser [nøtralize] *vt* to neutralize.

neutralité [nøtralite] *nf* neutrality.

neutre [nøtr] ◆ *nm* (LING) neuter. ◆ *adj* 1. (*gén*) neutral. 2. (LING) neuter.

neutron [nøtrɔ̃] *nm* neutron.

neuve → **neuf¹**.

neuvième [nœvjɛm] *adj num, nm & nmf* ninth; *voir aussi* **sixième**.

névé [neve] *nm* snowbank.

neveu [nəvø] *nm* nephew.

névralgie [nevralʒi] *nf* (MÉD) neuralgia.

névrose [nevroz] *nf* neurosis.

névrosé, -e [nevroze] *adj & nm, f* neurotic.

nez [ne] *nm* nose; **saigner du ~** to have a nosebleed; **~ aquilin** aquiline nose; **~ busqué** hooked nose; **~ à ~** face to face.

ni [ni] *conj*: **sans pull ~ écharpe** without a sweater or a scarf; **je ne peux ~ ne veux venir** I neither can nor want to come. ► **ni ... ni** *loc corrélative* neither ... nor; **~ lui ~ moi** neither of us; **~ l'un ~ l'autre n'a parlé** neither of them spoke; **je ne les aime ~ l'un ~ l'autre** I don't like either of them.

niais, -e [njɛ, njɛz] ◆ *adj* silly, foolish. ◆ *nm, f* fool.

Nicaragua [nikaragwa] *nm*: **le ~** Nicaragua.

niche [niʃ] *nf* 1. (*de chien*) kennel. 2. (*de statue*) niche.

nicher [niʃe] *vi* (*oiseaux*) to nest.

nickel [nikɛl] ◆ *nm* nickel. ◆ *adj inv fam* spotless, spick and span.

nicotine [nikɔtin] *nf* nicotine.

nid [ni] *nm* nest.

nièce [njɛs] *nf* niece.

nier [nje] *vt* to deny.

nigaud, -e [nigo, od] *nm, f* simpleton.

Niger [niʒɛr] *nm* 1. (*fleuve*): **le ~** the River Niger. 2. (*État*): **le ~** Niger.

Nigeria [niʒerja] *nm*: **le ~** Nigeria.

Nil [nil] *nm*: **le ~** the Nile.

n'importe → **importer**.

nippon, -one [nipɔ̃, ɔn] *adj* Japanese. ► **Nippon, -one** *nm, f* Japanese (person); **les Nippons** the Japanese.

nirvana [nirvana] *nm* nirvana.

nitrate [nitrat] *nm* nitrate.

nitroglycérine [nitrɔgliserin] *nf* nitroglycerine.

niveau, -x [nivo] *nm* (*gén*) level; **de même ~** *fig* of the same standard; **audessus du ~ de la mer** above sea level; **~ de vie** standard of living; **au ~ de** at the level of; *fig* (*en ce qui concerne*) as regards.

niveler [nivle] *vt* to level; *fig* to level out.

noble [nɔbl] ◆ *nmf* nobleman (*f* noblewoman). ◆ *adj* noble.

noblesse [nɔbles] *nf* nobility.

noce [nɔs] *nf* 1. (*mariage*) wedding. 2. (*invités*) wedding party. ► **noces** *nfpl* wedding (*sg*); **~s d'or/d'argent** golden/ silver wedding (anniversary).

nocif, -ive [nɔsif, iv] *adj* (*produit, gaz*) noxious.

noctambule [nɔktɑ̃byl] *nmf* night bird.

nocturne [nɔktyrn] ◆ *nm ou nf* (*d'un magasin*) late opening. ◆ *adj* 1. (*émission, attaque*) night (*avant n*). 2. (*animal*) nocturnal.

Noël [nɔɛl] *nm* Christmas; **joyeux ~!** happy ou merry Christmas!

NOËL

Christmas in France begins on Christmas Eve with a family supper, traditionally turkey with chestnuts followed by a Yule log. Children used to leave their shoes by the fireplace for Father Christmas to fill with presents but today presents are usually placed around the Christmas tree and given and received on Christmas Eve.

nœud [nø] *nm* 1. (*de fil, de bois*) knot; **double ~** double knot. 2. (NAVIG) knot. 3. (*de l'action, du problème*) crux. 4. (*ornement*) bow; **~ de cravate** knot (*in one's tie*); **~ papillon** bow tie. 5. (ANAT, ASTRON, ÉLECTR & RAIL) node.

noir, -e [nwar] *adj* 1. (*gén*) black; **~ de** (*poussière, suie*) black with. 2. (*pièce, couloir*) dark. ► **Noir, -e** *nm, f* black. ► **noir** *nm* 1. (*couleur*) black; **~ sur blanc** *fig* in black and white. 2. (*obscurité*) dark. 3. *loc*: **acheter qqch au ~** to buy sthg on the black market; **travail au ~** moonlighting. ► **noire** *nf* crotchet Br, quarter note Am.

noirâtre [nwaratr] *adj* blackish.

noirceur [nwarsœr] *nf fig* (*méchanceté*) wickedness.

noircir [nwarsir] ◆ *vi* to darken. ◆ *vt litt & fig* to blacken.

Noire → **mer.**

noisetier [nwaztje] *nm* hazel tree.

noisette [nwazet] *nf* (*fruit*) hazelnut.

noix [nwa] *nf* **1.** (*fruit*) walnut; **~ de cajou** cashew (nut); **~ de coco** coconut; **~ de muscade** nutmeg. **2.** *loc:* **à la ~** *fam* dreadful.

nom [nɔ̃] *nm* **1.** (*gén*) name; **au ~ de** in the name of; **~ déposé** trade name; **~ de famille** surname; **~ de jeune fille** maiden name. **2.** (*prénom*) (first) name. **3.** (GRAM) noun; **~ propre/commun** proper/common noun.

nomade [nɔmad] ◆ *nmf* nomad. ◆ *adj* nomadic.

nombre [nɔ̃br] *nm* number; **~ pair/impair** even/odd number.

nombreux, -euse [nɔ̃brø, øz] *adj* **1.** (*famille, foule*) large. **2.** (*erreurs, occasions*) numerous; **peu ~** few.

nombril [nɔ̃bril] *nm* navel; **il se prend pour le ~ du monde** he thinks the world revolves around him.

nominal, -e, -aux [nɔminal, o] *adj* **1.** (*liste*) of names. **2.** (*valeur, autorité*) nominal. **3.** (GRAM) noun (*avant n*).

nomination [nɔminasjɔ̃] *nf* nomination, appointment.

nommé, -e [nɔme] *adj* **1.** (*désigné*) named. **2.** (*choisi*) appointed.

nommément [nɔmemã] *adv* (*citer*) by name.

nommer [nɔme] *vt* **1.** (*appeler*) to name, to call. **2.** (*qualifier*) to call. **3.** (*promouvoir*) to appoint, to nominate. **4.** (*dénoncer, mentionner*) to name. ▸ **se nommer** *vp* **1.** (*s'appeler*) to be called. **2.** (*se désigner*) to give one's name.

non [nɔ̃] ◆ *adv* **1.** (*réponse négative*) no. **2.** (*se rapportant à une phrase précédente*) not; **moi ~** not me; **moi ~ plus** (and) neither am/do etc **1. 3.** (*sert à demander une confirmation*): **c'est une bonne idée, ~?** it's a good idea, isn't it? **4.** (*modifie un adjectif ou un adverbe*) not; **~ loin d'ici** not far from here. ◆ *nm inv* no. ▸ **non (pas) que ... mais** *loc corrélative* not that ... but.

nonagénaire [nɔnaʒenɛr] *nmf & adj* nonagenarian.

non-agression [nɔnagresjɔ̃] *nf* non-aggression.

nonante [nɔnãt] *adj num* Belg & Helv ninety.

nonchalance [nɔ̃ʃalãs] *nf* nonchalance, casualness.

non-fumeur, -euse [nɔ̃fymœr, øz] *nm, f* non-smoker.

non-lieu [nɔ̃ljø] (*pl* **non-lieux**) *nm* (JUR) dismissal through lack of evidence; **rendre un ~** to dismiss a case for lack of evidence.

nonne [nɔn] *nf* nun.

non-sens [nɔ̃sãs] *nm inv* **1.** (*absurdité*) nonsense. **2.** (*contresens*) meaningless word.

non-violence [nɔ̃vjɔlãs] *nf* non-violence.

non-voyant, -e [nɔ̃vwajã, ãt] *nm, f* visually handicapped.

nord [nɔr] ◆ *nm* north; **un vent du ~** a northerly wind; **au ~** in the north; **au ~ (de)** to the north (of); **le grand Nord** the frozen North. ◆ *adj inv* north; (*province, région*) northern.

nord-africain, -e [nɔrafrikɛ̃, ɛn] (*mpl* **nord-africains**, *fpl* **nord-africaines**) *adj* North African. ▸ **Nord-Africain, -e** *nm, f* North African.

nord-américain, -e [nɔramerikɛ̃, ɛn] (*mpl* **nord-américains**, *fpl* **nord-américaines**) *adj* North American. ▸ **Nord-Américain, -e** *nm, f* North American.

nord-est [nɔrɛst] *nm & adj inv* north-east.

nordique [nɔrdik] *adj* Nordic, Scandinavian. ▸ **Nordique** *nmf* **1.** (*Scandinave*) Scandinavian. **2.** Can North Canadian.

nord-ouest [nɔrwɛst] *nm & adj inv* north-west.

normal, -e, -aux [nɔrmal, o] *adj* normal. ▸ **normale** *nf* (*moyenne*): **la ~e** the norm.

normalement [nɔrmalmã] *adv* normally, usually; **~ il devrait déjà être arrivé** he should have arrived by now.

normalien, -enne [nɔrmaljɛ̃, ɛn] *nm, f* student at teacher training college.

normaliser [nɔrmalize] *vt* **1.** (*situation*) to normalize. **2.** (*produit*) to standardize.

normand, -e [nɔrmã, ãd] *adj* Norman. ▸ **Normand, -e** *nm, f* Norman.

Normandie [nɔrmãdi] *nf*: **la ~** Normandy.

norme [nɔrm] *nf* **1.** (*gén*) standard, norm. **2.** (*critère*) criterion.

Norvège [nɔrvɛʒ] *nf*: **la ~** Norway.

norvégien, -enne [nɔrveʒjɛ̃, ɛn] *adj* Norwegian. ▸ **norvégien** *nm* (*langue*) Norwegian. ▸ **Norvégien, -enne** *nm, f* Norwegian.

nos → **notre**.

nostalgie [nɔstalʒi] *nf* nostalgia.

nostalgique [nɔstalʒik] *adj* nostalgic.

notable [nɔtabl] ♦ *adj* noteworthy, notable. ♦ *nm* notable.

notaire [nɔtɛr] *nm* ≃ solicitor Br, ≃ lawyer.

notamment [nɔtamã] *adv* in particular.

note [nɔt] *nf* 1. (*gén* & MUS) note; **prendre des ~s** to take notes. 2. (SCOL & UNIV) mark, grade Am; **avoir une bonne/mauvaise ~** to have a good/bad mark. 3. (*facture*) bill.

noter [nɔte] *vt* 1. (*écrire*) to note down. 2. (*constater*) to note, to notice. 3. (SCOL & UNIV) to mark, to grade Am.

notice [nɔtis] *nf* instructions (*pl*).

notifier [nɔtifje] *vt*: **~ qqch à qqn** to notify sb of sthg.

notion [nɔsjõ] *nf* 1. (*conscience, concept*) notion, concept. 2. (*gén pl*) (*rudiment*) smattering (U).

notoire [nɔtwar] *adj* (*fait*) well-known; (*criminel*) notorious.

notre [nɔtr] (*pl* **nos** [no]) *adj poss* our.

nôtre [nɔtr] ▶ **le nôtre** (*f* **la nôtre**, *pl* **les nôtres**) *pron poss* ours; **les ~s** our family (*sg*); **serez-vous des ~s demain?** will you be joining us tomorrow?

nouer [nwe] *vt* 1. (*corde, lacet*) to tie; (*bouquet*) to tie up. 2. *fig* (*gorge, estomac*) to knot. ▶ **se nouer** *vp* 1. (*gorge*) to tighten up. 2. (*intrigue*) to start.

noueux, -euse [nwø, øz] *adj* (*bois*) knotty; (*mains*) gnarled.

nougat [nuga] *nm* nougat.

nouille [nuj] *nf fam péj* idiot. ▶ **nouilles** *nfpl* (*pâtes*) pasta (U), noodles (*pl*).

nourrice [nuris] *nf* (*garde d'enfants*) nanny, child-minder; (*qui allaite*) wet nurse.

nourrir [nurir] *vt* 1. (*gén*) to feed. 2. (*sentiment, projet*) to nurture. ▶ **se nourrir** *vp* to eat; **se ~ de qqch** *litt* & *fig* to live on sthg.

nourrissant, -e [nurisã, ãt] *adj* nutritious, nourishing.

nourrisson [nurisõ] *nm* infant.

nourriture [nurityr] *nf* food.

nous [nu] *pron pers* 1. (*sujet*) we. 2. (*objet*) us. ▶ **nous-mêmes** *pron pers* ourselves.

nouveau, -elle, -x [nuvo, ɛl, o] (**nouvel** *devant voyelle et h muet*) ♦ *adj* new; **~x mariés** newlyweds. ♦ *nm, f* new boy (*f* new girl). ▶ **nouveau** *nm*: **il y a du ~** there's something new. ▶ **nouvelle** *nf* 1. (*information*) (piece of) news (U). 2. (*court récit*) short story. ▶ **nouvelles** *nfpl* news; **les nouvelles** (MÉDIA) the news (*sg*); **il a donné de ses nouvelles** I/we *etc* have heard from him. ▶ **à nouveau** *loc adv* 1. (*encore*) again. 2. (*de manière différente*) afresh, anew. ▶ **de nouveau** *loc adv* again.

nouveau-né, -e [nuvone] (*mpl* **nouveau-nés**, *fpl* **nouveau-nées**) *nm, f* newborn baby.

nouveauté [nuvote] *nf* 1. (*actualité*) novelty. 2. (*innovation*) something new. 3. (*ouvrage*) new book/film *etc*.

nouvel, nouvelle → **nouveau**.

Nouvelle-Calédonie [nuvɛlkaledɔni] *nf*: **la ~** New Caledonia.

Nouvelle-Guinée [nuvɛlgine] *nf*: **la ~** New Guinea.

Nouvelle-Zélande [nuvɛlzelãd] *nf*: **la ~** New Zealand.

novateur, -trice [nɔvatœr, tris] ♦ *adj* innovative. ♦ *nm, f* innovator.

novembre [nɔvãbr] *nm* November; *voir aussi* **septembre**.

novice [nɔvis] ♦ *nmf* novice. ♦ *adj* inexperienced.

noyade [nwajad] *nf* drowning.

noyau, -x [nwajo] *nm* 1. (*de fruit*) stone, pit. 2. (ASTRON, BIOL & PHYS) nucleus. 3. *fig* (*d'amis*) group, circle; (*d'opposants, de résistants*) cell; **~ dur** hard core. 4. *fig* (*centre*) core.

noyauter [nwajote] *vt* to infiltrate.

noyé, -e [nwaje] ♦ *adj* 1. (*personne*) drowned. 2. (*inondé*) flooded; **yeux ~s de larmes** eyes swimming with tears. ♦ *nm, f* drowned person.

noyer [nwaje] *vt* 1. (*animal, personne*) to drown. 2. (*terre, moteur*) to flood. 3. (*estomper, diluer*) to swamp; (*contours*) to blur. ▶ **se noyer** *vp* 1. (*personne*) to drown. 2. *fig* (*se perdre*): **se ~ dans** to become bogged down in.

N/Réf (*abr de* **Notre référence**) O/Ref.

nu, -e [ny] *adj* 1. (*personne*) naked. 2. (*paysage, fil électrique*) bare. 3. (*style, vérité*) plain. ▶ **nu** *nm* nude; **à ~** stripped, bare; **mettre à ~** to strip bare.

nuage [nɥaʒ] *nm* 1. (*gén*) cloud. 2. (*petite quantité*): **un ~ de lait** a drop of milk.

nuageux, -euse [nɥaʒø, øz] *adj* 1. (*temps, ciel*) cloudy. 2. *fig* (*esprit*) hazy.

nuance [nɥãs] *nf* (*de couleur*) shade; (*de son, de sens*) nuance.

nubile [nybil] *adj* nubile.

nucléaire [nykleɛr] ◆ *nm* nuclear energy. ◆ *adj* nuclear.

nudisme [nydism] *nm* nudism, naturism.

nudité [nydite] *nf* 1. (*de personne*) nudity, nakedness. 2. (*de lieu, style*) bareness.

nuée [nɥe] *nf* 1. (*multitude*): **une ~ de** a horde of. 2. *littéraire* (*nuage*) cloud.

nues [ny] *nfpl*: **tomber des ~** to be completely taken aback.

nui [nɥi] *pp inv* → **nuire**.

nuire [nɥir] *vi*: **~ à** to harm, to injure.

nuisance [nɥizɑ̃s] *nf* (environmental) nuisance *ou* hazard.

nuisette [nɥizɛt] *nf* short nightgown, babydoll nightgown.

nuisible [nɥizibl] *adj* harmful.

nuit [nɥi] *nf* 1. (*laps de temps*) night; **cette ~** (*la nuit dernière*) last night; (*la nuit prochaine*) tonight; **de ~** at night; **bateau/vol de ~** night ferry/flight; **~ blanche** sleepless night. 2. (*obscurité*) darkness, night; **il fait ~** it's dark.

nuitée [nɥite] *nf* overnight stay.

nul, nulle [nyl] ◆ *adj indéf* (*avant n*) *littéraire* no. ◆ *adj* (*après n*) 1. (*égal à zéro*) nil. 2. (*sans valeur*) useless, hopeless; **être ~ en maths** to be hopeless *ou* useless in maths. 3. (*sans résultat*): **match ~** draw. ◆ *nm, f péj* nonentity. ◆ *pron indéf sout* no one, nobody. ▶ **nulle part** *adv* nowhere.

nullement [nylmɑ̃] *adv* by no means.

nullité [nylite] *nf* 1. (*médiocrité*) incompetence. 2. (JUR) invalidity, nullity.

numéraire [nymerɛr] *nm* cash.

numération [nymerasjɔ̃] *nf* (MÉD): **~ globulaire** blood count.

numérique [nymerik] *adj* 1. (*gén*) numerical. 2. (INFORM) digital.

numéro [nymero] *nm* 1. (*gén*) number; **composer** *ou* **faire un ~** to dial a number; **faire un faux ~** to dial a wrong number; **~ minéralogique** *ou* **d'immatriculation** registration *Br ou* license *Am* number; **~ de téléphone** telephone number; **~ vert** = freefone number. 2. (*de spectacle*) act, turn. 3. *fam* (*personne*): **quel ~!** what a character!

numéroter [nymerɔte] *vt* to number.

nu-pieds [nypje] *nm inv* (*sandale*) sandal.

nuptial, -e, -aux [nypsjal, o] *adj* nuptial.

nuque [nyk] *nf* nape.

nurse [nœrs] *nf* children's nurse, nanny.

nursery [nœrsəri] (*pl* **nurseries**) *nf* 1. (*dans un hôpital*) nursery. 2. (*dans un lieu public*) parent-and-baby facilities (*pl*).

nutritif, -ive [nytritif, iv] *adj* nutritious.

nutritionniste [nytrisjɔnist] *nmf* nutritionist, dietician.

Nylon® [nilɔ̃] *nm* nylon.

nymphe [nɛ̃f] *nf* nymph.

nymphomane [nɛ̃fɔman] *nf & adj* nymphomaniac.

o, O [o] *nm inv* (*lettre*) o, O. ▶ **O** (*abr de* **Ouest**) W.

ô [o] *interj* oh!, O!

oasis [ɔazis] *nf* 1. (*dans désert*) oasis. 2. *fig* (*de calme*) haven, oasis.

obéir [ɔbeir] *vi* 1. (*personne*): **~ à qqn/qqch** to obey sb/sthg. 2. (*freins*) to respond.

obéissant, -e [ɔbeisɑ̃, ɑ̃t] *adj* obedient.

obélisque [ɔbelisk] *nm* obelisk.

obèse [ɔbɛz] *adj* obese.

obésité [ɔbezite] *nf* obesity.

objecteur [ɔbʒɛktœr] *nm* objector; **~ de conscience** conscientious objector.

objectif, -ive [ɔbʒɛktif, iv] *adj* objective. ▶ **objectif** *nm* 1. (PHOT) lens. 2. (*but, cible*) objective, target.

objection [ɔbʒɛksjɔ̃] *nf* objection; **faire ~ à** to object to.

objectivité [ɔbʒɛktivite] *nf* objectivity.

objet [ɔbʒɛ] *nm* 1. (*chose*) object; **~ d'art** object d'art; **~ décoratif** ornament; **~ de valeur** valuable; **~s trouvés** lost property office *Br*, lost and found (office) *Am*. 2. (*sujet*) subject.

obligation [ɔbligasjɔ̃] *nf* 1. (*gén*) obligation; **être dans l'~ de faire qqch** to be obliged to do sthg. 2. (FIN) bond, debenture.

obligatoire [ɔbligatwar] *adj* 1. (*imposé*) compulsory, obligatory. 2. *fam* (*inéluctable*) inevitable.

obligeance [ɔbliʒɑ̃s] *nf sout* obligingness; **avoir l'~ de faire qqch** to be good *ou* kind enough to do sthg.

obliger [ɔbliʒe] *vt* 1. (*forcer*): ~ **qqn à qqch** to impose sthg on sb; ~ **qqn à faire qqch** to force sb to do sthg; **être obligé de faire qqch** to be obliged to do sthg. 2. (*rendre service à*) to oblige. ▶ **s'obliger** *vp*: **s'~ à qqch** to impose sthg on o.s.; **s'~ à faire qqch** to force o.s. to do sthg.

oblique [ɔblik] *adj* oblique.

obliquer [ɔblike] *vi* to turn off.

oblitération [ɔbliterasjɔ̃] *nf* (*d'un timbre*) cancelling.

oblitérer [ɔblitere] *vt* 1. (*tamponner*) to cancel. 2. (MÉD) to obstruct. 3. (*effacer*) to obliterate.

obnubiler [ɔbnybile] *vt* to obsess; **être obnubilé par** to be obsessed with ou by.

obole [ɔbɔl] *nf* small contribution.

obscène [ɔpsɛn] *adj* obscene.

obscénité [ɔpsenite] *nf* obscenity.

obscur, -e [ɔpskyr] *adj* 1. (*sombre*) dark. 2. (*confus*) vague. 3. (*inconnu, douteux*) obscure.

obscurantisme [ɔpskyrɑ̃tism] *nm* obscurantism.

obscurcir [ɔpskyrsir] *vt* 1. (*assombrir*) to darken. 2. (*embrouiller*) to confuse. ▶ **s'obscurcir** *vp* 1. (*s'assombrir*) to grow dark. 2. (*s'embrouiller*) to become confused.

obscurité [ɔpskyrite] *nf* (*nuit*) darkness.

obsédé, -e [ɔpsede] ◆ *adj* obsessed. ◆ *nm, f* obsessive.

obséder [ɔpsede] *vt* to obsess, to haunt.

obsèques [ɔpsɛk] *nfpl* funeral (*sg*).

obséquieux, -euse [ɔpsekjø, øz] *adj* obsequious.

observateur, -trice [ɔpsɛrvatœr, tris] ◆ *adj* observant. ◆ *nm, f* observer.

observation [ɔpsɛrvasjɔ̃] *nf* 1. (*gén*) observation; **être en ~** (MÉD) to be under observation. 2. (*critique*) remark.

observatoire [ɔpsɛrvatwar] *nm* (ASTRON) observatory.

observer [ɔpsɛrve] *vt* 1. (*regarder, remarquer, respecter*) to observe. 2. (*épier*) to watch. 3. (*constater*): **faire ~ qqch à qqn** to point sthg out to sb.

obsession [ɔpsesjɔ̃] *nf* obsession.

obsolète [ɔpsɔlɛt] *adj* obsolete.

obstacle [ɔpstakl] *nm* 1. (*entrave*) obstacle. 2. *fig* (*difficulté*) hindrance; **faire ~ à qqch/qqn** to hinder sthg/sb.

obstétrique [ɔpstetrik] *nf* obstetrics (U).

obstination [ɔpstinasjɔ̃] *nf* stubbornness, obstinacy.

obstiné, -e [ɔpstine] *adj* 1. (*entêté*) stubborn, obstinate. 2. (*acharné*) dogged.

obstiner [ɔpstine] ▶ **s'obstiner** *vp* to insist; **s'~ à faire qqch** to persist stubbornly in doing sthg; **s'~ dans qqch** to cling stubbornly to sthg.

obstruction [ɔpstryksjɔ̃] *nf* 1. (MÉD) obstruction, blockage. 2. (POLIT & SPORT) obstruction.

obstruer [ɔpstrye] *vt* to block, to obstruct. ▶ **s'obstruer** *vp* to become blocked.

obtempérer [ɔptɑ̃pere] *vi*: ~ **à** to comply with.

obtenir [ɔptənir] *vt* to get, to obtain; ~ **qqch de qqn** to get sthg from sb; ~ **qqch à ou pour qqn** to obtain sthg for sb.

obtention [ɔptɑ̃sjɔ̃] *nf* obtaining.

obtenu, -e [ɔptəny] *pp* → **obtenir**.

obturer [ɔptyre] *vt* to close, to seal; (*dent*) to fill.

obtus, -e [ɔpty, yz] *adj* obtuse.

obus [ɔby] *nm* shell.

OC (*abr de* **ondes courtes**) SW.

occasion [ɔkazjɔ̃] *nf* 1. (*possibilité, chance*) opportunity, chance; **saisir l'~ (de faire qqch)** to seize ou grab the chance (to do sthg); **à l'~** some time; (*de temps en temps*) sometimes, on occasion; **à la première ~** at the first opportunity. 2. (*circonstance*) occasion; **à l'~ de** on the occasion of. 3. (*bonne affaire*) bargain. ▶ **d'occasion** *loc adv & loc adj* second-hand.

occasionnel, -elle [ɔkazjɔnɛl] *adj* (*irrégulier - visite, problème*) occasional; (*- travail*) casual.

occasionner [ɔkazjɔne] *vt* to cause.

occident [ɔksidɑ̃] *nm* west. ▶ **Occident** *nm*: **l'Occident** the West.

occidental, -e, -aux [ɔksidɑ̃tal, o] *adj* western. ▶ **Occidental, -e, -aux** *nm, f* Westerner.

occlusion [ɔklyzjɔ̃] *nf* 1. (MÉD) blockage, obstruction. 2. (LING & CHIM) occlusion.

occulte [ɔkylt] *adj* occult.

occulter [ɔkylte] *vt* (*sentiments*) to conceal.

occupation [ɔkypasjɔ̃] *nf* 1. (*activité*) occupation, job. 2. (MIL) occupation.

occupé, -e [ɔkype] *adj* 1. (*personne*) busy; **être ~ à qqch** to be busy with sthg. 2. (*appartement, zone*) occupied. 3. (*place*) taken; (*toilettes*) engaged; **c'est ~** (*téléphone*) it's engaged Br ou busy Am.

occuper [ɔkype] vt 1. (gén) to occupy. 2. (espace) to take up. 3. (fonction, poste) to hold. 4. (main-d'œuvre) to employ. ▶ **s'occuper** vp 1. (s'activer) to keep o.s. busy; **s'~ à qqch/à faire qqch** to be busy with sthg/doing sthg. 2. **s'~ de qqch** (se charger de) to take care of sthg, to deal with sthg; (s'intéresser à) to take an interest in sthg, to be interested in sthg; **occupez-vous de vos affaires!** mind your own business! 3. (prendre soin): **s'~ de qqn** to take care of sb, to look after sb.

occurrence [ɔkyrɑ̃s] nf 1. (circonstance): **en l'~** in this case. 2. (LING) occurrence.

OCDE (abr de Organisation de coopération et de développement économique) nf OECD.

océan [ɔseɑ̃] nm ocean; **l'~ Antarctique** the Antarctic Ocean; **l'~ Arctique** the Arctic Ocean; **l'~ Atlantique** the Atlantic Ocean; **l'~ Indien** the Indian Ocean; **l'~ Pacifique** the Pacific Ocean.

Océanie [ɔseani] nf: **l'~** Oceania.

océanique [ɔseanik] adj ocean (avant n).

ocre [ɔkr] adj inv & nf ochre.

octante [ɔktɑ̃t] adj num Belg & Helv eighty.

octave [ɔktav] nf octave.

octet [ɔktɛ] nm (INFORM) byte.

octobre [ɔktɔbr] nm October; voir aussi **septembre**.

octogénaire [ɔktɔʒenɛr] nmf & adj octogenarian.

octroyer [ɔktrwaje] vt: **~ qqch à qqn** to grant sb sthg, to grant sthg to sb. ▶ **s'octroyer** vp to grant o.s., to treat o.s. to.

oculaire [ɔkylɛr] ◆ nm eyepiece. ◆ adj ocular, eye (avant n); **témoin ~** eyewitness.

oculiste [ɔkylist] nmf ophthalmologist.

ode [ɔd] nf ode.

odeur [ɔdœr] nf smell.

odieux, -euse [ɔdjø, øz] adj 1. (crime) odious, abominable. 2. (personne, attitude) unbearable, obnoxious.

odorant, -e [ɔdɔrɑ̃, ɑ̃t] adj sweet-smelling, fragrant.

odorat [ɔdɔra] nm (sense of) smell.

œdème [edɛm] nm oedema.

œil [œj] (pl **yeux** [jø]) nm 1. (gén) eye; **yeux bridés/exorbités/globuleux** slanting/bulging/protruding eyes; **avoir les yeux cernés** to have bags under one's eyes; **baisser/lever les yeux** to look down/up, to lower/raise one's eyes; **à**

l'~ nu to the naked eye; **à vue d'~** visibly. 2. loc: **avoir qqch/qqn à l'~** to have one's eye on sthg/sb; **n'avoir pas froid aux yeux** not to be afraid of anything, to have plenty of nerve; **mon ~!** fam like hell!; **cela saute aux yeux** it's obvious.

œillade [œjad] nf wink; **lancer une ~ à qqn** to wink at sb.

œillère [œjɛr] nf eyebath. ▶ **œillères** nfpl blinkers Br, blinders Am.

œillet [œjɛ] nm 1. (fleur) carnation. 2. (de chaussure) eyelet.

œnologue [enɔlɔg] nmf wine expert.

œsophage [ezɔfaʒ] nm oesophagus.

œstrogène [ɛstrɔʒɛn] nm oestrogen.

œuf [œf] nm egg; **~ à la coque/au plat/poché** boiled/fried/poached egg; **~ mollet/dur** soft-boiled/hard-boiled egg; **~s brouillés** scrambled eggs.

œuvre [œvr] nf 1. (travail) work; **être à l'~** to be working ou at work; **se mettre à l'~** to get down to work; **mettre qqch en ~** to make use of sthg; (loi, accord, projet) to implement sthg. 2. (d'artiste) work; (- ensemble de sa production) works (pl); **~ d'art** work of art. 3. (organisation) charity; **~ de bienfaisance** charity, charitable organization.

off [ɔf] adj inv (CIN) (voix, son) off.

offense [ɔfɑ̃s] nf 1. (insulte) insult. 2. (RELIG) trespass.

offenser [ɔfɑ̃se] vt 1. (personne) to offend. 2. (bon goût) to offend against. ▶ **s'offenser** vp: **s'~ de** to take offence at, to be offended by.

offensif, -ive [ɔfɑ̃sif, iv] adj offensive. ▶ **offensive** nf 1. (MIL) offensive; **passer à l'offensive** to go on the offensive; **prendre l'offensive** to take the offensive. 2. fig (du froid) (sudden) onset.

offert, -e [ɔfɛr, ɛrt] pp → **offrir**.

office [ɔfis] nm 1. (bureau) office, agency; **~ du tourisme** tourist office. 2. (fonction): **faire ~ de** to act as; **remplir son ~** to do its job, to fulfil its function. 3. (RELIG) service. ▶ **d'office** loc adv automatically, as a matter of course; **commis d'~** officially appointed.

officialiser [ɔfisjalize] vt to make official.

officiel, -elle [ɔfisjɛl] adj & nm, f official.

officiellement [ɔfisjɛlmɑ̃] adv officially.

officier¹ [ɔfisje] vi to officiate.

officier² [ɔfisje] nm officer.

officieux, -euse [ɔfisjø, øz] adj unofficial.

offrande [ɔfrɑ̃d] *nf* 1. (*don*) offering. 2. (RELIG) offertory.

offre [ɔfr] *nf* 1. (*proposition*) offer; (*aux enchères*) bid; (*pour contrat*) tender; **'~s d'emploi** 'situations vacant', 'vacancies'; **~ d'essai** trial offer; **~ de lancement** introductory offer; **~ publique d'achat** takeover bid. 2. (ÉCON) supply; **la loi de l'~ et de la demande** the law of supply and demand.

offrir [ɔfrir] *vt* 1. (*faire cadeau*): **~ qqch à qqn** to give sb sthg, to give sthg to sb. 2. (*proposer*): **~ qqch à qqn** to offer sb sthg ou sthg to sb. 3. (*présenter*) to offer, to present; **son visage n'offrait rien d'accueillant** his/her face showed no sign of welcome. ▶ **s'offrir** *vp* 1. (*croisière, livre*) to treat o.s. to. 2. (*se présenter*) to present itself. 3. (*se proposer*) to offer one's services, to offer o.s.

offusquer [ɔfyske] *vt* to offend. ▶ **s'offusquer** *vp*: **s'~ (de)** to take offence (at).

ogive [ɔʒiv] *nf* 1. (ARCHIT) ogive. 2. (MIL) (*d'obus*) head; (*de fusée*) nosecone; **~ nucléaire** nuclear warhead.

ogre, ogresse [ɔgr, ɔgres] *nm, f* ogre (*f* ogress).

oh [o] *interj* oh!; **~ la la!** dear oh dear!

ohé [ɔe] *interj* hey!

oie [wa] *nf* goose.

oignon [ɔɲɔ̃] *nm* 1. (*plante*) onion. 2. (*bulbe*) bulb. 3. (MÉD) bunion.

oiseau, -x [wazo] *nm* 1. (ZOOL) bird; **~ de proie** bird of prey. 2. *fam péj* (*individu*) character.

oisif, -ive [wazif, iv] ◆ *adj* idle. ◆ *nm, f* man of leisure (*f* woman of leisure).

oisillon [wazijɔ̃] *nm* fledgling.

oisiveté [wazivte] *nf* idleness.

O.K. [ɔke] *interj fam* okay.

oléoduc [ɔleɔdyk] *nm* (oil) pipeline.

olfactif, -ive [ɔlfaktif, iv] *adj* olfactory.

olive [ɔliv] *nf* olive.

olivier [ɔlivje] *nm* (*arbre*) olive tree; (*bois*) olive wood.

OLP (*abr de* **Organisation de libération de la Palestine**) *nf* PLO.

olympique [ɔlɛ̃pik] *adj* Olympic (*avant n*).

ombilical, -e, -aux [ɔ̃bilikal, o] *adj* umbilical.

ombrage [ɔ̃braʒ] *nm* shade.

ombragé, -e [ɔ̃braʒe] *adj* shady.

ombrageux, -euse [ɔ̃braʒø, øz] *adj* 1. (*personne*) touchy, prickly. 2. (*cheval*) nervous, skittish.

ombre [ɔ̃br] *nf* 1. (*zone sombre*) shade; **à**

l'~ de (*arbre*) in the shade of; **laisser qqch dans l'~** *fig* to deliberately ignore sthg. 2. (*forme, fantôme*) shadow. 3. (*trace*) hint.

ombrelle [ɔ̃brel] *nf* parasol.

omelette [ɔmlet] *nf* omelette.

omettre [ɔmetr] *vt* to omit; **~ de faire qqch** to omit to do sthg.

omis, -e [ɔmi, iz] *pp* → **omettre**.

omission [ɔmisjɔ̃] *nf* omission; **par ~** by omission.

omnibus [ɔmnibys] *nm* stopping ou local train.

omniprésent, -e [ɔmniprezɑ̃, ɑ̃t] *adj* omnipresent.

omnisports [ɔmnispɔr] *adj inv* sports (*avant n*).

omnivore [ɔmnivɔr] ◆ *nm* omnivore. ◆ *adj* omnivorous.

omoplate [ɔmɔplat] *nf* (*os*) shoulder blade; (*épaule*) shoulder.

OMS (*abr de* **Organisation mondiale de la santé**) *nf* WHO.

on [ɔ̃] *pron pers indéf* 1. (*indéterminé*) you, one; **~ n'a pas le droit de fumer ici** you're not allowed ou one isn't allowed to smoke here, smoking isn't allowed here. 2. (*les gens, l'espèce humaine*) they, people; **~ vit de plus en plus vieux en Europe** people in Europe are living longer and longer. 3. (*quelqu'un*) someone; **~ vous a appelé au téléphone ce matin** there was a telephone call for you this morning. 4. *fam* (*nous*) we; **~ s'en va** we're off, we're going.

oncle [ɔ̃kl] *nm* uncle.

onctueux, -euse [ɔ̃ktɥø, øz] *adj* smooth.

onde [ɔ̃d] *nf* (PHYS) wave. ▶ **ondes** *nfpl* (*radio*) air (*sg*).

ondée [ɔ̃de] *nf* shower (of rain).

ondoyer [ɔ̃dwaje] *vi* to ripple.

ondulation [ɔ̃dylasjɔ̃] *nf* 1. (*mouvement*) rippling; (*de sol, terrain*) undulation. 2. (*de coiffure*) wave.

onduler [ɔ̃dyle] *vi* (*drapeau*) to ripple, to wave; (*cheveux*) to be wavy; (*route*) to undulate.

onéreux, -euse [ɔnerø, øz] *adj* costly.

ongle [ɔ̃gl] *nm* 1. (*de personne*) fingernail, nail; **se ronger les ~s** to bite one's nails. 2. (*d'animal*) claw.

onglet [ɔ̃gle] *nm* 1. (*de reliure*) tab. 2. (*de lame*) thumbnail groove. 3. (CULIN) top skirt.

onguent [ɔ̃gɑ̃] *nm* ointment.

onomatopée [ɔnɔmatɔpe] *nf* onomatopoeia.

ont → **avoir**.

ONU, Onu [ɔny] (*abr de* **Organisation des Nations unies**) *nf* UN, UNO.

onyx [ɔniks] *nm* onyx.

onze [ɔ̃z] ◆ *adj num* eleven. ◆ *nm* (*chiffre &* SPORT) eleven; *voir aussi* **six**.

onzième [ɔ̃zjɛm] *adj num, nm & nmf* eleventh; *voir aussi* **sixième**.

OPA (*abr de* **offre publique d'achat**) *nf* takeover bid.

opacité [ɔpasite] *nf* opacity.

opale [ɔpal] *nf & adj inv* opal.

opaline [ɔpalin] *nf* opaline.

opaque [ɔpak] *adj*: ~ **(à)** opaque (to).

OPEP, Opep [ɔpɛp] (*abr de* **Organisation des pays exportateurs de pétrole**) *nf* OPEC.

opéra [ɔpera] *nm* **1.** (MUS) opera. **2.** (*théâtre*) opera house.

opéra-comique [ɔperakɔmik] *nm* light opera.

opérateur, -trice [ɔperatœr, tris] *nm, f* operator.

opération [ɔperasjɔ̃] *nf* **1.** (*gén*) operation. **2.** (COMM) deal, transaction.

opérationnel, -elle [ɔperasjɔnɛl] *adj* operational.

opérer [ɔpere] ◆ *vt* **1.** (MÉD) to operate on. **2.** (*exécuter*) to carry out, to implement; (*choix, tri*) to make. ◆ *vi* (*agir*) to take effect; (*personne*) to operate, to proceed. ▶ **s'opérer** *vp* to come about, to take place.

opérette [ɔperɛt] *nf* operetta.

ophtalmologiste [ɔftalmɔlɔʒist] *nmf* ophthalmologist.

Opinel® [ɔpinɛl] *nm* folding knife used especially for outdoor activities, scouting etc.

opiniâtre [ɔpinjatr] *adj* **1.** (*caractère, personne*) stubborn, obstinate. **2.** (*effort*) dogged; (*travail*) unrelenting; (*fièvre, toux*) persistent.

opinion [ɔpinjɔ̃] *nf* opinion; **avoir (une) bonne/mauvaise ~ de** to have a good/bad opinion of; **l'~ publique** public opinion.

opium [ɔpjɔm] *nm* opium.

opportun, -e [ɔpɔrtœ̃, yn] *adj* opportune, timely.

opportuniste [ɔpɔrtynist] ◆ *nmf* opportunist. ◆ *adj* opportunistic.

opportunité [ɔpɔrtynite] *nf* **1.** (*à-propos*) opportuneness, timeliness. **2.** (*occasion*) opportunity.

opposant, -e [ɔposɑ̃, ɑ̃t] ◆ *adj* opposing. ◆ *nm, f*: ~ **(à)** opponent (of).

opposé, -e [ɔpoze] *adj* **1.** (*direction, côté, angle*) opposite. **2.** (*intérêts, opinions*) conflicting; (*forces*) opposing. **3.** (*hostile*): ~ **à** opposed to. ▶ **opposé** *nm*: **l'~** the opposite; **à l'~ de** in the opposite direction from; *fig* unlike, contrary to.

opposer [ɔpoze] *vt* **1.** (*mettre en opposition - choses, notions*): ~ **qqch (à)** to contrast sthg (with). **2.** (*mettre en présence - personnes, armées*) to oppose; ~ **deux équipes** to bring two teams together; ~ **qqn à qqn** to pit ou set sb against sb. **3.** (*refus, protestation, objection*) to put forward. **4.** (*diviser*) to divide. ▶ **s'opposer** *vp* **1.** (*contraster*) to contrast. **2.** (*entrer en conflit*) to clash. **3.** **s'~ à** (*se dresser contre*) to oppose, to be opposed to; **s'~ à ce que qqn fasse qqch** to be opposed to sb's doing sthg.

opposition [ɔpozisjɔ̃] *nf* **1.** (*gén*) opposition; **faire ~ à** (*décision, mariage*) to oppose; (*chèque*) to stop; **entrer en ~ avec** to come into conflict with. **2.** (JUR): ~ **(à)** objection (to). **3.** (*contraste*) contrast; **par ~ à** in contrast with, as opposed to.

oppresser [ɔprese] *vt* **1.** (*étouffer*) to suffocate, to stifle. **2.** *fig* (*tourmenter*) to oppress.

oppresseur [ɔpresœr] *nm* oppressor.

oppressif, -ive [ɔpresif, iv] *adj* oppressive.

oppression [ɔpresjɔ̃] *nf* **1.** (*asservissement*) oppression. **2.** (*malaise*) tightness of the chest.

opprimé, -e [ɔprime] ◆ *adj* oppressed. ◆ *nm, f* oppressed person.

opprimer [ɔprime] *vt* **1.** (*asservir*) to oppress. **2.** (*étouffer*) to stifle.

opter [ɔpte] *vi*: ~ **pour** to opt for.

opticien, -enne [ɔptisjɛ̃, ɛn] *nm, f* optician.

optimal, -e, -aux [ɔptimal, o] *adj* optimal.

optimisme [ɔptimism] *nm* optimism.

optimiste [ɔptimist] ◆ *nmf* optimist. ◆ *adj* optimistic.

option [ɔpsjɔ̃] *nf* **1.** (*gén*) option; **prendre une ~ sur** (FIN) to take (out) an option on. **2.** (*accessoire*) optional extra.

optionnel, -elle [ɔpsjɔnɛl] *adj* optional.

optique [ɔptik] ◆ *nf* **1.** (*science, technique*) optics (U). **2.** (*perspective*) viewpoint. ◆ *adj* (*nerf*) optic; (*verre*) optical.

opulence [ɔpylɑ̃s] *nf* **1.** (*richesse*) opulence. **2.** (*ampleur*) fullness, ampleness.

opulent, -e [ɔpylɑ̃, ɑ̃t] *adj* **1.** (*riche*) rich. **2.** (*gros*) ample.

or¹ [ɔr] *nm* **1.** (*métal, couleur*) gold; **en ~** (*objet*) gold (*avant* n); **une occasion en ~** a golden opportunity; **une affaire en ~** (*achat*) an excellent bargain; (*commerce*) a lucrative line of business; **~ massif** solid gold. **2.** (*dorure*) gilding.

or² [ɔr] *conj* (*au début d'une phrase*) now; (*pour introduire un contraste*) well, but.

oracle [ɔrakl] *nm* oracle.

orage [ɔraʒ] *nm* (*tempête*) storm.

orageux, -euse [ɔraʒø, øz] *adj* stormy.

oraison [ɔrɛzɔ̃] *nf* prayer; **~ funèbre** funeral oration.

oral, -e, -aux [ɔral, o] *adj* oral.
▶ **oral** *nm* oral (*examination*). **~ de rattrapage** *oral examination taken after failing written exams.*

oralement [ɔralmɑ̃] *adv* orally.

orange [ɔrɑ̃ʒ] ◆ *nf* orange. ◆ *nm & adj inv* (*couleur*) orange.

orangé, -e [ɔrɑ̃ʒe] *adj* orangey.

orangeade [ɔrɑ̃ʒad] *nf* orange squash.

oranger [ɔrɑ̃ʒe] *nm* orange tree.

orang-outan, orang-outang [ɔrɑ̃utɑ̃] *nm* orangutang.

orateur, -trice [ɔratœr, tris] *nm, f* **1.** (*conférencier*) speaker. **2.** (*personne éloquente*) orator.

orbital, -e, -aux [ɔrbital, o] *adj* (*mouvement*) orbital; (*station*) orbiting.

orbite [ɔrbit] *nf* **1.** (ANAT) (eye) socket. **2.** (ASTRON & *fig*) orbit; **mettre sur ~** (AÉRON) to put into orbit; *fig* to launch.

orchestre [ɔrkɛstr] *nm* **1.** (MUS) orchestra. **2.** (CIN & THÉÂTRE) stalls (*pl*) Br, orchestra Am; **fauteuil d'~** seat in the stalls Br, orchestra seat Am.

orchestrer [ɔrkɛstre] *vt litt & fig* to orchestrate.

orchidée [ɔrkide] *nf* orchid.

ordinaire [ɔrdinɛr] ◆ *adj* **1.** (*usuel, standard*) ordinary, normal. **2.** *péj* (*commun*) ordinary, common. ◆ *nm* **1.** (*moyenne*): **l'~** the ordinary. **2.** (*alimentation*) usual diet. ▶ **d'ordinaire** *loc adv* normally, usually.

ordinal, -e, -aux [ɔrdinal, o] *adj* ordinal. ▶ **ordinal, -aux** *nm* ordinal (number).

ordinateur [ɔrdinatœr] *nm* computer; **~ individuel** personal computer, PC.

ordonnance [ɔrdɔnɑ̃s] ◆ *nf* **1.** (MÉD) prescription. **2.** (*de gouvernement, juge*) order. ◆ *nm ou nf* (MIL) orderly.

ordonné, -e [ɔrdɔne] *adj* (*maison, élève*) tidy.

ordonner [ɔrdɔne] *vt* **1.** (*ranger*) to organize, to put in order. **2.** (*enjoindre*) to order, to tell; **~ à qqn de faire qqch** to order sb to do sthg. **3.** (RELIG) to ordain. **4.** (MATHS) to arrange in order. ▶ **s'ordonner** *vp* to be arranged ou put in order.

ordre [ɔrdr] *nm* **1.** (*gén*, MIL & RELIG) order; **par ~ alphabétique/chronologique/décroissant** in alphabetical/chronological/descending order; **donner un ~ à qqn** to give sb an order; **être aux ~s de qqn** to be at sb's disposal; **jusqu'à nouvel ~** until further notice; **l'~ public** law and order. **2.** (*bonne organisation*) tidiness, orderliness; **en ~** orderly, tidy; **mettre en ~** to put in order, to tidy (up). **3.** (*catégorie*): **de premier ~** first-rate; **de second ~** second-rate; **d'~ privé/pratique** of a private/practical nature; **pouvez-vous me donner un ~ de grandeur?** can you give me some idea of the size/amount *etc*? **4.** (*corporation*) professional association; **l'Ordre des médecins** ≃ the British Medical Association Br, ≃ the American Medical Association Am. **5.** (FIN): **à l'~ de** payable to. ▶ **ordre du jour** *nm* **1.** (*de réunion*) agenda; **à l'~ du jour** (*de réunion*) on the agenda; *fig* topical. **2.** (MIL) order of the day.

ordure [ɔrdyr] *nf* **1.** *fig* (*grossièreté*) filth (U). **2.** *péj* (*personne*) scum (U), bastard. ▶ **ordures** *nfpl* (*déchets*) rubbish (U) Br, garbage (U) Am.

ordurier, -ère [ɔrdyrje, ɛr] *adj* filthy, obscene.

orée [ɔre] *nf* edge.

oreille [ɔrɛj] *nf* **1.** (ANAT) ear. **2.** (*ouïe*) hearing. **3.** (*de fauteuil, écrou*) wing; (*de marmite, tasse*) handle.

oreiller [ɔreje] *nm* pillow.

oreillette [ɔrɛjɛt] *nf* **1.** (*du cœur*) auricle. **2.** (*de casquette*) earflap.

oreillons [ɔrɛjɔ̃] *nmpl* mumps (*sg*).

ores [ɔr] ▶ **d'ores et déjà** *loc adv* from now on.

orfèvre [ɔrfɛvr] *nm* goldsmith; (*d'argent*) silversmith.

orfèvrerie [ɔrfɛvrəri] *nf* **1.** (*art*) goldsmith's art; (*d'argent*) silversmith's art. **2.** (*commerce*) goldsmith's trade; (*d'argent*) silversmith's trade.

organe [ɔrgan] *nm* **1.** (ANAT) organ. **2.** (*institution*) organ, body. **3.** *fig* (*porte-parole*) representative.

organigramme [ɔrganigram] *nm* **1.** (*hiérarchique*) organization chart.

2. (INFORM) flow chart.

organique [ɔrganik] *adj* organic.

organisateur, -trice [ɔrganizatœr, tris] ♦ *adj* organizing (*avant n*). ♦ *nm, f* organizer.

organisation [ɔrganizasjɔ̃] *nf* organization.

organisé, -e [ɔrganize] *adj* organized.

organiser [ɔrganize] *vt* to organize. ► **s'organiser** *vp* **1.** (*personne*) to be ou get organized. **2.** (*prendre forme*) to take shape.

organisme [ɔrganism] *nm* **1.** (BIOL & ZOOL) organism. **2.** (*institution*) body, organization.

organiste [ɔrganist] *nmf* organist.

orgasme [ɔrgasm] *nm* orgasm.

orge [ɔrʒ] *nf* barley.

orgie [ɔrʒi] *nf* orgy.

orgue [ɔrg] *nm* organ.

orgueil [ɔrgœj] *nm* pride.

orgueilleux, -euse [ɔrgœjø, øz] ♦ *adj* proud. ♦ *nm, f* proud person.

orient [ɔrjɑ̃] *nm* east. ► **Orient** *nm*: **l'Orient** the Orient, the East.

oriental, -e, -aux [ɔrjɑ̃tal, o] *adj* (*région, frontière*) eastern; (*d'Extrême-Orient*) oriental.

orientation [ɔrjɑ̃tasjɔ̃] *nf* **1.** (*direction*) orientation; **avoir le sens de l'~** to have a good sense of direction. **2.** (SCOL) career. **3.** (*de maison*) aspect. **4.** *fig* (*de politique, recherche*) direction, trend.

orienté, -e [ɔrjɑ̃te] *adj* (*tendancieux*) biased.

orienter [ɔrjɑ̃te] *vt* **1.** (*disposer*) to position. **2.** (*voyageur, élève, recherches*) to guide, to direct. ► **s'orienter** *vp* **1.** (*se repérer*) to find ou get one's bearings. **2.** *fig* (*se diriger*): **s'~ vers** to move towards.

orifice [ɔrifis] *nm* orifice.

originaire [ɔriʒinɛr] *adj* **1.** (*natif*): **être ~ de** to originate from; (*personne*) to be a native of. **2.** (*premier*) original.

original, -e, -aux [ɔriʒinal, o] ♦ *adj* **1.** (*premier, inédit*) original. **2.** (*singulier*) eccentric. ♦ *nm, f* (*personne*) (outlandish) character. ► **original, -aux** *nm* (*œuvre, document*) original.

originalité [ɔriʒinalite] *nf* **1.** (*nouveauté*) originality; (*caractéristique*) original feature. **2.** (*excentricité*) eccentricity.

origine [ɔriʒin] *nf* **1.** (*gén*) origin; **d'~** (*originel*) original; (*de départ*) of origin; **pays d'~** country of origin; **d'~ anglaise** of English origin; **à l'~** originally. **2.** (*souche*) origins (*pl*). **3.** (*provenance*) source.

ORL *nmf* (*abr de* **oto-rhino-laryngologiste**) ENT specialist.

orme [ɔrm] *nm* elm.

ornement [ɔrnəmɑ̃] *nm* **1.** (*gén* & MUS) ornament; **d'~** (*plante, arbre*) ornamental. **2.** (ARCHIT) embellishment.

orner [ɔrne] *vt* **1.** (*décorer*): **~ (de)** to decorate (with). **2.** (*agrémenter*) to adorn.

ornière [ɔrnjɛr] *nf* rut.

ornithologie [ɔrnitɔlɔʒi] *nf* ornithology.

orphelin, -e [ɔrfəlɛ̃, in] ♦ *adj* orphan (*avant n*), orphaned. ♦ *nm, f* orphan.

orphelinat [ɔrfəlina] *nm* orphanage.

orteil [ɔrtɛj] *nm* toe.

orthodontiste [ɔrtɔdɔ̃tist] *nmf* orthodontist.

orthodoxe [ɔrtɔdɔks] ♦ *adj* **1.** (RELIG) Orthodox. **2.** (*conformiste*) orthodox. ♦ *nmf* (RELIG) Orthodox Christian.

orthographe [ɔrtɔgraf] *nf* spelling.

orthopédiste [ɔrtɔpedist] *nmf* orthopaedist.

orthophoniste [ɔrtɔfɔnist] *nmf* speech therapist.

ortie [ɔrti] *nf* nettle.

os [ɔs, *pl* o] *nm* **1.** (*gén*) bone; **~ à moelle** marrowbone. **2.** *fam fig* (*difficulté*) snag, hitch.

oscillation [ɔsilasjɔ̃] *nf* oscillation; (*de navire*) rocking.

osciller [ɔsile] *vi* **1.** (*se balancer*) to swing; (*navire*) to rock. **2.** (*vaciller, hésiter*) to waver.

osé, -e [oze] *adj* daring, audacious.

oseille [ozɛj] *nf* (BOT) sorrel.

oser [oze] *vt* to dare; **~ faire qqch** to dare (to) do sthg.

osier [ozje] *nm* **1.** (BOT) osier. **2.** (*fibre*) wicker.

Oslo [ɔslo] *n* Oslo.

ossature [ɔsatyr] *nf* **1.** (ANAT) skeleton. **2.** *fig* (*structure*) framework.

ossements [ɔsmɑ̃] *nmpl* bones.

osseux, -euse [ɔsø, øz] *adj* **1.** (ANAT & MÉD) bone (*avant n*). **2.** (*maigre*) bony.

ossuaire [ɔsɥɛr] *nm* ossuary.

ostensible [ɔstɑ̃sibl] *adj* conspicuous.

ostentation [ɔstɑ̃tasjɔ̃] *nf* ostentation.

ostéopathe [ɔsteɔpat] *nmf* osteopath.

otage [ɔtaʒ] *nm* hostage; **prendre qqn en ~** to take sb hostage.

OTAN, Otan [ɔtɑ̃] (*abr de* **Organisation du traité de l'Atlantique Nord**) *nf* NATO.

otarie [ɔtari] *nf* sea lion.

ôter [ote] *vt* **1.** (*enlever*) to take off. **2.** (*soustraire*) to take away. **3.** (*retirer*, *prendre*): ~ **qqch à qqn** to take sthg away from sb.

otite [ɔtit] *nf* ear infection.

oto-rhino-laryngologie [ɔtɔrinɔlarēgɔlɔʒi] *nf* ear, nose and throat medicine, ENT.

ou [u] *conj* 1. (*indique une alternative, une approximation*) or. 2. (*sinon*): ~ (**bien**) or (else). ▶ **ou (bien) ... ou (bien)** *loc corrélative* either ... or; ~ **c'est elle,** ~ **c'est moi!** it's either her or me!

où [u] ◆ *pron rel* 1. (*spatial*) where; **le village** ~ **j'habite** the village where I live, the village I live in; **partout** ~ **vous irez** wherever you go. 2. (*temporel*) that; **le jour** ~ **je suis venu** the day (that) I came. ◆ *adv* where; **je vais** ~ **je veux** I go where I please; ~ **que vous alliez** wherever you go. ◆ *adv interr* where?; ~ **vas-tu?** where are you going?; **dites-moi** ~ **il est allé** tell me where he's gone. ▶ **d'où** *loc adv* (*conséquence*) hence.

ouaté, -e [wate] *adj* 1. (*garni d'ouate*) cotton wool (*avant n*) Br, cotton (*avant n*) Am; (*vêtement*) quilted. 2. *fig* (*feutré*) muffled.

oubli [ubli] *nm* 1. (*acte d'oublier*) forgetting. 2. (*négligence*) omission; (*étourderie*) oversight. 3. (*général*) oblivion; **tomber dans l'~** to sink into oblivion.

oublier [ublije] *vt* to forget; (*laisser quelque part*) to leave behind; ~ **de faire qqch** to forget to do sthg.

oubliettes [ublijɛt] *nfpl* dungeon (*sg*).

ouest [wɛst] ◆ *nm* west; **un vent d'~** a westerly wind; **à l'~** in the west; **à l'~ (de)** to the west (of). ◆ *adj inv* (*gén*) west; (*province, région*) western.

ouest-allemand, -e [wɛstalmɑ̃, ɑ̃d] *adj* West German.

ouf [uf] *interj* phew!

Ouganda [ugɑ̃da] *nm*: **l'~** Uganda.

oui [wi] ◆ *adv* yes; **tu viens,** ~ **ou non?** are you coming or not?, are you coming or aren't you?; **je crois que** ~ I think so; **faire signe que** ~ to nod; **mais** ~, **bien sûr que** ~ yes, of course. ◆ *nm inv* yes; **pour un** ~ **pour un non** for no apparent reason.

ouï-dire [widir] *nm inv*: **par** ~ by ou from hearsay.

ouïe [wi] *nf* hearing; **avoir l'~ fine** to have excellent hearing. ▶ **ouïes** *nfpl* (*de poisson*) gills.

ouragan [uragɑ̃] *nm* (MÉTÉOR) hurricane.

ourlet [urlɛ] *nm* (COUTURE) hem.

ours [urs] *nm* bear; ~ **(en peluche)** teddy (bear); ~ **polaire** polar bear.

ourse [urs] *nf* she-bear.

oursin [ursē] *nm* sea urchin.

ourson [ursɔ̃] *nm* bear cub.

outil [uti] *nm* tool.

outillage [utijaʒ] *nm* (*équipement*) tools (*pl*), equipment.

outrage [utraʒ] *nm* 1. *sout* (*insulte*) insult. 2. (JUR): ~ **à la pudeur** indecent behaviour (U).

outrager [utraʒe] *vt* (*offenser*) to insult.

outrance [utrɑ̃s] *nf* excess; **à** ~ excessively.

outrancier, -ère [utrɑ̃sje, ɛr] *adj* extravagant.

outre¹ [utr] *nf* wineskin.

outre² [utr] ◆ *prép* besides, as well as. ◆ *adv*: **passer** ~ to go on, to proceed further. ▶ **en outre** *loc adv* moreover, besides.

outre-Atlantique [utratlɑ̃tik] *loc adv* across the Atlantic.

outre-Manche [utrəmɑ̃ʃ] *loc adv* across the Channel.

outremer [utrəmɛr] ◆ *nm* (*pierre*) lapis lazuli; (*couleur*) ultramarine. ◆ *adj inv* ultramarine.

outre-mer [utrəmɛr] *loc adv* overseas.

outrepasser [utrəpase] *vt* to exceed.

outrer [utre] *vt* (*personne*) to outrage.

outre-Rhin [utrərē] *loc adv* across the Rhine.

outsider [awtsajdœr] *nm* outsider.

ouvert, -e [uvɛr, ɛrt] ◆ *pp* → **ouvrir**. ◆ *adj* 1. (*gén*) open; **grand** ~ wide open. 2. (*robinet*) on, running.

ouvertement [uvɛrtəmɑ̃] *adv* openly.

ouverture [uvɛrtyr] *nf* 1. (*gén*) opening; (*d'hostilités*) outbreak; ~ **d'esprit** open-mindedness. 2. (MUS) overture. 3. (PHOT) aperture. ▶ **ouvertures** *nfpl* (*propositions*) overtures.

ouvrable [uvrabl] *adj* working; **heures** ~**s** hours of business.

ouvrage [uvraʒ] *nm* 1. (*travail*) work (U), task; **se mettre à l'~** to start work. 2. (*objet produit*) (piece of) work; (COUTURE) work (U). 3. (*livre, écrit*) work; ~ **de référence** reference work.

ouvré, -e [uvre] *adj*: **jour** ~ working day.

ouvre-boîtes [uvrəbwat] *nm inv* tin opener Br, can opener.

ouvre-bouteilles [uvrəbutɛj] *nm inv* bottle opener.

ouvreuse [uvrøz] *nf* usherette.

ouvrier, -ère [uvrije, ɛr] ◆ *adj* (*quartier, enfance*) working-class; (*conflit*) industrial; (*questions, statut*) labour (*avant n*); **classe ouvrière** working class. ◆ *nm, f* worker; ~ **agricole** farm worker; ~ **qualifié** skilled worker; ~ **spécialisé** semi-skilled worker.

ouvrir [uvrir] ◆ *vt* 1. (*gén*) to open. 2. (*chemin, voie*) to open up. 3. (*gaz*) to turn on. ◆ *vi* to open; ~ **sur qqch** to open onto sthg. ▶ **s'ouvrir** *vp* 1. (*porte, fleur*) to open. 2. (*route, perspectives*) to open up. 3. (*personne*) **s'~ (à qqn)** to confide (in sb), to open up (to sb). 4. (*se blesser*) **s'~ le genou** to cut one's knee open; **s'~ les veines** to slash ou cut one's wrists.

ovaire [ɔvɛr] *nm* ovary.

ovale [ɔval] *adj & nm* oval.

ovation [ɔvasjɔ̃] *nf* ovation; **faire une ~ à qqn** to give sb an ovation.

overdose [ɔvœrdoz] *nf* overdose.

ovin, -e [ɔvɛ̃, in] *adj* ovine. ▶ **ovin** *nm* sheep.

OVNI, Ovni [ɔvni] (*abr de* **objet volant non identifié**) *nm* UFO.

oxydation [ɔksidasjɔ̃] *nf* oxidation, oxidization.

oxyde [ɔksid] *nm* oxide.

oxyder [ɔkside] *vt* to oxidize.

oxygène [ɔksiʒɛn] *nm* oxygen.

oxygéné, -e [ɔksiʒene] *adj* (CHIM) oxygenated; → **eau.**

ozone [ozon] *nm* ozone.

P

p¹, P [pe] *nm inv* p, P.

p² 1. (*abr de* **page**) p. 2. *abr de* **pièce**.

pacemaker [pɛsmekœr] *nm* pacemaker.

pachyderme [paʃidɛrm] *nm* elephant; **les ~s** (the) pachyderms.

pacifier [pasifje] *vt* to pacify.

pacifique [pasifik] *adj* peaceful.

Pacifique [pasifik] *nm*: **le ~** the Pacific (Ocean).

pacifiste [pasifist] *nmf & adj* pacifist.

pack [pak] *nm* pack.

pacotille [pakotij] *nf* shoddy goods (*pl*), rubbish; **de ~** cheap.

pacte [pakt] *nm* pact.

pactiser [paktize] *vi*: ~ **avec** (*faire un*

pacte avec) to make a pact with; (*transiger avec*) to come to terms with.

pactole [paktɔl] *nm* gold mine *fig*.

pagaie [page] *nf* paddle.

pagaille, pagaye, pagaïe [pagaj] *nf fam* mess.

pagayer [pageje] *vi* to paddle.

page [paʒ] ◆ *nf* 1. (*feuillet*) page; ~ **blanche** blank page; **mettre en ~s** (TYPO) to make up (into pages); ~ **d'accueil** (INFORM) home page. 2. *loc*: **être à la ~** to be up-to-date. ◆ *nm* page (boy).

pagne [paɲ] *nm* loincloth.

pagode [pagɔd] *nf* pagoda.

paie, paye [pɛ] *nf* pay (U), wages (*pl*).

paiement, payement [pɛmɑ̃] *nm* payment.

païen, -ïenne [pajɛ̃, ɛn] *adj & nm, f* pagan, heathen.

paillard, -e [pajar, ard] *adj* bawdy.

paillasse [pajas] *nf* 1. (*matelas*) straw mattress. 2. (*d'évier*) draining board.

paillasson [pajasɔ̃] *nm* (*tapis*) doormat.

paille [paj] *nf* 1. (BOT) straw. 2. (*pour boire*) straw. ▶ **paille de fer** *nf* steel wool.

pailleté, -e [pajte] *adj* sequined.

paillette [pajɛt] *nf* (*gén pl*) 1. (*sur vêtements*) sequin, spangle. 2. (*d'or*) grain of gold dust. 3. (*de lessive, savon*) flake; **savon en ~s** soap flakes (*pl*).

pain [pɛ̃] *nm* 1. (*aliment*) bread; **un ~** a loaf; **petit ~** (bread) roll; ~ **de campagne** ≃ farmhouse loaf; ~ **complet** wholemeal bread; ~ **d'épice** ≃ gingerbread; ~ **de mie** sandwich loaf. 2. (*de savon, cire*) bar.

PAIN

Bread is an essential element of every French meal. The basic French loaf is a long stick known as a 'baguette' but there are also other types: a 'ficelle' (long and thin), a 'bâtard' (short), and a 'pain de 400g' (long and fat). The traditional British sliced loaf is rarely found.

---

pair, -e [pɛr] *adj* even. ▶ **pair** *nm* peer. ▶ **paire** *nf* pair; **une ~e de** (*lunettes, ciseaux, chaussures*) a pair of. ▶ **au pair** *loc adv* for board and lodging, for one's keep; **jeune fille au ~** au pair (girl). ▶ **de pair** *loc adv*: **aller de ~ avec** to go hand in hand with.

paisible [pɛzibl] *adj* peaceful.

paître [pɛtr] *vi* to graze.

paix [pɛ] *nf* peace; **en ~** (*en harmonie*) at

peace; (*tranquillement*) in peace; **avoir la ~** to have peace and quiet; **faire la ~ avec qqn** to make peace with sb.

Pakistan [pakistɑ̃] nm: **le ~** Pakistan.

palace [palas] nm luxury hotel.

palais [palɛ] nm 1. (*château*) palace. 2. (*grand édifice*) centre; **~ de justice** (JUR) law courts (pl). 3. (ANAT) palate.

palan [palɑ̃] nm block and tackle, hoist.

pale [pal] nf (*de rame, d'hélice*) blade.

pâle [pal] adj pale.

paléontologie [paleɔ̃tɔlɔʒi] nf paleontology.

Palestine [palɛstin] nf: **la ~** Palestine.

palet [palɛ] nm (HOCKEY) puck.

palette [palɛt] nf (*de peintre*) palette.

pâleur [palœr] nf (*de visage*) pallor.

palier [palje] nm 1. (*d'escalier*) landing. 2. (*étape*) level. 3. (TECHNOL) bearing.

pâlir [palir] vi (*couleur, lumière*) to fade; (*personne*) to turn ou go pale.

palissade [palisad] nf (*clôture*) fence; (*de verdure*) hedge.

palliatif, -ive [paljatif, iv] adj palliative. ▸ **palliatif** nm 1. (MÉD) palliative. 2. *fig* stopgap measure.

pallier [palje] vt to make up for.

palmarès [palmarɛs] nm 1. (*de lauréats*) list of (medal) winners; (SCOL) list of prizewinners. 2. (*de succès*) record (of achievements).

palme [palm] nf 1. (*de palmier*) palm-leaf. 2. (*de nageur*) flipper. 3. (*décoration, distinction*): **avec ~** (MIL) = with bar.

palmé, -e [palme] adj 1. (BOT) palmate. 2. (ZOOL) web-footed; (*patte*) webbed.

palmeraie [palmərɛ] nf palm grove.

palmier [palmje] nm (BOT) palm tree.

palmipède [palmipɛd] nm web-footed bird.

palombe [palɔ̃b] nf woodpigeon.

pâlot, -otte [palo, ɔt] adj pale, sickly-looking.

palourde [palurd] nf clam.

palper [palpe] vt (*toucher*) to feel, to finger; (MÉD) to palpate.

palpitant, -e [palpitɑ̃, ɑ̃t] adj exciting, thrilling.

palpitation [palpitasjɔ̃] nf palpitation.

palpiter [palpite] vi (*paupières*) to flutter; (*cœur*) to pound.

paludisme [palydism] nm malaria.

pâmer [pame] ▸ **se pâmer** vp *littéraire* (*s'évanouir*) to swoon (away).

pamphlet [pɑ̃flɛ] nm satirical tract.

pamplemousse [pɑ̃pləmus] nm grapefruit.

pan [pɑ̃] ◆ nm 1. (*de vêtement*) tail. 2. (*d'affiche*) piece, bit; **~ de mur** section of wall. ◆ *interj* bang!

panache [panaʃ] nm 1. (*de plumes, fumée*) plume. 2. (*éclat*) panache.

panaché, -e [panaʃe] adj 1. (*de plusieurs couleurs*) multicoloured. 2. (*mélangé*) mixed. ▸ **panaché** nm shandy.

Panama [panama] nm (*pays*): **le ~** Panama.

panaris [panari] nm whitlow.

pancarte [pɑ̃kart] nf 1. (*de manifestant*) placard. 2. (*de signalisation*) sign.

pancréas [pɑ̃kreas] nm pancreas.

pané, -e [pane] adj breaded, in breadcrumbs.

panier [panje] nm basket; **~ à provisions** shopping basket.

panique [panik] ◆ nf panic. ◆ adj panicky; **être pris d'une peur ~** to be panic-stricken.

paniquer [panike] ◆ vt to panic; **il était complètement paniqué** he was in total ou complete panic. ◆ vi to panic.

panne [pan] nf (*arrêt*) breakdown; **tomber en ~** to break down; **tomber en ~ d'essence** ou **en ~ sèche** to run out of petrol; **~ de courant** ou **d'électricité** power failure.

panneau, -x [pano] nm 1. (*pancarte*) sign; **~ indicateur** signpost; **~ publicitaire** (advertising) hoarding Br, billboard Am; **~ de signalisation** road sign. 2. (*élément*) panel.

panonceau, -x [panɔ̃so] nm (*enseigne*) sign.

panoplie [panɔpli] nf 1. (*jouet*) outfit. 2. *fig* (*de mesures*) package.

panorama [panɔrama] nm (*vue*) view, panorama; *fig* overview.

panse [pɑ̃s] nf 1. (*d'estomac*) first stomach, rumen. 2. *fam* (*gros ventre*) belly, paunch. 3. (*partie arrondie*) bulge.

pansement [pɑ̃smɑ̃] nm dressing, bandage; **~ (adhésif)** (sticking) plaster Br, Bandaid® Am.

panser [pɑ̃se] vt 1. (*plaie*) to dress, to bandage; (*jambe*) to put a dressing on, to bandage; (*avec pansement adhésif*) to put a plaster Br ou Bandaid® Am on. 2. (*cheval*) to groom.

pantalon [pɑ̃talɔ̃] nm trousers (pl) Br, pants (pl) Am, pair of trousers Br ou pants Am.

pantelant, -e [pɑ̃tlɑ̃, ɑ̃t] adj panting, gasping.

panthère [pɑ̃tɛr] nf panther.

pantin [pɑ̃tɛ̃] nm 1. (jouet) jumping jack. 2. péj (personne) puppet.

pantomime [pɑ̃tɔmim] nf (art, pièce) mime.

pantoufle [pɑ̃tufl] nf slipper.

PAO (abr de **publication assistée par ordinateur**) nf DTP.

paon [pɑ̃] nm peacock.

papa [papa] nm dad, daddy.

papauté [papote] nf papacy.

pape [pap] nm (RELIG) pope.

paperasse [papras] nf péj 1. (papier sans importance) bumf (U) Br, papers (pl). 2. (papiers administratifs) paperwork (U).

papeterie [papɛtri] nf (magasin) stationer's; (fabrique) paper mill.

papetier, -ère [paptje, ɛr] nm, f (commerçant) stationer; (fabricant) paper manufacturer.

papier [papje] nm (matière, écrit) paper; ~ **alu** ou **aluminium** aluminium Br ou aluminum Am foil, tinfoil; ~ **carbone** carbon paper; ~ **crépon** crêpe paper; ~ **d'emballage** wrapping paper; ~ **en-tête** headed notepaper; ~ **hygiénique** ou **toilette** toilet paper; ~ **à lettres** writing paper, notepaper; ~ **peint** wallpaper; ~ **de verre** glasspaper, sandpaper. ▶ **papiers** nmpl: ~**s (d'identité)** (identity) papers.

papier-calque [papjekalk] (pl **papiers-calque**) nm tracing paper.

papille [papij] nf: ~**s gustatives** taste buds.

papillon [papijɔ̃] nm 1. (ZOOL) butterfly. 2. (écrou) wing nut. 3. (nage) butterfly (stroke).

papillonner [papijɔne] vi to flit about ou around.

papillote [papijɔt] nf 1. (de bonbon) sweet paper ou wrapper Br, candy paper Am. 2. (de cheveux) curl paper.

papilloter [papijɔte] vi (lumière) to twinkle; (yeux) to blink.

papoter [papɔte] vi fam to chatter.

paprika [paprika] nm paprika.

paquebot [pakbo] nm liner.

pâquerette [pakrɛt] nf daisy.

Pâques [pak] nfpl Easter (sg); **joyeuses ~** Happy Easter.

paquet [pakɛ] nm 1. (colis) parcel. 2. (emballage) packet; ~**-cadeau** gift-wrapped parcel.

paquetage [paktaʒ] nm (MIL) kit.

par [par] prép 1. (spatial) through, by (way of); **passer ~ la Suède et le Danemark** to go via Sweden and Denmark; **regarder ~ la fenêtre** to look out of the window; ~ **endroits** in places; ~ **ici/là** this/that way; **mon cousin habite ~ ici** my cousin lives round here. 2. (temporel) on; ~ **un beau jour d'été** on a lovely summer's day; ~ **le passé** in the past. 3. (moyen, manière, cause) by; ~ **bateau/train/avion** by boat/train/plane; ~ **pitié** out of ou from pity; ~ **accident** by accident, by chance. 4. (introduit le complément d'agent) by; **faire faire qqch ~ qqn** to have sthg done by sb. 5. (sens distributif) per, a; **une heure ~ jour** one hour a ou per day; **deux ~ deux** two at a time; **marcher deux ~ deux** to walk in twos. ▶ **par-ci par-là** loc adv here and there.

para [para] (abr de **parachutiste**) nm para.

parabole [parabɔl] nf 1. (récit) parable. 2. (MATHS) parabola.

parabolique [parabɔlik] adj parabolic; **antenne ~** dish ou parabolic aerial.

paracétamol [parasetamɔl] nm paracetamol.

parachever [paraʃve] vt to put the finishing touches to.

parachute [paraʃyt] nm parachute; ~ **ascensionnel** parachute (for parascending).

parachutiste [paraʃytist] nmf parachutist; (MIL) paratrooper.

parade [parad] nf 1. (spectacle) parade. 2. (défense) parry; fig riposte.

paradis [paradi] nm paradise.

paradoxal, -e, -aux [paradɔksal, o] adj paradoxical.

paradoxe [paradɔks] nm paradox.

parafe, paraphe [paraf] nm initials (pl).

parafer, parapher [parafe] vt to initial.

paraffine [parafin] nf paraffin Br, kerosene Am; (solide) paraffin wax.

parages [paraʒ] nmpl: **être** ou **se trouver dans les ~** fig to be in the area ou vicinity.

paragraphe [paragraf] nm paragraph.

Paraguay [paragwɛ] nm: **le ~** Paraguay.

paraître [parɛtr] ◆ v attr to look, to seem, to appear. ◆ vi 1. (se montrer) to appear. 2. (être publié) to come out, to be published. ◆ v impers: **il paraît/paraîtrait que** it appears/would appear that.

parallèle [paralɛl] ◆ nm parallel; **établir un ~ entre** fig to draw a parallel between. ◆ nf parallel (line). ◆ adj

1. (*action, en maths*) parallel. 2. (*marché*) unofficial; (*médecine, énergie*) alternative.

parallélisme [paralelism] *nm* parallelism; (*de roues*) alignment.

paralyser [paralize] *vt* to paralyse.

paralysie [paralizi] *nf* paralysis.

paramédical, -e, -aux [paramedikal, o] *adj* paramedical.

paramètre [parametr] *nm* parameter.

paranoïa [paranɔja] *nf* paranoia.

paranoïaque [paranɔjak] ◆ *adj* paranoid. ◆ *nmf* paranoiac.

parapente [parapɑ̃t] *nm* paragliding.

parapet [parapɛ] *nm* parapet.

paraphe = **parafe**.

parapher = **parafer**.

paraphrase [parafraz] *nf* paraphrase.

paraplégique [paraple3ik] *nmf & adj* paraplegic.

parapluie [paraplɥi] *nm* umbrella.

parasite [parazit] ◆ *nm* parasite. ◆ *adj* parasitic. ▶ **parasites** *nmpl* (RADIO & TÉLÉ) interference (U).

parasol [parasɔl] *nm* parasol, sunshade.

paratonnerre [paratɔnɛr] *nm* lightning conductor.

paravent [paravɑ̃] *nm* screen.

parc [park] *nm* 1. (*jardin*) park; (*de château*) grounds (*pl*); ~ **d'attractions** amusement park; ~ **de loisirs à thème** = theme park; ~ **national** national park. 2. (*pour l'élevage*) pen. 3. (*de bébé*) playpen. 4. (*de voitures*) fleet; **le ~ automobile** the number of cars on the roads.

PARCS NATIONAUX

There are six national parks in France, the best-known being la Vanoise (in the Alps), Cévennes (in the southeast) and Mercantour (in the southern Alps). There are stricter regulations on the protection of wildlife than in regional parks.

PARCS NATURELS RÉGIONAUX

There are 20 regional parks in France, including Brière (in southern Brittany), Camargue and Lubéron (in the southeast), and Morvan (to the southeast of Paris). Within these designated areas wildlife is protected and tourism is encouraged.

parcelle [parsɛl] *nf* 1. (*petite partie*) fragment, particle. 2. (*terrain*) parcel of land.

parce que [parsk(ə)] *loc conj* because.

parchemin [parʃəmɛ̃] *nm* parchment.

parcimonieux, -euse [parsimɔnjø, øz] *adj* parsimonious.

parcmètre [parkmɛtr] *nm* parking meter.

parcourir [parkurir] *vt* 1. (*région, route*) to cover. 2. (*journal, dossier*) to skim ou glance through, to scan.

parcours [parkur] *nm* 1. (*trajet, voyage*) journey; (*itinéraire*) route; ~ **santé** trail in the countryside where signs encourage people to do exercises for their health. 2. (GOLF) (*terrain*) course; (*trajet*) round.

parcouru, -e [parkury] *pp* → **parcourir**.

par-delà [pardəla] *prép* beyond.

par-derrière [parderjɛr] *adv* 1. (*par le côté arrière*) round the back. 2. (*en cachette*) behind one's back.

par-dessous [pardəsu] *prép & adv* under, underneath.

pardessus [pardəsy] *nm inv* overcoat.

par-dessus [pardəsy] ◆ *prép* over, over the top of; ~ **tout** above all. ◆ *adv* over, over the top.

par-devant [pardəvɑ̃] ◆ *prép* in front of. ◆ *adv* in front.

pardi [pardi] *interj fam* of course!

pardon [pardɔ̃] ◆ *nm* forgiveness; **demander ~** to say (one is) sorry. ◆ *interj* (*excuses*) (I'm) sorry!; (*pour attirer l'attention*) excuse me!; ~**?** (I beg your) pardon? Br, pardon me? Am.

PARDON

The Breton word for 'pilgrimage', 'pardon' has come to mean a celebration held in spring and summer in Brittany in honour of the patron saint of a village or town. People come from far around, often dressed in traditional costumes, to take part in processions and in the general festivities.

pardonner [pardɔne] ◆ *vt* to forgive; ~ **qqch à qqn** to forgive sb for sthg; ~ **à qqn d'avoir fait qqch** to forgive sb for doing sthg. ◆ *vi*: **ce genre d'erreur ne pardonne pas** this kind of mistake is fatal.

paré, -e [pare] *adj* (*prêt*) ready.

pare-balles [parbal] *adj inv* bulletproof.

pare-brise [parbriz] *nm inv* windscreen Br, windshield Am.

pare-chocs [parʃɔk] *nm inv* bumper.

pareil, -eille [parɛj] *adj* 1. (*semblable*):

~ (à) similar (to). **2.** (*tel*) such; **un ~ film** such a film, a film like this; **de ~s films** such films, films like these. ▶ **pareil** *adv fam* the same (way).

parent, -e [parã, ãt] ◆ *adj*: **~ (de)** related (to). ◆ *nm, f* relative, relation. ▶ **parents** *nmpl* (*père et mère*) parents, mother and father.

parenté [parãte] *nf* (*lien, affinité*) relationship.

parenthèse [parãtɛz] *nf* **1.** (*digression*) digression, parenthesis. **2.** (TYPO) bracket, parenthesis; **entre ~s** in brackets; *fig* incidentally, by the way; **ouvrir/fermer la ~** to open/close brackets.

parer [pare] ◆ *vt* **1.** *sout* (*orner*) to adorn. **2.** (*vêtir*): **~ qqn de qqch** to dress sb up in sthg, to deck sb out in sthg; *fig* to attribute sthg to sb. **3.** (*contrer*) to ward off, to parry. ◆ *vi*: **~ à** (*faire face à*) to deal with; (*pourvoir à*) to prepare for; **~ au plus pressé** to see to what is most urgent. ▶ **se parer** *vp* to dress up, to put on all one's finery.

pare-soleil [parsɔlɛj] *nm inv* sun visor.

paresse [parɛs] *nf* **1.** (*fainéantise*) laziness, idleness. **2.** (MÉD) sluggishness.

paresser [parese] *vi* to laze about ou around.

paresseux, -euse [paresø, øz] ◆ *adj* **1.** (*fainéant*) lazy. **2.** (MÉD) sluggish. ◆ *nm, f* (*personne*) lazy ou idle person. ▶ **paresseux** *nm* (*animal*) sloth.

parfaire [parfɛr] *vt* to complete, to perfect.

parfait, -e [parfɛ, ɛt] *adj* perfect. ▶ **parfait** *nm* (GRAM) perfect (tense).

parfaitement [parfɛtmã] *adv* **1.** (*admirablement, très*) perfectly. **2.** (*marque l'assentiment*) absolutely.

parfois [parfwa] *adv* sometimes.

parfum [parfœ̃] *nm* **1.** (*de fleur*) scent, fragrance. **2.** (*à base d'essences*) perfume, scent. **3.** (*de glace*) flavour.

parfumé, -e [parfyme] *adj* **1.** (*fleur*) fragrant. **2.** (*mouchoir*) perfumed. **3.** (*femme*): **elle est trop ~e** she's wearing too much perfume.

parfumer [parfyme] *vt* **1.** (*suj: fleurs*) to perfume. **2.** (*mouchoir*) to perfume, to scent. **3.** (CULIN) to flavour. ▶ **se parfumer** *vp* to put perfume on.

parfumerie [parfymri] *nf* perfumery.

pari [pari] *nm* **1.** (*entre personnes*) bet. **2.** (*jeu*) betting (U).

paria [parja] *nm* pariah.

parier [parje] *vt*: **~ (sur)** to bet (on).

parieur [parjœr] *nm* punter.

Paris [pari] *n* Paris.

parisien, -enne [parizjɛ̃, ɛn] *adj* (*vie, société*) Parisian; (*métro, banlieue, région*) Paris (*avant n*). ▶ **Parisien, -enne** *nm, f* Parisian.

paritaire [pariter] *adj*: **commission ~** joint commission (*with both sides equally represented*).

parité [parite] *nf* parity.

parjure [parʒyr] ◆ *nmf* (*personne*) perjurer. ◆ *nm* (*faux serment*) perjury.

parjurer [parʒyre] ▶ **se parjurer** *vp* to perjure o.s.

parka [parka] *nm ou nf* parka.

parking [parkiŋ] *nm* (*parc*) car park *Br*, parking lot *Am*.

parlant, -e [parlã, ãt] *adj* **1.** (*qui parle*): **le cinéma ~** talking pictures; **l'horloge ~e** (TÉLÉCOM) the speaking clock. **2.** *fig* (*chiffres, données*) eloquent; (*portrait*) vivid.

parlement [parləmã] *nm* parliament; **le Parlement européen** the European Parliament.

parlementaire [parləmɛ̃tɛr] ◆ *nmf* (*député*) member of parliament; (*négociateur*) negotiator. ◆ *adj* parliamentary.

parlementer [parləmãte] *vi* **1.** (*négocier*) to negotiate, to parley. **2.** (*parler longtemps*) to talk at length.

parler [parle] ◆ *vi* **1.** (*gén*) to talk, to speak; **~ à/avec qqn** to speak to/with sb, to talk to/with sb; **~ de qqch à qqn** to speak ou talk to sb about sthg; **~ de qqn/qqch** to talk about sb/sthg; **~ de faire qqch** to talk about doing sthg; **~ en français** to speak in French; **sans ~ de** apart from, not to mention; **à proprement ~** strictly speaking; **tu parles!** *fam* you can say that again!; **n'en parlons plus** we'll say no more about it. **2.** (*avouer*) to talk. ◆ *vt* (*langue*) to speak; **~ (le) français** to speak French.

parloir [parlwar] *nm* parlour.

parmi [parmi] *prép* among.

parodie [parɔdi] *nf* parody.

parodier [parɔdje] *vt* to parody.

paroi [parwa] *nf* **1.** (*mur*) wall; (*cloison*) partition; **~ rocheuse** rock face. **2.** (*de récipient*) inner side.

paroisse [parwas] *nf* parish.

paroissial, -e, -aux [parwasjal, o] *adj* parish (*avant n*).

paroissien, -enne [parwasjɛ̃, ɛn] *nm, f* parishioner.

parole [parɔl] *nf* **1.** (*faculté de parler*): **la ~** speech. **2.** (*propos, discours*): **adresser la ~ à qqn** to speak to sb; **couper la ~ à**

qqn to cut sb off; **prendre la ~** to speak. 3. (*promesse, mot*) word; **tenir ~** to keep one's word; **donner sa ~ (d'honneur)** to give one's word (of honour); **croire qqn sur ~** to take sb's word for it. ▶ **paroles** *nfpl* (MUS) words, lyrics.

paroxysme [parɔksism] *nm* height.

parquer [parke] *vt* 1. (*animaux*) to pen in ou up. 2. (*prisonniers*) to shut up ou in. 3. (*voiture*) to park.

parquet [parke] *nm* 1. (*plancher*) parquet floor. 2. (JUR) ≃ Crown Prosecution Service Br, ≃ District Attorney's office Am.

parqueter [parkəte] *vt* to lay a parquet floor in.

parrain [parɛ̃] *nm* 1. (*d'enfant*) godfather. 2. (*de festival, sportif*) sponsor.

parrainer [parɛne] *vt* to sponsor, to back.

parricide [parisid] *nm* (*crime*) parricide.

parsemer [parsəme] *vt*: **~ (de)** to strew (with).

part [par] *nf* 1. (*de gâteau*) portion; (*de bonheur, héritage*) share; (*partie*) part. 2. (*participation*): **prendre ~ à qqch** to take part in sthg. 3. *loc*: **de la ~ de** from; (*appeler, remercier*) on behalf of; **c'est de la ~ de qui?** (*au téléphone*) who's speaking ou calling?; **dites-lui de ma ~ que ...** tell him from me that ...; **ce serait bien aimable de votre ~** it would be very kind of you; **pour ma ~** as far as I'm concerned; **faire ~ à qqn de qqch** to inform sb of sthg. ▶ **à part** *loc adv* aside, separately. ◆ *loc adj* exceptional. ◆ *loc prép* apart from. ▶ **autre part** *loc adv* somewhere else. ▶ **d'autre part** *loc adv* besides, moreover. ▶ **de part et d'autre** *loc adv* on both sides. ▶ **d'une part ..., d'autre part** *loc corrélative* on the one hand ..., on the other hand.

part. *abr de* **particulier**.

partage [partaʒ] *nm* (*action*) sharing (out).

partager [partaʒe] *vt* 1. (*morceler*) to divide (up); **être partagé** *fig* to be divided. 2. (*mettre en commun*): **~ qqch avec qqn** to share sthg with sb. ▶ **se partager** *vp* 1. (*se diviser*) to be divided. 2. (*partager son temps*) to divide one's time. 3. (*se répartir*): **se ~ qqch** to share sthg between themselves/ourselves *etc.*

partance [partɑ̃s] *nf*: **en ~** outward bound; **en ~ pour** bound for.

partant, -e [partɑ̃, ɑ̃t] *adj*: **être ~ pour** to be ready for. ▶ **partant** *nm* starter.

partenaire [partənɛr] *nmf* partner.

partenariat [partənarja] *nm* partnership.

parterre [partɛr] *nm* 1. (*de fleurs*) (flower) bed. 2. (THÉÂTRE) stalls (*pl*) Br, orchestra Am.

parti, -e [parti] ◆ *pp* → **partir**. ◆ *adj fam* (*ivre*) tipsy. ▶ **parti** *nm* 1. (POLIT) party. 2. (*choix, décision*) course of action; **prendre ~** to make up one's mind; **prendre le ~ de faire qqch** to make up one's mind to do sthg; **en prendre son ~** to be resigned; **être de ~ pris** to be prejudiced ou biased; **tirer ~ de** to make (good) use of. 3. (*personne à marier*) match. ▶ **partie** *nf* 1. (*élément, portion*) part; **en grande ~e** largely; **en majeure ~e** for the most part; **faire ~e (intégrante) de qqch** to be (an integral) part of sthg. 2. (*domaine d'activité*) field, subject. 3. (SPORT) game. 4. (JUR) party; **la ~e adverse** the opposing party. 5. *loc*: **prendre qqn à ~e** to attack sb. ▶ **en partie** *loc adv* partly, in part.

partial, -e, -aux [parsjal, o] *adj* biased.

partialité [parsjalite] *nf* partiality, bias.

participant, -e [partisipɑ̃, ɑ̃t] ◆ *adj* participating. ◆ *nm, f* 1. (*à réunion*) participant. 2. (SPORT) competitor. 3. (*à concours*) entrant.

participation [partisipasjɔ̃] *nf* 1. (*collaboration*) participation. 2. (ÉCON) interest; **~ aux bénéfices** profit-sharing.

participe [partisip] *nm* participle; **~ passé/présent** past/present participle.

participer [partisipe] *vi*: **~ à** (*réunion, concours*) to take part in; (*frais*) to contribute to; (*bénéfices*) to share in.

particularité [partikylarite] *nf* distinctive feature.

particule [partikyl] *nf* 1. (*gén & LING*) particle. 2. (*nobiliaire*) nobiliary particle.

particulier, -ère [partikylje, ɛr] *adj* 1. (*personnel, privé*) private. 2. (*spécial*) particular, special; (*propre*) peculiar, characteristic; **~ à** peculiar to, characteristic of. 3. (*remarquable*) unusual, exceptional; **cas ~** special case. 4. (*assez bizarre*) peculiar. ▶ **particulier** *nm* (*personne*) private individual.

particulièrement [partikyljɛrmɑ̃] *adv* particularly; **tout ~** especially.

partie → **parti**.

partiel, -elle [parsjɛl] *adj* partial. ▶ **partiel** *nm* (UNIV) ≃ end-of-term exam.

partir [partir] *vi* **1.** (*personne*) to go, to leave; ~ **à** to go to; ~ **pour** to leave for; ~ **de** (*bureau*) to leave; (*aéroport, gare*) to leave from; (*hypothèse, route*) to start from; (*date*) to run from. **2.** (*voiture*) to start. **3.** (*coup de feu*) to go off; (*bouchon*) to pop. **4.** (*tache*) to come out, to go. ▶ **à partir de** *loc prép* from.

partisan, -e [partizã, an] *adj* (*partial*) partisan; **être ~ de** to be in favour of. ▶ **partisan** *nm* (*adepte*) supporter, advocate.

partition [partisjɔ̃] *nf* **1.** (*séparation*) partition. **2.** (MUS) score.

partout [partu] *adv* everywhere; **un peu ~** all over, everywhere.

paru, -e [pary] *pp* → **paraître.**

parure [paryr] *nf* (matching) set.

parution [parysjɔ̃] *nf* publication.

parvenir [parvənir] *vi*: ~ **à faire qqch** to manage to do sthg; **faire ~ qqch à qqn** to send sthg to sb.

parvenu, -e [parvəny] ◆ *pp* → **parvenir.** ◆ *nm, f péj* parvenu, upstart.

pas¹ [pa] *nm* **1.** (*gén*) step; **allonger le ~** to quicken one's pace; **revenir sur ses ~** to retrace one's steps; ~ **à ~** step by step; **à ~ de loup** *fig* stealthily. **2.** (TECHNOL) thread. **3.** *loc*: **c'est à deux ~ (d'ici)** it's very near (here); **faire les cent ~** to pace up and down; **faire un faux ~** to slip; *fig* to make a faux pas; **faire le premier ~** to make the first move; **franchir ou sauter le ~** to take the plunge; **(rouler) au ~** (to move) at a snail's pace; **sur le ~ de la porte** on the doorstep; **tirer qqn d'un mauvais ~** to get sb out of a tight spot.

pas² [pa] *adv* **1.** (*avec ne*) not; **elle ne vient ~** she's not ou she isn't coming; **elle n'a ~ mangé** she hasn't eaten; **je ne le connais ~** I don't know him; **il n'y a ~ de vin** there's no wine, there isn't any wine; **je préférerais ne ~ le rencontrer** I would prefer not to meet him, I would rather not meet him. **2.** (*sans ne*) not; **l'as-tu vu ou ~?** have you seen him or not?; **il est très satisfait, moi ~** he's very pleased, but I'm not; ~ **encore** not yet; ~ **du tout** not at all. **3.** (*avec pron indéf*): ~ **un** (*aucun*) none, not one; ~ **un d'eux n'est venu** none of them ou not one of them came.

pascal, -e [paskal] (*pl* **pascals** ou **pascaux** [pasko]) *adj* Easter (*avant n*).

passable [pasabl] *adj* passable, fair.

passage [pasaʒ] *nm* **1.** (*action - de passer*) going past; (*- de traverser*) crossing;

être de ~ to be passing through. **2.** (*endroit*) passage, way; '~ **interdit'** 'no entry'; ~ **clouté** ou **pour piétons** pedestrian crossing; ~ **à niveau** level crossing *Br*, grade crossing *Am*; ~ **protégé** priority given to traffic on the main road; ~ **souterrain** underpass *Br*, subway *Am*. **3.** (*extrait*) passage.

passager, -ère [pasaʒe, ɛr] ◆ *adj* (*bonheur*) fleeting, short-lived. ◆ *nm, f* passenger.

passant, -e [pasã, ãt] ◆ *adj* busy. ◆ *nm, f* passer-by. ▶ **passant** *nm* (*de ceinture*) (belt) loop.

passe [pas] ◆ *nm* passkey. ◆ *nf* **1.** (*au sport*) pass. **2.** (NAVIG) channel.

passé, -e [pase] *adj* **1.** (*qui n'est plus*) past; (*précédent*): **la semaine ~e** last week; **au cours de la semaine ~e** in the last week; **il est trois heures ~es** it's gone three *Br*, it's after three. **2.** (*fané*) faded. ▶ **passé** ◆ *nm* past; ~ **composé** perfect tense; ~ **simple** past historic. ◆ *prép* after.

passe-droit [pasdrwa] (*pl* **passe-droits**) *nm* privilege.

passe-montagne [pasmɔ̃taɲ] (*pl* **passe-montagnes**) *nm* Balaclava (helmet).

passe-partout [paspartu] *nm inv* **1.** (*clé*) passkey. **2.** (*en apposition*) (*tenue*) all-purpose; (*phrase*) stock (*avant n*).

passeport [paspɔr] *nm* passport.

passer [pase] ◆ *vi* (*aux: être*) **1.** (*se frayer un chemin*) to pass, to get past. **2.** (*défiler*) to go by ou past. **3.** (*aller*) to go; ~ **à** ou **au travers** ou **par** to come ou pass through; ~ **chez qqn** to call on sb, to drop in on sb; ~ **devant** (*bâtiment*) to pass; (*juge*) to come before; **en passant** in passing. **4.** (*venir - facteur*) to come, to call. **5.** (SCOL) to pass, to be admitted; ~ **dans la classe supérieure** to move up, to be moved up (a class). **6.** (*être accepté*) to be accepted. **7.** (*fermer les yeux*): ~ **sur qqch** to pass over sthg. **8.** (*temps*) to pass, to go by. **9.** (*disparaître - souvenir, couleur*) to fade; (*- douleur*) to pass, to go away. **10.** (CIN, TÉLÉ & THÉÂTRE) to be on; ~ **à la radio/télévision** to be on the radio/television. **11.** (CARTES) to pass. **12.** (*devenir*): ~ **président/directeur** to become president/director, to be appointed president/director. **13.** *loc*: ~ **inaperçu** to pass ou go unnoticed; **passons ...** let's move on ...; ~ **pour** to be regarded as; **se faire ~ pour qqn** to pass o.s. off as sb; **il y est passé** *fam* (*mort*) he

kicked the bucket. ◆ vt (aux: avoir)
1. (franchir - frontière, rivière) to cross;
(- douane) to go through. 2. (soirée,
vacances) to spend. 3. (sauter - ligne, tour)
to miss. 4. (défauts): ~ qqch à qqn to
overlook sthg in sb. 5. (faire aller - bras)
to pass, to put. 6. (filtrer - huile) to
strain; (- café) to filter. 7. (film, disque) to
put on. 8. (vêtement) to slip on.
9. (vitesses) to change; ~ la OU en
troisième to change into third (gear).
10. (donner): ~ qqch à qqn to pass sb
sthg; (MÉD) to give sb sthg. 11. (accord):
~ un contrat avec qqn to have an agreement with sb. 12. (SCOL & UNIV) (examen)
to sit, to take. 13. (au téléphone): je vous
passe Mme Ledoux (transmettre) I'll put
you through to Mme Ledoux; (donner
l'écouteur à) I'll hand you Mme Ledoux.
▶ se passer vp 1. (événement) to happen, to take place; comment ça s'est
passé? how did it go?; ça ne se passera
pas comme ça! I'm not putting up with
that! 2. (s'enduire - crème) to put on.
3. (s'abstenir): se ~ de qqch/de faire qqch
to do without sthg/doing sthg.

passerelle [pasʀɛl] nf 1. (pont) footbridge. 2. (passage mobile) gangway.

passe-temps [pastɑ̃] nm inv pastime.

passif, -ive [pasif, iv] adj passive.
▶ **passif** nm 1. (GRAM) passive. 2. (FIN)
liabilities (pl).

passion [pasjɔ̃] nf passion; avoir la ~
de qqch to have a passion for sthg.

passionnant, -e [pasjɔnɑ̃, ɑ̃t] adj
exciting, fascinating.

passionné, -e [pasjɔne] ◆ adj 1. (personne) passionate. 2. (récit, débat) impas-
sioned. ◆ nm, f passionate person; ~
de ski/d'échecs etc skiing/chess etc fanatic.

passionnel, -elle [pasjɔnɛl] adj
(crime) of passion.

passionner [pasjɔne] vt (personne) to
grip, to fascinate. ▶ se passionner vp:
se ~ pour to have a passion for.

passivité [pasivite] nf passivity.

passoire [paswaʀ] nf (à liquide) sieve;
(à légumes) colander.

pastel [pastɛl] ◆ nm pastel. ◆ adj inv
(couleur) pastel (avant n).

pastèque [pastɛk] nf watermelon.

pasteur [pastœʀ] nm 1. littéraire (berger)
shepherd. 2. (RELIG) pastor, minister.

pasteuriser [pastœʀize] vt to pasteurize.

pastille [pastij] nf (bonbon) pastille,
lozenge.

pastis [pastis] nm aniseed-flavoured aperitif.

patate [patat] nf 1. fam (pomme de terre)
spud. 2. fam (imbécile) fathead.

patauger [patoʒe] vi (barboter) to
splash about.

pâte [pat] nf 1. (à tarte) pastry; (à pain)
dough; ~ brisée shortcrust pastry; ~
feuilletée puff pastry; ~ à frire batter; ~
à pain bread dough. 2. (mélange) paste;
~ d'amandes almond paste; ~ de fruits
jelly made from fruit paste; ~ à modeler
modelling clay. ▶ **pâtes** nfpl pasta (sg).

pâté [pate] nm 1. (CULIN) pâté; ~ de
campagne farmhouse pâté; ~ en croûte
pâté baked in a pastry case; ~ de foie liver
pâté. 2. (tache) ink blot. 3. (bloc): ~ de
maisons block (of houses).

patelin [patlɛ̃] nm fam village, place.

patente [patɑ̃t] nf licence fee (for
traders and professionals).

patère [patɛʀ] nf (portemanteau) coat
hook.

paternalisme [patɛʀnalism] nm
paternalism.

paternel, -elle [patɛʀnɛl] adj (devoir,
autorité) paternal; (amour, ton) fatherly.

paternité [patɛʀnite] nf paternity,
fatherhood; fig authorship, paternity.

pâteux, -euse [patø, øz] adj (aliment)
doughy; (encre) thick.

pathétique [patetik] adj moving,
pathetic.

pathologie [patɔlɔʒi] nf pathology.

patibulaire [patibylɛʀ] adj péj sinister.

patience [pasjɑ̃s] nf 1. (gén) patience.
2. (jeu de cartes) patience Br, solitaire
Am.

patient, -e [pasjɑ̃, ɑ̃t] ◆ adj patient.
◆ nm, f (MÉD) patient.

patienter [pasjɑ̃te] vi to wait.

patin [patɛ̃] nm (SPORT) skate; ~ à
glace/à roulettes ice/roller skate; faire
du ~ à glace/à roulettes to go ice-/roller-
skating.

patinage [patinaʒ] nm (SPORT) skating;
~ artistique/de vitesse figure/speed
skating.

patiner [patine] ◆ vi 1. (SPORT) to
skate. 2. (véhicule) to skid. ◆ vt (objet)
to give a patina to; (avec vernis) to varnish. ▶ se patiner vp to take on a
patina.

patineur, -euse [patinœʀ, øz] nm, f
skater.

patinoire [patinwaʀ] nf ice OU skating
rink.

pâtisserie [patisʀi] nf 1. (gâteau) pas-

try. **2.** (*art, métier*) pastry-making.
3. (*commerce*) = cake shop.
pâtissier, -ère [patisje, ɛr] ◆ *adj*:
crème pâtissière confectioner's custard.
◆ *nm, f* pastrycook.
patois [patwa] *nm* patois.
patriarche [patrijarʃ] *nm* patriarch.
patrie [patri] *nf* country, homeland.
patrimoine [patrimwan] *nm* (*familial*)
inheritance; (*collectif*) heritage.
patriote [patrijɔt] *nmf* patriot.
patriotique [patrijɔtik] *adj* patriotic.
patron, -onne [patrɔ̃, ɔn] *nm, f*
1. (*d'entreprise*) head. **2.** (*chef*) boss.
3. (RELIG) patron saint. ▶ **patron** *nm*
(*modèle*) pattern.
patronage [patrɔnaʒ] *nm* **1.** (*protection*) patronage; (*de saint*) protection.
2. (*organisation*) youth club.
patronal, -e, -aux [patrɔnal, o] *adj*
(*organisation, intérêts*) employers' (*avant n*).
patronat [patrɔna] *nm* employers.
patronyme [patrɔnim] *nm* patronymic.
patrouille [patruj] *nf* patrol.
patte [pat] *nf* **1.** (*d'animal*) paw;
(*d'oiseau*) foot. **2.** *fam* (*jambe*) leg; (*pied*)
foot; (*main*) hand, paw. **3.** (*favori*) sideburn.
pâturage [patyraʒ] *nm* (*lieu*) pasture
land.
pâture [patyr] *nf* (*nourriture*) food, fodder; *fig* intellectual nourishment.
paume [pom] *nf* **1.** (*de main*) palm.
2. (SPORT) real tennis.
paumé, -e [pome] *fam* ◆ *adj* lost.
◆ *nm, f* down and out.
paumer [pome] *fam vt* to lose. ▶ **se**
paumer *vp* to get lost.
paupière [popjɛr] *nf* eyelid.
pause [poz] *nf* **1.** (*arrêt*) break; **~-café**
coffee-break. **2.** (MUS) pause.
pauvre [povr] ◆ *nmf* poor person.
◆ *adj* poor; **~ en** low in.
pauvreté [povrəte] *nf* poverty.
pavaner [pavane] ▶ **se pavaner** *vp*
to strut.
pavé, -e [pave] *adj* cobbled. ▶ **pavé**
nm **1.** (*chaussée*): **être sur le ~** *fig* to be out
on the streets; **battre le ~** *fig* to walk the
streets. **2.** (*de pierre*) cobblestone,
paving stone. **3.** *fam* (*livre*) tome.
4. (INFORM): **~ numérique** numeric keypad.
pavillon [pavijɔ̃] *nm* **1.** (*bâtiment*)
detached house. **2.** (*de trompette*) bell.
3. (*d'oreille*) pinna, auricle. **4.** (*drapeau*)
flag.

pavot [pavo] *nm* poppy.
payant, -e [pɛjɑ̃, ɑ̃t] *adj* **1.** (*hôte*) paying (*avant n*). **2.** (*spectacle*) with an admission charge. **3.** *fam* (*affaire*) profitable.
paye = **paie**.
payement = **paiement**.
payer [peje] ◆ *vt* **1.** (*gén*) to pay; (*achat*)
to pay for; **~ qqch à qqn** to buy sthg for
sb, to buy sb sthg, to treat sb to sthg.
2. (*expier - crime, faute*) to pay for. ◆ *vi*: **~**
(pour) to pay (for).
pays [pei] *nm* **1.** (*gén*) country.
2. (*région, province*) region. ▶ **pays de**
Galles *nm*: **le ~ de Galles** Wales.
paysage [peizaʒ] *nm* **1.** (*site, vue*) landscape, scenery. **2.** (*tableau*) landscape.
paysagiste [peizaʒist] *nmf* **1.** (*peintre*)
landscape artist. **2.** (*concepteur de parcs*)
landscape gardener.
paysan, -anne [peizɑ̃, an] ◆ *adj* (*vie,
coutume*) country (*avant n*), rural; (*organisation, revendication*) farmers' (*avant n*); *péj*
peasant (*avant n*). ◆ *nm, f* **1.** (*agriculteur*)
(small) farmer. **2.** *péj* (*rustre*) peasant.
Pays-Bas [peiba] *nmpl*: **les ~** the
Netherlands.
PC *nm* **1.** (*abr de* **Parti communiste**)
Communist Party. **2.** (*abr de* **personal**
computer) PC.
PCV (*abr de* **à percevoir**) *nm* reverse
charge call.
P-DG (*abr de* **président-directeur**
général) *nm* Chairman and Managing
Director Br, Chairman and President
Am.
péage [peaʒ] *nm* toll.
peau [po] *nf* **1.** (*gén*) skin; **~ d'orange**
orange peel; (MÉD) = cellulite. **2.** (*cuir*)
hide, leather (U).
peaufiner [pofine] *vt litt & fig* to polish
up.
péché [peʃe] *nm* sin.
pêche [pɛʃ] *nf* **1.** (*fruit*) peach. **2.** (*activité*) fishing; (*poissons*) catch; **aller à la ~**
to go fishing.
pécher [peʃe] *vi* to sin.
pêcher¹ [peʃe] *vt* **1.** (*poisson*) to catch.
2. *fam* (*trouver*) to dig up.
pêcher² [peʃe] *nm* peach tree.
pécheur, -eresse [peʃœr, peʃrɛs]
◆ *adj* sinful. ◆ *nm, f* sinner.
pêcheur, -euse [pɛʃœr, øz] *nm, f*
fisherman (*f* fisherwoman).
pectoral, -e, -aux [pɛktɔral, o] *adj*
(*sirop*) cough (*avant n*). ▶ **pectoraux**
nmpl pectorals.
pécuniaire [pekynjɛr] *adj* financial.
pédagogie [pedagɔʒi] *nf* **1.** (*science*)

education, pedagogy. **2.** (*qualité*) teaching ability.

pédagogique [pedagɔʒik] *adj* educational; (*méthode*) teaching (*avant n*).

pédagogue [pedagɔg] ♦ *nmf* teacher. ♦ *adj*: **être ~** to be a good teacher.

pédale [pedal] *nf* (*gén*) pedal.

pédaler [pedale] *vi* (*à bicyclette*) to pedal.

Pédalo® [pedalo] *nm* pedal boat.

pédant, -e [pedɑ̃, ɑ̃t] *adj* pedantic.

pédéraste [pederast] *nm* homosexual, pederast.

pédiatre [pedjatr] *nmf* pediatrician.

pédicure [pedikyr] *nmf* chiropodist.

peigne [pɛɲ] *nm* **1.** (*démêloir, barrette*) comb. **2.** (*de tissage*) card.

peigner [peɲe] *vt* **1.** (*cheveux*) to comb. **2.** (*fibres*) to card. ▶ **se peigner** *vp* to comb one's hair.

peignoir [peɲwar] *nm* dressing gown Br, robe Am, bathrobe Am.

peindre [pɛ̃dr] *vt* to paint; *fig* (*décrire*) to depict.

peine [pɛn] *nf* **1.** (*châtiment*) punishment, penalty; (JUR) sentence; **sous ~ de qqch** on pain of sthg; **~ capitale** ou **de mort** capital punishment, death sentence. **2.** (*chagrin*) sorrow, sadness (U); **faire de la ~ à qqn** to upset sb, to distress sb. **3.** (*effort*) trouble; **ça ne vaut pas** ou **ce n'est pas la ~** it's not worth it. **4.** (*difficulté*) difficulty; **avoir de la ~ à faire qqch** to have difficulty ou trouble doing sthg; **à grand-~** with great difficulty. ▶ **à peine** *loc adv* scarcely, hardly; **à ~ ... que** hardly ... than; **c'est à ~ si on se parle** we hardly speak (to each other).

peint, -e [pɛ̃, pɛ̃t] *pp* → **peindre**.

peintre [pɛ̃tr] *nm* painter.

peinture [pɛ̃tyr] *nf* **1.** (*gén*) painting. **2.** (*produit*) paint; '**~ fraîche**' 'wet paint'.

péjoratif, -ive [peʒɔratif, iv] *adj* pejorative.

Pékin [pekɛ̃] *n* Peking, Beijing.

pékinois, -e [pekinwa, az] *adj* of/from Peking. ▶ **pékinois** *nm* **1.** (*langue*) Mandarin. **2.** (*chien*) pekinese. ▶ **Pékinois, -e** *nm, f* native ou inhabitant of Peking.

pelage [pəlaʒ] *nm* coat, fur.

pêle-mêle [pɛlmɛl] *adv* pell-mell.

peler [pəle] *vt & vi* to peel.

pèlerin [pɛlrɛ̃] *nm* pilgrim.

pèlerinage [pɛlrinaʒ] *nm* **1.** (*voyage*) pilgrimage. **2.** (*lieu*) place of pilgrimage.

pélican [pelikɑ̃] *nm* pelican.

pelle [pɛl] *nf* **1.** (*instrument*) shovel. **2.** (*machine*) digger.

pelleter [pɛlte] *vt* to shovel.

pellicule [pelikyl] *nf* film. ▶ **pellicules** *nfpl* dandruff (U).

pelote [pəlɔt] *nf* (*de laine, ficelle*) ball.

peloter [pəlɔte] *vt fam* to paw.

peloton [pəlɔtɔ̃] *nm* **1.** (*de soldats*) squad; **~ d'exécution** firing squad. **2.** (*de concurrents*) pack.

pelotonner [pəlɔtɔne] ▶ **se pelotonner** *vp* to curl up.

pelouse [pəluz] *nf* **1.** (*de jardin*) lawn. **2.** (*de champ de courses*) public enclosure. **3.** (FOOTBALL & RUGBY) field.

peluche [pəlyʃ] *nf* **1.** (*jouet*) soft toy. **2.** (*d'étoffe*) piece of fluff.

pelure [pəlyr] *nf* (*fruit*) peel.

pénal, -e, -aux [penal, o] *adj* penal.

pénaliser [penalize] *vt* to penalize.

penalty [penalti] (*pl* **penaltys** ou **penalties**) *nm* penalty.

penaud, -e [pəno, od] *adj* sheepish.

penchant [pɑ̃ʃɑ̃] *nm* **1.** (*inclination*) tendency. **2.** (*sympathie*): **~ pour** liking ou fondness for.

pencher [pɑ̃ʃe] ♦ *vi* to lean; **~ vers/ pour** *fig* to incline towards/in favour of. ♦ *vt* to bend. ▶ **se pencher** *vp* (*s'incliner*) to lean over; (*se baisser*) to bend down; **se ~ sur qqn/qqch** to lean over sb/sthg.

pendaison [pɑ̃dezɔ̃] *nf* hanging.

pendant¹, -e [pɑ̃dɑ̃, ɑ̃t] *adj* (*bras*) hanging, dangling. ▶ **pendant** *nm* **1.** (*bijou*): **~ d'oreilles** (drop) earring. **2.** (*de paire*) counterpart.

pendant² [pɑ̃dɑ̃] *prép* during. ▶ **pendant que** *loc conj* while, whilst; **~ que j'y suis, ...** while I'm at it, ...

pendentif [pɑ̃dɑ̃tif] *nm* pendant.

penderie [pɑ̃dri] *nf* wardrobe.

pendre [pɑ̃dr] ♦ *vi* **1.** (*être fixé en haut*): **~ (à)** to hang (from). **2.** (*descendre trop bas*) to hang down. ♦ *vt* **1.** (*rideaux, tableau*) to hang (up), to put up. **2.** (*personne*) to hang. ▶ **se pendre** *vp* (*se suicider*) to hang o.s.

pendule [pɑ̃dyl] ♦ *nm* pendulum. ♦ *nf* clock.

pénétrer [penetre] ♦ *vi* to enter. ♦ *vt* (*mur, vêtement*) to penetrate.

pénible [penibl] *adj* **1.** (*travail*) laborious. **2.** (*nouvelle, maladie*) painful. **3.** *fam* (*personne*) tiresome.

péniche [peniʃ] *nf* barge.

pénicilline [penisilin] *nf* penicillin.

péninsule [penɛ̃syl] nf peninsula.
pénis [penis] nm penis.
pénitence [penitãs] nf 1. (repentir) penitence. 2. (peine, punition) penance.
pénitencier [penitãsje] nm prison, penitentiary Am.
pénombre [penɔ̃br] nf half-light.
pense-bête [pãsbɛt] (pl pense-bêtes) nm reminder.
pensée [pãse] nf 1. (idée, faculté) thought. 2. (esprit) mind, thoughts (pl). 3. (doctrine) thought, thinking. 4. (BOT) pansy.
penser [pãse] ◆ vi to think; ~ à qqn/qqch (avoir à l'esprit) to think of sb/sthg, to think about sb/sthg; (se rappeler) to remember sb/sthg; ~ à faire qqch (avoir à l'esprit) to think of doing sthg; (se rappeler) to remember to do sthg; qu'est-ce que tu en penses? what do you think (of it)? ◆ vt to think; je pense que oui I think so; je pense que non I don't think so; ~ faire qqch to be planning to do sthg.
pensif, -ive [pãsif, iv] adj pensive, thoughtful.
pension [pãsjɔ̃] nf 1. (allocation) pension; ~ alimentaire (dans un divorce) alimony. 2. (hébergement) board and lodgings; ~ complète full board; demi-~ half board. 3. (hôtel) guesthouse; ~ de famille guesthouse, boarding house. 4. (prix de l'hébergement) ≃ rent, keep. 5. (internat) boarding school; être en ~ to be a boarder ou at boarding school.
pensionnaire [pãsjɔnɛr] nmf 1. (élève) boarder. 2. (hôte payant) lodger.
pensionnat [pãsjɔna] nm (internat) boarding school.
pentagone [pɛ̃tagɔn] nm pentagon.
pente [pãt] nf slope; en ~ sloping, inclined.
pentecôte [pãtkot] nf (juive) Pentecost; (chrétienne) Whitsun.
pénurie [penyri] nf shortage.
pépier [pepje] vi to chirp.
pépin [pepɛ̃] nm 1. (graine) pip. 2. fam (ennui) hitch. 3. fam (parapluie) umbrella, brolly Br.
pépinière [pepinjɛr] nf tree nursery; fig (école, établissement) nursery.
pépite [pepit] nf nugget.
perçant, -e [pɛrsã, ãt] adj 1. (regard, son) piercing. 2. (froid) bitter, biting.
percepteur [pɛrsɛptœr] nm tax collector.
perception [pɛrsɛpsjɔ̃] nf 1. (d'impôts) collection. 2. (bureau) tax office. 3. (sensation) perception.

percer [pɛrse] ◆ vt 1. (mur, roche) to make a hole in; (coffre-fort) to crack. 2. (trou) to make; (avec perceuse) to drill. 3. (silence, oreille) to pierce. 4. (foule) to make one's way through. 5. fig (mystère) to penetrate. ◆ vi 1. (soleil) to break through. 2. (abcès) to burst; avoir une dent qui perce to be cutting a tooth. 3. (réussir) to make a name for o.s., to break through.
perceuse [pɛrsøz] nf drill.
percevoir [pɛrsəvwar] vt 1. (intention, nuance) to perceive. 2. (retraite, indemnité) to receive. 3. (impôts) to collect.
perche [pɛrʃ] nf 1. (poisson) perch. 2. (de bois, métal) pole.
percher [pɛrʃe] ◆ vi (oiseau) to perch. ◆ vt to perch. ▶ se percher vp to perch.
perchoir [pɛrʃwar] nm perch.
percolateur [pɛrkɔlatœr] nm percolator.
perçu, -e [pɛrsy] pp → percevoir.
percussion [pɛrkysjɔ̃] nf percussion.
percutant, -e [pɛrkytã, ãt] adj 1. (obus) explosive. 2. fig (argument) forceful.
percuter [pɛrkyte] ◆ vt to strike, to smash into. ◆ vi to explode.
perdant, -e [pɛrdã, ãt] ◆ adj losing. ◆ nm, f loser.
perdre [pɛrdr] ◆ vt 1. (gén) to lose. 2. (temps) to waste; (occasion) to miss, to waste. 3. (suj: bonté, propos) to be the ruin of. ◆ vi to lose. ▶ se perdre vp 1. (coutume) to die out, to become lost. 2. (personne) to get lost, to lose one's way.
perdrix [pɛrdri] nf partridge.
perdu, -e [pɛrdy] ◆ pp → perdre. ◆ adj 1. (égaré) lost. 2. (endroit) out-of-the-way. 3. (balle) stray. 4. (emballage) non-returnable. 5. (temps, occasion) wasted. 6. (malade) dying. 7. (récolte, robe) spoilt, ruined.
père [pɛr] nm (gén) father; ~ de famille father. ▶ père Noël nm: le ~ Noël Father Christmas, Santa Claus.
péremptoire [perãptwar] adj peremptory.
perfection [pɛrfɛksjɔ̃] nf (qualité) perfection.
perfectionnement [pɛrfɛksjɔnmã] nm improvement.
perfectionner [pɛrfɛksjɔne] vt to perfect. ▶ se perfectionner vp to improve.
perfide [pɛrfid] adj perfidious.

perforer [pɛrfɔre] *vt* to perforate.

performance [pɛrfɔrmãs] *nf* performance.

performant, -e [pɛrfɔrmã, ãt] *adj* 1. (*personne*) efficient. 2. (*machine*) high-performance (*avant n*).

perfusion [pɛrfyzjɔ̃] *nf* perfusion.

péridurale [peridyral] *nf* epidural.

péril [peril] *nm* peril.

périlleux, -euse [perijø, øz] *adj* perilous, dangerous.

périmé, -e [perime] *adj* out-of-date; *fig* (*idées*) outdated.

périmètre [perimɛtr] *nm* 1. (*contour*) perimeter. 2. (*contenu*) area.

période [perjɔd] *nf* period.

périodique [perjɔdik] ◆ *nm* periodical. ◆ *adj* periodic.

péripétie [peripesi] *nf* event.

périphérie [periferi] *nf* 1. (*de ville*) outskirts (*pl*). 2. (*bord*) periphery; (*de cercle*) circumference.

périphérique [periferik] ◆ *nm* 1. (*route*) ring road Br, beltway Am. 2. (INFORM) peripheral device. ◆ *adj* peripheral.

périphrase [perifraz] *nf* periphrasis.

périple [peripl] *nm* 1. (NAVIG) voyage. 2. (*voyage*) trip.

périr [perir] *vi* to perish.

périssable [perisabl] *adj* 1. (*denrée*) perishable. 2. *littéraire* (*sentiment*) transient.

perle [pɛrl] *nf* 1. (*de nacre*) pearl. 2. (*de bois, verre*) bead. 3. (*personne*) gem.

permanence [pɛrmanãs] *nf* 1. (*continuité*) permanence; **en ~** constantly. 2. (*service*): **être de ~** to be on duty. 3. (*bureau*) office. 4. (SCOL): **(salle de) ~** study room.

permanent, -e [pɛrmanã, ãt] *adj* permanent; (*cinéma*) with continuous showings; (*comité*) standing (*avant n*). ▶ **permanente** *nf* perm.

permettre [pɛrmɛtr] *vt* to permit, to allow; **~ à qqn de faire qqch** to permit ou allow sb to do sthg. ▶ **se permettre** *vp*: **se ~ qqch** to allow o.s sthg; (*avoir les moyens de*) to be able to afford sthg; **se ~ de faire qqch** to take the liberty of doing sthg.

permis, -e [pɛrmi, iz] *pp* → **permettre**. ▶ **permis** *nm* licence, permit; **~ de conduire** driving licence Br, driver's license Am; **~ de construire** planning permission Br, building permit Am; **~ de travail** work permit.

permission [pɛrmisjɔ̃] *nf* 1. (*autorisa-*

tion) permission. 2. (MIL) leave.

permuter [pɛrmyte] ◆ *vt* to change round; (*mots, figures*) to transpose. ◆ *vi* to change, to switch.

pérorer [perɔre] *vi péj* to hold forth.

Pérou [peru] *nm*: **le ~** Peru.

perpendiculaire [pɛrpãdikylɛr] ◆ *nf* perpendicular. ◆ *adj*: **~ (à)** perpendicular (to).

perpétrer [pɛrpetre] *vt* to perpetrate.

perpétuel, -elle [pɛrpetɥɛl] *adj* 1. (*fréquent, continu*) perpetual. 2. (*rente*) life (*avant n*); (*secrétaire*) permanent.

perpétuer [pɛrpetɥe] *vt* to perpetuate. ▶ **se perpétuer** *vp* to continue; (*espèce*) to perpetuate itself.

perpétuité [pɛrpetɥite] *nf* perpetuity; **à ~** for life; **être condamné à ~** to be sentenced to life imprisonment.

perplexe [pɛrplɛks] *adj* perplexed.

perquisition [pɛrkizisjɔ̃] *nf* search.

perron [pɛrɔ̃] *nm* steps (*pl*) (*at entrance to building*).

perroquet [pɛrɔkɛ] *nm* (*animal*) parrot.

perruche [peryʃ] *nf* budgerigar.

perruque [peryk] *nf* wig.

persan, -e [pɛrsã, an] *adj* Persian. ▶ **persan** *nm* (*chat*) Persian (cat).

persécuter [pɛrsekyte] *vt* 1. (*martyriser*) to persecute. 2. (*harceler*) to harass.

persécution [pɛrsekysjɔ̃] *nf* persecution.

persévérant, -e [pɛrseverã, ãt] *adj* persevering.

persévérer [pɛrsevere] *vi*: **~ (dans)** to persevere (in).

persienne [pɛrsjɛn] *nf* shutter.

persil [pɛrsi] *nm* parsley.

Persique [pɛrsik] → **golfe**.

persistant, -e [pɛrsistã, ãt] *adj* persistent; **arbre à feuillage ~** evergreen (tree).

persister [pɛrsiste] *vi* to persist; **~ à faire qqch** to persist in doing sthg.

personnage [pɛrsɔnaʒ] *nm* 1. (THÉÂTRE) character; (ART) figure. 2. (*personnalité*) image.

personnalité [pɛrsɔnalite] *nf* 1. (*gén*) personality. 2. (JUR) status.

personne [pɛrsɔn] ◆ *nf* person; **~s** people; **en ~** in person, personally; **~ âgée** elderly person. ◆ *pron indéf* 1. (*quelqu'un*) anybody, anyone. 2. (*aucune personne*) nobody, no one; **~ ne viendra** nobody will come; **il n'y a jamais ~** there's never anybody there, nobody is ever there.

personnel, -elle [pɛrsɔnɛl] *adj* 1. (*gén*) personal. 2. (*égoïste*) self-centred. ▶ **personnel** *nm* staff, personnel.

personnellement [pɛrsɔnɛlmã] *adv* personally.

personnifier [pɛrsɔnifje] *vt* to personify.

perspective [pɛrspɛktiv] *nf* 1. (ART & *point de vue*) perspective. 2. (*panorama*) view. 3. (*éventualité*) prospect.

perspicace [pɛrspikas] *adj* perspicacious.

persuader [pɛrsɥade] *vt*: ~ qqn de qqch/de faire qch to persuade sb of sthg/to do sthg, to convince sb of sthg/to do sthg.

persuasif, -ive [pɛrsɥazif, iv] *adj* persuasive.

persuasion [pɛrsɥazjɔ̃] *nf* persuasion.

perte [pɛrt] *nf* 1. (*gén*) loss. 2. (*gaspillage - de temps*) waste. 3. (*ruine, déchéance*) ruin. ▶ **pertes** *nfpl* (*morts*) losses. ▶ **à perte de vue** *loc adv* as far as the eye can see.

pertinent, -e [pɛrtinã, ãt] *adj* pertinent, relevant.

perturber [pɛrtyrbe] *vt* 1. (*gén*) to disrupt; ~ l'ordre public to disturb the peace. 2. (PSYCHOL) to disturb.

pervenche [pɛrvã ʃ] *nf* 1. (BOT) periwinkle. 2. *fam* (*contractuelle*) traffic warden Br, meter maid Am.

pervers, -e [pɛrvɛr, ɛrs] ♦ *adj* 1. (*vicieux*) perverted. 2. (*effet*) unwanted. ♦ *nm, f* pervert.

perversion [pɛrvɛrsjɔ̃] *nf* perversion.

perversité [pɛrvɛrsite] *nf* perversity.

pervertir [pɛrvɛrtir] *vt* to pervert.

pesamment [pəzamã] *adv* heavily.

pesant, -e [pəsã, ãt] *adj* 1. (*lourd*) heavy. 2. (*style, architecture*) ponderous.

pesanteur [pəzãtœr] *nf* 1. (PHYS) gravity. 2. (*lourdeur*) heaviness.

pesée [pəze] *nf* (*opération*) weighing.

pèse-personne [pɛzpɛrsɔn] (*pl inv* OU **pèse-personnes**) *nm* scales (*pl*).

peser [pəze] ♦ *vt* to weigh. ♦ *vi* 1. (*avoir un certain poids*) to weigh. 2. (*être lourd*) to be heavy. 3. (*appuyer*): ~ sur qqch to press (down) on sthg.

peseta [pezeta] *nf* peseta.

pessimisme [pesimism] *nm* pessimism.

pessimiste [pesimist] ♦ *nmf* pessimist. ♦ *adj* pessimistic.

peste [pɛst] *nf* 1. (MÉD) plague. 2. (*personne*) pest.

pestiféré, -e [pɛstifere] ♦ *adj* plague-stricken. ♦ *nm, f* plague victim.

pestilentiel, -elle [pɛstilãsjɛl] *adj* pestilential.

pet [pɛ] *nm fam* fart.

pétale [petal] *nm* petal.

pétanque [petãk] *nf* = bowls (U).

pétarader [petarade] *vi* to backfire.

pétard [petar] *nm* 1. (*petit explosif*) banger Br, firecracker. 2. *fam* (*revolver*) gun. 3. *fam* (*haschich*) joint.

péter [pete] ♦ *vi* 1. *tfam* (*personne*) to fart. 2. *fam* (*câble, élastique*) to snap. ♦ *vt fam* to bust.

pétiller [petije] *vi* 1. (*vin, eau*) to sparkle, to bubble. 2. (*feu*) to crackle. 3. *fig* (*yeux*) to sparkle.

petit, -e [pəti, it] ♦ *adj* 1. (*de taille, jeune*) small, little; ~ frère little OU younger brother; ~e sœur little OU younger sister. 2. (*voyage, visite*) short, little. 3. (*faible, infime - somme d'argent*) small; (- *bruit*) faint, slight. 4. (*de peu d'importance, de peu de valeur*) minor. 5. (*médiocre, mesquin*) petty. 6. (*de rang modeste - commerçant, propriétaire, pays*) small; (- *fonctionnaire*) minor. ♦ *nm, f* (*enfant*) little one, child; bonjour, mon ~/ma ~e good morning, my dear; pauvre ~! poor little thing!; la classe des ~s (SCOL) the infant class. ♦ *nm* (*jeune animal*) young (U); faire des ~s to have puppies/kittens *etc*. ▶ **petit à petit** *loc adv* little by little, gradually.

petit déjeuner [p(ə)tidezønœ] *nm* breakfast.

petite-fille [p(ə)titfij] *nf* granddaughter.

petitement [p(ə)titmã] *adv* 1. (*chichement - vivre*) poorly. 2. (*mesquinement*) pettily.

petite-nièce [p(ə)titnjɛs] *nf* great-niece.

petitesse [p(ə)titɛs] *nf* 1. (*de personne, de revenu*) smallness. 2. (*d'esprit*) pettiness.

petit-fils [p(ə)titfis] *nm* grandson.

petit-four [p(ə)titfur] *nm* petit-four.

pétition [petisjɔ̃] *nf* petition.

petit-lait [p(ə)titlɛ] *nm* whey.

petit-nègre [p(ə)titnɛgr] *nm inv fam* pidgin French.

petit-neveu [p(ə)titn(ə)vø] *nm* great-nephew.

petits-enfants [p(ə)titzãfã] *nmpl* grandchildren.

petit-suisse [p(ə)titsɥis] *nm* fresh soft cheese, eaten with sugar.

pétrifier [petrifje] *vt litt & fig* to petrify.

pétrin [petrɛ̃] *nm* **1.** (*de boulanger*) kneading machine. **2.** *fam* (*embarras*) pickle; **se fourrer/être dans le ~** to get into/to be in a pickle.

pétrir [petrir] *vt* (*pâte, muscle*) to knead.

pétrole [petrɔl] *nm* oil, petroleum.

pétrolier, -ère [petrɔlje, ɛr] *adj* oil (*avant n*), petroleum (*avant n*). ▶ **pétrolier** *nm* (*navire*) oil tanker.

pétrolifère [petrɔlifɛr] *adj* oil-bearing.

pétulant, -e [petylɑ̃, ɑ̃t] *adj* exuberant.

peu [pø] ♦ *adv* **1.** (*avec verbe, adjectif, adverbe*): **il a ~ dormi** he didn't sleep much, he slept little; **~ souvent** not very often, rarely; **très ~** very little. **2.** **~ de** (+ *nom sg*) little, not much; (+ *nom pl*) few, not many; **il a ~ de travail** he hasn't got much work, he has little work; **~ de gens le connaissent** few ou not many know him. ♦ *nm* **1.** (*petite quantité*): **le ~ de** (+ *nom sg*) the little; (+ *nom pl*) the few. **2.** **un ~** a little, a bit; **un (tout) petit ~** a little bit; **elle est un ~ sotte** she's a bit stupid; **un ~ de** a little; **un ~ de vin/patience** a little wine/patience. ▶ **avant peu** *loc adv* soon, before long. ▶ **depuis peu** *loc adv* recently. ▶ **peu à peu** *loc adv* gradually, little by little. ▶ **pour peu que** *loc conj* (+ *subjonctif*) if ever, if only. ▶ **pour un peu** *loc adv* nearly, almost. ▶ **si peu que** *loc conj* (+ *subjonctif*) however little. ▶ **sous peu** *loc adv* soon, shortly.

peuplade [pœplad] *nf* tribe.

peuple [pœpl] *nm* **1.** (*gén*) people; **le ~** the (common) people. **2.** *fam* (*multitude*): **quel ~!** what a crowd!

peuplement [pœpləmɑ̃] *nm* **1.** (*action*) populating. **2.** (*population*) population.

peupler [pœple] *vt* **1.** (*pourvoir d'habitants - région*) to populate; (- *bois, étang*) to stock. **2.** (*habiter, occuper*) to inhabit. **3.** *fig* (*remplir*) to fill. ▶ **se peupler** *vp* **1.** (*région*) to become populated. **2.** (*rue, salle*) to be filled.

peuplier [pøplije] *nm* poplar.

peur [pœr] *nf* fear; **avoir ~ de qqn/qqch** to be afraid of sb/sthg; **avoir ~ de faire qqch** to be afraid of doing sthg; **avoir ~ que** (+ *subjonctif*) to be afraid that; **j'ai ~ qu'il ne vienne pas** I'm afraid he won't come; **faire ~ à qqn** to frighten sb; **par** ou **de ~ de qqch** for fear of sthg; **par** ou **de ~ de faire qqch** for fear of doing sthg.

peureux, -euse [pœrø, øz] *adj* fearful, timid.

peut → **pouvoir**.

peut-être [pøtɛtr] *adv* perhaps, maybe; **~ qu'ils ne viendront pas, ils ne viendront ~ pas** perhaps ou maybe they won't come.

peux → **pouvoir**.

phalange [falɑ̃ʒ] *nf* (ANAT) phalanx.

phallocrate [falɔkrat] *nm* male chauvinist.

phallus [falys] *nm* phallus.

pharaon [faraɔ̃] *nm* pharaoh.

phare [far] ♦ *nm* **1.** (*tour*) lighthouse. **2.** (AUTOM) headlight; **~ antibrouillard** fog lamp. ♦ *adj* landmark (*avant n*); **une industrie ~** a flagship ou pioneering industry.

pharmaceutique [farmasøtik] *adj* pharmaceutical.

pharmacie [farmasi] *nf* **1.** (*science*) pharmacology. **2.** (*magasin*) chemist's Br, drugstore Am. **3.** (*meuble*): **(armoire à) ~** medicine cupboard.

pharmacien, -enne [farmasjɛ̃, ɛn] *nm, f* chemist Br, druggist Am.

pharyngite [farɛ̃ʒit] *nf* pharyngitis (U).

pharynx [farɛ̃ks] *nm* pharynx.

phase [faz] *nf* phase; **être en ~ avec qqn** to be on the same wavelength as sb.

phénoménal, -e, -aux [fenɔmenal, o] *adj* phenomenal.

phénomène [fenɔmɛn] *nm* **1.** (*fait*) phenomenon. **2.** (*être anormal*) freak. **3.** *fam* (*excentrique*) character.

philanthropie [filɑ̃trɔpi] *nf* philanthropy.

philatélie [filateli] *nf* philately, stamp-collecting.

philharmonique [filarmɔnik] *adj* philharmonic.

Philippines [filipin] *nfpl*: **les ~** the Philippines.

philologie [filɔlɔʒi] *nf* philology.

philosophe [filɔzɔf] ♦ *nmf* philosopher. ♦ *adj* philosophical.

philosophie [filɔzɔfi] *nf* philosophy.

phobie [fɔbi] *nf* phobia.

phonétique [fɔnetik] ♦ *nf* phonetics (U). ♦ *adj* phonetic.

phonographe [fɔnɔgraf] *nm vieilli* gramophone Br, phonograph Am.

phoque [fɔk] *nm* seal.

phosphate [fɔsfat] *nm* phosphate.

phosphore [fɔsfɔr] *nm* phosphorus.

phosphorescent, -e [fɔsfɔresɑ̃, ɑ̃t] *adj* phosphorescent.

photo 254

photo [fɔto] ◆ *nf* **1.** (*technique*) photography. **2.** (*image*) photo, picture; **prendre qqn en ~** to take a photo of sb; **~ d'identité** passport photo. ◆ *adj inv*: **appareil ~** camera.

photocopie [fɔtɔkɔpi] *nf* **1.** (*procédé*) photocopying. **2.** (*document*) photocopy.

photocopier [fɔtɔkɔpje] *vt* to photocopy.

photocopieur [fɔtɔkɔpjœr] *nm*, **photocopieuse** [fɔtɔkɔpjøz] *nf* photocopier.

photoélectrique [fɔtɔelektrik] *adj* photoelectric.

photogénique [fɔtɔʒenik] *adj* photogenic.

photographe [fɔtɔgraf] *nmf* **1.** (*artiste, technicien*) photographer. **2.** (*commerçant*) camera dealer.

photographie [fɔtɔgrafi] *nf* **1.** (*technique*) photography. **2.** (*cliché*) photograph.

photographier [fɔtɔgrafje] *vt* to photograph.

Photomaton® [fɔtɔmatɔ̃] *nm* photo booth.

photoreportage [fɔtɔrəpɔrtaʒ] *nm* (PRESSE) report (*consisting mainly of photographs*).

phrase [fraz] *nf* **1.** (LING) sentence; **~ toute faite** stock phrase. **2.** (MUS) phrase.

physicien, -enne [fizisjɛ̃, ɛn] *nm, f* physicist.

physiologie [fizjɔlɔʒi] *nf* physiology.

physiologique [fizjɔlɔʒik] *adj* physiological.

physionomie [fizjɔnɔmi] *nf* **1.** (*faciès*) face. **2.** (*apparence*) physiognomy.

physionomiste [fizjɔnɔmist] *adj*: **être ~** to have a good memory for faces.

physique [fizik] ◆ *adj* physical. ◆ *nf* (SCIENCE) physics (U). ◆ *nm* **1.** (*constitution*) physical well-being. **2.** (*apparence*) physique.

physiquement [fizikmã] *adv* physically.

piaffer [pjafe] *vi* **1.** (*cheval*) to paw the ground. **2.** (*personne*) to fidget.

piailler [pjaje] *vi* **1.** (*oiseaux*) to cheep. **2.** (*enfant*) to squawk.

pianiste [pjanist] *nmf* pianist.

piano [pjano] ◆ *nm* piano. ◆ *adv* **1.** (MUS) piano. **2.** (*doucement*) gently.

pianoter [pjanɔte] *vi* **1.** (*jouer du piano*) to plunk away (on the piano). **2.** (*sur table*) to drum one's fingers.

piaule [pjol] *nf fam* (*hébergement*) place; (*chambre*) room.

PIB (*abr de* **produit intérieur brut**) *nm* GDP.

pic [pik] *nm* **1.** (*outil*) pick, pickaxe. **2.** (*montagne*) peak. **3.** (*oiseau*) woodpecker. ▸ **à pic** *loc adv* **1.** (*verticalement*) vertically; **couler à ~** to sink like a stone. **2.** *fam fig* (*à point nommé*) just at the right moment.

pichenette [piʃnɛt] *nf* flick (of the finger).

pichet [piʃɛ] *nm* jug.

pickpocket [pikpɔkɛt] *nm* pickpocket.

picorer [pikɔre] *vi & vt* to peck.

picotement [pikɔtmã] *nm* prickling (U), prickle.

pie [pi] ◆ *nf* **1.** (*oiseau*) magpie. **2.** *fig & péj* (*bavard*) chatterbox. ◆ *adj inv* (*cheval*) piebald.

pièce [pjɛs] *nf* **1.** (*élément*) piece; (*de moteur*) part; **~ de collection** collector's item; **~ détachée** spare part. **2.** (*unité*): **quinze francs ~** fifteen francs each ou apiece; **acheter/vendre qqch à la ~** to buy/sell sthg singly, to buy/sell sthg separately; **travailler à la ~** to do piece work. **3.** (*document*) document, paper; **~ d'identité** identification papers (*pl*); **~ justificative** written proof (U), supporting document. **4.** (*œuvre littéraire ou musicale*) piece; **~ (de théâtre)** play. **5.** (*argent*): **~ (de monnaie)** coin. **6.** (*maison*) room. **7.** (COUTURE) patch.

pied [pje] *nm* **1.** (*gén*) foot; **à ~** on foot; **avoir ~** to be able to touch the bottom; **perdre ~** *litt & fig* to be out of one's depth; **être/marcher ~s nus** ou **nu-~s** to be/to go barefoot; **~ bot** (*handicap*) club-foot. **2.** (*base - de montagne, table*) foot; (*- de verre*) stem; (*- de lampe*) base. **3.** (*plant - de tomate*) stalk; (*- de vigne*) stock. **4.** *loc*: **être sur ~** to be (back) on one's feet, to be up and about; **faire du ~ à** ~ to play footsie with; **mettre qqch sur ~** to get sthg on its feet, to get sthg off the ground; **je n'ai jamais mis les ~s chez lui** I've never set foot in his house; **au ~ de la lettre** literally, to the letter.

pied-de-biche [pjedbiʃ] (*pl* **pieds-de-biche**) *nm* (*outil*) nail claw.

piédestal, -aux [pjedestal, o] *nm* pedestal.

pied-noir [pjenwar] *nmf French settler in Algeria.*

piège [pjɛʒ] *nm litt & fig* trap.

piéger [pjeʒe] *vt* **1.** (*animal, personne*) to trap. **2.** (*colis, véhicule*) to boobytrap.

pierraille [pjɛraj] *nf* loose stones (*pl*).

pierre [pjɛr] *nf* stone; ~ **d'achoppement** *fig* stumbling block; ~ **précieuse** precious stone.

pierreries [pjɛrri] *nfpl* precious stones, jewels.

piété [pjete] *nf* piety.

piétiner [pjetine] ◆ *vi* 1. (*trépigner*) to stamp (one's feet). 2. *fig* (*ne pas avancer*) to make no progress, to be at a standstill. ◆ *vt* (*personne, parterre*) to trample.

piéton, -onne [pjetɔ̃, ɔn] ◆ *nm, f* pedestrian. ◆ *adj* pedestrian (*avant n*).

piétonnier, -ère [pjetɔnje, ɛr] *adj* pedestrian (*avant n*).

piètre [pjɛtr] *adj* poor.

pieu, -x [pjø] *nm* 1. (*poteau*) post, stake. 2. *fam* (*lit*) pit Br, sack Am.

pieuvre [pjœvr] *nf* octopus.

pieux, pieuse [pjø, pjøz] *adj* (*personne, livre*) pious.

pif [pif] *nm fam* conk, hooter Br; **au ~** *fig* by guesswork.

pigeon [piʒɔ̃] *nm* 1. (*oiseau*) pigeon. 2. *fam fig* (*personne*) sucker.

pigeonnier [piʒɔnje] *nm* (*pour pigeons*) pigeon loft, dovecote.

pigment [pigmɑ̃] *nm* pigment.

pignon [piɲɔ̃] *nm* 1. (*de mur*) gable. 2. (*d'engrenage*) gearwheel. 3. (*de pomme de pin*) pine kernel.

pile [pil] ◆ *nf* 1. (*de livres, journaux*) pile. 2. (ÉLECTR) battery. 3. (*de pièce*) ~ **ou face** heads or tails. ◆ *adv fam* on the dot; **tomber/arriver ~** to come/to arrive at just the right time.

piler [pile] ◆ *vt* (*amandes*) to crush, to grind. ◆ *vi fam* (AUTOM) to jam on the brakes.

pileux, -euse [pilø, øz] *adj* hairy (*avant n*); **système ~** hair.

pilier [pilje] *nm* 1. (*de construction*) pillar. 2. *fig* (*soutien*) mainstay, pillar. 3. (RUGBY) prop (forward).

pillard, -e [pijar, ard] *nm, f* looter.

piller [pije] *vt* 1. (*ville, biens*) to loot. 2. *fig* (*ouvrage, auteur*) to plagiarize.

pilon [pilɔ̃] *nm* 1. (*instrument*) pestle. 2. (*de poulet*) drumstick. 3. (*jambe de bois*) wooden leg.

pilonner [pilɔne] *vt* to pound.

pilori [pilɔri] *nm* pillory; **mettre** ou **clouer qqn au ~** *fig* to pillory sb.

pilotage [pilɔtaʒ] *nm* piloting; ~ **automatique** automatic piloting.

pilote [pilɔt] ◆ *nm* (*d'avion*) pilot; (*de voiture*) driver; ~ **automatique** autopilot; ~ **de chasse** fighter pilot; ~ **de course** rac-

ing driver; ~ **d'essai** test pilot; ~ **de ligne** airline pilot. ◆ *adj* pilot (*avant n*), experimental.

piloter [pilɔte] *vt* 1. (*avion*) to pilot; (*voiture*) to drive. 2. (*personne*) to show around.

pilotis [pilɔti] *nm* pile.

pilule [pilyl] *nf* pill; **prendre la ~** to be on the pill.

piment [pimɑ̃] *nm* 1. (*plante*) pepper, capsicum; ~ **rouge** chilli pepper, hot red pepper. 2. *fig* (*piquant*) spice.

pimpant, -e [pɛ̃pɑ̃, ɑ̃t] *adj* smart.

pin [pɛ̃] *nm* pine; ~ **parasol** umbrella pine; ~ **sylvestre** Scots pine.

pince [pɛ̃s] *nf* 1. (*grande*) pliers (*pl*). 2. (*petite*): ~ (**à épiler**) tweezers (*pl*); ~ **à linge** clothes peg. 3. (*de crabe*) pincer. 4. (COUTURE) dart.

pinceau, -x [pɛ̃so] *nm* (*pour peindre*) brush.

pincée [pɛ̃se] *nf* pinch.

pincer [pɛ̃se] ◆ *vt* 1. (*serrer*) to pinch; (MUS) to pluck; (*lèvres*) to purse. 2. *fam fig* (*arrêter*) to nick Br, to catch. 3. (*suj: froid*) to nip. ◆ *vi fam* (*faire froid*): **ça pince!** it's a bit nippy!

pincettes [pɛ̃sɛt] *nfpl* (*ustensile*) tongs.

pingouin [pɛ̃gwɛ̃] *nm* penguin.

ping-pong [piŋpɔ̃g] *nm* ping pong, table tennis.

pin's [pinz] *nm inv* badge.

pinson [pɛ̃sɔ̃] *nm* chaffinch.

pintade [pɛ̃tad] *nf* guinea fowl.

pin-up [pinœp] *nf inv* pinup (girl).

pioche [pjɔʃ] *nf* 1. (*outil*) pick. 2. (JEU) pile.

piocher [pjɔʃe] ◆ *vt* 1. (*terre*) to dig. 2. (JEU) to take. 3. *fig* (*choisir*) to pick at random. ◆ *vi* 1. (*creuser*) to dig. 2. (JEU) to pick up; ~ **dans** (*tas*) to delve into; (*économies*) to dip into.

pion, pionne [pjɔ̃, pjɔn] *nm, f fam* (SCOL) supervisor (*often a student who does this as a part-time job*). ► **pion** *nm* (*aux échecs*) pawn; (*aux dames*) piece; **n'être qu'un ~** *fig* to be just a pawn in the game.

pionnier, -ère [pjɔnje, ɛr] *nm, f* pioneer.

pipe [pip] *nf* pipe.

pipeline, pipe-line [pajplajn, piplin] (*pl* **pipe-lines**) *nm* pipeline.

pipi [pipi] *nm fam* wee; **faire ~** to have a wee.

piquant, -e [pikɑ̃, ɑ̃t] *adj* 1. (*barbe, feuille*) prickly. 2. (*sauce*) spicy, hot. ► **piquant** *nm* 1. (*d'animal*) spine; (*de* *végétal*) thorn, prickle. **2.** *fig* (*d'histoire*) spice.

pique [pik] ◆ *nf* **1.** (*arme*) pike. **2.** *fig* (*mot blessant*) barbed comment. ◆ *nm* (*aux cartes*) spade.

pique-assiette [pikasjɛt] (*pl inv* OU **pique-assiettes**) *nmf péj* sponger.

pique-nique [piknik] (*pl* **pique-niques**) *nm* picnic.

piquer [pike] ◆ *vt* **1.** (*suj: guêpe, méduse*) to sting; (*suj: serpent, moustique*) to bite. **2.** (*avec pointe*) to prick. **3.** (MÉD) to give an injection to. **4.** (*animal*) to put down. **5.** (*fleur*): ~ **qqch dans** to stick sthg into. **6.** (*suj: tissu, barbe*) to prickle. **7.** (*suj: fumée, froid*) to sting. **8.** (COUTURE) to sew, to machine. **9.** *fam* (*voler*) to pinch. **10.** *fig* (*curiosité*) to excite, to arouse. **11.** *fam* (*voleur, escroc*) to nick Br, to catch. ◆ *vi* **1.** (*ronce*) to prick; (*ortie*) to sting. **2.** (*guêpe, méduse*) to sting; (*serpent, moustique*) to bite. **3.** (*épice*) to burn. **4.** *fam* (*voler*): ~ (**dans**) to pinch (from). **5.** (*avion*) to dive.

piquet [pikɛ] *nm* (*pieu*) peg, stake. ▶ **piquet de grève** *nm* picket.

piqûre [pikyr] *nf* **1.** (*de guêpe, méduse*) sting; (*de serpent, moustique*) bite. **2.** (*d'ortie*) sting. **3.** (*injection*) jab Br, shot.

piratage [pirataʒ] *nm* piracy; (INFORM) hacking.

pirate [pirat] ◆ *nm* (*corsaire*) pirate; ~ **de l'air** hijacker, skyjacker. ◆ *adj* pirate (*avant n*).

pire [pir] ◆ *adj* **1.** (*comparatif relatif*) worse. **2.** (*superlatif*): **le/la** ~ the worst. ◆ *nm*: **le** ~ (**de**) the worst (of).

pirogue [pirɔg] *nf* dugout canoe.

pirouette [pirwɛt] *nf* **1.** (*saut*) pirouette. **2.** *fig* (*faux-fuyant*) prevarication, evasive answer.

pis [pi] ◆ *adj littéraire* (*pire*) worse. ◆ *adv* worse; **de mal en** ~ from bad to worse. ◆ *nm* udder.

pis-aller [pizale] *nm inv* last resort.

pisciculture [pisikyltyr] *nf* fish farming.

piscine [pisin] *nf* swimming pool; ~ **couverte/découverte** indoor/open-air swimming pool.

pissenlit [pisɑ̃li] *nm* dandelion.

pisser [pise] *fam* ◆ *vt* (*suj: plaie*): **son genou pissait le sang** blood was gushing from his knee. ◆ *vi* to pee, to piss.

pissotière [pisɔtjɛr] *nf fam* public urinal.

pistache [pistaʃ] *nf* (*fruit*) pistachio (nut).

piste [pist] *nf* **1.** (*trace*) trail. **2.** (*zone aménagée*): ~ **d'atterrissage** runway; ~ **cyclable** cycle track; ~ **de danse** dance floor; ~ **de ski** ski run. **3.** (*chemin*) path, track. **4.** (*d'enregistrement*) track.

pisteur [pistœr] *nm* (*pour surveillance*) ski patrolman.

pistil [pistil] *nm* pistil.

pistolet [pistɔlɛ] *nm* **1.** (*arme*) pistol, gun. **2.** (*à peinture*) spray gun.

piston [pistɔ̃] *nm* **1.** (*de moteur*) piston. **2.** (MUS) (*d'instrument*) valve. **3.** *fig* (*appui*) string-pulling.

pistonner [pistɔne] *vt* to pull strings for; **se faire** ~ to have strings pulled for one.

pitance [pitɑ̃s] *nf péj & vieilli* sustenance.

piteux, -euse [pitø, øz] *adj* piteous.

pitié [pitje] *nf* pity; **avoir** ~ **de qqn** to have pity on sb, to pity sb.

piton [pitɔ̃] *nm* **1.** (*clou*) piton. **2.** (*pic*) peak.

pitoyable [pitwajabl] *adj* pitiful.

pitre [pitr] *nm* clown.

pitrerie [pitrəri] *nf* tomfoolery.

pittoresque [pitɔrɛsk] *adj* **1.** (*région*) picturesque. **2.** (*détail*) colourful, vivid.

pivot [pivo] *nm* **1.** (*de machine, au basket*) pivot. **2.** (*de dent*) post. **3.** (*centre*) *fig* mainspring.

pivoter [pivɔte] *vi* to pivot; (*porte*) to revolve.

pizza [pidza] *nf* pizza.

Pl., pl. *abr de* **place**.

placage [plakaʒ] *nm* (*de bois*) veneer.

placard [plakar] *nm* **1.** (*armoire*) cupboard. **2.** (*affiche*) poster, notice.

placarder [plakarde] *vt* (*affiche*) to put up, to stick up; (*mur*) to placard, to stick a notice on.

place [plas] *nf* **1.** (*espace*) space, room; **prendre de la** ~ to take up (a lot of) space; **il y a de la** ~? is there any room?; **faire** ~ **à** (*amour, haine*) to give way to. **2.** (*emplacement, position*) position; **changer qqch de** ~ to put sthg in a different place, to move sthg; **prendre la** ~ **de qqn** to take sb's place; **à la** ~ **de qqn** instead of sb, in sb's place; **à ta** ~ if I were you, in your place; **sur** ~ on the spot. **3.** (*siège*) seat; ~ **assise** seat. **4.** (*rang*) place. **5.** (*de ville*) square. **6.** (*emploi*) position, job. **7.** (MIL) (*de garnison*) garrison (town); ~ **forte** fortified town.

placement [plasmɑ̃] *nm* **1.** (*d'argent*) investment. **2.** (*d'employé*) placing.

placenta [plasɛ̃ta] nm (ANAT) placenta.
placer [plase] vt 1. (gén) to put, to place; (invités, spectateurs) to seat. 2. (mot, anecdote) to put in, to get in. 3. (argent) to invest. ▶ **se placer** vp 1. (prendre place - debout) to stand; (- assis) to sit (down). 2. fig (dans situation) to put o.s. 3. (se classer) to come, to be.
placide [plasid] adj placid.
plafond [plafɔ̃] nm litt & fig ceiling; **faux** ~ false ceiling.
plafonner [plafɔne] vi (prix, élève) to peak; (avion) to reach its ceiling.
plage [plaʒ] nf 1. (de sable) beach. 2. (d'ombre, de prix) band; fig (de temps) slot. 3. (de disque) track. 4. (dans voiture): ~ **arrière** back shelf.
plagiat [plaʒja] nm plagiarism.
plagier [plaʒje] vt to plagiarize.
plaider [plede] ◆ vt to plead. ◆ vi to plead; ~ **contre qqn** to plead against sb; ~ **pour qqn** (JUR) to plead for sb; (justifier) to plead sb's cause.
plaidoirie [plɛdwari] nf, **plaidoyer** [plɛdwaje] nm (JUR) speech for the defence; fig plea.
plaie [plɛ] nf 1. litt & fig wound. 2. fam (personne) pest.
plaindre [plɛ̃dr] vt to pity. ▶ **se plaindre** vp to complain.
plaine [plɛn] nf plain.
plain-pied [plɛ̃pje] ▶ **de plain-pied** loc adv 1. (pièce) on one floor; **de** ~ **avec** litt & fig on a level with. 2. fig (directement) straight.
plaint, -e [plɛ̃, plɛ̃t] pp → **plaindre**.
plainte [plɛ̃t] nf 1. (gémissement) moan, groan; fig & litt (du vent) moan. 2. (doléance & JUR) complaint; **porter** ~ to lodge a complaint; ~ **contre X** ≈ complaint against person or persons unknown.
plaintif, -ive [plɛ̃tif, iv] adj plaintive.
plaire [plɛr] vi to be liked; **il me plaît** I like him; **ça te plairait d'aller au cinéma?** would you like to go to the cinema?; **s'il vous/te plaît** please.
plaisance [plɛzɑ̃s] ▶ **de plaisance** loc adj pleasure (avant n); **navigation de** ~ sailing; **port de** ~ marina.
plaisancier, -ère [plɛzɑ̃sje, ɛr] nm, f (amateur) sailor.
plaisant, -e [plɛzɑ̃, ɑ̃t] adj pleasant.
plaisanter [plɛzɑ̃te] vi to joke; **tu plaisantes?** you must be joking!
plaisanterie [plɛzɑ̃tri] nf joke; **c'est une** ~? iron you must be joking!

plaisantin [plɛzɑ̃tɛ̃] nm joker.
plaisir [plezir] nm pleasure; **les** ~**s de la vie** life's pleasures; **avoir du/prendre** ~ **à faire qqch** to have/to take pleasure in doing sthg; **faire** ~ **à qqn** to please sb; **avec** ~ with pleasure; **j'ai le** ~ **de vous annoncer que ...** I have the (great) pleasure of announcing that ...
plan¹, -e [plɑ̃, plan] adj level, flat.
plan² [plɑ̃] nm 1. (dessin - de ville) map; (- de maison) plan. 2. (projet) plan; **faire des** ~**s** to make plans. 3. (domaine): **sur tous les** ~**s** in all respects; **sur le** ~ **familial** as far as the family is concerned. 4. (surface): ~ **d'eau** lake; ~ **de travail** work surface, worktop. 5. (GÉOM) plane. 6. (CINÉMA) take; **gros** ~ close-up. ▶ **à l'arrière-plan** loc adv in the background. ▶ **au premier plan** loc adv (dans l'espace) in the foreground. ▶ **en plan** loc adv: **laisser qqn en** ~ to leave sb stranded, to abandon sb; **il a tout laissé en** ~ he dropped everything. ▶ **sur le même plan** loc adj on the same level.
planche [plɑ̃ʃ] nf 1. (en bois) plank; ~ **à dessin** drawing board; ~ **à repasser** ironing board; ~ **à roulettes** skateboard; ~ **à voile** (planche) sailboard; (sport) windsurfing; **faire la** ~ fig to float. 2. (d'illustration) plate.
plancher [plɑ̃ʃe] nm 1. (de maison, de voiture) floor. 2. fig (limite) floor, lower limit.
plancton [plɑ̃ktɔ̃] nm plankton.
planer [plane] vi 1. (avion, oiseau) to glide. 2. (nuage, fumée, brouillard) to float. 3. fig (danger): ~ **sur qqn** to hang over sb. 4. fam fig (personne) to be out of touch with reality.
planétaire [planetɛr] adj 1. (ASTRON) planetary. 2. (mondial) world (avant n).
planétarium [planetarjɔm] nm planetarium.
planète [planɛt] nf planet.
planeur [planœr] nm glider.
planification [planifikasjɔ̃] nf (ÉCON) planning.
planisphère [planisfɛr] nm map of the world, planisphere.
planning [planiŋ] nm 1. (de fabrication) workflow schedule. 2. (agenda personnel) schedule; ~ **familial** (contrôle) family planning; (organisme) family planning clinic.
planque [plɑ̃k] nf fam 1. (cachette) hideout. 2. fig (situation, travail) cushy number.
plant [plɑ̃] nm (plante) seedling.

plantaire [plɑ̃tɛr] *adj* plantar.

plantation [plɑ̃tasjɔ̃] *nf* 1. (*exploitation - d'arbres, de coton, de café*) plantation; (- *de légumes*) patch. 2. (*action*) planting.

plante [plɑ̃t] *nf* 1. (BOT) plant; ~ verte ou d'appartement ou d'intérieur house ou pot plant. 2. (ANAT) sole.

planter [plɑ̃te] *vt* 1. (*arbre, terrain*) to plant. 2. (*clou*) to hammer in, to drive in; (*pieu*) to drive in; (*couteau, griffes*) to stick in. 3. (*tente*) to pitch. 4. *fam fig* (*laisser tomber*) to dump. 5. *fig* (*chapeau*) to stick; (*baiser*) to plant.

planteureux, -euse [plɑ̃tyrø, øz] *adj* 1. (*repas*) lavish. 2. (*femme*) buxom.

plaque [plak] *nf* 1. (*de métal, de verre, de verglas*) sheet; (*de marbre*) slab; ~ chauffante ou de cuisson hotplate; ~ de chocolat bar of chocolate. 2. (*gravée*) plaque; ~ d'immatriculation ou minéralogique number plate Br, license plate Am. 3. (*insigne*) badge. 4. (*sur la peau*) patch. 5. (*dentaire*) plaque.

plaqué, -e [plake] *adj* (*métal*) plated; ~ or/argent gold-/silver-plated. ► **plaqué** *nm* (*métal*): du ~ or/argent gold/silver plate.

plaquer [plake] *vt* 1. (*métal*) to plate. 2. (*bois*) to veneer. 3. (*aplatir*) to flatten; ~ qqn contre qqch to pin sb against sthg; ~ qqch contre qqch to stick sthg onto sthg. 4. (RUGBY) to tackle. 5. (MUS) (*accord*) to play. 6. *fam* (*travail, personne*) to chuck.

plaquette [plakɛt] *nf* 1. (*de métal*) plaque; (*de marbre*) tablet. 2. (*de chocolat*) bar; (*de beurre*) pat. 3. (*de comprimés*) packet, strip. 4. (*gén pl*) (BIOL) platelet. 5. (AUTOM): ~ de frein brake pad.

plasma [plasma] *nm* plasma.

plastique [plastik] *adj* & *nm* plastic.

plastiquer [plastike] *vt* to blow up (*with plastic explosives*).

plat, -e [pla, plat] *adj* 1. (*gén*) flat. 2. (*eau*) still. ► **plat** *nm* 1. (*partie plate*) flat. 2. (*récipient*) dish. 3. (*mets*) course; ~ cuisiné ready-cooked meal ou dish; ~ du jour today's special; ~ préparé ready meal; ~ principal ou de résistance main course. 4. (*plongeon*) belly-flop. ► **à plat** *loc adv* 1. (*horizontalement, dégonflé*) flat. 2. *fam* (*épuisé*) exhausted.

platane [platan] *nm* plane tree.

plateau [plato] *nm* 1. (*de cuisine*) tray; ~ de/à fromages cheese board. 2. (*de balance*) pan. 3. (GÉOGR & *fig*) plateau. 4. (THÉÂTRE) stage; (CIN & TÉLÉ) set. 5. (*de vélo*) chain wheel.

plateau-repas [platorəpa] *nm* tray (of food).

plate-bande [platbɑ̃d] *nf* flower bed.

plate-forme [platfɔrm] *nf* (*gén*) platform; ~ de forage drilling platform.

platine [platin] ◆ *adj inv* platinum. ◆ *nm* (*métal*) platinum. ◆ *nf* (*tourne-disque*) deck; ~ laser compact disc player.

platonique [platonik] *adj* (*amour, amitié*) platonic.

plâtras [platra] *nm* (*gravats*) rubble.

plâtre [platr] *nm* 1. (CONSTR & MÉD) plaster. 2. (*sculpture*) plaster cast. 3. *péj* (*fromage*): c'est du vrai ~ it's like sawdust.

plâtrer [platre] *vt* 1. (*mur*) to plaster. 2. (MÉD) to put in plaster.

plausible [plozibl] *adj* plausible.

play-back [plɛbak] *nm inv* miming; chanter en ~ to mime.

play-boy [plɛbɔj] (*pl* play-boys) *nm* playboy.

plébiscite [plebisit] *nm* plebiscite.

plein, -e [plɛ̃, plɛn] *adj* 1. (*rempli, complet*) full; c'est la ~e forme I am/they are *etc* in top form; en ~e nuit in the middle of the night; en ~ air in the open air. 2. (*non creux*) solid. 3. (*femelle*) pregnant. ► **plein** ◆ *adv fam*: il a de l'encre ~ les doigts he has ink all over his fingers; en ~ dans/sur qqch right in/on sthg. ◆ *nm* (*de réservoir*) full tank; le ~, s'il vous plaît fill her up please; faire le ~ to fill up.

plein-temps [plɛ̃tɑ̃] *nm* full-time job.

plénitude [plenityd] *nf* fullness.

pléonasme [pleonasm] *nm* pleonasm.

pleurer [plœre] ◆ *vi* 1. (*larmoyer*) to cry; ~ de joie to weep for joy, to cry with joy. 2. *péj* (*se plaindre*) to whinge. 3. (*se lamenter*): ~ sur to lament. ◆ *vt* to mourn.

pleurnicher [plœrniʃe] *vi* to whine, to whinge.

pleurs [plœr] *nmpl*: être en ~ to be in tears.

pleuvoir [pløvwar] *v impers litt* & *fig* to rain; il pleut it is raining.

Plexiglas® [plɛksiglas] *nm* Plexiglass®.

plexus [plɛksys] *nm* plexus; ~ solaire solar plexus.

pli [pli] *nm* 1. (*de tissu*) pleat; (*de pantalon*) crease; faux ~ crease. 2. (*du front*) line; (*du cou*) fold. 3. (*lettre*) envelope; (*enveloppe*) envelope; sous ~ séparé under separate cover. 4. (CARTES) trick. 5. (GÉOL) fold.

pliant, -e [plijɑ̃, ɑ̃t] *adj* folding (*avant n*).

plier [plije] ◆ vt 1. (*papier, tissu*) to fold. 2. (*vêtement, vélo*) to fold (up). 3. (*branche, bras*) to bend. ◆ vi 1. (*se courber*) to bend. 2. *fig* (*céder*) to bow. ▶ **se plier** vp 1. (*être pliable*) to fold (up). 2. *fig* (*se soumettre*): **se ~ à qqch** to bow to sthg.

plinthe [plɛ̃t] nf plinth.

plissé, -e [plise] adj 1. (*jupe*) pleated. 2. (*peau*) wrinkled.

plissement [plismɑ̃] nm 1. (*de front*) creasing; (*d'yeux*) screwing up. 2. (GÉOL) fold.

plisser [plise] ◆ vt 1. (COUTURE) to pleat. 2. (*front*) to crease; (*lèvres*) to pucker; (*yeux*) to screw up. ◆ vi (*étoffe*) to crease.

plomb [plɔ̃] nm 1. (*métal, de vitrail*) lead. 2. (*de chasse*) shot. 3. (ÉLECTR) fuse; **les ~s ont sauté** a fuse has blown ou gone. 4. (*de pêche*) sinker.

plombage [plɔ̃baʒ] nm (*de dent*) filling.

plomber [plɔ̃be] vt 1. (*ligne*) to weight (with lead). 2. (*dent*) to fill.

plombier [plɔ̃bje] nm plumber.

plonge [plɔ̃ʒ] nf dishwashing; **faire la ~** to wash dishes.

plongeant, -e [plɔ̃ʒɑ̃, ɑ̃t] adj 1. (*vue*) from above. 2. (*décolleté*) plunging.

plongée [plɔ̃ʒe] nf diving; **~ sous-marine** scuba- diving.

plongeoir [plɔ̃ʒwar] nm diving board.

plongeon [plɔ̃ʒɔ̃] nm (*dans l'eau, au football*) dive.

plonger [plɔ̃ʒe] ◆ vt 1. (*immerger, enfoncer*) to plunge; **~ la tête sous l'eau** to put one's head under the water. 2. *fig* (*précipiter*): **~ qqn dans qqch** to throw sb into sthg; **~ une pièce dans l'obscurité** to plunge a room into darkness. ◆ vi (*dans l'eau, gardien de but*) to dive. ▶ **se plonger** vp 1. (*s'immerger*) to submerge. 2. *fig* (*s'absorber*): **se ~ dans qqch** to immerse o.s. in sthg.

plongeur, -euse [plɔ̃ʒœr, øz] nm, f 1. (*dans l'eau*) diver. 2. (*dans restaurant*) dishwasher.

ployer [plwaje] vt & vi *litt & fig* to bend.

plu [ply] ◆ pp inv → **plaire**. ◆ pp inv → **pleuvoir**.

pluie [plɥi] nf 1. (*averse*) rain (U); **sous la ~** in the rain; **une ~ battante** driving rain; **une ~ fine** drizzle. 2. *fig* (*grande quantité*): **une ~ de** a shower of.

plume [plym] nf 1. (*d'oiseau*) feather. 2. (*pour écrire - d'oiseau*) quill pen; (*- de stylo*) nib.

plumeau, -x [plymo] nm feather duster.

plumer [plyme] vt 1. (*volaille*) to pluck. 2. *fam fig & péj* (*personne*) to fleece.

plumier [plymje] nm pencil box.

plupart [plypar] nf: **la ~ de** most of, the majority of; **la ~ du temps** most of the time, mostly; **pour la ~** mostly, for the most part.

pluriel, -elle [plyrjɛl] adj 1. (GRAM) plural. 2. (*société*) pluralist. ▶ **pluriel** nm plural; **au ~** in the plural.

plus [ply(s)] ◆ adv 1. (*quantité*) more; **je ne peux vous en dire ~** I can't tell you anything more; **beaucoup ~ de** (+ *nom sg*) a lot more, much more; (+ *nom pl*) a lot more, many more; **un peu ~ de** (+ *nom sg*) a little more; (+ *nom pl*) a few more; **~ j'y pense, ~ je me dis que ...** the more I think about it, the more I'm sure ... 2. (*comparaison*) more; **c'est ~ court par là** it's shorter that way; **viens ~ souvent** come more often; **c'est un peu ~ loin** it's a (little) bit further; **~ jeune (que)** younger (than); **c'est ~ simple qu'on ne le croit** it's simpler than you think. 3. (*superlatif*): **le ~** the most; **c'est lui qui travaille le ~** he's the hardest worker, he's the one who works (the) hardest; **le ~ souvent** the most often; **le ~ loin** the furthest; **le ~ vite possible** as quickly as possible. 4. (*négation*) no more; **~ un mot!** not another word!; **ne ... ~** no longer, no more; **il ne vient ~ me voir** he doesn't come to see me any more, he no longer comes to see me; **je n'y vais ~ du tout** I don't go there any more. ◆ nm 1. (*signe*) plus (sign). 2. *fig* (*atout*) plus. ◆ prép plus; **trois ~ trois font six** three plus three is six, three and three are six. ▶ **au plus** loc adv at the most; **tout au ~** at the very most. ▶ **de plus** loc adv 1. (*en supplément, en trop*) more; **elle a cinq ans de ~ que moi** she's five years older than me. 2. (*en outre*) furthermore, what's more. ▶ **de plus en plus** loc adv more and more. ▶ **de plus en plus de** loc prép more and more. ▶ **en plus** loc adv 1. (*en supplément*) extra. 2. (*d'ailleurs*) moreover, what's more. ▶ **en plus de** loc prép in addition to. ▶ **ni plus ni moins** loc adv no more no less. ▶ **plus ou moins** loc adv more or less. ▶ **sans plus** loc adv: **elle est gentille, sans ~** she's nice, but no more than that.

plusieurs [plyzjœr] adj indéf pl & pron indéf mfpl several.

plus-que-parfait [plyskəparfɛ] nm (GRAM) pluperfect.

plus-value [plyvaly] nf 1. (d'investissement) appreciation. 2. (excédent) surplus. 3. (bénéfice) profit.

plutôt [plyto] adv rather; ~ que de faire qqch instead of doing sthg, rather than doing ou do sthg.

pluvieux, -euse [plyvjø, øz] adj rainy.

PME (abr de petite et moyenne entreprise) nf SME.

PMI nf (abr de petite et moyenne industrie) small industrial firm.

PMU (abr de Pari mutuel urbain) nm system for betting on horses.

PNB (abr de produit national brut) nm GNP.

pneu [pnø] nm (de véhicule) tyre.

pneumatique [pnømatik] ◆ nf (PHYS) pneumatics (U). ◆ adj 1. (fonctionnant à l'air) pneumatic. 2. (gonflé à l'air) inflatable.

pneumonie [pnømɔni] nf pneumonia.

PO (abr de petites ondes) MW.

poche [pɔʃ] nf 1. (de vêtement, de sac, d'air) pocket; de ~ pocket (avant n). 2. (sac, sous les yeux) bag; faire des ~s (vêtement) to bag.

pocher [pɔʃe] vt 1. (CULIN) to poach. 2. (blesser): ~ l'œil à qqn to give sb a black eye.

pochette [pɔʃɛt] nf 1. (enveloppe) envelope; (d'allumettes) book; (de photos) packet. 2. (de disque) sleeve. 3. (mouchoir) (pocket) handkerchief.

pochoir [pɔʃwar] nm stencil.

podium [pɔdjɔm] nm podium.

poêle [pwal] ◆ nf pan; ~ à frire frying pan. ◆ nm stove.

poème [pɔɛm] nm poem.

poésie [pɔezi] nf 1. (genre, émotion) poetry. 2. (pièce écrite) poem.

poète [pɔɛt] nm 1. (écrivain) poet. 2. fig & hum (rêveur) dreamer.

pognon [pɔɲɔ̃] nm fam dosh.

pogrom(e) [pɔgrɔm] nm pogrom.

poids [pwa] nm 1. (gén) weight; quel ~ fait-il? how heavy is it/he?; perdre/prendre du ~ to lose/gain weight; vendre au ~ to sell by weight; ~ lourd (BOXE) heavyweight; (camion) heavy goods vehicle; de ~ (argument) weighty. 2. (SPORT) (lancer) shot.

poignant, -e [pwaɲɑ̃, ɑ̃t] adj poignant.

poignard [pwaɲar] nm dagger.

poignée [pwaɲe] nf 1. (quantité, petit nombre) handful. 2. (manche) handle. ▶ **poignée de main** nf handshake.

poignet [pwaɲɛ] nm 1. (ANAT) wrist.

2. (de vêtement) cuff.

poil [pwal] nm 1. (du corps) hair. 2. (d'animal) hair, coat. 3. (de pinceau) bristle; (de tapis) strand. 4. fam (peu): il s'en est fallu d'un ~ que je réussisse I came within a hair's breadth of succeeding.

poilu, -e [pwaly] adj hairy.

poinçon [pwɛ̃sɔ̃] nm 1. (outil) awl. 2. (marque) hallmark.

poinçonner [pwɛ̃sɔne] vt 1. (bijou) to hallmark. 2. (billet, tôle) to punch.

poing [pwɛ̃] nm fist.

point [pwɛ̃] ◆ nm 1. (COUTURE & TRICOT) stitch; ~s de suture (MÉD) stitches. 2. (de ponctuation): ~ (final) full stop Br, period Am; ~ d'interrogation/d'exclamation question/exclamation mark; ~s de suspension suspension points. 3. (petite tache) dot; ~ noir (sur la peau) blackhead; fig (problème) problem. 4. (endroit) spot, point; fig point; ~ culminant (en montagne) summit; fig climax; ~ de repère (temporel) reference point; (spatial) landmark; ~ de vente point of sale, sale outlet; ~ de vue (panorama) viewpoint; fig (opinion, aspect) point of view; avoir un ~ commun avec qqn to have something in common with sb. 5. (degré) point; au ~ que, à tel ~ que to such an extent that; je ne pensais pas que cela le vexerait à ce ~ I didn't think it would make him so cross; être ... au ~ de faire qqch to be so ... as to do sthg. 6. fig (position) position. 7. (réglage): mettre au ~ (machine) to adjust; (idée, projet) to finalize; à ~ (cuisson) just right; à ~ (nommé) just in time. 8. (question, détail) point, detail; ~ faible weak point. 9. (score) point. 10. (douleur) pain; ~ de côté stitch. 11. (début): être sur le ~ de faire qqch to be on the point of doing sthg, to be about to do sthg. 12. (AUTOM) au ~ mort in neutral. 13. (GÉOGR): ~s cardinaux points of the compass. ◆ adv vieilli: ne ~ not (at all).

pointe [pwɛ̃t] nf 1. (extrémité) point; (de nez) tip; se hausser sur la ~ des pieds to stand on tiptoe; se terminer en ~ to taper; ~ d'asperge asparagus tip. 2. (clou) tack. 3. (sommet) peak, summit; à la ~ de fig at the peak of; à la ~ de la technique at the forefront ou leading edge of technology. 4. fig (trait d'esprit) witticism. 5. fig (petite quantité): une ~ de a touch of. ▶ **pointes** nfpl (DANSE) points; faire des ou les ~s to dance on one's points. ▶ **de pointe** loc adj 1. (vitesse) maximum, top. 2. (industrie, secteur) leading; (technique) latest.

pointer [pwɛ̃te] ♦ vt **1.** (cocher) to tick (off). **2.** (employés - à l'entrée) to check in; (- à la sortie) to check out. **3.** (diriger): ~ qqch vers/sur to point sthg towards/at. ♦ vi **1.** (à l'usine - à l'entrée) to clock in; (- à la sortie) to clock out. **2.** (à la pétanque) to get as close to the jack as possible. **3.** (jour) to break.

pointillé [pwɛ̃tije] nm **1.** (ligne) dotted line; en ~ (ligne) dotted. **2.** (perforations) perforations (pl).

pointilleux, -euse [pwɛ̃tijø, øz] adj: ~ (sur) particular (about).

pointu, -e [pwɛ̃ty] adj **1.** (objet) pointed. **2.** (voix, ton) sharp. **3.** (étude, formation) specialized.

pointure [pwɛ̃tyr] nf (shoe) size.

point-virgule [pwɛ̃virgyl] nm semicolon.

poire [pwar] nf **1.** (fruit) pear. **2.** (MÉD): ~ à injections syringe. **3.** fam (visage) face. **4.** fam (naïf) dope.

poireau, -x [pwaro] nm leek.

poirier [pwarje] nm pear tree.

pois [pwa] nm **1.** (BOT) pea; ~ chiche chickpea; petits ~ garden peas, petits pois; ~ de senteur sweet pea. **2.** fig (motif) dot, spot; à ~ spotted, polkadot.

poison [pwazɔ̃] ♦ nm (substance) poison. ♦ nmf fam fig (personne) drag, pain; (enfant) brat.

poisse [pwas] nf fam bad luck; porter la ~ to be bad luck.

poisseux, -euse [pwasø, øz] adj sticky.

poisson [pwasɔ̃] nm fish; ~ d'avril (farce) April fool; (en papier) paper fish pinned to someone's back as a prank on April Fools' Day; ~ rouge goldfish. ► **Poissons** nmpl (ASTROL) Pisces (sg).

poissonnerie [pwasɔnri] nf (boutique) fish shop, fishmonger's (shop).

poissonnier, -ère [pwasɔnje, ɛr] nm, f fishmonger.

poitrine [pwatrin] nf (thorax) chest; (de femme) chest, bust.

poivre [pwavr] nm pepper; ~ blanc white pepper; ~ gris, ~ noir black pepper.

poivrier [pwavrije] nm, **poivrière** [pwavrijɛr] nf pepper pot.

poivron [pwavrɔ̃] nm pepper, capsicum; ~ rouge/vert red/green pepper.

poker [pɔkɛr] nm poker.

polaire [pɔlɛr] adj polar.

polar [pɔlar] nm fam thriller, whodunnit.

Polaroïd® [pɔlarɔid] nm Polaroid®.

polder [pɔldɛr] nm polder.

pôle [pol] nm pole; ~ Nord/Sud North/South Pole.

polémique [pɔlemik] ♦ nf controversy. ♦ adj (style, ton) polemical.

poli, -e [pɔli] adj **1.** (personne) polite. **2.** (surface) polished.

police [pɔlis] nf **1.** (force de l'ordre) police; être de ou dans la ~ to be in the police; ~ secours emergency service provided by the police. **2.** (contrat) policy; ~ d'assurance insurance policy.

polichinelle [pɔliʃinɛl] nm (personnage) Punch; secret de ~ fig open secret.

policier, -ère [pɔlisje, ɛr] adj **1.** (de la police) police (avant n). **2.** (film, roman) detective (avant n). ► **policier** nm police officer.

poliomyélite [pɔljɔmjelit] nf poliomyelitis.

polir [pɔlir] vt to polish.

polisson, -onne [pɔlisɔ̃, ɔn] ♦ adj **1.** (chanson, propos) lewd, suggestive. **2.** (enfant) naughty. ♦ nm, f (enfant) naughty child.

politesse [pɔlitɛs] nf **1.** (courtoisie) politeness. **2.** (action) polite action.

politicien, -enne [pɔlitisjɛ̃, ɛn] ♦ adj péj politicking, politically unscrupulous. ♦ nm, f politician, politico.

politique [pɔlitik] ♦ nf **1.** (de gouvernement, de personne) policy. **2.** (affaires publiques) politics (U). ♦ adj **1.** (pouvoir, théorie) political; homme ~ politician. **2.** littéraire (choix, réponse) politic.

politiser [pɔlitize] vt to politicize.

pollen [pɔlɛn] nm pollen.

polluant [pɔlɥɑ̃] nm pollutant.

polluer [pɔlɥe] vt to pollute.

pollution [pɔlysjɔ̃] nf pollution.

polo [pɔlo] nm **1.** (sport) polo. **2.** (chemise) polo shirt.

Pologne [pɔlɔɲ] nf: la ~ Poland.

polonais, -e [pɔlɔnɛ, ɛz] adj Polish. ► **polonais** nm (langue) Polish. ► **Polonais, -e** nm, f Pole.

poltron, -onne [pɔltrɔ̃, ɔn] ♦ nm, f coward. ♦ adj cowardly.

polychrome [pɔlikrom] adj polychrome, polychromatic.

polyclinique [pɔliklinik] nf general hospital.

polycopié, -e [pɔlikɔpje] adj duplicate (avant n). ► **polycopié** nm duplicated lecture notes (pl).

polyester [pɔliɛstɛr] nm polyester.

polygame [pɔligam] *adj* polygamous.
polyglotte [pɔliglɔt] *nmf & adj* polyglot.
polygone [pɔligɔn] *nm* (MATHS) polygon.
Polynésie [pɔlinezi] *nf*: **la ~** Polynesia.
polystyrène [pɔlistiʀɛn] *nm* polystyrene.
polytechnicien, -enne [pɔliteknisjɛ̃, ɛn] *nm, f* student or ex-student of the École Polytechnique.
Polytechnique [pɔliteknik] *n*: **l'École ~** prestigious engineering college.
polyvalent, -e [pɔlivalɑ̃, ɑ̃t] *adj* **1.** (*salle*) multi-purpose. **2.** (*personne*) versatile.
pommade [pɔmad] *nf* (*médicament*) ointment.
pomme [pɔm] *nf* **1.** (*fruit*) apple; **~ de pin** pine ou fir cone. **2.** (*pomme de terre*): **~s frites** chips *Br*, (French) fries *Am*; **~s vapeur** steamed potatoes. ▶ **pomme d'Adam** *nf* Adam's apple.
pomme de terre [pɔmdətɛʀ] *nf* potato.
pommette [pɔmɛt] *nf* cheekbone.
pommier [pɔmje] *nm* apple tree.
pompe [pɔ̃p] *nf* **1.** (*appareil*) pump; **~ à essence** petrol pump *Br*, gas pump *Am*. **2.** (*magnificence*) pomp, ceremony. **3.** *fam* (*chaussure*) shoe. ▶ **pompes funèbres** *nfpl* undertaker's (*sg*), funeral director's (*sg*) *Br*, mortician's (*sg*) *Am*.
pomper [pɔ̃pe] *vt* (*eau, air*) to pump.
pompeux, -euse [pɔ̃pø, øz] *adj* pompous.
pompier [pɔ̃pje] *nm* fireman *Br*, fire fighter *Am*.
pompiste [pɔ̃pist] *nmf* petrol *Br* ou gas *Am* pump attendant.
pompon [pɔ̃pɔ̃] *nm* pompom.
pomponner [pɔ̃pɔne] ▶ **se pomponner** *vp* to get dressed up.
ponce [pɔ̃s] *adj*: **pierre ~** pumice (stone).
poncer [pɔ̃se] *vt* (*bois*) to sand (down).
ponceuse [pɔ̃søz] *nf* sander, sanding machine.
ponction [pɔ̃ksjɔ̃] *nf* **1.** (MÉD - *lombaire*) puncture; (- *pulmonaire*) tapping. **2.** *fig* (*prélèvement*) withdrawal.
ponctualité [pɔ̃ktɥalite] *nf* punctuality.
ponctuation [pɔ̃ktɥasjɔ̃] *nf* punctuation.
ponctuel, -elle [pɔ̃ktɥɛl] *adj* **1.** (*action*) specific, selective. **2.** (*personne*) punctual.
ponctuer [pɔ̃ktɥe] *vt* to punctuate; **~ qqch de qqch** *fig* to punctuate sthg with sthg.
pondéré, -e [pɔ̃deʀe] *adj* **1.** (*personne*) level-headed. **2.** (ÉCON) weighted.
pondre [pɔ̃dʀ] *vt* **1.** (*œufs*) to lay. **2.** *fam fig* (*projet, texte*) to produce.
pondu, -e [pɔ̃dy] *pp* → **pondre**.
poney [pɔnɛ] *nm* pony.
pont [pɔ̃] *nm* **1.** (CONSTR) bridge; **~s et chaussées** (ADMIN) = highways department. **2.** (*lien*) link, connection; **~ aérien** airlift. **3.** (*congé*) day off granted by an employer to fill the gap between a national holiday and a weekend. **4.** (*de navire*) deck.
ponte [pɔ̃t] ◆ *nf* (*action*) laying; (*œufs*) clutch. ◆ *nm fam* (*autorité*) big shot.
pont-levis [pɔ̃ləvi] *nm* drawbridge.
ponton [pɔ̃tɔ̃] *nm* (*plate-forme*) pontoon.
pop [pɔp] ◆ *nm* pop. ◆ *adj* pop (*avant n*).
pop-corn [pɔpkɔʀn] *nm inv* popcorn (U).
populace [pɔpylas] *nf péj* mob.
populaire [pɔpylɛʀ] *adj* **1.** (*du peuple - volonté*) popular, of the people; (- *quartier*) working-class; (- *art, chanson*) folk. **2.** (*personne*) popular.
populariser [pɔpylarize] *vt* to popularize.
popularité [pɔpylarite] *nf* popularity.
population [pɔpylasjɔ̃] *nf* population; **~ active** working population.
porc [pɔʀ] *nm* **1.** (*animal*) pig, hog *Am*. **2.** *fig & péj* (*personne*) pig, swine. **3.** (*viande*) pork. **4.** (*peau*) pigskin.
porcelaine [pɔʀsəlɛn] *nf* **1.** (*matière*) china, porcelain. **2.** (*objet*) piece of china ou porcelain.
porc-épic [pɔʀkepik] *nm* porcupine.
porche [pɔʀʃ] *nm* porch.
porcherie [pɔʀʃəʀi] *nf litt & fig* pigsty.
porcin, -e [pɔʀsɛ̃, in] *adj* **1.** (*élevage*) pig (*avant n*). **2.** *fig & péj* (*yeux*) piggy.
pore [pɔʀ] *nm* pore.
poreux, -euse [pɔʀø, øz] *adj* porous.
pornographie [pɔʀnɔgʀafi] *nf* pornography.
port [pɔʀ] *nm* **1.** (*lieu*) port; **~ de commerce/pêche** commercial/fishing port. **2.** (*fait de porter sur soi - d'objet*) carrying; (- *de vêtement, décoration*) wearing; **~ d'armes** carrying of weapons. **3.** (*transport*) carriage; **franco de ~** carriage paid.
portable [pɔʀtabl] ◆ *nm* (TV) portable; (INFORM) laptop, portable. ◆ *adj* **1.** (*vêtement*) wearable. **2.** (*ordinateur, machine à écrire*) portable, laptop.

portail [portaj] nm portal.

portant, -e [portã, ãt] adj: être bien/mal ~ to be in good/poor health.

portatif, -ive [portatif, iv] adj portable.

porte [port] nf 1. (de maison, voiture) door; **mettre qqn à la ~** to throw sb out; **~ d'entrée** front door. 2. (AÉRON, SKI & de ville) gate. 3. fig (de région) gateway.

porte-à-faux [portafo] nm inv (roche) overhang; (CONSTR) cantilever; **en ~** overhanging; (CONSTR) cantilevered; fig in a delicate situation.

porte-à-porte [portaport] nm inv: **faire du ~** to sell from door to door.

porte-avions [portavjõ] nm inv aircraft carrier.

porte-bagages [portbagaʒ] nm inv luggage rack; (de voiture) roof rack.

porte-bonheur [portbonœr] nm inv lucky charm.

porte-clefs, porte-clés [portəkle] nm inv keyring.

porte-documents [portdokymã] nm inv attaché ou document case.

portée [porte] nf 1. (de missile) range; **à ~ de main** within reach; **à ~ de voix** within earshot; **à ~ de vue** in sight; **à ~ de qqn** fig within sb's reach. 2. (d'événement) impact, significance. 3. (MUS) stave, staff. 4. (de femelle) litter.

porte-fenêtre [portfənɛtr] nf French window ou door Am.

portefeuille [portfœj] nm 1. (pour billets) wallet. 2. (FIN & POLIT) portfolio.

porte-jarretelles [portʒartɛl] nm inv suspender belt Br, garter belt Am.

portemanteau, -x [portmãto] nm (au mur) coat-rack; (sur pied) coat stand.

porte-monnaie [portmone] nm inv purse.

porte-parole [portparol] nm inv spokesman (f spokeswoman).

porter [porte] ◆ vt 1. (gén) to carry. 2. (vêtement, lunettes, montre) to wear; (barbe) to have. 3. (nom, date, inscription) to bear. 4. (inscrire) to put down, to write down; **porté disparu** reported missing. ◆ vi 1. (remarque) to strike home. 2. (voix, tir) to carry. ▶ **se porter** ◆ vp (se sentir): **se ~ bien/mal** to be well/unwell. ◆ v attr: **se ~ garant de qqch** to guarantee sthg, to vouch for sthg; **se ~ candidat à** to stand for election to Br, to run for Am.

porte-savon [portsavõ] (pl inv ou **porte-savons**) nm soap dish.

porte-serviettes [portsɛrvjɛt] nm inv towel rail.

porteur, -euse [portœr, øz] ◆ adj: **marché ~** (COMM) growth market; **mère porteuse** surrogate mother; **mur ~** load-bearing wall. ◆ nm, f 1. (de message, nouvelle) bringer, bearer. 2. (de bagages) porter. 3. (détenteur - de papiers, d'actions) holder; (- de chèque) bearer. 4. (de maladie) carrier.

portier [portje] nm commissionaire.

portière [portjɛr] nf (de voiture, train) door.

portillon [portijõ] nm barrier, gate.

portion [porsjõ] nf (de gâteau) portion, helping.

portique [portik] nm 1. (ARCHIT) portico. 2. (SPORT) crossbeam (for hanging apparatus).

porto [porto] nm port.

Porto Rico [portoriko], **Puerto Rico** [pwertoriko] n Puerto Rico.

portrait [portre] nm portrait; (PHOT) photograph; **faire le ~ de qqn** fig to describe sb.

portraitiste [portretist] nmf portrait painter.

portrait-robot [portrerobo] nm Photofit® picture, Identikit® picture.

portuaire [portɥer] adj port (avant n), harbour (avant n).

portugais, -e [portyge, ɛz] adj Portuguese. ▶ **portugais** nm (langue) Portuguese. ▶ **Portugais, -e** nm, f Portuguese (person); **les Portugais** the Portuguese.

Portugal [portygal] nm: **le ~** Portugal.

pose [poz] nf 1. (de pierre, moquette) laying; (de papier peint, rideaux) hanging. 2. (position) pose. 3. (PHOT) exposure.

posé, -e [poze] adj sober, steady.

poser [poze] ◆ vt 1. (mettre) to put down; **~ qqch sur qqch** to put sthg on sthg. 2. (installer - rideaux, papier peint) to hang; (- étagère) to put up; (- moquette, carrelage) to lay. 3. (donner à résoudre - problème, difficulté) to pose; **~ une question** to ask a question; **~ sa candidature** to apply; (POLIT) to stand for election. ◆ vi to pose. ▶ **se poser** vp 1. (oiseau, avion) to land; fig (choix, regard): **se ~ sur** to fall on. 2. (question, problème) to arise, to come up.

positif, -ive [pozitif, iv] adj positive.

position [pozisjõ] nf position; **prendre ~** fig to take up a position, to take a stand.

posologie [pozoloʒi] nf dosage.

posséder [posede] vt 1. (détenir -

voiture, maison) to possess, to own; (- *diplôme*) to have; (- *capacités, connaissances*) to possess, to have. **2.** (*langue, art*) to have mastered. **3.** *fam* (*personne*) to have.

possesseur [pɔsesœr] *nm* **1.** (*de bien*) possessor, owner. **2.** (*de secret, diplôme*) holder.

possessif, -ive [pɔsesif, iv] *adj* possessive. ▶ **possessif** *nm* (GRAM) possessive.

possession [pɔsesjɔ̃] *nf* (*gén*) possession; **être en ma/ta** *etc* ~ to be in my/your *etc* possession.

possibilité [pɔsibilite] *nf* **1.** (*gén*) possibility. **2.** (*moyen*) chance, opportunity.

possible [pɔsibl] ♦ *adj* possible; **c'est/ce n'est pas** ~ that's possible/impossible; **dès que** ou **aussitôt que** ~ as soon as possible. ♦ *nm*: **faire tout son** ~ to do one's utmost, to do everything possible; **dans la mesure du** ~ as far as possible.

postal, -e, -aux [pɔstal, o] *adj* postal.

poste [pɔst] ♦ *nf* **1.** (*service*) post Br, mail Am; **envoyer/recevoir qqch par la** ~ to send/receive sthg by post. **2.** (*bureau*) post office; ~ **restante** poste restante Br, general delivery Am. ♦ *nm* **1.** (*emplacement*) post; ~ **de police** police station. **2.** (*emploi*) position, post. **3.** (*appareil*): ~ **de radio** radio; ~ **de télévision** television (set). **4.** (TÉLÉCOM) extension.

poster¹ [pɔstɛr] *nm* poster.

poster² [pɔste] *vt* **1.** (*lettre*) to post Br, to mail Am. **2.** (*sentinelle*) to post. ▶ **se poster** *vp* to position o.s., to station o.s.

postérieur, -e [pɔsterjœr] *adj* **1.** (*date*) later, subsequent. **2.** (*membre*) hind (*avant n*), back (*avant n*). ▶ **postérieur** *nm hum* posterior.

posteriori [pɔsterjɔri] ▶ **a posteriori** *loc adv* a posteriori.

postérité [pɔsterite] *nf* (*générations à venir*) posterity.

posthume [pɔstym] *adj* posthumous.

postiche [pɔstiʃ] *adj* false.

postier, -ère [pɔstje, ɛr] *nm, f* post-office worker.

postillonner [pɔstijɔne] *vi* to splutter.

post-scriptum [pɔstskriptɔm] *nm inv* postscript.

postulant, -e [pɔstylɑ̃, ɑ̃t] *nm, f* (*pour emploi*) applicant.

postuler [pɔstyle] *vt* **1.** (*emploi*) to apply for. **2.** (PHILO) to postulate.

posture [pɔstyr] *nf* posture; **être** ou **se trouver en mauvaise** ~ *fig* to be in a difficult position.

pot [po] *nm* **1.** (*récipient*) pot, jar; (*à eau, à lait*) jug; ~ **de chambre** chamber pot; ~ **de fleurs** flowerpot. **2.** (AUTOM): ~ **catalytique** catalytic convertor; ~ **d'échappement** exhaust (pipe); (*silencieux*) silencer Br, muffler Am. **3.** *fam* (*boisson*) drink.

potable [pɔtabl] *adj* **1.** (*liquide*) drinkable; **eau** ~ drinking water. **2.** *fam* (*travail*) acceptable.

potage [pɔtaʒ] *nm* soup.

potager, -ère [pɔtaʒe, ɛr] *adj*: **jardin** ~ vegetable garden; **plante potagère** vegetable. ▶ **potager** *nm* kitchen ou vegetable garden.

potasser [pɔtase] *vt fam* (*cours*) to swot up Br, to bone up on Am; (*examen*) to swot up for Br, to bone up for Am.

potassium [pɔtasjɔm] *nm* potassium.

pot-au-feu [pɔtofø] *nm inv* **1.** (*plat*) boiled beef with vegetables. **2.** (*viande*) ≃ piece of stewing steak.

pot-de-vin [podvɛ̃] (*pl* pots-de-vin) *nm* bribe.

pote [pɔt] *nm fam* mate Br, buddy Am.

poteau, -x [pɔto] *nm* post; ~ **de but** goalpost; ~ **indicateur** signpost; ~ **télégraphique** telegraph pole.

potelé, -e [pɔtle] *adj* plump, chubby.

potence [pɔtɑ̃s] *nf* **1.** (CONSTR) bracket. **2.** (*de pendaison*) gallows (*sg*).

potentiel, -elle [pɔtɑ̃sjɛl] *adj* potential. ▶ **potentiel** *nm* potential.

poterie [pɔtri] *nf* **1.** (*art*) pottery. **2.** (*objet*) piece of pottery.

potiche [pɔtiʃ] *nf* (*vase*) vase.

potier, -ère [pɔtje, ɛr] *nm, f* potter.

potin [pɔtɛ̃] *nm fam* (*bruit*) din. ▶ **potins** *nmpl fam* (*ragots*) gossip (U).

potion [pɔsjɔ̃] *nf* potion.

potiron [pɔtirɔ̃] *nm* pumpkin.

pot-pourri [popuri] *nm* potpourri.

pou, -x [pu] *nm* louse.

poubelle [pubɛl] *nf* dustbin Br, trashcan Am.

pouce [pus] *nm* **1.** (*de main*) thumb; (*de pied*) big toe. **2.** (*mesure*) inch.

poudre [pudr] *nf* powder; **prendre la** ~ **d'escampette** to make off.

poudreux, -euse [pudrø, øz] *adj* powdery. ▶ **poudreuse** *nf* powder (snow).

poudrier [pudrije] *nm* (*boîte*) powder compact.

poudrière [pudrijɛr] *nf* powder magazine; *fig* powder keg.

pouf [puf] ♦ *nm* pouffe. ♦ *interj* thud!
pouffer [pufe] *vi* : ~ **(de rire)** to snigger.
pouilleux, -euse [pujø, øz] *adj* 1. (*personne, animal*) flea-ridden. 2. (*endroit*) squalid.
poulailler [pulaje] *nm* 1. (*de ferme*) henhouse. 2. *fam* (THÉÂTRE) gods (*sg*).
poulain [pulɛ̃] *nm* foal; *fig* protégé.
poule [pul] *nf* 1. (ZOOL) hen. 2. *fam péj* (*femme*) bird Br, broad Am. 3. (SPORT) (*compétition*) round robin; (RUGBY) (*groupe*) pool.
poulet [pulɛ] *nm* 1. (ZOOL) chicken; ~ **fermier** free-range chicken. 2. *fam* (*policier*) cop.
pouliche [puliʃ] *nf* filly.
poulie [puli] *nf* pulley.
poulpe [pulp] *nm* octopus.
pouls [pu] *nm* pulse.
poumon [pumɔ̃] *nm* lung.
poupe [pup] *nf* stern; **avoir le vent en ~** *fig* to be going places.
poupée [pupe] *nf* (*jouet*) doll.
poupon [pupɔ̃] *nm* 1. (*bébé*) little baby. 2. (*jouet*) baby doll.
pouponnière [pupɔnjɛr] *nf* nursery.
pour [pur] ♦ *prép* 1. (*gén*) for. 2. (+ *infinitif*) : **faire** ~ in order to do, (so as) to do; **je suis venu** ~ **vous voir** I've come to see you; ~ **m'avoir aidé** for having helped me, for helping me. 3. (*indique un rapport*) for; **avancé** ~ **son âge** advanced for his/her age; ~ **moi** for my part, as far as I'm concerned; ~ **ce qui est de** as regards, with regard to. ♦ *adv* : **je suis** ~ I'm (all) for it. ♦ *nm* : **le** ~ **et le contre** the pros and cons (*pl*). ▸ **pour que** *loc conj* (+ subjonctif) so that, in order that.
pourboire [purbwar] *nm* tip.
pourcentage [pursɑ̃taʒ] *nm* percentage.
pourparlers [purparle] *nmpl* talks.
pourpre [purpr] *nm & adj* crimson.
pourquoi [purkwa] ♦ *adv* why; ~ **pas?** why not?; **c'est** ~ ... that's why ... ♦ *nm inv* : **le** ~ **(de)** the reason (for).
pourri, -e [puri] *adj* 1. (*fruit*) rotten. 2. (*personne, milieu*) corrupt. 3. (*enfant*) spoiled rotten, ruined.
pourrir [purir] ♦ *vt* 1. (*matière, aliment*) to rot, to spoil. 2. (*enfant*) to ruin, to spoil rotten. ♦ *vi* (*matière*) to rot; (*fruit, aliment*) to go rotten ou bad.
pourriture [purityr] *nf* 1. (*d'aliment*) rot. 2. *fig* (*de personne, de milieu*) corruption. 3. *injurieux* (*personne*) bastard.
poursuite [pursɥit] *nf* 1. (*de personne*)

chase. 2. (*d'argent, de vérité*) pursuit. 3. (*de négociations*) continuation. ▸ **poursuites** *nfpl* (JUR) (legal) proceedings.
poursuivi, -e [pursɥivi] *pp* → **poursuivre**.
poursuivre [pursɥivr] ♦ *vt* 1. (*voleur*) to pursue, to chase; (*gibier*) to hunt. 2. (*rêve, vengeance*) to pursue. 3. (*enquête, travail*) to carry on with, to continue. 4. (JUR) (*criminel*) to prosecute; (*voisin*) to sue. ♦ *vi* to go on, to carry on.
pourtant [purtɑ̃] *adv* nevertheless, even so.
pourtour [purtur] *nm* perimeter.
pourvoi [purvwa] *nm* (JUR) appeal.
pourvoir [purvwar] ♦ *vt* : ~ **qqn de** to provide sb with; ~ **qqch de** to equip ou fit sth with. ♦ *vi* : ~ **à** to provide for.
pourvu, -e [purvy] *pp* → **pourvoir**. ▸ **pourvu que** *loc conj* (+ subjonctif) 1. (*condition*) providing, provided (that). 2. (*souhait*) let's hope (that).
pousse [pus] *nf* 1. (*croissance*) growth. 2. (*bourgeon*) shoot.
poussé, -e [puse] *adj* 1. (*travail*) meticulous. 2. (*moteur*) souped-up.
pousse-café [puskafe] *nm inv fam* liqueur.
poussée [puse] *nf* 1. (*pression*) pressure. 2. (*coup*) push. 3. (*de fièvre, inflation*) rise.
pousse-pousse [puspus] *nm inv* 1. (*voiture*) rickshaw. 2. Helv (*poussette*) pushchair.
pousser [puse] ♦ *vt* 1. (*personne, objet*) to push. 2. (*moteur, voiture*) to drive hard. 3. (*recherches, études*) to carry on, to continue. 4. (*cri, soupir*) to give. 5. (*inciter*) : ~ **qqn à faire qqch** to urge sb to do sthg. 6. (*au crime, au suicide*) : ~ **qqn à** to drive sb to. ♦ *vi* 1. (*exercer une pression*) to push. 2. (*croître*) to grow. 3. *fam* (*exagérer*) to overdo it. ▸ **se pousser** *vp* to move up.
poussette [pusɛt] *nf* pushchair.
poussière [pusjɛr] *nf* (*gén*) dust.
poussiéreux, -euse [pusjerø, øz] *adj* 1. (*meuble*) dusty. 2. *fig* (*organisation*) old-fashioned.
poussif, -ive [pusif, iv] *adj fam* wheezy.
poussin [pusɛ̃] *nm* 1. (ZOOL) chick. 2. (SPORT) under-11.
poutre [putr] *nf* beam.
poutrelle [putrɛl] *nf* girder.
pouvoir [puvwar] ♦ *nm* (*gén*) power; ~ **d'achat** purchasing power; **les ~s publics** the authorities. ♦ *vt* 1. (*avoir la possibilité*

de, parvenir à): ~ **faire qqch** to be able to do sthg; **je ne peux pas venir ce soir** I can't come tonight; **pouvez-vous ...?** can you ...?, could you ...?; **je n'en peux plus** (*exaspéré*) I'm at the end of my tether; (*fatigué*) I'm exhausted; **je/tu n'y peux rien** there's nothing I/you can do about it; **tu aurais pu me le dire!** you might have ou could have told me! **2.** (*avoir la permission de*): **je peux prendre la voiture?** can I borrow the car?; **aucun élève ne peut partir** no pupil may leave. **3.** (*indiquant l'éventualité*): **vous pourriez rater votre train** you could ou might miss your train. ► **se pouvoir** *v impers*: **il se peut que je me trompe** I may be mistaken; **cela se peut/pourrait bien** that's quite possible.

pragmatique [pragmatik] *adj* pragmatic.

Prague [prag] *n* Prague.

prairie [preri] *nf* meadow; (*aux États-Unis*) prairie.

praline [pralin] *nf* **1.** (*amande*) sugared almond. **2.** Belg (*chocolat*) chocolate.

praticable [pratikabl] *adj* **1.** (*route*) passable. **2.** (*plan*) feasible, practicable.

praticien, -enne [pratisjɛ̃, ɛn] *nm, f* practitioner; (MÉD) medical practitioner.

pratiquant, -e [pratikɑ̃, ɑ̃t] *adj* practising.

pratique [pratik] ◆ *nf* **1.** (*expérience*) practical experience. **2.** (*usage*) practice; **mettre qqch en ~** to put sthg into practice. ◆ *adj* practical; (*gadget, outil*) handy.

pratiquement [pratikmɑ̃] *adv* **1.** (*en fait*) in practice. **2.** (*quasiment*) practically.

pratiquer [pratike] ◆ *vt* **1.** (*métier*) to practise Br, to practice Am; (*sport*) to do; (*jeu de ballon*) to play; (*méthode*) to apply. **2.** (*ouverture*) to make. ◆ *vi* (RELIG) to be a practising Christian/Jew/Muslim *etc*.

pré [pre] *nm* meadow.

préalable [prealabl] ◆ *adj* prior, previous. ◆ *nm* precondition. ► **au préalable** *loc adv* first, beforehand.

préambule [preɑ̃byl] *nm* **1.** (*introduction, propos*) preamble; **sans ~** immediately. **2.** (*prélude*): ~ **de** prelude to.

préau, -x [preo] *nm* (*d'école*) (covered) play area.

préavis [preavi] *nm inv* advance notice ou warning.

précaire [prekɛr] *adj* (*incertain*) precarious.

précaution [prekosjɔ̃] *nf* **1.** (*prévoyance*) precaution; **par ~** as a precaution; **prendre des ~s** to take precautions. **2.** (*prudence*) caution.

précédent, -e [presedɑ̃, ɑ̃t] *adj* previous. ► **précédent** *nm* precedent; **sans ~** unprecedented.

précéder [presede] *vt* **1.** (*dans le temps - gén*) to precede; (*- suj: personne*) to arrive before. **2.** (*marcher devant*) to go in front of. **3.** *fig* (*devancer*) to get ahead of.

précepte [presɛpt] *nm* precept.

précepteur, -trice [preseptœr, tris] *nm, f* (private) tutor.

prêcher [preʃe] *vt & vi* to preach.

précieux, -euse [presjø, øz] *adj* **1.** (*pierre, métal*) precious; (*objet*) valuable; (*collaborateur*) invaluable, valued. **2.** *péj* (*style*) precious, affected.

précipice [presipis] *nm* precipice.

précipitation [presipitasjɔ̃] *nf* **1.** (*hâte*) haste. **2.** (CHIM) precipitation. ► **précipitations** *nfpl* (MÉTÉOR) precipitation (U).

précipiter [presipite] *vt* **1.** (*objet, personne*) to throw, to hurl; ~ **qqn/qqch du haut de** to throw sb/sthg off, to hurl sb/sthg off. **2.** (*départ*) to hasten. ► **se précipiter** *vp* **1.** (*se jeter*) to throw o.s., to hurl o.s. **2.** (*s'élancer*): **se ~** (*vers qqn*) to rush ou hurry (towards sb). **3.** (*s'accélérer - gén*) to speed up; (*- choses, événements*) to move faster.

précis, -e [presi, iz] *adj* **1.** (*exact*) precise, accurate. **2.** (*fixé*) definite, precise. ► **précis** *nm* handbook.

précisément [presizemɑ̃] *adv* precisely, exactly.

préciser [presize] *vt* **1.** (*heure, lieu*) to specify. **2.** (*pensée*) to clarify. ► **se préciser** *vp* to become clear.

précision [presizjɔ̃] *nf* **1.** (*de style, d'explication*) precision. **2.** (*détail*) detail.

précoce [prekɔs] *adj* **1.** (*plante, fruit*) early. **2.** (*enfant*) precocious.

préconçu, -e [prekɔ̃sy] *adj* preconceived.

préconiser [prekɔnize] *vt* to recommend.

précurseur [prekyrsœr] ◆ *nm* precursor, forerunner. ◆ *adj* precursory.

prédateur, -trice [predatœr, tris] *adj* predatory. ► **prédateur** *nm* predator.

prédécesseur [predesesœr] *nm* predecessor.

prédestiner [predɛstine] *vt* to predestine; **être prédestiné à qqch/à faire qqch**

to be predestined for sthg/to do sthg.

prédicateur, -trice [predikatœr, tris] *nm, f* preacher.

prédiction [prediksjɔ̃] *nf* prediction.

prédilection [predileksjɔ̃] *nf* partiality, liking; **avoir une ~ pour** to have a partiality ou liking for.

prédire [predir] *vt* to predict.

prédit, -e [predi, it] *pp* → **prédire**.

prédominer [predɔmine] *vt* to predominate.

préfabriqué, -e [prefabrike] *adj* 1. (*maison*) prefabricated. 2. (*accusation, sourire*) false. ▶ **préfabriqué** *nm* prefabricated material.

préface [prefas] *nf* preface.

préfecture [prefektyr] *nf* prefecture.

préférable [preferabl] *adj* preferable.

préféré, -e [prefere] *adj & nm, f* favourite.

préférence [preferɑ̃s] *nf* preference; **de ~** preferably.

préférentiel, -elle [preferɑ̃sjɛl] *adj* preferential.

préférer [prefere] *vt*: **~ qqn/qqch (à)** to prefer sb/sthg (to); **je préfère rentrer** I would rather go home, I would prefer to go home; **je préfère ça!** I like that better!, I prefer that!

préfet [prefɛ] *nm* prefect.

préfixe [prefiks] *nm* prefix.

préhistoire [preistwar] *nf* prehistory.

préinscription [preɛ̃skripsjɔ̃] *nf* preregistration.

préjudice [preʒydis] *nm* harm (U), detriment (U); **porter ~ à qqn** to harm sb.

préjugé [preʒyʒe] *nm*: **~ (contre)** prejudice (against).

prélasser [prelase] ▶ **se prélasser** *vp* to lounge.

prélat [prela] *nm* prelate.

prélavage [prelavaʒ] *nm* pre-wash.

prélèvement [prelɛvmɑ̃] *nm* 1. (MÉD) removal; (*de sang*) sample. 2. (FIN) deduction; **~ automatique** direct debit; **~ mensuel** monthly standing order; **~s obligatoires** tax and social security contributions.

prélever [prelve] *vt* 1. (FIN): **~ de l'argent (sur)** to deduct money (from). 2. (MÉD) to remove; **~ du sang** to take a blood sample.

préliminaire [preliminɛr] *adj* preliminary. ▶ **préliminaires** *nmpl* 1. (*de paix*) preliminary talks. 2. (*de discours*) preliminaries.

prématuré, -e [prematyre] ◆ *adj* premature. ◆ *nm, f* premature baby.

préméditation [premeditasjɔ̃] *nf* premeditation; **avec ~** (*meurtre*) premeditated; (*agir*) with premeditation.

premier, -ère [prəmje, ɛr] ◆ *adj* 1. (*gén*) first; (*étage*) first Br, second Am. 2. (*qualité*) top. 3. (*état*) original. ◆ *nm, f* first; **jeune ~** (CIN) leading man. ▶ **première** *nf* 1. (CIN) première; (THÉÂTRE) première, first night. 2. (*exploit*) first. 3. (*première classe*) first class. 4. (SCOL) ≃ lower sixth year ou form Br, ≃ eleventh grade Am. 5. (AUTOM) first (gear). ▶ **premier de l'an** *nm*: **le ~ de l'an** New Year's Day. ▶ **en premier** *loc adv* first, firstly.

premièrement [prəmjɛrmɑ̃] *adv* first, firstly.

prémonition [premɔnisjɔ̃] *nf* premonition.

prémunir [premynir] *vt*: **~ qqn (contre)** to protect sb (against). ▶ **se prémunir** *vp* to protect o.s.; **se ~ contre qqch** to guard against sthg.

prénatal, -e [prenatal] (*pl* **prénatals** ou **prénataux** [prenato]) *adj* antenatal; (*allocation*) maternity (*avant n*).

prendre [prɑ̃dr] ◆ *vt* 1. (*gén*) to take. 2. (*enlever*) to take (away); **~ qqch à qqn** to take sthg from sb. 3. (*aller chercher - objet*) to get, to fetch; (*- personne*) to pick up. 4. (*repas, boisson*) to have; **vous prendrez quelque chose?** would you like something to eat/drink? 5. (*voleur*) to catch; **se faire ~** to get caught. 6. (*responsabilité*) to take (on). 7. (*aborder - personne*) to handle; (*- problème*) to tackle. 8. (*réserver*) to book; (*louer*) to rent, to take; (*acheter*) to buy. 9. (*poids*) to gain, to put on. ◆ *vi* 1. (*ciment, sauce*) to set. 2. (*plante, greffe*) to take; (*mode*) to catch on. 3. (*feu*) to catch. 4. (*se diriger*): **~ à droite** to turn right. ▶ **se prendre** *vp* 1. (*se considérer*): **pour qui se prend-il?** who does he think he is? 2. *loc*: **s'en ~ à qqn** (*physiquement*) to set about sb; (*verbalement*) to take it out on sb; **je sais comment m'y ~** I know how to do it ou go about it.

prénom [prenɔ̃] *nm* first name.

prénommer [prenɔme] *vt* to name, to call. ▶ **se prénommer** *vp* to be called.

prénuptial, -e, -aux [prenypsjal, o] *adj* premarital.

préoccupation [preɔkypasjɔ̃] *nf* preoccupation.

préoccuper [preɔkype] *vt* to preoccupy. ▶ **se préoccuper** *vp*: **se ~ de qqch** to be worried about sthg.

préparatifs [preparatif] *nmpl* preparations.

préparation [preparasjɔ̃] *nf* preparation.

préparer [prepare] *vt* 1. (*gén*) to prepare; (*plat, repas*) to cook, to prepare; ~ **qqn à qqch** to prepare sb for sthg. 2. (*réserver*): ~ **qqch à qqn** to have sthg in store for sb. 3. (*congrès*) to organize. ▶ **se préparer** *vp* 1. (*personne*): **se ~ à qqch/à faire qqch** to prepare for sthg/to do sthg. 2. (*tempête*) to be brewing.

prépondérant, -e [prepɔ̃derã, ãt] *adj* dominating.

préposé, -e [prepoze] *nm, f* (minor) official; (*de vestiaire*) attendant; (*facteur*) postman (*f* postwoman) Br, mailman (*f* mailwoman) Am; ~ **à qqch** person in charge of sthg.

préposition [prepozisjɔ̃] *nf* preposition.

préretraite [prerətrɛt] *nf* early retirement; (*allocation*) early retirement pension.

prérogative [prerɔgativ] *nf* prerogative.

près [prɛ] *adv* near, close. ▶ **de près** *loc adv* closely; **regarder qqch de ~** to watch sthg closely. ▶ **près de** *loc prép* 1. (*dans l'espace*) near, close to. 2. (*dans le temps*) close to. 3. (*presque*) nearly, almost. ▶ **à peu près** *loc adv* more or less, just about; **il est à peu ~ cinq heures** it's about five o'clock. ▶ **à ceci près que, à cela près que** *loc conj* except that, apart from the fact that. ▶ **à … près** *loc adv*: **à dix centimètres ~** to within ten centimetres; **il n'en est pas à un ou deux jours ~** a day or two more or less won't make any difference.

présage [prezaʒ] *nm* omen.

présager [prezaʒe] *vt* 1. (*annoncer*) to portend. 2. (*prévoir*) to predict.

presbytère [presbitɛr] *nm* presbytery.

presbytie [presbisi] *nf* longsightedness Br, farsightedness Am.

prescription [preskripsjɔ̃] *nf* 1. (MÉD) prescription. 2. (JUR) limitation.

prescrire [preskrir] *vt* 1. (*mesures, conditions*) to lay down, to stipulate. 2. (MÉD) to prescribe.

prescrit, -e [preskri, it] *pp* → **prescrire**.

préséance [preseãs] *nf* precedence.

présence [prezãs] *nf* 1. (*gén*) presence; **en ~** face to face; **en ~ de** in the presence of. 2. (*compagnie*) company (U). 3. (*assiduité*) attendance; **feuille de ~** attendance sheet. ▶ **présence d'es-**

prit *nf* presence of mind.

présent, -e [prezã, ãt] *adj* (*gén*) present; **le ~ ouvrage** this work; **la ~e loi** this law; **avoir qqch ~ à l'esprit** to remember sthg. ▶ **présent** *nm* 1. (*gén*) present; **à ~** at present; **à ~ que** now that; **jusqu'à ~** up to now, so far; **dès à ~** right away. 2. (GRAM): **le ~** the present tense.

présentable [prezãtabl] *adj* (*d'aspect*) presentable.

présentateur, -trice [prezãtatœr, tris] *nm, f* presenter.

présentation [prezãtasjɔ̃] *nf* 1. (*de personne*): **faire les ~s** to make the introductions. 2. (*aspect extérieur*) appearance. 3. (*de papiers, de produit, de film*) presentation. 4. (*de magazine*) layout.

présenter [prezãte] *vt* 1. (*gén*) to present; (*projet*) to present, to submit. 2. (*invité*) to introduce. 3. (*condoléances, félicitations, avantages*) to offer; (*hommages*) to pay; ~ **qqch à qqn** to offer sb sthg. ▶ **se présenter** *vp* 1. (*se faire connaître*): **se ~ (à)** to introduce o.s. (to). 2. (*être candidat*): **se ~ à** (*élection*) to stand in Br, to run in Am; (*examen*) to sit Br, to take. 3. (*paraître*) to appear. 4. (*occasion, situation*) to arise, to present itself. 5. (*affaire, contrat*): **se ~ bien/mal** to look good/bad.

présentoir [prezãtwar] *nm* display stand.

préservatif [prezɛrvatif] *nm* condom.

préserver [prezɛrve] *vt* to preserve. ▶ **se préserver** *vp*: **se ~ de** to protect o.s. from.

présidence [prezidãs] *nf* 1. (*de groupe*) chairmanship. 2. (*d'État*) presidency.

président, -e [prezidã, ãt] *nm, f* 1. (*d'assemblée*) chairman (*f* chairwoman). 2. (*d'État*) president; ~ **de la République** President (of the Republic) of France. 3. (JUR) (*de tribunal*) presiding judge; (*de jury*) foreman (*f* forewoman).

présider [prezide] ◆ *vt* 1. (*réunion*) to chair. 2. (*banquet, dîner*) to preside over. ◆ *vi*: ~ **à** to be in charge of; *fig* to govern, to preside at.

présomption [prezɔ̃psjɔ̃] *nf* 1. (*hypothèse*) presumption. 2. (JUR) presumption.

présomptueux, -euse [prezɔ̃ptɥø, øz] *adj* presumptuous.

presque [prɛsk] *adv* almost, nearly; ~ **rien** next to nothing, scarcely anything; ~ **jamais** hardly ever.

presqu'île [prɛskil] *nf* peninsula.

pressant, -e [presɑ̃, ɑ̃t] *adj* pressing.
presse [prɛs] *nf* press.
pressé, -e [prese] *adj* **1.** (*travail*) urgent. **2.** (*personne*): **être ~** to be in a hurry. **3.** (*citron, orange*) freshly squeezed.
pressentiment [presɑ̃timɑ̃] *nm* premonition.
pressentir [presɑ̃tir] *vt* (*événement*) to have a premonition of.
presse-papiers [prɛspapje] *nm inv* paperweight.
presser [prese] *vt* **1.** (*écraser - olives*) to press; (*- citron, orange*) to squeeze. **2.** (*bouton*) to press, to push. **3.** *sout* (*harceler*): **~ qqn de faire qqch** to press sb to do sthg. **4.** (*accélérer*) to speed up; **~ le pas** to speed up, to walk faster. ► **se presser** *vp* **1.** (*se dépêcher*) to hurry (up). **2.** (*s'agglutiner*): **se ~ (autour de)** to crowd (around). **3.** (*se serrer*) to huddle.
pressing [presiŋ] *nm* (*établissement*) dry cleaner's.
pression [presjɔ̃] *nf* **1.** (*gén*) pressure; **exercer une ~ sur qqch** to exert pressure on sthg; **sous ~** (*liquide & fig*) under pressure; (*cabine*) pressurized. **2.** (*sur vêtement*) press stud Br, popper Br, snap fastener Am. **3.** (*bière*) draught beer.
pressoir [preswar] *nm* **1.** (*machine*) press. **2.** (*lieu*) press house.
prestance [prestɑ̃s] *nf* bearing; **avoir de la ~** to have presence.
prestataire [prestatɛr] *nmf* **1.** (*bénéficiaire*) person in receipt of benefit, claimant. **2.** (*fournisseur*) provider; **~ de service** service provider.
prestation [prestasjɔ̃] *nf* **1.** (*allocation*) benefit; **~ en nature** payment in kind. **2.** (*de comédien*) performance. **3.** (COMM): **~ de service** provision ou delivery of a service.
preste [prest] *adj littéraire* nimble.
prestidigitateur, -trice [prestidiʒitatœr, tris] *nm, f* conjurer.
prestige [prestiʒ] *nm* prestige.
prestigieux, -euse [prestiʒjø, øz] *adj* (*réputé*) prestigious.
présumer [prezyme] ♦ *vt* to presume, to assume; **être présumé coupable/innocent** to be presumed guilty/innocent. ♦ *vi*: **~ de qqch** to overestimate sthg.
prêt, -e [prɛ, prɛt] *adj* ready; **~ à qqch/à faire qqch** ready for sthg/to do sthg; **~s? partez!** (SPORT) get set, go! ► **prêt** *nm* (*action*) lending (U); (*somme*) loan.
prêt-à-porter [prɛtaporte] (*pl* **prêts-à-porter**) *nm* ready-to-wear clothing (U).

prétendant [pretɑ̃dɑ̃] *nm* **1.** (*au trône*) pretender. **2.** (*amoureux*) suitor.
prétendre [pretɑ̃dr] *vt* **1.** (*affecter*): **~ faire qqch** to claim to do sthg. **2.** (*affirmer*): **~ que** to claim (that), to maintain (that).
prétendu, -e [pretɑ̃dy] ♦ *pp* → **prétendre**. ♦ *adj* (*avant n*) so-called.
prête-nom [prɛtnɔ̃] (*pl* **prête-noms**) *nm* front man.
prétentieux, -euse [pretɑ̃sjø, øz] *adj* pretentious.
prétention [pretɑ̃sjɔ̃] *nf* **1.** (*suffisance*) pretentiousness. **2.** (*ambition*) pretension, ambition; **avoir la ~ de faire qqch** to claim ou pretend to do sthg.
prêter [prete] *vt* **1.** (*fournir*): **~ qqch (à qqn)** (*objet, argent*) to lend (sb) sthg; *fig* (*concours, appui*) to lend (sb) sthg, to give (sb) sthg. **2.** (*attribuer*): **~ qqch à qqn** to attribute sthg to sb. ► **se prêter** *vp*: **se ~ à** (*participer à*) to go along with; (*convenir à*) to fit, to suit.
prétérit [preterit] *nm* preterite.
prêteur, -euse [prɛtœr, øz] *nm, f*: **~ sur gages** pawnbroker.
prétexte [pretɛkst] *nm* pretext, excuse; **sous ~ de faire qqch/que** on the pretext of doing sthg/that; **sous aucun ~** on no account.
prétexter [pretɛkste] *vt* to give as an excuse.
prêtre [prɛtr] *nm* priest.
preuve [prœv] *nf* **1.** (*gén*) proof. **2.** (JUR) evidence. **3.** (*témoignage*) sign, token; **faire ~ de qqch** to show sthg; **faire ses ~s** to prove o.s./itself.
prévaloir [prevalwar] *vi* (*dominer*): **~ (sur)** to prevail (over). ► **se prévaloir** *vp*: **se ~ de** to boast about.
prévalu [prevaly] *pp inv* → **prévaloir**.
prévenance [prevnɑ̃s] *nf* (*attitude*) thoughtfulness, consideration.
prévenant, -e [prevnɑ̃, ɑ̃t] *adj* considerate, attentive.
prévenir [prevnir] *vt* **1.** (*employé, élève*): **~ qqn (de)** to warn sb (about). **2.** (*police*) to inform. **3.** (*désirs*) to anticipate. **4.** (*maladie*) to prevent.
préventif, -ive [prevɑ̃tif, iv] *adj* **1.** (*mesure, médecine*) preventive. **2.** (JUR): **être en détention préventive** to be on remand.
prévention [prevɑ̃sjɔ̃] *nf* **1.** (*protection*): **~ (contre)** prevention (of); **~ routière** road safety (measures). **2.** (JUR) remand.

prévenu, -e [prevny] ♦ *pp* →
prévenir. ♦ *nm, f* accused, defendant.
prévision [previzjɔ̃] *nf* forecast, prediction; (*de coûts*) estimate; (ÉCON) forecast; **les ~s météorologiques** the weather
forecast. ▶ **en prévision de** *loc prép* in
anticipation of.
prévoir [prevwar] *vt* **1.** (*s'attendre à*)
to expect. **2.** (*prédire*) to predict.
3. (*anticiper*) to foresee, to anticipate.
4. (*programmer*) to plan; **comme prévu** as
planned, according to plan.
prévoyant, -e [prevwajɑ̃, ɑ̃t] *adj*
provident.
prévu, -e [prevy] *pp* → **prévoir.**
prier [prije] ♦ *vt* **1.** (RELIG) to pray to.
2. (*implorer*) to beg; **(ne pas) se faire ~**
(pour faire qqch) (not) to need to be
persuaded (to do sthg); **je vous en prie**
(*de grâce*) please, I beg you; (*de rien*)
don't mention it, not at all. **3.** *sout*
(*demander*): **~ qqn de faire qqch** to
request sb to do sthg. ♦ *vi* (RELIG) to
pray.
prière [prijɛr] *nf* **1.** (RELIG - *recueillement*)
prayer (U), praying (U); (- *formule*)
prayer. **2.** *littéraire* (*demande*) entreaty; **~**
de frapper avant d'entrer please knock
before entering.
primaire [primɛr] *adj* **1.** (*premier*):
études ~s primary education (U). **2.** *péj*
(*primitif*) limited.
prime [prim] ♦ *nf* **1.** (*d'employé*) bonus;
~ d'intéressement profit-related bonus.
2. (*allocation - de déménagement, de trans-*
port) allowance; (- *à l'exportation*) incentive. **3.** (*d'assurance*) premium. ♦ *adj*
1. (*premier*): **de ~ abord** at first glance;
de ~ jeunesse in the first flush of youth.
2. (MATHS) prime.
primer [prime] ♦ *vi* to take precedence, to come first. ♦ *vt* **1.** (*être*
supérieur à) to take precedence over.
2. (*récompenser*) to award a prize to; **le**
film a été primé au festival the film won
an award at the festival.
primeur [primœr] *nf* immediacy; **avoir**
la ~ de qqch to be the first to hear sthg.
▶ **primeurs** *nfpl* early produce (U).
primevère [primvɛr] *nf* primrose.
primitif, -ive [primitif, iv] ♦ *adj*
1. (*gén*) primitive. **2.** (*aspect*) original.
♦ *nm, f* primitive.
primordial, -e, -aux [primɔrdjal, o]
adj essential.
prince [prɛ̃s] *nm* prince.
princesse [prɛ̃sɛs] *nf* princess.
princier, -ère [prɛ̃sje, ɛr] *adj* princely.

principal, -e, -aux [prɛ̃sipal, o] ♦ *adj*
(*gén*) main, principal. ♦ *nm, f* **1.** (*important*):
le ~ the main thing. **2.** (SCOL) headmaster
(*f* headmistress) Br, principal Am.
principalement [prɛ̃sipalmɑ̃] *adv*
mainly, principally.
principauté [prɛ̃sipote] *nf* principality.
principe [prɛ̃sip] *nm* principle; **par ~**
on principle; **~ actif** active ingredient.
▶ **en principe** *loc adv* theoretically, in
principle.
printanier, -ère [prɛ̃tanje, ɛr] *adj*
(*temps*) spring-like.
printemps [prɛ̃tɑ̃] *nm* **1.** (*saison*)
spring. **2.** *fam* (*année*): **avoir 20 ~** to be
20.
priori [prijɔri] ▶ **a priori** ♦ *loc adv* in
principle. ♦ *nm inv* initial reaction.
prioritaire [prijɔritɛr] *adj* **1.** (*industrie,*
mesure) priority (*avant n*). **2.** (AUTOM) with
right of way.
priorité [prijɔrite] *nf* **1.** (*importance pri-*
mordiale) priority; **en ~** first. **2.** (AUTOM)
right of way; **~ à droite** give way to the
right.
pris, -e [pri, priz] ♦ *pp* → **prendre.**
♦ *adj* **1.** (*place*) taken; (*personne*) busy;
(*mains*) full. **2.** (*nez*) blocked; (*gorge*)
sore. ▶ **prise** *nf* **1.** (*sur barre, sur branche*)
grip, hold; **lâcher ~e** to let go; *fig* to give
up. **2.** (*action de prendre - de ville*) seizure,
capture; **~e en charge** (*par Sécurité sociale*)
(guaranteed) reimbursement; **~e de**
conscience realization; **~e d'otages**
hostage taking; **~e de sang** blood test;
~e de vue shot; **~e de vue** OU **vues** (*action*)
filming, shooting. **3.** (*à la pêche*) haul.
4. (ÉLECTR): **~e (de courant)** (*mâle*) plug;
(*femelle*) socket. **5.** (*de judo*) hold.
prisme [prism] *nm* prism.
prison [prizɔ̃] *nf* **1.** (*établissement*)
prison. **2.** (*réclusion*) imprisonment.
prisonnier, -ère [prizɔnje, ɛr] ♦ *nm, f*
prisoner; **faire qqn ~** to take sb prisoner, to capture sb. ♦ *adj* imprisoned; *fig*
trapped.
privation [privasjɔ̃] *nf* deprivation.
▶ **privations** *nfpl* privations, hard-
ships.
privatisation [privatizasjɔ̃] *nf* privati-
zation.
privatiser [privatize] *vt* to privatize.
privé, -e [prive] *adj* private. ▶ **privé**
nm **1.** (ÉCON) private sector. **2.** (*détective*)
private eye. **3.** (*intimité*): **en ~** in private; **dans le ~** in private life.
priver [prive] *vt*: **~ qqn (de)** to deprive
sb (of).

privilège [privilɛʒ] nm privilege.

privilégié, -e [privileʒje] ◆ adj 1. (personne) privileged. 2. (climat, site) favoured. ◆ nm, f privileged person.

prix [pri] nm 1. (coût) price; **à** ou **au ~ coûtant** at cost (price); **~ d'achat** purchase price; **à aucun ~** on no account; **à ~ fixe** set-price (avant n); **hors de ~** too expensive; **à moitié ~** at half price; **à tout ~** at all costs; **~ net** net (price); **~ de revient** cost price; **y mettre le ~** to pay a lot. 2. (importance) value. 3. (récompense) prize.

probabilité [prɔbabilite] nf 1. (chance) probability. 2. (vraisemblance) probability, likelihood; **selon toute ~** in all probability.

probable [prɔbabl] adj probable, likely.

probablement [prɔbabləmɑ̃] adv probably.

probant, -e [prɔbɑ̃, ɑ̃t] adj convincing, conclusive.

probité [prɔbite] nf integrity.

problème [prɔblɛm] nm problem; **sans ~!**, **(il n'y a) pas de ~!** fam no problem!; **ça ne lui pose aucun ~** hum that doesn't worry him/her.

procédé [prɔsede] nm 1. (méthode) process. 2. (conduite) behaviour (U).

procéder [prɔsede] vi 1. (agir) to proceed. 2. (exécuter): **~ à qqch** to set about sthg.

procédure [prɔsedyr] nf procedure; (démarche) proceedings (pl).

procès [prɔsɛ] nm (JUR) trial; **intenter un ~ à qqn** to sue sb.

processeur [prɔsesœr] nm processor.

procession [prɔsesjɔ̃] nf procession.

processus [prɔsesys] nm process.

procès-verbal [prɔsɛverbal] nm 1. (contravention - gén) ticket; (- pour stationnement interdit) parking ticket. 2. (compte-rendu) minutes.

prochain, -e [prɔʃɛ̃, ɛn] adj 1. (suivant) next; **la ~e fois** next time; **la semaine ~e** next week; **à la ~e!** fam see you! 2. (imminent) impending. ▶ **prochain** nm littéraire (semblable) fellow man.

prochainement [prɔʃɛnmɑ̃] adv soon, shortly.

proche [prɔʃ] adj 1. (dans l'espace) near; **~ de** near, close to; (semblable à) very similar to, closely related to. 2. (dans le temps) imminent, near; **dans un ~ avenir** in the immediate future. 3. (ami, parent) close. ▶ **proches** nmpl: **les ~s** close

friends and relatives. ▶ **de proche en proche** loc adv sout gradually.

Proche-Orient [prɔʃɔrjɑ̃] nm: **le ~** the Near East.

proclamation [prɔklamasjɔ̃] nf proclamation.

proclamer [prɔklame] vt to proclaim, to declare.

procréation [prɔkreasjɔ̃] nf procreation; **~ artificielle** artificial reproduction.

procréer [prɔkree] vt littéraire to procreate.

procuration [prɔkyrasjɔ̃] nf proxy; **par ~** by proxy.

procurer [prɔkyre] vt: **~ qqch à qqn** (suj: personne) to obtain sthg for sb; (suj: chose) to give ou bring sb sthg. ▶ **se procurer** vp: **se ~ qqch** to obtain sthg.

procureur [prɔkyrœr] nm: **Procureur de la République** = Attorney General.

prodige [prɔdiʒ] nm 1. (miracle) miracle. 2. (tour de force) marvel, wonder. 3. (génie) prodigy.

prodigieux, -euse [prɔdiʒjø, øz] adj fantastic, incredible.

prodigue [prɔdig] adj (dépensier) extravagant.

prodiguer [prɔdige] vt littéraire (soins, amitié): **~ qqch (à)** to lavish sthg (on).

producteur, -trice [prɔdyktœr, tris] ◆ nm, f 1. (gén) producer. 2. (AGRIC) producer, grower. ◆ adj: **~ de pétrole** oil-producing (avant n).

productif, -ive [prɔdyktif, iv] adj productive.

production [prɔdyksjɔ̃] nf 1. (gén) production; **la ~ littéraire d'un pays** the literature of a country. 2. (producteurs) producers (pl).

productivité [prɔdyktivite] nf productivity.

produire [prɔdɥir] vt 1. (gén) to produce. 2. (provoquer) to cause. ▶ **se produire** vp 1. (arriver) to occur, to take place. 2. (acteur, chanteur) to appear.

produit, -e [prɔdɥi, it] pp → **produire**. ▶ **produit** nm (gén) product; **~s alimentaires** foodstuffs, foods; **~ de beauté** cosmetic, beauty product; **~s chimiques** chemicals; **~s d'entretien** cleaning products; **~ de grande consommation** mass consumption product.

proéminent, -e [prɔeminɑ̃, ɑ̃t] adj prominent.

profane [prɔfan] ◆ nmf 1. (non religieux) non-believer. 2. (novice) layman. ◆ adj 1. (laïc) secular. 2. (ignorant) ignorant.

profaner [prɔfane] vt 1. (église) to desecrate. 2. fig (mémoire) to defile.

proférer [prɔfere] vt to utter.

professeur [prɔfesœr] nm (gén) teacher; (dans l'enseignement supérieur) lecturer; (titulaire) professor.

profession [prɔfesjɔ̃] nf 1. (métier) occupation; **sans ~** unemployed; **~ libérale** profession. 2. (corps de métier - libéral) profession; (- manuel) trade.

professionnel, -elle [prɔfesjɔnɛl] ◆ adj 1. (gén) professional. 2. (école) technical; (enseignement) vocational. ◆ nm, f professional.

professorat [prɔfesɔra] nm teaching.

profil [prɔfil] nm 1. (de personne, d'emploi) profile; (de bâtiment) outline; **de ~** (visage, corps) in profile; (objet) from the side. 2. (coupe) section.

profiler [prɔfile] vt to shape. ▶ **se profiler** vp 1. (bâtiment, arbre) to stand out. 2. (solution) to emerge.

profit [prɔfi] nm 1. (avantage) benefit; **au ~ de** in aid of; **tirer ~ de** to profit from, to benefit from. 2. (gain) profit.

profitable [prɔfitabl] adj profitable; **être ~ à qqn** to benefit sb, to be beneficial to sb.

profiter [prɔfite] vi (tirer avantage): **~ de** (vacances) to benefit from; (personne) to take advantage of; **~ de qqch pour faire qqch** to take advantage of sthg to do sthg; **en ~** to make the most of it.

profond, -e [prɔfɔ̃, ɔ̃d] adj 1. (gén) deep. 2. (pensée) deep, profound.

profondément [prɔfɔ̃demã] adv 1. (enfoui) deep. 2. (intensément - aimer, intéresser) deeply; (- dormir) soundly; **être ~ endormi** to be fast asleep. 3. (extrêmement - convaincu, ému) deeply, profoundly; (- différent) profoundly.

profondeur [prɔfɔ̃dœr] nf depth; **en ~** in depth.

profusion [prɔfyzjɔ̃] nf: **une ~ de** a profusion of; **à ~** in abundance, in profusion.

progéniture [prɔʒenityr] nf offspring.

programmable [prɔgramabl] adj programmable.

programmateur, -trice [prɔgramatœr, tris] nm, f programme planner. ▶ **programmateur** nm automatic control unit.

programmation [prɔgramasjɔ̃] nf 1. (INFORM) programming. 2. (RADIO & TÉLÉ) programme planning.

programme [prɔgram] nm 1. (gén) programme Br, program Am. 2. (INFORM) program. 3. (planning) schedule. 4. (SCOL) syllabus.

programmer [prɔgrame] vt 1. (organiser) to plan. 2. (RADIO & TÉLÉ) to schedule. 3. (INFORM) to program.

programmeur, -euse [prɔgramœr, øz] nm, f (INFORM) (computer) programmer.

progrès [prɔgrɛ] nm progress (U); **faire des ~** to make progress.

progresser [prɔgrese] vi 1. (avancer) to progress, to advance. 2. (maladie) to spread. 3. (élève) to make progress.

progressif, -ive [prɔgresif, iv] adj progressive; (difficulté) increasing.

progression [prɔgresjɔ̃] nf 1. (avancée) advance. 2. (de maladie, du nationalisme) spread.

prohiber [prɔibe] vt to ban, to prohibit.

proie [prwa] nf prey; **être la ~ de qqch** fig to be the victim of sthg; **être en ~ à** (sentiment) to be prey to.

projecteur [prɔʒɛktœr] nm 1. (de lumière) floodlight; (THÉÂTRE) spotlight. 2. (d'images) projector.

projectile [prɔʒɛktil] nm missile.

projection [prɔʒɛksjɔ̃] nf 1. (gén) projection. 2. (jet) throwing.

projectionniste [prɔʒɛksjɔnist] nmf projectionist.

projet [prɔʒɛ] nm 1. (perspective) plan; **avoir pour ~ de faire qqch** to plan to do sthg. 2. (étude, ébauche) draft; **~ de loi** bill.

projeter [prɔʃte] vt 1. (envisager) to plan; **~ de faire qqch** to plan to do sthg. 2. (missile, pierre) to throw. 3. (film, diapositives) to show.

prolétaire [prɔletɛr] nmf & adj proletarian.

prolétariat [prɔletarja] nm proletariat.

proliférer [prɔlifere] vi to proliferate.

prolifique [prɔlifik] adj prolific.

prologue [prɔlɔg] nm prologue.

prolongation [prɔlɔ̃gasjɔ̃] nf (extension) extension, prolongation. ▶ **prolongations** nfpl (SPORT) extra time (U).

prolongement [prɔlɔ̃ʒmã] nm (de mur, quai) extension; **être dans le ~ de** to be a continuation of. ▶ **prolongements** nmpl (conséquences) repercussions.

prolonger [prɔlɔ̃ʒe] vt 1. (dans le temps): **~ qqch (de)** to prolong sthg (by). 2. (dans l'espace): **~ qqch (de)** to extend sthg (by).

promenade [prɔmnad] nf 1. (balade)

walk, stroll; *fig* trip, excursion; ~ **en voiture** drive; ~ **à vélo** (bike) ride; **faire une** ~ to go for a walk. **2.** (*lieu*) promenade.

promener [prɔmne] *vt* **1.** (*personne*) to take out (for a walk); (*en voiture*) to take for a drive. **2.** *fig* (*regard, doigts*): ~ **qqch sur** to run sthg over. ▶ **se promener** *vp* to go for a walk.

promeneur, -euse [prɔmnœr, øz] *nm, f* walker, stroller.

promesse [prɔmɛs] *nf* **1.** (*serment*) promise; **tenir sa** ~ to keep one's promise. **2.** (*engagement*) undertaking; ~ **d'achat/de vente** (JUR) agreement to purchase/to sell. **3.** *fig* (*espérance*): **être plein de ~s** to be very promising.

prometteur, -euse [prɔmɛtœr, øz] *adj* promising.

promettre [prɔmɛtr] ◆ *vt* to promise; ~ **qqch à qqn** to promise sb sthg; ~ **de faire qqch** to promise to do sthg; ~ **à qqn que** to promise sb that. ◆ *vi* to be promising; **ça promet!** *iron* that bodes well!

promis, -e [prɔmi, iz] ◆ *pp* → **promettre**. ◆ *adj* promised. ◆ *nm, f hum* intended.

promiscuité [prɔmiskɥite] *nf* overcrowding; ~ **sexuelle** (sexual) promiscuity.

promontoire [prɔmɔ̃twar] *nm* promontory.

promoteur, -trice [prɔmɔtœr, tris] *nm, f* **1.** (*novateur*) instigator. **2.** (*constructeur*) property developer.

promotion [prɔmɔsjɔ̃] *nf* **1.** (*gén*) promotion; **en** ~ (*produit*) on special offer. **2.** (MIL & SCOL) year.

promouvoir [prɔmuvwar] *vt* to promote.

prompt, -e [prɔ̃, prɔ̃t] *adj sout*: ~ (**à faire qqch**) swift (to do sthg).

promu, -e [prɔmy] *pp* → **promouvoir**.

promulguer [prɔmylge] *vt* to promulgate.

prôner [prone] *vt sout* to advocate.

pronom [prɔnɔ̃] *nm* pronoun.

pronominal, -e, -aux [prɔnɔminal, o] *adj* pronominal.

prononcé, -e [prɔnɔ̃se] *adj* marked.

prononcer [prɔnɔ̃se] *vt* **1.** (JUR & LING) to pronounce. **2.** (*dire*) to utter. ▶ **se prononcer** *vp* **1.** (*se dire*) to be pronounced. **2.** (*trancher - assemblée*) to decide, to reach a decision; (- *magistrat*) to deliver a verdict; **se** ~ **sur** to give one's opinion of.

prononciation [prɔnɔ̃sjasjɔ̃] *nf* **1.** (LING) pronunciation. **2.** (JUR) pronouncement.

pronostic [prɔnɔstik] *nm* **1.** (*gén pl*) (*prévision*) forecast. **2.** (MÉD) prognosis.

propagande [prɔpagɑ̃d] *nf* **1.** (*endoctrinement*) propaganda. **2.** *fig & hum* (*publicité*): **faire de la** ~ **pour qqch** to plug sthg.

propager [prɔpaʒe] *vt* to spread. ▶ **se propager** *vp* to spread; (BIOL) to be propagated; (PHYS) to propagate.

propane [prɔpan] *nm* propane.

prophète [prɔfɛt], **prophétesse** [prɔfetɛs] *nm, f* prophet (*f* prophetess).

prophétie [prɔfesi] *nf* prophecy.

prophétiser [prɔfetize] *vt* to prophesy.

propice [prɔpis] *adj* favourable.

proportion [prɔpɔrsjɔ̃] *nf* proportion; **toutes ~s gardées** relatively speaking.

proportionné, -e [prɔpɔrsjɔne] *adj*: **bien/mal** ~ well-/badly-proportioned.

proportionnel, -elle [prɔpɔrsjɔnɛl] *adj*: ~ (**à**) proportional (to). ▶ **proportionnelle** *nf*: **la ~le** proportional representation.

propos [prɔpo] ◆ *nm* **1.** (*discours*) talk. **2.** (*but*) intention; **c'est à quel ~?** what is it about?; **hors de** ~ at the wrong time. ◆ *nmpl* (*paroles*) talk (U), words. ▶ **à propos** *loc adv* **1.** (*opportunément*) at (just) the right time. **2.** (*au fait*) by the way. ▶ **à propos de** *loc prép* about.

proposer [prɔpoze] *vt* **1.** (*offrir*) to offer, to propose; ~ **qqch à qqn** to offer sb sthg, to offer sthg to sb; ~ **à qqn de faire qqch** to offer to do sthg for sb. **2.** (*suggérer*) to suggest, to propose; ~ **de faire qqch** to suggest ou propose doing sthg. **3.** (*loi, candidat*) to propose.

proposition [prɔpozisjɔ̃] *nf* **1.** (*offre*) offer, proposal. **2.** (*suggestion*) suggestion, proposal. **3.** (GRAM) clause.

propre [prɔpr] ◆ *adj* **1.** (*nettoyé*) clean. **2.** (*soigné*) neat, tidy. **3.** (*éduqué - enfant*) toilet-trained; (- *animal*) house-trained Br, housebroken Am. **4.** (*personnel*) own. **5.** (*particulier*): ~ **à** peculiar to. **6.** (*de nature*): ~ **à faire qqch** capable of doing sthg. ◆ *nm* (*propreté*) cleanness, cleanliness; **recopier qqch au** ~ to make a fair copy of sthg, to copy sthg up. ▶ **au propre** *loc adv* (LING) literally.

proprement [prɔprəmɑ̃] *adv* **1.** (*convenablement - habillé*) neatly, tidily; (- *se tenir*) correctly. **2.** (*véritablement*) completely; **à** ~ **parler** strictly ou properly speaking; **l'événement ~ dit** the event itself, the actual event.

propreté [prɔprəte] *nf* cleanness, cleanliness.

propriétaire [prɔprijetɛr] *nmf* 1. (*possesseur*) owner; **~ terrien** landowner. 2. (*dans l'immobilier*) landlord.

propriété [prɔprijete] *nf* 1. (*gén*) property; **~ privée** private property. 2. (*droit*) ownership. 3. (*terres*) property (U). 4. (*convenance*) suitability. 5. (*caractéristique*) property, characteristic.

propulser [prɔpylse] *vt litt & fig* to propel. ▶ **se propulser** *vp* to move forward, to propel o.s. forward ou along; *fig* to shoot.

prorata [prɔrata] ▶ **au prorata de** *loc prép* in proportion to.

prosaïque [prɔzaik] *adj* prosaic, mundane.

proscrit, -e [prɔskri, it] *adj* (*interdit*) banned, prohibited.

prose [proz] *nf* prose; **en ~** in prose.

prospecter [prɔspɛkte] *vt* 1. (*pays, région*) to prospect. 2. (COMM) to canvass.

prospection [prɔspɛksjɔ̃] *nf* 1. (*de ressources*) prospecting. 2. (COMM) canvassing.

prospectus [prɔspɛktys] *nm* (advertising) leaflet.

prospérer [prɔspere] *vi* to prosper, to thrive; (*plante, insecte*) to thrive.

prospérité [prɔsperite] *nf* 1. (*richesse*) prosperity. 2. (*bien-être*) well-being.

prostate [prɔstat] *nf* prostate (gland).

prosterner [prɔstɛrne] ▶ **se prosterner** *vp* to bow down; **se ~ devant** to bow down before; *fig* to kowtow to.

prostituée [prɔstitɥe] *nf* prostitute.

prostituer [prɔstitɥe] ▶ **se prostituer** *vp* to prostitute o.s.

prostitution [prɔstitysjɔ̃] *nf* prostitution.

prostré, -e [prɔstre] *adj* prostrate.

protagoniste [prɔtagɔnist] *nmf* protagonist, hero (*f* heroine).

protecteur, -trice [prɔtɛktœr, tris] ◆ *adj* protective. ◆ *nm, f* 1. (*défenseur*) protector. 2. (*des arts*) patron. 3. (*souteneur*) pimp.

protection [prɔtɛksjɔ̃] *nf* 1. (*défense*) protection; **prendre qqn sous sa ~** to take sb under one's wing. 2. (*des arts*) patronage.

protectionnisme [prɔtɛksjɔnism] *nm* protectionism.

protégé, -e [prɔteʒe] ◆ *adj* protected. ◆ *nm, f* protégé.

protège-cahier [prɔtɛʒkaje] (*pl* **protège-cahiers**) *nm* exercise book cover.

protéger [prɔteʒe] *vt* (*gén*) to protect.

protéine [prɔtein] *nf* protein.

protestant, -e [prɔtɛstɑ̃, ɑ̃t] *adj & nm, f* Protestant.

protestation [prɔtɛstasjɔ̃] *nf* (*contestation*) protest.

protester [prɔtɛste] *vi* to protest; **~ contre qqch** to protest against sthg, to protest sthg Am.

prothèse [prɔtɛz] *nf* prosthesis; **~ dentaire** dentures (*pl*), false teeth (*pl*).

protide [prɔtid] *nm* protein.

protocolaire [prɔtɔkɔlɛr] *adj* (*poli*) conforming to etiquette.

protocole [prɔtɔkɔl] *nm* protocol.

proton [prɔtɔ̃] *nm* proton.

prototype [prɔtɔtip] *nm* prototype.

protubérance [prɔtyberɑ̃s] *nf* bulge, protuberance.

proue [pru] *nf* bows (*pl*), prow.

prouesse [pruɛs] *nf* feat.

prouver [pruve] *vt* 1. (*établir*) to prove. 2. (*montrer*) to demonstrate, to show.

provenance [prɔvnɑ̃s] *nf* origin; **en ~ de** from.

provençal, -e, -aux [prɔvɑ̃sal, o] *adj* 1. (*de Provence*) of/from Provence. 2. (CULIN) *with tomatoes, garlic and onions.* ▶ **provençal** *nm* (*langue*) Provençal.

Provence [prɔvɑ̃s] *nf*: **la ~** Provence.

provenir [prɔvnir] *vi*: **~ de** to come from; *fig* to be due to, to be caused by.

proverbe [prɔvɛrb] *nm* proverb.

proverbial, -e, -aux [prɔvɛrbjal, o] *adj* proverbial.

providence [prɔvidɑ̃s] *nf* providence.

providentiel, -elle [prɔvidɑ̃sjɛl] *adj* providential.

province [prɔvɛ̃s] *nf* 1. (*gén*) province. 2. (*campagne*) provinces (*pl*).

provincial, -e, -aux [prɔvɛ̃sjal, o] *adj & nm, f* provincial.

proviseur [prɔvizœr] *nm* ≃ head Br, ≃ headteacher Br, ≃ headmaster (*f* headmistress) Br, ≃ principal Am.

provision [prɔvizjɔ̃] *nf* 1. (*réserve*) stock, supply. 2. (FIN) retainer; → **chèque.** ▶ **provisions** *nfpl* provisions.

provisoire [prɔvizwar] ◆ *adj* temporary; (JUR) provisional. ◆ *nm*: **ce n'est que du ~** it's only a temporary arrangement.

provisoirement [prɔvizwarmɑ̃] *adv* temporarily.

provocant, -e [prɔvɔkɑ̃, ɑ̃t] *adj* provocative.

provocation [prɔvɔkasjɔ̃] nf provocation.

provoquer [prɔvɔke] vt 1. (entraîner) to cause. 2. (personne) to provoke.

proxénète [prɔksenɛt] nm pimp.

proximité [prɔksimite] nf (de lieu) proximity, nearness; à ~ de near.

prude [pryd] adj prudish.

prudence [prydãs] nf care, caution.

prudent, -e [prydã, ãt] adj careful, cautious.

prune [pryn] nf plum.

pruneau, -x [pryno] nm (fruit) prune.

prunelle [prynɛl] nf (ANAT) pupil.

prunier [prynje] nm plum tree.

PS¹ (abr de **Parti socialiste**) nm French socialist party.

PS², P-S (abr de post-scriptum) nm PS.

psaume [psom] nm psalm.

pseudonyme [psødɔnim] nm pseudonym.

psy [psi] fam nmf (abr de **psychiatre**) shrink.

psychanalyse [psikanaliz] nf psychoanalysis.

psychanalyste [psikanalist] nmf psychoanalyst, analyst.

psychédélique [psikedelik] adj psychedelic.

psychiatre [psikjatr] nmf psychiatrist.

psychiatrie [psikjatri] nf psychiatry.

psychique [psiʃik] adj psychic; (maladie) psychosomatic.

psychologie [psikɔlɔʒi] nf psychology.

psychologique [psikɔlɔʒik] adj psychological.

psychologue [psikɔlɔg] ◆ nmf psychologist. ◆ adj psychological.

psychose [psikoz] nf 1. (MÉD) psychosis. 2. (crainte) obsessive fear.

psychosomatique [psikɔsɔmatik] adj psychosomatic.

psychothérapie [psikɔterapi] nf psychotherapy.

Pte 1. abr de **porte**. 2. abr de **pointe**.

PTT (abr de **Postes, télécommunications et télédiffusion**) nfpl former French post office and telecommunications network.

pu [py] pp → **pouvoir**.

puant, -e [pɥã, ãt] adj 1. (fétide) smelly, stinking. 2. fam fig (personne) bumptious, full of oneself.

puanteur [pɥãtœr] nf stink, stench.

pub¹ [pyb] nf fam ad, advert Br; (métier) advertising.

pub² [pœb] nm pub.

pubère [pybɛr] adj pubescent.

puberté [pybɛrte] nf puberty.

pubis [pybis] nm (zone) pubis.

public, -ique [pyblik] adj public. ▶ **public** nm 1. (auditoire) audience; **en ~** in public. 2. (population) public.

publication [pyblikasjɔ̃] nf publication.

publicitaire [pyblisitɛr] ◆ nmf advertising executive. ◆ adj (campagne) advertising (avant n); (vente, film) promotional.

publicité [pyblisite] nf 1. (domaine) advertising; ~ comparative comparative advertising; ~ mensongère misleading advertising, deceptive advertising. 2. (réclame) advertisement, advert. 3. (autour d'une affaire) publicity (U).

publier [pyblije] vt (livre) to publish; (communiqué) to issue, to release.

publireportage [pyblirəpɔrtaʒ] nm free write-up Br, reading notice Am.

puce [pys] nf 1. (insecte) flea. 2. (INFORM) (silicon) chip. 3. fig (terme affectueux) pet, love. 4. loc: mettre la ~ à l'oreille de qqn to set sb thinking.

puceau, -elle, -x [pyso, ɛl, o] nm, f & adj fam virgin.

pudeur [pydœr] nf 1. (physique) modesty, decency. 2. (morale) restraint.

pudibond, -e [pydibɔ̃, ɔ̃d] adj prudish, prim and proper.

pudique [pydik] adj 1. (physiquement) modest, decent. 2. (moralement) restrained.

puer [pɥe] ◆ vi to stink; **ça pue ici!** it stinks in here! ◆ vt to reek of, to stink of.

puéricultrice [pɥerikyltris] nf nursery nurse.

puériculture [pɥerikyltyr] nf childcare.

puéril, -e [pɥeril] adj childish.

Puerto Rico = Porto Rico.

pugilat [pyʒila] nm fight.

puis [pɥi] adv then; **et ~** (d'ailleurs) and moreover ou besides.

puiser [pɥize] vt (liquide) to draw; ~ **qqch dans qqch** fig to draw ou take sthg from sthg.

puisque [pɥiskə] conj (gén) since.

puissance [pɥisãs] nf power. ▶ **en puissance** loc adj potential.

puissant, -e [pɥisã, ãt] adj powerful. ▶ **puissant** nm: **les ~s** the powerful.

puisse, puisses etc → **pouvoir**.

puits [pɥi] nm 1. (d'eau) well. 2. (de gisement) shaft; ~ **de pétrole** oil well.

pull [pyl], **pull-over** [pylɔvɛr] (pl **pull-overs**) nm jumper Br, sweater.

pulluler [pylyle] *vi* to swarm.

pulmonaire [pylmɔnɛr] *adj* lung (*avant n*), pulmonary.

pulpe [pylp] *nf* pulp.

pulsation [pylsasjɔ̃] *nf* beat, beating (U).

pulsion [pylsjɔ̃] *nf* impulse.

pulvérisation [pylverizasjɔ̃] *nf* **1.** (*d'insecticide*) spraying. **2.** (MÉD) spray; (*traitement*) spraying.

pulvériser [pylverize] *vt* **1.** (*projeter*) to spray. **2.** (*détruire*) to pulverize; *fig* to smash.

puma [pyma] *nm* puma.

punaise [pynɛz] *nf* **1.** (*insecte*) bug. **2.** (*clou*) drawing pin Br, thumbtack Am.

punch [pɔ̃ʃ] *nm* punch.

puni, -e [pyni] *adj* punished.

punir [pynir] *vt* : ~ **qqn (de)** to punish sb (with).

punition [pynisjɔ̃] *nf* punishment.

pupille [pypij] ◆ *nf* (ANAT) pupil. ◆ *nmf* (*orphelin*) ward; ~ **de l'État** ≃ child in care; ~ **de la Nation** war orphan (*in care*).

pupitre [pypitr] *nm* **1.** (*d'orateur*) lectern; (MUS) stand. **2.** (TECHNOL) console. **3.** (*d'écolier*) desk.

pur, -e [pyr] *adj* **1.** (*gén*) pure. **2.** *fig* (*absolu*) pure, sheer; ~ **et simple** pure and simple. **3.** *fig & littéraire* (*intention*) honourable. **4.** (*lignes*) pure, clean.

purée [pyre] *nf* purée; ~ **de pommes de terre** mashed potatoes (*pl*).

purement [pyrmɑ̃] *adv* purely; ~ **et simplement** purely and simply.

pureté [pyrte] *nf* **1.** (*gén*) purity. **2.** (*de sculpture, de diamant*) perfection. **3.** (*d'intention*) honourableness.

purgatoire [pyrgatwar] *nm* purgatory.

purge [pyrʒ] *nf* **1.** (MÉD & POLIT) purge. **2.** (*de radiateur*) bleeding.

purger [pyrʒe] *vt* **1.** (MÉD & POLIT) to purge. **2.** (*radiateur*) to bleed. **3.** (*peine*) to serve.

purifier [pyrifje] *vt* to purify.

purin [pyrɛ̃] *nm* slurry.

puritain, -e [pyritɛ̃, ɛn] ◆ *adj* (*pudibond*) puritanical. ◆ *nm, f* **1.** (*prude*) puritan. **2.** (RELIG) Puritan.

puritanisme [pyritanism] *nm* puritanism; (RELIG) Puritanism.

pur-sang [pyrsɑ̃] *nm inv* thoroughbred.

purulent, -e [pyrylɑ̃, ɑ̃t] *adj* purulent.

pus [py] *nm* pus.

pusillanime [pyzilanim] *adj* pusillanimous.

putain [pytɛ̃] *nf vulg* **1.** *péj* (*prostituée*)

whore. **2.** *fig* (*pour exprimer le mécontentement*): **(ce)** ~ **de ...** this/that sodding ... Br, this/that goddam ... Am.

putréfier [pytrefje] ▸ **se putréfier** *vp* to putrefy, to rot.

putsch [putʃ] *nm* uprising, coup.

puzzle [pœzl] *nm* jigsaw (puzzle).

P-V *nm abr de* **procès-verbal**.

pyjama [piʒama] *nm* pyjamas (*pl*).

pylône [pilon] *nm* pylon.

pyramide [piramid] *nf* pyramid.

Pyrénées [pirene] *nfpl*: **les** ~ the Pyrenees.

Pyrex® [pirɛks] *nm* Pyrex®.

pyromane [pirɔman] *nmf* arsonist; (MÉD) pyromaniac.

python [pitɔ̃] *nm* python.

q, Q [ky] *nm inv* (*lettre*) q, Q.

QCM (*abr de* **questionnaire à choix multiple**) *nm* multiple choice questionnaire.

QG (*abr de* **quartier général**) *nm* HQ.

QI (*abr de* **quotient intellectuel**) *nm* IQ.

qqch (*abr de* **quelque chose**) sthg.

qqn (*abr de* **quelqu'un**) s.o., sb.

qu' → **que**.

quadragénaire [kwadraʒenɛr] *nmf* forty year old.

quadrilatère [kwadrilatɛr] *nm* quadrilateral.

quadrillage [kadrijaʒ] *nm* **1.** (*de papier, de tissu*) criss-cross pattern. **2.** (*policier*) combing.

quadriller [kadrije] *vt* **1.** (*papier*) to mark with squares. **2.** (*ville - suj: rues*) to criss-cross; (- *suj: police*) to comb.

quadrimoteur [kwadrimɔtœr] *nm* four-engined plane.

quadrupède [k(w)adrypɛd] *nm & adj* quadruped.

quadruplés, -ées [k(w)adryple] *nm, f pl* quadruplets, quads.

quai [kɛ] *nm* **1.** (*de gare*) platform. **2.** (*de port*) quay, wharf. **3.** (*de rivière*) embankment.

qualificatif, -ive [kalifikatif, iv] *adj* qualifying. ▸ **qualificatif** *nm* term.

qualification [kalifikasjɔ̃] *nf* (*gén*) qualification.

qualifier [kalifje] vt 1. (gén) to qualify; être qualifié pour qqch/pour faire qqch to be qualified for sthg/to do sthg. 2. (caractériser): ~ qqn/qqch de qqch to describe sb/sthg as sthg, to call sb/sthg sthg. ▶ se qualifier vp to qualify.

qualitatif, -ive [kalitatif, iv] adj qualitative.

qualité [kalite] nf 1. (gén) quality; de bonne/mauvaise ~ of good/poor quality. 2. (condition) position, capacity.

quand [kɑ̃] ◆ conj (lorsque, alors que) when; ~ tu le verras, demande-lui de téléphoner when you see him, ask him to phone me. ◆ adv interr when; ~ arriveras-tu? when will you arrive?; jusqu'à ~ restez-vous? how long are you staying for? ▶ quand même ◆ loc adv all the same; je pense qu'il ne viendra pas, mais je l'inviterai ~ même I don't think he'll come but I'll invite him all the same; tu pourrais faire attention ~ même! you might at least be careful! ◆ interj: ~ même, à son âge! really, at his/her age! ▶ quand bien même loc conj sout even though, even if.

quant [kɑ̃] ▶ quant à loc prép as for.

quantifier [kɑ̃tifje] vt to quantify.

quantitatif, -ive [kɑ̃titatif, iv] adj quantitative.

quantité [kɑ̃tite] nf 1. (mesure) quantity, amount. 2. (abondance): (une) ~ de a great many, a lot of; en ~ in large numbers; des exemplaires en ~ a large number of copies.

quarantaine [karɑ̃tɛn] nf 1. (nombre): une ~ de about forty. 2. (âge): avoir la ~ to be in one's forties. 3. (isolement) quarantine.

quarante [karɑ̃t] adj num & nm forty; voir aussi six.

quarantième [karɑ̃tjɛm] adj num, nm & nmf fortieth; voir aussi sixième.

quart [kar] nm 1. (fraction) quarter; trois ~s three-quarters; deux heures moins le ~ (a) quarter to two, (a) quarter of two Am; deux heures et ~ (a) quarter past two, (a) quarter after two Am; il est moins le ~ it's (a) quarter to; un ~ de a quarter of; un ~ d'heure a quarter of an hour. 2. (NAVIG) watch. 3. ~ de finale quarter final.

quartier [kartje] nm 1. (de ville) area, district. 2. (de fruit) piece; (de viande) quarter. 3. (héraldique, de lune) quarter. 4. (gén pl) (MIL) quarters (pl); ~ général headquarters (pl).

QUARTIER LATIN

This district on the south bank of the Seine in Paris has long been associated with students and artists. It straddles the 5th and 6th 'arrondissements', with the Sorbonne university at its centre. It is also famous for its numerous book-shops, libraries, cafés and cinemas.

---

quartz [kwarts] nm quartz; montre à ~ quartz watch.

quasi [kazi] adv almost, nearly.

quasi- [kazi] préfixe near; ~collision near collision.

quasiment [kazimɑ̃] adv fam almost, nearly.

quatorze [katɔrz] adj num & nm fourteen; voir aussi six.

quatorzième [katɔrzjɛm] adj num, nm & nmf fourteenth; voir aussi sixième.

quatrain [katrɛ̃] nm quatrain.

quatre [katr] ◆ adj num four; monter l'escalier ~ à ~ to take the stairs four at a time; se mettre en ~ pour qqn to bend over backwards for sb. ◆ nm four; voir aussi six.

quatre-vingt = quatre-vingts.

quatre-vingt-dix [katrəvɛ̃dis] adj num & nm ninety; voir aussi six.

quatre-vingt-dixième [katrəvɛ̃dizjɛm] adj num, nm & nmf ninetieth; voir aussi sixième.

quatre-vingtième [katrəvɛ̃tjɛm] adj num, nm & nmf eightieth; voir aussi sixième.

quatre-vingts, quatre-vingt [katrəvɛ̃] adj num & nm eighty; voir aussi six.

quatrième [katrijɛm] ◆ adj num, nm & nmf fourth; voir aussi sixième. ◆ nf (SCOL) = third year ou form Br, = eighth grade Am.

quatuor [kwatɥɔr] nm quartet.

que [k(ə)] ◆ conj 1. (introduit une subordonnée) that; il a dit qu'il viendrait he said (that) he'd come; il veut ~ tu viennes he wants you to come. 2. (introduit une hypothèse) whether; ~ vous le vouliez ou non whether you like it or not. 3. (reprend une autre conjonction): s'il fait beau et que nous avons le temps ... if the weather is good and we have time ... 4. (indique un ordre, un souhait): qu'il entre! let him come in!; tout le monde sorte! everybody out! 5. (après un présentatif): voilà/voici ~ ça recommence! here we go again! 6. (comparatif - après moins, plus) than; (- après autant, aussi, même) as;

plus jeune ~ moi younger than I (am) ou than me; elle a la même robe ~ moi she has the same dress as I do ou as me. 7. (seulement): ne ... ~ only; je n'ai qu'une sœur I've only got one sister. ◆ pron rel (chose, animal) which, that; (personne) whom, that; la femme ~ j'aime the woman (whom ou that) I love; le livre qu'il m'a prêté the book (which ou that) he lent me. ◆ pron interr what; ~ savez-vous au juste? what exactly do you know?; ~ faire? what can I/we/one do?; je me demande ~ faire I wonder what I should do. ◆ adv excl: qu'elle est belle! how beautiful she is!; ~ de monde! what a lot of people! ▶ c'est que loc conj it's because; si je vais me coucher, c'est ~ j'ai sommeil if I'm going to bed, it's because I'm tired. ▶ qu'est-ce que pron interr what; qu'est-ce ~ tu veux encore? what else do you want? ▶ qu'est-ce qui pron interr what; qu'est-ce qui se passe? what's going on?

Québec [kebɛk] nm (province): le ~ Quebec.

québécois, -e [kebekwa, az] adj Quebec (avant n). ▶ québécois nm (langue) Quebec French. ▶ Québécois, -e nm, f Quebecker, Québécois.

quel [kɛl] (f quelle, mpl quels, fpl quelles) ◆ adj interr (personne) which; (chose) what, which; ~ homme? which man?; ~ livre voulez-vous? what ou which book do you want?; je ne sais ~s sont ses projets I don't know what his plans are; quelle heure est-il? what time is it?, what's the time? ◆ adj excl: ~ idiot! what an idiot!; quelle honte! the shame of it! ◆ adj indéf: ~ que (+ subjonctif) (chose, animal) whatever; (personne) whoever; il se baigne, ~ que soit le temps he goes swimming whatever the weather; il refuse de voir les nouveaux arrivants, ~s qu'ils soient he refuses to see new arrivals, whoever they may be. ◆ pron interr which (one); de vous trois, ~ est le plus jeune? which (one) of you three is the youngest?

quelconque [kɛlkɔ̃k] adj 1. (n'importe lequel) any; donner un prétexte ~ to give any old excuse; si pour une raison ~ ... if for any reason ...; une ~ observation some remark or other. 2. (après n) péj (banal) ordinary, mediocre.

quelque [kɛlk(ə)] ◆ adj indéf some; à ~ distance de là some way away (from there); j'ai ~s lettres à écrire I have some ou a few letters to write; vous n'avez pas ~s livres à me montrer? don't you have any books to show me?; les ~s fois où j'étais absent the few times I wasn't there; les ~s 200 francs qu'il m'a prêtés the 200 francs or so (that) he lent me; ~ route que je prenne whatever route I take; ~ peu somewhat, rather. ◆ adv (environ) about; 200 francs et ~ some ou about 200 francs; il est midi et ~ fam it's just after midday.

quelque chose [kɛlkəʃoz] pron indéf something; ~ de différent something different; ~ d'autre something else; tu veux boire ~? do you want something ou anything to drink?; apporter un petit ~ à qqn to give sb a little something; c'est ~! (ton admiratif) it's really something!; cela m'a fait ~ I really felt it.

quelquefois [kɛlkəfwa] adv sometimes, occasionally.

quelque part [kɛlkəpar] adv somewhere; l'as-tu vu ~? did you see him anywhere?, have you seen him anywhere?

quelques-uns, quelques-unes [kɛlkəzœ̃, yn] pron indéf some, a few.

quelqu'un [kɛlkœ̃] pron indéf m someone, somebody; c'est ~ d'ouvert/d'intelligent he's/she's a frank/an intelligent person.

quémander [kemɑ̃de] vt to beg for; ~ qqch à qqn to beg sb for sthg.

qu'en-dira-t-on [kɑ̃diratɔ̃] nm inv fam tittle-tattle.

quenelle [kənɛl] nf very finely chopped mixture of fish or chicken cooked in stock.

querelle [kərɛl] nf quarrel.

quereller [kərele] ▶ se quereller vp: se ~ (avec) to quarrel (with).

querelleur, -euse [kərɛlœr, øz] adj quarrelsome.

qu'est-ce que [kɛskə] → que.

qu'est-ce qui [kɛski] → que.

question [kɛstjɔ̃] nf question; poser une ~ à qqn to ask sb a question; il est ~ de faire qqch it's a question ou matter of doing sthg; il n'en est pas ~ there is no question of it; remettre qqn/qqch en ~ to question sb/sthg, to challenge sb/sthg; ~ subsidiaire tiebreaker.

questionnaire [kɛstjɔnɛr] nm questionnaire.

questionner [kɛstjɔne] vt to question.

quête [kɛt] nf 1. sout (d'objet, de personne) quest; se mettre en ~ de to go in search of. 2. (d'aumône): faire la ~ to take a collection.

quêter [kete] ◆ vi to collect. ◆ vt fig to seek, to look for.

queue [kø] nf 1. (d'animal) tail; **faire une ~ de poisson à qqn** (fig & AUTOM) to cut sb up. 2. (de fruit) stalk. 3. (de poêle) handle. 4. (de liste, de classe) bottom; (de file, peloton) rear. 5. (file) queue Br, line Am; **faire la ~** to queue Br, to stand in line Am; **à la ~ leu leu** in single file.

queue-de-cheval [kødʃəval] (pl queues-de-cheval) nf ponytail.

queue-de-pie [kødpi] (pl queues-de-pie) nf fam tails (pl).

qui [ki] ◆ pron rel 1. (sujet) (personne) who; (chose) which, that; **l'homme ~ parle** the man who's talking; **je l'ai vu ~ passait** I saw him pass; **le chien ~ aboie** the barking dog, the dog which ou that is barking; **~ plus est** (and) what's more. 2. (complément d'objet direct) who; **tu vois ~ je veux dire** you see who I mean; **invite ~ tu veux** invite whoever ou anyone you like. 3. (après une préposition) who, whom; **la personne à ~ je parle** the person I'm talking to, the person to whom I'm talking. 4. (indéfini): **~ que tu sois** whoever you are; **~ que ce soit** whoever it may be. ◆ pron interr 1. (sujet) who; **~ es-tu?** who are you?; **je voudrais savoir ~ est là** I would like to know who's there. 2. (complément d'objet, après une préposition) who, whom; **~ demandez-vous?** who do you want to see?; **dites-moi ~ vous demandez** tell me who you want to see; **à ~ vas-tu le donner?** who are you going to give it to?, to whom are you going to give it? ► **qui est-ce qui** pron interr who. ► **qui est-ce que** pron interr who, whom.

quiche [kiʃ] nf quiche.

quiconque [kikɔ̃k] ◆ pron indéf anyone, anybody. ◆ pron rel indéf sout anyone who, whoever.

quidam [kidam] nm fam chap Br, guy Am.

quiétude [kjetyd] nf tranquillity.

quignon [kiɲɔ̃] nm fam hunk.

quille [kij] nf (de bateau) keel. ► **quilles** nfpl (jeu): **(jeu de) ~s** skittles (U).

quincaillerie [kɛ̃kajri] nf 1. (magasin) ironmonger's (shop) Br, hardware shop. 2. fam fig (bijoux) jewellery.

quinconce [kɛ̃kɔ̃s] nm: **en ~** in a staggered arrangement.

quinine [kinin] nf quinine.

quinquagénaire [kɛ̃kaʒenɛr] nmf fifty year old.

quinquennal, -e, -aux [kɛ̃kenal, o] adj (plan) five-year (avant n); (élection) five-yearly.

quintal, -aux [kɛ̃tal, o] nm quintal.

quinte [kɛ̃t] nf (MUS) fifth. ► **quinte de toux** nf coughing fit.

quintuple [kɛ̃typl] nm & adj quintuple.

quinzaine [kɛ̃zɛn] nf 1. (nombre) fifteen (or so); **une ~ de** about fifteen. 2. (deux semaines) fortnight Br, two weeks (pl).

quinze [kɛ̃z] ◆ adj num fifteen; **dans ~ jours** in a fortnight Br, in two weeks. ◆ nm (chiffre) fifteen; voir aussi **six**.

quinzième [kɛ̃zjɛm] adj num, nm & nmf fifteenth; voir aussi **sixième**.

quiproquo [kiprɔko] nm misunderstanding.

quittance [kitɑ̃s] nf receipt.

quitte [kit] adj quits; **en être ~ pour qqch/pour faire qqch** to get off with sth/doing sth; **~ à faire qqch** even if it means doing sth.

quitter [kite] vt 1. (gén) to leave; **ne quittez pas!** (au téléphone) hold the line, please! 2. (fonctions) to give up. ► **se quitter** vp to part.

qui-vive [kiviv] nm inv: **être sur le ~** to be on the alert.

quoi [kwa] ◆ pron rel (après prép): **ce à ~ je me suis intéressé** what I was interested in; **après ~** after which; **avoir de ~ vivre** to have enough to live on; **avez-vous de ~ écrire?** have you got something to write with?; **merci – il n'y a pas de ~** thank you – don't mention it. ◆ pron interr what; **à ~ penses-tu?** what are you thinking about?; **je ne sais pas ~ dire** I don't know what to say; **à ~ bon?** what's the point ou use?; **~ de neuf?** what's new?; **décide-toi, ~!** fam make your mind up, will you?; **tu viens ou ~?** fam are you coming or what? ► **quoi que** loc conj (+ subjonctif) whatever; **~ qu'il arrive** whatever happens; **~ qu'il dise** whatever he says; **~ qu'il en soit** be that as it may.

quoique [kwakə] conj although, though.

quolibet [kɔlibɛ] nm sout jeer, taunt.

quota [k(w)ɔta] nm quota.

quotidien, -enne [kɔtidjɛ̃, ɛn] adj daily. ► **quotidien** nm 1. (routine) daily life; **au ~** on a day-to-day basis. 2. (journal) daily (newspaper).

quotient [kɔsjɑ̃] nm quotient; **~ intellectuel** intelligence quotient.

R

r¹, R [ɛr] *nm inv* (*lettre*) r, R.
r² *abr de* **rue**.
rabâchage [rabaʃaʒ] *nm fam* harping on (U).
rabâcher [rabaʃe] ◆ *vi fam* to harp on. ◆ *vt* to go over (and over).
rabais [rabɛ] *nm* reduction, discount; **au ~** *péj* (*artiste*) third-rate; (*travailler*) for a pittance.
rabaisser [rabese] *vt* 1. (*réduire*) to reduce; (*orgueil*) to humble. 2. (*personne*) to belittle. ▶ **se rabaisser** *vp* 1. (*se déprécier*) to belittle o.s. 2. (*s'humilier*): **se ~ à faire qqch** to demean o.s. by doing sthg.
rabat [raba] *nm* (*partie rabattue*) flap.
rabat-joie [rabaʒwa] ◆ *nm inv* killjoy. ◆ *adj inv*: **être ~** to be a killjoy.
rabattre [rabatr] *vt* 1. (*col*) to turn down. 2. (*siège*) to tilt back; (*couvercle*) to shut. 3. (*gibier*) to drive. ▶ **se rabattre** *vp* 1. (*siège*) to tilt back; (*couvercle*) to shut. 2. (*voiture, coureur*) to cut in. 3. (*se contenter*): **se ~ sur** to fall back on.
rabattu, -e [rabaty] *pp* → **rabattre**.
rabbin [rabɛ̃] *nm* rabbi.
râble [rabl] *nm* (*de lapin*) back; (CULIN) saddle.
râblé, -e [rable] *adj* stocky.
rabot [rabo] *nm* plane.
raboter [rabɔte] *vt* to plane.
rabougri, -e [rabugri] *adj* 1. (*plante*) stunted. 2. (*personne*) shrivelled, wizened.
rabrouer [rabrue] *vt* to snub.
raccommodage [rakɔmɔdaʒ] *nm* mending.
raccommoder [rakɔmɔde] *vt* 1. (*vêtement*) to mend. 2. *fam fig* (*personnes*) to reconcile, to get back together.
raccompagner [rakɔ̃paɲe] *vt* to see home, to take home.
raccord [rakɔr] *nm* 1. (*liaison*) join. 2. (*pièce*) connector, coupling. 3. (CIN) link.
raccordement [rakɔrdəmɑ̃] *nm* connection, linking.
raccorder [rakɔrde] *vt*: **~ qqch (à)** to connect sthg (to), to join sthg (to). ▶ **se raccorder** *vp*: **se ~ à** to be connected to; *fig* (*faits*) to tie in with.
raccourci [rakursi] *nm* shortcut.
raccourcir [rakursir] ◆ *vt* to shorten. ◆ *vi* to grow shorter.
raccrocher [rakrɔʃe] ◆ *vt* to hang back up. ◆ *vi* (*au téléphone*): **~ (au nez de qqn)** to hang up (on sb), to put the phone down (on sb). ▶ **se raccrocher** *vp*: **se ~ à** to cling to, to hang on to.
race [ras] *nf* (*humaine*) race; (*animale*) breed; **de ~** pedigree; (*cheval*) thoroughbred.
racé, -e [rase] *adj* 1. (*animal*) purebred. 2. (*voiture*) of distinction.
rachat [raʃa] *nm* 1. (*transaction*) repurchase. 2. *fig* (*de péchés*) atonement.
racheter [raʃte] *vt* 1. (*acheter en plus - gén*) to buy another; (*- pain, lait*) to buy some more. 2. (*acheter d'occasion*) to buy. 3. (*acheter après avoir vendu*) to buy back. 4. *fig* (*péché, faute*) to atone for; (*défaut, lapsus*) to make up for. 5. (*prisonnier*) to ransom. 6. (*honneur*) to redeem. 7. (COMM) (*société*) to buy out. ▶ **se racheter** *vp fig* to redeem o.s.
rachitique [raʃitik] *adj* suffering from rickets.
racial, -e, -aux [rasjal, o] *adj* racial.
racine [rasin] *nf* root; (*de nez*) base; **~ carrée/cubique** (MATHS) square/cube root.
racisme [rasism] *nm* racism.
raciste [rasist] *nmf & adj* racist.
racketter [rakɛte] *vt*: **~ qqn** to subject sb to a protection racket.
raclée [rakle] *nf fam* hiding, thrashing.
racler [rakle] *vt* to scrape. ▶ **se racler** *vp*: **se ~ la gorge** to clear one's throat.
raclette [raklɛt] *nf* (CULIN) *melted Swiss cheese served with jacket potatoes.*
racoler [rakɔle] *vt fam péj* (*suj: commerçant*) to tout for; (*suj: prostituée*) to solicit.
racoleur, -euse [rakɔlœr, øz] *adj fam péj* (*air, sourire*) come-hither; (*publicité*) strident.
racontar [rakɔ̃tar] *nm fam péj* piece of gossip. ▶ **racontars** *nmpl fam péj* tittletattle (U).
raconter [rakɔ̃te] *vt* 1. (*histoire*) to tell, to relate; (*événement*) to relate, to tell about; **~ qqch à qqn** to tell sb sthg, to relate sthg to sb. 2. (*ragot, mensonge*) to tell; **qu'est-ce que tu racontes?** what are you on about?
radar [radar] *nm* radar.
rade [rad] *nf* (natural) harbour.
radeau, -x [rado] *nm* (*embarcation*) raft.

radiateur [radjatœr] nm radiator.
radiation [radjasjɔ̃] nf 1. (PHYS) radiation. 2. (de liste, du barreau) striking off.
radical, -e, -aux [radikal, o] adj radical. ▶ **radical** nm 1. (gén) radical. 2. (LING) stem.
radier [radje] vt to strike off.
radieux, -euse [radjø, øz] adj radiant; (soleil) dazzling.
radin, -e [radɛ̃, in] fam péj ◆ adj stingy. ◆ nm, f skinflint.
radio [radjo] ◆ nf 1. (station, poste) radio; **à la ~** on the radio. 2. (MÉD): **passer une ~** to have an X-ray, to be X-rayed. ◆ nm radio operator.
radioactif, -ive [radjoaktif, iv] adj radioactive.
radioactivité [radjoaktivite] nf radioactivity.
radiodiffuser [radjodifyze] vt to broadcast.
radiographie [radjografi] nf 1. (technique) radiography. 2. (image) X-ray.
radiologue [radjolog], **radiologiste** [radjolɔʒist] nmf radiologist.
radioréveil, radio-réveil [radjorevɛj] nm radio alarm, clock radio.
radiotélévisé, -e [radjotelevize] adj broadcast on both radio and television.
radis [radi] nm radish.
radium [radjɔm] nm radium.
radoter [radɔte] vi to ramble.
radoucir [radusir] vt to soften. ▶ **se radoucir** vp (temps) to become milder; (personne) to calm down.
radoucissement [radusismɑ̃] nm 1. (d'attitude) softening. 2. (de température) rise; **un ~ du temps** a spell of milder weather.
rafale [rafal] nf 1. (de vent) gust; **en ~s** in gusts ou bursts. 2. (de coups de feu, d'applaudissements) burst.
raffermir [rafɛrmir] vt 1. (muscle) to firm up. 2. fig (pouvoir) to strengthen.
raffinage [rafinaʒ] nm refining.
raffiné, -e [rafine] adj refined.
raffinement [rafinmɑ̃] nm refinement.
raffiner [rafine] vt to refine.
raffinerie [rafinri] nf refinery.
raffoler [rafɔle] vi: **~ de qqn/qqch** to adore sb/sthg.
raffut [rafy] nm fam row, racket.
rafistoler [rafistɔle] vt fam to patch up.
rafle [rafl] nf raid.
rafler [rafle] vt to swipe.

rafraîchir [rafreʃir] vt 1. (nourriture, vin) to chill, to cool; (air) to cool. 2. (vêtement, appartement) to smarten up; fig (mémoire, idées) to refresh; (connaissances) to brush up. ▶ **se rafraîchir** vp 1. (se refroidir) to cool (down). 2. (en buvant) to have a drink.
rafraîchissant, -e [rafreʃisɑ̃, ɑ̃t] adj refreshing.
rafraîchissement [rafreʃismɑ̃] nm 1. (de climat) cooling. 2. (boisson) cold drink.
raft(ing) [raft(iŋ)] nm whitewater rafting.
ragaillardir [ragajardir] vt fam to buck up, to perk up.
rage [raʒ] nf 1. (fureur) rage; **faire ~** (tempête) to rage. 2. (maladie) rabies (U). ▶ **rage de dents** nf (raging) toothache.
rager [raʒe] vi fam to fume.
rageur, -euse [raʒœr, øz] adj bad-tempered.
raglan [raglɑ̃] adj inv raglan (avant n).
ragot [rago] nm (gén pl) fam (malicious) rumour, tittle-tattle.
ragoût [ragu] nm stew.
rai [rɛ] nm littéraire (de soleil) ray.
raï [raj] nm raï (type of Algerian popular music).
raid [rɛd] nm (AÉRON, BOURSE & MIL) raid; **~ aérien** air raid.
raide [rɛd] ◆ adj 1. (cheveux) straight. 2. (tendu - corde) taut; (- membre) stiff. 3. (pente) steep. 4. (personne - attitude physique) stiff, starchy; (- caractère) inflexible. 5. fam (histoire) hard to swallow, far-fetched. 6. fam (chanson) rude, blue. 7. fam (sans le sou) broke. ◆ adv 1. (abruptement) steeply. 2. loc: **tomber ~ mort** to fall down dead.
raideur [rɛdœr] nf 1. (de membre) stiffness. 2. (de personne - attitude physique) stiffness, starchiness; (- caractère) inflexibility.
raidir [rɛdir] vt (muscle) to tense; (corde) to tighten, to tauten. ▶ **se raidir** vp 1. (se contracter) to grow stiff, to stiffen. 2. fig (résister): **se ~ contre** to steel o.s. against.
raie [rɛ] nf 1. (rayure) stripe. 2. (dans les cheveux) parting Br, part Am. 3. (des fesses) crack. 4. (poisson) skate.
rail [raj] nm rail.
raillerie [rajri] nf sout mockery (U).
railleur, -euse [rajœr, øz] sout ◆ adj mocking. ◆ nm, f scoffer.
rainure [renyr] nf (longue) groove, channel; (courte) slot.

raisin [rɛzɛ̃] nm (fruit) grapes (pl); **~s secs** raisins.

raison [rɛzɔ̃] nf 1. (gén) reason; **à plus forte ~** all the more (so); **se faire une ~** to resign o.s.; **~ de plus pour faire qqch** all the more reason to do sthg. 2. (justesse, équité): **avoir ~** to be right; **avoir ~ de faire qqch** to be right to do sthg; **donner ~ à qqn** to prove sb right. ▶ **à raison de** loc prép at (the rate of). ▶ **en raison de** loc prép owing to, because of.

raisonnable [rɛzɔnabl] adj reasonable.

raisonnement [rɛzɔnmɑ̃] nm 1. (faculté) reason, power of reasoning. 2. (argumentation) reasoning, argument.

raisonner [rɛzɔne] ◆ vt (personne) to reason with. ◆ vi 1. (penser) to reason. 2. (discuter): **~ avec** to reason with.

rajeunir [raʒœnir] ◆ vt 1. (suj: couleur, vêtement): **~ qqn** to make sb look younger. 2. (suj: personne): **~ qqn de trois ans** to take three years off sb's age. 3. (vêtement, canapé) to renovate, to do up; (meubles) to modernize. 4. fig (parti) to rejuvenate. ◆ vi (personne) to look younger; (se sentir plus jeune) to feel younger ou rejuvenated.

rajouter [raʒute] vt to add; **en ~** fam to exaggerate.

rajuster [raʒyste], **réajuster** [reaʒyste] vt to adjust; (cravate) to straighten. ▶ **se rajuster** vp to straighten one's clothes.

râle [ral] nm moan; (de mort) death rattle.

ralenti, -e [ralɑ̃ti] adj slow. ▶ **ralenti** nm 1. (AUTOM) idling speed; **tourner au ~** (AUTOM) to idle; fig to tick over Br. 2. (CIN) slow motion.

ralentir [ralɑ̃tir] ◆ vt 1. (allure, expansion) to slow (down). 2. (rythme) to slacken. ◆ vi to slow down ou up.

ralentissement [ralɑ̃tismɑ̃] nm 1. (d'allure, d'expansion) slowing (down). 2. (de rythme) slackening. 3. (embouteillage) hold-up. 4. (PHYS) deceleration.

râler [rale] vi 1. (malade) to breathe with difficulty. 2. fam (grogner) to moan.

ralliement [ralimɑ̃] nm rallying.

rallier [ralje] vt 1. (poste, parti) to join. 2. (suffrages) to win. 3. (troupes) to rally. ▶ **se rallier** vp to rally; **se ~ à** (parti) to join; (cause) to rally to; (avis) to come round to.

rallonge [ralɔ̃ʒ] nf 1. (de table) leaf, extension. 2. (électrique) extension (lead).

rallonger [ralɔ̃ʒe] ◆ vt to lengthen. ◆ vi to lengthen, to get longer.

rallumer [ralyme] vt 1. (feu, cigarette) to relight; fig (querelle) to revive. 2. (appareil, lumière électrique) to switch (back) on again.

rallye [rali] nm rally.

ramadan [ramadɑ̃] nm Ramadan.

ramassage [ramasaʒ] nm collection; **~ scolaire** (action) pick-up (of school children); (service) school bus.

ramasser [ramase] vt 1. (récolter, réunir) to gather, to collect; fig (forces) to gather. 2. (prendre) to pick up. 3. fam (claque, rhume) to get. ▶ **se ramasser** vp 1. (se replier) to crouch. 2. fam (tomber, échouer) to come a cropper.

rambarde [rɑ̃bard] nf (guard) rail.

rame [ram] nf 1. (aviron) oar. 2. (RAIL) train. 3. (de papier) ream.

rameau, -x [ramo] nm branch.

ramener [ramne] vt 1. (remmener) to take back. 2. (rapporter, restaurer) to bring back. 3. (réduire): **~ qqch à qqch** to reduce sthg to sthg, to bring sthg down to sthg.

ramer [rame] vi (rameur) to row.

rameur, -euse [ramœr, øz] nm, f rower.

ramification [ramifikasjɔ̃] nf (division) branch.

ramolli, -e [ramɔli] adj soft; fig soft (in the head).

ramollir [ramɔlir] vt 1. (beurre) to soften. 2. fam fig (ardeurs) to cool. ▶ **se ramollir** vp 1. (beurre) to go soft, to soften. 2. fam fig (courage) to weaken.

ramoner [ramɔne] vt to sweep.

ramoneur [ramɔnœr] nm (chimney) sweep.

rampant, -e [rɑ̃pɑ̃, ɑ̃t] adj 1. (animal) crawling. 2. (plante) creeping.

rampe [rɑ̃p] nf 1. (d'escalier) banister, handrail. 2. (d'accès) ramp; **~ de lancement** launch pad. 3. (THÉÂTRE): **la ~** the footlights (pl).

ramper [rɑ̃pe] vi 1. (animal, soldat, enfant) to crawl. 2. (plante) to creep.

rance [rɑ̃s] adj (beurre) rancid.

rancir [rɑ̃sir] vi to go rancid.

rancœur [rɑ̃kœr] nf rancour, resentment.

rançon [rɑ̃sɔ̃] nf ransom; fig price.

rancune [rɑ̃kyn] nf rancour, spite; **garder** ou **tenir ~ à qqn de qqch** to hold a grudge against sb for sthg; **sans ~!** no hard feelings!

rancunier, -ère [rɑ̃kynje, ɛr] adj vindictive, spiteful.

randonnée [rɑ̃dɔne] *nf* **1.** (*promenade - à pied*) walk; (- *à cheval, à bicyclette*) ride; (- *en voiture*) drive. **2.** (*activité*): **la ~** (*à pied*) walking; (*à cheval*) riding.

randonneur, -euse [rɑ̃dɔnœr, øz] *nm, f* walker, rambler.

rang [rɑ̃] *nm* **1.** (*d'objets, de personnes*) row; **se mettre en ~ par deux** to line up in twos. **2.** (MIL) rank. **3.** (*position sociale*) station. **4.** Can (*peuplement rural*) rural district. **5.** Can (*chemin*) country road.

rangé, -e [rɑ̃ʒe] *adj* (*sérieux*) well-ordered, well-behaved.

rangée [rɑ̃ʒe] *nf* row.

rangement [rɑ̃ʒmɑ̃] *nm* (*mise en ordre*) tidying up; (*espace*) storage space.

ranger [rɑ̃ʒe] *vt* **1.** (*chambre*) to tidy. **2.** (*objets*) to arrange. **3.** (*voiture*) to park. **4.** *fig* (*livre, auteur*): **~ parmi** to rank among. ▶ **se ranger** *vp* **1.** (*élèves, soldats*) to line up. **2.** (*voiture*) to pull in. **3.** (*piéton*) to step aside. **4.** (*s'assagir*) to settle down.

ranimer [ranime] *vt* **1.** (*personne*) to revive, to bring round. **2.** (*feu*) to rekindle. **3.** *fig* (*sentiment*) to reawaken.

rapace [rapas] ◆ *nm* bird of prey. ◆ *adj* (*cupide*) rapacious, grasping.

rapatrier [rapatrije] *vt* to repatriate.

râpe [rap] *nf* **1.** (*de cuisine*) grater. **2.** Helv *fam* (*avare*) miser, skinflint.

râpé, -e [rape] *adj* **1.** (CULIN) grated. **2.** (*manteau*) threadbare. **3.** *fam* (*raté*): **c'est ~!** we've had it!

râper [rape] *vt* (CULIN) to grate.

râpeux, -euse [rapø, øz] *adj* **1.** (*tissu*) rough. **2.** (*vin*) harsh.

rapide [rapid] ◆ *adj* **1.** (*gén*) rapid. **2.** (*train, coureur*) fast. **3.** (*musique, intelligence*) lively, quick. ◆ *nm* **1.** (*train*) express (train). **2.** (*de fleuve*) rapid.

rapidement [rapidmɑ̃] *adv* rapidly.

rapidité [rapidite] *nf* rapidity.

rapiécer [rapjese] *vt* to patch.

rappel [rapɛl] *nm* **1.** (*de réservistes, d'ambassadeur*) recall. **2.** (*souvenir*) reminder; **~ à l'ordre** call to order. **3.** (*de paiement*) back pay. **4.** (*de vaccination*) booster. **5.** (*au spectacle*) curtain call, encore. **6.** (SPORT) abseiling; **descendre en ~ to** abseil (down).

rappeler [raple] *vt* **1.** (*gén*) to call back; **~ qqn à qqch** *fig* to bring sb back to sthg. **2.** (*faire penser à*): **~ qqch à qqn** to remind sb of sthg; **ça rappelle les vacances** it reminds me of my holidays. ▶ **se rappeler** *vp* to remember.

rapport [rapɔr] *nm* **1.** (*corrélation*) link, connection. **2.** (*compte-rendu*) report. **3.** (*profit*) return, yield. **4.** (MATHS) ratio. ▶ **rapports** *nmpl* **1.** (*relations*) relations. **2.** (*sexuels*): **~s (sexuels)** intercourse (*sg*). ▶ **par rapport à** *loc prép* (*comparativement à*) in comparison to, compared with; (*en ce qui concerne*) in relation to.

rapporter [rapɔrte] *vt* to bring back. ▶ **se rapporter** *vp*: **se ~ à** to refer ou relate to.

rapporteur, -euse [rapɔrtœr, øz] *nm, f* sneak, telltale. ▶ **rapporteur** *nm* **1.** (*de commission*) rapporteur. **2.** (GÉOM) protractor.

rapprochement [raprɔʃmɑ̃] *nm* **1.** (*d'objets, de personnes*) bringing together. **2.** *fig* (*entre événements*) link, connection. **3.** *fig* (*de pays, de parti*) rapprochement, coming together.

rapprocher [raprɔʃe] *vt* **1.** (*mettre plus près*): **~ qqn/qqch de qqch** to bring sb/sthg nearer to sthg, to bring sb/sthg closer to sthg. **2.** *fig* (*personnes*) to bring together. **3.** *fig* (*idée, texte*): **~ qqch (de)** to compare sthg (with). ▶ **se rapprocher** *vp* **1.** (*approcher*): **se ~ (de qqn/ qqch)** to approach (sb/sthg). **2.** (*se ressembler*): **se ~ de qqch** to be similar to sthg. **3.** (*se réconcilier*): **se ~ de qqn** to become closer to sb.

rapt [rapt] *nm* abduction.

raquette [rakɛt] *nf* **1.** (*de tennis, de squash*) racket; (*de ping-pong*) bat. **2.** (*à neige*) snowshoe.

rare [rar] *adj* **1.** (*peu commun, peu fréquent*) rare; **ses ~s amis** his few friends. **2.** (*peu dense*) sparse.

raréfier [rarefje] *vt* to rarefy. ▶ **se raréfier** *vp* to become rarefied.

rarement [rarmɑ̃] *adv* rarely.

rareté [rarte] *nf* **1.** (*de denrées, de nouvelles*) scarcity. **2.** (*de visites, de lettres*) infrequency. **3.** (*objet précieux*) rarity.

ras, -e [ra, raz] *adj* **1.** (*herbe, poil*) short. **2.** (*mesure*) full. ▶ **ras** *adv* short; **à ~ de** level with; **en avoir ~ le bol** *fam* to be fed up.

rasade [razad] *nf* glassful.

rasage [razaʒ] *nm* shaving.

rasant, -e [razɑ̃, ɑ̃t] *adj* **1.** (*lumière*) low-angled. **2.** *fam* (*film, discours*) boring.

raser [raze] *vt* **1.** (*barbe, cheveux*) to shave off. **2.** (*mur, sol*) to hug. **3.** (*village*) to raze. **4.** *fam* (*personne*) to bore. ▶ **se raser** *vp* (*avec rasoir*) to shave.

ras-le-bol [ralbɔl] *nm inv fam* discontent.

rasoir [razwar] ◆ *nm* razor; **~ électrique** electric shaver. ◆ *adj inv fam* boring.

rassasier [rasazje] *vt* to satisfy.

rassemblement [rasãbləmã] *nm* 1. (*d'objets*) collecting, gathering. 2. (*foule*) crowd, gathering. 3. (*union, parti*) union. 4. (MIL) parade; **~! fall in!**

rassembler [rasãble] *vt* 1. (*personnes, documents*) to collect, to gather. 2. (*courage*) to summon up; (*idées*) to collect. ► **se rassembler** *vp* 1. (*manifestants*) to assemble. 2. (*famille*) to get together.

rasseoir [raswar] ► **se rasseoir** *vp* to sit down again.

rasséréner [raserene] *vt sout* to calm down.

rassis, -e [rasi, iz] *adj* (*pain*) stale.

rassurant, -e [rasyrã, ãt] *adj* reassuring.

rassuré, -e [rasyre] *adj* confident, at ease.

rassurer [rasyre] *vt* to reassure.

rat [ra] ◆ *nm* rat; **petit ~** *fig* young ballet pupil. ◆ *adj fam* (*avare*) mean, stingy.

ratatiné, -e [ratatine] *adj* (*fruit, personne*) shrivelled.

rate [rat] *nf* 1. (*animal*) female rat. 2. (*organe*) spleen.

raté, -e [rate] *nm, f* (*personne*) failure. ► **raté** *nm* 1. (*gén pl*) (AUTOM) misfiring (U); **faire des ~s** to misfire. 2. *fig* (*difficulté*) problem.

râteau, -x [rato] *nm* rake.

rater [rate] ◆ *vt* 1. (*train, occasion*) to miss. 2. (*plat, affaire*) to make a mess of; (*examen*) to fail. ◆ *vi* to go wrong.

ratification [ratifikasjõ] *nf* ratification.

ratifier [ratifje] *vt* to ratify.

ration [rasjõ] *nf fig* share; **~ alimentaire** food intake.

rationaliser [rasjonalize] *vt* to rationalize.

rationnel, -elle [rasjonɛl] *adj* rational.

rationnement [rasjonmã] *nm* rationing.

rationner [rasjone] *vt* to ration.

ratissage [ratisaʒ] *nm* 1. (*de jardin*) raking. 2. (*de quartier*) search.

ratisser [ratise] *vt* 1. (*jardin*) to rake. 2. (*quartier*) to search, to comb.

raton [ratõ] *nm* (ZOOL) young rat. ► **raton laveur** *nm* racoon.

RATP (*abr de* **Régie autonome des transports parisiens**) *nf* Paris transport authority.

rattacher [rataʃe] *vt* 1. (*attacher de nou-*

veau) to do up, to fasten again. 2. (*relier*): **~ qqch à** to join sthg to; *fig* to link sthg with. 3. (*unir*): **~ qqn à** to bind sb to. ► **se rattacher** *vp*: **se ~ à** to be linked to.

rattrapage [ratrapaʒ] *nm* 1. (SCOL): **cours de ~** remedial class. 2. (*de salaires, prix*) adjustment.

rattraper [ratrape] *vt* 1. (*animal, prisonnier*) to recapture. 2. (*temps*): **~ le temps perdu** to make up for lost time. 3. (*rejoindre*) to catch up with. 4. (*erreur*) to correct. 5. (*personne qui tombe*) to catch. ► **se rattraper** *vp* 1. (*se retenir*): **se ~ à qqn/qqch** to catch hold of sb/sthg. 2. (*se faire pardonner*) to make amends.

rature [ratyr] *nf* alteration.

rauque [rok] *adj* hoarse, husky.

ravager [ravaʒe] *vt* (*gén*) to devastate, to ravage.

ravages [ravaʒ] *nmpl* (*de troupes*) ravages, devastation (*sg*); (*d'inondation*) devastation (*sg*); (*du temps*) ravages.

ravaler [ravale] *vt* 1. (*façade*) to clean, to restore. 2. (*personne*): **~ qqn au rang de** to lower sb to the level of. 3. *fig* (*larmes, colère*) to stifle, to hold back.

ravauder [ravode] *vt* to mend, to repair.

ravi, -e [ravi] *adj*: **~ (de)** delighted (with); **je suis ~ de l'avoir trouvé** I'm delighted that I found it, I'm delighted to have found it; **~ de vous connaître** pleased to meet you.

ravin [ravẽ] *nm* ravine, gully.

raviolis [ravjoli] *nmpl* ravioli (U).

ravir [ravir] *vt* 1. (*charmer*) to delight; **à ~** beautifully. 2. *littéraire* (*arracher*): **~ qqch à qqn** to rob sb of sthg.

raviser [ravize] ► **se raviser** *vp* to change one's mind.

ravissant, -e [ravisã, ãt] *adj* delightful, beautiful.

ravisseur, -euse [raviscer, øz] *nm, f* abductor.

ravitaillement [ravitajmã] *nm* (*en denrées*) resupplying; (*en carburant*) refuelling.

ravitailler [ravitaje] *vt* (*en denrées*) to resupply; (*en carburant*) to refuel.

raviver [ravive] *vt* 1. (*feu*) to rekindle. 2. (*couleurs*) to brighten up. 3. *fig* (*douleur*) to revive. 4. (*plaie*) to reopen.

rayé, -e [reje] *adj* 1. (*tissu*) striped. 2. (*disque, vitre*) scratched.

rayer [reje] *vt* 1. (*disque, vitre*) to scratch. 2. (*nom, mot*) to cross out.

rayon [rɛjɔ̃] *nm* 1. (*de lumière*) beam, ray; *fig* (*d'espoir*) ray. 2. (*gén pl*) (*radiation*) radiation (U); **~ laser** laser beam; **~s X** X-rays. 3. (*de roue*) spoke. 4. (GÉOM) radius; **dans un ~ de** *fig* within a radius of. 5. (*étagère*) shelf. 6. (*dans un magasin*) department.

rayonnant, -e [rɛjɔnɑ̃, ɑ̃t] *adj litt & fig* radiant.

rayonnement [rɛjɔnmɑ̃] *nm* 1. (*gén*) radiance; (*des arts*) influence. 2. (PHYS) radiation.

rayonner [rɛjɔne] *vi* 1. (*soleil*) to shine; **~ de joie** *fig* to radiate happiness. 2. (*culture*) to be influential. 3. (*avenues, lignes, chaleur*) to radiate. 4. (*touriste*) to tour around (*from a base*).

rayure [rɛjyr] *nf* 1. (*sur étoffe*) stripe. 2. (*sur disque, sur meuble*) scratch.

raz [ra] ► **raz de marée** *nm* tidal wave; (POLIT & *fig*) landslide.

razzia [razja] *nf fam* raid.

RDA (*abr de* **République démocratique allemande**) *nf* GDR.

RdC *abr de* **rez-de-chaussée**.

ré [re] *nm inv* (MUS) D; (*chanté*) re.

réacteur [reaktœr] *nm* (*d'avion*) jet engine; **~ nucléaire** nuclear reactor.

réaction [reaksjɔ̃] *nf:* **~ (à/contre)** reaction (to/against).

réactionnaire [reaksjɔnɛr] *nmf & adj péj* reactionary.

réactiver [reaktive] *vt* to reactivate.

réactualiser [reaktɥalize] *vt* (*moderniser*) to update, to bring up to date.

réadapter [readapte] *vt* to readapt; (*accidenté*) to rehabilitate.

réagir [reaʒir] *vi:* **~ (à/contre)** to react (to/against); **~ sur** to affect.

réajuster = **rajuster**.

réalisable [realizabl] *adj* 1. (*projet*) feasible. 2. (FIN) realizable.

réalisateur, -trice [realizatœr, tris] *nm, f* (CIN & TÉLÉ) director.

réalisation [realizasjɔ̃] *nf* 1. (*de projet*) carrying out. 2. (CIN & TÉLÉ) production.

réaliser [realize] *vt* 1. (*projet*) to carry out; (*ambitions, rêves*) to achieve, to realize. 2. (CIN & TÉLÉ) to produce. 3. (*s'apercevoir de*) to realize. ► **se réaliser** *vp* 1. (*ambition*) to be realized; (*rêve*) to come true. 2. (*personne*) to fulfil o.s.

réaliste [realist] ◆ *nmf* realist. ◆ *adj* 1. (*personne, objectif*) realistic. 2. (ART & LITTÉRATURE) realist.

réalité [realite] *nf* reality; **en ~** in reality.

réaménagement [reamenaʒmɑ̃] *nm*

(*de projet*) restructuring.

réamorcer [reamɔrse] *vt* to start up again.

réanimation [reanimasjɔ̃] *nf* resuscitation; **en ~** in intensive care.

réanimer [reanime] *vt* to resuscitate.

réapparaître [reaparɛtr] *vi* to reappear.

réassortiment [reasɔrtimɑ̃] *nm* restocking.

rébarbatif, -ive [rebarbatif, iv] *adj* (*travail*) daunting.

rebâtir [rəbatir] *vt* to rebuild.

rebattu, -e [rəbaty] *adj* overworked, hackneyed.

rebelle [rəbɛl] *adj* 1. (*personne*) rebellious; (*troupes*) rebel (*avant n*). 2. (*mèche, boucle*) unruly.

rebeller [rəbele] ► **se rebeller** *vp:* **~ (contre)** to rebel (against).

rébellion [rebeljɔ̃] *nf* rebellion.

rebiffer [rəbife] ► **se rebiffer** *vp fam:* **se ~ (contre)** to rebel (against).

reboiser [rəbwaze] *vt* to reafforest.

rebond [rəbɔ̃] *nm* bounce.

rebondir [rəbɔ̃dir] *vi* 1. (*objet*) to bounce; (*contre mur*) to rebound. 2. *fig* (*affaire*) to come to life (again).

rebondissement [rəbɔ̃dismɑ̃] *nm* (*d'affaire*) new development.

rebord [rəbɔr] *nm* (*de table*) edge; (*de fenêtre*) sill, ledge.

reboucher [rəbuʃe] *vt* (*bouteille*) to put the cork back in, to recork; (*trou*) to fill in.

rebours [rəbur] ► **à rebours** *loc adv* the wrong way.

reboutonner [rəbutɔne] *vt* to rebutton.

rebrousse-poil [rəbruspwal] ► **à rebrousse-poil** *loc adv* the wrong way; **prendre qqn à ~** *fig* to rub sb up the wrong way.

rebrousser [rəbruse] *vt* to brush back; **~ chemin** *fig* to retrace one's steps.

rébus [rebys] *nm* rebus.

rebut [rəby] *nm* scrap; **mettre qqch au ~** to get rid of sthg, to scrap sthg.

rebuter [rəbyte] *vt* (*suj: travail*) to dishearten.

récalcitrant, -e [rekalsitrɑ̃, ɑ̃t] *adj* recalcitrant, stubborn.

recaler [rəkale] *vt fam* to fail.

récapitulatif, -ive [rekapitylatif, iv] *adj* summary (*avant n*). ► **récapitulatif** *nm* summary.

récapituler [rekapityle] *vt* to recapitulate, to recap.

recel [rəsɛl] *nm* (*action*) receiving *ou*

handling stolen goods; (*délit*) possession of stolen goods.

receleur, -euse [rəsəlœr, øz] *nm, f* receiver (*of stolen goods*).

récemment [resamã] *adv* recently.

recensement [rəsãsmã] *nm* 1. (*de population*) census. 2. (*d'objets*) inventory.

recenser [rəsãse] *vt* 1. (*population*) to take a census of. 2. (*objets*) to take an inventory of.

récent, -e [resã, ãt] *adj* recent.

recentrer [rəsãtre] *vt* to refocus.

récépissé [resepise] *nm* receipt.

récepteur, -trice [reseptœr, tris] *adj* receiving. ▶ *nm* receiver.

réception [resepsjõ] *nf* 1. (*gén*) reception; **donner une ~** to hold a reception. 2. (*de marchandises*) receipt. 3. (*bureau*) reception (desk). 4. (SPORT) (*de sauteur, skieur*) landing; (*du ballon - avec la main*) catch; (*- avec le pied*): **bonne ~ de X qui ...** X traps the ball and ...

réceptionner [resepsjone] *vt* 1. (*marchandises*) to take delivery of. 2. (SPORT - *avec la main*) to catch; (*- avec le pied*) to control.

réceptionniste [resepsjonist] *nmf* receptionist.

récession [resesjõ] *nf* recession.

recette [rəset] *nf* 1. (COMM) takings (*pl*). 2. (CULIN) recipe; *fig* (*méthode*) recipe, formula.

recevable [rəsəvabl] *adj* 1. (*excuse, offre*) acceptable. 2. (JUR) admissible.

receveur, -euse [rəsəvœr, øz] *nm, f* 1. (ADMIN): **~ des impôts** tax collector; **~ des postes** postmaster (*f* postmistress). 2. (*de bus*) conductor (*f* conductress). 3. (*de greffe*) recipient.

recevoir [rəsəvwar] *vt* 1. (*gén*) to receive. 2. (*coup*) to get, to receive. 3. (*invités*) to entertain; (*client*) to see. 4. (SCOL & UNIV): **être reçu à un examen** to pass an exam. ▶ **se recevoir** *vp* (SPORT) to land.

rechange [rəʃãʒ] ▶ **de rechange** *loc adj* spare; *fig* alternative.

réchapper [reʃape] *vi*: **~ de** to survive.

recharge [rəʃarʒ] *nf* (*cartouche*) refill.

rechargeable [rəʃarʒabl] *adj* (*batterie*) rechargeable; (*briquet*) refillable.

réchaud [reʃo] *nm* (*portable*) stove.

réchauffé, -e [reʃofe] *adj* (*plat*) reheated; *fig* rehashed.

réchauffement [reʃofmã] *nm* warming (up).

réchauffer [reʃofe] *vt* 1. (*nourriture*) to reheat. 2. (*personne*) to warm up. ▶ **se**

réchauffer *vp* to warm up.

rêche [reʃ] *adj* rough.

recherche [rəʃɛrʃ] *nf* 1. (*quête &* INFORM) search; **être à la ~ de** to be in search of; **faire ou effectuer des ~s** to make inquiries. 2. (SCIENCE) research; **faire de la ~** to do research. 3. (*raffinement*) elegance.

recherché, -e [rəʃɛrʃe] *adj* 1. (*ouvrage*) sought-after. 2. (*raffiné - vocabulaire*) refined; (*- mets*) exquisite.

rechercher [rəʃɛrʃe] *vt* 1. (*objet, personne*) to search for, to hunt for. 2. (*compagnie*) to seek out.

rechigner [rəʃiɲe] *vi*: **~ à** to balk at.

rechute [rəʃyt] *nf* relapse.

récidive [residiv] *nf* 1. (JUR) repeat offence. 2. (MÉD) recurrence.

récidiver [residive] *vi* 1. (JUR) to commit another offence. 2. (MÉD) to recur.

récidiviste [residivist] *nmf* repeat ou persistent offender.

récif [resif] *nm* reef.

récipient [resipjã] *nm* container.

réciproque [resiprɔk] ◆ *adj* reciprocal. ◆ *nf*: **la ~** the reverse.

réciproquement [resiprɔkmã] *adv* mutually; **et ~** and vice versa.

récit [resi] *nm* story.

récital, -als [resital] *nm* recital.

récitation [resitasjõ] *nf* recitation.

réciter [resite] *vt* to recite.

réclamation [reklamasjõ] *nf* complaint; **faire/déposer une ~** to make/lodge a complaint.

réclame [reklam] *nf* 1. (*annonce*) advert, advertisement. 2. (*publicité*): **la ~** advertising. 3. (*promotion*): **en ~** on special offer.

réclamer [reklame] *vt* 1. (*demander*) to ask for, to request; (*avec insistance*) to demand. 2. (*nécessiter*) to require, to demand.

reclasser [rəklase] *vt* 1. (*dossiers*) to refile. 2. (ADMIN) to regrade.

réclusion [reklyzjõ] *nf* imprisonment; **~ à perpétuité** life imprisonment.

recoiffer [rəkwafe] ▶ **se recoiffer** *vp* to do one's hair again.

recoin [rəkwẽ] *nm* nook.

recoller [rəkɔle] *vt* (*objet brisé*) to stick back together.

récolte [rekɔlt] *nf* 1. (AGRIC - *action*) harvesting (U), gathering (U); (*- produit*) harvest, crop. 2. *fig* collection.

récolter [rekɔlte] *vt* to harvest; *fig* to collect.

recommandable [rəkɔmãdabl] *adj*

commendable; **peu ~** undesirable.

recommandation [rəkɔmɑ̃dasjɔ̃] *nf* recommendation.

recommandé, -e [rəkɔmɑ̃de] *adj* 1. (*envoi*) registered; **envoyer qqch en ~** to send sthg by registered post Br ou mail Am. 2. (*conseillé*) advisable.

recommander [rəkɔmɑ̃de] *vt* to recommend; **~ à qqn de faire qqch** to advise sb to do sthg; **~ qqn à qqn** to recommend sb to sb.

recommencer [rəkɔmɑ̃se] ♦ *vt* (*travail*) to start ou begin again; (*erreur*) to make again; **~ à faire qqch** to start ou begin doing sthg again. ♦ *vi* to start ou begin again; **ne recommence pas!** don't do that again!

récompense [rekɔ̃pɑ̃s] *nf* reward.

récompenser [rekɔ̃pɑ̃se] *vt* to reward.

recompter [rəkɔ̃te] *vt* to recount.

réconciliation [rekɔ̃siljasjɔ̃] *nf* reconciliation.

réconcilier [rekɔ̃silje] *vt* to reconcile.

reconduction [rəkɔ̃dyksjɔ̃] *nf* renewal.

reconduire [rəkɔ̃dɥir] *vt* 1. (*personne*) to accompany, to take. 2. (*politique, bail*) to renew.

reconduit, -e [rəkɔ̃dɥi, it] *pp* → **reconduire**.

réconfort [rekɔ̃fɔr] *nm* comfort.

réconfortant, -e [rekɔ̃fɔrtɑ̃, ɑ̃t] *adj* comforting.

réconforter [rekɔ̃fɔrte] *vt* to comfort.

reconnaissable [rəkɔnɛsabl] *adj* recognizable.

reconnaissance [rəkɔnɛsɑ̃s] *nf* 1. (*gén*) recognition. 2. (MIL) reconnaissance; **aller/partir en ~** to go out on reconnaissance. 3. (*gratitude*) gratitude; **exprimer sa ~ à qqn** to show ou express one's gratitude to sb.

reconnaissant, -e [rəkɔnɛsɑ̃, ɑ̃t] *adj* grateful; **je vous serais ~ de m'aider** I would be grateful if you would help me.

reconnaître [rəkɔnɛtr] *vt* 1. (*gén*) to recognize. 2. (*erreur*) to admit, to acknowledge. 3. (MIL) to reconnoitre.

reconnu, -e [rəkɔny] ♦ *pp* → **reconnaître**. ♦ *adj* well-known.

reconquérir [rəkɔ̃kerir] *vt* to reconquer.

reconquis, -e [rəkɔ̃ki, iz] *pp* → **reconquérir**.

reconsidérer [rəkɔ̃sidere] *vt* to reconsider.

reconstituant, -e [rəkɔ̃stitɥɑ̃, ɑ̃t] *adj*

invigorating. ▶ **reconstituant** *nm* tonic.

reconstituer [rəkɔ̃stitɥe] *vt* 1. (*puzzle*) to put together. 2. (*crime, délit*) to reconstruct.

reconstitution [rəkɔ̃stitysjɔ̃] *nf* 1. (*de puzzle*) putting together. 2. (*de crime, délit*) reconstruction.

reconstruction [rəkɔ̃stryksjɔ̃] *nf* reconstruction, rebuilding.

reconstruire [rəkɔ̃strɥir] *vt* to reconstruct, to rebuild.

reconstruit, -e [rəkɔ̃strɥi, it] *pp* → **reconstruire**.

reconversion [rəkɔ̃vɛrsjɔ̃] *nf* 1. (*d'employé*) redeployment. 2. (*d'usine, de société*) conversion; **~ économique/technique** economic/technical restructuring.

reconvertir [rəkɔ̃vɛrtir] *vt* 1. (*employé*) to redeploy. 2. (*économie*) to restructure. ▶ **se reconvertir** *vp*: **se ~ dans** to move into.

recopier [rəkɔpje] *vt* to copy out.

record [rəkɔr] ♦ *nm* record; **détenir/améliorer/battre un ~** to hold/improve/beat a record; **~ mondial** ou **du monde** world record. ♦ *adj inv* record (*avant n*).

recoucher [rəkuʃe] *vt* to put back to bed. ▶ **se recoucher** *vp* to go back to bed.

recoudre [rəkudr] *vt* to sew (up) again.

recoupement [rəkupmɑ̃] *nm* cross-check; **par ~** by cross-checking.

recouper [rəkupe] ▶ **se recouper** *vp* 1. (*lignes*) to intersect. 2. (*témoignages*) to match up.

recourir [rəkurir] *vi*: **~ à** (*médecin, agence*) to turn to; (*force, mensonge*) to resort to.

recours [rəkur] *nm* 1. (*emploi*): **avoir ~ à** (*médecin, agence*) to turn to; (*force, mensonge*) to resort to, to have recourse to. 2. (*solution*) solution, way out; **en dernier ~** as a last resort. 3. (JUR) action; **~ en cassation** appeal.

recouvert, -e [rəkuvɛr, ɛrt] *pp* → **recouvrir**.

recouvrir [rəkuvrir] *vt* 1. (*gén*) to cover; (*fauteuil*) to re-cover. 2. (*personne*) to cover (up). ▶ **se recouvrir** *vp* 1. (*tuiles*) to overlap. 2. (*surface*): **se ~ (de)** to be covered (with).

recracher [rəkraʃe] *vt* to spit out.

récréatif, -ive [rekreatif, iv] *adj* entertaining.

récréation [rekreasjɔ̃] *nf* 1. (*détente*)

relaxation, recreation. **2.** (SCOL) break.

recréer [rəkree] *vt* to recreate.

récrimination [rekriminasjɔ̃] *nf* complaint.

récrire [rekrir], **réécrire** [reekrir] *vt* to rewrite.

recroqueviller [rəkrɔkvije] ▸ **se recroqueviller** *vp* to curl up.

recru, -e [rəkry] *adj*: ~ **de fatigue** *littéraire* exhausted. ▸ **recrue** *nf* recruit.

recrudescence [rəkrydɛsɑ̃s] *nf* renewed outbreak.

recrutement [rəkrytmɑ̃] *nm* recruitment.

recruter [rəkryte] *vt* to recruit.

rectal, -e, -aux [rɛktal, o] *adj* rectal.

rectangle [rɛktɑ̃gl] *nm* rectangle.

rectangulaire [rɛktɑ̃gylɛr] *adj* rectangular.

recteur [rɛktœr] *nm* (SCOL) *chief administrative officer of an education authority,* ≃ (Chief) Education Officer Br.

rectificatif, -ive [rɛktifikatif, iv] *adj* correcting. ▸ **rectificatif** *nm* correction.

rectification [rɛktifikasjɔ̃] *nf* **1.** (*correction*) correction. **2.** (*de tir*) adjustment.

rectifier [rɛktifje] *vt* **1.** (*tir*) to adjust. **2.** (*erreur*) to rectify, to correct.

rectiligne [rɛktilɪɲ] *adj* rectilinear.

recto [rɛkto] *nm* right side; ~ **verso** on both sides.

rectorat [rɛktɔra] *nm* (SCOL) *offices of the education authority,* ≃ Education Offices Br.

reçu, -e [rəsy] *pp* → **recevoir.** ▸ **reçu** *nm* receipt.

recueil [rəkœj] *nm* collection.

recueillement [rəkœjmɑ̃] *nm* meditation.

recueillir [rəkœjir] *vt* **1.** (*fonds*) to collect. **2.** (*suffrages*) to win. **3.** (*enfant*) to take in. ▸ **se recueillir** *vp* to meditate.

recul [rəkyl] *nm* **1.** (*mouvement arrière*) step backwards; (MIL) retreat. **2.** (*d'arme à feu*) recoil. **3.** (*de civilisation*) decline; (*d'inflation, de chômage*): ~ **(de)** downturn (in). **4.** (*retrait*): **avec du** ~ with hindsight.

reculé, -e [rəkyle] *adj* distant.

reculer [rəkyle] ◆ *vt* **1.** (*voiture*) to back up. **2.** (*date*) to put back, to postpone. ◆ *vi* **1.** (*aller en arrière*) to move backwards; (*voiture*) to reverse. **2.** (*renoncer*) to retreat; **ne** ~ **devant rien** *fig* to stop at nothing. **3.** (*maladie, pauvreté*) to be brought under control.

reculons [rəkylɔ̃] ▸ **à reculons** *adv* backwards.

récupération [rekyperasjɔ̃] *nf* (*de déchets*) salvage.

récupérer [rekypere] ◆ *vt* **1.** (*objet*) to get back. **2.** (*déchets*) to salvage. **3.** (*idée*) to pick up. **4.** (*journée*) to make up. ◆ *vi* to recover, to recuperate.

récurer [rekyre] *vt* to scour.

récuser [rekyze] *vt* **1.** (JUR) to challenge. **2.** *sout* (*refuser*) to reject.

recyclage [rəsiklaʒ] *nm* **1.** (*d'employé*) retraining. **2.** (*de déchets*) recycling.

recycler [rəsikle] *vt* **1.** (*employé*) to retrain. **2.** (*déchets*) to recycle. ▸ **se recycler** *vp* (*employé*) to retrain.

rédacteur, -trice [redaktœr, tris] *nm, f* (*de journal*) subeditor; (*d'ouvrage de référence*) editor; ~ **en chef** editor-in-chief.

rédaction [redaksjɔ̃] *nf* **1.** (*de texte*) editing. **2.** (SCOL) essay. **3.** (*personnel*) editorial staff.

redécouvrir [rədekuvrir] *vt* to rediscover.

redéfinir [rədefinir] *vt* to redefine.

redéfinition [rədefinisjɔ̃] *nf* redefinition.

redemander [rədəmɑ̃de] *vt* to ask again for.

rédemption [redɑ̃psjɔ̃] *nf* redemption.

redescendre [rədesɑ̃dr] ◆ *vt* (*aux: avoir*) **1.** (*escalier*) to go/come down again. **2.** (*objet - d'une étagère*) to take down again. ◆ *vi* (*aux: être*) to go/come down again.

redevable [rədəvabl] *adj*: **être** ~ **de 10 francs à qqn** to owe sb 10 francs; **être** ~ **à qqn de qqch** (*service*) to be indebted to sb for sthg.

redevance [rədəvɑ̃s] *nf* (*de radio, télévision*) licence fee; (*téléphonique*) rental (fee).

redevenir [rədəvnir] *vi* to become again.

rédhibitoire [redibitwar] *adj* (*défaut*) crippling; (*prix*) prohibitive.

rediffusion [rədifyzjɔ̃] *nf* repeat.

rédiger [rediʒe] *vt* to write.

redire [rədir] *vt* to repeat; **avoir** OU **trouver à** ~ **à qqch** *fig* to find fault with sthg.

redistribuer [rədistribɥe] *vt* to redistribute.

redit, -e [rədi, it] *pp* → **redire.**

redite [rədit] *nf* repetition.

redondance [rədɔ̃dɑ̃s] *nf* redundancy.

redonner [rədɔne] *vt* to give back; (*confiance, forces*) to restore.

redoublant, -e [rədublɑ̃, ɑ̃t] nm, f pupil who is repeating a year.

redoubler [rəduble] ♦ vt 1. (syllabe) to reduplicate. 2. (efforts) to intensify. 3. (SCOL) to repeat. ♦ vi to intensify.

redoutable [rədutabl] adj formidable.

redouter [rədute] vt to fear.

redoux [rədu] nm thaw.

redressement [rədrɛsmɑ̃] nm 1. (de pays, d'économie) recovery. 2. (JUR): ~ fiscal payment of back taxes.

redresser [rədrɛse] ♦ vt 1. (poteau, arbre) to put ou set upright; ~ la tête to raise one's head; fig to hold up one's head. 2. (situation) to set right. ♦ vi (AUTOM) to straighten up. ▶ se redresser vp 1. (personne) to stand ou sit straight. 2. (pays) to recover.

réducteur, -trice [redyktœr, tris] adj (limitatif) simplistic.

réduction [redyksjɔ̃] nf 1. (gén) reduction. 2. (MÉD) setting.

réduire [redɥir] ♦ vt 1. (gén) to reduce; ~ en to reduce to. 2. (MÉD) to set. 3. Helv (ranger) to put away. ♦ vi (CULIN) to reduce.

réduit, -e [redɥi, it] ♦ pp → réduire. ♦ adj reduced. ▶ réduit nm (local) small room.

rééchelonner [reeʃlɔne] vt to reschedule.

réécrire = récrire.

réédition [reedisjɔ̃] nf new edition.

rééducation [reedykasjɔ̃] nf 1. (de membre) re-education. 2. (de délinquant, malade) rehabilitation.

réel, -elle [reɛl] adj real.

réélection [reelɛksjɔ̃] nf re-election.

réellement [reɛlmɑ̃] adv really.

rééquilibrer [reekilibre] vt to balance (again).

réessayer [reeseje] vt to try again.

réévaluer [reevalɥe] vt to revalue.

réexaminer [reɛgzamine] vt to re-examine.

réexpédier [reɛkspedje] vt to send back.

réf. (abr de référence) ref.

refaire [rəfɛr] vt 1. (faire de nouveau - travail, devoir) to do again; (- voyage) to make again. 2. (mur, toit) to repair.

refait, -e [rəfɛ, ɛt] pp → refaire.

réfection [refɛksjɔ̃] nf repair.

réfectoire [refɛktwar] nm refectory.

référence [referɑ̃s] nf reference; faire ~ à to refer to.

référendum [referɛ̃dɔm] nm referendum.

référer [refere] vi: en ~ à qqn to refer the matter to sb.

refermer [rəfɛrme] vt to close ou shut again.

réfléchi, -e [refleʃi] adj 1. (action) considered; c'est tout ~ I've made up my mind, I've decided. 2. (personne) thoughtful. 3. (GRAM) reflexive.

réfléchir [refleʃir] ♦ vt 1. (refléter) to reflect. 2. (penser): ~ que to think ou reflect that. ♦ vi to think, to reflect; ~ à ou sur qqch to think about sthg.

reflet [rəflɛ] nm 1. (image) reflection. 2. (de lumière) glint.

refléter [rəflete] vt to reflect. ▶ se refléter vp 1. (se réfléchir) to be reflected. 2. (transparaître) to be mirrored.

refleurir [rəflœrir] vi (fleurir à nouveau) to flower again.

réflexe [reflɛks] ♦ nm reflex. ♦ adj reflex (avant n).

réflexion [reflɛksjɔ̃] nf 1. (de lumière, d'ondes) reflection. 2. (pensée) reflection, thought. 3. (remarque) remark.

refluer [rəflye] vi 1. (liquide) to flow back. 2. (foule) to flow back; (avec violence) to surge back.

reflux [rəfly] nm 1. (d'eau) ebb. 2. (de personnes) backward surge.

refonte [rəfɔ̃t] nf 1. (de métal) remelting. 2. (d'ouvrage) recasting. 3. (d'institution, de système) overhaul, reshaping.

reforestation [rəfɔrɛstasjɔ̃] nf reforestation.

réformateur, -trice [reformatœr, tris] ♦ adj reforming. ♦ nm, f 1. (personne) reformer. 2. (RELIG) Reformer.

réforme [reform] nf reform.

reformer [rəforme] vt to re-form.

réformer [reforme] vt 1. (améliorer) to reform, to improve. 2. (MIL) to invalid out. 3. (matériel) to scrap.

réformiste [reformist] adj & nmf reformist.

refoulé, -e [rəfule] ♦ adj repressed, frustrated. ♦ nm, f repressed person.

refouler [rəfule] vt 1. (personnes) to repel, to repulse. 2. (PSYCHOL) to repress.

réfractaire [refrakter] ♦ adj 1. (rebelle) insubordinate; ~ à resistant to. 2. (matière) refractory. ♦ nmf insubordinate.

refrain [rəfrɛ̃] nm (MUS) refrain, chorus; c'est toujours le même ~ fam fig it's always the same old story.

refréner [rəfrene] *vt* to check, to hold back.

réfrigérant, -e [refriʒerɑ̃, ɑ̃t] *adj* 1. (*liquide*) refrigerating, refrigerant. 2. *fam* (*accueil*) icy.

réfrigérateur [refriʒeratœr] *nm* refrigerator.

refroidir [rəfrwadir] ◆ *vt* 1. (*plat*) to cool. 2. (*décourager*) to discourage. ◆ *vi* to cool.

refroidissement [rəfrwadismɑ̃] *nm* 1. (*de température*) drop, cooling. 2. (*grippe*) chill.

refuge [rəfyʒ] *nm* 1. (*abri*) refuge. 2. (*de montagne*) hut.

réfugié, -e [refyʒje] *nm, f* refugee.

réfugier [refyʒje] ▶ **se réfugier** *vp* to take refuge.

refus [rəfy] *nm inv* refusal; **ce n'est pas de ~** *fam* I wouldn't say no.

refuser [rəfyze] *vt* 1. (*repousser*) to refuse; **~ de faire qqch** to refuse to do sthg. 2. (*contester*): **~ qqch à qqn** to deny sb sthg. 3. (*clients, spectateurs*) to turn away. 4. (*candidat*): **être refusé** to fail. ▶ **se refuser** *vp*: **se ~ à faire qqch** to refuse to do sthg.

réfuter [refyte] *vt* to refute.

regagner [rəgaɲe] *vt* 1. (*reprendre*) to regain, to win back. 2. (*revenir à*) to get back to.

regain [rəgɛ̃] *nm* (*retour*): **un ~ de** a revival of, a renewal of; **un ~ de vie** a new lease of life.

régal, -als [regal] *nm* treat, delight.

régaler [regale] *vt* to treat; **c'est moi qui régale!** it's my treat! ▶ **se régaler** *vp*: **je me régale** (*nourriture*) I'm thoroughly enjoying it; (*activité*) I'm having the time of my life.

regard [rəgar] *nm* look.

regardant, -e [rəgardɑ̃, ɑ̃t] *adj* 1. *fam* (*économe*) mean. 2. (*minutieux*): **être très/ peu ~ sur qqch** to be very/not very particular about sthg.

regarder [rəgarde] ◆ *vt* 1. (*observer, examiner, consulter*) to look at; (*télévision, spectacle*) to watch; **~ qqn faire qqch** to watch sb doing sthg; **~ les trains passer** to watch the trains go by. 2. (*considérer*) to consider, to regard; **~ qqn/qqch comme** to regard sb/sthg as, to consider sb/sthg as. 3. (*concerner*) to concern; **cela ne te regarde pas** it's none of your business. ◆ *vi* 1. (*observer, examiner*) to look. 2. (*faire attention*): **sans ~ à la dépense** regardless of the expense; **y ~ à deux fois** to think twice about it.

régate [regat] *nf* (*gén pl*) regatta.

régénérer [reʒenere] *vt* to regenerate. ▶ **se régénérer** *vp* to regenerate.

régent, -e [reʒɑ̃, ɑ̃t] *nm, f* regent.

régenter [reʒɑ̃te] *vt*: **vouloir tout ~** *péj* to want to be the boss.

reggae [rege] *nm & adj inv* reggae.

régie [reʒi] *nf* 1. (*entreprise*) state-controlled company. 2. (RADIO & TÉLÉ) (*pièce*) control room; (CIN, THÉÂTRE & TÉLÉ) (*équipe*) production team.

regimber [rəʒɛ̃be] *vi* to balk.

régime [reʒim] *nm* 1. (*politique*) regime. 2. (*administratif*) system; **~ carcéral** prison regime. 3. (*alimentaire*) diet; **se mettre au/suivre un ~** to go on/to be on a diet. 4. (*de moteur*) speed. 5. (*de fleuve, des pluies*) cycle. 6. (*de bananes, dattes*) bunch.

régiment [reʒimɑ̃] *nm* 1. (MIL) regiment. 2. *fam* (*grande quantité*): **un ~ de** masses of, loads of.

région [reʒjɔ̃] *nf* region.

régional, -e, -aux [reʒjɔnal, o] *adj* regional.

régir [reʒir] *vt* to govern.

régisseur [reʒisœr] *nm* 1. (*intendant*) steward. 2. (*de théâtre*) stage manager.

registre [rəʒistr] *nm* (*gén*) register; **~ de comptabilité** ledger.

réglable [reglabl] *adj* 1. (*adaptable*) adjustable. 2. (*payable*) payable.

réglage [reglaʒ] *nm* adjustment, setting.

règle [regl] *nf* 1. (*instrument*) ruler. 2. (*principe, loi*) rule; **je suis en ~** my papers are in order. ▶ **en règle générale** *loc adv* as a general rule. ▶ **règles** *nfpl* (*menstruation*) period (*sg*).

réglé, -e [regle] *adj* (*organisé*) regular, well-ordered.

règlement [reglomɑ̃] *nm* 1. (*résolution*) settling; **~ de comptes** *fig* settling of scores. 2. (*règle*) regulation. 3. (*paiement*) settlement.

réglementaire [reglomɑ̃ter] *adj* 1. (*régulier*) statutory. 2. (*imposé*) regulation (*avant n*).

réglementation [reglomɑ̃tasjɔ̃] *nf* 1. (*action*) regulation. 2. (*ensemble de règles*) regulations (*pl*), rules (*pl*).

régler [regle] *vt* 1. (*affaire, conflit*) to settle, to sort out. 2. (*appareil*) to adjust. 3. (*payer - note*) to settle, to pay; (- *commerçant*) to pay.

réglisse [reglis] *nf* liquorice.

règne [rɛɲ] *nm* 1. (*de souverain*) reign; **sous le ~ de** in the reign of. 2. (*pouvoir*) rule. **3.** (BIOL) kingdom.

régner [reɲe] *vi* **1.** (*souverain*) to rule, to reign. **2.** (*silence*) to reign.

regonfler [rəgɔ̃fle] *vt* **1.** (*pneu, ballon*) to blow up again, to reinflate. **2.** *fam* (*personne*) to cheer up.

regorger [rəgɔrʒe] *vi*: **~ de** to be abundant in.

régresser [regrese] *vi* **1.** (*sentiment, douleur*) to diminish. **2.** (*personne*) to regress.

régression [regresjɔ̃] *nf* **1.** (*recul*) decline. **2.** (PSYCHOL) regression.

regret [rəgrɛ] *nm*: **~ (de)** regret (for); **à ~** with regret; **sans ~** with no regrets.

regrettable [rəgrɛtabl] *adj* regrettable.

regretter [rəgrɛte] ◆ *vt* **1.** (*époque*) to miss, to regret; (*personne*) to miss. **2.** (*faute*) to regret; **~ d'avoir fait qqch** to regret having done sthg. **3.** (*déplorer*): **~ que** + *subjonctif*) to be sorry *ou* to regret that. ◆ *vi* to be sorry.

regroupement [rəgrupmɑ̃] *nm* **1.** (*action*) bringing together. **2.** (*groupe*) group, assembly.

regrouper [rəgrupe] *vt* **1.** (*grouper à nouveau*) to regroup, to reassemble. **2.** (*réunir*) to group together. ► **se regrouper** *vp* to gather, to assemble.

régulariser [regylarize] *vt* **1.** (*documents*) to sort out, to put in order; (*situation*) to straighten out. **2.** (*circulation, fonctionnement*) to regulate.

régularité [regylarite] *nf* **1.** (*gén*) regularity. **2.** (*de travail, résultats*) consistency.

régulateur, -trice [regylatœr, tris] *adj* regulating.

régulation [regylasjɔ̃] *nf* (*contrôle*) control, regulation.

régulier, -ère [regylje, ɛr] *adj* **1.** (*gén*) regular. **2.** (*uniforme, constant*) steady, regular. **3.** (*travail, résultats*) consistent. **4.** (*légal*) legal; **être en situation régulière** to have all the legally required documents.

régulièrement [regyljɛrmɑ̃] *adv* **1.** (*gén*) regularly. **2.** (*uniformément*) steadily, regularly; (*étalé, façonné*) evenly.

réhabilitation [reabilitasjɔ̃] *nf* rehabilitation.

réhabiliter [reabilite] *vt* **1.** (*accusé*) to rehabilitate, to clear; *fig* (*racheter*) to restore to favour. **2.** (*rénover*) to restore.

rehausser [rəose] *vt* **1.** (*surélever*) to heighten. **2.** *fig* (*mettre en valeur*) to enhance.

rein [rɛ̃] *nm* kidney. ► **reins** *nmpl* small of the back (*sg*); **avoir mal aux ~s** to have backache.

réincarnation [reɛ̃karnasjɔ̃] *nf* reincarnation.

reine [rɛn] *nf* queen.

réinsertion [reɛ̃sɛrsjɔ̃] *nf* (*de délinquant*) rehabilitation; (*dans vie professionnelle*) reintegration.

réintégrer [reɛ̃tegre] *vt* **1.** (*rejoindre*) to return to. **2.** (JUR) to reinstate.

rejaillir [rəʒajir] *vi* to splash up; **~ sur qqn** *fig* to rebound on sb.

rejet [rəʒɛ] *nm* **1.** (*gén*) rejection. **2.** (*pousse*) shoot.

rejeter [rəʒte] *vt* **1.** (*relancer*) to throw back. **2.** (*offre, personne*) to reject. **3.** (*partie du corps*): **~ les bras en arrière** to throw back one's head/one's arms. **4.** (*imputer*): **~ la responsabilité de qqch sur qqn** to lay the responsibility for sthg at sb's door.

rejeton [rəʒtɔ̃] *nm* offspring (U).

rejoindre [rəʒwɛ̃dr] *vt* **1.** (*retrouver*) to join. **2.** (*regagner*) to return to. **3.** (*concorder avec*) to agree with. **4.** (*rattraper*) to catch up with. ► **se rejoindre** *vp* **1.** (*personnes, routes*) to meet. **2.** (*opinions*) to agree.

rejoint, -e [rəʒwɛ̃, ɛ̃t] *pp* → **rejoindre**.

réjoui, -e [reʒwi] *adj* joyful.

réjouir [reʒwir] *vt* to delight. ► **se réjouir** *vp* to be delighted; **se ~ de qqch** to be delighted at *ou* about sthg.

réjouissance [reʒwisɑ̃s] *nf* rejoicing. ► **réjouissances** *nfpl* festivities.

relâche [rəlaʃ] *nf* **1.** (*pause*): **sans ~** without respite *ou* a break. **2.** (THÉÂTRE): **faire ~** to be closed.

relâchement [rəlaʃmɑ̃] *nm* relaxation.

relâcher [rəlaʃe] *vt* **1.** (*étreinte, cordes*) to loosen. **2.** (*discipline, effort*) to relax, to slacken. **3.** (*prisonnier*) to release. ► **se relâcher** *vp* **1.** (*se desserrer*) to loosen. **2.** (*faiblir - discipline*) to become lax; (*- attention*) to flag. **3.** (*se laisser aller*) to slacken off.

relais [rəlɛ] *nm* **1.** (*auberge*) post house; **~ routier** transport cafe. **2.** (SPORT & TÉLÉ): **prendre/passer le ~** to take/hand over; (*course de*) **~** relay.

relance [rəlɑ̃s] *nf* (*économique*) revival, boost; (*de projet*) relaunch.

relancer [rəlɑ̃se] *vt* **1.** (*renvoyer*) to throw back. **2.** (*faire reprendre - économie*) to boost; (*- projet*) to relaunch; (*- moteur, machine*) to restart.

relater [rəlate] *vt littéraire* to relate.

relatif, -ive [rəlatif, iv] *adj* relative; **~ à** relating to; **tout est ~** it's all relative. ▶ **relative** nf (GRAM) relative clause.

relation [rəlasjɔ̃] *nf* relationship; **mettre qqn en ~ avec qqn** to put sb in touch with sb. ▶ **relations** *nfpl* 1. (*rapport*) relationship (*sg*); **~s sexuelles** sexual relations, intercourse (U). 2. (*connaissance*) acquaintance; **avoir des ~s** to have connections.

relationnel, -elle [rəlasjɔnɛl] *adj* (*problèmes*) relationship (*avant n*).

relative → relatif.

relativement [rəlativmɑ̃] *adv* relatively.

relativiser [rəlativize] *vt* to relativize.

relativité [rəlativite] *nf* relativity.

relax, relaxe [rəlaks] *adj fam* relaxed.

relaxation [rəlaksasjɔ̃] *nf* relaxation.

relaxe = **relax**.

relaxer [rəlakse] *vt* 1. (*reposer*) to relax. 2. (JUR) to discharge. ▶ **se relaxer** *vp* to relax.

relayer [rəleje] *vt* to relieve. ▶ **se relayer** *vp* to take over from one another.

relecture [rəlɛktyr] *nf* second reading, rereading.

reléguer [rəlege] *vt* to relegate.

relent [rəlɑ̃] *nm* 1. (*odeur*) stink, stench. 2. *fig* (*trace*) whiff.

relevé, -e [rəlve] *adj* (CULIN) spicy. ▶ **relevé** *nm* reading; **faire le ~ de qqch** to read sthg; **~ de compte** bank statement; **~ d'identité bancaire** bank account number.

relève [rəlɛv] *nf* relief; **prendre la ~** to take over.

relever [rəlve] ◆ *vt* 1. (*redresser - personne*) to help up; (*- pays, économie*) to rebuild; (*- moral, niveau*) to raise. 2. (*ramasser*) to collect. 3. (*tête, col, store*) to raise; (*manches*) to push up. 4. (CULIN - *mettre en valeur*) to bring out; (*- pimenter*) to season; *fig* (*récit*) to liven up, to spice up. 5. (*noter*) to note down; (*compteur*) to read. 6. (*relayer*) to take over from, to relieve. 7. (*erreur*) to note. ◆ *vi* 1. (*se rétablir*): **~ de** to recover from. 2. (*être du domaine*): **~ de** to come under. ▶ **se relever** *vp* (*se mettre debout*) to stand up; (*sortir du lit*) to get up.

relief [rəljɛf] *nm* relief; **en ~** in relief, raised; **une carte en ~** relief map; **mettre en ~** *fig* to enhance, to bring out.

relier [rəlje] *vt* 1. (*livre*) to bind. 2. (*joindre*) to connect. 3. *fig* (*associer*) to link up.

religieux, -euse [rəliʒjø, øz] *adj* 1. (*vie, chant*) religious; (*mariage*) religious, church (*avant n*). 2. (*respectueux*) reverent. ▶ **religieux** *nm* monk. ▶ **religieuse** *nf* 1. (RELIG) nun. 2. (*gâteau*) choux pastry with a chocolate or coffee filling.

religion [rəliʒjɔ̃] *nf* 1. (*culte*) religion. 2. (*croyance*) religion, faith.

relique [rəlik] *nf* relic.

relire [rəlir] *vt* 1. (*lire*) to reread. 2. (*vérifier*) to read over.

reliure [rəljyr] *nf* binding.

reloger [rələʒe] *vt* to rehouse.

relu, -e [rəly] *pp* → **relire**.

reluire [rəlɥir] *vi* to shine, to gleam.

reluisant, -e [rəlɥizɑ̃, ɑ̃t] *adj* shining, gleaming; **peu** OU **pas très** ~ *fig* (*avenir, situation*) not all that brilliant.

remaniement [rəmanimɑ̃] *nm* restructuring; **~ ministériel** cabinet reshuffle.

remarier [rəmarje] ▶ **se remarier** *vp* to remarry.

remarquable [rəmarkabl] *adj* remarkable.

remarque [rəmark] *nf* 1. (*observation*) remark; (*critique*) critical remark. 2. (*annotation*) note.

remarquer [rəmarke] ◆ *vt* 1. (*apercevoir*) to notice; **faire ~ qqch (à qqn)** to point sthg out (to sb); **se faire ~** *péj* to draw attention to o.s. 2. (*noter*) to remark, to comment. ◆ *vi*: **ce n'est pas l'idéal, remarque!** it's not ideal, mind you! ▶ **se remarquer** *vp* to be noticeable.

remballer [rɑ̃bale] *vt* (*marchandise*) to pack up again.

rembarrer [rɑ̃bare] *vt fam* to snub.

remblai [rɑ̃blɛ] *nm* embankment.

rembobiner [rɑ̃bɔbine] *vt* to rewind.

rembourrer [rɑ̃bure] *vt* to stuff, to pad.

remboursable [rɑ̃bursabl] *adj* refundable.

remboursement [rɑ̃bursəmɑ̃] *nm* refund, repayment.

rembourser [rɑ̃burse] *vt* 1. (*dette*) to pay back, to repay. 2. (*personne*) to pay back; **~ qqn de qqch** to reimburse sb for sthg.

rembrunir [rɑ̃brynir] ▶ **se rembrunir** *vp* to cloud over, to become gloomy.

remède [rəmɛd] *nm litt* & *fig* remedy, cure.

remédier [rəmedje] *vi*: **~ à qqch** to put

sthg right, to remedy sthg.

remembrement [rəmãbrəmã] *nm* land regrouping.

remerciement [rəmɛrsimã] *nm* thanks (*pl*); **une lettre de ~** a thank-you letter.

remercier [rəmɛrsje] *vt* 1. (*dire merci à*) to thank; **~ qqn de** ou **pour qqch** to thank sb for sthg; **non, je vous remercie** no, thank you. 2. (*congédier*) to dismiss.

remettre [rəmɛtr] *vt* 1. (*replacer*) to put back; **~ en question** to call into question; **~ qqn à sa place** to put sb in his place. 2. (*enfiler de nouveau*) to put back on. 3. (*rétablir - lumière, son*) to put back on; **~ qqch en marche** to restart sthg; **~ de l'ordre dans qqch** to tidy sthg up; **~ une montre à l'heure** to put a watch right; **~ qqch en état de marche** to put sthg back in working order. 4. (*donner*): **~ qqch à qqn** to hand sthg over to sb; (*médaille, prix*) to present sthg to sb. 5. (*ajourner*): **~ qqch (à)** to put sthg off (until). ▶ **se remettre** *vp* 1. (*recommencer*): **se ~ à qqch** to take up sthg again; **se ~ à fumer** to start smoking again. 2. (*se rétablir*) to get better; **se ~ de qqch** to get over sthg. 3. (*redevenir*): **se ~ debout** to stand up again; **le temps s'est remis au beau** the weather has cleared up.

réminiscence [reminisãs] *nf* reminiscence.

remis, -e [rəmi, iz] *pp* → **remettre**.

remise [rəmiz] *nf* 1. (*action*): **~ en forme** getting fit; **~ en jeu** throw-in; **~ en marche** restarting; **~ en question** ou **cause** calling into question. 2. (*de message, colis*) handing over; (*de médaille, prix*) presentation. 3. (*réduction*) discount; **~ de peine** (JUR) remission. 4. (*hangar*) shed.

rémission [remisjõ] *nf* remission; **sans ~** (*punir, juger*) without mercy.

remodeler [rəmɔdle] *vt* 1. (*forme*) to remodel. 2. (*remanier*) to restructure.

remontant, -e [rəmõtã, ãt] *adj* (*tonique*) invigorating. ▶ **remontant** *nm* tonic.

remonte-pente [rəmõtpãt] (*pl* **remonte-pentes**) *nm* ski-tow.

remonter [rəmõte] ◆ *vt* (*aux: avoir*) 1. (*escalier, pente*) to go/come back up. 2. (*assembler*) to put together again. 3. (*manches*) to turn up. 4. (*horloge, montre*) to wind up. 5. (*ragaillardir*) to put new life into, to cheer up. ◆ *vi* (*aux: être*) 1. (*monter à nouveau - personne*) to go/

come back up; (- *baromètre*) to rise again; (- *prix, température*) to go up again, to rise; (- *sur vélo*) to get back on; **~ dans une voiture** to get back into a car. 2. (*dater*): **~ à** to date ou go back to.

remontoir [rəmõtwar] *nm* winder.

remontrer [rəmõtre] *vt* to show again; **vouloir en ~ à qqn** to try to show sb up.

remords [rəmɔr] *nm* remorse.

remorque [rəmɔrk] *nf* trailer; **être en ~** to be on tow.

remorquer [rəmɔrke] *vt* (*voiture, bateau*) to tow.

remorqueur [rəmɔrkœr] *nm* tug, tugboat.

remous [rəmu] ◆ *nm* (*de bateau*) wash, backwash; (*de rivière*) eddy. ◆ *nmpl fig* stir, upheaval.

rempailler [rãpaje] *vt* to re-cane.

rempart [rãpar] *nm* (*gén pl*) rampart.

remplaçable [rãplasabl] *adj* replaceable.

remplaçant, -e [rãplasã, ãt] *nm, f* (*suppléant*) stand-in; (SPORT) substitute.

remplacement [rãplasmã] *nm* 1. (*changement*) replacing, replacement. 2. (*intérim*) substitution; **faire des ~s** to stand in; (*docteur*) to act as a locum.

remplacer [rãplase] *vt* 1. (*gén*) to replace. 2. (*prendre la place de*) to stand in for; (SPORT) to substitute.

remplir [rãplir] *vt* 1. (*gén*) to fill; **~ de** to fill with; **~ qqn de joie/d'orgueil** to fill sb with happiness/pride. 2. (*questionnaire*) to fill in ou out. 3. (*mission, fonction*) to complete, to fulfil.

remplissage [rãplisaʒ] *nm* 1. (*de récipient*) filling up. 2. *fig & péj* (*de texte*) padding out.

remporter [rãpɔrte] *vt* 1. (*repartir avec*) to take away again. 2. (*gagner*) to win.

remuant, -e [rəmɥã, ãt] *adj* restless, overactive.

remue-ménage [rəmymenaʒ] *nm inv* commotion, confusion.

remuer [rəmɥe] ◆ *vt* 1. (*bouger, émouvoir*) to move. 2. (*café, thé*) to stir; (*salade*) to toss. ◆ *vi* to move, to stir; **arrête de ~ comme ça** stop being so restless. ▶ **se remuer** *vp* 1. (*se mouvoir*) to move. 2. *fig* (*réagir*) to make an effort.

rémunération [remynerasjõ] *nf* remuneration.

rémunérer [remynere] *vt* 1. (*personne*) to remunerate, to pay. 2. (*activité*) to pay for.

renâcler [rənakle] *vi fam* to make a fuss; **~ devant** ou **à qqch** to balk at sthg.

renaissance [rənɛsɑ̃s] *nf* rebirth.
renaître [rənɛtr] *vi* 1. (*ressusciter*) to come back to life, to come to life again; **faire ~** (*passé, tradition*) to revive. 2. (*revenir - sentiment, printemps*) to return; (*- économie*) to revive, to recover.
renard [rənar] *nm* fox.
renchérir [rãʃerir] *vi* 1. (*augmenter*) to become more expensive; (*prix*) to go up. 2. (*surenchérir*) **~ sur** to add to.
rencontre [rãkõtr] *nf* (*gén*) meeting; **faire une bonne ~** to meet somebody interesting; **faire une mauvaise ~** to meet an unpleasant person; **aller/venir à la ~ de qqn** to go/come to meet sb.
rencontrer [rãkõtre] *vt* 1. (*gén*) to meet. 2. (*heurter*) to strike. ▶ **se rencontrer** *vp* 1. (*gén*) to meet. 2. (*opinions*) to agree.
rendement [rãdmã] *nm* (*de machine, travailleur*) output; (*de terre, placement*) yield.
rendez-vous [rãdevu] *nm inv* 1. (*rencontre*) appointment; (*amoureux*) date; **on a tous ~ au café** we're all meeting at the café; **lors de notre dernier ~** at our last meeting; **prendre ~ avec qqn** to make an appointment with sb; **donner ~ à qqn** to arrange to meet sb. 2. (*lieu*) meeting place.
rendormir [rãdɔrmir] ▶ **se rendormir** *vp* to go back to sleep.
rendre [rãdr] ♦ *vt* 1. (*restituer*): **~ qqch à qqn** to give sth back to sb, to return sth to sb. 2. (*donner en retour - invitation, coup*) to return; **~ la politesse** to return the favour. 3. (JUR - *jugement*) to pronounce. 4. (*produire - effet*) to produce. 5. (*vomir*) to vomit, to cough up. 6. (MIL) (*céder*) to surrender; **~ les armes** to lay down one's arms. 7. (+ *adj*) (*faire devenir*) to make; **~ qqn fou** to drive sb mad. 8. (*exprimer*) to render. ♦ *vi* 1. (*produire - champ*) to yield. 2. (*vomir*) to vomit, to be sick. ▶ **se rendre** *vp* 1. (*céder, capituler*) to give in; **j'ai dû me ~ à l'évidence** I had to face facts. 2. (*aller*): **se ~ à** to go to. 3. (+ *adj*) (*se faire tel*): **se ~ utile/malade** to make o.s. useful/ill.
rêne [rɛn] *nf* rein.
renégat, -e [rənega, at] *nm, f sout* renegade.
renégocier [rənegɔsje] *vt* to renegotiate.
renfermé, -e [rãfɛrme] *adj* introverted, withdrawn. ▶ **renfermé** *nm*: **ça sent le ~** it smells stuffy in here.
renfermer [rãfɛrme] *vt* (*contenir*) to contain. ▶ **se renfermer** *vp* to withdraw.
renflé, -e [rãfle] *adj* bulging.
renflouer [rãflue] *vt* 1. (*bateau*) to refloat. 2. *fig* (*entreprise, personne*) to bail out.
renfoncement [rãfõsmã] *nm* recess.
renforcer [rãfɔrse] *vt* to reinforce, to strengthen; **cela me renforce dans mon opinion** that confirms my opinion.
renfort [rãfɔr] *nm* reinforcement; **venir en ~** to come as reinforcements.
renfrogné, -e [rãfrɔɲe] *adj* scowling.
renfrogner [rãfrɔɲe] ▶ **se renfrogner** *vp* to scowl, to pull a face.
rengaine [rãgɛn] *nf* 1. (*formule répétée*) (*old*) story. 2. (*chanson*) (*old*) song.
rengorger [rãgɔrʒe] ▶ **se rengorger** *vp fig* to puff o.s. up.
renier [rənje] *vt* 1. (*famille, ami*) to disown. 2. (*foi, opinion*) to renounce, to repudiate.
renifler [rənifle] ♦ *vi* to sniff. ♦ *vt* to sniff; **~ quelque chose de louche** to smell a rat.
renne [rɛn] *nm* reindeer (*inv*).
renom [rənõ] *nm* renown, fame.
renommé, -e [rənɔme] *adj* renowned, famous. ▶ **renommée** *nf* renown, fame; **de ~e internationale** world-famous, internationally renowned.
renoncement [rənõsmã] *nm*: **~ (à)** renunciation (of).
renoncer [rənõse] *vi*: **~ à** to give up; **~ à comprendre qqch** to give up trying to understand sthg.
renouer [rənwe] ♦ *vt* 1. (*lacet, corde*) to re-tie, to tie up again. 2. (*contact, conversation*) to resume. ♦ *vi*: **~ avec qqn** to take up with sb again; **~ avec sa famille** to make it up with one's family again.
renouveau, -x [rənuvo] *nm* (*transformation*) revival.
renouvelable [rənuvlabl] *adj* renewable; (*expérience*) repeatable.
renouveler [rənuvle] *vt* (*gén*) to renew. ▶ **se renouveler** *vp* 1. (*être remplacé*) to be renewed. 2. (*changer, innover*) to have new ideas. 3. (*se répéter*) to be repeated, to recur.
renouvellement [rənuvɛlmã] *nm* renewal.
rénovation [renɔvasjõ] *nf* renovation, restoration.
rénover [renɔve] *vt* 1. (*immeuble*) to renovate, to restore. 2. (*système, méthodes*) to reform.
renseignement [rãsɛɲəmã] *nm* infor-

mation (U); **un ~** a piece of information; **prendre des ~s (sur)** to make enquiries (about). ▶ **renseignements** nmpl (service d'information) enquiries, information.

renseigner [rɑ̃seɲe] vt: **~ qqn (sur)** to give sb information (about), to inform sb (about). ▶ **se renseigner** vp 1. (s'enquérir) to make enquiries, to ask for information. 2. (s'informer) to find out.

rentabiliser [rɑ̃tabilize] vt to make profitable.

rentabilité [rɑ̃tabilite] nf profitability.

rentable [rɑ̃tabl] adj 1. (COMM) profitable. 2. fam (qui en vaut la peine) worthwhile.

rente [rɑ̃t] nf 1. (d'un capital) revenue, income. 2. (pension) pension, annuity.

rentier, -ère [rɑ̃tje, ɛr] nm, f person of independent means.

rentrée [rɑ̃tre] nf 1. (fait de rentrer) return. 2. (reprise des activités): **la ~ parlementaire** the reopening of parliament; **la ~ des classes** the start of the new school year. 3. (recette) income.

rentrer [rɑ̃tre] ◆ vi (aux: être) 1. (entrer de nouveau) to go/comeback in; **tout a fini par ~ dans l'ordre** everything returned to normal. 2. (entrer) to go/come in. 3. (revenir chez soi) to go/come back to, to go/come home. 4. (recouvrer, récupérer): **~ dans** to recover, to get back; **~ dans ses frais** to cover one's costs, to break even. 5. (se jeter avec violence): **~ dans** to crash into. 6. (s'emboîter) to go in, to fit; **~ les uns dans les autres** to fit together. 7. (être perçu - fonds) to come in. ◆ vt (aux: avoir) 1. (mettre ou remettre à l'intérieur) to bring in. 2. (ventre) to pull in; (griffes) to retract, to draw in; (chemise) to tuck in. 3. fig (rage, larmes) to hold back.

renversant, -e [rɑ̃versɑ̃, ɑ̃t] adj staggering, astounding.

renverse [rɑ̃vers] nf: **tomber à la ~** to fall over backwards.

renversement [rɑ̃versəmɑ̃] nm 1. (inversion) turning upside down. 2. (de situation) reversal.

renverser [rɑ̃verse] vt 1. (mettre à l'envers) to turn upside down. 2. (faire tomber) to knock over; (- piéton) to run over; (- liquide) to spill. 3. fig (régime) to overthrow; (ministre) to throw out of office. 4. (tête, buste) to tilt back. ▶ **se renverser** vp 1. (incliner le corps en arrière) to lean back. 2. (tomber) to overturn.

renvoi [rɑ̃vwa] nm 1. (licenciement) dis-

missal. 2. (de colis, lettre) return, sending back. 3. (ajournement) postponement. 4. (référence) cross-reference. 5. (JUR) referral. 6. (éructation) belch.

renvoyer [rɑ̃vwaje] vt 1. (faire retourner) to send back. 2. (congédier) to dismiss. 3. (colis, lettre) to send back, to return. 4. (balle) to throw back. 5. (réfléchir - lumière) to reflect; (- son) to echo. 6. (référer): **~ qqn à** to refer sb to. 7. (différer) to postpone, to put off.

réorganisation [reɔrganizasjɔ̃] nf reorganization.

réorganiser [reɔrganize] vt to reorganize.

réouverture [reuvɛrtyr] nf reopening.

repaire [rəpɛr] nm den.

répandre [repɑ̃dr] vt 1. (verser, renverser) to spill; (larmes) to shed. 2. (diffuser, dégager) to give off. 3. fig (bienfaits) to pour out; (effroi, terreur, nouvelle) to spread.

répandu, -e [repɑ̃dy] ◆ pp → **répandre**. ◆ adj (opinion, maladie) widespread.

réparable [reparabl] adj 1. (objet) repairable. 2. (erreur) that can be put right.

réparateur, -trice [reparatœr, tris] ◆ adj (sommeil) refreshing. ◆ nm, f repairer.

réparation [reparasjɔ̃] nf 1. (d'objet - action) repairing; (- résultat) repair; **en ~** under repair. 2. (de faute): **~ (de)** atonement (for). 3. (indemnité) reparation, compensation.

réparer [repare] vt 1. (objet) to repair. 2. (faute, oubli) to make up for; **~ ses torts** to make amends.

reparler [rəparle] vi: **~ de qqn/qqch** to talk about sb/sthg again.

repartie [rəparti] nf retort; **avoir de la ~** to be good at repartee.

repartir [rəpartir] ◆ vt littéraire to reply. ◆ vi 1. (retourner) to go back, to return. 2. (partir de nouveau) to set off again. 3. (recommencer) to start again.

répartir [repartir] vt 1. (partager) to share out, to divide up. 2. (dans l'espace) to spread out, to distribute. 3. (classer) to divide ou split up. ▶ **se répartir** vp to divide up.

répartition [repartisjɔ̃] nf 1. (partage) sharing out; (de tâches) allocation. 2. (dans l'espace) distribution.

repas [rəpa] nm meal; **prendre son ~** to eat; **~ de fête** celebratory meal.

repassage [rəpasaʒ] nm ironing.

repasser [rəpase] ◆ vi (aux: être) (passer

à nouveau) to go/come back; (*film*) to be on again. ◆ vt (aux: avoir) **1.** (*frontière, montagne*) to cross again, to recross. **2.** (*examen*) to resit. **3.** (*film*) to show again. **4.** (*linge*) to iron.

repêchage [rəpɛʃaʒ] nm (*de noyé, voiture*) recovery.

repêcher [rəpeʃe] vt **1.** (*noyé, voiture*) to fish out. **2.** fam (*candidat*) to let through.

repeindre [rəpɛ̃dr] vt to repaint.

repeint, -e [rəpɛ̃, ɛ̃t] pp → **repeindre**.

repenser [rəpɑ̃se] vt to rethink.

repentir [rəpɑ̃tir] nm repentance. ► **se repentir** vp to repent; **se ~ de qqch/d'avoir fait qqch** to be sorry for sthg/for having done sthg.

répercussion [repɛrkysjɔ̃] nf repercussion.

répercuter [repɛrkyte] vt **1.** (*lumière*) to reflect; (*son*) to throw back. **2.** (*ordre, augmentation*) to pass on. ► **se répercuter** vp **1.** (*lumière*) to be reflected; (*son*) to echo. **2.** (*influer*): **se ~ sur** to have repercussions on.

repère [rəpɛr] nm (*marque*) mark; (*objet concret*) landmark; **point de ~** point of reference.

repérer [rəpere] vt **1.** (*situer*) to locate, to pinpoint. **2.** fam (*remarquer*) to spot; **se faire ~** to be spotted.

répertoire [repɛrtwar] nm **1.** (*agenda*) thumb-indexed notebook. **2.** (*de théâtre, d'artiste*) repertoire. **3.** (INFORM) directory.

répertorier [repɛrtɔrje] vt to make a list of.

répéter [repete] ◆ vt **1.** (*gén*) to repeat. **2.** (*leçon*) to go over, to learn; (*rôle*) to rehearse. ◆ vi to rehearse. ► **se répéter** vp **1.** (*radoter*) to repeat o.s. **2.** (*se reproduire*) to be repeated; **que cela ne se répète pas!** don't let it happen again!

répétitif, -ive [repetitif, iv] adj repetitive.

répétition [repetisjɔ̃] nf **1.** (*réitération*) repetition. **2.** (MUS & THÉÂTRE) rehearsal.

repeupler [rəpœple] vt **1.** (*région, ville*) to repopulate. **2.** (*forêt*) to replant; (*étang*) to restock.

repiquer [rəpike] vt **1.** (*replanter*) to plant out. **2.** (*disque, cassette*) to tape.

répit [repi] nm respite; **sans ~** without respite.

replacer [rəplase] vt **1.** (*remettre*) to replace, to put back. **2.** (*situer*) to place, to put. ► **se replacer** vp to find new employment.

replanter [rəplɑ̃te] vt to replant.

replet, -ète [rəplɛ, ɛt] adj chubby.

repli [rəpli] nm **1.** (*de tissu*) fold; (*de rivière*) bend. **2.** (*de troupes*) withdrawal.

replier [rəplije] vt **1.** (*plier de nouveau*) to fold up again. **2.** (*ramener en pliant*) to fold back. **3.** (*armée*) to withdraw. ► **se replier** vp **1.** (*armée*) to withdraw. **2.** (*personne*): **se ~ sur soi-même** to withdraw into o.s. **3.** (*journal, carte*) to fold.

réplique [replik] nf **1.** (*riposte*) reply; **sans ~** (*argument*) irrefutable. **2.** (*d'acteur*) line; **donner la ~ à qqn** to play opposite sb. **3.** (*copie*) replica; (*sosie*) double.

répliquer [replike] ◆ vt: **~ à qqn que** to reply to sb that. ◆ vi **1.** (*répondre*) to reply; (*avec impertinence*) to answer back. **2.** fig (*riposter*) to retaliate.

replonger [rəplɔ̃ʒe] ◆ vt to plunge back. ◆ vi to dive back. ► **se replonger** vp: **se ~ dans qqch** to immerse o.s. in sthg again.

répondeur [repɔ̃dœr] nm: **~ (téléphonique** ou **automatique** ou **-enregistreur)** answering machine.

répondre [repɔ̃dr] ◆ vi: **~ à qqn** (*faire connaître sa pensée*) to answer sb, to reply to sb; (*riposter*) to answer sb back; **~ à qqch** (*faire une réponse*) to reply to sthg, to answer sthg; (*en se défendant*) to respond to sthg; **~ au téléphone** to answer the telephone; **ça ne répond pas** there's no answer. ◆ vt to answer, to reply. ► **répondre à** vt **1.** (*correspondre à - besoin*) to answer; (*- conditions*) to meet. **2.** (*ressembler à - description*) to match. ► **répondre de** vt to answer for.

répondu, -e [repɔ̃dy] pp → **répondre**.

réponse [repɔ̃s] nf **1.** (*action de répondre*) answer, reply; **en ~ à votre lettre ...** in reply ou in answer ou in response to your letter ... **2.** (*solution*) answer. **3.** (*réaction*) response.

report [rəpɔr] nm **1.** (*de réunion, rendez-vous*) postponement. **2.** (COMM) (*d'écritures*) carrying forward.

reportage [rəpɔrtaʒ] nm (*article, enquête*) report.

reporter¹ [rəpɔrter] nm reporter.

reporter² [rəpɔrte] vt **1.** (*rapporter*) to take back. **2.** (*différer*): **~ qqch à** to postpone sthg till, to put sthg off till. **3.** (*somme*): **~ (sur)** to carry forward (to). **4.** (*transférer*): **~ sur** to transfer to. ► **se reporter** vp: **se ~ à** (*se référer à*) to refer to.

repos [rəpo] nm **1.** (*gén*) rest; **prendre**

un jour de ~ to take a day off. **2.** (*tranquillité*) peace and quiet.

reposé, -e [rəpoze] *adj* rested; **à tête ~e** with a clear head.

reposer [rəpoze] ◆ *vt* **1.** (*poser à nouveau*) to put down again, to put back down. **2.** (*remettre*) to put back. **3.** (*poser de nouveau - question*) to ask again. **4.** (*appuyer*) to rest. **5.** (*délasser*) to rest, to relax. ◆ *vi* **1.** (*pâte*) to sit, to stand; (*vin*) to stand. **2.** (*théorie*): **~ sur** to rest on. ▶ **se reposer** *vp* **1.** (*se délasser*) to rest. **2.** (*faire confiance*): **se ~ sur qqn** to rely on sb.

repoussant, -e [rəpusɑ̃, ɑ̃t] *adj* repulsive.

repousser [rəpuse] ◆ *vi* to grow again, to grow back. ◆ *vt* **1.** (*écarter*) to push away, to push back; (*l'ennemi*) to repel, to drive back. **2.** (*éconduire*) to reject. **3.** (*proposition*) to reject, to turn down. **4.** (*différer*) to put back, to postpone.

répréhensible [repreɑ̃sibl] *adj* reprehensible.

reprendre [rəprɑ̃dr] ◆ *vt* **1.** (*prendre de nouveau*) to take again; **je passe te ~ dans une heure** I'll come by and pick you up again in an hour; **~ la route** to take to the road again; **~ haleine** to get one's breath back. **2.** (*récupérer - objet prêté*) to take back; (*- prisonnier, ville*) to recapture. **3.** (COMM) (*entreprise, affaire*) to take over. **4.** (*se resservir*): **~ un gâteau/de la viande** to take another cake/some more meat. **5.** (*recommencer*) to resume; **'et ainsi' reprit-il ...** 'and so', he continued ... **6.** (*retoucher*) to repair; (*jupe*) to alter. **7.** (*corriger*) to correct. ◆ *vi* **1.** (*affaires, plante*) to pick up. **2.** (*recommencer*) to start again.

représailles [rəprezaj] *nfpl* reprisals.

représentant, -e [rəprezɑ̃tɑ̃, ɑ̃t] *nm, f* representative.

représentatif, -ive [rəprezɑ̃tatif, iv] *adj* representative.

représentation [rəprezɑ̃tasjɔ̃] *nf* **1.** (*gén*) representation. **2.** (*spectacle*) performance.

représentativité [rəprezɑ̃tativite] *nf* representativeness.

représenter [rəprezɑ̃te] *vt* to represent. ▶ **se représenter** *vp* **1.** (*s'imaginer*): **se ~ qqch** to visualize sthg. **2.** (*se présenter à nouveau*): **se ~ à** (*aux élections*) to stand again at; (*à un examen*) to resit.

répression [represjɔ̃] *nf* **1.** (*de révolte*) repression. **2.** (*de criminalité, d'injustices*) suppression.

réprimande [reprimɑ̃d] *nf* reprimand.

réprimander [reprimɑ̃de] *vt* to reprimand.

réprimer [reprime] *vt* **1.** (*émotion, rire*) to repress, to check. **2.** (*révolte, crimes*) to put down, to suppress.

repris, -e [rəpri, iz] *pp* → **reprendre**. ▶ **repris** *nm*: **~ de justice** habitual criminal.

reprisage [rəprizaʒ] *nm* mending.

reprise [rəpriz] *nf* **1.** (*recommencement - des hostilités*) resumption, renewal; (*- des affaires*) recovery, recovery; (*- de pièce*) revival; **à plusieurs ~s** on several occasions, several times. **2.** (BOXE) round. **3.** (*raccommodage*) mending.

repriser [rəprize] *vt* to mend.

réprobateur, -trice [reprɔbatœr, tris] *adj* reproachful.

réprobation [reprɔbasjɔ̃] *nf* disapproval.

reproche [rəprɔʃ] *nm* reproach; **faire des ~s à qqn** to reproach sb.

reprocher [rəprɔʃe] *vt*: **~ qqch à qqn** to reproach sb for sthg. ▶ **se reprocher** *vp*: **se ~ (qqch)** to blame o.s. (for sthg).

reproducteur, -trice [rəprɔdyktœr, tris] *adj* reproductive.

reproduction [rəprɔdyksjɔ̃] *nf* reproduction; **~ interdite** all rights (of reproduction) reserved.

reproduire [rəprɔdɥir] *vt* to reproduce. ▶ **se reproduire** *vp* **1.** (BIOL) to reproduce, to breed. **2.** (*se répéter*) to recur.

reproduit, -e [rəprɔdɥi, it] *pp* → **reproduire**.

réprouver [repruve] *vt* (*blâmer*) to reprove.

reptile [rɛptil] *nm* reptile.

repu, -e [rəpy] *adj* full, sated.

républicain, -e [repyblikɛ̃, ɛn] *adj & nm, f* republican.

république [repyblik] *nf* republic; **la République française** the French Republic; **la République populaire de Chine** the People's Republic of China; **la République tchèque** the Czech Republic.

répudier [repydje] *vt* (*femme*) to repudiate.

répugnance [repyɲɑ̃s] *nf* **1.** (*horreur*) repugnance. **2.** (*réticence*) reluctance; **avoir** ou **éprouver de la ~ à faire qqch** to be reluctant to do sthg.

répugnant, -e [repyɲɑ̃, ɑ̃t] *adj* repugnant.

répugner [repyɲe] *vi*: **~ à qqn** to dis-

gust sb, to fill sb with repugnance; ~ à **faire qqch** to be reluctant to do sthg, to be loath to do sthg.
répulsion [repylsjɔ̃] nf repulsion.
réputation [repytasjɔ̃] nf reputation; **avoir une ~ de** to have a reputation for; **avoir bonne/mauvaise ~** to have a good/bad reputation.
réputé, -e [repyte] adj famous, well-known.
requérir [rəkerir] vt 1. (nécessiter) to require, to call for. 2. (solliciter) to solicit. 3. (JUR) (réclamer au nom de la loi) to demand.
requête [rəkɛt] nf 1. (prière) petition. 2. (JUR) appeal.
requiem [rekɥijɛm] nm inv requiem.
requin [rəkɛ̃] nm shark.
requis, -e [rəki, iz] ♦ pp → **requérir**. ♦ adj required, requisite.
réquisition [rekizisjɔ̃] nf 1. (MIL) requisition. 2. (JUR) closing speech for the prosecution.
réquisitionner [rekizisjɔne] vt to requisition.
réquisitoire [rekizitwar] nm (JUR) closing speech for the prosecution; ~ **(contre)** fig indictment (of).
RER (abr de réseau express régional) nm train service linking central Paris with its suburbs and airports.

RER

The RER is a rail network extending throughout the Paris region linking the centre with the suburbs and Orly and Charles de Gaulle airports. There are three main lines (A, B and C) which connect with Paris metro stations as well as train stations.

---

rescapé, -e [rɛskape] nm, f survivor.
rescousse [rɛskus] ▸ **à la rescousse** loc adv: **venir à la ~ de qqn** to come to sb's rescue; **appeler qqn à la ~** to call on sb for help.
réseau [rezo] nm network; ~ **ferroviaire/routier** rail/road network.
réservation [rezɛrvasjɔ̃] nf reservation, booking.
réserve [rezɛrv] nf 1. (gén) reserve, stock; **en ~** in reserve; **officier de ~** (MIL) reserve officer. 2. (restriction) reservation; **faire des ~s (sur)** to have reservations (about); **sous ~ de** subject to; **sans ~** unreservedly. 3. (territoire) reserve; (- d'Indiens) reservation; ~ **naturelle** nature reserve. 4. (local) storeroom.

réservé, -e [rezɛrve] adj reserved.
réserver [rezɛrve] vt 1. (destiner): ~ **qqch (à qqn)** (chambre, place) to reserve ou book sthg (for sb); fig (surprise, désagrément) to have sthg in store (for sb). 2. (mettre de côté, garder): ~ **qqch (pour)** to put sthg on one side (for), to keep sthg (for). ▸ **se réserver** vp 1. (s'accorder): ~ **qqch** to keep sthg for o.s.; **se ~ le droit de faire qqch** to reserve the right to do sthg. 2. (se ménager) to save o.s.
réservoir [rezɛrvwar] nm 1. (cuve) tank. 2. (bassin) reservoir.
résidence [rezidɑ̃s] nf 1. (habitation) residence; ~ **principale** main residence ou home; ~ **secondaire** second home; ~ **universitaire** hall of residence. 2. (immeuble) block of luxury flats Br, luxury apartment block Am. ▸ **résidence surveillée** nf: **en ~ surveillée** under house arrest.
résident, -e [rezidɑ̃, ɑ̃t] nm, f 1. (de pays): **les ~s français en Écosse** French nationals resident in Scotland. 2. (habitant d'une résidence) resident.
résidentiel, -elle [rezidɑ̃sjɛl] adj residential.
résider [rezide] vi 1. (habiter): ~ **à/dans/en** to reside in. 2. (consister): ~ **dans** to lie in.
résidu [rezidy] nm (reste) residue; (déchet) waste.
résignation [reziɲasjɔ̃] nf resignation.
résigné, -e [reziɲe] adj resigned.
résigner [reziɲe] ▸ **se résigner** vp: **se ~ (à)** to resign o.s. (to).
résilier [rezilje] vt to cancel, to terminate.
résille [rezij] nf 1. (pour cheveux) hairnet. 2. **bas ~** fishnet stockings.
résine [rezin] nf resin.
résistance [rezistɑ̃s] nf 1. (gén, ÉLECTR & PHYS) resistance; **manquer de ~** to lack stamina; **opposer une ~** to put up resistance. 2. (de radiateur, chaudière) element. ▸ **Résistance** nf: **la Résistance** (HIST) the Resistance.
résistant, -e [rezistɑ̃, ɑ̃t] ♦ adj (personne) tough; (tissu) hard-wearing, tough; **être ~ au froid/aux infections** to be resistant to the cold/to infection. ♦ nm, f (gén) resistance fighter; (de la Résistance) member of the Resistance.
résister [reziste] vi to resist; ~ **à** (attaque, désir) to resist; (tempête, fatigue) to withstand; (personne) to stand up to, to oppose.

résolu, -e [rezɔly] ◆ *pp* → **résoudre**. ◆ *adj* resolute; **être bien ~ à faire qqch** to be determined to do sthg.

résolument [rezɔlymɑ̃] *adv* resolutely.

résolution [rezɔlysjɔ̃] *nf* 1. (*décision*) resolution; **prendre la ~ de faire qqch** to make a resolution to do sthg. 2. (*détermination*) resolve, determination. 3. (*solution*) solving.

résonance [rezɔnɑ̃s] *nf* 1. (ÉLECTR & PHYS) resonance. 2. *fig* (*écho*) echo.

résonner [rezɔne] *vi* 1. (*retentir*) to resound; (*renvoyer le son*) to echo.

résorber [rezɔrbe] *vt* 1. (*déficit*) to absorb. 2. (MÉD) to resorb. ▶ **se résorber** *vp* 1. (*déficit*) to be absorbed. 2. (MÉD) to be resorbed.

résoudre [rezudr] *vt* (*problème*) to solve, to resolve. ▶ **se résoudre** *vp*: **se ~ à faire qqch** to make up one's mind to do sthg, to decide ou resolve to do sthg.

respect [rɛspɛ] *nm* respect.

respectable [rɛspɛktabl] *adj* respectable.

respecter [rɛspɛkte] *vt* (*honorer*) to respect; (*se conformer à*) to respect, to keep to; **faire ~ la loi** to enforce the law.

respectif, -ive [rɛspɛktif, iv] *adj* respective.

respectivement [rɛspɛktivmɑ̃] *adv* respectively.

respectueux, -euse [rɛspɛktɥø, øz] *adj* respectful; **être ~ de** to have respect for.

respiration [rɛspirasjɔ̃] *nf* breathing (U); **retenir sa ~** to hold one's breath.

respiratoire [rɛspiratwar] *adj* respiratory.

respirer [rɛspire] ◆ *vi* 1. (*inspirer-expirer*) to breathe. 2. *fig* (*se reposer*) to get one's breath; (*être soulagé*) to be able to breathe again. ◆ *vt* 1. (*aspirer*) to breathe in. 2. *fig* (*exprimer*) to exude.

resplendissant, -e [rɛsplɑ̃disɑ̃, ɑ̃t] *adj* radiant.

responsabiliser [rɛspɔ̃sabilize] *vt*: **~ qqn** to make sb aware of his/her responsibilities.

responsabilité [rɛspɔ̃sabilite] *nf* 1. (*morale*) responsibility; **avoir la ~ de** to be responsible for, to have the responsibility of. 2. (JUR) liability.

responsable [rɛspɔ̃sabl] ◆ *adj* 1. (*gén*): **~ (de)** responsible (for); (*légalement*) liable (for); (*chargé de*) in charge (of), responsible (for). 2. (*sérieux*) respon-

sible. ◆ *nmf* 1. (*auteur, coupable*) person responsible. 2. (*dirigeant*) official. 3. (*personne compétente*) person in charge.

resquiller [rɛskije] *vi* 1. (*au théâtre etc*) to sneak in without paying. 2. (*dans autobus etc*) to dodge paying the fare.

resquilleur, -euse [rɛskijœr, øz] *nm, f* 1. (*au théâtre etc*) person who sneaks in without paying. 2. (*dans autobus etc*) fare-dodger.

ressac [rəsak] *nm* undertow.

ressaisir [rəsezir] ▶ **se ressaisir** *vp* to pull o.s. together.

ressasser [rəsase] *vt* (*répéter*) to keep churning out.

ressemblance [rəsɑ̃blɑ̃s] *nf* (*gén*) resemblance, likeness; (*trait*) resemblance.

ressemblant, -e [rəsɑ̃blɑ̃, ɑ̃t] *adj* lifelike.

ressembler [rəsɑ̃ble] *vi*: **~ à** (*physiquement*) to resemble, to look like; (*moralement*) to be like, to resemble; **cela ne lui ressemble pas** that's not like him. ▶ **se ressembler** *vp* to look alike.

ressemeler [rəsəmle] *vt* to resole.

ressentiment [rəsɑ̃timɑ̃] *nm* resentment.

ressentir [rəsɑ̃tir] *vt* to feel.

resserrer [rəsere] *vt* 1. (*ceinture, boulon*) to tighten. 2. *fig* (*lien*) to strengthen. ▶ **se resserrer** *vp* 1. (*route*) to (become) narrow. 2. (*nœud, étreinte*) to tighten. 3. *fig* (*relations*) to grow stronger, to strengthen.

resservir [rəservir] ◆ *vt* 1. (*plat*) to serve again; *fig* (*histoire*) to trot out. 2. (*personne*) to give another helping to. ◆ *vi* to be used again. ▶ **se resservir** *vp*: **se ~ de qqch** (*ustensile*) to use sthg again; (*plat*) to take another helping of sthg.

ressort [rəsɔr] *nm* 1. (*mécanisme*) spring. 2. *fig* (*énergie*) spirit. 3. *fig* (*compétence*): **être du ~ de qqn** to be sb's area of responsibility, to come under sb's jurisdiction. ▶ **en dernier ressort** *loc adv* in the last resort, as a last resort.

ressortir [rəsɔrtir] ◆ *vi* (*aux: être*) 1. (*personne*) to go out again. 2. *fig* (*couleur*): **~ (sur)** to stand out (against); **faire ~** to highlight. 3. *fig* (*résulter de*): **~ de** to emerge from. ◆ *vt* (*aux: avoir*) to take ou get ou bring out again.

ressortissant, -e [rəsɔrtisɑ̃, ɑ̃t] *nm, f* national.

ressource [rəsurs] *nf* resort; **votre seule ~ est de ...** the only course open to you is to ... ▶ **ressources** nfpl 1. (*financières*) means. 2. (*énergétiques, de langue*) resources; **~s naturelles** natural resources. 3. (*de personne*) resourcefulness (U).

ressurgir [rəsyrʒir] vi to reappear.

ressusciter [resysite] vi to rise (from the dead); *fig* to revive.

restant, -e [rɛstɑ̃, ɑ̃t] adj remaining, left. ▶ **restant** nm rest, remainder.

restaurant [rɛstɔrɑ̃] nm restaurant; **manger au ~** to eat out; **~ d'entreprise** staff canteen.

restaurateur, -trice [rɛstɔratœr, tris] nm, f 1. (CULIN) restaurant owner. 2. (ART) restorer.

restauration [rɛstɔrasjɔ̃] nf 1. (CULIN) catering; **dans la ~** in the restaurant trade OU catering business; **~ rapide** fast food. 2. (ART & POLIT) restoration.

restaurer [rɛstɔre] vt to restore. ▶ **se restaurer** vp to have something to eat.

reste [rɛst] nm 1. (*de lait, temps*): **le ~ (de)** the rest (of). 2. (MATHS) remainder. ▶ **restes** nmpl 1. (*de repas*) leftovers. 2. (*de mort*) remains. ▶ **au reste, du reste** loc adv besides.

rester [rɛste] ◆ vi 1. (*dans lieu, état*) to stay, to remain; **restez calme!** stay OU keep calm! 2. (*subsister*) to remain, to be left; **le seul bien qui me reste** the only thing I have left. 3. (*s'arrêter*): **en ~ à qqch** to stop at sthg; **en ~ là** to finish there. 4. loc: **y ~** *fam* (*mourir*) to pop one's clogs. ◆ v impers: **il en reste un peu** there's still a little left; **il te reste de l'argent?** do you still have some money left?

restituer [rɛstitɥe] vt 1. (*objet volé*) to return, to restore; (*argent*) to refund, to return. 2. (*énergie*) to release. 3. (*son*) to reproduce.

resto [rɛsto] nm *fam* restaurant; **les ~s du cœur** charity food distribution centres; **~-U** (UNIV) refectory.

Restoroute® [rɛstorut] nm motorway cafe Br, highway restaurant Am.

restreindre [rɛstrɛ̃dr] vt to restrict. ▶ **se restreindre** vp 1. (*domaine, champ*) to narrow. 2. (*personne*) to cut back; **se ~ dans qqch** to restrict sthg.

restreint, -e [rɛstrɛ̃, ɛ̃t] pp → **restreindre**.

restrictif, -ive [rɛstriktif, iv] adj restrictive.

restriction [rɛstriksjɔ̃] nf 1. (*condition*) condition; **sans ~** unconditionally. 2. (*limitation*) restriction. ▶ **restrictions** nfpl (*alimentaires*) rationing (U).

restructurer [rəstryktyre] vt to restructure.

résultat [rezylta] nm result; (*d'action*) outcome.

résulter [rezylte] ◆ vi: **~ de** to be the result of, to result from. ◆ v impers: **il en résulte que ...** as a result, ...

résumé [rezyme] nm summary, résumé; **en ~** (*pour conclure*) to sum up; (*en bref*) in brief, summarized.

résumer [rezyme] vt to summarize. ▶ **se résumer** vp (*se réduire*): **se ~ à qqch/à faire qqch** to come down to sthg/to doing sthg.

résurgence [rezyrʒɑ̃s] nf resurgence.

résurrection [rezyrɛksjɔ̃] nf resurrection.

rétablir [retablir] vt 1. (*gén*) to restore; (*malade*) to restore (to health). 2. (*communications, contact*) to re-establish. ▶ **se rétablir** vp 1. (*silence*) to return, to be restored. 2. (*malade*) to recover. 3. (GYM) to pull o.s. up.

rétablissement [retablismɑ̃] nm 1. (*d'ordre*) restoration. 2. (*de communications*) re-establishment. 3. (*de malade*) recovery. 4. (GYM) pull-up.

retard [rətar] nm 1. (*délai*) delay; **être en ~** (*sur heure*) to be late; (*sur échéance*) to be behind; **avoir du ~** to be late OU delayed. 2. (*de pays, peuple, personne*) backwardness.

retardataire [rətardater] nmf (*en retard*) latecomer.

retardement [rətardəmɑ̃] nm: **à ~** belatedly; *voir aussi* **bombe**.

retarder [rətarde] ◆ vt 1. (*personne, train*) to delay; (*sur échéance*) to put back. 2. (*ajourner - rendez-vous*) to put back OU off; (*- départ*) to put back OU off, to delay. 3. (*montre*) to put back. ◆ vi 1. (*horloge*) to be slow. 2. *fam* (*ne pas être au courant*) to be behind the times. 3. (*être en décalage*): **~ sur** to be out of step OU tune with.

retéléphoner [rətelefone] vi to phone again.

retenir [rətnir] vt 1. (*physiquement - objet, personne, cri*) to hold back; (*- souffle*) to hold; **~ qqn de faire qqch** to stop OU restrain sb from doing sthg. 2. (*retarder*) to keep, to detain. 3. (*montant, impôt*) to keep back, to withhold. 4. (*chambre*) to reserve. 5. (*leçon, cours*) to remember. 6. (*projet*) to accept, to adopt. 7. (*eau, chaleur*) to retain. 8. (MATHS) to carry. 9. (*intérêt, attention*) to hold. ▶ **se retenir** vp 1. (*s'accrocher*):

se ~ à to hold onto. **2.** (*se contenir*) to hold on; **se ~ de faire qqch** to refrain from doing sthg.

rétention [retɑ̃sjɔ̃] *nf* (MÉD) retention.

retentir [rətɑ̃tir] *vi* **1.** (*son*) to ring (out). **2.** (*pièce, rue*): **~ de** to resound with. **3.** *fig* (*fatigue, blessure*): **~ sur** to have an effect on.

retentissant, -e [rətɑ̃tisɑ̃, ɑ̃t] *adj* resounding.

retentissement [rətɑ̃tismɑ̃] *nm* (*de mesure*) repercussions (*pl*).

retenu, -e [rətny] *pp* → **retenir**.

retenue [rətny] *nf* **1.** (*prélèvement*) deduction. **2.** (MATHS) amount carried. **3.** (SCOL) detention. **4.** *fig* (*de personne - dans relations*) reticence; (*- dans comportement*) restraint; **sans ~** without restraint.

réticence [retisɑ̃s] *nf* (*hésitation*) hesitation, reluctance; **avec ~** hesitantly.

réticent, -e [retisɑ̃, ɑ̃t] *adj* hesitant, reluctant.

rétine [retin] *nf* retina.

retiré, -e [rətire] *adj* (*lieu*) remote, isolated; (*vie*) quiet.

retirer [rətire] *vt* **1.** (*vêtement, emballage*) to take off, to remove; (*permis, jouet*) to take away; **~ qqch à qqn** to take sthg away from sb. **2.** (*plainte*) to withdraw, to take back. **3.** (*avantages, bénéfices*): **~ qqch de qqch** to get ou derive sthg from sthg. **4.** (*bagages, billet*) to collect; (*argent*) to withdraw. ▶ **se retirer** *vp* **1.** (*s'isoler*) to withdraw, to retreat. **2.** (*des affaires*): **se ~ (de)** to retire (from). **3.** (*refluer*) to recede.

retombées [rətɔ̃be] *nfpl* repercussions, fallout (*sg*).

retomber [rətɔ̃be] *vi* **1.** (*gymnaste, chat*) to land. **2.** (*redevenir*): **~ malade** to relapse. **3.** (*cheveux*) to hang down. **4.** *fig* (*responsabilité*): **~ sur** to fall on.

rétorquer [retɔrke] *vt* to retort; **~ à qqn que ...** to retort to sb that ...

retors, -e [rətɔr, ɔrs] *adj* wily.

rétorsion [retɔrsjɔ̃] *nf* retaliation; **mesures de ~** reprisals.

retouche [rətuʃ] *nf* **1.** (*de texte, vêtement*) alteration. **2.** (ART & PHOT) touching up.

retoucher [rətuʃe] *vt* **1.** (*texte, vêtement*) to alter. **2.** (ART & PHOT) to touch up.

retour [rətur] *nm* **1.** (*gén*) return; **à mon/ton ~** when I/you get back, on my/your return; **être de ~ (de)** to be back (from); **~ en arrière** flashback; **en ~** in return. **2.** (*trajet*) journey back, return journey.

retourner [rəturne] ◆ *vt* (*aux: avoir*) **1.** (*carte, matelas*) to turn over; (*terre*) to turn (over). **2.** (*compliment, objet prêté*): **~ qqch (à qqn)** to return sthg (to sb). **3.** (*lettre, colis*) to send back, to return. ◆ *vi* (*aux: être*) to come/go back; **~ en arrière** ou **sur ses pas** to retrace one's steps. ▶ **se retourner** *vp* **1.** (*basculer*) to turn over. **2.** (*pivoter*) to turn round. **3.** *fam fig* (*s'adapter*) to sort o.s. out. **4.** (*rentrer*): **s'en ~** to go back (home). **5.** *fig* (*s'opposer*): **se ~ contre** to turn against.

retracer [rətrase] *vt* **1.** (*ligne*) to redraw. **2.** (*événement*) to relate.

rétracter [retrakte] *vt* to retract. ▶ **se rétracter** *vp* **1.** (*se contracter*) to retract. **2.** (*se dédire*) to back down.

retrait [rətrɛ] *nm* **1.** (*gén*) withdrawal; **~ du permis** disqualification from driving. **2.** (*de bagages*) collection. **3.** (*des eaux*) ebbing. ▶ **en retrait** *loc adj & loc adv* **1.** (*maison*) set back from the road; **rester en ~** *fig* to hang back. **2.** (*texte*) indented.

retraite [rətrɛt] *nf* **1.** (*gén*) retreat. **2.** (*cessation d'activité*) retirement; **être à la** ou **en ~** to be retired. **3.** (*revenu*) (retirement) pension.

retraité, -e [rətrete] ◆ *adj* **1.** (*personne*) retired. **2.** (TECHNOL) reprocessed. ◆ *nm, f* retired person, pensioner.

retrancher [rətrɑ̃ʃe] *vt* **1.** (*passage*): **~ qqch (de)** to cut sthg out (from), to remove sthg (from). **2.** (*montant*): **~ qqch (de)** to take sthg away (from), to deduct sthg (from). ▶ **se retrancher** *vp* to entrench o.s.; **se ~ derrière/dans** *fig* to take refuge behind/in.

retransmettre [rətrɑ̃smɛtr] *vt* to broadcast.

retransmis, -e [rətrɑ̃smi, iz] *pp* → **retransmettre**.

retransmission [rətrɑ̃smisjɔ̃] *nf* broadcast.

retravailler [rətravaje] ◆ *vt*: **~ qqch** to work on sthg again. ◆ *vi* to start work again.

rétrécir [retresir] *vi* (*tissu*) to shrink.

rétrécissement [retresismɑ̃] *nm* **1.** (*de vêtement*) shrinkage. **2.** (MÉD) stricture.

rétribution [retribysjɔ̃] *nf* remuneration.

rétro [retro] ◆ *nm* **1.** (*style*) old style ou fashion. **2.** *fam* (*rétroviseur*) rear-view mirror. ◆ *adj inv* old-style.

rétroactif, -ive [retrɔaktif, iv] *adj* retrospective.

rétrograde [retrɔgrad] adj péj reactionary.

rétrograder [retrɔgrade] ◆ vt to demote. ◆ vi (AUTOM) to change down.

rétroprojecteur [retrɔprɔʒɛktœr] nm overhead projector.

rétrospectif, -ive [retrɔspɛktif, iv] adj retrospective. ▶ **rétrospective** nf retrospective.

rétrospectivement [retrɔspɛktivmɑ̃] adv retrospectively.

retrousser [rɔtruse] vt 1. (manches, pantalon) to roll up. 2. (lèvres) to curl.

retrouvailles [rɔtruvaj] nfpl reunion (sg).

retrouver [rɔtruve] vt 1. (gén) to find; (appétit) to recover, to regain. 2. (reconnaître) to recognize. 3. (ami) to meet, to see. ▶ **se retrouver** vp 1. (entre amis) to meet (up) again; **on se retrouve au café?** shall we meet up ou see each other at the cafe? 2. (être de nouveau) to find o.s. again. 3. (s'orienter) to find one's way; **ne pas s'y ~** (dans papiers) to be completely lost.

rétroviseur [retrɔvizœr] nm rear-view mirror.

réunification [reynifikasjɔ̃] nf reunification.

réunifier [reynifje] vt to reunify.

réunion [reynjɔ̃] nf 1. (séance) meeting. 2. (jonction) union, merging. 3. (d'amis, de famille) reunion.

Réunion [reynjɔ̃] nf: **(l'île de) la ~** Reunion.

réunir [reynir] vt 1. (fonds) to collect. 2. (extrémités) to put together, to bring together. 3. (qualités) to combine. 4. (personnes) to bring together; (- après séparation) to reunite. ▶ **se réunir** vp 1. (personnes) to meet. 2. (entreprises) to combine; (états) to unite. 3. (fleuves, rues) to converge.

réussi, -e [reysi] adj successful; **c'est ~!** fig & iron congratulations!, well done!

réussir [reysir] ◆ vi 1. (personne, affaire) to succeed, to be a success; **~ à faire qqch** to succeed in doing sthg. 2. (climat): **~ à** to agree with. ◆ vt 1. (portrait, plat) to make a success of. 2. (examen) to pass.

réussite [reysit] nf 1. (succès) success. 2. (jeu de cartes) patience Br, solitaire Am.

réutiliser [reytilize] vt to reuse.

revaloriser [rɔvalɔrize] vt (monnaie) to revalue; (salaires) to raise; fig (idée, doctrine) to rehabilitate.

revanche [rɔvɑ̃ʃ] nf 1. (vengeance) revenge; **prendre sa ~** to take one's revenge. 2. (SPORT) return (match). ▶ **en revanche** loc adv (par contre) on the other hand.

rêvasser [rɛvase] vi to daydream.

rêve [rɛv] nm dream.

rêvé, -e [rɛve] adj ideal.

revêche [rɔvɛʃ] adj surly.

réveil [revɛj] nm 1. (de personne) waking (up); fig awakening. 2. (pendule) alarm clock.

réveiller [reveje] vt 1. (personne) to wake up. 2. (courage) to revive. ▶ **se réveiller** vp 1. (personne) to wake (up). 2. (ambitions) to reawaken.

réveillon [revɛjɔ̃] nm (jour - de Noël) Christmas Eve; (- de nouvel an) New Year's Eve.

RÉVEILLON

The 'réveillon' in France refers to celebrations on both Christmas Eve and New Year's Eve. To celebrate New Year's Eve, also known as 'la Saint-Sylvestre', French people often have a large meal with friends. At midnight everyone kisses, drinks champagne and wishes one another 'bonne année' ('Happy New Year'). In the streets car drivers welcome in the New Year by hooting their horns.

---

réveillonner [revɛjɔne] vi to have a Christmas Eve/New Year's Eve meal.

révélateur, -trice [revelatœr, tris] adj revealing. ▶ **révélateur** nm (PHOT) developer; fig (ce qui révèle) indication.

révélation [revelasjɔ̃] nf 1. (gén) revelation. 2. (artiste) discovery.

révéler [revele] vt 1. (gén) to reveal. 2. (artiste) to discover. ▶ **se révéler** vp 1. (apparaître) to be revealed. 2. (s'avérer) to prove to be.

revenant [rɔvnɑ̃] nm 1. (fantôme) spirit, ghost. 2. fam (personne) stranger.

revendeur, -euse [rɔvɑ̃dœr, øz] nm, f retailer.

revendication [rɔvɑ̃dikasjɔ̃] nf claim, demand.

revendiquer [rɔvɑ̃dike] vt (dû, responsabilité) to claim; (avec force) to demand.

revendre [rɔvɑ̃dr] vt 1. (après utilisation) to resell. 2. (vendre plus de) to sell more of.

revendu, -e [rɔvɑ̃dy] pp → **revendre**.

revenir [rɔvnir] vi 1. (gén) to come back, to return; **~ de** to come back from, to return from; **~ à** to come back to, to return to; **~ sur** (sujet) to go over again; (*décision*) to go back on; ~ **à soi** to come to. 2. (*mot, sujet*) to crop up. 3. (*à l'esprit*): ~ **à** to come back to. 4. (*impliquer*): **cela revient au même/à dire que ...** it amounts to the same thing/to saying (that) ... 5. (*coûter*): ~ **à** to come to, to amount to; ~ **cher** to be expensive. 6. (*honneur, tâche*): ~ **à** to fall to; **c'est à lui qu'il revient de ...** it is up to him to ... 7. (CULIN): **faire ~** to brown. 8. *loc*: **sa tête ne me revient pas** I don't like the look of him/her; **il n'en revenait pas** he couldn't get over it.

revente [rəvãt] *nf* resale.

revenu, -e [rəvny] *pp* → **revenir**. ▶ **revenu** *nm* (*de pays*) revenue; (*de personne*) income.

rêver [reve] ◆ *vi* to dream; (*rêvasser*) to daydream; ~ **de/à** to dream of/about. ◆ *vt* to dream; ~ **que** to dream (that).

réverbération [reverberasjɔ̃] *nf* reverberation.

réverbère [reverber] *nm* street lamp ou light.

révérence [reverãs] *nf* 1. (*salut*) bow. 2. *littéraire* (*déférence*) reverence.

révérend, -e [reverã, ãd] *adj* reverend. ▶ **révérend** *nm* reverend.

révérer [revere] *vt* to revere.

rêverie [revri] *nf* reverie.

revers [rəver] *nm* 1. (*de main*) back; (*de pièce*) reverse. 2. (*de veste*) lapel; (*de pantalon*) turn-up *Br*, cuff *Am*. 3. (TENNIS) backhand. 4. *fig* (*de fortune*) reversal.

reverser [rəverse] *vt* 1. (*liquide*) to pour out more of. 2. (FIN): ~ **qqch sur** to pay sthg into.

réversible [reversibl] *adj* reversible.

revêtement [rəvetmã] *nm* surface.

revêtir [rəvetir] *vt* 1. (*mur, surface*): ~ **(de)** to cover (with). 2. (*aspect*) to take on, to assume. 3. (*vêtement*) to put on; (*personne*) to dress.

revêtu, -e [rəvety] *pp* → **revêtir**.

rêveur, -euse [rever, øz] ◆ *adj* dreamy. ◆ *nm, f* dreamer.

revient [rəvjɛ̃] → **prix**.

revigorer [rəvigore] *vt* to invigorate.

revirement [rəvirmã] *nm* change.

réviser [revize] *vt* 1. (*réexaminer, modifier*) to revise, to review. 2. (SCOL) to revise. 3. (*machine*) to check.

révision [revizjɔ̃] *nf* 1. (*réexamen, modification*) révision, review. 2. (SCOL) revision. 3. (*de machine*) checkup.

revisser [rəvise] *vt* to screw back again.

revivre [rəvivr] ◆ *vi* (*personne*) to come

back to life, to revive; *fig* (*espoir*) to be revived, to revive; **faire ~** to revive. ◆ *vt* to relive; **faire ~ qqch à qqn** to bring sthg back to sb.

revoici [rəvwasi] *prép*: **me ~!** it's me again!, I'm back!

revoir [rəvwar] *vt* 1. (*renouer avec*) to see again. 2. (*corriger, étudier*) to revise *Br*, to review *Am*. ▶ **se revoir** *vp* (*amis*) to see each other again; (*professionnellement*) to meet again. ▶ **au revoir** *interj* & *nm* goodbye.

révoltant, -e [revɔltã, ãt] *adj* revolting.

révolte [revɔlt] *nf* revolt.

révolter [revɔlte] *vt* to disgust. ▶ **se révolter** *vp*: **se ~ (contre)** to revolt (against).

révolu, -e [revɔly] *adj* past; **avoir 15 ans ~s** (ADMIN) to be over 15.

révolution [revɔlysjɔ̃] *nf* 1. (*gén*) revolution. 2. *fam* (*effervescence*) uproar.

révolutionnaire [revɔlysjɔner] *nmf* & *adj* revolutionary.

révolutionner [revɔlysjɔne] *vt* 1. (*transformer*) to revolutionize. 2. (*mettre en émoi*) to stir up.

revolver [revɔlver] *nm* revolver.

révoquer [revɔke] *vt* 1. (*fonctionnaire*) to dismiss. 2. (*loi*) to revoke.

revue [rəvy] *nf* 1. (*gén*) review; ~ **de presse** press review; **passer en ~** *fig* to review. 2. (*défilé*) march-past. 3. (*magazine*) magazine. 4. (*spectacle*) revue.

rez-de-chaussée [redʃose] *nm inv* ground floor *Br*, first floor *Am*.

RFA (*abr de* **République fédérale d'Allemagne**) *nf* FRG.

rhabiller [rabije] *vt* to dress again. ▶ **se rhabiller** *vp* to get dressed again.

rhésus [rezys] *nm* rhesus (factor); ~ **positif/négatif** rhesus positive/negative.

rhétorique [retɔrik] *nf* rhetoric.

Rhin [rɛ̃] *nm*: **le ~** the Rhine.

rhinite [rinit] *nf* rhinitis (U).

rhinocéros [rinɔserɔs] *nm* rhinoceros.

rhino-pharyngite [rinɔfarɛ̃ʒit] *nf* (*pl* **rhino-pharyngites**) *nf* throat infection.

rhododendron [rɔdɔdɛ̃drɔ̃] *nm* rhododendron.

Rhône [ron] *nm*: **le ~** the (River) Rhone.

rhubarbe [rybarb] *nf* rhubarb.

rhum [rɔm] *nm* rum.

rhumatisme [rymatism] *nm* rheumatism.

rhume [rym] *nm* cold; **attraper un ~** to catch a cold; **~ des foins** hay fever.

ri [ri] *pp inv* → **rire**.

riant, -e [rijã, ãt] *adj* smiling; *fig* cheerful.

RIB, Rib [rib] (*abr de* **relevé d'identité bancaire**) *nm* bank account identification slip.

ribambelle [ribãbɛl] *nf*: **~ de** string of.

ricaner [rikane] *vi* to snigger.

riche [riʃ] ◆ *adj* 1. (*gén*) rich; (*personne, pays*) rich, wealthy; **~ en** ou **de** rich in. 2. (*idée*) great. ◆ *nmf* rich person; **les ~s** the rich.

richesse [riʃɛs] *nf* 1. (*de personne, pays*) wealth (U). 2. (*de faune, flore*) abundance. ▶ **richesses** *nfpl* (*gén*) wealth (U).

ricochet [rikɔʃɛ] *nm litt & fig* rebound; (*de balle d'arme*) ricochet; **par ~** in an indirect way.

rictus [riktys] *nm* rictus.

ride [rid] *nf* wrinkle; (*de surface d'eau*) ripple.

rideau, -x [rido] *nm* curtain; **~ de fer** (*frontière*) Iron Curtain.

rider [ride] *vt* 1. (*peau*) to wrinkle. 2. (*surface*) to ruffle. ▶ **se rider** *vp* to become wrinkled.

ridicule [ridikyl] ◆ *adj* ridiculous. ◆ *nm*: **se couvrir de ~** to make o.s. look ridiculous; **tourner qqn/qqch en ~** to ridicule sb/sthg.

ridiculiser [ridikylize] *vt* to ridicule. ▶ **se ridiculiser** *vp* to make o.s. look ridiculous.

rien [rjɛ̃] ◆ *pron indéf* 1. (*en contexte négatif*): **ne ... rien** nothing, not ... anything; **je n'ai ~ fait** I've done nothing, I haven't done anything; **~ ne m'intéresse** nothing interests me; **il n'y a plus ~ dans le réfrigérateur** there's nothing left in the fridge. 2. (*aucune chose*) nothing; **que fais-tu? – ~** what are you doing? – nothing; **~ de nouveau** nothing new; **~ d'autre** nothing else; **~ du tout** nothing at all; **~ à faire** it's no good; **de ~!** don't mention it!, not at all!; **pour ~** for nothing. 3. (*quelque chose*) anything; **sans ~ dire** without saying anything. ◆ *nm*: **pour un ~** (*se fâcher, pleurer*) for nothing, at the slightest thing; **perdre son temps à des ~s** to waste one's time with trivia; **en un ~ de temps** in no time at all. ▶ **rien que** *loc adv* only, just; **la vérité, ~ que la vérité** the truth and nothing but the truth; **~ que l'idée des vacances la comblait** just thinking about the holiday filled her with joy.

rieur, rieuse [rijœr, rijøz] *adj* cheerful.

rigide [riʒid] *adj* rigid; (*muscle*) tense.

rigidité [riʒidite] *nf* rigidity; (*de muscle*) tenseness; (*de principes, mœurs*) strictness.

rigole [rigɔl] *nf* channel.

rigoler [rigɔle] *vi fam* 1. (*rire*) to laugh. 2. (*plaisanter*): **~ (de)** to joke (about).

rigolo, -ote [rigɔlo, ɔt] *fam* ◆ *adj* funny. ◆ *nm, f péj* phoney.

rigoureux, -euse [rigurø, øz] *adj* 1. (*discipline, hiver*) harsh. 2. (*analyse*) rigorous.

rigueur [rigœr] *nf* 1. (*de punition*) severity, harshness. 2. (*de climat*) harshness. 3. (*d'analyse*) rigour, exactness. ▶ **à la rigueur** *loc adv* if necessary, if need be.

rillettes [rijɛt] *nfpl* potted pork, duck or goose.

rime [rim] *nf* rhyme.

rimer [rime] *vi*: **~ (avec)** to rhyme (with).

rinçage [rɛ̃saʒ] *nm* rinsing.

rincer [rɛ̃se] *vt* (*bouteille*) to rinse out; (*cheveux, linge*) to rinse.

ring [riŋ] *nm* 1. (BOXE) ring. 2. *Belg* (*route*) bypass.

riposte [ripɔst] *nf* 1. (*réponse*) retort, riposte. 2. (*contre-attaque*) counterattack.

riposter [ripɔste] ◆ *vt*: **~ que** to retort ou riposte that. ◆ *vi* 1. (*répondre*) to riposte. 2. (*contre-attaquer*) to counter, to retaliate.

rire [rir] ◆ *nm* laugh; **éclater de ~** to burst out laughing. ◆ *vi* 1. (*gén*) to laugh. 2. (*plaisanter*): **pour ~** *fam* as a joke, for a laugh.

risée [rize] *nf* ridicule; **être la ~ de** to be the laughing stock of.

risible [rizibl] *adj* (*ridicule*) ridiculous.

risque [risk] *nm* risk; **prendre des ~s** to take risks; **à tes/vos ~s et périls** at your own risk.

risqué, -e [riske] *adj* 1. (*entreprise*) risky, dangerous. 2. (*plaisanterie*) risqué, daring.

risquer [riske] *vt* 1. (*vie, prison*) to risk; **~ de faire qqch** to be likely to do sthg; **je risque de perdre tout ce que j'ai** I'm running the risk of losing everything I have. 2. (*tenter*) to venture. ▶ **se risquer** *vp* to venture; **se ~ à faire qqch** to dare to do sthg.

rissoler [risɔle] *vi* to brown.

rite [rit] *nm* 1. (RELIG) rite. 2. (*cérémonial & fig*) ritual.

rituel, -elle [ritɥɛl] *adj* ritual. ▶ **rituel** *nm* ritual.

rivage [rivaʒ] *nm* shore.

rival, -e, -aux [rival, o] ◆ *adj* rival (*avant n*). ◆ *nm, f* rival.

rivaliser [rivalize] *vi*: ~ **avec** to compete with.

rivalité [rivalite] *nf* rivalry.

rive [riv] *nf* (*de rivière*) bank; **la ~ droite** (*à Paris*) the north bank of the Seine (*generally considered more affluent than the south bank*); **la ~ gauche** (*à Paris*) the south bank of the Seine (*traditionally associated with students and artists*).

river [rive] *vt* 1. (*fixer*): ~ **qqch à qqch** to rivet sthg to sthg. 2. (*clou*) to clinch; **être rivé à** *fig* to be riveted ou glued to.

riverain, -e [rivʀɛ̃, ɛn] *nm, f* resident.

rivet [rivɛ] *nm* rivet.

rivière [rivjɛʀ] *nf* river.

rixe [riks] *nf* fight, brawl.

riz [ri] *nm* rice.

rizière [rizjɛʀ] *nf* paddy (field).

RMI (*abr de revenu minimum d'insertion*) *nm* minimum guaranteed income (*for people with no other source of income*).

robe [ʀɔb] *nf* 1. (*de femme*) dress; ~ **de mariée** wedding dress. 2. (*peignoir*): ~ **de chambre** dressing gown. 3. (*de cheval*) coat. 4. (*de vin*) colour.

robinet [ʀɔbinɛ] *nm* tap.

robinetterie [ʀɔbinɛtʀi] *nf* (*installations*) taps (*pl*).

robot [ʀɔbo] *nm* 1. (*gén*) robot. 2. (*ménager*) food processor.

robotique [ʀɔbɔtik] *nf* robotics (U).

robotisation [ʀɔbɔtizasjɔ̃] *nf* automation.

robuste [ʀɔbyst] *adj* 1. (*personne, santé*) robust. 2. (*plante*) hardy. 3. (*voiture*) sturdy.

roc [ʀɔk] *nm* rock.

rocade [ʀɔkad] *nf* bypass.

rocaille [ʀɔkaj] *nf* 1. (*cailloux*) loose stones (*pl*). 2. (*dans jardin*) rockery.

rocailleux, -euse [ʀɔkajø, øz] *adj* 1. (*terrain*) rocky. 2. *fig* (*voix*) harsh.

rocambolesque [ʀɔkɑ̃bɔlɛsk] *adj* fantastic.

roche [ʀɔʃ] *nf* rock.

rocher [ʀɔʃe] *nm* rock.

rocheux, -euse [ʀɔʃø, øz] *adj* rocky. ▶ **Rocheuses** *nfpl*: **les Rocheuses** the Rockies.

rock [ʀɔk] *nm* rock ('n' roll).

rodage [ʀɔdaʒ] *nm* 1. (*de véhicule*) running-in; 'en ~' 'running in'. 2. *fig* (*de méthode*) running-in period.

rodéo [ʀɔdeo] *nm* rodeo; *fig & iron* free-for-all.

roder [ʀɔde] *vt* 1. (*véhicule*) to run in. 2. *fam* (*méthode*) to run in, to debug; (*personne*) to break in.

rôdeur, -euse [ʀodœʀ, øz] *nm, f* prowler.

rogne [ʀɔɲ] *nf fam* bad temper; **être/se mettre en ~** to be in/to get into a bad mood, to be in/to get into a temper.

rogner [ʀɔɲe] ◆ *vt* 1. (*ongles*) to trim. 2. (*revenus*) to eat into. ◆ *vi*: ~ **sur qqch** to cut down on sthg.

roi [ʀwa] *nm* king; **tirer les ~s** to celebrate Epiphany.

rôle [ʀol] *nm* role, part; **jeu de ~** role play.

romain, -e [ʀɔmɛ̃, ɛn] *adj* Roman. ▶ **Romain, -e** *nm, f* Roman.

roman, -e [ʀɔmɑ̃, an] *adj* 1. (*langue*) Romance. 2. (ARCHIT) Romanesque. ▶ **roman** *nm* (LITTÉRATURE) novel.

romance [ʀɔmɑ̃s] *nf* (*chanson*) love song.

romanche [ʀɔmɑ̃ʃ] *nm & adj* Romansh.

romancier, -ère [ʀɔmɑ̃sje, ɛʀ] *nm, f* novelist.

romand, -e [ʀɔmɑ̃, ɑ̃d] *adj* of/from French-speaking Switzerland.

romanesque [ʀɔmanɛsk] *adj* 1. (LITTÉRATURE) novelistic. 2. (*aventure*) fabulous, storybook (*avant n*).

roman-feuilleton [ʀɔmɑ̃fœjtɔ̃] *nm* serial; *fig* soap opera.

roman-photo [ʀɔmɑ̃fɔto] *nm* story told in photographs.

romantique [ʀɔmɑ̃tik] *nmf & adj* romantic.

romantisme [ʀɔmɑ̃tism] *nm* 1. (ART) Romantic movement. 2. (*sensibilité*) romanticism.

romarin [ʀɔmaʀɛ̃] *nm* rosemary.

rompre [ʀɔ̃pʀ] ◆ *vt* 1. *sout* (*objet*) to break. 2. (*charme, marché*) to break; (*fiançailles, relations*) to break off. ◆ *vi* to break; ~ **avec qqn** *fig* to break up with sb. ▶ **se rompre** *vp* to break; **se ~ le cou/les reins** to break one's neck/back.

ronce [ʀɔ̃s] *nf* (*arbuste*) bramble.

ronchonner [ʀɔ̃ʃɔne] *vi fam*: ~ **(après)** to grumble (at).

rond, -e [ʀɔ̃, ʀɔ̃d] *adj* 1. (*forme, chiffre*) round. 2. (*joue, ventre*) chubby, plump. 3. *fam* (*ivre*) tight. ▶ **rond** *nm* 1. (*cercle*) circle; **en ~** in a circle ou ring; **tourner en ~** *fig* to go round in circles. 2. (*anneau*) ring. 3. *fam* (*argent*): **je n'ai pas un ~** I haven't got a penny ou bean.

ronde [rɔ̃d] nf 1. (de surveillance) rounds (pl); (de policier) beat. 2. (danse) round. 3. (MUS) semibreve Br, whole note Am. ► **à la ronde** loc adv: **à des kilomètres à la ~** for miles around.

rondelle [rɔ̃dɛl] nf 1. (de saucisson) slice. 2. (de métal) washer.

rondement [rɔ̃dmɑ̃] adv (efficacement) efficiently, briskly.

rondeur [rɔ̃dœr] nf 1. (forme) roundness. 2. (partie charnue) curve.

rond-point [rɔ̃pwɛ̃] nm roundabout Br, traffic circle Am.

ronflant, -e [rɔ̃flɑ̃, ɑ̃t] adj péj grandiose.

ronflement [rɔ̃fləmɑ̃] nm 1. (de dormeur) snore. 2. (de poêle, moteur) hum, purr.

ronfler [rɔ̃fle] vi 1. (dormeur) to snore. 2. (poêle, moteur) to hum, to purr.

ronger [rɔ̃ʒe] vt (bois, os) to gnaw; (métal, falaise) to eat away at; fig to gnaw at, to eat away at. ► **se ronger** vp 1. (grignoter): **se ~ les ongles** to bite one's nails. 2. fig (se tourmenter) to worry, to torture o.s.

rongeur, -euse [rɔ̃ʒœr, øz] adj gnawing, rodent (avant n). ► **rongeur** nm rodent.

ronronner [rɔ̃rɔne] vi (chat) to purr; (moteur) to purr, to hum.

roquefort [rɔkfɔr] nm Roquefort (strong blue cheese).

rosace [rozas] nf 1. (ornement) rose. 2. (vitrail) rose window. 3. (figure géométrique) rosette.

rosbif [rɔsbif] nm 1. (viande) roast beef. 2. fam (Anglais) pejorative or humorous term used with reference to British people.

rose [roz] ◆ nf rose. ◆ nm pink. ◆ adj pink.

rosé, -e [roze] adj (teinte) rosy. ► **rosé** nm rosé. ► **rosée** nf dew.

roseau, -x [rozo] nm reed.

rosier [rozje] nm rose bush.

rosir [rozir] vt & vi to turn pink.

rosser [rɔse] vt to thrash.

rossignol [rɔsiɲɔl] nm (oiseau) nightingale.

rot [ro] nm burp.

rotatif, -ive [rɔtatif, iv] adj rotary.

rotation [rɔtasjɔ̃] nf rotation.

roter [rɔte] vi fam to burp.

rôti, -e [roti] adj roast. ► **rôti** nm roast, joint.

rotin [rɔtɛ̃] nm rattan.

rôtir [rotir] ◆ vt to roast. ◆ vi (CULIN) to roast.

rôtisserie [rotisri] nf 1. (restaurant) ≃ steakhouse. 2. (magasin) shop selling roast meat.

rotonde [rɔtɔ̃d] nf (bâtiment) rotunda.

rotule [rɔtyl] nf kneecap.

rouage [rwaʒ] nm cog, gearwheel; **les ~s de l'État** fig the wheels of State.

rouble [rubl] nm rouble.

roucouler [rukule] ◆ vt to warble; fig to coo. ◆ vi to coo; fig to bill and coo.

roue [ru] nf 1. (gén) wheel; **~ de secours** spare wheel; **un deux ~s** a two-wheeled vehicle. 2. (de paon): **faire la ~** to display. 3. (GYM) cartwheel.

rouer [rwe] vt: **~ qqn de coups** to thrash sb, to beat sb.

rouge [ruʒ] ◆ nm 1. (couleur) red. 2. fam (vin) red (wine). 3. (fard) rouge, blusher; **~ à lèvres** lipstick. 4. (AUTOM): **passer au ~** to turn red; (conducteur) to go through a red light. ◆ nmf (POLIT & péj) Red. ◆ adj 1. (gén) red. 2. (fer, tison) red-hot. 3. (POLIT & péj) Red.

rouge-gorge [ruʒgɔrʒ] nm robin.

rougeole [ruʒɔl] nf measles (sg).

rougeoyer [ruʒwaje] vi to turn red.

rougeur [ruʒœr] nf 1. (de visage, de chaleur, d'effort) flush; (de gêne) blush. 2. (sur peau) red spot ou blotch.

rougir [ruʒir] ◆ vt 1. (colorer) to turn red. 2. (chauffer) to make red-hot. ◆ vi 1. (devenir rouge) to turn red. 2. (d'émotion): **~ (de)** (de plaisir, colère) to flush (with); (de gêne) to blush (with). 3. fig (avoir honte): **~ de qqch** to be ashamed of sthg.

rougissant, -e [ruʒisɑ̃, ɑ̃t] adj (ciel) reddening; (jeune fille) blushing.

rouille [ruj] ◆ nf 1. (oxyde) rust. 2. (CULIN) spicy garlic sauce for fish soup. ◆ adj inv rust.

rouiller [ruje] ◆ vt to rust, to make rusty. ◆ vi to rust.

roulade [rulad] nf (galipette) roll.

rouleau, -x [rulo] nm 1. (gén & TECHNOL) roller; **~ compresseur** steamroller. 2. (de papier) roll. 3. (à pâtisserie) rolling pin.

roulement [rulmɑ̃] nm 1. (gén) rolling. 2. (de personnel) rotation; **travailler par ~** to work to a rota. 3. (de tambour, tonnerre) roll. 4. (TECHNOL) rolling bearing.

rouler [rule] ◆ vt 1. (déplacer) to wheel. 2. (enrouler - tapis) to roll up; (- cigarette) to roll. 3. fam (balancer) to sway. 4. (LING) to roll. 5. fam fig (duper) to swindle, to do. ◆ vi 1. (ballon, bateau) to roll.

2. (*véhicule*) to go, to run; (*suj: personne*) to drive. ► **se rouler** *vp* to roll about; **se ~ par terre** to roll on the ground; **se ~ en boule** to roll o.s. into a ball.

roulette [rulɛt] *nf* **1.** (*petite roue*) castor. **2.** (*de dentiste*) drill. **3.** (JEU) roulette.

roulis [ruli] *nm* roll.

roulotte [rulɔt] *nf* (*de gitan*) caravan; (*de tourisme*) caravan Br, trailer Am.

roumain, -e [rumɛ̃, ɛn] *adj* Romanian. ► **roumain** *nm* (*langue*) Romanian. ► **Roumain, -e** *nm, f* Romanian.

Roumanie [rumani] *nf*: **la ~** Romania.

rouquin, -e [rukɛ̃, in] *fam* ◆ *adj* red-headed. ◆ *nm, f* redhead.

rouspéter [ruspete] *vi fam* to grumble, to moan.

rousse → **roux**.

rousseur [rusœr] *nf* redness. ► **taches de rousseur** *nfpl* freckles.

roussir [rusir] ◆ *vt* **1.** (*rendre roux*) to turn brown; (CULIN) to brown. **2.** (*brûler légèrement*) to singe. ◆ *vi* to turn brown; (CULIN) to brown.

route [rut] *nf* **1.** (*gén*) road; **en ~** on the way; **en ~!** let's go!; **mettre en ~** (*démarrer*) to start up; *fig* to get under way; **la ~ européenne** the trans-Europe highway. **2.** (*itinéraire*) route.

routier, -ère [rutje, ɛr] *adj* road (*avant n*). ► **routier** *nm* **1.** (*chauffeur*) long-distance lorry driver Am ou trucker Am. **2.** (*restaurant*) ≃ transport cafe Br, ≃ truck stop Am.

routine [rutin] *nf* routine.

routinier, -ère [rutinje, ɛr] *adj* routine.

rouvert, -e [ruvɛr, ɛrt] *pp* → **rouvrir**.

rouvrir [ruvrir] *vt* to reopen, to open again. ► **se rouvrir** *vp* to reopen, to open again.

roux, rousse [ru, rus] ◆ *adj* **1.** (*cheveux*) red. **2.** (*sucre*) brown. ◆ *nm, f* (*personne*) redhead. ► **roux** *nm* (*couleur*) red, russet.

royal, -e, -aux [rwajal, o] *adj* **1.** (*de roi*) royal. **2.** (*magnifique*) princely.

royaliste [rwajalist] *nmf & adj* royalist.

royaume [rwajom] *nm* kingdom.

Royaume-Uni [rwajomyni] *nm*: **le ~** the United Kingdom.

royauté [rwajote] *nf* **1.** (*fonction*) kingship. **2.** (*régime*) monarchy.

RPR (*abr de* **Rassemblement pour la République**) *nm* French political party to the right of the political spectrum.

rte *abr de* **route**.

ruade [ryad] *nf* kick.

ruban [rybã] *nm* ribbon; **~ adhésif** adhesive tape.

rubéole [rybeɔl] *nf* German measles (*sg*), rubella.

rubis [rybi] *nm* (*pierre précieuse*) ruby.

rubrique [rybrik] *nf* **1.** (*chronique*) column. **2.** (*dans classement*) heading.

ruche [ryʃ] *nf* (*abri*) hive, beehive.

rude [ryd] *adj* **1.** (*surface*) rough. **2.** (*voix*) harsh. **3.** (*personne, manières*) rough, uncouth. **4.** (*hiver, épreuve*) harsh, severe; (*tâche, adversaire*) tough.

rudement [rydmã] *adv* **1.** (*brutalement - tomber*) hard; (*- répondre*) harshly. **2.** *fam* (*très*) damn.

rudesse [rydɛs] *nf* harshness, severity.

rudimentaire [rydimɑ̃tɛr] *adj* rudimentary.

rudoyer [rydwaje] *vt* to treat harshly.

rue [ry] *nf* street.

ruée [rɥe] *nf* rush.

ruelle [rɥɛl] *nf* (*rue*) alley, lane.

ruer [rɥe] *vi* to kick. ► **se ruer** *vp*: **se ~ sur** to pounce on.

rugby [rygbi] *nm* rugby.

rugir [ryʒir] *vi* to roar; (*vent*) to howl.

rugissement [ryʒismã] *nm* roar, roaring (U); (*de vent*) howling.

rugosité [rygozite] *nf* **1.** (*de surface*) roughness. **2.** (*aspérité*) rough patch.

rugueux, -euse [rygø, øz] *adj* rough.

ruine [rɥin] *nf* **1.** (*gén*) ruin. **2.** (*effondrement*) ruin, downfall. **3.** (*humaine*) wreck.

ruiner [rɥine] *vt* to ruin. ► **se ruiner** *vp* to ruin o.s., to bankrupt o.s.

ruineux, -euse [rɥinø, øz] *adj* ruinous.

ruisseau, -x [rɥiso] *nm* **1.** (*cours d'eau*) stream. **2.** *fig & péj* (*caniveau*) gutter.

ruisseler [rɥisle] *vi*: **~ (de)** to stream (with).

rumeur [rymœr] *nf* **1.** (*bruit*) murmur. **2.** (*nouvelle*) rumour.

ruminer [rymine] *vt* to ruminate; *fig* to mull over.

rupture [ryptyr] *nf* **1.** (*cassure*) breaking. **2.** *fig* (*changement*) abrupt change. **3.** (*de négociations, fiançailles*) breaking off; (*de contrat*) breach. **4.** (*amoureuse*) breakup, split.

rural, -e, -aux [ryral, o] *adj* country (*avant n*), rural.

ruse [ryz] *nf* **1.** (*habileté*) cunning, craftiness. **2.** (*subterfuge*) ruse.

rusé, -e [ryze] *adj* cunning, crafty.

russe [rys] ◆ *adj* Russian. ◆ *nm* (*langue*) Russian. ► **Russe** *nmf* Russian.

Russie [rysi] *nf*: **la ~** Russia.

rustine [rystin] nf small rubber patch for repairing bicycle tyres.

rustique [rystik] adj rustic.

rustre [rystr] péj ◆ nmf lout. ◆ adj loutish.

rutilant, -e [rytilā, āt] adj (brillant) gleaming.

rythme [ritm] nm 1. (MUS) rhythm; **en ~** in rhythm. 2. (de travail, production) pace, rate.

rythmique [ritmik] adj rhythmical.

S

s, S [ɛs] nm inv 1. (lettre) s, S. 2. (forme) zigzag. ▶ **S** (abr de **Sud**) S.

s' → **se, si.**

s/ abr de **sur.**

sa → **son².**

SA (abr de **société anonyme**) nf = Ltd Br, = Inc. Am.

sabbatique [sabatik] adj 1. (RELIG) Sabbath (avant n). 2. (congé) sabbatical.

sable [sabl] nm sand; **~s mouvants** quicksand (sg), quicksands.

sablé, -e [sable] adj (route) sandy. ▶ **sablé** nm = shortbread (U).

sabler [sable] vt 1. (route) to sand. 2. (boire): **~ le champagne** to crack a bottle of champagne.

sablier [sablije] nm hourglass.

sablonneux, -euse [sablɔnø, øz] adj sandy.

saborder [sabɔrde] vt (navire) to scuttle; fig (entreprise) to wind up; fig (projet) to scupper.

sabot [sabo] nm 1. (chaussure) clog. 2. (de cheval) hoof. 3. (AUTOM): **~ de Denver** wheel clamp, Denver boot.

sabotage [sabotaʒ] nm 1. (volontaire) sabotage. 2. (bâclage) bungling.

saboter [sabɔte] vt 1. (volontairement) to sabotage. 2. (bâcler) to bungle.

saboteur, -euse [sabɔtœr, øz] nm, f (MIL & POLIT) saboteur.

sabre [sabr] nm sabre.

sac [sak] nm 1. (gén) bag; (pour grains) sack; (contenu) bag, bagful, sack, sackful; **~ de couchage** sleeping bag; **~ à dos** rucksack; **~ à main** handbag. 2. fam (10 francs) 10 francs. 3. littéraire (pillage) sack.

saccade [sakad] nf jerk.

saccadé, -e [sakade] adj jerky.

saccage [sakaʒ] nm havoc.

saccager [sakaʒe] vt 1. (piller) to sack. 2. (dévaster) to destroy.

sachant ppr → **savoir.**

sache, saches etc → **savoir.**

sachet [saʃɛ] nm (de bonbons) bag; (de shampooing) sachet; **~ de thé** teabag.

sacoche [sakɔʃ] nf 1. (de médecin, d'écolier) bag. 2. (de cycliste) pannier.

sac-poubelle [sakpubɛl] (pl **sacs-poubelle**) nm (petit) dustbin liner; (grand) rubbish bag Br, garbage bag Am.

sacre [sakr] nm (de roi) coronation; (d'évêque) consecration.

sacré, -e [sakre] adj 1. (gén) sacred. 2. (RELIG) (ordres, écritures) holy. 3. (avant n) fam (maudit) bloody (avant n) Br, goddam (avant n) Am.

sacrement [sakrəmā] nm sacrament.

sacrément [sakremā] adv fam vieilli dashed.

sacrer [sakre] vt 1. (roi) to crown; (évêque) to consecrate. 2. fig (déclarer) to hail.

sacrifice [sakrifis] nm sacrifice.

sacrifié, -e [sakrifje] adj 1. (personne) sacrificed. 2. (prix) giveaway (avant n).

sacrifier [sakrifje] vt (gén) to sacrifice; **~ qqn/qqch à** to sacrifice sb/sthg to. ▶ **se sacrifier** vp: **se ~ à/pour** to sacrifice o.s. to/for.

sacrilège [sakrilɛʒ] ◆ nm sacrilege. ◆ adj sacrilegious.

sacristain [sakristē] nm sacristan.

sacristie [sakristi] nf sacristy.

sadique [sadik] ◆ nmf sadist. ◆ adj sadistic.

sadisme [sadism] nm sadism.

safari [safari] nm safari.

safran [safrā] nm (épice) saffron.

saga [saga] nf saga.

sage [saʒ] ◆ adj 1. (personne, conseil) wise, sensible. 2. (enfant, chien) good. 3. (goûts) modest; (propos, vêtement) sober. ◆ nm wise man, sage.

sage-femme [saʒfam] nf midwife.

sagement [saʒmā] adv 1. (avec bon sens) wisely, sensibly. 2. (docilement) like a good girl/boy.

sagesse [saʒɛs] nf 1. (bon sens) wisdom, good sense. 2. (docilité) good behaviour.

Sagittaire [saʒitɛr] nm (ASTROL) Sagittarius.

Sahara [saara] nm: **le ~** the Sahara.

saignant, -e [sɛɲā, āt] adj 1. (blessure) bleeding. 2. (viande) rare, underdone.

saignement [sɛɲmā] nm bleeding.

saloperie

saigner [seɲe] ♦ vt 1. (malade, animal) to bleed. 2. (financièrement): ~ qqn (à blanc) to bleed sb (white). ♦ vi to bleed; **je saigne du nez** my nose is bleeding, I've got a nosebleed.

saillant, -e [sajɑ̃, ɑ̃t] adj (proéminent) projecting, protruding; (muscles) bulging; (pommettes) prominent.

saillie [saji] nf (avancée) projection; **en ~** projecting.

saillir [sajir] vi (balcon) to project, to protrude; (muscles) to bulge.

sain, -e [sɛ̃, sɛn] adj 1. (gén) healthy; ~ **et sauf** safe and sound. 2. (lecture) wholesome. 3. (fruit) fit to eat; (mur, gestion) sound.

saint, -e [sɛ̃, sɛ̃t] ♦ adj 1. (sacré) holy. 2. (pieux) saintly. 3. (extrême): **avoir une ~e horreur de qqch** to detest sthg. ♦ nm, f saint.

saint-bernard [sɛ̃bɛrnar] nm inv 1. (chien) St Bernard. 2. fig (personne) good Samaritan.

saintement [sɛ̃tmɑ̃] adv: **vivre ~** to lead a saintly life.

sainte-nitouche [sɛ̃tnituʃ] nf péj: **c'est une ~** butter wouldn't melt in her mouth.

sainteté [sɛ̃te] nf holiness.

saint-glinglin [sɛ̃glɛ̃glɛ̃] ▸ **à la saint-glinglin** loc adv fam till Doomsday.

Saint-Père [sɛ̃pɛr] nm Holy Father.

sais, sait etc → **savoir**.

saisie [sezi] nf 1. (FISC & JUR) distraint, seizure. 2. (INFORM) input; ~ **de données** data capture.

saisir [sezir] vt 1. (empoigner) to take hold of; (avec force) to seize. 2. (FIN & JUR) to seize, to distrain. 3. (INFORM) to capture. 4. (comprendre) to grasp. 5. (suj: sensation, émotion) to grip, to seize. 6. (surprendre) **être saisi par** to be struck by. 7. (CULIN) to seal. ▸ **se saisir** vp: ~ **de qqn/qqch** to seize sb/sthg, to grab sb/sthg.

saisissant, -e [sezisɑ̃, ɑ̃t] adj 1. (spectacle) gripping; (ressemblance) striking. 2. (froid) biting.

saison [sɛzɔ̃] nf season; **en/hors ~** in/out of season; **la haute/basse/morte ~** the high/low/off season.

saisonnier, -ère [sɛzɔnje, ɛr] ♦ adj seasonal. ♦ nm, f seasonal worker.

salace [salas] adj salacious.

salade [salad] nf 1. (plante) lettuce. 2. (plat) (green) salad; ~ **de fruits** fruit salad.

saladier [saladje] nm salad bowl.

salaire [salɛr] nm 1. (rémunération) salary, wage; ~ **brut/net/de base** gross/net/basic salary, gross/net/basic wage. 2. fig (récompense) reward.

salant [salɑ̃] → **marais**.

salarial, -e, -aux [salarjal, o] adj wage (avant n).

salarié, -e [salarje] ♦ adj 1. (personne) wage-earning. 2. (travail) paid. ♦ nm, f salaried employee.

salaud [salo] vulg ♦ nm bastard. ♦ adj m shitty.

sale [sal] adj 1. (linge, mains) dirty; (couleur) dirty, dingy. 2. (avant n) (type, gueule, coup) nasty; (tour, histoire) dirty; (bête, temps) filthy.

salé, -e [sale] adj 1. (eau, saveur) salty; (beurre) salted; (viande, poisson) salt (avant n), salted. 2. fig (histoire) spicy. 3. fam fig (addition, facture) steep.

saler [sale] vt (gén) to salt. .

saleté [salte] nf 1. (malpropreté) dirtiness, filthiness. 2. (crasse) dirt (U), filth (U); **faire des ~s** to make a mess. 3. fam (maladie) bug. 4. (obscénité) dirty thing, obscenity; **il m'a dit des ~s** he used obscenities to me. 5. (action) disgusting thing; **faire une ~ à qqn** to play a dirty trick on sb. 6. fam péj (personne) nasty piece of work.

salière [saljɛr] nf saltcellar.

salir [salir] vt 1. (linge, mains) to (make) dirty, to soil. 2. fig (réputation, personne) to sully.

salissant, -e [salisɑ̃, ɑ̃t] adj 1. (tissu) easily soiled. 2. (travail) dirty, messy.

salive [saliv] nf saliva.

saliver [salive] vi to salivate.

salle [sal] nf 1. (pièce) room; **en ~** (dans un café) inside; ~ **d'attente** waiting room; ~ **de bains** bathroom; ~ **de cinéma** cinema; ~ **de classe** classroom; ~ **d'eau, ~ de douches** shower room; ~ **d'embarquement** departure lounge; ~ **à manger** dining room; ~ **d'opération** operating theatre; ~ **de séjour** living room; ~ **de spectacle** theatre; ~ **des ventes** saleroom. 2. (de spectacle) auditorium. 3. (public) audience, house; **faire ~ comble** to have a full house.

salon [salɔ̃] nm 1. (de maison) lounge Br, living room. 2. (commerce): ~ **de coiffure** hairdressing salon, hairdresser's; ~ **de thé** tearoom. 3. (foire-exposition) show.

salope [salɔp] nf vulg bitch.

saloperie [salɔpri] nf fam 1. (pacotille) rubbish (U). 2. (maladie) bug. 3. (saleté) junk (U), rubbish (U); **faire des ~s** to make a mess. **4.** (*action*) dirty trick; **faire des ~s à qqn** to play dirty tricks on sb. **5.** (*propos*) dirty comment.

salopette [salɔpɛt] *nf* (*d'ouvrier*) overalls (*pl*); (*à bretelles*) dungarees (*pl*).

saltimbanque [saltɛ̃bɑ̃k] *nmf* acrobat.

salubrité [salybrite] *nf* healthiness.

saluer [salɥe] *vt* **1.** (*accueillir*) to greet. **2.** (*dire au revoir à*) to take one's leave of. **3.** (MIL & *fig*) to salute. ▶ **se saluer** *vp* to say hello/goodbye (to one another).

salut [saly] ◆ *nm* **1.** (*de la main*) wave; (*de la tête*) nod; (*propos*) greeting. **2.** (MIL) salute. **3.** (*sauvegarde*) safety. **4.** (RELIG) salvation. ◆ *interj fam* (*bonjour*) hi!; (*au revoir*) bye!, see you too!

salutaire [salytɛr] *adj* **1.** (*conseil, expérience*) salutary. **2.** (*remède, repos*) beneficial.

salutation [salytasjɔ̃] *nf littéraire* salutation, greeting. ▶ **salutations** *nfpl*: **veuillez agréer, Monsieur, mes ~s distinguées** OU **mes sincères ~s** *sout* yours faithfully, yours sincerely.

salve [salv] *nf* salvo.

samaritain, -e [samaritɛ̃, ɛn] *adj* Samaritan.

samedi [samdi] *nm* Saturday; **nous sommes partis ~** we left on Saturday; **~ 13 septembre** Saturday 13th September; **~ dernier/prochain** last/next Saturday; **le ~** on Saturdays.

SAMU, Samu [samy] (*abr de* **Service d'aide médicale d'urgence**) *nm* French ambulance and emergency service, ≃ Ambulance Brigade Br, ≃ Paramedics Am.

sanatorium [sanatɔrjɔm] *nm* sanatorium.

sanctifier [sɑ̃ktifje] *vt* **1.** (*rendre saint*) to sanctify. **2.** (*révérer*) to hallow.

sanction [sɑ̃ksjɔ̃] *nf* sanction; *fig* (*conséquence*) penalty, price; **prendre des ~s contre** to impose sanctions on.

sanctionner [sɑ̃ksjɔne] *vt* to sanction.

sanctuaire [sɑ̃ktɥɛr] *nm* **1.** (*d'église*) sanctuary. **2.** (*lieu saint*) shrine.

sandale [sɑ̃dal] *nf* sandal.

sandalette [sɑ̃dalɛt] *nf* sandal.

sandwich [sɑ̃dwitʃ] (*pl* **sandwiches** OU **sandwichs**) *nm* sandwich.

sang [sɑ̃] *nm* blood.

sang-froid [sɑ̃frwa] *nm inv* calm; **de ~** in cold blood; **perdre/garder son ~** to lose/to keep one's head.

sanglant, -e [sɑ̃glɑ̃, ɑ̃t] *adj* bloody; *fig* cruel.

sangle [sɑ̃gl] *nf* strap; (*de selle*) girth.

sangler [sɑ̃gle] *vt* (*attacher*) to strap; (*cheval*) to girth.

sanglier [sɑ̃glije] *nm* boar.

sanglot [sɑ̃glo] *nm* sob; **éclater en ~s** to burst into sobs.

sangloter [sɑ̃glɔte] *vi* to sob.

sangsue [sɑ̃sy] *nf* leech; *fig* (*personne*) bloodsucker.

sanguin, -e [sɑ̃gɛ̃, in] *adj* **1.** (ANAT) blood (*avant n*). **2.** (*rouge - visage*) ruddy; (*- orange*) blood (*avant n*). **3.** (*emporté*) quick-tempered.

sanguinaire [sɑ̃ginɛr] *adj* **1.** (*tyran*) bloodthirsty. **2.** (*lutte*) bloody.

Sanisette® [sanizɛt] *nf automatic public toilet.*

sanitaire [sanitɛr] *adj* **1.** (*service, mesure*) health (*avant n*). **2.** (*installation, appareil*) bathroom (*avant n*). ▶ **sanitaires** *nmpl* toilets and showers.

sans [sɑ̃] ◆ *prép* without; **~ argent** without any money; **~ faire un effort** without making an effort. ◆ *adv*: **passe-moi mon manteau, je ne veux pas sortir ~** pass me my coat, I don't want to go out without it. ▶ **sans que** *loc conj*: **~ que vous le sachiez** without your knowing.

sans-abri [sɑ̃zabri] *nmf inv* homeless person.

sans-emploi [sɑ̃zɑ̃plwa] *nmf inv* unemployed person.

sans-gêne [sɑ̃ʒɛn] ◆ *nm inv* (*qualité*) rudeness, lack of consideration. ◆ *adj inv* rude, inconsiderate.

santé [sɑ̃te] *nf* health; **à ta/votre ~!** cheers!, good health!

santon [sɑ̃tɔ̃] *nm figure placed in Christmas crib.*

saoul = **soûl**.

saouler = **soûler**.

sapeur-pompier [sapœrpɔ̃pje] *nm* fireman, fire fighter.

saphir [safir] *nm* sapphire.

sapin [sapɛ̃] *nm* **1.** (*arbre*) fir, firtree; **~ de Noël** Christmas tree. **2.** (*bois*) fir, deal Br.

sarcasme [sarkasm] *nm* sarcasm.

sarcastique [sarkastik] *adj* sarcastic.

sarcler [sarkle] *vt* to weed.

sarcophage [sarkɔfaʒ] *nm* sarcophagus.

Sardaigne [sardɛɲ] *nf*: **la ~** Sardinia.

sardine [sardin] *nf* sardine.

SARL, Sarl (*abr de* **société à responsabilité limitée**) *nf* limited liability company; **Leduc, ~** ≃ Leduc Ltd.

sarment [sarmã] nm (de vigne) shoot.

sas [sas] nm 1. (AÉRON & NAVIG) airlock. 2. (d'écluse) lock. 3. (tamis) sieve.

satanique [satanik] adj satanic.

satelliser [satelize] vt 1. (fusée) to put into orbit. 2. (pays) to make a satellite.

satellite [satelit] nm satellite.

satiété [sasjete] nf: à ~ (boire, manger) one's fill; (répéter) ad nauseam.

satin [satɛ̃] nm satin.

satiné, -e [satine] adj satin (avant n); (peau) satiny-smooth. ▶ **satiné** nm satin-like quality.

satire [satir] nf satire.

satirique [satirik] adj satirical.

satisfaction [satisfaksjɔ̃] nf satisfaction.

satisfaire [satisfɛr] vt to satisfy. ▶ **se satisfaire** vp: se ~ de to be satisfied with.

satisfaisant, -e [satisfəzɑ̃, ɑ̃t] adj 1. (travail) satisfactory. 2. (expérience) satisfying.

satisfait, -e [satisfɛ, ɛt] ◆ pp → **satisfaire**. ◆ adj satisfied; être ~ de to be satisfied with.

saturation [satyrasjɔ̃] nf saturation.

saturé, -e [satyre] adj: ~ (de) saturated (with).

saturne [satyrn] nm vieilli lead. ▶ **Saturne** nf (ASTRON) Saturn.

satyre [satir] nm satyr; fig sex maniac.

sauce [sos] nf (CULIN) sauce.

saucière [sosjɛr] nf sauceboat.

saucisse [sosis] nf (CULIN) sausage.

saucisson [sosisɔ̃] nm slicing sausage.

sauf¹, sauve [sof, sov] adj (personne) safe, unharmed; fig (honneur) saved, intact.

sauf² [sof] prép 1. (à l'exclusion de) except, apart from. 2. (à moins de) unless; ~ erreur unless there is some mistake; ~ que except (that).

sauf-conduit [sofkɔ̃dɥi] (pl sauf-conduits) nm safe-conduct.

sauge [soʒ] nf (CULIN) sage.

saugrenu, -e [sogrəny] adj ridiculous, nonsensical.

saule [sol] nm willow; ~ pleureur weeping willow.

saumon [somɔ̃] nm salmon.

saumoné, -e [somɔne] adj salmon (avant n).

saumure [somyr] nf brine.

sauna [sona] nm sauna.

saupoudrer [sopudre] vt: ~ qqch de to sprinkle sthg with.

saurai, sauras etc → **savoir**.

saut [so] nm (bond) leap, jump; ~ en hauteur (SPORT) high jump; ~ en longueur (SPORT) long jump, broad jump Am; faire un ~ chez qqn fig to pop in and see sb.

sauté, -e [sote] adj sautéed.

saute-mouton [sotmutɔ̃] nm inv: jouer à ~ to play leapfrog.

sauter [sote] ◆ vi 1. (bondir) to jump, to leap; ~ à la corde to skip; ~ d'un sujet à l'autre fig to jump from one subject to another; ~ au cou de qqn fig to throw one's arms around sb. 2. (exploser) to blow up; (fusible) to blow. 3. (partir - bouchon) to fly out; (- serrure) to burst off; (- bouton) to fly off; (- chaîne de vélo) to come off. 4. fam (employé) to get the sack. ◆ vt 1. (fossé, obstacle) to jump ou leap over. 2. fig (page, repas) to skip.

sauterelle [sotrɛl] nf (ZOOL) grasshopper.

sauteur, -euse [sotœr, øz] ◆ adj (insecte) jumping (avant n). ◆ nm, f (athlète) jumper.

sautiller [sotije] vi to hop.

sautoir [sotwar] nm (bijou) chain.

sauvage [sovaʒ] ◆ adj 1. (plante, animal) wild. 2. (farouche - animal familier) shy, timid; (- personne) unsociable. 3. (conduite, haine) savage. ◆ nmf 1. (solitaire) recluse. 2. péj (brute, indigène) savage.

sauvagerie [sovaʒri] nf 1. (férocité) brutality, savagery. 2. (insociabilité) unsociableness.

sauve → **sauf¹**.

sauvegarde [sovgard] nf 1. (protection) safeguard. 2. (INFORM) saving; (copie) backup.

sauvegarder [sovgarde] vt 1. (protéger) to safeguard. 2. (INFORM) to save; (copier) to back up.

sauve-qui-peut [sovkipø] ◆ nm inv (débandade) stampede. ◆ interj every man for himself!

sauver [sove] vt 1. (gén) to save; ~ qqn/qqch de to save sb/sthg from, to rescue sb/sthg from. 2. (navire, biens) to salvage. ▶ **se sauver** vp: se ~ (de) to run away (from); (prisonnier) to escape (from).

sauvetage [sovtaʒ] nm 1. (de personne) rescue. 2. (de navire, biens) salvage.

sauveteur [sovtœr] nm rescuer.

sauvette [sovɛt] ▶ **à la sauvette** loc adv hurriedly, at great speed.

savamment [savamã] adv 1. (avec érudition) learnedly. 2. (avec habileté) skilfully, cleverly.

savane [savan] *nf* savanna.

savant, -e [savã, ãt] *adj* 1. (*érudit*) scholarly. 2. (*habile*) skilful, clever. 3. (*animal*) performing (*avant n*).
▶ **savant** *nm* scientist.

saveur [savœr] *nf* flavour; *fig* savour.

savoir [savwar] ◆ *vt* 1. (*gén*) to know; **faire ~ qqch à qqn** to tell sb sthg, to inform sb of sthg; **si j'avais su ...** had I but known ..., if I had only known ...; **sans le ~** unconsciously, without being aware of it; **tu (ne) peux pas ~** *fam* you have no idea; **pas que je sache** not as far as I know. 2. (*être capable de*) to know how to; **sais-tu conduire?** can you drive? ◆ *nm* learning. ▶ **à savoir** *loc conj* namely, that is.

savoir-faire [savwarfɛr] *nm inv* know-how, expertise.

savoir-vivre [savwarvivr] *nm inv* good manners (*pl*).

savon [savõ] *nm* 1. (*matière*) soap; (*pain*) cake ou bar of soap. 2. *fam* (*réprimande*) telling-off.

savonner [savone] *vt* (*linge*) to soap.
▶ **se savonner** *vp* to soap o.s.

savonnette [savonɛt] *nf* guest soap.

savourer [savure] *vt* to savour.

savoureux, -euse [savurø, øz] *adj* 1. (*mets*) tasty. 2. *fig* (*anecdote*) juicy.

saxophone [saksofon] *nm* saxophone.

s/c (*abr de* **sous couvert de**) c/o.

scabreux, -euse [skabrø, øz] *adj* 1. (*propos*) shocking, indecent. 2. (*entreprise*) risky.

scalpel [skalpɛl] *nm* scalpel.

scalper [skalpe] *vt* to scalp.

scandale [skãdal] *nm* 1. (*fait choquant*) scandal. 2. (*indignation*) uproar. 3. (*tapage*) scene; **faire du** ou **un ~** to make a scene.

scandaleux, -euse [skãdalø, øz] *adj* scandalous, outrageous.

scandaliser [skãdalize] *vt* to shock, to scandalize.

scander [skãde] *vt* 1. (*vers*) to scan. 2. (*slogan*) to chant.

scandinave [skãdinav] *adj* Scandinavian. ▶ **Scandinave** *nmf* Scandinavian.

Scandinavie [skãdinavi] *nf*: **la ~** Scandinavia.

scanner¹ [skane] *vt* to scan.

scanner² [skanɛr] *nm* scanner.

scaphandre [skafãdr] *nm* 1. (*de plongeur*) diving suit. 2. (*d'astronaute*) spacesuit.

scarabée [skarabe] *nm* beetle, scarab.

scatologique [skatɔlɔʒik] *adj* scatological.

sceau, -x [so] *nm* seal; *fig* stamp, hallmark.

scélérat, -e [selera, at] *littéraire* ◆ *adj* wicked. ◆ *nm, f* villain; *péj* rogue, rascal.

sceller [sele] *vt* 1. (*gén*) to seal. 2. (CONSTR) (*fixer*) to embed.

scénario [senarjo] *nm* 1. (CIN, LITTÉRATURE & THÉÂTRE) (*canevas*) scenario. 2. (CIN & TÉLÉ) (*découpage, synopsis*) screenplay, script. 3. *fig* (*rituel*) pattern.

scénariste [senarist] *nmf* scriptwriter.

scène [sɛn] *nf* 1. (*gén*) scene. 2. (*estrade*) stage; **entrée en ~** (THÉÂTRE) entrance; *fig* appearance; **mettre en ~** (THÉÂTRE) to stage; (CIN) to direct.

scepticisme [sɛptisism] *nm* scepticism.

sceptique [sɛptik] ◆ *nmf* sceptic. ◆ *adj* 1. (*incrédule*) sceptical. 2. (PHILO) sceptic.

sceptre [sɛptr] *nm* sceptre.

schéma [ʃema] *nm* (*diagramme*) diagram; (*résumé*) outline.

schématique [ʃematik] *adj* 1. (*dessin*) diagrammatic. 2. (*interprétation, exposé*) simplified.

schématiser [ʃematize] *vt péj* (*généraliser*) to oversimplify.

schisme [ʃism] *nm* 1. (RELIG) schism. 2. (*d'opinion*) split.

schizophrène [skizɔfrɛn] *nmf & adj* schizophrenic.

schizophrénie [skizɔfreni] *nf* schizophrenia.

sciatique [sjatik] ◆ *nf* sciatica. ◆ *adj* sciatic.

scie [si] *nf* (*outil*) saw.

sciemment [sjamã] *adv* knowingly.

science [sjãs] *nf* 1. (*connaissances scientifiques*) science; **~s humaines** ou **sociales** (UNIV) social sciences. 2. (*érudition*) knowledge. 3. (*art*) art.

science-fiction [sjãsfiksjõ] *nf* science fiction.

sciences-po [sjãspo] *nfpl* (UNIV) political science (*sg*). ▶ **Sciences-Po** *n* *grande école for political science*.

scientifique [sjãtifik] ◆ *nmf* scientist. ◆ *adj* scientific.

scier [sje] *vt* (*branche*) to saw.

scierie [siri] *nf* sawmill.

scinder [sɛ̃de] *vt*: **~ (en)** to split (into), to divide (into). ▶ **se scinder** *vp*: **se ~ (en)** to split (into), to divide (into).

scintiller [sɛ̃tije] *vi* to sparkle.

scission [sisjɔ̃] *nf* split.

sciure [sjyr] *nf* sawdust.

sclérose [skleroz] *nf* sclerosis; *fig* ossification; ~ **en plaques** multiple sclerosis.

sclérosé, -e [skleroze] *adj* sclerotic; *fig* ossified.

scolaire [skɔlɛr] *adj* school (*avant n*); *péj* bookish.

scolarisable [skɔlarizabl] *adj* of school age.

scolarité [skɔlarite] *nf* schooling; **frais de ~** (SCOL) school fees; (UNIV) tuition fees.

scooter [skutœr] *nm* scooter.

scorbut [skɔrbyt] *nm* scurvy.

score [skɔr] *nm* (SPORT) score.

scorpion [skɔrpjɔ̃] *nm* scorpion. ▶ **Scorpion** *nm* (ASTROL) Scorpio.

scotch [skɔtʃ] *nm* (*alcool*) whisky, Scotch.

Scotch® [skɔtʃ] *nm* (*adhésif*) ≃ Sellotape® Br, ≃ Scotch tape® Am.

scotcher [skɔtʃe] *vt* to sellotape Br, to scotch-tape Am.

scout, -e [skut] *adj* scout (*avant n*). ▶ **scout** *nm* scout.

scribe [skrib] *nm* (HIST) scribe.

script [skript] *nm* (CIN & TÉLÉ) script.

scripte [skript] *nmf* (CIN & TÉLÉ) continuity person.

scrupule [skrypyl] *nm* scruple; **avec ~** scrupulously; **sans ~s** (*être*) unscrupulous; (*agir*) unscrupulously.

scrupuleux, -euse [skrypylø, øz] *adj* scrupulous.

scrutateur, -trice [skrytatœr, tris] *adj* searching.

scruter [skryte] *vt* to scrutinize.

scrutin [skrytɛ̃] *nm* 1. (*vote*) ballot. 2. (*système*) voting system; ~ **majoritaire** first-past-the-post system; ~ **proportionnel** proportional representation system.

sculpter [skylte] *vt* to sculpt.

sculpteur [skyltœr] *nm* sculptor.

sculpture [skyltyr] *nf* sculpture.

SDF (*abr de* **sans domicile fixe**) *nmf*: **les ~** the homeless.

se [sə], **s'** (*devant voyelle ou h muet*) *pron pers* 1. (*réfléchi*) (*personne*) oneself, himself (*f* herself), (*pl*) themselves; (*chose, animal*) itself, (*pl*) themselves; **elle ~ regarde dans le miroir** she looks at herself in the mirror. 2. (*réciproque*) each other, one another; **ils ~ sont rencontrés hier** they met yesterday. 3. (*passif*): **ce produit ~ vend bien/partout** this product is selling well/is sold everywhere. 4. (*remplace l'adjectif possessif*): ~ **laver les mains** to wash one's hands; ~ **couper le doigt** to cut one's finger.

séance [seɑ̃s] *nf* 1. (*réunion*) meeting, sitting, session. 2. (*période*) session; (*de pose*) sitting. 3. (CIN & THÉÂTRE) performance. 4. *loc*: ~ **tenante** right away, forthwith.

seau, -x [so] *nm* 1. (*récipient*) bucket. 2. (*contenu*) bucketful.

sec, sèche [sɛk, sɛʃ] *adj* 1. (*gén*) dry. 2. (*fruits*) dried. 3. (*personne - maigre*) lean; (*- austère*) austere. 4. *fig* (*cœur*) hard; (*voix, ton*) sharp. ▶ **sec** ◆ *adv* 1. (*beaucoup*): **boire ~** to drink heavily. 2. (*démarrer*) sharply. ◆ *nm*: **tenir au ~** to keep in a dry place.

sécable [sekabl] *adj* divisible.

sécateur [sekatœr] *nm* secateurs (*pl*).

sécession [sesesjɔ̃] *nf* secession; **faire ~ (de)** to secede (from).

sèche-cheveux [sɛʃʃəvø] *nm inv* hairdryer.

sèche-linge [sɛʃlɛ̃ʒ] *nm inv* tumble-dryer.

sécher [seʃe] ◆ *vt* 1. (*linge*) to dry. 2. *arg scol* (*cours*) to skip, to skive off Br. ◆ *vi* 1. (*linge*) to dry. 2. (*peau*) to dry out; (*rivière*) to dry up. 3. *arg scol* (*ne pas savoir répondre*) to dry up.

sécheresse [seʃrɛs] *nf* 1. (*de terre, climat, style*) dryness. 2. (*absence de pluie*) drought. 3. (*de réponse*) curtness.

séchoir [seʃwar] *nm* 1. (*tringle*) airer, clotheshorse. 2. (*électrique*) dryer; ~ **à cheveux** hairdryer.

second, -e [səgɔ̃, ɔ̃d] ◆ *adj num* second; **dans un état ~** dazed. ◆ *nm, f* second; *voir aussi* **sixième**. ▶ **seconde** *nf* 1. (*unité de temps & MUS*) second. 2. (SCOL) ≃ fifth year *ou* form Br, ≃ tenth grade Am. 3. (TRANSPORT) second class.

secondaire [səgɔ̃dɛr] ◆ *nm*: **le ~** (GÉOL) the Mesozoic; (SCOL) secondary education; (ÉCON) the secondary sector. ◆ *adj* 1. (*gén* & SCOL) secondary; **effets ~s** (MÉD) side effects. 2. (GÉOL) Mesozoic.

seconder [səgɔ̃de] *vt* to assist.

secouer [səkwe] *vt* (*gén*) to shake. ▶ **se secouer** *vp fam* to snap out of it.

secourable [səkurabl] *adj* helpful; **main ~** helping hand.

secourir [səkurir] *vt* (*blessé, miséreux*) to help; (*personne en danger*) to rescue.

secouriste [səkurist] *nmf* first-aid worker.

secours [səkur] *nm* 1. (*aide*) help; **appeler au ~** to call for help; **les ~** emergency services; **au ~!** help! 2. (*dons*) aid, relief. 3. (*renfort*) relief, reinforcements (*pl*). 4. (*soins*) aid; **les premiers ~** first aid (U). ▶ **de secours** *loc adj* 1. (*trousse, poste*) first-aid (*avant n*). 2. (*éclairage, issue*) emergency (*avant n*). 3. (*roue*) spare.

secouru, -e [səkury] *pp* → **secourir**.

secousse [səkus] *nf* 1. (*mouvement*) jerk, jolt. 2. *fig* (*bouleversement*) upheaval; (*psychologique*) shock. 3. (*tremblement de terre*) tremor.

secret, -ète [səkrɛ, ɛt] *adj* 1. (*gén*) secret. 2. (*personne*) reticent. ▶ **secret** *nm* 1. (*gén*) secret. 2. (*discrétion*) secrecy; **dans le plus grand ~** in the utmost secrecy.

secrétaire [səkretɛr] ◆ *nmf* (*personne*) secretary; **~ de direction** executive secretary. ◆ *nm* (*meuble*) writing desk, secretaire.

secrétariat [səkretarja] *nm* 1. (*bureau*) secretary's office; (*d'organisation internationale*) secretariat. 2. (*personnel*) secretarial staff. 3. (*métier*) secretarial work.

sécréter [sekrete] *vt* to secrete; *fig* to exude.

sécrétion [sekresjɔ̃] *nf* secretion.

sectaire [sɛktɛr] *nmf & adj* sectarian.

secte [sɛkt] *nf* sect.

secteur [sɛktœr] *nm* 1. (*zone*) area; **se trouver dans le ~** *fam* to be somewhere around. 2. (ADMIN) district. 3. (ÉCON, GÉOM & MIL) sector; **~ privé/public** private/public sector; **~ primaire/secondaire/tertiaire** primary/secondary/tertiary sector. 4. (ÉLECTR) mains; **sur ~** off OU from the mains.

section [sɛksjɔ̃] *nf* 1. (*gén*) section; (*de parti*) branch. 2. (MIL) platoon.

sectionner [sɛksjɔne] *vt* 1. *fig* (*diviser*) to divide into sections. 2. (*trancher*) to sever.

Sécu [seky] *fam abr de* **Sécurité sociale**.

séculaire [sekylɛr] *adj* (*ancien*) age-old.

sécurisant, -e [sekyrizɑ̃, ɑ̃t] *adj* (*milieu*) secure; (*attitude*) reassuring.

sécurité [sekyrite] *nf* 1. (*d'esprit*) security. 2. (*absence de danger*) safety; **la ~ routière** road safety; **en toute ~** safe and sound. 3. (*dispositif*) safety catch. 4. (*organisme*): **la Sécurité sociale** = the DSS Br, = the Social Security Am.

sédatif, -ive [sedatif, iv] *adj* sedative. ▶ **sédatif** *nm* sedative.

sédentaire [sedɑ̃tɛr] *adj* (*personne,*

métier) sedentary; (*casanier*) stay-at-home.

sédentariser [sedɑ̃tarize] ▶ **se sédentariser** *vp* (*tribu*) to settle, to become settled.

sédiment [sedimɑ̃] *nm* sediment.

sédition [sedisjɔ̃] *nf* sedition.

séducteur, -trice [sedyktœr, tris] ◆ *adj* seductive. ◆ *nm, f* seducer (*f* seductress).

séduire [sedɥir] *vt* 1. (*plaire à*) to attract, to appeal to. 2. (*abuser de*) to seduce.

séduisant, -e [sedɥizɑ̃, ɑ̃t] *adj* attractive.

séduit, -e [sedɥi, it] *pp* → **séduire**.

segment [sɛgmɑ̃] *nm* (GÉOM) segment.

segmenter [sɛgmɑ̃te] *vt* to segment.

ségrégation [segregasjɔ̃] *nf* segregation.

seigle [sɛgl] *nm* rye.

seigneur [sɛɲœr] *nm* lord. ▶ **Seigneur** *nm*: **le Seigneur** the Lord.

sein [sɛ̃] *nm* breast; *fig* bosom; **donner le ~ (à un bébé)** to breast-feed (a baby). ▶ **au sein de** *loc prép* within.

Seine [sɛn] *nf*: **la ~** the (River) Seine.

séisme [seism] *nm* earthquake.

seize [sɛz] *adj num & nm* sixteen; *voir aussi* **six**.

seizième [sɛzjɛm] *adj num, nm & nmf* sixteenth; *voir aussi* **sixième**.

séjour [seʒur] *nm* 1. (*durée*) stay; **interdit de ~** = banned; **~ linguistique** stay abroad (*to develop language skills*). 2. (*pièce*) living room.

séjourner [seʒurne] *vi* to stay.

sel [sɛl] *nm* salt; *fig* piquancy.

sélection [selɛksjɔ̃] *nf* selection.

sélectionner [selɛksjɔne] *vt* to select, to pick.

self-service [sɛlfsɛrvis] (*pl* **self-services**) *nm* self-service cafeteria.

selle [sɛl] *nf* (*gén*) saddle.

seller [sele] *vt* to saddle.

selon [səlɔ̃] *prép* 1. (*conformément à*) in accordance with. 2. (*d'après*) according to. ▶ **selon que** *loc conj* depending on whether.

semaine [səmɛn] *nf* (*période*) week; **à la ~** (*être payé*) by the week.

sémantique [semɑ̃tik] *adj* semantic.

semblable [sɑ̃blabl] ◆ *nm* (*prochain*) fellow man; **il n'a pas son ~** there's nobody like him. ◆ *adj* 1. (*analogue*) similar; **~ à** like, similar to. 2. (*avant n*) (*tel*) such.

semblant [sɑ̃blɑ̃] *nm*: **un ~ de** a semblance of; **faire ~ (de faire qqch)** to pretend (to do sthg).

sembler [sɑ̃ble] ♦ *vi* to seem. ♦ *v impers*: **il (me/te) semble que** it seems (to me/you) that.

semelle [səmɛl] *nf* (*de chaussure - dessous*) sole; (- *à l'intérieur*) insole.

semence [səmɑ̃s] *nf* 1. (*graine*) seed. 2. (*sperme*) semen (U).

semer [səme] *vt* 1. (*planter & fig*) to sow. 2. (*répandre*) to scatter; **~ qqch de** to scatter sthg with, to strew sthg with. 3. *fam* (*se débarrasser de*) to shake off. 4. *fam* (*perdre*) to lose.

semestre [səmɛstr] *nm* half year, six-month period; (SCOL) semester.

semestriel, -elle [səmɛstrijɛl] *adj* 1. (*qui a lieu tous les six mois*) half-yearly, six-monthly. 2. (*qui dure six mois*) six months', six-month.

séminaire [seminɛr] *nm* 1. (RELIG) seminary. 2. (UNIV & *colloque*) seminar.

séminariste [seminarist] *nm* seminarist.

semi-remorque [səmirəmɔrk] (*pl* **semi-remorques**) *nm* articulated lorry *Br*, semitrailer *Am*.

semis [səmi] *nm* 1. (*méthode*) sowing broadcast. 2. (*plant*) seedling.

semoule [səmul] *nf* semolina.

sempiternel, -elle [sɑ̃pitɛrnɛl] *adj* eternal.

sénat [sena] *nm* senate; **le Sénat** *upper house of the French parliament*.

sénateur [senatœr] *nm* senator.

Sénégal [senegal] *nm*: **le ~** Senegal.

sénile [senil] *adj* senile.

sénilité [senilite] *nf* senility.

sens [sɑ̃s] *nm* 1. (*fonction, instinct, raison*) sense; **avoir le ~ de l'humour** to have a sense of humour; **bon ~** good sense. 2. (*direction*) direction; **dans le ~ de la longueur** lengthways; **dans le ~ des aiguilles d'une montre** clockwise; **dans le ~ contraire des aiguilles d'une montre** anticlockwise *Br*, counterclockwise *Am*; **~ dessus dessous** upside down; **~ interdit** ou **unique** one-way street. 3. (*signification*) meaning; **cela n'a pas de ~!** it's nonsensical!; **dans** ou **en un ~** in one sense.

sensation [sɑ̃sasjɔ̃] *nf* 1. (*perception*) sensation, feeling. 2. (*impression*) feeling.

sensationnel, -elle [sɑ̃sasjɔnɛl] *adj* sensational.

sensé, -e [sɑ̃se] *adj* sensible.

sensibiliser [sɑ̃sibilize] *vt* 1. (MÉD & PHOT) to sensitize. 2. *fig* (*public*): **~ (à)** to

make aware (of).

sensibilité [sɑ̃sibilite] *nf*: **~ (à)** sensitivity (to).

sensible [sɑ̃sibl] *adj* 1. (*gén*): **~ (à)** sensitive (to). 2. (*notable*) considerable, appreciable.

sensiblement [sɑ̃siblmɑ̃] *adv* 1. (*à peu près*) more or less. 2. (*notablement*) appreciably, considerably.

sensoriel, -elle [sɑ̃sɔrjɛl] *adj* sensory.

sensualité [sɑ̃syalite] *nf* (*lascivité*) sensuousness; (*charnelle*) sensuality.

sensuel, -elle [sɑ̃syɛl] *adj* 1. (*charnel*) sensual. 2. (*lascif*) sensuous.

sentence [sɑ̃tɑ̃s] *nf* 1. (*jugement*) sentence. 2. (*maxime*) adage.

sentencieux, -euse [sɑ̃tɑ̃sjø, øz] *adj péj* sententious.

senteur [sɑ̃tœr] *nf littéraire* perfume.

senti, -e [sɑ̃ti] ♦ *pp* → **sentir**. ♦ *adj*: **bien ~** (*mots*) well-chosen.

sentier [sɑ̃tje] *nm* path.

sentiment [sɑ̃timɑ̃] *nm* feeling; **veuillez agréer, Monsieur, l'expression de mes ~s distingués/cordiaux/les meilleurs** yours faithfully/sincerely/truly.

sentimental, -e, -aux [sɑ̃timɑ̃tal, o] ♦ *adj* 1. (*amoureux*) love (*avant n*). 2. (*sensible, romanesque*) sentimental. ♦ *nm, f* sentimentalist.

sentinelle [sɑ̃tinɛl] *nf* sentry.

sentir [sɑ̃tir] ♦ *vt* 1. (*percevoir - par l'odorat*) to smell; (- *par le goût*) to taste; (- *par le toucher*) to feel. 2. (*exhaler - odeur*) to smell of. 3. (*colère, tendresse*) to feel. 4. (*affectation, plagiat*) to smack of. 5. (*danger*) to sense, to be aware of; **~ que** to feel (that). 6. (*beauté*) to feel, to appreciate. ♦ *vi*: **~ bon/mauvais** to smell good/bad. ► **se sentir** ♦ *v attr*: **se ~ bien/fatigué** to feel well/tired. ♦ *vp* (*être perceptible*): **ça se sent!** you can really tell!

séparation [separasjɔ̃] *nf* separation.

séparatiste [separatist] *nmf* separatist.

séparé, -e [separe] *adj* 1. (*intérêts*) separate. 2. (*couple*) separated.

séparer [separe] *vt* 1. (*gén*): **~ (de)** to separate (from). 2. (*suj: divergence*) to divide. ► **se séparer** *vp* 1. (*se défaire*): **se ~ de** to part with. 2. (*conjoints*) to separate, to split up; **se ~ de** to separate from, to split up with. 3. (*participants*) to disperse. 4. (*route*): **se ~ (en)** to split (into), to divide (into).

sept [sɛt] *adj num & nm* seven; *voir aussi* **six**.

septembre [sɛptɑ̃br] *nm* September; **en ~, au mois de ~** in September; **début ~, au début du mois de ~** at the beginning of September; **fin ~, à la fin du mois de ~** at the end of September; **d'ici ~** by September; **(à la) mi-~** (in) mid-September; **le premier/deux/dix ~** the first/second/tenth of September.

septennat [sɛptena] *nm* seven-year term (of office).

septicémie [sɛptisemi] *nf* septicaemia, blood poisoning.

septième [sɛtjɛm] *adj num, nm & nmf* seventh; *voir aussi* **sixième**.

sépulcre [sepylkr] *nm* sepulchre.

sépulture [sepyltyr] *nf* 1. (*lieu*) burial place. 2. (*inhumation*) burial.

séquelle [sekɛl] *nf* (*gén pl*) aftermath; (MÉD) aftereffect.

séquence [sekɑ̃s] *nf* sequence.

séquestrer [sekɛstre] *vt* 1. (*personne*) to confine. 2. (*biens*) to impound.

serai, seras *etc* → **être.**

serbe [sɛrb] *adj* Serbian. ▸ **Serbe** *nmf* Serb.

Serbie [sɛrbi] *nf*: **la ~** Serbia.

serein [e [sərɛ̃, ɛn] *adj* (*calme*) serene.

sérénade [serenad] *nf* (MUS) serenade.

sérénité [serenite] *nf* serenity.

serf, serve [sɛrf, sɛrv] *nm, f* serf.

sergent [sɛrʒɑ̃] *nm* sergeant.

série [seri] *nf* 1. (*gén*) series (*sg*). 2. (SPORT) rank; (*au tennis*) seeding. 3. (COMM & IND): **produire qqch en ~** to mass-produce sthg; **hors ~** custommade; *fig* outstanding, extraordinary.

sérieusement [serjøzmɑ̃] *adv* seriously.

sérieux, -euse [serjø, øz] *adj* 1. (*grave*) serious. 2. (*digne de confiance*) reliable; (*client, offre*) genuine. 3. (*consciencieux*) responsible; **ce n'est pas ~** it's irresponsible. 4. (*considérable*) considerable. ▸ **sérieux** *nm* 1. (*application*) sense of responsibility. 2. (*gravité*) seriousness; **garder son ~** to keep a straight face; **prendre qqn/qqch au ~** to take sb/sthg seriously.

serin, -e [sərɛ̃, in] *nm, f* (*oiseau*) canary.

seringue [sərɛ̃g] *nf* syringe.

serment [sɛrmɑ̃] *nm* 1. (*affirmation solennelle*) oath; **sous ~** on ou under oath. 2. (*promesse*) vow, pledge.

sermon [sɛrmɔ̃] *nm litt & fig* sermon.

séronégatif, -ive [serɔnegatif, iv] *adj* HIV-negative.

séropositif, -ive [serɔpozitif, iv] *adj* HIV-positive.

séropositivité [serɔpozitivite] *nf* HIV infection.

serpe [sɛrp] *nf* billhook.

serpent [sɛrpɑ̃] *nm* (ZOOL) snake.

serpenter [sɛrpɑ̃te] *vi* to wind.

serpillière [sɛrpijɛr] *nf* floor cloth.

serre [sɛr] *nf* (*bâtiment*) greenhouse, glasshouse. ▸ **serres** *nfpl* (ZOOL) talons, claws.

serré, -e [sere] *adj* 1. (*écriture*) cramped; (*tissu*) closely-woven; (*rangs*) serried. 2. (*vêtement, chaussure*) tight. 3. (*discussion*) closely argued; (*match*) close-fought. 4. (*poing, dents*) clenched; **la gorge ~** with a lump in one's throat; **j'en avais le cœur ~** *fig* it was heartbreaking. 5. (*café*) strong.

serrer [sere] ◆ *vt* 1. (*saisir*) to grip, to hold tight; **~ la main à qqn** to shake sb's hand; **~ qqn dans ses bras** to hug sb. 2. *fig* (*rapprocher*) to bring together; **~ les rangs** to close ranks. 3. (*poing, dents*) to clench; (*lèvres*) to purse; *fig* (*cœur*) to wring. 4. (*suj: vêtement, chaussure*) to be too tight for. 5. (*vis, ceinture*) to tighten; (*frein à main*) to put on. 6. (*trottoir, bordure*) to hug. ◆ *vi* (AUTOM): **~ à droite/gauche** to keep right/left. ▸ **se serrer** *vp* 1. (*se blottir*): **se ~ contre** to huddle up to ou against. 2. (*se rapprocher*) to squeeze up.

serre-tête [sɛrtɛt] *nm inv* headband.

serrure [seryr] *nf* lock.

serrurier [seryrje] *nm* locksmith.

sertir [sɛrtir] *vt* 1. (*pierre précieuse*) to set. 2. (TECHNOL) (*assujettir*) to crimp.

sérum [serɔm] *nm* serum.

servage [sɛrvaʒ] *nm* serfdom; *fig* bondage.

servante [sɛrvɑ̃t] *nf* (*domestique*) maidservant.

serveur, -euse [sɛrvœr, øz] *nm, f* (*de restaurant*) waiter (*f* waitress); (*de bar*) barman (*f* barmaid). ▸ **serveur** *nm* (INFORM) server.

servi, -e [sɛrvi] *pp* → **servir.**

serviable [sɛrvjabl] *adj* helpful, obliging.

service [sɛrvis] *nm* 1. (*gén*) service; **être en ~** to be in use, to be set up; **hors ~** out of order. 2. (*travail*) duty; **pendant le ~** while on duty. 3. (*département*) department; **~ d'ordre** police and stewards (*at a demonstration*). 4. (MIL): **~ (militaire)** military ou national service. 5. (*aide, assistance*) favour; **rendre un ~ à qqn** to do sb a favour; **rendre ~** to be helpful; ~ **après-vente** after-sales service. **6.** (à table): **premier/deuxième** ~ first/second sitting. **7.** (pourboire) service (charge); ~ **compris/non compris** service included/not included. **8.** (assortiment - de porcelaine) service, set; (- de linge) service.

serviette [sɛrvjɛt] nf **1.** (de table) serviette, napkin. **2.** (de toilette) towel. **3.** (porte-documents) briefcase. ▸ **serviette hygiénique** nf sanitary towel Br, sanitary napkin Am.

serviette-éponge [sɛrvjɛtepɔ̃ʒ] nf terry towel.

servile [sɛrvil] adj **1.** (gén) servile. **2.** (traduction, imitation) slavish.

servir [sɛrvir] ◆ vt **1.** (gén) to serve; ~ **qqch à qqn** to serve sb sthg, to help sb to sthg. **2.** (avantager) to serve (well), to help. ◆ vi **1.** (avoir un usage) to be useful ou of use; **ça peut toujours/encore** ~ it may/may still come in useful. **2.** (être utile): ~ **à qqch/à faire qqch** to be used for sthg/for doing sthg; **ça ne sert à rien** it's pointless. **3.** (tenir lieu): ~ **de** (personne) to act as; (chose) to serve as. **4.** (MIL & SPORT) to serve. **5.** (CARTES) to deal. ▸ **se servir** vp **1.** (prendre): **se ~ (de)** to help o.s. (to); **servez-vous!** help yourself! **2.** (utiliser): **se ~ de qqn/qqch** to use sb/sthg.

serviteur [sɛrvitœr] nm servant.

servitude [sɛrvityd] nf **1.** (esclavage) servitude. **2.** (gén pl) (contrainte) constraint.

ses → **son²**.

session [sesjɔ̃] nf **1.** (d'assemblée) session, sitting. **2.** (UNIV) exam session. **3.** (INFORM): **ouvrir une** ~ to log in ou on; **fermer** ou **clore une** ~ to log out ou off.

set [sɛt] nm **1.** (TENNIS) set. **2.** (napperon): ~ **(de table)** set of table ou place mats.

seuil [sœj] nm litt & fig threshold.

seul, -e [sœl] ◆ adj **1.** (isolé) alone; ~ **à** ~ alone (together), privately. **2.** (sans compagnie) alone, by o.s.; **parler tout** ~ to talk to o.s. **3.** (sans aide) on one's own, by o.s. **4.** (unique): **le** ~ **...** the only ~; **un** ~ **...** a single ...; **pas un** ~ **...** not one ..., not a single ... **5.** (esseulé) lonely. ◆ nm, f: **le** ~ the only one; **un** ~ a single one, only one.

seulement [sœlmɑ̃] adv **1.** (gén) only; (exclusivement) only, solely. **2.** (même) even. ▸ **non seulement ... mais (encore)** loc corrélative not only ... but (also).

sève [sɛv] nf (BOT) sap.

sévère [sever] adj severe.

sévérité [severite] nf severity.

sévices [sevis] nmpl sout ill treatment (U).

sévir [sevir] vi **1.** (épidémie, guerre) to rage. **2.** (punir) to give out a punishment.

sevrer [səvre] vt to wean.

sexe [sɛks] nm **1.** (gén) sex. **2.** (organe) genitals (pl).

sexiste [sɛksist] nmf & adj sexist.

sexologue [sɛksɔlɔg] nmf sexologist.

sex-shop [sɛksʃɔp] (pl **sex-shops**) nm sex shop.

sextant [sɛkstɑ̃] nm sextant.

sexualité [sɛksyalite] nf sexuality.

sexuel, -elle [sɛksyɛl] adj sexual.

sexy [sɛksi] adj inv fam sexy.

seyant, -e [sɛjɑ̃, ɑ̃t] adj becoming.

shampooing [ʃɑ̃pwɛ̃] nm shampoo.

shérif [ʃerif] nm sheriff.

shopping [ʃɔpiŋ] nm shopping; **faire du** ~ to go (out) shopping.

short [ʃɔrt] nm shorts (pl), pair of shorts.

show-business [ʃobiznɛs] nm inv show business.

si¹ [si] nm inv (MUS) B; (chanté) ti.

si² [si] ◆ adv **1.** (tellement) so; **elle est** ~ **belle** she is so beautiful; **il roulait** ~ **vite qu'il a eu un accident** he was driving so fast (that) he had an accident; **ce n'est pas** ~ **facile que ça** it's not as easy as that; ~ **vieux qu'il soit** however old he may be, old as he is. **2.** (oui) yes; **tu n'aimes pas le café?** – ~ don't you like coffee? – yes, I do. ◆ conj **1.** (gén) if; ~ **tu veux, on y va** we'll go if you want; ~ **tu faisais cela, je te détesterais** I would hate you if you did that; ~ **seulement** if only. **2.** (dans une question indirecte) if, whether; **dites-moi** ~ **vous venez** tell me if ou whether you're coming. ▸ **si bien que** loc conj so that, with the result that.

SI nm (abr de **syndicat d'initiative**) tourist office.

siamois, -e [sjamwa, az] adj: **frères** ~, **sœurs** ~**es** (MÉD) Siamese twins.

Sibérie [siberi] nf: **la** ~ Siberia.

sibyllin, -e [sibilɛ̃, in] adj enigmatic.

SICAV, Sicav [sikav] (abr de **société d'investissement à capital variable**) nf **1.** (société) unit trust, mutual fund. **2.** (action) share in a unit trust.

Sicile [sisil] nf: **la** ~ Sicily.

SIDA, Sida [sida] (abr de **syndrome immunodéficitaire acquis**) nm AIDS.

side-car [sidkar] (*pl* **side-cars**) *nm* side-car.

sidéen, -enne [sideɛ̃, ɛn] *nm, f* person with AIDS.

sidérer [sidere] *vt fam* to stagger.

sidérurgie [sideryrʒi] *nf* (*industrie*) iron and steel industry.

siècle [sjɛkl] *nm* 1. (*cent ans*) century. 2. (*gén pl*) *fam* (*longue durée*) ages (*pl*).

siège [sjɛʒ] *nm* 1. (*meuble & POLIT*) seat. 2. (*MIL*) siege. 3. (*d'organisme*) head-quarters, head office; **~ social** registered office. 4. (*MÉD*): **se présenter par le ~** to be in the breech position.

siéger [sjeʒe] *vi* (*juge, assemblée*) to sit.

sien [sjɛ̃] ▶ **le sien** (*f* **la sienne** [lasjɛn], *mpl* **les siens** [lesjɛ̃], *fpl* **les siennes** [lesjɛn]) *pron poss* (*d'homme*) his; (*de femme*) hers; (*de chose, d'animal*) its; **les ~s** his/her family; **faire des siennes** to be up to one's usual tricks.

sieste [sjɛst] *nf* siesta.

sifflement [sifləmɑ̃] *nm* (*son*) whistling; (*de serpent*) hissing.

siffler [sifle] ◆ *vi* to whistle; (*serpent*) to hiss. ◆ *vt* 1. (*air de musique*) to whistle. 2. (*femme*) to whistle at. 3. (*chien*) to whistle (for). 4. (*acteur*) to boo, to hiss. 5. *fam* (*verre*) to knock back.

sifflet [siflɛ] *nm* whistle. ▶ **sifflets** *nmpl* hissing (U), boos.

siffloter [siflote] *vi & vt* to whistle.

sigle [sigl] *nm* acronym, (set of) initials.

signal, -aux [siɲal, o] *nm* 1. (*geste, son*) signal; **~ d'alarme** alarm (signal); **donner le ~ (de)** to give the signal (for). 2. (*panneau*) sign.

signalement [siɲalmɑ̃] *nm* description.

signaler [siɲale] *vt* 1. (*fait*) to point out; **rien à ~** nothing to report. 2. (*à la police*) to denounce.

signalétique [siɲaletik] *adj* identifying.

signalisation [siɲalizasjɔ̃] *nf* (*panneaux*) signs (*pl*); (*au sol*) (road) markings (*pl*); (*NAVIG*) signals (*pl*).

signataire [siɲatɛr] *nmf* signatory.

signature [siɲatyr] *nf* 1. (*nom, marque*) signature. 2. (*acte*) signing.

signe [siɲ] *nm* 1. (*gén*) sign; **être ~ de** to be a sign of; **être né sous le ~ de** (ASTROL) to be born under the sign of; **~ avant-coureur** advance indication. 2. (*trait*) mark; **~ particulier** distinguishing mark.

signer [siɲe] *vt* to sign. ▶ **se signer** *vp* to cross o.s.

signet [siɲɛ] *nm* bookmark (*attached to spine of book*).

significatif, -ive [siɲifikatif, iv] *adj* significant.

signification [siɲifikasjɔ̃] *nf* (*sens*) meaning.

signifier [siɲifje] *vt* 1. (*vouloir dire*) to mean. 2. (*faire connaître*) to make known. 3. (JUR) to serve notice of.

silence [silɑ̃s] *nm* 1. (*gén*) silence; **garder le ~ (sur)** to remain silent (about). 2. (MUS) rest.

silencieux, -euse [silɑ̃sjø, øz] *adj* (*lieu, appareil*) quiet; (*personne - taciturne*) quiet; (*- muet*) silent. ▶ **silencieux** *nm* silencer.

silex [silɛks] *nm* flint.

silhouette [silwɛt] *nf* 1. (*de personne*) silhouette; (*de femme*) figure; (*d'objet*) outline. 2. (ART) silhouette.

silicium [silisjɔm] *nm* silicon.

silicone [silikon] *nf* silicone.

sillage [sijaʒ] *nm* wake.

sillon [sijɔ̃] *nm* 1. (*tranchée, ride*) furrow. 2. (*de disque*) groove.

sillonner [sijone] *vt* 1. (*champ*) to furrow. 2. (*ciel*) to crisscross.

silo [silo] *nm* silo.

simagrées [simagre] *nfpl péj*: **faire des ~** to make a fuss.

similaire [similɛr] *adj* similar.

similicuir [similikɥir] *nm* imitation leather.

similitude [similityd] *nf* similarity.

simple [sɛ̃pl] ◆ *adj* 1. (*gén*) simple. 2. (*ordinaire*) ordinary. 3. (*billet*): **un aller ~** a single ticket. ◆ *nm* (TENNIS) singles (*sg*).

simplement [sɛ̃pləmɑ̃] *adv* simply; **tout ~** quite simply, just.

simplicité [sɛ̃plisite] *nf* simplicity.

simplifier [sɛ̃plifje] *vt* to simplify.

simpliste [sɛ̃plist] *adj péj* simplistic.

simulacre [simylakr] *nm* 1. (*semblant*): **un ~ de** a pretence of, a sham. 2. (*action simulée*) enactment.

simulateur, -trice [simylatœr, tris] *nm, f* pretender; (*de maladie*) malingerer. ▶ **simulateur** *nm* (TECHNOL) simulator.

simulation [simylasjɔ̃] *nf* 1. (*gén*) simulation. 2. (*comédie*) shamming, feigning; (*de maladie*) malingering.

simuler [simyle] *vt* 1. (*gén*) to simulate. 2. (*feindre*) to feign, to sham.

simultané, -e [simyltane] *adj* simultaneous.

sincère [sɛ̃sɛr] *adj* sincere.

sincèrement [sɛ̃sɛrmɑ̃] *adv* 1. (*franche-*

ment) honestly, sincerely. **2.** (*vraiment*) really, truly.

sincérité [sɛ̃serite] *nf* sincerity.

sine qua non [sinekwanɔn] *adj*: **condition ~** prerequisite.

Singapour [sɛ̃gapur] *n* Singapore.

singe [sɛ̃ʒ] *nm* (ZOOL) monkey; (*de grande taille*) ape.

singer [sɛ̃ʒe] *vt* **1.** (*personne*) to mimic, to ape. **2.** (*sentiment*) to feign.

singerie [sɛ̃ʒri] *nf* **1.** (*grimace*) face. **2.** (*manières*) fuss (U).

singulariser [sɛ̃gylarize] *vt* to draw ou call attention to. ▶ **se singulariser** *vp* to draw ou call attention to o.s.

singularité [sɛ̃gylarite] *nf* **1.** *littéraire* (*bizarrerie*) strangeness. **2.** (*particularité*) peculiarity.

singulier, -ère [sɛ̃gylje, ɛr] *adj* **1.** *sout* (*bizarre*) strange; **2.** (GRAM) singular. **3.** (*d'homme à homme*): **combat ~** single combat. ▶ **singulier** *nm* (GRAM) singular.

singulièrement [sɛ̃gyljɛrmɑ̃] *adv* **1.** *littéraire* (*bizarrement*) strangely. **2.** (*beaucoup, très*) particularly.

sinistre [sinistr] ◆ *nm* **1.** (*catastrophe*) disaster. **2.** (JUR) damage (U). ◆ *adj* **1.** (*personne, regard*) sinister; (*maison, ambiance*) gloomy. **2.** (*avant n*) *péj* (*crétin, imbécile*) dreadful, terrible.

sinistré, -e [sinistre] ◆ *adj* (*région*) disaster (*avant n*), disaster-stricken; (*famille*) disaster-stricken. ◆ *nm, f* disaster victim.

sinon [sinɔ̃] *conj* **1.** (*autrement*) or else, otherwise. **2.** (*sauf*) except, apart from. **3.** (*si ce n'est*) if not.

sinueux, -euse [sinɥø, øz] *adj* winding; *fig* tortuous.

sinuosité [sinɥozite] *nf* bend, twist.

sinus [sinys] *nm* **1.** (ANAT) sinus. **2.** (MATHS) sine.

sinusite [sinyzit] *nf* sinusitis (U).

sionisme [sjɔnism] *nm* Zionism.

siphon [sifɔ̃] *nm* **1.** (*tube*) siphon. **2.** (*bouteille*) soda siphon.

siphonner [sifɔne] *vt* to siphon.

sirène [sirɛn] *nf* siren.

sirop [siro] *nm* syrup; **~ d'érable** maple syrup; **~ de grenadine** (syrup of) grenadine; **~ de menthe** mint cordial.

siroter [sirɔte] *vt fam* to sip.

sis, -e [si, siz] *adj* (JUR) located.

sismique [sismik] *adj* seismic.

site [sit] *nm* **1.** (*emplacement*) site; **~ archéologique/historique** archaeological/historic site. **2.** (*paysage*) beauty

spot. **3.** (INFORM): **~ Web** Web site.

sitôt [sito] *adv*: **~ après** immediately after; **pas de ~** not for some time, not for a while; **~ arrivé, ...** as soon as I/he *etc* arrived, ...; **~ dit, ~ fait** no sooner said than done. ▶ **sitôt que** *loc conj* as soon as.

situation [sitɥasjɔ̃] *nf* **1.** (*position, emplacement*) position, location. **2.** (*contexte, circonstance*) situation; **~ de famille** marital status. **3.** (*emploi*) job, position. **4.** (FIN) financial statement.

situer [sitɥe] *vt* **1.** (*maison*) to site, to situate; **bien/mal situé** well/badly situated. **2.** (*sur carte*) to locate. ▶ **se situer** *vp* (*scène*) to be set; (*dans classement*) to be.

six [sis *en fin de phrase, si devant consonne ou h aspiré*, siz *devant voyelle ou h muet*] ◆ *adj num* six; **il a ~ ans** he is six (years old); **il est ~ heures** it's six (o'clock); **le ~ janvier** (on) the sixth of January; **daté du ~ septembre** dated the sixth of September; **Charles Six** Charles the Sixth; **page ~** page six. ◆ *nm inv* **1.** (*gén*) six; **~ de pique** six of spades. **2.** (*adresse*) (number) six. ◆ *pron* six; **ils étaient ~** there were six of them; **~ par ~** six at a time.

sixième [sizjɛm] ◆ *adj num* sixth. ◆ *nmf* sixth; **arriver/se classer ~** to come (in)/to be placed sixth. ◆ *nf* (SCOL) ≃ first year ou form Br, ≃ sixth grade Am; **être en ~** to be in the first year ou form Br, to be in sixth grade Am; **entrer en ~** to go to secondary school. ◆ *nm* **1.** (*part*): **le/un ~ de** one/a sixth of; **cinq ~s** five sixths. **2.** (*arrondissement*) sixth arrondissement. **3.** (*étage*) sixth floor Br, seventh floor Am.

skateboard [skɛtbɔrd] *nm* skateboard.

sketch [skɛtʃ] (*pl* **sketches**) *nm* sketch (*in a revue etc*).

ski [ski] *nm* **1.** (*objet*) ski. **2.** (*sport*) skiing; **faire du ~** to ski; **~ acrobatique/alpin/de fond** freestyle/alpine/cross-country skiing; **~ nautique** water-skiing.

skier [skje] *vi* to ski.

skieur, -euse [skjœr, øz] *nm, f* skier.

skipper [skipœr] *nm* **1.** (*capitaine*) skipper. **2.** (*barreur*) helmsman.

slalom [slalɔm] *nm* **1.** (SKI) slalom. **2.** (*zigzags*): **faire du ~** to zigzag.

slave [slav] *adj* Slavonic. ▶ **Slave** *nmf* Slav.

slip [slip] *nm* briefs (*pl*); **~ de bain** (*d'homme*) swimming trunks (*pl*); (*de* *femme*) bikini bottoms (*pl*).

slogan [slɔgã] *nm* slogan.

Slovaquie [slɔvaki] *nf*: **la ~** Slovakia.

Slovénie [slɔveni] *nf*: **la ~** Slovenia.

slow [slo] *nm* slow dance.

smasher [smaʃe] *vi* (TENNIS) to smash (the ball).

SME (*abr de* **Système monétaire européen**) *nm* EMS.

SMIC, Smic [smik] (*abr de* **salaire minimum interprofessionnel de croissance**) *nm* index-linked guaranteed minimum wage.

smoking [smɔkiŋ] *nm* dinner jacket, tuxedo Am.

SNCF (*abr de* **Société nationale des chemins de fer français**) *nf* French railways board, ≃ BR Br.

snob [snɔb] ♦ *nmf* snob. ♦ *adj* snobbish.

snober [snɔbe] *vt* to snub, to cold-shoulder.

snobisme [snɔbism] *nm* snobbery, snobbishness.

sobre [sɔbr] *adj* 1. (*personne*) temperate. 2. (*style*) sober; (*décor, repas*) simple.

sobriété [sɔbrijete] *nf* sobriety.

sobriquet [sɔbrike] *nm* nickname.

soc [sɔk] *nm* ploughshare.

sociable [sɔsjabl] *adj* sociable.

social, -e, -aux [sɔsjal, o] *adj* 1. (*rapports, classe, service*) social. 2. (COMM): **capital ~** share capital; **raison ~e** company name. ▶ **social** *nm*: **le ~** social affairs (*pl*).

socialisme [sɔsjalism] *nm* socialism.

socialiste [sɔsjalist] *nmf & adj* socialist.

sociétaire [sɔsjetɛr] *nmf* member.

société [sɔsjete] *nf* 1. (*communauté, classe sociale, groupe*) society; **en ~** in society. 2. (*présence*) company, society. 3. (COMM) company, firm.

sociologie [sɔsjɔlɔʒi] *nf* sociology.

sociologue [sɔsjɔlɔg] *nmf* sociologist.

socioprofessionnel, -elle [sɔsjɔprɔfesjɔnɛl] *adj* socioprofessional.

socle [sɔkl] *nm* 1. (*de statue*) plinth, pedestal. 2. (*de lampe*) base.

socquette [sɔkɛt] *nf* ankle ou short sock.

soda [sɔda] *nm* fizzy drink.

sodium [sɔdjɔm] *nm* sodium.

sodomiser [sɔdɔmize] *vt* to sodomize.

sœur [sœr] *nf* 1. (*gén*) sister; **grande/petite ~** big/little sister. 2. (RELIG) nun, sister.

sofa [sɔfa] *nm* sofa.

Sofia [sɔfja] *n* Sofia.

SOFRES [sɔfrɛs] (*abr de* **Société française d'enquêtes par sondages**) *nf* French opinion poll company.

software [sɔftwɛr] *nm* software.

soi [swa] *pron pers* oneself; **chacun pour ~** every man for himself; **cela va de ~** that goes without saying. ▶ **soi-même** *pron pers* oneself.

soi-disant [swadizã] ♦ *adj inv* (*avant n*) so-called. ♦ *adv fam* supposedly.

soie [swa] *nf* 1. (*textile*) silk. 2. (*poil*) bristle.

soierie [swari] *nf* (*gén pl*) (*textile*) silk.

soif [swaf] *nf* thirst; **~ (de)** *fig* thirst (for), craving (for); **avoir ~** to be thirsty.

soigné, -e [swaɲe] *adj* 1. (*travail*) meticulous. 2. (*personne*) well-groomed; (*jardin, mains*) well-cared-for.

soigner [swaɲe] *vt* 1. (*suj: médecin*) to treat; (*suj: infirmière, parent*) to nurse. 2. (*invités, jardin, mains*) to look after. 3. (*travail, présentation*) to take care over. ▶ **se soigner** *vp* to take care of o.s., to look after o.s.

soigneusement [swaɲøzmã] *adv* carefully.

soigneux, -euse [swaɲø, øz] *adj* 1. (*personne*) tidy, neat. 2. (*travail*) careful.

soin [swɛ̃] *nm* 1. (*attention*) care; **avoir ou prendre ~ de faire qqch** to be sure to do sthg; **avec ~** carefully; **sans ~** (*procéder*) carelessly; (*travail*) careless; **être aux petits ~s pour qqn** *fig* to wait on sb hand and foot. 2. (*souci*) concern. ▶ **soins** *nmpl* care (U); **les premiers ~s** first aid (*sg*).

soir [swar] *nm* evening; **demain ~** tomorrow evening ou night; **le ~** in the evening; **à ce ~!** see you tonight!

soirée [sware] *nf* 1. (*soir*) evening. 2. (*réception*) party.

sois → **être**.

soit¹ [swat] *adv* so be it.

soit² [swa] ♦ *vb* → **être**. ♦ *conj* 1. (*c'est-à-dire*) in other words, that is to say. 2. (MATHS) (*étant donné*): **~ une droite AB** given a straight line AB. ▶ **soit ... soit** *loc corrélative* either ... or. ▶ **soit que ... soit que** *loc corrélative* (+ subjonctif) whether ... or (whether).

soixante [swasãt] ♦ *adj num* sixty; **les années ~** the Sixties. ♦ *nm* sixty; *voir aussi* **six**.

soixante-dix [swasãtdis] ♦ *adj num* seventy; **les années ~** the Seventies. ♦ *nm* seventy; *voir aussi* **six**.

soixante-dixième [swasãtdizjɛm]

sommité

adj num, nm & *nmf* seventieth; *voir aussi*
sixième.

soixantième [swasɑ̃tjɛm] *adj num, nm*
& *nmf* sixtieth; *voir aussi* **sixième**.

soja [sɔʒa] *nm* soya.

sol [sɔl] *nm* **1.** (*terre*) ground. **2.** (*de maison*) floor. **3.** (*territoire*) soil. **4.** (MUS) G;
(*chanté*) so.

solaire [sɔlɛr] *adj* **1.** (*énergie, four*) solar.
2. (*crème*) sun (*avant n*).

solarium [sɔlarjɔm] *nm* solarium.

soldat [sɔlda] *nm* **1.** (MIL) soldier; (*grade*)
private; **le ~ inconnu** the Unknown
Soldier. **2.** (*jouet*) (toy) soldier.

solde [sɔld] ◆ *nm* **1.** (*de compte, facture*)
balance; **~ créditeur/débiteur** credit/
debit balance. **2.** (*rabais*): **en ~** (*acheter*)
in a sale. ◆ *nf* (MIL) pay. ▶ **soldes** *nmpl*
sales.

solder [sɔlde] *vt* **1.** (*compte*) to close.
2. (*marchandises*) to sell off. ▶ **se solder**
vp: **se ~ par** *fig* (*aboutir*) to end in.

sole [sɔl] *nf* sole.

soleil [sɔlɛj] *nm* **1.** (*astre, motif*) sun; **~
couchant/levant** setting/rising sun. **2.**
(*lumière, chaleur*) sun, sunlight; **au ~** in
the sun; **en plein ~** right in the sun; **il fait
(du) ~** it's sunny; **prendre le ~** to sunbathe.

solennel, -elle [sɔlanɛl] *adj* **1.** (*cérémonieux*) ceremonial. **2.** (*grave*) solemn.
3. *péj* (*pompeux*) pompous.

solennité [sɔlanite] *nf* **1.** (*gravité*)
solemnity. **2.** (*raideur*) stiffness, formality. **3.** (*fête*) special occasion.

solfège [sɔlfɛʒ] *nm*: **apprendre le ~** to
learn the rudiments of music.

solidaire [sɔlidɛr] *adj* **1.** (*lié*): **être ~ de
qqn** to be behind sb, to show solidar-
ity with sb. **2.** (*relié*) interdependent,
integral.

solidarité [sɔlidarite] *nf* (*entraide*) solidarity; **par ~** (*se mettre en grève*) in sympathy.

solide [sɔlid] ◆ *adj* **1.** (*état, corps*) solid.
2. (*construction*) solid, sturdy. **3.** (*personne*) sturdy, robust. **4.** (*argument*)
solid, sound. **5.** (*relation*) stable, strong.
◆ *nm* solid; **il nous faut du ~** *fig* we need
something solid ou concrete.

solidifier [sɔlidifje] *vt* **1.** (*ciment, eau*) to
solidify. **2.** (*structure*) to reinforce. ▶ **se
solidifier** *vp* to solidify.

solidité [sɔlidite] *nf* **1.** (*de matière,
construction*) solidity. **2.** (*de mariage*) stability, strength. **3.** (*de raisonnement, d'argument*) soundness.

soliloque [sɔlilɔk] *nm sout* soliloquy.

soliste [sɔlist] *nmf* soloist.

solitaire [sɔlitɛr] ◆ *adj* **1.** (*de caractère*)
solitary. **2.** (*esseulé, retiré*) lonely. ◆ *nmf*
(*personne*) loner, recluse. ◆ *nm* (*jeu, diamant*) solitaire.

solitude [sɔlityd] *nf* **1.** (*isolement*) loneliness. **2.** (*retraite*) solitude.

sollicitation [sɔlisitasjɔ̃] *nf* (*gén pl*)
entreaty.

solliciter [sɔlisite] *vt* **1.** (*demander -
entretien, audience*) to request; (*- attention,
intérêt*) to seek. **2.** (*s'intéresser à*): **être sol-
licité** to be in demand. **3.** (*faire appel à*):
~ qqn pour faire qqch to appeal to sb to
do sthg.

sollicitude [sɔlisityd] *nf* solicitude,
concern.

solo [sɔlo] *nm* solo; **en ~** solo.

solstice [sɔlstis] *nm*: **~ d'été/d'hiver**
summer/winter solstice.

soluble [sɔlybl] *adj* **1.** (*matière*) soluble;
(*café*) instant. **2.** *fig* (*problème*) solvable.

solution [sɔlysjɔ̃] *nf* **1.** (*résolution*) solution, answer. **2.** (*liquide*) solution.

solvable [sɔlvabl] *adj* solvent, credit-
worthy.

solvant [sɔlvɑ̃] *nm* solvent.

Somalie [sɔmali] *nf*: **la ~** Somalia.

sombre [sɔ̃br] *adj* **1.** (*couleur, costume,
pièce*) dark. **2.** *fig* (*pensées, avenir*) dark,
gloomy. **3.** (*avant n*) *fam* (*profond*): **c'est
un ~ crétin** he's a prize idiot.

sombrer [sɔ̃bre] *vi* to sink; **~ dans** *fig* to
sink into.

sommaire [sɔmɛr] ◆ *adj* **1.** (*explication*)
brief. **2.** (*exécution*) summary. **3.** (*installation*) basic. ◆ *nm* summary.

sommation [sɔmasjɔ̃] *nf* **1.** (*assignation*) summons (*sg*). **2.** (*ordre - de payer*)
demand; (*- de se rendre*) warning.

somme [sɔm] ◆ *nf* **1.** (*addition*) total,
sum. **2.** (*d'argent*) sum, amount. **3.**
(*ouvrage*) overview. ◆ *nm* nap. ▶ **en
somme** *loc adv* in short. ▶ **somme
toute** *loc adv* when all's said and done.

sommeil [sɔmɛj] *nm* sleep; **avoir ~** to
be sleepy.

sommeiller [sɔmeje] *vi* **1.** (*personne*) to
doze. **2.** *fig* (*qualité*) to be dormant.

sommelier, -ère [sɔməlje, ɛr] *nm, f*
wine waiter (*f* wine waitress).

sommes → **être**.

sommet [sɔmɛ] *nm* **1.** (*de montagne*)
summit, top. **2.** *fig* (*de hiérarchie*) top; (*de
perfection*) height. **3.** (GÉOM) apex.

sommier [sɔmje] *nm* base, bed base.

sommité [sɔmite] *nf* (*personne*) leading
light.

somnambule [sɔmnɑ̃byl] ◆ *nmf* sleepwalker. ◆ *adj*: **être ~** to be a sleepwalker.

somnifère [sɔmnifɛr] *nm* sleeping pill.

somnolent, -e [sɔmnɔlɑ̃, ɑ̃t] *adj* (*personne*) sleepy, drowsy; *fig* (*vie*) dull; *fig* (*économie*) sluggish.

somnoler [sɔmnɔle] *vi* to doze.

somptueux, -euse [sɔ̃ptɥø, øz] *adj* sumptuous, lavish.

somptuosité [sɔ̃ptɥozite] *nf* lavishness (U).

son¹ [sɔ̃] *nm* **1.** (*bruit*) sound; **au ~ de** to the sound of; **~ et lumière** son et lumière. **2.** (*céréale*) bran.

son² [sɔ̃] (*f* **sa** [sa], *pl* **ses** [se]) *adj poss* **1.** (*possesseur défini - homme*) his; (*- femme*) her; (*- chose, animal*) its; **il aime ~ père** he loves his father; **elle aime ses parents** she loves her parents; **la ville a perdu ~ charme** the town has lost its charm. **2.** (*possesseur indéfini*) one's; (*- après 'chacun', 'tout le monde' etc*) his/her, their.

sonate [sɔnat] *nf* sonata.

sondage [sɔ̃daʒ] *nm* **1.** (*enquête*) poll, survey; **~ d'opinion** opinion poll. **2.** (TECHNOL) drilling. **3.** (MÉD) probing.

sonde [sɔ̃d] *nf* **1.** (MÉTÉOR) sonde; (*spatiale*) probe. **2.** (MÉD) probe. **3.** (NAVIG) sounding line. **4.** (TECHNOL) drill.

sonder [sɔ̃de] *vt* **1.** (MÉD & NAVIG) to sound. **2.** (*terrain*) to drill. **3.** *fig* (*opinion, personne*) to sound out.

songe [sɔ̃ʒ] *nm littéraire* dream.

songer [sɔ̃ʒe] *sout* ◆ *vt*: **~ que** to consider that. ◆ *vi* **1.** (*penser*): **~ à** to think about. **2.** (*rêver*) to dream.

songeur, -euse [sɔ̃ʒœr, øz] *adj* pensive, thoughtful.

sonnant, -e [sɔnɑ̃, ɑ̃t] *adj*: **à six heures ~es** at six o'clock sharp.

sonné, -e [sɔne] *adj* **1.** (*passé*): **il est trois heures ~es** it's gone three o'clock; **il a quarante ans bien ~s** *fam fig* he's on the wrong side of forty. **2.** *fig* (*étourdi*) groggy.

sonner [sɔne] ◆ *vt* **1.** (*cloche*) to ring. **2.** (*retraite, alarme*) to sound. **3.** (*domestique*) to ring for. **4.** *fam fig* (*siffler*): **je ne t'ai pas sonné!** who asked you! ◆ *vi* (*gén*) to ring; **~ chez qqn** to ring sb's bell.

sonnerie [sɔnri] *nf* **1.** (*bruit*) ringing. **2.** (*mécanisme*) striking mechanism. **3.** (*signal*) call.

sonnet [sɔnɛ] *nm* sonnet.

sonnette [sɔnɛt] *nf* bell.

sono [sɔno] *nf fam* (*de salle*) P.A. (system); (*de discothèque*) sound system.

sonore [sɔnɔr] *adj* **1.** (CIN & PHYS) sound (*avant n*). **2.** (*voix, rire*) ringing, resonant. **3.** (*salle*) resonant.

sonorisation [sɔnɔrizasjɔ̃] *nf* **1.** (*action - de film*) addition of the soundtrack; (*- de salle*) wiring for sound. **2.** (*matériel - de salle*) public address system, P.A. (system); (*- de discothèque*) sound system.

sonoriser [sɔnɔrize] *vt* **1.** (*film*) to add the soundtrack to. **2.** (*salle*) to wire for sound.

sonorité [sɔnɔrite] *nf* **1.** (*de piano, voix*) tone. **2.** (*de salle*) acoustics (*pl*).

sont → **être.**

sophistiqué, -e [sɔfistike] *adj* sophisticated.

soporifique [sɔpɔrifik] ◆ *adj* soporific. ◆ *nm* sleeping drug, soporific.

soprano [sɔprano] (*pl* **sopranos** ou **soprani** [sɔprani]) *nm ou nmf* soprano.

sorbet [sɔrbɛ] *nm* sorbet.

Sorbonne [sɔrbɔn] *nf*: **la ~** the Sorbonne (*highly respected Paris university*).

sorcellerie [sɔrsɛlri] *nf* witchcraft, sorcery.

sorcier, -ère [sɔrsje, ɛr] *nm, f* sorcerer (*f* witch).

sordide [sɔrdid] *adj* squalid; *fig* sordid.

sornettes [sɔrnɛt] *nfpl* nonsense (U).

sort [sɔr] *nm* **1.** (*maléfice*) spell; **jeter un ~ (à qqn)** to cast a spell (on sb). **2.** (*destinée*) fate. **3.** (*condition*) lot. **4.** (*hasard*): **le ~ fate**; **tirer au ~** to draw lots.

sortant, -e [sɔrtɑ̃, ɑ̃t] *adj* **1.** (*numéro*) winning. **2.** (*président, directeur*) outgoing (*avant n*).

sorte [sɔrt] *nf* sort, kind; **une ~ de** a sort of, a kind of; **toutes ~s de** all kinds of, all sorts of.

sortie [sɔrti] *nf* **1.** (*issue*) exit, way out; (*d'eau, d'air*) outlet; **~ d'autoroute** motorway junction ou exit; **~ de secours** emergency exit. **2.** (*départ*): **c'est la ~ de l'école** it's home-time; **à la ~ du travail** when work finishes, after work. **3.** (*de produit*) launch, launching; (*de disque*) release; (*de livre*) publication. **4.** (*gén pl*) (*dépense*) outgoings (*pl*), expenditure (U). **5.** (*excursion*) outing; (*au cinéma, au restaurant*) evening ou night out; **faire une ~** to go out. **6.** (MIL) sortie. **7.** (INFORM): **~ imprimante** printout.

sortilège [sɔrtilɛʒ] *nm* spell.

sortir [sɔrtir] ◆ *vi* (*aux: être*) **1.** (*de la maison, du bureau etc*) to leave, to go/come out; **~ de** to go/come out of, to leave.

2. (*pour se distraire*) to go out. **3.** *fig* (*quitter*): ~ **de** (*réserve, préjugés*) to shed. **4.** *fig* (*de maladie*): ~ **de** to get over, to recover from; (*coma*) to come out of. **5.** (*film, livre, produit*) to come out; (*disque*) to be released. **6.** (*au jeu - carte, numéro*) to come up. **7.** (*s'écarter de*): ~ **de** (*sujet*) to get away from; (*légalité, compétence*) to be outside. **8.** *loc*: ~ **de l'ordinaire** to be out of the ordinary; **d'où il sort, celui-là**? where did HE spring from? ◆ *vt* (*aux: avoir*) **1.** (*gén*): ~ **qqch (de)** to take sth out (of). **2.** (*de situation difficile*) to get out, to extract. **3.** (*produit*) to launch; (*disque*) to bring out, to release; (*livre*) to bring out, to publish. ▶ **se sortir** *vp fig* (*de pétrin*) to get out; **s'en** ~ (*en réchapper*) to come out of it; (*y arriver*) to get through it.

SOS *nm* SOS; **lancer un** ~ to send out an SOS.

sosie [sɔzi] *nm* double.

sot, sotte [so, sɔt] ◆ *adj* silly, foolish. ◆ *nm, f* fool.

sottise [sɔtiz] *nf* stupidity (U), foolishness (U); **dire/faire une** ~ to say/do something stupid.

sou [su] *nm*: **être sans le** ~ to be penniless. ▶ **sous** *nmpl fam* money (U).

soubassement [subasmã] *nm* base.

soubresaut [subrəso] *nm* **1.** (*de voiture*) jolt. **2.** (*de personne*) start.

souche [suʃ] *nf* **1.** (*d'arbre*) stump. **2.** (*de carnet*) counterfoil, stub.

souci [susi] *nm* **1.** (*tracas*) worry; **se faire du** ~ to worry. **2.** (*préoccupation*) concern. **3.** (*fleur*) marigold.

soucier [susje] ▶ **se soucier** *vp*: **se** ~ **de** to care about.

soucieux, -euse [susjø, øz] *adj* **1.** (*préoccupé*) worried, concerned. **2.** (*concerné*): **être** ~ **de qqch/de faire qqch** to be concerned about sth/ about doing sth.

soucoupe [sukup] *nf* **1.** (*assiette*) saucer. **2.** (*vaisseau*): ~ **volante** flying saucer.

soudain, -e [sudɛ̃, ɛn] *adj* sudden. ▶ **soudain** *adv* suddenly, all of a sudden.

Soudan [sudã] *nm*: **le** ~ the Sudan.

soude [sud] *nf* soda.

souder [sude] *vt* **1.** (TECHNOL) to weld, to solder. **2.** (MÉD) to knit. **3.** *fig* (*unir*) to bind together.

soudoyer [sudwaje] *vt* to bribe.

soudure [sudyr] *nf* (TECHNOL) welding; (*résultat*) weld.

souffert, -e [sufɛr, ɛrt] *pp* → **souffrir**.

souffle [sufl] *nm* **1.** (*respiration*) breathing; (*expiration*) puff, breath; **un** ~ **d'air** *fig* a breath of air, a puff of wind. **2.** *fig* (*inspiration*) inspiration. **3.** (*d'explosion*) blast. **4.** (MÉD): ~ **au cœur** heart murmur. **5.** *loc*: **avoir le** ~ **coupé** to have one's breath taken away.

soufflé [sufle] *nm* soufflé.

souffler [sufle] ◆ *vt* **1.** (*bougie*) to blow out. **2.** (*vitre*) to blow out, to shatter. **3.** (*chuchoter*): ~ **qqch à qqn** to whisper sth to sb. **4.** *fam* (*prendre*): ~ **qqch à qqn** to pinch sth from sb. ◆ *vi* **1.** (*gén*) to blow. **2.** (*respirer*) to puff, to pant.

soufflet [sufle] *nm* **1.** (*instrument*) bellows (*sg*). **2.** (*de train*) connecting corridor, concertina vestibule. **3.** (COUTURE) gusset.

souffleur, -euse [suflœr, øz] *nm, f* (THÉÂTRE) prompt. ▶ **souffleur** *nm* (*de verre*) blower.

souffrance [sufrãs] *nf* suffering.

souffrant, -e [sufrã, ãt] *adj* poorly.

souffre-douleur [sufrədulœr] *nm inv* whipping boy.

souffrir [sufrir] ◆ *vi* to suffer; ~ **de** to suffer from; ~ **du dos/cœur** to have back/heart problems. ◆ *vt littéraire* (*supporter*) to stand, to bear.

soufre [sufr] *nm* sulphur.

souhait [swɛ] *nm* wish; **à tes/vos** ~**s!** bless you!

souhaiter [swete] *vt*: ~ **qqch** to wish for sth; ~ **faire qqch** to hope to do sth; ~ **qqch à qqn** to wish sb sth; ~ **à qqn de faire qqch** to hope that sb does sth; **souhaiter que ...** (+ *subjonctif*) to hope that ...

souiller [suje] *vt littéraire* (*salir*) to soil; *fig & sout* to sully.

soûl, -e, saoul, -e [su, sul] *adj* drunk.

soulagement [sulaʒmã] *nm* relief.

soulager [sulaʒe] *vt* (*gén*) to relieve.

soûler, saouler [sule] *vt* **1.** *fam* (*enivrer*): ~ **qqn** to get sb drunk; *fig* to intoxicate sb. **2.** *fig & péj* (*de plaintes*): ~ **qqn** to bore sb silly. ▶ **se soûler** *vp fam* to get drunk.

soulèvement [sulɛvmã] *nm* uprising.

soulever [sulve] *vt* **1.** (*fardeau, poids*) to lift; (*rideau*) to raise. **2.** *fig* (*question*) to raise, to bring up. **3.** *fig* (*enthousiasme*) to generate, to arouse; (*tollé*) to stir up; ~ **qqn contre** to stir sb up against. ▶ **se soulever** *vp* **1.** (*s'élever*) to raise o.s., to lift o.s. **2.** (*se révolter*) to rise up.

soulier [sulje] *nm* shoe.

souligner [suliɲe] vt 1. (par un trait) to underline. 2. fig (insister sur) to underline, to emphasize. 3. (mettre en valeur) to emphasize.

soumettre [sumɛtr] vt 1. (astreindre): ~ qqn à to subject sb to. 2. (ennemi, peuple) to subjugate. 3. (projet, problème): ~ qqch (à) to submit sthg (to). ► **se soumettre** vp: se ~ (à) to submit (to).

soumis, -e [sumi, iz] ◆ pp → **soumettre**. ◆ adj submissive.

soumission [sumisjɔ̃] nf submission.

soupape [supap] nf valve.

soupçon [supsɔ̃] nm (suspicion, intuition) suspicion.

soupçonner [supsɔne] vt (suspecter) to suspect; ~ qqn de qqch/de faire qqch to suspect sb of sthg/of doing sthg.

soupçonneux, -euse [supsɔnø, øz] adj suspicious.

soupe [sup] nf (CULIN) soup; ~ **populaire** soup kitchen.

souper [supe] ◆ nm supper. ◆ vi to have supper.

soupeser [supəze] vt 1. (poids) to feel the weight of. 2. (évaluer) to weigh up.

soupière [supjɛr] nf tureen.

soupir [supir] nm 1. (souffle) sigh; **pousser un ~** to let out ou give a sigh. 2. (MUS) crotchet rest Br, quarter-note rest Am.

soupirail, -aux [supiraj, o] nm barred basement window (for ventilation purposes).

soupirant [supirã] nm suitor.

soupirer [supire] vi (souffler) to sigh.

souple [supl] adj 1. (gymnaste) supple. 2. (pas) lithe. 3. (paquet, col) soft. 4. (tissu, cheveux) flowing. 5. (tuyau, horaire, caractère) flexible.

souplesse [suples] nf 1. (de gymnaste) suppleness. 2. (flexibilité - de tuyau) pliability, flexibility; (- de matière) suppleness. 3. (de personne) flexibility.

source [surs] nf 1. (gén) source. 2. (d'eau) spring; **prendre sa ~ à** to rise in.

sourcil [sursi] nm eyebrow; **froncer les ~s** to frown.

sourcilière [sursiljɛr] → **arcade**.

sourciller [sursije] vi: **sans ~** without batting an eyelid.

sourcilleux, -euse [sursijø, øz] adj fussy, finicky.

sourd, -e [sur, surd] ◆ adj 1. (personne) deaf. 2. (bruit, voix) muffled. 3. (douleur) dull. 4. (lutte, hostilité) silent. ◆ nm, f deaf person.

sourdement [surdəmã] adv 1. (avec un bruit sourd) dully. 2. fig (secrètement) silently.

sourdine [surdin] nf mute; **en ~** (sans bruit) softly; (secrètement) in secret.

sourd-muet, sourde-muette [surmɥe, surdmɥet] nm, f deaf-mute, deaf and dumb person.

sourdre [surdr] vi to well up.

souriant, -e [surjã, ãt] adj smiling, cheerful.

souricière [surisjɛr] nf mousetrap; fig trap.

sourire [surir] ◆ vi to smile; ~ **à qqn** to smile at sb; fig (destin, chance) to smile on sb. ◆ nm smile.

souris [suri] nf (INFORM & ZOOL) mouse.

sournois, -e [surnwa, az] adj 1. (personne) underhand. 2. fig (maladie, phénomène) unpredictable.

sous [su] prép 1. (gén) under; **nager ~ l'eau** to swim underwater; ~ **la pluie** in the rain; ~ **cet aspect** ou **angle** from that point of view. 2. (dans un délai de) within; ~ **huit jours** within a week.

sous-alimenté, -e [suzalimãte] adj malnourished, underfed.

sous-bois [subwa] nm inv undergrowth.

souscription [suskripsjɔ̃] nf subscription.

souscrire [suskrir] vi: ~ **à** to subscribe to.

sous-développé, -e [sudevlɔpe] adj (ÉCON) underdeveloped; fig & péj backward.

sous-directeur, -trice [sudirɛktœr, tris] nm, f assistant manager (f assistant manageress).

sous-ensemble [suzãsãbl] nm subset.

sous-entendu [suzãtãdy] nm insinuation.

sous-estimer [suzestime] vt to underestimate, to underrate.

sous-évaluer [suzevalɥe] vt to underestimate.

sous-jacent, -e [suʒasã, ãt] adj underlying.

sous-louer [sulwe] vt to sublet.

sous-marin, -e [sumarɛ̃, in] adj underwater (avant n). ► **sous-marin** nm submarine.

sous-officier [suzɔfisje] nm non-commissioned officer.

sous-préfecture [suprefɛktyr] nf sub-prefecture.

sous-préfet [suprefɛ] nm sub-prefect.
sous-produit [suprɔdɥi] nm **1.** (objet) by-product. **2.** fig (imitation) pale imitation.
soussigné, -e [susiɲe] ♦ adj: **je ~** I the undersigned. ♦ nm, f undersigned.
sous-sol [susɔl] nm **1.** (de bâtiment) basement. **2.** (naturel) subsoil.
sous-tasse [sutas] nf saucer.
sous-titre [sutitr] nm subtitle.
soustraction [sustraksjɔ̃] nf (MATHS) subtraction.
soustraire [sustrɛr] vt **1.** (retrancher): **~ qqch de** to subtract sthg from. **2.** sout (voler): **~ qqch à qqn** to take sthg away from sb. ▶ **se soustraire** vp: **se ~ à** to escape from.
sous-traitant, -e [sutrɛtɑ̃, ɑ̃t] adj subcontracting. ▶ **sous-traitant** nm subcontractor.
sous-verre [suvɛr] nm inv picture or document framed between a sheet of glass and a rigid backing.
sous-vêtement [suvɛtmɑ̃] nm undergarment; **~s** underwear (U), underclothes.
soutane [sutan] nf cassock.
soute [sut] nf hold.
soutenance [sutnɑ̃s] nf viva.
souteneur [sutnœr] nm procurer.
soutenir [sutnir] vt **1.** (immeuble, personne) to support, to hold up. **2.** (effort, intérêt) to sustain. **3.** (encourager) to support; (POLIT) to back, to support. **4.** (affirmer): **~ que** to maintain (that). **5.** (résister à) to withstand; (regard, comparaison) to bear.
soutenu, -e [sutny] adj **1.** (style, langage) elevated. **2.** (attention, rythme) sustained. **3.** (couleur) vivid.
souterrain, -e [sutɛrɛ̃, ɛn] adj underground. ▶ **souterrain** nm underground passage.
soutien [sutjɛ̃] nm support; **apporter son ~ à** to give one's support to.
soutien-gorge [sutjɛ̃gɔrʒ] (pl **soutiens-gorge**) nm bra.
soutirer [sutire] vt fig (tirer): **~ qqch à qqn** to extract sthg from sb.
souvenir [suvnir] nm **1.** (réminiscence, mémoire) memory. **2.** (objet) souvenir. ▶ **se souvenir** vp (ne pas oublier): **se ~ de qqch/de qqn** to remember sthg/sb; **se ~ que** to remember (that).
souvent [suvɑ̃] adv often.
souvenu, -e [suvny] pp → **souvenir**.
souverain, -e [suvrɛ̃, ɛn] ♦ adj **1.** (remède, état) sovereign. **2.** (indif-

férence) supreme. ♦ nm, f (monarque) sovereign, monarch.
souveraineté [suvrɛnte] nf sovereignty.
soviétique [sɔvjetik] adj Soviet. ▶ **Soviétique** nmf Soviet (citizen).
soyeux, -euse [swajø, øz] adj silky.
soyez → **être**.
SPA (abr de **Société protectrice des animaux**) nf French society for the protection of animals, ≃ RSPCA Br, ≃ SPCA Am.
spacieux, -euse [spasjø, øz] adj spacious.
spaghettis [spageti] nmpl spaghetti (U).
sparadrap [sparadra] nm sticking plaster.
spartiate [sparsjat] adj (austère) Spartan.
spasme [spasm] nm spasm.
spasmodique [spasmɔdik] adj spasmodic.
spatial, -e, -aux [spasjal, o] adj space (avant n).
spatule [spatyl] nf **1.** (ustensile) spatula. **2.** (de ski) tip.
speaker, speakerine [spikœr, spikrin] nm, f announcer.
spécial, -e, -aux [spesjal, o] adj **1.** (particulier) special. **2.** fam (bizarre) peculiar.
spécialiser [spesjalize] vt to specialize. ▶ **se spécialiser** vp: **se ~ (dans)** to specialize (in).
spécialiste [spesjalist] nmf specialist.
spécialité [spesjalite] nf speciality.
spécifier [spesifje] vt to specify.
spécifique [spesifik] adj specific.
spécimen [spesimɛn] nm **1.** (représentant) specimen. **2.** (exemplaire) sample.
spectacle [spɛktakl] nm **1.** (représentation) show. **2.** (domaine) show business, entertainment. **3.** (tableau) spectacle, sight.
spectaculaire [spɛktakylɛr] adj spectacular.
spectateur, -trice [spɛktatœr, tris] nm, f **1.** (témoin) witness. **2.** (de spectacle) spectator.
spectre [spɛktr] nm **1.** (fantôme) spectre. **2.** (PHYS) spectrum.
spéculateur, -trice [spekylatœr, tris] nm, f speculator.
spéculation [spekylasjɔ̃] nf speculation.
spéculer [spekyle] vi: **~ sur** (FIN) to speculate in; fig (miser) to count on.
speech [spitʃ] (pl **speeches**) nm speech.

spéléologie [speleɔlɔʒi] *nf* (*exploration*) potholing; (*science*) speleology.

spermatozoïde [spɛrmatɔzɔid] *nm* sperm, spermatozoon.

sperme [spɛrm] *nm* sperm, semen.

sphère [sfɛr] *nf* sphere.

sphérique [sferik] *adj* spherical.

spirale [spiral] *nf* spiral.

spirituel, -elle [spirituɛl] *adj* 1. (*de l'âme, moral*) spiritual. 2. (*vivant, drôle*) witty.

spiritueux [spirituø] *nm* spirit.

splendeur [splãdœr] *nf* 1. (*beauté, prospérité*) splendour. 2. (*merveille*): **c'est une ~!** it's magnificent!

splendide [splãdid] *adj* magnificent, splendid.

spongieux, -euse [spɔ̃ʒjø, øz] *adj* spongy.

sponsor [spɔ̃sɔr] *nm* sponsor.

sponsoriser [spɔ̃sɔrize] *vt* to sponsor.

spontané, -e [spɔ̃tane] *adj* spontaneous.

spontanéité [spɔ̃taneite] *nf* spontaneity.

sporadique [spɔradik] *adj* sporadic.

sport [spɔr] ◆ *nm* sport; **~s d'hiver** winter sports. ◆ *adj inv* 1. (*vêtement*) sports (*avant n*). 2. (*fair play*) sporting.

sportif, -ive [spɔrtif, iv] ◆ *adj* 1. (*association, résultats*) sports (*avant n*). 2. (*personne, physique*) sporty, athletic. 3. (*fair play*) sportsmanlike, sporting. ◆ *nm, f* sportsman (*f* sportswoman).

sportswear [spɔrtswɛr] *nm* sportswear.

spot [spɔt] *nm* 1. (*lampe*) spot, spotlight. 2. (*publicité*): **~ (publicitaire)** commercial, advert.

sprint [sprint] *nm* (SPORT - *accélération*) spurt; (- *course*) sprint.

square [skwar] *nm* small public garden.

squash [skwaʃ] *nm* squash.

squelette [skəlɛt] *nm* skeleton.

squelettique [skəletik] *adj* (*corps*) emaciated.

St (*abr de* **saint**) St.

stabiliser [stabilize] *vt* 1. (*gén*) to stabilize; (*meuble*) to steady. 2. (*terrain*) to make firm. ► **se stabiliser** *vp* 1. (*véhicule, prix, situation*) to stabilize. 2. (*personne*) to settle down.

stabilité [stabilite] *nf* stability.

stable [stabl] *adj* 1. (*gén*) stable. 2. (*meuble*) steady, stable.

stade [stad] *nm* 1. (*terrain*) stadium. 2. (*étape &* MÉD) stage; **en être au ~ de/**

où to reach the stage of/at which.

stage [staʒ] *nm* (SCOL) work placement; (*sur le temps de travail*) in-service training; **faire un ~** (*cours*) to go on a training course; (*expérience professionnelle*) to go on a work placement.

stagiaire [staʒjɛr] ◆ *nmf* trainee. ◆ *adj* trainee (*avant n*).

stagnant, -e [stagnã, ãt] *adj* stagnant.

stagner [stagne] *vi* to stagnate.

stalactite [stalaktit] *nf* stalactite.

stalagmite [stalagmit] *nf* stalagmite.

stand [stãd] *nm* 1. (*d'exposition*) stand. 2. (*de fête*) stall.

standard [stãdar] ◆ *adj inv* standard. ◆ *nm* 1. (*norme*) standard. 2. (*téléphonique*) switchboard.

standardiste [stãdardist] *nmf* switchboard operator.

standing [stãdiŋ] *nm* standing; **quartier de grand ~** select district.

star [star] *nf* (CIN) star.

starter [starter] *nm* (AUTOM) choke; **mettre le ~** to pull the choke out.

starting-block [startiŋblɔk] (*pl* **starting-blocks**) *nm* starting-block.

station [stasjɔ̃] *nf* 1. (*arrêt - de bus*) stop; (- *de métro*) station; **à quelle ~ dois-je descendre?** which stop do I get off at?; **~ de taxis** taxi stand. 2. (*installations*) station; **~ d'épuration** sewage treatment plant. 3. (*ville*) resort; **~ balnéaire** seaside resort; **~ de ski/de sports d'hiver** ski/winter sports resort; **~ thermale** spa (town). 4. (*position*) position. 5. (INFORM): **~ de travail** work station.

stationnaire [stasjɔnɛr] *adj* stationary.

stationnement [stasjɔnmã] *nm* parking; **'~ interdit'** 'no parking'.

stationner [stasjɔne] *vi* to park.

station-service [stasjɔ̃sɛrvis] (*pl* **stations-service**) *nf* service station, petrol station Br, gas station Am.

statique [statik] *adj* static.

statisticien, -enne [statistisjɛ̃, ɛn] *nm, f* statistician.

statistique [statistik] ◆ *adj* statistical. ◆ *nf* (*donnée*) statistic.

statue [staty] *nf* statue.

statuer [statɥe] *vi*: **~ sur** to give a decision on.

statuette [statɥɛt] *nf* statuette.

statu quo [statykwo] *nm inv* status quo.

stature [statyr] *nf* stature.

statut [staty] *nm* status. ► **statuts** *nmpl* statutes.

statutaire [statytɛr] *adj* statutory.

Ste (*abr de* **sainte**) St.

Sté (*abr de* **société**) Co.

steak [stɛk] *nm* steak; ~ **haché** mince.

stèle [stɛl] *nf* stele.

sténo [steno] ◆ *nmf* stenographer. ◆ *nf* shorthand.

sténodactylo [stenɔdaktilo] *nmf* shorthand typist.

sténodactylographie [stenɔdaktilɔgrafi] *nf* shorthand typing.

stentor [stɑ̃tɔr] → **voix**.

steppe [stɛp] *nf* steppe.

stéréo [stereo] ◆ *adj inv* stereo. ◆ *nf* stereo; **en ~** in stereo.

stéréotype [stereɔtip] *nm* stereotype.

stérile [steril] *adj* **1.** (*personne*) sterile, infertile; (*terre*) barren. **2.** *fig* (*inutile - discussion*) sterile; (*- efforts*) futile. **3.** (MÉD) sterile.

stérilet [sterilɛ] *nm* IUD, intra-uterine device.

stériliser [sterilize] *vt* to sterilize.

stérilité [sterilite] *nf litt & fig* sterility; (*d'efforts*) futility.

sterling [stɛrliŋ] *adj inv & nm inv* sterling.

sternum [stɛrnɔm] *nm* breastbone, sternum.

stéthoscope [stetɔskɔp] *nm* stethoscope.

steward [stiwart] *nm* steward.

stigmate [stigmat] *nm* (*gén pl*) mark, scar.

stimulant, -e [stimylɑ̃, ɑ̃t] *adj* stimulating. ▶ **stimulant** *nm* **1.** (*remontant*) stimulant. **2.** (*motivation*) incentive, stimulus.

stimulation [stimylasjɔ̃] *nf* stimulation.

stimuler [stimyle] *vt* to stimulate.

stipuler [stipyle] *vt*: ~ **que** to stipulate (that).

stock [stɔk] *nm* stock; **en ~** in stock.

stocker [stɔke] *vt* **1.** (*marchandises*) to stock. **2.** (INFORM) to store.

Stockholm [stɔkɔlm] *n* Stockholm.

stoïque [stɔik] *adj* stoical.

stop [stɔp] ◆ *interj* stop! ◆ *nm* **1.** (*panneau*) stop sign. **2.** (*auto-stop*) hitchhiking, hitching.

stopper [stɔpe] ◆ *vt* (*arrêter*) to stop, to halt. ◆ *vi* to stop.

store [stɔr] *nm* **1.** (*de fenêtre*) blind. **2.** (*de magasin*) awning.

strabisme [strabism] *nm* squint.

strangulation [strɑ̃gylasjɔ̃] *nf* strangulation.

strapontin [strapɔ̃tɛ̃] *nm* (*siège*) pull-down seat.

strass [stras] *nm* paste.

stratagème [strataʒɛm] *nm* stratagem.

stratégie [strateʒi] *nf* strategy.

stratégique [strateʒik] *adj* strategic.

stress [strɛs] *nm* stress.

stressant, -e [strɛsɑ̃, ɑ̃t] *adj* stressful.

stressé, -e [strɛse] *adj* stressed.

strict, -e [strikt] *adj* **1.** (*personne, règlement*) strict. **2.** (*sobre*) plain. **3.** (*absolu - minimum*) bare, absolute; (*- vérité*) absolute; **dans la plus ~e intimité** strictly in private; **au sens ~ du terme** in the strict sense of the word.

strident, -e [stridɑ̃, ɑ̃t] *adj* strident, shrill.

strié, -e [strije] *adj* (*rayé*) striped.

strier [strije] *vt* to streak.

strip-tease [striptiz] (*pl* **strip-teases**) *nm* striptease.

strophe [strɔf] *nf* verse.

structure [stryktyr] *nf* structure.

structurer [stryktyre] *vt* to structure.

studieux, -euse [stydjø, øz] *adj* (*personne*) studious.

studio [stydjo] *nm* **1.** (CIN, PHOT & TÉLÉ) studio. **2.** (*appartement*) studio flat Br, studio apartment Am.

stupéfaction [stypefaksjɔ̃] *nf* astonishment, stupefaction.

stupéfait, -e [stypefɛ, ɛt] *adj* astounded, stupefied.

stupéfiant, -e [stypefjɑ̃, ɑ̃t] *adj* astounding, stunning. ▶ **stupéfiant** *nm* narcotic, drug.

stupeur [stypœr] *nf* **1.** (*stupéfaction*) astonishment. **2.** (MÉD) stupor.

stupide [stypid] *adj* **1.** *péj* (*abruti*) stupid. **2.** (*insensé - mort*) senseless; (*- accident*) stupid.

stupidité [stypidite] *nf* stupidity.

style [stil] *nm* **1.** (*gén*) style. **2.** (GRAM): **~ direct/indirect** direct/indirect speech.

styliste [stilist] *nmf* (COUTURE) designer.

stylo [stilo] *nm* pen; **~ plume** fountain pen.

stylo-feutre [stiloføtr] *nm* felt-tip pen.

su, -e [sy] *pp* → **savoir**.

suave [sɥav] *adj* (*voix*) smooth; (*parfum*) sweet.

subalterne [sybaltɛrn] ◆ *nmf* subordinate, junior. ◆ *adj* (*rôle*) subordinate; (*employé*) junior.

subconscient, -e [sybkɔ̃sjɑ̃, ɑ̃t] *adj*

subconscious. ▶ **subconscient** *nm* subconscious.

subdiviser [sybdivize] *vt* to subdivide.

subir [sybir] *vt* 1. (*conséquences, colère*) to suffer; (*personne*) to put up with. 2. (*opération, épreuve, examen*) to undergo. 3. (*dommages, pertes*) to sustain, to suffer; ~ **une hausse** to be increased.

subit, -e [sybi, it] *adj* sudden.

subitement [sybitmã] *adv* suddenly.

subjectif, -ive [sybʒɛktif, iv] *adj* (*personnel, partial*) subjective.

subjonctif [sybʒɔ̃ktif] *nm* subjunctive.

subjuguer [sybʒyge] *vt* to captivate.

sublime [syblim] *adj* sublime.

submerger [sybmɛrʒe] *vt* 1. (*inonder*) to flood. 2. (*envahir*) to overcome, to overwhelm. 3. (*déborder*) to overwhelm; **être submergé de travail** to be swamped with work.

subordination [sybɔrdinasjɔ̃] *nf* subordination.

subordonné, -e [sybɔrdɔne] ◆ *adj* (GRAM) subordinate, dependent. ◆ *nm, f* subordinate.

subornation [sybɔrnasjɔ̃] *nf* bribing, subornation.

subrepticement [sybreptismã] *adv* surreptitiously.

subsidiaire [sybzidjɛr] *adj* subsidiary.

subsistance [sybzistãs] *nf* subsistence.

subsister [sybziste] *vi* 1. (*chose*) to remain. 2. (*personne*) to live, to subsist.

substance [sypstãs] *nf* 1. (*matière*) substance. 2. (*essence*) gist.

substantiel, -elle [sypstãsjɛl] *adj* substantial.

substantif [sypstãtif] *nm* noun.

substituer [sypstitɥe] *vt*: ~ **qqch à qqch** to substitute sthg for sthg. ▶ **se substituer** *vp*: **se** ~ **à** (*personne*) to stand in for, to substitute for; (*chose*) to take the place of.

substitut [sypstity] *nm* (*remplacement*) substitute.

substitution [sypstitysjɔ̃] *nf* substitution.

subterfuge [sypterfyʒ] *nm* subterfuge.

subtil, -e [syptil] *adj* subtle.

subtiliser [syptilize] *vt* to steal.

subtilité [syptilite] *nf* subtlety.

subvenir [sybvənir] *vi*: ~ **à** to meet, to cover.

subvention [sybvãsjɔ̃] *nf* grant, subsidy.

subventionner [sybvãsjɔne] *vt* to give a grant to, to subsidize.

subversif, -ive [sybvɛrsif, iv] *adj* subversive.

succédané [syksedane] *nm* substitute.

succéder [syksede] *vt*: ~ **à** (*suivre*) to follow; (*remplacer*) to succeed, to take over from. ▶ **se succéder** *vp* to follow one another.

succès [syksɛ] *nm* 1. (*gén*) success; **avoir du** ~ to be very successful; **sans** ~ (*essai*) unsuccessful; (*essayer*) unsuccessfully. 2. (*chanson, pièce*) hit.

successeur [syksesœr] *nm* 1. (*gén*) successor. 2. (JUR) successor, heir.

successif, -ive [syksesif, iv] *adj* successive.

succession [syksesjɔ̃] *nf* 1. (*gén*) succession; **une** ~ **de** a succession of; **prendre la** ~ **de qqn** to take over from sb, to succeed sb. 2. (JUR) succession, inheritance; **droits de** ~ death duties.

succinct, -e [syksɛ̃, ɛ̃t] *adj* 1. (*résumé*) succinct. 2. (*repas*) frugal.

succion [syksjɔ̃, sysjɔ̃] *nf* suction, sucking.

succomber [sykɔ̃be] *vi*: ~ **(à)** to succumb (to).

succulent, -e [sykylã, ãt] *adj* delicious.

succursale [sykyrsal] *nf* branch.

sucer [syse] *vt* to suck.

sucette [sysɛt] *nf* (*friandise*) lolly Br, lollipop.

sucre [sykr] *nm* sugar; ~ **en morceaux** lump sugar; ~ **en poudre**, ~ **semoule** caster sugar.

sucré, -e [sykre] *adj* (*goût*) sweet.

sucrer [sykre] *vt* 1. (*café, thé*) to sweeten, to sugar. 2. *fam* (*permission*) to withdraw; (*passage, réplique*) to cut; ~ **qqch à qqn** to take sthg away from sb.

sucrerie [sykrəri] *nf* 1. (*usine*) sugar refinery. 2. (*friandise*) sweet Br, candy Am.

sucrette [sykrɛt] *nf* sweetener.

sucrier [sykrije] *nm* sugar bowl.

sud [syd] ◆ *nm* south; **un vent du** ~ a southerly wind; **au** ~ in the south; **au** ~ **(de)** to the south (of). ◆ *adj inv* (*gén*) south; (*province, région*) southern.

sud-africain, -e [sydafrikɛ̃, ɛn] (*mpl* **sud-africains**, *fpl* **sud-africaines**) *adj* South African. ▶ **Sud-Africain, -e** *nm, f* South African.

sud-américain, -e [sydamerikɛ̃, ɛn] (*mpl* **sud-américains**, *fpl* **sud-américaines**) *adj* South American. ▶ **Sud-Américain, -e** *nm, f* South American.

sudation [sydasjɔ̃] *nf* sweating.

sud-est [sydɛst] *nm & adj inv* south-east.

sud-ouest [sydwɛst] *nm & adj inv* southwest.

Suède [sɥɛd] *nf*: **la ~** Sweden.

suédois, -e [sɥedwa, az] *adj* Swedish. ▶ **suédois** *nm* (*langue*) Swedish. ▶ **Suédois, -e** *nm, f* Swede.

suer [sɥe] ◆ *vi* (*personne*) to sweat. ◆ *vt* to exude.

sueur [sɥœr] *nf* sweat; **avoir des ~s froides** *fig* to be in a cold sweat.

Suez [sɥez] *n*: **le canal de ~** the Suez Canal.

suffi [syfi] *pp inv* → **suffire.**

suffire [syfir] ◆ *vi* 1. (*être assez*): **~ pour qqch/pour faire qqch** to be enough for sthg/to do sthg, to be sufficient for sthg/to do sthg; **ça suffit!** that's enough! 2. (*satisfaire*): **~ à** to be enough for. ◆ *v impers*: **il suffit de ...** all that is necessary is ..., all that you have to do is ...; **il suffit que** (+ *subjonctif*): **il suffit que vous lui écriviez** all (that) you need do is write to him. ▶ **se suffire** *vp*: **se ~ à soi-même** to be self-sufficient.

suffisamment [syfizamɑ̃] *adv* sufficiently.

suffisant, -e [syfizɑ̃, ɑ̃t] *adj* 1. (*satisfaisant*) sufficient. 2. (*vaniteux*) self-important.

suffixe [syfiks] *nm* suffix.

suffocation [syfɔkasjɔ̃] *nf* suffocation.

suffoquer [syfɔke] ◆ *vt* 1. (*suj: chaleur, fumée*) to suffocate. 2. *fig* (*suj: colère*) to choke; (*suj: nouvelle, révélation*) to astonish, to stun. ◆ *vi* to choke.

suffrage [syfraʒ] *nm* vote.

suggérer [sygʒere] *vt* 1. (*proposer*) to suggest; **~ qqch à qqn** to suggest sthg to sb; **~ à qqn de faire qqch** to suggest that sb (should) do sthg. 2. (*faire penser à*) to evoke.

suggestif, -ive [sygʒɛstif, iv] *adj* 1. (*musique*) evocative. 2. (*pose, photo*) suggestive.

suggestion [sygʒɛstjɔ̃] *nf* suggestion.

suicidaire [sɥisider] *adj* suicidal.

suicide [sɥisid] *nm* suicide.

suicider [sɥiside] ▶ **se suicider** *vp* to commit suicide, to kill o.s.

suie [sɥi] *nf* soot.

suinter [sɥɛ̃te] *vi* 1. (*eau, sang*) to ooze, to seep. 2. (*surface, mur*) to sweat; (*plaie*) to weep.

suis → **être.**

suisse [sɥis] ◆ *adj* Swiss. ◆ *nm* (RELIG) verger. ▶ **Suisse** ◆ *nf* (*pays*): **la ~** Switzerland; **la ~ allemande/italienne/romande** German-/Italian-/French-speaking Switzerland. ◆ *nmf* (*personne*) Swiss (person); **les Suisses** the Swiss.

suite [sɥit] *nf* 1. (*de liste, feuilleton*) continuation. 2. (*série - de maisons, de succès*) series; (*- d'événements*) sequence. 3. (*succession*): **prendre la ~ de** (*personne*) to succeed, to take over from; (*affaire*) to take over; **à la ~** one after the other; **à la ~ de** *fig* following. 4. (*escorte*) retinue. 5. (MUS) suite. 6. (*appartement*) suite. ▶ **suites** *nfpl* consequences. ▶ **par la suite** *loc adv* afterwards. ▶ **par suite de** *loc prép* owing to, because of.

suivant, -e [sɥivɑ̃, ɑ̃t] ◆ *adj* next, following. ◆ *nm, f* next *ou* following one; **au ~!** next!

suivi, -e [sɥivi] ◆ *pp* → **suivre.** ◆ *adj* (*visites*) regular; (*travail*) sustained; (*qualité*) consistent. ▶ **suivi** *nm* follow-up.

suivre [sɥivr] ◆ *vt* 1. (*gén*) to follow; **suivi de** followed by; **'faire ~'** 'please forward'; **à ~** to be continued. 2. (*traitement, formation*) to undergo. 3. (*suj: médecin*) to treat. ◆ *vi* 1. (SCOL) to keep up. 2. (*venir après*) to follow. ▶ **se suivre** *vp* to follow one another.

sujet, -ette [syʒɛ, ɛt] ◆ *adj*: **être ~ à qqch** to be subject *ou* prone to sthg. ◆ *nm, f* (*de souverain*) subject. ▶ **sujet** *nm* (*gén*) subject; **c'est à quel ~?** what is it about?; **~ de conversation** topic of conversation; **au ~ de** about, concerning.

sulfate [sylfat] *nm* sulphate.

sulfurique [sylfyrik] *adj* sulphuric.

super [syper] *fam* ◆ *adj inv* super, great. ◆ *nm* four star (petrol) *Br*, premium *Am*.

superbe [syperb] *adj* superb; (*enfant, femme*) beautiful.

supercherie [syperʃəri] *nf* deception, trickery.

superficie [syperfisi] *nf* 1. (*surface*) area. 2. *fig* (*aspect superficiel*) surface.

superficiel, -elle [syperfisjɛl] *adj* superficial.

superflu, -e [syperfly] *adj* superfluous. ▶ **superflu** *nm* superfluity.

supérieur, -e [syperjœr] ◆ *adj* 1. (*étage*) upper. 2. (*intelligence, qualité*) superior; **~ à** superior to; (*température*) higher than, above. **3.** (*dominant - équipe*) superior; (*- cadre*) senior. **4.** (SCOL *- classe*) upper, senior; (*- enseignement*) higher. **5.** *péj* (*air*) superior. ◆ *nm, f* superior.

supériorité [syperjorite] *nf* superiority.

superlatif [syperlatif] *nm* superlative.

supermarché [sypermarʃe] *nm* supermarket.

superposer [syperpoze] *vt* to stack. ▶ **se superposer** *vp* to be stacked.

superproduction [syperprodyksjɔ̃] *nf* spectacular.

superpuissance [syperpɥisɑ̃s] *nf* superpower.

supersonique [sypersɔnik] *adj* supersonic.

superstitieux, -euse [syperstisjø, øz] *adj* superstitious.

superstition [syperstisjɔ̃] *nf* (*croyance*) superstition.

superviser [sypervize] *vt* to supervise.

supplanter [syplɑ̃te] *vt* to supplant.

suppléant, -e [sypleɑ̃, ɑ̃t] ◆ *adj* acting (*avant n*), temporary. ◆ *nm, f* substitute, deputy.

suppléer [syplee] *vt* **1.** *littéraire* (*carence*) to compensate for. **2.** (*personne*) to stand in for.

supplément [syplemɑ̃] *nm* **1.** (*surplus*): **un ~ de détails** additional details, extra details. **2.** (PRESSE) supplement. **3.** (*de billet*) extra charge.

supplémentaire [syplemɑ̃tɛr] *adj* extra, additional.

supplication [syplikasjɔ̃] *nf* plea.

supplice [syplis] *nm* torture; *fig* (*souffrance*) torture, agony.

supplier [syplije] *vt*: **~ qqn de faire qqch** to beg sb to do sthg.

support [sypɔr] *nm* **1.** (*socle*) support, base. **2.** *fig* (*de communication*) medium; **~ pédagogique** teaching aid; **~ publicitaire** advertising medium.

supportable [sypɔrtabl] *adj* **1.** (*douleur*) bearable. **2.** (*conduite*) tolerable, acceptable.

supporter[1] [sypɔrte] *vt* **1.** (*soutenir, encourager*) to support. **2.** (*endurer*) to bear, to stand; **~ que** (+ *subjonctif*): **il ne supporte pas qu'on le contredise** he cannot bear being contradicted. **3.** (*résister à*) to withstand. ▶ **se supporter** *vp* (*se tolérer*) to bear ou stand each other.

supporter[2] [sypɔrter] *nm* supporter.

supposer [sypoze] *vt* **1.** (*imaginer*) to suppose, to assure; **en supposant que** (+ subjonctif), **à ~ que** (+ *subjonctif*) supposing (that). **2.** (*impliquer*) to imply, to presuppose.

supposition [sypozisjɔ̃] *nf* supposition, assumption.

suppositoire [sypozitwar] *nm* suppository.

suppression [sypresjɔ̃] *nf* **1.** (*de permis de conduire*) withdrawal; (*de document*) suppression. **2.** (*de mot, passage*) deletion. **3.** (*de loi, poste*) abolition.

supprimer [syprime] *vt* **1.** (*document*) to suppress; (*obstacle, difficulté*) to remove. **2.** (*mot, passage*) to delete. **3.** (*loi, poste*) to abolish. **4.** (*témoin*) to do away with, to eliminate. **5.** (*permis de conduire, revenus*): **~ qqch à qqn** to take sthg away from sb. **6.** (*douleur*) to take away, to suppress.

suprématie [sypremasi] *nf* supremacy.

suprême [syprɛm] *adj* (*gén*) supreme.

sur [syr] *prép* **1.** (*position - dessus*) on; (*- au-dessus de*) above, over; **~ la table** on the table. **2.** (*direction*) towards; **~ la droite/gauche** on the right/left, to the right/left. **3.** (*distance*): **travaux ~ 10 kilomètres** roadworks for 10 kilometres. **4.** (*d'après*) by; **juger qqn ~ sa mine** to judge sb by his/her appearance. **5.** (*grâce à*) on; **il vit ~ les revenus de ses parents** he lives on ou off his parents' income. **6.** (*au sujet de*) on, about. **7.** (*proportion*) out of; (*mesure*) by; **9 ~ 10** 9 out of 10; **un mètre ~ deux** one metre by two; **un jour ~ deux** every other day; **une fois ~ deux** every other time. ▶ **sur ce** *loc adv* whereupon.

sûr, -e [syr] *adj* **1.** (*sans danger*) safe. **2.** (*digne de confiance - personne*) reliable, trustworthy; (*- goût*) reliable, sound; (*- investissement*) sound. **3.** (*certain*) sure, certain; **~ de** sure of; **~ et certain** absolutely certain; **~ de soi** self-confident.

surabondance [syrabɔ̃dɑ̃s] *nf* overabundance.

suraigu, -ë [syregy] *adj* high-pitched, shrill.

suranné, -e [syrane] *adj littéraire* oldfashioned, outdated.

surcharge [syrʃarʒ] *nf* **1.** (*excès de poids*) excess load; (*- de bagages*) excess weight. **2.** *fig* (*surcroît*): **une ~ de travail** extra work. **3.** (*surabondance*) surfeit. **4.** (*de document*) alteration.

surcharger [syrʃarʒe] *vt* **1.** (*véhicule, personne*): **~ (de)** to overload (with).

2. (*texte*) to alter extensively.

surchauffer [syrʃofe] *vt* to overheat.

surcroît [syrkrwa] *nm*: **un ~ de travail/ d'inquiétude** additional work/anxiety.

surdité [syrdite] *nf* deafness.

surdoué, -e [syrdwe] *adj* exceptionally ou highly gifted.

sureffectif [syrefɛktif] *nm* overmanning, overstaffing.

surélever [syrelve] *vt* to raise, to heighten.

sûrement [syrmã] *adv* **1.** (*certainement*) certainly; **~ pas!** *fam* no way!, definitely not! **2.** (*sans doute*) certainly, surely. **3.** (*sans risque*) surely, safely.

surenchère [syrãʃɛr] *nf* higher bid; *fig* overstatement, exaggeration.

surenchérir [syrãʃerir] *vi* to bid higher; *fig* to try to go one better.

surendetté, -e [syrãdete] *adj* overindebted.

surendettement [syrãdetmã] *nm* overindebtedness.

surestimer [syrɛstime] *vt* **1.** (*exagérer*) to overestimate. **2.** (*surévaluer*) to overvalue. ▶ **se surestimer** *vp* to overestimate o.s.

sûreté [syrte] *nf* **1.** (*sécurité*) safety; **en ~** safe; **de ~** safety (*avant n*). **2.** (*fiabilité*) reliability. **3.** (JUR) surety.

surexposer [syrɛkspoze] *vt* to overexpose.

surf [sœrf] *nm* surfing.

surface [syrfas] *nf* **1.** (*extérieur, apparence*) surface. **2.** (*superficie*) surface area. ▶ **grande surface** *nf* hypermarket.

surfait, -e [syrfɛ, ɛt] *adj* overrated.

surfer [sœrfe] *vi* to go surfing.

surgelé, -e [syrʒəle] *adj* frozen. ▶ **surgelé** *nm* frozen food.

surgir [syrʒir] *vi* to appear suddenly; *fig* (*difficulté*) to arise, to come up.

surhumain, -e [syrymɛ̃, ɛn] *adj* superhuman.

surimpression [syrɛ̃presjɔ̃] *nf* double exposure.

surinfection [syrɛ̃fɛksjɔ̃] *nf* secondary infection.

sur-le-champ [syrləʃã] *loc adv* immediately, straightaway.

surlendemain [syrlãdmɛ̃] *nm*: **le ~** two days later; **le ~ de mon départ** two days after I left.

surligner [syrliɲe] *vt* to highlight.

surligneur [syrliɲœr] *nm* highlighter (pen).

surmenage [syrmənaʒ] *nm* overwork.

surmener [syrməne] *vt* to overwork. ▶ **se surmener** *vp* to overwork.

surmonter [syrmɔ̃te] *vt* **1.** (*obstacle, peur*) to overcome, to surmount. **2.** (*suj: statue, croix*) to surmount, to top.

surnager [syrnaʒe] *vi* (*flotter*) to float (on the surface).

surnaturel, -elle [syrnatyrɛl] *adj* supernatural. ▶ **surnaturel** *nm*: **le ~** the supernatural.

surnom [syrnɔ̃] *nm* nickname.

surnommer [syrnɔme] *vt* to nickname.

surpasser [syrpase] *vt* to surpass, to outdo. ▶ **se surpasser** *vp* to surpass ou excel o.s.

surpeuplé, -e [syrpœple] *adj* overpopulated.

surplomb [syrplɔ̃] ▶ **en surplomb** *loc adj* overhanging.

surplomber [syrplɔ̃be] ◆ *vt* to overhang. ◆ *vi* to be out of plumb.

surplus [syrply] *nm* (*excédent*) surplus.

surprenant, -e [syrprənã, ãt] *adj* surprising, amazing.

surprendre [syrprãdr] *vt* **1.** (*voleur*) to catch (in the act). **2.** (*secret*) to overhear. **3.** (*prendre à l'improviste*) to surprise, to catch unawares. **4.** (*étonner*) to surprise, to amaze.

surpris, -e [syrpri, iz] *pp* → **surprendre**.

surprise [syrpriz] ◆ *nf* surprise; **par ~** by surprise; **faire une ~ à qqn** to give sb a surprise. ◆ *adj* (*inattendu*) surprise (*avant n*); **grève ~** lightning strike.

surproduction [syrprodyksjɔ̃] *nf* overproduction.

surréalisme [syrrealism] *nm* surrealism.

sursaut [syrso] *nm* **1.** (*de personne*) jump, start; **en ~** with a start. **2.** (*d'énergie*) burst, surge.

sursauter [syrsote] *vi* to start, to give a start.

sursis [syrsi] *nm* (JUR & *fig*) reprieve; **six mois avec ~** six months' suspended sentence.

sursitaire [syrsitɛr] *nmf* (MIL) person whose call-up has been deferred.

surtaxe [syrtaks] *nf* surcharge.

surtout [syrtu] *adv* **1.** (*avant tout*) above all. **2.** (*spécialement*) especially, particularly; **~ pas** certainly not. ▶ **surtout que** *loc conj fam* especially as.

survécu [syrveky] *pp* → **survivre**.

surveillance [syrvejãs] *nf* supervision; (*de la police, de militaire*) surveillance.

surveillant, -e [syrvεjã, ãt] *nm, f* supervisor; (*de prison*) warder Br, guard.

surveiller [syrveje] *vt* 1. (*enfant*) to watch, to keep an eye on; (*suspect*) to keep a watch on. 2. (*travaux*) to supervise; (*examen*) to invigilate. 3. (*ligne, langage*) to watch. ▶ **se surveiller** *vp* to watch o.s.

survenir [syrvənir] *vi* (*incident*) to occur.

survenu, -e [syrvəny] *pp* → **survenir**.

survêtement [syrvεtmã] *nm* tracksuit.

survie [syrvi] *nf* (*de personne*) survival.

survivant, -e [syrvivã, ãt] ◆ *nm, f* survivor. ◆ *adj* surviving.

survivre [syrvivr] *vi* to survive; ~ à (*personne*) to outlive, to survive; (*accident, malheur*) to survive.

survoler [syrvɔle] *vt* 1. (*territoire*) to fly over. 2. (*texte*) to skim (through).

sus [sy(s)] *interj*: ~ à l'ennemi! at the enemy! ▶ **en sus** *loc adv* moreover, in addition; **en ~ de** over and above, in addition to.

susceptibilité [sysεptibilite] *nf* touchiness, sensitivity.

susceptible [sysεptibl] *adj* 1. (*ombrageux*) touchy, sensitive. 2. (*en mesure de*): ~ **de faire qqch** liable ou likely to do sthg; ~ **d'amélioration, ~ d'être amélioré** open to improvement.

susciter [sysite] *vt* 1. (*admiration, curiosité*) to arouse. 2. (*ennuis, problèmes*) to create.

suspect, -e [syspε, εkt] ◆ *adj* 1. (*personne*) suspicious. 2. (*douteux*) suspect. ◆ *nm, f* suspect.

suspecter [syspεkte] *vt* to suspect, to have one's suspicions about; ~ **qqn de qqch/de faire qqch** to suspect sb of sthg/of doing sthg.

suspendre [syspãdr] *vt* 1. (*lustre, tableau*) to hang (up). 2. (*pourparlers*) to suspend; (*séance*) to adjourn; (*journal*) to suspend publication of. 3. (*fonctionnaire, constitution*) to suspend. 4. (*jugement*) to postpone, to defer.

suspendu, -e [syspãdy] ◆ *pp* → **suspendre**. ◆ *adj* 1. (*fonctionnaire*) suspended. 2. (*séance*) adjourned. 3. (*lustre, tableau*): ~ **au plafond/au mur** hanging from the ceiling/on the wall.

suspens [syspã] ▶ **en suspens** *loc adv* in abeyance.

suspense [syspãs, syspεns] *nm* suspense.

suspension [syspãsjɔ̃] *nf* 1. (*gén*) suspension; **en ~** in suspension, suspended. 2. (*de combat*) halt; (*d'audience*) adjournment. 3. (*lustre*) light fitting.

suspicion [syspisjɔ̃] *nf* suspicion.

susurrer [sysyre] *vt & vi* to murmur.

suture [sytyr] *nf* suture.

svelte [zvεlt] *adj* slender.

SVP *abr de* **s'il vous plaît**.

sweat-shirt [switʃœrt] (*pl* **sweat-shirts**) *nm* sweatshirt.

syllabe [silab] *nf* syllable.

symbole [sε̃bɔl] *nm* symbol.

symbolique [sε̃bɔlik] *adj* 1. (*figure*) symbolic. 2. (*geste, contribution*) token (*avant n*). 3. (*rémunération*) nominal.

symboliser [sε̃bɔlize] *vt* to symbolize.

symétrie [simetri] *nf* symmetry.

symétrique [simetrik] *adj* symmetrical.

sympa [sε̃pa] *adj fam* (*personne*) likeable, nice; (*soirée, maison*) pleasant, nice; (*ambiance*) friendly.

sympathie [sε̃pati] *nf* 1. (*pour personne, projet*) liking; **accueillir un projet avec ~** to look sympathetically ou favourably on a project. 2. (*condoléances*) sympathy.

sympathique [sε̃patik] *adj* 1. (*personne*) likeable, nice; (*soirée, maison*) pleasant, nice; (*ambiance*) friendly. 2. (ANAT & MÉD) sympathetic.

sympathiser [sε̃patize] *vi* to get on well; ~ **avec qqn** to get on well with sb.

symphonie [sε̃fɔni] *nf* symphony.

symphonique [sε̃fɔnik] *adj* (*musique*) symphonic; (*concert, orchestre*) symphony (*avant n*).

symptomatique [sε̃ptɔmatik] *adj* symptomatic.

symptôme [sε̃ptom] *nm* symptom.

synagogue [sinagɔg] *nf* synagogue.

synchroniser [sε̃krɔnize] *vt* to synchronize.

syncope [sε̃kɔp] *nf* 1. (*évanouissement*) blackout. 2. (MUS) syncopation.

syndic [sε̃dik] *nm* (*de copropriété*) representative.

syndicaliste [sε̃dikalist] ◆ *nmf* trade unionist. ◆ *adj* (trade) union (*avant n*).

syndicat [sε̃dika] *nm* (*d'employés, d'agriculteurs*) (trade) union; (*d'employeurs, de propriétaires*) association. ▶ **syndicat d'initiative** *nm* tourist office.

syndiqué, -e [sε̃dike] *adj* unionized.

syndrome [sε̃drom] *nm* syndrome.

synonyme [sinɔnim] ◆ *nm* synonym. ◆ *adj* synonymous.

syntaxe [sε̃taks] *nf* syntax.

synthé [sɛte] nm fam synth.

synthèse [sɛtɛz] nf 1. (opération & CHIM) synthesis. 2. (exposé) overview.

synthétique [sɛtetik] adj 1. (vue) overall. 2. (produit) synthetic.

synthétiseur [sɛtetizœr] nm synthesizer.

syphilis [sifilis] nf syphilis.

Syrie [siri] nf: **la ~** Syria.

syrien, -enne [sirjɛ̃, ɛn] adj Syrian. ▶ **Syrien, -enne** nm, f Syrian.

systématique [sistematik] adj systematic.

systématiser [sistematize] vt to systematize.

système [sistɛm] nm system; **~ expert** (INFORM) expert system; **~ d'exploitation** (INFORM) operating system; **~ nerveux** nervous system; **~ solaire** solar system.

T

t, T [te] nm inv t, T.

t' → **te**.

ta → **ton²**.

tabac [taba] nm 1. (plante, produit) tobacco; **~ blond** mild ou Virginia tobacco; **~ brun** dark tobacco; **~ à priser** snuff. 2. (magasin) tobacconist's.

TABAC

As well as selling cigarettes, cigars and tobacco, 'tabacs' in France also sell stamps, road tax stickers and lottery tickets. In the countryside they may also stock newspapers.

tabagisme [tabaʒism] nm 1. (intoxication) nicotine addiction. 2. (habitude) smoking.

tabernacle [tabɛrnakl] nm tabernacle.

table [tabl] nf (meuble) table; **à ~!** lunch/dinner etc is ready!; **être à ~** to be at table, to be having a meal; **se mettre à ~** to sit down to eat; fig to come clean; **dresser** ou **mettre la ~** to lay the table; **~ de chevet** ou **de nuit** bedside table. ▶ **table des matières** nf contents (pl), table of contents. ▶ **table de multiplication** nf (multiplication) table.

tableau, -x [tablo] nm 1. (peinture) painting, picture; fig (description) picture. 2. (THÉÂTRE) scene. 3. (panneau) board; **~ d'affichage** notice board Br, bulletin board Am; **~ de bord** (AÉRON) instrument panel; (AUTOM) dashboard; **~ noir** blackboard. 4. (de données) table.

tabler [table] vi: **~ sur** to count ou bank on.

tablette [tablɛt] nf 1. (planchette) shelf. 2. (de chewing-gum) stick; (de chocolat) bar.

tableur [tablœr] nm (INFORM) spreadsheet.

tablier [tablije] nm 1. (de cuisinière) apron; (d'écolier) smock. 2. (de pont) roadway, deck.

tabloïd(e) [tablɔid] nm tabloid.

tabou, -e [tabu] adj taboo. ▶ **tabou** nm taboo.

tabouret [taburɛ] nm stool.

tabulateur [tabylatœr] nm tabulator, tab.

tac [tak] nm: **du ~ au ~** tit for tat.

tache [taʃ] nf 1. (de pelage) marking; (de peau) mark; **~ de rousseur** ou **de son** freckle. 2. (de couleur, lumière) spot, patch. 3. (sur nappe, vêtement) stain.

tâche [taʃ] nf task.

tacher [taʃe] vt 1. (nappe, vêtement) to stain, to mark. 2. fig (réputation) to tarnish.

tâcher [taʃe] vi: **~ de faire qqch** to try to do sthg.

tacheter [taʃte] vt to spot, to speckle.

tacite [tasit] adj tacit.

taciturne [tasityrn] adj taciturn.

tact [takt] nm (délicatesse) tact; **manquer de ~** to be tactless.

tactique [taktik] ◆ adj tactical. ◆ nf tactics (pl).

tag [tag] nm identifying name written with a spray can on walls, the sides of trains etc.

tagueur, -euse [tagœr, øz] nm, f person who sprays their 'tag' on walls, the sides of trains etc.

taie [tɛ] nf (enveloppe): **~ (d'oreiller)** pillowcase, pillow slip.

taille [taj] nf 1. (action - de pierre, diamant) cutting; (- d'arbre, de haie) pruning. 2. (stature) height. 3. (mesure, dimensions) size; **vous faites quelle ~?** what size are you?, what size do you take?; **ce n'est pas à ma ~** it doesn't fit me; **de ~** sizeable, considerable. 4. (milieu du corps) waist.

taille-crayon [tajkrejɔ̃] (pl **taille-crayons**) nm pencil sharpener.

tailler [taje] vt 1. (couper - chair, pierre,

diamant) to cut; (- *arbre, haie*) to prune; (- *crayon*) to sharpen; (- *bois*) to carve. **2.** (*vêtement*) to cut out.

tailleur [tajœr] *nm* **1.** (*couturier*) tailor. **2.** (*vêtement*) (lady's) suit. **3.** (*de diamants, pierre*) cutter.

taillis [taji] *nm* coppice, copse.

tain [tɛ̃] *nm* silvering; **miroir sans ~** two-way mirror.

taire [tɛr] *vt* to conceal. ► **se taire** *vp* **1.** (*rester silencieux*) to be silent ou quiet. **2.** (*cesser de s'exprimer*) to fall silent; **tais-toi!** shut up!

Taiwan [tajwan] *n* Taiwan.

talc [talk] *nm* talcum powder.

talent [talɑ̃] *nm* talent; **avoir du ~** to be talented, to have talent; **les jeunes ~s** young talent (U).

talentueux, -euse [talɑ̃tɥø, øz] *adj* talented.

talisman [talismɑ̃] *nm* talisman.

talkie-walkie [tɔkiwɔki] *nm* walkie-talkie.

talon [talɔ̃] *nm* **1.** (*gén*) heel; **~s aiguilles/hauts** stiletto/high heels; **~s plats** low ou flat heels. **2.** (*de chèque*) counterfoil, stub. **3.** (CARTES) stock.

talonner [talɔne] *vt* **1.** (*suj: poursuivant*) to be hard on the heels of. **2.** (*suj: créancier*) to harry, to hound.

talonnette [talɔnɛt] *nf* (*de chaussure*) heel cushion, heel-pad.

talquer [talke] *vt* to put talcum powder on.

talus [taly] *nm* embankment.

tambour [tɑ̃bur] *nm* **1.** (*instrument, cylindre*) drum. **2.** (*musicien*) drummer. **3.** (*porte à tourniquet*) revolving door.

tambourin [tɑ̃burɛ̃] *nm* **1.** (*à grelots*) tambourine. **2.** (*tambour*) tambourin.

tambouriner [tɑ̃burine] *vi:* **~ sur** ou **à** to drum on; **~ contre** to drum against.

tamis [tami] *nm* (*crible*) sieve.

Tamise [tamiz] *nf:* **la ~** the Thames.

tamisé, -e [tamize] *adj* (*éclairage*) subdued.

tamiser [tamize] *vt* **1.** (*farine*) to sieve. **2.** (*lumière*) to filter.

tampon [tɑ̃pɔ̃] *nm* **1.** (*bouchon*) stopper, plug. **2.** (*éponge*) pad; **~ à récurer** scourer. **3.** (*de coton, d'ouate*) pad; **~ hygiénique** ou **périodique** tampon. **4.** (*cachet*) stamp. **5.** litt & fig (*amortisseur*) buffer.

tamponner [tɑ̃pɔne] *vt* **1.** (*document*) to stamp. **2.** (*plaie*) to dab.

tam-tam [tamtam] (*pl* **tam-tams**) *nm* tom-tom.

tandem [tɑ̃dɛm] *nm* **1.** (*vélo*) tandem. **2.** (*duo*) pair; **en ~** together, in tandem.

tandis [tɑ̃di] ► **tandis que** *loc conj* **1.** (*pendant que*) while. **2.** (*alors que*) while, whereas.

tangage [tɑ̃gaʒ] *nm* pitching, pitch.

tangent, -e [tɑ̃ʒɑ̃, ɑ̃t] *adj:* **c'était ~** fig it was close, it was touch and go. ► **tangente** *nf* tangent.

tangible [tɑ̃ʒibl] *adj* tangible.

tango [tɑ̃go] *nm* tango.

tanguer [tɑ̃ge] *vi* to pitch.

tanière [tanjɛr] *nf* den, lair.

tank [tɑ̃k] *nm* tank.

tanner [tane] *vt* **1.** (*peau*) to tan. **2.** fam (*personne*) to pester, to annoy.

tant [tɑ̃] *adv* **1.** (*quantité*): **~ de** so much; **~ de travail** so much work. **2.** (*nombre*): **~ de** so many; **~ de livres/d'élèves** so many books/pupils. **3.** (*tellement*) such a lot, so much; **il l'aime ~** he loves her so much. **4.** (*quantité indéfinie*) so much; **ça coûte ~** it costs so much. **5.** (*un jour indéfini*): **votre lettre du ~** your letter of such-and-such a date. **6.** (*comparatif*): **~ que** as much as. **7.** (*valeur temporelle*): **~ que** (*aussi longtemps que*) as long as; (*pendant que*) while. ► **en tant que** *loc conj* as. ► **tant bien que mal** *loc adv* after a fashion, somehow or other. ► **tant mieux** *loc adv* so much the better; **~ mieux pour lui** good for him. ► **tant pis** *loc adv* too bad; **~ pis pour lui** too bad for him.

tante [tɑ̃t] *nf* (*parente*) aunt.

tantinet [tɑ̃tinɛ] *nm:* **un ~ exagéré/trop long** a bit exaggerated/too long.

tantôt [tɑ̃to] *adv* **1.** (*parfois*) sometimes. **2.** vieilli (*après-midi*) this afternoon.

tapage [tapaʒ] *nm* **1.** (*bruit*) row. **2.** fig (*battage*) fuss (U).

tapageur, -euse [tapaʒœr, øz] *adj* **1.** (*hôte, enfant*) rowdy. **2.** (*style*) flashy. **3.** (*liaison, publicité*) blatant.

tape [tap] *nf* slap.

tape-à-l'œil [tapalœj] *adj inv* flashy.

taper [tape] ♦ *vt* **1.** (*personne, cuisse*) to slap; **~ (un coup) à la porte** to knock at the door. **2.** (*à la machine*) to type. ♦ *vi* **1.** (*frapper*) to hit; **~ du poing sur** to bang one's fist on; **~ dans ses mains** to clap. **2.** (*à la machine*) to type. **3.** fam (*soleil*) to beat down. **4.** fig (*critiquer*): **~ sur qqn** to knock sb.

tapis [tapi] *nm* (*gén*) carpet; (*de gymnase*) mat; **~ de bain** bath mat; **~ roulant** (*pour bagages*) conveyor belt; (*pour personnes*) travolator.

tapisser [tapise] *vt*: ~ **(de)** to cover (with).

tapisserie [tapisri] *nf* (*de laine*) tapestry; (*papier peint*) wallpaper.

tapissier, -ère [tapisje, ɛr] *nm, f* 1. (*artisan*) tapestry maker. 2. (*décorateur*) (interior) decorator. 3. (*commerçant*) upholsterer.

tapoter [tapɔte] ◆ *vt* to tap; (*joue*) to pat. ◆ *vi*: ~ **sur** to tap on.

taquin, -e [takɛ̃, in] *adj* teasing.

taquiner [takine] *vt* 1. (*suj: personne*) to tease. 2. (*suj: douleur*) to worry.

tarabuster [tarabyste] *vt* 1. (*suj: personne*) to badger. 2. (*suj: idée*) to niggle at.

tard [tar] *adv* late; **plus** ~ later; **au plus** ~ at the latest.

tarder [tarde] ◆ *vi*: ~ **à faire qqch** (*attendre pour*) to delay ou put off doing sthg; (*être lent à*) to take a long time to do sthg; **le feu ne va pas** ~ **à s'éteindre** it won't be long before the fire goes out; **elle ne devrait plus** ~ **maintenant** she should be here any time now. ◆ *v impers*: **il me tarde de te revoir/qu'il vienne** I am longing to see you again/for him to come.

tardif, -ive [tardif, iv] *adj* (*heure*) late.

tare [tar] *nf* 1. (*défaut*) defect. 2. (*de balance*) tare.

tarif [tarif] *nm* 1. (*prix - de restaurant, café*) price; (*- de service*) rate, price; (*douanier*) tariff; **demi-**~ half rate ou price; ~ **réduit** reduced price; (*au cinéma, théâtre*) concession. 2. (*tableau*) price list.

tarir [tarir] *vi* to dry up; **elle ne tarit pas d'éloges sur son professeur** she never stops praising her teacher. ▶ **se tarir** *vp* to dry up.

tarot [taro] *nm* tarot. ▶ **tarots** *nmpl* tarot cards.

tartare [tartar] *adj* Tartar; **(steak)** ~ steak tartare.

tarte [tart] ◆ *nf* 1. (*gâteau*) tart; ~ **à la crème** (CULIN) custard tart; *fig* (*sujet, propos*) hackneyed. 2. *fam fig* (*gifle*) slap. ◆ *adj* (*avec ou sans accord*) *fam* (*idiot*) stupid.

tartine [tartin] *nf* (*de pain*) piece of bread and butter.

tartiner [tartine] *vt* 1. (*pain*) to spread; **chocolat/fromage à** ~ chocolate/cheese spread. 2. *fam fig* (*pages*) to cover.

tartre [tartr] *nm* 1. (*de dents, vin*) tartar. 2. (*de chaudière*) fur, scale.

tas [ta] *nm* heap; **un** ~ **de** a lot of.

tasse [tas] *nf* cup; ~ **à café/à thé** coffee/tea cup; ~ **de café/de thé** cup of coffee/tea.

tasser [tase] *vt* 1. (*neige*) to compress, to pack down. 2. (*vêtements, personnes*): ~ **qqn/qqch dans** to stuff sb/sthg into. ▶ **se tasser** *vp* 1. (*fondations*) to settle. 2. *fig* (*vieillard*) to shrink. 3. (*personnes*) to squeeze up. 4. *fam fig* (*situation*) to settle down.

tâter [tate] *vt* to feel; *fig* to sound out. ▶ **se tâter** *vp fam fig* (*hésiter*) to be in two minds.

tatillon, -onne [tatijɔ̃, ɔn] *adj* finicky.

tâtonner [tatɔne] *vi* to grope around.

tâtons [tatɔ̃] *loc adv*: **marcher/procéder à** ~ to feel one's way.

tatouage [tatwaʒ] *nm* (*dessin*) tattoo.

tatouer [tatwe] *vt* to tattoo.

taudis [todi] *nm* slum.

taupe [top] *nf litt & fig* mole.

taureau, -x [tɔro] *nm* (*animal*) bull. ▶ **Taureau** *nm* (ASTROL) Taurus.

tauromachie [tɔromaʃi] *nf* bullfighting.

taux [to] *nm* rate; (*de cholestérol, d'alcool*) level; ~ **de change** exchange rate; ~ **d'intérêt** interest rate; ~ **de natalité** birth rate.

taverne [tavɛrn] *nf* tavern.

taxe [taks] *nf* tax; **hors** ~ (COMM) exclusive of tax, before tax; (*boutique, achat*) duty-free; **toutes** ~s **comprises** inclusive of tax; ~ **sur la valeur ajoutée** value added tax.

taxer [takse] *vt* (*imposer*) to tax.

taxi [taksi] *nm* 1. (*voiture*) taxi. 2. (*chauffeur*) taxi driver.

TB, tb (*abr de* **très bien**) VG.

Tchad [tʃad] *nm*: **le** ~ Chad.

tchécoslovaque [tʃekɔslɔvak] *adj* Czechoslovakian. ▶ **Tchécoslovaque** *nmf* Czechoslovak.

Tchécoslovaquie [tʃekɔslɔvaki] *nf*: **la** ~ Czechoslovakia.

tchèque [tʃɛk] ◆ *adj* Czech. ◆ *nm* (*langue*) Czech. ▶ **Tchèque** *nmf* Czech.

TD (*abr de* **travaux dirigés**) *nmpl* supervised practical work.

te [tə], **t'** *pron pers* 1. (*complément d'objet direct*) you. 2. (*complément d'objet indirect*) (to) you. 3. (*réfléchi*) yourself. 4. (*avec un présentatif*): ~ **voici!** here you are!

technicien, -enne [tɛknisjɛ̃, ɛn] *nm, f* 1. (*professionnel*) technician. 2. (*spécialiste*): ~ **(de)** expert (in).

technico-commercial, -e [tɛknikɔkɔmɛrsjal] (*mpl* **technico-commerciaux**, *fpl*

technico-commerciales) *nm, f* sales engineer.

technique [tɛknik] ◆ *adj* technical. ◆ *nf* technique.

technocrate [tɛknɔkrat] *nmf* technocrat.

technologie [tɛknɔlɔʒi] *nf* technology.

technologique [tɛknɔlɔʒik] *adj* technological.

teckel [tekɛl] *nm* dachshund.

tee-shirt (*pl* **tee-shirts**), **T-shirt** (*pl* **T-shirts**) [tiʃœrt] *nm* T-shirt.

teigne [tɛɲ] *nf* 1. (*mite*) moth. 2. (MÉD) ringworm. 3. *fam fig & péj* (*femme*) cow; (*homme*) bastard.

teindre [tɛ̃dr] *vt* to dye.

teint, -e [tɛ̃, tɛ̃t] ◆ *pp* → **teindre**. ◆ *adj* dyed. ▶ **teint** *nm* (*carnation*) complexion. ▶ **teinte** *nf* colour.

teinté, -e [tɛ̃te] *adj* tinted; ~ **de** *fig* tinged with.

teinter [tɛ̃te] *vt* to stain.

teinture [tɛ̃tyr] *nf* 1. (*action*) dyeing. 2. (*produit*) dye. ▶ **teinture d'iode** *nf* tincture of iodine.

teinturerie [tɛ̃tyrri] *nf* 1. (*pressing*) dry cleaner's. 2. (*métier*) dyeing.

teinturier, -ère [tɛ̃tyrje, ɛr] *nm, f* (*de pressing*) dry cleaner.

tel [tɛl] (*f* **telle**, *mpl* **tels**, *fpl* **telles**) *adj* 1. (*valeur indéterminée*) such-and-such a; ~ **et** ~ such-and-such a. 2. (*semblable*) such; **un** ~ **homme** such a man; **de telles gens** such people; **je n'ai rien dit de** ~ I never said anything of the sort; **comme** ~ as such. 3. (*valeur emphatique ou intensive*) such; **un** ~ **génie** such a genius; **un** ~ **bonheur** such happiness. 4. (*introduit un exemple ou une énumération*): ~ **(que)** such as, like. 5. (*introduit une comparaison*) like; **il est** ~ **que je l'avais toujours rêvé** he's just like I always dreamt he would be; ~ **quel** as it is/was *etc*. ▶ **à tel point que** *loc conj* to such an extent that. ▶ **de telle manière que** *loc conj* in such a way that. ▶ **de telle sorte que** *loc conj* with the result that, so that.

tél. (*abr de* **téléphone**) tel.

télé [tele] *nf fam* TV, telly *Br*.

téléachat [teleaʃa] *nm* teleshopping.

téléacteur, -trice [teleaktœr, tris] *nm, f* telesalesperson.

télécabine [telekabin] *nf* cable car.

Télécarte® [telekart] *nf* phonecard.

télécharger [teleʃarʒe] *vt* to download.

télécommande [telekɔmɑ̃d] *nf* remote control.

télécommunication [telekɔmynikasjɔ̃] *nf* telecommunications (*pl*).

télécopie [telekɔpi] *nf* fax.

télécopieur [telekɔpjœr] *nm* fax (machine).

téléfilm [telefilm] *nm* film made for television.

télégramme [telegram] *nm* telegram.

télégraphe [telegraf] *nm* telegraph.

télégraphier [telegrafje] *vt* to telegraph.

téléguider [telegide] *vt* to operate by remote control; *fig* to mastermind.

télématique [telematik] *nf* telematics (U).

téléobjectif [teleɔbʒɛktif] *nm* telephoto lens (*sg*).

télépathie [telepati] *nf* telepathy.

téléphérique [teleferik] *nm* cableway.

téléphone [telefɔn] *nm* telephone; ~ **sans fil** cordless telephone.

téléphoner [telefɔne] *vi* to telephone, to phone; ~ **à qqn** to telephone sb, to phone sb (up).

téléphonique [telefɔnik] *adj* telephone (*avant n*), phone (*avant n*).

téléprospection [teleprɔspɛksjɔ̃] *nf* telemarketing.

télescope [teleskɔp] *nm* telescope.

télescoper [teleskɔpe] *vt* (*véhicule*) to crash into. ▶ **se télescoper** *vp* (*véhicules*) to concertina.

télescopique [teleskɔpik] *adj* (*antenne*) telescopic.

téléscripteur [teleskriptœr] *nm* teleprinter *Br*, teletypewriter *Am*.

télésiège [telesjɛʒ] *nm* chairlift.

téléski [teleski] *nm* ski tow.

téléspectateur, -trice [telespɛktatœr, tris] *nm, f* (television) viewer.

télétravail [teletravaj] *nm* teleworking.

téléviseur [televizœr] *nm* television (set).

télévision [televizjɔ̃] *nf* television; **à la** ~ on television.

télex [telɛks] *nm inv* telex.

tellement [tɛlmɑ̃] *adv* 1. (*si, à ce point*) so; (+ *comparatif*) so much; ~ **plus jeune que** so much younger than; **pas** ~ not especially, not particularly. 2. (*autant*): ~ **de** (*personnes, objets*) so many; (*gentillesse, travail*) so much. 3. (*tant*) so much; **elle a** ~ **changé** she's changed so much; **je ne comprends rien** ~ **il parle vite** he talks so quickly that I can't understand a word.

téméraire [temerɛr] ◆ *adj* 1. (*auda-*

cieux) bold. 2. (*imprudent*) rash. ◆ *nmf* hothead.

témérité [temerite] *nf* 1. (*audace*) boldness. 2. (*imprudence*) rashness.

témoignage [temwaɲaʒ] *nm* 1. (JUR) testimony, evidence (U); **faux** ~ perjury. 2. (*gage*) token, expression; **en** ~ **de** as a token of. 3. (*récit*) account.

témoigner [temwaɲe] ◆ *vt* 1. (*manifester*) to show, to display. 2. (JUR): ~ **que** to testify that. ◆ *vi* (JUR) to testify; ~ **contre** to testify against.

témoin [temwē] ◆ *nm* 1. (*gén*) witness; **être** ~ **de qqch** to be a witness to sthg, to witness sthg; ~ **oculaire** eyewitness. 2. *littéraire* (*marque*): ~ **de** evidence (U) of. 3. (SPORT) baton. ◆ *adj* (*appartement*) show (*avant n*).

tempe [tɑ̃p] *nf* temple.

tempérament [tɑ̃peramɑ̃] *nm* temperament; **avoir du** ~ to be hot-blooded.

température [tɑ̃peratyr] *nf* temperature; **avoir de la** ~ to have a temperature.

tempéré, -e [tɑ̃pere] *adj* (*climat*) temperate.

tempérer [tɑ̃pere] *vt* (*adoucir*) to temper; *fig* (*enthousiasme, ardeur*) to moderate.

tempête [tɑ̃pɛt] *nf* storm.

tempêter [tɑ̃pɛte] *vi* to rage.

temple [tɑ̃pl] *nm* 1. (HIST) temple. 2. (*protestant*) church.

tempo [tempo] *nm* tempo.

temporaire [tɑ̃pɔrɛr] *adj* temporary.

temporairement [tɑ̃pɔrɛrmɑ̃] *adv* temporarily.

temporel, -elle [tɑ̃pɔrɛl] *adj* 1. (*défini dans le temps*) time (*avant n*). 2. (*terrestre*) temporal.

temps [tɑ̃] *nm* 1. (*gén*) time; **à plein** ~ full-time; **à mi-~** half-time; **à** ~ **partiel** part-time; **en un** ~ **record** in record time; **au** ou **du** ~ **où** (in the days) when; **de mon** ~ in my day; **ça prend un certain** ~ it takes some time; **ces** ~**-ci, ces derniers** ~ these days; **pendant ce** ~ meanwhile; **en** ~ **utile** in due course; **en** ~ **de guerre/paix** in wartime/peacetime; **il était** ~! *iron* and about time too!; **avoir le** ~ **de faire qqch** to have time to do sthg; ~ **libre** free time; **à** ~ in time; **de** ~ **à autre** now and then ou again; **de** ~ **en** ~ from time to time; **en même** ~ at the same time; **tout le** ~ all the time, the whole time; **avoir tout son** ~ to have all the time in the world. 2. (MUS) beat. 3. (GRAM) tense. 4. (MÉTÉOR) weather; **par tous les** ~ in all weathers.

tenable [tənabl] *adj* bearable.

tenace [tənas] *adj* 1. (*gén*) stubborn. 2. *fig* (*odeur, rhume*) lingering.

ténacité [tenasite] *nf* (*de préjugé, personne*) stubbornness.

tenailler [tənaje] *vt* to torment.

tenailles [tənaj] *nfpl* pincers.

tenancier, -ère [tənɑ̃sje, ɛr] *nm, f* manager (*f* manageress).

tendance [tɑ̃dɑ̃s] *nf* 1. (*disposition*) tendency; **avoir** ~ **à qqch/à faire qqch** to have a tendency to sthg/to do sthg, to be inclined to sthg/to do sthg. 2. (*économique, de mode*) trend.

tendancieux, -euse [tɑ̃dɑ̃sjø, øz] *adj* tendentious.

tendeur [tɑ̃dœr] *nm* (*sangle*) elastic strap (*for fastening luggage etc*).

tendinite [tɑ̃dinit] *nf* tendinitis.

tendon [tɑ̃dɔ̃] *nm* tendon.

tendre¹ [tɑ̃dr] *adj* 1. (*gén*) tender. 2. (*matériau*) soft. 3. (*couleur*) delicate.

tendre² [tɑ̃dr] *vt* 1. (*corde*) to tighten. 2. (*muscle*) to tense. 3. (*objet, main*): ~ **qqch à qqn** to hold out sthg to sb. 4. (*bâche*) to hang. 5. (*piège*) to set (up). ▶ **se tendre** *vp* to tighten; *fig* (*relations*) to become strained.

tendresse [tɑ̃drɛs] *nf* 1. (*affection*) tenderness. 2. (*indulgence*) sympathy.

tendu, -e [tɑ̃dy] ◆ *pp* → **tendre²**. ◆ *adj* 1. (*fil, corde*) taut. 2. (*personne*) tense. 3. (*atmosphère, rapports*) strained. 4. (*main*) outstretched.

ténèbres [tenɛbr] *nfpl* darkness (*sg*), shadows; *fig* depths.

ténébreux, -euse [tenebrø, øz] *adj* 1. *fig* (*dessein, affaire*) mysterious. 2. (*personne*) serious, solemn.

teneur [tənœr] *nf* content; (*de traité*) terms (*pl*); ~ **en alcool/cuivre** alcohol/copper content.

tenir [tənir] ◆ *vt* 1. (*objet, personne, solution*) to hold. 2. (*garder, conserver, respecter*) to keep. 3. (*gérer - boutique*) to keep, to run. 4. (*apprendre*): ~ **qqch de qqn** to have sthg from sb. 5. (*considérer*): ~ **qqn pour** to regard sb as. ◆ *vi* 1. (*être solide*) to stay up, to hold together. 2. (*durer*) to last. 3. (*pouvoir être contenu*) to fit. 4. (*être attaché*): ~ **à** (*personne*) to care about; (*privilèges*) to value. 5. (*vouloir absolument*): ~ **à faire qqch** to insist on doing sthg. 6. (*ressembler*): ~ **de** to take after. 7. (*relever de*): ~ **de** to have something of. 8. (*dépendre de*): **il ne tient qu'à toi de ...** it's entirely up to you to ... 9. *loc*: ~ **bon** to stand firm; **tiens!** (*en don-*

nant) here!; (*surprise*) well, well!; (*pour attirer attention*) look! ▶ **se tenir** *vp* **1.** (*réunion*) to be held. **2.** (*personnes*) to hold one another; **se ~ par la main** to hold hands. **3.** (*être présent*) to be. **4.** (*être cohérent*) to make sense. **5.** (*se conduire*) to behave (o.s.). **6.** (*se retenir*): **se ~ (à)** to hold on (to). **7.** (*se borner*): **s'en ~ à** to stick to.

tennis [tenis] ◆ *nm* (*sport*) tennis. ◆ *nmpl* tennis shoes.

ténor [tenɔr] *nm* **1.** (*chanteur*) tenor. **2.** *fig* (*vedette*): **un ~ de la politique** a political star performer.

tension [tɑ̃sjɔ̃] *nf* **1.** (*contraction, désaccord*) tension. **2.** (MÉD) pressure; **avoir de la ~** to have high blood pressure. **3.** (ÉLECTR) voltage; **haute/basse ~** high/low voltage.

tentaculaire [tɑ̃takylɛr] *adj fig* sprawling.

tentant, -e [tɑ̃tɑ̃, ɑ̃t] *adj* tempting.

tentation [tɑ̃tasjɔ̃] *nf* temptation.

tentative [tɑ̃tativ] *nf* attempt; **~ de suicide** suicide attempt.

tente [tɑ̃t] *nf* tent.

tenter [tɑ̃te] *vt* **1.** (*entreprendre*): **~ qqch/de faire qqch** to attempt sthg/to do sthg. **2.** (*plaire*) to tempt; **être tenté par qqch/de faire qqch** to be tempted by sthg/to do sthg.

tenture [tɑ̃tyr] *nf* hanging.

tenu, -e [tɔny] ◆ *pp* → **tenir**. ◆ *adj* **1.** (*obligé*): **être ~ de faire qqch** to be required ou obliged to do sthg. **2.** (*en ordre*): **bien/mal ~** (*maison*) well/badly kept.

ténu, -e [teny] *adj* **1.** (*fil*) fine; *fig* (*distinction*) tenuous. **2.** (*voix*) thin.

tenue [tɔny] *nf* **1.** (*entretien*) running. **2.** (*manières*) good manners (*pl*). **3.** (*maintien du corps*) posture. **4.** (*costume*) dress; **être en petite ~** to be scantily dressed. ▶ **tenue de route** *nf* roadholding.

ter [tɛr] ◆ *adv* (MUS) three times. ◆ *adj*: **12 ~ 12B**.

Tergal® [tɛrgal] *nm* = Terylene®.

tergiverser [tɛrʒivɛrse] *vi* to shillyshally.

terme [tɛrm] *nm* **1.** (*fin*) end; **mettre un ~ à** to put an end ou a stop to. **2.** (*de grossesse*) term; **avant ~** prematurely. **3.** (*échéance*) time limit; (*de loyer*) rent day; **à court/moyen/long ~** (*calculer*) in the short/medium/long term; (*projet*) short-/medium-/long-term. **4.** (*mot, élément*) term. ▶ **termes** *nmpl* **1.** (*expressions*) words. **2.** (*de contrat*) terms.

terminaison [tɛrminɛzɔ̃] *nf* (GRAM) ending.

terminal, -e, -aux [tɛrminal, o] *adj* **1.** (*au bout*) final. **2.** (MÉD) (*phase*) terminal. ▶ **terminal, -aux** *nm* terminal. ▶ **terminale** *nf* (SCOL) = upper sixth year ou form Br, = twelfth grade Am.

terminer [tɛrmine] *vt* to end, to finish; (*travail, repas*) to finish. ▶ **se terminer** *vp* to end, to finish.

terminologie [tɛrminɔlɔʒi] *nf* terminology.

terminus [tɛrminys] *nm* terminus.

termite [tɛrmit] *nm* termite.

terne [tɛrn] *adj* dull.

ternir [tɛrnir] *vt* to dirty; (*métal, réputation*) to tarnish.

terrain [tɛrɛ̃] *nm* **1.** (*sol*) soil; **vélo tout ~** mountain bike. **2.** (*surface*) piece of land. **3.** (*emplacement - de football, rugby*) pitch; (*- de golf*) course; **~ d'aviation** airfield; **~ de camping** campsite. **4.** *fig* (*domaine*) ground.

terrasse [tɛras] *nf* terrace.

terrassement [tɛrasmɑ̃] *nm* (*action*) excavation.

terrasser [tɛrase] *vt* (*suj: personne*) to bring down; (*suj: émotion*) to overwhelm; (*suj: maladie*) to conquer.

terre [tɛr] *nf* **1.** (*monde*) world. **2.** (*sol*) ground; **par ~** on the ground; **~ à ~** *fig* down-to-earth. **3.** (*matière*) earth, soil. **4.** (*propriété*) land (U). **5.** (*territoire, continent*) land. **6.** (ÉLECTR) earth Br, ground Am. ▶ **Terre** *nf*: **la Terre** Earth.

terreau [tɛro] *nm* compost.

terre-plein [tɛrplɛ̃] (*pl* **terre-pleins**) *nm* platform.

terrer [tɛre] ▶ **se terrer** *vp* to go to earth.

terrestre [tɛrɛstr] *adj* **1.** (*croûte, atmosphère*) of the earth. **2.** (*animal, transport*) land (*avant n*). **3.** (*plaisir, paradis*) earthly. **4.** (*considérations*) worldly.

terreur [tɛrœr] *nf* terror.

terrible [tɛribl] *adj* **1.** (*gén*) terrible. **2.** (*appétit, soif*) terrific, enormous. **3.** *fam* (*excellent*) brilliant.

terriblement [tɛribləmɑ̃] *adv* terribly.

terrien, -enne [tɛrjɛ̃, ɛn] ◆ *adj* (*foncier*): **propriétaire ~** landowner. ◆ *nm, f* (*habitant de la Terre*) earthling.

terrier [tɛrje] *nm* **1.** (*tanière*) burrow. **2.** (*chien*) terrier.

terrifier [tɛrifje] *vt* to terrify.

terrine [tɛrin] *nf* terrine.

territoire [tɛritwar] *nm* **1.** (*pays, zone*) territory. **2.** (ADMIN) area. ▶ **territoire**

tiédir

d'outre-mer *nm* (French) overseas territory.

territorial, -e, -aux [tɛritɔrjal, o] *adj* territorial.

terroir [tɛrwar] *nm* 1. (*sol*) soil. 2. (*région rurale*) country.

terroriser [tɛrɔrize] *vt* to terrorize.

terrorisme [tɛrɔrism] *nm* terrorism.

terroriste [tɛrɔrist] *nmf* terrorist.

tertiaire [tɛrsjɛr] ◆ *nm* tertiary sector.
◆ *adj* tertiary.

tes → **ton²**.

tesson [tɛsɔ̃] *nm* piece of broken glass.

test [tɛst] *nm* test; **~ de grossesse** pregnancy test.

testament [tɛstamɑ̃] *nm* will.

tester [tɛste] *vt* to test.

testicule [tɛstikyl] *nm* testicle.

tétaniser [tetanize] *vt* to cause to go into spasm; *fig* to paralyse.

tétanos [tetanos] *nm* tetanus.

têtard [tetar] *nm* tadpole.

tête [tɛt] *nf* 1. (*gén*) head; **de la ~ aux pieds** from head to foot ou toe; **la ~ la première** head first; **calculer qqch de ~** to calculate sthg in one's head; **~ de lecture** (INFORM) read head; **~ de liste** (POLIT) main candidate; **être ~ en l'air** to have one's head in the clouds; **faire la ~** to sulk; **tenir ~ à qqn** to stand up to sb. 2. (*visage*) face. 3. (*devant - de cortège, peloton*) head, front; **en ~** (SPORT) in the lead.

tête-à-queue [tɛtakø] *nm inv* spin.

tête-à-tête [tɛtatɛt] *nm inv* tête-à-tête.

tête-bêche [tɛtbɛʃ] *loc adv* head to tail.

tétée [tete] *nf* feed.

tétine [tetin] *nf* 1. (*de biberon, mamelle*) teat. 2. (*sucette*) dummy Br, pacifier Am.

têtu, -e [tety] *adj* stubborn.

texte [tɛkst] *nm* 1. (*écrit*) wording. 2. (*imprimé*) text. 3. (*extrait*) passage.

textile [tɛkstil] ◆ *adj* textile (*avant n*).
◆ *nm* 1. (*matière*) textile. 2. (*industrie*): **le ~ textiles** (*pl*), the textile industry.

textuel, -elle [tɛkstɥɛl] *adj* 1. (*analyse*) textual; (*citation*) exact. 2. (*traduction*) literal.

texture [tɛkstyr] *nf* texture.

TF1 (*abr de* Télévision Française 1) *nf* French independent television company.

TGV (*abr de* train à grande vitesse) *nm* French high-speed train linking major cities.

TGV
This high-speed train, the fastest in the world, first ran on the Paris–Lyons line.

Today it connects Paris with many large French cities such as Nice, Marseilles, Rennes, Nantes, Bordeaux and Lille.

---

thaïlandais, -e [tajlɑ̃dɛ, ɛz] *adj* Thai.
▶ **Thaïlandais, -e** *nm, f* Thai.

Thaïlande [tajlɑ̃d] *nf*: **la ~** Thailand.

thalasso(thérapie) [talaso(terapi)] *nf* seawater therapy.

thé [te] *nm* tea.

théâtral, -e, -aux [teatral, o] *adj* (*ton*) theatrical.

théâtre [teatr] *nm* 1. (*bâtiment, représentation*) theatre. 2. (*art*): **faire du ~** to be on the stage; **adapté pour le ~** adapted for the stage. 3. (*œuvre*) plays (*pl*). 4. (*lieu*) scene; **~ d'opérations** (MIL) theatre of operations.

théière [tejɛr] *nf* teapot.

thématique [tematik] ◆ *adj* thematic.
◆ *nf* themes (*pl*).

thème [tɛm] *nm* 1. (*sujet & MUS*) theme. 2. (SCOL) prose.

théologie [teɔlɔʒi] *nf* theology.

théorème [teɔrɛm] *nm* theorem.

théoricien, -enne [teɔrisjɛ̃, ɛn] *nm, f* theoretician.

théorie [teɔri] *nf* theory; **en ~** in theory.

théorique [teɔrik] *adj* theoretical.

thérapeute [terapøt] *nmf* therapist.

thérapie [terapi] *nf* therapy.

thermal, -e, -aux [tɛrmal, o] *adj* thermal.

thermes [tɛrm] *nmpl* thermal baths.

thermique [tɛrmik] *adj* thermal.

thermomètre [tɛrmɔmɛtr] *nm* (*instrument*) thermometer.

Thermos® [tɛrmos] *nm ou nf* Thermos® (flask).

thermostat [tɛrmɔsta] *nm* thermostat.

thèse [tɛz] *nf* 1. (*opinion*) argument. 2. (PHILO & UNIV) thesis; **~ de doctorat** doctorate. 3. (*théorie*) theory.

thon [tɔ̃] *nm* tuna.

thorax [tɔraks] *nm* thorax.

thym [tɛ̃] *nm* thyme.

thyroïde [tirɔid] *nf* thyroid (gland).

Tibet [tibɛ] *nm*: **le ~** Tibet.

tibia [tibja] *nm* tibia.

tic [tik] *nm* tic.

ticket [tikɛ] *nm* ticket; **~ de caisse** (till) receipt; **~-repas** ≃ luncheon voucher.

tic-tac [tiktak] *nm inv* tick-tock.

tiède [tjɛd] *adj* 1. (*boisson, eau*) tepid, lukewarm. 2. (*vent*) mild. 3. *fig* (*accueil*) lukewarm.

tiédir [tjedir] ◆ *vt* to warm. ◆ *vi* to

become warm; **faire ~ qqch** to warm sthg.

tien [tjɛ̃] ▸ **le tien** (f **la tienne** [latjɛn], mpl **les tiens** [letjɛ̃], fpl **les tiennes** [letjɛn]) pron poss yours; **à la tienne!** cheers!

tierce [tjɛrs] ◆ nf **1.** (MUS) third. **2.** (CARTES & ESCRIME) tierce. ◆ adj → **tiers.**

tiercé [tjɛrse] nm system of betting involving the first three horses in a race.

tiers, tierce [tjɛr, tjɛrs] adj: **une tierce personne** a third party. ▸ **tiers** nm **1.** (étranger) outsider, stranger. **2.** (tierce personne) third party. **3.** (de fraction): **le ~ de** one-third of; **deux ~** two-thirds.

tiers-monde [tjɛrmɔ̃d] nm: **le ~** the Third World.

tiers-mondisation [tjɛrmɔ̃dizasjɔ̃] nf: **la ~ de ce pays** this country's economic degeneration to Third World levels.

tige [tiʒ] nf **1.** (de plante) stem, stalk. **2.** (de bois, métal) rod.

tignasse [tiɲas] nf fam mop (of hair).

tigre [tigr] nm tiger.

tigresse [tigrɛs] nf tigress.

tilleul [tijœl] nm lime (tree).

timbale [tɛ̃bal] nf **1.** (gobelet) (metal) cup. **2.** (MUS) kettledrum.

timbre [tɛ̃br] nm **1.** (gén) stamp. **2.** (de voix) timbre. **3.** (de bicyclette) bell.

timbrer [tɛ̃bre] vt to stamp.

timide [timid] ◆ adj **1.** (personne) shy. **2.** (protestation, essai) timid. **3.** (soleil) uncertain. ◆ nmf shy person.

timoré, -e [timɔre] adj fearful, timorous.

tintamarre [tɛ̃tamar] nm fam racket.

tintement [tɛ̃tmɑ̃] nm (de cloche, d'horloge) chiming; (de pièces) jingling.

tinter [tɛ̃te] vi **1.** (cloche, horloge) to chime. **2.** (pièces) to jingle.

tir [tir] nm **1.** (SPORT - activité) shooting; (- lieu): **(centre de) ~** shooting range. **2.** (trajectoire) shot. **3.** (salve) fire (U). **4.** (manière, action de tirer) firing.

tirage [tiraʒ] nm **1.** (de journal) circulation; (de livre) print run; **à grand ~** mass circulation. **2.** (du loto) draw; **~ au sort** drawing lots. **3.** (de cheminée) draught.

tiraillement [tirajmɑ̃] nm (gén pl) **1.** (crampe) cramp. **2.** fig (conflit) conflict.

tirailler [tiraje] ◆ vt **1.** (tirer sur) to tug (at). **2.** fig (écarteler): **être tiraillé par/entre qqch** to be torn by/between sthg. ◆ vi to fire wildly.

tiré, -e [tire] adj (fatigué): **avoir les traits ~s** ou **le visage ~** to look drawn.

tire-bouchon [tirbuʃɔ̃] (pl **tire-bouchons**) nm corkscrew. ▸ **en tire-bouchon** loc adv corkscrew (avant n).

tirelire [tirlir] nf moneybox.

tirer [tire] ◆ vt **1.** (gén) to pull; (rideaux) to draw; (tiroir) to pull open. **2.** (tracer - trait) to draw. **3.** (revue, livre) to print. **4.** (avec arme) to fire. **5.** (faire sortir - vin) to draw off; **~ qqn de** litt & fig to help ou to get sb out of; **~ un revolver/un mouchoir de sa poche** to pull a gun/a handkerchief out of one's pocket; **~ la langue** to stick out one's tongue. **6.** (aux cartes, au loto) to draw. **7.** (plaisir, profit) to derive. **8.** (déduire - conclusion) to draw; (- leçon) to learn. ◆ vi **1.** (tendre): **~ sur** to pull on ou at. **2.** (aspirer): **~ sur** (pipe) to draw ou pull on. **3.** (couleur): **bleu tirant sur le vert** greenish blue. **4.** (cheminée) to draw. **5.** (avec arme) to fire, to shoot. **6.** (SPORT) to shoot. ▸ **se tirer** vp **1.** fam (s'en aller) to push off. **2.** (se sortir): **se ~ de** to get o.s. out of; **s'en ~** fam to escape.

tiret [tire] nm dash.

tireur, -euse [tirœr, øz] nm, f (avec arme) gunman; **~ d'élite** marksman (f markswoman).

tiroir [tirwar] nm drawer.

tiroir-caisse [tirwarkɛs] nm till.

tisane [tizan] nf herb tea.

tisonnier [tizɔnje] nm poker.

tissage [tisaʒ] nm weaving.

tisser [tise] vt litt & fig to weave; (suj: araignée) to spin.

tissu [tisy] nm **1.** (étoffe) cloth, material. **2.** (BIOL) tissue.

titiller [titije] vt to titillate.

titre [titr] nm **1.** (gén) title. **2.** (de presse) headline; **gros ~** headline. **3.** (universitaire) diploma, qualification. **4.** (JUR) title; **~ de propriété** title deed. **5.** (FIN) security. ▸ **titre de transport** nm ticket. ▸ **à titre de** loc prép: **à ~ d'exemple** by way of example; **à ~ d'information** for information.

tituber [titybe] vi to totter.

titulaire [titylɛr] ◆ adj (employé) permanent; (UNIV) with tenure. ◆ nmf (de passeport, permis) holder; (de poste, chaire) occupant.

titulariser [titylarize] vt to give tenure to.

toast [tost] nm **1.** (pain grillé) toast (U). **2.** (discours) toast; **porter un ~ à** to drink a toast to.

toboggan [tɔbɔgɑ̃] nm **1.** (traîneau)

toboggan. **2.** (*de terrain de jeu*) slide; (*de piscine*) chute.

toc [tɔk] ♦ *interj*: **et ~!** so there! ♦ *nm fam*: **c'est du ~** it's fake; **en ~** fake (*avant n*).

Togo [tɔgo] *nm*: **le ~** Togo.

toi [twa] *pron pers* you. ▶ **toi-même** *pron pers* yourself.

toile [twal] *nf* **1.** (*étoffe*) cloth; (*de lin*) linen; **~ cirée** oilcloth. **2.** (*tableau*) canvas, picture. ▶ **toile d'araignée** *nf* spider's web.

toilette [twalɛt] *nf* **1.** (*de personne, d'animal*) washing; **faire sa ~** to (have a) wash. **2.** (*parure, vêtements*) outfit, clothes (*pl*). ▶ **toilettes** *nfpl* toilet (*sg*), toilets.

toise [twaz] *nf* height gauge.

toison [twazɔ̃] *nf* **1.** (*pelage*) fleece. **2.** (*chevelure*) mop (of hair).

toit [twa] *nm* roof; **~ ouvrant** sunroof.

toiture [twatyr] *nf* roof, roofing.

tôle [tol] *nf* (*de métal*) sheet metal; **~ ondulée** corrugated iron.

tolérance [tɔlerɑ̃s] *nf* **1.** (*gén*) tolerance. **2.** (*liberté*) concession.

tolérant, -e [tɔlerɑ̃, ɑ̃t] *adj* **1.** (*large d'esprit*) tolerant. **2.** (*indulgent*) liberal.

tolérer [tɔlere] *vt* to tolerate. ▶ **se tolérer** *vp* to put up with ou tolerate each other.

tollé [tɔle] *nm* protest.

tomate [tɔmat] *nf* tomato.

tombal, -e, -aux [tɔ̃bal, o] *adj*: **pierre ~e** gravestone.

tombant, -e [tɔ̃bɑ̃, ɑ̃t] *adj* (*moustaches*) drooping; (*épaules*) sloping.

tombe [tɔ̃b] *nf* (*fosse*) grave, tomb.

tombeau, -x [tɔ̃bo] *nm* tomb.

tombée [tɔ̃be] *nf* fall; **à la ~ du jour** ou **de la nuit** at nightfall.

tomber [tɔ̃be] *vi* (aux: être) **1.** (*gén*) to fall; **faire ~ qqn** to knock sb over ou down; **~ raide mort** to drop down dead; **~ bien** (*robe*) to hang well; *fig* (*visite, personne*) to come at a good time. **2.** (*cheveux*) to fall out. **3.** (*nouvelle*) to break. **4.** (*diminuer - prix*) to drop, to fall; (*- fièvre, vent*) to drop; (*- jour*) to come to an end; (*- colère*) to die down. **5.** (*devenir brusquement*): **~ malade** to fall ill; **~ amoureux** to fall in love; **être bien/mal tombé** to be lucky/unlucky. **6.** (*trouver*): **~ sur** to come across. **7.** (*date, événement*) to fall on.

tombola [tɔ̃bɔla] *nf* raffle.

tome [tɔm] *nm* volume.

ton¹ [tɔ̃] *nm* **1.** (*de voix*) tone; **hausser/baisser le ~** to raise/lower one's voice.

2. (MUS) key; **donner le ~** to give the chord; *fig* to set the tone.

ton² [tɔ̃] (f **ta** [ta], pl **tes** [te]) *adj poss* your.

tonalité [tɔnalite] *nf* **1.** (MUS) tonality. **2.** (*au téléphone*) dialling tone.

tondeuse [tɔ̃døz] *nf* (*à cheveux*) clippers (*pl*); **~ (à gazon)** mower, lawnmower.

tondre [tɔ̃dr] *vt* (*gazon*) to mow; (*mouton*) to shear; (*caniche, cheveux*) to clip.

tondu, -e [tɔ̃dy] *adj* (*caniche, cheveux*) clipped; (*pelouse*) mown.

tonicité [tɔnisite] *nf* (*des muscles*) tone.

tonifier [tɔnifje] *vt* (*peau*) to tone; (*esprit*) to stimulate.

tonique [tɔnik] *adj* **1.** (*boisson*) tonic (*avant n*); (*froid*) bracing; (*lotion*) toning. **2.** (LING & MUS) tonic.

tonitruant, -e [tɔnitryɑ̃, ɑ̃t] *adj* booming.

tonnage [tɔnaʒ] *nm* tonnage.

tonnant, -e [tɔnɑ̃, ɑ̃t] *adj* thundering, thunderous.

tonne [tɔn] *nf* (1000 kg) tonne.

tonneau, -x [tɔno] *nm* **1.** (*baril*) barrel, cask. **2.** (*de voiture*) roll. **3.** (NAVIG) ton.

tonnelle [tɔnɛl] *nf* bower, arbour.

tonner [tɔne] *vi* to thunder.

tonnerre [tɔnɛr] *nm* thunder; **coup de ~** thunderclap; *fig* bombshell.

tonte [tɔ̃t] *nf* (*de mouton*) shearing; (*de gazon*) mowing; (*de caniche, cheveux*) clipping.

tonus [tɔnys] *nm* **1.** (*dynamisme*) energy. **2.** (*de muscle*) tone.

top [tɔp] *nm* (*signal*) beep.

toper [tɔpe] *vi*: **tope-là!** right, you're on!

topographie [tɔpɔgrafi] *nf* topography.

toque [tɔk] *nf* (*de juge, de jockey*) cap; (*de cuisinier*) hat.

torche [tɔrʃ] *nf* torch.

torcher [tɔrʃe] *vt fam* **1.** (*assiette, fesses*) to wipe. **2.** (*travail*) to dash off.

torchon [tɔrʃɔ̃] *nm* **1.** (*serviette*) cloth. **2.** *fam* (*travail*) mess.

tordre [tɔrdr] *vt* (*gén*) to twist. ▶ **se tordre** *vp*: **se ~ la cheville** to twist one's ankle; **se ~ de rire** *fam fig* to double up with laughter.

tordu, -e [tɔrdy] ♦ *pp* → **tordre**. ♦ *adj fam* (*bizarre, fou*) crazy; (*esprit*) warped.

tornade [tɔrnad] *nf* tornado.

torpeur [tɔrpœr] *nf* torpor.

torpille [tɔrpij] *nf* (MIL) torpedo.

torpiller [tɔrpije] *vt* to torpedo.

torréfaction [tɔrefaksjɔ̃] *nf* roasting.

torrent [tɔrɑ̃] nm torrent; **un ~ de** fig (injures) a stream of; (lumière, larmes) a flood of.

torrentiel, -elle [tɔrɑ̃sjɛl] adj torrential.

torride [tɔrid] adj torrid.

torsade [tɔrsad] nf 1. (de cheveux) twist, coil. 2. (de pull) cable.

torsader [tɔrsade] vt to twist.

torse [tɔrs] nm chest.

torsion [tɔrsjɔ̃] nf twisting; (PHYS) torsion.

tort [tɔr] nm 1. (erreur) fault; **avoir ~** to be wrong; **être dans son** ou **en ~** to be in the wrong; **à ~** wrongly. 2. (préjudice) wrong.

torticolis [tɔrtikɔli] nm stiff neck.

tortiller [tɔrtije] vt (enrouler) to twist; (moustache) to twirl. ► **se tortiller** vp to writhe, to wriggle.

tortionnaire [tɔrsjɔnɛr] nmf torturer.

tortue [tɔrty] nf tortoise; fig slowcoach Br, slowpoke Am.

tortueux, -euse [tɔrtɥø, øz] adj winding, twisting; fig tortuous.

torture [tɔrtyr] nf torture.

torturer [tɔrtyre] vt to torture.

tôt [to] adv 1. (de bonne heure) early. 2. (vite) soon, early. ► **au plus tôt** loc adv at the earliest.

total, -e, -aux [tɔtal, o] adj total. ► **total** nm total.

totalement [tɔtalmã] adv totally.

totaliser [tɔtalize] vt 1. (additionner) to add up, to total. 2. (réunir) to have a total of.

totalitaire [tɔtalitɛr] adj totalitarian.

totalitarisme [tɔtalitarism] nm totalitarianism.

totalité [tɔtalite] nf whole; **en ~** entirely.

totem [tɔtɛm] nm totem.

toubib [tubib] nmf fam doc.

touchant, -e [tuʃã, ãt] adj touching.

touche [tuʃ] nf 1. (de clavier) key; **~ de fonction** function key. 2. (de peinture) stroke. 3. fig (note): **une ~ de** a touch of. 4. (PÊCHE) bite. 5. (FOOTBALL - ligne) touch line; (- remise en jeu) throw-in; (RUGBY - ligne) touch (line); (- remise en jeu) line-out. 6. (ESCRIME) hit.

toucher [tuʃe] ◆ nm: **le ~** the (sense of) touch; **au ~** to the touch. ◆ vt 1. (palper, émouvoir) to touch. 2. (rivage, correspondant) to reach; (cible) to hit. 3. (salaire) to get, to be paid; (chèque) to cash; (gros lot) to win. 4. (concerner) to affect, to concern. ◆ vi: **~ à** to touch; (problème) to touch on; (maison) to

adjoin; **~ à sa fin** to draw to a close. ► **se toucher** vp (maisons) to be adjacent (to each other), to adjoin (each other).

touffe [tuf] nf tuft.

touffu, -e [tufy] adj (forêt) dense; (barbe) bushy.

toujours [tuʒur] adv 1. (continuité, répétition) always; **ils s'aimeront ~** they will always love one another, they will love one another forever; **~ plus** more and more; **~ moins** less and less. 2. (encore) still. 3. (de toute façon) anyway, anyhow. ► **de toujours** loc adj: **ce sont des amis de ~** they are lifelong friends. ► **pour toujours** loc adv forever, for good. ► **toujours est-il que** loc conj the fact remains that.

toupet [tupɛ] nm 1. (de cheveux) quiff Br, tuft of hair. 2. fam fig (aplomb) cheek; **avoir du ~, ne pas manquer de ~** fam to have a cheek.

toupie [tupi] nf (spinning) top.

tour [tur] ◆ nm 1. (périmètre) circumference; **faire le ~ de** to go round; **faire un ~** to go for a walk/drive etc; **~ d'horizon** survey; **~ de piste** (SPORT) lap; **~ de taille** waist measurement. 2. (rotation) turn; **fermer à double ~** to double-lock. 3. (plaisanterie) trick. 4. (succession) turn; **c'est à mon ~** it's my turn; **à ~ de rôle** in turn; **~ à ~** alternately, in turn. 5. (d'événements) turn. 6. (de potier) wheel. ◆ nf 1. (monument, de château) tower; (immeuble) tower-block Br, high-rise Am; **la ~ Eiffel** the Eiffel Tower. 2. (ÉCHECS) rook, castle. ► **tour de contrôle** nf control tower.

TOUR EIFFEL

Built by Gustave Eiffel for the World Fair in 1889, the Eiffel Tower has come to symbolize Paris and is one of the most popular tourist attractions in the world. From the top, which can be reached by lift, there is a panoramic view over the whole city and beyond.

tourbe [turb] nf peat.

tourbillon [turbijɔ̃] nm 1. (de vent) whirlwind. 2. (de poussière, fumée) swirl. 3. (d'eau) whirlpool. 4. fig (agitation) hurly-burly.

tourbillonner [turbijɔne] vi to whirl, to swirl; fig to whirl (round).

tourelle [turɛl] nf turret.

tourisme [turism] nm tourism; **le ~ vert** country holidays (pl).

touriste [turist] nmf tourist.

touristique [turistik] adj tourist (avant n).

tourment [turmã] nm sout torment.

tourmente [turmãt] nf **1.** littéraire (tempête) storm, tempest. **2.** fig turmoil.

tourmenter [turmãte] vt to torment. ▶ **se tourmenter** vp to worry o.s., to fret.

tournage [turnaʒ] nm (CIN) shooting.

tournant, -e [turnã, ãt] adj (porte) revolving; (fauteuil) swivel (avant n); (pont) swing (avant n). ▶ **tournant** nm bend; fig turning point.

tourné, -e [turne] adj (lait) sour, off.

tourne-disque [turnədisk] (pl **tourne-disques**) nm record player.

tournée [turne] nf **1.** (voyage) tour. **2.** fam (consommations) round.

tourner [turne] ◆ vt **1.** (gén) to turn. **2.** (pas, pensées) to turn, to direct. **3.** (obstacle, loi) to get round. **4.** (CIN) to shoot. ◆ vi **1.** (gén) to turn; (moteur) to turn over; (planète) to revolve; ~ **autour de qqn** fig to hang around sb; ~ **autour du pot** ou **du sujet** fig to beat about the bush. **2.** fam (entreprise) to tick over; **ça tourne bien** it's going well. **3.** (lait) to go off. ▶ **se tourner** vp to turn (right) round; **se ~ vers** to turn towards.

tournesol [turnəsɔl] nm (plante) sunflower.

tournevis [turnəvis] nm screwdriver.

tourniquet [turnikɛ] nm **1.** (entrée) turnstile. **2.** (MÉD) tourniquet.

tournis [turni] nm fam: **avoir le ~** to feel dizzy ou giddy.

tournoi [turnwa] nm tournament.

tournoyer [turnwaje] vi to wheel, to whirl.

tournure [turnyr] nf **1.** (apparence) turn. **2.** (formulation) form; ~ **de phrase** turn of phrase.

tourteau, -x [turto] nm (crabe) crab.

tourterelle [turtərɛl] nf turtledove.

tous → **tout.**

Toussaint [tusɛ̃] nf: **la ~** All Saints' Day.

TOUSSAINT

In France on 1 November people celebrate All Saints' Day by laying flowers (typically chrysanthemums) on the graves of their relatives. Ironically, this is also the time of the year at which most deaths occur from road traffic accidents.

---

tousser [tuse] vi to cough.

toussotement [tusɔtmã] nm coughing.

toussoter [tusɔte] vi to cough.

tout [tu] (f **toute** [tut], mpl **tous** [tus], fpl **toutes** [tut]) ◆ adj qualificatif **1.** (avec substantif singulier déterminé) all; ~ **le vin** all the wine; ~ **un gâteau** a whole cake; **toute la journée/la nuit** all day/night, the whole day/night; **toute sa famille** all his family, his whole family. **2.** (avec pronom démonstratif): ~ **ceci/cela** all this/that; ~ **ce que je sais** all I know. ◆ adj indéf **1.** (exprime la totalité) all; **tous les gâteaux** all the cakes; **tous les deux** both of us/them etc; **tous les trois** all three of us/them etc. **2.** (chaque) every; **tous les jours** every day; **tous les deux ans** every two years; **tous les combien?** how often? **3.** (n'importe quel) any; **à toute heure** at any time. ◆ pron indéf everything, all; **je t'ai ~ dit** I've told you everything; **ils voulaient tous la voir** they all wanted to see her; **ce sera ~?** will that be all?; **c'est ~ que c'est** that's all. ▶ **tout** ◆ adv **1.** (entièrement, tout à fait) very, quite; ~ **jeune/près** very young/near; **ils étaient ~ seuls** they were all alone; ~ **en haut** right at the top. **2.** (avec un gérondif): ~ **en marchant** while walking. ◆ nm: **un** ~ a whole; **le** ~ **est de** ... the main thing is to ... ▶ **du tout au tout** loc adv completely, entirely. ▶ **pas du tout** loc adv not at all. ▶ **tout à fait** loc adv **1.** (complètement) quite, entirely. **2.** (exactement) exactly. ▶ **tout à l'heure** loc adv **1.** (futur) in a little while, shortly; **à ~ à l'heure!** see you later! **2.** (passé) a little while ago. ▶ **tout de suite** loc adv immediately, at once.

tout-à-l'égout [tutalegu] nm inv mains drainage.

toutefois [tutfwa] adv however.

tout-petit [tup(ə)ti] (pl **tout-petits**) nm toddler, tot.

tout-puissant, toute-puissante [tupɥisã, tutpɥisãt] (mpl **tout-puissants**, fpl **toutes-puissantes**) adj omnipotent, all-powerful.

toux [tu] nf cough.

toxicomane [tɔksikɔman] nmf drug addict.

toxine [tɔksin] nf toxin.

toxique [tɔksik] adj toxic.

trac [trak] nm nerves (pl); (THÉÂTRE) stage fright; **avoir le ~** to get nervous; (THÉÂTRE) to get stage fright.

tracas [traka] nm worry.

tracasser [trakase] *vt* to worry, to bother. ▶ **se tracasser** *vp* to worry.

tracasserie [trakasri] *nf* annoyance.

trace [tras] *nf* **1.** (*d'animal*) track. **2.** (*de brûlure, fatigue*) mark. **3.** (*gén pl*) (*vestige*) trace. **4.** (*très petite quantité*): **une ~ de** a trace of.

tracé [trase] *nm* (*lignes*) plan, drawing; (*de parcours*) line.

tracer [trase] *vt* **1.** (*dessiner, dépeindre*) to draw. **2.** (*route, piste*) to mark out.

trachéite [trakeit] *nf* throat infection.

tract [trakt] *nm* leaflet.

tractations [traktasjɔ̃] *nfpl* negotiations, dealings.

tracter [trakte] *vt* to tow.

tracteur [traktœr] *nm* tractor.

traction [traksjɔ̃] *nf* **1.** (*action de tirer*) towing, pulling; **~ avant/arrière** front-/rear-wheel drive. **2.** (TECHNOL) tensile stress. **3.** (SPORT - *au sol*) press-up Br, push-up Am; (- *à la barre*) pull-up.

tradition [tradisjɔ̃] *nf* tradition.

traditionnel, -elle [tradisjɔnɛl] *adj* **1.** (*de tradition*) traditional. **2.** (*habituel*) usual.

traducteur, -trice [tradyktœr, tris] *nm, f* translator.

traduction [tradyksjɔ̃] *nf* (*gén*) translation.

traduire [traduir] *vt* **1.** (*texte*) to translate; **~ qqch en français/anglais** to translate sthg into French/English. **2.** (*révéler - crise*) to reveal, to betray; (- *sentiments, pensée*) to render, to express. **3.** (JUR): **~ qqn en justice** to bring sb before the courts.

trafic [trafik] *nm* **1.** (*de marchandises*) traffic, trafficking. **2.** (*circulation*) traffic.

trafiquant, -e [trafikã, ãt] *nm, f* trafficker, dealer.

trafiquer [trafike] ◆ *vt* **1.** (*falsifier*) to tamper with. **2.** *fam* (*manigancer*): **qu'est-ce que tu trafiques?** what are you up to? ◆ *vi* to be involved in trafficking.

tragédie [traʒedi] *nf* tragedy.

tragique [traʒik] *adj* tragic.

tragiquement [traʒikmã] *adv* tragically.

trahir [trair] *vt* **1.** (*gén*) to betray. **2.** (*suj: moteur*) to let down; (*suj: forces*) to fail. ▶ **se trahir** *vp* to give o.s. away.

trahison [traizɔ̃] *nf* **1.** (*gén*) betrayal. **2.** (JUR) treason.

train [trɛ̃] *nm* **1.** (TRANSPORT) train. **2.** (*allure*) pace. **3.** *loc*: **être en ~** *fig* to be on form. ▶ **train de vie** *nm* lifestyle. ▶ **en train de** *loc prép*: **être en ~ de lire/**

travailler to be reading/working.

traînant, -e [trɛnã, ãt] *adj* (*voix*) drawling; (*démarche*) dragging.

traîne [trɛn] *nf* **1.** (*de robe*) train. **2.** *loc*: **être à la ~** to lag behind.

traîneau, -x [trɛno] *nm* sleigh, sledge.

traînée [trene] *nf* **1.** (*trace*) trail. **2.** *tfam péj* (*prostituée*) tart, whore.

traîner [trene] ◆ *vt* **1.** (*tirer, emmener*) to drag. **2.** (*trimbaler*) to lug around, to cart around. **3.** (*maladie*) to be unable to shake off. ◆ *vi* **1.** (*personne*) to dawdle. **2.** (*maladie, affaire*) to drag on; **~ en longueur** to drag. **3.** (*vêtements, livres*) to lie around OU about. ▶ **se traîner** *vp* **1.** (*personne*) to drag o.s. along. **2.** (*jour, semaine*) to drag.

train-train [trɛ̃trɛ̃] *nm fam* routine, daily grind.

traire [trɛr] *vt* (*vache*) to milk.

trait [trɛ] *nm* **1.** (*ligne*) line, stroke; **~ d'union** hyphen. **2.** (*gén pl*) (*de visage*) feature. **3.** (*caractéristique*) trait, feature. **4.** *loc*: **avoir ~ à** to be to do with, to concern. ▶ **d'un trait** *loc adv* (*boire, lire*) in one go.

traitant, -e [trɛtã, ãt] *adj* (*shampooing, crème*) medicated; → **médecin**.

traite [trɛt] *nf* **1.** (*de vache*) milking. **2.** (COMM) bill, draft. **3.** (*d'esclaves*): **la ~ des noirs** the slave trade; **la ~ des blanches** the white slave trade. ▶ **d'une seule traite** *loc adv* without stopping, in one go.

traité [trete] *nm* **1.** (*ouvrage*) treatise. **2.** (POLIT) treaty.

traitement [trɛtmã] *nm* **1.** (*gén* & MÉD) treatment; **mauvais ~** ill-treatment. **2.** (*rémunération*) wage. **3.** (IND & INFORM) processing; **~ de texte** word processing. **4.** (*de problème*) handling.

traiter [trete] ◆ *vt* **1.** (*gén* & MÉD) to treat; **bien/mal ~ qqn** to treat sb well/badly. **2.** (*qualifier*): **~ qqn d'imbécile/de lâche** *etc* to call sb an imbecile/a coward *etc*. **3.** (*question, thème*) to deal with. **4.** (IND & INFORM) to process. ◆ *vi* **1.** (*négocier*) to negotiate. **2.** (*livre*): **~ de** to deal with.

traiteur [trɛtœr] *nm* caterer.

traître, -esse [trɛtr, ɛs] ◆ *adj* treacherous. ◆ *nm, f* traitor.

traîtrise [trɛtriz] *nf* **1.** (*déloyauté*) treachery. **2.** (*acte*) act of treachery.

trajectoire [traʒɛktwar] *nf* trajectory, path; *fig* path.

trajet [traʒɛ] *nm* **1.** (*distance*) distance.

2. (*itinéraire*) route. **3.** (*voyage*) journey.
trame [tram] *nf* weft; *fig* framework.
tramer [trame] *vt sout* to plot. ▶ **se tramer** ◆ *vp* to be plotted. ◆ *v impers*: **il se trame quelque chose** there's something afoot.
tramontane [tramɔ̃tan] *nf strong cold wind that blows through Languedoc-Roussillon in southwest France*.
trampoline [trɑ̃pɔlin] *nm* trampoline.
tram(way) [tram(wε)] *nm* tram Br, streetcar Am.
tranchant, -e [trɑ̃ʃɑ̃, ɑ̃t] *adj* **1.** (*instrument*) sharp. **2.** (*personne*) assertive. **3.** (*ton*) curt. ▶ **tranchant** *nm* edge.
tranche [trɑ̃ʃ] *nf* **1.** (*de gâteau, jambon*) slice; **~ d'âge** *fig* age bracket. **2.** (*de livre, pièce*) edge. **3.** (*période*) part, section. **4.** (*de revenus*) portion; (*de paiement*) instalment; (*fiscale*) bracket.
trancher [trɑ̃ʃe] ◆ *vt* (*couper*) to cut; (*pain, jambon*) to slice; **~ la question** *fig* to settle the question. ◆ *vi* **1.** *fig* (*décider*) to decide. **2.** (*contraster*): **~ avec** ou **sur** to contrast with.
tranquille [trɑ̃kil] *adj* **1.** (*endroit, vie*) quiet; **laisser qqn/qqch ~** to leave sb/sth alone; **se tenir/rester ~** to keep/remain quiet. **2.** (*rassuré*) at ease, easy; **soyez ~** don't worry.
tranquillement [trɑ̃kilmɑ̃] *adv* **1.** (*sans s'agiter*) quietly. **2.** (*sans s'inquiéter*) calmly.
tranquillisant, -e [trɑ̃kilizɑ̃, ɑ̃t] *adj* **1.** (*nouvelle*) reassuring. **2.** (*médicament*) tranquillizing. ▶ **tranquillisant** *nm* tranquillizer.
tranquilliser [trɑ̃kilize] *vt* to reassure. ▶ **se tranquilliser** *vp* to set one's mind at rest.
tranquillité [trɑ̃kilite] *nf* **1.** (*calme*) peacefulness, quietness. **2.** (*sérénité*) peace, tranquillity.
transaction [trɑ̃zaksjɔ̃] *nf* transaction.
transat [trɑ̃zat] *nm* deckchair.
transatlantique [trɑ̃zatlɑ̃tik] ◆ *adj* transatlantic. ◆ *nm* transatlantic liner. ◆ *nf* transatlantic race.
transcription [trɑ̃skripsjɔ̃] *nf* (*de document & MUS*) transcription; (*dans un autre alphabet*) transliteration; **~ phonétique** phonetic transcription.
transcrire [trɑ̃skrir] *vt* (*document & MUS*) to transcribe; (*dans un autre alphabet*) to transliterate.
transcrit, -e [trɑ̃skri, it] *pp* → **transcrire**.

transe [trɑ̃s] *nf*: **être en ~** *fig* to be beside o.s.
transférer [trɑ̃sfere] *vt* to transfer.
transfert [trɑ̃sfεr] *nm* transfer.
transfigurer [trɑ̃sfigyre] *vt* to transfigure.
transformateur, -trice [trɑ̃sfɔrmatœr, tris] *adj* (IND) processing (*avant n*). ▶ **transformateur** *nm* transformer.
transformation [trɑ̃sfɔrmasjɔ̃] *nf* **1.** (*de pays, personne*) transformation. **2.** (IND) processing. **3.** (RUGBY) conversion.
transformer [trɑ̃sfɔrme] *vt* **1.** (*gén*) to transform; (*magasin*) to convert; **~ qqch en** to turn sthg into. **2.** (IND & RUGBY) to convert. ▶ **se transformer** *vp*: **se ~ en monstre/papillon** to turn into a monster/butterfly.
transfuge [trɑ̃sfyʒ] *nmf* renegade.
transfuser [trɑ̃sfyze] *vt* (*sang*) to transfuse.
transfusion [trɑ̃sfyzjɔ̃] *nf*: **~ (sanguine)** (blood) transfusion.
transgresser [trɑ̃sgrese] *vt* (*loi*) to infringe; (*ordre*) to disobey.
transhumance [trɑ̃zymɑ̃s] *nf* transhumance.
transi, -e [trɑ̃zi] *adj*: **être ~ de** to be paralysed ou transfixed with; **être ~ de froid** to be chilled to the bone.
transiger [trɑ̃ziʒe] *vi*: **~ (sur)** to compromise (on).
transistor [trɑ̃zistɔr] *nm* transistor.
transit [trɑ̃zit] *nm* transit.
transiter [trɑ̃zite] *vi* to pass in transit.
transitif, -ive [trɑ̃sitif, iv] *adj* transitive.
transition [trɑ̃zisjɔ̃] *nf* transition; **sans ~** with no transition, abruptly.
transitivité [trɑ̃zitivite] *nf* transitivity.
transitoire [trɑ̃zitwar] *adj* (*passager*) transitory.
translucide [trɑ̃slysid] *adj* translucent.
transmettre [trɑ̃smetr] *vt* **1.** (*message, salutations*): **~ qqch (à)** to pass sthg on (to). **2.** (*tradition, propriété*): **~ qqch (à)** to hand sthg down (to). **3.** (*fonction, pouvoir*): **~ qqch (à)** to hand sthg over (to). **4.** (*maladie*): **~ qqch (à)** to transmit sthg (to), to pass sthg on (to). **5.** (*concert, émission*) to broadcast. ▶ **se transmettre** *vp* **1.** (*maladie*) to be passed on, to be transmitted. **2.** (*nouvelle*) to be passed on. **3.** (*courant, onde*) to be transmitted. **4.** (*tradition*) to be handed down.
transmis, -e [trɑ̃smi, iz] *pp* → **transmettre**.

transmissible [trãsmisibl] *adj* 1. (*patrimoine*) transferable. 2. (*maladie*) transmissible.

transmission [trãsmisjɔ̃] *nf* 1. (*de biens*) transfer. 2. (*de maladie*) transmission. 3. (*de message*) passing on. 4. (*de tradition*) handing down.

transparaître [trãsparɛtr] *vi* to show.

transparence [trãsparãs] *nf* transparency.

transparent, -e [trãsparã, ãt] *adj* transparent. ▶ **transparent** *nm* transparency.

transpercer [trãspɛrse] *vt* to pierce; *fig* (*suj: froid, pluie*) to go right through.

transpiration [trãspirasjɔ̃] *nf* (*sueur*) perspiration.

transpirer [trãspire] *vi* (*suer*) to perspire.

transplanter [trãsplãte] *vt* to transplant.

transport [trãspɔr] *nm* transport (U); **~s en commun** public transport (*sg*).

transportable [trãspɔrtabl] *adj* (*marchandise*) transportable; (*blessé*) fit to be moved.

transporter [trãspɔrte] *vt* (*marchandises, personnes*) to transport.

transporteur [trãspɔrtœr] *nm* (*personne*) carrier; **~ routier** road haulier.

transposer [trãspoze] *vt* 1. (*déplacer*) to transpose. 2. (*adapter*): **~ qqch (à)** to adapt sthg (for).

transposition [trãspozisjɔ̃] *nf* 1. (*déplacement*) transposition. 2. (*adaptation*): **~ (à)** adaptation (for).

transsexuel, -elle [trãssɛksɥɛl] *adj & nm, f* transsexual.

transvaser [trãsvaze] *vt* to decant.

transversal, -e, -aux [trãsversal, o] *adj* 1. (*coupe*) cross (*avant n*). 2. (*chemin*) running at right angles, cross (*avant n*) *Am*. 3. (*vallée*) transverse.

trapèze [trapɛz] *nm* 1. (GÉOM) trapezium. 2. (GYM) trapeze.

trapéziste [trapezist] *nmf* trapeze artist.

trappe [trap] *nf* 1. (*ouverture*) trapdoor. 2. (*piège*) trap.

trapu, -e [trapy] *adj* 1. (*personne*) stocky, solidly built. 2. (*édifice*) squat.

traquenard [traknar] *nm* trap.

traquer [trake] *vt* (*animal*) to track; (*personne, faute*) to track ou hunt down.

traumatiser [tromatize] *vt* to traumatize.

traumatisme [tromatism] *nm* traumatism.

travail [travaj] *nm* 1. (*gén*) work (U); **se mettre au ~** to get down to work; **demander du ~** (*projet*) to require some work. 2. (*tâche, emploi*) job; **~ intérimaire** temporary work. 3. (*du métal, du bois*) working. 4. (*phénomène - du bois*) warping; (*- du temps, fermentation*) action. 5. (MÉD): **être/entrer en ~** to be in/go into labour. ▶ **travaux** *nmpl* 1. (*d'aménagement*) work (U); (*routiers*) roadworks; **travaux publics** civil engineering (*sg*). 2. (SCOL): **travaux dirigés** class work; **travaux manuels** arts and crafts; **travaux pratiques** practical work (U).

travaillé, -e [travaje] *adj* 1. (*matériau*) wrought, worked. 2. (*style*) laboured. 3. (*tourmenté*): **être ~ par** to be tormented by.

travailler [travaje] ♦ *vi* 1. (*gén*) to work; **~ chez/dans** to work at/in; **~ à qqch** to work on sthg. 2. (*métal, bois*) to warp. ♦ *vt* 1. (*étudier*) to work at ou on; (*piano*) to practise. 2. (*essayer de convaincre*) to work on. 3. (*suj: idée, remords*) to torment. 4. (*matière*) to work, to fashion.

travailleur, -euse [travajœr, øz] ♦ *adj* hard-working. ♦ *nm, f* worker.

travelling [travliŋ] *nm* (*mouvement*) travelling shot.

travers [traver] *nm* failing, fault. ▶ **à travers** *loc adv & loc prép* through. ▶ **au travers** *loc adv* through. ▶ **au travers de** *loc prép* through. ▶ **de travers** *loc adv* 1. (*irrégulièrement - écrire*) unevenly; **marcher de ~** to stagger. 2. (*nez, escalier*) crooked. 3. (*obliquement*) sideways. 4. (*mal*) wrong; **aller de ~** to go wrong; **comprendre qqch de ~** to misunderstand sthg. ▶ **en travers** *loc adv* crosswise. ▶ **en travers de** *loc prép* across.

traverse [travers] *nf* 1. (*de chemin de fer*) sleeper, tie *Am*. 2. (*chemin*) short cut.

traversée [traverse] *nf* crossing.

traverser [traverse] *vt* 1. (*rue, mer, montagne*) to cross; (*ville*) to go through. 2. (*peau, mur*) to go through, to pierce. 3. (*crise, période*) to go through.

traversin [traversɛ̃] *nm* bolster.

travestir [travestir] *vt* 1. (*déguiser*) to dress up. 2. *fig* (*vérité, idée*) to distort. ▶ **se travestir** *vp* 1. (*pour bal*) to wear fancy dress. 2. (*en femme*) to put on drag.

trébucher [trebyʃe] *vi*: **~ (sur/contre)** to stumble (over/against).

trèfle [trefl] *nm* 1. (*plante*) clover. 2. (*carte*) club; (*famille*) clubs (*pl*).

treille [trej] *nf* 1. (*vigne*) climbing vine.

2. (*tonnelle*) trellised vines (*pl*).

treillis [trɛji] *nm* 1. (*clôture*) trellis (fencing). 2. (*toile*) canvas. 3. (MIL) combat uniform.

treize [trɛz] *adj num & nm* thirteen; *voir aussi* **six**.

treizième [trɛzjɛm] *adj num, nm & nmf* thirteenth; **~ mois** *bonus corresponding to an extra month's salary which is paid annually; voir aussi* **sixième**.

trekking [trekiŋ] *nm* trek.

tréma [trema] *nm* diaeresis.

tremblant, -e [trãblã, ãt] *adj* 1. (*personne - de froid*) shivering; (*- d'émotion*) trembling, shaking. 2. (*voix*) quavering. 3. (*lumière*) flickering.

tremblement [trãbləmã] *nm* 1. (*de corps*) trembling. 2. (*de voix*) quavering. 3. (*de feuilles*) fluttering. ▸ **tremblement de terre** *nm* earthquake.

trembler [trãble] *vi* 1. (*personne - de froid*) to shiver; (*- d'émotion*) to tremble, to shake. 2. (*voix*) to quaver. 3. (*lumière*) to flicker. 4. (*terre*) to shake.

trembloter [trãblɔte] *vi* 1. (*personne*) to tremble. 2. (*voix*) to quaver. 3. (*lumière*) to flicker.

trémousser [tremuse] ▸ **se trémousser** *vp* to jig up and down.

trempe [trãp] *nf* 1. (*envergure*) calibre; **de sa ~** of his/her calibre. 2. *fam* (*coups*) thrashing.

tremper [trãpe] ◆ *vt* 1. (*mouiller*) to soak. 2. (*plonger*): **~ qqch dans** to dip sthg into. 3. (*métal*) to harden, to quench. ◆ *vi* (*linge*) to soak.

tremplin [trãplɛ̃] *nm litt & fig* springboard; (SKI) ski jump.

trentaine [trãten] *nf* 1. (*nombre*): **une ~ de** about thirty. 2. (*âge*): **avoir la ~** to be in one's thirties.

trente [trãt] ◆ *adj num* thirty. ◆ *nm* thirty; *voir aussi* **six**.

trentième [trãtjɛm] *adj num, nm & nmf* thirtieth; *voir aussi* **sixième**.

trépidant, -e [trepidã, ãt] *adj* (*vie*) hectic.

trépied [trepje] *nm* (*support*) tripod.

trépigner [trepiɲe] *vi* to stamp one's feet.

très [trɛ] *adv* very; **~ bien** very well; **être ~ aimé** to be much ou greatly liked; **j'ai ~ envie de ...** I'd very much like to ...; **je ne suis pas ~ chocolat** *fam* I'm not really into chocolate.

trésor [trezɔr] *nm* treasure. ▸ **Trésor** *nm*: **le Trésor public** the public revenue department.

trésorerie [trezɔrri] *nf* 1. (*service*) accounts department. 2. (*gestion*) accounts (*pl*). 3. (*fonds*) finances (*pl*), funds (*pl*).

trésorier, -ère [trezɔrje, ɛr] *nm, f* treasurer.

tressaillement [tresajmã] *nm* (*de joie*) thrill; (*de douleur*) wince.

tressaillir [tresajir] *vi* 1. (*de joie*) to thrill; (*de douleur*) to wince. 2. (*sursauter*) to start, to jump.

tressauter [tresote] *vi* (*sursauter*) to jump, to start; (*dans véhicule*) to be tossed about.

tresse [tres] *nf* 1. (*de cheveux*) plait. 2. (*de rubans*) braid.

tresser [trese] *vt* 1. (*cheveux*) to plait. 2. (*osier*) to braid. 3. (*panier, guirlande*) to weave.

tréteau, -x [treto] *nm* trestle.

treuil [trœj] *nm* winch, windlass.

trêve [trɛv] *nf* 1. (*cessez-le-feu*) truce. 2. *fig* (*répit*) rest, respite; **~ de plaisanteries/de sottises** that's enough joking/nonsense. ▸ **sans trêve** *loc adv* relentlessly, unceasingly.

tri [tri] *nm* (*de lettres*) sorting; (*de candidats*) selection; **faire le ~ dans qqch** *fig* to sort sthg out.

triage [trijaʒ] *nm* (*de lettres*) sorting; (*de candidats*) selection.

triangle [trijãgl] *nm* triangle.

triangulaire [trijãgylɛr] *adj* triangular.

triathlon [trijatlɔ̃] *nm* triathlon.

tribal, -e, -aux [tribal, o] *adj* tribal.

tribord [tribɔr] *nm* starboard; **à ~** on the starboard side, to starboard.

tribu [triby] *nf* tribe.

tribulations [tribylasjɔ̃] *nfpl* tribulations, trials.

tribunal, -aux [tribynal, o] *nm* (JUR) court; **~ correctionnel** ≃ Magistrates' Court *Br*, ≃ County Court *Am*; **~ de grande instance** ≃ Crown Court *Br*, ≃ Circuit Court *Am*.

tribune [tribyn] *nf* 1. (*d'orateur*) platform. 2. (*gén pl*) (*de stade*) stand.

tribut [triby] *nm littéraire* tribute.

tributaire [tribytɛr] *adj*: **être ~ de** to depend ou be dependent on.

tricher [trife] *vi* 1. (*au jeu, à examen*) to cheat. 2. (*mentir*): **~ sur** to lie about.

tricherie [trifri] *nf* cheating.

tricheur, -euse [trifœr, øz] *nm, f* cheat.

tricolore [trikɔlɔr] *adj* 1. (*à trois couleurs*) three-coloured. 2. (*français*) French.

tricot [triko] nm 1. (*vêtement*) jumper Br, sweater. 2. (*ouvrage*) knitting; **faire du ~** to knit. 3. (*étoffe*) knitted fabric, jersey.

tricoter [trikɔte] vi & vt to knit.

tricycle [trisikl] nm tricycle.

trier [trije] vt 1. (*classer*) to sort out. 2. (*sélectionner*) to select.

trilingue [trilɛ̃g] adj trilingual.

trimestre [trimɛstr] nm (*période*) term.

trimestriel, -elle [trimɛstrijɛl] adj (*loyer, magazine*) quarterly; (SCOL) end-of-term (*avant n*).

tringle [trɛ̃gl] nf rod; **~ à rideaux** curtain rod.

trinité [trinite] nf *littéraire* trinity. ▶ **Trinité** nf: **la Trinité** the Trinity.

trinquer [trɛ̃ke] vi (*boire*) to toast, to clink glasses; **~ à** to drink to.

trio [trijo] nm trio.

triomphal, -e, -aux [trijɔ̃fal, o] adj (*succès*) triumphal; (*accueil*) triumphant.

triomphant, -e [trijɔ̃fɑ̃, ɑ̃t] adj (*équipe*) winning; (*air*) triumphant.

triomphe [trijɔ̃f] nm triumph.

triompher [trijɔ̃fe] vi (*gén*) to triumph; **~ de** to triumph over.

tripes [trip] nfpl 1. (*d'animal, de personne*) guts. 2. (CULIN) tripe (*sg*).

triple [tripl] ◆ adj triple. ◆ nm: **le ~ (de)** three times as much (as).

triplé [triple] nm 1. (*au turf*) bet on three horses winning in three different races. 2. (SPORT) (*trois victoires*) hat-trick of victories. ▶ **triplés, -ées** nm, f pl triplets.

triste [trist] adj 1. (*personne, nouvelle*) sad; **être ~ de qqch/de faire qqch** to be sad about sthg/about doing sthg. 2. (*paysage, temps*) gloomy; (*couleur*) dull. 3. (*avant n*) (*lamentable*) sorry.

tristesse [tristɛs] nf 1. (*de personne, nouvelle*) sadness. 2. (*de paysage, temps*) gloominess.

triturer [trityre] vt fam (*mouchoir*) to knead. ▶ **se triturer** vp fam: **se ~ l'esprit** ou **les méninges** to rack one's brains.

trivial, -e, -aux [trivjal, o] adj 1. (*banal*) trivial. 2. *péj* (*vulgaire*) crude, coarse.

troc [trɔk] nm 1. (*échange*) exchange. 2. (*système économique*) barter.

trois [trwa] ◆ nm three. ◆ adj num three; *voir aussi* **six**.

troisième [trwazjɛm] ◆ adj num & nmf third. ◆ nm third; (*étage*) third floor Br, fourth floor Am. ◆ nf 1. (SCOL) ≃ fourth year ou form Br, ≃ ninth grade Am. 2.

(*vitesse*) third (gear); *voir aussi* **sixième**.

trombe [trɔ̃b] nf water spout.

trombone [trɔ̃bɔn] nm 1. (*agrafe*) paper clip. 2. (*instrument*) trombone.

trompe [trɔ̃p] nf 1. (*instrument*) trumpet. 2. (*d'éléphant*) trunk. 3. (*d'insecte*) proboscis. 4. (ANAT) tube.

trompe-l'œil [trɔ̃plœj] nm inv 1. (*peinture*) trompe-l'oeil; **en ~** done in trompe-l'oeil. 2. (*apparence*) deception.

tromper [trɔ̃pe] vt 1. (*personne*) to deceive; (*époux*) to be unfaithful to, to deceive. 2. (*vigilance*) to elude. ▶ **se tromper** vp to make a mistake, to be mistaken; **se ~ de jour/maison** to get the wrong day/house.

tromperie [trɔ̃pri] nf deception.

trompette [trɔ̃pɛt] nf trumpet.

trompettiste [trɔ̃petist] nmf trumpeter.

trompeur, -euse [trɔ̃pœr, øz] adj 1. (*personne*) deceitful. 2. (*calme, apparence*) deceptive.

tronc [trɔ̃] nm 1. (*d'arbre, de personne*) trunk. 2. (*d'église*) collection box. ▶ **tronc commun** nm (*de programmes*) common element ou feature; (SCOL) core syllabus.

tronçon [trɔ̃sɔ̃] nm 1. (*morceau*) piece, length. 2. (*de route, de chemin de fer*) section.

tronçonneuse [trɔ̃sɔnøz] nf chain saw.

trône [tron] nm throne.

trôner [trone] vi 1. (*personne*) to sit enthroned; (*objet*) to have pride of place. 2. *hum* (*faire l'important*) to lord it.

trop [tro] adv 1. (*devant adj, adv*) too; **avoir ~ chaud/froid/peur** to be too hot/cold/frightened. 2. (*avec verbe*) too much; **nous étions ~** there were too many of us; **je n'aime pas ~ le chocolat** I don't like chocolate very much; **sans ~ savoir pourquoi** without really knowing why. 3. (*avec complément*): **~ de** (*quantité*) too much; (*nombre*) too many. ▶ **en trop, de trop** loc adv too much/many; **10 francs de** ou **en ~** 10 francs too much; **une personne de** ou **en ~** one person too many; **être de ~** (*personne*) to be in the way, to be unwelcome.

trophée [trofe] nm trophy.

tropical, -e, -aux [trɔpikal, o] adj tropical.

tropique [trɔpik] nm tropic. ▶ **tropiques** nmpl tropics.

trop-plein [troplɛ̃] (*pl* trop-pleins) nm (*excès*) excess; *fig* excess, surplus.

troquer [trɔke] vt: ~ qqch (contre) to barter sthg (for); fig to swap sthg (for).

trot [tro] nm trot; au ~ at a trot.

trotter [trɔte] vi 1. (cheval) to trot. 2. (personne) to run around.

trotteur, -euse [trɔtœr, øz] nm, f trotter. ▶ **trotteuse** nf second hand.

trottiner [trɔtine] vi to trot.

trottoir [trɔtwar] nm pavement Br, sidewalk Am.

trou [tru] nm 1. (gén) hole; ~ d'air air pocket. 2. (manque, espace vide) gap; ~ de mémoire memory lapse.

troublant, -e [trublã, ãt] adj disturbing.

trouble [trubl] ◆ adj 1. (eau) cloudy. 2. (image, vue) blurred. 3. (affaire) shady. ◆ nm 1. (désordre) trouble, discord. 2. (gêne) confusion; (émoi) agitation. 3. (gén pl) (dérèglement) disorder. ▶ **troubles** nmpl (sociaux) unrest (U).

trouble-fête [trublefɛt] nmf inv spoilsport.

troubler [truble] vt 1. (eau) to cloud, to make cloudy. 2. (image, vue) to blur. 3. (sommeil, événement) to disrupt, to disturb. 4. (esprit, raison) to cloud. 5. (inquiéter, émouvoir) to disturb. 6. (rendre perplexe) to trouble. ▶ **se troubler** vp 1. (eau) to become cloudy. 2. (personne) to become flustered.

trouée [true] nf gap; (MIL) breach.

trouer [true] vt 1. (chaussette) to make a hole in. 2. fig (silence) to disturb.

trouille [truj] nf fam fear, terror.

troupe [trup] nf 1. (MIL) troop. 2. (d'amis) group, band. 3. (THÉÂTRE) theatre group.

troupeau, -x [trupo] nm (de vaches, d'éléphants) herd; (de moutons, d'oies) flock; péj (de personnes) herd.

trousse [trus] nf case, bag; ~ de secours first-aid kit; ~ de toilette toilet bag.

trousseau, -x [truso] nm 1. (de mariée) trousseau. 2. (de clefs) bunch.

trouvaille [truvaj] nf 1. (découverte) find, discovery. 2. (invention) new idea.

trouver [truve] ◆ vt to find; to feel (that); ~ bon/mauvais que ... to think (that) it is right/wrong that ...; ~ qqch à faire/à dire etc to find sthg to do/say etc. ◆ v impers: il se trouve que ... the fact is that ... ▶ **se trouver** vp 1. (dans un endroit) to be. 2. (dans un état) to find o.s. 3. (se sentir) to feel; se ~ mal (s'évanouir) to faint.

truand [tryã] nm crook.

truc [tryk] nm 1. (combine) trick. 2. fam (chose) thing, thingamajig.

trucage = truquage.

truculent, -e [trykylã, ãt] adj colourful.

truelle [tryɛl] nf trowel.

truffe [tryf] nf 1. (champignon) truffle. 2. (museau) muzzle.

truffer [tryfe] vt 1. (volaille) to garnish with truffles. 2. fig (discours): ~ de to stuff with.

truie [trɥi] nf sow.

truite [trɥit] nf trout.

truquage, trucage [trykaʒ] nm (CIN) (special) effect.

truquer [tryke] vt 1. (élections) to rig. 2. (CIN) to use special effects in.

trust [trœst] nm 1. (groupement) trust. 2. (entreprise) corporation.

tsar [tsar], **tzar** [dzar] nm tsar.

tsigane = tzigane.

TSVP (abr de tournez s'il vous plaît) PTO.

tt abr de tout.

tt conf. abr de tout confort.

ttes abr de toutes.

TTX (abr de traitement de texte) WP.

tu¹, -e [ty] pp → taire.

tu² [ty] pron pers you.

tuba [tyba] nm 1. (MUS) tuba. 2. (de plongée) snorkel.

tubaire [tybɛr] adj tubal.

tube [tyb] nm 1. (gén) tube; ~ cathodique cathode ray tube. 2. fam (chanson) hit. ▶ **tube digestif** nm digestive tract.

tubercule [tybɛrkyl] nm (BOT) tuber.

tuberculose [tybɛrkyloz] nf tuberculosis.

tuer [tɥe] vt to kill. ▶ **se tuer** vp 1. (se suicider) to kill o.s. 2. (par accident) to die.

tuerie [tyri] nf slaughter.

tue-tête [tytɛt] ▶ **à tue-tête** loc adv at the top of one's voice.

tueur, -euse [tɥœr, øz] nm, f (meurtrier) killer.

tuile [tɥil] nf 1. (de toit) tile. 2. fam (désagrément) blow.

tulipe [tylip] nf tulip.

tulle [tyl] nm tulle.

tuméfié, -e [tymefje] adj swollen.

tumeur [tymœr] nf tumour.

tumulte [tymylt] nm 1. (désordre) hubbub. 2. littéraire (trouble) tumult.

tunique [tynik] nf tunic.

Tunisie [tynizi] nf: la ~ Tunisia.

tunisien, -enne [tynizjɛ̃, ɛn] adj Tunisian. ▶ **Tunisien, -enne** nm, f Tunisian.

tunnel [tynɛl] *nm* tunnel; **le ~ sous la Manche** the Channel Tunnel.

LE TUNNEL SOUS LA MANCHE
The Channel Tunnel beneath the English Channel connects Coquelles near Calais and Cheriton near Folkestone. Vehicles are transported on a train known as 'Le Shuttle' and there is also a regular passenger service linking London with Paris, Lille and Brussels, on the 'Eurostar' train.

---

turban [tyrbɑ̃] *nm* turban.
turbine [tyrbin] *nf* turbine.
turbo [tyrbo] *nm ou nf* turbo.
turbulence [tyrbylɑ̃s] *nf* (MÉTÉOR) turbulence.
turbulent, -e [tyrbylɑ̃, ɑ̃t] *adj* boisterous.
turc, turque [tyrk] *adj* Turkish. ▶ **turc** *nm* (*langue*) Turkish. ▶ **Turc, Turque** *nm, f* Turk.
turf [tœrf] *nm* (*activité*): **le ~** racing.
turnover [tœrnɔvœr] *nm* turnover.
turque → **turc**.
Turquie [tyrki] *nf*: **la ~** Turkey.
turquoise [tyrkwaz] *nf & adj inv* turquoise.
tutelle [tytɛl] *nf* **1.** (JUR) guardianship. **2.** (*dépendance*) supervision.
tuteur, -trice [tytœr, tris] *nm, f* guardian. ▶ **tuteur** *nm* (*pour plante*) stake.
tutoyer [tytwaje] *vt*: **~ qqn** to use the 'tu' form to sb.
tuyau, -x [tɥijo] *nm* **1.** (*conduit*) pipe; **~ d'arrosage** hosepipe; **~ d'échappement** exhaust pipe. **2.** *fam* (*renseignement*) tip.
tuyauterie [tɥijotri] *nf* piping (U), pipes (*pl*).
TV (*abr de* **télévision**) *nf* TV.
TVA (*abr de* **taxe à la valeur ajoutée**) *nf* = VAT.
tweed [twid] *nm* tweed.
tympan [tɛ̃pɑ̃] *nm* (ANAT) eardrum.
type [tip] ◆ *nm* **1.** (*exemple caractéristique*) perfect example. **2.** (*genre*) type. **3.** *fam* (*individu*) guy, bloke. ◆ *adj inv* (*caractéristique*) typical.
typhoïde [tifɔid] *nf* typhoid.
typhon [tifɔ̃] *nm* typhoon.
typhus [tifys] *nm* typhus.
typique [tipik] *adj* typical.
typiquement [tipikmɑ̃] *adv* typically.
typographie [tipɔgrafi] *nf* typography.

tyran [tirɑ̃] *nm* tyrant.
tyrannique [tiranik] *adj* tyrannical.
tyranniser [tiranize] *vt* to tyrannize.
tzar = **tsar**.
tzigane [dzigan], **tsigane** [tsigan] *nmf* gipsy.

U

u, U [y] *nm inv* u, U.
UDF (*abr de* **Union pour la démocratie française**) *nf French political party to the right of the political spectrum*.
UE (*abr de* **Union européenne**) *nf* EU.
UFR (*abr de* **unité de formation et de recherche**) *nf* university department.
Ukraine [ykrɛn] *nf*: **l'~** the Ukraine.
ulcère [ylsɛr] *nm* ulcer.
ulcérer [ylsere] *vt* **1.** (MÉD) to ulcerate. **2.** *sout* (*mettre en colère*) to enrage.
ULM (*abr de* **ultra léger motorisé**) *nm* microlight.
ultérieur, -e [ylterjœr] *adj* later, subsequent.
ultimatum [yltimatɔm] *nm* ultimatum.
ultime [yltim] *adj* ultimate, final.
ultramoderne [yltramɔdɛrn] *adj* ultramodern.
ultrasensible [yltrasɑ̃sibl] *adj* (*personne*) ultra-sensitive; (*pellicule*) high-speed.
ultrason [yltrasɔ̃] *nm* ultrasound (U).
ultraviolet, -ette [yltravjɔlɛ, ɛt] *adj* ultraviolet. ▶ **ultraviolet** *nm* ultraviolet.
un [œ̃] (*f* **une** [yn]) ◆ *art indéf* a, an (*devant voyelle*); **~ homme** a man; **~ livre** a book; **une femme** a woman; **une pomme** an apple. ◆ *pron indéf* one; **l'~ de mes amis** one of my friends; **l'~ l'autre** each other; **les ~s les autres** one another; **l'~ ..., l'autre** one ..., the other; **les ~s ..., les autres** some ..., others; **l'~ et l'autre** both (of them); **l'~ ou l'autre** either (of them); **ni l'~ ni l'autre** neither one nor the other, neither (of them). ◆ *adj num* one; **une personne à la fois** one person at a time. ◆ *nm* one; *voir aussi* **six**. ▶ **une** *nf*: **faire la/être à la une** (PRESSE) to make the/to be on the front page.
unanime [ynanim] *adj* unanimous.

unanimité [ynanimite] *nf* unanimity; **faire l'~** to be unanimously approved; **à l'~** unanimously.

UNESCO, Unesco [ynɛsko] (*abr de* United Nations Educational, Scientific and Cultural Organization) *nf* UNESCO.

uni, -e [yni] *adj* 1. (*joint, réuni*) united. 2. (*famille, couple*) close. 3. (*surface, mer*) smooth; (*route*) even. 4. (*étoffe, robe*) plain.

UNICEF, Unicef [ynisɛf] (*abr de* United Nations International Children's Emergency Fund) *nm* UNICEF.

unifier [ynifje] *vt* 1. (*régions, parti*) to unify. 2. (*programmes*) to standardize.

uniforme [ynifɔrm] ◆ *adj* uniform; (*régulier*) regular. ◆ *nm* uniform.

uniformiser [ynifɔrmize] *vt* 1. (*couleur*) to make uniform. 2. (*programmes, lois*) to standardize.

unilatéral, -e, -aux [ynilateral, o] *adj* unilateral; **stationnement ~** parking on only one side of the street.

union [ynjɔ̃] *nf* 1. (*de couleurs*) blending. 2. (*mariage*) union; **~ libre** cohabitation. 3. (*de pays*) union; (*de syndicats*) confederation; **Union européenne** European Union. 4. (*entente*) unity. ▶ **Union soviétique** *nf*: **l'(ex-)Union soviétique** the (former) Soviet Union.

unique [ynik] *adj* 1. (*seul - enfant, veston*) only; (*- préoccupation*) sole. 2. (*principe, prix*) single. 3. (*exceptionnel*) unique.

uniquement [ynikmɑ̃] *adv* 1. (*exclusivement*) only, solely. 2. (*seulement*) only, just.

unir [ynir] *vt* 1. (*assembler - mots, qualités*) to put together, to combine; (*- pays*) to unite; **~ qqch à** (*pays*) to unite sthg with; (*mot, qualité*) to combine sthg with. 2. (*réunir - partis, familles*) to unite. 3. (*marier*) to unite, to join in marriage. ▶ **s'unir** *vp* 1. (*s'associer*) to unite, to join together. 2. (*se marier*) to be joined in marriage.

unitaire [yniter] *adj* (*à l'unité*): **prix ~** unit price.

unité [ynite] *nf* 1. (*cohésion*) unity. 2. (COMM, MATHS & MIL) unit. ▶ **unité centrale** *nf* (INFORM) central processing unit.

univers [yniver] *nm* universe; *fig* world.

universel, -elle [yniversɛl] *adj* universal.

universitaire [yniversiter] ◆ *adj* university (*avant n*). ◆ *nmf* academic.

université [yniversite] *nf* university.

uranium [yranjɔm] *nm* uranium.

urbain, -e [yrbɛ̃, ɛn] *adj* 1. (*de la ville*) urban. 2. *littéraire* (*affable*) urbane.

urbaniser [yrbanize] *vt* to urbanize.

urbanisme [yrbanism] *nm* town planning.

urgence [yrʒɑ̃s] *nf* 1. (*de mission*) urgency. 2. (MÉD) emergency; **(service des) ~s** accident and emergency department (*sg*) Br, emergency room (*sg*) Am. ▶ **d'urgence** *loc adv* immediately.

urgent, -e [yrʒɑ̃, ɑ̃t] *adj* urgent.

urine [yrin] *nf* urine.

uriner [yrine] *vi* to urinate.

urinoir [yrinwar] *nm* urinal.

urne [yrn] *nf* 1. (*vase*) urn. 2. (*de vote*) ballot box.

URSS (*abr de* Union des républiques socialistes soviétiques) *nf*: **l'(ex-)~** the (former) USSR.

urticaire [yrtiker] *nf* urticaria, hives (*pl*).

Uruguay [yrygwɛ] *nm*: **l'~** Uruguay.

USA (*abr de* United States of America) *nmpl* USA.

usage [yzaʒ] *nm* 1. (*gén*) use; **à ~ externe/interne** for external/internal use; **hors d'~** out of action. 2. (*coutume*) custom. 3. (LING) usage.

usagé, -e [yzaʒe] *adj* worn, old.

usager [yzaʒe] *nm* user.

usé, -e [yze] *adj* 1. (*détérioré*) worn; **eaux ~es** waste water (*sg*). 2. (*personne*) worn-out. 3. (*plaisanterie*) hackneyed, well-worn.

user [yze] ◆ *vt* 1. (*consommer*) to use. 2. (*vêtement*) to wear out. 3. (*forces*) to use up; (*santé*) to ruin; (*personne*) to wear out. ◆ *vi* (*se servir*): **~ de** (*charme*) to use; (*droit, privilège*) to exercise. ▶ **s'user** *vp* 1. (*chaussure*) to wear out. 2. (*amour*) to burn itself out.

usine [yzin] *nf* factory.

usiner [yzine] *vt* 1. (*façonner*) to machine. 2. (*fabriquer*) to manufacture.

usité, -e [yzite] *adj* in common use; **très/peu ~** commonly/rarely used.

ustensile [ystɑ̃sil] *nm* implement, tool.

usuel, -elle [yzɥɛl] *adj* common, usual.

usufruit [yzyfrɥi] *nm* usufruct.

usure [yzyr] *nf* 1. (*de vêtement, meuble*) wear. 2. (*intérêt*) usury.

usurier, -ère [yzyrje, ɛr] *nm, f* usurer.

usurpateur, -trice [yzyrpatœr, tris] *nm, f* usurper.

usurper [yzyrpe] *vt* to usurp.

ut [yt] *nm inv* C.

utérus [yterys] *nm* uterus, womb.

utile [ytil] *adj* useful; **être ~ à qqn** to be useful ou of help to sb, to help sb.

utilisateur, -trice [ytilizatœr, tris] *nm, f* user.

utilisation [ytilizasjɔ̃] *nf* use.

utiliser [ytilize] *vt* to use.

utilitaire [ytiliter] ♦ *adj* (*pratique*) utilitarian; (*véhicule*) commercial. ♦ *nm* (INFORM) utility (program).

utilité [ytilite] *nf* 1. (*usage*) usefulness. 2. (JUR): **entreprise d'~ publique** public utility; **organisme d'~ publique** registered charity.

utopie [ytɔpi] *nf* 1. (*idéal*) utopia. 2. (*projet irréalisable*) unrealistic idea.

utopiste [ytɔpist] *nmf* utopian.

UV ♦ *nf* (abr de **unité de valeur**) university course unit, = credit. ♦ (abr de **ultraviolet**) UV.

v, V [ve] *nm inv* v, V.

v. 1. (abr de **vers**) (LITTÉRATURE) v. 2. (abr de **verset**) v. 3. (abr de **vers**) (*environ*) approx.

va [va] ♦ → **aller**. ♦ *interj*: **courage, ~!** come on, cheer up!; **~ donc!** come on!; **~ pour 50 francs/demain** OK, let's say 50 francs/tomorrow.

vacance [vakɑ̃s] *nf* vacancy. ▶ **vacances** *nfpl* holiday (*sg*) Br, vacation (*sg*) Am; **être/partir en ~s** to be/go on holiday; **les grandes ~s** the summer holidays.

vacancier, -ère [vakɑ̃sje, ɛr] *nm, f* holiday-maker Br, vacationer Am.

vacant, -e [vakɑ̃, ɑ̃t] *adj* (*poste*) vacant; (*logement*) vacant, unoccupied.

vacarme [vakarm] *nm* racket, din.

vacataire [vakater] ♦ *adj* (*employé*) temporary. ♦ *nmf* temporary worker.

vacation [vakasjɔ̃] *nf* (*d'expert*) session.

vaccin [vaksɛ̃] *nm* vaccine.

vaccination [vaksinasjɔ̃] *nf* vaccination.

vacciner [vaksine] *vt*: **~ qqn (contre)** (MÉD) to vaccinate sb (against); *fam fig*

to make sb immune (to).

vache [vaʃ] ♦ *nf* 1. (ZOOL) cow. 2. (*cuir*) cowhide. 3. *fam péj* (*femme*) cow; (*homme*) pig. ♦ *adj fam* rotten.

vachement [vaʃmɑ̃] *adv fam* bloody Br, dead Br, real Am.

vacherin [vaʃrɛ̃] *nm* (*dessert*) meringue filled with ice cream and whipped cream.

vaciller [vasije] *vi* 1. (*jambes, fondations*) to shake; (*lumière*) to flicker; **~ sur ses jambes** to be unsteady on one's legs. 2. (*mémoire, santé*) to fail.

va-et-vient [vaevjɛ̃] *nm inv* 1. (*de personnes*) comings and goings (*pl*), toing and froing. 2. (*de balancier*) to-and-fro movement. 3. (ÉLECTR) two-way switch.

vagabond, -e [vagabɔ̃, ɔ̃d] ♦ *adj* 1. (*chien*) stray; (*vie*) vagabond (*avant n*). 2. (*humeur*) restless. ♦ *nm, f* (*rôdeur*) vagrant, tramp; *littéraire* (*voyageur*) wanderer.

vagabondage [vagabɔ̃daʒ] *nm* (*délit*) vagrancy; (*errance*) wandering, roaming.

vagin [vaʒɛ̃] *nm* vagina.

vagissement [vaʒismɑ̃] *nm* cry, wail.

vague [vag] ♦ *adj* 1. (*idée, promesse*) vague. 2. (*vêtement*) loose-fitting. 3. (*avant n*) (*quelconque*): **il a un ~ travail dans un bureau** he has some job or other in an office. 4. (*avant n*) (*cousin*) distant. ♦ *nf* wave; **une ~ de froid** a cold spell; **~ de chaleur** heatwave.

vaguement [vagmɑ̃] *adv* vaguely.

vaillant, -e [vajɑ̃, ɑ̃t] *adj* 1. (*enfant, vieillard*) hale and hearty. 2. *littéraire* (*héros*) valiant.

vain, -e [vɛ̃, vɛn] *adj* 1. (*inutile*) vain, useless; **en ~** in vain, to no avail. 2. *littéraire* (*vaniteux*) vain.

vaincre [vɛ̃kr] *vt* 1. (*ennemi*) to defeat. 2. (*obstacle, peur*) to overcome.

vaincu, -e [vɛ̃ky] ♦ *pp* → **vaincre**. ♦ *adj* defeated. ♦ *nm, f* defeated person.

vainement [vɛnmɑ̃] *adv* vainly.

vainqueur [vɛ̃kœr] ♦ *nm* 1. (*de combat*) conqueror, victor. 2. (SPORT) winner. ♦ *adj m* victorious, conquering.

vais → **aller**.

vaisseau, -x [vɛso] *nm* 1. (NAVIG) vessel, ship; **~ spatial** (AÉRON) spaceship. 2. (ANAT) vessel. 3. (ARCHIT) nave.

vaisselle [vɛsɛl] *nf* crockery; **faire** ou **laver la ~** to do the dishes, to wash up.

val [val] (*pl* **vals** ou **vaux** [vo]) *nm* valley.

valable [valabl] *adj* 1. (*passeport*) valid. 2. (*raison, excuse*) valid, legitimate.

3. (*œuvre*) good, worthwhile.
valet [valɛ] *nm* **1.** (*serviteur*) servant. **2.** (CARTES) jack, knave.
valeur [valœr] *nf* **1.** (*gén & MUS*) value; **avoir de la ~** to be valuable; **mettre en ~** (*talents*) to bring out; **~ ajoutée** (ÉCON) added value; **de (grande) ~** (*chose*) (very) valuable. **2.** (*gén pl*) (BOURSE) stocks and shares (*pl*), securities (*pl*). **3.** (*mérite*) worth, merit. **4.** *fig* (*importance*) value, importance. **5.** (*equivalent*): **la ~ de** the equivalent of.
valide [valid] *adj* **1.** (*personne - bien portant*) fit; (*- non blessé*) able-bodied; (*membre*) good. **2.** (*contrat*) valid.
valider [valide] *vt* to validate, to authenticate.
validité [validite] *nf* validity.
valise [valiz] *nf* case, suitcase; **faire sa ~/ses ~s** to pack one's case/cases; *fam fig* (*partir*) to pack one's bags.
vallée [vale] *nf* valley.
vallon [valɔ̃] *nm* small valley.
vallonné, -e [valɔne] *adj* undulating.
valoir [valwar] ◆ *vi* **1.** (*gén*) to be worth; **ça vaut combien?** how much is it?; **ne rien ~** not to be any good, to be worthless; **ça vaut mieux** *fam* that's best; **mieux vaut** ou **il vaut mieux lui dire** it's better to tell him; **ça ne vaut pas la peine** it's not worth it; **faire ~** (*vues*) to assert; (*talent*) to show. **2.** (*règle*): **~ pour** to apply to, to hold good for. ◆ *vt* (*médaille, gloire*) to bring, to earn. ◆ *v impers*: **il vaudrait mieux que nous partions** it would be better if we left, we'd better leave. ▶ **se valoir** *vp* to be equally good/bad.
valoriser [valɔrize] *vt* (*immeuble, région*) to develop; (*individu, société*) to improve the image of.
valse [vals] *nf* waltz.
valser [valse] *vi* to waltz; **envoyer ~ qqch** *fam fig* to send sthg flying.
valu [valy] *pp inv* → **valoir**.
valve [valv] *nf* valve.
vampire [vãpir] *nm* **1.** (*fantôme*) vampire. **2.** (ZOOL) vampire bat.
vandalisme [vãdalism] *nm* vandalism.
vanille [vanij] *nf* vanilla.
vanillé, -e [vanije] *adj* vanilla-flavoured.
vanité [vanite] *nf* vanity.
vaniteux, -euse [vanitø, øz] *adj* vain, conceited.
vanne [van] *nf* **1.** (*d'écluse*) lockgate. **2.** *fam* (*remarque*) gibe.

vannerie [vanri] *nf* basketwork, wickerwork.
vantard, -e [vãtar, ard] ◆ *adj* bragging, boastful. ◆ *nm, f* boaster.
vanter [vãte] *vt* to vaunt. ▶ **se vanter** *vp* to boast, to brag; **se ~ de faire qqch** to boast ou brag about doing sthg.
va-nu-pieds [vanypje] *nmf inv* *fam* beggar.
vapeur [vapœr] *nf* **1.** (*d'eau*) steam; **à la ~** steamed. **2.** (*émanation*) vapour. ▶ **vapeurs** *nfpl* **1.** (*malaise*): **avoir ses ~s** to have the vapours. **2.** (*émanations*) fumes.
vapocuiseur [vapɔkɥizœr] *nm* pressure cooker.
vaporisateur [vapɔrizatœr] *nm* **1.** (*atomiseur*) spray, atomizer. **2.** (IND) vaporizer.
vaporiser [vapɔrize] *vt* **1.** (*parfum, déodorant*) to spray. **2.** (PHYS) to vaporize.
vaquer [vake] *vi*: **~ à** to see to, to attend to.
varappe [varap] *nf* rock climbing.
variable [varjabl] ◆ *adj* **1.** (*temps*) changeable. **2.** (*distance, résultats*) varied, varying. **3.** (*température*) variable. ◆ *nf* variable.
variante [varjãt] *nf* variant.
variateur [varjatœr] *nm* (ÉLECTR) dimmer switch.
variation [varjasjɔ̃] *nf* variation.
varice [varis] *nf* varicose vein.
varicelle [varisɛl] *nf* chickenpox.
varié, -e [varje] *adj* **1.** (*divers*) various. **2.** (*non monotone*) varied, varying.
varier [varje] *vt & vi* to vary.
variété [varjete] *nf* variety. ▶ **variétés** *nfpl* variety show (*sg*).
variole [varjɔl] *nf* smallpox.
Varsovie [varsɔvi] *n* Warsaw; **le pacte de ~** the Warsaw Pact.
vas → **aller**.
vase [vaz] ◆ *nm* vase; **en ~ clos** *fig* in isolation. ◆ *nf* mud, silt.
vaseline [vazlin] *nf* Vaseline®, petroleum jelly.
vaseux, -euse [vazø, øz] *adj* (*fond*) muddy.
vaste [vast] *adj* vast, immense.
Vatican [vatikã] *nm*: **le ~** the Vatican.
vaudrait → **valoir**.
vaut → **valoir**.
vautour [votur] *nm* vulture.
vd *abr de* **vend**.
veau, -x [vo] *nm* **1.** (*animal*) calf. **2.** (*viande*) veal. **3.** (*peau*) calfskin.

vecteur [vɛktœr] nm 1. (GÉOM) vector. 2. (intermédiaire) vehicle; (MÉD) carrier.

vécu, -e [veky] ♦ pp → **vivre**. ♦ adj real.

vedette [vədɛt] nf 1. (NAVIG) patrol boat. 2. (star) star.

végétal, -e, -aux [veʒetal, o] adj (huile) vegetable (avant n); (cellule, fibre) plant (avant n).

végétalien, -enne [veʒetaljɛ̃, ɛn] adj & nm, f vegan.

végétarien, -enne [veʒetarjɛ̃, ɛn] adj & nm, f vegetarian.

végétation [veʒetasjɔ̃] nf vegetation. ▶ **végétations** nfpl adenoids.

végéter [veʒete] vi to vegetate.

véhémence [veemɑ̃s] nf vehemence.

véhicule [veikyl] nm vehicle.

veille [vɛj] nf 1. (jour précédent) day before, eve; **la ~ de mon anniversaire** the day before my birthday; **la ~ de Noël** Christmas Eve. 2. (éveil) wakefulness; (privation de sommeil) sleeplessness.

veillée [veje] nf 1. (soirée) evening. 2. (de mort) watch.

veiller [veje] ♦ vi 1. (rester éveillé) to stay up. 2. (rester vigilant): **~ à qqch** to look after sthg; **~ à faire qqch** to see that sthg is done; **~ sur** to watch over. ♦ vt to sit up with.

veilleur [vejœr] nm: **~ de nuit** night watchman.

veilleuse [vejøz] nf 1. (lampe) nightlight. 2. (AUTOM) sidelight. 3. (de chauffe-eau) pilot light.

veinard, -e [vɛnar, ard] fam ♦ adj lucky. ♦ nm, f lucky devil.

veine [vɛn] nf 1. (gén) vein. 2. (de bois) grain. 3. fam (chance) luck.

veineux, -euse [venø, øz] adj 1. (ANAT) venous. 2. (marbre) veined; (bois) grainy.

véliplanchiste [veliplɑ̃ʃist] nmf windsurfer.

velléité [veleite] nf whim.

vélo [velo] nm fam bike; **aller à ~** to go by bike, to cycle; **faire du ~** to go cycling.

vélocité [velɔsite] nf swiftness, speed.

vélodrome [velɔdrom] nm velodrome.

vélomoteur [velɔmɔtœr] nm light motorcycle.

velours [vəlur] nm velvet.

velouté, -e [vəlute] adj velvety. ▶ **velouté** nm 1. (de peau) velvetiness. 2. (potage) cream soup.

velu, -e [vəly] adj hairy.

vénal, -e, -aux [venal, o] adj venal.

vendange [vɑ̃dɑ̃ʒ] nf 1. (récolte) grape harvest, wine harvest. 2. (période): **les ~s** (grape) harvest time (sg).

vendanger [vɑ̃dɑ̃ʒe] vi to harvest the grapes.

vendeur, -euse [vɑ̃dœr, øz] nm, f salesman (f saleswoman).

vendre [vɑ̃dr] vt to sell; **'à ~'** 'for sale'.

vendredi [vɑ̃drədi] nm Friday; **Vendredi Saint** Good Friday; voir aussi **samedi**.

vendu, -e [vɑ̃dy] ♦ pp → **vendre**. ♦ adj 1. (cédé) sold. 2. (corrompu) corrupt. ♦ nm, f traitor.

vénéneux, -euse [venenø, øz] adj poisonous.

vénérable [venerabl] adj venerable.

vénération [venerasjɔ̃] nf veneration, reverence.

vénérer [venere] vt to venerate, to revere.

vénérien, -enne [venerjɛ̃, ɛn] adj venereal.

Venezuela [venezɥela] nm: **le ~** Venezuela.

vengeance [vɑ̃ʒɑ̃s] nf vengeance.

venger [vɑ̃ʒe] vt to avenge. ▶ **se venger** vp to get one's revenge; **se ~ de qqn** to take revenge on sb; **se ~ de qqch** to take revenge for sthg; **se ~ sur** to take it out on.

vengeur, vengeresse [vɑ̃ʒœr, vɑ̃ʒrɛs] ♦ adj vengeful. ♦ nm, f avenger.

venimeux, -euse [vənimø, øz] adj venomous.

venin [vənɛ̃] nm venom.

venir [vənir] vi to come; (plante, arbre) to come on; **~ de** (personne, mot) to come from; (échec) to be due to; **~ de faire qqch** to have just done sthg; **je viens de la voir** I've just seen her; **s'il venait à mourir ...** if he was to die ...; **où veux-tu en ~?** what are you getting at?; **dans les années à ~** in the coming years.

vent [vɑ̃] nm wind; **il fait** ou **il y a du ~** it's windy.

vente [vɑ̃t] nf 1. (cession, transaction) sale; **en ~** on sale; **en ~ libre** available over the counter; **~ par correspondance** mail order. 2. (technique) selling.

venteux, -euse [vɑ̃tø, øz] adj windy.

ventilateur [vɑ̃tilatœr] nm fan.

ventilation [vɑ̃tilasjɔ̃] nf 1. (de pièce) ventilation. 2. (FIN) breakdown.

ventouse [vɑ̃tuz] nf 1. (de caoutchouc) suction pad; (d'animal) sucker. 2. (MÉD) cupping glass. 3. (TECHNOL) air vent.

ventre [vãtr] *nm* (*de personne*) stomach; **avoir/prendre du ~** to have/be getting (a bit of) a paunch; **à plat ~** flat on one's stomach.

ventriloque [vãtrilɔk] *nmf* ventriloquist.

venu, -e [vəny] ♦ *pp →* **venir.** ♦ *adj:* **bien ~** welcome; **mal ~** unwelcome; **il serait mal ~ de faire cela** it would be improper to do that. ♦ *nm, f:* **nouveau ~** newcomer. ► **venue** *nf* coming, arrival.

vêpres [vɛpr] *nfpl* vespers.

ver [vɛr] *nm* worm.

véracité [verasite] *nf* truthfulness.

véranda [verãda] *nf* veranda.

verbal, -e, -aux [vɛrbal, o] *adj* 1. (*promesse, violence*) verbal. 2. (GRAM) verb (*avant n*).

verbaliser [vɛrbalize] ♦ *vt* to verbalize. ♦ *vi* to make out a report.

verbe [vɛrb] *nm* (GRAM) verb.

verdeur [vɛrdœr] *nf* 1. (*de personne*) vigour, vitality. 2. (*de langage*) crudeness.

verdict [vɛrdikt] *nm* verdict.

verdir [vɛrdir] *vt & vi* to turn green.

verdoyant, -e [vɛrdwajã, ãt] *adj* green.

verdure [vɛrdyr] *nf* 1. (*végétation*) greenery. 2. *fam* (*salade*) salad stuff.

véreux, -euse [verø, øz] *adj* worm-eaten, maggoty; *fig* shady.

verge [vɛrʒ] *nf* 1. (ANAT) penis. 2. *littéraire* (*baguette*) rod, stick.

verger [vɛrʒe] *nm* orchard.

vergeture [vɛrʒətyr] *nf* stretchmark.

verglas [vɛrgla] *nm* (black) ice.

véridique [veridik] *adj* truthful.

vérification [verifikasjɔ̃] *nf* (*contrôle*) check, checking.

vérifier [verifje] *vt* 1. (*contrôler*) to check. 2. (*confirmer*) to prove, to confirm.

véritable [veritabl] *adj* real; (*ami*) true.

vérité [verite] *nf* 1. (*chose vraie, réalité, principe*) truth (U). 2. (*sincérité*) sincerity. ► **en vérité** *loc adv* actually, really.

vermeil, -eille [vɛrmɛj] *adj* scarlet. ► **vermeil** *nm* silver-gilt.

vermicelle [vɛrmisɛl] *nm* vermicelli (U).

vermillon [vɛrmijɔ̃] *nm & adj inv* vermilion.

vermine [vɛrmin] *nf* (*parasites*) vermin.

vermoulu, -e [vɛrmuly] *adj* riddled with woodworm; *fig* moth-eaten.

verni, -e [vɛrni] *adj* 1. (*bois*) varnished. 2. (*souliers*): **chaussures ~es** patent-leather shoes. 3. *fam* (*chanceux*) lucky.

vernir [vɛrnir] *vt* to varnish.

vernis [vɛrni] *nm* varnish; *fig* veneer; **~ à ongles** nail polish ou varnish.

vernissage [vɛrnisaʒ] *nm* 1. (*de meuble*) varnishing. 2. (*d'exposition*) private viewing.

verre [vɛr] *nm* 1. (*matière, récipient*) glass; (*quantité*) glassful, glass; **~ dépoli** frosted glass. 2. (*optique*) lens; **~s de contact** contact lenses. 3. (*boisson*) drink; **boire un ~** to have a drink; **vin au ~** wine by the glass.

verrière [vɛrjɛr] *nf* (*toit*) glass roof.

verrou [vɛru] *nm* bolt.

verrouillage [vɛrujaʒ] *nm* (AUTOM): **~ central** central locking.

verrouiller [vɛruje] *vt* 1. (*porte*) to bolt. 2. (*personne*) to lock up.

verrue [vɛry] *nf* wart; **~ plantaire** verruca.

vers¹ [vɛr] ♦ *nm* line. ♦ *nmpl:* **en ~** in verse; **faire des ~** to write poetry.

vers² [vɛr] *prép* 1. (*dans la direction de*) towards. 2. (*aux environs de - temporel*) around, about; (*- spatial*) near; **~ la fin du mois** towards the end of the month.

Versailles [vɛrsaj] *n* Versailles.

VERSAILLES

Originally a hunting lodge used by Louis XIII, Versailles was transformed in the middle of the 17th century by Louis XIV into an imposing royal palace with architecture along classical lines. It is famous for the 'galerie des Glaces', a 75-metre long room with mirrors on the walls, and its elaborate gardens with ornamental fountains and pools.

---

versant [vɛrsã] *nm* side.

versatile [vɛrsatil] *adj* changeable, fickle.

verse [vɛrs] ► **à verse** *loc adv:* **pleuvoir à ~** to pour down.

Verseau [vɛrso] *nm* (ASTROL) Aquarius.

versement [vɛrsəmã] *nm* payment.

verser [vɛrse] ♦ *vt* 1. (*eau*) to pour; (*larmes, sang*) to shed. 2. (*argent*) to pay. ♦ *vi* to overturn, to tip over.

verset [vɛrsɛ] *nm* verse.

version [vɛrsjɔ̃] *nf* 1. (*gén*) version; **~ française/originale** French/original version. 2. (*traduction*) translation (*into mother tongue*).

verso [vɛrso] *nm* back.

vert, -e [vɛr, vɛrt] *adj* 1. (*couleur, fruit, légume, bois*) green. 2. *fig* (*vieillard*) spry, sprightly. 3. (*réprimande*) sharp. 4. (à la

campagne): **le tourisme** ~ country holidays (*pl*). ▶ **vert** *nm* (*couleur*) green.
▶ **Verts** *nmpl*: **les Verts** (POLIT) the Greens.

vertébral, -e, -aux [vertebral, o] *adj* vertebral.

vertèbre [vertebr] *nf* vertebra.

vertement [vertəmã] *adv* sharply.

vertical, -e, -aux [vertikal, o] *adj* vertical. ▶ **verticale** *nf* vertical; **à la ~e** (*descente*) vertical; (*descendre*) vertically.

vertige [vertiʒ] *nm* 1. (*peur du vide*) vertigo. 2. (*étourdissement*) dizziness; *fig* intoxication; **avoir des ~s** to suffer from ou have dizzy spells.

vertigineux, -euse [vertiʒinø, øz] *adj* 1. *fig* (*vue, vitesse*) breathtaking. 2. (*hauteur*) dizzy.

vertu [verty] *nf* 1. (*morale, chasteté*) virtue. 2. (*pouvoir*) properties (*pl*), power.

vertueux, -euse [vertyø, øz] *adj* virtuous.

verve [verv] *nf* eloquence.

vésicule [vezikyl] *nf* vesicle.

vessie [vesi] *nf* bladder.

veste [vest] *nf* (*vêtement*) jacket; ~ **croisée/droite** double-/single-breasted jacket.

vestiaire [vestjer] *nm* 1. (*au théâtre*) cloakroom. 2. (*gén pl*) (SPORT) changing-room, locker-room.

vestibule [vestibyl] *nm* (*pièce*) hall, vestibule.

vestige [vestiʒ] *nm* (*gén pl*) (*de ville*) remains (*pl*); *fig* (*de civilisation, grandeur*) vestiges (*pl*), relic.

vestimentaire [vestimãter] *adj* (*industrie*) clothing (*avant n*); (*dépense*) on clothes; **détail ~** accessory.

veston [vestɔ̃] *nm* jacket.

vêtement [vetmã] *nm* garment, article of clothing; **~s** clothing (U), clothes; **~s de dessus** outer garments.

vétéran [veterã] *nm* veteran.

vétérinaire [veteriner] *nmf* vet, veterinary surgeon.

vêtir [vetir] *vt* to dress. ▶ **se vêtir** *vp* to dress, to get dressed.

veto [veto] *nm inv* veto; **mettre son ~ à qqch** to veto sthg.

vêtu, -e [vety] ◆ *pp* → **vêtir**. ◆ *adj*: **~ (de)** dressed (in).

vétuste [vetyst] *adj* dilapidated.

veuf, veuve [vœf, vœv] ◆ *adj* widowed. ◆ *nm, f* widower (*f* widow).

veuille *etc* → **vouloir**.

veut → **vouloir**.

veuvage [vœvaʒ] *nm* (*de femme*) widowhood; (*d'homme*) widowerhood.

veuve → **veuf**.

veux → **vouloir**.

vexation [veksasjɔ̃] *nf* (*humiliation*) insult.

vexer [vekse] *vt* to offend. ▶ **se vexer** *vp* to take offence.

VF (*abr de* **version française**) *nf* indicates that a film has been dubbed into French.

via [vja] *prép* via.

viabiliser [vjabilize] *vt* to service.

viable [vjabl] *adj* viable.

viaduc [vjadyk] *nm* viaduct.

viager, -ère [vjaʒe, er] *adj* life (*avant n*). ▶ **viager** *nm* life annuity.

viande [vjãd] *nf* meat.

vibration [vibrasjɔ̃] *nf* vibration.

vibrer [vibre] *vi* 1. (*trembler*) to vibrate. 2. *fig* (*être ému*): **~ (de)** to be stirred (with).

vice [vis] *nm* 1. (*de personne*) vice. 2. (*d'objet*) fault, defect.

vice-président, -e [visprezidã, ãt] (*mpl* **vice-présidents**, *fpl* **vice-présidentes**) *nm, f* (POLIT) vice-president; (*de société*) vice-chairman (*f* vice-chairwoman).

vice versa [visversa] *loc adv* vice versa.

vicié, -e [visje] *adj* (*air*) polluted, tainted.

vicieux, -euse [visjø, øz] *adj* 1. (*personne, conduite*) perverted, depraved. 2. (*animal*) restive. 3. (*attaque*) underhand.

victime [viktim] *nf* victim; (*blessé*) casualty.

victoire [viktwar] *nf* (MIL) victory; (POLIT & SPORT) win, victory.

victorieux, -euse [viktɔrjø, øz] *adj* 1. (MIL) victorious; (POLIT & SPORT) winning (*avant n*), victorious. 2. (*air*) triumphant.

victuailles [viktɥaj] *nfpl* provisions.

vidange [vidãʒ] *nf* 1. (*action*) emptying, draining. 2. (AUTOM) oil change. 3. (*mécanisme*) waste outlet. ▶ **vidanges** *nfpl* sewage (U).

vidanger [vidãʒe] *vt* to empty, to drain.

vide [vid] ◆ *nm* 1. (*espace*) void; *fig* (*néant, manque*) emptiness. 2. (*absence d'air*) vacuum; **conditionné sous ~** vacuum-packed. 3. (*ouverture*) gap, space. ◆ *adj* empty.

vidéo [video] ◆ *nf* video. ◆ *adj inv* video (*avant n*).

vidéocassette [videokaset] *nf* video cassette.

vin

vidéodisque [videɔdisk] *nm* video-disc.

vide-ordures [vidɔrdyr] *nm inv* rubbish chute.

vidéothèque [videɔtɛk] *nf* video library.

vide-poches [vidpɔʃ] *nm inv* (*de voiture*) glove compartment.

vider [vide] *vt* 1. (*rendre vide*) to empty. 2. (*évacuer*): ~ **les lieux** to vacate the premises. 3. (*poulet*) to clean. 4. *fam* (*personne - épuiser*) to drain; (*- expulser*) to chuck out. ▶ **se vider** *vp* 1. (*eaux*): **se ~ dans** to empty into, to drain into. 2. (*baignoire, salle*) to empty.

videur [vidœr] *nm* bouncer.

vie [vi] *nf* 1. (*gén*) life; **sauver la ~ à qqn** to save sb's life; **être en ~** to be alive; **à ~ for life**. 2. (*subsistance*) cost of living; **gagner sa ~** to earn one's living.

vieil → **vieux**.

vieillard [vjejar] *nm* old man.

vieille → **vieux**.

vieillerie [vjɛjri] *nf* (*objet*) old thing.

vieillesse [vjɛjɛs] *nf* (*fin de la vie*) old age.

vieillir [vjejir] ◆ *vi* 1. (*personne*) to grow old, to age. 2. (CULIN) to mature, to age. 3. (*tradition, idée*) to become dated ou outdated. ◆ *vt* 1. (*suj: coiffure, vêtement*): ~ **qqn** to make sb look older. 2. (*suj: personne*): **ils m'ont vieilli de cinq ans** they said I was five years older than I actually am.

vieillissement [vjejismã] *nm* (*de personne*) ageing.

Vienne [vjɛn] *n* (*en Autriche*) Vienna.

vierge [vjɛrʒ] ◆ *nf* virgin; **la (Sainte) Vierge** the Virgin (Mary). ◆ *adj* 1. (*personne*) virgin. 2. (*terre*) virgin; (*page*) blank; (*casier judiciaire*) clean. ▶ **Vierge** *nf* (ASTROL) Virgo.

Viêt-nam [vjɛtnam] *nm*: **le ~** Vietnam.

vietnamien, -enne [vjɛtnamjɛ̃, ɛn] *adj* Vietnamese. ▶ **vietnamien** *nm* (*langue*) Vietnamese. ▶ **Vietnamien, -enne** *nm, f* Vietnamese person.

vieux, vieille [vjø, vjɛj] ◆ *adj* (*vieil devant voyelle ou h muet*) old; ~ **jeu** old-fashioned. ◆ *nm, f* 1. (*personne âgée*) old man (*f* woman); **les ~** the old. 2. *fam* (*ami*): **mon ~** old chap ou boy *Br*, old buddy *Am*; **ma vieille** old girl.

vif, vive [vif, viv] *adj* 1. (*preste - enfant*) lively; (*- imagination*) vivid. 2. (*couleur, œil*) bright; **rouge/jaune ~** bright red/yellow. 3. (*reproche*) sharp; (*discussion*) bitter. 4. *sout* (*vivant*) alive. 5. (*douleur, déception*) acute; (*intérêt*) keen; (*amour, haine*) intense, deep. ▶ **à vif** *loc adj* (*plaie*) open; **j'ai les nerfs à ~** *fig* my nerves are frayed.

vigie [viʒi] *nf* (NAVIG - *personne*) lookout; (*- poste*) crow's nest.

vigilant, -e [viʒilɑ̃, ɑ̃t] *adj* vigilant, watchful.

vigile [viʒil] *nm* watchman.

vigne [viɲ] *nf* 1. (*plante*) vine, grapevine. 2. (*plantation*) vineyard. ▶ **vigne vierge** *nf* Virginia creeper.

vigneron, -onne [viɲrɔ̃, ɔn] *nm, f* wine grower.

vignette [viɲɛt] *nf* 1. (*timbre*) label; (*de médicament*) price sticker (*for reimbursement by the social security services*); (AUTOM) tax disc *Br*, license sticker *Am*. 2. (*motif*) vignette.

vignoble [viɲɔbl] *nm* 1. (*plantation*) vineyard. 2. (*vignes*) vineyards (*pl*).

vigoureux, -euse [vigurø, øz] *adj* (*corps, personne*) vigorous; (*bras, sentiment*) strong.

vigueur [vigœr] *nf* vigour. ▶ **en vigueur** *loc adj* in force.

vilain, -e [vilɛ̃, ɛn] *adj* 1. (*gén*) nasty. 2. (*laid*) ugly.

vilebrequin [vilbrəkɛ̃] *nm* 1. (*outil*) brace and bit. 2. (AUTOM) crankshaft.

villa [vila] *nf* villa.

village [vilaʒ] *nm* village.

villageois, -e [vilaʒwa, az] *nm, f* villager.

ville [vil] *nf* (*petite, moyenne*) town; (*importante*) city; **aller en ~** to go into town; **habiter en ~** to live in town; ~ **d'eau** spa (town).

villégiature [vileʒjatyr] *nf* holiday.

vin [vɛ̃] *nm* wine; ~ **blanc/rosé/rouge** white/rosé/red wine; ~ **chaud** mulled wine. ▶ **vin d'honneur** *nm* reception.

VIN

France is one of the biggest producers of wine in the world. In the main wine-growing areas of Burgundy, Bordeaux, the Loire and Beaujolais, both red and white wines are produced. In Alsace white wine is more common and Provence is known for its rosé wines. French wine is classified according to four categories, the names of which appear on the label: 'AOC' (the highest-quality wines with the vineyard of origin identified), 'VDQS' (good-quality wine from a certain area), 'vins de pays' (table wines with the region of origin identified), and 'vins de table' (basic table wines which may be blended and have no mention of where they are produced).

vinaigre [vinεgr] *nm* vinegar.

vinaigrette [vinεgrεt] *nf* oil and vinegar dressing.

vinasse [vinas] *nf fam péj* plonk.

vindicatif, -ive [vɛ̃dikatif, iv] *adj* vindictive.

vingt [vɛ̃] *adj num & nm* twenty; *voir aussi* **six**.

vingtaine [vɛ̃tεn] *nf:* **une ~ de** about twenty.

vingtième [vɛ̃tjεm] *adj num, nm & nmf* twentieth; *voir aussi* **sixième**.

vinicole [vinikɔl] *adj* wine-growing, wine-producing.

viol [vjɔl] *nm* **1.** (*de femme*) rape. **2.** (*de sépulture*) desecration; (*de sanctuaire*) violation.

violation [vjɔlasjɔ̃] *nf* violation, breach.

violence [vjɔlɑ̃s] *nf* violence; **se faire ~** to force o.s.

violent, -e [vjɔlɑ̃, ɑ̃t] *adj* **1.** (*personne, tempête*) violent. **2.** *fig* (*douleur, angoisse, chagrin*) acute; (*haine, passion*) violent.

violer [vjɔle] *vt* **1.** (*femme*) to rape. **2.** (*loi, traité*) to break. **3.** (*sépulture*) to desecrate; (*sanctuaire*) to violate.

violet, -ette [vjɔlε, εt] *adj* purple; (*pâle*) violet. ▶ **violet** *nm* purple; (*pâle*) violet.

violette [vjɔlεt] *nf* violet.

violeur [vjɔlœr] *nm* rapist.

violon [vjɔlɔ̃] *nm* (*instrument*) violin.

violoncelle [vjɔlɔ̃sεl] *nm* (*instrument*) cello.

violoniste [vjɔlɔnist] *nmf* violinist.

vipère [vipεr] *nf* viper.

virage [viraʒ] *nm* **1.** (*sur route*) bend. **2.** (*changement*) turn.

viral, -e, -aux [viral, o] *adj* viral.

virement [virmɑ̃] *nm* (FIN) transfer; **~ bancaire/postal** bank/giro transfer.

virer [vire] ◆ *vi* **1.** (*tourner*): **~ à droite/à gauche** to turn right/left. **2.** (*étoffe*) to change colour; **~ au blanc/jaune** to go white/yellow. **3.** (MÉD) to react positively. ◆ *vt* **1.** (FIN) to transfer. **2.** *fam* (*renvoyer*) to kick out.

virevolter [virvɔlte] *vi* (*tourner*) to twirl ou spin round.

virginité [virʒinite] *nf* **1.** (*de personne*) virginity. **2.** (*de sentiment*) purity.

virgule [virgyl] *nf* (*entre mots*) comma; (*entre chiffres*) (decimal) point.

viril, -e [viril] *adj* virile.

virilité [virilite] *nf* virility.

virtuel, -elle [virtɥεl] *adj* potential.

virtuose [virtɥoz] *nmf* virtuoso.

virulence [virylɑ̃s] *nf* virulence.

virulent, -e [virylɑ̃, ɑ̃t] *adj* virulent.

virus [virys] *nm* (INFORM & MÉD) virus.

vis [vis] *nf* screw.

visa [viza] *nm* visa.

visage [vizaʒ] *nm* face.

vis-à-vis [vizavi] *nm* **1.** (*personne*) person sitting opposite. **2.** (*immeuble*): **avoir un ~** to have a building opposite. ▶ **vis-à-vis de** *loc prép* **1.** (*en face de*) opposite. **2.** (*en comparaison de*) beside, compared with. **3.** (*à l'égard de*) towards.

viscéral, -e, -aux [viseral, o] *adj* **1.** (ANAT) visceral. **2.** *fam* (*réaction*) gut (*avant n*); (*haine, peur*) deep-seated.

viscère [visεr] *nm* (*gén pl*) innards (*pl*).

viscose [viskɔz] *nf* viscose.

visé, -e [vize] *adj* **1.** (*concerné*) concerned. **2.** (*vérifié*) stamped.

visée [vize] *nf* **1.** (*avec arme*) aiming. **2.** (*gén pl*) *fig* (*intention, dessein*) aim.

viser [vize] ◆ *vt* **1.** (*cible*) to aim at. *fig* (*poste*) to aspire to, to aim for; (*personne*) to be directed ou aimed at. **3.** (*document*) to check, to stamp. ◆ *vi* to aim, to take aim; **~ à** to aim at; **~ à faire qqch** to aim to do sthg, to be intended to do sthg; **~ haut** *fig* to aim high.

viseur [vizœr] *nm* **1.** (*d'arme*) sights (*pl*). **2.** (PHOT) viewfinder.

visibilité [vizibilite] *nf* visibility.

visible [vizibl] *adj* **1.** (*gén*) visible. **2.** (*personne*): **il n'est pas ~** he's not seeing visitors.

visiblement [vizibləmɑ̃] *adv* visibly.

visière [vizjεr] *nf* **1.** (*de casque*) visor. **2.** (*de casquette*) peak. **3.** (*de protection*) eyeshade.

vision [vizjɔ̃] *nf* **1.** (*faculté*) eyesight, vision. **2.** (*représentation*) view, vision. **3.** (*mirage*) vision.

visionnaire [vizjɔnεr] *nmf & adj* visionary.

visionner [vizjɔne] *vt* to view.

visite [vizit] *nf* **1.** (*chez ami, officielle*) visit; **rendre ~ à qqn** to pay sb a visit. **2.** (MÉD - *à l'extérieur*) call, visit; (- *dans hôpital*) rounds (*pl*); **passer une ~ médicale** to have a medical. **3.** (*de monument*) tour. **4.** (*d'expert*) inspection.

visiter [vizite] *vt* **1.** (*en touriste*) to tour. **2.** (*malade, prisonnier*) to visit.

visiteur, -euse [vizitœr, øz] *nm, f* visitor.

vison [vizɔ̃] *nm* mink.

visqueux, -euse [viskø, øz] *adj* 1. (*liquide*) viscous. 2. (*surface*) sticky.

visser [vise] *vt* 1. (*planches*) to screw together. 2. (*couvercle*) to screw down. 3. (*bouchon*) to screw in; (*écrou*) to screw on.

visualiser [vizyalize] *vt* 1. (*gén*) to visualize. 2. (INFORM) to display; (TECHNOL) to make visible.

visuel, -elle [vizɥɛl] *adj* visual.

vital, -e, -aux [vital, o] *adj* vital.

vitalité [vitalite] *nf* vitality.

vitamine [vitamin] *nf* vitamin.

vitaminé, -e [vitamine] *adj* with added vitamins, vitamin-enriched.

vite [vit] *adv* 1. (*rapidement*) quickly, fast; **fais ~!** hurry up! 2. (*tôt*) soon.

vitesse [vites] *nf* 1. (*gén*) speed; **à toute ~** at top speed. 2. (AUTOM) gear.

viticole [vitikɔl] *adj* wine-growing.

viticulteur, -trice [vitikyltœr, tris] *nm, f* wine-grower.

vitrail, -aux [vitraj, o] *nm* stained-glass window.

vitre [vitr] *nf* 1. (*de fenêtre*) pane of glass, window pane; **faire les ~s** to clean the windows. 2. (*de voiture, train*) window.

vitré, -e [vitre] *adj* glass (*avant n*).

vitreux, -euse [vitrø, øz] *adj* 1. (*roche*) vitreous. 2. (*œil, regard*) glassy, glazed.

vitrine [vitrin] *nf* 1. (*de boutique*) (shop) window. 2. (*meuble*) display cabinet.

vivable [vivabl] *adj* (*appartement*) livable-in; (*situation*) bearable, tolerable; (*personne*): **il n'est pas ~** he's impossible to live with.

vivace [vivas] *adj* 1. (*plante*) perennial; (*arbre*) hardy. 2. *fig* (*haine, ressentiment*) deep-rooted, entrenched; (*souvenir*) enduring.

vivacité [vivasite] *nf* 1. (*promptitude - de personne*) liveliness, vivacity; **~ d'esprit** quick-wittedness. 2. (*de coloris, teint*) intensity, brightness. 3. (*de propos*) sharpness.

vivant, -e [vivɑ̃, ɑ̃t] *adj* 1. (*en vie*) alive, living. 2. (*enfant, quartier*) lively. 3. (*souvenir*) still fresh. ▶ **vivant** *nm* (*personne*): **les ~s** the living.

vive¹ [viv] *nf* (*poisson*) weever.

vive² [viv] *interj* three cheers for, **~ le roi!** long live the King!

vivement [vivmɑ̃] ◆ *adv* 1. (*agir*) quickly. 2. (*répondre*) sharply. 3. (*affecter*) deeply. ◆ *interj*: **~ les vacances!** roll on the holidays!; **~ que l'été arrive** I'll be glad when summer comes, summer can't come quick enough.

vivifiant, -e [vivifjɑ̃, ɑ̃t] *adj* invigorating, bracing.

vivisection [viviseksjɔ̃] *nf* vivisection.

vivre [vivr] ◆ *vi* to live; (*être en vie*) to be alive; **~ de** to live on; **faire ~ sa famille** to support one's family; **être difficile/facile à ~** to be hard/easy to get on with; **avoir vécu** to have seen life. ◆ *vt* 1. (*passer*) to spend. 2. (*éprouver*) to experience. ▶ **vivres** *nmpl* provisions.

vizir [vizir] *nm* vizier.

VO (*abr de* version originale) *nf* indicates that a film has not been dubbed.

vocable [vɔkabl] *nm* term.

vocabulaire [vɔkabylɛr] *nm* 1. (*gén*) vocabulary. 2. (*livre*) lexicon, glossary.

vocal, -e, -aux [vɔkal, o] *adj*: **ensemble ~** choir; → **corde**.

vocation [vɔkasjɔ̃] *nf* 1. (*gén*) vocation. 2. (*d'organisation*) mission.

vocifération [vɔsiferasjɔ̃] *nf* shout, scream.

vociférer [vɔsifere] *vt* to shout, to scream.

vodka [vɔdka] *nf* vodka.

vœu, -x [vø] *nm* 1. (RELIG & *résolution*) vow; **faire ~ de silence** to take a vow of silence. 2. (*souhait, requête*) wish. ▶ **vœux** *nmpl* greetings.

vogue [vɔg] *nf* vogue, fashion; **en ~** fashionable, in vogue.

voguer [vɔge] *vi littéraire* to sail.

voici [vwasi] *prép* 1. (*pour désigner, introduire*) here is/are; **le ~** here he/it is; **les ~** here they are; **~!** here you are!; **vous cherchiez des allumettes? - en ~** were you looking for matches? - there are some here; **~ ce qui s'est passé** this is what happened. 2. (*il y a*): **~ trois mois** three months ago; **~ quelques années que je ne l'ai pas vu** I haven't seen him for some years (now), it's been some years since I last saw him.

voie [vwa] *nf* 1. (*route*) road; **route à deux ~s** two-lane road; **la ~ publique** the public highway. 2. (RAIL) track, line; (*de gare*) platform; **~ ferrée** railway line *Br*, railroad line *Am*; **~ de garage** siding; *fig* dead-end job. 3. (*mode de transport*) route. 4. (ANAT) passage, tract; **par ~ buccale** *ou* **orale** orally, by mouth; **par ~ rectale** by rectum; **~ respiratoire** respiratory tract. 5. *fig* (*chemin*) way. 6. (*filière, moyen*) means (*pl*). ▶ **Voie lactée** *nf*: **la Voie lactée** the Milky Way. ▶ **en voie**

de *loc prép* on the way ou road to; **en ~ de développement** developing.

voilà *prép* **1.** *(pour désigner)* there is/are; **le ~** there he/it is; **les ~** there they are; **me ~** that's me, there I am; **~!** here ou there you are!; **vous cherchiez de l'encre – en ~** you were looking for ink – there is some (over) there; **nous ~ arrivés** we've arrived. **2.** *(reprend ce dont on a parlé)* that is; *(introduit ce dont on va parler)* this is; **~ ce que j'en pense** this is/that is what I think; **~ tout** that's all; **et ~!** there we are! **3.** *(il y a)*: **~ dix jours** ten days ago; **~ dix ans que je le connais** I've known him for ten years (now).

voile [vwal] ◆ *nf* **1.** *(de bateau)* sail. **2.** *(activité)* sailing. ◆ *nm* **1.** *(textile)* voile. **2.** *(coiffure)* veil. **3.** *(de brume)* mist.

voilé, -e [vwale] *adj* **1.** *(visage, allusion)* veiled. **2.** *(ciel, regard)* dull. **3.** *(roue)* buckled. **4.** *(son, voix)* muffled.

voiler [vwale] *vt* **1.** *(visage)* to veil. **2.** *(vérité, sentiment)* to hide. **3.** *(suj: brouillard, nuages)* to cover. ▶ **se voiler** *vp* **1.** *(femme)* to wear a veil. **2.** *(ciel)* to cloud over; *(yeux)* to mist over. **3.** *(roue)* to buckle.

voilier [vwalje] *nm* *(bateau)* sailing boat, sailboat *Am*.

voilure [vwalyr] *nf* *(de bateau)* sails *(pl)*.

voir [vwar] ◆ *vt* *(gén)* to see; **je l'ai vu tomber** I saw him fall; **faire ~ qqch à qqn** to show sb sthg; **ne rien avoir à ~ avec** *fig* to have nothing to do with; **voyons, ...** *(en réfléchissant)* let's see, ... ◆ *vi* to see. ▶ **se voir** *vp* **1.** *(se regarder)* to see o.s., to watch o.s. **2.** *(se rencontrer)* to see one another ou each other. **3.** *(se remarquer)* to be obvious, to show; **ça se voit!** you can tell!

voire [vwar] *adv* even.

voirie [vwari] *nf* (ADMIN) ≃ Department of Transport.

voisin, -e [vwazɛ̃, in] ◆ *adj* **1.** *(pays, ville)* neighbouring; *(maison)* next-door. **2.** *(idée)* similar. ◆ *nm, f* neighbour; **~ de palier** next-door neighbour *(in a flat)*.

voisinage [vwazinaʒ] *nm* **1.** *(quartier)* neighbourhood. **2.** *(relations)* neighbourliness. **3.** *(environs)* vicinity.

voiture [vwatyr] *nf* **1.** *(automobile)* car; **~ de fonction** company car; **~ de location** hire car; **~ d'occasion/de sport** second-hand/sports car. **2.** *(de train)* carriage.

voix [vwa] *nf* **1.** *(gén)* voice; **~ de stentor** stentorian voice; **à mi-~** in an undertone; **à ~ basse** in a low voice, quietly;

à ~ haute *(parler)* in a loud voice; *(lire)* aloud; **de vive ~** in person. **2.** *(suffrage)* vote.

vol [vɔl] *nm* **1.** *(d'oiseau, avion)* flight; **à ~ d'oiseau** as the crow flies; **en plein ~** in flight. **2.** *(groupe d'oiseaux)* flight, flock. **3.** *(délit)* theft.

vol. *(abr de volume)* vol.

volage [vɔlaʒ] *adj littéraire* fickle.

volaille [vɔlaj] *nf*: **la ~** poultry, (domestic) fowl.

volant, -e [vɔlɑ̃, ɑ̃t] *adj* **1.** *(qui vole)* flying. **2.** *(mobile)*: **feuille ~e** loose sheet. ▶ **volant** *nm* **1.** *(de voiture)* steering wheel. **2.** *(de robe)* flounce. **3.** *(de badminton)* shuttlecock.

volatiliser [vɔlatilize] ▶ **se volatiliser** *vp* to volatilize; *fig* to vanish into thin air.

volcan [vɔlkɑ̃] *nm* volcano; *fig* spitfire.

volcanique [vɔlkanik] *adj* volcanic; *fig* *(tempérament)* fiery.

volée [vɔle] *nf* **1.** *(de flèches)* volley; **une ~ de coups** a hail of blows. **2.** (FOOTBALL & TENNIS) volley.

voler [vɔle] ◆ *vi* to fly. ◆ *vt* *(personne)* to rob; *(chose)* to steal.

volet [vɔlɛ] *nm* **1.** *(de maison)* shutter. **2.** *(de dépliant)* leaf; *(d'émission)* part.

voleur, -euse [vɔlœr, øz] *nm, f* thief.

volière [vɔljɛr] *nf* aviary.

volley-ball [vɔlɛbol] *(pl* **volley-balls)** *nm* volleyball.

volontaire [vɔlɔ̃tɛr] ◆ *nmf* volunteer. ◆ *adj* **1.** *(omission)* deliberate; *(activité)* voluntary. **2.** *(enfant)* strong-willed.

volonté [vɔlɔ̃te] *nf* **1.** *(vouloir)* will; **à ~** unlimited, as much as you like. **2.** *(disposition)*: **bonne ~** willingness, good will; **mauvaise ~** unwillingness. **3.** *(détermination)* willpower.

volontiers [vɔlɔ̃tje] *adv* **1.** *(avec plaisir)* with pleasure, gladly, willingly. **2.** *(affable, bavard)* naturally.

volt [vɔlt] *nm* volt.

voltage [vɔltaʒ] *nm* voltage.

volte-face [vɔltəfas] *nf inv* about-turn *Br*, about-face *Am*; *fig* U-turn, about-turn *Br*, about-face *Am*.

voltige [vɔltiʒ] *nf* **1.** *(au trapèze)* trapeze work; **haute ~** flying trapeze act; *fam fig* mental gymnastics *(U)*. **2.** *(à cheval)* circus riding. **3.** *(en avion)* aerobatics *(U)*.

voltiger [vɔltiʒe] *vi* **1.** *(insecte, oiseau)* to flit ou flutter about. **2.** *(feuilles)* to flutter about.

volubile [vɔlybil] *adj* voluble.

volume [vɔlym] *nm* volume.

volumineux, -euse [vɔlyminø, øz] *adj* voluminous, bulky.

volupté [vɔlypte] *nf* (*sensuelle*) sensual ou voluptuous pleasure; (*morale, esthétique*) delight.

voluptueux, -euse [vɔlyptɥø, øz] *adj* voluptuous.

volute [vɔlyt] *nf* **1.** (*de fumée*) wreath. **2.** (ARCHIT) volute, helix.

vomi [vɔmi] *nm fam* vomit.

vomir [vɔmir] *vt* **1.** (*aliments*) to bring up. **2.** (*fumées*) to belch, to spew (out); (*injures*) to spit out.

vont → **aller**.

vorace [vɔras] *adj* voracious.

voracité [vɔrasite] *nf* voracity.

vos → **votre**.

vote [vɔt] *nm* vote.

voter [vɔte] ♦ *vi* to vote. ♦ *vt* (POLIT) to vote for; (*crédits*) to vote; (*loi*) to pass.

votre [vɔtr] (*pl* **vos** [vo]) *adj poss* your.

vôtre [votr] ▶ **le vôtre** (*f* **la vôtre**, *pl* **les vôtres**) *pron poss* yours; **les ~s** your family; **vous et les ~s** people like you; **à la ~!** your good health!

vouer [vwe] *vt* **1.** (*promettre, jurer*): **~ qqch à qqn** to swear ou vow sthg to sb. **2.** (*consacrer*) to devote. **3.** (*condamner*): **être voué à** to be doomed to.

vouloir [vulwar] ♦ *vt* **1.** (*gén*) to want; **veux-tu te taire!** will you be quiet!; **je voudrais savoir** I would like to know; **~ que** (+ *subjonctif*): **je veux qu'il parte** I want him to leave; **~ qqch de qqn/qqch** to want sthg from sb/sthg; **combien voulez-vous de votre maison?** how much do you want for your house?; **ne pas ~ de qqn/qqch** not to want sb/sthg; **je veux bien** I don't mind; **si vous voulez** if you like, if you want; **veuillez vous asseoir** please take a seat; **sans le ~** without meaning ou wishing to, unintentionally. **2.** (*suj: coutume*) to demand. **3.** (*s'attendre à*) to expect; **que voulez-vous que j'y fasse?** what do you want me to do about it? **4.** *loc*: **~ dire** to mean; **si on veut** more or less, if you like; **en ~ à qqn** to have a grudge against sb. ♦ *nm*: **le bon ~ de qqn** sb's good will. ▶ **se vouloir** *vp*: **elle se veut différente** she thinks she's different; **s'en ~ de faire qqch** to be cross with o.s. for doing sthg.

voulu, -e [vuly] ♦ *pp* → **vouloir** ♦ *adj* **1.** (*requis*) requisite **2.** (*délibéré*) intentional.

vous [vu] *pron pers* **1.** (*sujet, objet direct*) you. **2.** (*objet indirect*) (to) you. **3.** (*après*

préposition, comparatif) you; **à ~!** your turn! **4.** (*réfléchi*) yourself, (*pl*) yourselves. ▶ **vous-même** *pron pers* yourself. ▶ **vous-mêmes** *pron pers* yourselves.

voûte [vut] *nf* **1.** (ARCHIT) vault; *fig* arch. **2.** (ANAT): **~ du palais** roof of the mouth; **~ plantaire** arch (of the foot).

voûté, -e [vute] *adj* (*personne, dos*) hunched; (*galerie*) arched.

voûter [vute] *vt* to arch over, to vault. ▶ **se voûter** *vp* to be ou become stooped.

vouvoyer [vuvwaje] *vt*: **~ qqn** to use the 'vous' form to sb.

voyage [vwajaʒ] *nm* journey, trip; **les ~s** travel (*sg*), travelling (U); **partir en ~** to go away, to go on a trip; **~ d'affaires** business trip; **~ organisé** package tour; **~ de noces** honeymoon.

voyager [vwajaʒe] *vi* to travel.

voyageur, -euse [vwajaʒœr, øz] *nm, f* traveller.

voyagiste [vwajaʒist] *nm* tour operator.

voyance [vwajɑ̃s] *nf* clairvoyance.

voyant, -e [vwajɑ̃, ɑ̃t] ♦ *adj* loud, gaudy. ♦ *nm, f* (*devin*) seer. ▶ **voyant** *nm* (*lampe*) light; (AUTOM) indicator (light); **~ d'essence/d'huile** petrol/oil warning light.

voyelle [vwajɛl] *nf* vowel.

voyeur, -euse [vwajœr, øz] *nm, f* voyeur, Peeping Tom.

voyou [vwaju] *nm* **1.** (*garnement*) urchin. **2.** (*loubard*) lout.

vrac [vrak] ▶ **en vrac** *loc adv* **1.** (*sans emballage*) loose. **2.** (*en désordre*) higgledy-piggledy. **3.** (*au poids*) in bulk.

vrai, -e [vrɛ] *adj* **1.** (*histoire*) true; **c'est ou il est ~ que ...** it's true that ... **2.** (*or, perle, nom*) real. **3.** (*personne*) natural. **4.** (*ami, raison*) real, true. ▶ **vrai** *nm*: **à ~ dire, à dire ~** to tell the truth.

vraiment [vrɛmɑ̃] *adv* really.

vraisemblable [vrɛsɑ̃blabl] *adj* likely, probable; (*excuse*) plausible.

vraisemblance [vrɛsɑ̃blɑ̃s] *nf* likelihood, probability; (*d'excuse*) plausibility.

V/Réf (*abr de* **Votre référence**) your ref.

vrille [vrij] *nf* **1.** (BOT) tendril. **2.** (*outil*) gimlet. **3.** (*spirale*) spiral.

vrombir [vrɔ̃bir] *vi* to hum.

vrombissement [vrɔ̃bismɑ̃] *nm* humming (U).

VTT (*abr de* **vélo tout terrain**) *nm* mountain bike.

vu, -e [vy] ♦ *pp* → **voir**. ♦ *adj* **1.** (*perçu*):

être bien/mal ~ to be acceptable/unacceptable. **2.** (*compris*) clear. ► **vu** *prép* given, in view of. ► **vue** *nf* **1.** (*sens, vision*) sight, eyesight. **2.** (*regard*) gaze; à première ~e at first sight; de ~e by sight; en ~e (*vedette*) in the public eye; perdre qqn de ~e to lose touch with sb. **3.** (*panorama, idée*) view. **4.** (CIN) → **prise**. ► **en vue de** *loc prép* with a view to. ► **vu que** *loc conj* given that, seeing that.

vulgaire [vylgɛr] *adj* **1.** (*grossier*) vulgar, coarse. **2.** (*avant n*) *péj* (*quelconque*) common.

vulgarisation [vylgarizasjɔ̃] *nf* popularization.

vulgariser [vylgarize] *vt* to popularize.

vulgarité [vylgarite] *nf* vulgarity, coarseness.

vulnérable [vylnerabl] *adj* vulnerable.

vulve [vylv] *nf* vulva.

w, W [dubləve] *nm inv* w, W.

wagon [vagɔ̃] *nm* carriage; ~ de première/seconde classe first-class/second-class carriage.

wagon-lit [vagɔ̃li] *nm* sleeping car, sleeper.

wagon-restaurant [vagɔ̃rɛstorɑ̃] *nm* restaurant ou dining car.

Walkman® [wɔkman] *nm* personal stereo, Walkman®.

wallon, -onne [walɔ̃, ɔn] *adj* Walloon. ► **wallon** *nm* (*langue*) Walloon. ► **Wallon, -onne** *nm, f* Walloon.

Wallonie [walɔni] *nf*: la ~ southern Belgium (*where French and Walloon are spoken*).

Washington [waʃiŋtɔn] *n* **1.** (*ville*) Washington D.C. **2.** (*État*) Washington State.

water-polo [waterpolo] *nm* water polo.

watt [wat] *nm* watt.

W.-C. [vese] (*abr de* **water closet**) *nmpl* WC (*sg*), toilets.

week-end [wikɛnd] (*pl* **week-ends**) *nm* weekend.

western [wɛstɛrn] *nm* western.

whisky [wiski] (*pl* **whiskies**) *nm* whisky.

white-spirit [wajtspirit] (*pl* **white-spirits**) *nm* white spirit.

x, X [iks] *nm inv* x, X; l'X *prestigious engineering college in Paris.*

xénophobe [gzenɔfɔb] ◆ *nmf* xenophobe. ◆ *adj* xenophobic.

xénophobie [gzenɔfɔbi] *nf* xenophobia.

xérès [kzerɛs] *nm* sherry.

xylophone [ksilɔfɔn] *nm* xylophone.

y¹, Y [igrɛk] *nm inv* y, Y.

y² [i] ◆ *adv* (*lieu*) there; j'y vais demain I'm going there tomorrow; mets-y du sel put some salt in it; va voir sur la table si les clefs y sont go and see if the keys are on the table; ils ont ramené des vases anciens et y ont fait pousser des fleurs exotiques they brought back some antique vases and grew exotic flowers in them. ◆ *pron* (*la traduction varie selon la préposition utilisée avec le verbe*): pensez-y think about it; n'y comptez pas don't count on it; j'y suis! I've got it!; *voir aussi* aller, avoir *etc.*

yacht [jot] *nm* yacht.

yaourt [jaurt], **yogourt, yoghourt** [jɔgurt] *nm* yoghurt.

Yémen [jemɛn] *nm*: le ~ Yemen.

yen [jɛn] *nm* yen.

yeux → **œil**.

yiddish [jidiʃ] *nm inv & adj inv* Yiddish.

yoga [jɔga] *nm* yoga.

yoghourt = **yaourt**.

yogourt = **yaourt**.

yougoslave [jugɔslav] *adj* Yugoslav, Yugoslavian. ► **Yougoslave** *nmf* Yugoslav, Yugoslavian.

Yougoslavie [jugɔslavi] *nf*: la ~ Yugoslavia.

z, Z [zɛd] *nm inv* z, Z.

Zaïre [zair] *nm*: le ~ Zaïre.

zapper [zape] *vi* to zap, to channel-hop.

zapping [zapiŋ] *nm* zapping, channel-hopping.

zèbre [zɛbr] *nm* zebra; **un drôle de ~** *fam fig* an oddball.

zébrure [zebryr] *nf* **1.** (*de pelage*) stripe. **2.** (*marque*) weal.

zébu [zeby] *nm* zebu.

zèle [zɛl] *nm* zeal; **faire du ~** *péj* to be over-zealous.

zélé, -e [zele] *adj* zealous.

zénith [zenit] *nm* zenith.

zéro [zero] ♦ *nm* **1.** (*chiffre*) zero, nought; (*dans numéro de téléphone*) O Br, zero Am. **2.** (*nombre*) nought, nothing. **3.** (*de graduation*) freezing point, zero; **au-dessus/au-dessous de ~** above/below (zero); **avoir le moral à ~** *fig* to be ou feel down. ♦ *adj*: **~ faute** no mistakes.

zeste [zɛst] *nm* peel, zest.

zézayer [zezeje] *vi* to lisp.

zigzag [zigzag] *nm* zigzag; **en ~** winding.

zigzaguer [zigzage] *vi* to zigzag (along).

zinc [zɛ̃g] *nm* **1.** (*matière*) zinc. **2.** *fam* (*comptoir*) bar. **3.** *fam* (*avion*) crate.

zizi [zizi] *nm fam* willy Br, peter Am.

zodiaque [zɔdjak] *nm* zodiac.

zone [zon] *nf* **1.** (*région*) zone, area; **~ bleue** restricted parking zone; **~ industrielle** industrial estate; **~ piétonne** ou **piétonnière** pedestrian precinct Br ou zone Am. **2.** *fam* (*faubourg*): **la ~** the slum belt.

zoner [zone] *vi* to hang about, to hang around.

zoo [zo(o)] *nm* zoo.

zoologie [zɔɔlɔʒi] *nf* zoology.

zoom [zum] *nm* **1.** (*objectif*) zoom (lens). **2.** (*gros plan*) zoom.

zut [zyt] *interj fam* damn!

a¹ (pl **as** OR **a's**), **A** (pl **As** OR **A's**) [eɪ] n (letter) a m inv, A m inv; **to get from A to B** aller d'un point à un autre. ▶ **A** n 1. (MUS) la m inv. 2. (SCH) (mark) A m inv.

a² [stressed eɪ, unstressed ə] (before vowel or silent 'h' **an** [stressed æn, unstressed ən]) indef art 1. (gen) un (une); **a boy** un garçon; **a table** une table; **an orange** une orange. 2. (referring to occupation): **to be a doctor/lawyer/plumber** être médecin/avocat/plombier. 3. (instead of the number one) un (une); **a hundred/thousand pounds** cent/mille livres. 4. (to express prices, ratios etc): **20p a kilo** 20p le kilo; **£10 a person** 10 livres par personne; **twice a week/month** deux fois par semaine/mois; **50 km an hour** 50 km à l'heure.

AA n 1. (abbr of **Automobile Association**) automobile club britannique, ≃ ACF m, ≃ TCF m. 2. (abbr of **Alcoholics Anonymous**) Alcooliques Anonymes mpl.

AAA n (abbr of **American Automobile Association**) automobile club américain, ≃ ACF m, ≃ TCF m.

AB n Am abbr of **Bachelor of Arts**.

aback [ə'bæk] adv: **to be taken ~** être décontenancé(e).

abandon [ə'bændən] ◆ vt abandonner. ◆ n: **with ~** avec abandon.

abashed [ə'bæʃt] adj confus(e).

abate [ə'beɪt] vi (storm, fear) se calmer; (noise) faiblir.

abattoir ['æbətwɑːr] n abattoir m.

abbey ['æbɪ] n abbaye f.

abbot ['æbət] n abbé m.

abbreviate [ə'briːvɪeɪt] vt abréger.

abbreviation [ə,briːvɪ'eɪʃn] n abréviation f.

ABC n 1. (alphabet) alphabet m. 2. fig (basics) B.A.-Ba m, abc m.

abdicate ['æbdɪkeɪt] vt & vi abdiquer.

abdomen ['æbdəmen] n abdomen m.

abduct [əb'dʌkt] vt enlever.

aberration [,æbə'reɪʃn] n aberration f.

abet [ə'bet] vt → **aid**.

abhor [əb'hɔːr] vt exécrer, abhorrer.

abide [ə'baɪd] vt supporter, souffrir. ▶ **abide by** vt fus respecter, se soumettre à.

ability [ə'bɪlətɪ] n 1. (capacity, capability) aptitude f. 2. (skill) talent m.

abject ['æbdʒekt] adj 1. (poverty) noir(e). 2. (person) pitoyable; (apology) servile.

ablaze [ə'bleɪz] adj (on fire) en feu.

able ['eɪbl] adj 1. (capable): **to be ~ to do sthg** pouvoir faire qqch. 2. (accomplished) compétent(e).

able-bodied [-'bɒdɪd] adj valide.

ably ['eɪblɪ] adv avec compétence, habilement.

abnormal [æb'nɔːml] adj anormal(e).

aboard [ə'bɔːd] ◆ adv à bord. ◆ prep (ship, plane) à bord; (bus, train) dans.

abode [ə'bəʊd] n fml: **of no fixed ~** sans domicile fixe.

abolish [ə'bɒlɪʃ] vt abolir.

abolition [,æbə'lɪʃn] n abolition f.

abominable [ə'bɒmɪnəbl] adj abominable.

aborigine [,æbə'rɪdʒənɪ] n aborigène mf d'Australie.

abort [ə'bɔːt] vt (pregnancy) interrompre.

abortion [ə'bɔːʃn] n avortement m, interruption f (volontaire) de grossesse; **to have an ~** se faire avorter.

abortive [ə'bɔːtɪv] adj manqué(e).

abound [ə'baʊnd] vi 1. (be plentiful)

abonder. **2.** (*be full*): **to ~ with** OR **in** abonder en.

about [ə'baʊt] ◆ *adv* **1.** (*approximately*) environ, à peu près; **~ fifty/a hundred/ a thousand** environ cinquante/cent/ mille; **at ~ five o'clock** vers cinq heures; **I'm just ~ ready** je suis presque prêt. **2.** (*referring to place*): **to run ~** courir çà et là; **to leave things lying ~** laisser traîner des affaires; **to walk ~** aller et venir, se promener. **3.** (*on the point of*): **to be ~ to do sthg** être sur le point de faire qqch. ◆ *prep* **1.** (*relating to, concerning*) au sujet de; **a film ~ Paris** un film sur Paris; **what is it ~?** de quoi s'agit-il?; **to talk ~ sthg** parler de qqch. **2.** (*referring to place*): **his belongings were scattered ~ the room** ses affaires étaient éparpillées dans toute la pièce; **to wander ~ the streets** errer de par les rues.

about-turn, about-face *n* (MIL) demi-tour *m*; *fig* volte-face *f inv*.

above [ə'bʌv] ◆ *adv* **1.** (*on top, higher up*) au-dessus. **2.** (*in text*) ci-dessus, plus haut. **3.** (*more, over*) plus; **children aged 5 and ~** les enfants âgés de 5 ans et plus OR de plus de 5 ans. ◆ *prep* **1.** (*on top of, higher up than*) au-dessus de. **2.** (*more than*) plus de. ▶ **above all** *adv* avant tout.

aboveboard [ə,bʌv'bɔːd] *adj* honnête.

abrasive [ə'breɪsɪv] *adj* (*substance*) abrasif(ive); *fig* caustique, acerbe.

abreast [ə'brest] *adv* de front. ▶ **abreast of** *prep*: **to keep ~ of** se tenir au courant de.

abridged [ə'brɪdʒd] *adj* abrégé(e).

abroad [ə'brɔːd] *adv* à l'étranger.

abrupt [ə'brʌpt] *adj* **1.** (*sudden*) soudain(e), brusque. **2.** (*brusque*) abrupt(e).

abscess ['æbsɪs] *n* abcès *m*.

abscond [əb'skɒnd] *vi* s'enfuir.

abseil ['æbseɪl] *vi* descendre en rappel.

absence ['æbsəns] *n* absence *f*.

absent ['æbsənt] *adj*: **~ (from)** absent(e) (de).

absentee [,æbsən'tiː] *n* absent *m*, -e *f*.

absent-minded [-'maɪndɪd] *adj* distrait(e).

absolute ['æbsəluːt] *adj* **1.** (*complete - fool, disgrace*) complet(ète). **2.** (*totalitarian - ruler, power*) absolu(e).

absolutely ['æbsəluːtlɪ] *adv* absolument.

absolve [əb'zɒlv] *vt*: **to ~ sb (from)** absoudre qqn (de).

absorb [əb'sɔːb] *vt* absorber; (*information*) retenir, assimiler; **to be ~ed in sthg** être absorbé dans qqch.

absorbent [əb'sɔːbənt] *adj* absorbant(e).

absorption [əb'sɔːpʃn] *n* absorption *f*.

abstain [əb'steɪn] *vi*: **to ~ (from)** s'abstenir (de).

abstemious [æb'stiːmjəs] *adj fml* frugal(e), sobre.

abstention [əb'stenʃn] *n* abstention *f*.

abstract ['æbstrækt] ◆ *adj* abstrait(e). ◆ *n* (*summary*) résumé *m*, abrégé *m*.

absurd [əb'sɜːd] *adj* absurde.

ABTA ['æbtə] (*abbr of* **Association of British Travel Agents**) *n* association des agences de voyage britanniques.

abundant [ə'bʌndənt] *adj* abondant(e).

abundantly [ə'bʌndəntlɪ] *adv* **1.** (*clear, obvious*) parfaitement, tout à fait. **2.** (*exist, grow*) en abondance.

abuse [*n* ə'bjuːs, *vb* ə'bjuːz] ◆ *n* (U) **1.** (*offensive remarks*) insultes *fpl*, injures *fpl*. **2.** (*maltreatment*) mauvais traitement *m*; **child ~** mauvais traitements infligés aux enfants. **3.** (*of power, drugs etc*) abus *m*. ◆ *vt* **1.** (*insult*) insulter, injurier. **2.** (*maltreat*) maltraiter. **3.** (*power, drugs etc*) abuser de.

abusive [ə'bjuːsɪv] *adj* grossier(ère), injurieux(euse).

abysmal [ə'bɪzml] *adj* épouvantable, abominable.

abyss [ə'bɪs] *n* abîme *m*, gouffre *m*.

a/c (*abbr of* **account (current)**) cc.

AC *n* (*abbr of* **alternating current**) courant *m* alternatif.

academic [,ækə'demɪk] ◆ *adj* **1.** (*of college, university*) universitaire. **2.** (*person*) intellectuel(elle). **3.** (*question, discussion*) théorique. ◆ *n* universitaire *mf*.

academy [ə'kædəmɪ] *n* **1.** (*school, college*) école *f*; **~ of music** conservatoire *m*. **2.** (*institution, society*) académie *f*.

ACAS ['eɪkæs] (*abbr of* **Advisory Conciliation and Arbitration Service**) *n* organisme britannique de conciliation des conflits du travail.

accede [æk'siːd] *vi* **1.** (*agree*): **to ~ to** agréer, donner suite à. **2.** (*monarch*): **to ~ to the throne** monter sur le trône.

accelerate [ək'seləreɪt] *vi* **1.** (*car, driver*) accélérer. **2.** (*inflation, growth*) s'accélérer.

acceleration [ək,selə'reɪʃn] *n* accélération *f*.

accelerator [ək'seləreɪtər] *n* accélérateur *m*.

accent ['æksent] *n* accent *m*.

accept [ək'sept] *vt* 1. (*gen*) accepter; (*for job, as member of club*) recevoir, admettre. 2. (*agree*): **to ~ that ...** admettre que ...

acceptable [ək'septəbl] *adj* acceptable.

acceptance [ək'septəns] *n* 1. (*gen*) acceptation *f*. 2. (*for job, as member of club*) admission *f*.

access ['ækses] *n* 1. (*entry, way in*) accès *m*. 2. (*opportunity to use, see*): **to have ~ to sthg** avoir qqch à sa disposition, disposer de qqch.

accessible [ək'sesəbl] *adj* 1. (*reachable - place*) accessible. 2. (*available*) disponible.

accessory [ək'sesəri] *n* 1. (*of car, vacuum cleaner*) accessoire *m*. 2. (JUR) complice *mf*.

accident ['æksidənt] *n* accident *m*; **~ and emergency department** Br (service *m* des) urgences *fpl*; **by ~** par hasard, par accident.

accidental [,æksi'dentl] *adj* accidentel(elle).

accidentally [,æksi'dentəli] *adv* 1. (*drop, break*) par mégarde. 2. (*meet*) par hasard.

accident-prone *adj* prédisposé(e) aux accidents.

acclaim [ə'kleɪm] ◆ *n* (U) éloges *mpl*. ◆ *vt* louer.

acclimatize, -ise [ə'klaɪmətaɪz], **acclimate** Am ['ækləmeɪt] *vi*: **to ~ (to)** s'acclimater (à).

accommodate [ə'kɒmədeɪt] *vt* 1. (*provide room for*) loger. 2. (*oblige - person, wishes*) satisfaire.

accommodating [ə'kɒmədeɪtɪŋ] *adj* obligeant(e).

accommodation Br [ə,kɒmə'deɪʃn] *n*, **accommodations** Am [ə,kɒmə-'deɪʃnz] *npl* logement *m*.

accompany [ə'kʌmpəni] *vt* (*gen*) accompagner.

accomplice [ə'kʌmplis] *n* complice *mf*.

accomplish [ə'kʌmpliʃ] *vt* accomplir, achever.

accomplishment [ə'kʌmpliʃmənt] *n* 1. (*action*) accomplissement *m*. 2. (*achievement*) réussite *f*. ▶ **accomplishments** *npl* talents *mpl*.

accord [ə'kɔːd] *n*: **to do sthg of one's own ~** faire qqch de son propre chef OR de soi-même.

accordance [ə'kɔːdəns] *n*: **in ~ with** conformément à.

according [ə'kɔːdɪŋ] ▶ **according to** *prep* 1. (*as stated or shown by*) d'après; **to go ~ to plan** se passer comme prévu. 2. (*with regard to*) suivant, en fonction de.

accordingly [ə'kɔːdɪŋli] *adv* 1. (*appropriately*) en conséquence. 2. (*consequently*) par conséquent.

accordion [ə'kɔːdjən] *n* accordéon *m*.

accost [ə'kɒst] *vt* accoster.

account [ə'kaʊnt] *n* 1. (*with bank, shop, company*) compte *m*. 2. (*report*) compte-rendu *m*. 3. *phr*: **to take ~ of sthg, to take sthg into ~** prendre qqch en compte; **to be of no ~** n'avoir aucune importance; **on no ~** sous aucun prétexte, en aucun cas. ▶ **accounts** *npl* (*of business*) comptabilité *f*, comptes *mpl*. ▶ **by all accounts** *adv* d'après ce que l'on dit, au dire de tous. ▶ **on account of** *prep* à cause de. ▶ **account for** *vt fus* 1. (*explain*) justifier, expliquer. 2. (*represent*) représenter.

accountable [ə'kaʊntəbl] *adj* (*responsible*): **~ (for)** responsable (de).

accountancy [ə'kaʊntənsi] *n* comptabilité *f*.

accountant [ə'kaʊntənt] *n* comptable *mf*.

accrue [ə'kruː] *vi* (*money*) fructifier; (*interest*) courir.

accumulate [ə'kjuːmjʊleɪt] ◆ *vt* accumuler, amasser. ◆ *vi* s'accumuler.

accuracy ['ækjʊrəsi] *n* 1. (*of description, report*) exactitude *f*. 2. (*of weapon, typist, figures*) précision *f*.

accurate ['ækjʊrət] *adj* 1. (*description, report*) exact(e). 2. (*weapon, typist, figures*) précis(e).

accurately ['ækjʊrətli] *adv* 1. (*truthfully - describe, report*) fidèlement. 2. (*precisely - aim*) avec précision; (*- type*) sans faute.

accusation [,ækjuː'zeɪʃn] *n* accusation *f*.

accuse [ə'kjuːz] *vt*: **to ~ sb of sthg/of doing sthg** accuser qqn de qqch/de faire qqch.

accustomed [ə'kʌstəmd] *adj*: **to be ~ to sthg/to doing sthg** avoir l'habitude de qqch/de faire qqch.

ace [eɪs] *n* as *m*.

ache [eɪk] ◆ *n* douleur *f*. ◆ *vi* 1. (*back, limb*) faire mal; **my head ~s** j'ai mal à la tête. 2. *fig* (*want*): **to be aching for sthg** mourir d'envie de qqch.

achieve [ə'tʃiːv] *vt* (*success, victory*)

obtenir, remporter; (*goal*) atteindre; (*ambition*) réaliser; (*fame*) parvenir à.

achievement [ə'tʃiːvmənt] *n* (*success*) réussite *f*.

Achilles' tendon [ə'kɪliːz-] *n* tendon *m* d'Achille.

acid ['æsɪd] ◆ *adj lit & fig* acide. ◆ *n* acide *m*.

acid rain *n* (U) pluies *fpl* acides.

acknowledge [ək'nɒlɪdʒ] *vt* 1. (*fact, situation, person*) reconnaître. 2. (*letter*): to ~ (receipt of) accuser réception de. 3. (*greet*) saluer.

acknowledg(e)ment [ək'nɒlɪdʒmənt] *n* 1. (*gen*) reconnaissance *f*. 2. (*letter*) accusé *m* de réception. ▶ **acknowledg(e)ments** *npl* (*in book*) remerciements *mpl*.

acne ['ækni] *n* acné *f*.

acorn ['eɪkɔːn] *n* gland *m*.

acoustic [ə'kuːstɪk] *adj* acoustique. ▶ **acoustics** *npl* (*of room*) acoustique *f*.

acquaint [ə'kweɪnt] *vt*: to ~ sb with sthg mettre qqn au courant de qqch; to be ~ed with sb connaître qqn.

acquaintance [ə'kweɪntəns] *n* (*person*) connaissance *f*.

acquire [ə'kwaɪər] *vt* acquérir.

acquisitive [ə'kwɪzɪtɪv] *adj* avide de possessions.

acquit [ə'kwɪt] *vt* 1. (JUR) acquitter. 2. (*perform*): to ~ o.s. well/badly bien/mal se comporter.

acquittal [ə'kwɪtl] *n* acquittement *m*.

acre ['eɪkər] *n* = 4046,9 *m²*, ≃ demi-hectare *m*.

acrid ['ækrɪd] *adj* (*taste, smell*) âcre; *fig* acerbe.

acrimonious [ˌækrɪ'məʊnjəs] *adj* acrimonieux(euse).

acrobat ['ækrəbæt] *n* acrobate *mf*.

across [ə'krɒs] ◆ *adv* 1. (*from one side to the other*) en travers. 2. (*in measurements*): **the river is 2 km** ~ la rivière mesure 2 km de large. 3. (*in crossword*): 21 ~ 21 horizontalement. ◆ *prep* 1. (*from one side to the other*) d'un côté à l'autre de, en travers de; to walk ~ the road traverser la route; to run ~ the road traverser la route en courant. 2. (*on the other side of*) de l'autre côté de; **the house** ~ **the road** la maison d'en face. ▶ **across from** *prep* en face de.

acrylic [ə'krɪlɪk] ◆ *adj* acrylique. ◆ *n* acrylique *m*.

act [ækt] ◆ *n* 1. (*action, deed*) acte *m*; to catch sb in the ~ of doing sthg surprendre qqn en train de faire qqch. 2. (JUR)

loi *f*. 3. (*of play, opera*) acte *m*; (*in cabaret etc*) numéro *m*; *fig* (*pretence*): to put on an ~ jouer la comédie. 4. *phr*: to get one's ~ together se reprendre en main. ◆ *vi* 1. (*gen*) agir. 2. (*behave*) se comporter; to ~ as if se conduire comme si, se comporter comme si; to ~ like se conduire comme, se comporter comme. 3. (*in play, film*) jouer; *fig* (*pretend*) jouer la comédie. 4. (*function*): to ~ as (*person*) être; (*object*) servir de. ◆ *vt* (*part*) jouer.

ACT (*abbr of* **American College Test**) *n* examen américain de fin d'études secondaires.

acting ['æktɪŋ] ◆ *adj* par intérim, provisoire. ◆ *n* (*in play, film*) interprétation *f*.

action ['ækʃn] *n* 1. (*gen*) action *f*; to take ~ agir, prendre des mesures; to put sthg into ~ mettre qqch à exécution; in ~ (*person*) en action; (*machine*) en marche; out of ~ (*person*) hors de combat; (*machine*) hors service, hors d'usage. 2. (JUR) procès *m*, action *f*.

action replay *n* répétition *f* immédiate (au ralenti).

activate ['æktɪveɪt] *vt* mettre en marche.

active ['æktɪv] *adj* 1. (*gen*) actif(ive); (*encouragement*) vif (vive). 2. (*volcano*) en activité.

actively ['æktɪvlɪ] *adv* activement.

activity [æk'tɪvətɪ] *n* activité *f*.

actor ['æktər] *n* acteur *m*.

actress ['æktrɪs] *n* actrice *f*.

actual ['æktʃʊəl] *adj* réel(elle).

actually ['æktʃʊəlɪ] *adv* 1. (*really, in truth*) vraiment. 2. (*by the way*) au fait.

acumen ['ækjʊmen] *n* flair *m*.

acupuncture ['ækjʊpʌŋktʃər] *n* acuponcture *f*.

acute [ə'kjuːt] *adj* 1. (*severe - pain, illness*) aigu(ë); (- *danger*) sérieux(euse), grave. 2. (*perceptive - person, mind*) perspicace. 3. (*keen - eyesight*) perçant(e); (- *hearing*) fin(e); (- *sense of smell*) développé(e). 4. (MATH): ~ angle angle *m* aigu. 5. (LING): e ~ e accent aigu.

ad [æd] (*abbr of* **advertisement**) *n inf* (*in newspaper*) annonce *f*; (*on TV*) pub *f*.

AD (*abbr of* **Anno Domini**) ap. J.-C.

adamant ['ædəmənt] *adj*: to be ~ être inflexible.

Adam's apple [ˌædəmz-] *n* pomme *f* d'Adam.

adapt [ə'dæpt] ◆ *vt* adapter. ◆ *vi*: to ~ (to) s'adapter (à).

adaptable [ə'dæptəbl] *adj* (*person*) souple.

adapter, adaptor [ə'dæptər] n (ELEC - for several devices) prise f multiple; (- for foreign plug) adaptateur m.

add [æd] vt 1. (gen): **to ~ sthg (to)** ajouter qqch (à). 2. (numbers) additionner. ▶ **add on** vt sep: **to ~ sthg on (to)** ajouter qqch (à); (charge, tax) rajouter qqch (à). ▶ **add to** vt fus ajouter à, augmenter. ▶ **add up** vt sep additionner. ▶ **add up to** vt fus se monter à.

adder ['ædər] n vipère f.

addict ['ædɪkt] n lit & fig drogué m, -e f; **drug ~** drogué.

addicted [ə'dɪktɪd] adj: **~ (to)** drogué(e) (à); fig passionné(e) (de).

addiction [ə'dɪkʃn] n: **~ (to)** dépendance f (à); fig penchant m (pour).

addictive [ə'dɪktɪv] adj qui rend dépendant(e).

addition [ə'dɪʃn] n addition f; **in ~ (to)** en plus (de).

additional [ə'dɪʃənl] adj supplémentaire.

additive ['ædɪtɪv] n additif m.

address [ə'dres] ◆ n 1. (place) adresse f. 2. (speech) discours m. ◆ vt 1. (gen) adresser. 2. (meeting, conference) prendre la parole à. 3. (problem, issue) aborder, examiner.

address book n carnet m d'adresses.

adenoids ['ædɪnɔɪdz] npl végétations fpl.

adept ['ædept] adj: **~ (at)** doué(e) (pour).

adequate ['ædɪkwət] adj adéquat(e).

adhere [əd'hɪər] vi 1. (stick): **to ~ (to)** adhérer (à). 2. (observe): **to ~ to** obéir à. 3. (keep): **to ~ to** adhérer à.

adhesive [əd'hi:sɪv] ◆ adj adhésif(ive). ◆ n adhésif m.

adhesive tape n ruban m adhésif.

adjacent [ə'dʒeɪsənt] adj: **~ (to)** adjacent(e) (à), contigu(ë) (à).

adjective ['ædʒɪktɪv] n adjectif m.

adjoining [ə'dʒɔɪnɪŋ] ◆ adj voisin(e). ◆ prep attenant à.

adjourn [ə'dʒɜːn] ◆ vt ajourner. ◆ vi suspendre la séance.

adjudicate [ə'dʒu:dɪkeɪt] vi: **to ~ (on OR upon)** se prononcer (sur).

adjust [ə'dʒʌst] ◆ vt ajuster, régler. ◆ vi: **to ~ (to)** s'adapter (à).

adjustable [ə'dʒʌstəbl] adj réglable.

adjustment [ə'dʒʌstmənt] n 1. (modification) ajustement m; (TECH) réglage m. 2. (change in attitude): **~ (to)** adaptation f (à).

ad lib [,æd'lɪb] ◆ adj improvisé(e). ◆ adv à volonté. ▶ **ad-lib** vi improviser.

administer [əd'mɪnɪstər] vt 1. (company, business) administrer, gérer. 2. (justice, punishment) dispenser. 3. (drug, medication) administrer.

administration [əd,mɪnɪ'streɪʃn] n administration f.

administrative [əd'mɪnɪstrətɪv] adj administratif(ive).

admirable ['ædmərəbl] adj admirable.

admiral ['ædmərəl] n amiral m.

admiration [,ædmə'reɪʃn] n admiration f.

admire [əd'maɪər] vt admirer.

admirer [əd'maɪərər] n admirateur m, -trice f.

admission [əd'mɪʃn] n 1. (permission to enter) admission f. 2. (to museum etc) entrée f. 3. (confession) confession f, aveu m.

admit [əd'mɪt] ◆ vt 1. (confess) reconnaître; **to ~ (that)** ... reconnaître que ...; **to ~ doing sthg** reconnaître avoir fait qqch; **to ~ defeat** fig s'avouer vaincu(e). 2. (allow to enter, join) admettre; **to be admitted to hospital** Br OR **to the hospital** Am être admis(e) à l'hôpital. ◆ vi: **to ~ to** admettre, reconnaître.

admittance [əd'mɪtəns] n admission f; **'no ~'** 'entrée interdite'.

admittedly [əd'mɪtɪdlɪ] adv de l'aveu général.

admonish [əd'mɒnɪʃ] vt réprimander.

ad nauseam [,æd'nɔ:zɪæm] adv (talk) à n'en plus finir.

ado [ə'du:] n: **without further OR more ~** sans plus de cérémonie.

adolescence [,ædə'lesns] n adolescence f.

adolescent [,ædə'lesnt] ◆ adj adolescent(e); pej puéril(e). ◆ n adolescent m, -e f.

adopt [ə'dɒpt] vt adopter.

adoption [ə'dɒpʃn] n adoption f.

adore [ə'dɔ:r] vt adorer.

adrenalin [ə'drenəlɪn] n adrénaline f.

Adriatic [,eɪdrɪ'ætɪk] n: **the ~ (Sea)** l'Adriatique f, la mer Adriatique.

adrift [ə'drɪft] ◆ adj à la dérive. ◆ adv: **to go ~** fig aller à la dérive.

adult ['ædʌlt] ◆ adj 1. (gen) adulte. 2. (films, literature) pour adultes. ◆ n adulte mf.

adultery [ə'dʌltərɪ] n adultère m.

advance [əd'vɑ:ns] ◆ n 1. (gen) avance f. 2. (progress) progrès m. ◆ comp à l'avance. ◆ vt 1. (gen) avancer. 2. (improve) faire progresser OR avancer.

♦ vi **1.** (gen) avancer. **2.** (improve) progresser. ▶ **advances** npl: **to make ~ to sb** (sexual) faire des avances à qqn; (business) faire des propositions à qqn. ▶ **in advance** adv à l'avance.

advanced [əd'vɑːnst] adj avancé(e).

advantage [əd'vɑːntɪdʒ] n: **~ (over)** avantage m (sur); **to be to one's ~** être à son avantage; **to take ~ of sthg** profiter de qqch; **to take ~ of sb** exploiter qqn.

advent ['ædvənt] n avènement m. ▶ **Advent** n (RELIG) Avent m.

adventure [əd'ventʃəʳ] n aventure f.

adventure playground n terrain m d'aventures.

adventurous [əd'ventʃərəs] adj aventureux(euse).

adverb ['ædvɜːb] n adverbe m.

adverse ['ædvɜːs] adj défavorable.

advert ['ædvɜːt] Br = **advertisement**.

advertise ['ædvətaɪz] ♦ vt (COMM) faire de la publicité pour; (event) annoncer. ♦ vi faire de la publicité; **to ~ for sb/sthg** chercher qqn/qqch par voie d'annonce.

advertisement [əd'vɜːtɪsmənt] n (in newspaper) annonce f; (COMM & fig) publicité f.

advertiser ['ædvətaɪzəʳ] n annonceur m.

advertising ['ædvətaɪzɪŋ] n (U) publicité f.

advertising executive n publicitaire mf.

advice [əd'vaɪs] n (U) conseils mpl; **a piece of ~** un conseil; **to give sb ~** donner des conseils à qqn; **to take sb's ~** suivre les conseils de qqn.

advisable [əd'vaɪzəbl] adj conseillé(e), recommandé(e).

advise [əd'vaɪz] ♦ vt **1.** (give advice to): **to ~ sb to do sthg** conseiller à qqn de faire qqch; **to ~ sb against sthg** déconseiller qqch à qqn; **to ~ sb against doing sthg** déconseiller à qqn de faire qqch. **2.** (professionally): **to ~ sb on sthg** conseiller qqn sur qqch. **3.** (inform): **to ~ sb (of sthg)** aviser qqn (de qqch). ♦ vi **1.** (give advice): **to ~ against sthg/against doing sthg** déconseiller qqch/de faire qqch. **2.** (professionally): **to ~ on sthg** conseiller sur qqch.

advisedly [əd'vaɪzɪdlɪ] adv en connaissance de cause, délibérément.

adviser Br, **advisor** Am [əd'vaɪzəʳ] n conseiller m, -ère f.

advisory [əd'vaɪzərɪ] adj consultatif(ive).

advocate [n 'ædvəkət, vb 'ædvəkeɪt] ♦ n **1.** (JUR) avocat m, -e f. **2.** (supporter) partisan m. ♦ vt préconiser, recommander.

Aegean [iː'dʒiːən] n: **the ~ (Sea)** la mer Égée.

aerial ['eərɪəl] ♦ adj aérien(enne). ♦ n Br antenne f.

aerobics [eə'rəʊbɪks] n (U) aérobic m.

aerodynamic [ˌeərəʊdaɪ'næmɪk] adj aérodynamique. ▶ **aerodynamics** npl (aerodynamic qualities) aérodynamisme m.

aeroplane ['eərəpleɪn] n Br avion m.

aerosol ['eərəsɒl] n aérosol m.

aesthetic, esthetic Am [iːs'θetɪk] adj esthétique.

afar [ə'fɑːʳ] adv: **from ~** de loin.

affable ['æfəbl] adj affable.

affair [ə'feəʳ] n **1.** (gen) affaire f. **2.** (extra-marital relationship) liaison f.

affect [ə'fekt] vt **1.** (influence) avoir un effet OR des conséquences sur. **2.** (emotionally) affecter, émouvoir. **3.** (put on) affecter.

affection [ə'fekʃn] n affection f.

affectionate [ə'fekʃnət] adj affectueux(euse).

affirm [ə'fɜːm] vt **1.** (declare) affirmer. **2.** (confirm) confirmer.

affix [ə'fɪks] vt (stamp) coller.

afflict [ə'flɪkt] vt affliger; **to be ~ed with** souffrir de.

affluence ['æfluəns] n prospérité f.

affluent ['æfluənt] adj riche.

afford [ə'fɔːd] vt **1.** (buy, pay for): **to be able to ~ sthg** avoir les moyens d'acheter qqch. **2.** (spare): **to be able to ~ the time (to do sthg)** avoir le temps (de faire qqch). **3.** (harmful, embarrassing thing): **to be able to ~ sthg** pouvoir se permettre qqch. **4.** (provide, give) procurer.

affront [ə'frʌnt] ♦ n affront m, insulte f. ♦ vt insulter, faire un affront à.

Afghanistan [æf'gænɪstæn] n Afghanistan m.

afield [ə'fiːld] adv: **far ~** loin.

afloat [ə'fləʊt] adj lit & fig à flot.

afoot [ə'fʊt] adj en préparation.

afraid [ə'freɪd] adj **1.** (frightened): **to be ~ (of)** avoir peur (de); **to be ~ of doing** OR **to do sthg** avoir peur de faire qqch. **2.** (reluctant, apprehensive): **to be ~ of** craindre. **3.** (in apologies): **to be ~ (that) ...** regretter que ...; **I'm ~ so/not** j'ai bien peur que oui/non.

afresh [ə'freʃ] adv de nouveau.

Africa ['æfrɪkə] n Afrique f.

African ['æfrɪkən] ◆ *adj* africain(e). ◆ *n* Africain *m*, -e *f*.

aft [ɑːft] *adv* sur OR à l'arrière.

after ['ɑːftər] ◆ *prep* 1. (*gen*) après; ~ you! après vous!; to be ~ sb/sthg *inf* (*in search of*) chercher qqn/qqch; to name sb ~ sb Br donner à qqn le nom de qqn. 2. Am (*telling the time*): it's twenty ~ three il est trois heures vingt. ◆ *adv* après. ◆ *conj* après que. ▶ **afters** *npl* Br *inf* dessert *m*. ▶ **after all** *adv* après tout.

aftereffects ['ɑːftərɪˌfekts] *npl* suites *fpl*, répercussions *fpl*.

afterlife ['ɑːftəlaɪf] (*pl* **-lives** [-laɪvz]) *n* vie *f* future.

aftermath ['ɑːftəmæθ] *n* conséquences *fpl*, suites *fpl*.

afternoon [ˌɑːftəˈnuːn] *n* après-midi *m inv*; in the ~ l'après-midi; good ~ bonjour.

aftershave ['ɑːftəʃeɪv] *n* après-rasage *m*.

aftertaste ['ɑːftəteɪst] *n* lit & fig arrière-goût *m*.

afterthought ['ɑːftəθɔːt] *n* pensée *f* OR réflexion *f* coup.

afterward(s) ['ɑːftəwəd(z)] *adv* après.

again [əˈgen] *adv* encore une fois, de nouveau; to do ~ refaire; to say ~ répéter; to start ~ recommencer; ~ and ~ à plusieurs reprises; all over ~ une fois de plus; time and ~ maintes et maintes fois; half as much ~ à moitié autant; (twice) as much ~ deux fois autant; then OR there ~ d'autre part.

against [əˈgenst] *prep* & *adv* contre; (as) ~ contre.

age [eɪdʒ] (*cont* ageing OR aging) ◆ *n* 1. (*gen*) âge *m*; she's 20 years of ~ elle a 20 ans; what ~ are you? quel âge avez-vous?; to be under ~ être mineur; to come of ~ atteindre sa majorité. 2. (*old age*) vieillesse *f*. 3. (*in history*) époque *f*. ◆ *vt* & *vi* vieillir. ▶ **ages** *npl*: ~s ago il y a une éternité; I haven't seen him for ~s je ne l'ai pas vu depuis une éternité.

aged [*adj sense 1* eɪdʒd, *adj sense 2* & *npl* 'eɪdʒɪd] ◆ *adj* 1. (*of stated age*): ~ 15 âgé(e) de 15 ans. 2. (*very old*) âgé(e), vieux (vieille). ◆ *npl*: the ~ les personnes *fpl* âgées.

age group *n* tranche *f* d'âge.

agency ['eɪdʒənsɪ] *n* 1. (*business*) agence *f*. 2. (*organization*) organisme *m*.

agenda [əˈdʒendə] (*pl* **-s**) *n* ordre *m* du jour.

agent ['eɪdʒənt] *n* agent *m*.

aggravate ['ægrəveɪt] *vt* 1. (*make worse*) aggraver. 2. (*annoy*) agacer.

aggregate ['ægrɪgət] *n* (*total*) total *m*.

aggressive [əˈgresɪv] *adj* agressif(ive).

aggrieved [əˈgriːvd] *adj* blessé(e), froissé(e).

aghast [əˈgɑːst] *adj*: ~ (at sthg) atterré(e) (par qqch).

agile [Br 'ædʒaɪl, Am 'ædʒəl] *adj* agile.

agitate ['ædʒɪteɪt] ◆ *vt* 1. (*disturb*) inquiéter. 2. (*shake*) agiter. ◆ *vi*: to ~ for/against faire campagne pour/contre.

AGM (*abbr of* **annual general meeting**) *n* Br AGA *f*.

agnostic [ægˈnɒstɪk] ◆ *adj* agnostique. ◆ *n* agnostique *mf*.

ago [əˈgəʊ] *adv*: a long time ~ il y a longtemps; three days ~ il y a trois jours.

agonizing ['ægənaɪzɪŋ] *adj* déchirant(e).

agony ['ægənɪ] *n* 1. (*physical pain*) douleur *f* atroce; to be in ~ souffrir le martyre. 2. (*mental pain*) angoisse *f*; to be in ~ être angoissé(e).

agony aunt *n* Br *inf* personne qui tient la rubrique du courrier du cœur.

agree [əˈgriː] ◆ *vi* 1. (*concur*): to ~ (with/about) être d'accord (avec/au sujet de); to ~ on (*price, terms*) convenir de. 2. (*consent*): to ~ (to sthg) donner son consentement (à qqch). 3. (*be consistent*) concorder. 4. (*food*): to ~ with être bon (bonne) pour, réussir à. 5. (GRAMM): to ~ (with) s'accorder (avec). ◆ *vt* 1. (*price, conditions*) accepter, convenir de. 2. (*concur, concede*): to ~ (that) ... admettre que ... 3. (*arrange*): to ~ to do sthg se mettre d'accord pour faire qqch.

agreeable [əˈgriːəbl] *adj* 1. (*pleasant*) agréable. 2. (*willing*): to be ~ to consentir à.

agreed [əˈgriːd] *adj*: to be ~ (on sthg) être d'accord (à propos de qqch).

agreement [əˈgriːmənt] *n* 1. (*gen*) accord *m*; to be in ~ (with) être d'accord (avec). 2. (*consistency*) concordance *f*.

agricultural [ˌægrɪˈkʌltʃərəl] *adj* agricole.

agriculture ['ægrɪkʌltʃər] *n* agriculture *f*.

aground [əˈgraʊnd] *adv*: to run ~ s'échouer.

ahead [əˈhed] *adv* 1. (*in front*) devant, en avant, right ~, straight ~ droit devant. 2. (*in better position*) en avance; Scotland are ~ by two goals to one l'Écosse mène par deux à un; to get ~ (*be successful*) réussir. 3. (*in time*) à l'avance;

the months ~ les mois à venir. ▶ **ahead of** *prep* **1.** (*in front of*) devant. **2.** (*in time*) avant; ~ **of schedule** (*work*) en avance sur le planning.

aid [eɪd] ◆ *n* aide *f*; **with the ~ of** (*person*) avec l'aide de; (*thing*) à l'aide de; **in ~ of** au profit de. ◆ *vt* **1.** (*help*) aider. **2.** (JUR): **to ~ and abet** être complice de.

AIDS, Aids [eɪdz] (*abbr of* **acquired immune deficiency syndrome**) ◆ *n* SIDA *m*, Sida *m*. ◆ *comp*: ~ **patient** sidéen *m*, -enne *f*.

ailing ['eɪlɪŋ] *adj* **1.** (*ill*) souffrant(e). **2.** *fig* (*economy, industry*) dans une mauvaise passe.

ailment ['eɪlmənt] *n* maladie *f*.

aim [eɪm] ◆ *n* **1.** (*objective*) but *m*, objectif *m*. **2.** (*in firing gun, arrow*): **to take ~ at** viser. ◆ *vt* **1.** (*gun, camera*): **to ~ sthg at** braquer qqch sur. **2.** *fig*: **to be ~ed at** (*plan, campaign etc*) être destiné(e) à, viser; (*criticism*) être dirigé(e) contre. ◆ *vi*: **to ~ (at)** viser; **to ~ at OR for** *fig* viser; **to ~ to do sthg** viser à faire qqch.

aimless ['eɪmlɪs] *adj* (*person*) désœuvré(e); (*life*) sans but.

ain't [eɪnt] *inf* = **am not, are not, is not, have not, has not.**

air [eəʳ] ◆ *n* **1.** (*gen*) air *m*; **to throw sthg into the ~** jeter qqch en l'air; **by ~** (*travel*) par avion; **to be (up) in the ~** *fig* (*plans*) être vague. **2.** (RADIO & TV): **on the ~** à l'antenne. ◆ *comp* (*transport*) aérien(enne). ◆ *vt* **1.** (*gen*) aérer. **2.** (*make publicly known*) faire connaître OR communiquer. **3.** (*broadcast*) diffuser. ◆ *vi* sécher.

airbag ['eabæg] *n* (AUT) coussin *m* pneumatique (de sécurité).

airbase ['eəbeɪs] *n* base *f* aérienne.

airbed ['eəbed] *n* Br matelas *m* pneumatique.

airborne ['eəbɔːn] *adj* **1.** (*troops etc*) aéroporté(e); (*seeds*) emporté(e) par le vent. **2.** (*plane*) qui a décollé.

air-conditioned [-kən'dɪʃnd] *adj* climatisé(e), à air conditionné.

air-conditioning [-kən'dɪʃnɪŋ] *n* climatisation *f*.

aircraft ['eəkrɑːft] (*pl inv*) *n* avion *m*.

aircraft carrier *n* porte-avions *m inv*.

airfield ['eəfiːld] *n* terrain *m* d'aviation.

airforce ['eəfɔːs] *n* armée *f* de l'air.

airgun ['eəgʌn] *n* carabine *f* OR fusil *m* à air comprimé.

airhostess ['eə,həʊstɪs] *n* hôtesse *f* de l'air.

airlift ['eəlɪft] ◆ *n* pont *m* aérien. ◆ *vt* transporter par pont aérien.

airline ['eəlaɪn] *n* compagnie *f* aérienne.

airliner ['eəlaɪnəʳ] *n* (*short-distance*) (avion *m*) moyen-courrier *m*; (*long-distance*) (avion *m*) long-courrier *m*.

airlock ['eəlɒk] *n* **1.** (*in tube, pipe*) poche *f* d'air. **2.** (*airtight chamber*) sas *m*.

airmail ['eəmeɪl] *n* poste *f* aérienne; **by ~** par avion.

airplane ['eəpleɪn] *n* Am avion *m*.

airport ['eəpɔːt] *n* aéroport *m*.

air raid *n* raid *m* aérien, attaque *f* aérienne.

air rifle *n* carabine *f* à air comprimé.

airsick ['eəsɪk] *adj*: **to be ~** avoir le mal de l'air.

airspace ['eəspeɪs] *n* espace *m* aérien.

air steward *n* steward *m*.

airstrip ['eəstrɪp] *n* piste *f*.

air terminal *n* aérogare *f*.

airtight ['eətaɪt] *adj* hermétique.

air-traffic controller *n* aiguilleur *m* (du ciel).

airy ['eərɪ] *adj* **1.** (*room*) aéré(e). **2.** (*notions, promises*) chimérique, vain(e). **3.** (*nonchalant*) nonchalant(e).

aisle [aɪl] *n* allée *f*; (*in plane*) couloir *m*.

ajar [ə'dʒɑːʳ] *adj* entrouvert(e).

aka (*abbr of* **also known as**) alias.

alacrity [ə'lækrətɪ] *n* empressement *m*.

alarm [ə'lɑːm] ◆ *n* **1.** (*fear*) alarme *f*, inquiétude *f*. **2.** (*device*) alarme *f*; **to raise OR sound the ~** donner OR sonner l'alarme. ◆ *vt* alarmer, alerter.

alarm clock *n* réveil *m*, réveille-matin *m inv*.

alarming [ə'lɑːmɪŋ] *adj* alarmant(e), inquiétant(e).

alas [ə'læs] *excl* hélas!

Albania [æl'beɪnjə] *n* Albanie *f*.

Albanian [æl'beɪnjən] ◆ *adj* albanais(e). ◆ *n* **1.** (*person*) Albanais *m*, -e *f*. **2.** (*language*) albanais *m*.

albeit [ɔːl'biːɪt] *conj* bien que (+ *subjunctive*).

albino [æl'biːnəʊ] (*pl* -s) *n* albinos *mf*.

album ['ælbəm] *n* album *m*.

alcohol ['ælkəhɒl] *n* alcool *m*.

alcoholic [,ælkə'hɒlɪk] ◆ *adj* (*person*) alcoolique; (*drink*) alcoolisé(e). ◆ *n* alcoolique *mf*.

alcopop ['ælkəʊpɒp] *n* boisson gazeuse faiblement alcoolisée.

alcove ['ælkəʊv] n alcôve f.

alderman ['ɔːldəmən] (pl -men [-mən]) n conseiller m municipal.

ale [eɪl] n bière f.

alert [ə'lɜːt] ◆ adj 1. (vigilant) vigilant(e). 2. (perceptive) vif (vive), éveillé(e). 3. (aware): to be ~ to être conscient(e) de. ◆ n (warning) alerte f; on the ~ (watchful) sur le qui-vive; (MIL) en état d'alerte. ◆ vt alerter; to ~ sb to sthg avertir qqn de qqch.

A-level (abbr of Advanced level) n ≃ baccalauréat m.

alfresco [æl'freskəʊ] adj & adv en plein air.

algae ['ældʒiː] npl algues fpl.

algebra ['ældʒɪbrə] n algèbre f.

Algeria [æl'dʒɪərɪə] n Algérie f.

alias ['eɪlɪəs] (pl -es) ◆ adv alias. ◆ n faux nom m, nom d'emprunt.

alibi ['ælɪbaɪ] n alibi m.

alien ['eɪljən] ◆ adj 1. (gen) étranger(ère). 2. (from outer space) extraterrestre. ◆ n 1. (from outer space) extraterrestre mf. 2. (JUR) (foreigner) étranger m, -ère f.

alienate ['eɪljəneɪt] vt aliéner.

alight [ə'laɪt] ◆ adj allumé(e), en feu. ◆ vi 1. (bird etc) se poser. 2. (from bus, train): to ~ from descendre de.

align [ə'laɪn] vt (line up) aligner.

alike [ə'laɪk] ◆ adj semblable. ◆ adv de la même façon; to look ~ se ressembler.

alimony ['ælɪmənɪ] n pension f alimentaire.

alive [ə'laɪv] adj 1. (living) vivant(e), en vie. 2. (practice, tradition) vivace; to keep ~ préserver. 3. (lively) plein(e) de vitalité; to come ~ (story, description) prendre vie; (person, place) s'animer.

alkali ['ælkəlaɪ] (pl -s OR -es) n alcali m.

all [ɔːl] ◆ adj 1. (with sg noun) tout (toute); ~ day/night/evening toute la journée/la nuit/la soirée; ~ the drink toute la boisson; ~ the time tout le temps. 2. (with pl noun) tous (toutes); ~ the boxes toutes les boîtes; ~ men tous les hommes; ~ three died ils sont morts tous les trois, tous les trois sont morts. ◆ pron 1. (sg) (the whole amount) tout m; she drank it ~, she drank ~ of it elle a tout bu. 2. (pl) (everybody, everything) tous (toutes), ~ of them came, they ~ came ils sont tous venus. 3. (with superl): ... of ~ ... de tous (toutes); I like this one best of ~ je préfère celui-ci entre tous. 4. above ~ → above; after ~ → after; at

~ → at. ◆ adv 1. (entirely) complètement; I'd forgotten ~ about that j'avais complètement oublié cela; ~ alone tout seul (toute seule). 2. (in sport, competitions): the score is five ~ le score est cinq partout. 3. (with compar): to run ~ the faster courir d'autant plus vite; ~ the better d'autant mieux. ▶ all but adv presque, pratiquement. ▶ all in all adv dans l'ensemble. ▶ in all adv en tout.

Allah ['ælə] n Allah m.

all-around Am = all-round.

allay [ə'leɪ] vt (fears, anger) apaiser, calmer; (doubts) dissiper.

all clear n signal m de fin d'alerte; fig feu m vert.

allegation [,ælɪ'geɪʃn] n allégation f.

allege [ə'ledʒ] vt prétendre, alléguer; she is ~d to have done it on prétend qu'elle l'a fait.

allegedly [ə'ledʒɪdlɪ] adv prétendument.

allegiance [ə'liːdʒəns] n allégeance f.

allergic [ə'lɜːdʒɪk] adj: ~ (to) allergique (à).

allergy ['ælədʒɪ] n allergie f; to have an ~ to sthg être allergique à qqch.

alleviate [ə'liːvɪeɪt] vt apaiser, soulager.

alley(way) ['ælɪ(weɪ)] n (street) ruelle f; (in garden) allée f.

alliance [ə'laɪəns] n alliance f.

allied ['ælaɪd] adj 1. (MIL) allié(e). 2. (related) connexe.

alligator ['ælɪgeɪtər] (pl inv OR -s) n alligator m.

all-important adj capital(e), crucial(e).

all-in adj Br (price) global(e). ▶ all in adv (inclusive) tout compris.

all-night adj (party etc) qui dure toute la nuit; (bar etc) ouvert(e) toute la nuit.

allocate ['æləkeɪt] vt (money, resources): to ~ sthg (to sb) attribuer qqch (à qqn).

allot [ə'lɒt] vt (job) assigner; (money, resources) attribuer; (time) allouer.

allotment [ə'lɒtmənt] n 1. Br (garden) jardin m ouvrier (loué par la commune). 2. (sharing out) attribution f.

all-out adj (effort) maximum (inv); (war) total(e).

allow [ə'laʊ] vt 1. (permit - activity, behaviour) autoriser, permettre; to ~ sb to do sthg permettre à qqn de faire qqch, autoriser qqn à faire qqch. 2. (set aside - money, time) prévoir. 3. (officially accept) accepter. 4. (concede): to ~ that ...

admettre que ... ▶ **allow for** vt fus
tenir compte de.

allowance [ə'lauəns] n 1. (money
received) indemnité f. 2. Am (pocket
money) argent m de poche. 3. (excuse) to
make ~s for sb faire preuve d'indulgence envers qqn; to make ~s for sthg
prendre qqch en considération.

alloy ['ælɔɪ] n alliage m.

all right ◆ adv bien; (in answer - yes)
d'accord. ◆ adj 1. (healthy) en bonne
santé; (unharmed) sain et sauf (saine et
sauve). 2. inf (acceptable, satisfactory): it
was ~ c'était pas mal; that's ~ (never
mind) ce n'est pas grave.

all-round Br, **all-around** Am adj
(multi-skilled) doué(e) dans tous les
domaines.

all-time adj (record) sans précédent.

allude [ə'lu:d] vi: to ~ to faire allusion
à.

alluring [ə'ljuərɪŋ] adj séduisant(e).

allusion [ə'lu:ʒn] n allusion f.

ally [n 'ælaɪ, vb ə'laɪ] n allié m, -e f.
◆ vt: to ~ o.s. with s'allier à.

almighty [ɔ:l'maɪtɪ] adj inf (noise) terrible.

almond ['ɑ:mənd] n (nut) amande f.

almost ['ɔ:lməust] adv presque; I ~
missed the bus j'ai failli rater le bus.

alms [ɑ:mz] npl dated aumône f.

aloft [ə'lɒft] adv (in the air) en l'air.

alone [ə'ləun] ◆ adj seul(e). ◆ adv seul;
to leave sthg ~ ne pas toucher à qqch;
leave me ~! laisse-moi tranquille!

along [ə'lɒŋ] ◆ adv: to walk ~ se
promener; to move ~ avancer; can I
come ~ (with you)? est-ce que je peux
venir (avec vous)? ◆ prep le long de; to
run/walk ~ the street courir/marcher le
long de la rue. ▶ all along adv depuis
le début. ▶ along with prep ainsi que.

alongside [ə,lɒŋ'saɪd] ◆ prep le long
de, à côté de; (person) à côté de. ◆ adv
bord à bord.

aloof [ə'lu:f] ◆ adj distant(e). ◆ adv: to
remain ~ (from) garder ses distances
(vis-à-vis de).

aloud [ə'laud] adv à voix haute, tout
haut.

alphabet ['ælfəbet] n alphabet
m.

alphabetical [,ælfə'betɪkl] adj alphabétique.

Alps [ælps] npl: the ~ les Alpes fpl.

already [ɔ:l'redɪ] adv déjà.

alright [,ɔ:l'raɪt] = all right.

Alsace [æl'sæs] n Alsace f.

Alsatian [æl'seɪʃn] n (dog) berger m
allemand.

also ['ɔ:lsəu] adv aussi.

altar ['ɔ:ltər] n autel m.

alter ['ɔ:ltər] ◆ vt changer, modifier.
◆ vi changer.

alteration [,ɔ:ltə'reɪʃn] n modification
f, changement m.

alternate [adj Br ɔ:l'tɜ:nət, Am
'ɔ:ltərnət, vb 'ɔ:ltɜ:neɪt] ◆ adj alterné(e),
alternatif(ive); ~ days tous les deux
jours, un jour sur deux. ◆ vt faire
alterner. ◆ vi: to ~ (with) alterner (avec);
to ~ between sthg and sthg passer de
qqch à qqch.

alternately [ɔ:l'tɜ:nətlɪ] adv alternativement.

alternating current ['ɔ:ltəneɪtɪŋ-] n
courant m alternatif.

alternative [ɔ:l'tɜ:nətɪv] ◆ adj 1. (different) autre. 2. (non-traditional - society)
parallèle; (- art, energy) alternatif(ive).
◆ n 1. (between two solutions) alternative f.
2. (other possibility): ~ (to) solution f de
remplacement (à); to have no ~ but to
do sthg ne pas avoir d'autre choix que
de faire qqch.

alternatively [ɔ:l'tɜ:nətɪvlɪ] adv ou
bien.

alternative medicine n médecine f
parallèle OR douce.

alternator ['ɔ:ltəneɪtər] n (ELEC) alter-
nateur m.

although [ɔ:l'ðəu] conj bien que (+
subjunctive).

altitude ['æltɪtju:d] n altitude f.

alto ['æltəu] (pl -s) n 1. (male voice)
haute-contre f. 2. (female voice) contralto
m.

altogether [,ɔ:ltə'geðər] adv 1. (completely) entièrement, tout à fait. 2. (considering all things) tout compte fait. 3. (in
all) en tout.

aluminium Br [,ælju'mɪnɪəm], **aluminum** Am [ə'lu:mɪnəm] ◆ n aluminium m. ◆ comp en aluminium.

always ['ɔ:lweɪz] adv toujours.

am [æm] → be.

a.m. (abbr of ante meridiem): at 3 ~ à 3h
(du matin).

AM (abbr of amplitude modulation) n AM
f.

amalgamate [ə'mælgəmeɪt] vt & vi
(unite) fusionner.

amass [ə'mæs] vt amasser.

amateur ['æmətər] ◆ adj amateur
(inv); pej d'amateur. ◆ n amateur m.

amaze [ə'meɪz] vt étonner, stupéfier.

amazed [ə'meɪzd] adj stupéfait(e).
amazement [ə'meɪzmənt] n stupéfaction f.
amazing [ə'meɪzɪŋ] adj 1. (surprising) étonnant(e), ahurissant(e). 2. (wonderful) excellent(e).
Amazon ['æməzn] n 1. (river): **the ~** l'Amazone f. 2. (region): **the ~ (Basin)** l'Amazonie f; **the ~ rainforest** la forêt amazonienne.
ambassador [æm'bæsədəʳ] n ambassadeur m, -drice f.
amber ['æmbəʳ] ◆ adj 1. (amber-coloured) ambré(e). 2. Br (traffic light) orange (inv). ◆ n (substance) ambre m.
ambiguous [æm'bɪgjʊəs] adj ambigu(ë).
ambition [æm'bɪʃn] n ambition f.
ambitious [æm'bɪʃəs] adj ambitieux (euse).
amble ['æmbl] vi déambuler.
ambulance ['æmbjʊləns] n ambulance f.
ambush ['æmbʊʃ] ◆ n embuscade f. ◆ vt tendre une embuscade à.
amenable [ə'mi:nəbl] adj: **~ (to)** ouvert(e) (à).
amend [ə'mend] vt modifier; (law) amender. ▶ **amends** npl: **to .make ~s (for)** se racheter (pour).
amendment [ə'mendmənt] n modification f; (to law) amendement m.
amenities [ə'mi:nətɪz] npl aménagements mpl, équipements mpl.
America [ə'merɪkə] n Amérique f; **in ~** en Amérique.
American [ə'merɪkn] ◆ adj américain(e). ◆ n Américain m, -e f.
American Indian n Indien m, -enne f d'Amérique, Amérindien m, -enne f.
amiable ['eɪmjəbl] adj aimable.
amicable ['æmɪkəbl] adj amical(e).
amid(st) [ə'mɪd(st)] prep au milieu de, parmi.
amiss [ə'mɪs] ◆ adj: **is there anything ~?** y a-t-il quelque chose qui ne va pas? ◆ adv: **to take sthg ~** prendre qqch de travers.
ammonia [ə'məʊnjə] n (liquid) ammoniaque f.
ammunition [,æmjʊ'nɪʃn] n (U) 1. (MIL) munitions fpl. 2. fig (argument) argument m.
amnesia [æm'ni:zjə] n amnésie f.
amnesty ['æmnəstɪ] n amnistie f.
amok [ə'mɒk] adv: **to run ~** être pris(e) d'une crise de folie furieuse.
among(st) [ə'mʌŋ(st)] prep parmi,

entre; **~ other things** entre autres (choses).
amoral [,eɪ'mɒrəl] adj amoral(e).
amorous ['æmərəs] adj amoureux (euse).
amount [ə'maʊnt] n 1. (quantity) quantité f; **a great ~ of** beaucoup de. 2. (sum of money) somme f, montant m. ▶ **amount to** vt fus 1. (total) se monter à, s'élever à. 2. (be equivalent to) revenir à, équivaloir à.
amp [æmp] n abbr of **ampere**.
ampere ['æmpeəʳ] n ampère m.
amphibious [æm'fɪbɪəs] adj amphibie.
ample ['æmpl] adj 1. (enough) suffisamment de, assez de. 2. (large) ample.
amplifier ['æmplɪfaɪəʳ] n amplificateur m.
amputate ['æmpjʊteɪt] vt & vi amputer.
Amsterdam [,æmstə'dæm] n Amsterdam.
Amtrak ['æmtræk] n société nationale de chemins de fer aux États-Unis.
amuck [ə'mʌk] = **amok**.
amuse [ə'mju:z] vt 1. (make laugh) amuser, faire rire. 2. (entertain) divertir, distraire; **to ~ o.s. (by doing sthg)** s'occuper (à faire qqch).
amused [ə'mju:zd] adj 1. (laughing) amusé(e); **to be ~ at OR by sthg** trouver qqch amusant. 2. (entertained): **to keep o.s. ~** s'occuper.
amusement [ə'mju:zmənt] n 1. (laughter) amusement m. 2. (diversion, game) distraction f.
amusement arcade n galerie f de jeux.
amusement park n parc m d'attractions.
amusing [ə'mju:zɪŋ] adj amusant(e).
an [stressed æn, unstressed ən] → **a**.
anabolic steroid [,ænə'bɒlɪk-] n (stéroïde m) anabolisant m.
anaemic Br, **anemic** Am [ə'ni:mɪk] adj anémique; fig & pej fade, plat(e).
anaesthetic Br, **anesthetic** Am [,ænɪs'θetɪk] n anesthésique m; **under ~** sous anesthésie; **local/general ~** anesthésie f locale/générale.
analogy [ə'nælədʒɪ] n analogie f.
analyse Br, **analyze** Am ['ænəlaɪz] vt analyser.
analysis [ə'næləsɪs] (pl **analyses** [ə'næləsi:z]) n analyse f.
analyst ['ænəlɪst] n analyste mf.
analytic(al) [,ænə'lɪtɪk(l)] adj analytique.

analyze Am = **analyse**.

anarchist ['ænəkɪst] n anarchiste mf.

anarchy ['ænəkɪ] n anarchie f.

anathema [ə'næθəmə] n anathème m.

anatomy [ə'nætəmɪ] n anatomie f.

ANC (abbr of **African National Congress**) n ANC m.

ancestor ['ænsestər] n lit & fig ancêtre m.

anchor ['æŋkər] ◆ n ancre f; **to drop/weigh ~** jeter/lever l'ancre. ◆ vt 1. (secure) ancrer. 2. (TV) présenter. ◆ vi (NAUT) jeter l'ancre.

anchovy ['æntʃəvɪ] (pl inv OR **-ies**) n anchois m.

ancient ['eɪnʃənt] adj 1. (monument etc) historique; (custom) ancien(enne). 2. hum (car etc) antique; (person) vieux (vieille).

ancillary [æn'sɪlərɪ] adj auxiliaire.

and [stressed ænd, unstressed ənd, ən] conj 1. (as well as, plus) et. 2. (in numbers): **one hundred ~ eighty** cent quatre-vingts; **six ~ a half** six et demi. 3. (to): **come ~ see!** venez voir!; **try ~ come** essayez de venir; **wait ~ see** vous verrez bien. ▶ **and so on, and so forth** adv et ainsi de suite.

Andes ['ændi:z] npl: **the ~** les Andes fpl.

Andorra [æn'dɔ:rə] n Andorre f.

anecdote ['ænɪkdəʊt] n anecdote f.

anemic Am = **anaemic**.

anesthetic etc Am = **anaesthetic** etc.

anew [ə'nju:] adv: **to start ~** recommencer (à zéro).

angel ['eɪndʒəl] n ange m.

anger ['æŋgər] ◆ n colère f. ◆ vt fâcher, irriter.

angina [æn'dʒaɪnə] n angine f de poitrine.

angle ['æŋgl] n 1. (gen) angle m; **at an ~** de travers, en biais. 2. (point of view) point m de vue, angle m.

angler ['æŋglər] n pêcheur m (à la ligne).

Anglican ['æŋglɪkən] ◆ adj anglican(e). ◆ n anglican m, -e f.

angling ['æŋglɪŋ] n pêche f à la ligne.

angry ['æŋgrɪ] adj (person) en colère, fâché(e); (words, quarrel) violent(e); **to be ~ with OR at sb** être en colère OR fâché contre qqn; **to get ~** se mettre en colère, se fâcher.

anguish ['æŋgwɪʃ] n angoisse f.

angular ['æŋgjʊlər] adj anguleux (euse).

animal ['ænɪml] ◆ n animal m; pej brute f. ◆ adj animal(e).

animate ['ænɪmət] adj animé(e), vivant(e).

animated ['ænɪmeɪtɪd] adj animé(e).

aniseed ['ænɪsi:d] n anis m.

ankle ['æŋkl] ◆ n cheville f. ◆ comp: **~ socks** socquettes fpl; **~ boots** bottines fpl.

annex(e) ['æneks] ◆ n (building) annexe f. ◆ vt annexer.

annihilate [ə'naɪəleɪt] vt anéantir, annihiler.

anniversary [ˌænɪ'vɜ:sərɪ] n anniversaire m.

announce [ə'naʊns] vt annoncer.

announcement [ə'naʊnsmənt] n 1. (statement) déclaration f; (in newspaper) avis m. 2. (U) (act of stating) annonce f.

announcer [ə'naʊnsər] n (RADIO & TV) speaker m, speakerine f.

annoy [ə'nɔɪ] vt agacer, contrarier.

annoyance [ə'nɔɪəns] n contrariété f.

annoyed [ə'nɔɪd] adj mécontent(e), agacé(e); **to get ~** se fâcher; **to be ~ with sb** être fâché contre qqn.

annoying [ə'nɔɪɪŋ] adj agaçant(e).

annual ['ænjʊəl] ◆ adj annuel(elle). ◆ n 1. (plant) plante f annuelle. 2. (book - gen) publication f annuelle; (- for children) album m.

annual general meeting n assemblée f générale annuelle.

annul [ə'nʌl] vt annuler; (law) abroger.

annum ['ænəm] n: **per ~** par an.

anomaly [ə'nɒməlɪ] n anomalie f.

anonymous [ə'nɒnɪməs] adj anonyme.

anorak ['ænəræk] n anorak m.

anorexia (nervosa) [ˌænə'reksɪə (nɜ:'vəʊsə)] n anorexie f mentale.

anorexic [ˌænə'reksɪk] ◆ adj anorexique. ◆ n anorexique mf.

another [ə'nʌðər] ◆ adj 1. (additional): **~ apple** encore une pomme, une pomme de plus, une autre pomme; **in ~ few minutes** dans quelques minutes; **(would you like) ~ drink?** encore un verre? 2. (different): **~ job** un autre travail. ◆ pron 1. (additional one) un autre (une autre), encore un (encore une); **one after ~** l'un après l'autre (l'une après l'autre). 2. (different one) un autre (une autre); **one ~** l'un l'autre (l'une l'autre).

answer ['ɑ:nsər] ◆ n 1. (gen) réponse f; **there's no ~** (on phone) ça ne répond pas; **in ~ to** en réponse à. 2. (to problem) solution f. ◆ vt répondre à; **to ~ the door**

aller ouvrir la porte; **to ~ the phone** répondre au téléphone. ◆ *vi* (*reply*) répondre. ▶ **answer back** ◆ *vt sep* répondre à. ◆ *vi* répondre. ▶ **answer for** *vt fus* être responsable de, répondre de.

answerable ['ɑːnsərəbl] *adj*: ~ **to sb/ for sthg** responsable devant qqn/de qqch.

answering machine ['ɑːnsərɪŋ-] *n* répondeur *m*.

ant [ænt] *n* fourmi *f*.

antagonism [æn'tægənɪzm] *n* antagonisme *m*, hostilité *f*.

antagonize, -ise [æn'tægənaɪz] *vt* éveiller l'hostilité de.

Antarctic [æn'tɑːktɪk] ◆ *n*: **the ~** l'Antarctique *m*. ◆ *adj* antarctique.

antelope ['æntɪləʊp] (*pl inv* OR **-s**) *n* antilope *f*.

antenatal [,æntɪ'neɪtl] *adj* prénatal(e).

antenatal clinic *n* service *m* de consultation prénatale.

antenna [æn'tenə] (*pl sense 1* **-nae** [-niː], *pl sense 2* **-s**) *n* **1.** (*of insect*) antenne *f*. **2.** Am (*for* TV, *radio*) antenne *f*.

anthem ['ænθəm] *n* hymne *m*.

anthology [æn'θɒlədʒɪ] *n* anthologie *f*.

antibiotic [,æntɪbaɪ'ɒtɪk] *n* antibiotique *m*.

antibody ['æntɪ,bɒdɪ] *n* anticorps *m*.

anticipate [æn'tɪsɪpeɪt] *vt* **1.** (*expect*) s'attendre à, prévoir. **2.** (*request, movement*) anticiper; (*competitor*) prendre de l'avance sur. **3.** (*look forward to*) savourer à l'avance.

anticipation [æn,tɪsɪ'peɪʃn] *n* (*expectation*) attente *f*; (*eagerness*) impatience *f*; **in ~ of** en prévision de.

anticlimax [,æntɪ'klaɪmæks] *n* déception *f*.

anticlockwise [,æntɪ'klɒkwaɪz] *adj &* *adv* Br dans le sens inverse des aiguilles d'une montre.

antics ['æntɪks] *npl* **1.** (*of children, animals*) gambades *fpl*. **2.** *pej* (*of politicians etc*) bouffonneries *fpl*.

anticyclone [,æntɪ'saɪkləʊn] *n* anticyclone *m*.

antidepressant [,æntɪdɪ'presnt] *n* antidépresseur *m*.

antidote ['æntɪdəʊt] *n lit & fig*: ~ **(to)** antidote *m* (contre).

antifreeze ['æntɪfriːz] *n* antigel *m*.

antihistamine [,æntɪ'hɪstəmɪn] *n* antihistaminique *m*.

antiperspirant [,æntɪ'pɜːspərənt] *n* déodorant *m*.

antiquated ['æntɪkweɪtɪd] *adj* dépassé(e).

antique [æn'tiːk] ◆ *adj* ancien(enne). ◆ *n* (*object*) objet *m* ancien; (*piece of furniture*) meuble *m* ancien.

antique shop *n* magasin *m* d'antiquités.

anti-Semitism [,æntɪ'semɪtɪzəm] *n* antisémitisme *m*.

antiseptic [,æntɪ'septɪk] ◆ *adj* antiseptique. ◆ *n* désinfectant *m*.

antisocial [,æntɪ'səʊʃl] *adj* **1.** (*against society*) antisocial(e). **2.** (*unsociable*) peu sociable, sauvage.

antlers [,æntləz] *npl* bois *mpl*.

anus ['eɪnəs] *n* anus *m*.

anvil ['ænvɪl] *n* enclume *f*.

anxiety [æŋ'zaɪətɪ] *n* **1.** (*worry*) anxiété *f*. **2.** (*cause of worry*) souci *m*. **3.** (*keenness*) désir *m* farouche.

anxious ['æŋkʃəs] *adj* **1.** (*worried*) anxieux(euse), très inquiet(ète); **to be ~ about** se faire du souci au sujet de. **2.** (*keen*): **to be ~ to do sthg** tenir à faire qqch; **to be ~ that** tenir à ce que (+ *subjunctive*).

any ['enɪ] ◆ *adj* **1.** (*with negative*) de, d'; **I haven't got ~ money/tickets** je n'ai pas d'argent/de billets; **he never does ~ work** il ne travaille jamais. **2.** (*some - with sg noun*) du, de l', de la; (- *with pl noun*) des; **have you got ~ money/milk/cousins?** est-ce que vous avez de l'argent/du lait/des cousins? **3.** (*no matter which*) n'importe quel (n'importe quelle); **~ box will do** n'importe quelle boîte fera l'affaire; *see also* **case, day, moment, rate.** ◆ *pron* **1.** (*with negative*) en; **I didn't buy ~ (of them)** je n'en ai pas acheté; **I didn't know ~ of the guests** je ne connaissais aucun des invités. **2.** (*some*) en; **do you have ~?** est-ce que vous en avez? **3.** (*no matter which one or ones*) n'importe lequel (n'importe laquelle); **take ~ you like** prenez n'importe lequel/laquelle, prenez celui/celle que vous voulez. ◆ *adv* **1.** (*with negative*): **I can't see it ~ more** je ne le vois plus; **I can't stand it ~ longer** je ne peux plus le supporter. **2.** (*some, a little*) un peu; **do you want ~ more potatoes?** voulez-vous encore des pommes de terre?; **is that ~ better/different?** est-ce que c'est mieux/différent comme ça?

anybody ['enɪ,bɒdɪ] = **anyone.**

anyhow ['enɪhaʊ] *adv* **1.** (*in spite of that*) quand même, néanmoins. **2.** (*carelessly*) n'importe comment. **3.** (*in any case*) de toute façon.

anyone ['enɪwʌn] *pron* **1.** (*in negative sentences*): **I didn't see ~** je n'ai vu personne. **2.** (*in questions*) quelqu'un. **3.** (*any person*) n'importe qui.

anyplace *Am* = **anywhere**.

anything ['enɪθɪŋ] *pron* **1.** (*in negative sentences*): **I didn't see ~** je n'ai rien vu. **2.** (*in questions*) quelque chose; **~ else?** (*in shop*) et avec ceci? **3.** (*any object, event*) n'importe quoi; **if ~ happens ...** s'il arrive quoi que ce soit ...

anyway ['enɪweɪ] *adv* (*in any case*) de toute façon.

anywhere ['enɪweəʳ], **anyplace** *Am* ['enɪpleɪs] *adv* **1.** (*in negative sentences*): **I haven't seen him ~** je ne l'ai vu nulle part. **2.** (*in questions*) quelque part. **3.** (*any place*) n'importe où.

apart [ə'pɑːt] *adv* **1.** (*separated*) séparé(e), éloigné(e). **2.** (*to one side*) à l'écart. **3.** (*aside*) joking **~** sans plaisanter, plaisanterie à part. ▶ **apart from** *prep* **1.** (*except for*) à part, sauf. **2.** (*as well as*) en plus de, outre.

apartheid [ə'pɑːtheɪt] *n* apartheid *m*.

apartment [ə'pɑːtmənt] *n* appartement *m*.

apartment building *n Am* immeuble *m* (*d'habitation*).

apathy ['æpəθɪ] *n* apathie *f*.

ape [eɪp] ♦ *n* singe *m*. ♦ *vt* singer.

aperitif [əperə'tiːf] *n* apéritif *m*.

aperture ['æpə,tjuəʳ] *n* **1.** (*hole, opening*) orifice *m*, ouverture *f*. **2.** (PHOT) ouverture *f*.

APEX ['eɪpeks] (*abbr of* **advance purchase excursion**) *n Br*: **~ ticket** billet *m* APEX.

apiece [ə'piːs] *adv* (*for each person*) chacun(e), par personne; (*for each thing*) chacun(e), pièce (*inv*).

apocalypse [ə'pɒkəlɪps] *n* apocalypse *f*.

apologetic [ə,pɒlə'dʒetɪk] *adj* (*letter etc*) d'excuse; **to be ~ about sthg** s'excuser de qqch.

apologize, -ise [ə'pɒlədʒaɪz] *vi* s'excuser; **to ~ to sb (for sthg)** faire des excuses à qqn (pour qqch).

apology [ə'pɒlədʒɪ] *n* excuses *fpl*.

apostle [ə'pɒsl] *n* (RELIG) apôtre *m*.

apostrophe [ə'pɒstrəfɪ] *n* apostrophe *f*.

appal *Br*, **appall** *Am* [ə'pɔːl] *vt* horrifier.

appalling [ə'pɔːlɪŋ] *adj* épouvantable.

apparatus [,æpə'reɪtəs] (*pl inv* OR **-es**) *n* **1.** (*device*) appareil *m*, dispositif *m*. **2.** (U) (*in gym*) agrès *mpl*. **3.** (*system, organization*) appareil *m*.

apparel [ə'pærəl] *n Am* habillement *m*.

apparent [ə'pærənt] *adj* **1.** (*evident*) évident(e). **2.** (*seeming*) apparent(e).

apparently [ə'pærəntlɪ] *adv* **1.** (*it seems*) à ce qu'il paraît. **2.** (*seemingly*) apparemment, en apparence.

appeal [ə'piːl] ♦ *vi* **1.** (*request*): **to ~ (to sb for sthg)** lancer un appel (à qqn pour obtenir qqch). **2.** (*make a plea*): **to ~ to** faire appel à. **3.** (JUR): **to ~ (against)** faire appel (de). **4.** (*attract, interest*): **to ~ to sb** plaire à qqn; **it ~s to me** ça me plaît. ♦ *n* **1.** (*request*) appel *m*. **2.** (JUR) appel *m*. **3.** (*charm, interest*) intérêt *m*, attrait *m*.

appealing [ə'piːlɪŋ] *adj* (*attractive*) attirant(e), sympathique.

appear [ə'pɪəʳ] *vi* **1.** (*gen*) apparaître; (*book*) sortir, paraître. **2.** (*seem*) sembler, paraître; **to ~ to be/do** sembler être/faire; **it would ~ (that) ...** il semblerait que ... **3.** (*in play, film etc*) jouer. **4.** (JUR) comparaître.

appearance [ə'pɪərəns] *n* **1.** (*gen*) apparition *f*; **to make an ~** se montrer. **2.** (*look*) apparence *f*, aspect *m*.

appease [ə'piːz] *vt* apaiser.

append [ə'pend] *vt* ajouter; (*signature*) apposer.

appendices [ə'pendɪsiːz] *pl* → **appendix**.

appendicitis [ə,pendɪ'saɪtɪs] *n* (U) appendicite *f*.

appendix [ə'pendɪks] (*pl* **-dixes** OR **-dices**) *n* appendice *m*; **to have one's ~ out** OR **removed** se faire opérer de l'appendicite.

appetite ['æpɪtaɪt] *n* **1.** (*for food*): **~ (for)** appétit *m* (pour). **2.** *fig* (*enthusiasm*): **~ (for)** goût *m* (de OR pour).

appetizer, -iser ['æpɪtaɪzəʳ] *n* (*food*) amuse-gueule *m inv*; (*drink*) apéritif *m*.

appetizing, -ising ['æpɪtaɪzɪŋ] *adj* (*food*) appétissant(e).

applaud [ə'plɔːd] ♦ *vt* **1.** (*clap*) applaudir. **2.** (*approve*) approuver, applaudir à. ♦ *vi* applaudir.

applause [ə'plɔːz] *n* (U) applaudissements *mpl*.

apple ['æpl] *n* pomme *f*.

apple tree *n* pommier *m*.

appliance [ə'plaɪəns] *n* (*device*) appareil *m*.

applicable [ə'plɪkəbl] *adj*: **~ (to)** applicable (à).

applicant ['æplɪkənt] n: ~ **(for)** (job) candidat m, -e f (à); (state benefit) demandeur m, -euse f (de).

application [,æplɪ'keɪʃn] n 1. (gen) application f. 2. (for job etc): ~ **(for)** demande f (de). 3. (COMPUT): ~ **(program)** programme m d'application.

application form n formulaire m de demande.

applied [ə'plaɪd] adj (science) appliqué(e).

apply [ə'plaɪ] ♦ vt appliquer; to ~ the brakes freiner. ♦ vi 1. (for work, grant): to ~ **(for)** faire une demande (de); to ~ for a job faire une demande d'emploi; to ~ to sb (for sthg) s'adresser à qqn (pour obtenir qqch). 2. (be relevant): to ~ **(to)** s'appliquer (à), concerner.

appoint [ə'pɔɪnt] vt 1. (to job, position): to ~ sb (as sthg) nommer qqn (qqch); to ~ sb to sthg nommer qqn à qqch. 2. (time, place) fixer.

appointment [ə'pɔɪntmənt] n 1. (to job, position) nomination f, désignation f. 2. (job, position) poste m, emploi m. 3. (arrangement to meet) rendez-vous m; to make an ~ prendre un rendez-vous.

apportion [ə'pɔːʃn] vt répartir.

appraisal [ə'preɪzl] n évaluation f.

appreciable [ə'priːʃəbl] adj (difference) sensible; (amount) appréciable.

appreciate [ə'priːʃɪeɪt] ♦ vt 1. (value, like) apprécier, aimer. 2. (recognize, understand) comprendre, se rendre compte de. 3. (be grateful for) être reconnaissant(e) de. ♦ vi (FIN) prendre de la valeur.

appreciation [ə,priːʃɪ'eɪʃn] n 1. (liking) contentement m. 2. (understanding) compréhension f. 3. (gratitude) reconnaissance f.

appreciative [ə'priːʃjətɪv] adj (person) reconnaissant(e); (remark) élogieux (euse).

apprehensive [,æprɪ'hensɪv] adj inquiet(ète); to be ~ **about** sthg appréhender OR craindre qqch.

apprentice [ə'prentɪs] n apprenti m, -e f.

apprenticeship [ə'prentɪsʃɪp] n apprentissage m.

approach [ə'prəʊtʃ] ♦ n 1. (gen) approche f. 2. (method) démarche f, approche f. 3. (to person): to make an ~ to sb faire une proposition à qqn. ♦ vt 1. (come near to - place, person, thing) s'approcher de. 2. (ask): to ~ sb about sthg aborder qqch avec qqn; (COMM) entrer en contact avec qqn au sujet de qqch. 3. (tackle - problem) aborder. ♦ vi s'approcher.

approachable [ə'prəʊtʃəbl] adj accessible.

appropriate [adj ə'prəʊprɪət, vb ə'prəʊprɪeɪt] ♦ adj (clothing) convenable; (action) approprié(e); (moment) opportun(e). ♦ vt 1. (JUR) s'approprier. 2. (allocate) affecter.

approval [ə'pruːvl] n approbation f; on ~ (COMM) à condition, à l'essai.

approve [ə'pruːv] ♦ vi: to ~ **(of sthg)** approuver (qqch). ♦ vt (ratify) approuver, ratifier.

approx. [ə'prɒks] (abbr of approximately) approx., env.

approximate [ə'prɒksɪmət] adj approximatif(ive).

approximately [ə'prɒksɪmətlɪ] adv à peu près, environ.

apricot ['eɪprɪkɒt] n abricot m.

April ['eɪprəl] n avril m; see also **September**.

April Fools' Day n le premier avril.

apron ['eɪprən] n (clothing) tablier m.

apt [æpt] adj 1. (pertinent) pertinent(e), approprié(e). 2. (likely): to be ~ to do sthg avoir tendance à faire qqch.

aptitude ['æptɪtjuːd] n aptitude f, disposition f.

aptly ['æptlɪ] adv avec justesse, à propos.

aqualung ['ækwəlʌŋ] n scaphandre m autonome.

aquarium [ə'kweərɪəm] (pl -riums OR -ria [-rɪə]) n aquarium m.

Aquarius [ə'kweərɪəs] n Verseau m.

aquatic [ə'kwætɪk] adj 1. (animal, plant) aquatique. 2. (sport) nautique.

aqueduct ['ækwɪdʌkt] n aqueduc m.

Arab ['ærəb] ♦ adj arabe. ♦ n (person) Arabe mf.

Arabian [ə'reɪbjən] adj d'Arabie, arabe.

Arabic ['ærəbɪk] ♦ adj arabe. ♦ n arabe m.

Arabic numeral n chiffre m arabe.

arable ['ærəbl] adj arable.

arbitrary ['ɑːbɪtrərɪ] adj arbitraire.

arbitration [,ɑːbɪ'treɪʃn] n arbitrage m; to go to ~ recourir à l'arbitrage.

arcade [ɑː'keɪd] n 1. (for shopping) galerie f marchande. 2. (covered passage) arcades fpl.

arch [ɑːtʃ] ♦ adj malicieux(euse), espiègle. ♦ n 1. (ARCHIT) arc m, voûte f.

2. (*of foot*) voûte *f* plantaire, cambrure *f*. ◆ *vt* cambrer, arquer. ◆ *vi* former une voûte.

archaeologist [ˌɑːkɪˈɒlədʒɪst] *n* archéologue *mf*.

archaeology [ˌɑːkɪˈɒlədʒɪ] *n* archéologie *f*.

archaic [ɑːˈkeɪɪk] *adj* archaïque.

archbishop [ˌɑːtʃˈbɪʃəp] *n* archevêque *m*.

archenemy [ˌɑːtʃˈenɪmɪ] *n* ennemi *m* numéro un.

archeology *etc* [ˌɑːkɪˈɒlədʒɪ] = **archaeology** *etc*.

archer [ˈɑːtʃər] *n* archer *m*.

archery [ˈɑːtʃərɪ] *n* tir *m* à l'arc.

archetypal [ˌɑːkɪˈtaɪpl] *adj* typique.

architect [ˈɑːkɪtekt] *n* lit & fig architecte *m*.

architecture [ˈɑːkɪtektʃər] *n* (*gen* & COMPUT) architecture *f*.

archives [ˈɑːkaɪvz] *npl* archives *fpl*.

archway [ˈɑːtʃweɪ] *n* passage *m* voûté.

Arctic [ˈɑːktɪk] ◆ *adj* **1.** (GEOGR) arctique. **2.** *inf* (*very cold*) glacial(e). ◆ *n*: the ~ l'Arctique *m*.

ardent [ˈɑːdənt] *adj* fervent(e), passionné(e).

arduous [ˈɑːdjʊəs] *adj* ardu(e).

are [*weak form* ər, *strong form* ɑːr] → **be**.

area [ˈeərɪə] *n* **1.** (*region*) région *f*; **parking** ~ aire de stationnement; **in the** ~ **of** (*approximately*) environ, à peu près. **2.** (*surface size*) aire *f*, superficie *f*. **3.** (*of knowledge, interest etc*) domaine *m*.

area code *n* indicatif *m* de zone.

arena [əˈriːnə] *n* lit & fig arène *f*.

aren't [ɑːnt] = **are not**.

Argentina [ˌɑːdʒənˈtiːnə] *n* Argentine *f*.

Argentine [ˈɑːdʒəntaɪn], **Argentinian** [ˌɑːdʒənˈtɪnɪən] ◆ *adj* argentin(e). ◆ *n* Argentin *m*, -e *f*.

arguably [ˈɑːɡjʊəblɪ] *adv*: **she's ~ the best** on peut soutenir qu'elle est la meilleure.

argue [ˈɑːɡjuː] ◆ *vi* **1.** (*quarrel*): **to ~ (with sb about sthg)** se disputer (avec qqn à propos de qqch). **2.** (*reason*): **to ~ (for/against)** argumenter (pour/contre). ◆ *vt* débattre de, discuter de; **to ~ that** soutenir OR maintenir que.

argument [ˈɑːɡjʊmənt] *n* **1.** (*quarrel*) dispute *f*; **to have an ~ (with sb)** se disputer (avec qqn). **2.** (*reason*) argument *m*. **3.** (U) (*reasoning*) discussion *f*, débat *m*.

argumentative [ˌɑːɡjʊˈmentətɪv] *adj*

querelleur(euse), batailleur(euse).

arid [ˈærɪd] *adj* lit & fig aride.

Aries [ˈeəriːz] *n* Bélier *m*.

arise [əˈraɪz] (*pt* **arose** [əˈrɪzn]) *vi* (*appear*) surgir, survenir; **to ~ from** résulter de, provenir de; **if the need ~s** si le besoin se fait sentir.

aristocrat [Br ˈærɪstəkræt, Am əˈrɪstəkræt] *n* aristocrate *mf*.

arithmetic [əˈrɪθmətɪk] *n* arithmétique *f*.

ark [ɑːk] *n* arche *f*.

arm [ɑːm] ◆ *n* **1.** (*of person, chair*) bras *m*; **~ in ~** bras dessus bras dessous; **to twist sb's ~** fig forcer la main à qqn. **2.** (*of garment*) manche *f*. ◆ *vt* armer. ▶ **arms** *npl* armes *fpl*; **to take up ~s** prendre les armes; **to be up in ~s about sthg** s'élever contre qqch.

armaments [ˈɑːməmənts] *npl* (*weapons*) matériel *m* de guerre, armements *mpl*.

armchair [ˈɑːmtʃeər] *n* fauteuil *m*.

armed [ɑːmd] *adj* lit & fig: ~ **(with)** armé(e) (de).

armed forces *npl* forces *fpl* armées.

armhole [ˈɑːmhəʊl] *n* emmanchure *f*.

armour Br, **armor** Am [ˈɑːmər] *n* **1.** (*for person*) armure *f*. **2.** (*for military vehicle*) blindage *m*.

armoured car [ˌɑːməd-] *n* voiture *f* blindée.

armoury Br, **armory** Am [ˈɑːmərɪ] *n* arsenal *m*.

armpit [ˈɑːmpɪt] *n* aisselle *f*.

armrest [ˈɑːmrest] *n* accoudoir *m*.

arms control [ˈɑːmz-] *n* contrôle *m* des armements.

army [ˈɑːmɪ] *n* lit & fig armée *f*.

A road *n* Br route *f* nationale.

aroma [əˈrəʊmə] *n* arôme *m*.

arose [əˈrəʊz] *pt* → **arise**.

around [əˈraʊnd] ◆ *adv* **1.** (*about, round*): **to walk ~** marcher par-ci par-là, errer; **to lie ~** (*clothes etc*) traîner. **2.** (*on all sides*) (tout) autour. **3.** (*near*) dans les parages. **4.** (*in circular movement*): **to turn ~** se retourner. **5.** *phr*: **he has been ~** *inf* il n'est pas né d'hier, il a de l'expérience. ◆ *prep* **1.** (*gen*) autour de; **to walk ~ a garden/town** faire le tour d'un jardin/d'une ville; **all ~ the country** dans tout le pays. **2.** (*near*): ~ **here** par ici. **3.** (*approximately*) environ, à peu près.

arouse [əˈraʊz] *vt* **1.** (*excite - feeling*) éveiller, susciter; (*- person*) exciter. **2.** (*wake*) réveiller.

arrange [əˈreɪndʒ] *vt* **1.** (*flowers, books, furniture*) arranger, disposer. **2.** (*event,* *meeting etc*) organiser, fixer; **to ~ to do sthg** convenir de faire qqch. **3.** (MUS) arranger.

arrangement [əˈreɪndʒmənt] *n* **1.** (*agreement*) accord *m*, arrangement *m*; **to come to an ~** s'entendre, s'arranger. **2.** (*of furniture, books*) arrangement *m*. **3.** (MUS) arrangement *m*. ▶ **arrangements** *npl* dispositions *fpl*, préparatifs *mpl*.

array [əˈreɪ] ◆ *n* (*of objects*) étalage *m*. ◆ *vt* (*ornaments etc*) disposer.

arrears [əˈrɪəz] *npl* (*money owed*) arriéré *m*; **to be in ~** (*late*) être en retard; (*owing money*) avoir des arriérés.

arrest [əˈrest] ◆ *n* (*by police*) arrestation *f*; **under ~** en état d'arrestation. ◆ *vt* **1.** (*gen*) arrêter. **2.** *fml* (*sb's attention*) attirer, retenir.

arrival [əˈraɪvl] *n* **1.** (*gen*) arrivée *f*; **late ~** (*of train etc*) retard *m*. **2.** (*person - at airport, hotel*) arrivant *m*, -e *f*; **new ~** (*person*) nouveau venu *m*, nouvelle venue *f*; (*baby*) nouveau-né *m*, nouveau-née *f*.

arrive [əˈraɪv] *vi* arriver; (*baby*) être né(e); **to ~ at** (*conclusion, decision*) arriver à.

arrogant [ˈærəgənt] *adj* arrogant(e).

arrow [ˈærəʊ] *n* flèche *f*.

arse Br [ɑːs], **ass** Am [æs] *n v inf* cul *m*.

arsenic [ˈɑːsnɪk] *n* arsenic *m*.

arson [ˈɑːsn] *n* incendie *m* criminel OR volontaire.

art [ɑːt] ◆ *n* art *m*. ◆ *comp* (*exhibition*) d'art; (*college*) des beaux-arts; **~ student** étudiant *m*, -e *f* d'une école des beaux-arts. ▶ **arts** *npl* **1.** (SCH & UNIV) lettres *fpl*. **2.** (*fine arts*): **the ~s** les arts *mpl*.

artefact [ˈɑːtɪfækt] = **artifact**.

artery [ˈɑːtərɪ] *n* artère *f*.

art gallery *n* (*public*) musée *m* d'art; (*for selling paintings*) galerie *f* d'art.

arthritis [ɑːˈθraɪtɪs] *n* arthrite *f*.

artichoke [ˈɑːtɪtʃəʊk] *n* artichaut *m*.

article [ˈɑːtɪkl] *n* article *m*; **~ of clothing** vêtement *m*.

articulate [*adj* ɑːˈtɪkjʊlət, *vb* ɑːˈtɪkjʊleɪt] ◆ *adj* (*person*) qui sait s'exprimer; (*speech*) net (nette), distinct(e). ◆ *vt* (*thought, wish*) formuler.

articulated lorry [ɑːˈtɪkjʊleɪtɪd-] *n* Br semi-remorque *m*.

artifact [ˈɑːtɪfækt] *n* objet *m* fabriqué.

artificial [ˌɑːtɪˈfɪʃl] *adj* **1.** (*not natural*) artificiel(elle). **2.** (*insincere*) affecté(e).

artillery [ɑːˈtɪlərɪ] *n* artillerie *f*.

artist [ˈɑːtɪst] *n* artiste *mf*.

artiste [ɑːˈtiːst] *n* artiste *mf*.

artistic [ɑːˈtɪstɪk] *adj* (*person*) artiste; (*style etc*) artistique.

artistry [ˈɑːtɪstrɪ] *n* art *m*, talent *m* artistique.

artless [ˈɑːtlɪs] *adj* naturel(elle), ingénu(e).

as [*unstressed* əz, *stressed* æz] ◆ *conj* **1.** (*referring to time*) comme, alors que; **she rang (just) ~ I was leaving** elle m'a téléphoné au moment même où OR juste comme je partais; **~ time goes by** à mesure que le temps passe, avec le temps. **2.** (*referring to manner, way*) comme; **do ~ I say** fais ce que je (te) dis. **3.** (*introducing a statement*) comme; **~ you know, ...** comme tu le sais, ... **4.** (*because*) comme. ◆ *prep* **1.** (*referring to function, characteristic*) en, comme, en tant que; **I'm speaking ~ your friend** je te parle en ami; **she works ~ a nurse** elle est infirmière. **2.** (*referring to attitude, reaction*): **it came ~ a shock** cela nous a fait un choc. ◆ *adv* (*in comparisons*): **~ rich ~** aussi riche que; **~ red ~ a tomato** rouge comme une tomate; **he's ~ tall ~ I am** il est aussi grand que moi; **twice ~ big ~** deux fois plus gros que; **~ much/many ~** autant que; **~ much wine/many chocolates ~** autant de vin/de chocolats que. ▶ **as for** *prep* quant à. ▶ **as from, as of** *prep* dès, à partir de. ▶ **as if, as though** *conj* comme si; **it looks ~ if** OR **~ though it will rain** on dirait qu'il va pleuvoir. ▶ **as to** *prep* **1.** (*concerning*) en ce qui concerne, au sujet de. **2.** = **as for.**

a.s.a.p. (*abbr of* **as soon as possible**) d'urgence, dans les meilleurs délais.

asbestos [æsˈbestəs] *n* asbeste *m*, amiante *m*.

ascend [əˈsend] *vt & vi* monter.

ascendant [əˈsendənt] *n*: **to be in the ~** avoir le dessus.

ascent [əˈsent] *n lit & fig* ascension *f*.

ascertain [ˌæsəˈteɪn] *vt* établir.

ascribe [əˈskraɪb] *vt*: **to ~ sthg to** attribuer qqch à; (*blame*) imputer qqch à.

ash [æʃ] *n* **1.** (*from cigarette, fire*) cendre *f*. **2.** (*tree*) frêne *m*.

ashamed [əˈʃeɪmd] *adj* honteux (euse), confus(e); **to be ~ of** avoir honte de; **to be ~ to do sthg** avoir honte de faire qqch.

ashen-faced [ˌæʃnˈfeɪst] *adj* blême.

ashore [əˈʃɔːr] *adv* à terre.

ashtray [ˈæʃtreɪ] *n* cendrier *m*.

Ash Wednesday *n* le mercredi des Cendres.

Asia [Br 'eɪʃə, Am 'eɪʒə] n Asie f.
Asian [Br 'eɪʃn, Am 'eɪʒn] ◆ adj asiatique. ◆ n (person) Asiatique mf.
aside [ə'saɪd] ◆ adv 1. (to one side) de côté; **to move ~** s'écarter; **to take sb ~** prendre qqn à part. 2. (apart) à part; **~ from** à l'exception de. ◆ n 1. (in play) aparté m. 2. (remark) réflexion f, commentaire m.
ask [ɑːsk] ◆ vt 1. (gen) demander; **to ~ sb sthg** demander qqch à qqn; **he ~ed me my name** il m'a demandé mon nom; **to ~ sb for sthg** demander qqch à qqn; **to ~ sb to do sthg** demander à qqn de faire qqch. 2. (put - question) poser. 3. (invite) inviter. ◆ vi demander. ▶ **ask after** vt fus demander des nouvelles de. ▶ **ask for** vt fus 1. (person) demander à voir. 2. (thing) demander.
askance [ə'skæns] adv: **to look ~ at sb** regarder qqn d'un air désapprobateur.
askew [ə'skjuː] adj (not straight) de travers.
asking price ['ɑːskɪŋ-] n prix m demandé.
asleep [ə'sliːp] adj endormi(e); **to fall ~** s'endormir.
asparagus [ə'spærəgəs] n (U) asperges fpl.
aspect ['æspekt] n 1. (gen) aspect m. 2. (of building) orientation f.
aspersions [ə'spɜːʃnz] npl: **to cast ~ on** jeter le discrédit sur.
asphalt ['æsfælt] n asphalte m.
asphyxiate [əs'fɪksɪeɪt] vt asphyxier.
aspiration [ˌæspə'reɪʃn] n aspiration f.
aspire [ə'spaɪəʳ] vi: **to ~ to sthg/to do sthg** aspirer à qqch/à faire qqch.
aspirin ['æsprɪn] n aspirine f.
ass [æs] n 1. (donkey) âne m. 2. Am v inf = **arse**.
assailant [ə'seɪlənt] n assaillant m, -e f.
assassin [ə'sæsɪn] n assassin m.
assassinate [ə'sæsɪneɪt] vt assassiner.
assassination [əˌsæsɪ'neɪʃn] n assassinat m.
assault [ə'sɔːlt] ◆ n 1. (MIL): **~ (on)** assaut m (de), attaque f (de). 2. (physical attack): **~ (on sb)** agression f (contre qqn). ◆ vt (attack - physically) agresser; (- sexually) violenter.
assemble [ə'sembl] ◆ vt 1. (gather) réunir. 2. (fit together) assembler, monter. ◆ vi se réunir, s'assembler.
assembly [ə'semblɪ] n 1. (gen) assemblée f. 2. (fitting together) assemblage m.
assembly line n chaîne f de montage.

assent [ə'sent] ◆ n consentement m, assentiment m. ◆ vi: **to ~ (to)** donner son consentement OR assentiment (à).
assert [ə'sɜːt] vt 1. (fact, belief) affirmer, soutenir. 2. (authority) imposer.
assertive [ə'sɜːtɪv] adj assuré(e).
assess [ə'ses] vt évaluer, estimer.
assessment [ə'sesmənt] n 1. (opinion) opinion f. 2. (calculation) évaluation f, estimation f.
assessor [ə'sesəʳ] n (of tax) contrôleur m (des impôts).
asset ['æset] n avantage m, atout m. ▶ **assets** npl (COMM) actif m.
assign [ə'saɪn] vt 1. (allot): **to ~ sthg (to)** assigner qqch (à). 2. (give task to): **to ~ sb (to sthg/to do sthg)** nommer qqn (à qqch/pour faire qqch).
assignment [ə'saɪnmənt] n 1. (task) mission f; (SCH) devoir m. 2. (act of assigning) attribution f.
assimilate [ə'sɪmɪleɪt] vt assimiler.
assist [ə'sɪst] vt: **to ~ sb (with sthg/in doing sthg)** aider qqn (dans qqch/à faire qqch); (professionally) assister qqn (dans qqch/pour faire qqch).
assistance [ə'sɪstəns] n aide f; **to be of ~ (to)** être utile (à).
assistant [ə'sɪstənt] ◆ n assistant m, -e f; **(shop) ~** vendeur m, -euse f. ◆ comp: **~ editor** rédacteur en chef adjoint m, rédactrice en chef adjointe f; **~ manager** sous-directeur m, -trice f.
associate [adj & n ə'səʊʃɪət, vb ə'səʊʃɪeɪt] ◆ adj associé(e). ◆ n associé m, -e f. ◆ vt: **to ~ sb/sthg (with)** associer qqn/qqch (à); **to be ~d with** être associé(e) à. ◆ vi: **to ~ with sb** fréquenter qqn.
association [əˌsəʊsɪ'eɪʃn] n association f; **in ~ with** avec la collaboration de.
assorted [ə'sɔːtɪd] adj varié(e).
assortment [ə'sɔːtmənt] n mélange m.
assume [ə'sjuːm] vt 1. (suppose) supposer, présumer. 2. (power, responsibility) assumer. 3. (appearance, attitude) adopter.
assumed name [ə'sjuːmd-] n nom m d'emprunt.
assuming [ə'sjuːmɪŋ] conj en supposant que.
assumption [ə'sʌmpʃn] n (supposition) supposition f.
assurance [ə'ʃʊərəns] n 1. (gen) assurance f. 2. (promise) garantie f, promesse f.
assure [ə'ʃʊəʳ] vt: **to ~ sb (of)** assurer qqn (de).

assured [ə'ʃʊəd] adj assuré(e).

asterisk ['æstərɪsk] n astérisque m.

astern [ə'stɜːn] adv (NAUT) en poupe.

asthma ['æsmə] n asthme m.

astonish [ə'stɒnɪʃ] vt étonner.

astonishment [ə'stɒnɪʃmənt] n étonnement m.

astound [ə'staʊnd] vt stupéfier.

astray [ə'streɪ] adv: **to go ~** (become lost) s'égarer; **to lead sb ~** détourner qqn du droit chemin.

astride [ə'straɪd] prep à cheval OR califourchon sur.

astrology [ə'strɒlədʒɪ] n astrologie f.

astronaut ['æstrənɔːt] n astronaute mf.

astronomical [ˌæstrə'nɒmɪkl] adj astronomique.

astronomy [ə'strɒnəmɪ] n astronomie f.

astute [ə'stjuːt] adj malin(igne).

asylum [ə'saɪləm] n asile m.

at [unstressed ət, stressed æt] prep 1. (indicating place, position) à; **~ my father's** chez mon père; **~ home** à la maison, chez soi; **~ school** à l'école; **~ work** au travail. 2. (indicating direction) vers; **to look ~ sb** regarder qqn; **to smile ~ sb** sourire à qqn; **to shoot ~ sb** tirer sur qqn. 3. (indicating a particular time) à; **~ midnight/noon/eleven o'clock** à minuit/midi/onze heures; **~ night** la nuit; **~ Christmas/Easter** à Noël/Pâques. 4. (indicating age, speed, rate) à; **~ 52 (years of age)** à 52 ans; **~ 100 mph** à 160 km/h. 5. (indicating price): **~ £50 a pair** 50 livres la paire. 6. (indicating particular state, condition) en; **~ peace/war** en paix/guerre; **to be ~ lunch/dinner** être en train de déjeuner/dîner. 7. (after adjectives): **amused/appalled/puzzled ~ sthg** diverti/effaré/intrigué par qqch; **delighted ~ sthg** ravi de qqch; **to be bad/good ~ sthg** être mauvais/bon en qqch. ▶ **at all** adv 1. (with negative): **not ~ all** (when thanked) je vous en prie; (when answering a question) pas du tout; **she's not ~ all happy** elle n'est pas du tout contente. 2. (in the slightest): **anything ~ all will do** n'importe quoi fera l'affaire; **do you know her ~ all?** est-ce que vous la connaissez?

ate [Br et, Am eɪt] pt → **eat**.

atheist ['eɪθɪɪst] n athée mf.

Athens ['æθɪnz] n Athènes.

athlete ['æθliːt] n athlète mf.

athletic [æθ'letɪk] adj athlétique. ▶ **athletics** npl athlétisme m.

Atlantic [ət'læntɪk] ♦ adj atlantique. ♦ n: **the ~ (Ocean)** l'océan m Atlantique, l'Atlantique m.

atlas ['ætləs] n atlas m.

atmosphere ['ætməˌsfɪər] n atmosphère f.

atmospheric [ˌætməs'ferɪk] adj 1. (pressure, pollution etc) atmosphérique. 2. (film, music etc) d'ambiance.

atom ['ætəm] n 1. (TECH) atome m. 2. fig (tiny amount) grain m, parcelle f.

atom bomb n bombe f atomique.

atomic [ə'tɒmɪk] adj atomique.

atomic bomb = **atom bomb**.

atomizer, -iser ['ætəmaɪzər] n atomiseur m, vaporisateur m.

atone [ə'təʊn] vi: **to ~ for** racheter.

A to Z n plan m de ville.

atrocious [ə'trəʊʃəs] adj (very bad) atroce, affreux(euse).

atrocity [ə'trɒsətɪ] n (terrible act) atrocité f.

attach [ə'tætʃ] vt 1. (gen): **to ~ sthg (to)** attacher qqch (à). 2. (letter etc) joindre.

attaché case [ə'tæʃeɪ-] n attaché-case m.

attached [ə'tætʃt] adj (fond): **~ to** attaché(e) à.

attachment [ə'tætʃmənt] n 1. (device) accessoire m. 2. (fondness): **~ (to)** attachement m (à).

attack [ə'tæk] ♦ n 1. (physical, verbal): **~ (on)** attaque f (contre). 2. (of illness) crise f. ♦ vt 1. (gen) attaquer. 2. (job, problem) s'attaquer à. ♦ vi attaquer.

attacker [ə'tækər] n 1. (assailant) agresseur m. 2. (SPORT) attaquant m, -e f.

attain [ə'teɪn] vt atteindre, parvenir à.

attainment [ə'teɪnmənt] n 1. (of success, aims etc) réalisation f. 2. (skill) talent m.

attempt [ə'tempt] ♦ n: **~ (at)** tentative f (de); **~ on sb's life** tentative d'assassinat. ♦ vt tenter, essayer; **to ~ to do sthg** essayer OR tenter de faire qqch.

attend [ə'tend] ♦ vt 1. (meeting, party) assister à. 2. (school, church) aller à. ♦ vi 1. (be present) être présent(e). 2. (pay attention): **to ~ (to)** prêter attention (à). ▶ **attend to** vt fus 1. (deal with) s'occuper de, régler. 2. (look after - customer) s'occuper de; (- patient) soigner.

attendance [ə'tendəns] n 1. (number present) assistance f, public m. 2. (presence) présence f.

attendant [ə'tendənt] ♦ adj (problems) qui en découle. ♦ n (at museum, car *park*) gardien *m*, -enne *f*; (*at petrol station*) pompiste *mf*.

attention [ə'tenʃn] ◆ *n* (U) **1.** (*gen*) attention *f*; **to bring sthg to sb's ~, to draw sb's ~ to sthg** attirer l'attention de qqn sur qqch; **to attract** OR **catch sb's ~** attirer l'attention de qqn; **to pay ~ to** prêter attention à; **for the ~ of** (COMM) à l'attention de. **2.** (*care*) soins *mpl*, attentions *fpl*. ◆ *excl* (MIL) garde-à-vous!

attentive [ə'tentɪv] *adj* attentif(ive).

attic ['ætɪk] *n* grenier *m*.

attitude ['ætɪtjuːd] *n* **1.** (*gen*): ~ (**to** OR **towards**) attitude *f* (envers). **2.** (*posture*) pose *f*.

attn. (*abbr of* **for the attention of**) à l'attention de.

attorney [ə'tɜːnɪ] *n* Am avocat *m*, -e *f*.

attorney general (*pl* **attorneys general**) *n* ministre *m* de la Justice.

attract [ə'trækt] *vt* attirer.

attraction [ə'trækʃn] *n* **1.** (*gen*) attraction *f*; ~ **to sb** attirance *f* envers qqn. **2.** (*of thing*) attrait *m*.

attractive [ə'træktɪv] *adj* (*person*) attirant(e), séduisant(e); (*thing, idea*) attrayant, séduisant; (*investment*) intéressant(e).

attribute [*vb* ə'trɪbjuːt, *n* 'ætrɪbjuːt] ◆ *vt*: **to ~ sthg to** attribuer qqch à. ◆ *n* attribut *m*.

attrition [ə'trɪʃn] *n* usure *f*.

aubergine ['əʊbəʒiːn] *n* Br aubergine *f*.

auburn ['ɔːbən] *adj* auburn (*inv*).

auction ['ɔːkʃn] ◆ *n* vente *f* aux enchères; **at** OR **by ~** aux enchères; **to put sthg up for ~** mettre qqch (dans une vente) aux enchères. ◆ *vt* vendre aux enchères. ► **auction off** *vt sep* vendre aux enchères.

auctioneer [ˌɔːkʃə'nɪər] *n* commissaire-priseur *m*.

audacious [ɔː'deɪʃəs] *adj* audacieux (euse).

audible ['ɔːdəbl] *adj* audible.

audience ['ɔːdjəns] *n* **1.** (*of play, film*) public *m*, spectateurs *mpl*; (*of TV programme*) téléspectateurs *mpl*. **2.** (*formal meeting*) audience *f*.

audiovisual [ˌɔːdɪəʊvɪzjʊəl] *adj* audiovisuel(elle).

audit ['ɔːdɪt] ◆ *n* audit *m*, vérification *f* des comptes. ◆ *vt* vérifier, apurer.

audition [ɔː'dɪʃn] *n* (THEATRE) audition *f*; (CINEMA) bout *m* d'essai.

auditor ['ɔːdɪtər] *n* auditeur *m*, -trice *f*.

auditorium [ˌɔːdɪ'tɔːrɪəm] (*pl* **-riums** OR **-ria** [-rɪə]) *n* salle *f*.

augur ['ɔːgər] *vi*: **to ~ well/badly** être de bon/mauvais augure.

August ['ɔːgəst] *n* août *m*; *see also* **September**.

Auld Lang Syne [ˌɔːldlæŋ'saɪn] *n* chant traditionnel britannique correspondant à 'ce n'est qu'un au revoir, mes frères'.

aunt [ɑːnt] *n* tante *f*.

auntie, aunty ['ɑːntɪ] *n inf* tata *f*, tantine *f*.

au pair [ˌəʊ'peər] *n* jeune fille *f* au pair.

aura ['ɔːrə] *n* atmosphère *f*.

aural ['ɔːrəl] *adj* auditif(ive).

auspices ['ɔːspɪsɪz] *npl*: **under the ~ of** sous les auspices de.

auspicious [ɔː'spɪʃəs] *adj* prometteur (euse).

Aussie ['ɒzɪ] *inf* ◆ *adj* australien(enne). ◆ *n* Australien *m*, australienne *f*.

austere [ɒ'stɪər] *adj* austère.

austerity [ɒ'sterətɪ] *n* austérité *f*.

Australia [ɒ'streɪljə] *n* Australie *f*.

Australian [ɒ'streɪljən] ◆ *adj* australien(enne). ◆ *n* Australien *m*, -enne *f*.

Austria ['ɒstrɪə] *n* Autriche *f*.

Austrian ['ɒstrɪən] ◆ *adj* autrichien (enne). ◆ *n* Autrichien *m*, -enne *f*.

authentic [ɔː'θentɪk] *adj* authentique.

author ['ɔːθər] *n* auteur *m*.

authoritarian [ɔːˌθɒrɪ'teərɪən] *adj* autoritaire.

authoritative [ɔː'θɒrɪtətɪv] *adj* **1.** (*person, voice*) autoritaire. **2.** (*study*) qui fait autorité.

authority [ɔː'θɒrətɪ] *n* **1.** (*organization, power*) autorité *f*; **to be in ~** être le/la responsable. **2.** (*permission*) autorisation *f*. **3.** (*expert*): ~ (**on sthg**) expert *m*, -e *f* (en qqch). ► **authorities** *npl*: **the authorities** les autorités *fpl*.

authorize, -ise ['ɔːθəraɪz] *vt*: **to ~ sb (to do sthg)** autoriser qqn (à faire qqch).

autistic [ɔː'tɪstɪk] *adj* (*child*) autiste; (*behaviour*) autistique.

auto ['ɔːtəʊ] (*pl* **-s**) *n* Am auto *f*, voiture *f*.

autobiography [ˌɔːtəbaɪ'ɒgrəfɪ] *n* autobiographie *f*.

autocratic [ˌɔːtə'krætɪk] *adj* autocratique.

autograph ['ɔːtəgrɑːf] ◆ *n* autographe *m*. ◆ *vt* signer.

automate ['ɔːtəmeɪt] *vt* automatiser.

automatic [ˌɔːtə'mætɪk] ◆ *adj* (*gen*) automatique. ◆ *n* **1.** (*car*) voiture *f* à transmission automatique. **2.** (*gun*) automatique *m*. **3.** (*washing machine*)

lave-linge *m* automatique.
automatically [ˌɔːtəˈmætɪklɪ] *adv* (*gen*) automatiquement.
automation [ˌɔːtəˈmeɪʃn] *n* automatisation *f*, automation *f*.
automobile [ˈɔːtəməbiːl] *n* Am automobile *f*.
autonomy [ɔːˈtɒnəmɪ] *n* autonomie *f*.
autopsy [ˈɔːtɒpsɪ] *n* autopsie *f*.
autumn [ˈɔːtəm] *n* automne *m*.
auxiliary [ɔːgˈzɪljərɪ] ◆ *adj* auxiliaire. ◆ *n* auxiliaire *mf*.
Av. (*abbr of* **avenue**) av.
avail [əˈveɪl] ◆ *n*: **to no ~** en vain, sans résultat. ◆ *vt*: **to ~ o.s. of** profiter de.
available [əˈveɪləbl] *adj* disponible.
avalanche [ˈævəlɑːnʃ] *n* lit & fig avalanche *f*.
avarice [ˈævərɪs] *n* avarice *f*.
Ave. (*abbr of* **avenue**) av.
avenge [əˈvendʒ] *vt* venger.
avenue [ˈævənjuː] *n* avenue *f*.
average [ˈævərɪdʒ] ◆ *adj* moyen (enne). ◆ *n* moyenne *f*; **on ~** en moyenne. ◆ *vt*: **the cars were averaging 90 mph** les voitures roulaient en moyenne à 150 km/h. ▶ **average out** *vi*: **to ~ out at** donner la moyenne de.
aversion [əˈvɜːʃn] *n*: **~ (to)** aversion *f* (pour).
avert [əˈvɜːt] *vt* 1. (*avoid*) écarter; (*accident*) empêcher. 2. (*eyes, glance*) détourner.
aviary [ˈeɪvjərɪ] *n* volière *f*.
avid [ˈævɪd] *adj*: **~ (for)** avide (de).
avocado [ˌævəˈkɑːdəʊ] (*pl* **-s** OR **-es**) *n*: **~ (pear)** avocat *m*.
avoid [əˈvɔɪd] *vt* éviter; **to ~ doing sthg** éviter de faire qqch.
avoidance [əˈvɔɪdəns] *n* → **tax avoidance**.
await [əˈweɪt] *vt* attendre.
awake [əˈweɪk] (*pt* **awoke** OR **awaked**, *pp* **awoken**) ◆ *adj* (*not sleeping*) réveillé (e); **are you ~?** tu dors? ◆ *vt* 1. (*wake up*) réveiller. 2. *fig* (*feeling*) éveiller. ◆ *vi* 1. (*wake up*) se réveiller. 2. *fig* (*feeling*) s'éveiller.
awakening [əˈweɪknɪŋ] *n* 1. (*from sleep*) réveil *m*. 2. *fig* (*of feeling*) éveil *m*.
award [əˈwɔːd] ◆ *n* (*prize*) prix *m*. ◆ *vt*: **to ~ sb sthg**, **to ~ sthg to sb** (*prize*) décerner qqch à qqn; (*compensation, free kick*) accorder qqch à qqn.
aware [əˈweəʳ] *adj*: **to be ~ of sthg** se rendre compte de qqch, être conscient(e) de qqch; **to be ~ that** se rendre compte que, être conscient que.

awareness [əˈweənɪs] *n* (U) conscience *f*.
awash [əˈwɒʃ] *adj* lit & fig: **~ (with)** inondé(e) (de).
away [əˈweɪ] ◆ *adv* 1. (*in opposite direction*): **to move** OR **walk ~ (from)** s'éloigner (de); **to turn ~** se détourner. 2. (*in distance*): **we live 4 miles ~ (from here)** nous habitons à 6 kilomètres (d'ici). 3. (*in time*): **the elections are a month ~** les élections se dérouleront dans un mois. 4. (*absent*) absent(e); **she's ~ on holiday** elle est partie en vacances. 5. (*in safe place*): **to put sthg ~** ranger qqch. 6. (*so as to be gone or used up*): **to fade ~** disparaître; **to give sthg ~** donner qqch, faire don de qqch; **to take sthg ~** emporter qqch. 7. (*continuously*): **to be working ~** travailler sans arrêt. ◆ *adj* (SPORT) (*team, fans*) de l'équipe des visiteurs; **~ game** match *m* à l'extérieur.
awe [ɔː] *n* respect *m* mêlé de crainte; **to be in ~ of sb** être impressionné par qqn.
awesome [ˈɔːsəm] *adj* impressionnant(e).
awful [ˈɔːful] *adj* 1. (*terrible*) affreux (euse). 2. *inf* (*very great*): **an ~ lot (of)** énormément (de).
awfully [ˈɔːflɪ] *adv inf* (*bad, difficult*) affreusement; (*nice, good*) extrêmement.
awhile [əˈwaɪl] *adv* un moment.
awkward [ˈɔːkwəd] *adj* 1. (*clumsy*) gauche, maladroit(e). 2. (*embarrassed*) mal à l'aise, gêné(e). 3. (*difficult - person, problem, task*) difficile. 4. (*inconvenient*) incommode. 5. (*embarrassing*) embarrassant(e), gênant(e).
awning [ˈɔːnɪŋ] *n* 1. (*of tent*) auvent *m*. 2. (*of shop*) banne *f*.
awoke [əˈwəʊk] *pt* → **awake**.
awoken [əˈwəʊkn] *pp* → **awake**.
awry [əˈraɪ] ◆ *adj* de travers. ◆ *adv*: **to go ~** aller de travers, mal tourner.
axe Br, **ax** Am [æks] ◆ *n* hache *f*. ◆ *vt* (*project*) abandonner; (*jobs*) supprimer.
axes [ˈæksiːz] *pl* → **axis**.
axis [ˈæksɪs] (*pl* **axes**) *n* axe *m*.
axle [ˈæksl] *n* essieu *m*.
aye [aɪ] ◆ *adv* oui. ◆ *n* voix *f* pour.
azalea [əˈzeɪljə] *n* azalée *f*.
Azores [əˈzɔːz] *npl*: **the ~** les Açores *fpl*.

B

b (*pl* **b's** OR **bs**), **B** (*pl* **B's** OR **Bs**) [biː] *n* (*letter*) b *m inv*, B *m inv.* ▶ **B** *n* **1.** (MUS) si *m.* **2.** (SCH) (*mark*) B *m inv.*

BA *n abbr of* **Bachelor of Arts.**

babble ['bæbl] ◆ *n* (*of voices*) murmure *m*, rumeur *f.* ◆ *vi* (*person*) babiller.

baboon [bə'buːn] *n* babouin *m.*

baby ['beɪbɪ] *n* **1.** (*child*) bébé *m.* **2.** *inf* (*darling*) chéri *m*, -e *f.*

baby buggy *n* **1.** Br (*foldable pushchair*) poussette *f.* **2.** Am = **baby carriage.**

baby carriage *n* Am landau *m.*

baby-sit *vi* faire du baby-sitting.

baby-sitter [-ˌsɪtər] *n* baby-sitter *mf.*

bachelor ['bætʃələr] *n* célibataire *m.*

Bachelor of Arts *n* licencié *m*, -e *f* en OR ès Lettres.

Bachelor of Science *n* licencié *m*, -e *f* en OR ès Sciences.

back [bæk] ◆ *adv* **1.** (*backwards*) en arrière; **to step/move** ~ reculer; **to push** ~ repousser. **2.** (*to former position or state*): **I'll be** ~ **at five** je rentrerai OR serai de retour à dix-sept heures; **I'd like my money** ~ (*in shop*) je voudrais me faire rembourser; **to go** ~ retourner; **to come** ~ revenir, rentrer; **to go** ~ **to sleep** se rendormir; **to go** ~ **and forth** (*person*) faire des allées et venues; **to be** ~ (**in fashion**) revenir à la mode. **3.** (*in time*): **to think** ~ (**to**) se souvenir (de). **4.** (*in return*): **to phone** OR **call** ~ rappeler. ◆ *n* **1.** (*of person, animal*) dos *m*; **behind sb's** ~ *fig* derrière le dos de qqn. **2.** (*of door, book, hand*) dos *m*; (*of head*) derrière *m*; (*of envelope, cheque*) revers *m*; (*of page*) verso *m*; (*of chair*) dossier *m.* **3.** (*of room, fridge*) fond *m*; (*of car*) arrière *m.* **4.** (SPORT) arrière *m.* ◆ *adj* (*in compounds*) **1.** (*at the back*) de derrière; (*seat, wheel*) arrière (*inv*); (*page*) dernier(ère). **2.** (*overdue*): ~ **rent** arriéré *m* de loyer. ◆ *vt* **1.** (*reverse*) reculer. **2.** (*support*) appuyer. **3.** (*bet on*) parier sur, miser sur. ◆ *vi* reculer. ▶ **back to back** *adv* **1.** (*stand*) dos à dos. **2.** (*happen*) l'un après l'autre. ▶ **back to front** *adv* à l'envers. ▶ **back down** *vi* céder. ▶ **back out** *vi* (*of promise etc*) se dédire. ▶ **back up** ◆ *vt sep* **1.** (*support - claim*) appuyer, sou-

tenir; (- *person*) épauler, soutenir. **2.** (*reverse*) reculer. **3.** (COMPUT) sauvegarder. ◆ *vi* (*reverse*) reculer.

backache ['bækeɪk] *n*: **to have** ~ avoir mal aux reins OR au dos.

backbencher [ˌbæk'bentʃər] *n* Br (POL) député qui n'a aucune position officielle au gouvernement ni dans aucun parti.

backbone ['bækbəʊn] *n* épine *f* dorsale, colonne *f* vertébrale; *fig* (*main support*) pivot *m.*

backcloth ['bækklɒθ] Br = **backdrop.**

backdate [ˌbæk'deɪt] *vt* antidater.

back door *n* porte *f* de derrière.

backdrop ['bækdrɒp] *n lit & fig* toile *f* de fond.

backfire [ˌbæk'faɪər] *vi* **1.** (AUT) pétarader. **2.** (*plan*): **to** ~ (**on sb**) se retourner (contre qqn).

backgammon ['bækˌgæmən] *n* backgammon *m*, = jacquet *m.*

background ['bækgraʊnd] *n* **1.** (*in picture, view*) arrière-plan *m*; **in the** ~ dans le fond, à l'arrière-plan; *fig* au second plan. **2.** (*of event, situation*) contexte *m.* **3.** (*upbringing*) milieu *m.*

backhand ['bækhænd] *n* revers *m.*

backhanded ['bækhændɪd] *adj fig* ambigu(ë), équivoque.

backhander ['bækhændər] *n* Br *inf* pot-de-vin *m.*

backing ['bækɪŋ] *n* **1.** (*support*) soutien *m.* **2.** (*lining*) doublage *m.*

backlash ['bæklæʃ] *n* contrecoup *m*, choc *m* en retour.

backlog ['bæklɒg] *n*: ~ (**of work**) arriéré *m* de travail, travail *m* en retard.

back number *n* vieux numéro *m.*

backpack ['bækpæk] *n* sac *m* à dos.

back pay *n* rappel *m* de salaire.

back seat *n* (*in car*) siège *m* OR banquette *f* arrière; **to take a** ~ *fig* jouer un rôle secondaire.

backside [ˌbæk'saɪd] *n inf* postérieur *m*, derrière *m.*

backstage [ˌbæk'steɪdʒ] *adv* dans les coulisses.

back street *n* petite rue *f.*

backstroke ['bækstrəʊk] *n* dos *m* crawlé.

backup ['bækʌp] ◆ *adj* (*plan, team*) de secours, de remplacement. ◆ *n* **1.** (*gen*) aide *f*, soutien *m.* **2.** (COMPUT) (*copie f de*) sauvegarde *f.*

backward ['bækwəd] ◆ *adj* **1.** (*movement, look*) en arrière. **2.** (*country*) arriéré(e); (*person*) arriéré, attardé(e). ◆ *adv* Am = **backwards.**

backwards ['bækwədz], **backward** Am ['bækwərd] *adv* (*move, go*) en arrière, à reculons; (*read list*) à rebours, à l'envers; ~ **and forwards** (*movement*) de va-et-vient, d'avant en arrière et d'arrière en avant; **to walk ~ and forwards** aller et venir.

backwater ['bæk,wɔːtə^r] *n fig* désert *m*.

backyard [,bæk'jɑːd] *n* **1.** Br (*yard*) arrière-cour *f*. **2.** Am (*garden*) jardin *m* de derrière.

bacon ['beɪkən] *n* bacon *m*.

bacteria [bæk'tɪərɪə] *npl* bactéries *fpl*.

bad [bæd] (*compar* **worse**, *superl* **worst**) ♦ *adj* **1.** (*not good*) mauvais(e); **to be ~ at sthg** être mauvais en qqch; **too ~!** dommage!; **not ~** pas mal. **2.** (*unhealthy*) malade; **smoking is ~ for you** fumer est mauvais pour la santé; **I'm feeling ~** je ne suis pas dans mon assiette. **3.** (*serious*): **a ~ cold** un gros rhume. **4.** (*rotten*) pourri(e), gâté(e); **to go ~** se gâter, s'avarier. **5.** (*guilty*): **to feel ~ about sthg** se sentir coupable de qqch. **6.** (*naughty*) méchant(e). ♦ *adv* Am = **badly**.

badge [bædʒ] *n* **1.** (*metal, plastic*) badge *m*. **2.** (*sewn-on*) écusson *m*.

badger ['bædʒə^r] ♦ *n* blaireau *m*. ♦ *vt*: **to ~ sb (to do sthg)** harceler qqn (pour qu'il fasse qqch).

badly ['bædlɪ] (*compar* **worse**, *superl* **worst**) *adv* **1.** (*not well*) mal. **2.** (*seriously - wounded*) grièvement; (- *affected*) gravement, sérieusement; **to be ~ in need of sthg** avoir vraiment OR absolument besoin de qqch.

badly-off *adj* (*poor*) pauvre, dans le besoin.

bad-mannered [-'mænəd] *adj* (*child*) mal élevé(e); (*shop assistant*) impoli(e).

badminton ['bædmɪntən] *n* badminton *m*.

bad-tempered [-'tempəd] *adj* **1.** (*by nature*) qui a mauvais caractère. **2.** (*in a bad mood*) de mauvaise humeur.

baffle ['bæfl] *vt* déconcerter, confondre.

bag [bæg] ♦ *n* **1.** (*gen*) sac *m*; **to pack one's ~s** *fig* plier bagage. **2.** (*handbag*) sac *m* à main. ♦ *vt* Br *inf* (*reserve*) garder. ► **bags** *npl* **1.** (*under eyes*) poches *fpl*. **2.** *inf* (*lots*): **~s of** plein OR beaucoup de.

bagel ['beɪgəl] *n* petit pain en couronne.

baggage ['bægɪdʒ] *n* (*U*) bagages *mpl*.

baggage reclaim *n* retrait *m* des bagages.

baggy ['bægɪ] *adj* ample.

bagpipes ['bægpaɪps] *npl* cornemuse *f*.

Bahamas [bə'hɑːməz] *npl*: **the ~** les Bahamas *fpl*.

bail [beɪl] *n* (*U*) caution *f*; **on ~** sous caution. ► **bail out** ♦ *vt sep* **1.** (*pay bail for*) se porter garant de. **2.** *fig* (*rescue*) tirer d'affaire. ♦ *vi* (*from plane*) sauter (en parachute).

bailiff ['beɪlɪf] *n* huissier *m*.

bait [beɪt] ♦ *n* appât *m*. ♦ *vt* **1.** (*put bait on*) appâter. **2.** (*tease*) tourmenter.

bake [beɪk] ♦ *vt* **1.** (CULIN) faire cuire au four. **2.** (*clay, bricks*) cuire. ♦ *vi* (*food*) cuire au four.

baked beans [beɪkt-] *npl* haricots *mpl* blancs à la tomate.

baked potato [beɪkt-] *n* pomme *f* de terre en robe de chambre.

baker ['beɪkə^r] *n* boulanger *m*, -ère *f*; **~'s (shop)** boulangerie *f*.

bakery ['beɪkərɪ] *n* boulangerie *f*.

baking ['beɪkɪŋ] *n* cuisson *f*.

balaclava (helmet) [,bælə'klɑːvə-] *n* Br passe-montagne *m*.

balance ['bæləns] ♦ *n* **1.** (*equilibrium*) équilibre *m*; **to keep/lose one's ~** garder/perdre l'équilibre; **off ~** déséquilibré(e). **2.** *fig* (*counterweight*) contrepoids *m*; (*of evidence*) poids *m*, force *f*. **3.** (*scales*) balance *f*. **4.** (FIN) solde *m*. ♦ *vt* **1.** (*keep in balance*) maintenir en équilibre. **2.** (*compare*): **to ~ sthg against sthg** mettre qqch et qqch en balance. **3.** (*in accounting*): **to ~ a budget** équilibrer un budget; **to ~ the books** clôturer les comptes, dresser le bilan. ♦ *vi* **1.** (*maintain equilibrium*) se tenir en équilibre. **2.** (*budget, accounts*) s'équilibrer. ► **on balance** *adv* tout bien considéré.

balanced diet [,bælənst-] *n* alimentation *f* équilibrée.

balance of payments *n* balance *f* des paiements.

balance of trade *n* balance *f* commerciale.

balance sheet *n* bilan *m*.

balcony ['bælkənɪ] *n* balcon *m*.

bald [bɔːld] *adj* **1.** (*head, man*) chauve. **2.** (*tyre*) lisse. **3.** *fig* (*blunt*) direct(e).

bale [beɪl] *n* balle *f*. ► **bale out** Br ♦ *vt sep* (*boat*) écoper, vider. ♦ *vi* (*from plane*) sauter en parachute.

Balearic Islands [,bælɪ'ærɪk-], **Balearics** [,bælɪ'ærɪks] *npl*: **the ~** les Baléares *fpl*.

baleful ['beɪlfʊl] *adj* sinistre.

balk [bɔːk] *vi*: **to ~ (at)** hésiter OR reculer (devant).

Balkans ['bɔːlkənz], **Balkan States** ['bɔːlkən-] npl: **the ~** les Balkans mpl, les États mpl balkaniques.

ball [bɔːl] n **1.** (round shape) boule f; (in game) balle f; (football) ballon m; **to be on the ~** fig connaître son affaire, s'y connaître. **2.** (of foot) plante f. **3.** (dance) bal m. ▶ **balls** v inf ◆ npl (testicles) couilles fpl. ◆ n (U) (nonsense) conneries fpl.

ballad ['bæləd] n ballade f.

ballast ['bæləst] n lest m.

ball bearing n roulement m à billes.

ball boy n ramasseur m de balles.

ballerina [ˌbælə'riːnə] n ballerine f.

ballet ['bæleɪ] n **1.** (U) (art of dance) danse f. **2.** (work) ballet m.

ballet dancer n danseur m, -euse f de ballet.

ball game n **1.** Am (baseball match) match m de base-ball. **2.** inf (situation): **it's a whole new ~** c'est une autre paire de manches.

balloon [bə'luːn] n **1.** (gen) ballon m. **2.** (in cartoon) bulle f.

ballot ['bælət] ◆ n **1.** (voting paper) bulletin m de vote. **2.** (voting process) scrutin m. ◆ vt appeler à voter.

ballot box n **1.** (container) urne f. **2.** (voting process) scrutin m.

ballot paper n bulletin m de vote.

ball park n Am terrain m de base-ball.

ballpoint (pen) ['bɔːlpɔɪnt-] n stylo m à bille.

ballroom ['bɔːlrum] n salle f de bal.

ballroom dancing n (U) danse f de salon.

balm [bɑːm] n baume m.

balmy ['bɑːmɪ] adj doux (douce).

balti ['bɔːltɪ] n (pan) récipient métallique utilisé dans la cuisine indienne; (food) plat épicé préparé dans un 'balti'.

Baltic ['bɔːltɪk] ◆ adj (port, coast) de la Baltique. ◆ n: **the ~ (Sea)** la Baltique.

Baltic Republic n: **the ~s** les républiques fpl baltes.

bamboo [bæm'buː] n bambou m.

bamboozle [bæm'buːzl] vt inf embobiner.

ban [bæn] ◆ n interdiction f; **there is a ~ on smoking** il est interdit de fumer. ◆ vt interdire; **to ~ sb from doing sthg** interdire à qqn de faire qqch.

banal [bə'nɑːl] adj pej banal(e), ordinaire.

banana [bə'nɑːnə] n banane f.

band [bænd] n **1.** (MUS - rock) groupe m; (- military) fanfare f; (- jazz) orchestre m. **2.** (group, strip) bande f. **3.** (stripe) rayure f. **4.** (range) tranche f. ▶ **band together** vi s'unir.

bandage ['bændɪdʒ] ◆ n bandage m, bande f. ◆ vt mettre un pansement OR un bandage sur.

Band-Aid® n pansement m adhésif.

b and b, B and B n abbr of **bed and breakfast**.

bandit ['bændɪt] n bandit m.

bandstand ['bændstænd] n kiosque m à musique.

bandwagon ['bændwægən] n: **to jump on the ~** suivre le mouvement.

bandy ['bændɪ] adj qui a les jambes arquées. ▶ **bandy about, bandy around** vt sep répandre, faire circuler.

bandy-legged [-ˌlegd] adj = **bandy**.

bang [bæŋ] ◆ adv (exactly): **~ in the middle** en plein milieu; **to be ~ on time** être pile à l'heure. ◆ n **1.** (blow) coup m violent. **2.** (of gun etc) détonation f; (of door) claquement m. ◆ vt frapper violemment; (door) claquer; **to ~ one's head** se cogner la tête. ◆ vi **1.** (knock): **to ~ on** frapper à. **2.** (make a loud noise - gun etc) détoner; (- door) claquer. **3.** (crash): **to ~ into** se cogner contre. ◆ excl boum! ▶ **bangs** npl Am frange f.

banger ['bæŋər] n Br **1.** inf (sausage) saucisse f. **2.** inf (old car) vieille guimbarde f. **3.** (firework) pétard m.

bangle ['bæŋgl] n bracelet m.

banish ['bænɪʃ] vt bannir.

banister ['bænɪstər] n, **banisters** ['bænɪstəz] npl rampe f.

bank [bæŋk] ◆ n **1.** (FIN & fig) banque f. **2.** (of river, lake) rive f, bord m. **3.** (of earth) talus m. **4.** (of clouds) masse f; (of fog) nappe f. ◆ vt (FIN) mettre OR déposer à la banque. ◆ vi **1.** (FIN): **to ~ with** avoir un compte à. **2.** (plane) tourner. ▶ **bank on** vt fus compter sur.

bank account n compte m en banque.

bank balance n solde m bancaire.

bank card = **banker's card**.

bank charges npl frais mpl bancaires.

bank draft n traite f bancaire.

banker ['bæŋkər] n banquier m.

banker's card n Br carte f d'identité bancaire.

bank holiday n Br jour m férié.

banking ['bæŋkɪŋ] n: **to go into ~** travailler dans la banque.

bank manager n directeur m de banque.

bank note n billet m de banque.

bank rate n taux m d'escompte.

bankrupt ['bæŋkrʌpt] adj failli(e); **to go ~** faire faillite.

bankruptcy ['bæŋkrəptsɪ] n (gen) faillite f.

bank statement n relevé m de compte.

banner ['bænəʳ] n banderole f.

bannister(s) ['bænɪstə(z)] = **banister(s)**.

banquet ['bæŋkwɪt] n banquet m.

banter ['bæntəʳ] n (U) badinage m.

bap [bæp] n Br petit pain m.

baptism ['bæptɪzm] n baptême m.

Baptist ['bæptɪst] n baptiste mf.

baptize, -ise [Br bæp'taɪz, Am 'bæptaɪz] vt baptiser.

bar [bɑːʳ] ◆ n 1. (piece - of gold) lingot m; (- of chocolate) tablette f; **a ~ of soap** une savonnette. 2. (length of wood, metal) barre f; **to be behind ~s** être derrière les barreaux OR sous les verrous. 3. fig (obstacle) obstacle m. 4. (pub) bar m. 5. (counter of pub) comptoir m, zinc m. 6. (MUS) mesure f. ◆ vt 1. (door, road) barrer; (window) mettre des barreaux à; **to ~ sb's way** barrer la route OR le passage à qqn. 2. (ban) interdire, défendre; **to ~ sb (from)** interdire à qqn (de). ◆ prep sauf, excepté; **~ none** sans exception. ▶ **Bar** n (JUR): **the Bar** Br le barreau; Am les avocats mpl.

barbaric [bɑː'bærɪk] adj barbare.

barbecue ['bɑːbɪkjuː] n barbecue m.

barbed wire [bɑːbd-] n (U) fil m de fer barbelé.

barber ['bɑːbəʳ] n coiffeur m (pour hommes); **~'s (shop)** salon m de coiffure (pour hommes); **to go to the ~'s** aller chez le coiffeur.

barbiturate [bɑː'bɪtjʊrət] n barbiturique m.

bar code n code m (à) barres.

bare [beəʳ] ◆ adj 1. (feet, arms etc) nu(e); (trees, hills etc) dénudé(e). 2. (absolute, minimum): **the ~ facts** les simples faits; **the ~ minimum** le strict minimum. 3. (empty) vide. ◆ vt découvrir; **to ~ one's teeth** montrer les dents.

bareback ['beəbæk] adv à cru, à nu.

barefaced ['beəfeɪst] adj éhonté(e).

barefoot(ed) [,beə'fʊt(ɪd)] ◆ adj aux pieds nus. ◆ adv nu-pieds, pieds nus.

barely ['beəlɪ] adv (scarcely) à peine, tout juste.

bargain ['bɑːgɪn] ◆ n 1. (agreement) marché m; **into the ~** en plus, par-dessus le marché. 2. (good buy) affaire f, occasion f. ◆ vi négocier; **to ~ with sb for sthg** négocier qqch avec qqn. ▶ **bargain for, bargain on** vt fus compter sur, prévoir.

barge [bɑːdʒ] ◆ n péniche f. ◆ vi inf: **to ~ past sb** bousculer qqn. ▶ **barge in** vi inf: **to ~ in (on)** interrompre.

baritone ['bærɪtəʊn] n baryton m.

bark [bɑːk] ◆ n 1. (of dog) aboiement m. 2. (on tree) écorce f. ◆ vi (dog): **to ~ (at)** aboyer (après).

barley ['bɑːlɪ] n orge f.

barley sugar n Br sucre m d'orge.

barley water n Br orgeat m.

barmaid ['bɑːmeɪd] n barmaid f, serveuse f de bar.

barman ['bɑːmən] (pl -men [-mən]) n barman m, serveur m de bar.

barn [bɑːn] n grange f.

barometer [bə'rɒmɪtəʳ] n lit & fig baromètre m.

baron ['bærən] n baron m.

baroness ['bærənɪs] n baronne f.

barrack ['bærək] vt Br huer, conspuer. ▶ **barracks** npl caserne f.

barrage ['bærɑːʒ] n 1. (of firing) barrage m. 2. (of questions etc) avalanche f, déluge m. 3. Br (dam) barrage m.

barrel ['bærəl] n 1. (for beer, wine) tonneau m, fût m. 2. (for oil) baril m. 3. (of gun) canon m.

barren ['bærən] adj stérile.

barricade [,bærɪ'keɪd] n barricade f.

barrier ['bærɪəʳ] n lit & fig barrière f.

barring ['bɑːrɪŋ] prep sauf.

barrister ['bærɪstəʳ] n Br avocat m, -e f.

barrow ['bærəʊ] n brouette f.

bartender ['bɑːtendəʳ] n Am barman m.

barter ['bɑːtəʳ] ◆ n troc m. ◆ vt: **to ~ sthg (for)** troquer OR échanger qqch (contre). ◆ vi faire du troc.

base [beɪs] ◆ n base f. ◆ vt baser; **to ~ sthg on OR upon** baser OR fonder qqch sur. ◆ adj indigne, ignoble.

baseball ['beɪsbɔːl] n base-ball m.

baseball cap n casquette f de base-ball.

Basel ['bɑːzl] n Bâle.

basement ['beɪsmənt] n sous-sol m.

base rate n taux m de base.

bases ['beɪsiːz] pl → **basis**.

bash [bæʃ] inf ◆ n 1. (painful blow) coup m. 2. (attempt): **to have a ~** tenter le coup. ◆ vt (hit - gen) frapper, cogner; (- car) percuter.

bashful ['bæʃfʊl] adj timide.

basic ['beɪsɪk] adj fondamental(e); (vocabulary, salary) de base. ▸ **basics** npl (rudiments) éléments mpl, bases fpl.

BASIC ['beɪsɪk] (abbr of **Beginner's All-purpose Symbolic Instruction Code**) n basic m.

basically ['beɪsɪklɪ] adv 1. (essentially) au fond, fondamentalement. 2. (really) en fait.

basil ['bæzl] n basilic m.

basin ['beɪsn] n 1. Br (bowl - for cooking) terrine f; (- for washing) cuvette f. 2. (in bathroom) lavabo m. 3. (GEOGR) bassin m.

basis ['beɪsɪs] (pl -ses) n base f; on the ~ of sur la base de; on a regular ~ de façon régulière; to be paid on a weekly/monthly ~ toucher un salaire hebdomadaire/mensuel.

bask [bɑːsk] vi: to ~ in the sun se chauffer au soleil.

basket ['bɑːskɪt] n corbeille f; (with handle) panier m.

basketball ['bɑːskɪtbɔːl] n basketball m, basket m.

bass [beɪs] ◆ adj bas (basse). ◆ n 1. (singer) basse f. 2. (double bass) contrebasse f. 3. = **bass guitar**.

bass drum [beɪs-] n grosse caisse f.

bass guitar [beɪs-] n basse f.

bassoon [bə'suːn] n basson m.

bastard ['bɑːstəd] n 1. (illegitimate child) bâtard m, -e f, enfant naturel m, enfant naturelle f. 2. v inf (unpleasant person) salaud m, saligaud m.

bastion ['bæstɪən] n bastion m.

bat [bæt] n 1. (animal) chauve-souris f. 2. (for cricket, baseball) batte f; (for table-tennis) raquette f. 3. phr: to do sthg off one's own ~ faire qqch de son propre chef.

batch [bætʃ] n 1. (of papers) tas m, liasse f; (of letters, applicants) série f. 2. (of products) lot m.

bated ['beɪtɪd] adj: with ~ breath en retenant son souffle.

bath [bɑːθ] ◆ n 1. (bathtub) baignoire f. 2. (act of washing) bain m; to have OR take a bath prendre un bain. ◆ vt baigner, donner un bain à. ▸ **baths** npl Br piscine f.

bathe [beɪð] ◆ vt 1. (wound) laver. 2. (subj: light, sunshine): to be ~d in OR with être baigné(e) de. ◆ vi 1. (swim) se baigner. 2. Am (take a bath) prendre un bain.

bathing ['beɪðɪŋ] n (U) baignade f.

bathing cap n bonnet m de bain.

bathing costume, bathing suit n maillot m de bain.

bath mat n tapis m de bain.

bathrobe ['bɑːθrəʊb] n (made of towelling) sortie f de bain; (dressing gown) peignoir m.

bathroom ['bɑːθrʊm] n 1. Br (room with bath) salle f de bains. 2. Am (toilet) toilettes fpl.

bath towel n serviette f de bain.

bathtub ['bɑːθtʌb] n baignoire f.

baton ['bætən] n 1. (of conductor) baguette f. 2. (in relay race) témoin m. 3. Br (of policeman) bâton m, matraque f.

batsman ['bætsmən] (pl -men [-mən]) n batteur m.

battalion [bə'tæljən] n bataillon m.

batten ['bætn] n planche f, latte f.

batter ['bætər] ◆ n (U) pâte f. ◆ vt battre.

battered ['bætəd] adj 1. (child, woman) battu(e). 2. (car, hat) cabossé(e).

battery ['bætərɪ] n batterie f; (of calculator, toy) pile f.

battle ['bætl] ◆ n 1. (in war) bataille f. 2. (struggle): ~ (for/against/with) lutte f (pour/contre/avec), combat m (pour/contre/avec). ◆ vi: to ~ (for/against/with) se battre (pour/contre/avec), lutter (pour/contre/avec).

battlefield ['bætlfiːld], **battleground** ['bætlgraʊnd] n (MIL) champ m de bataille.

battlements ['bætlmənts] npl remparts mpl.

battleship ['bætlʃɪp] n cuirassé m.

bauble ['bɔːbl] n babiole f, colifichet m.

baulk [bɔːk] = **balk**.

bawdy ['bɔːdɪ] adj grivois(e), salé(e).

bawl [bɔːl] vt & vi brailler.

bay [beɪ] n 1. (GEOGR) baie f. 2. (for loading) aire f (de chargement). 3. (for parking) place f (de stationnement). 4. phr: to keep sb/sthg at ~ tenir qqn/qqch à distance, tenir qqn/qqch en échec.

bay leaf n feuille f de laurier.

bay window n fenêtre f en saillie.

bazaar [bə'zɑːr] n 1. (market) bazar m. 2. Br (charity sale) vente f de charité.

B & B n abbr of **bed and breakfast**.

BBC (abbr of **British Broadcasting Corporation**) n office national britannique de radiodiffusion.

BC (abbr of **before Christ**) av. J.-C.

be [biː] (pt was OR were, pp been) ◆ aux vb 1. (in combination with ppr: to form cont tense): what is he doing? qu'est-ce qu'il fait?; **it's snowing** il neige; **they've been promising reform for years** ça fait des années qu'ils nous promettent des réformes. **2.** (*in combination with pp: to form passive*) être; **to ~ loved** être aimé(e); **there was no one to ~ seen** il n'y avait personne. **3.** (*in question tags*): **she's pretty, isn't she?** elle est jolie, n'est-ce pas?; **the meal was delicious, wasn't it?** le repas était délicieux, non? OR vous n'avez pas trouvé? **4.** (*followed by 'to' + infin*): **I'm to ~ promoted** je vais avoir de l'avancement; **you're not to tell anyone** ne le dis à personne. ◆ *copulative vb* **1.** (*with adj, n*) être; **to ~ a doctor/lawyer/plumber** être médecin/avocat/plombier; **she's intelligent/attractive** elle est intelligente/jolie; **I'm hot/cold** j'ai chaud/froid; **1 and 1 are 2** 1 et 1 font 2. **2.** (*referring to health*) aller, se porter; **to ~ seriously ill** être gravement malade; **she's better now** elle va mieux maintenant; **how are you?** comment allez-vous? **3.** (*referring to age*): **how old are you?** quel âge avez-vous?; **I'm 20 (years old)** j'ai 20 ans. **4.** (*cost*) coûter, faire; **how much was it?** combien cela a-t-il coûté?, combien ça faisait?; **that will ~ £10, please** cela fait 10 livres, s'il vous plaît. ◆ *vi* **1.** (*exist*) être, exister; **~ that as it may** quoi qu'il en soit. **2.** (*referring to place*) être; **Toulouse is in France** Toulouse se trouve OR est en France; **he will ~ here tomorrow** il sera là demain. **3.** (*referring to movement*) aller, être; **I've been to the cinema** j'ai été OR je suis allé au cinéma. ◆ *v impers* **1.** (*referring to time, dates, distance*) être; **it's two o'clock** il est deux heures; **it's 3 km to the next town** la ville voisine est à 3 km. **2.** (*referring to the weather*) faire; **it's hot/cold** il fait chaud/froid; **it's windy** il fait du vent, il y a du vent. **3.** (*for emphasis*): **it's me/Paul/the milkman** c'est moi/Paul/le laitier.

beach [bi:tʃ] ◆ *n* plage *f*. ◆ *vt* échouer.

beacon ['bi:kən] *n* **1.** (*warning fire*) feu *m*, fanal *m*. **2.** (*lighthouse*) phare *m*. **3.** (*radio beacon*) radiophare *m*.

bead [bi:d] *n* **1.** (*of wood, glass*) perle *f*. **2.** (*of sweat*) goutte *f*.

beagle ['bi:gl] *n* beagle *m*.

beak [bi:k] *n* bec *m*.

beaker ['bi:kər] *n* gobelet *m*.

beam [bi:m] ◆ *n* **1.** (*of wood, concrete*) poutre *f*. **2.** (*of light*) rayon *m*. ◆ *vt* (*signal, news*) transmettre. ◆ *vi* (*smile*) faire un sourire radieux.

bean [bi:n] *n* (*gen*) haricot *m*; (*of coffee*) grain *m*; **to be full of ~s** *inf* péter le feu; **to spill the ~s** *inf* manger le morceau.

beanbag ['bi:nbæg] *n* (*chair*) sacco *m*.

beanshoot ['bi:nʃu:t], **beansprout** ['bi:nspraut] *n* germe *m* OR pousse *f* de soja.

bear [beər] (*pt* **bore**, *pp* **borne**) ◆ *n* (*animal*) ours *m*. ◆ *vt* **1.** (*carry*) porter. **2.** (*support, tolerate*) supporter; **to ~ responsibility (for)** assumer OR prendre la responsabilité (de). **3.** (*feeling*): **to ~ sb a grudge** garder rancune à qqn. ◆ *vi*: **to ~ left/right** se diriger vers la gauche/la droite; **to bring pressure/influence to ~ on sb** exercer une pression/une influence sur qqn. ▶ **bear out** *vt sep* confirmer, corroborer. ▶ **bear up** *vi* tenir le coup. ▶ **bear with** *vt fus* être patient(e) avec.

beard [biəd] *n* barbe *f*.

bearer ['beərər] *n* **1.** (*gen*) porteur *m*, -euse *f*. **2.** (*of passport*) titulaire *mf*.

bearing ['beəriŋ] *n* **1.** (*connection*): **~ (on)** rapport *m* (avec). **2.** (*deportment*) allure *f*, maintien *m*. **3.** (TECH) (*for shaft*) palier *m*. **4.** (*on compass*) orientation *f*; **to get one's ~s** s'orienter, se repérer.

beast [bi:st] *n* **1.** (*animal*) bête *f*. **2.** *inf pej* (*person*) brute *f*.

beastly ['bi:stli] *adj dated* (*person*) malveillant(e), cruel(elle); (*headache, weather*) épouvantable.

beat [bi:t] (*pt* **beat**, *pp* **beaten**) ◆ *n* **1.** (*of heart, drum, wings*) battement *m*. **2.** (MUS) (*rhythm*) mesure *f*, temps *m*. **3.** (*of policeman*) ronde *f*. ◆ *vt* **1.** (*gen*) battre; **it ~s me** *inf* ça me dépasse. **2.** (*be better than*) être bien mieux que, valoir mieux que. **3.** *phr*: **~ it!** *inf* décampe!, fiche le camp! ◆ *vi* battre. ▶ **beat off** *vt sep* (*resist*) repousser. ▶ **beat up** *vt sep inf* tabasser.

beating ['bi:tiŋ] *n* **1.** (*blows*) raclée *f*, rossée *f*. **2.** (*defeat*) défaite *f*.

beautiful ['bju:tiful] *adj* **1.** (*gen*) beau (belle). **2.** *inf* (*very good*) joli(e).

beautifully ['bju:təfli] *adv* **1.** (*attractively - dressed*) élégamment; (*- decorated*) avec goût. **2.** *inf* (*very well*) parfaitement, à la perfection.

beauty ['bju:ti] *n* (*gen*) beauté *f*.

beauty parlour *n* institut *m* de beauté.

beauty salon = **beauty parlour**.

beauty spot *n* **1.** (*picturesque place*) site *m* pittoresque. **2.** (*on skin*) grain *m* de beauté.

beaver ['biːvər] n castor m.

became [bɪ'keɪm] pt → **become**.

because [bɪ'kɒz] conj parce que. ► **because of** prep à cause de.

beck [bek] n: **to be at sb's ~ and call** être aux ordres OR à la disposition de qqn.

beckon ['bekən] ◆ vt (signal to) faire signe à. ◆ vi (signal): **to ~ to sb** faire signe à qqn.

become [bɪ'kʌm] (pt **became**, pp **become**) vi devenir; **to ~ quieter** se calmer; **to ~ irritated** s'énerver.

becoming [bɪ'kʌmɪŋ] adj 1. (attractive) seyant(e), qui va bien. 2. (appropriate) convenable.

bed [bed] n 1. (to sleep on) lit m; **to go to ~** se coucher; **to go to ~ with sb** euphemism coucher avec qqn. 2. (flowerbed) parterre m. 3. (of sea, river) lit m, fond m.

bed and breakfast n ≃ chambre f d'hôte.

bedclothes ['bedkləʊðz] npl draps mpl et couvertures fpl.

bedlam ['bedləm] n pagaille f.

bed linen n (U) draps mpl et taies fpl.

bedraggled [bɪ'drægld] adj (person) débraillé(e); (hair) embroussaillé(e).

bedridden ['bed,rɪdn] adj grabataire.

bedroom ['bedrum] n chambre f (à coucher).

bedside ['bedsaɪd] n chevet m.

bed-sit(ter) n Br chambre f meublée.

bedsore ['bedsɔːr] n escarre f.

bedspread ['bedspred] n couvre-lit m, dessus-de-lit m inv.

bedtime ['bedtaɪm] n heure f du coucher.

bee [biː] n abeille f.

beech [biːtʃ] n hêtre m.

beef [biːf] n bœuf m.

beefburger ['biːf,bɜːgər] n hamburger m.

Beefeater ['biːf,iːtər] n hallebardier m (de la Tour de Londres).

beefsteak ['biːf,steɪk] n bifteck m.

beehive ['biːhaɪv] n (for bees) ruche f.

beeline ['biːlaɪn] n: **to make a ~ for** inf aller tout droit OR directement vers.

been [biːn] pp → **be**.

beep [biːp] n (on answering machine) bip m sonore.

beer [bɪər] n bière f.

beet [biːt] n betterave f.

beetle ['biːtl] n scarabée m.

beetroot ['biːtruːt] n betterave f.

before [bɪ'fɔːr] ◆ adv auparavant, avant; **I've never been there ~** je n'y suis jamais allé; **I've seen it ~** je l'ai déjà vu; **the year ~** l'année d'avant OR précédente. ◆ prep 1. (in time) avant. 2. (in space) devant. ◆ conj avant de (+ infin), avant que (+ subjunctive); **~ leaving** avant de partir; **~ you leave** avant que vous ne partiez.

beforehand [bɪ'fɔːhænd] adv à l'avance.

befriend [bɪ'frend] vt prendre en amitié.

beg [beg] ◆ vt 1. (money, food) mendier. 2. (favour) solliciter, quémander; (forgiveness) demander; **to ~ sb to do sthg** prier OR supplier qqn de faire qqch. ◆ vi 1. (for money, food): **to ~ (for sthg)** mendier (qqch). 2. (plead) supplier; **to ~ for** (forgiveness etc) demander.

began [bɪ'gæn] pt → **begin**.

beggar ['begər] n mendiant m, -e f.

begin [bɪ'gɪn] (pt **began**, pp **begun**) ◆ vt commencer; **to ~ doing** OR **to do sthg** commencer OR se mettre à faire qqch. ◆ vi commencer; **to ~ with** pour commencer, premièrement.

beginner [bɪ'gɪnər] n débutant m, -e f.

beginning [bɪ'gɪnɪŋ] n début m, commencement m.

begrudge [bɪ'grʌdʒ] vt 1. (envy): **to ~ sb sthg** envier qqch à qqn. 2. (do unwillingly): **to ~ doing sthg** rechigner à faire qqch.

begun [bɪ'gʌn] pp → **begin**.

behalf [bɪ'hɑːf] n: **on ~ of** Br, **in ~ of** Am de la part de, au nom de.

behave [bɪ'heɪv] ◆ vt: **to ~ o.s.** se conduire OR se comporter bien. ◆ vi 1. (in a particular way) se conduire, se comporter. 2. (acceptably) se tenir bien.

behaviour Br, **behavior** Am [bɪ'heɪvjər] n conduite f, comportement m.

behead [bɪ'hed] vt décapiter.

beheld [bɪ'held] pt & pp → **behold**.

behind [bɪ'haɪnd] ◆ prep 1. (gen) derrière. 2. (in time) en retard sur. ◆ adv 1. (gen) derrière. 2. (in time) en retard; **to leave sthg ~** oublier qqch; **to stay ~** rester; **to be ~ with sthg** être en retard dans qqch. ◆ n inf derrière m, postérieur m.

behold [bɪ'həʊld] (pt & pp **beheld**) vt literary voir, regarder.

beige [beɪʒ] ◆ adj beige. ◆ n beige m.

being ['biːɪŋ] n 1. (creature) être m. 2. (existence): **in ~** existant(e); **to come into ~** voir le jour, prendre naissance.

Beirut [,beɪ'ruːt] n Beyrouth.

belated [bɪ'leɪtɪd] adj tardif(ive).

belch [beltʃ] ◆ n renvoi m, rot m. ◆ vi (person) éructer, roter.

beleaguered [bɪ'li:gəd] adj assiégé(e); fig harcelé(e), tracassé(e).

Belgian ['beldʒən] ◆ adj belge. ◆ n Belge mf.

Belgium ['beldʒəm] n Belgique f; in ~ en Belgique.

Belgrade [,bel'greɪd] n Belgrade.

belie [bɪ'laɪ] (cont belying) vt 1. (disprove) démentir. 2. (give false idea of) donner une fausse idée de.

belief [bɪ'li:f] n 1. (faith, certainty): ~ (in) croyance f (en). 2. (principle, opinion) opinion f, conviction f.

believe [bɪ'li:v] ◆ vt croire; ~ it or not tu ne me croiras peut-être pas. ◆ vi croire; to ~ in sb croire en qqn; to ~ in sthg croire à qqch.

believer [bɪ'li:vəʳ] n 1. (RELIG) croyant m, -e f. 2. (in idea, action): ~ in partisan m, -e f de.

belittle [bɪ'lɪtl] vt dénigrer, rabaisser.

bell [bel] n (of church) cloche f; (handbell) clochette f; (on door) sonnette f; (on bike) timbre m.

belligerent [bɪ'lɪdʒərənt] adj 1. (at war) belligérant(e). 2. (aggressive) belliqueux (euse).

bellow ['beləʊ] vi 1. (person) brailler, beugler. 2. (bull) beugler.

bellows ['beləʊz] npl soufflet m.

belly ['belɪ] n (of person) ventre m; (of animal) panse f.

bellyache ['belɪeɪk] n mal m de ventre.

belly button n inf nombril m.

belong [bɪ'lɒŋ] vi 1. (be property): to ~ to sb appartenir OR être à qqn. 2. (be member): to ~ to sthg être membre de qqch. 3. (be in right place) être à sa place; that chair ~s here ce fauteuil va ici.

belongings [bɪ'lɒŋɪŋz] npl affaires fpl.

beloved [bɪ'lʌvd] adj bien-aimé(e).

below [bɪ'ləʊ] ◆ adv 1. (lower) en dessous, en bas. 2. (in text) ci-dessous. 3. (NAUT) en bas. ◆ prep sous, au-dessous de.

belt [belt] ◆ n 1. (for clothing) ceinture f. 2. (TECH) courroie f. ◆ vt inf flanquer une raclée à.

beltway ['belt,weɪ] n Am route f périphérique.

bemused [bɪ'mju:zd] adj perplexe.

bench [bentʃ] n 1. (gen & POL) banc m. 2. (in lab, workshop) établi m.

bend [bend] (pt & pp bent) ◆ n 1. (in road) courbe f, virage m. 2. (in pipe, river) coude m. 3. phr: round the ~ inf dingue, fou (folle). ◆ vt 1. (arm, leg) plier. 2. (wire, fork etc) tordre, courber. ◆ vi (person) se baisser, se courber; (tree, rod) plier; to ~ over backwards for sb se mettre en quatre pour qqn.

beneath [bɪ'ni:θ] ◆ adv dessous, en bas. ◆ prep 1. (under) sous. 2. (unworthy of) indigne de.

benefactor ['benɪfæktəʳ] n bienfaiteur m.

beneficial [,benɪ'fɪʃl] adj: ~ (to sb) salutaire (à qqn); ~ (to sthg) utile (à qqch).

beneficiary [,benɪ'fɪʃərɪ] n bénéficiaire mf.

benefit ['benɪfɪt] ◆ n 1. (advantage) avantage m; for the ~ of dans l'intérêt de; to be to sb's ~, to be of ~ to sb être dans l'intérêt de qqn. 2. (ADMIN) (allowance of money) allocation f, prestation f. ◆ vt profiter à. ◆ vi: to ~ from tirer avantage de, profiter de.

Benelux ['benɪlʌks] n Bénélux m.

benevolent [bɪ'nevələnt] adj bienveillant(e).

benign [bɪ'naɪn] adj 1. (person) gentil (ille), bienveillant(e). 2. (MED) bénin (igne).

bent [bent] ◆ pt & pp → **bend**. ◆ adj 1. (wire, bar) tordu(e). 2. (person, body) courbé(e), voûté(e). 3. Br inf (dishonest) véreux(euse). 4. (determined): to be ~ on doing sthg vouloir absolument faire qqch, être décidé(e) à faire qqch. ◆ n: ~ (for) penchant m (pour).

bequeath [bɪ'kwi:ð] vt lit & fig léguer.

bequest [bɪ'kwest] n legs m.

berate [bɪ'reɪt] vt réprimander.

bereaved [bɪ'ri:vd] (pl inv) ◆ adj endeuillé(e), affligé(e). ◆ n: the ~ la famille du défunt.

beret ['bereɪ] n béret m.

berk [bɜ:k] n Br inf idiot m, -e f.

Berlin [bɜ:'lɪn] n Berlin.

berm [bɜ:m] n Am bas-côté m.

Bern [bɜ:n] n Berne.

berry ['berɪ] n baie f.

berserk [bə'zɜ:k] adj: to go ~ devenir fou furieux (folle furieuse).

berth [bɜ:θ] ◆ n 1. (in harbour) poste m d'amarrage, mouillage m. 2. (in ship, train) couchette f. ◆ vi (ship) accoster, se ranger à quai.

beseech [bɪ'si:tʃ] (pt & pp besought OR beseeched) vt literary: to ~ sb (to do sthg) supplier qqn (de faire qqch).

beset [bɪ'set] (*pt* & *pp* **beset**) ♦ *adj*: ~ **with** OR **by** (*doubts etc*) assailli(e) de. ♦ *vt* assaillir.

beside [bɪ'saɪd] *prep* 1. (*next to*) à côté de, auprès de. 2. (*compared with*) comparé(e) à, à côté de. 3. *phr*: **to be ~ o.s. with anger** être hors de soi; **to be ~ o.s. with joy** être fou (folle) de joie.

besides [bɪ'saɪdz] ♦ *adv* en outre, en plus. ♦ *prep* en plus de.

besiege [bɪ'siːdʒ] *vt* 1. (*town, fortress*) assiéger. 2. *fig* (*trouble, annoy*) assaillir, harceler.

besotted [bɪ'sɒtɪd] *adj*: ~ **(with sb)** entiché(e) (de qqn).

besought [bɪ'sɔːt] *pt* & *pp* → **beseech**.

best [best] ♦ *adj* le meilleur (la meilleure). ♦ *adv* le mieux. ♦ *n* le mieux; **to do one's ~** faire de son mieux; **all the ~!** meilleurs souhaits!; **to be for the ~** être pour le mieux; **to make the ~ of sthg** s'accommoder de qqch, prendre son parti de qqch. ▶ **at best** *adv* au mieux.

best man *n* garçon *m* d'honneur.

bestow [bɪ'stəʊ] *vt fml*: **to ~ sthg on sb** conférer qqch à qqn.

best-seller *n* (*book*) best-seller *m*.

bet [bet] (*pt* & *pp* **bet** OR **-ted**) ♦ *n* pari *m*. ♦ *vt* parier. ♦ *vi* parier; **I wouldn't ~ on it** *fig* je n'en suis pas si sûr.

betray [bɪ'treɪ] *vt* trahir.

betrayal [bɪ'treɪəl] *n* (*of person*) trahison *f*.

better ['betər] ♦ *adj* (*compar of* **good**) meilleur(e); **to get ~** s'améliorer; (*after illness*) se remettre, se rétablir. ♦ *adv* (*compar of* **well**) mieux; **I'd ~ leave** il faut que je parte, je dois partir. ♦ *n* meilleur *m*, -e *f*; **to get the ~ of sb** avoir raison de qqn. ♦ *vt* améliorer; **to ~ o.s.** s'élever.

better off *adj* 1. (*financially*) plus à son aise. 2. (*in better situation*) mieux.

betting ['betɪŋ] *n* (U) paris *mpl*.

betting shop *n* Br ≃ bureau *m* de P.M.U.

between [bɪ'twiːn] ♦ *prep* entre. ♦ *adv*: **(in) ~** (*in space*) au milieu; (*in time*) dans l'intervalle.

beverage ['bevərɪdʒ] *n fml* boisson *f*.

beware [bɪ'weər] *vi*: **to ~ (of)** prendre garde (à), se méfier (de); **~ of ...** attention à ...

bewildered [bɪ'wɪldəd] *adj* déconcerté(e), perplexe.

bewitching [bɪ'wɪtʃɪŋ] *adj* charmeur (euse), ensorcelant(e).

beyond [bɪ'jɒnd] ♦ *prep* 1. (*in space*) au-delà de. 2. (*in time*) après, plus tard que. 3. (*exceeding*) au-dessus de; **it's ~ my control** je n'y peux rien; **it's ~ my responsibility** cela n'entre pas dans le cadre de mes responsabilités. ♦ *adv* au-delà.

bias ['baɪəs] *n* 1. (*prejudice*) préjugé *m*, parti *m* pris. 2. (*tendency*) tendance *f*.

biased ['baɪəst] *adj* partial(e); **to be ~ towards sb/sthg** favoriser qqn/qqch; **to be ~ against sb/sthg** défavoriser qqn/qqch.

bib [bɪb] *n* (*for baby*) bavoir *m*, bavette *f*.

Bible ['baɪbl] *n*: **the ~** la Bible.

bicarbonate of soda [baɪ'kɑːbənət-] *n* bicarbonate *m* de soude.

biceps ['baɪseps] (*pl inv*) *n* biceps *m*.

bicker ['bɪkər] *vi* se chamailler.

bicycle ['baɪsɪkl] ♦ *n* bicyclette *f*, vélo *m*. ♦ *vi* aller en bicyclette OR vélo.

bicycle path *n* piste *f* cyclable.

bicycle pump *n* pompe *f* à vélo.

bid [bɪd] (*pt* & *pp* **bid**) ♦ *n* 1. (*attempt*) tentative *f*. 2. (*at auction*) enchère *f*. 3. (COMM) offre *f*. ♦ *vt* (*at auction*) faire une enchère de. ♦ *vi* 1. (*at auction*): **to ~ (for)** faire une enchère (pour). 2. (*attempt*): **to ~ for sthg** briguer qqch.

bidder ['bɪdər] *n* enchérisseur *m*, -euse *f*.

bidding ['bɪdɪŋ] *n* (U) enchères *fpl*.

bide [baɪd] *vt*: **to ~ one's time** attendre son heure OR le bon moment.

bifocals [,baɪ'fəʊklz] *npl* lunettes *fpl* bifocales.

big [bɪg] *adj* 1. (*gen*) grand(e). 2. (*in amount, bulk - box, problem, book*) gros (grosse).

bigamy ['bɪgəmɪ] *n* bigamie *f*.

big deal *inf* ♦ *n*: **it's no ~** ce n'est pas dramatique; **what's the ~?** où est le problème? ♦ *excl* tu parles!, et alors?

Big Dipper [-'dɪpər] *n* 1. Br (*rollercoaster*) montagnes *fpl* russes. 2. Am (ASTRON): **the ~** la Grande Ourse.

bigheaded [,bɪg'hedɪd] *adj inf* crâneur (euse).

bigot ['bɪgət] *n* sectaire *mf*.

bigoted ['bɪgətɪd] *adj* sectaire.

bigotry ['bɪgətrɪ] *n* sectarisme *m*.

big time *n inf*: **to make the ~** réussir, arriver en haut de l'échelle.

big toe *n* gros orteil *m*.

big top *n* chapiteau *m*.

big wheel *n* Br (*at fairground*) grande roue *f*.

bike [baɪk] *n inf* 1. (*bicycle*) vélo *m*.

2. (*motorcycle*) bécane f, moto f.
bikini [bɪˈkiːnɪ] n Bikini® m.
bile [baɪl] n **1.** (*fluid*) bile f. **2.** (*anger*) mauvaise humeur f.
bilingual [baɪˈlɪŋgwəl] adj bilingue.
bill [bɪl] ◆ n **1.** (*statement of cost*): ~ **(for)** note f OR facture f (de); (*in restaurant*) addition f (de). **2.** (*in parliament*) projet m de loi. **3.** (*of show, concert*) programme m. **4.** Am (*banknote*) billet m de banque. **5.** (*poster*): 'post OR stick no ~s' 'défense d'afficher'. **6.** (*beak*) bec m. ◆ vt (*invoice*): **to ~ sb (for)** envoyer une facture à qqn (pour).
billboard [ˈbɪlbɔːd] n panneau m d'affichage.
billet [ˈbɪlɪt] n logement m (chez l'habitant).
billfold [ˈbɪlfəʊld] n Am portefeuille m.
billiards [ˈbɪljədz] n billard m.
billion [ˈbɪljən] num **1.** Am (*thousand million*) milliard m. **2.** Br (*million million*) billion m.
Bill of Rights n: **the ~** les dix premiers amendements à la Constitution américaine.
bimbo [ˈbɪmbəʊ] (*pl* -s OR -es) n inf pej: **she's a bit of a ~** c'est le genre 'pin-up'.
bin [bɪn] n **1.** Br (*for rubbish*) poubelle f. **2.** (*for grain, coal*) coffre m.
bind [baɪnd] (*pt & pp* **bound**) vt **1.** (*tie up*) attacher, lier. **2.** (*unite - people*) lier. **3.** (*bandage*) panser. **4.** (*book*) relier. **5.** (*constrain*) contraindre, forcer.
binder [ˈbaɪndər] n (*cover*) classeur m.
binding [ˈbaɪndɪŋ] ◆ adj qui lie OR engage; (*agreement*) irrévocable. ◆ n (*on book*) reliure f.
binge [bɪndʒ] inf ◆ n: **to go on a ~** prendre une cuite. ◆ vi: **to ~ on sthg** se gaver OR se bourrer de qqch.
bingo [ˈbɪŋgəʊ] n bingo m, = loto m.
binoculars [bɪˈnɒkjʊləz] npl jumelles fpl.
biochemistry [ˌbaɪəʊˈkemɪstrɪ] n biochimie f.
biodegradable [ˌbaɪəʊdɪˈgreɪdəbl] adj biodégradable.
biography [baɪˈɒgrəfɪ] n biographie f.
biological [ˌbaɪəˈlɒdʒɪkl] adj biologique; (*washing powder*) aux enzymes.
biology [baɪˈɒlədʒɪ] n biologie f.
birch [bɜːtʃ] n (*tree*) bouleau m.
bird [bɜːd] n **1.** (*creature*) oiseau m. **2.** inf (*woman*) gonzesse f.
birdie [ˈbɜːdɪ] n **1.** (*bird*) petit oiseau m. **2.** (GOLF) birdie m.
bird's-eye view n vue f aérienne.
bird-watcher [-ˌwɒtʃər] n observa-

teur m, -trice f d'oiseaux.
Biro® [ˈbaɪərəʊ] n stylo m à bille.
birth [bɜːθ] n lit & fig naissance f; **to give ~ (to)** donner naissance (à).
birth certificate n acte m OR extrait m de naissance.
birth control n (U) régulation f OR contrôle m des naissances.
birthday [ˈbɜːθdeɪ] n anniversaire m.
birthmark [ˈbɜːθmɑːk] n tache f de vin.
birthrate [ˈbɜːθreɪt] n (taux m de) natalité f.
Biscay [ˈbɪskeɪ] n: **the Bay of ~** le golfe de Gascogne.
biscuit [ˈbɪskɪt] n Br gâteau m sec, biscuit m; Am scone m.
bisect [baɪˈsekt] vt couper OR diviser en deux.
bishop [ˈbɪʃəp] n **1.** (RELIG) évêque m. **2.** (*in chess*) fou m.
bison [ˈbaɪsn] (*pl inv* OR -s) n bison m.
bit [bɪt] ◆ pt → **bite**. ◆ n **1.** (*small piece - of paper, cheese etc*) morceau m, bout m; (- *of book, film*) passage m; **~s and pieces** Br petites affaires fpl OR choses fpl; **to take sthg to ~s** démonter qqch. **2.** (*amount*): **a ~ of** un peu de; **a ~ of shopping** quelques courses; **it's a ~ of a nuisance** c'est un peu embêtant; **a ~ of trouble** un petit problème; **quite a ~ of** pas mal de, beaucoup de. **3.** (*short time*): **for a ~** pendant quelque temps. **4.** (*of drill*) mèche f. **5.** (*of bridle*) mors m. **6.** (COMPUT) bit m. ► **a bit** adv un peu; **I'm a ~ tired** je suis un peu fatigué. ► **bit by bit** adv petit à petit.
bitch [bɪtʃ] n **1.** (*female dog*) chienne f. **2.** v inf pej (*woman*) salope f, garce f.
bitchy [ˈbɪtʃɪ] adj inf vache, rosse.
bite [baɪt] (*pt* **bit**, *pp* **bitten**) ◆ n **1.** (*act of biting*) morsure f, coup m de dent. **2.** inf (*food*): **to have a ~ (to eat)** manger un morceau. **3.** (*wound*) piqûre f. ◆ vt **1.** (*subj: person, animal*) mordre. **2.** (*subj: insect, snake*) piquer, mordre. ◆ vi **1.** (*animal, person*): **to ~ (into)** mordre (dans); **to ~ off sthg** arracher qqch d'un coup de dents. **2.** (*insect, snake*) mordre, piquer. **3.** (*grip*) adhérer, mordre. **4.** fig (*take effect*) se faire sentir.
biting [ˈbaɪtɪŋ] adj **1.** (*very cold*) cinglant(e), piquant(e). **2.** (*humour, comment*) mordant(e), caustique.
bitten [ˈbɪtn] pp → **bite**.
bitter [ˈbɪtər] ◆ adj **1.** (*gen*) amer(ère). **2.** (*icy*) glacial(e). **3.** (*argument*) violent(e). ◆ n Br bière relativement amère, à forte teneur en houblon.

bitter lemon n Schweppes® m au citron.

bitterness ['bɪtənɪs] n 1. (gen) amertume f. 2. (of wind, weather) âpreté f.

bizarre [bɪ'zɑːʳ] adj bizarre.

blab [blæb] vi inf lâcher le morceau.

black [blæk] ♦ adj noir(e). ♦ n 1. (colour) noir m. 2. (person) noir m, -e f. 3. phr: in ~ and white (in writing) noir sur blanc, par écrit; in the ~ (financially solvent) solvable, sans dettes. ♦ vt Br (boycott) boycotter. ▶ **black out** vi (faint) s'évanouir.

blackberry ['blækbərɪ] n mûre f.

blackbird ['blækbɜːd] n merle m.

blackboard ['blækbɔːd] n tableau m (noir).

blackcurrant [ˌblæk'kʌrənt] n cassis m.

blacken ['blækn] ♦ vt (make dark) noircir. ♦ vi s'assombrir.

black eye n œil m poché OR au beurre noir.

blackhead ['blækhed] n point m noir.

black ice n verglas m.

blackleg ['blækleg] n pej jaune m.

blacklist ['blæklɪst] ♦ n liste f noire. ♦ vt mettre sur la liste noire.

blackmail ['blækmeɪl] ♦ n lit & fig chantage m. ♦ vt 1. (for money) faire chanter. 2. fig (emotionally) faire du chantage à.

black market n marché m noir.

blackout ['blækaut] n 1. (MIL & PRESS) black-out m. 2. (power cut) panne f d'électricité. 3. (fainting fit) évanouissement m.

black pudding n Br boudin m.

Black Sea n: the ~ la mer Noire.

black sheep n brebis f galeuse.

blacksmith ['blæksmɪθ] n forgeron m; (for horses) maréchal-ferrant m.

black spot n (AUT) point m noir.

bladder ['blædəʳ] n vessie f.

blade [bleɪd] n 1. (of knife, saw) lame f. 2. (of propeller) pale f. 3. (of grass) brin m.

blame [bleɪm] ♦ n responsabilité f, faute f; to take the ~ for sthg endosser la responsabilité de qqch. ♦ vt blâmer, condamner; to ~ sthg on rejeter la responsabilité de qqch sur, imputer qqch à; to ~ sb/sthg for sthg reprocher qqch à qqn/qqch; to be to ~ for sthg être responsable de qqch.

bland [blænd] adj 1. (person) terne. 2. (food) fade, insipide. 3. (music, style) insipide.

blank [blæŋk] ♦ adj 1. (sheet of paper) blanc (blanche); (wall) nu(e). 2. fig (look) vide, sans expression. ♦ n 1. (empty space) blanc m. 2. (cartridge) cartouche f à blanc.

blank cheque n chèque m en blanc; fig carte f blanche.

blanket ['blæŋkɪt] n 1. (for bed) couverture f. 2. (of snow) couche f, manteau m; (of fog) nappe f.

blare [bleəʳ] vi hurler; (radio) beugler.

blasphemy ['blæsfəmɪ] n blasphème m.

blast [blɑːst] ♦ n 1. (explosion) explosion f. 2. (of air, from bomb) souffle m. ♦ vt (hole, tunnel) creuser à la dynamite. ♦ excl Br inf zut!, mince! ▶ **(at) full blast** adv (play music etc) à pleins gaz OR tubes; (work) d'arrache-pied.

blasted ['blɑːstɪd] adj inf fichu(e), maudit(e).

blast-off n (SPACE) lancement m.

blatant ['bleɪtənt] adj criant(e), flagrant(e).

blaze [bleɪz] ♦ n 1. (fire) incendie m. 2. fig (of colour, light) éclat m, flamboiement m. ♦ vi 1. (fire) flamber. 2. fig (with colour) flamboyer.

blazer ['bleɪzəʳ] n blazer m.

bleach [bliːtʃ] ♦ n eau f de Javel. ♦ vt (hair) décolorer; (clothes) blanchir.

bleached [bliːtʃt] adj décoloré(e).

bleachers ['bliːtʃəz] npl Am (SPORT) gradins mpl.

bleak [bliːk] adj 1. (future) sombre. 2. (place, weather, face) lugubre, triste.

bleary-eyed [ˌblɪərɪ'aɪd] adj aux yeux troubles OR voilés.

bleat [bliːt] ♦ n bêlement m. ♦ vi bêler; fig (person) se plaindre, geindre.

bleed [bliːd] (pt & pp bled [bled]) ♦ vt (radiator etc) purger. ♦ vi saigner.

bleeper ['bliːpəʳ] n bip m, bip-bip m.

blemish ['blemɪʃ] n lit & fig défaut m.

blend [blend] ♦ n mélange m. ♦ vt: to ~ sthg (with) mélanger qqch (avec OR à). ♦ vi: to ~ (with) se mêler (à OR avec).

blender ['blendəʳ] n mixer m.

bless [bles] (pt & pp -ed OR blest) vt bénir; ~ you! (after sneezing) à vos souhaits!; (thank you) merci mille fois!

blessing ['blesɪŋ] n bénédiction f.

blest [blest] pt & pp → **bless**.

blew [bluː] pt → **blow**.

blight [blaɪt] vt gâcher, briser.

blimey ['blaɪmɪ] excl Br inf zut alors!, mince alors!

blind [blaɪnd] ♦ adj lit & fig aveugle; to be ~ to sthg ne pas voir qqch. ♦ n (for window) store m. ♦ npl: the ~ les aveugles *mpl*. ◆ *vt* aveugler; **to ~ sb to sthg** *fig* cacher qqch à qqn.

blind alley *n lit & fig* impasse *f*.

blind corner *n* virage *m* sans visibilité.

blind date *n* rendez-vous avec quelqu'un qu'on ne connaît pas.

blinders ['blaɪndəz] *npl Am* œillères *fpl*.

blindfold ['blaɪndfəʊld] ◆ *adv* les yeux bandés. ◆ *n* bandeau *m*. ◆ *vt* bander les yeux à.

blindly ['blaɪndlɪ] *adv lit & fig* à l'aveuglette, aveuglément.

blindness ['blaɪndnɪs] *n* cécité *f*; **~ (to)** *fig* aveuglement *m* (devant).

blind spot *n* **1.** (AUT) angle *m* mort. **2.** *fig* (*inability to understand*) blocage *m*.

blink [blɪŋk] ◆ *n phr*: **on the ~** (*machine*) détraqué(e). ◆ *vt* (*eyes*) cligner. ◆ *vi* **1.** (*person*) cligner des yeux. **2.** (*light*) clignoter.

blinkered ['blɪŋkəd] *adj*: **to be ~** *lit & fig* avoir des œillères.

blinkers ['blɪŋkəz] *npl Br* œillères *fpl*.

bliss [blɪs] *n* bonheur *m* suprême, félicité *f*.

blissful ['blɪsfʊl] *adj* (*day, silence*) merveilleux(euse); (*ignorance*) total(e).

blister ['blɪstər] ◆ *n* (*on skin*) ampoule *f*, cloque *f*. ◆ *vi* **1.** (*skin*) se couvrir d'ampoules. **2.** (*paint*) cloquer, se boursoufler.

blithely ['blaɪðlɪ] *adv* gaiement, joyeusement.

blitz [blɪts] *n* (MIL) bombardement *m* aérien.

blizzard ['blɪzəd] *n* tempête *f* de neige.

bloated ['bləʊtɪd] *adj* **1.** (*face*) bouffi(e). **2.** (*with food*) ballonné(e).

blob [blɒb] *n* **1.** (*drop*) goutte *f*. **2.** (*indistinct shape*) forme *f*; **a ~ of colour** une tache de couleur.

block [blɒk] ◆ *n* **1.** (*building*): **office ~** immeuble *m* de bureaux; **~ of flats** *Br* immeuble *m*. **2.** *Am* (*of buildings*) pâté *m* de maisons. **3.** (*of stone, ice*) bloc *m*. **4.** (*obstruction*) blocage *m*. ◆ *vt* **1.** (*road, pipe, view*) boucher. **2.** (*prevent*) bloquer, empêcher.

blockade [blɒ'keɪd] ◆ *n* blocus *m*. ◆ *vt* faire le blocus de.

blockage ['blɒkɪdʒ] *n* obstruction *f*

blockbuster ['blɒkbʌstər] *n inf* (*book*) best-seller *m*; (*film*) film *m* à succès.

block capitals *npl* majuscules *fpl* d'imprimerie.

block letters *npl* majuscules *fpl* d'imprimerie.

bloke [bləʊk] *n Br inf* type *m*.

blond [blɒnd] *adj* blond(e).

blonde [blɒnd] ◆ *adj* blond(e). ◆ *n* (*woman*) blonde *f*.

blood [blʌd] *n* sang *m*; **in cold ~** de sang-froid.

bloodbath ['blʌdbɑːθ, *pl* -bɑːðz] *n* bain *m* de sang, massacre *m*.

blood cell *n* globule *m*.

blood donor *n* donneur *m*, -euse *f* de sang.

blood group *n* groupe *m* sanguin.

bloodhound ['blʌdhaʊnd] *n* limier *m*.

blood poisoning *n* septicémie *f*.

blood pressure *n* tension *f* artérielle; **to have high ~** faire de l'hypertension.

bloodshed ['blʌdʃed] *n* carnage *m*.

bloodshot ['blʌdʃɒt] *adj* (*eyes*) injecté(e) de sang.

bloodstream ['blʌdstriːm] *n* sang *m*.

blood test *n* prise *f* de sang.

bloodthirsty ['blʌdˌθɜːstɪ] *adj* sanguinaire.

blood transfusion *n* transfusion *f* sanguine.

bloody ['blʌdɪ] ◆ *adj* **1.** (*gen*) sanglant(e). **2.** *Br v inf* foutu(e); **you ~ idiot!** espèce de con! ◆ *adv Br v inf* vachement.

bloody-minded [-'maɪndɪd] *adj Br inf* contrariant(e).

bloom [bluːm] ◆ *n* fleur *f*. ◆ *vi* fleurir.

blooming ['bluːmɪŋ] ◆ *adj Br inf* (*to show annoyance*) sacré(e), fichu(e). ◆ *adv Br inf* sacrément.

blossom ['blɒsəm] ◆ *n* (*of tree*) fleurs *fpl*; **in ~** en fleur OR fleurs. ◆ *vi* **1.** (*tree*) fleurir. **2.** *fig* (*person*) s'épanouir.

blot [blɒt] ◆ *n lit & fig* tache *f*. ◆ *vt* **1.** (*paper*) faire des pâtés sur. **2.** (*ink*) sécher. ► **blot out** *vt sep* voiler, cacher; (*memories*) effacer.

blotchy ['blɒtʃɪ] *adj* couvert(e) de marbrures OR taches.

blotting paper ['blɒtɪŋ-] *n* (U) (papier *m*) buvard *m*.

blouse [blaʊz] *n* chemisier *m*.

blow [bləʊ] (*pt* blew, *pp* blown) ◆ *vi* **1.** (*gen*) souffler. **2.** (*in wind*): **to ~ off** s'envoler. **3.** (*fuse*) sauter. ◆ *vt* **1.** (*subj: wind*) faire voler, chasser. **2.** (*clear*): **to ~ one's nose** se moucher. **3.** (*trumpet*) jouer de, souffler dans; **to ~ a whistle** donner un coup de sifflet, siffler. ◆ *n* (*hit*) coup *m*. ► **blow out** ◆ *vt sep* souffler. ◆ vi 1. (candle) s'éteindre. 2. (tyre) éclater. ▶ **blow over** vi se calmer. ▶ **blow up** ◆ vt sep 1. (inflate) gonfler. 2. (with bomb) faire sauter. 3. (photograph) agrandir. ◆ vi exploser.

blow-dry ◆ n Brushing® m. ◆ vt faire un Brushing® à.

blowlamp Br ['bləʊlæmp], **blowtorch** ['bləʊtɔːtʃ] n chalumeau m, lampe f à souder.

blown [bləʊn] pp → **blow**.

blowout ['bləʊaʊt] n (of tyre) éclatement m.

blowtorch = **blowlamp**.

blubber ['blʌbər] ◆ n graisse f de baleine. ◆ vi pej chialer.

blue [bluː] ◆ adj 1. (colour) bleu(e). 2. inf (sad) triste, cafardeux(euse). 3. (pornographic) porno (inv). ◆ n bleu m; **out of the ~** (happen) subitement; (arrive) à l'improviste. ▶ **blues** npl: **the ~s** (MUS) le blues; inf (sad feeling) le blues, le cafard.

bluebell ['bluːbel] n jacinthe f des bois.

blueberry ['bluːbəri] n myrtille f.

bluebottle ['bluːbɒtl] n mouche f bleue, mouche de la viande.

blue cheese n (fromage m) bleu m.

blue-collar adj manuel(elle).

blue jeans npl Am blue-jean m, jean m.

blueprint ['bluːprint] n photocalque m; fig plan m, projet m.

bluff [blʌf] ◆ adj franc (franche). ◆ n 1. (deception) bluff m; **to call sb's ~** prendre qqn au mot. 2. (cliff) falaise f à pic. ◆ vt bluffer, donner le change à. ◆ vi faire du bluff, bluffer.

blunder ['blʌndər] ◆ n gaffe f, bévue f. ◆ vi (make mistake) faire une gaffe, commettre une bévue.

blunt [blʌnt] ◆ adj 1. (knife) émoussé(e); (pencil) épointé(e); (object, instrument) contondant(e). 2. (person, manner) direct(e), carré(e). ◆ vt lit & fig émousser.

blur [blɜːr] ◆ n forme f confuse, tache f floue. ◆ vt (vision) troubler, brouiller.

blurb [blɜːb] n texte m publicitaire.

blurt [blɜːt] ▶ **blurt out** vt sep laisser échapper.

blush [blʌʃ] ◆ n rougeur f. ◆ vi rougir.

blusher ['blʌʃər] n fard m à joues, blush m.

blustery ['blʌstəri] adj venteux(euse).

BMX (abbr of **bicycle motorcross**) n bicross m.

BO abbr of **body odour**.

boar [bɔːr] n 1. (male pig) verrat m. 2. (wild pig) sanglier m.

board [bɔːd] ◆ n 1. (plank) planche f. 2. (for notices) panneau m d'affichage. 3. (for games - gen) tableau m; (- for chess) échiquier m. 4. (blackboard) tableau m (noir). 5. (of company): ~ (**of directors**) conseil m d'administration. 6. (committee) comité m, conseil m. 7. Br (at hotel, guesthouse) pension f; ~ **and lodging** pension; **full** ~ pension complète; **half** ~ demi-pension f. 8. **on** ~ (on ship, plane, bus, train) à bord. 9. phr: **above** ~ régulier(ère), dans les règles. ◆ vt (ship, aeroplane) monter à bord de; (train, bus) monter dans.

boarder ['bɔːdər] n 1. (lodger) pensionnaire mf. 2. (at school) interne mf, pensionnaire mf.

boarding card ['bɔːdɪŋ-] n carte f d'embarquement.

boardinghouse ['bɔːdɪŋhaʊs, pl -haʊzɪz] n pension f de famille.

boarding school ['bɔːdɪŋ-] n pensionnat m, internat m.

Board of Trade n Br: **the ~** ≃ le ministère m du Commerce.

boardroom ['bɔːdrʊm] n salle f du conseil (d'administration).

boast [bəʊst] ◆ n vantardise f, fanfaronnade f. ◆ vi: **to ~** (**about**) se vanter (de).

boastful ['bəʊstfʊl] adj vantard(e), fanfaron(onne).

boat [bəʊt] n (large) bateau m; (small) canot m, embarcation f; **by** ~ en bateau.

boater ['bəʊtər] n (hat) canotier m.

boating ['bəʊtɪŋ] n canotage m; **to go** ~ faire du canotage.

boatswain ['bəʊsn] n maître m d'équipage.

bob [bɒb] ◆ n 1. (hairstyle) coupe f au carré. 2. Br inf dated (shilling) shilling m. 3. = **bobsleigh**. ◆ vi (boat, ship) tanguer.

bobbin ['bɒbɪn] n bobine f.

bobby ['bɒbɪ] n Br inf agent m de police.

bobsleigh ['bɒbsleɪ] n bobsleigh m.

bode [bəʊd] vi literary: **to ~ ill/well (for)** être de mauvais/bon augure (pour).

bodily ['bɒdɪlɪ] ◆ adj (needs) matériel (elle); (pain) physique. ◆ adv (lift, move) à bras-le-corps.

body ['bɒdɪ] n 1. (of person) corps m. 2. (corpse) corps m, cadavre m. 3. (organization) organisme m, organisation f.

4. (*of car*) carrosserie *f*; (*of plane*) fuselage *m*. **5.** (U) (*of wine*) corps *m*. **6.** (U) (*of hair*) volume *m*. **7.** (*garment*) body *m*.
body building *n* culturisme *m*.
bodyguard ['bɒdɪgɑːd] *n* garde *m* du corps.
body odour *n* odeur *f* corporelle.
bodywork ['bɒdɪwɜːk] *n* carrosserie *f*.
bog [bɒg] *n* **1.** (*marsh*) marécage *m*. **2.** Br *v inf* (*toilet*) chiottes *fpl*.
bogged down [‚bɒgd-] *adj* **1.** fig (*in work*): ~ **(in)** submergé(e) (de). **2.** (*car etc*): ~ **(in)** enlisé(e) (dans).
boggle ['bɒgl] *vi*: **the mind ~s!** ce n'est pas croyable!, on croit rêver!
bogus ['bəʊgəs] *adj* faux (fausse), bidon (*inv*).
boil [bɔɪl] ◆ *n* **1.** (MED) furoncle *m*. **2.** (*boiling point*): **to bring sthg to the ~** porter qqch à ébullition; **to come to the ~** venir à ébullition. ◆ *vt* **1.** (*water, food*) faire bouillir. **2.** (*kettle*) mettre sur le feu. ◆ *vi* (*water*) bouillir. ▶ **boil down to** *vt fus* fig revenir à, se résumer à. ▶ **boil over** *vi* **1.** (*liquid*) déborder. **2.** fig (*feelings*) exploser.
boiled ['bɔɪld] *adj*: ~ **egg** œuf *m* à la coque; ~ **sweet** Br bonbon *m* (dur).
boiler ['bɔɪlər] *n* chaudière *f*.
boiler suit *n* Br bleu *m* de travail.
boiling ['bɔɪlɪŋ] *adj* **1.** (*liquid*) bouillant(e). **2.** inf (*weather*) très chaud(e), torride; (*person*): **I'm ~ (hot)!** je crève de chaleur!
boiling point *n* point *m* d'ébullition.
boisterous ['bɔɪstərəs] *adj* turbulent(e), remuant(e).
bold [bəʊld] *adj* **1.** (*confident*) hardi(e), audacieux(euse). **2.** (*lines, design*) hardi(e); (*colour*) vif (vive), éclatant(e). **3.** (TYPO): ~ **type** OR **print** caractères *mpl* gras.
bollard ['bɒlɑːd] *n* (*on road*) borne *f*.
bollocks ['bɒləks] Br *v inf* ◆ *npl* couilles *fpl*. ◆ *excl* quelles conneries!
bolster ['bəʊlstər] ◆ *n* (*pillow*) traversin *m*. ◆ *vt* renforcer, affirmer. ▶ **bolster up** *vt sep* soutenir, appuyer.
bolt [bəʊlt] ◆ *n* **1.** (*on door, window*) verrou *m*. **2.** (*type of screw*) boulon *m*. ◆ *adv*: ~ **upright** droit(e) comme un piquet. ◆ *vt* **1.** (*fasten together*) boulonner. **2.** (*close - door, window*) verrouiller. **3.** (*food*) engouffrer, engloutir. ◆ *vi* (*run*) détaler.
bomb [bɒm] ◆ *n* bombe *f*. ◆ *vt* bombarder.
bombard [bɒm'bɑːd] *vt* (MIL & fig): **to ~ (with)** bombarder (de).

bombastic [bɒm'bæstɪk] *adj* pompeux (euse).
bomb disposal squad *n* équipe *f* de déminage.
bomber ['bɒmər] *n* **1.** (*plane*) bombardier *m*. **2.** (*person*) plastiqueur *m*.
bombing ['bɒmɪŋ] *n* bombardement *m*.
bombshell ['bɒmʃel] *n* fig bombe *f*.
bona fide [‚bəʊnə'faɪdɪ] *adj* véritable, authentique; (*offer*) sérieux(euse).
bond [bɒnd] ◆ *n* **1.** (*between people*) lien *m*. **2.** (*promise*) engagement *m*. **3.** (FIN) bon *m*, titre *m*. ◆ *vt* **1.** (*glue*): **to ~ sthg to sthg** coller qqch sur qqch. **2.** fig (*people*) unir.
bondage ['bɒndɪdʒ] *n* servitude *f*, esclavage *m*.
bone [bəʊn] ◆ *n* os *m*; (*of fish*) arête *f*. ◆ *vt* (*meat*) désosser; (*fish*) enlever les arêtes de.
bone-dry *adj* tout à fait sec (sèche).
bone-idle *adj* paresseux(euse) comme une couleuvre OR un lézard.
bonfire ['bɒnˌfaɪər] *n* (*for fun*) feu *m* de joie; (*to burn rubbish*) feu.
bonfire night *n* Br le 5 novembre (*commémoration de la tentative de Guy Fawkes de faire sauter le Parlement en 1605*).
Bonn [bɒn] *n* Bonn.
bonnet ['bɒnɪt] *n* **1.** Br (*of car*) capot *m*. **2.** (*hat*) bonnet *m*.
bonny ['bɒnɪ] *adj* Scot beau (belle), joli(e).
bonus ['bəʊnəs] (*pl* **-es**) *n* **1.** (*extra money*) prime *f*, gratification *f*. **2.** fig (*added advantage*) plus *m*.
bony ['bəʊnɪ] *adj* **1.** (*person, hand, face*) maigre, osseux(euse). **2.** (*meat*) plein(e) d'os; (*fish*) plein d'arêtes.
boo [buː] (*pl* **-s**) ◆ *excl* hou! ◆ *n* huée *f*. ◆ *vt & vi* huer.
boob [buːb] *n* inf (*mistake*) gaffe *f*, bourde *f*. ▶ **boobs** *npl* Br *v inf* nichons *mpl*.
booby trap ['buːbɪ-] *n* **1.** (*bomb*) objet *m* piégé. **2.** (*practical joke*) farce *f*.
book [bʊk] ◆ *n* **1.** (*for reading*) livre *m*. **2.** (*of stamps, tickets, cheques*) carnet *m*; (*of matches*) pochette *f*. ◆ *vt* **1.** (*reserve - gen*) réserver; (*- performer*) engager; **to be fully ~ed** être complet. **2.** inf (*subj: police*) coller un PV à. **3.** Br (FTBL) prendre le nom de. ◆ *vi* réserver. ▶ **books** *npl* (COMM) livres *mpl* de comptes. ▶ **book up** *vt sep* réserver, retenir.
bookcase ['bʊkkeɪs] *n* bibliothèque *f*.
bookie ['bʊkɪ] *n* inf bookmaker *m*.

booking ['bʊkɪŋ] n 1. (reservation) réservation f. 2. Br (FTBL): **to get a ~** recevoir un carton jaune.

booking office n bureau m de réservation OR location.

bookkeeping ['bʊk,kiːpɪŋ] n comptabilité f.

booklet ['bʊklɪt] n brochure f.

bookmaker ['bʊk,meɪkər] n bookmaker m.

bookmark ['bʊkmɑːk] n signet m.

bookseller ['bʊk,selər] n libraire mf.

bookshelf ['bʊkʃelf] (pl **-shelves** [-ʃelvz]) n rayon m OR étagère f à livres.

bookshop Br ['bʊkʃɒp], **bookstore** Am ['bʊkstɔːr] n librairie f.

book token n chèque-livre m.

boom [buːm] ◆ n 1. (loud noise) grondement m. 2. (in business, trade) boom m. 3. (NAUT) bôme f. 4. (for TV camera, microphone) girafe f, perche f. ◆ vi 1. (make noise) gronder. 2. (business, trade) être en plein essor OR en hausse.

boon [buːn] n avantage m.

boost [buːst] ◆ n (to production, sales) augmentation f; (to economy) croissance f. ◆ vt 1. (production, sales) stimuler. 2. (popularity) accroître, renforcer.

booster ['buːstər] n (MED) rappel m.

boot [buːt] ◆ n 1. (for walking, sport) chaussure f. 2. (fashion item) botte f. 3. Br (of car) coffre m. ◆ vt inf flanquer des coups de pied à.

booth [buːð] n 1. (at fair) baraque f foraine. 2. (telephone booth) cabine f. 3. (voting booth) isoloir m.

booty ['buːtɪ] n butin m.

booze [buːz] inf ◆ n (U) alcool m, boisson f alcoolisée. ◆ vi picoler.

bop [bɒp] inf n 1. (hit) coup m. 2. (disco, dance) boum f.

border ['bɔːdər] ◆ n 1. (between countries) frontière f. 2. (edge) bord m. 3. (in garden) bordure f. ◆ vt 1. (country) être limitrophe de. 2. (edge) border. ► **border on** vt fus frôler, être voisin(e) de.

borderline ['bɔːdəlaɪn] ◆ adj: **~ case** cas m limite. ◆ n fig limite f, ligne f de démarcation.

bore [bɔːr] ◆ pt → **bear**. ◆ n 1. (person) raseur m, -euse f; (situation, event) corvée f. 2. (of gun) calibre m. ◆ vt 1. (not interest) ennuyer, raser; **to ~ sb stiff** OR **to tears** OR **to death** ennuyer qqn à mourir. 2. (drill) forer, percer.

bored [bɔːd] adj (person) qui s'ennuie; (look) d'ennui; **to be ~ with** en avoir assez de.

boredom ['bɔːdəm] n (U) ennui m.

boring ['bɔːrɪŋ] adj ennuyeux(euse).

born [bɔːn] adj né(e); **to be ~** naître; **I was ~ in 1965** je suis né en 1965; **when were you ~?** quelle est ta date de naissance?

borne [bɔːn] pp → **bear**.

borough ['bʌrə] n municipalité f.

borrow ['bɒrəʊ] vt emprunter; **to ~ sthg (from sb)** emprunter qqch (à qqn).

Bosnia ['bɒznɪə] n Bosnie f.

Bosnia-Herzegovina [-,hɜːtsəgə-'viːnə] n Bosnie-Herzégovine f.

Bosnian ['bɒznɪən] ◆ adj bosniaque. ◆ n Bosniaque mf.

bosom ['bʊzəm] n poitrine f, seins mpl; fig sein m; **~ friend** ami m intime.

boss [bɒs] ◆ n patron m, -onne f, chef m. ◆ vt pej donner des ordres à, régenter. ► **boss about, boss around** vt sep pej donner des ordres à, régenter.

bossy ['bɒsɪ] adj autoritaire.

bosun ['bəʊsn] = **boatswain**.

botany ['bɒtənɪ] n botanique f.

botch [bɒtʃ] ► **botch up** vt sep inf bousiller, saboter.

both [bəʊθ] ◆ adj les deux. ◆ pron: **~ (of them)** (tous) les deux ((toutes) les deux); **~ of us are coming** on vient tous les deux. ◆ adv: **she is ~ intelligent and amusing** elle est à la fois intelligente et drôle.

bother ['bɒðər] ◆ vt 1. (worry) ennuyer, inquiéter; **to ~ o.s. (about)** se tracasser (au sujet de); **I can't be ~ed to do it** je n'ai vraiment pas envie de le faire. 2. (pester, annoy) embêter; **I'm sorry to ~ you** excusez-moi de vous déranger. ◆ vi: **to ~ about sthg** s'inquiéter de qqch; **don't ~ (to do it)** ce n'est pas la peine (de le faire). ◆ n (U) embêtement m; **it's no ~ at all** cela ne me dérange OR m'ennuie pas du tout.

bothered ['bɒðəd] adj inquiet(ète).

bottle ['bɒtl] ◆ n 1. (gen) bouteille f; (for medicine, perfume) flacon m; (for baby) biberon m. 2. (U) Br inf (courage) cran m, culot m. ◆ vt (wine etc) mettre en bouteilles; (fruit) mettre en bocal. ► **bottle up** vt sep (feelings) refouler, contenir.

bottle bank n container m pour verre usagé.

bottleneck ['bɒtlnek] n 1. (in traffic) bouchon m, embouteillage m. 2. (in production) goulet m d'étranglement.

bottle-opener n ouvre-bouteilles m inv, décapsuleur m.

bottom ['bɒtəm] ◆ adj 1. (lowest) du bas. 2. (in class) dernier(ère). ◆ n 1. (of bottle, lake, garden) fond m; (of page, ladder, street) bas m; (of hill) pied m. 2. (of scale) bas m; (of class) dernier m, -ère f. 3. (buttocks) derrière m. 4. (cause): **to get to the ~ of sthg** aller au fond de qqch, découvrir la cause de qqch. ▶ **bottom out** vi atteindre son niveau le plus bas.

bottom line n fig: **the ~** l'essentiel m.

bough [baʊ] n branche f.

bought [bɔːt] pt & pp → **buy**.

boulder ['bəʊldəʳ] n rocher m.

bounce [baʊns] ◆ vi 1. (ball) rebondir; (person) sauter. 2. inf (cheque) être sans provision. ◆ vt (ball) faire rebondir. ◆ n rebond m.

bouncer ['baʊnsəʳ] n inf videur m.

bound [baʊnd] ◆ pt & pp → **bind**. ◆ adj 1. (certain): **he's ~ to win** il va sûrement gagner; **she's ~ to see it** elle ne peut pas manquer de le voir. 2. (obliged): **to be ~ to do sthg** être obligé(e) OR tenu(e) de faire qqch; **I'm ~ to say/admit** je dois dire/reconnaître. 3. (for place): **to be ~ for** (subj: person) être en route pour; (subj: plane, train) être à destination de. ◆ n (leap) bond m, saut m. ◆ vt: **to be ~ed by** (subj: field) être limité(e) OR délimité(e) par; (subj: country) être limitrophe de. ▶ **bounds** npl limites fpl; **out of ~s** interdit, défendu.

boundary ['baʊndərɪ] n (gen) frontière f; (of property) limite f, borne f.

bourbon ['bɜːbən] n bourbon m.

bout [baʊt] n 1. (of illness) accès m; **a ~ of flu** une grippe. 2. (session) période f. 3. (boxing match) combat m.

bow¹ [baʊ] ◆ n 1. (in greeting) révérence f. 2. (of ship) proue f, avant m. ◆ vt (head) baisser, incliner. ◆ vi 1. (make a bow) saluer. 2. (defer): **to ~ to** s'incliner devant.

bow² [bəʊ] n 1. (weapon) arc m. 2. (MUS) archet m. 3. (knot) nœud m.

bowels ['baʊəlz] npl intestins mpl; fig entrailles fpl.

bowl [bəʊl] ◆ n 1. (container - gen) jatte f, saladier m; (- small) bol m; (- for washing up) cuvette f. 2. (of toilet, sink) cuvette f; (of pipe) fourneau m. ◆ vi (CRICKET) lancer la balle. ▶ **bowls** n (U) boules fpl (sur herbe).

bow-legged [ˌbəʊ'legɪd] adj aux jambes arquées.

bowler ['bəʊləʳ] n 1. (CRICKET) lanceur m. 2. **~ (hat)** chapeau m melon.

bowling ['bəʊlɪŋ] n (U) bowling m.

bowling alley n (building) bowling m; (alley) piste f de bowling.

bowling green n terrain m de boules (sur herbe).

bow tie [bəʊ-] n nœud m papillon.

box [bɒks] ◆ n 1. (gen) boîte f. 2. (THEATRE) loge f. ◆ vi boxer, faire de la boxe.

boxer ['bɒksəʳ] n 1. (fighter) boxeur m. 2. (dog) boxer m.

boxer shorts npl caleçon m.

boxing ['bɒksɪŋ] n boxe f.

Boxing Day n jour des étrennes en Grande-Bretagne (le 26 décembre).

boxing glove n gant m de boxe.

box office n bureau m de location.

boxroom ['bɒksrʊm] n Br débarras m.

boy [bɔɪ] ◆ n (male child) garçon m. ◆ excl inf: **(oh) ~!** ben, mon vieux!, ben, dis-donc!

boycott ['bɔɪkɒt] ◆ n boycott m, boycottage m. ◆ vt boycotter.

boyfriend ['bɔɪfrend] n copain m, petit ami m.

boyish ['bɔɪɪʃ] adj (appearance - of man) gamin(e); (- of woman) de garçon; (behaviour) garçonnier(ère).

BR (abbr of **British Rail**) n ≃ SNCF f.

bra [brɑː] n soutien-gorge m.

brace [breɪs] ◆ n 1. (on teeth) appareil m (dentaire). 2. (on leg) appareil m orthopédique. ◆ vt 1. (steady) soutenir, consolider; **to ~ o.s.** s'accrocher, se cramponner. 2. fig (prepare): **to ~ o.s. (for sthg)** se préparer (à qqch). ▶ **braces** npl Br bretelles fpl.

bracelet ['breɪslɪt] n bracelet m.

bracing ['breɪsɪŋ] adj vivifiant(e).

bracken ['brækn] n fougère f.

bracket ['brækɪt] ◆ n 1. (support) support m. 2. (parenthesis - round) parenthèse f; (- square) crochet m; **in ~s** entre parenthèses/crochets. 3. (group): **age/income ~** tranche f d'âge/de revenus. ◆ vt (enclose in brackets) mettre entre parenthèses/crochets.

brag [bræg] vi se vanter.

braid [breɪd] ◆ n 1. (on uniform) galon m. 2. (of hair) tresse f, natte f. ◆ vt (hair) tresser, natter.

brain [breɪn] n cerveau m. ▶ **brains** npl (intelligence) intelligence f.

brainchild ['breɪntʃaɪld] n inf idée f personnelle, invention f personnelle.

brainwash ['breɪnwɒʃ] vt faire un lavage de cerveau à.

brainwave ['breɪnweɪv] n idée f géniale OR de génie.

brainy ['breɪnɪ] *adj inf* intelligent(e).
brake [breɪk] ♦ *n lit & fig* frein *m*. ♦ *vi* freiner.
brake light *n* stop *m*, feu *m* arrière.
bramble ['bræmbl] *n* (*bush*) ronce *f*; (*fruit*) mûre *f*.
bran [bræn] *n* son *m*.
branch [brɑːntʃ] ♦ *n* 1. (*of tree, subject*) branche *f*. 2. (*of railway*) bifurcation *f*, embranchement *m*. 3. (*of company*) filiale *f*, succursale *f*; (*of bank*) agence *f*. ♦ *vi* bifurquer. ▶ **branch out** *vi* (*person, company*) étendre ses activités, se diversifier.
brand [brænd] ♦ *n* 1. (COMM) marque *f*. 2. *fig* (*type, style*) type *m*, genre *m*. ♦ *vt* 1. (*cattle*) marquer au fer rouge. 2. *fig* (*classify*): **to ~ sb (as) sthg** étiqueter qqn comme qqch, coller à qqn l'étiquette de qqch.
brandish ['brændɪʃ] *vt* brandir.
brand name *n* marque *f*.
brand-new *adj* flambant neuf (flambant neuve), tout neuf (toute neuve).
brandy ['brændɪ] *n* cognac *m*.
brash [bræʃ] *adj* effronté(e).
brass [brɑːs] *n* 1. (*metal*) laiton *m*, cuivre *m* jaune. 2. (MUS): **the ~** les cuivres *mpl*.
brass band *n* fanfare *f*.
brassiere [Br 'bræsɪər, Am brə'zɪr] *n* soutien-gorge *m*.
brat [bræt] *n inf pej* sale gosse *m*.
bravado [brə'vɑːdəʊ] *n* bravade *f*.
brave [breɪv] ♦ *adj* courageux(euse), brave. ♦ *n* guerrier *m* indien, brave *m*. ♦ *vt* braver, affronter.
bravery ['breɪvərɪ] *n* courage *m*, bravoure *f*.
brawl [brɔːl] *n* bagarre *f*, rixe *f*.
brawn [brɔːn] *n* (U) 1. (*muscle*) muscle *m*. 2. Br (*meat*) fromage *m* de tête.
bray [breɪ] *vi* (*donkey*) braire.
brazen ['breɪzn] *adj* (*person*) effronté(e), impudent(e); (*lie*) éhonté(e). ▶ **brazen out** *vt sep*: **to ~ it out** crâner.
brazier ['breɪzjər] *n* brasero *m*.
Brazil [brə'zɪl] *n* Brésil *m*.
Brazilian [brə'zɪljən] ♦ *adj* brésilien(enne). ♦ *n* Brésilien *m*, -enne *f*.
brazil nut *n* noix *f* du Brésil.
breach [briːtʃ] ♦ *n* 1. (*of law, agreement*) infraction *f*, violation *f*; (*of promise*) rupture *f*; **to be in ~ of sthg** enfreindre OR violer qqch; **~ of contract** rupture *f* de contrat. 2. (*opening, gap*) trou *m*, brèche *f*. ♦ *vt* 1. (*agreement, contract*) rompre. 2. (*make hole in*) faire une brèche dans.

breach of the peace *n* atteinte *f* à l'ordre public.
bread [bred] *n* pain *m*; **~ and butter** tartine *f* beurrée, pain beurré; *fig* gagne-pain *m*.
bread bin Br, **bread box** Am *n* boîte *f* à pain.
breadcrumbs ['bredkrʌmz] *npl* chapelure *f*.
breadline ['bredlaɪn] *n*: **to be on the ~** être sans ressources OR sans le sou.
breadth [bretθ] *n* 1. (*width*) largeur *f*. 2. *fig* (*scope*) ampleur *f*, étendue *f*.
breadwinner ['bred,wɪnər] *n* soutien *m* de famille.
break [breɪk] (*pt* broke, *pp* broken) ♦ *n* 1. (*gap*): **~ (in)** trouée *f* (dans). 2. (*fracture*) fracture *f*. 3. (*pause - gen*) pause *f*; (*- at school*) récréation *f*; **to take a ~** (*short*) faire une pause; (*longer*) prendre des jours de congé; **without a ~** sans interruption; **to have a ~ from doing sthg** arrêter de faire qqch. 4. *inf* (*luck*): **(lucky) ~** chance *f*, veine *f*. ♦ *vt* 1. (*gen*) casser, briser; **to ~ one's arm/leg** se casser le bras/la jambe; **to ~ a record** battre un record. 2. (*interrupt - journey*) interrompre; (*- contact, silence*) rompre. 3. (*not keep - law, rule*) enfreindre, violer; (*- promise*) manquer à. 4. (*tell*): **to ~ the news (of sthg to sb)** annoncer la nouvelle (de qqch à qqn). ♦ *vi* 1. (*gen*) se casser, se briser. 2. (*pause*) s'arrêter, faire une pause. 3. (*weather*) se gâter. 4. (*voice - with emotion*) se briser; (*- at puberty*) muer. 5. (*news*) se répandre, éclater. 6. *phr*: **to ~ even** rentrer dans ses frais. ▶ **break away** *vi* (*escape*) s'échapper. ▶ **break down** ♦ *vt sep* 1. (*destroy - barrier*) démolir; (*- door*) enfoncer. 2. (*analyse*) analyser. ♦ *vi* 1. (*car, machine*) tomber en panne; (*resistance*) céder; (*negotiations*) échouer. 2. (*emotionally*) fondre en larmes, éclater en sanglots. ▶ **break in** ♦ *vi* 1. (*burglar*) entrer par effraction. 2. (*interrupt*): **to ~ in (on sb/sthg)** interrompre (qqn/qqch). ♦ *vt sep* (*horse*) dresser. ▶ **break into** *vt fus* 1. (*subj: burglar*) entrer par effraction dans. 2. (*begin*): **to ~ into song/applause** se mettre à chanter/applaudir. ▶ **break off** ♦ *vt sep* 1. (*detach*) détacher. 2. (*talks, relationship*) rompre; (*holiday*) interrompre. ♦ *vi* 1. (*become detached*) se casser, se détacher. 2. (*stop talking*) s'interrompre, se taire. ▶ **break out** *vi* 1. (*begin - fire*) se déclarer; (*- fighting*) éclater. 2. (*escape*):

to ~ out (of) s'échapper (de), s'évader (de). ▶ **break up** ◆ vt sep 1. (into smaller pieces) mettre en morceaux. 2. (end - marriage, relationship) détruire; (- fight, party) mettre fin à. ◆ vi 1. (into smaller pieces - gen) se casser en morceaux. 2. (end - marriage, relationship) se briser; (- talks, party) prendre fin; (- school) finir, fermer; **to ~ up (with sb)** rompre (avec qqn). 3. (crowd) se disperser.

breakage ['breikidʒ] n bris m.

breakdown ['breikdaun] n 1. (of vehicle, machine) panne f; (of negotiations) échec m; (in communications) rupture f. 2. (analysis) détail m.

breakdown service n service m de dépannage.

breakfast ['brekfəst] n petit déjeuner m.

breakfast television n Br télévision f du matin.

break-in n cambriolage m.

breaking ['breikiŋ] n: ~ **and entering** (JUR) entrée f par effraction.

breakneck ['breiknek] adj: **at ~ speed** à fond de train.

breakthrough ['breikθru:] n percée f.

breakup ['breikʌp] n (of marriage, relationship) rupture f.

breast [brest] n 1. (of woman) sein m; (of man) poitrine f. 2. (meat of bird) blanc m.

breast-feed vt & vi allaiter.

breaststroke ['breststrəʊk] n brasse f.

breath [breθ] n souffle m, haleine f; **to take a deep ~** inspirer profondément; **out of ~** hors d'haleine, à bout de souffle; **to get one's ~ back** reprendre haleine OR son souffle.

breathalyse Br, **-yze** Am ['breθəlaiz] vt ≃ faire subir l'Alcootest® à.

breathe [bri:ð] ◆ vi respirer. ◆ vt 1. (inhale) respirer. 2. (exhale - smell) souffler des relents de. ▶ **breathe in** ◆ vi ◆ vt sep aspirer. ▶ **breathe out** vi expirer.

breather ['bri:ðər] n inf moment m de repos OR répit.

breathing ['bri:ðiŋ] n respiration f.

breathless ['breθlis] adj 1. (out of breath) hors d'haleine, essoufflé(e). 2. (with excitement) fébrile, fiévreux(euse).

breathtaking ['breθ,teikiŋ] adj à vous couper le souffle.

breed [bri:d] (pt & pp bred [bred]) ◆ n lit & fig race f, espèce f. ◆ vt 1. (animals, plants) élever. 2. fig (suspicion, contempt) faire naître, engendrer. ◆ vi se reproduire.

breeding ['bri:diŋ] n (U) 1. (of animals, plants) élevage m. 2. (manners) bonnes manières fpl, savoir-vivre m.

breeze [bri:z] n brise f.

breezy ['bri:zi] adj 1. (windy) venteux (euse). 2. (cheerful) jovial(e), enjoué(e).

brevity ['breviti] n brièveté f.

brew [bru:] ◆ vt (beer) brasser; (tea) faire infuser; (coffee) préparer, faire. ◆ vi 1. (tea) infuser; (coffee) se faire. 2. fig (trouble, storm) se préparer, couver.

brewer ['bru:ər] n brasseur m.

brewery ['bruəri] n brasserie f.

bribe [braib] ◆ n pot-de-vin m. ◆ vt: **to ~ sb (to do sthg)** soudoyer qqn (pour qu'il fasse qqch).

bribery ['braibəri] n corruption f.

brick [brik] n brique f.

bricklayer ['brik,leiər] n maçon m.

bridal ['braidl] adj (dress) de mariée; (suite etc) nuptial(e).

bride [braid] n mariée f.

bridegroom ['braidgrum] n marié m.

bridesmaid ['braidzmeid] n demoiselle f d'honneur.

bridge [bridʒ] ◆ n 1. (gen) pont m. 2. (on ship) passerelle f. 3. (of nose) arête f. 4. (card game, for teeth) bridge m. ◆ vt fig (gap) réduire.

bridle ['braidl] n bride f.

bridle path n piste f cavalière.

brief [bri:f] ◆ adj 1. (short) bref (brève), court(e); **in ~** en bref, en deux mots. 2. (revealing) très court(e). ◆ n 1. (JUR) affaire f, dossier m. 2. Br (instructions) instructions fpl. ◆ vt: **to ~ sb (on)** (bring up to date) mettre qqn au courant (de); (instruct) briefer qqn (sur). ▶ **briefs** npl slip m.

briefcase ['bri:fkeis] n serviette f.

briefing ['bri:fiŋ] n instructions fpl, briefing m.

briefly ['bri:fli] adv 1. (for a short time) un instant. 2. (concisely) brièvement.

brigade [bri'geid] n brigade f.

brigadier [,brigə'diər] n général m de brigade.

bright [brait] adj 1. (room) clair(e); (light, colour) vif (vive); (sunlight) éclatant(e); (eyes, future) brillant(e). 2. (intelligent) intelligent(e).

brighten ['braitn] vi 1. (become lighter) s'éclaircir. 2. (face, mood) s'éclairer. ▶ **brighten up** ◆ vt sep égayer. ◆ vi 1. (person) s'égayer, s'animer. 2. (weather) se dégager, s'éclaircir.

brilliance ['briljəns] n 1. (cleverness)

intelligence f. **2.** (of colour, light) éclat m.

brilliant ['brɪljənt] adj **1.** (gen) brillant(e). **2.** (colour) éclatant(e). **3.** inf (wonderful) super (inv), génial(e).

Brillo pad® ['brɪləʊ-] n ≃ tampon m Jex®.

brim [brɪm] ◆ n bord m. ◆ vi: **to ~ with** lit & fig être plein(e) de.

brine [braɪn] n saumure f.

bring [brɪŋ] (pt & pp **brought**) vt **1.** (person) amener; (object) apporter. **2.** (cause - happiness, shame) entraîner, causer; **to ~ sthg to an end** mettre fin à qqch. ▶ **bring about** vt sep causer, provoquer. ▶ **bring around** vt sep (make conscious) ranimer. ▶ **bring back** vt sep **1.** (object) rapporter; (person) ramener. **2.** (memories) rappeler. **3.** (reinstate) rétablir. ▶ **bring down** vt sep **1.** (plane) abattre; (government) renverser. **2.** (prices) faire baisser. ▶ **bring forward** vt sep **1.** (gen) avancer. **2.** (in bookkeeping) reporter. ▶ **bring in** vt sep **1.** (law) introduire. **2.** (money - subj: person) gagner; (- subj: deal) rapporter. ▶ **bring off** vt sep (plan) réaliser, réussir; (deal) conclure, mener à bien. ▶ **bring out** vt sep **1.** (product) lancer; (book) publier, faire paraître. **2.** (cause to appear) faire ressortir. ▶ **bring round, bring to** = **bring around.** ▶ **bring up** vt sep **1.** (raise - children) élever. **2.** (mention) mentionner. **3.** (vomit) rendre, vomir.

brink [brɪŋk] n: **on the ~ of** au bord de, à la veille de.

brisk [brɪsk] adj **1.** (quick) vif (vive), rapide. **2.** (manner, tone) déterminé(e).

bristle ['brɪsl] ◆ n poil m. ◆ vi lit & fig se hérisser.

Britain ['brɪtn] n Grande-Bretagne f; **in ~** en Grande-Bretagne.

British ['brɪtɪʃ] adj britannique.

British Isles npl: **the ~** les îles fpl Britanniques.

British Rail n société des chemins de fer britanniques, ≃ SNCF f.

British Telecom [-'telɪkɒm] n société britannique de télécommunications.

Briton ['brɪtn] n Britannique mf.

Brittany ['brɪtənɪ] n Bretagne f.

brittle ['brɪtl] adj fragile.

broach [brəʊtʃ] vt (subject) aborder.

broad [brɔːd] adj **1.** (wide) large; (- range, interests) divers(e), varié(e). **2.** (description) général(e). **3.** (hint) transparent(e); (accent) prononcé(e). ▶ **in broad daylight** adv en plein jour.

B road n Br route f départementale.

broad bean n fève f.

broadcast ['brɔːdkɑːst] (pt & pp **broadcast**) ◆ n (RADIO & TV) émission f. ◆ vt (RADIO) radiodiffuser; (TV) téléviser.

broaden ['brɔːdn] ◆ vt élargir. ◆ vi s'élargir.

broadly ['brɔːdlɪ] adv (generally) généralement.

broadminded [ˌbrɔːd'maɪndɪd] adj large d'esprit.

broccoli ['brɒkəlɪ] n brocoli m.

brochure ['brəʊʃər] n brochure f, prospectus m.

broil [brɔɪl] vt Am griller.

broke [brəʊk] ◆ pt → **break.** ◆ adj inf fauché(e).

broken ['brəʊkn] ◆ pp → **break.** ◆ adj **1.** (gen) cassé(e); **to have a ~ leg** avoir la jambe cassée. **2.** (interrupted - journey, sleep) interrompu(e); (- line) brisé(e). **3.** (marriage) brisé(e), détruit(e); (home) désuni(e). **4.** (hesitant): **to speak in ~ English** parler un anglais hésitant.

broker ['brəʊkər] n courtier m; (insurance) ~ assureur m, courtier m d'assurances.

brolly ['brɒlɪ] n Br inf pépin m.

bronchitis [brɒŋ'kaɪtɪs] n (U) bronchite f.

bronze [brɒnz] ◆ adj (colour) (couleur) bronze (inv). ◆ n (gen) bronze m.

brooch [brəʊtʃ] n broche f.

brood [bruːd] vi: **to ~ (over OR about sthg)** ressasser (qqch), remâcher (qqch).

brook [brʊk] n ruisseau m.

broom [bruːm] n balai m.

broomstick ['bruːmstɪk] n manche m à balai.

Bros, bros (abbr of **brothers**) Frères.

broth [brɒθ] n bouillon m.

brothel ['brɒθl] n bordel m.

brother ['brʌðər] n frère m.

brother-in-law (pl **brothers-in-law**) n beau-frère m.

brought [brɔːt] pt & pp → **bring.**

brow [braʊ] n **1.** (forehead) front m. **2.** (eyebrow) sourcil m. **3.** (of hill) sommet m.

brown [braʊn] ◆ adj **1.** (colour) brun(e), marron (inv); ~ **bread** pain m bis. **2.** (tanned) bronzé(e), hâlé(e). ◆ n (colour) marron m, brun m. ◆ vt (food) faire dorer.

Brownie (Guide) ['braʊnɪ-] n ≃ jeannette f.

brown paper n papier m d'emballage, papier kraft.

brown rice n riz m complet.

brown sugar n sucre m roux.

browse [brauz] vi 1. (look): **I'm just browsing** (in shop) je ne fais que regarder; **to ~ through** (magazines etc) feuilleter. 2. (animal) brouter.

bruise [bru:z] ◆ n bleu m. ◆ vt 1. (skin, arm) se faire un bleu à; (fruit) taler. 2. fig (pride) meurtrir, blesser.

brunch [brʌntʃ] n brunch m.

brunette [bru:'net] n brunette f.

brunt [brʌnt] n: **to bear** OR **take the ~ of** subir le plus gros de.

brush [brʌʃ] ◆ n 1. (gen) brosse f; (of painter) pinceau m. 2. (encounter): **to have a ~ with the police** avoir des ennuis avec la police. ◆ vt 1. (clean with brush) brosser. 2. (touch lightly) effleurer. ▶ **brush aside** vt sep fig écarter, repousser. ▶ **brush off** vt sep (dismiss) envoyer promener. ▶ **brush up** ◆ vt sep (revise) réviser. ◆ vi: **to ~ up on sthg** réviser qqch.

brush-off n inf: **to give sb the ~** envoyer promener qqn.

brushwood ['brʌʃwʊd] n (U) brindilles fpl.

brusque [bru:sk] adj brusque.

Brussels ['brʌslz] n Bruxelles,

brussels sprout n chou m de Bruxelles.

brutal ['bru:tl] adj brutal(e).

brute [bru:t] ◆ adj (force) brutal(e). ◆ n brute f.

BSc (abbr of Bachelor of Science) n (titulaire d'une) licence de sciences.

BT (abbr of British Telecom) n société britannique de télécommunications.

bubble ['bʌbl] ◆ n bulle f. ◆ vi (liquid) faire des bulles, bouillonner.

bubble bath n bain m moussant.

bubble gum n bubble-gum m.

bubblejet printer ['bʌbldʒet-] n imprimante f à bulle d'encre.

Bucharest [,bju:kə'rest] n Bucarest.

buck [bʌk] ◆ n 1. (male animal) mâle m. 2. inf (dollar) dollar m. 3. inf (responsibility): **to pass the ~** refiler la responsabilité. ◆ vi (horse) ruer. ▶ **buck up** inf vi 1. (hurry up) se remuer, se dépêcher. 2. (cheer up) ne pas se laisser abattre.

bucket ['bʌkɪt] n (gen) seau m.

Buckingham Palace ['bʌkɪŋəm-] n le palais de Buckingham (résidence officielle du souverain britannique).

buckle ['bʌkl] ◆ n boucle f. ◆ vt 1. (fasten) boucler. 2. (bend) voiler. ◆ vi (wheel) se voiler; (knees, legs) se plier.

bud [bʌd] ◆ n bourgeon m. ◆ vi bourgeonner.

Budapest [,bju:də'pest] n Budapest.

Buddha ['budə] n Bouddha m.

Buddhism ['budɪzm] n bouddhisme m.

budding ['bʌdɪŋ] adj (writer, artist) en herbe.

buddy ['bʌdɪ] n inf pote m.

budge [bʌdʒ] ◆ vt faire bouger. ◆ vi bouger.

budgerigar ['bʌdʒərɪgɑ:r] n perruche f.

budget ['bʌdʒɪt] ◆ adj (holiday, price) pour petits budgets. ◆ n budget m. ▶ **budget for** vt fus prévoir.

budgie ['bʌdʒɪ] n inf perruche f.

buff [bʌf] ◆ adj (brown) chamois (inv). ◆ n inf (expert) mordu m, -e f.

buffalo ['bʌfələʊ] (pl inv OR **-es** OR **-s**) n buffle m.

buffer ['bʌfər] n (gen) tampon m.

buffet[1] [Br 'bufeɪ, Am bə'feɪ] n (food, cafeteria) buffet m.

buffet[2] ['bʌfɪt] vt (physically) frapper.

buffet car ['bufeɪ-] n wagon-restaurant m.

bug [bʌg] ◆ n 1. (insect) punaise f. 2. inf (germ) microbe m. 3. inf (listening device) micro m. 4. (COMPUT) défaut m, bug m. ◆ vt 1. inf (telephone) mettre sur table d'écoute; (room) cacher des micros dans. 2. inf (annoy) embêter.

bugger ['bʌgər] Br v inf ◆ n (person) con m, conne f. ◆ excl merde! ▶ **bugger off** vi: **~ off!** fous le camp!

buggy ['bʌgɪ] n 1. (carriage) boghei m. 2. (pushchair) poussette f; Am (pram) landau m.

bugle ['bju:gl] n clairon m.

build [bɪld] (pt & pp **built**) ◆ vt lit & fig construire, bâtir. ◆ n carrure f. ▶ **build on, build upon** ◆ vt fus (success) tirer avantage de. ◆ vt sep (base on) baser sur. ▶ **build up** ◆ vt sep (business) développer; (reputation) bâtir. ◆ vi (clouds) s'amonceler; (traffic) augmenter.

builder ['bɪldər] n entrepreneur m.

building ['bɪldɪŋ] n bâtiment m.

building and loan association n Am société d'épargne et de financement immobilier.

building site n chantier m.

building society n Br société d'épargne et de financement immobilier.

buildup ['bɪldʌp] n (increase) accroissement m.

built [bɪlt] pt & pp → **build**.

built-in adj **1.** (CONSTR) encastré(e).
2. (inherent) inné(e).

built-up adj: ~ **area** agglomération f.

bulb [bʌlb] n **1.** (ELEC) ampoule f.
2. (BOT) oignon m.

Bulgaria [bʌl'geərɪə] n Bulgarie f.

Bulgarian [bʌl'geərɪən] ◆ adj bulgare.
◆ n **1.** (person) Bulgare mf. **2.** (language)
bulgare m.

bulge [bʌldʒ] ◆ n (lump) bosse f. ◆ vi:
to ~ (with) être gonflé (de).

bulk [bʌlk] ◆ n **1.** (mass) volume m.
2. (of person) corpulence f. **3.** (COMM): **in
~** en gros. **4.** (majority): **the ~ of** le plus
gros de. ◆ adj en gros.

bulky ['bʌlkɪ] adj volumineux(euse).

bull [bʊl] n (male cow) taureau m; (male
elephant, seal) mâle m.

bulldog ['bʊldɒg] n bouledogue m.

bulldozer ['bʊldəʊzər] n bulldozer m.

bullet ['bʊlɪt] n (for gun) balle f.

bulletin ['bʊlətɪn] n bulletin m.

bullet-proof adj pare-balles (inv).

bullfight ['bʊlfaɪt] n corrida f.

bullfighter ['bʊl,faɪtər] n toréador m.

bullfighting ['bʊl,faɪtɪŋ] n (U) courses
fpl de taureaux; (art) tauromachie f.

bullion ['bʊljən] n (U): **gold ~** or m en
barres.

bullock ['bʊlək] n bœuf m.

bullring ['bʊlrɪŋ] n arène f.

bull's-eye n centre m.

bully ['bʊlɪ] ◆ n tyran m. ◆ vt tyranniser, brutaliser.

bum [bʌm] n **1.** v inf (bottom) derrière
m. **2.** inf pej (tramp) clochard m.

bumblebee ['bʌmblbiː] n bourdon m.

bump [bʌmp] ◆ n **1.** (lump) bosse f.
2. (knock, blow) choc m. **3.** (noise) bruit m
sourd. ◆ vt (head etc) cogner; (car)
heurter. ▶ **bump into** vt fus (meet by
chance) rencontrer par hasard.

bumper ['bʌmpər] ◆ adj (harvest, edition)
exceptionnel(elle). ◆ n **1.** (AUT) pare-
chocs m inv. **2.** Am (RAIL) tampon m.

bumpy ['bʌmpɪ] adj **1.** (surface) défon-
cé(e). **2.** (ride) cahoteux(euse); (sea
crossing) agité(e).

bun [bʌn] n **1.** (cake) petit pain m aux
raisins; (bread roll) petit pain au lait.
2. (hairstyle) chignon m.

bunch [bʌntʃ] ◆ n (of people) groupe m;
(of flowers) bouquet m; (of grapes) grappe
f; (of bananas) régime m; (of keys)
trousseau m. ◆ vi se grouper.
▶ **bunches** npl (hairstyle) couettes fpl.

bundle ['bʌndl] ◆ n (of clothes) paquet
m; (of notes, newspapers) liasse f; (of wood)

fagot m. ◆ vt (put roughly - person)
entasser; (- clothes) fourrer, entasser.

bung [bʌŋ] ◆ n bonde f. ◆ vt Br inf
envoyer.

bungalow ['bʌŋgələʊ] n bungalow m.

bungle ['bʌŋgl] vt gâcher, bâcler.

bunion ['bʌnjən] n oignon m.

bunk [bʌŋk] n (bed) couchette f.

bunk bed n lit m superposé.

bunker ['bʌŋkər] n **1.** (GOLF & MIL)
bunker m. **2.** (for coal) coffre m.

bunny ['bʌnɪ] n: ~ **(rabbit)** lapin m.

bunting ['bʌntɪŋ] n (U) guirlandes fpl
(de drapeaux).

buoy [Br bɔɪ, Am 'buːɪ] n bouée f.
▶ **buoy up** vt sep (encourage) soutenir.

buoyant ['bɔɪənt] adj **1.** (able to float)
qui flotte. **2.** fig (person) enjoué(e);
(economy) florissant(e); (market) ferme.

burden ['bɜːdn] ◆ n lit & fig: ~ **(on)**
charge f (pour), fardeau m (pour). ◆ vt:
to ~ sb with (responsibilities, worries) accabler qqn de.

bureau ['bjʊərəʊ] (pl **-x**) n **1.** Br (desk)
bureau m; Am (chest of drawers) com-
mode f. **2.** (office) bureau m.

bureaucracy [bjʊə'rɒkrəsɪ] n bureaucratie f.

bureaux ['bjʊərəʊz] pl → **bureau.**

burger ['bɜːgər] n hamburger m.

burglar ['bɜːglər] n cambrioleur m,
-euse f.

burglar alarm n système m
d'alarme.

burglarize Am = **burgle.**

burglary ['bɜːglərɪ] n cambriolage m.

burgle ['bɜːgl], **burglarize** Am
['bɜːgləraɪz] vt cambrioler.

Burgundy ['bɜːgəndɪ] n Bourgogne f.

burial ['berɪəl] n enterrement m.

burly ['bɜːlɪ] adj bien charpenté(e).

Burma ['bɜːmə] n Birmanie f.

burn [bɜːn] (pt & pp **burnt** OR **-ed**) ◆ vt
brûler; **I've ~ed my hand** je me suis
brûlé la main. ◆ vi brûler. ◆ n brûlure f.
▶ **burn down** ◆ vt sep (building, town)
incendier. ◆ vi (building) brûler complètement.

burner ['bɜːnər] n brûleur m.

Burns' Night [bɜːnz-] n fête célébrée en
l'honneur du poète écossais Robert Burns, le
25 janvier.

burnt [bɜːnt] pt & pp → **burn.**

burp [bɜːp] inf ◆ n rot m. ◆ vi roter.

burrow ['bʌrəʊ] ◆ n terrier m. ◆ vi
1. (dig) creuser un terrier. **2.** fig (search)
fouiller.

bursar ['bɜːsər] n intendant m, -e f.

bursary ['bɜːsərɪ] n Br (scholarship, grant) bourse f.

burst [bɜːst] (pt & pp **burst**) ◆ vi (gen) éclater. ◆ vt faire éclater. ◆ n (of gunfire) rafale f; (of enthusiasm) élan m; **a ~ of applause** un tonnerre d'applaudissements. ▶ **burst into** vt fus 1. (room) faire irruption dans. 2. (begin suddenly): **to ~ into tears** fondre en larmes; **to ~ into flames** prendre feu. ▶ **burst out** vt fus (say suddenly) s'exclamer; **to ~ out laughing** éclater de rire.

bursting ['bɜːstɪŋ] adj 1. (full) plein(e), bourré(e). 2. (with emotion): **~ with** débordé(e) de. 3. (eager): **to be ~ to do sthg** mourir d'envie de faire qqch.

bury ['berɪ] vt 1. (in ground) enterrer. 2. (hide) cacher, enfouir.

bus [bʌs] n autobus m, bus m; (long-distance) car m; **by ~** en autobus/car.

bush [bʊʃ] n 1. (plant) buisson m. 2. (open country): **the ~** la brousse. 3. phr: **she doesn't beat about the ~** elle n'y va pas par quatre chemins.

bushy ['bʊʃɪ] adj touffu(e).

business ['bɪznɪs] n 1. (U) (commerce) affaires fpl; **we do a lot of ~ with them** nous travaillons beaucoup avec eux; **on ~** pour affaires; **to mean ~** inf ne pas plaisanter; **to go out of ~** fermer, faire faillite. 2. (company, duty) affaire f; **mind your own ~!** inf occupe-toi de tes oignons! 3. (affair, matter) histoire f, affaire f.

business class n classe f affaires.

businesslike ['bɪznɪslaɪk] adj efficace.

businessman ['bɪznɪsmæn] (pl **-men** [-men]) n homme m d'affaires.

business trip n voyage m d'affaires.

businesswoman ['bɪznɪsˌwʊmən] (pl **-women** [-ˌwɪmɪn]) n femme f d'affaires.

busker ['bʌskər] n Br chanteur m, -euse f des rues.

bus shelter n Abribus® m.

bus station n gare f routière.

bus stop n arrêt m de bus.

bust [bʌst] (pt & pp **bust** OR **-ed**) ◆ adj inf 1. (broken) foutu(e). 2. (bankrupt): **to go ~** faire faillite. ◆ n 1. (bosom) poitrine f. 2. (statue) buste m. ◆ vt inf (break) péter.

bustle ['bʌsl] ◆ n (U) (activity) remue-ménage m. ◆ vi s'affairer.

busy ['bɪzɪ] ◆ adj 1. (gen) occupé(e); **to be ~ doing sthg** être occupé à faire qqch. 2. (life, week) chargé(e); (town, office) animé(e). ◆ vt: **to ~ o.s. (doing sthg)** s'occuper (à faire qqch).

busybody ['bɪzɪˌbɒdɪ] n pej mouche f du coche.

busy signal n Am (TELEC) tonalité f 'occupé'.

but [bʌt] ◆ conj mais; **I'm sorry, ~ I don't agree** je suis désolé, mais je ne suis pas d'accord. ◆ prep sauf, excepté; **he has no one ~ himself to blame** il ne peut s'en prendre qu'à lui-même. ◆ adv fml seulement, ne … que; **had I ~ known!** si j'avais su!; **we can ~ try** on peut toujours essayer. ▶ **but for** prep sans.

butcher ['bʊtʃər] ◆ n boucher m; **~'s (shop)** boucherie f. ◆ vt 1. (animal) abattre. 2. fig (massacre) massacrer.

butler ['bʌtlər] n maître m d'hôtel (chez un particulier).

butt [bʌt] ◆ n 1. (of cigarette, cigar) mégot m. 2. (of rifle) crosse f. 3. (for water) tonneau m. 4. (of joke, criticism) cible f. ◆ vt donner un coup de tête à. ▶ **butt in** vi (interrupt): **to ~ in on sb** interrompre qqn; **to ~ in on sthg** s'immiscer OR s'imposer dans qqch.

butter ['bʌtər] ◆ n beurre m. ◆ vt beurrer.

buttercup ['bʌtəkʌp] n bouton m d'or.

butter dish n beurrier m.

butterfly ['bʌtəflaɪ] n (SWIMMING & ZOOL) papillon m.

buttocks ['bʌtəks] npl fesses fpl.

button ['bʌtn] ◆ n 1. (gen) bouton m. 2. Am (badge) badge m. ◆ vt = **button up**. ▶ **button up** vt sep boutonner.

button mushroom n champignon m de Paris.

buttress ['bʌtrɪs] n contrefort m.

buxom ['bʌksəm] adj bien en chair.

buy [baɪ] (pt & pp **bought**) ◆ vt acheter; **to ~ sthg from sb** acheter qqch à qqn. ◆ n: **a good ~** une bonne affaire. ▶ **buy up** vt sep acheter en masse.

buyer ['baɪər] n acheteur m, -euse f.

buyout ['baɪaʊt] n rachat m.

buzz [bʌz] ◆ n 1. (of insect) bourdonnement m. 2. inf (telephone call): **to give sb a ~** passer un coup de fil à qqn. ◆ vi: **to ~ (with)** bourdonner (de). ◆ vt (on intercom) appeler.

buzzer ['bʌzər] n sonnerie f.

buzzword ['bʌzwɜːd] n inf mot m à la mode.

by [baɪ] ◆ prep 1. (indicating cause, agent) par; **caused/written/killed ~** causé/écrit/tué par. 2. (indicating means, method, manner): **to pay ~ cheque** payer par chèque; **to travel ~ bus/train/plane/ship** voyager en bus/par le train/en avion/en bateau; **~ doing sthg** en faisant qqch; **~ nature** de nature, de tempérament. **3.** (*beside, close to*) près de; **~ the sea** au bord de la mer; **I sat ~ her bed** j'étais assis à son chevet. **4.** (*past*): **to pass ~ sb/sthg** passer devant qqn/qqch; **to drive ~ sb/sthg** passer en voiture devant qqn/qqch. **5.** (*via, through*) par; **come in ~ the back door** entrez par la porte de derrière. **6.** (*at or before a particular time*) avant, pas plus tard que; **I'll be there ~ eight** j'y serai avant huit heures; **~ now** déjà. **7.** (*during*): **~ day** le OR de jour; **~ night** la OR de nuit. **8.** (*according to*) selon, suivant; **~ law** conformément à la loi. **9.** (*in arithmetic*) par; **divide/multiply 20 ~ 2** divisez/ multipliez 20 par 2. **10.** (*in measurements*): **2 metres ~ 4** 2 mètres sur 4. **11.** (*in quantities, amounts*) à; **~ the yard** au mètre; **~ the thousands** par milliers; **paid ~ the day/week/month** payé à la journée/à la semaine/au mois; **to cut prices ~ 50%** réduire les prix de 50%. **12.** (*indicating gradual change*): **day ~ day** jour après jour, de jour en jour; **one ~ one** un à un, un par un. **13.** *phr*: **(all) ~ oneself** (tout) seul ((toute) seule). ◆ *adv* → **go, pass** *etc.*

bye(-bye) [baɪ(baɪ)] *excl inf* au revoir!, salut!

bye-election = by-election.

byelaw [ˈbaɪlɔː] = **bylaw.**

by-election *n* élection *f* partielle.

bygone [ˈbaɪgɒn] *adj* d'autrefois. ▶ **bygones** *npl*: **to let ~s be ~s** oublier le passé.

bylaw [ˈbaɪlɔː] *n* arrêté *m*.

bypass [ˈbaɪpɑːs] ◆ *n* **1.** (*road*) route *f* de contournement. **2.** (MED): **~ (operation)** pontage *m*. ◆ *vt* (*town, difficulty*) contourner; (*subject*) éviter.

by-product *n* **1.** (*product*) dérivé *m*. **2.** *fig* (*consequence*) conséquence *f*.

bystander [ˈbaɪˌstændər] *n* spectateur *m*, -trice *f*.

byte [baɪt] *n* (COMPUT) octet *m*.

byword [ˈbaɪwɜːd] *n* (*symbol*): **to be a ~ for** être synonyme de.

C

c (*pl* **c's** OR **cs**), **C** (*pl* **C's** OR **Cs**) [siː] *n* (*letter*) c *m inv*, C *m inv*. ▶ **C** *n* **1.** (MUS) do *m*. **2.** (SCH) (*mark*) C *m inv*. **3.** (*abbr of* **celsius, centigrade**) C.

c., ca. *abbr of* **circa.**

cab [kæb] *n* **1.** (*taxi*) taxi *m*. **2.** (*of lorry*) cabine *f*.

cabaret [ˈkæbəreɪ] *n* cabaret *m*.

cabbage [ˈkæbɪdʒ] *n* (*vegetable*) chou *m*.

cabin [ˈkæbɪn] *n* **1.** (*on ship, plane*) cabine *f*. **2.** (*house*) cabane *f*.

cabin class *n* seconde classe *f*.

cabinet [ˈkæbɪnɪt] *n* **1.** (*cupboard*) meuble *m*. **2.** (POL) cabinet *m*.

cable [ˈkeɪbl] ◆ *n* câble *m*. ◆ *vt* (*news*) câbler; (*person*) câbler à.

cable car *n* téléphérique *m*.

cable television, cable TV *n* télévision *f* par câble.

cache [kæʃ] *n* **1.** (*store*) cache *f*. **2.** (COMPUT) mémoire-cache *f*, antémémoire *f*.

cackle [ˈkækl] *vi* **1.** (*hen*) caqueter. **2.** (*person*) jacasser.

cactus [ˈkæktəs] (*pl* **-tuses** OR **-ti** [-taɪ]) *n* cactus *m*.

cadet [kəˈdet] *n* élève *m* officier.

cadge [kædʒ] *Br inf* ◆ *vt*: **to ~ sthg off** OR **from sb** taper qqn de qqch. ◆ *vi*: **to ~ off** OR **from sb** taper qqn.

caesarean (section) *Br*, **cesarean (section)** *Am* [sɪˈzeərɪən-] *n* césarienne *f*.

cafe, café [ˈkæfeɪ] *n* café *m*.

cafeteria [ˌkæfɪˈtɪərɪə] *n* cafétéria *f*.

caffeine [ˈkæfiːn] *n* caféine *f*.

cage [keɪdʒ] *n* (*for animal*) cage *f*.

cagey [ˈkeɪdʒɪ] (*compar* **-ier**, *superl* **-iest**) *adj inf* discret(ète).

cagoule [kəˈguːl] *n* Br K-way® *m inv*.

cajole [kəˈdʒəʊl] *vt*: **to ~ sb (into doing sthg)** enjôler qqn (pour qu'il fasse qqch).

cake [keɪk] *n* **1.** (CULIN) gâteau *m*; (*of fish, potato*) croquette *f*; **it's a piece of ~** *inf fig* c'est du gâteau. **2.** (*of soap*) pain *m*.

caked [keɪkt] *adj*: **~ with mud** recouvert(e) de boue séchée.

calcium [ˈkælsɪəm] *n* calcium *m*.

calculate [ˈkælkjʊleɪt] *vt* **1.** (*result,*

number) calculer; (*consequences*) évaluer. **2.** (*plan*): **to be ~d to do sthg** être calculé(e) pour faire qqch.

calculating ['kælkjʊleɪtɪŋ] *adj pej* calculateur(trice).

calculation [,kælkjʊ'leɪʃn] *n* calcul *m*.

calculator ['kælkjʊleɪtə^r] *n* calculatrice *f*.

calendar ['kælɪndə^r] *n* calendrier *m*.

calendar year *n* année *f* civile.

calf [kɑːf] (*pl* **calves**) *n* **1.** (*of cow, leather*) veau *m*; (*of elephant*) éléphanteau *m*; (*of seal*) bébé *m* phoque. **2.** (ANAT) mollet *m*.

calibre, caliber Am ['kælɪbə^r] *n* calibre *m*.

California [,kælɪ'fɔːnjə] *n* Californie *f*.

calipers Am = **callipers**.

call [kɔːl] ◆ *n* **1.** (*cry*) appel *m*, cri *m*. **2.** (TELEC) appel *m* (téléphonique). **3.** (*summons, invitation*) appel *m*; **to be on ~** (*doctor etc*) être de garde. **4.** (*visit*) visite *f*; **to pay a ~ on sb** rendre visite à qqn. **5.** (*demand*): **~ (for)** demande *f* (de). ◆ *vt* **1.** (*name, summon, phone*) appeler; **she's ~ed Joan** elle s'appelle Joan; **let's ~ it £10** disons 10 livres. **2.** (*label*): **he ~ed me a liar** il m'a traité de menteur. **3.** (*shout*) appeler, crier. **4.** (*announce - meeting*) convoquer; (*- strike*) lancer; (*- flight*) appeler; (*- election*) annoncer. ◆ *vi* **1.** (*shout - person*) crier; (*- animal, bird*) pousser un cri/des cris. **2.** (TELEC) appeler; **who's ~ing?** qui est à l'appareil? **3.** (*visit*) passer. ▶ **call back** ◆ *vt sep* rappeler. ◆ *vi* **1.** (TELEC) rappeler. **2.** (*visit again*) repasser. ▶ **call for** *vt fus* **1.** (*collect - person*) passer prendre; (*- package, goods*) passer chercher. **2.** (*demand*) demander. ▶ **call in** ◆ *vt sep* **1.** (*expert, police etc*) faire venir. **2.** (COMM) (*goods*) rappeler; (FIN) (*loan*) exiger le remboursement de. ◆ *vi* passer. ▶ **call off** *vt sep* **1.** (*cancel*) annuler. **2.** (*dog*) rappeler. ▶ **call on** *vt fus* **1.** (*visit*) passer voir. **2.** (*ask*): **to ~ on sb to do sthg** demander à qqn de faire qqch. ▶ **call out** ◆ *vt sep* **1.** (*police, doctor*) appeler. **2.** (*cry out*) crier. ◆ *vi* (*cry out*) crier. ▶ **call round** *vi* passer. ▶ **call up** *vt sep* **1.** (MIL & TELEC) appeler. **2.** (COMPUT) rappeler.

call box *n* Br cabine *f* (téléphonique).

caller ['kɔːlə^r] *n* **1.** (*visitor*) visiteur *m*, -euse *f*. **2.** (TELEC) demandeur *m*.

call-in *n* Am (RADIO & TV) programme *m* à ligne ouverte.

calling ['kɔːlɪŋ] *n* **1.** (*profession*) métier *m*. **2.** (*vocation*) vocation *f*.

calling card *n* Am carte *f* de visite.

callipers Br, **calipers** Am ['kælɪpəz] *npl* **1.** (MATH) compas *m*. **2.** (MED) appareil *m* orthopédique.

callous ['kæləs] *adj* dur(e).

callus ['kæləs] (*pl* **-es**) *n* cal *m*, durillon *m*.

calm [kɑːm] ◆ *adj* calme. ◆ *n* calme *m*. ◆ *vt* calmer. ▶ **calm down** ◆ *vt sep* calmer. ◆ *vi* se calmer.

Calor gas® ['kælə^r-] *n* Br butane *m*.

calorie ['kælərɪ] *n* calorie *f*.

calves [kɑːvz] *pl* → **calf**.

camber ['kæmbə^r] *n* (*of road*) bombement *m*.

Cambodia [kæm'bəʊdjə] *n* Cambodge *m*.

camcorder ['kæm,kɔːdə^r] *n* Caméscope® *m*.

came [keɪm] *pt* → **come**.

camel ['kæml] *n* chameau *m*.

cameo ['kæmɪəʊ] (*pl* **-s**) *n* **1.** (*jewellery*) camée *m*. **2.** (CINEMA & THEATRE) courte apparition *f* (d'une grande vedette).

camera ['kæmərə] *n* (PHOT) appareil-photo *m*; (CINEMA & TV) caméra *f*. ▶ **in camera** *adv* à huis clos.

cameraman ['kæmərəmæn] (*pl* **-men** [-men]) *n* cameraman *m*.

Cameroon [,kæmə'ruːn] *n* Cameroun *m*.

camouflage ['kæməflɑːʒ] ◆ *n* camouflage *m*. ◆ *vt* camoufler.

camp [kæmp] ◆ *n* camp *m*. ◆ *vi* camper. ▶ **camp out** *vi* camper.

campaign [kæm'peɪn] ◆ *n* campagne *f*. ◆ *vi*: **to ~ (for/against)** mener une campagne (pour/contre).

camp bed *n* lit *m* de camp.

camper ['kæmpə^r] *n* **1.** (*person*) campeur *m*, -euse *f*. **2.** (*vehicle*): **~ (van)** camping-car *m*.

campground ['kæmpgraʊnd] *n* Am terrain *m* de camping.

camping ['kæmpɪŋ] *n* camping *m*; **to go ~** faire du camping.

camping site, campsite ['kæmpsaɪt] *n* (terrain *m* de) camping *m*.

campus ['kæmpəs] (*pl* **-es**) *n* campus *m*.

can[1] [kæn] (*pt & pp* **-ned**, *cont* **-ning**) ◆ *n* (*of drink, food*) boîte *f*; (*of oil*) bidon *m*; (*of paint*) pot *m*. ◆ *vt* mettre en boîte.

can[2] [*weak form* kən, *strong form* kæn] (*pt & conditional* **could**, *negative* **cannot** OR **can't**) *modal vb* **1.** (*be able to*) pouvoir; **~ you come to lunch?** tu peux venir déjeuner?; ~ **you see/hear/smell something?** tu vois/entends/sens quelque chose? **2.** (*know how to*) savoir; ~ **you drive/cook?** tu sais conduire/cuisiner?; **I ~ speak French** je parle le français. **3.** (*indicating permission, in polite requests*) pouvoir; ~ **I speak to John, please?** est-ce que je pourrais parler à John, s'il vous plaît? **4.** (*indicating disbelief, puzzlement*) pouvoir; **what ~ she have done with it?** qu'est-ce qu'elle a bien pu en faire?; **you ~'t be serious!** tu ne parles pas sérieusement! **5.** (*indicating possibility*) **I could see you tomorrow** je pourrais vous voir demain; **the train could have been cancelled** peut-être que le train a été annulé.

Canada ['kænədə] *n* Canada *m*; **in ~** au Canada.

Canadian [kə'neɪdjən] ♦ *adj* canadien (enne). ♦ *n* Canadien *m*, -enne *f*.

canal [kə'næl] *n* canal *m*.

Canaries [kə'neərɪz] *npl*: **the ~** les Canaries *fpl*.

canary [kə'neərɪ] *n* canari *m*.

cancel ['kænsl] *vt* **1.** (*gen*) annuler; (*appointment, delivery*) décommander. **2.** (*stamp*) oblitérer; (*cheque*) faire opposition à. ► **cancel out** *vt sep* annuler; **to ~ each other out** s'annuler.

cancellation [,kænsə'leɪʃn] *n* annulation *f*.

cancer ['kænsəʳ] *n* cancer *m*. ► **Cancer** *n* Cancer *m*.

candelabra [,kændɪ'lɑːbrə] *n* candélabre *m*.

candid ['kændɪd] *adj* franc (franche).

candidate ['kændɪdət] *n*: ~ **(for)** candidat *m*, -e *f* (pour).

candle ['kændl] *n* bougie *f*, chandelle *f*.

candlelight ['kændllaɪt] *n* lueur *f* d'une bougie OR d'une chandelle.

candlelit ['kændllɪt] *adj* aux chandelles.

candlestick ['kændlstɪk] *n* bougeoir *m*.

candour Br, **candor** Am ['kændəʳ] *n* franchise *f*.

candy ['kændɪ] *n* **1.** (U) (*confectionery*) confiserie *f*. **2.** (*sweet*) bonbon *m*.

candyfloss ['kændɪflɒs] *n* Br barbe *f* à papa.

cane [keɪn] ♦ *n* **1.** (U) (*for furniture*) rotin *m*. **2.** (*walking stick*) canne *f*. **3.** (*for punishment*): **the ~** la verge. **4.** (*for supporting plant*) tuteur *m*. ♦ *vt* fouetter.

canine ['keɪnaɪn] ♦ *adj* canin(e). ♦ *n*: ~ **(tooth)** canine *f*.

canister ['kænɪstəʳ] *n* (*for film, tea*)

boîte *f*; (*for gas, smoke*) bombe *f*.

cannabis ['kænəbɪs] *n* cannabis *m*.

canned [kænd] *adj* (*food, drink*) en boîte.

cannibal ['kænɪbl] *n* cannibale *mf*.

cannon ['kænən] (*pl inv* OR **-s**) *n* canon *m*.

cannonball ['kænənbɔːl] *n* boulet *m* de canon.

cannot ['kænɒt] *fml* → **can²**.

canny ['kænɪ] *adj* (*shrewd*) adroit(e).

canoe [kə'nuː] *n* canoë *m*, kayak *m*.

canoeing [kə'nuːɪŋ] *n* (U) canoë-kayak *m*.

canon ['kænən] *n* canon *m*.

can opener *n* ouvre-boîtes *m inv*.

canopy ['kænəpɪ] *n* **1.** (*over bed*) baldaquin *m*; (*over seat*) dais *m*. **2.** (*of trees, branches*) voûte *f*.

can't [kɑːnt] = **cannot**.

cantankerous [kæn'tæŋkərəs] *adj* hargneux(euse).

canteen [kæn'tiːn] *n* **1.** (*restaurant*) cantine *f*. **2.** (*box of cutlery*) ménagère *f*.

canter ['kæntəʳ] ♦ *n* petit galop *m*. ♦ *vi* aller au petit galop.

cantilever ['kæntɪliːvəʳ] *n* cantilever *m*.

canvas ['kænvəs] *n* toile *f*.

canvass ['kænvəs] *vt* **1.** (POL) (*person*) solliciter la voix de. **2.** (*opinion*) sonder.

canyon ['kænjən] *n* cañon *m*.

cap [kæp] ♦ *n* **1.** (*hat - gen*) casquette *f*. **2.** (*of pen*) capuchon *m*; (*of bottle*) capsule *f*; (*of lipstick*) bouchon *m*. ♦ *vt* **1.** (*top*): **to be capped with** être coiffé(e) de. **2.** (*outdo*): **to ~ it all** pour couronner le tout.

capability [,keɪpə'bɪlətɪ] *n* capacité *f*.

capable ['keɪpəbl] *adj*: ~ **(of)** capable (de).

capacity [kə'pæsɪtɪ] *n* **1.** (U) (*limit*) capacité *f*, contenance *f*. **2.** (*ability*): ~ **(for)** aptitude *f* (à). **3.** (*role*) qualité *f*; **in an advisory ~** en tant que conseiller.

cape [keɪp] *n* **1.** (GEOGR) cap *m*. **2.** (*cloak*) cape *f*.

caper ['keɪpəʳ] *n* **1.** (CULIN) câpre *f*. **2.** *inf* (*dishonest activity*) coup *m*, combine *f*.

capita → **per capita**.

capital ['kæpɪtl] ♦ *adj* **1.** (*letter*) majuscule. **2.** (*offence*) capital(e). ♦ *n* **1.** (*of country*): ~ **(city)** capitale *f*. **2.** (TYPO): ~ **(letter)** majuscule *f*. **3.** (U) (*money*) capital *m*; **to make ~ (out) of** *fig* tirer profit de.

capital expenditure *n* (U) dépenses *fpl* d'investissement.

capital gains tax *n* impôt *m* sur les plus-values.

capital goods *npl* biens *mpl* d'équipement.

capitalism ['kæpɪtəlɪzm] *n* capitalisme *m*.

capitalist ['kæpɪtəlɪst] ◆ *adj* capitaliste. ◆ *n* capitaliste *mf*.

capitalize, -ise ['kæpɪtəlaɪz] *vi*: to ~ on tirer parti de.

capital punishment *n* peine *f* capitale OR de mort.

Capitol Hill ['kæpɪtl-] *n* siège du Congrès à Washington.

capitulate [kə'pɪtjʊleɪt] *vi* capituler.

Capricorn ['kæprɪkɔːn] *n* Capricorne *m*.

capsize [kæp'saɪz] ◆ *vt* faire chavirer. ◆ *vi* chavirer.

capsule ['kæpsjuːl] *n* 1. (*gen*) capsule *f*. 2. (MED) gélule *f*.

captain ['kæptɪn] *n* capitaine *m*.

caption ['kæpʃn] *n* légende *f*.

captivate ['kæptɪveɪt] *vt* captiver.

captive ['kæptɪv] ◆ *adj* captif(ive). ◆ *n* captif *m*, -ive *f*.

captor ['kæptər] *n* ravisseur *m*, -euse *f*.

capture ['kæptʃər] ◆ *vt* 1. (*person, animal*) capturer; (*city*) prendre; (*market*) conquérir. 2. (*attention, imagination*) captiver. 3. (COMPUT) saisir. ◆ *n* (*of person, animal*) capture *f*; (*of city*) prise *f*.

car [kɑːr] ◆ *n* 1. (AUT) voiture *f*. 2. (RAIL) wagon *m*, voiture *f*. ◆ *comp* (*door, accident*) de voiture; (*industry*) automobile.

carafe [kə'ræf] *n* carafe *f*.

caramel ['kærəmel] *n* caramel *m*.

carat ['kærət] *n* Br carat *m*; **24-~ gold** or à 24 carats.

caravan ['kærəvæn] *n* (*gen*) caravane *f*; (*towed by horse*) roulotte *f*.

caravan site *n* Br camping *m* pour caravanes.

carbohydrate [,kɑːbəʊ'haɪdreɪt] *n* (CHEM) hydrate *m* de carbone. ► **carbohydrates** *npl* (*in food*) glucides *mpl*.

carbon ['kɑːbən] *n* (*element*) carbone *m*.

carbonated ['kɑːbəneɪtɪd] *adj* (*mineral water*) gazeux(euse).

carbon copy *n* 1. (*document*) carbone *m*. 2. *fig* (*exact copy*) réplique *f*.

carbon dioxide [-daɪ'ɒksaɪd] *n* gaz *m* carbonique.

carbon monoxide [-mɒ'nɒksaɪd] *n* oxyde *m* de carbone.

carbon paper *n* (U) (papier *m*) carbone *m*.

car-boot sale *n* Br brocante en plein air où les coffres des voitures servent d'étal.

carburettor Br, **carburetor** Am [,kɑːbə'retər] *n* carburateur *m*.

carcass ['kɑːkəs] *n* (*of animal*) carcasse *f*.

card [kɑːd] *n* 1. (*gen*) carte *f*. 2. (U) (*cardboard*) carton *m*. ► **cards** *npl*: to play ~s jouer aux cartes. ► **on the cards** Br, **in the cards** Am *adv inf*: it's on the ~s that ... il y a de grandes chances pour que ...

cardboard ['kɑːdbɔːd] ◆ *n* (U) carton *m*. ◆ *comp* en carton.

cardboard box *n* boîte *f* en carton.

cardiac ['kɑːdɪæk] *adj* cardiaque.

cardigan ['kɑːdɪgən] *n* cardigan *m*.

cardinal ['kɑːdɪnl] ◆ *adj* cardinal(e). ◆ *n* (RELIG) cardinal *m*.

card index *n* Br fichier *m*.

card table *n* table *f* de jeu.

care [keər] ◆ *n* 1. (U) (*protection, attention*) soin *m*, attention *f*; to be in ~ Br être à l'Assistance publique; to take ~ of (*look after*) s'occuper de; to take ~ (to do sthg) prendre soin (de faire qqch); take ~! faites bien attention à vous! 2. (*cause of worry*) souci *m*. ◆ *vi* 1. (*be concerned*): to ~ about se soucier de. 2. (*mind*): I don't ~ ça m'est égal; who ~s? qu'est-ce que ça peut faire? ► **care of** *prep* chez. ► **care for** *vt fus dated* (*like*) aimer.

career [kə'rɪər] *n* carrière *f*.

careers adviser [kə'rɪəz-] *n* conseiller *m*, -ère *f* d'orientation.

carefree ['keəfriː] *adj* insouciant(e).

careful ['keəfʊl] *adj* 1. (*cautious*) prudent(e); to be ~ to do sthg prendre soin de faire qqch, faire attention à faire qqch; be ~! fais attention!; to be ~ with one's money regarder à la dépense. 2. (*work*) soigné(e); (*worker*) consciencieux(euse).

carefully ['keəflɪ] *adv* 1. (*cautiously*) prudemment. 2. (*thoroughly*) soigneusement.

careless ['keəlɪs] *adj* 1. (*work*) peu soigné(e); (*driver*) négligent(e). 2. (*unconcerned*) insouciant(e).

caress [kə'res] ◆ *n* caresse *f*. ◆ *vt* caresser.

caretaker ['keə,teɪkər] *n* Br gardien *m*, -enne *f*.

car ferry *n* ferry *m*.

cargo ['kɑːgəʊ] (*pl* **-es** OR **-s**) *n* cargaison *f*.

car hire *n* Br location *f* de voitures.

Caribbean [Br kærɪ'biːən, Am kə-'rɪbɪən] *n*: **the ~ (Sea)** la mer des

Caraïbes OR des Antilles.

caring ['keərɪŋ] *adj* bienveillant(e).

carnage ['kɑːnɪdʒ] *n* carnage *m*.

carnal ['kɑːnl] *adj literary* charnel(elle).

carnation [kɑːˈneɪʃn] *n* œillet *m*.

carnival ['kɑːnɪvl] *n* carnaval *m*.

carnivorous [kɑːˈnɪvərəs] *adj* carnivore.

carol ['kærəl] *n*: **(Christmas)** ~ chant *m* de Noël.

carousel [ˌkærəˈsel] *n* **1.** (*at fair*) manège *m*. **2.** (*at airport*) carrousel *m*.

carp [kɑːp] (*pl inv* OR **-s**) ◆ *n* carpe *f*. ◆ *vi*: **to** ~ **(about sthg)** critiquer (qqch).

car park *n* Br parking *m*.

carpenter ['kɑːpəntər] *n* (*on building site, in shipyard*) charpentier *m*; (*furniture-maker*) menuisier *m*.

carpentry ['kɑːpəntrɪ] *n* (*on building site, in shipyard*) charpenterie *f*; (*furniture-making*) menuiserie *f*.

carpet ['kɑːpɪt] ◆ *n lit & fig* tapis *m*; **(fitted)** ~ moquette *f*. ◆ *vt* (*floor*) recouvrir d'un tapis; (*with fitted carpet*) recouvrir de moquette, moquetter.

carpet sweeper [-ˌswiːpər] *n* balai *m* mécanique.

car phone *n* téléphone *m* pour automobile.

car rental *n* Am location *f* de voitures.

carriage ['kærɪdʒ] *n* **1.** (*of train, horse-drawn*) voiture *f*. **2.** (U) (*transport of goods*) transport *m*; ~ **paid** OR **free** Br franco de port.

carriage return *n* retour *m* chariot.

carriageway ['kærɪdʒweɪ] *n* Br chaussée *f*.

carrier ['kærɪər] *n* **1.** (COMM) transporteur *m*. **2.** (*of disease*) porteur *m*, -euse *f*. **3.** = **carrier bag**.

carrier bag *n* sac *m* (en plastique).

carrot ['kærət] *n* carotte *f*.

carry ['kærɪ] ◆ *vt* **1.** (*subj: person, wind, water*) porter; (- *subj: vehicle*) transporter. **2.** (*disease*) transmettre. **3.** (*responsibility*) impliquer; (*consequences*) entraîner. **4.** (*motion, proposal*) voter. **5.** (*baby*) attendre. **6.** (MATH) retenir. ◆ *vi* (*sound*) porter. ▶ **carry away** *vt fus*: **to get carried away** s'enthousiasmer. ▶ **carry forward** *vt sep* (FIN) reporter. ▶ **carry off** *vt sep* **1.** (*plan*) mener à bien. **2.** (*prize*) remporter. ▶ **carry on** ◆ *vt* **to** continuer; **to** ~ **on doing sthg** continuer à OR de faire qqch. ◆ *vi* **1.** (*continue*) continuer; **to** ~ **on with sthg** continuer qqch. **2.** *inf* (*make a fuss*) faire des histoires. ▶ **carry out** *vt fus* (*task*) remplir;

(*plan, order*) exécuter; (*experiment*) effectuer; (*investigation*) mener. ▶ **carry through** *vt sep* (*accomplish*) réaliser.

carryall ['kærɪɔːl] *n* Am fourre-tout *m inv*.

carrycot ['kærɪkɒt] *n* couffin *m*.

carry-out *n* plat *m* à emporter.

carsick ['kɑːˌsɪk] *adj*: **to be** ~ être malade en voiture.

cart [kɑːt] ◆ *n* charrette *f*. ◆ *vt inf* traîner.

carton ['kɑːtn] *n* **1.** (*box*) boîte *f* en carton. **2.** (*of cream, yoghurt*) pot *m*; (*of milk*) carton *m*.

cartoon [kɑːˈtuːn] *n* **1.** (*satirical drawing*) dessin *m* humoristique. **2.** (*comic strip*) bande *f* dessinée. **3.** (*film*) dessin *m* animé.

cartridge ['kɑːtrɪdʒ] *n* **1.** (*for gun, pen*) cartouche *f*. **2.** (*for camera*) chargeur *m*.

cartwheel ['kɑːtwiːl] *n* (*movement*) roue *f*.

carve [kɑːv] ◆ *vt* **1.** (*wood, stone*) sculpter; (*design, name*) graver. **2.** (*slice - meat*) découper. ◆ *vi* découper. ▶ **carve out** *vt sep fig* se tailler. ▶ **carve up** *vt sep fig* diviser.

carving ['kɑːvɪŋ] *n* (*of wood*) sculpture *f*; (*of stone*) ciselure *f*.

carving knife *n* couteau *m* à découper.

car wash *n* (*process*) lavage *m* de voitures; (*place*) station *f* de lavage de voitures.

case [keɪs] *n* **1.** (*gen*) cas *m*; **to be the** ~ être le cas; **in** ~ **of** en cas de; **in that** ~ dans ce cas; **in which** ~ auquel cas; **as** OR **whatever the** ~ **may be** selon le cas. **2.** (*argument*): ~ **(for/against)** arguments *mpl* (pour/contre). **3.** (JUR) affaire *f*, procès *m*. **4.** (*- for glasses - gen*) caisse *f*; (*- for glasses etc*) étui *m*. **5.** Br (*suitcase*) valise *f*. ▶ **in any case** *adv* quoi qu'il en soit, de toute façon. ▶ **in case** ◆ *conj* au cas où. ◆ *adv*: **(just) in** ~ à tout hasard.

cash [kæʃ] ◆ *n* (U) **1.** (*notes and coins*) liquide *m*; **to pay (in)** ~ payer comptant OR en espèces. **2.** *inf* (*money*) sous *mpl*, fric *m*. **3.** (*payment*): ~ **in advance** paiement *m* à l'avance; ~ **on delivery** paiement *m* à la livraison. ◆ *vt* encaisser.

cash and carry *n* libre-service *m* de gros, cash-and-carry *m*.

cashbook ['kæʃbʊk] *n* livre *m* de caisse.

cash box *n* caisse *f*.

cash card *n* carte *f* de retrait.

cash desk n Br caisse f.
cash dispenser [-dɪˌspensəʳ] n distributeur m automatique de billets.
cashew (nut) [ˈkæʃuː-] n noix f de cajou.
cashier [kæˈʃɪəʳ] n caissier m, -ère f.
cash machine n distributeur m de billets.
cashmere [kæʃˈmɪəʳ] n cachemire m.
cash register n caisse f enregistreuse.
casing [ˈkeɪsɪŋ] n revêtement m; (TECH) boîtier m.
casino [kəˈsiːnəʊ] (pl -s) n casino m.
cask [kɑːsk] n tonneau m.
casket [ˈkɑːskɪt] n 1. (for jewels) coffret m. 2. Am (coffin) cercueil m.
casserole [ˈkæsərəʊl] n 1. (stew) ragoût m. 2. (pan) cocotte f.
cassette [kæˈset] n (of magnetic tape) cassette f; (PHOT) recharge f.
cassette player n lecteur m de cassettes.
cassette recorder n magnétophone m à cassettes.
cast [kɑːst] (pt & pp cast) ◆ n (CINEMA & THEATRE - actors) acteurs mpl; (- list of actors) distribution f. ◆ vt 1. (throw) jeter; **to ~ doubt on sthg** jeter le doute sur qqch. 2. (CINEMA & THEATRE) donner un rôle à. 3. (vote): **to ~ one's vote** voter. 4. (metal) couler; (statue) mouler. ▶ **cast aside** vt sep fig écarter, rejeter. ▶ **cast off** vi (NAUT) larguer les amarres.
castaway [ˈkɑːstəweɪ] n naufragé m, -e f.
caster [ˈkɑːstəʳ] n (wheel) roulette f.
caster sugar n Br sucre m en poudre.
casting vote [ˈkɑːstɪŋ-] n voix f prépondérante.
cast iron n fonte f.
castle [ˈkɑːsl] n 1. (building) château m. 2. (CHESS) tour f.
castor [ˈkɑːstəʳ] = caster.
castor oil n huile f de ricin.
castor sugar n = caster sugar.
castrate [kæˈstreɪt] vt châtrer.
casual [ˈkæʒʊəl] adj 1. (relaxed, indifferent) désinvolte. 2. (offhand) sans-gêne. 3. (chance) fortuit(e). 4. (clothes) décontracté(e), sport (inv). 5. (work, worker) temporaire.
casually [ˈkæʒʊəlɪ] adv (in a relaxed manner) avec désinvolture; **~ dressed** habillé simplement.
casualty [ˈkæʒjʊəltɪ] n 1. (dead person) mort m, -e f, victime f; (injured person) blessé m, -e f; (of road accident) accidenté m, -e f. 2. = **casualty department**.
casualty department n service m des urgences.
cat [kæt] n 1. (domestic) chat m. 2. (wild) fauve m.
catalogue Br, **catalog** Am [ˈkætəlɒg] ◆ n (gen) catalogue m; (in library) fichier m. ◆ vt cataloguer.
catalyst [ˈkætəlɪst] n catalyseur m.
catalytic convertor [ˌkætəˈlɪtɪkkən-ˈvɜːtəʳ] n pot m catalytique.
catapult [ˈkætəpʌlt] Br n (hand-held) lance-pierres m inv.
cataract [ˈkætərækt] n cataracte f.
catarrh [kəˈtɑːʳ] n catarrhe m.
catastrophe [kəˈtæstrəfɪ] n catastrophe f.
catch [kætʃ] (pt & pp caught) ◆ vt 1. (gen) attraper; **to ~ sight** OR **a glimpse of** apercevoir; **to ~ sb's attention** attirer l'attention de qqn; **to ~ the post** Br arriver à temps pour la levée. 2. (discover, surprise) prendre, surprendre; **to ~ sb doing sthg** surprendre qqn à faire qqch. 3. (hear clearly) saisir, comprendre. 4. (trap): **I caught my finger in the door** je me suis pris le doigt dans la porte. 5. (strike) frapper. ◆ vi 1. (become hooked, get stuck) se prendre. 2. (fire) prendre, partir. ◆ n 1. (of ball, thing caught) prise f. 2. (fastener - of box) fermoir m; (- of window) loqueteau m; (- of door) loquet m. 3. (snag) hic m, entourloupette f. ▶ **catch on** vi 1. (become popular) prendre. 2. inf (understand): **to ~ on (to sthg)** piger (qqch). ▶ **catch out** vt sep (trick) prendre en défaut, coincer. ▶ **catch up** ◆ vt sep rattraper. ◆ vi: **to ~ up on sthg** rattraper qqch. ▶ **catch up with** vt fus rattraper.
catching [ˈkætʃɪŋ] adj contagieux (euse).
catchment area [ˈkætʃmənt-] n Br (of school) secteur m de recrutement scolaire.
catchphrase [ˈkætʃfreɪz] n rengaine f, scie f.
catchy [ˈkætʃɪ] adj facile à retenir, entraînant(e).
categorically [ˌkætɪˈgɒrɪklɪ] adv catégoriquement.
category [ˈkætəgərɪ] n catégorie f.
cater [ˈkeɪtəʳ] vi (provide food) s'occuper de la nourriture, prévoir les repas. ▶ **cater for** vt fus Br 1. (tastes, needs) pourvoir à, satisfaire; (customers) s'adresser à. 2. (anticipate) prévoir. ▶ **cater to** vt fus satisfaire.

caterer 50

caterer ['keɪtərəʳ] n traiteur m.

catering ['keɪtərɪŋ] n (trade) restauration f.

caterpillar ['kætəpɪləʳ] n chenille f.

caterpillar tracks npl chenille f.

cathedral [kəˈθiːdrəl] n cathédrale f.

Catholic ['kæθlɪk] ◆ adj catholique. ◆ n catholique mf. ▶ **catholic** adj (tastes) éclectique.

Catseyes® ['kætsaɪz] npl Br catadioptres mpl.

cattle ['kætl] npl bétail m.

catty ['kætɪ] adj inf pej (spiteful) rosse, vache.

catwalk ['kætwɔːk] n passerelle f.

caucus ['kɔːkəs] n 1. Am (POL) comité m électoral (d'un parti). 2. Br (POL) comité m (d'un parti).

caught [kɔːt] pt & pp → **catch**.

cauliflower ['kɒlɪˌflaʊəʳ] n chou-fleur m.

cause [kɔːz] ◆ n cause f; **I have no ~ for complaint** je n'ai pas à me plaindre, je n'ai pas lieu de me plaindre; **to have ~ to do sthg** avoir lieu OR des raisons de faire qqch. ◆ vt causer; **to ~ sb to do sthg** faire faire qqch à qqn; **to ~ sthg to be done** faire faire qqch.

caustic ['kɔːstɪk] adj caustique.

caution ['kɔːʃn] ◆ n 1. (U) (care) précaution f, prudence f. 2. (warning) avertissement m. 3. Br (JUR) réprimande f. ◆ vt 1. (warn): **to ~ sb against doing sthg** déconseiller à qqn de faire qqch. 2. Br (subj: policeman): **to ~ sb for sthg** réprimander qqn pour qqch.

cautious ['kɔːʃəs] adj prudent(e).

cavalry ['kævlrɪ] n cavalerie f.

cave [keɪv] n caverne f, grotte f. ▶ **cave in** vi (roof, ceiling) s'affaisser.

caveman ['keɪvmæn] (pl -men [-men]) n homme m des cavernes.

cavernous ['kævənəs] adj (room, building) immense.

caviar(e) ['kævɪɑːʳ] n caviar m.

cavity ['kævətɪ] n cavité f.

cavort [kəˈvɔːt] vi gambader.

CB n (abbr of **citizens' band**) CB f.

CBI n abbr of **Confederation of British Industry**.

cc ◆ n (abbr of **cubic centimetre**) cm³. ◆ (abbr of **carbon copy**) pcc.

CD n (abbr of **compact disc**) CD m.

CD player n lecteur m de CD.

CD-ROM [ˌsiːdiːˈrɒm] (abbr of **compact disc read only memory**) n CD-ROM m, CD-Rom m.

cease [siːs] fml ◆ vt cesser; **to ~ doing** OR **to do sthg** cesser de faire qqch. ◆ vi cesser.

cease-fire n cessez-le-feu m inv.

ceaseless ['siːslɪs] adj fml incessant(e), continuel(elle).

cedar (tree) ['siːdəʳ-] n cèdre m.

cedilla [sɪˈdɪlə] n cédille f.

ceiling ['siːlɪŋ] n lit & fig plafond m.

celebrate ['selɪbreɪt] ◆ vt (gen) célébrer, fêter. ◆ vi faire la fête.

celebrated ['selɪbreɪtɪd] adj célèbre.

celebration [ˌselɪˈbreɪʃn] n 1. (U) (activity, feeling) fête f, festivités fpl. 2. (event) festivités fpl.

celebrity [sɪˈlebrətɪ] n célébrité f.

celery ['selərɪ] n céleri m (en branches).

celibate ['selɪbət] adj célibataire.

cell [sel] n (gen & COMPUT) cellule f.

cellar ['seləʳ] n cave f.

cello ['tʃeləʊ] (pl -s) n violoncelle m.

Cellophane® ['seləfeɪn] n Cellophane® f.

Celsius ['selsɪəs] adj Celsius (inv).

Celt [kelt] n Celte mf.

Celtic ['keltɪk] ◆ adj celte. ◆ n (language) celte m.

cement [sɪˈment] n ciment m.

cement mixer n bétonnière f.

cemetery ['semɪtrɪ] n cimetière m.

censor ['sensəʳ] ◆ n censeur m. ◆ vt censurer.

censorship ['sensəʃɪp] n censure f.

censure ['senʃəʳ] ◆ n blâme m, critique f. ◆ vt blâmer, critiquer.

census ['sensəs] (pl **censuses**) n recensement m.

cent [sent] n cent m.

centenary Br [sen'tiːnərɪ], **centennial** Am [sen'tenjəl] n centenaire m.

center Am = **centre**.

centigrade ['sentɪgreɪd] adj centigrade.

centilitre Br, **centiliter** Am ['sentɪˌliːtəʳ] n centilitre m.

centimetre Br, **centimeter** Am ['sentɪˌmiːtəʳ] n centimètre m.

centipede ['sentɪpiːd] n mille-pattes m inv.

central ['sentrəl] adj central(e).

Central America n Amérique f centrale.

central heating n chauffage m central.

centralize, -ise ['sentrəlaɪz] vt centraliser.

central locking [-'lɒkɪŋ] n (AUT) verrouillage m centralisé.

central reservation n Br (AUT) terre-plein m central.

centre Br, **center** Am ['sentər] ◆ n centre m; ~ **of attention** centre d'attraction, point m de mire. ◆ adj 1. (middle) central(e); **a ~ parting** une raie au milieu. 2. (POL) du centre, centriste. ◆ vt centrer.

centre back n (FTBL) arrière m central.

centre forward n (FTBL) avant-centre m inv.

centre half n (FTBL) arrière m central.

century ['sentʃʊrɪ] n siècle m.

ceramic [sɪ'ræmɪk] adj en céramique.
▶ **ceramics** npl (objects) objets mpl en céramique.

cereal ['sɪərɪəl] n céréale f.

ceremonial [,serɪ'məʊnjəl] ◆ adj (dress) de cérémonie; (duties) honorifique. ◆ n cérémonial m.

ceremony ['serɪmənɪ] n 1. (event) cérémonie f. 2. (U) (pomp, formality) cérémonies fpl; **to stand on ~** faire des cérémonies.

certain ['sɜːtn] adj (gen) certain(e); **he is ~ to be late** il est certain qu'il sera en retard, il sera certainement en retard; **to be ~ of sthg/of doing sthg** être assuré de qqch/de faire qqch, être sûr de qqch/de faire qqch; **to make ~** vérifier; **to make ~ of** s'assurer de; **I know for ~ that ...** je suis sûr or certain que ...; **a ~ extent** jusqu'à un certain point, dans une certaine mesure.

certainly ['sɜːtnlɪ] adv certainement.

certainty ['sɜːtntɪ] n certitude f.

certificate [sə'tɪfɪkət] n certificat m.

certified ['sɜːtɪfaɪd] adj (teacher) diplômé(e); (document) certifié(e).

certified mail n Am envoi m recommandé.

certified public accountant n Am expert-comptable m.

certify ['sɜːtɪfaɪ] vt 1. (declare true): **to ~ (that)** certifier or attester que. 2. (declare insane) déclarer mentalement aliéné(e).

cervical [sə'vaɪkl] adj (cancer) du col de l'utérus.

cervical smear n frottis m vaginal.

cervix ['sɜːvɪks] (pl **-ices** [-ɪsiːz]) n col m de l'utérus.

cesarean (section) [sɪ'zeərɪən-] = **caesarean (section)**.

cesspit ['sespɪt], **cesspool** ['sespuːl] n fosse f d'aisance.

cf. (abbr of confer) cf.

CFC (abbr of chlorofluorocarbon) n CFC m.

ch. (abbr of chapter) chap.

chafe [tʃeɪf] vt (rub) irriter.

chaffinch ['tʃæfɪntʃ] n pinson m.

chain [tʃeɪn] ◆ n chaîne f; ~ **of events** suite f or série f d'événements. ◆ vt (person, animal) enchaîner; (object) attacher avec une chaîne.

chain reaction n réaction f en chaîne.

chain saw n tronçonneuse f.

chain-smoke vi fumer cigarette sur cigarette.

chain store n grand magasin m (à succursales multiples).

chair [tʃeər] ◆ n 1. (gen) chaise f; (armchair) fauteuil m. 2. (university post) chaire f. 3. (of meeting) présidence f. ◆ vt (meeting) présider; (discussion) diriger.

chair lift n télésiège m.

chairman ['tʃeəmən] (pl **-men** [-mən]) n président m.

chairperson ['tʃeə,pɜːsn] (pl **-s**) n président m, -e f.

chalet ['ʃæleɪ] n chalet m.

chalk [tʃɔːk] n craie f.

chalkboard ['tʃɔːkbɔːd] n Am tableau m (noir).

challenge ['tʃælɪndʒ] ◆ n défi m. ◆ vt 1. (to fight, competition): **she ~d me to a race/a game of chess** elle m'a défié à la course/aux échecs; **to ~ sb to do sthg** défier qqn de faire qqch. 2. (question) mettre en question or en doute.

challenging ['tʃælɪndʒɪŋ] adj 1. (task, job) stimulant(e). 2. (look, tone of voice) provocateur(trice).

chamber ['tʃeɪmbər] n (gen) chambre f.

chambermaid ['tʃeɪmbəmeɪd] n femme f de chambre.

chamber music n musique f de chambre.

chamber of commerce n chambre f de commerce.

chameleon [kə'miːljən] n caméléon m.

champagne [,ʃæm'peɪn] n champagne m.

champion ['tʃæmpjən] n champion m, -onne f.

championship ['tʃæmpjənʃɪp] n championnat m.

chance [tʃɑːns] ◆ n 1. (U) (luck) hasard m; **by ~** par hasard; **if by any ~** si par hasard. 2. (likelihood) chance f, **she didn't stand a ~ (of doing sthg)** elle n'avait aucune chance (de faire qqch); **on the off ~** à tout hasard. 3. (opportunity) occasion f. **4.** (*risk*) risque m; **to take a ~** risquer le coup; **to take a ~ on doing sthg** se risquer à faire qqch. ◆ *adj* fortuit(e), accidentel(elle). ◆ *vt* (*risk*) risquer; **to ~ it** tenter sa chance.

chancellor ['tʃɑːnsələʳ] *n* **1.** (*chief minister*) chancelier m. **2.** (UNIV) président m, -e f honoraire.

Chancellor of the Exchequer *n* Br Chancelier m de l'Échiquier, ≃ ministre m des Finances.

chandelier [ʃændə'lɪəʳ] *n* lustre m.

change [tʃeɪndʒ] ◆ *n* **1.** (*gen*): **~ (in sb/ in sthg)** changement m (en qqn/de qqch); **~ of clothes** vêtements mpl de rechange; **for a ~** pour changer (un peu). **2.** (*money*) monnaie f. ◆ *vt* **1.** (*gen*) changer; **to ~ sthg into sthg** changer OR transformer qqch en qqch; **to ~ one's mind** changer d'avis. **2.** (*jobs, trains, sides*) changer de. **3.** (*money - into smaller units*) faire la monnaie de; (*- into different currency*) changer. ◆ *vi* **1.** (*gen*) changer. **2.** (*change clothes*) se changer. **3.** (*be transformed*): **to ~ into** se changer en. ▶ **change over** *vi* (*convert*): **to ~ over from/to** passer de/à.

changeable ['tʃeɪndʒəbl] *adj* (*mood*) changeable; (*weather*) variable.

change machine *n* distributeur m de monnaie.

changeover ['tʃeɪndʒ,əʊvəʳ] *n*: **~ (to)** passage m (à), changement m (pour).

changing ['tʃeɪndʒɪŋ] *adj* changeant(e).

changing room *n* (SPORT) vestiaire m; (*in shop*) cabine f d'essayage.

channel ['tʃænl] ◆ *n* **1.** (TV) chaîne f; (RADIO) station f. **2.** (*for irrigation*) canal m; (*duct*) conduit m. **3.** (*on river, sea*) chenal m. ◆ *vt lit & fig* canaliser. ▶ **Channel** *n*: **the (English) Channel** la Manche. ▶ **channels** *npl*: **to go through the proper ~s** suivre OR passer la filière.

Channel Islands *npl*: **the ~** les îles fpl Anglo-Normandes.

Channel tunnel *n*: **the ~** le tunnel sous la Manche.

chant [tʃɑːnt] ◆ *n* chant m. ◆ *vt* **1.** (RELIG) chanter. **2.** (*words, slogan*) scander.

chaos ['keɪɒs] *n* chaos m.

chaotic [keɪ'ɒtɪk] *adj* chaotique.

chap [tʃæp] *n* Br inf (*man*) type m.

chapel ['tʃæpl] *n* chapelle f.

chaperone ['ʃæpərəʊn] *n* chaperon m.

chaplain ['tʃæplɪn] *n* aumônier m.

chapped [tʃæpt] *adj* (*skin, lips*) gercé(e).

chapter ['tʃæptəʳ] *n* chapitre m.

char [tʃɑːʳ] *vt* (*burn*) calciner.

character ['kærəktəʳ] *n* **1.** (*gen*) caractère m. **2.** (*in film, book, play*) personnage m. **3.** *inf* (*eccentric*) original m.

characteristic [,kærəktə'rɪstɪk] ◆ *adj* caractéristique. ◆ *n* caractéristique f.

characterize, -ise ['kærəktəraɪz] *vt* caractériser.

charade [ʃə'rɑːd] *n* farce f. ▶ **charades** *n* (U) charades fpl.

charcoal ['tʃɑːkəʊl] *n* (*for drawing*) charbon m; (*for burning*) charbon de bois.

charge [tʃɑːdʒ] ◆ *n* **1.** (*cost*) prix m; **free of ~** gratuit. **2.** (JUR) accusation f, inculpation f. **3.** (*responsibility*): **to take ~ of** se charger de; **to be in ~ of, to have ~ of** être responsable de, s'occuper de; **in ~** responsable. **4.** (ELEC & MIL) charge f. ◆ *vt* **1.** (*customer, sum*) faire payer; **how much do you ~?** vous prenez combien?; **to ~ sthg to sb** mettre qqch sur le compte de qqn. **2.** (*suspect, criminal*): **to ~ sb (with)** accuser qqn (de). **3.** (ELEC & MIL) charger. ◆ *vi* (*rush*) se précipiter, foncer.

charge card *n* carte f de compte crédit (*auprès d'un magasin*).

charger ['tʃɑːdʒəʳ] *n* (*for batteries*) chargeur m.

chariot ['tʃærɪət] *n* char m.

charisma [kə'rɪzmə] *n* charisme m.

charity ['tʃærətɪ] *n* charité f.

charm [tʃɑːm] ◆ *n* charme m. ◆ *vt* charmer.

charming ['tʃɑːmɪŋ] *adj* charmant(e).

chart [tʃɑːt] ◆ *n* **1.** (*diagram*) graphique m, diagramme m. **2.** (*map*) carte f. ◆ *vt* **1.** (*plot, map*) porter sur une carte. **2.** *fig* (*record*) retracer. ▶ **charts** *npl*: **the ~s** le hit-parade.

charter ['tʃɑːtəʳ] ◆ *n* (*document*) charte f. ◆ *vt* (*plane, boat*) affréter.

chartered accountant [,tʃɑːtəd-] *n* Br expert-comptable m.

charter flight *n* vol m charter.

chase [tʃeɪs] ◆ *n* (*pursuit*) poursuite f, chasse f. ◆ *vt* **1.** (*pursue*) poursuivre. **2.** (*drive away*) chasser. ◆ *vi*: **to ~ after sb/sthg** courir après qqn/qqch.

chasm ['kæzm] *n lit & fig* abîme m.

chassis ['ʃæsɪ] (*pl inv*) *n* châssis m.

chat [tʃæt] ◆ *n* causerie f, bavardage m; **to have a ~** causer, bavarder. ◆ *vi* causer, bavarder. ▶ **chat up** *vt sep* Br inf baratiner.

chat show *n* Br talk-show m.

chatter ['tʃætər] ◆ n 1. (of person) bavardage m. 2. (of animal, bird) caquetage m. ◆ vi 1. (person) bavarder. 2. (animal, bird) jacasser, caqueter. 3. (teeth): **his teeth were ~ing** il claquait des dents.

chatterbox ['tʃætəbɒks] n inf moulin m à paroles.

chatty ['tʃætɪ] adj (person) bavard(e); (letter) plein(e) de bavardages.

chauffeur ['ʃəʊfər] n chauffeur m.

chauvinist ['ʃəʊvɪnɪst] n 1. (sexist) macho m. 2. (nationalist) chauvin m, -e f.

cheap [tʃiːp] ◆ adj 1. (inexpensive) pas cher (chère), bon marché (inv). 2. (at a reduced price - fare, rate) réduit(e); (- ticket) à prix réduit. 3. (low-quality) de mauvaise qualité. 4. (joke, comment) facile. ◆ adv (à) bon marché.

cheapen ['tʃiːpn] vt (degrade) rabaisser.

cheaply ['tʃiːplɪ] adv à bon marché, pour pas cher.

cheat [tʃiːt] ◆ n tricheur m, -euse f. ◆ vt tromper; **to ~ sb out of sthg** escroquer qqch à qqn. ◆ vi 1. (in game, exam) tricher. 2. inf (be unfaithful): **to ~ on sb** tromper qqn.

check [tʃek] ◆ n 1. (inspection, test): ~ **(on)** contrôle m (de). 2. (restraint): ~ **(on)** frein m (à), restriction f (sur). 3. Am (bill) note f. 4. (pattern) carreaux mpl. 5. Am = **cheque.** ◆ vt 1. (test, verify) vérifier; (passport, ticket) contrôler. 2. (restrain, stop) enrayer, arrêter. ◆ vi: **to ~ (for sthg)** vérifier (qqch); **to ~ on sthg** vérifier OR contrôler qqch. ▶ **check in** ◆ vt sep (luggage, coat) enregistrer. ◆ vi 1. (at hotel) signer le registre. 2. (at airport) se présenter à l'enregistrement. ▶ **check out** ◆ vt sep 1. (luggage, coat) retirer. 2. (investigate) vérifier. ◆ vi (from hotel) régler sa note. ▶ **check up** vi: **to ~ up on sb** prendre des renseignements sur qqn; **to ~ up (on sthg)** vérifier (qqch).

checkbook Am = **chequebook.**

checked [tʃekt] adj à carreaux.

checkered Am = **chequered.**

checkers ['tʃekəz] n (U) Am jeu m de dames.

check-in n enregistrement m.

checking account ['tʃekɪŋ-] n Am compte m courant.

checkmate ['tʃekmeɪt] n échec et mat m.

checkout ['tʃekaʊt] n (in supermarket) caisse f.

checkpoint ['tʃekpɔɪnt] n (place) (poste m de) contrôle m.

checkup ['tʃekʌp] n (MED) bilan m de santé, check-up m.

Cheddar (cheese) ['tʃedər-] n (fromage m de) cheddar m.

cheek [tʃiːk] n 1. (of face) joue f. 2. inf (impudence) culot m.

cheekbone ['tʃiːkbəʊn] n pommette f.

cheeky ['tʃiːkɪ] adj insolent(e), effronté(e).

cheer [tʃɪər] ◆ n (shout) acclamation f. ◆ vt 1. (shout for) acclamer. 2. (gladden) réjouir. ◆ vi applaudir. ▶ **cheers** excl 1. (said before drinking) santé! 2. inf (goodbye) salut!, ciao!, tchao! ▶ **cheer up** ◆ vt sep remonter le moral à. ◆ vi s'égayer.

cheerful ['tʃɪəfʊl] adj joyeux(euse), gai(e).

cheerio [,tʃɪərɪ'əʊ] excl inf au revoir!, salut!

cheese [tʃiːz] n fromage m.

cheeseboard ['tʃiːzbɔːd] n plateau m à fromage.

cheeseburger ['tʃiːz,bɜːgər] n cheeseburger m, hamburger m au fromage.

cheesecake ['tʃiːzkeɪk] n (CULIN) gâteau m au fromage blanc, cheesecake m.

cheetah ['tʃiːtə] n guépard m.

chef [ʃef] n chef m.

chemical ['kemɪkl] ◆ adj chimique. ◆ n produit m chimique.

chemist ['kemɪst] n 1. Br (pharmacist) pharmacien m, -enne f; **~'s (shop)** pharmacie f. 2. (scientist) chimiste mf.

chemistry ['kemɪstrɪ] n chimie f.

cheque Br, **check** Am [tʃek] n chèque m.

chequebook Br, **checkbook** Am ['tʃekbʊk] n chéquier m, carnet m de chèques.

cheque card n Br carte f bancaire.

chequered Br ['tʃekəd], **checkered** Am ['tʃekerd] adj fig (career, life) mouvementé(e).

cherish ['tʃerɪʃ] vt chérir; (hope) nourrir, caresser.

cherry ['tʃerɪ] n (fruit) cerise f; **~ (tree)** cerisier m.

chess [tʃes] n échecs mpl.

chessboard ['tʃesbɔːd] n échiquier m.

chessman ['tʃesmæn] (pl **-men** [-men]) n pièce f.

chest [tʃest] n 1. (ANAT) poitrine f. 2. (box) coffre m.

chestnut ['tʃesnʌt] ◆ adj (colour) châtain (inv). ◆ n (nut) châtaigne f; **~ (tree)** châtaignier m.

chest of drawers (pl **chests of draw-**

chew

ers *n* commode *f*.

chew [tʃuː] ◆ *n* (*sweet*) bonbon *m* (à mâcher). ◆ *vt* mâcher. ► **chew up** *vt sep* mâchouiller.

chewing gum ['tʃuːɪŋ-] *n* chewing-gum *m*.

chic [ʃiːk] *adj* chic (*inv*).

chick [tʃɪk] *n* (*baby bird*) oisillon *m*.

chicken ['tʃɪkɪn] *n* **1.** (*bird, food*) poulet *m*. **2.** *inf* (*coward*) froussard *m*, -e *f*. ► **chicken out** *vi inf* se dégonfler.

chickenpox ['tʃɪkɪnpɒks] *n* (U) varicelle *f*.

chickpea ['tʃɪkpiː] *n* pois *m* chiche.

chicory ['tʃɪkərɪ] *n* (*vegetable*) endive *f*.

chief [tʃiːf] ◆ *adj* **1.** (*main - aim, problem*) principal(e). **2.** (*head*) en chef. ◆ *n* chef *m*.

chief executive *n* directeur général *m*, directrice générale *f*.

chiefly ['tʃiːflɪ] *adv* **1.** (*mainly*) principalement. **2.** (*above all*) surtout.

chiffon ['ʃɪfɒn] *n* mousseline *f*.

chilblain ['tʃɪlbleɪn] *n* engelure *f*.

child [tʃaɪld] (*pl* **children**) *n* enfant *mf*.

child benefit *n* (U) Br ≃ allocations *fpl* familiales.

childbirth ['tʃaɪldbɜːθ] *n* (U) accouchement *m*.

childhood ['tʃaɪldhʊd] *n* enfance *f*.

childish ['tʃaɪldɪʃ] *adj pej* puéril(e), enfantin(e).

childlike ['tʃaɪldlaɪk] *adj* enfantin(e), d'enfant.

childminder ['tʃaɪld,maɪndəʳ] *n* Br gardienne *f* d'enfants, nourrice *f*.

childproof ['tʃaɪldpruːf] *adj* (*container*) qui ne peut pas être ouvert par les enfants; ~ **lock** verrouillage *m* de sécurité pour enfants.

children ['tʃɪldrən] *pl* → **child**.

children's home *n* maison *f* d'enfants.

Chile ['tʃɪlɪ] *n* Chili *m*.

Chilean ['tʃɪlɪən] ◆ *adj* chilien(enne). ◆ *n* Chilien *m*, -enne *f*.

chili ['tʃɪlɪ] = **chilli**.

chill [tʃɪl] ◆ *adj* frais (fraîche). ◆ *n* **1.** (*illness*) coup *m* de froid. **2.** (*in temperature*): **there's a ~ in the air** le fond de l'air est frais. **3.** (*feeling of fear*) frisson *m*. ◆ *vt* **1.** (*drink, food*) mettre au frais. **2.** (*person*) faire frissonner. ◆ *vi* (*drink, food*) rafraîchir.

chilli ['tʃɪlɪ] (*pl* **-ies**) *n* (*vegetable*) piment *m*.

chilling ['tʃɪlɪŋ] *adj* **1.** (*very cold*) glacial(e). **2.** (*frightening*) qui glace le sang.

chilly ['tʃɪlɪ] *adj* froid(e); **to feel ~** avoir froid; **it's ~** il fait froid.

chime [tʃaɪm] ◆ *n* (*of bell, clock*) carillon *m*. ◆ *vt* (*time*) sonner. ◆ *vi* (*bell, clock*) carillonner.

chimney ['tʃɪmnɪ] *n* cheminée *f*.

chimneypot ['tʃɪmnɪpɒt] *n* mitre *f* de cheminée.

chimneysweep ['tʃɪmnɪswiːp] *n* ramoneur *m*.

chimp(anzee) [tʃɪmp(ənˈziː)] *n* chimpanzé *m*.

chin [tʃɪn] *n* menton *m*.

china ['tʃaɪnə] *n* porcelaine *f*.

China ['tʃaɪnə] *n* Chine *f*.

Chinese [,tʃaɪˈniːz] ◆ *adj* chinois(e). ◆ *n* (*language*) chinois *m*. ◆ *npl*: **the ~** les Chinois *mpl*.

Chinese cabbage *n* chou *m* chinois.

Chinese leaves *npl* Br = **Chinese cabbage**.

chink [tʃɪŋk] *n* **1.** (*narrow opening*) fente *f*. **2.** (*sound*) tintement *m*.

chip [tʃɪp] ◆ *n* **1.** Br (*fried potato*) frite *f*; Am (*potato crisp*) chip *m*. **2.** (*of glass, metal*) éclat *m*; (*of wood*) copeau *m*. **3.** (*flaw*) ébréchure *f*. **4.** (*microchip*) puce *f*. **5.** (*for gambling*) jeton *m*. ◆ *vt* (*cup, glass*) ébrécher. ► **chip in** *inf vi* **1.** (*contribute*) contribuer. **2.** (*interrupt*) mettre son grain de sel.

chipboard ['tʃɪpbɔːd] *n* aggloméré *m*.

chip shop *n* Br friterie *f*.

chiropodist [kɪˈrɒpədɪst] *n* pédicure *mf*.

chirp [tʃɜːp] *vi* (*bird*) pépier; (*cricket*) chanter.

chirpy ['tʃɜːpɪ] *adj* gai(e).

chisel ['tʃɪzl] ◆ *n* (*for wood*) ciseau *m*; (*for metal, rock*) burin *m*. ◆ *vt* ciseler.

chit [tʃɪt] *n* (*note*) note *f*, reçu *m*.

chitchat ['tʃɪttʃæt] *n* (U) *inf* bavardage *m*.

chivalry ['ʃɪvlrɪ] *n* (U) **1.** *literary* (*of knights*) chevalerie *f*. **2.** (*good manners*) galanterie *f*.

chives [tʃaɪvz] *npl* ciboulette *f*.

chlorine ['klɔːriːn] *n* chlore *m*.

choc-ice ['tʃɒkaɪs] *n* Br Esquimau® *m*.

chock [tʃɒk] *n* cale *f*.

chock-a-block, chock-full *adj inf*: ~ **(with)** plein(e) à craquer (de).

chocolate ['tʃɒkələt] ◆ *n* chocolat *m*. ◆ *comp* au chocolat.

choice [tʃɔɪs] ◆ *n* choix *m*. ◆ *adj* de choix.

choir ['kwaɪəʳ] *n* chœur *m*.

choirboy ['kwaɪəbɔɪ] n jeune choriste m.

choke [tʃəʊk] ◆ n (AUT) starter m. ◆ vt 1. (strangle) étrangler, étouffer. 2. (block) obstruer, boucher. ◆ vi s'étrangler.

cholera ['kɒlərə] n choléra m.

choose [tʃuːz] (pt chose, pp chosen) ◆ vt 1. (select) choisir. 2. (decide): **to ~ to do sthg** décider or choisir de faire qqch. ◆ vi (select): **to ~ (from)** choisir (parmi or entre).

choos(e)y ['tʃuːzɪ] (compar -ier, superl -iest) adj difficile.

chop [tʃɒp] ◆ n 1. (CULIN) côtelette f. ◆ vt 1. (wood) couper; (vegetables) hacher. 2. inf fig (funding, budget) réduire. 3. phr: **to ~ and change** changer sans cesse d'avis. ◆ **chops** npl inf babines fpl. ▶ **chop down** vt sep (tree) abattre. ▶ **chop up** vt sep couper en morceaux.

chopper ['tʃɒpər] n 1. (axe) couperet m. 2. inf (helicopter) hélico m.

choppy ['tʃɒpɪ] adj (sea) agité(e).

chopsticks ['tʃɒpstɪks] npl baguettes fpl.

chord [kɔːd] n (MUS) accord m.

chore [tʃɔːr] n corvée f; **household ~s** travaux mpl ménagers.

chortle ['tʃɔːtl] vi glousser.

chorus ['kɔːrəs] n 1. (part of song) refrain m. 2. (singers) chœur m. 3. fig (of praise, complaints) concert m.

chose [tʃəʊz] pt → **choose**.

chosen ['tʃəʊzn] pp → **choose**.

Christ [kraɪst] ◆ n Christ m. ◆ excl Seigneur!, bon Dieu!

christen ['krɪsn] vt 1. (baby) baptiser. 2. (name) nommer.

christening ['krɪsnɪŋ] n baptême m.

Christian ['krɪstʃən] ◆ adj (RELIG) chrétien(enne). ◆ n chrétien m, -enne f.

Christianity [ˌkrɪstɪˈænətɪ] n christianisme m.

Christian name n prénom m.

Christmas ['krɪsməs] n Noël m; **happy** OR **merry ~!** joyeux Noël!

Christmas card n carte f de Noël.

Christmas Day n jour m de Noël.

Christmas Eve n veille f de Noël.

Christmas pudding n Br pudding m (de Noël).

Christmas tree n arbre m de Noël.

chrome [krəʊm], **chromium** ['krəʊmɪəm] ◆ n chrome m. ◆ comp chromé(e).

chronic ['krɒnɪk] adj (illness, unemployment) chronique; (liar, alcoholic) invétéré(e).

chronicle ['krɒnɪkl] n chronique f.

chronological [ˌkrɒnəˈlɒdʒɪkl] adj chronologique.

chrysanthemum [krɪˈsænθəməm] (pl -s) n chrysanthème m.

chubby ['tʃʌbɪ] adj (cheeks, face) joufflu(e); (person, hands) potelé(e).

chuck [tʃʌk] vt inf 1. (throw) lancer, envoyer. 2. (job, boyfriend) laisser tomber. ▶ **chuck away, chuck out** vt sep inf jeter, balancer.

chuckle ['tʃʌkl] vi glousser.

chug [tʃʌg] vi (train) faire teuf-teuf.

chum [tʃʌm] n inf copain m, copine f.

chunk [tʃʌŋk] n gros morceau m.

church [tʃɜːtʃ] n (building) église f; **to go to ~** aller à l'église; (Catholics) aller à la messe.

Church of England n: **the ~** l'Église d'Angleterre.

churchyard ['tʃɜːtʃjɑːd] n cimetière m.

churlish ['tʃɜːlɪʃ] adj grossier(ère).

churn [tʃɜːn] ◆ n 1. (for making butter) baratte f. 2. (for milk) bidon m. ◆ vt (stir up) battre. ▶ **churn out** vt sep inf produire en série.

chute [ʃuːt] n glissière f; **rubbish ~** vide-ordures m inv.

chutney ['tʃʌtnɪ] n chutney m.

CIA (abbr of **Central Intelligence Agency**) n CIA f.

CID (abbr of **Criminal Investigation Department**) n la police judiciaire britannique.

cider ['saɪdər] n cidre m.

cigar [sɪˈgɑːr] n cigare m.

cigarette [ˌsɪgəˈret] n cigarette f.

cinder ['sɪndər] n cendre f.

Cinderella [ˌsɪndəˈrelə] n Cendrillon f.

cine-camera ['sɪnɪ-] n caméra f.

cine-film ['sɪnɪ-] n film m.

cinema ['sɪnəmə] n cinéma m.

cinnamon ['sɪnəmən] n cannelle f.

cipher ['saɪfər] n (secret writing) code m.

circa ['sɜːkə] prep environ.

circle ['sɜːkl] ◆ n 1. (gen) cercle m; **to go round in ~s** fig tourner en rond. 2. (in theatre, cinema) balcon m. 3. (family and friends) entourage m. ◆ vt 1. (draw a circle round) entourer (d'un cercle). 2. (move round) faire le tour de. ◆ vi (plane) tourner en rond.

circuit ['sɜːkɪt] n 1. (gen & ELEC) circuit m. 2. (lap) tour m; (movement round) révolution f.

circuitous [səˈkjuːɪtəs] adj indirect(e).

circular ['sɜːkjʊlər] ◆ adj (gen) circulaire. ◆ n (letter) circulaire f; (advertisement) prospectus m.

circulate ['sɜːkjʊleɪt] ◆ vi 1. (gen) cir-

culer. **2.** (*socialize*) se mêler aux invités.
♦ *vt* (*rumour*) propager; (*document*) faire
circuler.
circulation [ˌsɜːkjʊˈleɪʃn] *n* **1.** (*gen*) circulation *f*. **2.** (PRESS) tirage *m*.
circumcision [ˌsɜːkəmˈsɪʒn] *n* circoncision *f*.
circumference [səˈkʌmfərəns] *n* circonférence *f*.
circumflex [ˈsɜːkəmfleks] *n*: ~ **(accent)**
accent *m* circonflexe.
circumspect [ˈsɜːkəmspekt] *adj* cir-
conspect(e).
circumstances [ˈsɜːkəmstənsɪz] *npl*
circonstances *fpl*; **under** OR **in no ~** en
aucun cas; **under** OR **in the ~** en de telles
circonstances.
circumvent [ˌsɜːkəmˈvent] *vt fml* (*law,
rule*) tourner.
circus [ˈsɜːkəs] *n* cirque *m*.
CIS (*abbr of* **Commonwealth of
Independent States**) *n* CEI *f*.
cistern [ˈsɪstən] *n* **1.** *Br* (*inside roof*)
réservoir *m* d'eau. **2.** (*in toilet*) réservoir
m de chasse d'eau.
cite [saɪt] *vt* citer.
citizen [ˈsɪtɪzn] *n* **1.** (*of country*) citoyen
m, -enne *f*. **2.** (*of town*) habitant *m*, -e *f*.
Citizens' Advice Bureau *n service
britannique d'information et d'aide au
consommateur.*
Citizens' Band *n fréquence radio réservée
au public,* citizen band *f*.
citizenship [ˈsɪtɪznʃɪp] *n* citoyenneté
f.
citrus fruit [ˈsɪtrəs-] *n* agrume *m*.
city [ˈsɪti] *n* ville *f*, cité *f*. ▶ **City** *n Br*:
the City la City (*quartier financier de
Londres*).
city centre *n* centre-ville *m*.
city hall *n Am* ≃ mairie *f*, ≃ hôtel *m*
de ville.
city technology college *n Br établissement d'enseignement technique du secondaire subventionné par les entreprises.*
civic [ˈsɪvɪk] *adj* (*leader, event*) munici-
pal(e); (*duty, pride*) civique.
civic centre *n Br* centre *m* administratif municipal.
civil [ˈsɪvl] *adj* **1.** (*public*) civil(e).
2. (*polite*) courtois(e), poli(e).
civil engineering *n* génie *m* civil.
civilian [sɪˈvɪljən] ♦ *n* civil *m*, -e *f*.
♦ *comp* civil(e).
civilization [ˌsɪvəlaɪˈzeɪʃn] *n* civilisation *f*.
civilized [ˈsɪvəlaɪzd] *adj* civilisé(e).
civil law *n* droit *m* civil.

civil liberties *npl* libertés *fpl* civiques.
civil rights *npl* droits *mpl* civils.
civil servant *n* fonctionnaire *mf*.
civil service *n* fonction *f* publique.
civil war *n* guerre *f* civile.
cl (*abbr of* **centilitre**) cl.
clad [klæd] *adj literary* (*dressed*): ~ **in** vê-
tu(e) de.
claim [kleɪm] ♦ *n* **1.** (*for pay etc*) revendication *f*; (*for expenses, insurance*)
demande *f*. **2.** (*right*) droit *m*; **to lay ~ to
sthg** revendiquer qqch. **3.** (*assertion*)
affirmation *f*. ♦ *vt* **1.** (*ask for*) réclamer.
2. (*responsibility, credit*) revendiquer.
3. (*maintain*) prétendre. ♦ *vi*: **to ~ for
sthg** faire une demande d'indemnité
pour qqch; **to ~ (on one's insurance)** faire
une déclaration de sinistre.
claimant [ˈkleɪmənt] *n* (*to throne*) prétendant *m*, -e *f*; (*of state benefit*) demandeur *m*, -eresse *f*, requérant *m*, -e *f*.
clairvoyant [kleəˈvɔɪənt] *n* voyant *m*,
-e *f*.
clam [klæm] *n* palourde *f*.
clamber [ˈklæmbər] *vi* grimper.
clammy [ˈklæmɪ] *adj* (*skin*) moite;
(*weather*) lourd et humide.
clamour *Br*, **clamor** *Am* [ˈklæmər] ♦ *n*
(U) (*noise*) cris *mpl*. ♦ *vi*: **to ~ for sthg**
demander qqch à cor et à cri.
clamp [klæmp] ♦ *n* (*gen*) pince *f*, agrafe
f; (*for carpentry*) serre-joint *m*; (MED)
clamp *m*. ♦ *vt* **1.** (*gen*) serrer. **2.** (AUT)
poser un sabot de Denver à. ▶ **clamp
down** *vi*: **to ~ down (on)** sévir (contre).
clan [klæn] *n* clan *m*.
clandestine [klænˈdestɪn] *adj* clandes-
tin(e).
clang [klæŋ] *n* bruit *m* métallique.
clap [klæp] ♦ *vt* (*hands*): **to ~ one's hands**
applaudir, taper des mains. ♦ *vi*
applaudir, taper des mains.
clapping [ˈklæpɪŋ] *n* (U) applaudissements *mpl*.
claret [ˈklærət] *n* **1.** (*wine*) bordeaux *m*
rouge. **2.** (*colour*) bordeaux *m inv*.
clarify [ˈklærɪfaɪ] *vt* (*explain*) éclaircir,
clarifier.
clarinet [ˌklærəˈnet] *n* clarinette *f*.
clarity [ˈklærətɪ] *n* clarté *f*.
clash [klæʃ] ♦ *n* **1.** (*of interests, personal-
ities*) conflit *m*. **2.** (*fight, disagreement*) heurt
m, affrontement *m*. **3.** (*noise*) fracas *m*.
♦ *vi* **1.** (*fight, disagree*) se heurter. **2.** (*differ,
conflict*) entrer en conflit. **3.** (*coincide*): **to ~
(with sthg)** tomber en même temps (que
qqch). **4.** (*colours*) jurer.
clasp [klɑːsp] ♦ *n* (*on necklace etc*) fer-

moir m; (on belt) boucle f. ◆ vt (hold tight)
serrer.

class [klɑːs] ◆ n 1. (gen) classe f. 2. (lesson) cours m, classe f. 3. (category) catégorie f. ◆ vt classer.

classic ['klæsɪk] ◆ adj classique. ◆ n classique m.

classical ['klæsɪkl] adj classique.

classified ['klæsɪfaɪd] adj (information, document) classé secret (classée secrète).

classified ad n petite annonce f.

classify ['klæsɪfaɪ] vt classifier, classer.

classmate ['klɑːsmeɪt] n camarade mf de classe.

classroom ['klɑːsrʊm] n (salle f de) classe f.

classy ['klɑːsɪ] adj inf chic (inv).

clatter ['klætər] n cliquetis m; (louder) fracas m.

clause [klɔːz] n 1. (in document) clause f. 2. (GRAMM) proposition f.

claw [klɔː] ◆ n 1. (of cat, bird) griffe f. 2. (of crab, lobster) pince f. ◆ vt griffer. ◆ vi (person): **to ~ at** s'agripper à.

clay [kleɪ] n argile f.

clean [kliːn] ◆ adj 1. (not dirty) propre. 2. (sheet of paper, driving licence) vierge; (reputation) sans tache. 3. (joke) de bon goût. 4. (smooth) net (nette). ◆ vt nettoyer; **to ~ one's teeth** se brosser OR laver les dents. ◆ vi faire le ménage. ▶ **clean out** vt sep (room, drawer) nettoyer à fond. ▶ **clean up** vt sep (clear up) nettoyer.

cleaner ['kliːnər] n 1. (person) personne f qui fait le ménage. 2. (substance) produit m d'entretien.

cleaning ['kliːnɪŋ] n nettoyage m.

cleanliness ['klenlɪnɪs] n propreté f.

cleanse [klenz] vt 1. (skin, wound) nettoyer. 2. fig (make pure) purifier.

cleanser ['klenzər] n (detergent) détergent m; (for skin) démaquillant m.

clean-shaven [-'ʃeɪvn] adj rasé(e) de près.

clear [klɪər] ◆ adj 1. (gen) clair(e); (glass, plastic) transparent(e); (difference) net (nette); **to make sthg ~ (to sb)** expliquer qqch clairement (à qqn); **to make it ~ that** préciser que; **to make o.s. ~** bien se faire comprendre. 2. (voice, sound) clair(e). ◆ adv: **to stand ~** s'écarter; **to stay ~ of sb/sthg, to steer ~ of sb/sthg** éviter qqn/qqch. ◆ vt 1. (road, path) dégager; (table) débarrasser. 2. (obstacle, fallen tree) enlever.

3. (jump) sauter, franchir. 4. (debt) s'acquitter de. 5. (authorize) donner le feu vert à. 6. (JUR) innocenter. ◆ vi (fog, smoke) se dissiper; (weather, sky) s'éclaircir. ▶ **clear away** vt sep (plates) débarrasser; (books) enlever. ▶ **clear off** vi Br inf dégager. ▶ **clear out** ◆ vt sep (cupboard) vider; (room) ranger. ◆ vi inf (leave) dégager. ▶ **clear up** ◆ vt sep 1. (tidy) ranger. 2. (mystery, misunderstanding) éclaircir. ◆ vi 1. (weather) s'éclaircir. 2. (tidy up) tout ranger.

clearance ['klɪərəns] n 1. (of rubbish) enlèvement m; (of land) déblaiement m. 2. (permission) autorisation f.

clear-cut adj net (nette).

clearing ['klɪərɪŋ] n (in wood) clairière f.

clearing bank n Br banque f de clearing.

clearly ['klɪəlɪ] adv 1. (distinctly, lucidly) clairement. 2. (obviously) manifestement.

clearway ['klɪəweɪ] n Br route où le stationnement n'est autorisé qu'en cas d'urgence.

cleavage ['kliːvɪdʒ] n (between breasts) décolleté m.

cleaver ['kliːvər] n couperet m.

clef [klef] n clef f.

cleft [kleft] n fente f.

clench [klentʃ] vt serrer.

clergy ['klɜːdʒɪ] npl: **the ~** le clergé.

clergyman ['klɜːdʒɪmən] (pl -men [-mən]) n membre m du clergé.

clerical ['klerɪkl] adj 1. (ADMIN) de bureau. 2. (RELIG) clérical(e).

clerk [Br klɑːk, Am klɜːrk] n 1. (in office) employé m, -e f de bureau. 2. (JUR) clerc m. 3. Am (shop assistant) vendeur m, -euse f.

clever ['klevər] adj 1. (intelligent - person) intelligent(e); (- idea) ingénieux(euse). 2. (skilful) habile, adroit(e).

click [klɪk] ◆ n (of lock) déclic m; (of tongue, heels) claquement m. ◆ vt faire claquer. ◆ vi (heels) claquer; (camera) faire un déclic.

client ['klaɪənt] n client m, -e f.

cliff [klɪf] n falaise f.

climate ['klaɪmɪt] n climat m.

climatic [klaɪ'mætɪk] adj climatique.

climax ['klaɪmæks] n (culmination) apogée m.

climb [klaɪm] ◆ n ascension f, montée f. ◆ vt (tree, rope) monter à; (stairs) monter; (wall, hill) escalader. ◆ vi 1. (person) monter, grimper. 2. (plant) grimper; (road) monter; (plane) prendre de l'altitude. 3. (increase) augmenter.

climb-down n reculade f.

climber ['klaɪmə^r] n (person) alpiniste mf, grimpeur m, -euse f.

climbing ['klaɪmɪŋ] n (rock climbing) varappe f; (mountain climbing) alpinisme m; (rock climbing) escalade f.

climbing wall n mur m d'escalade.

clinch [klɪntʃ] vt (deal) conclure.

cling [klɪŋ] (pt & pp clung) vi 1. (hold tightly): to ~ (to) s'accrocher (à), se cramponner (à). 2. (clothes): to ~ (to) coller (à).

clingfilm ['klɪŋfɪlm] n Br film m alimentaire transparent.

clinic ['klɪnɪk] n (building) centre m médical, clinique f.

clinical ['klɪnɪkl] adj 1. (MED) clinique. 2. fig (attitude) froid(e).

clink [klɪŋk] vi tinter.

clip [klɪp] ♦ n 1. (for paper) trombone m; (for hair) pince f; (of earring) clip m. 2. (excerpt) extrait m. ♦ vt 1. (fasten) attacher. 2. (nails) couper; (hedge) tailler; (newspaper cutting) découper.

clipboard ['klɪpbɔːd] n écritoire f à pince, clipboard m.

clippers ['klɪpəz] npl (for hair) tondeuse f; (for nails) pince f à ongles; (for hedge) cisaille f à haie; (for pruning) sécateur m.

clipping ['klɪpɪŋ] n (from newspaper) coupure f.

cloak [kləʊk] n (garment) cape f.

cloakroom ['kləʊkrʊm] n 1. (for clothes) vestiaire m. 2. Br (toilets) toilettes fpl.

clock [klɒk] n 1. (large) horloge f; (small) pendule f; round the ~ (work, be open) 24 heures sur 24. 2. (AUT) (mileometer) compteur m. ► **clock in, clock on** vi Br (at work) pointer (à l'arrivée). ► **clock off, clock out** vi Br (at work) pointer (à la sortie).

clockwise ['klɒkwaɪz] adj & adv dans le sens des aiguilles d'une montre.

clockwork ['klɒkwɜːk] ♦ n: to go like ~ fig aller OR marcher comme sur des roulettes. ♦ comp (toy) mécanique.

clog [klɒg] vt boucher. ► **clogs** npl sabots mpl. ► **clog up** ♦ vt sep boucher. ♦ vi se boucher.

close¹ [kləʊs] ♦ adj 1. (near): ~ (to) proche (de), près (de); a ~ friend un ami intime (une amie intime); ~ up, ~ to de près; ~ by, ~ at hand tout près; that was a ~ shave OR thing OR call on l'a échappé belle. 2. (link, resemblance) fort(e); (cooperation, connection) étroit(e). 3. (questioning) serré(e); (examination)

minutieux(euse); to keep a ~ watch on sb/sthg surveiller qqn/qqch de près. 4. (weather) lourd(e); (air in room) renfermé(e). 5. (result, contest, race) serré(e). ♦ adv: ~ (to) près (de); to come ~r (together) se rapprocher. ► **close on, close to** prep (almost) près de.

close² [kləʊz] ♦ vt 1. (gen) fermer. 2. (end) clore. ♦ vi 1. (shop, bank) fermer; (door, lid) (se) fermer. 2. (end) se terminer, finir. ♦ n fin f. ► **close down** vt sep & vi fermer.

closed [kləʊzd] adj fermé(e).

close-knit [,kləʊs-] adj (très) uni(e).

closely ['kləʊslɪ] adv (listen, examine, watch) de près; (resemble) beaucoup; to be ~ related to OR with être proche parent de.

closet ['klɒzɪt] ♦ n Am (cupboard) placard m. ♦ adj inf non avoué(e).

close-up ['kləʊs-] n gros plan m.

closing time ['kləʊzɪŋ-] n heure f de fermeture.

closure ['kləʊʒə^r] n fermeture f.

clot [klɒt] ♦ n 1. (of blood, milk) caillot m. 2. Br inf (fool) empoté m, -e f. ♦ vi (blood) coaguler.

cloth [klɒθ] n 1. (U) (fabric) tissu m. 2. (duster) chiffon m; (for drying) torchon m.

clothe [kləʊð] vt fml (dress) habiller.

clothes [kləʊðz] npl vêtements mpl, habits mpl; to put one's ~ on s'habiller; to take one's ~ off se déshabiller.

clothes brush n brosse f à habits.

clothesline ['kləʊðzlaɪn] n corde f à linge.

clothes peg Br, **clothespin** Am ['kləʊðzpɪn] n pince f à linge.

clothing ['kləʊðɪŋ] n (U) vêtements mpl, habits mpl.

cloud [klaʊd] n nuage m. ► **cloud over** vi (sky) se couvrir.

cloudy ['klaʊdɪ] adj 1. (sky, day) nuageux(euse). 2. (liquid) trouble.

clout [klaʊt] inf ♦ n (U) (influence) poids m, influence f. ♦ vt donner un coup à.

clove [kləʊv] n: a ~ of garlic une gousse d'ail. ► **cloves** npl (spice) clous mpl de girofle.

clover ['kləʊvə^r] n trèfle m.

clown [klaʊn] ♦ n 1. (performer) clown m. 2. (fool) pitre m. ♦ vi faire le pitre.

cloying ['klɔɪɪŋ] adj 1. (smell) écœurant(e). 2. (sentimentality) à l'eau de rose.

club [klʌb] ♦ n 1. (organization, place) club m. 2. (weapon) massue f. 3. (golf) ~ club m. ♦ vt matraquer. ► **clubs** npl

coffee table

(CARDS) trèfle m. ▶ **club together** vi se cotiser.

club car n Am (RAIL) wagon-restaurant m.

clubhouse ['klʌbhaʊs, pl -haʊzɪz] n club m, pavillon m.

cluck [klʌk] vi glousser.

clue [kluː] n 1. (in crime) indice m; I haven't (got) a ~ (about) je n'ai aucune idée (sur). 2. (in crossword) définition f.

clued-up [kluːd-] adj Br inf calé(e).

clump [klʌmp] n (of trees, bushes) massif m, bouquet m.

clumsy ['klʌmzɪ] adj 1. (ungraceful) gauche, maladroit(e). 2. (tactless) sans tact.

clung [klʌŋ] pt & pp → **cling**.

cluster ['klʌstə**r**] ◆ n (group) groupe m. ◆ vi (people) se rassembler; (buildings etc) être regroupé(e).

clutch [klʌtʃ] ◆ n (AUT) embrayage m. ◆ vt agripper. ◆ vi: to ~ at s'agripper à.

clutter ['klʌtə**r**] n désordre m.

cm (abbr of **centimetre**) n cm.

CND (abbr of **Campaign for Nuclear Disarmament**) n mouvement pour le désarmement nucléaire.

c/o (abbr of **care of**) a/s.

Co. 1. (abbr of **Company**) Cie. 2. abbr of **County**.

coach [kəʊtʃ] ◆ n 1. (bus) car m, autocar m. 2. (RAIL) voiture f. 3. (horsedrawn) carrosse m. 4. (SPORT) entraîneur m. 5. (tutor) répétiteur m, -trice f. ◆ vt 1. (SPORT) entraîner. 2. (tutor) donner des leçons (particulières) à.

coal [kəʊl] n charbon m.

coalfield ['kəʊlfiːld] n bassin m houiller.

coalition [,kəʊə'lɪʃn] n coalition f.

coalman ['kəʊlmæn] (pl -men [-men]) n Br charbonnier m.

coalmine ['kəʊlmaɪn] n mine f de charbon.

coarse [kɔːs] adj 1. (rough - cloth) grossier(ère); (- hair) épais(aisse); (- skin) granuleux(euse). 2. (vulgar) grossier(ère).

coast [kəʊst] ◆ n côte f. ◆ vi (in car, on bike) avancer en roue libre.

coastal ['kəʊstl] adj côtier(ère).

coaster ['kəʊstə**r**] n (small mat) dessous m de verre.

coastguard ['kəʊstɡɑːd] n 1. (person) garde-côte m. 2. (organization): **the ~** la gendarmerie maritime.

coastline ['kəʊstlaɪn] n côte f.

coat [kəʊt] ◆ n 1. (garment) manteau m. 2. (of animal) pelage m. 3. (layer) couche f. ◆ vt: to ~ sthg (with) recouvrir qqch (de); (with paint etc) enduire qqch (de).

coat hanger n cintre m.

coating ['kəʊtɪŋ] n couche f; (CULIN) glaçage m.

coat of arms (pl coats of arms) n blason m.

coax [kəʊks] vt: to ~ sb (to do OR into doing sthg) persuader qqn (de faire qqch) à force de cajoleries.

cob [kɒb] n → **corn**.

cobbled ['kɒbld] adj pavé(e).

cobbler ['kɒblə**r**] n cordonnier m.

cobbles ['kɒblz], **cobblestones** ['kɒblstəʊnz] npl pavés mpl.

cobweb ['kɒbweb] n toile f d'araignée.

Coca-Cola® [,kəʊkə'kəʊlə] n Coca-Cola® m inv.

cocaine [kəʊ'keɪn] n cocaïne f.

cock [kɒk] ◆ n 1. (male chicken) coq m. 2. (male bird) mâle m. ◆ vt 1. (gun) armer. 2. (head) incliner. ▶ **cock up** vt sep Br v inf faire merder.

cockerel ['kɒkrəl] n jeune coq m.

cockeyed ['kɒkaɪd] adj inf 1. (lopsided) de travers. 2. (foolish) complètement fou (folle).

cockle ['kɒkl] n (shellfish) coque f.

Cockney ['kɒknɪ] (pl Cockneys) n (person) Cockney mf (personne issue des quartiers populaires de l'est de Londres).

cockpit ['kɒkpɪt] n (in plane) cockpit m.

cockroach ['kɒkrəʊtʃ] n cafard m.

cocksure [,kɒk'ʃɔː**r**] adj trop sûr(e) de soi.

cocktail ['kɒkteɪl] n cocktail m.

cock-up n v inf: to make a ~ se planter.

cocky ['kɒkɪ] adj inf suffisant(e).

cocoa ['kəʊkəʊ] n cacao m.

coconut ['kəʊkənʌt] n noix f de coco.

cod [kɒd] (pl inv) n morue f.

COD abbr of **cash on delivery**.

code [kəʊd] ◆ n code m. ◆ vt coder.

cod-liver oil n huile f de foie de morue.

coerce [kəʊ'ɜːs] vt: to ~ sb (into doing sthg) contraindre qqn (à faire qqch).

C of E abbr of **Church of England**.

coffee ['kɒfɪ] n café m.

coffee bar n Br café m.

coffee break n pause-café f.

coffee morning n Br réunion matinale pour prendre le café.

coffeepot ['kɒfɪpɒt] n cafetière f.

coffee shop n 1. Br (shop) café m. 2. Am (restaurant) ≃ café-restaurant m.

coffee table n table f basse.

coffin ['kɒfɪn] *n* cercueil *m*.

cog [kɒg] *n* (*tooth on wheel*) dent *f*; (*wheel*) roue *f* dentée.

coherent [kəʊ'hɪərənt] *adj* cohérent(e).

cohesive [kəʊ'hiːsɪv] *adj* cohésif(ive).

coil [kɔɪl] ◆ *n* **1.** (*of rope etc*) rouleau *m*; (*one loop*) boucle *f*. **2.** (ELEC) bobine *f*. **3.** Br (*contraceptive device*) stérilet *m*. ◆ *vt* enrouler. ◆ *vi* s'enrouler. ▶ **coil up** *vt sep* enrouler.

coin [kɔɪn] ◆ *n* pièce *f* (de monnaie). ◆ *vt* (*word*) inventer.

coinage ['kɔɪnɪdʒ] *n* (U) (*currency*) monnaie *f*.

coin-box *n* Br cabine *f* (publique) à pièces.

coincide [,kəʊɪn'saɪd] *vi* coïncider.

coincidence [kəʊ'ɪnsɪdəns] *n* coïncidence *f*.

coincidental [kəʊ,ɪnsɪ'dentl] *adj* de coïncidence.

coke [kəʊk] *n* **1.** (*fuel*) coke *m*. **2.** *drugs sl* coco *f*.

Coke® [kəʊk] *n* Coca® *m*.

cola ['kəʊlə] *n* cola *m*.

colander ['kʌləndər] *n* passoire *f*.

cold [kəʊld] ◆ *adj* froid(e); it's ~ il fait froid; to be ~ avoir froid; to get ~ (*person*) avoir froid; (*hot food*) refroidir; a ~ drink une boisson fraîche. ◆ *n* **1.** (*illness*) rhume *m*; to catch (a) ~ attraper un rhume, s'enrhumer. **2.** (*low temperature*) froid *m*.

cold-blooded [-'blʌdɪd] *adj fig* (*killer*) sans pitié; (*murder*) de sang-froid.

cold sore *n* bouton *m* de fièvre.

cold war *n*: the ~ la guerre froide.

coleslaw ['kəʊlslɔː] *n* chou *m* cru mayonnaise.

colic ['kɒlɪk] *n* colique *f*.

collaborate [kə'læbəreɪt] *vi* collaborer.

collapse [kə'læps] ◆ *n* (*gen*) écroulement *m*, effondrement *m*; (*of marriage*) échec *m*. ◆ *vi* **1.** (*building, person*) s'effondrer, s'écrouler; (*marriage*) échouer. **2.** (*fold up*) être pliant(e).

collapsible [kə'læpsəbl] *adj* pliant(e).

collar ['kɒlər] ◆ *n* **1.** (*on clothes*) col *m*. **2.** (*for dog*) collier *m*. **3.** (TECH) collier *m*, bague *f*. ◆ *vt inf* (*detain*) coincer.

collarbone ['kɒləbəʊn] *n* clavicule *f*.

collate [kə'leɪt] *vt* collationner.

collateral [kɒ'lætərəl] *n* (U) nantissement *m*.

colleague ['kɒliːg] *n* collègue *mf*.

collect [kə'lekt] ◆ *vt* **1.** (*gather together - gen*) rassembler, recueillir; (- *wood etc*) ramasser; to ~ o.s. se reprendre. **2.** (*as a hobby*) collectionner. **3.** (*go to get*) aller chercher, passer prendre. **4.** (*money*) recueillir; (*taxes*) percevoir. ◆ *vi* **1.** (*crowd, people*) se rassembler. **2.** (*dust, leaves, dirt*) s'amasser, s'accumuler. **3.** (*for charity, gift*) faire la quête. ◆ *adv* Am (TELEC): to call (sb) ~ téléphoner (à qqn) en PCV.

collection [kə'lekʃn] *n* **1.** (*of objects*) collection *f*. **2.** (LITERATURE) recueil *m*. **3.** (*of money*) quête *f*. **4.** (*of mail*) levée *f*.

collective [kə'lektɪv] ◆ *adj* collectif(ive). ◆ *n* coopérative *f*.

collector [kə'lektər] *n* **1.** (*as a hobby*) collectionneur *m*, -euse *f*. **2.** (*of debts, rent*) encaisseur *m*; ~ of taxes percepteur *m*.

college ['kɒlɪdʒ] *n* **1.** (*gen*) ≃ école *f* d'enseignement (technique) supérieur. **2.** (*of university*) maison communautaire d'étudiants sur un campus universitaire.

college of education *n* ≃ institut *m* de formation de maîtres.

collide [kə'laɪd] *vi*: to ~ (with) entrer en collision (avec).

collie ['kɒlɪ] *n* colley *m*.

colliery ['kɒljərɪ] *n* mine *f*.

collision [kə'lɪʒn] *n* (*crash*): ~ (with/ between) collision *f* (avec/entre); to be on a ~ course (with) *fig* aller au-devant de l'affrontement (avec).

colloquial [kə'ləʊkwɪəl] *adj* familier (ère).

collude [kə'luːd] *vi*: to ~ with sb comploter avec qqn.

Colombia [kə'lɒmbɪə] *n* Colombie *f*.

colon ['kəʊlən] *n* **1.** (ANAT) côlon *m*. **2.** (*punctuation mark*) deux-points *m inv*.

colonel ['kɜːnl] *n* colonel *m*.

colonial [kə'ləʊnjəl] *adj* colonial(e).

colonize, -ise ['kɒlənaɪz] *vt* coloniser.

colony ['kɒlənɪ] *n* colonie *f*.

color *etc* Am = **colour** *etc*.

colossal [kə'lɒsl] *adj* colossal(e).

colour Br, **color** Am ['kʌlər] ◆ *n* couleur *f*; in ~ en couleur. ◆ *adj* en couleur. ◆ *vt* **1.** (*food, liquid etc*) colorer; (*with pen, crayon*) colorier. **2.** (*dye*) teindre. **3.** *fig* (*judgment*) fausser. ◆ *vi* rougir.

colour bar *n* discrimination *f* raciale.

colour-blind *adj* daltonien(enne).

coloured Br, **colored** Am ['kʌləd] *adj* de couleur; brightly ~ de couleur vive.

colourful Br, **colorful** Am ['kʌləful] *adj* **1.** (*gen*) coloré(e). **2.** (*person, area*) haut(e) en couleur.

colouring Br, **coloring** Am ['kʌlərɪŋ]

n 1. (*dye*) colorant *m*. 2. (U) (*complexion*) teint *m*.

colour scheme *n* combinaison *f* de couleurs.

colt [kəʊlt] *n* (*young horse*) poulain *m*.

column ['kɒləm] *n* 1. (*gen*) colonne *f*. 2. (PRESS) (*article*) rubrique *f*.

columnist ['kɒləmnɪst] *n* chroniqueur *m*.

coma ['kəʊmə] *n* coma *m*.

comb [kəʊm] ◆ *n* (*for hair*) peigne *m*. ◆ *vt* 1. (*hair*) peigner. 2. (*search*) ratisser.

combat ['kɒmbæt] ◆ *n* combat *m*. ◆ *vt* combattre.

combination [,kɒmbɪ'neɪʃn] *n* combinaison *f*.

combine [*vb* kəm'baɪn, *n* 'kɒmbaɪn] ◆ *vt* (*gen*) rassembler; (*pieces*) combiner; **to ~ sthg with sthg** (*two substances*) mélanger qqch avec OR à qqch; *fig* allier qqch à qqch. ◆ *vi* (COMM & POL): **to ~ (with)** fusionner (avec). ◆ *n* 1. (*group*) cartel *m*. 2. = **combine harvester**.

combine harvester [-'hɑːvɪstə'] *n* moissonneuse-batteuse *f*.

come [kʌm] (*pt* came, *pp* come) *vi* 1. (*move*) venir; (*arrive*) arriver, venir; **the news came as a shock** la nouvelle m'a/lui a *etc* fait un choc; **coming!** j'arrive! 2. (*reach*): **to ~ up to** arriver à, monter jusqu'à; **to ~ down to** descendre OR tomber jusqu'à. 3. (*happen*) arriver, se produire; **~ what may** quoi qu'il arrive. 4. (*become*): **to ~ true** se réaliser; **to ~ undone** se défaire; **to ~ unstuck** se décoller. 5. (*begin gradually*): **to ~ to do sthg** en arriver à OR en venir à faire qqch. 6. (*be placed in order*) venir, être placé(e); **P ~s before Q** P vient avant Q, P précède Q; **she came second in the exam** elle était deuxième à l'examen. 7. *phr*: **~ to think of it** maintenant que j'y pense, réflexion faite. ▶ **to come** *adv* à venir; **in (the) days/years to ~** dans les jours/années à venir. ▶ **come about** *vi* (*happen*) arriver, se produire. ▶ **come across** *vt fus* tomber sur, trouver par hasard. ▶ **come along** *vi* 1. (*arrive by chance*) arriver. 2. (*improve - work*) avancer; (- *student*) faire des progrès. ▶ **come apart** *vi* 1. (*fall to pieces*) tomber en morceaux. 2. (*come off*) se détacher. ▶ **come at** *vt fus* (*attack*) attaquer. ▶ **come back** *vi* 1. (*in talk, writing*): **to ~ back to sthg** revenir à qqch. 2. (*memory*): **to ~ back (to sb)** revenir (à qqn). ▶ **come by** *vt fus* (*get, obtain*) trouver, dénicher. ▶ **come down** *vi*

1. (*decrease*) baisser. 2. (*descend*) descendre. ▶ **come down to** *vt fus* se résumer à, se réduire à. ▶ **come down with** *vt fus* (*cold, flu*) attraper. ▶ **come forward** *vi* se présenter. ▶ **come from** *vt fus* venir de. ▶ **come in** *vi* (*enter*) entrer. ▶ **come in for** *vt fus* (*criticism*) être l'objet de. ▶ **come into** *vt fus* 1. (*inherit*) hériter de. 2. (*begin to be*): **to ~ into being** prendre naissance, voir le jour. ▶ **come off** *vi* 1. (*button, label*) se détacher; (*stain*) s'enlever. 2. (*joke, attempt*) réussir. 3. *phr*: **~ off it!** *inf* et puis quoi encore!, non mais sans blague! ▶ **come on** *vi* 1. (*start*) commencer, apparaître. 2. (*start working - light, heating*) s'allumer. 3. (*progress, improve*) avancer, faire des progrès. 4. *phr*: **~ on!** (*expressing encouragement*) allez!; (*hurry up*) allez, dépêche-toi!; (*expressing disbelief*) allons donc! ▶ **come out** *vi* 1. (*become known*) être découvert (e). 2. (*appear - product, book, film*) sortir, paraître; (- *sun, moon, stars*) paraître. 3. (*go on strike*) faire grève. 4. (*declare publicly*): **to ~ out for/against sthg** se déclarer pour/contre qqch. ▶ **come round** *vi* (*regain consciousness*) reprendre connaissance, revenir à soi. ▶ **come through** *vt fus* survivre à. ▶ **come to** ◆ *vt fus* 1. (*reach*): **to ~ to an end** se terminer, prendre fin; **to ~ to a decision** arriver à OR prendre une décision. 2. (*amount to*) s'élever à. ◆ *vi* (*regain consciousness*) revenir à soi, reprendre connaissance. ▶ **come under** *vt fus* 1. (*be governed by*) être soumis(e) à. 2. (*suffer*): **to ~ under attack (from)** en butte aux attaques (de). ▶ **come up** *vi* 1. (*be mentioned*) survenir. 2. (*be imminent*) approcher. 3. (*happen unexpectedly*) se présenter. 4. (*sun*) se lever. ▶ **come up against** *vt fus* se heurter à. ▶ **come up to** *vt fus* 1. (*approach - in space*) s'approcher de. 2. (*equal*) répondre à. ▶ **come up with** *vt fus* (*answer, idea*) proposer.

comeback ['kʌmbæk] *n* come-back *m*; **to make a ~** (*fashion*) revenir à la mode; (*actor etc*) revenir à la scène.

comedian [kə'miːdjən] *n* (*comic*) comique *m*; (THEATRE) comédien *m*.

comedy ['kɒmədɪ] *n* comédie *f*.

comet ['kɒmɪt] *n* comète *f*.

come-uppance [,kʌm'ʌpəns] *n*: **to get one's ~** *inf* recevoir ce qu'on mérite.

comfort ['kʌmfət] ◆ *n* 1. (U) (*ease*) confort *m*. 2. (*luxury*) commodité *f*.

3. (*solace*) réconfort *m*, consolation *f*. ◆ *vt* réconforter, consoler.

comfortable ['kʌmftəbl] *adj* **1.** (*gen*) confortable. **2.** *fig* (*person - at ease, financially*) à l'aise. **3.** (*after operation, accident*): he's ~ son état est stationnaire.

comfortably ['kʌmftəbli] *adv* **1.** (*sit, sleep*) confortablement. **2.** (*without financial difficulty*) à l'aise. **3.** (*win*) aisément.

comfort station *n Am* toilettes *fpl* publiques.

comic ['kɒmik] ◆ *adj* comique, amusant(e). ◆ *n* **1.** (*comedian*) comique *m*, actrice *f* comique. **2.** (*magazine*) bande *f* dessinée.

comical ['kɒmikl] *adj* comique, drôle.

comic strip *n* bande *f* dessinée.

coming ['kʌmiŋ] ◆ *adj* (*future*) à venir, futur(e). ◆ *n*: ~s **and goings** allées et venues *fpl*.

comma ['kɒmə] *n* virgule *f*.

command [kə'mɑːnd] ◆ *n* **1.** (*order*) ordre *m*. **2.** (U) (*control*) commandement *m*. **3.** (*of language, subject*) maîtrise *f*; **to have at one's ~** (*language*) maîtriser; (*resources*) avoir à sa disposition. **4.** (COMPUT) commande *f*. ◆ *vt* **1.** (*order*): **to ~ sb to do sthg** ordonner OR commander à qqn de faire qqch. **2.** (MIL) (*control*) commander. **3.** (*deserve - respect*) inspirer; (- *attention, high price*) mériter.

commandeer [,kɒmən'diər] *vt* réquisitionner.

commander [kə'mɑːndər] *n* **1.** (*in army*) commandant *m*. **2.** (*in navy*) capitaine *m* de frégate.

commando [kə'mɑːndəʊ] (*pl* -s OR -es) *n* commando *m*.

commemorate [kə'meməreit] *vt* commémorer.

commemoration [kə,memə'reiʃn] *n* commémoration *f*.

commence [kə'mens] *fml* ◆ *vt* commencer, entamer; **to ~ doing sthg** commencer à faire qqch. ◆ *vi* commencer.

commend [kə'mend] *vt* **1.** (*praise*): **to ~ sb (on** OR **for)** féliciter qqn (de). **2.** (*recommend*): **to ~ sthg (to sb)** recommander qqch (à qqn).

commensurate [kə'menʃərət] *adj fml*: ~ **with** correspondant(e) à.

comment ['kɒment] ◆ *n* commentaire *m*, remarque *f*; **no ~!** sans commentaire! ◆ *vt*: **to ~ that** remarquer que. ◆ *vi*: **to ~ (on)** faire des commentaires OR remarques (sur).

commentary ['kɒməntri] *n* commentaire *m*.

commentator ['kɒmənteitər] *n* commentateur *m*, -trice *f*.

commerce ['kɒmɜːs] *n* (U) commerce *m*, affaires *fpl*.

commercial [kə'mɜːʃl] ◆ *adj* commercial(e). ◆ *n* publicité *f*, spot *m* publicitaire.

commercial break *n* publicités *fpl*.

commiserate [kə'mizəreit] *vi*: **to ~ with sb** témoigner de la compassion pour qqn.

commission [kə'miʃn] ◆ *n* **1.** (*money, investigative body*) commission *f*. **2.** (*order for work*) commande *f*. ◆ *vt* (*work*) commander; **to ~ sb to do sthg** charger qqn de faire qqch.

commissionaire [kə,miʃə'neər] *n Br* chasseur *m*.

commissioner [kə'miʃnər] *n* (*in police*) commissaire *m*.

commit [kə'mit] *vt* **1.** (*crime, sin etc*) commettre; **to ~ suicide** se suicider. **2.** (*promise - money, resources*) allouer; **to ~ o.s. (to sthg/to doing sthg)** s'engager (à qqch/à faire qqch). **3.** (*consign*): **to ~ sb to prison** faire incarcérer qqn; **to ~ sthg to memory** apprendre qqch par cœur.

commitment [kə'mitmənt] *n* **1.** (U) (*dedication*) engagement *m*. **2.** (*responsibility*) obligation *f*.

committee [kə'miti] *n* commission *f*, comité *m*.

commodity [kə'mɒdəti] *n* marchandise *f*.

common ['kɒmən] ◆ *adj* **1.** (*frequent*) courant(e). **2.** (*shared*): ~ **(to)** commun(e) (à). **3.** (*ordinary*) banal(e). **4.** *Br pej* (*vulgar*) vulgaire. ◆ *n* (*land*) terrain *m* communal. ▶ **in common** *adv* en commun.

common law *n* droit *m* coutumier. ▶ **common-law** *adj*: **common-law wife** concubine *f*.

commonly ['kɒmənli] *adv* (*generally*) d'une manière générale, généralement.

Common Market *n*: **the ~** le Marché commun.

commonplace ['kɒmənpleis] *adj* banal(e), ordinaire.

common room *n* (*staffroom*) salle *f* des professeurs; (*for students*) salle commune.

Commons ['kɒmənz] *npl Br*: **the ~** les Communes *fpl*, la Chambre des Communes.

common sense *n* (U) bon sens *m*.

Commonwealth ['kɒmənwelθ] *n*: **the ~** le Commonwealth.

Commonwealth of Independent States *n*: the ~ la Communauté des États Indépendants.

commotion [kə'məʊʃn] *n* remue-ménage *m*.

communal ['kɒmjʊnl] *adj* (*kitchen, garden*) commun(e); (*life etc*) communautaire, collectif(ive).

commune ['kɒmju:n] *n* communauté *f*.

communicate [kə'mju:nɪkeɪt] *vt & vi* communiquer.

communication [kə,mju:nɪ'keɪʃn] *n* contact *m*; (TELEC) communication *f*.

communication cord *n* Br sonnette *f* d'alarme.

communion [kə'mju:njən] *n* communion *f*. ▶ **Communion** *n* (U) (RELIG) communion *f*.

Communism ['kɒmjʊnɪzm] *n* communisme *m*.

Communist ['kɒmjʊnɪst] ♦ *adj* communiste. ♦ *n* communiste *mf*.

community [kə'mju:nətɪ] *n* communauté *f*.

community centre *n* foyer *m* municipal.

community charge *n* Br = impôts *mpl* locaux.

commutation ticket [,kɒmjʊ'teɪʃn-] *n* Am carte *f* de transport.

commute [kə'mju:t] ♦ *vt* (JUR) commuer. ♦ *vi* (*to work*) faire la navette pour se rendre à son travail.

commuter [kə'mju:tər] *n* personne qui fait tous les jours la navette de banlieue en ville pour se rendre à son travail.

compact [*adj* kəm'pækt, *n* 'kɒmpækt] ♦ *adj* compact(e). ♦ *n* 1. (*for face powder*) poudrier *m*. 2. Am (AUT) ~ (**car**) petite voiture *f*.

compact disc *n* compact *m* (disc *m*), disque *m* compact.

compact disc player *n* lecteur *m* de disques compacts.

companion [kəm'pænjən] *n* (*person*) camarade *mf*.

companionship [kəm'pænjənʃɪp] *n* compagnie *f*.

company ['kʌmpənɪ] *n* 1. (COMM - *gen*) société *f*; (- *insurance, airline, shipping company*) compagnie *f*. 2. (*companionship*) compagnie *f*; **to keep sb ~** tenir compagnie à qqn. 3. (*of actors*) troupe *f*.

company secretary *n* secrétaire général *m*, secrétaire générale *f*.

comparable ['kɒmprəbl] *adj*: ~ (**to** OR **with**) comparable (à).

comparative [kəm'pærətɪv] *adj* 1.

(*relative*) relatif(ive). 2. (*study, in grammar*) comparatif(ive).

comparatively [kəm'pærətɪvlɪ] *adv* (*relatively*) relativement.

compare [kəm'peər] ♦ *vt*: **to ~ sb/sthg (with), to ~ sb/sthg (to)** comparer qqn/qqch (avec), comparer qqn/qqch (à); **~d with** OR **to** par rapport à. ♦ *vi*: **to ~ (with)** être comparable (à).

comparison [kəm'pærɪsn] *n* comparaison *f*; **in ~ with** OR **to** en comparaison de, par rapport à.

compartment [kəm'pɑ:tmənt] *n* compartiment *m*.

compass ['kʌmpəs] *n* (*magnetic*) boussole *f*. ▶ **compasses** *npl*: (**a pair of**) **~es** un compas.

compassion [kəm'pæʃn] *n* compassion *f*.

compassionate [kəm'pæʃənət] *adj* compatissant(e).

compatible [kəm'pætəbl] *adj* (*gen &* COMPUT): ~ (**with**) compatible (avec).

compel [kəm'pel] *vt* (*force*): **to ~ sb (to do sthg)** obliger qqn (à faire qqch).

compelling [kəm'pelɪŋ] *adj* (*forceful*) irrésistible.

compensate ['kɒmpenseɪt] ♦ *vt*: **to ~ sb for sthg** (*financially*) dédommager OR indemniser qqn de qqch. ♦ *vi*: **to ~ for sthg** compenser qqch.

compensation [,kɒmpen'seɪʃn] *n* 1. (*money*): ~ (**for**) dédommagement *m* (pour). 2. (*way of compensating*): ~ (**for**) compensation *f* (pour).

compete [kəm'pi:t] *vi* 1. (*vie - people*): **to ~ with sb for sthg** disputer qqch à qqn; **to ~ for sthg** se disputer qqch. 2. (COMM): **to ~ (with)** être en concurrence (avec); **to ~ for sthg** se faire concurrence pour qqch. 3. (*take part*) être en compétition.

competence ['kɒmpɪtəns] *n* (U) (*proficiency*) compétence *f*, capacité *f*.

competent ['kɒmpɪtənt] *adj* compétent(e).

competition [,kɒmpɪ'tɪʃn] *n* 1. (U) (*rivalry*) rivalité *f*, concurrence *f*. 2. (COMM) concurrence *f*. 3. (*race, contest*) concours *m*, compétition *f*.

competitive [kəm'petətɪv] *adj* 1. (*person*) qui a l'esprit de compétition; (*match, sport*) de compétition. 2. (COMM - *goods*) compétitif(ive); (- *manufacturer*) concurrentiel(elle).

competitor [kəm'petɪtər] *n* concurrent *m*, -e *f*.

compile [kəm'paɪl] *vt* rédiger.

complacency [kəm'pleɪsnsɪ] *n* autosatisfaction *f*.

complain [kəm'pleɪn] *vi* 1. (*moan*): **to ~ (about)** se plaindre (de). 2. (MED): **to ~ of** se plaindre de.

complaint [kəm'pleɪnt] *n* 1. (*gen*) plainte *f*; (*in shop*) réclamation *f*. 2. (MED) affection *f*, maladie *f*.

complement [*n* 'komplɪmənt, *vb* 'komplɪ,ment] ◆ *n* 1. (*accompaniment*) accompagnement *m*. 2. (*number*) effectif *m*. 3. (GRAMM) complément *m*. ◆ *vt* aller bien avec.

complementary [,komplɪ'mentərɪ] *adj* complémentaire.

complete [kəm'pli:t] ◆ *adj* 1. (*gen*) complet(ète); **~ with** doté(e) de, muni(e) de. 2. (*finished*) achevé(e). ◆ *vt* 1. (*make whole*) compléter. 2. (*finish*) achever, terminer. 3. (*questionnaire, form*) remplir.

completely [kəm'pli:tlɪ] *adv* complètement.

completion [kəm'pli:ʃn] *n* achèvement *m*.

complex ['kompleks] ◆ *adj* complexe. ◆ *n* (*mental, of buildings*) complexe *m*.

complexion [kəm'plekʃn] *n* teint *m*.

compliance [kəm'plaɪəns] *n*: **~ (with)** conformité *f* (à).

complicate ['komplɪkeɪt] *vt* compliquer.

complicated ['komplɪkeɪtɪd] *adj* compliqué(e).

complication [,komplɪ'keɪʃn] *n* complication *f*.

compliment [*n* 'komplɪmənt, *vb* 'komplɪ,ment] ◆ *n* compliment *m*. ◆ *vt*: **to ~ sb (on)** féliciter qqn (de). ▶ **compliments** *npl fml* compliments *mpl*.

complimentary [,komplɪ'mentərɪ] *adj* 1. (*admiring*) flatteur(euse). 2. (*free*) gratuit(e).

complimentary ticket *n* billet *m* de faveur.

comply [kəm'plaɪ] *vi*: **to ~ with** se conformer à.

component [kəm'pəunənt] *n* composant *m*.

compose [kəm'pəuz] *vt* 1. (*gen*) composer; **to be ~d of** se composer de, être composé de. 2. (*calm*): **to ~ o.s.** se calmer.

composed [kəm'pəuzd] *adj* (*calm*) calme.

composer [kəm'pəuzər] *n* compositeur *m*, -trice *f*.

composition [,kompə'zɪʃn] *n* composition *f*.

compost [Br 'kompost, Am 'kompəust] *n* compost *m*.

composure [kəm'pəuʒər] *n* sang-froid *m*, calme *m*.

compound ['kompaund] *n* 1. (CHEM & LING) composé *m*. 2. (*enclosed area*) enceinte *f*.

comprehend [,komprɪ'hend] *vt* (*understand*) comprendre.

comprehension [,komprɪ'henʃn] *n* compréhension *f*.

comprehensive [,komprɪ'hensɪv] ◆ *adj* 1. (*account, report*) exhaustif(ive), détaillé(e). 2. (*insurance*) tous-risques (*inv*). ◆ *n* = **comprehensive school**.

comprehensive school *n* établissement secondaire britannique d'enseignement général.

compress [kəm'pres] *vt* 1. (*squeeze, press*) comprimer. 2. (*shorten - text*) condenser.

comprise [kəm'praɪz] *vt* comprendre; **to be ~d of** consister en, comprendre.

compromise ['komprəmaɪz] ◆ *n* compromis *m*. ◆ *vt* compromettre. ◆ *vi* transiger.

compulsion [kəm'pʌlʃn] *n* 1. (*strong desire*): **to have a ~ to do sthg** ne pas pouvoir s'empêcher de faire qqch. 2. (U) (*obligation*) obligation *f*.

compulsive [kəm'pʌlsɪv] *adj* 1. (*smoker, liar etc*) invétéré(e). 2. (*book, TV programme*) captivant(e).

compulsory [kəm'pʌlsərɪ] *adj* obligatoire.

computer [kəm'pju:tər] ◆ *n* ordinateur *m*. ◆ *comp*: **~ graphics** Infographie® *f*; **~ program** programme *m* informatique.

computer game *n* jeu *m* électronique.

computerized [kəm'pju:təraɪzd] *adj* informatisé(e).

computer science *n* informatique *f*.

computer scientist *n* informaticien *m*, -enne *f*.

computing [kəm'pju:tɪŋ] *n* informatique *f*.

comrade ['komreɪd] *n* camarade *mf*.

con [kon] *inf* ◆ *n* (*trick*) escroquerie *f*. ◆ *vt* (*trick*): **to ~ sb (out of)** escroquer qqn (de); **to ~ sb into doing sthg** persuader qqn de faire qqch (en lui mentant).

concave [,kon'keɪv] *adj* concave.

conceal [kən'si:l] *vt* cacher, dissimuler; **to ~ sthg from sb** cacher qqch à qqn.

concede [kən'si:d] ♦ vt concéder. ♦ vi céder.

conceit [kən'si:t] n (arrogance) vanité f.

conceited [kən'si:tɪd] adj vaniteux (euse).

conceive [kən'si:v] ♦ vt concevoir. ♦ vi 1. (MED) concevoir. 2. (imagine): to ~ of concevoir.

concentrate ['kɒnsəntreɪt] ♦ vt concentrer. ♦ vi: to ~ (on) se concentrer (sur).

concentration [,kɒnsən'treɪʃn] n concentration f.

concentration camp n camp m de concentration.

concept ['kɒnsept] n concept m.

concern [kən'sɜːn] ♦ n 1. (worry, anxiety) souci m, inquiétude f. 2. (COMM) (company) affaire f. ♦ vt 1. (worry) inquiéter; **to be ~ed (about)** s'inquiéter (de). 2. (involve) concerner, intéresser; **as far as I'm ~ed** en ce qui me concerne; **to be ~ed with** (subj: person) s'intéresser à; **to ~ o.s. with sthg** s'intéresser à, s'occuper de. 3. (subj: book, film) traiter de.

concerning [kən'sɜːnɪŋ] prep en ce qui concerne.

concert ['kɒnsət] n concert m.

concerted [kən'sɜːtɪd] adj (effort) concerté(e).

concert hall n salle f de concert.

concertina [,kɒnsə'ti:nə] n concertina m.

concerto [kən'tʃɜːtəʊ] (pl -s) n concerto m.

concession [kən'seʃn] n 1. (gen) concession f. 2. (special price) réduction f.

conciliatory [kən'sɪlɪətrɪ] adj conciliant(e).

concise [kən'saɪs] adj concis(e).

conclude [kən'klu:d] ♦ vt conclure. ♦ vi (meeting) prendre fin; (speaker) conclure.

conclusion [kən'klu:ʒn] n conclusion f.

conclusive [kən'klu:sɪv] adj concluant (e).

concoct [kən'kɒkt] vt préparer; fig concocter.

concoction [kən'kɒkʃn] n préparation f.

concourse ['kɒŋkɔ:s] n (hall) hall m.

concrete ['kɒŋkri:t] ♦ adj (definite) concret(ète). ♦ n (U) béton m. ♦ comp (made of concrete) en béton.

concubine ['kɒŋkjʊbaɪn] n maîtresse f.

concur [kən'kɜːr] vi (agree): **to ~ (with)** être d'accord (avec).

concurrently [kən'kʌrəntlɪ] adv simultanément.

concussion [kən'kʌʃn] n commotion f.

condemn [kən'dem] vt condamner.

condensation [,kɒnden'seɪʃn] n condensation f.

condense [kən'dens] ♦ vt condenser. ♦ vi se condenser.

condensed milk [kən'denst-] n lait m condensé.

condescending [,kɒndɪ'sendɪŋ] adj condescendant(e).

condition [kən'dɪʃn] ♦ n 1. (gen) condition f; **in (a) good/bad** ~ en bon/mauvais état; **out of** ~ pas en forme. 2. (MED) maladie f. ♦ vt (gen) conditionner.

conditional [kən'dɪʃənl] adj conditionnel(elle).

conditioner [kən'dɪʃnər] n 1. (for hair) après-shampooing m. 2. (for clothes) assouplissant m.

condolences [kən'dəʊlənsɪz] npl condoléances fpl.

condom ['kɒndəm] n préservatif m.

condominium [,kɒndə'mɪnɪəm] n Am 1. (apartment) appartement m dans un immeuble en copropriété. 2. (apartment block) immeuble m en copropriété.

condone [kən'dəʊn] vt excuser.

conducive [kən'dju:sɪv] adj: **to be ~ to sthg/to doing sthg** inciter à qqch/à faire qqch.

conduct [n 'kɒndʌkt, vb kən'dʌkt] ♦ n conduite f. ♦ vt 1. (carry out, transmit) conduire. 2. (behave): **to ~ o.s. well/badly** se conduire bien/mal. 3. (MUS) diriger.

conducted tour [kən'dʌktɪd-] n visite f guidée.

conductor [kən'dʌktər] n 1. (MUS) chef m d'orchestre. 2. (on bus) receveur m. 3. Am (on train) chef m de train.

conductress [kən'dʌktrɪs] n (on bus) receveuse f.

cone [kəʊn] n 1. (shape) cône m. 2. (for ice cream) cornet m. 3. (from tree) pomme f de pin.

confectioner [kən'fekʃnər] n confiseur m; **~'s (shop)** confiserie f.

confectionery [kən'fekʃnərɪ] n confiserie f.

confederation [kən,fedə'reɪʃn] n confédération f.

Confederation of British Industry n: **the** ~ ≃ le conseil du patronat.

confer [kən'fɜːr] ♦ vt: **to ~ sthg (on sb)**

conférer qqch (à qqn). ◆ *vi*: **to ~ (with sb on** OR **about sthg)** s'entretenir (avec qqn de qqch).

conference ['kɒnfərəns] *n* conférence *f*.

confess [kən'fes] ◆ *vt* **1.** (*admit*) avouer, confesser. **2.** (RELIG) confesser. ◆ *vi*: **to ~ (to sthg)** avouer (qqch).

confession [kən'feʃn] *n* confession *f*.

confetti [kən'feti] *n* (U) confettis *mpl*.

confide [kən'faid] *vi*: **to ~ in sb** se confier à qqn.

confidence ['kɒnfidəns] *n* **1.** (*self-assurance*) confiance *f* en soi, assurance *f*. **2.** (*trust*) confiance *f*; **to have ~ in** avoir confiance en. **3.** (*secrecy*): **in ~** en confidence. **4.** (*secret*) confidence *f*.

confidence trick *n* abus *m* de confiance.

confident ['kɒnfidənt] *adj* **1.** (*self-assured*): **to be ~** avoir confiance en soi. **2.** (*sure*) sûr(e).

confidential [,kɒnfi'denʃl] *adj* confidentiel(elle).

confine [kən'fain] *vt* **1.** (*limit*) limiter; **to ~ o.s. to** se limiter à. **2.** (*shut up*) enfermer, confiner.

confined [kən'faind] *adj* (*space, area*) restreint(e).

confinement [kən'fainmənt] *n* (*imprisonment*) emprisonnement *m*.

confines ['kɒnfainz] *npl* confins *mpl*.

confirm [kən'fɜːm] *vt* confirmer.

confirmation [,kɒnfə'meiʃn] *n* confirmation *f*.

confirmed [kən'fɜːmd] *adj* (*habitual*) invétéré(e); (*bachelor, spinster*) endurci(e).

confiscate ['kɒnfiskeit] *vt* confisquer.

conflict [*n* 'kɒnflikt, *vb* kən'flikt] ◆ *n* conflit *m*. ◆ *vi*: **to ~ (with)** s'opposer (à), être en conflit (avec).

conflicting [kən'fliktiŋ] *adj* contradictoire.

conform [kən'fɔːm] *vi*: **to ~ (to** OR **with)** se conformer (à).

confound [kən'faund] *vt* (*confuse, defeat*) déconcerter.

confront [kən'frʌnt] *vt* **1.** (*problem, enemy*) affronter. **2.** (*challenge*): **to ~ sb (with)** confronter qqn (avec).

confrontation [,kɒnfrʌn'teiʃn] *n* affrontement *m*.

confuse [kən'fjuːz] *vt* **1.** (*disconcert*) troubler; **to ~ the issue** brouiller les cartes. **2.** (*mix up*) confondre.

confused [kən'fjuːzd] *adj* **1.** (*not clear*) compliqué(e). **2.** (*disconcerted*) trou-

blé(e), désorienté(e); **I'm ~** je n'y comprends rien.

confusing [kən'fjuːziŋ] *adj* pas clair(e).

confusion [kən'fjuːʒn] *n* confusion *f*.

congeal [kən'dʒiːl] *vi* (*blood*) se coaguler.

congenial [kən'dʒiːnjəl] *adj* sympathique, agréable.

congested [kən'dʒestid] *adj* **1.** (*street, area*) encombré(e). **2.** (MED) congestionné(e).

congestion [kən'dʒestʃn] *n* **1.** (*of traffic*) encombrement *m*. **2.** (MED) congestion *f*.

conglomerate [,kən'glɒmərət] *n* (COMM) conglomérat *m*.

congratulate [kən'grætʃuleit] *vt*: **to ~ sb (on sthg/on doing sthg)** féliciter qqn (de qqch/d'avoir fait qqch).

congratulations [kən,grætʃu'leiʃənz] *npl* félicitations *fpl*.

congregate ['kɒŋgrigeit] *vi* se rassembler.

congregation [,kɒŋgri'geiʃn] *n* assemblée *f* des fidèles.

congress ['kɒŋgres] *n* (*meeting*) congrès *m*. ▶ **Congress** *n* Am (POL) le Congrès.

congressman ['kɒŋgresmən] (*pl* **-men** [-mən]) *n* Am (POL) membre *m* du Congrès.

conifer ['kɒnifər] *n* conifère *m*.

conjugation [,kɒndʒu'geiʃn] *n* (GRAMM) conjugaison *f*.

conjunction [kən'dʒʌŋkʃn] *n* (GRAMM) conjonction *f*.

conjunctivitis [kən,dʒʌŋkti'vaitis] *n* conjonctivite *f*.

conjure ['kʌndʒər] *vi* (*by magic*) faire des tours de prestidigitation. ▶ **conjure up** *vt sep* évoquer.

conjurer ['kʌndʒərər] *n* prestidigitateur *m*, -trice *f*.

conjuror ['kʌndʒərər] = **conjurer**.

conk [kɒŋk] *n inf* pif *m*. ▶ **conk out** *vi inf* tomber en panne.

conker ['kɒŋkər] *n* Br marron *m*.

conman ['kɒnmæn] (*pl* **-men** [-men]) *n* escroc *m*.

connect [kə'nekt] ◆ *vt* **1.** (*join*): **to ~ sthg (to)** relier qqch (à). **2.** (*on telephone*) mettre en communication. **3.** (*associate*) associer; **to ~ sb/sthg to, to ~ sb/sthg with** associer qqn/qqch à. **4.** (ELEC) (*to power supply*): **to ~ sthg to** brancher qqch à. ◆ *vi* (*train, plane, bus*): **to ~ (with)** assurer la correspondance (avec).

connected [kə'nektid] *adj* (*related*): **to be ~ with** avoir un rapport avec.

constant

connection [kə'nekʃn] n **1.** (relationship): ~ **(between/with)** rapport m (entre/avec); **in** ~ **with** à propos de. **2.** (ELEC) branchement m, connexion f. **3.** (on telephone) communication f. **4.** (plane, train, bus) correspondance f. **5.** (professional acquaintance) relation f.

connive [kə'naɪv] vi **1.** (plot) comploter. **2.** (allow to happen): **to** ~ **at sthg** fermer les yeux sur qqch.

connoisseur [ˌkɒnə'sɜːr] n connaisseur m, -euse f.

conquer ['kɒŋkər] vt **1.** (country etc) conquérir. **2.** (fears, inflation etc) vaincre.

conqueror ['kɒŋkərər] n conquérant m, -e f.

conquest ['kɒŋkwest] n conquête f.

cons [kɒnz] npl **1.** Br inf: **all mod** ~ tout confort. **2.** → **pro**.

conscience ['kɒnʃəns] n conscience f.

conscientious [ˌkɒnʃɪ'enʃəs] adj consciencieux(euse).

conscious ['kɒnʃəs] adj **1.** (not unconscious) conscient(e). **2.** (aware): ~ **of sthg** conscient(e) de qqch. **3.** (intentional - insult) délibéré(e), intentionnel(elle); (- effort) conscient(e).

consciousness ['kɒnʃəsnɪs] n conscience f.

conscript ['kɒnskrɪpt] (MIL) n conscrit m.

conscription [kən'skrɪpʃn] n conscription f.

consecutive [kən'sekjʊtɪv] adj consécutif(ive).

consent [kən'sent] ◆ n (U) **1.** (permission) consentement m. **2.** (agreement) accord m. ◆ vi: **to** ~ **(to)** consentir (à).

consequence ['kɒnsɪkwəns] n **1.** (result) conséquence f; **in** ~ par conséquent. **2.** (importance) importance f.

consequently ['kɒnsɪkwəntlɪ] adv par conséquent.

conservation [ˌkɒnsə'veɪʃn] n (of nature) protection f; (of buildings) conservation f; (of energy, water) économie f.

conservative [kən'sɜːvətɪv] ◆ adj **1.** (not modern) traditionnel(elle). **2.** (cautious) prudent(e). ◆ n traditionaliste mf. ▶ **Conservative** (POL) ◆ adj conservateur(trice). ◆ n conservateur m, -trice f.

Conservative Party n: **the** ~ le parti conservateur.

conservatory [kən'sɜːvətrɪ] n (of house) véranda f.

conserve [n 'kɒnsɜːv, vb kən'sɜːv] ◆ n confiture f. ◆ vt (energy, supplies) économiser; (nature, wildlife) protéger.

consider [kən'sɪdər] vt **1.** (think about) examiner. **2.** (take into account) prendre en compte; **all things ~ed** tout compte fait. **3.** (judge) considérer.

considerable [kən'sɪdrəbl] adj considérable.

considerably [kən'sɪdrəblɪ] adv considérablement.

considerate [kən'sɪdərət] adj prévenant(e).

consideration [kən,sɪdə'reɪʃn] n **1.** (U) (careful thought) réflexion f; **to take sthg into** ~ tenir compte de qqch, prendre qqch en considération; **under** ~ à l'étude. **2.** (U) (care) attention f. **3.** (factor) facteur m.

considering [kən'sɪdərɪŋ] ◆ prep étant donné. ◆ conj étant donné que.

consign [kən'saɪn] vt: **to** ~ **sb/sthg to** reléguer qqn/qqch à.

consignment [kən'saɪnmənt] n (load) expédition f.

consist [kən'sɪst] ▶ **consist in** vt fus: **to** ~ **in sthg** consister dans qqch; **to** ~ **in doing sthg** consister à faire qqch. ▶ **consist of** vt fus consister en.

consistency [kən'sɪstənsɪ] n **1.** (coherence) cohérence f. **2.** (texture) consistance f.

consistent [kən'sɪstənt] adj **1.** (regular - behaviour) conséquent(e); (- improvement) régulier(ère); (- supporter) constant(e). **2.** (coherent) cohérent(e); **to be** ~ **with** (with one's position) être compatible avec; (with the facts) correspondre avec.

consolation [ˌkɒnsə'leɪʃn] n réconfort m.

console [n 'kɒnsəʊl, vt kən'səʊl] ◆ n tableau m de commande; (COMPUT & MUS) console f. ◆ vt consoler.

consonant ['kɒnsənənt] n consonne f.

consortium [kən'sɔːtjəm] (pl **-tiums** OR **-tia** [-tjə]) n consortium m.

conspicuous [kən'spɪkjuəs] adj voyant(e), qui se remarque.

conspiracy [kən'spɪrəsɪ] n conspiration f, complot m.

conspire [kən'spaɪər] vt: **to** ~ **to do sthg** comploter de faire qqch; (subj: events) contribuer à faire qqch.

constable ['kʌnstəbl] n Br (policeman) agent m de police.

constabulary [kən'stæbjʊlərɪ] n police f.

constant ['kɒnstənt] adj **1.** (unvarying) constant(e). **2.** (recurring) continuel(elle).

constantly ['kɒnstəntlɪ] adv constamment.

consternation [ˌkɒnstə'neɪʃn] n consternation f.

constipated ['kɒnstɪpeɪtɪd] adj constipé(e).

constipation [ˌkɒnstɪ'peɪʃn] n constipation f.

constituency [kən'stɪtjʊənsɪ] n (area) circonscription f électorale.

constituent [kən'stɪtjʊənt] n 1. (voter) électeur m, -trice f. 2. (element) composant m.

constitute ['kɒnstɪtjuːt] vt 1. (form, represent) représenter, constituer. 2. (establish, set up) constituer.

constitution [ˌkɒnstɪ'tjuːʃn] n constitution f.

constraint [kən'streɪnt] n 1. (restriction): ~ (on) limitation f (à). 2. (U) (self-control) retenue f, réserve f. 3. (coercion) contrainte f.

construct [kən'strʌkt] vt construire.

construction [kən'strʌkʃn] n construction f.

constructive [kən'strʌktɪv] adj constructif(ive).

construe [kən'struː] vt fml (interpret): to ~ sthg as interpréter qqch comme.

consul ['kɒnsəl] n consul m.

consulate ['kɒnsjʊlət] n consulat m.

consult [kən'sʌlt] ◆ vt consulter. ◆ vi: to ~ with sb s'entretenir avec qqn.

consultant [kən'sʌltənt] n 1. (expert) expert-conseil m. 2. Br (hospital doctor) spécialiste mf.

consultation [ˌkɒnsəl'teɪʃn] n (meeting, discussion) entretien m.

consulting room [kən'sʌltɪŋ-] n cabinet m de consultation.

consume [kən'sjuːm] vt (food, fuel etc) consommer.

consumer [kən'sjuːməʳ] n consommateur m, -trice f.

consumer goods npl biens mpl de consommation.

consumer society n société f de consommation.

consuming [kən'sjuːmɪŋ] adj dévorant(e).

consummate ['kɒnsəmeɪt] vt consommer.

consumption [kən'sʌmpʃn] n (use) consommation f.

cont. abbr of **continued**.

contact ['kɒntækt] ◆ n 1. (U) (touch, communication) contact m; in ~ (with sb) en rapport OR contact (avec qqn); to

lose ~ with sb perdre le contact avec qqn. 2. (person) relation f, contact m. ◆ vt contacter, prendre contact avec; (by phone) joindre, contacter.

contact lens n verre m de contact, lentille f (cornéenne).

contagious [kən'teɪdʒəs] adj contagieux(euse).

contain [kən'teɪn] vt 1. (hold, include) contenir, renfermer. 2. fml (control) contenir; (epidemic) circonscrire.

container [kən'teɪnəʳ] n 1. (box, bottle etc) récipient m. 2. (for transporting goods) conteneur m, container m.

contaminate [kən'tæmɪneɪt] vt contaminer.

cont'd abbr of **continued**.

contemplate ['kɒntempleɪt] ◆ vt 1. (consider) envisager. 2. fml (look at) contempler. ◆ vi (consider) méditer.

contemporary [kən'tempərərɪ] ◆ adj contemporain(e). ◆ n contemporain m, -e f.

contempt [kən'tempt] n 1. (scorn): ~ (for) mépris m (pour). 2. (JUR): ~ (of court) outrage m à la cour.

contemptuous [kən'temptʃʊəs] adj méprisant(e); ~ of sthg dédaigneux (euse) de qqch.

contend [kən'tend] vi 1. (deal): to ~ with sthg faire face à qqch. 2. (compete): to ~ for (subj: several people) se disputer; (subj: one person) se battre pour; to ~ against lutter contre.

contender [kən'tendəʳ] n (in election) candidat m, -e f; (in competition) concurrent m, -e f; (in boxing etc) prétendant m, -e f.

content [n 'kɒntent, adj & vb kən'tent] ◆ adj: ~ (with) satisfait(e) (de), content (e) (de); to be ~ to do sthg ne pas demander mieux que de faire qqch. ◆ n 1. (amount) teneur f. 2. (subject matter) contenu m. ◆ vt: to ~ o.s. with sthg/ with doing sthg se contenter de qqch/ de faire qqch. ▶ **contents** npl 1. (of container, document) contenu m. 2. (at front of book) table f des matières.

contented [kən'tentɪd] adj satisfait(e).

contention [kən'tenʃn] n fml 1. (argument, assertion) assertion f, affirmation f. 2. (U) (disagreement) dispute f.

contest [n 'kɒntest, vb kən'test] ◆ n 1. (competition) concours m. 2. (for power, control) combat m, lutte f. ◆ vt 1. (compete for) disputer. 2. (dispute) contester.

contestant [kən'testənt] n concurrent m, -e f.

context ['kɒntekst] *n* contexte *m*.
continent ['kɒntɪnənt] *n* continent *m*.
▶ **Continent** *n* Br: **the Continent**
l'Europe *f* continentale.
continental [,kɒntɪ'nentl] *adj* (GEOGR)
continental(e).
continental breakfast *n* petit déjeuner *m* (*par opposition à 'English breakfast'*).
continental quilt *n* Br couette *f*.
contingency [kən'tɪndʒənsɪ] *n* éventualité *f*.
contingency plan *n* plan *m* d'urgence.
continual [kən'tɪnjʊəl] *adj* continuel
(elle).
continually [kən'tɪnjʊəlɪ] *adv* continuellement.
continuation [kən,tɪnjʊ'eɪʃn] *n* 1. (U)
(*act*) continuation *f*. 2. (*sequel*) suite *f*.
continue [kən'tɪnju:] ◆ *vt* 1. (*carry on*)
continuer, poursuivre; **to ~ doing** OR **to
do sthg** continuer à OR de faire qqch.
2. (*after an interruption*) reprendre. ◆ *vi*
1. (*carry on*) continuer; **to ~ with sthg**
poursuivre qqch, continuer qqch.
2. (*after an interruption*) reprendre, se
poursuivre.
continuous [kən'tɪnjʊəs] *adj* conti-
nu(e).
continuously [kən'tɪnjʊəslɪ] *adv* sans
arrêt, continuellement.
contort [kən'tɔ:t] *vt* tordre.
contortion [kən'tɔ:ʃn] *n* 1. (U) (*twisting*) torsion *f*. 2. (*position*) contorsion *f*.
contour ['kɒn,tʊər] *n* 1. (*outline*)
contour *m*. 2. (*on map*) courbe *f* de niveau.
contraband ['kɒntrəbænd] ◆ *adj* de
contrebande. ◆ *n* contrebande *f*.
contraception [,kɒntrə'sepʃn] *n*
contraception *f*.
contraceptive [,kɒntrə'septɪv] ◆ *adj*
(*method, device*) anticonceptionnel(elle),
contraceptif(ive); (*advice*) sur la contraception. ◆ *n* contraceptif *m*.
contract [*n* 'kɒntrækt, *vb* kən'trækt] ◆ *n*
contrat *m*. ◆ *vt* 1. (*gen*) contracter.
2. (COMM): **to ~ sb (to do sthg)** passer un
contrat avec qqn (pour faire qqch); **to ~
to do sthg** s'engager par contrat à faire
qqch. ◆ *vi* (*decrease in size, length*) se
contracter.
contraction [kən'trækʃn] *n* contraction *f*.
contractor [kən'træktər] *n* entrepreneur *m*.
contradict [,kɒntrə'dɪkt] *vt* contredire.

contradiction [,kɒntrə'dɪkʃn] *n*
contradiction *f*.
contraflow ['kɒntrəfləʊ] *n* circulation
f à contre-sens.
contraption [kən'træpʃn] *n* machin *m*,
truc *m*.
contrary ['kɒntrərɪ, *adj sense* 2 kən-
'treərɪ] ◆ *adj* 1. (*opposite*): **~ (to)** contraire
(à), opposé(e) (à). 2. (*awkward*) contra-
riant(e). ◆ *n* contraire *m*; **on the ~** au
contraire. ▶ **contrary to** *prep* contrairement à.
contrast [*n* 'kɒntrɑ:st, *vb* kən'trɑ:st]
◆ *n* contraste *m*; **by** OR **in ~** par
contraste; **in ~ with** OR **to sthg** par
contraste avec qqch. ◆ *vt* contraster.
◆ *vi*: **to ~ (with)** faire contraste (avec).
contravene [,kɒntrə'vi:n] *vt* enfreindre, transgresser.
contribute [kən'trɪbju:t] ◆ *vt* (*money*)
apporter; (*help, advice, ideas*) donner, apporter. ◆ *vi* 1. (*gen*): **to ~ (to)** contribuer
(à). 2. (*write material*): **to ~ to** collaborer
à.
contribution [,kɒntrɪ'bju:ʃn] *n* 1. (*of
money*): **~ (to)** cotisation *f* (à), contribution *f* (à). 2. (*article*) article *m*.
contributor [kən'trɪbjutər] *n* 1. (*of
money*) donateur *m*, -trice *f*. 2. (*to magazine, newspaper*) collaborateur *m*, -trice
f.
contrive [kən'traɪv] *vt fml* 1. (*engineer*)
combiner. 2. (*manage*): **to ~ to do sthg** se
débrouiller pour faire qqch.
contrived [kən'traɪvd] *adj* tiré(e) par
les cheveux.
control [kən'trəʊl] ◆ *n* (*gen*) contrôle
m; (*of traffic*) régulation *f*; **to get sb/sthg
under ~** maîtriser qqn/qqch; **to be in ~
of sthg** (*subj: boss, government*) diriger
qqch; (*subj: army*) avoir le contrôle de
qqch; (*of emotions, situation*) maîtriser
qqch; **to lose ~** (*of emotions*) perdre le
contrôle. ◆ *vt* 1. (*company, country*) être
à la tête de, diriger. 2. (*operate*) commander, faire fonctionner. 3. (*restrict,
restrain - disease*) enrayer, juguler; (*- inflation*) mettre un frein à, contenir; (*- children*) tenir; (*- crowd*) contenir; (*- emotions*)
maîtriser, contenir; **to ~ o.s.** se maîtriser, se contrôler. ▶ **controls** *npl* (*of
machine, vehicle*) commandes *fpl*.
controller [kən'trəʊlər] *n* (*person*)
contrôleur *m*.
control panel *n* tableau *m* de bord.
control tower *n* tour *f* de contrôle.
controversial [,kɒntrə'vɜ:ʃl] *adj* (*writer,
theory etc*) controversé(e); **to be ~** don-

ner matière à controverse.

controversy ['kɒntrəvɜːsɪ, Br kən-'trɒvəsɪ] n controverse f, polémique f.

convalesce [ˌkɒnvə'les] vi se remettre d'une maladie, relever de maladie.

convene [kən'viːn] ◆ vt convoquer, réunir. ◆ vi se réunir, s'assembler.

convenience [kən'viːnjəns] n 1. (usefulness) commodité f. 2. (personal comfort, advantage) agrément m, confort m; **at your earliest ~** fml dès que possible.

convenience store n Am petit supermarché de quartier.

convenient [kən'viːnjənt] adj 1. (suitable) qui convient. 2. (handy) pratique, commode.

convent ['kɒnvənt] n couvent m.

convention [kən'venʃn] n 1. (agreement, assembly) convention f. 2. (practice) usage m, convention f.

conventional [kən'venʃənl] adj conventionnel(elle).

converge [kən'vɜːdʒ] vi: **to ~ (on)** converger (sur).

conversant [kən'vɜːsənt] adj fml: **~ with sthg** familiarisé(e) avec qqch, qui connaît bien qqch.

conversation [ˌkɒnvə'seɪʃn] n conversation f.

converse [n 'kɒnvɜːs, vb kən'vɜːs] ◆ n (opposite): **the ~** le contraire, l'inverse m. ◆ vi fml converser.

conversely [kən'vɜːslɪ] adv fml inversement.

conversion [kən'vɜːʃn] n 1. (changing, in religious beliefs) conversion f. 2. (in building) aménagement m, transformation f. 3. (RUGBY) transformation f.

convert [vb kən'vɜːt, n 'kɒnvɜːt] ◆ vt 1. (change): **to ~ sthg to** OR **into** convertir qqch en; **to ~ sb (to)** (RELIG) convertir qqn (à). 2. (building, ship): **to ~ sthg to** OR **into** transformer qqch en, aménager qqch en. ◆ vi: **to ~ from sthg to sthg** passer de qqch à qqch. ◆ n converti m, -e f.

convertible [kən'vɜːtəbl] n (voiture) décapotable f.

convex [kɒn'veks] adj convexe.

convey [kən'veɪ] vt 1. fml (transport) transporter. 2. (express): **to ~ sthg (to sb)** communiquer qqch (à qqn).

conveyer belt [kən'veɪər-] n convoyeur m, tapis m roulant.

convict [n 'kɒnvɪkt, vb kən'vɪkt] ◆ n détenu m. ◆ vt: **to ~ sb of sthg** reconnaître qqn coupable de qqch.

conviction [kən'vɪkʃn] n 1. (belief, fervour) conviction f. 2. (JUR) (of criminal) condamnation f.

convince [kən'vɪns] vt convaincre, persuader; **to ~ sb of sthg/to do sthg** convaincre qqn de qqch/de faire qqch, persuader qqn de qqch/de faire qqch.

convincing [kən'vɪnsɪŋ] adj 1. (persuasive) convaincant(e). 2. (resounding - victory) retentissant(e), éclatant(e).

convoluted ['kɒnvəluːtɪd] adj (tortuous) compliqué(e).

convoy ['kɒnvɔɪ] n convoi m.

convulse [kən'vʌls] vt (person): **to be ~d with** se tordre de.

convulsion [kən'vʌlʃn] n (MED) convulsion f.

coo [kuː] vi roucouler.

cook [kʊk] ◆ n cuisinier m, -ère f. ◆ vt (food) faire cuire; (meal) préparer. ◆ vi (person) cuisiner, faire la cuisine; (food) cuire.

cookbook ['kʊk,bʊk] = **cookery book**.

cooker ['kʊkər] n (stove) cuisinière f.

cookery ['kʊkərɪ] n cuisine f.

cookery book n livre m de cuisine.

cookie ['kʊkɪ] n Am (biscuit) biscuit m, gâteau m sec.

cooking ['kʊkɪŋ] n cuisine f.

cool [kuːl] ◆ adj 1. (not warm) frais (fraîche); (dress) léger(ère). 2. (calm) calme. 3. (unfriendly) froid(e). 4. inf (excellent) génial(e); (trendy) branché(e). ◆ vt faire refroidir. ◆ vi (become less warm) refroidir. ◆ n (calm): **to keep/lose one's ~** garder/perdre son sang-froid, garder/perdre son calme. ▶ **cool down** vi (become less warm - food, engine) refroidir; (- person) se rafraîchir.

cool box n glacière f.

coop [kuːp] n poulailler m. ▶ **coop up** vt sep inf confiner.

cooperate [kəʊ'ɒpəreɪt] vi: **to ~ (with sb/sthg)** coopérer (avec qqn/à qqch), collaborer (avec qqn/à qqch).

cooperation [kəʊˌɒpə'reɪʃn] n (U) 1. (collaboration) coopération f, collaboration f. 2. (assistance) aide f, concours m.

cooperative [kəʊ'ɒpərətɪv] ◆ adj coopératif(ive). ◆ n coopérative f.

coordinate [n kəʊ'ɔːdɪnət, vt kəʊ-'ɔːdɪneɪt] ◆ n (on map, graph) coordonnée f. ◆ vt coordonner. ▶ **coordinates** npl (clothes) coordonnés mpl.

coordination [kəʊˌɔːdɪ'neɪʃn] n coordination f.

cop [kɒp] n inf flic m.

cope [kəʊp] *vi* se débrouiller; **to ~ with** faire face à.

Copenhagen [ˌkəʊpən'heɪgən] *n* Copenhague.

copier ['kɒpɪər] *n* copieur *m*, photocopieur *m*.

cop-out *n inf* dérobade *f*, échappatoire *f*.

copper ['kɒpər] *n* **1.** (*metal*) cuivre *m*. **2.** Br *inf* (*policeman*) flic *m*.

coppice ['kɒpɪs], **copse** [kɒps] *n* taillis *m*.

copy ['kɒpɪ] ◆ *n* **1.** (*imitation*) copie *f*, reproduction *f*. **2.** (*duplicate*) copie *f*. **3.** (*of book*) exemplaire *m*; (*of magazine*) numéro *m*. ◆ *vt* **1.** (*imitate*) copier, imiter. **2.** (*photocopy*) photocopier.

copyright ['kɒpɪraɪt] *n* copyright *m*, droit *m* d'auteur.

coral ['kɒrəl] *n* corail *m*.

cord [kɔːd] *n* **1.** (*string*) ficelle *f*; (*rope*) corde *f*. **2.** (*electric*) fil *m*, cordon *m*. **3.** (*fabric*) velours *m* côtelé. ▸ **cords** *npl* pantalon *m* en velours côtelé.

cordial ['kɔːdjəl] ◆ *adj* cordial(e), chaleureux(euse). ◆ *n* cordial *m*.

cordon ['kɔːdn] *n* cordon *m*. ▸ **cordon off** *vt sep* barrer (par un cordon de police).

corduroy ['kɔːdərɔɪ] *n* velours *m* côtelé.

core [kɔːr] ◆ *n* **1.** (*of apple etc*) trognon *m*, cœur *m*. **2.** (*of cable, Earth*) noyau *m*; (*of nuclear reactor*) cœur *m*. **3.** *fig* (*of people*) noyau *m*; (*of problem, policy*) essentiel *m*. ◆ *vt* enlever le cœur de.

Corfu [kɔː'fuː] *n* Corfou.

corgi ['kɔːgɪ] (*pl* -s) *n* corgi *m*.

coriander [ˌkɒrɪ'ændər] *n* coriandre *f*.

cork [kɔːk] *n* **1.** (*material*) liège *m*. **2.** (*stopper*) bouchon *m*.

corkscrew ['kɔːkskruː] *n* tirebouchon *m*.

corn [kɔːn] *n* **1.** Br (*wheat*) grain *m*; Am (*maize*) maïs *m*; **~ on the cob** épi *m* de maïs cuit. **2.** (*on foot*) cor *m*.

cornea ['kɔːnɪə] (*pl* -s) *n* cornée *f*.

corned beef [kɔːnd-] *n* corned-beef *m inv*.

corner ['kɔːnər] ◆ *n* **1.** (*angle*) coin *m*, angle *m*; **to cut ~s** *fig* brûler les étapes. **2.** (*bend in road*) virage *m*, tournant *m*. **3.** (FTBL) corner *m*. ◆ *vt* **1.** (*person, animal*) acculer. **2.** (*market*) accaparer.

corner shop *n* magasin *m* du coin OR du quartier.

cornerstone ['kɔːnəstəʊn] *n fig* pierre *f* angulaire.

cornet ['kɔːnɪt] *n* **1.** (*instrument*) cornet *m* à pistons. **2.** Br (*ice-cream cone*) cornet *m* de glace.

cornflakes ['kɔːnfleɪks] *npl* cornflakes *mpl*.

cornflour Br ['kɔːnflaʊər], **cornstarch** Am ['kɔːnstɑːtʃ] *n* ≃ Maïzena® *f*, fécule *f* de maïs.

Cornwall ['kɔːnwɔːl] *n* Cornouailles *f*.

corny ['kɔːnɪ] *adj inf* (*joke*) peu original(e); (*story, film*) à l'eau de rose.

coronary ['kɒrənrɪ], **coronary thrombosis** [-θrɒm'bəʊsɪs] (*pl* **coronary thromboses** [-siːz]) *n* infarctus *m* du myocarde.

coronation [ˌkɒrə'neɪʃn] *n* couronnement *m*.

coroner ['kɒrənər] *n* coroner *m*.

corporal ['kɔːpərəl] *n* (*gen*) caporal *m*; (*in artillery*) brigadier *m*.

corporal punishment *n* châtiment *m* corporel.

corporate ['kɔːpərət] *adj* **1.** (*business*) corporatif(ive), de société. **2.** (*collective*) collectif(ive).

corporation [ˌkɔːpə'reɪʃn] *n* **1.** (*town council*) conseil *m* municipal. **2.** (*large company*) compagnie *f*, société *f* enregistrée.

corps [kɔːr] (*pl inv*) *n* corps *m*.

corpse [kɔːps] *n* cadavre *m*.

correct [kə'rekt] ◆ *adj* **1.** (*accurate*) correct(e), exact(e); **you're quite ~** tu as parfaitement raison. **2.** (*proper, socially acceptable*) correct(e), convenable. ◆ *vt* corriger.

correction [kə'rekʃn] *n* correction *f*.

correlation [ˌkɒrə'leɪʃn] *n* corrélation *f*.

correspond [ˌkɒrɪ'spɒnd] *vi* **1.** (*gen*): **to ~ (with OR to)** correspondre (à). **2.** (*write letters*): **to ~ (with sb)** correspondre (avec qqn).

correspondence [ˌkɒrɪ'spɒndəns] *n*: **~ (with)** correspondance *f* (avec).

correspondence course *n* cours *m* par correspondance.

correspondent [ˌkɒrɪ'spɒndənt] *n* correspondant *m*, -e *f*.

corridor ['kɒrɪdɔːr] *n* (*in building*) couloir *m*, corridor *m*.

corroborate [kə'rɒbəreɪt] *vt* corroborer.

corrode [kə'rəʊd] ◆ *vt* corroder, attaquer. ◆ *vi* se corroder.

corrosion [kə'rəʊʒn] *n* corrosion *f*.

corrugated ['kɒrəgeɪtɪd] *adj* ondulé(e).

corrugated iron n tôle f ondulée.

corrupt [kə'rʌpt] ◆ adj (gen & COMPUT) corrompu(e). ◆ vt corrompre, dépraver.

corruption [kə'rʌpʃn] n corruption f.

corset ['kɔːsɪt] n corset m.

Corsica ['kɔːsɪkə] n Corse f.

cosh [kɒʃ] n matraque f, gourdin m.

cosmetic [kɒz'metɪk] ◆ n cosmétique m, produit m de beauté. ◆ adj fig superficiel(elle).

cosmopolitan [kɒzmə'pɒlɪtn] adj cosmopolite.

cosset ['kɒsɪt] vt dorloter, choyer.

cost [kɒst] (pt & pp cost OR -ed) ◆ n lit & fig coût m; **at all ~s** à tout prix, coûte que coûte. ◆ vt 1. lit & fig coûter; **it ~ me £10** ça m'a coûté 10 livres. 2. (COMM) (estimate) évaluer le coût de. ◆ vi coûter; **how much does it ~?** combien ça coûte?, combien cela coûte-t-il? ▶ **costs** npl (JUR) dépens mpl.

co-star ['kəʊ-] n partenaire mf.

Costa Rica [,kɒstə'riːkə] n Costa Rica m.

cost-effective adj rentable.

costing ['kɒstɪŋ] n évaluation f du coût.

costly ['kɒstlɪ] adj lit & fig coûteux (euse).

cost of living n: **the ~** le coût de la vie.

cost price n prix m coûtant.

costume ['kɒstjuːm] n 1. (gen) costume m. 2. (swimming costume) maillot m (de bain).

costume jewellery n (U) bijoux mpl fantaisie.

cosy Br, **cozy** Am ['kəʊzɪ] adj (house, room) douillet(ette); (atmosphere) chaleureux(euse); **to feel ~** se sentir bien au chaud.

cot [kɒt] n 1. Br (for child) lit m d'enfant, petit lit. 2. Am (folding bed) lit m de camp.

cottage ['kɒtɪdʒ] n cottage m, petite maison f (de campagne).

cottage cheese n fromage m blanc.

cottage pie n Br ≃ hachis m Parmentier.

cotton ['kɒtn] ◆ n (gen) coton m. ◆ comp de coton. ▶ **cotton on** vi inf: **to ~ on (to sthg)** piger (qqch), comprendre (qqch).

cotton candy n Am barbe f à papa.

cotton wool n ouate f, coton m hydrophile.

couch [kautʃ] n 1. (sofa) canapé m. 2. (in doctor's surgery) lit m.

cough [kɒf] ◆ n toux f. ◆ vi tousser.

cough mixture n Br sirop m pour la toux.

cough sweet n Br pastille f pour la toux.

cough syrup = **cough mixture**.

could [kud] pt → **can²**.

couldn't ['kudnt] = **could not**.

could've ['kudəv] = **could have**.

council ['kaunsl] n conseil m municipal.

council estate n quartier m de logements sociaux.

council house n Br maison f qui appartient à la municipalité, ≃ H.L.M. m or f.

councillor ['kaunsələr] n conseiller municipal m, conseillère municipale f.

council tax n Br ≃ impôts mpl locaux.

counsel ['kaunsl] n 1. (U) fml (advice) conseil m. 2. (lawyer) avocat m, -e f.

counsellor Br, **counselor** Am ['kaunsələr] n 1. (gen) conseiller m, -ère f. 2. (lawyer) avocat m.

count [kaunt] ◆ n 1. (total) total m; **to keep ~ of** tenir le compte de; **to lose ~ of sthg** ne plus savoir qqch, ne pas se rappeler qqch. 2. (aristocrat) comte m. ◆ vt 1. (gen) compter. 2. (consider): **to ~ sb as sthg** considérer qqn comme qqch. ◆ vi (gen) compter; **to ~ (up) to** compter jusqu'à. ▶ **count against** vt fus jouer contre. ▶ **count (up)on** vt fus 1. (rely on) compter sur. 2. (expect) s'attendre à, prévoir. ▶ **count up** vt fus compter.

countdown ['kauntdaun] n compte m à rebours.

counter ['kauntər] ◆ n 1. (in shop, bank) comptoir m. 2. (in board game) pion m. ◆ vt: **to ~ sthg (with)** (criticism etc) riposter à qqch (par). ◆ vi: **to ~ with sthg/by doing sthg** riposter par qqch/en faisant qqch. ▶ **counter to** adv contrairement à; **to run ~ to** aller à l'encontre de.

counteract [,kauntə'rækt] vt contrebalancer, compenser.

counterattack ['kauntərə,tæk] vt & vi contre-attaquer.

counterclockwise [,kauntə'klɒkwaɪz] adj & adv Am dans le sens inverse des aiguilles d'une montre.

counterfeit ['kauntəfɪt] ◆ adj faux (fausse). ◆ vt contrefaire.

counterfoil ['kauntəfɔɪl] n talon m, souche f.

countermand [,kauntə'maːnd] vt annuler.

counterpart ['kauntəpɑːt] n (person) homologue mf; (thing) équivalent m, -e f.

counterproductive [ˌkauntəprə'dʌktɪv] adj qui a l'effet inverse.

countess ['kauntɪs] n comtesse f.

countless ['kauntlɪs] adj innombrable.

country ['kʌntrɪ] n 1. (nation) pays m. 2. (countryside): **the ~** la campagne; **in the ~** à la campagne. 3. (region) région f; (terrain) terrain m.

country dancing n (U) danse f folklorique.

country house n manoir m.

countryman ['kʌntrɪmən] (pl -men [-mən]) n (from same country) compatriote m.

country park n Br parc m naturel.

countryside ['kʌntrɪsaɪd] n campagne f.

county ['kauntɪ] n comté m.

county council n Br conseil m général.

coup [kuː] n 1. (rebellion): **~ (d'état)** coup m d'État. 2. (success) coup m (de maître), beau coup m.

couple ['kʌpl] ◆ n 1. (in relationship) couple m. 2. (small number): **a ~ (of)** (two) deux; (a few) quelques, deux ou trois. ◆ vt (join): **to ~ sthg (to)** atteler qqch (à).

coupon ['kuːpɒn] n 1. (voucher) bon m. 2. (form) coupon m.

courage ['kʌrɪdʒ] n courage m; **to take ~ (from sthg)** être encouragé (par qqch).

courgette [kɔː'ʒet] n Br courgette f.

courier ['kʊrɪər] n 1. (on holiday) guide m, accompagnateur m, -trice f. 2. (to deliver letters, packages) courrier m, messager m.

course [kɔːs] n 1. (gen & SCH) cours m; **~ of action** ligne f de conduite; **in the ~ of** au cours de. 2. (MED) (of injections) série f; **~ of treatment** traitement m. 3. (of ship, plane) route f; **to be on ~** suivre le cap fixé; fig (on target) être dans la bonne voie; **to be off ~** faire fausse route. 4. (of meal) plat m. 5. (SPORT) terrain m. ► **of course** adv 1. (inevitably, not surprisingly) évidemment, naturellement. 2. (certainly) bien sûr; **of ~ not** bien sûr que non.

coursebook ['kɔːsbʊk] n livre m de cours.

coursework ['kɔːswɜːk] n (U) travail m personnel.

court [kɔːt] ◆ n 1. (JUR - building, room) cour f, tribunal m; (- judge, jury etc): **the ~** la justice; **to take sb to ~** faire un procès à qqn. 2. (SPORT - gen) court m; (- for

basketball, volleyball) terrain m. 3. (courtyard, of monarch) cour f. ◆ vi dated sortir ensemble, se fréquenter.

courteous ['kɜːtjəs] adj courtois(e), poli(e).

courtesy ['kɜːtɪsɪ] n courtoisie f, politesse f. ► **(by) courtesy of** prep avec la permission de.

courthouse ['kɔːthaʊs, pl -haʊzɪz] n Am palais m de justice, tribunal m.

courtier ['kɔːtjər] n courtisan m.

court-martial (pl **court-martials** OR **courts-martial**) n cour f martiale.

courtroom ['kɔːtrʊm] n salle f de tribunal.

courtyard ['kɔːtjɑːd] n cour f.

cousin ['kʌzn] n cousin m, -e f.

cove [kəʊv] n (bay) crique f.

covenant ['kʌvənənt] n (of money) engagement m contractuel.

cover ['kʌvər] ◆ n 1. (covering - of furniture) housse f; (- of pan) couvercle m; (- of book, magazine) couverture f. 2. (blanket) couverture f. 3. (protection, shelter) abri m; **to take ~** s'abriter, se mettre à l'abri; **under ~** à l'abri, à couvert. 4. (concealment) couverture f. 5. (insurance) couverture f, garantie f. ◆ vt 1. (gen): **to ~ sthg (with)** couvrir qqch (de). 2. (insure): **to ~ sb against** couvrir qqn en cas de. 3. (include) englober, comprendre. ► **cover up** vt sep fig (scandal etc) dissimuler, cacher.

coverage ['kʌvərɪdʒ] n (of news) reportage m.

cover charge n couvert m.

covering ['kʌvərɪŋ] n (of floor etc) revêtement m; (of snow, dust) couche f.

covering letter Br, **cover letter** Am n lettre f explicative OR d'accompagnement.

cover note n Br lettre f de couverture, attestation f provisoire d'assurance.

covert ['kʌvət] adj (activity) clandestin(e); (look, glance) furtif(ive).

cover-up n étouffement m.

covet ['kʌvɪt] vt convoiter.

cow [kaʊ] ◆ n 1. (female type of cattle) vache f. 2. (female elephant etc) femelle f. ◆ vt intimider, effrayer.

coward ['kaʊəd] n lâche mf.

cowardly ['kaʊədlɪ] adj lâche.

cowboy ['kaʊbɔɪ] n (cattlehand) cowboy m.

cower ['kaʊər] vi se recroqueviller.

cox [kɒks], **coxswain** ['kɒksən] n barreur m.

coy [kɔɪ] *adj* qui fait le/la timide.

cozy Am = **cosy**.

CPA *n abbr of* **certified public accountant**.

CPS (*abbr of* Crown Prosecution Service) *n* = ministère *m* public.

crab [kræb] *n* crabe *m*.

crab apple *n* pomme *f* sauvage.

crack [kræk] ◆ *n* 1. (*in glass, pottery*) fêlure *f*; (*in wall, wood, ground*) fissure *f*; (*in skin*) gerçure *f*. 2. (*gap - in door*) entrebâillement *m*; (*- in curtains*) interstice *m*. 3. (*noise - of whip*) claquement *m*; (*- of twigs*) craquement *m*. 4. *inf* (*attempt*): **to have a ~ at sthg** tenter qqch, essayer de faire qqch. 5. *drugs sl* crack *m*. ◆ *adj* (*troops etc*) de première classe. ◆ *vt* 1. (*glass, plate*) fêler; (*wood, wall*) fissurer. 2. (*egg, nut*) casser. 3. (*whip*) faire claquer. 4. (*bang, hit sharply*): **to ~ one's head** se cogner la tête. 5. (*solve - problem*) résoudre; (*- code*) déchiffrer. 6. *inf* (*make - joke*) faire. ◆ *vi* 1. (*glass, pottery*) se fêler; (*ground, wood, wall*) se fissurer; (*skin*) se crevasser, se gercer. 2. (*break down - person*) craquer, s'effondrer; (*- resistance*) se briser. ► **crack down** *vi*: **to ~ down (on)** sévir (contre). ► **crack up** *vi* craquer.

cracker [ˈkrækəʳ] *n* 1. (*biscuit*) cracker *m*, craquelin *m*. 2. Br (*for Christmas*) diablotin *m*.

crackers [ˈkrækəz] *adj* Br *inf* dingue, cinglé(e).

crackle [ˈkrækl] *vi* (*frying food*) grésiller; (*fire*) crépiter; (*radio etc*) crachoter.

cradle [ˈkreɪdl] ◆ *n* berceau *m*; (TECH) nacelle *f*. ◆ *vt* (*baby*) bercer; (*object*) tenir délicatement.

craft [krɑːft] (*pl sense 2 inv*) *n* 1. (*trade, skill*) métier *m*. 2. (*boat*) embarcation *f*.

craftsman [ˈkrɑːftsmən] (*pl -men* [-mən]) *n* artisan *m*, homme *m* de métier.

craftsmanship [ˈkrɑːftsmənʃɪp] *n* (U) 1. (*skill*) dextérité *f*, art *m*. 2. (*skilled work*) travail *m*, exécution *f*.

craftsmen *pl* → **craftsman**.

crafty [ˈkrɑːftɪ] *adj* rusé(e).

crag [kræg] *n* rocher *m* escarpé.

cram [kræm] ◆ *vt* 1. (*stuff*) fourrer. 2. (*overfill*): **to ~ sthg with** bourrer qqch de. ◆ *vi* bachoter.

cramp [kræmp] ◆ *n* crampe *f*. ◆ *vt* gêner, entraver.

cranberry [ˈkrænbərɪ] *n* canneberge *f*.

crane [kreɪn] *n* grue *f*.

crank [kræŋk] ◆ *n* 1. (TECH) manivelle *f*. 2. *inf* (*person*) excentrique *mf*. ◆ *vt* (*wind - handle*) tourner; (*- mechanism*) remonter (à la manivelle).

crankshaft [ˈkræŋkʃɑːft] *n* vilebrequin *m*.

cranny [ˈkrænɪ] *n* → **nook**.

crap [kræp] *n* (U) *v inf* merde *f*; **it's a load of ~** tout ça, c'est des conneries.

crash [kræʃ] ◆ *n* 1. (*accident*) accident *m*. 2. (*noise*) fracas *m*. ◆ *vt*: **I ~ed the car** j'ai eu un accident avec la voiture. ◆ *vi* 1. (*cars, trains*) se percuter, se rentrer dedans; (*car, train*) avoir un accident; (*plane*) s'écraser; **to ~ into** (*wall*) rentrer dans, emboutir. 2. (FIN - *business, company*) faire faillite; (*- stock market*) s'effondrer.

crash course *n* cours *m* intensif.

crash helmet *n* casque *m* de protection.

crash-land *vi* atterrir en catastrophe.

crass [kræs] *adj* grossier(ère).

crate [kreɪt] *n* cageot *m*, caisse *f*.

crater [ˈkreɪtəʳ] *n* cratère *m*.

cravat [krəˈvæt] *n* cravate *f*.

crave [kreɪv] ◆ *vt* (*affection, luxury*) avoir soif de; (*cigarette, chocolate*) avoir un besoin fou OR maladif de. ◆ *vi*: **to ~ for** (*affection, luxury*) avoir soif de; (*cigarette, chocolate*) avoir un besoin fou OR maladif de.

crawl [krɔːl] ◆ *vi* 1. (*baby*) marcher à quatre pattes; (*person*) se traîner. 2. (*insect*) ramper. 3. (*vehicle, traffic*) avancer au pas. 4. *inf* (*place, floor*): **to be ~ing with** grouiller de. ◆ *n* (*swimming stroke*): **the ~** le crawl.

crayfish [ˈkreɪfɪʃ] (*pl inv* OR -es) *n* écrevisse *f*.

crayon [ˈkreɪɒn] *n* crayon *m* de couleur.

craze [kreɪz] *n* engouement *m*.

crazy [ˈkreɪzɪ] *adj inf* 1. (*mad*) fou (folle). 2. (*enthusiastic*): **to be ~ about sb/sthg** être fou (folle) de qqn/qqch.

creak [kriːk] *vi* (*door, handle*) craquer; (*floorboard, bed*) grincer.

cream [kriːm] ◆ *adj* (*in colour*) crème (*inv*). ◆ *n* (*gen*) crème *f*.

cream cake *n* Br gâteau *m* à la crème.

cream cheese *n* fromage *m* frais.

cream cracker *n* Br biscuit *m* salé (*souvent mangé avec du fromage*).

cream tea *n* Br goûter *se composant de thé et de scones servis avec de la crème et de la confiture.*

crease [kriːs] ◆ *n* (*in fabric - deliberate*) pli *m*; (*- accidental*) (faux) pli. ◆ *vt* froisser. ◆ vi (fabric) se froisser.

create [kri:'eit] vt créer.

creation [kri:'eiʃn] n création f.

creative [kri:'eitiv] adj créatif(ive).

creature ['kri:tʃər] n créature f.

crèche [kreʃ] n Br crèche f.

credence ['kri:dns] n: **to give** OR **lend ~ to sthg** ajouter foi à qqch.

credentials [kri'denʃlz] npl 1. (papers) pièce f d'identité; fig (qualifications) capacités fpl. 2. (references) références fpl.

credibility [,kredə'biləti] n crédibilité f.

credit ['kredit] ◆ n 1. (FIN) crédit m; **to be in ~** (person) avoir un compte approvisionné; (account) être approvisionné; **on ~** à crédit. 2. (U) (praise) honneur m, mérite m; **to give sb ~ for sthg** reconnaître que qqn a fait qqch. 3. (UNIV) unité f de valeur. ◆ vt 1. (FIN): **to ~ £10 to an account, to ~ an account with £10** créditer un compte de 10 livres. 2. inf (believe) croire. 3. (give the credit to): **to ~ sb with sthg** accorder OR attribuer qqch à qqn. ▶ **credits** npl (CINEMA) générique m.

credit card n carte f de crédit.

credit note n avoir m; (FIN) note f de crédit.

creditor ['kreditər] n créancier m, -ère f.

creed [kri:d] n 1. (belief) principes mpl. 2. (RELIG) croyance f.

creek [kri:k] n 1. (inlet) crique f. 2. Am (stream) ruisseau m.

creep [kri:p] (pt & pp **crept**) ◆ vi 1. (insect) ramper; (traffic) avancer au pas. 2. (move stealthily) se glisser. ◆ n inf (nasty person) sale type m. ▶ **creeps** npl: **to give sb the ~s** inf donner la chair de poule à qqn.

creeper ['kri:pər] n (plant) plante f grimpante.

creepy ['kri:pi] adj inf qui donne la chair de poule.

creepy-crawly [-'krɔ:li] (pl creepy-crawlies) n inf bestiole f qui rampe.

cremate [kri'meit] vt incinérer.

cremation [kri'meiʃn] n incinération f.

crematorium [,kremə'tɔ:riəm] (pl -riums OR -ria [-riə]), **crematory** Am ['kremətri] n crématorium m.

crepe [kreip] n 1. (cloth, rubber) crêpe m. 2. (pancake) crêpe f.

crepe bandage n Br bande f Velpeau®.

crepe paper n (U) papier m crépon.

crept [krept] pt & pp → **creep.**

crescent ['kresnt] n 1. (shape) croissant. 2. (street) rue f en demi-cercle.

cress [kres] n cresson m.

crest [krest] n 1. (of bird, hill) crête f. 2. (on coat of arms) timbre m.

crestfallen ['krest,fɔ:ln] adj découragé(e).

Crete [kri:t] n Crète f.

cretin ['kretin] n inf (idiot) crétin m, -e f.

Creutzfeldt-Jakob disease [,krɔitsfelt'jækɔb-] n maladie f de Creutzfeldt-Jakob.

crevice ['krevis] n fissure f.

crew [kru:] n 1. (of ship, plane) équipage m. 2. (team) équipe f.

crew cut n coupe f en brosse.

crew-neck(ed) [-nek(t)] adj ras du cou.

crib [krib] ◆ n (cot) lit m d'enfant. ◆ vt inf (copy): **to ~ sthg off** OR **from sb** copier qqch sur qqn.

crick [krik] n (in neck) torticolis m.

cricket ['krikit] n 1. (game) cricket m. 2. (insect) grillon m.

crime [kraim] n crime m.

criminal ['kriminl] ◆ adj criminel (elle). ◆ n criminel m, -elle f.

crimson ['krimzn] ◆ adj (in colour) rouge foncé (inv); (with embarrassment) cramoisi(e). ◆ n cramoisi m.

cringe [krind3] vi 1. (in fear) avoir un mouvement de recul (par peur). 2. inf (with embarrassment): **to ~ (at sthg)** ne plus savoir où se mettre (devant qqch).

crinkle ['krinkl] vt (clothes) froisser.

cripple ['kripl] ◆ n dated & offensive infirme mf. ◆ vt 1. (MED) (disable) estropier. 2. (country) paralyser; (ship, plane) endommager.

crisis ['kraisis] (pl crises ['kraisi:z]) n crise f.

crisp [krisp] adj 1. (pastry) croustillant(e); (apple, vegetables) croquant(e); (snow) craquant(e). 2. (weather, manner) vif (vive). ▶ **crisps** npl Br chips fpl.

crisscross ['kriskrɒs] ◆ adj entrecroisé(e). ◆ vt entrecroiser.

criterion [krai'tiəriən] (pl -rions OR -ria [-riə]) n critère m.

critic ['kritik] n 1. (reviewer) critique m. 2. (detractor) détracteur m, -trice f.

critical ['kritikl] adj critique; **to be ~ of sb/sthg** critiquer qqn/qqch.

critically ['kritikli] adv 1. (ill) gravement; **~ important** d'une importance capitale. 2. (analytically) de façon critique.

criticism ['kritisizm] n critique f.

criticize, -ise ['krɪtɪsaɪz] vt & vi critiquer.

croak [krəʊk] vi 1. (frog) coasser; (raven) croasser. 2. (person) parler d'une voix rauque.

Croat ['krəʊæt], **Croatian** [krəʊ'eɪʃn] ◆ adj croate. ◆ n 1. (person) Croate mf. 2. (language) croate m.

Croatia [krəʊ'eɪʃə] n Croatie f.

Croatian = **Croat**.

crochet ['krəʊʃeɪ] n crochet m.

crockery ['krɒkərɪ] n vaisselle f.

crocodile ['krɒkədaɪl] (pl inv OR -s) n crocodile m.

crocus ['krəʊkəs] (pl -cuses) n crocus m.

croft [krɒft] n Br petite ferme f (particulièrement en Écosse).

crony ['krəʊnɪ] n inf copain m, copine f.

crook [krʊk] n 1. (criminal) escroc m. 2. (of arm, elbow) pliure f. 3. (shepherd's staff) houlette f.

crooked ['krʊkɪd] adj 1. (bent) courbé(e). 2. (teeth, tie) de travers. 3. inf (dishonest) malhonnête.

crop [krɒp] n 1. (kind of plant) culture f. 2. (harvested produce) récolte f. 3. (whip) cravache f. ▶ **crop up** vi survenir.

croquette [krɒ'ket] n croquette f.

cross [krɒs] ◆ adj (person) fâché(e); (look) méchant(e); **to get ~ (with sb)** se fâcher (contre qqn). ◆ n 1. (gen) croix f. 2. (hybrid) croisement m. ◆ vt 1. (gen) traverser. 2. (arms, legs) croiser. 3. Br (cheque) barrer. ◆ vi (intersect) se croiser. ▶ **cross off, cross out** vt sep rayer.

crossbar ['krɒsbɑːr] n 1. (SPORT) barre f transversale. 2. (on bicycle) barre f.

cross-Channel adj transManche.

cross-country ◆ adj: ~ **running** cross m; ~ **skiing** ski m de fond. ◆ n cross-country m, cross m.

cross-examine vt (JUR) faire subir un contre-interrogatoire à; fig questionner de près.

cross-eyed [-aɪd] adj qui louche.

crossfire ['krɒs,faɪər] n (U) feu m croisé.

crossing ['krɒsɪŋ] n 1. (on road) passage m clouté; (on railway line) passage à niveau. 2. (sea journey) traversée f.

cross-legged [-legd] adv en tailleur.

cross-purposes npl: **to talk at ~** ne pas parler de la même chose.

cross-reference n renvoi m.

crossroads ['krɒsrəʊdz] (pl inv) n croisement m.

cross-section n 1. (drawing) coupe f transversale. 2. (sample) échantillon m.

crosswalk ['krɒswɔːk] n Am passage m clouté, passage pour piétons.

crossways ['krɒsweɪz] = **crosswise**.

crosswind ['krɒswɪnd] n vent m de travers.

crosswise ['krɒswaɪz] adv en travers.

crossword (puzzle) ['krɒswɜːd-] n mots croisés mpl.

crotch [krɒtʃ] n entrejambe m.

crotchety ['krɒtʃɪtɪ] adj Br inf grognon (onne).

crouch [kraʊtʃ] vi s'accroupir.

crow [krəʊ] ◆ n corbeau m; **as the ~ flies** à vol d'oiseau. ◆ vi 1. (cock) chanter. 2. inf (person) frimer.

crowbar ['krəʊbɑːr] n pied-de-biche m.

crowd [kraʊd] ◆ n (mass of people) foule f. ◆ vi s'amasser. ◆ vt 1. (streets, town) remplir. 2. (force into small space) entasser.

crowded ['kraʊdɪd] adj: ~ **(with)** bondé(e) (de), plein(e) (de).

crown [kraʊn] ◆ n 1. (of king, on tooth) couronne f. 2. (of head, hill) sommet m; (of hat) fond m. ◆ vt couronner. ▶ **Crown** n: **the Crown** (monarchy) la Couronne.

crown jewels npl joyaux mpl de la Couronne.

crown prince n prince m héritier.

crow's feet npl pattes fpl d'oie.

crucial ['kruːʃl] adj crucial(e).

crucifix ['kruːsɪfɪks] n crucifix m.

Crucifixion [,kruːsɪ'fɪkʃn] n: **the ~** la Crucifixion.

crude [kruːd] adj 1. (material) brut(e). 2. (joke, drawing) grossier(ère).

crude oil n (U) brut m.

cruel [krʊəl] adj cruel(elle).

cruelty ['krʊəltɪ] n (U) cruauté f.

cruet ['kruːɪt] n service m à condiments.

cruise [kruːz] ◆ n croisière f. ◆ vi 1. (sail) croiser. 2. (car) rouler; (plane) voler.

cruiser ['kruːzər] n 1. (warship) croiseur m. 2. (cabin cruiser) yacht m de croisière.

crumb [krʌm] n (of food) miette f.

crumble ['krʌmbl] ◆ n crumble m (aux fruits). ◆ vt émietter. ◆ vi 1. (bread, cheese) s'émietter; (building, wall) s'écrouler; (cliff) s'ébouler; (plaster) s'effriter. 2. fig (society, relationship) s'effondrer.

crumbly ['krʌmblɪ] adj friable.

crumpet ['krʌmpɪt] n (CULIN) petite crêpe f épaisse.

crumple ['krʌmpl] vt (crease) froisser.

crunch [krʌntʃ] ◆ n crissement m; **when it comes to the ~** inf au moment crucial OR décisif; **if it comes to the ~** inf s'il le faut. ◆ vt 1. (with teeth) croquer. 2. (underfoot) crisser.

crunchy ['krʌntʃɪ] adj (food) croquant(e).

crusade [kruːˈseɪd] n lit & fig croisade f.

crush [krʌʃ] ◆ n 1. (crowd) foule f. 2. inf (infatuation): **to have a ~ on sb** avoir le béguin pour qqn. ◆ vt 1. (gen) écraser; (seeds, grain) broyer; (ice) piler. 2. fig (hopes) anéantir.

crust [krʌst] n croûte f.

crutch [krʌtʃ] n (stick) béquille f; fig soutien m.

crux [krʌks] n nœud m.

cry [kraɪ] ◆ n (of person, bird) cri m. ◆ vi 1. (weep) pleurer. 2. (shout) crier. ▶ **cry off** vi se dédire. ▶ **cry out** ◆ vt crier. ◆ vi crier; (in pain, dismay) pousser un cri.

cryptic ['krɪptɪk] adj mystérieux(euse), énigmatique.

crystal ['krɪstl] n cristal m.

crystal clear adj (obvious) clair(e) comme de l'eau de roche.

CSE (abbr of Certificate of Secondary Education) n ancien brevet de l'enseignement secondaire en Grande-Bretagne.

CTC abbr of **city technology college.**

cub [kʌb] n 1. (young animal) petit m. 2. (boy scout) louveteau m.

Cuba ['kjuːbə] n Cuba.

Cuban ['kjuːbən] ◆ adj cubain(e). ◆ n Cubain m, -e f.

cubbyhole ['kʌbɪhəʊl] n cagibi m.

cube [kjuːb] ◆ n cube m. ◆ vt (MATH) élever au cube.

cubic ['kjuːbɪk] adj cubique.

cubicle ['kjuːbɪkl] n cabine f.

Cub Scout n louveteau m.

cuckoo ['kʊkuː] n coucou m.

cuckoo clock n coucou m.

cucumber ['kjuːkʌmbər] n concombre m.

cuddle ['kʌdl] ◆ n caresse f, câlin m. ◆ vt caresser, câliner. ◆ vi s'enlacer.

cuddly toy ['kʌdlɪ-] n jouet m en peluche.

cue [kjuː] n 1. (RADIO, THEATRE & TV) signal m; **on ~** au bon moment. 2. (in snooker, pool) queue f (de billard).

cuff [kʌf] n 1. (of sleeve) poignet m; **off the ~** au pied levé. 2. Am (of trouser) revers m inv. 3. (blow) gifle f.

cuff link n bouton m de manchette.

cul-de-sac ['kʌldəsæk] n cul-de-sac m.

cull [kʌl] ◆ n massacre m. ◆ vt 1. (kill) massacrer. 2. (gather) recueillir.

culminate ['kʌlmɪneɪt] vi: **to ~ in sthg** se terminer par qqch, aboutir à qqch.

culmination [ˌkʌlmɪˈneɪʃn] n apogée m.

culottes [kjuːˈlɒts] npl jupe-culotte f.

culpable ['kʌlpəbl] adj coupable.

culprit ['kʌlprɪt] n coupable mf.

cult [kʌlt] ◆ n culte m. ◆ comp culte.

cultivate ['kʌltɪveɪt] vt cultiver.

cultivation [ˌkʌltɪˈveɪʃn] n (U) (farming) culture f.

cultural ['kʌltʃərəl] adj culturel(elle).

culture ['kʌltʃər] n culture f.

cultured ['kʌltʃəd] adj (educated) cultivé(e).

cumbersome ['kʌmbəsəm] adj (object) encombrant(e).

cunning ['kʌnɪŋ] ◆ adj (person) rusé(e); (plan, method, device) astucieux(euse). ◆ n (U) (of person) ruse f; (of plan, method, device) astuce f.

cup [kʌp] n 1. (container, unit of measurement) tasse f. 2. (prize, competition) coupe f. 3. (of bra) bonnet m.

cupboard ['kʌbəd] n placard m.

Cup Final n: **the ~** la finale de la coupe.

cup tie n Br match m de coupe.

curate ['kjʊərət] n vicaire m.

curator [ˌkjʊəˈreɪtər] n conservateur m.

curb [kɜːb] ◆ n 1. (control): **~ (on)** frein m (à). 2. Am (of road) bord m du trottoir. ◆ vt mettre un frein à.

curdle ['kɜːdl] vi cailler.

cure [kjʊər] ◆ n: **~ (for)** (MED) remède m (contre); fig remède (à). ◆ vt 1. (MED) guérir. 2. (solve - problem) éliminer. 3. (rid): **to ~ sb of sthg** guérir qqn de qqch, faire perdre l'habitude de qqch à qqn. 4. (preserve - by smoking) fumer; (- by salting) saler; (- tobacco, hide) sécher.

cure-all n panacée f.

curfew ['kɜːfjuː] n couvre-feu m.

curio ['kjʊərɪəʊ] (pl -s) n bibelot m.

curiosity [ˌkjʊərɪˈɒsɪtɪ] n curiosité f.

curious ['kjʊərɪəs] adj: **~ (about)** curieux(euse) (à propos de).

curl [kɜːl] ◆ n (of hair) boucle f. ◆ vt 1. (hair) boucler. 2. (roll up) enrouler. ◆ vi 1. (hair) boucler. 2. (roll up) s'enrouler. ▶ **curl up** vi (person, animal) se mettre en boule, se pelotonner.

curler ['kɜːlər] n bigoudi m.

curling tongs ['kɜːlɪŋ-] npl fer m à friser.

curly ['kɜːlɪ] adj (hair) bouclé(e).

currant ['kʌrənt] n (dried grape) raisin m

de Corinthe, raisin sec.

currency ['kʌrənsɪ] n **1.** (type of money) monnaie f. **2.** (U) (money) devise f. **3.** fml (acceptability): **to gain ~** s'accréditer.

current ['kʌrənt] ◆ adj (price, method) actuel(elle); (year, week) en cours; (boyfriend, girlfriend) du moment; **~ issue** dernier numéro. ◆ n (of water, air, electricity) courant m.

current account n Br compte m courant.

current affairs npl actualité f, questions fpl d'actualité.

currently ['kʌrəntlɪ] adv actuellement.

curriculum [kə'rɪkjələm] (pl **-lums** OR **-la** [-lə]) n programme m d'études.

curriculum vitae [-'viːtaɪ] (pl **curricula vitae**) n curriculum vitae m.

curry ['kʌrɪ] n curry m.

curse [kɜːs] ◆ n **1.** (evil spell) malédiction f; fig fléau m. **2.** (swearword) juron m. ◆ vt maudire. ◆ vi jurer.

cursor ['kɜːsər] n (COMPUT) curseur m.

cursory ['kɜːsərɪ] adj superficiel(elle).

curt [kɜːt] adj brusque.

curtail [kɜː'teɪl] vt (visit) écourter.

curtain ['kɜːtn] n rideau m.

curts(e)y ['kɜːtsɪ] (pt & pp curtsied) ◆ n révérence f. ◆ vi faire une révérence.

curve [kɜːv] ◆ n courbe f. ◆ vi faire une courbe.

cushion ['kʊʃn] ◆ n coussin m. ◆ vt (fall, blow, effects) amortir.

cushy ['kʊʃɪ] adj inf pépère, peinard(e).

custard ['kʌstəd] n crème f anglaise.

custard tart n tarte f à la crème.

custodian [kʌ'stəʊdjən] n (of building) gardien m, -enne f; (of museum) conservateur m.

custody ['kʌstədɪ] n **1.** (of child) garde f. **2.** (JUR): **in ~** en garde à vue.

custom ['kʌstəm] n **1.** (tradition, habit) coutume f. **2.** (COMM) clientèle f. ► **customs** n (place) douane f.

customary ['kʌstəmrɪ] adj (behaviour) coutumier(ère); (way, time) habituel (elle).

customer ['kʌstəmər] n **1.** (client) client m, -e f. **2.** inf (person) type m.

customize, -ise ['kʌstəmaɪz] vt (make) fabriquer OR assembler sur commande; (modify) modifier sur commande.

Customs and Excise n Br = service m des contributions indirectes.

customs duty n droit m de douane.

customs officer n douanier m, -ère f.

cut [kʌt] (pt & pp cut) ◆ n **1.** (in wood etc) entaille f; (in skin) coupure f. **2.** (of meat) morceau m. **3.** (reduction): **~ (in)** (taxes, salary, personnel) réduction f (de); (film, article) coupure f (dans). **4.** (of suit, hair) coupe f. ◆ vt **1.** (gen) couper; (taxes, costs, workforce) réduire; **to ~ one's finger** se couper le doigt. **2.** inf (lecture, class) sécher. ◆ vi **1.** (gen) couper. **2.** (intersect) se couper. ► **cut back** ◆ vt sep **1.** (prune) tailler. **2.** (reduce) réduire. ◆ vi: **to ~ back on** réduire, diminuer. ► **cut down** ◆ vt sep **1.** (chop down) couper. **2.** (reduce) réduire, diminuer. ◆ vi: **to ~ down on smoking/eating/ spending** fumer/manger/dépenser moins. ► **cut in** vi **1.** (interrupt): **to ~ in (on sb)** interrompre (qqn). **2.** (AUT & SPORT) se rabattre. ► **cut off** vt sep **1.** (piece, crust) couper; (finger, leg - subj: surgeon) amputer. **2.** (power, telephone, funding) couper. **3.** (separate): **to be ~ off (from)** (person) être coupé(e) (de); (village) être isolé(e) (de). ► **cut out** vt sep **1.** (photo, article) découper; (sewing pattern) couper; (dress) tailler. **2.** (stop): **to ~ out smoking/chocolates** arrêter de fumer/de manger des chocolats; **~ it out!** inf ça suffit! **3.** (exclude) exclure. ► **cut up** vt sep (chop up) couper, hacher.

cutback ['kʌtbæk] n: **~ (in)** réduction f (de).

cute [kjuːt] adj (appealing) mignon (onne).

cuticle ['kjuːtɪkl] n envie f.

cutlery ['kʌtlərɪ] n (U) couverts mpl.

cutlet ['kʌtlɪt] n côtelette f.

cutout ['kʌtaʊt] n **1.** (on machine) disjoncteur m. **2.** (shape) découpage m.

cut-price, cut-rate Am adj à prix réduit.

cutthroat ['kʌtθrəʊt] adj (ruthless) acharné(e).

cutting ['kʌtɪŋ] ◆ adj (sarcastic - remark) cinglant(e); (- wit) acerbe. ◆ n **1.** (of plant) bouture f. **2.** (from newspaper) coupure f. **3.** Br (for road, railway) tranchée f.

CV (abbr of curriculum vitae) n CV m.

cwt. abbr of **hundredweight**.

cyanide ['saɪənaɪd] n cyanure m.

cybercafe ['saɪbə,kæfeɪ] n cybercafé m.

cyberspace ['saɪbəspeɪs] n cyberespace m.

cycle ['saɪkl] ◆ n **1.** (of events, songs) cycle m. **2.** (bicycle) bicyclette f. ◆ comp (path, track) cyclable; (race) cycliste; (shop) de cycles. ◆ vi faire de la bicyclette.

cycling ['saɪklɪŋ] n cyclisme m.
cyclist ['saɪklɪst] n cycliste mf.
cygnet ['sɪgnɪt] n jeune cygne m.
cylinder ['sɪlɪndəʳ] n cylindre m.
cymbals ['sɪmblz] npl cymbales fpl.
cynic ['sɪnɪk] n cynique mf.
cynical ['sɪnɪkl] adj cynique.
cynicism ['sɪnɪsɪzm] n cynisme m.
cypress ['saɪprəs] n cyprès m.
Cypriot ['sɪprɪət] ◆ adj chypriote. ◆ n Chypriote mf.
Cyprus ['saɪprəs] n Chypre f.
cyst [sɪst] n kyste m.
cystitis [sɪs'taɪtɪs] n cystite f.
czar [zɑːʳ] n tsar m.
Czech [tʃek] ◆ adj tchèque. ◆ n 1. (person) Tchèque mf. 2. (language) tchèque m.
Czechoslovak [,tʃekə'sləuvæk] = **Czechoslovakian**.
Czechoslovakia [,tʃekəslə'vækɪə] n Tchécoslovaquie f.
Czechoslovakian [,tʃekəslə'vækɪən] ◆ adj tchécoslovaque. ◆ n Tchécoslovaque mf.

D

d (pl **d's** OR **ds**), **D** (pl **D's** OR **Ds**) [diː] n (letter) d m inv, D m inv. ▶ **D** n 1. (MUS) ré m. 2. (SCH) (mark) D m inv.
DA abbr of **district attorney**.
dab [dæb] ◆ n (of cream, powder, ointment) petit peu m; (of paint) touche f. ◆ vt 1. (skin, wound) tamponner. 2. (apply - cream, ointment): **to ~ sthg on** OR **onto** appliquer qqch sur.
dabble ['dæbl] vi: **to ~ in** toucher un peu à.
dachshund ['dækshʊnd] n teckel m.
dad [dæd], **daddy** ['dædɪ] n inf papa m.
daddy longlegs [-'lɒŋlegz] (pl inv) n faucheur m.
daffodil ['dæfədɪl] n jonquille f.
daft [dɑːft] adj inf stupide, idiot(e).
dagger ['dægəʳ] n poignard m.
daily ['deɪlɪ] ◆ adj 1. (newspaper, occurrence) quotidien(enne). 2. (rate, output) journalier(ère). ◆ adv (happen, write) quotidiennement; **twice ~** deux fois par jour. ◆ n (newspaper) quotidien m.
dainty ['deɪntɪ] adj délicat(e).
dairy ['deərɪ] n 1. (on farm) laiterie f. 2. (shop) crémerie f.
dairy products npl produits mpl laitiers.
dais ['deɪɪs] n estrade f.
daisy ['deɪzɪ] n (weed) pâquerette f; (cultivated) marguerite f.
daisy-wheel printer n imprimante f à marguerite.
dale [deɪl] n vallée f.
dam [dæm] ◆ n (across river) barrage m. ◆ vt construire un barrage sur.
damage ['dæmɪdʒ] ◆ n 1. (physical harm) dommage m, dégât m. 2. (harmful effect) tort m. ◆ vt 1. (harm physically) endommager, abîmer. 2. (have harmful effect on) nuire à. ▶ **damages** npl (JUR) dommages et intérêts mpl.
damn [dæm] ◆ adj inf fichu(e), sacré(e). ◆ adv inf sacrément. ◆ n inf: **not to give** OR **care a ~ (about sthg)** se ficher pas mal (de qqch). ◆ vt (RELIG) (condemn) damner. ◆ excl inf zut!
damned [dæmd] inf ◆ adj fichu(e), sacré(e); **well I'll be** OR **I'm ~!** c'est trop fort!, elle est bien bonne celle-là! ◆ adv sacrément.
damning ['dæmɪŋ] adj accablant(e).
damp [dæmp] ◆ adj humide. ◆ n humidité f. ◆ vt (make wet) humecter.
dampen ['dæmpən] vt 1. (make wet) humecter. 2. fig (emotion) abattre.
damson ['dæmzn] n prune f de Damas.
dance [dɑːns] ◆ n 1. (gen) danse f. 2. (social event) bal m. ◆ vi danser.
dancer ['dɑːnsəʳ] n danseur m, -euse f.
dancing ['dɑːnsɪŋ] n (U) danse f.
dandelion ['dændɪlaɪən] n pissenlit m.
dandruff ['dændrʌf] n (U) pellicules fpl.
Dane [deɪn] n Danois m, -e f.
danger ['deɪndʒəʳ] n 1. (U) (possibility of harm) danger m; **in ~** en danger; **out of ~** hors de danger. 2. (hazard, risk): **~ (to)** risque m (pour); **to be in ~ of doing sthg** risquer de faire qqch.
dangerous ['deɪndʒərəs] adj dangereux(euse).
dangle ['dæŋgl] ◆ vt laisser pendre. ◆ vi pendre.
Danish ['deɪnɪʃ] ◆ adj danois(e). ◆ n 1. (language) danois m. 2. Am = **Danish pastry**. ◆ npl: **the ~** les Danois mpl.
Danish pastry n gâteau feuilleté fourré aux fruits. ◆
dank [dæŋk] adj humide et froid(e).

dapper ['dæpə^r] adj pimpant(e).

dappled ['dæpld] adj 1. (light) tacheté(e). 2. (horse) pommelé(e).

dare [deə^r] ◆ vt 1. (be brave enough): to ~ to do sthg oser faire qqch. 2. (challenge): to ~ sb to do sthg défier qqn de faire qqch. 3. phr: I ~ say je suppose, sans doute. ◆ vi oser; how ~ you! comment osez-vous! ◆ n défi m.

daredevil ['deə,devl] n casse-cou m inv.

daring ['deərɪŋ] ◆ adj audacieux (euse). ◆ n audace f.

dark [dɑ:k] ◆ adj 1. (room, night) sombre; it's getting ~ il commence à faire nuit. 2. (in colour) foncé(e). 3. (dark-haired) brun(e); (dark-skinned) basané(e). ◆ n 1. (darkness): the ~ l'obscurité f; to be in the ~ about sthg ignorer tout de qqch. 2. (night): before/after ~ avant/après la tombée de la nuit.

darken ['dɑ:kn] ◆ vt assombrir. ◆ vi s'assombrir.

dark glasses npl lunettes fpl noires.

darkness ['dɑ:knɪs] n obscurité f.

darkroom ['dɑ:krʊm] n chambre f noire.

darling ['dɑ:lɪŋ] ◆ adj (dear) chéri(e). ◆ n 1. (loved person, term of address) chéri m, -e f. 2. (idol) chouchou m, idole f.

darn [dɑ:n] ◆ vt repriser. ◆ adj inf sacré(e), satané(e). ◆ adv inf sacrément.

dart [dɑ:t] ◆ n (arrow) fléchette f. ◆ vi se précipiter. ▶ **darts** n (game) jeu m de fléchettes.

dartboard ['dɑ:tbɔ:d] n cible f de jeu de fléchettes.

dash [dæʃ] ◆ n 1. (of milk, wine) goutte f; (of cream) soupçon m; (of salt) pincée f; (of colour, paint) touche f. 2. (in punctuation) tiret m. 3. (rush): to make a ~ for se ruer vers. ◆ vt (hopes) anéantir. ◆ vi se précipiter.

dashboard ['dæʃbɔ:d] n tableau m de bord.

dashing ['dæʃɪŋ] adj fringant(e).

data ['deɪtə] n (U) données fpl.

database ['deɪtəbeɪs] n base f de données.

data processing n traitement m de données.

date [deɪt] ◆ n 1. (in time) date f; to ~ à ce jour. 2. (appointment) rendez-vous m. 3. (person) petit ami m, petite amie f. 4. (fruit) datte f. ◆ vt 1. (gen) dater. 2. (go out with) sortir avec. ◆ vi (go out of fashion) dater.

dated ['deɪtɪd] adj qui date.

date of birth n date f de naissance.

daub [dɔ:b] vt: to ~ sthg with sthg barbouiller qqch de qqch.

daughter ['dɔ:tə^r] n fille f.

daughter-in-law (pl daughters-in-law) n belle-fille f.

daunting ['dɔ:ntɪŋ] adj intimidant(e).

dawdle ['dɔ:dl] vi flâner.

dawn [dɔ:n] ◆ n lit & fig aube f. ◆ vi 1. (day) poindre. 2. (era, period) naître. ▶ **dawn (up)on** vt fus venir à l'esprit de.

day [deɪ] n jour m; (duration) journée f; the ~ before la veille; the ~ after le lendemain; the ~ before yesterday avant-hier; the ~ after tomorrow après-demain; any ~ now d'un jour à l'autre; one ~, some ~, one of these ~s un jour (ou l'autre), un de ces jours; in my ~ de mon temps; to make sb's ~ réchauffer le cœur de qqn. ▶ **days** adv le jour.

daybreak ['deɪbreɪk] n aube f; at ~ à l'aube.

daycentre ['deɪsentə^r] n Br (for children) garderie f; (for elderly people) centre de jour pour les personnes du troisième âge.

daydream ['deɪdri:m] vi rêvasser.

daylight ['deɪlaɪt] n 1. (light) lumière f du jour. 2. (dawn) aube f.

day off (pl days off) n jour m de congé.

day return n Br billet aller et retour valable pour une journée.

daytime ['deɪtaɪm] ◆ n jour m, journée f. ◆ comp (television) pendant la journée; (job, flight) de jour.

day-to-day adj (routine, life) journalier (ère); on a ~ basis au jour le jour.

day trip n excursion f d'une journée.

daze [deɪz] ◆ n: in a ~ hébété(e), ahuri(e). ◆ vt 1. (subj: blow) étourdir. 2. fig (subj: shock, event) abasourdir, sidérer.

dazzle ['dæzl] vt éblouir.

DC n (abbr of direct current) courant m continu.

D-day ['di:deɪ] n le jour J.

DEA (abbr of Drug Enforcement Administration) n agence américaine de lutte contre la drogue.

deacon ['di:kn] n diacre m.

deactivate [,di:'æktɪveɪt] vt désarmocer.

dead [ded] ◆ adj 1. (not alive, not lively) mort(e); to shoot sb ~ abattre qqn. 2. (numb) engourdi(e). 3. (not operating - battery) à plat. 4. (complete - silence) de mort. ◆ adv 1. (directly, precisely): ~ ahead droit devant soi; ~ on time pile à l'heure. 2. inf (completely) tout à fait.

3. (*suddenly*): **to stop ~** s'arrêter net. ◆ *npl*: **the ~** les morts *mpl*.

deaden ['dedn] *vt* (*sound*) assourdir; (*pain*) calmer.

dead end *n* impasse *f*.

dead heat *n* arrivée *f* ex-aequo.

deadline ['dedlaɪn] *n* dernière limite *f*.

deadlock ['dedlɒk] *n* impasse *f*.

dead loss *n inf*: **to be a ~** (*person*) être bon (bonne) à rien; (*object*) ne rien valoir.

deadly ['dedlɪ] ◆ *adj* **1.** (*poison, enemy*) mortel(elle). **2.** (*accuracy*) imparable. ◆ *adv* (*boring, serious*) tout à fait.

deadpan ['dedpæn] ◆ *adj* pince-sans-rire (*inv*). ◆ *adv* impassiblement.

deaf [def] ◆ *adj* sourd(e); **to be ~ to sthg** être sourd à qqch. ◆ *npl*: **the ~** les sourds *mpl*.

deaf-aid *n* Br appareil *m* acoustique.

deaf-and-dumb *adj* sourd-muet (sourde-muette).

deafen ['defn] *vt* assourdir.

deaf-mute ◆ *adj* sourd-muet (sourde-muette). ◆ *n* sourd-muet *m*, sourde-muette *f*.

deafness ['defnɪs] *n* surdité *f*.

deal [di:l] (*pt* & *pp* **dealt**) ◆ *n* **1.** (*quantity*): **a good** OR **great ~** beaucoup; **a good** OR **great ~ of** beaucoup de, bien de/des. **2.** (*business agreement*) marché *m*, affaire *f*; **to do** OR **strike a ~ with sb** conclure un marché avec qqn. **3.** *inf* (*treatment*): **to get a bad ~** ne pas faire une affaire. ◆ *vt* **1.** (*strike*): **to ~ sb/sthg a blow, to ~ a blow to sb/sthg** porter un coup à qqn/qqch. **2.** (*cards*) donner, distribuer. ◆ *vi* **1.** (*at cards*) donner, distribuer. **2.** (*in drugs*) faire le trafic (de drogues). ▶ **deal out** *vt sep* distribuer. ▶ **deal with** *vt fus* **1.** (*handle*) s'occuper de. **2.** (*be about*) traiter de. **3.** (*be faced with*) avoir affaire à.

dealer ['di:lər] *n* **1.** (*trader*) négociant *m*; (*in drugs*) trafiquant *m*. **2.** (*cards*) donneur *m*.

dealing ['di:lɪŋ] *n* commerce *m*. ▶ **dealings** *npl* relations *fpl*, rapports *mpl*.

dealt [delt] *pt* & *pp* → **deal**.

dean [di:n] *n* doyen *m*.

dear [dɪər] ◆ *adj*: **~ (to)** cher (chère) (à); **Dear Sir** (*in letter*) Cher Monsieur; **Dear Madam** Chère Madame. ◆ *n* chéri *m*, -e *f*. ◆ *excl*: **oh ~!** mon Dieu!

dearly ['dɪəlɪ] *adv* (*love, wish*) de tout son cœur.

death [deθ] *n* mort *f*; **to frighten sb to ~**

faire une peur bleue à qqn; **to be sick to ~ of sthg/of doing sthg** en avoir marre de qqch/de faire qqch.

death certificate *n* acte *m* de décès.

death duty Br, **death tax** Am *n* droits *mpl* de succession.

deathly ['deθlɪ] *adj* de mort.

death penalty *n* peine *f* de mort.

death rate *n* taux *m* de mortalité.

death tax Am = **death duty**.

debar [di:'bɑːr] *vt*: **to ~ sb (from)** (*place*) exclure qqn (de); **to ~ sb from doing sthg** interdire à qqn de faire qqch.

debase [dɪ'beɪs] *vt* dégrader; **to ~ o.s.** s'avilir.

debate [dɪ'beɪt] ◆ *n* débat *m*; **open to ~** discutable. ◆ *vt* débattre, discuter; **to ~ whether** s'interroger pour savoir si. ◆ *vi* débattre.

debating society [dɪ'beɪtɪŋ-] *n* club *m* de débats.

debauchery [dɪ'bɔːtʃərɪ] *n* débauche *f*.

debit ['debɪt] ◆ *n* débit *m*. ◆ *vt* débiter.

debit note *n* note *f* de débit.

debris ['deɪbriː] *n* (U) débris *mpl*.

debt [det] *n* dette *f*; **to be in ~** avoir des dettes, être endetté(e); **to be in sb's ~** être redevable à qqn.

debt collector *n* agent *m* de recouvrements.

debtor ['detər] *n* débiteur *m*, -trice *f*.

debug [,di:'bʌg] *vt* (COMPUT) (*program*) mettre au point, déboguer.

debunk [,di:'bʌŋk] *vt* démentir.

debut ['deɪbjuː] *n* débuts *mpl*.

decade ['dekeɪd] *n* décennie *f*.

decadence ['dekədəns] *n* décadence *f*.

decadent ['dekədənt] *adj* décadent(e).

decaffeinated [dɪ'kæfɪneɪtɪd] *adj* décaféiné(e).

decanter [dɪ'kæntər] *n* carafe *f*.

decathlon [dɪ'kæθlɒn] *n* décathlon *m*.

decay [dɪ'keɪ] ◆ *n* **1.** (*of body, plant*) pourriture *f*, putréfaction *f*; (*of tooth*) carie *f*. **2.** *fig* (*of building*) délabrement *m*; (*of society*) décadence *f*. ◆ *vi* **1.** (*rot*) pourrir; (*tooth*) se carier. **2.** *fig* (*building*) se délabrer, tomber en ruines; (*society*) tomber en décadence.

deceased [dɪ'siːst] (*pl inv*) ◆ *adj* décédé(e). ◆ *n*: **the ~** le défunt, la défunte.

deceit [dɪ'siːt] *n* tromperie *f*, supercherie *f*.

deceitful [dɪ'siːtfʊl] *adj* trompeur (euse).

deceive [dɪ'siːv] *vt* (*person*) tromper, duper; (*subj: memory, eyes*) jouer des tours à; **to ~ o.s.** se leurrer, s'abuser.

December [dɪ'sembər] *n* décembre *m*; *see also* **September**.

decency ['diːsnsɪ] *n* décence *f*, bienséance *f*; **to have the ~ to do sthg** avoir la décence de faire qqch.

decent ['diːsnt] *adj* **1.** (*behaviour, dress*) décent(e). **2.** (*wage, meal*) correct(e), décent(e). **3.** (*person*) gentil(ille), brave.

deception [dɪ'sepʃn] *n* **1.** (*lie, pretence*) tromperie *f*, duperie *f*. **2.** (U) (*act of lying*) supercherie *f*.

deceptive [dɪ'septɪv] *adj* trompeur (euse).

decide [dɪ'saɪd] ◆ *vt* décider; **to ~ to do sthg** décider de faire qqch. ◆ *vi* se décider. ▸ **decide (up)on** *vt fus* se décider pour, choisir.

decided [dɪ'saɪdɪd] *adj* **1.** (*definite*) certain(e), incontestable. **2.** (*resolute*) décidé(e), résolu(e).

decidedly [dɪ'saɪdɪdlɪ] *adv* **1.** (*clearly*) manifestement, incontestablement. **2.** (*resolutely*) résolument.

deciduous [dɪ'sɪdjʊəs] *adj* à feuilles caduques.

decimal ['desɪml] ◆ *adj* décimal(e). ◆ *n* décimale *f*.

decimal point *n* virgule *f*.

decimate ['desɪmeɪt] *vt* décimer.

decipher [dɪ'saɪfər] *vt* déchiffrer.

decision [dɪ'sɪʒn] *n* décision *f*.

decisive [dɪ'saɪsɪv] *adj* **1.** (*person*) déterminé(e), résolu(e). **2.** (*factor, event*) décisif(ive).

deck [dek] *n* **1.** (*of ship*) pont *m*. **2.** (*of bus*) impériale *f*. **3.** (*of cards*) jeu *m*. **4.** Am (*of house*) véranda *f*.

deckchair ['dektʃeər] *n* chaise longue *f*, transat *m*.

declaration [,deklə'reɪʃn] *n* déclaration *f*.

Declaration of Independence *n*: **the ~** la Déclaration d'Indépendance des États-Unis d'Amérique (1776).

declare [dɪ'kleər] *vt* déclarer.

decline [dɪ'klaɪn] ◆ *n* déclin *m*; **to be in ~** être en déclin; **on the ~** en baisse. ◆ *vt* décliner; **to ~ to do sthg** refuser de faire qqch. ◆ *vi* **1.** (*deteriorate*) décliner. **2.** (*refuse*) refuser.

decode [,diː'kəʊd] *vt* décoder.

decompose [,diːkəm'pəʊz] *vi* se décomposer.

decongestant [,diːkən'dʒestənt] *n* décongestionnant *m*.

decorate ['dekəreɪt] *vt* décorer.

decoration [,dekə'reɪʃn] *n* décoration *f*.

decorator ['dekəreɪtər] *n* décorateur *m*, -trice *f*.

decoy [*n* 'diːkɔɪ, *vt* dɪ'kɔɪ] ◆ *n* (*for hunting*) appât *m*, leurre *m*; (*person*) compère *m*. ◆ *vt* attirer dans un piège.

decrease [*n* 'diːkriːs, *vb* dɪ'kriːs] ◆ *n*: **~ (in)** diminution *f* (de), baisse *f* (de). ◆ *vt* diminuer, réduire. ◆ *vi* diminuer, décroître.

decree [dɪ'kriː] ◆ *n* **1.** (*order, decision*) décret *m*. **2.** Am (*JUR*) arrêt *m*, jugement *m*. ◆ *vt* décréter, ordonner.

decree nisi [-'naɪsaɪ] (*pl* **decrees nisi**) *n* Br jugement *m* provisoire.

decrepit [dɪ'krepɪt] *adj* (*person*) décrépit(e); (*house*) délabré(e).

dedicate ['dedɪkeɪt] *vt* **1.** (*book etc*) dédier. **2.** (*life, career*) consacrer.

dedication [,dedɪ'keɪʃn] *n* **1.** (*commitment*) dévouement *m*. **2.** (*in book*) dédicace *f*.

deduce [dɪ'djuːs] *vt* déduire, conclure.

deduct [dɪ'dʌkt] *vt* déduire, retrancher.

deduction [dɪ'dʌkʃn] *n* déduction *f*.

deed [diːd] *n* **1.** (*action*) action *f*, acte *m*. **2.** (*JUR*) acte *m* notarié.

deem [diːm] *vt* juger, considérer; **to ~ it wise to do sthg** juger prudent de faire qqch.

deep [diːp] ◆ *adj* profond(e). ◆ *adv* profondément; **~ down** (*fundamentally*) au fond.

deepen ['diːpn] *vi* **1.** (*river, sea*) devenir profond(e). **2.** (*crisis, recession, feeling*) s'aggraver.

deep freeze *n* congélateur *m*.

deep fry *vt* faire frire.

deeply ['diːplɪ] *adv* profondément.

deep-sea *adj*: **~ diving** plongée *f* sous-marine; **~ fishing** pêche *f* hauturière.

deer [dɪər] (*pl inv*) *n* cerf *m*.

deface [dɪ'feɪs] *vt* barbouiller.

defamatory [dɪ'fæmətrɪ] *adj* diffamatoire, diffamant(e).

default [dɪ'fɔːlt] ◆ *n* **1.** (*failure*) défaillance *f*; **by ~** par défaut. **2.** (*COMPUT*) valeur *f* par défaut. ◆ *vi* manquer à ses engagements.

defeat [dɪ'fiːt] ◆ *n* défaite *f*; **to admit ~** s'avouer battu(e) OR vaincu(e). ◆ *vt* **1.** (*team, opponent*) vaincre, battre. **2.** (*motion, proposal*) rejeter.

defeatist [dɪ'fiːtɪst] ◆ *adj* défaitiste. ◆ *n* défaitiste *mf*.

defect [*n* 'di:fekt, *vi* dɪ'fekt] ◆ *n* défaut *m*. ◆ *vi*: **to ~ to** passer à.

defective [dɪ'fektɪv] *adj* défectueux (euse).

defence Br, **defense** Am [dɪ'fens] *n* 1. (*gen*) défense *f*. 2. (*protective device, system*) protection *f*. 3. (JUR): **the ~** la défense.

defenceless Br, **defenseless** Am [dɪ'fenslɪs] *adj* sans défense.

defend [dɪ'fend] *vt* défendre.

defendant [dɪ'fendənt] *n* défendeur *m*, -eresse *f*.

defender [dɪ'fendəʳ] *n* défenseur *m*.

defense Am = **defence**.

defenseless Am = **defenceless**.

defensive [dɪ'fensɪv] ◆ *adj* défensif (ive). ◆ *n*: **on the ~** sur la défensive.

defer [dɪ'fɜːʳ] ◆ *vt* différer. ◆ *vi*: **to ~ to sb** s'en remettre à (l'opinion de) qqn.

deferential [,defə'renʃl] *adj* respectueux(euse).

defiance [dɪ'faɪəns] *n* défi *m*; **in ~ of** au mépris de.

defiant [dɪ'faɪənt] *adj* (*person*) intraitable, intransigeant(e); (*action*) de défi.

deficiency [dɪ'fɪʃnsɪ] *n* 1. (*lack*) manque *m*; (*of vitamins etc*) carence *f*. 2. (*inadequacy*) imperfection *f*.

deficient [dɪ'fɪʃnt] *adj* 1. (*lacking*): **to be ~ in** manquer de. 2. (*inadequate*) insuffisant(e), médiocre.

deficit ['defɪsɪt] *n* déficit *m*.

define [dɪ'faɪn] *vt* définir.

definite ['defɪnɪt] *adj* 1. (*plan*) bien déterminé(e); (*date*) certain(e). 2. (*improvement, difference*) net (nette), marqué(e). 3. (*answer*) précis(e), catégorique. 4. (*confident - person*) assuré(e).

definitely ['defɪnɪtlɪ] *adv* 1. (*without doubt*) sans aucun doute, certainement. 2. (*for emphasis*) catégoriquement.

definition [defɪ'nɪʃn] *n* 1. (*gen*) définition *f*. 2. (*clarity*) clarté *f*, précision *f*.

deflate [dɪ'fleɪt] ◆ *vt* (*balloon, tyre*) dégonfler. ◆ *vi* (*balloon, tyre*) se dégonfler.

deflation [dɪ'fleɪʃn] *n* (ECON) déflation *f*.

deflect [dɪ'flekt] *vt* (*ball, bullet*) dévier; (*stream*) détourner, dériver; (*criticism*) détourner.

defogger [,di:'fɒgəʳ] *n* Am (AUT) dispositif *m* antibuée.

deformed [dɪ'fɔːmd] *adj* difforme.

defraud [dɪ'frɔːd] *vt* (*person*) escroquer; (*Inland Revenue etc*) frauder.

defrost [,di:'frɒst] ◆ *vt* 1. (*fridge*) dégivrer; (*frozen food*) décongeler. 2. Am (AUT - *de-ice*) dégivrer; (- *demist*) désembuer. ◆ *vi* (*fridge*) dégivrer; (*frozen food*) se décongeler.

deft [deft] *adj* adroit(e).

defunct [dɪ'fʌŋkt] *adj* qui n'existe plus; (*person*) défunt(e).

defuse [,di:'fjuːz] *vt* Br désamorcer.

defy [dɪ'faɪ] *vt* 1. (*gen*) défier; **to ~ sb to do sthg** mettre qqn au défi de faire qqch. 2. (*efforts*) résister à, faire échouer.

degenerate [*adj* dɪ'dʒenərət, *vb* dɪ'dʒenəreɪt] ◆ *adj* dégénéré(e). ◆ *vi*: **to ~ (into)** dégénérer (en).

degrading [dɪ'greɪdɪŋ] *adj* dégradant(e), avilissant(e).

degree [dɪ'griː] *n* 1. (*measurement*) degré *m*. 2. (UNIV) diplôme *m* universitaire; **to have/take a ~ (in)** avoir/faire une licence (de). 3. (*amount*): **to a certain ~** jusqu'à un certain point, dans une certaine mesure; **a ~ of risk** un certain risque; **a ~ of truth** une certaine part de vérité; **by ~s** progressivement, petit à petit.

dehydrated [,di:haɪ'dreɪtɪd] *adj* déshydraté(e).

de-ice [di:'aɪs] *vt* dégivrer.

deign [deɪn] *vt*: **to ~ to do sthg** daigner faire qqch.

deity ['di:ɪtɪ] *n* dieu *m*, déesse *f*, divinité *f*.

dejected [dɪ'dʒektɪd] *adj* abattu(e), découragé(e).

delay [dɪ'leɪ] ◆ *n* retard *m*, délai *m*. ◆ *vt* 1. (*cause to be late*) retarder. 2. (*defer*) différer; **to ~ doing sthg** tarder à faire qqch. ◆ *vi*: **to ~ (in doing sthg)** tarder (à faire qqch).

delayed [dɪ'leɪd] *adj*: **to be ~** (*person, train*) être retardé(e).

delectable [dɪ'lektəbl] *adj* délicieux (euse).

delegate [*n* 'delɪgət, *vb* 'delɪgeɪt] ◆ *n* délégué *m*, -e *f*. ◆ *vt* déléguer; **to ~ sb to do sthg** déléguer qqn pour faire qqch; **to ~ sthg to sb** déléguer qqch à qqn.

delegation [,delɪ'geɪʃn] *n* délégation *f*.

delete [dɪ'liːt] *vt* supprimer, effacer.

deli ['delɪ] *n* inf abbr of **delicatessen**.

deliberate [*adj* dɪ'lɪbərət, *vb* dɪ'lɪbəreɪt] ◆ *adj* 1. (*intentional*) voulu(e), délibéré(e). 2. (*slow*) lent(e), sans hâte. ◆ *vi* délibérer.

deliberately [dɪ'lɪbərətlɪ] *adv* (*on purpose*) exprès, à dessein.

delicacy ['delɪkəsɪ] n 1. (gen) délicatesse f. 2. (food) mets m délicat.

delicate ['delɪkət] adj délicat(e); (movement) gracieux(euse).

delicatessen [ˌdelɪkə'tesn] n épicerie f fine.

delicious [dɪ'lɪʃəs] adj délicieux(euse).

delight [dɪ'laɪt] ◆ n (great pleasure) délice m; **to take ~ in doing sthg** prendre grand plaisir à faire qqch. ◆ vt enchanter, charmer. ◆ vi: **to ~ in sthg/in doing sthg** prendre grand plaisir à qqch/à faire qqch.

delighted [dɪ'laɪtɪd] adj: **~ (by OR with)** enchanté(e) (de), ravi(e) (de); **to be ~ to do sthg** être enchanté OR ravi de faire qqch.

delightful [dɪ'laɪtfʊl] adj ravissant(e), charmant(e); (meal) délicieux(euse).

delinquent [dɪ'lɪŋkwənt] ◆ adj délinquant(e). ◆ n délinquant m, -e f.

delirious [dɪ'lɪrɪəs] adj délirant(e).

deliver [dɪ'lɪvər] vt 1. (distribute): **to ~ sthg (to sb)** (mail, newspaper) distribuer qqch (à qqn); (COMM) livrer qqch (à qqn). 2. (speech) faire; (warning) donner; (message) remettre; (blow, kick) donner, porter. 3. (baby) mettre au monde. 4. (free) délivrer. 5. Am (POL) (votes) obtenir.

delivery [dɪ'lɪvərɪ] n 1. (COMM) livraison f. 2. (way of speaking) élocution f. 3. (birth) accouchement m.

delude [dɪ'luːd] vt tromper, induire en erreur; **to ~ o.s.** se faire des illusions.

delusion [dɪ'luːʒn] n illusion f.

delve [delv] vi: **to ~ into** (past) fouiller; (bag etc) fouiller dans.

demand [dɪ'mɑːnd] ◆ n 1. (claim, firm request) revendication f, exigence f; **on ~** sur demande. 2. (need): **~ (for)** demande f (de); **in ~** demandé(e), recherché(e). ◆ vt 1. (ask for - justice, money) réclamer; (- explanation, apology) exiger; **to ~ to do sthg** exiger de faire qqch. 2. (require) demander, exiger.

demanding [dɪ'mɑːndɪŋ] adj 1. (exhausting) astreignant(e). 2. (not easily satisfied) exigeant(e).

demean [dɪ'miːn] vt: **to ~ o.s.** s'abaisser.

demeaning [dɪ'miːnɪŋ] adj avilissant(e), dégradant(e).

demeanour Br, **demeanor** Am [dɪ'miːnər] n (U) fml comportement m.

demented [dɪ'mentɪd] adj fou (folle), dément(e).

demise [dɪ'maɪz] n (U) décès m; fig mort f, fin f.

demister [ˌdiː'mɪstər] n Br dispositif m antibuée.

demo ['deməʊ] (abbr of **demonstration**) n inf manif f.

democracy [dɪ'mɒkrəsɪ] n démocratie f.

democrat ['deməkræt] n démocrate mf. ▶ **Democrat** n Am démocrate mf.

democratic [ˌdemə'krætɪk] adj démocratique. ▶ **Democratic** adj Am démocrate.

Democratic Party n Am: **the ~** le Parti démocrate.

demolish [dɪ'mɒlɪʃ] vt (destroy) démolir.

demonstrate ['demənstreɪt] ◆ vt 1. (prove) démontrer, prouver. 2. (machine, computer) faire une démonstration de. ◆ vi: **to ~ (for/against)** manifester (pour/contre).

demonstration [ˌdemən'streɪʃn] n 1. (of machine, emotions) démonstration f. 2. (public meeting) manifestation f.

demonstrator ['demənstreɪtər] n 1. (in march) manifestant m, -e f. 2. (of machine, product) démonstrateur m, -trice f.

demoralized [dɪ'mɒrəlaɪzd] adj démoralisé(e).

demote [ˌdiː'məʊt] vt rétrograder.

demure [dɪ'mjʊər] adj modeste, réservé(e).

den [den] n (of animal) antre m, tanière f.

denial [dɪ'naɪəl] n (of rights, facts, truth) dénégation f; (of accusation) démenti m.

denier ['denɪər] n denier m.

denigrate ['denɪgreɪt] vt dénigrer.

denim ['denɪm] n jean m. ▶ **denims** npl: **a pair of ~s** un jean.

denim jacket n veste f en jean.

Denmark ['denmɑːk] n Danemark m.

denomination [dɪˌnɒmɪ'neɪʃn] n 1. (RELIG) confession f. 2. (money) valeur f.

denounce [dɪ'naʊns] vt dénoncer.

dense [dens] adj 1. (crowd, forest) dense; (fog) dense, épais(aisse). 2. inf (stupid) bouché(e).

density ['densətɪ] n densité f.

dent [dent] ◆ n bosse f. ◆ vt cabosser.

dental ['dentl] adj dentaire; **~ appointment** rendez-vous m chez le dentiste.

dental floss n fil m dentaire.

dental surgeon n chirurgien-dentiste m.

dentist ['dentɪst] n dentiste mf.

dentures ['dentʃəz] npl dentier m.

deny [dɪ'naɪ] vt 1. (refute) nier. 2. fml

(*refuse*) nier, refuser; **to ~ sb sthg** refuser qqch à qqn.

deodorant [diːˈəudərənt] n déodorant m.

depart [dɪˈpɑːt] vi fml 1. (*leave*): **to ~ (from)** partir de. 2. (*differ*): **to ~ from sthg** s'écarter de qqch.

department [dɪˈpɑːtmənt] n 1. (*in organization*) service m. 2. (*in shop*) rayon m. 3. (SCH & UNIV) département m. 4. (*in government*) département m, ministère m.

department store n grand magasin m.

departure [dɪˈpɑːtʃər] n 1. (*leaving*) départ m. 2. (*change*) nouveau départ m; **a ~ from tradition** un écart par rapport à la tradition.

departure lounge n salle f d'embarquement.

depend [dɪˈpend] vi: **to ~ on** (*be dependent on*) dépendre de; (*rely on*) compter sur; (*emotionally*) se reposer sur; **it ~s** cela dépend; **~ing on** selon.

dependable [dɪˈpendəbl] adj (*person*) sur qui on peut compter; (*source of income*) sûr(e); (*car*) fiable.

dependant [dɪˈpendənt] n personne f à charge.

dependent [dɪˈpendənt] adj 1. (*reliant*): **~ (on)** dépendant(e) (de); **to be ~ on sb/sthg** dépendre de qqn/qqch. 2. (*addicted*) dépendant(e), accro. 3. (*contingent*): **to be ~ on** dépendre de.

depict [dɪˈpɪkt] vt 1. (*show in picture*) représenter. 2. (*describe*): **to ~ sb/sthg as** dépeindre qqn/qqch comme.

deplete [dɪˈpliːt] vt épuiser.

deplorable [dɪˈplɔːrəbl] adj déplorable.

deplore [dɪˈplɔːr] vt déplorer.

deploy [dɪˈplɔɪ] vt déployer.

depopulation [diːˌpɒpjuˈleɪʃn] n dépeuplement m.

deport [dɪˈpɔːt] vt expulser.

depose [dɪˈpəuz] vt déposer.

deposit [dɪˈpɒzɪt] ◆ n 1. (*gen*) dépôt m; **to make a ~** (*into bank account*) déposer de l'argent. 2. (*payment - as guarantee*) caution f; (*- as instalment*) acompte m; (*- on bottle*) consigne f. ◆ vt déposer.

deposit account n Br compte m sur livret.

depot [ˈdepəu] n 1. (*gen*) dépôt m. 2. Am (*station*) gare.

depreciate [dɪˈpriːʃɪeɪt] vi se déprécier.

depress [dɪˈpres] vt 1. (*sadden, discour-*

age) déprimer. 2. (*weaken - economy*) affaiblir; (*- prices*) faire baisser.

depressed [dɪˈprest] adj 1. (*sad*) déprimé(e). 2. (*run-down - area*) en déclin.

depressing [dɪˈpresɪŋ] adj déprimant(e).

depression [dɪˈpreʃn] n 1. (*gen*) dépression f. 2. (*sadness*) tristesse f.

deprivation [ˌdeprɪˈveɪʃn] n privation f.

deprive [dɪˈpraɪv] vt: **to ~ sb of sthg** priver qqn de qqch.

depth [depθ] n profondeur f; **in ~** (*study, analyse*) en profondeur; **to be out of one's ~** (*in water*) ne pas avoir pied; fig avoir perdu pied, être dépassé. ▶ **depths** npl: **the ~** (*of seas*) les profondeurs fpl; (*of memory, archives*) le fin fond; **in the ~s of winter** au cœur de l'hiver; **to be in the ~s of despair** toucher le fond du désespoir.

deputation [ˌdepjuˈteɪʃn] n délégation f.

deputize, -ise [ˈdepjutaɪz] vi: **to ~ for sb** assurer les fonctions de qqn, remplacer qqn.

deputy [ˈdepjutɪ] ◆ adj adjoint(e); **~ chairman** vice-président m; **~ head** (SCH) directeur m adjoint; **~ leader** (POL) vice-président m. ◆ n 1. (*second-in-command*) adjoint m, -e f. 2. Am (*deputy sheriff*) shérif m adjoint.

derail [dɪˈreɪl] vt (*train*) faire dérailler.

deranged [dɪˈreɪndʒd] adj dérangé(e).

derby [Br ˈdɑːbɪ, Am ˈdɜːbɪ] n 1. (SPORT) derby m. 2. Am (*hat*) chapeau m melon.

derelict [ˈderəlɪkt] adj en ruines.

deride [dɪˈraɪd] vt railler.

derisory [dəˈraɪzərɪ] adj 1. (*puny, trivial*) dérisoire. 2. (*derisive*) moqueur (euse).

derivative [dɪˈrɪvətɪv] ◆ adj pej pas original(e). ◆ n dérivé m.

derive [dɪˈraɪv] ◆ vt 1. (*draw, gain*): **to ~ sthg from sthg** tirer qqch de qqch. 2. (*originate*): **to be ~d from** venir de. ◆ vi: **to ~ from** venir de.

derogatory [dɪˈrɒgətrɪ] adj désobligeant(e).

derv [dɜːv] n Br gas-oil m.

descend [dɪˈsend] ◆ vt fml (*go down*) descendre. ◆ vi 1. fml (*go down*) descendre. 2. (*fall*): **to ~ (on)** (*enemy*) s'abattre (sur); (*subj: silence, gloom*) tomber (sur). 3. (*stoop*): **to ~ to sthg/to doing sthg** s'abaisser à qqch/à faire qqch.

descendant [dɪˈsendənt] n descendant m, -e f.

descended [dɪ'sendɪd] *adj*: **to be ~ from sb** descendre de qqn.

descent [dɪ'sent] *n* **1.** (*downwards movement*) descente *f*. **2.** (U) (*origin*) origine *f*.

describe [dɪ'skraɪb] *vt* décrire.

description [dɪ'skrɪpʃn] *n* **1.** (*account*) description *f*. **2.** (*type*) sorte *f*, genre *m*.

desecrate ['desɪkreɪt] *vt* profaner.

desert [*n* 'dezət, *vb & npl* dɪ'zɜːt] ♦ **désert** *m*. ♦ *vt* **1.** (*place*) déserter. **2.** (*person, group*) déserter, abandonner. ♦ *vi* (MIL) déserter. ▷ **deserts** *npl*: **to get one's just ~s** recevoir ce que l'on mérite.

deserted [dɪ'zɜːtɪd] *adj* désert(e).

deserter [dɪ'zɜːtər] *n* déserteur *m*.

desert island ['dezət-] *n* île *f* déserte.

deserve [dɪ'zɜːv] *vt* mériter; **to ~ to do sthg** mériter de faire qqch.

deserving [dɪ'zɜːvɪŋ] *adj* (*person*) méritant(e); (*cause, charity*) méritoire.

design [dɪ'zaɪn] ♦ *n* **1.** (*plan, drawing*) plan *m*, étude *f*. **2.** (U) (*art*) design *m*. **3.** (*pattern*) motif *m*, dessin *m*. **4.** (*shape*) ligne *f*; (*of dress*) style *m*. **5.** *fml* (*intention*) dessein *m*; **by ~** à dessein; **to have ~s on sb/sthg** avoir des desseins sur qqn/qqch. ♦ *vt* **1.** (*draw plans for - building, car*) faire les plans de, dessiner; (- *dress*) créer. **2.** (*plan*) concevoir, mettre au point; **to be ~ed for sthg/to do sthg** être conçu pour qqch/pour faire qqch.

designate [*adj* 'dezɪgnət, *vb* 'dezɪgneɪt] ♦ *adj* désigné(e). ♦ *vt* désigner.

designer [dɪ'zaɪnər] ♦ *adj* de marque. ♦ *n* (INDUSTRY) concepteur *m*, -trice *f*; (ARCHIT) dessinateur *m*, -trice *f*; (*of dresses etc*) styliste *mf*; (THEATRE) décorateur *m*, -trice *f*.

desirable [dɪ'zaɪərəbl] *adj* **1.** (*enviable, attractive*) désirable. **2.** *fml* (*appropriate*) désirable, souhaitable.

desire [dɪ'zaɪər] ♦ *n* désir *m*; **~ for sthg/to do sthg** désir de qqch/de faire qqch. ♦ *vt* désirer.

desist [dɪ'zɪst] *vi fml*: **to ~ (from doing sthg)** cesser (de faire qqch).

desk [desk] *n* bureau *m*; **reception ~** réception *f*; **information ~** bureau *m* de renseignements.

desktop publishing ['desk,tɒp-] *n* publication *f* assistée par ordinateur, PAO *f*.

desolate ['desələt] *adj* (*place*) abandonné(e).

despair [dɪ'speər] ♦ *n* (U) désespoir *m*. ♦ *vi* désespérer; **to ~ of** désespérer

de; **to ~ of doing sthg** désespérer de faire qqch.

despairing [dɪ'speərɪŋ] *adj* de désespoir.

despatch [dɪ'spætʃ] = **dispatch**.

desperate ['desprət] *adj* désespéré(e); **to be ~ for sthg** avoir absolument besoin de qqch.

desperately ['desprətlɪ] *adv* désespérément; **~ ill** gravement malade.

desperation [,despə'reɪʃn] *n* désespoir *m*; **in ~** de désespoir.

despicable [dɪ'spɪkəbl] *adj* ignoble.

despise [dɪ'spaɪz] *vt* (*person*) mépriser; (*racism*) exécrer.

despite [dɪ'spaɪt] *prep* malgré.

despondent [dɪ'spɒndənt] *adj* découragé(e).

dessert [dɪ'zɜːt] *n* dessert *m*.

dessertspoon [dɪ'zɜːtspuːn] *n* (*spoon*) cuillère *f* à dessert.

destination [,destɪ'neɪʃn] *n* destination *f*.

destined ['destɪnd] *adj* **1.** (*intended*): **~ for** destiné(e) à; **~ to do sthg** destiné à faire qqch. **2.** (*bound*): **~ for** à destination de.

destiny ['destɪnɪ] *n* destinée *f*.

destitute ['destɪtjuːt] *adj* indigent(e).

destroy [dɪ'strɔɪ] *vt* (*ruin*) détruire.

destruction [dɪ'strʌkʃn] *n* destruction *f*.

detach [dɪ'tætʃ] *vt* **1.** (*pull off*) détacher; **to ~ sthg from sthg** détacher qqch de qqch. **2.** (*dissociate*): **to ~ o.s. from sthg** (*from reality*) se détacher de qqch; (*from proceedings, discussions*) s'écarter de qqch.

detached [dɪ'tætʃt] *adj* (*unemotional*) détaché(e).

detached house *n* maison *f* individuelle.

detachment [dɪ'tætʃmənt] *n* détachement *m*.

detail ['diːteɪl] ♦ *n* **1.** (*small point*) détail *m*; **to go into ~** entrer dans les détails; **in ~** en détail. **2.** (MIL) détachement *m*. ♦ *vt* (*list*) détailler. ▷ **details** *npl* (*personal information*) coordonnées *fpl*.

detailed ['diːteɪld] *adj* détaillé(e).

detain [dɪ'teɪn] *vt* **1.** (*in police station*) détenir; (*in hospital*) garder. **2.** (*delay*) retenir.

detect [dɪ'tekt] *vt* **1.** (*subj: person*) déceler. **2.** (*subj: machine*) détecter.

detection [dɪ'tekʃn] *n* (U) **1.** (*of crime*) dépistage *m*. **2.** (*of aircraft, submarine*) détection *f*.

detective [dɪ'tektɪv] *n* détective *m*.

detective novel n roman m policier.

detention [dɪ'tenʃn] n 1. (of suspect, criminal) détention f. 2. (SCH) retenue f.

deter [dɪ'tɜːr] vt dissuader; **to ~ sb from doing sthg** dissuader qqn de faire qqch.

detergent [dɪ'tɜːdʒənt] n détergent m.

deteriorate [dɪ'tɪərɪəreɪt] vi se détériorer.

determination [dɪ,tɜːmɪ'neɪʃn] n détermination f.

determine [dɪ'tɜːmɪn] vt 1. (establish, control) déterminer. 2. fml (decide): **to ~ to do sthg** décider de faire qqch.

determined [dɪ'tɜːmɪnd] adj 1. (person) déterminé(e); **~ to do sthg** déterminé à faire qqch. 2. (effort) obstiné(e).

deterrent [dɪ'terənt] n moyen m de dissuasion.

detest [dɪ'test] vt détester.

detonate ['detəneɪt] ◆ vt faire détoner. ◆ vi détoner.

detour ['diː,tʊər] n détour m.

detract [dɪ'trækt] vi: **to ~ from** diminuer.

detriment ['detrɪmənt] n: **to the ~ of** au détriment de.

detrimental [,detrɪ'mentl] adj préjudiciable.

deuce [djuːs] n (TENNIS) égalité f.

devaluation [,diːvæljuː'eɪʃn] n dévaluation f.

devastated ['devəsteɪtɪd] adj 1. (area, city) dévasté(e). 2. fig (person) accablé(e).

devastating ['devəsteɪtɪŋ] adj 1. (hurricane, remark) dévastateur(trice). 2. (upsetting) accablant(e). 3. (attractive) irrésistible.

develop [dɪ'veləp] ◆ vt 1. (gen) développer. 2. (land, area) aménager, développer. 3. (illness, fault, habit) contracter. 4. (resources) développer, exploiter. ◆ vi 1. (grow, advance) se développer. 2. (appear - problem, trouble) se déclarer.

developing country [dɪ'veləpɪŋ-] n pays m en voie de développement.

development [dɪ'veləpmənt] n 1. (gen) développement m. 2. (U) (of land, area) exploitation f. 3. (land being developed) zone f d'aménagement; (developed area) zone aménagée. 4. (U) (of illness, fault) évolution f.

deviate ['diːvɪeɪt] vi: **to ~ (from)** dévier (de), s'écarter (de).

device [dɪ'vaɪs] n 1. (apparatus) appareil m, dispositif m. 2. (plan, method) moyen m.

devil ['devl] n 1. (evil spirit) diable m. 2. inf (person) type m; **poor ~!** pauvre diable! 3. (for emphasis): **who/where/why the ~ ...?** qui/où/pourquoi diable ...? ▶ **Devil** n (Satan): **the Devil** le Diable.

devious ['diːvjəs] adj 1. (dishonest - person) retors(e), à l'esprit tortueux; (- scheme, means) détourné(e). 2. (tortuous) tortueux(euse).

devise [dɪ'vaɪz] vt concevoir.

devoid [dɪ'vɔɪd] adj fml: **~ of** dépourvu(e) de, dénué(e) de.

devolution [,diːvə'luːʃn] n (POL) décentralisation f.

devote [dɪ'vəut] vt: **to ~ sthg to sthg** consacrer qqch à qqch.

devoted [dɪ'vəutɪd] adj dévoué(e); **a ~ mother** une mère dévouée à ses enfants.

devotee [,devə'tiː] n (fan) passionné m, -e f.

devotion [dɪ'vəuʃn] n 1. (commitment): **~ (to)** dévouement m (à). 2. (RELIG) dévotion f.

devour [dɪ'vauər] vt lit & fig dévorer.

devout [dɪ'vaut] adj dévot(e).

dew [djuː] n rosée f.

diabetes [,daɪə'biːtiːz] n diabète m.

diabetic [,daɪə'betɪk] ◆ adj (person) diabétique. ◆ n diabétique mf.

diabolic(al) [,daɪə'bɒlɪk(l)] adj 1. (evil) diabolique. 2. inf (very bad) atroce.

diagnose ['daɪəgnəuz] vt diagnostiquer.

diagnosis [,daɪəg'nəusɪs] (pl -oses [-əusiːz]) n diagnostic m.

diagonal [daɪ'ægənl] ◆ adj (line) diagonal(e). ◆ n diagonale f.

diagram ['daɪəgræm] n diagramme m.

dial ['daɪəl] ◆ n cadran m; (of radio) cadran de fréquences. ◆ vt (number) composer.

dialect ['daɪəlekt] n dialecte m.

dialling code ['daɪəlɪŋ-] n Br indicatif m.

dialling tone Br ['daɪəlɪŋ-], **dial tone** Am n tonalité f.

dialogue Br, **dialog** Am ['daɪəlɒg] n dialogue m.

dial tone Am = **dialling tone**.

dialysis [daɪ'ælɪsɪs] n dialyse f.

diameter [daɪ'æmɪtər] n diamètre m.

diamond ['daɪəmənd] n 1. (gem) diamant m. 2. (shape) losange m. ▶ **diamonds** npl carreau m.

diaper ['daɪəpər] n Am couche f.

diaphragm ['daɪəfræm] n diaphragme m.

diarrh(o)ea [,daɪə'rɪə] n diarrhée f.
diary ['daɪərɪ] n 1. (appointment book) agenda m. 2. (journal) journal m.
dice [daɪs] (pl inv) ◆ n (for games) dé m. ◆ vt couper en dés.
dictate [vb dɪk'teɪt, n 'dɪkteɪt] ◆ vt dicter. ◆ n ordre m.
dictation [dɪk'teɪʃn] n dictée f.
dictator [dɪk'teɪtəʳ] n dictateur m.
dictatorship [dɪk'teɪtəʃɪp] n dictature f.
dictionary ['dɪkʃənrɪ] n dictionnaire m.
did [dɪd] pt → **do**.
diddle ['dɪdl] vt inf escroquer, rouler.
didn't ['dɪdnt] = **did not**.
die [daɪ] (pl **dice**, pt & pp **died**, cont **dying**) ◆ vi mourir; **to be dying** se mourir; **to be dying to do sthg** mourir d'envie de faire qqch; **to be dying for a drink/cigarette** mourir d'envie de boire un verre/de fumer une cigarette. ◆ n (dice) dé m.
▶ **die away** vi (sound) s'éteindre; (wind) tomber. ▶ **die down** vi (sound) s'affaiblir; (wind) tomber; (fire) baisser.
▶ **die out** vi s'éteindre, disparaître.
diehard ['daɪhɑːd] n: **to be a ~** être coriace; (reactionary) être réactionnaire.
diesel ['diːzl] n diesel m.
diesel engine n (AUT) moteur m diesel; (RAIL) locomotive f diesel.
diesel fuel, diesel oil n diesel m.
diet ['daɪət] ◆ n 1. (eating pattern) alimentation f. 2. (to lose weight) régime m; **to be on a ~** être au régime, faire un régime. ◆ comp (low-calorie) de régime. ◆ vi suivre un régime.
differ ['dɪfəʳ] vi 1. (be different) être différent(e), différer; (people) être différent; **to ~ from** être différent de. 2. (disagree): **to ~ with sb (about sthg)** ne pas être d'accord avec qqn (à propos de qqch).
difference ['dɪfrəns] n différence f; **it doesn't make any ~** cela ne change rien.
different ['dɪfrənt] adj: **~ (from)** différent(e) (de).
differentiate [,dɪfə'renʃɪeɪt] ◆ vt: **to ~ sthg from sthg** différencier qqch de qqch, faire la différence entre qqch et qqch. ◆ vi: **to ~ (between)** faire la différence (entre).
difficult ['dɪfɪkəlt] adj difficile.
difficulty ['dɪfɪkəltɪ] n difficulté f; **to have ~ in doing sthg** avoir de la difficulté ou du mal à faire qqch.
diffident ['dɪfɪdənt] adj (person) qui manque d'assurance; (manner, voice, approach) hésitant(e).

diffuse [dɪ'fjuːz] vt diffuser, répandre.
dig [dɪg] (pt & pp **dug**) ◆ vi 1. (in ground) creuser. 2. (subj: belt, strap): **to ~ into sb** couper qqn. ◆ n 1. fig (unkind remark) pique f. 2. (ARCHEOL) fouilles fpl. ◆ vt 1. (hole) creuser. 2. (garden) bêcher.
▶ **dig out** vt sep inf (find) dénicher.
▶ **dig up** vt sep 1. (from ground) déterrer; (potatoes) arracher. 2. inf (information) dénicher.
digest [n 'daɪdʒest, vb dɪ'dʒest] ◆ n résumé m, digest m. ◆ vt digérer.
digestion [dɪ'dʒestʃn] n digestion f.
digestive biscuit [dɪ'dʒestɪv-] n Br ≃ sablé m (à la farine complète).
digit ['dɪdʒɪt] n 1. (figure) chiffre m. 2. (finger) doigt m; (toe) orteil m.
digital ['dɪdʒɪtl] adj numérique, digital(e).
dignified ['dɪgnɪfaɪd] adj digne, plein(e) de dignité.
dignity ['dɪgnətɪ] n dignité f.
digress [daɪ'gres] vi: **to ~ (from)** s'écarter (de).
digs [dɪgz] npl Br inf piaule f.
dike [daɪk] n (wall, bank) digue f.
dilapidated [dɪ'læpɪdeɪtɪd] adj délabré(e).
dilate [daɪ'leɪt] ◆ vt dilater. ◆ vi se dilater.
dilemma [dɪ'lemə] n dilemme m.
diligent ['dɪlɪdʒənt] adj appliqué(e).
dilute [daɪ'luːt] ◆ adj dilué(e). ◆ vt: **to ~ sthg (with)** diluer qqch (avec).
dim [dɪm] ◆ adj 1. (dark - light) faible; (- room) sombre. 2. (indistinct - memory, outline) vague. 3. (weak - eyesight) faible. 4. inf (stupid) borné(e). ◆ vt & vi baisser.
dime [daɪm] n Am (pièce f de) dix cents mpl.
dimension [dɪ'menʃn] n dimension f.
diminish [dɪ'mɪnɪʃ] vt & vi diminuer.
diminutive [dɪ'mɪnjutɪv] fml ◆ adj minuscule. ◆ n (GRAMM) diminutif m.
dimmers ['dɪmərz] npl Am (dipped headlights) phares mpl code (inv); (parking lights) feux mpl de position.
dimmer (switch) ['dɪmər-] n variateur m de lumière.
dimple ['dɪmpl] n fossette f.
din [dɪn] n inf barouf m.
dine [daɪn] vi fml dîner. ▶ **dine out** vi dîner dehors.
diner ['daɪnəʳ] n 1. (person) dîneur m, -euse f. 2. Am (café) = resto m routier.
dinghy ['dɪŋgɪ] n (for sailing) dériveur m; (for rowing) (petit) canot m.

dingy ['dɪndʒɪ] *adj* miteux(euse), crasseux(euse).

dining car ['daɪnɪŋ-] *n* wagon-restaurant *m*.

dining room ['daɪnɪŋ-] *n* **1.** (*in house*) salle *f* à manger. **2.** (*in hotel*) restaurant *m*.

dinner ['dɪnə^r] *n* dîner *m*.

dinner jacket *n* smoking *m*.

dinner party *n* dîner *m*.

dinnertime ['dɪnətaɪm] *n* heure *f* du dîner.

dinosaur ['daɪnəsɔː^r] *n* dinosaure *m*.

dint [dɪnt] *n fml*: **by ~ of** à force de.

dip [dɪp] ◆ *n* **1.** (*in road, ground*) déclivité *f*. **2.** (*sauce*) sauce *f*, dip *m*. **3.** (*swim*): **to go for a ~** aller se baigner en vitesse, aller faire trempette. ◆ *vt* **1.** (*into liquid*): **to ~ sthg in** OR **into** tremper OR plonger qqch dans. **2.** Br (AUT): **to ~ one's headlights** se mettre en code. ◆ *vi* **1.** (*sun*) baisser, descendre à l'horizon; (*wing*) plonger. **2.** (*road, ground*) descendre.

diploma [dɪ'pləʊmə] (*pl* **-s**) *n* diplôme *m*.

diplomacy [dɪ'pləʊməsɪ] *n* diplomatie *f*.

diplomat ['dɪpləmæt] *n* diplomate *m*.

diplomatic [,dɪplə'mætɪk] *adj* **1.** (*service, corps*) diplomatique. **2.** (*tactful*) diplomate.

dipstick ['dɪpstɪk] *n* (AUT) jauge *f* (*de niveau d'huile*).

dire ['daɪə^r] *adj* (*need, consequences*) extrême; (*warning*) funeste.

direct [dɪ'rekt] ◆ *adj* direct(e); (*challenge*) manifeste. ◆ *vt* **1.** (*gen*) diriger. **2.** (*aim*): **to ~ sthg at sb** (*question, remark*) adresser qqch à qqn; **the campaign is ~ed at teenagers** cette campagne vise les adolescents. **3.** (*order*): **to ~ sb to do sthg** ordonner à qqn de faire qqch. ◆ *adv* directement.

direct current *n* courant *m* continu.

direct debit *n* Br prélèvement *m* automatique.

direction [dɪ'rekʃn] *n* direction *f*. ▸ **directions** *npl* **1.** (*to find a place*) indications *fpl*. **2.** (*for use*) instructions *fpl*.

directly [dɪ'rektlɪ] *adv* **1.** (*in straight line*) directement. **2.** (*honestly, clearly*) sans détours. **3.** (*exactly - behind, above*) exactement. **4.** (*immediately*) immédiatement. **5.** (*very soon*) tout de suite.

director [dɪ'rektə^r] *n* **1.** (*of company*) directeur *m*, -trice *f*. **2.** (THEATRE) metteur *m* en scène; (CINEMA & TV) réalisateur *m*, -trice *f*.

directory [dɪ'rektərɪ] *n* **1.** (*annual publi-*

cation) annuaire *m*. **2.** (COMPUT) répertoire *m*.

directory enquiries *n* Br renseignements *mpl* (téléphoniques).

dire straits *npl*: **in ~** dans une situation désespérée.

dirt [dɜːt] *n* (U) **1.** (*mud, dust*) saleté *f*. **2.** (*earth*) terre *f*.

dirt cheap *inf* ◆ *adj* très bon marché, donné(e). ◆ *adv* pour trois fois rien.

dirty ['dɜːtɪ] ◆ *adj* **1.** (*not clean, not fair*) sale. **2.** (*smutty - language, person*) grossier(ère); (- *book, joke*) cochon(onne). ◆ *vt* salir.

disability [,dɪsə'bɪlətɪ] *n* infirmité *f*.

disabled [dɪs'eɪbld] ◆ *adj* (*person*) handicapé(e), infirme. ◆ *npl*: **the ~** les handicapés, les infirmes.

disadvantage [,dɪsəd'vɑːntɪdʒ] *n* désavantage *m*, inconvénient *m*; **to be at a ~** être désavantagé.

disadvantaged [,dɪsəd'vɑːntɪdʒd] *adj* défavorisé(e).

disagree [,dɪsə'griː] *vi* **1.** (*have different opinions*): **to ~ (with)** ne pas être d'accord (avec). **2.** (*differ*) ne pas concorder. **3.** (*subj: food, drink*): **to ~ with sb** ne pas réussir à qqn.

disagreeable [,dɪsə'griːəbl] *adj* désagréable.

disagreement [,dɪsə'griːmənt] *n* **1.** (*in opinion*) désaccord *m*. **2.** (*argument*) différend *m*.

disallow [,dɪsə'laʊ] *vt* **1.** *fml* (*appeal, claim*) rejeter. **2.** (*goal*) refuser.

disappear [,dɪsə'pɪə^r] *vi* disparaître.

disappearance [,dɪsə'pɪərəns] *n* disparition *f*.

disappoint [,dɪsə'pɔɪnt] *vt* décevoir.

disappointed [,dɪsə'pɔɪntɪd] *adj*: **~ (in** OR **with)** déçu(e) (par).

disappointing [,dɪsə'pɔɪntɪŋ] *adj* décevant(e).

disappointment [,dɪsə'pɔɪntmənt] *n* déception *f*.

disapproval [,dɪsə'pruːvl] *n* désapprobation *f*.

disapprove [,dɪsə'pruːv] *vi*: **to ~ of sb/sthg** désapprouver qqn/qqch.

disarm [dɪs'ɑːm] *vt* & *vi* désarmer.

disarmament [dɪs'ɑːməmənt] *n* désarmement *m*.

disarray [,dɪsə'reɪ] *n*: **in ~** en désordre; (*government*) en pleine confusion.

disaster [dɪ'zɑːstə^r] *n* **1.** (*damaging event*) catastrophe *f*. **2.** (U) (*misfortune*) échec *m*, désastre *m*. **3.** *inf* (*failure*) désastre *m*.

disastrous [dɪ'zɑːstrəs] adj désastreux (euse).

disband [dɪs'bænd] ◆ vt dissoudre. ◆ vi se dissoudre.

disbelief [ˌdɪsbɪ'liːf] n: **in** OR **with ~** avec incrédulité.

disc Br, **disk** Am [dɪsk] n disque m.

discard [dɪ'skɑːd] vt mettre au rebut.

discern [dɪ'sɜːn] vt discerner, distinguer.

discerning [dɪ'sɜːnɪŋ] adj judicieux (euse).

discharge [n 'dɪstʃɑːdʒ, vt dɪs'tʃɑːdʒ] ◆ n **1.** (of patient) autorisation f de sortie, décharge f; (JUR) relaxe f; **to get one's ~** (MIL) être rendu à la vie civile. **2.** (emission - of smoke) émission f; (- of sewage) déversement m; (MED) écoulement m. ◆ vt **1.** (allow to leave - patient) signer la décharge de; (- prisoner, defendant) relaxer; (- soldier) rendre à la vie civile. **2.** fml (fulfil) assumer. **3.** (emit - smoke) émettre; (- sewage, chemicals) déverser.

disciple [dɪ'saɪpl] n disciple m.

discipline ['dɪsɪplɪn] ◆ n discipline f. ◆ vt **1.** (control) discipliner. **2.** (punish) punir.

disc jockey n disc-jockey m.

disclaim [dɪs'kleɪm] vt fml nier.

disclose [dɪs'kləʊz] vt révéler, divulguer.

disclosure [dɪs'kləʊʒər] n révélation f, divulgation f.

disco ['dɪskəʊ] (pl -s) (abbr of **discotheque**) n discothèque f.

discomfort [dɪs'kʌmfət] n **1.** (U) (physical pain) douleur f. **2.** (U) (anxiety, embarrassment) malaise m.

disconcert [ˌdɪskən'sɜːt] vt déconcerter.

disconnect [ˌdɪskə'nekt] vt **1.** (detach) détacher. **2.** (from gas, electricity - appliance) débrancher; (- house) couper. **3.** (TELEC) couper.

disconsolate [dɪs'kɒnsələt] adj inconsolable.

discontent [ˌdɪskən'tent] n: **~ (with)** mécontentement m (à propos de).

discontented [ˌdɪskən'tentɪd] adj mécontent(e).

discontinue [ˌdɪskən'tɪnjuː] vt cesser, interrompre.

discord ['dɪskɔːd] n **1.** (U) (disagreement) discorde f, désaccord m. **2.** (MUS) dissonance f.

discotheque ['dɪskəʊtek] n discothèque f.

discount [n 'dɪskaʊnt, vb Br dɪs'kaʊnt, Am 'dɪskaʊnt] ◆ n remise f. ◆ vt (report, claim) ne pas tenir compte de.

discourage [dɪs'kʌrɪdʒ] vt décourager; **to ~ sb from doing sthg** dissuader qqn de faire qqch.

discover [dɪ'skʌvər] vt découvrir.

discovery [dɪ'skʌvərɪ] n découverte f.

discredit [dɪs'kredɪt] ◆ n discrédit m. ◆ vt discréditer.

discreet [dɪ'skriːt] adj discret(ète).

discrepancy [dɪs'krepənsɪ] n: **~ (in/ between)** divergence f (entre).

discretion [dɪ'skreʃn] n (U) **1.** (tact) discrétion f. **2.** (judgment) jugement m, discernement m; **at the ~ of** avec l'autorisation de.

discriminate [dɪ'skrɪmɪneɪt] vi **1.** (distinguish) différencier, distinguer; **to ~ between** faire la distinction entre. **2.** (be prejudiced): **to ~ against sb** faire de la discrimination envers qqn.

discriminating [dɪ'skrɪmɪneɪtɪŋ] adj avisé(e).

discrimination [dɪˌskrɪmɪ'neɪʃn] n **1.** (prejudice) discrimination f. **2.** (judgment) discernement m, jugement m.

discus ['dɪskəs] (pl -es) n disque m.

discuss [dɪ'skʌs] vt discuter (de); **to ~ sthg with sb** discuter de qqch avec qqn.

discussion [dɪ'skʌʃn] n discussion f; **under ~** en discussion.

disdain [dɪs'deɪn] n: **~ (for)** dédain m (pour).

disease [dɪ'ziːz] n (illness) maladie f.

disembark [ˌdɪsɪm'bɑːk] vi débarquer.

disenchanted [ˌdɪsɪn'tʃɑːntɪd] adj: **~ (with)** désenchanté(e) (de).

disengage [ˌdɪsɪn'geɪdʒ] vt **1.** (release): **to ~ sthg (from)** libérer OR dégager qqch (de). **2.** (TECH) déclencher; **to ~ the gears** débrayer.

disfavour Br, **disfavor** Am [dɪs-'feɪvər] n (dislike, disapproval) désapprobation f.

disfigure [dɪs'fɪgər] vt défigurer.

disgrace [dɪs'greɪs] ◆ n **1.** (shame) honte f; **to bring ~ on sb** jeter la honte sur qqn; **in ~** en défaveur. **2.** (cause of shame - thing) honte f, scandale m; (- person) honte f. ◆ vt faire honte à; **to ~ o.s.** se couvrir de honte.

disgraceful [dɪs'greɪsfʊl] adj honteux (euse), scandaleux(euse).

disgruntled [dɪs'grʌntld] adj mécontent(e).

disguise [dɪs'gaɪz] ◆ n déguisement m; **in ~** déguisé(e). ◆ vt **1.** (person, voice) déguiser. **2.** (hide - fact, feelings) dissimuler.

disgust [dɪs'gʌst] ◆ n: **~ (at)** (behaviour, violence etc) dégoût m (pour); (decision) dégoût (devant). ◆ vt dégoûter, écœurer.

disgusting [dɪs'gʌstɪŋ] adj dégoûtant(e).

dish [dɪʃ] n plat m; Am (plate) assiette f. ▶ **dishes** npl vaisselle f; **to do** OR **wash the ~es** faire la vaisselle.

dish aerial Br, **dish antenna** Am n antenne f parabolique.

dishcloth ['dɪʃklɒθ] n lavette f.

disheartened [dɪs'hɑːtnd] adj découragé(e).

dishevelled Br, **disheveled** Am [dɪ-'ʃevəld] adj (person) échevelé(e); (hair) en désordre.

dishonest [dɪs'ɒnɪst] adj malhonnête.

dishonor etc Am = **dishonour** etc.

dishonour Br, **dishonor** Am [dɪs-'ɒnər] ◆ n déshonneur m. ◆ vt déshonorer.

dishonourable Br, **dishonorable** Am [dɪs'ɒnərəbl] adj (person) peu honorable; (behaviour) déshonorant(e).

dish soap n Am liquide m pour la vaisselle.

dish towel n Am torchon m.

dishwasher ['dɪʃ,wɒʃər] n (machine) lave-vaisselle m inv.

disillusioned [,dɪsɪ'luːʒnd] adj désillusionné(e), désenchanté(e); **to be ~ with** ne plus avoir d'illusions sur.

disincentive [,dɪsɪn'sentɪv] n: **to be a ~** avoir un effet dissuasif; (in work context) être démotivant(e).

disinclined [,dɪsɪn'klaɪnd] adj: **to be ~ to do sthg** être peu disposé(e) à faire qqch.

disinfect [,dɪsɪn'fekt] vt désinfecter.

disinfectant [,dɪsɪn'fektənt] n désinfectant m.

disintegrate [dɪs'ɪntɪgreɪt] vi (object) se désintégrer, se désagréger.

disinterested [,dɪs'ɪntrəstɪd] adj **1.** (objective) désintéressé(e). **2.** inf (uninterested): **~ (in)** indifférent(e) (à).

disjointed [dɪs'dʒɔɪntɪd] adj décousu(e).

disk [dɪsk] n **1.** (COMPUT) disque m, disquette f. **2.** Am = **disc.**

disk drive Br, **diskette drive** Am n (COMPUT) lecteur m de disques OR de disquettes.

diskette [dɪs'ket] n (COMPUT) disquette f.

diskette drive n Am = **disk drive.**

dislike [dɪs'laɪk] ◆ n: **~ (of)** aversion f (pour); **to take a ~ to sb/sthg** prendre qqn/qqch en grippe. ◆ vt ne pas aimer.

dislocate ['dɪsləkeɪt] vt **1.** (MED) se démettre. **2.** (disrupt) désorganiser.

dislodge [dɪs'lɒdʒ] vt: **to ~ sthg (from)** déplacer qqch (de); (free) décoincer qqch (de).

disloyal [,dɪs'lɔɪəl] adj: **~ (to)** déloyal(e) (envers).

dismal ['dɪzml] adj **1.** (gloomy, depressing) lugubre. **2.** (unsuccessful - attempt) infructueux(euse); (- failure) lamentable.

dismantle [dɪs'mæntl] vt démanteler.

dismay [dɪs'meɪ] ◆ n consternation f. ◆ vt consterner.

dismiss [dɪs'mɪs] vt **1.** (from job): **to ~ sb (from)** congédier qqn (de). **2.** (refuse to take seriously - idea, person) écarter; (- plan, challenge) rejeter. **3.** (allow to leave - class) laisser sortir; (- troops) faire rompre les rangs à.

dismissal [dɪs'mɪsl] n **1.** (from job) licenciement m, renvoi m. **2.** (refusal to take seriously) rejet m.

dismount [,dɪs'maʊnt] vi: **to ~ (from)** descendre (de).

disobedience [,dɪsə'biːdjəns] n désobéissance f.

disobedient [,dɪsə'biːdjənt] adj désobéissant(e).

disobey [,dɪsə'beɪ] vt désobéir à.

disorder [dɪs'ɔːdər] n **1.** (disarray): **in ~** en désordre. **2.** (U) (rioting) troubles mpl. **3.** (MED) trouble m.

disorderly [dɪs'ɔːdəlɪ] adj **1.** (untidy - room) en désordre; (- appearance) désordonné(e). **2.** (unruly) indiscipliné(e).

disorganized, -ised [dɪs'ɔːgənaɪzd] adj (person) désordonné(e), brouillon (onne); (system) mal conçu(e).

disorientated Br [dɪs'ɔːrɪənteɪtɪd], **disoriented** Am [dɪs'ɔːrɪəntɪd] adj désorienté(e).

disown [dɪs'əʊn] vt désavouer.

disparaging [dɪ'spærɪdʒɪŋ] adj désobligeant(e).

dispassionate [dɪ'spæʃnət] adj impartial(e).

dispatch [dɪ'spætʃ] ◆ n (message) dépêche f. ◆ vt (send) envoyer, expédier.

dispel [dɪ'spel] vt (feeling) dissiper, chasser.

dispensary [dɪ'spensərɪ] n officine f.

dispense [dɪ'spens] vt (*justice, medicine*) administrer. ▶ **dispense with** vt fus 1. (*do without*) se passer de. 2. (*make unnecessary*) rendre superflu(e).

dispensing chemist Br, **dispensing pharmacist** Am [dɪ'spensɪŋ-] n pharmacien m, -enne f.

disperse [dɪ'spɜːs] ◆ vt 1. (*crowd*) disperser. 2. (*knowledge, news*) répandre, propager. ◆ vi se disperser.

dispirited [dɪ'spɪrɪtɪd] adj découragé(e), abattu(e).

displace [dɪs'pleɪs] vt 1. (*cause to move*) déplacer. 2. (*supplant*) supplanter.

display [dɪ'spleɪ] ◆ n 1. (*arrangement*) exposition f. 2. (*demonstration*) manifestation f. 3. (*public event*) spectacle m. 4. (COMPUT - *device*) écran m; (- *information displayed*) affichage m, visualisation f. ◆ vt 1. (*arrange*) exposer. 2. (*show*) faire preuve de, montrer.

displease [dɪs'pliːz] vt déplaire à, mécontenter; **to be ~d with** être mécontent(e) de.

displeasure [dɪs'pleʒər] n mécontentement m.

disposable [dɪ'spəʊzəbl] adj 1. (*throw away*) jetable. 2. (*income*) disponible.

disposal [dɪ'spəʊzl] n 1. (*removal*) enlèvement m. 2. (*availability*): **at sb's ~** à la disposition de qqn.

dispose [dɪ'spəʊz] ▶ **dispose of** vt fus (*get rid of*) se débarrasser de; (*problem*) résoudre.

disposed [dɪ'spəʊzd] adj 1. (*willing*): **to be ~ to do sthg** être disposé(e) à faire qqch. 2. (*friendly*): **to be well ~ to** OR **towards sb** être bien disposé(e) envers qqn.

disposition [,dɪspə'zɪʃn] n 1. (*temperament*) caractère m, tempérament m. 2. (*tendency*): **~ to do sthg** tendance f à faire qqch.

disprove [,dɪs'pruːv] vt réfuter.

dispute [dɪ'spjuːt] ◆ n 1. (*quarrel*) dispute f. 2. (U) (*disagreement*) désaccord m. 3. (INDUSTRY) conflit m. ◆ vt contester.

disqualify [,dɪs'kwɒlɪfaɪ] vt 1. (*subj: authority*): **to ~ sb (from doing sthg)** interdire à qqn (de faire qqch); **to ~ sb from driving** Br retirer le permis de conduire à qqn. 2. (SPORT) disqualifier.

disquiet [dɪs'kwaɪət] n inquiétude f.

disregard [,dɪsrɪ'gɑːd] ◆ n (U): **~ (for)** (*money, danger*) mépris m (pour); (*feelings*) indifférence f (à). ◆ vt (*fact*) ignorer; (*danger*) mépriser; (*warning*) ne pas tenir compte de.

disrepair [,dɪsrɪ'peər] n délabrement m; **to fall into ~** tomber en ruines.

disreputable [dɪs'repjʊtəbl] adj peu respectable.

disrepute [,dɪsrɪ'pjuːt] n: **to bring sthg into ~** discréditer qqch; **to fall into ~** acquérir une mauvaise réputation.

disrupt [dɪs'rʌpt] vt perturber.

dissatisfaction ['dɪs,sætɪs'fækʃn] n mécontentement m.

dissatisfied [,dɪs'sætɪsfaɪd] adj: **~ (with)** mécontent(e) (de), pas satisfait(e) (de).

dissect [dɪ'sekt] vt lit & fig disséquer.

dissent [dɪ'sent] ◆ n dissentiment m. ◆ vi: **to ~ (from)** être en désaccord (avec).

dissertation [,dɪsə'teɪʃn] n dissertation f.

disservice [,dɪs'sɜːvɪs] n: **to do sb a ~** rendre un mauvais service à qqn.

dissimilar [,dɪ'sɪmɪlər] adj: **~ (to)** différent(e) (de).

dissipate ['dɪsɪpeɪt] vt 1. (*heat*) dissiper. 2. (*efforts, money*) gaspiller.

dissociate [dɪ'səʊʃɪeɪt] vt dissocier; **to ~ o.s. from** se désolidariser de.

dissolute ['dɪsəluːt] adj dissolu(e).

dissolve [dɪ'zɒlv] ◆ vt dissoudre. ◆ vi 1. (*substance*) se dissoudre. 2. fig (*disappear*) disparaître.

dissuade [dɪ'sweɪd] vt: **to ~ sb (from)** dissuader qqn (de).

distance ['dɪstəns] n distance f; **at a ~** assez loin; **from a ~** de loin; **in the ~** au loin.

distant ['dɪstənt] adj 1. (*gen*): **~ (from)** éloigné(e) (de). 2. (*reserved - person, manner*) distant(e).

distaste [dɪs'teɪst] n: **~ (for)** dégoût m (pour).

distasteful [dɪs'teɪstful] adj répugnant(e), déplaisant(e).

distended [dɪ'stendɪd] adj (*stomach*) distendu(e).

distil Br, **distill** Am [dɪ'stɪl] vt 1. (*liquid*) distiller. 2. fig (*information*) tirer.

distillery [dɪ'stɪlərɪ] n distillerie f.

distinct [dɪ'stɪŋkt] adj 1. (*different*): **~ (from)** distinct(e) (de), différent(e) (de); **as ~ from** par opposition à. 2. (*definite - improvement*) net (nette).

distinction [dɪ'stɪŋkʃn] n 1. (*difference*) distinction f, différence f; **to draw** OR **make a ~ between** faire une distinction entre. 2. (U) (*excellence*) distinction f. 3. (*exam result*) mention f très bien.

distinctive [dɪ'stɪŋktɪv] adj caractéristique.

do

distinguish [dɪ'stɪŋgwɪʃ] vt **1.** (tell apart): **to ~ sthg from sthg** distinguer qqch de qqch, faire la différence entre qqch et qqch. **2.** (perceive) distinguer. **3.** (characterize) caractériser.

distinguished [dɪ'stɪŋgwɪʃt] adj distingué(e).

distinguishing [dɪ'stɪŋgwɪʃɪŋ] adj (feature, mark) caractéristique.

distort [dɪ'stɔːt] vt déformer.

distract [dɪ'strækt] vt: **to ~ sb (from)** distraire qqn (de).

distracted [dɪ'stræktɪd] adj (preoccupied) soucieux(euse).

distraction [dɪ'strækʃn] n (interruption, diversion) distraction f.

distraught [dɪ'strɔːt] adj éperdu(e).

distress [dɪ'stres] ◆ n (anxiety) détresse f; (pain) douleur f, souffrance f. ◆ vt affliger.

distressing [dɪ'stresɪŋ] adj (news, image) pénible.

distribute [dɪ'strɪbjuːt] vt **1.** (gen) distribuer. **2.** (spread out) répartir.

distribution [ˌdɪstrɪ'bjuːʃn] n **1.** (gen) distribution f. **2.** (spreading out) répartition f.

distributor [dɪ'strɪbjutər] n (AUT & COMM) distributeur m.

district [dɪ'strɪkt] n **1.** (area - of country) région f; (- of town) quartier m. **2.** (ADMIN) district m.

district attorney n Am ≃ procureur m de la République.

district council n Br ≃ conseil m général.

district nurse n Br infirmière f visiteuse or à domicile.

distrust [dɪs'trʌst] ◆ n méfiance f. ◆ vt se méfier de.

disturb [dɪ'stɜːb] vt **1.** (interrupt) déranger. **2.** (upset, worry) inquiéter. **3.** (sleep, surface) troubler.

disturbance [dɪ'stɜːbəns] n **1.** (POL) troubles mpl; (fight) tapage m. **2.** (interruption) dérangement m. **3.** (of mind, emotions) trouble m.

disturbed [dɪ'stɜːbd] adj **1.** (emotionally, mentally) perturbé(e). **2.** (worried) inquiet(ète).

disturbing [dɪ'stɜːbɪŋ] adj (image) bouleversant(e); (news) inquiétant(e).

disuse [ˌdɪs'juːs] n: **to fall into ~** (factory) être à l'abandon; (regulation) tomber en désuétude.

disused [ˌdɪs'juːzd] adj désaffecté(e).

ditch [dɪtʃ] ◆ n fossé m. ◆ vt inf (boyfriend, girlfriend) plaquer; (old car, clothes) se débarrasser de; (plan) abandonner.

dither ['dɪðər] vi hésiter.

ditto ['dɪtəu] adv idem.

dive [daɪv] (Br pt & pp **-d**, Am pt & pp **-d** OR **dove**) ◆ vi plonger; (bird, plane) piquer. ◆ n **1.** (gen) plongeon m. **2.** (of plane) piqué m. **3.** inf pej (bar, restaurant) bouge m.

diver ['daɪvər] n plongeur m, -euse f.

diverge [daɪ'vɜːdʒ] vi: **to ~ (from)** diverger (de).

diversify [daɪ'vɜːsɪfaɪ] ◆ vt diversifier. ◆ vi se diversifier.

diversion [daɪ'vɜːʃn] n **1.** (amusement) distraction f; (tactical) diversion f. **2.** (of traffic) déviation f. **3.** (of river, funds) détournement m.

diversity [daɪ'vɜːsətɪ] n diversité f.

divert [daɪ'vɜːt] vt **1.** (traffic) dévier. **2.** (river, funds) détourner. **3.** (person - amuse) distraire; (- tactically) détourner.

divide [dɪ'vaɪd] ◆ vt **1.** (separate) séparer. **2.** (share out) diviser, partager. **3.** (split up): **to ~ sthg (into)** diviser qqch (en). **4.** (MATH): **89 ~d by 3** 89 divisé par 3. **5.** (people - in disagreement) diviser. ◆ vi se diviser.

dividend ['dɪvɪdend] n dividende m.

divine [dɪ'vaɪn] adj divin(e).

diving ['daɪvɪŋ] n (U) plongeon m; (with breathing apparatus) plongée f (sousmarine).

divingboard ['daɪvɪŋbɔːd] n plongeoir m.

divinity [dɪ'vɪnətɪ] n **1.** (godliness, god) divinité f. **2.** (study) théologie f.

division [dɪ'vɪʒn] n **1.** (gen) division f. **2.** (separation) séparation f.

divorce [dɪ'vɔːs] ◆ n divorce m. ◆ vt (husband, wife) divorcer.

divorced [dɪ'vɔːst] adj divorcé(e).

divorcee [dɪvɔː'siː] n divorcé m, -e f.

divulge [daɪ'vʌldʒ] vt divulguer.

DIY (abbr of **do-it-yourself**) n Br bricolage m.

dizzy ['dɪzɪ] adj (giddy): **to feel ~** avoir la tête qui tourne.

DJ n (abbr of **disc jockey**) disc-jockey m.

DNA (abbr of **deoxyribonucleic acid**) n ADN m.

do [duː] (pt **did**, pp **done**, pl **dos** OR **do's**) ◆ aux vb **1.** (in negatives): **don't leave it there** ne le laisse pas là. **2.** (in questions): **~ you think she'll come?** tu crois qu'elle viendra? **3.** (referring back to previous verb): **she reads more than I ~** elle lit plus que moi; **I like reading – so ~ I** j'aime lire – moi aussi. **4.** (*in question tags*): **so you think you can dance, ~ you?** alors tu t'imagines que tu sais danser, c'est ça? **5.** (*for emphasis*): **I did tell you but you've forgotten** je te l'avais bien dit, mais tu l'as oublié; **~ come in** entrez donc. ◆ *vt* **1.** (*perform an activity, a service*) faire; **to ~ the cooking/housework** faire la cuisine/ le ménage; **to ~ one's hair** se coiffer; **to ~ one's teeth** se laver OR se brosser les dents. **2.** (*take action*) faire; **to ~ something about sthg** trouver une solution pour qqch. **3.** (*referring to job*): **what do you ~?** qu'est-ce que vous faites dans la vie? **4.** (*study*) faire; **I did physics at school** j'ai fait de la physique à l'école. **5.** (*travel at a particular speed*) faire, rouler; **the car can ~ 110 mph** = la voiture peut faire du 180 à l'heure. ◆ *vi* **1.** (*act*) faire; **~ as I tell you** fais comme je te dis. **2.** (*perform in a particular way*): **they're ~ing really well** leurs affaires marchent bien; **he could ~ better** il pourrait mieux faire; **how did you ~ in the exam?** comment ça a marché à l'examen? **3.** (*be good enough, be sufficient*) suffire, aller; **will £6 ~?** est-ce que 6 livres suffiront?, 6 livres, ça ira?; **that will ~** ça suffit. ◆ *n* (*party*) fête *f*, soirée *f*. ▶ **dos** *npl*: **~s and don'ts** ce qu'il faut faire et ne pas faire. ▶ **do away with** *vt fus* supprimer. ▶ **do out of** *vt sep inf*: **to ~ sb out of sthg** escroquer OR carotter qqch à qqn. ▶ **do up** *vt sep* **1.** (*fasten - shoelaces, shoes*) attacher; (*- buttons, coat*) boutonner. **2.** (*decorate - room, house*) refaire. **3.** (*wrap up*) emballer. ▶ **do with** *vt fus* **1.** (*need*) avoir besoin de. **2.** (*have connection with*): **that has nothing to ~ with it** ça n'a rien à voir, ça n'a aucun rapport; **I had nothing to ~ with it** je n'y étais pour rien. ▶ **do without** ◆ *vt fus* se passer de. ◆ *vi* s'en passer.

Doberman ['dəʊbəmən] (*pl* **-s**) *n*: **~ (pinscher)** doberman *m*.

docile [Br 'dəʊsaɪl, Am 'dɒsəl] *adj* docile.

dock [dɒk] ◆ *n* **1.** (*in harbour*) docks *mpl*. **2.** (JUR) banc *m* des accusés. ◆ *vi* (*ship*) arriver à quai.

docker ['dɒkəʳ] *n* docker *m*.

docklands ['dɒkləndz] *npl* Br docks *mpl*.

dockworker ['dɒkwɜːkəʳ] = **docker**.

dockyard ['dɒkjɑːd] *n* chantier *m* naval.

doctor ['dɒktəʳ] ◆ *n* **1.** (MED) docteur *m*, médecin *m*; **to go to the ~'s** aller chez le docteur. **2.** (UNIV) docteur *m*. ◆ *vt* (*results, report*) falsifier; (*text, food*) altérer.

doctorate ['dɒktərət], **doctor's degree** *n* doctorat *m*.

doctrine ['dɒktrɪn] *n* doctrine *f*.

document ['dɒkjumənt] *n* document *m*.

documentary [,dɒkju'mentərɪ] ◆ *adj* documentaire. ◆ *n* documentaire *m*.

dodge [dɒdʒ] ◆ *n inf* combine *f*. ◆ *vt* éviter, esquiver. ◆ *vi* s'esquiver.

dodgy ['dɒdʒɪ] *adj* Br inf (*plan, deal*) douteux(euse).

doe [dəʊ] *n* **1.** (*deer*) biche *f*. **2.** (*rabbit*) lapine *f*.

does [*weak form* dəz, *strong form* dʌz] → **do**.

doesn't ['dʌznt] = **does not**.

dog [dɒg] ◆ *n* (*animal*) chien *m*, chienne *f*. ◆ *vt* **1.** (*subj: person - follow*) suivre de près. **2.** (*subj: problems, bad luck*) poursuivre.

dog collar *n* **1.** (*of dog*) collier *m* de chien. **2.** (*of priest*) col *m* d'ecclésiastique.

dog-eared [-ɪəd] *adj* écorné(e).

dog food *n* nourriture *f* pour chiens.

dogged ['dɒgɪd] *adj* opiniâtre.

dogsbody ['dɒgz,bɒdɪ] *n* Br inf (*woman*) bonne *f* à tout faire; (*man*) factotum *m*.

doing ['duːɪŋ] *n*: **is this your ~?** c'est toi qui es cause de tout cela? ▶ **doings** *npl* actions *fpl*.

do-it-yourself *n* (U) bricolage *m*.

doldrums ['dɒldrəmz] *npl*: **to be in the ~** *fig* être dans le marasme.

dole [dəʊl] *n* Br (*unemployment benefit*) allocation *f* de chômage; **to be on the ~** être au chômage. ▶ **dole out** *vt sep* (*food, money*) distribuer au compte-gouttes.

doleful ['dəʊlfʊl] *adj* morne.

doll [dɒl] *n* poupée *f*.

dollar ['dɒləʳ] *n* dollar *m*.

dollop ['dɒləp] *n inf* bonne cuillerée *f*.

dolphin ['dɒlfɪn] *n* dauphin *m*.

domain [də'meɪn] *n lit & fig* domaine *m*.

dome [dəʊm] *n* dôme *m*.

domestic [də'mestɪk] ◆ *adj* **1.** (*policy, politics, flight*) intérieur(e). **2.** (*chores, animal*) domestique. **3.** (*home-loving*) casanier(ère). ◆ *n* domestique *mf*.

domestic appliance *n* appareil *m* ménager.

dominant ['dɒmɪnənt] *adj* dominant(e);

(*personality, group*) dominateur(trice).
dominate ['dɒmɪneɪt] *vt* dominer.
domineering [,dɒmɪ'nɪərɪŋ] *adj* autoritaire.
dominion [də'mɪnjən] *n* **1.** (U) (*power*) domination *f*. **2.** (*land*) territoire *m*.
domino ['dɒmɪnəʊ] (*pl* **-es**) *n* domino *m*. ▶ **dominoes** *npl* dominos *mpl*.
don [dɒn] *n* Br (UNIV) professeur *m* d'université.
donate [də'neɪt] *vt* faire don de.
done [dʌn] ◆ *pp* → **do**. ◆ *adj* **1.** (*job, work*) achevé(e); **I'm nearly ~** j'ai presque fini. **2.** (*cooked*) cuit(e). ◆ *excl* (*to conclude deal*) tope!
donkey ['dɒŋkɪ] (*pl* **donkeys**) *n* âne *m*, ânesse *f*.
donor ['dəʊnə^r] *n* **1.** (MED) donneur *m*, -euse *f*. **2.** (*to charity*) donateur *m*, -trice *f*.
donor card *n* carte *f* de donneur.
don't [dəʊnt] = **do not**.
doodle ['du:dl] ◆ *n* griffonnage *m*. ◆ *vi* griffonner.
doom [du:m] *n* (*fate*) destin *m*.
doomed [du:md] *adj* condamné(e); **the plan was ~ to failure** le plan était voué à l'échec.
door [dɔ:^r] *n* porte *f*; (*of vehicle*) portière *f*.
doorbell ['dɔ:bel] *n* sonnette *f*.
doorknob ['dɔ:nɒb] *n* bouton *m* de porte.
doorman ['dɔ:mən] (*pl* **-men** [-mən]) *n* portier *m*.
doormat ['dɔ:mæt] *n* paillasson *m*.
doorstep ['dɔ:step] *n* pas *m* de la porte.
doorway ['dɔ:weɪ] *n* embrasure *f* de la porte.
dope [dəʊp] ◆ *n inf* **1.** *drugs sl* dope *f*. **2.** (*for athlete, horse*) dopant *m*. **3.** *inf* (*fool*) imbécile *mf*. ◆ *vt* (*horse*) doper.
dormant ['dɔ:mənt] *adj* **1.** (*volcano*) endormi(e). **2.** (*law*) inappliqué(e).
dormitory ['dɔ:mətrɪ] *n* **1.** (*gen*) dortoir *m*. **2.** Am (*in university*) ≃ cité *f* universitaire.
Dormobile® ['dɔ:mə,bi:l] *n* Br camping-car *m*.
DOS [dɒs] (*abbr of* **disk operating system**) *n* DOS *m*.
dose [dəʊs] *n* **1.** (MED) dose *f*. **2.** *fig* (*amount*): **a ~ of the measles** la rougeole.
dosser ['dɒsə^r] *n* Br *inf* clochard *m*, -e *f*.
dosshouse ['dɒshaʊs, *pl* -haʊzɪz] *n* Br *inf* asile *m* de nuit.
dot [dɒt] ◆ *n* point *m*; **on the ~** à l'heure

pile. ◆ *vt*: **dotted with** parsemé(e) de.
dote [dəʊt] ▶ **dote (up)on** *vt fus* adorer.
dot-matrix printer *n* imprimante *f* matricielle.
dotted line ['dɒtɪd-] *n* ligne *f* pointillée.
double ['dʌbl] ◆ *adj* double; **~ doors** porte *f* à deux battants. ◆ *adv* **1.** (*twice*): **~ the amount** deux fois plus; **to see ~** voir double. **2.** (*in two*) en deux; **to bend ~** se plier en deux. ◆ *n* **1.** (*twice as much*): **I earn ~ what I used to** je gagne le double de ce que je gagnais auparavant. **2.** (*drink, look-alike*) double *m*. **3.** (CINEMA) doublure *f*. ◆ *vt* doubler. ◆ *vi* (*increase twofold*) doubler. ▶ **doubles** *npl* (TENNIS) double *m*.
double-barrelled Br, **double-barreled** Am [-'bærəld] *adj* **1.** (*shotgun*) à deux coups. **2.** (*name*) à rallonge.
double bass [-beɪs] *n* contrebasse *f*.
double bed *n* lit *m* pour deux personnes, grand lit.
double-breasted [-'brestɪd] *adj* (*jacket*) croisé(e).
double-check *vt* & *vi* revérifier.
double chin *n* double menton *m*.
double cream *n* Br crème *f* fraîche épaisse.
double-cross *vt* trahir.
double-decker [-'dekə^r] *n* (*bus*) autobus *m* à impériale.
double-dutch *n* Br charabia *m*.
double-glazing [-'gleɪzɪŋ] *n* double vitrage *m*.
double room *n* chambre *f* pour deux personnes.
double vision *n* vue *f* double.
doubly ['dʌblɪ] *adv* doublement.
doubt [daʊt] ◆ *n* doute *m*; **there is no ~ that** il n'y a aucun doute que; **without (a) ~** sans aucun doute; **to be in ~** (*person*) ne pas être sûr(e); (*outcome*) être incertain(e); **to cast ~ on sthg** mettre qqch en doute; **no ~** sans aucun doute. ◆ *vt* douter; **to ~ whether** OR **if** douter que.
doubtful ['daʊtfʊl] *adj* **1.** (*decision, future*) incertain(e). **2.** (*person, value*) douteux(euse).
doubtless ['daʊtlɪs] *adv* sans aucun doute.
dough [dəʊ] *n* (U) **1.** (CULIN) pâte *f*. **2.** *v inf* (*money*) fric *m*.
doughnut ['dəʊnʌt] *n* beignet *m*.
douse [daʊs] *vt* **1.** (*fire, flames*) éteindre. **2.** (*drench*) tremper.
dove[1] [dʌv] *n* (*bird*) colombe *f*.

dove² [dəʊv] Am pt → **dive**.

Dover ['dəʊvə'] n Douvres.

dovetail ['dʌvteɪl] fig vi coïncider.

dowdy ['daʊdɪ] adj sans chic.

down [daʊn] ◆ adv 1. (downwards) en bas, vers le bas; **to bend ~** se pencher; **to climb ~** descendre; **to fall ~** tomber (par terre); **to pull ~** tirer vers le bas. 2. (along): **we went ~ to have a look** on est allé jeter un coup d'œil; **I'm going ~ to the shop** je vais au magasin. 3. (southwards): **we travelled ~ to London** on est descendu à Londres. 4. (lower in amount): **prices are coming ~** les prix baissent; **~ to the last detail** jusqu'au moindre détail. ◆ prep 1. (downwards): **they ran ~ the hill/stairs** ils ont descendu la colline/l'escalier en courant. 2. (along): **to walk ~ the street** descendre la rue. ◆ adj 1. inf (depressed): **to feel ~** avoir le cafard. 2. (computer, telephones) en panne. ◆ n (U) duvet m. ◆ vt 1. (knock over) abattre. 2. (drink) avaler d'un trait. ▶ **downs** npl Br collines fpl.

down-and-out ◆ adj indigent(e). ◆ n personne f dans le besoin.

down-at-heel adj déguenillé(e).

downbeat ['daʊnbiːt] adj inf pessimiste.

downcast ['daʊnkɑːst] adj (sad) démoralisé(e).

downfall ['daʊnfɔːl] n (U) ruine f.

downhearted [ˌdaʊn'hɑːtɪd] adj découragé(e).

downhill [ˌdaʊn'hɪl] ◆ adj (downward) en pente. ◆ adv: **to walk ~** descendre la côte; **her career is going ~** fig sa carrière est sur le déclin.

Downing Street ['daʊnɪŋ-] n rue du centre de Londres où réside le premier ministre.

down payment n acompte m.

downpour ['daʊnpɔː'] n pluie f torrentielle.

downright ['daʊnraɪt] ◆ adj franc (franche); (lie) effronté(e). ◆ adv franchement.

downstairs [ˌdaʊn'steəz] ◆ adj du bas; (on floor below) à l'étage en-dessous. ◆ adv en bas; (on floor below) à l'étage en-dessous; **to come** OR **go ~** descendre.

downstream [ˌdaʊn'striːm] adv en aval.

down-to-earth adj pragmatique, terre-à-terre (inv).

downtown [ˌdaʊn'taʊn] ◆ adj: **~ New York** le centre de New York. ◆ adv en ville.

downturn ['daʊntɜːn] n: **~ (in)** baisse f (de).

down under adv en Australie/Nouvelle-Zélande.

downward ['daʊnwəd] ◆ adj 1. (towards ground) vers le bas. 2. (trend) à la baisse. ◆ adv Am = **downwards**.

downwards ['daʊnwədz] adv (look, move) vers le bas.

dowry ['daʊərɪ] n dot f.

doz. (abbr of **dozen**) douz.

doze [dəʊz] ◆ n somme m. ◆ vi sommeiller. ▶ **doze off** vi s'assoupir.

dozen ['dʌzn] ◆ num adj: **a ~ eggs** une douzaine d'œufs. ◆ n douzaine f; **50p a ~** 50p la douzaine; **~s of** inf des centaines de.

dozy ['dəʊzɪ] adj 1. (sleepy) somnolent(e). 2. Br inf (stupid) lent(e).

Dr. 1. (abbr of **Drive**) av. 2. (abbr of **Doctor**) Dr.

drab [dræb] adj terne.

draft [drɑːft] ◆ n 1. (early version) premier jet m, ébauche f; (of letter) brouillon m. 2. (money order) traite f. 3. Am (MIL): **the ~** la conscription f. 4. Am = **draught**. ◆ vt 1. (speech) ébaucher, faire le plan de; (letter) faire le brouillon de. 2. Am (MIL) appeler. 3. (staff) muter.

draftsman Am = **draughtsman**.

drafty Am = **draughty**.

drag [dræg] ◆ vt 1. (gen) traîner. 2. (lake, river) draguer. ◆ vi 1. (dress, coat) traîner. 2. fig (time, action) traîner en longueur. ◆ n 1. inf (bore) plaie f. 2. inf (on cigarette) bouffée f. 3. (cross-dressing): **in ~** en travesti. ▶ **drag on** vi (meeting, time) s'éterniser, traîner en longueur.

dragon ['drægən] n lit & fig dragon m.

dragonfly ['drægnflaɪ] n libellule f.

drain [dreɪn] ◆ n 1. (pipe) égout m. 2. (depletion - of resources, funds): **~ on** épuisement m de. ◆ vt 1. (vegetables) égoutter; (land) assécher, drainer. 2. (strength, resources) épuiser. 3. (drink, glass) boire. ◆ vi (dishes) égoutter.

drainage ['dreɪnɪdʒ] n 1. (pipes, ditches) (système m du) tout-à-l'égout m. 2. (draining - of land) drainage m.

draining board Br ['dreɪnɪŋ-], **drainboard** Am ['dreɪnbɔːrd] n égouttoir m.

drainpipe ['dreɪnpaɪp] n tuyau m d'écoulement.

dram [dræm] n goutte f (de whisky).

drama ['drɑːmə] n 1. (play, excitement) drame m. 2. (U) (art) théâtre m.

dramatic [drə'mætɪk] adj 1. (gen) dramatique. 2. (sudden, noticeable) spectaculaire.

dramatist ['dræmətɪst] n dramaturge mf.

dramatize, -ise ['dræmətaɪz] vt 1. (rewrite as play, film) adapter pour la télévision/la scène/l'écran. 2. pej (make exciting) dramatiser.

drank [dræŋk] pt → drink.

drape [dreɪp] vt draper; **to be ~d with** OR **in** être drapé(e) de. ► **drapes** npl Am rideaux mpl.

drastic ['dræstɪk] adj 1. (measures) drastique, radical(e). 2. (improvement, decline) spectaculaire.

draught Br, **draft** Am [drɑːft] n 1. (air current) courant m d'air. 2. (from barrel): **on ~** (beer) à la pression. ► **draughts** n Br jeu m de dames.

draught beer n Br bière f à la pression.

draughtboard ['drɑːftbɔːd] n Br damier m.

draughtsman Br, **draftsman** Am ['drɑːftsmən] (pl -men [-mən]) n dessinateur m, -trice f.

draughty Br, **drafty** Am ['drɑːftɪ] adj plein(e) de courants d'air.

draw [drɔː] (pt drew, pp drawn) ◆ vt 1. (gen) tirer. 2. (sketch) dessiner. 3. (comparison, distinction) établir, faire. 4. (attract) attirer, entraîner; **to ~ sb's attention to** attirer l'attention de qqn sur. ◆ vi 1. (sketch) dessiner. 2. (move): **to ~ near** (person) s'approcher; (time) approcher; **to ~ away** reculer. 3. (SPORT) faire match nul; **to be ~ing** être à égalité. ◆ n 1. (SPORT) (result) match m nul. 2. (lottery) tirage m. 3. (attraction) attraction f. ► **draw out** vt sep 1. (encourage - person) faire sortir de sa coquille. 2. (prolong) prolonger. 3. (money) faire un retrait de, retirer. ► **draw up** ◆ vt sep (contract, plan) établir, dresser. ◆ vi (vehicle) s'arrêter.

drawback ['drɔːbæk] n inconvénient m, désavantage m.

drawbridge ['drɔːbrɪdʒ] n pont-levis m.

drawer [drɔːr] n (in desk, chest) tiroir m.

drawing ['drɔːɪŋ] n dessin m.

drawing board n planche f à dessin.

drawing pin n Br punaise f.

drawing room n salon m.

drawl [drɔːl] n voix f traînante.

drawn [drɔːn] pp → draw.

dread [dred] ◆ n (U) épouvante f. ◆ vt appréhender; **to ~ doing sthg** appréhender de faire qqch.

dreadful ['dredful] adj affreux(euse), épouvantable.

dreadfully ['dredfulɪ] adv 1. (badly) terriblement. 2. (extremely) extrêmement; **I'm ~ sorry** je regrette infiniment.

dream [driːm] (pt & pp -ed OR dreamt) ◆ n rêve m. ◆ adj de rêve. ◆ vt: **to ~ (that)** ... rêver que ... ◆ vi: **to ~ (of** OR **about)** rêver (de); **I wouldn't ~ of it** cela ne me viendrait même pas à l'idée. ► **dream up** vt sep inventer.

dreamt [dremt] pt & pp → dream.

dreamy ['driːmɪ] adj 1. (distracted) rêveur(euse). 2. (dreamlike) de rêve.

dreary ['drɪərɪ] adj 1. (weather) morne. 2. (dull, boring) ennuyeux(euse).

dredge [dredʒ] vt draguer. ► **dredge up** vt sep 1. (with dredger) draguer. 2. fig (from past) déterrer.

dregs [dregz] npl lit & fig lie f.

drench [drentʃ] vt tremper; **to be ~ed in** OR **with** être inondé(e) de.

dress [dres] ◆ n 1. (woman's garment) robe f. 2. (U) (clothing) costume m, tenue f. ◆ vt 1. (clothe) habiller; **to be ~ed** être habillé(e); **to be ~ed in** être vêtu(e) de; **to get ~ed** s'habiller. 2. (bandage) panser. 3. (CULIN) (salad) assaisonner. ◆ vi s'habiller. ► **dress up** vi 1. (in costume) se déguiser. 2. (in best clothes) s'habiller (élégamment).

dress circle n premier balcon m.

dresser ['dresər] n 1. (for dishes) vaisselier m. 2. Am (chest of drawers) commode f.

dressing ['dresɪŋ] n 1. (bandage) pansement m. 2. (for salad) assaisonnement m. 3. Am (for turkey etc) farce f.

dressing gown n robe f de chambre.

dressing room n 1. (THEATRE) loge f. 2. (SPORT) vestiaire m.

dressing table n coiffeuse f.

dressmaker ['dres,meɪkər] n couturier m, -ère f.

dressmaking ['dres,meɪkɪŋ] n couture f.

dress rehearsal n générale f.

dressy ['dresɪ] adj habillé(e).

drew [druː] pt → draw.

dribble ['drɪbl] ◆ n 1. (saliva) bave f. 2. (trickle) traînée f. ◆ vt (SPORT) dribbler. ◆ vi 1. (drool) baver. 2. (liquid) tomber goutte à goutte, couler.

dried [draɪd] adj (milk, eggs) en poudre; (fruit) sec (sèche); (flowers) séché(e).

drier ['draɪər] = dryer.

drift [drɪft] ◆ *n* **1.** (*movement*) mouvement *m*; (*direction*) direction *f*, sens *m*. **2.** (*meaning*) sens *m* général. **3.** (*of snow*) congère *f*; (*of sand, leaves*) amoncellement *m*, entassement *m*. ◆ *vi* **1.** (*boat*) dériver. **2.** (*snow, sand, leaves*) s'amasser, s'amonceler.

driftwood ['drɪftwʊd] *n* bois *m* flottant.

drill [drɪl] ◆ *n* **1.** (*tool*) perceuse *f*; (*dentist's*) fraise *f*; (*in mine etc*) perforatrice *f*. **2.** (*exercise, training*) exercice *m*. ◆ *vt* **1.** (*wood, hole*) percer; (*tooth*) fraiser; (*well*) forer. **2.** (*soldiers*) entraîner. ◆ *vi* (*excavate*): **to ~ for oil** forer à la recherche de pétrole.

drink [drɪŋk] (*pt* **drank**, *pp* **drunk**) ◆ *n* **1.** (*gen*) boisson *f*; **to have a ~** boire un verre. **2.** (U) (*alcohol*) alcool *m*. ◆ *vt* boire. ◆ *vi* boire.

drink-driving Br, **drunk-driving** Am *n* conduite *f* en état d'ivresse.

drinker ['drɪŋkə^r] *n* buveur *m*, -euse *f*.

drinking water ['drɪŋkɪŋ-] *n* eau *f* potable.

drip [drɪp] ◆ *n* **1.** (*drop*) goutte *f*. **2.** (MED) goutte-à-goutte *m inv*. ◆ *vi* (*gen*) goutter, tomber goutte à goutte.

drip-dry *adj* qui ne se repasse pas.

drive [draɪv] (*pt* **drove**, *pp* **driven**) ◆ *n* **1.** (*in car*) trajet *m* (en voiture); **to go for a ~** faire une promenade (en voiture). **2.** (*urge*) désir *m*, besoin *m*. **3.** (*campaign*) campagne *f*. **4.** (U) (*energy*) dynamisme *m*, énergie *f*. **5.** (*road to house*) allée *f*. **6.** (SPORT) drive *m*. ◆ *vt* **1.** (*vehicle, passenger*) conduire. **2.** (TECH) entraîner, actionner. **3.** (*animals, people*) pousser. **4.** (*motivate*) pousser. **5.** (*force*): **to ~ sb to sthg/to do sthg** pousser qqn à qqch/à faire qqch; **to ~ sb mad** OR **crazy** rendre qqn fou. **6.** (*nail, stake*) enfoncer. ◆ *vi* (*driver*) conduire; (*travel by car*) aller en voiture.

drivel ['drɪvl] *n* (U) *inf* foutaises *fpl*, idioties *fpl*.

driven ['drɪvn] *pp* → **drive**.

driver ['draɪvə^r] *n* (*of vehicle - gen*) conducteur *m*, -trice *f*; (*- of taxi*) chauffeur *m*.

driver's license Am = **driving licence**.

drive shaft *n* arbre *m* de transmission.

driveway ['draɪvweɪ] *n* allée *f*.

driving ['draɪvɪŋ] ◆ *adj* (*rain*) battant(e); (*wind*) cinglant(e). ◆ *n* (U) conduite *f*.

driving instructor *n* moniteur *m*, -trice *f* d'auto-école.

driving lesson *n* leçon *f* de conduite.

driving licence Br, **driver's license** Am *n* permis *m* de conduire.

driving mirror *n* rétroviseur *m*.

driving school *n* auto-école *f*.

driving test *n* (examen *m* du) permis *m* de conduire.

drizzle ['drɪzl] ◆ *n* bruine *f*. ◆ *v impers* bruiner.

droll [drəʊl] *adj* drôle.

drone [drəʊn] *n* **1.** (*of traffic, voices*) ronronnement *m*; (*of insect*) bourdonnement *m*. **2.** (*male bee*) abeille *f* mâle, faux-bourdon *m*.

drool [druːl] *vi* baver; **to ~ over** *fig* baver (d'admiration) devant.

droop [druːp] *vi* (*head*) pencher; (*shoulders, eyelids*) tomber.

drop [drɒp] ◆ *n* **1.** (*of liquid*) goutte *f*. **2.** (*sweet*) pastille *f*. **3.** (*decrease*): **~ (in)** baisse *f* (de). **4.** (*distance down*) dénivellation *f*; **sheer ~** à-pic *m inv*. ◆ *vt* **1.** (*let fall*) laisser tomber. **2.** (*voice, speed, price*) baisser. **3.** (*abandon*) abandonner; (*player*) exclure. **4.** (*let out of car*) déposer. **5.** (*utter*): **to ~ a hint that** laisser entendre que. **6.** (*write*): **to ~ sb a note** OR **line** écrire un petit mot à qqn. ◆ *vi* **1.** (*fall*) tomber. **2.** (*temperature, demand*) baisser; (*voice, wind*) tomber. ▶ **drops** *npl* (MED) gouttes *fpl*. ▶ **drop in** *vi inf*: **to ~ in (on sb)** passer (chez qqn). ▶ **drop off** ◆ *vt sep* déposer. ◆ *vi* **1.** (*fall asleep*) s'endormir. **2.** (*interest, sales*) baisser. ▶ **drop out** *vi*: **to ~ out (of** OR **from sthg)** abandonner (qqch); **to ~ out of society** vivre en marge de la société.

dropout ['drɒpaʊt] *n* (*from society*) marginal *m*, -e *f*; (*from college*) étudiant *m*, -e *f* qui abandonne ses études.

droppings ['drɒpɪŋz] *npl* (*of bird*) fiente *f*; (*of animal*) crottes *fpl*.

drought [draʊt] *n* sécheresse *f*.

drove [drəʊv] *pt* → **drive**.

drown [draʊn] ◆ *vt* (*in water*) noyer. ◆ *vi* se noyer.

drowsy ['draʊzɪ] *adj* assoupi(e), somnolent(e).

drudgery ['drʌdʒərɪ] *n* (U) corvée *f*.

drug [drʌg] ◆ *n* **1.** (*medicine*) médicament *m*. **2.** (*narcotic*) drogue *f*. ◆ *vt* droguer.

drug abuse *n* usage *m* de stupéfiants.

drug addict *n* drogué *m*, -e *f*.

druggist ['drʌgɪst] *n* Am pharmacien *m*, -enne *f*.

drug test *n* (*of athlete, horse*) contrôle *m* antidopage.

drum [drʌm] ◆ *n* **1.** (MUS) tambour *m*. **2.** (*container*) bidon *m*. ◆ *vt* & *vi* tambouriner. ▶ **drums** *npl* batterie *f*. ▶ **drum up** *vt sep* (*support, business*) rechercher, solliciter.

drummer ['drʌmər] *n* (*gen*) (joueur *m*, -euse *f* de) tambour *m*; (*in pop group*) batteur *m*, -euse *f*.

drumstick ['drʌmstɪk] *n* **1.** (*for drum*) baguette *f* de tambour. **2.** (*of chicken*) pilon *m*.

drunk [drʌŋk] ◆ *pp* → **drink**. ◆ *adj* (*on alcohol*) ivre, soûl(e); **to get ~** se soûler, s'enivrer. ◆ *n* soûlard *m*, -e *f*.

drunkard ['drʌŋkəd] *n* alcoolique *mf*.

drunk-driving Am = **drink-driving**.

drunken ['drʌŋkn] *adj* (*person*) ivre; (*quarrel*) d'ivrognes.

drunken driving = **drink-driving**.

dry [draɪ] ◆ *adj* **1.** (*gen*) sec (sèche); (*day*) sans pluie. **2.** (*river, earth*) asséché(e). **3.** (*wry*) pince-sans-rire (*inv*). ◆ *vt* (*gen*) sécher; (*with cloth*) essuyer. ◆ *vi* sécher. ▶ **dry up** *vt sep* (*dishes*) essuyer. ◆ *vi* **1.** (*river, lake*) s'assécher. **2.** (*supply*) se tarir. **3.** (*actor, speaker*) avoir un trou, sécher. **4.** (*dry dishes*) essuyer.

dry cleaner *n* : **~'s** pressing *m*.

dryer ['draɪər] *n* (*for clothes*) séchoir *m*.

dry land *n* terre *f* ferme.

dry rot *n* pourriture *f* sèche.

dry ski slope *n* piste *f* de ski artificielle.

DSS (*abbr of* **Department of Social Security**) *n* ministère britannique de la sécurité sociale.

DTI (*abbr of* **Department of Trade and Industry**) *n* ministère britannique du commerce et de l'industrie.

DTP (*abbr of* **desktop publishing**) *n* PAO *f*.

dual ['djuːəl] *adj* double.

dual carriageway *n* Br route *f* à quatre voies.

dubbed [dʌbd] *adj* **1.** (CINEMA) doublé(e). **2.** (*nicknamed*) surnommé(e).

dubious ['djuːbjəs] *adj* **1.** (*suspect*) douteux(euse). **2.** (*uncertain*) hésitant(e), incertain(e); **to be ~ about doing sthg** hésiter à faire qqch.

Dublin ['dʌblɪn] *n* Dublin.

duchess ['dʌtʃɪs] *n* duchesse *f*.

duck [dʌk] ◆ *n* canard *m*. ◆ *vt* **1.** (*head*) baisser. **2.** (*responsibility*) esquiver, se dérober à. ◆ *vi* (*lower head*) se baisser.

duckling ['dʌklɪŋ] *n* caneton *m*.

duct [dʌkt] *n* **1.** (*pipe*) canalisation *f*. **2.** (ANAT) canal *m*.

dud [dʌd] ◆ *adj* (*bomb*) non éclaté(e); (*cheque*) sans provision, en bois. ◆ *n* obus *m* non éclaté.

dude [djuːd] *n* Am *inf* (*man*) gars *m*, type *m*.

due [djuː] ◆ *adj* **1.** (*expected*): **she's ~ back shortly** elle devrait rentrer sous peu; **when is the train ~?** à quelle heure le train doit-il arriver? **2.** (*appropriate*) dû (due), qui convient; **in ~ course** (*at the appropriate time*) en temps voulu; (*eventually*) à la longue. **3.** (*owed, owing*) dû (due). ◆ *adv*: **~ west** droit vers l'ouest. ◆ *n* dû *m*. ▶ **dues** *npl* cotisation *f*. ▶ **due to** *prep* (*owing to*) dû à; (*because of*) provoqué par, à cause de.

duel ['djuːəl] ◆ *n* duel *m*. ◆ *vi* se battre en duel.

duet [djuːˈet] *n* duo *m*.

duffel bag ['dʌfl-] *n* sac *m* marin.

duffel coat ['dʌfl-] *n* duffel-coat *m*.

duffle bag ['dʌfl-] = **duffel bag**.

duffle coat ['dʌfl-] = **duffel coat**.

dug [dʌg] *pt* & *pp* → **dig**.

duke [djuːk] *n* duc *m*.

dull [dʌl] ◆ *adj* **1.** (*boring - book, conversation*) ennuyeux(euse); (*- person*) terne. **2.** (*colour, light*) terne. **3.** (*weather*) maussade. **4.** (*sound, ache*) sourd(e). ◆ *vt* **1.** (*pain*) atténuer; (*senses*) émousser. **2.** (*make less bright*) ternir.

duly ['djuːlɪ] *adv* **1.** (*properly*) dûment. **2.** (*as expected*) comme prévu.

dumb [dʌm] *adj* **1.** (*unable to speak*) muet(ette). **2.** *inf* (*stupid*) idiot(e).

dumbfound [dʌmˈfaʊnd] *vt* stupéfier, abasourdir; **to be ~ed** ne pas en revenir.

dummy ['dʌmɪ] ◆ *adj* faux (fausse). ◆ *n* **1.** (*of tailor*) mannequin *m*. **2.** (*copy*) maquette *f*. **3.** Br (*for baby*) sucette *f*, tétine *f*. **4.** (SPORT) feinte *f*.

dump [dʌmp] ◆ *n* **1.** (*for rubbish*) décharge *f*. **2.** (MIL) dépôt *m*. ◆ *vt* **1.** (*put down*) déposer. **2.** (*dispose of*) jeter. **3.** *inf* (*boyfriend, girlfriend*) laisser tomber, plaquer.

dumper (truck) Br ['dʌmpər-], **dump truck** Am *n* tombereau *m*, dumper *m*.

dumping ['dʌmpɪŋ] *n* décharge *f*; **'no ~'** 'décharge interdite'.

dumpling ['dʌmplɪŋ] *n* boulette *f* de pâte.

dump truck Am = **dumper (truck)**.

dumpy ['dʌmpɪ] *adj inf* boulot(otte).

dunce [dʌns] n cancre m.

dune [djuːn] n dune f.

dung [dʌŋ] n fumier m.

dungarees [ˌdʌŋɡəˈriːz] npl Br (for work) bleu m de travail; (fashion garment) salopette f.

dungeon [ˈdʌndʒən] n cachot m.

Dunkirk [dʌnˈkɜːk] n Dunkerque.

duo [ˈdjuːəʊ] n duo m.

duplex [ˈdjuːpleks] n Am 1. (apartment) duplex m. 2. (house) maison f jumelée.

duplicate [adj & n ˈdjuːplɪkət, vb ˈdjuːplɪkeɪt] ◆ adj (key, document) en double. ◆ n double m; in ~ en double. ◆ vt (copy - gen) faire un double de; (- on photocopier) photocopier.

durable [ˈdjʊərəbl] adj solide, résistant(e).

duration [djʊˈreɪʃn] n durée f; for the ~ of jusqu'à la fin de.

duress [djʊˈres] n: under ~ sous la contrainte.

Durex® [ˈdjʊəreks] n préservatif m.

during [ˈdjʊərɪŋ] prep pendant, au cours de.

dusk [dʌsk] n crépuscule m.

dust [dʌst] ◆ n (U) poussière f. ◆ vt 1. (clean) épousseter. 2. (cover with powder): to ~ sthg (with) saupoudrer qqch (de).

dustbin [ˈdʌstbɪn] n Br poubelle f.

dustcart [ˈdʌstkɑːt] n Br camion m des boueux.

duster [ˈdʌstər] n (cloth) chiffon m (à poussière).

dust jacket n (on book) jaquette f.

dustman [ˈdʌstmən] (pl -men [-mən]) n Br éboueur m.

dustpan [ˈdʌstpæn] n pelle f à poussière.

dusty [ˈdʌstɪ] adj poussiéreux(euse).

Dutch [dʌtʃ] ◆ adj néerlandais(e), hollandais(e). ◆ n (language) néerlandais m, hollandais m. ◆ npl: the ~ les Néerlandais, les Hollandais. ◆ adv: to go ~ partager les frais.

dutiful [ˈdjuːtɪfʊl] adj obéissant(e).

duty [ˈdjuːtɪ] n 1. (U) (responsibility) devoir m; to do one's ~ faire son devoir. 2. (work): to be on/off ~ être/ne pas être de service. 3. (tax) droit m. ▶ **duties** npl fonctions fpl.

duty-free adj hors taxe.

duvet [ˈduːveɪ] n Br couette f.

duvet cover n Br housse f de couette.

dwarf [dwɔːf] (pl -s OR dwarves [dwɔːvz]) ◆ n nain m, -e f. ◆ vt (tower over) écraser.

dwell [dwel] (pt & pp dwelt OR -ed) vi literary habiter. ▶ **dwell on** vt fus s'étendre sur.

dwelling [ˈdwelɪŋ] n literary habitation f.

dwelt [dwelt] pt & pp → **dwell**.

dwindle [ˈdwɪndl] vi diminuer.

dye [daɪ] ◆ n teinture f. ◆ vt teindre.

dying [ˈdaɪɪŋ] ◆ cont → **die**. ◆ adj (person) mourant(e), moribond(e); (plant, language, industry) moribond.

dyke [daɪk] = **dike**.

dynamic [daɪˈnæmɪk] adj dynamique.

dynamite [ˈdaɪnəmaɪt] n (U) lit & fig dynamite f.

dynamo [ˈdaɪnəməʊ] (pl -s) n dynamo f.

dynasty [Br ˈdɪnəstɪ, Am ˈdaɪnəstɪ] n dynastie f.

dyslexia [dɪsˈleksɪə] n dyslexie f.

dyslexic [dɪsˈleksɪk] adj dyslexique.

E

e (pl e's OR es), **E** (pl E's OR Es) [iː] n (letter) e m inv, E m inv. ▶ **E** n 1. (MUS) mi m. 2. (abbr of east) E.

each [iːtʃ] ◆ adj chaque. ◆ pron chacun(e); the books cost £10.99 ~ les livres coûtent 10,99 livres (la) pièce; ~ other l'un l'autre (l'une l'autre), les uns les autres (les unes les autres); they love ~ other ils s'aiment; we've known ~ other for years nous nous connaissons depuis des années.

eager [ˈiːɡər] adj passionné(e), avide; to be ~ for être avide de; to be ~ to do sthg être impatient de faire qqch.

eagle [ˈiːɡl] n (bird) aigle m.

ear [ɪər] n 1. (gen) oreille f. 2. (of corn) épi m.

earache [ˈɪəreɪk] n: to have ~ avoir mal à l'oreille.

eardrum [ˈɪədrʌm] n tympan m.

earl [ɜːl] n comte m.

earlier [ˈɜːlɪər] ◆ adj (previous) précédent(e); (more early) plus tôt. ◆ adv plus tôt; ~ on plus tôt.

earliest [ˈɜːlɪəst] ◆ adj (first) premier (ère); (most early) le plus tôt. ◆ n: at the ~ au plus tôt.

earlobe ['ɪələʊb] n lobe m de l'oreille.
early ['ɜːlɪ] ◆ adj 1. (before expected time) en avance. 2. (in day) de bonne heure; **the ~ train** le premier train; **to make an ~ start** partir de bonne heure. 3. (at beginning): **in the ~ sixties** au début des années soixante. ◆ adv 1. (before expected time) en avance; **I was ten minutes ~** j'étais en avance de dix minutes. 2. (in day) tôt, de bonne heure; **as ~ as** dès; **~ on** tôt.
early retirement n retraite f anticipée.
earmark ['ɪəmɑːk] vt: **to be ~ed for** être réservé(e) à.
earn [ɜːn] vt 1. (as salary) gagner. 2. (COMM) rapporter. 3. fig (respect, praise) gagner, mériter.
earnest ['ɜːnɪst] adj sérieux(euse).
▶ **in earnest** ◆ adj sérieux(euse).
◆ adv pour de bon, sérieusement.
earnings ['ɜːnɪŋz] npl (of person) salaire m, gains mpl; (of company) bénéfices mpl.
earphones ['ɪəfəʊnz] npl casque m.
earplugs ['ɪəplʌgz] npl boules fpl Quiès®.
earring ['ɪərɪŋ] n boucle f d'oreille.
earshot ['ɪəʃɒt] n: **within ~** à portée de voix; **out of ~** hors de portée de voix.
earth [ɜːθ] ◆ n (gen & ELEC) terre f; **how/what/where/why on ~ ...?** mais comment/que/où/pourquoi donc ...?; **to cost the ~** Br coûter les yeux de la tête. ◆ vt Br: **to be ~ed** être à la masse.
earthenware ['ɜːθnweər] n (U) poteries fpl.
earthquake ['ɜːθkweɪk] n tremblement m de terre.
earthworm ['ɜːθwɜːm] n ver m de terre.
earthy ['ɜːθɪ] adj 1. fig (humour, person) truculent(e). 2. (taste, smell) de terre, terreux(euse).
earwig ['ɪəwɪg] n perce-oreille m.
ease [iːz] ◆ n (U) 1. (lack of difficulty) facilité f; **to do sthg with ~** faire qqch sans difficulté OR facilement. 2. (comfort): **at ~** à l'aise; **ill at ~** mal à l'aise.
◆ vt 1. (pain) calmer; (restrictions) modérer. 2. (move carefully): **to ~ sthg in/out** faire entrer/sortir qqch délicatement.
◆ vi (problem) s'arranger; (pain) s'atténuer; (rain) diminuer. ▶ **ease off** vi (pain) s'atténuer; (rain) diminuer.
▶ **ease up** vi 1. (rain) diminuer. 2. (relax) se détendre.
easel ['iːzl] n chevalet m.
easily ['iːzɪlɪ] adv 1. (without difficulty)

facilement. 2. (without doubt) de loin. 3. (in a relaxed manner) tranquillement.
east [iːst] ◆ n 1. (direction) est m. 2. (region): **the ~** l'est m. ◆ adj est (inv); (wind) d'est. ◆ adv à l'est, vers l'est; **~ of** à l'est de. ▶ **East** n: **the East** (gen & POL) l'Est m; (Asia) l'Orient m.
East End n: **the ~** les quartiers est de Londres.
Easter ['iːstər] n Pâques m.
Easter egg n œuf m de Pâques.
easterly ['iːstəlɪ] adj à l'est, de l'est; (wind) de l'est.
eastern ['iːstən] adj de l'est.
▶ **Eastern** adj (gen & POL) de l'Est; (from Asia) oriental(e).
East German ◆ adj d'Allemagne de l'Est. ◆ n Allemand m, -e f de l'Est.
East Germany n: (former) **~** (l'ex-)Allemagne f de l'Est.
eastward ['iːstwəd] ◆ adj à l'est, vers l'est. ◆ adv = **eastwards**.
eastwards ['iːstwədz] adv vers l'est.
easy ['iːzɪ] ◆ adj 1. (not difficult, comfortable) facile. 2. (relaxed - manner) naturel (elle). ◆ adv: **to take it** OR **things ~** inf ne pas se fatiguer.
easy chair n fauteuil m.
easygoing [ˌiːzɪˈgəʊɪŋ] adj (person) facile à vivre; (manner) complaisant(e).
eat [iːt] (pt ate, pp eaten) vt & vi manger.
▶ **eat away**, **eat into** vt fus 1. (subj: acid, rust) ronger. 2. (deplete) grignoter.
eaten ['iːtn] pp → **eat**.
eaves ['iːvz] npl avant-toit m.
eavesdrop ['iːvzdrɒp] vi: **to ~ (on sb)** écouter (qqn) de façon indiscrète.
ebb [eb] ◆ n reflux m. ◆ vi (tide, sea) se retirer, refluer.
ebony ['ebənɪ] ◆ adj (colour) noir(e) d'ébène. ◆ n ébène f.
EC (abbr of European Community) n CE f.
eccentric [ɪkˈsentrɪk] ◆ adj (odd) excentrique. ◆ n (person) excentrique mf.
echo ['ekəʊ] (pl -es) ◆ n lit & fig écho m.
◆ vt (words) répéter; (opinion) faire écho à. ◆ vi retentir, résonner.
éclair [eɪˈkleər] n éclair m.
eclipse [ɪˈklɪps] ◆ n lit & fig éclipse f.
◆ vt fig éclipser.
ecological [ˌiːkəˈlɒdʒɪkl] adj écologique.
ecology [ɪˈkɒlədʒɪ] n écologie f.
economic [ˌiːkəˈnɒmɪk] adj 1. (ECON) économique. 2. (profitable) rentable.
economical [ˌiːkəˈnɒmɪkl] adj 1. (cheap) économique. 2. (person) économe.
economics [ˌiːkəˈnɒmɪks] ◆ n (U)

économie *f* (politique), sciences *fpl* économiques. ◆ *npl* (*of plan, business*) aspect *m* financier.

economize, -ise [ı'kɒnəmaız] *vi* économiser.

economy [ı'kɒnəmı] *n* économie *f*; **economies of scale** économies d'échelle.

economy class *n* classe *f* touriste.

ecstasy ['ekstəsı] *n* 1. (*pleasure*) extase *f*, ravissement *m*. 2. (*drug*) ecstasy *m* or *f*.

ecstatic [ek'stætık] *adj* (*person*) en extase; (*feeling*) extatique.

ECU, Ecu ['ekju:] (*abbr of* **European Currency Unit**) *n* ECU *m*, écu *m*.

eczema ['eksımə] *n* eczéma *m*.

Eden ['i:dn] *n*: **(the Garden of)** ~ le jardin *m* d'Éden, l'Éden *m*.

edge [edʒ] ◆ *n* 1. (*gen*) bord *m*; (*of coin, book*) tranche *f*; (*of knife*) tranchant *m*; **to be on the** ~ **of** *fig* être à deux doigts de. 2. (*advantage*): **to have an** ~ **over** OR **the** ~ **on** avoir un léger avantage sur. ◆ *vi*: **to** ~ **forward** avancer tout doucement. ▶ **on edge** *adj* contracté(e), tendu(e).

edgeways ['edʒweız], **edgewise** ['edʒwaız] *adv* latéralement, de côté.

edgy ['edʒı] *adj* contracté(e), tendu(e).

edible ['edıbl] *adj* (*safe to eat*) comestible.

edict ['i:dıkt] *n* décret *m*.

Edinburgh ['edınbrə] *n* Édimbourg.

edit ['edıt] *vt* 1. (*correct - text*) corriger. 2. (CINEMA) monter; (RADIO & TV) réaliser. 3. (*magazine*) diriger; (*newspaper*) être le rédacteur en chef de.

edition [ı'dıʃn] *n* édition *f*.

editor ['edıtər] *n* 1. (*of magazine*) directeur *m*, -trice *f*; (*of newspaper*) rédacteur *m*, -trice *f* en chef. 2. (*of text*) correcteur *m*, -trice *f*. 3. (CINEMA) monteur *m*, -euse *f*; (RADIO & TV) réalisateur *m*, -trice *f*.

editorial [,edı'tɔ:rıəl] ◆ *adj* (*department, staff*) de la rédaction; (*style, policy*) éditorial(e). ◆ *n* éditorial *m*.

educate ['edʒukeıt] *vt* 1. (SCH & UNIV) instruire. 2. (*inform*) informer, éduquer.

education [,edʒu'keıʃn] *n* 1. (*gen*) éducation *f*. 2. (*teaching*) enseignement *m*, instruction *f*.

educational [,edʒu'keıʃənl] *adj* 1. (*establishment, policy*) pédagogique. 2. (*toy, experience*) éducatif(ive).

EEC (*abbr of* **European Economic Community**) *n* ancien nom de la Communauté Européenne.

eel [i:l] *n* anguille *f*.

eerie ['ıərı] *adj* inquiétant(e), sinistre.

efface [ı'feıs] *vt* effacer.

effect [ı'fekt] ◆ *n* (*gen*) effet *m*; **to have an** ~ **on** avoir OR produire un effet sur; **for** ~ pour attirer l'attention, pour se faire remarquer; **to take** ~ (*law*) prendre effet, entrer en vigueur; **to put sthg into** ~ (*policy, law*) mettre qqch en application. ◆ *vt* (*repairs, change*) effectuer; (*reconciliation*) amener. ▶ **effects** *npl*: **(special)** ~**s** effets *mpl* spéciaux.

effective [ı'fektıv] *adj* 1. (*successful*) efficace. 2. (*actual, real*) effectif(ive).

effectively [ı'fektıvlı] *adv* 1. (*successfully*) efficacement. 2. (*in fact*) effectivement.

effectiveness [ı'fektıvnıs] *n* efficacité *f*.

effeminate [ı'femınət] *adj* efféminé(e).

effervescent [,efə'vesənt] *adj* (*liquid*) effervescent(e); (*drink*) gazeux(euse).

efficiency [ı'fıʃənsı] *n* (*of person, method*) efficacité *f*; (*of factory, system*) rendement *m*.

efficient [ı'fıʃənt] *adj* efficace.

effluent ['efluənt] *n* effluent *m*.

effort ['efət] *n* effort *m*; **to be worth the** ~ valoir la peine; **with** ~ avec peine; **to make the** ~ **to do sthg** s'efforcer de faire qqch; **to make an/no** ~ **to do sthg** faire un effort/ne faire aucun effort pour faire qqch.

effortless ['efətlıs] *adj* (*easy*) facile; (*natural*) aisé(e).

effusive [ı'fju:sıv] *adj* (*person*) démonstratif(ive).

e.g. (*abbr of* **exempli gratia**) *adv* par exemple.

egg [eg] *n* œuf *m*. ▶ **egg on** *vt sep* pousser, inciter.

eggcup ['egkʌp] *n* coquetier *m*.

eggplant ['egplɑ:nt] *n* Am aubergine *f*.

eggshell ['egʃel] *n* coquille *f* d'œuf.

egg white *n* blanc *m* d'œuf.

egg yolk [-jəuk] *n* jaune *m* d'œuf.

ego ['i:gəu] (*pl* **-s**) *n* moi *m*.

egoism ['i:gəuızm] *n* égoïsme *m*.

egoistic [,i:gəu'ıstık] *adj* égoïste.

egotistic(al) [,i:gə'tıstık(l)] *adj* égotiste.

Egypt ['i:dʒıpt] *n* Égypte *f*.

Egyptian [ı'dʒıpʃn] ◆ *adj* égyptien (enne). ◆ *n* Égyptien *m*, -enne *f*.

eiderdown ['aıdədaun] *n* (*bed cover*) édredon *m*.

eliminate

eight [eɪt] *num* huit; *see also* **six**.
eighteen [ˌeɪˈtiːn] *num* dix-huit; *see also* **six**.
eighth [eɪtθ] *num* huitième; *see also* **sixth**.
eighty [ˈeɪtɪ] *num* quatre-vingts; *see also* **sixty**.
Eire [ˈeərə] *n* République *f* d'Irlande.
either [ˈaɪðəʳ, ˈiːðəʳ] ◆ *adj* **1.** (*one or the other*) l'un ou l'autre (l'une ou l'autre) (des deux); **she couldn't find ~ jumper** elle ne trouva ni l'un ni l'autre des pulls; **~ way** de toute façon. **2.** (*each*) chaque; **on ~ side** de chaque côté. ◆ *pron:* **~** (**of them**) l'un ou l'autre *m*, l'une ou l'autre *f*; **I don't like ~** (**of them**) je n'aime aucun des deux, je n'aime ni l'un ni l'autre. ◆ *adv* (*in negatives*) non plus; **I don't ~** moi non plus. ◆ *conj:* **~ ... or** soit ... soit, ou ... ou; **I'm not fond of ~ him or his wife** je ne les aime ni lui ni sa femme.
eject [ɪˈdʒekt] *vt* **1.** (*object*) éjecter, émettre. **2.** (*person*) éjecter, expulser.
eke [iːk] ► **eke out** *vt sep* (*money, food*) économiser, faire durer.
elaborate [*adj* ɪˈlæbrət, *vb* ɪˈlæbəreɪt] ◆ *adj* (*ceremony, procedure*) complexe; (*explanation, plan*) détaillé(e), minutieux (euse). ◆ *vi:* **to ~** (**on**) donner des précisions (sur).
elapse [ɪˈlæps] *vi* s'écouler.
elastic [ɪˈlæstɪk] ◆ *adj lit & fig* élastique. ◆ *n* (U) élastique *m*.
elasticated [ɪˈlæstɪkeɪtɪd] *adj* élastique.
elastic band *n* Br élastique *m*, caoutchouc *m*.
elated [ɪˈleɪtɪd] *adj* transporté(e) (de joie).
elbow [ˈelbəʊ] *n* coude *m*.
elder [ˈeldəʳ] ◆ *adj* aîné(e). ◆ *n* **1.** (*older person*) aîné *m*, -e *f*. **2.** (*of tribe, church*) ancien *m*. **3. ~** (**tree**) sureau *m*.
elderly [ˈeldəlɪ] ◆ *adj* âgé(e). ◆ *npl:* **the ~** les personnes *fpl* âgées.
eldest [ˈeldɪst] *adj* aîné(e).
elect [ɪˈlekt] ◆ *adj* élu(e). ◆ *vt* (*by voting*) élire.
election [ɪˈlekʃn] *n* élection *f*.
electioneering [ɪˌlekʃəˈnɪərɪŋ] *n* (U) *usu pej* propagande *f* électorale.
elector [ɪˈlektəʳ] *n* électeur *m*, -trice *f*.
electorate [ɪˈlektərət] *n:* **the ~** l'électorat *m*.
electric [ɪˈlektrɪk] *adj lit & fig* électrique. ► **electrics** *npl* Br *inf* (*in car, machine*) installation *f* électrique.

electrical [ɪˈlektrɪkl] *adj* électrique.
electrical shock Am = **electric shock**.
electric blanket *n* couverture *f* chauffante.
electric cooker *n* cuisinière *f* électrique.
electric fire *n* radiateur *m* électrique.
electrician [ˌɪlekˈtrɪʃn] *n* électricien *m*, -enne *f*.
electricity [ˌɪlekˈtrɪsətɪ] *n* électricité *f*.
electric shock Br, **electrical shock** Am *n* décharge *f* électrique.
electrify [ɪˈlektrɪfaɪ] *vt* **1.** (TECH) électrifier. **2.** *fig* (*excite*) galvaniser, électriser.
electrocute [ɪˈlektrəkjuːt] *vt* électrocuter.
electrolysis [ˌɪlekˈtrɒləsɪs] *n* électrolyse *f*.
electron [ɪˈlektrɒn] *n* électron *m*.
electronic [ˌɪlekˈtrɒnɪk] *adj* électronique. ► **electronics** ◆ *n* (U) (*technology, science*) électronique *f*. ◆ *npl* (*equipment*) (équipement *m*) électronique *f*.
electronic data processing *n* traitement *m* électronique de données.
electronic mail *n* courrier *m* électronique.
elegant [ˈelɪgənt] *adj* élégant(e).
element [ˈelɪmənt] *n* **1.** (*gen*) élément *m*; **an ~ of truth** une part de vérité. **2.** (*in heater, kettle*) résistance *f*. ► **elements** *npl* **1.** (*basics*) rudiments *mpl*. **2.** (*weather*): **the ~s** les éléments *mpl*.
elementary [ˌelɪˈmentərɪ] *adj* élémentaire.
elementary school *n* Am école *f* primaire.
elephant [ˈelɪfənt] (*pl inv* OR **-s**) *n* éléphant *m*.
elevate [ˈelɪveɪt] *vt* **1.** (*give importance to*): **to ~ sb/sthg** (**to**) élever qqn/qqch (à). **2.** (*raise*) soulever.
elevator [ˈelɪveɪtəʳ] *n* Am ascenseur *m*.
eleven [ɪˈlevn] *num* onze; *see also* **six**.
elevenses [ɪˈlevnzɪz] *n* (U) Br ≃ pause-café *f*.
eleventh [ɪˈlevnθ] *num* onzième; *see also* **sixth**.
elicit [ɪˈlɪsɪt] *vt fml:* **to ~ sthg** (**from sb**) arracher qqch (à qqn).
eligible [ˈelɪdʒəbl] *adj* (*suitable, qualified*) admissible; **to be ~ for sthg** avoir droit à qqch; **to be ~ to do sthg** avoir le droit de faire qqch.
eliminate [ɪˈlɪmɪneɪt] *vt:* **to ~ sb/sthg** (**from**) éliminer qqn/qqch (de).

elite [r'li:t] ♦ adj d'élite. ♦ n élite f.

elitist [r'li:tɪst] ♦ adj élitiste. ♦ n élitiste mf.

elk [elk] (pl inv OR **-s**) n élan m.

elm [elm] n: ~ **(tree)** orme m.

elocution [ˌeləˈkjuːʃn] n élocution f,
diction f.

elongated [ˈiːlɒŋgeɪtɪd] adj allon-
gé(e); (fingers) long (longue).

elope [r'ləʊp] vi: **to ~ (with)** s'enfuir
(avec).

eloquent [ˈeləkwənt] adj éloquent(e).

El Salvador [ˌelˈsælvədɔːr] n Salvador
m.

else [els] adv: **anything ~** n'importe
quoi d'autre; **anything ~?** (in shop) et
avec ça?, ce sera tout?; **he doesn't want
anything ~** il n'a besoin de rien d'autre;
everyone ~ tous les autres; **nothing ~**
rien d'autre; **someone ~** quelqu'un
d'autre; **something ~** quelque chose
d'autre; **somewhere ~** autre part; **who/
what ~?** qui/quoi d'autre?; **where ~?** (à)
quel autre endroit? ▶ **or else** conj (or if
not) sinon, sans quoi.

elsewhere [els'weər] adv ailleurs,
autre part.

elude [r'luːd] vt échapper à.

elusive [r'luːsɪv] adj insaisissable; (success) qui échappe.

emaciated [r'meɪʃeɪtɪd] adj (face)
émacié(e); (person, limb) décharné(e).

E-mail (abbr of **electronic mail**) n BAL f.

emanate [ˈeməneɪt] fml vi: **to ~ from**
émaner de.

emancipate [r'mænsɪpeɪt] vt: **to ~ sb
(from)** affranchir OR émanciper qqn
(de).

embankment [ɪm'bæŋkmənt] n (of
river) berge f; (of railway) remblai m; (of
road) banquette f.

embark [ɪm'bɑːk] vi 1. (board ship): **to ~
(on)** embarquer (sur). 2. (start): **to ~ on
OR upon sthg** s'embarquer dans qqch.

embarkation [ˌembɑːˈkeɪʃn] n embarquement m.

embarrass [ɪm'bærəs] vt embarrasser.

embarrassed [ɪm'bærəst] adj embar-
rassé(e).

embarrassing [ɪm'bærəsɪŋ] adj
embarrassant(e).

embarrassment [ɪm'bærəsmənt] n
embarras m.

embassy [ˈembəsɪ] n ambassade f.

embedded [ɪm'bedɪd] adj 1. (buried): ~
in (in rock, wood) incrusté(e) dans; (in
mud) noyé(e) dans. 2. (ingrained) enra-
ciné(e).

embellish [ɪm'belɪʃ] vt 1. (decorate): **to ~
sthg (with)** (room, house) décorer qqch
(de); (dress) orner qqch (de). 2. (story)
enjoliver.

embers [ˈembəz] npl braises fpl.

embezzle [ɪm'bezl] vt détourner.

embittered [ɪm'bɪtəd] adj aigri(e).

emblem [ˈembləm] n emblème m.

embody [ɪm'bɒdɪ] vt incarner; **to be
embodied in sthg** être exprimé dans
qqch.

embossed [ɪm'bɒst] adj 1. (heading,
design): ~ **(on)** inscrit(e) (sur), gravé(e)
en relief (sur). 2. (wallpaper) gaufré(e);
(leather) frappé(e).

embrace [ɪm'breɪs] ♦ n étreinte f. ♦ vt
embrasser. ♦ vi s'embrasser, s'étreindre.

embroider [ɪm'brɔɪdər] ♦ vt 1. (SEW-
ING) broder. 2. pej (embellish) enjoliver.
♦ vi (SEWING) broder.

embroidery [ɪm'brɔɪdərɪ] n (U)
broderie f.

embroil [ɪm'brɔɪl] vt: **to be ~ed (in)** être
mêlé(e) (à).

embryo [ˈembrɪəʊ] (pl **-s**) n embryon
m.

emerald [ˈemərəld] ♦ adj (colour) émeraude (inv). ♦ n (stone) émeraude f.

emerge [r'mɜːdʒ] ♦ vi 1. (come out): **to ~
(from)** émerger (de). 2. (from experience,
situation): **to ~ from** sortir de. 3. (become
known) apparaître. 4. (come into existence - poet, artist) percer; (- movement,
organization) émerger. ♦ vt: **it ~s that ...** il
ressort OR il apparaît que ...

emergence [r'mɜːdʒəns] n émergence
f.

emergency [r'mɜːdʒənsɪ] ♦ adj d'urgence. ♦ n urgence f; **in an ~, in emer-
gencies** en cas d'urgence.

emergency exit n sortie f de secours.

emergency landing n atterrissage
m forcé.

emergency services npl = police-
secours f.

emery board [ˈemərɪ-] n lime f à
ongles.

emigrant [ˈemɪgrənt] n émigré m, -e f.

emigrate [ˈemɪgreɪt] vi: **to ~ (to)** émigrer (en/à).

eminent [ˈemɪnənt] adj éminent(e).

emission [r'mɪʃn] n émission f.

emit [r'mɪt] vt émettre.

emotion [r'məʊʃn] n 1. (U) (strength of
feeling) émotion f. 2. (particular feeling)
sentiment m.

emotional [ɪ'məʊʃənl] *adj* **1.** (*sensitive, demonstrative*) émotif(ive). **2.** (*moving*) émouvant(e). **3.** (*psychological*) émotionnel(elle).

emperor ['empərər] *n* empereur *m*.

emphasis ['emfəsɪs] (*pl* **-ases** [-əsi:z]) *n*: ~ **(on)** accent *m* (sur); **to lay** OR **place** ~ **on sthg** insister sur OR souligner qqch.

emphasize, -ise ['emfəsaɪz] *vt* insister sur.

emphatic [ɪm'fætɪk] *adj* (*forceful*) catégorique.

emphatically [ɪm'fætɪklɪ] *adv* **1.** (*with emphasis*) catégoriquement. **2.** (*certainly*) absolument.

empire ['empaɪər] *n* empire *m*.

employ [ɪm'plɔɪ] *vt* employer; **to be ~ed as** être employé comme; **to ~ sthg as sthg/to do sthg** employer qqch comme qqch/pour faire qqch.

employee [ɪm'plɔɪi:] *n* employé *m*, -e *f*.

employer [ɪm'plɔɪər] *n* employeur *m*, -euse *f*.

employment [ɪm'plɔɪmənt] *n* emploi *m*, travail *m*.

employment agency *n* bureau *m* OR agence *f* de placement.

empower [ɪm'paʊər] *vt* *fml*: **to be ~ed to do sthg** être habilité(e) à faire qqch.

empress ['emprɪs] *n* impératrice *f*.

empty ['emptɪ] ◆ *adj* **1.** (*containing nothing*) vide. **2.** *pej* (*meaningless*) vain(e). ◆ *vt* vider; **to ~ sthg into/out of** vider qqch dans/de. ◆ *vi* se vider. ◆ *n* *inf* bouteille *f* vide.

empty-handed [-'hændɪd] *adv* les mains vides.

EMS (*abbr of* European Monetary System) *n* SME *m*.

emulate ['emjʊleɪt] *vt* imiter.

emulsion [ɪ'mʌlʃn] *n*: ~ **(paint)** peinture *f* mate OR à émulsion.

enable [ɪ'neɪbl] *vt*: **to ~ sb to do sthg** permettre à qqn de faire qqch.

enact [ɪ'nækt] *vt* **1.** (JUR) promulguer. **2.** (THEATRE) jouer.

enamel [ɪ'næml] *n* **1.** (*material*) émail *m*. **2.** (*paint*) peinture *f* laquée.

encampment [ɪn'kæmpmənt] *n* campement *m*.

encapsulate [ɪn'kæpsjʊleɪt] *vt*: **to ~ sthg (in)** résumer qqch (en).

encase [ɪn'keɪs] *vt*: **to be ~d in** (*armour*) être enfermé(e) dans; (*leather*) être bardé(e) de.

enchanted [ɪn'tʃɑ:ntɪd] *adj*: ~ **(by/ with)** enchanté(e) (par/de).

enchanting [ɪn'tʃɑ:ntɪŋ] *adj* enchanteur(eresse).

encircle [ɪn'sɜ:kl] *vt* entourer; (*subj: troops*) encercler.

enclose [ɪn'kləʊz] *vt* **1.** (*surround, contain*) entourer. **2.** (*put in envelope*) joindre; **please find ~d ...** veuillez trouver ci-joint ...

enclosure [ɪn'kləʊʒər] *n* **1.** (*place*) enceinte *f*. **2.** (*in letter*) pièce *f* jointe.

encompass [ɪn'kʌmpəs] *vt* *fml* **1.** (*include*) contenir. **2.** (*surround*) entourer; (*subj: troops*) encercler.

encore ['ɒŋkɔ:r] ◆ *n* rappel *m*. ◆ *excl* bis!

encounter [ɪn'kaʊntər] ◆ *n* rencontre *f*. ◆ *vt* *fml* rencontrer.

encourage [ɪn'kʌrɪdʒ] *vt* **1.** (*give confidence to*): **to ~ sb (to do sthg)** encourager qqn (à faire qqch). **2.** (*promote*) encourager, favoriser.

encouragement [ɪn'kʌrɪdʒmənt] *n* encouragement *m*.

encroach [ɪn'krəʊtʃ] *vi*: **to ~ on** OR **upon** empiéter sur.

encyclop(a)edia [ɪn,saɪklə'pi:djə] *n* encyclopédie *f*.

end [end] ◆ *n* **1.** (*gen*) fin *f*; **at an** ~ terminé, fini; **to come to an** ~ se terminer, s'arrêter; **to put an** ~ **to sthg** mettre fin à qqch; **in the** ~ (*finally*) finalement. **2.** (*of rope, path, garden, table etc*) bout *m*, extrémité *f*; (*of box*) côté *m*. **3.** (*leftover part - of cigarette*) mégot *m*; (*- of pencil*) bout *m*. ◆ *vt* mettre fin à; (*day*) finir; **to ~ sthg with** terminer OR finir qqch par. ◆ *vi* se terminer; **to ~ in** se terminer par; **to ~ with** se terminer par OR avec. ▶ **on end** *adv* **1.** (*upright*) debout. **2.** (*continuously*) d'affilée. ▶ **end up** *vi* finir; **to ~ up doing sthg** finir par faire qqch.

endanger [ɪn'deɪndʒər] *vt* mettre en danger.

endearing [ɪn'dɪərɪŋ] *adj* engageant(e).

endeavour Br, **endeavor** Am [ɪn'devər] *fml* ◆ *n* effort *m*, tentative *f*. ◆ *vt*: **to ~ to do sthg** s'efforcer OR tenter de faire qqch.

ending ['endɪŋ] *n* fin *f*, dénouement *m*.

endive ['endaɪv] *n* **1.** (*salad vegetable*) endive *f*. **2.** (*chicory*) chicorée *f*.

endless ['endlɪs] *adj* **1.** (*unending*) interminable; (*patience, possibilities*) infini(e); (*resources*) inépuisable. **2.** (*vast*) infini(e).

endorse [ɪn'dɔ:s] *vt* **1.** (*approve*) approuver. **2.** (*cheque*) endosser.

endorsement [ɪn'dɔ:smənt] *n* **1.**

(approval) approbation f. **2.** Br (on driving licence) contravention portée au permis de conduire.

endow [ɪn'dau] vt **1.** (equip): **to be ~ed with sthg** être doté(e) de qqch. **2.** (donate money to) faire des dons à.

endurance [ɪn'djuərəns] n endurance f.

endure [ɪn'djuər] ◆ vt supporter, endurer. ◆ vi perdurer.

endways Br ['endweɪz], **endwise** Am ['endwaɪz] adv **1.** (not sideways) en long. **2.** (with ends touching) bout à bout.

enemy ['enɪmɪ] ◆ n ennemi m, -e f. ◆ comp ennemi(e).

energetic [,enə'dʒetɪk] adj énergique; (person) plein(e) d'entrain.

energy ['enədʒɪ] n énergie f.

enforce [ɪn'fɔːs] vt appliquer, faire respecter.

enforced [ɪn'fɔːst] adj forcé(e).

engage [ɪn'geɪdʒ] ◆ vt **1.** (attention, interest) susciter, éveiller. **2.** (TECH) engager. **3.** fml (employ) engager; **to be ~d in** OR **on sthg** prendre part à qqch. ◆ vi (be involved): **to ~ in** s'occuper de.

engaged [ɪn'geɪdʒd] adj **1.** (to be married): **~ (to sb)** fiancé(e) (à qqn); **to get ~** se fiancer. **2.** (busy) occupé(e); **~ in sthg** engagé dans qqch. **3.** (telephone, toilet) occupé(e).

engaged tone n Br tonalité f 'occupé'.

engagement [ɪn'geɪdʒmənt] n **1.** (to be married) fiançailles fpl. **2.** (appointment) rendez-vous m inv.

engagement ring n bague f de fiançailles.

engaging [ɪn'geɪdʒɪŋ] adj engageant(e); (personality) attirant(e).

engine ['endʒɪn] n **1.** (of vehicle) moteur m. **2.** (RAIL) locomotive f.

engine driver n Br mécanicien m.

engineer [,endʒɪ'nɪər] n **1.** (of roads) ingénieur m; (of machinery, on ship) mécanicien m; (of electrical equipment) technicien m. **2.** Am (engine driver) mécanicien m.

engineering [,endʒɪ'nɪərɪŋ] n ingénierie f.

England ['ɪŋglənd] n Angleterre f; **in ~** en Angleterre.

English ['ɪŋglɪʃ] ◆ adj anglais(e). ◆ n (language) anglais m. ◆ npl: **the ~** les Anglais.

English breakfast n petit déjeuner m anglais traditionnel.

English Channel n: **the ~** la Manche.

Englishman ['ɪŋglɪʃmən] (pl -men [-mən]) n Anglais m.

Englishwoman ['ɪŋglɪʃ,wumən] (pl -women [-wɪmɪn]) n Anglaise f.

engrave [ɪn'greɪv] vt: **to ~ sthg (on stone/in one's memory)** graver qqch (sur la pierre/dans sa mémoire).

engraving [ɪn'greɪvɪŋ] n gravure f.

engrossed [ɪn'grəust] adj: **to be ~ (in sthg)** être absorbé(e) (par qqch).

engulf [ɪn'gʌlf] vt engloutir.

enhance [ɪn'hɑːns] vt accroître.

enjoy [ɪn'dʒɔɪ] vt **1.** (like) aimer; **to ~ doing sthg** avoir plaisir à OR aimer faire qqch; **to ~ o.s.** s'amuser. **2.** fml (possess) jouir de.

enjoyable [ɪn'dʒɔɪəbl] adj agréable.

enjoyment [ɪn'dʒɔɪmənt] n (gen) plaisir m.

enlarge [ɪn'lɑːdʒ] vt agrandir.
▶ **enlarge (up)on** vt fus développer.

enlargement [ɪn'lɑːdʒmənt] n **1.** (expansion) extension f. **2.** (PHOT) agrandissement m.

enlighten [ɪn'laɪtn] vt éclairer.

enlightened [ɪn'laɪtnd] adj éclairé(e).

enlightenment [ɪn'laɪtnmənt] n (U) éclaircissement m.

enlist [ɪn'lɪst] ◆ vt **1.** (MIL) enrôler. **2.** (recruit) recruter. **3.** (obtain) s'assurer. ◆ vi (MIL): **to ~ (in)** s'enrôler (dans).

enmity ['enmɪtɪ] n hostilité f.

enormity [ɪ'nɔːmɪtɪ] n (extent) étendue f.

enormous [ɪ'nɔːməs] adj énorme; (patience, success) immense.

enough [ɪ'nʌf] ◆ adj assez de; **~ money/time** assez d'argent/de temps. ◆ pron assez; **more than ~** largement, bien assez; **to have had ~ (of sthg)** en avoir assez (de qqch). ◆ adv **1.** (sufficiently) assez; **big ~ for sthg/to do sthg** assez grand pour qqch/pour faire qqch; **to be good ~ to do sthg** fml être assez gentil pour OR de faire qqch, être assez aimable pour OR de faire qqch. **2.** (rather) plutôt; **strangely ~** bizarrement, c'est bizarre.

enquire [ɪn'kwaɪər] ◆ vt: **to ~ when/whether/how ...** demander quand/si/comment ... ◆ vi: **to ~ (about)** se renseigner (sur).

enquiry [ɪn'kwaɪərɪ] n **1.** (question) demande f de renseignements; **'Enquiries'** 'renseignements'. **2.** (investigation) enquête f.

enraged [ɪn'reɪdʒd] adj déchaîné(e); (animal) enragé(e).

enrol, enroll Am [ɪn'rəʊl] ♦ vt inscrire.
♦ vi: **to ~ (in)** s'inscrire (à).

ensign ['ensaɪn] n (flag) pavillon m.

ensue [ɪn'sjuː] vi s'ensuivre.

ensure [ɪn'ʃʊəʳ] vt assurer; **to ~ (that) ...** s'assurer que ...

ENT (abbr of **Ear, Nose & Throat**) n ORL f.

entail [ɪn'teɪl] vt entraîner; **what does the work ~?** en quoi consiste le travail?

enter ['entəʳ] ♦ vt 1. (room, vehicle) entrer dans. 2. (university, army) entrer à; (school) s'inscrire à, s'inscrire dans. 3. (competition, race) s'inscrire à; (politics) se lancer dans. 4. (register): **to ~ sb/sthg for sthg** inscrire qqn/qqch à qqch. 5. (write down) inscrire. 6. (COMPUT) entrer. ♦ vi 1. (come or go in) entrer. 2. (register): **to ~ (for)** s'inscrire (à). ▶ **enter into** vt fus (negotiations, correspondence) entamer.

enter key n (COMPUT) (touche f) entrée f.

enterprise ['entəpraɪz] n entreprise f.

enterprise zone n Br zone dans une région défavorisée qui bénéficie de subsides de l'État.

enterprising ['entəpraɪzɪŋ] adj qui fait preuve d'initiative.

entertain [,entə'teɪn] vt 1. (amuse) divertir. 2. (invite - guests) recevoir. 3. fml (thought, proposal) considérer.

entertainer [,entə'teɪnəʳ] n fantaisiste mf.

entertaining [,entə'teɪnɪŋ] adj divertissant(e).

entertainment [,entə'teɪnmənt] n 1. (U) (amusement) divertissement m. 2. (show) spectacle m.

enthral, enthrall Am [ɪn'θrɔːl] vt captiver.

enthrone [ɪn'θrəʊn] vt introniser.

enthusiasm [ɪn'θjuːzɪæzm] n 1. (passion, eagerness): **~ (for)** enthousiasme m (pour). 2. (interest) passion f.

enthusiast [ɪn'θjuːzɪæst] n amateur m, -trice f.

enthusiastic [ɪn,θjuːzɪ'æstɪk] adj enthousiaste.

entice [ɪn'taɪs] vt entraîner.

entire [ɪn'taɪəʳ] adj entier(ère).

entirely [ɪn'taɪəlɪ] adv totalement.

entirety [ɪn'taɪrətɪ] n: **in its ~** en entier.

entitle [ɪn'taɪtl] vt (allow): **to ~ sb to sthg** donner droit à qqch à qqn; **to ~ sb to do sthg** autoriser qqn à faire qqch.

entitled [ɪn'taɪtld] adj 1. (allowed) autorisé(e); **to be ~ to sthg** avoir droit à qqch; **to be ~ to do sthg** avoir le droit de faire qqch. 2. (called) intitulé(e).

entitlement [ɪn'taɪtlmənt] n droit m.

entrance [n 'entrəns, vt ɪn'trɑːns] ♦ n 1. (way in): **~ (to)** entrée f (de). 2. (arrival) entrée f. 3. (entry): **to gain ~ to** (building) obtenir l'accès à; (society, university) être admis(e) dans. ♦ vt ravir, enivrer.

entrance examination n examen m d'entrée.

entrance fee n 1. (to cinema, museum) droit m d'entrée. 2. (for club) droit m d'inscription.

entrant ['entrənt] n (in race, competition) concurrent m, -e f.

entreat [ɪn'triːt] vt: **to ~ sb (to do sthg)** supplier qqn (de faire qqch).

entrenched [ɪn'trentʃt] adj ancré(e).

entrepreneur [,ɒntrəprə'nɜːʳ] n entrepreneur m.

entrust [ɪn'trʌst] vt: **to ~ sthg to sb, to ~ sb with sthg** confier qqch à qqn.

entry ['entrɪ] n 1. (gen) entrée f; **to gain ~ to** avoir accès à; **'no ~'** 'défense d'entrer'; (AUT) 'sens interdit'. 2. (in competition) inscription f. 3. (in dictionary) entrée f; (in diary, ledger) inscription f.

entry form n formulaire m OR feuille f d'inscription.

entry phone n portier m électronique.

envelop [ɪn'veləp] vt envelopper.

envelope ['envələʊp] n enveloppe f.

envious ['envɪəs] adj envieux(euse).

environment [ɪn'vaɪərənmənt] n 1. (surroundings) milieu m, cadre m. 2. (natural world): **the ~** l'environnement m.

environmental [ɪn,vaɪərən'mentl] adj (pollution, awareness) de l'environnement; (impact) sur l'environnement.

environmentally [ɪn,vaɪərən'mentəlɪ] adv (damaging) pour l'environnement; **~ friendly** qui préserve l'environnement.

envisage [ɪn'vɪzɪdʒ], **envision** Am [ɪn'vɪʒn] vt envisager.

envoy ['envɔɪ] n émissaire m.

envy ['envɪ] ♦ n envie f, jalousie f. ♦ vt envier; **to ~ sb sthg** envier qqch à qqn.

epic ['epɪk] ♦ adj épique. ♦ n épopée f.

epidemic [,epɪ'demɪk] n épidémie f.

epileptic [,epɪ'leptɪk] ♦ adj épileptique. ♦ n épileptique mf.

episode ['epɪsəʊd] n épisode m.

epistle [ɪ'pɪsl] n épître f.

epitaph ['epɪtɑːf] n épitaphe f.

epitome [ɪ'pɪtəmɪ] n: **the ~ of** le modèle de.

epitomize, -ise [ɪ'pɪtəmaɪz] vt incarner.

epoch ['iːpɒk] n époque f.

equable ['ekwəbl] adj égal(e), constant(e).

equal ['iːkwəl] ♦ adj 1. (gen): ~ (to) égal(e) (à); **on ~ terms** d'égal à égal. 2. (capable): ~ **to sthg** à la hauteur de qqch. ♦ n égal m, -e f. ♦ vt égaler.

equality [iːˈkwɒlətɪ] n égalité f.

equalize, -ise ['iːkwəlaɪz] ♦ vt niveler. ♦ vi (SPORT) égaliser.

equalizer ['iːkwəlaɪzə^r] n (SPORT) but m égalisateur.

equally ['iːkwəlɪ] adv 1. (important, stupid etc) tout aussi. 2. (in amount) en parts égales. 3. (also) en même temps.

equal opportunities npl égalité f des chances.

equanimity [ˌekwəˈnɪmətɪ] n sérénité f, égalité f d'âme.

equate [ɪˈkweɪt] vt: **to ~ sthg with** assimiler qqch à.

equation [ɪˈkweɪʒn] n équation f.

equator [ɪˈkweɪtə^r] n: **the ~** l'équateur m.

equilibrium [ˌiːkwɪˈlɪbrɪəm] n équilibre m.

equip [ɪˈkwɪp] vt équiper; **to ~ sb/sthg with** équiper qqn/qqch de, munir qqn/qqch de; **he's well equipped for the job** il est bien préparé pour ce travail.

equipment [ɪˈkwɪpmənt] n (U) équipement m, matériel m.

equities ['ekwətɪz] npl (ST EX) actions fpl ordinaires.

equivalent [ɪˈkwɪvələnt] ♦ adj équivalent(e); **to be ~ to** être équivalent à, équivaloir à. ♦ n équivalent m.

equivocal [ɪˈkwɪvəkl] adj équivoque.

er [ɜː^r] excl euh!

era ['ɪərə] (pl -s) n ère f, période f.

eradicate [ɪˈrædɪkeɪt] vt éradiquer.

erase [ɪˈreɪz] vt 1. (rub out) gommer. 2. fig (memory) effacer; (hunger, poverty) éliminer.

eraser [ɪˈreɪzə^r] n gomme f.

erect [ɪˈrekt] ♦ adj 1. (person, posture) droit(e). 2. (penis) en érection. ♦ vt 1. (statue) ériger; (building) construire. 2. (tent) dresser.

erection [ɪˈrekʃn] n 1. (U) (of statue) érection f; (of building) construction f. 2. (erect penis) érection f.

ERM (abbr of Exchange Rate Mechanism) n mécanisme m des changes (du SME).

ermine ['ɜːmɪn] n (fur) hermine f.

erode [ɪˈrəʊd] ♦ vt 1. (rock, soil) éroder. 2. fig (confidence, rights) réduire. ♦ vi 1. (rock, soil) s'éroder. 2. fig (confidence)

diminuer; (rights) se réduire.

erosion [ɪˈrəʊʒn] n 1. (of rock, soil) érosion f. 2. fig (of confidence) baisse f; (of rights) diminution f.

erotic [ɪˈrɒtɪk] adj érotique.

err [ɜː^r] vi se tromper.

errand ['erənd] n course f, commission f; **to go on** OR **run an ~** faire une course.

erratic [ɪˈrætɪk] adj irrégulier(ère).

error ['erə^r] n erreur f; **a spelling/typing ~** une faute d'orthographe/de frappe; **an ~ of judgment** une erreur de jugement; **in ~** par erreur.

erupt [ɪˈrʌpt] vi 1. (volcano) entrer en éruption. 2. fig (violence, war) éclater.

eruption [ɪˈrʌpʃn] n 1. (of volcano) éruption f. 2. (of violence) explosion f; (of war) déclenchement m.

escalate ['eskəleɪt] vi 1. (conflict) s'intensifier. 2. (costs) monter en flèche.

escalator ['eskəleɪtə^r] n escalier m roulant.

escapade [ˌeskəˈpeɪd] n aventure f, exploit m.

escape [ɪˈskeɪp] ♦ n 1. (gen) fuite f, évasion f; **to make one's ~** s'échapper; **to have a lucky ~** l'échapper belle. 2. (leakage - of gas, water) fuite f. ♦ vt échapper à. ♦ vi 1. (gen) s'échapper, fuir; (from prison) s'évader; **to ~ from** (place) s'échapper de; (danger, person) échapper à. 2. (survive) s'en tirer.

escapism [ɪˈskeɪpɪzm] n (U) évasion f (de la réalité).

escort [n 'eskɔːt, vb ɪˈskɔːt] ♦ n 1. (guard) escorte f; **under ~** sous escorte. 2. (companion - male) cavalier m; (- female) hôtesse f. ♦ vt escorter, accompagner.

Eskimo ['eskɪməʊ] (pl -s) n (person) Esquimau m, -aude f (attention: le terme 'Eskimo', comme son équivalent français, est souvent considéré comme injurieux en Amérique du Nord. On préférera le terme 'Inuit').

espadrille [ˌespəˈdrɪl] n espadrille f.

especially [ɪˈspeʃəlɪ] adv 1. (in particular) surtout. 2. (more than usually) particulièrement. 3. (specifically) spécialement.

espionage ['espɪəˌnɑːʒ] n espionnage m.

esplanade [ˌespləˈneɪd] n esplanade f.

Esquire [ɪˈskwaɪə^r] n: **G. Curry ~** Monsieur G. Curry.

essay ['eseɪ] n 1. (SCH & UNIV) dissertation f. 2. (LITERATURE) essai m.

essence ['esns] n 1. (nature) essence f,

nature f; **in ~** par essence. **2.** (CULIN) extrait m.

essential [ɪ'senʃl] adj **1.** (absolutely necessary): **~ (to** OR **for)** indispensable (à). **2.** (basic) essentiel(elle), de base. ▶ **essentials** npl **1.** (basic commodities) produits mpl de première nécessité. **2.** (most important elements) essentiel m.

essentially [ɪ'senʃəlɪ] adv fondamentalement, avant tout.

establish [ɪ'stæblɪʃ] vt **1.** (gen) établir; **to ~ contact with** établir le contact avec. **2.** (organization, business) fonder, créer.

establishment [ɪ'stæblɪʃmənt] n **1.** (gen) établissement m. **2.** (of organization, business) fondation f, création f. ▶ **Establishment** n (status quo): **the Establishment** l'ordre m établi, l'Establishment m.

estate [ɪ'steɪt] n **1.** (land, property) propriété f, domaine m. **2. (housing) ~** lotissement m. **3. (industrial) ~** zone f industrielle. **4.** (JUR) (inheritance) biens mpl.

estate agency n Br agence f immobilière.

estate agent n Br agent m immobilier.

estate car n Br break m.

esteem [ɪ'stiːm] ◆ n estime f. ◆ vt estimer.

esthetic etc Am = **aesthetic** etc.

estimate [n 'estɪmət, vb 'estɪmeɪt] ◆ n **1.** (calculation, judgment) estimation f, évaluation f. **2.** (COMM) devis m. ◆ vt estimer, évaluer.

estimation [,estɪ'meɪʃn] n **1.** (opinion) opinion f. **2.** (calculation) estimation f, évaluation f.

Estonia [e'stəʊnɪə] n Estonie f.

estranged [ɪ'streɪndʒd] adj (couple) séparé(e); (husband, wife) dont on s'est séparé.

estuary ['estjʊərɪ] n estuaire m.

etc. (abbr of et cetera) etc.

etching ['etʃɪŋ] n gravure f à l'eau forte.

eternal [ɪ'tɜːnl] adj **1.** (life) éternel (elle). **2.** fig (complaints, whining) sempiternel(elle). **3.** (truth, value) immuable.

eternity [ɪ'tɜːnətɪ] n éternité f.

ethic ['eθɪk] n éthique f, morale f. ▶ **ethics** ◆ n (U) (study) éthique f, morale f. ◆ npl (morals) morale f.

ethical ['eθɪkl] adj moral(e).

Ethiopia [,iːθɪ'əʊpɪə] n Éthiopie f.

ethnic ['eθnɪk] adj **1.** (traditions, groups) ethnique. **2.** (clothes) folklorique.

ethos ['iːθɒs] n génie m (d'un peuple/ d'une civilisation).

etiquette ['etɪket] n convenances fpl, étiquette f.

EU (abbr of **European Union**) n UE f.

eulogy ['juːlədʒɪ] n panégyrique m.

euphemism ['juːfəmɪzm] n euphémisme m.

euphoria [juː'fɔːrɪə] n euphorie f.

Eurocheque ['jʊərəʊ,tʃek] n eurochèque m.

Euro MP n député m européen.

Europe ['jʊərəp] n Europe f.

European [,jʊərə'pɪən] ◆ adj européen(enne). ◆ n Européen m, -enne f.

European Community n: **the ~** la Communauté européenne.

European Monetary System n: **the ~** le Système monétaire européen.

European Parliament n: **the ~** le Parlement européen.

European Union n Union f européenne.

euthanasia [,juːθə'neɪzjə] n euthanasie f.

evacuate [ɪ'vækjʊeɪt] vt évacuer.

evade [ɪ'veɪd] vt **1.** (gen) échapper à. **2.** (issue, question) esquiver, éluder.

evaluate [ɪ'væljʊeɪt] vt évaluer.

evaporate [ɪ'væpəreɪt] vi **1.** (liquid) s'évaporer. **2.** fig (hopes, fears) s'envoler; (confidence) disparaître.

evaporated milk [ɪ'væpəreɪtɪd-] n lait m condensé (non sucré).

evasion [ɪ'veɪʒn] n **1.** (of responsibility) dérobade f. **2.** (lie) faux-fuyant m.

evasive [ɪ'veɪsɪv] adj évasif(ive).

eve [iːv] n veille f.

even ['iːvn] ◆ adj **1.** (speed, rate) régulier (ère); (temperature, temperament) égal(e). **2.** (flat, level) plat(e), régulier(ère). **3.** (equal - contest) équilibré(e); (- teams, players) de la même force; (- scores) à égalité; **to get ~ with sb** se venger de qqn. **4.** (not odd - number) pair(e). ◆ adv **1.** (gen) même; **~ now** encore maintenant; **~ then** même alors. **2.** (in comparisons): **~ bigger/better/more stupid** encore plus grand/mieux/plus bête. ▶ **even if** conj même si. ▶ **even so** adv quand même. ▶ **even though** conj bien que (+ subjunctive). ▶ **even out** ◆ vt sep égaliser. ◆ vi s'égaliser.

evening ['iːvnɪŋ] n soir m; (duration, entertainment) soirée f; **in the ~** le soir. ▶ **evenings** adv Am le soir. ◆

evening class n cours m du soir.

evening dress n (worn by man) habit m de soirée; (worn by woman) robe f du soir.

event [ɪ'vent] n 1. (happening) événement m. 2. (SPORT) épreuve f. 3. (case): in the ~ of en cas de; in the ~ that au cas où. ▶ **in any event** adv en tout cas, de toute façon. ▶ **in the event** adv Br en l'occurrence, en réalité.

eventful [ɪ'ventful] adj mouvementé(e).

eventual [ɪ'ventʃʊəl] adj final(e).

eventuality [ɪ,ventʃʊ'ælətɪ] n éventualité f.

eventually [ɪ'ventʃʊəlɪ] adv finalement, en fin de compte.

ever ['evər] adv 1. (at any time) jamais; have you ~ been to Paris? êtes-vous déjà allé à Paris?; I hardly ~ see him je ne le vois presque jamais. 2. (all the time) toujours; as ~ comme toujours; for ~ pour toujours. 3. (for emphasis): ~ so tellement; ~ such vraiment; why/how ~? pourquoi/comment donc? ▶ **ever since** ◆ adv depuis (ce moment-là). ◆ conj depuis que. ◆ prep depuis.

evergreen ['evəgri:n] ◆ adj à feuilles persistantes. ◆ n arbre m à feuilles persistantes.

everlasting [,evə'lɑːstɪŋ] adj éternel (elle).

every ['evrɪ] adj chaque; ~ morning chaque matin, tous les matins. ▶ **every now and then, every so often** adv de temps en temps, de temps à autre. ▶ **every other** adj: ~ other day tous les deux jours, un jour sur deux; ~ other street une rue sur deux.

everybody ['evrɪ,bɒdɪ] = **everyone**.

everyday ['evrɪdeɪ] adj quotidien (enne).

everyone ['evrɪwʌn] pron chacun, tout le monde.

everyplace Am = **everywhere**.

everything ['evrɪθɪŋ] pron tout.

everywhere ['evrɪweər], **everyplace** Am ['evrɪ,pleɪs] adv partout.

evict [ɪ'vɪkt] vt expulser.

evidence ['evɪdəns] n (U) 1. (proof) preuve f. 2. (JUR) (of witness) témoignage m; to give ~ témoigner.

evident ['evɪdənt] adj évident(e), manifeste.

evidently ['evɪdəntlɪ] adv 1. (seemingly) apparemment. 2. (obviously) de toute évidence, manifestement.

evil ['i:vl] ◆ adj (person) mauvais(e),

malveillant(e). ◆ n mal m.

evoke [ɪ'vəuk] vt (memory) évoquer; (emotion, response) susciter.

evolution [,i:və'lu:ʃn] n évolution f.

evolve [ɪ'vɒlv] ◆ vt développer. ◆ vi: to ~ (into/from) se développer (en/à partir de).

ewe [ju:] n brebis f.

ex- [eks] prefix ex-.

exacerbate [ɪg'zæsəbeɪt] vt (feeling) exacerber; (problems) aggraver.

exact [ɪg'zækt] ◆ adj exact(e), précis(e); to be ~ pour être exact OR précis, exactement. ◆ vt: to ~ sthg (from) exiger qqch (de).

exacting [ɪg'zæktɪŋ] adj (job, standards) astreignant(e); (person) exigeant(e).

exactly [ɪg'zæktlɪ] ◆ adv exactement. ◆ excl exactement!, parfaitement!

exaggerate [ɪg'zædʒəreɪt] vt & vi exagérer.

exaggeration [ɪg,zædʒə'reɪʃn] n exagération f.

exalted [ɪg'zɔːltɪd] adj haut placé(e).

exam [ɪg'zæm] n examen m; to take OR sit an ~ passer un examen.

examination [ɪg,zæmɪ'neɪʃn] n examen m.

examine [ɪg'zæmɪn] vt 1. (gen) examiner; (passport) contrôler. 2. (JUR, SCH & UNIV) interroger.

examiner [ɪg'zæmɪnər] n examinateur m, -trice f.

example [ɪg'zɑːmpl] n exemple m; for ~ par exemple.

exasperate [ɪg'zæspəreɪt] vt exaspérer.

exasperation [ɪg,zæspə'reɪʃn] n exaspération f.

excavate ['ekskəveɪt] vt 1. (land) creuser. 2. (object) déterrer.

exceed [ɪk'siːd] vt 1. (amount, number) excéder. 2. (limit, expectations) dépasser.

exceedingly [ɪk'siːdɪŋlɪ] adv extrêmement.

excel [ɪk'sel] vi: to ~ (in OR at) exceller (dans); to ~ o.s. Br se surpasser.

excellence ['eksələns] n excellence f, supériorité f.

excellent ['eksələnt] adj excellent(e).

except [ɪk'sept] ◆ prep & conj: ~ (for) à part, sauf. ◆ vt: to ~ sb (from) exclure qqn (de).

excepting [ɪk'septɪŋ] prep & conj = **except**.

exception [ɪk'sepʃn] n 1. (exclusion): ~ (to) exception f (à); with the ~ of à l'exception de. 2. (offence): to take ~ to s'offenser de, se froisser de.

exceptional [ɪk'sɛpʃənl] *adj* exceptionnel(elle).

excerpt ['eksɜ:pt] *n*: ~ **(from)** extrait *m* (de), passage *m* (de).

excess [ɪk'ses, *before nouns* 'ekses] ◆ *adj* excédentaire. ◆ *n* excès *m*.

excess baggage *n* excédent *m* de bagages.

excess fare *n* Br supplément *m*.

excessive [ɪk'sesɪv] *adj* excessif(ive).

exchange [ɪks'tʃeɪndʒ] ◆ *n* 1. (*gen*) échange *m*; **in ~ (for)** en échange (de). 2. (TELEC): **(telephone)** ~ central *m* (téléphonique). ◆ *vt* (*swap*) échanger; **to ~ sthg for sthg** échanger qqch contre qqch.

exchangeable [ɪks'tʃeɪndʒəbl] *adj* échangeable.

exchange rate *n* (FIN) taux *m* de change.

Exchequer [ɪks'tʃekər] *n* Br: **the ~** ≃ le ministère des Finances.

excise ['eksaɪz] *n* (U) contributions *fpl* indirectes.

excite [ɪk'saɪt] *vt* exciter.

excited [ɪk'saɪtɪd] *adj* excité(e).

excitement [ɪk'saɪtmənt] *n* (*state*) excitation *f*.

exciting [ɪk'saɪtɪŋ] *adj* passionnant(e); (*prospect*) excitant(e).

exclaim [ɪk'skleɪm] ◆ *vt* s'écrier. ◆ *vi* s'exclamer.

exclamation [,eksklə'meɪʃn] *n* exclamation *f*.

exclamation mark Br, **exclamation point** Am *n* point *m* d'exclamation.

exclude [ɪk'sklu:d] *vt*: **to ~ sb/sthg (from)** exclure qqn/qqch (de).

excluding [ɪk'sklu:dɪŋ] *prep* sans compter, à l'exclusion de.

exclusive [ɪk'sklu:sɪv] ◆ *adj* 1. (*high-class*) fermé(e). 2. (*unique - use, news story*) exclusif(ive). ◆ *n* (PRESS) exclusivité *f*. ▶ **exclusive of** *prep*: ~ **of interest** intérêts non compris.

excrement ['ekskrɪmənt] *n* excrément *m*.

excruciating [ɪk'skru:ʃieɪtɪŋ] *adj* atroce.

excursion [ɪk'skɜ:ʃn] *n* (*trip*) excursion *f*.

excuse [*n* ɪk'skju:s, *vb* ɪk'skju:z] ◆ *n* excuse *f*. ◆ *vt* 1. (*gen*) excuser; **to ~ sb for sthg/for doing sthg** excuser qqn de qqch/de faire qqch; ~ **me** (*to attract attention*) excusez-moi; (*forgive me*) par-

don, excusez-moi; Am (*sorry*) pardon. 2. (*let off*): **to ~ sb (from)** dispenser qqn (de).

ex-directory *adj* Br qui est sur la liste rouge.

execute ['eksɪkju:t] *vt* exécuter.

execution [,eksɪ'kju:ʃn] *n* exécution *f*.

executioner [,eksɪ'kju:ʃnər] *n* bourreau *m*.

executive [ɪg'zekjutɪv] ◆ *adj* (*power, board*) exécutif(ive). ◆ *n* 1. (COMM) cadre *m*. 2. (*of government*) exécutif *m*; (*of political party*) comité *m* central, bureau *m*.

executive director *n* cadre *m* supérieur.

executor [ɪg'zekjutər] *n* exécuteur *m* testamentaire.

exemplify [ɪg'zemplɪfaɪ] *vt* 1. (*typify*) exemplifier. 2. (*give example of*) exemplifier, illustrer.

exempt [ɪg'zempt] ◆ *adj*: ~ **(from)** exempt(e) (de). ◆ *vt*: **to ~ sb (from)** exempter qqn (de).

exercise ['eksəsaɪz] ◆ *n* exercice *m*. ◆ *vt* (*gen*) exercer. ◆ *vi* prendre de l'exercice.

exercise book *n* (*notebook*) cahier *m* d'exercices; (*published book*) livre *m* d'exercices.

exert [ɪg'zɜ:t] *vt* exercer; (*strength*) employer; **to ~ o.s.** se donner du mal.

exertion [ɪg'zɜ:ʃn] *n* effort *m*.

exhale [eks'heɪl] ◆ *vt* exhaler. ◆ *vi* expirer.

exhaust [ɪg'zɔ:st] ◆ *n* 1. (U) (*fumes*) gaz *mpl* d'échappement. 2. ~ **(pipe)** pot *m* d'échappement. ◆ *vt* épuiser.

exhausted [ɪg'zɔ:stɪd] *adj* épuisé(e).

exhausting [ɪg'zɔ:stɪŋ] *adj* épuisant(e).

exhaustion [ɪg'zɔ:stʃn] *n* épuisement *m*.

exhaustive [ɪg'zɔ:stɪv] *adj* complet(ète), exhaustif(ive).

exhibit [ɪg'zɪbɪt] ◆ *n* 1. (ART) objet *m* exposé. 2. (JUR) pièce *f* à conviction. ◆ *vt* 1. (*demonstrate - feeling*) montrer; (- *skill*) faire preuve de. 2. (ART) exposer.

exhibition [,eksɪ'bɪʃn] *n* 1. (ART) exposition *f*. 2. (*of feeling*) démonstration *f*. 3. *phr*: **to make an ~ of o.s.** Br se donner en spectacle.

exhilarating [ɪg'zɪləreɪtɪŋ] *adj* (*experience*) grisant(e); (*walk*) vivifiant(e).

exile ['eksaɪl] ◆ *n* 1. (*condition*) exil *m*; **in ~** en exil. 2. (*person*) exilé *m*, -e *f*. ◆ *vt*: **to ~ sb (from/to)** exiler qqn (de/vers).

exist [ɪg'zɪst] *vi* exister.

existence [ɪgˈzɪstəns] n existence f; **in ~** qui existe, existant(e); **to come into ~** naître.

existing [ɪgˈzɪstɪŋ] adj existant(e).

exit [ˈeksɪt] ♦ n sortie f. ♦ vi sortir.

exodus [ˈeksədəs] n exode m.

exonerate [ɪgˈzɒnəreɪt] vt: **to ~ sb (from)** disculper qqn (de).

exorbitant [ɪgˈzɔːbɪtənt] adj exorbitant(e).

exotic [ɪgˈzɒtɪk] adj exotique.

expand [ɪkˈspænd] ♦ vt (production, influence) accroître; (business, department, area) développer. ♦ vi (population, influence) s'accroître; (business, department, market) se développer; (metal) se dilater. ▶ **expand (up)on** vt fus développer.

expanse [ɪkˈspæns] n étendue f.

expansion [ɪkˈspænʃn] n (of production, population) accroissement m; (of business, department, area) développement m; (of metal) dilatation f.

expect [ɪkˈspekt] ♦ vt 1. (anticipate) s'attendre à; (event, letter, baby) attendre; **when do you ~ it to be ready?** quand pensez-vous que cela sera prêt?; **to ~ sb to do sthg** s'attendre à ce que qqn fasse qqch. 2. (count on) compter sur. 3. (demand) exiger, demander; **to ~ sb to do sthg** attendre de qqn qu'il fasse qqch; **to ~ sthg from sb** exiger qqch de qqn. 4. (suppose) supposer; **I ~ so** je crois que oui. ♦ vi 1. (anticipate): **to ~ to do sthg** compter faire qqch. 2. (be pregnant): **to be ~ing** être enceinte, attendre un bébé.

expectancy → **life expectancy**.

expectant [ɪkˈspektənt] adj qui est dans l'expectative.

expectant mother n femme f enceinte.

expectation [ˌekspekˈteɪʃn] n 1. (hope) espoir m, attente f. 2. (belief): **it's my ~ that ...** à mon avis, ...; **against all ~ or ~s, contrary to all ~ or ~s** contre toute attente.

expedient [ɪkˈspiːdjənt] fml ♦ adj indiqué(e). ♦ n expédient m.

expedition [ˌekspɪˈdɪʃn] n expédition f.

expel [ɪkˈspel] vt 1. (gen) expulser. 2. (SCH) renvoyer.

expend [ɪkˈspend] vt: **to ~ time/money (on)** consacrer du temps/de l'argent (à).

expendable [ɪkˈspendəbl] adj dont on peut se passer, qui n'est pas indispensable.

expenditure [ɪkˈspendɪtʃər] n (U) dépense f.

expense [ɪkˈspens] n 1. (amount spent) dépense f. 2. (U) (cost) frais mpl; **at the ~ of** au prix de; **at sb's ~** (financial) aux frais de qqn; fig aux dépens de qqn. ▶ **expenses** npl (COMM) frais mpl.

expense account n frais mpl de représentation.

expensive [ɪkˈspensɪv] adj 1. (financially - gen) cher (chère), coûteux(euse); (- tastes) dispendieux(euse). 2. (mistake) qui coûte cher.

experience [ɪkˈspɪərɪəns] ♦ n expérience f. ♦ vt (difficulty) connaître; (disappointment) éprouver, ressentir; (loss, change) subir.

experienced [ɪkˈspɪərɪənst] adj expérimenté(e); **to be ~ at** or **in sthg** avoir de l'expérience en or en matière de qqch.

experiment [ɪkˈsperɪmənt] ♦ n expérience f; **to carry out an ~** faire une expérience. ♦ vi: **to ~ (with sthg)** expérimenter (qqch).

expert [ˈekspɜːt] ♦ adj expert(e); (advice) d'expert. ♦ n expert m, -e f.

expertise [ˌekspɜːˈtiːz] n (U) compétence f.

expire [ɪkˈspaɪər] vi expirer.

expiry [ɪkˈspaɪərɪ] n expiration f.

explain [ɪkˈspleɪn] ♦ vt expliquer; **to ~ sthg to sb** expliquer qqch à qqn. ♦ vi s'expliquer; **to ~ to sb (about sthg)** expliquer (qqch) à qqn.

explanation [ˌekspləˈneɪʃn] n: **~ (for)** explication f (de).

explicit [ɪkˈsplɪsɪt] adj explicite.

explode [ɪkˈspləʊd] ♦ vt (bomb) faire exploser. ♦ vi lit & fig exploser.

exploit [n ˈeksplɔɪt, vb ɪkˈsplɔɪt] ♦ n exploit m. ♦ vt exploiter.

exploitation [ˌeksplɔɪˈteɪʃn] n (U) exploitation f.

exploration [ˌekspləˈreɪʃn] n exploration f.

explore [ɪkˈsplɔːr] vt & vi explorer.

explorer [ɪkˈsplɔːrər] n explorateur m, -trice f.

explosion [ɪkˈspləʊʒn] n explosion f; (of interest) débordement m.

explosive [ɪkˈspləʊsɪv] ♦ adj lit & fig explosif(ive). ♦ n explosif m.

exponent [ɪkˈspəʊnənt] n (of theory) défenseur m.

export [n & comp ˈekspɔːt, vb ɪkˈspɔːt] ♦ n exportation f. ♦ comp d'exportation. ♦ vt exporter.

exporter [ek'spɔːtəʳ] n exportateur m, -trice f.

expose [ɪk'spəʊz] vt 1. (uncover) exposer, découvrir; **to be ~d to sthg** être exposé à qqch. 2. (unmask - corruption) révéler; (- person) démasquer.

exposed [ɪk'spəʊzd] adj (land, house, position) exposé(e).

exposure [ɪk'spəʊʒəʳ] n 1. (to light, radiation) exposition f. 2. (MED): **to die of ~** mourir de froid. 3. (PHOT - time) temps m de pose; (- photograph) pose f. 4. (U) (publicity) publicité f; (coverage) couverture f.

exposure meter n posemètre m.

expound [ɪk'spaʊnd] fml ◆ vt exposer. ◆ vi: **to ~ on** faire un exposé sur.

express [ɪk'spres] ◆ adj 1. Br (letter, delivery) exprès (inv). 2. (train, coach) express (inv). 3. fml (specific) exprès (esse). ◆ adv exprès. ◆ n (train) rapide m, express m. ◆ vt exprimer.

expression [ɪk'spreʃn] n expression f.

expressive [ɪk'spresɪv] adj expressif(ive).

expressly [ɪk'spresli] adv expressément.

expressway [ɪk'spresweɪ] n Am voie f express.

exquisite [ɪk'skwɪzɪt] adj exquis(e).

ext., extn. (abbr of extension): **~ 4174** p. 4174.

extend [ɪk'stend] ◆ vt 1. (enlarge - building) agrandir. 2. (make longer - gen) prolonger; (- visa) proroger; (- deadline) repousser. 3. (expand - rules, law) étendre (la portée de); (- power) accroître. 4. (stretch out - arm, hand) étendre. 5. (offer - help) apporter, offrir; (- credit) accorder. ◆ vi (stretch - in space) s'étendre; (- in time) continuer.

extension [ɪk'stenʃn] n 1. (to building) agrandissement m. 2. (lengthening - gen) prolongement m; (- of visit) prolongation f; (- of visa) prorogation f; (- of deadline) report m. 3. (of power) accroissement m; (of law) élargissement m. 4. (TELEC) poste m. 5. (ELEC) prolongateur m.

extension cable n rallonge f.

extensive [ɪk'stensɪv] adj 1. (in amount) considérable. 2. (in area) vaste. 3. (in range - discussions) approfondi(e); (- changes, use) considérable.

extensively [ɪk'stensɪvli] adv 1. (in amount) considérablement. 2. (in range) abondamment, largement.

extent [ɪk'stent] n 1. (of land, area) étendue f, superficie f; (of problem, damage) étendue f. 2. (degree): **to what ~ ...?** dans

quelle mesure ...?; **to the ~ that** (in so far as) dans la mesure où; (to the point where) au point que; **to a certain ~** jusqu'à un certain point; **to a large ~** en grande partie; **to some ~** en partie.

extenuating circumstances [ɪk-'stenjʊeɪtɪŋ-] npl circonstances fpl atténuantes.

exterior [ɪk'stɪərɪəʳ] ◆ adj extérieur(e). ◆ n 1. (of house, car) extérieur m. 2. (of person) dehors m, extérieur m.

exterminate [ɪk'stɜːmɪneɪt] vt exterminer.

external [ɪk'stɜːnl] adj externe.

extinct [ɪk'stɪŋkt] adj 1. (species) disparu(e). 2. (volcano) éteint(e).

extinguish [ɪk'stɪŋgwɪʃ] vt (fire, cigarette) éteindre.

extinguisher [ɪk'stɪŋgwɪʃəʳ] n extincteur m.

extn. = ext.

extol, extoll Am [ɪk'stəʊl] vt louer.

extort [ɪk'stɔːt] vt: **to ~ sthg from sb** extorquer qqch à qqn.

extortionate [ɪk'stɔːʃnət] adj exorbitant(e).

extra ['ekstrə] ◆ adj supplémentaire. ◆ n 1. (addition) supplément m; **optional ~** option f. 2. (CINEMA & THEATRE) figurant m, -e f. ◆ adv (hard, big etc) extra; (pay, charge etc) en plus.

extra- ['ekstrə] prefix extra-.

extract [n 'ekstrækt, vb ɪk'strækt] ◆ n extrait m. ◆ vt 1. (take out - tooth) arracher; **to ~ sthg from** tirer qqch de. 2. (confession, information): **to ~ sthg (from sb)** arracher qqch (à qqn), tirer qqch (de qqn). 3. (coal, oil) extraire.

extradite ['ekstrədaɪt] vt: **to ~ sb (from/to)** extrader qqn (de/vers).

extramarital [,ekstrə'mærɪtl] adj extraconjugal(e).

extramural [,ekstrə'mjʊərəl] adj (UNIV) hors faculté.

extraordinary [ɪk'strɔːdnrɪ] adj extraordinaire.

extraordinary general meeting n assemblée f générale extraordinaire.

extravagance [ɪk'strævəgəns] n 1. (U) (excessive spending) gaspillage m, prodigalités fpl. 2. (luxury) extravagance f, folie f.

extravagant [ɪk'strævəgənt] adj 1. (wasteful - person) dépensier(ère); (- use, tastes) dispendieux(euse). 2. (elaborate, exaggerated) extravagant(e).

extreme [ɪk'striːm] ◆ adj extrême. ◆ n extrême m.

extremely [ɪk'striːmlɪ] *adv* extrêmement.

extremist [ɪk'striːmɪst] ◆ *adj* extrémiste. ◆ *n* extrémiste *mf*.

extricate ['ekstrɪkeɪt] *vt*: **to ~ sthg (from)** dégager qqch (de); **to ~ o.s. (from)** (*from seat belt etc*) s'extirper (de); (*from difficult situation*) se tirer (de).

extrovert ['ekstrəvɜːt] ◆ *adj* extraverti(e). ◆ *n* extraverti *m*, -e *f*.

exuberance [ɪg'zjuːbərəns] *n* exubérance *f*.

exultant [ɪg'zʌltənt] *adj* triomphant(e).

eye [aɪ] (*cont* eyeing OR eying) ◆ *n* **1.** (*gen*) œil *m*; **to cast** OR **run one's ~ over sthg** jeter un coup d'œil sur qqch; **to catch sb's ~** attirer l'attention de qqn; **to have one's ~ on sb** avoir qqn à l'œil; **to keep one's ~s open for sthg** (*try to find*) essayer de repérer qqch; **to keep an ~ on sthg** surveiller qqch, garder l'œil sur qqch. **2.** (*of needle*) chas *m*. ◆ *vt* regarder, reluquer.

eyeball ['aɪbɔːl] *n* globe *m* oculaire.

eyebath ['aɪbɑːθ] *n* œillère *f* (*pour bains d'œil*).

eyebrow ['aɪbraʊ] *n* sourcil *m*.

eyebrow pencil *n* crayon *m* à sourcils.

eyedrops ['aɪdrɒps] *npl* gouttes *fpl* pour les yeux.

eyelash ['aɪlæʃ] *n* cil *m*.

eyelid ['aɪlɪd] *n* paupière *f*.

eyeliner ['aɪ,laɪnər] *n* eye-liner *m*.

eye-opener *n inf* révélation *f*.

eye shadow *n* fard *m* à paupières.

eyesight ['aɪsaɪt] *n* vue *f*.

eyesore ['aɪsɔːr] *n* horreur *f*.

eyestrain ['aɪstreɪn] *n* fatigue *f* des yeux.

eyewitness [,aɪ'wɪtnɪs] *n* témoin *m* oculaire.

F

f (*pl* f's OR fs), **F** (*pl* F's OR Fs) [ef] *n* (*letter*) f *m inv*, F *m inv*. ▶ **F** *n* **1.** (MUS) fa *m*. **2.** (*abbr of* **Fahrenheit**) F.

fable ['feɪbl] *n* fable *f*.

fabric ['fæbrɪk] *n* **1.** (*cloth*) tissu *m*.

2. (*of building, society*) structure *f*.

fabrication [,fæbrɪ'keɪʃn] *n* **1.** (*lie, lying*) fabrication *f*, invention *f*. **2.** (*manufacture*) fabrication *f*.

fabulous ['fæbjʊləs] *adj* **1.** (*gen*) fabuleux(euse). **2.** *inf* (*excellent*) sensationnel(elle), fabuleux(euse).

façade [fə'sɑːd] *n* façade *f*.

face [feɪs] ◆ *n* **1.** (*of person*) visage *m*, figure *f*; **~ to ~** face à face; **to say sthg to sb's ~** dire qqch à qqn en face. **2.** (*expression*) visage *m*, mine *f*; **to make** OR **pull a ~** faire la grimace. **3.** (*of cliff, mountain*) face *f*, paroi *f*; (*of building*) façade *f*; (*of clock, watch*) cadran *m*; (*of coin, shape*) face *f*. **4.** (*surface - of planet*) surface *f*; **on the ~ of it** à première vue. **5.** (*respect*): **to save/lose ~** sauver/perdre la face. ◆ *vt* **1.** (*look towards - subj: person*) faire face à; **the house ~s the sea/south** la maison donne sur la mer/est orientée vers le sud. **2.** (*decision, crisis*) être confronté(e) à; (*problem, danger*) faire face à. **3.** (*facts, truth*) faire face à, admettre. **4.** *inf* (*cope with*) affronter. ▶ **face down** *adv* (*person*) face contre terre; (*object*) à l'envers; (*card*) face en dessous. ▶ **face up** *adv* (*person*) sur le dos; (*object*) à l'endroit; (*card*) face en dessus. ▶ **face up to** *vt fus* faire face à.

facecloth ['feɪsklɒθ] *n Br* gant *m* de toilette.

face cream *n* crème *f* pour le visage.

face-lift *n* lifting *m*; *fig* restauration *f*, rénovation *f*.

face powder *n* poudre *f* de riz, poudre pour le visage.

face-saving [-,seɪvɪŋ] *adj* qui sauve la face.

facet ['fæsɪt] *n* facette *f*.

facetious [fə'siːʃəs] *adj* facétieux(euse).

face value *n* (*of coin, stamp*) valeur *f* nominale; **to take sthg at ~** prendre qqch au pied de la lettre.

facility [fə'sɪlətɪ] *n* (*feature*) fonction *f*. ▶ **facilities** *npl* (*amenities*) équipement *m*, aménagement *m*.

facing ['feɪsɪŋ] *adj* d'en face; (*sides*) opposé(e).

facsimile [fæk'sɪmɪlɪ] *n* **1.** (*fax*) télécopie *f*, fax *m*. **2.** (*copy*) fac-similé *m*.

fact [fækt] *n* **1.** (*true piece of information*) fait *m*. **2.** (U) (*truth*) faits *mpl*, réalité *f*. ▶ **in fact** ◆ *adv* de fait, effectivement. ◆ *conj* en fait.

fact of life *n* fait *m*, réalité *f*; **the facts of life** *euphemism* les choses *fpl* de la vie.

factor ['fæktər] n facteur m.

factory ['fæktərɪ] n fabrique f, usine f.

fact sheet n Br résumé m, brochure f.

factual ['fæktʃʊəl] adj factuel(elle), basé(e) sur les faits.

faculty ['fækltɪ] n 1. (gen) faculté f. 2. Am (in college): **the ~** le corps enseignant.

FA Cup n en Angleterre, championnat de football dont la finale se joue à Wembley.

fad [fæd] n engouement m, mode f; (personal) marotte f.

fade [feɪd] ◆ vt (jeans, curtains, paint) décolorer. ◆ vi 1. (jeans, curtains, paint) se décolorer; (colour) passer; (flower) se flétrir. 2. (light) baisser, diminuer. 3. (sound) diminuer, s'affaiblir. 4. (memory) s'effacer; (feeling, interest) diminuer.

faeces Br, **feces** Am ['fiːsiːz] npl fèces fpl.

fag [fæg] n inf 1. Br (cigarette) clope m. 2. Am pej (homosexual) pédé m.

Fahrenheit ['færənhaɪt] adj Fahrenheit (inv).

fail [feɪl] ◆ vt 1. (exam, test) rater, échouer à. 2. (not succeed): **to ~ to do sthg** ne pas arriver à faire qqch. 3. (neglect): **to ~ to do sthg** manquer OR omettre de faire qqch. 4. (candidate) refuser. ◆ vi 1. (not succeed) ne pas réussir OR y arriver. 2. (not pass exam) échouer. 3. (stop functioning) lâcher. 4. (weaken - health, daylight) décliner; (- eyesight) baisser.

failing ['feɪlɪŋ] ◆ n (weakness) défaut m, point m faible. ◆ prep à moins de; **~ that** à défaut.

failure ['feɪljər] n 1. (lack of success, unsuccessful thing) échec m. 2. (person) raté m, -e f. 3. (of engine, brake etc) défaillance f; (of crop) perte f.

faint [feɪnt] ◆ adj 1. (smell) léger(ère); (memory) vague; (sound, hope) faible. 2. (slight - chance) petit(e), faible. 3. (dizzy): **I'm feeling a bit ~** je ne me sens pas bien. ◆ vi s'évanouir.

fair [feər] ◆ adj 1. (just) juste, équitable; **it's not ~!** ce n'est pas juste! 2. (quite large) grand(e), important(e). 3. (quite good) assez bon (assez bonne). 4. (hair) blond(e). 5. (skin, complexion) clair(e). 6. (weather) beau (belle). ◆ n 1. Br (funfair) fête f foraine. 2. (trade fair) foire f. ◆ adv (fairly) loyalement. ► **fair enough** adv Br inf OK, d'accord.

fair-haired [-'heəd] adj (person) blond(e).

fairly ['feəlɪ] adv 1. (rather) assez; **~ certain** presque sûr. 2. (justly) équitable-

ment; (describe) avec impartialité; (fight, play) loyalement.

fairness ['feənɪs] n (justness) équité f.

fairy ['feərɪ] n (imaginary creature) fée f.

fairy tale n conte m de fées.

faith [feɪθ] n 1. (belief) foi f, confiance f. 2. (RELIG) foi f.

faithful ['feɪθfʊl] adj fidèle.

faithfully ['feɪθfʊlɪ] adv (loyally) fidèlement; **Yours ~** Br (in letter) je vous prie d'agréer mes salutations distinguées.

fake [feɪk] ◆ adj faux (fausse). ◆ n 1. (object, painting) faux m. 2. (person) imposteur m. ◆ vt 1. (results) falsifier; (signature) imiter. 2. (illness, emotions) simuler.

falcon ['fɔːlkən] n faucon m.

Falkland Islands ['fɔːklənd-], **Falklands** ['fɔːkləndz] npl: **the ~** les îles fpl Falkland, les Malouines fpl.

fall [fɔːl] (pt fell, pp fallen) ◆ vi 1. (gen) tomber; **to ~ flat** (joke) tomber à plat. 2. (decrease) baisser. 3. (become): **to ~ asleep** s'endormir; **to ~ in love** tomber amoureux(euse). ◆ n 1. (gen): **~ (in)** chute (de). 2. Am (autumn) automne m. ► **falls** npl chutes fpl. ► **fall apart** vi 1. (disintegrate - book, chair) tomber en morceaux. 2. fig (country) tomber en ruine; (person) s'effondrer. ► **fall back** vi (person, crowd) reculer. ► **fall back on** vt fus (resort to) se rabattre sur. ► **fall behind** vi 1. (in race) se faire distancer. 2. (with rent) être en retard; **to ~ behind with one's work** avoir du retard dans son travail. ► **fall for** vt fus 1. inf (fall in love with) tomber amoureux(euse) de. 2. (trick, lie) se laisser prendre à. ► **fall in** vi 1. (roof, ceiling) s'écrouler, s'affaisser. 2. (MIL) former les rangs. ► **fall off** vi 1. (branch, handle) se détacher, tomber. 2. (demand, numbers) baisser, diminuer. ► **fall out** vi 1. (hair, tooth) tomber. 2. (friends) se brouiller. 3. (MIL) rompre les rangs. ► **fall over** vt fus: **to ~ over sthg** trébucher sur qqch et tomber. ◆ vi (person, chair etc) tomber. ► **fall through** vi (plan, deal) échouer.

fallacy ['fæləsɪ] n erreur f, idée f fausse.

fallen ['fɔːln] pp → fall.

fallible ['fæləbl] adj faillible.

fallout ['fɔːlaʊt] n (U) (radiation) retombées fpl.

fallout shelter n abri m anti-atomique.

fallow ['fæləʊ] adj: **to lie ~** être en jachère.

false [fɔːls] *adj* faux (fausse).

false alarm *n* fausse alerte *f*.

falsely ['fɔːlslɪ] *adv* à tort; (*smile, laugh*) faussement.

false teeth *npl* dentier *m*.

falsify ['fɔːlsɪfaɪ] *vt* falsifier.

falter ['fɔːltər] *vi* 1. (*move unsteadily*) chanceler. 2. (*steps, voice*) devenir hésitant(e). 3. (*hesitate, lose confidence*) hésiter.

fame [feɪm] *n* gloire *f*, renommée *f*.

familiar [fə'mɪljər] *adj* familier(ère); ~ **with sthg** familiarisé(e) avec qqch.

familiarity [fə,mɪlɪ'ærətɪ] *n* (U) (*knowledge*): ~ **with sthg** connaissance *f* de qqch, familiarité *f* avec qqch.

familiarize, -ise [fə'mɪljəraɪz] *vt*: **to ~ o.s. with sthg** se familiariser avec qqch; **to ~ sb with sthg** familiariser qqn avec qqch.

family ['fæmlɪ] *n* famille *f*.

family credit *n* (U) Br ≃ complément *m* familial.

family doctor *n* médecin *m* de famille.

family planning *n* planning *m* familial; ~ **clinic** centre *m* de planning familial.

famine ['fæmɪn] *n* famine *f*.

famished ['fæmɪʃt] *adj inf* (*very hungry*) affamé(e); **I'm ~!** je meurs de faim!

famous ['feɪməs] *adj*: ~ **(for)** célèbre (pour).

famously ['feɪməslɪ] *adv dated*: **to get on ~** s'entendre comme larrons en foire.

fan [fæn] ◆ *n* 1. (*of paper, silk*) éventail *m*. 2. (*electric or mechanical*) ventilateur *m*. 3. (*enthusiast*) fan *mf*. ◆ *vt* 1. (*face*) éventer. 2. (*fire, feelings*) attiser. ▶ **fan out** *vi* se déployer.

fanatic [fə'nætɪk] *n* fanatique *mf*.

fan belt *n* courroie *f* de ventilateur.

fanciful ['fænsɪful] *adj* 1. (*odd*) bizarre, fantasque. 2. (*elaborate*) extravagant(e).

fancy ['fænsɪ] ◆ *adj* 1. (*elaborate - hat, clothes*) extravagant(e); (- *food, cakes*) raffiné(e). 2. (*expensive - restaurant, hotel*) de luxe; (- *prices*) fantaisiste. ◆ *n* (*desire, liking*) envie *f*, lubie *f*; **to take a ~ to sb** se prendre d'affection pour qqn; **to take a ~ to sthg** se mettre à aimer qqch; **to take sb's ~** faire envie à qqn, plaire à qqn. ◆ *vt* 1. (*want*) avoir envie de; **to ~ doing sthg** avoir envie de faire qqch. 2. *inf* (*like*): **I ~ her** elle me plaît. 3. (*imagine*): ~ **that!** ça alors!

fancy dress *n* (U) déguisement *m*.

fancy-dress party *n* bal *m* costumé.

fanfare ['fænfeər] *n* fanfare *f*.

fang [fæŋ] *n* (*of wolf*) croc *m*; (*of snake*) crochet *m*.

fan heater *n* radiateur *m* soufflant.

fanny ['fænɪ] *n* Am inf (*buttocks*) fesses *fpl*.

fantasize, -ise ['fæntəsaɪz] *vi*: **to ~ (about sthg/about doing sthg)** fantasmer (sur qqch/sur le fait de faire qqch).

fantastic [fæn'tæstɪk] *adj* 1. *inf* (*wonderful*) fantastique, formidable. 2. (*incredible*) extraordinaire, incroyable.

fantasy ['fæntəsɪ] *n* 1. (*dream, imaginary event*) rêve *m*, fantasme *m*. 2. (U) (*fiction*) fiction *f*. 3. (*imagination*) fantaisie *f*.

fantasy football *n* jeu où chaque participant se constitue une équipe virtuelle avec les noms de footballeurs réels, chaque but marqué par ceux-ci dans la réalité valant un point dans le jeu.

fao (*abbr of* **for the attention of**) à l'attention de.

far [fɑːr] (*compar* **farther** OR **further**, *superl* **farthest** OR **furthest**) ◆ *adv* 1. (*in distance*) loin; **how ~ is it?** c'est à quelle distance?, (est-ce que) c'est loin?; **have you come ~?** vous venez de loin?; ~ **away** OR **off** loin; ~ **and wide** partout; **as ~ as** jusqu'à. 2. (*in time*): ~ **away** OR **off** loin; **so ~** jusqu'à maintenant, jusqu'ici. 3. (*in degree or extent*) bien; **as ~ as** autant que; **as ~ as I'm concerned** en ce qui me concerne; **as ~ as possible** autant que possible, dans la mesure du possible; ~ **and away, by ~** de loin; ~ **from it** loin de là, au contraire. ◆ *adj* (*extreme*): **the ~ end of the street** l'autre bout de la rue; **the ~ right of the party** l'extrême droite du parti; **the door on the ~ left** la porte la plus à gauche.

faraway ['fɑːrəweɪ] *adj* lointain(e).

farce [fɑːs] *n* 1. (THEATRE) farce *f*. 2. *fig* (*disaster*) pagaille *f*, vaste rigolade *f*.

farcical ['fɑːsɪkl] *adj* grotesque.

fare [feər] *n* 1. (*payment*) prix *m*, tarif *m*. 2. *dated* (*food*) nourriture *f*.

Far East *n*: **the ~** l'Extrême-Orient *m*.

farewell [,feə'wel] ◆ *n* adieu *m*. ◆ *excl literary* adieu!

farm [fɑːm] ◆ *n* ferme *f*. ◆ *vt* cultiver.

farmer ['fɑːmər] *n* fermier *m*.

farmhand ['fɑːmhænd] *n* ouvrier *m*, -ère *f* agricole.

farmhouse ['fɑːmhaʊs, *pl* -haʊzɪz] *n* ferme *f*.

farming ['fɑːmɪŋ] *n* (U) agriculture *f*; (*of animals*) élevage *m*.

farm labourer = **farmhand**.

farmland ['fɑːmlænd] *n* (U) terres *fpl* cultivées OR arables.

farmstead ['fɑːmsted] *n* Am ferme *f*.

farm worker = farmhand.

farmyard ['fɑːmjɑːd] *n* cour *f* de ferme.

far-reaching [-'riːtʃɪŋ] *adj* d'une grande portée.

farsighted [ˌfɑː'saɪtɪd] *adj* 1. (*person*) prévoyant(e); (*plan*) élaboré(e) avec clairvoyance. 2. Am (*longsighted*) hypermétrope.

fart [fɑːt] *v inf* ◆ *n* (*air*) pet *m*. ◆ *vi* péter.

farther ['fɑːðə'] *compar* → far.

farthest ['fɑːðəst] *superl* → far.

fascinate ['fæsɪneɪt] *vt* fasciner.

fascinating ['fæsɪneɪtɪŋ] *adj* (*person*, *country*) fascinant(e); (*job*) passionnant(e); (*idea, thought*) très intéressant(e).

fascination [ˌfæsɪ'neɪʃn] *n* fascination *f*.

fascism ['fæʃɪzm] *n* fascisme *m*.

fashion ['fæʃn] ◆ *n* 1. (*clothing, style*) mode *f*; to be in/out of ~ être/ne plus être à la mode. 2. (*manner*) manière *f*. ◆ *vt fml* façonner, fabriquer.

fashionable ['fæʃnəbl] *adj* à la mode.

fashion show *n* défilé *m* de mode.

fast [fɑːst] ◆ *adj* 1. (*rapid*) rapide. 2. (*clock, watch*) qui avance. ◆ *adv* 1. (*rapidly*) vite. 2. (*firmly*) solidement; to hold ~ to sthg *lit & fig* s'accrocher à qqch; ~ asleep profondément endormi. ◆ *n* jeûne *m*. ◆ *vi* jeûner.

fasten ['fɑːsn] ◆ *vt* (*jacket, bag*) fermer; (*seat belt*) attacher; to ~ sthg to sthg attacher qqch à qqch. ◆ *vi*: to ~ on to sb/sthg se cramponner à qqn/qqch.

fastener ['fɑːsnə'] *n* (*of bag, necklace*) fermoir *m*; (*of dress*) fermeture *f*.

fastening ['fɑːsnɪŋ] *n* fermeture *f*.

fast food *n* fast food *m*.

fastidious [fə'stɪdɪəs] *adj* (*fussy*) méticuleux(euse).

fat [fæt] ◆ *adj* 1. (*overweight*) gros (grosse), gras (grasse); to get ~ grossir. 2. (*not lean - meat*) gras (grasse). 3. (*thick - file, wallet*) gros (grosse), épais(aisse). ◆ *n* 1. (*flesh, on meat, in food*) graisse *f*. 2. (U) (*for cooking*) matière *f* grasse.

fatal ['feɪtl] *adj* 1. (*serious - mistake*) fatal(e); (*- decision, words*) fatidique. 2. (*accident, illness*) mortel(elle).

fatality [fə'tælətɪ] *n* (*accident victim*) mort *m*.

fate [feɪt] *n* 1. (*destiny*) destin *m*; to tempt ~ tenter le diable. 2. (*result, end*) sort *m*.

fateful ['feɪtfʊl] *adj* fatidique.

father ['fɑːðə'] *n* père *m*.

Father Christmas *n* Br le Père Noël.

father-in-law (*pl* father-in-laws OR fathers-in-law) *n* beau-père *m*.

fatherly ['fɑːðəlɪ] *adj* paternel(elle).

fathom ['fæðəm] ◆ *n* brasse *f*. ◆ *vt*: to ~ sb/sthg (out) comprendre qqn/qqch.

fatigue [fə'tiːg] *n* 1. (*exhaustion*) épuisement *m*. 2. (*in metal*) fatigue *f*.

fatten ['fætn] *vt* engraisser.

fattening ['fætnɪŋ] *adj* qui fait grossir.

fatty ['fætɪ] ◆ *adj* gras (grasse). ◆ *n inf pej* gros *m*, grosse *f*.

fatuous ['fætjʊəs] *adj* stupide, niais(e).

faucet ['fɔːsɪt] *n* Am robinet *m*.

fault ['fɔːlt] ◆ *n* 1. (*responsibility, in tennis*) faute *f*; **it's my** ~ c'est de ma faute. 2. (*mistake, imperfection*) défaut *m*; **to find** ~ **with sb/sthg** critiquer qqn/qqch; **at** ~ fautif(ive). 3. (GEOL) faille *f*. ◆ *vt*: **to** ~ **sb (on sthg)** prendre qqn en défaut (sur qqch).

faultless ['fɔːltlɪs] *adj* impeccable.

faulty ['fɔːltɪ] *adj* défectueux(euse).

fauna ['fɔːnə] *n* faune *f*.

favour Br, **favor** Am ['feɪvə'] ◆ *n* 1. (*approval*) faveur *f*, approbation *f*; **in sb's** ~ en faveur de qqn; **to be in/out of** ~ **with sb** avoir/ne pas avoir les faveurs de qqn, avoir/ne pas avoir la cote avec qqn. 2. (*kind act*) service *m*; **to do sb a** ~ rendre (un) service à qqn; **to return the** ~ rendre la politesse. 3. (*favouritism*) favoritisme *m*. ◆ *vt* 1. (*prefer*) préférer, privilégier. 2. (*treat better, help*) favoriser. ▶ **in favour** *adv* (*in agreement*) pour, d'accord. ▶ **in favour of** *prep* 1. (*in preference to*) au profit de. 2. (*in agreement with*): **to be in** ~ **of sthg/of doing sthg** être partisan(e) de qqch/de faire qqch.

favourable Br, **favorable** Am ['feɪvrəbl] *adj* (*positive*) favorable.

favourite Br, **favorite** Am ['feɪvrɪt] ◆ *adj* favori(ite). ◆ *n* favori *m*, -ite *f*.

favouritism Br, **favoritism** Am ['feɪvrɪtɪzm] *n* favoritisme *m*.

fawn [fɔːn] ◆ *adj* fauve (*inv*). ◆ *n* (*animal*) faon *m*. ◆ *vi*: **to** ~ **on sb** flatter qqn servilement.

fax [fæks] ◆ *n* fax *m*, télécopie *f*. ◆ *vt* 1. (*person*) envoyer un fax à. 2. (*document*) envoyer en fax.

fax machine *n* fax *m*, télécopieur *m*.

fax modem *n* modem *m* fax.

FBI (*abbr of* **Federal Bureau of Investigation**) *n* FBI *m*.

fear [fɪə'] ◆ *n* 1. (U) (*feeling*) peur *f*. 2. (*object of fear*) crainte *f*. 3. (*risk*) risque *m*; **for ~ of** de peur de (+ *infin*), de peur que (+ *subjunctive*). ◆ *vt* 1. (*be afraid of*) craindre, avoir peur de. 2. (*anticipate*) craindre; **to ~ (that)** ... craindre que ..., avoir peur que ...

fearful ['fɪəful] *adj* 1. *fml* (*frightened*) peureux(euse); **to be ~ of sthg** avoir peur de qqch. 2. (*frightening*) effrayant(e).

fearless ['fɪəlɪs] *adj* intrépide.

feasible ['fiːzəbl] *adj* faisable.

feast [fiːst] ◆ *n* (*meal*) festin *m*, banquet *m*. ◆ *vi*: **to ~ on** OR **off sthg** se régaler de qqch.

feat [fiːt] *n* exploit *m*, prouesse *f*.

feather ['feðə'] *n* plume *f*.

feature ['fiːtʃə'] ◆ *n* 1. (*characteristic*) caractéristique *f*. 2. (GEOGR) particularité *f*. 3. (*article*) article *m* de fond. 4. (RADIO & TV) émission *f* spéciale, spécial *m*. 5. (CINEMA) long métrage *m*. ◆ *vt* 1. (*subj: film, exhibition*) mettre en vedette. 2. (*comprise*) présenter, comporter. ◆ *vi*: **to ~ (in)** figurer en vedette (dans). ▶ **features** *npl* (*of face*) traits *mpl*.

feature film *n* long métrage *m*.

February ['februəri] *n* février *m; see also* **September**.

feces Am = **faeces**.

fed [fed] *pt & pp* → **feed**.

federal ['fedrəl] *adj* fédéral(e).

federation [,fedə'reɪʃn] *n* fédération *f*.

fed up *adj*: **to be ~ (with)** en avoir marre (de).

fee [fiː] *n* (*of school*) frais *mpl*; (*of doctor*) honoraires *mpl*; (*for membership*) cotisation *f*; (*for entrance*) tarif *m*, prix *m*.

feeble ['fiːbl] *adj* faible.

feed [fiːd] (*pt & pp* **fed**) ◆ *vt* 1. (*give food to*) nourrir. 2. (*fire, fears etc*) alimenter. 3. (*put, insert*): **to ~ sthg into sthg** mettre OR insérer qqch dans qqch. ◆ *vi* (*take food*): **to ~ (on** OR **off)** se nourrir (de). ◆ *n* 1. (*for baby*) repas *m*. 2. (*animal food*) nourriture *f*.

feedback ['fiːdbæk] *n* (U) 1. (*reaction*) réactions *fpl*. 2. (ELEC) réaction *f*, rétroaction *f*.

feeding bottle ['fiːdɪŋ-] *n* Br biberon *m*.

feel [fiːl] (*pt & pp* **felt**) ◆ *vt* 1. (*touch*) toucher. 2. (*sense, experience, notice*) sentir; (*emotion*) ressentir; **to ~ o.s. doing sthg** se sentir faire qqch. 3. (*believe*): **to ~ (that)** ... croire que ..., penser que ... 4.

phr: **I'm not ~ing myself today** je ne suis pas dans mon assiette aujourd'hui. ◆ *vi* 1. (*have sensation*): **to ~ cold/hot/sleepy** avoir froid/chaud/sommeil; **to ~ like sthg/like doing sthg** (*be in mood for*) avoir envie de qqch/de faire qqch. 2. (*have emotion*) se sentir; **to ~ angry** être en colère. 3. (*seem*) sembler; **it ~s strange** ça fait drôle. 4. (*by touch*): **to ~ for sthg** chercher qqch. ◆ *n* 1. (*sensation, touch*) toucher *m*, sensation *f*. 2. (*atmosphere*) atmosphère *f*.

feeler ['fiːlə'] *n* antenne *f*.

feeling ['fiːlɪŋ] *n* 1. (*emotion*) sentiment *m*. 2. (*physical sensation*) sensation *f*. 3. (*intuition, sense*) sentiment *m*, impression *f*. 4. (*understanding*) sensibilité *f*. ▶ **feelings** *npl* sentiments *mpl*; **to hurt sb's ~s** blesser (la sensibilité de) qqn.

feet [fiːt] *pl* → **foot**.

feign [feɪn] *vt fml* feindre.

fell [fel] ◆ *pt* → **fall**. ◆ *vt* (*tree, person*) abattre. ▶ **fells** *npl* (GEOGR) lande *f*.

fellow ['feləʊ] ◆ *n* 1. *dated* (*man*) homme *m*. 2. (*comrade, peer*) camarade *m*, compagnon *m*. 3. (*of society, college*) membre *m*, associé *m*. ◆ *adj*: **one's ~ men** ses semblables; **~ passenger** compagnon *m*, compagne *f* (de voyage); **~ student** camarade *mf* (d'études).

fellowship ['feləʊʃɪp] *n* 1. (*comradeship*) amitié *f*, camaraderie *f*. 2. (*society*) association *f*, corporation *f*. 3. (*of society, college*) titre *m* de membre OR d'associé.

felony ['feləni] *n* (JUR) crime *m*, forfait *m*.

felt [felt] ◆ *pt & pp* → **feel**. ◆ *n* (U) feutre *m*.

felt-tip pen *n* stylo-feutre *m*.

female ['fiːmeɪl] ◆ *adj* (*person*) de sexe féminin; (*animal, plant*) femelle; (*sex, figure*) féminin(e); **~ student** étudiante *f*. ◆ *n* femelle *f*.

feminine ['feminin] ◆ *adj* féminin(e). ◆ *n* (GRAMM) féminin *m*.

feminist ['feminist] *n* féministe *mf*.

fence [fens] ◆ *n* (*barrier*) clôture *f*; **to sit on the ~** *fig* ménager la chèvre et le chou. ◆ *vt* clôturer, entourer d'une clôture.

fencing ['fensɪŋ] *n* (SPORT) escrime *f*.

fend [fend] *vi*: **to ~ for o.s.** se débrouiller tout seul. ▶ **fend off** *vt sep* (*blows*) parer; (*questions, reporters*) écarter.

fender ['fendə'] *n* 1. (*round fireplace*) pare-feu *m inv*. 2. (*on boat*) défense *f*. 3. Am (*on car*) aile *f*.

ferment [*n* 'fɜːment, *vb* fə'ment] ◆ *n*

(U) (*unrest*) agitation *f*, effervescence *f*.
◆ *vi* (*wine, beer*) fermenter.

fern [fɜːn] *n* fougère *f*.

ferocious [fəˈrəʊʃəs] *adj* féroce.

ferret [ˈferɪt] *n* furet *m*. ▸ **ferret about, ferret around** *vi inf* fureter un peu partout.

ferris wheel [ˈferɪs-] *n* grande roue *f*.

ferry [ˈferɪ] ◆ *n* ferry *m*, ferry-boat *m*; (*smaller*) bac *m*. ◆ *vt* transporter.

ferryboat [ˈferɪbəʊt] *n* = **ferry**.

fertile [ˈfɜːtaɪl] *adj* 1. (*land, imagination*) fertile, fécond(e). 2. (*woman*) féconde.

fertilizer [ˈfɜːtɪlaɪzəʳ] *n* engrais *m*.

fester [ˈfestəʳ] *vi* (*wound, sore*) suppurer.

festival [ˈfestəvl] *n* 1. (*event, celebration*) festival *m*. 2. (*holiday*) fête *f*.

festive [ˈfestɪv] *adj* de fête.

festive season *n*: **the ~** la période des fêtes.

festivities [fesˈtɪvətɪz] *npl* réjouissances *fpl*.

festoon [feˈstuːn] *vt* décorer de guirlandes; **to be ~ed with** être décoré de.

fetch [fetʃ] *vt* 1. (*go and get*) aller chercher. 2. (*raise - money*) rapporter.

fete, fête [feɪt] *n* fête *f*, kermesse *f*.

fetish [ˈfetɪʃ] *n* 1. (*sexual obsession*) objet *m* de fétichisme. 2. (*mania*) manie *f*, obsession *f*.

fetus [ˈfiːtəs] = **foetus**.

feud [fjuːd] ◆ *n* querelle *f*. ◆ *vi* se quereller.

feudal [ˈfjuːdl] *adj* féodal(e).

fever [ˈfiːvəʳ] *n* fièvre *f*.

feverish [ˈfiːvərɪʃ] *adj* fiévreux(euse).

few [fjuː] ◆ *adj* peu de; **the first ~ pages** les toutes premières pages; **quite a ~, a good ~** pas mal de, un bon nombre de; **~ and far between** rares. ◆ *pron* peu; **a ~** quelques-uns *mpl*, quelques-unes *fpl*.

fewer [ˈfjuːəʳ] ◆ *adj* moins (de). ◆ *pron* moins.

fewest [ˈfjuːəst] *adj* le moins (de).

fiancé [fɪˈɒnseɪ] *n* fiancé *m*.

fiancée [fɪˈɒnseɪ] *n* fiancée *f*.

fiasco [fɪˈæskəʊ] (*Br pl* **-s**, *Am pl* **-es**) *n* fiasco *m*.

fib [fɪb] *inf* ◆ *n* bobard *m*, blague *f*. ◆ *vi* raconter des bobards OR des blagues.

fibre *Br*, **fiber** *Am* [ˈfaɪbəʳ] *n* fibre *f*.

fibreglass *Br*, **fiberglass** *Am* [ˈfaɪbəɡlɑːs] *n* (U) fibre *f* de verre.

fickle [ˈfɪkl] *adj* versatile.

fiction [ˈfɪkʃn] *n* fiction *f*.

fictional [ˈfɪkʃənl] *adj* fictif(ive).

fictitious [fɪkˈtɪʃəs] *adj* (*false*) fictif(ive).

fiddle [ˈfɪdl] ◆ *vi* (*play around*): **to ~ with** sthg tripoter qqch. ◆ *vt Br inf* truquer. ◆ *n* 1. (*violin*) violon *m*. 2. *Br inf* (*fraud*) combine *f*, escroquerie *f*.

fiddly [ˈfɪdlɪ] *adj Br inf* délicat(e).

fidget [ˈfɪdʒɪt] *vi* remuer.

field [fiːld] *n* 1. (*gen* & COMPUT) champ *m*. 2. (*for sports*) terrain *m*. 3. (*of knowledge*) domaine *m*.

field day *n*: **to have a ~** s'en donner à cœur joie.

field glasses *npl* jumelles *fpl*.

field marshal *n* ≃ maréchal *m* (de France).

field trip *n* voyage *m* d'étude.

fieldwork [ˈfiːldwɜːk] *n* (U) recherches *fpl* sur le terrain.

fiend [fiːnd] *n* 1. (*cruel person*) monstre *m*. 2. *inf* (*fanatic*) fou *m*, folle *f*, mordu *m*, -e *f*.

fiendish [ˈfiːndɪʃ] *adj* 1. (*evil*) abominable. 2. *inf* (*very difficult, complex*) compliqué(e), complexe.

fierce [fɪəs] *adj* féroce; (*heat*) torride; (*storm, temper*) violent(e).

fiery [ˈfaɪərɪ] *adj* 1. (*burning*) ardent(e). 2. (*volatile - speech*) enflammé(e); (- *temper, person*) fougueux(euse).

fifteen [fɪfˈtiːn] *num* quinze; *see also* **six**.

fifth [fɪfθ] *num* cinquième; *see also* **sixth**.

fifty [ˈfɪftɪ] *num* cinquante; *see also* **sixty**.

fifty-fifty ◆ *adj* moitié-moitié, fifty-fifty; **to have a ~ chance** avoir cinquante pour cent de chances. ◆ *adv* moitié-moitié, fifty-fifty.

fig [fɪɡ] *n* figue *f*.

fight [faɪt] (*pt* & *pp* **fought**) ◆ *n* 1. (*physical*) bagarre *f*; **to have a ~ (with sb)** se battre (avec qqn), se bagarrer (avec qqn); **to put up a ~** se battre, se défendre. 2. *fig* (*battle, struggle*) lutte *f*, combat *m*. 3. (*argument*) dispute *f*; **to have a ~ (with sb)** se disputer (avec qqn). ◆ *vt* 1. (*physically*) se battre contre OR avec. 2. (*conduct - war*) mener. 3. (*enemy, racism*) combattre. ◆ *vi* 1. (*in war, punch-up*) se battre. 2. *fig* (*struggle*): **to ~ for/against** sthg lutter pour/contre qqch. 3. (*argue*): **to ~ (about OR over)** se battre OR se disputer (à propos de). ▸ **fight back** ◆ *vt fus* refouler. ◆ *vi* riposter.

fighter [ˈfaɪtəʳ] *n* 1. (*plane*) avion *m* de chasse, chasseur *m*. 2. (*soldier*) combattant *m*. 3. (*combative person*) battant *m*, -e *f*.

fighting ['faɪtɪŋ] *n* (U) (*punch-up*) bagarres *fpl*; (*in war*) conflits *mpl*.

figment ['fɪgmənt] *n*: **a ~ of sb's imagination** le fruit de l'imagination de qqn.

figurative ['fɪgərətɪv] *adj* (*meaning*) figuré(e).

figure [*Br* 'fɪgəʳ, *Am* 'fɪgjər] ◆ *n* 1. (*statistic, number*) chiffre *m*. 2. (*human shape, outline*) silhouette *f*, forme *f*. 3. (*personality, diagram*) figure *f*. 4. (*shape of body*) ligne *f*. ◆ *vt* (*suppose*) penser, supposer. ◆ *vi* (*feature*) figurer, apparaître. ► **figure out** *vt sep* (*understand*) comprendre; (*find*) trouver.

figurehead ['fɪgəhed] *n* 1. (*on ship*) figure *f* de proue. 2. *fig & pej* (*leader*) homme *m* de paille.

figure of speech *n* figure *f* de rhétorique.

Fiji ['fiːdʒiː] *n* Fidji *fpl*.

file [faɪl] ◆ *n* 1. (*folder, report*) dossier *m*; **on ~, on the ~s** répertorié dans les dossiers. 2. (COMPUT) fichier *m*. 3. (*tool*) lime *f*. 4. (*line*) **in single ~** en file indienne. ◆ *vt* 1. (*document*) classer. 2. (JUR - *accusation, complaint*) porter, déposer; (- *lawsuit*) intenter. 3. (*fingernails, wood*) limer. ◆ *vi* 1. (*walk in single file*) marcher en file indienne. 2. (JUR): **to ~ for divorce** demander le divorce.

filet *Am* = **fillet**.

filing cabinet ['faɪlɪŋ-] *n* classeur *m*, fichier *m*.

Filipino [ˌfɪlɪ'piːnəu] (*pl* -s) ◆ *adj* philippin(e). ◆ *n* Philippin *m*, -e *f*.

fill [fɪl] ◆ *vt* 1. (*gen*) remplir; **to ~ sthg with sthg** remplir qqch de qqch. 2. (*gap, hole*) boucher. 3. (*vacancy - subj: employer*) pourvoir à; (- *subj: employee*) prendre. ◆ *n*: **to eat one's ~** manger à sa faim. ► **fill in** ◆ *vt sep* 1. (*form*) remplir. 2. (*inform*): **to ~ sb in (on)** mettre qqn au courant (de). ◆ *vi* (*substitute*): **to ~ in for sb** remplacer qqn. ► **fill out** ◆ *vt sep* (*form*) remplir. ► **fill up** ◆ *vt sep* remplir. ◆ *vi* se remplir.

fillet *Br*, **filet** *Am* ['fɪlɪt] *n* filet *m*.

fillet steak *n* filet *m* de bœuf.

filling ['fɪlɪŋ] ◆ *adj* très nourrissant(e). ◆ *n* 1. (*in tooth*) plombage *m*. 2. (*in cake, sandwich*) garniture *f*.

filling station *n* station-service *f*.

film [fɪlm] ◆ *n* 1. (*movie*) film *m*. 2. (*layer, for camera*) pellicule *f*. 3. (*footage*) images *fpl*. ◆ *vt & vi* filmer.

film star *n* vedette *f* de cinéma.

Filofax® ['faɪləufæks] *n* Filofax® *m*.

filter ['fɪltəʳ] ◆ *n* filtre *m*. ◆ *vt* (*coffee*) passer; (*water, oil, air*) filtrer.

filter coffee *n* café *m* filtre.

filter lane *n Br* ≃ voie *f* de droite.

filter-tipped [-'tɪpt] *adj* à bout filtre.

filth [fɪlθ] *n* (U) 1. (*dirt*) saleté *f*, crasse *f*. 2. (*obscenity*) obscénités *fpl*.

filthy ['fɪlθɪ] *adj* 1. (*very dirty*) dégoûtant(e), répugnant(e). 2. (*obscene*) obscène.

fin [fɪn] *n* (*of fish*) nageoire *f*.

final ['faɪnl] ◆ *adj* 1. (*last*) dernier(ère). 2. (*at end*) final(e). 3. (*definitive*) définitif (ive). ◆ *n* finale *f*. ► **finals** *npl* (UNIV) examens *mpl* de dernière année.

finale [fɪ'nɑːlɪ] *n* finale *m*.

finalize, -ise ['faɪnəlaɪz] *vt* mettre au point.

finally ['faɪnəlɪ] *adv* enfin.

finance [*n* 'faɪnæns, *vb* faɪ'næns] ◆ *n* (U) finance *f*. ◆ *vt* financer. ► **finances** *npl* finances *fpl*.

financial [fɪ'nænʃl] *adj* financier(ère).

find [faɪnd] (*pt & pp* **found**) ◆ *vt* 1. (*gen*) trouver. 2. (*realize*): **to ~ (that)** ... s'apercevoir que ... 3. (JUR): **to be found guilty/not guilty (of)** être déclaré(e) coupable/non coupable (de). ◆ *n* trouvaille *f*. ► **find out** ◆ *vi* se renseigner. ◆ *vt fus* 1. (*information*) se renseigner sur. 2. (*truth*) découvrir, apprendre. ◆ *vt sep* démasquer.

findings ['faɪndɪŋz] *npl* conclusions *fpl*.

fine [faɪn] ◆ *adj* 1. (*good - work*) excellent(e); (- *building, weather*) beau (belle). 2. (*perfectly satisfactory*) très bien; **I'm ~** ça va bien. 3. (*thin, smooth*) fin(e). 4. (*minute - detail, distinction*) subtil(e); (- *adjustment, tuning*) délicat(e). ◆ *adv* (*very well*) très bien. ◆ *n* amende *f*. ◆ *vt* condamner à une amende.

fine arts *npl* beaux-arts *mpl*.

finely ['faɪnlɪ] *adv* 1. (*chopped, ground*) fin. 2. (*tuned, balanced*) délicatement.

finery ['faɪnərɪ] *n* (U) parure *f*.

fine-tune *vt* (*mechanism*) régler au quart de tour; *fig* régler minutieusement.

finger ['fɪŋgəʳ] ◆ *n* doigt *m*. ◆ *vt* (*feel*) palper.

fingernail ['fɪŋgəneɪl] *n* ongle *m* (de la main).

fingerprint ['fɪŋgəprɪnt] *n* empreinte *f* (digitale).

fingertip ['fɪŋgətɪp] *n* bout *m* du doigt; **at one's ~s** sur le bout des doigts.

finicky ['fɪnɪkɪ] *adj pej* (*eater, task*) difficile; (*person*) tatillon(onne).

finish ['fɪnɪʃ] ◆ n 1. (end) fin f; (of race) arrivée f. 2. (texture) finition f. ◆ vt finir, terminer; **to ~ doing sthg** finir OR terminer de faire qqch. ◆ vi finir, terminer; (school, film) se terminer. ▶ **finish off** vt sep finir, terminer. ▶ **finish up** vi finir.

finishing line ['fɪnɪʃɪŋ-] n ligne f d'arrivée.

finishing school ['fɪnɪʃɪŋ-] n école privée pour jeunes filles surtout axée sur l'enseignement de bonnes manières.

finite ['faɪnaɪt] adj fini(e).

Finland ['fɪnlənd] n Finlande f.

Finn [fɪn] n Finlandais m, -e f.

Finnish ['fɪnɪʃ] ◆ adj finlandais(e), finnois(e). ◆ n (language) finnois m.

fir [fɜːʳ] n sapin m.

fire ['faɪəʳ] ◆ n 1. (gen) feu m; **on ~** en feu; **to catch ~** prendre feu; **to set ~ to sthg** mettre le feu à qqch. 2. (out of control) incendie m. 3. Br (heater) appareil m de chauffage. 4. (U) (shooting) coups mpl de feu; **to open ~ (on)** ouvrir le feu (sur). ◆ vt 1. (shoot) tirer. 2. (dismiss) renvoyer. ◆ vi: **to ~ (on OR at)** faire feu (sur), tirer (sur).

fire alarm n avertisseur m d'incendie.

firearm ['faɪərɑːm] n arme f à feu.

firebomb ['faɪəbɒm] n bombe f incendiaire.

fire brigade Br, **fire department** Am n sapeurs-pompiers mpl.

fire door n porte f coupe-feu.

fire engine n voiture f de pompiers.

fire escape n escalier m de secours.

fire extinguisher n extincteur m d'incendie.

fireguard ['faɪəgɑːd] n garde-feu m inv.

firelighter ['faɪəlaɪtəʳ] n allume-feu m inv.

fireman ['faɪəmən] (pl **-men** [-mən]) n pompier m.

fireplace ['faɪəpleɪs] n cheminée f.

fireproof ['faɪəpruːf] adj ignifugé(e).

fireside ['faɪəsaɪd] n: **by the ~** au coin du feu.

fire station n caserne f des pompiers.

firewood ['faɪəwʊd] n bois m de chauffage.

firework ['faɪəwɜːk] n fusée f de feu d'artifice. ▶ **fireworks** npl (outburst of anger) étincelles fpl.

firing ['faɪərɪŋ] n (U) (MIL) tir m, fusillade f.

firing squad n peloton m d'exécution.

firm [fɜːm] ◆ adj 1. (gen) ferme; **to stand ~** tenir bon. 2. (support, structure) solide. 3. (evidence, news) certain(e). ◆ n firme f, société f.

first [fɜːst] ◆ adj premier(ère); **for the ~ time** pour la première fois; **~ thing in the morning** tôt le matin. ◆ adv 1. (before anyone else) en premier. 2. (before anything else) d'abord; **~ of all** tout d'abord. 3. (for the first time) (pour) la première fois. ◆ n 1. (person) premier m, -ère f. 2. (unprecedented event) première f. 3. Br (UNIV) diplôme universitaire avec mention très bien. ▶ **at first** adv d'abord. ▶ **at first hand** adv de première main.

first aid n (U) premiers secours mpl.

first-aid kit n trousse f de premiers secours.

first-class adj 1. (excellent) excellent(e). 2. (ticket, compartment) de première classe; (stamp, letter) tarif normal.

first floor n Br premier étage m; Am rez-de-chaussée m inv.

firsthand [fɜːstˈhænd] adj & adv de première main.

first lady n première dame f du pays.

firstly ['fɜːstlɪ] adv premièrement.

first name n prénom m.

first-rate adj excellent(e).

firtree ['fɜːtriː] = **fir**.

fish [fɪʃ] (pl inv) ◆ n poisson m. ◆ vt (river, sea) pêcher dans. ◆ vi (fisherman): **to ~ (for sthg)** pêcher (qqch).

fish and chips npl Br poisson m frit avec frites.

fish and chip shop n Br endroit où l'on vend du poisson frit et des frites.

fishbowl ['fɪʃbəʊl] n bocal m (à poissons).

fishcake ['fɪʃkeɪk] n croquette f de poisson.

fisherman ['fɪʃəmən] (pl **-men** [-mən]) n pêcheur m.

fish farm n centre m de pisciculture.

fish fingers Br, **fish sticks** Am npl bâtonnets mpl de poisson panés.

fishing ['fɪʃɪŋ] n pêche f; **to go ~** aller à la pêche.

fishing boat n bateau m de pêche.

fishing line n ligne f.

fishing rod n canne f à pêche.

fishmonger ['fɪʃˌmʌŋgəʳ] n poissonnier m, -ère f; **~'s (shop)** poissonnerie f.

fish sticks Am = **fish fingers**.

fishy ['fɪʃɪ] adj 1. (smell, taste) de poisson. 2. (suspicious) louche.

fist [fɪst] n poing m.

fit [fɪt] ◆ adj 1. (suitable) convenable; **to be ~ for sthg** être bon (bonne) à qqch; **to be ~ to do sthg** être apte à faire qqch. 2. (healthy) en forme; **to keep ~** se maintenir en forme. ◆ n 1. (of clothes, shoes etc) ajustement m; **it's a tight ~** c'est un peu juste; **it's a good ~** c'est la bonne taille. 2. (epileptic seizure) crise f; **to have a ~** avoir une crise; fig piquer une crise. 3. (bout - of crying) crise f; (- of rage) accès m; (- of sneezing) suite f; **in ~s and starts** par à-coups. ◆ vt 1. (be correct size for) aller à. 2. (place): **to ~ sthg into sthg** insérer qqch dans qqch. 3. (provide): **to ~ sthg with sthg** équiper OR munir qqch de qqch. 4. (be suitable for) correspondre à. ◆ vi (be correct size, go) aller; (into container) entrer. ▶ **fit in** ◆ vt sep (accommodate) prendre. ◆ vi s'intégrer; **to ~ in with sthg** correspondre à qqch; **to ~ in with sb** s'accorder à qqn.

fitful ['fɪtfʊl] adj (sleep) agité(e); (wind, showers) intermittent(e).

fitment ['fɪtmənt] n meuble m encastré.

fitness ['fɪtnɪs] n (U) 1. (health) forme f. 2. (suitability): **~ (for)** aptitude f (pour).

fitted carpet [,fɪtəd-] n moquette f.

fitted kitchen [,fɪtəd-] n Br cuisine f intégrée OR équipée.

fitter ['fɪtər] n (mechanic) monteur m.

fitting ['fɪtɪŋ] ◆ adj fml approprié(e). ◆ n 1. (part) appareil m. 2. (for clothing) essayage m. ▶ **fittings** npl installations fpl.

fitting room n cabine f d'essayage.

five [faɪv] num cinq; see also **six**.

fiver ['faɪvər] n inf 1. Br (amount) cinq livres fpl; (note) billet m de cinq livres. 2. Am (amount) cinq dollars mpl; (note) billet m de cinq dollars.

fix [fɪks] ◆ vt 1. (gen) fixer; **to ~ sthg to sthg** fixer qqch à qqch. 2. (in memory) graver. 3. (repair) réparer. 4. inf (rig) truquer. 5. (food, drink) préparer. ◆ n 1. inf (difficult situation): **to be in a ~** être dans le pétrin. 2. drugs sl piqûre f. ▶ **fix up** vt sep 1. (provide): **to ~ sb up with sthg** obtenir qqch pour qqn. 2. (arrange) arranger.

fixation [fɪk'seɪʃn] n: **~ (on OR about)** obsession f (de).

fixed [fɪkst] adj 1. (attached) fixé(e). 2. (set, unchanging) fixe; (smile) figé(e).

fixture ['fɪkstʃər] n 1. (furniture) installation f. 2. (permanent feature) tradition f

bien établie. 3. (SPORT) rencontre f (sportive).

fizz [fɪz] vi (lemonade, champagne) pétiller; (fireworks) crépiter.

fizzle ['fɪzl] ▶ **fizzle out** vi (fire) s'éteindre; (firework) se terminer; (interest, enthusiasm) se dissiper.

fizzy ['fɪzɪ] adj pétillant(e).

flabbergasted ['flæbəgɑːstɪd] adj sidéré(e).

flabby ['flæbɪ] adj mou (molle).

flag [flæg] ◆ n drapeau m. ◆ vi (person, energy) faiblir; (conversation) traîner. ▶ **flag down** vt sep (taxi) héler; **to ~ sb down** faire signe à qqn de s'arrêter.

flagpole ['flægpəʊl] n mât m.

flagrant ['fleɪɡrənt] adj flagrant(e).

flagstone ['flægstəʊn] n dalle f.

flair [fleər] n 1. (talent) don m. 2. (U) (stylishness) style m.

flak [flæk] n (U) inf (criticism) critiques fpl sévères.

flake [fleɪk] ◆ n (of paint, plaster) écaille f; (of snow) flocon m; (of skin) petit lambeau m. ◆ vi (paint, plaster) s'écailler; (skin) peler.

flamboyant [flæm'bɔɪənt] adj 1. (showy, confident) extravagant(e). 2. (brightly coloured) flamboyant(e).

flame [fleɪm] n flamme f; **in ~s** en flammes; **to burst into ~s** s'enflammer.

flamingo [flə'mɪŋɡəʊ] (pl **-s** OR **-es**) n flamant m rose.

flammable ['flæməbl] adj inflammable.

flan [flæn] n tarte f.

flank [flæŋk] ◆ n flanc m. ◆ vt: **to be ~ed by** être flanqué(e) de.

flannel ['flænl] n 1. (fabric) flanelle f. 2. Br (facecloth) gant m de toilette.

flap [flæp] ◆ n 1. (of envelope, pocket) rabat m. 2. inf (panic): **in a ~** paniqué(e). ◆ vt & vi battre.

flapjack ['flæpdʒæk] n 1. Br (biscuit) biscuit m à l'avoine. 2. Am (pancake) crêpe f épaisse.

flare [fleər] ◆ n (distress signal) fusée f éclairante. ◆ vi 1. (burn brightly): **to ~ (up)** s'embraser. 2. (intensify): **to ~ (up)** (war, revolution) s'intensifier soudainement; (person) s'emporter. 3. (widen - trousers, skirt) s'évaser; (- nostrils) se dilater. ▶ **flares** npl Br pantalon m à pattes d'éléphant.

flash [flæʃ] ◆ n 1. (of light, colour) éclat m; **~ of lightning** éclair m. 2. (PHOT) flash m. 3. (sudden moment) éclair m; **in a ~** en un rien de temps. ◆ vt 1. (shine) projeter; **to ~ one's headlights** faire un appel de phares. **2.** (*send out - signal, smile*) envoyer; (*- look*) jeter. **3.** (*show*) montrer. ◆ *vi* **1.** (*torch*) briller. **2.** (*light - on and off*) clignoter; (*eyes*) jeter des éclairs. **3.** (*rush*): **to ~ by** OR **past** passer comme un éclair.

flashback ['flæʃbæk] *n* flashback *m*, retour *m* en arrière.

flashbulb ['flæʃbʌlb] *n* ampoule *f* de flash.

flashgun ['flæʃgʌn] *n* flash *m*.

flashlight ['flæʃlaɪt] *n* (*torch*) lampe *f* électrique.

flashy ['flæʃɪ] *adj inf* tape-à-l'œil (*inv*).

flask [flɑːsk] *n* (*thermos flask*) Thermos® *m or f*.

flat [flæt] ◆ *adj* **1.** (*gen*) plat(e). **2.** (*tyre*) crevé(e). **3.** (*refusal, denial*) catégorique. **4.** (*business, trade*) calme. **5.** (*dull - voice, tone*) monotone; (*- performance, writing*) terne. **6.** (MUS *- person*) qui chante trop grave; (*- note*) bémol. **7.** (*fare, price*) fixe. **8.** (*beer, lemonade*) éventé(e). **9.** (*battery*) à plat. ◆ *adv* **1.** (*level*) à plat. **2.** (*exactly*): **two hours ~** deux heures pile. ◆ *n* **1.** Br (*apartment*) appartement *m*. **2.** (MUS) bémol *m*. ▶ **flat out** *adv* (*work*) d'arrache-pied; (*travel - subj: vehicle*) le plus vite possible.

flatly ['flætlɪ] *adv* **1.** (*absolutely*) catégoriquement. **2.** (*dully - say*) avec monotonie; (*- perform*) de façon terne.

flatmate ['flætmeɪt] *n* Br personne avec laquelle on partage un appartement.

flat rate *n* tarif *m* forfaitaire.

flatten ['flætn] *vt* **1.** (*make flat - steel, paper*) aplatir; (*- wrinkles, bumps*) aplanir. **2.** (*destroy*) raser. ▶ **flatten out** ◆ *vi* s'aplanir. ◆ *vt sep* aplanir.

flatter ['flætəʳ] *vt* flatter.

flattering ['flætərɪŋ] *adj* **1.** (*complimentary*) flatteur(euse). **2.** (*clothes*) seyant(e).

flattery ['flætərɪ] *n* flatterie *f*.

flaunt [flɔːnt] *vt* faire étalage de.

flavour Br, **flavor** Am ['fleɪvəʳ] ◆ *n* **1.** (*of food*) goût *m*; (*of ice cream, yoghurt*) parfum *m*. **2.** *fig* (*atmosphere*) atmosphère *f*. ◆ *vt* parfumer.

flavouring Br, **flavoring** Am ['fleɪvərɪŋ] *n* (U) parfum *m*.

flaw [flɔː] *n* (*in material, character*) défaut *m*; (*in plan, argument*) faille *f*.

flawless ['flɔːlɪs] *adj* parfait(e).

flax [flæks] *n* lin *m*.

flea [fliː] *n* puce *f*.

flea market *n* marché *m* aux puces.

fleck [flek] ◆ *n* moucheture *f*, petite tache *f*. ◆ *vt*: **~ed with** moucheté(e) de.

fled [fled] *pt & pp* → **flee**.

flee [fliː] (*pt & pp* **fled**) *vt & vi* fuir.

fleece [fliːs] ◆ *n* toison *f*. ◆ *vt inf* escroquer.

fleet [fliːt] *n* **1.** (*of ships*) flotte *f*. **2.** (*of cars, buses*) parc *m*.

fleeting ['fliːtɪŋ] *adj* (*moment*) bref (brève); (*look*) fugitif(ive); (*visit*) éclair (*inv*).

Fleet Street *n* rue de Londres dont le nom est utilisé pour désigner la presse britannique.

Flemish ['flemɪʃ] ◆ *adj* flamand(e). ◆ *n* (*language*) flamand *m*. ◆ *npl*: **the ~** les Flamands *mpl*.

flesh [fleʃ] *n* chair *f*; **his/her ~ and blood** (*family*) les siens.

flew [fluː] *pt* → **fly**.

flex [fleks] ◆ *n* (ELEC) fil *m*. ◆ *vt* (*bend*) fléchir.

flexible ['fleksəbl] *adj* flexible.

flexitime ['fleksɪtaɪm] *n* (U) horaire *m* à la carte OR flexible.

flick [flɪk] ◆ *n* **1.** (*of whip, towel*) petit coup *m*. **2.** (*with finger*) chiquenaude *f*. ◆ *vt* (*switch*) appuyer sur. ▶ **flick through** *vt fus* feuilleter.

flicker ['flɪkəʳ] *vi* **1.** (*candle, light*) vaciller. **2.** (*shadow*) trembler; (*eyelids*) ciller.

flick knife *n* Br couteau *m* à cran d'arrêt.

flight [flaɪt] *n* **1.** (*gen*) vol *m*. **2.** (*of steps, stairs*) volée *f*. **3.** (*escape*) fuite *f*.

flight attendant *n* steward *m*, hôtesse *f* de l'air.

flight crew *n* équipage *m*.

flight deck *n* **1.** (*of aircraft carrier*) pont *m* d'envol. **2.** (*of plane*) cabine *f* de pilotage.

flight recorder *n* enregistreur *m* de vol.

flimsy ['flɪmzɪ] *adj* (*dress, material*) léger (ère); (*building, bookcase*) peu solide; (*excuse*) piètre.

flinch [flɪntʃ] *vi* tressaillir.

fling [flɪŋ] (*pt & pp* **flung**) ◆ *n* (*affair*) aventure *f*, affaire *f*. ◆ *vt* lancer.

flint [flɪnt] *n* **1.** (*rock*) silex *m*. **2.** (*in lighter*) pierre *f*.

flip [flɪp] ◆ *vt* **1.** (*turn - pancake*) faire sauter; (*- record*) tourner. **2.** (*switch*) appuyer sur. ◆ *vi inf* (*become angry*) piquer une colère. ◆ *n* **1.** (*flick*) chiquenaude *f*. **2.** (*somersault*) saut *m* périlleux. ▶ **flip through** *vt fus* feuilleter.

flip-flop *n* (*shoe*) tong *f*.

flippant ['flɪpənt] *adj* désinvolte.

flipper ['flɪpəʳ] *n* 1. (*of animal*) nageoire *f*. 2. (*for swimmer, diver*) palme *f*.

flirt [flɜːt] ◆ *n* flirt *m*. ◆ *vi* (*with person*): to ~ (**with sb**) flirter (avec qqn).

flirtatious [flɜːˈteɪʃəs] *adj* flirteur (euse).

flit [flɪt] *vi* (*bird*) voleter.

float [fləʊt] ◆ *n* 1. (*for buoyancy*) flotteur *m*. 2. (*in procession*) char *m*. 3. (*money*) petite caisse *f*. ◆ *vt* (*on water*) faire flotter. ◆ *vi* (*on water*) flotter; (*through air*) glisser.

flock [flɒk] *n* 1. (*of birds*) vol *m*; (*of sheep*) troupeau *m*. 2. *fig* (*of people*) foule *f*.

flog [flɒg] *vt* 1. (*whip*) flageller. 2. *Br inf* (*sell*) refiler.

flood [flʌd] ◆ *n* 1. (*of water*) inondation *f*. 2. (*great amount*) déluge *m*, avalanche *f*. ◆ *vt* 1. (*with water, light*) inonder. 2. (*overwhelm*): to ~ sthg (**with**) inonder qqch (de).

flooding ['flʌdɪŋ] *n* (U) inondations *fpl*.

floodlight ['flʌdlaɪt] *n* projecteur *m*.

floor [flɔːʳ] ◆ *n* 1. (*of room*) sol *m*; (*of club, disco*) piste *f*. 2. (*of valley, sea, forest*) fond *m*. 3. (*storey*) étage *m*. 4. (*at meeting, debate*) auditoire *m*. ◆ *vt* 1. (*knock down*) terrasser. 2. (*baffle*) dérouter.

floorboard ['flɔːbɔːd] *n* plancher *m*.

floor show *n* spectacle *m* de cabaret.

flop [flɒp] *inf n* (*failure*) fiasco *m*.

floppy ['flɒpɪ] *adj* (*flower*) flasque; (*collar*) lâche.

floppy (disk) *n* disquette *f*, disque *m* souple.

flora ['flɔːrə] *n* flore *f*.

florid ['flɒrɪd] *adj* 1. (*red*) rougeaud(e). 2. (*extravagant*) fleuri(e).

florist ['flɒrɪst] *n* fleuriste *mf*; ~'s (*shop*) magasin *m* de fleuriste.

flotsam ['flɒtsəm] *n* (U): ~ and jetsam débris *mpl*; *fig* épaves *fpl*.

flounder ['flaʊndəʳ] *vi* 1. (*in water, mud, snow*) patauger. 2. (*in conversation*) bredouiller.

flour ['flaʊəʳ] *n* farine *f*.

flourish ['flʌrɪʃ] ◆ *vi* (*plant, flower*) bien pousser; (*children*) être en pleine santé; (*company, business*) prospérer; (*arts*) s'épanouir. ◆ *vt* brandir. ◆ *n* grand geste *m*.

flout [flaʊt] *vt* bafouer.

flow [fləʊ] ◆ *n* 1. (*movement - of water, information*) circulation *f*; (*- of funds*) mouvement *m*; (*- of words*) flot *m*. 2. (*of tide*) flux *m*. ◆ *vi* 1. (*gen*) couler. 2. (*traffic,*

days, weeks) s'écouler. 3. (*hair, clothes*) flotter.

flow chart, flow diagram *n* organigramme *m*.

flower ['flaʊəʳ] ◆ *n* fleur *f*. ◆ *vi* (*bloom*) fleurir.

flowerbed ['flaʊəbed] *n* parterre *m*.

flowerpot ['flaʊəpɒt] *n* pot *m* de fleurs.

flowery ['flaʊərɪ] *adj* 1. (*dress, material*) à fleurs. 2. *pej* (*style*) fleuri(e).

flown [fləʊn] *pp* → **fly**.

flu [fluː] *n* (U) grippe *f*.

fluctuate ['flʌktʃueɪt] *vi* fluctuer.

fluency ['fluːənsɪ] *n* aisance *f*.

fluent ['fluːənt] *adj* 1. (*in foreign language*): to speak ~ French parler couramment le français. 2. (*writing, style*) coulant(e), aisé(e).

fluff [flʌf] *n* (U) 1. (*down*) duvet *m*. 2. (*dust*) moutons *mpl*.

fluffy ['flʌfɪ] *adj* duveteux(euse); (*toy*) en peluche.

fluid ['fluːɪd] ◆ *n* fluide *m*; (*in diet, for cleaning*) liquide *m*. ◆ *adj* 1. (*flowing*) fluide. 2. (*unfixed*) changeant(e).

fluid ounce *n* = 0,03 litre.

fluke [fluːk] *n inf* (*chance*) coup *m* de bol.

flummox ['flʌməks] *vt inf* désarçonner.

flung [flʌŋ] *pt & pp* → **fling**.

flunk [flʌŋk] *inf vt* 1. (*exam, test*) rater. 2. (*student*) recaler.

fluorescent [fluəˈresənt] *adj* fluorescent(e).

fluoride ['fluəraɪd] *n* fluorure *m*.

flurry ['flʌrɪ] *n* 1. (*of snow*) rafale *f*. 2. *fig* (*of objections*) concert *m*; (*of activity, excitement*) débordement *m*.

flush [flʌʃ] ◆ *adj* (*level*): ~ with niveau avec. ◆ *n* 1. (*in lavatory*) chasse *f* d'eau. 2. (*blush*) rougeur *f*. 3. (*sudden feeling*) accès *m*. ◆ *vt* (*toilet*): to ~ the toilet tirer la chasse d'eau. ◆ *vi* (*blush*) rougir.

flushed [flʌʃt] *adj* 1. (*red-faced*) rouge. 2. (*excited*): ~ with exalté(e) par.

flustered ['flʌstəd] *adj* troublé(e).

flute [fluːt] *n* (MUS) flûte *f*.

flutter ['flʌtəʳ] ◆ *n* 1. (*of wings*) battement *m*. 2. *inf* (*of excitement*) émoi *m*. ◆ *vi* 1. (*bird, insect*) voleter; (*wings*) battre. 2. (*flag, dress*) flotter.

flux [flʌks] *n* (*change*): to be in a state of ~ être en proie à des changements permanents.

fly [flaɪ] (*pt* flew, *pp* flown) ◆ *n* 1. (*insect*) mouche *f*. 2. (*of trousers*) braguette *f*.

♦ *vt* **1.** (*kite, plane*) faire voler. **2.** (*passengers, supplies*) transporter par avion. **3.** (*flag*) faire flotter. ♦ *vi* **1.** (*bird, insect, plane*) voler. **2.** (*pilot*) faire voler un avion. **3.** (*passenger*) voyager en avion. **4.** (*move fast, pass quickly*) filer. **5.** (*flag*) flotter. ▶ **fly away** *vi* s'envoler.

fly-fishing *n* pêche *f* à la mouche.

flying ['flaɪɪŋ] ♦ *adj* volant(e). ♦ *n* aviation *f*; **to like ~** aimer prendre l'avion.

flying colours *npl*: **to pass (sthg) with ~** réussir (qqch) haut la main.

flying picket *n* piquet *m* de grève volant.

flying saucer *n* soucoupe *f* volante.

flying squad *n* Br force *d'intervention rapide de la police.*

flying start *n*: **to get off to a ~** prendre un départ sur les chapeaux de roue.

flying visit *n* visite *f* éclair.

flyover ['flaɪ,əʊvər] *n* Br autopont *m*.

flysheet ['flaɪʃiːt] *n* auvent *m*.

fly spray *n* insecticide *m*.

FM *n* (*abbr of* **frequency modulation**) FM *f*.

foal [fəʊl] *n* poulain *m*.

foam [fəʊm] ♦ *n* (U) **1.** (*bubbles*) mousse *f*. **2. ~** (*rubber*) caoutchouc *m* Mousse®. ♦ *vi* (*water, champagne*) mousser.

fob [fɒb] ▶ **fob off** *vt sep* repousser; **to ~ sthg off on sb** refiler qqch à qqn; **to ~ sb off with sthg** se débarrasser de qqn à l'aide de qqch.

focal point ['fəʊkl-] *n* foyer *m*; *fig* point *m* central.

focus ['fəʊkəs] (*pl* **-cuses** OR **-ci** [-kaɪ]) ♦ *n* **1.** (PHOT) mise *f* au point; **in ~** net; **out of ~** flou. **2.** (*centre - of rays*) foyer *m*; (*- of earthquake*) centre *m*. ♦ *vt* (*lens, camera*) mettre au point. ♦ *vi* **1.** (*with camera, lens*) se fixer; (*eyes*) accommoder; **to ~ on sthg** (*with camera, lens*) se fixer sur qqch; (*with eyes*) fixer qqch. **2.** (*attention*): **to ~ on sthg** se concentrer sur qqch.

fodder ['fɒdər] *n* (U) fourrage *m*.

foe [fəʊ] *n literary* ennemi *m*.

foetus ['fiːtəs] *n* fœtus *m*.

fog [fɒg] *n* (U) brouillard *m*.

foggy ['fɒgɪ] *adj* (*misty*) brumeux (euse).

foghorn ['fɒghɔːn] *n* sirène *f* de brume.

fog lamp *n* feu *m* de brouillard.

foible ['fɔɪbl] *n* marotte *f*.

foil [fɔɪl] ♦ *n* (U) (*metal sheet - of tin, silver*) feuille *f*; (*- CULIN*) papier *m* d'aluminium. ♦ *vt* déjouer.

fold [fəʊld] ♦ *vt* **1.** (*bend, close up*) plier;

to ~ one's arms croiser les bras. **2.** (*wrap*) envelopper. ♦ *vi* **1.** (*close up - table, chair*) se plier. **2.** *inf* (*company, project*) échouer; (THEATRE) quitter l'affiche. ♦ *n* **1.** (*in material, paper*) pli *m*. **2.** (*for animals*) parc *m*. **3.** *fig* (*spiritual home*): **the ~** le bercail. ▶ **fold up** ♦ *vt sep* plier. ♦ *vi* **1.** (*close up - table, map*) se plier; (*- petals, leaves*) se refermer. **2.** (*company, project*) échouer.

folder ['fəʊldər] *n* (*for papers - wallet*) chemise *f*; (*- binder*) classeur *m*.

folding ['fəʊldɪŋ] *adj* (*table, umbrella*) pliant(e); (*doors*) en accordéon.

foliage ['fəʊlɪɪdʒ] *n* feuillage *m*.

folk [fəʊk] ♦ *adj* (*art, dancing*) folklorique; (*medicine*) populaire. ♦ *npl* (*people*) gens *mpl*. ▶ **folks** *npl inf* (*relatives*) famille *f*.

folklore ['fəʊklɔːr] *n* folklore *m*.

folk music *n* musique *f* folk.

folk song *n* chanson *f* folk.

follow ['fɒləʊ] ♦ *vt* suivre. ♦ *vi* **1.** (*gen*) suivre. **2.** (*be logical*) tenir debout; **it ~s that ...** il s'ensuit que ... ▶ **follow up** *vt sep* **1.** (*pursue - idea, suggestion*) prendre en considération; (*- advertisement*) donner suite à. **2.** (*complete*): **to ~ sthg up with** faire suivre qqch de.

follower ['fɒləʊər] *n* (*believer*) disciple *mf*.

following ['fɒləʊɪŋ] ♦ *adj* suivant(e). ♦ *n* groupe *m* d'admirateurs. ♦ *prep* après.

folly ['fɒlɪ] *n* (U) (*foolishness*) folie *f*.

fond [fɒnd] *adj* (*affectionate*) affectueux (euse); **to be ~ of** aimer beaucoup.

fondle ['fɒndl] *vt* caresser.

font [fɒnt] *n* **1.** (*in church*) fonts *mpl* baptismaux. **2.** (COMPUT & TYPO) police *f* (de caractères).

food [fuːd] *n* nourriture *f*.

food mixer *n* mixer *m*.

food poisoning [-,pɔɪznɪŋ] *n* intoxication *f* alimentaire.

food processor [-,prəʊsesər] *n* robot *m* ménager.

foodstuffs ['fuːdstʌfs] *npl* denrées *fpl* alimentaires.

fool [fuːl] ♦ *n* **1.** (*idiot*) idiot *m*, -e *f*. Br (*dessert*) = mousse *f*. ♦ *vt* duper; **to ~ sb into doing sthg** amener qqn à faire qqch en le dupant. ♦ *vi* faire l'imbécile. ▶ **fool about, fool around** *vi* **1.** (*behave foolishly*) faire l'imbécile. **2.** (*be unfaithful*) être infidèle.

foolhardy ['fuːl,hɑːdɪ] *adj* téméraire.

foolish ['fuːlɪʃ] *adj* idiot(e), stupide.

foolproof ['fuːlpruːf] *adj* infaillible.

foot [fʊt] (*pl sense 1* **feet**, *pl sense 2 inv* OR **feet**) ◆ *n* **1.** (*gen*) pied *m*; (*of animal*) patte *f*; (*of page, stairs*) bas *m*; **to be on one's feet** être debout; **to get to one's feet** se mettre debout, se lever; **on** ~ **à** pied; **to put one's** ~ **in it** mettre les pieds dans le plat; **to put one's feet up** se reposer. **2.** (*unit of measurement*) = 30,48 *cm*, = pied *m*. ◆ *vt inf:* **to** ~ **the bill** payer la note.

footage ['fʊtɪdʒ] *n* (U) séquences *fpl*.

football ['fʊtbɔːl] *n* **1.** (*game - soccer*) football *m*, foot *m*; (- *American football*) football américain. **2.** (*ball*) ballon *m* de football OR foot.

footballer ['fʊtbɔːləʳ] *n* Br joueur *m*, -euse *f* de football, footballeur *m*, -euse *f*.

football ground *n* Br terrain *m* de football.

football player = **footballer**.

footbrake ['fʊtbreɪk] *n* frein *m* (à pied).

footbridge ['fʊtbrɪdʒ] *n* passerelle *f*.

foothills ['fʊthɪlz] *npl* contreforts *mpl*.

foothold ['fʊthəʊld] *n* prise *f* (de pied).

footing ['fʊtɪŋ] *n* **1.** (*foothold*) prise *f*; **to lose one's** ~ trébucher. **2.** *fig* (*basis*) position *f*.

footlights ['fʊtlaɪts] *npl* rampe *f*.

footnote ['fʊtnəʊt] *n* note *f* en bas de page.

footpath ['fʊtpɑːθ, *pl* -pɑːðz] *n* sentier *m*.

footprint ['fʊtprɪnt] *n* empreinte *f* (de pied), trace *f* (de pas).

footstep ['fʊtstep] *n* **1.** (*sound*) bruit *m* de pas. **2.** (*footprint*) empreinte *f* (de pied).

footwear ['fʊtweəʳ] *n* (U) chaussures *fpl*.

for [fɔːʳ] ◆ *prep* **1.** (*referring to intention, destination, purpose*) pour; **this is** ~ **you** c'est pour vous; **the plane** ~ **Paris** l'avion à destination de Paris; **let's meet** ~ **a drink** retrouvons-nous pour prendre un verre; **what's it** ~? ça sert à quoi? **2.** (*representing, on behalf of*) pour; **the MP** ~ **Barnsley** le député de Barnsley; **let me do that** ~ **you** laissez-moi faire, je vais vous le faire. **3.** (*because of*) pour, en raison de; ~ **various reasons** pour plusieurs raisons; **a prize** ~ **swimming** un prix de natation; ~ **fear of being ridiculed** de OR par peur d'être ridiculisé. **4.** (*with regard to*) pour; **to be ready** ~ **sthg** être prêt à OR pour qqch;

it's not ~ **me to say** ce n'est pas à moi à le dire; **to feel sorry** ~ **sb** plaindre qqn. **5.** (*indicating amount of time, space*): **there's no time** ~ **that** now on n'a pas le temps de faire cela OR de s'occuper de cela maintenant; **there's room** ~ **another person** il y a de la place pour encore une personne. **6.** (*indicating period of time*): **she'll be away** ~ **a month** elle sera absente (pendant) un mois; **we talked** ~ **hours** on a parlé pendant des heures; **I've lived here** ~ **3 years** j'habite ici depuis 3 ans, cela fait 3 ans que j'habite ici; **I can do it for you** ~ **tomorrow** je peux vous le faire pour demain. **7.** (*indicating distance*) pendant, sur; ~ **50 kilometres** pendant OR sur 50 kilomètres; **I walked** ~ **miles** j'ai marché (pendant) des kilomètres. **8.** (*indicating particular occasion*) pour; ~ **Christmas** pour Noël. **9.** (*indicating amount of money, price*): **they're 50p** ~ **ten** cela coûte 50p les dix; **I bought/sold it** ~ **£10** je l'ai acheté/vendu 10 livres. **10.** (*in favour of, in support of*) pour; **to vote** ~ **sthg** voter pour qqch; **to be all** ~ **sthg** être tout à fait pour OR en faveur de qqch. **11.** (*in ratios*) pour. **12.** (*indicating meaning*): **P** ~ **Peter** P comme Peter; **what's the Greek** ~ **'mother'?** comment dit-on 'mère' en grec? ◆ *conj fml* (*as, since*) car. ▶ **for all** ◆ *prep:* malgré; ~ **all his money ...** malgré tout son argent ... ◆ *conj:* ~ **all I know** pour autant que je sache.

forage ['fɒrɪdʒ] *vi:* **to** ~ **(for)** fouiller (pour trouver).

foray ['fɒreɪ] *n:* ~ **(into)** *lit & fig* incursion *f* (dans).

forbad [fə'bæd], **forbade** [fə'beɪd] *pt* → **forbid**.

forbid [fə'bɪd] (*pt* -**bade** OR -**bad**, *pp* **forbid** OR -**bidden**) *vt* interdire, défendre; **to** ~ **sb to do sthg** interdire OR défendre à qqn de faire qqch.

forbidden [fə'bɪdn] ◆ *pp* → **forbid**. ◆ *adj* interdit(e), défendu(e).

forbidding [fə'bɪdɪŋ] *adj* (*severe, unfriendly*) austère; (*threatening*) sinistre.

force [fɔːs] ◆ *n* **1.** (*gen*) force *f*; **by** ~ **de** force. **2.** (*effect*): **to be in/to come into** ~ être/entrer en vigueur. ◆ *vt* **1.** (*gen*) forcer; **to** ~ **sb to do sthg** forcer qqn à faire qqch. **2.** (*press*): **to** ~ **sthg on sb** imposer qqch à qqn. ▶ **forces** *npl:* **the** ~**s** les forces *fpl* armées; **to join** ~**s** joindre ses efforts.

force-feed *vt* nourrir de force.

forceful ['fɔːsfʊl] *adj* (*person*)

énergique; (speech) vigoureux(euse).

forceps ['fɔːseps] npl forceps m.

forcibly ['fɔːsəblɪ] adv 1. (using physical force) de force. 2. (powerfully) avec vigueur.

ford [fɔːd] n gué m.

fore [fɔːʳ] ◆ adj (NAUT) à l'avant. ◆ n: to come to the ~ s'imposer.

forearm ['fɔːrɑːm] n avant-bras m inv.

foreboding [fɔː'bəʊdɪŋ] n pressentiment m.

forecast ['fɔːkɑːst] (pt & pp forecast OR -ed) ◆ n prévision f; (weather) ~ prévisions météorologiques. ◆ vt prévoir.

foreclose [fɔː'kləʊz] ◆ vt saisir. ◆ vi: to ~ on sb saisir qqn.

forecourt ['fɔːkɔːt] n (of petrol station) devant m; (of building) avant-cour f.

forefinger ['fɔːˌfɪŋgəʳ] n index m.

forefront ['fɔːfrʌnt] n: in OR at the ~ of au premier plan de.

forego [fɔː'gəʊ] = forgo.

foregone conclusion ['fɔːgɒn-] n: it's a ~ c'est couru.

foreground ['fɔːgraʊnd] n premier plan m.

forehand ['fɔːhænd] n (TENNIS) coup m droit.

forehead ['fɔːhed] n front m.

foreign ['fɒrən] adj 1. (gen) étranger (ère); (correspondent) à l'étranger. 2. (policy, trade) extérieur(e).

foreign affairs npl affaires fpl étrangères.

foreign currency n (U) devises fpl étrangères.

foreigner ['fɒrənəʳ] n étranger m, -ère f.

foreign minister n ministre m des Affaires étrangères.

Foreign Office n Br: the ~ ≃ le ministère des Affaires étrangères.

Foreign Secretary n Br ≃ ministre m des Affaires étrangères.

foreleg ['fɔːleg] n (of horse) membre m antérieur; (of other animals) patte f de devant.

foreman ['fɔːmən] (pl -men [-mən]) n 1. (of workers) contremaître m. 2. (JUR) président m du jury.

foremost ['fɔːməʊst] ◆ adj principal(e). ◆ adv: first and ~ tout d'abord.

forensic [fə'rensɪk] adj (department, investigation) médico-légal(e).

forensic medicine, forensic science n médecine f légale.

forerunner ['fɔːˌrʌnəʳ] n précurseur m.

foresee [fɔː'siː] (pt -saw [-'sɔː], pp -seen) vt prévoir.

foreseeable [fɔː'siːəbl] adj prévisible; for the ~ future pour tous les jours/mois etc à venir.

foreseen [fɔː'siːn] pp → foresee.

foreshadow [fɔː'ʃædəʊ] vt présager.

foresight ['fɔːsaɪt] n (U) prévoyance f.

forest ['fɒrɪst] n forêt f.

forestall [fɔː'stɔːl] vt (attempt, discussion) prévenir; (person) devancer.

forestry ['fɒrɪstrɪ] n sylviculture f.

foretaste ['fɔːteɪst] n avant-goût m.

foretell [fɔː'tel] (pt & pp -told) vt prédire.

foretold [fɔː'təʊld] pt & pp → foretell.

forever [fə'revəʳ] adv (eternally) (pour) toujours.

forewarn [fɔː'wɔːn] vt avertir.

foreword ['fɔːwɜːd] n avant-propos m inv.

forfeit ['fɔːfɪt] ◆ n amende f; (in game) gage m. ◆ vt perdre.

forgave [fə'geɪv] pt → forgive.

forge [fɔːdʒ] ◆ n forge f. ◆ vt 1. (INDUSTRY & fig) forger. 2. (signature, money) contrefaire; (passport) falsifier. ► **forge ahead** vi prendre de l'avance.

forger ['fɔːdʒəʳ] n faussaire mf.

forgery ['fɔːdʒərɪ] n 1. (U) (crime) contrefaçon f. 2. (forged article) faux m.

forget [fə'get] (pt -got, pp -gotten) ◆ vt oublier; to ~ to do sthg oublier de faire qqch; ~ it! laisse tomber! ◆ vi: to ~ (about sthg) oublier (qqch).

forgetful [fə'getful] adj distrait(e), étourdi(e).

forget-me-not n myosotis m.

forgive [fə'gɪv] (pt -gave, pp -given [-'gɪvən]) vt pardonner; to ~ sb for sthg/ for doing sthg pardonner qqch à qqn/à qqn d'avoir fait qqch.

forgiveness [fə'gɪvnɪs] n (U) pardon m.

forgo [fɔː'gəʊ] (pt -went, pp -gone [-'gɒn]) vt renoncer à.

forgot [fə'gɒt] pt → forget.

forgotten [fə'gɒtn] pp → forget.

fork [fɔːk] ◆ n 1. (for eating) fourchette f. 2. (for gardening) fourche f. 3. (in road) bifurcation f; (of river) embranchement m. ◆ vi bifurquer. ► **fork out** inf ◆ vt fus allonger, débourser. ◆ vi: to ~ out (for) casquer (pour).

forklift truck ['fɔːklɪft-] n chariot m élévateur.

forlorn [fə'lɔːn] adj 1. (person, face) malheureux(euse), triste. 2. (place, land-

scape) désolé(e). **3.** (*hope, attempt*) désespéré(e).

form [fɔ:m] ◆ *n* **1.** (*shape, fitness, type*) forme *f*; **on ~** Br, **in ~** Am en forme; **off ~** pas en forme; **in the ~ of** sous forme de. **2.** (*questionnaire*) formulaire *m*. **3.** Br (SCH) classe *f*. ◆ *vt* former. ◆ *vi* se former.

formal ['fɔ:ml] *adj* **1.** (*person*) formaliste; (*language*) soutenu(e). **2.** (*dinner party, announcement*) officiel(elle); (*dress*) de cérémonie.

formality [fɔ:'mælətɪ] *n* formalité *f*.

format ['fɔ:mæt] ◆ *n* (*gen* & COMPUT) format *m*. ◆ *vt* (COMPUT) formater.

formation [fɔ:'meɪʃn] *n* **1.** (*gen*) formation *f*. **2.** (*of idea, plan*) élaboration *f*.

formative ['fɔ:mətɪv] *adj* formateur (trice).

former ['fɔ:mə^r] ◆ *adj* **1.** (*previous*) ancien(enne); **~ husband** ex-mari *m*; **~ pupil** ancien élève *m*, ancienne élève *f*. **2.** (*first of two*) premier(ère). ◆ *n*: **the ~** le premier (la première), celui-là (celle-là).

formerly ['fɔ:məlɪ] *adv* autrefois.

formidable ['fɔ:mɪdəbl] *adj* impressionnant(e).

formula ['fɔ:mjʊlə] (*pl* **-as** OR **-ae** [-i:]) *n* formule *f*.

formulate ['fɔ:mjʊleɪt] *vt* formuler.

forsake [fə'seɪk] (*pt* **forsook**, *pp* **forsaken**) *vt* literary (*person*) abandonner; (*habit*) renoncer à.

forsaken [fə'seɪkn] *adj* abandonné(e).

forsook [fə'sʊk] *pt* → **forsake**.

fort [fɔ:t] *n* fort *m*.

forte ['fɔ:tɪ] *n* point *m* fort.

forth [fɔ:θ] *adv* literary en avant.

forthcoming [fɔ:θ'kʌmɪŋ] *adj* **1.** (*imminent*) à venir. **2.** (*helpful*) communicatif (ive).

forthright ['fɔ:θraɪt] *adj* franc (franche), direct(e).

fortified wine ['fɔ:tɪfaɪd-] *n* vin *m* de liqueur.

fortify ['fɔ:tɪfaɪ] *vt* **1.** (MIL) fortifier. **2.** *fig* (*resolve etc*) renforcer.

fortnight ['fɔ:tnaɪt] *n* quinze jours *mpl*, quinzaine *f*.

fortnightly ['fɔ:t,naɪtlɪ] ◆ *adj* bimensuel(elle). ◆ *adv* tous les quinze jours.

fortress ['fɔ:trɪs] *n* forteresse *f*.

fortunate ['fɔ:tʃnət] *adj* heureux (euse); **to be ~** avoir de la chance.

fortunately ['fɔ:tʃnətlɪ] *adv* heureusement.

fortune ['fɔ:tʃu:n] *n* **1.** (*wealth*) fortune *f*. **2.** (*luck*) fortune *f*, chance *f*. **3.** (*future*):

to tell sb's ~ dire la bonne aventure à qqn.

fortune-teller [-,telə^r] *n* diseuse *f* de bonne aventure.

forty ['fɔ:tɪ] *num* quarante; *see also* **sixty**.

forward ['fɔ:wəd] ◆ *adj* **1.** (*movement*) en avant. **2.** (*planning*) à long terme. **3.** (*impudent*) effronté(e). ◆ *adv* **1.** (*ahead*) en avant; **to go** OR **move ~** avancer. **2.** (*in time*): **to bring a meeting ~** avancer la date d'une réunion. ◆ *n* (SPORT) avant *m*. ◆ *vt* (*letter*) faire suivre; (*goods*) expédier.

forwarding address ['fɔ:wədɪŋ-] *n* adresse *f* où faire suivre le courrier.

forwards ['fɔ:wədz] *adv* = **forward**.

forwent [fɔ:'went] *pt* → **forgo**.

fossil ['fɒsl] *n* fossile *m*.

foster ['fɒstə^r] ◆ *adj* (*family*) d'accueil. ◆ *vt* **1.** (*child*) accueillir. **2.** *fig* (*nurture*) nourrir, entretenir.

foster child *n* enfant *m* placé en famille d'accueil.

foster parent *n* parent *m* nourricier.

fought [fɔ:t] *pt* & *pp* → **fight**.

foul [faʊl] ◆ *adj* **1.** (*gen*) infect(e); (*water*) croupi(e). **2.** (*language*) ordurier (ère). ◆ *n* (SPORT) faute *f*. ◆ *vt* **1.** (*make dirty*) souiller, salir. **2.** (SPORT) commettre une faute contre.

found [faʊnd] ◆ *pt* & *pp* → **find**. ◆ *vt* **1.** (*hospital, town*) fonder. **2.** (*base*): **to ~ sthg on** fonder OR baser qqch sur.

foundation [faʊn'deɪʃn] *n* **1.** (*creation, organization*) fondation *f*. **2.** (*basis*) fondement *m*, base *f*. **3.** **~ (cream)** fond *m* de teint. ▶ **foundations** *npl* (CONSTR) fondations *fpl*.

founder ['faʊndə^r] ◆ *n* fondateur *m*, -trice *f*. ◆ *vi* (*ship*) sombrer.

foundry ['faʊndrɪ] *n* fonderie *f*.

fountain ['faʊntɪn] *n* fontaine *f*.

fountain pen *n* stylo *m* à encre.

four [fɔ:^r] *num* quatre; **on all ~s** à quatre pattes; *see also* **six**.

four-letter word *n* mot *m* grossier.

four-poster (bed) *n* lit *m* à baldaquin.

foursome ['fɔ:səm] *n* groupe *m* de quatre.

fourteen [,fɔ:'ti:n] *num* quatorze; *see also* **six**.

fourth [fɔ:θ] *num* quatrième; *see also* **sixth**.

Fourth of July *n*: **the ~** Fête de l'Indépendance américaine.

four-wheel drive *n*: **with ~** à quatre

roues motrices.

fowl [faʊl] (*pl inv* OR **-s**) *n* volaille *f*.

fox [fɒks] ◆ *n* renard *m*. ◆ *vt* laisser perplexe.

foxglove ['fɒksglʌv] *n* digitale *f*.

foyer ['fɔɪeɪ] *n* **1.** (*of hotel, theatre*) foyer *m*. **2.** Am (*of house*) hall *m* d'entrée.

fracas ['fræka:, Am 'freɪkəs] (Br *pl inv*, Am *pl* **-cases**) *n* bagarre *f*.

fraction ['frækʃn] *n* fraction *f*.

fractionally ['frækʃnəlɪ] *adv* un tout petit peu.

fracture ['fræktʃər] ◆ *n* fracture *f*. ◆ *vt* fracturer.

fragile ['frædʒaɪl] *adj* fragile.

fragment ['frægmənt] *n* fragment *m*.

fragrance ['freɪgrəns] *n* parfum *m*.

fragrant ['freɪgrənt] *adj* parfumé(e).

frail [freɪl] *adj* fragile.

frame [freɪm] ◆ *n* **1.** (*gen*) cadre *m*; (*of glasses*) monture *f*; (*of door, window*) encadrement *m*; (*of boat*) carcasse *f*. **2.** (*physique*) charpente *f*. ◆ *vt* **1.** (*gen*) encadrer. **2.** (*express*) formuler. **3.** *inf* (*set up*) monter un coup contre.

frame of mind *n* état *m* d'esprit.

framework ['freɪmwɜːk] *n* **1.** (*structure*) armature *f*, carcasse *f*. **2.** *fig* (*basis*) structure *f*, cadre *m*.

France [frɑ:ns] *n* France *f*; **in ~** en France.

franchise ['fræntʃaɪz] *n* **1.** (POL) droit *m* de vote. **2.** (COMM) franchise *f*.

frank [fræŋk] ◆ *adj* franc (franche). ◆ *vt* affranchir.

frankly ['fræŋklɪ] *adv* franchement.

frantic ['fræntɪk] *adj* frénétique.

fraternity [frə'tɜːnətɪ] *n* **1.** (*community*) confrérie *f*. **2.** (U) (*friendship*) fraternité *f*. **3.** Am (*of students*) club *m* d'étudiants.

fraternize, -ise ['frætənaɪz] *vi* fraterniser.

fraud [frɔ:d] *n* **1.** (U) (*crime*) fraude *f*. **2.** *pej* (*impostor*) imposteur *m*.

fraught [frɔ:t] *adj* **1.** (*full*): **~ with** plein(e) de. **2.** Br (*person*) tendu(e); (*time, situation*) difficile.

fray [freɪ] ◆ *vt fig*: **my nerves were ~ed** j'étais extrêmement tendu(e). ◆ *vi* (*material, sleeves*) s'user; **tempers ~ed** *fig* l'atmosphère était tendue OR électrique. ◆ *n literary* bagarre *f*.

frayed [freɪd] *adj* (*jeans, collar*) élimé(e).

freak [fri:k] ◆ *adj* bizarre, insolite. ◆ *n* **1.** (*strange creature*) monstre *m*, phénomène *m*. **2.** (*unusual event*) accident *m* bizarre. **3.** *inf* (*fanatic*) fana *mf*. ▸ **freak**

out *inf* *vi* (*get angry*) exploser (de colère); (*panic*) paniquer.

freckle ['frekl] *n* tache *f* de rousseur.

free [fri:] (*compar* **freer**, *superl* **freest**, *pt* & *pp* **freed**) ◆ *adj* **1.** (*gen*) libre; **to be ~ to do sthg** être libre de faire qqch; **feel ~!** je t'en prie!; **to set ~** libérer. **2.** (*not paid for*) gratuit(e); **~ of charge** gratuitement. ◆ *adv* **1.** (*without payment*) gratuitement; **for ~** gratuitement. **2.** (*run, live*) librement. ◆ *vt* **1.** (*gen*) libérer. **2.** (*trapped person, object*) dégager.

freedom ['fri:dəm] *n* **1.** (*gen*) liberté *f*; **~ of speech** liberté d'expression. **2.** (*exception*): **~ (from)** exemption *f* (de).

Freefone® ['fri:fəʊn] *n* (U) Br = numéro *m* vert.

free-for-all *n* mêlée *f* générale.

free gift *n* prime *f*.

freehand ['fri:hænd] *adj* & *adv* à main levée.

freehold ['fri:həʊld] *n* propriété *f* foncière inaliénable.

free house *n* pub *m* en gérance libre.

free kick *n* coup *m* franc.

freelance ['fri:lɑ:ns] ◆ *adj* indépendant(e), free-lance (*inv*). ◆ *n* indépendant *m*, -e *f*, free-lance *mf*.

freely ['fri:lɪ] *adv* **1.** (*gen*) librement. **2.** (*generously*) sans compter.

Freemason ['fri:,meɪsn] *n* franc-maçon *m*.

Freephone® ['fri:fəʊn] = **Freefone®**.

Freepost® ['fri:pəʊst] *n* port *m* payé.

free-range *adj* de ferme.

freestyle ['fri:staɪl] *n* (SWIMMING) nage *f* libre.

free trade *n* (U) libre-échange *m*.

freeway ['fri:weɪ] *n* Am autoroute *f*.

freewheel [,fri:'wi:l] *vi* (*on bicycle*) rouler en roue libre; (*in car*) rouler au point mort.

free will *n* (U) libre arbitre *m*; **to do sthg of one's own ~** faire qqch de son propre gré.

freeze [fri:z] (*pt* **froze**, *pp* **frozen**) ◆ *vt* **1.** (*gen*) geler; (*food*) congeler. **2.** (*wages, prices*) bloquer. ◆ *vi* **1.** (*gen*) geler. **2.** (*stop moving*) s'arrêter. ◆ *n* **1.** (*cold weather*) gel *m*. **2.** (*of wages, prices*) blocage *m*.

freeze-dried [-'draɪd] *adj* lyophilisé(e).

freezer ['fri:zər] *n* congélateur *m*.

freezing ['fri:zɪŋ] ◆ *adj* glacé(e); **I'm ~** je gèle. ◆ *n* = **freezing point**.

freezing point *n* point *m* de congélation.

freight [freɪt] n (goods) fret m.

freight train n train m de marchandises.

French [frentʃ] ◆ adj français(e). ◆ n (language) français m. ◆ npl: **the ~** les Français mpl.

French bean n haricot m vert.

French bread n (U) baguette f.

French Canadian ◆ adj canadien français (canadienne française). ◆ n Canadien français m, Canadienne française f.

French doors = **French windows**.

French dressing n (in UK) vinaigrette f; (in US) sauce-salade à base de mayonnaise et de ketchup.

French fries npl frites fpl.

Frenchman ['frentʃmən] (pl **-men** [-mən]) n Français m.

French stick n Br baguette f.

French windows npl porte-fenêtre f.

Frenchwoman ['frentʃˌwumən] (pl **-women** [-ˌwɪmɪn]) n Française f.

frenetic [frə'netɪk] adj frénétique.

frenzy ['frenzɪ] n frénésie f.

frequency ['friːkwənsɪ] n fréquence f.

frequent [adj 'friːkwənt, vb frɪ'kwent] ◆ adj fréquent(e). ◆ vt fréquenter.

frequently ['friːkwəntlɪ] adv fréquemment.

fresh [freʃ] adj 1. (gen) frais (fraîche). 2. (not salty) doux (douce). 3. (new - drink, piece of paper) autre; (- look, approach) nouveau(elle). 4. inf dated (cheeky) familier(ère).

freshen ['freʃn] ◆ vt rafraîchir. ◆ vi (wind) devenir plus fort. ▶ **freshen up** vi faire un brin de toilette.

fresher ['freʃər] n Br inf bleu m, -e f.

freshly ['freʃlɪ] adv (squeezed, ironed) fraîchement.

freshman ['freʃmən] (pl **-men** [-mən]) n étudiant m, -e f de première année.

freshness ['freʃnɪs] n (U) 1. (gen) fraîcheur f. 2. (originality) nouveauté f.

freshwater ['freʃˌwɔːtər] adj d'eau douce.

fret [fret] vi (worry) s'inquiéter.

friar ['fraɪər] n frère m.

friction ['frɪkʃn] n (U) friction f.

Friday ['fraɪdɪ] n vendredi m; see also **Saturday**.

fridge [frɪdʒ] n frigo m.

fridge-freezer n Br réfrigérateur-congélateur m.

fried [fraɪd] adj frit(e); **~ egg** œuf m au plat.

friend [frend] n ami m, -e f; **to be ~s**

with sb être ami avec qqn; **to make ~s (with sb)** se lier d'amitié (avec qqn).

friendly ['frendlɪ] adj (person, manner, match) amical(e); (nation) ami(e); (argument) sans conséquence; **to be ~ with sb** être ami avec qqn.

friendship ['frendʃɪp] n amitié f.

fries [fraɪz] = **French fries**.

frieze [friːz] n frise f.

fright [fraɪt] n peur f; **to give sb a ~** faire peur à qqn; **to take ~** prendre peur.

frighten ['fraɪtn] vt faire peur à, effrayer.

frightened ['fraɪtnd] adj apeuré(e); **to be ~ of sthg/of doing sthg** avoir peur de qqch/de faire qqch.

frightening ['fraɪtnɪŋ] adj effrayant(e).

frightful ['fraɪtful] adj dated effroyable.

frigid ['frɪdʒɪd] adj (sexually) frigide.

frill [frɪl] n 1. (decoration) volant m. 2. inf (extra) supplément m.

fringe [frɪndʒ] n 1. (gen) frange f. 2. (edge - of village) bordure f; (- of wood, forest) lisière f.

fringe benefit n avantage m extrasalarial.

frisk [frɪsk] vt fouiller.

frisky ['frɪskɪ] adj inf vif (vive).

fritter ['frɪtər] n beignet m. ▶ **fritter away** vt sep gaspiller.

frivolous ['frɪvələs] adj frivole.

frizzy ['frɪzɪ] adj crépu(e).

fro [frəu] → **to**.

frock [frɒk] n dated robe f.

frog [frɒg] n (animal) grenouille f; **to have a ~ in one's throat** avoir un chat dans la gorge.

frogman ['frɒgmən] (pl **-men**) n homme-grenouille m.

frogmen ['frɒgmən] pl → **frogman**.

frolic ['frɒlɪk] (pt & pp **-ked**, cont **-king**) vi folâtrer.

from [weak form frəm, strong form frɒm] prep 1. (indicating source, origin, removal) de; **where are you ~?** d'où venez-vous?, d'où êtes-vous?; **a flight ~ Paris** un vol en provenance de Paris; **to translate ~ Spanish into English** traduire du espagnol en anglais; **to drink ~ a glass** boire dans un verre; **to take sthg (away) ~ sb** prendre qqch à qqn. 2. (indicating a deduction) de; **to deduct sthg ~ sthg** retrancher qqch de qqch. 3. (indicating escape, separation) de; **he ran away ~ home** il a fait une fugue, il s'est sauvé de chez lui. 4. (indicating position) de; **seen ~ above/below** vu d'en haut/d'en bas. 5. (indicat-

ing distance) de; **it's 60 km ~ here** c'est à 60 km d'ici. **6.** (*indicating material object is made out of*) en; **it's made ~ wood/plastic** c'est en bois/plastique. **7.** (*starting at a particular time*) de; **~ 2 pm to** OR **till 6 pm** de 14 h à 18 h; **~ the moment I saw him** dès que OR dès l'instant où je l'ai vu. **8.** (*indicating difference*) de; **to be different ~ sb/sthg** être différent de qqn/qqch. **9.** (*indicating change*): **~ ... to** de ... à; **the price went up ~ £100 to £150** le prix est passé OR monté de 100 livres à 150 livres. **10.** (*because of, as a result of*) de; **to suffer ~ cold/hunger** souffrir du froid/de la faim. **11.** (*on the evidence of*) d'après, à. **12.** (*indicating lowest amount*) depuis, à partir de; **prices start ~ £50** le premier prix est de 50 livres.

front [frʌnt] ◆ *n* **1.** (*most forward part - gen*) avant *m*; (*- of dress, envelope, house*) devant *m*; (*- of class*) premier rang *m*. **2.** (METEOR & MIL) front *m*. **3.** (**sea**) **~** front *m* de mer. **4.** (*outward appearance - of person*) contenance *f*; *pej* (*- of business*) façade *f*. ◆ *adj* (*tooth, garden*) de devant; (*row, page*) premier(ère). ▶ **in front** *adv* **1.** (*further forward - walk, push*) devant; (*- people*) à l'avant. **2.** (*winning*): **to be in ~** mener. ▶ **in front of** *prep* devant.

frontbench [ˌfrʌnt'bentʃ] *n* à la chambre des Communes, bancs occupés respectivement par les ministres du gouvernement en exercice et ceux du gouvernement fantôme.

front door *n* porte *f* d'entrée.

frontier ['frʌntɪər, *Am* frʌn'tɪər] *n* (*border*) frontière *f*; *fig* limite *f*.

front man *n* **1.** (*of company, organization*) porte-parole *m inv*. **2.** (TV) présentateur *m*.

front room *n* salon *m*.

front-runner *n* favori *m*, -ite *f*.

front-wheel drive *n* traction *f* avant.

frost [frɒst] *n* gel *m*.

frostbite ['frɒstbaɪt] *n* (U) gelure *f*.

frosted ['frɒstɪd] *adj* **1.** (*glass*) dépoli(e). **2.** *Am* (CULIN) glacé(e).

frosty ['frɒstɪ] *adj* **1.** (*weather, welcome*) glacial(e). **2.** (*field, window*) gelé(e).

froth [frɒθ] *n* (*on beer*) mousse *f*; (*on sea*) écume *f*.

frown [fraun] *vi* froncer les sourcils. ▶ **frown (up)on** *vt fus* désapprouver.

froze [frəuz] *pt* → **freeze.**

frozen ['frəuzn] ◆ *pp* → **freeze.** ◆ *adj* gelé(e); (*food*) congelé(e).

frugal ['fruːgl] *adj* **1.** (*meal*) frugal(e). **2.** (*person, life*) économe.

fruit [fruːt] (*pl inv* OR **fruits**) *n* fruit *m*.

fruitcake ['fruːtkeɪk] *n* cake *m*.

fruiterer ['fruːtərər] *n Br* fruitier *m*.

fruitful ['fruːtful] *adj* (*successful*) fructueux(euse).

fruition [fruː'ɪʃn] *n*: **to come to ~** se réaliser.

fruit juice *n* jus *m* de fruits.

fruitless ['fruːtlɪs] *adj* vain(e).

fruit machine *n Br* machine *f* à sous.

fruit salad *n* salade *f* de fruits.

frumpy ['frʌmpɪ] *adj* mal attifé(e).

frustrate [frʌ'streɪt] *vt* **1.** (*annoy, disappoint*) frustrer. **2.** (*prevent*) faire échouer.

frustrated [frʌ'streɪtɪd] *adj* **1.** (*person, artist*) frustré(e). **2.** (*effort, love*) vain(e).

frustration [frʌ'streɪʃn] *n* frustration *f*.

fry [fraɪ] (*pt & pp* **fried**) *vt & vi* frire.

frying pan ['fraɪɪŋ-] *n* poêle *f* à frire.

ft. *abbr of* **foot, feet.**

fuck [fʌk] *vulg vt & vi* baiser. ▶ **fuck off** *vi vulg*: **~ off!** fous le camp!

fudge [fʌdʒ] *n* (U) (*sweet*) caramel *m* (mou).

fuel [fjuəl] ◆ *n* combustible *m*; (*for engine*) carburant *m*. ◆ *vt* **1.** (*supply with fuel*) alimenter (en combustible/carburant). **2.** *fig* (*speculation*) nourrir.

fuel pump *n* pompe *f* d'alimentation.

fuel tank *n* réservoir *m* à carburant.

fugitive ['fjuːdʒətɪv] *n* fugitif *m*, -ive *f*.

fulfil, fulfill *Am* [ful'fɪl] *vt* **1.** (*duty, role*) remplir; (*hope*) répondre à; (*ambition, prophecy*) réaliser. **2.** (*satisfy - need*) satisfaire.

fulfilment, fulfillment *Am* [ful-'fɪlmənt] *n* (U) **1.** (*satisfaction*) grande satisfaction *f*. **2.** (*of ambition, dream*) réalisation *f*; (*of role, promise*) exécution *f*; (*of need*) satisfaction *f*.

full [ful] ◆ *adj* **1.** (*gen*) plein(e); (*bus, car park*) complet(ète); (*with food*) gavé(e), repu(e). **2.** (*complete - recovery, control*) total(e); (*- explanation, day*) entier(ère); (*- volume*) maximum. **3.** (*busy - life*) rempli(e); (*- timetable, day*) chargé(e). **4.** (*flavour*) riche. **5.** (*plump - figure*) rondelet(ette); (*- mouth*) charnu(e). **6.** (*skirt, sleeve*) ample. ◆ *adv* (*very*): **you know ~ well that ...** tu sais très bien que ... ◆ *n*: **in ~** complètement, entièrement.

full-blown [-'bləun] *adj* général(e); **to have ~ AIDS** avoir le Sida avéré.

full board *n* pension *f* complète.

full-fledged *Am* = **fully-fledged.**

full moon *n* pleine lune *f*.

full-scale *adj* **1.** (*life-size*) grandeur nature (*inv*). **2.** (*complete*) de grande envergure.

full stop n point m.

full time n Br (SPORT) fin f de match.
▶ **full-time** adj & adv (work, worker) à temps plein.

full up adj (bus, train) complet(ète); (with food) gavé(e), repu(e).

fully ['fʊlɪ] adv (understand, satisfy) tout à fait; (trained, describe) entièrement.

fully-fledged Br, **full-fledged** Am [-'fledʒd] adj diplômé(e).

fulsome ['fʊlsəm] adj excessif(ive).

fumble ['fʌmbl] vi fouiller, tâtonner; to ~ for fouiller pour trouver.

fume [fjuːm] vi (with anger) rager.
▶ **fumes** npl (from paint) émanations fpl; (from smoke) fumées fpl; (from car) gaz mpl d'échappement.

fumigate ['fjuːmɪgeɪt] vt fumiger.

fun [fʌn] n (U) 1. (pleasure, amusement): to have ~ s'amuser; for ~, for the ~ of it pour s'amuser. 2. (playfulness): to be full of ~ être plein(e) d'entrain. 3. (ridicule): to make ~ of OR poke ~ at sb se moquer de qqn.

function ['fʌŋkʃn] ◆ n 1. (gen) fonction f. 2. (formal social event) réception f officielle. ◆ vi fonctionner; to ~ as servir de.

functional ['fʌŋkʃnəl] adj 1. (practical) fonctionnel(elle). 2. (operational) en état de marche.

fund [fʌnd] ◆ n fonds m; fig (of knowledge) puits m. ◆ vt financer. ▶ **funds** npl fonds mpl.

fundamental [,fʌndə'mentl] adj: ~ (to) fondamental(e) (à).

funding ['fʌndɪŋ] n (U) financement m.

funeral ['fjuːnərəl] n obsèques fpl.

funeral parlour n entreprise f de pompes funèbres.

funfair ['fʌnfeər] n fête f foraine.

fungus ['fʌŋgəs] (pl -gi [-gaɪ] OR -guses) n champignon m.

funnel ['fʌnl] n 1. (tube) entonnoir m. 2. (of ship) cheminée f.

funny ['fʌnɪ] adj 1. (amusing, odd) drôle. 2. (ill) tout drôle (toute drôle).

fur [fɜːr] n fourrure f.

fur coat n (manteau m de) fourrure f.

furious ['fjʊərɪəs] adj 1. (very angry) furieux(euse). 2. (wild - effort, battle) acharné(e); (- temper) déchaîné(e).

furlong ['fɜːlɒŋ] n = 201,17 mètres.

furnace ['fɜːnɪs] n (fire) fournaise f.

furnish ['fɜːnɪʃ] vt 1. (fit out) meubler. 2. fml (provide) fournir; to ~ sb with sthg fournir qqch à qqn.

furnished ['fɜːnɪʃt] adj meublé(e).

furnishings ['fɜːnɪʃɪŋz] npl mobilier m.

furniture ['fɜːnɪtʃər] n (U) meubles mpl; a piece of ~ un meuble.

furrow ['fʌrəʊ] n 1. (in field) sillon m. 2. (on forehead) ride f.

furry ['fɜːrɪ] adj 1. (animal) à fourrure. 2. (material) recouvert(e) de fourrure.

further ['fɜːðər] ◆ compar → far. ◆ adv 1. (gen) plus loin; how much ~ is it? combien de kilomètres y a-t-il?; ~ on plus loin. 2. (more - complicate, develop) davantage; (- enquire) plus avant. 3. (in addition) de plus. ◆ adj nouveau(elle), supplémentaire; until ~ notice jusqu'à nouvel ordre. ◆ vt (career, aims) faire avancer; (cause) encourager.

further education n Br éducation f post-scolaire.

furthermore [,fɜːðə'mɔːr] adv de plus.

furthest ['fɜːðɪst] ◆ superl → far. ◆ adj le plus éloigné (la plus éloignée). ◆ adv le plus loin.

furtive ['fɜːtɪv] adj (person) sournois(e); (glance) furtif(ive).

fury ['fjʊərɪ] n fureur f.

fuse, fuze Am [fjuːz] ◆ n 1. (ELEC) fusible m, plomb m. 2. (of bomb) détonateur m; (of firework) amorce f. ◆ vt 1. (join by heat) réunir par la fusion. 2. (combine) fusionner. ◆ vi 1. (ELEC): the lights have ~d les plombs ont sauté. 2. (join by heat) fondre. 3. (combine) fusionner.

fuse-box n boîte f à fusibles.

fused [fjuːzd] adj (plug) avec fusible incorporé.

fuselage ['fjuːzəlɑːʒ] n fuselage m.

fuss [fʌs] ◆ n 1. (excitement, anxiety) agitation f; to make a ~ faire des histoires. 2. (U) (complaints) protestations fpl. ◆ vi faire des histoires.

fussy ['fʌsɪ] adj 1. (fastidious - person) tatillon(onne); (- eater) difficile. 2. (over-decorated) tarabiscoté(e).

futile ['fjuːtaɪl] adj vain(e).

futon ['fuːtɒn] n futon m.

future ['fjuːtʃər] ◆ n 1. (gen) avenir m; in ~ à l'avenir; in the ~ dans le futur, à l'avenir. 2. (GRAMM): ~ (tense) futur m. ◆ adj futur(e).

fuze Am = **fuse**.

fuzzy ['fʌzɪ] adj 1. (hair) crépu(e). 2. (photo) flou(e). 3. (mind) confus(e).

G

g[1] (*pl* **g's** OR **gs**), **G** (*pl* **G's** OR **Gs**) [dʒiː] *n* (*letter*) g *m inv*, G *m inv*. ▶ **G** ◆ *n* (MUS) sol *m*. ◆ (*abbr of* **good**) B.

g[2] (*abbr of* **gram**) g.

gab [gæb] → **gift**.

gabble ['gæbl] ◆ *vt & vi* baragouiner. ◆ *n* charabia *m*.

gable ['geɪbl] *n* pignon *m*.

gadget ['gædʒɪt] *n* gadget *m*.

Gaelic ['geɪlɪk] ◆ *adj* gaélique. ◆ *n* gaélique *m*.

gag [gæg] ◆ *n* **1.** (*for mouth*) bâillon *m*. **2.** *inf* (*joke*) blague *f*, gag *m*. ◆ *vt* (*put gag on*) bâillonner.

gage Am = **gauge**.

gaiety ['geɪətɪ] *n* gaieté *f*.

gaily ['geɪlɪ] *adv* **1.** (*cheerfully*) gaiement. **2.** (*thoughtlessly*) allègrement.

gain [geɪn] ◆ *n* **1.** (*gen*) profit *m*. **2.** (*improvement*) augmentation *f*. ◆ *vt* **1.** (*acquire*) gagner. **2.** (*increase in - speed, weight*) prendre; (*- confidence*) gagner en. ◆ *vi* **1.** (*advance*): **to ~ in sthg** gagner en qqch. **2.** (*benefit*): **to ~ from** OR **by sthg** tirer un avantage de qqch. **3.** (*watch, clock*) avancer. ▶ **gain on** *vt fus* rattraper.

gait [geɪt] *n* démarche *f*.

gal. *abbr of* **gallon**.

gala ['gɑːlə] *n* (*celebration*) gala *m*.

galaxy ['gæləksɪ] *n* galaxie *f*.

gale [geɪl] *n* (*wind*) grand vent *m*.

gall [gɔːl] *n* (*nerve*): **to have the ~ to do sthg** avoir le toupet de faire qqch.

gallant [*sense 1* 'gælənt, *sense 2* gə'lænt, 'gælənt] *adj* **1.** (*courageous*) courageux (euse). **2.** (*polite to women*) galant.

gall bladder *n* vésicule *f* biliaire.

gallery ['gælərɪ] *n* **1.** (*gen*) galerie *f*. **2.** (*for displaying art*) musée *m*. **3.** (*in theatre*) paradis *m*.

galley ['gælɪ] (*pl* **galleys**) *n* **1.** (*ship*) galère *f*. **2.** (*kitchen*) coquerie *f*.

Gallic ['gælɪk] *adj* français(e).

galling ['gɔːlɪŋ] *adj* humiliant(e).

gallivant [,gælɪ'vænt] *vi inf* mener une vie de patachon.

gallon ['gælən] *n* = 4,546 litres, gallon *m*.

gallop ['gæləp] ◆ *n* galop *m*. ◆ *vi* galoper.

gallows ['gæləʊz] (*pl inv*) *n* gibet *m*.

gallstone ['gɔːlstəʊn] *n* calcul *m* biliaire.

galore [gə'lɔːʳ] *adj* en abondance.

galvanize, -ise ['gælvənaɪz] *vt* **1.** (TECH) galvaniser. **2.** (*impel*): **to ~ sb into action** pousser qqn à agir.

gambit ['gæmbɪt] *n* entrée *f* en matière.

gamble ['gæmbl] ◆ *n* (*calculated risk*) risque *m*. ◆ *vi* **1.** (*bet*) jouer; **to ~ on** jouer de l'argent sur. **2.** (*take risk*): **to ~ on** miser sur.

gambler ['gæmbləʳ] *n* joueur *m*, -euse *f*.

gambling ['gæmblɪŋ] *n* (U) jeu *m*.

game [geɪm] ◆ *n* **1.** (*gen*) jeu *m*. **2.** (*match*) match *m*. **3.** (U) (*hunted animals*) gibier *m*. ◆ *adj* **1.** (*brave*) courageux(euse). **2.** (*willing*): **~ (for sthg/to do sthg)** partant(e) (pour qqch/pour faire qqch). ▶ **games** ◆ *n* (SCH) éducation *f* physique. ◆ *npl* (*sporting contest*) jeux *mpl*.

gamekeeper ['geɪm,kiːpəʳ] *n* garde-chasse *m*.

game reserve *n* réserve *f* (de chasse).

gammon ['gæmən] *n* jambon *m* fumé.

gamut ['gæmət] *n* gamme *f*.

gang [gæŋ] *n* **1.** (*of criminals*) gang *m*. **2.** (*of young people*) bande *f*. ▶ **gang up** *vi inf*: **to ~ up (on)** se liguer (contre).

gangland ['gæŋlænd] *n* (U) milieu *m*.

gangrene ['gæŋgriːn] *n* gangrène *f*.

gangster ['gæŋstəʳ] *n* gangster *m*.

gangway ['gæŋweɪ] *n* **1.** Br (*aisle*) allée *f*. **2.** (*gangplank*) passerelle *f*.

gantry ['gæntrɪ] *n* portique *m*.

gaol [dʒeɪl] Br = **jail**.

gap [gæp] *n* **1.** (*empty space*) trou *m*; (*text*) blanc *m*; *fig* (*in knowledge, report*) lacune *f*. **2.** (*interval of time*) période *f*. **3.** *fig* (*great difference*) fossé *m*.

gape [geɪp] *vi* **1.** (*person*) rester bouche bée. **2.** (*hole, shirt*) bâiller.

gaping ['geɪpɪŋ] *adj* **1.** (*open-mouthed*) bouche bée (*inv*). **2.** (*wide-open*) béant(e); (*shirt*) grand ouvert (grande ouverte).

garage [Br 'gærɑːʒ, 'gærɪdʒ, Am gə'rɑːʒ] *n* **1.** (*gen*) garage *m*. **2.** Br (*for fuel*) station-service *f*.

garbage [gɑːbɪdʒ] *n* (U) **1.** (*refuse*) détritus *mpl*. **2.** *inf* (*nonsense*) idioties *fpl*.

garbage can *n* Am poubelle *f*.

garbage truck *n* Am camion-poubelle *m*.

garbled ['gɑːbld] *adj* confus(e).

garden ['gɑːdn] ♦ n jardin m. ♦ vi jardiner.

garden centre n jardinerie f, garden centre m.

gardener ['gɑːdnəʳ] n (professional) jardinier m, -ère f; (amateur) personne f qui aime jardiner.

gardening ['gɑːdnɪŋ] n jardinage m.

garden shed n abri m de jardin.

gargle ['gɑːgl] vi se gargariser.

gargoyle ['gɑːgɔɪl] n gargouille f.

garish ['geərɪʃ] adj criard(e).

garland ['gɑːlənd] n guirlande f de fleurs.

garlic ['gɑːlɪk] n ail m.

garlic bread n pain m à l'ail.

garment ['gɑːmənt] n vêtement m.

garnish ['gɑːnɪʃ] ♦ n garniture f. ♦ vt garnir.

garrison ['gærɪsn] n (soldiers) garnison f.

garrulous ['gærələs] adj volubile.

garter ['gɑːtəʳ] n 1. (for socks) support-chaussette m; (for stockings) jarretière f. 2. Am (suspender) jarretelle f.

gas [gæs] (pl -es OR -ses) ♦ n 1. (gen) gaz m inv. 2. Am (for vehicle) essence f. ♦ vt gazer.

gas cooker n Br cuisinière f à gaz.

gas cylinder n bouteille f de gaz.

gas fire n Br appareil m de chauffage à gaz.

gas gauge n Am jauge f d'essence.

gash [gæʃ] ♦ n entaille f. ♦ vt entailler.

gasket ['gæskɪt] n joint m d'étanchéité.

gasman ['gæsmæn] (pl -men [-men]) n (who reads meter) employé m du gaz; (for repairs) installateur m de gaz.

gas mask n masque m à gaz.

gas meter n compteur m à gaz.

gasoline ['gæsəliːn] n Am essence f.

gasp [gɑːsp] ♦ n halètement m. ♦ vi 1. (breathe quickly) haleter. 2. (in shock, surprise) avoir le souffle coupé.

gas pedal n Am accélérateur m.

gas station n Am station-service f.

gas stove = **gas cooker**.

gas tank n Am réservoir m.

gas tap n (for mains supply) robinet m de gaz; (on gas fire) prise f de gaz.

gastroenteritis ['gæstrəʊˌentəˈraɪtɪs] n gastro-entérite f.

gastronomic [ˌgæstrəˈnɒmɪk] adj gastronomique.

gastronomy [gæsˈtrɒnəmɪ] n gastronomie f.

gasworks ['gæswɜːks] (pl inv) n usine f à gaz.

gate [geɪt] n (of garden, farm) barrière f; (of town, at airport) porte f; (of park) grille f.

gatecrash ['geɪtkræʃ] inf vt & vi prendre part à une réunion, une réception sans y avoir été convié.

gateway ['geɪtweɪ] n 1. (entrance) entrée f. 2. (means of access): ~ to porte f de; fig clé f de.

gather ['gæðəʳ] ♦ vt 1. (collect) ramasser; (flowers) cueillir; (information) recueillir; (courage, strength) rassembler; to ~ together rassembler. 2. (increase - speed, force) prendre. 3. (understand): to ~ (that) ... croire comprendre que ... 4. (cloth - into folds) plisser. ♦ vi (come together) se rassembler; (clouds) s'amonceler.

gathering ['gæðərɪŋ] n (meeting) rassemblement m.

gaudy ['gɔːdɪ] adj voyant(e).

gauge, gage Am [geɪdʒ] ♦ n 1. (for rain) pluviomètre m; (for fuel) jauge f (d'essence); (for tyre pressure) manomètre m. 2. (of gun, wire) calibre m. 3. (RAIL) écartement m. ♦ vt 1. (measure) mesurer. 2. (evaluate) jauger.

Gaul [gɔːl] n 1. (country) Gaule f. 2. (person) Gaulois m, -e f.

gaunt [gɔːnt] adj 1. (thin) hâve. 2. (bare, grim) désolé(e).

gauntlet ['gɔːntlɪt] n gant m (de protection); to run the ~ of sthg endurer qqch; to throw down the ~ (to sb) jeter le gant (à qqn).

gauze [gɔːz] n gaze f.

gave [geɪv] pt → **give**.

gawky ['gɔːkɪ] adj (person) dégingandé(e); (movement) désordonné(e).

gawp [gɔːp] vi: to ~ (at) rester bouche bée (devant).

gay [geɪ] ♦ adj 1. (gen) gai(e). 2. (homosexual) homo (inv), gay (inv). ♦ n homo mf, gay mf.

gaze [geɪz] ♦ n regard m (fixe). ♦ vi: to ~ at sb/sthg regarder qqn/qqch (fixement).

gazelle [gəˈzel] (pl inv OR -s) n gazelle f.

gazetteer [ˌgæzɪˈtɪəʳ] n index m géographique.

gazump [gəˈzʌmp] vt Br inf: to be ~ed être victime d'une suroffre.

GB (abbr of Great Britain) n G-B f.

GCE (abbr of General Certificate of Education) n certificat de fin d'études secondaires en Grande-Bretagne.

GCSE (abbr of General Certificate of Secondary Education) n examen de fin d'études secondaires en Grande-Bretagne.

GDP (*abbr of* **gross domestic product**) *n* PIB *m*.

gear [gɪə**ʳ**] ♦ *n* **1.** (TECH) (*mechanism*) embrayage *m*. **2.** (*speed - of car, bicycle*) vitesse *f*; **to be in/out of ~** être en prise/au point mort. **3.** (U) (*equipment, clothes*) équipement *m*. ♦ *vt*: **to ~ sthg to sb/sthg** destiner qqch à qqn/qqch. ▶ **gear up** *vi*: **to ~ up for sthg/to do sthg** se préparer pour qqch/à faire qqch.

gearbox [ˈgɪəbɒks] *n* boîte *f* de vitesses.

gear lever, gear stick Br, **gear shift** Am *n* levier *m* de changement de vitesse.

gear wheel *n* pignon *m*, roue *f* d'engrenage.

geese [giːs] *pl* → **goose**.

gel [dʒel] ♦ *n* (*for hair*) gel *m*. ♦ *vi* **1.** (*thicken*) prendre. **2.** *fig* (*take shape*) prendre tournure.

gelatin [ˈdʒelətɪn], **gelatine** [ˌdʒeləˈtiːn] *n* gélatine *f*.

gelignite [ˈdʒelɪgnaɪt] *n* gélignite *f*.

gem [dʒem] *n* **1.** (*jewel*) pierre *f* précieuse, gemme *f*. **2.** *fig* (*person, thing*) perle *f*.

Gemini [ˈdʒemɪnaɪ] *n* Gémeaux *mpl*.

gender [ˈdʒendə**ʳ**] *n* **1.** (*sex*) sexe *m*. **2.** (GRAMM) genre *m*.

gene [dʒiːn] *n* gène *m*.

general [ˈdʒenərəl] ♦ *adj* général(e). ♦ *n* général *m*. ▶ **in general** *adv* en général.

general anaesthetic *n* anesthésie *f* générale.

general delivery *n* Am poste *f* restante.

general election *n* élection *f* générale.

generalization [ˌdʒenərəlaɪˈzeɪʃn] *n* généralisation *f*.

general knowledge *n* culture *f* générale.

generally [ˈdʒenərəlɪ] *adv* **1.** (*usually, in most cases*) généralement. **2.** (*unspecifically*) en général; (*describe*) en gros.

general practitioner *n* (médecin *m*) généraliste *m*.

general public *n*: **the ~** le grand public.

general strike *n* grève *f* générale.

generate [ˈdʒenəreɪt] *vt* (*energy, jobs*) générer; (*electricity, heat*) produire; (*interest, excitement*) susciter.

generation [ˌdʒenəˈreɪʃn] *n* **1.** (*gen*) génération *f*. **2.** (*creation - of jobs*) création *f*; (*- of interest, excitement*) induction *f*; (*- of electricity*) production *f*.

generator [ˈdʒenəreɪtə**ʳ**] *n* générateur *m*; (ELEC) génératrice *f*, générateur.

generosity [ˌdʒenəˈrɒsətɪ] *n* générosité *f*.

generous [ˈdʒenərəs] *adj* généreux (euse).

genetic [dʒɪˈnetɪk] *adj* génétique. ▶ **genetics** *n* (U) génétique *f*.

Geneva [dʒɪˈniːvə] *n* Genève.

genial [ˈdʒiːnjəl] *adj* affable.

genitals [ˈdʒenɪtlz] *npl* organes *mpl* génitaux.

genius [ˈdʒiːnjəs] (*pl* **-es**) *n* génie *m*.

gent [dʒent] *n* Br *inf* gentleman *m*. ▶ **gents** *n* Br (*toilets*) toilettes *fpl* pour hommes; (*sign on door*) messieurs.

genteel [dʒenˈtiːl] *adj* raffiné(e).

gentle [ˈdʒentl] *adj* doux (douce); (*hint*) discret(ète); (*telling-off*) léger(ère).

gentleman [ˈdʒentlmən] (*pl* **-men** [-mən]) *n* **1.** (*well-behaved man*) gentleman *m*. **2.** (*man*) monsieur *m*.

gently [ˈdʒentlɪ] *adv* (*gen*) doucement; (*speak, smile*) avec douceur.

gentry [ˈdʒentrɪ] *n* petite noblesse *f*.

genuine [ˈdʒenjuɪn] *adj* authentique; (*interest, customer*) sérieux(euse); (*person, concern*) sincère.

geography [dʒɪˈɒgrəfɪ] *n* géographie *f*.

geological [ˌdʒɪəˈlɒdʒɪkl] *adj* géologique.

geology [dʒɪˈɒlədʒɪ] *n* géologie *f*.

geometric(al) [ˌdʒɪəˈmetrɪk(l)] *adj* géométrique.

geometry [dʒɪˈɒmətrɪ] *n* géométrie *f*.

geranium [dʒɪˈreɪnjəm] (*pl* **-s**) *n* géranium *m*.

gerbil [ˈdʒɜːbɪl] *n* gerbille *f*.

geriatric [ˌdʒerɪˈætrɪk] *adj* **1.** (MED) gériatrique. **2.** *pej* (*person*) décrépit(e); (*object*) vétuste.

germ [dʒɜːm] *n* **1.** (*bacterium*) germe *m*. **2.** *fig* (*of idea, plan*) embryon *m*.

German [ˈdʒɜːmən] ♦ *adj* allemand(e). ♦ *n* **1.** (*person*) Allemand *m*, -e *f*. **2.** (*language*) allemand *m*.

German measles *n* (U) rubéole *f*.

Germany [ˈdʒɜːmənɪ] *n* Allemagne *f*.

germinate [ˈdʒɜːmɪneɪt] *vi* germer.

gerund [ˈdʒerənd] *n* gérondif *m*.

gesticulate [dʒesˈtɪkjuleɪt] *vi* gesticuler.

gesture [ˈdʒestʃə**ʳ**] ♦ *n* geste *m*. ♦ *vi*: **to ~ to** OR **towards sb** faire signe à qqn.

get [get] (Br *pt* & *pp* **got**, Am *pt* **got**, *pp* gotten) ♦ *vt* **1.** (*cause to do*): **to ~ sb to do sthg** faire faire qqch à qqn; **I'll ~ my sister to help** je vais demander à ma sœur de nous aider. **2.** (*cause to be done*): **to ~ sthg done** faire faire qqch; **I got the car fixed** j'ai fait réparer la voiture. **3.** (*cause to become*): **to ~ sb pregnant** rendre qqn enceinte; **I can't ~ the car started** je n'arrive pas à mettre la voiture en marche. **4.** (*cause to move*): **to ~ sb/sthg through sthg** faire passer qqn/qqch par qqch; **to ~ sb/sthg out of sthg** faire sortir qqn/qqch de qqch. **5.** (*bring, fetch*) aller chercher; **can I ~ you something to eat/drink?** est-ce que je peux vous offrir quelque chose à manger/boire? **6.** (*obtain - gen*) obtenir; (*- job, house*) trouver. **7.** (*receive*) recevoir, avoir; **what did you ~ for your birthday?** qu'est-ce que tu as eu pour ton anniversaire?; **she ~s a good salary** elle touche un bon traitement. **8.** (*experience a sensation*) avoir; **do you ~ the feeling he doesn't like us?** tu n'as pas l'impression qu'il ne nous aime pas? **9.** (*be infected with, suffer from*) avoir, attraper; **to ~ a cold** attraper un rhume. **10.** (*understand*) comprendre, saisir. **11.** (*catch - bus, train, plane*) prendre. **12.** (*capture*) prendre, attraper. **13.** (*find*): **you ~ a lot of artists here** on trouve *OR* il y a beaucoup d'artistes ici; *see also* **have**. ♦ *vi* **1.** (*become*) devenir; **to ~ suspicious** devenir méfiant; **I'm getting cold/bored** je commence à avoir froid/à m'ennuyer; **it's getting late** il se fait tard. **2.** (*arrive*) arriver; **I only got back yesterday** je suis rentré hier seulement. **3.** (*eventually succeed in*): **to ~ to do sthg** parvenir à *OR* finir par faire qqch; **did you ~ to see him?** est-ce que tu as réussi à le voir? **4.** (*progress*): **how far have you got?** où en es-tu?; **we're getting nowhere** on n'arrive à rien. ♦ *aux vb*: **to ~ excited** s'exciter; **to ~ hurt** se faire mal; **to ~ beaten up** se faire tabasser; **let's ~ going** *OR* **moving** allons-y; *see also* **have**. ▶ **get about** *vi* **1.** (*move from place to place*) se déplacer. **2.** (*circulate - news, rumour*) circuler, se répandre; *see also* **get around**. ▶ **get along** *vi* **1.** (*manage*) se débrouiller. **2.** (*progress*) avancer, faire des progrès. **3.** (*have a good relationship*) s'entendre. ▶ **get around, get round** ♦ *vt fus* (*overcome*) venir à bout de, surmonter. ♦ *vi* **1.** (*circulate*) circuler, se répandre. **2.** (*eventually do*): **to ~ around to (doing) sthg** trouver le temps de faire qqch; *see also* **get**

about. ▶ **get at** *vt fus* **1.** (*reach*) parvenir à. **2.** (*imply*) vouloir dire; **what are you getting at?** où veux-tu en venir? **3.** *inf* (*criticize*) critiquer, dénigrer. ▶ **get away** *vi* **1.** (*leave*) partir, s'en aller. **2.** (*go on holiday*) partir en vacances. **3.** (*escape*) s'échapper, s'évader. ▶ **get away with** *vt fus*: **to let sb ~ away with sthg** passer qqch à qqn. ▶ **get back** ♦ *vt sep* (*recover, regain*) retrouver, récupérer. ♦ *vi* (*move away*) s'écarter. ▶ **get back to** *vt fus* **1.** (*return to previous state, activity*) revenir à; **to ~ back to sleep** se rendormir; **to ~ back to work** (*after pause*) se remettre au travail; (*after illness*) reprendre son travail. **2.** *inf* (*phone back*) rappeler; **I'll ~ back to you on that** je te reparlerai de ça plus tard. ▶ **get by** *vi* se débrouiller, s'en sortir. ▶ **get down** *vt sep* **1.** (*depress*) déprimer. **2.** (*fetch from higher level*) descendre. ▶ **get down to** *vt fus*: **to ~ down to doing sthg** se mettre à faire qqch. ▶ **get in** *vi* **1.** (*enter - gen*) entrer; (*- referring to vehicle*) monter. **2.** (*arrive*) arriver; (*arrive home*) rentrer. ▶ **get into** *vt fus* **1.** (*car*) monter dans. **2.** (*become involved in*) se lancer dans; **to ~ into an argument with sb** se disputer avec qqn. **3.** (*enter into a particular situation, state*): **to ~ into trouble** s'attirer des ennuis; **to ~ into the habit of doing sthg** prendre l'habitude de faire qqch. ▶ **get off** ♦ *vt sep* (*remove*) enlever. ♦ *vt fus* **1.** (*go away from*) partir de. **2.** (*train, bus etc*) descendre de. ♦ *vi* **1.** (*leave bus, train*) descendre. **2.** (*escape punishment*) s'en tirer. **3.** (*depart*) partir. ▶ **get on** ♦ *vt fus* **1.** (*bus, train, plane*) monter dans. **2.** (*horse*) monter sur. ♦ *vi* **1.** (*enter bus, train*) monter. **2.** (*have good relationship*) s'entendre, s'accorder. **3.** (*progress*) avancer, progresser; **how are you getting on?** comment ça va? **4.** (*proceed*): **to ~ on (with sthg)** continuer (qqch), poursuivre (qqch). **5.** (*be successful professionally*) réussir. ▶ **get out** ♦ *vt sep* **1.** (*take out*) sortir. **2.** (*remove*) enlever. ♦ *vi* **1.** (*from car, bus, train*) descendre. **2.** (*news*) s'ébruiter. ▶ **get out of** *vt fus* **1.** (*car etc*) descendre de. **2.** (*escape from*) s'évader de, s'échapper de. **3.** (*avoid*) éviter, se dérober à; **to ~ out of doing sthg** se dispenser de faire qqch. ▶ **get over** *vt fus* **1.** (*recover from*) se remettre de. **2.** (*overcome*) surmonter, venir à bout de. **3.** (*communicate*) communiquer. ▶ **get round** = **get around**. ▶ **get through**

◆ vt fus 1. (job, task) arriver au bout de. 2. (exam) réussir à. 3. (food, drink) consommer. 4. (unpleasant situation) endurer, supporter. ◆ vi 1. (make o.s. understood): **to ~ through (to sb)** se faire comprendre (de qqn). 2. (TELEC) obtenir la communication. ▶ **get to** vt fus inf (annoy) taper sur les nerfs à. ▶ **get together** ◆ vt sep (organize - team, belongings) rassembler; (- project, report) préparer. ◆ vi se réunir. ▶ **get up** ◆ vi se lever. ◆ vt fus (petition, demonstration) organiser. ▶ **get up to** vt fus inf faire.

getaway ['getǝweɪ] n fuite f.

get-together n inf réunion f.

geyser ['giːzǝʳ] n 1. (hot spring) geyser m. 2. Br (water heater) chauffe-eau m inv.

Ghana ['gɑːnǝ] n Ghana m.

ghastly ['gɑːstlɪ] adj 1. inf (very bad, unpleasant) épouvantable. 2. (horrifying, macabre) effroyable.

gherkin ['gɜːkɪn] n cornichon m.

ghetto ['getǝʊ] (pl **-s** OR **-es**) n ghetto m.

ghetto blaster [-ˌblɑːstǝʳ] n inf grand radiocassette m portatif.

ghost [gǝʊst] n (spirit) spectre m.

giant ['dʒaɪǝnt] ◆ adj géant(e). ◆ n géant m.

gibberish ['dʒɪbǝrɪʃ] n (U) charabia m, inepties fpl.

gibe [dʒaɪb] n insulte f.

giblets ['dʒɪblɪts] npl abats mpl.

Gibraltar [dʒɪ'brɔːltǝʳ] n Gibraltar m.

giddy ['gɪdɪ] adj (dizzy): **to feel ~** avoir la tête qui tourne.

gift [gɪft] n 1. (present) cadeau m. 2. (talent) don m; **to have a ~ for sthg/for doing sthg** avoir un don pour qqch/pour faire qqch; **the ~ of the gab** le bagou.

gift certificate Am = **gift token**.

gifted ['gɪftɪd] adj doué(e).

gift token, gift voucher n Br chèque-cadeau m.

gig [gɪg] n inf (concert) concert m.

gigabyte ['gaɪgǝbaɪt] n (COMPUT) gigaoctet m.

gigantic [dʒaɪ'gæntɪk] adj énorme, gigantesque.

giggle ['gɪgl] ◆ n 1. (laugh) gloussement m. 2. Br inf (fun): **to be a ~** être marrant(e) OR tordant(e); **to have a ~** bien s'amuser. ◆ vi (laugh) glousser.

gilded ['gɪldɪd] adj = **gilt**.

gill [dʒɪl] n (unit of measurement) = 0,142 litre, quart m de pinte.

gills [gɪlz] npl (of fish) branchies fpl.

gilt [gɪlt] ◆ adj (covered in gold) doré(e).

◆ n (U) (gold layer) dorure f.

gimmick ['gɪmɪk] n pej artifice m.

gin [dʒɪn] n gin m; **~ and tonic** gin tonic.

ginger ['dʒɪndʒǝʳ] ◆ n 1. (root) gingembre m. 2. (powder) gingembre m en poudre. ◆ adj Br (colour) roux (rousse).

ginger ale n boisson gazeuse au gingembre.

ginger beer n boisson non-alcoolisée au gingembre.

gingerbread ['dʒɪndʒǝbred] n pain m d'épice.

ginger-haired [-'heǝd] adj roux (rousse).

gingerly ['dʒɪndʒǝlɪ] adv avec précaution.

gipsy ['dʒɪpsɪ] ◆ adj gitan(e). ◆ n gitan m, -e f; Br pej bohémien m, -enne f.

giraffe [dʒɪ'rɑːf] (pl inv OR **-s**) n girafe f.

girder ['gɜːdǝʳ] n poutrelle f.

girdle ['gɜːdl] n (corset) gaine f.

girl [gɜːl] n 1. (gen) fille f. 2. (girlfriend) petite amie f.

girlfriend ['gɜːlfrend] n 1. (female lover) petite amie f. 2. (female friend) amie f.

girl guide Br, **girl scout** Am n éclaireuse f, guide f.

giro ['dʒaɪrǝʊ] (pl **-s**) n Br 1. (U) (system) virement m postal. 2. ~ (cheque) chèque m d'indemnisation f (chômage OR maladie).

girth [gɜːθ] n 1. (circumference - of tree) circonférence f; (- of person) tour m de taille. 2. (of horse) sangle f.

gist [dʒɪst] n substance f; **to get the ~ of sthg** comprendre l'essentiel de qqch.

give [gɪv] (pt **gave**, pp **given**) ◆ vt 1. (gen) donner; (message) transmettre; (attention, time) consacrer; **to ~ sb/sthg sthg** donner qqch à qqn/qqch; **to ~ sb a fright/a smile** faire peur/un sourire à qqn; **to ~ a sigh** pousser un soupir; **to ~ a speech** faire un discours. 2. (as present): **to ~ sb sthg, to ~ sthg to sb** donner qqch à qqn, offrir qqch à qqn. ◆ vi (collapse, break) céder, s'affaisser. ◆ n (elasticity) élasticité f, souplesse f. ▶ **give or take** prep: **~ or take a day/£10** à un jour/10 livres près. ▶ **give away** vt sep 1. (get rid of) donner. 2. (reveal) révéler. ▶ **give back** vt sep (return) rendre. ▶ **give in** vi 1. (admit defeat) abandonner, se rendre. 2. (agree unwillingly): **to ~ in to sthg** céder à qqch. ▶ **give off** vt fus (smell) exhaler; (smoke) faire; (heat) produire. ▶ **give out** ◆ vt sep (distribute) distribuer. ◆ vi (supplies) s'épuiser; (car) lâcher. ▶ **give up** ◆ vt sep 1. (stop) renoncer à; **to ~ up drinking/smoking** arrêter de boire/de fumer. **2.** (*surrender*): **to ~ o.s. up** (**to sb**) se rendre (à qqn). ◆ *vi* abandonner, se rendre.

given ['gɪvn] ◆ *adj* **1.** (*set, fixed*) convenu(e), fixé(e). **2.** (*prone*): **to be ~ to sthg/to doing sthg** être enclin(e) à qqch/à faire qqch. ◆ *prep* étant donné; **~ that** étant donné que.

given name *n Am* prénom *m*.

glacier ['glæsjə^r] *n* glacier *m*.

glad [glæd] *adj* **1.** (*happy, pleased*) content(e); **to be ~ about sthg** être content de qqch. **2.** (*willing*): **to be ~ to do sthg** faire qqch volontiers OR avec plaisir. **3.** (*grateful*): **to be ~ of sthg** être content(e) de qqch.

gladly ['glædlɪ] *adv* **1.** (*happily, eagerly*) avec joie. **2.** (*willingly*) avec plaisir.

glamor *Am* = **glamour**.

glamorous ['glæmərəs] *adj* (*person*) séduisant(e); (*appearance*) élégant(e); (*job, place*) prestigieux(euse).

glamour *Br*, **glamor** *Am* ['glæmə^r] *n* (*of person*) charme *m*; (*of appearance*) élégance *f*, chic *m*; (*of job, place*) prestige *m*.

glance [glɑːns] ◆ *n* (*quick look*) regard *m*, coup d'œil *m*; **at a ~** d'un coup d'œil; **at first ~** au premier coup d'œil. ◆ *vi* (*look quickly*): **to ~ at sb/sthg** jeter un coup d'œil à qqn/qqch. ▶ **glance off** *vt fus* (*subj: ball, bullet*) ricocher sur.

glancing ['glɑːnsɪŋ] *adj* de côté, oblique.

gland [glænd] *n* glande *f*.

glandular fever [ˌglændjʊlə^r-] *n* mononucléose *f* infectieuse.

glare [gleə^r] ◆ *n* **1.** (*scowl*) regard *m* mauvais. **2.** (U) (*of headlights, publicity*) lumière *f* aveuglante. ◆ *vi* **1.** (*scowl*): **to ~ at sb/sthg** regarder qqn/qqch d'un œil mauvais. **2.** (*sun, lamp*) briller d'une lumière éblouissante.

glaring ['gleərɪŋ] *adj* **1.** (*very obvious*) flagrant(e). **2.** (*blazing, dazzling*) aveuglant(e).

glasnost ['glæznɒst] *n* glasnost *f*, transparence *f*.

glass [glɑːs] ◆ *n* **1.** (*gen*) verre *m*. **2.** (U) (*glassware*) verrerie *f*. ◆ *comp* (*bottle, jar*) en OR de verre; (*door, partition*) vitré(e). ▶ **glasses** *npl* (*spectacles*) lunettes *fpl*.

glassware ['glɑːsweə^r] *n* (U) verrerie *f*.

glassy ['glɑːsɪ] *adj* **1.** (*smooth, shiny*) lisse comme un miroir. **2.** (*blank, lifeless*) vitreux(euse).

glaze [gleɪz] ◆ *n* (*on pottery*) vernis *m*; (*on pastry, flan*) glaçage *m*. ◆ *vt* (*pottery,*

tiles, bricks) vernisser; (*pastry, flan*) glacer.

glazier ['gleɪzjə^r] *n* vitrier *m*.

gleam [gliːm] ◆ *n* (*of gold*) reflet *m*; (*of fire, sunset, disapproval*) lueur *f*. ◆ *vi* **1.** (*surface, object*) luire. **2.** (*light, eyes*) briller.

gleaming ['gliːmɪŋ] *adj* brillant(e).

glean [gliːn] *vt* (*gather*) glaner.

glee [gliː] *n* (U) (*joy*) joie *f*, jubilation *f*.

glen [glen] *n Scot* vallée *f*.

glib [glɪb] *adj pej* (*salesman, politician*) qui a du bagout; (*promise, excuse*) facile.

glide [glaɪd] *vi* **1.** (*move smoothly - dancer, boat*) glisser sans effort; (*- person*) se mouvoir sans effort. **2.** (*fly*) planer.

glider ['glaɪdə^r] *n* (*plane*) planeur *m*.

gliding ['glaɪdɪŋ] *n* (*sport*) vol *m* à voile.

glimmer ['glɪmə^r] *n* (*faint light*) faible lueur *f*; *fig* signe *m*, lueur.

glimpse [glɪmps] ◆ *n* **1.** (*look, sight*) aperçu *m*. **2.** (*idea, perception*) idée *f*. ◆ *vt* **1.** (*catch sight of*) apercevoir, entrevoir. **2.** (*perceive*) pressentir.

glint [glɪnt] ◆ *n* **1.** (*flash*) reflet *m*. **2.** (*in eyes*) éclair *m*. ◆ *vi* étinceler.

glisten ['glɪsn] *vi* briller.

glitter ['glɪtə^r] ◆ *n* (U) scintillement *m*. ◆ *vi* **1.** (*object, light*) scintiller. **2.** (*eyes*) briller.

gloat [gləʊt] *vi*: **to ~ (over sthg)** se réjouir (de qqch).

global ['gləʊbl] *adj* (*worldwide*) mondial(e).

global warming [-ˈwɔːmɪŋ] *n* réchauffement *m* de la planète.

globe [gləʊb] *n* **1.** (*Earth*): **the ~** la terre. **2.** (*spherical map*) globe *m* terrestre. **3.** (*spherical object*) globe *m*.

gloom [gluːm] *n* (U) **1.** (*darkness*) obscurité *f*. **2.** (*unhappiness*) tristesse *f*.

gloomy ['gluːmɪ] *adj* **1.** (*room, sky, prospects*) sombre. **2.** (*person, atmosphere, mood*) triste, lugubre.

glorious ['glɔːrɪəs] *adj* **1.** (*beautiful, splendid*) splendide. **2.** (*very enjoyable*) formidable. **3.** (*successful, impressive*) magnifique.

glory ['glɔːrɪ] *n* **1.** (U) (*fame, admiration*) gloire *f*. **2.** (U) (*beauty*) splendeur *f*. ▶ **glory in** *vt fus* (*relish*) savourer.

gloss [glɒs] *n* **1.** (U) (*shine*) brillant *m*, lustre *m*. **2.** **~ (paint)** peinture *f* brillante. ▶ **gloss over** *vt fus* passer sur.

glossary ['glɒsərɪ] *n* glossaire *m*.

glossy ['glɒsɪ] *adj* **1.** (*hair, surface*) brillant(e). **2.** (*book, photo*) sur papier glacé.

glove [glʌv] *n* gant *m*.

glove compartment *n* boîte *f* à gants.

glow [gləʊ] ♦ *n* (U) (*of fire, light, sunset*) lueur *f*. ♦ *vi* **1.** (*shine out - fire*) rougeoyer; (*light, stars, eyes*) flamboyer. **2.** (*shine in light*) briller.

glower [ˈglaʊəʳ] *vi*: **to ~ (at)** lancer des regards noirs (à).

glucose [ˈgluːkəʊs] *n* glucose *m*.

glue [gluː] (*cont* glueing OR gluing) ♦ *n* (U) colle *f*. ♦ *vt* (*stick with glue*) coller; **to ~ sthg to sthg** coller qqch à OR avec qqch.

glum [glʌm] *adj* (*unhappy*) morne.

glut [glʌt] *n* surplus *m*.

glutton [ˈglʌtn] *n* (*greedy person*) glouton *m*, -onne *f*; **to be a ~ for punishment** être maso, être masochiste.

gnarled [nɑːld] *adj* (*tree, hands*) noueux (euse).

gnash [næʃ] *vt*: **to ~ one's teeth** grincer des dents.

gnat [næt] *n* moucheron *m*.

gnaw [nɔː] ♦ *vt* (*chew*) ronger. ♦ *vi* (*worry*): **to ~ (away) at sb** ronger qqn.

gnome [nəʊm] *n* gnome *m*, lutin *m*.

GNP (*abbr of* **gross national product**) *n* PNB *m*.

go [gəʊ] (*pt* went, *pp* gone, *pl* goes) ♦ *vi* **1.** (*move, travel*) aller; **where are you ~ing?** où vas-tu?; **we went by bus/train** nous sommes allés en bus/par le train; **where does this path ~?** où mène ce chemin?; **to ~ and do sthg** aller faire qqch; **to ~ swimming/shopping/jogging** aller nager/faire les courses/faire du jogging; **to ~ for a walk** aller se promener, faire une promenade. **2.** (*depart*) partir, s'en aller; **I must ~, I have to ~** il faut que je m'en aille; **what time does the bus ~?** à quelle heure part le bus?; **let's ~!** allons-y! **3.** (*become*) devenir; **to ~ grey** grisonner, devenir gris; **to ~ mad** devenir fou. **4.** (*pass - time*) passer. **5.** (*progress*) marcher, se dérouler; **the conference went very smoothly** la conférence s'est déroulée sans problème or s'est très bien passée; **to ~ well/badly** aller bien/mal; **how's it ~ing?** *inf* comment ça va? **6.** (*function, work*) marcher; **the car won't ~** la voiture ne veut pas démarrer. **7.** (*indicating intention, expectation*): **to be ~ing to do sthg** aller faire qqch; **he said he was ~ing to be late** il a prévenu qu'il allait arriver en retard; **we're ~ing (to ~) to America in June** on va (aller) en

Amérique en juin; **she's ~ing to have a baby** elle attend un bébé. **8.** (*bell, alarm*) sonner. **9.** (*stop working, break - light bulb, fuse*) sauter. **10.** (*deteriorate - hearing, sight etc*) baisser. **11.** (*match, be compatible*): **to ~ (with)** aller (avec); **those colours don't really ~** ces couleurs ne vont pas bien ensemble. **12.** (*fit*) aller. **13.** (*belong*) aller, se mettre; **the plates ~ in the cupboard** les assiettes vont or se mettent dans le placard. **14.** (*in division*): **three into two won't ~** deux divisé par trois n'y va pas. **15.** *inf* (*expressing irritation, surprise*): **now what's he gone and done?** qu'est-ce qu'il a fait encore? ♦ *n* **1.** (*turn*) tour *m*; **it's my ~** c'est à moi (de jouer). **2.** *inf* (*attempt*): **to have a ~ (at sthg)** essayer (de faire qqch). **3.** *phr*: **to have a ~ at sb** *inf* s'en prendre à qqn, engueuler qqn; **to be on the ~** *inf* être sur la brèche. ▶ **to go** *adv* (*remaining*): **there are only three days to ~** il ne reste que trois jours. ▶ **go ahead** *vi* **1.** (*proceed*): **to ~ ahead with sthg** mettre qqch à exécution; **~ ahead!** allez-y! **2.** (*take place*) avoir lieu. ▶ **go along** *vi* (*proceed*) avancer; **as you ~ along** au fur et à mesure. ▶ **go along with** *vt fus* (*suggestion, idea*) appuyer, soutenir; (*person*) suivre. ▶ **go around** *vi* **1.** (*frequent*): **to ~ around with sb** fréquenter qqn. **2.** (*spread*) circuler, courir. ▶ **go back on** *vt fus* (*one's word, promise*) revenir sur. ▶ **go back to** *vt fus* **1.** (*return to activity*) reprendre, se remettre à; **to ~ back to sleep** se rendormir. **2.** (*date from*) remonter à, dater de. ▶ **go by** ♦ *vi* (*time*) s'écouler, passer. ♦ *vt fus* **1.** (*be guided by*) suivre. **2.** (*judge from*) juger d'après. ▶ **go down** ♦ *vi* **1.** (*get lower - prices etc*) baisser. **2.** (*be accepted*): **to ~ down well/badly** être bien/mal accueilli. **3.** (*sun*) se coucher. **4.** (*tyre, balloon*) se dégonfler. ♦ *vt fus* descendre. ▶ **go for** *vt fus* **1.** (*choose*) choisir. **2.** (*be attracted to*) être attiré(e) par. **3.** (*attack*) tomber sur, attaquer. **4.** (*try to obtain - job, record*) essayer d'obtenir. ▶ **go in** *vi* entrer. ▶ **go in for** *vt fus* **1.** (*competition*) prendre part à; (*exam*) se présenter à. **2.** (*activity - enjoy*) aimer; (- *participate in*) faire, s'adonner à. ▶ **go into** *vt fus* **1.** (*investigate*) étudier, examiner. **2.** (*take up as a profession*) entrer dans. ▶ **go off** ♦ *vi* **1.** (*explode*) exploser. **2.** (*alarm*) sonner. **3.** (*go bad - food*) se gâter. **4.** (*lights, heating*) s'éteindre. ♦ *vt fus* (*lose interest in*) ne plus aimer. ▶ **go on** ♦ *vi* **1.** (*take* place, happen) se passer. **2.** (heating etc) se mettre en marche. **3.** (continue): **to ~ on (doing)** continuer (à faire). **4.** (proceed to further activity): **to ~ on to sthg** passer à qqch; **to ~ on to do sthg** faire qqch après. **5.** (talk for too long) parler à n'en plus finir; **to ~ on about sthg** ne pas arrêter de parler de qqch. ◆ vt fus (be guided by) se fonder sur. ▶ **go on at** vt fus (nag) harceler. ▶ **go out** vi **1.** (leave) sortir. **2.** (for amusement): **to ~ out (with sb)** sortir (avec qqn). **3.** (light, fire, cigarette) s'éteindre. ▶ **go over** vt fus **1.** (examine) examiner, vérifier. **2.** (repeat, review) repasser. ▶ **go round** vi (revolve) tourner; see also **go around.** ▶ **go through** vt fus **1.** (experience) subir, souffrir. **2.** (study, search through) examiner; **she went through his pockets** elle lui a fait les poches, elle a fouillé dans ses poches. ▶ **go through with** vt fus (action, threat) aller jusqu'au bout de. ▶ **go towards** vt fus contribuer à. ▶ **go under** vi lit & fig couler. ▶ **go up** ◆ vi **1.** (gen) monter. **2.** (prices) augmenter. ◆ vt fus monter. ▶ **go without** ◆ vt fus se passer de. ◆ vi s'en passer.

goad [gəʊd] vt (provoke) talonner.

go-ahead ◆ adj (dynamic) dynamique. ◆ n (U) (permission) feu m vert.

goal [gəʊl] n but m.

goalkeeper ['gəʊl,kiːpər] n gardien m de but.

goalmouth ['gəʊlmaʊθ, pl -maʊðz] n but m.

goalpost ['gəʊlpəʊst] n poteau m de but.

goat [gəʊt] n chèvre f.

gob [gɒb] v inf ◆ n Br (mouth) gueule f. ◆ vi (spit) mollarder.

gobble ['gɒbl] vt engloutir. ▶ **gobble down, gobble up** vt sep engloutir.

go-between n intermédiaire mf.

gobsmacked ['gɒbsmækt] adj Br inf bouche bée (inv).

go-cart = go-kart.

god [gɒd] n dieu m, divinité f. ▶ **God** ◆ n Dieu m; **God knows** Dieu seul le sait; **for God's sake** pour l'amour de Dieu; **thank God** Dieu merci. ◆ excl: **(my) God!** mon Dieu!

godchild ['gɒdtʃaɪld] (pl -children [-,tʃɪldrən]) n filleul m, -e f.

goddaughter ['gɒd,dɔːtər] n filleule f.

goddess ['gɒdɪs] n déesse f.

godfather ['gɒd,fɑːðər] n parrain m.

godforsaken ['gɒdfə,seɪkn] adj morne, désolé(e).

godmother ['gɒd,mʌðər] n marraine f.

godsend ['gɒdsend] n aubaine f.

godson ['gɒdsʌn] n filleul m.

goes [gəʊz] pl → **go.**

goggles ['gɒglz] npl lunettes fpl.

going ['gəʊɪŋ] ◆ n (U) **1.** (rate of advance) allure f. **2.** (travel conditions) conditions fpl. ◆ adj **1.** Br (available) disponible. **2.** (rate, salary) en vigueur.

go-kart [-kɑːt] n kart m.

gold [gəʊld] ◆ n (U) (metal, jewellery) or m. ◆ comp (made of gold) en or. ◆ adj (gold-coloured) doré(e).

golden ['gəʊldən] adj **1.** (made of gold) en or. **2.** (gold-coloured) doré(e).

goldfish ['gəʊldfɪʃ] (pl inv) n poisson m rouge.

gold leaf n (U) feuille f d'or.

gold medal n médaille f d'or.

goldmine ['gəʊldmaɪn] n lit & fig mine f d'or.

gold-plated [-'pleɪtɪd] adj plaqué(e) or.

goldsmith ['gəʊldsmɪθ] n orfèvre m.

golf [gɒlf] n golf m.

golf ball n **1.** (for golf) balle f de golf. **2.** (for typewriter) boule f.

golf club n (stick, place) club m de golf.

golf course n terrain m de golf.

golfer ['gɒlfər] n golfeur m, -euse f.

gone [gɒn] ◆ pp → **go.** ◆ adj (no longer here) parti(e). ◆ prep: **it's ~ ten (o'clock)** il est dix heures passées.

gong [gɒŋ] n gong m.

good [gʊd] (compar **better,** superl **best**) ◆ adj **1.** (gen) bon (bonne); **it's ~ to see you again** ça fait plaisir de te revoir; **to be ~ at sthg** être bon en qqch; **to be ~ with** (animals, children) savoir y faire avec; (one's hands) être habile de; **it's ~ for you** c'est bon pour toi or pour la santé; **to feel ~** (person) se sentir bien; **it's ~ that ...** c'est bien que ...; **~!** très bien! **2.** (kind - person) gentil(ille); **to be ~ to sb** être très attentionné envers qqn; **to be ~ enough to do sthg** avoir l'amabilité de faire qqch. **3.** (well-behaved - child) sage; (- behaviour) correct(e); **be ~!** sois sage!, tiens-toi tranquille! ◆ n **1.** (U) (benefit) bien m; **it will do him ~** ça lui fera du bien. **2.** (use) utilité f; **what's the ~ of doing that?** à quoi bon faire ça?; **it's no ~** ça ne sert à rien; **it's no ~ crying/worrying** ça ne sert à rien de pleurer/de s'en faire. **3.** (U) (morally correct behaviour) bien m; **to be up to no ~** préparer un sale coup. ▶ **goods** npl (merchandise) marchandises *fpl*, articles *mpl*. ► **as good as** *adv* pratiquement, pour ainsi dire. ► **for good** *adv* (*forever*) pour de bon, définitivement. ► **good afternoon** *excl* bonjour! ► **good evening** *excl* bonsoir! ► **good morning** *excl* bonjour! ► **good night** *excl* bonsoir!; (*at bedtime*) bonne nuit!

goodbye [ˌgʊdˈbaɪ] ◆ *excl* au revoir! ◆ *n* au revoir *m*.

Good Friday *n* Vendredi *m* saint.

good-humoured [-ˈhjuːməd] *adj* (*person*) de bonne humeur; (*smile, remark, rivalry*) bon enfant.

good-looking [-ˈlʊkɪŋ] *adj* (*person*) beau (belle).

good-natured [-ˈneɪtʃəd] *adj* (*person*) d'un naturel aimable; (*rivalry, argument*) bon enfant.

goodness [ˈgʊdnɪs] ◆ *n* (U) **1.** (*kindness*) bonté *f*. **2.** (*nutritive quality*) valeur *f* nutritive. ◆ *excl*: **(my) ~!** mon Dieu!, Seigneur!; **for ~' sake!** par pitié!, pour l'amour de Dieu!; **thank ~!** grâce à Dieu!

goods train *n* Br train *m* de marchandises.

goodwill [ˌgʊdˈwɪl] *n* bienveillance *f*.

goody [ˈgʊdɪ] *inf* ◆ *n* (*person*) bon *m*. ◆ *excl* chouette!

goose [guːs] (*pl* **geese**) *n* (*bird*) oie *f*.

gooseberry [ˈgʊzbərɪ] *n* **1.** (*fruit*) groseille *f* à maquereau. **2.** Br *inf* (*third person*): **to play ~** tenir la chandelle.

gooseflesh [ˈguːsfleʃ] *n*, **goose pimples** Br, **goosebumps** Am [ˈguːsbʌmps] *npl* chair *f* de poule.

gore [gɔːʳ] ◆ *n* (U) *literary* (*blood*) sang *m*. ◆ *vt* encorner.

gorge [gɔːdʒ] ◆ *n* gorge *f*, défilé *m*. ◆ *vt*: **to ~ o.s. on** OR **with sthg** se bourrer OR se goinfrer de qqch.

gorgeous [ˈgɔːdʒəs] *adj* divin(e); *inf* (*good-looking*) magnifique, splendide.

gorilla [gəˈrɪlə] *n* gorille *m*.

gormless [ˈgɔːmlɪs] *adj* Br *inf* bêta (bêtasse).

gorse [gɔːs] *n* (U) ajonc *m*.

gory [ˈgɔːrɪ] *adj* sanglant(e).

gosh [gɒʃ] *excl inf* ça alors!

go-slow *n* Br grève *f* du zèle.

gospel [ˈgɒspl] *n* (*doctrine*) évangile *m*. ► **Gospel** *n* Évangile *m*.

gossip [ˈgɒsɪp] ◆ *n* **1.** (*conversation*) bavardage *m*; *pej* commérage *m*. **2.** (*person*) commère *f*. ◆ *vi* (*talk*) bavarder, papoter; *pej* cancaner.

gossip column *n* échos *mpl*.

got [gɒt] *pt* & *pp* → **get**.

gotten [ˈgɒtn] Am *pp* → **get**.

goulash [ˈguːlæʃ] *n* goulache *m*.

gourmet [ˈgʊəmeɪ] ◆ *n* gourmet *m*. ◆ *comp* (*food, restaurant*) gastronomique; (*cook*) gastronome.

gout [gaʊt] *n* (U) goutte *f*.

govern [ˈgʌvən] ◆ *vt* **1.** (*gen*) gouverner. **2.** (*control*) régir. ◆ *vi* (POL) gouverner.

governess [ˈgʌvənɪs] *n* gouvernante *f*.

government [ˈgʌvnmənt] *n* gouvernement *m*.

governor [ˈgʌvənəʳ] *n* **1.** (POL) gouverneur *m*. **2.** (*of school*) = membre *m* du conseil d'établissement; (*of bank*) gouverneur *m*. **3.** (*of prison*) directeur *m*.

gown [gaʊn] *n* **1.** (*for woman*) robe *f*. **2.** (*for surgeon*) blouse *f*; (*for judge, academic*) robe *f*, toge *f*.

GP *n abbr of* **general practitioner**.

grab [græb] ◆ *vt* **1.** (*seize*) saisir. **2.** *inf* (*sandwich*) avaler en vitesse; **to ~ a few hours' sleep** dormir quelques heures. **3.** *inf* (*appeal to*) emballer. ◆ *vi*: **to ~ at sthg** faire un geste pour attraper qqch.

grace [greɪs] ◆ *n* **1.** (*elegance*) grâce *f*. **2.** (U) (*extra time*) répit *m*. **3.** (*prayer*) grâces *fpl*. ◆ *vt fml* **1.** (*honour*) honorer de sa présence. **2.** (*decorate*) orner, décorer.

graceful [ˈgreɪsfʊl] *adj* gracieux(euse), élégant(e).

gracious [ˈgreɪʃəs] ◆ *adj* (*polite*) courtois(e). ◆ *excl*: **(good) ~!** juste ciel!

grade [greɪd] ◆ *n* **1.** (*quality - of worker*) catégorie *f*; (*- of wool, paper*) qualité *f*; (*- of petrol*) type *m*; (*- of eggs*) calibre *m*. **2.** Am (*class*) classe *f*. **3.** (*mark*) note *f*. ◆ *vt* **1.** (*classify*) classer. **2.** (*mark, assess*) noter.

grade crossing *n* Am passage *m* à niveau.

grade school *n* Am école *f* primaire.

gradient [ˈgreɪdjənt] *n* pente *f*, inclinaison *f*.

gradual [ˈgrædʒʊəl] *adj* graduel(elle), progressif(ive).

gradually [ˈgrædʒʊəlɪ] *adv* graduellement, petit à petit.

graduate [*n* ˈgrædʒʊət, *vb* ˈgrædʒʊeɪt] ◆ *n* **1.** (*from university*) diplômé *m*, -e *f*. **2.** Am (*of high school*) = titulaire *mf* du baccalauréat. ◆ *vi* **1.** (*from university*): **to ~ (from)** = obtenir son diplôme (à). **2.** Am (*from high school*): **to ~ (from)** = obtenir son baccalauréat (à).

graduation [ˌgrædʒʊˈeɪʃn] *n* (U) (*ceremony*) remise *f* des diplômes.

graffiti [grəˈfiːtɪ] *n* (U) graffiti *mpl*.

graft [grɑːft] ◆ n 1. (from plant) greffe f, greffon m. 2. (MED) greffe f. 3. Br (hard work) boulot m. 4. Am inf (corruption) graissage m de patte. ◆ vt (plant, skin) greffer.

grain [greɪn] n 1. (gen) grain m. 2. (U) (crops) céréales fpl. 3. (U) (pattern - in wood) fil m; (- in material) grain m; (- in stone, marble) veines fpl.

gram [græm] n gramme m.

grammar ['græmər] n grammaire f.

grammar school n (in UK) = lycée m; (in US) école f primaire.

grammatical [grə'mætɪkl] adj grammatical(e).

gramme [græm] Br = **gram**.

gramophone ['græməfəʊn] n dated gramophone m, phonographe m.

gran [græn] n Br inf mamie f, mémé f.

grand [grænd] ◆ adj 1. (impressive) grandiose, imposant(e). 2. (ambitious) grand(e). 3. (important) important(e); (socially) distingué(e). 4. inf dated (excellent) sensationnel(elle), formidable. ◆ n inf (thousand pounds) mille livres fpl; (thousand dollars) mille dollars mpl.

grand(d)ad ['grændæd] n inf papi m, pépé m.

grandchild ['græntʃaɪld] (pl -children [-,tʃɪldrən]) n (boy) petit-fils m; (girl) petite-fille f. ▶ **grandchildren** npl petits-enfants mpl.

granddaughter ['græn,dɔːtər] n petite-fille f.

grandeur ['grændʒər] n (splendour) splendeur f, magnificence f.

grandfather ['grænd,fɑːðər] n grand-père m.

grandma ['grænmɑː] n inf mamie f, mémé f.

grandmother ['græn,mʌðər] n grand-mère f.

grandpa ['grænpɑː] n inf papi m, pépé m.

grandparents ['græn,peərənts] npl grands-parents mpl.

grand piano n piano m à queue.

grand slam n (SPORT) grand chelem m.

grandson ['grænsʌn] n petit-fils m.

grandstand ['grændstænd] n tribune f.

grand total n somme f globale, total m général.

granite ['grænɪt] n granit m.

granny ['grænɪ] n inf mamie f, mémé f.

grant [grɑːnt] ◆ n subvention f; (for study) bourse f. ◆ vt 1. (wish, appeal) accorder; (request) accéder à. 2. (admit) admettre, reconnaître. 3. (give) accorder; **to take sb for ~ed** (not appreciate sb's help) penser que tout ce que qqn fait va de soi; (not value sb's presence) penser que qqn fait partie des meubles; **to take sthg for ~ed** (result, sb's agreement) considérer qqch comme acquis.

granulated sugar ['grænjʊleɪtɪd-] n sucre m cristallisé.

granule ['grænjuːl] n granule m; (of sugar) grain m.

grape [greɪp] n (grain m de) raisin m; **a bunch of ~s** une grappe de raisin.

grapefruit ['greɪpfruːt] (pl inv OR -s) n pamplemousse m.

grapevine ['greɪpvaɪn] n vigne f; **on the ~** fig par le téléphone arabe.

graph [grɑːf] n graphique m.

graphic ['græfɪk] adj 1. (vivid) vivant(e). 2. (ART) graphique. ▶ **graphics** npl graphique f.

graphic design n graphisme m.

graphic designer n graphiste mf.

graphite ['græfaɪt] n (U) graphite m, mine f de plomb.

graph paper n (U) papier m millimétré.

grapple ['græpl] ▶ **grapple with** vt fus 1. (person, animal) lutter avec. 2. (problem) se débattre avec, se colleter avec.

grasp [grɑːsp] ◆ n 1. (grip) prise f. 2. (understanding) compréhension f; **to have a good ~ of sthg** avoir une bonne connaissance de qqch. ◆ vt 1. (grip, seize) saisir, empoigner. 2. (understand) saisir, comprendre. 3. (opportunity) saisir.

grasping ['grɑːspɪŋ] adj pej avide, cupide.

grass [grɑːs] ◆ n (BOT & drugs sl) herbe f. ◆ vi Br crime sl moucharder; **to ~ on sb** dénoncer qqn.

grasshopper ['grɑːs,hɒpər] n sauterelle f.

grass roots ◆ npl fig base f. ◆ comp du peuple.

grass snake n couleuvre f.

grate [greɪt] ◆ n grille f de foyer. ◆ vt râper. ◆ vi grincer, crisser.

grateful ['greɪtfʊl] adj: **to be ~ to sb (for sthg)** être reconnaissant(e) à qqn (de qqch).

grater ['greɪtər] n râpe f.

gratify ['grætɪfaɪ] vt 1. (please - person): **to be gratified** être content(e), être satisfait(e). 2. (satisfy - wish) satisfaire, assouvir.

grating ['greɪtɪŋ] ◆ adj grinçant(e); (voix) de crécelle. ◆ n (grille) grille f.

gratitude ['grætɪtjuːd] n (U): ~ (to sb for sthg) gratitude f OR reconnaissance f (envers qqn de qqch).

gratuitous [grə'tjuːɪtəs] adj fml gratuit(e).

grave¹ [greɪv] ◆ adj grave; (concern) sérieux(euse). ◆ n tombe f.

grave² [graːv] adj (LING): e ~ e m accent grave.

gravel ['grævl] n (U) gravier m.

gravestone ['greɪvstəun] n pierre f tombale.

graveyard ['greɪvjaːd] n cimetière m.

gravity ['grævətɪ] n 1. (force) gravité f, pesanteur f. 2. (seriousness) gravité f.

gravy ['greɪvɪ] n (U) (meat juice) jus m de viande.

gray Am = **grey.**

graze [greɪz] ◆ vt 1. (subj: cows, sheep) brouter, paître. 2. (subj: farmer) faire paître. 3. (skin) écorcher, égratigner. 4. (touch lightly) frôler, effleurer. ◆ vi brouter, paître. ◆ n écorchure f, égratignure f.

grease [griːs] ◆ n graisse f. ◆ vt graisser.

greaseproof paper [ˌgriːspruːf-] n (U) Br papier m sulfurisé.

greasy ['griːzɪ] adj 1. (covered in grease) graisseux(euse); (clothes) taché(e) de graisse. 2. (food, skin, hair) gras (grasse).

great [greɪt] adj 1. (gen) grand(e); ~ big énorme. 2. inf (splendid) génial(e), formidable; **to feel** ~ se sentir en pleine forme; ~! super!, génial!

Great Britain n Grande-Bretagne f; in ~ en Grande-Bretagne.

greatcoat ['greɪtkəut] n pardessus m.

Great Dane n danois m.

great-grandchild n (boy) arrière-petit-fils m; (girl) arrière-petite-fille f. ► **great-grandchildren** npl arrière-petits-enfants mpl.

great-grandfather n arrière-grand-père m.

great-grandmother n arrière-grand-mère f.

greatly ['greɪtlɪ] adv beaucoup; (different) très.

greatness ['greɪtnɪs] n grandeur f.

Greece [griːs] n Grèce f.

greed [griːd] n (U) 1. (for food) gloutonnerie f. 2. fig (for money, power): ~ (for) avidité f (de).

greedy ['griːdɪ] adj 1. (for food) glouton

(onne). 2. (for money, power): ~ for sthg avide de qqch.

Greek [griːk] ◆ adj grec (grecque). ◆ n 1. (person) Grec m, Grecque f. 2. (language) grec m.

green [griːn] ◆ adj 1. (in colour, unripe) vert(e). 2. (ecological - issue, politics) écologique; (- person) vert(e). 3. inf (inexperienced) inexpérimenté(e), jeune. ◆ n 1. (colour) vert m. 2. (GOLF) green m. 3. **village** ~ pelouse f communale. ► **Green** n (POL) vert m, -e f, écologiste mf; **the Greens** les Verts, les Écologistes. ► **greens** npl (vegetables) légumes mpl verts.

green belt n Br ceinture f verte.

green card n 1. Br (for vehicle) carte f verte. 2. Am (residence permit) carte f de séjour.

greenery ['griːnərɪ] n verdure f.

greenfly ['griːnflaɪ] (pl inv OR -ies) n puceron m.

greengage ['griːngeɪdʒ] n reine-claude f.

greengrocer ['griːnˌgrəusəʳ] n marchand m, -e f de légumes; ~'s (shop) magasin m de fruits et légumes.

greenhouse ['griːnhaus, pl -hauzɪz] n serre f.

greenhouse effect n: **the** ~ l'effet m de serre.

Greenland ['griːnlənd] n Groenland m.

green salad n salade f verte.

greet [griːt] vt 1. (say hello to) saluer. 2. (receive) accueillir.

greeting ['griːtɪŋ] n salutation f, salut m. ► **greetings** npl: **Christmas/birthday** ~s vœux mpl de Noël/d'anniversaire.

greetings card Br, **greeting card** Am n carte f de vœux.

grenade [grə'neɪd] n: (hand) ~ grenade f (à main).

grew [gruː] pt → **grow.**

grey Br, **gray** Am [greɪ] ◆ adj 1. (in colour) gris(e). 2. (grey-haired): **to go** ~ grisonner. 3. (dull, gloomy) morne, triste. ◆ n gris m.

grey-haired [-'head] adj aux cheveux gris.

greyhound ['greɪhaund] n lévrier m.

grid [grɪd] n 1. (grating) grille f. 2. (system of squares) quadrillage m.

griddle ['grɪdl] n plaque f à cuire.

gridlock ['grɪdlɒk] n Am embouteillage m.

grief [griːf] n (U) 1. (sorrow) chagrin m, peine f. 2. inf (trouble) ennuis mpl. 3. phr: **to come to** ~ (person) avoir de gros problèmes; (*project*) échouer, tomber à l'eau; **good ~!** Dieu du ciel!, mon Dieu!

grievance ['griːvns] *n* grief *m*, doléance *f*.

grieve [griːv] *vi* (*at death*) être en deuil; **to ~ for sb/sthg** pleurer qqn/qqch.

grievous ['griːvəs] *adj fml* grave; (*shock*) cruel(elle).

grievous bodily harm *n* (U) coups *mpl* et blessures *fpl*.

grill [gril] ◆ *n* (*on cooker, fire*) gril *m*. ◆ *vt* 1. (*cook on grill*) griller, faire griller. 2. *inf* (*interrogate*) cuisiner.

grille [gril] *n* grille *f*.

grim [grim] *adj* 1. (*stern - face, expression*) sévère; (- *determination*) inflexible. 2. (*cheerless - truth, news*) sinistre; (- *room, walls*) lugubre; (- *day*) morne, triste.

grimace [grɪ'meɪs] ◆ *n* grimace *f*. ◆ *vi* grimacer, faire la grimace.

grime [graɪm] *n* (U) crasse *f*, saleté *f*.

grimy ['graɪmɪ] *adj* sale, encrassé(e).

grin [grin] ◆ *n* (*large*) sourire *m*. ◆ *vi*: **to ~ (at sb/sthg)** adresser un large sourire (à qqn/qqch).

grind [graɪnd] (*pt & pp* **ground**) ◆ *vt* (*crush*) moudre. ◆ *vi* (*scrape*) grincer. ◆ *n* (*hard, boring work*) corvée *f*. ▶ **grind down** *vt sep* (*oppress*) opprimer. ▶ **grind up** *vt sep* pulvériser.

grinder ['graɪndəʳ] *n* moulin *m*.

grip [grip] ◆ *n* 1. (*grasp, hold*) prise *f*. 2. (*control*) contrôle *m*; **he's got a good ~ on the situation** il a la situation bien en main; **to get to ~s with sthg** s'attaquer à qqch; **to get a ~ on o.s.** se ressaisir. 3. (*adhesion*) adhérence *f*. 4. (*handle*) poignée *f*. 5. (*bag*) sac *m* (de voyage). ◆ *vt* 1. (*grasp*) saisir; (*subj: tyres*) adhérer à. 2. *fig* (*imagination, country*) captiver.

gripe [graɪp] *inf* ◆ *n* (*complaint*) plainte *f*. ◆ *vi*: **to ~ (about sthg)** râler OR rouspéter (contre qqch).

gripping ['grɪpɪŋ] *adj* passionnant(e).

grisly ['grɪzlɪ] *adj* (*horrible, macabre*) macabre.

gristle ['grɪsl] *n* (U) nerfs *mpl*.

grit [grit] ◆ *n* (U) 1. (*stones*) gravillon *m*; (*in eye*) poussière *f*. 2. *inf* (*courage*) cran *m*. ◆ *vt* sabler.

gritty ['grɪtɪ] *adj* 1. (*stony*) couvert(e) de gravillon. 2. *inf* (*brave - person*) qui a du cran; (- *performance, determination*) courageux(euse).

groan [grəʊn] ◆ *n* gémissement *m*. ◆ *vi* 1. (*moan*) gémir. 2. (*creak*) grincer, gémir.

grocer ['grəʊsəʳ] *n* épicier *m*, -ère *f*; **~'s**

(*shop*) épicerie *f*.

groceries ['grəʊsəriz] *npl* (*foods*) provisions *fpl*.

grocery ['grəʊsəri] *n* (*shop*) épicerie *f*.

groggy ['grɒgɪ] *adj* groggy (*inv*).

groin [grɔɪn] *n* aine *f*.

groom [gruːm] ◆ *n* 1. (*of horses*) palefrenier *m*, garçon *m* d'écurie. 2. (*bridegroom*) marié *m*. ◆ *vt* 1. (*brush*) panser. 2. *fig* (*prepare*): **to ~ sb (for sthg)** préparer OR former qqn (pour qqch).

groove [gruːv] *n* (*in metal, wood*) rainure *f*; (*in record*) sillon *m*.

grope [grəʊp] *vi*: **to ~ (about) for sthg** chercher qqch à tâtons.

gross [grəʊs] (*pl inv* OR **-es**) ◆ *adj* 1. (*total*) brut(e). 2. *fml* (*serious - negligence*) coupable; (- *misconduct*) choquant(e); (- *inequality*) flagrant(e). 3. (*coarse, vulgar*) grossier(ère). 4. *inf* (*obese*) obèse, énorme. ◆ *n* grosse *f*, douze douzaines *fpl*.

grossly ['grəʊslɪ] *adv* (*seriously*) extrêmement, énormément.

grotesque [grəʊ'tesk] *adj* grotesque.

grotto ['grɒtəʊ] (*pl* **-es** OR **-s**) *n* grotte *f*.

grotty ['grɒtɪ] *adj Br inf* minable.

ground [graʊnd] ◆ *pt & pp* → **grind**. ◆ *n* 1. (U) (*surface of earth*) sol *m*, terre *f*; **above ~** en surface; **below ~** sous terre; **on the ~** par terre, au sol. 2. (U) (*area of land*) terrain *m*. 3. (*for sport etc*) terrain *m*. 4. (*advantage*): **to gain/lose ~** gagner/perdre du terrain. ◆ *vt* 1. (*base*): **to be ~ed on** OR **in sthg** être fondé(e) sur qqch. 2. (*aircraft, pilot*) interdire de vol. 3. *inf* (*child*) priver de sortie. 4. Am (ELEC): **to be ~ed** être à la masse. ▶ **grounds** *npl* 1. (*reason*) motif *m*, raison *f*; **~s for sthg** motifs de qqch; **~s for doing sthg** raisons de faire qqch. 2. (*land round building*) parc *m*. 3. (*of coffee*) marc *m*.

ground crew *n* personnel *m* au sol.

ground floor *n* rez-de-chaussée *m inv*.

grounding ['graʊndɪŋ] *n*: **~ (in)** connaissances *fpl* de base (en).

groundless ['graʊndlɪs] *adj* sans fondement.

groundsheet ['graʊndʃiːt] *n* tapis *m* de sol.

ground staff *n* 1. (*at sports ground*) personnel *m* d'entretien (*d'un terrain de sport*). 2. Br = **ground crew**.

groundswell ['graʊndswel] *n* vague *f* de fond.

groundwork ['graʊndwɜːk] *n* (U) travail *m* préparatoire.

group [gru:p] ◆ n groupe m. ◆ vt grouper, réunir. ◆ vi: **to ~ (together)** se grouper.

groupie ['gru:pɪ] n inf groupie f.

grouse [graus] (pl inv OR -s) ◆ n (bird) grouse f, coq m de bruyère. ◆ vi inf râler, rouspéter.

grove [grəʊv] n (group of trees) bosquet m.

grovel ['grɒvl] vi: **to ~ (to sb)** ramper (devant qqn).

grow [grəʊ] (pt grew, pp grown) ◆ vi 1. (gen) pousser; (person, animal) grandir; (company, city) s'agrandir; (fears, influence, traffic) augmenter, s'accroître; (problem, idea, plan) prendre de l'ampleur; (economy) se développer. 2. (become) devenir; **to ~ old** vieillir; **to ~ tired of sthg** se fatiguer de qqch. ◆ vt 1. (plants) faire pousser. 2. (hair, beard) laisser pousser. ▶ **grow on** vt fus inf plaire de plus en plus à; **it'll ~ on you** cela finira par te plaire. ▶ **grow out of** vt fus 1. (clothes, shoes) devenir trop grand pour. 2. (habit) perdre. ▶ **grow up** vi 1. (become adult) grandir, devenir adulte; **~ up!** ne fais pas l'enfant! 2. (develop) se développer.

grower ['grəʊəʳ] n cultivateur m, -trice f.

growl [graʊl] vi (animal) grogner, gronder; (engine) vrombir, gronder; (person) grogner.

grown [grəʊn] ◆ pp → **grow**. ◆ adj adulte.

grown-up ◆ adj 1. (fully grown) adulte, grand(e). 2. (mature) mûr(e). ◆ n adulte mf, grande personne f.

growth [grəʊθ] n 1. (increase - gen) croissance f; (- of opposition, company) développement m; (- of population) augmentation f, accroissement m. 2. (MED) (lump) tumeur f, excroissance f.

grub [grʌb] n 1. (insect) larve f. 2. inf (food) bouffe f.

grubby ['grʌbɪ] adj sale, malpropre.

grudge [grʌdʒ] ◆ n rancune f; **to bear sb a ~, to bear a ~ against sb** garder rancune à qqn. ◆ vt: **to ~ sb sthg** donner qqch à qqn à contrecœur; (success) en vouloir à qqn à cause de qqch.

gruelling Br, **grueling** Am ['grʊəlɪŋ] adj épuisant(e), exténuant(e).

gruesome ['gru:səm] adj horrible.

gruff [grʌf] adj 1. (hoarse) gros (grosse). 2. (rough, unfriendly) brusque, bourru(e).

grumble ['grʌmbl] vi 1. (complain): **to ~ about sthg** rouspéter OR grommeler

contre qqch. 2. (rumble - thunder, train) gronder; (- stomach) gargouiller.

grumpy ['grʌmpɪ] adj inf renfrogné(e).

grunt [grʌnt] ◆ n grognement m. ◆ vi grogner.

G-string n cache-sexe m inv.

guarantee [,gærən'ti:] ◆ n garantie f. ◆ vt garantir.

guard [gɑ:d] ◆ n 1. (person) garde m; (in prison) gardien m. 2. (group of guards) garde f. 3. (defensive operation) garde f; **to be on ~** être de garde OR de faction; **to catch sb off ~** prendre qqn au dépourvu. 4. Br (RAIL) chef m de train. 5. (protective device - for body) protection f; (- for fire) garde-feu m inv. ◆ vt 1. (protect - building) protéger, garder; (- person) protéger. 2. (prisoner) garder, surveiller. 3. (hide - secret) garder.

guard dog n chien m de garde.

guarded ['gɑ:dɪd] adj prudent(e).

guardian ['gɑ:djən] n 1. (of child) tuteur m, -trice f. 2. (protector) gardien m, -enne f, protecteur m, -trice f.

guardrail ['gɑ:dreɪl] n Am (on road) barrière f de sécurité.

guard's van n Br wagon m du chef de train.

guerilla [gə'rɪlə] = **guerrilla**.

Guernsey ['gɜ:nzɪ] n (place) Guernesey f.

guerrilla [gə'rɪlə] n guérillero m; **urban ~** guérillero m des villes.

guerrilla warfare n (U) guérilla f.

guess [ges] ◆ n conjecture f. ◆ vt deviner; **~ what?** tu sais quoi? ◆ vi 1. (conjecture) deviner; **to ~ at sthg** deviner qqch. 2. (suppose): **I ~ (so)** je suppose (que oui).

guesswork ['geswɜ:k] n (U) conjectures fpl, hypothèses fpl.

guest [gest] n 1. (gen) invité m, -e f. 2. (at hotel) client m, -e f.

guesthouse ['gesthaʊs, pl -haʊzɪz] n pension f de famille.

guestroom ['gestrʊm] n chambre f d'amis.

guffaw [gʌ'fɔ:] ◆ n gros rire m. ◆ vi rire bruyamment.

guidance ['gaɪdəns] n (U) 1. (help) conseils mpl. 2. (leadership) direction f.

guide [gaɪd] ◆ n 1. (person, book) guide m. 2. (indication) indication f. ◆ vt 1. (show by leading) guider. 2. (control) diriger. 3. (influence): **to be ~d by sb/sthg** se laisser guider par qqn/qqch. ▶ **Guide** n = **Girl Guide**.

guide book n guide m.

guide dog n chien m d'aveugle.

guidelines ['gaɪdlaɪnz] npl directives fpl, lignes fpl directrices.

guild [gɪld] n 1. (HISTORY) corporation f, guilde f. 2. (association) association f.

guile [gaɪl] n (U) literary ruse f, astuce f.

guillotine ['gɪlə,tiːn] ♦ n 1. (for executions) guillotine f. 2. (for paper) massicot m. ♦ vt (execute) guillotiner.

guilt [gɪlt] n culpabilité f.

guilty ['gɪltɪ] adj coupable; **to be ~ of sthg** être coupable de qqch; **to be found ~/not ~** (JUR) être reconnu coupable/non coupable.

guinea pig ['gɪnɪ-] n cobaye m.

guise [gaɪz] n fml apparence f.

guitar [gɪ'tɑːr] n guitare f.

guitarist [gɪ'tɑːrɪst] n guitariste mf.

gulf [gʌlf] n 1. (sea) golfe m. 2. (breach, chasm): ~ (between) abîme m (entre). ► **Gulf** n: **the Gulf** le Golfe.

gull [gʌl] n mouette f.

gullet ['gʌlɪt] n œsophage m; (of bird) gosier m.

gullible ['gʌləbl] adj crédule.

gully ['gʌlɪ] n 1. (valley) ravine f. 2. (ditch) rigole f.

gulp [gʌlp] ♦ n (of drink) grande gorgée f; (of food) grosse bouchée f. ♦ vt avaler. ♦ vi avoir la gorge nouée. ► **gulp down** vt sep avaler.

gum [gʌm] ♦ n 1. (chewing gum) chewing-gum m. 2. (adhesive) colle f, gomme f. 3. (ANAT) gencive f. ♦ vt coller.

gumboots ['gʌmbuːts] npl Br bottes fpl de caoutchouc.

gun [gʌn] n 1. (weapon - small) revolver m; (- rifle) fusil m; (- large) canon m. 2. (starting pistol) pistolet m. 3. (tool) pistolet m; (for staples) agrafeuse f. ► **gun down** vt sep abattre.

gunboat ['gʌnbəʊt] n canonnière f.

gunfire ['gʌnfaɪər] n (U) coups mpl de feu.

gunman ['gʌnmən] (pl -men [-mən]) n personne f armée.

gunpoint ['gʌnpɔɪnt] n: **at ~** sous la menace d'un fusil OR pistolet.

gunpowder ['gʌn,paʊdər] n poudre f à canon.

gunshot ['gʌnʃɒt] n (firing of gun) coup m de feu.

gunsmith ['gʌnsmɪθ] n armurier m.

gurgle ['gɜːgl] vi 1. (water) glouglouter. 2. (baby) gazouiller.

guru ['gʊruː] n gourou m, guru m.

gush [gʌʃ] ♦ n jaillissement m. ♦ vi 1. (flow out) jaillir. 2. pej (enthuse) s'exprimer de façon exubérante.

gusset ['gʌsɪt] n gousset m.

gust [gʌst] n rafale f, coup m de vent.

gusto ['gʌstəʊ] n: **with ~** avec enthousiasme.

gut [gʌt] ♦ n (MED) intestin m. ♦ vt 1. (remove organs from) vider. 2. (destroy) éventrer. ► **guts** npl inf 1. (intestines) intestins mpl; **to hate sb's ~s** ne pas pouvoir piffer qqn. 2. (courage) cran m.

gutter ['gʌtər] n 1. (ditch) rigole f. 2. (on roof) gouttière f.

gutter press n presse f à sensation.

guy [gaɪ] n 1. inf (man) type m. 2. (person) copain m, copine f. 3. Br (dummy) effigie de Guy Fawkes.

Guy Fawkes' Night [-'fɔːks-] n fête célébrée le 5 novembre pendant laquelle sont tirés des feux d'artifice et allumés des feux de joie.

guy rope n corde f de tente.

guzzle ['gʌzl] ♦ vt bâfrer; (drink) lamper. ♦ vi s'empiffrer.

gym [dʒɪm] n inf 1. (gymnasium) gymnase m. 2. (exercises) gym f.

gymnasium [dʒɪm'neɪzjəm] (pl -iums OR -ia [-jə]) n gymnase m.

gymnast ['dʒɪmnæst] n gymnaste mf.

gymnastics [dʒɪm'næstɪks] n (U) gymnastique f.

gym shoes npl (chaussures fpl de) tennis mpl.

gymslip ['dʒɪm,slɪp] n Br tunique f.

gynaecologist Br, **gynecologist** Am [,gaɪnə'kɒlədʒɪst] n gynécologue mf.

gynaecology Br, **gynecology** Am [,gaɪnə'kɒlədʒɪ] n gynécologie f.

gypsy ['dʒɪpsɪ] = gipsy.

gyrate [dʒaɪ'reɪt] vi tournoyer.

H

h (pl h's OR hs), **H** (pl H's OR Hs) [eɪtʃ] n (letter) h m inv, H m inv.

haberdashery ['hæbədæʃərɪ] n mercerie f.

habit ['hæbɪt] n 1. (customary practice) habitude f; **out of ~** par habitude; **to make a ~ of doing sthg** avoir l'habitude de faire qqch. 2. (garment) habit m.

habitat ['hæbɪtæt] n habitat m.

habitual [hə'bɪtʃʊəl] *adj* 1. (*usual, characteristic*) habituel(elle). 2. (*regular*) invétéré(e).

hack [hæk] ◆ *n* (*writer*) écrivailleur *m*, -euse *f*. ◆ *vt* (*cut*) tailler. ▶ **hack into** *vt fus* (COMPUT) pirater.

hacker ['hækər] *n*: (**computer**) ~ pirate *m* informatique.

hackneyed ['hæknɪd] *adj* rebattu(e).

hacksaw ['hæksɔː] *n* scie *f* à métaux.

had [*weak form* həd, *strong form* hæd] *pt & pp* → **have**.

haddock ['hædək] (*pl inv*) *n* églefin *m*, aiglefin *m*.

hadn't ['hædnt] = **had not**.

haemophiliac [ˌhiːməˈfɪlɪæk] = **hemophiliac**.

haemorrhage ['hemərɪdʒ] = **hemorrhage**.

haemorrhoids ['heməroɪdz] = **hemorrhoids**.

haggard ['hægəd] *adj* (*face*) défait(e); (*person*) abattu(e).

haggis ['hægɪs] *n* plat typique écossais fait d'une panse de brebis farcie, le plus souvent servie avec des navets et des pommes de terre.

haggle ['hægl] *vi* marchander; **to ~ over** OR **about sthg** marchander qqch.

Hague [heɪg] *n*: **The ~** La Haye.

hail [heɪl] ◆ *n* grêle *f*; *fig* pluie *f*. ◆ *vt* 1. (*call*) héler. 2. (*acclaim*): **to ~ sb/sthg as sthg** acclamer qqn/qqch comme qqch. ◆ *v impers* grêler.

hailstone ['heɪlstəʊn] *n* grêlon *m*.

hair [heər] *n* 1. (U) (*on human head*) cheveux *mpl*; **to do one's ~** se coiffer. 2. (U) (*on animal, human skin*) poils *mpl*. 3. (*individual hair – on head*) cheveu *m*; (*– on skin*) poil *m*.

hairbrush ['heəbrʌʃ] *n* brosse *f* à cheveux.

haircut ['heəkʌt] *n* coupe *f* de cheveux.

hairdo ['heəduː] (*pl* -s) *n inf* coiffure *f*.

hairdresser ['heəˌdresər] *n* coiffeur *m*, -euse *f*; ~**'s** (*salon*) salon *m* de coiffure.

hairdryer ['heəˌdraɪər] *n* (*handheld*) sèche-cheveux *m inv*; (*with hood*) casque *m*.

hair gel *n* gel *m* coiffant.

hairgrip ['heəgrɪp] *n* Br pince *f* à cheveux.

hairpin ['heəpɪn] *n* épingle *f* à cheveux.

hairpin bend *n* virage *m* en épingle à cheveux.

hair-raising [-ˌreɪzɪŋ] *adj* à faire dresser les cheveux sur la tête; (*jour-*

ney) effrayant(e).

hair remover [-rɪˌmuːvər] *n* (crème *f*) dépilatoire *m*.

hair slide *n* Br barrette *f*.

hairspray ['heəspreɪ] *n* laque *f*.

hairstyle ['heəstaɪl] *n* coiffure *f*.

hairy ['heərɪ] *adj* 1. (*covered in hair*) velu(e), poilu(e). 2. *inf* (*frightening*) à faire dresser les cheveux sur la tête.

Haiti ['heɪtɪ] *n* Haïti.

hake [heɪk] (*pl inv* OR -s) *n* colin *m*, merluche *f*.

half [Br hɑːf, Am hæf] (*pl senses 1 and 2* **halves**, *pl senses 3, 4 and 5* **halves** OR **halfs**) ◆ *adj* demi(e); ~ **a dozen** une demi-douzaine; ~ **an hour** une demi-heure; ~ **a pound** une demi-livre; ~ **English** à moitié anglais. ◆ *adv* 1. (*gen*) à moitié; ~**-and-**~ moitié-moitié. 2. (*by half*) de moitié. 3. (*in telling the time*): ~ **past ten** Br, ~ **after ten** Am dix heures et demie; **it's ~ past** il est la demie. ◆ *n* 1. (*gen*) moitié *f*; **in ~** en deux; **to go halves (with sb)** partager (avec qqn). 2. (SPORT) (*of match*) mi-temps *f*. 3. (SPORT) (*halfback*) demi *m*. 4. (*of beer*) demi *m*. 5. (*child's ticket*) demi-tarif *m*, tarif *m* enfant. ◆ *pron* la moitié; ~ **of them** la moitié d'entre eux.

halfback ['hɑːfbæk] *n* demi *m*.

half board *n* demi-pension *f*.

half-breed ◆ *adj* métis(isse). ◆ *n* métis *m*, -isse *f* (*attention: le terme 'half-breed' est considéré raciste*).

half-caste [-kɑːst] ◆ *adj* métis(isse). ◆ *n* métis *m*, -isse *f* (*attention: le terme 'half-caste' est considéré raciste*).

half-hearted [-'hɑːtɪd] *adj* sans enthousiasme.

half hour *n* demi-heure *f*.

half-mast *n*: **at ~** (*flag*) en berne.

half moon *n* demi-lune *f*.

half note *n* Am (MUS) blanche *f*.

halfpenny ['heɪpnɪ] (*pl* -**pennies** OR -**pence**) *n* demi-penny *m*.

half-price *adj* à moitié prix.

half term *n* Br congé *m* de mi-trimestre.

half time *n* (U) mi-temps *f*.

halfway [hɑːf'weɪ] ◆ *adj* à mi-chemin. ◆ *adv* 1. (*in space*) à mi-chemin. 2. (*in time*) à la moitié.

halibut ['hælɪbət] (*pl inv* OR -s) *n* flétan *m*.

hall [hɔːl] *n* 1. (*in house*) vestibule *m*, entrée *f*. 2. (*meeting room, building*) salle *f*. 3. (*country house*) manoir *m*.

hallmark ['hɔːlmɑːk] *n* 1. (*typical fea-*

ture) marque *f*. **2.** (*on metal*) poinçon *m*.

hallo [hə'ləʊ] = **hello**.

hall of residence (*pl* **halls of residence**) *n* Br (UNIV) résidence *f* universitaire.

Hallowe'en [,hæləʊ'iːn] *n* Halloween *f* (*fête des sorcières et des fantômes*).

hallucinate [hə'luːsɪneɪt] *vi* avoir des hallucinations.

hallway ['hɔːlweɪ] *n* vestibule *m*.

halo ['heɪləʊ] (*pl* -**es** OR -**s**) *n* nimbe *m*; (ASTRON) halo *m*.

halt [hɔːlt] ◆ *n* (*stop*): **to come to a ~** (*vehicle*) s'arrêter, s'immobiliser; (*activity*) s'interrompre; **to call a ~ to** sthg mettre fin à qqch. ◆ *vt* arrêter. ◆ *vi* s'arrêter.

halterneck ['hɔːltənek] *adj* dos nu (*inv*).

halve [Br hɑːv, Am hæv] *vt* **1.** (*reduce by half*) réduire de moitié. **2.** (*divide*) couper en deux.

halves [Br hɑːvz, Am hævz] *pl* → **half**.

ham [hæm] ◆ *n* (*meat*) jambon *m*. ◆ *comp* au jambon.

hamburger ['hæmbɜːgəʳ] *n* (*burger*) hamburger *m*.

hamlet ['hæmlɪt] *n* hameau *m*.

hammer ['hæməʳ] ◆ *n* marteau *m*. ◆ *vt* **1.** (*with tool*) marteler; (*nail*) enfoncer à coups de marteau. **2.** (*with fist*) marteler du poing. **3.** *fig*: **to ~ sthg into sb** faire entrer qqch dans la tête de qqn. **4.** *inf* (*defeat*) battre à plates coutures. ◆ *vi* (*with fist*): **to ~ (on)** cogner du poing (à). ▶ **hammer out** *vt fus* (*agreement, solution*) parvenir finalement à.

hammock ['hæmək] *n* hamac *m*.

hamper ['hæmpəʳ] ◆ *n* **1.** (*for food*) panier *m* d'osier. **2.** Am (*for laundry*) coffre *m* à linge. ◆ *vt* gêner.

hamster ['hæmstəʳ] *n* hamster *m*.

hamstring ['hæmstrɪŋ] *n* tendon *m* du jarret.

hand [hænd] ◆ *n* **1.** (*part of body*) main *f*; **to hold ~s** se tenir la main; **by ~** à la main; **to get** OR **lay one's ~s on** mettre la main sur; **to get out of ~** échapper à tout contrôle; **to have one's ~s full** avoir du pain sur la planche; **to try one's ~ at** sthg s'essayer à qqch. **2.** (*help*) coup *m* de main; **to give** OR **lend sb a ~ (with** sthg) donner un coup de main à qqn (pour faire qqch). **3.** (*worker*) ouvrier *m*, -ère *f*. **4.** (*of clock, watch*) aiguille *f*. **5.** (*handwriting*) écriture *f*. **6.** (*of cards*) jeu *m*, main *f*. ◆ *vt*: **to ~ sthg to sb, to ~ sb sthg** passer qqch à qqn. ▶ **(close) at hand**

adv proche. ▶ **on hand** *adv* disponible. ▶ **on the other hand** *conj* d'autre part. ▶ **out of hand** *adv* (*completely*) d'emblée. ▶ **to hand** *adv* à portée de la main, sous la main. ▶ **hand down** *vt sep* transmettre. ▶ **hand in** *vt sep* remettre. ▶ **hand out** *vt sep* distribuer. ▶ **hand over** *vt sep* **1.** (*baton, money*) remettre. **2.** (*responsibility, power*) transmettre. ◆ *vi*: **to ~ over (to)** passer le relais (à).

handbag ['hændbæg] *n* sac *m* à main.

handball ['hændbɔːl] *n* (*game*) handball *m*.

handbook ['hændbʊk] *n* manuel *m*; (*for tourist*) guide *m*.

handbrake ['hændbreɪk] *n* frein *m* à main.

handcuffs ['hændkʌfs] *npl* menottes *fpl*.

handful ['hændfʊl] *n* (*of sand, grass, people*) poignée *f*.

handgun ['hændgʌn] *n* revolver *m*, pistolet *m*.

handicap ['hændɪkæp] ◆ *n* handicap *m*. ◆ *vt* handicaper; (*progress, work*) entraver.

handicapped ['hændɪkæpt] ◆ *adj* handicapé(e). ◆ *npl*: **the ~** les handicapés *mpl*.

handicraft ['hændɪkrɑːft] *n* activité *f* artisanale.

handiwork ['hændɪwɜːk] *n* (U) ouvrage *m*.

handkerchief ['hæŋkətʃɪf] (*pl* -**chiefs** OR -**chieves** [-tʃiːvz]) *n* mouchoir *m*.

handle ['hændl] ◆ *n* (*of jug, cup*) anse *f*; (*of knife, pan*) manche *m*. ◆ *vt* **1.** (*with hands*) manipuler; (*without permission*) toucher à. **2.** (*deal with, be responsible for*) s'occuper de; (*difficult situation*) faire face à. **3.** (*treat*) traiter, s'y prendre avec.

handlebars ['hændlbɑːz] *npl* guidon *m*.

handler ['hændləʳ] *n* **1.** (*of dog*) maître-chien *m*. **2.** (*at airport*): **(baggage) ~** bagagiste *m*.

hand luggage *n* (U) Br bagages *mpl* à main.

handmade [,hænd'meɪd] *adj* fait(e) (à la) main.

handout ['hændaʊt] *n* **1.** (*gift*) don *m*. **2.** (*leaflet*) prospectus *m*.

handrail ['hændreɪl] *n* rampe *f*.

handset ['hændset] *n* combiné *m*.

handshake ['hændʃeɪk] *n* serrement *m* OR poignée *f* de main.

handsome ['hænsəm] *adj* **1.** (*good-looking*) beau (belle). **2.** (*reward, profit*) beau (belle); (*gift*) généreux(euse).

handstand ['hændstænd] *n* équilibre *m* (*sur les mains*).

handwriting ['hænd,raɪtɪŋ] *n* écriture *f*.

handy ['hændɪ] *adj inf* **1.** (*useful*) pratique; **to come in ~** être utile. **2.** (*skilful*) adroit(e). **3.** (*near*) tout près, à deux pas.

handyman ['hændɪmæn] (*pl* **-men** [-men]) *n* bricoleur *m*.

hang [hæŋ] (*pt & pp sense* 1 **hung**, *pt & pp sense* 2 **hung** OR **hanged**) ◆ *vt* **1.** (*fasten*) suspendre. **2.** (*execute*) pendre. ◆ *vi* **1.** (*be fastened*) pendre, être accroché(e). **2.** (*be executed*) être pendu(e). ◆ *n*: **to get the ~ of sthg** *inf* saisir le truc OR attraper le coup pour faire qqch. ▶ **hang about, hang around** *vi* traîner. ▶ **hang on** *vi* **1.** (*keep hold*): **to ~ on (to)** s'accrocher OR se cramponner (à). **2.** *inf* (*continue waiting*) attendre. **3.** (*persevere*) tenir bon. ▶ **hang out** *vi inf* (*spend time*) traîner. ▶ **hang round** = **hang about.** ▶ **hang up** ◆ *vt sep* pendre. ◆ *vi* (*on telephone*) raccrocher.

hangar ['hæŋə^r] *n* hangar *m*.

hanger ['hæŋə^r] *n* cintre *m*.

hanger-on (*pl* **hangers-on**) *n* parasite *m*.

hang gliding *n* deltaplane *m*, vol *m* libre.

hangover ['hæŋ,əʊvə^r] *n* (*from drinking*) gueule *f* de bois.

hang-up *n inf* complexe *m*.

hanker ['hæŋkə^r] ▶ **hanker after, hanker for** *vt fus* convoiter.

hankie, hanky ['hæŋkɪ] (*abbr of* **handkerchief**) *n inf* mouchoir *m*.

haphazard [,hæp'hæzəd] *adj* fait(e) au hasard.

happen ['hæpən] *vi* **1.** (*occur*) arriver, se passer; **to ~ to sb** arriver à qqn. **2.** (*chance*): **I just ~ed to meet him** je l'ai rencontré par hasard; **as it ~s** en fait.

happening ['hæpənɪŋ] *n* événement *m*.

happily ['hæpɪlɪ] *adv* **1.** (*with pleasure*) de bon cœur. **2.** (*contentedly*): **to be ~ doing sthg** être bien tranquillement en train de faire qqch. **3.** (*fortunately*) heureusement.

happiness ['hæpɪnɪs] *n* bonheur *m*.

happy ['hæpɪ] *adj* **1.** (*gen*) heureux (euse); **to be ~ to do sthg** être heureux de faire qqch; **~ Christmas/birthday!** joyeux Noël/anniversaire!; **~ New Year!**

bonne année! **2.** (*satisfied*) heureux (euse), content(e); **to be ~ with** OR **about sthg** être heureux de qqch.

happy-go-lucky *adj* décontracté(e).

happy medium *n* juste milieu *m*.

harangue [hə'ræŋ] ◆ *n* harangue *f*. ◆ *vt* haranguer.

harass ['hærəs] *vt* harceler.

harbour Br, **harbor** Am ['hɑ:bə^r] ◆ *n* port *m*. ◆ *vt* **1.** (*feeling*) entretenir; (*doubt, grudge*) garder. **2.** (*person*) héberger.

hard [hɑ:d] ◆ *adj* **1.** (*gen*) dur(e); **to be ~ on sb/sthg** être dur avec qqn/pour qqch. **2.** (*winter, frost*) rude. **3.** (*water*) calcaire. **4.** (*fact*) concret(ète); (*news*) sûr(e), vérifié(e). **5.** Br (POL): **~ left/right** extrême gauche/droite. ◆ *adv* **1.** (*strenuously - work*) dur; (- *listen, concentrate*) avec effort; **to try ~ (to do sthg)** faire de son mieux (pour faire qqch). **2.** (*forcefully*) fort. **3.** (*heavily - rain*) à verse; (- *snow*) dru. **4.** *phr*: **to be ~ pushed** OR **put** OR **pressed to do sthg** avoir bien de la peine à faire qqch; **to feel ~ done by** avoir l'impression d'avoir été traité injustement.

hardback ['hɑ:dbæk] ◆ *adj* relié(e). ◆ *n* livre *m* relié.

hardboard ['hɑ:dbɔ:d] *n* panneau *m* de fibres.

hard-boiled *adj* (CULIN): **~ egg** œuf *m* dur.

hard cash *n* (U) espèces *fpl*.

hard copy *n* (COMPUT) sortie *f* papier.

hard disk *n* (COMPUT) disque *m* dur.

harden ['hɑ:dn] ◆ *vt* durcir; (*steel*) tremper. ◆ *vi* **1.** (*glue, concrete*) durcir. **2.** (*attitude, opposition*) se durcir.

hard-headed [-'hedɪd] *adj* (*decision*) pragmatique; **to be ~** (*person*) avoir la tête froide.

hard-hearted [-'hɑ:tɪd] *adj* insensible, impitoyable.

hard labour *n* (U) travaux *mpl* forcés.

hard-liner *n* partisan *m* de la manière forte.

hardly ['hɑ:dlɪ] *adv* **1.** (*scarcely*) à peine, ne … guère; **~ ever/anything** presque jamais/rien; **I can ~ move/wait** je peux à peine bouger/attendre. **2.** (*only just*) à peine.

hardness ['hɑ:dnɪs] *n* **1.** (*firmness*) dureté *f*. **2.** (*difficulty*) difficulté *f*.

hardship ['hɑ:dʃɪp] *n* **1.** (U) (*difficult conditions*) épreuves *fpl*. **2.** (*difficult circumstance*) épreuve *f*.

hard shoulder *n* Br (AUT) bande *f*

d'arrêt d'urgence.

hard up adj inf fauché(e); ~ **for sthg** à court de qqch.

hardware ['hɑːdweəʳ] n (U) **1.** (tools, equipment) quincaillerie f. **2.** (COMPUT) hardware m, matériel m.

hardware shop n quincaillerie f.

hardwearing [,hɑːd'weərɪŋ] adj Br résistant(e).

hardworking [,hɑːd'wɜːkɪŋ] adj travailleur(euse).

hardy ['hɑːdɪ] adj **1.** (person, animal) vigoureux(euse), robuste. **2.** (plant) résistant(e), vivace.

hare [heəʳ] n lièvre m.

harebrained ['heə,breɪnd] adj inf (person) écervelé(e); (scheme, idea) insensé(e).

harelip [,heə'lɪp] n bec-de-lièvre m.

haricot (bean) ['hærɪkəʊ-] n haricot m blanc.

harm [hɑːm] ◆ n **1.** (injury) mal m. **2.** (damage - to clothes, plant) dommage m; (- to reputation) tort m; **to do ~ to sb, to do sb ~** faire du tort à qqn; **to do ~ to sthg, to do sthg ~** endommager qqch; **to be out of ~'s way** (person) être en sûreté OR lieu sûr; (thing) être en lieu sûr. ◆ vt **1.** (injure) faire du mal à. **2.** (damage - clothes, plant) endommager; (- reputation) faire du tort à.

harmful ['hɑːmfʊl] adj nuisible, nocif (ive).

harmless ['hɑːmlɪs] adj **1.** (not dangerous) inoffensif(ive). **2.** (inoffensive) innocent(e).

harmonica [hɑː'mɒnɪkə] n harmonica m.

harmonize, -ise ['hɑːmənaɪz] ◆ vt harmoniser. ◆ vi s'harmoniser.

harmony ['hɑːmənɪ] n harmonie f.

harness ['hɑːnɪs] ◆ n (for horse, child) harnais m. ◆ vt **1.** (horse) harnacher. **2.** (energy, resources) exploiter.

harp [hɑːp] n harpe f. ▶ **harp on** vi: **to ~ on (about sthg)** rabâcher (qqch).

harpoon [hɑː'puːn] ◆ n harpon m. ◆ vt harponner.

harpsichord ['hɑːpsɪkɔːd] n clavecin m.

harrowing ['hærəʊɪŋ] adj (experience) éprouvant(e); (report, film) déchirant(e).

harsh [hɑːʃ] adj **1.** (life, conditions) rude; (criticism, treatment) sévère. **2.** (to senses - sound) discordant(e); (- light, voice) criard(e); (- surface) rugueux (euse), rêche; (- taste) âpre.

harvest ['hɑːvɪst] ◆ n (of cereal crops)

moisson f; (of fruit) récolte f; (of grapes) vendange f, vendanges fpl. ◆ vt (cereals) moissonner; (fruit) récolter; (grapes) vendanger.

has [weak form həz, strong form hæz] → **have**.

has-been n inf pej ringard m, -e f.

hash [hæʃ] n **1.** (meat) hachis m. **2.** inf (mess): **to make a ~ of sthg** faire un beau gâchis de qqch.

hashish ['hæʃiːʃ] n haschich m.

hasn't ['hæznt] = **has not**.

hassle ['hæsl] inf ◆ n (annoyance) tracas m, embêtement m. ◆ vt tracasser.

haste [heɪst] n hâte f; **to do sthg in ~** faire qqch à la hâte; **to make ~** dated se hâter.

hasten ['heɪsn] fml ◆ vt hâter, accélérer. ◆ vi se hâter, se dépêcher; **to ~ to do sthg** s'empresser de faire qqch.

hastily ['heɪstɪlɪ] adv **1.** (quickly) à la hâte. **2.** (rashly) sans réfléchir.

hasty ['heɪstɪ] adj **1.** (quick) hâtif(ive). **2.** (rash) irréfléchi(e).

hat [hæt] n chapeau m.

hatch [hætʃ] ◆ vt **1.** (chick) faire éclore; (egg) couver. **2.** fig (scheme, plot) tramer. ◆ vi (chick, egg) éclore. ◆ n (for serving food) passe-plats m inv.

hatchback ['hætʃ,bæk] n voiture f avec hayon.

hatchet ['hætʃɪt] n hachette f.

hatchway ['hætʃ,weɪ] n passe-plats m inv, guichet m.

hate [heɪt] ◆ n (U) haine f. ◆ vt **1.** (detest) haïr. **2.** (dislike) détester; **to ~ doing sthg** avoir horreur de faire qqch.

hateful ['heɪtfʊl] adj odieux(euse).

hatred ['heɪtrɪd] n (U) haine f.

hat trick n (SPORT): **to score a ~** marquer trois buts.

haughty ['hɔːtɪ] adj hautain(e).

haul [hɔːl] ◆ n **1.** (of drugs, stolen goods) prise f, butin m. **2.** (distance): **long ~** long voyage m OR trajet m. ◆ vt (pull) traîner, tirer.

haulage ['hɔːlɪdʒ] n transport m routier, camionnage m.

haulier Br ['hɔːlɪəʳ], **hauler** Am ['hɔːlər] n entrepreneur m de transports routiers.

haunch [hɔːntʃ] n (of person) hanche f; (of animal) derrière m, arrière-train m.

haunt [hɔːnt] ◆ n repaire m. ◆ vt hanter.

have [hæv] (pt & pp **had**) ◆ aux vb (to form perfect tenses - gen) avoir; (- with many intransitive verbs) être; **to ~ eaten** avoir mangé; **to ~ left** être parti(e); **I was out of breath, having run all the way** j'étais essoufflé d'avoir couru tout le long du chemin. ◆ vt 1. (*possess, receive*): **to ~ (got)** avoir; **I ~ no money, I haven't got any money** je n'ai pas d'argent; **I've got things to do** j'ai (des choses) à faire. 2. (*experience illness*) avoir; **to ~ flu** avoir la grippe. 3. (*referring to an action, instead of another verb*): **to ~ a read** lire; **to ~ a swim** nager; **to ~ a bath/shower** prendre un bain/une douche; **to ~ a cigarette** fumer une cigarette; **to ~ a meeting** tenir une réunion. 4. (*give birth to*): **to ~ a baby** avoir un bébé. 5. (*cause to be done*): **to ~ sb do sthg** faire faire qqch à qqn; **to ~ sthg done** faire faire qqch; **to ~ one's hair cut** se faire couper les cheveux. 6. (*be treated in a certain way*): **I had my car stolen** je me suis fait voler ma voiture, on m'a volé ma voiture. 7. *inf* (*cheat*): **to be had** se faire avoir. 8. *phr*: **to ~ it in for sb** en avoir après qqn, en vouloir à qqn; **to ~ had it** (*car, machine, clothes*) avoir fait son temps. ◆ *modal vb* (*be obliged*): **to ~ (got) to do sthg** devoir faire qqch, être obligé(e) de faire qqch; **do you ~ to go?, ~ you got to go?** est-ce que tu dois partir?, est-ce que tu es obligé de partir?; **I've got to go to work** il faut que j'aille travailler. ▶ **have on** vt sep 1. (*be wearing*) porter. 2. (*tease*) faire marcher. ▶ **have out** vt sep 1. (*have removed*): **to ~ one's appendix/tonsils out** se faire opérer de l'appendicite/des amygdales. 2. (*discuss frankly*): **to ~ it out with sb** s'expliquer avec qqn.

haven ['heɪvn] n havre m.

haven't ['hævnt] = **have not**.

haversack ['hævəsæk] n sac m à dos.

havoc ['hævək] n (U) dégâts mpl; **to play ~ with** (*gen*) abîmer; (*with plans*) ruiner.

Hawaii [hə'waɪiː] n Hawaii m.

hawk [hɔːk] n faucon m.

hawker ['hɔːkər] n colporteur m.

hay [heɪ] n foin m.

hay fever n (U) rhume m des foins.

haystack ['heɪˌstæk] n meule f de foin.

haywire ['heɪˌwaɪər] adj inf: **to go ~** (*person*) perdre la tête; (*machine*) se détraquer.

hazard ['hæzəd] ◆ n hasard m. ◆ vt hasarder.

hazardous ['hæzədəs] adj hasardeux (euse).

hazard warning lights npl Br (AUT)

feux mpl de détresse.

haze [heɪz] n brume f.

hazel ['heɪzl] adj noisette (*inv*).

hazelnut ['heɪzlˌnʌt] n noisette f.

hazy ['heɪzɪ] adj 1. (*misty*) brumeux (euse). 2. (*memory, ideas*) flou(e), vague.

he [hiː] pers pron 1. (*unstressed*) il; **~'s tall** il est grand; **there ~ is** le voilà. 2. (*stressed*) lui; **HE can't do it** lui ne peut pas le faire.

head [hed] ◆ n 1. (*of person, animal*) tête f; **a** OR **per ~** par tête, par personne; **to laugh one's ~ off** rire à gorge déployée; **to be off one's ~** Br, **to be out of one's ~** Am être dingue; **to be soft in the ~** être débile; **to go to one's ~** (*alcohol, praise*) monter à la tête; **to keep one's ~** garder son sang-froid; **to lose one's ~** perdre la tête. 2. (*of table, bed, hammer*) tête f; (*of stairs, page*) haut m. 3. (*of flower*) tête f; (*of cabbage*) pomme f. 4. (*leader*) chef m; **~ of state** chef m d'État. 5. (*head teacher*) directeur m, -trice f. ◆ vt 1. (*procession, list*) être en tête de. 2. (*be in charge of*) être à la tête de. 3. (FTBL): **to ~ the ball** faire une tête. ◆ vi: **where are you ~ing?** où allez-vous? ▶ **heads** npl (*on coin*) face f; **~s or tails?** pile ou face? ▶ **head for** vt fus 1. (*place*) se diriger vers. 2. fig (*trouble, disaster*) aller au devant de.

headache ['hedeɪk] n mal m de tête; **to have a ~** avoir mal à la tête.

headband ['hedbænd] n bandeau m.

head boy n Br élève chargé de la discipline et qui siège aux conseils de son école.

headdress ['hedˌdres] n coiffe f.

header ['hedər] n (FTBL) tête f.

headfirst [ˌhed'fɜːst] adv (la) tête la première.

head girl n Br élève chargée de la discipline et qui siège aux conseils de son école.

heading ['hedɪŋ] n titre m, intitulé m.

headlamp ['hedlæmp] n Br phare m.

headland ['hedlənd] n cap m.

headlight ['hedlaɪt] n phare m.

headline ['hedlaɪn] n (*in newspaper*) gros titre m; (TV & RADIO) grand titre m.

headlong ['hedlɒŋ] adv 1. (*quickly*) à toute allure. 2. (*unthinkingly*) tête baissée. 3. (*headfirst*) (la) tête la première.

headmaster [ˌhed'mɑːstər] n directeur m (d'une école).

headmistress [ˌhed'mɪstrɪs] n directrice f (d'une école).

head office n siège m social.

head-on ◆ adj (*collision*) de plein

fouet; (confrontation) de front. ◆ adv de plein fouet.

headphones ['hedfəʊnz] npl casque m.

headquarters [‚hed'kwɔːtəz] npl (of business, organization) siège m; (of armed forces) quartier m général.

headrest ['hedrest] n appui-tête m.

headroom ['hedrʊm] n (U) hauteur f.

headscarf ['hedskɑːf] (pl **-scarves** [-skɑːvz] OR **-scarfs**) n foulard m.

headset ['hedset] n casque m.

head start n avantage m au départ; ~ on OR over avantage sur.

headstrong ['hedstrɒŋ] adj volontaire, têtu(e).

head waiter n maître m d'hôtel.

headway ['hedweɪ] n: to make ~ faire des progrès.

headwind ['hedwɪnd] n vent m contraire.

heady ['hedɪ] adj 1. (exciting) grisant(e). 2. (causing giddiness) capiteux(euse).

heal [hiːl] ◆ vt 1. (cure) guérir. 2. fig (troubles, discord) apaiser. ◆ vi se guérir.

healing ['hiːlɪŋ] ◆ adj curatif(ive). ◆ n (U) guérison f.

health [helθ] n santé f.

health centre n = centre m médico-social.

health food n produits mpl diététiques.

health food shop n magasin m de produits diététiques.

health service n = sécurité f sociale.

healthy ['helθɪ] adj 1. (gen) sain(e). 2. (well) en bonne santé, bien portant(e). 3. fig (economy, company) qui se porte bien. 4. (profit) bon (bonne).

heap [hiːp] ◆ n tas m. ◆ vt (pile up) entasser. ► **heaps** npl inf: ~s of (people, objects) des tas de; (time, money) énormément de.

hear [hɪər] (pt & pp heard [hɜːd]) ◆ vt 1. (gen & JUR) entendre. 2. (learn of) apprendre; to ~ (that) ... apprendre que ... ◆ vi 1. (perceive sound) entendre. 2. (know): to ~ about entendre parler de. 3. (receive news): to ~ about avoir des nouvelles de; to ~ from sb recevoir des nouvelles de qqn. 4. phr: to have heard of avoir entendu parler de.

hearing ['hɪərɪŋ] n 1. (sense) ouïe f; hard of ~ dur(e) d'oreille. 2. (trial) audience f.

hearing aid n audiophone m.

hearsay ['hɪəseɪ] n ouï-dire m.

hearse [hɜːs] n corbillard m.

heart [hɑːt] n lit & fig cœur m; from the ~ du fond du cœur; it's close to my ~ ça me tient à cœur; to lose ~ perdre courage; to break sb's ~ briser le cœur à qqn. ► **hearts** npl cœur m. ► **at heart** adv au fond (de soi). ► **by heart** adv par cœur.

heartache ['hɑːteɪk] n peine f de cœur.

heart attack n crise f cardiaque.

heartbeat ['hɑːtbiːt] n battement m de cœur.

heartbroken ['hɑːt‚brəʊkn] adj qui a le cœur brisé.

heartburn ['hɑːtbɜːn] n (U) brûlures fpl d'estomac.

heart failure n arrêt m cardiaque.

heartfelt ['hɑːtfelt] adj sincère.

hearth [hɑːθ] n foyer m.

heartless ['hɑːtlɪs] adj sans cœur.

heartwarming ['hɑːt‚wɔːmɪŋ] adj réconfortant(e).

hearty ['hɑːtɪ] adj 1. (greeting, person) cordial(e). 2. (substantial - meal) copieux (euse); (- appetite) gros (grosse).

heat [hiːt] ◆ n 1. (U) (warmth) chaleur f. 2. (U) fig (pressure) pression f. 3. (eliminating round) éliminatoire f. 4. (ZOOL): on Br OR in ~ en chaleur. ◆ vt chauffer. ► **heat up** ◆ vt sep réchauffer. ◆ vi chauffer.

heated ['hiːtɪd] adj (argument, discussion, person) animé(e); (issue) chaud(e).

heater ['hiːtər] n appareil m de chauffage.

heath [hiːθ] n lande f.

heathen ['hiːðn] ◆ adj païen(enne). ◆ n païen m, -enne f.

heather ['heðər] n bruyère f.

heating ['hiːtɪŋ] n chauffage m.

heatstroke ['hiːtstrəʊk] n (U) coup m de chaleur.

heat wave n canicule f, vague f de chaleur.

heave [hiːv] ◆ vt 1. (pull) tirer (avec effort); (push) pousser (avec effort). 2. inf (throw) lancer. ◆ vi 1. (pull) tirer. 2. (rise and fall) se soulever. 3. (retch) avoir des haut-le-cœur.

heaven ['hevn] n paradis m. ► **heavens** ◆ npl: the ~s literary les cieux mpl. ◆ excl: (good) ~s! juste ciel!!

heavenly ['hevnlɪ] adj inf (delightful) délicieux(euse), merveilleux(euse).

heavily ['hevɪlɪ] adv 1. (booked, in debt) lourdement; (rain, smoke, drink) énormément. 2. (solidly - built) solidement. 3. (breathe, sigh) péniblement, bruyamment. **4.** (*fall, sit down*) lourdement.

heavy ['hevɪ] *adj* **1.** (*gen*) lourd(e); **how ~ is it?** ça pèse combien? **2.** (*traffic*) dense; (*rain*) battant(e); (*fighting*) acharné(e); (*casualties, corrections*) nombreux(euses); (*smoker, drinker*) gros (grosse). **3.** (*noisy - breathing*) bruyant(e). **4.** (*schedule*) chargé(e). **5.** (*physically exacting - work, job*) pénible.

heavy cream *n* Am crème *f* fraîche épaisse.

heavy goods vehicle *n* Br poids lourd *m*.

heavyweight ['hevɪweɪt] (SPORT) ◆ *adj* poids lourd. ◆ *n* poids lourd *m*.

Hebrew ['hiːbruː] ◆ *adj* hébreu, hébraïque. ◆ *n* **1.** (*person*) Hébreu *m*, Israélite *mf*. **2.** (*language*) hébreu *m*.

Hebrides ['hebrɪdiːz] *npl*: **the ~** les (îles *fpl*) Hébrides.

heck [hek] *excl inf*: **what/where/why the ~ ...?** que/où/pourquoi diable ...?; **a ~ of a nice guy** un type vachement sympa.

heckle ['hekl] ◆ *vt* interpeller. ◆ *vi* interrompre bruyamment.

hectic ['hektɪk] *adj* (*meeting, day*) agité(e), mouvementé(e).

he'd [hiːd] = **he had, he would.**

hedge [hedʒ] ◆ *n* haie *f*. ◆ *vi* (*prevaricate*) répondre de façon détournée.

hedgehog ['hedʒhɒg] *n* hérisson *m*.

heed [hiːd] ◆ *n*: **to take ~ of sthg** tenir compte de qqch. ◆ *vt fml* tenir compte de.

heel [hiːl] *n* talon *m*.

hefty ['heftɪ] *adj* **1.** (*well-built*) costaud(e). **2.** (*large*) gros (grosse).

heifer ['hefər] *n* génisse *f*.

height [haɪt] *n* **1.** (*of building, mountain*) hauteur *f*; (*of person*) taille *f*; **5 metres in ~** 5 mètres de haut; **what ~ is it?** ça fait quelle hauteur?; **what ~ are you?** combien mesurez-vous? **2.** (*above ground - of aircraft*) altitude *f*. **3.** (*zenith*): **at the ~ of the summer/season** au cœur de l'été/de la saison; **at the ~ of his fame** au sommet de sa gloire.

heighten ['haɪtn] *vt & vi* augmenter.

heir [eər] *n* héritier *m*.

heiress ['eərɪs] *n* héritière *f*.

heirloom ['eəluːm] *n* meuble *m* /bijou *m* de famille.

heist [haɪst] *n inf* casse *m*.

held [held] *pt & pp* → **hold.**

helicopter ['helɪkɒptər] *n* hélicoptère *m*.

helium ['hiːlɪəm] *n* hélium *m*.

hell [hel] ◆ *n* **1.** *lit & fig* enfer *m*. **2.** *inf* (*for emphasis*): **he's a ~ of a nice guy** c'est un type vachement sympa; **what/where/why the ~ ...?** que/où/pourquoi ..., bon sang? **3.** *phr*: **to do sthg for the ~ of it** *inf* faire qqch pour le plaisir, faire qqch juste comme ça; **to give sb ~** *inf* (*verbally*) engueuler qqn; **go to ~!** *v inf* va te faire foutre! ◆ *excl inf* merde!, zut!

he'll [hiːl] = **he will.**

hellish ['helɪʃ] *adj inf* infernal(e).

hello [hə'ləʊ] *excl* **1.** (*as greeting*) bonjour!; (*on phone*) allô! **2.** (*to attract attention*) hé!

helm [helm] *n lit & fig* barre *f*.

helmet ['helmɪt] *n* casque *m*.

help [help] ◆ *n* **1.** (U) (*assistance*) aide *f*; **he gave me a lot of ~** il m'a beaucoup aidé; **with the ~ of sthg** à l'aide de qqch; **with sb's ~** avec l'aide de qqn; **to be of ~** rendre service. **2.** (U) (*emergency aid*) secours *m*. **3.** (*useful person or object*): **to be a ~** aider, rendre service. ◆ *vi* aider. ◆ *vt* **1.** (*assist*) aider; **to ~ sb (to) do sthg** aider qqn à faire qqch; **to ~ sb with sthg** aider qqn à faire qqch. **2.** (*avoid*): **I can't ~ it** je n'y peux rien; **I couldn't ~ laughing** je ne pouvais pas m'empêcher de rire. **3.** *phr*: **to ~ o.s. (to sthg)** se servir (de qqch). ◆ *excl* au secours!, à l'aide!
▶ **help out** *vt sep & vi* aider.

helper ['helpər] *n* **1.** (*gen*) aide *mf*. **2.** Am (*to do housework*) femme *f* de ménage.

helpful ['helpful] *adj* **1.** (*person*) serviable. **2.** (*advice, suggestion*) utile.

helping ['helpɪŋ] *n* portion *f*; (*of cake, tart*) part *f*.

helpless ['helplɪs] *adj* impuissant(e); (*look, gesture*) d'impuissance.

helpline ['helplaɪn] *n* ligne *f* d'assistance téléphonique.

Helsinki ['helsɪŋkɪ] *n* Helsinki.

hem [hem] ◆ *n* ourlet *m*. ◆ *vt* ourler.
▶ **hem in** *vt sep* encercler.

hemisphere ['hemɪsfɪər] *n* hémisphère *m*.

hemline ['hemlaɪn] *n* ourlet *m*.

hemophiliac [ˌhiːməˈfɪlɪæk] *n* hémophile *mf*.

hemorrhage ['hemərɪdʒ] *n* hémorragie *f*.

hemorrhoids ['hemərɔɪdz] *npl* hémorroïdes *fpl*.

hen [hen] *n* **1.** (*female chicken*) poule *f*. **2.** (*female bird*) femelle *f*.

hence [hens] *adv fml* **1.** (*therefore*) d'où. **2.** (*from now*) d'ici.

henceforth [ˌhensˈfɔːθ] adv fml dorénavant.

henchman [ˈhentʃmən] (pl -men [-mən]) n pej acolyte m.

henna [ˈhenə] ◆ n henné m. ◆ vt (hair) appliquer du henné sur.

henpecked [ˈhenpekt] adj pej dominé par sa femme.

her [hɜːʳ] ◆ pers pron 1. (direct - unstressed) la, l' (+ vowel or silent 'h'); (- stressed) elle; **I know/like ~** je la connais/l'aime; **it's ~** c'est elle. 2. (referring to animal, car, ship etc) follow the gender of your translation. 3. (indirect) lui; **we spoke to ~** nous lui avons parlé; **he sent ~ a letter** il lui a envoyé une lettre. 4. (after prep, in comparisons etc) elle; **I'm shorter than ~** je suis plus petit qu'elle. ◆ poss adj son (sa), ses (pl); **~ coat** son manteau; **~ bedroom** sa chambre; **~ children** ses enfants; **it was HER fault** c'était de sa faute à elle.

herald [ˈherəld] ◆ vt fml annoncer. ◆ n (messenger) héraut m.

herb [hɜːb] n herbe f.

herd [hɜːd] ◆ n troupeau m. ◆ vt 1. (cattle, sheep) mener. 2. fig (people) conduire, mener; (into confined space) parquer.

here [hɪəʳ] adv 1. (in this place) ici; **~ he is/they are** le/les voici; **~ it is** le/la voici; **~ is/are** voici; **~ and there** çà et là. 2. (present) là.

hereabouts Br [ˌhɪərəˈbaʊts], **hereabout** Am [ˌhɪərəˈbaʊt] adv par ici.

hereafter [ˌhɪərˈɑːftəʳ] ◆ adv fml ci-après. ◆ n: **the ~** l'au-delà m.

hereby [ˌhɪəˈbaɪ] adv fml par la présente.

hereditary [hɪˈredɪtrɪ] adj héréditaire.

heresy [ˈherəsɪ] n hérésie f.

herewith [ˌhɪəˈwɪð] adv fml (with letter) ci-joint, ci-inclus.

heritage [ˈherɪtɪdʒ] n héritage m, patrimoine m.

hermetically [hɜːˈmetɪklɪ] adv: **~ sealed** fermé(e) hermétiquement.

hermit [ˈhɜːmɪt] n ermite m.

hernia [ˈhɜːnjə] n hernie f.

hero [ˈhɪərəʊ] (pl -es) n héros m.

heroic [hɪˈrəʊɪk] adj héroïque.

heroin [ˈherəʊɪn] n héroïne f.

heroine [ˈherəʊɪn] n héroïne f.

heron [ˈherən] (pl inv OR -s) n héron m.

herring [ˈherɪŋ] (pl inv OR -s) n hareng m.

hers [hɜːz] poss pron le sien (la sienne), les siens (les siennes) (pl); **that money is ~** cet argent est à elle OR est le sien;

a friend of ~ un ami à elle, un de ses amis.

herself [hɜːˈself] pron 1. (reflexive) se; (after prep) elle. 2. (for emphasis) elle-même.

he's [hiːz] = **he is, he has.**

hesitant [ˈhezɪtənt] adj hésitant(e).

hesitate [ˈhezɪteɪt] vi hésiter; **to ~ to do sthg** hésiter à faire qqch.

hesitation [ˌhezɪˈteɪʃn] n hésitation f.

heterogeneous [ˌhetərəˈdʒiːnjəs] adj fml hétérogène.

heterosexual [ˌhetərəʊˈsekʃʊəl] ◆ adj hétérosexuel(elle). ◆ n hétérosexuel m, -elle f.

hexagon [ˈheksəgən] n hexagone m.

hey [heɪ] excl hé!

heyday [ˈheɪdeɪ] n âge m d'or.

HGV (abbr of **heavy goods vehicle**) n PL m.

hi [haɪ] excl inf salut!

hiatus [haɪˈeɪtəs] (pl -es) n fml pause f.

hibernate [ˈhaɪbəneɪt] vi hiberner.

hiccough, hiccup [ˈhɪkʌp] ◆ n hoquet m; fig (difficulty) accroc m; **to have ~s** avoir le hoquet. ◆ vi hoqueter.

hid [hɪd] pt → **hide.**

hidden [ˈhɪdn] ◆ pp → **hide.** ◆ adj caché(e).

hide [haɪd] (pt **hid**, pp **hidden**) ◆ vt: **to ~ sthg (from sb)** cacher qqch (à qqn); (information) taire qqch (à qqn). ◆ vi se cacher. ◆ n 1. (animal skin) peau f. 2. (for watching birds, animals) cachette f.

hide-and-seek n cache-cache m.

hideaway [ˈhaɪdəweɪ] n cachette f.

hideous [ˈhɪdɪəs] adj hideux(euse); (error, conditions) abominable.

hiding [ˈhaɪdɪŋ] n 1. (concealment): **to be in ~** se tenir caché(e). 2. inf (beating): **to give sb a (good) ~** donner une (bonne) raclée OR correction à qqn.

hiding place n cachette f.

hierarchy [ˈhaɪərɑːkɪ] n hiérarchie f.

hi-fi [ˈhaɪfaɪ] n hi-fi f inv.

high [haɪ] ◆ adj 1. (gen) haut(e); **it's 3 feet/6 metres ~** cela fait 3 pieds/6 mètres de haut; **how ~ is it?** cela fait combien de haut? 2. (speed, figure, altitude, office) élevé(e). 3. (high-pitched) aigu (uë). 4. drugs sl qui plane, défoncé(e). 5. inf (drunk) bourré(e). ◆ adv haut. ◆ n (highest point) maximum m.

highbrow [ˈhaɪbraʊ] adj intellectuel (elle).

high chair n chaise f haute (d'enfant).

high-class adj de premier ordre; (hotel, restaurant) de grande classe.

High Court n Br (JUR) Cour f suprême.
higher ['haɪəʳ] adj (exam, qualification) supérieur(e). ▶ **Higher** n: **Higher (Grade)** (SCH) examen de fin d'études secondaires en Écosse.

higher education n (U) études fpl supérieures.

high-handed [-'hændɪd] adj despotique.

high jump n saut m en hauteur.

Highland Games ['haɪlənd-] npl jeux mpl écossais.

Highlands ['haɪləndz] npl: **the ~** les Highlands fpl (région montagneuse du nord de l'Écosse).

highlight ['haɪlaɪt] ◆ n (of event, occasion) moment m or point m fort. ◆ vt souligner; (with highlighter) surligner. ▶ **highlights** npl (in hair) reflets mpl, mèches fpl.

highlighter (pen) ['haɪlaɪtəʳ-] n surligneur m.

highly ['haɪlɪ] adv 1. (very) extrêmement, très. 2. (in important position): ~ **placed** haut placé(e). 3. (favourably): **to think ~ of sb/sthg** penser du bien de qqn/qqch.

highly-strung adj nerveux(euse).

Highness ['haɪnɪs] n: **His/Her/Your (Royal) ~** Son/Votre Altesse (Royale); **their (Royal) ~es** leurs Altesses (Royales).

high-pitched [-'pɪtʃt] adj aigu(uë).

high point n (of occasion) point m fort.

high-powered [-'paʊəd] adj 1. (powerful) de forte puissance. 2. (prestigious - activity, place) de haut niveau; (- job, person) très important(e).

high-ranking [-'ræŋkɪŋ] adj de haut rang.

high-rise adj: ~ **block of flats** tour f.

high school n Br lycée m; Am établissement m d'enseignement supérieur.

high season n haute saison f.

high spot n point m fort.

high street n Br rue f principale.

high-tech [-'tek] adj (method, industry) de pointe.

high tide n marée f haute.

highway ['haɪweɪ] n 1. Am (motorway) autoroute f. 2. (main road) grande route f.

Highway Code n Br: **the ~** le code de la route.

hijack ['haɪdʒæk] ◆ n détournement m. ◆ vt détourner.

hijacker ['haɪdʒækəʳ] n (of aircraft)

pirate m de l'air; (of vehicle) pirate m de la route.

hike [haɪk] ◆ n (long walk) randonnée f. ◆ vi faire une randonnée.

hiker ['haɪkəʳ] n randonneur m, -euse f.

hiking ['haɪkɪŋ] n marche f.

hilarious [hɪ'leərɪəs] adj hilarant(e).

hill [hɪl] n 1. (mound) colline f. 2. (slope) côte f.

hillside ['hɪlsaɪd] n coteau m.

hilly ['hɪlɪ] adj vallonné(e).

hilt [hɪlt] n garde f; **to support/defend sb to the ~** soutenir/défendre qqn à fond.

him [hɪm] pers pron 1. (direct - unstressed) le, l' (+ vowel or silent 'h'); (- stressed) lui; **I know/like ~** je le connais/l'aime; **it's ~** c'est lui. 2. (indirect) lui; **we spoke to ~** nous lui avons parlé; **she sent ~ a letter** elle lui a envoyé une lettre. 3. (after prep, in comparisons etc) lui; **I'm shorter than ~** je suis plus petit que lui.

Himalayas [ˌhɪmə'leɪəz] npl: **the ~** l'Himalaya m.

himself [hɪm'self] pron 1. (reflexive) se; (after prep) lui. 2. (for emphasis) lui-même.

hind [haɪnd] (pl inv OR -s) ◆ adj de derrière. ◆ n biche f.

hinder ['hɪndəʳ] vt gêner, entraver.

Hindi ['hɪndɪ] n hindi m.

hindrance ['hɪndrəns] n obstacle m.

hindsight ['haɪndsaɪt] n: **with the benefit of ~** avec du recul.

Hindu ['hɪnduː] (pl -s) ◆ adj hindou(e). ◆ n Hindou m, -e f.

hinge [hɪndʒ] n (whole fitting) charnière f; (pin) gond m. ▶ **hinge (up)on** vt fus (depend on) dépendre de.

hint [hɪnt] ◆ n 1. (indication) allusion f; **to drop a ~** faire une allusion. 2. (piece of advice) conseil m, indication f. 3. (small amount) soupçon m. ◆ vi: **to ~ at sthg** faire allusion à qqch. ◆ vt: **to ~ that ...** insinuer que ...

hip [hɪp] n hanche f.

hippie ['hɪpɪ] = **hippy**.

hippo ['hɪpəʊ] (pl -s) n hippopotame m.

hippopotamus [ˌhɪpə'pɒtəməs] (pl -muses OR -mi [-maɪ]) n hippopotame m.

hippy ['hɪpɪ] n hippie mf.

hire ['haɪəʳ] ◆ n (U) (of car, equipment) location f; **for ~** (bicycles etc) à louer; (taxi) libre. ◆ vt 1. (rent) louer. 2. (employ) employer les services de. ▶ **hire out** vt sep louer.

hire car n Br voiture f de location.

hire purchase n (U) Br achat m à

crédit OR à tempérament.

his [hɪz] ◆ *poss adj* son (sa), ses (*pl*); ~ **house** sa maison; ~ **money** son argent; ~ **children** ses enfants; ~ **name** is Joe il s'appelle Joe. ◆ *poss pron* le sien (la sienne), les siens (les siennes) (*pl*); **that money is** ~ cet argent est à lui OR est le sien; **it wasn't her fault, it was** HIS ce n'était pas de sa faute à elle, c'était de sa faute à lui; **a friend of** ~ un ami à lui, un de ses amis.

hiss [hɪs] ◆ *n* (*of animal, gas etc*) sifflement *m*; (*of crowd*) sifflet *m*. ◆ *vi* (*animal, gas etc*) siffler.

historic [hɪ'stɒrɪk] *adj* historique.

historical [hɪ'stɒrɪkəl] *adj* historique.

history ['hɪstərɪ] *n* 1. (*gen*) histoire *f*. 2. (*past record*) antécédents *mpl*; **medical** ~ passé *m* médical.

hit [hɪt] (*pt & pp* hit) ◆ *n* 1. (*blow*) coup *m*. 2. (*successful strike*) coup *m* OR tir *m* réussi; (*in fencing*) touche *f*. 3. (*success*) succès *m*; **to be a** ~ **with** plaire à. ◆ *comp* à succès. ◆ *vt* 1. (*strike*) frapper; (*nail*) taper sur. 2. (*crash into*) heurter, percuter. 3. (*reach*) atteindre. 4. (*affect badly*) toucher, affecter. 5. *phr*: **to** ~ **it off (with sb)** bien s'entendre (avec qqn).

hit-and-miss = hit-or-miss.

hit-and-run *adj* (*accident*) avec délit de fuite; ~ **driver** chauffard *m* (*qui a commis un délit de fuite*).

hitch [hɪtʃ] ◆ *n* (*problem, snag*) ennui *m*. ◆ *vt* 1. (*catch*): **to** ~ **a lift** faire du stop. 2. (*fasten*): **to** ~ **sthg on** OR **onto** accrocher OR attacher qqch à. ◆ *vi* (*hitchhike*) faire du stop. ▶ **hitch up** *vt sep* (*pull up*) remonter.

hitchhike ['hɪtʃhaɪk] *vi* faire de l'autostop.

hitchhiker ['hɪtʃhaɪkə^r] *n* autostoppeur *m*, -euse *f*.

hi-tech [,haɪ'tek] = high-tech.

hitherto [,hɪðə'tuː] *adv fml* jusqu'ici.

hit-or-miss *adj* aléatoire.

HIV (*abbr of* **human immunodeficiency virus**) *n* VIH *m*, HIV *m*; **to be** ~-**positive** être séropositif.

hive [haɪv] *n* ruche *f*. ▶ **hive off** *vt sep* (*assets*) séparer.

HNC (*abbr of* **Higher National Certificate**) *n brevet de technicien en Grande-Bretagne.*

HND (*abbr of* **Higher National Diploma**) *n brevet de technicien supérieur en Grande-Bretagne.*

hoard [hɔːd] ◆ *n* (*store*) réserves *fpl*; (*of useless items*) tas *m*. ◆ *vt* amasser; (*food, petrol*) faire des provisions de.

hoarding ['hɔːdɪŋ] *n Br* (*for advertisements*) panneau *m* d'affichage publicitaire.

hoarse [hɔːs] *adj* (*person, voice*) enroué(e); (*shout, whisper*) rauque.

hoax [həʊks] *n* canular *m*.

hob [hɒb] *n Br* (*on cooker*) rond *m*, plaque *f*.

hobble ['hɒbl] *vi* (*limp*) boitiller.

hobby ['hɒbɪ] *n* passe-temps *m inv*, hobby *m*.

hobbyhorse ['hɒbɪhɔːs] *n* 1. (*toy*) cheval *m* à bascule. 2. *fig* (*favourite topic*) dada *m*.

hobo ['həʊbəʊ] (*pl* -es OR -s) *n Am* clochard *m*, -e *f*.

hockey ['hɒkɪ] *n* 1. (*on grass*) hockey *m*. 2. *Am* (*ice hockey*) hockey *m* sur glace.

hoe [həʊ] ◆ *n* houe *f*. ◆ *vt* biner.

hog [hɒg] ◆ *n* 1. *Am* (*pig*) cochon *m*. 2. *inf* (*greedy person*) goinfre *m*. 3. *phr*: **to go the whole** ~ aller jusqu'au bout. ◆ *vt inf* (*monopolize*) accaparer, monopoliser.

Hogmanay ['hɒgməneɪ] *n* la Saint-Sylvestre en Écosse.

hoist [hɔɪst] ◆ *n* (*device*) treuil *m*. ◆ *vt* hisser.

hold [həʊld] (*pt & pp* held) ◆ *vt* 1. (*gen*) tenir. 2. (*keep in position*) maintenir. 3. (*as prisoner*) détenir; **to** ~ **sb prisoner/hostage** détenir qqn prisonnier/comme otage. 4. (*have, possess*) avoir. 5. *fml* (*consider*) considérer, estimer; **to** ~ **sb responsible for sthg** rendre qqn responsable de qqch, tenir qqn pour responsable de qqch. 6. (*on telephone*): **please** ~ **the line** ne quittez pas, je vous prie. 7. (*keep, maintain*) retenir. 8. (*sustain, support*) supporter. 9. (*contain*) contenir. 10. *phr*: ~ **it!**, ~ **everything!** attendez!, arrêtez!; **to** ~ **one's own** se défendre. ◆ *vi* 1. (*remain unchanged - gen*) tenir; (- *luck*) persister; (- *weather*) se maintenir; **to** ~ **still** OR **steady** ne pas bouger, rester tranquille. 2. (*on phone*) attendre. ◆ *n* 1. (*grasp, grip*) prise *f*, étreinte *f*; **to take** OR **lay** ~ **of sthg** saisir qqch; **to get** ~ **of sthg** (*obtain*) se procurer qqch; **to get** ~ **of sb** (*find*) joindre. 2. (*of ship, aircraft*) cale *f*. 3. (*control, influence*) prise *f*. ▶ **hold back** *vt sep* 1. (*restrain, prevent*) retenir; (*anger*) réprimer. 2. (*keep secret*) cacher. ▶ **hold down** *vt sep* (*job*) garder. ▶ **hold off** *vt sep* (*fend off*) tenir à distance. ▶ **hold on** *vi* 1. (*wait*) attendre; (*on phone*) ne pas quitter. 2. (*grip*): **to** ~ **on (to sthg)** se tenir (à qqch). ▶ **hold out** ◆ *vt sep* (*hand, arms*) tendre.

♦ *vi* **1.** (*last*) durer. **2.** (*resist*): **to ~ out (against sb/sthg)** résister (à qqn/qqch). ► **hold up** *vt sep* **1.** (*raise*) lever. **2.** (*delay*) retarder.

holdall ['həʊldɔːl] *n* Br fourre-tout *m inv*.

holder ['həʊldəʳ] *n* **1.** (*for cigarette*) porte-cigarettes *m inv*. **2.** (*owner*) détenteur *m*, -trice *f*; (*of position, title*) titulaire *mf*.

holding ['həʊldɪŋ] *n* **1.** (*investment*) effets *mpl* en portefeuille. **2.** (*farm*) ferme *f*.

holdup ['həʊldʌp] *n* **1.** (*robbery*) hold-up *m*. **2.** (*delay*) retard *m*.

hole [həʊl] *n* **1.** (*gen*) trou *m*. **2.** *inf* (*predicament*) pétrin *m*.

holiday ['hɒlɪdeɪ] *n* **1.** (*vacation*) vacances *fpl*; **to be/go on ~** être/partir en vacances. **2.** (*public holiday*) jour *m* férié.

holiday camp *n* Br camp *m* de vacances.

holidaymaker ['hɒlɪdɪˌmeɪkəʳ] *n* Br vacancier *m*, -ère *f*.

holiday pay *n* Br *salaire payé pendant les vacances*.

holiday resort *n* Br lieu *m* de vacances.

holistic [həʊ'lɪstɪk] *adj* holistique.

Holland ['hɒlənd] *n* Hollande *f*.

holler ['hɒləʳ] *vi & vt inf* gueuler, brailler.

hollow ['hɒləʊ] ♦ *adj* creux (creuse); (*eyes*) cave; (*promise, victory*) faux (fausse); (*laugh*) qui sonne faux. ♦ *n* creux *m*. ► **hollow out** *vt sep* creuser, évider.

holly ['hɒlɪ] *n* houx *m*.

holocaust ['hɒləkɔːst] *n* (*destruction*) destruction *f*, holocauste *m*. ► **Holocaust** *n*: **the Holocaust** l'holocauste *m*.

holster ['həʊlstəʳ] *n* étui *m*.

holy ['həʊlɪ] *adj* saint(e); (*ground*) sacré(e).

Holy Ghost *n*: **the ~** le Saint-Esprit.

Holy Land *n*: **the ~** la Terre sainte.

Holy Spirit *n*: **the ~** le Saint-Esprit.

home [həʊm] ♦ *n* **1.** (*house, institution*) maison *f*; **to make one's ~** s'établir, s'installer. **2.** (*own country*) patrie *f*; (*city*) ville *f* natale. **3.** (*one's family*) foyer *m*; **to leave ~** quitter la maison. **4.** *fig* (*place of origin*) berceau *m*. ♦ *adj* **1.** (*not foreign*) intérieur(e); (~ *product*) national(e). **2.** (*in one's own home - cooking*) familial(e); (~ *life*) de famille; (~ *improvements*) domes-

tique. **3.** (SPORT - *game*) sur son propre terrain; (~ *team*) qui reçoit. ♦ *adv* (*to or at one's house*) chez soi, à la maison. ► **at home** *adv* **1.** (*in one's house, flat*) chez soi, à la maison. **2.** (*comfortable*) à l'aise; **at ~ with sthg** à l'aise dans qqch; **to make o.s. at ~** faire comme chez soi. **3.** (*in one's own country*) chez nous.

home address *n* adresse *f* du domicile.

home brew *n* (U) (*beer*) bière *f* faite à la maison.

home computer *n* ordinateur *m* domestique.

Home Counties *npl*: **the ~** *les comtés entourant Londres*.

home economics *n* (U) économie *f* domestique.

home help *n* Br aide *f* ménagère.

homeland ['həʊmlænd] *n* **1.** (*country of birth*) patrie *f*. **2.** (*in South Africa*) homeland *m*, bantoustan *m*.

homeless ['həʊmlɪs] ♦ *adj* sans abri. ♦ *npl*: **the ~** les sans-abri *mpl*.

homely ['həʊmlɪ] *adj* **1.** (*simple*) simple. **2.** (*unattractive*) ordinaire.

homemade [ˌhəʊm'meɪd] *adj* fait(e) (à la) maison.

Home Office *n* Br: **the ~** le ministère de l'Intérieur.

homeopathic [ˌhəʊmɪəʊ'pæθɪk] *adj* homéopathique.

homeopathy [ˌhəʊmɪ'ɒpəθɪ] *n* homéopathie *f*.

home page *n* (COMPUT) page *f* d'accueil.

Home Secretary *n* Br = ministre *m* de l'Intérieur.

homesick ['həʊmsɪk] *adj* qui a le mal du pays.

hometown ['həʊmtaʊn] *n* ville *f* natale.

homeward ['həʊmwəd] ♦ *adj* de retour. ♦ *adv* = **homewards**.

homewards ['həʊmwədz] *adv* vers la maison.

homework ['həʊmwɜːk] *n* (U) **1.** (SCH) devoirs *mpl*. **2.** *inf* (*preparation*) boulot *m*.

homicide ['hɒmɪsaɪd] *n* homicide *m*.

homoeopathy *etc* [ˌhəʊmɪ'ɒpəθɪ] = **homeopathy** *etc*.

homogeneous [ˌhɒmə'dʒiːnjəs] *adj* homogène.

homosexual [ˌhɒmə'sekʃʊəl] ♦ *adj* homosexuel(elle). ♦ *n* homosexuel *m*, -elle *f*.

hone [həʊn] *vt* aiguiser.

honest ['ɒnɪst] ♦ *adj* **1.** (*trustworthy*)

honnête, probe. **2.** (*frank*) franc (franche), sincère; **to be ~ ...** pour dire la vérité ..., à dire vrai ... **3.** (*legal*) légitime. ◆ *adv inf* = **honestly 2.**

honestly ['ɒnɪstlɪ] ◆ *adv* **1.** (*truthfully*) honnêtement. **2.** (*expressing sincerity*) je vous assure. ◆ *excl* (*expressing impatience, disapproval*) franchement!

honesty ['ɒnɪstɪ] *n* honnêteté *f*, probité *f*.

honey ['hʌnɪ] *n* **1.** (*food*) miel *m*. **2.** (*dear*) chéri *m*, -e *f*.

honeycomb ['hʌnɪkəʊm] *n* gâteau *m* de miel.

honeymoon ['hʌnɪmuːn] *n lit & fig* lune *f* de miel.

honeysuckle ['hʌnɪˌsʌkl] *n* chèvre-feuille *m*.

Hong Kong [ˌhɒŋ'kɒŋ] *n* Hong Kong, Hongkong.

honk [hɒŋk] ◆ *vi* **1.** (*motorist*) klaxonner. **2.** (*goose*) cacarder. ◆ *vt*: **to ~ the horn** klaxonner.

honor *etc Am* = **honour** *etc*.

honorary [Br 'ɒnərərɪ, Am ɒnə'reərɪ] *adj* honoraire.

honour *Br*, **honor** *Am* ['ɒnər] ◆ *n* honneur *m*; **in ~ of sb/sthg** en l'honneur de qqn/qqch. ◆ *vt* honorer. ▶ **honours** *npl* **1.** (*tokens of respect*) honneurs *mpl*. **2.** (*of university degree*) ≃ licence *f*.

honourable *Br*, **honorable** *Am* ['ɒnrəbl] *adj* honorable.

hood [hʊd] *n* **1.** (*on cloak, jacket*) capuchon *m*. **2.** (*of cooker*) hotte *f*. **3.** (*of pram; convertible car*) capote *f*. **4.** *Am* (*car bonnet*) capot *m*.

hoodlum ['huːdləm] *n Am inf* gangster *m*, truand *m*.

hoof [huːf, hʊf] (*pl* **-s** OR **hooves**) *n* sabot *m*.

hook [hʊk] ◆ *n* **1.** (*for hanging things on*) crochet *m*. **2.** (*for catching fish*) hameçon *m*. **3.** (*fastener*) agrafe *f*. **4.** (*of telephone*): **off the ~** décroché. ◆ *vt* **1.** (*attach with hook*) accrocher. **2.** (*catch with hook*) prendre. ▶ **hook up** *vt sep*: **to ~ sthg up to sthg** connecter qqch à qqch.

hooked [hʊkt] *adj* **1.** (*shaped like a hook*) crochu(e). **2.** *inf* (*addicted*): **to be ~ (on)** être accro (à); (*music, art*) être mordu(e) (de).

hook(e)y ['hʊkɪ] *n Am inf*: **to play ~** faire l'école buissonnière.

hooligan ['huːlɪgən] *n* hooligan *m*, vandale *m*.

hoop [huːp] *n* **1.** (*circular band*) cercle *m*. **2.** (*toy*) cerceau *m*.

hooray [hʊ'reɪ] = **hurray**.

hoot [huːt] ◆ *n* **1.** (*of owl*) hululement *m*. **2.** (*of horn*) coup *m* de Klaxon®. **3.** *Br inf* (*something amusing*): **to be a ~** être tordant(e). ◆ *vi* **1.** (*owl*) hululer. **2.** (*horn*) klaxonner. ◆ *vt*: **to ~ the horn** klaxonner.

hooter ['huːtər] *n* (*horn*) Klaxon® *m*.

Hoover® *Br* ['huːvər] *n* aspirateur *m*. ▶ **hoover** *vt* (*room*) passer l'aspirateur dans; (*carpet*) passer à l'aspirateur.

hooves [huːvz] *pl* → **hoof**.

hop [hɒp] ◆ *n* saut *m*; (*on one leg*) saut à cloche-pied. ◆ *vi* sauter; (*on one leg*) sauter à cloche-pied; (*bird*) sautiller. ▶ **hops** *npl* houblon *m*.

hope [həʊp] ◆ *vi* espérer; **to ~ for sthg** espérer qqch; **I ~ so** j'espère bien; **I ~ not** j'espère bien que non. ◆ *vt*: **to ~ (that)** espérer que; **to ~ to do sthg** espérer faire qqch. ◆ *n* espoir *m*; **in the ~ of** dans l'espoir de.

hopeful ['həʊpfʊl] *adj* **1.** (*optimistic*) plein(e) d'espoir; **to be ~ of doing sthg** avoir l'espoir de faire qqch; **to be ~ of sthg** espérer qqch. **2.** (*promising*) encourageant(e), qui promet.

hopefully ['həʊpfəlɪ] *adv* **1.** (*in a hopeful way*) avec bon espoir, avec optimisme. **2.** (*with luck*) ... espérons que ...

hopeless ['həʊpləs] *adj* **1.** (*gen*) désespéré(e); (*tears*) de désespoir. **2.** *inf* (*useless*) nul (nulle).

hopelessly ['həʊpləslɪ] *adv* **1.** (*despairingly*) avec désespoir. **2.** (*completely*) complètement.

horizon [hə'raɪzn] *n* horizon *m*; **on the ~** *lit & fig* à l'horizon.

horizontal [ˌhɒrɪ'zɒntl] ◆ *adj* horizontal(e). ◆ *n*: **the ~** l'horizontale *f*.

hormone ['hɔːməʊn] *n* hormone *f*.

horn [hɔːn] *n* **1.** (*of animal*) corne *f*. **2.** (MUS) (*instrument*) cor *m*. **3.** (*on car*) Klaxon® *m*; (*on ship*) sirène *f*.

hornet ['hɔːnɪt] *n* frelon *m*.

horny ['hɔːnɪ] *adj* **1.** (*hard*) corné(e); (*hand*) calleux(euse). **2.** *v inf* (*sexually excited*) excité(e) (sexuellement).

horoscope ['hɒrəskəʊp] *n* horoscope *m*.

horrendous [hɒ'rendəs] *adj* horrible.

horrible ['hɒrəbl] *adj* horrible.

horrid ['hɒrɪd] *adj* (*unpleasant*) horrible.

horrific [hɒ'rɪfɪk] *adj* horrible.

horrify ['hɒrɪfaɪ] *vt* horrifier.

horror ['hɒrər] *n* horreur *f*.

horror film *n* film *m* d'épouvante.

horse [hɔːs] *n* (*animal*) cheval *m*.

horseback ['hɔːsbæk] ◆ *adj* à cheval;

~ riding Am équitation f. ◆ n: **on ~ à cheval.**

horse chestnut n (nut) marron m d'Inde; **~ (tree)** marronnier m d'Inde.

horseman ['hɔ:smən] (pl **-men** [-mən]) n cavalier m.

horsepower ['hɔ:ˌspaʊəʳ] n puissance f en chevaux.

horse racing n (U) courses fpl de chevaux.

horseradish ['hɔ:sˌrædɪʃ] n (plant) raifort m.

horse riding n équitation f.

horseshoe ['hɔ:sʃu:] n fer m à cheval.

horsewoman ['hɔ:sˌwʊmən] (pl **-women** [-ˌwɪmɪn]) n cavalière f.

horticulture ['hɔ:tɪkʌltʃəʳ] n horticulture f.

hose [həʊz] ◆ n (hosepipe) tuyau m. ◆ vt arroser au jet.

hosepipe ['həʊzpaɪp] n = **hose**.

hosiery ['həʊzɪərɪ] n bonneterie f.

hospitable [hɒ'spɪtəbl] adj hospitalier (ère), accueillant(e).

hospital ['hɒspɪtl] n hôpital m.

hospitality [ˌhɒspɪ'tælətɪ] n hospitalité f.

host [həʊst] ◆ n 1. (gen) hôte m. 2. (compere) animateur m, -trice f. 3. (large number): **a ~ of** une foule de. ◆ vt présenter, animer.

hostage ['hɒstɪdʒ] n otage m.

hostel ['hɒstl] n 1. (basic accommodation) foyer m. 2. (youth hostel) auberge f de jeunesse.

hostess ['həʊstes] n hôtesse f.

hostile [Br 'hɒstaɪl, Am 'hɒstl] adj: **~ (to)** hostile (à).

hostility [hɒ'stɪlətɪ] n (antagonism, unfriendliness) hostilité f. ▶ **hostilities** npl hostilités fpl.

hot [hɒt] adj 1. (gen) chaud(e); **I'm ~** j'ai chaud; **it's ~** il fait chaud. 2. (spicy) épicé(e). 3. inf (expert) fort(e), calé(e). 4. (recent) de dernière heure OR minute. 5. (temper) colérique.

hot-air balloon n montgolfière f.

hotbed ['hɒtbed] n foyer m.

hot-cross bun n petit pain sucré que l'on mange le vendredi saint.

hot dog n hot dog m.

hotel [həʊ'tel] n hôtel m.

hot flush Br, **hot flash** Am n bouffée f de chaleur.

hotfoot ['hɒtˌfʊt] adv à toute vitesse.

hotheaded [ˌhɒt'hedɪd] adj impulsif (ive).

hothouse ['hɒthaʊs, pl -haʊzɪz] n (greenhouse) serre f.

hot line n 1. (between government heads) téléphone m rouge. 2. (special line) ligne ouverte 24 heures sur 24.

hotly ['hɒtlɪ] adv 1. (passionately) avec véhémence. 2. (closely) de près.

hotplate ['hɒtpleɪt] n plaque f chauffante.

hot-tempered [-'tempəd] adj colérique.

hot-water bottle n bouillotte f.

hound [haʊnd] ◆ n (dog) chien m. ◆ vt 1. (persecute) poursuivre, pourchasser. 2. (drive): **to ~ sb out (of)** chasser qqn (de).

hour ['aʊəʳ] n heure f; **half an ~** une demi-heure; **70 miles per** OR **an ~** 110 km à l'heure; **on the ~** à l'heure juste. ▶ **hours** npl (of business) heures fpl d'ouverture.

hourly ['aʊəlɪ] ◆ adj 1. (happening every hour) toutes les heures. 2. (per hour) à l'heure. ◆ adv 1. (every hour) toutes les heures. 2. (per hour) à l'heure.

house [n & adj haʊs, pl 'haʊzɪz, vb haʊz] ◆ n 1. (gen) maison f; **on the ~** aux frais de la maison. 2. (POL) chambre f. 3. (in debates) assistance f. 4. (THEATRE) (audience) auditoire m, salle f; **to bring the ~ down** faire crouler la salle sous les applaudissements. ◆ vt (accommodate) loger, héberger; (department, store) abriter. ◆ adj 1. (within business) d'entreprise; (style) de la maison. 2. (wine) maison (inv).

house arrest n: **under ~** en résidence surveillée.

houseboat ['haʊsbəʊt] n péniche f aménagée.

housebreaking ['haʊsˌbreɪkɪŋ] n (U) cambriolage m.

housecoat ['haʊskəʊt] n peignoir m.

household ['haʊshəʊld] ◆ adj 1. (domestic) ménager(ère). 2. (word, name) connu(e) de tous. ◆ n maison f, ménage m.

housekeeper ['haʊsˌki:pəʳ] n gouvernante f.

housekeeping ['haʊsˌki:pɪŋ] n (U) 1. (work) ménage m. 2. **~ (money)** argent m du ménage.

house music n house music f.

House of Commons n Br: **the ~** la Chambre des communes.

House of Lords n Br: **the ~** la Chambre des lords.

House of Representatives n Am: **the ~** la Chambre des représentants.

houseplant ['haʊsplɑ:nt] n plante f

d'appartement.

Houses of Parliament *npl*: **the ~** le Parlement britannique (*où se réunissent la Chambre des communes et la Chambre des lords*).

housewarming (party) ['haus-,wɔːmɪŋ-] *n* pendaison *f* de crémaillère.

housewife ['hauswaɪf] (*pl* **-wives** [-waɪvz]) *n* femme *f* au foyer.

housework ['hauswɜːk] *n* (U) ménage *m*.

housing ['hauzɪŋ] *n* (U) (*accommodation*) logement *m*.

housing association *n* Br association *f* d'aide au logement.

housing benefit *n* (U) Br allocation *f* logement.

housing estate Br, **housing project** Am *n* cité *f*.

hovel ['hɒvl] *n* masure *f*, taudis *m*.

hover ['hɒvə^r] *vi* (*fly*) planer.

hovercraft ['hɒvəkrɑːft] (*pl inv* OR **-s**) *n* aéroglisseur *m*, hovercraft *m*.

how [hau] *adv* **1.** (*gen*) comment; **~ do you do it?** comment fait-on?; **~ are you?** comment allez-vous?; **~ do you do?** enchanté(e) (de faire votre connaissance). **2.** (*referring to degree, amount*): **~ high is it?** combien cela fait-il de haut?, quelle en est la hauteur?; **~ long have you been waiting?** cela fait combien de temps que vous attendez?; **~ many people came?** combien de personnes sont venues?; **~ old are you?** quel âge as-tu? **3.** (*in exclamations*): **~ nice!** que c'est bien!; **~ awful!** quelle horreur! ▶ **how about** *adv*: **~ about a drink?** si on prenait un verre?; **~ about you?** et toi? ▶ **how much** ◆ *pron* combien; **~ much does it cost?** combien ça coûte? ◆ *adj* combien de; **~ much bread?** combien de pain?

however [hau'evə^r] ◆ *adv* **1.** (*nevertheless*) cependant, toutefois. **2.** (*no matter how*) quelque … que (+ *subjunctive*), si … que (+ *subjunctive*); **~ many/much** peu importe la quantité de. **3.** (*how*) comment. ◆ *conj* (*in whatever way*) de quelque manière que (+ *subjunctive*).

howl [haul] ◆ *n* hurlement *m*; (*of laughter*) éclat *m*. ◆ *vi* hurler; (*with laughter*) rire aux éclats.

hp (*abbr of* **horsepower**) *n* CV *m*.

HP *n* **1.** Br (*abbr of* **hire purchase**): **to buy sthg on ~** acheter qqch à crédit. **2.** = **hp**.

HQ (*abbr of* **headquarters**) *n* QG *m*.

hr (*abbr of* **hour**) h.

hub [hʌb] *n* **1.** (*of wheel*) moyeu *m*. **2.** (*of activity*) centre *m*.

hubbub ['hʌbʌb] *n* vacarme *m*, brouhaha *m*.

hubcap ['hʌbkæp] *n* enjoliveur *m*.

huddle ['hʌdl] ◆ *vi* se blottir. ◆ *n* petit groupe *m*.

hue [hjuː] *n* (*colour*) teinte *f*, nuance *f*.

huff [hʌf] *n*: **in a ~** froissé(e).

hug [hʌg] ◆ *n* étreinte *f*; **to give sb a ~** serrer qqn dans ses bras. ◆ *vt* **1.** (*embrace*) étreindre, serrer dans ses bras. **2.** (*hold*) tenir. **3.** (*stay close to*) serrer.

huge [hjuːdʒ] *adj* énorme; (*subject*) vaste; (*success*) fou (folle).

hulk [hʌlk] *n* **1.** (*of ship*) carcasse *f*. **2.** (*person*) malabar *m*, mastodonte *m*.

hull [hʌl] *n* coque *f*.

hullo [hə'ləu] *excl* = **hello**.

hum [hʌm] ◆ *vi* **1.** (*buzz*) bourdonner; (*machine*) vrombir, ronfler. **2.** (*sing*) fredonner, chantonner. ◆ *vt* fredonner, chantonner.

human ['hjuːmən] ◆ *adj* humain(e). ◆ *n*: **~ (being)** être *m* humain.

humane [hjuː'meɪn] *adj* humain(e).

humanitarian [hjuːˌmænɪ'teərɪən] *adj* humanitaire.

humanity [hjuː'mænətɪ] *n* humanité *f*. ▶ **humanities** *npl*: **the humanities** les humanités *fpl*, les sciences *fpl* humaines.

human race *n*: **the ~** la race humaine.

human rights *npl* droits *mpl* de l'homme.

humble ['hʌmbl] ◆ *adj* humble; (*origins, employee*) modeste. ◆ *vt* humilier.

humbug ['hʌmbʌg] *n* **1.** *dated* (*hypocrisy*) hypocrisie *f*. **2.** Br (*sweet*) type de bonbon dur.

humdrum ['hʌmdrʌm] *adj* monotone.

humid ['hjuːmɪd] *adj* humide.

humidity [hjuː'mɪdətɪ] *n* humidité *f*.

humiliate [hjuː'mɪlɪeɪt] *vt* humilier.

humiliation [hjuːˌmɪlɪ'eɪʃn] *n* humiliation *f*.

humility [hjuː'mɪlətɪ] *n* humilité *f*.

humor Am = **humour**.

humorous ['hjuːmərəs] *adj* humoristique; (*person*) plein(e) d'humour.

humour Br, **humor** Am ['hjuːmə^r] ◆ *n* **1.** (*sense of fun*) humour *m*. **2.** (*of situation, remark*) côté *m* comique. **3.** *dated* (*mood*) humeur *f*. ◆ *vt* se montrer conciliant(e) envers.

hump [hʌmp] *n* bosse *f*.

humpbacked bridge ['hʌmpbækt-] *n* pont *m* en dos d'âne.

hunch [hʌntʃ] *n inf* pressentiment *m*, intuition *f*.

hunchback ['hʌntʃbæk] *n* bossu *m*, -e *f*.

hunched [hʌntʃt] *adj* voûté(e).

hundred ['hʌndrəd] *num* cent; **a** OR **one** ~ cent; *see also* **six**. ▶ **hundreds** *npl* des centaines.

hundredth ['hʌndrətθ] *num* centième; *see also* **sixth**.

hundredweight ['hʌndrədweɪt] *n* (*in* UK) poids *m* de 112 livres, = 50,8 *kg*; (*in* US) poids *m* de 100 livres, = 45,3 *kg*.

hung [hʌŋ] *pt & pp* → **hang**.

Hungarian [hʌŋˈgeərɪən] ◆ *adj* hongrois(e). ◆ *n* 1. (*person*) Hongrois *m*, -e *f*. 2. (*language*) hongrois *m*.

Hungary ['hʌŋgərɪ] *n* Hongrie *f*.

hunger ['hʌŋgər] *n* 1. (*gen*) faim *f*. 2. (*strong desire*) soif *f*. ▶ **hunger after**, **hunger for** *vt fus* avoir faim de.

hunger strike *n* grève *f* de la faim.

hung over *adj inf:* **to be** ~ avoir la gueule de bois.

hungry ['hʌŋgrɪ] *adj* 1. (*for food*): **to be** ~ avoir faim; (*starving*) être affamé(e). 2. (*eager*): **to be** ~ **for** être avide de.

hung up *adj inf:* **to be** ~ (**on** OR **about**) être obsédé(e) (par).

hunk [hʌŋk] *n* 1. (*large piece*) gros morceau *m*. 2. *inf* (*man*) beau mec *m*.

hunt [hʌnt] ◆ *n* chasse *f*; (*for missing person*) recherches *fpl*. ◆ *vi* 1. (*chase animals, birds*) chasser. 2. *Br* (*chase foxes*) chasser le renard. 3. (*search*): **to** ~ (**for sthg**) chercher partout (qqch). ◆ *vt* 1. (*animals, birds*) chasser. 2. (*person*) poursuivre, pourchasser.

hunter ['hʌntər] *n* (*of animals, birds*) chasseur *m*.

hunting ['hʌntɪŋ] *n* 1. (*of animals*) chasse *f*. 2. *Br* (*of foxes*) chasse *f* au renard.

hurdle ['hɜːdl] ◆ *n* 1. (*in race*) haie *f*. 2. (*obstacle*) obstacle *m*. ◆ *vt* (*jump over*) sauter.

hurl [hɜːl] *vt* 1. (*throw*) lancer avec violence. 2. (*shout*) lancer.

hurray [huˈreɪ] *excl* hourra!

hurricane ['hʌrɪkən] *n* ouragan *m*.

hurried ['hʌrɪd] *adj* (*hasty*) précipité(e).

hurriedly ['hʌrɪdlɪ] *adv* précipitamment; (*eat, write*) vite, en toute hâte.

hurry ['hʌrɪ] ◆ *vt* (*person*) faire se dépêcher; (*process*) hâter, **to** ~ **to do sthg** se dépêcher OR se presser de faire qqch. ◆ *vi* se dépêcher, se presser. ◆ *n* hâte *f*, précipitation *f*; **to be in a** ~ être

pressé; **to do sthg in a** ~ faire qqch à la hâte. ▶ **hurry up** *vi* se dépêcher.

hurt [hɜːt] (*pt & pp* **hurt**) ◆ *vt* 1. (*physically, emotionally*) blesser; (*one's leg, arm*) se faire mal à; **to** ~ **o.s.** se faire mal. 2. *fig* (*harm*) faire du mal à. ◆ *vi* 1. (*gen*) faire mal; **my leg** ~**s** ma jambe me fait mal. 2. *fig* (*do harm*) faire du mal. ◆ *adj* blessé(e); (*voice*) offensé(e).

hurtful ['hɜːtfʊl] *adj* blessant(e).

hurtle ['hɜːtl] *vi* aller à toute allure.

husband ['hʌzbənd] *n* mari *m*.

hush [hʌʃ] ◆ *n* silence *m*. ◆ *excl* silence!, chut!

husk [hʌsk] *n* (*of seed, grain*) enveloppe *f*.

husky ['hʌskɪ] ◆ *adj* (*hoarse*) rauque. ◆ *n* chien *m* esquimau.

hustle ['hʌsl] ◆ *vt* (*hurry*) pousser, bousculer. ◆ *n* agitation *f*.

hut [hʌt] *n* 1. (*rough house*) hutte *f*. 2. (*shed*) cabane *f*.

hutch [hʌtʃ] *n* clapier *m*.

hyacinth ['haɪəsɪnθ] *n* jacinthe *f*.

hydrant ['haɪdrənt] *n* bouche *f* d'incendie.

hydraulic [haɪˈdrɔːlɪk] *adj* hydraulique.

hydroelectric [ˌhaɪdrəʊɪˈlektrɪk] *adj* hydro-électrique.

hydrofoil ['haɪdrəfɔɪl] *n* hydrofoil *m*.

hydrogen ['haɪdrədʒən] *n* hydrogène *m*.

hyena [haɪˈiːnə] *n* hyène *f*.

hygiene ['haɪdʒiːn] *n* hygiène *f*.

hygienic [haɪˈdʒiːnɪk] *adj* hygiénique.

hymn [hɪm] *n* hymne *m*, cantique *m*.

hype [haɪp] *n* (U) *inf* battage *m* publicitaire.

hyperactive [ˌhaɪpərˈæktɪv] *adj* hyperactif(ive).

hypermarket [ˈhaɪpəˌmɑːkɪt] *n* hypermarché *m*.

hyphen ['haɪfn] *n* trait *m* d'union.

hypnosis [hɪpˈnəʊsɪs] *n* hypnose *f*.

hypnotic [hɪpˈnɒtɪk] *adj* hypnotique.

hypnotize, -ise ['hɪpnətaɪz] *vt* hypnotiser.

hypocrisy [hɪˈpɒkrəsɪ] *n* hypocrisie *f*.

hypocrite ['hɪpəkrɪt] *n* hypocrite *mf*.

hypocritical [ˌhɪpəˈkrɪtɪkl] *adj* hypocrite.

hypothesis [haɪˈpɒθɪsɪs] (*pl* **-theses** [-θɪsiːz]) *n* hypothèse *f*.

hypothetical [ˌhaɪpəˈθetɪkl] *adj* hypothétique.

hysteria [hɪsˈtɪərɪə] *n* hystérie *f*.

hysterical [hɪsˈterɪkl] *adj* 1. (*gen*) hystérique. 2. *inf* (*very funny*) désopilant(e).
hysterics [hɪsˈterɪks] *npl* 1. (*panic, excitement*) crise *f* de nerfs. 2. *inf* (*laughter*) fou rire *m*.

I

i (*pl* **i's** OR **is**), **I** (*pl* **I's** OR **Is**) [aɪ] *n* (*letter*) i *m inv*, I *m inv*.
I [aɪ] *pers pron* 1. (*unstressed*) je, j' (*before vowel or silent 'h'*); **he and I are leaving for Paris** lui et moi (nous) partons pour Paris. 2. (*stressed*) moi; **I can't do it** moi je ne peux pas le faire.
ice [aɪs] ◆ *n* 1. (*frozen water, ice cream*) glace *f*. 2. (U) (*on road*) verglas *m*. 3. (U) (*ice cubes*) glaçons *mpl*. ◆ *vt Br* glacer.
▶ **ice over, ice up** *vi* (*lake, pond*) geler; (*window, windscreen*) givrer; (*road*) se couvrir de verglas.
iceberg [ˈaɪsbɜːg] *n* iceberg *m*.
iceberg lettuce *n* laitue *f* iceberg.
icebox [ˈaɪsbɒks] *n* 1. *Br* (*in refrigerator*) freezer *m*. 2. *Am* (*refrigerator*) réfrigérateur *m*.
ice cream *n* glace *f*.
ice cube *n* glaçon *m*.
ice hockey *n* hockey *m* sur glace.
Iceland [ˈaɪslənd] *n* Islande *f*.
Icelandic [aɪsˈlændɪk] ◆ *adj* islandais(e). ◆ *n* (*language*) islandais *m*.
ice lolly *n Br* sucette *f* glacée.
ice pick *n* pic *m* à glace.
ice rink *n* patinoire *f*.
ice skate *n* patin *m* à glace. ▶ **ice-skate** *vi* faire du patin (à glace).
ice-skating *n* patinage *m* (sur glace).
icicle [ˈaɪsɪkl] *n* glaçon *m* (naturel).
icing [ˈaɪsɪŋ] *n* (U) glaçage *m*, glace *f*.
icing sugar *n Br* sucre *m* glace.
icon [ˈaɪkɒn] *n* (*gen* & COMPUT) icône *f*.
icy [ˈaɪsɪ] *adj* 1. (*weather, manner*) glacial(e). 2. (*covered in ice*) verglacé(e).
I'd [aɪd] = **I would**, **I had**.
ID *n* (U) (*abbr of* **identification**) papiers *mpl*.
idea [aɪˈdɪə] *n* idée *f*; (*intention*) intention *f*; **to have an ~ (that)** ... avoir idée que ...; **to have no ~** n'avoir aucune idée; **to get the ~** *inf* piger.

ideal [aɪˈdɪəl] ◆ *adj* idéal(e). ◆ *n* idéal *m*.
ideally [aɪˈdɪəlɪ] *adv* idéalement; (*suited*) parfaitement.
identical [aɪˈdentɪkl] *adj* identique.
identification [aɪˌdentɪfɪˈkeɪʃn] *n* (U) 1. (*gen*): **~ (with)** identification *f* (à). 2. (*documentation*) pièce *f* d'identité.
identify [aɪˈdentɪfaɪ] ◆ *vt* 1. (*recognize*) identifier. 2. (*subj: document, card*) permettre de reconnaître. 3. (*associate*): **to ~ sb with sthg** associer qqn à qqch. ◆ *vi* (*empathize*): **to ~ with** s'identifier à.
Identikit picture® [aɪˈdentɪkɪt-] *n* portrait-robot *m*.
identity [aɪˈdentətɪ] *n* identité *f*.
identity card *n* carte *f* d'identité.
identity parade *n* séance d'identification d'un suspect dans un échantillon de plusieurs personnes.
ideology [ˌaɪdɪˈɒlədʒɪ] *n* idéologie *f*.
idiom [ˈɪdɪəm] *n* 1. (*phrase*) expression *f* idiomatique. 2. *fml* (*style*) langue *f*.
idiomatic [ˌɪdɪəˈmætɪk] *adj* idiomatique.
idiosyncrasy [ˌɪdɪəˈsɪŋkrəsɪ] *n* particularité *f*, caractéristique *f*.
idiot [ˈɪdɪət] *n* idiot *m*, -e *f*, imbécile *mf*.
idiotic [ˌɪdɪˈɒtɪk] *adj* idiot(e).
idle [ˈaɪdl] ◆ *adj* 1. (*lazy*) oisif(ive), désœuvré(e). 2. (*not working - machine, factory*) arrêté(e); (*- worker*) qui chôme, en chômage. 3. (*threat*) vain(e). 4. (*curiosity*) simple, pur(e). ◆ *vi* tourner au ralenti. ▶ **idle away** *vt sep* (*time*) perdre à ne rien faire.
idol [ˈaɪdl] *n* idole *f*.
idolize, -ise [ˈaɪdəlaɪz] *vt* idolâtrer, adorer.
idyllic [ɪˈdɪlɪk] *adj* idyllique.
i.e. (*abbr of* **id est**) c-à-d.
if [ɪf] *conj* 1. (*gen*) si; **~ I were you** à ta place, si j'étais toi. 2. (*though*) bien que. 3. (*that*) que. ▶ **if not** *conj* sinon.
▶ **if only** ◆ *conj* 1. (*naming a reason*) ne serait-ce que. 2. (*expressing regret*) si seulement. ◆ *excl* si seulement!
igloo [ˈɪgluː] *n* (*pl* **-s**) igloo *m*, iglou *m*.
ignite [ɪgˈnaɪt] ◆ *vt* mettre le feu à, enflammer; (*firework*) tirer. ◆ *vi* prendre feu, s'enflammer.
ignition [ɪgˈnɪʃn] *n* 1. (*act of igniting*) ignition *f*. 2. (AUT) allumage *m*; **to switch on the ~** mettre le contact.
ignition key *n* clef *f* de contact.
ignorance [ˈɪgnərəns] *n* ignorance *f*.
ignorant [ˈɪgnərənt] *adj* 1. (*uneducated, unaware*) ignorant(e); **to be ~ of sthg** être

ignorant de qqch. **2.** (*rude*) mal élevé(e).

ignore [ɪgˈnɔːr] *vt* (*advice, facts*) ne pas tenir compte de; (*person*) faire semblant de ne pas voir.

ilk [ɪlk] *n*: **of that ~** (*of that sort*) de cet acabit, de ce genre.

ill [ɪl] ◆ *adj* **1.** (*unwell*) malade; **to feel ~** se sentir malade OR souffrant; **to be taken ~**, **to fall ~** tomber malade. **2.** (*bad*) mauvais(e); **~ luck** malchance f. ◆ *adv* mal; **to speak/think ~ of sb** dire/penser du mal de qqn.

I'll [aɪl] = **I will, I shall**.

ill-advised [-ədˈvaɪzd] *adj* (*remark, action*) peu judicieux(euse); (*person*) malavisé(e).

ill at ease *adj* mal à l'aise.

illegal [ɪˈliːgl] *adj* illégal(e); (*immigrant*) en situation irrégulière.

illegible [ɪˈledʒəbl] *adj* illisible.

illegitimate [ˌɪlɪˈdʒɪtɪmət] *adj* illégitime.

ill-equipped [-ɪˈkwɪpt] *adj*: **to be ~ to do sthg** être mal placé(e) pour faire qqch.

ill-fated [-ˈfeɪtɪd] *adj* fatal(e), funeste.

ill feeling *n* animosité f.

ill health *n* mauvaise santé f.

illicit [ɪˈlɪsɪt] *adj* illicite.

illiteracy [ɪˈlɪtərəsɪ] *n* analphabétisme *m*, illettrisme *m*.

illiterate [ɪˈlɪtərət] ◆ *adj* analphabète, illettré(e). ◆ *n* analphabète *mf*, illettré *m*, -e *f*.

illness [ˈɪlnɪs] *n* maladie f.

illogical [ɪˈlɒdʒɪkl] *adj* illogique.

ill-suited *adj* mal assorti(e); **to be ~ for sthg** être inapte à qqch.

ill-timed [-ˈtaɪmd] *adj* déplacé(e), mal à propos.

ill-treat *vt* maltraiter.

illuminate [ɪˈluːmɪneɪt] *vt* éclairer.

illumination [ɪˌluːmɪˈneɪʃn] *n* (*lighting*) éclairage *m*. ▶ **illuminations** *npl* Br illuminations *fpl*.

illusion [ɪˈluːʒn] *n* illusion f; **to have no ~s about** ne se faire OR n'avoir aucune illusion sur; **to be under the ~ that** croire OR s'imaginer que, avoir l'illusion que.

illustrate [ˈɪləstreɪt] *vt* illustrer.

illustration [ˌɪləˈstreɪʃn] *n* illustration f.

illustrious [ɪˈlʌstrɪəs] *adj* illustre, célèbre.

ill will *n* animosité f.

I'm [aɪm] = **I am**.

image [ˈɪmɪdʒ] *n* **1.** (*gen*) image f. **2.** (*of company, politician*) image f de marque.

imagery [ˈɪmɪdʒrɪ] *n* (U) images *fpl*.

imaginary [ɪˈmædʒɪnrɪ] *adj* imaginaire.

imagination [ɪˌmædʒɪˈneɪʃn] *n* **1.** (*ability*) imagination f. **2.** (*fantasy*) invention f.

imaginative [ɪˈmædʒɪnətɪv] *adj* imaginatif(ive); (*solution*) plein(e) d'imagination.

imagine [ɪˈmædʒɪn] *vt* imaginer; **to ~ doing sthg** s'imaginer OR se voir faisant qqch; **~ (that)!** tu t'imagines!

imbalance [ˌɪmˈbæləns] *n* déséquilibre *m*.

imbecile [ˈɪmbɪsiːl] *n* imbécile *mf*, idiot *m*, -e *f*.

IMF (*abbr of* **International Monetary Fund**) *n* FMI *m*.

imitate [ˈɪmɪteɪt] *vt* imiter.

imitation [ˌɪmɪˈteɪʃn] ◆ *n* imitation f. ◆ *adj* (*leather*) imitation (*before n*); (*jewellery*) en toc.

immaculate [ɪˈmækjʊlət] *adj* impeccable.

immature [ˌɪməˈtjʊər] *adj* **1.** (*lacking judgment*) qui manque de maturité. **2.** (*not fully grown*) jeune, immature.

immediate [ɪˈmiːdjət] *adj* **1.** (*urgent*) immédiat(e); (*problem, meeting*) urgent(e). **2.** (*very near*) immédiat(e); (*family*) le plus proche.

immediately [ɪˈmiːdjətlɪ] ◆ *adv* **1.** (*at once*) immédiatement. **2.** (*directly*) directement. ◆ *conj* dès que.

immense [ɪˈmens] *adj* immense; (*improvement, change*) énorme.

immerse [ɪˈmɜːs] *vt*: **to ~ sthg in sthg** immerger OR plonger qqch dans qqch; **to ~ o.s. in sthg** *fig* se plonger dans qqch.

immersion heater [ɪˈmɜːʃn-] *n* chauffe-eau *m* électrique.

immigrant [ˈɪmɪgrənt] *n* immigré *m*, -e *f*.

immigration [ˌɪmɪˈgreɪʃn] *n* immigration f.

imminent [ˈɪmɪnənt] *adj* imminent(e).

immobilize, -ise [ɪˈməʊbɪlaɪz] *vt* immobiliser.

immobilizer [ɪˈməʊbɪlaɪzər] *n* (AUT) système *m* antidémarrage.

immoral [ɪˈmɒrəl] *adj* immoral(e).

immortal [ɪˈmɔːtl] ◆ *adj* immortel (elle). ◆ *n* immortel *m*, -elle *f*.

immortalize, -ise [ɪˈmɔːtəlaɪz] *vt* immortaliser.

immovable [ɪˈmuːvəbl] *adj* **1.** (*fixed*) fixe. **2.** (*determined*) inébranlable.

immune [ɪˈmjuːn] *adj* **1.** (MED): **~ (to)** immunisé(e) (contre). **2.** *fig* (*protected*):

to be ~ to OR from être à l'abri de.

immunity [ɪ'mjuːnətɪ] n 1. (MED): ~ (to) immunité f (contre). 2. fig (protection): ~ to OR from immunité f contre.

immunize, -ise ['ɪmjuːnaɪz] vt: to ~ sb (against) immuniser qqn (contre).

imp [ɪmp] n 1. (creature) lutin m. 2. (naughty child) petit diable m.

impact [n 'ɪmpækt, vb ɪm'pækt] ◆ n impact m; to make an ~ on OR upon sb faire une forte impression sur qqn; to make an ~ on OR upon sthg avoir un impact sur qqch. ◆ vt 1. (collide with) entrer en collision avec. 2. (influence) avoir un impact sur.

impair [ɪm'peəʳ] vt affaiblir, abîmer; (efficiency) réduire.

impart [ɪm'pɑːt] vt fml 1. (information): to ~ sthg (to sb) communiquer OR transmettre qqch (à qqn). 2. (feeling, quality): to ~ sthg (to) donner qqch (à).

impartial [ɪm'pɑːʃl] adj impartial(e).

impassable [ɪm'pɑːsəbl] adj impraticable.

impassive [ɪm'pæsɪv] adj impassible.

impatience [ɪm'peɪʃns] n 1. (gen) impatience f. 2. (irritability) irritation f.

impatient [ɪm'peɪʃnt] adj 1. (gen) impatient(e); to be ~ to do sthg être impatient de faire qqch; to be ~ for sthg attendre qqch avec impatience. 2. (irritable): to become OR get ~ s'impatienter.

impeccable [ɪm'pekəbl] adj impeccable.

impede [ɪm'piːd] vt entraver, empêcher; (person) gêner.

impediment [ɪm'pedɪmənt] n 1. (obstacle) obstacle m. 2. (disability) défaut m.

impel [ɪm'pel] vt: to ~ sb to do sthg inciter qqn à faire qqch.

impending [ɪm'pendɪŋ] adj imminent(e).

imperative [ɪm'perətɪv] ◆ adj (essential) impératif(ive), essentiel(elle). ◆ n impératif m.

imperfect [ɪm'pɜːfɪkt] ◆ adj imparfait(e). ◆ n (GRAMM): ~ (tense) imparfait m.

imperial [ɪm'pɪərɪəl] adj 1. (of empire) impérial(e). 2. (system of measurement) qui a cours légal dans le Royaume-Uni.

imperil [ɪm'perɪl] vt mettre en péril OR en danger; (project) compromettre.

impersonal [ɪm'pɜːsnl] adj impersonnel(elle).

impersonate [ɪm'pɜːsəneɪt] vt se faire passer pour.

impersonation [ɪm.pɜːsə'neɪʃn] n usurpation f d'identité; (by mimic) imitation f.

impertinent [ɪm'pɜːtɪnənt] adj impertinent(e).

impervious [ɪm'pɜːvjəs] adj (not influenced): ~ to indifférent(e) à.

impetuous [ɪm'petʃʊəs] adj impétueux(euse).

impetus ['ɪmpɪtəs] n (U) 1. (momentum) élan m. 2. (stimulus) impulsion f.

impinge [ɪm'pɪndʒ] vi: to ~ on sb/sthg affecter qqn/qqch.

implant [n 'ɪmplɑːnt, vb ɪm'plɑːnt] ◆ n implant m. ◆ vt: to ~ sthg in OR into sb implanter qqch dans qqn.

implausible [ɪm'plɔːzəbl] adj peu plausible.

implement [n 'ɪmplɪmənt, vb 'ɪmplɪment] ◆ n outil m, instrument m. ◆ vt exécuter, appliquer.

implication [.ɪmplɪ'keɪʃn] n implication f; by ~ par voie de conséquence.

implicit [ɪm'plɪsɪt] adj 1. (inferred) implicite. 2. (belief, faith) absolu(e).

implore [ɪm'plɔːʳ] vt: to ~ sb (to do sthg) implorer qqn (de faire qqch).

imply [ɪm'plaɪ] vt 1. (suggest) sous-entendre, laisser supposer OR entendre. 2. (involve) impliquer.

impolite [.ɪmpə'laɪt] adj impoli(e).

import [n 'ɪmpɔːt, vb ɪm'pɔːt] ◆ n (product, action) importation f. ◆ vt (gen & COMPUT) importer.

importance [ɪm'pɔːtns] n importance f.

important [ɪm'pɔːtnt] adj important(e); to be ~ to sb importer à qqn.

importer [ɪm'pɔːtəʳ] n importateur m, -trice f.

impose [ɪm'pəʊz] ◆ vt (force): to ~ sthg (on) imposer qqch (à). ◆ vi (cause trouble): to ~ (on sb) abuser (de la gentillesse de qqn).

imposing [ɪm'pəʊzɪŋ] adj imposant(e).

imposition [.ɪmpə'zɪʃn] n 1. (of tax, limitations etc) imposition f. 2. (cause of trouble): it's an ~ c'est abuser de ma/ notre gentillesse.

impossible [ɪm'pɒsəbl] adj impossible.

impostor, imposter Am [ɪm'pɒstəʳ] n imposteur m.

impotent ['ɪmpətənt] adj impuissant(e).

impound [ɪm'paʊnd] vt confisquer.

impoverished [ɪm'pɒvərɪʃt] adj appauvri(e).

impractical [ɪm'præktɪkl] *adj* pas pratique.

impregnable [ɪm'pregnəbl] *adj* 1. (*fortress, defences*) imprenable. 2. *fig* (*person*) inattaquable.

impregnate ['ɪmpregneɪt] *vt* 1. (*introduce substance into*): **to ~ sthg with** imprégner qqch de. 2. *fml* (*fertilize*) féconder.

impress [ɪm'pres] *vt* 1. (*person*) impressionner. 2. (*stress*): **to ~ sthg on sb** faire bien comprendre qqch à qqn.

impression [ɪm'preʃn] *n* 1. (*gen*) impression *f*; **to be under the ~ (that)** ... avoir l'impression que ...; **to make an ~** faire impression. 2. (*by mimic*) imitation *f*. 3. (*of stamp, book*) impression *f*, empreinte *f*.

impressive [ɪm'presɪv] *adj* impressionnant(e).

imprint ['ɪmprɪnt] *n* 1. (*mark*) empreinte *f*. 2. (*publisher's name*) nom *m* de l'éditeur.

imprison [ɪm'prɪzn] *vt* emprisonner.

improbable [ɪm'prɒbəbl] *adj* (*story, excuse*) improbable.

impromptu [ɪm'prɒmptjuː] *adj* impromptu(e).

improper [ɪm'prɒpər] *adj* 1. (*unsuitable*) impropre. 2. (*incorrect, illegal*) incorrect(e). 3. (*rude*) indécent(e).

improve [ɪm'pruːv] ♦ *vi* s'améliorer; (*patient*) aller mieux; **to ~ on OR upon sthg** améliorer qqch. ♦ *vt* améliorer.

improvement [ɪm'pruːvmənt] *n*: **~ (in/on)** amélioration *f* (de/par rapport à).

improvise ['ɪmprəvaɪz] *vt & vi* improviser.

impudent ['ɪmpjʊdənt] *adj* impudent(e).

impulse ['ɪmpʌls] *n* impulsion *f*; **on ~** par impulsion.

impulsive [ɪm'pʌlsɪv] *adj* impulsif(ive).

impunity [ɪm'pjuːnətɪ] *n*: **with ~** avec impunité.

impurity [ɪm'pjʊərətɪ] *n* impureté *f*.

in [ɪn] ♦ *prep* 1. (*indicating place, position*) dans; **~ a box/bag/drawer** dans une boîte/un sac/un tiroir; **~ Paris** à Paris; **~ Belgium** en Belgique; **~ Canada** au Canada; **~ the United States** aux États-Unis; **~ the country** à la campagne; **to be ~ hospital/prison** être à l'hôpital/en prison; **~ here** ici; **~ there** là. 2. (*wearing*) en; **dressed ~ a suit** vêtu d'un costume. 3. (*at a particular time, season*): **~ 1994** en 1994; **~ April** en avril; **~ (the) spring** au printemps; **~ (the) winter** en hiver; **at two o'clock ~ the afternoon** à deux heures de l'après-midi. 4. (*period of time - within*) en; (*- after*) dans; **he learned to type ~ two weeks** il a appris à taper à la machine en deux semaines; **I'll be ready ~ five minutes** je serai prêt dans 5 minutes. 5. (*during*): **it's my first decent meal ~ weeks** c'est mon premier repas correct depuis des semaines. 6. (*indicating situation, circumstances*): **~ the sun** au soleil; **~ the rain** sous la pluie; **~ danger/difficulty** en danger/difficulté. 7. (*indicating manner, condition*): **~ a loud/soft voice** d'une voix forte/douce; **to write ~ pencil/ink** écrire au crayon/à l'encre; **to speak ~ English/French** parler (en) anglais/français. 8. (*indicating emotional state*): **~ anger** sous le coup de la colère; **~ joy/delight** avec joie/plaisir. 9. (*specifying area of activity*): **he's ~ computers** il est dans l'informatique. 10. (*referring to quantity, numbers, age*): **~ large/small quantities** en grande/petite quantité; **~ (their) thousands** par milliers; **she's ~ her sixties** elle a la soixantaine. 11. (*describing arrangement*): **~ twos** par deux; **~ a line/row/circle** en ligne/rang/cercle. 12. (*as regards*): **to be three metres ~ length/width** faire trois mètres de long/large; **a change ~ direction** un changement de direction. 13. (*in ratios*): **5 pence ~ the pound** 5 pence par livre sterling; **one ~ ten** un sur dix. 14. (*after superl*) de; **the longest river ~ the world** le fleuve le plus long du monde. 15. (*+ present participle*): **~ doing sthg** en faisant qqch. ♦ *adv* 1. (*inside*) dedans, à l'intérieur. 2. (*at home, work*) là; **I'm staying ~ tonight** je reste à la maison OR chez moi ce soir; **is Judith ~?** est-ce que Judith est là? 3. (*of train, boat, plane*): **to be ~** être arrivé(e). 4. (*of tide*): **the tide's ~** c'est la marée haute. 5. *phr*: **we're ~ for some bad weather** nous allons avoir du mauvais temps. ♦ *adj inf* à la mode. ▶ **ins** *npl*: **the ~s and outs** les tenants et les aboutissants *mpl*.

in. *abbr of* **inch.**

inability [ˌɪnə'bɪlətɪ] *n*: **~ (to do sthg)** incapacité *f* (à faire qqch).

inaccessible [ˌɪnək'sesəbl] *adj* inaccessible.

inaccurate [ɪn'ækjʊrət] *adj* inexact(e).

inadequate [ɪn'ædɪkwət] *adj* insuffisant(e).

inadvertently [ˌɪnəd'vɜːtəntlɪ] *adv* par inadvertance.

inadvisable [ˌɪnəd'vaɪzəbl] *adj* déconseillé(e).

inane [ɪ'neɪn] *adj* inepte; (*person*) stupide.

inanimate [ɪn'ænɪmət] *adj* inanimé(e).

inappropriate [ˌɪnə'prəʊprɪət] *adj* inopportun(e); (*expression, word*) impropre; (*clothing*) peu approprié(e).

inarticulate [ˌɪnɑː'tɪkjʊlət] *adj* inarticulé(e), indistinct(e); (*person*) qui s'exprime avec difficulté; (*explanation*) mal exprimé(e).

inasmuch [ˌɪnəz'mʌtʃ] ▶ **inasmuch as** *conj fml* attendu que.

inaudible [ɪ'nɔːdɪbl] *adj* inaudible.

inaugural [ɪ'nɔːgjʊrəl] *adj* inaugural(e).

inauguration [ɪˌnɔːgjʊ'reɪʃn] *n* (*of leader, president*) investiture *f*; (*of building, system*) inauguration *f*.

in-between *adj* intermédiaire.

inborn [ˌɪn'bɔːn] *adj* inné(e).

inbound ['ɪnbaʊnd] *adj Am* qui arrive.

inbred [ˌɪn'bred] *adj* **1.** (*closely related*) consanguin(e); (*animal*) croisé(e). **2.** (*inborn*) inné(e).

inbuilt [ˌɪn'bɪlt] *adj* (*inborn*) inné(e).

inc. (*abbr of* **inclusive**): **12-15 April ~** du 12 au 15 avril inclus.

Inc. [ɪŋk] (*abbr of* **incorporated**) ≃ SARL.

incapable [ɪn'keɪpəbl] *adj* incapable; **to be ~ of sthg/of doing sthg** être incapable de qqch/de faire qqch.

incapacitated [ˌɪnkə'pæsɪteɪtɪd] *adj* inapte physiquement; **~ for work** mis(e) dans l'incapacité de travailler.

incarcerate [ɪn'kɑːsəreɪt] *vt* incarcérer.

incendiary device [ɪn'sendjərɪ-] *n* dispositif *m* incendiaire.

incense [*n* 'ɪnsens, *vb* ɪn'sens] ◆ *n* encens *m*. ◆ *vt* (*anger*) mettre en colère.

incentive [ɪn'sentɪv] *n* **1.** (*encouragement*) motivation *f*. **2.** (COMM) récompense *f*, prime *f*.

incentive scheme *n* programme *m* d'encouragement.

inception [ɪn'sepʃn] *n fml* commencement *m*.

incessant [ɪn'sesnt] *adj* incessant(e).

incessantly [ɪn'sesntlɪ] *adv* sans cesse.

incest ['ɪnsest] *n* inceste *m*.

inch [ɪntʃ] ◆ *n* = 2,5 *cm*, ≃ pouce *m*. ◆ *vi*: **to ~ forward** avancer petit à petit.

incidence ['ɪnsɪdəns] *n* (*of disease, theft*) fréquence *f*.

incident ['ɪnsɪdənt] *n* incident *m*.

incidental [ˌɪnsɪ'dentl] *adj* accessoire.

incidentally [ˌɪnsɪ'dentəlɪ] *adv* à propos.

incinerate [ɪn'sɪnəreɪt] *vt* incinérer.

incisive [ɪn'saɪsɪv] *adj* incisif(ive).

incite [ɪn'saɪt] *vt* inciter; **to ~ sb to do sthg** inciter qqn à faire qqch.

inclination [ˌɪnklɪ'neɪʃn] *n* **1.** (U) (*liking, preference*) inclination *f*, goût *m*. **2.** (*tendency*): **~ to do sthg** inclination *f* à faire qqch.

incline [*n* 'ɪnklaɪn, *vb* ɪn'klaɪn] ◆ *n* inclinaison *f*. ◆ *vt* (*head*) incliner.

inclined [ɪn'klaɪnd] *adj* **1.** (*tending*): **to be ~ to sthg/to do sthg** avoir tendance à qqch/à faire qqch. **2.** (*wanting*): **to be ~ to do sthg** être enclin(e) à faire qqch. **3.** (*sloping*) incliné(e).

include [ɪn'kluːd] *vt* inclure.

included [ɪn'kluːdɪd] *adj* inclus(e).

including [ɪn'kluːdɪŋ] *prep* y compris.

inclusive [ɪn'kluːsɪv] *adj* inclus(e); (*including all costs*) tout compris; **~ of VAT** TVA incluse OR comprise.

incoherent [ˌɪnkəʊ'hɪərənt] *adj* incohérent(e).

income ['ɪŋkʌm] *n* revenu *m*.

income support *n Br* allocations supplémentaires accordées aux personnes ayant un faible revenu.

income tax *n* impôt *m* sur le revenu.

incompatible [ˌɪnkəm'pætɪbl] *adj*: **~ (with)** incompatible (avec).

incompetent [ɪn'kɒmpɪtənt] *adj* incompétent(e).

incomplete [ˌɪnkəm'pliːt] *adj* incomplet(ète).

incomprehensible [ɪnˌkɒmprɪ'hensəbl] *adj* incompréhensible.

inconceivable [ˌɪnkən'siːvəbl] *adj* inconcevable.

inconclusive [ˌɪnkən'kluːsɪv] *adj* peu concluant(e).

incongruous [ɪn'kɒŋgrʊəs] *adj* incongru(e).

inconsequential [ˌɪnkɒnsɪ'kwenʃl] *adj* sans importance.

inconsiderable [ˌɪnkən'sɪdərəbl] *adj*: **not ~** non négligeable.

inconsiderate [ˌɪnkən'sɪdərət] *adj* inconsidéré(e); (*person*) qui manque de considération.

inconsistency [ˌɪnkən'sɪstənsɪ] *n* inconsistance *f*.

inconsistent [ˌɪnkən'sɪstənt] *adj* **1.** (*not agreeing, contradictory*) contradictoire; (*person*) inconséquent(e); **~ with sthg** en contradiction avec qqch. **2.** (*erratic*) inconsistant(e).

inconspicuous [ˌɪnkən'spɪkjʊəs] *adj* qui passe inaperçu(e).

inconvenience [ˌɪnkən'viːnjəns] ◆ *n* désagrément *m*. ◆ *vt* déranger.

inconvenient [ˌɪnkən'viːnjənt] *adj* inopportun(e).

incorporate [ɪn'kɔːpəreɪt] *vt* **1.** (*integrate*): **to ~ sb/sthg (into)** incorporer qqn/qqch (dans). **2.** (*comprise*) contenir, comprendre.

incorporated [ɪn'kɔːpəreɪtɪd] *adj* (COMM) constitué(e) en société commerciale.

incorrect [ˌɪnkə'rekt] *adj* incorrect(e).

incorrigible [ɪn'kɒrɪdʒəbl] *adj* incorrigible.

increase [*n* 'ɪnkriːs, *vb* ɪn'kriːs] ◆ *n*: **~ (in)** augmentation *f* (de); **to be on the ~** aller en augmentant. ◆ *vt & vi* augmenter.

increasing [ɪn'kriːsɪŋ] *adj* croissant(e).

increasingly [ɪn'kriːsɪŋlɪ] *adv* de plus en plus.

incredible [ɪn'kredəbl] *adj* incroyable.

incredulous [ɪn'kredjʊləs] *adj* incrédule.

increment ['ɪnkrɪmənt] *n* augmentation *f*.

incriminating [ɪn'krɪmɪneɪtɪŋ] *adj* compromettant(e).

incubator ['ɪnkjʊbeɪtəʳ] *n* (*for baby*) incubateur *m*, couveuse *f*.

incumbent [ɪn'kʌmbənt] *fml* ◆ *adj*: **to be ~ on OR upon sb to do sthg** incomber à qqn de faire qqch. ◆ *n* (*of post*) titulaire *m*.

incur [ɪn'kɜːʳ] *vt* encourir.

indebted [ɪn'detɪd] *adj* (*grateful*): **~ to sb** redevable à qqn.

indecent [ɪn'diːsnt] *adj* **1.** (*improper*) indécent(e). **2.** (*unreasonable*) malséant(e).

indecent assault *n* attentat *m* à la pudeur.

indecent exposure *n* outrage *m* public à la pudeur.

indecisive [ˌɪndɪ'saɪsɪv] *adj* indécis(e).

indeed [ɪn'diːd] *adv* **1.** (*certainly, to express surprise*) vraiment; **yes ~ I am, yes ~** certainement. **2.** (*in fact*) en effet. **3.** (*for emphasis*): **very big/bad ~** extrêmement grand/mauvais, vraiment grand/mauvais.

indefinite [ɪn'defɪnɪt] *adj* **1.** (*not fixed*) indéfini(e). **2.** (*imprecise*) vague.

indefinitely [ɪn'defɪnətlɪ] *adv* **1.** (*for unfixed period*) indéfiniment. **2.** (*imprecisely*) vaguement.

indemnity [ɪn'demnətɪ] *n* indemnité *f*.

indent [ɪn'dent] *vt* **1.** (*dent*) entailler. **2.** (*text*) mettre en retrait.

independence [ˌɪndɪ'pendəns] *n* indépendance *f*.

Independence Day *n* fête de l'indépendance américaine, le 4 juillet.

independent [ˌɪndɪ'pendənt] *adj*: **~ (of)** indépendant(e) (de).

independent school *n* Br école *f* privée.

in-depth *adj* approfondi(e).

indescribable [ˌɪndɪ'skraɪbəbl] *adj* indescriptible.

indestructible [ˌɪndɪ'strʌktəbl] *adj* indestructible.

index ['ɪndeks] (*pl* senses 1 and 2 **-es**, sense 3 **-es** OR **indices**) *n* **1.** (*of book*) index *m*. **2.** (*in library*) répertoire *m*, fichier *m*. **3.** (ECON) indice *m*.

index card *n* fiche *f*.

index finger *n* index *m*.

index-linked [-ˌlɪŋkt] *adj* indexé(e).

India ['ɪndjə] *n* Inde *f*.

Indian ['ɪndjən] ◆ *adj* indien(enne). ◆ *n* Indien *m*, -enne *f*.

Indian Ocean *n*: **the ~** l'océan *m* Indien.

indicate ['ɪndɪkeɪt] ◆ *vt* indiquer. ◆ *vi* (AUT) mettre son clignotant.

indication [ˌɪndɪ'keɪʃn] *n* **1.** (*suggestion*) indication *f*. **2.** (*sign*) signe *m*.

indicative [ɪn'dɪkətɪv] ◆ *adj*: **~ of** indicatif(ive) de. ◆ *n* (GRAMM) indicatif *m*.

indicator ['ɪndɪkeɪtəʳ] *n* **1.** (*sign*) indicateur *m*. **2.** (AUT) clignotant *m*.

indices ['ɪndɪsiːz] *pl* → **index**.

indict [ɪn'daɪt] *vt*: **to ~ sb (for)** accuser qqn (de).

indictment [ɪn'daɪtmənt] *n* **1.** (JUR) acte *m* d'accusation. **2.** (*criticism*) mise *f* en accusation.

indifference [ɪn'dɪfrəns] *n* indifférence *f*.

indifferent [ɪn'dɪfrənt] *adj* **1.** (*uninterested*): **~ (to)** indifférent(e) (à). **2.** (*mediocre*) médiocre.

indigenous [ɪn'dɪdʒɪnəs] *adj* indigène.

indigestion [ˌɪndɪ'dʒestʃn] *n* (U) indigestion *f*.

indignant [ɪn'dɪgnənt] *adj*: **~ (at)** indigné(e) (de).

indignity [ɪn'dɪgnətɪ] *n* indignité *f*.

indigo ['ɪndɪgəʊ] ◆ *adj* indigo (*inv*). ◆ *n* indigo *m*.

indirect [ˌɪndɪ'rekt] *adj* indirect(e).

indiscreet [ˌɪndɪ'skriːt] *adj* indiscret (ète).

indiscriminate [ˌɪndɪˈskrɪmɪnət] *adj*
(*person*) qui manque de discernement;
(*treatment*) sans distinction; (*killing*)
commis au hasard.

indispensable [ˌɪndɪˈspensəbl] *adj*
indispensable.

indisputable [ˌɪndɪˈspjuːtəbl] *adj*
indiscutable.

indistinguishable [ˌɪndɪˈstɪŋgwɪʃəbl]
adj: ~ **(from)** que l'on ne peut distinguer
(de).

individual [ˌɪndɪˈvɪdʒʊəl] ◆ *adj* 1. (*separate, for one person*) individuel(elle). 2. (*distinctive*) personnel(elle). ◆ *n* individu *m*.

indoctrination [ɪnˌdɒktrɪˈneɪʃn] *n*
endoctrinement *m*.

Indonesia [ˌɪndəˈniːzjə] *n* Indonésie *f*.

indoor [ˈɪndɔːr] *adj* d'intérieur; (*swimming pool*) couvert(e); (*sports*) en salle.

indoors [ˌɪnˈdɔːz] *adv* à l'intérieur.

induce [ɪnˈdjuːs] *vt* 1. (*persuade*): **to ~ sb
to do sthg** inciter OR pousser qqn à faire
qqch. 2. (*bring about*) provoquer.

inducement [ɪnˈdjuːsmənt] *n* (*incentive*)
incitation *f*, encouragement *m*.

induction [ɪnˈdʌkʃn] *n* 1. (*into official
position*): ~ **(into)** installation *f* (à).
2. (*introduction to job*) introduction *f*.
3. (ELEC) induction *f*.

induction course *n* stage *m* d'initiation.

indulge [ɪnˈdʌldʒ] ◆ *vt* 1. (*whim, passion*) céder à. 2. (*child, person*) gâter. ◆ *vi*:
to ~ in sthg se permettre qqch.

indulgence [ɪnˈdʌldʒəns] *n* 1. (*act of
indulging*) indulgence *f*. 2. (*special treat*)
gâterie *f*.

indulgent [ɪnˈdʌldʒənt] *adj* indul-
gent(e).

industrial [ɪnˈdʌstrɪəl] *adj* industriel
(elle).

industrial action *n*: **to take ~** se mettre en grève.

industrial estate Br, **industrial
park** Am *n* zone *f* industrielle.

industrialist [ɪnˈdʌstrɪəlɪst] *n* industriel *m*.

industrial park Am = **industrial
estate.**

industrial relations *npl* relations *fpl*
patronat-syndicats.

industrial revolution *n* révolution *f*
industrielle.

industrious [ɪnˈdʌstrɪəs] *adj* indus-
trieux(euse).

industry [ˈɪndəstrɪ] *n* 1. (*gen*) industrie
f. 2. (U) (*hard work*) assiduité *f*, application *f*.

inebriated [ɪˈniːbrɪeɪtɪd] *adj fml* ivre.

inedible [ɪnˈedɪbl] *adj* 1. (*meal, food*)
immangeable. 2. (*plant, mushroom*) non
comestible.

ineffective [ˌɪnɪˈfektɪv] *adj* inefficace.

ineffectual [ˌɪnɪˈfektʃʊəl] *adj* inefficace;
(*person*) incapable, incompétent(e).

inefficiency [ˌɪnɪˈfɪʃnsɪ] *n* inefficacité *f*;
(*of person*) incapacité *f*, incompétence *f*.

inefficient [ˌɪnɪˈfɪʃnt] *adj* inefficace;
(*person*) incapable, incompétent(e).

ineligible [ɪnˈelɪdʒəbl] *adj* inéligible; **to
be ~ for sthg** ne pas avoir droit à qqch.

inept [ɪˈnept] *adj* inepte; (*person*) stupide.

inequality [ˌɪnɪˈkwɒlətɪ] *n* inégalité
f.

inert [ɪˈnɜːt] *adj* inerte.

inertia [ɪˈnɜːʃə] *n* inertie *f*.

inescapable [ˌɪnɪˈskeɪpəbl] *adj*
inéluctable.

inevitable [ɪnˈevɪtəbl] ◆ *adj* inévitable. ◆ *n*: **the ~** l'inévitable *m*.

inevitably [ɪnˈevɪtəblɪ] *adv* inévitablement.

inexcusable [ˌɪnɪkˈskjuːzəbl] *adj* inexcusable, impardonnable.

inexhaustible [ˌɪnɪgˈzɔːstəbl] *adj*
inépuisable.

inexpensive [ˌɪnɪkˈspensɪv] *adj* bon
marché (*inv*), pas cher (chère).

inexperienced [ˌɪnɪkˈspɪərɪənst] *adj*
inexpérimenté(e), qui manque d'expérience.

inexplicable [ˌɪnɪkˈsplɪkəbl] *adj* inexplicable.

infallible [ɪnˈfæləbl] *adj* infaillible.

infamous [ˈɪnfəməs] *adj* infâme.

infancy [ˈɪnfənsɪ] *n* petite enfance *f*; **in
its ~** *fig* à ses débuts.

infant [ˈɪnfənt] *n* 1. (*baby*) nouveau-né
m, nouveau-née *f*, nourrisson *m*.
2. (*young child*) enfant *mf* en bas âge.

infantry [ˈɪnfəntrɪ] *n* infanterie *f*.

infant school *n* Br école *f* maternelle
(*de 5 à 7 ans*).

infatuated [ɪnˈfætjʊeɪtɪd] *adj*: ~ **(with)**
entiché(e) (de).

infatuation [ɪnˌfætjʊˈeɪʃn] *n*: ~ **(with)**
béguin *m* (pour).

infect [ɪnˈfekt] *vt* 1. (MED) infecter. 2. *fig*
(*subj: enthusiasm etc*) se propager à.

infection [ɪnˈfekʃn] *n* infection *f*.

infectious [ɪnˈfekʃəs] *adj* 1. (*disease*)
infectieux(euse). 2. *fig* (*feeling, laugh*)
contagieux(euse).

infer [ɪnˈfɜːr] *vt* (*deduce*): **to ~ sthg (from)**
déduire qqch (de).

inferior [ɪnˈfɪərɪəʳ] ♦ adj 1. (in status) inférieur(e). 2. (product) de qualité inférieure; (work) médiocre. ♦ n (in status) subalterne mf.

inferiority [ɪnˌfɪərɪˈɒrətɪ] n infériorité f.

inferiority complex n complexe m d'infériorité.

inferno [ɪnˈfɜːnəʊ] (pl -s) n brasier m.

infertile [ɪnˈfɜːtaɪl] adj 1. (woman) stérile. 2. (soil) infertile.

infested [ɪnˈfestɪd] adj: ~ with infesté(e) de.

infighting [ˈɪnˌfaɪtɪŋ] n (U) querelles fpl intestines.

infiltrate [ˈɪnfɪltreɪt] vt infiltrer.

infinite [ˈɪnfɪnət] adj infini(e).

infinitive [ɪnˈfɪnɪtɪv] n infinitif m.

infinity [ɪnˈfɪnətɪ] n infini m.

infirm [ɪnˈfɜːm] ♦ adj infirme. ♦ npl: the ~ les infirmes mpl.

infirmary [ɪnˈfɜːmərɪ] n (hospital) hôpital m.

infirmity [ɪnˈfɜːmətɪ] n infirmité f.

inflamed [ɪnˈfleɪmd] adj (MED) enflammé(e).

inflammable [ɪnˈflæməbl] adj inflammable.

inflammation [ˌɪnfləˈmeɪʃn] n (MED) inflammation f.

inflatable [ɪnˈfleɪtəbl] adj gonflable.

inflate [ɪnˈfleɪt] vt 1. (tyre, life jacket etc) gonfler. 2. (ECON) (prices, salaries) hausser, gonfler.

inflation [ɪnˈfleɪʃn] n (ECON) inflation f.

inflationary [ɪnˈfleɪʃnrɪ] adj (ECON) inflationniste.

inflict [ɪnˈflɪkt] vt: to ~ sthg on sb infliger qqch à qqn.

influence [ˈɪnflʊəns] ♦ n influence f; under the ~ of (person, group) sous l'influence de; (alcohol, drugs) sous l'effet OR l'empire de. ♦ vt influencer.

influential [ˌɪnflʊˈenʃl] adj influent(e).

influenza [ˌɪnflʊˈenzə] n (U) grippe f.

influx [ˈɪnflʌks] n afflux m.

inform [ɪnˈfɔːm] vt: to ~ sb (of) informer qqn (de); to ~ sb about renseigner qqn sur. ▶ **inform on** vt fus dénoncer.

informal [ɪnˈfɔːml] adj 1. (party, person) simple; (clothes) de tous les jours. 2. (negotiations, visit) officieux(euse); (meeting) informel(elle).

informant [ɪnˈfɔːmənt] n informateur m, -trice f.

information [ˌɪnfəˈmeɪʃn] n (U): ~ (on OR about) renseignements mpl OR informations fpl (sur); a piece of ~ un ren-

seignement; for your ~ fml à titre d'information.

information desk n bureau m de renseignements.

information technology n informatique f.

informative [ɪnˈfɔːmətɪv] adj informatif(ive).

informer [ɪnˈfɔːməʳ] n indicateur m, -trice f.

infrared [ˌɪnfrəˈred] adj infrarouge.

infrastructure [ˈɪnfrəˌstrʌktʃəʳ] n infrastructure f.

infringe [ɪnˈfrɪndʒ] ♦ vt 1. (right) empiéter sur. 2. (law, agreement) enfreindre. ♦ vi 1. (on right): to ~ on empiéter sur. 2. (on law, agreement): to ~ on enfreindre.

infringement [ɪnˈfrɪndʒmənt] n 1. (of right): ~ (of) atteinte f (à). 2. (of law, agreement) transgression f.

infuriating [ɪnˈfjʊərɪeɪtɪŋ] adj exaspérant(e).

ingenious [ɪnˈdʒiːnjəs] adj ingénieux (euse).

ingenuity [ˌɪndʒɪˈnjuːətɪ] n ingéniosité f.

ingenuous [ɪnˈdʒenjʊəs] adj ingénu(e), naïf (naïve).

ingot [ˈɪŋgət] n lingot m.

ingrained [ˌɪnˈgreɪnd] adj 1. (dirt) incrusté(e). 2. fig (belief, hatred) enraciné(e).

ingratiating [ɪnˈgreɪʃɪeɪtɪŋ] adj doucereux(euse), mielleux(euse).

ingredient [ɪnˈgriːdjənt] n ingrédient m; fig élément m.

inhabit [ɪnˈhæbɪt] vt habiter.

inhabitant [ɪnˈhæbɪtənt] n habitant m, -e f.

inhale [ɪnˈheɪl] ♦ vt inhaler, respirer. ♦ vi (breathe in) respirer.

inhaler [ɪnˈheɪləʳ] n (MED) inhalateur m.

inherent [ɪnˈhɪərənt, ɪnˈherənt] adj: ~ (in) inhérent(e) (à).

inherently [ɪnˈhɪərəntlɪ, ɪnˈherəntlɪ] adv fondamentalement, en soi.

inherit [ɪnˈherɪt] ♦ vt: to ~ sthg (from sb) hériter qqch (de qqn). ♦ vi hériter.

inheritance [ɪnˈherɪtəns] n héritage m.

inhibit [ɪnˈhɪbɪt] vt 1. (prevent) empêcher. 2. (PSYCH) inhiber.

inhibition [ˌɪnhɪˈbɪʃn] n inhibition f.

inhospitable [ˌɪnhɒˈspɪtəbl] adj inhospitalier(ère).

in-house ♦ adj interne; (staff) de la maison. ♦ adv (produce, work) sur place.

inhuman [ɪnˈhjuːmən] adj inhumain(e).

initial [ɪ'nɪʃl] ◆ adj initial(e), premier (ère); ~ **letter** initiale f. ◆ vt parapher. ▶ **initials** npl initiales fpl.

initially [ɪ'nɪʃəlɪ] adv initialement, au début.

initiate [ɪ'nɪʃɪeɪt] vt 1. (talks) engager; (scheme) ébaucher, inaugurer. 2. (teach): **to ~ sb into sthg** initier qqn à qqch.

initiative [ɪ'nɪʃətɪv] n 1. (gen) initiative f. 2. (advantage): **to have the ~** avoir l'avantage m.

inject [ɪn'dʒekt] vt 1. (MED): **to ~ sb with sthg, to ~ sthg into sb** injecter qqch à qqn. 2. fig (excitement) insuffler; (money) injecter.

injection [ɪn'dʒekʃn] n injection f.

injure ['ɪndʒəʳ] vt 1. (limb, person) blesser; **to ~ one's arm** se blesser au bras. 2. fig (reputation, chances) compromettre.

injured [ɪn'dʒəd] ◆ adj (limb, person) blessé(e). ◆ npl: **the ~** les blessés mpl.

injury ['ɪndʒərɪ] n 1. (to limb, person) blessure f; **to do o.s. an ~** se blesser. 2. fig (to reputation) coup m, atteinte f.

injury time n (U) arrêts mpl de jeu.

injustice [ɪn'dʒʌstɪs] n injustice f; **to do sb an ~** se montrer injuste envers qqn.

ink [ɪŋk] n encre f.

ink-jet printer n (COMPUT) imprimante f à jet d'encre.

inkling ['ɪŋklɪŋ] n: **to have an ~ of** avoir une petite idée de.

inlaid [ˌɪn'leɪd] adj: **~ (with)** incrusté(e) (de).

inland [adj 'ɪnlənd, adv ɪn'lænd] ◆ adj intérieur(e). ◆ adv à l'intérieur.

Inland Revenue n Br: **the ~** ≃ le fisc.

in-laws npl inf (parents-in-law) beaux-parents mpl; (others) belle-famille f.

inlet ['ɪnlet] n 1. (of lake, sea) avancée f. 2. (TECH) arrivée f.

inmate ['ɪnmeɪt] n (of prison) détenu m, -e f; (of mental hospital) interné m, -e f.

inn [ɪn] n auberge f.

innate [ɪ'neɪt] adj inné(e).

inner ['ɪnəʳ] adj 1. (on inside) interne, intérieur(e). 2. (feelings) intime.

inner city n: **the ~** les quartiers mpl pauvres.

inner tube n chambre f à air.

innings ['ɪnɪŋz] (pl inv) n Br (CRICKET) tour m de batte.

innocence ['ɪnəsəns] n innocence f.

innocent ['ɪnəsənt] ◆ adj innocent(e); **~ of** (crime) non coupable de. ◆ n innocent m, -e f.

innocuous [ɪ'nɒkjʊəs] adj inoffensif (ive).

innovation [ˌɪnə'veɪʃn] n innovation f.

innovative ['ɪnəvətɪv] adj 1. (idea, design) innovateur(trice). 2. (person, company) novateur(trice).

innuendo [ˌɪnjuː'endəʊ] (pl -es OR -s) n insinuation f.

innumerable [ɪ'njuːmərəbl] adj innombrable.

inoculate [ɪ'nɒkjʊleɪt] vt: **to ~ sb (with sthg)** inoculer (qqch à) qqn.

inordinately [ɪ'nɔːdɪnətlɪ] adv excessivement.

in-patient n malade hospitalisé m, malade hospitalisée f.

input ['ɪnpʊt] (pt & pp input OR -ted) ◆ n 1. (contribution) contribution f, concours m. 2. (COMPUT & ELEC) entrée f. ◆ vt (COMPUT) entrer.

inquest ['ɪnkwest] n enquête f.

inquire [ɪn'kwaɪəʳ] ◆ vt: **to ~ when/ whether/how ...** demander quand/si/ comment ... ◆ vi: **to ~ (about)** se renseigner (sur). ▶ **inquire after** vt fus s'enquérir de. ▶ **inquire into** vt fus enquêter sur.

inquiry [ɪn'kwaɪərɪ] n 1. (question) demande f de renseignements; **'Inquiries'** 'renseignements'. 2. (investigation) enquête f.

inquiry desk n bureau m de renseignements.

inquisitive [ɪn'kwɪzətɪv] adj inquisiteur(trice).

inroads ['ɪnrəʊdz] npl: **to make ~ into** (savings) entamer.

insane [ɪn'seɪn] adj fou (folle).

insanity [ɪn'sænətɪ] n folie f.

insatiable [ɪn'seɪʃəbl] adj insatiable.

inscription [ɪn'skrɪpʃn] n 1. (engraved) inscription f. 2. (written) dédicace f.

inscrutable [ɪn'skruːtəbl] adj impénétrable.

insect ['ɪnsekt] n insecte m.

insecticide [ɪn'sektɪsaɪd] n insecticide m.

insect repellent n crème f anti-insectes.

insecure [ˌɪnsɪ'kjʊəʳ] adj 1. (person) anxieux(euse). 2. (job, investment) incertain(e).

insensible [ɪn'sensəbl] adj 1. (unconscious) inconscient(e). 2. (unaware, not feeling): **~ of/to** insensible à.

insensitive [ɪn'sensətɪv] adj: **~ (to)** insensible (à).

inseparable [ɪn'seprəbl] adj inséparable.

insert [vb ɪn'sɜːt, n 'ɪnsɜːt] ◆ vt: **to ~**

sthg (in OR into) insérer qqch (dans). ◆ n (in newspaper) encart m.

insertion [ɪn'sɜːʃn] n insertion f.

in-service training n Br formation f en cours d'emploi.

inshore [adj 'ɪnʃɔːr, adv ɪn'ʃɔːr] ◆ adj côtier(ère). ◆ adv (be situated) près de la côte; (move) vers la côte.

inside [ɪn'saɪd] ◆ prep 1. (building, object) à l'intérieur de, dans; (group, organization) au sein de. 2. (time): ~ **three weeks** en moins de trois semaines. ◆ adv 1. (gen) dedans, à l'intérieur; **to go** ~ entrer; **come** ~! entrez! 2. prison sl en taule. ◆ adj intérieur(e). ◆ n 1. (interior): **the** ~ **l'intérieur** m; (clothes) à l'envers; **to know sthg** ~ **out** connaître qqch à fond. 2. (AUT): **the** ~ (in UK) la gauche; (in Europe, US etc) la droite.

inside lane n (AUT) (in UK) voie f de gauche; (in Europe, US etc) voie de droite.

insight ['ɪnsaɪt] n 1. (wisdom) sagacité f, perspicacité f. 2. (glimpse): ~ (into) aperçu m (de).

insignificant [ˌɪnsɪg'nɪfɪkənt] adj insignifiant(e).

insincere [ˌɪnsɪn'sɪər] adj pas sincère.

insinuate [ɪn'sɪnjʊeɪt] vt insinuer, laisser entendre.

insipid [ɪn'sɪpɪd] adj insipide.

insist [ɪn'sɪst] ◆ vt 1. (claim): **to** ~ (that) ... insister sur le fait que ... 2. (demand): **to** ~ (that) ... insister pour que (+ subjunctive) ... ◆ vi: **to** ~ (on sthg) exiger (qqch); **to** ~ **on doing sthg** tenir à faire qqch, vouloir absolument faire qqch.

insistent [ɪn'sɪstənt] adj 1. (determined) insistant(e); **to be** ~ **on** insister sur. 2. (continual) incessant(e).

insofar [ˌɪnsəʊ'fɑːr] ▶ **insofar as** conj dans la mesure où.

insole ['ɪnsəʊl] n semelle f intérieure.

insolent ['ɪnsələnt] adj insolent(e).

insolvent [ɪn'sɒlvənt] adj insolvable.

insomnia [ɪn'sɒmnɪə] n insomnie f.

inspect [ɪn'spekt] vt 1. (letter, person) examiner. 2. (factory, troops etc) inspecter.

inspection [ɪn'spekʃn] n 1. (investigation) examen m. 2. (official check) inspection f.

inspector [ɪn'spektər] n inspecteur m, -trice f.

inspiration [ˌɪnspə'reɪʃn] n inspiration f.

inspire [ɪn'spaɪər] vt: **to** ~ **sb to do sthg** pousser OR encourager qqn à faire

qqch; **to** ~ **sb with sthg, to** ~ **sthg in sb** inspirer qqch à qqn.

install Br, **instal** Am [ɪn'stɔːl] vt (fit) installer.

installation [ˌɪnstə'leɪʃn] n installation f.

instalment Br, **installment** Am [ɪn'stɔːlmənt] n 1. (payment) acompte m; **in** ~**s** par acomptes. 2. (episode) épisode m.

instance ['ɪnstəns] n exemple m; **for** ~ par exemple.

instant ['ɪnstənt] ◆ adj 1. (immediate) instantané(e), immédiat(e). 2. (coffee) soluble; (food) à préparation rapide. ◆ n instant m; **the** ~ **(that)** ... dès OR aussitôt que ...; **this** ~ tout de suite, immédiatement.

instantly ['ɪnstəntlɪ] adv immédiatement.

instead [ɪn'sted] adv au lieu de cela. ▶ **instead of** prep au lieu de; ~ **of him** à sa place.

instep ['ɪnstep] n cou-de-pied m.

instigate ['ɪnstɪgeɪt] vt être à l'origine de, entreprendre.

instil Br, **instill** Am [ɪn'stɪl] vt: **to** ~ **sthg in** OR **into sb** instiller qqch à qqn.

instinct ['ɪnstɪŋkt] n 1. (intuition) instinct m. 2. (impulse) réaction f, mouvement m.

instinctive [ɪn'stɪŋktɪv] adj instinctif (ive).

institute ['ɪnstɪtjuːt] ◆ n institut m. ◆ vt instituer.

institution [ˌɪnstɪ'tjuːʃn] n institution f.

instruct [ɪn'strʌkt] vt 1. (tell, order): **to** ~ **sb to do sthg** charger qqn de faire qqch. 2. (teach) instruire; **to** ~ **sb in sthg** enseigner qqch à qqn.

instruction [ɪn'strʌkʃn] n instruction f. ▶ **instructions** npl mode m d'emploi, instructions fpl.

instructor [ɪn'strʌktər] n 1. (gen) instructeur m, -trice f, moniteur m, -trice f. 2. Am (SCH) enseignant m, -e f.

instrument ['ɪnstrʊmənt] n lit & fig instrument m.

instrumental [ˌɪnstrʊ'mentl] adj (important, helpful): **to be** ~ **in** contribuer à.

instrument panel n tableau m de bord.

insubordinate [ˌɪnsə'bɔːdɪnət] adj insubordonné(e).

insubstantial [ˌɪnsəb'stænʃl] adj (structure) peu solide; (meal) peu substantiel (elle).

insufficient [ˌɪnsəˈfɪʃnt] *adj fml* insuffisant(e).

insular [ˈɪnsjʊlər] *adj* (*outlook*) borné(e); (*person*) à l'esprit étroit.

insulate [ˈɪnsjʊleɪt] *vt* 1. (*loft, cable*) isoler; (*hot water tank*) calorifuger. 2. (*protect*): **to ~ sb against** OR **from sthg** protéger qqn de qqch.

insulating tape [ˈɪnsjʊleɪtɪŋ-] *n Br* chatterton *m*.

insulation [ˌɪnsjʊˈleɪʃn] *n* isolation *f*.

insulin [ˈɪnsjʊlɪn] *n* insuline *f*.

insult [*vt* ɪnˈsʌlt, *n* ˈɪnsʌlt] ◆ *vt* insulter, injurier. ◆ *n* insulte *f*, injure *f*.

insuperable [ɪnˈsuːprəbl] *adj fml* insurmontable.

insurance [ɪnˈʃʊərəns] *n* 1. (*against fire, accident, theft*) assurance *f*. 2. *fig* (*safeguard, protection*) protection *f*, garantie *f*.

insurance policy *n* police *f* d'assurance.

insure [ɪnˈʃʊər] ◆ *vt* 1. (*against fire, accident, theft*): **to ~ sb/sthg against sthg** assurer qqn/qqch contre qqch. 2. *Am* (*make certain*) s'assurer. ◆ *vi* (*prevent*): **to ~ against** se protéger de.

insurer [ɪnˈʃʊərər] *n* assureur *m*.

insurmountable [ˌɪnsəˈmaʊntəbl] *adj fml* insurmontable.

intact [ɪnˈtækt] *adj* intact(e).

intake [ˈɪnteɪk] *n* 1. (*amount consumed*) consommation *f*. 2. (*people recruited*) admission *f*. 3. (*inlet*) prise *f*, arrivée *f*.

integral [ˈɪntɪɡrəl] *adj* intégral(e); **to be ~ to sthg** faire partie intégrante de qqch.

integrate [ˈɪntɪɡreɪt] ◆ *vi* s'intégrer. ◆ *vt* intégrer.

integrity [ɪnˈteɡrətɪ] *n* 1. (*honour*) intégrité *f*, honnêteté *f*. 2. *fml* (*wholeness*) intégrité *f*, totalité *f*.

intellect [ˈɪntəlekt] *n* 1. (*ability to think*) intellect *m*. 2. (*cleverness*) intelligence *f*.

intellectual [ˌɪntəˈlektjʊəl] ◆ *adj* intellectuel(elle). ◆ *n* intellectuel *m*, -elle *f*.

intelligence [ɪnˈtelɪdʒəns] *n* (U) 1. (*ability to think*) intelligence *f*. 2. (*information service*) service *m* de renseignements. 3. (*information*) informations *fpl*, renseignements *mpl*.

intelligent [ɪnˈtelɪdʒənt] *adj* intelligent(e).

intelligent card *n* carte *f* à puce OR à mémoire.

intend [ɪnˈtend] *vt* (*mean*) avoir l'intention de; **to be ~ed for** être destiné à; **to be ~ed to do sthg** être destiné à faire qqch, viser à faire qqch; **to ~ to do sthg** avoir l'intention de faire qqch.

intended [ɪnˈtendɪd] *adj* (*result*) voulu(e); (*victim*) visé(e).

intense [ɪnˈtens] *adj* 1. (*gen*) intense. 2. (*serious - person*) sérieux(euse).

intensely [ɪnˈtenslɪ] *adv* 1. (*irritating, boring*) extrêmement; (*suffer*) énormément. 2. (*look*) intensément.

intensify [ɪnˈtensɪfaɪ] ◆ *vt* intensifier, augmenter. ◆ *vi* s'intensifier.

intensity [ɪnˈtensətɪ] *n* intensité *f*.

intensive [ɪnˈtensɪv] *adj* intensif(ive).

intensive care *n* réanimation *f*.

intent [ɪnˈtent] ◆ *adj* 1. (*absorbed*) absorbé(e). 2. (*determined*): **to be ~ on** OR **upon doing sthg** être résolu(e) OR décidé(e) à faire qqch. ◆ *n fml* intention *f*, dessein *m*; **to all ~s and purposes** pratiquement, virtuellement.

intention [ɪnˈtenʃn] *n* intention *f*.

intentional [ɪnˈtenʃənl] *adj* intentionnel(elle), voulu(e).

intently [ɪnˈtentlɪ] *adv* avec attention, attentivement.

interact [ˌɪntərˈækt] *vi* 1. (*communicate, work together*): **to ~ (with sb)** communiquer (avec qqn). 2. (*react*): **to ~ (with sthg)** interagir (avec qqch).

intercede [ˌɪntəˈsiːd] *vi fml*: **to ~ (with sb)** intercéder (auprès de qqn).

intercept [ˌɪntəˈsept] *vt* intercepter.

interchange [*n* ˈɪntətʃeɪndʒ, *vb* ˌɪntəˈtʃeɪndʒ] ◆ *n* 1. (*exchange*) échange *m*. 2. (*road junction*) échangeur *m*. ◆ *vt* échanger.

interchangeable [ˌɪntəˈtʃeɪndʒəbl] *adj*: **~ (with)** interchangeable (avec).

intercity [ˌɪntəˈsɪtɪ] *n* système de trains rapides reliant les grandes villes en Grande-Bretagne; **Intercity 125®** train rapide pouvant rouler à 125 miles (200 km) à l'heure.

intercom [ˈɪntəkɒm] *n* Interphone® *m*.

intercourse [ˈɪntəkɔːs] *n* (U) (*sexual*) rapports *mpl* (sexuels).

interest [ˈɪntrəst] ◆ *n* 1. (*gen*) intérêt *m*; **to lose ~** se désintéresser. 2. (*hobby*) centre *m* d'intérêt. 3. (U) (FIN) intérêt *m*, intérêts *mpl*. ◆ *vt* intéresser.

interested [ˈɪntrəstɪd] *adj* intéressé(e); **to be ~ in** s'intéresser à; **I'm not ~ in that** cela ne m'intéresse pas; **to be ~ in doing sthg** avoir envie de faire qqch.

interesting [ˈɪntrəstɪŋ] *adj* intéressant(e).

interest rate *n* taux *m* d'intérêt.

interface [ˈɪntəfeɪs] *n* 1. (COMPUT) interface *f*. 2. *fig* (*junction*) rapports *mpl*, relations *fpl*.

interfere [ˌɪntəˈfɪəʳ] vi 1. (meddle): **to ~ in** sthg s'immiscer dans qqch, se mêler de qqch. 2. (damage): **to ~ with** sthg gêner qqch; (routine) déranger qqch.

interference [ˌɪntəˈfɪərəns] n (U) 1. (meddling): **~ (with** OR **in)** ingérence f (dans), intrusion f (dans). 2. (TELEC) parasites mpl.

interim [ˈɪntərɪm] ◆ adj provisoire. ◆ n: **in the ~** dans l'intérim, entre-temps.

interior [ɪnˈtɪərɪəʳ] ◆ adj 1. (inner) intérieur(e). 2. (POL) de l'Intérieur. ◆ n intérieur m.

interlock [ˌɪntəˈlɒk] vi (gears) s'enclencher, s'engrener; (fingers) s'entrelacer.

interloper [ˈɪntələʊpəʳ] n intrus m, -e f.

interlude [ˈɪntəluːd] n 1. (pause) intervalle m. 2. (interval) interlude m.

intermediary [ˌɪntəˈmiːdjərɪ] n intermédiaire mf.

intermediate [ˌɪntəˈmiːdjət] adj 1. (transitional) intermédiaire. 2. (post-beginner - level) moyen(enne); (- student, group) de niveau moyen.

interminable [ɪnˈtɜːmɪnəbl] adj interminable, sans fin.

intermission [ˌɪntəˈmɪʃn] n entracte m.

intermittent [ˌɪntəˈmɪtənt] adj intermittent(e).

intern [vb ɪnˈtɜːn, n ˈɪntɜːn] ◆ vt interner. ◆ n Am (gen) stagiaire mf; (MED) interne mf.

internal [ɪnˈtɜːnl] adj 1. (gen) interne. 2. (within country) intérieur(e).

internally [ɪnˈtɜːnəlɪ] adv 1. (within the body): **to bleed ~** faire une hémorragie interne. 2. (within country) à l'intérieur. 3. (within organization) intérieurement.

Internal Revenue n Am: **the ~** ≃ le fisc.

international [ˌɪntəˈnæʃənl] ◆ adj international(e). ◆ n Br (SPORT) 1. (match) match m international. 2. (player) international m, -e f.

Internet [ˈɪntənet] n: **the ~** l'Internet m.

interpret [ɪnˈtɜːprɪt] ◆ vt: **to ~** sthg **(as)** interpréter qqch (comme). ◆ vi (translate) faire l'interprète.

interpreter [ɪnˈtɜːprɪtəʳ] n interprète mf.

interracial [ˌɪntəˈreɪʃl] adj entre des races différentes, racial(e).

interrelate [ˌɪntərɪˈleɪt] ◆ vt mettre en corrélation. ◆ vi: **to ~ (with)** être lié(e)

(à), être en corrélation (avec).

interrogate [ɪnˈterəgeɪt] vt interroger.

interrogation [ɪnˌterəˈgeɪʃn] n interrogatoire m.

interrogation mark n Am point m d'interrogation.

interrogative [ˌɪntəˈrɒgətɪv] (GRAMM) ◆ adj interrogatif(ive). ◆ n interrogatif m.

interrupt [ˌɪntəˈrʌpt] ◆ vt interrompre; (calm) rompre. ◆ vi interrompre.

interruption [ˌɪntəˈrʌpʃn] n interruption f.

intersect [ˌɪntəˈsekt] ◆ vi s'entrecroiser, s'entrecouper. ◆ vt croiser, couper.

intersection [ˌɪntəˈsekʃn] n (in road) croisement m, carrefour m.

intersperse [ˌɪntəˈspɜːs] vt: **to be ~d with** être émaillé(e) de, être entremêlé(e) de.

interstate (highway) [ˈɪntəsteɪt-] n Am autoroute f.

interval [ˈɪntəvl] n 1. (gen) intervalle m; **at ~s** par intervalles; **at monthly/yearly ~s** tous les mois/ans. 2. Br (at play, concert) entracte m.

intervene [ˌɪntəˈviːn] vi 1. (person, police): **to ~ (in)** intervenir (dans), s'interposer (dans). 2. (event, war, strike) survenir. 3. (time) s'écouler.

intervention [ˌɪntəˈvenʃn] n intervention f.

interview [ˈɪntəvjuː] ◆ n 1. (for job) entrevue f, entretien m. 2. (PRESS) interview f. ◆ vt 1. (for job) faire passer une entrevue OR un entretien à. 2. (PRESS) interviewer.

interviewer [ˈɪntəvjuːəʳ] n 1. (for job) personne f qui fait passer une entrevue. 2. (PRESS) interviewer m.

intestine [ɪnˈtestɪn] n intestin m.

intimacy [ˈɪntɪməsɪ] n (closeness): **~ (between/with)** intimité f (entre/avec).

intimate [adj ˈɪntɪmət, vb ˈɪntɪmeɪt] ◆ adj 1. (gen) intime. 2. (detailed - knowledge) approfondi(e). ◆ vt fml faire savoir, faire connaître.

intimately [ˈɪntɪmətlɪ] adv 1. (very closely) étroitement. 2. (as close friends) intimement. 3. (in detail) à fond.

intimidate [ɪnˈtɪmɪdeɪt] vt intimider.

into [ˈɪntʊ] prep 1. (inside) dans. 2. (against): **to bump ~** sthg se cogner contre qqch; **to crash ~** rentrer dans. 3. (referring to change in state) en; **to translate** sthg **~ Spanish** traduire qqch en espagnol. 4. (concerning): **research/investigation ~** recherche/enquête sur. 5. (MATH): **3 ~ 2** 2 divisé par 3. 6. inf (*interested in*): **to be ~ sthg** être passionné(e) par qqch.

intolerable [ɪn'tɒlrəbl] *adj* intolérable, insupportable.

intolerance [ɪn'tɒlərəns] *n* intolérance *f.*

intolerant [ɪn'tɒlərənt] *adj* intolérant(e).

intoxicated [ɪn'tɒksɪkeɪtɪd] *adj* **1.** (*drunk*) ivre. **2.** *fig* (*excited*): **to be ~ by** OR **with sthg** être grisé(e) OR enivré(e) par qqch.

intransitive [ɪn'trænzətɪv] *adj* intransitif(ive).

intravenous [ˌɪntrə'viːnəs] *adj* intraveineux(euse).

in-tray *n* casier *m* des affaires à traiter.

intricate ['ɪntrɪkət] *adj* compliqué(e).

intrigue [ɪn'triːg] ♦ *n* intrigue *f.* ♦ *vt* intriguer, exciter la curiosité de.

intriguing [ɪn'triːgɪŋ] *adj* fascinant(e).

intrinsic [ɪn'trɪnsɪk] *adj* intrinsèque.

introduce [ˌɪntrə'djuːs] *vt* **1.** (*present*) présenter; **to ~ sb to sb** présenter qqn à qqn. **2.** (*bring in*): **to ~ sthg (to** OR **into)** introduire qqch (dans). **3.** (*allow to experience*): **to ~ sb to sthg** initier qqn à qqch, faire découvrir qqch à qqn. **4.** (*signal beginning of*) annoncer.

introduction [ˌɪntrə'dʌkʃn] *n* **1.** (*in book, of new method etc*) introduction *f.* **2.** (*of people*): **~ (to sb)** présentation *f* (à qqn).

introductory [ˌɪntrə'dʌktrɪ] *adj* d'introduction, préliminaire.

introvert ['ɪntrəvɜːt] *n* introverti *m*, -e *f.*

introverted ['ɪntrəvɜːtɪd] *adj* introverti(e).

intrude [ɪn'truːd] *vi* faire intrusion; **to ~ on sb** déranger qqn.

intruder [ɪn'truːdəʳ] *n* intrus *m*, -e *f.*

intrusive [ɪn'truːsɪv] *adj* gênant(e), importun(e).

intuition [ˌɪntjuː'ɪʃn] *n* intuition *f.*

inundate ['ɪnʌndeɪt] *vt* **1.** *fml* (*flood*) inonder. **2.** (*overwhelm*): **to be ~d with** être submergé(e) de.

invade [ɪn'veɪd] *vt* **1.** (MIL & *fig*) envahir. **2.** (*disturb - privacy etc*) violer.

invalid [*adj* ɪn'vælɪd, *n* 'ɪnvəlɪd] ♦ *adj* **1.** (*illegal, unacceptable*) non valide, non valable. **2.** (*not reasonable*) non valable. ♦ *n* invalide *mf.*

invaluable [ɪn'væljʊəbl] *adj*: **~ (to)** (*help, advice, person*) précieux(euse) (pour); (*experience, information*) inestimable (pour).

invariably [ɪn'veərɪəblɪ] *adv* invariablement, toujours.

invasion [ɪn'veɪʒn] *n lit* & *fig* invasion *f.*

invent [ɪn'vent] *vt* inventer.

invention [ɪn'venʃn] *n* invention *f.*

inventive [ɪn'ventɪv] *adj* inventif(ive).

inventor [ɪn'ventəʳ] *n* inventeur *m*, -trice *f.*

inventory ['ɪnvəntrɪ] *n* **1.** (*list*) inventaire *m*. **2.** Am (*goods*) stock *m.*

invert [ɪn'vɜːt] *vt* retourner.

inverted commas [ɪnˌvɜːtɪd-] *npl* Br guillemets *mpl.*

invest [ɪn'vest] ♦ *vt* **1.** (*money*): **to ~ sthg (in)** investir qqch (dans). **2.** (*time, energy*): **to ~ sthg in sthg/in doing sthg** consacrer qqch à qqch/à faire qqch, employer qqch à qqch/à faire qqch. ♦ *vi* **1.** (FIN): **to ~ (in sthg)** investir (dans qqch). **2.** *fig* (*buy*): **to ~ in sthg** se payer qqch, s'acheter qqch.

investigate [ɪn'vestɪgeɪt] *vt* enquêter sur, faire une enquête sur; (*subj: scientist*) faire des recherches sur.

investigation [ɪnˌvestɪ'geɪʃn] *n* **1.** (*enquiry*): **~ (into)** enquête *f* (sur); (*scientific*) recherches *fpl* (sur). **2.** (U) (*investigating*) investigation *f.*

investment [ɪn'vestmənt] *n* **1.** (FIN) investissement *m*, placement *m*. **2.** (*of energy*) dépense *f.*

investor [ɪn'vestəʳ] *n* investisseur *m.*

inveterate [ɪn'vetərət] *adj* invétéré(e).

invidious [ɪn'vɪdɪəs] *adj* (*task*) ingrat(e); (*comparison*) injuste.

invigilate [ɪn'vɪdʒɪleɪt] Br ♦ *vi* surveiller les candidats (à un examen). ♦ *vt* surveiller.

invigorating [ɪn'vɪgəreɪtɪŋ] *adj* tonifiant(e), vivifiant(e).

invincible [ɪn'vɪnsɪbl] *adj* (*army, champion*) invincible; (*record*) imbattable.

invisible [ɪn'vɪzɪbl] *adj* invisible.

invitation [ˌɪnvɪ'teɪʃn] *n* (*request*) invitation *f.*

invite [ɪn'vaɪt] *vt* **1.** (*ask to come*): **to ~ sb (to)** inviter qqn (à). **2.** (*ask politely*): **to ~ sb to do sthg** inviter qqn à faire qqch. **3.** (*encourage*): **to ~ trouble** aller au devant des ennuis; **to ~ gossip** faire causer.

inviting [ɪn'vaɪtɪŋ] *adj* attrayant(e), agréable; (*food*) appétissant(e).

invoice ['ɪnvɔɪs] ♦ *n* facture *f.* ♦ *vt* **1.** (*client*) envoyer la facture à. **2.** (*goods*) facturer.

invoke [ɪn'vəʊk] *vt* **1.** *fml* (*law, act*) invoquer. **2.** (*feelings*) susciter, faire naître; (*help*) demander, implorer.

involuntary [ɪn'vɒləntrɪ] *adj* involontaire.

involve [ɪn'vɒlv] *vt* **1.** (*entail*) nécessiter; **what's ~d?** de quoi s'agit-il?; **to ~ doing sthg** nécessiter de faire qqch. **2.** (*concern, affect*) toucher. **3.** (*person*): **to ~ sb in sthg** impliquer qqn dans qqch.

involved [ɪn'vɒlvd] *adj* **1.** (*complex*) complexe, compliqué(e). **2.** (*participating*): **to be ~ in sthg** participer OR prendre part à qqch. **3.** (*in relationship*): **to be ~ with sb** avoir des relations intimes avec qqn.

involvement [ɪn'vɒlvmənt] *n* **1.** (*participation*): **~ (in)** participation *f* (à). **2.** (*concern, enthusiasm*): **~ (in)** engagement *m* (dans).

inward ['ɪnwəd] ◆ *adj* **1.** (*inner*) intérieur(e). **2.** (*towards the inside*) vers l'intérieur. ◆ *adv* Am = **inwards**.

inwards ['ɪnwədz] *adv* vers l'intérieur.

iodine [Br 'aɪədiːn, Am 'aɪədaɪn] *n* iode *m*.

iota [aɪ'əʊtə] *n* brin *m*, grain *m*.

IOU (*abbr of* **I owe you**) *n* reconnaissance *f* de dette.

IQ (*abbr of* **intelligence quotient**) *n* QI *m*.

IRA *n* (*abbr of* **Irish Republican Army**) IRA *f*.

Iran [ɪ'rɑːn] *n* Iran *m*.

Iranian [ɪ'reɪnjən] ◆ *adj* iranien(enne). ◆ *n* Iranien *m*, -enne *f*.

Iraq [ɪ'rɑːk] *n* Iraq *m*, Irak *m*.

Iraqi [ɪ'rɑːkɪ] ◆ *adj* iraquien(enne), irakien(enne). ◆ *n* Iraquien *m*, -enne *f*, Irakien *m*, -enne *f*.

irate [aɪ'reɪt] *adj* furieux(euse).

Ireland ['aɪələnd] *n* Irlande *f*.

iris ['aɪərɪs] (*pl* **-es**) *n* iris *m*.

Irish ['aɪrɪʃ] ◆ *adj* irlandais(e). ◆ *n* (*language*) irlandais *m*. ◆ *npl*: **the ~** les Irlandais.

Irishman ['aɪrɪʃmən] (*pl* **-men** [-mən]) *n* Irlandais *m*.

Irish Sea *n*: **the ~** la mer d'Irlande.

Irishwoman ['aɪrɪʃ,wʊmən] (*pl* **-women** [-,wɪmɪn]) *n* Irlandaise *f*.

irksome ['ɜːksəm] *adj* ennuyeux (euse), assommant(e).

iron ['aɪən] ◆ *adj* **1.** (*made of iron*) de OR en fer. **2.** *fig* (*very strict*) de fer. ◆ *n* **1.** (*metal, golf club*) fer *m*. **2.** (*for clothes*) fer *m* à repasser. ◆ *vt* repasser. ▶ **iron out** *vt sep fig* (*difficulties*) aplanir; (*problems*) résoudre.

Iron Curtain *n*: **the ~** le rideau de fer.

ironic(al) [aɪ'rɒnɪk(l)] *adj* ironique.

ironing ['aɪənɪŋ] *n* repassage *m*.

ironing board *n* planche *f* OR table *f* à repasser.

ironmonger ['aɪən,mʌŋgər] *n* Br quincaillier *m*; **~'s (shop)** quincaillerie *f*.

irony ['aɪrənɪ] *n* ironie *f*.

irrational [ɪ'ræʃənl] *adj* irrationnel (elle), déraisonnable; (*person*) non rationnel(elle).

irreconcilable [ɪ,rekən'saɪləbl] *adj* inconciliable.

irregular [ɪ'regjʊlər] *adj* irrégulier (ère).

irrelevant [ɪ'reləvənt] *adj* sans rapport.

irreparable [ɪ'repərəbl] *adj* irréparable.

irreplaceable [,ɪrɪ'pleɪsəbl] *adj* irremplaçable.

irrepressible [,ɪrɪ'presəbl] *adj* (*enthusiasm*) que rien ne peut entamer; **he's ~** il est d'une bonne humeur à toute épreuve.

irresistible [,ɪrɪ'zɪstəbl] *adj* irrésistible.

irrespective [,ɪrɪ'spektɪv] ▶ **irrespective of** *prep* sans tenir compte de.

irresponsible [,ɪrɪ'spɒnsəbl] *adj* irresponsable.

irrigate ['ɪrɪgeɪt] *vt* irriguer.

irrigation [,ɪrɪ'geɪʃn] *n* irrigation *f*.

irritable ['ɪrɪtəbl] *adj* irritable.

irritate ['ɪrɪteɪt] *vt* irriter.

irritating ['ɪrɪteɪtɪŋ] *adj* irritant(e).

irritation [ɪrɪ'teɪʃn] *n* **1.** (*anger, soreness*) irritation *f*. **2.** (*cause of anger*) source *f* d'irritation.

IRS (*abbr of* **Internal Revenue Service**) *n* Am: **the ~** = le fisc.

is [ɪz] → **be**.

Islam ['ɪzlɑːm] *n* islam *m*.

island ['aɪlənd] *n* **1.** (*isle*) île *f*. **2.** (AUT) refuge *m* pour piétons.

islander ['aɪləndər] *n* habitant *m*, -e *f* d'une île.

isle [aɪl] *n* île *f*.

Isle of Man *n*: **the ~** l'île *f* de Man.

Isle of Wight [-waɪt] *n*: **the ~** l'île *f* de Wight.

isn't ['ɪznt] = **is not**.

isobar ['aɪsəbɑːr] *n* isobare *f*.

isolate ['aɪsəleɪt] *vt*: **to ~ sb/sthg (from)** isoler qqn/qqch (de).

isolated ['aɪsəleɪtɪd] *adj* isolé(e).

Israel ['ɪzreɪəl] *n* Israël *m*.

Israeli [ɪz'reɪlɪ] ◆ *adj* israélien(enne). ◆ *n* Israélien *m*, -enne *f*.

issue [ˈɪʃuː] ♦ n 1. (important subject) question f, problème m; **to make an ~ of sthg** faire toute une affaire de qqch; **at ~** en question, en cause. 2. (edition) numéro m. 3. (bringing out - of banknotes, shares) émission f. ♦ vt 1. (make public - decree, statement) faire; (- warning) lancer. 2. (bring out - banknotes, shares) émettre; (- book) publier. 3. (passport etc) délivrer.

isthmus [ˈɪsməs] n isthme m.

it [ɪt] pron 1. (referring to specific person or thing - subj) il (elle); (- direct object) le (la), l' (+ vowel or silent 'h'); (- indirect object) lui; **did you find ~?** tu l'as trouvé(e) ?; **give ~ to me at once** donne-moi ça tout de suite. 2. (with prepositions): **in/to/at ~** y; **put the vegetables in ~** mettez-y les légumes; **on ~** dessus; **about ~** en; **under ~** dessous; **beside ~** à côté; **from/of ~** en; **he's very proud of ~** il en est très fier. 3. (impersonal use) il, ce; **~ is cold today** il fait froid aujourd'hui; **~'s two o'clock** il est deux heures; **who is ~? – ~'s me** qui est-ce? – c'est moi.

IT n abbr of **information technology.**

Italian [ɪˈtæljən] ♦ adj italien(enne). ♦ n 1. (person) Italien m, -enne f. 2. (language) italien m.

italic [ɪˈtælɪk] adj italique. ▶ **italics** npl italiques fpl.

Italy [ˈɪtəlɪ] n Italie f.

itch [ɪtʃ] ♦ n démangeaison f. ♦ vi 1. (be itchy): **my arm ~es** mon bras me démange. 2. fig (be impatient): **to be ~ing to do sthg** mourir d'envie de faire qqch.

itchy [ˈɪtʃɪ] adj qui démange.

it'd [ˈɪtəd] = **it would, it had.**

item [ˈaɪtəm] n 1. (gen) chose f, article m; (on agenda) question f, point m. 2. (PRESS) article m.

itemize, -ise [ˈaɪtəmaɪz] vt détailler.

itinerary [aɪˈtɪnərərɪ] n itinéraire m.

it'll [ɪtl] = **it will.**

its [ɪts] poss adj son (sa), ses (pl).

it's [ɪts] = **it is, it has.**

itself [ɪtˈself] pron 1. (reflexive) se; (after prep) soi. 2. (for emphasis) lui-même (elle-même); **in ~** en soi.

ITV (abbr of **Independent Television**) n sigle désignant les programmes diffusés par les chaînes relevant de l'IBA.

I've [aɪv] = **I have.**

ivory [ˈaɪvərɪ] n ivoire m.

ivy [ˈaɪvɪ] n lierre m.

Ivy League n Am les huit grandes universités de l'est des États-Unis.

J

j (pl **j's** OR **js**), **J** (pl **J's** OR **Js**) [dʒeɪ] n (letter) j m inv, J m inv.

jab [dʒæb] ♦ n 1. Br inf (injection) piqûre f. 2. (BOXING) direct m. ♦ vt: **to ~ sthg into** planter OR enfoncer qqch dans.

jabber [ˈdʒæbər] vt & vi baragouiner.

jack [dʒæk] n 1. (device) cric m. 2. (playing card) valet m. ▶ **jack up** vt sep 1. (car) soulever avec un cric. 2. fig (prices) faire grimper.

jackal [ˈdʒækəl] n chacal m.

jackdaw [ˈdʒækdɔː] n choucas m.

jacket [ˈdʒækɪt] n 1. (garment) veste f. 2. (of potato) peau f, pelure f. 3. (of book) jaquette f. 4. Am (of record) pochette f.

jacket potato n pomme de terre f en robe de chambre.

jack knife n canif m. ▶ **jack-knife** vi (lorry) se mettre en travers de la route.

jack plug n jack m.

jackpot [ˈdʒækpɒt] n gros lot m.

Jacuzzi® [dʒəˈkuːzɪ] n Jacuzzi® m, bain m à remous.

jaded [ˈdʒeɪdɪd] adj blasé(e).

jagged [ˈdʒægɪd] adj déchiqueté(e), dentelé(e).

jail [dʒeɪl] ♦ n prison f. ♦ vt emprisonner, mettre en prison.

jailer [ˈdʒeɪlər] n geôlier m, -ère f.

jam [dʒæm] ♦ n 1. (preserve) confiture f. 2. (of traffic) embouteillage m, bouchon m. 3. inf (difficult situation): **to get into/be in a ~** se mettre/être dans le pétrin. ♦ vt 1. (mechanism, door) bloquer, coincer. 2. (push tightly): **to ~ sthg into** entasser OR tasser qqch dans; **to ~ sthg onto** enfoncer qqch sur. 3. (block - streets) embouteiller; (- switchboard) surcharger. 4. (RADIO) brouiller. ♦ vi (lever, door) se coincer; (brakes) se bloquer.

Jamaica [dʒəˈmeɪkə] n la Jamaïque.

jam-packed [-ˈpækt] adj inf plein(e) à craquer.

jangle [ˈdʒæŋgl] ♦ vt (keys) faire cliqueter; (bells) faire retentir. ♦ vi (keys) cliqueter; (bells) retentir.

janitor [ˈdʒænɪtər] n Am & Scot concierge mf.

January [ˈdʒænjʊərɪ] n janvier m; see also **September.**

Japan [dʒə'pæn] n Japon m.
Japanese [ˌdʒæpə'niːz] (pl inv) ◆ adj japonais(e). ◆ n (language) japonais m. ◆ npl (people): **the ~** les Japonais mpl.
jar [dʒɑːʳ] ◆ n pot m. ◆ vt (shake) secouer. ◆ vi **1.** (noise, voice): **to ~ (on sb)** irriter (qqn), agacer (qqn). **2.** (colours) jurer.
jargon ['dʒɑːɡən] n jargon m.
jaundice ['dʒɔːndɪs] n jaunisse f.
jaundiced ['dʒɔːndɪst] adj fig (attitude, view) aigri(e).
jaunt [dʒɔːnt] n balade f.
jaunty ['dʒɔːntɪ] adj désinvolte, insouciant(e).
javelin ['dʒævlɪn] n javelot m.
jaw [dʒɔː] n mâchoire f.
jawbone ['dʒɔːbəʊn] n (os m) maxillaire m.
jay [dʒeɪ] n geai m.
jaywalker ['dʒeɪwɔːkəʳ] n piéton m qui traverse en dehors des clous.
jazz [dʒæz] n (MUS) jazz m. ► **jazz up** vt sep inf égayer.
jazzy ['dʒæzɪ] adj (bright) voyant(e).
jealous ['dʒeləs] adj jaloux(ouse).
jealousy ['dʒeləsɪ] n jalousie f.
jeans [dʒiːnz] npl jean m, blue-jean m.
Jeep® ['dʒiːp] n Jeep® f.
jeer [dʒɪəʳ] ◆ vt huer, conspuer. ◆ vi: **to ~ (at sb)** huer (qqn), conspuer (qqn).
Jehovah's Witness [dʒɪ,həʊvəz-] n témoin m de Jéhovah.
Jello® ['dʒeləʊ] n Am gelée f.
jelly ['dʒelɪ] n gelée f.
jellyfish ['dʒelɪfɪʃ] (pl inv OR -es) n méduse f.
jeopardize, -ise ['dʒepədaɪz] vt compromettre, mettre en danger.
jerk [dʒɜːk] ◆ n **1.** (movement) secousse f, saccade f. **2.** v inf (fool) abruti m, -e f. ◆ vi (person) sursauter; (vehicle) cahoter.
jersey ['dʒɜːzɪ] (pl jerseys) n **1.** (sweater) pull m. **2.** (cloth) jersey m.
Jersey ['dʒɜːzɪ] n Jersey f.
jest [dʒest] n plaisanterie f; **in ~** pour rire.
Jesus (Christ) ['dʒiːzəs-] n Jésus m, Jésus-Christ m.
jet [dʒet] n **1.** (plane) jet m, avion m à réaction. **2.** (of fluid) jet m. **3.** (nozzle, outlet) ajutage m.
jet-black adj noir(e) comme (du) jais.
jet engine n moteur m à réaction.
jetfoil ['dʒetfɔɪl] n hydroglisseur m.
jet lag n fatigue f due au décalage horaire.
jetsam ['dʒetsəm] → **flotsam**.

jettison ['dʒetɪsən] vt **1.** (cargo) jeter, larguer. **2.** fig (ideas) abandonner, renoncer à.
jetty ['dʒetɪ] n jetée f.
Jew [dʒuː] n Juif m, -ive f.
jewel ['dʒuːəl] n bijou m; (in watch) rubis m.
jeweller Br, **jeweler** Am ['dʒuːələʳ] n bijoutier m; **~'s (shop)** bijouterie f.
jewellery Br, **jewelry** Am ['dʒuːəlrɪ] n (U) bijoux mpl.
Jewess ['dʒuːɪs] n juive f.
Jewish ['dʒuːɪʃ] adj juif(ive).
jib [dʒɪb] n **1.** (of crane) flèche f. **2.** (sail) foc m.
jibe [dʒaɪb] n sarcasme m, moquerie f.
jiffy ['dʒɪfɪ] n inf: **in a ~** en un clin d'œil.
Jiffy bag® n enveloppe f matelassée.
jig [dʒɪɡ] n gigue f.
jigsaw (puzzle) ['dʒɪɡsɔː-] n puzzle m.
jilt [dʒɪlt] vt laisser tomber.
jingle ['dʒɪŋɡl] ◆ n **1.** (sound) cliquetis m. **2.** (song) jingle m, indicatif m. ◆ vi (bell) tinter; (coins, bracelets) cliqueter.
jinx [dʒɪŋks] n poisse f.
jitters ['dʒɪtəz] npl inf: **the ~** le trac.
job [dʒɒb] n **1.** (employment) emploi m. **2.** (task) travail m, tâche f. **3.** (difficult task): **to have a ~ doing sthg** avoir du mal à faire qqch. **4.** phr: **that's just the ~** Br inf c'est exactement OR tout à fait ce qu'il faut.
job centre n Br agence f pour l'emploi.
jobless ['dʒɒblɪs] adj au chômage.
jobsharing ['dʒɒbʃeərɪŋ] n partage m de l'emploi.
jockey ['dʒɒkɪ] (pl jockeys) ◆ n jockey m. ◆ vi: **to ~ for position** manœuvrer pour devancer ses concurrents.
jocular ['dʒɒkjʊləʳ] adj **1.** (cheerful) enjoué(e), jovial(e). **2.** (funny) amusant(e).
jodhpurs ['dʒɒdpəz] npl jodhpurs mpl, culotte f de cheval.
jog [dʒɒɡ] ◆ n: **to go for a ~** faire du jogging. ◆ vt pousser; **to ~ sb's memory** rafraîchir la mémoire de qqn. ◆ vi faire du jogging, jogger.
jogging ['dʒɒɡɪŋ] n jogging m.
john [dʒɒn] n Am inf petit coin m, cabinets mpl.
join [dʒɔɪn] ◆ n raccord m, joint m. ◆ vt **1.** (connect - gen) unir, joindre; (- towns etc) relier. **2.** (get together with) rejoindre, retrouver. **3.** (political party) devenir

membre de; (club) s'inscrire à; (army) s'engager dans; **to ~ a queue** Br, **to ~ a line** Am prendre la queue. ◆ vi **1.** (connect) se joindre. **2.** (become a member - gen) devenir membre; (- of club) s'inscrire. ▶ **join in** ◆ vt fus prendre part à, participer à. ◆ vi participer. ▶ **join up** vi (MIL) s'engager dans l'armée.

joiner ['dʒɔɪnər] n menuisier m.

joinery ['dʒɔɪnərɪ] n menuiserie f.

joint [dʒɔɪnt] ◆ adj (effort) conjugué(e); (responsibility) collectif(ive). ◆ n **1.** (gen & TECH) joint m. **2.** (ANAT) articulation f. **3.** Br (of meat) rôti m. **4.** inf (place) bouge m. **5.** drugs sl joint m.

joint account n compte m joint.

jointly ['dʒɔɪntlɪ] adv conjointement.

joke [dʒəʊk] ◆ n blague f, plaisanterie f; **to play a ~ on sb** faire une blague à qqn, jouer un tour à qqn; **it's no ~** inf (not easy) ce n'est pas de la tarte. ◆ vi plaisanter, blaguer; **to ~ about sthg** plaisanter sur qqch, se moquer de qqch.

joker ['dʒəʊkər] n **1.** (person) blagueur m, -euse f. **2.** (playing card) joker m.

jolly ['dʒɒlɪ] ◆ adj (person) jovial(e), enjoué(e); (time, party) agréable. ◆ adv Br inf drôlement, rudement.

jolt [dʒəʊlt] ◆ n **1.** (jerk) secousse f, soubresaut m. **2.** (shock) choc m. ◆ vt secouer.

Jordan ['dʒɔːdn] n Jordanie f.

jostle ['dʒɒsl] ◆ vt bousculer. ◆ vi se bousculer.

jot [dʒɒt] n (of truth) grain m, brin m. ▶ **jot down** vt sep noter, prendre note de.

jotter ['dʒɒtər] n (notepad) bloc-notes m.

journal ['dʒɜːnl] n **1.** (magazine) revue f. **2.** (diary) journal m.

journalism ['dʒɜːnəlɪzm] n journalisme m.

journalist ['dʒɜːnəlɪst] n journaliste mf.

journey ['dʒɜːnɪ] (pl **journeys**) n voyage m.

jovial ['dʒəʊvjəl] adj jovial(e).

jowls [dʒaʊlz] npl bajoues fpl.

joy [dʒɔɪ] n joie f.

joyful ['dʒɔɪfʊl] adj joyeux(euse).

joyride ['dʒɔɪraɪd] (pt -**rode**, pp -**ridden**) vi une virée dans une voiture volée.

joyrode ['dʒɔɪrəʊd] pt→ **joyride**.

joystick ['dʒɔɪstɪk] n (AERON) manche m (à balai); (COMPUT) manette f.

JP n abbr of **Justice of the Peace**.

Jr. (abbr of **Junior**) Jr.

jubilant ['dʒuːbɪlənt] adj (person) débordant(e) de joie, qui jubile; (shout) de joie.

jubilee ['dʒuːbɪliː] n jubilé m.

judge [dʒʌdʒ] ◆ n juge m. ◆ vt **1.** (gen) juger. **2.** (estimate) évaluer, juger. ◆ vi juger; **to ~ from** OR **by, judging from** OR **by** à en juger par.

judg(e)ment ['dʒʌdʒmənt] n jugement m.

judicial [dʒuː'dɪʃl] adj judiciaire.

judiciary [dʒuː'dɪʃərɪ] n: **the ~** la magistrature.

judicious [dʒuː'dɪʃəs] adj judicieux(euse).

judo ['dʒuːdəʊ] n judo m.

jug [dʒʌg] n pot m, pichet m.

juggernaut ['dʒʌgənɔːt] n poids m lourd.

juggle ['dʒʌgl] ◆ vt lit & fig jongler avec. ◆ vi jongler.

juggler ['dʒʌglər] n jongleur m, -euse f.

jugular (vein) ['dʒʌgjʊlər-] n (veine f) jugulaire f.

juice [dʒuːs] n jus m.

juicy ['dʒuːsɪ] adj (fruit) juteux(euse).

jukebox ['dʒuːkbɒks] n juke-box m.

July [dʒuː'laɪ] n juillet m; see also **September**.

jumble ['dʒʌmbl] ◆ n (mixture) mélange m, fatras m. ◆ vt: **to ~ (up)** mélanger, embrouiller.

jumble sale n Br vente f de charité (où sont vendus des articles d'occasion).

jumbo jet ['dʒʌmbəʊ-] n jumbo-jet m.

jumbo-sized [-saɪzd] adj géant(e), énorme.

jump [dʒʌmp] ◆ n **1.** (leap) saut m, bond m. **2.** (fence) obstacle m. **3.** (rapid increase) flambée f, hausse f brutale. ◆ vt **1.** (fence, stream etc) sauter, franchir d'un bond. **2.** inf (attack) sauter sur, tomber sur. ◆ vi **1.** (gen) sauter, bondir; (in surprise) sursauter. **2.** (increase rapidly) grimper en flèche, faire un bond. ▶ **jump at** vt fus fig sauter sur.

jumper ['dʒʌmpər] n **1.** Br (pullover) pull m. **2.** Am (dress) robe f chasuble.

jump leads npl câbles mpl de démarrage.

jump-start vt: **to ~ a car** faire démarrer une voiture en la poussant.

jumpsuit ['dʒʌmpsuːt] n combinaison-pantalon f.

jumpy ['dʒʌmpɪ] adj nerveux(euse).

Jun. = **Junr**.

junction ['dʒʌŋkʃn] n (of roads) car-

refour *m*; (RAIL) embranchement *m*.
June [dʒuːn] *n* juin *m*; *see also*
September.
jungle ['dʒʌŋgl] *n lit & fig* jungle *f*.
junior ['dʒuːnjərᵣ] ◆ *adj* **1.** (*gen*) jeune.
2. Am (*after name*) junior. ◆ *n* **1.** (*in rank*)
subalterne *mf*. **2.** (*in age*) cadet *m*, -ette
f. **3.** Am (SCH) = élève *mf* de première;
(UNIV) = étudiant *m*, -e *f* de deuxième
année.
junior high school *n* Am = collège
m d'enseignement secondaire.
junior school *n* Br école *f* primaire.
junk [dʒʌŋk] *n* (*unwanted objects*) bric-à-
brac *m*.
junk food *n* (U) *pej* cochonneries *fpl*.
junkie ['dʒʌŋkɪ] *n drugs sl* drogué *m*, -e
f.
junk mail *n* (U) *pej* prospectus *mpl*
publicitaires envoyés par la poste.
junk shop *n* boutique *f* de brocanteur.
Junr (*abbr of* **Junior**) Jr.
Jupiter ['dʒuːpɪtərᵣ] *n* (*planet*) Jupiter *f*.
jurisdiction [,dʒʊərɪs'dɪkʃn] *n* juridiction *f*.
juror ['dʒʊərərᵣ] *n* juré *m*, -e *f*.
jury ['dʒʊərɪ] *n* jury *m*.
just [dʒʌst] ◆ *adv* **1.** (*recently*): **he's ~ left**
il vient de partir. **2.** (*at that moment*): **I
was ~ about to go** j'allais juste partir,
j'étais sur le point de partir; **I'm ~ going
to do it now** je vais le faire tout de suite
OR à l'instant; **she arrived ~ as I was leaving** elle est arrivée au moment même
où je partais OR juste comme je par-
tais. **3.** (*only, simply*): **it's ~ a rumour** ce
n'est qu'une rumeur; **~ add water** vous
n'avez plus qu'à ajouter de l'eau; **~ a
minute** OR **moment** OR **second!** un (petit)
instant! **4.** (*almost not*) tout juste, à
peine; **I only ~ missed the train** j'ai manqué le train de peu; **we have ~ enough
time** on a juste assez de temps. **5.** (*for
emphasis*): **the coast is ~ marvellous** la
côte est vraiment magnifique; **~ look at
this mess!** non, mais regarde un peu ce
désordre! **6.** (*exactly, precisely*) tout à fait,
exactement; **it's ~ what I need** c'est tout
à fait ce qu'il me faut. **7.** (*in requests*):
could you ~ move over please? pourriez-
vous vous pousser un peu s'il vous
plaît? ◆ *adj* juste, équitable. ▶ **just
about** *adv* à peu près, plus ou moins.
▶ **just as** *adv* (*in comparison*) tout aussi;
you're ~ as clever as he is tu es tout
aussi intelligent que lui. ▶ **just now**
adv **1.** (*a short time ago*) il y a un moment,

tout à l'heure. **2.** (*at this moment*) en ce
moment.
justice ['dʒʌstɪs] *n* **1.** (*gen*) justice *f*.
2. (*of claim, cause*) bien-fondé *m*.
Justice of the Peace (*pl* **Justices of
the Peace**) *n* juge *m* de paix.
justify ['dʒʌstɪfaɪ] *vt* (*give reasons for*)
justifier.
jut [dʒʌt] *vi*: **to ~ (out)** faire saillie,
avancer.
juvenile ['dʒuːvənaɪl] ◆ *adj* **1.** (JUR) mi-
neur(e), juvénile. **2.** (*childish*) puéril(e).
◆ *n* (JUR) mineur *m*, -e *f*.
juxtapose [,dʒʌkstə'pəʊz] *vt* juxtaposer.

K

k (*pl* **k's** OR **ks**), **K** (*pl* **K's** OR **Ks**) [keɪ] *n*
(*letter*) k *m inv*, K *m inv*. ▶ **K 1.** (*abbr of*
kilobyte) Ko. **2.** (*abbr of* **thousand**) K.
kaleidoscope [kə'laɪdəskəʊp] *n* kaléidoscope *m*.
kangaroo [,kæŋgə'ruː] *n* kangourou
m.
kaput [kə'pʊt] *adj inf* fichu(e), foutu(e).
karat ['kærət] *n* Am carat *m*.
karate [kə'rɑːtɪ] *n* karaté *m*.
kayak ['kaɪæk] *n* kayak *m*.
KB (*abbr of* **kilobyte(s)**) *n* (COMPUT) Ko *m*.
kcal (*abbr of* **kilocalorie**) Kcal.
kebab [kɪ'bæb] *n* brochette *f*.
keel [kiːl] *n* quille *f*; **on an even ~** stable. ▶ **keel over** *vi* (*ship*) chavirer; (*person*) tomber dans les pommes.
keen [kiːn] *adj* **1.** (*enthusiastic*) enthousiaste, passionné(e); **to be ~ on sthg**
avoir la passion de qqch; **he's ~ on her**
elle lui plaît; **to be ~ to do** OR **on doing
sthg** tenir à faire qqch. **2.** (*interest, desire,
mind*) vif (vive); (*competition*) âpre,
acharné(e). **3.** (*sense of smell*) fin(e); (*eyesight*) perçant(e).
keep [kiːp] (*pt & pp* **kept**) ◆ *vt* **1.** (*retain,
store*) garder; **~ the change!** gardez la
monnaie!; **to ~ sthg warm** garder OR
tenir qqch au chaud. **2.** (*prevent*): **to
keep sb/sthg from doing sthg** empêcher
qqn/qqch de faire qqch. **3.** (*detain*)
retenir; (*prisoner*) détenir; **to ~ sb waiting** faire attendre qqn. **4.** (*promise*)

tenir; (*appointment*) aller à; (*vow*) être fidèle à. **5.** (*not disclose*): **to ~ sthg from sb** cacher qqch à qqn; **to ~ sthg to o.s.** garder qqch pour soi. **6.** (*diary, record, notes*) tenir. **7.** (*own - sheep, pigs etc*) élever; (*- shop*) tenir; (*- car*) avoir, posséder. **8.** *phr*: **they ~ themselves to themselves** ils restent entre eux, ils se tiennent à l'écart. ◆ *vi* **1.** (*remain*): **to ~ warm** se tenir au chaud; **to ~ quiet** garder le silence; **~ quiet!** taisez-vous! **2.** (*continue*): **he ~ interrupting me** il n'arrête pas de m'interrompre; **to ~ talking/walking** continuer à parler/à marcher. **3.** (*continue moving*): **to ~ left/right** garder sa gauche/sa droite; **to ~ north/south** continuer vers le nord/le sud. **4.** (*food*) se conserver. **5.** Br (*in health*): **how are you ~ing?** comment allez-vous? ◆ *n*: **to earn one's ~** gagner sa vie. ◆ **keeps** *n*: **for ~s** pour toujours. ▶ **keep back** *vt sep* (*information*) cacher, ne pas divulguer; (*money*) retenir. ▶ **keep off** *vt fus*: **'~ off the grass'** '(il est) interdit de marcher sur la pelouse'. ▶ **keep on** *vi* **1.** (*continue*): **to ~ on (doing sthg)** (*without stopping*) continuer (de OR à faire qqch); (*repeatedly*) ne pas arrêter (de faire qqch). **2.** (*talk incessantly*): **to ~ on (about sthg)** ne pas arrêter de parler (de qqch). ▶ **keep out** ◆ *vt sep* empêcher d'entrer. ◆ *vi*: **'~ out'** 'défense d'entrer'. ▶ **keep to** *vt fus* (*rules, deadline*) respecter, observer. ▶ **keep up** ◆ *vt sep* (*continue to do*) continuer; (*maintain*) maintenir. ◆ *vi* (*maintain pace, level etc*): **to ~ up (with sb)** aller aussi vite (que qqn).

keeper ['kiːpər] *n* gardien *m*, -enne *f*.

keep-fit *n* (U) Br gymnastique *f*.

keeping ['kiːpɪŋ] *n* **1.** (*care*) garde *f*. **2.** (*conformity, harmony*): **to be in/out of ~ with** (*rules etc*) être/ne pas être conforme à; (*subj: clothes, furniture*) aller/ne pas aller avec.

keepsake ['kiːpseɪk] *n* souvenir *m*.

keg [keg] *n* tonnelet *m*, baril *m*.

kennel ['kenl] *n* **1.** (*shelter for dog*) niche *f*. **2.** Am = **kennels**. ▶ **kennels** *npl* Br chenil *m*.

Kenya ['kenjə] *n* Kenya *m*.

Kenyan ['kenjən] ◆ *adj* kenyan(e). ◆ *n* Kenyan *m*, -e *f*.

kept [kept] *pt & pp* → **keep**.

kerb [kɜːb] *n* Br bordure *f* du trottoir.

kernel ['kɜːnl] *n* amande *f*.

kerosene ['kerəsiːn] *n* kérosène *m*.

ketchup ['ketʃəp] *n* ketchup *m*.

kettle ['ketl] *n* bouilloire *f*.

key [kiː] ◆ *n* **1.** (*gen & MUS*) clef *f*, clé *f*; **the ~ (to sthg)** *fig* la clé (de qqch). **2.** (*of typewriter, computer, piano*) touche *f*. **3.** (*of map*) légende *f*. ◆ *adj* clé (*after n*). ▶ **key in** *vt sep* (*text, data*) saisir; (*code*) composer.

keyboard ['kiːbɔːd] *n* (*gen & COMPUT*) clavier *m*.

keyed up [ˌkiːd-] *adj* tendu(e), énervé(e).

keyhole ['kiːhəʊl] *n* trou *m* de serrure.

keynote ['kiːnəʊt] ◆ *n* note *f* dominante. ◆ *comp*: **~ speech** discours-programme *m*.

keypad ['kiːpæd] *n* (COMPUT) pavé *m* numérique.

key ring *n* porte-clés *m inv*.

kg (*abbr of* **kilogram**) kg.

khaki ['kɑːkɪ] ◆ *adj* kaki (*inv*). ◆ *n* (*colour*) kaki *m*.

kick [kɪk] ◆ *n* **1.** (*with foot*) coup *m* de pied. **2.** *inf* (*excitement*): **to get a ~ from sthg** trouver qqch excitant; **to do sthg for ~s** faire qqch pour le plaisir. ◆ *vt* **1.** (*with foot*) donner un coup de pied à; **to ~ o.s.** *fig* se donner des gifles OR des claques. **2.** *inf* (*give up*): **to ~ the habit** arrêter. ◆ *vi* (*person - repeatedly*) donner des coups de pied; (*- once*) donner un coup de pied; (*baby*) gigoter; (*animal*) ruer. ▶ **kick about, kick around** *vi* Br *inf* traîner. ▶ **kick off** *vi* **1.** (FTBL) donner le coup d'envoi. **2.** *inf fig* (*start*) démarrer. ▶ **kick out** *vt sep inf* vider, jeter dehors.

kid [kɪd] ◆ *n* **1.** *inf* (*child*) gosse *mf*, gamin *m*, -e *f*. **2.** *inf* (*young person*) petit jeune *m*, petite jeune *f*. **3.** (*goat, leather*) chevreau *m*. ◆ *comp inf* (*brother, sister*) petit(e). ◆ *vt inf* **1.** (*tease*) faire marcher. **2.** (*delude*): **to ~ o.s.** se faire des illusions. ◆ *vi inf*: **to be kidding** plaisanter.

kidnap ['kɪdnæp] *vt* kidnapper, enlever.

kidnapper Br, **kidnaper** Am ['kɪdnæpər] *n* kidnappeur *m*, -euse *f*, ravisseur *m*, -euse *f*.

kidnapping Br, **kidnaping** Am ['kɪdnæpɪŋ] *n* enlèvement *m*.

kidney ['kɪdnɪ] (*pl* **kidneys**) *n* **1.** (ANAT) rein *m*. **2.** (CULIN) rognon *m*.

kidney bean *n* haricot *m* rouge.

kill [kɪl] ◆ *vt* **1.** (*cause death of*) tuer. **2.** *fig* (*hope, chances*) mettre fin à; (*pain*) supprimer. ◆ *vi* tuer. ◆ *n* mise *f* à mort.

killer ['kɪlər] *n* (*person*) meurtrier *m*, -ère *f*; (*animal*) tueur *m*, -euse *f*.

killing ['kɪlɪŋ] *n* meurtre *m*.

killjoy ['kɪldʒɔɪ] n rabat-joie m inv.

kiln [kɪln] n four m.

kilo ['ki:ləʊ] (pl **-s**) (abbr of **kilogram**) n kilo m.

kilobyte ['kɪləbaɪt] n (COMPUT) kilo-octet m.

kilogram(me) ['kɪləgræm] n kilo-gramme m.

kilohertz ['kɪləhɜːtz] (pl inv) n kilo-hertz m.

kilometre Br ['kɪlə,mi:tər], **kilometer** Am [kɪ'lɒmɪtər] n kilomètre m.

kilowatt ['kɪləwɒt] n kilowatt m.

kilt [kɪlt] n kilt m.

kin [kɪn] n → **kith**.

kind [kaɪnd] ◆ adj gentil(ille), aimable. ◆ n genre m, sorte f; **they're two of a** ~ ils se ressemblent; **in** ~ (payment) en nature; **a** ~ **of** une espèce de, une sorte de; ~ **of** Am inf un peu.

kindergarten ['kɪndə,gɑːtn] n jardin m d'enfants.

kind-hearted [-'hɑːtɪd] adj qui a bon cœur, bon (bonne).

kindle ['kɪndl] vt 1. (fire) allumer. 2. fig (feeling) susciter.

kindly ['kaɪndlɪ] ◆ adj 1. (person) plein(e) de bonté, bienveillant(e). 2. (gesture) plein(e) de gentillesse. ◆ adv 1. (speak, smile etc) avec gen-tillesse. 2. (please): ~ **leave the room!** veuillez sortir, s'il vous plaît!; **will you** ~ **...?** veuillez ..., je vous prie de ...

kindness ['kaɪndnɪs] n gentillesse f.

kindred ['kɪndrɪd] adj (similar) sem-blable, similaire; ~ **spirit** âme f sœur.

king [kɪŋ] n roi m.

kingdom ['kɪŋdəm] n 1. (country) royaume m. 2. (of animals, plants) règne m.

kingfisher ['kɪŋ,fɪʃər] n martin-pêcheur m.

king-size(d) [-saɪz(d)] adj (cigarette) long (longue); (pack) géant(e); **a** ~ **bed** un grand lit (de 195 cm).

kinky ['kɪŋkɪ] adj inf vicieux(euse).

kiosk ['ki:ɒsk] n 1. (small shop) kiosque m. 2. Br (telephone box) cabine f (télé-phonique).

kip [kɪp] Br inf ◆ n somme m, roupillon m. ◆ vi faire OR piquer un petit somme.

kipper ['kɪpər] n hareng m fumé OR saur.

kiss [kɪs] ◆ n baiser m; **to give sb a** ~ embrasser qqn, donner un baiser à qqn. ◆ vt embrasser. ◆ vi s'embrasser.

kiss of life n: **the** ~ le bouche-à-bouche.

kit [kɪt] n 1. (set) trousse f. 2. (U) (SPORT) affaires fpl, équipement m. 3. (to be assembled) kit m.

kit bag n sac m de marin.

kitchen ['kɪtʃɪn] n cuisine f.

kitchenette [,kɪtʃɪ'net] n kitchenette f, cuisinette f.

kitchen sink n évier m.

kitchen unit n élément m de cuisine.

kite [kaɪt] n (toy) cerf-volant m.

kith [kɪθ] n: ~ **and kin** parents et amis mpl.

kitten ['kɪtn] n chaton m.

kitty ['kɪtɪ] n (shared fund) cagnotte f.

kiwi ['ki:wi:] n 1. (bird) kiwi m, aptéryx m. 2. inf (New Zealander) Néo-Zélandais m, -e f.

kiwi fruit n kiwi m.

km (abbr of **kilometre**) km.

km/h (abbr of **kilometres per hour**) km/h.

knack [næk] n: **to have a** OR **the** ~ **(for doing sthg)** avoir le coup (pour faire qqch).

knackered ['nækəd] adj Br v inf cre-vé(e), claqué(e).

knapsack ['næpsæk] n sac m à dos.

knead [niːd] vt pétrir.

knee [niː] n genou m.

kneecap ['niːkæp] n rotule f.

kneel [niːl] (Br pt & pp **knelt**, Am pt & pp **knelt** OR **-ed**) vi se mettre à genoux, s'agenouiller. ▶ **kneel down** vi se mettre à genoux, s'agenouiller.

knelt [nelt] pt & pp → **kneel**.

knew [njuː] pt → **know**.

knickers ['nɪkəz] npl Br (underwear) culotte f.

knick-knack ['nɪknæk] n babiole f, bibelot m.

knife [naɪf] (pl **knives**) ◆ n couteau m. ◆ vt donner un coup de couteau à, poignarder.

knight [naɪt] ◆ n 1. (in history, member of nobility) chevalier m. 2. (in chess) cavalier m. ◆ vt faire chevalier.

knighthood ['naɪthʊd] n titre m de chevalier.

knit [nɪt] (pt & pp **knit** OR **-ted**) ◆ adj: **closely** OR **tightly** ~ fig très uni(e). ◆ vt tri-coter. ◆ vi 1. (with wool) tricoter. 2. (bro-ken bones) se souder.

knitting ['nɪtɪŋ] n (U) tricot m.

knitting needle n aiguille f à tricoter.

knitwear ['nɪtweər] n (U) tricots mpl.

knives [naɪvz] pl → **knife**.

knob [nɒb] n 1. (on door) poignée f, bouton m; (on drawer) poignée; (on bedstead) pomme f. **2.** (on TV, radio etc) bouton m.

knock [nɒk] ◆ n **1.** (hit) coup m. **2.** inf (piece of bad luck) coup m dur. ◆ vt **1.** (hit) frapper, cogner; **to ~ sb/sthg over** renverser qqn/qqch. **2.** inf (criticize) critiquer, dire du mal de. ◆ vi **1.** (on door): **to ~ (at OR on)** frapper (à). **2.** (car engine) cogner, avoir des ratés. ▶ **knock down** vt sep **1.** (subj: car, driver) renverser. **2.** (building) démolir. ▶ **knock off** vi inf (stop working) finir son travail OR sa journée. ▶ **knock out** vt sep **1.** (make unconscious) assommer. **2.** (from competition) éliminer.

knocker ['nɒkər] n (on door) heurtoir m.

knock-kneed [-'niːd] adj cagneux (euse), qui a les genoux cagneux.

knock-on effect n Br réaction f en chaîne.

knockout ['nɒkaʊt] n knock-out m, K.-O. m.

knot [nɒt] ◆ n **1.** (gen) nœud m; **to tie/untie a ~** faire/défaire un nœud. **2.** (of people) petit attroupement m. ◆ vt nouer, faire un nœud à.

knotty ['nɒtɪ] adj fig épineux(euse).

know [nəʊ] (pt knew, pp known) ◆ vt **1.** (gen) savoir; (language) savoir parler; **to ~ (that)** ... savoir que ...; **to let sb ~ (about sthg)** faire savoir (qqch) à qqn, informer qqn (de qqch); **to ~ how to do sthg** savoir faire qqch; **to get to ~ sthg** apprendre qqch. **2.** (person, place) connaître; **to get to ~ sb** apprendre à mieux connaître qqn. ◆ vi savoir; **to ~ of sthg** connaître qqch; **to ~ about** (be aware of) être au courant de; (be expert in) s'y connaître en. ◆ n: **to be in the ~** être au courant.

know-all n Br (monsieur) je-sais-tout m, (madame) je-sais-tout f.

know-how n savoir-faire m, technique f.

knowing ['nəʊɪŋ] adj (smile, look) entendu(e).

knowingly ['nəʊɪŋlɪ] adv **1.** (smile, look) d'un air entendu. **2.** (intentionally) sciemment.

know-it-all = **know-all**.

knowledge ['nɒlɪdʒ] n (U) **1.** (gen) connaissance f; **without my ~** à mon insu; **to the best of my ~** à ma connaissance, autant que je sache. **2.** (learning, understanding) savoir m, connaissances fpl.

knowledgeable ['nɒlɪdʒəbl] adj bien informé(e).

known [nəʊn] pp → **know**.

knuckle ['nʌkl] n **1.** (ANAT) articulation f OR jointure f du doigt. **2.** (of meat) jarret m.

knuckle-duster n coup-de-poing m américain.

koala (bear) [kəʊ'ɑːlə-] n koala m.

Koran [kɒ'rɑːn] n: **the ~** le Coran.

Korea [kə'rɪə] n Corée f.

Korean [kə'rɪən] ◆ adj coréen(enne). ◆ n **1.** (person) Coréen m, -enne f. **2.** (language) coréen m.

kosher ['kəʊʃər] adj (meat) kasher (inv).

Koweit = **Kuwait**.

kung fu [ˌkʌŋ'fuː] n kung-fu m.

Kurd [kɜːd] n Kurde mf.

Kuwait [kʊ'weɪt], **Koweit** [kəʊ'weɪt] n **1.** (country) Koweït m. **2.** (city) Koweït City.

L

l¹ (pl **l's** OR **ls**), **L** (pl **L's** OR **Ls**) [el] n (letter) l m inv, L m inv.

l² (abbr of litre) l.

lab [læb] n inf labo m.

label ['leɪbl] ◆ n **1.** (identification) étiquette f. **2.** (of record) label m, maison f de disques. ◆ vt **1.** (fix label to) étiqueter. **2.** (describe): **to ~ sb (as)** cataloguer OR étiqueter qqn (comme).

labor etc Am = **labour** etc.

laboratory [Br lə'bɒrətrɪ, Am 'læbrəˌtɔːrɪ] n laboratoire m.

laborious [lə'bɔːrɪəs] adj laborieux (euse).

labor union n Am syndicat m.

labour Br, **labor** Am ['leɪbər] ◆ n **1.** (gen & MED) travail m. **2.** (workers, work carried out) main d'œuvre f. ◆ vi travailler dur; **to ~ at OR over** peiner sur. ▶ **Labour** (POL) ◆ adj travailliste. ◆ n (U) Br les travaillistes mpl.

laboured Br, **labored** Am ['leɪbəd] adj (breathing) pénible; (style) lourd(e), laborieux(euse).

labourer Br, **laborer** Am ['leɪbərər] n travailleur manuel m, travailleuse manuelle f; (agricultural) ouvrier agricole m, ouvrière agricole f.

Labour Party n Br: **the ~** le parti travailliste.

Labrador ['læbrədɔ:ʳ] n (dog) labrador m.

labyrinth ['læbərɪnθ] n labyrinthe m.

lace [leɪs] ◆ n **1.** (fabric) dentelle f. **2.** (of shoe etc) lacet m. ◆ vt **1.** (shoe etc) lacer. **2.** (drink) verser de l'alcool dans. ► **lace up** vt sep lacer.

lace-up n Br chaussure f à lacets.

lack [læk] ◆ n manque m; **for** OR **through ~ of** par manque de; **no ~ of** bien assez de. ◆ vt manquer de. ◆ vi: **to be ~ing in sthg** manquer de qqch; **to be ~ing** manquer, faire défaut.

lackadaisical [ˌlækə'deɪzɪkl] adj pej nonchalant(e).

lacklustre Br, **lackluster** Am ['læk-ˌlʌstəʳ] adj terne.

laconic [lə'kɒnɪk] adj laconique.

lacquer ['lækəʳ] ◆ n (for wood) vernis m, laque f; (for hair) laque f. ◆ vt laquer.

lacrosse [lə'krɒs] n crosse f.

lad [læd] n inf (boy) garçon m, gars m.

ladder ['lædəʳ] ◆ n **1.** (for climbing) échelle f. **2.** Br (in tights) maille f filée, estafilade f. ◆ vt & vi Br (tights) filer.

laden ['leɪdn] adj: **~ (with)** chargé(e) (de).

ladies Br ['leɪdɪz], **ladies' room** Am n toilettes fpl (pour dames).

ladle ['leɪdl] ◆ n louche f. ◆ vt servir (à la louche).

lady ['leɪdɪ] ◆ n (gen) dame f; **ladies and gentlemen** (in speech, announcement) messieurs-dames. ◆ comp: **a ~ doctor** une femme docteur. ► **Lady** n Lady f.

ladybird Br ['leɪdɪbɜ:d], **ladybug** Am ['leɪdɪbʌg] n coccinelle f.

lady-in-waiting [-'weɪtɪŋ] (pl ladies-in-waiting) n dame f d'honneur.

ladylike ['leɪdɪlaɪk] adj distingué(e).

Ladyship ['leɪdɪʃɪp] n: **her/your ~** Madame la baronne/la duchesse etc.

lag [læg] ◆ vi: **to ~ (behind)** (person, runner) traîner; (economy, development) être en retard, avoir du retard. ◆ vt (roof, pipe) calorifuger. ◆ n (timelag) décalage m.

lager ['lɑ:gəʳ] n (bière f) blonde f.

lagoon [lə'gu:n] n lagune f.

laid [leɪd] pt & pp → **lay.**

laid-back adj inf relaxe, décontracté(e).

lain [leɪn] pp → **lie.**

lair [leəʳ] n repaire m, antre m.

lake [leɪk] n lac m.

Lake District n: **the ~** la région des lacs (au nord-ouest de l'Angleterre).

Lake Geneva n le lac Léman OR de Genève.

lamb [læm] n agneau m.

lambswool ['læmzwʊl] ◆ n lambswool m. ◆ comp en lambswool, en laine d'agneau.

lame [leɪm] adj lit & fig boiteux(euse).

lament [lə'ment] ◆ n lamentation f. ◆ vt se lamenter sur.

lamentable ['læməntəbl] adj lamentable.

laminated ['læmɪneɪtɪd] adj (wood) stratifié(e); (glass) feuilleté(e); (steel) laminé(e).

lamp [læmp] n lampe f.

lampoon [læm'pu:n] ◆ n satire f. ◆ vt faire la satire de.

lamppost ['læmppəʊst] n réverbère m.

lampshade ['læmpʃeɪd] n abat-jour m.

lance [lɑ:ns] ◆ n lance f. ◆ vt (boil) percer.

lance corporal n caporal m.

land [lænd] ◆ n **1.** (solid ground) terre f (ferme); (farming ground) terre, terrain m. **2.** (property) terres fpl, propriété f. **3.** (nation) pays m. ◆ vt **1.** (from ship, plane) débarquer. **2.** (catch - fish) prendre. **3.** (plane) atterrir. **4.** inf (obtain) décrocher. **5.** inf (place): **to ~ sb in trouble** attirer des ennuis à qqn; **to be ~ed with sthg** se coltiner qqch. ◆ vi **1.** (plane) atterrir. **2.** (fall) tomber. ► **land up** vi inf atterrir.

landing ['lændɪŋ] n **1.** (of stairs) palier m. **2.** (AERON) atterrissage m. **3.** (of goods from ship) débarquement m.

landing card n carte f de débarquement.

landing gear n (U) train m d'atterrissage.

landing stage n débarcadère m.

landing strip n piste f d'atterrissage.

landlady ['lænd,leɪdɪ] n (living in) logeuse f; (owner) propriétaire f.

landlord ['lændlɔ:d] n **1.** (of rented property) propriétaire m. **2.** (of pub) patron m.

landmark ['lændmɑ:k] n point m de repère; fig événement m marquant.

landowner ['lænd,əʊnəʳ] n propriétaire foncier m, propriétaire foncière f.

landscape ['lændskeɪp] n paysage m.

landslide ['lændslaɪd] n **1.** (of earth) glissement m de terrain; (of rocks) éboulement m. **2.** fig (election victory) victoire f écrasante.

lane [leɪn] n **1.** (in country) petite route f, chemin m. **2.** (in town) ruelle f. **3.** (for traffic) voie f; **'keep in ~'** 'ne changez pas de file'. **4.** (AERON & SPORT) couloir m.

language ['læŋgwɪdʒ] *n* 1. (*of people, country*) langue *f*. 2. (*terminology, ability to speak*) langage *m*.

language laboratory *n* laboratoire *m* de langues.

languid ['læŋgwɪd] *adj* indolent(e).

languish ['læŋgwɪʃ] *vi* languir.

lank [læŋk] *adj* terne.

lanky ['læŋkɪ] *adj* dégingandé(e).

lantern ['læntən] *n* lanterne *f*.

lap [læp] ◆ *n* 1. (*of person*): **on sb's ~** sur les genoux de qqn. 2. (*of race*) tour *m* de piste. ◆ *vt* 1. (*subj: animal*) laper. 2. (*in race*) prendre un tour d'avance sur. ◆ *vi* (*water, waves*) clapoter.

lapel [lə'pel] *n* revers *m*.

Lapland ['læplænd] *n* Laponie *f*.

lapse [læps] ◆ *n* 1. (*failing*) défaillance *f*. 2. (*in behaviour*) écart *m* de conduite. 3. (*of time*) intervalle *m*, laps *m* de temps. ◆ *vi* 1. (*passport*) être périmé(e); (*membership*) prendre fin; (*tradition*) se perdre. 2. (*person*): **to ~ into bad habits** prendre de mauvaises habitudes.

lap-top (computer) *n* (ordinateur *m*) portable *m*.

larceny ['lɑːsənɪ] *n* (*U*) vol *m* (simple).

lard [lɑːd] *n* saindoux *m*.

larder ['lɑːdər] *n* garde-manger *m*.

large [lɑːdʒ] *adj* grand(e); (*person, animal, book*) gros (grosse). ► **at large** *adv* 1. (*as a whole*) dans son ensemble. 2. (*prisoner, animal*) en liberté. ► **by and large** *adv* dans l'ensemble.

largely ['lɑːdʒlɪ] *adv* en grande partie.

lark [lɑːk] *n* 1. (*bird*) alouette *f*. 2. *inf* (*joke*) blague *f*. ► **lark about** *vi* s'amuser.

laryngitis [ˌlærɪn'dʒaɪtɪs] *n* (*U*) laryngite *f*.

larynx ['lærɪŋks] *n* larynx *m*.

lasagna, lasagne [lə'zænjə] *n* (*U*) lasagnes *fpl*.

laser ['leɪzər] *n* laser *m*.

laser printer *n* imprimante *f* (à) laser.

lash [læʃ] ◆ *n* 1. (*eyelash*) cil *m*. 2. (*with whip*) coup *m* de fouet. ◆ *vt* 1. (*gen*) fouetter. 2. (*tie*) attacher. ► **lash out** *vi* 1. (*physically*): **to ~ out (at OR against)** envoyer un coup (à). 2. *Br inf* (*spend money*): **to ~ out (on sthg)** faire une folie (en s'achetant qqch).

lass [læs] *n* jeune fille *f*.

lasso [læ'suː] (*pl* -s) ◆ *n* lasso *m*. ◆ *vt* attraper au lasso.

last [lɑːst] ◆ *adj* dernier(ère); **~ week/year** la semaine/l'année dernière, la semaine/l'année passée; **~ night** hier soir; **~ but one** avant-dernier (avant-dernière); **down to the ~ detail/penny** jusqu'au moindre détail/dernier sou. ◆ *adv* 1. (*most recently*) la dernière fois. 2. (*finally*) en dernier, le dernier (la dernière). ◆ *pron*: **the Saturday before ~** pas samedi dernier, mais le samedi d'avant; **the year before ~** il y a deux ans; **the ~ but one** l'avant-dernier *m*, l'avant-dernière *f*; **to leave sthg till ~** faire qqch en dernier. ◆ *n*: **the ~ I saw of him** la dernière fois que je l'ai vu. ◆ *vi* durer; (*food*) se garder, se conserver; (*feeling*) persister. ► **at (long) last** *adv* enfin.

last-ditch *adj* ultime, désespéré(e).

lasting ['lɑːstɪŋ] *adj* durable.

lastly ['lɑːstlɪ] *adv* pour terminer, finalement.

last-minute *adj* de dernière minute.

last name *n* nom *m* de famille.

latch [lætʃ] *n* loquet *m*. ► **latch onto** *vt fus inf* s'accrocher à.

late [leɪt] ◆ *adj* 1. (*not on time*): **to be ~ (for sthg)** être en retard (pour qqch). 2. (*near end of*): **in ~ December** vers la fin décembre. 3. (*later than normal*) tardif (ive). 4. (*former*) ancien(enne). 5. (*dead*) feu(e). ◆ *adv* 1. (*not on time*) en retard; **to arrive 20 minutes ~** arriver avec 20 minutes de retard. 2. (*later than normal*) tard; **to work/go to bed ~** travailler/se coucher tard. ► **of late** *adv* récemment, dernièrement.

latecomer ['leɪtˌkʌmər] *n* retardataire *mf*.

lately ['leɪtlɪ] *adv* ces derniers temps, dernièrement.

latent ['leɪtənt] *adj* latent(e).

later ['leɪtər] ◆ *adj* (*date*) ultérieur(e); (*edition*) postérieur(e). ◆ *adv*: **~ (on)** plus tard.

lateral ['lætərəl] *adj* latéral(e).

latest ['leɪtɪst] ◆ *adj* dernier(ère). ◆ *n*: **at the ~** au plus tard.

lathe [leɪð] *n* tour *m*.

lather ['lɑːðər] ◆ *n* mousse *f* (de savon). ◆ *vt* savonner.

Latin ['lætɪn] ◆ *adj* latin(e). ◆ *n* (*language*) latin *m*.

Latin America *n* Amérique *f* latine.

Latin American ◆ *adj* latino-américain(e). ◆ *n* (*person*) Latino-Américain *m*, -e *f*.

latitude ['lætɪtjuːd] *n* latitude *f*.

latter ['lætər] ◆ *adj* 1. (*later*) dernier (ère). 2. (*second*) deuxième. ◆ *n*: **the ~**

celui-ci (celle-ci), ce dernier (cette dernière).

latterly [ˈlætəlɪ] *adv* récemment.

lattice [ˈlætɪs] *n* treillis *m*, treillage *m*.

Latvia [ˈlætvɪə] *n* Lettonie *f*.

laudable [ˈlɔːdəbl] *adj* louable.

laugh [lɑːf] ◆ *n* rire *m*; **we had a good ~** *inf* on a bien rigolé, on s'est bien amusé; **to do sthg for ~s** OR **a ~** *inf* faire qqch pour rire OR rigoler. ◆ *vi* rire. ▶ **laugh at** *vt fus* (*mock*) se moquer de, rire de. ▶ **laugh off** *vt sep* tourner en plaisanterie.

laughable [ˈlɑːfəbl] *adj* ridicule, risible.

laughingstock [ˈlɑːfɪŋstɒk] *n* risée *f*.

laughter [ˈlɑːftə`r`] *n* (U) rire *m*, rires *mpl*.

launch [lɔːntʃ] ◆ *n* 1. (*gen*) lancement *m*. 2. (*boat*) chaloupe *f*. ◆ *vt* lancer.

launch(ing) pad [ˈlɔːntʃ(ɪŋ)-] *n* pas *m* de tir.

launder [ˈlɔːndə`r`] *vt lit & fig* blanchir.

laund(e)rette [lɔːnˈdret], **Laundromat®** *Am* [ˈlɔːndrəmæt] *n* laverie *f* automatique.

laundry [ˈlɔːndrɪ] *n* 1. (U) (*clothes*) lessive *f*. 2. (*business*) blanchisserie *f*.

laurel [ˈlɒrəl] *n* laurier *m*.

lava [ˈlɑːvə] *n* lave *f*.

lavatory [ˈlævətrɪ] *n* toilettes *fpl*.

lavender [ˈlævəndə`r`] *n* (*plant*) lavande *f*.

lavish [ˈlævɪʃ] ◆ *adj* 1. (*generous*) généreux(euse); **to be ~ with** être prodigue de. 2. (*sumptuous*) somptueux (euse). ◆ *vt*: **to ~ sthg on sb** prodiguer qqch à qqn.

law [lɔː] *n* 1. (*gen*) loi *f*; **against the ~** contraire à la loi, illégal(e); **to break the ~** enfreindre OR transgresser la loi; **~ and order** ordre *m* public. 2. (JUR) droit *m*.

law-abiding [-əˌbaɪdɪŋ] *adj* respectueux(euse) des lois.

law court *n* tribunal *m*, cour *f* de justice.

lawful [ˈlɔːfʊl] *adj* légal(e), licite.

lawn [lɔːn] *n* pelouse *f*, gazon *m*.

lawnmower [ˈlɔːnˌməʊə`r`] *n* tondeuse *f* à gazon.

lawn tennis *n* tennis *m*.

law school *n* faculté *f* de droit.

lawsuit [ˈlɔːsuːt] *n* procès *m*.

lawyer [ˈlɔːjə`r`] *n* (*in court*) avocat *m*; (*of company*) conseiller *m* juridique; (*for wills, sales*) notaire *m*.

lax [læks] *adj* relâché(e).

laxative [ˈlæksətɪv] *n* laxatif *m*.

lay [leɪ] (*pt & pp* **laid**) ◆ *pt* → **lie**. ◆ *vt* 1. (*gen*) poser, mettre; *fig*: **to ~ the blame for sthg on sb** rejeter la responsabilité de qqch sur qqn. 2. (*trap, snare*) tendre, dresser; (*plans*) faire; **to ~ the table** mettre la table OR le couvert. 3. (*egg*) pondre. ◆ *adj* 1. (RELIG) laïque. 2. (*untrained*) profane. ▶ **lay aside** *vt sep* mettre de côté. ▶ **lay down** *vt sep* 1. (*guidelines, rules*) imposer, stipuler. 2. (*put down*) déposer. ▶ **lay off** ◆ *vt sep* (*make redundant*) licencier. ◆ *vt fus inf* 1. (*leave alone*) ficher la paix à. 2. (*give up*) arrêter. ▶ **lay on** *vt sep Br* (*provide, supply*) organiser. ▶ **lay out** *vt sep* 1. (*arrange*) arranger, disposer. 2. (*design*) concevoir.

layabout [ˈleɪəbaʊt] *n Br inf* fainéant *m*, -e *f*.

lay-by (*pl* **lay-bys**) *n Br* aire *f* de stationnement.

layer [ˈleɪə`r`] *n* couche *f*; *fig* (*level*) niveau *m*.

layman [ˈleɪmən] (*pl* **-men** [-mən]) *n* 1. (*untrained person*) profane *m*. 2. (RELIG) laïc *m*.

layout [ˈleɪaʊt] *n* (*of office, building*) agencement *m*; (*of garden*) plan *m*; (*of page*) mise *f* en page.

laze [leɪz] *vi*: **to ~ (about** OR **around)** paresser.

lazy [ˈleɪzɪ] *adj* (*person*) paresseux (euse), fainéant(e); (*action*) nonchalant(e).

lazybones [ˈleɪzɪbəʊnz] (*pl inv*) *n* paresseux *m*, -euse *f*, fainéant *m*, -e *f*.

lb (*abbr of* **pound**) livre (*unité de poids*).

LCD (*abbr of* **liquid crystal display**) *n* affichage à cristaux liquides.

lead¹ [liːd] (*pt & pp* **led**) ◆ *n* 1. (*winning position*): **to be in** OR **have the ~** mener, être en tête. 2. (*amount ahead*): **to have a ~ of ...** devancer de ... 3. (*initiative, example*) initiative *f*, exemple *m*; **to take the ~** montrer l'exemple. 4. (THEATRE): **the ~** le rôle principal. 5. (*clue*) indice *m*. 6. (*for dog*) laisse *f*. 7. (*wire, cable*) câble *m*, fil *m*. ◆ *adj* (*role etc*) principal(e). ◆ *vt* 1. (*be at front of*) mener, être à la tête de. 2. (*guide*) guider, conduire. 3. (*be in charge of*) être à la tête de, diriger. 4. (*organize - protest etc*) mener, organiser. 5. (*life*) mener. 6. (*cause*): **to ~ sb to do sthg** inciter OR pousser qqn à faire qqch. ◆ *vi* 1. (*path, cable etc*) mener, conduire. 2. (*give access*): **to ~ to/into** donner sur, donner accès à. 3. (*in race, match*) mener. 4. (*result in*): **to ~ to sthg**

aboutir à qqch, causer qqch. ► **lead up to** vt fus **1.** (*precede*) conduire à, aboutir à. **2.** (*build up to*) amener.

lead² [led] ◆ n plomb m; (*in pencil*) mine f. ◆ comp en or de plomb.

leaded ['ledɪd] adj (*petrol*) au plomb; (*window*) à petits carreaux.

leader ['liːdər] n **1.** (*head, chief*) chef m; (POL) leader m. **2.** (*in race, competition*) premier m, -ère f. **3.** Br (PRESS) éditorial m.

leadership ['liːdəʃɪp] n **1.** (*people in charge*): **the ~** les dirigeants mpl. **2.** (*position of leader*) direction f. **3.** (*qualities of leader*) qualités fpl de chef.

lead-free [led-] adj sans plomb.

leading ['liːdɪŋ] adj **1.** (*most important*) principal(e). **2.** (*at front*) de tête.

leading light n personnage m très important or influent.

leaf [liːf] (pl **leaves**) n **1.** (*of tree, plant*) feuille f. **2.** (*of table - hinged*) abattant m; (- *pull-out*) rallonge f. **3.** (*of book*) feuille f, page f. ► **leaf through** vt fus (*magazine etc*) parcourir, feuilleter.

leaflet ['liːflɪt] n prospectus m.

league [liːg] n ligue f; (SPORT) championnat m; **to be in ~ with** être de connivence avec.

leak [liːk] ◆ n lit & fig fuite f. ◆ vt fig (*secret, information*) divulguer. ◆ vi fuir. ► **leak out** vi **1.** (*liquid*) fuir. **2.** fig (*secret, information*) transpirer, être divulgué(e).

leakage ['liːkɪdʒ] n fuite f.

lean [liːn] (pt & pp **leant** or **-ed**) ◆ adj **1.** (*slim*) mince. **2.** (*meat*) maigre. **3.** fig (*month, time*) mauvais(e). ◆ vt (*rest*): **to ~ sthg against** appuyer qqch contre, adosser qqch à. ◆ vi **1.** (*bend, slope*) se pencher. **2.** (*rest*): **to ~ on/against** s'appuyer sur/contre.

leaning ['liːnɪŋ] n: **~ (towards)** penchant m (pour).

leant [lent] pt & pp → **lean**.

lean-to (pl **lean-tos**) n appentis m.

leap [liːp] (pt & pp **leapt** or **-ed**) ◆ n lit & fig bond m. ◆ vi **1.** (*gen*) bondir. **2.** fig (*increase*) faire un bond.

leapfrog ['liːpfrɒg] ◆ n saute-mouton m. ◆ vt dépasser (d'un bond). ◆ vi: **to ~ over** sauter par-dessus.

leapt [lept] pt & pp → **leap**.

leap year n année f bissextile.

learn [lɜːn] (pt & pp **-ed** or **learnt**) vt: **to ~ (that) ...** apprendre que ...; **to ~ (how) to do sthg** apprendre à faire qqch. ◆ vi: **to ~ (of or about sthg)** apprendre (qqch).

learned ['lɜːnɪd] adj savant(e).

learner ['lɜːnər] n débutant m, -e f.

learner (driver) n conducteur débutant m, conductrice débutante f (qui n'a pas encore son permis).

learning ['lɜːnɪŋ] n savoir m, érudition f.

learnt [lɜːnt] pt & pp → **learn**.

lease [liːs] ◆ n bail m. ◆ vt louer; **to ~ sthg from sb** louer qqch à qqn; **to ~ sthg to sb** louer qqch à qqn.

leasehold ['liːshəʊld] ◆ adj loué(e) à bail, tenu(e) à bail. ◆ adv à bail.

leash [liːʃ] n laisse f.

least [liːst] (superl of **little**) ◆ adj: **the ~** le moindre (la moindre), le plus petit (la plus petite). ◆ pron (*smallest amount*): **the ~** le moins; **it's the ~ (that) he can do** c'est la moindre des choses qu'il puisse faire; **not in the ~** pas du tout, pas le moins du monde; **to say the ~** c'est le moins qu'on puisse dire. ◆ adv: **(the) ~** le moins (la moins). ► **at least** adv au moins; (*to correct*) du moins. ► **least of all** adv surtout pas, encore moins. ► **not least** adv fml notamment.

leather ['leðər] ◆ n cuir m. ◆ comp en cuir.

leave [liːv] (pt & pp **left**) ◆ vt **1.** (*gen*) laisser; **to ~ sb alone** laisser qqn tranquille. **2.** (*go away from*) quitter. **3.** (*bequeath*): **to ~ sb sthg, to ~ sthg to sb** léguer or laisser qqch à qqn; see also **left.** ◆ vi partir. ◆ n congé m; **to be on ~** (*from work*) être en congé; (*from army*) être en permission. ► **leave behind** vt sep **1.** (*abandon*) abandonner, laisser. **2.** (*forget*) oublier, laisser. ► **leave out** vt sep omettre, exclure.

leave of absence n congé m.

leaves [liːvz] pl → **leaf**.

Lebanon ['lebənən] n Liban m.

lecherous ['letʃərəs] adj lubrique, libidineux(euse).

lecture ['lektʃər] ◆ n **1.** (*talk - gen*) conférence f; (- UNIV) cours m magistral. **2.** (*scolding*): **to give sb a ~** réprimander qqn, sermonner qqn. ◆ vt (*scold*) réprimander, sermonner. ◆ vi: **to ~ on sthg** faire un cours sur qqch; **to ~ in sthg** être professeur de qqch.

lecturer ['lektʃərər] n (*speaker*) conférencier m, -ère f; (UNIV) maître assistant m.

led [led] pt & pp → **lead¹**.

ledge [ledʒ] n **1.** (*of window*) rebord m. **2.** (*of mountain*) corniche f.

ledger ['ledʒər] n grand livre m.

leech [liːtʃ] *n lit & fig* sangsue *f*.

leek [liːk] *n* poireau *m*.

leer [lɪəʳ] ◆ *n* regard *m* libidineux.
◆ *vi*: **to ~ at** reluquer.

leeway [ˈliːweɪ] *n* (*room to manoeuvre*)
marge *f* de manœuvre.

left [left] ◆ *pt & pp* → **leave**. ◆ *adj*
1. (*remaining*): **to be ~** rester; **have you
any money ~?** il te reste de l'argent?
2. (*not right*) gauche. ◆ *adv* à gauche.
◆ *n*: **on** OR **to the ~** à gauche. ▶ **Left** *n*
(POL): **the Left** la Gauche.

left-hand *adj* de gauche; **~ side**
gauche *f*, côté *m* gauche.

left-hand drive *adj* (*car*) avec la
conduite à gauche.

left-handed [-ˈhændɪd] *adj* **1.** (*person*)
gaucher(ère). **2.** (*implement*) pour
gaucher.

left luggage (office) *n Br* consigne *f*.

leftover [ˈleftəʊvəʳ] *adj* qui reste, en
surplus. ▶ **leftovers** *npl* restes *mpl*.

left wing *n* (POL) gauche *f*. ▶ **left-
wing** *adj* (POL) de gauche.

leg [leg] *n* **1.** (*of person, trousers*) jambe *f*;
(*of animal*) patte *f*; **to pull sb's ~** faire
marcher qqn. **2.** (CULIN) (*of lamb*) gigot *m*;
(*of pork, chicken*) cuisse *f*. **3.** (*of furniture*)
pied *m*. **4.** (*of journey, match*) étape *f*.

legacy [ˈlegəsɪ] *n* legs *m*, héritage *m*.

legal [ˈliːgl] *adj* **1.** (*concerning the law*)
juridique. **2.** (*lawful*) légal(e).

legalize, -ise [ˈliːgəlaɪz] *vt* légaliser,
rendre légal.

legal tender *n* monnaie *f* légale.

legend [ˈledʒənd] *n lit & fig* légende *f*.

leggings [ˈlegɪŋz] *npl* jambières *fpl*,
leggings *mpl* or *fpl*.

legible [ˈledʒəbl] *adj* lisible.

legislation [ˌledʒɪsˈleɪʃn] *n* législation *f*.

legislature [ˈledʒɪsleɪtʃəʳ] *n* corps *m*
législatif.

legitimate [lɪˈdʒɪtɪmət] *adj* légitime.

legless [ˈleglɪs] *adj Br inf* (*drunk*) bour-
ré(e), rond(e).

legroom [ˈlegrʊm] *n* (U) place *f* pour
les jambes.

leg-warmers [-ˌwɔːməz] *npl* jambières *fpl*.

leisure [Br ˈleʒəʳ, Am ˈliːʒəʳ] *n* loisir *m*,
temps *m* libre; **at (one's) ~** à loisir, tout
à loisir.

leisure centre *n* centre *m* de loisirs.

leisurely [Br ˈleʒəlɪ, Am ˈliːʒərlɪ] ◆ *adj*
(*pace*) lent(e), tranquille. ◆ *adv* (*walk*)
sans se presser.

leisure time *n* (U) temps *m* libre,
loisirs *mpl*.

lemon [ˈlemən] *n* (*fruit*) citron *m*.

lemonade [ˌleməˈneɪd] *n* **1.** *Br* (*fizzy*)
limonade *f*. **2.** (*still*) citronnade *f*.

lemon juice *n* jus *m* de citron.

lemon sole *n* limande-sole *f*.

lemon squash *n Br* citronnade *f*.

lemon squeezer [-ˈskwiːzəʳ] *n*
presse-citron *m inv*.

lemon tea *n* thé *m* (au) citron.

lend [lend] (*pt & pp* **lent**) *vt* **1.** (*loan*)
prêter; **to ~ sb sthg, to ~ sthg to sb** prêter
qqch à qqn. **2.** (*offer*): **to ~ support (to sb)**
offrir son soutien (à qqn); **to ~ assistance (to sb)** prêter assistance (à qqn).
3. (*add*): **to ~ sthg to sthg** (*quality etc*)
ajouter qqch à qqch.

lending rate [ˈlendɪŋ-] *n* taux *m* de
crédit.

length [leŋθ] *n* **1.** (*gen*) longueur *f*; **what
~ is it?** ça fait quelle longueur?; **it's five
metres in ~** cela fait cinq mètres de
long. **2.** (*piece - of string, wood*) morceau
m, bout *m*; (*- of cloth*) coupon *m*. **3.** (*duration*) durée *f*. **4.** *phr*: **to go to great ~s to
do sthg** tout faire pour faire qqch. ▶ **at
length** *adv* **1.** (*eventually*) enfin. **2.** (*in
detail*) à fond.

lengthen [ˈleŋθən] ◆ *vt* (*dress etc*) rallonger; (*life*) prolonger. ◆ *vi* allonger.

lengthways [ˈleŋθweɪz] *adv* dans le
sens de la longueur.

lengthy [ˈleŋθɪ] *adj* très long (longue).

lenient [ˈliːnjənt] *adj* (*person*) indul-
gent(e); (*laws*) clément(e).

lens [lenz] *n* **1.** (*of camera*) objectif *m*; (*of
glasses*) verre *m*. **2.** (*contact lens*) verre *m*
de contact, lentille *f* (cornéenne).

lent [lent] *pt & pp* → **lend**.

Lent [lent] *n* Carême *m*.

lentil [ˈlentɪl] *n* lentille *f*.

Leo [ˈliːəʊ] *n* le Lion.

leopard [ˈlepəd] *n* léopard *m*.

leotard [ˈliːətɑːd] *n* collant *m*.

leper [ˈlepəʳ] *n* lépreux *m*, -euse *f*.

leprosy [ˈleprəsɪ] *n* lèpre *f*.

lesbian [ˈlezbɪən] *n* lesbienne *f*.

less [les] (*compar of* **little**) ◆ *adj* moins
de; **~ money/time than me** moins d'ar-
gent/de temps que moi. ◆ *pron* moins;
it costs ~ than you think ça coûte moins
cher que tu ne le crois; **no ~ than £50**
pas moins de 50 livres; **the ~ ... the ~ ...**
moins ... moins ... ◆ *adv* moins; **~ than
five** moins de cinq; **~ and ~** de moins
en moins. ◆ *prep* (*minus*) moins.

lessen [ˈlesn] ◆ *vt* (*risk, chance*) diminuer, réduire; (*pain*) atténuer. ⬩ *vi* (*gen*)
diminuer; (*pain*) s'atténuer.

lesser ['lesə^r] *adj* moindre; **to a ~ extent** OR **degree** à un degré moindre.

lesson ['lesn] *n* leçon *f*, cours *m*; **to teach sb a ~** *fig* donner une (bonne) leçon à qqn.

let [let] (*pt & pp* **let**) *vt* 1. (*allow*): **to ~ sb do sthg** laisser qqn faire qqch; **to ~ sb know sthg** dire qqch à qqn; **to ~ go of sb/sthg** lâcher qqn/qqch; **to ~ sb go** (*gen*) laisser (partir) qqn; (*prisoner*) libérer qqn. 2. (*in verb forms*): **~ them wait** qu'ils attendent; **~'s go!** allons-y!; **~'s see** voyons. 3. (*rent out*) louer; **'to ~'** 'à louer'. ▶ **let alone** *conj* encore moins, sans parler de. ▶ **let down** *vt sep* 1. (*deflate*) dégonfler. 2. (*disappoint*) décevoir. ▶ **let in** *vt sep* (*admit*) laisser OR faire entrer. ▶ **let off** *vt sep* 1. (*excuse*): **to ~ sb off sthg** dispenser qqn de qqch. 2. (*not punish*) ne pas punir. 3. (*bomb*) faire éclater; (*gun, firework*) faire partir. ▶ **let on** *vi*: **don't ~ on!** ne dis rien (à personne)! ▶ **let out** *vt sep* 1. (*allow to go out*) laisser sortir. 2. (*laugh, scream*) laisser échapper. ▶ **let up** *vi* 1. (*rain*) diminuer. 2. (*person*) s'arrêter.

letdown ['letdaʊn] *n inf* déception *f*.

lethal ['li:θl] *adj* mortel(elle), fatal(e).

lethargic [lə'θɑ:dʒɪk] *adj* léthargique.

let's [lets] = **let us**.

letter ['letə^r] *n* lettre *f*.

letter bomb *n* lettre *f* piégée.

letterbox ['letəbɒks] *n Br* boîte *f* aux OR à lettres.

letter of credit *n* lettre *f* de crédit.

lettuce ['letɪs] *n* laitue *f*, salade *f*.

letup ['letʌp] *n* (*in fighting*) répit *m*; (*in work*) relâchement *m*.

leuk(a)emia [lu:'ki:mɪə] *n* leucémie *f*.

level ['levl] ◆ *adj* 1. (*equal in height*) à la même hauteur; (*horizontal*) horizontal(e); **to be ~ with** être au niveau de. 2. (*equal in standard*) à égalité. 3. (*flat*) plat(e), plan(e). ◆ *n* 1. (*gen*) niveau *m*; **to be on the ~** *inf* être réglo. 2. *Am* (*spirit level*) niveau *m* à bulle. ◆ *vt* 1. (*make flat*) niveler, aplanir. 2. (*demolish*) raser. ▶ **level off, level out** *vi* 1. (*inflation etc*) se stabiliser. 2. (*aeroplane*) se mettre en palier. ▶ **level with** *vt fus inf* être franc (franche) OR honnête avec.

level crossing *n Br* passage *m* à niveau.

level-headed [-'hedɪd] *adj* raisonnable.

lever [*Br* 'li:və^r, *Am* 'levər] *n* levier *m*.

leverage [*Br* 'li:vərɪdʒ, *Am* 'levərɪdʒ] *n* (U) 1. (*force*): **to get ~ on sthg** avoir une prise sur qqch. 2. *fig* (*influence*) influence *f*.

levy ['levɪ] ◆ *n* prélèvement *m*, impôt *m*. ◆ *vt* prélever, percevoir.

lewd [lju:d] *adj* obscène.

liability [,laɪə'bɪlətɪ] *n* responsabilité *f*; *fig* (*person*) danger *m* public. ▶ **liabilities** *npl* (FIN) dettes *fpl*, passif *m*.

liable ['laɪəbl] *adj* 1. (*likely*): **to be ~ to do sthg** risquer de faire qqch, être susceptible de faire qqch. 2. (*prone*): **to be ~ to sthg** être sujet(ette) à qqch. 3. (JUR): **to be ~ (for)** être responsable (de); **to be ~ to** être passible de.

liaise [lɪ'eɪz] *vi*: **to ~ with** assurer la liaison avec.

liar ['laɪə^r] *n* menteur *m*, -euse *f*.

libel ['laɪbl] ◆ *n* diffamation *f*. ◆ *vt* diffamer.

liberal ['lɪbərəl] ◆ *adj* 1. (*tolerant*) libéral(e). 2. (*generous*) généreux(euse). ◆ *n* libéral *m*, -e *f*. ▶ **Liberal** (POL) ◆ *adj* libéral(e). ◆ *n* libéral *m*, -e *f*.

Liberal Democrat *n* adhérent du principal parti centriste britannique.

liberate ['lɪbəreɪt] *vt* libérer.

liberation [,lɪbə'reɪʃn] *n* libération *f*.

liberty ['lɪbətɪ] *n* liberté *f*; **at ~** en liberté; **to be at ~ to do sthg** être libre de faire qqch; **to take liberties (with sb)** prendre des libertés (avec qqn).

Libra ['li:brə] *n* Balance *f*.

librarian [laɪ'breərɪən] *n* bibliothécaire *mf*.

library ['laɪbrərɪ] *n* bibliothèque *f*.

library book *n* livre *m* de bibliothèque.

libretto [lɪ'bretəʊ] (*pl* **-s**) *n* livret *m*.

Libya ['lɪbɪə] *n* Libye *f*.

lice [laɪs] *pl* → **louse**.

licence ['laɪsəns] ◆ *n* 1. (*gen*) permis *m*, autorisation *f*; **driving ~** permis *m* de conduire; **TV ~** redevance *f* télé. 2. (COMM) licence *f*. ◆ *vt Am* = **license**.

license ['laɪsəns] ◆ *vt* autoriser. ◆ *n Am* = **licence**.

licensed ['laɪsənst] *adj* 1. (*person*): **to be ~ to do sthg** avoir un permis pour OR l'autorisation de faire qqch. 2. *Br* (*premises*) qui détient une licence de débit de boissons.

license plate *n Am* plaque *f* d'immatriculation.

lick [lɪk] *vt* 1. (*gen*) lécher. 2. *inf* (*defeat*) écraser.

licorice ['lɪkərɪs] = **liquorice**.

lid [lɪd] *n* 1. (*cover*) couvercle *m*. 2. (*eyelid*) paupière *f*.

lie [laɪ] (*pt sense* 1 **lied**, *pt senses* 2-6 **lay**, *pp sense* 1 **lied**, *pp senses* 2-6 **lain**, *cont all senses* **lying**) ◆ *n* mensonge *m*; **to tell ~s** mentir, dire des mensonges. ◆ *vi* 1. (*tell lie*): **to ~ (to sb)** mentir (à qqn). 2. (*be horizontal*) être allongé(e), être couché(e). 3. (*lie down*) s'allonger, se coucher. 4. (*be situated*) se trouver, être. 5. (*difficulty, solution etc*) résider. 6. *phr*: **to ~ low** se planquer, se tapir. ▶ **lie about, lie around** *vi* traîner. ▶ **lie down** *vi* s'allonger, se coucher. ▶ **lie in** *vi* Br rester au lit, faire la grasse matinée.

Liechtenstein ['lɪktənstaɪn] *n* Liechtenstein *m*.

lie-down *n* Br: **to have a ~** faire une sieste OR un (petit) somme.

lie-in *n* Br: **to have a ~** faire la grasse matinée.

lieutenant [Br lef'tenənt, Am lu:-'tenənt] *n* lieutenant *m*.

life [laɪf] (*pl* **lives**) *n* 1. (*gen*) vie *f*; **that's ~!** c'est la vie!; **for ~** à vie; **to come to ~** s'éveiller, s'animer. 2. (U) *inf* (*life imprisonment*) emprisonnement *m* à perpétuité.

life assurance = **life insurance**.

life belt *n* bouée *f* de sauvetage.

lifeboat ['laɪfbəut] *n* canot *m* de sauvetage.

life buoy *n* bouée *f* de sauvetage.

life expectancy [-ɪk'spektənsɪ] *n* espérance *f* de vie.

lifeguard ['laɪfgɑːd] *n* (*at swimming pool*) maître-nageur sauveteur *m*; (*at beach*) gardien *m* de plage.

life imprisonment [-ɪm'prɪznmənt] *n* emprisonnement *m* à perpétuité.

life insurance *n* assurance-vie *f*.

life jacket *n* gilet *m* de sauvetage.

lifeless ['laɪflɪs] *adj* 1. (*dead*) sans vie, inanimé(e). 2. (*listless - performance*) qui manque de vie; (*- voice*) monotone.

lifelike ['laɪflaɪk] *adj* 1. (*statue, doll*) qui semble vivant(e). 2. (*portrait*) ressemblant(e).

lifeline ['laɪflaɪn] *n* corde *f* (de sauvetage); *fig* lien *m* vital (avec l'extérieur).

lifelong ['laɪflɒŋ] *adj* de toujours.

life preserver [-prɪ,zɜːvəʳ] *n* Am (*life belt*) bouée *f* de sauvetage; (*life jacket*) gilet *m* de sauvetage.

life raft *n* canot *m* pneumatique (de sauvetage).

lifesaver ['laɪf,seɪvəʳ] *n* (*person*) maître-nageur sauveteur *m*.

life sentence *n* condamnation *f* à perpétuité.

life-size(d) [-saɪz(d)] *adj* grandeur nature (*inv*).

lifespan ['laɪfspæn] *n* 1. (*of person, animal*) espérance *f* de vie. 2. (*of product, machine*) durée *f* de vie.

lifestyle ['laɪfstaɪl] *n* style *m* de vie.

life-support system *n* respirateur *m* artificiel.

lifetime ['laɪftaɪm] *n* vie *f*; **in my ~** de mon vivant.

lift [lɪft] ◆ *n* 1. (*in car*): **to give sb a ~** emmener OR prendre qqn en voiture. 2. Br (*elevator*) ascenseur *m*. ◆ *vt* 1. (*gen*) lever; (*weight*) soulever. 2. (*plagiarize*) plagier. 3. *inf* (*steal*) voler. ◆ *vi* 1. (*lid etc*) s'ouvrir. 2. (*fog etc*) se lever.

lift-off *n* décollage *m*.

light [laɪt] (*pt & pp* **lit** OR **-ed**) ◆ *adj* 1. (*not dark*) clair(e). 2. (*not heavy*) léger (ère). 3. (*traffic*) fluide; (*corrections*) peu nombreux(euses). 4. (*work*) facile. ◆ *n* 1. (U) (*brightness*) lumière *f*. 2. (*device*) lampe *f*; (AUT - *gen*) feu *m*; (- *headlamp*) phare *m*. 3. (*for cigarette*) feu *m*; **have you got a ~?** vous avez du feu?; **to set ~ to sthg** mettre le feu à qqch. 4. (*perspective*): **in the ~ of** Br, **in light of** Am à la lumière de. 5. *phr*: **to come to ~** être découvert(e) OR dévoilé(e). ◆ *vt* 1. (*fire, cigarette*) allumer. 2. (*room, stage*) éclairer. ◆ *adv*: **to travel ~** voyager léger. ▶ **light up** ◆ *vt sep* 1. (*illuminate*) éclairer. 2. (*cigarette etc*) allumer. ◆ *vi* 1. (*face*) s'éclairer. 2. *inf* (*start smoking*) allumer une cigarette.

light bulb *n* ampoule *f*.

lighten ['laɪtn] ◆ *vt* 1. (*give light to*) éclairer; (*make less dark*) éclaircir. 2. (*make less heavy*) alléger. ◆ *vi* (*brighten*) s'éclaircir.

lighter ['laɪtəʳ] *n* (*cigarette lighter*) briquet *m*.

light-headed [-'hedɪd] *adj*: **to feel ~** avoir la tête qui tourne.

light-hearted [-'hɑːtɪd] *adj* 1. (*cheerful*) joyeux(euse), gai(e). 2. (*amusing*) amusant(e).

lighthouse ['laɪthaus, *pl* -hauzɪz] *n* phare *m*.

lighting ['laɪtɪŋ] *n* éclairage *m*.

light meter *n* posemètre *m*, cellule *f* photoélectrique.

lightning ['laɪtnɪŋ] *n* (U) éclair *m*, foudre *f*.

lightweight ['laɪtweɪt] ◆ *adj* (*object*) léger(ère). ◆ *n* (*boxer*) poids *m* léger.

likable ['laɪkəbl] *adj* sympathique.

like [laɪk] ◆ *prep* 1. (*gen*) comme; **to**

look ~ sb/sthg ressembler à qqn/qqch; **to taste ~ sthg** avoir un goût de qqch; **~ this/that** comme ci/ça. **2.** (*such as*) tel que, comme. ◆ *vt* **1.** (*gen*) aimer; **I ~ her** elle me plaît; **to ~ doing** OR **to do sthg** aimer faire qqch. **2.** (*expressing a wish*): **would you ~ some more cake?** vous prendrez encore du gâteau?; **I'd ~ to go** je voudrais bien OR j'aimerais y aller; **I'd ~ you to come** je voudrais bien OR j'aimerais que vous veniez; **if you ~** si vous voulez. ◆ *n*: **the ~** une chose pareille. ► **likes** *npl*: **~s and dislikes** goûts *mpl*.

likeable ['laɪkəbl] = **likable**.

likelihood ['laɪklɪhʊd] *n* (U) chances *fpl*, probabilité *f*.

likely ['laɪklɪ] *adj* **1.** (*probable*) probable; **he's ~ to get angry** il risque de se fâcher; **a ~ story!** *iro* à d'autres! **2.** (*candidate*) prometteur(euse).

liken ['laɪkn] *vt*: **to ~ sb/sthg to** assimiler qqn/qqch à.

likeness ['laɪknɪs] *n* **1.** (*resemblance*): **~ (to)** ressemblance *f* (avec). **2.** (*portrait*) portrait *m*.

likewise ['laɪkwaɪz] *adv* (*similarly*) de même; **to do ~** faire pareil OR de même.

liking ['laɪkɪŋ] *n* (*for person*) affection *f*, sympathie *f*; (*for food, music*) goût *m*, penchant *m*; **to be to sb's ~** être du goût de qqn, plaire à qqn.

lilac ['laɪlək] ◆ *adj* (*colour*) lilas (*inv*). ◆ *n* lilas *m*.

Lilo® ['laɪləʊ] (*pl* **-s**) *n* Br matelas *m* pneumatique.

lily ['lɪlɪ] *n* lis *m*.

lily of the valley (*pl* **lilies of the valley**) *n* muguet *m*.

limb [lɪm] *n* **1.** (*of body*) membre *m*. **2.** (*of tree*) branche *f*.

limber ['lɪmbər] ► **limber up** *vi* s'échauffer.

limbo ['lɪmbəʊ] (*pl* **-s**) *n* (U) (*uncertain state*): **to be in ~** être dans les limbes.

lime [laɪm] *n* **1.** (*fruit*) citron *m* vert. **2.** (*drink*): **~ (juice)** jus *m* de citron vert. **3.** (*linden tree*) tilleul *m*. **4.** (*substance*) chaux *f*.

limelight ['laɪmlaɪt] *n*: **to be in the ~** être au premier plan.

limerick ['lɪmərɪk] *n* poème humoristique en cinq vers.

limestone ['laɪmstəʊn] *n* (U) pierre *f* à chaux, calcaire *m*.

limey ['laɪmɪ] (*pl* **limeys**) *n* Am *inf* terme péjoratif désignant un Anglais.

limit ['lɪmɪt] ◆ *n* limite *f*; **off ~s** d'accès

interdit; **within ~s** (*to an extent*) dans une certaine mesure. ◆ *vt* limiter, restreindre.

limitation [ˌlɪmɪ'teɪʃn] *n* limitation *f*, restriction *f*.

limited ['lɪmɪtɪd] *adj* limité(e), restreint(e).

limited (liability) company *n* société *f* anonyme.

limousine ['lɪməziːn] *n* limousine *f*.

limp [lɪmp] ◆ *adj* mou (molle). ◆ *n*: **to have a ~** boiter. ◆ *vi* boiter.

limpet ['lɪmpɪt] *n* patelle *f*, bernique *f*.

line [laɪn] ◆ *n* **1.** (*gen*) ligne *f*. **2.** (*row*) rangée *f*. **3.** (*queue*) file *f*, queue *f*; **to stand** OR **wait in ~** faire la queue. **4.** (RAIL - *track*) voie *f*; (- *route*) ligne *f*. **5.** (*of poem, song*) vers *m*. **6.** (*wrinkle*) ride *f*. **7.** (*string, wire etc*) corde *f*; **a fishing ~** une ligne. **8.** (TELEC) ligne *f*; **hold the ~!** ne quittez pas! **9.** *inf* (*short letter*): **to drop sb a ~** écrire un (petit) mot à qqn. **10.** *inf* (*work*): **~ of business** branche *f*. **11.** (*borderline*) frontière *f*. **12.** (COMM) gamme *f*. **13.** *phr*: **to draw the ~ at sthg** refuser de faire OR d'aller jusqu'à faire qqch; **to step out of ~** faire cavalier seul. ◆ *vt* (*drawer, box*) tapisser; (*clothes*) doubler. ► **out of line** *adj* (*remark, behaviour*) déplacé(e). ► **line up** ◆ *vt sep* **1.** (*in rows*) aligner. **2.** (*organize*) prévoir. ◆ *vi* (*in row*) s'aligner; (*in queue*) faire la queue.

lined [laɪnd] *adj* **1.** (*paper*) réglé(e). **2.** (*wrinkled*) ridé(e).

linen ['lɪnɪn] *n* (U) **1.** (*cloth*) lin *m*. **2.** (*tablecloths, sheets*) linge *m* (de maison).

liner ['laɪnər] *n* (*ship*) paquebot *m*.

linesman ['laɪnzmən] (*pl* **-men** [-mən]) *n* (TENNIS) juge *m* de ligne; (FTBL) juge de touche.

lineup ['laɪnʌp] *n* **1.** (SPORT) équipe *f*. **2.** Am (*identification parade*) rangée *f* de suspects (*pour identification par un témoin*).

linger ['lɪŋgər] *vi* **1.** (*person*) s'attarder. **2.** (*doubt, pain*) persister.

lingo ['lɪŋgəʊ] (*pl* **-es**) *n* *inf* jargon *m*.

linguist ['lɪŋgwɪst] *n* linguiste *mf*.

linguistics [lɪŋ'gwɪstɪks] *n* (U) linguistique *f*.

lining ['laɪnɪŋ] *n* **1.** (*of coat, curtains, box*) doublure *f*. **2.** (*of stomach*) muqueuse *f*. **3.** (AUT) (*of brakes*) garniture *f*.

link [lɪŋk] ◆ *n* **1.** (*of chain*) maillon *m*. **2.** (*connection*): **~ (between/with)** lien *m* (entre/avec). ◆ *vt* (*cities, parts*) relier; (*events etc*) lier; **to ~ arms** se donner le bras. ▶ **link up** vt sep relier; **to ~ sthg up with sthg** relier qqch avec OR à qqch.

links [lɪŋks] (pl inv) n terrain m de golf (au bord de la mer).

lino ['laɪnəʊ], **linoleum** [lɪ'nəʊlɪəm] n lino m, linoléum m.

lintel ['lɪntl] n linteau m.

lion ['laɪən] n lion m.

lioness ['laɪənes] n lionne f.

lip [lɪp] n **1.** (of mouth) lèvre f. **2.** (of container) bord m.

lip-read vi lire sur les lèvres.

lip salve [-sælv] n Br pommade f pour les lèvres.

lipstick ['lɪpstɪk] n rouge m à lèvres.

liqueur [lɪ'kjʊər] n liqueur f.

liquid ['lɪkwɪd] ◆ adj liquide. ◆ n liquide m.

liquidation [ˌlɪkwɪ'deɪʃn] n liquidation f.

liquidize, -ise ['lɪkwɪdaɪz] vt Br (CULIN) passer au mixer.

liquidizer ['lɪkwɪdaɪzər] n Br mixer m.

liquor ['lɪkər] n (U) alcool m, spiritueux mpl.

liquorice ['lɪkərɪʃ, 'lɪkərɪs] n réglisse f.

liquor store n Am magasin m de vins et d'alcools.

Lisbon ['lɪzbən] n Lisbonne.

lisp [lɪsp] ◆ n zézaiement m. ◆ vi zézayer.

list [lɪst] ◆ n liste f. ◆ vt (in writing) faire la liste de; (in speech) énumérer.

listed building [ˌlɪstɪd-] n Br monument m classé.

listen ['lɪsn] vi: **to ~ to** (sb/sthg) écouter (qqn/qqch); **to ~ for sthg** guetter qqch.

listener ['lɪsnər] n auditeur m, -trice f.

listless ['lɪstlɪs] adj apathique, mou (molle).

lit [lɪt] pt & pp → **light**.

liter Am = **litre**.

literacy ['lɪtərəsɪ] n fait m de savoir lire et écrire.

literal ['lɪtərəl] adj littéral(e).

literally ['lɪtərəlɪ] adv littéralement; **to take sthg ~** prendre qqch au pied de la lettre.

literary ['lɪtərərɪ] adj littéraire.

literate ['lɪtərət] adj **1.** (able to read and write) qui sait lire et écrire. **2.** (well-read) cultivé(e).

literature ['lɪtrətʃər] n littérature f; (printed information) documentation f.

lithe [laɪð] adj souple, agile.

Lithuania [ˌlɪθjʊ'eɪnɪə] n Lituanie f.

litigation [ˌlɪtɪ'geɪʃn] n litige m; **to go to ~** aller en justice.

litre Br, **liter** Am ['liːtər] n litre m.

litter ['lɪtər] ◆ n **1.** (U) (rubbish) ordures fpl, détritus mpl. **2.** (of animals) portée f. ◆ vt: **to be ~ed with** être couvert(e) de.

litterbin ['lɪtəˌbɪn] n Br boîte f à ordures.

little ['lɪtl] (compar sense 2 **less**, superl sense 2 **least**) ◆ adj **1.** (not big) petit(e); **a ~ while** un petit moment. **2.** (not much) peu de; **~ money** peu d'argent; **a ~ money** un peu d'argent. ◆ pron: **~ of the money was left** il ne restait pas beaucoup d'argent, il restait peu d'argent; **a ~** un peu. ◆ adv peu, pas beaucoup; **~ by ~** peu à peu.

little finger n petit doigt m, auriculaire m.

live¹ [lɪv] ◆ vi **1.** (gen) vivre. **2.** (have one's home) habiter, vivre; **to ~ in Paris** habiter (à) Paris. ◆ vt: **to ~ a quiet life** mener une vie tranquille; **to ~ it up** inf faire la noce. ▶ **live down** vt sep faire oublier. ▶ **live off** vt fus (savings, the land) vivre de; (family) vivre aux dépens de. ▶ **live on** ◆ vt fus vivre de. ◆ vi (memory, feeling) rester, survivre. ▶ **live together** vi vivre ensemble. ▶ **live up to** vt fus: **to ~ up to sb's expectations** répondre à l'attente de qqn; **to ~ up to one's reputation** faire honneur à sa réputation. ▶ **live with** vt fus **1.** (cohabit with) vivre avec. **2.** inf (accept) se faire à, accepter.

live² [laɪv] adj **1.** (living) vivant(e). **2.** (coal) ardent(e). **3.** (bullet, bomb) non explosé(e). **4.** (ELEC) sous tension. **5.** (RADIO & TV) en direct; (performance) en public.

livelihood ['laɪvlɪhʊd] n gagne-pain m.

lively ['laɪvlɪ] adj **1.** (person) plein(e) d'entrain. **2.** (debate, meeting) animé(e). **3.** (mind) vif (vive).

liven ['laɪvn] ▶ **liven up** ◆ vt sep (person) égayer; (place) animer. ◆ vi s'animer.

liver ['lɪvər] n foie m.

livery ['lɪvərɪ] n livrée f.

lives [laɪvz] pl → **life**.

livestock ['laɪvstɒk] n (U) bétail m.

livid ['lɪvɪd] adj **1.** (angry) furieux (euse). **2.** (bruise) violacé(e).

living ['lɪvɪŋ] ◆ adj vivant(e), en vie. ◆ n: **to earn** OR **make a ~** gagner sa vie; **what do you do for a ~?** qu'est-ce que vous faites dans la vie?

living conditions npl conditions fpl de vie.

living room n salle f de séjour, living m.

living standards npl niveau m de vie.

living wage n minimum m vital.

lizard ['lɪzəd] n lézard m.

llama ['lɑːmə] (pl inv OR -s) n lama m.

load [ləud] ◆ n 1. (something carried) chargement m, charge f. 2. (large amount): ~s of, a ~ of inf des tas de, plein de; a ~ of rubbish inf de la foutaise. ◆ vt (gen & COMPUT) charger; (video recorder) mettre une vidéo-cassette dans; to ~ sb/sthg with charger qqn/qqch de; to ~ a gun/camera (with) charger un fusil/un appareil (avec). ▶ **load up** vt sep & vi charger.

loaded ['ləudɪd] adj 1. (question) insidieux(euse). 2. inf (rich) plein(e) aux as.

loading bay ['ləudɪŋ-] n aire f de chargement.

loaf [ləuf] (pl **loaves**) n: a ~ (of bread) un pain.

loan [ləun] ◆ n prêt m; on ~ prêté(e). ◆ vt prêter; to ~ sthg to sb, to ~ sb sthg prêter qqch à qqn.

loath [ləuθ] adj: to be ~ to do sthg ne pas vouloir faire qqch, hésiter à faire qqch.

loathe [ləuð] vt détester; to ~ doing sthg avoir horreur de OR détester faire qqch.

loathsome ['ləuðsəm] adj dégoûtant(e), répugnant(e).

loaves [ləuvz] pl → **loaf**.

lob [lɒb] ◆ n (TENNIS) lob m. ◆ vt 1. (throw) lancer. 2. (TENNIS): to ~ a ball lober, faire un lob.

lobby ['lɒbɪ] ◆ n 1. (of hotel) hall m. 2. (pressure group) lobby m, groupe m de pression. ◆ vt faire pression sur.

lobe [ləub] n lobe m.

lobster ['lɒbstər] n homard m.

local ['ləukl] ◆ adj local(e). ◆ n inf 1. (person): **the ~s** les gens mpl du coin OR du pays. 2. Br (pub) café m OR bistro m du coin.

local authority n Br autorités fpl locales.

local call n communication f urbaine.

local government n administration f municipale.

locality [ləu'kælətɪ] n endroit m.

localized, -ised ['ləukəlaɪzd] adj localisé(e).

locally ['ləukəlɪ] adv 1. (on local basis) localement. 2. (nearby) dans les environs, à proximité.

locate [Br ləu'keɪt, Am 'ləukeɪt] vt 1. (find - position) trouver, repérer; (- source, problem) localiser. 2. (situate - business, factory) implanter, établir; to be ~d être situé.

location [ləu'keɪʃn] n 1. (place) emplacement m. 2. (CINEMA): on ~ en extérieur.

loch [lɒk, lɒx] n Scot loch m, lac m.

lock [lɒk] ◆ n 1. (of door etc) serrure f. 2. (on canal) écluse f. 3. (AUT) (steering lock) angle m de braquage. 4. (of hair) mèche f. ◆ vt 1. (door, car, drawer) fermer à clef; (bicycle) cadenasser. 2. (immobilize) bloquer. ◆ vi 1. (door, suitcase) fermer à clef. 2. (become immobilized) se bloquer. ▶ **lock in** vt sep enfermer (à clef). ▶ **lock out** vt sep 1. (accidentally) enfermer dehors, laisser dehors; to ~ o.s. out s'enfermer dehors. 2. (deliberately) empêcher d'entrer, mettre à la porte. ▶ **lock up** vt sep (person - in prison) mettre en prison OR sous les verrous; (- in asylum) enfermer; (house) fermer à clef; (valuables) enfermer, mettre sous clef.

locker ['lɒkər] n casier m.

locker room n Am vestiaire m.

locket ['lɒkɪt] n médaillon m.

locksmith ['lɒksmɪθ] n serrurier m.

locomotive ['ləukə,məutɪv] n locomotive f.

locum ['ləukəm] (pl -s) n remplaçant m, -e f.

locust ['ləukəst] n sauterelle f, locuste f.

lodge [lɒdʒ] ◆ n 1. (of caretaker, freemasons) loge f. 2. (of manor house) pavillon m (de gardien). 3. (for hunting) pavillon m de chasse. ◆ vi 1. (stay): to ~ with sb loger chez qqn. 2. (become stuck) se loger, se coincer. 3. fig (in mind) s'enraciner, s'ancrer. ◆ vt (complaint) déposer; to ~ an appeal interjeter OR faire appel.

lodger ['lɒdʒər] n locataire mf.

lodging ['lɒdʒɪŋ] n → **board**. ▶ **lodgings** npl chambre f meublée.

loft [lɒft] n grenier m.

lofty ['lɒftɪ] adj 1. (noble) noble. 2. pej (haughty) hautain(e), arrogant(e). 3. literary (high) haut(e), élevé(e).

log [lɒg] ◆ n 1. (of wood) bûche f. 2. (of ship) journal m de bord; (of plane) carnet m de vol. ◆ vt consigner, enregistrer. ▶ **log in** vi (COMPUT) ouvrir une session. ▶ **log out** vi (COMPUT) fermer une session.

logbook ['lɒgbuk] n 1. (of ship) journal m de bord; (of plane) carnet m de vol. 2. (of car) ≃ carte f grise.

look

loggerheads ['lɒgəhedz] n: **at ~ en désaccord.**

logic ['lɒdʒɪk] n logique f.

logical ['lɒdʒɪkl] adj logique.

logistics [lə'dʒɪstɪks] ◆ n (U) (MIL) logistique f. ◆ npl fig organisation f.

logo ['ləʊgəʊ] (pl -s) n logo m.

loin [lɔɪn] n filet m.

loiter ['lɔɪtər] vi traîner.

loll [lɒl] vi 1. (sit, lie about) se prélasser. 2. (hang down - head, tongue) pendre.

lollipop ['lɒlɪpɒp] n sucette f.

lollipop lady n Br dame qui fait traverser la rue aux enfants à la sortie des écoles.

lollipop man n Br monsieur qui fait traverser la rue aux enfants à la sortie des écoles.

lolly ['lɒlɪ] n 1. (lollipop) sucette f. 2. Br (ice lolly) sucette f glacée.

London ['lʌndən] n Londres.

Londoner ['lʌndənər] n Londonien m, -enne f.

lone [ləʊn] adj solitaire.

loneliness ['ləʊnlɪnɪs] n (of person) solitude f; (of place) isolement m.

lonely ['ləʊnlɪ] adj 1. (person) solitaire, seul(e). 2. (childhood) solitaire. 3. (place) isolé(e).

loner ['ləʊnər] n solitaire mf.

lonesome ['ləʊnsəm] adj Am inf 1. (person) solitaire, seul(e). 2. (place) isolé(e).

long [lɒŋ] ◆ adj long (longue); **two days/years ~** de deux jours/ans, qui dure deux jours/ans; **10 metres/miles ~** long de 10 mètres/miles, de 10 mètres/miles (de long). ◆ adv longtemps; **how ~ will it take?** combien de temps cela va-t-il prendre?; **how ~ will you be?** tu en as pour combien de temps?; **how ~ is the book?** le livre fait combien de pages?; **I no ~er like him** je ne l'aime plus; **I can't wait any ~er** je ne peux pas attendre plus longtemps; **so ~!** inf au revoir!, salut!; **before ~** sous peu. ◆ vt: **to ~ to do sthg** avoir très envie de faire qqch. ▶ **as long as, so long as** conj tant que. ▶ **long for** vt fus (peace and quiet) désirer ardemment; (holidays) attendre avec impatience.

long-distance adj (runner, race) de fond; **~ lorry driver** routier m.

long-distance call n communication f interurbaine.

longhand ['lɒŋhænd] n écriture f normale.

long-haul adj long-courrier

longing ['lɒŋɪŋ] ◆ adj plein(e) de convoitise. ◆ n 1. (desire) envie f, convoitise f; **a ~ for** un grand désir or

une grande envie de. 2. (nostalgia) nostalgie f, regret m.

longitude ['lɒndʒɪtjuːd] n longitude f.

long jump n saut m en longueur.

long-life adj (milk) longue conservation (inv); (battery) longue durée (inv).

long-playing record [-'pleɪɪŋ-] n 33 tours m.

long-range adj 1. (missile, bomber) à longue portée. 2. (plan, forecast) à long terme.

long shot n (guess) coup m à tenter (sans grand espoir de succès).

longsighted [,lɒŋ'saɪtɪd] adj presbyte.

long-standing adj de longue date.

longsuffering [,lɒŋ'sʌfərɪŋ] adj (person) à la patience infinie.

long term n: **in the ~** à long terme.

long wave n (U) grandes ondes fpl.

longwinded [,lɒŋ'wɪndɪd] adj (person) prolixe; (speech) interminable.

loo [luː] (pl -s) n Br inf cabinets mpl, petit coin m.

look [lʊk] ◆ n 1. (with eyes) regard m; **to take** OR **have a ~ (at sthg)** regarder (qqch), jeter un coup d'œil (à qqch); **to give sb a ~** jeter un regard à qqn, regarder qqn de travers. 2. (search): **to have a ~ (for sthg)** chercher (qqch). 3. (appearance) aspect m, air m; **by the ~** OR **~s of it, by the ~** OR **~s of things** vraisemblablement, selon toute probabilité. ◆ vi 1. (with eyes) regarder. 2. (search) chercher. 3. (building, window): **to ~ (out) onto** donner sur. 4. (seem) avoir l'air, sembler; **it ~s like rain** OR **as if it will rain** on dirait qu'il va pleuvoir; **she ~s like her mother** elle ressemble à sa mère. ▶ **looks** npl (attractiveness) beauté f. ▶ **look after** vt fus s'occuper de. ▶ **look at** vt fus 1. (see, glance at) regarder; (examine) examiner. 2. (judge) considérer. ▶ **look down on** vt fus (condescend to) mépriser. ▶ **look for** vt fus chercher. ▶ **look forward to** vt fus attendre avec impatience. ▶ **look into** vt fus examiner, étudier. ▶ **look out** vi prendre garde, faire attention; **~ out!** attention! ▶ **look out for** vt fus (person) guetter; (new book) être à l'affût de, essayer de repérer. ▶ **look round** ◆ vt fus (house, shop, town) faire le tour de. ◆ vi 1. (turn) se retourner. 2. (browse) regarder. ▶ **look up** ◆ vt sep 1. (in book) chercher. 2. (visit - person) aller OR passer voir. ◆ vi (improve - business) reprendre; **things are ~ing up** ça va mieux, la situation s'améliore. ▶ **look**

up to vt fus admirer.

lookout ['lʊkaʊt] n 1. (place) poste m de guet. 2. (person) guetteur m. 3. (search): **to be on the ~ for** être à la recherche de.

loom [luːm] ◆ n métier m à tisser. ◆ vi (building, person) se dresser; fig (date, threat) être imminent(e). ▶ **loom up** vi surgir.

loony ['luːnɪ] inf ◆ adj cinglé(e), timbré(e). ◆ n cinglé m, -e f, fou m, folle f.

loop [luːp] n 1. (gen & COMPUT) boucle f. 2. (contraceptive) stérilet m.

loophole ['luːphəʊl] n faille f, échappatoire f.

loose [luːs] adj 1. (not firm - joint) desserré(e); (- handle, post) branlant(e); (- tooth) qui bouge OR branle; (- knot) défait(e). 2. (unpackaged - sweets, nails) en vrac, au poids. 3. (clothes) ample, large. 4. (not restrained - hair) dénoué(e); (- animal) en liberté, détaché(e). 5. pej & dated (woman) facile; (living) dissolu(e). 6. (inexact - translation) approximatif(ive).

loose change n petite OR menue monnaie f.

loose end n: **to be at a ~** Br, **to be at ~s** Am être désœuvré, n'avoir rien à faire.

loosely ['luːslɪ] adv 1. (not firmly) sans serrer. 2. (inexactly) approximativement.

loosen ['luːsn] vt desserrer, défaire. ▶ **loosen up** vi 1. (before game, race) s'échauffer. 2. inf (relax) se détendre.

loot [luːt] ◆ n butin m. ◆ vt piller.

looting ['luːtɪŋ] n pillage m.

lop [lɒp] vt élaguer, émonder. ▶ **lop off** vt sep couper.

lop-sided [-'saɪdɪd] adj (table) bancal(e), boiteux(euse); (picture) de travers.

lord [lɔːd] n Br seigneur m. ▶ **Lord** n 1. (RELIG): **the Lord** (God) le Seigneur; **good Lord!** Br Seigneur!, mon Dieu! 2. (in titles) Lord m; (as form of address): **my Lord** Monsieur le duc/comte etc. ▶ **Lords** npl Br (POL): **the (House of) Lords** la Chambre des lords.

Lordship ['lɔːdʃɪp] n: **your/his ~** Monsieur le duc/comte etc.

lore [lɔːr] n (U) traditions fpl.

lorry ['lɒrɪ] n Br camion m.

lorry driver n Br camionneur m, conducteur m de poids lourd.

lose [luːz] (pt & pp lost) ◆ vt 1. (gen) perdre; **to ~ sight of** lit & fig perdre de vue; **to ~ one's way** se perdre, perdre son chemin; fig être un peu perdu.

2. (subj: clock, watch) retarder de; **to ~ time** retarder. 3. (pursuers) semer. ◆ vi perdre. ▶ **lose out** vi être perdant(e).

loser ['luːzər] n 1. (gen) perdant m, -e f. 2. inf pej (unsuccessful person) raté m, -e f.

loss [lɒs] n 1. (gen) perte f. 2. phr: **to be at a ~** être perplexe, être embarrassé(e).

lost [lɒst] ◆ pt & pp → **lose**. ◆ adj (gen) perdu(e); **to get ~** se perdre; **get ~!** inf fous/foutez le camp!

lost-and-found office n Am bureau m des objets trouvés.

lost property office n Br bureau m des objets trouvés.

lot [lɒt] n 1. (large amount): **a ~ (of)**, **~s (of)** beaucoup (de); (entire amount): **the ~** le tout. 2. (at auction) lot m. 3. (destiny) sort m. 4. Am (of land) terrain m; (car park) parking m. 5. phr: **to draw ~s** tirer au sort. ▶ **a lot** adv beaucoup.

lotion ['ləʊʃn] n lotion f.

lottery ['lɒtərɪ] n lit & fig loterie f.

loud [laʊd] ◆ adj 1. (not quiet, noisy - gen) fort(e); (- person) bruyant(e). 2. (colour, clothes) voyant(e). ◆ adv fort; **out ~** tout haut.

loudhailer [ˌlaʊd'heɪlər] n Br mégaphone m, porte-voix m.

loudly ['laʊdlɪ] adv 1. (noisily) fort. 2. (gaudily) de façon voyante.

loudspeaker [ˌlaʊd'spiːkər] n haut-parleur m.

lounge [laʊndʒ] ◆ n 1. (in house) salon m. 2. (in airport) hall m, salle f. 3. Br = **lounge bar**. ◆ vi se prélasser.

lounge bar n Br l'une des deux salles d'un bar, la plus confortable.

louse [laʊs] (pl sense 1 lice, pl sense 2 -s) n 1. (insect) pou m. 2. inf pej (person) salaud m.

lousy ['laʊzɪ] adj inf minable, nul(le); (weather) pourri(e).

lout [laʊt] n rustre m.

louvre Br, **louver** Am ['luːvər] n persienne f.

lovable ['lʌvəbl] adj adorable.

love [lʌv] ◆ n 1. (gen) amour m; **to be in ~** être amoureux(euse); **to fall in ~** tomber amoureux(euse); **to make ~** faire l'amour; **give her my ~** embrasse-la pour moi; **~ from** (at end of letter) affectueusement, grosses bises. 2. inf (form of address) mon chéri (ma chérie). 3. (TENNIS) zéro m. ◆ vt aimer; **to ~ to do sthg** OR **doing sthg** aimer OR adorer faire qqch.

love affair n liaison f.

love life n vie f amoureuse.

lovely ['lʌvlɪ] adj 1. (beautiful) très joli(e). 2. (pleasant) très agréable, excellent(e).

lover ['lʌvə^r] n 1. (sexual partner) amant m, -e f. 2. (enthusiast) passionné m, -e f, amoureux m, -euse f.

loving ['lʌvɪŋ] adj (person, relationship) affectueux(euse); (care) tendre.

low [ləʊ] ◆ adj 1. (not high - gen) bas (basse); (- wall, building) peu élevé(e); (- standard, quality) mauvais(e); (- intelligence) faible; (- neckline) décolleté(e). 2. (little remaining) presque épuisé(e). 3. (not loud - voice) bas (basse); (- whisper, moan) faible. 4. (depressed) déprimé(e). 5. (not respectable) bas (basse). ◆ adv 1. (not high) bas. 2. (not loudly - speak) à voix basse; (- whisper) faiblement. ◆ n 1. (low point) niveau m OR point m bas. 2. (METEOR) dépression f.

low-calorie adj à basses calories.

low-cut adj décolleté(e).

lower ['ləʊə^r] ◆ adj inférieur(e). ◆ vt 1. (gen) baisser; (flag) abaisser. 2. (reduce - price, level) baisser; (- age of consent) abaisser; (- resistance) diminuer.

low-fat adj (yoghurt, crisps) allégé(e); (milk) demi-écrémé(e).

low-key adj discret(ète).

lowly ['ləʊlɪ] adj modeste, humble.

low-lying adj bas (basse).

loyal ['lɔɪəl] adj loyal(e).

loyalty ['lɔɪəltɪ] n loyauté f.

lozenge ['lɒzɪndʒ] n 1. (tablet) pastille f. 2. (shape) losange m.

LP (abbr of **long-playing record**) n 33 tours m.

L-plate n Br plaque signalant que le conducteur du véhicule est en conduite accompagnée.

Ltd, ltd (abbr of **limited**) = SARL; Smith and Sons, ~ = Smith & Fils, SARL.

lubricant ['luːbrɪkənt] n lubrifiant m.

lubricate ['luːbrɪkeɪt] vt lubrifier.

lucid ['luːsɪd] adj lucide.

luck [lʌk] n chance f; good ~ chance; good ~! bonne chance!; bad ~ malchance f; bad OR hard ~! pas de chance!; to be in ~ avoir de la chance; with (any) ~ avec un peu de chance.

luckily ['lʌkɪlɪ] adv heureusement.

lucky ['lʌkɪ] adj 1. (fortunate - person) qui a de la chance; (- event) heureux (euse). 2. (bringing good luck) porte-bonheur (inv).

lucrative ['luːkrətɪv] adj lucratif(ive).

ludicrous ['luːdɪkrəs] adj ridicule.

lug [lʌg] vt inf traîner.

luggage ['lʌgɪdʒ] n (U) Br bagages mpl.

luggage rack n Br porte-bagages m inv.

lukewarm ['luːkwɔːm] adj lit & fig tiède.

lull [lʌl] ◆ n: ~ (in) (storm) accalmie f (de); (fighting, conversation) arrêt m (de). ◆ vt: to ~ sb to sleep endormir qqn en le berçant; to ~ sb into a false sense of security endormir les soupçons de qqn.

lullaby ['lʌləbaɪ] n berceuse f.

lumber ['lʌmbə^r] n (U) 1. Am (timber) bois m de charpente. 2. Br (bric-a-brac) bric-à-brac m inv. ▶ **lumber with** vt sep Br inf: to ~ sb with sthg coller qqch à qqn.

lumberjack ['lʌmbədʒæk] n bûcheron m, -onne f.

luminous ['luːmɪnəs] adj (dial) lumineux(euse); (paint, armband) phosphorescent(e).

lump [lʌmp] ◆ n 1. (gen) morceau m; (of earth, clay) motte f; (in sauce) grumeau m. 2. (on body) grosseur f. ◆ vt: to ~ sthg together réunir qqch; to ~ it inf faire avec, s'en accommoder.

lump sum n somme f globale.

lunacy ['luːnəsɪ] n folie f.

lunar ['luːnə^r] adj lunaire.

lunatic ['luːnətɪk] ◆ adj pej dément(e), démentiel(elle). ◆ n 1. pej (fool) fou m, folle f. 2. (insane person) fou m, folle f, aliéné m, -e f.

lunch [lʌntʃ] n déjeuner m.

luncheon ['lʌntʃən] n fml déjeuner m.

luncheon meat n sorte de saucisson.

luncheon voucher n Br ticket-restaurant m.

lunch hour n pause f de midi.

lunchtime ['lʌntʃtaɪm] n heure f du déjeuner.

lung [lʌŋ] n poumon m.

lunge [lʌndʒ] vi faire un brusque mouvement (du bras) en avant; to ~ at sb s'élancer sur qqn.

lurch [lɜːtʃ] ◆ n (of person) écart m brusque; (of car) embardée f; to leave sb in the ~ laisser qqn dans le pétrin. ◆ vi (person) tituber; (car) faire une embardée.

lure [ljʊə^r] ◆ n charme m trompeur. ◆ vt attirer OR persuader par la ruse.

lurid ['ljʊərɪd] adj 1. (outfit) aux couleurs criardes. 2. (story, details) affreux(euse).

lurk [lɜːk] vi 1. (person) se cacher, se dissimuler. 2. (memory, danger) subsister.

luscious ['lʌʃəs] *adj* **1.** (*delicious*) succulent(e). **2.** *fig* (*woman*) appétissant(e).

lush [lʌʃ] *adj* **1.** (*luxuriant*) luxuriant(e). **2.** (*rich*) luxueux(euse).

lust [lʌst] *n* **1.** (*sexual desire*) désir *m*. **2.** *fig*: ~ **for sthg** soif de qqch. ▶ **lust after, lust for** *vt fus* **1.** (*wealth, power etc*) être assoiffé(e) de. **2.** (*person*) désirer.

lusty ['lʌstɪ] *adj* vigoureux(euse).

Luxembourg ['lʌksəmbɜːg] *n* **1.** (*country*) Luxembourg *m*. **2.** (*city*) Luxembourg.

luxurious [lʌg'ʒʊərɪəs] *adj* **1.** (*expensive*) luxueux(euse). **2.** (*pleasurable*) voluptueux(euse).

luxury ['lʌkʃərɪ] ◆ *n* luxe *m*. ◆ *comp* de luxe.

LW (*abbr of* **long wave**) GO.

Lycra® ['laɪkrə] ◆ *n* Lycra® *m*. ◆ *comp* en Lycra®.

lying ['laɪɪŋ] ◆ *adj* (*person*) menteur (euse). ◆ *n* (U) mensonges *mpl*.

lynch [lɪntʃ] *vt* lyncher.

lyric ['lɪrɪk] *adj* lyrique.

lyrical ['lɪrɪkl] *adj* lyrique.

lyrics ['lɪrɪks] *npl* paroles *fpl*.

M

m¹ (*pl* **m's** OR **ms**), **M** (*pl* **M's** OR **Ms**) [em] *n* (*letter*) m *m inv*, M *m inv*. ▶ **M** Br *abbr of* **motorway**.

m² **1.** (*abbr of* **metre**) m. **2.** (*abbr of* **million**) M. **3.** *abbr of* **mile**.

MA *n abbr of* **Master of Arts**.

mac [mæk] (*abbr of* **mackintosh**) *n* Br *inf* (*coat*) imper *m*.

macaroni [,mækə'rəʊnɪ] *n* (U) macaronis *mpl*.

mace [meɪs] *n* **1.** (*ornamental rod*) masse *f*. **2.** (*spice*) macis *m*.

machine [mə'ʃiːn] ◆ *n lit & fig* machine *f*. ◆ *vt* **1.** (SEWING) coudre à la machine. **2.** (TECH) usiner.

machinegun [mə'ʃiːngʌn] *n* mitrailleuse *f*.

machinery [mə'ʃiːnərɪ] *n* (U) machines *fpl*; *fig* mécanisme *m*.

macho ['mætʃəʊ] *adj* macho (*inv*).

mackerel ['mækrəl] (*pl inv* OR **-s**) *n* maquereau *m*.

mackintosh ['mækɪntɒʃ] *n* Br imperméable *m*.

mad [mæd] *adj* **1.** (*insane*) fou (folle); **to go** ~ devenir fou. **2.** (*foolish*) insensé(e). **3.** (*furious*) furieux(euse). **4.** (*hectic - rush, pace*) fou (folle). **5.** (*very enthusiastic*): **to be** ~ **about sb/sthg** être fou (folle) de qqn/qqch.

Madagascar [,mædə'gæskə⁺] *n* Madagascar *m*.

madam ['mædəm] *n* madame *f*.

madcap ['mædkæp] *adj* risqué(e), insensé(e).

madden ['mædn] *vt* exaspérer.

made [meɪd] *pt & pp* → **make**.

Madeira [mə'dɪərə] *n* **1.** (*wine*) madère *m*. **2.** (GEOGR) Madère *f*.

made-to-measure *adj* fait(e) sur mesure.

made-up *adj* **1.** (*with make-up*) maquillé(e). **2.** (*invented*) fabriqué(e).

madly ['mædlɪ] *adv* (*frantically*) comme un fou; ~ **in love** follement amoureux.

madman ['mædmən] (*pl* **-men** [-mən]) *n* fou *m*.

madness ['mædnɪs] *n lit & fig* folie *f*, démence *f*.

Madrid [mə'drɪd] *n* Madrid.

Mafia ['mæfɪə] *n*: **the** ~ la Mafia.

magazine [,mægə'ziːn] *n* **1.** (PRESS) revue *f*, magazine *m*; (RADIO & TV) magazine. **2.** (*of gun*) magasin *m*.

maggot ['mægət] *n* ver *m*, asticot *m*.

magic ['mædʒɪk] ◆ *adj* magique. ◆ *n* magie *f*.

magical ['mædʒɪkl] *adj* magique.

magician [mə'dʒɪʃn] *n* magicien *m*.

magistrate ['mædʒɪstreɪt] *n* magistrat *m*, juge *m*.

magistrates' court *n* Br ≃ tribunal *m* d'instance.

magnanimous [mæg'nænɪməs] *adj* magnanime.

magnate ['mægneɪt] *n* magnat *m*.

magnesium [mæg'niːzɪəm] *n* magnésium *m*.

magnet ['mægnɪt] *n* aimant *m*.

magnetic [mæg'netɪk] *adj lit & fig* magnétique.

magnetic tape *n* bande *f* magnétique.

magnificent [mæg'nɪfɪsənt] *adj* magnifique, superbe.

magnify ['mægnɪfaɪ] *vt* (*in vision*) grossir; (*sound*) amplifier; *fig* exagérer.

magnifying glass ['mægnɪfaɪɪŋ-] *n* loupe *f*.

magnitude ['mægnɪtjuːd] n envergure f, ampleur f.

magpie ['mægpaɪ] n pie f.

mahogany [mə'hɒgənɪ] n acajou m.

maid [meɪd] n (servant) domestique f.

maiden ['meɪdn] ♦ adj (flight, voyage)
premier(ère). ♦ n literary jeune fille f.

maiden aunt n tante f célibataire.

maiden name n nom m de jeune
fille.

mail [meɪl] ♦ n 1. (letters, parcels) courrier m. 2. (system) poste f. ♦ vt poster.

mailbox ['meɪlbɒks] n Am boîte f à OR
aux lettres.

mailing list ['meɪlɪŋ-] n liste f
d'adresses.

mailman ['meɪlmən] (pl -men [-mən]) n
Am facteur m.

mail order n vente f par correspondance.

mailshot ['meɪlʃɒt] n publipostage m.

maim [meɪm] vt estropier.

main [meɪn] ♦ adj principal(e). ♦ n
(pipe) conduite f. ► **mains** npl: **the ~s** le
secteur. ► **in the main** adv dans
l'ensemble.

main course n plat m principal.

mainframe (computer) ['meɪn-
freɪm-] n ordinateur m central.

mainland ['meɪnlənd] ♦ adj continen-
tal(e). ♦ n: **the ~** le continent.

main line n (RAIL) grande ligne f.

mainly ['meɪnlɪ] adv principalement.

main road n route f à grande circulation.

mainstay ['meɪnsteɪ] n pilier m, élément m principal.

mainstream ['meɪnstriːm] ♦ adj do-
minant(e). ♦ n: **the ~** la tendance
générale.

maintain [meɪn'teɪn] vt 1. (preserve,
keep constant) maintenir. 2. (provide for,
look after) entretenir. 3. (assert): **to ~ (that)**
... maintenir que ..., soutenir que ...

maintenance ['meɪntənəns] n 1. (of
public order) maintien m. 2. (care) entretien m, maintenance f. 3. (JUR) pension
f alimentaire.

maize [meɪz] n maïs m.

majestic [mə'dʒestɪk] adj majestueux
(euse).

majesty ['mædʒəstɪ] n (grandeur)
majesté f. ► **Majesty** n: **His/Her
Majesty** Sa Majesté le roi/la reine.

major ['meɪdʒər] ♦ adj 1. (important)
majeur(e). 2. (main) principal(e).
3. (MUS) majeur(e). ♦ n 1. (in army) =
chef m de bataillon; (in air force) com-

mandant m. 2. (UNIV) (subject) matière f.

Majorca [mə'dʒɔːkə, mə'jɔːkə] n
Majorque f.

majority [mə'dʒɒrətɪ] n majorité f; **in a**
OR **the ~** dans la majorité.

make [meɪk] (pt & pp made) ♦ vt 1.
(gen - produce) faire; (- manufacture)
faire, fabriquer; **to ~ a meal** préparer un
repas; **to ~ a film** tourner OR réaliser un
film. 2. (perform an action) faire; **to ~ a
decision** prendre une décision; **to ~ a
mistake** faire une erreur, se tromper.
3. (cause to be) rendre; **to ~ sb happy/sad**
rendre qqn heureux/triste. 4. (force,
cause to do): **to ~ sb do sthg** faire faire
qqch à qqn, obliger qqn à faire qqch;
to ~ sb laugh faire rire qqn. 5. (be con-
structed): **to be made of** être en; **what's it
made of?** c'est en quoi? 6. (add up to)
faire; **2 and 2 ~ 4** 2 et 2 font 4. 7. (calculate): **I ~ it 50** d'après moi il y en a 50,
j'en ai compté 50; **what time do you ~ it?**
quelle heure as-tu?; **I ~ it 6 o'clock** il est
6 heures (à ma montre). 8. (earn) gagner, se faire; **to ~ a profit** faire des
bénéfices; **to ~ a loss** essuyer des
pertes. 9. (reach) arriver à. 10. (gain
- friend, enemy) se faire; **to ~ friends (with
sb)** se lier d'amitié (avec qqn). 11. phr:
to ~ it (reach in time) arriver à temps; (be a
success) réussir, arriver; (be able to attend)
se libérer, pouvoir venir; **to ~ do with** se
contenter de. ♦ n (brand) marque f.
► **make for** vt fus 1. (move towards) se
diriger vers. 2. (contribute to, be conducive
to) rendre probable, favoriser. ► **make
of** vt sep 1. (understand) comprendre.
2. (have opinion of) penser de. ► **make
off** vi filer. ► **make out** ♦ vt sep 1. (see,
hear) discerner; (understand) comprendre. 2. (fill out - cheque) libeller; (- bill,
receipt) faire; (- form) remplir. ♦ vt fus (pretend, claim): **to ~ out (that)** ... prétendre
que ... ► **make up** ♦ vt sep 1. (compose,
constitute) composer, constituer. 2. (story,
excuse) inventer. 3. (apply cosmetics to)
maquiller. 4. (prepare - gen) faire; (- prescription) préparer, exécuter. 5. (make
complete) compléter. ♦ vi (become friends
again) se réconcilier. ► **make up for** vt
fus compenser. ► **make up to** vt sep: **to
~ it up to sb** (for sthg) se racheter auprès
de qqn (pour qqch).

make-believe n: **it's all ~** c'est (de la)
pure fantaisie.

maker ['meɪkər] n (of product) fabricant
m, -e f; (of film) réalisateur m, -trice f.

makeshift ['meɪkʃɪft] adj de fortune.

make-up n 1. (cosmetics) maquillage m; ~ **remover** démaquillant m. 2. (person's character) caractère m. 3. (of team, group, object) constitution f.

making ['meɪkɪŋ] n fabrication f; **his problems are of his own ~** ses problèmes sont de sa faute; **in the ~** en formation; **to have the ~s of** avoir l'étoffe de.

malaise [məˈleɪz] n fml malaise m.

malaria [məˈleərɪə] n malaria f.

Malaya [məˈleɪə] n Malaisie f, Malaysia f Occidentale.

Malaysia [məˈleɪzɪə] n Malaysia f.

male [meɪl] ◆ adj (gen) mâle; (sex) masculin(e). ◆ n mâle m.

male nurse n infirmier m.

malevolent [məˈlevələnt] adj malveillant(e).

malfunction [mælˈfʌŋkʃn] vi mal fonctionner.

malice ['mælɪs] n méchanceté f.

malicious [məˈlɪʃəs] adj malveillant(e).

malign [məˈlaɪn] ◆ adj pernicieux (euse). ◆ vt calomnier.

malignant [məˈlɪɡnənt] adj (MED) malin(igne).

mall [mɔːl] n: (shopping) ~ centre m commercial.

mallet ['mælɪt] n maillet m.

malnutrition [ˌmælnjuːˈtrɪʃn] n malnutrition f.

malpractice [ˌmælˈpræktɪs] n (U) (JUR) faute f professionnelle.

malt [mɔːlt] n malt m.

Malta ['mɔːltə] n Malte f.

mammal ['mæml] n mammifère m.

mammoth ['mæməθ] ◆ adj gigantesque. ◆ n mammouth m.

man [mæn] (pl **men** [men]) ◆ n 1. homme m; **the ~ in the street** l'homme de la rue. 2. (as form of address) mon vieux. ◆ vt (ship, spaceship) fournir du personnel pour; (telephone) répondre au; (switchboard) assurer le service de.

manage ['mænɪdʒ] ◆ vi 1. (cope) se débrouiller, y arriver. 2. (survive, get by) s'en sortir. ◆ vt 1. (succeed): **to ~ to do sthg** arriver à faire qqch. 2. (be responsible for, control) gérer.

manageable ['mænɪdʒəbl] adj maniable.

management ['mænɪdʒmənt] n 1. (control, running) gestion f. 2. (people in control) direction f.

manager ['mænɪdʒəʳ] n (of organization) directeur m, -trice f; (of shop, restaurant,

hotel) gérant m, -e f; (of football team, pop star) manager m.

manageress [ˌmænɪdʒəˈres] n Br (of organization) directrice f; (of shop, restaurant, hotel) gérante f.

managerial [ˌmænɪˈdʒɪərɪəl] adj directorial(e).

managing director ['mænɪdʒɪŋ-] n directeur général m, directrice générale f.

mandarin ['mændərɪn] n (fruit) mandarine f.

mandate ['mændeɪt] n mandat m.

mandatory ['mændətrɪ] adj obligatoire.

mane [meɪn] n crinière f.

maneuver Am = manoeuvre.

manfully ['mænfʊlɪ] adv courageusement, vaillamment.

mangle ['mæŋɡl] vt mutiler, déchirer.

mango ['mæŋɡəʊ] (pl **-es** OR **-s**) n mangue f.

mangy ['meɪndʒɪ] adj galeux(euse).

manhandle ['mæn,hændl] vt malmener.

manhole ['mænhəʊl] n regard m, trou m d'homme.

manhood ['mænhʊd] n: **to reach ~** devenir un homme.

mania ['meɪnjə] n: ~ **(for)** manie f (de).

maniac ['meɪnɪæk] n fou m, folle f; **a sex ~** un obsédé sexuel (une obsédée sexuelle).

manic ['mænɪk] adj fig (person) surexcité(e); (behaviour) de fou.

manicure ['mænɪ,kjʊəʳ] n manucure f.

manifest ['mænɪfest] fml ◆ adj manifeste, évident(e). ◆ vt manifester.

manifesto [ˌmænɪˈfestəʊ] (pl **-s** OR **-es**) n manifeste m.

manipulate [məˈnɪpjʊleɪt] vt lit & fig manipuler.

manipulative [məˈnɪpjʊlətɪv] adj (person) rusé(e); (behaviour) habile, subtil(e).

mankind [mænˈkaɪnd] n humanité f, genre m humain.

manly ['mænlɪ] adj viril(e).

man-made adj (fabric, fibre) synthétique; (environment) artificiel(elle); (problem) causé(e) par l'homme.

manner ['mænəʳ] n 1. (method) manière f, façon f. 2. (attitude) attitude f, comportement m. ▶ **manners** npl manières fpl.

mannerism ['mænərɪzm] n tic m, manie f.

mannish ['mænɪʃ] adj masculin(e).

manoeuvre Br, **maneuver** Am [mə-

'nu:vəʳ] ♦ n manœuvre f. ♦ vt & vi manœuvrer.

manor ['mænəʳ] n manoir m.

manpower ['mæn,pauəʳ] n main-d'œuvre f.

mansion ['mænʃn] n château m.

manslaughter ['mæn,slɔ:təʳ] n homicide m involontaire.

mantelpiece ['mæntlpi:s] n (dessus m de) cheminée f.

manual ['mænjuəl] ♦ adj manuel (elle). ♦ n manuel m.

manual worker n travailleur manuel m, travailleuse manuelle f.

manufacture [,mænjuˈfæktʃəʳ] ♦ n fabrication f; (of cars) construction f. ♦ vt fabriquer; (cars) construire.

manufacturer [,mænjuˈfæktʃərəʳ] n fabricant m; (of cars) constructeur m.

manure [məˈnjuəʳ] n fumier m.

manuscript ['mænjuskript] n manuscrit m.

many ['meni] (compar **more**, superl **most**) ♦ adj beaucoup de; **how ~ ...?** combien de ...?; **too ~** trop de; **as ~ ... as** autant de ... que; **so ~** autant de; **a good** OR **great ~** un grand nombre de. ♦ pron (a lot, plenty) beaucoup.

map [mæp] n carte f. ▶ **map out** vt sep (plan) élaborer; (timetable) établir; (task) définir.

maple ['meipl] n érable m.

mar [mɑːʳ] vt gâter, gâcher.

marathon ['mærəθn] ♦ adj marathon (inv). ♦ n marathon m.

marauder [məˈrɔːdəʳ] n maraudeur m, -euse f.

marble ['mɑːbl] n 1. (stone) marbre m. 2. (for game) bille f.

march [mɑːtʃ] ♦ n marche f. ♦ vi 1. (soldiers etc) marcher au pas. 2. (demonstrators) manifester, faire une marche de protestation. 3. (quickly): **to ~ up to sb** s'approcher de qqn d'un pas décidé.

March [mɑːtʃ] n mars m; see also **September**.

marcher ['mɑːtʃəʳ] n (protester) marcheur m, -euse f.

mare [meəʳ] n jument f.

margarine [,mɑːdʒəˈriːn, ,mɑːgəˈriːn] n margarine f.

marge [mɑːdʒ] n inf margarine f.

margin ['mɑːdʒin] n 1. (gen) marge f; **to win by a narrow ~** gagner de peu OR de justesse. 2. (edge - of an area) bord m.

marginal ['mɑːdʒinl] adj 1. (unimportant) marginal(e), secondaire. 2. Br

(POL): **~ seat** circonscription électorale où la majorité passe facilement d'un parti à un autre.

marginally ['mɑːdʒinəli] adv très peu.

marigold ['mærigəuld] n souci m.

marihuana, marijuana [,mæriˈwɑːnə] n marihuana f.

marine [məˈriːn] ♦ adj marin(e). ♦ n marine m.

marital ['mæritl] adj (sex, happiness) conjugal(e); (problems) matrimonial(e).

marital status n situation f de famille.

maritime ['mæritaim] adj maritime.

mark [mɑːk] ♦ n 1. (stain) tache f, marque f. 2. (sign, written symbol) marque f. 3. (in exam) note f, point m. 4. (stage, level) barre f. 5. (currency) mark m. ♦ vt 1. (gen) marquer. 2. (stain) marquer, tacher. 3. (exam, essay) noter, corriger. ▶ **mark off** vt sep (cross off) cocher.

marked [mɑːkt] adj (change, difference) marqué(e); (improvement, deterioration) sensible.

marker ['mɑːkəʳ] n (sign) repère m.

marker pen n marqueur m.

market ['mɑːkit] ♦ n marché m. ♦ vt commercialiser.

market garden n jardin m maraîcher.

marketing ['mɑːkitiŋ] n marketing m.

marketplace ['mɑːkitpleis] n 1. (in a town) place f du marché. 2. (COMM) marché m.

market research n étude f de marché.

market value n valeur f marchande.

marking ['mɑːkiŋ] n (SCH) correction f. ▶ **markings** npl (on animal, flower) taches fpl, marques fpl; (on road) signalisation f horizontale.

marksman ['mɑːksmən] (pl -men [-mən]) n tireur m d'élite.

marmalade ['mɑːməleid] n confiture f d'oranges amères.

maroon [məˈruːn] adj bordeaux (inv).

marooned [məˈruːnd] adj abandonné(e).

marquee [mɑːˈkiː] n grande tente f.

marriage ['mæridʒ] n mariage m.

marriage bureau n Br agence f matrimoniale.

marriage certificate n acte m de mariage.

marriage guidance n conseil m conjugal.

married ['mærid] adj 1. (person) marié(e); **to get ~** se marier. 2. (life) conjugal(e).

marrow ['mærəʊ] n 1. Br (vegetable) courge f. 2. (in bones) moelle f.

marry ['mæri] ◆ vt 1. (become spouse of) épouser, se marier avec. 2. (subj: priest, registrar) marier. ◆ vi se marier.

Mars [mɑːz] n (planet) Mars f.

marsh [mɑːʃ] n marais m, marécage m.

marshal ['mɑːʃl] ◆ n 1. (MIL) maréchal m. 2. (steward) membre m du service d'ordre. 3. Am (law officer) officier m de police fédérale. ◆ vt rassembler.

martial arts [ˌmɑːʃl-] npl arts mpl martiaux.

martial law [ˌmɑːʃl-] n loi f martiale.

martyr ['mɑːtər] n martyr m, -e f.

martyrdom ['mɑːtədəm] n martyre m.

marvel ['mɑːvl] ◆ n merveille f. ◆ vi: to ~ (at) s'émerveiller (de), s'étonner (de).

marvellous Br, **marvelous** Am ['mɑːvələs] adj merveilleux(euse).

Marxism ['mɑːksɪzm] n marxisme m.

Marxist ['mɑːksɪst] ◆ adj marxiste. ◆ n marxiste mf.

marzipan ['mɑːzɪpæn] n (U) pâte f d'amandes.

mascara [mæs'kɑːrə] n mascara m.

masculine ['mæskjʊlɪn] adj masculin(e).

mash [mæʃ] vt faire une purée de.

mashed potatoes [mæʃt-] npl purée f de pommes de terre.

mask [mɑːsk] lit & fig ◆ n masque m. ◆ vt masquer.

masochist ['mæsəkɪst] n masochiste mf.

mason ['meɪsn] n 1. (stonemason) maçon m. 2. (freemason) franc-maçon m.

masonry ['meɪsnrɪ] n (stones) maçonnerie f.

masquerade [ˌmæskə'reɪd] vi: to ~ as se faire passer pour.

mass [mæs] ◆ n (gen & PHYSICS) masse f. ◆ adj (protest, meeting) en masse, en nombre; (unemployment, support) massif (ive). ◆ vi se masser. ▶ **Mass** n (RELIG) messe f. ▶ **masses** npl 1. inf (lots): ~es (of) des masses (de); (food) des tonnes (de). 2. (workers): the ~es les masses fpl.

massacre ['mæsəkər] ◆ n massacre m. ◆ vt massacrer.

massage [Br 'mæsɑːʒ, Am mə'sɑːʒ] ◆ n massage m. ◆ vt masser.

massive ['mæsɪv] adj massif(ive), énorme.

mass media n or npl: the ~ les (mass) media mpl.

mass production n fabrication f OR production f en série.

mast [mɑːst] n 1. (on boat) mât m. 2. (RADIO & TV) pylône m.

master ['mɑːstər] ◆ n 1. (gen) maître m. 2. Br (SCH - in primary school) instituteur m, maître m; (- in secondary school) professeur m. ◆ adj maître. ◆ vt maîtriser; (difficulty) surmonter, vaincre; (situation) se rendre maître de.

master key n passe m, passepartout m.

masterly ['mɑːstəlɪ] adj magistral(e).

mastermind ['mɑːstəmaɪnd] ◆ n cerveau m. ◆ vt organiser, diriger.

Master of Arts (pl **Masters of Arts**) n 1. (degree) maîtrise f ès lettres. 2. (person) titulaire mf d'une maîtrise ès lettres.

Master of Science (pl **Masters of Science**) n 1. (degree) maîtrise f ès sciences. 2. (person) titulaire mf d'une maîtrise ès sciences.

masterpiece ['mɑːstəpiːs] n chef-d'œuvre m.

master's degree n ≃ maîtrise f.

mastery ['mɑːstərɪ] n maîtrise f.

mat [mæt] n 1. (on floor) petit tapis m; (at door) paillasson m. 2. (on table) set m de table; (coaster) dessous m de verre.

match [mætʃ] ◆ n 1. (game) match m. 2. (for lighting) allumette f. 3. (equal): to be no ~ for sb ne pas être de taille à lutter contre qqn. ◆ vt 1. (be the same as) correspondre à, s'accorder avec. 2. (pair off) faire correspondre. 3. (be equal with) égaler, rivaliser avec. ◆ vi 1. (be the same) correspondre. 2. (go together well) être assorti(e).

matchbox ['mætʃbɒks] n boîte f à allumettes.

matching ['mætʃɪŋ] adj assorti(e).

mate [meɪt] ◆ n 1. inf (friend) copain m, copine f, pote m. 2. Br inf (term of address) mon vieux. 3. (of female animal) mâle m; (of male animal) femelle f. 4. (NAUT): (first) ~ second m. ◆ vi s'accoupler.

material [mə'tɪərɪəl] ◆ adj 1. (goods, benefits, world) matériel(elle). 2. (important) important(e), essentiel(elle). ◆ n 1. (substance) matière f, substance f; (type of substance) matériau m, matière f. 2. (fabric) tissu m, étoffe f; (type of fabric) tissu. 3. (U) (information - for book, article etc) matériaux mpl. ▶ **materials** npl matériaux mpl.

materialistic [mə,tɪərɪə'lɪstɪk] adj matérialiste.

materialize, -ise [mə'tɪərɪəlaɪz] vi

1. (*offer, threat*) se concrétiser, se réaliser. **2.** (*person, object*) apparaître.

maternal [mə'tɜ:nl] *adj* maternel (elle).

maternity [mə'tɜ:nəti] *n* maternité *f*.

maternity dress *n* robe *f* de grossesse.

maternity hospital *n* maternité *f*.

math Am = **maths**.

mathematical [,mæθə'mætɪkl] *adj* mathématique.

mathematics [,mæθə'mætɪks] *n* (U) mathématiques *fpl*.

maths Br [mæθs], **math** Am [mæθ] (*abbr of* **mathematics**) *inf n* (U) maths *fpl*.

matinée ['mætɪneɪ] *n* matinée *f*.

mating season ['meɪtɪŋ-] *n* saison *f* des amours.

matrices ['meɪtrɪsi:z] *pl* → **matrix**.

matriculation [mə,trɪkjʊ'leɪʃn] *n* inscription *f*.

matrimonial [,mætrɪ'məʊnjəl] *adj* matrimonial(e), conjugal(e).

matrimony ['mætrɪmənɪ] *n* (U) mariage *m*.

matrix ['meɪtrɪks] (*pl* **matrices** OR **-es**) *n* **1.** (*context, framework*) contexte *m*, structure *f*. **2.** (MATH & TECH) matrice *f*.

matron ['meɪtrən] *n* **1.** Br (*in hospital*) infirmière *f* en chef. **2.** (*in school*) infirmière *f*.

matronly ['meɪtrənlɪ] *adj euphemism* (*woman*) qui a l'allure d'une matrone; (*figure*) de matrone.

matt Br, **matte** Am [mæt] *adj* mat(e).

matted ['mætɪd] *adj* emmêlé(e).

matter ['mætər] ◆ *n* **1.** (*question, situation*) question *f*, affaire *f*; **that's another** OR **a different ~** c'est tout autre chose, c'est une autre histoire; **as a ~ of course** automatiquement; **to make ~s worse** aggraver la situation; **and to make ~s worse ...** pour tout arranger ... **2.** (*trouble, cause of pain*): **there's something the ~ with my radio** il y a quelque chose qui cloche OR ne va pas dans ma radio; **what's the ~?** qu'est-ce qu'il y a?; **what's the ~ with him?** qu'est-ce qu'il a? **3.** (PHYSICS) matière *f*. **4.** (U) (*material*) matière *f*; **reading ~** choses *fpl* à lire. ◆ *vi* (*be important*) importer, avoir de l'importance; **it doesn't ~** cela n'a pas d'importance. ▶ **as a matter of fact** *adv* en fait, à vrai dire. ▶ **for that matter** *adv* d'ailleurs. ▶ **no matter** *adv*: **no ~ what** coûte que coûte, à tout prix; **no ~ how hard I try to explain ...** j'ai beau essayer de lui expliquer ...

Matterhorn ['mætə,hɔ:n] *n*: **the ~** le mont Cervin.

matter-of-fact *adj* terre-à-terre, neutre.

mattress ['mætrɪs] *n* matelas *m*.

mature [mə'tjʊər] ◆ *adj* **1.** (*person, attitude*) mûr(e). **2.** (*cheese*) fait(e); (*wine*) arrivé(e) à maturité. ◆ *vi* **1.** (*person*) mûrir. **2.** (*cheese, wine*) se faire.

mature student *n* Br (UNIV) étudiant qui a commencé ses études sur le tard.

maul [mɔ:l] *vt* mutiler.

mauve [məʊv] ◆ *adj* mauve. ◆ *n* mauve *m*.

max. [mæks] (*abbr of* **maximum**) max.

maxim ['mæksɪm] (*pl* **-s**) *n* maxime *f*.

maxima ['mæksɪmə] *pl* → **maximum**.

maximum ['mæksɪməm] (*pl* **maxima** OR **-s**) ◆ *adj* maximum (*inv*). ◆ *n* maximum *m*.

may [meɪ] *modal vb* **1.** (*expressing possibility*): **it ~ rain** il se peut qu'il pleuve, il va peut-être pleuvoir; **be that as it ~** quoi qu'il en soit. **2.** (*can*) pouvoir; **on a clear day the coast ~ be seen** on peut voir la côte par temps clair. **3.** (*asking permission*): **~ I come in?** puis-je entrer? **4.** (*as contrast*): **it ~ be expensive but ...** c'est peut-être cher, mais ... **5.** *fml* (*expressing wish, hope*): **~ they be happy!** qu'ils soient heureux!; *see also* **might**.

May [meɪ] *n* mai *m*; *see also* **September**.

maybe ['meɪbi:] *adv* peut-être; **~ I'll come** je viendrai peut-être.

May Day *n* le Premier mai.

mayhem ['meɪhem] *n* pagaille *f*.

mayonnaise [,meɪə'neɪz] *n* mayonnaise *f*.

mayor [meər] *n* maire *m*.

mayoress ['meərɪs] *n* **1.** (*female mayor*) femme *f* maire. **2.** (*mayor's wife*) femme *f* du maire.

maze [meɪz] *n* labyrinthe *m*, dédale *m*.

MB (*abbr of* **megabyte**) Mo.

MD *n abbr of* **managing director**.

me [mi:] *pers pron* **1.** (*direct, indirect*) me, m' (+ *vowel or silent 'h'*); **can you see/hear ~?** tu me vois/m'entends?; **it's ~** c'est moi; **they spoke to ~** ils m'ont parlé; **she gave it to ~** elle me l'a donné. **2.** (*stressed, after prep, in comparisons etc*) moi; **you can't expect ME to do it** tu ne peux pas exiger que ce soit moi qui le fasse; **she's shorter than ~** elle est plus petite que moi.

meadow ['medəʊ] *n* prairie *f*, pré *m*.

meagre Br, **meager** Am ['mi:gər] *adj* maigre.

meal [miːl] n repas m.

mealtime ['miːltaɪm] n heure f du repas.

mean [miːn] (pt & pp **meant**) ◆ vt 1. (signify) signifier, vouloir dire; **money ~s nothing to him** l'argent ne compte pas pour lui. 2. (intend): **to ~ to do sthg** vouloir faire qqch, avoir l'intention de faire qqch; **I didn't ~ to drop it** je n'ai pas fait exprès de le laisser tomber; **to be meant for sb/sthg** être destiné(e) à qqn/qqch; **to be meant to do sthg** être censé(e) faire qqch; **to ~ well** agir dans une bonne intention. 3. (be serious about): **I ~ it** je suis sérieux(euse). 4. (entail) occasionner, entraîner. 5. phr: **I ~** (as explanation) c'est vrai; (as correction) je veux dire. ◆ adj 1. (miserly) radin(e), chiche; **to be ~ with sthg** être avare de qqch. 2. (unkind) mesquin(e), méchant(e); **to be ~ to sb** être mesquin envers qqn. 3. (average) moyen(enne). ◆ n (average) moyenne f; see also **means**.

meander [mɪ'ændər] vi (river, road) serpenter; (person) errer.

meaning ['miːnɪŋ] n sens m, signification f.

meaningful ['miːnɪŋfʊl] adj (look) significatif(ive); (relationship, discussion) important(e).

meaningless ['miːnɪŋlɪs] adj (gesture, word) dénué(e) OR vide de sens; (proposal, discussion) sans importance.

means [miːnz] ◆ n (method, way) moyen m; **by ~ of** au moyen de. ◆ npl (money) moyens mpl, ressources fpl. ▶ **by all means** adv mais certainement, bien sûr. ▶ **by no means** adv fml nullement, en aucune façon.

meant [ment] pt & pp → **mean**.

meantime ['miːntaɪm] n: **in the ~** en attendant.

meanwhile ['miːnwaɪl] adv 1. (at the same time) pendant ce temps. 2. (between two events) en attendant.

measles ['miːzlz] n: **(the) ~** la rougeole.

measly ['miːzlɪ] adj inf misérable, minable.

measure ['meʒər] ◆ n 1. (gen) mesure f. 2. (indication): **it is a ~ of her success that** ... la preuve de son succès, c'est que ... ◆ vt & vi mesurer.

measurement ['meʒəmənt] n mesure f.

meat [miːt] n viande f.

meatball ['miːtbɔːl] n boulette f de viande.

meat pie n Br tourte f à la viande.

meaty ['miːtɪ] adj fig important(e).

Mecca ['mekə] n La Mecque.

mechanic [mɪ'kænɪk] n mécanicien m, -enne f. ▶ **mechanics** ◆ n (U) (study) mécanique f. ◆ npl fig mécanisme m.

mechanical [mɪ'kænɪkl] adj 1. (device) mécanique. 2. (person, mind) fort(e) en mécanique. 3. (routine, automatic) machinal(e).

mechanism ['mekənɪzm] n lit & fig mécanisme m.

medal ['medl] n médaille f.

medallion [mɪ'dæljən] n médaillon m.

meddle ['medl] vi: **to ~ in** se mêler de.

media ['miːdjə] ◆ pl → **medium**. ◆ n or npl: **the ~** les médias mpl.

mediaeval [,medɪ'iːvl] = **medieval**.

mediate ['miːdɪeɪt] ◆ vt négocier. ◆ vi: **to ~ (for/between)** servir de médiateur (pour/entre).

mediator ['miːdɪeɪtər] n médiateur m, -trice f.

Medicaid ['medɪkeɪd] n Am assistance médicale aux personnes sans ressources.

medical ['medɪkl] ◆ adj médical(e). ◆ n examen m médical.

medical officer n (in factory etc) médecin m du travail; (MIL) médecin militaire.

Medicare ['medɪkeər] n Am programme fédéral d'assistance médicale pour personnes âgées.

medicated ['medɪkeɪtɪd] adj traitant(e).

medicine ['medsɪn] n 1. (subject, treatment) médecine f; **Doctor of Medicine** (UNIV) docteur m en médecine. 2. (substance) médicament m.

medieval [,medɪ'iːvl] adj médiéval(e).

mediocre [,miːdɪ'əʊkər] adj médiocre.

meditate ['medɪteɪt] vi: **to ~ (on** OR **upon)** méditer (sur).

Mediterranean [,medɪtə'reɪnjən] ◆ n (sea): **the ~ (Sea)** la (mer) Méditerranée. ◆ adj méditerranéen(enne).

medium ['miːdjəm] (pl sense 1 **media**, pl sense 2 **mediums**) ◆ adj moyen(enne). ◆ n 1. (way of communicating) moyen m. 2. (spiritualist) médium m.

medium-size(d) [-saɪz(d)] adj de taille moyenne.

medium wave n onde f moyenne.

medley ['medlɪ] (pl **medleys**) n 1. (mixture) mélange m. 2. (MUS) pot-pourri m.

meek [miːk] adj docile.

meet [miːt] (pt & pp **met**) ◆ vt 1. (gen) rencontrer; (by arrangement) retrouver. 2.

(*go to meet - person*) aller/venir attendre, aller/venir chercher; (*- train, plane*) aller attendre. **3.** (*need, requirement*) satisfaire, répondre à. **4.** (*problem*) résoudre; (*challenge*) répondre à. **5.** (*costs*) payer. **6.** (*join*) rejoindre. ◆ *vi* **1.** (*gen*) se rencontrer; (*by arrangement*) se retrouver; (*for a purpose*) se réunir. **2.** (*join*) se joindre. ◆ *n* Am (*meeting*) meeting *m*.
▶ **meet up** *vi* se retrouver; **to ~ up with sb** rencontrer qqn, retrouver qqn.
▶ **meet with** *vt fus* **1.** (*encounter - disapproval*) être accueilli(e) par; (*- success*) remporter; (*- failure*) essuyer. **2.** Am (*by arrangement*) retrouver.

meeting ['mi:tɪŋ] *n* **1.** (*for discussions, business*) réunion *f*. **2.** (*by chance*) rencontre *f*; (*by arrangement*) entrevue *f*.

megabyte ['megəbaɪt] *n* (COMPUT) méga-octet *m*.

megaphone ['megəfəʊn] *n* mégaphone *m*, porte-voix *m*.

melancholy ['melənkəlɪ] ◆ *adj* (*person*) mélancolique; (*news, facts*) triste. ◆ *n* mélancolie *f*.

mellow ['meləʊ] ◆ *adj* (*light, voice*) doux (douce); (*taste, wine*) moelleux(euse). ◆ *vi* s'adoucir.

melody ['melədɪ] *n* mélodie *f*.

melon ['melən] *n* melon *m*.

melt [melt] ◆ *vt* faire fondre. ◆ *vi* **1.** (*become liquid*) fondre. **2.** *fig*: **his heart ~ed at the sight** il fut tout attendri devant ce spectacle. **3.** (*disappear*): **to ~ (away)** fondre. ▶ **melt down** *vt sep* fondre.

meltdown ['meltdaʊn] *n* fusion *f* du cœur (du réacteur).

melting pot ['meltɪŋ-] *n fig* creuset *m*.

member ['membər] *n* membre *m*; (*of club*) adhérent *m*, -e *f*.

Member of Congress (*pl* **Members of Congress**) *n* Am membre *m* du Congrès.

Member of Parliament (*pl* **Members of Parliament**) *n* Br ≃ député *m*.

membership ['membəʃɪp] *n* **1.** (*of organization*) adhésion *f*. **2.** (*number of members*) nombre *m* d'adhérents. **3.** (*members*): **the ~** les membres *mpl*.

membership card *n* carte *f* d'adhésion.

memento [mɪ'mentəʊ] (*pl* **-s**) *n* souvenir *m*.

memo ['meməʊ] (*pl* **-s**) *n* note *f* de service.

memoirs ['memwɑːz] *npl* mémoires *mpl*.

memorandum [,memə'rændəm] (*pl* **-da** [-də] OR **-dums**) *n* note *f* de service.

memorial [mɪ'mɔːrɪəl] ◆ *adj* commémoratif(ive). ◆ *n* monument *m*.

memorize, -ise ['meməraɪz] *vt* (*phone number, list*) retenir; (*poem*) apprendre par cœur.

memory ['memərɪ] *n* **1.** (*gen & COMPUT*) mémoire *f*; **from ~** de mémoire. **2.** (*event, experience*) souvenir *m*.

men [men] *pl* → **man**.

menace ['menəs] ◆ *n* **1.** (*gen*) menace *f*. **2.** *inf* (*nuisance*) plaie *f*. ◆ *vt* menacer.

menacing ['menəsɪŋ] *adj* menaçant(e).

mend [mend] ◆ *n inf*: **to be on the ~** aller mieux. ◆ *vt* réparer; (*clothes*) raccommoder; (*sock, pullover*) repriser.

menial ['mi:njəl] *adj* avilissant(e).

meningitis [,menɪn'dʒaɪtɪs] *n* (U) méningite *f*.

menopause ['menəpɔːz] *n*: **the ~** la ménopause.

men's room *n* Am: **the ~** les toilettes *fpl* pour hommes.

menstruation [,menstrʊ'eɪʃn] *n* menstruation *f*.

menswear ['menzweər] *n* (U) vêtements *mpl* pour hommes.

mental ['mentl] *adj* mental(e); (*image, picture*) dans la tête.

mental hospital *n* hôpital *m* psychiatrique.

mentality [men'tælətɪ] *n* mentalité *f*.

mentally handicapped ['mentəlɪ-] *npl*: **the ~** les handicapés *mpl* mentaux.

mention ['menʃn] ◆ *vt* mentionner, signaler; **not to ~** sans parler de; **don't ~ it!** je vous en prie! ◆ *n* mention *f*.

menu ['menjuː] *n* (*gen & COMPUT*) menu *m*.

meow Am = **miaow**.

MEP (*abbr of* Member of the European Parliament) *n* parlementaire *m* européen.

mercenary ['mɜːsɪnrɪ] ◆ *adj* mercenaire. ◆ *n* mercenaire *m*.

merchandise ['mɜːtʃəndaɪz] *n* (U) marchandises *fpl*.

merchant ['mɜːtʃənt] *n* marchand *m*, -e *f*, commerçant *m*, -e *f*.

merchant bank *n* Br banque *f* d'affaires.

merchant navy Br, **merchant marine** Am *n* marine *f* marchande.

merciful ['mɜːsɪful] *adj* **1.** (*person*) clément(e). **2.** (*death, release*) qui est une délivrance.

merciless ['mɜːsɪlɪs] *adj* impitoyable.

mercury ['mɜːkjʊrɪ] *n* mercure *m*.

Mercury ['mɜːkjʊrɪ] *n* (*planet*) Mercure *f*.

mercy ['mɜːsɪ] *n* **1.** (*kindness, pity*) pitié *f*; **at the ~ of** *fig* à la merci de. **2.** (*blessing*): **what a ~ that** ... quelle chance que ...

mere [mɪə] *adj* seul(e); **she's a ~ child** ce n'est qu'une enfant; **it cost a ~ £10** cela n'a coûté que 10 livres.

merely ['mɪəlɪ] *adv* seulement, simplement.

merge [mɜːdʒ] ♦ *vt* (COMM & COMPUT) fusionner. ♦ *vi* **1.** (COMM): **to ~ (with)** fusionner (avec). **2.** (*roads, lines*): **to ~ (with)** se joindre (à). **3.** (*colours*) se fondre. ♦ *n* (COMPUT) fusion *f*.

merger ['mɜːdʒə] *n* fusion *f*.

meringue [mə'ræŋ] *n* meringue *f*.

merit ['merɪt] ♦ *n* (*value*) mérite *m*, valeur *f*. ♦ *vt* mériter. ▶ **merits** *npl* (*advantages*) qualités *fpl*.

mermaid ['mɜːmeɪd] *n* sirène *f*.

merry ['merɪ] *adj* **1.** *literary* (*happy*) joyeux(euse); **Merry Christmas!** joyeux Noël! **2.** *inf* (*tipsy*) gai(e), éméché(e).

merry-go-round *n* manège *m*.

mesh [meʃ] ♦ *n* maille *f* (du filet); **wire ~ grillage** *m*. ♦ *vi* (*gears*) s'engrener.

mesmerize, -ise ['mezməraɪz] *vt*: **to be ~d by** être fasciné(e) par.

mess [mes] *n* **1.** (*untidy state*) désordre *m*; *fig* gâchis *m*. **2.** (MIL) mess *m*. ▶ **mess about, mess around** *inf* ♦ *vt sep*: **to ~ sb about** traiter qqn par-dessus OR par-dessous la jambe. ♦ *vi* **1.** (*fool around*) perdre OR gaspiller son temps. **2.** (*interfere*): **to ~ about with sthg** s'immiscer dans qqch. ▶ **mess up** *vt sep inf* **1.** (*room*) mettre en désordre; (*clothes*) salir. **2.** *fig* (*spoil*) gâcher.

message ['mesɪdʒ] *n* message *m*.

messenger ['mesɪndʒə] *n* messager *m*, -ère *f*.

Messrs, Messrs. ['mesəz] (*abbr of* messieurs) MM.

messy ['mesɪ] *adj* **1.** (*dirty*) sale; (*untidy*) désordonné(e); **a ~ job** un travail salissant. **2.** *inf* (*divorce*) difficile; (*situation*) embrouillé(e).

met [met] *pt & pp* → **meet**.

metal ['metl] ♦ *n* métal *m*. ♦ *comp* en OR de métal.

metallic [mɪ'tælɪk] *adj* **1.** (*sound, ore*) métallique. **2.** (*paint, finish*) métallisé(e).

metalwork ['metlwɜːk] *n* (*craft*) ferronnerie *f*.

metaphor ['metəfə] *n* métaphore *f*.

mete [miːt] ▶ **mete out** *vt sep* (*punishment*) infliger.

meteor ['miːtɪə] *n* météore *m*.

meteorology [ˌmiːtjə'rɒlədʒɪ] *n* météorologie *f*.

meter ['miːtə] ♦ *n* **1.** (*device*) compteur *m*. **2.** Am = **metre**. ♦ *vt* (*gas, electricity*) établir la consommation de.

method ['meθəd] *n* méthode *f*.

methodical [mɪ'θɒdɪkl] *adj* méthodique.

Methodist ['meθədɪst] ♦ *adj* méthodiste. ♦ *n* méthodiste *mf*.

meths [meθs] *n* Br *inf* alcool *m* à brûler.

methylated spirits ['meθɪleɪtɪd-] *n* alcool *m* à brûler.

meticulous [mɪ'tɪkjʊləs] *adj* méticuleux(euse).

metre Br, **meter** Am ['miːtə] *n* mètre *m*.

metric ['metrɪk] *adj* métrique.

metronome ['metrənəʊm] *n* métronome *m*.

metropolitan [ˌmetrə'pɒlɪtn] *adj* métropolitain(e).

Metropolitan Police *npl*: **the ~** la police de Londres.

mettle ['metl] *n*: **to be on one's ~** être d'attaque; **to show** OR **prove one's ~** montrer ce dont on est capable.

mew [mjuː] = **miaow**.

mews [mjuːz] (*pl inv*) *n* Br ruelle *f*.

Mexican ['meksɪkn] ♦ *adj* mexicain(e). ♦ *n* Mexicain *m*, -e *f*.

Mexico ['meksɪkəʊ] *n* Mexique *m*.

MI5 (*abbr of* **Military Intelligence 5**) *n* service de contre-espionnage britannique.

MI6 (*abbr of* **Military Intelligence 6**) *n* service de renseignements britannique.

miaow Br [miː'aʊ], **meow** Am [mɪ'aʊ] ♦ *n* miaulement *m*, miaou *m*. ♦ *vi* miauler.

mice [maɪs] *pl* → **mouse**.

mickey ['mɪkɪ] *n*: **to take the ~ out of sb** Br *inf* se payer la tête de qqn, faire marcher qqn.

microchip ['maɪkrəʊtʃɪp] *n* (COMPUT) puce *f*.

microcomputer [ˌmaɪkrəʊkəm'pjuːtə] *n* micro-ordinateur *m*.

microfilm ['maɪkrəʊfɪlm] *n* microfilm *m*.

microphone ['maɪkrəfəʊn] *n* microphone *m*, micro *m*.

microscope ['maɪkrəskəʊp] *n* microscope *m*.

microscopic [ˌmaɪkrə'skɒpɪk] *adj* microscopique.

microwave (oven) ['maɪkrəweɪv-] *n*

(four *m* à) micro-ondes *m*.
mid- [mɪd] *prefix*: **~height** mi-hauteur; **~morning** milieu de la matinée; **~winter** plein hiver.
midair [mɪd'eəʳ] ♦ *adj* en plein ciel. ♦ *n*: **in ~** en plein ciel.
midday [mɪd'deɪ] *n* midi *m*.
middle [mɪdl] ♦ *adj* (*centre*) du milieu, du centre. ♦ *n* **1.** (*centre*) milieu *m*, centre *m*; **in the ~ (of)** au milieu (de). **2.** (*in time*) milieu *m*; **to be in the ~ of doing sthg** être en train de faire qqch; **to be in the ~ of a meeting** être en pleine réunion; **in the ~ of the night** au milieu de la nuit, en pleine nuit. **3.** (*waist*) taille *f*.
middle-aged *adj* d'une cinquantaine d'années.
Middle Ages *npl*: **the ~** le Moyen Âge.
middle-class *adj* bourgeois(e).
middle classes *npl*: **the ~** la bourgeoisie.
Middle East *n*: **the ~** le Moyen-Orient.
middleman [mɪdlmæn] (*pl* **-men** [-men]) *n* intermédiaire *mf*.
middle name *n* second prénom *m*.
middleweight [mɪdlweɪt] *n* poids *m* moyen.
middling [mɪdlɪŋ] *adj* moyen(enne).
Mideast [mɪd'iːst] *n* Am: **the ~** le Moyen-Orient.
midfield [mɪd'fiːld] *n* (FTBL) milieu *m* de terrain.
midge [mɪdʒ] *n* moucheron *m*.
midget [mɪdʒɪt] *n* nain *m*, -e *f*.
midi system [mɪdɪ-] *n* chaîne *f* midi.
Midlands [mɪdləndz] *npl*: **the ~** *les comtés du centre de l'Angleterre*.
midnight [mɪdnaɪt] *n* minuit *m*.
midriff [mɪdrɪf] *n* diaphragme *m*.
midst [mɪdst] *n* **1.** (*in space*): **in the ~ of** au milieu de. **2.** (*in time*): **to be in the ~ of doing sthg** être en train de faire qqch.
midsummer [mɪd,sʌməʳ] *n* cœur *m* de l'été.
Midsummer Day *n* la Saint-Jean.
midway [mɪd'weɪ] *adv* **1.** (*in space*): **~ (between)** à mi-chemin (entre). **2.** (*in time*): **~ through the meeting** en pleine réunion.
midweek [*adj* mɪd'wiːk, *adv* mɪd'wiːk] ♦ *adj* du milieu de la semaine. ♦ *adv* en milieu de semaine.
midwife [mɪdwaɪf] (*pl* **-wives** [-waɪvz]) *n* sage-femme *f*.
midwifery [mɪd,wɪfərɪ] *n* obstétrique *f*.

might [maɪt] ♦ *modal vb* **1.** (*expressing possibility*): **the criminal ~ be armed** il est possible que le criminel soit armé. **2.** (*expressing suggestion*): **it ~ be better to wait** il vaut peut-être mieux attendre. **3.** *fml* (*asking permission*): **he asked if he ~ leave the room** il demanda s'il pouvait sortir de la pièce. **4.** (*expressing concession*): **you ~ well be right** vous avez peut-être raison. **5.** *phr*: **I ~ have known** OR **guessed** j'aurais dû m'en douter. ♦ *n* (U) force *f*.
mighty [maɪtɪ] ♦ *adj* (*powerful*) puissant(e). ♦ *adv* Am *inf* drôlement, vachement.
migraine [miːgreɪn, maɪgreɪn] *n* migraine *f*.
migrant [maɪgrənt] ♦ *adj* **1.** (*bird, animal*) migrateur(trice). **2.** (*workers*) émigré(e). ♦ *n* **1.** (*bird, animal*) migrateur *m*. **2.** (*person*) émigré *m*, -e *f*.
migrate [Br maɪ'greɪt, Am 'maɪgreɪt] *vi* **1.** (*bird, animal*) migrer. **2.** (*person*) émigrer.
mike [maɪk] (*abbr of* **microphone**) *n inf* micro *m*.
mild [maɪld] *adj* **1.** (*disinfectant, reproach*) léger(ère). **2.** (*tone, weather*) doux (douce). **3.** (*illness*) bénin(igne).
mildew [mɪldjuː] *n* (U) moisissure *f*.
mildly [maɪldlɪ] *adv* **1.** (*gently*) doucement; **to put it ~, ...**, c'est le moins qu'on puisse dire. **2.** (*not strongly*) légèrement. **3.** (*slightly*) un peu.
mile [maɪl] *n* mile *m*; (NAUT) mille *m*; **to be ~s away** *fig* être très loin.
mileage [maɪlɪdʒ] *n* distance *f* en miles, ≈ kilométrage *m*.
mileometer [maɪ'lɒmɪtəʳ] *n* compteur *m* de miles, ≈ compteur kilométrique.
milestone [maɪlstəʊn] *n* (*marker stone*) borne *f*; *fig* événement *m* marquant.
militant [mɪlɪtənt] ♦ *adj* militant(e). ♦ *n* militant *m*, -e *f*.
military [mɪlɪtrɪ] ♦ *adj* militaire. ♦ *n*: **the ~** les militaires *mpl*, l'armée *f*.
militia [mɪ'lɪʃə] *n* milice *f*.
milk [mɪlk] ♦ *n* lait *m*. ♦ *vt* **1.** (*cow*) traire. **2.** *fig* (*use to own ends*) exploiter.
milk chocolate *n* chocolat *m* au lait.
milkman [mɪlkmən] (*pl* **-men** [-mən]) *n* laitier *m*.
milk shake *n* milk-shake *m*.
milky [mɪlkɪ] *adj* **1.** Br (*coffee*) avec beaucoup de lait. **2.** (*pale white*) laiteux (euse).
Milky Way *n*: **the ~** la Voie lactée.
mill [mɪl] ♦ *n* **1.** (*flour-mill, grinder*)

moulin m. **2.** (factory) usine f. ◆ vt moudre. ▶ **mill about**, **mill around** vi grouiller.

millennium [mɪˈlenɪəm] (pl **-nnia** [-nɪə]) n millénaire m.

miller [ˈmɪləʳ] n meunier m.

millet [ˈmɪlɪt] n millet m.

milligram(me) [ˈmɪlɪgræm] n milligramme m.

millimetre Br, **millimeter** Am [ˈmɪlɪˌmiːtəʳ] n millimètre m.

millinery [ˈmɪlɪnrɪ] n chapellerie f féminine.

million [ˈmɪljən] n million m; a ~, ~s of fig des milliers de, un million de.

millionaire [ˌmɪljəˈneəʳ] n millionnaire mf.

millstone [ˈmɪlstəʊn] n meule f.

milometer [maɪˈlɒmɪtəʳ] = **mileometer**.

mime [maɪm] ◆ n mime m. ◆ vt & vi mimer.

mimic [ˈmɪmɪk] (pt & pp **-ked**, cont **-king**) ◆ n imitateur m, -trice f. ◆ vt imiter.

mimicry [ˈmɪmɪkrɪ] n imitation f.

min. [mɪn] **1.** (abbr of **minute**) mn, min. **2.** (abbr of **minimum**) min.

mince [mɪns] ◆ n Br viande f hachée. ◆ vt (meat) hacher. ◆ vi marcher à petits pas maniérés.

mincemeat [ˈmɪnsmiːt] n **1.** (fruit) mélange de pommes, raisins secs et épices utilisé en pâtisserie. **2.** Am (meat) viande f hachée.

mince pie n tartelette f de Noël.

mincer [ˈmɪnsəʳ] n hachoir m.

mind [maɪnd] ◆ n **1.** (gen) esprit m; state of ~ état d'esprit; to bear sthg in ~ ne pas oublier qqch; to come into/cross sb's ~ venir à/traverser l'esprit de qqn; to have sthg on one's ~ avoir l'esprit préoccupé, être préoccupé par qqch; to keep an open ~ réserver son jugement; to have sthg in ~ avoir qqch dans l'idée; to make one's ~ up se décider. **2.** (attention): to put one's ~ to sthg s'appliquer à qqch; to keep one's ~ on sthg se concentrer sur qqch. **3.** (opinion): to change one's ~ changer d'avis; to my ~ à mon avis; to speak one's ~ parler franchement; to be in two ~s (about sthg) se tâter OR être indécis (à propos de qqch). **4.** (person) cerveau m. ◆ vi (be bothered): I don't ~ ça m'est égal; I hope you don't ~ j'espère que vous n'y voyez pas d'inconvénient; never ~ (don't worry) ne t'en fais pas; (it's not important) ça ne fait rien. ◆ vt **1.** (be bothered about, dislike): I don't ~ waiting ça ne me gêne OR

dérange pas d'attendre; do you ~ if ...? cela ne vous ennuie pas si ...?; I wouldn't ~ a beer je prendrais bien une bière. **2.** (pay attention to) faire attention à, prendre garde à. **3.** (take care of - luggage) garder, surveiller; (- shop) tenir. ▶ **mind you** adv remarquez.

minder [ˈmaɪndəʳ] n Br inf (bodyguard) ange m gardien.

mindful [ˈmaɪndfʊl] adj: ~ of (risks) attentif(ive) à; (responsibility) soucieux (euse) de.

mindless [ˈmaɪndlɪs] adj stupide, idiot(e).

mine¹ [maɪn] poss pron le mien (la mienne), les miens (les miennes) (pl); that money is ~ cet argent est à moi; it wasn't your fault, it was MINE ce n'était pas de votre faute, c'était de la mienne OR de ma faute à moi; a friend of ~ un ami à moi, un de mes amis.

mine² [maɪn] ◆ n mine f. ◆ vt **1.** (coal, gold) extraire. **2.** (road, beach, sea) miner.

minefield [ˈmaɪnfiːld] n champ m de mines; fig situation f explosive.

miner [ˈmaɪnəʳ] n mineur m.

mineral [ˈmɪnərəl] ◆ adj minéral(e). ◆ n minéral m.

mineral water n eau f minérale.

minesweeper [ˈmaɪnˌswiːpəʳ] n dragueur m de mines.

mingle [ˈmɪŋgl] vi: to ~ (with) (sounds, fragrances) se mélanger (à); (people) se mêler (à).

miniature [ˈmɪnətʃəʳ] ◆ adj miniature. ◆ n **1.** (painting) miniature f. **2.** (of alcohol) bouteille f miniature. **3.** (small scale): in ~ en miniature.

minibus [ˈmɪnɪbʌs] (pl **-es**) n minibus m.

minicab [ˈmɪnɪkæb] n Br radiotaxi m.

minima [ˈmɪnɪmə] pl → **minimum**.

minimal [ˈmɪnɪml] adj (cost) insignifiant(e); (damage) minime.

minimum [ˈmɪnɪməm] (pl **-mums** OR **-ma**) ◆ adj minimum (inv). ◆ n minimum m.

mining [ˈmaɪnɪŋ] ◆ n exploitation f minière. ◆ adj minier(ère).

miniskirt [ˈmɪnɪskɜːt] n minijupe f.

minister [ˈmɪnɪstəʳ] n **1.** (POL) ministre m. **2.** (RELIG) pasteur m. ▶ **minister to** vt fus (person) donner OR prodiguer ses soins à; (needs) pourvoir à.

ministerial [ˌmɪnɪˈstɪərɪəl] adj ministériel(elle).

minister of state n secrétaire mf d'État.

miss

ministry ['mɪnɪstrɪ] n 1. (POL) ministère m. 2. (RELIG): **the ~** le saint ministère.

mink [mɪŋk] (pl inv) n vison m.

minnow ['mɪnəʊ] n vairon m.

minor ['maɪnər] ◆ adj (gen & MUS) mineur(e); (detail) petit(e); (role) secondaire. ◆ n mineur m, -e f.

minority [maɪ'nɒrətɪ] n minorité f.

mint [mɪnt] ◆ n 1. (herb) menthe f. 2. (sweet) bonbon m à la menthe. 3. (for coins): **the Mint** l'hôtel de la Monnaie; **in ~ condition** en parfait état. ◆ vt (coins) battre.

minus ['maɪnəs] (pl **-es**) ◆ prep moins. ◆ adj (answer, quantity) négatif(ive). ◆ n 1. (MATH) signe m moins. 2. (disadvantage) handicap m.

minus sign n signe m moins.

minute[1] ['mɪnɪt] n minute f; **at any ~** à tout moment, d'une minute à l'autre; **stop that this ~!** arrête tout de suite OR immédiatement! ► **minutes** npl procès-verbal m, compte m rendu.

minute[2] [maɪ'njuːt] adj minuscule.

miracle ['mɪrəkl] n miracle m.

miraculous [mɪ'rækjʊləs] adj miraculeux(euse).

mirage [mɪ'rɑːʒ] n lit & fig mirage m.

mire [maɪər] n fange f, boue f.

mirror ['mɪrər] ◆ n miroir m, glace f. ◆ vt refléter.

mirth [mɜːθ] n hilarité f, gaieté f.

misadventure [mɪsəd'ventʃər] n: **death by ~** (JUR) mort f accidentelle.

misapprehension ['mɪs,æprɪ'henʃn] n idée f fausse.

misbehave [mɪsbɪ'heɪv] vi se conduire mal.

miscalculate [mɪs'kælkjʊleɪt] ◆ vt mal calculer. ◆ vi se tromper.

miscarriage [mɪs'kærɪdʒ] n (MED) fausse couche f; **to have a ~** faire une fausse couche.

miscarriage of justice n erreur f judiciaire.

miscellaneous [mɪsə'leɪnjəs] adj varié(e), divers(e).

mischief ['mɪstʃɪf] n (U) 1. (playfulness) malice f, espièglerie f. 2. (naughty behaviour) sottises fpl, bêtises fpl. 3. (harm) dégât m.

mischievous ['mɪstʃɪvəs] adj 1. (playful) malicieux(euse). 2. (naughty) espiègle, coquin(e).

misconception [mɪskən'sepʃn] n idée f fausse.

misconduct [mɪs'kɒndʌkt] n inconduite f.

misconstrue [mɪskən'struː] vt fml mal interpréter.

miscount [mɪs'kaʊnt] vt & vi mal compter.

misdeed [mɪs'diːd] n méfait m.

misdemeanour Br, **misdemeanor** Am [mɪsdɪ'miːnər] n (JUR) délit m.

miser ['maɪzər] n avare mf.

miserable ['mɪzrəbl] adj 1. (person) malheureux(euse), triste. 2. (conditions, life) misérable; (pay) dérisoire; (weather) maussade. 3. (failure) pitoyable, lamentable.

miserly ['maɪzəlɪ] adj avare.

misery ['mɪzərɪ] n 1. (of person) tristesse f. 2. (of conditions, life) misère f.

misfire [mɪs'faɪər] vi 1. (gun, plan) rater. 2. (car engine) avoir des ratés.

misfit ['mɪsfɪt] n inadapté m, -e f.

misfortune [mɪs'fɔːtʃuːn] n 1. (bad luck) malchance f. 2. (piece of bad luck) malheur m.

misgivings [mɪs'gɪvɪŋz] npl craintes fpl, doutes mpl.

misguided [mɪs'gaɪdɪd] adj (person) malavisé(e); (attempt) malencontreux (euse); (opinion) peu judicieux(euse).

mishandle [mɪs'hændl] vt 1. (person, animal) manier sans précaution. 2. (negotiations) mal mener; (business) mal gérer.

mishap ['mɪshæp] n mésaventure f.

misinterpret [mɪsɪn'tɜːprɪt] vt mal interpréter.

misjudge [mɪs'dʒʌdʒ] vt 1. (distance, time) mal évaluer. 2. (person, mood) méjuger, se méprendre sur.

mislay [mɪs'leɪ] (pt & pp **-laid** [-'leɪd]) vt égarer.

mislead [mɪs'liːd] (pt & pp **-led**) vt induire en erreur.

misleading [mɪs'liːdɪŋ] adj trompeur (euse).

misled [mɪs'led] pt & pp → **mislead**.

misnomer [mɪs'nəʊmər] n nom m mal approprié.

misplace [mɪs'pleɪs] vt égarer.

misprint ['mɪsprɪnt] n faute f d'impression.

miss [mɪs] ◆ vt 1. (gen) rater, manquer; **not to be ~ed** ne pas manquer. 2. (home, person): **I ~ my family/her** ma famille/elle me manque. 3. (avoid, escape) échapper à; **I just ~ed being run over** j'ai failli me faire écraser ◆ vi rater. ◆ n: **to give sthg a ~** inf ne pas aller à qqch. ► **miss out** ◆ vt sep (omit - *by accident*) oublier; (- *deliberately*) omettre. ◆ *vi*: **to ~ out on sthg** ne pas pouvoir profiter de qqch.

Miss [mɪs] *n* Mademoiselle *f*.

misshapen [ˌmɪsˈʃeɪpn] *adj* difforme.

missile [Br 'mɪsaɪl, Am 'mɪsəl] *n* 1. (*weapon*) missile *m*. 2. (*thrown object*) projectile *m*.

missing ['mɪsɪŋ] *adj* 1. (*lost*) perdu(e), égaré(e). 2. (*not present*) manquant(e), qui manque.

mission ['mɪʃn] *n* mission *f*.

missionary ['mɪʃənrɪ] *n* missionnaire *mf*.

misspend [ˌmɪsˈspend] (*pt & pp* -**spent** [-'spent]) *vt* gaspiller.

mist [mɪst] *n* brume *f*. ► **mist over, mist up** *vi* s'embuer.

mistake [mɪˈsteɪk] (*pt* -**took**, *pp* -**taken**) ◆ *n* erreur *f*; **by ~** par erreur; **to make a ~** faire une erreur, se tromper. ◆ *vt* 1. (*misunderstand - meaning*) mal comprendre; (- *intention*) se méprendre sur. 2. (*fail to recognize*): **to ~ sb/sthg for** prendre qqn/qqch pour, confondre qqn/qqch avec.

mistaken [mɪˈsteɪkn] ◆ *pp* → **mistake**. ◆ *adj* 1. (*person*): **to be ~ (about)** se tromper (en ce qui concerne OR sur). 2. (*belief, idea*) erroné(e), faux (fausse).

mister ['mɪstər] *n inf* monsieur *m*. ► **Mister** *n* Monsieur *m*.

mistletoe ['mɪsltəʊ] *n* gui *m*.

mistook [mɪˈstʊk] *pt* → **mistake**.

mistreat [ˌmɪsˈtriːt] *vt* maltraiter.

mistress ['mɪstrɪs] *n* maîtresse *f*.

mistrust [ˌmɪsˈtrʌst] ◆ *n* méfiance *f*. ◆ *vt* se méfier de.

misty ['mɪstɪ] *adj* brumeux(euse).

misunderstand [ˌmɪsʌndəˈstænd] (*pt & pp* -**stood**) *vt & vi* mal comprendre.

misunderstanding [ˌmɪsʌndəˈstændɪŋ] *n* malentendu *m*.

misunderstood [ˌmɪsʌndəˈstʊd] *pt & pp* → **misunderstand**.

misuse [*n* ˌmɪsˈjuːs, *vb* ˌmɪsˈjuːz] ◆ *n* 1. (*of one's time, resources*) mauvais emploi *m*. 2. (*of power*) abus *m*; (*of funds*) détournement *m*. ◆ *vt* 1. (*one's time, resources*) mal employer. 2. (*power*) abuser de; (*funds*) détourner.

miter Am = **mitre**.

mitigate ['mɪtɪɡeɪt] *vt* atténuer, mitiger.

mitre Br, **miter** Am ['maɪtər] *n* 1. (*hat*) mitre *f*. 2. (*joint*) onglet *m*.

mitt [mɪt] *n* 1. = **mitten**. 2. (*in baseball*) gant *m*.

mitten ['mɪtn] *n* moufle *f*.

mix [mɪks] ◆ *vt* 1. (*gen*) mélanger. 2. (*activities*): **to ~ sthg with sthg** combiner OR associer qqch et qqch. 3. (*drink*) préparer; (*cement*) malaxer. ◆ *vi* 1. (*gen*) se mélanger. 2. (*socially*): **to ~ with** fréquenter. ◆ *n* 1. (*gen*) mélange *m*. 2. (MUS) mixage *m*. ► **mix up** *vt sep* 1. (*confuse*) confondre. 2. (*disorganize*) mélanger.

mixed [mɪkst] *adj* 1. (*assorted*) assortis (ies). 2. (*education*) mixte.

mixed-ability *adj* Br (*class*) tous niveaux confondus.

mixed grill *n* assortiment *m* de grillades.

mixed up *adj* 1. (*confused - person*) qui ne sait plus où il en est, paumé(e); (- *mind*) embrouillé(e). 2. (*involved*): **to be ~ in sthg** être mêlé(e) à qqch.

mixer ['mɪksər] *n* (*for food*) mixer *m*.

mixture ['mɪkstʃər] *n* 1. (*gen*) mélange *m*. 2. (MED) préparation *f*.

mix-up *n inf* confusion *f*.

mm (*abbr of* **millimetre**) mm.

moan [məʊn] ◆ *n* (*of pain, sadness*) gémissement *m*. ◆ *vi* 1. (*in pain, sadness*) gémir. 2. *inf* (*complain*): **to ~ (about)** rouspéter OR râler (à propos de).

moat [məʊt] *n* douves *fpl*.

mob [mɒb] ◆ *n* foule *f*. ◆ *vt* assaillir.

mobile ['məʊbaɪl] ◆ *adj* 1. (*gen*) mobile. 2. (*able to travel*) motorisé(e). ◆ *n* mobile *m*.

mobile home *n* auto-caravane *f*.

mobile phone *n* téléphone *m* portatif.

mobilize, -ise ['məʊbɪlaɪz] *vt & vi* mobiliser.

mock [mɒk] ◆ *adj* faux (fausse); **~ exam** examen blanc. ◆ *vt* se moquer de. ◆ *vi* se moquer.

mockery ['mɒkərɪ] *n* moquerie *f*.

mod cons [mɒd-] (*abbr of* **modern conveniences**) *npl* Br *inf*: **all ~** tout confort, tt. conf.

mode [məʊd] *n* mode *m*.

model ['mɒdl] ◆ *n* 1. (*gen*) modèle *m*. 2. (*fashion model*) mannequin *m*. ◆ *adj* 1. (*perfect*) modèle. 2. (*reduced-scale*) (en) modèle réduit. ◆ *vt* 1. (*clay*) modeler. 2. (*clothes*): **to ~ a dress** présenter un modèle de robe. 3. (*copy*): **to ~ o.s. on sb** prendre modèle sur qqn, se modeler sur qqn. ◆ *vi* être mannequin.

modem ['məʊdem] *n* (COMPUT) modem *m*.

moderate [*adj* 'mɒdərət, *vb* 'mɒdəreɪt]

◆ *adj* modéré(e). ◆ *vt* modérer. ◆ *vi* se modérer.

moderation [,mɒdə'reɪʃn] *n* modération *f*; **in ~** avec modération.

modern ['mɒdən] *adj* moderne.

modernize, -ise ['mɒdənaɪz] ◆ *vt* moderniser. ◆ *vi* se moderniser.

modern languages *npl* langues *fpl* vivantes.

modest ['mɒdɪst] *adj* modeste.

modesty ['mɒdɪstɪ] *n* modestie *f*.

modicum ['mɒdɪkəm] *n* minimum *m*.

modify ['mɒdɪfaɪ] *vt* modifier.

module ['mɒdjuːl] *n* module *m*.

mogul ['məʊɡl] *n fig* magnat *m*.

mohair ['məʊheəʳ] *n* mohair *m*.

moist [mɔɪst] *adj* (*soil, climate*) humide; (*cake*) moelleux(euse).

moisten ['mɔɪsn] *vt* humecter.

moisture ['mɔɪstʃəʳ] *n* humidité *f*.

moisturizer ['mɔɪstʃəraɪzəʳ] *n* crème *f* hydratante, lait *m* hydratant.

molar ['məʊləʳ] *n* molaire *f*.

molasses [mə'læsɪz] *n* (U) mélasse *f*.

mold *etc* Am = **mould**.

mole [məʊl] *n* **1.** (*animal, spy*) taupe *f*. **2.** (*on skin*) grain *m* de beauté.

molecule ['mɒlɪkjuːl] *n* molécule *f*.

molest [mə'lest] *vt* **1.** (*attack sexually*) attenter à la pudeur de. **2.** (*attack*) molester.

mollusc, mollusk Am ['mɒləsk] *n* mollusque *m*.

mollycoddle ['mɒlɪ,kɒdl] *vt inf* chouchouter.

molt Am = **moult**.

molten ['məʊltn] *adj* en fusion.

mom [mɒm] *n* Am *inf* maman *f*.

moment ['məʊmənt] *n* moment *m*, instant *m*; **at any ~** d'un moment à l'autre; **at the ~** en ce moment; **for the ~** pour le moment.

momentarily ['məʊməntərɪlɪ] *adv* **1.** (*for a short time*) momentanément. **2.** Am (*soon*) très bientôt.

momentary ['məʊməntrɪ] *adj* momentané(e), passager(ère).

momentous [mə'mentəs] *adj* capital(e), très important(e).

momentum [mə'mentəm] *n* (U) **1.** (PHYSICS) moment *m*. **2.** *fig* (*speed, force*) vitesse *f*; **to gather ~** prendre de la vitesse.

momma ['mɒmə], **mommy** ['mɒmɪ] *n* Am maman *f*.

Monaco ['mɒnəkəʊ] *n* Monaco.

monarch ['mɒnək] *n* monarque *m*.

monarchy ['mɒnəkɪ] *n* monarchie *f*.

monastery ['mɒnəstrɪ] *n* monastère *m*.

Monday ['mʌndɪ] *n* lundi *m*; *see also* **Saturday**.

monetary ['mʌnɪtrɪ] *adj* monétaire.

money ['mʌnɪ] *n* argent *m*; **to make ~** gagner de l'argent; **to get one's ~'s worth** en avoir pour son argent.

moneybox ['mʌnɪbɒks] *n* tirelire *f*.

moneylender ['mʌnɪ,lendəʳ] *n* prêteur *m*, -euse *f* sur gages.

money order *n* mandat *m* postal.

money-spinner [-,spɪnəʳ] *n inf* mine *f* d'or.

mongol ['mɒŋɡəl] *dated & offensive n* mongolien *m*, -enne *f*.

Mongolia [mɒŋ'ɡəʊlɪə] *n* Mongolie *f*.

mongrel ['mʌŋɡrəl] *n* (*dog*) bâtard *m*.

monitor ['mɒnɪtəʳ] ◆ *n* (COMPUT, MED & TV) moniteur *m*. ◆ *vt* **1.** (*check*) contrôler, suivre de près. **2.** (*broadcasts, messages*) être à l'écoute de.

monk [mʌŋk] *n* moine *m*.

monkey ['mʌŋkɪ] *n* (*pl* **monkeys**) *n* singe *m*.

monkey nut *n* cacahuète *f*.

monkey wrench *n* clef *f* à molette.

mono ['mɒnəʊ] ◆ *adj* mono (*inv*). ◆ *n* (*sound*) monophonie *f*.

monochrome ['mɒnəkrəʊm] *adj* monochrome.

monocle ['mɒnəkl] *n* monocle *m*.

monologue, monolog Am ['mɒnəlɒɡ] *n* monologue *m*.

monoplane ['mɒnəpleɪn] *n* monoplan *m*.

monopolize, -ise [mə'nɒpəlaɪz] *vt* monopoliser.

monopoly [mə'nɒpəlɪ] *n*: **~ (on OR of)** monopole *m* (de).

monotone ['mɒnətəʊn] *n* ton *m* monocorde.

monotonous [mə'nɒtənəs] *adj* monotone.

monotony [mə'nɒtənɪ] *n* monotonie *f*.

monsoon [mɒn'suːn] *n* mousson *f*.

monster ['mɒnstəʳ] *n* **1.** (*creature, cruel person*) monstre *m*. **2.** (*huge thing, person*) colosse *m*.

monstrosity [mɒn'strɒsətɪ] *n* monstruosité *f*.

monstrous ['mɒnstrəs] *adj* monstrueux(euse).

Mont Blanc [,mɔ̃'blɑ̃] *n* le mont Blanc.

month [mʌnθ] *n* mois *m*.

monthly ['mʌnθlɪ] ◆ *adj* mensuel (elle). ◆ *adv* mensuellement. ◆ *n* (*publication*) mensuel *m*.

Montreal [,mɒntrɪ'ɔːl] *n* Montréal.

monument ['mɒnjʊmənt] *n* monument *m*.

monumental [ˌmɒnjʊ'mentl] *adj* monumental(e).

moo [muː] (*pl* **-s**) ♦ *n* meuglement *m*, beuglement *m*. ♦ *vi* meugler, beugler.

mood [muːd] *n* humeur *f*; **in a (bad) ~** de mauvaise humeur; **in a good ~** de bonne humeur.

moody ['muːdɪ] *adj pej* **1.** (*changeable*) lunatique. **2.** (*bad-tempered*) de mauvaise humeur, mal luné(e).

moon [muːn] *n* lune *f*.

moonlight ['muːnlaɪt] (*pt & pp* **-ed**) ♦ *n* clair *m* de lune. ♦ *vi* travailler au noir.

moonlighting ['muːnlaɪtɪŋ] *n* (U) travail *m* (au) noir.

moonlit ['muːnlɪt] *adj* (*countryside*) éclairé(e) par la lune; (*night*) de lune.

moor [mɔːʳ] ♦ *n* lande *f*. ♦ *vt* amarrer. ♦ *vi* mouiller.

moorland ['mɔːlənd] *n* lande *f*.

moose [muːs] (*pl inv*) *n* (North American) orignal *m*.

mop [mɒp] ♦ *n* **1.** (*for cleaning*) balai *m* à laver. **2.** *inf* (*hair*) tignasse *f*. ♦ *vt* **1.** (*floor*) laver. **2.** (*sweat*) essuyer; **to ~ one's face** s'essuyer le visage. ▶ **mop up** *vt sep* (*clean up*) éponger.

mope [məʊp] *vi* broyer du noir.

moped ['məʊped] *n* vélomoteur *m*.

moral ['mɒrəl] ♦ *adj* moral(e). ♦ *n* (*lesson*) morale *f*. ▶ **morals** *npl* moralité *f*.

morale [mə'rɑːl] *n* (U) moral *m*.

morality [mə'rælətɪ] *n* moralité *f*.

morass [mə'ræs] *n fig* (*of detail, paperwork*) fatras *m*.

morbid ['mɔːbɪd] *adj* morbide.

more [mɔːʳ] ♦ *adv* **1.** (*with adjectives and adverbs*) plus; **~ important (than)** plus important (que); **~ often/quickly (than)** plus souvent/rapidement (que). **2.** (*to a greater degree*) plus, davantage. **3.** (*another time*): **once/twice ~** une fois/deux fois de plus, encore une fois/deux fois. ♦ *adj* **1.** (*larger number, amount of*) plus de, davantage de; **~ than 70 people died** plus de 70 personnes ont péri. **2.** (*an extra amount of*) encore (de); **have some ~ tea** prends encore du thé; **I finished two ~ chapters today** j'ai fini deux autres OR encore deux chapitres aujourd'hui; **we need ~ money/time** il nous faut plus d'argent/de temps, il nous faut davantage d'argent/de temps. ♦ *pron* plus, davantage; **~ than five** plus de cinq; **he's got ~ than I have** il en a plus que moi; **there's no ~ (left)** il

n'y en a plus, il n'en reste plus; **(and) what's ~** de plus, qui plus est. ▶ **any more** *adv*: **not ... any ~** ne ... plus. ▶ **more and more** ♦ *adv & pron* de plus en plus; **~ and ~ depressed** de plus en plus déprimé. ♦ *adj* de plus en plus de; **there are ~ and ~ cars on the roads** il y a de plus en plus de voitures sur les routes. ▶ **more or less** *adv* **1.** (*almost*) plus ou moins. **2.** (*approximately*) environ, à peu près.

moreover [mɔː'rəʊvəʳ] *adv* de plus.

morgue [mɔːg] *n* morgue *f*.

Mormon ['mɔːmən] *n* mormon *m*, -e *f*.

morning ['mɔːnɪŋ] *n* matin *m*; (*duration*) matinée *f*; **I work in the ~** je travaille le matin; **I'll do it tomorrow ~** OR **in the ~** je le ferai demain. ▶ **mornings** *adv Am* le matin.

Moroccan [mə'rɒkən] ♦ *adj* marocain(e). ♦ *n* Marocain *m*, -e *f*.

Morocco [mə'rɒkəʊ] *n* Maroc *m*.

moron ['mɔːrɒn] *n inf* idiot *m*, -e *f*, crétin *m*, -e *f*.

morose [mə'rəʊs] *adj* morose.

morphine ['mɔːfiːn] *n* morphine *f*.

Morse (code) [mɔːs-] *n* morse *m*.

morsel ['mɔːsl] *n* bout *m*, morceau *m*.

mortal ['mɔːtl] ♦ *adj* mortel(elle). ♦ *n* mortel *m*, -elle *f*.

mortality [mɔː'tælətɪ] *n* mortalité *f*.

mortar ['mɔːtəʳ] *n* mortier *m*.

mortgage ['mɔːgɪdʒ] ♦ *n* empruntlogement *m*. ♦ *vt* hypothéquer.

mortified ['mɔːtɪfaɪd] *adj* mortifié(e).

mortuary ['mɔːtʃʊərɪ] *n* morgue *f*.

mosaic [mə'zeɪɪk] *n* mosaïque *f*.

Moscow ['mɒskəʊ] *n* Moscou.

Moslem ['mɒzləm] = **Muslim**.

mosque [mɒsk] *n* mosquée *f*.

mosquito [mə'skiːtəʊ] (*pl* **-es** OR **-s**) *n* moustique *m*.

moss [mɒs] *n* mousse *f*.

most [məʊst] (*superl of* **many**) ♦ *adj* **1.** (*the majority of*) la plupart de; **~ tourists here are German** la plupart des touristes ici sont allemands. **2.** (*largest amount of*): **(the) ~** le plus de; **she's got (the) ~ money/sweets** c'est elle qui a le plus d'argent/de bonbons. ♦ *pron* **1.** (*the majority*) la plupart; **~ of the tourists here are German** la plupart des touristes ici sont allemands; **~ of them** la plupart d'entre eux. **2.** (*largest amount*): **(the) ~** le plus; **at ~** au maximum, tout au plus. **3.** *phr*: **to make the ~ of sthg** profiter de qqch au maximum. ♦ *adv* **1.** (*to greatest extent*): **(the) ~** le plus. **2.** *fml* (*very*) très, fort. **3.** *Am* (*almost*) presque.

mostly ['məʊstlɪ] *adv* principalement, surtout.

MOT *n* (*abbr of* **Ministry of Transport (test)**) contrôle technique annuel obligatoire pour les véhicules de plus de trois ans.

motel [məʊ'tel] *n* motel *m*.

moth [mɒθ] *n* papillon *m* de nuit; (*in clothes*) mite *f*.

mothball ['mɒθbɔːl] *n* boule *f* de naphtaline.

mother ['mʌðəʳ] ◆ *n* mère *f*. ◆ *vt* (*child*) materner, dorloter.

motherhood ['mʌðəhʊd] *n* maternité *f*.

mother-in-law (*pl* **mothers-in-law** OR **mother-in-laws**) *n* belle-mère *f*.

motherly ['mʌðəlɪ] *adj* maternel(elle).

mother-of-pearl *n* nacre *f*.

mother-to-be (*pl* **mothers-to-be**) *n* future maman *f*.

mother tongue *n* langue *f* maternelle.

motif [məʊ'tiːf] *n* motif *m*.

motion ['məʊʃn] ◆ *n* **1.** (*gen*) mouvement *m*; **to set sthg in ~** mettre qqch en branle. **2.** (*in debate*) motion *f*. ◆ *vt*: **to ~ sb to do sthg** faire signe à qqn de faire qqch. ◆ *vi*: **to ~ to sb** faire signe à qqn.

motionless ['məʊʃənlɪs] *adj* immobile.

motion picture *n Am* film *m*.

motivated ['məʊtɪveɪtɪd] *adj* motivé(e).

motivation [,məʊtɪ'veɪʃn] *n* motivation *f*.

motive ['məʊtɪv] *n* motif *m*.

motley ['mɒtlɪ] *adj pej* hétéroclite.

motor ['məʊtəʳ] ◆ *adj Br* automobile. ◆ *n* (*engine*) moteur *m*.

motorbike ['məʊtəbaɪk] *n inf* moto *f*.

motorboat ['məʊtəbəʊt] *n* canot *m* automobile.

motorcar ['məʊtəkɑːʳ] *n Br* automobile *f*, voiture *f*.

motorcycle ['məʊtə,saɪkl] *n* moto *f*.

motorcyclist ['məʊtə,saɪklɪst] *n* motocycliste *mf*.

motoring ['məʊtərɪŋ] ◆ *adj Br* (*magazine, correspondent*) automobile. ◆ *n* tourisme *m* automobile.

motorist ['məʊtərɪst] *n* automobiliste *mf*.

motor racing *n* (U) course *f* automobile.

motor scooter *n* scooter *m*.

motor vehicle *n* véhicule *m* automobile.

motorway ['məʊtəweɪ] *Br n* autoroute *f*.

mottled ['mɒtld] *adj* (*leaf*) tacheté(e); (*skin*) marbré(e).

motto ['mɒtəʊ] (*pl* **-s** OR **-es**) *n* devise *f*.

mould, mold *Am* [məʊld] ◆ *n* **1.** (*growth*) moisissure *f*. **2.** (*shape*) moule *m*. ◆ *vt* **1.** (*shape*) mouler, modeler. **2.** *fig* (*influence*) former, façonner.

moulding, molding *Am* ['məʊldɪŋ] *n* (*decoration*) moulure *f*.

mouldy, moldy *Am* ['məʊldɪ] *adj* moisi(e).

moult, molt *Am* [məʊlt] *vi* muer.

mound [maʊnd] *n* **1.** (*small hill*) tertre *m*, butte *f*. **2.** (*pile*) tas *m*, monceau *m*.

mount [maʊnt] ◆ *n* **1.** (*support - for jewel*) monture *f*; (*- for photograph*) carton *m* de montage; (*- for machine*) support *m*. **2.** (*horse*) monture *f*. **3.** (*mountain*) mont *m*. ◆ *vt* monter; **to ~ a horse** monter sur un cheval; **to ~ a bike** monter sur OR enfourcher un vélo. ◆ *vi* **1.** (*increase*) monter, augmenter. **2.** (*climb on horse*) se mettre en selle.

mountain ['maʊntɪn] *n* montagne *f*.

mountain bike *n* VTT *m*.

mountaineer [,maʊntɪ'nɪəʳ] *n* alpiniste *mf*.

mountaineering [,maʊntɪ'nɪərɪŋ] *n* alpinisme *m*.

mountainous ['maʊntɪnəs] *adj* (*region*) montagneux(euse).

mounted police ['maʊntɪd-] *n*: **the ~** la police montée.

mourn [mɔːn] ◆ *vt* pleurer. ◆ *vi*: **to ~ (for sb)** pleurer (qqn).

mourner ['mɔːnəʳ] *n* (*related*) parent *m* du défunt; (*unrelated*) ami *m*, -e *f* du défunt.

mournful ['mɔːnfʊl] *adj* (*face*) triste; (*sound*) lugubre.

mourning ['mɔːnɪŋ] *n* deuil *m*; **in ~** en deuil.

mouse [maʊs] (*pl* **mice**) *n* (COMPUT & ZOOL) souris *f*.

mousetrap ['maʊstræp] *n* souricière *f*.

mousse [muːs] *n* mousse *f*.

moustache *Br* [mə'stɑːʃ], **mustache** *Am* ['mʌstæʃ] *n* moustache *f*.

mouth [maʊθ] *n* **1.** (*of person, animal*) bouche *f*; (*of dog, cat, lion*) gueule *f*. **2.** (*of cave*) entrée *f*; (*of river*) embouchure *f*.

mouthful ['maʊθfʊl] *n* (*of food*) bouchée *f*; (*of drink*) gorgée *f*.

mouthorgan ['maʊθ,ɔːgən] *n* harmonica *m*.

mouthpiece ['maʊθpiːs] *n* **1.** (*of tele-*

phone) microphone *m*; (*of musical instrument*) bec *m*. **2.** (*spokesperson*) porteparole *m inv*.

mouthwash ['mauθwɒʃ] *n* eau *f* dentifrice.

mouth-watering [-,wɔːtərɪŋ] *adj* alléchant(e).

movable ['muːvəbl] *adj* mobile.

move [muːv] ◆ *n* **1.** (*movement*) mouvement *m*; **to get a ~ on** *inf* se remuer, se grouiller. **2.** (*change - of house*) déménagement *m*; (*- of job*) changement *m* d'emploi. **3.** (*in game - action*) coup *m*; (*- turn to play*) tour *m*; *fig* démarche *f*. ◆ *vt* **1.** (*shift*) déplacer, bouger. **2.** (*change - job, office*) changer de; **to ~ house** déménager. **3.** (*cause*): **to ~ sb to do sthg** inciter qqn à faire qqch. **4.** (*emotionally*) émouvoir. **5.** (*propose*): **to ~ sthg/that ...** proposer qqch/que ... ◆ *vi* **1.** (*shift*) bouger. **2.** (*act*) agir. **3.** (*to new house*) déménager; (*to new job*) changer d'emploi. ▶ **move about** *vi* **1.** (*fidget*) remuer. **2.** (*travel*) voyager. ▶ **move along** ◆ *vt sep* faire avancer. ◆ *vi* se déplacer; **the police asked him to ~ along** la police lui a demandé de circuler. ▶ **move around** *vi* = **move about**. ▶ **move away** *vi* (*leave*) partir. ▶ **move in** *vi* (*to house*) emménager. ▶ **move on** *vi* **1.** (*after stopping*) se remettre en route. **2.** (*in discussion*) changer de sujet. ▶ **move out** *vi* (*from house*) déménager. ▶ **move over** *vi* s'écarter, se pousser. ▶ **move up** *vi* (*on bench etc*) se déplacer.

moveable ['muːvəbl] = **movable**.

movement ['muːvmənt] *n* mouvement *m*.

movie ['muːvɪ] *n* film *m*.

movie camera *n* caméra *f*.

moving ['muːvɪŋ] *adj* **1.** (*emotionally*) émouvant(e), touchant(e). **2.** (*not fixed*) mobile.

mow [məʊ] (*pt* **-ed**, *pp* **-ed** OR **mown**) *vt* faucher; (*lawn*) tondre. ▶ **mow down** *vt sep* faucher.

mower ['məʊəʳ] *n* tondeuse *f* à gazon.

mown [məʊn] *pp* → **mow**.

mozzarella [,mɒtsə'relə] *n* mozzarelle *f*.

MP *n* **1.** (*abbr of* **Military Police**) PM. **2.** *Br* (*abbr of* **Member of Parliament**) ≃ député *m*.

mpg (*abbr of* **miles per gallon**) *n* miles au gallon.

mph (*abbr of* **miles per hour**) *n* miles à l'heure.

Mr ['mɪstəʳ] *n* Monsieur *m*; (*on letter*) M.

Mrs ['mɪsɪz] *n* Madame *f*; (*on letter*) Mme.

Ms [mɪz] *n* titre que les femmes peuvent utiliser au lieu de madame ou mademoiselle pour éviter la distinction entre les femmes mariées et les célibataires.

MS *n* (*abbr of* **multiple sclerosis**) SEP *f*.

MSc (*abbr of* **Master of Science**) *n* (*titulaire d'une*) maîtrise de sciences.

much [mʌtʃ] (*compar* **more**, *superl* **most**) ◆ *adj* beaucoup de; **there isn't ~ rice left** il ne reste pas beaucoup de riz; **as ~ money as ...** autant d'argent que ...; **too ~** trop de; **how ~ ...?** combien de ...?; **how ~ money do you earn?** tu gagnes combien? ◆ *pron* beaucoup; **I don't think ~ of his new house** sa nouvelle maison ne me plaît pas trop; **as ~ as** autant que; **too ~** trop; **how ~?** combien?; **I'm not ~ of a cook** je suis un piètre cuisinier; **so ~ for all my hard work** tout ce travail pour rien; **I thought as ~** c'est bien ce que je pensais. ◆ *adv* beaucoup; **I don't go out ~** je ne sors pas beaucoup OR souvent; **as ~ as** autant que; **thank you very ~** merci beaucoup; **without so ~ as ...** sans même ... ▶ **much as** *conj* bien que (+ subjunctive).

muck [mʌk] *n* (U) *inf* **1.** (*dirt*) saletés *fpl*. **2.** (*manure*) fumier *m*. ▶ **muck about**, **muck around** *Br inf* ◆ *vt sep*: **to ~ sb about** traiter qqn par-dessus OR pardessous la jambe. ◆ *vi* traîner. ▶ **muck up** *vt sep Br inf* gâcher.

mucky ['mʌkɪ] *adj* sale.

mucus ['mjuːkəs] *n* mucus *m*.

mud [mʌd] *n* boue *f*.

muddle ['mʌdl] ◆ *n* désordre *m*, fouillis *m*. ◆ *vt* **1.** (*papers*) mélanger. **2.** (*person*) embrouiller. ▶ **muddle along** *vi* se débrouiller tant bien que mal. ▶ **muddle through** *vi* se tirer d'affaire, s'en sortir tant bien que mal. ▶ **muddle up** *vt sep* mélanger.

muddy ['mʌdɪ] ◆ *adj* boueux(euse). ◆ *vt fig* embrouiller.

mudguard ['mʌdgɑːd] *n* garde-boue *m inv*.

mudslinging ['mʌd,slɪŋɪŋ] *n* (U) *fig* attaques *fpl*.

muesli ['mjuːzlɪ] *n Br* muesli *m*.

muff [mʌf] ◆ *n* manchon *m*. ◆ *vt inf* louper.

muffin ['mʌfɪn] *n* muffin *m*.

muffle ['mʌfl] *vt* étouffer.

mug [mʌg] ◆ *n* **1.** (*cup*) (grande) tasse

f. **2.** *inf (fool)* andouille *f.* ◆ *vt (attack)* agresser.

mugging ['mʌgɪŋ] *n* agression *f.*

muggy ['mʌgɪ] *adj* lourd(e), moite.

mule [mju:l] *n* mule *f.*

mull [mʌl] ▶ **mull over** *vt sep* ruminer, réfléchir à.

mulled [mʌld] *adj*: ~ **wine** vin *m* chaud.

multicoloured Br, **multicolored** Am ['mʌltɪˌkʌləd] *adj* multicolore.

multigym ['mʌltɪdʒɪm] *n* appareil *m* de musculation.

multilateral [ˌmʌltɪ'lætərəl] *adj* multilatéral(e).

multinational [ˌmʌltɪ'næʃənl] *n* multinationale *f.*

multiple ['mʌltɪpl] ◆ *adj* multiple. ◆ *n* multiple *m.*

multiple sclerosis [-sklɪ'rəʊsɪs] *n* sclérose *f* en plaques.

multiplex cinema ['mʌltɪpleks-] *n* grand cinéma *m* à plusieurs salles.

multiplication [ˌmʌltɪplɪ'keɪʃn] *n* multiplication *f.*

multiply ['mʌltɪplaɪ] ◆ *vt* multiplier. ◆ *vi* se multiplier.

multistorey Br, **multistory** Am [ˌmʌltɪ'stɔːrɪ] ◆ *adj* à étages. ◆ *n (car park)* parking *m* à étages.

multitude ['mʌltɪtjuːd] *n* multitude *f.*

mum [mʌm] Br *inf* ◆ *n* maman *f.* ◆ *adj*: **to keep** ~ ne pas piper mot.

mumble ['mʌmbl] *vt & vi* marmotter.

mummy ['mʌmɪ] *n* **1.** Br *inf (mother)* maman *f.* **2.** *(preserved body)* momie *f.*

mumps [mʌmps] *n (U)* oreillons *mpl.*

munch [mʌntʃ] *vt & vi* croquer.

mundane [mʌn'deɪn] *adj* banal(e), ordinaire.

municipal [mjuː'nɪsɪpl] *adj* municipal(e).

municipality [mjuːˌnɪsɪ'pælətɪ] *n* municipalité *f.*

mural ['mjʊərəl] *n* peinture *f* murale.

murder ['mɜːdər] ◆ *n* meurtre *m.* ◆ *vt* assassiner.

murderer ['mɜːdərər] *n* meurtrier *m*, assassin *m.*

murderous ['mɜːdərəs] *adj* meurtrier (ère).

murky ['mɜːkɪ] *adj* **1.** *(place)* sombre. **2.** *(water, past)* trouble.

murmur ['mɜːmər] ◆ *n* murmure *m*; (MED) souffle *m* au cœur. ◆ *vt & vi* murmurer.

muscle ['mʌsl] *n* muscle *m.* ▶ **muscle in** *vi* intervenir, s'immiscer.

muscular ['mʌskjʊlər] *adj* **1.** *(spasm,*

pain) musculaire. **2.** *(person)* musclé(e).

muse [mjuːz] ◆ *n* muse *f.* ◆ *vi* méditer, réfléchir.

museum [mjuː'ziːəm] *n* musée *m.*

mushroom ['mʌʃrʊm] ◆ *n* champignon *m.* ◆ *vi (organization, party)* se développer, grandir; *(houses)* proliférer.

music ['mjuːzɪk] *n* musique *f.*

musical ['mjuːzɪkl] ◆ *adj* **1.** *(event, voice)* musical(e). **2.** *(child)* doué(e) pour la musique, musicien(enne). ◆ *n* comédie *f* musicale.

musical instrument *n* instrument *m* de musique.

music centre *n* chaîne *f* compacte.

music hall *n* Br music-hall *m.*

musician [mjuː'zɪʃn] *n* musicien *m*, -enne *f.*

Muslim ['mʊzlɪm] ◆ *adj* musulman(e). ◆ *n* Musulman *m*, -e *f.*

muslin ['mʌzlɪn] *n* mousseline *f.*

mussel ['mʌsl] *n* moule *f.*

must [mʌst] ◆ *modal vb* **1.** *(expressing obligation)* devoir; **I** ~ **go** il faut que je m'en aille, je dois partir; **you** ~ **come and visit** il faut absolument que tu viennes nous voir. **2.** *(expressing likelihood)*: **they** ~ **have known** ils devaient le savoir. ◆ *n inf*: **a** ~ un must, un impératif.

mustache Am = **moustache**.

mustard ['mʌstəd] *n* moutarde *f.*

muster ['mʌstər] ◆ *vt* rassembler. ◆ *vi* se réunir, se rassembler.

mustn't ['mʌsnt] = **must not**.

must've ['mʌstəv] = **must have**.

musty ['mʌstɪ] *adj (smell)* de moisi; *(room)* qui sent le renfermé OR le moisi.

mute [mjuːt] ◆ *adj* muet(ette). ◆ *n* muet *m*, -ette *f.*

muted ['mjuːtɪd] *adj* **1.** *(colour)* sourd(e). **2.** *(reaction)* peu marqué(e); *(protest)* voilé(e).

mutilate ['mjuːtɪleɪt] *vt* mutiler.

mutiny ['mjuːtɪnɪ] ◆ *n* mutinerie *f.* ◆ *vi* se mutiner.

mutter ['mʌtər] ◆ *vt (threat, curse)* marmonner. ◆ *vi* marmotter, marmonner.

mutton ['mʌtn] *n* mouton *m.*

mutual ['mjuːtʃʊəl] *adj* **1.** *(feeling, help)* réciproque, mutuel(elle). **2.** *(friend, interest)* commun(e).

muzzle ['mʌzl] ◆ *n* **1.** *(of dog - mouth)* museau *m*; *(- guard)* muselière *f.* **2.** *(of gun)* gueule *f.* ◆ *vt lit & fig* museler.

MW *(abbr of medium wave)* PO.

my [maɪ] *poss adj* **1.** *(referring to oneself)* mon (ma), mes *(pl)*; ~ **dog** mon chien; ~

house ma maison; ~ **children** mes enfants; ~ **name is Joe/Sarah** je m'appelle Joe/Sarah; **it wasn't MY fault** ce n'était pas de ma faute à moi. **2.** (*in titles*): **yes, ~ Lord** oui, monsieur le comte/duc *etc.*

myriad ['mɪrɪəd] *literary* ♦ *adj* innombrable. ♦ *n* myriade *f.*

myself [maɪ'self] *pron* **1.** (*reflexive*) me; (*after prep*) moi. **2.** (*for emphasis*) moi-même; **I did it ~** je l'ai fait tout seul.

mysterious [mɪ'stɪərɪəs] *adj* mystérieux(euse).

mystery ['mɪstərɪ] *n* mystère *m.*

mystical ['mɪstɪkl] *adj* mystique.

mystified ['mɪstɪfaɪd] *adj* perplexe.

mystifying ['mɪstɪfaɪɪŋ] *adj* inexplicable, déconcertant(e).

mystique [mɪ'stiːk] *n* mystique *f.*

myth [mɪθ] *n* mythe *m.*

mythical ['mɪθɪkl] *adj* mythique.

mythology [mɪ'θɒlədʒɪ] *n* mythologie *f.*

N

n (*pl* **n's** OR **ns**), **N** (*pl* **N's** OR **Ns**) [en] *n* (*letter*) n *m inv*, N *m inv.* ▶ **N** (*abbr of* **north**) N.

n/a, N/A (*abbr of* **not applicable**) s.o.

nab [næb] *vt inf* **1.** (*arrest*) pincer. **2.** (*get quickly*) attraper, accaparer.

nag [næg] ♦ *vt* harceler. ♦ *n inf* (*horse*) canasson *m.*

nagging ['nægɪŋ] *adj* **1.** (*doubt*) persistant(e), tenace. **2.** (*husband, wife*) enquiquineur(euse).

nail [neɪl] ♦ *n* **1.** (*for fastening*) clou *m.* **2.** (*of finger, toe*) ongle *m.* ♦ *vt* clouer. ▶ **nail down** *vt sep* **1.** (*lid*) clouer. **2.** *fig* (*person*): **to ~ sb down to sthg** faire préciser qqch à qqn.

nailbrush ['neɪlbrʌʃ] *n* brosse *f* à ongles.

nail file *n* lime *f* à ongles.

nail polish *n* vernis *m* à ongles.

nail scissors *npl* ciseaux *mpl* à ongles.

nail varnish *n* vernis *m* à ongles.

nail varnish remover [-rɪ'muːvəʳ] *n* dissolvant *m.*

naive, naïve [naɪ'iːv] *adj* naïf(ïve).

naked ['neɪkɪd] *adj* **1.** (*body, flame*) nu(e); **with the ~ eye** à l'œil nu. **2.** (*emotions*) manifeste, évident(e); (*aggression*) non déguisé(e).

name [neɪm] ♦ *n* **1.** (*identification*) nom *m*; **what's your ~?** comment vous appelez-vous?; **to know sb by ~** connaître qqn de nom; **in my/his ~** à mon/son nom; **in the ~ of peace** au nom de la paix; **to call sb ~s** traiter qqn de tous les noms, injurier qqn. **2.** (*reputation*) réputation *f.* **3.** (*famous person*) grand nom *m*, célébrité *f.* ♦ *vt* **1.** (*gen*) nommer; **to ~ sb/sthg after** Br, **to ~ sb/sthg for** Am donner à qqn/à qqch le nom de. **2.** (*date, price*) fixer.

nameless ['neɪmlɪs] *adj* inconnu(e), sans nom; (*author*) anonyme.

namely ['neɪmlɪ] *adv* à savoir, c'est-à-dire.

namesake ['neɪmseɪk] *n* homonyme *m.*

nanny ['nænɪ] *n* nurse *f*, bonne *f* d'enfants.

nap [næp] ♦ *n*: **to have** OR **take a ~** faire un petit somme. ♦ *vi* faire un petit somme; **to be caught napping** *inf fig* être pris au dépourvu.

nape [neɪp] *n* nuque *f.*

napkin ['næpkɪn] *n* serviette *f.*

nappy ['næpɪ] *n* Br couche *f.*

nappy liner *n* change *m* (jetable).

narcissi [nɑː'sɪsaɪ] *pl* → **narcissus**.

narcissus [nɑː'sɪsəs] (*pl* **-cissuses** OR **-cissi**) *n* narcisse *m.*

narcotic [nɑː'kɒtɪk] *n* stupéfiant *m.*

narrative ['nærətɪv] ♦ *adj* narratif (ive). ♦ *n* **1.** (*story*) récit *m*, narration *f.* **2.** (*skill*) art *m* de la narration.

narrator [Br nə'reɪtəʳ, Am 'næreɪtər] *n* narrateur *m*, -trice *f.*

narrow ['nærəʊ] ♦ *adj* **1.** (*gen*) étroit(e); **to have a ~ escape** l'échapper belle. **2.** (*victory, majority*) de justesse. ♦ *vt* **1.** (*reduce*) réduire, limiter. **2.** (*eyes*) fermer à demi, plisser. ♦ *vi lit & fig* se rétrécir. ▶ **narrow down** *vt sep* réduire, limiter.

narrowly ['nærəʊlɪ] *adv* **1.** (*win, lose*) de justesse. **2.** (*miss*) de peu.

narrow-minded [-'maɪndɪd] *adj* (*person*) à l'esprit étroit, borné(e); (*attitude*) étroit(e), borné(e).

nasal ['neɪzl] *adj* nasal(e).

nasty ['nɑːstɪ] *adj* **1.** (*unpleasant - smell, feeling*) mauvais(e); (*- weather*) vilain(e), mauvais(e). **2.** (*unkind*) méchant(e). **3.** (*problem*) difficile, délicat(e). **4.** (*in-*

jury) vilain(e); (*accident*) grave; (*fall*) mauvais(e).

nation ['neɪʃn] *n* nation *f.*

national ['næʃənl] ◆ *adj* national(e); (*campaign, strike*) à l'échelon national; (*custom*) du pays, de la nation. ◆ *n* ressortissant *m*, -e *f.*

national anthem *n* hymne *m* national.

national dress *n* costume *m* national.

National Health Service *n*: **the ~** *le service national de santé britannique.*

National Insurance *n* (U) Br **1.** (*system*) système *m* de sécurité sociale (*maladie, retraite*) et d'assurance chômage. **2.** (*payment*) ≃ contributions *fpl* à la Sécurité sociale.

nationalism ['næʃnəlɪzm] *n* nationalisme *m.*

nationalist ['næʃnəlɪst] ◆ *adj* nationaliste. ◆ *n* nationaliste *mf.*

nationality [,næʃə'nælətɪ] *n* nationalité *f.*

nationalize, -ise ['næʃnəlaɪz] *vt* nationaliser.

national park *n* parc *m* national.

national service *n* Br (MIL) service *m* national OR militaire.

National Trust *n* Br: **the ~** *organisme non gouvernemental assurant la conservation de certains sites et monuments historiques.*

nationwide ['neɪʃənwaɪd] ◆ *adj* dans tout le pays; (*campaign, strike*) à l'échelon national. ◆ *adv* à travers tout le pays.

native ['neɪtɪv] ◆ *adj* **1.** (*country, area*) natal(e). **2.** (*language*) maternel(elle); **an English ~ speaker** une personne de langue maternelle anglaise. **3.** (*plant, animal*) indigène; **~ to** originaire de. ◆ *n* autochtone *mf*; (*of colony*) indigène *mf.*

Native American *n* Indien *m*, -enne *f* d'Amérique, Amérindien *m*, -enne *f.*

Nativity [nə'tɪvətɪ] *n*: **the ~** la Nativité.

NATO ['neɪtəʊ] (*abbr of* North Atlantic Treaty Organization) *n* OTAN *f.*

natural ['nætʃrəl] *adj* **1.** (*gen*) naturel (elle). **2.** (*instinct, talent*) inné(e). **3.** (*footballer, musician*) né(e).

natural gas *n* gaz *m* naturel.

natural history *n* histoire *f* naturelle.

naturalize, -ise ['nætʃrəlaɪz] *vt* naturaliser; **to be ~d** se faire naturaliser.

naturally ['nætʃrəlɪ] *adv* **1.** (*gen*) naturellement. **2.** (*unaffectedly*) sans affectation, avec naturel.

natural wastage *n* (U) départs *mpl* volontaires.

nature ['neɪtʃər] *n* nature *f*; **by ~** (*basically*) par essence; (*by disposition*) de nature, naturellement.

nature reserve *n* réserve *f* naturelle.

naughty ['nɔːtɪ] *adj* **1.** (*badly behaved*) vilain(e), méchant(e). **2.** (*rude*) grivois(e).

nausea ['nɔːsjə] *n* nausée *f.*

nauseam ['nɔːzɪæm] → **ad nauseam.**

nauseating ['nɔːsɪeɪtɪŋ] *adj* lit & fig écœurant(e).

nautical ['nɔːtɪkl] *adj* nautique.

naval ['neɪvl] *adj* naval(e).

nave [neɪv] *n* nef *f.*

navel ['neɪvl] *n* nombril *m.*

navigate ['nævɪgeɪt] ◆ *vt* **1.** (*plane*) piloter; (*ship*) gouverner. **2.** (*seas, river*) naviguer sur. ◆ *vi* (AERON & NAUT) naviguer; (AUT) lire la carte.

navigation [,nævɪ'geɪʃn] *n* navigation *f.*

navigator ['nævɪgeɪtər] *n* navigateur *m.*

navvy ['nævɪ] *n* Br inf terrassier *m.*

navy ['neɪvɪ] ◆ *n* marine *f.* ◆ *adj* (*in colour*) bleu marine (*inv*).

navy blue ◆ *adj* bleu marine (*inv*). ◆ *n* bleu *m* marine.

Nazareth ['næzərɪθ] *n* Nazareth.

Nazi ['nɑːtsɪ] (*pl* **-s**) ◆ *adj* nazi(e). ◆ *n* Nazi *m*, -e *f.*

NB (*abbr of* nota bene) NB.

near [nɪər] ◆ *adj* proche; **a ~ disaster** une catastrophe évitée de justesse OR de peu; **in the ~ future** dans un proche avenir, dans un avenir prochain; **it was a ~ thing** il était moins cinq. ◆ *adv* **1.** (*close*) près. **2.** (*almost*): **~ impossible** presque impossible; **nowhere ~ ready/ enough** loin d'être prêt/assez. ◆ *prep*: **~ (to)** (*in space*) près de; (*in time*) près de, vers; **~ to tears** au bord des larmes; **~ (to) death** sur le point de mourir; **~ (to) the truth** proche de la vérité. ◆ *vt* approcher de. ◆ *vi* approcher.

nearby [nɪə'baɪ] ◆ *adj* proche. ◆ *adv* tout près, à proximité.

nearly ['nɪəlɪ] *adv* presque; **I ~ fell** j'ai failli tomber; **not ~ enough/as good** loin d'être suffisant/aussi bon.

near miss *n* **1.** (SPORT) coup *m* qui a raté de peu. **2.** (*between planes, vehicles*) quasi-collision *f.*

nearside ['nɪəsaɪd] *n* (*right-hand drive*) côté *m* gauche; (*left-hand drive*) côté droit.

nearsighted [,nɪə'saɪtɪd] *adj* Am myope.

neat [niːt] *adj* **1.** (*room, house*) bien

tenu(e), en ordre; (work) soigné(e); (handwriting) net (nette); (appearance) soigné(e), net (nette). **2.** (solution, manoeuvre) habile, ingénieux(euse). **3.** (alcohol) pur(e), sans eau. **4.** Am inf (very good) chouette, super (inv).

neatly ['niːtlɪ] adv **1.** (arrange) avec ordre; (write) soigneusement; (dress) avec soin. **2.** (skilfully) habilement, adroitement.

nebulous ['nebjʊləs] adj nébuleux (euse).

necessarily [Br 'nesəsrəlɪ, ˌnesə'serɪlɪ] adv forcément, nécessairement.

necessary ['nesəsrɪ] adj **1.** (required) nécessaire, indispensable; **to make the ~ arrangements** faire le nécessaire. **2.** (inevitable) inévitable, inéluctable.

necessity [nɪ'sesətɪ] n nécessité f; **of ~** inévitablement, fatalement.

neck [nek] ◆ n **1.** (ANAT) cou m. **2.** (of shirt, dress) encolure f. **3.** (of bottle) col m, goulot m. ◆ vi inf se bécoter.

necklace ['neklɪs] n collier m.

neckline ['neklaɪn] n encolure f.

necktie ['nektaɪ] n Am cravate f.

nectarine ['nektərɪn] n brugnon m, nectarine f.

need [niːd] ◆ n besoin m; **there's no ~ to get up** ce n'est pas la peine de te lever; **there's no ~ for such language** tu n'as pas besoin d'être grossier; **~ for sthg/to do sthg** besoin de qqch/de faire qqch; **to be in** OR **have ~ of sthg** avoir besoin de qqch; **if ~ be** si besoin est, si nécessaire; **in ~** dans le besoin. ◆ vt **1.** (require): **to ~ sthg/to do sthg** avoir besoin de qqch/de faire qqch; **I ~ to go to the doctor** il faut que j'aille chez le médecin. **2.** (be obliged): **to ~ to do sthg** être obligé(e) de faire qqch. ◆ modal vb: **~ we go?** faut-il qu'on y aille?; **it ~ not happen** cela ne doit pas forcément se produire.

needle ['niːdl] ◆ n **1.** (gen) aiguille f. **2.** (stylus) saphir m. ◆ vt inf (annoy) asticoter, lancer des piques à.

needless ['niːdlɪs] adj (risk, waste) inutile; (remark) déplacé(e); **~ to say ...** bien entendu …

needlework ['niːdlwɜːk] n **1.** (embroidery) travail m d'aiguille. **2.** (U) (activity) couture f.

needn't ['niːdnt] = **need not**.

needy ['niːdɪ] adj nécessiteux(euse), indigent(e).

negative ['negətɪv] ◆ adj négatif(ive).

◆ n **1.** (PHOT) négatif m. **2.** (LING) négation f.

neglect [nɪ'glekt] ◆ n (of garden) mauvais entretien m; (of children) manque m de soins; (of duty) manquement m. ◆ vt négliger; (garden) laisser à l'abandon; **to ~ to do sthg** négliger OR omettre de faire qqch.

neglectful [nɪ'glektfʊl] adj négligent(e).

negligee ['neglɪʒeɪ] n déshabillé m, négligé m.

negligence ['neglɪdʒəns] n négligence f.

negligible ['neglɪdʒəbl] adj négligeable.

negotiable [nɪ'gəʊʃjəbl] adj négociable; **'price ~'** 'prix à débattre'.

negotiate [nɪ'gəʊʃɪeɪt] ◆ vt **1.** (COMM & POL) négocier. **2.** (obstacle) franchir; (bend) prendre, négocier. ◆ vi négocier; **to ~ with sb (for sthg)** engager des négociations avec qqn (pour obtenir qqch).

negotiation [nɪˌgəʊʃɪ'eɪʃn] n négociation f.

Negress ['niːgrɪs] n négresse f (attention: le terme 'Negress' est considéré raciste).

Negro ['niːgrəʊ] (pl -es) ◆ adj noir(e). ◆ n Noir m (attention: le terme 'Negro' est considéré raciste).

neigh [neɪ] vi (horse) hennir.

neighbour Br, **neighbor** Am ['neɪbər] n voisin m, -e f.

neighbourhood Br, **neighborhood** Am ['neɪbəhʊd] n **1.** (of town) voisinage m, quartier m. **2.** (approximate figure): **in the ~ of £300** environ 300 livres, dans les 300 livres.

neighbouring Br, **neighboring** Am ['neɪbərɪŋ] adj avoisinant(e).

neighbourly Br, **neighborly** Am ['neɪbəlɪ] adj bon voisin (bonne voisine).

neither ['naɪðər, 'niːðər] ◆ adv: **~ good nor bad** ni bon ni mauvais; **that's ~ here nor there** cela n'a rien à voir. ◆ pron & adj ni l'un ni l'autre (ni l'une ni l'autre). ◆ conj: **~ do I** moi non plus.

neon ['niːɒn] n néon m.

neon light n néon m, lumière f au néon.

nephew ['nefjuː] n neveu m.

Neptune ['neptjuːn] n (planet) Neptune f.

nerve [nɜːv] n **1.** (ANAT) nerf m. **2.** (courage) courage m, sang-froid m; **to lose one's ~** se dégonfler, flancher. **3.** (cheek) culot m, toupet m. ▶ **nerves**

npl nerfs *mpl*; **to get on sb's ~s** taper sur les nerfs OR le système de qqn.

nerve-racking [-ˌrækɪŋ] *adj* angoissant(e), éprouvant(e).

nervous ['nɜːvəs] *adj* 1. *(gen)* nerveux (euse). 2. *(apprehensive - smile, person etc)* inquiet(ète); *(- performer)* qui a le trac; **to be ~ about sthg** appréhender qqch.

nervous breakdown *n* dépression *f* nerveuse.

nest [nest] ◆ *n* nid *m*; **~ of tables** table *f* gigogne. ◆ *vi* *(bird)* faire son nid, nicher.

nest egg *n* pécule *m*, bas *m* de laine.

nestle ['nesl] *vi* se blottir.

net [net] ◆ *adj* net (nette); **~ result** résultat final. ◆ *n* 1. *(gen)* filet *m*. 2. *(fabric)* voile *m*, tulle *m*. ◆ *vt* 1. *(fish)* prendre au filet. 2. *(money - subj: person)* toucher net, gagner net; *(- subj: deal)* rapporter net.

Net [net] *n* (COMPUT): **the ~** le Net; **to surf the ~** surfer sur le Net.

netball ['netbɔːl] *n* netball *m*.

net curtains *npl* voilage *m*.

Netherlands ['neðələndz] *npl*: **the ~** les Pays-Bas *mpl*.

net profit *n* bénéfice *m* net.

net revenue *n* Am chiffre *m* d'affaires.

nett [net] *adj* = **net**.

netting ['netɪŋ] *n* 1. *(metal, plastic)* grillage *m*. 2. *(fabric)* voile *m*, tulle *m*.

nettle ['netl] *n* ortie *f*.

network ['netwɜːk] ◆ *n* réseau *m*. ◆ *vt* (RADIO & TV) diffuser.

neurosis [ˌnjʊəˈrəʊsɪs] *(pl* -ses) *n* névrose *f*.

neurotic [ˌnjʊəˈrɒtɪk] ◆ *adj* névrosé(e). ◆ *n* névrosé *m*, -e *f*.

neuter ['njuːtər] ◆ *adj* neutre. ◆ *vt* *(cat)* châtrer.

neutral ['njuːtrəl] ◆ *adj* *(gen)* neutre. ◆ *n* (AUT) point *m* mort.

neutrality [njuːˈtrælətɪ] *n* neutralité *f*.

neutralize, -ise ['njuːtrəlaɪz] *vt* neutraliser.

never ['nevər] *adv* jamais … ne, ne … jamais; **~ ever** jamais, au grand jamais; **well I ~!** ça par exemple!

never-ending *adj* interminable.

nevertheless [ˌnevəðəˈles] *adv* néanmoins, pourtant.

new [*adj* njuː, *n* njuːz] *adj* 1. *(gen)* nouveau(elle). 2. *(not used)* neuf (neuve); **as good as ~** comme neuf. ▶ **news** *n* (U) 1. *(information)* nouvelle *f*; **a piece of ~s** une nouvelle; **that's ~s to me** première nouvelle. 2. (RADIO) informations

fpl. 3. (TV) journal *m* télévisé, actualités *fpl*.

newborn ['njuːbɔːn] *adj* nouveau-né(e).

newcomer ['njuːˌkʌmər] *n*: **~ (to sthg)** nouveau-venu *m*, nouvelle-venue *f* (dans qqch).

newfangled [ˌnjuːˈfæŋgld] *adj inf pej* ultramoderne, trop moderne.

new-found *adj* récent(e), de fraîche date.

newly ['njuːlɪ] *adv* récemment, fraîchement.

newlyweds ['njuːlɪwedz] *npl* nouveaux OR jeunes mariés *mpl*.

new moon *n* nouvelle lune *f*.

news agency *n* agence *f* de presse.

newsagent Br ['njuːzeɪdʒənt], **newsdealer** Am ['njuːzdiːlər] *n* marchand *m* de journaux.

newscaster ['njuːzkɑːstər] *n* présentateur *m*, -trice *f*.

newsdealer Am = **newsagent**.

newsflash ['njuːzflæʃ] *n* flash *m* d'information.

newsletter ['njuːzˌletər] *n* bulletin *m*.

newspaper ['njuːzˌpeɪpər] *n* journal *m*.

newsreader ['njuːzˌriːdər] *n* présentateur *m*, -trice *f*.

newsreel ['njuːzriːl] *n* actualités *fpl* filmées.

newsstand ['njuːzstænd] *n* kiosque *m* à journaux.

newt [njuːt] *n* triton *m*.

new town *n* Br ville *f* nouvelle.

New Year *n* nouvel an *m*, nouvelle année *f*; **Happy ~!** bonne année!

New Year's Day *n* jour *m* de l'an, premier *m* de l'an.

New Year's Eve *n* la Saint-Sylvestre.

New York [-'jɔːk] *n* 1. *(city)*: **~ (City)** New York. 2. *(state)*: **~ (State)** l'État *m* de New York.

New Zealand [-'ziːlənd] *n* Nouvelle-Zélande *f*.

New Zealander [-'ziːləndər] *n* Néo-Zélandais *m*, -e *f*.

next [nekst] ◆ *adj* prochain(e); *(room)* d'à côté; *(page)* suivant(e); **~ Tuesday** mardi prochain; **~ time** la prochaine fois; **~ week** la semaine prochaine; **the ~ week** la semaine suivante OR d'après; **~ year** l'année prochaine; **~, please!** au suivant!; **the day after ~** le surlendemain; **the week after ~** dans deux semaines. ◆ *adv* 1. *(afterwards)* ensuite, après. 2. *(again)* la prochaine fois. 3. *(with superlatives)*: **he's the ~ biggest**

after Dan c'est le plus grand après OR à part Dan. ◆ *prep* Am à côté de. ► **next to** *prep* à côté de; **it cost ~ to nothing** cela a coûté une bagatelle OR trois fois rien; **I know ~ to nothing** je ne sais presque OR pratiquement rien.

next door *adv* à côté. ► **next-door** *adj*: **next-door neighbour** voisin *m*, -e *f* d'à côté.

next of kin *n* plus proche parent *m*.

NHS (*abbr of* **National Health Service**) *n* service national de santé en Grande-Bretagne, ≃ sécurité sociale *f*.

NI *n abbr of* **National Insurance**.

nib [nɪb] *n* plume *f*.

nibble ['nɪbl] *vt* grignoter, mordiller.

Nicaragua [ˌnɪkə'rægjuə] *n* Nicaragua *m*.

nice [naɪs] *adj* 1. (*holiday, food*) bon (bonne); (*day, picture*) beau (belle); (*dress*) joli(e). 2. (*person*) gentil(ille), sympathique; **to be ~ to sb** être gentil OR aimable avec qqn.

nice-looking [-'lʊkɪŋ] *adj* joli(e), beau (belle).

nicely ['naɪslɪ] *adv* 1. (*made, manage etc*) bien; (*dressed*) joliment; **that will do ~** cela fera très bien l'affaire. 2. (*politely - ask*) poliment, gentiment; (*- behave*) bien.

niche [niːʃ] *n* (*in wall*) niche *f*; *fig* bonne situation *f*, voie *f*.

nick [nɪk] ◆ *n* 1. (*cut*) entaille *f*, coupure *f*. 2. Br *inf* (*condition*): **in good/bad ~** en bon/mauvais état. 3. *phr*: **in the ~ of time** juste à temps. ◆ *vt* 1. (*cut*) couper, entailler. 2. Br *inf* (*steal*) piquer, faucher. 3. Br *inf* (*arrest*) pincer, choper.

nickel ['nɪkl] *n* 1. (*metal*) nickel *m*. 2. Am (*coin*) pièce *f* de cinq cents.

nickname ['nɪkneɪm] ◆ *n* sobriquet *m*, surnom *m*. ◆ *vt* surnommer.

nicotine ['nɪkətiːn] *n* nicotine *f*.

niece [niːs] *n* nièce *f*.

Nigeria [naɪ'dʒɪərɪə] *n* Nigeria *m*.

Nigerian [naɪ'dʒɪərɪən] ◆ *adj* nigérian(e). ◆ *n* Nigérian *m*, -e *f*.

niggle ['nɪgl] *vt* Br 1. (*worry*) tracasser. 2. (*criticize*) faire des réflexions à, critiquer.

night [naɪt] *n* 1. (*not day*) nuit *f*; **at ~** la nuit. 2. (*evening*) soir *m*; **at ~** le soir. 3. *phr*: **to have an early ~** se coucher de bonne heure; **to have a late ~** veiller, se coucher tard. ► **nights** *adv* 1. Am (*at night*) la nuit. 2. Br (*nightshift*): **to work ~s** travailler OR être de nuit.

nightcap ['naɪtkæp] *n* (*drink*) boisson

alcoolisée prise avant de se coucher.

nightclub ['naɪtklʌb] *n* boîte *f* de nuit, night-club *m*.

nightdress ['naɪtdres] *n* chemise *f* de nuit.

nightfall ['naɪtfɔːl] *n* tombée *f* de la nuit OR du jour.

nightgown ['naɪtgaʊn] *n* chemise *f* de nuit.

nightie ['naɪtɪ] *n inf* chemise *f* de nuit.

nightingale ['naɪtɪŋgeɪl] *n* rossignol *m*.

nightlife ['naɪtlaɪf] *n* vie *f* nocturne, activités *fpl* nocturnes.

nightly ['naɪtlɪ] ◆ *adj* (de) toutes les nuits OR tous les soirs. ◆ *adv* toutes les nuits, tous les soirs.

nightmare ['naɪtmeəʳ] *n lit & fig* cauchemar *m*.

night porter *n* veilleur *m* de nuit.

night school *n* (U) cours *mpl* du soir.

night shift *n* (*period*) poste *m* de nuit.

nightshirt ['naɪtʃɜːt] *n* chemise *f* de nuit d'homme.

nighttime ['naɪttaɪm] *n* nuit *f*.

nil [nɪl] *n* néant *m*; Br (SPORT) zéro *m*.

Nile [naɪl] *n*: **the ~** le Nil.

nimble ['nɪmbl] *adj* agile, leste.

nine [naɪn] *num* neuf; *see also* **six**.

nineteen [ˌnaɪn'tiːn] *num* dix-neuf; *see also* **six**.

ninety ['naɪntɪ] *num* quatre-vingt-dix; *see also* **sixty**.

ninth [naɪnθ] *num* neuvième; *see also* **sixth**.

nip [nɪp] ◆ *n* 1. (*pinch*) pinçon *m*; (*bite*) morsure *f*. 2. (*of drink*) goutte *f*, doigt *m*. ◆ *vt* (*pinch*) pincer; (*bite*) mordre.

nipple ['nɪpl] *n* 1. (ANAT) bout *m* de sein, mamelon *m*. 2. (*of bottle*) tétine *f*.

nit [nɪt] *n* 1. (*in hair*) lente *f*. 2. Br *inf* (*idiot*) idiot *m*, -e *f*, crétin *m*, -e *f*.

nitpicking ['nɪtpɪkɪŋ] *n inf* ergotage *m*, pinaillage *m*.

nitrogen ['naɪtrədʒən] *n* azote *m*.

nitty-gritty [ˌnɪtɪ'grɪtɪ] *n inf*: **to get down to the ~** en venir à l'essentiel OR aux choses sérieuses.

no [nəʊ] (*pl* **-es**) ◆ *adv* 1. (*gen*) non; (*expressing disagreement*) mais non. 2. (*not any*): **~ bigger/smaller** pas plus grand/petit; **~ better** pas mieux. ◆ *adj* aucun(e), pas de; **there's ~ telling what will happen** impossible de dire ce qui va se passer; **he's ~ friend of mine** je ne le compte pas parmi mes amis. ◆ *n* non *m*; **she won't take ~ for an answer** elle n'accepte pas de refus.

No., no. (*abbr of* **number**) No, no.

nobility [nə'bɪlətɪ] *n* noblesse *f*.

noble ['nəʊbl] ◆ *adj* noble. ◆ *n* noble *m*.

nobody ['nəʊbədɪ] ◆ *pron* personne, aucun(e). ◆ *n pej* rien-du-tout *mf*, moins que rien *mf*.

nocturnal [nɒk'tɜ:nl] *adj* nocturne.

nod [nɒd] ◆ *vt*: **to ~ one's head** incliner la tête, faire un signe de tête. ◆ *vi* **1.** (*in agreement*) faire un signe de tête affirmatif, faire signe que oui. **2.** (*to indicate sthg*) faire un signe de tête. **3.** (*as greeting*): **to ~ to sb** saluer qqn d'un signe de tête. ▶ **nod off** *vi* somnoler, s'assoupir.

noise [nɔɪz] *n* bruit *m*.

noisy ['nɔɪzɪ] *adj* bruyant(e).

no-man's-land *n* no man's land *m*.

nominal ['nɒmɪnl] *adj* **1.** (*in name only*) de nom seulement, nominal(e). **2.** (*very small*) nominal(e), insignifiant(e).

nominate ['nɒmɪneɪt] *vt* **1.** (*propose*): **to ~ sb (for/as sthg)** proposer qqn (pour/comme qqch). **2.** (*appoint*): **to ~ sb (as sthg)** nommer qqn (qqch); **to ~ sb (to sthg)** nominer qqn (à qqch).

nominee [,nɒmɪ'ni:] *n* personne *f* nommée OR désignée.

non- [nɒn] *prefix* non-.

nonalcoholic [,nɒnælkə'hɒlɪk] *adj* non-alcoolisé(e).

nonaligned [,nɒnə'laɪnd] *adj* non-aligné(e).

nonchalant [Br 'nɒnʃələnt, Am ,nɒnʃə'lɑ:nt] *adj* nonchalant(e).

noncommittal [,nɒnkə'mɪtl] *adj* évasif (ive).

nonconformist [,nɒnkən'fɔ:mɪst] ◆ *adj* non-conformiste. ◆ *n* non-conformiste *mf*.

nondescript [Br 'nɒndɪskrɪpt, Am ,nɒndɪ'skrɪpt] *adj* quelconque, terne.

none [nʌn] ◆ *pron* **1.** (*gen*) aucun(e); **there was ~ left** il n'y en avait plus, il n'en restait plus; **I'll have ~ of your nonsense** je ne tolérerai pas de bêtises de ta part. **2.** (*nobody*) personne, nul (nulle). ◆ *adv*: **~ the worse/wiser** pas plus mal/avancé; **~ the better** pas mieux. ▶ **none too** *adv* pas tellement OR trop.

nonentity [nɒ'nentətɪ] *n* nullité *f*, zéro *m*.

nonetheless [,nʌnðə'les] *adv* néanmoins, pourtant.

non-event *n* événement *m* raté OR décevant.

nonexistent [,nɒnɪg'zɪstənt] *adj* inexistant(e).

nonfiction [,nɒn'fɪkʃn] *n* (U) ouvrages *mpl* généraux.

no-nonsense *adj* direct(e), sérieux (euse).

nonpayment [,nɒn'peɪmənt] *n* non-paiement *m*.

nonplussed, nonplused Am [,nɒn-'plʌst] *adj* déconcerté(e), perplexe.

nonreturnable [,nɒnrɪ'tɜ:nəbl] *adj* (*bottle*) non consigné(e).

nonsense ['nɒnsəns] ◆ *n* (U) **1.** (*meaningless words*) charabia *m*. **2.** (*foolish idea*): **it was ~ to suggest ...** il était absurde de suggérer ... **3.** (*foolish behaviour*) bêtises *fpl*, idioties *fpl*; **to make (a) ~ of sthg** gâcher OR saboter qqch. ◆ *excl* quelles bêtises OR foutaises!

nonsensical [nɒn'sensɪkl] *adj* absurde, qui n'a pas de sens.

nonsmoker [,nɒn'sməʊkər] *n* non-fumeur *m*, -euse *f*, personne *f* qui ne fume pas.

nonstick [,nɒn'stɪk] *adj* qui n'attache pas, téflonisé(e).

nonstop [,nɒn'stɒp] ◆ *adj* (*flight*) direct(e), sans escale; (*activity*) continu (e); (*rain*) continuel(elle). ◆ *adv* (*talk, work*) sans arrêt; (*rain*) sans discontinuer.

noodles ['nu:dlz] *npl* nouilles *fpl*.

nook [nʊk] *n* (*of room*) coin *m*, recoin *m*; **every ~ and cranny** tous les coins, les coins et les recoins.

noon [nu:n] *n* midi *m*.

no one *pron* = **nobody**.

noose [nu:s] *n* nœud *m* coulant.

no-place Am = **nowhere**.

nor [nɔ:r] *conj*: **~ do I** moi non plus; → **neither**.

norm [nɔ:m] *n* norme *f*.

normal ['nɔ:ml] *adj* normal(e).

normality [nɔ:'mælɪtɪ], **normalcy** Am ['nɔ:mlsɪ] *n* normalité *f*.

normally ['nɔ:məlɪ] *adv* normalement.

Normandy ['nɔ:məndɪ] *n* Normandie *f*.

north [nɔ:θ] ◆ *n* **1.** (*direction*) nord *m*. **2.** (*region*): **the ~** le nord. ◆ *adj* nord (*inv*); (*wind*) du nord. ◆ *adv* au nord, vers le nord; **~ of** au nord de.

North Africa *n* Afrique *f* du Nord.

North America *n* Amérique *f* du Nord.

North American ◆ *adj* nord-américain(e). ◆ *n* Nord-Américain *m*, -e *f*.

northeast [ˌnɔːθˈiːst] ◆ n **1.** (direction) nord-est m. **2.** (region): **the ~** le nord-est. ◆ adj nord-est (inv); (wind) du nord-est. ◆ adv au nord-est, vers le nord-est; **~ of** au nord-est de.

northerly [ˈnɔːðəlɪ] adj du nord; **in a ~ direction** vers le nord, en direction du nord.

northern [ˈnɔːðən] adj du nord, nord (inv).

Northern Ireland n Irlande f du Nord.

northernmost [ˈnɔːðənməʊst] adj le plus au nord (la plus au nord), à l'extrême nord.

North Korea n Corée f du Nord.

North Pole n: **the ~** le pôle Nord.

North Sea n: **the ~** la mer du Nord.

northward [ˈnɔːθwəd] ◆ adj au nord. ◆ adv = **northwards**.

northwards [ˈnɔːθwədz] adv au nord, vers le nord.

northwest [ˌnɔːθˈwest] ◆ n **1.** (direction) nord-ouest m. **2.** (region): **the ~** le nord-ouest. ◆ adj nord-ouest (inv); (wind) du nord-ouest. ◆ adv au nord-ouest, vers le nord-ouest; **~ of** au nord-ouest de.

Norway [ˈnɔːweɪ] n Norvège f.

Norwegian [nɔːˈwiːdʒən] ◆ adj norvégien(enne). ◆ n **1.** (person) Norvégien m, -enne f. **2.** (language) norvégien m.

nose [nəʊz] n nez m; **keep your ~ out of my business** occupe-toi OR mêle-toi de tes affaires, occupe-toi OR mêle-toi de tes oignons; **to look down one's ~ at sb** fig traiter qqn de haut (en bas); **to look down one's ~ at sthg** fig considérer qqch avec mépris; **to poke** OR **stick one's ~ into sthg** mettre OR fourrer son nez dans qqch; **to turn up one's ~ at sthg** dédaigner qqch. ▶ **nose about, nose around** vi fouiner, fureter.

nosebleed [ˈnəʊzbliːd] n: **to have a ~** saigner du nez.

nosedive [ˈnəʊzdaɪv] ◆ n (of plane) piqué m. ◆ vi **1.** (plane) descendre en piqué, piquer du nez. **2.** fig (prices) dégringoler; (hopes) s'écrouler.

nosey [ˈnəʊzɪ] = **nosy**.

nostalgia [nɒˈstældʒə] n: **~ (for sthg)** nostalgie f (de qqch).

nostril [ˈnɒstrəl] n narine f.

nosy [ˈnəʊzɪ] adj curieux(euse), fouinard(e).

not [nɒt] adv ne pas, pas; **I think ~** je ne crois pas; **I'm afraid ~** je crains que

non; **~ always** pas toujours; **~ that ...** ce n'est pas que ..., non pas que ...; **~ at all** (no) pas du tout; (to acknowledge thanks) de rien, je vous en prie.

notable [ˈnəʊtəbl] adj notable, remarquable; **to be ~ for sthg** être célèbre pour qqch.

notably [ˈnəʊtəblɪ] adv **1.** (in particular) notamment, particulièrement. **2.** (noticeably) sensiblement, nettement.

notary [ˈnəʊtərɪ] n: **~ (public)** notaire m.

notch [nɒtʃ] n **1.** (cut) entaille f, encoche f. **2.** fig (on scale) cran m.

note [nəʊt] ◆ n **1.** (gen & MUS) note f; (short letter) mot m; **to take ~ of sthg** prendre note de qqch. **2.** (money) billet m (de banque). ◆ vt **1.** (notice) remarquer, constater. **2.** (mention) mentionner, signaler. ▶ **notes** npl (in book) notes fpl. ▶ **note down** vt sep noter, inscrire.

notebook [ˈnəʊtbʊk] n **1.** (for notes) carnet m, calepin m. **2.** (COMPUT) ordinateur m portable compact.

noted [ˈnəʊtɪd] adj célèbre, éminent(e).

notepad [ˈnəʊtpæd] n bloc-notes m.

notepaper [ˈnəʊtpeɪpər] n papier m à lettres.

noteworthy [ˈnəʊtˌwɜːðɪ] adj remarquable, notable.

nothing [ˈnʌθɪŋ] ◆ pron rien; **I've got ~ to do** je n'ai rien à faire; **for ~** pour rien; **~ but ne ... que**, rien que; **there's ~ for it (but to do sthg)** Br il n'y a rien d'autre à faire (que de faire qqch). ◆ adv: **you're ~ like your brother** tu ne ressembles pas du tout OR en rien à ton frère; **I'm ~ like finished** je suis loin d'avoir fini.

notice [ˈnəʊtɪs] ◆ n **1.** (written announcement) affiche f, placard m. **2.** (attention): **to take ~ (of sb/sthg)** faire OR prêter attention (à qqn/qqch); **to take no ~ (of sb/sthg)** ne pas faire attention (à qqn/qqch). **3.** (warning) avis m, avertissement m; **at short ~** dans un bref délai; **until further ~** jusqu'à nouvel ordre. **4.** (at work): **to be given one's ~** recevoir son congé, être renvoyé(e); **to hand in one's ~** donner sa démission, demander son congé. ◆ vt remarquer, s'apercevoir de.

noticeable [ˈnəʊtɪsəbl] adj sensible, perceptible.

notice board n panneau m d'affichage.

notify [ˈnəʊtɪfaɪ] vt: **to ~ sb (of sthg)** avertir OR aviser qqn (de qqch).

notion ['nəʊʃn] n idée f, notion f.
notorious [nəʊ'tɔːrɪəs] adj (criminal) notoire; (place) mal famé(e).
notwithstanding [,nɒtwɪθ'stændɪŋ] fml ◆ prep malgré; en dépit de. ◆ adv néanmoins, malgré tout.
nought [nɔːt] num zéro m; **~s and crosses** morpion m.
noun [naʊn] n nom m.
nourish ['nʌrɪʃ] vt nourrir.
nourishing ['nʌrɪʃɪŋ] adj nourrissant(e).
nourishment ['nʌrɪʃmənt] n (U) nourriture f, aliments mpl.
novel ['nɒvl] ◆ adj nouveau (nouvelle), original(e). ◆ n roman m.
novelist ['nɒvəlɪst] n romancier m, -ère f.
novelty ['nɒvltɪ] n 1. (gen) nouveauté f. 2. (cheap object) gadget m.
November [nə'vembər] n novembre m; see also **September**.
novice ['nɒvɪs] n novice mf.
now [naʊ] ◆ adv 1. (at this time, at once) maintenant; **any day/time ~** d'un jour/moment à l'autre; **~ and then** OR **again** de temps en temps, de temps à autre. 2. (in past) à ce moment-là, alors. 3. (to introduce statement): **~ let's just calm down** bon, on se calme maintenant. ◆ conj: **~ (that)** maintenant que. ◆ n: **for ~** pour le présent; **from ~ on** à partir de maintenant, désormais; **up until ~** jusqu'à présent; **by ~** déjà.
nowadays ['naʊədeɪz] adv actuellement, aujourd'hui.
nowhere Br ['nəʊweər], **no-place** Am adv nulle part; **~ near** loin de; **we're getting ~** on n'avance pas.
nozzle ['nɒzl] n ajutage m, buse f.
nuance [nju:'ɑːns] n nuance f.
nuclear ['nju:klɪər] adj nucléaire.
nuclear bomb n bombe f nucléaire.
nuclear disarmament n désarmement m nucléaire.
nuclear energy n énergie f nucléaire.
nuclear power n énergie f nucléaire.
nuclear reactor n réacteur m nucléaire.
nucleus ['nju:klɪəs] (pl **-lei** [-lɪaɪ]) n lit & fig noyau m.
nude [nju:d] ◆ adj nu(e). ◆ n nu m; **in the ~** nu(e).
nudge [nʌdʒ] vt pousser du coude; fig encourager, pousser.
nudist ['nju:dɪst] ◆ adj nudiste. ◆ n nudiste mf.

nugget ['nʌgɪt] n pépite f.
nuisance ['nju:sns] n ennui m, embêtement m; **to make a ~ of o.s.** embêter le monde; **what a ~!** quelle plaie!
nuke [nju:k] inf ◆ n bombe f nucléaire. ◆ vt atomiser.
null [nʌl] adj: **~ and void** nul et non avenu.
numb [nʌm] ◆ adj engourdi(e); **to be ~ with** (fear) être paralysé par; (cold) être transi de. ◆ vt engourdir.
number ['nʌmbər] ◆ n 1. (numeral) chiffre m. 2. (of telephone, house, car) numéro m. 3. (quantity) nombre m; **a ~ of** un certain nombre de, plusieurs; **any ~ of** un grand nombre de, bon nombre de. 4. (song) chanson f. ◆ vt 1. (amount to, include) compter; **to ~ among** compter parmi. 2. (give number to) numéroter.
number one ◆ adj premier(ère), principal(e). ◆ n inf (oneself) soi, sa pomme.
numberplate ['nʌmbəpleɪt] n plaque f d'immatriculation.
Number Ten n la résidence officielle du premier ministre britannique.
numeral ['nju:mərəl] n chiffre m.
numerate ['nju:mərət] adj Br (person) qui sait compter.
numerical [nju:'merɪkl] adj numérique.
numerous ['nju:mərəs] adj nombreux (euse).
nun [nʌn] n religieuse f, sœur f.
nurse [nɜːs] ◆ n infirmière f; (male) ~ infirmier m. ◆ vt 1. (patient, cold) soigner. 2. fig (desires, hopes) nourrir. 3. (subj: mother) allaiter.
nursery ['nɜːsərɪ] n 1. (for children) garderie f. 2. (for plants) pépinière f.
nursery rhyme n comptine f.
nursery school n (école f) maternelle f.
nursery slopes npl pistes fpl pour débutants.
nursing ['nɜːsɪŋ] n métier m d'infirmière.
nursing home n (for old people) maison f de retraite privée; (for childbirth) maternité f privée.
nurture ['nɜːtʃər] vt 1. (children) élever; (plants) soigner. 2. fig (hopes etc) nourrir.
nut [nʌt] n 1. (to eat) terme générique désignant les fruits tels que les noix, noisettes etc. 2. (of metal) écrou m. 3. inf (mad person) cinglé m, -e f. ► **nuts** ◆ adj inf: **to be ~s** être dingue. ◆ excl Am inf zut!

nutcrackers ['nʌt,krækəz] *npl* casse-noix *m inv*, casse-noisettes *m inv*.

nutmeg ['nʌtmeg] *n* noix *f* (de) muscade.

nutritious [nju:'trɪʃəs] *adj* nourrissant(e).

nutshell ['nʌtʃel] *n*: in a ~ en un mot.

nuzzle ['nʌzl] ◆ *vt* frotter son nez contre. ◆ *vi*: to ~ (up) against se frotter contre, frotter son nez contre.

nylon ['naɪlɒn] ◆ *n* Nylon® *m*. ◆ *comp* en Nylon®.

O

o (*pl* o's OR os), **O** (*pl* O's OR Os) [əʊ] *n* 1. (*letter*) o *m inv*, O *m inv*. 2. (*zero*) zéro *m*.

oak [əʊk] ◆ *n* chêne *m*. ◆ *comp* de OR en chêne.

OAP (*abbr of* **old age pensioner**) *n* retraité *m*, -e *f*.

oar [ɔː*r*] *n* rame *f*, aviron *m*.

oasis [əʊ'eɪsɪs] (*pl* **oases** [əʊ'eɪsi:z]) *n* oasis *f*.

oatcake ['əʊtkeɪk] *n* galette *f* d'avoine.

oath [əʊθ] *n* 1. (*promise*) serment *m*; on OR under ~ sous serment. 2. (*swearword*) juron *m*.

oatmeal ['əʊtmi:l] *n* (U) flocons *mpl* d'avoine.

oats [əʊts] *npl* (*grain*) avoine *f*.

obedience [ə'bi:djəns] *n* obéissance *f*.

obedient [ə'bi:djənt] *adj* obéissant(e), docile.

obese [əʊ'bi:s] *adj fml* obèse.

obey [ə'beɪ] ◆ *vt* obéir à. ◆ *vi* obéir.

obituary [ə'bɪtʃʊərɪ] *n* nécrologie *f*.

object [*n* 'ɒbdʒɪkt, *vb* əb'dʒekt] ◆ *n* 1. (*gen*) objet *m*. 2. (*aim*) objectif *m*, but *m*. 3. (GRAMM) complément *m* d'objet. ◆ *vt* objecter. ◆ *vi* protester; to ~ to sthg faire objection à qqch, s'opposer à qqch; to ~ to doing sthg se refuser à faire qqch.

objection [əb'dʒekʃn] *n* objection *f*; to have no ~ to sthg/to doing sthg ne voir aucune objection à qqch/à faire qqch.

objectionable [əb'dʒekʃənəbl] *adj* (*person, behaviour*) désagréable; (*language*) choquant(e).

objective [əb'dʒektɪv] ◆ *adj* objectif (ive). ◆ *n* objectif *m*.

obligation [,ɒblɪ'geɪʃn] *n* obligation *f*.

obligatory [ə'blɪgətrɪ] *adj* obligatoire.

oblige [ə'blaɪdʒ] *vt* 1. (*force*): to ~ sb to do sthg forcer OR obliger qqn à faire qqch. 2. *fml* (*do a favour to*) obliger.

obliging [ə'blaɪdʒɪŋ] *adj* obligeant(e).

oblique [ə'bli:k] ◆ *adj* oblique; (*reference, hint*) indirect(e). ◆ *n* (TYPO) barre *f* oblique.

obliterate [ə'blɪtəreɪt] *vt* (*destroy*) détruire, raser.

oblivion [ə'blɪvɪən] *n* oubli *m*.

oblivious [ə'blɪvɪəs] *adj*: to be ~ to OR of être inconscient(e) de.

oblong ['ɒblɒŋ] ◆ *adj* rectangulaire. ◆ *n* rectangle *m*.

obnoxious [əb'nɒkʃəs] *adj* (*person*) odieux(euse); (*smell*) infect(e), fétide; (*comment*) désobligeant(e).

oboe ['əʊbəʊ] *n* hautbois *m*.

obscene [əb'si:n] *adj* obscène.

obscure [əb'skjʊə*r*] ◆ *adj* obscur(e). ◆ *vt* 1. (*gen*) obscurcir. 2. (*view*) masquer.

observance [əb'zɜ:vəns] *n* observation *f*.

observant [əb'zɜ:vnt] *adj* observateur (trice).

observation [,ɒbzə'veɪʃn] *n* observation *f*.

observatory [əb'zɜ:vətrɪ] *n* observatoire *m*.

observe [əb'zɜ:v] *vt* 1. (*gen*) observer. 2. (*remark*) remarquer, faire observer.

observer [əb'zɜ:və*r*] *n* observateur *m*, -trice *f*.

obsess [əb'ses] *vt* obséder; to be ~ed by OR with sb/sthg être obsédé par qqn/qqch.

obsessive [əb'sesɪv] *adj* (*person*) obsessionnel(elle); (*need etc*) qui est une obsession.

obsolescent [,ɒbsə'lesnt] *adj* (*system*) qui tombe en désuétude; (*machine*) obsolescent(e).

obsolete ['ɒbsəli:t] *adj* obsolète.

obstacle ['ɒbstəkl] *n* obstacle *m*.

obstetrics [ɒb'stetrɪks] *n* obstétrique *f*.

obstinate ['ɒbstənət] *adj* 1. (*stubborn*) obstiné(e). 2. (*cough*) persistant(e); (*stain, resistance*) tenace.

obstruct [əb'strʌkt] *vt* 1. (*block*) obstruer. 2. (*hinder*) entraver, gêner.

obstruction [əb'strʌkʃn] *n* 1. (*in road*) encombrement *m*; (*in pipe*) engorgement *m*. 2. (SPORT) obstruction *f*.

obtain [əb'teɪn] vt obtenir.

obtainable [əb'teɪnəbl] adj que l'on peut obtenir.

obtrusive [əb'truːsɪv] adj (behaviour) qui attire l'attention; (smell) fort(e).

obtuse [əb'tjuːs] adj obtus(e).

obvious ['ɒbvɪəs] adj évident(e).

obviously ['ɒbvɪəslɪ] adv 1. (of course) bien sûr. 2. (clearly) manifestement.

occasion [ə'keɪʒn] ♦ n 1. (gen) occasion f. 2. (important event) événement m; **to rise to the ~** se montrer à la hauteur de la situation. ♦ vt (cause) provoquer, occasionner.

occasional [ə'keɪʒənl] adj (showers) passager(ère); (visit) occasionnel(elle); **I have the ~ drink/cigarette** je bois un verre/jc fumc une cigarette de temps à autre.

occasionally [ə'keɪʒnəlɪ] adv de temps en temps, quelquefois.

occult [ɒ'kʌlt] adj occulte.

occupant ['ɒkjʊpənt] n occupant m, -e f; (of vehicle) passager m.

occupation [ˌɒkjʊ'peɪʃn] n 1. (job) profession f. 2. (pastime, by army) occupation f.

occupational hazard [ɒkjʊ,peɪʃnl-] n risque m du métier.

occupational therapy [ɒkjʊ,peɪʃnl-] n thérapeutique f occupationnelle, ergothérapie f.

occupier ['ɒkjʊpaɪər] n occupant m, -e f.

occupy ['ɒkjʊpaɪ] vt occuper; **to ~ o.s.** s'occuper.

occur [ə'kɜːr] vi 1. (happen - gen) avoir lieu, se produire; (- difficulty) se présenter. 2. (be present) se trouver, être présent(e). 3. (thought, idea): **to ~ to sb** venir à l'esprit de qqn.

occurrence [ə'kʌrəns] n (event) événement m, circonstance f.

ocean ['əʊʃn] n océan m; Am (sea) mer f.

oceangoing ['əʊʃn,gəʊɪŋ] adj au long cours.

ochre Br, **ocher** Am ['əʊkər] adj ocre (inv).

o'clock [ə'klɒk] adv: **two ~** deux heures.

octave ['ɒktɪv] n octave f.

October [ɒk'təʊbər] n octobre m; see also **September**.

octopus ['ɒktəpəs] (pl **-puses** OR **-pi** [-paɪ]) n pieuvre f.

OD 1. abbr of **overdose**. 2. abbr of **overdrawn**.

odd [ɒd] adj 1. (strange) bizarre, étrange. 2. (leftover) qui reste. 3. (occasional): **I play the ~ game of tennis** je joue au tennis de temps en temps. 4. (not part of pair) dépareillé(e). 5. (number) impair(e). 6. phr: **twenty ~ years** une vingtaine d'années. ► **odds** npl: **the ~** les chances fpl; **against the ~s** envers et contre tout; **~s and ends** petites choses fpl, petits bouts mpl; **to be at ~s with sb** être en désaccord avec qqn.

oddity ['ɒdɪtɪ] n 1. (person) personne f bizarre; (thing) chose f bizarre. 2. (strangeness) étrangeté f.

odd jobs npl petits travaux mpl.

oddly ['ɒdlɪ] adv curieusement; **~ enough** chose curieuse.

oddments ['ɒdmənts] npl fins fpl de série.

odds-on ['ɒdz-] adj inf: **~ favourite** grand favori.

odometer [əʊ'dɒmɪtər] n odomètre m.

odour Br, **odor** Am ['əʊdər] n odeur f.

of [unstressed əv, stressed ɒv] prep 1. (gen) de; **the cover ~ a book** la couverture d'un livre; **to die ~ cancer** mourir d'un cancer. 2. (expressing quantity, amount, age etc) de; **thousands ~ people** des milliers de gens; **a piece ~ cake** un morceau de gâteau; **a pound ~ tomatoes** une livre de tomates; **a child ~ five** un enfant de cinq ans; **a cup ~ coffee** une tasse de café. 3. (made from) en. 4. (with dates, periods of time): **the 12th ~ February** le 12 février.

off [ɒf] ♦ adv 1. (at a distance, away): **10 miles ~** à 16 kilomètres; **two days ~** dans deux jours; **far ~** au loin; **to be ~** partir, s'en aller. 2. (so as to remove): **to take ~** enlever; **to cut sthg ~** couper qqch. 3. (so as to complete): **to finish ~** terminer; **to kill ~** achever. 4. (not at work etc): **a day/week ~** un jour/une semaine de congé. 5. (discounted): **£10 ~** 10 livres de remise OR réduction. ♦ prep 1. (at a distance from, away from) de; **to get ~ a bus** descendre d'un bus; **to take a book ~ a shelf** prendre un livre sur une étagère; **~ the coast** près de la côte. 2. (not attending): **to be ~ work** ne pas travailler; **~ school** absent de l'école. 3. (no longer liking): **she's ~ her food** elle n'a pas d'appétit. 4. (deducted from) sur. 5. inf (from): **to buy sthg ~ sb** acheter qqch à qqn. ♦ adj 1. (food) avarié(e), gâté(e); (milk) tourné(e). 2. (TV, light) éteint(e); (engine) coupé(e). 3. (cancelled) annulé(e). 4. (not at work etc) absent(e). 5. inf (off-

hand): **he was a bit ~ with me** il n'a pas été sympa avec moi.

offal ['ɒfl] *n* (U) abats *mpl*.

off-chance *n*: **on the ~ that ...** au cas où ...

off colour *adj* (*ill*) patraque.

off duty *adj* qui n'est pas de service; (*doctor, nurse*) qui n'est pas de garde.

offence Br, **offense** Am [ə'fens] *n* **1.** (*crime*) délit *m*. **2.** (*upset*): **to cause sb ~** vexer qqn; **to take ~** se vexer.

offend [ə'fend] *vt* offenser.

offender [ə'fendər] *n* **1.** (*criminal*) criminel *m*, -elle *f*. **2.** (*culprit*) coupable *mf*.

offense [*sense* 2 'ɒfens] *n* Am **1.** = **offence**. **2.** (SPORT) attaque *f*.

offensive [ə'fensɪv] ◆ *adj* **1.** (*behaviour, comment*) blessant(e). **2.** (*weapon, action*) offensif(ive). ◆ *n* offensive *f*.

offer ['ɒfər] ◆ *n* **1.** (*gen*) offre *f*, proposition *f*. **2.** (*price, bid*) offre *f*. **3.** (*in shop*) promotion *f*; **on ~** (*available*) en vente; (*at a special price*) en réclame, en promotion. ◆ *vt* **1.** (*gen*) offrir; **to ~ sthg to sb**, **to ~ sb sthg** offrir qqch à qqn; **to ~ to do sthg** proposer OR offrir de faire qqch. **2.** (*provide - services etc*) proposer; (*- hope*) donner. ◆ *vi* s'offrir.

offering ['ɒfərɪŋ] *n* (RELIG) offrande *f*.

off-guard *adv* au dépourvu.

offhand [,ɒf'hænd] ◆ *adj* cavalier(ère). ◆ *adv* tout de suite.

office ['ɒfɪs] *n* **1.** (*place, staff*) bureau *m*. **2.** (*department*) département *m*, service *m*. **3.** (*position*) fonction *f*, poste *m*; **in ~** en fonction; **to take ~** entrer en fonction.

office automation *n* bureautique *f*.

office block *n* immeuble *m* de bureaux.

office hours *npl* heures *fpl* de bureau.

officer ['ɒfɪsər] *n* **1.** (*in armed forces*) officier *m*. **2.** (*in organization*) agent *m*, fonctionnaire *mf*. **3.** (*in police force*) officier *m* (de police).

office worker *n* employé *m*, -e *f* de bureau.

official [ə'fɪʃl] ◆ *adj* officiel(elle). ◆ *n* fonctionnaire *mf*.

officially [ə'fɪʃəlɪ] *adv* **1.** (*formally*) officiellement. **2.** (*supposedly*) en principe.

offing ['ɒfɪŋ] *n*: **in the ~** en vue, en perspective.

off-licence *n* Br magasin autorisé à vendre des boissons alcoolisées à emporter.

off-line *adj* (COMPUT) non connecté(e).

off-peak *adj* (*electricity*) utilisé(e) aux heures creuses; (*fare*) réduit(e) aux heures creuses.

off-putting [-,pʊtɪŋ] *adj* désagréable, rébarbatif(ive).

off season *n*: **the ~** la morte-saison.

offset ['ɒfset] (*pt & pp* **offset**) *vt* (*losses*) compenser.

offshoot ['ɒfʃuːt] *n*: **to be an ~ of sthg** être né(e) OR provenir de qqch.

offshore ['ɒfʃɔːr] ◆ *adj* (*oil rig*) offshore (*inv*); (*island*) proche de la côte; (*fishing*) côtier(ère). ◆ *adv* au large.

offside [*adj & adv* ,ɒf'saɪd, *n* 'ɒfsaɪd] ◆ *adj* **1.** (*right-hand drive*) de droite; (*left-hand drive*) de gauche. **2.** (SPORT) hors-jeu (*inv*). ◆ *adv* (SPORT) hors-jeu. ◆ *n* (*right-hand drive*) côté *m* droit; (*left-hand drive*) côté gauche.

offspring ['ɒfsprɪŋ] (*pl inv*) *n* rejeton *m*.

offstage [,ɒf'steɪdʒ] *adj & adv* dans les coulisses.

off-the-peg *adj* Br de prêt-à-porter.

off-the-record ◆ *adj* officieux(euse). ◆ *adv* confidentiellement.

off-white *adj* blanc cassé (*inv*).

often ['ɒfn, 'ɒftn] *adv* souvent, fréquemment; **how ~ do you visit her?** vous la voyez tous les combien?; **as ~ as not** assez souvent; **every so ~** de temps en temps; **more ~ than not** le plus souvent, la plupart du temps.

ogle ['əʊgl] *vt* reluquer.

oh [əʊ] *excl* oh!; (*expressing hesitation*) euh!

oil [ɔɪl] ◆ *n* **1.** (*gen*) huile *f*. **2.** (*for heating*) mazout *m*. **3.** (*petroleum*) pétrole *m*. ◆ *vt* graisser, lubrifier.

oilcan ['ɔɪlkæn] *n* burette *f* d'huile.

oilfield ['ɔɪlfiːld] *n* gisement *m* pétrolifère.

oil filter *n* filtre *m* à huile.

oil-fired [-,faɪəd] *adj* au mazout.

oil painting *n* peinture *f* à l'huile.

oilrig ['ɔɪlrɪg] *n* (*at sea*) plate-forme *f* de forage OR pétrolière; (*on land*) derrick *m*.

oilskins ['ɔɪlskɪnz] *npl* ciré *m*.

oil slick *n* marée *f* noire.

oil tanker *n* **1.** (*ship*) pétrolier *m*, tanker *m*. **2.** (*lorry*) camion-citerne *m*.

oil well *n* puits *m* de pétrole.

oily ['ɔɪlɪ] *adj* (*rag etc*) graisseux(euse); (*food*) gras (grasse).

ointment ['ɔɪntmənt] *n* pommade *f*.

OK (*pt & pp* **OKed**, *cont* **OKing**), **okay** [,əʊ'keɪ] *inf* ◆ *adj*: **is it ~ with** OR **by you?** ça vous va?, vous êtes d'accord?; **are you ~?** ça va? ◆ *excl* **1.** (*expressing agree-*

ment) d'accord, O.K. **2.** (to introduce new topic): **~, can we start now?** bon, on commence? ♦ vt approuver, donner le feu vert à.

old [əʊld] ♦ adj **1.** (gen) vieux (vieille), âgé(e); **I'm 20 years ~** j'ai 20 ans; **how ~ are you?** quel âge as-tu? **2.** (former) ancien(enne). **3.** inf (as intensifier): **any ~** n'importe quel (n'importe quelle). ♦ npl: **the ~** les personnes fpl âgées.

old age n vieillesse f.

old age pensioner n Br retraité m, -e f.

Old Bailey [-'beɪlɪ] n: **the ~** la Cour d'assises de Londres.

old-fashioned [-'fæʃnd] adj **1.** (outmoded) démodé(e), passé(e) de mode. **2.** (traditional) vieux jeu (inv).

old people's home n hospice m de vieillards.

O level n Br examen optionnel destiné, jusqu'en 1988, aux élèves de niveau seconde ayant obtenu de bons résultats.

olive ['ɒlɪv] ♦ adj olive (inv). ♦ n olive f.

olive green adj vert olive (inv).

olive oil n huile f d'olive.

Olympic [ə'lɪmpɪk] adj olympique. ► **Olympics** npl: **the ~s** les Jeux mpl Olympiques.

Olympic Games npl: **the ~** les Jeux mpl Olympiques.

ombudsman ['ɒmbʊdzmən] (pl -men [-mən]) n ombudsman m.

omelet(te) ['ɒmlɪt] n omelette f; **mushroom ~** omelette aux champignons.

omen ['əʊmen] n augure m, présage m.

ominous ['ɒmɪnəs] adj (event, situation) de mauvais augure; (sign) inquiétant(e); (look, silence) menaçant(e).

omission [ə'mɪʃn] n omission f.

omit [ə'mɪt] vt omettre; **to ~ to do sthg** oublier de faire qqch.

omnibus ['ɒmnɪbəs] n **1.** (book) recueil m. **2.** Br (RADIO & TV) diffusion groupée des épisodes de la semaine.

on [ɒn] ♦ prep **1.** (indicating position, location) sur; **~ a chair/the wall** sur une chaise/le mur; **~ the ceiling** au plafond; **the information is ~ disk** l'information est sur disquette; **~ the left/right** à gauche/droite. **2.** (indicating means): **the car runs ~ petrol** la voiture marche à l'essence; **to be shown ~ TV** passer à la télé; **~ the radio** à la radio; **~ the telephone** au téléphone; **to live ~ fruit** vivre OR se nourrir de fruits; **to hurt o.s. ~ sthg** se faire mal avec qqch. **3.** (indicating mode of transport): **to travel ~ a bus/train/**

ship voyager en bus/par le train/en bateau; **I was ~ the bus** j'étais dans le bus; **~ foot** à pied. **4.** (concerning) sur; **a book ~ astronomy** un livre sur l'astronomie. **5.** (indicating time, activity): **~ Thursday** jeudi; **~ the 10th of February** le 10 février; **~ my birthday** le jour de mon anniversaire; **~ my return, ~ returning** à mon retour; **~ holiday** en vacances. **6.** (indicating influence) sur; **the impact ~ the environment** l'impact sur l'environnement. **7.** (using, supported by): **to be ~ social security** recevoir l'aide sociale; **he's ~ tranquillizers** il prend des tranquillisants; **to be ~ drugs** se droguer. **8.** (earning): **to be ~ £25,000 a year** gagner 25 000 livres par an; **to be ~ a low income** avoir un faible revenu. **9.** (referring to musical instrument): **to play sthg ~ the violin/flute/guitar** jouer qqch au violon/à la flûte/à la guitare. **10.** inf (paid by): **the drinks are ~ me** c'est moi qui régale, c'est ma tournée. ♦ adv **1.** (indicating covering, clothing): **put the lid ~** mettez le couvercle; **to put a sweater ~** mettre un pull; **what did she have ~?** qu'est-ce qu'elle portait?; **he had nothing ~** il était tout nu. **2.** (being shown): **what's ~ at the Ritz?** qu'est-ce qu'on joue OR donne au Ritz? **3.** (working - radio, TV, light) allumé(e); (- machine) en marche; (- tap) ouvert(e); **turn ~ the power** mets le courant. **4.** (indicating continuing action): **he kept ~ walking** il continua à marcher. **5.** (forward): **send my mail ~ (to me)** faites suivre mon courrier; **later ~** plus tard; **earlier ~** plus tôt. **6.** inf (referring to behaviour): **it's just not ~!** cela ne se fait pas! ► **from ... on** adv: **from now ~** dorénavant, désormais; **from then ~** à partir de ce moment-là. ► **on and off** adv de temps en temps. ► **on to, onto** prep (only written as **onto** for senses 4 and 5) **1.** (to a position on top of) sur; **she jumped ~ to the chair** elle a sauté sur la chaise. **2.** (to a position on a vehicle) dans; **she got ~ to the bus** elle est montée dans le bus; **he jumped ~ to his bicycle** il a sauté sur sa bicyclette. **3.** (to a position attached to): **stick the photo ~ to the page with glue** colle la photo sur la page. **4.** (aware of wrongdoing): **to be onto sb** être sur la piste de qqn. **5.** (in contact with): **get onto the factory** contactez l'usine.

once [wʌns] ♦ adv **1.** (on one occasion) une fois; **~ a day** une fois par jour; **~ again** OR **more** encore une fois; **~ and for all** une fois pour toutes; **~ in a while**

de temps en temps; ~ **or twice** une ou deux fois; **for** ~ pour une fois. **2.** (*previously*) autrefois, jadis; ~ **upon a time** il était une fois. ◆ *conj* dès que. ▶ **at once** *adv* **1.** (*immediately*) immédiatement. **2.** (*at the same time*) en même temps; **all at** ~ tout d'un coup.

oncoming ['ɒn,kʌmɪŋ] *adj* (*traffic*) venant en sens inverse.

one [wʌn] ◆ *num* (*the number* 1) un (une); **page** ~ page un; ~ **of my friends** l'un de mes amis, un ami à moi; ~ **fifth** un cinquième. ◆ *adj* **1.** (*only*) seul(e), unique; **it's her** ~ **ambition/love** c'est son unique ambition/son seul amour. **2.** (*indefinite*): ~ **of these days** un de ces jours. ◆ *pron* **1.** (*referring to a particular thing or person*): **which** ~ **do you want?** lequel voulez-vous?; **this** ~ celui-ci; **that** ~ celui-là; **she's the** ~ **I told you about** c'est celle dont je vous ai parlé. **2.** *fml* (*you, anyone*) on; **to do** ~**'s duty** faire son devoir. ▶ **for one** *adv*: **I for** ~ **remain unconvinced** pour ma part je ne suis pas convaincu.

one-armed bandit *n* machine *f* à sous.

one-man *adj* (*business*) dirigé(e) par un seul homme.

one-man band *n* (*musician*) homme-orchestre *m*.

one-off *inf* ◆ *adj* (*offer, event, product*) unique. ◆ *n*: **a** ~ (*product*) un exemplaire unique; (*event*) un événement unique.

one-on-one Am = **one-to-one**.

one-parent family *n* famille *f* monoparentale.

oneself [wʌn'self] *pron* **1.** (*reflexive*) se; (*after prep*) soi. **2.** (*emphatic*) soi-même.

one-sided [-'saɪdɪd] *adj* **1.** (*unequal*) inégal(e). **2.** (*biased*) partial(e).

one-to-one Br, **one-on-one** Am *adj* (*discussion*) en tête-à-tête; ~ **tuition** cours *mpl* particuliers.

one-upmanship [,wʌn'ʌpmənʃɪp] *n* art *m* de faire toujours mieux que les autres.

one-way *adj* **1.** (*street*) à sens unique. **2.** (*ticket*) simple.

ongoing ['ɒn,gəʊɪŋ] *adj* en cours, continu(e).

onion ['ʌnjən] *n* oignon *m*.

online ['ɒnlaɪn] *adj* & *adv* (COMPUT) en ligne, connecté(e).

onlooker ['ɒn,lʊkəʳ] *n* spectateur *m*, -trice *f*.

only ['əʊnlɪ] ◆ *adj* seul(e), unique; **an** ~

child un enfant unique. ◆ *adv* **1.** (*gen*) ne … que, seulement; **he** ~ **reads science fiction** il ne lit que de la science fiction; **it's** ~ **a scratch** c'est juste une égratignure; **he left** ~ **a few minutes ago** il est parti il n'y a pas deux minutes. **2.** (*for emphasis*): **I** ~ **wish I could** je voudrais bien; **it's** ~ **natural (that)** … c'est tout à fait normal que …; **I was** ~ **too willing to help** je ne demandais qu'à aider; **not** ~ **… but also** non seulement … mais encore; **I** ~ **just caught the train** j'ai eu le train de justesse. ◆ *conj* seulement, mais.

onset ['ɒnset] *n* début *m*, commencement *m*.

onshore ['ɒnʃɔːʳ] *adj* & *adv* (*from sea*) du large; (*on land*) à terre.

onslaught ['ɒnslɔːt] *n* attaque *f*.

onto [*unstressed before consonant* 'ɒntə, *unstressed before vowel* 'ɒntʊ, *stressed* 'ɒntuː] = **on to**.

onus ['əʊnəs] *n* responsabilité *f*, charge *f*.

onward ['ɒnwəd] *adj* & *adv* en avant.

onwards ['ɒnwədz] *adv* en avant; **from now** ~ dorénavant, désormais; **from then** ~ à partir de ce moment-là.

ooze [uːz] ◆ *vt fig* (*charm, confidence*) respirer. ◆ *vi*: **to** ~ **from** OR **out of sthg** suinter de qqch.

opaque [əʊ'peɪk] *adj* opaque; *fig* obscur(e).

OPEC ['əʊpek] (*abbr of* **Organization of Petroleum Exporting Countries**) *n* OPEP *f*.

open ['əʊpn] ◆ *adj* **1.** (*gen*) ouvert(e). **2.** (*receptive*): **to be** ~ **(to)** être réceptif(ive) (à). **3.** (*view, road, space*) dégagé(e). **4.** (*uncovered - car*) découvert(e). **5.** (*meeting*) public(ique); (*competition*) ouvert(e) à tous. **6.** (*disbelief, honesty*) manifeste, évident(e). **7.** (*unresolved*) non résolu(e). ◆ *n*: **in the** ~ (*sleep*) à la belle étoile; (*eat*) au grand air; **to bring sthg out into the** ~ divulguer qqch, exposer qqch au grand jour. ◆ *vt* **1.** (*gen*) ouvrir. **2.** (*inaugurate*) inaugurer. ◆ *vi* **1.** (*door, flower*) s'ouvrir. **2.** (*shop, library etc*) ouvrir. **3.** (*meeting, play etc*) commencer. ▶ **open on to** *vt fus* (*subj: room, door*) donner sur. ▶ **open up** ◆ *vt sep* (*develop*) exploiter, développer. ◆ *vi* **1.** (*possibilities etc*) s'offrir, se présenter. **2.** (*unlock door*) ouvrir.

opener ['əʊpnəʳ] *n* (*for cans*) ouvre-boîtes *m inv*; (*for bottles*) ouvre-bouteilles *m inv*, décapsuleur *m*.

opening ['əʊpnɪŋ] ◆ *adj* (*first*) premier (ère); (*remarks*) préliminaire. ◆ *n* **1.**

(*beginning*) commencement *m*, début *m*.
2. (*in fence*) trou *m*, percée *f*; (*in clouds*) trouée *f*, déchirure *f*. **3.** (*opportunity - gen*) occasion *f*; (*- COMM*) débouché *m*. **4.** (*job vacancy*) poste *m*.

opening hours *npl* heures *fpl* d'ouverture.

openly ['əupənlɪ] *adv* ouvertement, franchement.

open-minded [-'maɪndɪd] *adj* (*person*) qui a l'esprit large; (*attitude*) large.

open-plan *adj* non cloisonné(e).

Open University *n* Br: the ~ = centre *m* national d'enseignement à distance.

opera ['ɒpərə] *n* opéra *m*.

opera house *n* opéra *m*.

operate ['ɒpəreɪt] ◆ *vt* **1.** (*machine*) faire marcher, faire fonctionner. **2.** (*COMM*) diriger. ◆ *vi* **1.** (*rule, law, system*) jouer, être appliqué(e); (*machine*) fonctionner, marcher. **2.** (*COMM*) opérer, travailler. **3.** (*MED*) opérer; **to ~ on sb/sthg** opérer qqn/de qqch.

operating theatre Br, **operating room** Am ['ɒpəreɪtɪŋ-] *n* salle *f* d'opération.

operation [,ɒpə'reɪʃn] *n* **1.** (*gen & MED*) opération *f*; **to have an ~ (for)** se faire opérer (de). **2.** (*of machine*) marche *f*, fonctionnement *m*; **to be in ~** (*machine*) être en marche or en service; (*law, system*) être en vigueur. **3.** (*COMM - company*) exploitation *f*; (*- management*) administration *f*, gestion *f*.

operative ['ɒprətɪv] ◆ *adj* en vigueur. ◆ *n* ouvrier *m*, -ère *f*.

operator ['ɒpəreɪtər] *n* **1.** (*TELEC*) standardiste *mf*. **2.** (*of machine*) opérateur *m*, -trice *f*. **3.** (*COMM*) directeur *m*, -trice *f*.

opinion [ə'pɪnjən] *n* opinion *f*, avis *m*; **to be of the ~ that** être d'avis que, estimer que; **in my ~** à mon avis.

opinionated [ə'pɪnjəneɪtɪd] *adj pej* dogmatique.

opinion poll *n* sondage *m* d'opinion.

opponent [ə'pəunənt] *n* adversaire *mf*.

opportune ['ɒpətjuːn] *adj* opportun(e).

opportunist [,ɒpə'tjuːnɪst] *n* opportuniste *mf*.

opportunity [,ɒpə'tjuːnətɪ] *n* occasion *f*; **to take the ~ to do** or **of doing sthg** profiter de l'occasion pour faire qqch.

oppose [ə'pəuz] *vt* s'opposer à.

opposed [ə'pəuzd] *adj* opposé(e); **to be ~ to** être contre, être opposé à; **as ~ to** par opposition à.

opposing [ə'pəuzɪŋ] *adj* opposé(e).

opposite ['ɒpəzɪt] ◆ *adj* opposé(e); (*house*) d'en face. ◆ *adv* en face. ◆ *prep* en face de. ◆ *n* contraire *m*.

opposite number *n* homologue *mf*.

opposition [,ɒpə'zɪʃn] *n* **1.** (*gen*) opposition *f*. **2.** (*opposing team*) adversaire *mf*. ► **Opposition** *n* Br (*POL*): **the Opposition** l'opposition.

oppress [ə'pres] *vt* **1.** (*persecute*) opprimer. **2.** (*depress*) oppresser.

oppressive [ə'presɪv] *adj* **1.** (*unjust*) oppressif(ive). **2.** (*weather, heat*) étouffant(e), lourd(e). **3.** (*silence*) oppressant(e).

opt [ɒpt] ◆ *vt*: **to ~ to do sthg** choisir de faire qqch. ◆ *vi*: **to ~ for** opter pour. ► **opt in** *vi*: **to ~ in (to)** choisir de participer (à). ► **opt out** *vi*: **to ~ out (of)** (*gen*) choisir de ne pas participer (à); (*of responsibility*) se dérober (à); (*of NHS*) ne plus faire partie (de).

optical ['ɒptɪkl] *adj* optique.

optician [ɒp'tɪʃn] *n* **1.** (*who sells glasses*) opticien *m*, -enne *f*. **2.** (*ophthalmologist*) ophtalmologiste *mf*.

optimism ['ɒptɪmɪzm] *n* optimisme *m*.

optimist ['ɒptɪmɪst] *n* optimiste *mf*.

optimistic [,ɒptɪ'mɪstɪk] *adj* optimiste.

optimum ['ɒptɪməm] *adj* optimum.

option ['ɒpʃn] *n* option *f*, choix *m*; **to have the ~ to do** or **of doing sthg** pouvoir faire qqch, avoir la possibilité de faire qqch.

optional ['ɒpʃnl] *adj* facultatif(ive); **an ~ extra** un accessoire.

or [ɔːr] *conj* **1.** (*gen*) ou. **2.** (*after negative*): **he can't read ~ write** il ne sait ni lire ni écrire. **3.** (*otherwise*) sinon. **4.** (*as correction*) ou plutôt.

oral ['ɔːrəl] ◆ *adj* **1.** (*spoken*) oral(e). **2.** (*MED - medicine*) par voie orale, par la bouche; (*- hygiene*) buccal(e). ◆ *n* oral *m*, épreuve *f* orale.

orally ['ɔːrəlɪ] *adv* **1.** (*in spoken form*) oralement. **2.** (*MED*) par voie orale.

orange ['ɒrɪndʒ] ◆ *adj* orange (*inv*). ◆ *n* **1.** (*fruit*) orange *f*. **2.** (*colour*) orange *m*.

orator ['ɒrətər] *n* orateur *m*, -trice *f*.

orbit ['ɔːbɪt] ◆ *n* orbite *f*. ◆ *vt* décrire une orbite autour de.

orchard ['ɔːtʃəd] *n* verger *m*; **apple ~** champ *m* de pommiers, pommeraie *f*.

orchestra ['ɔːkɪstrə] *n* orchestre *m*.

orchestral [ɔː'kestrəl] *adj* orchestral(e).

orchid ['ɔːkɪd] *n* orchidée *f*.

ordain [ɔː'deɪn] *vt* **1.** (*decree*) ordonner,

décréter. **2.** (RELIG): **to be ~ed** être ordonné prêtre.

ordeal [ɔːˈdiːl] *n* épreuve *f*.

order [ˈɔːdəʳ] ◆ *n* **1.** (*gen*) ordre *m*; **to be under ~s to do sthg** avoir (reçu) l'ordre de faire qqch. **2.** (COMM) commande *f*; **to place an ~ with sb for sthg** passer une commande de qqch à qqn; **to ~** sur commande. **3.** (*sequence*) ordre *m*; **in ~** dans l'ordre; **in ~ of importance** par ordre d'importance. **4.** (*fitness for use*): **in working ~** en état de marche; **out of ~** (*machine*) en panne; (*behaviour*) déplacé(e); **in ~** (*correct*) en ordre. **5.** (U) (*discipline - gen*) ordre *m*; (*- in classroom*) discipline *f*. **6.** Am (*portion*) part *f*. ◆ *vt* **1.** (*command*) ordonner; **to ~ sb to do sthg** ordonner à qqn de faire qqch; **to ~ that** ordonner que. **2.** (COMM) commander. ▶ **in the order of** Br, **on the order of** Am *prep* environ, de l'ordre de. ▶ **in order that** *conj* pour que, afin que (+ *subjunctive*). ▶ **in order to** *conj* pour, afin de. ▶ **order about, order around** *vt sep* commander.

order form *n* bulletin *m* de commande.

orderly [ˈɔːdəlɪ] ◆ *adj* (*person*) ordonné(e); (*crowd*) discipliné(e); (*office, room*) en ordre. ◆ *n* (*in hospital*) garçon *m* de salle.

ordinarily [ˈɔːdənrəlɪ] *adv* d'habitude, d'ordinaire.

ordinary [ˈɔːdnrɪ] ◆ *adj* **1.** (*normal*) ordinaire. **2.** *pej* (*unexceptional*) ordinaire, quelconque. ◆ *n*: **out of the ~** qui sort de l'ordinaire, exceptionnel(elle).

ordnance [ˈɔːdnəns] *n* (U) **1.** (*supplies*) matériel *m* militaire. **2.** (*artillery*) artillerie *f*.

ore [ɔːʳ] *n* minerai *m*.

oregano [ˌɒrɪˈɡɑːnəʊ] *n* origan *m*.

organ [ˈɔːɡən] *n* **1.** (*gen*) organe *m*. **2.** (MUS) orgue *m*.

organic [ɔːˈɡænɪk] *adj* **1.** (*of animals, plants*) organique. **2.** (*farming, food*) biologique.

organization [ˌɔːɡənaɪˈzeɪʃn] *n* organisation *f*.

organize, -ise [ˈɔːɡənaɪz] *vt* organiser.

organizer [ˈɔːɡənaɪzəʳ] *n* organisateur *m*, -trice *f*.

orgasm [ˈɔːɡæzm] *n* orgasme *m*.

orgy [ˈɔːdʒɪ] *n* lit & fig orgie *f*.

Orient [ˈɔːrɪənt] *n*: **the ~** l'Orient *m*.

oriental [ˌɔːrɪˈentl] *adj* oriental(e).

orienteering [ˌɔːrɪənˈtɪərɪŋ] *n* (U)

course *f* d'orientation.

origami [ˌɒrɪˈɡɑːmɪ] *n* origami *m*.

origin [ˈɒrɪdʒɪn] *n* **1.** (*of river*) source *f*; (*of word, conflict*) origine *f*. **2.** (*birth*): **country of ~** pays *m* d'origine. ▶ **origins** *npl* origines *fpl*.

original [əˈrɪdʒənl] ◆ *adj* original(e); (*owner*) premier(ère). ◆ *n* original *m*.

originally [əˈrɪdʒənəlɪ] *adv* à l'origine, au départ.

originate [əˈrɪdʒəneɪt] ◆ *vt* être l'auteur de, être à l'origine de. ◆ *vi* (*belief, custom*): **to ~ (in)** prendre naissance (dans); **to ~ from** provenir de.

Orkney Islands [ˈɔːknɪ-], **Orkneys** [ˈɔːknɪz] *npl*: **the ~** les Orcades *fpl*.

ornament [ˈɔːnəmənt] *n* **1.** (*object*) bibelot *m*. **2.** (U) (*decoration*) ornement *m*.

ornamental [ˌɔːnəˈmentl] *adj* (*garden, pond*) d'agrément; (*design*) décoratif (ive).

ornate [ɔːˈneɪt] *adj* orné(e).

ornithology [ˌɔːnɪˈθɒlədʒɪ] *n* ornithologie *f*.

orphan [ˈɔːfn] ◆ *n* orphelin *m*, -e *f*. ◆ *vt*: **to be ~ed** devenir orphelin(e).

orphanage [ˈɔːfənɪdʒ] *n* orphelinat *m*.

orthodox [ˈɔːθədɒks] *adj* **1.** (*conventional*) orthodoxe. **2.** (RELIG) (*traditional*) traditionaliste.

orthopaedic [ˌɔːθəˈpiːdɪk] *adj* orthopédique.

orthopedic *etc* [ˌɔːθəˈpiːdɪk] = **orthopaedic** *etc*.

oscillate [ˈɒsɪleɪt] *vi* lit & fig osciller.

Oslo [ˈɒzləʊ] *n* Oslo.

ostensible [ɒˈstensəbl] *adj* prétendu(e).

ostentatious [ˌɒstənˈteɪʃəs] *adj* ostentatoire.

osteopath [ˈɒstɪəpæθ] *n* ostéopathe *mf*.

ostracize, -ise [ˈɒstrəsaɪz] *vt* frapper d'ostracisme, mettre au ban.

ostrich [ˈɒstrɪtʃ] *n* autruche *f*.

other [ˈʌðəʳ] ◆ *adj* autre; **the ~ one** l'autre; **the ~ day/week** l'autre jour/ semaine. ◆ *adv*: **there was nothing to do ~** than confess il ne pouvait faire autrement que d'avouer; **~ than John** John à part. ◆ *pron*: **~s** d'autres; **the ~** l'autre; **the ~s** les autres; **one after the ~** l'un après l'autre; **one or ~ of you** l'un (l'une) de vous deux; **none ~ than** nul (nulle) autre que. ▶ **something or other** *pron* quelque chose, je ne sais quoi. ▶ **somehow or other** *adv* d'une manière ou d'une autre.

otherwise ['ʌðəwaɪz] ♦ adv autrement; **or ~** (or not) ou non. ♦ conj sinon.
otter ['ɒtər] n loutre f.
ouch [aʊtʃ] excl aïe!, ouïe!
ought [ɔːt] aux vb 1. (sensibly): **I really ~ to go** il faut absolument que je m'en aille; **you ~ to see a doctor** tu devrais aller chez le docteur. 2. (morally): **you ~ not to have done that** tu n'aurais pas dû faire cela; **you ~ to look after your children better** tu devrais t'occuper un peu mieux de tes enfants. 3. (expressing probability): **she ~ to pass her exam** elle devrait réussir à son examen.
ounce [aʊns] n = 28,35 g, once f.
our ['aʊər] poss adj notre, nos (pl); **~ money/house** notre argent/maison; **~ children** nos enfants; **it wasn't OUR fault** ce n'était pas de notre faute à nous.
ours ['aʊəz] poss pron le nôtre (la nôtre), les nôtres (pl); **that money is ~** cet argent est à nous OR est le nôtre; **it wasn't their fault, it was OURS** ce n'était pas de leur faute, c'était de notre faute à nous OR de la nôtre; **a friend of ~** un ami à nous, un de nos amis.
ourselves [aʊə'selvz] pron pl 1. (reflexive) nous. 2. (for emphasis) nous-mêmes; **we did it by ~** nous l'avons fait tout seuls.
oust [aʊst] vt: **to ~ sb (from)** évincer qqn (de).
out [aʊt] adv 1. (not inside, out of doors) dehors; **I'm going ~ for a walk** je sors me promener; **to run ~** sortir en courant; **~ here** ici; **~ there** là-bas. 2. (away from home, office, published) sorti(e); **John's ~ at the moment** John est sorti, John n'est pas là en ce moment; **an afternoon ~** une sortie l'après-midi. 3. (extinguished) éteint(e); **the lights went ~** les lumières se sont éteintes. 4. (of tides): **the tide is ~** la marée est basse. 5. (out of fashion) démodé(e), passé(e) de mode. 6. (in flower) en fleur. 7. inf (on strike) en grève. 8. (determined): **to be ~ to do sthg** être résolu(e) OR décidé(e) à faire qqch. ▶ **out of** prep 1. (outside) en dehors de; **to go ~ of the room** sortir de la pièce; **to be ~ of the country** être à l'étranger. 2. (indicating cause) par; **~ of spite/love/boredom** par dépit/amour/ennui. 3. (indicating origin, source) de, dans; **a page ~ of a book** une page d'un livre; **it's made ~ of plastic** c'est en plastique. 4. (without) sans; **~ of petrol/money** à court d'essence/d'argent. 5. (sheltered from) à l'abri de; **we're ~ of**

the wind here nous sommes à l'abri du vent ici. 6. (to indicate proportion) sur; **one ~ of ten people** une personne sur dix; **ten ~ of ten** dix sur dix.
out-and-out adj (liar) fieffé(e); (disgrace) complet(ète).
outback ['aʊtbæk] n: **the ~** l'intérieur m du pays (en Australie).
outboard (motor) ['aʊtbɔːd-] n (moteur m) hors-bord m.
outbreak ['aʊtbreɪk] n (of war, crime) début m, déclenchement m; (of spots etc) éruption f.
outburst ['aʊtbɜːst] n explosion f.
outcast ['aʊtkɑːst] n paria m.
outcome ['aʊtkʌm] n issue f, résultat m.
outcrop ['aʊtkrɒp] n affleurement m.
outcry ['aʊtkraɪ] n tollé m.
outdated [,aʊt'deɪtɪd] adj démodé(e), vieilli(e).
outdid [,aʊt'dɪd] pt → outdo.
outdo [,aʊt'duː] (pt **-did**, pp **-done** [-'dʌn]) vt surpasser.
outdoor ['aʊtdɔːr] adj (life, swimming pool) en plein air; (activities) de plein air.
outdoors [aʊt'dɔːz] adv dehors.
outer ['aʊtər] adj extérieur(e).
outer space n cosmos m.
outfit ['aʊtfɪt] n 1. (clothes) tenue f. 2. inf (organization) équipe f.
outfitters ['aʊt,fɪtəz] n Br dated (for clothes) magasin m spécialisé de confection pour hommes.
outgoing ['aʊt,gəʊɪŋ] adj 1. (chairman etc) sortant(e); (mail) à expédier; (train) en partance. 2. (friendly, sociable) ouvert(e). ▶ **outgoings** npl Br dépenses fpl.
outgrow [,aʊt'grəʊ] (pt **-grew**, pp **-grown**) vt 1. (clothes) devenir trop grand(e) pour. 2. (habit) se défaire de.
outhouse ['aʊthaʊs, pl -haʊzɪz] n appentis m.
outing ['aʊtɪŋ] n (trip) sortie f.
outlandish [aʊt'lændɪʃ] adj bizarre.
outlaw ['aʊtlɔː] ♦ n hors-la-loi m inv. ♦ vt (practice) proscrire.
outlay ['aʊtleɪ] n dépenses fpl.
outlet ['aʊtlet] n 1. (for emotion) exutoire m. 2. (hole, pipe) sortie f. 3. (shop): **retail ~** point m de vente. 4. Am (ELEC) prise f (de courant).
outline ['aʊtlaɪn] ♦ n 1. (brief description) grandes lignes fpl; **in ~** en gros. 2. (silhouette) silhouette f. ♦ vt (describe briefly) exposer les grandes lignes de.
outlive [,aʊt'lɪv] vt (subj: person) survivre à.

outlook ['aʊtlʊk] n 1. (disposition) attitude f, conception f. 2. (prospect) perspective f.

outlying ['aʊtˌlaɪɪŋ] adj (village) reculé(e); (suburbs) écarté(e).

outmoded [ˌaʊt'məʊdɪd] adj démodé(e).

outnumber [ˌaʊt'nʌmbər] vt surpasser en nombre.

out-of-date adj (passport) périmé(e); (clothes) démodé(e); (belief) dépassé(e).

out of doors adv dehors.

out-of-the-way adj (village) perdu(e); (pub) peu fréquenté(e).

outpatient ['aʊtˌpeɪʃnt] n malade mf en consultation externe.

outpost ['aʊtpəʊst] n avant-poste m.

output ['aʊtpʊt] n 1. (production) production f. 2. (COMPUT) sortie f.

outrage ['aʊtreɪdʒ] ◆ n 1. (emotion) indignation f. 2. (act) atrocité f. ◆ vt outrager.

outrageous [aʊt'reɪdʒəs] adj 1. (offensive, shocking) scandaleux(euse), monstrueux(euse). 2. (very unusual) choquant(e).

outright [adj 'aʊtraɪt, adv ˌaʊt'raɪt] ◆ adj absolu(e), total(e). ◆ adv 1. (deny) carrément, franchement. 2. (win, fail) complètement, totalement.

outset ['aʊtset] n: **at the ~** au commencement, au début; **from the ~** depuis le commencement OR début.

outside [adv ˌaʊt'saɪd, adj, prep & n 'aʊtsaɪd] ◆ adj 1. (gen) extérieur(e); **an ~ opinion** une opinion indépendante. 2. (unlikely - chance, possibility) faible. ◆ adv à l'extérieur; **to go/run/look ~** aller/courir/regarder dehors. ◆ prep 1. (not inside) à l'extérieur de, en dehors de. 2. (beyond): **~ office hours** en dehors des heures de bureau. ◆ n extérieur m. ▶ **outside of** prep Am (apart from) à part.

outside lane n (AUT) (in UK) voie f de droite; (in Europe, US) voie f de gauche.

outside line n (TELEC) ligne f extérieure.

outsider [ˌaʊt'saɪdər] n 1. (in race) outsider m. 2. (from society) étranger m, -ère f.

outsize ['aʊtsaɪz] adj 1. (bigger than usual) énorme, colossal(e). 2. (clothes) grande taille (inv).

outskirts ['aʊtskɜːts] npl: **the ~** la banlieue.

outspoken [ˌaʊt'spəʊkn] adj franc (franche).

outstanding [ˌaʊt'stændɪŋ] adj 1. (excellent) exceptionnel(elle), remarquable. 2. (example) marquant(e). 3. (not paid) impayé(e). 4. (unfinished - work, problem) en suspens.

outstay [ˌaʊt'steɪ] vt: **I don't want to ~ my welcome** je ne veux pas abuser de votre hospitalité.

outstretched [ˌaʊt'stretʃt] adj (arms, hands) tendu(e); (wings) déployé(e).

outstrip [ˌaʊt'strɪp] vt devancer.

out-tray n corbeille f pour le courrier à expédier.

outward ['aʊtwəd] ◆ adj 1. (going away): **~ journey** aller m. 2. (apparent, visible) extérieur(e). ◆ adv Am = **outwards**.

outwardly ['aʊtwədlɪ] adv (apparently) en apparence.

outwards Br ['aʊtwədz], **outward** Am adv vers l'extérieur.

outweigh [ˌaʊt'weɪ] vt fig primer sur.

outwit [ˌaʊt'wɪt] vt se montrer plus malin(igne) que.

oval ['əʊvl] ◆ adj ovale. ◆ n ovale m.

Oval Office n: **the ~** bureau du président des États-Unis à la Maison-Blanche.

ovary ['əʊvərɪ] n ovaire m.

ovation [əʊ'veɪʃn] n ovation f; **the audience gave her a standing ~** le public l'a ovationnée.

oven ['ʌvn] n (for cooking) four m.

ovenproof ['ʌvnpruːf] adj qui va au four.

over ['əʊvər] ◆ prep 1. (above) au-dessus de. 2. (on top of) sur. 3. (on other side of) de l'autre côté de; **they live ~ the road** ils habitent en face. 4. (to other side of) par-dessus; **to go ~ the border** franchir la frontière. 5. (more than) plus de; **~ and above** en plus de. 6. (concerning) à propos de, au sujet de. 7. (during) pendant. ◆ adv 1. (distance away): **~ here** ici; **~ there** là-bas. 2. (across): **they flew ~ to America** ils se sont envolés pour les États-Unis; **we invited them ~** nous les avons invités chez nous. 3. (more) plus. 4. (remaining): **there's nothing (left) ~** il ne reste rien. 5. (RADIO): **~ and out!** à vous! 6. (involving repetitions): **(all) ~ again** (tout) au début; **~ and ~ again** à maintes reprises, maintes fois. ◆ adj (finished) fini(e), terminé(e). ▶ **all over** ◆ prep (throughout) partout, dans tout; **all ~ the world** dans le monde entier. ◆ adv (everywhere) partout. ◆ adj (finished) fini(e).

overall [adj & n 'əʊvərɔːl, adv ˌəʊvər'ɔːl] ◆ adj (general) d'ensemble. ◆ adv en général. ◆ *n* **1.** (*gen*) tablier *m*. **2.** Am (*for work*) bleu *m* de travail. ▶ **overalls** *npl* **1.** (*for work*) bleu *m* de travail. **2.** Am (*dungarees*) salopette *f*.

overawe [,əʊvər'ɔː] *vt* impressionner.

overbalance [,əʊvə'bæləns] *vi* basculer.

overbearing [,əʊvə'beərɪŋ] *adj* autoritaire.

overboard ['əʊvəbɔːd] *adv*: **to fall ~** tomber par-dessus bord.

overbook [,əʊvə'bʊk] *vi* surréserver.

overcame [,əʊvə'keɪm] *pt* → **overcome**.

overcast [,əʊvə'kɑːst] *adj* couvert(e).

overcharge [,əʊvə'tʃɑːdʒ] *vt*: **to ~ sb (for sthg)** faire payer (qqch) trop cher à qqn.

overcoat ['əʊvəkəʊt] *n* pardessus *m*.

overcome [,əʊvə'kʌm] (*pt* **-came**, *pp* **-come**) *vt* **1.** (*fears, difficulties*) surmonter. **2.** (*overwhelm*): **to be ~ (by OR with)** (*emotion*) être submergé(e) (de); (*grief*) être accablé(e) (de).

overcrowded [,əʊvə'kraʊdɪd] *adj* bondé(e).

overcrowding [,əʊvə'kraʊdɪŋ] *n* surpeuplement *m*.

overdo [,əʊvə'duː] (*pt* **-did** [-'dɪd], *pp* **-done**) *vt* **1.** (*exaggerate*) exagérer. **2.** (*do too much*) trop faire; **to ~ it** se surmener. **3.** (*overcook*) trop cuire.

overdone [,əʊvə'dʌn] ◆ *pp* → **overdo**. ◆ *adj* (*food*) trop cuit(e).

overdose ['əʊvədəʊs] *n* overdose *f*.

overdraft ['əʊvədrɑːft] *n* découvert *m*.

overdrawn [,əʊvə'drɔːn] *adj* à découvert.

overdue [,əʊvə'djuː] *adj* **1.** (*late*): **~ (for)** en retard (pour). **2.** (*change, reform*): (**long**) **~** attendu(e) (depuis longtemps). **3.** (*unpaid*) arriéré(e), impayé(e).

overestimate [,əʊvər'estɪmeɪt] *vt* surestimer.

overflow [*vb* ,əʊvə'fləʊ, *n* 'əʊvəfləʊ] ◆ *vi* **1.** (*gen*) déborder. **2.** (*streets, box*): **to be ~ing (with)** regorger (de). ◆ *n* (*pipe, hole*) trop-plein *m*.

overgrown [,əʊvə'grəʊn] *adj* (*garden*) envahi(e) par les mauvaises herbes.

overhaul [*n* 'əʊvəhɔːl, *vb* ,əʊvə'hɔːl] ◆ *n* **1.** (*of car, machine*) révision *f*. **2.** *fig* (*of system*) refonte *f*, remaniement *m*. ◆ *vt* **1.** (*car, machine*) réviser. **2.** *fig* (*system*) refondre, remanier.

overhead [*adv* ,əʊvə'hed, *adj* & *n* 'əʊvəhed] ◆ *adj* aérien(enne). ◆ *adv* au-dessus. ◆ *n* (U) Am frais *mpl* généraux.

▶ **overheads** *npl* Br frais *mpl* généraux.

overhead projector *n* rétroprojecteur *m*.

overhear [,əʊvə'hɪər] (*pt* & *pp* **-heard** [-'hɜːd]) *vt* entendre par hasard.

overheat [,əʊvə'hiːt] ◆ *vt* surchauffer. ◆ *vi* (*engine*) chauffer.

overjoyed [,əʊvə'dʒɔɪd] *adj*: **~ (at)** transporté(e) de joie (à).

overkill ['əʊvəkɪl] *n* (*excess*): **that would be ~** ce serait de trop.

overladen [,əʊvə'leɪdn] ◆ *pp* → **overload**. ◆ *adj* surchargé(e).

overland ['əʊvəlænd] *adj* & *adv* par voie de terre.

overlap [,əʊvə'læp] *vi* lit & fig se chevaucher.

overleaf [,əʊvə'liːf] *adv* au verso, au dos.

overload [,əʊvə'ləʊd] (*pp* **-loaded** OR **-laden**) *vt* surcharger.

overlook [,əʊvə'lʊk] *vt* **1.** (*subj: building, room*) donner sur. **2.** (*disregard, miss*) oublier, négliger. **3.** (*excuse*) passer sur, fermer les yeux sur.

overnight [*adj* 'əʊvənaɪt, *adv* ,əʊvə'naɪt] ◆ *adj* **1.** (*journey, parking*) de nuit; (*stay*) d'une nuit. **2.** *fig* (*sudden*): **~ success** succès *m* immédiat. ◆ *adv* **1.** (*stay, leave*) la nuit. **2.** (*suddenly*) du jour au lendemain.

overpass ['əʊvəpɑːs] *n* Am ≃ Toboggan® *m*.

overpower [,əʊvə'paʊər] *vt* **1.** (*in fight*) vaincre. **2.** *fig* (*overwhelm*) accabler, terrasser.

overpowering [,əʊvə'paʊərɪŋ] *adj* (*desire*) irrésistible; (*smell*) entêtant(e).

overran [,əʊvə'ræn] *pt* → **overrun**.

overrated [,əʊvə'reɪtɪd] *adj* surfait(e).

override [,əʊvə'raɪd] (*pt* **-rode**, *pp* **-ridden**) *vt* **1.** (*be more important than*) l'emporter sur, prévaloir sur. **2.** (*overrule - decision*) annuler.

overriding [,əʊvə'raɪdɪŋ] *adj* (*need, importance*) primordial(e).

overrode [,əʊvə'rəʊd] *pt* → **override**.

overrule [,əʊvə'ruːl] *vt* (*person*) prévaloir contre; (*decision*) annuler; (*objection*) rejeter.

overrun [,əʊvə'rʌn] (*pt* **-ran**, *pp* **-run**) ◆ *vt* **1.** (MIL) (*occupy*) occuper. **2.** *fig* (*cover, fill*): **to be ~ with** (*weeds*) être envahi(e) de; (*rats*) être infesté(e) de. ◆ *vi* dépasser (le temps alloué).

oversaw [,əʊvə'sɔː] *pt* → **oversee**.

overseas [*adj* 'əʊvəsiːz, *adv* ,əʊvə'siːz]

♦ *adj* (*sales, company*) à l'étranger; (*market*) extérieur(e); (*visitor, student*) étranger(ère); **~ aid** aide *f* aux pays étrangers. ♦ *adv* à l'étranger.

oversee [,əʊvə'siː] (*pt* **-saw**, *pp* **-seen** [-'siːn]) *vt* surveiller.

overseer ['əʊvə,siːə'] *n* contremaître *m*.

overshadow [,əʊvə'ʃædəʊ] *vt* (*subj: building, tree*) dominer; *fig* éclipser.

overshoot [,əʊvə'ʃuːt] (*pt & pp* **-shot**) *vt* dépasser, rater.

oversight ['əʊvəsaɪt] *n* oubli *m*; **through ~** par mégarde.

oversleep [,əʊvə'sliːp] (*pt & pp* **-slept** [-'slept]) *vi* ne pas se réveiller à temps.

overspill ['əʊvəspɪl] *n* (*of population*) excédent *m*.

overstep [,əʊvə'step] *vt* dépasser; **to ~ the mark** dépasser la mesure.

overt ['əʊvɜːt] *adj* déclaré(e), non déguisé(e).

overtake [,əʊvə'teɪk] (*pt* **-took**, *pp* **-taken** [-'teɪkn]) ♦ *vt* **1.** (AUT) doubler, dépasser. **2.** (*subj: misfortune, emotion*) frapper. ♦ *vi* (AUT) doubler.

overthrow [*n* 'əʊvəθrəʊ, *vb* ,əʊvə'θrəʊ] (*pt* **-threw** [-'θruː], *pp* **-thrown** [-'θrəʊn]) ♦ *n* (*of government*) coup *m* d'État. ♦ *vt* (*government*) renverser.

overtime ['əʊvətaɪm] ♦ *n* (U) (*extra work*) heures *fpl* supplémentaires. ♦ *adv*: **to work ~** faire des heures supplémentaires.

overtones ['əʊvətəʊnz] *npl* notes *fpl*, accents *mpl*.

overtook [,əʊvə'tʊk] *pt* → **overtake**.

overture ['əʊvə,tjʊə'] *n* (MUS) ouverture *f*.

overturn [,əʊvə'tɜːn] ♦ *vt* **1.** (*gen*) renverser. **2.** (*decision*) annuler. ♦ *vi* (*vehicle*) se renverser; (*boat*) chavirer.

overweight [,əʊvə'weɪt] *adj* trop gros (grosse).

overwhelm [,əʊvə'welm] *vt* **1.** (*subj: grief, despair*) accabler; **to be ~ed with joy** être au comble de la joie. **2.** (MIL) (*gain control of*) écraser.

overwhelming [,əʊvə'welmɪŋ] *adj* **1.** (*overpowering*) irrésistible, irrépressible. **2.** (*defeat, majority*) écrasant(e).

overwork [,əʊvə'wɜːk] ♦ *n* surmenage *m*. ♦ *vt* (*person, staff*) surmener.

overwrought [,əʊvə'rɔːt] *adj* excédé(e), à bout.

owe [əʊ] *vt*: **to ~ sthg to sb, to ~ sb sthg** devoir qqch à qqn.

owing ['əʊɪŋ] *adj* dû (due). ▶ **owing to** *prep* à cause de, en raison de.

owl [aʊl] *n* hibou *m*.

own [əʊn] ♦ *adj* propre; **my ~ car** ma propre voiture; **she has her ~ style** elle a son style à elle. ♦ *pron*: **I've got my ~** j'ai le mien; **he has a house of his ~** il a une maison à lui, il a sa propre maison; **on one's ~** tout seul (toute seule); **to get one's ~ back** *inf* prendre sa revanche. ♦ *vt* posséder. ▶ **own up** *vi*: **to ~ up (to sthg)** avouer OR confesser (qqch).

owner ['əʊnə'] *n* propriétaire *mf*.

ownership ['əʊnəʃɪp] *n* propriété *f*.

ox [ɒks] (*pl* **oxen**) *n* bœuf *m*.

Oxbridge ['ɒksbrɪdʒ] *n* désignation collective des universités d'Oxford et de Cambridge.

oxen ['ɒksn] *pl* → **ox**.

oxtail soup ['ɒksteɪl-] *n* soupe *f* à la queue de bœuf.

oxygen ['ɒksɪdʒən] *n* oxygène *m*.

oxygen mask *n* masque *m* à oxygène.

oxygen tent *n* tente *f* à oxygène.

oyster ['ɔɪstə'] *n* huître *f*.

oz. *abbr of* **ounce**.

ozone ['əʊzəʊn] *n* ozone *m*.

ozone-friendly *adj* qui préserve la couche d'ozone.

ozone layer *n* couche *f* d'ozone.

P

p¹ (*pl* **p's** OR **ps**), **P** (*pl* **P's** OR **Ps**) [piː] *n* (*letter*) p *m inv*, P *m inv*.

p² **1.** (*abbr of* **page**) p. **2.** *abbr of* **penny**, **pence**.

pa [paː] *n inf* papa *m*.

p.a. (*abbr of* **per annum**) p.a.

PA *n* **1.** Br *abbr of* **personal assistant**. **2.** (*abbr of* **public address system**) sono *f*.

pace [peɪs] ♦ *n* **1.** (*speed, rate*) vitesse *f*, allure *f*; **to keep ~ (with sb)** marcher à la même allure (que qqn); **to keep ~ (with sthg)** se maintenir au même niveau (que qqch). **2.** (*step*) pas *m*. ♦ *vi*: **to ~ (up and down)** faire les cent pas.

pacemaker ['peɪs,meɪkə'] *n* **1.** (MED) stimulateur *m* cardiaque, pacemaker *m*. **2.** (SPORT) meneur *m*, -euse *f*.

Pacific [pə'sɪfɪk] ♦ *adj* du Pacifique.

♦ *n*: **the ~ (Ocean)** l'océan *m* Pacifique, le Pacifique.

pacifier ['pæsɪfaɪəʳ] *n* Am (*for child*) tétine *f*, sucette *f*.

pacifist ['pæsɪfɪst] *n* pacifiste *mf*.

pacify ['pæsɪfaɪ] *vt* 1. (*person, baby*) apaiser. 2. (*country*) pacifier.

pack [pæk] ♦ *n* 1. (*bag*) sac *m*. 2. (*packet*) paquet *m*. 3. (*of cards*) jeu *m*. 4. (*of dogs*) meute *f*; (*of wolves, thieves*) bande *f*. ♦ *vt* 1. (*clothes, belongings*) emballer; **to ~ one's bags** faire ses bagages. 2. (*fill*) remplir; **to be ~ed into** être entassé dans. ♦ *vi* (*for journey*) faire ses bagages OR sa valise. ► **pack in** ♦ *vt sep* Br *inf* (*stop*) plaquer; **~ it in!** (*stop annoying me*) arrête!, ça suffit maintenant!; (*shut up*) la ferme! ♦ *vi* tomber en panne. ► **pack off** *vt sep inf* (*send away*) expédier.

package ['pækɪdʒ] ♦ *n* 1. (*of books, goods*) paquet *m*. 2. *fig* (*of proposals etc*) ensemble *m*, série *f*. 3. (COMPUT) progiciel *m*. ♦ *vt* (*wrap up*) conditionner.

package deal *n* contrat *m* global.

package tour *n* vacances *fpl* organisées.

packaging ['pækɪdʒɪŋ] *n* conditionnement *m*.

packed [pækt] *adj*: **~ (with)** bourré(e) (de).

packed lunch *n* Br panier-repas *m*.

packet ['pækɪt] *n* (*gen*) paquet *m*.

packing ['pækɪŋ] *n* (*material*) emballage *m*.

packing case *n* caisse *f* d'emballage.

pact [pækt] *n* pacte *m*.

pad [pæd] ♦ *n* 1. (*of cotton wool etc*) morceau *m*. 2. (*of paper*) bloc *m*. 3. (SPACE): (**launch**) **~** pas *m* de tir. 4. (*of cat, dog*) coussinet *m*. 5. *inf* (*home*) pénates *mpl*. ♦ *vt* (*furniture, jacket*) rembourrer; (*wound*) tamponner. ♦ *vi* (*walk softly*) marcher à pas feutrés.

padding ['pædɪŋ] *n* 1. (*material*) rembourrage *m*. 2. *fig* (*in speech, letter*) délayage *m*.

paddle ['pædl] ♦ *n* 1. (*for canoe etc*) pagaie *f*. 2. (*in sea*): **to have a ~** faire trempette. ♦ *vi* 1. (*in canoe etc*) avancer en pagayant. 2. (*in sea*) faire trempette.

paddle boat, paddle steamer *n* bateau *m* à aubes.

paddling pool ['pædlɪŋ-] *n* Br 1. (*in park etc*) pataugeoire *f*. 2. (*inflatable*) piscine *f* gonflable.

paddock ['pædək] *n* 1. (*small field*) enclos *m*. 2. (*at racecourse*) paddock *m*.

paddy field ['pædɪ-] *n* rizière *f*.

padlock ['pædlɒk] ♦ *n* cadenas *m*. ♦ *vt* cadenasser.

paediatrics [ˌpiːdɪˈætrɪks] = **pediatrics**.

pagan ['peɪɡən] ♦ *adj* païen(enne). ♦ *n* païen *m*, -enne *f*.

page [peɪdʒ] ♦ *n* 1. (*of book*) page *f*. 2. (*sheet of paper*) feuille *f*. ♦ *vt* (*in airport*) appeler au micro.

pageant ['pædʒənt] *n* (*show*) spectacle *m* historique.

pageantry ['pædʒəntrɪ] *n* apparat *m*.

paid [peɪd] ♦ *pt* & *pp* → **pay**. ♦ *adj* (*work, holiday, staff*) rémunéré(e), payé(e).

pail [peɪl] *n* seau *m*.

pain [peɪn] *n* 1. (*hurt*) douleur *f*; **to be in ~** souffrir. 2. *inf* (*annoyance*): **it's/he is such a ~** c'est/il est vraiment assommant. ► **pains** *npl* (*effort, care*): **to be at ~s to do sthg** vouloir absolument faire qqch; **to take ~s to do sthg** se donner beaucoup de mal OR peine pour faire qqch.

pained [peɪnd] *adj* peiné(e).

painful ['peɪnfʊl] *adj* 1. (*physically*) douloureux(euse). 2. (*emotionally*) pénible.

painfully ['peɪnfʊlɪ] *adv* 1. (*fall, hit*) douloureusement. 2. (*remember, feel*) péniblement.

painkiller ['peɪnˌkɪləʳ] *n* calmant *m*, analgésique *m*.

painless ['peɪnlɪs] *adj* 1. (*without hurt*) indolore, sans douleur. 2. *fig* (*changeover*) sans heurt.

painstaking ['peɪnzˌteɪkɪŋ] *adj* (*worker*) assidu(e); (*detail, work*) soigné(e).

paint [peɪnt] ♦ *n* peinture *f*. ♦ *vt* (*gen*) peindre.

paintbrush ['peɪntbrʌʃ] *n* pinceau *m*.

painter ['peɪntəʳ] *n* peintre *m*.

painting ['peɪntɪŋ] *n* 1. (U) (*gen*) peinture *f*. 2. (*picture*) toile *f*, tableau *m*.

paint stripper *n* décapant *m*.

paintwork ['peɪntwɜːk] *n* (U) surfaces *fpl* peintes.

pair [peəʳ] *n* 1. (*of shoes, wings etc*) paire *f*; **a ~ of trousers** un pantalon. 2. (*couple*) couple *m*.

pajamas [pəˈdʒɑːməz] = **pyjamas**.

Pakistan [Br ˌpɑːkɪˈstɑːn, Am ˈpækɪstæn] *n* Pakistan *m*.

Pakistani [Br ˌpɑːkɪˈstɑːnɪ, Am ˌpækɪˈstænɪ] ♦ *adj* pakistanais(e). ♦ *n* Pakistanais *m*, -e *f*.

pal [pæl] *n inf* 1. (*friend*) copain *m*, copine *f*. 2. (*as term of address*) mon vieux *m*.

palace ['pælɪs] *n* palais *m*.

palatable ['pælətəbl] *adj* 1. (*food*)

agréable au goût. **2.** *fig* (*idea*) acceptable, agréable.

palate ['pælət] *n* palais *m*.

palaver [pə'lɑ:vər] *n* (U) *inf* **1.** (*talk*) palabres *fpl*. **2.** (*fuss*) histoire *f*, affaire *f*.

pale [peɪl] *adj* pâle.

Palestine ['pælə,staɪn] *n* Palestine *f*.

Palestinian [,pælə'stɪnɪən] ♦ *adj* palestinien(enne). ♦ *n* Palestinien *m*, -enne *f*.

palette ['pælət] *n* palette *f*.

palings ['peɪlɪŋz] *npl* palissade *f*.

pall [pɔ:l] ♦ *n* (*of smoke*) voile *m*. ♦ *vi* perdre de son charme.

pallet ['pælɪt] *n* palette *f*.

pallor ['pælər] *n literary* pâleur *f*.

palm [pɑ:m] *n* **1.** (*tree*) palmier *m*. **2.** (*of hand*) paume *f*. ▶ **palm off** *vt sep inf*: **to ~ sthg off on sb** refiler qqch à qqn; **to ~ sb off with sthg** se débarrasser de qqn avec qqch.

Palm Sunday *n* dimanche *m* des Rameaux.

palm tree *n* palmier *m*.

palpable ['pælpəbl] *adj* évident(e), manifeste.

paltry ['pɔ:ltrɪ] *adj* dérisoire.

pamper ['pæmpər] *vt* choyer, dorloter.

pamphlet ['pæmflɪt] *n* brochure *f*.

pan [pæn] ♦ *n* **1.** (*gen*) casserole *f*. **2.** *Am* (*for bread, cakes etc*) moule *m*. ♦ *vt inf* (*criticize*) démolir. ♦ *vi* (CINEMA) faire un panoramique.

panacea [,pænə'sɪə] *n* panacée *f*.

panama [,pænə'mɑ:] *n*: **~ (hat)** panama *m*.

Panama [,pænəmɑ:] *n* Panama *m*.

Panama Canal *n*: **the ~** le canal de Panama.

pancake ['pænkeɪk] *n* crêpe *f*.

Pancake Day *n Br* mardi gras *m*.

Pancake Tuesday *n* mardi gras *m*.

panda ['pændə] (*pl inv* OR **-s**) *n* panda *m*.

Panda car *n Br* voiture *f* de patrouille.

pandemonium [,pændɪ'məʊnjəm] *n* tohu-bohu *m inv*.

pander ['pændər] *vi*: **to ~ to sb** se prêter aux exigences de qqn; **to ~ to sthg** se plier à qqch.

pane [peɪn] *n* vitre *f*, carreau *m*.

panel ['pænl] *n* **1.** (TV & RADIO) invités *mpl*; (*of experts*) comité *m*. **2.** (*of wood*) panneau *m*. **3.** (*of machine*) tableau *m* de bord.

panelling *Br*, **paneling** *Am* ['pænəlɪŋ] *n* (U) lambris *m*.

pang [pæŋ] *n* tiraillement *m*.

panic ['pænɪk] (*pt* & *pp* **-ked**, *cont* **-king**) ♦ *n* panique *f*. ♦ *vi* paniquer.

panicky ['pænɪkɪ] *adj* (*person*) paniqué(e); (*feeling*) de panique.

panic-stricken *adj* affolé(e), pris(e) de panique.

panorama [,pænə'rɑ:mə] *n* panorama *m*.

pansy ['pænzɪ] *n* (*flower*) pensée *f*.

pant [pænt] *vi* haleter.

panther ['pænθər] (*pl inv* OR **-s**) *n* panthère *f*.

panties ['pæntɪz] *npl inf* culotte *f*.

pantihose ['pæntɪhəʊz] = **panty hose**.

pantomime ['pæntəmaɪm] *n Br spectacle de Noël pour enfants, généralement inspiré de contes de fée*.

pantry ['pæntrɪ] *n* garde-manger *m inv*.

pants [pænts] *npl* **1.** *Br* (*underpants - for men*) slip *m*; (*- for women*) culotte *f*, slip. **2.** *Am* (*trousers*) pantalon *m*.

panty hose ['pæntɪhəʊz] *npl Am* collant *m*.

papa [*Br* pə'pɑ:, *Am* 'pæpə] *n* papa *m*.

paper ['peɪpər] ♦ *n* **1.** (U) (*for writing on*) papier *m*; **a piece of ~** (*sheet*) une feuille de papier; (*scrap*) un bout de papier; **on ~** (*written down*) par écrit; (*in theory*) sur le papier. **2.** (*newspaper*) journal *m*. **3.** (*in exam - test*) épreuve *f*; (*- answers*) copie *f*. **4.** (*essay*): **~ (on)** essai *m* (sur). ♦ *adj* (*hat, bag etc*) en papier; *fig* (*profits*) théorique. ♦ *vt* tapisser. ▶ **papers** *npl* (*official documents*) papiers *mpl*.

paperback ['peɪpəbæk] *n*: **~ (book)** livre *m* de poche.

paper clip *n* trombone *m*.

paper handkerchief *n* mouchoir *m* en papier.

paper knife *n* coupe-papier *m inv*.

paper shop *n Br* marchand *m* de journaux.

paperweight ['peɪpəweɪt] *n* presse-papiers *m inv*.

paperwork ['peɪpəwɜːk] *n* paperasserie *f*.

paprika ['pæprɪkə] *n* paprika *m*.

par [pɑ:r] *n* **1.** (*parity*): **on a ~ with** à égalité avec. **2.** (GOLF) par *m*, normale *f* Can. **3.** (*good health*): **below** OR **under ~** pas en forme.

parable ['pærəbl] *n* parabole *f*.

paracetamol [,pærə'si:təmɒl] *n* paracétamol *m*.

parachute ['pærəʃu:t] ♦ *n* parachute *m*. ♦ *vi* sauter en parachute.

parade [pə'reɪd] ♦ *n* **1.** (*celebratory*)

parade f, revue f. **2.** (MIL) défilé m. ◆ vt **1.** (*people*) faire défiler. **2.** (*object*) montrer. **3.** *fig* (*flaunt*) afficher. ◆ vi défiler.

paradise ['pærədaɪs] n paradis m.

paradox ['pærədɒks] n paradoxe m.

paradoxically [,pærə'dɒksɪklɪ] adv paradoxalement.

paraffin ['pærəfɪn] n paraffine f.

paragon ['pærəgən] n modèle m, parangon m.

paragraph ['pærəgrɑːf] n paragraphe m.

Paraguay ['pærəgwaɪ] n Paraguay m.

parallel ['pærəlel] ◆ adj lit & fig: ~ (**to** OR **with**) parallèle (à). ◆ n **1.** (GEOM) parallèle f. **2.** (*similarity* & GEOGR) parallèle m. **3.** *fig* (*similar person, object*) équivalent m.

paralyse Br, **paralyze** Am ['pærəlaɪz] vt lit & fig paralyser.

paralysis [pə'rælɪsɪs] (pl -lyses [-lɪsiːz]) n paralysie f.

paramedic [,pærə'medɪk] n auxiliaire médical m, auxiliaire médicale f.

parameter [pə'ræmɪtər] n paramètre m.

paramount ['pærəmaʊnt] adj primordial(e); **of ~ importance** d'une importance suprême.

paranoid ['pærənɔɪd] adj paranoïaque.

paraphernalia [,pærəfə'neɪljə] n (U) attirail m, bazar m.

parasite ['pærəsaɪt] n parasite m.

parasol ['pærəsɒl] n (*above table*) parasol m; (*hand-held*) ombrelle f.

paratrooper ['pærətruːpər] n parachutiste m.

parcel ['pɑːsl] n paquet m. ▶ **parcel up** vt sep empaqueter.

parched [pɑːtʃt] adj **1.** (*gen*) desséché(e). **2.** inf (*very thirsty*) assoiffé(e), mort(e) de soif.

parchment ['pɑːtʃmənt] n parchemin m.

pardon ['pɑːdn] ◆ n **1.** (JUR) grâce f. **2.** (U) (*forgiveness*) pardon m; **I beg your ~?** (*showing surprise, asking for repetition*) comment?, pardon?; **I beg your ~!** (*to apologize*) je vous demande pardon! ◆ vt **1.** (*forgive*) pardonner; **to ~ sb for sthg** pardonner qqch à qqn; **~ me!** pardon!, excusez-moi! **2.** (JUR) gracier. ◆ excl comment?

parent ['peərənt] n père m, mère f. ▶ **parents** npl parents mpl.

parental [pə'rentl] adj parental(e).

parenthesis [pə'renθɪsɪs] (pl -theses [-θɪsiːz]) n parenthèse f.

Paris ['pærɪs] n Paris.

parish ['pærɪʃ] n **1.** (RELIG) paroisse f. **2.** Br (*area of local government*) commune f.

Parisian [pə'rɪzjən] ◆ adj parisien (enne). ◆ n Parisien m, -enne f.

parity ['pærətɪ] n égalité f.

park [pɑːk] ◆ n parc m, jardin m public. ◆ vt garer. ◆ vi se garer, stationner.

parking ['pɑːkɪŋ] n stationnement m; **'no ~'** 'défense de stationner', 'stationnement interdit'.

parking lot n Am parking m.

parking meter n parcmètre m.

parking ticket n contravention f, PV m.

parlance ['pɑːləns] n: **in common/legal** etc **~** en langage courant/juridique etc.

parliament ['pɑːləmənt] n parlement m.

parliamentary [,pɑːlə'mentərɪ] adj parlementaire.

parlour Br, **parlor** Am ['pɑːlər] n dated salon m.

parochial [pə'rəʊkjəl] adj pej de clocher.

parody ['pærədɪ] ◆ n parodie f. ◆ vt parodier.

parole [pə'rəʊl] n (U) parole f; **on ~** en liberté conditionnelle.

parrot ['pærət] n perroquet m.

parry ['pærɪ] vt **1.** (*blow*) parer. **2.** (*question*) éluder.

parsley ['pɑːslɪ] n persil m.

parsnip ['pɑːsnɪp] n panais m.

parson ['pɑːsn] n pasteur m.

part [pɑːt] ◆ n **1.** (*gen*) partie f; **for the most ~** dans l'ensemble. **2.** (*of TV serial* etc) épisode m. **3.** (*component*) pièce f. **4.** (*in proportions*) mesure f. **5.** (THEATRE) rôle m. **6.** (*involvement*): **~ in** participation f à; **to play an important ~ in** jouer un rôle important dans; **to take ~ in** participer à; **for my ~** en ce qui me concerne. ◆ adv en partie. ◆ vt: **to ~ one's hair** se faire une raie. ◆ vi **1.** (*couple*) se séparer. **2.** (*curtains*) s'écarter, s'ouvrir. ▶ **parts** npl: **in these ~s** dans cette région. ▶ **part with** vt fus (*money*) débourser; (*possession*) se défaire de.

part exchange n reprise f; **to take sthg in ~** reprendre qqch.

partial ['pɑːʃl] adj **1.** (*incomplete*) partiel (elle). **2.** (*biased*) partial(e). **3.** (*fond*): **to be ~ to** avoir un penchant pour.

participant [pɑː'tɪsɪpənt] n participant m, -e f.

participate [pɑː'tɪsɪpeɪt] vi: **to ~ (in)** participer (à).

participation [pɑːˌtɪsɪˈpeɪʃn] *n* participation *f*.

participle [ˈpɑːtɪsɪpl] *n* participe *m*.

particle [ˈpɑːtɪkl] *n* particule *f*.

parti-coloured [ˈpɑːtɪ-] *adj* bariolé(e).

particular [pəˈtɪkjʊləʳ] *adj* **1.** (*gen*) particulier(ère). **2.** (*fussy*) pointilleux(euse); ~ **about** exigeant(e) à propos de. ▶ **particulars** *npl* renseignements *mpl.* ▶ **in particular** *adv* en particulier.

particularly [pəˈtɪkjʊləlɪ] *adv* particulièrement.

parting [ˈpɑːtɪŋ] *n* **1.** (*separation*) séparation *f*. **2.** Br (*in hair*) raie *f*.

partisan [ˌpɑːtɪˈzæn] ◆ *adj* partisan(e). ◆ *n* partisan *m*, -e *f*.

partition [pɑːˈtɪʃn] ◆ *n* (*wall, screen*) cloison *f*. ◆ *vt* **1.** (*room*) cloisonner. **2.** (*country*) partager.

partly [ˈpɑːtlɪ] *adv* partiellement, en partie.

partner [ˈpɑːtnəʳ] ◆ *n* **1.** (*in game, dance*) partenaire *mf*; (*spouse*) conjoint *m*, -e *f*; (*not married*) compagnon *m*, compagne *f*. **2.** (*in a business, crime*) associé *m*, -e *f*. ◆ *vt* être le partenaire de.

partnership [ˈpɑːtnəʃɪp] *n* association *f*.

partridge [ˈpɑːtrɪdʒ] *n* perdrix *f*.

part-time *adj & adv* à temps partiel.

party [ˈpɑːtɪ] ◆ *n* **1.** (POL) parti *m*. **2.** (*social gathering*) fête *f*, réception *f*; **to have** OR **throw a** ~ donner une fête. **3.** (*group*) groupe *m*. **4.** (JUR) partie *f*. ◆ *vi inf* faire la fête.

party line *n* **1.** (POL) ligne *f* du parti. **2.** (TELEC) ligne *f* commune à deux abonnés.

pass [pɑːs] ◆ *n* **1.** (SPORT) passe *f*. **2.** (*document - for security*) laissez-passer *m inv*; (*- for travel*) carte *f* d'abonnement. **3.** Br (*in exam*) mention *f* passable. **4.** (*between mountains*) col *m*. **5.** *phr*: **to make a** ~ **at sb** faire du plat à qqn. ◆ *vt* **1.** (*object, time*) passer; **to** ~ **sthg to sb, to** ~ **sb sthg** passer qqch à qqn. **2.** (*person in street etc*) croiser. **3.** (*place*) passer devant. **4.** (AUT) dépasser, doubler. **5.** (*exceed*) dépasser. **6.** (*exam*) réussir (à); (*driving test*) passer. **7.** (*candidate*) recevoir, admettre. **8.** (*law, motion*) voter. **9.** (*opinion*) émettre; (*judgment*) rendre, prononcer. ◆ *vi* **1.** (*gen*) passer. **2.** (AUT) doubler, dépasser. **3.** (*in exam*) réussir, être reçu(e). ▶ **pass as** *vt fus* passer pour. ▶ **pass away** *vi* s'éteindre. ▶ **pass by** ◆ *vt sep*: **the news ~ed him by**

la nouvelle ne l'a pas affecté. ◆ *vi* passer à côté. ▶ **pass for** = **pass as**. ▶ **pass on** ◆ *vt sep*: **to** ~ **sthg on (to)** (*object*) faire passer qqch (à); (*tradition, information*) transmettre qqch (à). ◆ *vi* **1.** (*move on*) continuer son chemin. **2.** = **pass away**. ▶ **pass out** *vi* **1.** (*faint*) s'évanouir. **2.** Br (MIL) finir OR terminer les classes. ▶ **pass over** *vt fus* (*problem, topic*) passer sous silence. ▶ **pass up** *vt sep* (*opportunity, invitation*) laisser passer.

passable [ˈpɑːsəbl] *adj* **1.** (*satisfactory*) passable. **2.** (*road*) praticable; (*river*) franchissable.

passage [ˈpæsɪdʒ] *n* **1.** (*gen*) passage *m*. **2.** (*between rooms*) couloir *m*. **3.** (*sea journey*) traversée *f*.

passageway [ˈpæsɪdʒweɪ] *n* (*between houses*) passage *m*; (*between rooms*) couloir *m*.

passbook [ˈpɑːsbʊk] *n* livret *m* (d'épargne).

passenger [ˈpæsɪndʒəʳ] *n* passager *m*, -ère *f*.

passerby [ˌpɑːsəˈbaɪ] (*pl* **passersby** [ˌpɑːsəzˈbaɪ]) *n* passant *m*, -e *f*.

passing [ˈpɑːsɪŋ] *adj* (*remark*) en passant; (*trend*) passager(ère). ▶ **in passing** *adv* en passant.

passion [ˈpæʃn] *n* passion *f*.

passionate [ˈpæʃənət] *adj* passionné(e).

passive [ˈpæsɪv] *adj* passif(ive).

Passover [ˈpɑːsˌəʊvəʳ] *n*: (**the**) ~ la Pâque juive.

passport [ˈpɑːspɔːt] *n* (*document*) passeport *m*.

passport control *n* contrôle *m* des passeports.

password [ˈpɑːswɜːd] *n* mot *m* de passe.

past [pɑːst] ◆ *adj* **1.** (*former*) passé(e); **for the** ~ **five years** ces cinq dernières années; **the** ~ **week** la semaine passée OR dernière. **2.** (*finished*) fini(e). ◆ *adv* **1.** (*in times*): **it's ten** ~ il est dix. **2.** (*in front*): **to drive** ~ passer (devant) en voiture; **to run** ~ passer (devant) en courant. ◆ *n* passé *m*; **in the** ~ dans le temps. ◆ *prep* **1.** (*in times*): **it's half** ~ **eight** il est huit heures et demie; **it's five** ~ **nine** il est neuf heures cinq. **2.** (*in front of*) devant; **we drove** ~ **them** nous les avons dépassés en voiture. **3.** (*beyond*) après, au-delà de.

pasta [ˈpæstə] *n* (U) pâtes *fpl*.

paste [peɪst] ◆ *n* **1.** (*gen*) pâte *f*.

2. (CULIN) pâté m. 3. (U) (glue) colle f.
♦ vt coller.

pastel ['pæstl] ♦ adj pastel (inv). ♦ n pastel m.

pasteurize, -ise ['pɑːstʃəraɪz] vt pasteuriser.

pastille ['pæstɪl] n pastille f.

pastime ['pɑːstaɪm] n passe-temps m inv.

pastor ['pɑːstər] n pasteur m.

past participle n participe m passé.

pastry ['peɪstrɪ] n 1. (mixture) pâte f. 2. (cake) pâtisserie f.

past tense n passé m.

pasture ['pɑːstʃər] n pâturage m, pré m.

pasty¹ ['peɪstɪ] adj blafard(e), terreux (euse).

pasty² ['pæstɪ] n Br petit pâté m, friand m.

pat [pæt] ♦ n 1. (light stroke) petite tape f; (to animal) caresse f. 2. (of butter) noix f, noisette f. ♦ vt (person) tapoter, donner une tape à; (animal) caresser.

patch [pætʃ] ♦ n 1. (piece of material) pièce f; (to cover eye) bandeau m. 2. (small area - of snow, ice) plaque f. 3. (of land) parcelle f, lopin m; **vegetable ~** carré m de légumes. 4. (period of time): **a difficult ~** une mauvaise passe. ♦ vt rapiécer. ▶ **patch up** vt sep 1. (mend) rafistoler, bricoler. 2. fig (quarrel) régler, arranger; **to ~ up a relationship** se raccommoder.

patchwork ['pætʃwɜːk] n patchwork m.

patchy ['pætʃɪ] adj (gen) inégal(e); (knowledge) insuffisant(e), imparfait(e).

pâté ['pæteɪ] n pâté m.

patent [Br 'peɪtənt, Am 'pætənt] ♦ adj (obvious) évident(e), manifeste. ♦ n brevet m (d'invention). ♦ vt faire breveter.

patent leather n cuir m verni.

paternal [pə'tɜːnl] adj paternel(elle).

path [pɑːθ, pl pɑːðz] n 1. (track) chemin m, sentier m. 2. (way ahead, course of action) voie f, chemin m. 3. (trajectory) trajectoire f.

pathetic [pə'θetɪk] adj 1. (causing pity) pitoyable, attendrissant(e). 2. (useless - efforts, person) pitoyable, minable.

pathological [ˌpæθə'lɒdʒɪkl] adj pathologique.

pathology [pə'θɒlədʒɪ] n pathologie f.

pathos ['peɪθɒs] n pathétique m.

pathway ['pɑːθweɪ] n chemin m, sentier m.

patience ['peɪʃns] n 1. (of person) patience f. 2. (card game) réussite f.

patient ['peɪʃnt] ♦ adj patient(e). ♦ n (in hospital) patient m, -e f, malade mf; (of doctor) patient.

patio ['pætɪəʊ] (pl -s) n patio m.

patriotic [Br ˌpætrɪ'ɒtɪk, Am ˌpeɪtrɪ'ɒtɪk] adj (gen) patriotique; (person) patriote.

patrol [pə'trəʊl] ♦ n patrouille f. ♦ vt patrouiller dans, faire une patrouille dans.

patrol car n voiture f de police.

patrolman [pə'trəʊlmən] (pl -men [-mən]) n Am agent m de police.

patron ['peɪtrən] n 1. (of arts) mécène m, protecteur m, -trice f. 2. Br (of charity) patron m, -onne f. 3. fml (customer) client m, -e f.

patronize, -ise ['pætrənaɪz] vt 1. (talk down to) traiter avec condescendance. 2. fml (back financially) patronner, protéger.

patronizing ['pætrənaɪzɪŋ] adj condescendant(e).

patter ['pætər] ♦ n 1. (sound - of rain) crépitement m. 2. (talk) baratin m, bavardage m. ♦ vi (feet, paws) trottiner; (rain) frapper, fouetter.

pattern ['pætən] n 1. (design) motif m, dessin m. 2. (of distribution, population) schéma m; (of life, behaviour) mode m. 3. (diagram): **~ patron** m. 4. (model) modèle m.

paunch [pɔːntʃ] n bedaine f.

pauper ['pɔːpər] n indigent m, -e f, nécessiteux m, -euse f.

pause [pɔːz] ♦ n 1. (short silence) pause f, silence m. 2. (break) pause f, arrêt m. ♦ vi 1. (stop speaking) marquer un temps. 2. (stop moving, doing) faire une pause, s'arrêter.

pave [peɪv] vt paver; **to ~ the way for sb/sthg** ouvrir la voie à qqn/qqch.

pavement ['peɪvmənt] n 1. Br (at side of road) trottoir m. 2. Am (roadway) chaussée f.

pavilion [pə'vɪljən] n pavillon m.

paving ['peɪvɪŋ] n (U) pavé m.

paving stone n pavé m.

paw [pɔː] n patte f.

pawn [pɔːn] ♦ n lit & fig pion m. ♦ vt mettre en gage.

pawnbroker ['pɔːnˌbrəʊkər] n prêteur m, -euse f sur gages.

pawnshop ['pɔːnʃɒp] n boutique f de prêteur sur gages.

pay [peɪ] (pt & pp paid) ♦ vt 1. (gen) payer; **to ~ sb for sthg** payer qqn pour qqch, payer qqch à qqn; **I paid £20 for that shirt** j'ai payé cette chemise 20 livres; **to ~ money into an account** Br verser de l'argent sur un compte; **to ~ a cheque into an account** déposer un chèque sur un compte. **2.** (*be profitable to*) rapporter à. **3.** (*give, make*): **to ~ attention (to sb/sthg)** prêter attention (à qqn/qqch); **to ~ sb a compliment** faire un compliment à qqn; **to ~ sb a visit** rendre visite à qqn. ◆ *vi* payer; **to ~ dearly for sthg** *fig* payer qqch cher. ◆ *n* salaire *m*, traitement *m*. ▶ **pay back** *vt sep* **1.** (*return loan of money*) rembourser. **2.** (*revenge oneself on*) revaloir; **I'll ~ you back for that** tu me le paieras, je te le revaudrai. ▶ **pay off** ◆ *vt sep* **1.** (*repay - debt*) s'acquitter de, régler; (- *loan*) rembourser. **2.** (*dismiss*) licencier, congédier. **3.** (*bribe*) soudoyer, acheter. ◆ *vi* (*course of action*) être payant(e). ▶ **pay up** *vi* payer.

payable ['peɪəbl] *adj* **1.** (*gen*) payable. **2.** (*on cheque*): **~ to** à l'ordre de.

paycheck ['peɪtʃek] *n* Am paie *f*.

payday ['peɪdeɪ] *n* jour *m* de paie.

payee [peɪ'iː] *n* bénéficiaire *mf*.

pay envelope *n* Am salaire *m*.

payment ['peɪmənt] *n* paiement *m*.

pay packet *n* Br **1.** (*envelope*) enveloppe *f* de paie. **2.** (*wages*) paie *f*.

pay phone, pay station Am *n* téléphone *m* public, cabine *f* téléphonique.

payroll ['peɪrəʊl] *n* registre *m* du personnel.

payslip ['peɪslɪp] *n* Br feuille *f* OR bulletin *m* de paie.

pay station Am = **pay phone**.

pc (*abbr of* **per cent**) p. cent.

PC *n* **1.** (*abbr of* **personal computer**) PC *m*, micro *m*. **2.** *abbr of* **police constable**.

PE (*abbr of* **physical education**) *n* EPS *f*.

pea [piː] *n* pois *m*.

peace [piːs] *n* (U) paix *f*; (*quiet, calm*) calme *m*, tranquillité *f*; **to make (one's) ~ with sb** faire la paix avec qqn.

peaceable ['piːsəbl] *adj* paisible, pacifique.

peaceful ['piːsfʊl] *adj* **1.** (*quiet, calm*) paisible, calme. **2.** (*not aggressive - person*) pacifique; (- *demonstration*) non-violent(e).

peacetime ['piːstaɪm] *n* temps *m* de paix.

peach [piːtʃ] ◆ *adj* couleur pêche (*inv*). ◆ *n* pêche *f*.

peacock ['piːkɒk] *n* paon *m*.

peak [piːk] ◆ *n* **1.** (*mountain top*) sommet *m*, cime *f*. **2.** *fig* (*of career, success*) apogée *m*, sommet *m*. **3.** (*of cap*) visière

f. ◆ *adj* (*condition*) optimum. ◆ *vi* atteindre un niveau maximum.

peaked [piːkt] *adj* (*cap*) à visière.

peak hours *npl* heures *fpl* d'affluence OR de pointe.

peak period *n* période *f* de pointe.

peak rate *n* tarif *m* normal.

peal [piːl] ◆ *n* (*of bells*) carillonnement *m*; (*of laughter*) éclat *m*; (*of thunder*) coup *m*. ◆ *vi* (*bells*) carillonner.

peanut ['piːnʌt] *n* cacahuète *f*.

peanut butter *n* beurre *m* de cacahuètes.

pear [peəʳ] *n* poire *f*.

pearl [pɜːl] *n* perle *f*.

peasant ['peznt] *n* (*in countryside*) paysan *m*, -anne *f*.

peat [piːt] *n* tourbe *f*.

pebble ['pebl] *n* galet *m*, caillou *m*.

peck [pek] ◆ *n* **1.** (*with beak*) coup *m* de bec. **2.** (*kiss*) bise *f*. ◆ *vt* **1.** (*with beak*) picoter, becqueter. **2.** (*kiss*): **to ~ sb on the cheek** faire une bise à qqn.

pecking order ['pekɪŋ-] *n* hiérarchie *f*.

peckish ['pekɪʃ] *adj* Br *inf*: **to feel ~** avoir un petit creux.

peculiar [pɪ'kjuːljəʳ] *adj* **1.** (*odd*) bizarre, curieux(euse). **2.** (*slightly ill*): **to feel ~** se sentir tout drôle (toute drôle) OR tout chose (toute chose). **3.** (*characteristic*): **~ to** propre à, particulier(ère) à.

peculiarity [pɪˌkjuːlɪ'ærətɪ] *n* **1.** (*oddness*) bizarrerie *f*, singularité *f*. **2.** (*characteristic*) particularité *f*, caractéristique *f*.

pedal ['pedl] ◆ *n* pédale *f*. ◆ *vi* pédaler.

pedal bin *n* poubelle *f* à pédale.

pedantic [pɪ'dæntɪk] *adj pej* pédant(e).

peddle ['pedl] *vt* **1.** (*drugs*) faire le trafic de. **2.** (*gossip, rumour*) colporter, répandre.

pedestal ['pedɪstl] *n* piédestal *m*.

pedestrian [pɪ'destrɪən] *n* piéton *m*.

pedestrian crossing *n* Br passage *m* pour piétons, passage clouté.

pedestrian precinct Br, **pedestrian zone** Am *n* zone *f* piétonne.

pediatrics [ˌpiːdɪ'ætrɪks] *n* pédiatrie *f*.

pedigree ['pedɪgriː] ◆ *adj* (*animal*) de race. ◆ *n* **1.** (*of animal*) pedigree *m*. **2.** (*of person*) ascendance *f*, généalogie *f*.

pedlar Br, **peddler** Am ['pedləʳ] *n* colporteur *m*.

pee [piː] *inf* ◆ *n* pipi *m*, pisse *f*. ◆ *vi* faire pipi, pisser.

peek [piːk] *inf* ◆ *n* coup *m* d'œil furtif. ◆ *vi* jeter un coup d'œil furtif.

peel [piːl] ◆ *n* (*of apple, potato*) peau *f*; (*of*

orange, lemon) écorce f. ◆ vt éplucher, peler. ◆ vi **1.** (*paint*) s'écailler. **2.** (*wallpaper*) se décoller. **3.** (*skin*) peler.

peelings ['pi:lɪŋz] npl épluchures fpl.

peep [pi:p] ◆ n **1.** (*look*) coup m d'œil OR regard m furtif. **2.** inf (*sound*) bruit m. ◆ vi jeter un coup d'œil furtif. ▶ **peep out** vi apparaître, se montrer.

peephole ['pi:phəʊl] n judas m.

peer [pɪər] ◆ n pair m. ◆ vi scruter, regarder attentivement.

peerage ['pɪərɪdʒ] n (*rank*) pairie f; **the ~** les pairs mpl.

peer group n pairs mpl.

peeved [pi:vd] adj inf fâché(e), irrité(e).

peevish ['pi:vɪʃ] adj grincheux(euse).

peg [peg] ◆ n **1.** (*hook*) cheville f. **2.** (*for clothes*) pince f à linge. **3.** (*for tent*) piquet m. ◆ vt fig (*prices*) bloquer.

pejorative [pɪ'dʒɒrətɪv] adj péjoratif (ive).

pekinese [,pi:kə'ni:z], **pekingese** [,pi:kɪŋ'i:z] (pl inv OR **-s**) n (*dog*) pékinois m.

Peking [pi:'kɪŋ] n Pékin.

pekingese = **pekinese**.

pelican ['pelɪkən] (pl inv OR **-s**) n pélican m.

pelican crossing n Br passage pour piétons avec feux de circulation.

pellet ['pelɪt] n **1.** (*small ball*) boulette f. **2.** (*for gun*) plomb m.

pelmet ['pelmɪt] n Br lambrequin m.

pelt [pelt] ◆ n (*animal skin*) peau f, fourrure f. ◆ vt: **to ~ sb (with sthg)** bombarder qqn (de qqch). ◆ vi (*run fast*): **to ~ along** courir ventre à terre; **to ~ down the stairs** dévaler l'escalier. ▶ **pelt down** v impers (*rain*): **it's ~ing down** il pleut à verse.

pelvis ['pelvɪs] (pl **-vises** OR **-ves** [-vi:z]) n pelvis m, bassin m.

pen [pen] ◆ n **1.** (*for writing*) stylo m. **2.** (*enclosure*) parc m, enclos m. ◆ vt (*enclose*) parquer.

penal ['pi:nl] adj pénal(e).

penalize, -ise ['pi:nəlaɪz] vt **1.** (*gen*) pénaliser. **2.** (*put at a disadvantage*) désavantager.

penalty ['penltɪ] n **1.** (*punishment*) pénalité f; **to pay the ~ (for sthg)** fig supporter OR subir les conséquences (de qqch). **2.** (*fine*) amende f. **3.** (HOCKEY) pénalité f; **~ (kick)** (FTBL) penalty m; (RUGBY) (coup m de pied de) pénalité f.

penance ['penəns] n **1.** (RELIG) péni-

tence f. **2.** fig (*punishment*) corvée f, pensum m.

pence [pens] Br pl → **penny**.

penchant [Br pɑ̃ʃɑ̃, Am 'pentʃənt] n: **to have a ~ for sthg** avoir un faible pour qqch; **to have a ~ for doing sthg** avoir tendance à OR bien aimer faire qqch.

pencil ['pensl] ◆ n crayon m; **in ~** au crayon. ◆ vt griffonner au crayon, crayonner.

pencil case n trousse f (d'écolier).

pencil sharpener n taille-crayon m.

pendant ['pendənt] n (*jewel on chain*) pendentif m.

pending ['pendɪŋ] fml ◆ adj **1.** (*imminent*) imminent(e). **2.** (*court case*) en instance. ◆ prep en attendant.

pendulum ['pendjʊləm] (pl **-s**) n balancier m.

penetrate ['penɪtreɪt] vt **1.** (*gen*) pénétrer dans; (subj: *light*) percer; (subj: *rain*) s'infiltrer dans. **2.** (subj: *spy*) infiltrer.

pen friend n correspondant m, -e f.

penguin ['peŋgwɪn] n manchot m.

penicillin [,penɪ'sɪlɪn] n pénicilline f.

peninsula [pə'nɪnsjʊlə] (pl **-s**) n péninsule f.

penis ['pi:nɪs] (pl **penises** ['pi:nɪsɪz]) n pénis m.

penitentiary [,penɪ'tenʃərɪ] n Am prison f.

penknife ['pennaɪf] (pl **-knives** [-naɪvz]) n canif m.

pen name n pseudonyme m.

pennant ['penənt] n fanion m.

penniless ['penɪlɪs] adj sans le sou.

penny ['penɪ] (pl sense 1 **-ies**, pl sense 2 **pence**) n **1.** (*coin*) Br penny m; Am cent m. **2.** Br (*value*) pence m.

pen pal n inf correspondant m, -e f.

pension ['penʃn] n **1.** Br (*on retirement*) retraite f. **2.** (*from disability*) pension f.

pensioner ['penʃənər] n Br: **(old-age) ~** retraité m, -e f.

pensive ['pensɪv] adj songeur(euse).

pentagon ['pentəgən] n pentagone m. ▶ **Pentagon** n Am: **the Pentagon** le Pentagone (siège du ministère américain de la Défense).

Pentecost ['pentɪkɒst] n Pentecôte f.

penthouse ['penthaʊs, pl **-hauzɪz**] n appartement m de luxe (au dernier étage).

pent up ['pent-] adj (*emotions*) refoulé(e); (*energy*) contenu(e).

penultimate [pe'nʌltɪmət] adj avant-dernier(ère).

people ['pi:pl] ♦ n (nation, race) nation f, peuple m. ♦ npl 1. (persons) personnes fpl; **few/a lot of** ~ peu/beaucoup de monde, peu/beaucoup de gens; **there were a lot of** ~ present il y avait beaucoup de monde. 2. (in general) gens mpl; ~ **say that ...** on dit que ... 3. (inhabitants) habitants mpl. 4. (POL): **the** ~ le peuple. ♦ vt: **to be** ~**d by** OR **with** être peuplé(e) de.

pep [pep] n (U) inf entrain m, pep m. ▶ **pep up** vt sep inf 1. (person) remonter, requinquer. 2. (party, event) animer.

pepper ['pepər] n 1. (spice) poivre m. 2. (vegetable) poivron m.

pepperbox n Am = **pepper pot**.

peppermint ['pepəmɪnt] n 1. (sweet) bonbon m à la menthe. 2. (herb) menthe f poivrée.

pepper pot Br, **pepperbox** Am ['pepəbɒks] n poivrier m.

pep talk n inf paroles fpl OR discours m d'encouragement.

per [pɜːr] prep: ~ **person** par personne; **to be paid £10** ~ **hour** être payé 10 livres de l'heure; ~ **kilo** le kilo; **as** ~ **instructions** conformément aux instructions.

per annum adv par an.

per capita [pə'kæpɪtə] adj & adv par habitant OR tête.

perceive [pə'siːv] vt 1. (notice) percevoir. 2. (understand, realize) remarquer, s'apercevoir de. 3. (consider): **to** ~ **sb/sthg as** considérer qqn/qqch comme.

per cent adv pour cent.

percentage [pə'sentɪdʒ] n pourcentage m.

perception [pə'sepʃn] n 1. (aural, visual) perception f. 2. (insight) perspicacité f, intuition f.

perceptive [pə'septɪv] adj perspicace.

perch [pɜːtʃ] (pl sense 2 only inv OR -es) ♦ n 1. lit & fig (position) perchoir m. 2. (fish) perche f. ♦ vi se percher.

percolator ['pɜːkəleɪtər] n cafetière f à pression.

percussion [pə'kʌʃn] n (MUS) percussion f.

perennial [pə'renjəl] ♦ adj permanent(e), perpétuel(elle); (BOT) vivace. ♦ n (BOT) plante f vivace.

perfect [adj & n 'pɜːfɪkt, vb pə'fekt] ♦ adj parfait(e); **he's a** ~ **nuisance** il est absolument insupportable. ♦ n (GRAMM): ~ **(tense)** parfait m. ♦ vt parfaire, mettre au point.

perfection [pə'fekʃn] n perfection f; **to** ~ parfaitement (bien).

perfectionist [pə'fekʃənɪst] n perfectionniste mf.

perfectly ['pɜːfɪktlɪ] adv parfaitement; **you know** ~ **well** tu sais très bien.

perforate ['pɜːfəreɪt] vt perforer.

perforations [,pɜːfə'reɪʃnz] npl (in paper) pointillés mpl.

perform [pə'fɔːm] ♦ vt 1. (carry out) exécuter; (- function) remplir. 2. (play, concert) jouer. ♦ vi 1. (machine) marcher, fonctionner; (team, person): **to** ~ **well/ badly** avoir de bons/mauvais résultats. 2. (actor) jouer; (singer) chanter.

performance [pə'fɔːməns] n 1. (carrying out) exécution f. 2. (show) représentation f. 3. (by actor, singer etc) interprétation f. 4. (of car, engine) performance f.

performer [pə'fɔːmər] n artiste mf, interprète mf.

perfume ['pɜːfjuːm] n parfum m.

perfunctory [pə'fʌŋktərɪ] adj rapide, superficiel(elle).

perhaps [pə'hæps] adv peut-être; ~ **so/not** peut-être que oui/non.

peril ['perɪl] n danger m, péril m.

perimeter [pə'rɪmɪtər] n périmètre m; ~ **fence** clôture f; ~ **wall** mur m d'enceinte.

period ['pɪərɪəd] ♦ n 1. (gen) période f. 2. (SCH) ≃ heure f. 3. (menstruation) règles fpl. 4. Am (full stop) point m. ♦ comp (dress, house) d'époque.

periodic [,pɪərɪ'ɒdɪk] adj périodique.

periodical [,pɪərɪ'ɒdɪkl] ♦ adj = **periodic**. ♦ n (magazine) périodique m.

peripheral [pə'rɪfərəl] ♦ adj 1. (unimportant) secondaire. 2. (at edge) périphérique. ♦ n (COMPUT) périphérique m.

perish ['perɪʃ] vi 1. (die) périr, mourir. 2. (food) pourrir, se gâter; (rubber) se détériorer.

perishable ['perɪʃəbl] adj périssable. ▶ **perishables** npl denrées fpl périssables.

perjury ['pɜːdʒərɪ] n (U) (JUR) parjure m, faux serment m.

perk [pɜːk] n inf à-côté m, avantage m. ▶ **perk up** vi se ragaillardir.

perky ['pɜːkɪ] adj inf (cheerful) guilleret (ette); (lively) plein(e) d'entrain.

perm [pɜːm] n permanente f.

permanent ['pɜːmənənt] ♦ adj permanent(e). ♦ n Am (perm) permanente f.

permeate ['pɜːmɪeɪt] vt 1. (subj: liquid, smell) s'infiltrer dans, pénétrer. 2. (subj: feeling, idea) se répandre dans.

permissible [pə'mɪsəbl] adj acceptable, admissible.

permission [pə'mɪʃn] n permission f, autorisation f.

permissive [pə'mɪsɪv] adj permissif (ive).

permit [vb pə'mɪt, n 'pɜːmɪt] ◆ vt permettre; **to ~ sb to do sthg** permettre à qqn de faire qqch, autoriser qqn à faire qqch; **to ~ sb sthg** permettre qqch à qqn. ◆ n permis m.

pernicious [pə'nɪʃəs] adj fml (harmful) pernicieux(euse).

pernickety [pə'nɪkətɪ] adj inf (fussy) tatillon(onne), pointilleux(euse).

perpendicular [,pɜːpən'dɪkjulər] ◆ adj perpendiculaire. ◆ n perpendiculaire f.

perpetrate ['pɜːpɪtreɪt] vt perpétrer, commettre.

perpetual [pə'petʃuəl] adj 1. pej (continuous) continuel(elle), incessant(e). 2. (long-lasting) perpétuel(elle).

perplex [pə'pleks] vt rendre perplexe.

perplexing [pə'pleksɪŋ] adj déroutant(e), déconcertant(e).

persecute ['pɜːsɪkjuːt] vt persécuter, tourmenter.

perseverance [,pɜːsɪ'vɪərəns] n persévérance f, ténacité f.

persevere [,pɜːsɪ'vɪər] vi 1. (with difficulty) persévérer, persister; **to ~ with** persévérer OR persister dans. 2. (with determination): **to ~ in doing sthg** persister à faire qqch.

Persian ['pɜːʃn] adj persan(e); (HISTORY) perse.

persist [pə'sɪst] vi: **to ~ (in doing sthg)** persister OR s'obstiner (à faire qqch).

persistence [pə'sɪstəns] n persistance f.

persistent [pə'sɪstənt] adj 1. (noise, rain) continuel(elle); (problem) constant(e). 2. (determined) tenace, obstiné(e).

person ['pɜːsn] (pl people OR persons fml) n 1. (man or woman) personne f; **in ~** en personne. 2. fml (body): **about one's ~** sur soi.

personable ['pɜːsnəbl] adj sympathique, agréable.

personal ['pɜːsənl] adj 1. (gen) personnel(elle). 2. pej (rude) désobligeant(e).

personal assistant n secrétaire mf de direction.

personal column n petites annonces fpl.

personal computer n ordinateur m personnel OR individuel.

personality [,pɜːsə'nælətɪ] n personnalité f.

personally ['pɜːsnəlɪ] adv personnellement; **to take sthg ~** se sentir visé par qqch.

personal organizer n agenda m modulaire multifonction.

personal property n (U) (JUR) biens mpl personnels.

personal stereo n baladeur m, Walkman® m.

personify [pə'sɒnɪfaɪ] vt personnifier.

personnel [,pɜːsə'nel] ◆ n (U) (department) service m du personnel. ◆ npl (staff) personnel m.

perspective [pə'spektɪv] n 1. (ART) perspective f. 2. (view, judgment) point m de vue, optique f.

Perspex® ['pɜːspeks] n Br ≃ Plexiglas® m.

perspiration [,pɜːspə'reɪʃn] n 1. (sweat) sueur f. 2. (act of perspiring) transpiration f.

persuade [pə'sweɪd] vt: **to ~ sb to do sthg** persuader OR convaincre qqn de faire qqch; **to ~ sb that** convaincre qqn que; **to ~ sb of** convaincre qqn de.

persuasion [pə'sweɪʒn] n 1. (act of persuading) persuasion f. 2. (belief - religious) confession f; (- political) opinion f, conviction f.

persuasive [pə'sweɪsɪv] adj (person) persuasif(ive); (argument) convaincant(e).

pert [pɜːt] adj mutin(e), coquin(e).

pertain [pə'teɪn] vi fml: **~ing to** concernant, relatif(ive) à.

pertinent ['pɜːtɪnənt] adj pertinent(e), approprié(e).

perturb [pə'tɜːb] vt inquiéter, troubler.

Peru [pə'ruː] n Pérou m.

peruse [pə'ruːz] vt lire attentivement.

pervade [pə'veɪd] vt (subj: smell) se répandre dans; (subj: feeling, influence) envahir.

perverse [pə'vɜːs] adj (contrary - person) contrariant(e); (- enjoyment) malin(igne).

perversion [Br pə'vɜːʃn, Am pə'vɜːrʒn] n 1. (sexual) perversion f. 2. (of truth) travestissement m.

pervert [n 'pɜːvɜːt, vb pə'vɜːt] ◆ n pervers m, -e f. ◆ vt 1. (truth, meaning) travestir, déformer; (course of justice) entraver. 2. (sexually) pervertir.

pessimist ['pesɪmɪst] n pessimiste mf.

pessimistic [,pesɪ'mɪstɪk] adj pessimiste.

pest [pest] n 1. (insect) insecte m nuisible; (*animal*) animal *m* nuisible. **2.** *inf* (*nuisance*) casse-pieds *mf inv*.

pester ['pestər] *vt* harceler, importuner.

pet [pet] ◆ *adj* (*favourite*): ~ **subject** dada *m*; ~ **hate** bête *f* noire. ◆ *n* **1.** (*animal*) animal *m* (familier). **2.** (*favourite person*) chouchou *m*, -oute *f*. ◆ *vt* caresser, câliner. ◆ *vi* se peloter, se caresser.

petal ['petl] *n* pétale *m*.

peter ['pi:tər] ► **peter out** *vi* (*path*) s'arrêter, se perdre; (*interest*) diminuer, décliner.

petite [pə'ti:t] *adj* menu(e).

petition [pɪ'tɪʃn] ◆ *n* pétition *f*. ◆ *vt* adresser une pétition à.

petrified ['petrɪfaɪd] *adj* (*terrified*) paralysé(e) OR pétrifié(e) de peur.

petrol ['petrəl] *n* Br essence *f*.

petrol bomb *n* Br cocktail *m* Molotov.

petrol can *n* Br bidon *m* à essence.

petroleum [pɪ'trəʊljəm] *n* pétrole *m*.

petrol pump *n* Br pompe *f* à essence.

petrol station *n* Br station-service *f*.

petrol tank *n* Br réservoir *m* d'essence.

pet shop *n* animalerie *f*.

petticoat ['petɪkəʊt] *n* jupon *m*.

petty ['petɪ] *adj* **1.** (*small-minded*) mesquin(e). **2.** (*trivial*) insignifiant(e), sans importance.

petty cash *n* (U) caisse *f* des dépenses courantes.

petty officer *n* second maître *m*.

petulant ['petjʊlənt] *adj* irritable.

pew [pju:] *n* banc *m* d'église.

pewter ['pju:tər] *n* étain *m*.

phantom ['fæntəm] ◆ *adj* fantomatique, spectral(e). ◆ *n* (*ghost*) fantôme *m*.

pharmaceutical [,fɑːmə'sjuːtɪkl] *adj* pharmaceutique.

pharmacist ['fɑːməsɪst] *n* pharmacien *m*, -enne *f*.

pharmacy ['fɑːməsɪ] *n* pharmacie *f*.

pharyngitis [,færɪn'dʒaɪtɪs] *n* (U) pharyngite *f*.

phase [feɪz] *n* phase *f*. ► **phase in** *vt sep* introduire progressivement. ► **phase out** *vt sep* supprimer progressivement.

PhD (*abbr of* **Doctor of Philosophy**) *n* (*titulaire d'un*) doctorat de 3ᵉ cycle.

pheasant ['feznt] (*pl inv* OR **-s**) *n* faisan *m*.

phenomena [fɪ'nɒmɪnə] *pl* → **phenomenon**.

phenomenal [fɪ'nɒmɪnl] *adj* phénoménal(e), extraordinaire.

phenomenon [fɪ'nɒmɪnən] (*pl* **-mena**) *n* phénomène *m*.

phial ['faɪəl] *n* fiole *f*.

philanthropist [fɪ'lænθrəpɪst] *n* philanthrope *mf*.

philately [fɪ'lætəlɪ] *n* philatélie *f*.

Philippine ['fɪlɪpiːn] *adj* philippin(e). ► **Philippines** *npl*: **the ~s** les Philippines *fpl*.

philosopher [fɪ'lɒsəfər] *n* philosophe *mf*.

philosophical [,fɪlə'sɒfɪkl] *adj* **1.** (*gen*) philosophique. **2.** (*stoical*) philosophe.

philosophy [fɪ'lɒsəfɪ] *n* philosophie *f*.

phlegm [flem] *n* flegme *m*.

phlegmatic [fleg'mætɪk] *adj* flegmatique.

phobia ['fəʊbjə] *n* phobie *f*.

phone [fəʊn] ◆ *n* téléphone *m*; **to be on the ~** (*speaking*) être au téléphone; Br (*connected to network*) avoir le téléphone. ◆ *comp* téléphonique. ◆ *vt* téléphoner à, appeler. ◆ *vi* téléphoner. ► **phone up** *vt sep* & *vi* téléphoner.

phone book *n* annuaire *m* (du téléphone).

phone booth *n* cabine *f* téléphonique.

phone box *n* Br cabine *f* téléphonique.

phone call *n* coup *m* de téléphone OR fil; **to make a ~** passer OR donner un coup de fil.

phonecard ['fəʊnkɑːd] *n* ≃ Télécarte® *f*.

phone-in *n* (RADIO & TV) programme *m* à ligne ouverte.

phone number *n* numéro *m* de téléphone.

phonetics [fə'netɪks] *n* (U) phonétique *f*.

phoney Br, **phony** Am ['fəʊnɪ] *inf* ◆ *adj* **1.** (*passport, address*) bidon (*inv*). **2.** (*person*) hypocrite, pas franc (pas franche). ◆ *n* poseur *m*, -euse *f*.

phosphorus ['fɒsfərəs] *n* phosphore *m*.

photo ['fəʊtəʊ] *n* photo *f*; **to take a ~ of sb/sthg** photographier qqn/qqch, prendre qqn/qqch en photo.

photocopier ['fəʊtəʊ,kɒpɪər] *n* photocopieur *m*, copieur *m*.

photocopy ['fəʊtəʊ,kɒpɪ] ◆ *n* photocopie *f*. ◆ *vt* photocopier.

photograph ['fəʊtəgrɑːf] ◆ *n* photographie *f*; **to take a ~ (of sb/sthg)** prendre (qqn/qqch) en photo, photographier (qqn/qqch). ◆ *vt* photographier, prendre en photo.

photographer [fə'tɒgrəfər] *n* photographe *mf*.

photography [fə'tɒgrəfɪ] *n* photographie *f*.

phrasal verb ['freɪzl-] *n* verbe *m* à postposition.

phrase [freɪz] ◆ *n* expression *f*. ◆ *vt* exprimer, tourner.

phrasebook ['freɪzbʊk] *n* guide *m* de conversation (*pour touristes*).

physical ['fɪzɪkl] ◆ *adj* 1. (*gen*) physique. 2. (*world, objects*) matériel(elle). ◆ *n* (*examination*) visite *f* médicale.

physical education *n* éducation *f* physique.

physically ['fɪzɪklɪ] *adv* physiquement.

physically handicapped ◆ *adj:* to be ~ être handicapé(e) physique. ◆ *npl:* the ~ les handicapés *mpl* physiques.

physician [fɪ'zɪʃn] *n* médecin *m*.

physicist ['fɪzɪsɪst] *n* physicien *m*, -enne *f*.

physics ['fɪzɪks] *n* (U) physique *f*.

physiotherapy [ˌfɪzɪəʊ'θerəpɪ] *n* kinésithérapie *f*.

physique [fɪ'zi:k] *n* physique *m*.

pianist ['pɪənɪst] *n* pianiste *mf*.

piano [pɪ'ænəʊ] (*pl* -s) *n* piano *m*.

pick [pɪk] ◆ *n* 1. (*tool*) pioche *f*, pic *m*. 2. (*selection*): to take one's ~ choisir, faire son choix. 3. (*best*): the ~ of le meilleur (la meilleure) de. ◆ *vt* 1. (*select, choose*) choisir, sélectionner. 2. (*gather*) cueillir. 3. (*remove*) enlever. 4. (*nose*): to ~ one's nose se décrotter le nez; to ~ one's teeth se curer les dents. 5. (*fight, quarrel*) chercher; to ~ a fight (with sb) chercher la bagarre (à qqn). 6. (*lock*) crocheter. ▶ **pick on** *vt fus* s'en prendre à, être sur le dos de. ▶ **pick out** *vt sep* 1. (*recognize*) repérer, reconnaître. 2. (*select, choose*) choisir, désigner. ▶ **pick up** ◆ *vt sep* 1. (*lift up*) ramasser. 2. (*collect*) aller chercher, passer prendre. 3. (*collect in car*) prendre, chercher. 4. (*skill, language*) apprendre; (*habit*) prendre; (*bargain*) découvrir; to ~ up speed prendre de la vitesse. 5. *inf* (*sexually - woman, man*) draguer. 6. (RADIO & TELEC) (*detect, receive*) capter, recevoir. 7. (*conversation, work*) reprendre, continuer. ◆ *vi* (*improve, start again*) reprendre.

pickaxe Br, **pickax** Am ['pɪkæks] *n* pioche *f*, pic *m*.

picket ['pɪkɪt] ◆ *n* piquet *m* de grève.

◆ *vt* mettre un piquet de grève devant.

picket line *n* piquet *m* de grève.

pickle ['pɪkl] ◆ *n* pickles *mpl*; to be in a ~ être dans le pétrin. ◆ *vt* conserver dans du vinaigre, de la saumure *etc*.

pickpocket ['pɪkˌpɒkɪt] *n* pickpocket *m*, voleur *m* à la tire.

pick-up *n* 1. (*of record player*) pick-up *m*. 2. (*truck*) camionnette *f*.

picnic ['pɪknɪk] (*pt & pp* -ked, *cont* -king) ◆ *n* pique-nique *m*. ◆ *vi* pique-niquer.

pictorial [pɪk'tɔ:rɪəl] *adj* illustré(e).

picture ['pɪktʃər] ◆ *n* 1. (*painting*) tableau *m*, peinture *f*; (*drawing*) dessin *m*. 2. (*photograph*) photo *f*, photographie *f*. 3. (TV) image *f*. 4. (CINEMA) film *m*. 5. (*in mind*) tableau *m*, image *f*. 6. *fig* (*situation*) tableau *m*. 7. *phr:* to get the ~ *inf* piger; to put sb in the ~ mettre qqn au courant. ◆ *vt* 1. (*in mind*) imaginer, s'imaginer, se représenter. 2. (*in photo*) photographier. 3. (*in painting*) représenter, peindre. ▶ **pictures** *npl* Br: the ~s le cinéma.

picture book *n* livre *m* d'images.

picturesque [ˌpɪktʃə'resk] *adj* pittoresque.

pie [paɪ] *n* (*savoury*) tourte *f*; (*sweet*) tarte *f*.

piece [pi:s] *n* 1. (*gen*) morceau *m*; (*of string*) bout *m*; a ~ of furniture un meuble; a ~ of clothing un vêtement; a ~ of advice un conseil; a ~ of information un renseignement; to fall to ~s tomber en morceaux; to take sthg to ~s démonter qqch; in ~s en morceaux; in one ~ (*intact*) intact(e); (*unharmed*) sain et sauf (saine et sauve). 2. (*coin, item, in chess*) pièce *f*; (*in draughts*) pion *m*. 3. (PRESS) article *m*. ▶ **piece together** *vt sep* (*facts*) coordonner.

piecemeal ['pi:smi:l] ◆ *adj* fait(e) petit à petit. ◆ *adv* petit à petit, peu à peu.

piecework ['pi:swɜ:k] *n* (U) travail *m* à la pièce OR aux pièces.

pie chart *n* camembert *m*, graphique *m* rond.

pier [pɪər] *n* (*at seaside*) jetée *f*.

pierce [pɪəs] *vt* percer, transpercer; to have one's ears ~d se faire percer les oreilles.

piercing ['pɪəsɪŋ] *adj* 1. (*sound, look*) perçant(e). 2. (*wind*) pénétrant(e).

pig [pɪg] *n* 1. (*animal*) porc *m*, cochon *m*. 2. *inf pej* (*greedy eater*) goinfre *m*, glouton *m*. 3. *inf pej* (*unkind person*) sale type *m*.

pigeon ['pɪdʒɪn] *n* pigeon *m*.

pigeonhole ['pɪdʒɪnhəʊl] ◆ n (compartment) casier m. ◆ vt (classify) étiqueter, cataloguer.

piggybank ['pɪgɪbæŋk] n tirelire f.

pigheaded [,pɪg'hedɪd] adj têtu(e).

pigment ['pɪgmənt] n pigment m.

pigpen Am = **pigsty**.

pigskin ['pɪgskɪn] n (peau f de) porc m.

pigsty ['pɪgstaɪ], **pigpen** Am ['pɪgpen] n lit & fig porcherie f.

pigtail ['pɪgteɪl] n natte f.

pike [paɪk] (pl sense 1 only inv OR -s) n 1. (fish) brochet m. 2. (spear) pique f.

pilchard ['pɪltʃəd] n pilchard m.

pile [paɪl] ◆ n 1. (heap) tas m; a ~ of, ~s of un tas OR des tas de. 2. (neat stack) pile f. 3. (of carpet) poil m. ◆ vt empiler. ▶ **piles** npl (MED) hémorroïdes fpl. ▶ **pile into** vt fus inf s'entasser dans, s'empiler dans. ▶ **pile up** ◆ vt sep empiler, entasser. ◆ vi 1. (form a heap) s'entasser. 2. fig (work, debts) s'accumuler.

pileup ['paɪlʌp] n (AUT) carambolage m.

pilfer ['pɪlfə'] ◆ vt chaparder. ◆ vi: to ~ (from) faire du chapardage (dans).

pilgrim ['pɪlgrɪm] n pèlerin m.

pilgrimage ['pɪlgrɪmɪdʒ] n pèlerinage m.

pill [pɪl] n 1. (gen) pilule f. 2. (contraceptive): the ~ la pilule; to be on the ~ prendre la pilule.

pillage ['pɪlɪdʒ] vt piller.

pillar ['pɪlə'] n lit & fig pilier m.

pillar box n Br boîte f aux lettres.

pillion ['pɪljən] n siège m arrière; to ride ~ monter derrière.

pillow ['pɪləʊ] n 1. (for bed) oreiller m. 2. Am (on sofa, chair) coussin m.

pillowcase ['pɪləʊkeɪs], **pillowslip** ['pɪləʊslɪp] n taie f d'oreiller.

pilot ['paɪlət] ◆ n 1. (AERON & NAUT) pilote m. 2. (TV) émission f pilote. ◆ comp pilote. ◆ vt piloter.

pilot burner, pilot light n veilleuse f.

pilot study n étude f pilote OR expérimentale.

pimp [pɪmp] n inf maquereau m, souteneur m.

pimple ['pɪmpl] n bouton m.

pin [pɪn] ◆ n 1. (for sewing) épingle f; to have ~s and needles avoir des fourmis. 2. (drawing pin) punaise f. 3. (safety pin) épingle f de nourrice OR de sûreté. 4. (of plug) fiche f. 5. (TECH) goupille f, cheville f. ◆ vt: to ~ sthg to/on sthg épingler qqch à/sur qqch; to ~ sb

against OR to clouer qqn contre; to ~ sthg on sb (blame) mettre OR coller qqch sur le dos de qqn; to ~ one's hopes on sb/sthg mettre tous ses espoirs en qqn/dans qqch. ▶ **pin down** vt sep 1. (identify) définir, identifier. 2. (force to make a decision): to ~ sb down obliger qqn à prendre une décision.

pinafore ['pɪnəfɔ:'] n 1. (apron) tablier m. 2. Br (dress) chasuble f.

pinball ['pɪnbɔ:l] n flipper m.

pincers ['pɪnsəz] npl 1. (tool) tenailles fpl. 2. (of crab) pinces fpl.

pinch [pɪntʃ] ◆ n 1. (nip) pincement m. 2. (of salt) pincée f. ◆ vt 1. (nip) pincer. 2. (subj: shoes) serrer. 3. inf (steal) piquer, faucher. ▶ **at a pinch** Br, **in a pinch** Am adv à la rigueur.

pincushion ['pɪn,kuʃn] n pelote f à épingles.

pine [paɪn] ◆ n pin m. ◆ vi: to ~ for désirer ardemment. ▶ **pine away** vi languir.

pineapple ['paɪnæpl] n ananas m.

pinetree ['paɪntri:] n pin m.

ping [pɪŋ] n (of bell) tintement m; (of metal) bruit m métallique.

Ping-Pong® [-pɒŋ] n ping-pong m.

pink [pɪŋk] ◆ adj rose; to go OR turn ~ rosir, rougir. ◆ n (colour) rose m.

pinnacle ['pɪnəkl] n 1. (mountain peak, spire) pic m, cime f. 2. fig (high point) apogée m.

pinpoint ['pɪnpɔɪnt] vt 1. (cause, problem) définir, mettre le doigt sur. 2. (position) localiser.

pin-striped [-,straɪpt] adj à très fines rayures.

pint [paɪnt] n 1. Br (unit of measurement) = 0,568 litre, ≃ demi-litre. 2. Am (unit of measurement) = 0,473 litre, ≃ demi-litre m. 3. Br (beer) ≃ demi m.

pioneer [,paɪə'nɪə'] ◆ n lit & fig pionnier m. ◆ vt: to ~ sthg être un des premiers (une des premières) à faire qqch.

pious ['paɪəs] adj 1. (RELIG) pieux (pieuse). 2. pej (sanctimonious) moralisateur(trice).

pip [pɪp] n 1. (seed) pépin m. 2. Br (RADIO) top m.

pipe [paɪp] ◆ n 1. (for gas, water) tuyau m. 2. (for smoking) pipe f. ◆ vt acheminer par tuyau. ▶ **pipes** npl (MUS) cornemuse f. ▶ **pipe down** vi inf se taire, la fermer. ▶ **pipe up** vi inf se faire entendre.

pipe cleaner n cure-pipe m.

pipe dream *n* projet *m* chimérique.

pipeline ['paɪplaɪn] *n* (*for gas*) gazoduc *m*; (*for oil*) oléoduc *m*, pipeline *m*.

piper ['paɪpəʳ] *n* joueur *m*, -euse *f* de cornemuse.

piping hot ['paɪpɪŋ-] *adj* bouillant(e).

pique [piːk] *n* dépit *m*.

pirate ['paɪrət] ◆ *adj* (*video, program*) pirate. ◆ *n* pirate *m*. ◆ *vt* (*video, program*) pirater.

pirate radio *n* Br radio *f* pirate.

pirouette [ˌpɪruˈet] ◆ *n* pirouette *f*. ◆ *vi* pirouetter.

Pisces ['paɪsiːz] *n* Poissons *mpl*.

piss [pɪs] *vulg* ◆ *n* (*urine*) pisse *f*. ◆ *vi* pisser.

pissed [pɪst] *adj vulg* 1. Br (*drunk*) bourré(e). 2. Am (*annoyed*) en boule.

pissed off *adj vulg* qui en a plein le cul.

pistol ['pɪstl] *n* pistolet *m*.

piston ['pɪstən] *n* piston *m*.

pit [pɪt] ◆ *n* 1. (*hole*) trou *m*; (*in road*) petit trou; (*on face*) marque *f*. 2. (*for orchestra*) fosse *f*. 3. (*mine*) mine *f*. 4. Am (*of fruit*) noyau *m*. ◆ *vt*: **to ~ sb against sb** opposer qqn à qqn. ▶ **pits** *npl* (*in motor racing*): **the ~s** les stands *mpl*.

pitch [pɪtʃ] ◆ *n* 1. (SPORT) terrain *m*. 2. (MUS) ton *m*. 3. (*level, degree*) degré *m*. 4. (*selling place*) place *f*. 5. *inf* (*sales talk*) baratin *m*. ◆ *vt* 1. (*throw*) lancer. 2. (*set-price*) fixer; (*-speech*) adapter. 3. (*tent*) dresser; (*camp*) établir. ◆ *vi* 1. (*ball*) rebondir. 2. (*fall*): **to ~ forward** être projeté(e) en avant. 3. (AERON & NAUT) tanguer.

pitch-black *adj*: **it's ~ in here** il fait noir comme dans un four.

pitched battle [ˌpɪtʃt-] *n* bataille *f* rangée.

pitcher ['pɪtʃəʳ] *n* Am 1. (*jug*) cruche *f*. 2. (*in baseball*) lanceur *m*.

pitchfork ['pɪtʃfɔːk] *n* fourche *f*.

piteous ['pɪtɪəs] *adj* pitoyable.

pitfall ['pɪtfɔːl] *n* piège *m*.

pith [pɪθ] *n* 1. (*in plant*) moelle *f*. 2. (*of fruit*) peau *f* blanche.

pithy ['pɪθɪ] *adj* (*brief*) concis(e); (*terse*) piquant(e).

pitiful ['pɪtɪful] *adj* (*condition*) pitoyable; (*excuse, effort*) lamentable.

pitiless ['pɪtɪlɪs] *adj* sans pitié, impitoyable.

pit stop *n* (*in motor racing*) arrêt *m* aux stands.

pittance ['pɪtəns] *n* (*wage*) salaire *m* de misère.

pity ['pɪtɪ] ◆ *n* pitié *f*; **what a ~!** quel dommage!; **it's a ~** c'est dommage; **to take OR have ~ on sb** prendre qqn en pitié, avoir pitié de qqn. ◆ *vt* plaindre.

pivot ['pɪvət] *n lit & fig* pivot *m*.

pizza ['piːtsə] *n* pizza *f*.

placard ['plækɑːd] *n* placard *m*, affiche *f*.

placate [pləˈkeɪt] *vt* calmer, apaiser.

place [pleɪs] ◆ *n* 1. (*location*) endroit *m*, lieu *m*; **~ of birth** lieu de naissance. 2. (*proper position, seat, vacancy, rank*) place *f*. 3. (*home*): **at/to my ~** chez moi. 4. (*in book*): **to lose one's ~** perdre sa page. 5. (MATH): **decimal ~** décimale *f*. 6. (*instance*): **in the first ~** tout de suite; **in the first ~ ... and in the second ~ ...** premièrement ... et deuxièmement ... 7. *phr*: **to take ~** avoir lieu; **to take the ~ of** prendre la place de, remplacer. ◆ *vt* 1. (*position, put*) placer, mettre. 2. (*apportion*): **to ~ the responsibility for sthg on sb** tenir qqn pour responsable de qqch. 3. (*identify*) remettre. 4. (*an order*) passer; **to ~ a bet** parier. 5. (*in race*): **to be ~d** être placé(e). ▶ **all over the place** *adv* (*everywhere*) partout. ▶ **in place** *adv* 1. (*in proper position*) à sa place. 2. (*established*) mis en place. ▶ **in place of** *prep* à la place de. ▶ **out of place** *adv* pas à sa place; *fig* déplacé(e).

place mat *n* set *m* (de table).

placement ['pleɪsmənt] *n* placement *m*.

placid ['plæsɪd] *adj* 1. (*person*) placide. 2. (*sea, place*) calme.

plagiarize, -ise ['pleɪdʒəraɪz] *vt* plagier.

plague [pleɪg] ◆ *n* 1. (MED) peste *f*. 2. *fig* (*nuisance*) fléau *m*. ◆ *vt*: **to be ~d by** (*bad luck*) être poursuivi(e) par; (*doubt*) être rongé(e) par; **to ~ sb with questions** harceler qqn de questions.

plaice [pleɪs] (*pl inv*) *n* carrelet *m*.

plaid [plæd] *n* plaid *m*.

Plaid Cymru [ˌplaɪdˈkʌmrɪ] *n* parti nationaliste gallois.

plain [pleɪn] ◆ *adj* 1. (*not patterned*) uni(e). 2. (*simple*) simple. 3. (*clear*) clair(e), évident(e). 4. (*blunt*) carré(e), franc (franche). 5. (*absolute*) pur(e) (et simple). 6. (*not pretty*) quelconque, ordinaire. ◆ *adv inf* complètement. ◆ *n* (GEOGR) plaine *f*.

plain chocolate *n* Br chocolat *m* à croquer.

plain-clothes *adj* en civil.

plain flour *n* Br farine *f* (sans levure).

plainly ['pleɪnlɪ] *adv* 1. (*obviously*) manifestement. **2.** (*distinctly*) clairement. **3.** (*frankly*) carrément, sans détours. **4.** (*simply*) simplement.

plaintiff ['pleɪntɪf] *n* demandeur *m*, -eresse *f*.

plait [plæt] ◆ *n* natte *f*. ◆ *vt* natter, tresser.

plan [plæn] ◆ *n* plan *m*, projet *m*; **to go according to ~** se passer OR aller comme prévu. ◆ *vt* **1.** (*organize*) préparer. **2.** (*propose*): **to ~ to do sthg** projeter de faire qqch, avoir l'intention de faire qqch. **3.** (*design*) concevoir. ◆ *vi*: **to ~ (for sthg)** faire des projets (pour qqch). ► **plans** *npl* plans *mpl*, projets *mpl*; **have you any ~s for tonight?** avez-vous prévu quelque chose pour ce soir? ► **plan on** *vt fus*: **to ~ on doing sthg** prévoir de faire qqch.

plane [pleɪn] ◆ *adj* plan(e). ◆ *n* **1.** (*aircraft*) avion *m*. **2.** (GEOM) plan *m*. **3.** *fig* (*level*) niveau *m*. **4.** (*tool*) rabot *m*. **5.** (*tree*) platane *m*.

planet ['plænɪt] *n* planète *f*.

plank [plæŋk] *n* **1.** (*of wood*) planche *f*. **2.** (POL) (*policy*) point *m*.

planning ['plænɪŋ] *n* **1.** (*designing*) planification *f*. **2.** (*preparation*) préparation *f*, organisation *f*.

planning permission *n* permis *m* de construire.

plant [plɑːnt] ◆ *n* **1.** (BOT) plante *f*. **2.** (*factory*) usine *f*. **3.** (U) (*heavy machinery*) matériel *m*. ◆ *vt* **1.** (*gen*) planter. **2.** (*bomb*) poser.

plantation [plæn'teɪʃn] *n* plantation *f*.

plaque [plɑːk] *n* **1.** (*commemorative sign*) plaque *f*. **2.** (U) (*on teeth*) plaque *f* dentaire.

plaster ['plɑːstər] ◆ *n* **1.** (*material*) plâtre *m*. **2.** Br (*bandage*) pansement *m* adhésif. ◆ *vt* **1.** (*wall, ceiling*) plâtrer. **2.** (*cover*): **to ~ sthg (with)** couvrir qqch (de).

plaster cast *n* **1.** (*for broken bones*) plâtre *m*. **2.** (*model, statue*) moule *m*.

plastered ['plɑːstəd] *adj inf* (*drunk*) bourré(e).

plasterer ['plɑːstərər] *n* plâtrier *m*.

plaster of Paris *n* plâtre *m* de moulage.

plastic ['plæstɪk] ◆ *adj* plastique. ◆ *n* plastique *m*.

Plasticine® Br ['plæstɪsiːn], **play dough** Am *n* pâte *f* à modeler.

plastic surgery *n* chirurgie *f* esthétique OR plastique.

plate [pleɪt] ◆ *n* **1.** (*dish*) assiette *f*. **2.** (*sheet of metal, plaque*) tôle *f*. **3.** (U)

(*metal covering*): **gold/silver ~** plaqué *m* or/argent. **4.** (*in book*) planche *f*. **5.** (*in dentistry*) dentier *m*. ◆ *vt*: **to be ~d (with)** être plaqué(e) (de).

plateau ['plætəʊ] (*pl* -**s** OR -**x** [-z]) *n* plateau *m*; *fig* phase *f* OR période *f* de stabilité.

plate-glass *adj* vitré(e).

platform ['plætfɔːm] *n* **1.** (*stage*) estrade *f*; (*for speaker*) tribune *f*. **2.** (*raised structure, of bus, of political party*) plateforme *f*. **3.** (RAIL) quai *m*.

platform ticket *n* Br ticket *m* de quai.

platinum ['plætɪnəm] *n* platine *m*.

platoon [plə'tuːn] *n* section *f*.

platter ['plætər] *n* (*dish*) plat *m*.

plausible ['plɔːzəbl] *adj* plausible.

play [pleɪ] ◆ *n* **1.** (U) (*amusement*) jeu *m*, amusement *m*. **2.** (THEATRE) pièce *f* (de théâtre); **a radio ~** une pièce radiophonique. **3.** (*game*): **~ on words** jeu *m* de mots. **4.** (TECH) jeu *m*. ◆ *vt* **1.** (*gen*) jouer; **to ~ a part** OR **role in** *fig* jouer un rôle dans. **2.** (*game, sport*) jouer à. **3.** (*team, opponent*) jouer contre. **4.** (MUS) (*instrument*) jouer de. **5.** *phr*: **to ~ it safe** ne pas prendre de risques. ◆ *vi* jouer. ► **play along** *vi*: **to ~ along (with sb)** entrer dans le jeu (de qqn). ► **play down** *vt sep* minimiser. ► **play up** ◆ *vt sep* (*emphasize*) insister sur. ◆ *vi* **1.** (*machine*) faire des siennes. **2.** (*child*) ne pas être sage.

play-act *vi* jouer la comédie.

playboy ['pleɪbɔɪ] *n* playboy *m*.

play dough Am = **Plasticine®**.

player ['pleɪər] *n* **1.** (*gen*) joueur *m*, -euse *f*. **2.** (THEATRE) acteur *m*, -trice *f*.

playful ['pleɪfʊl] *adj* **1.** (*person, mood*) taquin(e). **2.** (*kitten, puppy*) joueur(euse).

playground ['pleɪgraʊnd] *n* cour *f* de récréation.

playgroup ['pleɪgruːp] *n* jardin *m* d'enfants.

playing card ['pleɪɪŋ-] *n* carte *f* à jouer.

playing field ['pleɪɪŋ-] *n* terrain *m* de sport.

playmate ['pleɪmeɪt] *n* camarade *mf*.

play-off *n* (SPORT) belle *f*.

playpen ['pleɪpen] *n* parc *m*.

playschool ['pleɪskuːl] *n* jardin *m* d'enfants.

plaything ['pleɪθɪŋ] *n lit & fig* jouet *m*.

playtime ['pleɪtaɪm] *n* récréation *f*.

playwright ['pleɪraɪt] *n* dramaturge *m*.

plc *abbr of* **public limited company**.

plea [pli:] *n* **1.** (*for forgiveness, mercy*) supplication *f*; (*for help, quiet*) appel *m*. **2.** (JUR): **to enter a ~ of not guilty** plaider non coupable.

plead [pli:d] (*pt & pp* **-ed** OR **pled**) ◆ *vt* **1.** (JUR) plaider. **2.** (*give as excuse*) invoquer. ◆ *vi* **1.** (*beg*): **to ~ with sb** (**to do sthg**) supplier qqn (de faire qqch); **to ~ for sthg** implorer qqch. **2.** (JUR) plaider.

pleasant ['pleznt] *adj* agréable.

pleasantry ['plezntrɪ] *n*: **to exchange pleasantries** échanger des propos aimables.

please [pli:z] ◆ *vt* plaire à, faire plaisir à; **to ~ o.s.** faire comme on veut; **~ yourself!** comme vous voulez! ◆ *vi* plaire, faire plaisir; **to do as one ~s** faire comme on veut. ◆ *adv* s'il vous plaît.

pleased [pli:zd] *adj* **1.** (*satisfied*): **to be ~** (**with**) être content(e) (de). **2.** (*happy*): **to be ~** (**about**) être heureux(euse) (de); **~ to meet you!** enchanté(e)!

pleasing ['pli:zɪŋ] *adj* plaisant(e).

pleasure ['pleʒər] *n* plaisir *m*; **with ~** avec plaisir, volontiers; **it's a ~, my ~** je vous en prie.

pleat [pli:t] ◆ *n* pli *m*. ◆ *vt* plisser.

pled [pled] *pt & pp →* **plead**.

pledge [pledʒ] ◆ *n* **1.** (*promise*) promesse *f*. **2.** (*token*) gage *m*. ◆ *vt* **1.** (*promise*) promettre. **2.** (*make promise*): **to ~ o.s. to** s'engager à; **to ~ sb to secrecy** faire promettre le secret à qqn. **3.** (*pawn*) mettre en gage.

plentiful ['plentɪfʊl] *adj* abondant(e).

plenty ['plentɪ] ◆ *n* (U) abondance *f*. ◆ *pron*: **~ of** beaucoup de; **we've got ~ of time** nous avons largement le temps.

pliable ['plaɪəbl], **pliant** ['plaɪənt] *adj* **1.** (*material*) pliable, souple. **2.** *fig* (*person*) docile.

pliers ['plaɪəz] *npl* tenailles *fpl*, pinces *fpl*.

plight [plaɪt] *n* condition *f* critique.

plimsoll ['plɪmsəl] *n* Br tennis *m*.

plinth [plɪnθ] *n* socle *m*.

PLO (*abbr of* **Palestine Liberation Organization**) *n* OLP *f*.

plod [plɒd] *vi* **1.** (*walk slowly*) marcher lentement OR péniblement. **2.** (*work slowly*) peiner.

plodder ['plɒdər] *n pej* bûcheur *m*, -euse *f*.

plonk [plɒŋk] *n* (U) Br *inf* (*wine*) pinard *m*, vin *m* ordinaire. ▶ **plonk down** *vt sep inf* poser brutalement.

plot [plɒt] ◆ *n* **1.** (*plan*) complot *m*, conspiration *f*. **2.** (*story*) intrigue *f*. **3.** (*of*

land) (*parcelle f de*) terrain *m*, lopin *m*. ◆ *vt* **1.** (*plan*) comploter; **to ~ to do sthg** comploter de faire qqch. **2.** (*chart*) déterminer, marquer. **3.** (MATH) tracer, marquer. ◆ *vi* comploter.

plotter ['plɒtər] *n* (*schemer*) conspirateur *m*, -trice *f*.

plough Br, **plow** Am [plaʊ] ◆ *n* charrue *f*. ◆ *vt* (*field*) labourer. ▶ **plough into** ◆ *vt sep* (*money*) investir. ◆ *vt fus* (*subj: car*) rentrer dans.

ploughman's ['plaʊmənz] (*pl inv*) *n* Br: **~ (lunch)** repas de pain, fromage et pickles.

plow *etc* Am = **plough** *etc*.

ploy [plɔɪ] *n* stratagème *m*, ruse *f*.

pluck [plʌk] ◆ *vt* **1.** (*flower, fruit*) cueillir. **2.** (*pull sharply*) arracher. **3.** (*chicken, turkey*) plumer. **4.** (*eyebrows*) épiler. **5.** (MUS) pincer. ◆ *n* (U) *dated* courage *m*, cran *m*. ▶ **pluck up** *vt fus*: **to ~ up the courage to do sthg** rassembler son courage pour faire qqch.

plucky ['plʌkɪ] *adj dated* qui a du cran, courageux(euse).

plug [plʌg] ◆ *n* **1.** (ELEC) prise *f* de courant. **2.** (*for bath, sink*) bonde *f*. ◆ *vt* **1.** (*hole*) boucher, obturer. **2.** *inf* (*new book, film etc*) faire de la publicité pour. ▶ **plug in** *vt sep* brancher.

plughole ['plʌghəʊl] *n* bonde *f*, trou *m* d'écoulement.

plum [plʌm] ◆ *adj* **1.** (*colour*) prune (*inv*). **2.** (*very good*): **a ~ job** un poste en or. ◆ *n* (*fruit*) prune *f*.

plumb [plʌm] ◆ *adv* **1.** Br (*exactly*) exactement, en plein. **2.** Am (*completely*) complètement. ◆ *vt*: **to ~ the depths of** toucher le fond de.

plumber ['plʌmər] *n* plombier *m*.

plumbing ['plʌmɪŋ] *n* (U) **1.** (*fittings*) plomberie *f*, tuyauterie *f*. **2.** (*work*) plomberie *f*.

plume [plu:m] *n* **1.** (*feather*) plume *f*. **2.** (*on hat*) panache *m*. **3.** (*column*): **a ~ of smoke** un panache de fumée.

plummet ['plʌmɪt] *vi* **1.** (*bird, plane*) plonger. **2.** *fig* (*decrease*) dégringoler.

plump [plʌmp] *adj* bien en chair, grassouillet(ette). ▶ **plump for** *vt fus* opter pour, choisir. ▶ **plump up** *vt sep* (*cushion*) secouer.

plum pudding *n* pudding *m* de Noël.

plunder ['plʌndər] ◆ *n* (U) **1.** (*stealing, raiding*) pillage *m*. **2.** (*stolen goods*) butin *m*. ◆ *vt* piller.

plunge [plʌndʒ] ◆ *n* **1.** (*dive*) plongeon *m*; **to take the ~** se jeter à l'eau. **2.** *fig* (*decrease*) dégringolade *f*, chute *f*. ◆ *vt*: **to ~ sthg into** plonger qqch dans. ◆ *vi* **1.** (*dive*) plonger, tomber. **2.** *fig* (*decrease*) dégringoler.

plunger ['plʌndʒər] *n* débouchoir *m* à ventouse.

pluperfect [,pluː'pɜːfɪkt] *n*: **~ (tense)** plus-que-parfait *m*.

plural ['pluərəl] ◆ *adj* **1.** (GRAMM) pluriel(elle). **2.** (*not individual*) collectif (ive). **3.** (*multicultural*) multiculturel (elle). ◆ *n* pluriel *m*.

plus [plʌs] (*pl* **-es** OR **-ses**) ◆ *adj*: **30 ~ 30** ou plus. ◆ *n* **1.** (MATH) signe *m* plus. **2.** *inf* (*bonus*) plus *m*, atout *m*. ◆ *prep* et. ◆ *conj* (*moreover*) de plus.

plush [plʌʃ] *adj* luxueux(euse), somptueux(euse).

plus sign *n* signe *m* plus.

Pluto ['pluːtəu] *n* (*planet*) Pluton *f*.

plutonium [pluː'təunɪəm] *n* plutonium *m*.

ply [plaɪ] ◆ *n* (*of wool*) fil *m*; (*of wood*) pli *m*. ◆ *vt* **1.** (*trade*) exercer. **2.** (*supply*): **to ~ sb with drink** ne pas arrêter de remplir le verre de qqn. ◆ *vi* (*ship etc*) faire la navette.

plywood ['plaɪwud] *n* contreplaqué *m*.

p.m., pm (*abbr of* **post meridiem**): **at 3 ~** à 15 h.

PM *abbr of* **prime minister**.

PMT *abbr of* **premenstrual tension**.

pneumatic [njuː'mætɪk] *adj* pneumatique.

pneumatic drill *n* marteau piqueur *m*.

pneumonia [njuː'məunjə] *n* (U) pneumonie *f*.

poach [pəutʃ] ◆ *vt* **1.** (*fish*) pêcher sans permis; (*deer etc*) chasser sans permis. **2.** *fig* (*idea*) voler. **3.** (CULIN) pocher. ◆ *vi* braconner.

poacher ['pəutʃər] *n* braconnier *m*.

poaching ['pəutʃɪŋ] *n* braconnage *m*.

PO Box (*abbr of* **Post Office Box**) *n* BP *f*.

pocket ['pɒkɪt] ◆ *n lit & fig* poche *f*; **to be out of ~** en être de sa poche; **to pick sb's ~** faire les poches à qqn. ◆ *adj* de poche. ◆ *vt* empocher.

pocketbook ['pɒkɪtbuk] *n* **1.** (*notebook*) carnet *m*. **2.** *Am* (*handbag*) sac *m* à main.

pocketknife ['pɒkɪtnaɪf] (*pl* **-knives** [-naɪvz]) *n* canif *m*.

pocket money *n* argent *m* de poche.

pod [pɒd] *n* **1.** (*of plants*) cosse *f*. **2.** (*of spacecraft*) nacelle *f*.

podgy ['pɒdʒɪ] *adj inf* boulot(otte),

rondelet(ette).

podiatrist [pə'daɪətrɪst] *n Am* pédicure *mf*.

podium ['pəudɪəm] (*pl* **-diums** OR **-dia** [-dɪə]) *n* podium *m*.

poem ['pəuɪm] *n* poème *m*.

poet ['pəuɪt] *n* poète *m*.

poetic [pəu'etɪk] *adj* poétique.

poetry ['pəuɪtrɪ] *n* poésie *f*.

poignant ['pɔɪnjənt] *adj* poignant(e).

point [pɔɪnt] ◆ *n* **1.** (*tip*) pointe *f*. **2.** (*place*) endroit *m*, point *m*. **3.** (*time*) stade *m*, moment *m*. **4.** (*detail, argument*) question *f*, détail *m*; **you have a ~** il y a du vrai dans ce que vous dites; **to make a ~** faire une remarque; **to make one's ~** dire ce qu'on a à dire, dire son mot. **5.** (*main idea*) point *m* essentiel; **to get** OR **come to the ~** en venir au fait; **to miss the ~** ne pas comprendre; **beside the ~** à côté de la question. **6.** (*feature*): **good ~** qualité *f*; **bad ~** défaut *m*. **7.** (*purpose*): **what's the ~ in buying a new car?** à quoi bon acheter une nouvelle voiture?; **there's no ~ in having a meeting** cela ne sert à rien d'avoir une réunion. **8.** (*on scale, in scores*) point *m*. **9.** (MATH): **two ~ six** deux virgule six. **10.** (*of compass*) aire *f* du vent. **11.** *Br* (ELEC) prise *f* (de courant). **12.** *Am* (*full stop*) point *m* (final). **13.** *phr*: **to make a ~ of doing sthg** ne pas manquer de faire qqch. ◆ *vt*: **to ~ sthg (at)** (*gun, camera*) braquer qqch (sur); (*finger, hose*) pointer qqch (sur). ◆ *vi* **1.** (*indicate with finger*): **to ~ (at sb/ sthg)**, **to ~ (to sb/sthg)** montrer (qqn/ qqch) du doigt, indiquer (qqn/qqch) du doigt. **2.** *fig* (*suggest*): **to ~ to sthg** suggérer qqch, laisser supposer qqch. ▶ **points** *npl Br* (RAIL) aiguillage *m*. ▶ **up to a point** *adv* jusqu'à un certain point, dans une certaine mesure. ▶ **on the point of** *prep* sur le point de. ▶ **point out** *vt sep* (*person, place*) montrer, indiquer; (*fact, mistake*) signaler.

point-blank *adv* **1.** (*refuse*) catégoriquement; (*ask*) de but en blanc. **2.** (*shoot*) à bout portant.

pointed ['pɔɪntɪd] *adj* **1.** (*sharp*) pointu(e). **2.** *fig* (*remark*) mordant(e), incisif (ive).

pointer ['pɔɪntər] *n* **1.** (*piece of advice*) tuyau *m*, conseil *m*. **2.** (*needle*) aiguille *f*. **3.** (*stick*) baguette *f*. **4.** (COMPUT) pointeur *m*.

pointless ['pɔɪntlɪs] *adj* inutile, vain(e).

point of view (*pl* **points of view**) *n* point *m* de vue.

poise [pɔɪz] *n fig* calme *m*, sang-froid *m*.
poised [pɔɪzd] *adj* **1.** (*ready*): ~ **(for)** prêt(e) (pour); **to be ~ to do sthg** se tenir prêt à faire qqch. **2.** *fig* (*calm*) calme, posé(e).
poison ['pɔɪzn] ◆ *n* poison *m*. ◆ *vt* **1.** (*gen*) empoisonner. **2.** (*pollute*) polluer.
poisoning ['pɔɪznɪŋ] *n* empoisonnement *m*; **food ~** intoxication *f* alimentaire.
poisonous ['pɔɪznəs] *adj* **1.** (*fumes*) toxique; (*plant*) vénéneux(euse). **2.** (*snake*) venimeux(euse).
poke [pəʊk] ◆ *vt* **1.** (*prod*) pousser, donner un coup de coude à. **2.** (*put*) fourrer. **3.** (*fire*) attiser, tisonner. ◆ *vi* (*protrude*) sortir, dépasser. ▶ **poke about, poke around** *vi inf* fouiller, fourrager.
poker ['pəʊkəʳ] *n* **1.** (*game*) poker *m*. **2.** (*for fire*) tisonnier *m*.
poker-faced [-,feɪst] *adj* au visage impassible.
poky ['pəʊkɪ] *adj pej* (*room*) exigu(ë), minuscule.
Poland ['pəʊlənd] *n* Pologne *f*.
polar ['pəʊləʳ] *adj* polaire.
Polaroid® ['pəʊlərɔɪd] *n* **1.** (*camera*) Polaroïd® *m*. **2.** (*photograph*) photo *f* polaroïd.
pole [pəʊl] *n* **1.** (*rod, post*) perche *f*, mât *m*. **2.** (ELEC & GEOGR) pôle *m*.
Pole [pəʊl] *n* Polonais *m*, -e *f*.
pole vault *n*: **the ~** le saut à la perche.
police [pə'liːs] ◆ *npl* **1.** (*police force*): **the ~** la police. **2.** (*policemen*) agents *mpl* de police. ◆ *vt* maintenir l'ordre dans.
police car *n* voiture *f* de police.
police constable *n Br* agent *m* de police.
police force *n* police *f*.
policeman [pə'liːsmən] (*pl* **-men** [-mən]) *n* agent *m* de police.
police officer *n* policier *m*.
police record *n* casier *m* judiciaire.
police station *n* commissariat *m* (de police).
policewoman [pə'liːs,wʊmən] (*pl* **-women** [-,wɪmɪn]) *n* femme *f* agent de police.
policy ['pɒləsɪ] *n* **1.** (*plan*) politique *f*. **2.** (*document*) police *f*.
polio ['pəʊlɪəʊ] *n* polio *f*.
polish ['pɒlɪʃ] ◆ *n* **1.** (*for shoes*) cirage *m*; (*for floor*) cire *f*, encaustique *f*. **2.** (*shine*) brillant *m*, lustre *m*. **3.** *fig* (*refinement*) raffinement *m*. ◆ *vt* (*shoes, floor*) cirer; (*car*) astiquer; (*cutlery, glasses*)

faire briller. ▶ **polish off** *vt sep inf* expédier. ▶ **polish up** *vt sep* (*maths, language*) perfectionner; (*work*) peaufiner.
Polish ['pəʊlɪʃ] ◆ *adj* polonais(e). ◆ *n* (*language*) polonais *m*. ◆ *npl*: **the ~** les Polonais *mpl*.
polished ['pɒlɪʃt] *adj* **1.** (*refined*) raffiné(e). **2.** (*accomplished*) accompli(e), parfait(e).
polite [pə'laɪt] *adj* (*courteous*) poli(e).
politic ['pɒlətɪk] *adj* politique.
political [pə'lɪtɪkl] *adj* politique.
politically correct [pə,lɪtɪklɪ-] *adj* conforme au mouvement qui préconise le remplacement de termes jugés discriminants par d'autres 'politiquement corrects'.
politician [,pɒlɪ'tɪʃn] *n* homme *m* politique, femme *f* politique.
politics ['pɒlətɪks] ◆ *n* (U) politique *f*. ◆ *npl* **1.** (*personal beliefs*): **what are his ~?** de quel bord est-il? **2.** (*of group, area*) politique *f*.
polka ['pɒlkə] *n* polka *f*.
polka dot *n* pois *m*.
poll [pəʊl] ◆ *n* vote *m*, scrutin *m*. ◆ *vt* **1.** (*people*) interroger, sonder. **2.** (*votes*) obtenir. ▶ **polls** *npl*: **to go to the ~s** aller aux urnes.
pollen ['pɒlən] *n* pollen *m*.
polling booth ['pəʊlɪŋ-] *n* isoloir *m*.
polling day ['pəʊlɪŋ-] *n Br* jour *m* du scrutin OR des élections.
polling station ['pəʊlɪŋ-] *n* bureau *m* de vote.
pollutant [pə'luːtnt] *n* polluant *m*.
pollute [pə'luːt] *vt* polluer.
pollution [pə'luːʃn] *n* pollution *f*.
polo ['pəʊləʊ] *n* polo *m*.
polo neck *n Br* **1.** (*neck*) col *m* roulé. **2.** (*jumper*) pull *m* à col roulé.
polyethylene *Am* = **polythene**.
Polynesia [,pɒlɪ'niːzjə] *n* Polynésie *f*.
polystyrene [,pɒlɪ'staɪriːn] *n* polystyrène *m*.
polytechnic [,pɒlɪ'teknɪk] *n Br établissement d'enseignement supérieur; en 1993, les 'polytechnics' ont été transformés en universités.*
polythene *Br* ['pɒlɪθiːn], **polyethylene** *Am* [,pɒlɪ'eθɪliːn] *n* polyéthylène *m*.
polythene bag *n Br* sac *m* en plastique.
pomegranate ['pɒmɪ,grænɪt] *n* grenade *f*.
pomp [pɒmp] *n* pompe *f*, faste *m*.
pompom ['pɒmpɒm] *n* pompon *m*.
pompous ['pɒmpəs] *adj* **1.** (*person*) fat,

suffisant(e). **2.** (*style, speech*) pompeux (euse).

pond [pɒnd] *n* étang *m*, mare *f*.

ponder ['pɒndə'] *vt* considérer, peser.

ponderous ['pɒndərəs] *adj* **1.** (*dull*) lourd(e). **2.** (*large, heavy*) pesant(e).

pong [pɒŋ] *Br inf n* puanteur *f*.

pontoon [pɒn'tu:n] *n* **1.** (*bridge*) ponton *m*. **2.** *Br* (*game*) vingt-et-un *m*.

pony ['pəʊni] *n* poney *m*.

ponytail ['pəʊnɪteɪl] *n* queue-de-cheval *f*.

pony-trekking [-,trekɪŋ] *n* randonnée *f* à cheval OR en poney.

poodle ['pu:dl] *n* caniche *m*.

pool [pu:l] ◆ *n* **1.** (*pond, of blood*) mare *f*; (*of rain, light*) flaque *f*. **2.** (*swimming pool*) piscine *f*. **3.** (SPORT) billard *m* américain. ◆ *vt* (*resources etc*) mettre en commun. ▶ **pools** *npl Br*: **the ~s** ≃ le loto sportif.

poor [pɔ:'] ◆ *adj* **1.** (*gen*) pauvre. **2.** (*not very good*) médiocre, mauvais(e). ◆ *npl*: **the ~** les pauvres *mpl*.

poorly ['pɔ:lɪ] ◆ *adj Br* souffrant(e). ◆ *adv* mal, médiocrement.

pop [pɒp] ◆ *n* **1.** (U) (*music*) pop *m*. **2.** (U) *inf* (*fizzy drink*) boisson *f* gazeuse. **3.** *inf* (*father*) papa *m*. **4.** (*sound*) pan *m*. ◆ *vt* **1.** (*burst*) faire éclater, crever. **2.** (*put quickly*) mettre, fourrer. ◆ *vi* **1.** (*balloon*) éclater, crever; (*cork, button*) sauter. **2.** (*eyes*): **his eyes popped** il a écarquillé les yeux. ▶ **pop in** *vi* faire une petite visite. ▶ **pop up** *vi* surgir.

pop concert *n* concert *m* pop.

popcorn ['pɒpkɔ:n] *n* pop-corn *m*.

pope [pəʊp] *n* pape *m*.

pop group *n* groupe *m* pop.

poplar ['pɒplə'] *n* peuplier *m*.

poppy ['pɒpɪ] *n* coquelicot *m*, pavot *m*.

Popsicle® ['pɒpsɪkl] *n Am* sucette *f* glacée.

populace ['pɒpjʊləs] *n*: **the ~** le peuple.

popular ['pɒpjʊlə'] *adj* **1.** (*gen*) populaire. **2.** (*name, holiday resort*) à la mode.

popularize, -ise ['pɒpjʊləraɪz] *vt* **1.** (*make popular*) populariser. **2.** (*simplify*) vulgariser.

population [,pɒpjʊ'leɪʃn] *n* population *f*.

porcelain ['pɔ:səlɪn] *n* porcelaine *f*.

porch [pɔ:tʃ] *n* **1.** (*entrance*) porche *m*. **2.** *Am* (*verandah*) véranda *f*.

porcupine ['pɔ:kjʊpaɪn] *n* porc-épic *m*.

pore [pɔ:'] *n* pore *m*. ▶ **pore over** *vt fus* examiner de près.

pork [pɔ:k] *n* porc *m*.

pork pie *n* pâté *m* de porc en croûte.

pornography [pɔ:'nɒgrəfɪ] *n* pornographie *f*.

porous ['pɔ:rəs] *adj* poreux(euse).

porridge ['pɒrɪdʒ] *n* porridge *m*.

port [pɔ:t] *n* **1.** (*town, harbour*) port *m*. **2.** (NAUT) (*left-hand side*) bâbord *m*. **3.** (*drink*) porto *m*. **4.** (COMPUT) port *m*.

portable ['pɔ:təbl] *adj* portatif(ive).

portent ['pɔ:tənt] *n* présage *m*.

porter ['pɔ:tə'] *n* **1.** *Br* (*doorman*) concierge *m*, portier *m*. **2.** (*for luggage*) porteur *m*. **3.** *Am* (*on train*) employé *m*, -e *f* des wagons-lits.

portfolio [,pɔ:t'fəʊljəʊ] (*pl* **-s**) *n* **1.** (*case*) serviette *f*. **2.** (*sample of work*) portfolio *m*. **3.** (FIN) portefeuille *m*.

porthole ['pɔ:thəʊl] *n* hublot *m*.

portion ['pɔ:ʃn] *n* **1.** (*section*) portion *f*, part *f*. **2.** (*of food*) portion *f*.

portly ['pɔ:tlɪ] *adj* corpulent(e).

portrait ['pɔ:treɪt] *n* portrait *m*.

portray [pɔ:'treɪ] *vt* **1.** (CINEMA & THEATRE) jouer, interpréter. **2.** (*describe*) dépeindre. **3.** (*paint*) faire le portrait de.

Portugal ['pɔ:tʃʊgl] *n* Portugal *m*.

Portuguese [,pɔ:tʃʊ'gi:z] ◆ *adj* portugais(e). ◆ *n* (*language*) portugais *m*. ◆ *npl*: **the ~** les Portugais *mpl*.

pose [pəʊz] ◆ *n* (*stance*) pose *f*. ◆ *vt* **1.** (*danger*) présenter. **2.** (*problem, question*) poser. ◆ *vi* (ART & *pej*) poser. (*pretend to be*): **to ~ as** se faire passer pour.

posh [pɒʃ] *adj inf* **1.** (*hotel, clothes etc*) chic (*inv*). **2.** *Br* (*accent, person*) de la haute.

position [pə'zɪʃn] ◆ *n* **1.** (*gen*) position *f*. **2.** (*job*) poste *m*, emploi *m*. **3.** (*state*) situation *f*. ◆ *vt* placer, mettre en position.

positive ['pɒzətɪv] *adj* **1.** (*gen*) positif (ive). **2.** (*sure*) sûr(e), certain(e); **to be ~ about sthg** être sûr de qqch. **3.** (*optimistic*) positif(ive), optimiste; **to be ~ about sthg** avoir une attitude positive au sujet de qqch. **4.** (*definite*) formel(elle), précis(e). **5.** (*evidence*) irréfutable, indéniable. **6.** (*downright*) véritable.

posse ['pɒsɪ] *n Am* détachement *m*, troupe *f*.

possess [pə'zes] *vt* posséder.

possession [pə'zeʃn] *n* possession *f*. ▶ **possessions** *npl* possessions *fpl*, biens *mpl*.

possessive [pə'zesɪv] ◆ *adj* possessif (ive). ◆ *n* (GRAMM) possessif *m*.

possibility [,pɒsə'bɪlətɪ] *n* **1.** (*chance, likelihood*) possibilité *f*, chances *fpl*; **there**

is a ~ that ... il se peut que … (+ *subjunctive*). 2. (*option*) possibilité f, option f.

possible ['pɒsəbl] ◆ *adj* possible; **as much as** ~ autant que possible; **as soon as** ~ dès que possible. ◆ *n* possible *m*.

possibly ['pɒsəblɪ] *adv* 1. (*perhaps*) peut-être. 2. (*expressing surprise*): **how could he** ~ **have known?** mais comment a-t-il pu le savoir? 3. (*for emphasis*): **I can't** ~ **accept your money** je ne peux vraiment pas accepter cet argent.

post [pəʊst] ◆ *n* 1. (*service*): **the** ~ la poste; **by** ~ par la poste. 2. (*letters, delivery*) courrier *m*. 3. Br (*collection*) levée f. 4. (*pole*) poteau *m*. 5. (*position, job*) poste *m*, emploi *m*. 6. (MIL) poste *m*. ◆ *vt* 1. (*by mail*) poster, mettre à la poste. 2. (*employee*) muter.

postage ['pəʊstɪdʒ] *n* affranchissement *m*; ~ **and packing** frais *mpl* de port et d'emballage.

postal ['pəʊstl] *adj* postal(e).

postal order *n* mandat *m* postal.

postbox ['pəʊstbɒks] *n* Br boîte f aux lettres.

postcard ['pəʊstkɑːd] *n* carte f postale.

postcode ['pəʊstkəʊd] *n* Br code *m* postal.

postdate [ˌpəʊst'deɪt] *vt* postdater.

poster ['pəʊstər] *n* (*for advertising*) affiche f; (*for decoration*) poster *m*.

poste restante [ˌpəʊst'restɑːnt] *n* poste f restante.

posterior [pɒ'stɪərɪər] ◆ *adj* postérieur(e). ◆ *n* hum postérieur *m*, derrière *m*.

postgraduate [ˌpəʊst'grædʒʊət] ◆ *adj* de troisième cycle. ◆ *n* étudiant *m*, -e f de troisième cycle.

posthumous ['pɒstjʊməs] *adj* posthume.

postman ['pəʊstmən] (*pl* -**men** [-mən]) *n* facteur *m*.

postmark ['pəʊstmɑːk] ◆ *n* cachet *m* de la poste. ◆ *vt* timbrer, tamponner.

postmaster ['pəʊstˌmɑːstər] *n* receveur *m* des postes.

postmortem [ˌpəʊst'mɔːtəm] *n* lit & fig autopsie f.

post office *n* 1. (*organization*): **the Post Office** les Postes et Télécommunications *fpl*. 2. (*building*) (bureau *m* de) poste f

post office box *n* boîte f postale.

postpone [ˌpəʊst'pəʊn] *vt* reporter, remettre.

postscript ['pəʊstskrɪpt] *n* post-scriptum *m inv*.

posture ['pɒstʃər] *n* 1. (U) (*pose*) position f, posture f. 2. fig (*attitude*) attitude f.

postwar [ˌpəʊst'wɔːr] *adj* d'après-guerre.

posy ['pəʊzɪ] *n* petit bouquet *m* de fleurs.

pot [pɒt] ◆ *n* 1. (*for cooking*) marmite f, casserole f. 2. (*for tea*) théière f; (*for coffee*) cafetière f. 3. (*for paint, jam, plant*) pot *m*. 4. (U) inf (*cannabis*) herbe f. ◆ *vt* (*plant*) mettre en pot.

potassium [pə'tæsɪəm] *n* potassium *m*.

potato [pə'teɪtəʊ] (*pl* -**es**) *n* pomme f de terre.

potato peeler [-ˌpiːlər] *n* (couteau *m*) éplucheur *m*.

potent ['pəʊtənt] *adj* 1. (*powerful, influential*) puissant(e). 2. (*drink*) fort(e).

potential [pə'tenʃl] ◆ *adj* (*energy, success*) potentiel(elle); (*uses, danger*) possible; (*enemy*) en puissance. ◆ *n* (U) (*of person*) capacités *fpl* latentes; **to have** ~ (*person*) promettre; (*company*) avoir de l'avenir; (*scheme*) offrir des possibilités.

potentially [pə'tenʃəlɪ] *adv* potentiellement.

pothole ['pɒthəʊl] *n* 1. (*in road*) nid-de-poule *m*. 2. (*underground*) caverne f, grotte f.

potholing ['pɒtˌhəʊlɪŋ] *n* Br: **to go** ~ faire de la spéléologie.

potion ['pəʊʃn] *n* (*magic*) breuvage *m*; **love** ~ philtre *m*.

potluck [ˌpɒt'lʌk] *n*: **to take** ~ (*gen*) choisir au hasard; (*at meal*) manger à la fortune du pot.

potshot ['pɒtˌʃɒt] *n*: **to take a** ~ (**at sthg**) tirer (sur qqch) sans viser.

potted ['pɒtɪd] *adj* 1. (*plant*): ~ **plant** plante f d'appartement. 2. (*food*) conservé(e) en pot.

potter ['pɒtər] *n* potier *m*. ▶ **potter about, potter around** *vi* Br bricoler.

pottery ['pɒtərɪ] *n* poterie f; **a piece of** ~ une poterie.

potty ['pɒtɪ] Br inf ◆ *adj*: ~ (**about**) toqué(e) (de). ◆ *n* pot *m* (de chambre).

pouch [paʊtʃ] *n* 1. (*small bag*) petit sac *m*; **tobacco** ~ blague f à tabac. 2. (*of kangaroo*) poche f ventrale.

poultry ['pəʊltrɪ] ◆ *n* (U) (*meat*) volaille f. ◆ *npl* (*birds*) volailles *fpl*.

pounce [paʊns] *vi*: **to** ~ (**on**) (*bird*) fondre (sur); (*person*) se jeter (sur).

pound [paʊnd] ◆ *n* **1.** Br (*money*) livre *f*.
2. (*weight*) = 453,6 *grammes*, ≃ livre *f*.
3. (*for cars, dogs*) fourrière *f*. ◆ *vt* **1.** (*strike loudly*) marteler. **2.** (*crush*) piler, broyer.
◆ *vi* **1.** (*strike loudly*): **to ~ on** donner de grands coups à. **2.** (*heart*) battre fort;
my head is ~ing j'ai des élancements dans la tête.

pound sterling *n* livre *f* sterling.

pour [pɔːʳ] ◆ *vt* verser; **shall I ~ you a drink?** je te sers quelque chose à boire? ◆ *vi* **1.** (*liquid*) couler à flots. **2.** *fig* (*rush*): **to ~ in/out** entrer/sortir en foule. ◆ *v impers* (*rain hard*) pleuvoir à verse. ▶ **pour in** *vi* (*letters, news*) affluer.
▶ **pour out** *vt sep* **1.** (*empty*) vider.
2. (*serve - drink*) verser, servir.

pouring ['pɔːrɪŋ] *adj* (*rain*) torrentiel (elle).

pout [paʊt] *vi* faire la moue.

poverty ['pɒvətɪ] *n* pauvreté *f*; *fig* (*of ideas*) indigence *f*, manque *m*.

poverty-stricken *adj* (*person*) dans la misère; (*area*) misérable, très pauvre.

powder ['paʊdəʳ] ◆ *n* poudre *f*. ◆ *vt* (*face, body*) poudrer.

powder compact *n* poudrier *m*.

powdered ['paʊdəd] *adj* **1.** (*milk, eggs*) en poudre. **2.** (*face*) poudré(e).

powder puff *n* houppette *f*.

powder room *n* toilettes *fpl* pour dames.

power ['paʊəʳ] ◆ *n* **1.** (U) (*authority, ability*) pouvoir *m*; **to take ~** prendre le pouvoir; **to come to ~** parvenir au pouvoir; **to be in ~** être au pouvoir; **to be in** OR **within one's ~ to do sthg** être en son pouvoir de faire qqch. **2.** (*strength, powerful person*) puissance *f*, force *f*. **3.** (U) (*energy*) énergie *f*. **4.** (*electricity*) courant *m*, électricité *f*. ◆ *vt* faire marcher, actionner.

powerboat ['paʊəbəʊt] *n* hors-bord *m inv*.

power cut *n* coupure *f* de courant.

power failure *n* panne *f* de courant.

powerful ['paʊəfʊl] *adj* **1.** (*gen*) puissant(e). **2.** (*smell, voice*) fort(e). **3.** (*speech, novel*) émouvant(e).

powerless ['paʊəlɪs] *adj* impuissant(e); **to be ~ to do sthg** être dans l'impossibilité de faire qqch, ne pas pouvoir faire qqch.

power point *n* Br prise *f* de courant.

power station *n* centrale *f* électrique.

power steering *n* direction *f* assistée.

pp (*abbr of* **per procurationem**) pp.

p & p *abbr of* **postage and packing**.

PR *n* **1.** *abbr of* **proportional representation**. **2.** *abbr of* **public relations**.

practicable ['præktɪkəbl] *adj* réalisable, faisable.

practical ['præktɪkl] ◆ *adj* **1.** (*gen*) pratique. **2.** (*plan, solution*) réalisable. ◆ *n* épreuve *f* pratique.

practical joke *n* farce *f*.

practically ['præktɪklɪ] *adv* **1.** (*in a practical way*) d'une manière pratique.
2. (*almost*) presque, pratiquement.

practice, practise Am ['præktɪs] *n* **1.** (U) (*at sport*) entraînement *m*; (*at music etc*) répétition *f*; **to be out of ~** être rouillé(e). **2.** (*training session - at sport*) séance *f* d'entraînement; (- *at music etc*) répétition *f*. **3.** (*act of doing*): **to put sthg into practice** mettre qqch en pratique; **in ~** (*in fact*) en réalité, en fait. **4.** (*habit*) pratique *f*, coutume *f*. **5.** (U) (*of profession*) exercice *m*. **6.** (*of doctor*) cabinet *m*; (*of lawyer*) étude *f*.

practicing Am = **practising**.

practise, practice Am ['præktɪs] ◆ *vt* **1.** (*sport*) s'entraîner à; (*piano etc*) s'exercer à. **2.** (*custom*) suivre, pratiquer; (*religion*) pratiquer. **3.** (*profession*) exercer.
◆ *vi* **1.** (SPORT) s'entraîner; (MUS) s'exercer. **2.** (*doctor, lawyer*) exercer.

practising, practicing Am ['præktɪsɪŋ] *adj* (*doctor, lawyer*) en exercice; (*Christian etc*) pratiquant(e); (*homosexual*) déclaré(e).

practitioner [præk'tɪʃnəʳ] *n* praticien *m*, -enne *f*.

Prague [prɑːg] *n* Prague.

prairie ['preərɪ] *n* prairie *f*.

praise [preɪz] ◆ *n* (U) louange *f*, louanges *fpl*, éloge *m*, éloges *mpl*. ◆ *vt* louer, faire l'éloge de.

praiseworthy ['preɪz,wɜːðɪ] *adj* louable, méritoire.

pram [præm] *n* landau *m*.

prance [prɑːns] *vi* **1.** (*person*) se pavaner. **2.** (*horse*) caracoler.

prank [præŋk] *n* tour *m*, niche *f*.

prawn [prɔːn] *n* crevette *f* rose.

pray [preɪ] *vi*: **to ~ (to sb)** prier (qqn).

prayer [preəʳ] *n lit & fig* prière *f*.

prayer book *n* livre *m* de messe.

preach [priːtʃ] ◆ *vt* (*gen*) prêcher; (*sermon*) prononcer. ◆ *vi* **1.** (RELIG): **to ~ (to sb)** prêcher (qqn). **2.** *pej* (*pontificate*): **to ~ (at sb)** sermonner (qqn).

preacher ['priːtʃəʳ] *n* prédicateur *m*, pasteur *m*.

precarious [prɪ'keərɪəs] *adj* précaire.
precaution [prɪ'kɔːʃn] *n* précaution *f*.
precede [prɪ'siːd] *vt* précéder.
precedence ['presɪdəns] *n*: **to take ~ over sthg** avoir la priorité sur qqch; **to have** OR **take ~ over sb** avoir la préséance sur qqn.
precedent ['presɪdənt] *n* précédent *m*.
precinct ['priːsɪŋkt] *n* **1.** Br (*area*): **pedestrian ~** zone *f* piétonne; **shopping ~** centre *m* commercial. **2.** Am (*district*) circonscription *f* (administrative). ▶ **precincts** *npl* (*of institution*) enceinte *f*.
precious ['preʃəs] *adj* **1.** (*gen*) précieux (euse). **2.** *inf iro* (*damned*) sacré(e). **3.** (*affected*) affecté(e).
precipice ['presɪpɪs] *n* précipice *m*, paroi *f* à pic.
precipitate [*adj* prɪ'sɪpɪtət, *vb* prɪ'sɪpɪteɪt] *fml* ◆ *adj* hâtif(ive). ◆ *vt* (*hasten*) hâter, précipiter.
precise [prɪ'saɪs] *adj* précis(e); (*measurement, date*) exact(e).
precisely [prɪ'saɪslɪ] *adv* précisément, exactement.
precision [prɪ'sɪʒn] *n* précision *f*, exactitude *f*.
preclude [prɪ'kluːd] *vt fml* empêcher; (*possibility*) écarter; **to ~ sb from doing sthg** empêcher qqn de faire qqch.
precocious [prɪ'kəʊʃəs] *adj* précoce.
preconceived [,priːkən'siːvd] *adj* préconçu(e).
precondition [,priːkən'dɪʃn] *n fml* condition *f* sine qua non.
predator ['predətə'] *n* **1.** (*animal, bird*) prédateur *m*, rapace *m*. **2.** *fig* (*person*) corbeau *m*.
predecessor ['priːdɪsesə'] *n* **1.** (*person*) prédécesseur *m*. **2.** (*thing*) précédent *m*, -e *f*.
predicament [prɪ'dɪkəmənt] *n* situation *f* difficile; **to be in a ~** être dans de beaux draps.
predict [prɪ'dɪkt] *vt* prédire.
predictable [prɪ'dɪktəbl] *adj* prévisible.
prediction [prɪ'dɪkʃn] *n* prédiction *f*.
predispose [,priːdɪs'pəʊz] *vt*: **to be ~d to sthg/to do sthg** être prédisposé(e) à qqch/à faire qqch.
predominant [prɪ'dɒmɪnənt] *adj* prédominant(e).
predominantly [prɪ'dɒmɪnəntlɪ] *adv* principalement, surtout.
preempt [,priː'empt] *vt* (*action, decision*) devancer, prévenir.

preemptive [,priː'emptɪv] *adj* préventif(ive).
preen [priːn] *vt* **1.** (*subj: bird*) lisser, nettoyer. **2.** *fig* (*subj: person*): **to ~ o.s.** se faire beau (belle).
prefab ['priːfæb] *n inf* maison *f* préfabriquée.
preface ['prefɪs] *n*: **~ (to)** préface *f* (de), préambule *m* (de).
prefect ['priːfekt] *n* Br (*pupil*) élève de terminale qui aide les professeurs à maintenir la discipline.
prefer [prɪ'fɜː'] *vt* préférer; **to ~ sthg to sthg** préférer qqch à qqch, aimer mieux qqch que qqch; **to ~ to do sthg** préférer faire qqch, aimer mieux faire qqch.
preferable ['prefrəbl] *adj*: **~ (to)** préférable (à).
preferably ['prefrəblɪ] *adv* de préférence.
preference ['prefərəns] *n* préférence *f*.
preferential [,prefə'renʃl] *adj* préférentiel(elle).
prefix ['priːfɪks] *n* préfixe *m*.
pregnancy ['pregnənsɪ] *n* grossesse *f*.
pregnant ['pregnənt] *adj* (*woman*) enceinte; (*animal*) pleine, gravide.
prehistoric [,priːhɪ'stɒrɪk] *adj* préhistorique.
prejudice ['predʒʊdɪs] ◆ *n* **1.** (*biased view*): **~ (in favour of/against)** préjugé *m* (en faveur de/contre), préjugés *mpl* (en faveur de/contre). **2.** (U) (*harm*) préjudice *m*, tort *m*. ◆ *vt* **1.** (*bias*): **to ~ sb (in favour of/against)** prévenir qqn (en faveur de/contre), influencer qqn (en faveur de/contre). **2.** (*harm*) porter préjudice à.
prejudiced ['predʒʊdɪst] *adj* (*person*) qui a des préjugés; (*opinion*) préconçu(e); **to be ~ in favour of/against** avoir des préjugés en faveur de/contre.
prejudicial [,predʒʊ'dɪʃl] *adj*: **~ (to)** préjudiciable (à), nuisible (à).
preliminary [prɪ'lɪmɪnərɪ] *adj* préliminaire.
prelude ['preljuːd] *n* (*event*): **~ to sthg** prélude *m* de qqch.
premarital [,priː'mærɪtl] *adj* avant le mariage.
premature ['premə,tjʊə'] *adj* prématuré(e).
premeditated [,priː'medɪteɪtɪd] *adj* prémédité(e).
premenstrual syndrome, premenstrual tension [priː'menstrʊəl-]

n syndrome *m* prémenstruel.

premier ['premjəʳ] ◆ *adj* primordial(e), premier(ère). ◆ *n* premier ministre *m*.

premiere ['premɪeəʳ] *n* première *f*.

premise ['premɪs] *n* prémisse *f*. ▶ **premises** *npl* local *m*, locaux *mpl*; **on the ~s** sur place, sur les lieux.

premium ['priːmjəm] *n* prime *f*; **at a ~** *(above usual value)* à prix d'or; *(in great demand)* très recherché OR demandé.

premium bond *n* Br = billet *m* de loterie.

premonition [,premə'nɪʃn] *n* prémonition *f*, pressentiment *m*.

preoccupied [priː'ɒkjʊpaɪd] *adj*: **~ (with)** préoccupé(e) (de).

prep [prep] *n* (U) Br *inf* devoirs *mpl*.

prepaid ['priːpeɪd] *adj* payé(e) d'avance; *(envelope)* affranchi(e).

preparation [,prepə'reɪʃn] *n* préparation *f*. ▶ **preparations** *npl* préparatifs *mpl*; **to make ~s for** faire des préparatifs pour, prendre ses dispositions pour.

preparatory [prɪ'pærətrɪ] *adj* *(work, classes)* préparatoire; *(actions, measures)* préliminaire.

preparatory school *n* *(in UK)* école *f* primaire privée; *(in US)* école privée qui prépare à l'enseignement supérieur.

prepare [prɪ'peəʳ] ◆ *vt* préparer. ◆ *vi*: **to ~ for sthg/to do sthg** se préparer à qqch/à faire qqch.

prepared [prɪ'peəd] *adj* **1.** *(done beforehand)* préparé(e) d'avance. **2.** *(willing)*: **to be ~ to do sthg** être prêt(e) OR disposé(e) à faire qqch. **3.** *(ready)*: **to be ~ for sthg** être prêt(e) pour qqch.

preposition [,prepə'zɪʃn] *n* préposition *f*.

preposterous [prɪ'pɒstərəs] *adj* ridicule, absurde.

prep school *abbr of* **preparatory school**.

prerequisite [,priː'rekwɪzɪt] *n* condition *f* préalable.

prerogative [prɪ'rɒɡətɪv] *n* prérogative *f*, privilège *m*.

Presbyterian [,prezbɪ'tɪərɪən] ◆ *adj* presbytérien(enne). ◆ *n* presbytérien *m*, -enne *f*.

preschool [,priː'skuːl] ◆ *adj* préscolaire. ◆ *n* Am école *f* maternelle.

prescribe [prɪ'skraɪb] *vt* **1.** *(MED)* prescrire. **2.** *(order)* ordonner, imposer.

prescription [prɪ'skrɪpʃn] *n* *(MED - written form)* ordonnance *f*; *(- medicine)* médicament *m*.

presence ['prezns] *n* présence *f*; **to be**

in sb's ~ OR **in the ~ of sb** être en présence de qqn.

presence of mind *n* présence *f* d'esprit.

present [*adj & n* 'preznt, *vb* prɪ'zent] ◆ *adj* **1.** *(current)* actuel(elle). **2.** *(in attendance)* présent(e); **to be ~ at** assister à. ◆ *n* **1.** *(current time)*: **the ~** le présent. **2.** *(gift)* cadeau *m*. **3.** *(GRAMM)*: **~ (tense)** présent *m*. ◆ *vt* **1.** *(gen)* présenter; *(opportunity)* donner. **2.** *(give)* donner, remettre; **to ~ sb with sthg, to ~ sthg to sb** donner OR remettre qqch à qqn. **3.** *(portray)* représenter, décrire. **4.** *(arrive)*: **to ~ o.s.** se présenter.

presentable [prɪ'zentəbl] *adj* présentable.

presentation [,prezn'teɪʃn] *n* **1.** *(gen)* présentation *f*. **2.** *(ceremony)* remise *f* *(de récompense/prix)*. **3.** *(talk)* exposé *m*. **4.** *(of play)* représentation *f*.

present day *n*: **the ~** aujourd'hui. ▶ **present-day** *adj* d'aujourd'hui, contemporain(e).

presenter [prɪ'zentəʳ] *n* Br présentateur *m*, -trice *f*.

presently ['prezntlɪ] *adv* **1.** *(soon)* bientôt, tout à l'heure. **2.** *(at present)* actuellement, en ce moment.

preservation [,prezə'veɪʃn] *n* (U) **1.** *(maintenance)* maintien *m*. **2.** *(protection)* protection *f*, conservation *f*.

preservative [prɪ'zɜːvətɪv] *n* conservateur *m*.

preserve [prɪ'zɜːv] ◆ *vt* **1.** *(maintain)* maintenir. **2.** *(protect)* conserver. **3.** *(food)* conserver, mettre en conserve. ◆ *n* *(jam)* confiture *f*. ▶ **preserves** *npl* *(jam)* confiture *f*; *(vegetables)* pickles *mpl*, condiments *mpl*.

preset [,priː'set] *(pt & pp* **preset**) *vt* prérégler.

president ['prezɪdənt] *n* **1.** *(gen)* président *m*. **2.** Am *(company chairman)* P-DG *m*.

presidential [,prezɪ'denʃl] *adj* présidentiel(elle).

press [pres] ◆ *n* **1.** *(push)* pression *f*. **2.** *(journalism)*: **the ~** *(newspapers)* la presse, les journaux *mpl*; *(reporters)* les journalistes *mpl*. **3.** *(printing machine)* presse *f*; *(for wine)* pressoir *m*. ◆ *vt* **1.** *(push)* appuyer sur; **to ~ sthg against sthg** appuyer qqch sur qqch. **2.** *(squeeze)* serrer. **3.** *(iron)* repasser, donner un coup de fer à. **4.** *(urge)*: **to ~ sb (to do sthg OR into doing sthg)** presser qqn (de faire qqch). **5.** (*pursue - claim*) insister sur. ◆ vi **1.** (*push*): **to ~ (on sthg)** appuyer (sur qqch). **2.** (*squeeze*): **to ~ (on sthg)** serrer (qqch). **3.** (*crowd*) se presser. ▶ **press for** vt fus demander avec insistance. ▶ **press on** vi (*continue*): **to ~ on (with sthg)** continuer (qqch), ne pas abandonner (qqch).

press agency n agence f de presse.

press conference n conférence f de presse.

pressed [prest] adj: **to be ~ for time/money** être à court de temps/d'argent.

pressing ['presɪŋ] adj urgent(e).

press officer n attaché m de presse.

press release n communiqué m de presse.

press-stud n Br pression f.

press-up n Br pompe f, traction f.

pressure ['preʃər] n (U) **1.** (*gen*) pression f; **to put ~ on sb (to do sthg)** faire pression sur qqn (pour qu'il fasse qqch). **2.** (*stress*) tension f.

pressure cooker n Cocotte-Minute® f, autocuiseur m.

pressure gauge n manomètre m.

pressure group n groupe m de pression.

pressurize, -ise ['preʃəraɪz] vt **1.** (TECH) pressuriser. **2.** Br (*force*): **to ~ sb to do** OR **into doing sthg** forcer qqn à faire qqch.

prestige [pre'stiːʒ] n prestige m.

presumably [prɪ'zjuːməblɪ] adv vraisemblablement.

presume [prɪ'zjuːm] vt présumer; **to ~ (that)** ... supposer que ...

presumption [prɪ'zʌmpʃn] n **1.** (*assumption*) supposition f, présomption f. **2.** (U) (*audacity*) présomption f.

presumptuous [prɪ'zʌmptʃʊəs] adj présomptueux(euse).

pretence, pretense Am [prɪ'tens] n prétention f; **to make a ~ of doing sthg** faire semblant de faire qqch; **under false ~s** sous des prétextes fallacieux.

pretend [prɪ'tend] ◆ vt: **to ~ to do sthg** faire semblant de faire qqch. ◆ vi faire semblant.

pretense Am = **pretence**.

pretension [prɪ'tenʃn] n prétention f.

pretentious [prɪ'tenʃəs] adj prétentieux(euse).

pretext ['priːtekst] n prétexte m; **on** OR **under the ~ that** ... sous prétexte que ...; **on** OR **under the ~ of doing sthg** sous prétexte de faire qqch.

pretty ['prɪtɪ] ◆ adj joli(e). ◆ adv (*quite*)

plutôt; **~ much** OR **well** pratiquement, presque.

prevail [prɪ'veɪl] vi **1.** (*be widespread*) avoir cours, régner. **2.** (*triumph*): **to ~ (over)** prévaloir (sur), l'emporter (sur). **3.** (*persuade*): **to ~ on** OR **upon sb to do sthg** persuader qqn de faire qqch.

prevailing [prɪ'veɪlɪŋ] adj **1.** (*current*) actuel(elle). **2.** (*wind*) dominant(e).

prevalent ['prevələnt] adj courant(e), répandu(e).

prevent [prɪ'vent] vt: **to ~ sb/sthg (from doing sthg)** empêcher qqn/qqch (de faire qqch).

preventive [prɪ'ventɪv] adj préventif (ive).

preview ['priːvjuː] n avant-première f.

previous ['priːvjəs] adj **1.** (*earlier*) antérieur(e). **2.** (*preceding*) précédent(e).

previously ['priːvjəslɪ] adv avant, auparavant.

prewar [ˌpriː'wɔːr] adj d'avant-guerre.

prey [preɪ] n proie f. ▶ **prey on** vt fus **1.** (*live off*) faire sa proie de. **2.** (*trouble*): **to ~ on sb's mind** ronger qqn, tracasser qqn.

price [praɪs] ◆ n (*cost*) prix m; **at any ~** à tout prix. ◆ vt fixer le prix de.

priceless ['praɪslɪs] adj sans prix, inestimable.

price list n tarif m.

price tag n (*label*) étiquette f.

pricey ['praɪsɪ] adj inf chérot.

prick [prɪk] ◆ n **1.** (*scratch, wound*) piqûre f. **2.** vulg (*stupid person*) con m, conne f. ◆ vt piquer. ▶ **prick up** vt fus: **to ~ up one's ears** (*animal*) dresser les oreilles; (*person*) dresser OR tendre l'oreille.

prickle ['prɪkl] ◆ n **1.** (*thorn*) épine f. **2.** (*sensation on skin*) picotement m. ◆ vi picoter.

prickly ['prɪklɪ] adj **1.** (*plant, bush*) épineux(euse). **2.** fig (*person*) irritable.

prickly heat n (U) boutons mpl de chaleur.

pride [praɪd] ◆ n (U) **1.** (*satisfaction*) fierté f; **to take ~ in sthg/in doing sthg** être fier de qqch/de faire qqch. **2.** (*self-esteem*) orgueil m, amour-propre m. **3.** pej (*arrogance*) orgueil m. ◆ vt: **to ~ o.s. on sthg** être fier (fière) de qqch.

priest [priːst] n prêtre m.

priestess ['priːstɪs] n prêtresse f.

priesthood ['priːsthʊd] n **1.** (*position, office*): **the ~** le sacerdoce. **2.** (*priests*): **the ~** le clergé.

prig [prɪg] n petit saint m, petite sainte f.

prim [prɪm] adj guindé(e).

primarily ['praɪmərɪlɪ] adv principalement.

primary ['praɪmərɪ] ◆ adj 1. (main) premier(ère), principal(e). 2. (SCH) primaire. ◆ n Am (POL) primaire f.

primary school n école f primaire.

primate ['praɪmeɪt] n 1. (ZOOL) primate m. 2. (RELIG) primat m.

prime [praɪm] ◆ adj 1. (main) principal(e), primordial(e). 2. (excellent) excellent(e); ~ quality première qualité. ◆ n: to be in one's ~ être dans la fleur de l'âge. ◆ vt 1. (gun, pump) amorcer. 2. (paint) apprêter. 3. (inform): to ~ sb about sthg mettre qqn au courant de qqch.

prime minister n premier ministre m.

primer ['praɪmə'] n 1. (paint) apprêt m. 2. (textbook) introduction f.

primeval [praɪ'miːvl] adj (ancient) primitif(ive).

primitive ['prɪmɪtɪv] adj primitif(ive).

primrose ['prɪmrəʊz] n primevère f.

Primus stove® ['praɪməs-] n réchaud m de camping.

prince [prɪns] n prince m.

princess [prɪn'ses] n princesse f.

principal ['prɪnsəpl] ◆ adj principal(e). ◆ n (SCH) directeur m, -trice f; (UNIV) doyen m, -enne f.

principle ['prɪnsəpl] n principe m; on ~, as a matter of ~ par principe. ▶ in principle adv en principe.

print [prɪnt] ◆ n 1. (U) (type) caractères mpl; to be in ~ être disponible; to be out of ~ être épuisé. 2. (ART) gravure f. 3. (photograph) épreuve f. 4. (fabric) imprimé m. 5. (mark) empreinte f. ◆ vt 1. (produce by printing) imprimer. 2. (publish) publier. 3. (write in block letters) écrire en caractères d'imprimerie. ◆ vi (printer) imprimer. ▶ print out vt sep (COMPUT) imprimer.

printed matter ['prɪntɪd-] n (U) imprimés mpl.

printer ['prɪntə'] n 1. (person, firm) imprimeur m. 2. (COMPUT) imprimante f.

printing ['prɪntɪŋ] n (U) 1. (act of printing) impression f. 2. (trade) imprimerie f.

printout ['prɪntaʊt] n (COMPUT) sortie f d'imprimante, listing m.

prior ['praɪə'] ◆ adj antérieur(e), précédent(e). ◆ n (monk) prieur m. ▶ prior to prep avant; ~ to doing sthg avant de faire qqch.

priority [praɪ'ɒrətɪ] n priorité f; to have

or take ~ (over) avoir la priorité (sur).

prise [praɪz] vt: to ~ sthg away from sb arracher qqch à qqn; to ~ sthg open forcer qqch.

prison ['prɪzn] n prison f.

prisoner ['prɪznə'] n prisonnier m, -ère f.

prisoner of war (pl prisoners of war) n prisonnier m, -ère f de guerre.

privacy [Br 'prɪvəsɪ, Am 'praɪvəsɪ] n intimité f.

private ['praɪvɪt] ◆ adj 1. (not public) privé(e). 2. (confidential) confidentiel (elle). 3. (personal) personnel(elle). 4. (unsociable - person) secret(ète). ◆ n 1. (soldier) (simple) soldat m. 2. (secrecy): in ~ en privé.

private enterprise n (U) entreprise f privée.

private eye n détective m privé.

privately ['praɪvɪtlɪ] adv 1. (not by the state): ~ owned du secteur privé. 2. (confidentially) en privé. 3. (personally) intérieurement, dans son for intérieur.

private property n propriété f privée.

private school n école f privée.

privatize, -ise ['praɪvɪtaɪz] vt privatiser.

privet ['prɪvɪt] n troène m.

privilege ['prɪvɪlɪdʒ] n privilège m.

privy ['prɪvɪ] adj: to be ~ to sthg être dans le secret de qqch.

prize [praɪz] ◆ adj (possession) très précieux(euse); (animal) primé(e); (idiot, example) parfait(e). ◆ n prix m. ◆ vt priser.

prize-giving [-ˌgɪvɪŋ] n Br distribution f des prix.

prizewinner ['praɪzˌwɪnə'] n gagnant m, -e f.

pro [prəʊ] (pl -s) n 1. inf (professional) pro mf. 2. (advantage): the ~s and cons le pour et le contre.

probability [ˌprɒbə'bɪlətɪ] n probabilité f.

probable ['prɒbəbl] adj probable.

probably ['prɒbəblɪ] adv probablement.

probation [prə'beɪʃn] n (U) 1. (JUR) mise f à l'épreuve; to put sb on ~ mettre qqn en sursis avec mise à l'épreuve. 2. (trial period) essai m; to be on ~ être à l'essai.

probe [prəʊb] ◆ n 1. (investigation): ~ (into) enquête f (sur). 2. (MED & TECH) sonde f. ◆ vt sonder.

problem ['prɒbləm] ◆ n problème m;

no ~! *inf* pas de problème! ◆ *comp* difficile.

procedure [prə'siːdʒəʳ] *n* procédure *f*.

proceed [*vb* prə'siːd, *npl* 'prəusiːdz] ◆ *vt* (*do subsequently*): **to ~ to do sthg** se mettre à faire qqch. ◆ *vi* **1.** (*continue*): **to ~ (with sthg)** continuer (qqch), poursuivre (qqch). **2.** *fml* (*advance*) avancer. ➤ **proceeds** *npl* recette *f*.

proceedings [prə'siːdɪŋz] *npl* **1.** (*of meeting*) débats *mpl*. **2.** (JUR) poursuites *fpl*.

process ['prəuses] ◆ *n* **1.** (*series of actions*) processus *m*; **in the ~** ce faisant; **to be in the ~ of doing sthg** être en train de faire qqch. **2.** (*method*) procédé *m*. ◆ *vt* (*raw materials, food, data*) traiter, transformer; (*application*) s'occuper de.

processing ['prəusesɪŋ] *n* traitement *m*, transformation *f*.

procession [prə'seʃn] *n* cortège *m*, procession *f*.

proclaim [prə'kleɪm] *vt* (*declare*) proclamer.

procrastinate [prə'kræstɪneɪt] *vi* faire traîner les choses.

procure [prə'kjuəʳ] *vt* (*for oneself*) se procurer; (*for someone else*) procurer; (*release*) obtenir.

prod [prɒd] *vt* (*push, poke*) pousser doucement.

prodigal ['prɒdɪgl] *adj* prodigue.

prodigy ['prɒdɪdʒɪ] *n* prodige *m*.

produce [*n* 'prɒdjuːs, *vb* prə'djuːs] ◆ *n* (U) produits *mpl*. ◆ *vt* **1.** (*gen*) produire. **2.** (*cause*) provoquer, causer. **3.** (*show*) présenter. **4.** (THEATRE) mettre en scène.

producer [prə'djuːsəʳ] *n* **1.** (*of film, manufacturer*) producteur *m*, -trice *f*. **2.** (THEATRE) metteur en scène.

product ['prɒdʌkt] *n* produit *m*.

production [prə'dʌkʃn] *n* **1.** (U) (*manufacture, of film*) production *f*. **2.** (U) (*output*) rendement *m*. **3.** (U) (THEATRE) (*of play*) mise *f* en scène. **4.** (*show - gen*) production *f*; (- THEATRE) pièce *f*.

production line *n* chaîne *f* de fabrication.

productive [prə'dʌktɪv] *adj* **1.** (*land, business, workers*) productif(ive). **2.** (*meeting, experience*) fructueux(euse).

productivity [,prɒdʌk'tɪvətɪ] *n* productivité *f*.

profane [prə'feɪn] *adj* impie.

profession [prə'feʃn] *n* profession *f*; **by ~** de son métier.

professional [prə'feʃənl] ◆ *adj* **1.** (*gen*) professionnel(elle). **2.** (*of high standard*) de (haute) qualité. ◆ *n* professionnel *m*, -elle *f*.

professor [prə'fesəʳ] *n* **1.** Br (UNIV) professeur *m* (de faculté). **2.** Am & Can (*teacher*) professeur *m*.

proficiency [prə'fɪʃənsɪ] *n*: **~ (in)** compétence *f* (en).

profile ['prəufaɪl] *n* profil *m*.

profit ['prɒfɪt] ◆ *n* **1.** (*financial*) bénéfice *m*, profit *m*; **to make a ~** faire un bénéfice. **2.** (*advantage*) profit *m*. ◆ *vi* (*financially*) être le bénéficiaire; (*gain advantage*) tirer avantage OR profit.

profitability [,prɒfɪtə'bɪlətɪ] *n* rentabilité *f*.

profitable ['prɒfɪtəbl] *adj* **1.** (*financially*) rentable, lucratif(ive). **2.** (*beneficial*) fructueux(euse), profitable.

profiteering [,prɒfɪ'tɪərɪŋ] *n* affairisme *m*, mercantilisme *m*.

profound [prə'faund] *adj* profond(e).

profusely [prə'fjuːslɪ] *adv* (*sweat, bleed*) abondamment; **to apologize ~** se confondre en excuses.

profusion [prə'fjuːʒn] *n* profusion *f*.

progeny ['prɒdʒənɪ] *n* progéniture *f*.

prognosis [prɒg'nəusɪs] (*pl* **-noses** [-'nəusiːz]) *n* pronostic *m*.

program ['prəugræm] (*pt & pp* **-med** OR **-ed**, *cont* **-ming** OR **-ing**) ◆ *n* **1.** (COMPUT) programme *m*. **2.** Am = **programme**. ◆ *vt* **1.** (COMPUT) programmer. **2.** Am = **programme**.

programer Am = **programmer**.

programme Br, **program** Am ['prəugræm] ◆ *n* **1.** (*schedule, booklet*) programme *m*. **2.** (RADIO & TV) émission *f*. ◆ *vt* programmer; **to ~ sthg to do sthg** programmer qqch pour faire qqch.

programmer Br, **programer** Am ['prəugræməʳ] *n* (COMPUT) programmeur *m*, -euse *f*.

programming ['prəugræmɪŋ] *n* programmation *f*.

progress [*n* 'prəugres, *vb* prə'gres] ◆ *n* progrès *m*; **to make ~** (*improve*) faire des progrès; **to make ~ in sthg** avancer dans qqch; **in ~** en cours. ◆ *vi* **1.** (*improve - gen*) progresser, avancer; (- *person*) faire des progrès. **2.** (*continue*) avancer.

progressive [prə'gresɪv] *adj* **1.** (*enlightened*) progressiste. **2.** (*gradual*) progressif(ive).

prohibit [prə'hɪbɪt] *vt* prohiber; **to ~ sb from doing sthg** interdire OR défendre à qqn de faire qqch.

project [*n* 'prɒdʒekt, *vb* prə'dʒekt] ◆ *n* **1.** (*plan, idea*) projet *m*, plan *m*. **2.** (SCH) (study): ~ **(on)** dossier m (sur), projet m (sur). ◆ vt **1.** (gen) projeter. **2.** (estimate) prévoir. ◆ vi (jut out) faire saillie.

projectile [prə'dʒektaıl] n projectile m.

projection [prə'dʒekʃn] n **1.** (estimate) prévision f. **2.** (protrusion) saillie f. **3.** (U) (display, showing) projection f.

projector [prə'dʒektər] n projecteur m.

proletariat [,prəʊlı'teərıət] n prolétariat m.

prolific [prə'lıfık] adj prolifique.

prologue, prolog Am ['prəʊlɒg] n lit & fig prologue m.

prolong [prə'lɒŋ] vt prolonger.

prom [prɒm] n **1.** Br inf (abbr of **promenade**) promenade f, front m de mer. **2.** Am (ball) bal m d'étudiants. **3.** Br inf (abbr of **promenade concert**) concert m promenade.

promenade [,prɒmə'nɑːd] n Br (road by sea) promenade f, front m de mer.

promenade concert n Br concert m promenade.

prominent ['prɒmınənt] adj **1.** (important) important(e). **2.** (noticeable) proéminent(e).

promiscuous [prɒ'mıskjʊəs] adj (person) aux mœurs légères; (behaviour) immoral(e).

promise ['prɒmıs] ◆ n promesse f. ◆ vt: **to ~ (sb) to do sthg** promettre (à qqn) de faire qqch; **to ~ sb sthg** promettre qqch à qqn. ◆ vi promettre.

promising ['prɒmısıŋ] adj prometteur (euse).

promontory ['prɒməntrı] n promontoire m.

promote [prə'məʊt] vt **1.** (foster) promouvoir. **2.** (push, advertise) promouvoir, lancer. **3.** (in job) promouvoir.

promoter [prə'məʊtər] n **1.** (organizer) organisateur m, -trice f. **2.** (supporter) promoteur m, -trice f.

promotion [prə'məʊʃn] n promotion f, avancement m.

prompt [prɒmpt] ◆ adj rapide, prompt(e). ◆ adv: **at nine o'clock ~** à neuf heures précises ou tapantes. ◆ vt **1.** (motivate, encourage): **to ~ sb (to do sthg)** pousser ou inciter qqn (à faire qqch). **2.** (THEATRE) souffler sa réplique à. ◆ n (THEATRE) réplique f.

promptly ['prɒmptlı] adv **1.** (immediately) rapidement, promptement. **2.** (punctually) ponctuellement.

prone [prəʊn] adj **1.** (susceptible): **to be ~ to sthg** être sujet(ette) à qqch; **to be ~ to do sthg** avoir tendance à faire qqch.

2. (lying flat) étendu(e) face contre terre.

prong [prɒŋ] n (of fork) dent f.

pronoun ['prəʊnaʊn] n pronom m.

pronounce [prə'naʊns] ◆ vt prononcer. ◆ vi: **to ~ on** se prononcer sur.

pronounced [prə'naʊnst] adj prononcé(e).

pronunciation [prə,nʌnsı'eıʃn] n prononciation f.

proof [pruːf] n **1.** (evidence) preuve f. **2.** (of book etc) épreuve f. **3.** (of alcohol) teneur f en alcool.

prop [prɒp] ◆ n **1.** (physical support) support m, étai m. **2.** fig (supporting thing, person) soutien m. ◆ vt: **to ~ sthg against** appuyer qqch contre ou à. ▶ **props** npl accessoires mpl. ▶ **prop up** vt sep **1.** (physically support) soutenir, étayer. **2.** fig (sustain) soutenir.

propaganda [,prɒpə'gændə] n propagande f.

propel [prə'pel] vt propulser; fig pousser.

propeller [prə'pelər] n hélice f.

propelling pencil [prə'pelıŋ-] n Br porte-mine m inv.

propensity [prə'pensətı] n: ~ **(for ou to)** propension f (à).

proper ['prɒpər] adj **1.** (real) vrai(e). **2.** (correct) correct(e), bon (bonne). **3.** (decent - behaviour etc) convenable.

properly ['prɒpəlı] adv **1.** (satisfactorily, correctly) correctement, comme il faut. **2.** (decently) convenablement, comme il faut.

proper noun n nom m propre.

property ['prɒpətı] n **1.** (U) (possessions) biens mpl, propriété f. **2.** (building) bien m immobilier; (land) terres fpl. **3.** (quality) propriété f.

property owner n propriétaire m (foncier).

prophecy ['prɒfısı] n prophétie f.

prophesy ['prɒfısaı] vt prédire.

prophet ['prɒfıt] n prophète m.

proportion [prə'pɔːʃn] n **1.** (part) part f, partie f. **2.** (ratio) rapport m, proportion f. **3.** (ART): **in ~** proportionné(e); **out of ~** mal proportionné; **a sense of ~** fig le sens de la mesure.

proportional [prə'pɔːʃənl] adj proportionnel(elle).

proportional representation n représentation f proportionnelle.

proportionate [prə'pɔːʃnət] adj proportionnel(elle).

proposal [prə'pəʊzl] n **1.** (suggestion)

proposition f, offre f. **2.** (offer of marriage) demande f en mariage.

propose [prə'pəʊz] ♦ vt **1.** (suggest) proposer. **2.** (intend): **to ~ to do** OR **doing sthg** avoir l'intention de faire qqch, se proposer de faire qqch. **3.** (toast) porter. ♦ vi faire une demande en mariage; **to ~ to sb** demander qqn en mariage.

proposition [,prɒpə'zɪʃn] n proposition f.

proprietor [prə'praɪətər] n propriétaire mf.

propriety [prə'praɪətɪ] n (U) fml (moral correctness) bienséance f.

pro rata [-'rɑːtə] ♦ adj proportionnel (elle). ♦ adv au prorata.

prose [prəʊz] n (U) prose f.

prosecute ['prɒsɪkjuːt] ♦ vt poursuivre (en justice). ♦ vi (police) engager des poursuites judiciaires; (lawyer) représenter la partie plaignante.

prosecution [,prɒsɪ'kjuːʃn] n poursuites fpl judiciaires, accusation f; **the ~** la partie plaignante; (in Crown case) = le ministère public.

prosecutor ['prɒsɪkjuːtər] n plaignant m, -e f.

prospect [n 'prɒspekt, vb prə'spekt] ♦ n **1.** (hope) possibilité f, chances fpl. **2.** (probability) perspective f. ♦ vi: **to ~ (for sthg)** prospecter (pour chercher qqch). ► **prospects** npl: **~s (for)** chances fpl (de), perspectives fpl (de).

prospecting [prə'spektɪŋ] n prospection f.

prospective [prə'spektɪv] adj éventuel(elle).

prospectus [prə'spektəs] (pl -es) n prospectus m.

prosper ['prɒspər] vi prospérer.

prosperity [prɒ'sperətɪ] n prospérité f.

prosperous ['prɒspərəs] adj prospère.

prostitute ['prɒstɪtjuːt] n prostituée f.

prostrate ['prɒstreɪt] adj **1.** (lying down) à plat ventre. **2.** (with grief etc) prostré(e).

protagonist [prə'tægənɪst] n protagoniste mf.

protect [prə'tekt] vt: **to ~ sb/sthg (against)**, **to ~ sb/sthg (from)** protéger qqn/qqch (contre), protéger qqn/qqch (de).

protection [prə'tekʃn] n: **~ (from** OR **against)** protection f (contre), défense f (contre).

protective [prə'tektɪv] adj **1.** (layer, clothing) de protection. **2.** (person, feel-

ings) protecteur(trice).

protein ['prəʊtiːn] n protéine f.

protest [n 'prəʊtest, vb prə'test] ♦ n protestation f. ♦ vt **1.** (state) protester de. **2.** Am (protest against) protester contre. ♦ vi: **to ~ (about/against)** protester (à propos de/contre).

Protestant ['prɒtɪstənt] ♦ adj protestant(e). ♦ n protestant m, -e f.

protester [prə'testər] n (on march, at demonstration) manifestant m, -e f.

protest march n manifestation f, marche f de protestation.

protocol ['prəʊtəkɒl] n protocole m.

prototype ['prəʊtətaɪp] n prototype m.

protracted [prə'træktɪd] adj prolongé(e).

protrude [prə'truːd] vi avancer, dépasser.

protuberance [prə'tjuːbərəns] n protubérance f.

proud [praʊd] adj **1.** (satisfied, dignified) fier (fière). **2.** pej (arrogant) orgueilleux (euse), fier (fière).

prove [pruːv] (pp -d OR proven) vt **1.** (show to be true) prouver. **2.** (turn out): **to ~ (to be) false/useful** s'avérer faux/utile; **to ~ o.s. to be sthg** se révéler être qqch.

proven ['pruːvn, 'prəʊvn] ♦ pp → **prove**. ♦ adj (fact) avéré(e), établi(e); (liar) fieffé(e).

Provence [prɒ'vɑːns] n Provence f.

proverb ['prɒvɜːb] n proverbe m.

provide [prə'vaɪd] vt fournir; **to ~ sb with sthg** fournir qqch à qqn; **to ~ sthg for sb** fournir qqch à qqn. ► **provide for** vt fus **1.** (support) subvenir aux besoins de. **2.** fml (make arrangements for) prévoir.

provided [prə'vaɪdɪd] ► **provided (that)** conj à condition que (+ subjunctive), pourvu que (+ subjunctive).

providing [prə'vaɪdɪŋ] ► **providing (that)** conj à condition que (+ subjunctive), pourvu que (+ subjunctive).

province ['prɒvɪns] n **1.** (part of country) province f. **2.** (speciality) domaine m, compétence f.

provincial [prə'vɪnʃl] adj **1.** (town, newspaper) de province. **2.** pej (narrow-minded) provincial(e).

provision [prə'vɪʒn] n **1.** (U) (act of supplying): **~ (of)** approvisionnement m (en), fourniture f (de). **2.** (supply) provision f, réserve f. **3.** (U) (arrangements): **to make ~ for** (the future) prendre des mesures pour. **4.** (*in agreement, law*) clause *f*, disposition *f*. ▶ **provisions** *npl* (*supplies*) provisions *fpl*.

provisional [prə'vɪʒənl] *adj* provisoire.

proviso [prə'vaɪzəʊ] (*pl* **-s**) *n* condition *f*, stipulation *f*; **with the ~ that** à (la) condition que (+ *subjunctive*).

provocative [prə'vɒkətɪv] *adj* provocant(e).

provoke [prə'vəʊk] *vt* **1.** (*annoy*) agacer, contrarier. **2.** (*cause - fight, argument*) provoquer; (*- reaction*) susciter.

prow [praʊ] *n* proue *f*.

prowess ['praʊɪs] *n* prouesse *f*.

prowl [praʊl] ◆ *n*: **to be on the ~** rôder. ◆ *vt* (*streets etc*) rôder dans. ◆ *vi* rôder.

prowler ['praʊlər] *n* rôdeur *m*, -euse *f*.

proxy ['prɒksɪ] *n*: **by ~** par procuration.

prudent ['pruːdnt] *adj* prudent(e).

prudish ['pruːdɪʃ] *adj* prude, pudibond(e).

prune [pruːn] ◆ *n* (*fruit*) pruneau *m*. ◆ *vt* (*tree, bush*) tailler.

pry [praɪ] *vi* se mêler de ce qui ne vous regarde pas; **to ~ into sthg** chercher à découvrir qqch.

PS (*abbr of* **postscript**) *n* PS *m*.

psalm [sɑːm] *n* psaume *m*.

pseudonym ['sjuːdənɪm] *n* pseudonyme *m*.

psyche ['saɪkɪ] *n* psyché *f*.

psychiatric [ˌsaɪkɪ'ætrɪk] *adj* psychiatrique.

psychiatrist [saɪ'kaɪətrɪst] *n* psychiatre *mf*.

psychiatry [saɪ'kaɪətrɪ] *n* psychiatrie *f*.

psychic ['saɪkɪk] ◆ *adj* **1.** (*clairvoyant - person*) doué(e) de seconde vue; (*- powers*) parapsychique. **2.** (MED) psychique. ◆ *n* médium *m*.

psychoanalysis [ˌsaɪkəʊə'næləsɪs] *n* psychanalyse *f*.

psychoanalyst [ˌsaɪkəʊ'ænəlɪst] *n* psychanalyste *mf*.

psychological [ˌsaɪkə'lɒdʒɪkl] *adj* psychologique.

psychologist [saɪ'kɒlədʒɪst] *n* psychologue *mf*.

psychology [saɪ'kɒlədʒɪ] *n* psychologie *f*.

psychopath ['saɪkəpæθ] *n* psychopathe *mf*.

psychotic [saɪ'kɒtɪk] ◆ *adj* psychotique. ◆ *n* psychotique *mf*.

pt 1. *abbr of* **pint**. **2.** *abbr of* **point**.

PT (*abbr of* **physical training**) *n* EPS *f*.

PTO (*abbr of* **please turn over**) TSVP.

pub [pʌb] *n* pub *m*.

puberty ['pjuːbətɪ] *n* puberté *f*.

pubic ['pjuːbɪk] *adj* du pubis.

public ['pʌblɪk] ◆ *adj* public(ique); (*library*) municipal(e). ◆ *n*: **the ~** le public; **in ~** en public.

public-address system *n* système *m* de sonorisation.

publican ['pʌblɪkən] *n* Br gérant *m*, -e *f* d'un pub.

publication [ˌpʌblɪ'keɪʃn] *n* publication *f*.

public bar *n* Br bar *m*.

public company *n* société *f* anonyme (*cotée en Bourse*).

public convenience *n* Br toilettes *fpl* publiques.

public holiday *n* jour *m* férié.

public house *n* Br pub *m*.

publicity [pʌb'lɪsɪtɪ] *n* (U) publicité *f*.

publicize, -ise ['pʌblɪsaɪz] *vt* faire connaître au public.

public limited company *n* société *f* anonyme (*cotée en Bourse*).

public opinion *n* (U) opinion *f* publique.

public prosecutor *n* ≃ procureur *m* de la République.

public relations ◆ *n* (U) relations *fpl* publiques. ◆ *npl* relations *fpl* publiques.

public school *n* **1.** Br (*private school*) école *f* privée. **2.** Am (*state school*) école *f* publique.

public-spirited *adj* qui fait preuve de civisme.

public transport *n* (U) transports *mpl* en commun.

publish ['pʌblɪʃ] *vt* publier.

publisher ['pʌblɪʃər] *n* éditeur *m*, -trice *f*.

publishing ['pʌblɪʃɪŋ] *n* (U) (*industry*) édition *f*.

pub lunch *n* repas de midi servi dans un pub.

pucker ['pʌkər] *vt* plisser.

pudding ['pʊdɪŋ] *n* **1.** (*food - sweet*) entremets *m*; (*- savoury*) pudding *m*. **2.** (U) Br (*course*) dessert *m*.

puddle ['pʌdl] *n* flaque *f*.

puff [pʌf] ◆ *n* **1.** (*of cigarette, smoke*) bouffée *f*. **2.** (*gasp*) souffle *m*. ◆ *vt* (*cigarette etc*) tirer sur. ◆ *vi* **1.** (*smoke*): **to ~ at** OR **on sthg** fumer qqch. **2.** (*pant*) haleter. ▶ **puff out** *vt sep* (*cheeks, chest*) gonfler.

puffed [pʌft] *adj* (*swollen*): **~ (up)** gonflé(e).

puffin ['pʌfɪn] *n* macareux *m*.

puff pastry, puff paste Am *n* (U) pâte *f* feuilletée.

puffy ['pʌfɪ] *adj* gonflé(e), bouffi(e).

pull [pʊl] ◆ *vt* 1. (*gen*) tirer. 2. (*strain - muscle, hamstring*) se froisser. 3. (*tooth*) arracher. 4. (*attract*) attirer. 5. (*gun*) sortir. ◆ *vi* tirer. ◆ *n* 1. (*tug with hand*): **to give sthg a ~** tirer sur qqch. 2. (U) (*influence*) influence *f*. ▶ **pull apart** *vt sep* (*separate*) séparer. ▶ **pull at** *vt fus* tirer sur. ▶ **pull away** *vi* 1. (AUT) démarrer. 2. (*in race*) prendre de l'avance. ▶ **pull down** *vt sep* (*building*) démolir. ▶ **pull in** *vi* (AUT) se ranger. ▶ **pull off** *vt sep* 1. (*take off*) enlever, ôter. 2. (*succeed in*) réussir. ▶ **pull out** ◆ *vt sep* (*troops etc*) retirer. ◆ *vi* 1. (RAIL) partir, démarrer. 2. (AUT) déboîter. 3. (*withdraw*) se retirer. ▶ **pull over** *vi* (AUT) se ranger. ▶ **pull through** *vi* s'en sortir, s'en tirer. ▶ **pull together** *vt sep*: **to ~ o.s. together** se ressaisir, se reprendre. ▶ **pull up** ◆ *vt sep* 1. (*raise*) remonter. 2. (*chair*) avancer. ◆ *vi* s'arrêter.

pulley ['pʊlɪ] (*pl* **pulleys**) *n* poulie *f*.

pullover ['pʊl,əʊvəʳ] *n* pull *m*.

pulp [pʌlp] ◆ *adj* (*fiction, novel*) de quatre sous. ◆ *n* 1. (*for paper*) pâte *f* à papier. 2. (*of fruit*) pulpe *f*.

pulpit ['pʊlpɪt] *n* chaire *f*.

pulsate [pʌl'seɪt] *vi* (*heart*) battre fort; (*air, music*) vibrer.

pulse [pʌls] ◆ *n* 1. (MED) pouls *m*. 2. (TECH) impulsion *f*. ◆ *vi* battre, palpiter. ▶ **pulses** *npl* (*food*) légumes *mpl* secs.

puma ['pjuːmə] (*pl inv* OR **-s**) *n* puma *m*.

pumice (stone) ['pʌmɪs-] *n* pierre *f* ponce.

pummel ['pʌml] *vt* bourrer de coups.

pump [pʌmp] ◆ *n* pompe *f*. ◆ *vt* 1. (*water, gas etc*) pomper. 2. *inf* (*interrogate*) essayer de tirer les vers du nez à. ◆ *vi* (*heart*) battre fort. ▶ **pumps** *npl* (*shoes*) escarpins *mpl*.

pumpkin ['pʌmpkɪn] *n* potiron *m*.

pun [pʌn] *n* jeu *m* de mots, calembour *m*.

punch [pʌntʃ] ◆ *n* 1. (*blow*) coup *m* de poing. 2. (*tool*) poinçonneuse *f*. 3. (*drink*) punch *m*. ◆ *vt* 1. (*hit - once*) donner un coup de poing à; (*- repeatedly*) donner des coups de poing à. 2. (*ticket*) poinçonner; (*paper*) perforer.

Punch-and-Judy show [-'dʒuːdɪ-] *n* guignol *m*.

punch(ed) card [pʌntʃ(t)-] *n* carte *f* perforée.

punch line *n* chute *f*.

punch-up *n* Br *inf* bagarre *f*.

punchy ['pʌntʃɪ] *adj inf* (*style*) incisif (ive).

punctual ['pʌŋktʃʊəl] *adj* ponctuel (elle).

punctuation [,pʌŋktʃʊ'eɪʃn] *n* ponctuation *f*.

punctuation mark *n* signe *m* de ponctuation.

puncture ['pʌŋktʃəʳ] ◆ *n* crevaison *f*. ◆ *vt* (*tyre, ball*) crever; (*skin*) piquer.

pundit ['pʌndɪt] *n* pontife *m*.

pungent ['pʌndʒənt] *adj* 1. (*smell*) âcre; (*taste*) piquant(e). 2. *fig* (*criticism*) caustique, acerbe.

punish ['pʌnɪʃ] *vt* punir; **to ~ sb for sthg/for doing sthg** punir qqn pour qqch/pour avoir fait qqch.

punishing ['pʌnɪʃɪŋ] *adj* (*schedule, work*) épuisant(e), éreintant(e); (*defeat*) cuisant(e).

punishment ['pʌnɪʃmənt] *n* punition *f*, châtiment *m*.

punk [pʌŋk] ◆ *adj* punk (*inv*). ◆ *n* 1. (U) (*music*): **~ (rock)** punk *m*. 2. **~ (rocker)** punk *mf*. 3. Am *inf* (*lout*) loubard *m*.

punt [pʌnt] *n* (*boat*) bateau *m* à fond plat.

punter ['pʌntəʳ] *n* Br 1. (*gambler*) parieur *m*, -euse *f*. 2. *inf* (*customer*) client *m*, -e *f*.

puny ['pjuːnɪ] *adj* chétif(ive).

pup [pʌp] *n* 1. (*young dog*) chiot *m*. 2. (*young seal*) bébé phoque *m*.

pupil ['pjuːpl] *n* 1. (*student*) élève *mf*. 2. (*of eye*) pupille *f*.

puppet ['pʌpɪt] *n* 1. (*toy*) marionnette *f*. 2. *pej* (*person, country*) fantoche *m*, pantin *m*.

puppy ['pʌpɪ] *n* chiot *m*.

purchase ['pɜːtʃəs] ◆ *n* achat *m*. ◆ *vt* acheter.

purchaser ['pɜːtʃəsəʳ] *n* acheteur *m*, -euse *f*.

purchasing power ['pɜːtʃəsɪŋ-] *n* pouvoir *m* d'achat.

pure [pjʊəʳ] *adj* pur(e).

puree ['pjʊəreɪ] *n* purée *f*.

purely ['pjʊəlɪ] *adv* purement.

purge [pɜːdʒ] ◆ *n* (POL) purge *f*. ◆ *vt* 1. (POL) purger. 2. (*rid*) débarrasser, purger.

purify ['pjʊərɪfaɪ] *vt* purifier, épurer.

purist ['pjʊərɪst] *n* puriste *mf*.

puritan ['pjʊərɪtən] ♦ adj puritain(e).
♦ n puritain m, -e f.

purity ['pjʊərɪtɪ] n pureté f.

purl [pɜːl] ♦ n maille f à l'envers. ♦ vt
tricoter à l'envers.

purple ['pɜːpl] ♦ adj violet(ette). ♦ n
violet m.

purport [pə'pɔːt] vi fml: **to ~ to do/be
sthg** prétendre faire/être qqch.

purpose ['pɜːpəs] n 1. (reason) raison f,
motif m. 2. (aim) but m, objet m; **to no ~**
en vain, pour rien. 3. (determination)
détermination f. ▶ **on purpose** adv
exprès.

purr [pɜːr] vi ronronner.

purse [pɜːs] ♦ n 1. (for money) porte-
monnaie m inv, bourse f. 2. Am (handbag) sac m à main. ♦ vt (lips) pincer.

purser ['pɜːsər] n commissaire m de
bord.

pursue [pə'sjuː] vt 1. (follow) poursuivre, pourchasser. 2. (policy, aim) poursuivre; (question) continuer à débattre;
(matter) approfondir; (project) donner
suite à; **to ~ an interest in sthg** se livrer à
qqch.

pursuer [pə'sjuːər] n poursuivant m,
-e f.

pursuit [pə'sjuːt] n 1. (U) fml (attempt to
obtain) recherche f, poursuite f. 2. (chase,
in sport) poursuite f. 3. (occupation) occupation f, activité f.

pus [pʌs] n pus m.

push [pʊʃ] ♦ vt 1. (press, move - gen)
pousser; (- button) appuyer sur. 2.
(encourage): **to ~ sb (to do sthg)** inciter OR
pousser qqn (à faire qqch). 3. (force): **to
~ sb (into doing sthg)** forcer OR obliger
qqn (à faire qqch). 4. inf (promote) faire
de la réclame pour. ♦ vi 1. (gen) pousser; (on button) appuyer. 2. (campaign): **to
~ for sthg** faire pression pour obtenir
qqch. ♦ n 1. (with hand) poussée f. 2.
(forceful effort) effort m. ▶ **push around**
vt sep inf fig marcher sur les pieds de.
▶ **push in** vi (in queue) resquiller.
▶ **push off** vi inf filer, se sauver.
▶ **push on** vi continuer. ▶ **push
through** vt sep (law, reform) faire
accepter.

pushchair ['pʊʃtʃeər] n Br poussette f.

pushed [pʊʃt] adj inf: **to be ~ for sthg**
être à court de qqch; **to be hard ~ to do
sthg** avoir du mal OR de la peine à faire
qqch.

pusher ['pʊʃər] n drugs sl dealer m.

pushover ['pʊʃ,əʊvər] n inf: **it's a ~**
c'est un jeu d'enfant.

push-up n pompe f, traction f.

pushy ['pʊʃɪ] adj pej qui se met toujours en avant.

puss [pʊs], **pussy (cat)** ['pʊsɪ-] n inf
minet m, minou m.

put [pʊt] (pt & pp put) vt 1. (gen) mettre.
2. (place) mettre, poser, placer; **to ~ the
children to bed** coucher les enfants.
3. (express) dire, exprimer. 4. (question)
poser. 5. (estimate) estimer, évaluer.
6. (invest): **to ~ money into** investir de
l'argent dans. ▶ **put across** vt sep
(ideas) faire comprendre. ▶ **put away**
vt sep 1. (tidy away) ranger. 2. inf (lock up)
enfermer. ▶ **put back** vt sep 1. (replace)
remettre (à sa place OR en place).
2. (postpone) remettre. 3. (clock, watch)
retarder. ▶ **put by** vt sep (money) mettre
de côté. ▶ **put down** vt sep 1. (lay
down) poser, déposer. 2. (quell - rebellion) réprimer. 3. (write down) inscrire,
noter. 4. Br (kill): **to have a dog/cat ~
down** faire piquer un chien/chat. ▶ **put
down to** vt sep attribuer à. ▶ **put forward** vt sep 1. (propose) proposer,
avancer. 2. (meeting, clock, watch)
avancer. ▶ **put in** vt sep 1. (spend - time)
passer. 2. (submit) présenter. ▶ **put off**
vt sep 1. (postpone) remettre (à plus
tard). 2. (cause to wait) décommander.
3. (discourage) dissuader. 4. (disturb)
déconcerter, troubler. 5. (cause to dislike)
dégoûter. 6. (switch off - radio, TV) éteindre. ▶ **put on** vt sep 1. (clothes) mettre,
enfiler. 2. (arrange - exhibition etc) organiser; (- play) monter. 3. (gain): **to ~ on
weight** prendre du poids, grossir.
4. (switch on - radio, TV) allumer, mettre;
to ~ the light on allumer (la lumière); **to
~ the brake on** freiner. 5. (record, CD,
tape) passer, mettre. 6. (start cooking)
mettre à cuire. 7. (pretend - gen) feindre;
(- accent etc) prendre. 8. (bet) parier,
miser. 9. (add) ajouter. ▶ **put out** vt sep
1. (place outside) mettre dehors. 2. (book,
statement) publier; (record) sortir. 3. (fire,
cigarette) éteindre; **to ~ the light out**
éteindre (la lumière). 4. (extend - hand)
tendre. 5. (annoy, upset): **to be ~ out** être
contrarié(e). 6. (inconvenience) déranger.
▶ **put through** vt sep (TELEC) passer.
▶ **put up** vt sep 1. (build - gen) ériger;
(- tent) dresser. 2. (umbrella) ouvrir;
(flag) hisser. 3. (fix to wall) accrocher.
4. (provide - money) fournir. 5. (propose
- candidate) proposer. 6. (increase) augmenter. 7. (provide accommodation for)
loger, héberger. ♦ vt fus: **to ~ up a fight**

se défendre. ▶ **put up with** vt fus supporter.

putrid ['pju:trɪd] adj putride.

putt [pʌt] ◆ n putt m. ◆ vt & vi putter.

putting green ['pʌtɪŋ-] n green m.

putty ['pʌtɪ] n mastic m.

puzzle ['pʌzl] ◆ n 1. (toy) casse-tête m inv; (mental) devinette f. 2. (mystery) mystère m, énigme f. ◆ vt rendre perplexe. ◆ vi: **to ~ over sthg** essayer de comprendre qqch. ▶ **puzzle out** vt sep comprendre.

puzzling ['pʌzlɪŋ] adj curieux(euse).

pyjamas [pə'dʒɑ:məz] npl pyjama m; **a pair of ~** un pyjama.

pylon ['paɪlən] n pylône m.

pyramid ['pɪrəmɪd] n pyramide f.

Pyrenees [ˌpɪrə'ni:z] npl: **the ~** les Pyrénées fpl.

Pyrex® ['paɪreks] n Pyrex® m.

python ['paɪθn] (pl inv OR -s) n python m.

Q

q (pl **q's** OR **qs**), **Q** (pl **Q's** OR **Qs**) [kju:] n (letter) q m inv, Q m inv.

quack [kwæk] n 1. (noise) coin-coin m inv. 2. inf pej (doctor) charlatan m.

quad [kwɒd] abbr of **quadrangle**.

quadrangle ['kwɒdræŋgl] n 1. (figure) quadrilatère m. 2. (courtyard) cour f.

quadruple [kwɒ'dru:pl] ◆ adj quadruple. ◆ vt & vi quadrupler.

quadruplets ['kwɒdruplɪts] npl quadruplés mpl.

quads [kwɒdz] npl inf quadruplés mpl.

quagmire ['kwægmaɪər] n bourbier m.

quail [kweɪl] (pl inv OR -s) ◆ n caille f. ◆ vi literary reculer.

quaint [kweɪnt] adj pittoresque.

quake [kweɪk] vi trembler.

Quaker ['kweɪkər] n quaker m, -eresse f.

qualification [ˌkwɒlɪfɪ'keɪʃn] n 1. (certificate) diplôme m. 2. (quality, skill) compétence f. 3. (qualifying statement) réserve f.

qualified ['kwɒlɪfaɪd] adj 1. (trained) diplômé(e). 2. (able): **to be ~ to do sthg** avoir la compétence nécessaire pour faire qqch. 3. (limited) restreint(e), modéré(e).

qualify ['kwɒlɪfaɪ] ◆ vt 1. (modify) apporter des réserves à. 2. (entitle): **to ~ sb to do sthg** qualifier qqn pour faire qqch. ◆ vi 1. (pass exams) obtenir un diplôme. 2. (be entitled): **to ~ (for sthg)** avoir droit (à qqch), remplir les conditions requises (pour qqch). 3. (SPORT) se qualifier.

quality ['kwɒlɪtɪ] ◆ n qualité f. ◆ comp de qualité.

qualms [kwɑ:mz] npl doutes mpl.

quandary ['kwɒndərɪ] n embarras m; **to be in a ~ about** OR **over sthg** être bien embarrassé à propos de qqch.

quantify ['kwɒntɪfaɪ] vt quantifier.

quantity ['kwɒntətɪ] n quantité f.

quantity surveyor n métreur m, -euse f.

quarantine ['kwɒrənti:n] ◆ n quarantaine f. ◆ vt mettre en quarantaine.

quarrel ['kwɒrəl] ◆ n querelle f, dispute f. ◆ vi: **to ~ (with)** se quereller (avec), se disputer (avec).

quarrelsome ['kwɒrəlsəm] adj querelleur(euse).

quarry ['kwɒrɪ] n 1. (place) carrière f. 2. (prey) proie f.

quart [kwɔ:t] n = 1,136 litre Br, = 0,946 litre Am, = litre m.

quarter ['kwɔ:tər] n 1. (fraction, weight) quart m; **a ~ past two** Br, **a ~ after two** Am deux heures et quart; **a ~ to two** Br, **a ~ of two** Am deux heures moins le quart. 2. (of year) trimestre m. 3. Am (coin) pièce f de 25 cents. 4. (area in town) quartier m. 5. (direction): **from all ~s** de tous côtés. ▶ **quarters** npl (rooms) quartiers mpl. ▶ **at close quarters** adv de près.

quarterfinal [ˌkwɔ:tə'faɪnl] n quart m de finale.

quarterly ['kwɔ:təlɪ] ◆ adj trimestriel (elle). ◆ adv trimestriellement. ◆ n publication f trimestrielle.

quartet [kwɔ:'tet] n quatuor m.

quartz [kwɔ:ts] n quartz m.

quartz watch n montre f à quartz.

quash [kwɒʃ] vt 1. (sentence) annuler, casser. 2. (rebellion) réprimer.

quasi- ['kweɪzaɪ] prefix quasi-.

quaver ['kweɪvər] ◆ n 1. (MUS) croche f. 2. (in voice) tremblement m, chevrotement m. ◆ vi trembler, chevroter.

quay [ki:] n quai m.

quayside ['ki:saɪd] n bord m du quai.

queasy ['kwiːzɪ] adj: to feel ~ avoir mal au cœur.

Quebec [kwɪ'bek] n (province) Québec m.

queen [kwiːn] n 1. (gen) reine f. 2. (playing card) dame f.

Queen Mother n: the ~ la reine mère.

queer [kwɪəʳ] ◆ adj (odd) étrange, bizarre. ◆ n inf pej pédé m, homosexuel m.

quell [kwel] vt réprimer, étouffer.

quench [kwentʃ] vt: to ~ one's thirst se désaltérer.

querulous ['kwerʊləs] adj (child) ronchonneur(euse); (voice) plaintif(ive).

query ['kwɪərɪ] ◆ n question f. ◆ vt mettre en doute, douter de.

quest [kwest] n literary: ~ (for) quête f (de).

question ['kwestʃn] ◆ n 1. (gen) question f; to ask (sb) a ~ poser une question (à qqn). 2. (doubt) doute m; to call OR bring sth into ~ mettre qqch en doute; without ~ incontestablement, sans aucun doute; beyond ~ (know) sans aucun doute. 3. phr: there's no ~ of ... il n'est pas question de ... ◆ vt 1. (interrogate) questionner. 2. (express doubt about) mettre en question OR doute. ▶ in question adv: the ... in ~ le/la/les ... en question. ▶ out of the question adv hors de question.

questionable ['kwestʃənəbl] adj 1. (uncertain) discutable. 2. (not right, not honest) douteux(euse).

question mark n point m d'interrogation.

questionnaire [ˌkwestʃə'neəʳ] n questionnaire m.

queue [kjuː] Br ◆ n queue f, file f. ◆ vi faire la queue.

quibble ['kwɪbl] pej ◆ n chicane f. ◆ vi: to ~ (over OR about) chicaner (à propos de).

quiche [kiːʃ] n quiche f.

quick [kwɪk] ◆ adj 1. (gen) rapide. 2. (response, decision) prompt(e), rapide. ◆ adv vite, rapidement.

quicken ['kwɪkn] ◆ vt accélérer, presser. ◆ vi s'accélérer.

quickly ['kwɪklɪ] adv 1. (rapidly) vite, rapidement. 2. (without delay) promptement, immédiatement.

quicksand ['kwɪksænd] n sables mpl mouvants.

quick-witted [-'wɪtɪd] adj (person) à l'esprit vif.

quid [kwɪd] (pl inv) n Br inf livre f.

quiet ['kwaɪət] ◆ adj 1. (not noisy) tranquille; (voice) bas (basse); (engine) silencieux(euse); be ~! taisez-vous! 2. (not busy) calme. 3. (silent) silencieux(euse); to keep ~ about sth ne rien dire à propos de qqch, garder qqch secret. 4. (intimate) intime. 5. (colour) discret (ète), sobre. ◆ n tranquillité f; on the ~ inf en douce. ◆ vt Am calmer, apaiser. ▶ quiet down ◆ vt sep calmer, apaiser. ◆ vi se calmer.

quieten ['kwaɪətn] vt calmer, apaiser. ▶ quieten down ◆ vt sep calmer, apaiser. ◆ vi se calmer.

quietly ['kwaɪətlɪ] adv 1. (without noise) sans faire de bruit, silencieusement; (say) doucement. 2. (without excitement) tranquillement, calmement. 3. (without fuss - leave) discrètement.

quilt [kwɪlt] n (padded) édredon m; (continental) ~ couette f.

quinine [kwɪ'niːn] n quinine f.

quins Br [kwɪnz], **quints** Am [kwɪnts] npl inf quintuplés mpl.

quintet [kwɪn'tet] n quintette m.

quints Am = quins.

quintuplets [kwɪn'tjuːplɪts] npl quintuplés mpl.

quip [kwɪp] ◆ n raillerie f. ◆ vi railler.

quirk [kwɜːk] n bizarrerie f.

quit [kwɪt] (Br pt & pp quit OR -ted, Am pt & pp quit) ◆ vt 1. (resign from) quitter. 2. (stop): to ~ smoking arrêter de fumer. ◆ vi 1. (resign) démissionner. 2. (give up) abandonner.

quite [kwaɪt] adv 1. (completely) tout à fait, complètement; I ~ agree je suis entièrement d'accord; not ~ pas tout à fait; I don't ~ understand je ne comprends pas bien. 2. (fairly) assez, plutôt. 3. (for emphasis): she's ~ a singer c'est une chanteuse formidable. 4. (to express agreement): ~ (so)! exactement!

quits [kwɪts] adj inf: to be ~ (with sb) être quitte (envers qqn); to call it ~ en rester là.

quiver ['kwɪvəʳ] ◆ n 1. (shiver) frisson m. 2. (for arrows) carquois m. ◆ vi frissonner.

quiz [kwɪz] (pl -zes) ◆ n 1. (gen) quiz m, jeu-concours m. 2. Am (SCH) interrogation f. ◆ vt: to ~ sb (about sth) interroger qqn (au sujet de qqch).

quizzical ['kwɪzɪkl] adj narquois(e), moqueur(euse).

quota ['kwəʊtə] n quota m.

quotation [kwəʊ'teɪʃn] n 1. (citation) citation f. 2. (COMM) devis m.

quotation marks *npl* guillemets *mpl*;
in ~ entre guillemets.

quote [kwəʊt] ◆ *n* 1. (*citation*) citation
f. 2. (COMM) devis *m*. ◆ *vt* 1. (*cite*) citer.
2. (COMM) indiquer, spécifier. ◆ *vi*
1. (*cite*): **to ~ (from sthg)** citer (qqch).
2. (COMM): **to ~ for sthg** établir un devis
pour qqch.

quotient ['kwəʊʃnt] *n* quotient *m*.

R

r (*pl* **r's** OR **rs**), **R** (*pl* **R's** OR **Rs**) [ɑːr] *n* (*letter*) r *m inv*, R *m inv*.

rabbi ['ræbaɪ] *n* rabbin *m*.

rabbit ['ræbɪt] *n* lapin *m*.

rabbit hutch *n* clapier *m*.

rabble ['ræbl] *n* cohue *f*.

rabies ['reɪbiːz] *n* rage *f*.

RAC (*abbr of* **Royal Automobile Club**) *n*
club automobile britannique, ≃ TCF *m*, ≃
ACF *m*.

race [reɪs] ◆ *n* 1. (*competition*) course *f*.
2. (*people, ethnic background*) race *f*. ◆ *vt*
1. (*compete against*) faire la course avec.
2. (*horse*) faire courir. ◆ *vi* 1. (*compete*)
courir; **to ~ against sb** faire la course
avec qqn. 2. (*rush*): **to ~ in/out** entrer/
sortir à toute allure. 3. (*pulse*) être très
rapide. 4. (*engine*) s'emballer.

race car Am = **racing car**.

racecourse ['reɪskɔːs] *n* champ *m* de
courses.

race driver Am = **racing driver**.

racehorse ['reɪshɔːs] *n* cheval *m* de
course.

racetrack ['reɪstræk] *n* piste *f*.

racial discrimination ['reɪʃl-] *n* discrimination *f* raciale.

racing ['reɪsɪŋ] *n* (U): (**horse**) ~ les
courses *fpl*.

racing car Br, **race car** Am *n* voiture
f de course.

racing driver Br, **race driver** Am *n*
coureur *m* automobile, pilote *m* de
course.

racism ['reɪsɪzm] *n* racisme *m*.

racist ['reɪsɪst] ◆ *adj* raciste. ◆ *n*
raciste *mf*.

rack [ræk] *n* (*for bottles*) casier *m*; (*for
luggage*) porte-bagages *m inv*; (*for plates*)

racket ['rækɪt] *n* 1. (*noise*) boucan *m*.
2. (*illegal activity*) racket *m*. 3. (SPORT)
raquette *f*.

racquet ['rækɪt] *n* raquette *f*.

racy ['reɪsɪ] *adj* (*novel, style*) osé(e).

radar ['reɪdɑːr] *n* radar *m*.

radial (tyre) ['reɪdjəl-] *n* pneu *m* à
carcasse radiale.

radiant ['reɪdjənt] *adj* (*happy*) radieux
(euse).

radiate ['reɪdɪeɪt] ◆ *vt* 1. (*heat, light*)
émettre, dégager. 2. *fig* (*confidence,
health*) respirer. ◆ *vi* 1. (*heat, light*)
irradier. 2. (*roads, lines*) rayonner.

radiation [,reɪdɪ'eɪʃn] *n* (*radioactive*)
radiation *f*.

radiator ['reɪdɪeɪtər] *n* radiateur *m*.

radical ['rædɪkl] ◆ *adj* radical(e). ◆ *n*
(POL) radical *m*, -e *f*.

radii ['reɪdɪaɪ] *pl* → **radius**.

radio ['reɪdɪəʊ] (*pl* **-s**) ◆ *n* radio *f*; **on
the ~** à la radio. ◆ *comp* de radio. ◆ *vt*
(*person*) appeler par radio; (*information*)
envoyer par radio.

radioactive [,reɪdɪəʊ'æktɪv] *adj*
radioactif(ive).

radio alarm *n* radio-réveil *m*.

radio-controlled [-kən'trəʊld] *adj*
téléguidé(e).

radiography [,reɪdɪ'ɒgrəfɪ] *n* radiographie *f*.

radiology [,reɪdɪ'ɒlədʒɪ] *n* radiologie
f.

radiotherapy [,reɪdɪəʊ'θerəpɪ] *n*
radiothérapie *f*.

radish ['rædɪʃ] *n* radis *m*.

radius ['reɪdɪəs] (*pl* **radii**) *n* 1. (MATH)
rayon *m*. 2. (ANAT) radius *m*.

RAF [ɑːreɪ'ef, ræf] *n abbr of* **Royal Air
Force**.

raffle ['ræfl] ◆ *n* tombola *f*. ◆ *vt* mettre
en tombola.

raft [rɑːft] *n* (*of wood*) radeau *m*.

rafter ['rɑːftər] *n* chevron *m*.

rag [ræg] *n* 1. (*piece of cloth*) chiffon *m*. 2.
pej (*newspaper*) torchon *m*. ▶ **rags** *npl*
(*clothes*) guenilles *fpl*.

rag-and-bone man *n* chiffonnier *m*.

rag doll *n* poupée *f* de chiffon.

rage [reɪdʒ] ◆ *n* 1. (*fury*) rage *f*, fureur
f. 2. *inf* (*fashion*): **to be (all) the ~** faire
fureur. ◆ *vi* 1. (*person*) être furieux
(euse). 2. (*storm, argument*) faire rage.

ragged ['rægɪd] *adj* 1. (*person*) en haillons; (*clothes*) en lambeaux. 2. (*line, edge,
performance*) inégal(e).

rag week *n* Br semaine de carnaval

organisée par des étudiants afin de collecter des fonds pour des œuvres charitables.

raid [reɪd] ◆ n 1. (MIL) raid m. 2. (by criminals) hold-up m inv; (by police) descente f. ◆ vt 1. (MIL) faire un raid sur. 2. (subj: criminals) faire un hold-up dans; (subj: police) faire une descente dans.

raider ['reɪdər] n 1. (attacker) agresseur m. 2. (thief) braqueur m.

rail [reɪl] ◆ n 1. (on ship) bastingage m; (on staircase) rampe f; (on walkway) garde-fou m. 2. (bar) barre f. 3. (RAIL) rail m; **by ~** en train. ◆ comp (transport, travel) par le train; (strike) des cheminots.

railcard ['reɪlkɑːd] n Br carte donnant droit à des tarifs préférentiels sur les chemins de fer.

railing ['reɪlɪŋ] n (fence) grille f; (on ship) bastingage m; (on staircase) rampe f; (on walkway) garde-fou m.

railway Br ['reɪlweɪ], **railroad** Am ['reɪlrəʊd] n (system, company) chemin m de fer; (track) voie f ferrée.

railway line n (route) ligne f de chemin de fer; (track) voie f ferrée.

railwayman ['reɪlweɪmən] (pl **-men** [-mən]) n Br cheminot m.

railway station n gare f.

railway track n voie f ferrée.

rain [reɪn] ◆ n pluie f. ◆ v impers (METEOR) pleuvoir; **it's ~ing** il pleut. ◆ vi (fall like rain) pleuvoir.

rainbow ['reɪnbəʊ] n arc-en-ciel m.

raincoat ['reɪnkəʊt] n imperméable m.

raindrop ['reɪndrɒp] n goutte f de pluie.

rainfall ['reɪnfɔːl] n (shower) chute f de pluie; (amount) précipitations fpl.

rain forest n forêt f tropicale humide.

rainy ['reɪnɪ] adj pluvieux(euse).

raise [reɪz] ◆ vt 1. (lift up) lever; **to ~ o.s.** se lever. 2. (increase - gen) augmenter; (- standards) élever; **to ~ one's voice** élever la voix. 3. (obtain): **to ~ money** (from donations) collecter des fonds; (by selling, borrowing) se procurer de l'argent. 4. (subject, doubt) soulever; (memories) évoquer. 5. (children, cattle) élever. 6. (crops) cultiver. 7. (build) ériger, élever. ◆ n Am augmentation f (de salaire).

raisin ['reɪzn] n raisin m sec.

rake [reɪk] ◆ n 1. (implement) râteau m. 2. dated & literary (immoral man) débauché m. ◆ vt (path, lawn) ratisser; (leaves) râteler.

rally ['rælɪ] ◆ n 1. (meeting) rassemblement m. 2. (car race) rallye m. 3. (SPORT) (exchange of shots) échange m. ◆ vt rallier. ◆ vi 1. (supporters) se rallier. 2. (patient) aller mieux; (prices) remonter. ▶ **rally round** ◆ vt fus apporter son soutien à. ◆ vi inf venir en aide.

ram [ræm] ◆ n bélier m. ◆ vt 1. (crash into) percuter contre, emboutir. 2. (force) tasser.

RAM [ræm] (abbr of **random access memory**) n RAM f.

ramble ['ræmbl] ◆ n randonnée f, promenade f à pied. ◆ vi 1. (walk) faire une randonnée à pied. 2. pej (talk) radoter. ▶ **ramble on** vi pej radoter.

rambler ['ræmblər] n (walker) randonneur m, -euse f.

rambling ['ræmblɪŋ] adj 1. (house) plein(e) de coins et recoins. 2. (speech) décousu(e).

ramp [ræmp] n 1. (slope) rampe f. 2. (AUT) (to slow traffic down) ralentisseur m.

rampage [ræm'peɪdʒ] n: **to go on the ~** tout saccager.

rampant ['ræmpənt] adj qui sévit.

ramparts ['ræmpɑːts] npl rempart m.

ramshackle ['ræm,ʃækl] adj branlant(e).

ran [ræn] pt → **run**.

ranch [rɑːntʃ] n ranch m.

rancid ['rænsɪd] adj rance.

rancour Br, **rancor** Am ['ræŋkər] n rancœur f.

random ['rændəm] ◆ adj fait(e) au hasard; (number) aléatoire. ◆ n: **at ~** au hasard.

random access memory n (COMPUT) mémoire f vive.

R and R (abbr of **rest and recreation**) n Am permission f.

randy ['rændɪ] adj inf excité(e).

rang [ræŋ] → **ring**.

range [reɪndʒ] ◆ n 1. (of plane, telescope etc) portée f; **at close ~** à bout portant. 2. (of subjects, goods) gamme f; **price ~** éventail m des prix. 3. (of mountains) chaîne f. 4. (shooting area) champ m de tir. 5. (MUS) (of voice) tessiture f. ◆ vt (place in row) mettre en rang. ◆ vi 1. (vary): **to ~ between ... and ...** varier entre ... et ...; **to ~ from ... to ...** varier de ... à ... 2. (include): **to ~ over sthg** couvrir qqch.

ranger ['reɪndʒər] n garde m forestier.

rank [ræŋk] ◆ adj 1. (absolute - disgrace, stupidity) complet(ète); (- injustice) flagrant(e); **he's a ~ outsider** il n'a aucune chance. 2. (smell) fétide. ◆ n 1. (in army, *police etc*) grade *m*. **2.** (*social class*) rang *m*. **3.** (*row*) rangée *f*. **4.** *phr*: **the ~ and file** la masse; (*of union*) la base. ◆ *vt* (*classify*) classer. ◆ *vi*: **to ~ among** compter parmi; **to ~ as** être aux rangs de. ▶ **ranks** *npl* **1.** (*MIL*): **the ~s** le rang. **2.** *fig* (*members*) rangs *mpl*.

rankle ['ræŋkl] *vi*: **it ~d with him** ça lui est resté sur l'estomac OR le cœur.

ransack ['rænsæk] *vt* (*search through*) mettre tout sens dessus dessous dans; (*damage*) saccager.

ransom ['rænsəm] *n* rançon *f*; **to hold sb to ~** *fig* exercer un chantage sur qqn.

rant [rænt] *vi* déblatérer.

rap [ræp] ◆ *n* **1.** (*knock*) coup *m* sec. **2.** (*MUS*) rap *m*. ◆ *vt* (*table*) frapper sur; (*knuckles*) taper sur.

rape [reɪp] ◆ *n* **1.** (*crime, attack*) viol *m*. **2.** *fig* (*of countryside etc*) destruction *f*. **3.** (*plant*) colza *m*. ◆ *vt* violer.

rapeseed ['reɪpsiːd] *n* graine *f* de colza.

rapid ['ræpɪd] *adj* rapide. ▶ **rapids** *npl* rapides *mpl*.

rapidly ['ræpɪdlɪ] *adv* rapidement.

rapist ['reɪpɪst] *n* violeur *m*.

rapport [ræ'pɔːr] *n* rapport *m*.

rapture ['ræptʃər] *n* ravissement *m*.

rapturous ['ræptʃərəs] *adj* (*applause, welcome*) enthousiaste.

rare [reər] *adj* **1.** (*gen*) rare. **2.** (*meat*) saignant(e).

rarely ['reəlɪ] *adv* rarement.

raring ['reərɪŋ] *adj*: **to be ~ to go** être impatient(e) de commencer.

rarity ['reərətɪ] *n* rareté *f*.

rascal ['rɑːskl] *n* polisson *m*, -onne *f*.

rash [ræʃ] ◆ *adj* irréfléchi(e), imprudent(e). ◆ *n* **1.** (*MED*) éruption *f*. **2.** (*spate*) succession *f*, série *f*.

rasher ['ræʃər] *n* tranche *f*.

rasp [rɑːsp] *n* (*harsh sound*) grincement *m*.

raspberry ['rɑːzbərɪ] *n* **1.** (*fruit*) framboise *f*. **2.** (*rude sound*): **to blow a ~** faire pfft.

rat [ræt] *n* **1.** (*animal*) rat *m*. **2.** *inf pej* (*person*) ordure *f*, salaud *m*.

rate [reɪt] ◆ *n* **1.** (*speed*) vitesse *f*; (*of pulse*) fréquence *f*; **at this ~** à ce train-là. **2.** (*ratio, proportion*) taux *m*. **3.** (*price*) tarif *m*. ◆ *vt* **1.** (*consider*): **I ~ her very highly** je la tiens en haute estime; **to ~ sb/sthg as** considérer qqn/qqch comme; **to ~ sb/sthg among** classer qqn/qqch parmi. **2.** (*deserve*) mériter. ▶ **rates** *npl* Br impôts *mpl* locaux. ▶ **at any rate**

adv en tout cas.

ratepayer ['reɪtˌpeɪər] *n* Br contribuable *mf*.

rather ['rɑːðər] *adv* **1.** (*somewhat, more exactly*) plutôt. **2.** (*to small extent*) un peu. **3.** (*preferably*): **I'd ~ wait** je préférerais attendre; **she'd ~ not go** elle préférerait ne pas y aller. **4.** (*on the contrary*): (**but**) **~ ...** au contraire ... ▶ **rather than** *conj* plutôt que.

ratify ['rætɪfaɪ] *vt* ratifier, approuver.

rating ['reɪtɪŋ] *n* (*of popularity etc*) cote *f*.

ratio ['reɪʃɪəʊ] (*pl* -s) *n* rapport *m*.

ration ['ræʃn] ◆ *n* ration *f*. ◆ *vt* rationner. ▶ **rations** *npl* vivres *mpl*.

rational ['ræʃənl] *adj* rationnel(elle).

rationale [ˌræʃə'nɑːl] *n* logique *f*.

rationalize, -ise ['ræʃənəlaɪz] *vt* rationaliser.

rat race *n* jungle *f*.

rattle ['rætl] ◆ *n* **1.** (*of bottles, typewriter keys*) cliquetis *m*; (*of engine*) bruit *m* de ferraille. **2.** (*toy*) hochet *m*. ◆ *vt* **1.** (*bottles*) faire s'entrechoquer; (*keys*) faire cliqueter. **2.** (*unsettle*) secouer. ◆ *vi* (*bottles*) s'entrechoquer; (*keys, machine*) cliqueter; (*engine*) faire un bruit de ferraille.

rattlesnake ['rætlsneɪk], **rattler** Am ['rætlər] *n* serpent *m* à sonnettes.

raucous ['rɔːkəs] *adj* (*voice, laughter*) rauque; (*behaviour*) bruyant(e).

ravage ['rævɪdʒ] *vt* ravager. ▶ **ravages** *npl* ravages *mpl*.

rave [reɪv] ◆ *adj* (*review*) élogieux (euse). ◆ *n* Br *inf* (*party*) rave *f*. ◆ *vi* **1.** (*talk angrily*): **to ~ at** OR **against** tempêter OR fulminer contre. **2.** (*talk enthusiastically*): **to ~ about** parler avec enthousiasme de.

raven ['reɪvn] *n* corbeau *m*.

ravenous ['rævənəs] *adj* (*person*) affamé(e); (*animal, appetite*) vorace.

ravine [rə'viːn] *n* ravin *m*.

raving ['reɪvɪŋ] *adj*: **~ lunatic** fou furieux (folle furieuse).

ravioli [ˌrævɪ'əʊlɪ] *n* (U) ravioli *mpl*.

ravishing ['rævɪʃɪŋ] *adj* ravissant(e), enchanteur(eresse).

raw [rɔː] *adj* **1.** (*uncooked*) cru(e). **2.** (*untreated*) brut(e). **3.** (*painful*) à vif. **4.** (*inexperienced*) novice; **~ recruit** bleu *m*. **5.** (*weather*) froid(e); (*wind*) âpre.

raw deal *n*: **to get a ~** être défavorisé(e).

raw material *n* matière *f* première.

ray [reɪ] *n* (*beam*) rayon *m*; *fig* (*of hope*) lueur *f*.

rayon ['reɪɒn] n rayonne f.

raze [reɪz] vt raser.

razor ['reɪzəʳ] n rasoir m.

razor blade n lame f de rasoir.

RC abbr of **Roman Catholic**.

Rd abbr of **Road**.

R & D (abbr of **research and development**) n R-D f.

re [riː] prep concernant.

RE n (abbr of **religious education**) instruction f religieuse.

reach [riːtʃ] ◆ vt 1. (gen) atteindre; (place, destination) arriver à; (agreement, decision) parvenir à. 2. (contact) joindre, contacter. ◆ vi (land) s'étendre; **to ~ out** tendre le bras; **to ~ down to pick sthg up** se pencher pour ramasser qqch. ◆ n (of arm, boxer) allonge f; **within ~** (object) à portée; (place) à proximité; **out of** OR **beyond sb's ~** (object) hors de portée; (place) d'accès difficile, difficilement accessible.

react [rɪ'ækt] vi (gen) réagir.

reaction [rɪ'ækʃn] n réaction f.

reactionary [rɪ'ækʃənrɪ] ◆ adj réactionnaire. ◆ n réactionnaire mf.

reactor [rɪ'æktəʳ] n réacteur m.

read [riːd] (pt & pp **read** [red]) ◆ vt 1. (gen) lire. 2. (subj: sign, letter) dire. 3. (interpret, judge) interpréter. 4. (subj: meter, thermometer etc) indiquer. 5. Br (UNIV) étudier. ◆ vi lire; **the book ~s well** le livre se lit bien. ▶ **read out** vt sep lire à haute voix. ▶ **read up on** vt fus étudier.

readable ['riːdəbl] adj agréable à lire.

reader ['riːdəʳ] n (of book, newspaper) lecteur m, -trice f.

readership ['riːdəʃɪp] n (of newspaper) nombre m de lecteurs.

readily ['redɪlɪ] adv 1. (willingly) volontiers. 2. (easily) facilement.

reading ['riːdɪŋ] n 1. (U) (gen) lecture f. 2. (interpretation) interprétation f. 3. (on thermometer, meter etc) indications fpl.

readjust [,riːə'dʒʌst] ◆ vt (instrument) régler (de nouveau); (mirror) rajuster; (policy) rectifier. ◆ vi (person): **to ~ (to)** se réadapter (à).

readout ['riːdaut] n (COMPUT) affichage m.

ready ['redɪ] ◆ adj 1. (prepared) prêt(e); **to be ~ to do sthg** être prêt à faire qqch; **to get ~** se préparer; **to get sthg ~** préparer qqch. 2. (willing): **to be ~ to do sthg** être prêt(e) OR disposé(e) à faire qqch. ◆ vt préparer.

ready cash n liquide m.

ready-made adj lit & fig tout fait (toute faite).

ready meal n plat m préparé.

ready money n liquide m.

ready-to-wear adj prêt-à-porter.

reafforestation ['riːəˌfɒrɪ'steɪʃn] n reboisement m.

real ['rɪəl] ◆ adj 1. (gen) vrai(e), véritable; **~ life** réalité f; **for ~** pour de vrai; **this is the ~ thing** (object) c'est de l'authentique; (situation) c'est pour de vrai OR de bon. 2. (actual) réel(elle); **in ~ terms** dans la pratique. ◆ adv Am très.

real estate n (U) biens mpl immobiliers.

realign [,riːə'laɪn] vt (POL) regrouper.

realism ['rɪəlɪzm] n réalisme m.

realistic [,rɪə'lɪstɪk] adj réaliste.

reality [rɪ'ælətɪ] n réalité f.

realization [,rɪəlaɪ'zeɪʃn] n réalisation f.

realize, -ise ['rɪəlaɪz] vt 1. (understand) se rendre compte de, réaliser. 2. (sum of money, idea, ambition) réaliser.

really ['rɪəlɪ] ◆ adv 1. (gen) vraiment. 2. (in fact) en réalité. ◆ excl 1. (expressing doubt) vraiment? 2. (expressing surprise) pas possible! 3. (expressing disapproval) franchement!, ça alors!

realm [relm] n 1. fig (subject area) domaine m. 2. (kingdom) royaume m.

realtor ['rɪəltəʳ] n Am agent m immobilier.

reap [riːp] vt 1. (harvest) moissonner. 2. fig (obtain) récolter.

reappear [,riːə'pɪəʳ] vi réapparaître, reparaître.

rear [rɪəʳ] ◆ adj arrière (inv), de derrière. ◆ n 1. (back) arrière m; **to bring up the ~** fermer la marche. 2. inf (bottom) derrière m. ◆ vt (children, animals) élever. ◆ vi (horse): **to ~ (up)** se cabrer.

rearm [riː'ɑːm] vt & vi réarmer.

rearmost ['rɪəməust] adj dernier(ère).

rearrange [,riːə'reɪndʒ] vt 1. (furniture, room) réarranger; (plans) changer. 2. (meeting - to new time) changer l'heure de; (- to new date) changer la date de.

rearview mirror ['rɪəvjuː-] n rétroviseur m.

reason ['riːzn] ◆ n 1. (cause): **~ (for)** raison f (de); **for some ~** pour une raison ou pour une autre. 2. (U) (justification): **to have ~ to do sthg** avoir de bonnes raisons de faire qqch. 3. (common sense) bon sens m; **he won't listen to ~** on ne peut pas lui faire entendre raison; **it stands to ~** c'est logique. ◆ vt déduire.

♦ *vi* raisonner. ▶ **reason with** *vt fus* raisonner (avec).
reasonable ['riːznəbl] *adj* raisonnable.
reasonably ['riːznəblɪ] *adv* 1. (*quite*) assez. 2. (*sensibly*) raisonnablement.
reasoned ['riːznd] *adj* raisonné(e).
reasoning ['riːznɪŋ] *n* raisonnement *m*.
reassess [ˌriːə'ses] *vt* réexaminer.
reassurance [ˌriːə'ʃʊərəns] *n* 1. (*comfort*) réconfort *m*. 2. (*promise*) assurance *f*.
reassure [ˌriːə'ʃʊəʳ] *vt* rassurer.
reassuring [ˌriːə'ʃʊərɪŋ] *adj* rassurant(e).
rebate ['riːbeɪt] *n* (*on product*) rabais *m*; **tax ~** ≃ dégrèvement *m* fiscal.
rebel [*n* 'rebl, *vb* rɪ'bel] ♦ *n* rebelle *mf*. ♦ *vi*: **to ~ (against)** se rebeller (contre).
rebellion [rɪ'beljən] *n* rébellion *f*.
rebellious [rɪ'beljəs] *adj* rebelle.
rebound [*n* 'riːbaʊnd, *vb* rɪ'baʊnd] ♦ *n* (*of ball*) rebond *m*. ♦ *vi* (*ball*) rebondir.
rebuff [rɪ'bʌf] *n* rebuffade *f*.
rebuild [ˌriː'bɪld] (*pt & pp* **rebuilt** [ˌriː'bɪlt]) *vt* reconstruire.
rebuke [rɪ'bjuːk] ♦ *n* réprimande *f*. ♦ *vt* réprimander.
rebuttal [riː'bʌtl] *n* réfutation *f*.
recalcitrant [rɪ'kælsɪtrənt] *adj* récalcitrant(e).
recall [rɪ'kɔːl] ♦ *n* (*memory*) rappel *m*. ♦ *vt* 1. (*remember*) se rappeler, se souvenir de. 2. (*summon back*) rappeler.
recant [rɪ'kænt] *vi* se rétracter; (RELIG) abjurer.
recap ['riːkæp] ♦ *n* récapitulation *f*. ♦ *vt* (*summarize*) récapituler. ♦ *vi* récapituler.
recapitulate [ˌriːkə'pɪtjʊleɪt] *vt & vi* récapituler.
recd, rec'd *abbr of* **received**.
recede [riː'siːd] *vi* (*person, car etc*) s'éloigner; (*hopes*) s'envoler.
receding [rɪ'siːdɪŋ] *adj* (*hairline*) dégarni(e); (*chin, forehead*) fuyant(e).
receipt [rɪ'siːt] *n* 1. (*piece of paper*) reçu *m*. 2. (U) (*act of receiving*) réception *f*. ▶ **receipts** *npl* recettes *fpl*.
receive [rɪ'siːv] *vt* 1. (*gen*) recevoir; (*news*) apprendre. 2. (*welcome*) accueillir, recevoir.
receiver [rɪ'siːvəʳ] *n* 1. (*of telephone*) récepteur *m*, combiné *m*. 2. (*radio, TV set*) récepteur *m*. 3. (*criminal*) receleur *m*, -euse *f*. 4. (FIN) (*official*) administrateur *m*, -trice *f* judiciaire.
recent ['riːsnt] *adj* récent(e).

recently ['riːsntlɪ] *adv* récemment; **until ~** jusqu'à ces derniers temps.
receptacle [rɪ'septəkl] *n* récipient *m*.
reception [rɪ'sepʃn] *n* 1. (*gen*) réception *f*. 2. (*welcome*) accueil *m*, réception *f*.
reception desk *n* réception *f*.
receptionist [rɪ'sepʃənɪst] *n* réceptionniste *mf*.
recess ['riːses, Br rɪ'ses] *n* 1. (*alcove*) niche *f*. 2. (*secret place*) recoin *m*. 3. (POL): **to be in ~** être en vacances. 4. Am (SCH) récréation *f*.
recession [rɪ'seʃn] *n* récession *f*.
recharge [ˌriː'tʃɑːdʒ] *vt* recharger.
recipe ['resɪpɪ] *n lit & fig* recette *f*.
recipient [rɪ'sɪpɪənt] *n* (*of letter*) destinataire *mf*; (*of cheque*) bénéficiaire *mf*; (*of award*) récipiendaire *mf*.
reciprocal [rɪ'sɪprəkl] *adj* réciproque.
recital [rɪ'saɪtl] *n* récital *m*.
recite [rɪ'saɪt] *vt* 1. (*say aloud*) réciter. 2. (*list*) énumérer.
reckless ['reklɪs] *adj* imprudent(e).
reckon ['rekn] *vt* 1. *inf* (*think*) penser. 2. (*consider, judge*) considérer. 3. (*calculate*) calculer. ▶ **reckon on** *vt fus* compter sur. ▶ **reckon with** *vt fus* (*expect*) s'attendre à.
reckoning ['rekənɪŋ] *n* (U) (*calculation*) calculs *mpl*.
reclaim [rɪ'kleɪm] *vt* 1. (*claim back*) réclamer. 2. (*land*) assécher.
recline [rɪ'klaɪn] *vi* (*person*) être allongé(e).
reclining [rɪ'klaɪnɪŋ] *adj* (*chair*) à dossier réglable.
recluse [rɪ'kluːs] *n* reclus *m*, -e *f*.
recognition [ˌrekəg'nɪʃn] *n* reconnaissance *f*; **in ~ of** en reconnaissance de; **the town has changed beyond** OR **out of all ~** la ville est méconnaissable.
recognizable ['rekəgnaɪzəbl] *adj* reconnaissable.
recognize, -ise ['rekəgnaɪz] *vt* reconnaître.
recoil [*vb* rɪ'kɔɪl, *n* 'riːkɔɪl] ♦ *vi*: **to ~ (from)** reculer (devant). ♦ *n* (*of gun*) recul *m*.
recollect [ˌrekə'lekt] *vt* se rappeler.
recollection [ˌrekə'lekʃn] *n* souvenir *m*.
recommend [ˌrekə'mend] *vt* 1. (*commend*): **to ~ sb/sthg (to sb)** recommander qqn/qqch (à qqn). 2. (*advise*) conseiller, recommander.
recompense ['rekəmpens] ♦ *n* dédommagement *m*. ♦ *vt* dédommager.
reconcile ['rekənsaɪl] *vt* 1. (*beliefs, ideas*) concilier. 2. (*people*) réconcilier. 3.

(accept): **to ~ o.s. to sthg** se faire à l'idée de qqch.

reconditioned [ˌriːkən'dɪʃnd] adj remis(e) en état.

reconnaissance [rɪ'kɒnɪsəns] n reconnaissance f.

reconnoitre Br, **reconnoiter** Am [ˌrekə'nɔɪtəʳ] ◆ vt reconnaître. ◆ vi aller en reconnaissance.

reconsider [ˌriːkən'sɪdəʳ] ◆ vt reconsidérer. ◆ vi reconsidérer la question.

reconstruct [ˌriːkən'strʌkt] vt 1. (gen) reconstruire. 2. (crime, event) reconstituer.

record [n & adj 'rekɔːd, vb rɪ'kɔːd] ◆ n 1. (written account) rapport m; (file) dossier m; **to keep sthg on ~** archiver qqch; **(police) ~** casier m judiciaire; **off the ~** non officiel. 2. (vinyl disc) disque m. 3. (best achievement) record m. ◆ adj record (inv). ◆ vt 1. (write down) noter. 2. (put on tape) enregistrer.

recorded delivery [rɪ'kɔːdɪd-] n: **to send sthg by ~** envoyer qqch en recommandé.

recorder [rɪ'kɔːdəʳ] n (musical instrument) flûte f à bec.

record holder n détenteur m, -trice f du record.

recording [rɪ'kɔːdɪŋ] n enregistrement m.

record player n tourne-disque m.

recount [n 'riːkaʊnt, vt sense 1 rɪ'kaʊnt, sense 2 ˌriː'kaʊnt] ◆ n (of vote) deuxième dépouillement m du scrutin. ◆ vt 1. (narrate) raconter. 2. (count again) recompter.

recoup [rɪ'kuːp] vt récupérer.

recourse [rɪ'kɔːs] n: **to have ~ to** avoir recours à.

recover [rɪ'kʌvəʳ] ◆ vt 1. (retrieve) récupérer; **to ~ sthg from sb** reprendre qqch à qqn. 2. (one's balance) retrouver; (consciousness) reprendre. ◆ vi 1. (from illness) se rétablir; (from shock, divorce) se remettre. 2. fig (economy) se redresser; (trade) reprendre.

recovery [rɪ'kʌvərɪ] n 1. (from illness) guérison f, rétablissement m. 2. fig (of economy) redressement m, reprise f. 3. (retrieval) récupération f.

recreation [ˌrekrɪ'eɪʃn] n (U) (leisure) récréation f, loisirs mpl.

recrimination [rɪˌkrɪmɪ'neɪʃn] n récrimination f.

recruit [rɪ'kruːt] ◆ n recrue f. ◆ vt recruter; **to ~ sb to do sthg** fig embaucher qqn pour faire qqch. ◆ vi recruter.

recruitment [rɪ'kruːtmənt] n recrutement m.

rectangle ['rek,tæŋgl] n rectangle m.

rectangular [rek'tæŋgjʊləʳ] adj rectangulaire.

rectify ['rektɪfaɪ] vt (mistake) rectifier.

rector ['rektəʳ] n 1. (priest) pasteur m. 2. Scot (head - of school) directeur m; (- of college, university) président élu par les étudiants.

rectory ['rektərɪ] n presbytère m.

recuperate [rɪ'kuːpəreɪt] vi se rétablir.

recur [rɪ'kɜːʳ] vi (error, problem) se reproduire; (dream) revenir; (pain) réapparaître.

recurrence [rɪ'kʌrəns] n répétition f.

recurrent [rɪ'kʌrənt] adj (error, problem) qui se reproduit souvent; (dream) qui revient souvent.

recycle [ˌriː'saɪkl] vt recycler.

red [red] ◆ adj rouge; (hair) roux (rousse). ◆ n rouge m; **to be in the ~** inf être à découvert.

red card n (FTBL): **to be shown the ~, to get a ~** recevoir un carton rouge.

red carpet n: **to roll out the ~ for sb** dérouler le tapis rouge pour qqn. ▶ **red-carpet** adj: **to give sb the red-carpet treatment** recevoir qqn en grande pompe.

Red Cross n: **the ~** la Croix-Rouge.

redcurrant ['redkʌrənt] n (fruit) groseille f; (bush) groseillier m.

redden ['redn] vt & vi rougir.

redecorate [ˌriː'dekəreɪt] ◆ vt repeindre et retapisser. ◆ vi refaire la peinture et les papiers peints.

redeem [rɪ'diːm] vt 1. (save, rescue) racheter. 2. (from pawnbroker) dégager.

redeeming [rɪ'diːmɪŋ] adj qui rachète (les défauts).

redeploy [ˌriːdɪ'plɔɪ] vt (MIL) redéployer; (staff) réorganiser, réaffecter.

red-faced [-'feɪst] adj rougeaud(e), rubicond(e); (with embarrassment) rouge de confusion.

red-haired [-'heəd] adj roux (rousse).

red-handed [-'hændɪd] adj: **to catch sb ~** prendre qqn en flagrant délit OR la main dans le sac.

redhead ['redhed] n roux m, rousse f.

red herring n fig fausse piste f.

red-hot adj 1. (extremely hot) brûlant(e); (metal) chauffé(e) au rouge. 2. (very enthusiastic) ardent(e).

redid [ˌriː'dɪd] pt → redo.

redirect [ˌriːdɪ'rekt] vt 1. (energy, money) réorienter. 2. (traffic) détourner. 3. (let-

ters) faire suivre.

rediscover [ˌriːdɪˈskʌvər] *vt* redécouvrir.

red light *n* (*traffic signal*) feu *m* rouge.

red-light district *n* quartier *m* chaud.

redo [ˌriːˈduː] (*pt* -did, *pp* -done) *vt* refaire.

redolent [ˈredələnt] *adj literary* 1. (*reminiscent*): ~ of qui rappelle, évocateur (trice) de. 2. (*smelling*): ~ of qui sent.

redone [ˌriːˈdʌn] *pp* → redo.

redouble [ˌriːˈdʌbl] *vt*: to ~ one's efforts (to do sthg) redoubler d'efforts (pour faire qqch).

redraft [ˌriːˈdrɑːft] *vt* rédiger à nouveau.

redress [rɪˈdres] ◆ *n* (U) *fml* réparation *f*. ◆ *vt*: to ~ the balance rétablir l'équilibre.

Red Sea *n*: the ~ la mer Rouge.

red tape *n fig* paperasserie *f* administrative.

reduce [rɪˈdjuːs] *vt* réduire; to be ~d to doing sthg en être réduit à faire qqch; to ~ sb to tears faire pleurer qqn.

reduction [rɪˈdʌkʃn] *n* 1. (*decrease*): ~ (in) réduction *f* (de), baisse *f* (de). 2. (*discount*) rabais *m*, réduction *f*.

redundancy [rɪˈdʌndənsɪ] *n* Br (*dismissal*) licenciement *m*; (*unemployment*) chômage *m*.

redundant [rɪˈdʌndənt] *adj* 1. Br (*jobless*): to be made ~ être licencié(e). 2. (*not required*) superflu(e).

reed [riːd] *n* 1. (*plant*) roseau *m*. 2. (MUS) anche *f*.

reef [riːf] *n* récif *m*, écueil *m*.

reek [riːk] ◆ *n* relent *m*. ◆ *vi*: to ~ (of sthg) puer (qqch), empester (qqch).

reel [riːl] ◆ *n* 1. (*roll*) bobine *f*. 2. (*on fishing rod*) moulinet *m*. ◆ *vi* (*stagger*) chanceler. ▶ **reel in** *vt sep* remonter. ▶ **reel off** *vt sep* (*list*) débiter.

reenact [ˌriːɪˈnækt] *vt* (*play*) reproduire; (*event*) reconstituer.

ref [ref] *n* 1. *inf* (*abbr of* referee) arbitre *m*. 2. (*abbr of* reference) (ADMIN) réf. *f*.

refectory [rɪˈfektərɪ] *n* réfectoire *m*.

refer [rɪˈfɜːr] *vt* 1. (*person*): to ~ sb to (*hospital*) envoyer qqn à; (*specialist*) adresser qqn à; (ADMIN) renvoyer qqn à. 2. (*report, case, decision*): to ~ sthg to soumettre qqch à. ▶ **refer to** *vt fus* 1. (*speak about*) parler de, faire allusion à OR mention de. 2. (*apply to*) s'appliquer à, concerner. 3. (*consult*) se référer à, se reporter à.

referee [ˌrefəˈriː] ◆ *n* 1. (SPORT) arbitre

m. 2. Br (*for job application*) répondant *m*, -e *f*. ◆ *vt* (SPORT) arbitrer. ◆ *vi* (SPORT) être arbitre.

reference [ˈrefrəns] *n* 1. (*mention*): ~ (to) allusion *f* (à), mention *f* (de); with ~ to comme suite à. 2. (U) (*for advice, information*): ~ (to) consultation *f* (de), référence *f* (à). 3. (COMM) référence *f*. 4. (*in book*) renvoi *m*; map ~ coordonnées *fpl*. 5. (*for job application - letter*) référence *f*; (- *person*) répondant *m*, -e *f*.

reference book *n* ouvrage *m* de référence.

reference number *n* numéro *m* de référence.

referendum [ˌrefəˈrendəm] (*pl* -s OR -da [-də]) *n* référendum *m*.

refill [*n* ˈriːfɪl, *vb* ˌriːˈfɪl] ◆ *n* 1. (*for pen*) recharge *f*. 2. *inf* (*drink*): would you like a ~? vous voulez encore un verre? ◆ *vt* remplir à nouveau.

refine [rɪˈfaɪn] *vt* raffiner; *fig* peaufiner.

refined [rɪˈfaɪnd] *adj* raffiné(e); (*system, theory*) perfectionné(e).

refinement [rɪˈfaɪnmənt] *n* 1. (*improvement*) perfectionnement *m*. 2. (U) (*gentility*) raffinement *m*.

reflect [rɪˈflekt] ◆ *vt* 1. (*be a sign of*) refléter. 2. (*light, image*) réfléchir, refléter; (*heat*) réverbérer. 3. (*think*): to ~ that ... se dire que ... ◆ *vi* (*think*): to ~ (on OR upon) réfléchir (sur), penser (à).

reflection [rɪˈflekʃn] *n* 1. (*sign*) indication *f*, signe *m*. 2. (*criticism*): ~ on critique *f* de. 3. (*image*) reflet *m*. 4. (U) (*of light, heat*) réflexion *f*. 5. (*thought*) réflexion *f*; on ~ réflexion faite.

reflector [rɪˈflektər] *n* réflecteur *m*.

reflex [ˈriːfleks] *n*: ~ (action) réflexe *m*.

reflexive [rɪˈfleksɪv] *adj* (GRAMM) (*pronoun*) réfléchi(e); ~ verb verbe *m* pronominal réfléchi.

reforestation [riːˌfɒrɪˈsteɪʃn] = **reafforestation.**

reform [rɪˈfɔːm] ◆ *n* réforme *f*. ◆ *vt* (*gen*) réformer; (*person*) corriger. ◆ *vi* (*behave better*) se corriger, s'amender.

Reformation [ˌrefəˈmeɪʃn] *n*: the ~ la Réforme.

reformer [rɪˈfɔːmər] *n* réformateur *m*, -trice *f*.

refrain [rɪˈfreɪn] ◆ *n* refrain *m*. ◆ *vi*: to ~ from doing sthg s'abstenir de faire qqch.

refresh [rɪˈfreʃ] *vt* rafraîchir, revigorer.

refreshed [rɪˈfreʃt] *adj* reposé(e).

refresher course [rɪˈfreʃər-]*n* cours *m* de recyclage OR remise à niveau.

refreshing [rɪ'freʃɪŋ] *adj* **1.** (*pleasantly different*) agréable, réconfortant(e). **2.** (*drink, swim*) rafraîchissant(e).

refreshments [rɪ'freʃmənts] *npl* rafraîchissements *mpl.*

refrigerator [rɪ'frɪdʒəreɪtər] *n* réfrigérateur *m*, Frigidaire® *m.*

refuel [,riː'fjʊəl] ◆ *vt* ravitailler. ◆ *vi* se ravitailler en carburant.

refuge ['refjuːdʒ] *n lit & fig* refuge *m*, abri *m*; **to take ~ in** se réfugier dans.

refugee [,refjʊ'dʒiː] *n* réfugié *m*, -e *f.*

refund [*n* 'riːfʌnd, *vb* rɪ'fʌnd] ◆ *n* remboursement *m.* ◆ *vt*: **to ~ sthg to sb, to ~ sb sthg** rembourser qqch à qqn.

refundable [riː'fʌndəbl] *adj* remboursable.

refurbish [,riː'fɜːbɪʃ] *vt* remettre à neuf, rénover.

refusal [rɪ'fjuːzl] *n*: **~ (to do sthg)** refus *m* (de faire qqch).

refuse¹ [rɪ'fjuːz] ◆ *vt* refuser; **to ~ to do sthg** refuser de faire qqch. ◆ *vi* refuser.

refuse² ['refjuːs] *n* (U) (*rubbish*) ordures *fpl*, détritus *mpl.*

refuse collection ['refjuːs-] *n* enlèvement *m* des ordures ménagères.

refute [rɪ'fjuːt] *vt* réfuter.

regain [rɪ'geɪn] *vt* (*composure, health*) retrouver; (*leadership*) reprendre.

regal ['riːgl] *adj* majestueux(euse), royal(e).

regalia [rɪ'geɪljə] *n* (U) insignes *mpl.*

regard [rɪ'gɑːd] ◆ *n* **1.** (U) (*respect*) estime *f*, respect *m.* **2.** (*aspect*): **in this/that ~** à cet égard. ◆ *vt* considérer; **to ~ o.s. as** se considérer comme; **to be highly ~ed** être tenu(e) en haute estime. ▶ **regards** *npl*: **(with best) ~s** bien amicalement; **give her my ~s** faites-lui mes amitiés. ▶ **as regards** *prep* en ce qui concerne. ▶ **in regard to, with regard to** *prep* en ce qui concerne, relativement à.

regarding [rɪ'gɑːdɪŋ] *prep* concernant, en ce qui concerne.

regardless [rɪ'gɑːdlɪs] *adv* quand même. ▶ **regardless of** *prep* sans tenir compte de, sans se soucier de.

regime [reɪ'ʒiːm] *n* régime *m.*

regiment ['redʒɪmənt] *n* régiment *m.*

region ['riːdʒən] *n* région *f*; **in the ~ of** environ.

regional ['riːdʒənl] *adj* régional(e).

register ['redʒɪstər] ◆ *n* (*record*) registre *m.* ◆ *vt* **1.** (*record officially*) déclarer. **2.** (*show, measure*) indiquer, montrer. **3.** (*express*) exprimer. ◆ *vi* **1.** (*on official*

list) s'inscrire, se faire inscrire. **2.** (*at hotel*) signer le registre. **3.** *inf* (*advice, fact*): **it didn't ~** je n'ai pas compris.

registered ['redʒɪstəd] *adj* **1.** (*person*) inscrit(e); (*car*) immatriculé(e); (*charity*) agréé(e) par le gouvernement. **2.** (*letter, parcel*) recommandé(e).

registered trademark *n* marque *f* déposée.

registrar [,redʒɪ'strɑːr] *n* **1.** (*keeper of records*) officier *m* de l'état civil. **2.** (UNIV) secrétaire *m* général. **3.** *Br* (*doctor*) chef *m* de clinique.

registration [,redʒɪ'streɪʃn] *n* **1.** (*gen*) enregistrement *m*, inscription *f.* **2.** (AUT) = **registration number.**

registration number *n* (AUT) numéro *m* d'immatriculation.

registry ['redʒɪstrɪ] *n* bureau *m* de l'enregistrement.

registry office *n* bureau *m* de l'état civil.

regret [rɪ'gret] ◆ *n* regret *m.* ◆ *vt* (*be sorry about*): **to ~ sthg/doing sthg** regretter qqch/d'avoir fait qqch.

regretfully [rɪ'gretfʊlɪ] *adv* à regret.

regrettable [rɪ'gretəbl] *adj* regrettable, fâcheux(euse).

regroup [,riː'gruːp] *vi* se regrouper.

regular ['regjʊlər] ◆ *adj* **1.** (*gen*) régulier(ère); (*customer*) fidèle. **2.** (*usual*) habituel(elle). **3.** *Am* (*normal - size*) standard (*inv*). **4.** *Am* (*pleasant*) sympa (*inv*). ◆ *n* (*at pub*) habitué *m*, -e *f*; (*at shop*) client *m*, -e *f* fidèle.

regularly ['regjʊləlɪ] *adv* régulièrement.

regulate ['regjʊleɪt] *vt* régler.

regulation [,regjʊ'leɪʃn] ◆ *adj* (*standard*) réglementaire. ◆ *n* **1.** (*rule*) règlement *m.* **2.** (U) (*control*) réglementation *f.*

rehabilitate [,riːə'bɪlɪteɪt] *vt* (*criminal*) réinsérer, réhabiliter; (*patient*) rééduquer.

rehearsal [rɪ'hɜːsl] *n* répétition *f.*

rehearse [rɪ'hɜːs] *vt & vi* répéter.

reign [reɪn] ◆ *n* règne *m.* ◆ *vi*: **to ~ (over)** *lit & fig* régner (sur).

reimburse [,riːɪm'bɜːs] *vt*: **to ~ sb (for)** rembourser qqn (de).

rein [reɪn] *n fig*: **to give (a) free ~ to sb, to give sb free ~** laisser la bride sur le cou à qqn. ▶ **reins** *npl* (*for horse*) rênes *fpl.*

reindeer ['reɪn,dɪər] (*pl inv*) *n* renne *m.*

reinforce [,riːɪn'fɔːs] *vt* **1.** (*strengthen*) renforcer. **2.** (*back up, confirm*) appuyer, étayer.

reinforced concrete [ˌriːɪnˈfɔːst-] n béton m armé.

reinforcement [ˌriːɪnˈfɔːsmənt] n **1.** (U) (strengthening) renforcement m. **2.** (strengthener) renfort m. ► **reinforcements** npl renforts mpl.

reinstate [ˌriːɪnˈsteɪt] vt (employee) rétablir dans ses fonctions, réintégrer; (policy, method) rétablir.

reissue [riːˈɪʃuː] ◆ n (of book) réédition f. ◆ vt (book) rééditer; (film, record) ressortir.

reiterate [riːˈɪtəreɪt] vt réitérer, répéter.

reject [n ˈriːdʒekt, vb rɪˈdʒekt] ◆ n (product) article m de rebut. ◆ vt **1.** (not accept) rejeter. **2.** (candidate, coin) refuser.

rejection [rɪˈdʒekʃn] n **1.** (non-acceptance) rejet m. **2.** (of candidate) refus m.

rejoice [rɪˈdʒɔɪs] vi: **to ~ (at OR in)** se réjouir (de).

rejuvenate [rɪˈdʒuːvəneɪt] vt rajeunir.

rekindle [ˌriːˈkɪndl] vt fig ranimer, raviver.

relapse [rɪˈlæps] ◆ n rechute f. ◆ vi: **to ~ into** retomber dans.

relate [rɪˈleɪt] ◆ vt **1.** (connect): **to ~ sthg to sthg** établir un lien OR rapport entre qqch et qqch. **2.** (tell) raconter. ◆ vi **1.** (be connected): **to ~ to** avoir un rapport avec. **2.** (concern): **to ~ to** se rapporter à. **3.** (empathize): **to ~ (to sb)** s'entendre (avec qqn). ► **relating to** prep concernant.

related [rɪˈleɪtɪd] adj **1.** (people) apparenté(e). **2.** (issues, problems etc) lié(e).

relation [rɪˈleɪʃn] n **1.** (connection): **~ (to/between)** rapport m (avec/entre); **in ~ to** par rapport à. **2.** (person) parent m, -e f. ► **relations** npl (relationship) relations fpl, rapports mpl.

relationship [rɪˈleɪʃnʃɪp] n **1.** (between people, countries) relations fpl, rapports mpl; (romantic) liaison f. **2.** (connection) rapport m, lien m.

relative [ˈrelətɪv] ◆ adj relatif(ive). ◆ n parent m, -e f. ► **relative to** prep (compared with) relativement à; (connected with) se rapportant à, relatif(ive) à.

relatively [ˈrelətɪvlɪ] adv relativement.

relax [rɪˈlæks] ◆ vt **1.** (person) détendre, relaxer. **2.** (muscle, body) décontracter, relâcher; (one's grip) desserrer. **3.** (rule) relâcher. ◆ vi **1.** (person) se détendre, se décontracter. **2.** (muscle, body) se relâcher, se décontracter. **3.** (one's grip) se desserrer.

relaxation [ˌriːlækˈseɪʃn] n **1.** (of person) relaxation f, détente f. **2.** (of rule) relâchement m.

relaxed [rɪˈlækst] adj détendu(e), décontracté(e).

relaxing [rɪˈlæksɪŋ] adj relaxant(e), qui détend.

relay [ˈriːleɪ] ◆ n **1.** (SPORT): **~ (race)** course f de relais. **2.** (RADIO & TV) (broadcast) retransmission f. ◆ vt **1.** (RADIO & TV) (broadcast) relayer. **2.** (message, information) transmettre, communiquer.

release [rɪˈliːs] ◆ n **1.** (from prison, cage) libération f. **2.** (from pain, misery) délivrance f. **3.** (statement) communiqué m. **4.** (of gas, heat) échappement m. **5.** (U) (of film, record) sortie f. **6.** (film) nouveau film m; (record) nouveau disque m. ◆ vt **1.** (set free) libérer. **2.** (lift restriction on): **to ~ sb from** dégager qqn de. **3.** (make available - supplies) libérer; (- funds) débloquer. **4.** (let go of) lâcher. **5.** (TECH) (brake, handle) desserrer; (mechanism) déclencher. **6.** (gas, heat): **to be ~d (from/into)** se dégager (de/dans), s'échapper (de/dans). **7.** (film, record) sortir; (statement, report) publier.

relegate [ˈrelɪgeɪt] vt reléguer; **to be ~d** Br (SPORT) être relégué à la division inférieure.

relent [rɪˈlent] vi (person) se laisser fléchir; (wind, storm) se calmer.

relentless [rɪˈlentlɪs] adj implacable.

relevant [ˈreləvənt] adj **1.** (connected): **~ (to)** qui a un rapport (avec). **2.** (significant): **~ (to)** important(e) (pour). **3.** (appropriate - information) utile; (- document) justificatif(ive).

reliable [rɪˈlaɪəbl] adj (person) sur qui on peut compter, fiable; (device) fiable; (company, information) sérieux(euse).

reliably [rɪˈlaɪəblɪ] adv de façon fiable; **to be ~ informed (that)** ... savoir de source sûre que ...

reliant [rɪˈlaɪənt] adj: **to be ~ on** être dépendant(e) de.

relic [ˈrelɪk] n relique f; (of past) vestige m.

relief [rɪˈliːf] n **1.** (comfort) soulagement m. **2.** (for poor, refugees) aide f, assistance f. **3.** Am (social security) aide f sociale.

relieve [rɪˈliːv] vt **1.** (pain, anxiety) soulager; **to ~ sb of sthg** (take away from) délivrer qqn de qqch. **2.** (take over from) relayer. **3.** (give help to) secourir, venir en aide à.

religion [rɪˈlɪdʒn] n religion f.

religious [rɪˈlɪdʒəs] adj religieux(euse);

(*book*) de piété.

relinquish [rɪ'lɪŋkwɪʃ] *vt* (*power*) abandonner; (*claim, plan*) renoncer à; (*post*) quitter.

relish ['relɪʃ] ◆ *n* 1. (*enjoyment*): with (great) ~ avec délectation. 2. (*pickle*) condiment *m*. ◆ *vt* (*enjoy*) prendre plaisir à; I don't ~ the thought OR idea OR prospect of seeing him la perspective de le voir ne m'enchante guère.

relocate [ˌriːləʊ'keɪt] ◆ *vt* installer ailleurs, transférer. ◆ *vi* s'installer ailleurs, déménager.

reluctance [rɪ'lʌktəns] *n* répugnance *f*.

reluctant [rɪ'lʌktənt] *adj* peu enthousiaste; to be ~ to do sthg rechigner à faire qqch.

reluctantly [rɪ'lʌktəntlɪ] *adv* à contrecœur, avec répugnance.

rely [rɪ'laɪ] ▶ **rely on** *vt fus* 1. (*count on*) compter sur; to ~ on sb to do sthg compter sur qqn OR faire confiance à qqn pour faire qqch. 2. (*be dependent on*) dépendre de.

remain [rɪ'meɪn] ◆ *vt* rester; to ~ to be done rester à faire. ◆ *vi* rester. ▶ **remains** *npl* 1. (*remnants*) restes *mpl*. 2. (*antiquities*) ruines *fpl*, vestiges *mpl*.

remainder [rɪ'meɪndəʳ] *n* reste *m*.

remaining [rɪ'meɪnɪŋ] *adj* qui reste.

remand [rɪ'mɑːnd] (JUR) ◆ *n*: on ~ en détention préventive. ◆ *vt*: to ~ sb (in custody) placer qqn en détention préventive.

remark [rɪ'mɑːk] ◆ *n* (*comment*) remarque *f*, observation *f*. ◆ *vt* (*comment*): to ~ that ... faire remarquer que ...

remarkable [rɪ'mɑːkəbl] *adj* remarquable.

remarry [ˌriː'mærɪ] *vi* se remarier.

remedial [rɪ'miːdjəl] *adj* 1. (*pupil, class*) de rattrapage. 2. (*exercise*) correctif(ive); (*action*) de rectification.

remedy ['remədɪ] ◆ *n*: ~ (for) (MED) remède *m* (pour OR contre); *fig* remède (à OR contre). ◆ *vt* remédier à.

remember [rɪ'membəʳ] ◆ *vt* (*gen*) se souvenir de, se rappeler; to ~ to do sthg ne pas oublier de faire qqch, penser à faire qqch; to ~ doing sthg se souvenir d'avoir fait qqch, se rappeler avoir fait qqch. ◆ *vi* se souvenir, se rappeler.

remembrance [rɪ'membrəns] *n*: in ~ of en souvenir OR mémoire de.

Remembrance Day *n* l'Armistice *m*.

remind [rɪ'maɪnd] *vt*: to ~ sb of OR about sthg rappeler qqch à qqn; to ~ sb to do sthg rappeler à qqn de faire

qqch, faire penser à qqn à faire qqch.

reminder [rɪ'maɪndəʳ] *n* 1. (*to jog memory*): to give sb a ~ (to do sthg) faire penser à qqn (à faire qqch). 2. (*letter, note*) rappel *m*.

reminisce [ˌremɪ'nɪs] *vi* évoquer des souvenirs; to ~ about sthg évoquer qqch.

reminiscent [ˌremɪ'nɪsnt] *adj*: ~ of qui rappelle, qui fait penser à.

remiss [rɪ'mɪs] *adj* négligent(e).

remit[1] [rɪ'mɪt] *vt* (*money*) envoyer, verser.

remit[2] ['riːmɪt] *n Br* (*responsibility*) attributions *fpl*.

remittance [rɪ'mɪtns] *n* 1. (*amount of money*) versement *m*. 2. (COMM) règlement *m*, paiement *m*.

remnant ['remnənt] *n* 1. (*remaining part*) reste, restant *m*. 2. (*of cloth*) coupon *m*.

remold *Am* = remould.

remorse [rɪ'mɔːs] *n* (U) remords *m*.

remorseful [rɪ'mɔːsful] *adj* plein(e) de remords.

remorseless [rɪ'mɔːslɪs] *adj* implacable.

remote [rɪ'məʊt] *adj* 1. (*far-off - place*) éloigné(e); (*- time*) lointain(e). 2. (*person*) distant(e). 3. (*possibility, chance*) vague.

remote control *n* télécommande *f*.

remotely [rɪ'məʊtlɪ] *adv* 1. (*in the slightest*): not ~ pas le moins du monde, absolument pas. 2. (*far off*) au loin.

remould *Br*, **remold** *Am* ['riːməʊld] *n* pneu *m* rechapé.

removable [rɪ'muːvəbl] *adj* (*detachable*) détachable, amovible.

removal [rɪ'muːvl] *n* 1. (U) (*act of removing*) enlèvement *m*. 2. *Br* (*change of house*) déménagement *m*.

removal van *n Br* camion *m* de déménagement.

remove [rɪ'muːv] *vt* 1. (*take away - gen*) enlever; (*- stain*) faire partir, enlever; (*- problem*) résoudre; (*- suspicion*) dissiper. 2. (*clothes*) ôter, enlever. 3. (*employee*) renvoyer.

remuneration [rɪˌmjuːnə'reɪʃn] *n* rémunération *f*.

Renaissance [rə'neɪsəns] *n*: the ~ la Renaissance.

render ['rendəʳ] *vt* rendre; (*assistance*) porter; (FIN) (*account*) présenter.

rendering ['rendərɪŋ] *n* (*of play, music etc*) interprétation *f*.

rendezvous ['rɒndɪvuː] (*pl inv*) *n* rendez-vous *m inv*.

renegade ['renɪgeɪd] *n* renégat *m*, -e *f*.

renew [rɪ'njuː] vt 1. (gen) renouveler; (negotiations, strength) reprendre; (interest) faire renaître; **to ~ acquaintance with sb** renouer connaissance avec qqn. 2. (replace) remplacer.

renewable [rɪ'njuːəbl] adj renouvelable.

renewal [rɪ'njuːəl] n 1. (of activity) reprise f. 2. (of contract, licence etc) renouvellement m.

renounce [rɪ'naʊns] vt (reject) renoncer à.

renovate ['renəveɪt] vt rénover.

renown [rɪ'naʊn] n renommée f, renom m.

renowned [rɪ'naʊnd] adj: **~ (for)** renommé(e) (pour).

rent [rent] ◆ n (for house) loyer m. ◆ vt louer.

rental ['rentl] ◆ adj de location. ◆ n (for car, television, video) prix m de location; (for house) loyer m.

renunciation [rɪ,nʌnsɪ'eɪʃn] n renonciation f.

reorganize, -ise [,riː'ɔːɡənaɪz] vt réorganiser.

rep [rep] n 1. (abbr of representative) VRP m. 2. abbr of repertory.

repaid [riː'peɪd] pt & pp → repay.

repair [rɪ'peər] ◆ n réparation f; in good/bad ~ en bon/mauvais état. ◆ vt réparer.

repair kit n trousse f à outils.

repartee [,repɑː'tiː] n repartie f.

repatriate [,riː'pætrɪeɪt] vt rapatrier.

repay [riː'peɪ] (pt & pp repaid) vt 1. (money): **to ~ sb sthg, to ~ sthg to sb** rembourser qqch à qqn. 2. (favour) payer de retour, récompenser.

repayment [riː'peɪmənt] n remboursement m.

repeal [rɪ'piːl] ◆ n abrogation f. ◆ vt abroger.

repeat [rɪ'piːt] ◆ vt 1. (gen) répéter. 2. (RADIO & TV) rediffuser. ◆ n (RADIO & TV) reprise f, rediffusion f.

repeatedly [rɪ'piːtɪdlɪ] adv à maintes reprises, très souvent.

repel [rɪ'pel] vt repousser.

repellent [rɪ'pelənt] ◆ adj répugnant(e), repoussant(e). ◆ n: insect ~ crème f anti-insecte.

repent [rɪ'pent] ◆ vt se repentir de. ◆ vi: **to ~ (of)** se repentir (de).

repentance [rɪ'pentəns] n (U) repentir m.

repercussions [,riːpə'kʌʃnz] npl répercussions fpl.

repertoire ['repətwɑːr] n répertoire m.

repertory ['repətrɪ] n répertoire m.

repetition [,repɪ'tɪʃn] n répétition f.

repetitious [,repɪ'tɪʃəs], **repetitive** [rɪ'petɪtɪv] adj (action, job) répétitif(ive); (article, speech) qui a des redites.

replace [rɪ'pleɪs] vt 1. (gen) remplacer. 2. (put back) remettre (à sa place).

replacement [rɪ'pleɪsmənt] n 1. (substituting) remplacement m; (putting back) replacement m. 2. (new person): **~ (for sb)** remplaçant m, -e f (de qqn).

replay [n 'riː,pleɪ, vb ,riː'pleɪ] ◆ n match m rejoué. ◆ vt 1. (match, game) rejouer. 2. (film, tape) repasser.

replenish [rɪ'plenɪʃ] vt: **to ~ one's supply of sthg** se réapprovisionner en qqch.

replica ['replɪkə] n copie f exacte, réplique f.

reply [rɪ'plaɪ] ◆ n: **~ (to)** réponse f (à). ◆ vt & vi répondre.

reply coupon n coupon-réponse m.

report [rɪ'pɔːt] ◆ n 1. (account) rapport m, compte m rendu; (PRESS) reportage m. 2. Br (SCH) bulletin m. ◆ vt 1. (news, crime) rapporter, signaler. 2. (make known): **to ~ that ...** annoncer que ... 3. (complain about): **to ~ sb (to)** dénoncer qqn (à). ◆ vi 1. (give account): **to ~ (on)** faire un rapport (sur); (PRESS) faire un reportage (sur). 2. (present oneself): **to ~ (to sb/for sthg)** se présenter (à qqn/ pour qqch).

report card n bulletin m scolaire.

reportedly [rɪ'pɔːtɪdlɪ] adv à ce qu'il paraît.

reporter [rɪ'pɔːtər] n reporter m.

repose [rɪ'pəʊz] n literary repos m.

repossess [,riːpə'zes] vt saisir.

reprehensible [,reprɪ'hensəbl] adj répréhensible.

represent [,reprɪ'zent] vt (gen) représenter.

representation [,reprɪzen'teɪʃn] n (gen) représentation f. ▶ **representations** npl: **to make ~s to sb** faire une démarche auprès de qqn.

representative [,reprɪ'zentətɪv] ◆ adj représentatif(ive). ◆ n représentant m, -e f.

repress [rɪ'pres] vt réprimer.

repression [rɪ'preʃn] n répression f; (sexual) refoulement m.

reprieve [rɪ'priːv] ◆ n 1. fig (delay) sursis m, répit m. 2. (JUR) sursis m. ◆ vt accorder un sursis à.

reprimand ['reprɪmɑːnd] ◆ n réprimande f. ◆ vt réprimander.

reprisal [rɪ'praɪzl] n représailles fpl.
reproach [rɪ'prəʊtʃ] ◆ n reproche m.
◆ vt : **to ~ sb for** OR **with sthg** reprocher qqch à qqn.
reproachful [rɪ'prəʊtʃfʊl] adj (look, words) de reproche.
reproduce [ˌriːprə'djuːs] ◆ vt reproduire. ◆ vi se reproduire.
reproduction [ˌriːprə'dʌkʃn] n reproduction f.
reproof [rɪ'pruːf] n reproche m, blâme m.
reprove [rɪ'pruːv] vt : **to ~ sb (for)** blâmer qqn (pour OR de), réprimander qqn (pour).
reptile ['reptaɪl] n reptile m.
republic [rɪ'pʌblɪk] n république f.
republican [rɪ'pʌblɪkən] ◆ adj républicain(e). ◆ n républicain m, -e f. ▶ **Republican** ◆ adj républicain(e); **the Republican Party** Am le parti républicain. ◆ n républicain m, -e f.
repudiate [rɪ'pjuːdɪeɪt] vt fml (offer, suggestion) rejeter; (friend) renier.
repulse [rɪ'pʌls] vt repousser.
repulsive [rɪ'pʌlsɪv] adj repoussant(e).
reputable ['repjutəbl] adj de bonne réputation.
reputation [ˌrepjʊ'teɪʃn] n réputation f.
repute [rɪ'pjuːt] n : **of good ~** de bonne réputation.
reputed [rɪ'pjuːtɪd] adj réputé(e); **to be ~ to be sthg** être réputé pour être qqch, avoir la réputation d'être qqch.
reputedly [rɪ'pjuːtɪdlɪ] adv à OR d'après ce qu'on dit.
request [rɪ'kwest] ◆ n : **~ (for)** demande f (de); **on ~** sur demande. ◆ vt demander; **to ~ sb to do sthg** demander à qqn de faire qqch.
request stop n Br arrêt m facultatif.
require [rɪ'kwaɪəʳ] vt (subj: person) avoir besoin de; (subj: situation) nécessiter; **to ~ sb to do sthg** exiger de qqn qu'il fasse qqch.
requirement [rɪ'kwaɪəmənt] n besoin m.
requisition [ˌrekwɪ'zɪʃn] vt réquisitionner.
reran [ˌriː'ræn] pt → **rerun**.
rerun [n 'riːrʌn, vb ˌriː'rʌn] (pt **-ran**, pp **-run**) ◆ n (of TV programme) rediffusion f, reprise f; fig répétition f. ◆ vt **1.** (race) réorganiser. **2.** (TV programme) rediffuser; (tape) passer à nouveau, repasser.
resat [ˌriː'sæt] pt & pp → **resit**.

rescind [rɪ'sɪnd] vt (contract) annuler; (law) abroger.
rescue ['reskjuː] ◆ n **1.** (U) (help) secours mpl. **2.** (successful attempt) sauvetage m. ◆ vt sauver, secourir.
rescuer ['reskjʊəʳ] n sauveteur m.
research [ˌrɪ'sɜːtʃ] ◆ n (U): **~ (on** OR **into)** recherche f (sur), recherches fpl (sur). ◆ vt faire des recherches sur.
researcher [rɪ'sɜːtʃəʳ] n chercheur m, -euse f.
resemblance [rɪ'zembləns] n : **~ (to)** ressemblance f (avec).
resemble [rɪ'zembl] vt ressembler à.
resent [rɪ'zent] vt être indigné(e) par.
resentful [rɪ'zentfʊl] adj plein(e) de ressentiment.
resentment [rɪ'zentmənt] n ressentiment m.
reservation [ˌrezə'veɪʃn] n **1.** (booking) réservation f. **2.** (uncertainty): **without ~** sans réserve. **3.** Am (for Native Americans) réserve f indienne. ▶ **reservations** npl (doubts) réserves fpl.
reserve [rɪ'zɜːv] ◆ n **1.** (gen) réserve f; **in ~** en réserve. **2.** (SPORT) remplaçant m, -e f. ◆ vt **1.** (save) garder, réserver. **2.** (book) réserver. **3.** (retain): **to ~ the right to do sthg** se réserver le droit de faire qqch.
reserved [rɪ'zɜːvd] adj réservé(e).
reservoir ['rezəvwɑːʳ] n réservoir m.
reset [ˌriː'set] (pt & pp reset) vt **1.** (clock, watch) remettre à l'heure; (meter, controls) remettre à zéro. **2.** (COMPUT) réinitialiser.
reshape [ˌriː'ʃeɪp] vt (policy, thinking) réorganiser.
reshuffle [ˌriː'ʃʌfl] ◆ n : **cabinet ~** remaniement ministériel. ◆ vt remanier.
reside [rɪ'zaɪd] vi fml résider.
residence ['rezɪdəns] n résidence f.
residence permit n permis m de séjour.
resident ['rezɪdənt] ◆ adj résidant(e); (chaplain, doctor) à demeure. ◆ n résident m, -e f.
residential [ˌrezɪ'denʃl] adj: **~ course** stage ou formation avec logement sur place; **~ institution** internat m.
residential area n quartier m résidentiel.
residue ['rezɪdjuː] n reste m; (CHEM) résidu m.
resign [rɪ'zaɪn] ◆ vt **1.** (job) démissionner de. **2.** (accept calmly): **to ~ o.s. to** se résigner à. ◆ vi: **to ~ (from)** démissionner (de).

resignation [,rezɪg'neɪʃn] *n* **1.** (*from job*) démission *f*. **2.** (*calm acceptance*) résignation *f*.

resigned [rɪ'zaɪnd] *adj*: ~ **(to)** résigné(e) (à).

resilient [rɪ'zɪlɪənt] *adj* (*material*) élastique; (*person*) qui a du ressort.

resin ['rezɪn] *n* résine *f*.

resist [rɪ'zɪst] *vt* résister à.

resistance [rɪ'zɪstəns] *n* résistance *f*.

resit [*n* 'ri:sɪt, *vb* ,ri:'sɪt] (*pt & pp* **-sat**) Br ◆ *n* deuxième session *f*. ◆ *vt* repasser, se représenter à.

resolute ['rezəlu:t] *adj* résolu(e).

resolution [,rezə'lu:ʃn] *n* résolution *f*.

resolve [rɪ'zɒlv] ◆ *n* (U) (*determination*) résolution *f*. ◆ *vt* **1.** (*decide*): **to ~ (that)** ... décider que ...; **to ~ to do sthg** résoudre OR décider de faire qqch. **2.** (*solve*) résoudre.

resort [rɪ'zɔ:t] *n* **1.** (*for holidays*) lieu *m* de vacances. **2.** (*recourse*) recours *m*; **as a last ~, in the last ~** en dernier ressort OR recours. ► **resort to** *vt fus* recourir à, avoir recours à.

resounding [rɪ'zaʊndɪŋ] *adj* retentissant(e).

resource [rɪ'sɔ:s] *n* ressource *f*.

resourceful [rɪ'sɔ:sfʊl] *adj* plein(e) de ressources, débrouillard(e).

respect [rɪ'spekt] ◆ *n* **1.** (*gen*): ~ **(for)** respect *m* (pour); **with ~** avec respect; **with ~, ...** sauf votre respect, ... **2.** (*aspect*): **in this** OR **that ~** à cet égard; **in some ~s** à certains égards. ◆ *vt* respecter; **to ~ sb for sthg** respecter qqn pour qqch. ► **respects** *npl* respects *mpl*, hommages *mpl*. ► **with respect to** *prep* en ce qui concerne, quant à.

respectable [rɪ'spektəbl] *adj* **1.** (*morally correct*) respectable. **2.** (*adequate*) raisonnable, honorable.

respectful [rɪ'spektfʊl] *adj* respectueux(euse).

respective [rɪ'spektɪv] *adj* respectif (ive).

respectively [rɪ'spektɪvlɪ] *adv* respectivement.

respite ['respaɪt] *n* répit *m*.

resplendent [rɪ'splendənt] *adj* resplendissant(e).

respond [rɪ'spɒnd] *vi*: **to ~ (to)** répondre (à).

response [rɪ'spɒns] *n* réponse *f*.

responsibility [rɪ,spɒnsə'bɪlətɪ] *n*: ~ **(for)** responsabilité *f* (de).

responsible [rɪ'spɒnsəbl] *adj* **1.** (*gen*):

~ **(for sthg)** responsable (de qqch); **to be ~ to sb** être responsable devant qqn. **2.** (*job, position*) qui comporte des responsabilités.

responsibly [rɪ'spɒnsəblɪ] *adv* de façon responsable.

responsive [rɪ'spɒnsɪv] *adj* **1.** (*quick to react*) qui réagit bien. **2.** (*aware*): ~ **(to)** attentif(ive) (à).

rest [rest] ◆ *n* **1.** (*remainder*): **the ~ (of)** le reste (de); **the ~ (of them)** les autres *mfpl*. **2.** (*relaxation, break*) repos *m*; **to have a ~** se reposer. **3.** (*support*) support *m*, appui *m*. ◆ *vt* **1.** (*relax*) faire OR laisser reposer. **2.** (*support*): **to ~ sthg on/against** appuyer qqch sur/contre. **3.** *phr*: ~ **assured** soyez certain(e). ◆ *vi* **1.** (*relax*) se reposer. **2.** (*be supported*): **to ~ on/against** s'appuyer sur/contre. **3.** *fig* (*argument, result*): **to ~ on** reposer sur.

restaurant ['restərɒnt] *n* restaurant *m*.

restaurant car *n* Br wagon-restaurant *m*.

restful ['restfʊl] *adj* reposant(e).

rest home *n* maison *f* de repos.

restive ['restɪv] *adj* agité(e).

restless ['restlɪs] *adj* agité(e).

restoration [,restə'reɪʃn] *n* **1.** (*of law and order, monarchy*) rétablissement *m*. **2.** (*renovation*) restauration *f*.

restore [rɪ'stɔ:r] *vt* **1.** (*law and order, monarchy*) rétablir; (*confidence*) redonner. **2.** (*renovate*) restaurer. **3.** (*give back*) rendre, restituer.

restrain [rɪ'streɪn] *vt* (*person, crowd*) contenir, retenir; (*emotions*) maîtriser, contenir; **to ~ o.s. from doing sthg** se retenir de faire qqch.

restrained [rɪ'streɪnd] *adj* (*tone*) mesuré(e); (*person*) qui se domine.

restraint [rɪ'streɪnt] *n* **1.** (*restriction*) restriction *f*, entrave *f*. **2.** (U) (*self-control*) mesure *f*, retenue *f*.

restrict [rɪ'strɪkt] *vt* restreindre, limiter.

restriction [rɪ'strɪkʃn] *n* restriction *f*, limitation *f*.

restrictive [rɪ'strɪktɪv] *adj* restrictif (ive).

rest room *n* Am toilettes *fpl*.

result [rɪ'zʌlt] ◆ *n* résultat *m*; **as a ~** en conséquence; **as a ~ of** (*as a consequence of*) à la suite de; (*because of*) à cause de. ◆ *vi* **1.** (*cause*): **to ~ in** aboutir à. **2.** (*be caused*): **to ~ (from)** résulter (de).

resume [rɪ'zju:m] *vt & vi* reprendre.

résumé ['rezju:meɪ] *n* **1.** (*summary*) résumé *m*. **2.** Am (*curriculum vitae*) curriculum vitae *m inv*, CV *m*.

resumption [rɪ'zʌmpʃn] *n* reprise *f*.

resurgence [rɪ'sɜːdʒəns] *n* réapparition *f*.

resurrection [,rezə'rekʃn] *n fig* résurrection *f*.

resuscitation [rɪ,sʌsɪ'teɪʃn] *n* réanimation *f*.

retail ['riːteɪl] ◆ *n* (U) détail *m*. ◆ *adv* au détail.

retailer ['riːteɪləʳ] *n* détaillant *m*, -e *f*.

retail price *n* prix *m* de détail.

retain [rɪ'teɪn] *vt* conserver.

retainer [rɪ'teɪnəʳ] *n* (*fee*) provision *f*.

retaliate [rɪ'tælɪeɪt] *vi* rendre la pareille, se venger.

retaliation [rɪ,tælɪ'eɪʃn] *n* (U) vengeance *f*, représailles *fpl*.

retarded [rɪ'tɑːdɪd] *adj* retardé(e).

retch [retʃ] *vi* avoir des haut-le-cœur.

reticent ['retɪsənt] *adj* peu communicatif(ive); **to be ~ about sthg** ne pas beaucoup parler de qqch.

retina ['retɪnə] (*pl* -**nas** OR -**nae** [-niː]) *n* rétine *f*.

retinue ['retɪnjuː] *n* suite *f*.

retire [rɪ'taɪəʳ] *vi* **1.** (*from work*) prendre sa retraite. **2.** (*withdraw*) se retirer. **3.** (*to bed*) (aller) se coucher.

retired [rɪ'taɪəd] *adj* à la OR en retraite, retraité(e).

retirement [rɪ'taɪəmənt] *n* retraite *f*.

retiring [rɪ'taɪərɪŋ] *adj* (*shy*) réservé(e).

retort [rɪ'tɔːt] ◆ *n* (*sharp reply*) riposte *f*. ◆ *vt* riposter.

retrace [rɪ'treɪs] *vt*: **to ~ one's steps** revenir sur ses pas.

retract [rɪ'trækt] ◆ *vt* **1.** (*statement*) rétracter. **2.** (*undercarriage*) rentrer, escamoter; (*claws*) rentrer. ◆ *vi* (*undercarriage*) rentrer, s'escamoter.

retrain [,riː'treɪn] *vt* recycler.

retraining [,riː'treɪnɪŋ] *n* recyclage *m*.

retread ['riːtred] *n* pneu *m* rechapé.

retreat [rɪ'triːt] ◆ *n* retraite *f*. ◆ *vi* (*move away*) se retirer; (MIL) battre en retraite.

retribution [,retrɪ'bjuːʃn] *n* châtiment *m*.

retrieval [rɪ'triːvl] *n* (U) (COMPUT) recherche *f* et extraction *f*.

retrieve [rɪ'triːv] *vt* **1.** (*get back*) récupérer. **2.** (COMPUT) rechercher et extraire. **3.** (*situation*) sauver.

retriever [rɪ'triːvəʳ] *n* (*dog*) retriever *m*.

retrograde ['retrəgreɪd] *adj* rétrograde.

retrospect ['retrəspekt] *n*: **in ~** après coup.

retrospective [,retrə'spektɪv] *adj* **1.** (*mood, look*) rétrospectif(ive). **2.** (JUR) (*law, pay rise*) rétroactif(ive).

return [rɪ'tɜːn] ◆ *n* **1.** (U) (*arrival back, giving back*) retour *m*. **2.** (TENNIS) renvoi *m*. **3.** Br (*ticket*) aller (et) retour *m*. **4.** (*profit*) rapport *m*, rendement *m*. ◆ *vt* **1.** (*gen*) rendre; (*a loan*) rembourser; (*library book*) rapporter. **2.** (*send back*) renvoyer. **3.** (*replace*) remettre. **4.** (POL) élire. ◆ *vi* (*come back*) revenir; (*go back*) retourner. ► **returns** *npl* (COMM) recettes *fpl*; **many happy ~s (of the day)!** bon anniversaire! ► **in return** *adv* en retour, en échange. ► **in return for** *prep* en échange de.

return ticket *n* Br aller (et) retour *m*.

reunification [,riːjuːnɪfɪ'keɪʃn] *n* réunification *f*.

reunion [,riː'juːnjən] *n* réunion *f*.

reunite [,riːjuː'naɪt] *vt*: **to be ~d with sb** retrouver qqn.

rev [rev] *inf* ◆ *n* (*abbr of* revolution) tour *m*. ◆ *vt*: **to ~ the engine (up)** emballer le moteur. ◆ *vi*: **to ~ (up)** s'emballer.

revamp [,riː'væmp] *vt inf* (*system, department*) réorganiser; (*house*) retaper.

reveal [rɪ'viːl] *vt* révéler.

revealing [rɪ'viːlɪŋ] *adj* **1.** (*clothes - lowcut*) décolleté(e); (- *transparent*) qui laisse deviner le corps. **2.** (*comment*) révélateur(trice).

reveille [Br rɪ'vælɪ, Am 'revəlɪ] *n* réveil *m*.

revel ['revl] *vi*: **to ~ in sthg** se délecter de qqch.

revelation [,revə'leɪʃn] *n* révélation *f*.

revenge [rɪ'vendʒ] ◆ *n* vengeance *f*; **to take ~ (on sb)** se venger (de qqn). ◆ *vt* venger; **to ~ o.s. on sb** se venger de qqn.

revenue ['revənjuː] *n* revenu *m*.

reverberate [rɪ'vɜːbəreɪt] *vi* retentir, se répercuter; *fig* avoir des répercussions.

reverberations [rɪ,vɜːbə'reɪʃnz] *npl* réverbérations *fpl*; *fig* répercussions *fpl*.

revere [rɪ'vɪəʳ] *vt* révérer, vénérer.

reverence ['revərəns] *n* révérence *f*, vénération *f*.

Reverend ['revərənd] *n* révérend *m*.

reverie ['revərɪ] *n* rêverie *f*.

reversal [rɪ'vɜːsl] *n* **1.** (*of policy, decision*) revirement *m*. **2.** (*ill fortune*) revers *m* de fortune.

reverse [rɪ'vɜːs] ◆ *adj* (*order, process*) inverse. ◆ *n* **1.** (AUT): **~ (gear)** marche *f* arrière. **2.** (*opposite*): **the ~** le contraire.

3. (back): **the ~** (of paper) le verso, le dos; (of coin) le revers. ◆ vt **1.** (order, positions) inverser; (decision, trend) renverser. **2.** (turn over) retourner. **3.** Br (TELEC): **to ~ the charges** téléphoner en PCV. ◆ vi (AUT) faire marche arrière.

reverse-charge call n Br appel m en PCV.

reversing light [rɪ'vɜːsɪŋ-] n Br feu m de marche arrière.

revert [rɪ'vɜːt] vi: **to ~ to** retourner à.

review [rɪ'vjuː] ◆ n **1.** (of salary, spending) révision f; (of situation) examen m. **2.** (of book, play etc) critique f, compte rendu m. ◆ vt **1.** (salary) réviser; (situation) examiner. **2.** (book, play etc) faire la critique de. **3.** (troops) passer en revue. **4.** Am (study again) réviser.

reviewer [rɪ'vjuːəʳ] n critique mf.

revile [rɪ'vaɪl] vt injurier.

revise [rɪ'vaɪz] ◆ vt **1.** (reconsider) modifier. **2.** (rewrite) corriger. **3.** Br (study again) réviser. ◆ vi Br: **to ~ (for)** réviser (pour).

revision [rɪ'vɪʒn] n révision f.

revitalize, -ise [ˌriː'vaɪtəlaɪz] vt revitaliser.

revival [rɪ'vaɪvl] n (of economy, trade) reprise f; (of interest) regain m.

revive [rɪ'vaɪv] ◆ vt **1.** (person) ranimer. **2.** fig (economy) relancer; (interest) faire renaître; (tradition) rétablir; (musical, play) reprendre; (memories) ranimer, raviver. ◆ vi **1.** (person) reprendre connaissance. **2.** fig (economy) repartir, reprendre; (hopes) renaître.

revolt [rɪ'vəʊlt] ◆ n révolte f. ◆ vt révolter, dégoûter. ◆ vi se révolter.

revolting [rɪ'vəʊltɪŋ] adj dégoûtant(e); (smell) infect(e).

revolution [ˌrevə'luːʃn] n **1.** (gen) révolution f. **2.** (TECH) tour m, révolution f.

revolutionary [ˌrevə'luːʃnəri] ◆ adj révolutionnaire. ◆ n révolutionnaire mf.

revolve [rɪ'vɒlv] vi: **to ~ (around)** tourner (autour de).

revolver [rɪ'vɒlvəʳ] n revolver m.

revolving [rɪ'vɒlvɪŋ] adj tournant(e); (chair) pivotant(e).

revolving door n tambour m.

revue [rɪ'vjuː] n revue f.

revulsion [rɪ'vʌlʃn] n répugnance f.

reward [rɪ'wɔːd] ◆ n récompense f. ◆ vt: **to ~ sb (for/with sthg)** récompenser qqn (de/par qqch).

rewarding [rɪ'wɔːdɪŋ] adj (job) qui donne de grandes satisfactions.

rewind [ˌriː'waɪnd] (pt & pp rewound) vt (tape) rembobiner.

rewire [ˌriː'waɪəʳ] vt (house) refaire l'installation électrique de.

reword [ˌriː'wɜːd] vt reformuler.

rewound [ˌriː'waʊnd] pt & pp → rewind.

rewrite [ˌriː'raɪt] (pt rewrote [ˌriː'rəʊt], pp rewritten [ˌriː'rɪtn]) vt récrire.

Reykjavik ['rekjəvɪk] n Reykjavik.

rhapsody ['ræpsədɪ] n rhapsodie f; **to go into rhapsodies about sthg** s'extasier sur qqch.

rhetoric ['retərɪk] n rhétorique f.

rhetorical question [rɪ'tɒrɪkl-] n question f pour la forme.

rheumatism ['ruːmətɪzm] n (U) rhumatisme m.

Rhine [raɪn] n: **the ~** le Rhin.

rhino ['raɪnəʊ] (pl inv OR -s), **rhinoceros** [raɪ'nɒsərəs] (pl inv OR -es) n rhinocéros m.

rhododendron [ˌrəʊdə'dendrən] n rhododendron m.

Rhône [rəʊn] n: **the (River) ~** le Rhône.

rhubarb ['ruːbɑːb] n rhubarbe f.

rhyme [raɪm] ◆ n **1.** (word, technique) rime f. **2.** (poem) poème m. ◆ vi: **to ~ (with)** rimer (avec).

rhythm ['rɪðm] n rythme m.

rib [rɪb] n **1.** (ANAT) côte f. **2.** (of umbrella) baleine f; (of structure) membrure f.

ribbed [rɪbd] adj (jumper, fabric) à côtes.

ribbon ['rɪbən] n ruban m.

rice [raɪs] n riz m.

rice pudding n riz m au lait.

rich [rɪtʃ] ◆ adj riche; (clothes, fabrics) somptueux(euse); **to be ~ in** être riche en. ◆ npl: **the ~** les riches mpl. ▶ **riches** npl richesses fpl, richesse f.

richly ['rɪtʃlɪ] adv **1.** (rewarded) largement; (provided) très bien. **2.** (sumptuously) richement.

richness ['rɪtʃnɪs] n (U) richesse f.

rickets ['rɪkɪts] n (U) rachitisme m.

rickety ['rɪkətɪ] adj branlant(e).

rickshaw ['rɪkʃɔː] n pousse-pousse m inv.

ricochet ['rɪkəʃeɪ] (pt & pp -ed OR -ted, cont -ing OR -ting) ◆ n ricochet m. ◆ vi: **to ~ (off)** ricocher (sur).

rid [rɪd] (pt rid OR -ded, pp rid) vt: **to ~ sb/sthg of** débarrasser qqn/qqch de; **to get ~ of** se débarrasser de.

ridden ['rɪdn] pp → ride.

riddle ['rɪdl] n énigme f.

riddled ['rɪdld] adj: **to be ~ with** être criblé(e) de.

ride [raɪd] (pt **rode**, pp **ridden**) ◆ n promenade f, tour m; **to go for a ~** (on horse) faire une promenade à cheval; (on bike) faire une promenade à vélo; (in car) faire un tour en voiture; **to take sb for a ~** inf fig faire marcher qqn. ◆ vt 1. (travel on): **to ~ a horse/a bicycle** monter à cheval/à bicyclette. 2. Am (travel in - bus, train, elevator) prendre. 3. (distance) parcourir, faire. ◆ vi (on horseback) monter à cheval, faire du cheval; (on bicycle) faire de la bicyclette OR du vélo; **to ~ in a car/bus** aller en voiture/bus.

rider [ˈraɪdər] n (of horse) cavalier m, -ère f; (of bicycle) cycliste mf; (of motorbike) motocycliste mf.

ridge [rɪdʒ] n 1. (of mountain, roof) crête f, arête f. 2. (on surface) strie f.

ridicule [ˈrɪdɪkjuːl] ◆ n ridicule m. ◆ vt ridiculiser.

ridiculous [rɪˈdɪkjʊləs] adj ridicule.

riding [ˈraɪdɪŋ] n équitation f.

riding school n école f d'équitation.

rife [raɪf] adj répandu(e).

riffraff [ˈrɪfræf] n racaille f.

rifle [ˈraɪfl] ◆ n fusil m. ◆ vt (drawer, bag) vider.

rifle range n (indoor) stand m de tir; (outdoor) champ m de tir.

rift [rɪft] n 1. (GEOL) fissure f. 2. (quarrel) désaccord m.

rig [rɪg] ◆ n: (oil) ~ (on land) derrick m; (at sea) plate-forme f de forage. ◆ vt (match, election) truquer. ▶ **rig up** vt sep installer avec les moyens du bord.

rigging [ˈrɪgɪŋ] n (of ship) gréement m.

right [raɪt] ◆ adj 1. (correct - answer, time) juste, exact(e); (- decision, direction, idea) bon (bonne); **to be ~ (about)** avoir raison (au sujet de). 2. (morally correct) bien (inv); **to be ~ to do sthg** avoir raison de faire qqch. 3. (appropriate) qui convient. 4. (not left) droit(e). 5. Br inf (complete) véritable. ◆ n 1. (U) (moral correctness) bien m; **to be in the ~** avoir raison. 2. (entitlement, claim) droit m; **by ~s** en toute justice. 3. (not left) droite f. ◆ adv 1. (correctly) correctement. 2. (not left) à droite. 3. (emphatic use): ~ **down/ up** tout en bas/en haut; ~ **here** ici (même); ~ **in the middle** en plein milieu; **go ~ to the end of the street** allez tout au bout de la rue; ~ **now** tout de suite; ~ **away** immédiatement. ◆ vt 1. (injustice, wrong) réparer. 2. (ship) redresser. ◆ excl bon! ▶ **Right** n (POL): **the Right** la droite.

right angle n angle m droit; **to be at**

~**s (to)** faire un angle droit (avec).

righteous [ˈraɪtʃəs] adj (person) droit(e); (indignation) justifié(e).

rightful [ˈraɪtfʊl] adj légitime.

right-hand adj de droite; ~ **side** droite f, côté m droit.

right-hand drive adj avec conduite à droite.

right-handed [-ˈhændɪd] adj (person) droitier(ère).

right-hand man n bras m droit.

rightly [ˈraɪtlɪ] adv 1. (answer, believe) correctement. 2. (behave) bien. 3. (angry, worried etc) à juste titre.

right of way n 1. (AUT) priorité f. 2. (access) droit m de passage.

right-on adj inf branché(e).

right wing n: **the ~** la droite. ▶ **right-wing** adj de droite.

rigid [ˈrɪdʒɪd] adj 1. (gen) rigide. 2. (harsh) strict(e).

rigmarole [ˈrɪgmərəʊl] n pej 1. (process) comédie f. 2. (story) galimatias m.

rigor Am = **rigour**.

rigorous [ˈrɪgərəs] adj rigoureux(euse).

rigour Br, **rigor** Am [ˈrɪgər] n rigueur f.

rile [raɪl] vt agacer.

rim [rɪm] n (of container) bord m; (of wheel) jante f; (of spectacles) monture f.

rind [raɪnd] n (of fruit) peau f; (of cheese) croûte f; (of bacon) couenne f.

ring [rɪŋ] (pt rang, pp vt senses 1 & 2 & vi **rung**, pt & pp vt sense 3 only **ringed**) ◆ n 1. (telephone call): **to give sb a ~** donner OR passer un coup de téléphone à qqn. 2. (sound of bell) sonnerie f. 3. (circular object) anneau m; (on finger) bague f; (for napkin) rond m. 4. (of people, trees etc) cercle m. 5. (for boxing) ring m. 6. (of criminals, spies) réseau m. ◆ vt 1. Br (make phone call to) téléphoner à, appeler. 2. (bell) (faire) sonner; **to ~ the doorbell** sonner à la porte. 3. (draw a circle round, surround) entourer. ◆ vi 1. Br (make phone call) téléphoner. 2. (bell, telephone, person) sonner; **to ~ for sb** sonner qqn. 3. (resound): **to ~ with** résonner de. ▶ **ring back** vt sep & vi Br rappeler. ▶ **ring off** vi Br raccrocher. ▶ **ring up** vt sep Br téléphoner à, appeler.

ring binder n classeur m à anneaux.

ringing [ˈrɪŋɪŋ] n (of bell) sonnerie f; (in ears) tintement m.

ringing tone n sonnerie f.

ringleader [ˈrɪŋˌliːdər] n chef m.

ringlet [ˈrɪŋlɪt] n anglaise f.

ring road n Br (route f) périphérique m.

rink [rɪŋk] n (for ice skating) patinoire f; (for roller-skating) skating m.

rinse [rɪns] vt rincer; **to ~ one's mouth out** se rincer la bouche.

riot ['raɪət] ◆ n émeute f; **to run ~** se déchaîner. ◆ vi participer à une émeute.

rioter ['raɪətəʳ] n émeutier m, -ère f.

riotous ['raɪətəs] adj (crowd) tapageur (euse); (behaviour) séditieux(euse); (party) bruyant(e).

riot police npl = CRS mpl.

rip [rɪp] ◆ n déchirure f, accroc m. ◆ vt 1. (tear) déchirer. 2. (remove violently) arracher. ◆ vi se déchirer.

RIP (abbr of **rest in peace**) qu'il/elle repose en paix.

ripe [raɪp] adj mûr(e).

ripen ['raɪpn] vt & vi mûrir.

rip-off n inf: **that's a ~!** c'est de l'escroquerie OR de l'arnaque!

ripple ['rɪpl] ◆ n ondulation f, ride f. ◆ vt rider.

rise [raɪz] (pt **rose**, pp **risen** ['rɪzn]) ◆ n 1. Br (increase) augmentation f, hausse f; (in temperature) élévation f, hausse. 2. Br (increase in salary) augmentation f (de salaire). 3. (to power, fame) ascension f. 4. (slope) côte f, pente f. 5. phr: **to give ~ to** donner lieu à. ◆ vi 1. (move upwards) s'élever, monter; **to ~ to power** arriver au pouvoir; **to ~ to a challenge/to the occasion** se montrer à la hauteur d'un défi/de la situation. 2. (from chair, bed) se lever. 3. (increase - gen) monter, augmenter; (- voice, level) s'élever. 4. (rebel) se soulever.

rising ['raɪzɪŋ] ◆ adj 1. (ground, tide) montant(e). 2. (prices, inflation, temperature) en hausse. 3. (star, politician etc) à l'avenir prometteur. ◆ n (revolt) soulèvement m.

risk [rɪsk] ◆ n risque m, danger m; **at one's own ~** à ses risques et périls; **to run the ~ of doing sthg** courir le risque de faire qqch; **to take a ~** prendre un risque; **at ~** en danger. ◆ vt (health, life etc) risquer; **to ~ doing sthg** courir le risque de faire qqch.

risky ['rɪskɪ] adj risqué(e).

risqué ['riːskeɪ] adj risqué(e), osé(e).

rissole ['rɪsəʊl] n Br rissole f.

rite [raɪt] n rite m.

ritual ['rɪtʃʊəl] ◆ adj rituel(elle). ◆ n rituel m.

rival ['raɪvl] ◆ adj rival(e), concurrent(e). ◆ n rival m, -e f. ◆ vt rivaliser avec.

rivalry ['raɪvlrɪ] n rivalité f.

river ['rɪvəʳ] n rivière f, fleuve m.

river bank n berge f, rive f.

riverbed ['rɪvəbed] n lit m (de rivière OR de fleuve).

riverside ['rɪvəsaɪd] n: **the ~** le bord de la rivière OR du fleuve.

rivet ['rɪvɪt] ◆ n rivet m. ◆ vt 1. (fasten with rivets) river, riveter. 2. fig (fascinate): **to be ~ed by** être fasciné(e) par.

Riviera [ˌrɪvɪ'eərə] n: **the French ~** la Côte d'Azur; **the Italian ~** la Riviera italienne.

road [rəʊd] n route f; (small) chemin m; (in town) rue f; **by ~** par la route; **on the ~ to** fig sur le chemin de.

roadblock ['rəʊdblɒk] n barrage m routier.

road hog n inf pej chauffard m.

road map n carte f routière.

road rage n accès de colère de la part d'un automobiliste, se traduisant parfois par un acte de violence.

road safety n sécurité f routière.

roadside ['rəʊdsaɪd] n: **the ~** le bord de la route.

road sign n panneau m routier OR de signalisation.

road tax n = vignette f.

roadway ['rəʊdweɪ] n chaussée f.

road works [-wɜːks] npl travaux mpl (de réfection des routes).

roadworthy ['rəʊdˌwɜːðɪ] adj en bon état de marche.

roam [rəʊm] ◆ vt errer dans. ◆ vi errer.

roar [rɔːʳ] ◆ vi (person, lion) rugir; (wind) hurler; (car) gronder; (plane) vrombir; **to ~ with laughter** se tordre de rire. ◆ vt hurler. ◆ n (of person, lion) rugissement m; (of traffic) grondement m; (of plane, engine) vrombissement m.

roaring ['rɔːrɪŋ] adj: **a ~ fire** une belle flambée; **~ drunk** complètement saoul(e); **to do a ~ trade** faire des affaires en or.

roast [rəʊst] ◆ adj rôti(e). ◆ n rôti m. ◆ vt 1. (meat, potatoes) rôtir. 2. (coffee, nuts etc) griller.

roast beef n rôti m de bœuf, rosbif m.

rob [rɒb] vt (person) voler; (bank) dévaliser; **to ~ sb of sthg** (money, goods) voler OR dérober qqch à qqn; (opportunity, glory) enlever qqch à qqn.

robber ['rɒbəʳ] n voleur m, -euse f.

robbery ['rɒbərɪ] n vol m.

robe [rəʊb] n 1. (gen) robe f. 2. Am (dressing gown) peignoir m.

robin ['rɒbɪn] n rouge-gorge m.

robot ['rəʊbɒt] n robot m.

robust [rəʊ'bʌst] adj robuste.

rock [rɒk] ♦ n 1. (U) (substance) roche f. 2. (boulder) rocher m. 3. Am (pebble) caillou m. 4. (music) rock m. 5. Br (sweet) sucre m d'orge. ♦ comp (music, band) de rock. ♦ vt 1. (baby) bercer; (cradle, boat) balancer. 2. (shock) secouer. ♦ vi (se) balancer. ▶ **on the rocks** adv 1. (drink) avec de la glace OR des glaçons. 2. (marriage, relationship) près de la rupture.

rock and roll n rock m, rock and roll m.

rock bottom n: at ~ au plus bas; **to hit** ~ toucher le fond. ▶ **rock-bottom** adj (price) sacrifié(e).

rockery ['rɒkərɪ] n rocaille f.

rocket ['rɒkɪt] ♦ n 1. (gen) fusée f. 2. (MIL) fusée f, roquette f. ♦ vi monter en flèche.

rocket launcher [-,lɔːntʃər] n lance-fusées m inv, lance-roquettes m inv.

rocking chair ['rɒkɪŋ-] n fauteuil m à bascule, rocking-chair m.

rocking horse ['rɒkɪŋ-] n cheval m à bascule.

rock'n'roll [,rɒkən'rəʊl] = **rock and roll**.

rocky ['rɒkɪ] adj 1. (ground, road) rocailleux(euse), caillouteux(euse). 2. fig (economy, marriage) précaire.

Rocky Mountains npl: **the** ~ les montagnes fpl Rocheuses.

rod [rɒd] n (metal) tige f; (wooden) baguette f; (fishing) ~ canne f à pêche.

rode [rəʊd] pt → **ride**.

rodent ['rəʊdənt] n rongeur m.

roe [rəʊ] n (U) œufs mpl de poisson.

roe deer n chevreuil m.

rogue [rəʊg] n 1. (likeable rascal) coquin m. 2. dated (dishonest person) filou m.

role [rəʊl] n rôle m.

role play n jeu m de rôle.

roll [rəʊl] ♦ n 1. (of material, paper etc) rouleau m. 2. (of bread) petit pain m. 3. (list) liste f. 4. (of drums, thunder) roulement m. ♦ vt rouler; (log, ball etc) faire rouler. ♦ vi rouler. ▶ **roll about**, **roll around** vi (person) se rouler; (object) rouler çà et là. ▶ **roll over** vi se retourner. ▶ **roll up** ♦ vt sep 1. (carpet, paper etc) rouler. 2. (sleeves) retrousser. ♦ vi inf (arrive) s'amener, se pointer.

roll call n appel m.

roller ['rəʊlər] n rouleau m.

roller coaster n montagnes fpl russes.

roller skate n patin m à roulettes.

rolling ['rəʊlɪŋ] adj 1. (hills) onduleux (euse). 2. phr: **to be** ~ **in it** inf rouler sur l'or.

rolling pin n rouleau m à pâtisserie.

rolling stock n matériel m roulant.

roll-on adj (deodorant) à bille.

ROM [rɒm] (abbr of read only memory) n ROM f.

Roman ['rəʊmən] ♦ adj romain(e). ♦ n Romain m, -e f.

Roman Catholic ♦ adj catholique. ♦ n catholique mf.

romance [rəʊ'mæns] n 1. (U) (romantic quality) charme m. 2. (love affair) idylle f. 3. (book) roman m (d'amour).

Romania [ruː'meɪnjə] n Roumanie f.

Romanian [ruː'meɪnjən] ♦ adj roumain(e). ♦ n 1. (person) Roumain m, -e f. 2. (language) roumain m.

Roman numerals npl chiffres mpl romains.

romantic [rəʊ'mæntɪk] adj romantique.

Rome [rəʊm] n Rome.

romp [rɒmp] ♦ n ébats mpl. ♦ vi s'ébattre.

rompers ['rɒmpəz] npl, **romper suit** ['rɒmpər-] n barboteuse f.

roof [ruːf] n toit m; (of cave, tunnel) plafond m; **the** ~ **of the mouth** la voûte du palais; **to go through** OR **hit the** ~ fig exploser.

roofing ['ruːfɪŋ] n toiture f.

roof rack n galerie f.

rooftop ['ruːftɒp] n toit m.

rook [rʊk] n 1. (bird) freux m. 2. (chess piece) tour f.

rookie ['rʊkɪ] n Am inf bleu m.

room [ruːm, rʊm] n 1. (in building) pièce f. 2. (bedroom) chambre f. 3. (U) (space) place f.

rooming house ['ruːmɪŋ-] n Am maison f de rapport.

roommate ['ruːmeɪt] n camarade mf de chambre.

room service n service m dans les chambres.

roomy ['ruːmɪ] adj spacieux(euse).

roost [ruːst] ♦ n perchoir m, juchoir m. ♦ vi se percher, se jucher.

rooster ['ruːstər] n coq m.

root [ruːt] n racine f; fig (of problem) origine f; **to take** ~ lit & fig prendre racine. ♦ vi: **to** ~ **through** fouiller dans. ▶ **roots** npl racines fpl. ▶ **root for** vt fus Am inf encourager. ▶ **root out** vt sep (eradicate) extirper.

rope [rəup] ◆ *n* corde *f*; **to know the ~s** connaître son affaire, être au courant. ◆ *vt* corder; (*climbers*) encorder. ▶ **rope in** *vt sep inf fig* enrôler.

rosary ['rəuzərɪ] *n* rosaire *m*.

rose [rəuz] ◆ *pt* → **rise**. ◆ *adj* (*pink*) rose. ◆ *n* (*flower*) rose *f*.

rosé ['rəuzeɪ] *n* rosé *m*.

rosebud ['rəuzbʌd] *n* bouton *m* de rose.

rose bush *n* rosier *m*.

rosemary ['rəuzmərɪ] *n* romarin *m*.

rosette [rəu'zet] *n* rosette *f*.

roster ['rɒstər] *n* liste *f*, tableau *m*.

rostrum ['rɒstrəm] (*pl* **-trums** OR **-tra** [-trə]) *n* tribune *f*.

rosy ['rəuzɪ] *adj* rose.

rot [rɒt] ◆ *n* (U) **1.** (*decay*) pourriture *f*. **2.** Br dated (*nonsense*) bêtises *fpl*, balivernes *fpl*. ◆ *vt* & *vi* pourrir.

rota ['rəutə] *n* liste *f*, tableau *m*.

rotary ['rəutərɪ] ◆ *adj* rotatif(ive). ◆ *n* Am (*roundabout*) rond-point *m*.

rotate [rəu'teɪt] ◆ *vt* (*turn*) faire tourner. ◆ *vi* (*turn*) tourner.

rotation [rəu'teɪʃn] *n* (*turning movement*) rotation *f*.

rote [rəut] *n*: **by ~** de façon machinale.

rotten ['rɒtn] *adj* **1.** (*decayed*) pourri(e). **2.** inf (*bad*) moche. **3.** inf (*unwell*): **to feel ~** se sentir mal fichu(e).

rouge [ru:ʒ] *n* rouge *m* à joues.

rough [rʌf] ◆ *adj* **1.** (*not smooth - surface*) rugueux(euse), rêche; (- *road*) accidenté(e); (- *sea*) agité(e), houleux(euse); (- *crossing*) mauvais(e). **2.** (*person, treatment*) brutal(e); (*manners, conditions*) rude; (*area*) mal fréquenté(e). **3.** (*guess*) approximatif(ive); ~ **copy**, ~ **draft** brouillon *m*; ~ **sketch** ébauche *f*. **4.** (*harsh - voice, wine*) âpre; (- *life*) dur(e); **to have a ~ time** en baver. ◆ *adv*: **to sleep ~** coucher à la dure. ◆ *n* **1.** (GOLF) rough *m*. **2.** (*undetailed form*): **in ~** au brouillon. ◆ *vt phr*: **to ~ it** vivre à la dure.

roughage ['rʌfɪdʒ] *n* (U) fibres *fpl* alimentaires.

rough and ready *adj* rudimentaire.

roughcast ['rʌfkɑ:st] *n* crépi *m*.

roughen ['rʌfn] *vt* rendre rugueux(euse) OR rêche.

roughly ['rʌflɪ] *adv* **1.** (*approximately*) approximativement. **2.** (*handle, treat*) brutalement. **3.** (*made*) grossièrement.

roulette [ru:'let] *n* roulette *f*.

round [raund] ◆ *adj* rond(e). ◆ *prep* autour de; ~ **here** par ici; **all ~ the coun-** try dans tout le pays; **just ~ the corner** au coin de la rue; *fig* tout près; **to go ~ sthg** (*obstacle*) contourner qqch; **to go ~ a museum** visiter un musée. ◆ *adv* **1.** (*surrounding*): **all ~** tout autour. **2.** (*near*): ~ **about** dans le coin. **3.** (*in measurements*): **10 metres ~** 10 mètres de diamètre. **4.** (*to other side*): **to go ~** faire le tour; **to turn ~** se retourner; **to look ~** se retourner (pour regarder). **5.** (*at or to nearby place*): **come ~ and see us** venez OR passez nous voir; **he's ~ at her house** il est chez elle. **6.** (*approximately*): ~ **(about)** vers, environ. ◆ *n* **1.** (*of talks etc*) série *f*; **a ~ of applause** une salve d'applaudissements. **2.** (*of competition*) manche *f*. **3.** (*of doctor*) visites *fpl*; (*of postman, milkman*) tournée *f*. **4.** (*of ammunition*) cartouche *f*. **5.** (*of drinks*) tournée *f*. **6.** (BOXING) reprise *f*, round *m*. **7.** (GOLF) partie *f*. ◆ *vt* (*corner*) tourner; (*bend*) prendre. ▶ **rounds** *npl* (*of doctor*) visites *fpl*; **to do** OR **go the ~s** (*story, joke*) circuler; (*illness*) faire des ravages. ▶ **round off** *vt sep* terminer, conclure. ▶ **round up** *vt sep* **1.** (*gather together*) rassembler. **2.** (MATH) arrondir.

roundabout ['raundəbaut] ◆ *adj* détourné(e). ◆ *n* Br **1.** (*on road*) rond-point *m*. **2.** (*at fairground*) manège *m*.

rounders ['raundəz] *n* Br sorte de baseball.

roundly ['raundlɪ] *adv* (*beaten*) complètement; (*condemned etc*) franchement, carrément.

round-shouldered [-'ʃəuldəd] *adj* voûté(e).

round trip *n* aller et retour *m*.

roundup ['raundʌp] *n* (*summary*) résumé *m*.

rouse [rauz] *vt* **1.** (*wake up*) réveiller. **2.** (*impel*): **to ~ o.s. to do sthg** se forcer à faire qqch; **to ~ sb to action** pousser OR inciter qqn à agir. **3.** (*emotions*) susciter, provoquer.

rousing ['rauzɪŋ] *adj* (*speech*) vibrant(e), passionné(e); (*welcome*) enthousiaste.

rout [raut] ◆ *n* déroute *f*. ◆ *vt* mettre en déroute.

route [ru:t] ◆ *n* **1.** (*gen*) itinéraire *m*. **2.** *fig* (*way*) chemin *m*, voie *f*. ◆ *vt* (*goods*) acheminer.

route map *n* (*for journey*) croquis *m* d'itinéraire; (*for buses, trains*) carte *f* du réseau.

routine [ru:'ti:n] ◆ *adj* **1.** (*normal*) habituel(elle), de routine. **2.** *pej* (*uninteresting*) de routine. ◆ *n* routine *f*.

roving ['rəʊvɪŋ] adj itinérant(e).

row¹ [rəʊ] ◆ n 1. (line) rangée f; (of seats) rang m. 2. fig (of defeats, victories) série f; in a ~ d'affilée, de suite. ◆ vt (boat) faire aller à la rame; (person) transporter en canot OR bateau. ◆ vi ramer.

row² [raʊ] ◆ n 1. (quarrel) dispute f, querelle f. 2. inf (noise) vacarme m, raffut m. ◆ vi (quarrel) se disputer, se quereller.

rowboat ['rəʊbəʊt] n Am canot m.

rowdy ['raʊdɪ] adj chahuteur(euse), tapageur(euse).

rowing ['rəʊɪŋ] n (SPORT) aviron m.

rowing boat n Br canot m.

royal ['rɔɪəl] ◆ adj royal(e). ◆ n inf membre m de la famille royale.

Royal Air Force n: the ~ l'armée f de l'air britannique.

royal family n famille f royale.

Royal Mail n Br: the ~ ≃ la Poste.

Royal Navy n: the ~ la marine de guerre britannique.

royalty ['rɔɪəltɪ] n royauté f. ▶ **royalties** npl droits mpl d'auteur.

rpm npl (abbr of revolutions per minute) tours mpl par minute, tr/min.

RSPCA (abbr of Royal Society for the Prevention of Cruelty to Animals) n société britannique protectrice des animaux, ≃ SPA f.

RSVP (abbr of répondez s'il vous plaît) RSVP.

Rt Hon (abbr of Right Honourable) expression utilisée pour des titres nobiliaires.

rub [rʌb] ◆ vt frotter; to ~ sthg in (cream etc) faire pénétrer qqch (en frottant); to ~ one's eyes/hands se frotter les yeux/les mains; to ~ sb up the wrong way Br, to ~ sb the wrong way Am fig prendre qqn à rebrousse-poil. ◆ vi frotter. ▶ **rub off on** vt fus (subj: quality) déteindre sur. ▶ **rub out** vt sep (erase) effacer.

rubber ['rʌbər] ◆ adj en caoutchouc. ◆ n 1. (substance) caoutchouc m. 2. Br (eraser) gomme f. 3. Am inf (condom) préservatif m. 4. (in bridge) robre m, rob m.

rubber band n élastique m.

rubber plant n caoutchouc m.

rubber stamp n tampon m. ▶ **rubber-stamp** vt fig approuver sans discussion.

rubbish ['rʌbɪʃ] ◆ n (U) 1. (refuse) détritus mpl, ordures fpl. 2. inf fig (worthless objects) camelote f; the play was ~ la

pièce était nulle. 3. inf (nonsense) bêtises fpl, inepties fpl. ◆ vt inf débiner.

rubbish bin n Br poubelle f.

rubbish dump n Br dépotoir m.

rubble ['rʌbl] n (U) décombres mpl.

ruby ['ru:bɪ] n rubis m.

rucksack ['rʌksæk] n sac m à dos.

ructions ['rʌkʃnz] npl inf grabuge m.

rudder ['rʌdər] n gouvernail m.

ruddy ['rʌdɪ] adj 1. (complexion, face) coloré(e). 2. Br inf dated (damned) sacré(e).

rude [ru:d] adj 1. (impolite - gen) impoli(e); (- word) grossier(ère); (- noise) incongru(e). 2. (sudden): it was a ~ awakening le réveil fut pénible.

rudimentary [,ru:dɪ'mentərɪ] adj rudimentaire.

rueful ['ru:fʊl] adj triste.

ruffian ['rʌfjən] n voyou m.

ruffle ['rʌfl] vt 1. (hair) ébouriffer; (water) troubler. 2. (person) froisser; (composure) faire perdre.

rug [rʌg] n 1. (carpet) tapis m. 2. (blanket) couverture f.

rugby ['rʌgbɪ] n rugby m.

rugged ['rʌgɪd] adj 1. (landscape) accidenté(e); (features) rude. 2. (vehicle etc) robuste.

ruin ['ru:ɪn] ◆ n ruine f. ◆ vt ruiner; (clothes, shoes) abîmer. ▶ **in ruin(s)** adv lit & fig en ruine.

rule [ru:l] ◆ n 1. (gen) règle f; as a ~ en règle générale. 2. (regulation) règlement m. 3. (U) (control) autorité f. ◆ vt 1. (control) dominer. 2. (govern) gouverner. 3. (decide): to ~ (that) ... décider que ... ◆ vi 1. (give decision - gen) décider; (- JUR) statuer. 2. fml (be paramount) prévaloir. 3. (king, queen) régner; (POL) gouverner. ▶ **rule out** vt sep exclure, écarter.

ruled [ru:ld] adj (paper) réglé(e).

ruler ['ru:lər] n 1. (for measurement) règle f. 2. (leader) chef m d'État.

ruling ['ru:lɪŋ] ◆ adj au pouvoir. ◆ n décision f.

rum [rʌm] n rhum m.

Rumania [ru:'meɪnjə] = Romania.

Rumanian [ru:'meɪnjən] = Romanian.

rumble ['rʌmbl] ◆ n (of thunder, traffic) grondement m; (in stomach) gargouillement m. ◆ vi (thunder, traffic) gronder; (stomach) gargouiller.

rummage ['rʌmɪdʒ] vi fouiller.

rumour Br, **rumor** Am ['ru:mər] n rumeur f.

rumoured Br, **rumored** Am ['ru:məd] adj: he is ~ to be very wealthy le bruit court OR on dit qu'il est très riche.

rump [rʌmp] n **1.** (of animal) croupe f. **2.** inf (of person) derrière m.

rump steak n romsteck m.

rumpus ['rʌmpəs] n inf chahut m.

run [rʌn] (pt ran, pp run) ◆ n **1.** (on foot) course f; **to go for a ~** faire un petit peu de course à pied; **on the ~** en fuite, en cavale. **2.** (in car - for pleasure) tour m; (- journey) trajet m. **3.** (series) suite f, série f; **a ~ of bad luck** une période de déveine; **in the short/long ~** à court/long terme. **4.** (THEATRE): **to have a long ~** tenir longtemps l'affiche. **5.** (great demand): **~ on** ruée f sur. **6.** (in tights) échelle f. **7.** (in cricket, baseball) point m. **8.** (track - for skiing, bobsleigh) piste f. ◆ vt **1.** (race, distance) courir. **2.** (manage - business) diriger; (- shop, hotel) tenir; (- course) organiser. **3.** (operate) faire marcher. **4.** (car) avoir, entretenir. **5.** (water, bath) faire couler. **6.** (publish) publier. **7.** inf (drive): **can you ~ me to the station?** tu peux m'amener OR me conduire à la gare? **8.** (move): **to ~ sthg along/over sthg** passer qqch le long de/sur qqch. ◆ vi **1.** (on foot) courir. **2.** (pass - road, river, pipe) passer; **to ~ through sthg** traverser qqch. **3.** Am (in election): **to ~ (for)** être candidat (à). **4.** (operate - machine, factory) marcher; (- engine) tourner; **everything is running smoothly** tout va comme sur des roulettes, tout va bien; **to ~ on sthg** marcher à qqch; **to ~ off sthg** marcher sur qqch. **5.** (bus, train) faire le service; **trains ~ every hour** il y a un train toutes les heures. **6.** (flow) couler; **my nose is running** j'ai le nez qui coule. **7.** (colour) déteindre; (ink) baver. **8.** (continue - contract, insurance policy) être valide; (- THEATRE) se jouer. ▶ **run away** vi (flee): **to ~ away (from)** s'enfuir (de); **to ~ away from home** faire une fugue. ▶ **run down** ◆ vt sep **1.** (in vehicle) renverser. **2.** (criticize) dénigrer. **3.** (production) restreindre; (industry) réduire l'activité de. ◆ vi (clock) s'arrêter; (battery) se décharger. ▶ **run into** vt fus **1.** (encounter - problem) se heurter à; (- person) tomber sur. **2.** (in vehicle) rentrer dans. ▶ **run off** ◆ vt sep (a copy) tirer. ◆ vi: **to ~ off (with)** s'enfuir (avec). ▶ **run out** vi **1.** (food, supplies) s'épuiser; **time is running out** il ne reste plus beaucoup de temps. **2.** (licence, contract) expirer. ▶ **run out of** vt fus manquer de; **to ~ out of petrol** tomber en panne d'essence, tomber

en panne sèche. ▶ **run over** vt sep renverser. ▶ **run through** vt fus **1.** (practise) répéter. **2.** (read through) parcourir. ▶ **run to** vt fus (amount to) monter à, s'élever à. ▶ **run up** vt fus (bill, debt) laisser accumuler. ▶ **run up against** vt fus se heurter à.

runaway ['rʌnəweɪ] ◆ adj (train, lorry) fou (folle); (horse) emballé(e); (victory) haut la main; (inflation) galopant(e). ◆ n fuyard m, fugitif m, -ive f.

rundown ['rʌndaʊn] n **1.** (report) bref résumé m. **2.** (of industry) réduction f délibérée. ▶ **run-down** adj **1.** (building) délabré(e). **2.** (person) épuisé(e).

rung [rʌŋ] ◆ pp → **ring**. ◆ n échelon m, barreau m.

runner ['rʌnər] n **1.** (athlete) coureur m, -euse f. **2.** (of guns, drugs) contrebandier m. **3.** (of sledge) patin m; (for car seat) glissière f; (for drawer) coulisseau m.

runner bean n Br haricot m à rames.

runner-up (pl runners-up) n second m, -e f.

running ['rʌnɪŋ] ◆ adj **1.** (argument, battle) continu(e). **2.** (consecutive): **three weeks ~** trois semaines de suite. **3.** (water) courant(e). ◆ n **1.** (U) (SPORT) course f; **to go ~** faire de la course. **2.** (management) direction f, administration f. **3.** (of machine) marche f, fonctionnement m. **4.** phr: **to be in the ~ (for)** avoir des chances de réussir (dans); **to be out of the ~ (for)** n'avoir aucune chance de réussir (dans).

runny ['rʌnɪ] adj **1.** (food) liquide. **2.** (nose) qui coule.

run-of-the-mill adj banal(e), ordinaire.

runt [rʌnt] n avorton m.

run-up n **1.** (preceding time): **in the ~ to sthg** dans la période qui précède qqch. **2.** (SPORT) course f d'élan.

runway ['rʌnweɪ] n piste f.

rupture ['rʌptʃər] n rupture f.

rural ['rʊərəl] adj rural(e).

ruse [ruːz] n ruse f.

rush [rʌʃ] ◆ n **1.** (hurry) hâte f. **2.** (surge) ruée f, bousculade f; **to make a ~ for sthg** se ruer OR se précipiter vers qqch; **a ~ of air** une bouffée d'air. **3.** (demand): **~ (on OR for)** ruée f (sur). ◆ vt **1.** (hurry - work) faire à la hâte; (- person) bousculer, (- meal) expédier. **2.** (send quickly) transporter OR envoyer d'urgence. **3.** (attack suddenly) prendre d'assaut. ◆ vi **1.** (hurry) se dépêcher; **to ~ into sthg** faire qqch sans réfléchir.

2. (*move quickly, suddenly*) se précipiter, se ruer; **the blood ~ed to her head** le sang lui monta à la tête. ▶ **rushes** *npl* (BOT) joncs *mpl*.

rush hour *n* heures *fpl* de pointe OR d'affluence.

rusk [rʌsk] *n* biscotte *f*.

Russia ['rʌʃə] *n* Russie *f*.

Russian ['rʌʃn] ♦ *adj* russe. ♦ *n* **1.** (*person*) Russe *mf*. **2.** (*language*) russe *m*.

rust [rʌst] ♦ *n* rouille *f*. ♦ *vi* se rouiller.

rustic ['rʌstɪk] *adj* rustique.

rustle ['rʌsl] ♦ *vt* **1.** (*paper*) froisser. **2.** Am (*cattle*) voler. ♦ *vi* (*leaves*) bruire; (*papers*) produire un froissement.

rusty ['rʌstɪ] *adj* lit & fig rouillé(e).

rut [rʌt] *n* ornière *f*; **to get into a ~** s'encroûter; **to be in a ~** être prisonnier de la routine.

ruthless ['ru:θlɪs] *adj* impitoyable.

RV *n* Am (*abbr of* **recreational vehicle**) camping-car *m*.

rye [raɪ] *n* (*grain*) seigle *m*.

rye bread *n* pain *m* de seigle.

S

s (*pl* **ss** OR **s's**), **S** (*pl* **Ss** OR **S's**) [es] *n* (*letter*) s *m inv*, S *m inv*. ▶ **S** (*abbr of* **south**) S.

Sabbath ['sæbəθ] *n*: **the ~** le sabbat.

sabbatical [sə'bætɪkl] *n* année *f* sabbatique.

sabotage ['sæbətɑ:ʒ] ♦ *n* sabotage *m*. ♦ *vt* saboter.

saccharin(e) ['sækərɪn] *n* saccharine *f*.

sachet ['sæʃeɪ] *n* sachet *m*.

sack [sæk] ♦ *n* **1.** (*bag*) sac *m*. **2.** Br inf (*dismissal*): **to get** OR **be given the ~** être renvoyé(e), se faire virer. ♦ *vt* Br inf (*dismiss*) renvoyer.

sacking ['sækɪŋ] *n* (*fabric*) toile *f* à sac.

sacred ['seɪkrɪd] *adj* sacré(e).

sacrifice ['sækrɪfaɪs] lit & fig ♦ *n* sacrifice *m*. ♦ *vt* sacrifier.

sacrilege ['sækrɪlɪdʒ] *n* sacrilège *m*.

sacrosanct ['sækrəʊsæŋkt] *adj* sacrosaint(e).

sad [sæd] *adj* triste.

sadden ['sædn] *vt* attrister, affliger.

saddle ['sædl] ♦ *n* selle *f*. ♦ *vt* **1.** (*horse*) seller. **2.** fig (*burden*): **to ~ sb with sthg**

saddlebag ['sædlbæg] *n* sacoche *f*.

sadistic [sə'dɪstɪk] *adj* sadique.

sadly ['sædlɪ] *adv* **1.** (*unhappily*) tristement. **2.** (*unfortunately*) malheureusement.

sadness ['sædnɪs] *n* tristesse *f*.

s.a.e., sae *abbr of* **stamped addressed envelope**.

safari [sə'fɑːrɪ] *n* safari *m*.

safe [seɪf] ♦ *adj* **1.** (*not dangerous - gen*) sans danger; (- *driver, play, guess*) prudent(e); **it's ~ to say (that)** ... on peut dire à coup sûr que ... **2.** (*not in danger*) hors de danger, en sécurité; **~ and sound** sain et sauf (saine et sauve). **3.** (*not risky - bet, method*) sans risque; (- *investment*) sûr(e); **to be on the ~ side** par précaution. ♦ *n* coffre-fort *m*.

safe-conduct *n* sauf-conduit *m*.

safe-deposit box *n* coffre-fort *m*.

safeguard ['seɪfgɑːd] ♦ *n*: **~ (against)** sauvegarde *f* (contre). ♦ *vt*: **to ~ sb/ sthg (against)** sauvegarder qqn/qqch (contre), protéger qqn/qqch (contre).

safekeeping [seɪf'kiːpɪŋ] *n* bonne garde *f*.

safely ['seɪflɪ] *adv* **1.** (*not dangerously*) sans danger. **2.** (*not in danger*) en toute sécurité, à l'abri du danger. **3.** (*arrive - person*) à bon port, sain et sauf (saine et sauve); (- *parcel*) à bon port. **4.** (*for certain*): **I can ~ say (that)** ... je peux dire à coup sûr que ...

safe sex *n* sexe *m* sans risques, S.S.R. *m*.

safety ['seɪftɪ] *n* sécurité *f*.

safety belt *n* ceinture *f* de sécurité.

safety pin *n* épingle *f* de sûreté OR de nourrice.

saffron ['sæfrən] *n* safran *m*.

sag [sæg] *vi* (*sink downwards*) s'affaisser, fléchir.

sage [seɪdʒ] ♦ *adj* sage. ♦ *n* **1.** (U) (*herb*) sauge *f*. **2.** (*wise man*) sage *m*.

Sagittarius [sædʒɪ'teərɪəs] *n* Sagittaire *m*.

Sahara [sə'hɑːrə] *n*: **the ~ (Desert)** le (désert du) Sahara.

said [sed] *pt* & *pp* → **say**.

sail [seɪl] ♦ *n* **1.** (*of boat*) voile *f*; **to set ~** faire voile, prendre la mer. **2.** (*journey*) tour *m* en bateau. ♦ *vt* **1.** (*boat*) piloter, manœuvrer. **2.** (*sea*) parcourir. ♦ *vi* **1.** (*person - gen*) aller en bateau; (- SPORT) faire de la voile. **2.** (*boat - move*) naviguer; (- *leave*) partir, prendre la mer. fig (*through air*) voler. ▶ **sail through** *vt* *fus fig* réussir les doigts dans le nez.

sailboat *Am* = **sailing boat**.

sailing ['seɪlɪŋ] *n* **1.** (U) (SPORT) voile *f*; **to go ~** faire de la voile. **2.** (*departure*) départ *m*.

sailing boat *Br*, **sailboat** *Am* ['seɪlbəʊt] *n* bateau *m* à voiles, voilier *m*.

sailing ship *n* voilier *m*.

sailor ['seɪləʳ] *n* marin *m*, matelot *m*.

saint [seɪnt] *n* saint *m*, -e *f*.

saintly ['seɪntlɪ] *adj* (*person*) saint(e); (*life*) de saint.

sake [seɪk] *n*: **for the ~ of sb** par égard pour qqn, pour (l'amour de) qqn; **for the ~ of argument** à titre d'exemple; **for God's** OR **heaven's ~** pour l'amour de Dieu OR du ciel.

salad ['sæləd] *n* salade *f*.

salad bowl *n* saladier *m*.

salad cream *n Br sorte de mayonnaise douce.*

salad dressing *n* vinaigrette *f*.

salami [sə'lɑːmɪ] *n* salami *m*.

salary ['sælərɪ] *n* salaire *m*, traitement *m*.

sale [seɪl] *n* **1.** (*gen*) vente *f*; **on ~** en vente; **(up) for ~** à vendre. **2.** (*at reduced prices*) soldes *mpl*. ▶ **sales** *npl* **1.** (*quantity sold*) ventes *fpl*. **2.** (*at reduced prices*): **the ~s** les soldes *mpl*.

saleroom *Br* ['seɪlrʊm], **salesroom** *Am* ['seɪlzrʊm] *n* salle *f* des ventes.

sales assistant ['seɪlz-], **salesclerk** ['seɪlzklɜːrk] *Am n* vendeur *m*, -euse *f*.

salesman ['seɪlzmən] (*pl* **-men** [-mən]) *n* (*in shop*) vendeur *m*; (*travelling*) représentant *m* de commerce.

sales rep *n inf* représentant *m* de commerce.

salesroom *Am* = **saleroom**.

saleswoman ['seɪlz,wʊmən] (*pl* **-women** [-,wɪmɪn]) *n* (*in shop*) vendeuse *f*; (*travelling*) représentante *f* de commerce.

salient ['seɪljənt] *adj fml* qui ressort.

saliva [sə'laɪvə] *n* salive *f*.

sallow ['sæləʊ] *adj* cireux(euse).

salmon ['sæmən] (*pl inv* OR **-s**) *n* saumon *m*.

salmonella [,sælmə'nelə] *n* salmonelle *f*.

salon ['sælɒn] *n* salon *m*.

saloon [sə'luːn] *n* **1.** *Br* (*car*) berline *f*. **2.** *Am* (*bar*) saloon *m*. **3.** *Br* (*in pub*): **~ (bar)** bar *m*. **4.** (*in ship*) salon *m*.

salt [sɔːlt, sɒlt] ◆ *n* sel *m*. ◆ *vt* (*food*) saler; (*roads*) mettre du sel sur.

saltcellar *Br*, **salt shaker** *Am* [-,ʃeɪkəʳ] *n* salière *f*.

saltwater ['sɔːlt,wɔːtəʳ] ◆ *n* eau *f* de mer. ◆ *adj* de mer.

salty ['sɔːltɪ] *adj* (*food*) salé(e); (*water*) saumâtre.

salutary ['sæljʊtrɪ] *adj* salutaire.

salute [sə'luːt] ◆ *n* salut *m*. ◆ *vt* saluer. ◆ *vi* faire un salut.

salvage ['sælvɪdʒ] ◆ *n* (U) **1.** (*rescue of ship*) sauvetage *m*. **2.** (*property rescued*) biens *mpl* sauvés. ◆ *vt* sauver.

salvation [sæl'veɪʃn] *n* salut *m*.

Salvation Army *n*: **the ~** l'Armée *f* du Salut.

same [seɪm] ◆ *adj* même; **she was wearing the ~ jumper as I was** elle portait le même pull que moi; **at the ~ time** en même temps; **one and the ~** un seul et même (une seule et même). ◆ *pron*: **the ~** le même (la même), les mêmes (*pl*); **I'll have the ~ as you** je prendrai la même chose que toi; **she earns the ~ as I do** elle gagne autant que moi; **to do the ~** faire de même, en faire autant; **all** OR **just the ~** (*anyway*) quand même, tout de même; **it's all the ~ to me** ça m'est égal; **it's not the ~** ce n'est pas pareil. ◆ *adv*: **the ~** (*treat, spelled*) de la même manière.

sample ['sɑːmpl] ◆ *n* échantillon *m*. ◆ *vt* (*taste*) goûter.

sanatorium, sanitorium *Am* [,sænə-'tɔːrɪəm] (*pl* **-riums** OR **-ria** [-rɪə]) *n* sanatorium *m*.

sanctimonious [,sæŋktɪ'məʊnjəs] *adj* moralisateur(trice).

sanction ['sæŋkʃn] ◆ *n* sanction *f*. ◆ *vt* sanctionner.

sanctity ['sæŋktətɪ] *n* sainteté *f*.

sanctuary ['sæŋktʃʊərɪ] *n* **1.** (*for birds, wildlife*) réserve *f*. **2.** (*refuge*) asile *m*.

sand [sænd] ◆ *n* sable *m*. ◆ *vt* (*wood*) poncer.

sandal ['sændl] *n* sandale *f*.

sandalwood ['sændlwʊd] *n* (bois *m* de) santal *m*.

sandbox *Am* = **sandpit**.

sandcastle ['sænd,kɑːsl] *n* château *m* de sable.

sand dune *n* dune *f*.

sandpaper ['sænd,peɪpəʳ] *n* (U) papier *m* de verre.

sandpit *Br* ['sændpɪt], **sandbox** *Am* ['sændbɒks] *n* bac *m* à sable.

sandstone ['sændstəʊn] *n* grès *m*.

sandwich ['sænwɪdʒ] ◆ *n* sandwich *m*. ◆ *vt fig*: **to be ~ed between** être (pris(e)) en sandwich entre.

sandwich board n panneau m publicitaire (d'homme sandwich ou posé comme un tréteau).

sandwich course n Br stage m de formation professionnelle.

sandy ['sændɪ] adj 1. (beach) de sable; (earth) sableux(euse). 2. (sand-coloured) sable (inv).

sane [seɪn] adj 1. (not mad) sain(e) d'esprit. 2. (sensible) raisonnable, sensé(e).

sang [sæŋ] pt → sing.

sanitary ['sænɪtrɪ] adj 1. (method, system) sanitaire. 2. (clean) hygiénique, salubre.

sanitary towel, sanitary napkin Am n serviette f hygiénique.

sanitation [,sænɪ'teɪʃn] n (U) (in house) installations fpl sanitaires.

sanitorium Am = sanatorium.

sanity ['sænətɪ] n (U) 1. (saneness) santé f mentale, raison f. 2. (good sense) bon sens m.

sank [sæŋk] pt → sink.

Santa (Claus) ['sæntə(,klɔːz)] n le père Noël.

sap [sæp] ◆ n (of plant) sève f. ◆ vt (weaken) saper.

sapling ['sæplɪŋ] n jeune arbre m.

sapphire ['sæfaɪər] n saphir m.

sarcastic [sɑː'kæstɪk] adj sarcastique.

sardine [sɑː'diːn] n sardine f.

Sardinia [sɑː'dɪnjə] n Sardaigne f.

sardonic [sɑː'dɒnɪk] adj sardonique.

SAS (abbr of Special Air Service) n commando d'intervention spéciale de l'armée britannique.

SASE abbr of self-addressed stamped envelope.

sash [sæʃ] n (of cloth) écharpe f.

sat [sæt] pt & pp → sit.

SAT [sæt] n 1. (abbr of Standard Assessment Test) examen national en Grande-Bretagne pour les élèves de 7 ans, 11 ans et 14 ans. 2. (abbr of Scholastic Aptitude Test) examen d'entrée à l'université aux États-Unis.

Satan ['seɪtn] n Satan m.

satchel ['sætʃəl] n cartable m.

satellite ['sætəlaɪt] ◆ n satellite m. ◆ comp 1. (link) par satellite; ~ **dish** antenne f parabolique. 2. (country, company) satellite.

satellite TV n télévision f par satellite.

satin ['sætɪn] ◆ n satin m. ◆ comp (sheets, pyjamas) de OR en satin; (wallpaper, finish) satiné(e).

satire ['sætaɪər] n satire f.

satisfaction [,sætɪs'fækʃn] n satisfaction f.

satisfactory [,sætɪs'fæktərɪ] adj satisfaisant(e).

satisfied ['sætɪsfaɪd] adj (happy): ~ (with) satisfait(e) (de).

satisfy ['sætɪsfaɪ] vt 1. (gen) satisfaire. 2. (convince) convaincre, persuader; to ~ sb that convaincre qqn que.

satisfying ['sætɪsfaɪɪŋ] adj satisfaisant(e).

satsuma [,sæt'suːmə] n satsuma f.

saturate ['sætʃəreɪt] vt: to ~ sthg (with) saturer qqch (de).

Saturday ['sætədɪ] ◆ n samedi m; it's ~ on est samedi; on ~ samedi; on ~s le samedi; last ~ samedi dernier; this ~ ce samedi; next ~ samedi prochain; every ~ tous les samedis; every other ~ un samedi sur deux; the ~ before l'autre samedi; the ~ before last pas samedi dernier, mais le samedi d'avant; the ~ after next, ~ week, a week on ~ samedi en huit. ◆ comp (paper) du OR de samedi; ~ morning/afternoon/evening samedi matin/après-midi/soir.

sauce [sɔːs] n (CULIN) sauce f.

saucepan ['sɔːspən] n casserole f.

saucer ['sɔːsər] n sous-tasse f, soucoupe f.

saucy ['sɔːsɪ] adj inf coquin(e).

Saudi Arabia [,saudɪə'reɪbjə] n Arabie f Saoudite.

Saudi (Arabian) ['saudɪ-] ◆ adj saoudien(enne). ◆ n (person) Saoudien m, -enne f.

sauna ['sɔːnə] n sauna m.

saunter ['sɔːntər] vi flâner.

sausage ['sɒsɪdʒ] n saucisse f.

sausage meat n chair f à saucisse.

sausage roll n Br feuilleté m à la saucisse.

sauté [Br 'səuteɪ, Am sɔː'teɪ] (pt & pp **sautéed** OR **sautéd**) ◆ adj sauté(e). ◆ vt (potatoes) faire sauter; (onions) faire revenir.

savage ['sævɪdʒ] ◆ adj (fierce) féroce. ◆ n sauvage mf. ◆ vt attaquer avec férocité.

save [seɪv] ◆ vt 1. (rescue) sauver; to ~ sb's life sauver la vie à OR de qqn. 2. (time) gagner; (strength) économiser; (food) garder; (money - set aside) mettre de côté; (- spend less) économiser. 3. (avoid) éviter, épargner; to ~ sb sthg épargner qqch à qqn; to ~ sb from doing sthg éviter à qqn de faire qqch. 4. (SPORT) arrêter. 5. (COMPUT) sauvegarder. ◆ vi (*save money*) mettre de l'argent de côté. ◆ *n* (SPORT) arrêt *m*. ◆ *prep fml*: **~ (for)** sauf, à l'exception de. ▶ **save up** *vi* mettre de l'argent de côté.

saving grace ['seivin-] *n*: **its ~ was …** ce qui le rachetait, c'était …

savings ['seivinz] *npl* économies *fpl*.

savings account *n* Am compte *m* d'épargne.

savings and loan association *n* Am société *f* de crédit immobilier.

savings bank *n* caisse *f* d'épargne.

saviour Br, **savior** Am ['seivjər] *n* sauveur *m*.

savour Br, **savor** Am ['seivər] *vt lit & fig* savourer.

savoury Br, **savory** Am ['seivəri] ◆ *adj* 1. (*food*) salé(e). 2. (*respectable*) recommandable. ◆ *n* petit plat *m* salé.

saw [sɔ:] (Br *pt* -**ed**, *pp* **sawn**, Am *pt* & *pp* -**ed**) ◆ *pt* → **see**. ◆ *n* scie *f*. ◆ *vt* scier.

sawdust ['sɔ:dʌst] *n* sciure *f* (de bois).

sawed-off shotgun Am = **sawn-off shotgun**.

sawmill ['sɔ:mɪl] *n* scierie *f*, moulin *m* à scie Can.

sawn [sɔ:n] Br *pp* → **saw**.

sawn-off shotgun Br, **sawed-off shotgun** ['sɔ:d-] Am *n* carabine *f* à canon scié.

saxophone ['sæksəfəun] *n* saxophone *m*.

say [sei] (*pt* & *pp* **said**) ◆ *vt* 1. (*gen*) dire; **could you ~ that again?** vous pouvez répéter ce que vous venez de dire?; **(let's) ~ you won a lottery …** supposons que tu gagnes le gros lot …; **it ~s a lot about him** cela en dit long sur lui; **she's said to be …** on dit qu'elle est …; **that goes without ~ing** cela va sans dire; **it has a lot to be said for it** cela a beaucoup d'avantages. 2. (*subj: clock, watch*) indiquer. ◆ *n*: **to have a/no ~** avoir/ne pas avoir voix au chapitre; **to have a ~ in sthg** avoir son mot à dire sur qqch; **to have one's ~** dire ce que l'on a à dire, dire son mot. ▶ **that is to say** *adv* c'est-à-dire.

saying ['seiiŋ] *n* dicton *m*.

scab [skæb] *n* 1. (*of wound*) croûte *f*. 2. *inf pej* (*non-striker*) jaune *m*.

scaffold ['skæfəuld] *n* échafaud *m*.

scaffolding ['skæfəldiŋ] *n* échafaudage *m*.

scald [skɔ:ld] ◆ *n* brûlure *f*. ◆ *vt* ébouillanter; **to ~ one's arm** s'ébouillanter le bras.

scale [skeil] ◆ *n* 1. (*gen*) échelle *f*; **to ~**

(*map, drawing*) à l'échelle. 2. (*of ruler, thermometer*) graduation *f*. 3. (MUS) gamme *f*. 4. (*of fish, snake*) écaille *f*. 5. Am = **scales**. ◆ *vt* 1. (*cliff, mountain, fence*) escalader. 2. (*fish*) écailler. ▶ **scales** *npl* balance *f*. ▶ **scale down** *vt fus* réduire.

scale model *n* modèle *m* réduit.

scallop ['skɒləp] ◆ *n* (*shellfish*) coquille *f* Saint-Jacques. ◆ *vt* (*edge, garment*) festonner.

scalp [skælp] ◆ *n* 1. (ANAT) cuir *m* chevelu. 2. (*trophy*) scalp *m*. ◆ *vt* scalper.

scalpel ['skælpəl] *n* scalpel *m*.

scamper ['skæmpər] *vi* trottiner.

scampi ['skæmpi] *n* (U) scampi *mpl*.

scan [skæn] ◆ *n* (MED) scanographie *f*; (*during pregnancy*) échographie *f*. ◆ *vt* 1. (*examine carefully*) scruter. 2. (*glance at*) parcourir. 3. (TECH) balayer. 4. (COMPUT) faire un scannage de.

scandal ['skændl] *n* 1. (*gen*) scandale *m*. 2. (*gossip*) médisance *f*.

scandalize, -ise ['skændəlaiz] *vt* scandaliser.

Scandinavia [ˌskændɪ'neivjə] *n* Scandinavie *f*.

Scandinavian [ˌskændɪ'neivjən] ◆ *adj* scandinave. ◆ *n* (*person*) Scandinave *mf*.

scant [skænt] *adj* insuffisant(e).

scanty ['skænti] *adj* (*amount, resources*) insuffisant(e); (*income*) maigre; (*dress*) minuscule.

scapegoat ['skeipgəut] *n* bouc *m* émissaire.

scar [skɑ:r] *n* cicatrice *f*.

scarce ['skeəs] *adj* rare, peu abondant(e).

scarcely ['skeəsli] *adv* à peine; **~ anyone** presque personne; **I ~ ever go there now** je n'y vais presque or pratiquement plus jamais.

scare [skeər] ◆ *n* 1. (*sudden fear*): **to give sb a ~** faire peur à qqn. 2. (*public fear*) panique *f*; **bomb ~** alerte *f* à la bombe. ◆ *vt* faire peur à, effrayer. ▶ **scare away, scare off** *vt sep* faire fuir.

scarecrow ['skeəkrəu] *n* épouvantail *m*.

scared ['skeəd] *adj* apeuré(e); **to be ~** avoir peur; **to be ~ stiff** or **to death** être mort de peur.

scarf [skɑ:f] (*pl* -**s** or **scarves**) *n* (*wool*) écharpe *f*; (*silk etc*) foulard *m*.

scarlet ['skɑ:lət] ◆ *adj* écarlate. ◆ *n* écarlate *f*.

scarlet fever *n* scarlatine *f*.

scarves [skɑ:vz] pl → **scarf**.

scathing ['skeɪðɪŋ] adj (criticism) acerbe; (reply) cinglant(e).

scatter ['skætər] ♦ vt (clothes, paper etc) éparpiller; (seeds) semer à la volée. ♦ vi se disperser.

scatterbrained ['skætəbreɪnd] adj inf écervelé(e).

scavenger ['skævɪndʒər] n 1. (animal) animal m nécrophage. 2. (person) personne f qui fait les poubelles.

scenario [sɪ'nɑ:rɪəʊ] (pl -s) n 1. (possible situation) hypothèse f, scénario m. 2. (of film, play) scénario m.

scene [si:n] n 1. (in play, film, book) scène f; **behind the ~s** dans les coulisses. 2. (sight) spectacle m, vue f; (picture) tableau m. 3. (location) lieu m, endroit m. 4. (area of activity): **the political ~** la scène politique; **the music ~** le monde de la musique. 5. phr: **to set the ~ for sthg** préparer la voie à qqch.

scenery ['si:nərɪ] n (U) 1. (of countryside) paysage m. 2. (THEATRE) décor m, décors mpl.

scenic ['si:nɪk] adj (tour) touristique; **a ~ view** un beau panorama.

scent [sent] n 1. (smell - of flowers) senteur f, parfum m; (- of animal) odeur f, fumet m. 2. (U) (perfume) parfum m.

scepter Am = **sceptre**.

sceptic Br, **skeptic** Am ['skeptɪk] n sceptique mf.

sceptical Br, **skeptical** Am ['skeptɪkl] adj: **~ (about)** sceptique (sur).

sceptre Br, **scepter** Am ['septər] n sceptre m.

schedule [Br 'ʃedju:l, Am 'skedʒʊl] ♦ n 1. (plan) programme m, plan m; **on ~** (at expected time) à l'heure (prévue); (on expected day) à la date prévue; **ahead of/behind ~** en avance/en retard (sur le programme). 2. (list - of times) horaire m; (- of prices) tarif m. ♦ vt: **to ~ sthg (for)** prévoir qqch (pour).

scheduled flight [Br 'ʃedju:ld-, Am 'skedjʊld-] n vol m régulier.

scheme [ski:m] ♦ n 1. (plan) plan m, projet m. 2. pej (dishonest plan) combine f. 3. (arrangement) arrangement m; **colour ~** combinaison f de couleurs. ♦ vi pej conspirer.

scheming ['ski:mɪŋ] adj intrigant(e).

schism ['sɪzm, 'skɪzm] n schisme m.

schizophrenic [ˌskɪtsə'frenɪk] ♦ adj schizophrène. ♦ n schizophrène mf.

scholar ['skɒlər] n 1. (expert) érudit m, -e f, savant m, -e f. 2. dated (student) éco-

lier m, -ère f, élève mf. 3. (holder of scholarship) boursier m, -ère f.

scholarship ['skɒləʃɪp] n 1. (grant) bourse f (d'études). 2. (learning) érudition f.

school [sku:l] n 1. (gen) école f; (secondary school) lycée m, collège m. 2. (university department) faculté f. 3. Am (university) université f.

school age n âge m scolaire.

schoolbook ['sku:lbʊk] n livre m scolaire OR de classe.

schoolboy ['sku:lbɔɪ] n écolier m, élève m.

schoolchild ['sku:ltʃaɪld] (pl -children [-tʃɪldrən]) n écolier m, -ère f, élève mf.

schooldays ['sku:ldeɪz] npl années fpl d'école.

schoolgirl ['sku:lgɜ:l] n écolière f, élève f.

schooling ['sku:lɪŋ] n instruction f.

school-leaver [-,li:vər] n Br élève qui a fini ses études secondaires.

schoolmaster ['sku:l,mɑ:stər] n (primary) instituteur m, maître m d'école; (secondary) professeur m.

schoolmistress ['sku:l,mɪstrɪs] n (primary) institutrice f, maîtresse f d'école; (secondary) professeur m.

school of thought n école f (de pensée).

schoolteacher ['sku:l,ti:tʃər] n (primary) instituteur m, -trice f; (secondary) professeur m.

school year n année f scolaire.

schooner ['sku:nər] n (ship) schooner m, goélette f.

sciatica [saɪ'ætɪkə] n sciatique f.

science ['saɪəns] n science f.

science fiction n science-fiction f.

scientific [ˌsaɪən'tɪfɪk] adj scientifique.

scientist ['saɪəntɪst] n scientifique mf.

scintillating ['sɪntɪleɪtɪŋ] adj brillant(e).

scissors ['sɪzəz] npl ciseaux mpl; **a pair of ~** une paire de ciseaux.

sclerosis [sklɪ'rəʊsɪs] → **multiple sclerosis**.

scoff [skɒf] ♦ vt Br inf bouffer, boulotter. ♦ vi: **to ~ (at)** se moquer (de).

scold [skəʊld] vt gronder, réprimander.

scone [skɒn] n scone m.

scoop [sku:p] ♦ n 1. (for sugar) pelle f à main; (for ice cream) cuiller f à glace. 2. (of ice cream) boule f. 3. (news report) exclusivité f, scoop m. ♦ vt (with hands) prendre avec les mains; (with scoop) prendre avec une pelle à main.
▶ **scoop out** vt sep évider.

scooter ['sku:tə^r] n **1.** (toy) trottinette f. **2.** (motorcycle) scooter m.

scope [skəʊp] n (U) **1.** (opportunity) occasion f, possibilité f. **2.** (of report, inquiry) étendue f, portée f.

scorch [skɔ:tʃ] vt (clothes) brûler légèrement, roussir; (skin) brûler; (land, grass) dessécher.

scorching ['skɔ:tʃɪŋ] adj inf (day) torride; (sun) brûlant(e).

score [skɔ:^r] ◆ n **1.** (SPORT) score m. **2.** (in test) note f. **3.** dated (twenty). **4.** (MUS) partition f. **5.** (subject): **on that ~** à ce sujet, sur ce point. ◆ vt **1.** (goal, point etc) marquer; **to ~ 100%** avoir 100 sur 100. **2.** (success, victory) remporter. **3.** (cut) entailler. ◆ vi (SPORT) marquer (un but/point etc). ▶ **score out** vt sep Br barrer, rayer.

scoreboard ['skɔ:bɔ:d] n tableau m.

scorer ['skɔ:rə^r] n marqueur m.

scorn [skɔ:n] ◆ n (U) mépris m, dédain m. ◆ vt **1.** (person, attitude) mépriser. **2.** (help, offer) rejeter, dédaigner.

scornful ['skɔ:nful] adj méprisant(e); **to be ~ of sthg** mépriser qqch, dédaigner qqch.

Scorpio ['skɔ:pɪəʊ] (pl -s) n Scorpion m.

scorpion ['skɔ:pjən] n scorpion m.

Scot [skɒt] n Écossais m, -e f.

scotch [skɒtʃ] vt (rumour) étouffer; (plan) faire échouer.

Scotch [skɒtʃ] ◆ adj écossais(e). ◆ n scotch m, whisky m.

Scotch (tape)® n Am Scotch® m.

scot-free adj inf: **to get off ~** s'en tirer sans être puni(e).

Scotland ['skɒtlənd] n Écosse f.

Scots [skɒts] ◆ adj écossais(e). ◆ n (dialect) écossais m.

Scotsman ['skɒtsmən] (pl -men [-mən]) n Écossais m.

Scotswoman ['skɒtswʊmən] (pl -women [-,wɪmɪn]) n Écossaise f.

Scottish ['skɒtɪʃ] adj écossais(e).

scoundrel ['skaʊndrəl] n dated gredin m.

scour [skaʊə^r] vt **1.** (clean) récurer. **2.** (search - town etc) parcourir; (- countryside) battre.

scourge [skɜ:dʒ] n fléau m.

scout [skaʊt] n (MIL) éclaireur m. ▶ **Scout** n (boy scout) scout m. ▶ **scout around** vi: **to ~ around (for)** aller à la recherche (de).

scowl [skaʊl] ◆ n regard m noir. ◆ vi se renfrogner, froncer les sourcils; **to ~ at**

sb jeter des regards noirs à qqn.

scrabble ['skræbl] vi **1.** (scrape): **to ~ at sthg** gratter qqch. **2.** (feel around): **to ~ around for sthg** tâtonner pour trouver qqch.

scraggy ['skrægɪ] adj décharné(e), maigre.

scramble ['skræmbl] ◆ n (rush) bousculade f, ruée f. ◆ vi **1.** (climb): **to ~ up a hill** grimper une colline en s'aidant des mains OR à quatre pattes. **2.** (compete): **to ~ for sthg** se disputer qqch.

scrambled eggs ['skræmbld-] npl œufs mpl brouillés.

scrap [skræp] ◆ n **1.** (of paper, material) bout m; (of information) fragment m; (of conversation) bribe f. **2.** (metal) ferraille f. **3.** inf (fight, quarrel) bagarre f. ◆ vt (car) mettre à la ferraille; (plan, system) abandonner, laisser tomber. ▶ **scraps** npl (food) restes mpl.

scrapbook ['skræpbʊk] n album m (de coupures de journaux etc).

scrap dealer n ferrailleur m, marchand m de ferraille.

scrape [skreɪp] ◆ n **1.** (scraping noise) raclement m, grattement m. **2.** dated (difficult situation): **to get into a ~** se fourrer dans le pétrin. ◆ vt **1.** (clean, rub) gratter, racler; **to ~ sthg off sthg** enlever qqch de qqch en grattant OR raclant. **2.** (surface, car, skin) érafler. ◆ vi gratter. ▶ **scrape through** vt fus réussir de justesse.

scraper ['skreɪpə^r] n grattoir m, racloir m.

scrap merchant n Br ferrailleur m, marchand m de ferraille.

scrap paper Br, **scratch paper** Am n (papier m) brouillon m.

scrapyard ['skræpjɑ:d] n parc m à ferraille.

scratch [skrætʃ] ◆ n **1.** (wound) égratignure f, éraflure f. **2.** (on glass, paint etc) éraflure f. **3.** phr: **to be up to ~** être à la hauteur; **to do sthg from ~** faire qqch à partir de rien. ◆ vt **1.** (wound) écorcher, égratigner. **2.** (mark - paint, glass etc) rayer, érafler. **3.** (rub) gratter. ◆ vi gratter; (person) se gratter.

scratch card n carte f à gratter.

scratch paper Am = **scrap paper**.

scrawl [skrɔ:l] ◆ n griffonnage m, gribouillage m. ◆ vt griffonner, gribouiller.

scrawny ['skrɔ:nɪ] adj (person) efflanqué(e); (body, animal) décharné(e).

scream [skri:m] ◆ n (cry) cri m perçant, hurlement m; (of laughter) éclat

m. ◆ *vt* hurler. ◆ *vi* (*cry out*) crier, hurler.
scree [skri:] *n* éboulis *m.*
screech [skri:tʃ] ◆ *n* **1.** (*cry*) cri *m* perçant. **2.** (*of tyres*) crissement *m.* ◆ *vt* hurler. ◆ *vi* **1.** (*cry out*) pousser des cris perçants. **2.** (*tyres*) crisser.
screen [skri:n] ◆ *n* **1.** (*gen*) écran *m.* **2.** (*panel*) paravent *m.* ◆ *vt* **1.** (CINEMA) projeter, passer; (TV) téléviser, passer. **2.** (*hide*) cacher, masquer. **3.** (*shield*) protéger. **4.** (*candidate, employee*) passer au crible, filtrer.
screening ['skri:nɪŋ] *n* **1.** (CINEMA) projection *f*; (TV) passage *m* à la télévision. **2.** (*for security*) sélection *f*, tri *m*. **3.** (MED) dépistage *m.*
screenplay ['skri:npleɪ] *n* scénario *m.*
screw [skru:] ◆ *n* (*for fastening*) vis *f.* ◆ *vt* **1.** (*fix with screws*): **to ~ sthg to sthg** visser qqch à OR sur qqch. **2.** (*twist*) visser. **3.** *vulg* (*woman*) baiser. ◆ *vi* (*bolt, lid*) se visser. ► **screw up** *vt sep* **1.** (*crumple up*) froisser, chiffonner. **2.** (*eyes*) plisser; (*face*) tordre. **3.** *v inf* (*ruin*) gâcher, bousiller.
screwdriver ['skru:ˌdraɪvər] *n* (*tool*) tournevis *m.*
scribble ['skrɪbl] ◆ *n* gribouillage *m*, griffonnage *m.* ◆ *vt & vi* gribouiller, griffonner.
script [skrɪpt] *n* **1.** (*of play, film etc*) scénario *m*, script *m*. **2.** (*writing system*) écriture *f*. **3.** (*handwriting*) (écriture *f*) script *m.*
Scriptures ['skrɪptʃəz] *npl*: **the ~** les (Saintes) Écritures *fpl.*
scriptwriter ['skrɪptˌraɪtər] *n* scénariste *mf.*
scroll [skrəʊl] ◆ *n* rouleau *m.* ◆ *vt* (COMPUT) faire défiler.
scrounge [skraʊndʒ] *inf vt*: **to ~ money off sb** taper qqn; **can I ~ a cigarette off you?** je peux te piquer une cigarette?
scrounger ['skraʊndʒər] *n inf* parasite *m.*
scrub [skrʌb] ◆ *n* **1.** (*rub*): **to give sthg a ~** nettoyer qqch à la brosse. **2.** (U) (*undergrowth*) broussailles *fpl.* ◆ *vt* (*floor, clothes etc*) laver OR nettoyer à la brosse; (*hands, back*) frotter; (*saucepan*) récurer.
scruff [skrʌf] *n*: **by the ~ of the neck** par la peau du cou.
scruffy ['skrʌfɪ] *adj* mal soigné(e), débraillé(e).
scrum(mage) ['skrʌm(ɪdʒ)] *n* (RUGBY) mêlée *f.*
scruples ['skru:plz] *npl* scrupules *mpl.*
scrutinize, -ise ['skru:tɪnaɪz] *vt*

scruter, examiner attentivement.
scrutiny ['skru:tɪnɪ] *n* (U) examen *m* attentif.
scuba diving ['sku:bə-] *n* plongée *f* sous-marine (*autonome*).
scuff [skʌf] *vt* **1.** (*damage*) érafler. **2.** (*drag*): **to ~ one's feet** traîner les pieds.
scuffle ['skʌfl] *n* bagarre *f.*
scullery ['skʌlərɪ] *n* arrière-cuisine *f.*
sculptor ['skʌlptər] *n* sculpteur *m.*
sculpture ['skʌlptʃər] ◆ *n* sculpture *f.* ◆ *vt* sculpter.
scum [skʌm] *n* **1.** (U) (*froth*) écume *f*, mousse *f.* **2.** *v inf pej* (*person*) salaud *m.* **3.** (U) *v inf pej* (*people*) déchets *mpl.*
scupper ['skʌpər] *vt* **1.** (NAUT) couler. **2.** *Br fig* (*plan*) saboter, faire tomber à l'eau.
scurrilous ['skʌrələs] *adj* calomnieux (euse).
scurry ['skʌrɪ] *vi* se précipiter; **to ~ away** OR **off** se sauver, détaler.
scuttle ['skʌtl] ◆ *n* seau *m* à charbon. ◆ *vi* courir précipitamment OR à pas précipités.
scythe [saɪð] *n* faux *f.*
SDLP (*abbr of* **Social Democratic and Labour Party**) *n* parti travailliste d'Irlande du Nord.
sea [si:] ◆ *n* **1.** (*gen*) mer *f*; **at ~** en mer; **by ~** par mer; **by the ~** au bord de la mer; **out to ~** au large. **2.** *phr*: **to be all at ~** nager complètement. ◆ *comp* (*voyage*) en mer; (*animal*) marin(e), de mer.
seabed ['si:bed] *n*: **the ~** le fond de la mer.
seaboard ['si:bɔːd] *n* littoral *m*, côte *f.*
sea breeze *n* brise *f* de mer.
seafood ['si:fu:d] *n* (U) fruits *mpl* de mer.
seafront ['si:frʌnt] *n* front *m* de mer.
seagull ['si:gʌl] *n* mouette *f.*
seal [si:l] (*pl inv* OR **-s**) ◆ *n* **1.** (*animal*) phoque *m.* **2.** (*official mark*) cachet *m*, sceau *m.* **3.** (*official fastening*) cachet *m.* ◆ *vt* **1.** (*envelope*) coller, fermer. **2.** (*document, letter*) sceller, cacheter. **3.** (*block off*) obturer, boucher. ► **seal off** *vt sep* (*area, entrance*) interdire l'accès de.
sea level *n* niveau *m* de la mer.
sea lion (*pl inv* OR **-s**) *n* otarie *f.*
seam [si:m] *n* **1.** (SEWING) couture *f.* **2.** (*of coal*) couche *f*, veine *f.*
seaman ['si:mən] (*pl* **-men** [-mən]) *n* marin *m.*
seamy ['si:mɪ] *adj* sordide.
séance ['seɪɒns] *n* séance *f* de spiritisme.

seaplane ['si:pleɪn] *n* hydravion *m*.

seaport ['si:pɔ:t] *n* port *m* de mer.

search [sɜ:tʃ] ♦ *n* (*of person, luggage, house*) fouille *f*; (*for lost person, thing*) recherche *f*, recherches *fpl*; **~ for** recherche de; **in ~ of** à la recherche de. ♦ *vt* (*house, area, person*) fouiller; (*memory, mind, drawer*) fouiller dans. ♦ *vi*: **to ~ (for sb/sthg)** chercher (qqn/qqch).

searching ['sɜ:tʃɪŋ] *adj* (*question*) poussé(e), approfondi(e); (*look*) pénétrant(e); (*examination*) minutieux(euse).

searchlight ['sɜ:tʃlaɪt] *n* projecteur *m*.

search party *n* équipe *f* de secours.

search warrant *n* mandat *m* de perquisition.

seashell ['si:ʃel] *n* coquillage *m*.

seashore ['si:ʃɔ:r] *n*: **the ~** le rivage, la plage.

seasick ['si:sɪk] *adj*: **to be** OR **feel ~** avoir le mal de mer.

seaside ['si:saɪd] *n*: **the ~** le bord de la mer.

seaside resort *n* station *f* balnéaire.

season ['si:zn] ♦ *n* 1. (*gen*) saison *f*; **in ~** (*food*) de saison; **out of ~** (*holiday*) hors saison; (*food*) hors de saison. 2. (*of films*) cycle *m*. ♦ *vt* assaisonner, relever.

seasonal ['si:zənl] *adj* saisonnier(ère).

seasoned ['si:znd] *adj* (*traveller, campaigner*) chevronné(e), expérimenté(e); (*soldier*) aguerri(e).

seasoning ['si:znɪŋ] *n* assaisonnement *m*.

season ticket *n* carte *f* d'abonnement.

seat [si:t] ♦ *n* 1. (*gen*) siège *m*; (*in theatre*) fauteuil *m*; **take a ~!** asseyez-vous! 2. (*place to sit - in bus, train*) place *f*. 3. (*of trousers*) fond *m*. ♦ *vt* (*sit down*) faire asseoir, placer; **please be ~ed** veuillez vous asseoir.

seat belt *n* ceinture *f* de sécurité.

seawater ['si:,wɔ:tər] *n* eau *f* de mer.

seaweed ['si:wi:d] *n* (U) algue *f*.

seaworthy ['si:,wɜ:ðɪ] *adj* en bon état de navigabilité.

sec. *abbr of* **second**.

secede [sɪ'si:d] *vi fml*: **to ~ (from)** se séparer (de), faire sécession (de).

secluded [sɪ'klu:dɪd] *adj* retiré(e), écarté(e).

seclusion [sɪ'klu:ʒn] *n* solitude *f*, retraite *f*.

second ['sekənd] ♦ *n* 1. (*gen*) seconde *f*; **wait a ~!** une seconde!, (attendez) un instant!; **~ (gear)** seconde *f*. 2. Br (UNIV)

≃ licence *f* avec mention assez bien. ♦ *num* deuxième, second(e); **his score was ~ only to hers** il n'y a qu'elle qui ait fait mieux que lui OR qui l'ait surpassé; *see also* **sixth**. ♦ *vt* (*proposal, motion*) appuyer. ▶ **seconds** *npl* 1. (COMM) articles *mpl* de second choix. 2. (*of food*) rabiot *m*.

secondary ['sekəndrɪ] *adj* secondaire; **to be ~** être moins important(e) que.

secondary school *n* école *f* secondaire, lycée *m*.

second-class ['sekənd-] *adj* 1. *pej* (*citizen*) de deuxième zone; (*product*) de second choix. 2. (*ticket*) de seconde OR deuxième classe. 3. (*stamp*) à tarif réduit. 4. Br (UNIV) (*degree*) ≃ avec mention assez bien.

second-hand ['sekənd-] ♦ *adj* 1. (*goods, shop*) d'occasion. 2. *fig* (*information*) de seconde main. ♦ *adv* (*not new*) d'occasion.

second hand ['sekənd-] *n* (*of clock*) trotteuse *f*.

secondly ['sekəndlɪ] *adv* deuxièmement, en second lieu.

secondment [sɪ'kɒndmənt] *n* Br affectation *f* temporaire.

second-rate ['sekənd-] *adj pej* de deuxième ordre, médiocre.

second thought ['sekənd-] *n*: **to have ~s about sthg** avoir des doutes sur qqch; **on ~s** Br, **on ~** Am réflexion faite, tout bien réfléchi.

secrecy ['si:krəsɪ] *n* (U) secret *m*.

secret ['si:krɪt] ♦ *adj* secret(ète). ♦ *n* secret *m*; **in ~** en secret.

secretarial [,sekrə'teərɪəl] *adj* (*course, training*) de secrétariat, de secrétaire; **~ staff** secrétaires *mpl*.

secretary [Br 'sekrətrɪ, Am 'sekrə,terɪ] *n* 1. (*gen*) secrétaire *mf*. 2. (POL) (*minister*) ministre *m*.

Secretary of State *n* 1. Br: **~ (for)** ministre *m* (de). 2. Am ≃ ministre *m* des Affaires étrangères.

secretive ['si:krətɪv] *adj* secret(ète), dissimulé(e).

secretly ['si:krɪtlɪ] *adv* secrètement.

sect [sekt] *n* secte *f*.

sectarian [sek'teərɪən] *adj* (*killing, violence*) d'ordre religieux.

section ['sekʃn] ♦ *n* 1. (*portion - gen*) section *f*, partie *f*; (*- of road, pipe*) tronçon *m*; (*- of document, law*) article *m*. 2. (GEOM) coupe *f*, section *f*. ♦ *vt* sectionner.

sector ['sektər] *n* secteur *m*.

secular ['sekjʊlər] *adj* (*life*) séculier

(ère); (*education*) laïque; (*music*) profane.

secure [sɪ'kjʊər] ◆ *adj* 1. (*fixed - gen*) fixe; (- *windows, building*) bien fermé(e). 2. (*safe - job, future*) sûr(e); (- *valuable object*) en sécurité, en lieu sûr. 3. (*free of anxiety - childhood*) sécurisant(e); (- *marriage*) solide. ◆ *vt* 1. (*obtain*) obtenir. 2. (*fasten - gen*) attacher; (- *door, window*) bien fermer. 3. (*make safe*) assurer la sécurité de.

security [sɪ'kjʊərətɪ] *n* sécurité *f*. ► **securities** *npl* (FIN) titres *mpl*, valeurs *fpl*.

security guard *n* garde *m* de sécurité.

sedan [sɪ'dæn] *n* Am berline *f*.

sedate [sɪ'deɪt] ◆ *adj* posé(e), calme. ◆ *vt* donner un sédatif à.

sedation [sɪ'deɪʃn] *n* (U) sédation *f*; under ~ sous calmants.

sedative ['sedətɪv] *n* sédatif *m*, calmant *m*.

sediment ['sedɪmənt] *n* sédiment *m*, dépôt *m*.

seduce [sɪ'dju:s] *vt* séduire; to ~ sb into doing sthg amener OR entraîner qqn à faire qqch.

seductive [sɪ'dʌktɪv] *adj* séduisant(e).

see [si:] (*pt* saw, *pp* seen) ◆ *vt* 1. (*gen*) voir; ~ you! au revoir!; ~ you soon/later/tomorrow! *etc* à bientôt/tout à l'heure/demain! *etc*. 2. (*accompany*): I saw her to the door je l'ai accompagnée OR reconduite jusqu'à la porte; I saw her onto the train je l'ai accompagnée au train. 3. (*make sure*): to ~ (that) ... s'assurer que ... ◆ *vi* voir; you ~, ... voyez-vous, ...; I ~ je vois, je comprends; let's ~, let me ~ voyons, voyons voir. ► **seeing as, seeing that** *conj inf* vu que, étant donné que. ► **see about** *vt fus* (*arrange*) s'occuper de. ► **see off** *vt sep* 1. (*say goodbye to*) accompagner (pour dire au revoir). 2. Br (*chase away*) faire partir OR fuir. ► **see through** ◆ *vt fus* (*scheme*) voir clair dans; to ~ through sb voir dans le jeu de qqn. ◆ *vt sep* (*deal, project*) mener à terme, mener à bien. ► **see to** *vt fus* s'occuper de, se charger de.

seed [si:d] ◆ *n* 1. (*of plant*) graine *f*. 2. (SPORT): **fifth ~** joueur classé cinquième *m*, joueuse classée cinquième *f*. ◆ *vt* (*fruit*) épépiner. ► **seeds** *npl fig* germes *mpl*, semences *fpl*.

seedling ['si:dlɪŋ] *n* jeune plant *m*, semis *m*.

seedy ['si:dɪ] *adj* miteux(euse).

seek [si:k] (*pt & pp* sought) *vt* 1. (*gen*) chercher; (*peace, happiness*) rechercher; to ~ to do sthg chercher à faire qqch. 2. (*advice, help*) demander.

seem [si:m] ◆ *vi* sembler, paraître; to ~ bored avoir l'air de s'ennuyer; to ~ sad/tired avoir l'air triste/fatigué. ◆ *v impers*: it ~s (that) ... il semble OR paraît que ...

seemingly ['si:mɪŋlɪ] *adv* apparemment.

seen [si:n] *pp* → **see**.

seep [si:p] *vi* suinter.

seesaw ['si:sɔ:] *n* bascule *f*.

seethe [si:ð] *vi* 1. (*person*) bouillir, être furieux(euse). 2. (*place*): **to be seething with** grouiller de.

see-through *adj* transparent(e).

segment ['segmənt] *n* 1. (*section*) partie *f*, section *f*. 2. (*of fruit*) quartier *m*.

segregate ['segrɪgeɪt] *vt* séparer.

Seine [seɪn] *n*: **the (River) ~** la Seine.

seize [si:z] *vt* 1. (*grab*) saisir, attraper. 2. (*capture*) s'emparer de, prendre. 3. (*arrest*) arrêter. 4. *fig* (*opportunity, chance*) saisir, sauter sur. ► **seize (up)on** *vt fus* saisir, sauter sur. ► **seize up** *vi* 1. (*body*) s'ankyloser. 2. (*engine, part*) se gripper.

seizure ['si:ʒər] *n* 1. (MED) crise *f*, attaque *f*. 2. (U) (*of town*) capture *f*; (*of power*) prise *f*.

seldom ['seldəm] *adv* peu souvent, rarement.

select [sɪ'lekt] ◆ *adj* 1. (*carefully chosen*) choisi(e). 2. (*exclusive*) de premier ordre, d'élite. ◆ *vt* sélectionner, choisir.

selection [sɪ'lekʃn] *n* sélection *f*, choix *m*.

selective [sɪ'lektɪv] *adj* sélectif(ive); (*person*) difficile.

self [self] (*pl* selves) *n* moi *m*; she's her old ~ again elle est redevenue elle-même.

self-addressed stamped envelope [-ə'drest-] *n* Am enveloppe *f* affranchie pour la réponse.

self-assured *adj* sûr(e) de soi, plein(e) d'assurance.

self-catering *adj* (*holiday - in house*) en maison louée; (- *in flat*) en appartement loué.

self-centred [-'sentəd] *adj* égocentrique.

self-confessed [-kən'fest] *adj* de son propre aveu.

self-confident *adj* sûr(e) de soi, plein(e) d'assurance.

self-conscious *adj* timide.

self-contained [-kən'teɪnd] *adj* (*flat*)

indépendant(e), avec entrée particulière; (*person*) qui se suffit à soi-même.

self-control *n* maîtrise *f* de soi.

self-defence *n* autodéfense *f*.

self-discipline *n* autodiscipline *f*.

self-employed [-ɪmˈplɔɪd] *adj* qui travaille à son propre compte.

self-esteem *n* respect *m* de soi, estime *f* de soi.

self-evident *adj* qui va de soi, évident(e).

self-explanatory *adj* évident(e), qui ne nécessite pas d'explication.

self-government *n* autonomie *f*.

self-important *adj* suffisant(e).

self-indulgent *adj pej* (*person*) qui ne se refuse rien; (*film, book, writer*) nombriliste.

self-interest *n* (U) *pej* intérêt *m* personnel.

selfish [ˈselfɪʃ] *adj* égoïste.

selfishness [ˈselfɪʃnɪs] *n* égoïsme *m*.

selfless [ˈselflɪs] *adj* désintéressé(e).

self-made *adj*: ~ man self-made-man *m*.

self-medication [-ˌmedɪˈkeɪʃn] *n* automédication *f*.

self-opinionated *adj* opiniâtre.

self-pity *n* apitoiement *m* sur soi-même.

self-portrait *n* autoportrait *m*.

self-possessed [-pəˈzest] *adj* maître (maîtresse) de soi.

self-raising flour *Br* [-ˌreɪzɪŋ-], **self-rising flour** *Am n* farine *f* avec levure incorporée.

self-reliant *adj* indépendant(e), qui ne compte que sur soi.

self-respect *n* respect *m* de soi.

self-respecting [-rɪsˈpektɪŋ] *adj* qui se respecte.

self-restraint *n* (U) retenue *f*, mesure *f*.

self-righteous *adj* satisfait(e) de soi.

self-rising flour *Am* = **self-raising flour**.

self-sacrifice *n* abnégation *f*.

self-satisfied *adj* suffisant(e), content(e) de soi.

self-service *n* libre-service *m*, self-service *m*.

self-sufficient *adj* autosuffisant(e); **to be ~ in** satisfaire à ses besoins en.

self-taught *adj* autodidacte.

sell [sel] (*pt & pp* **sold**) ◆ *vt* 1. (*gen*) vendre; **to ~ sthg for £100** vendre qqch 100 livres; **to ~ sthg to sb, to ~ sb sthg** vendre qqch à qqn. 2. *fig* (*make acceptable*): **to ~ sthg to sb, to ~ sb sthg** faire accepter

qqch à qqn. ◆ *vi* 1. (*person*) vendre. 2. (*product*) se vendre; **it ~s for** OR **at £10** il se vend 10 livres. ▶ **sell off** *vt sep* vendre, liquider. ▶ **sell out** ◆ *vt sep*: **the performance is sold out** il ne reste plus de places, tous les billets ont été vendus. ◆ *vi* 1. (*shop*): **we've sold out** on n'en a plus. 2. (*betray one's principles*) être infidèle à ses principes.

sell-by date *n Br* date *f* limite de vente.

seller [ˈseləʳ] *n* vendeur *m*, -euse *f*.

selling price [ˈselɪŋ-] *n* prix *m* de vente.

Sellotape® [ˈseləteɪp] *n Br* ≃ Scotch® *m*, ruban *m* adhésif.

sell-out *n*: **the match was a ~** on a joué à guichets fermés.

selves [selvz] *pl* → **self**.

semaphore [ˈseməfɔːʳ] *n* (U) signaux *mpl* à bras.

semblance [ˈsembləns] *n* semblant *m*.

semen [ˈsiːmen] *n* (U) sperme *m*, semence *f*.

semester [sɪˈmestəʳ] *n* semestre *m*.

semicircle [ˈsemɪˌsɜːkl] *n* demi-cercle *m*.

semicolon [ˌsemɪˈkəʊlən] *n* point-virgule *m*.

semidetached [ˌsemɪdɪˈtætʃt] ◆ *adj* jumelé(e). ◆ *n Br* maison *f* jumelée.

semifinal [ˌsemɪˈfaɪnl] *n* demi-finale *f*.

seminar [ˈsemɪnɑːʳ] *n* séminaire *m*.

seminary [ˈsemɪnərɪ] *n* (RELIG) séminaire *m*.

semolina [ˌseməˈliːnə] *n* semoule *f*.

Senate [ˈsenɪt] *n* (POL): **the ~** le sénat; **the United States ~** le Sénat américain.

senator [ˈsenətəʳ] *n* sénateur *m*.

send [send] (*pt & pp* **sent**) *vt* (*gen*) envoyer; (*letter*) expédier, envoyer; **to ~ sb sthg, to ~ sthg to sb** envoyer qqch à qqn; **~ her my love** embrasse-la pour moi; **to ~ sb for sthg** envoyer qqn chercher qqch. ▶ **send for** *vt fus* 1. (*person*) appeler, faire venir. 2. (*by post*) commander par correspondance. ▶ **send in** *vt sep* (*report, application*) envoyer, soumettre. ▶ **send off** *vt sep* 1. (*by post*) expédier. 2. (SPORT) expulser. ▶ **send off for** *vt fus* commander par correspondance. ▶ **send up** *vt sep Br inf* (*imitate*) parodier, ridiculiser.

sender [ˈsendəʳ] *n* expéditeur *m*, -trice *f*.

send-off *n* fête *f* d'adieu.

senile [ˈsiːnaɪl] *adj* sénile.

senior ['siːnjə^r] ◆ *adj* **1.** (*highest-ranking*) plus haut placé(e). **2.** (*higher-ranking*): ~ **to sb** d'un rang plus élevé que qqn. **3.** (SCH) (*pupils, classes*) grand (e). ◆ *n* **1.** (*older person*) aîné *m*, -e *f*. **2.** (SCH) grand *m*, -e *f*.

senior citizen *n* personne *f* âgée OR du troisième âge.

sensation [sen'seɪʃn] *n* sensation *f*.

sensational [sen'seɪʃənl] *adj* (*gen*) sensationnel(elle).

sensationalist [sen'seɪʃnəlɪst] *adj pej* à sensation.

sense [sens] ◆ *n* **1.** (*ability, meaning*) sens *m*; **to make** ~ (*have meaning*) avoir un sens; ~ **of humour** sens de l'humour; ~ **of smell** odorat *m*. **2.** (*feeling*) sentiment *m*. **3.** (*wisdom*) bon sens *m*, intelligence *f*; **to make** ~ (*be sensible*) être logique. **4.** *phr*: **to come to one's** ~**s** (*be sensible again*) revenir à la raison; (*regain consciousness*) reprendre connaissance. ◆ *vt* (*feel*) sentir. ▶ **in a sense** *adv* dans un sens.

senseless ['senslɪs] *adj* **1.** (*stupid*) stupide. **2.** (*unconscious*) sans connaissance.

sensibilities [,sensɪ'bɪlətɪz] *npl* susceptibilité *f*.

sensible ['sensəbl] *adj* (*reasonable*) raisonnable, judicieux(euse).

sensitive ['sensɪtɪv] *adj* **1.** (*gen*): ~ **(to)** sensible (à). **2.** (*subject*) délicat(e). **3.** (*easily offended*): ~ **(about)** susceptible (en ce qui concerne).

sensual ['sensjʊəl] *adj* sensuel(elle).

sensuous ['sensjʊəs] *adj* qui affecte les sens.

sent [sent] *pt & pp* → **send.**

sentence ['sentəns] ◆ *n* **1.** (GRAMM) phrase *f*. **2.** (JUR) condamnation *f*, sentence *f*. ◆ *vt*: **to** ~ **sb (to)** condamner qqn (à).

sentiment ['sentɪmənt] *n* **1.** (*feeling*) sentiment *m*. **2.** (*opinion*) opinion *f*, avis *m*.

sentimental [,sentɪ'mentl] *adj* sentimental(e).

sentry ['sentrɪ] *n* sentinelle *f*.

separate [*adj & n* 'seprət, *vb* 'sepəreɪt] ◆ *adj* **1.** (*not joined*): ~ **(from)** séparé(e) (de). **2.** (*individual, distinct*) distinct(e). ◆ *vt* **1.** (*gen*): **to** ~ **sb/sthg (from)** séparer qqn/qqch (de); **to** ~ **sthg into** diviser OR séparer qqch en. **2.** (*distinguish*): **to** ~ **sb/sthg (from)** distinguer qqn/qqch (de). ◆ *vi* se séparer; **to** ~ **into** se diviser OR se séparer en. ▶ **separates** *npl* Br

coordonnés *mpl*.

separately ['seprətlɪ] *adv* séparément.

separation [,sepə'reɪʃn] *n* séparation *f*.

September [sep'tembə^r] *n* septembre *m*; **in** ~ en septembre; **last** ~ en septembre dernier; **this** ~ en septembre de cette année; **next** ~ en septembre prochain; **by** ~ en septembre, d'ici septembre; **every** ~ tous les ans en septembre; **during** ~ pendant le mois de septembre; **at the beginning of** ~ au début du mois de septembre, début septembre; **at the end of** ~ à la fin du mois de septembre, fin septembre; **in the middle of** ~ au milieu du mois de septembre, à la mi-septembre.

septic ['septɪk] *adj* infecté(e).

septic tank *n* fosse *f* septique.

sequel ['siːkwəl] *n* **1.** (*book, film*): ~ **(to)** suite *f* (de). **2.** (*consequence*): ~ **(to)** conséquence *f* (de).

sequence ['siːkwəns] *n* **1.** (*series*) suite *f*, succession *f*. **2.** (*order*) ordre *m*. **3.** (*of film*) séquence *f*.

Serb = **Serbian.**

Serbia ['sɜːbjə] *n* Serbie *f*.

Serbian ['sɜːbjən], **Serb** [sɜːb] ◆ *adj* serbe. ◆ *n* **1.** (*person*) Serbe *mf*. **2.** (*dialect*) serbe *m*.

serene [sɪ'riːn] *adj* (*calm*) serein(e), tranquille.

sergeant ['sɑːdʒənt] *n* **1.** (MIL) sergent *m*. **2.** (*in police*) brigadier *m*.

sergeant major *n* sergent-major *m*.

serial ['sɪərɪəl] *n* feuilleton *m*.

serial number *n* numéro *m* de série.

series ['sɪəriːz] (*pl inv*) *n* série *f*.

serious ['sɪərɪəs] *adj* sérieux(euse); (*illness, accident, trouble*) grave; **to be** ~ **about doing sthg** songer sérieusement à faire qqch.

seriously ['sɪərɪəslɪ] *adv* sérieusement; (*ill*) gravement; (*wounded*) grièvement, gravement; **to take sb/sthg** ~ prendre qqn/qqch au sérieux.

seriousness ['sɪərɪəsnɪs] *n* **1.** (*of mistake, illness*) gravité *f*. **2.** (*of person, speech*) sérieux *m*.

sermon ['sɜːmən] *n* sermon *m*.

serrated [sɪ'reɪtɪd] *adj* en dents de scie.

servant ['sɜːvənt] *n* domestique *mf*.

serve [sɜːv] ◆ *vt* **1.** (*work for*) servir. **2.** (*have effect*): **to** ~ **to do sthg** servir à faire qqch; **to** ~ **a purpose** (*subj: device etc*) servir à un usage. **3.** (*provide for*) desservir. **4.** (*meal, drink, customer*) servir; **to ~ sthg to sb, to ~ sb sthg** servir qqch à qqn. **5.** (JUR): **to ~ sb with a summons/writ, to ~ a summons/writ on sb** signifier une assignation/une citation à qqn. **6.** (*prison sentence*) purger, faire; (*apprenticeship*) faire. **7.** (SPORT) servir. **8.** *phr:* **it ~s him/you right** c'est bien fait pour lui/toi. ◆ *vi* servir; **to ~ as** servir de. ◆ *n* (SPORT) service *m*. ▶ **serve out, serve up** *vt sep* (*food*) servir.

service ['sɜːvɪs] ◆ *n* **1.** (*gen*) service *m*; **in/out of ~** en/hors service; **to be of ~ (to sb)** être utile (à qqn), rendre service (à qqn). **2.** (*of car*) révision *f*; (*of machine*) entretien *m*. ◆ *vt* (*car*) réviser; (*machine*) assurer l'entretien de. ▶ **services** *npl* **1.** (*on motorway*) aire *f* de services. **2.** (*armed forces*): **the ~s** les forces *fpl* armées. **3.** (*help*) service *m*.

serviceable ['sɜːvɪsəbl] *adj* pratique.

service area *n* aire *f* de services.

service charge *n* service *m*.

serviceman ['sɜːvɪsmən] (*pl* **-men** [-mən]) *n* soldat *m*, militaire *m*.

service station *n* station-service *f*.

serviette [ˌsɜːvɪ'et] *n* serviette *f* (de table).

sesame ['sesəmɪ] *n* sésame *m*.

session ['seʃn] *n* **1.** (*gen*) séance *f*. **2.** *Am* (*school term*) trimestre *m*.

set [set] (*pt* & *pp* **set**) ◆ *adj* **1.** (*fixed - gen*) fixe; (*- phrase*) figé(e). **2.** *Br* (SCH) (*book*) au programme. **3.** (*ready*): **~ (for sthg/to do sthg)** prêt(e) (à qqch/à faire qqch). **4.** (*determined*): **to be ~ on sthg** vouloir absolument qqch; **to be ~ on doing sthg** être résolu(e) à faire qqch; **to be dead ~ against sthg** s'opposer formellement à qqch. ◆ *n* **1.** (*of keys, tools, golf clubs etc*) jeu *m*; (*of stamps, books*) collection *f*; (*of saucepans*) série *f*; (*of tyres*) train *m*; **a ~ of teeth** (*natural*) une dentition, une denture; (*false*) un dentier. **2.** (*television, radio*) poste *m*. **3.** (CINEMA) plateau *m*; (THEATRE) scène *f*. **4.** (TENNIS) manche *f*, set *m*. ◆ *vt* **1.** (*place*) placer, poser, mettre; (*jewel*) sertir, monter. **2.** (*cause to be*): **to ~ sb free** libérer qqn, mettre qqn en liberté; **to ~ sthg in motion** mettre qqch en branle OR en route; **to ~ sthg on fire** mettre le feu à qqch. **3.** (*prepare - trap*) tendre; (*- table*) mettre. **4.** (*adjust*) régler. **5.** (*fix - date, deadline, target*) fixer. **6.** (*establish - example*) donner; (*- trend*) lancer; (*- record*) établir. **7.** (*homework, task*) donner; (*problem*) poser. **8.** (MED) (*bone, leg*) remettre. **9.** (*story*): **to be ~** se passer, se dérouler. ◆ *vi* **1.** (*sun*) se

coucher. **2.** (*jelly*) prendre; (*glue, cement*) durcir. ▶ **set about** *vt fus* (*start*) entreprendre, se mettre à; **to ~ about doing sthg** se mettre à faire qqch. ▶ **set aside** *vt sep* **1.** (*save*) mettre de côté. **2.** (*not consider*) rejeter, écarter. ▶ **set back** *vt sep* (*delay*) retarder. ▶ **set off** ◆ *vt sep* **1.** (*cause*) déclencher, provoquer. **2.** (*bomb*) faire exploser; (*firework*) faire partir. ◆ *vi* se mettre en route, partir. ▶ **set out** ◆ *vt sep* **1.** (*arrange*) disposer. **2.** (*explain*) présenter, exposer. ◆ *vt fus* (*intend*): **to ~ out to do sthg** entreprendre OR tenter de faire qqch. ◆ *vi* (*on journey*) se mettre en route, partir. ▶ **set up** *vt sep* **1.** (*organization*) créer, fonder; (*committee, procedure*) constituer, mettre en place; (*meeting*) arranger, organiser. **2.** (*roadblock*) placer, installer. **3.** (*equipment*) préparer, installer. **4.** *inf* (*make appear guilty*) monter un coup contre.

setback ['setbæk] *n* contretemps *m*, revers *m*.

set menu *n* menu *m* fixe.

settee [se'tiː] *n* canapé *m*.

setting ['setɪŋ] *n* **1.** (*surroundings*) décor *m*, cadre *m*. **2.** (*of dial, machine*) réglage *m*.

settle ['setl] ◆ *vt* **1.** (*argument*) régler; **that's ~d then** (c'est) entendu. **2.** (*bill, account*) régler, payer. **3.** (*calm - nerves*) calmer; **to ~ one's stomach** calmer les douleurs d'estomac. **4.** (*make comfortable*) installer. ◆ *vi* **1.** (*make one's home*) s'installer, se fixer. **2.** (*make oneself comfortable*) s'installer. **3.** (*dust*) retomber; (*sediment*) se déposer; (*bird, insect*) se poser. ▶ **settle down** *vi* **1.** (*give one's attention*): **to ~ down to sthg/to doing sthg** se mettre à qqch/à faire qqch. **2.** (*make oneself comfortable*) s'installer. **3.** (*become respectable*) se ranger. **4.** (*become calm*) calmer. ▶ **settle for** *vt fus* accepter, se contenter de. ▶ **settle in** *vi* s'adapter. ▶ **settle on** *vt fus* (*choose*) fixer son choix sur, se décider pour. ▶ **settle up** *vi*: **to ~ up (with sb)** régler (qqn).

settlement ['setlmənt] *n* **1.** (*agreement*) accord *m*. **2.** (*colony*) colonie *f*. **3.** (*payment*) règlement *m*.

settler ['setlər] *n* colon *m*.

set-up *n inf* **1.** (*system*): **what's the ~?** comment est-ce que c'est organisé? **2.** (*deception*) coup *m* monté.

seven ['sevn] *num* sept; *see also* **six**.

seventeen [ˌsevn'tiːn] *num* dix-sept; *see also* **six**.

seventeenth [ˌsevn'tiːnθ] *num* dix-septième; *see also* **sixth**.

seventh ['sevnθ] *num* septième; *see also* **sixth**.

seventy ['sevntɪ] *num* soixante-dix; *see also* **sixty**.

sever ['sevə**r**] *vt* **1.** (*cut through*) couper. **2.** *fig* (*relationship, ties*) rompre.

several ['sevrəl] ◆ *adj* plusieurs. ◆ *pron* plusieurs *mfpl*.

severance ['sevrəns] *n* (*of relations*) rupture *f*.

severance pay *n* indemnité *f* de licenciement.

severe [sɪ'vɪə**r**] *adj* **1.** (*weather*) rude, rigoureux(euse); (*shock*) gros (grosse), dur(e); (*pain*) violent(e); (*illness, injury*) grave. **2.** (*person, criticism*) sévère.

severity [sɪ'verɪtɪ] *n* **1.** (*of storm*) violence *f*; (*of problem, illness*) gravité *f*. **2.** (*sternness*) sévérité *f*.

sew [səʊ] (Br *pp* **sewn**, Am *pp* **sewed** OR **sewn**) *vt & vi* coudre. ▸ **sew up** *vt sep* (*join*) recoudre.

sewage ['suːɪdʒ] *n* (U) eaux *fpl* d'égout, eaux usées.

sewer ['suə**r**] *n* égout *m*.

sewing ['səʊɪŋ] *n* (U) **1.** (*activity*) couture *f*. **2.** (*work*) ouvrage *m*.

sewing machine *n* machine *f* à coudre.

sewn [səʊn] *pp* → **sew**.

sex [seks] *n* **1.** (*gender*) sexe *m*. **2.** (U) (*sexual intercourse*) rapports *mpl* (sexuels); **to have ~ with** avoir des rapports (sexuels) avec.

sexist ['seksɪst] ◆ *adj* sexiste. ◆ *n* sexiste *mf*.

sexual ['sekʃʊəl] *adj* sexuel(elle).

sexual harassment *n* harcèlement *m* sexuel.

sexual intercourse *n* (U) rapports *mpl* (sexuels).

sexy ['seksɪ] *adj inf* sexy (*inv*).

shabby ['ʃæbɪ] *adj* **1.** (*clothes*) élimé(e), râpé(e); (*furniture*) minable; (*person, street*) miteux(euse). **2.** (*behaviour*) moche, méprisable.

shack [ʃæk] *n* cabane *f*, hutte *f*.

shackle ['ʃækl] *vt* enchaîner; *fig* entraver. ▸ **shackles** *npl* fers *mpl*; *fig* entraves *fpl*.

shade [ʃeɪd] ◆ *n* **1.** (U) (*shadow*) ombre *f*. **2.** (*lampshade*) abat-jour *m inv*. **3.** (*colour*) nuance *f*, ton *m*. **4.** (*of meaning, opinion*) nuance *f*. ◆ *vt* (*from light*) abriter. ▸ **shades** *npl inf* (*sunglasses*) lunettes *fpl* de soleil.

shadow ['ʃædəʊ] *n* ombre *f*.

shadow cabinet *n* cabinet *m* fantôme.

shadowy ['ʃædəʊɪ] *adj* **1.** (*dark*) ombreux(euse). **2.** (*sinister*) mystérieux(euse).

shady ['ʃeɪdɪ] *adj* **1.** (*garden, street etc*) ombragé(e); (*tree*) qui donne de l'ombre. **2.** *inf* (*dishonest*) louche.

shaft [ʃɑːft] *n* **1.** (*vertical passage*) puits *m*; (*of lift*) cage *f*. **2.** (TECH) arbre *m*. **3.** (*of light*) rayon *m*. **4.** (*of tool, golf club*) manche *m*.

shaggy ['ʃægɪ] *adj* hirsute.

shake [ʃeɪk] (*pt* **shook**, *pp* **shaken**) ◆ *vt* **1.** (*move vigorously - gen*) secouer; (*- bottle*) agiter; **to ~ sb's hand** serrer la main de OR à qqn; **to ~ hands** se serrer la main; **to ~ one's head** secouer la tête; (*to say no*) faire non de la tête. **2.** (*shock*) ébranler, secouer. ◆ *vi* trembler. ◆ *n* (*tremble*) tremblement *m*; **to give sthg a ~** secouer qqch. ▸ **shake off** *vt sep* (*police, pursuers*) semer; (*illness*) se débarrasser de.

shaken ['ʃeɪkn] *pp* → **shake**.

shaky ['ʃeɪkɪ] *adj* (*building, table*) branlant(e); (*hand*) tremblant(e); (*person*) faible; (*argument, position*) incertain(e).

shall [*weak form* ʃəl, *strong form* ʃæl] *aux vb* **1.** (1st person sg & 1st person pl) (*to express future tense*): **I ~ be ...** je serai ... **2.** (*esp 1st person sg & 1st person pl*) (*in questions*): **~ we have lunch now?** tu veux qu'on déjeune maintenant?; **where ~ I put this?** où est-ce qu'il faut mettre ça? **3.** (*in orders*): **you ~ tell me!** tu vas OR dois me le dire!

shallow ['ʃæləʊ] *adj* **1.** (*water, dish, hole*) peu profond(e). **2.** *pej* (*superficial*) superficiel(elle).

sham [ʃæm] ◆ *adj* feint(e), simulé(e). ◆ *n* comédie *f*.

shambles ['ʃæmblz] *n* désordre *m*, pagaille *f*.

shame [ʃeɪm] ◆ *n* **1.** (U) (*remorse, humiliation*) honte *f*; **to bring ~ on** OR **upon sb** faire la honte de qqn. **2.** (*pity*): **it's a ~ (that ...)** c'est dommage (que ... (+ *subjunctive*)); **what a ~!** quel dommage! ◆ *vt* faire honte à, mortifier; **to ~ sb into doing sthg** obliger qqn à faire qqch en lui faisant honte.

shamefaced [ˌʃeɪm'feɪst] *adj* honteux(euse), penaud(e).

shameful ['ʃeɪmfʊl] *adj* honteux(euse), scandaleux(euse).

shameless ['ʃeɪmlɪs] *adj* effronté(e), éhonté(e).

shampoo [ʃæm'puː] (pl -s, pt & pp -ed, cont -ing) ♦ n shampooing m. ♦ vt: **to ~ sb's hair** faire un shampooing à qqn.

shamrock ['ʃæmrɒk] n trèfle m.

shandy ['ʃændɪ] n panaché m.

shan't [ʃɑːnt] = **shall not**.

shantytown ['ʃæntɪtaʊn] n bidonville m.

shape [ʃeɪp] ♦ n 1. (gen) forme f; **to take ~** prendre forme OR tournure. 2. (health): **to be in good/bad ~** être en bonne/mauvaise forme. ♦ vt 1. (pastry, clay etc): **to ~ sthg (into)** façonner OR modeler qqch (en). 2. (ideas, project, character) former. ► **shape up** vi (person, plans) se développer, progresser; (job, events) prendre tournure OR forme.

-shaped ['ʃeɪpt] suffix: **egg~** en forme d'œuf; **L~** en forme de L.

shapeless ['ʃeɪpləs] adj informe.

shapely ['ʃeɪplɪ] adj bien fait(e).

share [ʃeəʳ] ♦ n (portion, contribution) part f. ♦ vt partager. ♦ vi: **to ~ (in sthg)** partager (qqch). ► **shares** npl actions fpl. ► **share out** vt sep partager, répartir.

shareholder ['ʃeə,həʊldəʳ] n actionnaire mf.

shark [ʃɑːk] (pl inv OR -s) n (fish) requin m.

sharp [ʃɑːp] ♦ adj 1. (knife, razor) tranchant(e), affilé(e); (needle, pencil, teeth) pointu(e). 2. (image, outline, contrast) net (nette). 3. (person, mind) vif (vive); (eyesight) perçant(e). 4. (sudden - change, rise) brusque, soudain(e); (- hit, tap) sec (sèche). 5. (words, order, voice) cinglant(e). 6. (cry, sound) perçant(e); (pain, cold) vif (vive); (taste) piquant(e). 7. (MUS): **C/D ~** do/ré dièse. ♦ adv 1. (punctually): **at 8 o'clock ~** à 8 heures pile OR tapantes. 2. (immediately): **~ left/right** tout à fait à gauche/droite. ♦ n (MUS) dièse m.

sharpen ['ʃɑːpn] vt (knife, tool) aiguiser; (pencil) tailler.

sharpener ['ʃɑːpnəʳ] n (for pencil) taille-crayon m; (for knife) aiguisoir m (pour couteaux).

sharp-eyed [-'aɪd] adj: **she's very ~** elle remarque tout, rien ne lui échappe.

sharply ['ʃɑːplɪ] adv 1. (distinctly) nettement. 2. (suddenly) brusquement. 3. (harshly) sévèrement, durement.

shat [ʃæt] pt & pp → **shit**.

shatter ['ʃætəʳ] ♦ vt 1. (window, glass) briser, fracasser. 2. fig (hopes, dreams) détruire. ♦ vi se fracasser, voler en éclats.

shattered ['ʃætəd] adj 1. (upset) bouleversé(e). 2. Br inf (very tired) flapi(e).

shave [ʃeɪv] ♦ n: **to have a ~** se raser. ♦ vt 1. (remove hair from) raser. 2. (wood) planer, raboter. ♦ vi se raser.

shaver ['ʃeɪvəʳ] n rasoir m électrique.

shaving brush ['ʃeɪvɪŋ-] n blaireau m.

shaving cream ['ʃeɪvɪŋ-] n crème f à raser.

shaving foam ['ʃeɪvɪŋ-] n mousse f à raser.

shavings ['ʃeɪvɪŋz] npl (of wood, metal) copeaux mpl.

shawl [ʃɔːl] n châle m.

she [ʃiː] ♦ pers pron 1. (referring to woman, girl, animal) elle; **~'s tall** elle est grande; **SHE can't do it** elle, elle ne peut pas le faire; **there ~ is** la voilà; **if I were** OR **was ~** fml si j'étais elle, à sa place. 2. (referring to boat, car, country) follow the gender of your translation. ♦ comp: **~-elephant** éléphant m femelle; **~-wolf** louve f.

sheaf [ʃiːf] (pl **sheaves**) n 1. (of papers, letters) liasse f. 2. (of corn, grain) gerbe f.

shear [ʃɪəʳ] (pt -ed, pp -ed OR **shorn**) vt (sheep) tondre. ► **shears** npl 1. (for garden) sécateur m, cisaille f. 2. (for dressmaking) ciseaux mpl. ► **shear off** ♦ vt sep (branch) couper; (piece of metal) cisailler. ♦ vi se détacher.

sheath [ʃiːθ] (pl **sheaths** [ʃiːðz]) n 1. (for knife, cable) gaine f. 2. Br (condom) préservatif m.

sheaves [ʃiːvz] pl → **sheaf**.

shed [ʃed] (pt & pp **shed**) ♦ n (small) remise f, cabane f; (larger) hangar m. ♦ vt 1. (hair, skin, leaves) perdre. 2. (tears) verser, répandre. 3. (employees) se défaire de, congédier.

she'd [weak form ʃɪd, strong form ʃiːd] = **she had, she would**.

sheen [ʃiːn] n lustre m, éclat m.

sheep [ʃiːp] (pl inv) n mouton m.

sheepdog ['ʃiːpdɒg] n chien m de berger.

sheepish ['ʃiːpɪʃ] adj penaud(e).

sheepskin ['ʃiːpskɪn] n peau f de mouton.

sheer [ʃɪəʳ] adj 1. (absolute) pur(e). 2. (very steep) à pic, abrupt(e). 3. (material) fin(e).

sheet [ʃiːt] n 1. (for bed) drap m. 2. (of paper, glass, wood) feuille f; (of metal) plaque f.

sheik(h) [ʃeɪk] n cheik m.

shelf [ʃelf] (pl **shelves**) n (for storage) rayon m, étagère f.

shell [ʃel] ◆ n **1.** (of egg, nut, snail) coquille f. **2.** (of tortoise, crab) carapace f. **3.** (on beach) coquillage m. **4.** (of building, car) carcasse f. **5.** (MIL) obus m. ◆ vt **1.** (peas) écosser; (nuts, prawns) décortiquer; (eggs) enlever la coquille de, écaler. **2.** (MIL) bombarder.

she'll [ʃiːl] = **she will, she shall**.

shellfish [ˈʃelfɪʃ] (pl inv) n **1.** (creature) crustacé m, coquillage m. **2.** (U) (food) fruits mpl de mer.

shelter [ˈʃeltər] ◆ n abri m. ◆ vt **1.** (protect) abriter, protéger. **2.** (refugee, homeless person) offrir un asile à; (criminal, fugitive) cacher. ◆ vi s'abriter, se mettre à l'abri.

sheltered [ˈʃeltəd] adj **1.** (from weather) abrité(e). **2.** (life, childhood) protégé(e), sans soucis.

shelve [ʃelv] vt fig mettre au Frigidaire®, mettre en sommeil.

shelves [ʃelvz] pl → **shelf**.

shepherd [ˈʃepəd] ◆ n berger m. ◆ vt fig conduire.

shepherd's pie [ˈʃepədz-] n ≃ hachis m Parmentier.

sheriff [ˈʃerɪf] n Am shérif m.

sherry [ˈʃerɪ] n xérès m, sherry m.

she's [ʃiːz] = **she is, she has**.

Shetland [ˈʃetlənd] n: **(the) ~ (Islands)** les (îles) Shetland fpl.

sh(h) [ʃ] excl chut!

shield [ʃiːld] ◆ n **1.** (armour) bouclier m. **2.** Br (sports trophy) plaque f. ◆ vt: **to ~ sb (from)** protéger qqn (de OR contre).

shift [ʃɪft] ◆ n **1.** (change) changement m, modification f. **2.** (period of work) poste m; (workers) équipe f. ◆ vt **1.** (move) déplacer, changer de place. **2.** (change) changer, modifier. ◆ vi **1.** (move - gen) changer de place; (- wind) tourner, changer. **2.** (change) changer, se modifier. **3.** Am (AUT) changer de vitesse.

shiftless [ˈʃɪftlɪs] adj fainéant(e), paresseux(euse).

shifty [ˈʃɪftɪ] adj inf sournois(e), louche.

shilling [ˈʃɪlɪŋ] n shilling m.

shilly-shally [ˈʃɪlɪˌʃælɪ] vi hésiter, être indécis(e).

shimmer [ˈʃɪmər] ◆ n reflet m, miroitement m. ◆ vi miroiter.

shin [ʃɪn] n tibia m.

shinbone [ˈʃɪnbəʊn] n tibia m.

shine [ʃaɪn] (pt & pp shone) ◆ n brillant m. ◆ vt **1.** (direct): **to ~ a torch on sthg** éclairer qqch. **2.** (polish) faire briller, astiquer. ◆ vi briller.

shingle [ˈʃɪŋgl] n (U) (on beach) galets mpl. ▶ **shingles** n (U) zona m.

shiny [ˈʃaɪnɪ] adj brillant(e).

ship [ʃɪp] ◆ n bateau m; (larger) navire m. ◆ vt (goods) expédier; (troops, passengers) transporter.

shipbuilding [ˈʃɪpˌbɪldɪŋ] n construction f navale.

shipment [ˈʃɪpmənt] n (cargo) cargaison f, chargement m.

shipper [ˈʃɪpər] n affréteur m, chargeur m.

shipping [ˈʃɪpɪŋ] n (U) **1.** (transport) transport m maritime. **2.** (ships) navires mpl.

shipshape [ˈʃɪpʃeɪp] adj bien rangé(e), en ordre.

shipwreck [ˈʃɪprek] ◆ n **1.** (destruction of ship) naufrage m. **2.** (wrecked ship) épave f. ◆ vt: **to be ~ed** faire naufrage.

shipyard [ˈʃɪpjɑːd] n chantier m naval.

shire [ʃaɪər] n (county) comté m.

shirk [ʃɜːk] vt se dérober à.

shirt [ʃɜːt] n chemise f.

shirtsleeves [ˈʃɜːtsliːvz] npl: **to be in (one's) ~** être en manches OR en bras de chemise.

shit [ʃɪt] (pt & pp **shit** OR **-ted** OR **shat**) vulg ◆ n **1.** (excrement) merde f. **2.** (U) (nonsense) conneries fpl. ◆ vi chier. ◆ excl merde!

shiver [ˈʃɪvər] ◆ n frisson m. ◆ vi: **to ~ (with)** trembler (de), frissonner (de).

shoal [ʃəʊl] n (of fish) banc m.

shock [ʃɒk] ◆ n **1.** (surprise) choc m, coup m. **2.** (U) (MED): **to be suffering from ~, to be in (a state of) ~** être en état de choc. **3.** (impact) choc m, heurt m. **4.** (ELEC) décharge f électrique. ◆ vt **1.** (upset) bouleverser. **2.** (offend) choquer, scandaliser.

shock absorber [-əbˌzɔːbər] n amortisseur m.

shocking [ˈʃɒkɪŋ] adj **1.** (very bad) épouvantable, terrible. **2.** (outrageous) scandaleux(euse).

shod [ʃɒd] ◆ pt & pp → **shoe**. ◆ adj chaussé(e).

shoddy [ˈʃɒdɪ] adj (goods, work) de mauvaise qualité; (treatment) indigne, méprisable.

shoe [ʃuː] (pt & pp **-ed** OR **shod**) ◆ n chaussure f, soulier m. ◆ vt (horse) ferrer.

shoebrush [ˈʃuːbrʌʃ] n brosse f à chaussures.

shoehorn [ˈʃuːhɔːn] n chausse-pied m.

shoelace [ˈʃuːleɪs] n lacet m de soulier.

shoe polish n cirage m.

shoe shop n magasin m de chaussures.

shoestring ['ʃuːstrɪŋ] n fig: **on a ~** à peu de frais.

shone [ʃɒn] pt & pp → **shine**.

shoo [ʃuː] ◆ vt chasser. ◆ excl ouste!

shook [ʃʊk] pt → **shake**.

shoot [ʃuːt] (pt & pp **shot**) ◆ vt **1.** (kill with gun) tuer d'un coup de feu; (wound with gun) blesser d'un coup de feu; **to ~ o.s.** (kill o.s.) se tuer avec une arme à feu. **2.** Br (hunt) chasser. **3.** (arrow) décocher, tirer. **4.** (CINEMA) tourner. ◆ vi **1.** (fire gun): **to ~ (at)** tirer (sur). **2.** Br (hunt) chasser. **3.** (move quickly): **to ~ in/out/past** entrer/sortir/passer en trombe, entrer/sortir/passer comme un bolide. **4.** (CINEMA) tourner. **5.** (SPORT) tirer, shooter. ◆ n **1.** Br (hunting expedition) partie f de chasse. **2.** (of plant) pousse f. ▶ **shoot down** vt sep **1.** (aeroplane) descendre, abattre. **2.** (person) abattre. ▶ **shoot up** vi **1.** (child, plant) pousser vite. **2.** (price, inflation) monter en flèche.

shooting ['ʃuːtɪŋ] n **1.** (killing) meurtre m. **2.** (U) (hunting) chasse f.

shooting star n étoile f filante.

shop [ʃɒp] ◆ n **1.** (store) magasin m, boutique f. **2.** (workshop) atelier m. ◆ vi faire ses courses; **to go shopping** aller faire les courses OR commissions.

shop assistant n Br vendeur m, -euse f.

shop floor n: **the ~** fig les ouvriers mpl.

shopkeeper ['ʃɒp,kiːpər] n commerçant m, -e f.

shoplifting ['ʃɒp,lɪftɪŋ] n (U) vol m à l'étalage.

shopper ['ʃɒpər] n personne f qui fait ses courses.

shopping ['ʃɒpɪŋ] n (U) (purchases) achats mpl.

shopping bag n sac m à provisions.

shopping centre Br, **shopping mall** Am, **shopping plaza** Am [-,plɑːzə] n centre m commercial.

shopsoiled Br ['ʃɒpsɔɪld], **shopworn** Am ['ʃɒpwɔːn] adj qui a fait l'étalage, abîmé(e) (en magasin).

shop steward n délégué syndical m, déléguée syndicale f.

shopwindow [,ʃɒp'wɪndəʊ] n vitrine f.

shopworn Am = **shopsoiled**.

shore [ʃɔːr] n rivage m, bord m; **on ~** à terre. ▶ **shore up** vt sep étayer, étançonner; fig consolider.

shorn [ʃɔːn] ◆ pp → **shear**. ◆ adj tondu(e).

short [ʃɔːt] ◆ adj **1.** (not long - in time) court(e), bref (brève); (- in space) court. **2.** (not tall) petit(e). **3.** (curt) brusque, sec (sèche). **4.** (lacking): **time/money is ~** nous manquons de temps/d'argent; **to be ~ of** manquer de. **5.** (abbreviated): **to be ~ for** être le diminutif de. ◆ adv: **to be running ~ of** (running out of) commencer à manquer de, commencer à être à court de; **to cut sthg ~** (visit, speech) écourter qqch; (discussion) couper court à qqch; **to stop ~** s'arrêter net. ◆ n **1.** Br (alcoholic drink) alcool m fort. **2.** (film) court métrage m. ▶ **shorts** npl **1.** (gen) short m. **2.** Am (underwear) caleçon m. ▶ **for short** adv: **he's called Bob for ~** Bob est son diminutif. ▶ **in short** adv (enfin) bref. ▶ **nothing short of** prep rien moins que, pratiquement. ▶ **short of** prep (unless, without): **~ of doing sthg** à moins de faire qqch, à part faire qqch.

shortage ['ʃɔːtɪdʒ] n manque m, insuffisance f.

shortbread ['ʃɔːtbred] n sablé m.

short-change vt **1.** (subj: shopkeeper): **to ~ sb** ne pas rendre assez à qqn. **2.** fig (cheat) tromper, rouler.

short circuit n court-circuit m.

shortcomings ['ʃɔːt,kʌmɪŋz] npl défauts mpl.

shortcrust pastry ['ʃɔːtkrʌst-] n pâte f brisée.

short cut n **1.** (quick route) raccourci m. **2.** (quick method) solution f miracle.

shorten ['ʃɔːtn] ◆ vt **1.** (holiday, time) écourter. **2.** (skirt, rope etc) raccourcir. ◆ vi (days) raccourcir.

shortfall ['ʃɔːtfɔːl] n déficit m.

shorthand ['ʃɔːthænd] n (U) (writing system) sténographie f.

shorthand typist n Br sténodactylo f.

short list n Br liste f des candidats sélectionnés.

shortly ['ʃɔːtlɪ] adv (soon) bientôt.

shortsighted [,ʃɔːt'saɪtɪd] adj myope; fig imprévoyant(e).

short-staffed [-'stɑːft] adj: **to be ~** manquer de personnel.

short story n nouvelle f.

short-tempered [-'tempəd] adj emporté(e), irascible.

short-term adj (effects, solution) à court terme; (problem) de courte durée.

short wave n (U) ondes fpl courtes.

shot [ʃɒt] ◆ *pt & pp* → **shoot**. ◆ *n*
1. (*gunshot*) coup *m* de feu; **like a ~** sans
tarder, sans hésiter. 2. (*marksman*)
tireur *m*. 3. (SPORT) coup *m*. 4. (*photograph*) photo *f*; (CINEMA) plan *m*. 5. *inf*
(*attempt*): **to have a ~ at sthg** essayer de
faire qqch. 6. (*injection*) piqûre *f*.
shotgun [ʃɒtɡʌn] *n* fusil *m* de chasse.
should [ʃʊd] *aux vb* 1. (*indicating duty*):
we ~ leave now il faudrait partir maintenant. 2. (*seeking advice, permission*): **~ I
go too?** est-ce que je devrais y aller
aussi? 3. (*as suggestion*): **I ~ deny everything** moi, je nierais tout. 4. (*indicating
probability*): **she ~ be home soon** elle
devrait être de retour bientôt, elle va
bientôt rentrer. 5. (*was or were expected*):
they ~ have won the match ils auraient
dû gagner le match. 6. (*indicating intention, wish*): **I ~ like to come with you**
j'aimerais bien venir avec vous. 7. (*as
conditional*): **you ~ go if you're invited** tu
devrais y aller si tu es invité. 8. (*in subordinate clauses*): **we decided that you ~
meet him** nous avons décidé que ce
serait toi qui irais le chercher.
9. (*expressing uncertain opinion*): **I ~ think
he's about 50 (years old)** je pense qu'il
doit avoir dans les 50 ans.
shoulder [ʃəʊldər] ◆ *n* épaule *f*.
◆ *vt* 1. (*carry*) porter. 2. (*responsibility*)
endosser.
shoulder blade *n* omoplate *f*.
shoulder strap *n* 1. (*on dress*)
bretelle *f*. 2. (*on bag*) bandoulière *f*.
shouldn't [ʃʊdnt] = **should not**.
should've [ʃʊdəv] = **should have**.
shout [ʃaʊt] ◆ *n* (*cry*) cri *m*. ◆ *vt & vi*
crier. ▶ **shout down** *vt sep* huer.
shouting [ʃaʊtɪŋ] *n* (U) cris *mpl*.
shove [ʃʌv] ◆ *n*: **to give sb/sthg a ~**
pousser qqn/qqch. ◆ *vt* pousser; **to ~
clothes into a bag** fourrer des vêtements dans un sac. ▶ **shove off** *vi*
1. (*in boat*) pousser au large. 2. *inf* (*go
away*) ficher le camp, filer.
shovel [ʃʌvl] ◆ *n* (*tool*) pelle *f*. ◆ *vt*
enlever à la pelle, pelleter.
show [ʃəʊ] (*pt* -ed, *pp* shown OR -ed)
◆ *n* 1. (*display*) démonstration *f*, manifestation *f*. 2. (*at theatre*) spectacle *m*;
(*on radio, TV*) émission *f*. 3. (CINEMA)
séance *f*. 4. (*exhibition*) exposition *f*. ◆ *vt*
1. (*gen*) montrer; (*profit, loss*) indiquer;
(*respect*) témoigner; (*courage, mercy*) faire
preuve de; **to ~ sb sthg, to ~ sthg to sb**
montrer qqch à qqn. 2. (*escort*): **to ~ sb
to his seat/table** conduire qqn à sa

place/sa table. 3. (*film*) projeter, passer; (TV *programme*) donner, passer. ◆ *vi*
1. (*indicate*) indiquer, montrer. 2. (*be visible*) se voir, être visible. 3. (CINEMA):
what's ~ing tonight? qu'est-ce qu'on
joue comme film ce soir? ▶ **show off**
◆ *vt sep* exhiber. ◆ *vi* faire l'intéres-
sant(e). ▶ **show up** ◆ *vt sep* (*embarrass*)
embarrasser, faire honte à. ◆ *vi*
1. (*stand out*) se voir, ressortir. 2. (*arrive*)
s'amener, rappliquer.
show business *n* (U) monde *m* du
spectacle, show-business *m*.
showdown [ʃəʊdaʊn] *n*: **to have a ~
with sb** s'expliquer avec qqn.
shower [ʃaʊər] ◆ *n* 1. (*device, act*)
douche *f*; **to have OR take a ~** prendre
une douche, se doucher. 2. (*of rain*)
averse *f*. 3. *fig* (*of questions, confetti*)
avalanche *f*, déluge *m*. ◆ *vt*: **to ~ sb with**
couvrir qqn de. ◆ *vi* (*wash*) prendre une
douche, se doucher.
shower cap *n* bonnet *m* de douche.
shower room *n* salle *f* d'eau.
showing [ʃəʊɪŋ] *n* (CINEMA) projection
f.
show jumping [-,dʒʌmpɪŋ] *n* jumping *m*.
shown [ʃəʊn] *pp* → **show**.
show-off *n inf* m'as-tu-vu *m*, -e *f*.
showpiece [ʃəʊpiːs] *n* (*main attraction*)
joyau *m*, trésor *m*.
showroom [ʃəʊrʊm] *n* salle *f* OR magasin *m* d'exposition; (*for cars*) salle de
démonstration.
shrank [ʃræŋk] *pt* → **shrink**.
shrapnel [ʃræpnl] *n* (U) éclats *mpl*
d'obus.
shred [ʃred] ◆ *n* 1. (*of material, paper*)
lambeau *m*, brin *m*. 2. *fig* (*of evidence*)
parcelle *f*; (*of truth*) once *f*, grain *m*. ◆ *vt*
(*food*) râper; (*paper*) déchirer en lambeaux.
shredder [ʃredər] *n* (*machine*) destructeur *m* de documents.
shrewd [ʃruːd] *adj* fin(e), astucieux
(euse).
shriek [ʃriːk] ◆ *n* cri *m* perçant,
hurlement *m*; (*of laughter*) éclat *m*. ◆ *vi*
pousser un cri perçant.
shrill [ʃrɪl] *adj* (*sound, voice*) aigu(ë);
(*whistle*) strident(e).
shrimp [ʃrɪmp] *n* crevette *f*.
shrine [ʃraɪn] *n* (*place of worship*) lieu *m*
saint.
shrink [ʃrɪŋk] (*pt* shrank, *pp* shrunk)
◆ *vt* rétrécir. ◆ *vi* 1. (*cloth, garment*) rétrécir; (*person*) rapetisser; *fig* (*income, popu-*

larity etc) baisser, diminuer. **2.** (*recoil*): **to ~ away from sthg** reculer devant qqch; **to ~ from doing sthg** rechigner OR répugner à faire qqch.

shrinkage ['ʃrɪŋkɪdʒ] *n* rétrécissement *m*; *fig* diminution *f*, baisse *f*.

shrink-wrap *vt* emballer sous film plastique.

shrivel ['ʃrɪvl] ◆ *vt*: **to ~ (up)** rider, flétrir. ◆ *vi*: **to ~ (up)** se rider, se flétrir.

shroud [ʃraʊd] ◆ *n* (*cloth*) linceul *m*. ◆ *vt*: **to be ~ed in** (*darkness, fog*) être enseveli(e) sous; (*mystery*) être enveloppé(e) de.

Shrove Tuesday ['ʃrəʊv-] *n* Mardi *m* gras.

shrub [ʃrʌb] *n* arbuste *m*.

shrubbery ['ʃrʌbərɪ] *n* massif *m* d'arbustes.

shrug [ʃrʌg] ◆ *vt*: **to ~ one's shoulders** hausser les épaules. ◆ *vi* hausser les épaules. ▶ **shrug off** *vt sep* ignorer.

shrunk [ʃrʌŋk] *pp* → **shrink**.

shudder ['ʃʌdər] *vi* **1.** (*tremble*): **to ~ (with)** frémir (de), frissonner (de). **2.** (*shake*) vibrer, trembler.

shuffle ['ʃʌfl] *vt* **1.** (*drag*): **to ~ one's feet** traîner les pieds. **2.** (*cards*) mélanger, battre.

shun [ʃʌn] *vt* fuir, éviter.

shunt [ʃʌnt] *vt* (RAIL) aiguiller.

shut [ʃʌt] (*pt & pp* **shut**) ◆ *adj* (*closed*) fermé(e). ◆ *vt* fermer. ◆ *vi* **1.** (*door, window*) se fermer. **2.** (*shop*) fermer. ▶ **shut away** *vt sep* (*valuables, papers*) mettre sous clef. ▶ **shut down** *vt sep & vi* fermer. ▶ **shut out** *vt sep* (*noise*) supprimer; (*light*) ne pas laisser entrer; **to ~ sb out** laisser qqn à la porte. ▶ **shut up** *inf* ◆ *vt sep* (*silence*) faire taire. ◆ *vi* se taire.

shutter ['ʃʌtər] *n* **1.** (*on window*) volet *m*. **2.** (*in camera*) obturateur *m*.

shuttle ['ʃʌtl] ◆ *adj*: **~ service** (*service m de*) navette *f*. ◆ *n* (*train, bus, plane*) navette *f*.

shuttlecock ['ʃʌtlkɒk] *n* volant *m*.

shy [ʃaɪ] ◆ *adj* (*timid*) timide. ◆ *vi* (*horse*) s'effaroucher.

Siberia [saɪ'bɪərɪə] *n* Sibérie *f*.

sibling ['sɪblɪŋ] *n* (*brother*) frère *m*; (*sister*) sœur *f*.

Sicily ['sɪsɪlɪ] *n* Sicile *f*

sick [sɪk] *adj* **1.** (*ill*) malade. **2.** (*nauseous*): **to feel ~** avoir envie de vomir, avoir mal au cœur; **to be ~** Br (*vomit*) vomir. **3.** (*fed up*): **to be ~ of** en avoir

assez OR marre de. **4.** (*joke, humour*) macabre.

sickbay ['sɪkbeɪ] *n* infirmerie *f*.

sicken ['sɪkn] ◆ *vt* écœurer, dégoûter. ◆ *vi* Br: **to be ~ing for sthg** couver qqch.

sickening ['sɪknɪŋ] *adj* (*disgusting*) écœurant(e), dégoûtant(e).

sickle ['sɪkl] *n* faucille *f*.

sick leave *n* (U) congé *m* de maladie.

sickly ['sɪklɪ] *adj* **1.** (*unhealthy*) maladif(ive), souffreteux(euse). **2.** (*smell, taste*) écœurant(e).

sickness ['sɪknɪs] *n* **1.** (*illness*) maladie *f*. **2.** Br (U) (*nausea*) nausée *f*, nausées *fpl*; (*vomiting*) vomissement *m*, vomissements *mpl*.

sick pay *n* (U) indemnité *f* OR allocation *f* de maladie.

side [saɪd] ◆ *n* **1.** (*gen*) côté *m*; **at** OR **by my/her** *etc* **~** à mes/ses *etc* côtés; **on every ~, on all ~s** de tous côtés; **from ~ to ~** d'un côté à l'autre; **~ by ~** côte à côte. **2.** (*of table, river*) bord *m*. **3.** (*of hill, valley*) versant *m*, flanc *m*. **4.** (*in war, debate*) camp *m*, côté *m*; (SPORT) équipe *f*, camp; (*of argument*) point *m* de vue; **to take sb's ~** prendre le parti de qqn. **5.** (*aspect - gen*) aspect *m*; (*- of character*) facette *f*; **to be on the safe ~** pour plus de sûreté, par précaution. ◆ *adj* (*situated on side*) latéral(e). ▶ **side with** *vt fus* prendre le parti de, se ranger du côté de.

sideboard ['saɪdbɔːd] *n* (*cupboard*) buffet *m*.

sideboards Br ['saɪdbɔːdz], **sideburns** Am ['saɪdbɜːnz] *npl* favoris *mpl*, rouflaquettes *fpl*.

side effect *n* **1.** (MED) effet *m* secondaire OR indésirable. **2.** (*unplanned result*) effet *m* secondaire, répercussion *f*.

sidelight ['saɪdlaɪt] *n* (AUT) feu *m* de position.

sideline ['saɪdlaɪn] *n* **1.** (*extra business*) activité *f* secondaire. **2.** (SPORT) ligne *f* de touche.

sidelong ['saɪdlɒŋ] *adj & adv* de côté.

sidesaddle ['saɪd,sædl] *adv*: **to ride ~** monter en amazone.

sideshow ['saɪdʃəʊ] *n* spectacle *m* forain.

sidestep ['saɪdstep] *vt* faire un pas de côté pour éviter OR esquiver; *fig* éviter.

side street *n* (*not main street*) petite rue *f*; (*off main street*) rue transversale.

sidetrack ['saɪdtræk] *vt*: **to be ~ed** se laisser distraire.

sidewalk ['saɪdwɔːk] *n* Am trottoir *m*.

sideways ['saɪdweɪz] *adj* & *adv* de côté.

siding ['saɪdɪŋ] *n* voie *f* de garage.

sidle ['saɪdl] ▶ **sidle up** *vi*: to ~ up to sb se glisser vers qqn.

siege [siːdʒ] *n* siège *m*.

sieve [sɪv] ◆ *n* (*for flour, sand etc*) tamis *m*; (*for liquids*) passoire *f*. ◆ *vt* (*flour etc*) tamiser; (*liquid*) passer.

sift [sɪft] ◆ *vt* 1. (*flour, sand*) tamiser. 2. *fig* (*evidence*) passer au crible. ◆ *vi*: to ~ through examiner, éplucher.

sigh [saɪ] ◆ *n* soupir *m*. ◆ *vi* (*person*) soupirer, pousser un soupir.

sight [saɪt] ◆ *n* 1. (*seeing*) vue *f*; in ~ en vue; in/out of ~ en/hors de vue; at first ~ à première vue, au premier abord. 2. (*spectacle*) spectacle *m*. 3. (*on gun*) mire *f*. ◆ *vt* apercevoir. ▶ **sights** *npl* (*of city*) attractions *fpl* touristiques.

sightseeing ['saɪt,siːɪŋ] *n* tourisme *m*; to go ~ faire du tourisme.

sightseer ['saɪt,siːə^r] *n* touriste *mf*.

sign [saɪn] ◆ *n* 1. (*gen*) signe *m*; no ~ of aucune trace de. 2. (*notice*) enseigne *f*; (AUT) panneau *m*. ◆ *vt* signer. ▶ **sign on** *vi* 1. (*enrol* - MIL) s'engager; (- *for course*) s'inscrire. 2. (*register as unemployed*) s'inscrire au chômage. ▶ **sign up** ◆ *vt sep* (*worker*) embaucher; (*soldier*) engager. ◆ *vi* (MIL) s'engager; (*for course*) s'inscrire.

signal ['sɪgnl] ◆ *n* signal *m*. ◆ *vt* 1. (*indicate*) indiquer. 2. (*gesture to*): to ~ sb (to do sthg) faire signe à qqn (de faire qqch). ◆ *vi* 1. (AUT) clignoter, mettre son clignotant. 2. (*gesture*): to ~ sb (to do sthg) faire signe à qqn (de faire qqch).

signalman ['sɪgnlmən] (*pl* -men [-mən]) *n* (RAIL) aiguilleur *m*.

signature ['sɪgnətʃə^r] *n* (*name*) signature *f*.

signature tune *n* indicatif *m*.

signet ring ['sɪgnɪt-] *n* chevalière *f*.

significance [sɪg'nɪfɪkəns] *n* 1. (*importance*) importance *f*, portée *f*. 2. (*meaning*) signification *f*.

significant [sɪg'nɪfɪkənt] *adj* 1. (*considerable*) considérable. 2. (*important*) important(e). 3. (*meaningful*) significatif (ive).

signify ['sɪgnɪfaɪ] *vt* signifier, indiquer.

signpost ['saɪnpəʊst] *n* poteau *m* indicateur.

Sikh [siːk] ◆ *adj* sikh (*inv*). ◆ *n* (*person*) Sikh *mf*.

silence ['saɪləns] ◆ *n* silence *m*. ◆ *vt*

réduire au silence, faire taire.

silencer ['saɪlənsə^r] *n* silencieux *m*.

silent ['saɪlənt] *adj* 1. (*person, place*) silencieux(euse). 2. (CINEMA & LING) muet(ette).

silhouette [,sɪluː'et] *n* silhouette *f*.

silicon chip [,sɪlɪkən-] *n* puce *f*, pastille *f* de silicium.

silk [sɪlk] ◆ *n* soie *f*. ◆ *comp* en OR de soie.

silky ['sɪlkɪ] *adj* soyeux(euse).

sill [sɪl] *n* (*of window*) rebord *m*.

silly ['sɪlɪ] *adj* stupide, bête.

silo ['saɪləʊ] (*pl* -s) *n* silo *m*.

silt [sɪlt] *n* vase *f*, limon *m*.

silver ['sɪlvə^r] ◆ *adj* (*colour*) argenté(e). ◆ *n* (U) 1. (*metal*) argent *m*. 2. (*coins*) pièces *fpl* d'argent. 3. (*silverware*) argenterie *f*. ◆ *comp* en argent, d'argent.

silver foil, silver paper *n* (U) papier *m* d'argent OR d'étain.

silver-plated [-'pleɪtɪd] *adj* plaqué(e) argent.

silversmith ['sɪlvəsmɪθ] *n* orfèvre *mf*.

silverware ['sɪlvəweə^r] *n* (U) 1. (*dishes, spoons, etc*) argenterie *f*. 2. *Am* (*cutlery*) couverts *mpl*.

similar ['sɪmɪlə^r] *adj*: ~ (to) semblable (à), similaire (à).

similarly ['sɪmɪləlɪ] *adv* de la même manière, pareillement.

simmer ['sɪmə^r] *vt* faire cuire à feu doux, mijoter.

simpering ['sɪmpərɪŋ] *adj* affecté(e).

simple ['sɪmpl] *adj* 1. (*gen*) simple. 2. *dated (mentally retarded)* simplet(ette), simple d'esprit.

simplicity [sɪm'plɪsətɪ] *n* simplicité *f*.

simplify ['sɪmplɪfaɪ] *vt* simplifier.

simply ['sɪmplɪ] *adv* 1. (*gen*) simplement; quite ~ tout simplement. 2. (*for emphasis*) absolument.

simulate ['sɪmjʊleɪt] *vt* simuler.

simultaneous [Br ,sɪml'teɪnjəs, Am ,saɪməl'teɪnjəs] *adj* simultané(e).

sin [sɪn] ◆ *n* péché *m*. ◆ *vi*: to ~ (against) pécher (contre).

since [sɪns] ◆ *adv* depuis. ◆ *prep* depuis. ◆ *conj* 1. (*in time*) depuis que. 2. (*because*) comme, puisque.

sincere [sɪn'sɪə^r] *adj* sincère.

sincerely [sɪn'sɪəlɪ] *adv* sincèrement; Yours ~ (*at end of letter*) veuillez agréer, Monsieur/Madame, l'expression de mes sentiments les meilleurs.

sincerity [sɪn'serətɪ] *n* sincérité *f*.

sinew ['sɪnjuː] *n* tendon *m*.

sinful ['sɪnfʊl] *adj* (*thought*) mauvais(e);

(desire, act) coupable; ~ **person** pécheur *m*, -eresse *f*.

sing [sɪŋ] *(pt* **sang**, *pp* **sung)** *vt & vi* chanter.

Singapore [ˌsɪŋəˈpɔːʳ] *n* Singapour *m*.

singe [sɪndʒ] *vt* brûler légèrement; *(cloth)* roussir.

singer [ˈsɪŋəʳ] *n* chanteur *m*, -euse *f*.

singing [ˈsɪŋɪŋ] *n* (U) chant *m*.

single [ˈsɪŋgl] ◆ *adj* **1.** *(only one)* seul(e), unique; **every** ~ chaque. **2.** *(unmarried)* célibataire. **3.** Br *(ticket)* simple. ◆ *n* **1.** Br *(one-way ticket)* billet *m* simple, aller *m* (simple). **2.** (MUS) *(disque m)* 45 tours *m*. ▶ **singles** *npl* (TENNIS) simples *mpl.* ▶ **single out** *vt sep*: **to** ~ **sb out (for)** choisir qqn (pour).

single bed *n* lit *m* à une place.

single-breasted [-ˈbrestɪd] *adj (jacket)* droit(e).

single cream *n* Br crème *f* liquide.

single file *n*: **in** ~ en file indienne, à la file.

single-handed [-ˈhændɪd] *adv* tout seul (toute seule).

single-minded [-ˈmaɪndɪd] *adj* résolu(e).

single-parent family *n* famille *f* monoparentale.

single room *n* chambre *f* pour une personne OR à un lit.

singlet [ˈsɪŋglɪt] *n* Br tricot *m* de peau; (SPORT) maillot *m*.

singular [ˈsɪŋgjʊləʳ] ◆ *adj* singulier (ère). ◆ *n* singulier *m*.

sinister [ˈsɪnɪstəʳ] *adj* sinistre.

sink [sɪŋk] *(pt* **sank**, *pp* **sunk)** ◆ *n (in kitchen)* évier *m*; *(in bathroom)* lavabo *m*. ◆ *vt* **1.** *(ship)* couler. **2.** *(teeth, claws)*: **to** ~ **sthg into** enfoncer qqch dans. ◆ *vi* **1.** *(in water - ship)* couler, sombrer; *(- person, object)* couler. **2.** *(ground)* s'affaisser; *(sun)* baisser; **to** ~ **into poverty/despair** sombrer dans la misère/le désespoir. **3.** *(value, amount)* baisser, diminuer; *(voice)* faiblir. ▶ **sink in** *vi*: **it hasn't sunk in yet** je n'ai pas encore réalisé.

sink unit *n* bloc-évier *m*.

sinner [ˈsɪnəʳ] *n* pécheur *m*, -eresse *f*.

sinus [ˈsaɪnəs] *(pl* **-es)** *n* sinus *m inv*.

sip [sɪp] ◆ *n* petite gorgée *f*. ◆ *vt* siroter, boire à petits coups.

siphon [ˈsaɪfn] *n* siphon *m*. ▶ **siphon off** *vt sep* **1.** *(liquid)* siphonner. **2.** *fig (money)* canaliser.

sir [sɜːʳ] *n* **1.** *(form of address)* monsieur *m*. **2.** *(in titles)*: **Sir Phillip Holden** sir Phillip Holden.

siren [ˈsaɪərən] *n* sirène *f*.

sirloin (steak) [ˈsɜːlɔɪn-] *n* bifteck *m* dans l'aloyau or d'aloyau.

sissy [ˈsɪsɪ] *n inf* poule *f* mouillée, dégonflé *m*, -e *f*.

sister [ˈsɪstəʳ] *n* **1.** *(sibling)* sœur *f*. **2.** *(nun)* sœur *f*, religieuse *f*. **3.** Br *(senior nurse)* infirmière *f* chef.

sister-in-law *(pl* **sisters-in-law** OR **sister-in-laws)** *n* belle-sœur *f*.

sit [sɪt] *(pt & pp* **sat)** ◆ *vt* Br *(exam)* passer. ◆ *vi* **1.** *(person)* s'asseoir; **to be sitting** être assis(e); **to** ~ **on a committee** faire partie OR être membre d'un comité. **2.** *(court, parliament)* siéger, être en séance. ▶ **sit about, sit around** *vi* rester assis(e) à ne rien faire. ▶ **sit down** *vi* s'asseoir. ▶ **sit in on** *vt fus* assister à. ▶ **sit through** *vt fus* rester jusqu'à la fin de. ▶ **sit up** *vi* **1.** *(sit upright)* se redresser, s'asseoir. **2.** *(stay up)* veiller.

sitcom [ˈsɪtkɒm] *n inf* sitcom *f*.

site [saɪt] ◆ *n (of town, building)* emplacement *m*; *(archaeological)* site *m*; (CONSTR) chantier *m*. ◆ *vt* situer, placer.

sit-in *n* sit-in *m*, occupation *f* des locaux.

sitting [ˈsɪtɪŋ] *n* **1.** *(of meal)* service *m*. **2.** *(of court, parliament)* séance *f*.

sitting room *n* salon *m*.

situated [ˈsɪtjʊeɪtɪd] *adj*: **to be** ~ être situé(e), se trouver.

situation [ˌsɪtjʊˈeɪʃn] *n* **1.** *(gen)* situation *f*. **2.** *(job)* situation *f*, emploi *m*; ʼ**Situations Vacant**ʼ Br ʼoffres d'emploiʼ.

six [sɪks] ◆ *num adj* six *(inv)*; **she's** ~ **(years old)** elle a six ans. ◆ *num pron* six *mfpl*; **I want** ~ j'en veux six; **there were** ~ **of us** nous étions six. ◆ *num n* **1.** *(gen)* six *m inv*; **two hundred and** ~ deux cent six. **2.** *(six o'clock)*: **it's** ~ il est six heures; **we arrived at** ~ nous sommes arrivés à six heures.

sixteen [sɪksˈtiːn] *num* seize; *see also* **six**.

sixteenth [sɪksˈtiːnθ] *num* seizième; *see also* **sixth**.

sixth [sɪksθ] ◆ *num adj* sixième. ◆ *num adv* **1.** *(in race, competition)* sixième, en sixième place. **2.** *(in list)* sixièmement. ◆ *num pron* sixième *mf*. ◆ *n* **1.** *(fraction)* sixième *m*. **2.** *(in dates)*: **the** ~ **(of September)** le six (septembre).

sixth form *n* Br (SCH) = (classe *f*) terminale *f*.

sixth form college *n* Br *établissement préparant aux A-levels.*

sixty ['sɪkstɪ] *num* soixante; *see also* **six**. ▶ **sixties** *npl* **1.** (*decade*): **the sixties** les années *fpl* soixante. **2.** (*in ages*): **to be in one's sixties** être sexagénaire.

size [saɪz] *n* (*of person, clothes, company*) taille *f*; (*of building*) grandeur *f*, dimensions *fpl*; (*of problem*) ampleur *f*, taille; (*of shoes*) pointure *f*. ▶ **size up** *vt sep* (*person*) jauger; (*situation*) apprécier, peser.

sizeable ['saɪzəbl] *adj* assez important(e).

sizzle ['sɪzl] *vi* grésiller.

skate [skeɪt] (*pl sense 2 only inv* OR **-s**) ◆ *n* **1.** (*ice skate, roller skate*) patin *m*. **2.** (*fish*) raie *f*. ◆ *vi* (*on ice skates*) faire du patin sur glace, patiner; (*on roller skates*) faire du patin à roulettes.

skateboard ['skeɪtbɔːd] *n* planche *f* à roulettes, skateboard *m*, skate *m*.

skater ['skeɪtər] *n* (*on ice*) patineur *m*, -euse *f*; (*on roller skates*) patineur à roulettes.

skating ['skeɪtɪŋ] *n* (*on ice*) patinage *m*; (*on roller skates*) patinage à roulettes.

skating rink *n* patinoire *f*.

skeleton ['skelɪtn] *n* squelette *m*.

skeleton key *n* passe *m*, passepartout *m inv*.

skeleton staff *n* personnel *m* réduit.

skeptic *etc* Am = **sceptic** *etc*.

sketch [sketʃ] ◆ *n* **1.** (*drawing*) croquis *m*, esquisse *f*. **2.** (*description*) aperçu *m*, résumé *f*. **3.** (*by comedian*) sketch *m*. ◆ *vt* **1.** (*draw*) dessiner, faire un croquis de. **2.** (*describe*) donner un aperçu de, décrire à grands traits.

sketchbook ['sketʃbʊk] *n* carnet *m* à dessins.

sketchpad ['sketʃpæd] *n* bloc *m* à dessins.

sketchy ['sketʃɪ] *adj* incomplet(ète).

skewer ['skjʊər] ◆ *n* brochette *f*, broche *f*. ◆ *vt* embrocher.

ski [skiː] (*pt & pp* **skied**, *cont* **skiing**) ◆ *n* ski *m*. ◆ *vi* skier, faire du ski.

ski boots *npl* chaussures *fpl* de ski.

skid [skɪd] ◆ *n* dérapage *m*; **to go into a ~** déraper. ◆ *vi* déraper.

skier ['skiːər] *n* skieur *m*, -euse *f*.

skies [skaɪz] *pl* → **sky**.

skiing ['skiːɪŋ] *n* (U) ski *m*; **to go ~** faire du ski.

ski jump *n* (*slope*) tremplin *m*; (*event*) saut *m* à OR en skis.

skilful, skillful Am ['skɪlfʊl] *adj* habile, adroit(e).

ski lift *n* remonte-pente *m*.

skill [skɪl] *n* **1.** (U) (*ability*) habileté *f*,

adresse *f*. **2.** (*technique*) technique *f*, art *m*.

skilled [skɪld] *adj* **1.** (*skilful*): **~ (in** OR **at doing sthg)** habile OR adroit(e) (pour faire qqch). **2.** (*trained*) qualifié(e).

skillful *etc* Am = **skilful** *etc*.

skim [skɪm] ◆ *vt* **1.** (*cream*) écrémer; (*soup*) écumer. **2.** (*move above*) effleurer, raser. ◆ *vi*: **to ~ through sthg** (*newspaper, book*) parcourir qqch.

skim(med) milk [skɪm(d)-] *n* lait *m* écrémé.

skimp [skɪmp] ◆ *vt* lésiner sur. ◆ *vi*: **to ~ on** lésiner sur.

skimpy ['skɪmpɪ] *adj* (*meal*) maigre; (*clothes*) étriqué(e); (*facts*) insuffisant(e).

skin [skɪn] ◆ *n* peau *f*. ◆ *vt* **1.** (*dead animal*) écorcher, dépouiller; (*fruit*) éplucher, peler. **2.** (*graze*): **to ~ one's knee** s'érafler OR s'écorcher le genou.

skin-deep *adj* superficiel(elle).

skin diving *n* plongée *f* sous-marine.

skinny ['skɪnɪ] *adj* maigre.

skin-tight *adj* moulant(e), collant(e).

skip [skɪp] ◆ *n* **1.** (*jump*) petit saut *m*. **2.** Br (*container*) benne *f*. ◆ *vt* (*page, class, meal*) sauter. ◆ *vi* **1.** (*gen*) sauter, sautiller. **2.** Br (*over rope*) sauter à la corde.

ski pants *npl* fuseau *m*.

ski pole *n* bâton *m* de ski.

skipper ['skɪpər] *n* (NAUT & SPORT) capitaine *m*.

skipping rope ['skɪpɪŋ-] *n* Br corde *f* à sauter.

skirmish ['skɜːmɪʃ] *n* escarmouche *f*.

skirt [skɜːt] ◆ *n* (*garment*) jupe *f*. ◆ *vt* **1.** (*town, obstacle*) contourner. **2.** (*problem*) éviter. ▶ **skirt round** *vt fus* **1.** (*town, obstacle*) contourner. **2.** (*problem*) éviter.

skit [skɪt] *n* sketch *m*.

skittle ['skɪtl] *n* Br quille *f*. ▶ **skittles** *n* (U) (*game*) quilles *fpl*.

skive [skaɪv] *vi* Br *inf*: **to ~ (off)** s'esquiver, tirer au flanc.

skulk [skʌlk] *vi* (*hide*) se cacher; (*prowl*) rôder.

skull [skʌl] *n* crâne *m*.

skunk [skʌŋk] *n* (*animal*) mouffette *f*.

sky [skaɪ] *n* ciel *m*.

skylight ['skaɪlaɪt] *n* lucarne *f*.

skyscraper ['skaɪ,skreɪpər] *n* gratteciel *m inv*.

slab [slæb] *n* (*of concrete*) dalle *f*; (*of stone*) bloc *m*; (*of cake*) pavé *m*.

slack [slæk] ◆ *adj* **1.** (*not tight*) lâche. **2.** (*not busy*) calme. **3.** (*person*) négligent(e), pas sérieux(euse). ◆ *n* (*in rope*) mou *m*.

slacken ['slækn] ◆ *vt* (*speed, pace*) ralentir; (*rope*) relâcher. ◆ *vi* (*speed, pace*) ralentir.

slag [slæg] *n* (U) (*waste material*) scories *fpl*.

slagheap ['slæghi:p] *n* terril *m*.

slain [sleɪn] *pp* → **slay**.

slam [slæm] ◆ *vt* 1. (*shut*) claquer. 2. (*place with force*): **to ~ sthg on** OR **onto** jeter qqch brutalement sur, flanquer qqch sur. ◆ *vi* claquer.

slander ['slɑːndər] ◆ *n* calomnie *f*; (JUR) diffamation *f*. ◆ *vt* calomnier; (JUR) diffamer.

slang [slæŋ] *n* (U) argot *m*.

slant [slɑːnt] ◆ *n* 1. (*angle*) inclinaison *f*. 2. (*perspective*) point *m* de vue, perspective *f*. ◆ *vt* (*bias*) présenter d'une manière tendancieuse. ◆ *vi* (*slope*) être incliné(e), pencher.

slanting ['slɑːntɪŋ] *adj* (*roof*) en pente.

slap [slæp] ◆ *n* claque *f*, tape *f*; (*on face*) gifle *f*. ◆ *vt* 1. (*person, face*) gifler; (*back*) donner une claque OR une tape à. 2. (*place with force*): **to ~ sthg on** OR **onto** jeter qqch brutalement sur, flanquer qqch sur. ◆ *adv inf* (*directly*) en plein.

slapdash ['slæpdæʃ], **slaphappy** ['slæp,hæpɪ] *adj inf* (*work*) bâclé(e); (*person, attitude*) insouciant(e).

slapstick ['slæpstɪk] *n* (U) grosse farce *f*.

slap-up *adj* Br *inf* (*meal*) fameux(euse).

slash [slæʃ] ◆ *n* 1. (*long cut*) entaille *f*. 2. (*oblique stroke*) barre *f* oblique. ◆ *vt* 1. (*cut*) entailler. 2. *inf* (*prices*) casser; (*budget, unemployment*) réduire considérablement.

slat [slæt] *n* lame *f*; (*wooden*) latte *f*.

slate [sleɪt] ◆ *n* ardoise *f*. ◆ *vt inf* (*criticize*) descendre en flammes.

slaughter ['slɔːtər] ◆ *n* 1. (*of animals*) abattage *m*. 2. (*of people*) massacre *m*, carnage *m*. ◆ *vt* 1. (*animals*) abattre. 2. (*people*) massacrer.

slaughterhouse ['slɔːtəhaus, *pl* -haʊzɪz] *n* abattoir *m*.

slave [sleɪv] ◆ *n* esclave *mf*. ◆ *vi* travailler comme un nègre; **to ~ over sthg** peiner sur qqch.

slavery ['sleɪvərɪ] *n* esclavage *m*.

slay [sleɪ] (*pt* **slew**, *pp* **slain**) *vt literary* tuer.

sleazy ['sliːzɪ] *adj* (*disreputable*) mal famé(e).

sledge [sledʒ], **sled** Am [sled] *n* luge *f*;

(*larger*) traîneau *m*.

sledgehammer ['sledʒ,hæmər] *n* masse *f*.

sleek [sliːk] *adj* 1. (*hair, fur*) lisse, luisant(e). 2. (*shape*) aux lignes pures.

sleep [sliːp] (*pt & pp* **slept**) ◆ *n* sommeil *m*; **to go to ~** s'endormir. ◆ *vi* 1. (*be asleep*) dormir. 2. (*spend night*) coucher.
▶ **sleep in** *vi* faire la grasse matinée.
▶ **sleep with** *vt fus* coucher avec.

sleeper ['sliːpər] *n* 1. (*person*): **to be a heavy/light ~** avoir le sommeil lourd/léger. 2. (RAIL - *berth*) couchette *f*; (- *carriage*) wagon-lit *m*; (- *train*) train-couchettes *m*. 3. Br (*on railway track*) traverse *f*.

sleeping bag ['sliːpɪŋ-] *n* sac *m* de couchage.

sleeping car ['sliːpɪŋ-] *n* wagon-lit *m*.

sleeping pill ['sliːpɪŋ-] *n* somnifère *m*.

sleepless ['sliːplɪs] *adj*: **to have a ~ night** passer une nuit blanche.

sleepwalk ['sliːpwɔːk] *vi* être somnambule.

sleepy ['sliːpɪ] *adj* (*person*) qui a envie de dormir.

sleet [sliːt] ◆ *n* neige *f* fondue. ◆ *v impers*: **it's ~ing** il tombe de la neige fondue.

sleeve [sliːv] *n* 1. (*of garment*) manche *f*. 2. (*for record*) pochette *f*.

sleigh [sleɪ] *n* traîneau *m*.

sleight of hand [,slaɪt-] *n* (U) 1. (*skill*) habileté *f*. 2. (*trick*) tour *m* de passe-passe.

slender ['slendər] *adj* 1. (*thin*) mince. 2. *fig* (*resources, income*) modeste, maigre; (*hope, chance*) faible.

slept [slept] *pt & pp* → **sleep**.

slew [sluː] *pt* → **slay**.

slice [slaɪs] ◆ *n* 1. (*thin piece*) tranche *f*. 2. *fig* (*of profits, glory*) part *f*. 3. (SPORT) slice *m*. ◆ *vt* 1. (*cut into slices*) couper en tranches. 2. (*cut cleanly*) trancher. 3. (SPORT) slicer.

slick [slɪk] ◆ *adj* 1. (*skilful*) bien mené(e), habile. 2. *pej* (*superficial - talk*) facile; (- *person*) rusé(e). ◆ *n* nappe *f* de pétrole, marée *f* noire.

slide [slaɪd] (*pt & pp* **slid** [slɪd]) ◆ *n* 1. (*in playground*) toboggan *m*. 2. (PHOT) diapositive *f*, diapo *f*. 3. Br (*for hair*) barrette *f*. 4. (*decline*) déclin *m*; (*in prices*) baisse *f*. ◆ *vt* faire glisser. ◆ *vi* glisser.

sliding door [,slaɪdɪŋ-] *n* porte *f* coulissante.

sliding scale [,slaɪdɪŋ-] *n* échelle *f* mobile.

slight [slaɪt] ◆ adj **1.** (minor) léger(ère); **the ~est** le moindre (la moindre); **not in the ~est** pas du tout. **2.** (thin) mince. ◆ n affront m. ◆ vt offenser.

slightly ['slaɪtlɪ] adv (to small extent) légèrement.

slim [slɪm] ◆ adj **1.** (person, object) mince. **2.** (chance, possibility) faible. ◆ vi maigrir; (diet) suivre un régime amaigrissant.

slime [slaɪm] n (U) substance f visqueuse; (of snail) bave f.

slimming ['slɪmɪŋ] ◆ n amaigrissement m. ◆ adj (product) amaigrissant(e).

sling [slɪŋ] (pt & pp **slung**) ◆ n **1.** (for arm) écharpe f. **2.** (for loads) élingue f. ◆ vt **1.** (hammock etc) suspendre. **2.** inf (throw) lancer.

slip [slɪp] ◆ n **1.** (mistake) erreur f; **a ~ of the tongue** un lapsus. **2.** (of paper - gen) morceau m; (- strip) bande f. **3.** (underwear) combinaison f. **4.** phr: **to give sb the ~** inf fausser compagnie à qqn. ◆ vt glisser; **to ~ sthg on** enfiler qqch. ◆ vi **1.** (slide) glisser; **to ~ into sthg** se glisser dans qqch. **2.** (decline) décliner. ▶ **slip up** vi fig faire une erreur.

slipped disc [ˌslɪpt-] n hernie f discale.

slipper ['slɪpər] n pantoufle f, chausson m.

slippery ['slɪpərɪ] adj glissant(e).

slip road n Br bretelle f.

slipshod ['slɪpʃɒd] adj peu soigné(e).

slip-up n inf gaffe f.

slipway ['slɪpweɪ] n cale f de lancement.

slit [slɪt] (pt & pp **slit**) ◆ n (opening) fente f; (cut) incision f. ◆ vt (make opening in) faire une fente dans, fendre; (cut) inciser.

slither ['slɪðər] vi (person) glisser; (snake) onduler.

sliver ['slɪvər] n (of glass, wood) éclat m; (of meat, cheese) lamelle f.

slob [slɒb] n inf (in habits) saligaud m; (in appearance) gros lard m.

slog [slɒg] inf ◆ n (tiring work) corvée f. ◆ vi (work) travailler comme un bœuf OR un nègre.

slogan ['sləʊgən] n slogan m.

slop [slɒp] ◆ vt renverser. ◆ vi déborder.

slope [sləʊp] ◆ n pente f. ◆ vi (land) être en pente; (handwriting, table) pencher.

sloping ['sləʊpɪŋ] adj (land, shelf) en pente; (handwriting) penché(e).

sloppy ['slɒpɪ] adj (careless) peu soigné(e).

slot [slɒt] n **1.** (opening) fente f. **2.** (groove) rainure f. **3.** (in schedule) créneau m.

slot machine n **1.** (vending machine) distributeur m automatique. **2.** (for gambling) machine f à sous.

slouch [slaʊtʃ] vi être avachi(e).

Slovakia [sləˈvækɪə] n Slovaquie f.

slovenly ['slʌvnlɪ] adj négligé(e).

slow [sləʊ] ◆ adj **1.** (gen) lent(e). **2.** (clock, watch): **to be ~** retarder. ◆ adv lentement; **to go ~** (driver) aller lentement; (workers) faire la grève perlée. ◆ vt & vi ralentir. ▶ **slow down, slow up** vt sep & vi ralentir.

slowdown ['sləʊdaʊn] n ralentissement m.

slowly ['sləʊlɪ] adv lentement.

slow motion n: **in ~** au ralenti m.

sludge [slʌdʒ] n boue f.

slug [slʌg] n **1.** (animal) limace f. **2.** inf (of alcohol) rasade f. **3.** Am inf (bullet) balle f.

sluggish ['slʌgɪʃ] adj (person) apathique; (movement, growth) lent(e); (business) calme, stagnant(e).

sluice [sluːs] n écluse f.

slum [slʌm] n (area) quartier m pauvre.

slumber ['slʌmbər] literary ◆ n sommeil m. ◆ vi dormir paisiblement.

slump [slʌmp] ◆ n **1.** (decline): **~ (in)** baisse f (de). **2.** (period of poverty) crise f (économique). ◆ vi lit & fig s'effondrer.

slung [slʌŋ] pt & pp → **sling**.

slur [slɜːr] ◆ n **1.** (slight): **~ (on)** atteinte f (à). **2.** (insult) affront m, insulte f. ◆ vt mal articuler.

slush [slʌʃ] n (snow) neige f fondue.

slush fund, slush money Am n fonds mpl secrets, caisse f noire.

slut [slʌt] n **1.** inf (dirty, untidy) souillon f. **2.** v inf (sexually immoral) salope f.

sly [slaɪ] (compar **slyer** OR **slier**, superl **slyest** OR **sliest**) adj **1.** (look, smile) entendu(e). **2.** (person) rusé(e), sournois(e).

smack [smæk] ◆ n **1.** (slap) claque f; (on face) gifle f. **2.** (impact) claquement m. ◆ vt **1.** (slap) donner une claque à; (face) gifler. **2.** (place violently) poser violemment.

small [smɔːl] adj **1.** (gen) petit(e). **2.** (trivial) petit, insignifiant(e).

small ads [-ædz] npl Br petites annonces fpl.

small change n petite monnaie f.

smallholder ['smɔːlˌhəʊldər] n Br petit cultivateur m.

small hours *npl*: **in the ~** au petit jour OR matin.

smallpox ['smɔːlpɒks] *n* variole *f*, petite vérole *f*.

small print *n*: **the ~** les clauses *fpl* écrites en petits caractères.

small talk *n* (U) papotage *m*, bavardage *m*.

smarmy ['smɑːmɪ] *adj* mielleux(euse).

smart [smɑːt] ◆ *adj* **1.** (*stylish - person, clothes, car*) élégant(e). **2.** (*clever*) intelligent(e). **3.** (*fashionable - club, society, hotel*) à la mode, in (*inv*). **4.** (*quick - answer, tap*) vif (vive), rapide. ◆ *vi* **1.** (*eyes, skin*) brûler, piquer. **2.** (*person*) être blessé(e).

smarten ['smɑːtn] ▶ **smarten up** *vt sep* (*room*) arranger; **to ~ o.s. up** se faire beau (belle).

smash [smæʃ] ◆ *n* **1.** (*sound*) fracas *m*. **2.** *inf* (*car crash*) collision *f*, accident *m*. **3.** (SPORT) smash *m*. ◆ *vt* **1.** (*glass, plate etc*) casser, briser. **2.** *fig* (*defeat*) détruire. ◆ *vi* **1.** (*glass, plate etc*) se briser. **2.** (*crash*): **to ~ into sthg** s'écraser contre qqch.

smashing ['smæʃɪŋ] *adj inf* super (*inv*).

smattering ['smætərɪŋ] *n*: **to have a ~ of German** savoir quelques mots d'allemand.

smear [smɪəʳ] ◆ *n* **1.** (*dirty mark*) tache *f*. **2.** (MED) frottis *m*. **3.** (*slander*) diffamation *f*. ◆ *vt* **1.** (*smudge*) barbouiller, maculer. **2.** (*spread*): **to ~ sthg onto sthg** étaler qqch sur qqch; **to ~ sthg with sthg** enduire qqch de qqch. **3.** (*slander*) calomnier.

smell [smel] (*pt & pp* **-ed** OR **smelt**) ◆ *n* **1.** (*odour*) odeur *f*. **2.** (*sense of smell*) odorat *m*. ◆ *vt* sentir. ◆ *vi* **1.** (*flower, food*) sentir; **to ~ of sthg** sentir qqch; **to ~ good/bad** sentir bon/mauvais. **2.** (*smell unpleasantly*) sentir (mauvais), puer.

smelly ['smelɪ] *adj* qui sent mauvais, qui pue.

smelt [smelt] ◆ *pt & pp* → **smell**. ◆ *vt* (*metal*) extraire par fusion; (*ore*) fondre.

smile [smaɪl] ◆ *n* sourire *m*. ◆ *vi* sourire.

smirk [smɜːk] *n* sourire *m* narquois.

smock [smɒk] *n* blouse *f*.

smog [smɒg] *n* smog *m*.

smoke [sməʊk] ◆ *n* (U) (*from fire*) fumée *f*. ◆ *vt & vi* fumer.

smoked [sməʊkt] *adj* (*food*) fumé(e).

smoker ['sməʊkəʳ] *n* **1.** (*person*) fumeur *m*, -euse *f*. **2.** (RAIL) compartiment *m* fumeurs.

smokescreen ['sməʊkskriːn] *n fig* couverture *f*.

smoke shop *n* Am bureau *m* de tabac.

smoking ['sməʊkɪŋ] *n* tabagisme *m*; **'no ~'** 'défense de fumer'.

smoky ['sməʊkɪ] *adj* **1.** (*room, air*) enfumé(e). **2.** (*taste*) fumé(e).

smolder Am = **smoulder**.

smooth [smuːð] ◆ *adj* **1.** (*surface*) lisse. **2.** (*sauce*) homogène, onctueux(euse). **3.** (*movement*) régulier(ère). **4.** (*taste*) moelleux(euse). **5.** (*flight, ride*) confortable; (*landing, take-off*) en douceur. **6.** *pej* (*person, manner*) doucereux(euse), mielleux(euse). **7.** (*operation, progress*) sans problèmes. ◆ *vt* (*hair*) lisser; (*clothes, tablecloth*) défroisser.

smother ['smʌðəʳ] *vt* **1.** (*cover thickly*): **to ~ sb/sthg with** couvrir qqn/qqch de. **2.** (*person, fire*) étouffer.

smoulder Br, **smolder** Am ['sməʊldəʳ] *vi lit & fig* couver.

smudge [smʌdʒ] ◆ *n* tache *f*; (*of ink*) bavure *f*. ◆ *vt* (*drawing, painting*) maculer; (*paper*) faire une marque OR trace sur; (*face*) salir.

smug [smʌg] *adj* suffisant(e).

smuggle ['smʌgl] *vt* (*across frontiers*) faire passer en contrebande.

smuggler ['smʌgləʳ] *n* contrebandier *m*, -ère *f*.

smuggling ['smʌglɪŋ] *n* (U) contrebande *f*.

smutty ['smʌtɪ] *adj pej* (*book, language*) cochon(onne).

snack [snæk] *n* casse-croûte *m inv*.

snack bar *n* snack *m*, snack-bar *m*.

snag [snæg] ◆ *n* (*problem*) inconvénient *m*, écueil *m*. ◆ *vi*: **to ~ (on)** s'accrocher (à).

snail [sneɪl] *n* escargot *m*.

snake [sneɪk] *n* serpent *m*.

snap [snæp] ◆ *adj* (*decision, election*) subit(e); (*judgment*) irréfléchi(e). ◆ *n* **1.** (*of branch*) craquement *m*; (*of fingers*) claquement *m*. **2.** (*photograph*) photo *f*. **3.** (*card game*) = bataille *f*. ◆ *vt* **1.** (*break*) casser net. **2.** (*speak sharply*) dire d'un ton sec. ◆ *vi* **1.** (*break*) se casser net. **2.** (*dog*): **to ~ at** essayer de mordre. **3.** (*speak sharply*): **to ~ (at sb)** parler (à qqn) d'un ton sec. ▶ **snap up** *vt sep* (*bargain*) sauter sur.

snap fastener *n* pression *f*.

snappy ['snæpɪ] *adj inf* **1.** (*stylish*) chic. **2.** (*quick*) prompt(e); **make it ~!** dépêche-toi!, et que ça saute!

snapshot ['snæpʃɒt] n photo f.

snare [sneə^r] ◆ n piège m, collet m.
◆ vt prendre au piège, attraper.

snarl [snɑːl] ◆ n grondement m. ◆ vi
gronder.

snatch [snætʃ] ◆ n (of conversation)
bribe f; (of song) extrait m. ◆ vt (grab)
saisir.

sneak [sniːk] (Am pt snuck) ◆ n Br inf
rapporteur m, -euse f. ◆ vt: **to ~ a look
at sb/sthg** regarder qqn/qqch à la
dérobée. ◆ vi (move quietly) se glisser.

sneakers ['sniːkəz] npl Am tennis mpl,
baskets fpl.

sneaky ['sniːkɪ] adj inf sournois(e).

sneer [snɪə^r] ◆ n (smile) sourire m
dédaigneux; (laugh) ricanement m. ◆ vi
(smile) sourire dédaigneusement.

sneeze [sniːz] ◆ n éternuement m.
◆ vi éternuer.

snide [snaɪd] adj sournois(e).

sniff [snɪf] ◆ vt (smell) renifler. ◆ vi (to
clear nose) renifler.

snigger ['snɪgə^r] ◆ n rire m en
dessous. ◆ vi ricaner.

snip [snɪp] ◆ n inf (bargain) bonne
affaire f. ◆ vt couper.

sniper ['snaɪpə^r] n tireur m isolé.

snippet ['snɪpɪt] n fragment m.

snivel ['snɪvl] vi geindre.

snob [snɒb] n snob mf.

snobbish ['snɒbɪʃ], **snobby** ['snɒbɪ]
adj snob (inv).

snooker ['snuːkə^r] n (game) ≃ jeu m
de billard.

snoop [snuːp] vi inf fureter.

snooty ['snuːtɪ] adj inf prétentieux
(euse).

snooze [snuːz] ◆ n petit somme m.
◆ vi faire un petit somme.

snore [snɔː^r] ◆ n ronflement m. ◆ vi
ronfler.

snoring ['snɔːrɪŋ] n (U) ronflement m,
ronflements mpl.

snorkel ['snɔːkl] n tuba m.

snort [snɔːt] ◆ n (of person) grognement
m; (of horse, bull) ébrouement m. ◆ vi
(person) grogner; (horse) s'ébrouer.

snout [snaʊt] n groin m.

snow [snəʊ] ◆ n neige f. ◆ v impers
neiger.

snowball ['snəʊbɔːl] ◆ n boule f de
neige. ◆ vi fig faire boule de neige.

snowbound ['snəʊbaʊnd] adj blo-
qué(e) par la neige.

snowdrift ['snəʊdrɪft] n congère f.

snowdrop ['snəʊdrɒp] n perce-neige
m inv.

snowfall ['snəʊfɔːl] n chute f de
neige.

snowflake ['snəʊfleɪk] n flocon m de
neige.

snowman ['snəʊmæn] (pl -men
[-men]) n bonhomme m de neige.

snowmobile ['snəʊməbiːl] n chenillette f, motoneige f.

snowplough Br, **snowplow** Am
['snəʊplaʊ] n chasse-neige m inv.

snowshoe ['snəʊʃuː] n raquette
f.

snowstorm ['snəʊstɔːm] n tempête f
de neige.

SNP (abbr of Scottish National Party) n
parti nationaliste écossais.

Snr, snr abbr of **senior**.

snub [snʌb] ◆ n rebuffade f. ◆ vt
snober, ignorer.

snuck [snʌk] Am pt → **sneak**.

snuff [snʌf] n tabac m à priser.

snug [snʌg] adj 1. (person) à l'aise,
confortable; (in bed) bien au chaud.
2. (place) douillet(ette). 3. (close-fitting)
bien ajusté(e).

snuggle ['snʌgl] vi se blottir.

so [səʊ] ◆ adv 1. (to such a degree) si,
tellement; ~ **difficult (that)** ... si OR tellement difficile que ...; **don't be ~ stupid!**
ne sois pas si bête!; **I've never seen ~
much money/many cars** je n'ai jamais
vu autant d'argent/de voitures. 2. (in
referring back to previous statement, event etc):
~ **what's the point then?** alors à quoi
bon?; ~ **you knew already?** alors tu le
savais déjà?; **I don't think** ~ je ne crois
pas; **I'm afraid** ~ je crains bien que oui;
if ~ si oui; **is that** ~? vraiment? 3. (also)
aussi; ~ **can/do/would** etc **I** moi aussi;
**she speaks French and ~ does her hus-
band** elle parle français et son mari
aussi. 4. (in this way): **(like)** ~ comme
cela OR ça, de cette façon. 5. (in expressing agreement): ~ **there is** en effet, c'est
vrai; ~ **I see** c'est ce que je vois.
6. (unspecified amount, limit): **they pay us** ~
much a week ils nous payent tant par
semaine; **or** ~ environ, à peu près.
◆ conj alors; **I'm away next week** ~ **I
won't be there** je suis en
voyage la semaine prochaine donc OR
par conséquent je ne serai pas là; ~
what have you been up to? alors, qu'est-
ce que vous devenez?; ~ **what?** inf et
alors?, et après?; ~ **there!** inf là!, et
voilà! ▶ **so as** conj afin de, pour; **we
didn't knock ~ as not to disturb them** nous
n'avons pas frappé pour ne pas les

déranger. ▶ **so that** *conj* (*for the purpose that*) pour que (+ *subjunctive*).

soak [səʊk] ◆ *vt* laisser OR faire tremper. ◆ *vi* **1.** (*become thoroughly wet*): **to leave sthg to ~, to let sthg ~** laisser OR faire tremper qqch. **2.** (*spread*): **to ~ into** sthg tremper dans qqch; **to ~ through** (sthg) traverser (qqch). ▶ **soak up** *vt sep* absorber.

soaking ['səʊkɪŋ] *adj* trempé(e).

so-and-so *n inf* **1.** (*to replace a name*): **Mr ~** Monsieur un tel. **2.** (*annoying person*) enquiquineur *m*, -euse *f*.

soap [səʊp] *n* **1.** (U) (*for washing*) savon *m*. **2.** (TV) soap opera *m*.

soap flakes *npl* savon *m* en paillettes.

soap opera *n* soap opera *m*.

soap powder *n* lessive *f*.

soapy ['səʊpɪ] *adj* **1.** (*water*) savonneux (euse); (*taste*) de savon.

soar [sɔːʳ] *vi* **1.** (*bird*) planer. **2.** (*balloon, kite*) monter. **3.** (*prices, temperature*) monter en flèche.

sob [sɒb] ◆ *n* sanglot *m*. ◆ *vi* sangloter.

sober ['səʊbəʳ] *adj* **1.** (*not drunk*) qui n'est pas ivre. **2.** (*serious*) sérieux (euse). **3.** (*plain - clothes, colours*) sobre. ▶ **sober up** *vi* dessoûler.

sobering ['səʊbərɪŋ] *adj* qui donne à réfléchir.

so-called [-kɔːld] *adj* **1.** (*misleadingly named*) soi-disant (*inv*). **2.** (*widely known as*) ainsi appelé(e).

soccer ['sɒkəʳ] *n* football *m*.

sociable ['səʊʃəbl] *adj* sociable.

social ['səʊʃl] *adj* social(e).

social club *n* club *m*.

socialism ['səʊʃəlɪzm] *n* socialisme *m*.

socialist ['səʊʃəlɪst] ◆ *adj* socialiste. ◆ *n* socialiste *mf*.

socialize, -ise ['səʊʃəlaɪz] *vi* fréquenter des gens; **to ~ with sb** fréquenter qqn, frayer avec qqn.

social security *n* aide *f* sociale.

social services *npl* services *mpl* sociaux.

social worker *n* assistant social *m*, assistante sociale *f*.

society [sə'saɪətɪ] *n* **1.** (*gen*) société *f*. **2.** (*club*) association *f*, club *m*.

sociology [,səʊsɪ'ɒlədʒɪ] *n* sociologie *f*.

sock [sɒk] *n* chaussette *f*.

socket ['sɒkɪt] *n* **1.** (*for light bulb*) douille *f*; (*for plug*) prise *f* de courant. **2.** (*of eye*) orbite *f*; (*for bone*) cavité *f* articulaire.

sod [sɒd] *n* **1.** (*of turf*) motte *f* de gazon. **2.** *v inf* (*person*) con *m*.

soda ['səʊdə] *n* **1.** (CHEM) soude *f*. **2.** (*soda water*) eau *f* de Seltz. **3.** Am (*fizzy drink*) soda *m*.

soda water *n* eau *f* de Seltz.

sodden ['sɒdn] *adj* trempé(e), détrempé(e).

sodium ['səʊdɪəm] *n* sodium *m*.

sofa ['səʊfə] *n* canapé *m*.

Sofia ['səʊfjə] *n* Sofia.

soft [sɒft] *adj* **1.** (*not hard*) doux (douce), mou (molle). **2.** (*smooth, not loud, not bright*) doux (douce). **3.** (*without force*) léger(ère). **4.** (*caring*) tendre. **5.** (*lenient*) faible, indulgent(e).

soft drink *n* boisson *f* non alcoolisée.

soften ['sɒfn] ◆ *vt* **1.** (*fabric*) assouplir; (*substance*) ramollir; (*skin*) adoucir. **2.** (*shock, blow*) atténuer, adoucir. **3.** (*attitude*) modérer, adoucir. ◆ *vi* **1.** (*substance*) se ramollir. **2.** (*attitude, person*) s'adoucir, se radoucir.

softhearted [,sɒft'hɑːtɪd] *adj* au cœur tendre.

softly ['sɒftlɪ] *adv* **1.** (*gently, quietly*) doucement. **2.** (*not brightly*) faiblement. **3.** (*leniently*) avec indulgence.

soft-spoken *adj* à la voix douce.

software ['sɒftweəʳ] *n* (U) (COMPUT) logiciel *m*.

soggy ['sɒgɪ] *adj* trempé(e), détrempé(e).

soil [sɔɪl] ◆ *n* (U) **1.** (*earth*) sol *m*, terre *f*. **2.** *fig* (*territory*) sol *m*, territoire *m*. ◆ *vt* souiller, salir.

soiled [sɔɪld] *adj* sale.

solace ['sɒləs] *n literary* consolation *f*, réconfort *m*.

solar ['səʊləʳ] *adj* solaire.

sold [səʊld] *pt & pp* → **sell**.

solder ['səʊldəʳ] ◆ *n* (U) soudure *f*. ◆ *vt* souder.

soldier ['səʊldʒəʳ] *n* soldat *m*.

sold-out *adj* (*tickets*) qui ont tous été vendus; (*play, concert*) qui joue à guichets fermés.

sole [səʊl] (*pl sense 2 only inv* OR *-s*) ◆ *adj* **1.** (*only*) seul(e), unique. **2.** (*exclusive*) exclusif(ive). ◆ *n* **1.** (*of foot*) semelle *f*. **2.** (*fish*) sole *f*.

solemn ['sɒləm] *adj* solennel(elle); (*person*) sérieux(euse).

solicit [sə'lɪsɪt] ◆ *vt* (*request*) solliciter. ◆ *vi* (*prostitute*) racoler.

solicitor [sə'lɪsɪtəʳ] *n Br* (JUR) notaire *m*.

solid ['sɒlɪd] ◆ *adj* **1.** (*not fluid, sturdy, reliable*) solide. **2.** (*not hollow - tyres*)

plein(e); (~ *wood, rock, gold*) massif(ive).
3. (*without interruption*): **two hours ~** deux
heures d'affilée. ♦ n solide m.

solidarity [ˌsɒlɪˈdærətɪ] n solidarité f.

solitaire [ˌsɒlɪˈteəʳ] n **1.** (*jewel, board
game*) solitaire m. **2.** Am (*card game*)
réussite f, patience f.

solitary [ˈsɒlɪtrɪ] adj **1.** (*lonely, alone*)
solitaire. **2.** (*just one*) seul(e).

solitary confinement n isolement
m cellulaire.

solitude [ˈsɒlɪtjuːd] n solitude f.

solo [ˈsəʊləʊ] (pl -s) ♦ adj solo (inv). ♦ n
solo m. ♦ adv en solo.

soloist [ˈsəʊləʊɪst] n soliste mf.

soluble [ˈsɒljʊbl] adj soluble.

solution [səˈluːʃn] n **1.** (*to problem*): ~
(to) solution f (de). **2.** (*liquid*) solution f.

solve [sɒlv] vt résoudre.

solvent [ˈsɒlvənt] ♦ adj (FIN) solvable.
♦ n dissolvant m, solvant m.

Somalia [səˈmɑːlɪə] n Somalie f.

sombre Br, **somber** Am [ˈsɒmbəʳ] adj
sombre.

some [sʌm] ♦ adj **1.** (*a certain amount,
number of*): ~ **meat** de la viande; ~
money de l'argent; ~ **coffee** du café; ~
sweets des bonbons. **2.** (*fairly large number or quantity of*) quelque; **I had ~ difficulty getting here** j'ai eu quelque mal à
venir ici; **I've known him for ~ years** je le
connais depuis plusieurs années or pas
mal d'années. **3.** (*contrastive use*)
(*certain*): ~ **jobs are better paid than others** certains boulots sont mieux
rémunérés que d'autres; ~ **people like
his music** il y en a qui aiment sa
musique. **4.** (*in imprecise statements*)
quelque, quelconque; **she married ~
writer or other** elle a épousé un écrivain
quelconque or quelque écrivain; **there
must be ~ mistake** il doit y avoir erreur.
5. inf (*very good*): **that was ~ party!** c'était
une soirée formidable!, quelle soirée!
♦ pron **1.** (*a certain amount*) **can I have ~?**
(*money, milk, coffee etc*) est-ce que je peux
en prendre?; ~ **of it is mine** une partie
est à moi. **2.** (*a certain number*)
quelques-uns (quelques-unes), certains (certaines); **can I have ~?** (*books,
pens, potatoes etc*) est-ce que je peux en
prendre (quelques-uns)?; ~ **(of them)**
left early quelques-uns d'entre eux
sont partis tôt. ♦ adv quelque, environ;
there were ~ 7,000 people there il y avait
quelque or environ 7 000 personnes.

somebody [ˈsʌmbədɪ] pron
quelqu'un.

someday [ˈsʌmdeɪ] adv un jour, un de
ces jours.

somehow [ˈsʌmhaʊ], **someway** Am
[ˈsʌmweɪ] adv **1.** (*by some action*) d'une
manière ou d'une autre. **2.** (*for some reason*) pour une raison ou pour une autre.

someone [ˈsʌmwʌn] pron quelqu'un.

someplace Am = **somewhere**.

somersault [ˈsʌməsɔːlt] ♦ n cabriole
f, culbute f. ♦ vi faire une cabriole or
culbute.

something [ˈsʌmθɪŋ] ♦ pron (*unknown
thing*) quelque chose; ~ **odd/interesting**
quelque chose de bizarre/d'intéressant; **or ~** inf ou quelque chose comme
ça. ♦ adv: ~ **like**, ~ **in the region of** environ, à peu près.

sometime [ˈsʌmtaɪm] ♦ adj ancien
(enne). ♦ adv un de ces jours; ~ **last
week** la semaine dernière.

sometimes [ˈsʌmtaɪmz] adv quelquefois, parfois.

someway Am = **somehow**.

somewhat [ˈsʌmwɒt] adv quelque
peu.

somewhere Br [ˈsʌmweəʳ], **someplace** Am [ˈsʌmpleɪs] adv **1.** (*unknown
place*) quelque part; ~ **else** ailleurs; ~
near here près d'ici. **2.** (*used in approxi-
mations*) environ, à peu près.

son [sʌn] n fils m.

song [sɒŋ] n chanson f; (*of bird*) chant
m, ramage m.

sonic [ˈsɒnɪk] adj sonique.

son-in-law (pl **sons-in-law** or **son-in-
laws**) n gendre m, beau-fils m.

sonnet [ˈsɒnɪt] n sonnet m.

soon [suːn] adv **1.** (*before long*) bientôt;
~ **after** peu après. **2.** (*early*) tôt; **write
back ~** réponds-moi vite; **how ~ will it
be ready?** ce sera prêt quand?, dans
combien de temps est-ce que ce sera
prêt?; **as ~ as** dès que, aussitôt que.

sooner [ˈsuːnəʳ] adv **1.** (*in time*) plus
tôt; **no ~ ... than ...** à peine ... que ...;
~ **or later** tôt ou tard; **the ~ the better** le
plus tôt sera le mieux. **2.** (*expressing preference*): **I would ~ ...** je préférerais ...,
j'aimerais mieux ...

soot [sʊt] n suie f.

soothe [suːð] vt calmer, apaiser.

sophisticated [səˈfɪstɪkeɪtɪd] adj
1. (*stylish*) raffiné(e), sophistiqué(e).
2. (*intelligent*) averti(e). **3.** (*complicated*)
sophistiqué(e), très perfectionné(e).

sophomore [ˈsɒfəmɔːʳ] n Am étudiant
m, -e f de seconde année.

soporific [ˌsɒpəˈrɪfɪk] adj soporifique.

sopping ['sɒpɪŋ] adj: ~ **(wet)** tout trempé (toute trempée).

soppy ['sɒpɪ] adj inf 1. (sentimental - book, film) à l'eau de rose; (- person) sentimental(e). 2. (silly) bêta(asse), bête.

soprano [sə'prɑːnəʊ] (pl -s) n (person) soprano mf; (voice) soprano m.

sorbet ['sɔːbeɪ] n sorbet m.

sorcerer ['sɔːsərər] n sorcier m.

sordid ['sɔːdɪd] adj sordide.

sore [sɔːr] ◆ adj 1. (painful) douloureux(euse); **to have a ~ throat** avoir mal à la gorge. 2. Am (upset) fâché(e), contrarié(e). ◆ n plaie f.

sorely ['sɔːlɪ] adv literary (needed) grandement.

sorrow ['sɒrəʊ] n peine f, chagrin m.

sorry ['sɒrɪ] ◆ adj 1. (expressing apology, disappointment, sympathy) désolé(e); **to be ~ about sthg** s'excuser pour qqch; **to be ~ for sthg** regretter qqch; **to be ~ to do sthg** être désolé OR regretter de faire qqch; **to be** OR **feel ~ for sb** plaindre qqn. 2. (poor): **in a ~ state** en piteux état, dans un triste état. ◆ excl 1. (expressing apology) pardon!, excusez-moi!; **~, we're sold out** désolé, on n'en a plus. 2. (asking for repetition) pardon?, comment? 3. (to correct oneself) non, pardon OR je veux dire.

sort [sɔːt] ◆ n genre m, sorte f, espèce f; **~ of** (rather) plutôt, quelque peu; **a ~ of** une espèce OR sorte de. ◆ vt trier, classer. ▶ **sort out** vt sep 1. (classify) ranger, classer. 2. (solve) résoudre.

sorting office ['sɔːtɪŋ-] n centre m de tri.

SOS (abbr of **save our souls**) n SOS m.

so-so inf ◆ adj quelconque. ◆ adv comme ci comme ça.

soufflé ['suːfleɪ] n soufflé m.

sought [sɔːt] pt & pp → **seek**.

soul [səʊl] n 1. (gen) âme f. 2. (music) soul m.

soul-destroying [-dɪ,strɔɪɪŋ] adj abrutissant(e).

soulful ['səʊlfʊl] adj (look) expressif (ive); (song etc) sentimental(e).

sound [saʊnd] ◆ adj 1. (healthy - body) sain(e), en bonne santé; (- mind) sain. 2. (sturdy) solide. 3. (reliable - advice) judicieux(euse), sage; (- investment) sûr(e). ◆ vt: **to be ~ asleep** dormir à poings fermés, dormir d'un sommeil profond. ◆ n son m; (particular sound) bruit m, son m; **by the ~ of it ...** d'après ce que j'ai compris ... ◆ vt (alarm, bell)

sonner. ◆ vi 1. (make a noise) sonner, retentir; **to ~ like sthg** ressembler à qqch. 2. (seem) sembler, avoir l'air; **to ~ like sthg** avoir l'air de qqch, sembler être qqch. ▶ **sound out** vt sep: **to ~ sb out (on** OR **about)** sonder qqn (sur).

sound barrier n mur m du son.

sound effects npl bruitage m, effets mpl sonores.

sounding ['saʊndɪŋ] n (NAUT & fig) sondage m.

soundly ['saʊndlɪ] adv 1. (beaten) à plates coutures. 2. (sleep) profondément.

soundproof ['saʊndpruːf] adj insonorisé(e).

soundtrack ['saʊndtræk] n bande-son f.

soup [suːp] n soupe f, potage m.

soup plate n assiette f creuse OR à soupe.

soup spoon n cuiller f à soupe.

sour ['saʊər] ◆ adj 1. (taste, fruit) acide, aigre. 2. (milk) aigre. 3. (ill-tempered) aigre, acerbe. ◆ vt fig faire tourner au vinaigre, faire mal tourner.

source [sɔːs] n 1. (gen) source f. 2. (cause) origine f, cause f.

sour grapes n (U) inf: **what he said was just ~** il a dit ça par dépit.

south [saʊθ] ◆ n 1. (direction) sud m. 2. (region): **the ~** le sud; **the South of France** le Sud de la France, le Midi (de la France). ◆ adj sud (inv); (wind) du sud. ◆ adv au sud, vers le sud; **~ of** au sud de.

South Africa n Afrique f du Sud.

South African ◆ adj sud-africain(e). ◆ n (person) Sud-Africain m, -e f.

South America n Amérique f du Sud.

South American ◆ adj sud-américain(e). ◆ n (person) Sud-Américain m, -e f.

southeast [,saʊθ'iːst] ◆ n 1. (direction) sud-est m. 2. (region): **the ~** le sud-est. ◆ adj sud-est; (wind) du sud-est. ◆ adv au sud-est, vers le sud-est; **~ of** au sud-est de.

southerly ['sʌðəlɪ] adj au sud, du sud; (wind) du sud.

southern ['sʌðən] adj du sud; (France) du Midi.

South Korea n Corée f du Sud.

South Pole n: **the ~** le pôle Sud.

southward ['saʊθwəd] ◆ adj au sud, du sud. ◆ adv = **southwards**.

southwards ['saʊθwədz] adv vers le sud.

southwest [ˌsaʊθˈwest] ◆ n **1.** (direction) sud-ouest m. **2.** (region): **the ~** le sud-ouest. ◆ adj au sud-ouest, du sud-ouest; (wind) du sud-ouest. ◆ adv au sud-ouest, vers le sud-ouest; **~ of** au sud-ouest de.

souvenir [ˌsuːvəˈnɪər] n souvenir m.

sovereign [ˈsɒvrɪn] ◆ adj souverain(e). ◆ n **1.** (ruler) souverain m, -e f. **2.** (coin) souverain m.

soviet [ˈsəʊvɪət] n soviet m. ▶ **Soviet** ◆ adj soviétique. ◆ n (person) Soviétique mf.

Soviet Union n: **the (former) ~** l'(ex-)Union f soviétique.

sow¹ [səʊ] (pt **-ed**, pp **sown** OR **-ed**) vt lit & fig semer.

sow² [saʊ] n truie f.

sown [səʊn] pp → **sow¹**.

soya [ˈsɔɪə] n soja m.

soy(a) bean [ˈsɔɪ(ə)-] n graine f de soja.

spa [spɑː] n station f thermale.

space [speɪs] ◆ n **1.** (gap, roominess, outer space) espace m; (on form) blanc m, espace. **2.** (room) place f. **3.** (of time): **within** OR **in the ~ of ten minutes** en l'espace de dix minutes. ◆ comp spatial(e). ▶ **space out** vt sep espacer.

spacecraft [ˈspeɪskrɑːft] (pl inv) n vaisseau m spatial.

spaceman [ˈspeɪsmæn] (pl **-men** [-men]) n astronaute m, cosmonaute m.

spaceship [ˈspeɪsʃɪp] n vaisseau m spatial.

space shuttle n navette f spatiale.

spacesuit [ˈspeɪssuːt] n combinaison f spatiale.

spacing [ˈspeɪsɪŋ] n (TYPO) espacement m.

spacious [ˈspeɪʃəs] adj spacieux(euse).

spade [speɪd] n **1.** (tool) pelle f. **2.** (playing card) pique m. ▶ **spades** npl pique m.

spaghetti [spəˈgetɪ] n (U) spaghettis mpl.

Spain [speɪn] n Espagne f.

span [spæn] ◆ pt → **spin**. ◆ n **1.** (in time) espace m de temps, durée f. **2.** (range) éventail m, gamme f. **3.** (of bird, plane) envergure f. **4.** (of bridge) travée f; (of arch) ouverture f. ◆ vt **1.** (in time) embrasser, couvrir. **2.** (subj: bridge) franchir.

Spaniard [ˈspænjəd] n Espagnol m, -e f.

spaniel [ˈspænjəl] n épagneul m.

Spanish [ˈspænɪʃ] ◆ adj espagnol(e).

◆ n (language) espagnol m. ◆ npl: **the ~** les Espagnols.

spank [spæŋk] vt donner une fessée à, fesser.

spanner [ˈspænər] n clé f à écrous.

spar [spɑːr] ◆ n espar m. ◆ vi (BOXING) s'entraîner à la boxe.

spare [speər] ◆ adj **1.** (surplus) de trop; (component, clothing etc) de réserve, de rechange; **~ bed** lit m d'appoint. **2.** (available - seat, time, tickets) disponible. ◆ n (part) pièce f détachée OR de rechange. ◆ vt **1.** (make available - staff, money) se passer de; (- time) disposer de; **to have an hour to ~** avoir une heure de battement or de libre; **with a minute to ~** avec une minute d'avance. **2.** (not harm) épargner. **3.** (not use) épargner, ménager; **to ~ no expense** ne pas regarder à la dépense. **4.** (save from): **to ~ sb sthg** épargner qqch à qqn, éviter qqch à qqn.

spare part n pièce f détachée OR de rechange.

spare time n (U) temps m libre, loisirs mpl.

spare wheel n roue f de secours.

sparing [ˈspeərɪŋ] adj: **to be ~ with** OR **of sthg** être économe de qqch, ménager qqch.

sparingly [ˈspeərɪŋlɪ] adv (use) avec modération; (spend) avec parcimonie.

spark [spɑːk] n lit & fig étincelle f.

sparking plug [ˈspɑːkɪŋ-] Br = **spark plug**.

sparkle [ˈspɑːkl] ◆ n (U) (of eyes, jewel) éclat m; (of stars) scintillement m. ◆ vi étinceler, scintiller.

sparkling wine [ˈspɑːklɪŋ-] n vin m mousseux.

spark plug n bougie f.

sparrow [ˈspærəʊ] n moineau m.

sparse [spɑːs] adj clairsemé(e), épars(e).

spasm [ˈspæzm] n **1.** (MED) spasme m; (of coughing) quinte f. **2.** (of emotion) accès m.

spastic [ˈspæstɪk] (MED) n handicapé m, -e f moteur.

spat [spæt] pt & pp → **spit**.

spate [speɪt] n (of attacks etc) série f.

spatter [ˈspætər] vt éclabousser.

spawn [spɔːn] ◆ n (U) frai m, œufs mpl. ◆ vt fig donner naissance à, engendrer. ◆ vi (fish, frog) frayer.

speak [spiːk] (pt **spoke**, pp **spoken**) ◆ vt **1.** (say) dire. **2.** (language) parler. ◆ vi parler; **to ~ to** OR **with sb** parler à qqn; **to**

~ to sb about sthg parler de qqch à qqn; **to ~ about sb/sthg** parler de qqn/qqch. ▶ **so to speak** adv pour ainsi dire. ▶ **speak for** vt fus (represent) parler pour, parler au nom de. ▶ **speak up** vi 1. (support): **to ~ up for sb/sthg** parler en faveur de qqn/qqch, soutenir qqn/ qqch. 2. (speak louder) parler plus fort.

speaker ['spiːkə^r] n 1. (person talking) personne f qui parle. 2. (person making speech) orateur m. 3. (of language): **a German ~** une personne qui parle allemand. 4. (loudspeaker) haut-parleur m.

speaking ['spiːkɪŋ] adv: **relatively/ politically ~** relativement/politiquement parlant.

spear [spɪə^r] ◆ n lance f. ◆ vt transpercer d'un coup de lance.

spearhead ['spɪəhed] ◆ n fer m de lance. ◆ vt (campaign) mener; (attack) être le fer de lance de.

spec [spek] n Br inf: **on ~** à tout hasard.

special ['speʃl] adj 1. (gen) spécial(e). 2. (needs, effort, attention) particulier(ère).

special delivery n (U) (service) exprès m, envoi m par exprès; **by ~** en exprès.

specialist ['speʃəlɪst] ◆ adj spécialisé(e). ◆ n spécialiste mf.

speciality [,speʃɪ'ælətɪ], **specialty** Am ['speʃltɪ] n spécialité f.

specialize, -ise ['speʃəlaɪz] vi: **to ~ (in)** se spécialiser (dans).

specially ['speʃəlɪ] adv 1. (specifically) spécialement; (on purpose) exprès. 2. (particularly) particulièrement.

specialty n Am = **speciality**.

species ['spiːʃiːz] (pl inv) n espèce f.

specific [spə'sɪfɪk] adj 1. (particular) particulier(ère), précis(e). 2. (precise) précis(e). 3. (unique): **to ~ to** propre à.

specifically [spə'sɪfɪklɪ] adv 1. (particularly) particulièrement, spécialement. 2. (precisely) précisément.

specify ['spesɪfaɪ] vt préciser, spécifier.

specimen ['spesɪmən] n 1. (example) exemple m, spécimen m. 2. (of blood) prélèvement m; (of urine) échantillon m.

speck [spek] n 1. (small stain) toute petite tache f. 2. (of dust) grain m.

speckled ['spekld] adj: **~ (with)** tacheté(e) de.

specs [speks] npl inf (glasses) lunettes fpl.

spectacle ['spektəkl] n spectacle m. ▶ **spectacles** npl Br (glasses) lunettes fpl.

spectacular [spek'tækjʊlə^r] adj spectaculaire.

spectator [spek'teɪtə^r] n spectateur m, -trice f.

spectre Br, **specter** Am ['spektə^r] n spectre m.

spectrum ['spektrəm] (pl -tra [-trə]) n 1. (PHYSICS) spectre m. 2. fig (variety) gamme f.

speculation [,spekjʊ'leɪʃn] n 1. (gen) spéculation f. 2. (conjecture) conjectures fpl.

sped [sped] pt & pp → **speed**.

speech [spiːtʃ] n 1. (U) (ability) parole f. 2. (formal talk) discours m. 3. (THEATRE) texte m. 4. (manner of speaking) façon f de parler. 5. (dialect) parler m.

speechless ['spiːtʃlɪs] adj: **~ (with)** muet(ette) (de).

speed [spiːd] (pt & pp -ed OR sped) ◆ n vitesse f; (of reply, action) vitesse, rapidité f. ◆ vi 1. (move fast): **to ~ along** aller à toute allure OR vitesse; **to ~ away** démarrer à toute allure. 2. (AUT) (go too fast) rouler trop vite, faire un excès de vitesse. ▶ **speed up** vt sep (person) faire aller plus vite; (work, production) accélérer. ◆ vi aller plus vite; (car) accélérer.

speedboat ['spiːdbəʊt] n hors-bord m inv.

speeding ['spiːdɪŋ] n (U) excès m de vitesse.

speed limit n limitation f de vitesse.

speedometer [spɪ'dɒmɪtə^r] n compteur m (de vitesse).

speedway ['spiːdweɪ] n 1. (U) (SPORT) course f de motos. 2. Am (road) voie f express.

speedy ['spiːdɪ] adj rapide.

spell [spel] (Br pt & pp spelt OR -ed, Am pt & pp -ed) ◆ n 1. (period of time) période f. 2. (enchantment) charme m; (words) formule f magique; **to cast** OR **put a ~ on sb** jeter un sort à qqn, envoûter qqn. ◆ vt 1. (word, name) écrire. 2. fig (signify) signifier. ◆ vi épeler. ▶ **spell out** vt sep 1. (read aloud) épeler. 2. (explain): **to ~ sthg out (for** OR **to sb)** expliquer qqch clairement (à qqn).

spellbound ['spelbaʊnd] adj subjugué(e).

spelling ['spelɪŋ] n orthographe f.

spelt [spelt] Br pt & pp → **spell**.

spend [spend] (pt & pp spent) vt 1. (pay out): **to ~ money (on)** dépenser de l'argent (pour). 2. (time, life) passer; (effort) consacrer.

spendthrift ['spendθrɪft] n dépensier m, -ère f.

spent [spent] ◆ pt & pp → **spend**. ◆ adj (fuel, match, ammunition) utilisé(e); (patience, energy) épuisé(e).

sperm [spɜ:m] (pl inv OR -s) n sperme m.

spew [spju:] vt & vi vomir.

sphere [sfɪəʳ] n sphère f.

spice [spaɪs] n 1. (CULIN) épice f. 2. (U) fig (excitement) piment m.

spick-and-span [ˌspɪkən'spæn] adj impeccable, nickel (inv).

spicy [ˈspaɪsɪ] adj 1. (CULIN) épicé(e). 2. fig (story) pimenté(e), piquant(e).

spider [ˈspaɪdəʳ] n araignée f.

spike [spaɪk] n (metal) pointe f, lance f; (of plant) piquant m; (of hair) épi m.

spill [spɪl] (Br pt & pp spilt OR -ed, Am pt & pp -ed) ◆ vt renverser. ◆ vi (liquid) se répandre.

spilt [spɪlt] Br pt & pp → **spill**.

spin [spɪn] (pt span OR spun, pp spun) ◆ n 1. (turn): **to give sthg a ~** faire tourner qqch. 2. (AERON) vrille f. 3. inf (in car) tour m. 4. (SPORT) effet m. ◆ vt 1. (wheel) faire tourner; **to ~ a coin** jouer à pile ou face. 2. (washing) essorer. 3. (thread, wool, cloth) filer. 4. (SPORT) (ball) donner de l'effet à. ◆ vi tourner, tournoyer. ▶ **spin out** vt sep (money, story) faire durer.

spinach [ˈspɪnɪdʒ] n (U) épinards mpl.

spinal column [ˈspaɪnl-] n colonne f vertébrale.

spinal cord [ˈspaɪnl-] n moelle f épinière.

spindly [ˈspɪndlɪ] adj grêle, chétif(ive).

spin-dryer n Br essoreuse f.

spine [spaɪn] n 1. (ANAT) colonne f vertébrale. 2. (of book) dos m. 3. (of plant, hedgehog) piquant m.

spinning [ˈspɪnɪŋ] n (of thread) filage m.

spinning top n toupie f.

spin-off n (by-product) dérivé m.

spinster [ˈspɪnstəʳ] n célibataire f; pej vieille fille f.

spiral [ˈspaɪərəl] ◆ adj spiral(e). ◆ n spirale f. ◆ vi (staircase, smoke) monter en spirale.

spiral staircase n escalier m en colimaçon.

spire [ˈspaɪəʳ] n flèche f.

spirit [ˈspɪrɪt] n 1. (gen) esprit m. 2. (U) (determination) caractère m, courage m. ▶ **spirits** npl 1. (mood) humeur f; **to be in high ~s** être gai(e); **to be in low ~s** être déprimé(e). 2. (alcohol) spiritueux mpl.

spirited [ˈspɪrɪtɪd] adj fougueux(euse);

(performance) interprété(e) avec brio.

spirit level n niveau m à bulle d'air.

spiritual [ˈspɪrɪtʃʊəl] adj spirituel(elle).

spit [spɪt] (Br pt & pp spat, Am pt & pp spit) ◆ n 1. (U) (spittle) crachat m; (saliva) salive f. 2. (skewer) broche f. ◆ v cracher. ◆ v impers Br: **it's spitting** il tombe quelques gouttes.

spite [spaɪt] ◆ n rancune f. ◆ vt contrarier. ▶ **in spite of** prep en dépit de, malgré.

spiteful [ˈspaɪtfʊl] adj malveillant(e).

spittle [ˈspɪtl] n (U) crachat m.

splash [splæʃ] ◆ n 1. (sound) plouf m. 2. (of colour, light) tache f. ◆ vt éclabousser. ◆ vi 1. (person): **to ~ about** OR **around** barboter. 2. (liquid) jaillir. ▶ **splash out** inf vi: **to ~ out (on)** dépenser une fortune (pour).

spleen [spli:n] n 1. (ANAT) rate f. 2. (U) fig (anger) mauvaise humeur f.

splendid [ˈsplendɪd] adj splendide; (work, holiday, idea) excellent(e).

splint [splɪnt] n attelle f.

splinter [ˈsplɪntəʳ] ◆ n éclat m. ◆ vi (wood) se fendre en éclats; (glass) se briser en éclats.

split [splɪt] (pt & pp split, cont -ting) ◆ n 1. (in wood) fente f; (in garment - tear) déchirure f; (- by design) échancrure f. 2. (POL) ~ (in) division f OR scission f (au sein de). 3. (difference): ~ **between** écart m entre. ◆ vt 1. (wood) fendre; (clothes) déchirer. 2. (POL) diviser. 3. (share) partager; **to ~ the difference** fig couper la poire en deux. ◆ vi 1. (wood) se fendre; (clothes) se déchirer. 2. (POL) se diviser; (road, path) se séparer. ▶ **split up** vi (group, couple) se séparer.

split second n fraction f de seconde.

splutter [ˈsplʌtəʳ] vi (person) bredouiller, bafouiller; (engine) tousser; (fire) crépiter.

spoil [spɔɪl] (pt & pp -ed OR spoilt) vt 1. (ruin - holiday) gâcher, gâter; (- view) gâter; (- food) gâter, abîmer. 2. (over-indulge, treat well) gâter. ▶ **spoils** npl butin m.

spoiled [spɔɪld] adj = **spoilt**.

spoilsport [ˈspɔɪlspɔːt] n trouble-fête mf inv.

spoilt [spɔɪlt] ◆ pt & pp → **spoil**. ◆ adj (child) gâté(e).

spoke [spəʊk] ◆ pt → **speak**. ◆ n rayon m.

spoken [ˈspəʊkn] pp → **speak**.

spokesman [ˈspəʊksmən] (pl -men

[-mən]) n porte-parole m inv.

spokeswoman ['spəuks,wumən] (pl **-women** [-,wimin]) n porte-parole m inv.

sponge [spʌndʒ] (Br cont **spongeing**, Am cont **sponging**) ◆ n 1. (for cleaning, washing) éponge f. 2. (cake) gâteau m OR biscuit m de Savoie. ◆ vt éponger. ◆ vi inf: **to ~ off sb** taper qqn.

sponge bag n Br trousse f de toilette.

sponge cake n gâteau m OR biscuit m de Savoie.

sponsor ['spɒnsər] ◆ n sponsor m. ◆ vt 1. (finance, for charity) sponsoriser, parrainer. 2. (support) soutenir.

sponsored walk [,spɒnsəd-] n marche organisée pour recueillir des fonds.

sponsorship ['spɒnsəʃip] n sponsoring m, parrainage m.

spontaneous [spɒn'teinjəs] adj spontané(e).

spooky ['spuːki] adj inf qui donne la chair de poule.

spool [spuːl] n (gen & COMPUT) bobine f.

spoon [spuːn] n cuillère f, cuiller f.

spoon-feed vt nourrir à la cuillère; **to ~ sb** fig mâcher le travail à qqn.

spoonful ['spuːnful] (pl **-s** OR **spoonsful**) n cuillerée f.

sporadic [spə'rædik] adj sporadique.

sport [spɔːt] n 1. (game) sport m. 2. dated (cheerful person) chic type m /fille f.

sporting ['spɔːtiŋ] adj 1. (relating to sport) sportif(ive). 2. (generous, fair) chic (inv); **to have a ~ chance of doing sthg** avoir des chances de faire qqch.

sports car ['spɔːts-] n voiture f de sport.

sports jacket ['spɔːts-] n veste f sport.

sportsman ['spɔːtsmən] (pl **-men** [-mən]) n sportif m.

sportsmanship ['spɔːtsmənʃip] n sportivité f, esprit m sportif.

sportswear ['spɔːtsweər] n (U) vêtements mpl de sport.

sportswoman ['spɔːts,wumən] (pl **-women** [-,wimin]) n sportive f.

sporty ['spɔːti] adj inf (person) sportif (ive).

spot [spɒt] ◆ n 1. (mark, dot) tache f. 2. (pimple) bouton m. 3. (drop) goutte f. 4. inf (small amount): **to have a ~ of bother** avoir quelques ennuis. 5. (place) endroit m; **on the ~** sur place; **to do sthg on the ~** faire qqch immédiatement OR sur-le-champ. 6. (RADIO & TV) numéro m. ◆ vt (notice) apercevoir.

spot check n contrôle m au hasard OR intermittent.

spotless ['spɒtlis] adj (clean) impeccable.

spotlight ['spɒtlait] n (in theatre) projecteur m, spot m; (in home) spot m; **to be in the ~** fig être en vedette.

spotted ['spɒtid] adj (pattern, material) à pois.

spotty ['spɒti] adj Br (skin) boutonneux (euse).

spouse [spaus] n époux m, épouse f.

spout [spaut] ◆ n bec m. ◆ vi: **to ~ from** OR **out of** jaillir de.

sprain [sprein] ◆ n entorse f. ◆ vt: **to ~ one's ankle/wrist** se faire une entorse à la cheville/au poignet, se fouler la cheville/le poignet.

sprang [spræŋ] pt → **spring**.

sprawl [sprɔːl] vi 1. (person) être affalé(e). 2. (city) s'étaler.

spray [sprei] ◆ n 1. (U) (of water) gouttelettes fpl; (from sea) embruns mpl. 2. (container) bombe f, pulvérisateur m. 3. (of flowers) gerbe f. ◆ vt (product) pulvériser; (plants, crops) pulvériser de l'insecticide sur.

spread [spred] (pt & pp spread) ◆ n 1. (U) (food) pâte f à tartiner. 2. (of fire, disease) propagation f. 3. (of opinions) gamme f. ◆ vt 1. (map, rug) étaler, étendre; (fingers, arms, legs) écarter. 2. (butter, jam etc): **to ~ sthg (over)** étaler qqch (sur). 3. (disease, rumour, germs) répandre, propager. 4. (wealth, work) distribuer, répartir. ◆ vi 1. (disease, rumour) se propager, se répandre. 2. (water, cloud) s'étaler. ▶ **spread out** vi se disperser.

spread-eagled [-,iːgld] adj affalé(e).

spreadsheet ['spredʃiːt] n (COMPUT) tableur m.

spree [spriː] n: **to go on a spending** OR **shopping ~** faire des folies.

sprightly ['spraitli] adj alerte, fringant(e).

spring [spriŋ] (pt sprang, pp sprung) ◆ n 1. (season) printemps m; **in ~** au printemps. 2. (coil) ressort m. 3. (water source) source f. ◆ vi 1. (jump) sauter, bondir. 2. (originate): **to ~ from** provenir de. ▶ **spring up** vi (problem) surgir, se présenter; (friendship) naître; (wind) se lever.

springboard ['spriŋbɔːd] n lit & fig tremplin m.

spring-clean vt nettoyer de fond en comble.

spring onion n Br ciboule f.

springtime ['sprɪŋtaɪm] n: **in (the) ~** au printemps.

springy ['sprɪŋɪ] adj (carpet) moelleux (euse); (mattress, rubber) élastique.

sprinkle ['sprɪŋkl] vt: **to ~ water over** OR **on sthg, to ~ sthg with water** asperger qqch d'eau; **to ~ salt** etc **over** OR **on sthg, to ~ sthg with salt** etc saupoudrer qqch de sel etc.

sprinkler ['sprɪŋklər] n (for water) arroseur m.

sprint [sprɪnt] ◆ n sprint m. ◆ vi sprinter.

sprout [spraut] ◆ n 1. (vegetable): **(Brussels) ~s** choux mpl de Bruxelles. 2. (shoot) pousse f. ◆ vt (leaves) produire; **to ~ shoots** germer. ◆ vi (grow) pousser.

spruce [spru:s] ◆ adj net (nette), pimpant(e). ◆ n épicéa m. ▶ **spruce up** vt sep astiquer, briquer.

sprung [sprʌŋ] pp → **spring**.

spry [spraɪ] adj vif (vive).

spun [spʌn] pt & pp → **spin**.

spur [spɜ:r] ◆ n 1. (incentive) incitation f. 2. (on rider's boot) éperon m. ◆ vt (encourage): **to ~ sb to do sthg** encourager OR inciter qqn à faire qqch. ▶ **on the spur of the moment** adv sur un coup de tête, sous l'impulsion du moment. ▶ **spur on** vt sep encourager.

spurious ['spuərɪəs] adj 1. (affection, interest) feint(e). 2. (argument, logic) faux (fausse).

spurn [spɜ:n] vt repousser.

spurt [spɜ:t] ◆ n 1. (gush) jaillissement m. 2. (of activity, energy) sursaut m. 3. (burst of speed) accélération f. ◆ vi (gush): **to ~ (out of** OR **from)** jaillir (de).

spy [spaɪ] ◆ n espion m. ◆ vt inf apercevoir. ◆ vi espionner, faire de l'espionnage; **to ~ on sb** espionner qqn.

spying ['spaɪɪŋ] n (U) espionnage m.

Sq., sq. abbr of **square**.

squabble ['skwɒbl] ◆ n querelle f. ◆ vi: **to ~ (about** OR **over)** se quereller (à propos de).

squad [skwɒd] n 1. (of police) brigade f. 2. (MIL) peloton m. 3. (SPORT) (group of players) équipe f (parmi laquelle la sélection sera faite).

squadron ['skwɒdrən] n escadron m.

squalid ['skwɒlɪd] adj sordide, ignoble.

squall [skwɔ:l] n (storm) bourrasque f.

squalor ['skwɒlər] n (U) conditions fpl sordides.

squander ['skwɒndər] vt gaspiller.

square [skweər] ◆ adj 1. (in shape) carré(e); **one ~ metre** Br un mètre carré; **three metres ~** trois mètres sur trois. 2. (not owing money): **to be ~** être quitte. ◆ n 1. (shape) carré m. 2. (in town) place f. 3. inf (unfashionable person): **he's a ~** il est vieux jeu. ◆ vt 1. (MATH) élever au carré. 2. (reconcile) accorder. ▶ **square up** vi (settle up): **to ~ up with sb** régler ses comptes avec qqn.

squarely ['skweəlɪ] adv 1. (directly) carrément. 2. (honestly) honnêtement.

square meal n bon repas m.

squash [skwɒʃ] ◆ n 1. (SPORT) squash m. 2. (drink): **orange ~** orangeade f. 3. Am (vegetable) courge f. ◆ vt écraser.

squat [skwɒt] ◆ adj courtaud(e), ramassé(e). ◆ vi (crouch): **to ~ (down)** s'accroupir.

squatter ['skwɒtər] n Br squatter m.

squawk [skwɔ:k] n cri m strident OR perçant.

squeak [skwi:k] n 1. (of animal) petit cri m aigu. 2. (of door, hinge) grincement m.

squeal [skwi:l] vi (person, animal) pousser des cris aigus.

squeamish ['skwi:mɪʃ] adj facilement dégoûté(e).

squeeze [skwi:z] ◆ n (pressure) pression f. ◆ vt 1. (press firmly) presser. 2. (liquid, toothpaste) exprimer. 3. (cram): **to ~ sthg into sthg** entasser qqch dans qqch.

squelch [skweltʃ] vi: **to ~ through mud** patauger dans la boue.

squid [skwɪd] (pl inv OR **-s**) n calmar m.

squiggle ['skwɪgl] n gribouillis m.

squint [skwɪnt] ◆ n: **to have a ~** loucher, être atteint(e) de strabisme. ◆ vi: **to ~ at sthg** regarder qqch en plissant les yeux.

squire ['skwaɪər] n (landowner) propriétaire m.

squirm [skwɜ:m] vi (wriggle) se tortiller.

squirrel [Br 'skwɪrəl, Am 'skwɜ:rəl] n écureuil m.

squirt [skwɜ:t] ◆ vt (water, oil) faire jaillir, faire gicler. ◆ vi: **to ~ (out of)** jaillir (de), gicler (de).

Sr abbr of **senior**.

Sri Lanka [ˌsri:'læŋkə] n Sri Lanka m.

St 1. (abbr of **saint**) St, Ste. 2. abbr of **Street**.

stab [stæb] ◆ n 1. (with knife) coup m de couteau. 2. inf (attempt): **to have a ~ (at sthg)** essayer (qqch), tenter (qqch).

3. (*twinge*): ~ **of pain** élancement *m*; ~ **of guilt** remords *m*. ◆ *vt* **1.** (*person*) poignarder. **2.** (*food*) piquer.

stable ['steɪbl] ◆ *adj* stable. ◆ *n* écurie *f*.

stack [stæk] ◆ *n* (*pile*) pile *f*. ◆ *vt* (*pile up*) empiler.

stadium ['steɪdjəm] (*pl* **-diums** OR **-dia** [-djə]) *n* stade *m*.

staff [stɑːf] ◆ *n* (*employees*) personnel *m*; (*of school*) personnel enseignant, professeurs *mpl*. ◆ *vt* pourvoir en personnel.

stag [stæg] (*pl inv* OR **-s**) *n* cerf *m*.

stage [steɪdʒ] ◆ *n* **1.** (*phase*) étape *f*, phase *f*, stade *m*. **2.** (*platform*) scène *f*. **3.** (*acting profession*): **the ~** le théâtre. ◆ *vt* **1.** (THEATRE) monter, mettre en scène. **2.** (*organize*) organiser.

stagecoach ['steɪdʒkəʊtʃ] *n* diligence *f*.

stage fright *n* trac *m*.

stage-manage *vt lit & fig* mettre en scène.

stagger ['stægər] ◆ *vt* **1.** (*astound*) stupéfier. **2.** (*working hours*) échelonner; (*holidays*) étaler. ◆ *vi* tituber.

stagnant ['stægnənt] *adj* stagnant(e).

stagnate [stæg'neɪt] *vi* stagner.

stag party *n* soirée *f* entre hommes; (*before wedding*) soirée où un futur marié enterre sa vie de garçon avec ses amis.

staid [steɪd] *adj* guindé(e), collet monté.

stain [steɪn] ◆ *n* (*mark*) tache *f*. ◆ *vt* (*discolour*) tacher.

stained glass [,steɪnd-] *n* (U) (*windows*) vitraux *mpl*.

stainless steel ['steɪnlɪs-] *n* acier *m* inoxydable, Inox® *m*.

stain remover [-rɪ,muːvər] *n* détachant *m*.

stair [steər] *n* marche *f*. ▶ **stairs** *npl* escalier *m*.

staircase ['steəkeɪs] *n* escalier *m*.

stairway ['steəweɪ] *n* escalier *m*.

stairwell ['steəwel] *n* cage *f* d'escalier.

stake [steɪk] ◆ *n* **1.** (*share*): **to have a ~ in sthg** avoir des intérêts dans qqch. **2.** (*wooden post*) poteau *m*. **3.** (*in gambling*) enjeu *m*. ◆ *vt*: **to ~ money (on** OR **upon)** jouer OR miser de l'argent (sur); **to ~ one's reputation (on)** jouer OR risquer sa réputation (sur). ▶ **at stake** *adv* en jeu.

stale [steɪl] *adj* (*food, water*) pas frais (fraîche); (*bread*) rassis(e); (*air*) qui sent le renfermé.

stalemate ['steɪlmeɪt] *n* **1.** (*deadlock*) impasse *f*. **2.** (CHESS) pat *m*.

stalk [stɔːk] ◆ *n* **1.** (*of flower, plant*) tige *f*. **2.** (*of leaf, fruit*) queue *f*. ◆ *vt* (*hunt*) traquer. ◆ *vi*: **to ~ in/out** entrer/sortir d'un air hautain.

stall [stɔːl] ◆ *n* **1.** (*in street, market*) éventaire *m*, étal *m*; (*at exhibition*) stand *m*. **2.** (*in stable*) stalle *f*. ◆ *vt* (AUT) caler. ◆ *vi* **1.** (AUT) caler. **2.** (*delay*) essayer de gagner du temps. ▶ **stalls** *npl Br* (*in cinema, theatre*) orchestre *m*.

stallion ['stæljən] *n* étalon *m*.

stalwart ['stɔːlwət] *n* pilier *m*.

stamina ['stæmɪnə] *n* (U) résistance *f*.

stammer ['stæmər] ◆ *n* bégaiement *m*. ◆ *vi* bégayer.

stamp [stæmp] ◆ *n* **1.** (*for letter*) timbre *m*. **2.** (*tool*) tampon *m*. **3.** *fig* (*of authority etc*) marque *f*. ◆ *vt* **1.** (*mark by stamping*) tamponner. **2.** (*stomp*): **to ~ one's foot** taper du pied. ◆ *vi* **1.** (*stomp*) taper du pied. **2.** (*tread heavily*): **to ~ on sthg** marcher sur qqch.

stamp album *n* album *m* de timbres.

stamp-collecting [-kə,lektɪŋ] *n* philatélie *f*.

stamped addressed envelope ['stæmptə,drest-] *n Br* enveloppe *f* affranchie pour la réponse.

stampede [stæm'piːd] *n* débandade *f*.

stance [stæns] *n lit & fig* position *f*.

stand [stænd] (*pt & pp* **stood**) ◆ *n* **1.** (*stall*) stand *m*; (*selling newspapers*) kiosque *m*. **2.** (*supporting object*): **umbrella ~** porte-parapluies *m inv*; **hat ~** porte-chapeaux *m inv*. **3.** (SPORT) tribune *f*. **4.** (MIL) résistance *f*; **to make a ~** résister. **5.** (*public position*) position *f*. **6.** *Am* (JUR) barre *f*. ◆ *vt* **1.** (*place*) mettre (debout), poser (debout). **2.** (*withstand, tolerate*) supporter. ◆ *vi* **1.** (*be upright - person*) être OR se tenir debout; (*- object*) se trouver; (*- building*) se dresser; **~ still!** ne bouge pas!, reste tranquille! **2.** (*stand up*) se lever. **3.** (*liquid*) reposer. **4.** (*offer*) tenir toujours; (*decision*) demeurer valable. **5.** (*be in particular state*): **as things ~ ...** vu l'état actuel des choses ... **6.** *Br* (POL) se présenter. **7.** *Am* (*park car*): **'no ~ing'** 'stationnement interdit'. ▶ **stand back** *vi* reculer. ▶ **stand by** ◆ *vt fus* **1.** (*person*) soutenir. **2.** (*statement, decision*) s'en tenir à. ◆ *vi* **1.** (*in readiness*): **to ~ by (for sthg/to do sthg)** être prêt(e) (pour qqch/pour faire qqch). **2.** (*remain inactive*) rester là. ▶ **stand down** *vi* (*resign*) démissionner. ▶ **stand for** vt fus 1. (signify) représenter. 2. (tolerate) supporter, tolérer. ▶ **stand in** vi: **to ~ in for sb** remplacer qqn. ▶ **stand out** vi ressortir. ▶ **stand up** ◆ vt sep inf (boyfriend, girlfriend) poser un lapin à. ◆ vi (rise from seat) se lever; **~ up!** debout! ▶ **stand up for** vt fus défendre. ▶ **stand up to** vt fus 1. (weather, heat etc) résister à. 2. (person, boss) tenir tête à.

standard ['stændəd] ◆ adj 1. (normal - gen) normal(e); (- size) standard (inv). 2. (accepted) correct(e). ◆ n 1. (level) niveau m. 2. (point of reference) critère m; (TECH) norme f. 3. (flag) étendard m. ▶ **standards** npl (principles) valeurs fpl.

standard lamp n Br lampadaire m.

standard of living (pl **standards of living**) n niveau m de vie.

standby ['stændbaɪ] (pl **standbys**) ◆ n (person) remplaçant m, -e f; **on ~** prêt à intervenir. ◆ comp (ticket, flight) stand-by (inv).

stand-in n remplaçant m, -e f.

standing ['stændɪŋ] ◆ adj (invitation, army) permanent(e); (joke) continuel (elle). ◆ n 1. (reputation) importance f, réputation f. 2. (duration): **of long ~** de longue date; **we're friends of 20 years' ~** nous sommes amis depuis 20 ans.

standing order n prélèvement m automatique.

standing room n (U) places fpl debout.

standoffish [ˌstænd'ɒfɪʃ] adj distant(e).

standpoint ['stændpɔɪnt] n point m de vue.

standstill ['stændstɪl] n: **at a ~** (traffic, train) à l'arrêt; (negotiations, work) paralysé(e); **to come to a ~** (traffic, train) s'immobiliser; (negotiations, work) cesser.

stank [stæŋk] pt → stink.

staple ['steɪpl] ◆ adj (principal) principal(e), de base. ◆ n 1. (for paper) agrafe f. 2. (principal commodity) produit m de base. ◆ vt agrafer.

stapler ['steɪplə'] n agrafeuse f.

star [stɑː'] ◆ n 1. (gen) étoile f. 2. (celebrity) vedette f, star f. ◆ comp (quality) de star; **~ performer** vedette f. ◆ vi: **to ~ (in)** être la vedette (de). ▶ **stars** npl horoscope m.

starboard ['stɑːbəd] ◆ adj de tribord. ◆ n: **to ~** à tribord.

starch [stɑːtʃ] n amidon m.

stardom ['stɑːdəm] n (U) célébrité f.

stare [steə'] ◆ n regard m fixe. ◆ vi: to

~ at sb/sthg fixer qqn/qqch du regard.

stark [stɑːk] ◆ adj 1. (room, decoration) austère; (landscape) désolé(e). 2. (reality, fact) à l'état brut; (contrast) dur(e). ◆ adv: **~ naked** tout nu (toute nue), à poil.

starling ['stɑːlɪŋ] n étourneau m.

starry ['stɑːrɪ] adj étoilé(e).

starry-eyed [-'aɪd] adj innocent(e).

Stars and Stripes n: **the ~** le drapeau des États-Unis, la bannière étoilée.

start [stɑːt] ◆ n 1. (beginning) début m. 2. (jump) sursaut m. 3. (starting place) départ m. 4. (time advantage) avance f. ◆ vt 1. (begin) commencer; **to ~ doing** OR **to do sthg** commencer à faire qqch. 2. (turn on - machine) mettre en marche; (- engine, vehicle) démarrer, mettre en marche. 3. (set up - business, band) créer. ◆ vi 1. (begin) commencer, débuter; **to ~ with** pour commencer, d'abord. 2. (function - machine) se mettre en marche; (- car) démarrer. 3. (begin journey) partir. 4. (jump) sursauter. ▶ **start off** ◆ vt sep (meeting) ouvrir, commencer; (rumour) faire naître; (discussion) entamer, commencer. ◆ vi 1. (begin) commencer; (begin job) débuter. 2. (leave on journey) partir. ▶ **start out** vi 1. (in job) débuter. 2. (leave on journey) partir. ▶ **start up** ◆ vt sep 1. (business) créer; (shop) ouvrir. 2. (car, engine) mettre en marche. ◆ vi 1. (begin) commencer. 2. (machine) se mettre en route; (car, engine) démarrer.

starter ['stɑːtə'] n 1. Br (of meal) hors-d'œuvre m inv. 2. (AUT) démarreur m. 3. (to begin race) starter m.

starting point ['stɑːtɪŋ-] n point m de départ.

startle ['stɑːtl] vt faire sursauter.

startling ['stɑːtlɪŋ] adj surprenant(e).

starvation [stɑː'veɪʃn] n faim f.

starve [stɑːv] ◆ vt (deprive of food) affamer. ◆ vi 1. (have no food) être affamé(e); **to ~ to death** mourir de faim. 2. inf (be hungry) avoir très faim, crever OR mourir de faim.

state [steɪt] ◆ n état m; **to be in a ~** être dans tous ses états. ◆ comp d'État. ◆ vt 1. (express - reason) donner; (- name and address) décliner; **to ~ that ...** déclarer que ... 2. (specify) préciser. ▶ **State** n: **the State** l'État m. ▶ **States** npl: **the States** les États-Unis mpl.

State Department n Am ≃ ministère m des Affaires étrangères.

stately ['steɪtlɪ] adj majestueux(euse).

statement ['steɪtmənt] n 1. (declaration) déclaration f. 2. (JUR) déposition f. 3. (from bank) relevé m de compte.

state of mind (pl states of mind) n humeur f.

statesman ['steɪtsmən] (pl -men [-mən]) n homme m d'État.

static ['stætɪk] ♦ adj statique. ♦ n (U) parasites mpl.

static electricity n électricité f statique.

station ['steɪʃn] ♦ n 1. (RAIL) gare f; (for buses, coaches) gare routière. 2. (RADIO) station f. 3. (building) poste m. 4. fml (rank) rang m. ♦ vt 1. (position) placer, poster. 2. (MIL) poster.

stationary ['steɪʃnərɪ] adj immobile.

stationer ['steɪʃnər] n papetier m, -ère f; ~'s (shop) papeterie f.

stationery ['steɪʃnərɪ] n (U) (equipment) fournitures fpl de bureau; (paper) papier m à lettres.

stationmaster ['steɪʃn,mɑːstər] n chef m de gare.

station wagon n Am break m.

statistic [stə'tɪstɪk] n statistique f. ▶ **statistics** n (U) (science) statistique f.

statistical [stə'tɪstɪkl] adj statistique; (expert) en statistiques; (report) de statistiques.

statue ['stætʃuː] n statue f.

stature ['stætʃər] n 1. (height, size) stature f, taille f. 2. (importance) envergure f.

status ['steɪtəs] n (U) 1. (legal or social position) statut m. 2. (prestige) prestige m.

status symbol n signe m extérieur de richesse.

statute ['stætjuːt] n loi f.

statutory ['stætjutrɪ] adj statutaire.

staunch [stɔːntʃ] ♦ adj loyal(e). ♦ vt (flow) arrêter; (blood) étancher.

stave [steɪv] (pt & pp -d OR stove) n (MUS) portée f. ▶ **stave off** vt sep (disaster, defeat) éviter; (hunger) tromper.

stay [steɪ] ♦ vi 1. (not move away) rester. 2. (as visitor - with friends) passer quelques jours; (- in town, country) séjourner; to ~ in a hotel descendre à l'hôtel. 3. (continue, remain) rester, demeurer; to ~ out of sthg ne pas se mêler de qqch. ♦ n (visit) séjour m. ▶ **stay in** vi rester chez soi, ne pas sortir. ▶ **stay on** vi rester (plus longtemps). ▶ **stay out** vi (from home) ne pas rentrer. ▶ **stay up** vi ne pas se coucher, veiller; to ~ up late se coucher tard.

staying power ['steɪŋ-] n endurance f.

stead [sted] n: to stand sb in good ~ être utile à qqn.

steadfast ['stedfɑːst] adj ferme, résolu(e); (supporter) loyal(e).

steadily ['stedɪlɪ] adv 1. (gradually) progressivement. 2. (regularly - breathe) régulièrement; (- move) sans arrêt. 3. (calmly) de manière imperturbable.

steady ['stedɪ] ♦ adj 1. (gradual) progressif(ive). 2. (regular) régulier(ère). 3. (not shaking) ferme. 4. (calm - voice) calme; (- stare) imperturbable. 5. (stable - job, relationship) stable. 6. (sensible) sérieux(euse). ♦ vt 1. (stop from shaking) empêcher de bouger; to ~ o.s. se remettre d'aplomb. 2. (control - nerves) calmer.

steak [steɪk] n steak m, bifteck m; (of fish) darne f.

steal [stiːl] (pt **stole**, pp **stolen**) ♦ vt voler, dérober. ♦ vi (move secretly) se glisser.

stealthy ['stelθɪ] adj furtif(ive).

steam [stiːm] ♦ n (U) vapeur f. ♦ vt (CULIN) cuire à la vapeur. ♦ vi (give off steam) fumer. ▶ **steam up** vt sep (mist up) embuer. ♦ vi se couvrir de buée.

steamboat ['stiːmbəʊt] n (bateau m à) vapeur m.

steam engine n locomotive f à vapeur.

steamer ['stiːmər] n (ship) (bateau m à) vapeur m.

steamroller ['stiːm,rəʊlər] n rouleau m compresseur.

steamy ['stiːmɪ] adj 1. (full of steam) embué(e). 2. inf (erotic) érotique.

steel [stiːl] ♦ n (U) acier m. ♦ comp en acier, d'acier.

steelworks ['stiːlwɜːks] (pl inv) n aciérie f.

steep [stiːp] adj 1. (hill, road) raide, abrupt(e). 2. (increase, decline) énorme. 3. inf (expensive) excessif(ive).

steeple ['stiːpl] n clocher m, flèche f.

steeplechase ['stiːpltʃeɪs] n 1. (horse race) steeple-chase m. 2. (athletics race) steeple m.

steer ['stɪər] ♦ n bœuf m. ♦ vt 1. (ship) gouverner; (car, aeroplane) conduire, diriger. 2. (person) diriger, guider. ♦ vi: to ~ well (ship) gouverner bien; (car) être facile à manœuvrer; to ~ clear of sb/sthg éviter qqn/qqch.

steering ['stɪərɪŋ] n (U) direction f.

steering wheel n volant m.

stem [stem] ◆ n 1. (of plant) tige f. 2. (of glass) pied m. 3. (of pipe) tuyau m. 4. (GRAMM) radical m. ◆ vt (stop) arrêter. ▶ **stem from** vt fus provenir de.

stench [stentʃ] n puanteur f.

stencil ['stensl] ◆ n pochoir m. ◆ vt faire au pochoir.

stenographer [stə'nɒgrəfər] n Am sténographe mf.

step [step] ◆ n 1. (pace) pas m; in/out of ~ with fig en accord/désaccord avec. 2. (action) mesure f. 3. (stage) étape f; ~ by ~ petit à petit, progressivement. 4. (stair) marche f. 5. (of ladder) barreau m, échelon m. ◆ vi 1. (move foot): to ~ forward avancer; to ~ off OR down from sthg descendre de qqch; to ~ back reculer. 2. (tread): to ~ on/in sthg marcher sur/dans qqch. ▶ **steps** npl 1. (stairs) marches fpl. 2. Br (stepladder) escabeau m. ▶ **step down** vi (leave job) démissionner. ▶ **step in** vi intervenir. ▶ **step up** vt sep intensifier.

stepbrother ['step,brʌðər] n demi-frère m.

stepdaughter ['step,dɔːtər] n belle-fille f.

stepfather ['step,fɑːðər] n beau-père m.

stepladder ['step,lædər] n escabeau m.

stepmother ['step,mʌðər] n belle-mère f.

stepping-stone ['stepɪŋ-] n pierre f de gué; fig tremplin m.

stepsister ['step,sɪstər] n demi-sœur f.

stepson ['stepsʌn] n beau-fils m.

stereo ['steriəu] (pl -s) ◆ adj stéréo (inv). ◆ n 1. (appliance) chaîne f stéréo. 2. (sound): in ~ en stéréo.

stereotype ['steriətaip] n stéréotype m.

sterile ['sterail] adj stérile.

sterilize, -ise ['sterəlaiz] vt stériliser.

sterling ['stɜːlɪŋ] ◆ adj 1. (of British money) sterling (inv). 2. (excellent) exceptionnel(elle). ◆ n (U) livre f sterling.

sterling silver n argent m fin.

stern [stɜːn] ◆ adj sévère. ◆ n (NAUT) arrière m.

steroid ['stiərɔid] n stéroïde m.

stethoscope ['steθəskəup] n stéthoscope m.

stew [stjuː] ◆ n ragoût m. ◆ vt (meat) cuire en ragoût; (fruit) faire cuire.

steward ['stjuəd] n 1. (on plane, ship, train) steward m. 2. Br (at demonstration, meeting) membre m du service d'ordre.

stewardess ['stjuədis] n hôtesse f.

stick [stik] (pt & pp stuck) ◆ n 1. (of wood, dynamite, candy) bâton m. 2. (walking stick) canne f. 3. (SPORT) crosse f. ◆ vt 1. (push): to ~ sthg in OR into planter qqch dans. 2. (with glue, Sellotape®): to ~ sthg (on OR to) coller qqch (sur). 3. (put) mettre. 4. Br inf (tolerate) supporter. ◆ vi 1. (adhere): to ~ (to) coller (à). 2. (jam) se coincer. ▶ **stick out** vt sep 1. (head) sortir; (hand) lever; (tongue) tirer. 2. inf (endure): to ~ it out tenir le coup. ◆ vi 1. (protrude) dépasser. 2. inf (be noticeable) se remarquer. ▶ **stick to** vt fus 1. (follow closely) suivre. 2. (principles) rester fidèle à; (decision) s'en tenir à; (promise) tenir. ▶ **stick up** vi dépasser. ▶ **stick up for** vt fus défendre.

sticker ['stikər] n (label) autocollant m.

sticking plaster ['stikiŋ-] n sparadrap m.

stickler ['stiklər] n: to be a ~ for être à cheval sur.

stick shift n Am levier m de vitesses.

stick-up n inf vol m à main armée.

sticky ['stiki] adj 1. (hands, sweets) poisseux(euse); (label, tape) adhésif(ive). 2. inf (awkward) délicat(e).

stiff [stif] ◆ adj 1. (rod, paper, material) rigide; (shoes, brush) dur(e); (fabric) raide. 2. (door, drawer, window) dur(e) (à ouvrir/fermer); (joint) ankylosé(e); to have a ~ back avoir des courbatures dans le dos; to have a ~ neck avoir le torticolis. 3. (formal) guindé(e). 4. (severe - penalty) sévère; (- resistance) tenace; (- competition) serré(e). 5. (difficult - task) difficile. ◆ adv inf: to be bored ~ s'ennuyer à mourir; to be frozen/scared ~ mourir de froid/peur.

stiffen ['stifn] ◆ vt 1. (material) raidir; (with starch) empeser. 2. (resolve) renforcer. ◆ vi 1. (body) se raidir; (joints) s'ankyloser. 2. (competition, resistance) s'intensifier.

stifle ['staifl] vt & vi étouffer.

stifling ['staiflɪŋ] adj étouffant(e).

stigma ['stigmə] n 1. (disgrace) honte f, stigmate m. 2. (BOT) stigmate m.

stile [stail] n échalier m.

stiletto heel [sti'letəu-] n Br talon m aiguille.

still [stil] ◆ adv 1. (up to now, up to then) encore, toujours; I've ~ got £5 left il me reste encore 5 livres. 2. (even now) encore. 3. (nevertheless) tout de même. 4. (with comparatives): ~ bigger/more

important encore plus grand/plus important. ◆ adj 1. (not moving) immobile. 2. (calm) calme, tranquille. 3. (not windy) sans vent. 4. (not fizzy - gen) non gazeux(euse); (- mineral water) plat(e). ◆ n 1. (PHOT) photo f. 2. (for making alcohol) alambic m.

stillborn ['stɪlbɔːn] adj mort-né(e).

still life (pl -s) n nature f morte.

stilted ['stɪltɪd] adj emprunté(e), qui manque de naturel.

stilts ['stɪlts] npl 1. (for person) échasses fpl. 2. (for building) pilotis mpl.

stimulate ['stɪmjʊleɪt] vt stimuler.

stimulating ['stɪmjʊleɪtɪŋ] adj stimulant(e).

stimulus ['stɪmjʊləs] (pl -li [-laɪ]) n 1. (encouragement) stimulant m. 2. (BIOL & PSYCH) stimulus m.

sting [stɪŋ] (pt & pp stung) ◆ n 1. (by bee) piqûre f; (of bee) dard m. 2. (sharp pain) brûlure f. ◆ vt (gen) piquer. ◆ vi piquer.

stingy ['stɪndʒɪ] adj inf radin(e).

stink [stɪŋk] (pt stank OR stunk, pp stunk) ◆ n puanteur f. ◆ vi (smell) puer, empester.

stinking ['stɪŋkɪŋ] inf adj (cold) gros (grosse); (weather) pourri(e); (place) infect(e).

stint [stɪnt] ◆ n (period of work) part f de travail. ◆ vi: to ~ on lésiner sur.

stipulate ['stɪpjʊleɪt] vt stipuler.

stir [stɜːʳ] ◆ n (public excitement) sensation f. ◆ vt 1. (mix) remuer. 2. (move gently) agiter. 3. (move emotionally) émouvoir. ◆ vi bouger, remuer. ► **stir up** vt sep 1. (dust) soulever. 2. (trouble) provoquer; (resentment, dissatisfaction) susciter; (rumour) faire naître.

stirrup ['stɪrəp] n étrier m.

stitch [stɪtʃ] ◆ n 1. (SEWING) point m; (in knitting) maille f. 2. (MED) point m de suture. 3. (stomach pain): to have a ~ avoir un point de côté. ◆ vt 1. (SEWING) coudre. 2. (MED) suturer.

stoat [stəʊt] n hermine f.

stock [stɒk] ◆ n 1. (supply) réserve f. 2. (U) (COMM) stock m, réserve f; in ~ en stock; **out of ~** épuisé(e). 3. (FIN) valeurs fpl; **~s and shares** titres mpl. 4. (ancestry) souche f. 5. (CULIN) bouillon m. 6. (livestock) cheptel m. 7. phr: to take ~ (of) faire le point (de). ◆ adj classique. ◆ vt 1. (COMM) vendre, avoir en stock. 2. (fill - shelves) garnir. ► **stock up** vi: to ~ up (with) faire des provisions (de).

stockbroker ['stɒk,brəʊkəʳ] n agent m de change.

stock cube n Br bouillon-cube m.

stock exchange n Bourse f.

stockholder ['stɒk,həʊldəʳ] n Am actionnaire mf.

Stockholm ['stɒkhəʊm] n Stockholm.

stocking ['stɒkɪŋ] n (for woman) bas m.

stockist ['stɒkɪst] n Br dépositaire m, stockiste m.

stock market n Bourse f.

stock phrase n cliché m.

stockpile ['stɒkpaɪl] ◆ n stock m. ◆ vt (weapons) amasser; (food) stocker.

stocktaking ['stɒk,teɪkɪŋ] n (U) inventaire m.

stocky ['stɒkɪ] adj trapu(e).

stodgy ['stɒdʒɪ] adj (food) lourd(e) (à digérer).

stoical ['stəʊɪkl] adj stoïque.

stoke [stəʊk] vt (fire) entretenir.

stole [stəʊl] ◆ pt → steal. ◆ n étole f.

stolen ['stəʊln] pp → steal.

stolid ['stɒlɪd] adj impassible.

stomach ['stʌmək] ◆ n (organ) estomac m; (abdomen) ventre m. ◆ vt (tolerate) encaisser, supporter.

stomachache ['stʌmɪkeɪk] n: to have ~ avoir mal au ventre.

stomach upset n embarras m gastrique.

stone [stəʊn] (pl sense 3 only inv OR -s) ◆ n 1. (rock) pierre f; (smaller) caillou m. 2. (seed) noyau m. 3. Br (unit of measurement) = 6,348 kg. ◆ comp de OR en pierre. ◆ vt (person, car etc) jeter des pierres sur.

stone-cold adj complètement froid(e) OR glacé(e).

stonewashed ['stəʊnwɒʃt] adj délavé(e).

stonework ['stəʊnwɜːk] n maçonnerie f.

stood [stʊd] pt & pp → stand.

stool [stuːl] n (seat) tabouret m.

stoop [stuːp] ◆ n (bent back): to walk with a ~ marcher le dos voûté. ◆ vi 1. (bend down) se pencher. 2. (hunch shoulders) être voûté(e).

stop [stɒp] ◆ n 1. (gen) arrêt m; to put a ~ to sthg mettre un terme à qqch. 2. (full stop) point m. ◆ vt 1. (gen) arrêter; (end) mettre fin à; to ~ doing sthg arrêter de faire qqch; to ~ work arrêter de travailler, cesser le travail. 2. (prevent): to ~ sb/sthg (from doing sthg) empêcher qqn/qqch (de faire qqch). 3. (block) boucher. ◆ vi s'arrêter, cesser.

▶ **stop off** *vi* s'arrêter, faire halte.

▶ **stop up** *vt sep* (*block*) boucher.

stopgap ['stɒpgæp] *n* bouche-trou *m*.

stopover ['stɒp,əʊvəʳ] *n* halte *f*.

stoppage ['stɒpɪdʒ] *n* **1.** (*strike*) grève *f*. **2.** Br (*deduction*) retenue *f*.

stopper ['stɒpəʳ] *n* bouchon *m*.

stop press *n* nouvelles *fpl* de dernière heure.

stopwatch ['stɒpwɒtʃ] *n* chronomètre *m*.

storage ['stɔːrɪdʒ] *n* **1.** (*of goods*) entreposage *m*, emmagasinage *m*; (*of household objects*) rangement *m*. **2.** (COMPUT) stockage *m*, mémorisation *f*.

storage heater *n* Br radiateur *m* à accumulation.

store [stɔːʳ] ◆ *n* **1.** (*shop*) magasin *m*. **2.** (*supply*) provision *f*. **3.** (*place of storage*) réserve *f*. ◆ *vt* **1.** (*save*) mettre en réserve; (*goods*) entreposer, emmagasiner. **2.** (COMPUT) stocker, mémoriser.

▶ **store up** *vt sep* (*provisions*) mettre en réserve; (*goods*) emmagasiner; (*information*) mettre en mémoire, noter.

storekeeper ['stɔː,kiːpəʳ] *n* Am commerçant *m*, -e *f*.

storeroom ['stɔːrʊm] *n* magasin *m*.

storey Br (*pl* **storeys**), **story** Am (*pl* **-ies**) ['stɔːrɪ] *n* étage *m*.

stork [stɔːk] *n* cigogne *f*.

storm [stɔːm] ◆ *n* **1.** (*bad weather*) orage *m*. **2.** *fig* (*of abuse*) torrent *m*; (*of applause*) tempête *f*. ◆ *vt* (MIL) prendre d'assaut. ◆ *vi* **1.** (*go angrily*): **to ~ in/out** entrer/sortir comme un ouragan. **2.** (*speak angrily*) fulminer.

stormy ['stɔːmɪ] *adj lit & fig* orageux (euse).

story ['stɔːrɪ] *n* **1.** (*gen*) histoire *f*. **2.** (PRESS) article *m*; (RADIO & TV) nouvelle *f*. **3.** Am = **storey**.

storybook ['stɔːrɪbʊk] *adj* (*romance etc*) de conte de fées.

storyteller ['stɔːrɪ,teləʳ] *n* **1.** (*narrator*) conteur *m*, -euse *f*. **2.** *euphemism* (*liar*) menteur *m*, -euse *f*.

stout [staʊt] ◆ *adj* **1.** (*rather fat*) corpulent(e). **2.** (*strong*) solide. **3.** (*resolute*) ferme, résolu(e). ◆ *n* (U) stout *m*, bière *f* brune.

stove [stəʊv] ◆ *pt & pp* → **stave**. ◆ *n* (*for cooking*) cuisinière *f*; (*for heating*) poêle *m*, calorifère *m* Can.

stow [stəʊ] *vt*: **to ~ sthg (away)** ranger qqch.

stowaway ['stəʊəweɪ] *n* passager *m* clandestin.

straddle ['strædl] *vt* enjamber; (*chair*) s'asseoir à califourchon sur.

straggle ['strægl] *vi* **1.** (*buildings*) s'étendre, s'étaler; (*hair*) être en désordre. **2.** (*person*) traîner, lambiner.

straggler ['strægləʳ] *n* traînard *m*, -e *f*.

straight [streɪt] ◆ *adj* **1.** (*not bent*) droit (e); (*hair*) raide. **2.** (*frank*) franc (franche), honnête. **3.** (*tidy*) en ordre. **4.** (*choice, exchange*) simple. **5.** (*alcoholic drink*) sec, sans eau. **6.** *phr*: **let's get this ~** entendons-nous bien. ◆ *adv* **1.** (*in a straight line*) droit. **2.** (*directly, immediately*) droit, tout de suite. **3.** (*frankly*) carrément, franchement. **4.** (*undiluted*) sec, sans eau. ▶ **straight off** *adv* tout de suite, sur-le-champ. ▶ **straight out** *adv* sans mâcher ses mots.

straightaway [,streɪtə'weɪ] *adv* tout de suite, immédiatement.

straighten ['streɪtn] *vt* **1.** (*tidy - hair, dress*) arranger; (*- room*) mettre de l'ordre dans. **2.** (*make straight - horizontally*) rendre droit(e); (*- vertically*) redresser.

▶ **straighten out** *vt sep* (*problem*) résoudre.

straight face *n*: **to keep a ~** garder son sérieux.

straightforward [,streɪt'fɔːwəd] *adj* **1.** (*easy*) simple. **2.** (*frank*) honnête, franc (franche).

strain [streɪn] ◆ *n* **1.** (*mental*) tension *f*, stress *m*. **2.** (MED) foulure *f*. **3.** (TECH) contrainte *f*, effort *m*. ◆ *vt* **1.** (*work hard - eyes*) plisser fort; **to ~ one's ears** tendre l'oreille. **2.** (MED - *muscle*) se froisser; (*- eyes*) se fatiguer; **to ~ one's back** se faire un tour de reins. **3.** (*patience*) mettre à rude épreuve; (*budget*) grever. **4.** (*drain*) passer. **5.** (TECH) exercer une contrainte sur. ◆ *vi* (*try very hard*): **to ~ to do sthg** faire un gros effort pour faire qqch, se donner du mal pour faire qqch. ▶ **strains** *npl* (*of music*) accords *mpl*, airs *mpl*.

strained [streɪnd] *adj* **1.** (*worried*) contracté(e), tendu(e). **2.** (*relations, relationship*) tendu(e). **3.** (*unnatural*) forcé(e).

strainer ['streɪnəʳ] *n* passoire *f*.

strait [streɪt] *n* détroit *m*. ▶ **straits** *npl*: **in dire** OR **desperate ~s** dans une situation désespérée.

straitjacket ['streɪt,dʒækɪt] *n* camisole *f* de force.

straitlaced [,streɪt'leɪst] *adj* collet monté (*inv*).

strand [strænd] *n* **1.** (*of cotton, wool*)

brin *m*, fil *m*; (*of hair*) mèche *f*. **2.** (*theme*) fil *m*.

stranded ['strændɪd] *adj* (*boat*) échoué(e); (*people*) abandonné(e), en rade.

strange [streɪndʒ] *adj* **1.** (*odd*) étrange, bizarre. **2.** (*unfamiliar*) inconnu(e).

stranger ['streɪndʒəʳ] *n* **1.** (*unfamiliar person*) inconnu *m*, -e *f*. **2.** (*from another place*) étranger *m*, -ère *f*.

strangle ['stræŋgl] *vt* étrangler; *fig* étouffer.

stranglehold ['stræŋglhəʊld] *n* **1.** (*round neck*) étranglement *m*. **2.** *fig* (*control*): ~ **(on)** domination *f* (de).

strap [stræp] ◆ *n* (*for fastening*) sangle *f*, courroie *f*; (*of bag*) bandoulière *f*; (*of rifle, dress, bra*) bretelle *f*; (*of watch*) bracelet *m*. ◆ *vt* (*fasten*) attacher.

strapping ['stræpɪŋ] *adj* bien bâti(e), robuste.

Strasbourg ['stræzbɜ:g] *n* Strasbourg.

strategic [strə'ti:dʒɪk] *adj* stratégique.

strategy ['strætɪdʒɪ] *n* stratégie *f*.

straw [strɔ:] *n* paille *f*; **that's the last ~!** ça c'est le comble!

strawberry ['strɔ:bərɪ] ◆ *n* (*fruit*) fraise *f*. ◆ *comp* (*tart, yoghurt*) aux fraises; (*jam*) de fraises.

stray [streɪ] ◆ *adj* **1.** (*animal*) errant(e), perdu(e). **2.** (*bullet*) perdu(e); (*example*) isolé(e). ◆ *vi* **1.** (*person, animal*) errer, s'égarer. **2.** (*thoughts*) vagabonder, errer.

streak [stri:k] ◆ *n* **1.** (*line*) bande *f*, marque *f*; ~ **of lightning** éclair *m*. **2.** (*in character*) côté *m*. ◆ *vi* (*move quickly*) se déplacer comme un éclair.

stream [stri:m] ◆ *n* **1.** (*small river*) ruisseau *m*. **2.** (*of liquid, light*) flot *m*, jet *m*. **3.** (*of people, cars*) flot *m*; (*of complaints, abuse*) torrent *m*. **4.** Br (SCH) classe *f* de niveau. ◆ *vi* **1.** (*liquid*) couler à flots, ruisseler; (*light*) entrer à flots. **2.** (*people, cars*) affluer; **to ~ past** passer à flots. ◆ *vt* Br (SCH) répartir par niveau.

streamer ['stri:məʳ] *n* (*for party*) serpentin *m*.

streamlined ['stri:mlaɪnd] *adj* **1.** (*aerodynamic*) au profil aérodynamique. **2.** (*efficient*) rationalisé(e).

street [stri:t] *n* rue *f*.

streetcar ['stri:tkɑ:ʳ] *n* Am tramway *m*.

street lamp, street light *n* réverbère *m*.

street plan *n* plan *m*.

streetwise ['stri:twaɪz] *adj* *inf* averti(e), futé(e).

strength [streŋθ] *n* **1.** (*gen*) force *f*. **2.** (*power, influence*) puissance *f*. **3.** (*solidity, of currency*) solidité *f*.

strengthen ['streŋθn] *vt* **1.** (*structure, team, argument*) renforcer. **2.** (*economy, currency, friendship*) consolider. **3.** (*resolve, dislike*) fortifier, affermir. **4.** (*person*) enhardir.

strenuous ['strenjʊəs] *adj* (*exercise, activity*) fatigant(e), dur(e); (*effort*) vigoureux(euse), acharné(e).

stress [stres] ◆ *n* **1.** (*emphasis*): ~ **(on)** accent *m* (sur). **2.** (*mental*) stress *m*, tension *f*. **3.** (TECH): ~ **(on)** contrainte *f* (sur), effort *m* (sur). **4.** (LING) accent *m*. ◆ *vt* **1.** (*emphasize*) souligner, insister sur. **2.** (LING) accentuer.

stressed [strest] *adj* stressé(e).

stressful ['stresfʊl] *adj* stressant(e).

stretch [stretʃ] ◆ *n* **1.** (*of land, water*) étendue *f*; (*of road, river*) partie *f*, section *f*. **2.** (*of time*) période *f*. ◆ *vt* **1.** (*arms*) allonger; (*legs*) se dégourdir; (*muscles*) distendre. **2.** (*pull taut*) tendre, étirer. **3.** (*overwork - person*) surmener. **4.** (*resources, budget*) grever. **4.** (*challenge*): **to ~ sb** pousser qqn à la limite de ses capacités. ◆ *vi* **1.** (*area*): **to ~ over** s'étendre sur; **to ~ from ...** **to** s'étendre de ... à. **2.** (*person, animal*) s'étirer. **3.** (*material, elastic*) se tendre, s'étirer.

▶ **stretch out** ◆ *vt sep* (*arm, leg, hand*) tendre. ◆ *vi* (*lie down*) s'étendre, s'allonger.

stretcher ['stretʃəʳ] *n* brancard *m*, civière *f*.

strew [stru:] (*pt* **-ed**, *pp* **strewn** [stru:n] OR **-ed**) *vt*: **to be strewn with** être jonché(e) de.

stricken ['strɪkn] *adj*: **to be ~ by** OR **with panic** être pris(e) de panique; **to be ~ by an illness** souffrir OR être atteint(e) d'une maladie.

strict [strɪkt] *adj* (*gen*) strict(e).

strictly ['strɪktlɪ] *adv* **1.** (*gen*) strictement; ~ **speaking** à proprement parler. **2.** (*severely*) d'une manière stricte, sévèrement.

stride [straɪd] (*pt* **strode**, *pp* **stridden** ['strɪdn]) ◆ *n* (*long step*) grand pas *m*, enjambée *f*. ◆ *vi* marcher à grandes enjambées OR à grands pas.

strident ['straɪdnt] *adj* **1.** (*voice, sound*) strident(e). **2.** (*demand, attack*) véhément(e), bruyant(e).

strife [straɪf] *n* (U) conflit *m*, lutte *f*.

strike [straɪk] (*pt* & *pp* **struck**) ◆ *n* **1.** (*by workers*) grève *f*; **to be (out) on ~** être en grève; **to go on ~** faire grève, se mettre en grève. **2.** (MIL) raid *m*. **3.** (*of oil, gold*) découverte *f*. ◆ *vt* **1.** (*hit - deliberately*) frapper; (*- accidentally*) heurter. **2.** (*subj: thought*) venir à l'esprit de. **3.** (*conclude - deal, bargain*) conclure. **4.** (*light - match*) frotter. ◆ *vi* **1.** (*workers*) faire grève. **2.** (*hit*) frapper. **3.** (*attack*) attaquer. **4.** (*chime*) sonner. ▶ **strike down** *vt sep* terrasser. ▶ **strike out** ◆ *vt sep* rayer, barrer. ◆ *vi* (*head out*) se mettre en route, partir. ▶ **strike up** *vt fus* **1.** (*conversation*) commencer, engager; **to ~ up a friendship (with)** se lier d'amitié (avec). **2.** (*music*) commencer à jouer.

striker ['straɪkə*] *n* **1.** (*person on strike*) gréviste *mf*. **2.** (FTBL) buteur *m*.

striking ['straɪkɪŋ] *adj* **1.** (*noticeable*) frappant(e), saisissant(e). **2.** (*attractive*) d'une beauté frappante.

string [strɪŋ] (*pt & pp* **strung**) *n* **1.** (U) (*thin rope*) ficelle *f*. **2.** (*piece of thin rope*) bout *m* de ficelle; **to pull ~s** faire jouer le piston. **3.** (*of beads, pearls*) rang *m*. **4.** (*series*) série *f*, suite *f*. **5.** (*of musical instrument*) corde *f*. ▶ **strings** *npl* (MUS): **the ~s** les cordes *fpl*. ▶ **string out** *vt fus* échelonner. ▶ **string together** *vt sep fig* aligner.

string bean *n* haricot *m* vert.

stringed instrument [ˌstrɪŋd-] *n* instrument *m* à cordes.

stringent ['strɪndʒənt] *adj* strict(e), rigoureux(euse).

strip [strɪp] ◆ *n* **1.** (*narrow piece*) bande *f*. **2.** Br (SPORT) tenue *f*. ◆ *vt* **1.** (*undress*) déshabiller, dévêtir. **2.** (*paint, wallpaper*) enlever. ◆ *vi* (*undress*) se déshabiller, se dévêtir. ▶ **strip off** *vi* se déshabiller, se dévêtir.

strip cartoon *n* Br bande *f* dessinée.

stripe [straɪp] *n* **1.** (*band of colour*) rayure *f*. **2.** (*sign of rank*) galon *m*.

striped [straɪpt] *adj* à rayures, rayé(e).

strip lighting *n* éclairage *m* au néon.

stripper ['strɪpə*] *n* **1.** (*performer of striptease*) strip-teaseuse *f*, effeuilleuse *f*. **2.** (*for paint*) décapant *m*.

striptease ['striptiːz] *n* strip-tease *m*.

strive [straɪv] (*pt* **strove**, *pp* **striven** ['strɪvn]) *vi*: **to ~ for sthg** essayer d'obtenir qqch; **to ~ to do sthg** s'efforcer de faire qqch.

strode [strəʊd] *pt* → **stride**.

stroke [strəʊk] ◆ *n* **1.** (MED) attaque *f* cérébrale. **2.** (*of pen, brush*) trait *m*. **3.** (*in swimming - movement*) mouvement *m* des bras; (*- style*) nage *f*; (*in rowing*) coup *m*

d'aviron; (*in golf, tennis etc*) coup *m*. **4.** (*of clock*): **on the third ~** ≃ au quatrième top. **5.** Br (TYPO) (*oblique*) barre *f*. **6.** (*piece*): **a ~ of genius** un trait de génie; **a ~ of luck** un coup de chance or de veine; **at a ~** d'un seul coup. ◆ *vt* caresser.

stroll [strəʊl] ◆ *n* petite promenade *f*, petit tour *m*. ◆ *vi* se promener, flâner.

stroller ['strəʊlə*] *n* Am (*for baby*) poussette *f*.

strong [strɒŋ] *adj* **1.** (*gen*) fort(e); **~ point** point *m* fort. **2.** (*structure, argument, friendship*) solide. **3.** (*healthy*) robuste, vigoureux(euse). **4.** (*policy, measures*) énergique. **5.** (*in numbers*): **the crowd was 2,000 ~** il y avait une foule de 2 000 personnes. **6.** (*team, candidate*) sérieux(euse), qui a des chances de gagner.

strongbox ['strɒŋbɒks] *n* coffre-fort *m*.

stronghold ['strɒŋhəʊld] *n fig* bastion *m*.

strongly ['strɒŋlɪ] *adv* **1.** (*gen*) fortement. **2.** (*solidly*) solidement.

strong room *n* chambre *f* forte.

strove [strəʊv] *pt* → **strive**.

struck [strʌk] *pt & pp* → **strike**.

structure ['strʌktʃə*] *n* **1.** (*organization*) structure *f*. **2.** (*building*) construction *f*.

struggle ['strʌgl] ◆ *n* **1.** (*great effort*): **~ (for sthg/to do sthg)** lutte *f* (pour qqch/ pour faire qqch). **2.** (*fight*) bagarre *f*. ◆ *vi* **1.** (*make great effort*): **to ~ (for)** lutter (pour); **to ~ to do sthg** s'efforcer de faire qqch. **2.** (*to free oneself*) se débattre; (*fight*) se battre.

strum [strʌm] *vt* (*guitar*) gratter de; (*tune*) jouer.

strung [strʌŋ] *pt & pp* → **string**.

strut [strʌt] ◆ *n* (CONSTR) étai *m*, support *m*. ◆ *vi* se pavaner.

stub [stʌb] ◆ *n* **1.** (*of cigarette*) mégot *m*; (*of pencil*) morceau *m*. **2.** (*of ticket, cheque*) talon *m*. ◆ *vt*: **to ~ one's toe** se cogner le doigt de pied. ▶ **stub out** *vt sep* écraser.

stubble ['stʌbl] *n* (U) **1.** (*in field*) chaume *m*. **2.** (*on chin*) barbe *f* de plusieurs jours.

stubborn ['stʌbən] *adj* **1.** (*person*) têtu(e), obstiné(e). **2.** (*stain*) qui ne veut pas partir, rebelle.

stuck [stʌk] ◆ *pt & pp* → **stick**. ◆ *adj* **1.** (*jammed, trapped*) coincé(e). **2.** (*stumped*): **to be ~** sécher. **3.** (*stranded*) bloqué(e), en rade.

stuck-up *adj inf pej* bêcheur(euse).

stud [stʌd] *n* **1.** (*metal decoration*) clou *m* décoratif. **2.** (*earring*) clou *m* d'oreille. **3.** Br (*on boot, shoe*) clou *m*; (*on sports boots*) crampon *m*. **4.** (*of horses*) haras *m*.

studded ['stʌdɪd] *adj*: ~ **(with)** parsemé(e) (de), constellé(e) (de).

student ['stju:dnt] ◆ *n* étudiant *m*, -e *f*. ◆ *comp* (*life*) estudiantin(e); (*politics*) des étudiants; (*disco*) pour étudiants.

studio ['stju:dɪəʊ] (*pl* **-s**) *n* studio *m*; (*of artist*) atelier *m*.

studio flat Br, **studio apartment** Am *n* studio *m*.

studious ['stju:djəs] *adj* studieux (euse).

studiously ['stju:djəslɪ] *adv* studieusement.

study ['stʌdɪ] ◆ *n* **1.** (*gen*) étude *f*. **2.** (*room*) bureau *m*. ◆ *vt* **1.** (*learn*) étudier, faire des études de. **2.** (*examine*) examiner, étudier. ◆ *vi* étudier, faire ses études.

stuff [stʌf] ◆ *n* (U) **1.** *inf* (*things*) choses *fpl*. **2.** (*substance*) substance *f*. **3.** *inf* (*belongings*) affaires *fpl*. ◆ *vt* **1.** (*push*) fourrer. **2.** (*fill*): **to ~ sthg (with)** remplir OR bourrer qqch (de). **3.** (CULIN) farcir.

stuffed [stʌft] *adj* **1.** (*filled*): ~ **with** bourré(e) de. **2.** *inf* (*with food*) gavé(e). **3.** (CULIN) farci(e). **4.** (*preserved - animal*) empaillé(e).

stuffing ['stʌfɪŋ] *n* (U) **1.** (*filling*) bourre *f*, rembourrage *m*. **2.** (CULIN) farce *f*.

stuffy ['stʌfɪ] *adj* **1.** (*room*) mal aéré(e), qui manque d'air. **2.** (*person, club*) vieux jeu (*inv*).

stumble ['stʌmbl] *vi* trébucher. ▸ **stumble across, stumble on** *vt fus* tomber sur.

stumbling block ['stʌmblɪŋ-] *n* pierre *f* d'achoppement.

stump [stʌmp] ◆ *n* (*of tree*) souche *f*; (*of arm, leg*) moignon *m*. ◆ *vt* (*subj: question, problem*) dérouter, rendre perplexe.

stun [stʌn] *vt* **1.** (*knock unconscious*) étourdir, assommer. **2.** (*surprise*) stupéfier, renverser.

stung [stʌŋ] *pt* & *pp* → **sting**.

stunk [stʌŋk] *pt* & *pp* → **stink**.

stunning ['stʌnɪŋ] *adj* **1.** (*very beautiful*) ravissant(e); (*scenery*) merveilleux (euse). **2.** (*surprising*) stupéfiant(e), renversant(e).

stunt [stʌnt] ◆ *n* **1.** (*for publicity*) coup *m*. **2.** (CINEMA) cascade *f*. ◆ *vt* retarder, arrêter.

stunted ['stʌntɪd] *adj* rabougri(e).

stunt man *n* cascadeur *m*.

stupefy ['stju:pɪfaɪ] *vt* **1.** (*tire*) abrutir. **2.** (*surprise*) stupéfier, abasourdir.

stupendous [stju:'pendəs] *adj* extraordinaire, prodigieux(euse).

stupid ['stju:pɪd] *adj* **1.** (*foolish*) stupide, bête. **2.** *inf* (*annoying*) fichu(e).

stupidity [stju:'pɪdətɪ] *n* (U) bêtise *f*, stupidité *f*.

sturdy ['stɜ:dɪ] *adj* (*person*) robuste; (*furniture, structure*) solide.

stutter ['stʌtəʳ] *vi* bégayer.

sty [staɪ] *n* (*pigsty*) porcherie *f*.

stye [staɪ] *n* orgelet *m*, compère-loriot *m*.

style [staɪl] ◆ *n* **1.** (*characteristic manner*) style *m*. **2.** (U) (*elegance*) chic *m*, élégance *f*. **3.** (*design*) genre *m*, modèle *m*. ◆ *vt* (*hair*) coiffer.

stylish ['staɪlɪʃ] *adj* chic (*inv*), élégant(e).

stylist ['staɪlɪst] *n* (*hairdresser*) coiffeur *m*, -euse *f*.

stylus ['staɪləs] (*pl* **-es**) *n* (*on record player*) pointe *f* de lecture, saphir *m*.

suave [swɑ:v] *adj* doucereux(euse).

sub [sʌb] *n inf* **1.** (SPORT) (*abbr of* **substitute**) remplaçant *m*, -e *f*. **2.** (*abbr of* **submarine**) sous-marin *m*. **3.** Br (*abbr of* **subscription**) cotisation *f*.

subconscious [ˌsʌb'kɒnʃəs] ◆ *adj* inconscient(e). ◆ *n*: **the ~** l'inconscient *m*.

subcontract [ˌsʌbkən'trækt] *vt* sous-traiter.

subdivide [ˌsʌbdɪ'vaɪd] *vt* subdiviser.

subdue [səb'dju:] *vt* (*control - rioters, enemy*) soumettre, subjuguer; (- *temper, anger*) maîtriser, réprimer.

subdued [səb'dju:d] *adj* **1.** (*person*) abattu(e). **2.** (*anger, emotion*) contenu(e). **3.** (*colour*) doux (douce); (*light*) tamisé(e).

subject [*adj, n* & *prep* 'sʌbdʒekt, *vt* səb-'dʒekt] ◆ *adj* soumis(e); **to be ~ to** (*tax, law*) être soumis à; (*disease, headaches*) être sujet (sujette) à. ◆ *n* **1.** (*gen*) sujet *m*. **2.** (SCH & UNIV) matière *f*. ◆ *vt* **1.** (*control*) soumettre, assujettir. **2.** (*force to experience*): **to ~ sb to sthg** exposer OR soumettre qqn à qqch. ▸ **subject to** *prep* sous réserve de.

subjective [səb'dʒektɪv] *adj* subjectif (ive).

subject matter *n* (U) sujet *m*.

subjunctive [səb'dʒʌŋktɪv] *n* (GRAMM): ~ **(mood)** (mode *m*) subjonctif *m*.

sublet [,sʌb'let] (pt & pp **sublet**) vt sous-louer.

sublime [sə'blaɪm] adj sublime.

submachine gun [,sʌbmə'ʃiːn-] n mitraillette f.

submarine [,sʌbmə'riːn] n sous-marin m.

submerge [səb'mɜːdʒ] ◆ vt immerger, plonger. ◆ vi s'immerger, plonger.

submission [səb'mɪʃn] n 1. (obedience) soumission f. 2. (presentation) présentation f, soumission f.

submissive [səb'mɪsɪv] adj soumis(e), docile.

submit [səb'mɪt] ◆ vt soumettre. ◆ vi: **to ~ (to)** se soumettre (à).

subnormal [,sʌb'nɔːml] adj arriéré(e), attardé(e).

subordinate [sə'bɔːdɪnət] ◆ adj fml (less important): **~ (to)** subordonné(e) (à), moins important(e) (que). ◆ n subordonné m, -e f.

subpoena [sə'piːnə] (pt & pp **-ed**) (JUR) ◆ n citation f, assignation f. ◆ vt citer OR assigner à comparaître.

subscribe [səb'skraɪb] vi 1. (to magazine, newspaper) s'abonner, être abonné(e). 2. (to view, belief): **to ~ to** être d'accord avec, approuver.

subscriber [səb'skraɪbə*r*] n (to magazine, service) abonné m, -e f.

subscription [səb'skrɪpʃn] n 1. (to magazine) abonnement m. 2. (to charity, campaign) souscription f. 3. (to club) cotisation f.

subsequent ['sʌbsɪkwənt] adj ultérieur(e), suivant(e).

subsequently ['sʌbsɪkwəntlɪ] adv par la suite, plus tard.

subservient [səb'sɜːvjənt] adj (servile): **~ (to)** servile (vis-à-vis de), obséquieux (euse) (envers).

subside [səb'saɪd] vi 1. (pain, anger) se calmer, s'atténuer; (noise) diminuer. 2. (CONSTR - building) s'affaisser; (- ground) se tasser.

subsidence [səb'saɪdns, 'sʌbsɪdns] n (CONSTR - of building) affaissement m; (- of ground) tassement m.

subsidiary [səb'sɪdjərɪ] ◆ adj subsidiaire. ◆ n: **~ (company)** filiale f.

subsidize, -ise ['sʌbsɪdaɪz] vt subventionner.

subsidy ['sʌbsɪdɪ] n subvention f, subside m.

substance ['sʌbstəns] n 1. (gen) substance f. 2. (importance) importance f.

substantial [səb'stænʃl] adj 1. (consid-

erable) considérable, important(e); (meal) substantiel(elle). 2. (solid, well-built) solide.

substantially [səb'stænʃəlɪ] adv 1. (considerably) considérablement. 2. (mainly) en grande partie.

substantiate [səb'stænʃɪeɪt] vt fml prouver, établir.

substitute ['sʌbstɪtjuːt] ◆ n 1. (replacement): **~ (for)** (person) remplaçant m, -e f (de); (thing) succédané m (de). 2. (SPORT) remplaçant m, -e f. ◆ vt: **to ~ A for B** substituer A à B, remplacer B par A.

subtitle ['sʌb,taɪtl] n sous-titre m.

subtle ['sʌtl] adj subtil(e).

subtlety ['sʌtltɪ] n subtilité f.

subtract [səb'trækt] vt: **to ~ sthg (from)** soustraire qqch (de).

subtraction [səb'trækʃn] n soustraction f.

suburb ['sʌbɜːb] n faubourg m. ▶ **suburbs** npl: **the ~s** la banlieue.

suburban [sə'bɜːbn] adj 1. (of suburbs) de banlieue. 2. pej (life) étriqué(e); (person) à l'esprit étroit.

suburbia [sə'bɜːbɪə] n (U) la banlieue.

subversive [səb'vɜːsɪv] ◆ adj subversif(ive). ◆ n personne f qui agit de façon subversive.

subway ['sʌbweɪ] n 1. Br (underground walkway) passage m souterrain. 2. Am (underground railway) métro m.

succeed [sək'siːd] ◆ vt succéder à. ◆ vi réussir; **to ~ in doing sthg** réussir à faire qqch.

succeeding [sək'siːdɪŋ] adj fml (in future) à venir; (in past) suivant(e).

success [sək'ses] n succès m, réussite f.

successful [sək'sesful] adj 1. (attempt) couronné(e) de succès. 2. (film, book etc) à succès; (person) qui a du succès.

succession [sək'seʃn] n succession f.

successive [sək'sesɪv] adj successif(ive).

succinct [sək'sɪŋkt] adj succinct(e).

succumb [sə'kʌm] vi: **to ~ (to)** succomber (à).

such [sʌtʃ] ◆ adj tel (telle), pareil (eille); **~ nonsense** de telles inepties; **do you have ~ a thing as a tin-opener?** est-ce que tu aurais un ouvre-boîtes par hasard?; **~ money/books as I have** le peu d'argent/de livres que j'ai; **~ ... that** tel ... que. ◆ adv 1. (for emphasis) si, tellement; **it's ~ a horrible day!** quelle journée épouvantable!; **~ a lot of books**

tellement de livres; ~ **a long time** si OR tellement longtemps. **2.** (*in comparisons*) aussi. ◆ *pron:* **and ~** (**like**) et autres choses de ce genre. ▶ **as such** *adv* en tant que tel (telle), en soi. ▶ **such and such** *adj* tel et tel (telle et telle).

suck [sʌk] *vt* **1.** (*with mouth*) sucer. **2.** (*draw in*) aspirer.

sucker ['sʌkər] *n* **1.** (*suction pad*) ventouse *f*. **2.** *inf* (*gullible person*) poire *f*.

suction ['sʌkʃn] *n* succion *f*.

Sudan [suːˈdɑːn] *n* Soudan *m*.

sudden ['sʌdn] *adj* soudain(e), brusque; **all of a ~** tout d'un coup, soudain.

suddenly ['sʌdnlɪ] *adv* soudainement, tout d'un coup.

suds [sʌdz] *npl* mousse *f* de savon.

sue [suː] *vt*: **to ~ sb (for)** poursuivre qqn (pour).

suede [sweɪd] *n* daim *m*.

suet ['suɪt] *n* graisse *f* de rognon.

suffer ['sʌfər] ◆ *vt* **1.** (*pain, injury*) souffrir de. **2.** (*consequences, setback, loss*) subir. ◆ *vi* souffrir; **to ~ from** (MED) souffrir de.

sufferer ['sʌfrər] *n* (MED) malade *mf*.

suffering ['sʌfrɪŋ] *n* souffrance *f*.

suffice [səˈfaɪs] *vi fml* suffire.

sufficient [səˈfɪʃnt] *adj* suffisant(e).

sufficiently [səˈfɪʃntlɪ] *adv* suffisamment.

suffocate ['sʌfəkeɪt] *vt & vi* suffoquer.

suffrage ['sʌfrɪdʒ] *n* suffrage *m*.

suffuse [səˈfjuːz] *vt* baigner.

sugar ['ʃʊgər] ◆ *n* sucre *m*. ◆ *vt* sucrer.

sugar beet *n* betterave *f* à sucre.

sugarcane ['ʃʊgəkeɪn] *n* (U) canne *f* à sucre.

sugary ['ʃʊgərɪ] *adj* (*food*) sucré(e).

suggest [səˈdʒest] *vt* **1.** (*propose*) proposer, suggérer. **2.** (*imply*) suggérer.

suggestion [səˈdʒestʃn] *n* **1.** (*proposal*) proposition *f*, suggestion *f*. **2.** (U) (*implication*) suggestion *f*.

suggestive [səˈdʒestɪv] *adj* suggestif (ive); **to be ~ of sthg** suggérer qqch.

suicide ['suːɪsaɪd] *n* suicide *m*; **to commit ~** se suicider.

suit [suːt] ◆ *n* **1.** (*for man*) costume *m*, complet *m*; (*for woman*) tailleur *m*. **2.** (*in cards*) couleur *f*. **3.** (JUR) procès *m*, action *f*. ◆ *vt* **1.** (*subj: clothes, hairstyle*) aller à. **2.** (*be convenient, appropriate to*) convenir à. ◆ *vi* convenir, aller.

suitable ['suːtəbl] *adj* qui convient, qui va.

suitably ['suːtəblɪ] *adv* convenablement.

suitcase ['suːtkeɪs] *n* valise *f*.

suite [swiːt] *n* **1.** (*of rooms*) suite *f*. **2.** (*of furniture*) ensemble *m*.

suited ['suːtɪd] *adj* **1.** (*suitable*): **to be ~ to/for** convenir à/pour, aller à/pour. **2.** (*couple*): **well ~** très bien assortis.

suitor ['suːtər] *n dated* soupirant *m*.

sulfur Am = **sulphur**.

sulk [sʌlk] *vi* bouder.

sulky ['sʌlkɪ] *adj* boudeur(euse).

sullen ['sʌlən] *adj* maussade.

sulphur Br, **sulfur** Am ['sʌlfər] *n* soufre *m*.

sultana [səlˈtɑːnə] *n* Br (*dried grape*) raisin *m* sec.

sultry ['sʌltrɪ] *adj* **1.** (*weather*) lourd(e). **2.** (*sexual*) sensuel(elle).

sum [sʌm] *n* **1.** (*amount of money*) somme *f*. **2.** (*calculation*) calcul *m*. ▶ **sum up** ◆ *vt sep* (*summarize*) résumer. ◆ *vi* récapituler.

summarize, -ise ['sʌməraɪz] ◆ *vt* résumer. ◆ *vi* récapituler.

summary ['sʌmərɪ] *n* résumé *m*.

summer ['sʌmər] ◆ *n* été *m*; **in ~** en été. ◆ *comp* d'été; **the ~ holidays** les grandes vacances *fpl*.

summerhouse ['sʌməhaʊs, *pl* -haʊzɪz] *n* pavillon *m* (de verdure).

summer school *n* université *f* d'été.

summertime ['sʌmətaɪm] *n* été *m*.

summit ['sʌmɪt] *n* sommet *m*.

summon ['sʌmən] *vt* appeler, convoquer. ▶ **summon up** *vt sep* rassembler.

summons ['sʌmənz] (*pl* **summonses**) (JUR) ◆ *n* assignation *f*. ◆ *vt* assigner.

sump [sʌmp] *n* carter *m*.

sumptuous ['sʌmptʃʊəs] *adj* somptueux(euse).

sun [sʌn] *n* soleil *m*; **in the ~** au soleil.

sunbathe ['sʌnbeɪð] *vi* prendre un bain de soleil.

sunbed ['sʌnbed] *n* lit *m* à ultra-violets.

sunburn ['sʌnbɜːn] *n* (U) coup *m* de soleil.

sunburned ['sʌnbɜːnd], **sunburnt** ['sʌnbɜːnt] *adj* brûlé(e) par le soleil, qui a attrapé un coup de soleil.

Sunday ['sʌndɪ] *n* dimanche *m*; **~ lunch** déjeuner *m* du dimanche OR dominical; *see also* **Saturday**.

Sunday school *n* catéchisme *m*.

sundial ['sʌndaɪəl] *n* cadran *m* solaire.

sundown ['sʌndaʊn] *n* coucher *m* du soleil.

sundries ['sʌndrɪz] *npl fml* articles *mpl*

divers, objets *mpl* divers.

sundry ['sʌndrɪ] *adj fml* divers; **all and** ~ tout le monde, n'importe qui.

sunflower ['sʌn,flaʊəʳ] *n* tournesol *m*.

sung [sʌŋ] *pp* → **sing**.

sunglasses ['sʌn,glɑːsɪz] *npl* lunettes *fpl* de soleil.

sunk [sʌŋk] *pp* → **sink**.

sunlight ['sʌnlaɪt] *n* lumière *f* du soleil.

sunny ['sʌnɪ] *adj* **1.** (*day, place*) ensoleillé(e); **it's** ~ il fait beau, il fait (du) soleil. **2.** (*cheerful*) radieux(euse), heureux(euse).

sunrise ['sʌnraɪz] *n* lever *m* du soleil.

sunroof ['sʌnruːf] *n* toit *m* ouvrant.

sunset ['sʌnset] *n* coucher *m* du soleil.

sunshade ['sʌnʃeɪd] *n* parasol *m*.

sunshine ['sʌnʃaɪn] *n* lumière *f* du soleil.

sunstroke ['sʌnstrəʊk] *n* (U) insolation *f*.

suntan ['sʌntæn] ◆ *n* bronzage *m*. ◆ *comp* (*lotion, cream*) solaire.

suntrap ['sʌntræp] *n* endroit très ensoleillé.

super ['suːpəʳ] *adj inf* génial(e), super (*inv*).

superannuation ['suːpə,rænjʊ'eɪʃn] *n* (U) pension *f* de retraite.

superb [suː'pɜːb] *adj* superbe.

supercilious [,suːpə'sɪlɪəs] *adj* hautain(e).

superficial [,suːpə'fɪʃl] *adj* superficiel (elle).

superfluous [suː'pɜːfluəs] *adj* superflu(e).

superhuman [,suːpə'hjuːmən] *adj* surhumain(e).

superimpose [,suːpərɪm'pəʊz] *vt*: **to** ~ **sthg (on)** superposer qqch (à).

superintendent [,suːpərɪn'tendənt] *n* **1.** Br (*of police*) ≃ commissaire *m*. **2.** (*of department*) directeur *m*, -trice *f*.

superior [suː'pɪərɪəʳ] ◆ *adj* **1.** (*gen*): ~ **(to)** supérieur(e) (à). **2.** (*goods, craftsmanship*) de qualité supérieure. ◆ *n* supérieur *m*, -e *f*.

superlative [suː'pɜːlətɪv] ◆ *adj* exceptionnel(elle), sans pareil(eille). ◆ *n* (GRAMM) superlatif *m*.

supermarket ['suːpə,mɑːkɪt] *n* supermarché *m*.

supernatural [,suːpə'nætʃrəl] *adj* surnaturel(elle).

superpower ['suːpə,paʊəʳ] *n* superpuissance *f*.

supersede [,suːpə'siːd] *vt* remplacer.

supersonic [,suːpə'sɒnɪk] *adj* supersonique.

superstitious [,suːpə'stɪʃəs] *adj* superstitieux(euse).

superstore ['suːpəstɔːʳ] *n* hypermarché *m*.

supertanker ['suːpə,tæŋkəʳ] *n* supertanker *m*.

supervise ['suːpəvaɪz] *vt* surveiller; (*work*) superviser.

supervisor ['suːpəvaɪzəʳ] *n* surveillant *m*, -e *f*.

supper ['sʌpəʳ] *n* (*evening meal*) dîner *m*.

supple ['sʌpl] *adj* souple.

supplement [*n* 'sʌplɪmənt, *vb* 'sʌplɪment] ◆ *n* supplément *m*. ◆ *vt* compléter.

supplementary [,sʌplɪ'mentərɪ] *adj* supplémentaire.

supplementary benefit *n* Br ancien nom des allocations supplémentaires accordées aux personnes ayant un faible revenu.

supplier [sə'plaɪəʳ] *n* fournisseur *m*.

supply [sə'plaɪ] ◆ *n* **1.** (*store*) réserve *f*, provision *f*. **2.** (*system*) alimentation *f*. **3.** (U) (ECON) offre *f*. ◆ *vt* **1.** (*provide*): **to** ~ **sthg (to sb)** fournir qqch (à qqn). **2.** (*provide to*): **to** ~ **sb (with)** fournir qqn (en), approvisionner qqn (en); **to** ~ **sthg with sthg** alimenter qqch en qqch. ▶ **supplies** *npl* (*food*) vivres *mpl*; (MIL) approvisionnements *mpl*; **office supplies** fournitures *fpl* de bureau.

support [sə'pɔːt] ◆ *n* **1.** (U) (*physical help*) appui *m*. **2.** (U) (*emotional, financial help*) soutien *m*. **3.** (*object*) support *m*, appui *m*. ◆ *vt* **1.** (*physically*) soutenir, supporter; (*weight*) supporter. **2.** (*emotionally*) soutenir. **3.** (*financially*) subvenir aux besoins de. **4.** (*theory*) être en faveur de, être partisan de; (*political party, candidate*) appuyer; (SPORT) être un supporter de.

supporter [sə'pɔːtəʳ] *n* **1.** (*of person, plan*) partisan *m*, -e *f*. **2.** (SPORT) supporter *m*.

suppose [sə'pəʊz] ◆ *vt* supposer. ◆ *vi* supposer; **I** ~ **(so)** je suppose que oui; **I** ~ **not** je suppose que non.

supposed [sə'pəʊzd] *adj* **1.** (*doubtful*) supposé(e). **2.** (*reputed, intended*): **to be** ~ **to be** être censé(e) être.

supposedly [sə'pəʊzɪdlɪ] *adv* soidisant.

supposing [sə'pəʊzɪŋ] *conj* et si, à supposer que (+ *subjunctive*).

suppress [sə'pres] *vt* **1.** (*uprising*)

réprimer. **2.** (*information*) supprimer. **3.** (*emotions*) réprimer, étouffer.

supreme [so'pri:m] *adj* suprême.

Supreme Court *n* (*in US*): **the ~** la Cour Suprême.

surcharge ['sɜːtʃɑːdʒ] *n* (*extra payment*) surcharge *f*; (*extra tax*) surtaxe *f*.

sure [ʃʊəʳ] ◆ *adj* **1.** (*gen*) sûr(e); **to be ~ of o.s.** être sûr de soi. **2.** (*certain*): **to be ~ (of sthg/of doing sthg)** être sûr(e) (de qqch/de faire qqch), être certain(e) (de qqch/de faire qqch); **to make ~ (that)** ... s'assurer OR vérifier que ... **3.** *phr*: **I am** OR **I'm ~ (that)** ... je suis bien certain que ..., je ne doute pas que ... ◆ *adv* **1.** *inf* (*yes*) bien sûr. **2.** *Am* (*really*) vraiment. ▶ **for sure** *adv* sans aucun doute. ▶ **sure enough** *adv* en effet, effectivement.

surely ['ʃʊəlɪ] *adv* sûrement.

surety ['ʃʊərətɪ] *n* (U) caution *f*.

surf [sɜːf] *n* ressac *m*.

surface ['sɜːfɪs] ◆ *n* surface *f*; **on the ~** *fig* à première vue, vu de l'extérieur. ◆ *vi* **1.** (*diver*) remonter à la surface; (*submarine*) faire surface. **2.** (*problem, rumour*) apparaître OR s'étaler au grand jour.

surface mail *n* courrier *m* par voie de terre/de mer.

surfboard ['sɜːfbɔːd] *n* planche *f* de surf.

surfeit ['sɜːfɪt] *n fml* excès *m*.

surfing ['sɜːfɪŋ] *n* surf *m*.

surge [sɜːdʒ] ◆ *n* **1.** (*of people, vehicles*) déferlement *m*; (ELEC) surtension *f*. **2.** (*of emotion, interest*) vague *f*, montée *f*; (*of anger*) bouffée *f*; (*of sales, applications*) afflux *m*. ◆ *vi* (*people, vehicles*) déferler.

surgeon ['sɜːdʒən] *n* chirurgien *m*.

surgery ['sɜːdʒərɪ] *n* **1.** (U) (MED) (*performing operations*) chirurgie *f*. **2.** Br (MED) (*place*) cabinet *m* de consultation.

surgical ['sɜːdʒɪkl] *adj* chirurgical(e); **~ stocking** bas *m* orthopédique.

surgical spirit *n* Br alcool *m* à 90°.

surly ['sɜːlɪ] *adj* revêche, renfrogné(e).

surmount [sɜː'maʊnt] *vt* surmonter.

surname ['sɜːneɪm] *n* nom *m* de famille.

surpass [sə'pɑːs] *vt fml* dépasser.

surplus ['sɜːpləs] ◆ *adj* en surplus. ◆ *n* surplus *m*.

surprise [sə'praɪz] ◆ *n* surprise *f*. ◆ *vt* surprendre.

surprised [sə'praɪzd] *adj* surpris(e).

surprising [sə'praɪzɪŋ] *adj* surprenant(e).

surprisingly [sə'praɪzɪŋlɪ] *adv* étonnamment.

surrender [sə'rendəʳ] ◆ *n* reddition *f*, capitulation *f*. ◆ *vi* **1.** (*stop fighting*): **to ~ (to)** se rendre (à). **2.** *fig* (*give in*): **to ~ (to)** se laisser aller (à), se livrer (à).

surreptitious [ˌsʌrəp'tɪʃəs] *adj* subreptice.

surrogate ['sʌrəgeɪt] ◆ *adj* de substitution. ◆ *n* substitut *m*.

surrogate mother *n* mère *f* porteuse.

surround [sə'raʊnd] *vt* entourer; (*subj: police, army*) cerner.

surrounding [sə'raʊndɪŋ] *adj* environnant(e).

surroundings [sə'raʊndɪŋz] *npl* environnement *m*.

surveillance [sɜː'veɪləns] *n* surveillance *f*.

survey [*n* 'sɜːveɪ, *vb* sə'veɪ] ◆ *n* **1.** (*investigation*) étude *f*; (*of public opinion*) sondage *m*. **2.** (*of land*) levé *m*; (*of building*) inspection *f*. ◆ *vt* **1.** (*contemplate*) passer en revue. **2.** (*investigate*) faire une étude de, enquêter sur. **3.** (*land*) faire le levé de; (*building*) inspecter.

surveyor [sə'veɪəʳ] *n* (*of building*) expert *m*; (*of land*) géomètre *m*.

survival [sə'vaɪvl] *n* (*continuing to live*) survie *f*.

survive [sə'vaɪv] ◆ *vt* survivre à. ◆ *vi* survivre.

survivor [sə'vaɪvəʳ] *n* survivant *m*, -e *f*; *fig* battant *m*, -e *f*.

susceptible [sə'septəbl] *adj*: **~ (to)** sensible (à).

suspect [*adj* & *n* 'sʌspekt, *vb* sə'spekt] ◆ *adj* suspect(e). ◆ *n* suspect *m*, -e *f*. ◆ *vt* **1.** (*distrust*) douter de. **2.** (*think likely, consider guilty*) soupçonner; **to ~ sb of sthg** soupçonner qqn de qqch.

suspend [sə'spend] *vt* **1.** (*gen*) suspendre. **2.** (*from school*) renvoyer temporairement.

suspended sentence [sə'spendɪd-] *n* condamnation *f* avec sursis.

suspender belt [sə'spendəʳ-] *n* Br porte-jarretelles *m inv*.

suspenders [sə'spendəz] *npl* **1.** Br (*for stockings*) jarretelles *fpl*. **2.** *Am* (*for trousers*) bretelles *fpl*.

suspense [sə'spens] *n* suspense *m*.

suspension [sə'spenʃn] *n* **1.** (*gen* & AUT) suspension *f*. **2.** (*from school*) renvoi *m* temporaire.

suspension bridge *n* pont *m* suspendu.

suspicion [sə'spɪʃn] n soupçon m.
suspicious [sə'spɪʃəs] adj 1. (having suspicions) soupçonneux(euse). 2. (causing suspicion) suspect(e), louche.
sustain [sə'steɪn] vt 1. (maintain) soutenir. 2. fml (suffer - damage) subir; (- injury) recevoir. 3. fml (weight) supporter.
sustenance ['sʌstɪnəns] n (U) fml nourriture f.
SW (abbr of short wave) OC.
swab [swɒb] n (MED) tampon m.
swagger ['swægər] vi parader.
Swahili [swɑː'hiːlɪ] n (language) swahili m.
swallow ['swɒləʊ] ◆ n (bird) hirondelle f. ◆ vt avaler; fig (anger, tears) ravaler. ◆ vi avaler.
swam [swæm] pt → swim.
swamp [swɒmp] ◆ n marais m. ◆ vt 1. (flood) submerger. 2. (overwhelm) déborder, submerger.
swan [swɒn] n cygne m.
swap [swɒp] vt: to ~ sthg (with sb/for sthg) échanger qqch (avec qqn/contre qqch).
swarm [swɔːm] ◆ n essaim m. ◆ vi fig (people) grouiller; to be ~ing (with) (place) grouiller (de).
swarthy ['swɔːðɪ] adj basané(e).
swastika ['swɒstɪkə] n croix f gammée.
swat [swɒt] vt écraser.
sway [sweɪ] ◆ vt (influence) influencer. ◆ vi se balancer.
swear [sweər] (pt swore, pp sworn) ◆ vt jurer; to ~ to do sthg jurer de faire qqch. ◆ vi jurer.
swearword ['sweəwɜːd] n juron m, gros mot m.
sweat [swet] ◆ n (perspiration) transpiration f, sueur f. ◆ vi 1. (perspire) transpirer, suer. 2. inf (worry) se faire du mouron.
sweater ['swetər] n pullover m.
sweatshirt ['swetʃɜːt] n sweat-shirt m.
sweaty ['swetɪ] adj (skin, clothes) mouillé(e) de sueur.
swede [swiːd] n Br rutabaga m.
Swede [swiːd] n Suédois m, -e f.
Sweden ['swiːdn] n Suède f.
Swedish ['swiːdɪʃ] ◆ adj suédois(e). ◆ n (language) suédois m. ◆ npl: the ~ les Suédois mpl.
sweep [swiːp] (pt & pp swept) ◆ n 1. (sweeping movement) grand geste m. 2. (with brush): to give sthg a ~ donner un

coup de balai à qqch, balayer qqch. 3. (chimney sweep) ramoneur m. ◆ vt (gen) balayer; (scan with eyes) parcourir des yeux. ▶ **sweep away** ◆ vt sep (destroy) emporter, entraîner. ▶ **sweep up** ◆ vt sep (with brush) balayer. ◆ vi balayer.
sweeping ['swiːpɪŋ] adj 1. (effect, change) radical(e). 2. (statement) hâtif (ive).
sweet [swiːt] ◆ adj 1. (gen) doux (douce); (cake, flavour, pudding) sucré(e). 2. (kind) gentil(ille). 3. (attractive) adorable, mignon(onne). ◆ n Br 1. (candy) bonbon m. 2. (dessert) dessert m.
sweet corn n maïs m.
sweeten ['swiːtn] vt sucrer.
sweetheart ['swiːthɑːt] n 1. (term of endearment) chéri m, -e f, mon cœur m. 2. (boyfriend, girlfriend) petit ami m, petite amie f.
sweetness ['swiːtnɪs] n 1. (gen) douceur f; (of taste) goût m sucré, douceur. 2. (attractiveness) charme m.
sweet pea n pois m de senteur.
swell [swel] (pt -ed, pp swollen OR -ed) ◆ vi 1. (leg, face etc) enfler; (lungs, balloon) se gonfler; to ~ with pride se gonfler d'orgueil. 2. (crowd, population etc) grossir, augmenter; (sound) grossir, s'enfler. ◆ vt grossir, augmenter. ◆ n (of sea) houle f. ◆ adj Am inf chouette, épatant(e).
swelling ['swelɪŋ] n enflure f.
sweltering ['sweltərɪŋ] adj étouffant(e), suffocant(e).
swept [swept] pt & pp → sweep.
swerve [swɜːv] vi faire une embardée.
swift [swɪft] ◆ adj 1. (fast) rapide. 2. (prompt) prompt(e). ◆ n (bird) martinet m.
swig [swɪg] inf n lampée f.
swill [swɪl] ◆ n (U) (pig food) pâtée f. ◆ vt Br (wash) laver à grande eau.
swim [swɪm] (pt swam, pp swum) ◆ n: to have a ~ nager; to go for a ~ aller se baigner, aller nager. ◆ vi 1. (person, fish, animal) nager. 2. (room) tourner; my head was swimming j'avais la tête qui tournait.
swimmer ['swɪmər] n nageur m, -euse f.
swimming ['swɪmɪŋ] n natation f; to go ~ aller nager.
swimming cap n bonnet m de bain.
swimming costume n Br maillot m de bain.

swimming pool n piscine f.

swimming trunks npl maillot m OR slip m de bain.

swimsuit ['swɪmsuːt] n maillot m de bain.

swindle ['swɪndl] ◆ n escroquerie f. ◆ vt escroquer, rouler; **to ~ sb out of sthg** escroquer qqch à qqn.

swine [swaɪn] n inf (person) salaud m.

swing [swɪŋ] (pt & pp **swung**) ◆ n 1. (child's toy) balançoire f. 2. (change - of opinion) revirement m; (- of mood) changement m, saute f. 3. (sway) balancement m. 4. phr: **to be in full ~** battre son plein. ◆ vt 1. (move back and forth) balancer. 2. (move in a curve) faire virer. ◆ vi 1. (move back and forth) se balancer. 2. (turn - vehicle) virer, tourner; **to ~ round** (person) se retourner. 3. (change) changer.

swing bridge n pont m tournant.

swing door n porte f battante.

swingeing ['swɪndʒɪŋ] adj très sévère.

swipe [swaɪp] ◆ vt inf (steal) faucher, piquer. ◆ vi: **to ~ at** envoyer OR donner un coup à.

swirl [swɜːl] ◆ n tourbillon m. ◆ vi tourbillonner, tournoyer.

swish [swɪʃ] vt (tail) battre l'air de.

Swiss [swɪs] ◆ adj suisse. ◆ n (person) Suisse mf. ◆ npl: **the ~** les Suisses mpl.

switch [swɪtʃ] ◆ n 1. (control device) interrupteur m, commutateur m; (on radio, stereo etc) bouton m. 2. (change) changement m. ◆ vt (swap) échanger; (jobs) changer de. ► **switch off** vt sep éteindre. ► **switch on** vt sep allumer.

switchboard ['swɪtʃbɔːd] n standard m.

Switzerland ['swɪtsələnd] n Suisse f; **in ~** en Suisse.

swivel ['swɪvl] ◆ vt (chair) faire pivoter; (head, eyes) faire tourner. ◆ vi (chair) pivoter; (head, eyes) tourner.

swivel chair n fauteuil m pivotant OR tournant.

swollen ['swəʊln] ◆ pp → **swell**. ◆ adj (ankle, face) enflé(e); (river) en crue.

swoop [swuːp] ◆ n (raid) descente f. ◆ vi 1. (bird, plane) piquer. 2. (police, army) faire une descente.

swop [swɒp] = **swap**.

sword [sɔːd] n épée f.

swordfish ['sɔːdfɪʃ] (pl inv OR -es) n espadon m.

swore [swɔːr] pt → **swear**.

sworn [swɔːn] ◆ pp → **swear**. ◆ adj (JUR) sous serment.

swot [swɒt] Br inf ◆ n pej bûcheur m, -euse f. ◆ vi: **to ~ (for)** bûcher (pour).

swum [swʌm] pp → **swim**.

swung [swʌŋ] pt & pp → **swing**.

sycamore ['sɪkəmɔːr] n sycomore m.

syllable ['sɪləbl] n syllabe f.

syllabus ['sɪləbəs] (pl -buses OR -bi [-baɪ]) n programme m.

symbol ['sɪmbl] n symbole m.

symbolize, -ise ['sɪmbəlaɪz] vt symboliser.

symmetry ['sɪmətrɪ] n symétrie f.

sympathetic [ˌsɪmpə'θetɪk] adj 1. (understanding) compatissant(e), compréhensif(ive). 2. (willing to support): **~ (to)** bien disposé(e) à l'égard de).

sympathize, -ise ['sɪmpəθaɪz] vi 1. (feel sorry) compatir; **to ~ with sb** plaindre qqn; (in grief) compatir à la douleur de qqn. 2. (understand): **to ~ with sthg** comprendre qqch. 3. (support): **to ~ with sthg** approuver qqch, soutenir qqch.

sympathizer, -iser ['sɪmpəθaɪzər] n sympathisant m, -e f.

sympathy ['sɪmpəθɪ] n (U) 1. (understanding): **~ (for)** compassion f (pour), sympathie f (pour). 2. (agreement) approbation f, sympathie f. ► **sympathies** npl (to bereaved person) condoléances fpl.

symphony ['sɪmfənɪ] n symphonie f.

symposium [sɪm'pəʊzjəm] (pl -siums OR -sia [-zjə]) n symposium m.

symptom ['sɪmptəm] n symptôme m.

synagogue ['sɪnəgɒg] n synagogue f.

syndicate ['sɪndɪkət] n syndicat m, consortium m.

syndrome ['sɪndrəʊm] n syndrome m.

synonym ['sɪnənɪm] n: **~ (for OR of)** synonyme m (de).

synopsis [sɪ'nɒpsɪs] (pl -ses [-siːz]) n résumé m.

syntax ['sɪntæks] n syntaxe f.

synthesis ['sɪnθəsɪs] (pl -ses [-siːz]) n synthèse f.

synthetic [sɪn'θetɪk] adj 1. (man-made) synthétique. 2. pej (insincere) artificiel (elle), forcé(e).

syphilis ['sɪfɪlɪs] n syphilis f.

syphon ['saɪfn] = **siphon**.

Syria ['sɪrɪə] n Syrie f.

syringe [sɪ'rɪndʒ] n seringue f.

syrup ['sɪrəp] n (U) 1. (sugar and water) sirop m. 2. Br (golden syrup) mélasse f raffinée.

system ['sɪstəm] n 1. (gen) système m; **road/railway ~** réseau m routier/de chemins de fer. **2.** (*equipment - gen*) installation *f*; (*- electric, electronic*) appareil *m*. **3.** (U) (*methodical approach*) système *m*, méthode *f*.

systematic [,sɪstə'mætɪk] *adj* systématique.

system disk *n* (COMPUT) disque *m* système.

systems analyst ['sɪstəmz-] *n* (COMPUT) analyste fonctionnel *m*, analyste fonctionnelle *f*.

T

t (*pl* **t's** OR **ts**), **T** (*pl* **T's** OR **Ts**) [ti:] *n* (*letter*) t *m inv*, T *m inv*.

ta [tɑː] *excl Br inf* merci!

tab [tæb] *n* **1.** (*of cloth*) étiquette *f*. **2.** (*of metal*) languette *f*. **3.** Am (*bill*) addition *f*. **4.** *phr*: **to keep ~s on sb** tenir OR avoir qqn à l'œil, surveiller qqn.

tabby ['tæbɪ] *n*: **~ (cat)** chat tigré *m*, chatte tigrée *f*.

table ['teɪbl] ◆ *n* table *f*. ◆ *vt Br* (*propose*) présenter, proposer.

tablecloth ['teɪblklɒθ] *n* nappe *f*.

table lamp *n* lampe *f*.

tablemat ['teɪblmæt] *n* dessous-de-plat *m inv*.

tablespoon ['teɪblspuːn] *n* **1.** (*spoon*) cuiller *f* de service. **2.** (*spoonful*) cuillerée *f* à soupe.

tablet ['tæblɪt] *n* **1.** (*pill*) comprimé *m*, cachet *m*. **2.** (*of stone*) plaque *f* commémorative. **3.** (*of soap*) savonnette *f*, pain *m* de savon.

table tennis *n* ping-pong *m*, tennis *m* de table.

table wine *n* vin *m* de table.

tabloid ['tæblɔɪd] *n*: **~ (newspaper)** tabloïd *m*, tabloïde *m*; **the ~ press** la presse populaire.

tabulate ['tæbjʊleɪt] *vt* présenter sous forme de tableau.

tacit ['tæsɪt] *adj* tacite.

taciturn ['tæsɪtɜːn] *adj* taciturne.

tack [tæk] ◆ *n* **1.** (*nail*) clou *m*. **2.** (NAUT) bord *m*, bordée *f*. **3.** *fig* (*course of action*) tactique *f*, méthode *f*. ◆ *vt* **1.** (*fasten with nail - gen*) clouer; (*- notice*) punaiser. **2.** (SEWING) faufiler. ◆ *vi* (NAUT)

tirer une bordée.

tackle ['tækl] ◆ *n* **1.** (FTBL) tacle *m*; (RUGBY) plaquage *m*. **2.** (*equipment*) équipement *m*, matériel *m*. **3.** (*for lifting*) palan *m*, appareil *m* de levage. ◆ *vt* **1.** (*deal with*) s'attaquer à. **2.** (FTBL) tacler; (RUGBY) plaquer. **3.** (*attack*) empoigner.

tacky ['tækɪ] *adj* **1.** *inf* (*film, remark*) d'un goût douteux; (*jewellery*) de pacotille. **2.** (*sticky*) collant(e), pas encore sec (sèche).

tact [tækt] *n* (U) tact *m*, délicatesse *f*.

tactful ['tæktfʊl] *adj* (*remark*) plein(e) de tact; (*person*) qui a du tact OR de la délicatesse.

tactic ['tæktɪk] *n* tactique *f*. ▶ **tactics** *n* (U) (MIL) tactique *f*.

tactical ['tæktɪkl] *adj* tactique.

tactless ['tæktlɪs] *adj* qui manque de tact OR délicatesse.

tadpole ['tædpəʊl] *n* têtard *m*.

tag [tæg] *n* **1.** (*of cloth*) marque *f*. **2.** (*of paper*) étiquette *f*. ▶ **tag along** *vi inf* suivre.

tail [teɪl] ◆ *n* **1.** (*gen*) queue *f*. **2.** (*of coat*) basque *f*, pan *m*; (*of shirt*) pan. ◆ *vt inf* (*follow*) filer. ▶ **tails** ◆ *n* (*side of coin*) pile *f*. ◆ *npl* (*formal dress*) queue-de-pie *f*, habit *m*. ▶ **tail off** *vi* (*voice*) s'affaiblir; (*noise*) diminuer.

tailback ['teɪlbæk] *n Br* bouchon *m*.

tailcoat [,teɪl'kəʊt] *n* habit *m*, queue-de-pie *f*.

tail end *n* fin *f*.

tailgate ['teɪlgeɪt] *n* (AUT) hayon *m*.

tailor ['teɪlə'] ◆ *n* tailleur *m*. ◆ *vt fig* adapter.

tailor-made *adj fig* sur mesure.

tailwind ['teɪlwɪnd] *n* vent *m* arrière.

tainted ['teɪntɪd] *adj* **1.** (*reputation*) souillé(e), entaché(e). **2.** Am (*food*) avarié(e).

Taiwan [,taɪ'wɑːn] *n* Taiwan.

take [teɪk] (*pt* **took**, *pp* **taken**) ◆ *vt* **1.** (*gen*) prendre; **to ~ an exam** passer un examen; **to ~ a walk** se promener, faire une promenade; **to ~ a bath/photo** prendre un bain/une photo; **to ~ offence** se vexer, s'offenser. **2.** (*lead, drive*) emmener. **3.** (*accept*) accepter. **4.** (*contain*) contenir, avoir une capacité de. **5.** (*tolerate*) supporter. **6.** (*require*) demander; **how long will it ~?** combien de temps cela va-t-il prendre? **7.** (*wear*): **what size do you ~?** (*clothes*) quelle taille faites-vous?; (*shoes*) vous chaussez du combien? **8.** (*assume*): **I ~ it**

(that) ... je suppose que ..., je pense que ... 9. (rent) prendre, louer. ◆ n (CINEMA) prise f de vues. ▶ **take after** vt fus tenir de, ressembler à. ▶ **take apart** vt sep (dismantle) démonter. ▶ **take away** vt sep 1. (remove) enlever. 2. (deduct) retrancher, soustraire. ▶ **take back** vt sep 1. (return) rendre, rapporter. 2. (accept) reprendre. 3. (statement, accusation) retirer. ▶ **take down** vt sep 1. (dismantle) démonter. 2. (write down) prendre. 3. (lower) baisser. ▶ **take in** vt sep 1. (deceive) rouler, tromper. 2. (understand) comprendre. 3. (include) englober, couvrir. 4. (provide accommodation for) recueillir. ▶ **take off** ◆ vt sep 1. (remove) enlever, ôter. 2. (have as holiday): **to ~ a week/day off** prendre une semaine/un jour de congé. 3. Br (imitate) imiter. ◆ vi 1. (plane) décoller. 2. (go away suddenly) partir. ▶ **take on** vt sep 1. (accept) accepter, prendre. 2. (employ) embaucher, prendre. 3. (confront) s'attaquer à; (competitor) faire concurrence à; (SPORT) jouer contre. ▶ **take out** vt sep 1. (from container) sortir; (from pocket) prendre. 2. (go out with) emmener, sortir avec. ▶ **take over** ◆ vt sep 1. (take control of) reprendre, prendre la direction de. 2. (job): **to ~ over sb's job** remplacer qqn, prendre la suite de qqn. ◆ vi 1. (take control) prendre le pouvoir. 2. (in job) prendre la relève. ▶ **take to** vt fus 1. (person) éprouver de la sympathie pour, sympathiser avec; (activity) prendre goût à. 2. (begin): **to ~ to doing sthg** se mettre à faire qqch. ▶ **take up** vt sep 1. (begin - job) prendre; **to ~ up singing** se mettre au chant. 2. (use up) prendre, occuper. ▶ **take up on** vt sep (accept): **to ~ sb up on an offer** accepter l'offre de qqn.

takeaway Br ['teɪkə,weɪ], **takeout** Am ['teɪkaʊt] n (food) plat m à emporter.

taken ['teɪkn] pp → **take**.

takeoff ['teɪkɒf] n (of plane) décollage m.

takeout Am = **takeaway**.

takeover ['teɪk,əʊvər] n 1. (of company) prise f de contrôle, rachat m. 2. (of government) prise f de pouvoir.

takings ['teɪkɪŋz] npl recette f.

talc [tælk], **talcum (powder)** ['tælkəm-] n talc m.

tale [teɪl] n 1. (fictional story) histoire f, conte m. 2. (anecdote) récit m, histoire f.

talent ['tælənt] n: ~ **(for)** talent m (pour).

talented ['tæləntɪd] adj qui a du talent, talentueux(euse).

talk [tɔːk] ◆ n 1. (conversation) discussion f, conversation f. 2. (U) (gossip) bavardages mpl, racontars mpl. 3. (lecture) conférence f, causerie f. ◆ vi 1. (speak): **to ~ (to sb)** parler (à qqn); **to ~ about** parler de. 2. (gossip) bavarder, jaser. 3. (make a speech) faire un discours, parler; **to ~ on** OR **about** parler de. ◆ vt parler. ▶ **talks** npl entretiens mpl, pourparlers mpl. ▶ **talk into** vt sep: **to ~ sb into doing sthg** persuader qqn de faire qqch. ▶ **talk out of** vt sep: **to ~ sb out of doing sthg** dissuader qqn de faire qqch. ▶ **talk over** vt sep discuter de.

talkative ['tɔːkətɪv] adj bavard(e), loquace.

talk show n Am talk-show m, causerie f.

tall [tɔːl] adj grand(e); **how ~ are you?** combien mesurez-vous?; **she's 5 feet ~** elle mesure 1,50 m.

tall story n histoire f à dormir debout.

tally ['tælɪ] ◆ n compte m. ◆ vi correspondre, concorder.

talon ['tælən] n serre f, griffe f.

tambourine [,tæmbə'riːn] n tambourin m.

tame [teɪm] ◆ adj 1. (animal, bird) apprivoisé(e). 2. pej (person) docile; (party, story, life) terne, morne. ◆ vt 1. (animal, bird) apprivoiser. 2. (people) mater, dresser.

tamper ['tæmpər] ▶ **tamper with** vt fus (machine) toucher à; (records, file) altérer, falsifier; (lock) essayer de crocheter.

tampon ['tæmpɒn] n tampon m.

tan [tæn] ◆ adj brun clair (inv). ◆ n bronzage m, hâle m. ◆ vi bronzer.

tang [tæŋ] n (taste) saveur f forte OR piquante; (smell) odeur f forte OR piquante.

tangent ['tændʒənt] n (GEOM) tangente f; **to go off at a ~** fig changer de sujet, faire une digression.

tangerine [,tændʒə'riːn] n mandarine f.

tangible ['tændʒəbl] adj tangible.

Tangier [tæn'dʒɪər] n Tanger.

tangle ['tæŋgl] n 1. (mass) enchevêtrement m, emmêlement m. 2. fig (confusion): **to get into a ~** s'empêtrer, s'embrouiller.

tank [tæŋk] n 1. (container) réservoir m;

fish ~ aquarium m. **2.** (MIL) tank m, char m (d'assaut).

tanker ['tæŋkər] n **1.** (ship - for oil) pétrolier m. **2.** (truck) camion-citerne m. **3.** (train) wagon-citerne m.

tanned [tænd] adj bronzé(e), hâlé(e).

Tannoy® ['tænɔɪ] n système m de haut-parleurs.

tantalizing ['tæntəlaɪzɪŋ] adj (smell) très appétissant(e); (possibility, thought) très tentant(e).

tantamount ['tæntəmaʊnt] adj: **~ to** équivalent(e) à.

tantrum ['tæntrəm] (pl -s) n crise f de colère; **to have** OR **throw a ~** faire OR piquer une colère.

Tanzania [ˌtænzə'nɪə] n Tanzanie f.

tap [tæp] ◆ n **1.** (device) robinet m. **2.** (light blow) petite tape f, petit coup m. ◆ vt **1.** (hit) tapoter, taper. **2.** (resources, energy) exploiter, utiliser. **3.** (telephone, wire) mettre sur écoute.

tap dance n claquettes fpl.

tape [teɪp] ◆ n **1.** (magnetic tape) bande f magnétique; (cassette) cassette f. **2.** (strip of cloth, adhesive material) ruban m. ◆ vt **1.** (record) enregistrer; (on video) magnétoscoper, enregistrer au magnétoscope. **2.** (stick) scotcher.

tape measure n centimètre m, mètre m.

taper ['teɪpər] vi s'effiler; (trousers) se terminer en fuseau.

tape recorder n magnétophone m.

tapestry ['tæpɪstrɪ] n tapisserie f.

tar [tɑːr] n (U) goudron m.

target ['tɑːgɪt] ◆ n **1.** (of missile, bomb) objectif m; (for archery, shooting) cible f. **2.** fig (for criticism) cible f. **3.** fig (goal) objectif m. ◆ vt **1.** (city, building) viser. **2.** fig (subj: policy) s'adresser à, viser; (subj: advertising) cibler.

tariff ['tærɪf] n **1.** (tax) tarif m douanier. **2.** (list) tableau m OR liste f des prix.

Tarmac® ['tɑːmæk] n (material) macadam m. ▶ **tarmac** n (AERON): **the tarmac** la piste.

tarnish ['tɑːnɪʃ] vt lit & fig ternir.

tarpaulin [tɑː'pɔːlɪn] n (material) toile f goudronnée; (sheet) bâche f.

tart [tɑːt] ◆ adj **1.** (bitter) acide. **2.** (sarcastic) acide, acerbe. ◆ n **1.** (CULIN) tarte f. **2.** v inf (prostitute) pute f. ▶ **tart up** vt sep Br inf pej (room) retaper, rénover; **to ~ o.s. up** se faire beau (belle).

tartan ['tɑːtn] ◆ n tartan m. ◆ comp écossais(e).

tartar(e) sauce ['tɑːtər-] n sauce f tartare.

task [tɑːsk] n tâche f, besogne f.

task force n (MIL) corps m expéditionnaire.

tassel ['tæsl] n pompon m, gland m.

taste [teɪst] ◆ n **1.** (gen) goût m; **have a ~!** goûte!; **in good/bad ~** de bon/mauvais goût. **2.** fig (liking): **~ (for)** penchant m (pour), goût m (pour). **3.** fig (experience) aperçu m. ◆ vt **1.** (sense - food) sentir. **2.** (test, try) déguster, goûter. **3.** fig (experience) tâter de, goûter de. ◆ vi: **to ~ of** OR **like** avoir le goût de; **to ~ good/odd** etc avoir bon goût OR un drôle de goût etc.

tasteful ['teɪstfʊl] adj de bon goût.

tasteless ['teɪstlɪs] adj **1.** (object, decor, remark) de mauvais goût. **2.** (food) qui n'a aucun goût, fade.

tasty ['teɪstɪ] adj (delicious) délicieux (euse), succulent(e).

tatters ['tætəz] npl: **in ~** (clothes) en lambeaux; (confidence) brisé(e); (reputation) ruiné(e).

tattoo [tə'tuː] (pl -s) ◆ n **1.** (design) tatouage m. **2.** Br (military display) parade f OR défilé m militaire. ◆ vt tatouer.

tatty ['tætɪ] adj Br inf pej (clothes) défraîchi(e), usé(e); (flat, area) miteux (euse), minable.

taught [tɔːt] pt & pp → **teach**.

taunt [tɔːnt] ◆ vt railler, se moquer de. ◆ n raillerie f, moquerie f.

Taurus ['tɔːrəs] n Taureau m.

taut [tɔːt] adj tendu(e).

tawdry ['tɔːdrɪ] adj pej (jewellery) clinquant(e); (clothes) voyant(e), criard(e).

tax [tæks] ◆ n taxe f, impôt m. ◆ vt **1.** (goods) taxer. **2.** (profits, business, person) imposer. **3.** (strain) mettre à l'épreuve.

taxable ['tæksəbl] adj imposable.

tax allowance n abattement m fiscal.

taxation [tæk'seɪʃn] n (U) **1.** (system) imposition f. **2.** (amount) impôts mpl.

tax avoidance [-ə'vɔɪdəns] n évasion f fiscale.

tax collector n percepteur m.

tax disc n Br vignette f.

tax evasion n fraude f fiscale.

tax-free Br, **tax-exempt** Am adj exonéré(e) (d'impôt).

taxi ['tæksɪ] ◆ n taxi m. ◆ vi (plane) rouler au sol.

taxi driver n chauffeur m de taxi.

tax inspector n inspecteur m des impôts.

taxi rank Br, **taxi stand** n station f de taxis.

taxpayer ['tæks,peɪəʳ] n contribuable mf.

tax relief n allègement m OR dégrèvement m fiscal.

tax return n déclaration f d'impôts.

TB n abbr of **tuberculosis**.

tea [tiː] n 1. (drink, leaves) thé m. 2. Br (afternoon meal) goûter m; (evening meal) dîner m.

teabag ['tiːbæg] n sachet m de thé.

tea break n Br pause-café f.

teach [tiːtʃ] (pt & pp **taught**) ◆ vt 1. (instruct) apprendre; **to ~ sb sthg, to ~ sthg to sb** apprendre qqch à qqn; **to ~ sb to do sthg** apprendre à qqn à faire qqch. 2. (subj: teacher) enseigner; **to ~ sb sthg, to ~ sthg to sb** enseigner qqch à qqn. ◆ vi enseigner.

teacher ['tiːtʃəʳ] n (in primary school) instituteur m, -trice f, maître m, maîtresse f; (in secondary school) professeur m.

teacher training college Br, **teachers college** Am n = institut m universitaire de formation de maîtres, = IUFM m.

teaching ['tiːtʃɪŋ] n enseignement m.

teaching aid n support m pédagogique.

tea cloth n Br 1. (tablecloth) nappe f. 2. (tea towel) torchon m.

tea cosy Br, **tea cozy** Am n couvre-théière m inv, cosy m.

teacup ['tiːkʌp] n tasse f à thé.

teak [tiːk] n teck m.

team [tiːm] n équipe f.

teammate ['tiːmmeɪt] n co-équipier m, -ère f.

teamwork ['tiːmwɜːk] n (U) travail m d'équipe, collaboration f.

teapot ['tiːpɒt] n théière f.

tear¹ [tɪəʳ] n larme f.

tear² [teəʳ] (pt **tore**, pp **torn**) ◆ vt 1. (rip) déchirer. 2. (remove roughly) arracher. ◆ vi 1. (rip) se déchirer. 2. (move quickly) foncer, aller à toute allure. ◆ n déchirure f, accroc m. ▶ **tear apart** vt sep 1. (rip up) déchirer, mettre en morceaux. 2. fig (country, company) diviser; (person) déchirer. ▶ **tear down** vt sep (building) démolir; (poster) arracher. ▶ **tear up** vt sep déchirer.

teardrop ['tɪədrɒp] n larme f.

tearful ['tɪəfʊl] adj (person) en larmes.

tear gas [tɪəʳ-] n (U) gaz m lacrymogène.

tearoom ['tiːrʊm] n salon m de thé.

tease [tiːz] ◆ n taquin m, -e f. ◆ vt (mock): **to ~ sb (about sthg)** taquiner qqn (à propos de qqch).

tea service, tea set n service m à thé.

teaspoon ['tiːspuːn] n 1. (utensil) petite cuillère f, cuillère à café. 2. (amount) cuillerée f à café.

teat [tiːt] n tétine f.

teatime ['tiːtaɪm] n Br l'heure f du thé.

tea towel n torchon m.

technical ['teknɪkl] adj technique.

technical college n Br collège m technique.

technicality [,teknɪ'kælətɪ] n 1. (intricacy) technicité f. 2. (detail) détail m technique.

technically ['teknɪklɪ] adv 1. (gen) techniquement. 2. (theoretically) en théorie.

technician [tek'nɪʃn] n technicien m, -enne f.

technique [tek'niːk] n technique f.

technological [,teknə'lɒdʒɪkl] adj technologique.

technology [tek'nɒlədʒɪ] n technologie f.

teddy ['tedɪ] n: **~ (bear)** ours m en peluche, nounours m.

tedious ['tiːdjəs] adj ennuyeux(euse).

tee [tiː] n (GOLF) tee m.

teem [tiːm] vi 1. (rain) pleuvoir à verse. 2. (place): **to be ~ing with** grouiller de.

teenage ['tiːneɪdʒ] adj adolescent(e).

teenager ['tiːn,eɪdʒəʳ] n adolescent m, -e f.

teens [tiːnz] npl adolescence f.

tee shirt n tee-shirt m.

teeter ['tiːtəʳ] vi vaciller; **to ~ on the brink of** fig être au bord de.

teeth [tiːθ] pl → **tooth**.

teethe [tiːð] vi (baby) percer ses dents.

teething troubles ['tiːðɪŋ-] npl fig difficultés fpl initiales.

teetotaller Br, **teetotaler** Am [tiː'təʊtləʳ] n personne f qui ne boit jamais d'alcool.

TEFL ['tefl] (abbr of **teaching of English as a foreign language**) n enseignement de l'anglais langue étrangère.

tel. (abbr of **telephone**) tél.

telecommunications ['telɪkə,mjuːnɪ'keɪʃnz] npl télécommunications fpl.

telegram ['telɪgræm] n télégramme m.

telegraph ['telɪɡrɑːf] ◆ n télégraphe m. ◆ vt télégraphier.

telegraph pole, telegraph post
Br n poteau m télégraphique.

telepathy [tɪ'lepəθɪ] n télépathie f.

telephone ['telɪfəʊn] ◆ n téléphone
m; **to be on the ~** Br (connected) avoir le
téléphone; (speaking) être au téléphone. ◆ vt téléphoner à. ◆ vi téléphoner.

telephone book n annuaire m.

telephone booth n cabine f téléphonique.

telephone box n Br cabine f téléphonique.

telephone call n appel m téléphonique, coup m de téléphone.

telephone directory n annuaire m.

telephone number n numéro m de
téléphone.

telephonist [tɪ'lefənɪst] n Br télé-
phoniste mf.

telephoto lens [,telɪ'fəʊtəʊ-] n
téléobjectif m.

telescope ['telɪskəʊp] n télescope m.

teletext ['telɪtekst] n télétexte m.

televise ['telɪvaɪz] vt téléviser.

television ['telɪ,vɪʒn] n 1. (U) (medium,
industry) télévision f; **on ~** à la télévision. 2. (apparatus) (poste m de) télévision f, téléviseur m.

television set n poste m de télévision, téléviseur m.

teleworking ['telɪ,wɜːkɪŋ] n télétravail m.

telex ['teleks] ◆ n télex m. ◆ vt (message) envoyer par télex, télexer; (person)
envoyer un télex à.

tell [tel] (pt & pp **told**) ◆ vt 1. (gen) dire;
(story) raconter; **to ~ sb (that)** ... dire à
qqn que ...; **to ~ sb sthg, to ~ sthg to sb**
dire qqch à qqn; **to ~ sb to do sthg** dire
OR ordonner à qqn de faire qqch.
2. (judge, recognize) savoir, voir; **could you
~ me the time?** tu peux me dire l'heure
(qu'il est)? ◆ vi 1. (speak) parler.
2. (judge) savoir. 3. (have effect) se faire
sentir. ▶ **tell apart** vt sep distinguer.
▶ **tell off** vt sep gronder.

telling ['telɪŋ] adj (remark) révélateur
(trice).

telltale ['telteɪl] ◆ adj révélateur
(trice). ◆ n rapporteur m, -euse f,
mouchard m, -e f.

telly ['telɪ] (abbr of **television**) n Br inf
télé f; **on ~** à la télé.

temp [temp] inf ◆ n (abbr of **temporary**
(**employee**)) intérimaire mf. ◆ vi travailler comme intérimaire.

temper ['tempər] ◆ n 1. (angry state): **to**
be in a ~ être en colère; **to lose one's ~**
se mettre en colère. 2. (mood) humeur
f. 3. (temperament) tempérament m. ◆ vt
(moderate) tempérer.

temperament ['tempərəmənt] n tempérament m.

temperamental [,temprə'mentl] adj
(volatile, unreliable) capricieux(euse).

temperate ['temprət] adj tempéré(e).

temperature ['temprətʃər] n température f; **to have a ~** avoir de la température OR de la fièvre.

tempestuous [tem'pestjʊəs] adj lit &
fig orageux(euse).

template ['templɪt] n gabarit m.

temple ['templ] n 1. (RELIG) temple m.
2. (ANAT) tempe f.

temporarily [,tempə'rerəlɪ] adv temporairement, provisoirement.

temporary ['tempərərɪ] adj temporaire, provisoire.

tempt [tempt] vt tenter; **to ~ sb to do**
sthg donner à qqn l'envie de faire
qqch.

temptation [temp'teɪʃn] n tentation f.

tempting ['temptɪŋ] adj tentant(e).

ten [ten] num dix; see also **six**.

tenable ['tenəbl] adj (argument, position)
défendable.

tenacious [tɪ'neɪʃəs] adj tenace.

tenancy ['tenənsɪ] n location f.

tenant ['tenənt] n locataire mf.

tend [tend] vt 1. (have tendency): **to ~ to**
do sthg avoir tendance à faire qqch.
2. (look after) s'occuper de, garder.

tendency ['tendənsɪ] n: **~ (to do sthg)**
tendance f (à faire qqch).

tender ['tendər] ◆ adj tendre; (bruise,
part of body) sensible, douloureux
(euse). ◆ n (COMM) soumission f. ◆ vt
fml (apology, money) offrir; (resignation)
donner.

tendon ['tendən] n tendon m.

tenement ['tenəmənt] n immeuble m.

Tenerife [,tenə'riːf] n Tenerife.

tenet ['tenɪt] n fml principe m.

tennis ['tenɪs] n (U) tennis m.

tennis ball n balle f de tennis.

tennis court n court m de tennis.

tennis racket n raquette f de tennis.

tenor ['tenər] n (singer) ténor m.

tense [tens] ◆ adj tendu(e). ◆ n temps
m. ◆ vt tendre.

tension ['tenʃn] n tension f.

tent [tent] n tente f.

tentacle ['tentəkl] n tentacule m.

tentative ['tentətɪv] adj 1. (hesitant)
hésitant(e). 2. (not final) provisoire.

tenterhooks ['tentəhʊks] *npl*: **to be on ~** être sur des charbons ardents.

tenth [tenθ] *num* dixième; *see also* **sixth**.

tent peg *n* piquet *m* de tente.

tent pole *n* montant *m* OR mât *m* de tente.

tenuous ['tenjʊəs] *adj* ténu(e).

tenure ['tenjəʳ] *n* (U) *fml* **1.** (*of property*) bail *m*. **2.** (*of job*): **to have ~** être titulaire.

tepid ['tepɪd] *adj* tiède.

term [tɜːm] ◆ *n* **1.** (*word, expression*) terme *m*. **2.** (SCH & UNIV) trimestre *m*. **3.** (*period of time*) durée *f*, période *f*; **in the long/short ~** à long/court terme. ◆ *vt* appeler. ▶ **terms** *npl* **1.** (*of contract, agreement*) conditions *fpl*. **2.** (*basis*): **in international/real ~s** en termes internationaux/réels; **to be on good ~s (with sb)** être en bons termes (avec qqn); **to come to ~s with sthg** accepter qqch. ▶ **in terms of** *prep* sur le plan de, en termes de.

terminal ['tɜːmɪnl] ◆ *adj* (MED) en phase terminale. ◆ *n* **1.** (AERON, COMPUT & RAIL) terminal *m*. **2.** (ELEC) borne *f*.

terminate ['tɜːmɪneɪt] ◆ *vt* **1.** *fml* (*end - gen*) terminer, mettre fin à; (*- contract*) résilier. **2.** (*pregnancy*) interrompre. ◆ *vi* **1.** (*bus, train*) s'arrêter. **2.** (*contract*) se terminer.

termini ['tɜːmɪnaɪ] *pl* → **terminus**.

terminus ['tɜːmɪnəs] (*pl* **-ni** OR **-nuses**) *n* terminus *m*.

terrace ['terəs] *n* **1.** (*patio, on hillside*) terrasse *f*. **2.** Br (*of houses*) rangée *f* de maisons. ▶ **terraces** *npl* (FTBL): **the ~s** les gradins *mpl*.

terraced ['terəst] *adj* (*hillside*) en terrasses.

terraced house *n* Br maison attenante aux maisons voisines.

terrain [te'reɪn] *n* terrain *m*.

terrible ['terəbl] *adj* terrible; (*holiday, headache, weather*) affreux(euse), épouvantable.

terribly ['terəblɪ] *adv* terriblement; (*sing, write, organized*) affreusement mal; (*injured*) affreusement.

terrier ['terɪəʳ] *n* terrier *m*.

terrific [tə'rɪfɪk] *adj* **1.** (*wonderful*) fantastique, formidable. **2.** (*enormous*) énorme, fantastique.

terrified ['terɪfaɪd] *adj* terrifié(e); **to be ~ of** avoir une terreur folle OR peur folle de.

terrifying ['terɪfaɪɪŋ] *adj* terrifiant(e).

territory ['terətrɪ] *n* territoire *m*.

terror ['terəʳ] *n* terreur *f*.

terrorism ['terərɪzm] *n* terrorisme *m*.

terrorist ['terərɪst] *n* terroriste *mf*.

terrorize, -ise ['terəraɪz] *vt* terroriser.

terse [tɜːs] *adj* brusque.

Terylene® ['terɪliːn] *n* Térylène® *m*.

test [test] ◆ *n* **1.** (*trial*) essai *m*; (*of friendship, courage*) épreuve *f*. **2.** (*examination - of aptitude, psychological*) test *m*; (- SCH & UNIV) interrogation *f* écrite/orale; (*- of driving*) (examen *m* du) permis *m* de conduire. **3.** (MED *- of blood, urine*) analyse *f*; (*- of eyes*) examen *m*. ◆ *vt* **1.** (*try*) essayer; (*determination, friendship*) mettre à l'épreuve. **2.** (SCH & UNIV) faire faire une interrogation écrite/orale à; **to ~ sb on sthg** interroger qqn sur qqch. **3.** (MED *- blood, urine*) analyser; (*- eyes, reflexes*) faire un examen de.

testament ['testəmənt] *n* (*will*) testament *m*.

test-drive *vt* essayer.

testicles ['testɪklz] *npl* testicules *mpl*.

testify ['testɪfaɪ] ◆ *vt*: **to ~ that ...** témoigner que ... ◆ *vi* **1.** (JUR) témoigner. **2.** (*be proof*): **to ~ to sthg** témoigner de qqch.

testimony [Br 'testɪmənɪ, Am 'testəməʊnɪ] *n* témoignage *m*.

testing ['testɪŋ] *adj* éprouvant(e).

test match *n* Br match *m* international.

test pilot *n* pilote *m* d'essai.

test tube *n* éprouvette *f*.

test-tube baby *n* bébé-éprouvette *m*.

tetanus ['tetənəs] *n* tétanos *m*.

tether ['teðəʳ] ◆ *vt* attacher. ◆ *n*: **to be at the end of one's ~** être au bout du rouleau.

text [tekst] *n* texte *m*.

textbook ['tekstbʊk] *n* livre *m* OR manuel *m* scolaire.

textile ['tekstaɪl] *n* textile *m*.

texture ['tekstʃəʳ] *n* texture *f*; (*of paper, wood*) grain *m*.

Thai [taɪ] ◆ *adj* thaïlandais(e). ◆ *n* **1.** (*person*) Thaïlandais *m*, -e *f*. **2.** (*language*) thaï *m*.

Thailand ['taɪlænd] *n* Thaïlande *f*.

Thames [temz] *n*: **the ~** la Tamise.

than [*weak form* ðən, *strong form* ðæn] *conj* que; **Sarah is younger ~ her sister** Sarah est plus jeune que sa sœur; **more ~ three days/50 people** plus de trois jours/50 personnes.

thank [θæŋk] *vt*: **to ~ sb (for)** remercier qqn (pour OR de); **~ God** OR **goodness** OR

heavens! Dieu merci! ▶ **thanks** ♦ *npl*
remerciements *mpl*. ♦ *excl* merci!
▶ **thanks to** *prep* grâce à.
thankful ['θæŋkful] *adj* **1.** (*grateful*): ~
(for) reconnaissant(e) (de). **2.** (*relieved*)
soulagé(e).
thankless ['θæŋklɪs] *adj* ingrat(e).
thanksgiving ['θæŋks.ɡɪvɪŋ] *n* action *f*
de grâce. ▶ **Thanksgiving (Day)** *n fête
nationale américaine commémorant, le 4ᵉ jeudi
de novembre, l'installation des premiers colons
en Amérique.*
thank you *excl*: ~ **(for)** merci (pour or
de).
that [ðæt, *weak form of pron sense 2 & conj*
ðət] (*pl* those) ♦ *pron* **1.** (*demonstrative use:
pl 'those'*) ce, cela, ça; (*as opposed to 'this'*)
celui-là (celle-là); **who's ~?** qui est-ce?;
is ~ Maureen? c'est Maureen?; **what's ~?**
qu'est-ce que c'est que ça?; **~'s a
shame** c'est dommage; **which shoes are
you going to wear, these or those?**
quelles chaussures vas-tu mettre,
celles-ci ou celles-là?; **those who** ceux
(celles) qui. **2.** (*to introduce relative clauses
- subject*) que; (*- object*) que; (*- with
prep*) lequel (laquelle), lesquels (lesquelles) (*pl*); **we came to a path ~ led
into the woods** nous arrivâmes à un sentier qui menait dans les bois; **show me
the book ~ you bought** montre-moi le
livre que tu as acheté; **on the day ~ we
left** le jour où nous sommes partis.
♦ *adj* (*demonstrative: pl 'those'*) ce (cette),
cet (*before vowel or silent 'h'*), ces (*pl*); (*as
opposed to 'this'*) ce (cette) ...-là, ces
...-là (*pl*); **those chocolates are delicious**
ces chocolats sont délicieux; **later ~
day** plus tard ce jour-là; **I prefer ~ book**
je préfère ce livre-là; **I'll have ~ one** je
prendrai celui-là. ♦ *adv* aussi, si; **it
wasn't ~ bad/good** ce n'était pas si mal/
bien que ça. ♦ *conj* que; **tell him ~ the
children aren't coming** dites-lui que les
enfants ne viennent pas; **he recommended ~ I phone you** il m'a conseillé
de vous appeler. ▶ **that is (to say)**
adv c'est-à-dire.
thatched [θætʃt] *adj* de chaume.
that's [ðæts] = **that is.**
thaw [θɔː] ♦ *vt* (*ice*) faire fondre or
dégeler; (*frozen food*) décongeler. ♦ *vi*
1. (*ice*) dégeler, fondre; (*frozen food*)
décongeler. **2.** *fig* (*people, relations*) se
dégeler. ♦ *n* dégel *m*.
the [*weak form* ðə, *before vowel* ðɪ, *strong
form* ðiː] *def art* **1.** (*gen*) le (la), l' (+ *vowel
or silent 'h'*), les (*pl*); ~ **book** le livre; ~ **sea**

la mer; ~ **man** l'homme; ~ **boys/girls** les
garçons/filles; ~ **Joneses are coming to
supper** les Jones viennent dîner; **to play
~ piano** jouer du piano. **2.** (*with an adjective to form a noun*): ~ **British** les
Britanniques; ~ **old/young** les vieux/
jeunes; ~ **impossible** l'impossible. **3.** (*in
dates*): ~ **twelfth of May** le douze mai; ~
forties les années quarante. **4.** (*in comparisons*): ~ **more ... ~ less** plus ... moins;
~ **sooner ~ better** le plus tôt sera le
mieux. **5.** (*in titles*): **Alexander ~ Great**
Alexandre le Grand; **George ~ First**
Georges Premier.
theatre, theater *Am* ['θɪətər] *n*
1. (THEATRE) théâtre *m*. **2.** *Br* (MED) salle
f d'opération. **3.** *Am* (*cinema*) cinéma *m*.
theatregoer, theatergoer *Am*
['θɪətə.ɡəuər] *n* habitué *m*, -e *f* du
théâtre.
theatrical [θɪˈætrɪkl] *adj* théâtral(e);
(*company*) de théâtre.
theft [θeft] *n* vol *m*.
their [ðeər] *poss adj* leur, leurs (*pl*); ~
house leur maison; ~ **children** leurs
enfants; **it wasn't THEIR fault** ce n'était
pas de leur faute à eux.
theirs [ðeəz] *poss pron* le leur (la leur),
les leurs (*pl*); **that house is ~** cette maison est la leur, cette maison est à eux/
elles; **it wasn't our fault, it was THEIRS** ce
n'était pas de notre faute, c'était de la
leur; **a friend of ~** un de leurs amis, un
ami à eux/elles.
them [*weak form* ðəm, *strong form* ðem]
pers pron pl **1.** (*direct*) les; **I know ~** je les
connais; **if I were** OR **was ~** si j'étais eux/
elles, à leur place. **2.** (*indirect*) leur; **we
spoke to ~** nous leur avons parlé; **she
sent ~ a letter** elle leur a envoyé une
lettre; **I gave it to ~** je le leur ai donné.
3. (*stressed, after prep, in comparisons etc*)
eux (elles); **you can't expect THEM to do it**
tu ne peux pas exiger que ce soit eux
qui le fassent; **with ~** avec eux/elles;
without ~ sans eux/elles; **we're not as
wealthy as ~** nous ne sommes pas aussi
riches qu'eux/qu'elles.
theme [θiːm] *n* **1.** (*topic, motif*) thème
m, sujet *m*. **2.** (MUS) thème *m*; (*signature
tune*) indicatif *m*.
theme park *n* parc *m* à thème.
theme tune *n* chanson *f* principale.
themselves [ðəmˈselvz] *pron* **1.** (*reflexive*) se; (*after prep*) eux (elles). **2.** (*for
emphasis*) eux-mêmes *mpl*, elles-mêmes
fpl; **they did it ~** ils l'ont fait tout seuls.
then [ðen] *adv* **1.** (*not now*) alors, à cette

époque. **2.** (*next*) puis, ensuite. **3.** (*in that case*) alors, dans ce cas. **4.** (*therefore*) donc. **5.** (*also*) d'ailleurs, et puis.

theology [θɪˈɒlədʒɪ] n théologie f.

theoretical [θɪəˈretɪkl] adj théorique.

theorize, -ise [ˈθɪəraɪz] vi: **to ~ (about)** émettre une théorie (sur), théoriser (sur).

theory [ˈθɪərɪ] n théorie f; **in ~** en théorie.

therapist [ˈθerəpɪst] n thérapeute mf, psychothérapeute mf.

therapy [ˈθerəpɪ] n (U) thérapie f.

there [ðeəʳ] ♦ pron (*indicating existence of sthg*): **~ is/are** il y a; **~'s someone at the door** il y a quelqu'un à la porte; **~ must be some mistake** il doit y avoir erreur. ♦ adv **1.** (*in existence, available*) y, là; **is anybody ~?** il y a quelqu'un?; **is John ~, please?** (*when telephoning*) est-ce que John est là, s'il vous plaît? **2.** (*referring to place*) y, là; **I'm going ~ next week** j'y vais la semaine prochaine; **~ it is** c'est là; **~ he is!** le voilà!; **over ~** là-bas; **it's six kilometres ~ and back** cela fait six kilomètres aller-retour. ♦ excl: **~, I knew he'd turn up** tiens OR voilà, je savais bien qu'il s'amènerait; **~, ~** allons, allons. ▶ **there and then, then and there** adv immédiatement, sur-le-champ.

thereabouts [ðeərəˈbaʊts], **thereabout** Am [ðeərəˈbaʊt] adv: **or ~** (*nearby*) par là; (*approximately*) environ.

thereafter [ðeərˈɑːftəʳ] adv fml après cela, par la suite.

thereby [ˌðeərˈbaɪ] adv fml ainsi, de cette façon.

therefore [ˈðeəfɔːʳ] adv donc, par conséquent.

there's [ðeəz] = **there is**.

thermal [ˈθɜːml] adj thermique; (*clothes*) en Thermolactyl®.

thermometer [θəˈmɒmɪtəʳ] n thermomètre m.

Thermos (flask)® [ˈθɜːməs-] n (bouteille f) Thermos® m or f.

thermostat [ˈθɜːməstæt] n thermostat m.

thesaurus [θɪˈsɔːrəs] (pl -es) n dictionnaire m de synonymes.

these [ðiːz] pl → **this**.

thesis [ˈθiːsɪs] (pl **theses** [ˈθiːsiːz]) n thèse f.

they [ðeɪ] pers pron pl **1.** (*people, things, animals - unstressed*) ils (elles); (*- stressed*) eux (elles); **~'re pleased** ils sont contents (elles sont contentes); **~'re**

pretty earrings ce sont de jolies boucles d'oreille; **THEY can't do it** eux (elles), ils (elles) ne peuvent pas le faire; **there ~ are** les voilà. **2.** (*unspecified people*) on, ils; **~ say it's going to snow** on dit qu'il va neiger.

they'd [ðeɪd] = **they had, they would**.

they'll [ðeɪl] = **they shall, they will**.

they're [ðeəʳ] = **they are**.

they've [ðeɪv] = **they have**.

thick [θɪk] ♦ adj **1.** (*gen*) épais (épaisse); (*forest, hedge, fog*) dense; (*voice*) indistinct(e); **to be 6 inches ~** avoir 15 cm d'épaisseur. **2.** inf (*stupid*) bouché(e). ♦ n: **in the ~ of** au plus fort de, en plein OR au beau milieu de.

thicken [ˈθɪkn] ♦ vt épaissir. ♦ vi s'épaissir.

thicket [ˈθɪkɪt] n fourré m.

thickness [ˈθɪknɪs] n épaisseur f.

thickset [ˌθɪkˈset] adj trapu(e).

thick-skinned [-ˈskɪnd] adj qui a la peau dure.

thief [θiːf] (pl **thieves**) n voleur m, -euse f.

thieve [θiːv] vt & vi voler.

thieves [θiːvz] pl → **thief**.

thigh [θaɪ] n cuisse f.

thimble [ˈθɪmbl] n dé m (à coudre).

thin [θɪn] adj **1.** (*slice, layer, paper*) mince; (*cloth*) léger(ère); (*person*) maigre. **2.** (*liquid, sauce*) clair(e), peu épais (peu épaisse). **3.** (*sparse - crowd*) épars(e); (*- vegetation, hair*) clairsemé(e). ▶ **thin down** vt sep (*liquid, paint*) délayer, diluer; (*sauce*) éclaircir.

thing [θɪŋ] n **1.** (*gen*) chose f; **the (best) ~ to do would be ...** le mieux serait de ...; **the ~ is ...** le problème, c'est que ... **2.** (*anything*): **I don't know a ~** je n'y connais absolument rien. **3.** (*object*) chose f, objet m. **4.** (*person*): **you poor ~!** mon pauvre! ▶ **things** npl **1.** (*clothes, possessions*) affaires fpl. **2.** inf (*life*): **how are ~s?** comment ça va?

think [θɪŋk] (pt & pp **thought**) ♦ vt **1.** (*believe*): **to ~ (that)** croire que, penser que; **I ~ so/not** je crois que oui/non, je pense que oui/non. **2.** (*have in mind*) penser à. **3.** (*imagine*) s'imaginer. **4.** (*in polite requests*): **do you ~ you could help me?** tu pourrais m'aider? ♦ vi **1.** (*use mind*) réfléchir, penser. **2.** (*have stated opinion*): **what do you ~ of OR about his new film?** que pensez-vous de son dernier film?; **to ~ a lot of sb/sthg** penser beaucoup de bien de qqn/qqch. **3.** phr: **to ~ twice** y réfléchir à deux fois. ▶ **think about** vt fus: **to ~ about sb/sthg** songer à OR penser à qqn/qqch; **to ~ about doing sthg** songer à faire qqch; **I'll ~ about it** je vais y réfléchir. ▶ **think of** vt fus **1.** (consider) = **think about. 2.** (remember) se rappeler. **3.** (conceive) penser à, avoir l'idée de; **to ~ of doing sthg** avoir l'idée de faire qqch. ▶ **think over** vt sep réfléchir à. ▶ **think up** vt sep imaginer.

think tank n comité m d'experts.

third [θɜ:d] ◆ num troisième; see also **sixth.** ◆ n (UNIV) ≃ licence f mention passable.

thirdly ['θɜ:dlɪ] adv troisièmement, tertio.

third party insurance n assurance f de responsabilité civile.

third-rate adj pej de dernier OR troisième ordre.

Third World n: **the ~** le tiers-monde.

thirst [θɜ:st] n soif f; **~ for** fig soif de.

thirsty ['θɜ:stɪ] adj **1.** (person): **to be** OR **feel ~** avoir soif. **2.** (work) qui donne soif.

thirteen [ˌθɜ:'ti:n] num treize; see also **six.**

thirty ['θɜ:tɪ] num trente; see also **sixty.**

this [ðɪs] (pl **these**) ◆ pron (demonstrative use) ce, ceci; (as opposed to 'that') celui-ci (celle-ci); **~ is for you** c'est pour vous; **who's ~?** qui est-ce?; **what's ~?** qu'est-ce que c'est?; **which sweets does she prefer, these or those?** quels bonbons préfère-t-elle, ceux-ci ou ceux-là?; **~ is Daphne Logan** (introducing another person) je vous présente Daphne Logan; (introducing oneself on phone) ici Daphne Logan, Daphne Logan à l'appareil. ◆ adj **1.** (demonstrative use) ce (cette), cet (before vowel or silent 'h'), ces (pl); (as opposed to 'that') ce (cette) ...-ci, ces ...-ci (pl); **these chocolats are delicious** ces chocolats sont délicieux; **I prefer ~ book** je préfère ce livre-ci; **I'll have ~ one** je prendrai celui-ci; **~ afternoon** cet après-midi; **~ morning** ce matin; **~ week** cette semaine. **2.** inf (a certain) un certain (une certaine). ◆ adv aussi; **it was ~ big** c'était aussi grand que ça; **you'll need about ~ much** il vous en faudra à peu près comme ceci.

thistle ['θɪsl] n chardon m.

thong [θɒŋ] n (of leather) lanière f.

thorn [θɔ:n] n épine f.

thorny ['θɔ:nɪ] adj lit & fig épineux (euse).

thorough ['θʌrə] adj **1.** (exhaustive - search, inspection) minutieux(euse); (- investigation, knowledge) approfondi(e). **2.** (meticulous) méticuleux(euse). **3.** (complete, utter) complet(ète), absolu(e).

thoroughbred ['θʌrəbred] n pur-sang m inv.

thoroughfare ['θʌrəfeə'] n fml rue f, voie f publique.

thoroughly ['θʌrəlɪ] adv **1.** (fully, in detail) à fond. **2.** (completely, utterly) absolument, complètement.

those [ðəʊz] pl → **that.**

though [ðəʊ] ◆ conj bien que (+ subjunctive), quoique (+ subjunctive). ◆ adv pourtant, cependant.

thought [θɔ:t] ◆ pt & pp → **think.** ◆ n **1.** (gen) pensée f; (idea) idée f, pensée; **after much ~** après avoir mûrement réfléchi. **2.** (intention) intention f. ▶ **thoughts** npl **1.** (reflections) pensées fpl, réflexions fpl. **2.** (views) opinions fpl, idées fpl.

thoughtful ['θɔ:tfʊl] adj **1.** (pensive) pensif(ive). **2.** (considerate - person) prévenant(e), attentionné(e); (- remark, act) plein(e) de gentillesse.

thoughtless ['θɔ:tlɪs] adj (person) qui manque d'égards (pour les autres); (remark, behaviour) irréfléchi(e).

thousand ['θaʊznd] num mille; **a** OR **one ~** mille; **~s of** des milliers de; see also **six.**

thousandth ['θaʊzntθ] num millième; see also **sixth.**

thrash [θræʃ] vt **1.** (hit) battre, rosser. **2.** inf (defeat) écraser, battre à plates coutures. ▶ **thrash about, thrash around** vi s'agiter. ▶ **thrash out** vt sep (problem) débrouiller, démêler; (idea) débattre, discuter.

thread [θred] ◆ n **1.** (gen) fil m. **2.** (of screw) filet m, pas m. ◆ vt (needle) enfiler.

threadbare ['θredbeə'] adj usé(e) jusqu'à la corde.

threat [θret] n: **~ (to)** menace f (pour).

threaten ['θretn] ◆ vt: **to ~ sb (with)** menacer qqn (de); **to ~ to do sthg** menacer de faire qqch. ◆ vi menacer.

three [θri:] num trois; see also **six.**

three-dimensional [-dɪ'menʃənl] adj (film, picture) en relief; (object) à trois dimensions.

threefold ['θri:fəʊld] ◆ adj triple. ◆ adv: **to increase ~** tripler.

three-piece adj: **~ suit** (costume m) trois pièces m; **~ suite** canapé m et deux fauteuils assortis.

three-ply adj (wool) à trois fils.

three-quarters *npl* (*fraction*) trois quarts *mpl*.

thresh [θreʃ] *vt* battre.

threshold ['θreʃhəʊld] *n* seuil *m*.

threw [θru:] *pt* → **throw**.

thrifty ['θrɪftɪ] *adj* économe.

thrill [θrɪl] ◆ *n* **1.** (*sudden feeling*) frisson *m*, sensation *f*. **2.** (*enjoyable experience*) plaisir *m*. ◆ *vt* transporter, exciter.

thrilled [θrɪld] *adj*: ~ **(with sthg/to do sthg)** ravi(e) (de qqch/de faire qqch), enchanté(e) (de qqch/de faire qqch).

thriller ['θrɪlər] *n* thriller *m*.

thrilling ['θrɪlɪŋ] *adj* saisissant(e), palpitant(e).

thrive [θraɪv] (*pt* -**d** OR **throve**, *pp* -**d**) *vi* (*person*) bien se porter; (*plant*) pousser bien; (*business*) prospérer.

thriving ['θraɪvɪŋ] *adj* (*person*) bien portant(e); (*plant*) qui pousse bien; (*business*) prospère.

throat [θrəʊt] *n* gorge *f*.

throb [θrɒb] *vi* (*heart*) palpiter, battre fort; (*engine*) vibrer; (*music*) taper; **my head is throbbing** j'ai des élancements dans la tête.

throes [θrəʊz] *npl*: **to be in the ~ of** (*war, disease*) être en proie à; **to be in the ~ of an argument** être en pleine dispute.

throne [θrəʊn] *n* trône *m*.

throng [θrɒŋ] ◆ *n* foule *f*, multitude *f*. ◆ *vt* remplir, encombrer.

throttle ['θrɒtl] ◆ *n* (*valve*) papillon *m* des gaz; (*lever*) commande *f* des gaz. ◆ *vt* (*strangle*) étrangler.

through [θru:] ◆ *adj* (*finished*): **are you ~?** tu as fini?; **to be ~ with sthg** avoir fini qqch. ◆ *adv*: **to let sb ~** laisser passer qqn; **to read sthg ~** lire qqch jusqu'au bout; **to sleep ~ till ten** dormir jusqu'à dix heures. ◆ *prep* **1.** (*relating to place, position*) à travers; **to travel ~ sthg** traverser qqch; **to cut ~ sthg** couper qqch. **2.** (*during*) pendant. **3.** (*because of*) à cause de. **4.** (*by means of*) par l'intermédiaire de, par l'entremise de. **5.** *Am* (*up till and including*): **Monday ~ Friday** du lundi au vendredi. ▶ **through and through** *adv* (*completely*) jusqu'au bout des ongles; (*thoroughly*) par cœur, à fond.

throughout [θru:'aʊt] ◆ *prep* **1.** (*during*) pendant, durant; ~ **the meeting** pendant toute la réunion. **2.** (*everywhere in*) partout dans. ◆ *adv* **1.** (*all the time*) tout le temps. **2.** (*everywhere*) partout.

throve [θrəʊv] *pt* → **thrive**.

throw [θrəʊ] (*pt* **threw**, *pp* **thrown**) ◆ *vt* **1.** (*gen*) jeter; (*ball, javelin*) lancer. **2.** (*rider*) désarçonner. **3.** *fig* (*confuse*) déconcerter, décontenancer. ◆ *n* lancement *m*, jet *m*. ▶ **throw away** *vt sep* **1.** (*discard*) jeter. **2.** *fig* (*money*) gaspiller; (*opportunity*) perdre. ▶ **throw out** *vt sep* **1.** (*discard*) jeter. **2.** *fig* (*reject*) rejeter. **3.** (*from house*) mettre à la porte; (*from army, school*) expulser, renvoyer. ▶ **throw up** *vi inf* (*vomit*) dégobiller, vomir.

throwaway ['θrəʊə,weɪ] *adj* **1.** (*disposable*) jetable, à jeter. **2.** (*remark*) désinvolte.

throw-in *n* *Br* (FTBL) rentrée *f* en touche.

thrown [θrəʊn] *pp* → **throw**.

thru [θru:] *Am inf* = **through**.

thrush [θrʌʃ] *n* **1.** (*bird*) grive *f*. **2.** (MED) muguet *m*.

thrust [θrʌst] ◆ *n* **1.** (*forward movement*) poussée *f*; (*of knife*) coup *m*. **2.** (*main aspect*) idée *f* principale, aspect *m* principal. ◆ *vt* (*shove*) enfoncer, fourrer.

thud [θʌd] ◆ *n* bruit *m* sourd. ◆ *vi* tomber en faisant un bruit sourd.

thug [θʌg] *n* brute *f*, voyou *m*.

thumb [θʌm] ◆ *n* pouce *m*. ◆ *vt inf* (*hitch*): **to ~ a lift** faire du stop OR de l'auto-stop. ▶ **thumb through** *vt fus* feuilleter, parcourir.

thumbs down [,θʌmz-] *n*: **to get** OR **be given the ~** être rejeté(e).

thumbs up [,θʌmz-] *n* (*go-ahead*): **to give sb the ~** donner le feu vert à qqn.

thumbtack ['θʌmtæk] *n* *Am* punaise *f*.

thump [θʌmp] ◆ *n* **1.** (*blow*) grand coup *m*. **2.** (*thud*) bruit *m* sourd. ◆ *vt* (*hit*) cogner, taper sur. ◆ *vi* (*heart*) battre fort.

thunder ['θʌndər] ◆ *n* (U) **1.** (METEOR) tonnerre *m*. **2.** *fig* (*of traffic*) vacarme *m*; (*of applause*) tonnerre *m*. ◆ *v impers* (METEOR) tonner.

thunderbolt ['θʌndəbəʊlt] *n* coup *m* de foudre.

thunderclap ['θʌndəklæp] *n* coup *m* de tonnerre.

thunderstorm ['θʌndəstɔ:m] *n* orage *m*.

thundery ['θʌndərɪ] *adj* orageux (euse).

Thursday ['θɜ:zdɪ] *n* jeudi *m*; *see also* **Saturday**.

thus [ðʌs] *adv fml* **1.** (*therefore*) par conséquent, donc, ainsi. **2.** (*in this way*) ainsi, de cette façon, comme ceci.

thwart [θwɔ:t] *vt* contrecarrer, contrarier.

thyme [taɪm] n thym m.

thyroid ['θaɪrɔɪd] n thyroïde f.

tiara [tɪ'ɑːrə] n (worn by woman) diadème m.

Tibet [tɪ'bet] n Tibet m.

tic [tɪk] n tic m.

tick [tɪk] ◆ n 1. (written mark) coche f. 2. (sound) tic-tac m. 3. (insect) tique f. ◆ vt cocher. ◆ vi faire tic-tac. ▶ **tick off** vt sep 1. (mark off) cocher. 2. (tell off) enguirlander. ▶ **tick over** vi (engine, business) tourner au ralenti.

ticket ['tɪkɪt] n 1. (for access, train, plane) billet m; (for bus) ticket m; (for library) carte f; (label on product) étiquette f. 2. (for traffic offence) P.-V. m, papillon m.

ticket collector n Br contrôleur m, -euse f.

ticket inspector n Br contrôleur m, -euse f.

ticket machine n distributeur m de billets.

ticket office n bureau m de vente des billets.

tickle ['tɪkl] ◆ vt 1. (touch lightly) chatouiller. 2. fig (amuse) amuser. ◆ vi chatouiller.

ticklish ['tɪklɪʃ] adj (person) qui craint les chatouilles, chatouilleux(euse).

tidal ['taɪdl] adj (force) de la marée; (river) à marées; (barrier) contre la marée.

tidal wave n raz-de-marée m inv.

tidbit Am = titbit.

tiddlywinks ['tɪdlɪwɪŋks], **tiddledywinks** Am ['tɪdldɪwɪŋks] n jeu m de puce.

tide [taɪd] n 1. (of sea) marée f. 2. fig (of opinion, fashion) courant m, tendance f; (of protest) vague f.

tidy ['taɪdɪ] ◆ adj 1. (room, desk) en ordre, bien rangé(e); (hair, dress) soigné(e). 2. (person - in habits) ordonné(e); (- in appearance) soigné(e). ◆ vt ranger, mettre de l'ordre dans. ▶ **tidy up** ◆ vt sep ranger, mettre de l'ordre dans. ◆ vi ranger.

tie [taɪ] (pt & pp **tied**, cont **tying**) ◆ n 1. (necktie) cravate f. 2. (in game, competition) égalité f de points. ◆ vt 1. (fasten) attacher. 2. (shoelaces) nouer, attacher; **to ~ a knot** faire un nœud. 3. fig (link): **to be ~d to** être lié(e) à. ◆ vi (draw) être à égalité. ▶ **tie down** vt sep fig (restrict) restreindre la liberté de. ▶ **tie in with** vt sep concorder avec, coïncider avec. ▶ **tie up** vt sep 1. (with string, rope) attacher. 2. (shoelaces) nouer, attacher.

3. fig (money, resources) immobiliser. 4. fig (link): **to be ~d up with** être lié(e) à.

tiebreak(er) ['taɪbreɪk(ər)] n 1. (TENNIS) tie-break m. 2. (in game, competition) question f subsidiaire.

tiepin ['taɪpɪn] n épingle f de cravate.

tier [tɪər] n (of seats) gradin m; (of cake) étage m.

tiff [tɪf] n bisbille f, petite querelle f.

tiger ['taɪgər] n tigre m.

tight [taɪt] ◆ adj 1. (clothes, group, competition, knot) serré(e). 2. (taut) tendu(e). 3. (schedule) serré(e), minuté(e). 4. (strict) strict(e), sévère. 5. (corner, bend) raide. 6. inf (drunk) soûl(e), rond(e). 7. inf (miserly) radin(e), avare. ◆ adv 1. (firmly, securely) bien, fort; **to hold ~** tenir bien; **hold ~!** tiens bon!; **to shut** OR **close sthg ~** bien fermer qqch. 2. (tautly) à fond. ▶ **tights** npl collant m, collants mpl.

tighten ['taɪtn] ◆ vt 1. (belt, knot, screw) resserrer; **to ~ one's hold** OR **grip on** resserrer sa prise sur. 2. (pull tauter) tendre. 3. (make stricter) renforcer. ◆ vi 1. (rope) se tendre. 2. (grip, hold) se resserrer.

tightfisted [,taɪt'fɪstɪd] adj pej radin(e), pingre.

tightly ['taɪtlɪ] adv (firmly) bien, fort.

tightrope ['taɪtrəʊp] n corde f raide.

tile [taɪl] n (on roof) tuile f; (on floor, wall) carreau m.

tiled [taɪld] adj (floor, wall) carrelé(e); (roof) couvert de tuiles.

till [tɪl] ◆ prep jusqu'à; **from six ~ ten o'clock** de six heures à dix heures. ◆ conj jusqu'à ce que (+ subjunctive); **wait ~ I come back** attends que je revienne; (after negative) avant que (+ subjunctive); **it won't be ready ~ tomorrow** ça ne sera pas prêt avant demain. ◆ n tiroir-caisse m.

tiller ['tɪlər] n (NAUT) barre f.

tilt [tɪlt] ◆ vt incliner, pencher. ◆ vi s'incliner, pencher.

timber ['tɪmbər] n 1. (U) (wood) bois m de charpente OR de construction. 2. (beam) poutre f, madrier m.

time [taɪm] ◆ n 1. (gen) temps m; **a long ~** longtemps; **in a short ~** dans peu de temps, sous peu; **to take ~** prendre du temps; **to be ~ for sthg** être l'heure de qqch; **to have a good ~** s'amuser bien; **in good ~** de bonne heure; **ahead of ~** en avance, avant l'heure; **on ~** à l'heure; **to have no ~ for sb/sthg** ne pas supporter qqn/qqch; **to pass the ~**

passer le temps; **to play for ~** essayer de gagner du temps. **2.** (*as measured by clock*) heure *f*; **what's the ~?** quelle heure est-il?; **in a week's/year's ~** dans une semaine/un an. **3.** (*point in time in past*) époque *f*; **before my ~** avant que j'arrive ici. **4.** (*occasion*) fois *f*; **from ~ to ~** de temps en temps, de temps à autre; **~ after ~ and again** à maintes reprises, maintes et maintes fois. **5.** (MUS) mesure *f*. ◆ *vt* **1.** (*schedule*) fixer, prévoir. **2.** (*race, runner*) chronométrer. **3.** (*arrival, remark*) choisir le moment de. ▶ **times** ◆ *npl* fois *fpl*; **four ~s as much as me** quatre fois plus que moi. ◆ *prep* (MATH) fois. ▶ **at a time** *adv* d'affilée; **one at a ~** un par un, un seul à la fois; **months at a ~** des mois et des mois. ▶ **at times** *adv* quelquefois, parfois. ▶ **at the same time** *adv* en même temps. ▶ **about time** *adv*: **it's about ~ (that)** ... il est grand temps que ...; **about ~ too!** ce n'est pas trop tôt! ▶ **for the time being** *adv* pour le moment. ▶ **in time** *adv* **1.** (*not late*): **in ~ (for)** à l'heure (pour). **2.** (*eventually*) à la fin, à la longue; (*after a while*) avec le temps, à la longue.

time bomb *n lit & fig* bombe *f* à retardement.

time lag *n* décalage *m*.

timeless ['taɪmlɪs] *adj* éternel(elle).

time limit *n* délai *m*.

timely ['taɪmlɪ] *adj* opportun(e).

time off *n* temps *m* libre.

time out *n* (SPORT) temps *m* mort.

timer ['taɪmə] *n* minuteur *m*.

time scale *n* période *f*; (*of project*) délai *m*.

time-share *n Br* logement *m* en multipropriété.

time switch *n* minuterie *f*.

timetable ['taɪm,teɪbl] *n* **1.** (SCH) emploi *m* du temps. **2.** (*of buses, trains*) horaire *m*. **3.** (*schedule*) calendrier *m*.

time zone *n* fuseau *m* horaire.

timid ['tɪmɪd] *adj* timide.

timing ['taɪmɪŋ] *n* (U) **1.** (*of remark*) à-propos *m*. **2.** (*scheduling*): **the ~ of the election** le moment choisi pour l'élection. **3.** (*measuring*) chronométrage *m*.

timpani ['tɪmpənɪ] *npl* timbales *fpl*.

tin [tɪn] *n* **1.** (U) (*metal*) étain *m*; (*in sheets*) fer-blanc *m*. **2.** Br (*can*) boîte *f* de conserve. **3.** (*small container*) boîte *f*.

tin can *n* boîte *f* de conserve.

tinfoil ['tɪnfɔɪl] *n* (U) papier *m* (d')aluminium.

tinge [tɪndʒ] *n* **1.** (*of colour*) teinte *f*, nuance *f*. **2.** (*of feeling*) nuance *f*.

tinged [tɪndʒd] *adj*: **~ with** teinté(e) de.

tingle ['tɪŋgl] *vi* picoter.

tinker ['tɪŋkə] ◆ *n Br pej* (*gypsy*) romanichel *m*, -elle *f*. ◆ *vi*: **to ~ (with sthg)** bricoler (qqch).

tinkle ['tɪŋkl] *vi* (*ring*) tinter.

tinned [tɪnd] *adj Br* en boîte.

tin opener *n Br* ouvre-boîtes *m inv*.

tinsel ['tɪnsl] *n* (U) guirlandes *fpl* de Noël.

tint [tɪnt] *n* teinte *f*, nuance *f*; (*in hair*) rinçage *m*.

tinted ['tɪntɪd] *adj* (*glasses, windows*) teinté(e).

tiny ['taɪnɪ] *adj* minuscule.

tip [tɪp] ◆ *n* **1.** (*end*) bout *m*. **2.** Br (*dump*) décharge *f*. **3.** (*to waiter etc*) pourboire *m*. **4.** (*piece of advice*) tuyau *m*. ◆ *vt* **1.** (*tilt*) faire basculer. **2.** (*spill*) renverser. **3.** (*waiter etc*) donner un pourboire à. ◆ *vi* **1.** (*tilt*) basculer. **2.** (*spill*) se renverser. ▶ **tip over** ◆ *vt sep* renverser. ◆ *vi* se renverser.

tip-off *n* tuyau *m*; (*to police*) dénonciation *f*.

tipped ['tɪpt] *adj* (*cigarette*) à bout filtre.

tipsy ['tɪpsɪ] *adj inf* gai(e).

tiptoe ['tɪptəʊ] ◆ *n*: **on ~** sur la pointe des pieds. ◆ *vi* marcher sur la pointe des pieds.

tip-top *adj inf* dated excellent(e).

tire ['taɪə] ◆ *n Am* = **tyre**. ◆ *vt* fatiguer. ◆ *vi* **1.** (*get tired*) se fatiguer. **2.** (*get fed up*): **to ~ of** se lasser de.

tired ['taɪəd] *adj* **1.** (*sleepy*) fatigué(e), las (lasse). **2.** (*fed up*): **to be ~ of sthg/of doing sthg** en avoir assez de qqch/de faire qqch.

tireless ['taɪəlɪs] *adj* infatigable.

tiresome ['taɪəsəm] *adj* ennuyeux (euse).

tiring ['taɪərɪŋ] *adj* fatigant(e).

tissue ['tɪʃuː] *n* **1.** (*paper handkerchief*) mouchoir *m* en papier. **2.** (U) (BIOL) tissu *m*.

tissue paper *n* (U) papier *m* de soie.

tit [tɪt] *n* **1.** (*bird*) mésange *f*. **2.** *vulg* (*breast*) nichon *m*, néné *m*.

titbit Br ['tɪtbɪt], **tidbit** Am ['tɪdbɪt] *n* **1.** (*of food*) bon morceau *m*. **2.** *fig* (*of news*) petite nouvelle *f*.

tit for tat [-'tæt] *n* un prêté pour un rendu.

titillate ['tɪtɪleɪt] *vt* titiller.

title ['taɪtl] *n* titre *m*.

title deed *n* titre *m* de propriété.

title role n rôle m principal.

titter ['tɪtə'] vi rire bêtement.

TM abbr of **trademark**.

to [unstressed before consonant tə, unstressed before vowel tʊ, stressed tuː] ◆ prep **1.** (indicating place, direction) à; **to go ~ Liverpool/Spain/school** aller à Liverpool/en Espagne/à l'école; **to go ~ the butcher's** aller chez le boucher; **~ the left/right** à gauche/droite. **2.** (to express indirect object) à; **to give sthg ~ sb** donner qqch à qqn; **we were listening ~ the radio** nous écoutions la radio. **3.** (indicating reaction, effect) à; **~ my delight/surprise** à ma grande joie/surprise. **4.** (in stating opinion): **~ me, ...** à mon avis, ...; **it seemed quite unnecessary ~ me/him** etc cela me/lui etc semblait tout à fait inutile. **5.** (indicating state, process): **to drive sb ~ drink** pousser qqn à boire; **it could lead ~ trouble** cela pourrait causer des ennuis. **6.** (as far as) à, jusqu'à; **to count ~ 10** compter jusqu'à 10; **we work from 9 ~ 5** nous travaillons de 9 heures à 17 heures. **7.** (in expressions of time): **it's ten ~ three/quarter ~ one** il est trois heures moins dix/une heure moins le quart. **8.** (per) à; **40 miles ~ the gallon** = 7 litres aux cent (km). **9.** (of, for) de; **the key ~ the car** la clef de la voiture; **a letter ~ my daughter** une lettre à ma fille. ◆ adv (shut): **push the door ~** fermez la porte. ◆ with infinitive **1.** (forming simple infinitive): **~ walk** marcher; **~ laugh** rire. **2.** (following another verb): **to begin ~ do sthg** commencer à faire qqch; **to try ~ do sthg** essayer de faire qqch; **to want ~ do sthg** vouloir faire qqch. **3.** (following an adjective): **difficult ~ do** difficile à faire; **ready ~ go** prêt à partir. **4.** (indicating purpose) pour; **he worked hard ~ pass his exam** il a travaillé dur pour réussir son examen. **5.** (substituting for a relative clause): **I have a lot ~ do** j'ai beaucoup à faire; **he told me ~ leave** il m'a dit de partir. **6.** (to avoid repetition of infinitive): **I meant to call him but I forgot ~** je voulais l'appeler, mais j'ai oublié. **7.** (in comments): **~ be honest ...** en toute franchise ...; **~ sum up, ...** en résumé, ..., pour récapituler, ...

toad [təʊd] n crapaud m.

toadstool ['təʊdstuːl] n champignon m vénéneux.

to and fro adv: **to go ~** aller et venir; **to walk ~** marcher de long en large. ► **to-and-fro** adj de va-et-vient.

toast [təʊst] ◆ n **1.** (U) (bread) pain m

grillé, toast m. **2.** (drink) toast m. ◆ vt **1.** (bread) (faire) griller. **2.** (person) porter un toast à.

toasted sandwich [,təʊstɪd-] n sandwich m grillé.

toaster ['təʊstə'] n grille-pain m inv.

tobacco [tə'bækəʊ] n (U) tabac m.

tobacconist [tə'bækənɪst] n buraliste mf; **~'s (shop)** bureau m de tabac.

toboggan [tə'bɒgən] n luge f, traîne f sauvage Can.

today [tə'deɪ] ◆ n aujourd'hui m. ◆ adv aujourd'hui.

toddler ['tɒdlə'] n tout-petit m (qui commence à marcher).

toddy ['tɒdɪ] n grog m.

to-do (pl **-s**) n inf dated histoire f.

toe [təʊ] ◆ n (of foot) orteil m, doigt m de pied; (of sock, shoe) bout m. ◆ vt: **to ~ the line** se plier.

toenail ['təʊneɪl] n ongle m d'orteil.

toffee ['tɒfɪ] n caramel m.

toga ['təʊgə] n toge f.

together [tə'geðə'] adv **1.** (gen) ensemble. **2.** (at the same time) en même temps. ► **together with** prep ainsi que.

toil [tɔɪl] literary ◆ n labeur m. ◆ vi travailler dur.

toilet ['tɔɪlɪt] n (lavatory) toilettes fpl, cabinets mpl; **to go to the ~** aller aux toilettes OR aux cabinets.

toilet bag n trousse f de toilette.

toilet paper n (U) papier m hygiénique.

toiletries ['tɔɪlɪtrɪz] npl articles mpl de toilette.

toilet roll n rouleau m de papier hygiénique.

toilet water n eau f de toilette.

token ['təʊkn] ◆ adj symbolique. ◆ n **1.** (voucher) bon m. **2.** (symbol) marque f. ► **by the same token** adv de même.

told [təʊld] pt & pp → **tell**.

tolerable ['tɒlərəbl] adj passable.

tolerance ['tɒlərəns] n tolérance f.

tolerant ['tɒlərənt] adj tolérant(e).

tolerate ['tɒləreɪt] vt **1.** (put up with) supporter. **2.** (permit) tolérer.

toll [təʊl] ◆ n **1.** (number) nombre m. **2.** (fee) péage m. **3.** phr: **to take its ~** se faire sentir. ◆ vt & vi sonner.

toll-free Am adv: **to call ~** appeler un numéro vert.

tomato [Br tə'mɑːtəʊ, Am tə'meɪtəʊ] (pl **-es**) n tomate f.

tomb [tuːm] n tombe f.

tomboy ['tɒmbɔɪ] n garçon m manqué.

tombstone ['tu:mstəʊn] *n* pierre *f* tombale.

tomcat ['tɒmkæt] *n* matou *m*.

tomorrow [tə'mɒrəʊ] ◆ *n* demain *m*. ◆ *adv* demain.

ton [tʌn] (*pl inv* OR **-s**) *n* **1.** (*imperial*) = 1016 *kg* Br, = 907,2 *kg* Am, = tonne *f*. **2.** (*metric*) = 1000 *kg*, tonne *f*. ▶ **tons** *npl inf*: **-s** (**of**) des tas (de), plein (de).

tone [təʊn] *n* **1.** (*gen*) ton *m*. **2.** (*on phone*) tonalité *f*; (*on answering machine*) bip *m* sonore. ▶ **tone down** *vt sep* modérer. ▶ **tone up** *vt sep* tonifier.

tone-deaf *adj* qui n'a aucune oreille.

tongs [tɒŋz] *npl* pinces *fpl*; (*for hair*) fer *m* à friser.

tongue [tʌŋ] *n* **1.** (*gen*) langue *f*; **to hold one's** ~ *fig* tenir sa langue. **2.** (*of shoe*) languette *f*.

tongue-in-cheek *adj* ironique.

tongue-tied [-,taɪd] *adj* muet(ette).

tongue twister [-,twɪstəʳ] *n* phrase *f* difficile à dire.

tonic ['tɒnɪk] *n* **1.** (*tonic water*) Schweppes® *m*. **2.** (*medicine*) tonique *m*.

tonic water *n* Schweppes® *m*.

tonight [tə'naɪt] ◆ *n* ce soir *m*; (*late*) cette nuit *f*. ◆ *adv* ce soir; (*late*) cette nuit.

tonnage ['tʌnɪdʒ] *n* tonnage *m*.

tonne [tʌn] (*pl inv* OR **-s**) *n* tonne *f*.

tonsil ['tɒnsl] *n* amygdale *f*.

tonsil(l)itis [,tɒnsɪ'laɪtɪs] *n* (U) amygdalite *f*.

too [tu:] *adv* **1.** (*also*) aussi. **2.** (*excessively*) trop; ~ **many people** trop de gens; **it was over all** ~ **soon** ça s'était terminé bien trop tôt; **I'd be only** ~ **happy to help** je serais trop heureux de vous aider; **I wasn't** ~ **impressed** ça ne m'a pas impressionné outre mesure.

took [tʊk] *pt* → **take**.

tool [tu:l] *n lit & fig* outil *m*.

tool box *n* boîte *f* à outils.

tool kit *n* trousse *f* à outils.

toot [tu:t] ◆ *n* coup *m* de Klaxon®. ◆ *vi* klaxonner.

tooth [tu:θ] (*pl* teeth) *n* dent *f*.

toothache ['tu:θeɪk] *n* mal *m* OR rage *f* de dents; **to have** ~ avoir mal aux dents.

toothbrush ['tu:θbrʌʃ] *n* brosse *f* à dents.

toothpaste ['tu:θpeɪst] *n* (pâte *f*) dentifrice *m*.

toothpick ['tu:θpɪk] *n* cure-dents *m inv*.

top [tɒp] ◆ *adj* **1.** (*highest*) du haut.

2. (*most important, successful - officials*) important(e); (- *executives*) supérieur(e); (- *pop singer*) fameux(euse); (- *sportsman, sportswoman*) meilleur(e); (- *in exam*) premier(ère). **3.** (*maximum*) maximum. ◆ *n* **1.** (*highest point - of hill*) sommet *m*; (- *of page, pile*) haut *m*; (- *of tree*) cime *f*; (- *of list*) début *m*, tête *f*; **on** ~ dessus; **at the** ~ **of one's voice** à tue-tête. **2.** (*lid - of bottle, tube*) bouchon *m*; (- *of pen*) capuchon *m*; (- *of jar*) couvercle *m*. **3.** (*of table, box*) dessus *m*. **4.** (*clothing*) haut *m*. **5.** (*toy*) toupie *f*. **6.** (*highest rank - in league*) tête *f*; (- *in scale*) haut *m*; (- SCH) premier *m*, -ère *f*. ◆ *vt* **1.** (*be first in*) être en tête de. **2.** (*better*) surpasser. **3.** (*exceed*) dépasser. ▶ **on top of** *prep* **1.** (*in space*) sur. **2.** (*in addition to*) en plus de. ▶ **top up** Br, **top off** Am *vt sep* remplir.

top floor *n* dernier étage *m*.

top hat *n* haut-de-forme *m*.

top-heavy *adj* mal équilibré(e).

topic ['tɒpɪk] *n* sujet *m*.

topical ['tɒpɪkl] *adj* d'actualité.

topless ['tɒplɪs] *adj* (*woman*) aux seins nus.

top-level *adj* au plus haut niveau.

topmost ['tɒpməʊst] *adj* le plus haut (la plus haute).

topping ['tɒpɪŋ] *n* garniture *f*.

topple ['tɒpl] ◆ *vt* renverser. ◆ *vi* basculer.

top-secret *adj* top secret (top secrète).

topspin ['tɒpspɪn] *n* lift *m*.

topsy-turvy [,tɒpsɪ'tɜːvɪ] *adj* **1.** (*messy*) sens dessus dessous. **2.** (*confused*): **to be** ~ ne pas tourner rond.

torch [tɔːtʃ] *n* **1.** Br (*electric*) lampe *f* électrique. **2.** (*burning*) torche *f*.

tore [tɔːʳ] *pt* → **tear²**.

torment [*n* 'tɔːment, *vb* tɔː'ment] ◆ *n* tourment *m*. ◆ *vt* tourmenter.

torn [tɔːn] *pp* → **tear²**.

tornado [tɔː'neɪdəʊ] (*pl* **-es** OR **-s**) *n* tornade *f*.

torpedo [tɔː'piːdəʊ] (*pl* **-es**) *n* torpille *f*.

torrent ['tɒrənt] *n* torrent *m*.

torrid ['tɒrɪd] *adj* **1.** (*hot*) torride. **2.** *fig* (*passionate*) ardent(e).

tortoise ['tɔːtəs] *n* tortue *f*.

tortoiseshell ['tɔːtəʃel] ◆ *adj*: ~ **cat** chat *m* roux tigré. ◆ *n* (U) (*material*) écaille *f*.

torture ['tɔːtʃəʳ] ◆ *n* torture *f*. ◆ *vt* torturer.

Tory ['tɔːrɪ] ◆ *adj* tory, conservateur

(trice). ◆ n tory mf, conservateur m, -trice f.

toss [tɒs] ◆ vt 1. (throw) jeter; **to ~ a coin** jouer à pile ou face; **to ~ one's head** rejeter la tête en arrière. 2. (salad) remuer; (pancake) faire sauter. 3. (throw about) ballotter. ◆ vi (move about): **to ~ and turn** se tourner et se retourner. ▶ **toss up** vi jouer à pile ou face.

tot [tɒt] n 1. inf (small child) tout-petit m. 2. (of drink) larme f, goutte f.

total ['təʊtl] ◆ adj total(e); (disgrace, failure) complet(ète). ◆ n total m. ◆ vt 1. (add up) additionner. 2. (amount to) s'élever à.

totalitarian [ˌtəʊtælɪ'teərɪən] adj totalitaire.

totally ['təʊtəlɪ] adv totalement; **I agree** je suis totalement d'accord.

totter ['tɒtər] vi lit & fig chanceler.

touch [tʌtʃ] ◆ n 1. (U) (sense) toucher m. 2. (detail) touche f. 3. (U) (skill) marque f, note f. 4. (contact): **to keep in ~ (with sb)** rester en contact (avec qqn); **to get in ~ with sb** entrer en contact avec qqn; **to lose ~ with sb** perdre qqn de vue; **to be out of ~ with** ne plus être au courant de. 5. (SPORT): **in ~** en touche. 6. (small amount): **a ~** un petit peu. ◆ vt toucher. ◆ vi (be in contact) se toucher. ▶ **touch down** vi (plane) atterrir. ▶ **touch on** vt fus effleurer.

touch-and-go adj incertain(e).

touchdown ['tʌtʃdaʊn] n 1. (of plane) atterrissage m. 2. (in American football) but m.

touched [tʌtʃt] adj 1. (grateful) touché(e). 2. inf (slightly mad) fêlé(e).

touching ['tʌtʃɪŋ] adj touchant(e).

touchline ['tʌtʃlaɪn] n ligne f de touche.

touchy ['tʌtʃɪ] adj 1. (person) susceptible. 2. (subject, question) délicat(e).

tough [tʌf] adj 1. (material, vehicle, person) solide; (character, life) dur(e). 2. (meat) dur(e). 3. (decision, problem, task) difficile. 4. (rough - area of town) dangereux(euse). 5. (strict) sévère.

toughen ['tʌfn] vt 1. (character) endurcir. 2. (material) renforcer.

toupee ['tu:peɪ] n postiche m.

tour [tʊər] ◆ n 1. (journey) voyage m; (by pop group etc) tournée f. 2. (of town, museum) visite f, tour m. ◆ vt visiter.

touring ['tʊərɪŋ] n tourisme m.

tourism ['tʊərɪzm] n tourisme m.

tourist ['tʊərɪst] n touriste mf.

tourist (information) office n

office m de tourisme.

tournament ['tɔ:nəmənt] n tournoi m.

tour operator n voyagiste m.

tousle ['taʊzl] vt ébouriffer.

tout [taʊt] ◆ n revendeur m de billets. ◆ vt (tickets) revendre; (goods) vendre. ◆ vi: **to ~ for trade** racoler les clients.

tow [təʊ] ◆ n: **'on ~'** Br 'véhicule en remorque'. ◆ vt remorquer.

towards Br [tə'wɔ:dz], **toward** Am [tə'wɔ:d] prep 1. (gen) vers; (movement) vers, en direction de. 2. (in attitude) envers. 3. (for the purpose of) pour.

towel ['taʊəl] n serviette f; (tea towel) torchon m.

towelling Br, **toweling** Am ['taʊəlɪŋ] n (U) tissu m éponge.

towel rail n porte-serviettes m inv.

tower ['taʊər] ◆ n tour f. ◆ vi s'élever; **to ~ over sb/sthg** dominer qqn/qqch.

tower block n Br tour f.

towering ['taʊərɪŋ] adj imposant(e).

town [taʊn] n ville f; **to go out on the ~** faire la tournée des grands ducs; **to go to ~ on sthg** fig ne pas lésiner sur qqch.

town centre n centre-ville m.

town council n conseil m municipal.

town hall n mairie f.

town plan n plan m de ville.

town planning n urbanisme m.

township ['taʊnʃɪp] n 1. (in South Africa) township f. 2. (in US) ≃ canton m.

towpath ['təʊpɑ:θ, pl -pɑ:ðz] n chemin m de halage.

towrope ['təʊrəʊp] n câble m de remorquage.

tow truck n Am dépanneuse f.

toxic ['tɒksɪk] adj toxique.

toy [tɔɪ] n jouet m. ▶ **toy with** vt fus 1. (idea) caresser. 2. (coin etc) jouer avec; **to ~ with one's food** manger du bout des dents.

toy shop n magasin m de jouets.

trace [treɪs] ◆ n trace f. ◆ vt 1. (relatives, criminal) retrouver; (development, progress) suivre; (history, life) retracer. 2. (on paper) tracer.

tracing paper ['treɪsɪŋ-] n (U) papier-calque m.

track [træk] ◆ n 1. (path) chemin m. 2. (SPORT) piste f. 3. (RAIL) voie f ferrée. 4. (of animal, person) trace f. 5. (on record, tape) piste f. 6. phr: **to keep ~ of sb** rester en contact avec qqn; **to lose ~ of sb** perdre contact avec qqn; **to be on the right ~** être sur la bonne voie; **to be on the wrong ~** être sur la mauvaise piste. ◆ vt suivre la trace de. ▶ **track down** vt sep (criminal, animal) dépister; (object, address etc) retrouver.

track record n palmarès m.

tracksuit ['træksu:t] n survêtement m.

tract [trækt] n 1. (pamphlet) tract m. 2. (of land, forest) étendue f.

traction ['trækʃn] n (U) 1. (PHYSICS) traction f. 2. (MED): **in ~** en extension.

tractor ['træktər] n tracteur m.

trade [treɪd] ◆ n 1. (U) (commerce) commerce m. 2. (job) métier m; **by ~** de son état. ◆ vt (exchange): **to ~ sthg (for)** échanger qqch (contre). ◆ vi (COMM): **to ~ (with sb)** commercer (avec qqn). ▶ **trade in** vt sep (exchange) échanger, faire reprendre.

trade fair n exposition f commerciale.

trade-in n reprise f.

trademark ['treɪdmɑ:k] n 1. (COMM) marque f de fabrique. 2. fig (characteristic) marque f.

trade name n nom m de marque.

trader ['treɪdər] n marchand m, -e f, commerçant m, -e f.

tradesman ['treɪdzmən] (pl **-men** [-mən]) n commerçant m.

trade(s) union n Br syndicat m.

Trades Union Congress n Br: **the ~** la Confédération des syndicats britanniques.

trade(s) unionist [-'ju:njənɪst] n Br syndicaliste mf.

trading ['treɪdɪŋ] n (U) commerce m.

trading estate n Br zone f industrielle.

tradition [trə'dɪʃn] n tradition f.

traditional [trə'dɪʃənl] adj traditionnel(elle).

traffic ['træfɪk] (pt & pp **-ked**, cont **-king**) ◆ n (U) 1. (vehicles) circulation f. 2. (illegal trade): **~ (in)** trafic m (de). ◆ vi: **to ~ in** faire le trafic de.

traffic circle n Am rond-point m.

traffic jam n embouteillage m.

trafficker ['træfɪkər] n: **~ (in)** trafiquant m, -e f (de).

traffic lights npl feux mpl de signalisation.

traffic warden n Br contractuel m, -elle f.

tragedy ['trædʒədɪ] n tragédie f.

tragic ['trædʒɪk] adj tragique.

trail [treɪl] ◆ n 1. (path) sentier m. 2. (trace) piste f. ◆ vt 1. (drag) traîner. 2. (follow) suivre. ◆ vi 1. (drag, move slowly) traîner. 2. (SPORT) (lose): **to be ~ing**

être mené(e). ▶ **trail away, trail off** vi s'estomper.

trailer ['treɪlər] n 1. (vehicle - for luggage) remorque f; (- for living in) caravane f. 2. (CINEMA) bande-annonce f.

train [treɪn] ◆ n 1. (RAIL) train m. 2. (of dress) traîne f. ◆ vt 1. (teach): **to ~ sb to do sthg** apprendre à qqn à faire qqch. 2. (for job) former; **to ~ sb as/in** former qqn comme/dans. 3. (SPORT): **to ~ sb (for)** entraîner qqn (pour). 4. (gun, camera) braquer. ◆ vi 1. (for job): **to ~ (as)** recevoir OR faire une formation (de). 2. (SPORT): **to ~ (for)** s'entraîner (pour).

trained [treɪnd] adj formé(e).

trainee [treɪ'ni:] n stagiaire mf.

trainer ['treɪnər] n 1. (of animals) dresseur m, -euse f. 2. (SPORT) entraîneur m. ▶ **trainers** npl Br chaussures fpl de sport.

training ['treɪnɪŋ] n (U) 1. (for job): **~ (in)** formation f (de). 2. (SPORT) entraînement m.

training college n Br école f professionnelle.

training shoes npl Br chaussures fpl de sport.

train of thought n: **my/his ~** le fil de mes/ses pensées.

traipse [treɪps] vi traîner.

trait [treɪt] n trait m.

traitor ['treɪtər] n traître m.

trajectory [trə'dʒektərɪ] n trajectoire f.

tram [træm], **tramcar** ['træmkɑ:r] n Br tram m, tramway m.

tramp [træmp] ◆ n (homeless person) clochard m, -e f. ◆ vi marcher d'un pas lourd.

trample ['træmpl] vt piétiner.

trampoline ['træmpəli:n] n trampoline m.

trance [trɑ:ns] n transe f.

tranquil ['træŋkwɪl] adj tranquille.

tranquillizer Br, **tranquilizer** Am ['træŋkwɪlaɪzər] n tranquillisant m, calmant m.

transaction [træn'zækʃn] n transaction f.

transcend [træn'send] vt transcender.

transcript ['trænskrɪpt] n transcription f.

transfer [n 'trænsfɜ:r, vb træns'fɜ:r] ◆ n 1. (gen) transfert m; (of power) passation f; (of money) virement m. 2. (design) décalcomanie f. ◆ vt 1. (gen) transférer; (power) faire passer; (money) virer. 2. (employee) transférer, muter. ◆ vi être transféré.

transfix [træns'fɪks] vt: **to be ~ed with**

fear être paralysé(e) par la peur.

transform [træns'fɔːm] *vt*: **to ~ sb/sthg (into)** transformer qqn/qqch (en).

transfusion [træns'fjuːʒn] *n* transfusion *f*.

transient ['trænzɪənt] *adj* passager (ère).

transistor [træn'zɪstər] *n* transistor *m*.

transistor radio *n* transistor *m*.

transit ['trænsɪt] *n*: **in ~** en transit.

transition [træn'zɪʃn] *n* transition *f*.

transitive ['trænzɪtɪv] *adj* (GRAMM) transitif(ive).

transitory ['trænzɪtrɪ] *adj* transitoire.

translate [træns'leɪt] *vt* traduire.

translation [træns'leɪʃn] *n* traduction *f*.

translator [træns'leɪtər] *n* traducteur *m*, -trice *f*.

transmission [trænz'mɪʃn] *n* **1.** (gen) transmission *f*. **2.** (RADIO & TV) (programme) émission *f*.

transmit [trænz'mɪt] *vt* transmettre.

transmitter [trænz'mɪtər] *n* émetteur *m*.

transparency [trans'pærənsɪ] *n* (PHOT) diapositive *f*; (for overhead projector) transparent *m*.

transparent [træns'pærənt] *adj* transparent(e).

transpire [træn'spaɪər] *fml* ◆ *vt*: **it ~s that ...** on a appris que ... ◆ *vi* (happen) se passer, arriver.

transplant [*n* 'trænsplɑːnt, *vb* træns-'plɑːnt] ◆ *n* (MED) greffe *f*, transplantation *f*. ◆ *vt* **1.** (MED) greffer, transplanter. **2.** (seedlings) repiquer.

transport [*n* 'trænspɔːt, *vb* træn'spɔːt] ◆ *n* transport *m*. ◆ *vt* transporter.

transportation [ˌtrænspɔː'teɪʃn] *n* transport *m*.

transport cafe *n* Br restaurant *m* de routiers, routier *m*.

transpose [træns'pəuz] *vt* transposer.

trap [træp] ◆ *n* piège *m*. ◆ *vt* prendre au piège; **to be trapped** être coincé.

trapdoor [ˌtræp'dɔːr] *n* trappe *f*.

trapeze [trə'piːz] *n* trapèze *m*.

trappings ['træpɪŋz] *npl* signes *mpl* extérieurs.

trash [træʃ] *n* (U) **1.** Am (refuse) ordures *fpl*. **2.** *inf pej* (poor-quality thing) camelote *f*.

trashcan ['træʃkæn] *n* Am poubelle *f*.

traumatic [trɔː'mætɪk] *adj* traumatisant(e).

travel ['trævl] ◆ *n* (U) voyage *m*, voyages *mpl*. ◆ *vt* parcourir. ◆ *vi* **1.** (make journey) voyager. **2.** (move - current, signal) aller, passer; (- news) se répandre, circuler.

travel agency *n* agence *f* de voyages.

travel agent *n* agent *m* de voyages; **to/at the ~'s** à l'agence *f* de voyages.

traveller Br, **traveler** Am ['trævlər] *n* **1.** (person on journey) voyageur *m*, -euse *f*. **2.** (sales representative) représentant *m*.

traveller's cheque *n* chèque *m* de voyage.

travelling Br, **traveling** Am ['trævlɪŋ] *adj* **1.** (theatre, circus) ambulant(e). **2.** (clock, bag etc) de voyage; (allowance) de déplacement.

travelsick ['trævəlsɪk] *adj*: **to be ~** avoir le mal de la route/de l'air/de mer.

travesty ['trævəstɪ] *n* parodie *f*.

trawler ['trɔːlər] *n* chalutier *m*.

tray [treɪ] *n* plateau *m*.

treacherous ['tretʃərəs] *adj* traître (traîtresse).

treachery ['tretʃərɪ] *n* traîtrise *f*.

treacle ['triːkl] *n* Br mélasse *f*.

tread [tred] (*pt* **trod**, *pp* **trodden**) ◆ *n* **1.** (on tyre) bande *f* de roulement; (of shoe) semelle *f*. **2.** (way of walking) pas *m*; (sound) bruit *m* de pas. ◆ *vi*: **to ~ (on)** marcher (sur).

treason ['triːzn] *n* trahison *f*.

treasure ['treʒər] ◆ *n* trésor *m*. ◆ *vt* (object) garder précieusement; (memory) chérir.

treasurer ['treʒərər] *n* trésorier *m*, -ère *f*.

treasury ['treʒərɪ] *n* (room) trésorerie *f*. ▶ **Treasury** *n*: **the Treasury** le ministère des Finances.

treat [triːt] ◆ *vt* **1.** (gen) traiter. **2.** (on special occasion): **to ~ sb to sthg** offrir OR payer qqch à qqn. ◆ *n* **1.** (gift) cadeau *m*. **2.** (delight) plaisir *m*.

treatise ['triːtɪz] *n*: **~ (on)** traité *m* (de).

treatment ['triːtmənt] *n* traitement *m*.

treaty ['triːtɪ] *n* traité *m*.

treble ['trebl] ◆ *adj* **1.** (MUS - voice) de soprano; (- recorder) aigu (aiguë). **2.** (triple) triple. ◆ *n* (on stereo control) aigu *m*; (boy singer) soprano *m*. ◆ *vt* & *vi* tripler.

treble clef *n* clef *f* de sol.

tree [triː] *n* **1.** (gen) arbre *m*. **2.** (COMPUT) arbre *m*, arborescence *f*.

treetop ['triːtɒp] *n* cime *f*.

tree-trunk *n* tronc *m* d'arbre.

trek [trek] *n* randonnée *f*.

trellis ['trelɪs] *n* treillis *m*.

tremble ['trembl] vi trembler.

tremendous [trɪ'mendəs] adj 1. (size, success, difference) énorme; (noise) terrible. 2. inf (really good) formidable.

tremor ['tremər] n tremblement m.

trench [trentʃ] n tranchée f.

trench coat n trench-coat m.

trend [trend] n (tendency) tendance f.

trendy ['trendɪ] inf adj branché(e), à la mode.

trepidation [ˌtrepɪ'deɪʃn] n fml: **in** OR **with ~** avec inquiétude.

trespass ['trespəs] vi (on land) entrer sans permission; **'no ~ing'** 'défense d'entrer'.

trespasser ['trespəsər] n intrus m, -e f; **'~s will be prosecuted'** 'défense d'entrer sous peine de poursuites'.

trestle ['tresl] n tréteau m.

trestle table n table f à tréteaux.

trial ['traɪəl] n 1. (JUR) procès m; **to be on ~ (for)** passer en justice (pour). 2. (test, experiment) essai m; **on ~** à l'essai; **by ~ and error** en tâtonnant. 3. (unpleasant experience) épreuve f.

triangle ['traɪæŋgl] n (gen) triangle m.

tribe [traɪb] n tribu f.

tribunal [traɪ'bjuːnl] n tribunal m.

tributary ['trɪbjutrɪ] n affluent m.

tribute ['trɪbjuːt] n tribut m, hommage m; **to pay ~** to payer tribut à, rendre hommage à; **to be a ~ to** sthg témoigner de qqch.

trice [traɪs] n: **in a ~** en un clin d'œil.

trick [trɪk] ◆ n 1. (to deceive) tour m, farce f; **to play a ~ on sb** jouer un tour à qqn. 2. (to entertain) tour m. 3. (knack) truc m; **that will do the ~** inf ça fera l'affaire. ◆ vt attraper, rouler; **to ~ sb into doing sthg** amener qqn à faire qqch (par la ruse).

trickery ['trɪkərɪ] n (U) ruse f.

trickle ['trɪkl] ◆ n (of liquid) filet m. ◆ vi (liquid) dégouliner; **to ~ in/out** (people) entrer/sortir par petits groupes.

tricky ['trɪkɪ] adj (difficult) difficile.

tricycle ['traɪsɪkl] n tricycle m.

tried [traɪd] adj: **~ and tested** (method, system) qui a fait ses preuves.

trifle ['traɪfl] n 1. Br (CULIN) = diplomate m. 2. (unimportant thing) bagatelle f. ▶ **a trifle** adv un peu, un tantinet.

trifling ['traɪflɪŋ] adj insignifiant(e).

trigger ['trɪgər] n (on gun) détente f, gâchette f. ▶ **trigger off** vt sep déclencher, provoquer.

trill [trɪl] n trille m.

trim [trɪm] ◆ adj 1. (neat and tidy) net (nette). 2. (slim) svelte. ◆ n (of hair) coupe f. ◆ vt 1. (cut - gen) couper; (- hedge) tailler. 2. (decorate): **to ~ sthg (with)** garnir OR orner qqch (de).

trimming ['trɪmɪŋ] n 1. (on clothing) parement m. 2. (CULIN) garniture f.

trinket ['trɪŋkɪt] n bibelot m.

trio ['triːəʊ] (pl -s) n trio m.

trip [trɪp] ◆ n 1. (journey) voyage m. 2. drugs sl trip m. ◆ vt (make stumble) faire un croche-pied à. ◆ vi (stumble): **to ~ (over)** trébucher (sur). ▶ **trip up** vt sep (make stumble) faire un croche-pied à.

tripe [traɪp] n (U) 1. (CULIN) tripe f. 2. inf (nonsense) bêtises fpl, idioties fpl.

triple ['trɪpl] ◆ adj triple. ◆ vt & vi tripler.

triple jump n: **the ~** le triple saut.

triplets ['trɪplɪts] npl triplés mpl, triplées fpl.

triplicate ['trɪplɪkət] n: **in ~** en trois exemplaires.

tripod ['traɪpɒd] n trépied m.

trite [traɪt] adj pej banal(e).

triumph ['traɪəmf] ◆ n triomphe m. ◆ vi: **to ~ (over)** triompher (de).

trivia ['trɪvɪə] n (U) (trifles) vétilles fpl, riens mpl.

trivial ['trɪvɪəl] adj insignifiant(e).

trod [trɒd] pt → **tread**.

trodden ['trɒdn] pp → **tread**.

trolley ['trɒlɪ] (pl **trolleys**) n 1. Br (for shopping, luggage) chariot m, Caddie® m. 2. Br (for food, drinks) chariot m, table f roulante. 3. Am (tram) tramway m, tram m.

trombone [trɒm'bəʊn] n (MUS) trombone m.

troop [truːp] ◆ n bande f, troupe f. ◆ vi: **to ~ in/out/off** entrer/sortir/partir en groupe. ▶ **troops** npl troupes fpl.

trophy ['trəʊfɪ] n trophée m.

tropical ['trɒpɪkl] adj tropical(e).

tropics ['trɒpɪks] npl: **the ~** les tropiques mpl.

trot [trɒt] ◆ n (of horse) trot m. ◆ vi trotter. ▶ **on the trot** adv inf de suite, d'affilée.

trouble ['trʌbl] ◆ n (U) 1. (difficulty) problème m, difficulté f; **to be in ~** avoir des ennuis. 2. (bother) peine f, mal m; **to take the ~ to do sthg** se donner la peine de faire qqch; **it's no ~!** ça ne me dérange pas! 3. (pain, illness) mal m, ennui m. 4. (fighting) bagarre f; (POL) troubles mpl, conflits mpl. ◆ vt 1. (worry, upset) peiner, troubler. 2. (bother) déranger. 3. (give pain to) faire mal à.

▶ **troubles** *npl* **1.** (*worries*) ennuis *mpl*. **2.** (POL) troubles *mpl*, conflits *mpl*.

troubled ['trʌbld] *adj* **1.** (*worried*) inquiet(ète). **2.** (*disturbed - period*) de troubles, agité(e); (- *country*) qui connaît une période de troubles.

troublemaker ['trʌbl,meɪkər] *n* fauteur *m*, -trice *f* de troubles.

troubleshooter ['trʌbl,ʃuːtər] *n* expert *m*, spécialiste *mf*.

troublesome ['trʌblsəm] *adj* (*job*) pénible; (*cold*) gênant(e); (*back, knee*) qui fait souffrir.

trough [trɒf] *n* **1.** (*for animals - with water*) abreuvoir *m*; (- *with food*) auge *f*. **2.** (*low point - of wave*) creux *m*; *fig* point *m* bas.

troupe [truːp] *n* troupe *f*.

trousers ['trauzəz] *npl* pantalon *m*.

trout [traut] (*pl inv* OR **-s**) *n* truite *f*.

trowel ['trauəl] *n* (*for gardening*) déplantoir *m*; (*for cement, plaster*) truelle *f*.

truant ['truːənt] *n* (*child*) élève *mf* absentéiste; **to play ~** faire l'école buissonnière.

truce [truːs] *n* trêve *f*.

truck [trʌk] *n* **1.** (*lorry*) camion *m*. **2.** (RAIL) wagon *m* à plate-forme.

truck driver *n* routier *m*.

trucker ['trʌkər] *n* Am routier *m*.

truck farm *n* Am jardin *m* maraîcher.

truculent ['trʌkjulənt] *adj* agressif (ive).

trudge [trʌdʒ] *vi* marcher péniblement.

true ['truː] *adj* **1.** (*factual*) vrai(e); **to come ~** se réaliser. **2.** (*genuine*) vrai(e), authentique; **~ love** le grand amour. **3.** (*exact*) exact(e). **4.** (*faithful*) fidèle, loyal(e).

truffle ['trʌfl] *n* truffe *f*.

truly ['truːlɪ] *adv* **1.** (*gen*) vraiment. **2.** (*sincerely*) vraiment, sincèrement. **3.** *phr:* **yours ~** (*at end of letter*) croyez à l'expression de mes sentiments distingués.

trump [trʌmp] *n* atout *m*.

trumped-up ['trʌmpt-] *adj pej* inventé(e) de toutes pièces.

trumpet ['trʌmpɪt] *n* trompette *f*.

truncheon ['trʌntʃən] *n* matraque *f*.

trundle ['trʌndl] *vi* aller lentement.

trunk [trʌŋk] *n* **1.** (*of tree, person*) tronc *m*. **2.** (*of elephant*) trompe *f*. **3.** (*box*) malle *f*. **4.** Am (*of car*) coffre *m*. ▶ **trunks** *npl* maillot *m* de bain.

trunk call *n* Br communication *f* interurbaine.

trunk road *n* (route *f*) nationale *f*.

truss [trʌs] *n* (MED) bandage *m* herniaire.

trust [trʌst] ◆ *vt* **1.** (*have confidence in*) avoir confiance en, se fier à; **to ~ sb to do sthg** compter sur qqn pour faire qqch. **2.** (*entrust*): **to ~ sb with sthg** confier qqch à qqn. **3.** *fml* (*hope*): **to ~ (that)** ... espérer que ... ◆ *n* **1.** (U) (*faith*): **~ (in sb/sthg)** confiance *f* (en qqn/dans qqch). **2.** (U) (*responsibility*) responsabilité *f*. **3.** (FIN): **in ~** en dépôt. **4.** (COMM) trust *m*.

trusted ['trʌstɪd] *adj* (*person*) de confiance; (*method*) qui a fait ses preuves.

trustee [trʌsˈtiː] *n* (FIN & JUR) fidéicommissaire *mf*; (*of institution*) administrateur *m*, -trice *f*.

trust fund *n* fonds *m* en fidéicommis.

trusting ['trʌstɪŋ] *adj* confiant(e).

trustworthy ['trʌst,wɜːðɪ] *adj* digne de confiance.

truth [truːθ] *n* vérité *f*; **in (all) ~** à dire vrai, en vérité.

truthful ['truːθful] *adj* (*person, reply*) honnête; (*story*) véridique.

try [traɪ] ◆ *vt* **1.** (*attempt, test*) essayer; (*food, drink*) goûter; **to ~ to do sthg** essayer de faire qqch. **2.** (JUR) juger. **3.** (*put to the test*) éprouver, mettre à l'épreuve. ◆ *vi* essayer; **to ~ for sthg** essayer d'obtenir qqch. ◆ *n* **1.** (*attempt*) essai *m*, tentative *f*; **to give sthg a ~** essayer qqch. **2.** (RUGBY) essai *m*. ▶ **try on** *vt sep* (*clothes*) essayer. ▶ **try out** *vt sep* essayer.

trying ['traɪɪŋ] *adj* pénible, éprouvant(e).

T-shirt *n* tee-shirt *m*.

T-square *n* té *m*.

tub [tʌb] *n* **1.** (*of ice cream - large*) boîte *f*; (- *small*) petit pot *m*; (*of margarine*) barquette *f*. **2.** (*bath*) baignoire *f*.

tubby ['tʌbɪ] *adj inf* rondouillard(e), boulot(otte).

tube [tjuːb] *n* **1.** (*cylinder, container*) tube *m*. **2.** Br (*underground train*) métro *m*; **the ~** (*system*) le métro; **by ~** en métro.

tuberculosis [tjuː,bɜːkjuˈləusɪs] *n* tuberculose *f*.

tubing ['tjuːbɪŋ] *n* (U) tubes *mpl*, tuyaux *mpl*.

tubular ['tjuːbjulər] *adj* tubulaire.

TUC *n abbr of* **Trades Union Congress**.

tuck [tʌk] *vt* (*place neatly*) ranger. ▶ **tuck away** *vt sep* (*store*) mettre de

côté OR en lieu sûr. ▶ **tuck in** ◆ vt
1. (child, patient) border. 2. (clothes) rentrer. ◆ vi inf boulotter. ▶ **tuck up** vt sep
(child, patient) border.

tuck shop n Br (at school) petite boutique
qui vend des bonbons et des gâteaux.

Tuesday ['tju:zdɪ] n mardi m; see also
Saturday.

tuft [tʌft] n touffe f.

tug [tʌg] ◆ n 1. (pull): **to give sthg a ~**
tirer sur qqch. 2. (boat) remorqueur m.
◆ vt tirer. ◆ vi: **to ~ (at)** tirer (sur).

tug-of-war n lutte f de traction à la
corde; fig lutte acharnée.

tuition [tju:'ɪʃn] n (U) cours mpl.

tulip ['tju:lɪp] n tulipe f.

tumble ['tʌmbl] ◆ vi 1. (person)
tomber, faire une chute; (water) tomber
en cascades. 2. fig (prices) tomber,
chuter. ◆ n chute f, culbute f. ▶ **tumble to** vt fus Br inf piger.

tumbledown ['tʌmbldaʊn] adj déla-
bré(e), qui tombe en ruines.

tumble-dryer [-,draɪər] n sèche-linge
m inv.

tumbler ['tʌmblər] n (glass) verre m
(droit).

tummy ['tʌmɪ] n inf ventre m.

tumour Br, **tumor** Am ['tju:mər] n
tumeur f.

tuna [Br 'tju:nə, Am 'tu:nə] (pl inv OR **-s**)
n thon m.

tune [tju:n] ◆ n 1. (song, melody) air m.
2. (harmony): **in ~** (instrument) accor-
dé(e), juste; (play, sing) juste; **out of ~**
(instrument) mal accordé(e); (play, sing)
faux; **to be in/out of ~ (with)** fig être en
accord/désaccord (avec). ◆ vt 1. (MUS)
accorder. 2. (RADIO & TV) régler. 3.
(engine) régler. ▶ **tune in** vi (RADIO & TV)
être à l'écoute; **to ~ in to** se mettre sur.
▶ **tune up** vi (MUS) accorder son instrument.

tuneful ['tju:nfʊl] adj mélodieux
(euse).

tuner ['tju:nər] n 1. (RADIO & TV) syn-
toniseur m, tuner m. 2. (MUS) (person)
accordeur m.

tunic ['tju:nɪk] n tunique f.

tuning fork ['tju:nɪŋ-] n diapason m.

Tunisia [tju:'nɪzɪə] n Tunisie f.

tunnel ['tʌnl] ◆ n tunnel m. ◆ vi faire
OR creuser un tunnel.

turban ['tɜ:bən] n turban m.

turbine ['tɜ:baɪn] n turbine f.

turbocharged ['tɜ:bəʊtʃɑ:dʒd] adj
turbo (inv).

turbulence ['tɜ:bjʊləns] n (U) 1. (in air,

water) turbulence f. 2. fig (unrest) agitation f.

turbulent ['tɜ:bjʊlənt] adj 1. (air, water)
agité(e). 2. fig (disorderly) tumultueux
(euse), agité(e).

tureen [tə'ri:n] n soupière f.

turf [tɜ:f] (pl **-s** OR **turves**) ◆ n (grass surface) gazon m; (clod) motte f de gazon.
◆ vt gazonner. ▶ **turf out** vt sep Br inf
(person) virer; (old clothes) balancer,
bazarder.

turgid ['tɜ:dʒɪd] adj fml (style, writing)
pompeux(euse), ampoulé(e).

Turk [tɜ:k] n Turc m, Turque f.

turkey ['tɜ:kɪ] (pl **turkeys**) n dinde f.

Turkey ['tɜ:kɪ] n Turquie f.

Turkish ['tɜ:kɪʃ] ◆ adj turc (turque).
◆ n (language) turc m. ◆ npl: **the ~** les
Turcs mpl.

Turkish delight n loukoum m.

turmoil ['tɜ:mɔɪl] n agitation f, trouble
m.

turn ['tɜ:n] ◆ n 1. (in road) virage m,
tournant m; (in river) méandre m.
2. (revolution, twist) tour m. 3. (change)
tournure f, tour m. 4. (in game): **it's my ~** c'est (à) mon tour; **in ~** tour à
tour, chacun (à) son tour. 5. (perfor-
mance) numéro m. 6. (MED) crise f,
attaque f. 7. phr: **to do sb a good ~** rendre (un) service à qqn. ◆ vt 1. (gen)
tourner; (omelette, steak etc) retourner; **to
~ sthg inside out** retourner qqch; **to ~
one's thoughts/attention to sthg** tourner
ses pensées/son attention vers qqch.
2. (change): **to ~ sthg into** changer qqch
en. 3. (become): **to ~ red** rougir. ◆ vi
1. (gen) tourner; (person) se tourner, se
retourner. 2. (in book): **to ~ to a page** se
reporter OR aller à une page. 3. (for consolation): **to ~ to sb/sthg** se tourner vers
qqn/qqch. 4. (change): **to ~ into** se
changer en, se transformer en. ▶ **turn
around** = **turn round**. ▶ **turn away**
◆ vt sep (refuse entry to) refuser. ◆ vi se
détourner. ▶ **turn back** ◆ vt sep (sheets)
replier; (person, vehicle) refouler. ◆ vi
rebrousser chemin. ▶ **turn down** vt
sep 1. (reject) rejeter, refuser. 2. (radio,
volume, gas) baisser. ▶ **turn in** vi inf (go
to bed) se pieuter. ▶ **turn off** ◆ vt fus
(road, path) quitter. ◆ vt sep (radio, TV,
engine, gas) éteindre; (tap) fermer. ◆ vi
(leave path, road) tourner. ▶ **turn on** ◆ vt
sep 1. (radio, TV, engine, gas) allumer; (tap)
ouvrir; **to ~ the light on** allumer la
lumière. 2. inf (excite sexually) exciter.
◆ vt fus (attack) attaquer. ▶ **turn out**

◆ vt sep 1. (light, gas fire) éteindre. 2. (empty - pocket, bag) retourner, vider. ◆ vt fus: **to ~ out to be** s'avérer; **it ~s out that ...** il s'avère OR se trouve que ... ◆ vi 1. (end up) finir. 2. (arrive - person) venir. ▶ **turn over** ◆ vt sep 1. (playing card, stone) retourner; (page) tourner. 2. (consider) retourner dans sa tête. 3. (hand over) rendre, remettre. ◆ vi 1. (roll over) se retourner. 2. Br (TV) changer de chaîne. ▶ **turn round** ◆ vt sep 1. (reverse) retourner. 2. (wheel, words) tourner. ◆ vi se retourner. ▶ **turn up** ◆ vt sep (TV, radio) mettre plus fort; (gas) monter. ◆ vi 1. (arrive - person) se pointer. 2. (be found - person, object) être retrouvé; (- opportunity) se présenter.

turning ['tɜːnɪŋ] n (off road) route f latérale.

turning point n tournant m, moment m décisif.

turnip ['tɜːnɪp] n navet m.

turnout ['tɜːnaʊt] n (at election) taux m de participation; (at meeting) assistance f.

turnover ['tɜːnˌəʊvə'] n (U) 1. (of personnel) renouvellement m. 2. (FIN) chiffre m d'affaires.

turnpike ['tɜːnpaɪk] n Am autoroute f à péage.

turnstile ['tɜːnstaɪl] n tourniquet m.

turntable ['tɜːnˌteɪbl] n platine f.

turn-up n Br (on trousers) revers m inv; **a ~ for the books** inf une sacrée surprise.

turpentine ['tɜːpəntaɪn] n térébenthine f.

turquoise ['tɜːkwɔɪz] ◆ adj turquoise (inv). ◆ n 1. (mineral, gem) turquoise f. 2. (colour) turquoise m.

turret ['tʌrɪt] n tourelle f.

turtle ['tɜːtl] n (pl inv OR -s) n tortue f de mer.

turtleneck ['tɜːtlnek] n (garment) pull m à col montant; (neck) col m montant.

turves [tɜːvz] Br pl → **turf**.

tusk [tʌsk] n défense f.

tussle ['tʌsl] ◆ n lutte f. ◆ vi se battre; **to ~ over sthg** se disputer qqch.

tutor ['tjuːtə'] n 1. (private) professeur m particulier. 2. (UNIV) directeur m, -trice f d'études.

tutorial [tjuːˈtɔːrɪəl] n travaux mpl dirigés.

tuxedo [tʌkˈsiːdəʊ] (pl -s) n smoking m.

TV (abbr of **television**) n 1. (U) (medium, industry) télé f. 2. (apparatus) (poste m de) télé f.

twang [twæŋ] n 1. (sound) bruit m de pincement. 2. (accent) nasillement m.

tweed [twiːd] n tweed m.

tweezers ['twiːzəz] npl pince f à épiler.

twelfth [twelfθ] num douzième; see also sixth.

twelve [twelv] num douze; see also six.

twentieth ['twentɪəθ] num vingtième; see also sixth.

twenty ['twentɪ] num vingt; see also six.

twice [twaɪs] adv deux fois; **~ a day** deux fois par jour; **he earns ~ as much as me** il gagne deux fois plus que moi OR le double de moi; **~ as big** deux fois plus grand; **~ my size/age** le double de ma taille/mon âge.

twiddle ['twɪdl] ◆ vt jouer avec. ◆ vi: **to ~ with sthg** jouer avec qqch.

twig [twɪg] n brindille f, petite branche f.

twilight ['twaɪlaɪt] n crépuscule m.

twin [twɪn] ◆ adj jumeau (jumelle); (town) jumelé(e); **~ beds** lits mpl jumeaux. ◆ n jumeau m, jumelle f.

twin-bedded [-'bedɪd] adj à deux lits.

twine [twaɪn] ◆ n (U) ficelle f. ◆ vt: **to ~ sthg round sthg** enrouler qqch autour de qqch.

twinge [twɪndʒ] n (of pain) élancement m; **a ~ of guilt** un remords.

twinkle ['twɪŋkl] vi (star, lights) scintiller; (eyes) briller, pétiller.

twin room n chambre f à deux lits.

twin town n ville f jumelée.

twirl [twɜːl] ◆ vt faire tourner. ◆ vi tournoyer.

twist [twɪst] ◆ n 1. (in road) zigzag m, tournant m; (in river) méandre m, coude m; (in rope) entortillement m. 2. fig (in plot) tour m. ◆ vt 1. (wind, curl) entortiller. 2. (contort) tordre. 3. (turn) tourner; (lid - to open) dévisser; (- to close) visser. 4. (sprain): **to ~ one's ankle** se tordre OR se fouler la cheville. 5. (words, meaning) déformer. ◆ vi 1. (river, path) zigzaguer. 2. (be contorted) se tordre. 3. (turn): **to ~ round** se retourner.

twit [twɪt] n Br inf crétin m, -e f.

twitch [twɪtʃ] ◆ n tic m. ◆ vi (muscle, eye, face) se contracter.

two [tuː] num deux; **in ~** en deux; see also six.

two-door adj (car) à deux portes.

twofaced [ˌtuːˈfeɪst] adj pej fourbe.

twofold ['tuːfəʊld] ◆ adj double. ◆ adv doublement; **to increase ~** doubler.

two-piece adj: **~ swimsuit** deux-pièces

m inv; ~ **suit** (*for man*) costume *m* (deux-pièces).

twosome ['tuːsəm] *n inf* couple *m*.

two-thirds *npl* (*fraction*) deux tiers *mpl*.

two-way *adj* (*traffic, trade*) dans les deux sens.

tycoon [taɪˈkuːn] *n* magnat *m*.

type [taɪp] ◆ *n* **1.** (*sort, kind*) genre *m*, sorte *f*; (*model*) modèle *m*; (*in classification*) type *m*. **2.** (U) (TYPO) caractères *mpl*. ◆ *vt* (*letter, reply*) taper (à la machine). ◆ *vi* taper (à la machine).

typecast ['taɪpkɑːst] (*pt & pp* typecast) *vt*: **to be ~ as** être cantonné(e) dans le rôle de; **to be ~** être cantonné(e) aux mêmes rôles.

typeface ['taɪpfeɪs] *n* (TYPO) œil *m* de caractère.

typescript ['taɪpskrɪpt] *n* texte *m* dactylographié.

typeset ['taɪpset] (*pt & pp* typeset) *vt* composer.

typewriter ['taɪpˌraɪtər] *n* machine *f* à écrire.

typhoid (fever) ['taɪfɔɪd-] *n* typhoïde *f*.

typhoon [taɪˈfuːn] *n* typhon *m*.

typical ['tɪpɪkl] *adj*: ~ **(of)** typique (de), caractéristique (de); **that's ~ (of him/her)!** c'est bien de lui/d'elle!

typically ['tɪpɪklɪ] *adv* typiquement.

typing ['taɪpɪŋ] *n* dactylo *f*, dactylographie *f*.

typist ['taɪpɪst] *n* dactylo *mf*, dactylographe *mf*.

typography [taɪˈpɒɡrəfɪ] *n* typographie *f*.

tyranny ['tɪrənɪ] *n* tyrannie *f*.

tyrant ['taɪrənt] *n* tyran *m*.

tyre *Br*, **tire** *Am* ['taɪər] *n* pneu *m*.

tyre pressure *n* pression *f* (de gonflage).

U

u (*pl* u's OR us), **U** (*pl* U's OR Us) [juː] *n* (*letter*) u *m inv*, U *m inv*.

U-bend *n* siphon *m*.

udder ['ʌdər] *n* mamelle *f*.

UFO (*abbr of* **unidentified flying object**) *n* OVNI *m*, ovni *m*.

Uganda [juːˈɡændə] *n* Ouganda *m*.

ugh [ʌɡ] *excl* pouah!, beurk!

ugly ['ʌɡlɪ] *adj* **1.** (*unattractive*) laid(e). **2.** *fig* (*unpleasant*) pénible, désagréable.

UHF (*abbr of* **ultra-high frequency**) *n* UHF.

UK (*abbr of* **United Kingdom**) *n* Royaume-Uni *m*, R.U. *m*.

Ukraine [juːˈkreɪn] *n*: **the ~** l'Ukraine *f*.

ulcer ['ʌlsər] *n* ulcère *m*.

ulcerated ['ʌlsəreɪtɪd] *adj* ulcéré(e).

Ulster ['ʌlstər] *n* Ulster *m*.

ulterior [ʌlˈtɪərɪər] *adj*: ~ **motive** arrière-pensée *f*.

ultimata [ʌltɪˈmeɪtə] *pl* → **ultimatum**.

ultimate ['ʌltɪmət] ◆ *adj* **1.** (*final*) final(e), ultime. **2.** (*most powerful*) ultime, suprême. ◆ *n*: **the ~ in** le fin du fin dans.

ultimately ['ʌltɪmətlɪ] *adv* (*finally*) finalement.

ultimatum [ʌltɪˈmeɪtəm] (*pl* -**tums** OR -**ta** [-tə]) *n* ultimatum *m*.

ultrasound ['ʌltrəsaʊnd] *n* (U) ultrasons *mpl*.

ultraviolet [ʌltrəˈvaɪələt] *adj* ultraviolet(ette).

umbilical cord [ʌmˈbɪlɪkl-] *n* cordon *m* ombilical.

umbrella [ʌmˈbrelə] ◆ *n* (*portable*) parapluie *m*; (*fixed*) parasol *m*. ◆ *adj* (*organization*) qui en regroupe plusieurs autres.

umpire ['ʌmpaɪər] ◆ *n* arbitre *m*. ◆ *vt* arbitrer.

umpteen [ʌmpˈtiːn] *num adj inf* je ne sais combien de.

umpteenth [ʌmpˈtiːnθ] *num adj inf* énième.

UN (*abbr of* **United Nations**) *n*: **the ~** l'ONU *f*, l'Onu *f*.

unabated [ʌnəˈbeɪtɪd] *adj*: **the rain continued ~** la pluie continua de tomber sans répit.

unable [ʌnˈeɪbl] *adj*: **to be ~ to do sthg** ne pas pouvoir faire qqch, être incapable de faire qqch.

unacceptable [ʌnəkˈseptəbl] *adj* inacceptable.

unaccompanied [ʌnəˈkʌmpənɪd] *adj* **1.** (*child*) non accompagné(e); (*luggage*) sans surveillance. **2.** (*song*) a cappella, sans accompagnement.

unaccountably [ʌnəˈkaʊntəblɪ] *adv* (*inexplicably*) de façon inexplicable, inexplicablement.

unaccounted [ʌnəˈkaʊntɪd] *adj*: **to be ~ for** manquer.

unaccustomed [ˌʌnəˈkʌstəmd] adj (unused): **to be ~ to sthg/to doing sthg** ne pas être habitué(e) à qqch/à faire qqch.

unadulterated [ˌʌnəˈdʌltəreɪtɪd] adj 1. (unspoilt - wine) non frelaté(e); (- food) naturel(elle). 2. (absolute - joy) sans mélange; (- nonsense, truth) pur et simple (pure et simple).

unanimous [juːˈnænɪməs] adj unanime.

unanimously [juːˈnænɪməslɪ] adv à l'unanimité.

unanswered [ˌʌnˈɑːnsəd] adj qui reste sans réponse.

unappetizing, -ising [ˌʌnˈæpɪtaɪzɪŋ] adj peu appétissant(e).

unarmed [ˌʌnˈɑːmd] adj non armé(e).

unarmed combat n combat m sans armes.

unashamed [ˌʌnəˈʃeɪmd] adj (luxury) insolent(e); (liar, lie) effronté(e), éhonté(e).

unassuming [ˌʌnəˈsjuːmɪŋ] adj modeste, effacé(e).

unattached [ˌʌnəˈtætʃt] adj 1. (not fastened, linked): **~ (to)** indépendant(e) (de). 2. (without partner) libre, sans attaches.

unattended [ˌʌnəˈtendɪd] adj (luggage, shop) sans surveillance; (child) seul(e).

unattractive [ˌʌnəˈtræktɪv] adj 1. (not beautiful) peu attrayant(e), peu séduisant(e). 2. (not pleasant) déplaisant(e).

unauthorized, -ised [ˌʌnˈɔːθəraɪzd] adj non autorisé(e).

unavailable [ˌʌnəˈveɪləbl] adj qui n'est pas disponible, indisponible.

unavoidable [ˌʌnəˈvɔɪdəbl] adj inévitable.

unaware [ˌʌnəˈweər] adj ignorant(e), inconscient(e); **to be ~ of sthg** ne pas avoir conscience de qqch, ignorer qqch.

unawares [ˌʌnəˈweəz] adv: **to catch OR take sb ~** prendre qqn au dépourvu.

unbalanced [ˌʌnˈbælənst] adj 1. (biased) tendancieux(euse), partial(e). 2. (deranged) déséquilibré(e).

unbearable [ʌnˈbeərəbl] adj insupportable.

unbeatable [ʌnˈbiːtəbl] adj imbattable.

unbeknown(st) [ˌʌnbɪˈnəʊn(st)] adv: **~ to** à l'insu de.

unbelievable [ˌʌnbɪˈliːvəbl] adj incroyable.

unbending [ʌnˈbendɪŋ] adj inflexible, intransigeant(e).

unbia(s)sed [ʌnˈbaɪəst] adj impartial(e).

unborn [ʌnˈbɔːn] adj (child) qui n'est pas encore né(e).

unbreakable [ʌnˈbreɪkəbl] adj incassable.

unbridled [ʌnˈbraɪdld] adj effréné(e), débridé(e).

unbutton [ʌnˈbʌtn] vt déboutonner.

uncalled-for [ʌnˈkɔːld-] adj (remark) déplacé(e); (criticism) injustifié(e).

uncanny [ʌnˈkænɪ] adj étrange, mystérieux(euse); (resemblance) troublant(e).

unceasing [ʌnˈsiːsɪŋ] adj fml incessant(e), continuel(elle).

unceremonious [ˈʌnˌserɪˈməʊnjəs] adj brusque.

uncertain [ʌnˈsɜːtn] adj incertain(e); **in no ~ terms** sans mâcher ses mots.

unchanged [ˌʌnˈtʃeɪndʒd] adj inchangé(e).

unchecked [ˌʌnˈtʃekt] adj non maîtrisé(e), sans frein.

uncivilized, -ised [ˌʌnˈsɪvɪlaɪzd] adj non civilisé(e), barbare.

uncle [ˈʌŋkl] n oncle m.

unclear [ˌʌnˈklɪər] adj 1. (message, meaning, motive) qui n'est pas clair(e). 2. (uncertain - person, future) incertain(e).

uncomfortable [ʌnˈkʌmftəbl] adj 1. (shoes, chair, clothes etc) inconfortable; fig (fact, truth) désagréable. 2. (person - physically) qui n'est pas à l'aise; (- ill at ease) mal à l'aise.

uncommon [ʌnˈkɒmən] adj 1. (rare) rare. 2. fml (extreme) extraordinaire.

uncompromising [ʌnˈkɒmprəmaɪzɪŋ] adj intransigeant(e).

unconcerned [ˌʌnkənˈsɜːnd] adj (not anxious) qui ne s'inquiète pas.

unconditional [ˌʌnkənˈdɪʃənl] adj inconditionnel(elle).

unconscious [ʌnˈkɒnʃəs] ♦ adj 1. (having lost consciousness) sans connaissance. 2. fig (unaware): **to be ~ of** ne pas avoir conscience de, ne pas se rendre compte de. 3. (unnoticed - desires, feelings) inconscient(e). ♦ n (PSYCH) inconscient m.

unconsciously [ʌnˈkɒnʃəslɪ] adv inconsciemment.

uncontrollable [ˌʌnkənˈtrəʊləbl] adj 1. (unrestrainable - emotion, urge) irrépressible, irrésistible; (- increase, epidemic) qui ne peut être enrayé(e). 2. (un-

manageable - person) impossible, difficile.

unconventional [ˌʌnkən'venʃənl] *adj* peu conventionnel(elle), original(e).

unconvinced [ˌʌnkən'vɪnst] *adj* qui n'est pas convaincu(e), sceptique.

uncouth [ʌn'kuːθ] *adj* grossier(ère).

uncover [ʌn'kʌvəʳ] *vt* découvrir.

undecided [ˌʌndɪ'saɪdɪd] *adj* (*person*) indécis(e), irrésolu(e); (*issue*) indécis(e).

undeniable [ˌʌndɪ'naɪəbl] *adj* indéniable, incontestable.

under ['ʌndəʳ] ◆ *prep* 1. (*gen*) sous. 2. (*less than*) moins de; **children ~ five** les enfants de moins de cinq ans. 3. (*subject to - effect, influence*) sous; **~ the circumstances** dans ces circonstances, étant donné les circonstances; **to be ~ the impression that** ... avoir l'impression que ... 4. (*undergoing*): **~ discussion** en discussion; **~ consideration** à l'étude, à l'examen. 5. (*according to*) selon, conformément à. ◆ *adv* 1. (*underneath*) dessous; (*underwater*) sous l'eau; **to go ~** (*company*) couler, faire faillite. 2. (*less*) au-dessous.

underage [ˌʌndər'eɪdʒ] *adj* mineur(e).

undercarriage ['ʌndəˌkærɪdʒ] *n* train *m* d'atterrissage.

undercharge [ˌʌndə'tʃɑːdʒ] *vt* ne pas faire assez payer à.

underclothes ['ʌndəkləʊðz] *npl* sous-vêtements *mpl*.

undercoat ['ʌndəkəʊt] *n* (*of paint*) couche *f* de fond.

undercover ['ʌndəˌkʌvəʳ] *adj* secret (ète).

undercurrent ['ʌndəˌkʌrənt] *n* fig (*tendency*) courant *m* sous-jacent.

undercut [ˌʌndə'kʌt] (*pt & pp* **undercut**) *vt* (*in price*) vendre moins cher que.

underdeveloped [ˌʌndədɪ'veləpt] *adj* (*country*) sous-développé(e); (*person*) qui n'est pas complètement développé(e) OR formé(e).

underdog ['ʌndədɒg] *n*: **the ~** l'opprimé *m*; (SPORT) celui (celle) que l'on donne perdant(e).

underdone [ˌʌndə'dʌn] *adj* (*food*) pas assez cuit(e); (*steak*) saignant(e).

underestimate [ˌʌndər'estɪmeɪt] *vt* sous-estimer.

underexposed [ˌʌndərɪk'spəʊzd] *adj* (PHOT) sous-exposé(e).

underfoot [ˌʌndə'fʊt] *adv* sous les pieds.

undergo [ˌʌndə'gəʊ] (*pt* -**went**, *pp* -**gone** [-'gɒn]) *vt* subir; (*pain, difficulties*) éprouver.

undergraduate [ˌʌndə'grædjʊət] *n* étudiant *m*, -e *f* qui prépare la licence.

underground [*adj & n* 'ʌndəgraʊnd, *adv* ˌʌndə'graʊnd] ◆ *adj* 1. (*below the ground*) souterrain(e). 2. fig (*secret*) clandestin(e). ◆ *adv*: **to go/be forced ~** entrer dans la clandestinité. ◆ *n* 1. Br (*subway*) métro *m*. 2. (*activist movement*) résistance *f*.

undergrowth ['ʌndəgrəʊθ] *n* (U) sous-bois *m inv*.

underhand [ˌʌndə'hænd] *adj* sournois(e), en dessous.

underline [ˌʌndə'laɪn] *vt* souligner.

underlying [ˌʌndə'laɪɪŋ] *adj* sous-jacent(e).

undermine [ˌʌndə'maɪn] *vt* fig (*weaken*) saper, ébranler.

underneath [ˌʌndə'niːθ] ◆ *prep* 1. (*beneath*) sous, au-dessous de. 2. (*in movements*) sous. ◆ *adv* 1. (*beneath*) en dessous, dessous. 2. fig (*fundamentally*) au fond. ◆ *inf* inf en dessous. ◆ *n* (*underside*): **the ~** le dessous.

underpaid ['ʌndəpeɪd] *adj* sous-payé(e).

underpants ['ʌndəpænts] *npl* slip *m*.

underpass ['ʌndəpɑːs] *n* (*for cars*) passage *m* inférieur; (*for pedestrians*) passage *m* souterrain.

underprivileged [ˌʌndə'prɪvɪlɪdʒd] *adj* défavorisé(e), déshérité(e).

underrated [ˌʌndə'reɪtɪd] *adj* sous-estimé(e).

undershirt ['ʌndəʃɜːt] *n* Am maillot *m* de corps.

underside ['ʌndəsaɪd] *n*: **the ~** le dessous.

underskirt ['ʌndəskɜːt] *n* jupon *m*.

understand [ˌʌndə'stænd] (*pt & pp* -**stood**) ◆ *vt* 1. (*gen*) comprendre. 2. fml (*be informed*): **I ~ (that)** ... je crois comprendre que ..., il paraît que ... ◆ *vi* comprendre.

understandable [ˌʌndə'stændəbl] *adj* compréhensible.

understanding [ˌʌndə'stændɪŋ] ◆ *n* 1. (*knowledge, sympathy*) compréhension *f*. 2. (*agreement*) accord *m*, arrangement *m*. ◆ *adj* (*sympathetic*) compréhensif (ive).

understatement [ˌʌndə'steɪtmənt] *n* 1. (*inadequate statement*) affirmation *f* en dessous de la vérité. 2. (U) (*quality of understating*) euphémisme *m*.

understood [ˌʌndə'stʊd] *pt & pp* → **understand**.

understudy ['ʌndə,stʌdɪ] n doublure f.

undertake [,ʌndə'teɪk] (pt **-took**, pp **-taken** [-'teɪkn]) vt **1.** (take on - gen) entreprendre; (- responsibility) assumer. **2.** (promise): **to ~ to do sthg** promettre de faire qqch, s'engager à faire qqch.

undertaker ['ʌndə,teɪkəʳ] n entrepreneur m des pompes funèbres.

undertaking [,ʌndə'teɪkɪŋ] n **1.** (task) entreprise f. **2.** (promise) promesse f.

undertone ['ʌndətəʊn] n **1.** (quiet voice) voix f basse. **2.** (vague feeling) courant m.

undertook [,ʌndə'tʊk] pt → **undertake**.

underwater [,ʌndə'wɔːtəʳ] ◆ adj sous-marin(e). ◆ adv sous l'eau.

underwear ['ʌndəweəʳ] n (U) sous-vêtements mpl.

underwent [,ʌndə'went] pt → **undergo**.

underworld ['ʌndə,wɜːld] n (criminal society): **the ~** le milieu, la pègre.

underwriter ['ʌndə,raɪtəʳ] n assureur m.

undid [,ʌn'dɪd] pt → **undo**.

undies ['ʌndɪz] npl inf dessous mpl, lingerie f.

undisputed [,ʌndɪ'spjuːtɪd] adj incontesté(e).

undistinguished [,ʌndɪ'stɪŋgwɪʃt] adj médiocre, quelconque.

undo [,ʌn'duː] (pt **-did**, pp **-done**) vt **1.** (unfasten) défaire. **2.** (nullify) annuler, détruire.

undoing [,ʌn'duːɪŋ] n (U) fml perte f, ruine f.

undone [,ʌn'dʌn] ◆ pp → **undo**. ◆ adj **1.** (unfastened) défait(e). **2.** (task) non accompli(e).

undoubted [ʌn'daʊtɪd] adj indubitable, certain(e).

undoubtedly [ʌn'daʊtɪdlɪ] adv sans aucun doute.

undress [,ʌn'dres] ◆ vt déshabiller. ◆ vi se déshabiller.

undue [,ʌn'djuː] adj fml excessif(ive).

undulate ['ʌndjʊleɪt] vi onduler.

unduly [,ʌn'djuːlɪ] adv fml trop, excessivement.

unearth [,ʌn'ɜːθ] vt **1.** (dig up) déterrer. **2.** fig (discover) découvrir, dénicher.

unearthly [ʌn'ɜːθlɪ] adj inf (uncivilized - time of day) indu(e), impossible.

unease [ʌn'iːz] n (U) malaise m.

uneasy [ʌn'iːzɪ] adj (person, feeling) mal à l'aise, gêné(e); (peace) troublé(e), incertain(e); (silence) gêné(e).

uneconomic ['ʌn,iːkə'nɒmɪk] adj peu économique, peu rentable.

uneducated [,ʌn'edjʊkeɪtɪd] adj (person) sans instruction.

unemployed [,ʌnɪm'plɔɪd] ◆ adj au chômage, sans travail. ◆ npl: **the ~** sans-travail mpl, les chômeurs mpl.

unemployment [,ʌnɪm'plɔɪmənt] n chômage m.

unemployment benefit Br, **unemployment compensation** Am n allocation f de chômage.

unerring [,ʌn'ɜːrɪŋ] adj sûr(e), infaillible.

uneven [,ʌn'iːvn] adj **1.** (not flat - surface) inégal(e); (- ground) accidenté(e). **2.** (inconsistent) inégal(e). **3.** (unfair) injuste.

unexpected [,ʌnɪk'spektɪd] adj inattendu(e), imprévu(e).

unexpectedly [,ʌnɪk'spektɪdlɪ] adv subitement, d'une manière imprévue.

unfailing [ʌn'feɪlɪŋ] adj qui ne se dément pas, constant(e).

unfair [,ʌn'feəʳ] adj injuste.

unfaithful [,ʌn'feɪθfʊl] adj infidèle.

unfamiliar [,ʌnfə'mɪljəʳ] adj **1.** (not well-known) peu familier(ère), peu connu(e). **2.** (not acquainted): **to be ~ with sb/sthg** mal connaître qqn/qqch, ne pas connaître qqn/qqch.

unfashionable [,ʌn'fæʃnəbl] adj démodé(e), passé(e) de mode; (person) qui n'est plus à la mode.

unfasten [,ʌn'fɑːsn] vt défaire.

unfavourable Br, **unfavorable** Am [,ʌn'feɪvrəbl] adj défavorable.

unfeeling [ʌn'fiːlɪŋ] adj impitoyable, insensible.

unfinished [,ʌn'fɪnɪʃt] adj inachevé(e).

unfit [,ʌn'fɪt] adj **1.** (not in good health) qui n'est pas en forme. **2.** (not suitable): **~ (for)** impropre (à); (person) inapte (à).

unfold [ʌn'fəʊld] ◆ vt (map, newspaper) déplier. ◆ vi (become clear) se dérouler.

unforeseen [,ʌnfɔː'siːn] adj imprévu(e).

unforgettable [,ʌnfə'getəbl] adj inoubliable.

unforgivable [,ʌnfə'gɪvəbl] adj impardonnable.

unfortunate [ʌn'fɔːtʃnət] adj **1.** (unlucky) malheureux(euse), malchanceux(euse). **2.** (regrettable) regrettable, fâcheux(euse).

unfortunately [ʌn'fɔːtʃnətlɪ] adv malheureusement.

unfounded [ʌn'faʊndɪd] adj sans fondement, dénué(e) de tout fondement.

unfriendly [ʌn'frendlɪ] adj hostile, malveillant(e).

unfurnished [ʌn'fɜːnɪʃt] adj non meublé(e).

ungainly [ʌn'geɪnlɪ] adj gauche.

ungodly [ˌʌn'gɒdlɪ] adj inf (unreasonable) indu(e), impossible.

ungrateful [ʌn'greɪtfʊl] adj ingrat(e), peu reconnaissant(e).

unhappy [ʌn'hæpɪ] adj 1. (sad) triste, malheureux(euse). 2. (uneasy): **to be ~ (with** OR **about)** être inquiet(ète) (au sujet de). 3. (unfortunate) malheureux (euse), regrettable.

unharmed [ʌn'hɑːmd] adj indemne, sain et sauf (saine et sauve).

unhealthy [ʌn'helθɪ] adj 1. (person, skin) maladif(ive); (conditions, place) insalubre, malsain(e); (habit) malsain. 2. fig (undesirable) malsain(e).

unheard-of [ʌn'hɜːdɒv] adj 1. (unknown) inconnu(e). 2. (unprecedented) sans précédent, inouï(e).

unhook [ʌn'hʊk] vt 1. (dress, bra) dégrafer. 2. (coat, picture, trailer) décrocher.

unhurt [ʌn'hɜːt] adj indemne, sain et sauf (saine et sauve).

unhygienic [ˌʌnhaɪ'dʒiːnɪk] adj non hygiénique.

unidentified flying object [ˌʌnaɪ'dentɪfaɪd-] n objet m volant non identifié.

unification [ˌjuːnɪfɪ'keɪʃn] n unification f.

uniform ['juːnɪfɔːm] ◆ adj (rate, colour) uniforme; (size) même. ◆ n uniforme m.

unify ['juːnɪfaɪ] vt unifier.

unilateral [ˌjuːnɪ'lætərəl] adj unilatéral(e).

unimportant [ˌʌnɪm'pɔːtənt] adj sans importance, peu important(e).

uninhabited [ˌʌnɪn'hæbɪtɪd] adj inhabité(e).

uninjured [ʌn'ɪndʒəd] adj qui n'est pas blessé(e), indemne.

unintelligent [ˌʌnɪn'telɪdʒənt] adj inintelligent(e).

unintentional [ˌʌnɪn'tenʃənl] adj involontaire, non intentionnel(elle).

union ['juːnjən] ◆ n 1. (trade union) syndicat m. 2. (alliance) union f. ◆ comp syndical(e).

Union Jack n: **the ~** l'Union Jack m, le drapeau britannique.

unique [juː'niːk] adj 1. (exceptional)

unique, exceptionnel(elle). 2. (exclusive): **~ to** propre à. 3. (very special) unique.

unison ['juːnɪzn] n unisson m; **in ~** à l'unisson; (say) en chœur, en même temps.

unit ['juːnɪt] n 1. (gen) unité f. 2. (machine part) élément m, bloc m. 3. (of furniture) élément m. 4. (department) service m.

unite [juː'naɪt] ◆ vt unifier. ◆ vi s'unir.

united [juː'naɪtɪd] adj 1. (in harmony) uni(e). 2. (unified) unifié(e).

United Kingdom n: **the ~** le Royaume-Uni.

United Nations n: **the ~** les Nations fpl Unies.

United States n: **the ~ (of America)** les États-Unis mpl (d'Amérique); **in the ~** aux États-Unis.

unit trust n Br société f d'investissement à capital variable.

unity ['juːnətɪ] n (U) unité f.

universal [ˌjuːnɪ'vɜːsl] adj universel (elle).

universe ['juːnɪvɜːs] n univers m.

university [ˌjuːnɪ'vɜːsətɪ] ◆ n université f. ◆ comp universitaire; (lecturer) d'université; **~ student** étudiant m, -e f à l'université.

unjust [ʌn'dʒʌst] adj injuste.

unkempt [ʌn'kempt] adj (clothes, person) négligé(e), débraillé(e); (hair) mal peigné(e).

unkind [ʌn'kaɪnd] adj (uncharitable) méchant(e), pas gentil(ille).

unknown [ʌn'nəʊn] adj inconnu(e).

unlawful [ʌn'lɔːfʊl] adj illégal(e).

unleaded [ʌn'ledɪd] adj sans plomb.

unleash [ʌn'liːʃ] vt literary déchaîner.

unless [ən'les] conj à moins que (+ subjunctive); **~ I'm mistaken** à moins que je (ne) me trompe.

unlike [ʌn'laɪk] prep 1. (different from) différent(e) de. 2. (in contrast to) contrairement à, à la différence de. 3. (not typical of): **it's ~ you to complain** cela ne te ressemble pas de te plaindre.

unlikely [ʌn'laɪklɪ] adj 1. (event, result) peu probable, improbable; (story) invraisemblable. 2. (bizarre - clothes etc) invraisemblable.

unlisted [ʌn'lɪstɪd] adj Am (phone number) qui est sur la liste rouge.

unload [ʌn'ləʊd] vt décharger.

unlock [ʌn'lɒk] vt ouvrir.

unlucky [ʌn'lʌkɪ] adj 1. (unfortu-

nate - person) malchanceux(euse), qui n'a pas de chance; (*- experience, choice*) malheureux(euse). **2.** (*object, number etc*) qui porte malheur.

unmarried [ˌʌnˈmærɪd] *adj* célibataire, qui n'est pas marié(e).

unmistakable [ˌʌnmɪˈsteɪkəbl] *adj* qu'on ne peut pas ne pas reconnaître.

unmitigated [ʌnˈmɪtɪgeɪtɪd] *adj* (*disaster*) total(e); (*evil*) non mitigé(e).

unnatural [ʌnˈnætʃrəl] *adj* **1.** (*unusual*) anormal(e), qui n'est pas naturel(elle). **2.** (*affected*) peu naturel(elle); (*smile*) forcé(e).

unnecessary [ʌnˈnesəsəri] *adj* (*remark, expense, delay*) inutile.

unnerving [ˌʌnˈnɜːvɪŋ] *adj* troublant(e).

unnoticed [ˌʌnˈnəʊtɪst] *adj* inaperçu(e).

unobtainable [ˌʌnəbˈteɪnəbl] *adj* impossible à obtenir.

unobtrusive [ˌʌnəbˈtruːsɪv] *adj* (*person*) effacé(e); (*object*) discret(ète); (*building*) que l'on remarque à peine.

unofficial [ˌʌnəˈfɪʃl] *adj* non officiel (elle).

unorthodox [ʌnˈɔːθədɒks] *adj* peu orthodoxe.

unpack [ˌʌnˈpæk] ◆ *vt* (*suitcase*) défaire; (*box*) vider; (*clothes*) déballer. ◆ *vi* défaire ses bagages.

unpalatable [ʌnˈpælətəbl] *adj* d'un goût désagréable; *fig* dur(e) à avaler.

unparalleled [ʌnˈpærəleld] *adj* (*success, crisis*) sans précédent; (*beauty*) sans égal.

unpleasant [ʌnˈpleznt] *adj* désagréable.

unplug [ʌnˈplʌg] *vt* débrancher.

unpopular [ˌʌnˈpɒpjʊləʳ] *adj* impopulaire.

unprecedented [ʌnˈpresɪdəntɪd] *adj* sans précédent.

unpredictable [ˌʌnprɪˈdɪktəbl] *adj* imprévisible.

unprofessional [ˌʌnprəˈfeʃənl] *adj* (*person, work*) peu professionnel(elle); (*attitude*) contraire à l'éthique de la profession.

unqualified [ʌnˈkwɒlɪfaɪd] *adj* **1.** (*person*) non qualifié(e); (*teacher, doctor*) non diplômé(e). **2.** (*success*) formidable; (*support*) inconditionnel(elle).

unquestionable [ʌnˈkwestʃənəbl] *adj* (*fact*) incontestable; (*honesty*) certain(e).

unquestioning [ʌnˈkwestʃənɪŋ] *adj* aveugle, absolu(e).

unravel [ʌnˈrævl] *vt* **1.** (*undo - knitting*) défaire; (*- fabric*) effiler; (*- threads*) démêler. **2.** *fig* (*solve*) éclaircir.

unreal [ˌʌnˈrɪəl] *adj* (*strange*) irréel (elle).

unrealistic [ˌʌnrɪəˈlɪstɪk] *adj* irréaliste.

unreasonable [ʌnˈriːznəbl] *adj* qui n'est pas raisonnable, déraisonnable.

unrelated [ˌʌnrɪˈleɪtɪd] *adj*: **to be ~ (to)** n'avoir aucun rapport (avec).

unrelenting [ˌʌnrɪˈlentɪŋ] *adj* implacable.

unreliable [ˌʌnrɪˈlaɪəbl] *adj* (*machine, method*) peu fiable; (*person*) sur qui on ne peut pas compter.

unremitting [ˌʌnrɪˈmɪtɪŋ] *adj* inlassable.

unrequited [ˌʌnrɪˈkwaɪtɪd] *adj* non partagé(e).

unreserved [ˌʌnrɪˈzɜːvd] *adj* (*support, admiration*) sans réserve.

unresolved [ˌʌnrɪˈzɒlvd] *adj* non résolu(e).

unrest [ʌnˈrest] *n* (U) troubles *mpl*.

unrivalled Br, **unrivaled** Am [ʌnˈraɪvld] *adj* sans égal(e).

unroll [ˌʌnˈrəʊl] *vt* dérouler.

unruly [ʌnˈruːlɪ] *adj* (*crowd, child*) turbulent(e); (*hair*) indisciplinés.

unsafe [ˌʌnˈseɪf] *adj* **1.** (*dangerous*) dangereux(euse). **2.** (*in danger*): **to feel ~** ne pas se sentir en sécurité.

unsaid [ˌʌnˈsed] *adj*: **to leave sthg ~** passer qqch sous silence.

unsatisfactory [ˈʌnˌsætɪsˈfæktəri] *adj* qui laisse à désirer, peu satisfaisant(e).

unsavoury, unsavory Am [ˌʌnˈseɪvəri] *adj* (*person*) peu recommandable; (*district*) mal famé(e).

unscathed [ˌʌnˈskeɪðd] *adj* indemne.

unscrew [ˌʌnˈskruː] *vt* dévisser.

unscrupulous [ʌnˈskruːpjʊləs] *adj* sans scrupules.

unseemly [ʌnˈsiːmlɪ] *adj* inconvenant(e).

unselfish [ˌʌnˈselfɪʃ] *adj* désintéressé(e).

unsettled [ˌʌnˈsetld] *adj* **1.** (*person*) perturbé(e), troublé(e). **2.** (*weather*) variable, incertain(e). **3.** (*argument*) qui n'a pas été résolu(e); (*situation*) incertain(e).

unshak(e)able [ʌnˈʃeɪkəbl] *adj* inébranlable.

unshaven [ˌʌnˈʃeɪvn] *adj* non rasé(e).

unsightly [ʌnˈsaɪtlɪ] *adj* laid(e).

unskilled [ˌʌnˈskɪld] *adj* non qualifié(e).

unsociable [ʌn'səʊʃəbl] adj sauvage.

unsocial [,ʌn'səʊʃl] adj: **to work ~ hours** travailler en dehors des heures normales.

unsound [,ʌn'saʊnd] adj 1. (theory) mal fondé(e); (decision) peu judicieux (euse). 2. (building, structure) en mauvais état.

unspeakable [ʌn'spiːkəbl] adj indescriptible.

unstable [,ʌn'steɪbl] adj instable.

unsteady [,ʌn'stedɪ] adj (hand) tremblant(e); (table, ladder) instable.

unstoppable [ʌn'stɒpəbl] adj qu'on ne peut pas arrêter.

unstuck [,ʌn'stʌk] adj: **to come ~** (notice, stamp, label) se décoller; fig (plan, system) s'effondrer; fig (person) essuyer un échec.

unsuccessful [,ʌnsək'sesfʊl] adj (attempt) vain(e); (meeting) infructueux (euse); (candidate) refusé(e).

unsuccessfully [,ʌnsək'sesfʊlɪ] adv en vain, sans succès.

unsuitable [,ʌn'suːtəbl] adj qui ne convient pas; (clothes) peu approprié(e); **to be ~ for** ne pas convenir à.

unsure [,ʌn'ʃɔːr] adj 1. (not certain): **to be ~ (about/of)** ne pas être sûr(e) (de). 2. (not confident): **to be ~ (of o.s.)** ne pas être sûr(e) de soi.

unsuspecting [,ʌnsə'spektɪŋ] adj qui ne se doute de rien.

unsympathetic ['ʌn,sɪmpə'θetɪk] adj (unfeeling) indifférent(e).

untangle [,ʌn'tæŋgl] vt (string, hair) démêler.

untapped [,ʌn'tæpt] adj inexploité(e).

untenable [,ʌn'tenəbl] adj indéfendable.

unthinkable [ʌn'θɪŋkəbl] adj impensable.

untidy [ʌn'taɪdɪ] adj (room, desk) en désordre; (work, handwriting) brouillon (inv); (person, appearance) négligé(e).

untie [,ʌn'taɪ] (cont **untying**) vt (knot, parcel, shoelaces) défaire; (prisoner) détacher.

until [ən'tɪl] ◆ prep 1. (gen) jusqu'à; **~ now** jusqu'ici. 2. (after negative) avant; **not ~ tomorrow** pas avant demain. ◆ conj 1. (gen) jusqu'à ce que (+ subjunctive). 2. (after negative) avant que (+ subjunctive).

untimely [ʌn'taɪmlɪ] adj (death) prématuré(e); (arrival) intempestif(ive); (remark) mal à propos; (moment) mal choisi(e).

untold [,ʌn'təʊld] adj (amount, wealth) incalculable; (suffering, joy) indescriptible.

untoward [,ʌntə'wɔːd] adj malencontreux(euse).

untrue [,ʌn'truː] adj (not accurate) faux (fausse), qui n'est pas vrai(e).

unused [sense 1 ,ʌn'juːzd, sense 2 ʌn'juːst] adj 1. (clothes) neuf (neuve); (machine) qui n'a jamais servi; (land) qui n'est pas exploité. 2. (unaccustomed): **to be ~ to sthg/to doing sthg** ne pas avoir l'habitude de qqch/de faire qqch.

unusual [ʌn'juːʒl] adj rare, inhabituel (elle).

unusually [ʌn'juːʒəlɪ] adv exceptionnellement.

unveil [,ʌn'veɪl] vt lit & fig dévoiler.

unwanted [,ʌn'wɒntɪd] adj (object) dont on ne se sert pas; (child) non désiré(e); **to feel ~** se sentir mal-aimé(e).

unwavering [ʌn'weɪvərɪŋ] adj (determination) inébranlable.

unwelcome [ʌn'welkəm] adj (news, situation) fâcheux(euse); (visitor) importun(e).

unwell [,ʌn'wel] adj: **to be/feel ~** ne pas être/se sentir bien.

unwieldy [ʌn'wiːldɪ] adj 1. (cumbersome) peu maniable. 2. fig (system) lourd(e); (method) trop complexe.

unwilling [,ʌn'wɪlɪŋ] adj: **to be ~ to do sthg** ne pas vouloir faire qqch.

unwind [,ʌn'waɪnd] (pt & pp -**wound**) ◆ vt dérouler. ◆ vi fig (person) se détendre.

unwise [,ʌn'waɪz] adj imprudent(e), peu sage.

unwitting [ʌn'wɪtɪŋ] adj fml involontaire.

unworkable [,ʌn'wɜːkəbl] adj impraticable.

unworthy [ʌn'wɜːðɪ] adj (undeserving): **~ (of)** indigne (de).

unwound [,ʌn'waʊnd] pt & pp → **unwind**.

unwrap [,ʌn'ræp] vt défaire.

unwritten law [,ʌnrɪtn-] n droit m coutumier.

up [ʌp] ◆ adv 1. (towards or in a higher position) en haut; **she's ~ in her bedroom** elle est en haut dans sa chambre; **we walked ~ to the top** on est montés jusqu'au haut; **prices are going ~** les prix augmentent; **~ there** là-haut. 2. (into an upright position): **to stand ~** se lever; **to sit ~** s'asseoir (bien droit).

3. (*northwards*): **I'm coming ~ to York next week** je viens à York la semaine prochaine; **~ north** dans le nord. 4. (*along a road, river*): **their house is a little further ~** leur maison est un peu plus loin. ◆ *prep* 1. (*towards or in a higher position*) en haut de; **~ a hill/mountain** en haut d'une colline/d'une montagne; **~ a ladder** sur une échelle; **I went ~ the stairs** j'ai monté l'escalier. 2. (*at far end of*): **they live ~ the road from us** ils habitent un peu plus haut ou loin que nous (dans la même rue). 3. (*against current of river*): **to sail ~ the Amazon** remonter l'Amazone en bateau. ◆ *adj* 1. (*out of bed*) levé(e); **I was ~ at six today** je me suis levé à six heures aujourd'hui. 2. (*at an end*): **time's ~** c'est l'heure. 3. *inf* (*wrong*): **is something ~?** il y a quelque chose qui ne va pas?; **what's ~?** qu'est-ce qui ne va pas?, qu'est-ce qu'il y a? ◆ *n*: **~s and downs** hauts et bas *mpl*. ▶ **up and down** ◆ *adv*: **to jump ~ and down** sauter; **to walk ~ and down** faire les cent pas. ◆ *prep*: **we walked ~ and down the avenue** nous avons arpenté l'avenue. ▶ **up to** *prep* 1. (*as far as*) jusqu'à. 2. (*indicating level*) jusqu'à; **it could take ~ to six weeks** cela peut prendre jusqu'à six semaines; **it's not ~ to standard** ce n'est pas de la qualité voulue, ceci n'a pas le niveau requis. 3. (*well or able enough for*): **to be ~ to doing sthg** (*able to*) être capable de faire qqch; (*well enough for*) être en état de faire qqch; **my French isn't ~ to much** mon français ne vaut pas grand-chose ou n'est pas fameux. 4. *inf* (*secretly doing something*): **what are you ~ to?** qu'est-ce que tu fabriques?; **they're ~ to something** ils mijotent quelque chose, ils préparent un coup. 5. (*indicating responsibility*): **it's not ~ to me to decide** ce n'est pas moi qui décide, ce n'est pas à moi de décider; **it's ~ to you** c'est à vous de voir. ▶ **up until** *prep* jusqu'à.

up-and-coming *adj* à l'avenir prometteur.

upbringing [ˈʌpˌbrɪŋɪŋ] *n* éducation *f*.

update [ˌʌpˈdeɪt] *vt* mettre à jour.

upheaval [ʌpˈhiːvl] *n* bouleversement *m*.

upheld [ʌpˈheld] *pt & pp* → uphold.

uphill [ˌʌpˈhɪl] ◆ *adj* 1. (*slope, path*) qui monte. 2. *fig* (*task*) ardu(e). ◆ *adv*: **to go ~** monter.

uphold [ʌpˈhəʊld] (*pt & pp* -held) *vt*

(*law*) maintenir; (*decision, system*) soutenir.

upholstery [ʌpˈhəʊlstərɪ] *n* rembourrage *m*; (*of car*) garniture *f* intérieure.

upkeep [ˈʌpkiːp] *n* entretien *m*.

uplifting [ʌpˈlɪftɪŋ] *adj* édifiant(e).

up-market *adj* haut de gamme (*inv*).

upon [əˈpɒn] *prep fml* sur; **~ hearing the news ...** à ces nouvelles ...; **summer/the weekend is ~ us** l'été/le week-end approche.

upper [ˈʌpəʳ] ◆ *adj* supérieur(e). ◆ *n* (*of shoe*) empeigne *f*.

upper class *n*: **the ~** la haute société. ▶ **upper-class** *adj* (*accent, person*) aristocratique.

upper hand *n*: **to have the ~** avoir le dessus; **to gain** ou **get the ~** prendre le dessus.

uppermost [ˈʌpəməʊst] *adj* le plus haut (la plus haute); **it was ~ in his mind** c'était sa préoccupation majeure.

upright [*adj sense 1 & adv* ˌʌpˈraɪt, *adj sense 2 & n* ˈʌpraɪt] ◆ *adj* 1. (*person*) droit (e); (*structure*) vertical(e); (*chair*) à dossier droit. 2. *fig* (*honest*) droit(e). ◆ *adv* (*stand, sit*) droit. ◆ *n* montant *m*.

uprising [ˈʌpˌraɪzɪŋ] *n* soulèvement *m*.

uproar [ˈʌprɔːʳ] *n* 1. (U) (*commotion*) tumulte *m*. 2. (*protest*) protestations *fpl*.

uproot [ʌpˈruːt] *vt lit & fig* déraciner.

upset [ʌpˈset] (*pt & pp* upset) ◆ *adj* 1. (*distressed*) peiné(e), triste; (*offended*) vexé(e). 2. (MED): **to have an ~ stomach** avoir l'estomac dérangé. ◆ *n*: **to have a stomach ~** avoir l'estomac dérangé. ◆ *vt* 1. (*distress*) faire de la peine à. 2. (*plan, operation*) déranger. 3. (*overturn*) renverser.

upshot [ˈʌpʃɒt] *n* résultat *m*.

upside down [ˌʌpsaɪd-] ◆ *adj* à l'envers. ◆ *adv* à l'envers; **to turn sthg ~** *fig* mettre qqch sens dessus dessous.

upstairs [ˌʌpˈsteəz] ◆ *adj* d'en haut, du dessus. ◆ *adv* en haut. ◆ *n* étage *m*.

upstart [ˈʌpstɑːt] *n* parvenu *m*, -e *f*.

upstream [ˌʌpˈstriːm] ◆ *adj* d'amont; **to be ~ (from)** être en amont (de). ◆ *adv* vers l'amont; (*swim*) contre le courant.

upsurge [ˈʌpsɜːdʒ] *n*: **~ (of/in)** recrudescence *f* (de).

uptake [ˈʌpteɪk] *n*: **to be quick on the ~** saisir vite; **to be slow on the ~** être lent(e) à comprendre.

uptight [ʌpˈtaɪt] *adj inf* tendu(e).

up-to-date *adj* 1. (*modern*) moderne. 2. (*most recent - news*) tout dernier (toute dernière). 3. (*informed*): **to keep ~ with**

se tenir au courant de.

upturn ['ʌptɜ:n] n: ~ **(in)** reprise f (de).

upward ['ʌpwəd] ♦ adj (movement) ascendant(e); (look, rise) vers le haut. ♦ adv Am = **upwards**.

upwards ['ʌpwədz] adv vers le haut.
▶ **upwards of** prep plus de.

uranium [jʊ'reɪnjəm] n uranium m.

urban ['ɜ:bən] adj urbain(e).

urbane [ɜ:'beɪn] adj courtois(e).

urchin ['ɜ:tʃɪn] n dated gamin m, -e f.

Urdu ['ʊədu:] n ourdou m.

urge [ɜ:dʒ] ♦ n forte envie f; **to have an ~ to do sthg** avoir une forte envie de faire qqch. ♦ vt **1.** (try to persuade): **to ~ sb to do sthg** pousser qqn à faire qqch, presser qqn de faire qqch. **2.** (advocate) conseiller.

urgency ['ɜ:dʒənsɪ] n (U) urgence f.

urgent ['ɜ:dʒənt] adj (letter, case, request) urgent(e); (plea, voice, need) pressant(e).

urinal [,jʊə'raɪnl] n urinoir m.

urinate ['jʊərɪneɪt] vi uriner.

urine ['jʊərɪn] n urine f.

urn [ɜ:n] n **1.** (for ashes) urne f. **2.** (for tea): **tea ~** fontaine f à thé.

Uruguay ['jʊərəgwaɪ] n Uruguay m.

us [ʌs] pers pron nous; **can you see ~?** vous nous voyez/entendez?; **it's ~** c'est nous; **you can't expect us to do it** vous ne pouvez pas exiger que ce soit nous qui le fassions; **she gave it to ~** elle nous l'a donné; **with/without ~** avec/sans nous; **they are more wealthy than ~** ils sont plus riches que nous; **some of ~** quelques-uns d'entre nous.

US n abbr of **United States**.

USA n abbr of **United States of America**.

usage ['ju:zɪdʒ] n **1.** (LING) usage m. **2.** (U) (handling, treatment) traitement m.

use [n & aux vb ju:s, vt ju:z] ♦ n **1.** (act of using) utilisation f, emploi m; **to be in ~** être utilisé; **to be out of ~** être hors d'usage; **to make ~ of sthg** utiliser qqch. **2.** (ability to use) usage m. **3.** (usefulness): **to be of ~** être utile; **it's no ~** ça ne sert à rien; **what's the ~ (of doing sthg)?** à quoi bon (faire qqch)? ♦ aux vb: **I ~d to live in London** avant j'habitais à Londres; **he didn't ~ to be so fat** il n'était pas si gros avant; **there ~d to be a tree here** (autrefois) il y avait un arbre ici. ♦ vt **1.** (gen) utiliser, se servir de, employer. **2.** pej (exploit) se servir de.
▶ **use up** vt sep (supply) épuiser; (food) finir; (money) dépenser.

used [senses 1 and 2 ju:zd, sense 3 ju:st]

adj **1.** (handkerchief, towel) sale. **2.** (car) d'occasion. **3.** (accustomed): **to be ~ to sthg/to doing sthg** avoir l'habitude de qqch/de faire qqch; **to get ~ to sthg** s'habituer à qqch.

useful ['ju:sfʊl] adj utile.

useless ['ju:slɪs] adj **1.** (gen) inutile. **2.** inf (person) incompétent(e), nul (nulle).

user ['ju:zər] n (of product, machine) utilisateur m, -trice f; (of service) usager m.

user-friendly adj convivial(e), facile à utiliser.

usher ['ʌʃər] ♦ n placeur m. ♦ vt: **to ~ sb in/out** faire entrer/sortir qqn.

usherette [,ʌʃə'ret] n ouvreuse f.

USSR (abbr of **Union of Soviet Socialist Republics**) n: **the (former) ~** l'(ex-)URSS f.

usual ['ju:ʒəl] adj habituel(elle); **as ~** comme d'habitude.

usually ['ju:ʒəlɪ] adv d'habitude, d'ordinaire.

usurp [ju:'zɜ:p] vt usurper.

utensil [ju:'tensl] n ustensile m.

uterus ['ju:tərəs] (pl **-ri** [-raɪ] OR **-ruses**) n utérus m.

utility [ju:'tɪlətɪ] n **1.** (U) (usefulness) utilité f. **2.** (public service) service m public. **3.** (COMPUT) utilitaire m.

utility room n buanderie f.

utilize, -ise ['ju:təlaɪz] vt utiliser; (resources) exploiter, utiliser.

utmost ['ʌtməʊst] ♦ adj le plus grand (la plus grande). ♦ n: **to do one's ~** faire tout son possible, faire l'impossible; **to the ~** au plus haut point.

utter ['ʌtər] ♦ adj total(e), complet (ète). ♦ vt prononcer; (cry) pousser.

utterly ['ʌtəlɪ] adv complètement.

U-turn n demi-tour m; fig revirement m.

v¹ (pl **v's** OR **vs**), **V** (pl **V's** OR **Vs**) [vi:] n (letter) v m inv, V m inv.

v² **1.** (abbr of **verse**) v. **2.** (abbr of **vide**) (cross-reference) v. **3.** abbr of **versus**. **4.** (abbr of **volt**) v.

vacancy ['veɪkənsɪ] n **1.** (job) poste m vacant. **2.** (room available) chambre f à louer; **'vacancies'** 'chambres à louer';

'no vacancies' 'complet'.

vacant ['veɪkənt] adj 1. (room) inoccupé(e); (chair, toilet) libre. 2. (job, post) vacant(e). 3. (look, expression) distrait(e).

vacant lot n terrain m inoccupé; (for sale) terrain m à vendre.

vacate [və'keɪt] vt quitter.

vacation [və'keɪʃn] n Am vacances fpl.

vacationer [və'keɪʃənər] n Am vacancier m, -ère f.

vaccinate ['væksɪneɪt] vt vacciner.

vaccine [Br 'væksiːn, Am væk'siːn] n vaccin m.

vacuum ['vækjʊəm] ◆ n 1. (TECH & fig) vide m. 2. (cleaner) aspirateur m. ◆ vt (room) passer l'aspirateur dans; (carpet) passer à l'aspirateur.

vacuum cleaner n aspirateur m.

vacuum-packed adj emballé(e) sous vide.

vagina [və'dʒaɪnə] n vagin m.

vagrant ['veɪgrənt] n vagabond m, -e f.

vague [veɪg] adj 1. (gen) vague, imprécis(e). 2. (absent-minded) distrait(e).

vaguely ['veɪglɪ] adv vaguement.

vain [veɪn] adj 1. (futile, worthless) vain(e). 2. pej (conceited) vaniteux(euse).
▶ **in vain** adv en vain, vainement.

valentine card ['væləntaɪn-] n carte f de la Saint-Valentin.

Valentine's Day ['væləntaɪnz-] n: (St) ~ la Saint-Valentin.

valet ['væleɪ, 'vælɪt] n valet m de chambre.

valiant ['væljənt] adj vaillant(e).

valid ['vælɪd] adj 1. (reasonable) valable. 2. (legally usable) valide.

valley ['vælɪ] n (pl valleys) n vallée f.

valour Br, **valor** Am ['vælər] n (U) fml & literary bravoure f.

valuable ['væljʊəbl] adj 1. (advice, time, information) précieux(euse). 2. (object, jewel) de valeur. ▶ **valuables** npl objets mpl de valeur.

valuation [,væljʊ'eɪʃn] n 1. (U) (pricing) estimation f, expertise f. 2. (estimated price) valeur f estimée.

value ['væljuː] ◆ n valeur f; **to be good ~** être d'un bon rapport qualité-prix; **to get ~ for money** en avoir pour son argent. ◆ vt 1. (estimate price of) expertiser. 2. (cherish) apprécier. ▶ **values** npl (morals) valeurs fpl.

value-added tax [-'ædɪd-] n taxe f sur la valeur ajoutée.

valued ['væljuːd] adj précieux(euse).

valve [vælv] n (on tyre) valve f; (TECH) soupape f.

van [væn] n 1. (AUT) camionnette f. 2. Br (RAIL) fourgon m.

vandal ['vændl] n vandale mf.

vandalism ['vændəlɪzm] n vandalisme m.

vandalize, -ise ['vændəlaɪz] vt saccager.

vanguard ['vængɑːd] n avant-garde f; **in the ~ of** à l'avant-garde de.

vanilla [və'nɪlə] n vanille f.

vanish ['vænɪʃ] vi disparaître.

vanity ['vænətɪ] n (U) pej vanité f.

vantagepoint ['væntɪdʒ,pɔɪnt] n (for view) bon endroit m; fig position f avantageuse.

vapour Br, **vapor** Am ['veɪpər] n (U) vapeur f; (condensation) buée f.

variable ['veərɪəbl] adj variable; (mood) changeant(e).

variance ['veərɪəns] n fml: **at ~ (with)** en désaccord (avec).

variation [,veərɪ'eɪʃn] n: ~ **(in)** variation f (de).

varicose veins ['værɪkəʊs-] npl varices fpl.

varied ['veərɪd] adj varié(e).

variety [və'raɪətɪ] n 1. (gen) variété f. 2. (type) variété f, sorte f.

variety show n spectacle m de variétés.

various ['veərɪəs] adj 1. (several) plusieurs. 2. (different) divers.

varnish ['vɑːnɪʃ] ◆ n vernis m. ◆ vt vernir.

vary ['veərɪ] ◆ vt varier. ◆ vi: **to ~ (in/with)** varier (en/selon), changer (en/selon).

vase [Br vɑːz, Am veɪz] n vase m.

Vaseline® ['væsəliːn] n vaseline f.

vast [vɑːst] adj vaste, immense.

vat [væt] n cuve f.

VAT [væt, viːeɪ'tiː] (abbr of value added tax) n TVA f.

Vatican ['vætɪkən] n: **the ~** le Vatican.

vault [vɔːlt] ◆ n 1. (in bank) chambre f forte. 2. (roof) voûte f. 3. (in church) caveau m. ◆ vt sauter. ◆ vi: **to ~ over** sthg sauter (par-dessus) qqch.

VCR (abbr of video cassette recorder) n magnétoscope m.

VD n abbr of venereal disease.

VDU (abbr of visual display unit) n moniteur m.

veal [viːl] n (U) veau m.

veer [vɪər] vi virer.

vegan ['viːgən] ◆ adj végétalien (enne). ◆ n végétalien m, -enne f.

vegetable ['vedʒtəbl] ◆ n légume m.

veto

♦ adj (matter, protein) végétal(e); (soup, casserole) de OR aux légumes.

vegetarian [ˌvedʒɪˈteərɪən] ♦ adj végétarien(enne). ♦ n végétarien m, -enne f.

vegetation [ˌvedʒɪˈteɪʃn] n (U) végétation f.

vehement [ˈviːəmənt] adj véhément(e).

vehicle [ˈviːəkl] n lit & fig véhicule m.

veil [veɪl] n lit & fig voile m.

vein [veɪn] n 1. (ANAT) veine f. 2. (of leaf) nervure f. 3. (of mineral) filon m.

velocity [vɪˈlɒsətɪ] n vélocité f.

velvet [ˈvelvɪt] n velours m.

vendetta [venˈdetə] n vendetta f.

vending machine [ˈvendɪŋ-] n distributeur m automatique.

vendor [ˈvendər] n 1. fml (salesperson) marchand m, -e f. 2. (JUR) vendeur m, -eresse f.

veneer [vəˈnɪər] n placage m; fig apparence f.

venereal disease [vɪˈnɪərɪəl-] n maladie f vénérienne.

venetian blind [vɪˌniːʃn-] n store m vénitien.

Venezuela [ˌvenɪzˈweɪlə] n Venezuela m.

vengeance [ˈvendʒəns] n vengeance f; **it began raining with a ~** il a commencé à pleuvoir très fort.

venison [ˈvenɪzn] n venaison f.

venom [ˈvenəm] n lit & fig venin m.

vent [vent] ♦ n (pipe) tuyau m; (opening) orifice m; **to give ~ to** donner libre cours à. ♦ vt (anger, feelings) donner libre cours à; **to ~ sthg on sb** décharger qqch sur qqn.

ventilate [ˈventɪleɪt] vt ventiler.

ventilator [ˈventɪleɪtər] n ventilateur m.

ventriloquist [venˈtrɪləkwɪst] n ventriloque mf.

venture [ˈventʃər] ♦ n entreprise f. ♦ vt risquer; **to ~ to do sthg** se permettre de faire qqch. ♦ vi s'aventurer.

venue [ˈvenjuː] n lieu m.

veranda(h) [vəˈrændə] n véranda f.

verb [vɜːb] n verbe m.

verbal [ˈvɜːbl] adj verbal(e).

verbatim [vɜːˈbeɪtɪm] adj & adv mot pour mot.

verbose [vɜːˈbəʊs] adj verbeux(euse).

verdict [ˈvɜːdɪkt] n 1. (JUR) verdict m. 2. (opinion): **~ (on)** avis m (sur).

verge [vɜːdʒ] n 1. (of lawn) bordure f; (of road) bas-côté m, accotement m. 2. (brink): **on the ~ of sthg** au bord de

qqch; **on the ~ of doing sthg** sur le point de faire qqch. ▶ **verge (up)on** vt fus friser, approcher de.

verify [ˈverɪfaɪ] vt vérifier.

veritable [ˈverɪtəbl] adj hum or fml véritable.

vermin [ˈvɜːmɪn] npl vermine f.

vermouth [ˈvɜːməθ] n vermouth m.

versa [ˈvɜːsə] → **vice versa**.

versatile [ˈvɜːsətaɪl] adj (person, player) aux talents multiples; (machine, tool, food) souple d'emploi.

verse [vɜːs] n 1. (U) (poetry) vers mpl. 2. (stanza) strophe f. 3. (in Bible) verset m.

versed [vɜːst] adj: **to be well ~ in sthg** être versé(e) dans qqch.

version [ˈvɜːʃn] n version f.

versus [ˈvɜːsəs] prep 1. (SPORT) contre. 2. (as opposed to) par opposition à.

vertebra [ˈvɜːtɪbrə] (pl **-brae** [-briː]) n vertèbre f.

vertical [ˈvɜːtɪkl] adj vertical(e).

vertigo [ˈvɜːtɪɡəʊ] n (U) vertige m.

verve [vɜːv] n verve f.

very [ˈverɪ] ♦ adv 1. (as intensifier) très; **~ much** beaucoup. 2. (as euphemism): **not ~** pas très. ♦ adj: **the ~ room/book** la pièce/le livre même; **the ~ man/thing I've been looking for** juste l'homme/la chose que je cherchais; **at the ~ least** tout au moins; **~ last/first** tout dernier/premier; **of one's ~ own** bien à soi. ▶ **very well** adv très bien; **I can't ~ well tell him …** je ne peux tout de même pas lui dire que …

vessel [ˈvesl] n fml 1. (boat) vaisseau m. 2. (container) récipient m.

vest [vest] n 1. Br (undershirt) maillot m de corps. 2. Am (waistcoat) gilet m.

vested interest [ˈvestɪd-] n: **~ (in)** intérêt m particulier (à).

vestibule [ˈvestɪbjuːl] n fml (entrance hall) vestibule m.

vestige [ˈvestɪdʒ] n vestige m.

vestry [ˈvestrɪ] n sacristie f.

vet [vet] ♦ n Br (abbr of **veterinary surgeon**) vétérinaire mf. ♦ vt (candidates) examiner avec soin.

veteran [ˈvetrən] ♦ adj (experienced) chevronné(e). ♦ n 1. (MIL) ancien combattant m, vétéran m. 2. (experienced person) vétéran m.

veterinarian [ˌvetərɪˈneərɪən] n Am vétérinaire mf.

veterinary surgeon [ˈvetərɪnrɪ-] n Br fml vétérinaire mf.

veto [ˈviːtəʊ] (pl **-es**, pt & pp **-ed**, cont

-ing) ◆ *n* veto *m*. ◆ *vt* opposer son veto à.

vex [veks] *vt* contrarier.

vexed question [ˌvekst-] *n* question *f* controversée.

vg (*abbr of* **very good**) tb.

VHF (*abbr of* **very high frequency**) VHF.

VHS (*abbr of* **video home system**) *n* VHS *m*.

via ['vaɪə] *prep* 1. (*travelling through*) via, par. 2. (*by means of*) au moyen de.

viable ['vaɪəbl] *adj* viable.

vibrate [vaɪ'breɪt] *vi* vibrer.

vicar ['vɪkər] *n* (*in Church of England*) pasteur *m*.

vicarage ['vɪkərɪdʒ] *n* presbytère *m*.

vicarious [vɪ'keərɪəs] *adj*: **to take a ~ pleasure in sthg** retirer du plaisir indirectement de qqch.

vice [vaɪs] *n* 1. (*immorality, fault*) vice *m*. 2. (*tool*) étau *m*.

vice-chairman *n* vice-président *m*, -e *f*.

vice-chancellor *n* (UNIV) président *m*, -e *f*.

vice-president *n* vice-président *m*, -e *f*.

vice versa [ˌvaɪsɪ-] *adv* vice versa.

vicinity [vɪ'sɪnətɪ] *n*: **in the ~ (of)** aux alentours (de), dans les environs (de).

vicious ['vɪʃəs] *adj* violent(e), brutal(e).

vicious circle *n* cercle *m* vicieux.

victim ['vɪktɪm] *n* victime *f*.

victimize, -ise ['vɪktɪmaɪz] *vt* faire une victime de.

victor ['vɪktər] *n* vainqueur *m*.

victorious [vɪk'tɔːrɪəs] *adj* victorieux(euse).

victory ['vɪktərɪ] *n*: **~ (over)** victoire *f* (sur).

video ['vɪdɪəʊ] (*pl* **-es**, *pt & pp* **-ed**, *cont* **-ing**) ◆ *n* 1. (*medium, recording*) vidéo *f*. 2. (*machine*) magnétoscope *m*. 3. (*cassette*) vidéocassette *f*. ◆ *comp* vidéo (*inv*). ◆ *vt* 1. (*using video recorder*) magnétoscoper. 2. (*using camera*) faire une vidéo de, filmer.

video camera *n* caméra *f* vidéo.

video cassette *n* vidéocassette *f*.

video game *n* jeu *m* vidéo.

videorecorder ['vɪdɪəʊrɪˌkɔːdər] *n* magnétoscope *m*.

video shop *n* vidéoclub *m*.

videotape ['vɪdɪəʊteɪp] *n* 1. (*cassette*) vidéocassette *f*. 2. (U) (*ribbon*) bande *f* vidéo.

vie [vaɪ] (*pt & pp* **vied**, *cont* **vying**) *vi*: **to ~ for sthg** lutter pour qqch; **to ~ with sb (for sthg/to do sthg)** rivaliser avec qqn (pour qqch/pour faire qqch).

Vienna [vɪ'enə] *n* Vienne.

Vietnam [Br ˌvjet'næm, Am ˌvjet'nɑːm] *n* Viêt-nam *m*.

Vietnamese [ˌvjetnə'miːz] ◆ *adj* vietnamien(enne). ◆ *n* (*language*) vietnamien *m*. ◆ *npl*: **the ~** les Vietnamiens *mpl*.

view [vjuː] ◆ *n* 1. (*opinion*) opinion *f*, avis *m*; **in my ~** à mon avis. 2. (*scene, ability to see*) vue *f*; **to come into ~** apparaître. ◆ *vt* 1. (*consider*) considérer. 2. (*examine - gen*) examiner; (- *house*) visiter. ► **in view of** *prep* vu, étant donné. ► **with a view to** *conj* dans l'intention de, avec l'idée de.

viewer ['vjuːər] *n* 1. (TV) téléspectateur *m*, -trice *f*. 2. (*for slides*) visionneuse *f*.

viewfinder ['vjuːˌfaɪndər] *n* viseur *m*.

viewpoint ['vjuːpɔɪnt] *n* point *m* de vue.

vigil ['vɪdʒɪl] *n* veille *f*; (RELIG) vigile *f*.

vigilante [ˌvɪdʒɪ'læntɪ] *n* membre *m* d'un groupe d'autodéfense.

vigorous ['vɪgərəs] *adj* vigoureux(euse).

vile [vaɪl] *adj* (*mood*) massacrant(e), exécrable; (*person, act*) vil(e), ignoble; (*food*) infect(e), exécrable.

villa ['vɪlə] *n* villa *f*; (*bungalow*) pavillon *m*.

village ['vɪlɪdʒ] *n* village *m*.

villager ['vɪlɪdʒər] *n* villageois *m*, -e *f*.

villain ['vɪlən] *n* 1. (*of film, book*) méchant *m*, -e *f*; (*of play*) traître *m*. 2. (*criminal*) bandit *m*.

vindicate ['vɪndɪkeɪt] *vt* justifier.

vindictive [vɪn'dɪktɪv] *adj* vindicatif(ive).

vine [vaɪn] *n* vigne *f*.

vinegar ['vɪnɪgər] *n* vinaigre *m*.

vineyard ['vɪnjəd] *n* vignoble *m*.

vintage ['vɪntɪdʒ] ◆ *adj* 1. (*wine*) de grand cru. 2. (*classic*) typique. ◆ *n* année *f*, millésime *m*.

vintage wine *n* vin *m* de grand cru.

vinyl ['vaɪnɪl] *n* vinyle *m*.

viola [vɪ'əʊlə] *n* alto *m*.

violate ['vaɪəleɪt] *vt* violer.

violence ['vaɪələns] *n* violence *f*.

violent ['vaɪələnt] *adj* (*gen*) violent(e).

violet ['vaɪələt] ◆ *adj* violet(ette). ◆ *n* 1. (*flower*) violette *f*. 2. (*colour*) violet *m*.

violin [ˌvaɪə'lɪn] *n* violon *m*.

violinist [,vaɪə'lɪnɪst] n violoniste mf.

VIP (abbr of **very important person**) n VIP mf.

viper ['vaɪpər] n vipère f.

virgin ['vɜːdʒɪn] ◆ adj literary (land, forest, soil) vierge. ◆ n (woman) vierge f; (man) garçon m/homme m vierge.

Virgo ['vɜːgəʊ] n (pl -s) n Vierge f.

virile ['vɪraɪl] adj viril(e).

virtually ['vɜːtʃʊəlɪ] adv virtuellement, pratiquement.

virtual reality n réalité f virtuelle.

virtue ['vɜːtjuː] n 1. (good quality) vertu f. 2. (benefit): ~ (in doing sthg) mérite m (à faire qqch). ▶ **by virtue of** prep fml en vertu de.

virtuous ['vɜːtʃʊəs] adj vertueux (euse).

virus ['vaɪrəs] n (COMPUT & MED) virus m.

visa ['viːzə] n visa m.

vis-à-vis [,viːzɑː'viː] prep fml par rapport à.

viscose ['vɪskəʊs] n viscose f.

visibility [,vɪzɪ'bɪlətɪ] n visibilité f.

visible ['vɪzəbl] adj visible.

vision ['vɪʒn] n 1. (U) (ability to see) vue f. 2. (foresight, dream) vision f.

visit ['vɪzɪt] ◆ n visite f; on a ~ en visite. ◆ vt (person) rendre visite à; (place) visiter.

visiting hours ['vɪzɪtɪŋ-] npl heures fpl de visite.

visitor ['vɪzɪtər] n (to person) invité m, -e f; (to place) visiteur m, -euse f; (to hotel) client m, -e f.

visitors' book n livre m d'or; (in hotel) registre m.

visitor's passport n Br passeport m temporaire.

visor ['vaɪzər] n visière f.

vista ['vɪstə] n (view) vue f.

visual ['vɪʒʊəl] adj visuel(elle).

visual aids npl supports mpl visuels.

visual display unit n écran m de visualisation.

visualize, -ise ['vɪʒʊəlaɪz] vt se représenter, s'imaginer.

vital ['vaɪtl] adj 1. (essential) essentiel(elle). 2. (full of life) plein(e) d'entrain.

vitally ['vaɪtəlɪ] adv absolument.

vital statistics npl inf (of woman) mensurations fpl.

vitamin [Br 'vɪtəmɪn, Am 'vaɪtəmɪn] n vitamine f.

vivacious [vɪ'veɪʃəs] adj enjoué(e).

vivid ['vɪvɪd] adj 1. (bright) vif (vive). 2. (clear - description) vivant(e); (- memory) net (nette), précis(e).

vividly ['vɪvɪdlɪ] adv (describe) d'une manière vivante; (remember) clairement.

vixen ['vɪksn] n (fox) renarde f.

VLF (abbr of **very low frequency**) n très basse fréquence.

V-neck n (neck) décolleté m en V; (sweater) pull m à décolleté en V.

vocabulary [və'kæbjʊlərɪ] n vocabulaire m.

vocal ['vəʊkl] adj 1. (outspoken) qui se fait entendre. 2. (of the voice) vocal(e).

vocal cords npl cordes fpl vocales.

vocation [vəʊ'keɪʃn] n vocation f.

vocational [vəʊ'keɪʃənl] adj professionnel(elle).

vociferous [və'sɪfərəs] adj bruyant(e).

vodka ['vɒdkə] n vodka f.

vogue [vəʊg] n vogue f, mode f; in ~ en vogue, à la mode.

voice [vɔɪs] ◆ n (gen) voix f. ◆ vt (opinion, emotion) exprimer.

voice mail n (COMPUT) messagerie f vocale; to send/receive ~ envoyer/recevoir un message sur une boîte vocale.

void [vɔɪd] ◆ adj 1. (invalid) nul (nulle); → **null**. 2. fml (empty): ~ **of** dépourvu(e) de, dénué(e) de. ◆ n vide m.

volatile [Br 'vɒlətaɪl, Am 'vɒlətl] adj (situation) explosif(ive); (person) lunatique, versatile; (market) instable.

volcano [vɒl'keɪnəʊ] (pl -es OR -s) n volcan m.

volition [və'lɪʃn] n fml: of one's own ~ de son propre gré.

volley ['vɒlɪ] (pl volleys) ◆ n 1. (of gunfire) salve f. 2. fig (of questions, curses) torrent m; (of blows) volée f, pluie f. 3. (SPORT) volée f. ◆ vt frapper à la volée, reprendre de volée.

volleyball ['vɒlɪbɔːl] n volley-ball m.

volt [vəʊlt] n volt m.

voltage ['vəʊltɪdʒ] n voltage m, tension f.

voluble ['vɒljʊbl] adj volubile, loquace.

volume ['vɒljuːm] n 1. (gen) volume m. 2. (of work, letters) quantité f; (of traffic) densité f.

voluntarily [Br 'vɒləntrɪlɪ, Am ,vɒlən'terəlɪ] adv volontairement.

voluntary ['vɒləntrɪ] adj 1. (not obligatory) volontaire. 2. (unpaid) bénévole.

volunteer [,vɒlən'tɪər] ◆ n 1. (gen & MIL) volontaire mf. 2. (unpaid worker) bénévole *mf.* ◆ *vt* **1.** (*offer*): **to ~ to do sthg** se proposer OR se porter volontaire pour faire qqch. **2.** (*information, advice*) donner spontanément. ◆ *vi* **1.** (*offer one's services*): **to ~ (for)** se porter volontaire (pour), proposer ses services (pour). **2.** (MIL) s'engager comme volontaire.

vomit ['vɒmɪt] ◆ *n* vomi *m.* ◆ *vi* vomir.

vote [vəʊt] ◆ *n* **1.** (*individual decision*): **~ (for/against)** vote *m* (pour/contre), voix *f* (pour/contre). **2.** (*ballot*) vote *m.* **3.** (*right to vote*) droit *m* de vote. ◆ *vt* **1.** (*declare*) élire. **2.** (*choose*): **to ~ to do sthg** voter OR se prononcer pour faire qqch; **they ~d to return to work** ils ont voté le retour au travail. ◆ *vi*: **to ~ (for/against)** voter (pour/contre).

vote of thanks (*pl* **votes of thanks**) *n* discours *m* de remerciement.

voter ['vəʊtər] *n* électeur *m*, -trice *f.*

voting ['vəʊtɪŋ] *n* scrutin *m.*

vouch [vaʊtʃ] ► **vouch for** *vt fus* répondre de, se porter garant de.

voucher ['vaʊtʃər] *n* bon *m*, coupon *m.*

vow [vaʊ] ◆ *n* vœu *m*, serment *m.* ◆ *vt*: **to ~ to do sthg** jurer de faire qqch; **to ~ (that)** ... jurer que ...

vowel ['vaʊəl] *n* voyelle *f.*

voyage ['vɔɪɪdʒ] *n* voyage *m* en mer; (*in space*) vol *m.*

vs *abbr of* **versus**.

VSO (*abbr of* **Voluntary Service Overseas**) *n organisation britannique envoyant des travailleurs bénévoles dans des pays en voie de développement pour contribuer à leur développement technique.*

vulgar ['vʌlgər] *adj* **1.** (*in bad taste*) vulgaire. **2.** (*offensive*) grossier(ère).

vulnerable ['vʌlnərəbl] *adj* vulnérable; **~ to** (*attack*) exposé(e) à; (*colds*) sensible à.

vulture ['vʌltʃər] *n lit & fig* vautour *m.*

w (*pl* **w's** OR **ws**), **W** (*pl* **W's** OR **Ws**) ['dʌbljuː] *n* (*letter*) w *m inv*, W *m inv.* ► **W 1.** (*abbr of* **west**) O, W. **2.** (*abbr of* **watt**) w.
wad [wɒd] *n* **1.** (*of cotton wool, paper*) tampon *m.* **2.** (*of banknotes, documents*) liasse *f.* **3.** (*of tobacco*) chique *f*; (*of chewing-gum*) boulette *f.*

waddle ['wɒdl] *vi* se dandiner.

wade [weɪd] *vi* patauger. ► **wade through** *vt fus fig* se taper.

wading pool ['weɪdɪŋ-] *n Am* pataugeoire *f.*

wafer ['weɪfər] *n* (*thin biscuit*) gaufrette *f.*

waffle ['wɒfl] ◆ *n* **1.** (CULIN) gaufre *f.* **2.** *Br inf* (*vague talk*) verbiage *m.* ◆ *vi* parler pour ne rien dire.

waft [wɑːft, wɒft] *vi* flotter.

wag [wæg] ◆ *vt* remuer, agiter. ◆ *vi* (*tail*) remuer.

wage [weɪdʒ] ◆ *n* salaire *m*, paie *f*, paye *f.* ◆ *vt*: **to ~ war against** faire la guerre à. ► **wages** *npl* salaire *m.*

wage earner [-,ɜːnər] *n* salarié *m*, -e *f.*

wage packet *n Br* **1.** (*envelope*) enveloppe *f* de paye. **2.** *fig* (*pay*) paie *f*, paye *f.*

wager ['weɪdʒər] *n* pari *m.*

waggle ['wægl] *inf vt* agiter, remuer; (*ears*) remuer.

waggon ['wægən] *Br* = **wagon**.

wagon ['wægən] *n* **1.** (*horse-drawn*) chariot *m*, charrette *f.* **2.** *Br* (RAIL) wagon *m.*

wail [weɪl] ◆ *n* gémissement *m.* ◆ *vi* gémir.

waist [weɪst] *n* taille *f.*

waistcoat ['weɪskəʊt] *n* gilet *m.*

waistline ['weɪstlaɪn] *n* taille *f.*

wait [weɪt] ◆ *n* attente *f.* ◆ *vi* attendre; **I can't ~ to see you** je brûle d'impatience de te voir; **~ and see!** tu vas bien voir! ► **wait for** *vt fus* attendre; **to ~ for sb to do sthg** attendre que qqn fasse qqch. ► **wait on** *vt fus* (*serve food to*) servir. ► **wait up** *vi* veiller, ne pas se coucher.

waiter ['weɪtər] *n* garçon *m*, serveur *m.*

waiting list ['weɪtɪŋ-] *n* liste *f* d'attente.

waiting room ['weɪtɪŋ-] *n* salle *f* d'attente.

waitress ['weɪtrɪs] *n* serveuse *f.*

waive [weɪv] *vt* (*fee*) renoncer à; (*rule*) prévoir une dérogation à.

wake [weɪk] (*pt* **woke** OR **-d**, *pp* **woken** OR **-d**) ◆ *n* (*of ship*) sillage *m.* ◆ *vt* réveiller. ◆ *vi* se réveiller. ► **wake up** ◆ *vt sep* réveiller. ◆ *vi* (*wake*) se réveiller.

waken ['weɪkən] *fml* ◆ *vt* réveiller. ◆ *vi* se réveiller.

Wales [weɪlz] *n* pays *m* de Galles.

walk [wɔːk] ♦ n 1. (*way of walking*) démarche f, façon f de marcher. 2. (*journey - for pleasure*) promenade f; (- *long distance*) marche f; **it's a long ~** c'est loin à pied; **to go for a ~** aller se promener, aller faire une promenade. ♦ vt 1. (*accompany - person*) accompagner; (- *dog*) promener. 2. (*distance*) faire à pied. ♦ vi 1. (*gen*) marcher. 2. (*for pleasure*) se promener. ▶ **walk out** vi 1. (*leave suddenly*) partir. 2. (*go on strike*) se mettre en grève, faire grève. ▶ **walk out on** vt fus quitter.

walker ['wɔːkər] n 1. (*for pleasure*) promeneur m, -euse f; (*long-distance*) marcheur m, -euse f.

walkie-talkie [ˌwɔːkɪ'tɔːkɪ] n talkie-walkie m.

walking ['wɔːkɪŋ] n (U) marche f à pied, promenade f.

walking shoes npl chaussures fpl de marche.

walking stick n canne f.

Walkman® ['wɔːkmən] n baladeur m, Walkman® m.

walk of life (*pl* **walks of life**) n milieu m.

walkout ['wɔːkaʊt] n (*strike*) grève f, débrayage m.

walkover ['wɔːkˌəʊvər] n victoire f facile.

walkway ['wɔːkweɪ] n passage m; (*between buildings*) passerelle f.

wall [wɔːl] n 1. (*of room, building*) mur m; (*of rock, cave*) paroi f. 2. (ANAT) paroi f.

wallchart ['wɔːltʃɑːt] n planche f murale.

walled [wɔːld] adj fortifié(e).

wallet ['wɒlɪt] n portefeuille m.

wallflower ['wɔːlˌflaʊər] n 1. (*plant*) giroflée f. 2. inf fig (*person*): **to be a ~** faire tapisserie.

wallop ['wɒləp] inf vt (*person*) flanquer un coup à; (*ball*) taper fort dans.

wallow ['wɒləʊ] vi (*in liquid*) se vautrer.

wallpaper ['wɔːlˌpeɪpər] ♦ n papier peint. ♦ vt tapisser.

Wall Street n Wall Street m (*quartier financier de New York*).

wally ['wɒlɪ] n Br inf idiot m, -e f, andouille f.

walnut ['wɔːlnʌt] n 1. (*nut*) noix f. 2. (*tree, wood*) noyer m.

walrus ['wɔːlrəs] (*pl inv* OR **-es**) n morse m.

waltz [wɔːls] ♦ n valse f. ♦ vi (*dance*) valser, danser la valse.

wan [wɒn] adj pâle, blême.

wand [wɒnd] n baguette f.

wander ['wɒndər] vi 1. (*person*) errer. 2. (*mind*) divaguer; (*thoughts*) vagabonder.

wane [weɪn] vi 1. (*influence, interest*) diminuer, faiblir. 2. (*moon*) décroître.

wangle ['wæŋgl] vt inf se débrouiller pour obtenir.

want [wɒnt] ♦ n 1. (*need*) besoin m. 2. (*lack*) manque m; **for ~ of** faute de, par manque de. 3. (*deprivation*) pauvreté f, besoin m. ♦ vt 1. (*desire*) vouloir; **to ~ to do sthg** vouloir faire qqch; **to ~ sb to do sthg** vouloir que qqn fasse qqch. 2. inf (*need*) avoir besoin de.

wanted ['wɒntɪd] adj: **to be ~ (by the police)** être recherché(e) (par la police).

wanton ['wɒntən] adj (*destruction, neglect*) gratuit(e).

war [wɔːr] n guerre f.

ward [wɔːd] n 1. (*in hospital*) salle f. 2. Br (POL) circonscription f électorale. 3. (JUR) pupille mf. ▶ **ward off** vt fus (*danger*) écarter; (*disease, blow*) éviter; (*evil spirits*) éloigner.

warden ['wɔːdn] n 1. (*of park etc*) gardien m, -enne f. 2. Br (*of youth hostel, hall of residence*) directeur m, -trice f. 3. Am (*of prison*) directeur m, -trice f.

warder ['wɔːdər] n (*in prison*) gardien m, -enne f.

wardrobe ['wɔːdrəʊb] n garde-robe f.

warehouse ['weəhaʊs, pl -haʊzɪz] n entrepôt m, magasin m.

wares [weəz] npl marchandises fpl.

warfare ['wɔːfeər] n (U) guerre f.

warhead ['wɔːhed] n ogive f, tête f.

warily ['weərəlɪ] adv avec précaution OR circonspection.

warm [wɔːm] ♦ adj 1. (*gen*) chaud(e); **it's ~ today** il fait chaud aujourd'hui. 2. (*friendly*) chaleureux(euse). ♦ vt chauffer. ▶ **warm to** vt fus (*person*) se prendre de sympathie pour; (*idea, place*) se mettre à aimer. ▶ **warm up** ♦ vt sep réchauffer. ♦ vi 1. (*person, room*) se réchauffer. 2. (*machine, engine*) chauffer. 3. (SPORT) s'échauffer.

warm-hearted [-'hɑːtɪd] adj chaleureux(euse), affectueux(euse).

warmly ['wɔːmlɪ] adv 1. (*in warm clothes*): **to dress ~** s'habiller chaudement. 2. (*in a friendly way*) chaleureusement.

warmth [wɔːmθ] n chaleur f.

warn [wɔːn] vt avertir, prévenir; **to ~ sb**

of sthg avertir qqn de qqch; **to ~ sb not to do sthg** conseiller à qqn de ne pas faire qqch, déconseiller à qqn de faire qqch.

warning ['wɔːnɪŋ] n avertissement m.

warning light n voyant m, avertisseur m lumineux.

warning triangle n Br triangle m de signalisation.

warp [wɔːp] ◆ vt 1. (wood) gauchir, voiler. 2. (personality) fausser, pervertir. ◆ vi (wood) gauchir, se voiler.

warrant ['wɒrənt] ◆ n (JUR) mandat m. ◆ vt 1. (justify) justifier. 2. (guarantee) garantir.

warranty ['wɒrəntɪ] n garantie f.

warren ['wɒrən] n terrier m.

warrior ['wɒrɪər] n guerrier m, -ère f.

Warsaw ['wɔːsɔː] n Varsovie; **the ~ Pact** le pacte de Varsovie.

warship ['wɔːʃɪp] n navire m de guerre.

wart [wɔːt] n verrue f.

wartime ['wɔːtaɪm] n: **in ~** en temps de guerre.

wary ['weərɪ] adj prudent(e), circonspect(e); **to be ~ of** se méfier de; **to be ~ of doing sthg** hésiter à faire qqch.

was [weak form wəz, strong form wɒz] pt → **be**.

wash [wɒʃ] ◆ n 1. (act) lavage m; **to have a ~** se laver; **to give sthg a ~** laver qqch. 2. (clothes) lessive f. 3. (from boat) remous m. ◆ vt (clean) laver; **to ~ one's hands** se laver les mains. ◆ vi se laver. ▶ **wash away** vt sep emporter. ▶ **wash up** vt sep Br: **to ~ the dishes up** faire OR laver la vaisselle. ◆ vi 1. Br (wash dishes) faire OR laver la vaisselle. 2. Am (wash oneself) se laver.

washable ['wɒʃəbl] adj lavable.

washbasin Br ['wɒʃ,beɪsn], **washbowl** Am ['wɒʃbəʊl] n lavabo m.

washcloth ['wɒʃ,klɒθ] n Am gant m de toilette.

washer ['wɒʃər] n 1. (TECH) rondelle f. 2. (washing machine) machine f à laver.

washing ['wɒʃɪŋ] n (U) 1. (action) lessive f. 2. (clothes) linge m, lessive f.

washing line n corde f à linge.

washing machine n machine f à laver.

washing powder n Br lessive f, détergent m.

Washington ['wɒʃɪŋtən] n (city): **~ D.C.** Washington.

washing-up n Br vaisselle f.

washing-up liquid n Br liquide m

pour la vaisselle.

washout ['wɒʃaʊt] n inf fiasco m.

washroom ['wɒʃrʊm] n Am toilettes fpl.

wasn't [wɒznt] = **was not**.

wasp [wɒsp] n guêpe f.

wastage ['weɪstɪdʒ] n gaspillage m.

waste [weɪst] ◆ adj (material) de rebut; (fuel) perdu(e); (area of land) en friche. ◆ n 1. (misuse) gaspillage m; **it's a ~ of money** (extravagance) c'est du gaspillage; (bad investment) c'est de l'argent perdu; **a ~ of time** une perte de temps. 2. (U) (refuse) déchets mpl, ordures fpl. ◆ vt (money, food, energy) gaspiller; (time, opportunity) perdre. ▶ **wastes** npl literary étendues fpl désertes.

wastebasket Am = **wastepaper basket**.

waste disposal unit n broyeur m d'ordures.

wasteful ['weɪstfʊl] adj (person) gaspilleur(euse); (activity) peu économique.

waste ground n (U) terrain m vague.

wastepaper basket, wastepaper bin [,weɪst'peɪpər-], **wastebasket** Am ['weɪst,bɑːskɪt] n corbeille f à papier.

watch [wɒtʃ] ◆ n 1. (timepiece) montre f. 2. (act of watching): **to keep ~** faire le guet, monter la garde; **to keep ~ on sb/sthg** surveiller qqn/qqch. 3. (guard) garde f; (NAUT) (shift) quart m. ◆ vt 1. (look at) regarder. 2. (spy on, guard) surveiller. 3. (be careful about) faire attention à. ◆ vi regarder. ▶ **watch out** vi faire attention, prendre garde.

watchdog ['wɒtʃdɒg] n 1. (dog) chien m de garde. 2. fig (organization) organisation f de contrôle.

watchful ['wɒtʃfʊl] adj vigilant(e).

watchmaker ['wɒtʃ,meɪkər] n horloger m.

watchman ['wɒtʃmən] (pl -men [-mən]) n gardien m.

water ['wɔːtər] ◆ n (liquid) eau f. ◆ vt arroser. ◆ vi 1. (eyes) pleurer, larmoyer. 2. (mouth): **my mouth was ~ing** j'en avais l'eau à la bouche. ▶ **waters** npl (sea) eaux fpl. ▶ **water down** vt sep 1. (dilute) diluer; (alcohol) couper d'eau. 2. usu pej (plan, demand) atténuer, modérer; (play, novel) édulcorer.

water bottle n gourde f, bidon m (à eau).

water closet n dated toilettes fpl, waters mpl.

watercolour ['wɔːtə,kʌlər] n 1. (pic-

ture) aquarelle *f*. **2.** (*paint*) peinture *f* à l'eau, couleur *f* pour aquarelle.

watercress ['wɔːtəkres] *n* cresson *m*.

waterfall ['wɔːtəfɔːl] *n* chute *f* d'eau, cascade *f*.

water heater *n* chauffe-eau *m inv*.

waterhole ['wɔːtəhəʊl] *n* mare *f*, point *m* d'eau.

watering can ['wɔːtərɪŋ-] *n* arrosoir *m*.

water level *n* niveau *m* de l'eau.

water lily *n* nénuphar *m*.

waterline ['wɔːtəlaɪn] *n* (NAUT) ligne *f* de flottaison.

waterlogged ['wɔːtəlɒgd] *adj* **1.** (*land*) détrempé(e). **2.** (*vessel*) plein(e) d'eau.

water main *n* conduite *f* principale d'eau.

watermark ['wɔːtəmɑːk] *n* **1.** (*in paper*) filigrane *m*. **2.** (*showing water level*) laisse *f*.

watermelon ['wɔːtə,melən] *n* pastèque *f*.

water polo *n* water-polo *m*.

waterproof ['wɔːtəpruːf] ◆ *adj* imperméable. ◆ *n* imperméable *m*.

watershed ['wɔːtəʃed] *n fig* (*turning point*) tournant *m*, moment *m* critique.

water skiing *n* ski *m* nautique.

water tank *n* réservoir *m* d'eau, citerne *f*.

watertight ['wɔːtətaɪt] *adj* **1.** (*waterproof*) étanche. **2.** *fig* (*excuse, contract*) parfait(e); (*argument*) irréfutable; (*plan*) infaillible.

waterway ['wɔːtəweɪ] *n* voie *f* navigable.

waterworks ['wɔːtəwɜːks] (*pl inv*) *n* (*building*) installation *f* hydraulique, usine *f* de distribution d'eau.

watery ['wɔːtərɪ] *adj* **1.** (*food, drink*) trop dilué(e); (*tea, coffee*) pas assez fort(e). **2.** (*pale*) pâle.

watt [wɒt] *n* watt *m*.

wave [weɪv] ◆ *n* **1.** (*of hand*) geste *m*, signe *m*. **2.** (*of water, emotion, nausea*) vague *f*. **3.** (*of light, sound*) onde *f*; (*of heat*) bouffée *f*. **4.** (*in hair*) cran *m*, ondulation *f*. ◆ *vt* (*arm, handkerchief*) agiter; (*flag, stick*) brandir. ◆ *vi* **1.** (*with hand*) faire signe de la main; **to ~ at** OR **to sb** faire signe à qqn, saluer qqn de la main. **2.** (*flags, trees*) flotter.

wavelength ['weɪvleŋθ] *n* longueur *f* d'ondes; **to be on the same ~** *fig* être sur la même longueur d'ondes.

waver ['weɪvər] *vi* **1.** (*falter*) vaciller, chanceler. **2.** (*hesitate*) hésiter, vaciller.

3. (*fluctuate*) fluctuer, varier.

wavy ['weɪvɪ] *adj* (*hair*) ondulé(e); (*line*) onduleux(euse).

wax [wæks] ◆ *n* (U) **1.** (*in candles, polish*) cire *f*; (*for skis*) fart *m*. **2.** (*in ears*) cérumen *m*. ◆ *vt* cirer; (*skis*) farter. ◆ *vi* (*moon*) croître.

wax paper *n* Am papier *m* sulfurisé.

waxworks ['wækswɜːks] (*pl inv*) *n* (*museum*) musée *m* de cire.

way [weɪ] ◆ *n* **1.** (*means, method*) façon *f*; **to get** OR **have one's ~** obtenir ce qu'on veut. **2.** (*manner, style*) façon *f*, manière *f*; **in the same ~** de la même manière OR façon; **this/that ~** comme ça, de cette façon; **in a ~** d'une certaine manière, en quelque sorte. **3.** (*route, path*) chemin *m*; **~ in** entrée *f*; **~ out** sortie *f*; **to be out of one's ~** (*place*) ne pas être sur sa route; **on** OR **one's ~** sur le OR son chemin; **to be under ~** (*ship*) faire route; *fig* (*meeting*) être en cours; **to get under ~** (*ship*) se mettre en route; *fig* (*meeting*) démarrer; **'give ~'** Br (AUT) 'vous n'avez pas la priorité'; **to be in the ~** gêner; **to go out of one's ~ to do sthg** se donner du mal pour faire qqch; **to keep out of sb's ~** éviter qqn; **keep out of the ~!** restez à l'écart!; **to make ~ for** faire place à. **4.** (*direction*): **to go/look/come this ~** aller/regarder/venir par ici; **the right/wrong ~ round** (*in sequence*) dans le bon/mauvais ordre; **she had her hat on the wrong ~ round** elle avait mis son chapeau à l'envers; **the right/wrong ~ up** dans le bon/mauvais sens. **5.** (*distance*): **all the ~** tout le trajet; *fig* (*support etc*) jusqu'au bout; **a long ~** loin. **6.** *phr*: **to give ~** (*under weight, pressure*) céder; **no ~!** pas question! ◆ *adv inf* (*a lot*) largement; **~ better** bien mieux. ▶ **ways** *npl* (*customs, habits*) coutumes *fpl*. ▶ **by the way** *adv* au fait.

waylay [,weɪ'leɪ] (*pt & pp* -**laid** [-'leɪd]) *vt* arrêter (au passage).

wayward ['weɪwəd] *adj* qui n'en fait qu'à sa tête; (*behaviour*) capricieux(euse).

WC (*abbr of* **water closet**) *n* W.-C. *mpl*.

we [wiː] *pers pron* nous; **we can't do it** nous, nous ne pouvons pas le faire; **as ~ say in France** comme on dit en France; **~ British** nous autres Britanniques.

weak [wiːk] *adj* **1.** (*gen*) faible. **2.** (*delicate*) fragile. **3.** (*unconvincing*) peu convaincant(e). **4.** (*drink*) léger(ère).

weaken ['wiːkn] ◆ *vt* **1.** (*undermine*)

affaiblir. **2.** (*reduce*) diminuer. **3.** (*physically - person*) affaiblir; (*- structure*) fragiliser. ♦ *vi* faiblir.

weakling ['wiːklɪŋ] *n pej* mauviette *f*.

weakness ['wiːknɪs] *n* **1.** (U) (*physical - of person*) faiblesse *f*; (*- of structure*) fragilité *f*. **2.** (*imperfect point*) point *m* faible, faiblesse *f*.

wealth [welθ] *n* **1.** (U) (*riches*) richesse *f*. **2.** (*abundance*): **a ~ of** une profusion de.

wealthy ['welθɪ] *adj* riche.

wean [wiːn] *vt* (*baby, lamb*) sevrer.

weapon ['wepən] *n* arme *f*.

weaponry ['wepənrɪ] *n* (U) armement *m*.

wear [weəʳ] (*pt* **wore**, *pp* **worn**) ♦ *n* (U) **1.** (*type of clothes*) tenue *f*. **2.** (*damage*) usure *f*; **~ and tear** usure. **3.** (*use*): **these shoes have had a lot of ~** ces chaussures ont fait beaucoup d'usage. ♦ *vt* **1.** (*clothes, hair*) porter. **2.** (*damage*) user. ♦ *vi* **1.** (*deteriorate*) s'user. **2.** (*last*): **to ~ well** durer longtemps, faire de l'usage; **to ~ badly** ne pas durer longtemps. ▶ **wear away** ♦ *vt sep* (*rock, wood*) user; (*grass*) abîmer. ♦ *vi* (*rock, wood*) s'user; (*grass*) s'abîmer. ▶ **wear down** *vt sep* **1.** (*material*) user. **2.** (*person, resistance*) épuiser. ▶ **wear off** *vi* disparaître. ▶ **wear out** ♦ *vt sep* **1.** (*shoes, clothes*) user. **2.** (*person*) épuiser. ♦ *vi* s'user.

weary ['wɪərɪ] *adj* **1.** (*exhausted*) las (lasse); (*sigh*) de lassitude. **2.** (*fed up*): **to be ~ of sthg/of doing sthg** être las de qqch/de faire qqch.

weasel ['wiːzl] *n* belette *f*.

weather ['weðəʳ] ♦ *n* temps *m*; **in all ~s** par tous les temps; **to be under the ~** être patraque. ♦ *vt* (*crisis, problem*) surmonter.

weather-beaten [-,biːtn] *adj* (*face, skin*) tanné(e).

weathercock ['weðəkɒk] *n* girouette *f*.

weather forecast *n* météo *f*, prévisions *fpl* météorologiques.

weatherman ['weðəmæn] (*pl* **-men** [-men]) *n* météorologue *m*.

weather vane [-veɪn] *n* girouette *f*.

weave [wiːv] (*pt* **wove**, *pp* **woven**) ♦ *vt* (*using loom*) tisser. ♦ *vi* (*move*) se faufiler.

weaver ['wiːvəʳ] *n* tisserand *m*, -e *f*.

web [web] *n* **1.** (*cobweb*) toile *f* (d'araignée). **2.** *fig* (*of lies*) tissu *m*.

Web site *n* (COMPUT) site *m* Web.

wed [wed] (*pt & pp* **wed** OR **-ded**) *literary*

♦ *vt* épouser. ♦ *vi* se marier.

we'd [wiːd] = **we had, we would**.

wedding ['wedɪŋ] *n* mariage *m*.

wedding anniversary *n* anniversaire *m* de mariage.

wedding cake *n* pièce *f* montée.

wedding dress *n* robe *f* de mariée.

wedding ring *n* alliance *f*.

wedge [wedʒ] ♦ *n* **1.** (*for steadying*) cale *f*. **2.** (*for splitting*) coin *m*. **3.** (*of cake, cheese*) morceau *m*. ♦ *vt* caler.

Wednesday ['wenzdɪ] *n* mercredi *m*; *see also* **Saturday**.

wee [wiː] ♦ *adj* Scot petit(e). ♦ *n v inf* pipi *m*. ♦ *vi v inf* faire pipi.

weed [wiːd] ♦ *n* **1.** (*plant*) mauvaise herbe *f*. **2.** Br inf (*feeble person*) mauviette *f*. ♦ *vt* désherber.

weedkiller ['wiːd,kɪləʳ] *n* désherbant *m*.

weedy ['wiːdɪ] *adj* Br inf (*feeble*) qui agit comme une mauviette.

week [wiːk] *n* semaine *f*.

weekday ['wiːkdeɪ] *n* jour *m* de semaine.

weekend [,wiːk'end] *n* week-end *m*; **on** OR **at the ~** le week-end.

weekly ['wiːklɪ] ♦ *adj* hebdomadaire. ♦ *adv* chaque semaine. ♦ *n* hebdomadaire *m*.

weep [wiːp] (*pt & pp* **wept**) *vt & vi* pleurer.

weeping willow [,wiːpɪŋ-] *n* saule *m* pleureur.

weigh [weɪ] *vt* **1.** (*gen*) peser. **2.** (NAUT): **to ~ anchor** lever l'ancre. ▶ **weigh down** *vt sep* **1.** (*physically*): **to be ~ed down with sthg** plier sous le poids de qqch. **2.** (*mentally*): **to be ~ed down by** OR **with sthg** être accablé par qqch. ▶ **weigh up** *vt sep* **1.** (*consider carefully*) examiner. **2.** (*size up*) juger, évaluer.

weight [weɪt] *n lit & fig* poids *m*; **to put on** OR **gain ~** prendre du poids, grossir; **to lose ~** perdre du poids, maigrir; **to pull one's ~** faire sa part du travail, participer à la tâche.

weighted ['weɪtɪd] *adj*: **to be ~ in favour of/against** être favorable/défavorable à.

weighting ['weɪtɪŋ] *n* indemnité *f*.

weightlifting ['weɪt,lɪftɪŋ] *n* haltérophilie *f*.

weighty ['weɪtɪ] *adj* (*serious*) important(e), de poids.

weir [wɪəʳ] *n* barrage *m*.

weird [wɪəd] *adj* bizarre.

welcome ['welkəm] ♦ *adj* **1.** (*guest, help*

etc) bienvenu(e). **2.** (*free*): **you're ~ to ...** n'hésitez pas à ... **3.** (*in reply to thanks*): **you're ~** il n'y a pas de quoi, de rien. ♦ *n* accueil *m*. ♦ *vt* **1.** (*receive*) accueillir. **2.** (*approve of*) se réjouir de. ♦ *excl* bienvenue!

weld [weld] ♦ *n* soudure *f*. ♦ *vt* souder.

welfare ['welfeə'] ♦ *adj* social(e). ♦ *n* **1.** (*well-being*) bien-être *m*. **2.** *Am* (*income support*) assistance *f* publique.

welfare state *n* État-providence *m*.

well [wel] (*compar* **better**, *superl* **best**) ♦ *adj* bien; **I'm very ~, thanks** je vais très bien, merci; **all is ~** tout va bien; **just as ~** aussi bien. ♦ *adv* bien; **the team was ~ beaten** l'équipe a été battue à plates coutures; **to go ~** aller bien; **~ done!** bravo!; **~ and truly** bel et bien. ♦ *n* (*for water, oil*) puits *m*. ♦ *excl* **1.** (*in hesitation*) heu!, eh bien! **2.** (*to correct oneself*) bon!, enfin! **3.** (*to express resignation*): **oh ~!** eh bien! **4.** (*in surprise*) tiens! ▶ **as well** *adv* **1.** (*in addition*) aussi, également. **2.** (*with same result*): **I/you** *etc* **may** OR **might as ~** (**do sthg**) je/tu *etc* ferais aussi bien (de faire qqch). ▶ **as well as** *conj* en plus de, aussi bien que. ▶ **well up** *vi*: **tears ~ed up in her eyes** les larmes lui montaient aux yeux.

we'll [wi:l] = **we shall, we will**.

well-advised [-əd'vaɪzd] *adj* sage; **you would be ~ to do sthg** tu ferais bien de faire qqch.

well-behaved [-bɪ'heɪvd] *adj* sage.

wellbeing [,wel'bi:ɪŋ] *n* bien-être *m*.

well-built *adj* bien bâti(e).

well-done *adj* (CULIN) bien cuit(e).

well-dressed [-'drest] *adj* bien habillé(e).

well-earned [-ɜ:nd] *adj* bien mérité(e).

well-heeled [-'hi:ld] *adj inf* nanti(e).

wellington boots ['welɪŋtən-], **wellingtons** ['welɪŋtənz] *npl* bottes *fpl* de caoutchouc.

well-kept *adj* **1.** (*building, garden*) bien tenu(e). **2.** (*secret*) bien gardé(e).

well-known *adj* bien connu(e).

well-mannered [-'mænəd] *adj* bien élevé(e).

well-meaning *adj* bien intentionné(e).

well-nigh [-naɪ] *adv* presque, pratiquement.

well-off *adj* **1.** (*rich*) riche. **2.** (*well-provided*): **to be ~ for sthg** être bien pourvu(e) en qqch.

well-read [-'red] *adj* cultivé(e).

well-rounded [-'raundɪd] *adj* (*education, background*) complet(ète).

well-timed [-'taɪmd] *adj* bien calculé(e), qui vient à point nommé.

well-to-do *adj* riche.

wellwisher ['wel,wɪʃə'] *n* admirateur *m*, -trice *f*.

Welsh [welʃ] ♦ *adj* gallois(e). ♦ *n* (*language*) gallois *m*. ♦ *npl*: **the ~** les Gallois *mpl*.

Welshman ['welʃmən] (*pl* **-men** [-mən]) *n* Gallois *m*.

Welshwoman ['welʃ,wumən] (*pl* **-women** [-,wɪmɪn]) *n* Galloise *f*.

went [went] *pt* → **go**.

wept [wept] *pt & pp* → **weep**.

were [wɜ:'] → **be**.

we're [wɪə'] = **we are**.

weren't [wɜ:nt] = **were not**.

west [west] ♦ *n* **1.** (*direction*) ouest *m*. **2.** (*region*): **the ~** l'ouest *m*. ♦ *adj* ouest (*inv*) d'ouest. ♦ *adv* de l'ouest, vers l'ouest; **~ of** à l'ouest de. ▶ **West** *n* (POL): **the West** l'Occident *m*.

West Bank *n*: **the ~** la Cisjordanie.

West Country *n Br*: **the ~** le sud-ouest de l'Angleterre.

West End *n Br*: **the ~** le West-End (*quartier des grands magasins et des théâtres, à Londres*).

westerly ['westəlɪ] *adj* à l'ouest; (*wind*) de l'ouest; **in a ~ direction** vers l'ouest.

western ['westən] ♦ *adj* **1.** (*gen*) de l'ouest. **2.** (POL) occidental(e). ♦ *n* (*book, film*) western *m*.

West German ♦ *adj* ouest-allemand(e). ♦ *n* Allemand *m*, -e *f* de l'Ouest.

West Germany *n*: (**former**) **~** (ex-)Allemagne *f* de l'Ouest.

West Indian ♦ *adj* antillais(e). ♦ *n* Antillais *m*, -e *f*.

West Indies [-'ɪndi:z] *npl*: **the ~** les Antilles *fpl*.

Westminster ['westmɪnstə'] *n* quartier de Londres où se situe le Parlement britannique.

westward ['westwəd] *adj & adv* vers l'ouest.

westwards ['westwədz] *adv* vers l'ouest.

wet [wet] (*pt & pp* **wet** OR **-ted**) ♦ *adj* **1.** (*damp, soaked*) mouillé(e). **2.** (*rainy*) pluvieux(euse). **3.** (*not dry-paint, cement*) frais (fraîche). **4.** *Br inf pej* (*weak, feeble*) ramolli(e). ♦ *n inf* (POL) modéré *m*, -e *f*. ♦ *vt* mouiller.

wet blanket n inf pej rabat-joie m inv.

wet suit n combinaison f de plongée.

we've [wi:v] = **we have.**

whack [wæk] inf ◆ n 1. (share) part f. 2. (hit) grand coup m. ◆ vt donner un grand coup à, frapper fort.

whale [weɪl] n baleine f.

wharf [wɔ:f] (pl -s OR **wharves** [wɔ:vz]) n quai m.

what [wɒt] ◆ adj 1. (in direct, indirect questions) quel (quelle), quels (quelles) (pl); ~ **colour is it?** c'est de quelle couleur?; **he asked me ~ colour it was** il m'a demandé de quelle couleur c'était. 2. (in exclamations) quel (quelle), quels (quelles) (pl); ~ **a surprise!** quelle surprise!; ~ **an idiot I am!** ce que je peux être bête! ◆ pron 1. (interrogative - subject) qu'est-ce qui; (- object) qu'est-ce que, que; (- after prep) quoi; ~ **are they doing?** qu'est-ce qu'ils font?, que font-ils?; ~ **is going on?** qu'est-ce qui se passe?; ~ **are they talking about?** de quoi parlent-ils?; ~ **about another drink/going out for a meal?** et si on prenait un autre verre/allait manger au restaurant?; ~ **about the rest of us?** et nous alors?; ~ **if ...?** et si ...? 2. (relative - subject) ce qui; (- object) ce que; **I saw ~ happened/fell** j'ai vu ce qui s'était passé/était tombé; **you can't have ~ you want** tu ne peux pas avoir ce que tu veux. ◆ excl (expressing disbelief) comment!, quoi!

whatever [wɒt'evər] ◆ adj quel (quelle) que soit; **any book ~** n'importe quel livre; **no chance ~** pas la moindre chance; **nothing ~** rien du tout. ◆ pron quoi que (+ subjunctive); **I'll do ~ I can** je ferai tout ce que je peux; ~ **can this be?** qu'est-ce que cela peut-il bien être?; ~ **that may mean** quoi que cela puisse bien vouloir dire; **or ~** ou n'importe quoi d'autre.

whatsoever [ˌwɒtsəʊ'evər] adj: **I had no interest ~** je n'éprouvais pas le moindre intérêt; **nothing ~** rien du tout.

wheat [wi:t] n blé m.

wheedle [ˈwi:dl] vt: **to ~ sb into doing sthg** enjôler qqn pour qu'il fasse qqch; **to ~ sthg out of sb** enjôler qqn pour obtenir qqch.

wheel [wi:l] ◆ n 1. (gen) roue f. 2. (steering wheel) volant m. ◆ vt pousser. ◆ vi: **to ~ (round)** se retourner brusquement.

wheelbarrow [ˈwi:lˌbærəʊ] n brouette f.

wheelchair [ˈwi:lˌtʃeər] n fauteuil m roulant.

wheelclamp [ˈwi:lˌklæmp] ◆ n sabot m de Denver. ◆ vt: **my car was ~ed** on a mis un sabot à ma voiture.

wheeze [wi:z] ◆ n (sound) respiration f sifflante. ◆ vi respirer avec un bruit sifflant.

whelk [welk] n bulot m, buccin m.

when [wen] ◆ adv (in direct, indirect questions) quand; ~ **does the plane arrive?** quand OR à quelle heure arrive l'avion?; **he asked me ~ I would be in London** il m'a demandé quand je serais à Londres. ◆ conj 1. (referring to time) quand, lorsque; **he came to see me ~ I was abroad** il est venu me voir quand j'étais à l'étranger; **one day ~ I was on my own** un jour que OR où j'étais tout seul; **on the day ~ it happened** le jour où cela s'est passé. 2. (whereas, considering that) alors que.

whenever [wen'evər] ◆ conj quand; (each time that) chaque fois que. ◆ adv n'importe quand.

where [weər] ◆ adv (in direct, indirect questions) où; ~ **do you live?** où habitez-vous?; **do you know ~ he lives?** est-ce que vous savez où il habite? ◆ conj 1. (referring to place, situation) où; **this is ~ ...** c'est là que ... 2. (whereas) alors que.

whereabouts [adv ˌweərə'baʊts, n 'weərəbaʊts] ◆ adv où. ◆ npl: **their ~ are still unknown** on ne sait toujours pas où ils se trouvent.

whereas [weər'æz] conj alors que.

whereby [weə'baɪ] conj fml par lequel (laquelle), au moyen duquel (de laquelle).

whereupon [ˌweərə'pɒn] conj fml après quoi, sur quoi.

wherever [weər'evər] ◆ conj où que (+ subjunctive). ◆ adv 1. (no matter where) n'importe où. 2. (where) où donc; ~ **did you hear that?** mais où donc as-tu entendu dire cela?

wherewithal [ˈweəwɪðɔ:l] n fml: **to have the ~ to do sthg** avoir les moyens de faire qqch.

whet [wet] vt: **to ~ sb's appetite for sthg** donner à qqn envie de qqch.

whether [ˈweðər] conj 1. (indicating choice, doubt) si. 2. (no matter if): ~ **I want to or not** que je le veuille ou non.

which [wɪtʃ] ◆ adj 1. (in direct, indirect questions) quel (quelle), quels (quelles) (pl); ~ **house is yours?** quelle maison est la tienne?; ~ **one?** lequel (laquelle)?

2. (to refer back to sthg): **in ~ case** auquel cas. ◆ pron **1.** (in direct, indirect questions) lequel (laquelle), lesquels (lesquelles) (pl); **~ do you prefer?** lequel préférez-vous? **I can't decide ~ to have** je ne sais vraiment pas lequel prendre. **2.** (in relative clauses - subject) qui; (- object) que; (- after prep) lequel (laquelle), lesquels (lesquelles) (pl); **take the slice ~ is nearer to you** prends la tranche qui est le plus près de toi; **the television ~ we bought** le téléviseur que nous avons acheté; **the settee on ~ I am sitting** le canapé sur lequel je suis assis; **the film of ~ you spoke** le film dont vous avez parlé. **3.** (referring back - subject) ce qui; (- object) ce que; **why did you say you were ill, ~ nobody believed?** pourquoi as-tu dit que tu étais malade, ce que personne n'a cru?

whichever [wɪtʃ'evər] ◆ adj quel (quelle) que soit; **choose ~ colour you prefer** choisissez la couleur que vous préférez, n'importe laquelle. ◆ pron n'importe lequel (laquelle).

whiff [wɪf] n (of perfume, smoke) bouffée f; (of food) odeur f.

while [waɪl] ◆ n moment m; **let's stay here for a ~** restons ici un moment; **for a long ~** longtemps; **after a ~** après quelque temps. ◆ conj **1.** (during the time that) pendant que. **2.** (as long as) tant que. **3.** (whereas) alors que. ▶ **while away** vt sep passer.

whilst [waɪlst] conj = **while**.

whim [wɪm] n lubie f.

whimper ['wɪmpər] vt & vi gémir.

whimsical ['wɪmzɪkl] adj saugrenu(e).

whine [waɪn] vi (make sound) gémir.

whinge [wɪndʒ] vi Br: **to ~ (about)** se plaindre (de).

whip [wɪp] ◆ n **1.** (for hitting) fouet m. **2.** Br (POL) chef m de file (d'un groupe parlementaire). ◆ vt **1.** (gen) fouetter. **2.** (take quickly): **to ~ sthg out** sortir qqch brusquement; **to ~ sthg off** ôter OR enlever qqch brusquement.

whipped cream [wɪpt-] n crème f fouettée.

whip-round n Br inf: **to have a ~** faire une collecte.

whirl [wɜːl] ◆ n lit & fig tourbillon m. ◆ vt: **to ~ sb/sthg round** (spin round) faire tourbillonner qqn/qqch. ◆ vi tourbillonner; fig (head, mind) tourner.

whirlpool ['wɜːlpuːl] n tourbillon m.

whirlwind ['wɜːlwɪnd] n tornade f.

whirr [wɜːr] vi (engine) ronronner.

whisk [wɪsk] ◆ n (CULIN) fouet m, batteur m (à œufs). ◆ vt **1.** (move quickly) emmener OR emporter rapidement. **2.** (CULIN) battre.

whisker ['wɪskər] n moustache f. ▶ **whiskers** npl favoris mpl.

whisky Br, **whiskey** Am & Irish (pl whiskeys) ['wɪskɪ] n whisky m.

whisper ['wɪspər] ◆ vt murmurer, chuchoter. ◆ vi chuchoter.

whistle ['wɪsl] ◆ n **1.** (sound) sifflement m. **2.** (device) sifflet m. ◆ vt & vi siffler.

white [waɪt] ◆ adj **1.** (in colour) blanc (blanche). **2.** (coffee, tea) au lait. ◆ n **1.** (colour, of egg, eye) blanc m. **2.** (person) Blanc m, Blanche f.

white-collar adj de bureau.

white elephant n fig objet m coûteux et inutile.

Whitehall ['waɪthɔːl] n rue de Londres, centre administratif du gouvernement britannique.

white-hot adj chauffé(e) à blanc.

White House n: **the ~** la Maison-Blanche.

white lie n pieux mensonge m.

whiteness ['waɪtnɪs] n blancheur f.

white paper n (POL) livre m blanc.

white sauce n sauce f blanche.

white spirit n Br white-spirit m.

whitewash ['waɪtwɒʃ] ◆ n **1.** (U) (paint) chaux f. **2.** pej (cover-up): **a government ~** une combine du gouvernement pour étouffer l'affaire. ◆ vt (paint) blanchir à la chaux.

whiting ['waɪtɪŋ] (pl inv OR -s) n merlan m.

Whitsun ['wɪtsn] n Pentecôte f.

whittle ['wɪtl] vt (reduce): **to ~ sthg away** OR **down** réduire qqch.

whiz, whizz [wɪz] vi (go fast) aller à toute allure.

whiz(z) kid n inf petit prodige m.

who [huː] pron **1.** (in direct, indirect questions) qui; **~ are you?** qui êtes-vous?; **I didn't know ~ she was** je ne savais pas qui c'était. **2.** (in relative clauses) qui; **he's the doctor ~ treated me** c'est le médecin qui m'a soigné; **I don't know the person ~ came to see you** je ne connais pas la personne qui est venue vous voir.

who'd [huːd] = **who had**, **who would**.

whodu(n)nit [ˌhuːˈdʌnɪt] n inf polar m.

whoever [huːˈevər] pron **1.** (unknown person) quiconque. **2.** (indicating surprise, astonishment) qui donc. **3.** (no matter who) qui que (+ *subjunctive*); ~ **you are** qui que vous soyez; ~ **wins** qui que ce soit qui gagne.

whole [həʊl] ◆ *adj* **1.** (*entire, complete*) entier(ère). **2.** (*for emphasis*): **a** ~ **lot bigger** bien plus gros; **a** ~ **new idea** une idée tout à fait nouvelle. ◆ *n* **1.** (*all*): **the** ~ **of the school** toute l'école; **the** ~ **of the summer** tout l'été. **2.** (*unit, complete thing*) tout *m*. ► **as a whole** *adv* dans son ensemble. ► **on the whole** *adv* dans l'ensemble.

wholefood ['həʊlfuːd] *n* Br aliments *mpl* complets.

whole-hearted [-'hɑːtɪd] *adj* sans réserve, total(e).

wholemeal ['həʊlmiːl] Br, **whole wheat** Am *adj* complet(ète).

wholesale ['həʊlseɪl] ◆ *adj* **1.** (*buying, selling*) en gros; (*price*) de gros. **2.** *pej* (*excessive*) en masse. ◆ *adv* **1.** (*in bulk*) en gros. **2.** *pej* (*excessively*) en masse.

wholesaler ['həʊl,seɪlər] *n* marchand *m* de gros, grossiste *mf*.

wholesome ['həʊlsəm] *adj* sain(e).

whole wheat Am = wholemeal.

who'll [huːl] = who will.

wholly ['həʊlɪ] *adv* totalement.

whom [huːm] *pron fml* **1.** (*in direct, indirect questions*) qui; ~ **did you phone?** qui avez-vous appelé au téléphone?; **for/of/to** ~ pour/de/à qui. **2.** (*in relative clauses*) que; **the girl** ~ **he married** la jeune fille qu'il a épousée; **the man of** ~ **you speak** l'homme dont vous parlez; **the man to** ~ **you were speaking** l'homme à qui vous parliez.

whooping cough ['huːpɪŋ-] *n* coqueluche *f*.

whopping ['wɒpɪŋ] *inf* ◆ *adj* énorme. ◆ *adv*: **a** ~ **great lorry/lie** un camion/mensonge absolument énorme.

whore [hɔːr] *n offensive* putain *f*.

who're ['huːər] = who are.

whose [huːz] ◆ *pron* (*in direct, indirect questions*) à qui; ~ **is this?** à qui est ceci? ◆ *adj* **1.** à qui; ~ **car is that?** à qui est cette voiture?; ~ **son is he?** de qui est-il le fils? **2.** (*in relative clauses*) dont; **that's the boy** ~ **father's an MP** c'est le garçon dont le père est député; **the girl** ~ **mother you phoned yesterday** la fille à la mère de qui OR de laquelle tu as téléphoné hier.

who's who [huːz-] *n* (*book*) Bottin® *m* mondain.

who've [huːv] = who have.

why [waɪ] ◆ *adv* (*in direct questions*) pourquoi; ~ **did you lie to me?** pourquoi m'as-tu menti?; ~ **don't you all come?** pourquoi ne pas tous venir?, pourquoi est-ce que vous ne viendriez pas tous?; ~ **not?** pourquoi pas? ◆ *conj* pourquoi; **I don't know** ~ **he said that** je ne sais pas pourquoi il a dit cela. ◆ *pron*: **there are several reasons** ~ **he left** il est parti pour plusieurs raisons, les raisons pour lesquelles il est parti sont nombreuses; **I don't know the reason** ~ je ne sais pas pourquoi. ◆ *excl* tiens! ► **why ever** *adv* pourquoi donc.

wick [wɪk] *n* (*of candle, lighter*) mèche *f*.

wicked ['wɪkɪd] *adj* **1.** (*evil*) mauvais(e). **2.** (*mischievous, devilish*) malicieux(euse).

wicker ['wɪkər] *adj* en osier.

wickerwork ['wɪkəwɜːk] *n* vannerie *f*.

wicket ['wɪkɪt] *n* (CRICKET) **1.** (*stumps, dismissal*) guichet *m*. **2.** (*pitch*) terrain *m* entre les guichets.

wide [waɪd] ◆ *adj* **1.** (*gen*) large; **how** ~ **is the room?** quelle est la largeur de la pièce?; **to be six metres** ~ faire six mètres de large OR de largeur. **2.** (*gap, difference*) grand(e). **3.** (*experience, knowledge, issue*) vaste. ◆ *adv* **1.** (*broadly*) largement; **open** ~! ouvrez grand! **2.** (*off-target*): **the shot went** ~ le coup est passé loin du but OR à côté.

wide-angle lens *n* (PHOT) objectif *m* grand angle.

wide-awake *adj* tout à fait réveillé(e).

widely ['waɪdlɪ] *adv* **1.** (*smile, vary*) largement. **2.** (*extensively*) beaucoup; **to be** ~ **read** avoir beaucoup lu; **it is** ~ **believed that ...** beaucoup pensent que ..., nombreux sont ceux qui pensent que ...

widen ['waɪdn] *vt* **1.** (*make broader*) élargir. **2.** (*gap, difference*) agrandir, élargir.

wide open *adj* grand ouvert (grande ouverte).

wide-ranging [-'reɪndʒɪŋ] *adj* varié(e); (*consequences*) de grande envergure.

widespread ['waɪdspred] *adj* très répandu(e).

widow ['wɪdəʊ] *n* veuve *f*.

widowed ['wɪdəʊd] *adj* veuf (veuve).

widower ['wɪdəʊər] *n* veuf *m*.

width [wɪdθ] *n* largeur *f*; **in** ~ de large.

wield [wiːld] *vt* **1.** (*weapon*) manier. **2.** (*power*) exercer.

wife [waɪf] (pl **wives**) n femme f, épouse f.

wig [wɪg] n perruque f.

wiggle ['wɪgl] inf vt remuer.

wild [waɪld] adj 1. (animal, attack, scenery, flower) sauvage. 2. (weather, sea) déchaîné(e). 3. (laughter, hope, plan) fou (folle). 4. (random - estimate) fantaisiste; I made a ~ guess j'ai dit ça au hasard. ▶ **wilds** npl: **the ~s of** le fin fond de; **to live in the ~s** habiter en pleine nature.

wilderness ['wɪldənɪs] n étendue f sauvage.

wild-goose chase n inf: **it turned out to be a ~** ça s'est révélé être totalement inutile.

wildlife ['waɪldlaɪf] n (U) faune f et flore f.

wildly ['waɪldlɪ] adv 1. (enthusiastically, fanatically) frénétiquement. 2. (guess, suggest) au hasard; (shoot) dans tous les sens. 3. (very - different, impractical) tout à fait.

wilful Br, **willful** Am ['wɪlful] adj 1. (determined) obstiné(e). 2. (deliberate) délibéré(e).

will¹ [wɪl] ◆ n 1. (mental) volonté f; **against one's ~** contre son gré. 2. (document) testament m. ◆ vt: **to ~ sthg to happen** prier de toutes ses forces pour que qqch se passe; **to ~ sb to do sthg** concentrer toute sa volonté sur qqn pour qu'il fasse qqch.

will² [wɪl] modal vb 1. (to express future tense): I ~ **see you next week** je te verrai la semaine prochaine; **when ~ you have finished it?** quand est-ce que vous l'aurez fini?; ~ **you be here next week?** – **yes I ~/no I won't** est-ce que tu seras là la semaine prochaine? – oui/non. 2. (indicating willingness): ~ **you have some more tea?** voulez-vous encore du thé?; I **won't do it** je refuse de le faire, je ne veux pas le faire. 3. (in commands, requests): **you ~ leave this house at once** tu vas quitter cette maison tout de suite; **close that window, ~ you?** ferme cette fenêtre, veux-tu?; ~ **you be quiet!** veux-tu te taire!, tu vas te taire! 4. (indicating possibility, what usually happens): **the hall ~ hold up to 1000 people** la salle peut abriter jusqu'à 1 000 personnes. 5. (expressing an assumption): **that'll be your father** cela doit être ton père. 6. (indicating irritation): **she ~ keep phoning me** elle n'arrête pas de me téléphoner.

willful Am = **wilful**.

willing ['wɪlɪŋ] adj 1. (prepared): **if you're ~** si vous voulez bien; **to be ~ to do sthg** être disposé(e) OR prêt(e) à faire qqch. 2. (eager) enthousiaste.

willingly ['wɪlɪŋlɪ] adv volontiers.

willow (tree) ['wɪləʊ-] n saule m.

willpower ['wɪl,paʊəʳ] n volonté f.

willy-nilly [,wɪlɪ'nɪlɪ] adv 1. (at random) n'importe comment. 2. (wanting to or not) bon gré mal gré.

wilt [wɪlt] vi (plant) se faner; fig (person) dépérir.

wily ['waɪlɪ] adj rusé(e).

wimp [wɪmp] n pej inf mauviette f.

win [wɪn] (pt & pp **won**) ◆ n victoire f. ◆ vt 1. (game, prize, competition) gagner. 2. (support, approval) obtenir; (love, friendship) gagner. ◆ vi gagner. ▶ **win over, win round** vt sep convaincre, gagner à sa cause.

wince [wɪns] vi: **to ~ (at/with)** (with body) tressaillir (à/de); (with face) grimacer (à/de).

winch [wɪntʃ] n treuil m.

wind¹ [wɪnd] ◆ n 1. (METEOR) vent m. 2. (breath) souffle m. 3. (U) (in stomach) gaz mpl. ◆ vt (knock breath out of) couper le souffle à.

wind² [waɪnd] (pt & pp **wound**) ◆ vt 1. (string, thread) enrouler. 2. (clock) remonter. ◆ vi (river, road) serpenter. ▶ **wind down** ◆ vt sep 1. (car window) baisser. 2. (business) cesser graduellement. ◆ vi (relax) se détendre. ▶ **wind up** vt sep 1. (finish - meeting) clôturer; (- business) liquider. 2. (clock, car window) remonter. 3. Br inf (deliberately annoy) faire marcher. 4. inf (end up): **to ~ up doing sthg** finir par faire qqch.

windfall ['wɪndfɔːl] n (unexpected gift) aubaine f.

winding ['waɪndɪŋ] adj sinueux(euse).

wind instrument [wɪnd-] n instrument m à vent.

windmill ['wɪndmɪl] n moulin m à vent.

window ['wɪndəʊ] n 1. (gen & COMPUT) fenêtre f. 2. (pane of glass, in car) vitre f. 3. (of shop) vitrine f.

window box n jardinière f.

window cleaner n laveur m, -euse f de vitres.

window ledge n rebord m de fenêtre.

window pane n vitre f.

windowsill ['wɪndəʊsɪl] n (outside) rebord m de fenêtre; (inside) appui m de fenêtre.

windpipe ['wɪndpaɪp] *n* trachée *f*.
windscreen *Br* ['wɪndskriːn], **wind-shield** *Am* ['wɪndʃiːld] *n* pare-brise *m inv*.
windscreen washer *n* lave-glace *m*.
windscreen wiper [-,waɪpəʳ] *n* essuie-glace *m*.
windshield *Am* = **windscreen**.
windsurfing ['wɪndsɜːfɪŋ] *n*: **to go ~** faire de la planche à voile.
windswept ['wɪndswept] *adj* (*scenery*) balayé(e) par les vents.
windy ['wɪndɪ] *adj* venteux(euse); **it's ~** il fait *OR* il y a du vent.
wine [waɪn] *n* vin *m*.
wine bar *n Br* bar *m* à vin.
wine cellar *n* cave *f* (à vin).
wineglass ['waɪnglɑːs] *n* verre *m* à vin.
wine list *n* carte *f* des vins.
wine merchant *n Br* marchand *m* de vins.
wine tasting [-,teɪstɪŋ] *n* dégustation *f* (de vins).
wine waiter *n* sommelier *m*.
wing [wɪŋ] *n* aile *f*. ► **wings** *npl* (THEA-TRE): **the ~s** les coulisses *fpl*.
winger ['wɪŋəʳ] *n* (SPORT) ailier *m*.
wink [wɪŋk] ◆ *n* clin *m* d'œil. ◆ *vi* (*with eyes*): **to ~ (at sb)** faire un clin d'œil (à qqn).
winkle ['wɪŋkl] *n* bigorneau *m*. ► **winkle out** *vt sep* extirper; **to ~ sthg out of sb** arracher qqch à qqn.
winner ['wɪnəʳ] *n* (*person*) gagnant *m*, -e *f*.
winning ['wɪnɪŋ] *adj* (*victorious, success-ful*) gagnant(e). ► **winnings** *npl* gains *mpl*.
winning post *n* poteau *m* d'arrivée.
winter ['wɪntəʳ] ◆ *n* hiver *m*; **in ~** en hiver. ◆ *comp* d'hiver.
winter sports *npl* sports *mpl* d'hiver.
wintertime ['wɪntətaɪm] *n* (U) hiver *m*.
wint(e)ry ['wɪntrɪ] *adj* d'hiver.
wipe [waɪp] ◆ *n*: **to give sthg a ~** essuyer qqch, donner un coup de torchon à qqch. ◆ *vt* essuyer. ► **wipe out** *vt sep* 1. (*erase*) effacer. 2. (*eradicate*) anéantir. ► **wipe up** *vt sep & vi* essuyer.
wire ['waɪəʳ] ◆ *n* 1. (U) (*metal*) fil *m* de fer. 2. (*cable etc*) fil *m*. 3. (*telegram*) télégramme *m*. ◆ *vt* 1. (ELEC - *plug*) installer; (- *house*) faire l'installation électrique de. 2. (*send telegram to*) télégraphier à.
wireless ['waɪəlɪs] *n dated* T.S.F. *f*.

wiring ['waɪərɪŋ] *n* (U) installation *f* électrique.
wiry ['waɪərɪ] *adj* 1. (*hair*) crépu(e). 2. (*body, man*) noueux(euse).
wisdom ['wɪzdəm] *n* sagesse *f*.
wisdom tooth *n* dent *f* de sagesse.
wise [waɪz] *adj* sage.
wisecrack ['waɪzkræk] *n pej* vanne *f*.
wish [wɪʃ] ◆ *n* 1. (*desire*) souhait *m*, désir *m*; **~ for sthg/to do sthg** désir de qqch/de faire qqch. 2. (*magic request*) vœu *m*. ◆ *vt* 1. (*want*): **to ~ to do sthg** souhaiter faire qqch; **I ~ (that) he'd come** j'aimerais bien qu'il vienne; **I ~ I could** si seulement je pouvais. 2. (*expressing hope*): **to ~ sb sthg** souhaiter qqch à qqn. ◆ *vi* (*by magic*): **to ~ for sthg** souhaiter qqch. ► **wishes** *npl*: **best ~es** meilleurs vœux; **(with) best ~es** (*at end of letter*) bien amicalement.
wishful thinking [,wɪʃful-] *n*: **that's just ~** c'est prendre mes/ses *etc* désirs pour des réalités.
wishy-washy ['wɪʃɪ,wɒʃɪ] *adj inf pej* (*person*) sans personnalité; (*ideas*) vague.
wisp [wɪsp] *n* 1. (*tuft*) mèche *f*. 2. (*small cloud*) mince filet *m* OR volute *f*.
wistful ['wɪstful] *adj* nostalgique.
wit [wɪt] *n* 1. (*humour*) esprit *m*. 2. (*intelligence*): **to have the ~ to do sthg** avoir l'intelligence de faire qqch. ► **wits** *npl*: **to have** OR **keep one's ~s about one** être attentif(ive) OR sur ses gardes.
witch [wɪtʃ] *n* sorcière *f*.
with [wɪð] *prep* 1. (*in company of*) avec; **I play tennis ~ his wife** je joue au tennis avec sa femme; **we stayed ~ them for a week** nous avons passé une semaine chez eux. 2. (*indicating opposition*) avec; **to argue ~ sb** discuter avec qqn; **the war ~ Germany** la guerre avec OR contre l'Allemagne. 3. (*indicating means, manner, feelings*) avec; **I washed it ~ detergent** je l'ai lavé avec un détergent; **she was trembling ~ fright** elle tremblait de peur. 4. (*having*) avec; **a man ~ a beard** un homme avec une barbe, un barbu; **the man ~ the moustache** l'homme à la moustache. 5. (*regarding*): **he's very mean ~ money** il est très près de ses sous, il est très avare; **the trouble ~ her is that ...** l'ennui avec elle OR ce qu'il y a avec elle c'est que ... 6. (*indicating simultaneity*): **I can't do it ~ you watching me** je ne peux pas le faire quand OR pendant que tu me regardes.

word

7. (*because of*): ~ **my luck, I'll probably lose** avec ma chance habituelle, je suis sûr de perdre. **8.** *phr:* **I'm ~ you** (*I understand*) je vous suis; (*I'm on your side*) je suis des vôtres; (*I agree*) je suis d'accord avec vous.

withdraw [wɪð'drɔ:] (*pt* -**drew**, *pp* -**drawn**) ◆ *vt* **1.** *fml* (*remove*): **to ~ sthg (from)** enlever qqch (de). **2.** (*money, troops, remark*) retirer. ◆ *vi* **1.** *fml* (*leave*): **to ~ (from)** se retirer (de). **2.** (MIL) se replier; **to ~ from** évacuer. **3.** (*quit, give up*): **to ~ (from)** se retirer (de).

withdrawal [wɪð'drɔ:əl] *n* **1.** (*gen*): ~ **(from)** retrait *m* (de). **2.** (MIL) repli *m*.

withdrawal symptoms *npl* crise *f* de manque.

withdrawn [wɪð'drɔ:n] ◆ *pp* → **withdraw**. ◆ *adj* (*shy, quiet*) renfermé(e).

withdrew [wɪð'dru:] *pt* → **withdraw**.

wither [wɪðə⁻] *vi* **1.** (*dry up*) se flétrir. **2.** (*weaken*) mourir.

withhold [wɪð'həʊld] (*pt & pp* -**held** [-'held]) *vt* (*services*) refuser; (*information*) cacher; (*salary*) retenir.

within [wɪ'ðɪn] ◆ *prep* **1.** (*inside*) à l'intérieur de, dans; ~ **her** en elle, à l'intérieur d'elle-même. **2.** (*budget, comprehension*) dans les limites de; (*limits*) dans. **3.** (*less than - distance*) à moins de; (*- time*) d'ici, en moins de; ~ **the week** avant la fin de la semaine. ◆ *adv* à l'intérieur.

without [wɪð'aʊt] ◆ *prep* sans; ~ **a coat** sans manteau; **I left ~ seeing him** je suis parti sans l'avoir vu; **I left ~ him seeing me** je suis parti sans qu'il m'ait vu; **to go ~ sthg** se passer de qqch. ◆ *adv*: **to go** OR **do ~** s'en passer.

withstand [wɪð'stænd] (*pt & pp* -**stood** [-'stʊd]) *vt* résister à.

witness [wɪtnɪs] ◆ *n* **1.** (*gen*) témoin *m*. **2.** (*testimony*): **to bear ~ to sthg** témoigner de qqch. ◆ *vt* **1.** (*accident, crime*) être témoin de. **2.** *fig* (*changes, rise in birth rate*) assister à. **3.** (*countersign*) contresigner.

witness box *Br*, **witness stand** *Am n* barre *f* des témoins.

witticism [wɪtɪsɪzm] *n* mot *m* d'esprit.

witty [wɪtɪ] *adj* plein(e) d'esprit, spirituel(elle).

wives [waɪvz] *pl* → **wife**.

wizard [wɪzəd] *n* magicien *m*; *fig* as *m*, champion *m*, -onne *f*.

wobble [wɒbl] *vi* (*hand, wings*) trembler; (*chair, table*) branler.

woe [wəʊ] *n literary* malheur *m*.

woke [wəʊk] *pt* → **wake**.

woken [wəʊkn] *pp* → **wake**.

wolf [wʊlf] (*pl* **wolves**) *n* (*animal*) loup *m*.

woman [wʊmən] (*pl* **women**) ◆ *n* femme *f*. ◆ *comp:* ~ **doctor** femme *f* médecin; ~ **teacher** professeur *m* femme.

womanly [wʊmənlɪ] *adj* féminin(e).

womb [wu:m] *n* utérus *m*.

women [wɪmɪn] *pl* → **woman**.

women's lib *n* libération *f* de la femme.

women's liberation *n* libération *f* de la femme.

won [wʌn] *pt & pp* → **win**.

wonder [wʌndə⁻] ◆ *n* **1.** (U) (*amazement*) étonnement *m*. **2.** (*cause for surprise*): **it's a ~ (that)** ... c'est un miracle que ...; **it's no** OR **little** OR **small ~ (that)** ... il n'est pas étonnant que ... **3.** (*amazing thing, person*) merveille *f*. ◆ *vt* **1.** (*speculate*): **to ~ (if** OR **whether)** se demander (si). **2.** (*in polite requests*): **I ~ whether you would mind shutting the window?** est-ce que cela ne vous ennuierait pas de fermer la fenêtre? ◆ *vi* (*speculate*) se demander; **to ~ about sthg** s'interroger sur qqch.

wonderful [wʌndəfʊl] *adj* merveilleux(euse).

wonderfully [wʌndəfʊlɪ] *adv* **1.** (*very well*) merveilleusement, à merveille. **2.** (*for emphasis*) extrêmement.

won't [wəʊnt] = **will not**.

woo [wu:] *vt* **1.** *literary* (*court*) courtiser. **2.** (*try to win over*) chercher à rallier (à soi OR à sa cause).

wood [wʊd] ◆ *n* bois *m*. ◆ *comp* en bois. ▶ **woods** *npl* bois *mpl*.

wooded [wʊdɪd] *adj* boisé(e).

wooden [wʊdn] *adj* **1.** (*of wood*) en bois. **2.** *pej* (*actor*) gauche.

woodpecker [wʊd,pekə⁻] *n* pivert *m*.

woodwind [wʊdwɪnd] *n:* **the ~** les bois *mpl*.

woodwork [wʊdwɜ:k] *n* menuiserie *f*.

woodworm [wʊdwɜ:m] *n* ver *m* du bois.

wool [wʊl] *n* laine *f*; **to pull the ~ over sb's eyes** *inf* rouler qqn (dans la farine).

woollen *Br*, **woolen** *Am* [wʊlən] *adj* en laine, de laine. ▶ **woollens** *npl* lainages *mpl*.

woolly [wʊlɪ] *adj* **1.** (*woollen*) en laine, de laine. **2.** *inf* (*idea, thinking*) confus(e).

word [wɜ:d] ◆ *n* **1.** (LING) mot *m*; **too**

stupid for ~s vraiment trop bête; ~ for ~ (repeat, copy) mot pour mot; (translate) mot à mot; in other ~s en d'autres mots OR termes; in a ~ en un mot; to have a ~ (with sb) parler à qqn; she doesn't mince her ~s elle ne mâche pas ses mots; I couldn't get a ~ in edgeways je n'ai pas réussi à placer un seul mot. 2. (U) (news) nouvelles fpl. 3. (promise) parole f; to give sb one's ~ donner sa parole à qqn; to take sb's ~ for it croire qqn sur parole. ◆ vt (letter, reply) rédiger.

wording ['wɜːdɪŋ] n (U) termes mpl.

word processing n (U) (COMPUT) traitement m de texte.

word processor [-ˌprəʊsesəʳ] n (COMPUT) machine f à traitement de texte.

wore [wɔːʳ] pt → wear.

work [wɜːk] ◆ n 1. (U) (employment) travail m, emploi m; out of ~ sans emploi, au chômage; at ~ au travail. 2. (activity, tasks) travail m. 3. (ART & LITERATURE) œuvre f. ◆ vt 1. (person, staff) faire travailler. 2. (machine) faire marcher. 3. (wood, metal, land) travailler. ◆ vi 1. (do a job) travailler; to ~ on sthg travailler à qqch. 2. (function) fonctionner, marcher. 3. (succeed) marcher. 4. (become): to ~ loose se desserrer. ▶ **works** ◆ n (factory) usine f. ◆ npl 1. (mechanism) mécanisme m. 2. (digging, building) travaux mpl. ▶ **work on** vt fus 1. (pay attention to) travailler à. 2. (take as basis) se baser sur. ▶ **work out** ◆ vt sep 1. (plan, schedule) mettre au point. 2. (total, answer) trouver. ◆ vi 1. (figure, total): to ~ out at se monter à. 2. (turn out) se dérouler. 3. (be successful) (bien) marcher. 4. (train, exercise) s'entraîner. ▶ **work up** vt sep 1. (excite): to ~ o.s. up se mettre dans. 2. (generate): to ~ up an appetite s'ouvrir l'appétit; to ~ up enthusiasm s'enthousiasmer.

workable ['wɜːkəbl] adj (plan) réalisable; (system) fonctionnel(elle).

workaholic [ˌwɜːkə'hɒlɪk] n bourreau m de travail.

workday ['wɜːkdeɪ] n (not weekend) jour m ouvrable.

worked up [ˌwɜːkt-] adj dans tous ses états.

worker ['wɜːkəʳ] n travailleur m, -euse f, ouvrier m, -ère f.

workforce ['wɜːkfɔːs] n main f d'œuvre.

working ['wɜːkɪŋ] adj 1. (in operation) qui marche. 2. (having employment) qui travaille. 3. (conditions, clothes, hours) de travail. ▶ **workings** npl (of system, machine) mécanisme m.

working class n: the ~ la classe ouvrière. ▶ **working-class** adj ouvrier (ère).

working order n: in ~ en état de marche.

workload ['wɜːkləʊd] n quantité f de travail.

workman ['wɜːkmən] (pl -men [-mən]) n ouvrier m.

workmanship ['wɜːkmənʃɪp] n (U) travail m.

workmate ['wɜːkmeɪt] n camarade mf OR collègue mf de travail.

work permit [-ˌpɜːmɪt] n permis m de travail.

workplace ['wɜːkpleɪs] n lieu m de travail.

workshop ['wɜːkʃɒp] n atelier m.

workstation ['wɜːkˌsteɪʃn] n (COMPUT) poste m de travail.

worktop ['wɜːktɒp] n Br plan m de travail.

work-to-rule n Br grève f du zèle.

world [wɜːld] ◆ n 1. (gen) monde m. 2. loc: to think the ~ of sb admirer qqn énormément, ne jurer que par qqn; a ~ of difference une énorme différence. ◆ comp (power) mondial(e); (language) universel(elle); (tour) du monde.

world-class adj de niveau international.

world-famous adj de renommée mondiale.

worldly ['wɜːldlɪ] adj de ce monde, matériel(elle).

World War I n la Première Guerre mondiale.

World War II n la Deuxième Guerre mondiale.

worldwide ['wɜːldwaɪd] ◆ adj mondial(e). ◆ adv dans le monde entier.

worm [wɜːm] n (animal) ver m.

worn [wɔːn] ◆ pp → wear. ◆ adj 1. (threadbare) usé(e). 2. (tired) las (lasse).

worn-out adj 1. (old, threadbare) usé(e). 2. (tired) épuisé(e).

worried ['wʌrɪd] adj soucieux(euse), inquiet(ète).

worry ['wʌrɪ] ◆ n 1. (feeling) souci m. 2. (problem) souci m, ennui m. ◆ vt inquiéter, tracasser. ◆ vi s'inquiéter; to ~ about se faire du souci au sujet de; don't ~!, not to ~! ne vous en faites pas!

worrying ['wʌrɪɪŋ] adj inquiétant(e).

worse [wɜːs] ◆ *adj* **1.** (*not as good*) pire; **to get ~** (*situation*) empirer. **2.** (*more ill*) he's **~ today** il va plus mal aujourd'hui. ◆ *adv* plus mal; **they're even ~ off** c'est encore pire pour eux; **~ off** (*financially*) plus pauvre. ◆ *n* pire *m*; **for the ~** pour le pire.

worsen ['wɜːsn] *vt & vi* empirer.

worship ['wɜːʃɪp] ◆ *vt* adorer. ◆ *n* **1.** (U) (RELIG) culte *m*. **2.** (*adoration*) adoration *f*. ▶ **Worship** *n*: **Your/Her/His Worship** Votre/Son Honneur *m*.

worst [wɜːst] ◆ *adj*: **the ~** le pire (la pire), le plus mauvais (la plus mauvaise). ◆ *adv* le plus mal; **the ~ affected area** la zone la plus touchée. ◆ *n*: **the ~** le pire; **if the ~ comes to the ~** au pire. ▶ **at (the) worst** *adv* au pire.

worth [wɜːθ] ◆ *prep* **1.** (*in value*): **to be ~ sthg** valoir qqch; **how much is it ~?** combien cela vaut-il? **2.** (*deserving of*): **it's ~ a visit** cela vaut une visite; **to be ~ doing sthg** valoir la peine de faire qqch. ◆ *n* valeur *f*; **a week's/£20 ~ of groceries** pour une semaine/20 livres d'épicerie.

worthless ['wɜːθlɪs] *adj* **1.** (*object*) sans valeur, qui ne vaut rien. **2.** (*person*) qui n'est bon à rien.

worthwhile [,wɜːθ'waɪl] *adj* (*job, visit*) qui en vaut la peine; (*charity*) louable.

worthy ['wɜːðɪ] *adj* **1.** (*deserving of respect*) digne. **2.** (*deserving*): **to be ~ of sthg** mériter qqch. **3.** *pej* (*good but unexciting*) méritant(e).

would [wʊd] *modal vb* **1.** (*in reported speech*): **she said she ~ come** elle a dit qu'elle viendrait. **2.** (*indicating likelihood*): **what ~ you do?** que ferais-tu?; **what ~ you have done?** qu'aurais-tu fait?; **I ~ be most grateful** je vous en serais très reconnaissant. **3.** (*indicating willingness*): **she ~n't go** elle ne voulait pas y aller; **he ~ do anything for her** il ferait n'importe quoi pour elle. **4.** (*in polite questions*): **~ you like a drink?** voulez-vous OR voudriez-vous à boire?; **~ you mind closing the window?** cela vous ennuierait de fermer la fenêtre? **5.** (*indicating inevitability*): **he ~ say that** j'étais sûr qu'il allait dire ça, ça ne m'étonne pas de lui. **6.** (*giving advice*): **I ~ report it if I were you** si j'étais vous je préviendrais les autorités. **7.** (*expressing opinions*): **I ~ prefer** je préférerais; **I ~ have thought (that) ...** j'aurais pensé que ... **8.** (*indicating habit*): **he ~ smoke a cigar after dinner** il fumait un cigare après le dîner; **she ~**

often complain about the neighbours elle se plaignait souvent des voisins.

would-be *adj* prétendu(e).

wouldn't ['wʊdnt] = **would not**.

would've ['wʊdəv] = **would have**.

wound¹ [wuːnd] ◆ *n* blessure *f*. ◆ *vt* blesser.

wound² [waʊnd] *pt & pp* → **wind²**.

wove [wəʊv] *pt* → **weave**.

woven ['wəʊvn] *pp* → **weave**.

WP *n* (*abbr of* **word processing, word processor**) TTX *m*.

wrangle ['ræŋgl] ◆ *n* dispute *f*. ◆ *vi*: **to ~ (with sb over sthg)** se disputer (avec qqn à propos de qqch).

wrap [ræp] ◆ *vt* (*cover in paper, cloth*): **to ~ sthg (in)** envelopper OR emballer qqch (dans); **to ~ sthg around** OR **round sthg** enrouler qqch autour de qqch. ◆ *n* (*garment*) châle *m*. ▶ **wrap up** ◆ *vt sep* (*cover in paper or cloth*) envelopper, emballer. ◆ *vi* (*put warm clothes on*): **~ up well** OR **warmly!** couvrez-vous bien!

wrapper ['ræpə'] *n* papier *m*; Br (*of book*) jaquette *f*, couverture *f*.

wrapping ['ræpɪŋ] *n* emballage *m*.

wrapping paper *n* (U) papier *m* d'emballage.

wrath [rɒθ] *n* (U) *literary* courroux *m*.

wreak [riːk] *vt* (*destruction, havoc*) entraîner.

wreath [riːθ] *n* couronne *f*.

wreck [rek] ◆ *n* **1.** (*car, plane, ship*) épave *f*. **2.** *inf* (*person*) loque *f*. ◆ *vt* **1.** (*destroy*) détruire. **2.** (NAUT) provoquer le naufrage de; **to be ~ed** s'échouer. **3.** (*spoil - holiday*) gâcher; (- *health, hopes, plan*) ruiner.

wreckage ['rekɪdʒ] *n* (U) débris *mpl*.

wren [ren] *n* roitelet *m*.

wrench [rentʃ] ◆ *n* (*tool*) clef *f* anglaise. ◆ *vt* **1.** (*pull violently*) tirer violemment; **to ~ sthg off** arracher qqch. **2.** (*arm, leg, knee*) se tordre.

wrestle ['resl] *vi* **1.** (*fight*): **to ~ (with sb)** lutter (contre qqn). **2.** *fig* (*struggle*): **to ~ with sthg** se débattre OR lutter contre qqch.

wrestler ['reslə'] *n* lutteur *m*, -euse *f*.

wrestling ['reslɪŋ] *n* lutte *f*.

wretch [retʃ] *n* pauvre diable *m*.

wretched ['retʃɪd] *adj* **1.** (*miserable*) misérable. **2.** *inf* (*damned*) fichu(e).

wriggle ['rɪgl] *vi* remuer, se tortiller.

wring [rɪŋ] (*pt & pp* **wrung**) *vt* (*washing*) essorer, tordre.

wringing ['rɪŋɪŋ] *adj*: **~ (wet)** (*person*) trempé(e); (*clothes*) mouillé(e), à tordre.

wrinkle ['rɪŋkl] ◆ n 1. (on skin) ride f.
2. (in cloth) pli m. ◆ vt plisser. ◆ vi se
plisser, faire des plis.
wrist [rɪst] n poignet m.
wristwatch ['rɪstwɒtʃ] n montre-
bracelet f.
writ [rɪt] n acte m judiciaire.
write [raɪt] (pt **wrote**, pp **written**) ◆ vt
1. (gen & COMPUT) écrire. 2. Am (person)
écrire à. 3. (cheque, prescription) faire. ◆ vi
(gen & COMPUT) écrire. ▶ **write back** vi
répondre. ▶ **write down** vt sep écrire,
noter. ▶ **write into** vt sep: **to ~ a clause
into a contract** insérer une clause dans
un contrat. ▶ **write off** vt sep 1. (project)
considérer comme fichu. 2. (debt, investment) passer aux profits et pertes.
3. (person) considérer comme fini. 4. Br
inf (vehicle) bousiller. ▶ **write up** vt sep
(notes) mettre au propre.
write-off n (vehicle): **to be a ~** être complètement démoli(e).
writer ['raɪtər] n 1. (as profession)
écrivain m. 2. (of letter, article, story)
auteur m.
writhe [raɪð] vi se tordre.
writing ['raɪtɪŋ] n (U) 1. (handwriting,
activity) écriture f; **in ~** par écrit. 2. (something written) écrit m.
writing paper n (U) papier m à lettres.
written ['rɪtn] ◆ pp → **write**. ◆ adj
écrit(e).
wrong [rɒŋ] ◆ adj 1. (not normal, not satisfactory) qui ne va pas; **is something ~?** y
a-t-il quelque chose qui ne va pas?;
what's ~? qu'est-ce qui ne va pas?;
there's something ~ with the switch l'interrupteur ne marche pas bien. 2. (not
suitable) qui ne convient pas. 3. (not correct - answer, address) faux (fausse), mau-
vais(e); (- decision) mauvais; **to be ~** (person) avoir tort; **to be ~ to do sthg** avoir
tort de faire qqch. 4. (morally bad): **it's ~
to ...** c'est mal de ... ◆ adv (incorrectly)
mal; **to get sthg ~** se tromper à propos
de qqch; **to go ~** (make a mistake) se
tromper, faire une erreur; (stop functioning) se détraquer. ◆ n mal m; **to be in
the ~** être dans son tort. ◆ vt faire du
tort à.
wrongful ['rɒŋful] adj (unfair) injuste;
(arrest, dismissal) injustifié(e).
wrongly ['rɒŋlɪ] adv 1. (unsuitably) mal.
2. (mistakenly) à tort.
wrong number n faux numéro m.
wrote [rəut] pt → **write**.
wrought iron [rɔːt-] n fer m forgé.

wrung [rʌŋ] pt & pp → **wring**.
wry [raɪ] adj 1. (amused - smile, look)
amusé(e); (- humour) ironique. 2. (dis-
pleased) désabusé(e).
WWW (abbr of **World Wide Web**) n
WWW m.

XYZ

x (pl **x's** OR **xs**), **X** (pl **X's** OR **Xs**) [eks] n
1. (letter) x m inv, X m inv. 2. (unknown
thing) x m inv. 3. (to mark place) croix f.
4. (at end of letter): **XXX** grosses bises.
xenophobia [ˌzenə'fəubjə] n xénophobie f.
xenophobic [ˌzenə'fəubɪk] adj xénophobe.
Xmas ['eksməs] n Noël m.
X-ray ◆ n 1. (ray) rayon m X. 2. (picture) radiographie f, radio f. ◆ vt radio-
graphier.
xylophone ['zaɪləfəun] n xylophone
m.

y (pl **y's** OR **ys**), **Y** (pl **Y's** OR **Ys**) [waɪ] n
(letter) y m inv, Y m inv.
yacht [jɒt] n yacht m.
yachting ['jɒtɪŋ] n yachting m.
yachtsman ['jɒtsmən] (pl **-men**
[-mən]) n yachtman m.
yam [jæm] n igname f.
Yank [jæŋk] n Br inf terme péjoratif désignant un Américain, Amerloque mf.
Yankee ['jæŋkɪ] n Br inf (American)
terme péjoratif désignant un Américain,
Amerloque mf.
yap [jæp] vi (dog) japper.
yard [jɑːd] n 1. (unit of measurement) =
91,44 cm, yard m. 2. (walled area) cour f.
3. (area of work) chantier m. 4. Am
(attached to house) jardin m.
yardstick ['jɑːdstɪk] n mesure f.
yarn [jɑːn] n (thread) fil m.
yawn [jɔːn] ◆ n (when tired) bâillement
m. ◆ vi (when tired) bâiller.
yd abbr of **yard**.
yeah [jeə] adv inf ouais.
year [jɪər] n 1. (calendar year) année f;
all (the) ~ round toute l'année. 2. (period
of 12 months) année f, an m; **to be 21 ~s
old** avoir 21 ans. 3. (financial year) année

f; **the ~** 1992-93 l'exercice 1992-93. ▶ **years** *npl* (*long time*) années *fpl.*

yearly ['jɪəlɪ] ♦ *adj* annuel(elle). ♦ *adv* **1.** (*once a year*) annuellement. **2.** (*every year*) chaque année; **twice ~** deux fois par an.

yearn [jɜːn] *vi*: **to ~ for sthg/to do sthg** aspirer à qqch/à faire qqch.

yearning ['jɜːnɪŋ] *n*: **~** (*for sb/sthg*) désir *m* ardent (pour qqn/de qqch).

yeast [jiːst] *n* levure *f.*

yell [jel] ♦ *n* hurlement *m.* ♦ *vi & vt* hurler.

yellow ['jeləʊ] ♦ *adj* (*colour*) jaune. ♦ *n* jaune *m.*

yellow card *n* (FTBL) carton *m* jaune.

yelp [jelp] *vi* japper.

yeoman of the guard ['jəʊmən-] (*pl* **yeomen of the guard** ['jəʊmən-]) *n* hallebardier *m* de la garde royale.

yes [jes] ♦ *adv* **1.** (*gen*) oui; **~, please** oui, s'il te/vous plaît. **2.** (*expressing disagreement*) si. ♦ *n* oui *m inv.*

yesterday ['jestədɪ] ♦ *n* hier *m*; **the day before ~** avant-hier. ♦ *adv* hier.

yet [jet] ♦ *adv* **1.** (*gen*) encore; **~ faster** encore plus vite; **not ~** pas encore; **~ again** encore une fois; **as ~** jusqu'ici. **2.** (*in questions*) déjà; **have they finished ~?** est-ce qu'ils ont déjà fini? ♦ *conj* et cependant, mais.

yew [juː] *n* if *m.*

yield [jiːld] ♦ *n* rendement *m.* ♦ *vt* **1.** (*produce*) produire. **2.** (*give up*) céder. ♦ *vi* **1.** (*gen*): **to ~ (to)** céder (à). **2.** Am (AUT) (*give way*): '~' 'cédez le passage'.

YMCA (*abbr of* **Young Men's Christian Association**) *n* union *chrétienne de jeunes gens* (*proposant notamment des services d'hébergement*).

yoga ['jəʊgə] *n* yoga *m.*

yoghourt, yoghurt, yogurt [Br 'jɒgət, Am 'jəʊgərt] *n* yaourt *m.*

yoke [jəʊk] *n lit & fig* joug *m.*

yolk [jəʊk] *n* jaune *m* (d'œuf).

you [juː] *pers pron* **1.** (*subject - sg*) tu; (*- polite form, pl*) vous; **~'re a good cook** tu es/vous êtes bonne cuisinière; **are ~ French?** tu es/vous êtes français?; **~ French** vous autres Français; **~ idiot!** espèce d'idiot!; **if I were ou was ~** si j'étais toi/vous, à ta/votre place; **there ~ are** (*you've appeared*) te/vous voilà; (*have this*) voilà, tiens/tenez; **that jacket really isn't ~** cette veste n'est pas vraiment ton/votre style. **2.** (*object - unstressed, sg*) te; (*- polite form, pl*) vous; **I can see ~** je te/vous vois; **I gave it to ~** je te/vous l'ai

donné. **3.** (*object - stressed, sg*) toi; (*- polite form, pl*) vous; **I don't expect YOU to do it** je n'exige pas que ce soit toi qui le fasses/vous qui le fassiez. **4.** (*after prep, in comparisons etc, sg*) toi; (*- polite form, pl*) vous; **we shall go without ~** nous irons sans toi/vous; **I'm shorter than ~** je suis plus petit que toi/vous. **5.** (*anyone, one*) on; **~ have to be careful** on doit faire attention; **exercise is good for ~** l'exercice est bon pour la santé.

you'd [juːd] = **you had**, **you would**.

you'll [juːl] = **you will**.

young [jʌŋ] ♦ *adj* jeune. ♦ *npl* **1.** (*young people*): **the ~** les jeunes *mpl.* **2.** (*baby animals*) les petits *mpl.*

younger ['jʌŋgər] *adj* plus jeune.

youngster ['jʌŋstər] *n* jeune *m.*

your [jɔːr] *poss adj* **1.** (*referring to one person*) ton (ta), tes (*pl*); (*polite form, pl*) votre, vos (*pl*); **~ dog** ton/votre chien; **~ house** ta/votre maison; **~ children** tes/vos enfants; **what's ~ name?** comment t'appelles-tu/vous appelez-vous?; **it wasn't YOUR fault** ce n'était pas de ta faute à toi/de votre faute à vous. **2.** (*impersonal - one's*) son (sa), ses (*pl*); **~ attitude changes as you get older** on change sa manière de voir en vieillissant; **it's good for ~ teeth/hair** c'est bon pour les dents/les cheveux; **~ average Englishman** l'Anglais moyen.

you're [jɔːr] = **you are**.

yours [jɔːz] *poss pron* (*referring to one person*) le tien (la tienne), les tiens (les tiennes) (*pl*); (*polite form, pl*) le vôtre (la vôtre), les vôtres (*pl*); **that desk is ~** ce bureau est à toi/à vous, ce bureau est le tien/le vôtre; **it wasn't her fault, it was YOURS** ce n'était pas de sa faute, c'était de ta faute à toi/de votre faute à vous; **a friend of ~** un ami à toi/vous, un de tes/vos amis. ▶ **Yours** *adv* (*in letter*) → **faithfully, sincerely** *etc.*

yourself [jɔːˈself] (*pl* **-selves** [-ˈselvz]) *pron* **1.** (*reflexive - sg*) te; (*- polite form, pl*) vous; (*after preposition - sg*) toi; (*- polite form, pl*) vous. **2.** (*for emphasis - sg*) toi-même; (*- polite form*) vous-même; (*- pl*) vous-mêmes; **did you do it ~?** tu l'as/vous l'avez fait tout seul?

youth [juːθ] *n* **1.** (U) (*period, quality*) jeunesse *f.* **2.** (*young man*) jeune homme *m.* **3.** (U) (*young people*) jeunesse *f*, jeunes *mpl.*

youth club *n* centre *m* de jeunes.

youthful ['juːθfʊl] *adj* **1.** (*eager, innocent*) de jeunesse, juvénile. **2.** (*young*) jeune.

youth hostel *n* auberge *f* de jeunesse.

you've [ju:v] = **you have**.

YTS (*abbr of* **Youth Training Scheme**) *n* programme gouvernemental britannique d'insertion des jeunes dans la vie professionnelle.

Yugoslav = **Yugoslavian**.

Yugoslavia [ˌjuːgəˈslɑːvɪə] *n* Yougoslavie *f*.

Yugoslavian [ˌjuːgəˈslɑːvɪən], **Yugoslav** [ˌjuːgəˈslɑːv] ◆ *adj* yougoslave. ◆ *n* Yougoslave *mf*.

yuppie, yuppy [ˈjʌpɪ] *n inf* yuppie *mf*.

YWCA (*abbr of* **Young Women's Christian Association**) *n* union chrétienne de jeunes filles (*proposant notamment des services d'hébergement*).

z (*pl* **z's** OR **zs**), **Z** (*pl* **Z's** OR **Zs**) [Br zed, Am ziː] *n* (*letter*) z *m inv*, Z *m inv*.

Zambia [ˈzæmbɪə] *n* Zambie *f*.

zany [ˈzeɪnɪ] *adj inf* dingue.

zap [zæp] *vi inf*: **to ~ (off)** somewhere foncer quelque part.

zeal [ziːl] *n* zèle *m*.

zealous [ˈzeləs] *adj* zélé(e).

zebra [Br ˈzebrə, Am ˈziːbrə] (*pl inv* OR **-s**) *n* zèbre *m*.

zebra crossing *n* Br passage *m* pour piétons.

zenith [Br ˈzenɪθ, Am ˈziːnəθ] *n lit & fig* zénith *m*.

zero [Br ˈzɪərəʊ, Am ˈziːrəʊ] (*pl inv* OR **-es**) ◆ *adj* zéro, aucun(e). ◆ *n* zéro *m*.

zest [zest] *n* (U) **1.** (*excitement*) piquant *m*. **2.** (*eagerness*) entrain *m*. **3.** (*of orange, lemon*) zeste *m*.

zigzag [ˈzɪgzæg] *vi* zigzaguer.

Zimbabwe [zɪmˈbɑːbwɪ] *n* Zimbabwe *m*.

zinc [zɪŋk] *n* zinc *m*.

zip [zɪp] *n* Br (*fastener*) fermeture *f* Éclair®. ▶ **zip up** *vt sep* (*jacket*) remonter la fermeture Éclair® de; (*bag*) fermer la fermeture Éclair® de.

zip code *n* Am code *m* postal.

zip fastener *n* Br = **zip**.

zipper [ˈzɪpər] *n* Am = **zip**.

zodiac [ˈzəʊdɪæk] *n*: **the ~** le zodiaque.

zone [zəʊn] *n* zone *f*.

zoo [zuː] *n* zoo *m*.

zoology [zəʊˈɒlədʒɪ] *n* zoologie *f*.

zoom [zuːm] ◆ *vi inf* (*move quickly*) aller en trombe. ◆ *n* (PHOT) zoom *m*.

zoom lens *n* zoom *m*.

zucchini [zuːˈkiːnɪ] (*pl inv*) *n* Am courgette *f*.